EUROPE

59TH EDITION

Where to Stay and Eat
for All Budgets

Must-See Sights
and Local Secrets

Ratings You Can Trust

Fodor's Travel Publications   New York, Toronto, London, Sydney, Auckland
www.fodors.com

FODOR'S EUROPE

Editor: Paul Eisenberg

Editorial Contributors: Robert Andrews, Nuha Ansari, John Babb, Catherine Belonogoff, Carissa Bluestone, Graham Bolger, Muriel Bolger, Ryan Bradley, Stephen Brewer, Jacqueline Brown, Linda Cabasin, Susan Carroll, Jeffrey Carson, Naomi Coleman, Joyce Dalton, Coral Davenport, Bonnie Dodson, Lisa Dunford, Giovanna Dunmall, Elaine Eliah, Robert Fisher, Jane Foster, Sarah Fraser, James Gracie, Alexandre Sousa Guedes, Katrin Gygax, Valerie Hamilton, Louise Hart, Simon Hewitt, Rob Hincks, Lee Hogan, Julius Honnor, Alannah Hopkin, Anto Howard, Kate Hughes, Satu Hummasti, Georgi Iliev, Gareth Jenkins, Raymond Johnston, Nicola Keegan, Laura Kidder, Christina Knight, Anthony Grant Lechtman, Joan Lofgren, Matt Lombardi, Taryn Luciani, Eduardo Luzuriaga, Betsy Maury, Jennifer McDermott, Diane Mehta, Tom Mercer, Olivia Mollet, Christopher Mooney, Karin Palmquist, Anneliese Paull, Jennifer Paull, Sonya Procenko, Patricia Rucidlo, George Semler, Jonette Stabbert, Douglas Stallings, Melia Tatakis, Mei-Yin Teo, Amanda Theunissen, Mark Walters, Dorota Wasik, Alex Wijeratna, Megan Williams, Kay Winzenried

Maps: David Lindroth, *cartographer;* Rebecca Baer and Robert Blake, *map editors*

Design: Fabrizio La Rocca, *creative director;* Guido Caroti, *art director;* Melanie Marin, *senior picture editor*

Production/Manufacturing: Robert B. Shields

Cover Photo (Old-fashioned sign, Hautvilliers, Champagne): Catherine Karnow

COPYRIGHT

Copyright © 2004 by Fodors LLC

Fodor's is a registered trademark of Random House, Inc.

All rights reserved under International and Pan-American Copyright Conventions. Published in the United States by Fodor's Travel Publications, a unit of Fodors LLC, a subsidiary of Random House, Inc., and simultaneously in Canada by Random House of Canada Limited, Toronto. Distributed by Random House, Inc., New York. *No maps, illustrations, or other portions of this book may be reproduced in any form without written permission from the publisher.*

Fifty-ninth Edition

ISBN 1–4000–1275–9

ISSN 0362–0204

SPECIAL SALES

Fodor's Travel Publications are available at special discounts for bulk purchases for sales promotions or premiums. Special editions, including personalized covers, excerpts of existing guides, and corporate imprints, can be created in large quantities for special needs. For more information, contact your local bookseller or write to Special Markets, Fodor's Travel Publications, 1745 Broadway, New York, NY 10019. Inquiries from Canada should be directed to your local Canadian bookseller or sent to Random House of Canada, Ltd., Marketing Department, 2775 Matheson Boulevard East, Mississauga, Ontario L4W 4P7. Inquiries from the United Kingdom should be sent to Fodor's Travel Publications, 20 Vauxhall Bridge Road, London SW1V 2SA, England.

AN IMPORTANT TIP & AN INVITATION

Although all prices, opening times, and other details in this book are based on information supplied to us at press time, changes occur all the time in the travel world, and Fodor's cannot accept responsibility for facts that become outdated or for inadvertent errors or omissions. So **always confirm information when it matters,** especially if you're making a detour to visit a specific place. Your experiences—positive and negative—matter to us. If we have missed or misstated something, **please write to us.** We follow up on all suggestions. Contact the Europe editor at editors @fodors.com or c/o Fodor's at 1745 Broadway, New York, New York 10019.

PRINTED IN THE UNITED STATES OF AMERICA

10 9 8 7 6 5 4 3 2 1

CONTENTS

DESTINATION EUROPE

A trip takes you out of yourself. Concerns of life at home completely disappear, driven away by more immediate thoughts—about, say, what marvels will beguile the next day, or where you'll have dinner. That's where Fodor's comes in. We make sure that you know all your options, so that you don't miss something that's around the next bend just because you didn't know it was there. Because the best memories of your trip might well have nothing to do with what you came to Europe to see, we guide you to sights large and small all over the continent. You might set out to see every art museum in your path, but back at home you find yourself unable to forget that boisterous bistro or quirky boutique you chanced upon on your way back from the gallery. With Fodor's at your side, serendipitous discoveries are never far away. Bon voyage!

Karen Cure, Editorial Director

ABOUT THIS BOOK

There's no doubt that the best source for travel advice is a like-minded friend who's just been where you're headed. But with or without that friend, you'll have a better trip with a Fodor's guide in hand. Once you've learned to find your way around its pages, you'll be in great shape to find your way around your destination.

SELECTION

Our goal is to cover the best properties, sights, and activities in their category, as well as the most interesting communities to visit. We make a point of including local food-lovers' hot spots as well as neighborhood options, and we avoid all that's touristy unless it's really worth your time. You can go on the assumption that everything you read about in this book is recommended wholeheartedly by our writers and editors. It goes without saying that no property mentioned in the book has paid to be included.

RATINGS

Orange stars ★ denote sights and properties that our editors and writers consider the very best in the area covered by the entire book. These, the best of the best, denote Fodor's Choice. Black stars ★ highlight the sights and properties we deem Highly Recommended, the don't-miss sights within any region. In cities, sights pinpointed with numbered map bullets ❶ in the margins tend to be more important than those without bullets.

BUDGET WELL

Hotel and restaurant price categories from ¢ to $$$$ or £ to £££££ are defined in the opening pages of each chapter—expect to find a balanced selection for every budget. For attractions, we always give standard adult admission fees; reductions are usually available for children, students, and senior citizens. Look in Discounts & Deals in Smart Travel Tips for information on destination-wide ticket schemes. Want to pay with plastic? AE, D, DC, MC, V following restaurant and hotel listings indicate whether American Express, Discover, Diners Club, MasterCard, or Visa are accepted.

BASIC INFO

Smart Travel Tips lists travel essentials for the entire area covered by the book; city- and region-specific basics end each chapter. To find the best way to get around, see the transportation section; see individual modes of travel ("By Car," "By Train") for details. We assume you'll check Web sites or call for particulars.

ON THE MAPS

Maps throughout the book show you what's where and help you find your way around. Black and orange numbered bullets ❶ ❶ in the text correlate to bullets on maps.

FIND IT FAST

Chapters are in alphabetical order by country. Each covers the country's essential information from A to Z, exploring, dining, lodging, nightlife and the arts, shopping, and side trips in cities and regions. Sites in major cities accompanied by maps are arranged alphabetically. Within regional sections, all restaurants and lodgings are grouped with the town. The Essentials list that ends all city or regional sections covers getting there and getting around. It also provides helpful contacts and resources.

DON'T FORGET | Restaurants are open for lunch and dinner daily unless we state otherwise; we mention dress only when there's a specific requirement and reservations only when they're essential or not accepted—it's always best to book ahead. Hotels have private baths, phone, TVs, and air-conditioning and operate on the European Plan (a.k.a. EP, meaning without meals). We always list facilities but not whether you'll be charged extra to use them, so when pricing accommodations, find out what's included.

SYMBOLS

Many Listings

★ Fodor's Choice
★ Highly recommended
⊠ Physical address
✛ Directions
🏛 Mailing address
☎ Telephone
🖷 Fax
⊕ On the Web
✎ E-mail
🎟 Admission fee
☉ Open/closed times
⚑ Start of walk/itinerary
Ⓜ Metro stations
▭ Credit cards

Outdoors

⛳ Golf
⛺ Camping

Hotels & Restaurants

🏨 Hotel
🛏 Number of rooms
♨ Facilities
🍴 Meal plans
✗ Restaurant
🖋 Reservations
👔 Dress code
🚭 Smoking
🍶 BYOB
✗🏨 Hotel with restaurant that warrants a visit

Other

☕ Family-friendly
🛈 Contact information
⇨ See also
⊠ Branch address
☞ Take note

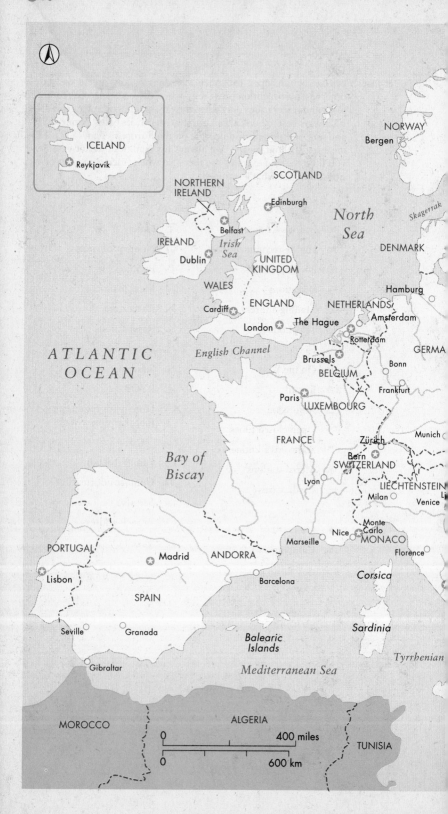

ICELAND
Reykjavík

NORWAY
Bergen

NORTHERN
IRELAND

SCOTLAND
Edinburgh

North
Sea

Skagerrak

Belfast

IRELAND

Irish
Sea

DENMARK

Dublin

UNITED
KINGDOM

WALES

Hamburg

NETHERLANDS

ENGLAND

Cardiff

The Hague   Amsterdam

London   Rotterdam

GERMA

ATLANTIC
OCEAN

English Channel

Brussels

Bonn

BELGIUM

Frankfurt

Paris

LUXEMBOURG

FRANCE

Zürich   Munich

Bern

SWITZERLAND

Bay of
Biscay

Lyon

LIECHTENSTEIN

Li

Milan   Venice

Monte
Carlo

Nice

PORTUGAL

Marseille   MONACO

Madrid

ANDORRA

Florence

Lisbon

Corsica

SPAIN

Barcelona

Seville   Granada

Sardinia

Balearic
Islands

Tyrrhenian

Gibraltar

Mediterranean Sea

MOROCCO

ALGERIA

0   400 miles

0   600 km

TUNISIA

Europe

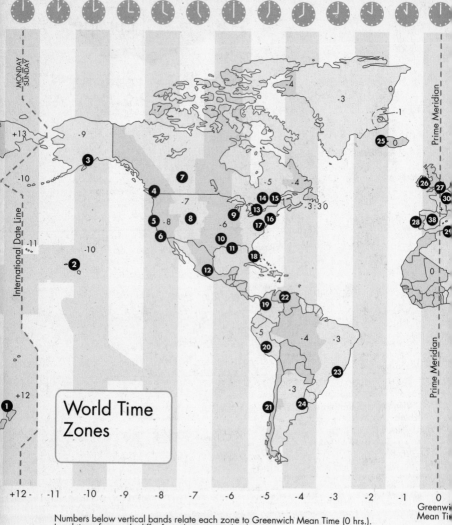

World Time Zones

Numbers below vertical bands relate each zone to Greenwich Mean Time (0 hrs.).
Local times frequently differ from these general indications,
as indicated by light-face numbers on map.

Algiers **29**	Berlin **34**	Delhi **48**	Jerusalem **42**
Anchorage **3**	Bogotá **19**	Denver **8**	Johannesburg **44**
Athens **41**	Budapest **37**	Dublin **26**	Lima **20**
Auckland **1**	Buenos Aires **24**	Edmonton **7**	Lisbon **28**
Baghdad **46**	Caracas **22**	Hong Kong **56**	London
Bangkok **50**	Chicago **9**	Honolulu **2**	(Greenwich) **27**
Beijing **54**	Copenhagen **33**	Istanbul **40**	Los Angeles **6**
	Dallas **10**	Jakarta **53**	Madrid **38**

SMART TRAVEL TIPS

Finding out about your destination before you leave home means you won't squander time organizing everyday minutiae once you've arrived. You'll be more streetwise when you hit the ground as well, better prepared to explore the aspects of Europe that drew you here in the first place. The organizations in this section can provide information to supplement this guide; contact them for up-to-the-minute details, and consult the A to Z sections at the start of each chapter for facts on the various topics as they relate to each country. Happy landings!

AIR TRAVEL

Before booking, **compare different modes of transportation.** Many city pairs are so close together that flying hardly makes sense. For instance, it may take just half an hour to fly between London and Paris, but you must factor in time spent getting to and from the airports, plus check-in time. A three-hour train ride from city center to city center seems a better alternative. It makes sense to **save air travel for longer distances**—say, between London and Rome, Paris and Vienna, Brussels and Stockholm—and do your local traveling from these hubs.

If you're flying so-called **national carriers,** full-fare tickets often remain the only kind available for one-way trips and restriction-free round-trips, and they are prohibitively expensive for most leisure travelers. On most European flights, your choice is between Business Class (which is what you get when paying full fare) and Economy (coach). Some flights are all Economy. First Class has ceased to exist in Europe. The most reasonable fares have long been nonrefundable and nontransferable round-trips (APEX fares), which require a Saturday night at the destination. But the near-monopoly that used to be enjoyed by these airlines is crumbling, and they have had to start offering less restrictive fares. Check before you fly.

Some national carriers reward transatlantic passengers with fixed-price flight coupons (priced at $100–$120) to destinations from their respective hubs and/or domestic or area air passes. These must be bought before leaving home. If you're young, **ask about youth standby fares,** which are available on a number of domestic and some international services.

Over the last few years, a substantial number of local airlines have been created to provide feeder services to major hubs and services between secondary city pairs. Do not, however, expect rock-bottom prices. **Seek advice from local branches of international travel agencies** like American Express or Carlson/Wagonlit.

Low-cost no-frills airlines base their fares on one-way travel, and a return ticket is simply twice the price. Advertised fares are always preceded by the word "from." To get the lowest fare, book two weeks ahead of time; it also helps to be flexible about your date of travel. In general, you have to book directly by calling the airline, credit card in hand. Some also accept reservations by fax. Reservation via Internet is available with companies such as the SABRE-powered Travelocity (⊕ www. travelocity.com) and Microsoft's Expedia (⊕ www.expedia.com). You can make secure payments via the Net and hunt the cheapest flight deals, as well as reserve hotels. You get a reservation number and pick up your boarding pass at the airport. Note that some flights use relatively distant secondary airports.

ARRIVALS

Passport control has become a perfunctory affair within most of the European Union (EU). The nine signatories to the Schengen Agreement (Austria, Belgium, France, Germany, Italy, Luxembourg, the Netherlands, Portugal, and Spain) have abolished passport controls for travelers between countries in that area, but individual countries can temporarily suspend it.

The most notable exception is Great Britain; when a number of flights from the United States arrive at Heathrow or Gatwick close together in the morning, **be prepared for a longish wait** (though rarely as long as Europeans have to wait at JFK in New York).

The Green Channel/Red Channel customs system in operation at most Western European airports and other borders is basically an honor system. If you have nothing to declare, walk through the Green Channel, where there are only spot luggage checks; if in doubt, go through the Red Channel. If you fly between two EU-member countries, go through the new **Blue Channel,** where there are no customs officers except the one who glances at baggage labels to make sure only people off EU flights get through. On average, you need to **count on at least half an hour from deplaning to getting out of the airport.**

BOOKING

When you book, **look for nonstop flights** and **remember that "direct" flights stop at least once.** Try to avoid connecting flights, which require a change of plane. Two airlines may operate a connecting flight jointly, so ask whether your airline operates every segment of the trip; you may find that the carrier you prefer flies you only part of the way. To find more booking tips and to check prices and make online flight reservations, log on to www. fodors.com.

CARRIERS

🛫 **U.S. Airlines American** ☎ 800/433-7300 in U.S.; 0845/778-9789 in U.K. ⊕ www.aa.com. **Continental** ☎ 800/525-0280 in U.S.; 0800/776-464 in U.K. ⊕ www.continental.com. **Delta** ☎ 800/221-1212 in U.S., 0800/414-767 in U.K. ⊕ www.delta. com. **Northwest** ☎ 800/225-2525 in U.S.; c/o alliance partner KLM, call 0990/750-9000 in U.K. ⊕ www.klm.com. **United** ☎ 800/538-2929 in U.S.; 0845/844-4777 in U.K. ⊕ www.ual.com. **US Airways** ☎ 800/428-4322 in U.S.; 0800/783-5556 in U.K. ⊕ www.usairways.com.

🛫 **European Airlines Austria: Austrian Airlines** ☎ 800/843-0002 in U.S.; 0845/601-0948 in U.K. ⊕ www.aua.com. **Belgium: Sabena Belgian World Airlines** ☎ 800/955-2000 in U.S.; 020/7494-2629 in U.K. ⊕ www.brussels-airlines.com. **The Czech Republic and Slovakia: Czech Airlines (CSA)** ☎ 212/765-6022 in U.S.; 0870/444-3747 in U.K. ⊕ www. csa.cz. **Denmark: Scandinavian Airlines (SAS)** ☎ 800/221-2350 in U.S.; 0870/6072-7727 in U.K. ⊕ www.scandinavian.net. **Finland: Finnair** ☎ 800/950-5000 in U.S., 0207/514-2429 in U.K. ⊕ www. finnair.com. **France: Air France** ☎ 800/237-2747 in U.S.; 0845/084-5111 in U.K. ⊕ www.airfrance.com. **Germany: LTU International Airways** ☎ 800/888-0200 in U.S. ⊕ www.ltu.com. **Lufthansa** ☎ 800/645-3880 in U.S.; 0845/7737-747 in U.K. ⊕ www. lufthansa.com. **Great Britain: British Airways** ☎ 800/247-9297 in U.S.; 0845/773-3377 in U.K. ⊕ www.ba.com. **Virgin Atlantic** ☎ 800/862-8621 in U.S.; 0129/345-0150 in U.K. ⊕ www.virgin-atlantic.com. **Greece: Olympic Airways** ☎ 800/223-1226 in U.S.; 0870/606-0460 in U.K. ⊕ www. olympic-airways.gr. **Hungary: Malév Hungarian Airlines** ☎ 212/757-6446; 800/223-6884 outside NY in U.S. ⊕ www.malev.hu. **Iceland: Icelandair** ☎ 800/223-5500 in U.S.; 020/7874-1000 in U.K. ⊕ www.icelandair.com. **Ireland: Aer Lingus** ☎ 888/474-7424 or 800/223-6537 in U.S.; 0845/

084-4444 in U.K. ⊕ www.aerlingus.com. Italy: **Alitalia** ☏ 800/223-5730 in U.S.; 020/8745-8200 in U.K. ⊕ www.alitalia.it. The Netherlands: **KLM Royal Dutch Airlines** ☏ 800/447-4747 in U.S.; 0870/507-4074 in U.K. ⊕ www.klm.com. Norway: **SAS** ☏ 800/221-2350 in U.S.; 0845/600-7767 in U.K. ⊕ www.scandinavian.net. Poland: **LOT Polish Airlines** ☏ 800/223-0593 in U.S.; 0845/601-0949 in U.K. ⊕ www.lot.com. Portugal: **TAP Air Portugal** ☏ 800/221-7370 in U.S.; 0807/457273 in U.K. ⊕ www.tap-airportugal.pt. Romania: **Tarom Romanian Air Transport** ☏ 212/560-0840 in U.S.; 020/7224-3693 in U.K. ⊕ www.tarom.ro. Spain: **Iberia Airlines** ☏ 800/772-4642 in U.S.; 0845/601-2854 in U.K. ⊕ www.iberia.es. Sweden: **SAS** ☏ 800/221-2350 in U.S.; 0845/600-7767 in U.K. ⊕ www.scandinavian.net. Turkey: **THY Turkish Airlines** ☏ 212/339-9662 in U.S.; 0845/601-0956 in U.K. ⊕ www.turkishairlines.com.

From Australia Qantas Airways ☏ 13-13-13 in Australia; 0845/774-7767 in U.K. ⊕ www.qantas.com.

From Canada Air Canada ☏ 888/247-2262 ⊕ www.aircanada.com. **Air Transat** ☏ 877/872-6728 ⊕ www.airtransat.com.

From Ireland Aer Lingus ☏ 081/836-5000 in Ireland; 0845/084-4444 in U.K. ⊕ www.aerlingus.com.

From New Zealand Air New Zealand ☏ 09/9357-3000 or 0800/028-4149 in New Zealand; 020/8741-2299 in U.K. ⊕ www.airnewzealand.com.

From the U.K. British Airways ✉ Box 5619, Sudbury, Suffolk, C010 2PG ☏ 0845/773-3377 ⊕ www.ba.com. **British Midland** ☏ 0870/607-0555 ⊕ www.flybmi.com. **EasyJet** ☏ 0870/600-0000 ⊕ www.easyjet.com. **KLM U.K.** ☏ 0870/507-4074 ⊕ www.klm.com. **Ryanair** ☏ 0871/246-0000 ⊕ www.ryanair.com. **Virgin Express** ☏ 020/7744-0004 ⊕ www.virgin-express.com.

No-Frills Carrier Reservations Within Europe Belgium: **Virgin Express** ☏ 020/744-0004 in U.K. ⊕ www.virgin-express.com from Brussels to Milan, Rome, Nice, Madrid, Barcelona, Copenhagen, and London (Gatwick, Heathrow, Stansted); from Rome to Barcelona and Madrid; from London (Stansted) to Berlin and Shannon. Ireland: **Ryanair** ☏ 0818/303030 in Ireland; 0871/246-0000 in U.K. ⊕ www.ryanair.com from Dublin to 12 U.K. destinations, to Paris (Beauvais) and Brussels (Charleroi); from London (Stansted, Luton, and Gatwick) to Dublin; from London (Stansted) to four other Irish destinations, five French destinations, four Scandinavian destinations, six Italian destinations, and Frankfurt. United Kingdom: **Buzz** ☏ 0870/240-7070 ⊕ www.buzzaway.com from London (Stansted) to Bordeaux, Düsseldorf, Berlin, Frankfurt, Hamburg, Helsinki, Jerez (Spain), Lyon, Marseilles, Milan, Paris, and Vienna. **EasyJet** ☏ 0870/600-0000 ⊕ www.easyjet.

com from London (Luton) and Liverpool to Amsterdam, Barcelona, Belfast, Geneva, Madrid, Malaga, Nice; from London (Luton) to Athens, Palma de Mallorca, Zurich, and four Scottish destinations; from Geneva to Amsterdam, Barcelona, Liverpool, London (Luton, Gatwick, and Stansted), and Nice.

CHECK-IN & BOARDING

Always **ask your carrier about its check-in policy.** Plan to arrive at the airport about two hours before your scheduled departure time for domestic flights and 2½ to 3 hours before international flights. You may need to arrive earlier if you're flying from one of the busier airports or during peak air-traffic times. To avoid delays at airport-security checkpoints, try not to wear any metal. Jewelry, belt and other buckles, steel-toe shoes, barrettes, and underwire bras are among the items that can set off detectors.

Assuming that not everyone with a ticket will show up, airlines routinely overbook planes. When everyone does, airlines ask for volunteers to give up their seats. In return, these volunteers usually get a several-hundred-dollar flight voucher, which can be used toward the purchase of another ticket, and are rebooked on the next flight out. If there are not enough volunteers, the airline must choose who will be denied boarding. The first to get bumped are passengers who checked in late and those flying on discounted tickets, so **get to the gate and check in as early as possible,** especially during peak periods.

Always **bring a government-issued photo ID to the airport;** even when it's not required, a passport is best.

CUTTING COSTS

The least expensive airfares to Europe are priced for round-trip travel and must usually be purchased in advance. Airlines generally allow you to change your return date for a fee; most low-fare tickets, however, are nonrefundable. It's smart to **call a number of airlines and check the Internet;** when you are quoted a good price, **book it on the spot**—the same fare may not be available the next day, or even the next hour. Always **check different routings** and look into using alternate airports. Also, price off-peak flights, which may be significantly less expensive than others. Travel agents, especially low-fare specialists (⇨ Discounts & Deals), are helpful.

Consolidators are another good source. They buy tickets for scheduled flights at reduced rates from the airlines, then sell them at prices that beat the best fare available directly from the airlines. Sometimes you can even get your money back if you need to return the ticket. Carefully read the fine print detailing penalties for changes and cancellations, purchase the ticket with a credit card, and **confirm your consolidator reservation with the airline.**

When you **fly as a courier,** you trade your checked-luggage space for a ticket deeply subsidized by a courier service. There are restrictions on when you can book and how long you can stay. Some courier companies list with membership organizations, such as the Air Courier Association and the International Association of Air Travel Couriers; these require you to become a member before you can book a flight.

Many airlines, singly or in collaboration, offer discount air passes that allow foreigners to travel economically in a particular country or region. Ask your airline about purchasing discount passes for intra-European flights before you leave home to save significantly on travel between European cities. If you're going to be covering a lot of ground, consider Europebyair.com, which sells intra-European flights to more than 150 cities for $99 per segment. They also offer unlimited flight passes good for 15 or 21 days.

Information about passes often can be found on most airlines' international Web pages, which tend to be aimed at travelers from outside the carrier's home country. The name of the pass into a search engine, or search for "pass" within the carrier's Web site.

⚑ Consolidators **AirlineConsolidator.com** ☎ 888/468-5385 ⊕ www.airlineconsolidator.com; for international tickets. **Best Fares** ☎ 800/576-8255 or 800/576-1600 ⊕ www.bestfares.com; $59.90 annual membership. **Cheap Tickets** ☎ 800/377-1000 or 888/922-8849 ⊕ www.cheaptickets.com. **Expedia** ☎ 800/397-3342 or 404/728-8787 ⊕ www.expedia.com. **Hotwire** ☎ 866/468-9473 or 920/330-9418 ⊕ www.hotwire.com. **Now Voyager Travel** ✉ 45 W. 21st St., 5th fl., New York, NY 10010 ☎ 212/459-1616 🖷 212/243-2711 ⊕ www.nowvoyagertravel.com. **Onetravel.com** ⊕ www.onetravel.com. **Orbitz** ☎ 888/656-4546 ⊕ www.orbitz.com. **Priceline.com** ⊕ www.priceline.com. **Travelocity** ☎ 888/709-5983; 877/282-2925 in Canada; 0870/876-3876 in U.K. ⊕ www.travelocity.com.

⚑ Courier Resources **Air Courier Association/Cheaptrips.com** ☎ 800/282-1202 ⊕ www.aircourier.org or www.cheaptrips.com. **International Association of Air Travel Couriers** ☎ 308/632-3273 ⊕ www.courier.org.
⚑ Discount Passes **FlightPass** EuropebyAir, ☎ 888/387-2479 ⊕ www.europebyair.com. **SAS Air Passes** Scandinavian Airlines, ☎ 800/221-2350; 0845/6072-7727 in U.K.; 1300/727707 in Australia ⊕ www.scandinavian.net.

ENJOYING THE FLIGHT

State your seat preference when purchasing your ticket, and then repeat it when you confirm and when you check in. For more legroom, you can request one of the few emergency-aisle seats at check-in, if you are capable of lifting at least 50 pounds—a Federal Aviation Administration requirement of passengers in these seats. Seats behind a bulkhead also offer more legroom, but they don't have under-seat storage. Don't sit in the row in front of the emergency aisle or in front of a bulkhead, where seats may not recline.

Ask the airline whether a snack or meal is served on the flight. If you have dietary concerns, **request special meals when booking.** These can be vegetarian, low-cholesterol, or kosher, for example. It's a good idea to pack some healthful snacks and a small (plastic) bottle of water in your carry-on bag. On long flights, try to maintain a normal routine, to help fight jet lag. At night, **get some sleep.** By day, **eat light meals, drink water** (not alcohol), and **move around the cabin** to stretch your legs. For additional jet-lag tips consult *Fodor's FYI: Travel Fit & Healthy* (available at bookstores everywhere).

Smoking policies vary from carrier to carrier. Many airlines prohibit smoking on all of their flights; others allow smoking only on certain routes or certain departures. Ask your carrier about its policy.

FLYING TIMES

Flights from New York to London take about 6½ hours, to Paris 7½ hours, to Frankfurt 7½ hours, and to Rome 8½ hours. From Sydney to London, flights take about 23 hours via Bangkok, to Paris 22¾ hours via Singapore, to Frankfurt 22 hours via Singapore, and to Rome 25 hours via Bangkok.

HOW TO COMPLAIN

If your baggage goes astray or your flight goes awry, complain right away. Most carriers require that you **file a claim immediately.** The Aviation Consumer Protection Division of the Department of Transportation publishes *Fly-Rights*, which discusses airlines and consumer issues and is available on-line.

Airline Complaints Aviation Consumer Protection Division ⊠ U.S. Department of Transportation, C-75, Room 4107, 400 7th St. NW, Washington, DC 20590 ☎ 202/366-2220 ⊕ www.dot.gov/airconsumer. **Federal Aviation Administration Consumer Hotline** ⊠ for inquiries: FAA, 800 Independence Ave. SW, Room 810, Washington, DC 20591 ☎ 800/322-7873 ⊕ www.faa.gov.

RECONFIRMING

Check the status of your flight before you leave for the airport. You can do this on your carrier's Web site, by linking to a flight-status checker (many Web booking services offer these), or by calling your carrier or travel agent. Always confirm international flights at least 72 hours ahead of the scheduled departure time.

AIRPORTS

See Essentials *in* city sections of country chapters.

DUTY-FREE SHOPPING

Duty-free shopping was eliminated for travelers between EU countries as of July 1, 1999. However, duty-free shopping still applies in non-EU countries, and tax-free shopping is available for tourists returning to non-EU countries from the EU. If you're looking for good deals associated with duty-free airport shopping, **check out liquor and beauty products,** although prices vary considerably. The amount of liquor you may buy is restricted, generally to two bottles.

Some airport concourses, notably in Amsterdam, Copenhagen, and Shannon, have practically been transformed into shopping malls, selling everything from electronics and chocolates to fashion and furs. These are tax-free rather than duty-free shops; if this is your last stop before leaving the EU, there's no value-added-tax (V.A.T.) and you can **avoid the tax-refund rigmarole** (⇨ Taxes).

BIKE TRAVEL

BIKES IN FLIGHT

Most airlines accommodate bikes as luggage, provided they are dismantled and boxed; check with individual airlines about packing requirements. Some airlines sell bike boxes, which are often free at bike shops, for about $15 (bike bags can be considerably more expensive). International travelers often can substitute a bike for a piece of checked luggage at no charge; otherwise, the cost is about $100. U.S. and Canadian airlines charge $40–$80 each way.

BOAT & FERRY TRAVEL

Ferry routes for passengers and vehicles link the countries surrounding the North Sea, the Irish Sea, and the Baltic Sea; Italy with Greece; and Spain, France, Italy, and Greece with their respective islands in the Mediterranean. Longer ferry routes—between, for instance, Britain and Spain or Scandinavia—can help you **reduce the amount of driving and often save time.** A number of modern ships offer improved comfort and entertainment ranging from one-armed bandits to gourmet dining.

FARES & SCHEDULES

See individual country chapters, or contact operators for specific information on fares and schedules.

Boat & Ferry Information Ferry operators between the British Isles and the Continent include **Brittany Ferries** ⊠ Millbay Docks, Plymouth PL1 3EW ☎ 0870/3665-3333 ⊕ www.brittanyferries.com, from Plymouth to Roscoff (Brittany) and Santander (Spain), from Poole to Cherbourg, and from Portsmouth to Caen and St. Malo. **DFDS Seaways** ⊠ Scandinavia House, Parkeston Quay, Harwich, Essex CO12 4QG ☎ 0870/533-3000; 800/533-3755 in U.S. ⊕ www.dfdsseaways.com, from Harwich to Esbjerg (Denmark), Hamburg, and Gothenburg and from Newcastle-upon-Tyne to IJmuiden, 20 mi west of Amsterdam and (summer season) to Gothenburg and Hamburg. **Fjord Line** ⊠ International Ferry Terminal, Royal Quays, North Shields NE29 6EE ☎ 0191/296-1313 ⊕ www.fjordline.co.uk, from Newcastle to Bergen/Stavanger/Haugesund (Norway). **Hoverspeed** ⊠ International Hoverport, Marine Parade, Dover, Kent CT17 9TG ☎ 0870/240-8070 ⊕ www.hoverspeed.com, Dover-Calais, Dover-Oostende, Folkestone-Boulogne, and Newhaven-Dieppe. **Irish Ferries** ⊠ Corn Exchange Building, Ground fl., Bunswick St., Liverpool L2 7TP ☎ 8705/171717 ⊕ www.irishferries.ie, Holyhead-Dublin and

Pembroke–Rosslare; also Rosslare (Ireland; reservations 1890/313131) to Cherbourg, and Roscoff. **P&O European Ferries** ⊠ Peninsular House, Wharf Rd., Portsmouth, PO2 8TA ☎ 0870/242-4999 or 0870/520-2020 ⊕ ww1.poferries.com sails Portsmouth to Cherbourg, Le Havre, and Bilbao (Spain), and Cairnyarn (Scotland)–Larne (Belfast). **P&O North Sea Ferries** ⊠ King George Dock, Hedon Rd., Hull HU9 5QA ☎ 0870/242-4999 ⊕ ww1.poferries.com, from Hull to Rotterdam and Zeebrugge. **P&O Stena Line** ⊠ Channel House, Channel View Rd., Dover, Kent CT17 9TJ ☎ 0870/242-4999 ⊕ ww1.poferries.com, Dover–Calais. **SeaFrance** ⊠ Eastern Docks, Dover, Kent CT16 1JA ☎ 0870/571-1711 ⊕ www.seafrance.co.uk, Dover–Calais. **Stena Line** ⊠ Charter House, Park St., Ashford, Kent TN24 8EX ☎ 0870/574-7474 or 0870/570-7070 ⊕ www.stenaline.co.uk, Harwich–Hook of Holland, Holyhead–Dun Laoghaire (Dublin), Fishguard–Rosslare, and Stranraer (Scotland)–Belfast. **Swansea Cork Ferries** ⊠ Harbour Office, Kings Dock, Swansea SA1 1SF ☎ 01792/456-116 ⊕ www.swansea-cork.ie, Swansea–Cork (mid-Mar.–early Nov.).

BUS TRAVEL

International bus travel is rapidly expanding in Europe, thanks to changing EU rules and the Channel Tunnel, but it still has some way to go before it achieves the status of a natural choice, except in Britain and Sweden. In other northern European countries, bus services exist mostly to supplement railroads.

Within several southern European countries—including Portugal, Greece, parts of Spain, and Turkey—the bus has supplanted the train as the main means of public transportation, and is often quicker and more comfortable, with more frequent service, than the antiquated national rolling stock. Be prepared to discover that the bus is more expensive. Competition among lines is keen, so **ask about air-conditioning and reclining seats before you book.**

Eurolines comprises 30 motor-coach operators of international scheduled services, all no-smoking. They also transport passengers within each country. The 30-nation network serves more than 500 destinations with services ranging from twice weekly to five times daily. Eurolines has its own coach stations in Paris (28 av. du Général de Gaulle at Bagnelot; métro: Gallieni), Brussels (80 rue du Progrès, next to the Gare du Nord), and Amsterdam (adjacent to the Amstel Railway Station).

In other cities, coaches depart from railway stations or municipal bus terminals.

From the U.K., Eurolines links London with 400 destinations on the European Continent and Ireland, from Stockholm to Rome, from Dublin to Bucharest. All are via Calais, using either ferry services or Le Shuttle/Eurotunnel under the English Channel. Buses leave from Victoria Coach Station (adjoining the railway station). Services link up with the National Express network covering the U.K.

National or regional tourist offices have information about bus services. For reservations on major lines before you go, **contact your travel agent at home.**

CUTTING COSTS

The **Busabout** service can take you to more than 85 cities in Europe with two options: the consecutive pass or the flexipass. If you're planning a whirlwind European tour on a small budget, two weeks of consecutive travel will run you $359; three weeks $479; and one month $589. For a more leisurely pace, the flexipass gives you 12 nonconsecutive traveling days in a two-month period for $579 or up to 20 days of nonconsecutive travel in a four-month period for $839. There are also links to Budpest ($49 supplement), Athens (a Greek Island Pass takes you to five islands for a $89 supplement), and Morocco ($59 supplement). There's an on-board guide who provides local information and, with notice, can book campsites, bungalows, budget hotels, or hostels.

The **Eurolines Pass** allows unlimited travel between 31 European cities on scheduled bus services. A 30-day summer pass costs $369 ($299 for those under 26 or over 60); a 60-day pass costs $429 ($329). Passes can be purchased from Eurolines offices and travel agents in Europe and from the companies listed below.

🚌 Discount Passes In the U.S.: Eurolines Passes can be purchased from **Destination Europe Resources (DER)** ⊠ 9501 W. Devon Ave., Rosemont, IL 60018 ☎ 800/782-2424 ⊕ www.der.com and from most Hostelling International and all STA offices (⇨ Students in Europe).

🚌 Bus Information **Busabout (U.K.) Ltd.** ⊠ Victoria Bus Station, 258 Vauxhall Bridge Rd., London, SW1V 1BS ☎ 020/7950-1661 🖷 020/7950-1662 ⊕ www.busabout.com. **Eurolines (U.K.)** ⊠ 4 Cardiff Rd., Luton LU1 1PP ☎ 0990/143219 🖷 01582/400-694 ⊕ www.eurolines.com. For brochures, timetables, and sales agents in the U.S. and Canada, contact the **Eurolines Pass Organization** ✉ Keizersgracht 317, 1016 EE Amsterdam, The Netherlands ☎ 020/625-3010 🖷 020/420-6904.

CAMERAS & PHOTOGRAPHY

The *Kodak Guide to Shooting Great Travel Pictures* (available at bookstores everywhere) is loaded with tips.

📷 Photo Help **Kodak Information Center** ☎ 800/242-2424 🌐 www.kodak.com.

EQUIPMENT PRECAUTIONS

Don't pack film and equipment in checked luggage, where it is much more susceptible to damage. X-ray machines used to view checked luggage are extremely powerful and therefore are likely to ruin your film. Try to **ask for hand inspection of film,** which becomes clouded after repeated exposure to airport X-ray machines, and **keep videotapes and computer disks away from metal detectors.** Always **keep film, tape, and computer disks out of the sun.** Carry an extra supply of batteries, and **be prepared to turn on your camera, camcorder, or laptop** to prove to airport security personnel that the device is real.

CAR RENTAL

The great attraction of renting is obviously that you become independent of public transport. Cost-wise, you should **consider renting a car only if you are with at least one other person;** single travelers pay a tremendous premium. Car rental costs vary from country to country; rates in Scandinavia and Eastern Europe are particularly high. If you're visiting a number of countries with varying rates, it makes sense to **rent a vehicle in the cheapest country.** For instance, if you plan to visit Normandy, the same company that rents you a car for a weekly rate of $246 in Paris will rent you one for $159 in Brussels, adding a few hours to your trip but at a 35% savings.

Picking up a car at an airport is convenient but often costs extra (up to 10%), as rental companies pass along the fees charged to them by airports.

Sample rates: London, $39 a day and $136 a week for an economy car with air-conditioning, a manual transmission, and unlimited mileage; Paris, $60 a day and $196 a week; Madrid, $37 a day and $132 a week; Rome, $49 a day and $167 a week; Frankfurt, $18 a day and $91 a week. These figures do not include tax on car rentals, which ranges from 15% to 21%.

🚗 Major Agencies **Alamo** ☎ 800/522-9696 🌐 www.alamo.com. **Avis** ☎ 800/331-1084; 800/879-2847 in Canada; 0870/606-0100 in U.K.; 02/9353-9000 in Australia; 09/526-2847 in New Zealand 🌐 www.avis.com. **Budget** ☎ 800/527-0700; 0870/156-5656 in U.K. 🌐 www.budget.com. **Dollar** ☎ 800/800-6000; 0124/622-0111 in U.K., where it's affiliated with Sixt; 02/9223-1444 in Australia 🌐 www.dollar.com. **Hertz** ☎ 800/654-3001; 800/263-0600 in Canada; 0870/844-8844 in U.K.; 02/9669-2444 in Australia; 09/256-8690 in New Zealand 🌐 www.hertz.com. **National Car Rental** ☎ 800/227-7368; 0870/600-6666 in U.K. 🌐 www.nationalcar.com.

CUTTING COSTS

For a good deal, **book through a travel agent who will shop around.** If you think you'll need a car in Europe but are unsure about when or where, ask your travel agent to check out Kemwel's CarPass. This gives the benefit of prepaid vouchers with the flexibility of last-minute bookings in Europe. Unused vouchers are refunded. Do **look into wholesalers,** companies that do not own fleets but rent in bulk from those that do and often offer better rates than traditional car-rental operations. Prices are best during off-peak periods. Rentals booked through wholesalers often must be paid for before you leave home.

Short-term leasing can save money if you need a rental for more than 17 days. Kemwel and Europe by Car are among the wholesalers offering such deals.

Also consider renting a diesel car, as it's more fuel efficient, the fuel is cheaper, and the rates can be less expensive as well.

🚗 Wholesalers **Auto Europe** ☎ 207/842-2000 or 800/223-5555 🖷 207/842-2222 🌐 www.autoeurope.com. **Europe by Car** ☎ 212/581-3040 or 800/223-1516 🖷 212/246-1458 🌐 www.europebycar.com. **Destination Europe Resources** (DER) ✉ 9501 W. Devon Ave., Rosemont, IL 60018 ☎ 800/782-2424 🌐 www.der.com. **Kemwel** ☎ 800/678-0678 🖷 207/842-2124 🌐 www.kemwel.com.

INSURANCE

When driving a rented car you are generally responsible for any damage to or loss of the vehicle. Collision policies that car-rental companies sell for European rentals typically do not cover stolen vehicles. Before you rent—and purchase collision or theft coverage—see what coverage you already have under the terms of your personal auto-insurance policy and credit cards.

In Italy, when driving a rented car, you are generally responsible for any damage to or loss of the vehicle. Collision policies that car-rental companies sell for European rentals typically don't cover stolen vehicles. Indeed, all car-rental agencies operating in Italy require that you buy a theft-protection policy. Before you rent—and purchase collision coverage—see what coverage you already have under the terms of your personal auto-insurance policy and credit cards.

SURCHARGES

Before you pick up a car in one city and leave it in another, **ask about drop-off charges or one-way service fees,** which can be substantial. Note, too, that some rental agencies charge extra if you return the car before the time specified in your contract. To avoid a hefty refueling fee, **fill the tank just before you turn in the car,** but be aware that gas stations near the rental outlet may overcharge. It's almost never a deal to buy the tank of gas that's in the car when you rent it; the understanding is that you'll return it empty, but some fuel usually remains.

CAR TRAVEL

Your driver's license may not be recognized outside your home country. International driving permits (IDPs) are available from the American and Canadian automobile associations and, in the United Kingdom, from the Automobile Association and Royal Automobile Club. These international permits, valid only in conjunction with your regular driver's license, are universally recognized; having one may save you a problem with local authorities.

Unless you're in a rush to get to your next destination, you'll find it rewarding to **avoid the freeways and use alternative routes.**

Motorway tolls can easily add $25 a day to your costs in driving through France, and there are toll roads throughout southern Europe, as well as charges for many

tunnels. When crossing borders into Switzerland, you'll be charged approximately €27.50 (about $30) for a *vignette* that entitles you to use Swiss freeways for 14 months; in Austria, a vignette begins at about €31 and you can choose its duration. To get a handle on toll costs, consult the national tourist office or car rental firm before you travel.

If you are driving a rented car, **be sure to carry the necessary papers provided by the rental company.** For U.K. citizens, if the vehicle is your own, you will need proof of ownership, a certificate of roadworthiness (known as a Ministry of Transport, or MOT, road vehicle certificate), up-to-date vehicle registration or tax certificate, and a Green Card proof of insurance, available from your insurance company (fees vary depending on destination and length of stay).

Border controls have been abolished within the EU (except in the U.K., Ireland, Scandinavia, and Greece). The border posts are still standing, but drivers whiz through them without slowing down. Truck traffic is generally routed to separate checkpoints.

Drivers traveling between Great Britain and the Continent can now **consider using the Eurotunnel,** the train carrying cars, buses, motorbikes, and trucks, plus their passengers, through the Channel Tunnel between Folkestone and Calais in 35 minutes. The shuttle trains operate continuously—three to four trains per hour—and reservations are not needed, but to avoid queueing, tickets can be bought in advance from travel agents or by credit card from **Eurotunnel** (☎ 03/2100–6100 in France; 0870/535–3535 in the U.K., www. eurotunnel.com). Prices vary according to length of stay on the Continent, as well as the season and time of travel. Prices given are for return fares, with the maximum rate applying in the peak July and August holiday period. A short break (less than five days) costs £83–£117, and a standard return costs £193–£227. Club Class gives you the right to priority queueing and entry to the Club Class lounge for a premium of 25%–35%. To calculate single fares simply divide by two. Note that you must make advance reservations to benefit from promotional fares and special offers. *See* The Channel Tunnel.

AUTO CLUBS

🚗 In Australia **Australian Automobile Association** ☎ 02/6247-7311 ⊕ www.aaa.asn.au.

🚗 In Canada **Canadian Automobile Association (CAA)** ☎ 613/247-0117 for membership ⊕ www.caa.ca.

🚗 In New Zealand **New Zealand Automobile Association** ☎ 09/377-4660 ⊕ www.nzaa.co.nz.

🚗 In the U.K. **Automobile Association (AA)** ☎ 0870/600-0371 ⊕ www.theaa.com. **Royal Automobile Club (RAC)** ☎ 0800/015-4435 for membership; 0800/092-2222 for insurance ⊕ www.rac.co.uk.

🚗 In the U.S. **American Automobile Association** ☎ 800/763-9900 ⊕ www.aaa.com.

EMERGENCY SERVICES

You must carry a reflecting red triangle (to be placed 30 meters behind your car in case of breakdown). A first-aid kit and fire extinguisher are strongly recommended.

GASOLINE

Be prepared: gasoline costs three to four times more than in the United States, due to heavy taxes. The better fuel economy of European cars offsets the higher price to some extent.

ROAD CONDITIONS

During peak vacation periods, main routes can be jammed with holiday traffic. In the United Kingdom, **try to avoid driving during any of the long bank-holiday (public holiday) weekends,** when motorways are invariably clogged. The tunnels carrying traffic between Italy and the countries to the north are often overburdened with truck traffic; cross the Alps on a weekend, if you can. In France, Greece, Spain, and Italy, huge numbers of people still take a fixed one-month vacation in August, so **avoid driving** during le départ, the first weekend in August, when vast numbers of drivers head south; or le retour, when they head back.

RULES OF THE ROAD

Establishing a speed limit for German motorways has proved a tougher nut than any government could crack. On the rest of the Continent, the limit is generally 120 kph (74 mph), but the cruising speed is mostly about 140 kph (about 87 mph). In the United Kingdom, the speed limit is 112 kph (70 mph), but there, too, passing at considerably higher speeds is not uncommon. In suburban and urban zones, the speed limit is much lower. For safe driving, **stay in the slower lane unless you want to pass, and make way for faster cars wanting to pass you.**

In the United Kingdom, the Republic of Ireland, Cyprus, and Gibraltar, cars drive on the left. In other European countries, traffic is on the right. If you're coming off the Eurotunnel's shuttle, or ferries from Britain or Ireland to the Continent (or vice versa), beware the transition. See individual country chapters for national speed limits and rules of the road.

THE CHANNEL TUNNEL

Short of flying, taking the "Chunnel" is the fastest way to cross the English Channel: 35 minutes from Folkestone to Calais, 60 minutes from motorway to motorway, or 3 hours from London's Waterloo Station to Paris's Gare du Nord.

🚗 Car Transport **Eurotunnel** ☎ 0870/535-3535 in U.K.; 070/223210 in Belgium; 03-21-00-61-00 in France ⊕ www.eurotunnel.com. **French Motorail/Rail Europe** ☎ 0870/241-5415 ⊕ www.frenchmotorail.com.

🚗 Passenger Service **Eurostar** ☎ 1233/617575; 0870/518-6186 in U.K. ⊕ www.eurostar.co.uk. **Rail Europe** ☎ 800/942-4866 or 800/274-8724; 0870/584-8848 U.K. inquiries and credit-card bookings ⊕ www.raileurope.com.

CHILDREN IN EUROPE

If you are renting a car, don't forget to **arrange for a car seat** when you reserve. For general advice about traveling with children, consult Fodor's FYI: Travel with Your Baby (available in bookstores everywhere).

FLYING

If your children are two or older, **ask about children's airfares.** As a general rule, infants under two not occupying a seat fly at greatly reduced fares or even for free. But if you want to guarantee a seat for an infant, you have to pay full fare. Consider flying during off-peak days and times; most airlines will grant an infant a seat without a ticket if there are available seats. When booking, **confirm carry-on allowances** if you're traveling with infants. In general, for babies charged 10% to 50% of the adult fare you are allowed one carry-on bag and a collapsible stroller; if the flight is full, the stroller may have to be checked or you may be limited to less.

Experts agree that it's a good idea to use safety seats aloft for children weighing less than 40 pounds. Airlines set their own policies: if you use a safety seat, U.S. carriers usually require that the child be ticketed, even if he or she is young enough to ride free, because the seats must be strapped into regular seats. And even if you pay the full adult fare for the seat, it may be worth it, especially on longer trips. Do **check your airline's policy about using safety seats during takeoff and landing.** Safety seats are not allowed everywhere in the plane, so get your seat assignments as early as possible.

When reserving, **request children's meals or a freestanding bassinet** (not available at all airlines) if you need them. But note that bulkhead seats, where you must sit to use the bassinet, may lack an overhead bin or storage space on the floor.

LODGING

Most hotels in Europe allow children under a certain age to stay in their parents' room at no extra charge, but others charge for them as extra adults; be sure to **find out the cutoff age for children's discounts.**

SIGHTS & ATTRACTIONS

Places that are especially appealing to children are indicated by a rubber-duckie icon (🦆) in the margin.

CONSUMER PROTECTION

Whether you're shopping for gifts or purchasing travel services, **pay with a major credit card** whenever possible, so you can cancel payment or get reimbursed if there's a problem (and you can provide documentation). If you're doing business with a particular company for the first time, **contact your local Better Business Bureau and the attorney general's offices** in your state and (for U.S. businesses) the company's home state as well. Have any complaints been filed? Finally, if you're buying a package or tour, always **consider travel insurance** that includes default coverage (⇨ Insurance).

🏢 BBBs **Council of Better Business Bureaus** ✉ 4200 Wilson Blvd., Suite 800, Arlington, VA 22203 ☎ 703/276-0100 🖷 703/525-8277 ⊕ www. bbb.org.

CRUISE TRAVEL

Europe is a major cruise center, with eight seas (Adriatic, Aegean, Baltic, Black, Ionian, Mediterranean, North, and Tyrrhenian) and the Atlantic Ocean. From the majesty of Norway's fjords to the ruins of ancient Greece, the region has more than one could possibly hope to see on one cruise vacation. **Select your ship as carefully as you choose your itinerary.** Cruises sail in Europe from April through November.

To learn how to plan, choose, and book a cruise-ship voyage, consult *Fodor's FYI: Plan & Enjoy Your Cruise* (available in bookstores everywhere).

🚢 Cruise Lines **Abercrombie & Kent** ✉ 1520 Kensington Rd., Suite 212, Oak Brook, IL 60523 ☎ 630/954-2944 or 800/323-7308 ⊕ www. abercrombiekent.com. **Celebrity Cruises** ✉ 1050 Caribbean Way, Miami, FL 33132 ☎ 305/539-6000 or 800/437-3111 ⊕ www.celebritycruises.com. **Clipper Cruise Line** ✉ 11969 Westline Industrial Dr., St. Louis, MO 63146 ☎ 314/655-6700 or 800/325-0010 ⊕ www.clippercruise.com. **Crystal Cruises** ✉ 2049 Century Park E, Suite 1400, Los Angeles, CA 90067 ☎ 800/446-6620 ⊕ www.crystalcruises.com. **Cunard Line Limited** ✉ 6100 Blue Lagoon Dr., Suite 400, Miami, FL 33126 ☎ 800/728-6273 ⊕ www. cunardline.com. **Holland America Line** ✉ 300 Elliott Ave. W, Seattle, WA 98119 ☎ 877/932-4259 ⊕ www.hollandamerica.com. **Orient Lines** ✉ 1510 S.E. 17th St., Suite 400, Fort Lauderdale, FL 33316 ☎ 954/527-6660 or 800/333-7300 ⊕ www. orientlines.com. **Princess Cruises** ✉ 24844 Avenue Rockefeller, Santa Clarita, CA 91355 ☎ 310/553-1770; 800/774-6237 for brochures ⊕ www.princess. com. **Radisson Seven Seas Cruises** ✉ 600 Corporate Dr., Suite 410, Fort Lauderdale, FL 33334 ☎ 877/505-5370 ⊕ www.rscc.com. **Royal Caribbean International** ✉ 1080 Caribbean Way, Miami, FL 33132 ☎ 305/539-6000 or 800/398-9819 ⊕ www. royalcaribbean.com. **Royal Olympic Cruises** ✉ 805 3rd Ave., 18th fl., New York, NY 10022 ☎ 212/397-6400; 800/872-6400 in U.S. and Canada ⊕ www. royalolympiccruises.com. **Silversea Cruises** ✉ 110 E. Broward Blvd., Fort Lauderdale, FL 33301 ☎ 954/522-4499 or 800/722-9955 ⊕ www.silversea.com. **Special Expeditions** ✉ 720 5th Ave., New York, NY 10019 ☎ 212/765-7740 or 800/397-3348 ⊕ www. specialexpeditions.com. **Windstar Cruises** ✉ 300 Elliott Ave. W, Seattle, WA 98119 ☎ 800/258-7245 ⊕ www.windstarcruises.com.

CUSTOMS & DUTIES

When shopping abroad, **keep receipts** for all purchases. Upon reentering the country,

be ready to show customs officials what you've bought. Pack purchases together in an easily accessible place. If you think a duty is incorrect, appeal the assessment. If you object to the way your clearance was handled, note the inspector's badge number. In either case, first ask to see a supervisor. If the problem isn't resolved, write to the appropriate authorities, beginning with the port director at your point of entry.

IN AUSTRALIA

Australian residents who are 18 or older may bring home A$400 worth of souvenirs and gifts (including jewelry), 250 cigarettes or 250 grams of cigars or other tobacco products, and 1,125 ml of alcohol (including wine, beer, and spirits). Residents under 18 may bring back A$200 worth of goods. Members of the same family traveling together may pool their allowances. Prohibited items include meat products. Seeds, plants, and fruits need to be declared upon arrival.

Australian Customs Service ⌾ Regional Director, Box 8, Sydney, NSW 2001 ☎ 02/9213-2000 or 1300/363263; 02/9364-7222 or 1800/803006 quarantine-inquiry line 🖶 02/9213-4043 ⊕ www.customs. gov.au.

IN CANADA

Canadian residents who have been out of Canada for at least seven days may bring in C$750 worth of goods duty-free. If you've been away fewer than seven days but more than 48 hours, the duty-free allowance drops to C$200. If your trip lasts 24 to 48 hours, the allowance is C$50. You may not pool allowances with family members. Goods claimed under the C$750 exemption may follow you by mail; those claimed under the lesser exemptions must accompany you. Alcohol and tobacco products may be included in the seven-day and 48-hour exemptions but not in the 24-hour exemption. If you meet the age requirements of the province or territory through which you reenter Canada, you may bring in, duty-free, 1.5 liters of wine *or* 1.14 liters (40 imperial ounces) of liquor *or* 24 12-ounce cans or bottles of beer or ale. Also, if you meet the local age requirement for tobacco products, you may bring in, duty-free, 200 cigarettes and 50 cigars. Check ahead of time with the Canada Customs and Revenue Agency or the Department of Agriculture for policies regarding meat products, seeds, plants, and fruits.

You may send an unlimited number of gifts (only one gift per recipient, however) worth up to C$60 each duty-free to Canada. Label the package UNSOLICITED GIFT—VALUE UNDER $60. Alcohol and tobacco are excluded.

Canada Customs and Revenue Agency ✉ 2265 St. Laurent Blvd., Ottawa, Ontario K1G 4K3 ☎ 800/461-9999, 204/983-3500, or 506/636-5064 ⊕ www. ccra.gc.ca.

IN NEW ZEALAND

All homeward-bound residents may bring back NZ$700 worth of souvenirs and gifts; passengers may not pool their allowances, and children can claim only the concession on goods intended for their own use. For those 17 or older, the duty-free allowance also includes 4.5 liters of wine or beer; one 1,125-ml bottle of spirits; and either 200 cigarettes, 250 grams of tobacco, 50 cigars, *or* a combination of the three up to 250 grams. Meat products, seeds, plants, and fruits must be declared upon arrival to the Agricultural Services Department.

New Zealand Customs ✉ Head office: The Customhouse, 17–21 Whitmore St., Box 2218, Wellington ☎ 09/300-5399 or 0800/428-786 ⊕ www.customs. govt.nz.

IN THE U.K.

If you are a U.K. resident and your journey was wholly within the European Union, you probably won't have to pass through customs when you return to the United Kingdom. If you plan to bring back large quantities of alcohol or tobacco, check EU limits beforehand. In most cases, if you bring back more than 200 cigars, 3,200 cigarettes, 10 liters of spirits, 110 liters of beer, and/or 90 liters of wine, you have to declare the goods upon return.

HM Customs and Excise ✉ Portcullis House, 21 Cowbridge Rd. E, Cardiff CF11 9SS ☎ 0845/010-9000 or 0208/929-0152; 0208/929-6731 or 0208/910-3602 complaints ⊕ www.hmce.gov.uk.

IN THE U.S.

U.S. residents who have been out of the country for at least 48 hours may bring home, for personal use, $800 worth of foreign goods duty-free, as long as they haven't used the $800 allowance or any part of it in the past 30 days. This exemption may include 1 liter of alcohol (for travelers 21 and older), 200 cigarettes, and 100 non-Cuban cigars. Family members from the same household who are traveling together may pool their $800 personal exemptions. For fewer than 48 hours, the duty-free allowance drops to $200, which may include 50 cigarettes, 10 non-Cuban cigars, and 150 ml of alcohol (or 150 ml of perfume containing alcohol). The $200 allowance cannot be combined with other individuals' exemptions, and if you exceed it, the full value of all the goods will be taxed. Antiques, which the U.S. Bureau of Customs and Border Protection defines as objects more than 100 years old, enter duty-free, as do original works of art done entirely by hand, including paintings, drawings, and sculptures. This doesn't apply to folk art or handicrafts, which are in general dutiable.

You may also send packages home duty-free, with a limit of one parcel per addressee per day (except alcohol or tobacco products or perfume worth more than $5). You can mail up to $200 worth of goods for personal use; label the package PERSONAL USE and attach a list of its contents and their retail value. If the package contains your used personal belongings, mark it AMERICAN GOODS RETURNED to avoid paying duties. You may send up to $100 worth of goods as a gift; mark the package UNSOLICITED GIFT. Mailed items do not affect your duty-free allowance on your return.

To avoid paying duty on foreign-made high-ticket items you already own and will take on your trip, register them with Customs before you leave the country. Consider filing a Certificate of Registration for laptops, cameras, watches, and other digital devices identified with serial numbers or other permanent markings; you can keep the certificate for other trips. Otherwise, bring a sales receipt or insurance form to show that you owned the item before you left the United States.

🛈 **U.S. Bureau of Customs and Border Protection** ✉ For inquiries and equipment registration, 1300 Pennsylvania Ave. NW, Washington, DC 20229 🌐 www.customs.gov ☎ 202/354-1000 ✉ For complaints, Customer Satisfaction Unit, 1300 Pennsylvania Ave. NW, Room 5.5D, Washington, DC 20229.

IN EUROPE

Since the EU's 1992 agreement on a unified European market, the same customs regulations apply to all 15 member states (Austria, Belgium, Denmark, Finland, France, Germany, Great Britain, Greece, Ireland, Italy, Luxembourg, the Netherlands, Portugal, Spain, and Sweden). If you arrive from another EU country, you do not have to pass through customs.

Duty-free allowances for visitors from outside the EU are the same whatever your nationality (but you have to be over 17): 200 cigarettes or 50 cigars or 100 cigarillos or 250 grams of pipe tobacco; 1 liter of spirits or 2 liters of fortified or sparkling wine or liqueurs; 2 liters of still table wine; 60 milliliters of perfume; 250 milliliters of toilet water (note: 1 U.S. quart equals 0.946 liters); plus $200 worth of other goods, including gifts and souvenirs. Unless otherwise noted in individual country chapters, there are no restrictions on the import or export of currency. These limits remained in force after June 30, 1999, when duty-free shopping for travel within the EU was abolished.

See individual country chapters on non-EU countries for information on their import limits.

DINING

See discussions of dining in individual country chapters. The restaurants we list are the cream of the crop in each price category.

Reservations are always a good idea: we mention them only when they're essential or not accepted. We mention dress only when men are required to wear a jacket or a jacket and tie.

CUTTING COSTS

To save money on meals, consider eating at restaurants and cafeterias in department stores; the food and selection are surprisingly good. The stores also often have deli counters with local specialties and basics, so you can load up and nibble on the go or head out to the park for a picnic.

Many universities have cafeterias, usually called *mensas*, subsidized by the government and open to the public. Don't expect a grand buffet, but you'll find several choices daily accommodating most appetites.

Street vendors are popular throughout Europe, with stands reading *donor-kebab* or some variation thereof. These stands pop up on the street, in small take-out windows in buildings, even vans. The food is cheap, hot, and usually very good; food might range from pizza and french fries to lamb kebabs and falafel.

When in Spain, savor local flavors without going over-budget by ordering *tapas,* small appetizer-size plates of meats, vegetables, or cheeses. At many bars, a serving comes free when you order a drink.

As you walk around, the cost of buying sodas and juices throughout the day will certainly add up. Consider buying bottled water and iced tea mix, for instance, to create your own brew, and reuse the bottles with tap water (destination permitting) to save even more.

DISABILITIES & ACCESSIBILITY

Getting around in many European cities and towns can be difficult if you're using a wheelchair, as cobblestone-paved streets and sidewalks are common in older, historic districts. Generally, newer facilities (including museums, transportation, hotels) provide easier access for people with disabilities.

LODGING

Contact a support organization at home to see whether they have publications with lists of approved accommodations. The U.S.–based Society for the Advancement of Travel for the Handicapped (SATH) is dedicated to promoting access for travelers with disabilities. The British nonprofit Holiday Care Service produces an annual guide, *The Holiday Care Service Guide to Accessible Accommodation and Travel,* which lists more than 1,000 establishments inspected for access by Holiday Care in association with the National Tourist Boards. It has sections on accessible transportation, identifies accessible tourist attractions, and suggests sample itineraries.

Support Organizations Holiday Care Service ⊠ 7th fl., Sunley House, 4 Bedford Pk., Croydon, Surrey, CR0 2AP ☎ 0845/124-9971 🖷 0845/124-9922 ⊕ www.holidaycare.org.uk. **The Society for the Advancement of Travel for the Handicapped (SATH)** ⊠ 347 5th Ave., Suite 610, New York, NY 10016 ☎ 212/447-7284 🖷 212/725-8253 ⊕ www.sath.org.

RESERVATIONS

When discussing accessibility with an operator or reservations agent, **ask hard questions.** Are there any stairs, inside *or* out? Are there grab bars next to the toilet *and* in the shower/tub? How wide is the doorway to the room? To the bathroom? For the most extensive facilities meeting the latest legal specifications, **opt for newer accommodations.** If you reserve through a toll-free number, consider also calling the hotel's local number to confirm the information from the central reservations office. Get confirmation in writing when you can.

Complaints Aviation Consumer Protection Division (⇨ Air Travel) for airline-related problems. **Departmental Office of Civil Rights** ⊠ For general inquiries, U.S. Department of Transportation, S-30, 400 7th St. SW, Room 10215, Washington, DC 20590 ☎ 202/366-4648 🖷 202/366-9371 ⊕ www.dot.gov/ost/docr/index.htm. **Disability Rights Section** ⊠ NYAV, U.S. Department of Justice, Civil Rights Division, 950 Pennsylvania Ave. NW, Washington, DC 20530 🖷 ADA information line 202/514-0301; 800/514-0301; 202/514-0383 TTY; 800/514-0383 TTY ⊕ www.ada.gov. **U.S. Department of Transportation Hotline** ☎ For disability-related air-travel problems, 800/778-4838; 800/455-9880 TTY.

TRAVEL AGENCIES

In the United States, the Americans with Disabilities Act requires that travel firms serve the needs of all travelers. Some agencies specialize in working with people with disabilities.

Travelers with Mobility Problems CareVacations ⊠ No. 5, 5110-50 Ave., Leduc, Alberta T9E 6V4, Canada ☎ 780/986-6404 or 877/478-7827 🖷 780/986-8332 ⊕ www.carevacations.com, for group tours and cruise vacations. **Flying Wheels Travel** ⊠ 143 W. Bridge St., Box 382, Owatonna, MN 55060 ☎ 507/451-5005 or 800/535-6790 🖷 507/451-1685 ⊕ www.flyingwheelstravel.com. **Melwood** ⊠ 5606 Dower House Rd., Upper Marlboro, MD 20772 ☎ 301/599-8000 🖷 301/599-0180 ⊕ www.melwood.com.

Travelers with Developmental Disabilities New Directions ⊠ 5276 Hollister Ave., Suite 207, Santa Barbara, CA 93111 ☎ 805/967-2841 or 888/967-2841 🖷 805/964-7344 ⊕ www.newdirectionstravel.com. **Sprout** ⊠ 893 Amsterdam Ave., New York, NY 10025 ☎ 212/222-9575 or 888/222-9575 🖷 212/222-9768 ⊕ www.gosprout.org.

DISCOUNTS & DEALS

Be a smart shopper and **compare all your options** before making decisions. A plane ticket bought with a promotional coupon from travel clubs, coupon books, and direct-mail offers or purchased on the Internet may not be cheaper than the least expensive fare from a discount ticket agency. And always keep in mind that what you get is just as important as what you save.

If you're looking to plan your trip around some free activities, try to be in town for a festival or other seasonal event that could yield street performances, concerts, and other goings-on. Year-round, check bulletin boards in tourist offices and churches for free concert announcements.

Many countries throughout Europe offer museum passes that can save you money and sometimes time if the pass enables you to circumvent long lines. In Paris, the *Cart Musees et Monuments* pass, available at major museums or métro stops, permits entry—usually without waiting in line—to 70 museums in greater Paris for €15 per day; you can buy a one-, three-, or five-day pass. In Berlin, one- or three-day *Tageskarte* or *Drei-Tage-Karte* passes, on sale at any of the state-owned museums, are good for all 20 museums run by the Staatliche Museen zu Berlin and cost €6 and €8, respectively. In Munich, you can buy a €15 day pass for all state-owned museums at any of the affiliated museums, or at a tourist office. The *Paseo del Arte* pass (€7.66) in Madrid gets you into the three most popular museums in the city— the Museo del Prado, the Centro de Arte Reina Sofia, and the Musee Thyssen-Bornemisza—and is available at any one of them.

There are also often free admission days at the state-owned museums in many countries, sometimes once a week but usually once a month, and often on Sunday. Inquire at tourist offices and museums when you visit for more information. There are usually student discounts at museums with proof of your student status; there are also discounts for teachers if you can present your dated union card.

Outlet malls have only recently become popular in Europe, and the leading provider of them is McArthur Glen (🌐 www.mcarthurglen.com). There are currently 12 locations: Ashford, Swindon, York, Mansfield, Cheshire Oaks, and Bridgend in England; Livingston, Scotland; Roermond, Holland; Roubaix and Troyes in France; Serravalle, Italy; and Parndorf, Austria. And if you're eager to get those gifts home and they happen to be paper products, save postage by mailing them through the media mail category; it does take longer than first-class but can be about a third of the price.

DISCOUNT RESERVATIONS

To save money, **look into discount reservations services** with Web sites and toll-free numbers, which use their buying power to get a better price on hotels, airline tickets (⇨ Air Travel), even car rentals. When booking a room, always **call the hotel's local toll-free number** (if one is available) rather than the central reservations number—you'll often get a better price. Always ask about special packages or corporate rates.

When shopping for the best deal on hotels and car rentals, **look for guaranteed exchange rates**, which protect you against a falling dollar. With your rate locked in, you won't pay more, even if the price goes up in the local currency.

🖪 Airline Tickets **Air 4 Less** ☎ 800/AIR4LESS; low-fare specialist. 🖪 Hotel Rooms **Accommodations Express** ☎ 800/444-7666 or 800/277-1064 🌐 www. accommodationsexpress.com. **Hotel Reservations Network** ☎ 800/964-6835 🌐 www.hotels.com. **Hotels.com** ☎ 800/246-8357 or 214/369-1246 🌐 www.hotels.com. **International Marketing & Travel Concepts** ☎ 800/790-4682 🌐 www.imtc-travel.com. **Steigenberger Reservation Service** ☎ 800/223-5652 🌐 www.srs-worldhotels.com. **Travel Interlink** ☎ 800/888-5898 🌐 www. travelinterlink.com. **Turbotrip.com** ☎ 800/473-7829 🌐 www.turbotrip.com.

PACKAGE DEALS

Don't confuse packages and guided tours. When you buy a package, you travel on your own, just as though you had planned the trip yourself. Fly/drive packages, which combine airfare and car rental, are often a good deal. In cities, ask the local visitor's bureau about hotel packages that include tickets to major museum exhibits or other special events. If you **buy a rail/drive pass,** you may save on train tickets and car rentals. All Eurailpass holders get a discount on Eurostar fares through the

Channel Tunnel and often receive reduced rates for buses, hotels, ferries, and car rentals. A German Rail Pass is also good for travel aboard some KD German Rhine Line steamers and on certain ferries to Finland, Denmark, and Sweden (if the pass includes those countries). Discounts are available on some Deutsche Touring/Europabus routes. Greek Flexipass Rail 'n Fly includes two flight vouchers for selected air-travel routes within Greece and free or reduced fares on some ferries.

ELECTRICITY

To use electric-powered equipment purchased in the United States or Canada, **bring a converter and adapter.**

If your appliances are dual-voltage, you'll need only an adapter. Don't use 110-volt outlets marked FOR SHAVERS ONLY for high-wattage appliances such as blow-dryers. Most laptops operate equally well on 110 and 220 volts and so require only an adapter.

GAY & LESBIAN TRAVEL

Although big cities like Amsterdam, London, and Paris have a visible and happening gay scene (the newly elected mayor of Paris is openly gay), most of Europe has a view of homosexuality similar to that found away from big cities in the United States.

⚐ Gay~ & Lesbian-Friendly Travel Agencies **Different Roads Travel** ✉ 8383 Wilshire Blvd., Suite 520, Beverly Hills, CA 90211 ☎ 323/651-5557 or 800/429-8747 (Ext. 14 for both) 🖷 323/651-3678 ✉ lgernert@tzell.com. **Kennedy Travel** ✉ 130 W. 42nd St., Suite 401, New York, NY 10036 ☎ 212/840-8659 or 800/237-7433 🖷 212/730-2269 ⊕ www.kennedytravel.com. **Now, Voyager** ✉ 4406 18th St., San Francisco, CA 94114 ☎ 415/626-1169 or 800/255-6951 🖷 415/626-8626 ⊕ www.nowvoyager.com. **Skylink Travel and Tour** ✉ 1455 N. Dutton Ave., Suite A, Santa Rosa, CA 95401 ☎ 707/546-9888 or 800/225-5759 🖷 707/636-0951; serving lesbian travelers.

INSURANCE

The most useful travel-insurance plan is a comprehensive policy that includes coverage for trip cancellation and interruption, default, trip delay, and medical expenses (with a waiver for preexisting conditions).

Without insurance you'll lose all or most of your money if you cancel your trip, regardless of the reason. Default insurance covers you if your tour operator, airline, or cruise line goes out of business. Trip-delay covers expenses that arise because of bad weather or mechanical delays. Study the fine print when comparing policies.

If you're traveling internationally, a key component of travel insurance is coverage for medical bills incurred if you get sick on the road. Such expenses aren't generally covered by Medicare or private policies. U.K. residents can buy a travel-insurance policy valid for most vacations taken during the year in which it's purchased (but check preexisting-condition coverage). British and Australian citizens need extra medical coverage when traveling overseas.

Always **buy travel policies directly from the insurance company;** if you buy them from a cruise line, airline, or tour operator that goes out of business, you probably won't be covered for the agency or operator's default, a major risk. Before making any purchase, **review your existing health and home-owner's policies** to find what they cover away from home.

⚐ Travel Insurers In the U.S.: **Access America** ✉ 6600 W. Broad St., Richmond, VA 23230 ☎ 800/284-8300 🖷 804/673-1491 or 800/346-9265 ⊕ www.accessamerica.com. **Travel Guard International** ✉ 1145 Clark St., Stevens Point, WI 54481 ☎ 715/345-0505 or 800/826-1300 🖷 800/955-8785 ⊕ www.travelguard.com.

⚐ In the U.K.: **Association of British Insurers** ✉ 51 Gresham St., London EC2V 7HQ ☎ 020/7600-3333 🖷 020/7696-8999 ⊕ www.abi.org.uk. In Canada: **RBC Insurance** ✉ 6880 Financial Dr., Mississauga, Ontario L5N 7Y5 ☎ 800/565-3129 🖷 905/813-4704 ⊕ www.rbcinsurance.com. In Australia: **Insurance Council of Australia** ✉ Insurance Enquiries and Complaints, Level 3, 56 Pitt St., Sydney, NSW 2000 ☎ 1300/363683 or 02/9251-4456 🖷 02/9251-4453 ⊕ www.iecltd.com.au. In New Zealand: **Insurance Council of New Zealand** ✉ Level 7, 111-115 Customhouse Quay, Box 474, Wellington ☎ 04/472-5230 🖷 04/473-3011 ⊕ www.icnz.org.nz.

LANGUAGE

A phrase book and language-tape set can help get you started. *Fodor's French for Travelers, Fodor's German for Travelers, Fodor's Italian for Travelers,* and *Fodor's Spanish for Travelers* (available at bookstores everywhere) are excellent.

LODGING

For discussions of accommodations in Europe, *see* the Lodging sections *in* individual country chapters. The lodgings we list are the cream of the crop in each price category. When pricing accommodations, always ask what facilities are included and what costs extra.

CUTTING COSTS

When booking a room, always **call the hotel's local toll-free number** (if one is available) rather than the central reservations number—you'll often get a better price. Always ask about special packages or corporate rates.

When looking for inexpensive lodging, consider asking local tourist offices about university dorms or religious housing. When schools are on break, many rent dorm rooms or convert other buildings into housing to bring in revenue. The spaces are comparable to hostel accommodations. For information on university housing in the U.K. contact Venuemasters. Religious housing is another alternative; convents and monasteries often allow guests as long as they are respectful of their rules. Such rules can include a curfew, no drinking, or single-sex guests only. This housing is popular in Spain and Italy—in fact, many paradors in Spain were once monasteries or convents. For information on lodging in Italy contact Italia SIXTINA. For more on lodging in Spain contact the Spanish Tourist Board, *see* Visitor Information.

There is also an accommodations network for teachers called Educators B&B Travel Network that helps find lodging with host teachers worldwide for $32 a night for a membership fee of $36 per year

Another option are campgrounds, especially in southern Europe during the summer. You can bring your own tent or find sites with cabins or RVs for rent, some stocked with utensils and other amenities. The grounds can be extensive, including souvenir shops, food stores, pools, and gyms, and can offer multiple forms of entertainment. The rates are based on the season, the accommodations, and the number of people, but are almost uniformly inexpensive. The best resource for campground information is the European Federation of Campingsite Organization.

When traveling long distances by rail, consider reserving a bunk on a night train, not only to help pass the time more quickly but to save on lodging expenses; it isn't much more than a regular ticket.

▣ European Federation of Campingsite Organization ✉ EFCO Secretariat, 6 Pullman Ct., Great Western Rd., Gloucester, England GL1 3ND ☎ 01452/526911 ⊕ www.campingeurope.com. **Italia SIXTINA** ✉ Siege Social: R.R.B., 15 rue de pas Perdus, B.P. 8338-95804, Cergy Saint Christophe Cedex France ☎ 01/3425-4444 🖷 01/3425-4445 ⊕ www.sixtina.com. **Venuemasters** ✉ The Workstation, Paternoster Row, Sheffield, England S1 2BX ☎ 011/4449-3090 ⊕ www.venuemasters.com.

APARTMENT & VILLA RENTALS

If you want a home base that's roomy enough for a family and comes with cooking facilities, **consider a furnished rental.** These can save you money, especially if you're traveling with a group. Home-exchange directories sometimes list rentals as well as exchanges.

▣ International Agents At Home Abroad ✉ 405 E. 56th St., Suite 6H, New York, NY 10022 ☎ 212/421-9165 🖷 212/752-1591 ⊕ www.athomeabroadinc.com. **Drawbridge to Europe** ✉ 98 Granite St., Ashland, OR 97520 ☎ 541/482-7778 or 888/268-1148 🖷 541/482-7779 ⊕ www.drawbridgetoeurope.com. **Hideaways International** ✉ 767 Islington St., Portsmouth, NH 03802 ☎ 603/430-4433 or 800/843-4433 🖷 603/430-4444 ⊕ www.hideaways.com; membership $129. **Hometours International** ✉ 1108 Scottie La., Knoxville, TN 37919 ☎ 865/690-8484 or 866/367-4668 ⊕ http://thor.he.net/~hometour. **Interhome** ✉ 1990 N.E. 163rd St., Suite 110, North Miami Beach, FL 33162 ☎ 305/940-2299 or 800/882-6864 🖷 305/940-2911 ⊕ www.interhome.us. **Vacation Home Rentals Worldwide** ✉ 235 Kensington Ave., Norwood, NJ 07648 ☎ 201/767-9393 or 800/633-3284 🖷 201/767-5510 ⊕ www.vhrww.com. **Villanet** ✉ 1251 N.W. 116th St., Seattle, WA 98177 ☎ 206/417-3444 or 800/964-1891 🖷 206/417-1832 ⊕ www.rentavilla.com. **Villas and Apartments Abroad** ✉ 370 Lexington Ave., Suite 1401, New York, NY 10017 ☎ 212/897-5045 or 800/433-3020 🖷 212/897-5039 ⊕ www.ideal-villas.com. **Villas International** ✉ 4340 Redwood Hwy., Suite D309, San Rafael, CA 94903 ☎ 415/499-9490 or 800/221-2260 🖷 415/499-9491 ⊕ www.villasintl.com.

HOME EXCHANGES

If you would like to exchange your home for someone else's, **join a home-exchange organization,** which will send you its updated listings of available exchanges for a year and will include your own listing in at least one of them. It's up to you to make specific arrangements. There is also a Web site that hosts a home exchange but is completely free, called Global-Freeloaders; after signing up as a host for a six-month period you are given access to a database with more than 3,000 people in more than 100 countries who will host you for free in turn.

Exchange Clubs Educators B&B Travel Network Box 5279, Eugene, OR 97405 800/956-4822; 0800/895891 from the U.K. 541/686-5818 www.edubabnet.com. **GlobalFreeloaders** www.globalfreeloaders.com. **HomeLink International** Box 47747, Tampa, FL 33647 813/975-9825 or 800/638-3841 813/910-8144 www.homelink.org; $110 yearly for a listing, on-line access, and catalog; $40 without catalog. **Intervac U.S.** 30 Corte San Fernando, Tiburon, CA 94920 800/756-4663 415/435-7440 www.intervacus.com; $105 yearly for a listing, on-line access, and a catalog; $50 without catalog.

HOSTELS

No matter what your age, you can **save on lodging costs by staying at hostels.** In some 4,500 locations in more than 70 countries around the world, Hostelling International (HI), the umbrella group for a number of national youth-hostel associations, offers single-sex, dorm-style beds and, at many hostels, rooms for couples and family accommodations. Membership in any HI national hostel association, open to travelers of all ages, allows you to stay in HI-affiliated hostels at member rates; one-year membership is about $28 for adults (C$35 for a two-year minimum membership in Canada, £13.50 in the U.K., A$52 in Australia, and NZ$40 in New Zealand); hostels charge about $10–$30 per night. Members have priority if the hostel is full; they're also eligible for discounts around the world, even on rail and bus travel in some countries.

Organizations Hostelling International–USA 8401 Colesville Rd., Suite 600, Silver Spring, MD 20910 301/495-1240 301/495-6697 www.hiayh.org. **Hostelling International–Canada** 400–205 Catherine St., Ottawa, Ontario K2P 1C3 613/237-7884 or 800/663-5777 613/237-7868 www.hihostels.ca. **YHA England and Wales** Trevelyan House, Dimple Rd., Matlock, Derbyshire DE4 3YH, U.K. 0870/870-8808 0870/770-6127 www.yha.org.uk. **YHA Australia** 422 Kent St., Sydney, NSW 2001 02/9261-1111 02/

9261-1969 www.yha.com.au. **YHA New Zealand** Level 3, 193 Cashel St., Box 436, Christchurch 03/379-9970 or 0800/278-299 03/365-4476 www.yha.org.nz.

HOTELS

All hotels listed have private baths unless otherwise noted.

RESERVING A ROOM

See individual country chapters for details on last-minute reservation services.

Toll-Free Numbers Best Western 800/528-1234 www.bestwestern.com. **Choice** 800/424-6423 www.choicehotels.com. **Clarion** 800/424-6423 www.choicehotels.com. **Comfort Inn** 800/424-6423 www.choicehotels.com. **Days Inn** 800/325-2525 www.daysinn.com. **Forte** 800/225-5843 www.roccofortehotels.com. **Four Seasons** 800/332-3442 www.fourseasons.com. **Hilton** 800/445-8667 www.hilton.com. **Holiday Inn** 800/465-4329 www.sixcontinentshotels.com. **Howard Johnson** 800/446-4656 www.hojo.com. **Hyatt Hotels & Resorts** 800/233-1234 www.hyatt.com. **Inter-Continental** 800/327-0200 www.intercontinental.com. **Marriott** 800/228-9290 www.marriott.com. **Le Meridien** 800/543-4300 www.lemeridien-hotels.com. **Nikko Hotels International** 800/645-5687 www.nikkohotels.com. **Quality Inn** 800/424-6423 www.choicehotels.com. **Radisson** 800/333-3333 www.radisson.com. **Ramada** 800/228-2828; 800/854-7854 international reservations www.ramada.com or www.ramadahotels.com. **Renaissance Hotels & Resorts** 800/468-3571 www.renaissancehotels.com. **Ritz-Carlton** 800/241-3333 www.ritzcarlton.com. **Sheraton** 800/325-3535 www.starwood.com/sheraton. **Westin Hotels & Resorts** 800/228-3000 www.starwood.com/westin.

MONEY MATTERS

Admission prices throughout this guide are included for attractions that charge more than $10 or the equivalent. Prices throughout this guide are given for adults. Substantially reduced fees are almost always available for children, students, and senior citizens. For information on taxes, *see* Taxes.

ATMS

ATMs are ubiquitous throughout Europe; you can draw local currency from an ATM in most airports as soon as you deplane.

CREDIT CARDS

Throughout this guide, the following abbreviations are used: **AE**, American Express; **DC**, Diners Club; **MC**, MasterCard; and **V**, Visa.

CURRENCY

On January 1, 2002, the new single European Union (EU) currency, the (€), finally became the official currency of the 11 countries participating in the European Monetary Union: Austria, Belgium, Finland, France, Germany, Ireland, Italy, Luxembourg, the Netherlands, Portugal, and Spain. Denmark, Great Britain, Greece, and Sweden, although a part of the EU, are not yet part of the monetary union, and therefore will retain the use of their local currencies, though some will accept euros while giving you local currency as change.

The euro makes life for the European traveler much, much easier. Gone are the days when a day trip to Belgium from France meant changing money into yet another currency and paying additional commissions. To make things even easier for travelers from the United States, the euro was created as a direct competitor with the U.S. dollar, which means that their values are quite similar. At press time, one euro was equal to US$1.15; 1.56 Canadian dollars, 1.73 Australian dollars, 1.97 New Zealand dollars, and .70 pounds sterling.

In the euro system there are eight coins: 1 and 2 euros, plus 1, 2, 5, 10, 20, and 50 centimes, or cents, of the euro. All coins have one side that has the value of the euro on it and the other side with one member country's unique national symbol. There are seven colorful notes: 5, 10, 20, 50, 100, 200, and 500 euros. Notes have the principal architectural styles from antiquity onward on one side and the map and the flag of Europe on the other and are the same for all countries.

CURRENCY EXCHANGE

For the most favorable rates, **change money through banks.** Although ATM transaction fees may be higher abroad than at home, ATM rates are excellent because they're based on wholesale rates offered only by major banks. You won't do as well at exchange booths in airports or rail and bus stations, in hotels, in restaurants, or in stores. To avoid lines at airport exchange booths, **get a bit of local currency before you leave home.**

⚡ Exchange Services International Currency Express ✉ 427 N. Camden Dr., Suite F, Beverly Hills, CA 90210 ☎ 888/278-6628 orders 🖷 310/278-6410 🌐 www.foreignmoney.com. **Thomas Cook Currency Services** ☎ 800/287-7362 orders and retail locations 🌐 www.us.thomascook.com.

TRAVELER'S CHECKS

Do you need traveler's checks? It depends on where you're headed. If you're going to rural areas and small towns, go with cash; traveler's checks are best used in cities. Lost or stolen checks can usually be replaced within 24 hours. To ensure a speedy refund, buy your own traveler's checks—don't let someone else pay for them: irregularities like this can cause delays. The person who bought the checks should make the call to request a refund.

PACKING

You should **pack more for the season than for any particular dress code.** In general, northern and central Europe have cold, snowy winters, and the Mediterranean countries have mild winters, though parts of southern Europe can be bitterly cold, too. In the Mediterranean resorts **bring a warm jacket for mornings and evenings,** even in summer. The mountains usually are warm on summer days, but the weather is unpredictable, and the nights are generally cool.

For European cities, **pack as you would for an American city:** formal outfits for first-class restaurants and nightclubs, casual clothes elsewhere. Jeans are perfectly acceptable for sightseeing and informal dining. Sturdy walking shoes are appropriate for the cobblestone streets and gravel paths that fill many of the parks and surround some of the historic buildings. For visits to churches, cathedrals, and mosques, **avoid shorts and revealing outfits.** In Italy, women cover their shoulders and arms (a shawl will do). Women, however, no longer need to cover their heads in Roman Catholic churches. In Greece many monasteries bar women wearing pants; long skirts are often provided at the entrance as a cover-up for both women wearing pants and men dressed in shorts. In Turkey, women must have a head covering; a long-sleeve shirt and a long skirt or slacks are required.

To discourage purse snatchers and pickpockets, **take a handbag with long straps** that you can sling across your body, bandolier-style, and with a zippered compartment for money.

If you stay in budget hotels, **take your own soap.**

In your carry-on luggage, **pack an extra pair of eyeglasses or contact lenses and enough of any medication** you take to last a few days longer than the entire trip. You may also ask your doctor to write a spare prescription using the drug's generic name, as brand names may vary from country to country. In luggage to be checked, **never pack prescription drugs, valuables, or undeveloped film.** And don't forget to carry with you the addresses of offices that handle refunds of lost traveler's checks. Check *Fodor's How to Pack* (available at on-line retailers and bookstores everywhere) for more tips.

To avoid customs and security delays, carry medications in their original packaging. Don't pack any sharp objects in your carry-on luggage, including knives of any size or material, scissors, and corkscrews, or anything else that might arouse suspicion.

To avoid having your checked luggage chosen for hand inspection, don't cram bags full. The U.S. Transportation Security Administration suggests packing shoes on top and placing personal items you don't want touched in clear plastic bags.

CHECKING LUGGAGE

You're allowed to carry aboard one bag and one personal article, such as a purse or a laptop computer. Make sure what you carry on fits under your seat or in the overhead bin. Get to the gate early, so you can board as soon as possible, before the overhead bins fill up.

Baggage allowances vary by carrier, destination, and ticket class. On international flights, you're usually allowed to check two bags weighing up to 70 pounds (32 kilograms) each, although a few airlines allow checked bags of up to 88 pounds (40 kilograms) in first class. Some international carriers don't allow more than 66 pounds (30 kilograms) per bag in business class and 44 pounds (20 kilograms) in economy. On domestic flights, the limit may be 50 pounds (23 kilograms) per bag. Most airlines won't accept bags that weigh more than 100 pounds (45 kilograms) on domestic or international flights. Check baggage restrictions with your carrier before you pack.

Airline liability for baggage is limited to $2,500 per person on flights within the United States. On international flights it amounts to $9.07 per pound or $20 per kilogram for checked baggage (roughly $640 per 70-pound bag) and $400 per passenger for unchecked baggage. You can buy additional coverage at check-in for about $10 per $1,000 of coverage, but it often excludes a rather extensive list of items, shown on your airline ticket.

Before departure, **itemize your bags' contents** and their worth, and label the bags with your name, address, and phone number. (If you use your home address, cover it so potential thieves can't see it readily.) Include a label inside each bag and **pack a copy of your itinerary.** At check-in, **make sure each bag is correctly tagged** with the destination airport's three-letter code. Because some checked bags will be opened for hand inspection, the U.S. Transportation Security Administration recommends that you leave luggage unlocked or use the plastic locks offered at check-in. TSA screeners place an inspection notice inside searched bags, which are resealed with a special lock.

If your bag has been searched and contents are missing or damaged, file a claim with the TSA Consumer Response Center as soon as possible. If your bags arrive damaged or fail to arrive at all, file a written report with the airline before leaving the airport.

📱 Complaints **U.S. Transportation Security Administration Consumer Response Center** ☎ 866/289–9673 ⊕ www.tsa.gov.

PASSPORTS & VISAS

When traveling internationally, **carry your passport** even if you don't need one (it's always the best form of ID), and **make two photocopies of the data page** (one for someone at home and another for you, carried separately from your passport). If you lose your passport, promptly call the nearest embassy or consulate and the local police.

U.S. passport applications for children under age 14 require consent from both parents or legal guardians; both parents must appear together to sign the application. If only one parent appears, he or she must submit a written statement from the other parent authorizing passport issuance for the child. A parent with sole authority must present evidence of it when applying; acceptable documentation includes the child's certified birth certificate listing only the applying parent, a court order specifically permitting this parent's travel with the child, or a death certificate for the nonapplying parent. Application forms and instructions are available on the Web site of the U.S. State Department's Bureau of Consular Affairs (⊕ www.travel.state.gov).

ENTERING EUROPE

Citizens of the United States, Canada, United Kingdom, Ireland, Australia, and New Zealand need passports for travel in Europe. Visas may also be required for visits to or through Turkey, Poland, Estonia, Latvia, Romania, Hungary, and the Czech and Slovak Republics even for short stays or train trips, and in some cases must be obtained before you'll be allowed to enter. Check with the nearest consulate of the country you'll be visiting for visa requirements and any other applicable information.

PASSPORT OFFICES

The best time to apply for a passport or to renew is in fall and winter. Before any trip, check your passport's expiration date, and, if necessary, renew it as soon as possible.

🛂 Australian Citizens **Passports Australia** ☎ 131-232 ⊕ www.passports.gov.au.

🛂 Canadian Citizens **Passport Office** ✉ To mail in applications: 200 Promenade du Portage, Hull, Québec J8X 4B7 ☎ 819/994-3500 or 800/567-6868 ⊕ www.ppt.gc.ca.

🛂 New Zealand Citizens **New Zealand Passports Office** ☎ 0800/22-5050 or 04/474-8100 ⊕ www.passports.govt.nz.

🛂 U.K. Citizens **U.K. Passport Service** ☎ 0870/521-0410 ⊕ www.passport.gov.uk.

🛂 U.S. Citizens **National Passport Information Center** ☎ 900/225-5674; 900/225-7778 TTY (calls are 55¢ per minute for automated service or $1.50 per minute for operator service); 888/362-8668; 888/498-3648 TTY (calls are $5.50 each) ⊕ www.travel.state.gov.

SAFETY

Europe, and Great Britain in particular, has been plagued in recent years by what has now become an agricultural crisis. The first cases of bovine spongiform encephalopathy (BSE), commonly known as "mad cow disease," surfaced in Great Britain in the mid-1980s. BSE is a fatal degenerative disease contracted by cattle. When contaminated beef is eaten by humans, it can result in Creutzfeldt-Jakob Disease (CJD), an extremely rare brainwasting illness fatal to humans.

Europe reacted swiftly to the threat, placing a ban on all beef exported from Great Britain for a short period and immediately banning all use of feed prepared with animal by-products. People are still wary, but at press time the risk of contracting the disease was considered extremely remote. The Centers for Disease Control and Prevention (⊕ www.cdc.gov) reported "The current risk for infection with the BSE agent among travelers to Europe is extremely small, if it exists at all." But, as always, stay informed.

In summer 2001, Great Britain, and to a much lesser extent France and the Netherlands, was affected by yet another crisis, foot-and-mouth disease. Foot-and-mouth disease affects animals almost exclusively; human cases are extremely rare, and the United Kingdom Ministry of Agriculture, Fisheries, and Food considers it harmless to humans. Nevertheless, it had a catastrophic effect on the British economy due to the fact that all animals suspected of being infected must be slaughtered immediately.

To limit the spread of foot-and-mouth disease, some hiking routes and coastal footpaths were closed, especially in north and southwestern England, and certain festivities were canceled. Some rural tourist attractions were also closed due to the crisis, though many have since reopened. Expect stringent border controls, with an enforced ban on carrying English dairy and farm products out of the territory, and you might have to disinfect your luggage and shoes before leaving the country. The British Tourist Authority Web site (⊕ www.travelbritain.org) will have the latest information on any safety issues, so check before you go.

WOMEN IN EUROPE

If you carry a purse, choose one with a zipper and a thick strap that you can drape across your body; adjust the length so that the purse sits in front of you at or above hip level. (Don't wear a money belt or a waist pack.) Store only enough money in the purse to cover casual spending. Distribute the rest of your cash and any valuables between deep front pockets, inside jacket or vest pockets, and a concealed money pouch.

SENIOR-CITIZEN TRAVEL

Radisson SAS Hotels in Europe offer discounts of 25% or more to senior citizens, subject to availability. You need a confirmed reservation.

To qualify for age-related discounts, **mention your senior-citizen status up front** when booking hotel reservations (not when checking out) and before you're seated in restaurants (not when paying the bill). Be sure to have identification on hand. When renting a car, ask about promotional car-rental discounts, which can be cheaper than senior-citizen rates. Train and bus passes are sometimes discounted for senior citizens as well.

Educational Programs Elderhostel ⊠ 11 Ave. de Lafayette, Boston, MA 02111-1746 ☎ 877/426-8056; 978/323-4141 international callers; 877/426-2167 TTY 🖷 877/426-2166 ⊕ www.elderhostel.org. **Interhostel** ⊠ University of New Hampshire, 6 Garrison Ave., Durham, NH 03824 ☎ 603/862-1147 or 800/733-9753 🖷 603/862-1113 ⊕ www.learn.unh.edu.

STUDENTS IN EUROPE

Students in Europe are entitled to a wide range of discounts on admission and transportation. An **International Student Identity Card,** issued by Council Travel (⇨ IDs & Services), will help you to procure these discounts. The globally recognized ISIC card is issued by local student travel organizations that are members of the International Student Travel Confederation, best found by consulting their Web site (⊕ www.istc.org).

Many U.S. colleges and universities have study-abroad programs or can connect you with one, and numerous institutions of higher learning in Europe accept foreign students for a semester or year's study. Check with your college administration or contact the CIEE for contacts and brochures.

If you're between 18 and 26, the Ibis hotel chain will let you have a room for $50 or less, provided you show up after 9 PM and they have a room free. You'll be asked for

your student ID. Your chances are best on weekends. There are more than 400 Ibis hotels in Europe, most of them in France.

IDs & Services STA Travel ⊠ 10 Downing St., New York, NY 10014 ☎ 212/627-3111 or 800/777-0112 🖷 212/627-3387 ⊕ www.sta.com. **Travel Cuts** ⊠ 187 College St., Toronto, Ontario M5T 1P7, Canada ☎ 416/979-2406; 800/592-2887; 866/246-9762 in Canada 🖷 416/979-8167 ⊕ www.travelcuts.com.

TAXES

VALUE-ADDED TAX

Information about national tax-refund programs is given in the A to Z section at the beginning of each country chapter. When making a purchase, **ask for a V.A.T. refund form** and find out whether the merchant gives refunds—not all stores do, nor are they required to. Have the form stamped like any customs form by customs officials when you leave the country or, if you're visiting several European Union countries, when you leave the EU. Be ready to show customs officials what you've bought (pack purchases together, in your carry-on luggage); budget extra time for this. After you're through passport control, take the form to a refund-service counter for an on-the-spot refund, or mail it back to the store or a refund service after you arrive home.

A refund service can save you some hassle, for a fee. Global Refund is a Europe-wide service with 190,000 affiliated stores and more than 700 refund counters—located at every major airport and border crossing. Its refund form is called a Tax Free Check. The service issues refunds in the form of cash, check, or credit-card adjustment, minus a processing fee. If you don't have time to wait at the refund counter, you can mail in the form instead.

V.A.T. Refunds Global Refund ⊠ 99 Main St., Suite 307, Nyack, NY 10960 ☎ 800/566-9828 🖷 845/348-1549 ⊕ www.globalrefund.com.

TELEPHONES

Telephone systems in Europe are in flux; expect new area codes and extra digits in numbers. Keep in mind that some countries now rely on phone cards; it's a good idea to buy one. Country codes appear in the A to Z section at the beginning of each country chapter. Cellular telephone companies unfortunately opted for different standards in the United States and Europe, so only the most sophisticated models with dual or triple band possibilities will function on both sides of the Atlantic. Functionality of both cell phones and pagers will also depend on the kind of subscription you have with your cell-phone company.

LONG-DISTANCE SERVICES

AT&T, MCI, and Sprint access codes make calling long distance relatively convenient, but you may find the local access number blocked in many hotel rooms. First ask the hotel operator to connect you. If the hotel operator balks, ask for an international operator, or dial the international operator yourself. One way to improve your odds of getting connected to your long-distance carrier is to travel with more than one company's calling card (a hotel may block Sprint, for example, but not MCI). If all else fails, call from a pay phone.

TIME

Most of continental Europe ticks at Central European Time (CET), one hour ahead of Greenwich Mean Time (GMT), which prevails in Great Britain, Ireland, Iceland, Portugal, and Madeira. Eastern European countries, including the Baltic States (Estonia, Latvia, and Lithuania), Romania, Bulgaria, Greece, and Turkey are two hours ahead of GMT. In most of mainland Europe clocks are turned back one hour during the night of the last Saturday/Sunday in March and put forward one hour on the last Saturday/Sunday night in October.

Europe uses the 24-hour (or "military") clock for everything from airplane departures to opening arias. After noon continue counting forward: 13:00 is 1 PM, 14:00 is 2 PM, etc.

TOURS & PACKAGES

Because everything is prearranged on a prepackaged tour or independent vacation, you spend less time planning—and often get it all at a good price.

BOOKING WITH AN AGENT

Travel agents are excellent resources. But it's a good idea to collect brochures from several agencies, as some agents' suggestions may be influenced by relationships with tour and package firms that reward them for volume sales. If you have a special interest, **find an agent with expertise in that area**; the American Society of Travel Agents (ASTA; ⇨ Travel Agencies) has a database of specialists worldwide.

Make sure your travel agent knows the accommodations and other services of the place being recommended. Ask about the hotel's location, room size, beds, and whether it has a pool, room service, or programs for children, if you care about these. Has your agent been there in person or sent others whom you can contact?

Do some homework on your own, too: local tourism boards can provide information about lesser-known and small-niche operators, some of which may sell only direct.

BUYER BEWARE

Each year consumers are stranded or lose their money when tour operators—even large ones with excellent reputations—go out of business. So **check out the operator**. Ask several travel agents about its reputation, and try to **book with a company that has a consumer-protection program**. (Look for information in the company's brochure.) In the United States, members of the National Tour Association and the United States Tour Operators Association are required to set aside funds to cover payments and travel arrangements in the event that the company defaults. It's also a good idea to choose a company that participates in the American Society of Travel Agents' Tour Operator Program; ASTA will act as mediator in any disputes between you and your tour operator.

Remember that the more your package or tour includes, the better you can predict the ultimate cost of your vacation. Make sure you know exactly what is covered, and **beware of hidden costs**. Are taxes, tips, and transfers included? Entertainment and excursions? These can add up.

⚑ Tour-Operator Recommendations **American Society of Travel Agents** (⇨ Travel Agencies). **National Tour Association (NTA)** ✉ 546 E. Main St., Lexington, KY 40508 ☎ 859/226-4444 or 800/682-8886 🖷 859/226-4404 ⊕ www.ntaonline.com. **United States Tour Operators Association** (USTOA) ✉ 275 Madison Ave., Suite 2014, New York, NY 10016 ☎ 212/599-6599 or 800/468-7862 🖷 212/599-6744 ⊕ www.ustoa.com.

TRAIN TRAVEL

Some national high-speed train systems have begun to link up to form the nucleus of a pan-European system. On a long journey, you still have to change trains a couple of times, for the national railways are jealously guarding their prerogatives. Deregulation, so far achieved only in Britain and the Netherlands, is vigorously pushed by the European Commission. French TGV (Trains à Grande Vitesse), which serve most major cities in France, have been extended to Geneva, Lausanne, Bern, Zürich, Turin, and Milan. They connect with the latest generation of Italy's tilting Pendolino trains, also called Eurostar Italia. Italy's service extends beyond the country's borders with a service from Turin to Lyon and, in a joint venture with the Swiss Railways, from Milan to Geneva and Zürich. Express Thalys trains operate from Brussels to Paris on high-speed tracks and from Brussels to Amsterdam and Cologne on conventional track. Germany's equally fast ICE trains connect Hamburg and points in between with Basel, and Mannheim with Munich.

High-speed trains travel at speeds of up to 190 mph on dedicated track and more than 150 mph on old track, covering the distance from Paris to Marseille in just over four hours, Hamburg to Munich in less than six. They have made both expensive sleeper compartments and budget *couchettes* (seats that convert into bunks) all but obsolete. Their other attraction is the comfort of a super-smooth ride. The flip side is the reservations requirement; rather than just hopping on the next train, you need to **reserve in advance or allow enough time to make a reservation at the station.**

The **Orient Express,** a glamorous re-creation of a sumptuous past, takes two days to cover the distance from London to Venice, and if you want to know the price, you can't afford it. The Swiss Railways operate special services that allow you to enjoy superb scenery and railway buffs to admire the equally superb railroad technology. The **Panoramic Express** takes 3 hours to travel from Montreux via Gstaad to Interlaken; the **Glacier Express** (7½ hours) runs from Zermatt to St. Moritz and also offers en route gourmet dining as befits these famous resorts; and the **Bernina Express,** the most spectacular, runs from Chur over the 7,400-foot Bernina Pass (where you can turn around; each leg takes 2½ hours), or you can continue to Tirano in Italy (four hours, with connections to Lugano and Milan). Holders of a Swisspass can travel on all three, but reservations are needed. For additional information on rail services and special fares, contact the national tourist office of the country (⇨ Visitor Information).

CLASSES

Virtually all European systems, including the high-speed ones, operate a two-class system. First class costs substantially more and is usually a luxury rather than a necessity. Some of the poorer European countries retain a third class, but avoid it unless you're an adventure-minded budget traveler.

CUTTING COSTS

To save money, **look into rail passes.** But be aware that if you don't plan to cover many miles you may come out ahead by buying individual tickets.

Before you invest in a discount pass, compare the cost against the point-to-point fares on your actual itinerary. EurailPasses provide unlimited first-class rail travel for the duration of the pass in 17 European countries: Austria, Belgium, Denmark, Finland, France, Germany, Greece, Hungary, the Irish Republic, Italy, Luxembourg, the Netherlands, Norway, Portugal, Spain, Sweden, and Switzerland (but not the United Kingdom). If you plan to rack up miles, get a standard pass. These are available for 15 days ($588, £380), 21 days ($762, £492), one month ($946, £610), two months ($1,338, £863), and three months ($1,654, £1,067). Note that you will have to pay a supplement for certain high-speed trains—half the fare on Eurostar.

In addition to standard EurailPasses, check out special rail-pass plans. Among these are the Eurail Youthpass (in second class for those under 26, from $414 [£267] to $1,160 [£748]), the Eurail Saverpass (which gives a discount for two to five people traveling together; a minimum of two people; from $498 [£321] to $1,408 [£908] per person), and the Eurail Flexipass (which allows 10 or 15 travel days within a two-month period, $694 [£448] and $914 [£590], respectively). This is also available at a youth rate. If you're going to travel in just one part of Europe, look into a regional pass, such as the East Europe Pass.

If your plans call for only limited train travel, consider Eurail Selectpass, which costs less money than a EurailPass and is available in first class only. It has a number of conditions. You can travel through three, four, or five countries, depending on the pass, but they must all be adjoining. You also get from 5 to 15 travel days during a two-month time period, which can be used consecutively or nonconsecutively. The other side of the coin is that a Europass costs a couple of hundred dollars less than the least expensive EurailPass. A Eurail Selectpass ranges in price from $356 (£230) to $794 (£512), a Eurail Selectpass Youth from $379 (£245) to $437 (£282). Also, if you are traveling with a total of two or more people you can buy the Eurail Select Saver pass, which ranges from $460 (£297) to $530 (£342).

It used to be the rule that non-Europeans had to **purchase Eurail passes before leaving** for Europe. This remains the recommended option, but you can now buy a pass in person within six months of your arrival in Europe from Rail Europe (⇨ Train Information) in London. Also remember that you need to **book seats ahead even if you are using a rail pass**; seat reservations are required on the cross-channel Eurostar service and European high-speed trains, and are a good idea on other trains that may be crowded—particularly around Easter and at the beginning and end of European vacation periods. You will also need to purchase sleeper or couchette (sleeping berth) reservations separately.

European nationals and others who have resided in Europe for at least six months qualify for the **InterRail Pass**. It used to be exclusively for young people but can now also be purchased, at a premium, by older travelers. This entitles you to unlimited second-class travel within up to eight zones you have preselected. One zone for 22 days, for instance, costs £149 for travelers under 26 (£219 for over 26); all zones for one month, £265 (£319). InterRail Passes can be bought only in Europe at main railway stations, or in the United Kingdom from Rail Europe in London (⇨ Train Information).

FROM THE U.K.

Sleek, high-speed Eurostar trains use the Channel Tunnel to link London (Waterloo) with Paris (Gare du Nord) in three hours and with Brussels (Gare du Midi) in 2 hours, 40 minutes. When the British build their high-speed rail link to London (St. Pancras), another half hour will be shaved off travel time. There are a minimum of 14 daily services to Paris and 10 to Brussels.

Many of the trains stop at Ashford (Kent), and all at the Lille-Europe station in northern France, where you can change to French TGV trains to Brittany, southwest France, Lyon, the Alps, and the Riviera, eliminating the need to transfer between stations in Paris.

Passengers headed for Germany and the Netherlands can buy through tickets via Brussels to Cologne (5½ hours) and Amsterdam (5 hours, 45 minutes). Eurostar does not accept EurailPasses but allows discounts of 40%–50% to passholders. Check for special prices and deals before you book. Or, if money is no object, you can choose the Premium First Class (to Paris only), complete with limo delivery and pick-up at the stations, improved catering, and greater comfort.

Conventional boat trains from London are timed to dovetail with ferry departures at Channel ports. The ferries connect with onward trains at the main French, Belgian, Dutch, and Irish ports. Be sure to ask when making your reservation which London railway station to use.

INDIVIDUAL COUNTRY PASSES

Single-country passes are issued by most national railways, and the majority are sold by Rail Europe (⇨ Train Information *and* individual country chapters). Almost all countries have national passes or passes that include a couple of other countries; the France N'Italy pass, for example, can save you money if you plan to travel by rail often. Also ask about discount passes before buying your tickets, as many countries have weekend rates, and some offer lower rates if you're traveling in groups.

FARES & SCHEDULES

A good rail timetable is indispensable if you're doing extensive rail traveling. The Thomas Cook Timetables are updated monthly. There's also an annual summer edition (limited to Britain, France, and the Benelux).

Train Information CIT Tours Corp. ✉ 15 W. 44th St., 10th fl., New York, NY 10036 ☎ 800/248-7245 for rail; 800/248-8687 for tours and hotels ✐ rail@cit-rail.com for rail; tour@cittours.com for tours and hotels, ⊕ www.cit-tours.com. **DER Travel Services** (⇨ Discount Passes, Eurolines, *in* Bus Travel). **Eurostar** ☎ 800/356-6711; 202/659-2973 in U.S.; 0345/303030 in U.K.; 0123/361-7575 to the U.K. from other countries ⊕ www.eurostar.com. **Rail Europe** ✉ 226-230 Westchester Ave., White Plains, NY 10604 ☎ 877/257-2887 ⊟ 800/432-1329 ✐ info@raileurope.com ⊕ www.raileurope.com ✉ 2087 Dundas E, Suite 105, Mississauga, Ontario L4X 1M2 Canada ☎ 800/361-7245 ✉ 179 Piccadilly, and Victoria Station, London W1V 8BA U.K. ☎ 0990/848-848 in U.K.; 020/7647-4900 to the U.K. from other countries. **Venice Simplon-Orient Express** ✉ Sea Containers House, 20 Upper Ground, London SE1 9PF ☎ 800/524-2420 in U.S.; 020/7805-5100 in U.K.; 0870/161-5060 brochures ⊕ www.orient-express.com.

TRAVEL AGENCIES

A good travel agent puts your needs first. Look for an agency that has been in business at least five years, emphasizes customer service, and has someone on staff who specializes in your destination. In addition, **make sure the agency belongs to a professional trade organization.** The American Society of Travel Agents (ASTA)—the largest and most influential in the field with more than 20,000 members in some 140 countries—maintains and enforces a strict code of ethics and will step in to help mediate any agent-client disputes involving ASTA members if necessary. ASTA (whose motto is "Without a travel agent, you're on your own") also maintains a Web site that includes a directory of agents. (If a travel agency is also acting as your tour operator, *see* Buyer Beware *in* Tours & Packages.)

Local Agent Referrals American Society of Travel Agents (ASTA) ✉ 1101 King St., Suite 200, Alexandria, VA 22314 ☎ 703/739-2782; 800/965-2782 24-hr hot line ⊟ 703/739-3268 ⊕ www. astanet.com. **Association of British Travel Agents** ✉ 68-71 Newman St., London W1T 3AH ☎ 020/ 7637-2444 ⊟ 020/7637-0713 ⊕ www.abtanet.com. **Association of Canadian Travel Agents** ✉ 130 Albert St., Suite 1705, Ottawa, Ontario K1P 5G4 ☎ 613/ 237-3657 ⊟ 613/237-7052 ⊕ www.acta.ca. **Australian Federation of Travel Agents** ✉ Level 3, 309 Pitt St., Sydney, NSW 2000 ☎ 02/9264-3299 ⊟ 02/ 9264-1085 ⊕ www.afta.com.au. **Travel Agents' As-**sociation of New Zealand ✉ Level 5, Tourism and Travel House, 79 Boulcott St., Box 1888, Wellington 6001 ☎ 04/499-0104 ⊟ 04/499-0786 ⊕ www. taanz.org.nz.

VISITOR INFORMATION

Learn more about foreign destinations by checking government-issued travel advisories and country information. For a broader picture, consider information from more than one country.

Austrian National Tourist Office U.S. ✉ 500 5th Ave., #800, New York, NY 10110 ☎ 212/944-6880 ⊟ 212/730-4568 ⊕ www.austria-tourism.at. **Canada** ✉ 2 Bloor St. E, Suite 3330, Toronto, Ontario M4W 1A8 ☎ 416/967-3381 ⊟ 416/967-4101. **U.K.** ✉ 14 Cork St., London, W1X 1PF ☎ 020/ 7629-0461 ⊟ 020/7499-6038. **Australia and New Zealand** ✉ 36 Carrington St., 1st fl., Sydney, NSW 2000 ☎ 02/9299-3621 ⊟ 02/9299-3808. **Ireland** ✉ Merrion Center, Nutley La., Dublin 4 ☎ 01/283-0488 ⊟ 01/283-0531.

Belgian National Tourist Office U.S. ✉ 780 3rd Ave., Suite 1501, New York, NY 10017 ☎ 212/758-8130 ⊟ 212/355-7675 ⊕ www.visitbelgium.com. **Canada** ✐ Box 760, Station NDG, Montréal, Québec H4A 3S2 ☎ 514/484-3594 ⊟ 514/489-8965. **U.K.** ✉ 29 Princess St., London W1R 7RG ☎ 0891/ 887799 ⊟ 0171/629-0454.

British Tourist Authority U.S. ✉ 551 5th Ave., Suite 701, New York, NY 10176 ☎ 212/986-2200 or 800/462-2748 ⊟ 212/986-1188; 818/441-8265 24-hour fax information line ⊕ www.visitbritain.com ✉ walk-in service only, 625 N. Michigan Ave., Suite 1510, Chicago, IL 60611. **Canada** ✉ 5915 Airport Rd., Suite 120, Mississauga, Ontario L4V 1T1 ☎ 905/405-1720 or 888/847-4885 ⊟ 905/405-1835. **U.K.** ✉ Britain Visitors Centre, 1 Regent St., London SW1Y 4XT ☎ 020/7808-3864; 0891/600-109 for 24-hour brochure line, costs 60p per minute ✉ Thames Tower, Black's Rd., London, W6 9EL ☎ No phone. **Australia** ✉ Level 16, Gateway, 1 Macquarie Pl., Sydney, NSW 2000 ☎ 02/9377-4400 ⊟ 02/9377-4499. **New Zealand** ✉ Level 17, NZI House, 151 Queen St., Auckland 1 ☎ 09/303-1446 ⊟ 09/377-6965. **Ireland** ✉ 18-19 College Green, Dublin 2 ☎ 01/670-8000 ⊟ 01/670-8244.

Bulgaria U.S. and Canada Balkan Tourist USA, authorized agent, ✉ 20 E. 46th St., Suite 1003, New York, NY 10017 ☎ 212/338-6838 or 800/822-1106 ⊟ 212/822-5910. **U.K.** Balkan Tourist U.K., ✉ 111 Bartholomew Rd., London NW2 BJ ☎ 0500/245165 for 24-hour brochure line ✉ Balkan Holidays, 19 Conduit St., Sofia House, London W1S 2BH ☎ 020/ 7491-4499 ⊟ 020/7543-5577.

Cyprus Tourist Office U.S. and Canada ✉ 13 E. 40th St., New York, NY 10016 ☎ 212/683-5280 ⊟ 212/683-5282 ⊕ www.cyprustourism.org. **U.K.**

✉ 17 Hanover St., London W1R 0H8 ☎ 020/
7569-8800 🖷 020/7499-4935 ✉ Turkish Republic
of Northern Cyprus Tourist Office, 29 Bedford Sq.,
London WC1B 3EG ☎ 020/7631-1920 🖷 020/
7631-1948.

🇫 Czech Center **U.S. and Canada** ✉ 1109 Madison
Ave., New York, NY 10028 ☎ 212/288-0830 🖷 212/
288-0971 ⊕ www.czechcenter.com. **Canada** Czech
Tourist Authority, ✉ c/o Czech Airlines, 401 Bay St.,
Suite 1510, Toronto, Ontario M5H 2Y4 ☎ 416/363-
9928 🖷 416/363-0239. **U.K.** ✉ 26-30 Kensington
Palace Gardens, London W8 4QY ☎ 020/7243-1115
🖷 020/7727-9654 ✉ Czech and Slovak Tourist
Centre, 16 Frognal Parade, Finchley Rd., London
NW3 5HG ☎ 020/7794-3263 🖷 020/7794-3265.

🇫 Danish Tourist Board **U.S. and Canada** ✉ 655
3rd Ave., 18th fl., New York, NY 10017 ☎ 212/885-
9700 🖷 212/885-9726 ⊕ www.dt.dk. **U.K.** ✉ 55
Sloane St., London SW1X 9SY ☎ 020/7259-5959;
0900/160-0109 for 24-hour brochure line, costs 60p
per minute 🖷 020/7259-5955.

🇫 Estonian Tourist Office **U.S.** Consulate, ✉ 600
3rd Ave., 26th fl., New York, NY 10016 ☎ 212/883-
0636 🖷 212/883-0648 ⊕ www.tourism.ee. **Canada**
Consulate, ✉ 958 Broadview Ave., Suite 202,
Toronto, Ontario M4K 2R6 ☎ 416/461-0764 🖷 416/
461-0353. **U.K.** Embassy, ✉ 16 Hyde Park Gate, London, SW7 5DG ☎ 020/7589-3428 🖷 020/
7589-3430. **Australia** Consulate, ✉ 86 Louisa Rd.,
Birchgrove, NSW 2041 ☎ 02/9810-7468 🖷 02/
9818-1779.

🇫 Finnish Tourist Board **U.S. and Canada** ✉ 655
3rd Ave., 18th fl., New York, NY 10017 ☎ 212/885-
9700 🖷 212/885-9710 ⊕ www.mek.fi. **U.K.** ✉ 66
Haymarket, London SW1Y 4RF ☎ 020/7930-5871
🖷 020/7321-0696. **Australia** ✉ c/o Finnesse Communications, Level 4, 81 York St., Sydney, NSW 2000
☎ 02/9290-1980 🖷 02/9290-1981.

🇫 French Government Tourist Office **U.S.** ✉ 444
Madison Ave., 16th fl., New York, NY 10022 ☎ 212/
838-7800 🖷 212/838-7855 ⊕ www.francetourism.
com ✉ 676 N. Michigan Ave., Suite 3360 Chicago,
IL 60611 ☎ 312/751-7800 ✉ 9454 Wilshire Blvd.,
Suite 715, Beverly Hills, CA 90212 ☎ 310/271-6665
🖷 310/276-2835. **Canada** ✉ 1981 Ave. McGill College, Suite 490, Montréal, Québec H3A 2W9 ☎ 514/
288-4264 🖷 514/845-4868. **U.K.** ✉ 178 Piccadilly,
London W1J 9AL ☎ 068/244123, 60p per minute
🖷 020/7493-6594. **Australia** ✉ 10 Suffolk St., Sydney, NSW 2000 ☎ 02/9231-5244 🖷 02/9221-8682.
Ireland ✉ 10 Suffolk St., Dublin 1 ☎ 01/679-0813
🖷 01/874-7324.

🇫 German National Tourist Office **U.S.** ✉ 122 E.
42nd St., 52nd fl., New York, NY 10168 ☎ 212/661-
7200 🖷 212/661-7174 ⊕ www.deutschland-
tourismus.de ✉ Box 59594, Chicago, IL 60659
☎ 773/539-6303 🖷 773/539-6378. **Canada** ✉ Box
65162, Toronto, Ontario M4K 3Z2 ☎ 416/968-1570
🖷 416/968-1986. **U.K.** ☏ Box 2695, London W1A

3TN ☎ 020/7317-0908; 0891/600-100 for brochures,
50p per minute 🖷 020/7495-6129. **Australia**
☏ GPO Box 1461, Sydney, NSW 2001 ☎ 02/
8296-0488 🖷 02/8296-0487.

🇫 Gibraltar Information Bureau **U.S. and Canada**
✉ 1155 15th St. NW, Washington, DC 20005 ☎ 202/
452-1108 🖷 202/452-1109 ⊕ www.gibraltar.gi. **U.K.**
Gibraltar Tourist Board, ✉ Arundel Great Court, 179
The Strand, London WC2R 1EH ☎ 020/7836-0777
🖷 020/7240-6612.

🇫 Greek National Tourist Organization **U.S.**
✉ 645 5th Ave., New York, NY 10022 ☎ 212/421-
5777 🖷 212/826-6940 ⊕ www.gnto.gr. **Canada**
✉ 91 Scollard St., 2nd fl., Toronto, Ontario M5R IG4
☎ 416/968-2220 🖷 416/968-6533. **U.K.** ✉ 4 Conduit St., London W1R 0DJ ☎ 020/7734-5997 🖷 020/
7287-1369. **Australia** ✉ 51-57 Pitt St., Sydney, NSW
2000 ☎ 02/9241-1663 🖷 02/9235-2174.

🇫 Hungarian National Tourist Office **U.S. and
Canada** ✉ 150 E. 58th St., 33rd fl., New York, NY
10155 ☎ 212/355-0240 🖷 212/207-4103 ⊕ www.
hungarytourism.hu. **U.K.** ✉ Embassy of the Republic of Hungary, Commercial Section, 35B Eaton Pl.,
London SW1X 8BY ☎ 020/7235-2664 🖷 020/
7235-8630.

🇫 Iceland Tourist Board **U.S. and Canada**
✉ Scandinavia Tourism Inc., 655 3rd Ave., New
York, NY 10017 ☎ 212/885-9700 🖷 212/885-9710
⊕ www.goscandinavia.com. **U.K.** ✉ 1 Eaton Terr.,
London SW1W 8EY ☎ 0170/590-1100; 020/
7874-1000 for IcelandAir.

🇫 Irish Tourist Board **U.S.** ✉ 345 Park Ave., New
York, NY 10154 ☎ 212/418-0800 or 800/223-6470
🖷 212/371-9052 ⊕ www.ireland.travel.ie. **Canada**
✉ 2 Bloor St. E, Suite 1501, Toronto, Ontario M4W
3E2 ☎ 800/223-6470. **U.K.** ✉ Ireland Desk, British
Visitor Centre 1 Regent St., London SW1Y 4XT
☎ 020/7493-3201 🖷 020/7493-9065. **Australia**
✉ 36 Carrington St., 5th fl., Sydney, NSW 2000
☎ 02/9299-6177 🖷 02/9299-6323. **Ireland**
✉ Bishops Square, Redmonds Hill, Dublin 2 ☎ 01/
476-3400.

🇫 Italian Government Travel Office (ENIT) **U.S.**
✉ 630 5th Ave., Suite 1565, New York, NY 10111
☎ 212/245-4822 🖷 212/586-9249 ⊕ www.
italiantourism.com ✉ 500 N. Michigan Ave., Suite
2240, Chicago, IL 60611 ☎ 312/644-0996 🖷 312/
644-3019 ✉ 12400 Wilshire Blvd., Suite 550, Los
Angeles, CA 90025 ☎ 310/820-1898 🖷 310/820-
6357. **Canada** ✉ 175 Bloor St. E, Suite 907 South
Tower, Toronto, Ontario H4W 3R8 ☎ 416/925-4882
🖷 416/925-4799. **U.K.** ✉ Italian State Tourist
Board, 1 Princess St., London W1B 2AY ☎ 020/
7399-3562. **Australia** ✉ c/o Italian Chamber of
Commerce, Level 26, 44 Market St., Sydney, NSW
2000 ☎ 02/9262-1666 🖷 02/9262-1677.

🇫 Lithuanian Tourist Board **U.S.** Lithuanian
Tourist Information Center, ✉ 40-24 235th St., Dou-
glaston, NY 11363 ☎ 718/423-6161 🖷 718/423-3979

🌐 www.tourism.lt. **Canada** Embassy, ✉ 130 Albert St., Suite 204, Ottawa, Ontario K1P 5G4 ☎ 613/567-5458 📠 613/567-5315. **U.K.** Embassy, ✉ 84 Gloucester Pl., London W1U 6AU ☎ 020/7486-6401 📠 020/7468-6403.

🏛 Luxembourg National Tourist Office **U.S. and Canada** ✉ 17 Beekman Pl., New York, NY 10022 ☎ 212/935-8888 📠 212/935-5896 🌐 www.ont.lu. **U.K.** ✉ 122 Regent St., London W1B 5SA ☎ 020/7434-2800 📠 020/7734-1205.

🏛 Monaco Government Tourist Office & Convention Bureau **U.S. and Canada** ✉ 565 5th Ave., New York, NY 10017 ☎ 212/286-3330 📠 212/286-9890 🌐 www.monaco-tourism.com. **U.K.** ✉ The Chambers, Chelsea Harbour, London SW10 0XF ☎ 020/7352-9962 or 0500/006-114 📠 020/7352-2103.

🏛 Netherlands Board of Tourism **U.S.** ✉ 225 N. Michigan Ave., Suite 1854, Chicago, IL 60601 ☎ 312/819-1500 or 888/464-6552 📠 312/819-1740 🌐 www.holland.com. **Canada** ✉ Adelaide St. E, Box 1078, Toronto, Ontario M5C 2K5 ☎ 888/464-6552 in English; 888/729-7227 in French 📠 416/363-1470. **U.K.** ✉ Box 523, London SW1E 6NT ☎ 020/7539-7950; 0906/871-7777 for 24-hour brochure line, costs 60p per minute 📠 020/7828-7941.

🏛 Norwegian Tourist Board **U.S. and Canada** ✉ 655 3rd Ave., Suite 1810, New York, NY 10017 ☎ 212/885-9700 📠 212/885-9710 🌐 www.goscandinavia.com. **U.K.** ✉ Charles House, 5 Lower Regent St., London SW1Y 4LR ☎ 020/7839-6255 📠 020/7839-6014.

🏛 Polish National Tourist Office **U.S. and Canada** ✉ 275 Madison Ave., Suite 1711, New York, NY 10016 ☎ 212/338-9412 📠 212/338-9283 🌐 www.polandtour.org. **U.K.** ✉ Remo House, 1st fl., 310-312 Regent St., London W1R 5AJ ☎ 020/7580-8811 📠 020/7580-8866.

🏛 Portuguese National Tourist Office **U.S.** ✉ 590 5th Ave., 3rd fl., New York, NY 10036 ☎ 212/354-4610 📠 212/575-4737 🌐 www.portugal.org. **Canada** ✉ 60 Bloor St. W, Suite 1005, Toronto, Ontario M4W 3B8 ☎ 416/921-7376 📠 416/921-1353. **Ireland** ✉ 54 Dawson St., Dublin 2 ☎ 01/670-9133 📠 01/670-9141. **U.K.** ✉ 2nd fl., 22-25A Sackville St., London W1S 3LY ☎ 020/7494-5720; 0900/160-0370 24-hour brochure line, costs 65p per minute 📠 020/7494-1868.

🏛 Romanian National Tourist Office **U.S. and Canada** ✉ 14 E. 38th St., 12th fl., New York, NY 10016 ☎ 212/545-8484 📠 212/251-0429. **U.K.** ✉ 22 New Cavendish St., London W1M 74T ☎ 020/7224-3692 📠 020/7935-6435.

🏛 Slovak Tourist Office **U.S. and Canada** Embassy, ✉ 3523 International Ct., NW, Washington, DC 20008 ☎ 202/237-1054 📠 202/237-6438 🌐 www.sacr.sk. **U.K.** Czech and Slovak Tourist Center, ✉ 16 Frognal Parade, Finchley Rd., London NW3 5HG ☎ 020/7794-3263 📠 020/7794-3265.

🏛 Slovenian Tourist Office **U.S.** ✉ 345 E. 12th St., New York, NY 10003 ☎ 212/358-9686 📠 212/358-9025 🌐 www.slovenia-tourism.si. **U.K.** ✉ New Barn Farm, Tadlow, Royston, Herts 5G8 0EP ☎ 0870/225-5305 📠 0176/763-1166.

🏛 Tourist Office of Spain **U.S.** ✉ 666 5th Ave., 35th fl., New York, NY 10103 ☎ 212/265-8822 📠 212/265-8864 🌐 www.okspain.org ✉ 845 N. Michigan Ave., Suite 915 E, Chicago, IL 60611 ☎ 312/642-1992 📠 312/642-9817 ✉ 8383 Wilshire Blvd., Suite 956, Los Angeles, CA 90211 ☎ 323/658-7188 📠 323/658-1061 ✉ 1221 Brickell Ave., Suite 1850, Miami, FL 33131 ☎ 305/358-1992 📠 305/358-8223. **Canada** ✉ 2 Bloor St. W, Suite 3402, Toronto, Ontario M4W 3E2 ☎ 416/961-3131 📠 416/961-1992. **U.K.** ✉ 22-23 Manchester Sq., London W1M 5AP ☎ 020/7486-8077; 0891/669920 24-hour brochure line, costs 60p per minute 📠 020/7486-8034.

🏛 Swedish Travel & Tourism Council **U.S. and Canada** ✉ Box 4649, Grand Central Station, New York, NY 10163-4649 ☎ 212/885-9700 📠 212/885-9764. **U.K.** ✉ 11 Montagu Pl., London W1H 2AL ☎ 0147/657-8811 24-hour brochure line 📠 020/7724-5872.

🏛 Switzerland Tourism **U.S.** ✉ 608 5th Ave., New York, NY 10020 ☎ 877/794-8037 📠 212/262-6116 🌐 www.switzerlandtourism.ch ✉ 501 Santa Monica Blvd., Suite 607, Santa Monica, CA 90401 ☎ 310/260-2421 📠 310/260-2923. **Canada** ✉ 926 The East Mall, Etobicoke (Toronto), Ontario M9B 6KI ☎ International toll-free 800/1002-0030 📠 416/695-2774. **U.K.** ✉ Swiss Centre, 1 New Coventry St., London W1V 8EE ☎ 020/7734-1921 📠 020/7851-1720. **Australia** ✉ Swissair Building, 33 Pitt St., Level 8, Sydney, NSW 2000 ☎ 02/9231-3744 📠 02/9251-6531.

🏛 Turkish Tourist Office **U.S.** ✉ 821 UN Plaza, New York, NY 10017 ☎ 212/687-2194 📠 212/599-7568 🌐 www.turkey.org ✉ 2525 Massachusetts Ave. NW, Washington, DC 20008 ☎ 202/429-9844 📠 202/429-5649. **Canada** ✉ 360 Albert St., Suite 801, Ottawa, Ontario K1R 7X7 ☎ 613/612-6800 📠 613/319-7446. **U.K.** ✉ Egyptian House, 170-173 Piccadilly, London W1V 9DD ☎ 020/7355-4207; 0900/188-7755, 24-hour brochure line, costs 65p per minute 📠 020/7491-0773.

🏛 U.S. Government Advisories **U.S. Department of State** ✉ Public Communication Division, PA/PL Room 2206, U.S. Department of State, 2201 C St. NW, Washington, DC 20520 ☎ 202/647-5225 for interactive hot line 🌐 http://travel.state.gov; enclose a self-addressed, stamped, business-size envelope.

WEB SITES

Do check out the World Wide Web when planning your trip. You'll find everything from weather forecasts to virtual tours of famous cities. Be sure to **visit Fodors.com**

(⊕ www.fodors.com), a complete travel-planning site. You can research prices and book plane tickets, hotel rooms, rental cars, vacation packages, and more. In addition, you can post your pressing questions in the Travel Talk section. Other planning tools include a currency converter and weather reports, and there are loads of links to travel resources.

Also check out the European Travel Commission's site, ⊕ www.visiteurope.com.

WHEN TO GO

For information about travel seasons and for the average daily maximum and minimum temperatures of the major European cities, *see* the A to Z section *in* each country chapter.

🔲 Forecasts **Weather Channel Connection** ☎ 900/932–8437, 95¢ per minute from a Touch-Tone phone ⊕ www.weather.com.

ANDORRA
ANDORRA LA VELLA & BEYOND

1

THE PRINCIPALITY OF ANDORRA has carved itself a niche in the world's imagination as the place to go for hiking, skiing, and trout fishing. This perception may cause some disappointment when you find yourself in a 20-mi traffic jam of bargain hunters on the one road through the country, but don't give up: if you avoid Spanish and French holidays, you will find that Andorra's upper reaches are still pristine.

In 1993, this 464-square-km (278-square-mi) tax haven, commercial oasis, winter-sports station, and mountain hideaway drafted a constitution and held elections, converting one of Europe's last pockets of feudalism into a modern democratic state and member of the United Nations. The bishop of Urgell and the president of France assumed symbolic roles as the co-heads of state of this unique Pyrenean country. Andorra originally fell through the cracks between France and Spain when Charlemagne founded the valley as an independent entity during his 8th-century battles with the Moors. In the 9th century, his heir, Charles the Bald, made the bishop of Urgell overlord of Andorra, a role contested by the French counts of Foix until a treaty providing for joint suzerainty was agreed upon in 1278. During the 16th century, the French monarchy inherited these rights and eventually passed them on to the presidents of France.

This dual protection long allowed Andorra to thrive as a low-tax, duty-free haven. Europe's new semiborderless unity, however, has changed this special status, and Andorra is now in the process of developing an improved tourist industry and a more conventional economy. Andorra is administratively divided into seven parishes—Sant Julià de Lòria, the capital Andorra la Vella, La Massana, Escaldes-Engordany, Encamp, Ordino, and Canillo—and each of these entities has its own tourist office.

Winter sports, mountain climbing and hiking, and the architectural and cultural heritage of its many Romanesque chapels, bridges, and medieval farms and town houses are Andorra's once and future stock in trade, although numbered bank accounts will surely not be disappearing anytime soon.

ANDORRA A TO Z

To research prices, get advice from other travelers, and book travel arrangements, visit www.fodors.com.

AIR TRAVEL
The nearest international airports are at Barcelona (210 km/130 mi) and in France, at Perpignan (128 km/79 mi) and Toulouse-Blagnac (196 km/122 mi).

BUS TRAVEL

Barcelona is connected with Andorra la Vella by Eurolines buses, which leave Barcelona's El Prat Airport's Terminal B (from in front of the Miró mural at the south end of the terminal) at 11 AM, 3 PM, and 8 PM. Buses to El Prat Airport leave Andorra at 9:45, 2, and 7. Buses from Barcelona's Sants Station to Andorra leave at 6:15, 11:30, 3:30, and 8:30. Return buses to Sants Station leave Andorra's Hotel Diplomatic at 9:15 AM, 1:30 PM, 6:30 PM, and 10:30 PM. In summer direct buses run from Perpignan and Toulouse to Andorra. The ride from Barcelona, Perpignan, or Toulouse to Andorra la Vella takes about three hours.

Minibuses connect Andorra's towns and villages, and fares are low; 150 ptas./€0.90 will take you 5 km (3 mi). Details on fares and services are available at hotels and from tourist offices.

BUSINESS HOURS

Banks are open weekdays 9–1 and 3–5, and Saturday 9–noon. They are closed Sunday. Andorra is predominantly Catholic; most chapels and churches are kept locked around the clock, the key being left at the closest house. Check with the local tourist office. Shops are open daily 9–8, though many are closed between 1 and 4.

CAR TRAVEL

The N-20 road from France into Spain via Andorra la Vella is curvy but well maintained, and handles the heaviest traffic. The spur north toward the ski resorts at La Massana and Ordino is also excellent. Once you leave the valley floor, the roads are narrow, winding, and best suited to four-wheel-drive vehicles, especially in snow. In winter, snow tires or chains are essential. Although the Puymorens Tunnel does not surface in Andorra, it does eliminate the switchbacks of the Puymorens mountain pass going through toward Spain from the northern entrance at L'Hospitalet, France. This pass is either dangerous or closed in bad weather.

The fastest, most direct route from Barcelona to Andorra la Vella (with about €30 in tolls) runs through Terrassa, Manresa, the Tunel del Cadí, and the Cerdanya Valley via Bellver de Cerdanya and La Seu d'Urgell. Slightly longer but toll-free is the western approach to La Seu d'Urgell via N-11 to Igualada through Cervera and Oliana on C-1311. The eastern entrance into Andorra through Puigcerdà to Pas de la Casa is often a good way to avoid traffic. Andorra is 625 km (375 mi) from Madrid via Zaragoza, Lleida, and Seu d' Urgell, a six-hour drive. Barcelona to Andorra is 220 km (132 mi), Perpignan to Andorra is 170 km (102 mi), and Toulouse to Andorra is 185 km (111 mi).

CONSULATES

🏴 Canada ✉ Elisenda de Pinós 10 (Pedralbes), Barcelona, Spain ☎ 93/204-2700.

🏴 United Kingdom ✉ Av. Diagonal 477, Barcelona, Spain ☎ 93/366-6200.

🏴 United States ✉ Pg. Reina Elisenda 23 (Pedralbes), Barcelona, Spain ☎ 93/280-2227.

CUSTOMS & DUTIES

Crossing out of Andorra can be a problem. The French customs officers between Pas de la Casa and the Puymorens Tunnel sporadically stage mammoth roadblocks and may search anything. Spanish customs between Andorra la Vella and Seu d'Urgell can also be tricky. The established limits for all varieties of goods are specified in "Franquicias dels Viatgers," a leaflet distributed by the Andorra National Tourist Office in Barcelona or Andorra la Vella. No one seems to mind how often you pass through customs on a given day, however. So one way to score significant savings is to stay in a hotel on the Spanish side and make a half dozen trips back and forth.

EATING & DRINKING

Andorra is not famous for fine dining, but there are good restaurants serving French, Spanish, or Catalan cuisine, and plenty of spots where you can eat hearty Pyrenean fare at no great cost. Local dishes to look for include *escudella* (a hearty mountain stew); *trinchat* (mashed potatoes and cabbage with bacon); *estofat d'isard* (stewed mountain goat); *truite de carreroles* (omelet with wild mushrooms); *truite de ríu* (river trout); local cheeses, such as *formatge de tupí*; and *rostes amb mel* (ham baked with honey). Most restaurants offer both prix-fixe and à la carte menus.

WHAT IT COSTS In Euros			
	$$$$	**$$$**	**$$**	**$**
AT DINNER	over €18	€12–€18	€6–€12	under €6

Prices are for a main course at dinner.

MEALTIMES Andorrans eat late: dinner doesn't usually get under way until 8 or 9, and lunch is a substantial meal served between 1:30 and 4.

RESERVATIONS & DRESS Casual dress is acceptable in all restaurants in Andorra, regardless of price category.

HOLIDAYS

January 1; March 14 (Constitution Day); Easter Monday; April 23 (St. George's Day); May 1 (Labor Day); Pentecost Monday (in May or June); June 24 (St. John's Day); September 8 (La Verge de Meritxell); November 1 (All Saints' Day); December 8 (Immaculate Conception); December 25; December 26 (St. Stephen's Feast).

LANGUAGE

Although less than half of the country's population of nearly 62,400 are native speakers of Catalan, this Romance language, with roots in Provençal, France, is the principality's official language. Spanish, French, and English are also spoken by hotel and commercial personnel.

LODGING

The number of Andorran hotels continues to increase, and standards are also rising. Furnishings are usually functional, but service is friendly and the facilities are excellent. Most hotels are open year-round. Reservations are necessary during July and August. Hotel rates often include at least two meals.

WHAT IT COSTS In Euros			
$$$$	**$$$**	**$$**	**$**
FOR 2 PEOPLE over €150	€90–€150	€60–€90	under €60

Prices are for a standard double room in high season, excluding tax.

MAIL & SHIPPING

There are no postal codes in Andorra, but from Spain be sure to include "Principat d'Andorra" when you address your letter, to distinguish the country from the Spanish town of the same name.
Post Offices **Spanish post office** ⊠ Carrer Joan Maragall 10. **French post office** ⊠ 1 rue Père d'Urg.

POSTAL RATES Postal service within the country is free.

MONEY MATTERS

Prices in Andorra are similar to those in neighboring France and Spain. The best bargains still available are products subject to state tax, such as tobacco, alcohol, perfume, and gasoline. Such staples as butter, cheese, and milk, which are sold as surplus by member countries of the European Union (EU), are also cheaper in Andorra.

Here are some sample prices: soft drink, €1; cup of coffee, €0.75–€0.90; 1½-km (1-mi) taxi ride, €2; ham sandwich, €3.

CURRENCY The main currency in Andorra is the European monetary unit, the euro (€).

SPORTS & THE OUTDOORS

Mountainous Andorra is a playground for hikers and backpackers. The mountains are high and the terrain is wild, so a degree of care and experience is advisable. There are three long-distance trails: the GR7, which runs from the French border near Pas de la Casa to Les Escaldes on the road from Andorra la Vella to Spain; the GR11, also called the Ordino Route, a high-mountain trail that stretches across the central range; and the GR P1, a potentially 5- to 10-day perimeter route running the crests around the Andorran border. There are 26 mountain refuges distributed throughout Andorra, so you can plan day treks and travel light. Some of the best hikes include the Estanys de Tristaina route from Ordino; the Vall de Madriu walk (six hours each way) from Escaldes to Pas de la Casa's upper reaches; the hike to the Cirque de Pessons from Cortals above Encamp; the walk from Sant Julià de Lòria to the Canòlic sanctuary; and the Vall d'Incles walk up to the Estanys (tarns, or Pyrenean glacial ponds) de Juclar. Get details on treks and walks from local tourist offices.

PASSPORTS & VISAS

Non-Europeans need a passport to cross the border; Europeans enter with only an identity card.

SHOPPING

Shopping has traditionally been one of Andorra's main attractions, but be careful: not all the goods displayed are at bargain prices. Good buys are such consumables as gasoline, perfume, butter, cheese, cigarettes, wine, whiskey, and gin. For cameras, tape recorders, and other imported items, compare prices and models carefully. Ask for the *precio último* (final price) and insist politely on *el descuento*, the 10% discount to which you are entitled as a visitor to Andorra.

The main shopping area is **Andorra la Vella.** There are also stores in all the new developments and in the towns close to the frontiers, namely Pas de la Casa and Sant Julià de Lòria. The **Punt de Trobada Center** (✉ Ctra. d'Espanya ☎ 843433), a mall 2 km (1 mi) from the Spanish border, is bright, modern, and immense. **La Casa del Formatge** (✉ Av. Carlemany s/n ☎ 821689) in Les Escaldes has more than 500 different kinds of cheeses from all over the world. (The abbreviation s/n, which means *sin numero,* is used when there is no street number for an address.)

TELEPHONES

COUNTRY & AREA CODES
The country code for Andorra is 376.

INTERNATIONAL CALLS
For assistance, call the local operator at 111. To call Andorra from Spain or France dial 00–376 and the six-digit local number. To dial long distance from Andorra dial 00, the country code of the country you are calling, and the local number.

LOCAL CALLS
For local directory assistance, dial 111. Andorra has no regional area codes. Most pay phones take phone cards issued by the telephone company and available at *tabacs* (stores that sell tobacco and stamps).

TIPPING

Restaurant and café prices always include a 10%–15% service charge; it's customary to leave 5%–10% in addition to the charge, but this is completely optional.

TRAIN TRAVEL

From Barcelona, take the train to Puigcerdà, then the bus to La Seu d'Urgell and Andorra la Vella; from Madrid, take the train to Lleida and then a bus to La Seu d'Urgell and Andorra la Vella. From Toulouse, take the train to Ax-les-Thermes and L'Hospitalet, where the bus to Pas de la Casa and Andorra la Vella meets the morning train. Alternatively, go on to Latour-de-Carol and take the bus from Puigcerdà to La Seu d'Urgell and Andorra la Vella.

TIMING

With reliable snowfall from December to early April, Andorra has excellent ski resorts at Soldeu, Arinsal, Pal, Pas de la Casa–Grau Roig, and Ordino–Arcalis and a cross-country center at La Rabassa. Winter brings a huge influx of ski buffs, but consumers are eager to take advantage of Andorra's tax- and duty-free shopping all year long, making weekends and holidays a traffic nightmare any time of year. In early April, the first flush of spring flowers enlivens the slopes and valleys.

CLIMATE   Keep in mind that even in summer the nighttime temperatures can drop to freezing. The following are the average daily maximum and minimum temperatures for Andorra.

Jan.	43F	6C	May	62F	17C	Sept.	71F	22C
	30	1		43	6		49	10
Feb.	45F	7C	June	73F	23C	Oct.	60F	16C
	30	1		39	4		42	6
Mar.	54F	12C	July	79F	26C	Nov.	51F	10C
	35	2		54	12		35	2
Apr.	58F	14C	Aug.	76F	24C	Dec.	42F	6C
	39	4		53	12		31	1

EXPLORING ANDORRA

Exploring Andorra takes time. The roads are narrow and steep, the views compel frequent stops, and every village has its secret treasures. Do as much sightseeing on foot as time permits. Key sites to visit include Andorra la Vella's Casa de la Vall, Ordino's aristocratic Casa d'Areny Plandolit, Sispony's bourgeois Museu Casa Rull, and Encamp's Cal Cristo, a typical farmer's dwelling. Andorra's Romanesque patrimony, surprisingly abundant, has two bridges and 34 chapels. Natural treasures include Pyrenean ponds and peaks such as the 9,708-foot Pic de Coma Pedrosa.

Andorra la Vella

The capital's pivotal attraction, outside its shops and restaurants, is the **Casa de la Vall** (House of the Valley), overlooking the town's main square. Constructed in 1580, this massive and medieval stone building is the seat of the Andorran government and the repository of notable Gothic frescoes, some of which were carefully moved here from village churches high in the Pyrenees. The kitchen is particularly interesting, with its collection of ancient copper pots and other culinary implements. ⊠ *Carrer de la Vall s/n* ☉ *Mon.–Sat. 9–1 and 3–7, Sun. 10–2.*

★ **$$–$$$** ✕ **Molí dels Fanals.** This quiet restaurant occupies an antique borda with a fireplace and wooden paneling. The Catalan cuisine here uses consistently high-quality ingredients. Try the *magret de canard* (breast of duck) with grapes and port. ⊠ *Carrer Dr. Vilanova 9 (Borda Casadet)* ☎ *821381* ▤ *AE, DC, MC, V* ☉ *Closed Mon. and last 2 wks in Aug. No dinner Sun.*

$$–$$$ ✕ **Versailles.** This tiny and authentic French bistro with only 10 tables is nearly always packed. The cuisine is primarily French with occasional Andorran specialties, such as *escudella barrejada* (a thick vegetable and meat soup) and *civet de jabalí* (stewed wild boar). ⊠ *Cap de Carrer 1* ☎ *821331* ▤ *AE, DC, MC, V.*

$$ ✕ **Borda Estevet.** A *borda* (a typical stone Andorran mountain refuge) with a very Pyrenean feel, this simple spot offers a selection of Spanish and Andorran dishes, beef cooked and served *à la llosa* (on hot slabs of slate), and three private dining rooms in addition to the main dining room. ⊠ *Ctra. Comella 2* ☎ *864026* ▤ *AE, DC, MC, V* ☉ *Closed Sun. in Aug.*

★ **$–$$** ✕▥ **Celler d'En Toni.** This small, rustic restaurant in the center of Andorra la Vella serves some of the best food in the principality, a blend of Mediterranean and Pyrenean cuisines. Known primarily as a restaurant, Celler d'En Toni also rents rooms, which are adequate but not luxurious. The quality of the restaurant more than compensates. ⊠ *Verge del Pilar 4* ☎ *821252* 🖷 *821872* ⇌ *17 rooms* ⚹ *Restaurant* ▤ *AE, DC, MC, V.*

$$$$ ⬚ **Hotel Crowne Plaza.** The Crowne Plaza is the pinnacle of Andorra's lodging options, combining the finest service and most comprehensive comfort in the principality. The rooms (all suites) are spacious and flawlessly decorated in bright colors. ✉ *Carrer Prat de la Creu 88* ☎ 874444 ⎙ 874445 ⊕ *www.uha.ad* ↝ *133 suites* ⚐ *Restaurant, pool* ▭ *AE, DC, MC, V.*

★ **$$$$** ⬚ **Hotel Mercure.** This large, modern hotel is widely considered one of the capital's best. The rooms are spacious and the furnishings smartly contemporary. The outdoor terrace is a pleasant spot to relax and watch the bustle below. ✉ *Carrer de la Roda* ☎ 873602 ⎙ 873652 ⊕ *www. mercure.com* ↝ *164 rooms, 9 suites* ⚐ *Restaurant, pool* ▭ *AE, DC, MC, V.*

$$$–$$$$ ⬚ **Andorra Park.** Stay here if you want a grand building away from the city's congestion. The hotel bar is a popular watering hole for local society. Outside are a pretty garden, a pitching and putting green, and an ample terrace. The deluxe guest rooms have private balconies. ✉ *Carrer Les Canals 24* ☎ 877777 ⎙ 820983 ⊕ *www.uha.ad* ↝ *40 rooms* ⚐ *Restaurant, pool* ▭ *AE, DC, MC, V.*

$$$–$$$$ ⬚ **Hotel Plaza.** With glass elevators whipping up and down the atrium and a jungly patio and panoramic views from rooms overlooking the Pyrenean heights, this hotel, in the center of the city, is a bright postmodern hub. The restaurant, La Cúpula, serves creditable international fare. ✉ *María Plá 19* ☎ 879444 ⎙ 821721 ↝ *100 rooms* ⚐ *Restaurant* ▭ *AE, DC, MC, V.*

$$$ ⬚ **Hotel Eden Roc.** Besides having all the comforts of larger hotels, this smaller spot has an exceptional dining room, a terrace, and attentive personal service. ✉ *Av. Dr. Mitjavila 1* ☎ 821000 ⎙ 860319 ↝ *56 rooms* ⚐ *Restaurant* ▭ *AE, V.*

Les Escaldes

The spa town, now virtually one with Andorra la Vella, is a 15-minute walk from the Casa de la Vall. The Romanesque church of **Sant Miquel d'Engolasters** stands on a ridge northeast of the capital and can be reached on foot—allow a half day for the round-trip—or by automobile up a mountain road. The views are well worth the climb.

★ **Caldea** is an elaborate thermal spa complex barely 1 km (½ mi) from the center of Andorra la Vella, complete with steam rooms, Turkish baths, and snow patios. There are three restaurants, boutiques, an art gallery, and a cocktail bar open until 2 AM. Charges for the treatments vary; a five-day Andorra ski ticket will get you in for free. ✉ *Parc de la Mola 10* ☎ 865777 ⎙ 865656.

★ **$$$$** ✕⬚ **Roc Blanc.** Sleek, modern, and luxurious, with a wealth of facilities to pamper the body, from mud baths to acupuncture—that's what the Roc Blanc is all about. The rooms are large, there's a terrace, and the hotel's restaurants, Brasserie L'Entrecôte and El Pí, serve Andorran and international specialties. ✉ *Plaça dels Co-Prínceps 5* ☎ 871400 ⎙ 871444 ⊕ *www.rocblanc.com* ↝ *180 rooms* ⚐ *2 restaurants, 2 pools* ▭ *AE, DC, MC, V.*

Encamp

Just beyond Encamp, which is 6 km (4 mi) northeast of Andorra la Vella, is the 12th-century church of **Sant Romà de les Bons,** in a picturesque context of medieval buildings and mountain scenery.

★ **Cal Cristo** is a must-visit—it's a 19th-century farmer's dwelling that has been perfectly preserved, down to the tiniest utensil. ✉ *Carrer dels Cavallers* ☎ 831405 ⊙ *Tues.–Sat. 9:30–1:30, 3–6:30, Sun. 10–2.*

The **funicamp telecabina** (cable car) carries hikers and sightseers from Encamp up to the Grau Roig ski resort. The telecabina also connects hotels in the valley with the upper slopes and ski runs, alleviating the wicked winter traffic jams for which Andorra has become famous.

$ ⊞ **Hotel La Mola.** This friendly spot, midway between the ski slopes and the bright lights of Andorra la Vella, is a comfortable choice that has all the basic facilities at half the price of some of the better-known Andorran hotels. ⊠ *Av. Co-Princep Episcopal 62* ☎ *831181* 🖷 *833046* 🛏 *46 rooms* ⚲ *Restaurant, pool* 🖃 *AE, DC, MC, V.*

Canillo

The **Santuari de Meritxell,** built by Barcelona architect Ricardo Bofill, in the shape of a Greek cross, occupies the site of the original chapel burned in 1972. A replica of the carving of Andorra's patron saint, Nuestra Senyora de Meritxell, discovered here in the 12th century, stands over the main altar. ⊠ *N-2, between Encamp and Canillo* ☉ *Wed.–Mon. 9–1 and 3–7.*

Just outside Canillo, on the road from Canillo to Prats, stands a 15th-century **seven-arm Gothic cross** of stone. It has an image of Christ on one side and of the Virgin on the other. One of the arms has been broken off, according to legend, by the devil. The Romanesque church of **Sant Joan de Caselles,** 2 km (1 mi) east of Canillo, is one of Andorra's treasures, with ancient walls of stone that have turned a lovely dappled gingerbread color over the centuries. The bell tower is stunning: three stories of weathered stone punctuated by rows of round-arch windows. Inside, a fine reredos (a wall or screen behind an altar), dating from 1525, depicts the life of St. John the Evangelist.

La Massana

★ Check out **Pont de Sant Antoni** (St. Anthony Bridge), a Romanesque stone bridge spanning a narrow river, just 3 km (2 mi) north of Andorra la Vella on the N-3 road toward La Massana. The rustic streets of the mountain town of La Massana are good for a picturesque stroll, too.

In Sispony, visit the **Museu Casa Rull** to see what a typical wealthy burgher's house of the 17th century looks like. ⊠ *Carrer Major, Sispony* ☎ *836919* ☉ *Tues.–Sat. 9:30–1:30, 3–6:30, Sun. 10–2.*

★ **$$$–$$$$** ✕ **El Rusc.** This smallish flower-covered chalet 1 km (½ mi) from La Massana may be Andorra's top restaurant—both in cost and quality. Basque and international specialties range from foie gras with onions to *besugo* (baked sea bream), a standard Cantabrican feast. ⊠ *Ctra. de Arinsal* ☎ *838200* 🖷 *835180* ⚲ *Reservations essential* 🖃 *AE, DC, MC, V* ☉ *Closed Mon. No dinner Sun.*

★ **$$–$$$** ✕ **La Borda de l'Avi.** This popular place specializes in lamb, goat, beef, quail, partridge, and trout cooked over coals. The three dining rooms can hold some 200 diners and, during the high season, often do. ⊠ *Ctra. de Arinsal* ☎ *835154* 🖃 *AE, DC, MC, V.*

Ordino

The tiny village of Ordino, 5 km (3 mi) northeast of La Massana, is known for its medieval church, **Sant Martíde la Cortinada.** Romanesque with baroque altarpieces, the church also has 12th-century frescoes and unusual wooden furnishings.

Museu Casa d'Areny Plandolit is an aristocratic 18th-century manor house affording a rare glimpse into the life and luxuries of a noble Andorran family. ⊠ *Carrer Major* ☎ *836908* ☉ *Tues.–Sat. 9:30–1:30, 3–6:30, Sun. 10–2.*

$$–$$$ 🏨 **Hotel Coma.** Surrounded by woods and meadows, this Swiss chalet–style hideaway just outside the village offers scenery, silence, and simple Andorran food at affordable prices. ✉ *Ctra. General* ☎ *736100* 📠 *736101* 🛏 *48 rooms* ⚲ *Restaurant, pool* ▭ *AE, DC, MC, V.*

La Cortinada

In this village is **Can Pal**, a fine example of medieval Andorran architecture. It's a privately owned manor house (strictly no admittance) with a dovecote attached. Note the turret perched high on the far side.

Santa Coloma

★ Santa Coloma's pre-Romanesque **Santa Coloma de les Bons** hermitage, the only Andorran church with a round tower, is the main attraction in this village 4 km (2½ mi) south of Andorra la Vella on CG-1. Parts of the church date from the 9th and 10th centuries. Twelfth-century Romanesque frescoes adorn the interior walls, while an 18th-century baroque altarpiece presides.

$$–$$$ ✗ **El Bon Racó.** Expect exactly what the name says it is—a good corner, nook, or retreat. A traditional borda in design, the place turns out fine Pyrenean home cooking at encouraging prices. Try to arrive early; it fills quickly, especially on weekends. ✉ *Av. Salou 86* ☎ *722085* ▭ *AE, DC, MC, V.*

Pas de la Casa

This conglomeration of high-rises and supermarkets is an Andorran Smuggler's Notch, traditionally a place for French and Spanish shoppers to effect a quick sting while the kids are skiing and then retreat back to their respective countries. Known to be colder and snowier than any other point around, Pas de la Casa is a favorite ski resort, especially for visitors from the Cerdanya Valley in Spain.

$$–$$$ 🏨 **Kandahar.** At the very foot of the lift of the ski resort, this modern hotel is wonderfully convenient; try to get a room overlooking the slopes. The menu evolves from buffet breakfast and lunch to serious cuisine at dinner. ✉ *Catalunya 9* ☎ *855127* 📠 *855178* 🌐 *www.hotelkandahar. ad* 🛏 *62 rooms* ⚲ *Restaurant, pool, bar* ▭ *AE, DC, MC, V.*

Sant Julià de Lòria

Sant Julià de Lòria is the first parish you encounter if you enter Andorra from Spain. It is the site of Andorra's only Nordic skiing facility. Around and above it are a number of unspoiled small villages. Fontaneda and its rustic Sant Miquel de Fontaneda chapel, in particular, are among Sant Julià de Lòria's finest sights.

★ **$$** 🏨 **Pol.** Gracefully modern surroundings and a friendly staff help make this hotel popular. A garden and terrace are part of the Pol's appeal, and its dance club is a busy nightspot. ✉ *Av. Verge de Canólich 52* ☎ *841122* 📠 *841852* ✉ *hotelpolandorra@andorra.ad* 🛏 *80 rooms* ⚲ *Restaurant* ▭ *AE, MC, V.*

ANDORRA ESSENTIALS

EMERGENCIES

🅵 Emergency Services **Ambulance** ☎ 118. **Medical and dental emergencies** ☎ 116. **Mountain rescue** ☎ 112. **Police** ☎ 110.

TOURS

Tours of Andorra la Vella and the surrounding countryside are offered by several firms; check with the tourist office for details or call Excursion Nadal or Sol i Neu Excursion.

🅵 Fees & Schedules **Excursion Nadal** ☎ 821138. **Sol i Neu Excursion** ☎ 823653.

TRAVEL AGENCY

⚑ **Relax Travel Agency/American Express** ⊠ Mossen Tremosa 12, Andorra la Vella
☎ 822044 🖷 827055.

VISITOR INFORMATION

⚑ **Andorra La Vella** Sindicat d'Iniciativa/National Tourist Office ⊠ Carrer Dr. Vilanova
☎ 820214 🖷 825823 ⊠ Barcelona office, World Trade Center BCN, Moll de Barcelona,
Ed. Nord, Planta Baixa 27, 08039 ☎ 93/508-8448 or 93/508-8449 ⊠ city tourist office, Plaça de la Rotonda ☎ 827117. **Canillo** Unió Pro-Turisme ⊠ Caseta Pro-Turisme
☎🖷 851002. **Encamp** Unió Pro-Foment i Turisme ⊠ Plaça Consell General ☎ 831405
🖷 831878. **Escaldes-Engordany** Unió Pro-Turisme ⊠ Plaça dels Co-Prínceps ☎ 820963.
La Massana Unió Pro-Turisme ⊠ Plaça del Quart ☎ 835693. **Ordino** Oficina de Turisme ⊠ Cruïlla d'Ordino ☎ 737080. **Pas de la Casa** Unió Pro-Turisme ⊠ C. Bernat III
☎ 855292. **Sant Julià de Lòria** Unió Pro-Turisme ⊠ Plaça de la Germandat ☎ 844345.

AUSTRIA
VIENNA, DANUBE VALLEY, SALZBURG, INNSBRUCK

2

AN OFT-TOLD STORY concerns an airline pilot whose prelanding announcement advised, "Ladies and gentlemen, we are on the final approach to Vienna Airport. Please make sure your seat belts are fastened, please refrain from smoking until you are inside the terminal, and please set your watches back 100 years."

Apocryphal or not, the pilot's observation suggests the allure of a country where visitors can sense something of what Europe was like before the pulse of the 20th century quickened to a beat that would have dizzied our great-grandparents. Today, the occasional gentleman will kiss a lady's hand just as in the days of the Habsburgs, and Lipizzan stallions still dance to Mozart minuets—in other words, Austria is a country that has not forgotten the elegance of its past.

Look beyond the postcard clichés of dancing white horses, the zither strains, and the singing of the Vienna Boys Choir, however, and you'll find a conservative-mannered yet modern country, one of Europe's richest, in which the juxtaposition of old and new often creates excitement— even controversy. Vienna has its sumptuous palaces, but it is also home to an assemblage of UN organizations housed in a wholly modern complex. Tucked away between storybook villages are giant industrial plants, one of which turns out millions of compact discs for Sony. The world's largest penicillin producer is hidden away in a Tyrolean valley. And those countless glittering crystal objects you see in jewelry and gift stores around the world originate in a small village outside Innsbruck. By no means is the country frozen in a time warp: rather, it is the contrast between the old and the new that makes Austria such a fascinating place to visit.

Poised as it is on the northeastern edge of the Alps, Austria shares a culture with Europe but has deep roots as well in the lands that lie beyond to the east. It was Metternich who declared that "Asia begins at the Landstrasse," referring to Vienna's role as a meeting place of East and West. In recent years, Austria's unique position as a crossroads has shown shaky resilience in the face of the meteoric rise and precipitous fall of the anti-immigrant and extremist Freedom Party. In fact, the success of the euro came as a bit of a surprise in Austria. The Austrian schilling was considered to be a symbol of national identity, like the national flag, and thus hard to surrender. The Austrians' quick acceptance of the euro could be a corroboration of a decline in national sentiment, a sign of willingness to be part of the new European community, or simply an acceptance of basic economic interest.

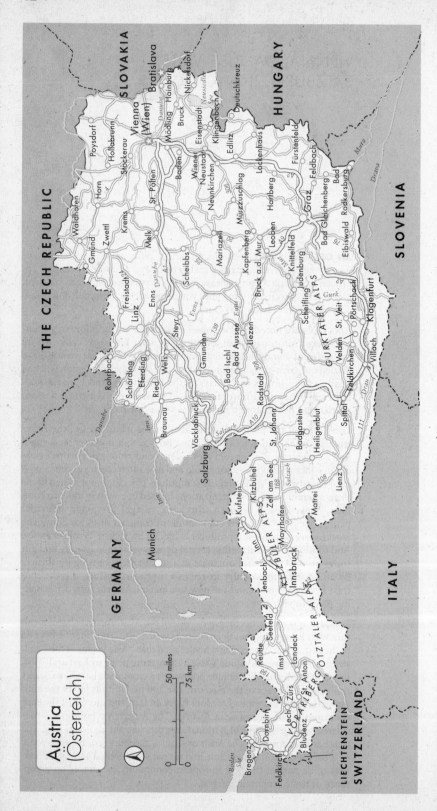

Austria
(Österreich)

Vienna's spectacular historical and artistic heritage—exemplified by the legacies of Beethoven, Freud, Klimt, and Mahler—remains to lure travelers. A fascinating mélange of Apfelstrudel and psychoanalysis, Schubert and sausages, Vienna possesses a definite old-world charm that natives would be the last to underplay. But as with most countries, the capital is only a small part of what Austria has to offer. A grand tour of the country reveals considerably more faces of Austria than the nine provinces would suggest: Salzburg—home every summer to one of the world's ritziest music festivals—is a departure point for the Salzkammergut lake country and the mountains of Land Salzburg; as the hub of the Alps, Innsbruck beckons skiers to explore the resorts of Lech, St. Anton, and Kitzbühel; finally, there's the scenic Wachau stretch of the Danube Valley.

AUSTRIA A TO Z

To research prices, get advice from other travelers, and book travel arrangements, visit www.fodors.com.

AIR TRAVEL

Austria's national airline, Austrian Airlines, flies to major worldwide destinations. Tyrolean Airlines offers service from Vienna to Graz, Linz, Innsbruck, Salzburg, and points outside Austria. Rheintalflug has service between Vienna and Altenrhein (Switzerland, near Bregenz), with bus connections to points in Voralberg. Be aware, though, that travel by air within the country is expensive.

Austrian Airlines (main office) ⊠ Kärtner Ring 18, 1010 Vienna ☎ 05/1789. **Rheintalflug** ☎ 00800-48800-000 in Voralberg. **Tyrolean Airlines** ☎ 05/1789.

BUS TRAVEL

Austria has an extensive national bus network run by the post office and railroads. Where trains don't go, buses do, and you'll find them (bright yellow for easy recognition) in the remotest regions. You can buy tickets onboard, and in the off-season there is no problem getting a seat, but on routes to favored ski areas during holiday periods reservations are essential. Bookings can be handled at the ticket office (there's one in most towns with bus service) or by travel agents. In most communities, bus routes begin and end at or near the railroad station, making transfers easy. Increasingly, coordination of bus service with railroads means that many of the discounts and special tickets available for trains apply to buses as well.

BUSINESS HOURS

BANKS & OFFICES Banks are open weekdays 8–noon or 12:30 and 1:30–3; until 5 on Thursday; closed Saturday. Hours vary from one city to another. Principal offices in cities stay open during lunch.

MUSEUMS & SIGHTS Museum opening days and times vary considerably from one city to another and depend on the season and other factors. Monday is often a closing day. Your hotel or the local tourist office will have current details.

SHOPS Shops are open weekdays from 8 or 9 until 6, in shopping centers until 7:30, and Saturday until 5, although some may still close at noon or 1. Many smaller shops close for one or two hours at midday. Larger food markets are open weekdays from 7:30 to 7:30, Saturday to 5.

CAR TRAVEL

GASOLINE Gas prices are among the most expensive in Europe, though eventually they will have to be lowered to conform with other EU countries. Currently it costs roughly €0.98 cents a liter for unleaded gasoline and €0.80

cents a liter for diesel, and at nearly 4 liters to the gallon, the final tally can be quite hefty.

PARKING   Traffic congestion in major cities means that driving generally takes longer than taking public transportation. City planners' solutions have been to make driving as difficult as possible, with one-way streets and other tricks, and a car in town is far more of a burden than a pleasure. Daytime parking is very difficult. In Vienna, a *Parkschein*, available at most tobacconists and magazine stands, allows you to park for up to 90 minutes—€0.40 for each 30-minute interval in units of 30, 60, and 90 minutes. You can park 10 minutes free of charge, but you must get a violet "gratis" sticker to put in your windshield. You can also park free in the First District on Saturday and Sunday, but not overnight. Overnight street parking in the First and Sixth through Ninth districts is restricted to residents with special permits; all other cars are subject to expensive ticketing or even towing, so in these districts be sure you have off-street garage parking. Parking in smaller towns and villages is much easier and not as restricted.

ROAD CONDITIONS   The Austrian highway network is excellent, and roads are well maintained and well marked. Secondary roads may be narrow and winding, albeit very picturesque. The main routes (Autobahns), especially the A2 down to Carinthia and Italy, are packed during both Austrian and German school holidays.

RULES OF THE ROAD   Drive on the right. Seat belts are compulsory in front. Children under 12 must sit in the back, and smaller children must be seated in a restraining seat. Speed limits are 130 kph (80 mph) on expressways, 100 kph (62 mph) on other main roads, 50 kph (31 mph) in built-up areas, or as posted. Some city areas have speed limits of 30 kph (19 mph). Be aware that speed is checked by radar, even in small towns, and fines are heavy. The right-of-way is for those coming from the right (especially in traffic circles) unless otherwise marked. All vehicles using the Autobahn (divided, mostly limited-access main highways, including the main highway from Vienna airport to the city) must display an Autobahn-Vignette toll sticker on the inside of the windshield. If you're renting a car in Austria, it's already included, but if you're coming from another country, you need to buy a 10-day sticker for €7.50. Two-month stickers cost €21.80. If you're caught without a sticker, the fine is a hefty €120. To apply for an Autobahn-Vignette, contact the ÖAMTC/Österreichischer Automobile-, Motorrad- und Touringclub.

🚗 **ÖAMTC/Österreichischer Automobile-, Motorrad- und Touringclub** ✉ Schubertring 3, A-1010, Vienna ☎ 01/71199–55 🌐 www.oemtc.at.

CUSTOMS & DUTIES

Austria's duty-free allowances are as follows: 200 cigarettes or 50 cigars or 250 grams of tobacco; 2 liters of wine and 1 liter of spirits; 1 bottle of toilet water (about 250-milliliter size); and 50 milliliters of perfume for those age 17 and over arriving from non–European Union countries. Tourists also do not have to pay duty on personal articles brought into Austria temporarily for their own use.

EATING & DRINKING

Take your choice among full-fledged restaurants in every price category, plus sidewalk *Würstel* (sausage) stands, *Imbissstuben* (quick-lunch stops), cafés, *Heurigen* (wine taverns), self-service restaurants, and modest *Gasthäuser* (neighborhood establishments serving local specialties). Most places post their menus outside. Shops (such as Eduscho) that sell coffee beans also offer coffee by the cup at prices considerably lower than those in cafés, though you can't sit down. Many Anker bakery shops also offer tasty *Schmankerl* (snacks) and coffee, and some offer a full breakfast. Würstel stands offer a tempting selection of grilled sausages, including *Käsekrainer* (beef and melted cheese), served with a roll and mustard. A growing number of shops and snack bars offer pizza by the slice.

WHAT IT COSTS In euros			
$$$$	**$$$**	**$$**	**$**
VIENNA			
PER PERSON over €22	€16–€22	€10–€15	under €10
OTHER AREAS			
AT DINNER over €20	€15–€20	€10–€14	under €10

Prices are for a main course.

MEALTIMES   The day begins with a very early Continental breakfast of rolls and coffee. *Gabelfrühstück* is a slightly more substantial breakfast with eggs or cold meat. A main meal is usually served between noon and 2, and an afternoon *Jause* (coffee with cake) is taken at teatime. Unless dining out, a light supper ends the day, usually between 6 and 9, but tending toward the later hour.

RESERVATIONS   A jacket and tie are generally advised for restaurants in the top two price
& DRESS   categories. Otherwise casual dress is acceptable. When in doubt, it's best to dress up.

EMBASSIES

For consulates, *see* Vienna Essentials.

🔲 Canada ✉ Laurenzerberg 2, 3rd floor of Hauptpost building complex, Vienna ☏ 01/53138-3000.

🔲 United Kingdom ✉ Jauresg. 12, near Schloss Belvedere, Vienna ☏ 01/71613-5151.

🔲 United States ✉ Boltzmanng. 16, Vienna ☏ 01/313-39.

HOLIDAYS

All banks and shops are closed on national holidays: New Year's Day; Epiphany (January 6); Easter Sunday and Monday; May Day (May 1); Ascension Day (mid-May); Pentecost Sunday and Monday (late May); Corpus Christi; Assumption (August 15); National Day (October 26); All Saints' Day (November 1); Immaculate Conception (December 8); December 25–26. On the December 8 holiday, banks and offices are closed but most shops are open.

LANGUAGE

German is the official national language. In larger cities and most resort areas you will have no problem finding English speakers; hotel and restaurant employees, in particular, speak English reasonably well. Most younger Austrians speak at least passable English.

LODGING

Although exact rates vary, a single room generally costs more than half the price of a comparable double. Breakfast at the roll-and-coffee level is often included in the room rate; full and sumptuous breakfast buffets, however, can involve a supplementary charge. Keep in mind that hotels outside Vienna may offer comprehensive rates that include breakfast *and* dinner; these are often excellent values.

WHAT IT COSTS In euros			
$$$$	**$$$**	**$$**	**$**
VIENNA			
FOR 2 PEOPLE	over €250	€175–€250	€100–€175	under €100
OTHER AREAS			
HOTELS	over €200	€150–€200	€100–€150	under €100

Prices are for a standard double room in high season, including local taxes (usually 10%), service (15%), and breakfast (except in the most expensive hotels).

CAMPING Most campsites are well equipped, with water and toilet facilities. Some have hookups for RVs. Few campsites are open year-round. Summer or winter, make reservations well in advance to be sure of a site. In addition to campsites, mountain cabins are available on an overnight basis to Alpine hikers. For information, contact Österreichischer Alpenverein. Information on camping is also available from the National Tourist Office (⇨ Visitor Information).
🏢 **Österreichischer Alpenverein** ✉ Wilhelm-Greil-Str. 15, A-6020 Innsbruck ☎ 0512/59547-19 🖷 0512/575528 🌐 www.alpenverein.at.

HOSTELS Hosteling is well developed, although most locations are outside city centers. For information, contact Österreichischer Jugendherbergsverband (Austrian Hostel Association).
🏢 **Österreichischer Jugendherbergsverband** ✉ Schottenring 28, A-1010, Vienna ☎ 01/533-5353 🖷 01/535-0861.

HOTELS Austrian hotels and pensions are officially classified using from one to five stars. These grades broadly coincide with our own four-point rating system. No matter what the category, standards for service and cleanliness are high. All hotels in the upper three categories have either a bath or shower in the room; even the most inexpensive accommodations provide hot and cold water. Accommodations include castles and palaces, conventional hotels, *Gasthöfe* (country inns), and the more modest pensions. In summer, student dormitories offer a reasonably priced option to guests of all ages.

MAIL & SHIPPING
American Express offices will hold mail at no charge for those carrying an American Express credit card or American Express traveler's checks.
🏢 **American Express** ✉ Kärntnerstr. 21–23, Vienna ☎ 01/515-40-0 ✉ Mozartpl. 5–7, Salzburg ☎ 0662/8080-0.

POSTAL RATES Airmail letters and postcards to the United States and Canada cost €1.09 minimum. Airmail letters and postcards to the United Kingdom cost €0.51.

MONEY MATTERS
Austria has become expensive, but as inflation is relatively low, the currency has remained fairly stable. Vienna and Salzburg are the most expensive cities, along with fashionable resorts at Kitzbühel, Seefeld, Badgastein, Velden, Zell am See, Pörtschach, St. Anton, Zürs, and Lech. Many smaller towns near these resorts offer virtually identical facilities at half the price. Drinks in bars and clubs cost considerably more than in cafés or restaurants. Austrian prices include service and tax.

Sample prices include a cup of coffee in a café or restaurant, €3–€4; half a liter of draft beer, €3–€4; small glass of wine, €4–€8; Coca-Cola, €3; open-face sandwich, €3.50; midrange theater ticket, €20; concert ticket, €30–€50; opera ticket, €40 and up; 2-km (1.6-mi) taxi ride, €6.

CREDIT CARDS Credit cards are not as widely used in Austria as they are in other European countries, and not all establishments that accept plastic take all cards. Some may require a minimum purchase if payment is to be made by card. Many restaurants take cash only. American Express has money machines in Vienna at its main office and at the airport. Many of the Bankomat money dispensers will also accept Visa cards if you have an encoded, international personal identification number.

🏠 **American Express** (main office) ✉ Kärntnerstr. 21-23.

CURRENCY As it is a member of the European Union (EU), Austria's unit of currency is the euro.

Exchange traveler's checks at banks, post offices, or American Express offices to get the best rate. All charge a small commission; some smaller banks or "change" offices may give a poorer rate *and* charge a higher fee. All change offices at airports and at main train stations in major cities cash traveler's checks. In Vienna, bank-operated change offices with extended hours are found on Stephansplatz and at the main rail stations. Bank Austria machines on Stephansplatz, at Kärntnerstrasse 51 (to the right of the Opera), and at the Raiffeisenbank on Kohlmarkt (at Michaelerplatz) change bills from other currencies into euros, but rates are poor and the commission hefty.

VALUE-ADDED A value-added tax (VAT) of 20% is charged on all sales and is auto-
TAX (VAT) matically included in prices. If you purchase goods worth €75 or more and are not a citizen of an EU country, you can claim a refund of the tax either as you leave or after you've returned home. Ask the store clerk to fill out the necessary papers. Get them stamped at the airport or border crossing by customs officials (who may ask to see the goods). You can get an immediate refund of the VAT, less a service charge, at international airports or at main border crossings, or you can return the papers by mail to the shop(s). The VAT refund can be credited to your credit card account or remitted by check.

TELEPHONES

COUNTRY & The country code for Austria is 43. When dialing an Austrian number
AREA CODES from abroad, drop the initial 0 from the local area code.

INTERNATIONAL It costs considerably more to telephone *from* Austria than it does *to* Aus-
CALLS tria. Calls from post offices are least expensive. To avoid hotel charges, call overseas and ask to be called back; use an international credit card, available from AT&T and MCI. Use the AT&T access code to reach an operator. Another option for long-distance access is MCI WorldPhone. To make a collect call—you can't do this from pay phones—dial the operator and ask for an *R*-Gespräch (pronounced "air-ga-*shprayk*"). For international information dial 118200 for numbers in Germany, 118202 for numbers in other European countries, and 118202 for overseas numbers. Most operators speak English; if yours doesn't, you'll be passed along to one who does.

🏠 **Access Codes AT&T** ☎ 0800-200-288. **MCI WorldPhone** ☎ 0800-200-235.

LOCAL CALLS Pay telephones take €1, €0.50, €0.20, and €0.10 coins. Emergency calls are free. Instructions are in English in most booths. The initial connection for a local call costs €0.20. Insert €0.10 or more to continue the connection when you hear the tone warning that your time is up. Phone cards, available at post offices, work in all phones marked WERTKARTENTELEFON. The cost of the call will be deducted from the card automatically. Phone numbers throughout Austria are currently being changed. A sharp tone indicates either no connection or that the number has been changed. Dial 118200 for numbers in Austria.

TIPPING

In restaurants, 10% service is included. Give a 5% tip, or 7% if you really liked the service. Leave the actual tip by telling the waiter the total amount you wish to pay—that is, the bill plus the tip—then remit the tip with the payment to the waiter (do not leave it on the table). Railroad porters and hotel porters or bellhops get €1 per bag. Doormen get €1–€2 for hailing a cab and assisting. Room service gets €1.50 for snacks and €2–€4 for full meals; in more expensive establishments, expect to tip on the higher side. Maids get no tip unless you stay a week or more, or unless a special service is rendered.

TRAIN TRAVEL

Austrian train service is excellent and efficient. The IC (InterCity) and EC (EuroCity) trains are the fastest, and an added charge of about €5 is usually included in the price of the ticket. It's a good idea to pay the extra €3.40 per ticket for a seat reservation, especially at peak holiday times, and year-round for travel to major destinations. If you're planning on doing a lot of traveling within Austria, it might be best to purchase a *Vorteilskarte,* which enables you to travel for a 45% discount on all trains within Austria. It's good for one year and costs €94.

VISITOR INFORMATION

🚩 **Central Tourist Office** (national tourist office) ✉ Margaretenstr. 1, A-1040, Vienna ☎ 01/211140 🖷 01/216–8492.

WHEN TO GO

Austria has two tourist seasons. The summer season technically starts around Easter, reaches its peak in July, and winds down in September. In summer, Vienna moves outdoors. May, June, September, and October are the most temperate months, and the most affordable. The winter cultural season starts in October and runs into June; winter sports get under way in December and last until the end of April, although you can ski in certain areas well into June and on some of the highest glaciers year-round. Some events—the Salzburg Festival is a prime example—occasion a substantial increase in hotel and other prices.

CLIMATE Summer can be warm; winter, bitterly cold. The southern region is usually several degrees warmer in summer, several degrees colder in winter. Winters north of the Alps can be overcast and dreary, whereas the south basks in winter sunshine. The following are the average daily maximum and minimum temperatures for Vienna.

Jan.	34F	1C	May	67F	19C	Sept.	68F	20C
	25	−4		50	10		53	11
Feb.	38F	3C	June	73F	23C	Oct.	56F	14C
	28	−3		56	14		44	7
Mar.	47F	8C	July	76F	25C	Nov.	45F	7C
	30	−1		60	15		37	3
Apr.	58F	15C	Aug.	75F	24C	Dec.	37F	3C
	43	6		59	15		30	−1

VIENNA

Vienna has been characterized as an "old dowager of a town"—an Austro-Hungarian empress widowed in 1918 by the Great War. It's not just the aristocratic and courtly atmosphere, with monumental doorways and facades of former palaces at every turn. Nor is it just that Vienna (Wien in German) has a higher proportion of middle-aged and older citizens than any other city in Europe, with a concomitant air of stability, quiet, and respectability. Rather, it's these factors—combined with a love of music; a discreet weakness for rich food (especially cakes); an adherence to old-fashioned and formal forms of address; a high regard for the arts; and a gentle mourning for lost glories—that preserve the city's enchanting elegance and dignity.

Exploring Vienna

Numbers in the margin correspond to points of interest on the Vienna map.

Most main sights are in the inner zone, the oldest part of the city, encircled by the Ringstrasse (Ring Road), once the course of the city walls and today a broad, tree-lined boulevard. As you wander around, train yourself to look upward; some of the most memorable architectural delights are found on upper stories and along rooflines. Note that addresses throughout the chapter ending with "-strasse" or "-gasse" (both meaning "street") are abbreviated "str." or "g." respectively (Augustinerstrasse will be "Augustinerstr."; Dorotheergasse will be "Dorotheerg").

Vienna addresses include a roman numeral that designates in which of the city's 23 districts the address is located. The First District (I, the inner city) is bounded by the Ringstrasse and the Danube Canal. The 2nd through 9th (II–IX) districts surround the inner city, starting with the 2nd district across the Danube Canal and running clockwise; the 10th through the 23rd (X–XXIII) districts form a second concentric ring of suburbs.

The Heart of Vienna

The Inner Stadt (Inner City), or First District, comprised the entire city in medieval times, and for more than eight centuries the enormous bulk of the Stephansdom (St. Stephen's Cathedral) remained the nucleus around which the city grew. Beginning in the 1870s, when Vienna reached the zenith of its imperial prosperity, the medieval walls were replaced by the Ringstrasse, along which a series of magnificent buildings were erected: the Staatsoper (opera house), the Hofburg Palace, the Kunsthistorisches Museum, the Parliament building, and the Rathaus (city hall). The pedestrian zone around the Stephansdom is lined with designer boutiques, cafés, and upscale restaurants.

❶ Albertina. After years of renovation, this museum has reopened and once again exhibits one of the world's largest collection of drawings, sketches, engravings, and etchings. Originally a 17th-century palace, the original structure has been expanded to include halls for temporary exhibitions and a vast study area. The permanent collection contains some of the greatest old master drawings, including Dürer's *Praying Hands*. Other highlights include works by Rembrandt, Michelangelo, and Correggio. ⊠ *Augustinerstr. 1* ☎ *01/53483–544* ⊕ *www.albertina.at* ☉ *Thurs.–Tues. 10–6, Wed. 10–9* Ⓤ *U3/Herreng.*

❸ Augustinerkirche (St. Augustine's Church). The interior of this 14th-century church has undergone restoration. Much of the earlier baroque ornamentation was removed in the 1780s, but the gilt organ decoration and main altar remain as visual sensations. This was the court church; the Habsburg rulers' hearts are preserved in a chamber here. On Sunday, the 11 AM mass is sung in Latin. ⊠ *Josefspl.* Ⓤ *U3/Herreng.*

㉓ Figarohaus (Mozart Memorial Rooms). A commemorative museum occupies the small apartment in the house on a narrow street just east of St. Stephen's Cathedral where Mozart lived from 1784 to 1787. It was here that the composer wrote *The Marriage of Figaro* (hence the nick-

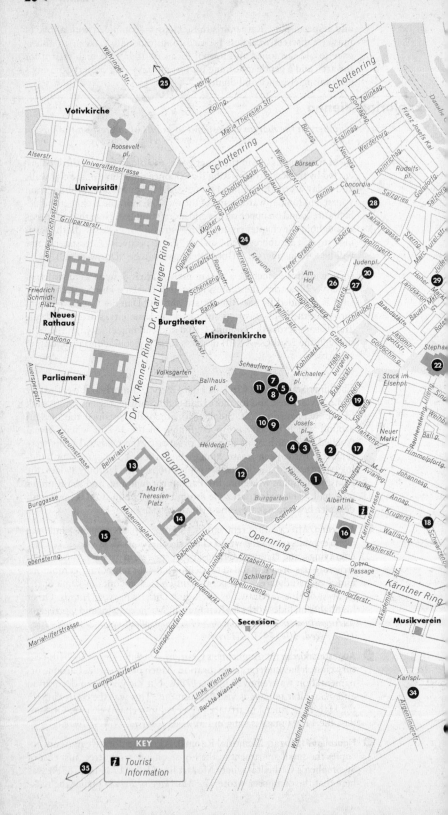

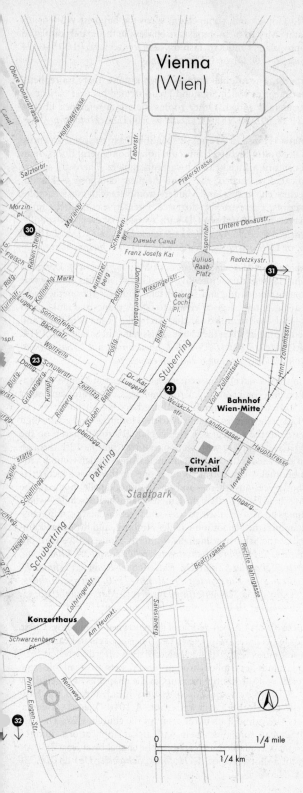

Vienna (Wien)

name Figaro House) and, some claim, spent the happiest years of his life. Fascinating Mozart memorabilia are on view, unfortunately displayed in an inappropriately modern fashion. ⊠ *Domg. 5* ☎ *01/513–6294* ⊗ *Tues.–Sun. 9–6* Ⓤ *U1 or U3/Stephanspl.*

㉕ Freud Apartment. The original famous couch is gone (there's a replica), but the apartment in which Sigmund Freud treated his first patients is otherwise generally intact. Other rooms include a reference library. ⊠ *Bergg. 19* ☎ *01/319–1596* ⊗ *Daily 9–5* Ⓤ *U2/Schottentor.*

Ⓒ **⑱ Haus der Musik** (House of Music). It would be easy to spend an entire day at this new, ultra high-tech museum housed on several floors of an early-19th-century palace near Schwarzenbergplatz. There are special rooms dedicated to each of the great Viennese composers—Haydn, Mozart, Beethoven, Strauss, and Mahler—complete with music samples and manuscripts. There are also dozens of interactive computer games. You can even record your own CD with a variety of everyday sounds. ⊠ *Seilerstätte 30* ☎ *01/51648–51* ⊕ *www.hdm.at* ⊗ *Daily 10–10* Ⓤ *U1, U2, or U4/Karlsplatz, then Streetcar D to Schwarzenbergpl.*

Ⓒ **㉜ Heeresgeschichtliches Museum** (Museum of Military History). Designed by Theophil Hansen, this impressive neo-Gothic building houses war artifacts ranging from armor and Turkish tents confiscated from the Turks during the 16th-century siege of Vienna to fighter planes and tanks. Also on display is the bullet-riddled car that Archduke Franz Ferdinand and his wife were riding in when they were assassinated in Sarajevo in 1914. ⊠ *Arsenal 3, Bldg. 18* ☎ *01/795–610* ⊕ *www.bmlv.gv.at* ⊗ *Sat.–Thurs. 9–5* Ⓤ *Tram 18/Ghegastr., near the Belvedere.*

★ **❼ Hofburg** (Imperial Palace). This centerpiece of Imperial Vienna is actually a vast complex comprising numerous buildings, courtyards, and other must-sees. Start with the magnificent domed entry—Michaelertor (St. Michael's Gate), the principal gateway to the Hofburg—and go through the courtyards to the vast, grassy Heldenplatz (Hero's Square), on the front. The palace complex, with sections dating from the 13th through 18th centuries, includes the **Augustinerkirche** (Augustianian Church), the **Nationalbibliothek**—its central room is one of the most spectacular baroque showpieces anywhere—and the **Hofburgkapelle**, home to the Vienna Boys Choir. Here, too, are the famous **Spanische Reitschule**—where the Lipizzaners go through their paces—and three fascinating museums: the **Silberkammer**, the **Schauräume in der Hofburg**, and the **Schatzkammer**, as well as the **Schmetterlinghaus** (Butterfly House), alive with unusual butterflies. ⊠ *Hofburg: main streets circling complex—Opernring, Augustinerstr., Schauflerg., and Dr. Karl Renner-Ring;* ⊠ *Schmetterlinghaus: entrance in Burggarten* ☎ *01/533–7570* ⊕ *www.hofburg-wien.at* ⊗ *Daily 9–5; Schmetterlinghaus: Nov.–Mar., daily 10–3:45; Apr.–Oct., weekdays 10–4:45, weekends 10–6:15* Ⓤ *U3/Herreng.*

❿ Hofburgkapelle (Court Chapel). Home of the renowned Vienna Boys Choir, this Gothic chapel dates from 1449. You'll need tickets to hear the angelic boys sing mass (only 10 side balcony seats afford views) at 9:15 AM on Sunday, mid-September through June; tickets are available from travel agencies at a substantial markup, at the chapel itself (open daily 11–1 and 3–5), or by writing two months in advance to the **Hofmusikkapelle** (⊡ Hofburg, Schweizerhof, A-1010, Vienna). General seating costs €5; prime seats in the front of the church, €29. The City Tourist Office can sometimes help with ticket applications. Limited standing room is available for free; get to the chapel by at least 8:30 AM on Sunday for a shot at a spot. ⊠ *Hofburg, Schweizer Hof* ☎ *01/533–9927* Ⓤ *U3/Herreng.*

㉑ Judenplatz Museum. In what was once the old Jewish ghetto, construction workers discovered the remains of a 13th-century synagogue while digging for a new parking garage. Simon Wiesenthal (a Vienna resident) helped to turn it into a museum dedicated to the Austrian Jews who died in World War II. Marking the outside is a rectangular concrete cube resembling library shelves, signifying Jewish love of learning, designed by Rachel Whiteread. Downstairs are three exhibition rooms on medieval Jewish life and the synagogue excavations. ⊠ *Judenpl. 8* ☎ *01/535–0431* ☽ *Sun.–Thurs. 10–6, Fri. 10–2* Ⓤ *U1 or U4/Schwedenpl.*

⑲ Jüdisches Museum der Stadt Wien (Jewish Museum). Housed in the former Eskeles town palace, the city's Jewish Museum offers exhibits that portray the richness of the Jewish culture and heritage that contributed so much to Vienna and Austria. On the top floor is a staggering collection of Judaica. ⊠ *Dorotheerg. 11* ☎ *01/535–0431* ⊕ *www.jmw.at* ☽ *Sun.–Wed. and Fri. 10–6, Thurs. 10–8* Ⓤ *U1 or U3/Stephanspl.*

⑰ Kapuzinerkirche (Capuchin Church). The ground-level church is nothing unusual, but the basement crypt holds the imperial vault, the Kaisergruft, a final resting place for many sarcophagi of long-dead Habsburgs. The oldest tomb is that of Ferdinand II; it dates from 1633. The most recent one is that of Empress Zita, widow of the last of the Kaisers, who died in 1989. ⊠ *Neuer Markt 1* ☎ *01/512–6853–12* ☽ *Daily 9:30–4* Ⓤ *U1 or U3/Stephanspl., or U1 or U4/Karlspl.*

★ **㉞ Karlskirche** (St. Charles's Church). The classical baroque facade and dome flanked by vast twin columns instantly identify the Karlskirche, one of the city's best-known landmarks. The church was built around 1715 by Fischer von Erlach. In the surprisingly small oval interior, the ceiling has airy frescoes, while the baroque altar is adorned with a magnificent sunburstlike array of gilded shafts. ⊠ *Karlspl.* Ⓤ *U1, U2, or U4/Karlspl.*

⑭ Kunsthistorisches Museum (Art History Museum). One of the finest art collections in the world, housed in palatial splendor, this is the crown jewel of Vienna's museums. Its glories are the Italian and Flemish collections, assembled by the Habsburgs over many centuries. The group of paintings by Pieter Brueghel the Elder is the largest in existence. The large-scale works concentrated in the main galleries shouldn't distract you from the masterworks in the more intimate side wings. One level down is the remarkable Kunstkammer (Art Cabinet), which displays priceless objects created for the Habsburg emperors. These include curiosities made of gold, silver, and crystal. ⊠ *Maria-Theresien-Pl.* ☎ *01/ 525–240* ⊕ *www.khm.at* ☽ *Tues. and Wed. and Fri.–Sun. 10–6, Thurs. 10–9* Ⓤ *U2/MuseumsQuartier, U2 or U3/Volkstheater.*

Fodor'sChoice ★

⑥ Lipizzaner Museum. To learn more about the extraordinary Lipizzan horses of the Spanish Riding School, visit the adjacent museum set in what used to be the imperial pharmacy. Exhibits document the history of the Lipizzaners through paintings, photographs, and videos giving an overview from the 16th century to the present. A visit to the nearby stables—part of the Spanish Riding School complex—allows you to see the horses up close through a window. ⊠ *Reitschulg. 2* ☎ *01/533–7811* ▨ *Combination ticket with morning training session at the Spanish Riding School €14.50* ☽ *Daily 9–6* Ⓤ *U3/Herreng.*

㉑ Museum für angewandte Kunst (MAK) (Museum of Applied Arts). A large collection of Austrian furniture, porcelain, art objects, and priceless Oriental carpets is housed in this fascinating museum. The museum puts on changing exhibitions of contemporary art, with artists ranging from Chris Burden to Nam June Paik. The museum also houses the popular

MAK Café. ✉ *Stubenring 5* ☎ *01/711–36–0* ⊕ *www.mak.at* ⊘ *Tues. 10 AM–midnight; Wed.–Sun. 10–6* Ⓤ *U3/Stubentor.*

🔵 **⑮ Museumsquartier** (Museum Quarter). Baroque and modern styles collide dazzlingly in this vast culture center. The MuseumsQuartier is housed in the 250-year-old Imperial Court Stables designed by Fischer von Erlach, with sleek modern wings added on to house the five museums, which exhibit thousands of artworks from the 18th to the 21st century. The **Leopold Museum** contains one of the greatest collections of Egon Schiele in the world, as well as works by Gustav Klimt and Oskar Kokoschka. Adjacent, in an eight-story whale-like edifice, the **Museum moderner Kunst Stiftung Ludwig (MUMOK)** houses Austria's national collection of modern art, which is notable for its emphasis on American Pop Art. The **Kunsthalle** is used for temporary exhibitions of avant-garde art, while the **ZOOM Kinder Museum** lets children 7 and up explore the fine line between the real and virtual world. In **Quartier21**, the latest addition in the sprawling baroque wing facing the Museumsplatz, a collection of artists' studios is open to the public for free. ✉ *Museumspl. 1–5* ☎ *01/ 523–5881; ZOOM Kinder Museum: 01/524–7908* ⊕ *www.mqw.at* ⊘ *Leopold Museum: Mon., Wed., Thurs. 11–7, Fri. 11–9, weekends 10–7, closed Tues.; MUMOK: Tues.–Sun. 10–6, Thurs. 10–9; Kunsthalle: Fri.–Wed. 10–7, Thurs. 10–10; ZOOM: weekdays 8:30–5, weekends 10–5:30* Ⓤ *U2/MuseumsQuartier, U2 or U3/Volkstheater.*

❹ Nationalbibliothek (National Library). The focus here is on the stunning baroque central hall—one of Europe's most magnificently decorated spaces. Look for the collection of globes on the third floor. ✉ *Josefspl. 1* ☎ *01/534–10 or 01/534–10–297* ⊘ *May–Oct., Fri.–Wed. 10–4, Thurs. 10–7; Nov.–Apr., Fri.–Wed. 10–2, Thurs. 10–7* Ⓤ *U3/Herreng.*

⑬ Naturhistorisches Museum (Natural History Museum). The twin building opposite the art-filled Kunsthistorisches Museum houses ranks of showcases filled with preserved animals, but such special collections as butterflies are better presented. Here, too, is the Venus of Willendorf, a 25,000-year-old statuette discovered in Lower Austria. ✉ *Maria-Theresien-Pl.* ☎ *01/521–77–0* ⊕ *www.khm.at* ⊘ *Thurs.–Mon. 9–6:30, Wed. 9–9* Ⓤ *U2 or U3/Volkstheater.*

⑫ Neue Burg (New Wing of the Imperial Palace). This 19th-century edifice—Hitler announced the annexation of Austria from its balcony in 1938—now houses a series of museums whose exhibits range from musical instruments (Beethoven's piano) to weapons (tons of armor) to the collections of the Völkerkunde (Ethnological) and Ephesus (Classical Antiquity) museums. ✉ *Heldenpl. 1* ☎ *01/525–240* ⊕ *www.khm.at* ⊘ *Wed.–Mon. 10–6* Ⓤ *U2/MuseumsQuartier.*

❾ Schatzkammer (Imperial Treasury). An almost overpowering display includes the magnificent crown jewels, the imperial crowns, the treasure of the Order of the Golden Fleece, regal robes, and other secular and ecclesiastical treasures. The imperial crown of the Holy Roman Empire is more than 1,000 years old. ✉ *Hofburg, Schweizer Hof* ☎ *01/52524–0* ⊘ *Wed.–Mon. 10–6* Ⓤ *U3/Herreng.*

❽ Schauräume in der Hofburg (Imperial Apartments). The long, repetitive suite of conventionally luxurious rooms is decorated (19th-century imitation of 18th-century rococo) to look regal but ends up looking merely official. Among the few signs of genuine life are Emperor Franz Josef's spartan, iron field bed, and Empress Elizabeth's wooden gymnastics equipment. Obsessed with her looks, she suffered from anorexia and was fanatically devoted to exercise. ✉ *Michaelerpl. 1; entrance under Michaelertor dome* ☎ *01/533–7570* ⊕ *www.hofburg-wien.at* ⊘ *Daily 9–4:30* Ⓤ *U3/Herreng.*

⓫ Silberkammer (Court Silver and Tableware Museum). See how royalty dined in this brilliant showcase of imperial table settings. Little wonder Marie-Antoinette—who, as a child of Maria Theresa, grew up in Schloss Schönbrunn—had a taste for extreme luxury. A combination ticket includes the imperial apartments around the corner. ✉ *Burghof inner court, Michaelertrakt* ☎ *01/533–7570* 🕐 *Daily 9–4:30* Ⓤ *U3/Herreng.*

★ ❺ Spanische Reitschule (Spanish Riding School). Probably the most famous interior in Vienna, the riding arena of the Spanish Riding School—wedding-cake white and crystal-chandeliered—is where the beloved white Lipizzaner horses train and perform dressage when they are not stabled in stalls across the Reitschulgasse to the east side of the school. For performance schedules and tickets, write to the Spanische Reitschule *at least* three months in advance. The AmEx office sometimes has a few last-minute tickets, but expect a 22% service charge. Performances are usually March–December, with the school on vacation in July and August. Generally, the full 80-minute show takes place Sunday at 11 AM plus selected Fridays at 6 PM. Morning training sessions with music are held Tuesday–Saturday from 10 to noon, and tickets can be bought *only* at the Josefplatz entrance, between 9:40 and 12:30. ✉ *Michaelerpl. 1, Hofburg, A-1010, Vienna* ☎ *01/533–9031–0* 🖷 *01/535–0186* 🌐 *www.srs.at* ✐ *€35–€105, standing room €24–€28; morning training sessions €11.50; Sat. classical dressage final rehearsal, €20* 🕐 *Mar.–June and late Aug.-mid-Dec.; closed tour wks* Ⓤ *U3/Herreng.*

⓰ Staatsoper (State Opera House). Considered one of the best opera houses in the world, the Staatsoper is a focus of Viennese social life as well. Almost totally destroyed in the last days of World War II (only the walls and front foyers were saved), it was rebuilt in its present, simpler elegance and reopened in 1955. Tickets for seats can be expensive and scarce, but among the very best bargains in Vienna are the Staatsoper standing-room tickets, available for each performance at delightfully affordable prices—as low as €3.50. Backstage tours are also available. ✉ *Opernring 2* ☎ *01/514–4426–13* 🌐 *www.wiener-staatsoper.at* Ⓤ *U1, U2, or U4/Karlspl.*

★ ㉒ Stephansdom (St. Stephen's Cathedral). The towering Gothic spires and gaudy 19th-century tile roof of the city's central landmark dominate the skyline. The oldest parts of the structure are the 13th-century entrance, the soaring Riesentor (Great Entry), and the Heidentürme (Heathens' Towers). Inside, the church is mysteriously shadowy, filled with monuments, tombs, sculptures, paintings, and pulpits. Despite numerous baroque additions—and extensive wartime damage—the cathedral seems authentically medieval. Climb the 343 steps of the south tower—der alte Steffl (Old Stephen) as the Viennese call it—for a stupendous view over the city. If you take a 30-minute tour of the crypt, you can see the copper jars in which the entrails of the Habsburgs are carefully preserved. ✉ *Stephanspl.* ☎ *01/515–5237–67* 🕐 *Daily 6 AM–10 PM. Guided tour in English daily, Apr.–Oct. at 3:45; catacombs tour (minimum 5 people) Mon.–Sat. every half hr 10–11:30 and 1:30–4:30, Sun. every half hr 1:30–4:30; North Tower elevator to Pummerin bell, Apr.–Oct., daily 9–6; July and Aug., daily 9–6:30; Nov.–Mar., daily 8:30–5* Ⓤ *U1 or U3/Stephanspl.*

☾ ❷ Theater Museum. Housed in the noted 18th-century Palais Lobkowitz—Beethoven was a regular visitor here—this museum covers the history of Austrian theater. A children's museum in the basement is reached, appropriately, by a slide. The facility is short-staffed, so have your hotel or the tourist office check first to see if it's open. Personnel speak only German. ✉ *Lobkowitzpl. 2* ☎ *01/512–8800–610* 🌐 *www.*

theatermuseum.at ☉ *Tues.–Sun. 10–5, Wed. 10–8; Kindermuseum Tues.–Sun. 10–10:30 and 2–2:30* Ⓤ *U3/Herreng.*

Other Corners of Vienna

City planning in the late 1800s and early 1900s was essential to manage the growth of the burgeoning imperial capital. Within a short walk of Stephansdom are other sights that give a sense of the history of old Vienna, with colorful cobblestone squares, statues, and baroque churches. A little farther out, the glories of imperial Austria are nowhere shown off more than in Shönnbrunn Palace, the summer residence of the court, and Belvedere Palace. Both palaces and their extensive gardens are in what was once the countryside, but the land is now incorporated into the city proper.

㉖ Am Hof. The name of this remarkable square translates simply as "at court." On the east side of Am Hof is the massive **Kirche am Hof** (also known as the Church of the Nine Choirs of Angels); most of the building's baroque overlay both inside and out dates from the 1600s. In style, the somewhat dreary interior is reminiscent of those of many Dutch churches. In the northeast corner of the square check out what is possibly the most ornate fire station in the world. You'll find an open-air antiques market in the square on Thursday and Friday in summer and frequent seasonal markets at other times. ☒ *Bounded by Tiefer Graben on west, Naglerg. on south, and Seitzerg. on east* Ⓤ *U3/Herreng.*

㉙ Hoher Markt. This ancient cobblestone square with its imposing central monument celebrating the betrothal of Mary and Joseph sits atop **Roman ruins** (☒ Hoher Markt 3 ☎ 01/535–5606), remains of the 2nd-century Roman legion encampment. On the north side of Hoher Markt is the amusing **Anker-Uhr,** a clock that marks the hour with a parade of moving figures. The figures are identified on a plaque at the lower left of the clock. ☒ *Judeng. and Fisch-hof Str.* Ⓤ *U1 or U4/Schwedenpl.*

㉛ Hundertwasserhaus (Hundertwasser House). This structure is an eccentric modern masterpiece envisioned by the late Austrian avant-garde artist Friedensreich Hundertwasser—an astonishing apartment complex marked by turrets, towers, unusual windows, and uneven floors. The nearby **KunstHaus Wien** (Vienna House of Art; ☒ Untere Weissgerberstr. 13 ☎ 01/712–0491 ⊕ www.kunsthauswien.com) is an art museum designed by the artist; it offers a floor of his work plus changing exhibits of other modern art. ☒ *Kegelg. and Löweng.* ⊕ *www.hundertwasserhaus. at* ☉ *Daily 10–7* Ⓤ *U1 or U4/Schwedenpl., then Tram N or O to Radetzkypl.*

㉘ Maria am Gestade (St. Mary's on the Bank). When built around 1400, this was a church for fishermen from the nearby canal, hence the name. Note the arched stone doorway and the ornate carved-stone-latticework "folded hands" spire. ☒ *Salvatorg. and Passauer Pl.* Ⓤ *U1 or U3/ Stephanspl.*

㉚ Ruprechtskirche (St. Rupert's Church). Vienna's oldest church, dating from the 11th century, is usually closed but sometimes opens for local art shows and summer evening classical concerts. ☒ *Ruprechtspl.* Ⓤ *U1 or U4/ Schwedenpl.*

㉝ Schloss Belvedere (Belvedere Palace). On a rise overlooking the city, this baroque palace is one of the showpieces of Vienna. It was commissioned by Prince Eugene of Savoy and built by Johann Lukas von Hildebrandt in 1721–22. The palace consists of two separate buildings, one at the foot of the hill and the other at the top. The Upper Belvedere houses a gallery of 19th- and 20th-century Viennese art, with works by Klimt (including his world-famous painting *The Kiss*), Schiele, Waldmüller, and Makart; the Lower Belvedere has a baroque museum together with exhibits of Austrian art of the Middle Ages. ⊠ *Prinz-Eugen-Str. 27* ☎ *01/79557-100* ⊕ *www.belvedere.at* ☉ *Tues.–Sun. 10–6* Ⓤ *U1, U2, or U4/Karlspl., then Tram D/Schloss Belvedere.*

㉟ Schloss Schönbrunn (Schönbrunn Palace). The Versailles of Vienna, this magnificent baroque residence with grandly formal gardens was built for the Habsburgs between 1696 and 1713. The complex was also a summer residence for Maria Theresa and Napoléon. Kaiser Franz Josef I was born and died here. His "office" (kept as he left it in 1916) is a touching reminder of his spartan life. In contrast, other rooms are filled with spectacular imperial elegance. The ornate reception areas are still used for state occasions. A guided tour leading through more than 40 of the palace's 1,441 rooms is the best way to see inside the palace (the most dazzling salons start at No. 21). Ask to see the Berglzimmer, ornately decorated ground-floor rooms generally not included in tours. ⊠ *Schönbrunner Schloss-Str.* ☎ *01/81113–239* ⊕ *www.schoenbrunn. at* ⊠ *€12.30 with guided tour (40 rooms)* ☉ *Apr.–June and Sept. and Oct., daily 8:30–5; July and Aug., daily 8:30–7; Nov.–Mar., daily 8:30–4:30* Ⓤ *U4/Schönbrunn.*

On the grounds of the Schönbrunn Palace is the **Tiergarten** (zoo), Europe's oldest menagerie, established in 1752 to amuse and educate the court. It houses an extensive assortment of animals; the original baroque enclosures now serve as viewing pavilions, with the animals housed in effective, modern settings. ☎ *01/877-9294-0* ⊕ *www.zoovienna.at* ☉ *Nov.–Jan., daily 9–4:30; Feb., daily 9–5; Mar. and Oct., daily 9–5:30; Apr., daily 9–6; May–Sept., daily 9–6:30.*

Pathways lead up through the formal gardens to the **Gloriette,** an 18th-century baroque folly on the rise behind Schloss Schönbrunn built to afford superb views of the city. A café is inside. ☉ *Apr.–June and Sept., daily 9–6; July and Aug., daily 9–7; Oct., daily 9–5.*

The **Wagenburg** (Imperial Coach Collection), near the entrance to the palace grounds, displays splendid examples of bygone conveyances, from ornate children's sleighs to the grand carriages built to carry the coffins of deceased emperors in state funerals. ☎ *01/877-3244* ☉ *Nov.–Mar., daily 10–4; Apr.–Oct., daily 9–6.*

Wander the grounds to discover the **Schöner Brunnen** (Beautiful Fountain) for which the Schönbrunn Palace is named; the re-created but convincing massive **Römische Ruinen** (Roman Ruins); and the great glass **Palmenhaus** (Palm House), with its orchids and exotic plants. ⊠ *Palm House: nearest entrance Hietzing* ☎ *01/877-5087* ⊕ *www.federalgardens.at* ☉ *May–Sept., daily 9:30–6.*

㉔ Schottenkirche, Museum im Schottenstift (Scottish Church and Museum). Despite its name, this church was founded in 1177 by monks who were Irish, not Scots. The present imposing building dates from the mid-1600s. In contrast to the plain exterior, the interior bubbles with cherubs and angels. The Benedictines have set up a small but worthwhile museum of mainly religious art, including a late-Gothic winged altarpiece removed from the church when the interior was given a baroque overlay. The museum entrance is in the courtyard. ⊠ *Freyung 6* ☎ *01/534–98–600* ⊕ *www.schottenstift.at* ☉ *Mon.–Sat. 10–5, Sun. 2–5* Ⓤ *U2/Schottentor.*

㉗ Uhrenmuseum (Clock Museum). Tucked away on several floors of a lovely Renaissance structure is an amazing collection of clocks and watches. Try to be here when the hundreds of clocks strike the noon hour. ✉ *Schulhof 2* ☎ *01/533–2265* ⏲ *Tues.–Sun. 9–4:30* Ⓤ *U3/Herreng.*

Vienna Environs

Wienerwald (Vienna Woods). You can reach a small corner of the historic Vienna Woods by streetcar and bus: take a streetcar or the U2 subway line to Schottentor/University and, from there, Streetcar 38 (Grinzing) to the end of the line. To get into the woods, change in Grinzing to Bus 38A. This will take you to the Kahlenberg, which provides a superb view out over the Danube and the city. You can take the bus or hike to the Leopoldsberg, the promontory over the Danube from which Turkish invading forces were repulsed during the 16th and 17th centuries. Grinzing itself is a village out of a picture book. Unfortunately, it also attracts its fair share of tour buses. For less touristy wine villages, try Sievering (Bus 39A), Neustift am Walde (U4, U6 subway to Spittelau, then Bus 35A), or the suburb of Nussdorf (Streetcar D).

Where to Eat

In the mid-1990s Vienna, once a culinary backwater, produced a new generation of chefs willing to slaughter sacred cows and create a *Neue Küche*, a new Vienna cuisine. This trend relies on lighter versions of the old standbys and combinations of such traditional ingredients as *Kürbiskernöl* (pumpkin-seed oil) and fruit sauces instead of butter and cream.

In a first-class restaurant you will pay as much as in most other Western European capitals. But you can still find good food at refreshingly low prices in the simpler neighborhood Gasthäuser (rustic inns). If you eat your main meal at noon (as the Viennese do), you can take advantage of the luncheon specials available at most restaurants.

$$$$
Fodor'sChoice
★
✗ **Steirereck.** Plans are under way for the new Steirereck am Stadtpark to be housed in the former Milk Drinking Hall, which was built in 1901 and stands next to a pretty pond in Vienna's city park. The haute cuisine Steirereck is known for will remain the same, such as delicate smoked catfish, turbot in an avocado crust, or tender lamb with crepes. At the end of the meal, be sure to sample the outstanding selection of cheeses from the cheese cellar. ✉ *Stadtpark* ☎ *01/713–3168* ⌐ *Reservations essential* 🏛 *Jacket and tie* ▭ *AE, DC, MC, V* ⏲ *Closed weekends* Ⓤ *U3/Stubentor or Tram 1 or 2.*

$$$–$$$$
✗ **Fabio's.** Though not much on decor, this minimalist, super-trendy, always crowded hot spot just off the Graben offers plenty in the way of people-watching. In summer it's especially agreeable with floor-to-ceiling windows opening onto a charming, narrow street. Start with an appetizer of marinated octopus, calamari, and mussels, then try the buttery risotto with grilled shrimp or lasagna stuffed with tender strips of steak and vegetables. Don't forget to order the luscious crème caramel for dessert. Service is pleasant, though it can be uneven. ✉ *Tuchlauben 6* ☎ *01/532–2222* ▭ *AE, DC, MC, V* ⏲ *Closed Sun.* Ⓤ *U1, U3/Stephanspl.*

★ **$$–$$$**
✗ **Artner.** This sleek restaurant with discreet lighting has one of the most innovative menus in the city, and it showcases exceptional wines from its own 350-year-old winery in the Carnuntum region east of Vienna. Delicious appetizers include a salad of field greens and grilled goat cheese (another house specialty), and recommended main courses are crispy pike perch with black-olive risotto or wild boar schnitzel with a potato-and-greens salad. You can choose to sit at the bar and have a glass of wine and the Artner sandwich—crusty grilled bread stuffed with melted goat cheese and grilled steak strips. ✉ *Florag. 6 (entrance on Neumanng.)* ☎ *01/503–5033* ▭ *AE, DC, MC, V* ⏲ *No lunch weekends* Ⓤ *U1/Taubstummeng.*

\$\$–\$\$\$ ✕ **Barbaro's.** The downstairs bistro with an open kitchen is *the* place to go in the city for superb pizzas and pastas. Settle into comfortable red leather chairs and wait for the wood-fired oven to turn out foccaccia and thin-crust pizzas topped with arugula and shaved Parmesan or ham and buffalo mozzarella. ⊠ *Neuer Markt 8* ☎ *01/955–2525* ▭ *AE, DC, MC, V* Ⓤ *U1 or U4/Karlspl.*

\$\$ ✕ **Palmenhaus.** Twenty-foot-high palm trees and exotic plants decorate this large, contemporary restaurant in the Hofburg Palace conservatory, at the back of the Burggarten and next to the Schmetterlinghaus. Seafood is the focus here, and it's temptingly featured in soups and risottos or simply grilled with lemon. A blackboard lists daily fish specials, and several vegetarian dishes are offered, such as pumpkin gnocchi. In fine weather, tables are set outside on the terrace overlooking the park. Service can be slow. ⊠ *Burggarten (or through Goetheg. gate after 8 PM)* ☎ *01/533–1033* 🖎 *Reservations essential* ▭ *DC, MC, V* Ⓤ *U2/MuseumsQuartier or Trams 1, 2, and D/Burgring.*

\$–\$\$ ✕ **Brezl Gwölb.** Housed in a medieval pretzel factory between Am Hof and Judenplatz, this snug restaurant fills up fast at night. Try the scrumptious *Tyroler G'röstl*, home-fried potatoes with slivered ham and onions served in a blackened skillet. Best tables are downstairs in the authentic medieval cellar, which looks like a set from *Phantom of the Opera*. ⊠ *Ledererhof 9* ☎ *01/533–8811* ▭ *AE, DC, MC, V* Ⓤ *U2/Schottentor.*

\$–\$\$ ✕ **Figlmüller.** Known for its gargantuan Wiener schnitzel—so large it usually overflows the plate—Figlmüller is always packed with diners sharing benches and long tables. Food choices are limited, and everything is à la carte. Try to get a table in the greenhouse passageway area. ⊠ *Wollzeile 5 (passageway from Stephansdom)* ☎ *01/512–6177* ▭ *No credit cards* ☉ *Closed Aug.* Ⓤ *U1/Stephanspl.*

\$–\$\$ ✕ **Frank's.** A cavernous cellar-like restaurant with aged brick walls, arches, and candlelight is not exactly what you'd expect to find inside the ultramodern central post office building. People come to Frank's for fun, and to choose from the vast selection of pizzas, burgers (both chicken and beef), salads, and pastas. There are also plenty of vegetarian and fresh-fish items. From October to April, Frank's offers a popular Sunday brunch with, among other American-style staples, bagels and Bloody Marys. ⊠ *Laurenzerberg 2 (entrance Postpassage Schwedenpl.)* ☎ *01/533–7805* 🖎 *Reservations essential* ▭ *D, MC, V* ☉ *No lunch Sat., no dinner Sun.* Ⓤ *U1, U4/Schwedenpl.*

\$–\$\$ ✕ **Hansen.** Housed downstairs in the Börse (Vienna Stock Exchange), this unique restaurant is also an exotic, upscale flower market. The decor is elegant, with close-set tables covered in white linen. The menu highlights Mediterranean-inspired dishes such as scampi risotto or spaghettini with oven-dried tomatoes in a black-olive cream sauce. There are also Austrian dishes done with a fresh, light slant. Lunch is the main event here, though you can also come for breakfast or a pretheater dinner. ⊠ *Wipplingerstr. 34* ☎ *01/532–0542* 🖎 *Reservations essential* ▭ *AE, DC, MC, V* ☉ *Closed Sun. and after 8 PM* Ⓤ *Tram 2 or D/Börse.*

\$–\$\$ ✕ **Lebenbauer.** Vienna's premier vegetarian restaurant has a no-smoking room, rare in this part of Europe. Specialties include soy and fennel in a curry sauce with ginger, pineapple, and wild rice, and spinach tortellini in a Gorgonzola sauce. ⊠ *Teinfaltstr. 3, near Freyung* ☎ *01/533–5556–0* ▭ *AE, DC, MC, V* ☉ *Closed weekends and first 2 wks in Aug.* Ⓤ *U2/Schottentor.*

\$ ✕ **Beim Czaak.** Pronounced "bime chalk," this simple spot with friendly service is a favorite with locals. It's long and narrow, with forest-green walls, framed caricatures of a few well-known Viennese on the walls, and limited seating outdoors. Choose a glass of Austrian wine to go along with Waldviertler pork stuffed with bacon, onions, and mushrooms, or spinach dumplings drizzled with Parmesan and browned butter. ⊠ *Postg. 15, corner of Fleischmarkt* ☎ *01/513–7215* ▭ *No credit cards* ⊘ *Closed Sun.* Ⓤ *U1 or U4/Schwedenpl.*

$ ╳ **Salzgries.** A typical old Viennese *Beisl,* which is a cross between a café and a pub, the Salzgries has an unpretentious, rather worn look. It's known for having good schnitzels, and you can get pork, milk-fed veal, or chicken breast, all fried to a golden crispness, with potato salad on the side. The *Vanillerostbraten* (garlicky rump steak) is also worth trying, and the *Moor im Hemd,* warm chocolate cake with whipped cream, is scrumptious. ⊠ *Marc-Aurel-Str. 6* ☎ *01/968–9645* ▭ *No credit cards* Ⓤ *U1 or U4/ Schwedenpl.*

Cafés

A quintessential Viennese institution, the coffeehouse, or café, is club, pub, and bistro all rolled into one. To savor the atmosphere of the coffeehouses you must take your time: set aside an afternoon, a morning, or at least a couple of hours, and settle down in one of your choice. There is no need to worry about overstaying your welcome, even over a single small cup of Mokka—although in some of the more opulent coffeehouses this cup of coffee and a pastry can cost as much as a meal.

Alte Backstube (⊠ Langeg. 34 ☎ 01/406–1101), in a gorgeous baroque house—with a café in front and restaurant in back—was once a bakery and is now a museum as well. **Café Central** (⊠ Herreng. 14, in Palais Ferstel ☎ 01/533–3763–26) is where Trotsky played chess; in the Palais Ferstel, it's one of Vienna's most beautiful cafés. **Cafe Landtmann** (⊠ Dr. Karl Leuger Str. 4 ☎ 01/532–0621), next to the dignified Burgtheater, with front-row views of the Ringstrasse, was reputedly Freud's favorite café. A 200-year-old institution, **Demel** (⊠ Kohlmarkt 14 ☎ 01/535–1717–0) is the grande dame of Viennese cafés. The elegant front rooms have more atmosphere than the airy modern atrium, while the first room is reserved for nonsmokers. Order the famous coffee and compare the Sacher torte with the one served up at the Sacher—for more than 100 years there has been an ongoing feud over who owns the original recipe. **Gerstner** (⊠ Kärntnerstr. 11–15 ☎ 01/512–496377) is in the heart of the bustling Kärntnerstrasse and is one of the more modern Viennese cafés, though it has been going strong since the mid-18th century. **Museum** (⊠ Friedrichstr. 6 ☎ 01/586–5202), with its original interior by the architect Adolf Loos, draws a mixed crowd and has an ample supply of newspapers. The **Sacher** (⊠ Philharmonikerstr. 4 ☎ 01/514560) is hardly a typical Vienna café; more a shrine to plush gilt and marzipan, it's both a must-see and a must-eat, despite the crowds of tourists here to order the world's ultimate chocolate cake.

Where to Stay

Vienna's first district (A-1010) is the best base for visitors because it's so close to most of the major sights, restaurants, and shops. This accessibility translates, of course, into higher prices. Try bargaining for discounts at the larger international chain hotels during the off-season.

$$$$ ▦ **Bristol.** This venerable landmark, dating from 1892, has one of the finest locations in the city, on the Ring next to the Opera House. The accent here is on tradition, and guest rooms are sumptuously furnished in Biedermeier style with decorative fireplaces, thick carpets, wing chairs, crystal chandeliers, and lace curtains. Penthouse rooms have terraces with staggering views of the Opera. The Bristol also houses the acclaimed Korso restaurant, the convivial Café Sirk, and a music salon complete with a pianist lulling the after-theater crowd with tunes on a time-burnished Boesendorfer. ⊠ *Kärntner Ring 1 A-1010* ☎ *01/515–*

16–0 🖶 *01/515–16–550* 🌐 *www.westin.com* 🛏 *141 rooms* ♨ *2 restaurants* 🖃 *AE, DC, MC, V.*

$$$$ 🏨 **Imperial.** The hotel is as much a palace today as when it was formally
FodorśChoice opened in 1873 by Emperor Franz Josef. The emphasis is on Old Vi-
★ enna elegance and privacy; the guest list is littered with famous names,
from heads of state to Michael Jackson. The beautiful rooms are furnished in antique style, though only the first three floors are part of the
original house and have high ceilings; subsequent floors were added in
the late 1930s. Suites include your own personal butler. ⊠ *Kärntner Ring
16, A-1010* 🖀 *01/501–10–0* 🖶 *01/501–10–410* 🌐 *www.luxurycollection.
com* 🛏 *138 rooms* ♨ *Restaurant* 🖃 *AE, DC, MC, V.*

$$$$ 🏨 **Palais Schwarzenberg.** Set against a vast formal park, the palace,
built in the early 1700s, seems like a country estate though it's just a
few minutes' walk from the heart of the city. The public salons are grand
and glorious, while each guest room is individual and luxuriously appointed, with original artwork adorning the walls. A renovated wing
has ultramodern suites by Italian designer Paolo Piva. You don't have
to be a guest here to come for a drink, coffee, or light lunch, served outside on the terrace in summer or beside a roaring fireplace in the main
sitting room in winter. ⊠ *Schwarzenbergpl. 9 A-1030* 🖀 *01/798–
4515–0* 🖶 *01/798–4714* 🌐 *www.palais-schwarzenberg.com* 🛏 *44
rooms* ♨ *Restaurant, pool, bar* 🖃 *AE, DC, MC, V.*

★ **$$$$** 🏨 **Sacher.** The grand old Sacher dates from 1876, and it has retained
its sense of history over the years while providing luxurious, modern-
day comfort. The corridors are a veritable art gallery, and the exquisitely
furnished bedrooms also contain original artwork. The location directly behind the Opera House could hardly be more central, and the
ratio of staff to guests is more than two to one. Meals in the Red Room
or Anna Sacher Room are first-rate; the Café Sacher, of course, is legendary. ⊠ *Philharmonikerstr. 4, A-1010* 🖀 *01/514–56–0* 🖶 *01/514–
57–810* 🌐 *www.sacher.com* 🛏 *113 rooms* ♨ *Restaurant, bar* 🖃 *AE,
DC, MC, V.*

$$$ 🏨 **König von Ungarn.** In a dormered, 16th-century house in the shadow
of St. Stephen's Cathedral, this hotel began catering to court nobility in
1815. The hotel radiates charm—rooms (some with Styrian wood-pan-
eled walls) are furnished with country antiques and have walk-in clos-
ets and double sinks in the sparkling bathrooms. The eight suites are
two-storied, and two have balconies with rooftop views. The inviting
atrium bar, bedecked with marble columns, ferns, and hunting trophies,
beckons you in to sit and have a drink. Insist on written confirmation
of bookings. ⊠ *Schulerstr. 10, A-1010* 🖀 *01/515–84–0* 🖶 *01/515–
848* 🌐 *www.kvu.at* 🛏 *33 rooms* ♨ *Restaurant* 🖃 *DC, MC, V.*

$$–$$$ 🏨 **Regina.** This dignified old hotel with grand reception rooms sits re-
gally on the edge of the Altstadt, commanding a view of Sigmund Freud
Park. It's near the Votivkirche, and about a 10-minute walk from the
center. The high-ceiling rooms are quiet, spacious, and attractively dec-
orated with contemporary furniture, and most have charming sitting areas.
Freud, who lived nearby, used to eat breakfast in the hotel's café every
morning. Buffet breakfast is included. ⊠ *Rooseveltpl. 15, A-1090* 🖀 *01/
404–460* 🖶 *01/408–8392* 🌐 *www.hotelregina.at* 🛏 *125 rooms* ♨ *Restau-
rant* 🖃 *AE, DC, MC, V.*

★ **$$** 🏨 **Altstadt.** A cognoscenti favorite, this small hotel set in one of Vienna's
most pampered neighborhoods was once a patrician home. Close to the
shops of Spittelberg and one streetcar stop from the main museums, this
place is known for its personable and helpful management. Palm trees,
a Secession-style wrought-iron staircase, modernist fabrics, and halogen lighting make for a design-style interior. Rooms are large with all
the modern comforts, and upper floors have views of the city roofline.

The English-style lounge has a fireplace and plump floral sofas. ☒ *Kircheng. 41, A-1070* ☎ *01/526–3399–0* 🖷 *01/523–4901* ⊕ *www.altstadt.at* ⤶ *25 rooms* ⊟ *AE, DC, MC, V.*

$$ 🏨 **Austria.** Tucked away on a tiny cul-de-sac, this older house offers the ultimate in quiet only five minutes' walk from the heart of the city. The high-ceiling rooms are pleasing in their combination of dark wood and lighter walls, and Oriental carpets cover many floors. The courtyard terrace is a perfect place to sip coffee. ☒ *Wolfeng. 3/Fleischmarkt 20, A-1010* ☎ *01/515–23–0* 🖷 *01/515–23–506* ⊕ *www.hotelaustria-wien.at* ⤶ *46 rooms* ⊟ *AE, DC, MC, V.*

$$ 🏨 **Museum.** In a beautiful belle epoque mansion just a five-minute walk from the Art History and Natural History museums, this elegant pension offers large, comfortable rooms with TV. There is also a sunny sitting room with deep, stuffed sofas and wing chairs, perfect for curling up in with a good book. This is a popular place, so book ahead. ☒ *Museumstr. 3 A-1070* ☎ *01/523–44–260* 🖷 *01/523–44–2630* ⤶ *15 rooms* ⊟ *AE, DC, MC, V.*

$$ 🏨 **Zur Wiener Staatsoper.** A great deal of loving care has gone into this family-owned hotel near the State Opera, reputed to be one of the Viennese settings in John Irving's *Hotel New Hampshire*. Rooms are small but have high ceilings and are charmingly decorated with pretty fabrics. ☒ *Krugerstr. 11, A-1010* ☎ *01/513–1274* 🖷 *01/513–1274–15* ⊕ *www.zurwienerstaatsoper.at* ⤶ *22 rooms* ⊟ *AE, MC, V.*

$ 🏨 **Pension Riedl.** Across the square from the Postsparkasse—the famous 19th-century postal savings bank designed by Otto Wagner—this small establishment offers pleasant rooms with cable TV. Breakfast is delivered to your room. Friendly owner Maria Felser is happy to arrange concert tickets and tours. ☒ *Georg-Coch-Pl. 3/4/10 (near Julius-Raab Pl.), A-1010* ☎ *01/512–7919* 🖷 *01/512–7919–8* ⤶ *8 rooms* ⊟ *DC, MC, V* ☉ *Closed last wk in Jan. and first 2 wks in Feb.*

$ 🏨 **Reimer.** The cheery, comfortable Reimer is in a prime location just off the Mariahilferstrasse. Rooms have high ceilings and large windows. Breakfast is included. ☒ *Kircheng. 18, A-1070* ☎ *01/523–6162* 🖷 *01/524–3782* ⤶ *14 rooms* ⊟ *MC, V.*

Nightlife & the Arts

The Arts

MUSIC Classical concerts are held in the **Konzerthaus** (☒ Lothringerstr. 20 ☎ 01/242002 ⊕ www.konzerthaus.at), featuring the Vienna Symphonic Orchestra, which also occasionally plays modern and jazz pieces. The **Musikverein** (☒ Bösendorferstr. 12 ☎ 01/505–8190–0 ⊕ www.musikverein.at) is the home of the acclaimed Vienna Philharmonic Orchestra. Tickets can be bought at their box offices or ordered by phone. Tickets to various musical events are sold through the **Vienna Ticket Service** (☎ 01/534–130).

THEATER & Check the monthly program published by the city; posters also show
OPERA opera and theater schedules. The **Staatsoper,** one of the world's great opera houses, presents major stars in its almost-nightly original-language performances. The **Volksoper** offers operas, operettas, and musicals, also in original-language performances. Performances at the **Akadamietheater** and **Burgtheater** are in German. Tickets for the Staatsoper, the Volksoper, and the Burg and Akademie theaters are available at the **central ticket office** (☒ Bundestheaterkassen, Hanuschg. 3 ☎ 01/514–440 or 01/513–1513 🖷 Staatsoper and Volkstheater 01/51444–3669; Akadamietheater and Burgtheater 01/514444–4147), or you can go in person to the office at the left rear of the Opera, open weekdays 8–6, Saturday 9–2, Sunday and holidays 9–noon. Tickets go on sale a month

before performances. Unsold tickets can be obtained at the evening box office. Tickets can be ordered three weeks or more in advance in writing, by fax, or a month in advance by phone. Standing-room tickets for the Staatsoper are a great bargain.

Theater is offered in English at **Vienna's English Theater** (✉ Josefsg. 12 ☎ 01/402–1260–0). The **International Theater** (✉ Porzellang. 8 ☎ 01/319–6272) is also a popular choice for seeing plays in English.

Nightlife

The central district for nightlife in Vienna is nicknamed the **Bermuda-Dreieck** (Bermuda Triangle). Centered on Judengasse/Seitenstettengasse, next to St. Ruprecht's, a small Romanesque church, the area is jammed with everything from good bistros to jazz clubs.

CABARETS   Cabaret has a long tradition in Vienna. To get much from any of it, you'll need good German with a smattering of Viennese vernacular as well, plus some knowledge of local affairs. A popular cabaret-nightclub is **Moulin Rouge** (✉ Walfischg. 11 ☎ 01/512–2130), where there are floor shows and some striptease. **Simpl** (✉ Wollzeile 36 ☎ 01/512–4742) continues earning its reputation for barbed political wit.

DISCOS   **Atrium** (✉ Schwarzenbergpl. 10, A-1040 ☎ 01/505–3594) offers everything from hip-hop and rap to pop-rock. **Eden Bar** (✉ Lilieng. 2 ☎ 01/512–7450) is the leading spot for the well-heeled, mature crowd with a live band playing most nights. **Havana** (✉ Mahlerstr. 11 ☎ 01/513–2075) is great for salsa and dancing and draws the young adult crowd. The **U-4** (✉ Schönbrunnerstr. 222 ☎ 01/815–8307) has a different theme every night, including gay night on Thursday.

NIGHTCLUBS   A former 1950s cinema just off the Kärntnerstrasse, **Kruger** (✉ Krugerstr. 5 ☎ 01/512–2455) now draws crowds with its deep leather sofas and English gentleman's club atmosphere. Near the Vienna Stock Exchange is the **Planter's Club** (✉ Zelinkag. 4 ☎ 01/533–3393–16), offering a nice selection of rums in a tropical colonial atmosphere. An outdoor glass elevator whisks you up to the **Skybar** (✉ Kärntnerstr. 19 ☎ 01/513–1712) at the top of the Steffl department store, where dramatic views and piano music set the mood.

WINE TAVERNS   Some of the city's atmospheric *Heurige,* or wine taverns, date from the 12th century. Open at lunchtime as well as evenings, the **Augustinerkeller** (✉ Augustinerstr. 1 ☎ 01/533–1026), in the Albertina Building, is a cheery wine tavern with live, schmaltzy music after 6 PM. The **Esterházykeller** (✉ Haarhof 1 ☎ 01/533–3482), in a particularly mazelike network of rooms, has good wines. The **Zwölf Apostelkeller** (✉ Sonnenfelsg. 3 ☎ 01/512–6777), near St. Stephen's, has rooms that are down, down, down underground.

Shopping

Boutiques
Famous names line the **Kohlmarkt** and **Graben** and their respective side streets, as well as the side streets off **Kärntnerstrasse.**

Folk Costumes
The main resource for exquisite Austrian *Trachten* (native dress) is **Loden-Plankl** (✉ Michaelerpl. 6 ☎ 01/533–8032).

Food & Flea Markets
The **Naschmarkt** (foodstuffs market; ✉ between Rechte and Linke Wienzeile) is a sensational open-air market offering specialties from around the world. The fascinating **Flohmarkt** (flea market; Ⓤ U-4 to Ketten-

brückeng.), open Saturday 8–4, operates year-round beyond the Naschmarkt. An **Arts and Antiques Market** (⊹ beside Danube Canal near Salztorbrücke) has a mixed selection, including some high-quality offerings. It's open May–September, weekends 10–6. Check Am Hof Square for antiques and collectibles on Thursday and Friday from late spring to early fall. Also try the seasonal markets in Freyung Square.

Shopping Districts

Kärntnerstrasse is lined with luxury boutiques and large emporiums. The Viennese do much of their in-town shopping in the many department and specialty stores of **Mariahilferstrasse**.

Vienna Essentials

AIRPORTS & TRANSFERS

All flights use Schwechat Airport, about 16 km (10 mi) southwest of Vienna.
🛈 **Schwechat Airport** ☎ 01/7007–0.

TRANSFERS A new super-fast double-decker train will run from Vienna's Schwechat Airport to Wien-Mitte in the center of the city, beginning in December 2003. The ride will take only 15 minutes and will operate every 30 minutes between 5:30 AM and midnight. The cost is estimated €8. Otherwise, the cheapest way into town is the S7 train (called the *Schnellbahn*), which shuttles every half hour between the airport and the Landstrasse/Wien-Mitte (city center) and Wien-Nord (north Vienna) stations; the fare is about €3, and the trip takes 35 minutes. Follow the picture signs of a train to the basement of the airport. Your ticket is also good for an immediate transfer to your destination within the city on the streetcar, bus, or U-Bahn.

Buses from the airport go to the City Air Terminal at the Hilton every 20 minutes between 6:30 AM and 11 PM, and every 30 minutes after that; traveling time is 20 minutes. Another line goes to the South and West train stations (Südbahnhof and Westbahnhof) in 20 and 35 minutes respectively. Departure times are every 30 minutes from 8:10 AM to 7:10 PM, hourly thereafter, and not at all 12:10–3:30 AM. Fare is €5.80 one-way, €10.90 for a round-trip. A taxi from the airport to downtown Vienna costs about €30–€40; agree on a price in advance. The cheapest cab service to the airport is C+K Airport Service, charging a set price of €23 (don't forget to tip, usually a couple of euros). C+K will also meet your plane at no extra charge if you let them know your flight information in advance.
🛈 **C+K Airport Service** ☎ 01/44444. **City Air Terminal** ✉ Am Stadtpark ☎ 05/1717.

BIKE TRAVEL

Vienna has hundreds of miles of marked bike routes, including reserved routes through the center of the city. Paved routes parallel the Danube. For details, get the city brochure on biking. Bicycles can be rented at a number of locations and can be taken on the Vienna subway year-round all day Sunday and holidays from 9 to 3, after 6:30 on weekdays, and, from May through September, after 9 AM Saturday. You'll need a half-fare ticket for the bike.

BUS TRAVEL WITHIN VIENNA

Inner-city buses are numbered 1A through 3A and operate weekdays until about 8 PM, Saturday until 7 PM. Reduced fares are available for these routes (buy a *Kurzstreckenkarte*; it allows you four trips for €3) as well as designated shorter stretches (roughly two to four stops) on all other bus and streetcar lines. Streetcars and buses are numbered or lettered according to route, and they run until midnight. Night buses marked "N" follow 22 special routes every half hour between 12:30 AM and 4:30 AM. Get a route plan from the public transport or VORVERKAUF offices. The fare is the same as for a regular daytime ticket, €1.50. The central terminus is Schwedenplatz. Streetcars 1 and 2 run the circular route around the Ring clockwise and counterclockwise, respectively.

CAR TRAVEL

The main access routes are the expressways to the west and south (Westautobahn A1, Südautobahn A2). Routes leading to the downtown area are marked ZENTRUM.

Unless you know your way around the city, a car is more of a nuisance than a help. The center of the city is a pedestrian zone, and city on-street parking is a problem. Observe signs; tow-away is expensive. In winter, overnight parking is forbidden on city streets with streetcar lines. Overnight street parking in Districts I, VI, VII, VIII, and IX is restricted to residents with stickers; check before you leave a car on the street, even for a brief period. You can park in the inner city for free on weekends and holidays and at night from 7 PM until midnight, but check street signs first.

CONSULATES

🛈 United Kingdom ✉ Jauresg. 10, near Schloss Belvedere ☎ 01/71613-5151.
🛈 United States ✉ Gartenbaupromenade, Parkring 12A, in Marriott building ☎ 01/313-39.

EMERGENCIES

If you need a doctor, ask your hotel, or in an emergency, phone your embassy or consulate. In each neighborhood, one pharmacy (*Apotheke*) in rotation is open all night and weekends; the address is posted on each area pharmacy.
🛈 Emergency Services **Ambulance** ☎ 144. **Police** ☎ 133.

ENGLISH-LANGUAGE MEDIA

🛈 Bookstores **British Bookshop** ✉ Weihburgg. 24-26 ☎ 01/512-1945-0 ✉ Mariahilferstr. 4 ☎ 01/522-6730. **Shakespeare & Co.** ✉ Sterng. 2 ☎ 01/535-5053.

SUBWAY TRAVEL

Subway (U-Bahn) lines—stations are marked with a huge blue "U"—are designated U-1, U-2, U-3, U-4, and U-6, and are clearly marked and color-coded. Trains run daily until about 12:30 AM. Additional services are provided by fast suburban trains, the S-bahn, indicated by a stylized blue "S" symbol. Both are tied into the general city fare system.

TAXIS

Cabs can be flagged on the street if the FREI (free) sign is lit. You can also dial ☎ 60160, 31300, or 40100 to request one. All rides around town are metered. The initial fare is €2, but expect to pay €5–€9 for an average city ride. There are additional charges for luggage, and a surcharge of €1 is added at night, on Sunday, and for telephone orders. Tip the driver by rounding up the fare.

TOURS

BUS TOURS Tours will take you to cultural events and nightclubs, and there are daytime bus trips to the Danube Valley, Salzburg, and Budapest, among other spots. Check with the City Tourist Office or your hotel.

The following are city orientation tours. Prices are similar, but find out whether you will visit or just drive past Schönbrunn and Belvedere palaces and whether admission fees are included. Cityrama provides city tours with hotel pickup. Vienna Sightseeing Tours offers a short highlights tour or a lengthier one to the Vienna Woods, Mayerling, and other sights near Vienna. Tours start in front of or beside the Staatsoper on the Operngasse.

🏛 **Cityrama** ☎ 01/534–130. **Vienna Sightseeing Tours** ☎ 01/712–4683–0.

WALKING TOURS Guided walking tours in English are available almost daily and include such topics as "Jewish Vienna." Check with the City Tourist Office or your hotel.

TRAIN TRAVEL

Vienna has four train stations. The Westbahnhof is for trains to and from Linz, Salzburg, and Innsbruck and to and from Germany, France, and Switzerland. The Südbahnhof is for trains to and from Graz, Klagenfurt, Villach, and Italy. The Franz-Josefs-Bahnhof, or Nordbahnhof, is for trains to and from Prague, Berlin, and Warsaw. Go to the Wien-Mitte/Landstrasse Hauptstrasse station for local trains to and from the north of the city. Budapest trains use both the Westbahnhof and Südbahnhof, and Bratislava trains both Wien-Mitte and the Südbahnhof, so check.

TRANSPORTATION AROUND VIENNA

Vienna is fairly easy to explore on foot; much of the heart of the city—the area within the Ringstrasse—is a pedestrian zone. Public transportation is comfortable, convenient, and frequent, though not cheap. Tickets for buses, subways, and streetcars are available in subway stations and from dispensers on buses and streetcars. Tickets in multiples of five are sold at cigarette shops—look for the sign TABAK-TRAFIK—or at the window marked VORVERKAUF at such central stations as Karlsplatz or Stephansplatz. A block of five tickets costs €7.50, a single ticket €1.50, a 24-hour ticket €5, a three-day tourist ticket €12, and an eight-day ticket €24. Maps and information in English are available at the Stephansplatz, Karlsplatz, and Praterstern U-Bahn stations.

The Vienna Card, available for €15.25 at tourist offices and most hotels, combines 72 hours' use of public transportation with discounts at certain museums and shops throughout the city.

TRAVEL AGENCIES

🏛 **American Express** ✉ Kärntnerstr. 21–23 ☎ 01/515–40–0. **Ökista** ✉ Garnisong. 7, A-1090 ☎ 01/401–480. **Österreichisches Verkehrsbüro** (Austrian Travel Agency) ✉ Friedrichstr. 7, A-1010 ☎ 01/588–000 🖷 01/58800–280.

VISITOR INFORMATION

🏛 **City Tourist Office** ✉ Am Albertinapl. 1, A-1010 ☎ 01/24555 🖷 01/216–84–92 ⊕ www.info.wien.at.

THE DANUBE VALLEY

Austria contains some of the most beautiful stretches of the Danube (Donau), extending about 88 km (55 mi) west of Vienna. The river rolls through the celebrated Wachau, a gloriously scenic valley with magnificent countryside, some of Austria's best food and wine, and comfortable—in some cases elegant—accommodations. Above the river are the ruins of ancient castles. The abbeys at Melk and Göttweig, with their magnificent libraries, dominate their settings. Vineyards sweep down to the river, which is lined with fruit trees that burst into blossom every spring. People here live close to the land, and at certain times of year vintners open their homes to sell their own wines and produce. Roadside stands offer flowers, fruits, vegetables, and wines. This is also a region of legend: the Danube shares with the Rhine the story of the mythical Nibelungen, defenders of Siegfried, hero of German myth.

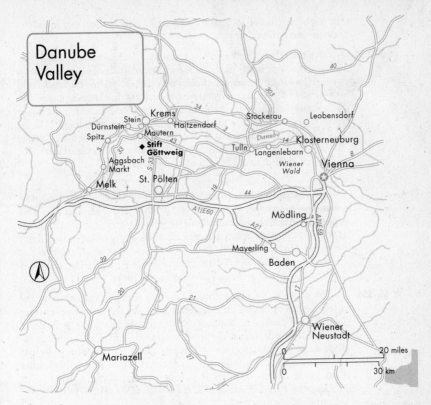

Danube
Valley

The most delightful way to approach the Wachau is by boat, but car
and train routes are also scenically splendid. From Vienna you can follow the southern Danube bank, crossing at Melk and returning along
the north bank. Vienna to Melk is about 112 km (70 mi), the return
along the north bank about 109 km (68 mi).

Klosterneuburg

The massive **Stift Klosterneuburg** (abbey) dominating this market town
was established in 1114; treasures in its museum include an enameled
altar dating from 1181. The abbey is a major agricultural landowner
in the region, and its extensive vineyards produce excellent wines.
✉ *Stiftspl. 1* ☎ *02243/411–0* ⊕ *www.stift-klosterneuburg.at* ✆ *Weekdays 9–6, weekends 10–5; tours in English Sun. and holidays at 2.*

Designed by Heinz Tesar, the **Sammlung Essl** contemporary art museum
displays post–World War II works. The permanent collection includes
pieces by regional artists, such as Hermann Nietsch and Arnulf Rainer,
and changing exhibits have celebrated contemporary notables like Nam
June Paik. The museum also hosts special evening concerts highlighting the work of various modern composers. ✉ *An der Donau–Au 1*
☎ *0800/232–800* ⊕ *www.sammlung-essl.at* ✆ *Tues., Thurs.–Sun. 10–7,
Wed. 10–9.*

Göttweig

You will see **Stift Göttweig** high above the Danube Valley long before you
reach it. This impressive 11th-century Benedictine abbey affords sensational panoramas of the Danube Valley; you can stroll the grounds
and visit the chapel. ✉ *Rte. 303, on south bank of Danube, opposite
Krems, Furth bei Göttweig* ☎ *02732/85581–231* ⊕ *www.stiftgoettweig.
or.at* ✆ *June–Sept., daily 9–6, Oct.–May, daily 10–6, last admittance 5*

PM; *tours (minimum 10 people) daily at 11 and 3; tours in English require a reservation.*

★ **$$–$$$** ✕▣ **Schickh.** This rambling yellow restaurant, tucked away beside a clear brook and among lovely old trees below the north side of Göttweig Abbey, is worth looking for. Seasonal choices may include creamy *Bärlauch* (wild wood garlic) soup, organic Waldviertler duck and homemade dumplings, or delicately seasoned fried chicken. Be sure to save room for the house dessert, *Cremeschnitte*, a light cream pastry. There are a handful of inexpensive guest rooms available for overnighters. ✉ *Furth bei Göttweig* ☎ *02736/7218–0* 🖷 *02736/7218–0* ⚑ *Reservations essential* ▭ *MC, V* ☺ *Closed Wed. and Thurs. and mid-Jan.–Mar.*

Melk

The **Benediktinerstift Melk** (Benedictine Abbey of Melk) is one of the most impressive in Europe, commandingly perched above the Danube. This is one of Austria's monumental, major sights, with its library rich in art as well as books; the ceiling frescoes are particularly memorable. ✉ *Abt Berthold Dietmayr-Str. 1* ☎ *02752/555-232* ⊕ *www.stiftmelk.at* ☺ *May–Sept., daily 9–5 (ticket office closes at 4); Oct.–Apr., daily 9–4 (ticket office closes at 3); call for tours in English.*

★ **$$–$$$** ✕▣ **Stadt Melk.** Nestled below the golden abbey in the center of the village square, this elegant restaurant has been well known ever since the duke and duchess of Windsor dined here long ago. Though the decor is decidedly Biedermeier, the food is nouvelle Austrian, and may include duck in a honey glaze or chicken breast stuffed with leeks and accompanied by corn and potato croquettes. There are also 16 rather plain guest rooms upstairs if you feel like making a night of it. ✉ *Hauptpl. 1, A-3390* ☎ *02752/52475* 🖷 *02752/52475–19* ▭ *AE, DC, MC, V.*

Dürnstein

Across the river from Melk, the romantic road hugs the Danube, heading north toward Dürnstein and Krems. The beautiful medieval town of Dürnstein is associated with Richard the Lion-Hearted, who was imprisoned in its now-ruined castle for 13 months in 1192–93. The town is also known for its fine hotels, restaurants, and wines, and for its gloriously baroque Stiftskirche (church).

$$$–$$$$ ▣ **Richard Löwenherz.** The impressive, vaulted reception rooms of this FodorśChoice former convent are beautifully furnished with antiques, and the invit-
★ ing open fire, stone floors, grandfather clock, and bowls of fresh roses make this one of the most romantic of the Romantic Hotels group. Though all rooms are spacious and comfortable, the balconied guest rooms in the newer part of the house have more modern furnishings. Wander the grounds among the roses, oleanders, and fig trees, all set against the backdrop of 600-year-old stone walls. ✉ *Dürnstein 8, A-3061* ☎ *02711/ 222* 🖷 *02711/222–18* ⊕ *www.loewenherz.cc* ⇜ *38 rooms* ⚐ *Restaurant, pool, bar* ▭ *AE, DC, MC, V* ☺ *Closed Nov.–Mar.*

Krems/Stein an der Donau

Remnants of the ancient city wall are prominent in this 1,000-year-old town, with its Renaissance, Gothic, and baroque monuments. Krems and Stein sit at the center of Austria's foremost wine-growing region. You can explore the town center, the churches, and view the Danube from lookout points perched high above the town.

Stein, with its 16th-century houses, is virtually part of adjacent Krems. Look for the former Imperial Toll House and the 14th-century Minoritenkirche, a church that now serves as a museum with temporary exhibitions, just off the main street.

$$ ▣ **Alte Post.** You're allowed to drive into the pedestrian zone to this 16th-century house in the heart of the Old Town, next to the Steinener Tor (Stone Gate). The rooms are in country style, and most have full baths, but the real highlight here is the lovely courtyard, used for dining in summer. ✉ *Obere Landstr. 32, A–3500, Krems* ☎ *02732/82276–0* 🖷 *02732/ 84396* ⊕ *www.altepost-krems.at* 🛏 *23 rooms, 9 with bath* 🍴 *Restaurant* 🗏 *No credit cards* ⊙ *Closed Jan.–mid-Mar.*

The Danube Valley Essentials

BOAT & FERRY TRAVEL

Travel upstream, with stops at Krems, Dürnstein, Melk, and points between. Return to Vienna by boat or by train from Melk (combination tickets available). Check in Vienna with DDSG Blue Danube Schiffahrt for ferry schedules.

🚢 **DDSG Blue Danube Schiffahrt** ✉ Friedrichstr. 7, Vienna ☎ 01/588-800 🖷 01/588-80-440 ⊕ www.ddsg-blue-danube.at.

CAR TRAVEL

If you're pressed for time, take the Autobahn to St. Pölten, turn north onto Route S-33, and follow the signs to Melk. For a more scenic route, follow the south shore of the Danube via Klosterneuburg and Greifenstein, taking Routes 14, 19, 43, and 33. Cross the Danube at Melk, and then return to Vienna along the north bank of the river (Route 3).

TOURS

Vienna travel agencies offer tours of the Wachau ranging from one-day outings to longer excursions.

TRAIN TRAVEL

Depart from the Westbahnhof for Melk, and then take the bus along the north bank of the Danube to Dürnstein and Krems. Side bus trips can be made from Krems to Göttweig.

VISITOR INFORMATION

🚉 **Lower Austria Tourist Office** ✉ Fischhof 3/3, Vienna ☎ 01/53610-6200 🖷 01/53610-6060 ⊕ www.niederoesterreich.at. **Dürnstein** ✉ Parkpl. Ost ☎ 02711/219 ⊕ www.duernstein.at. **Klosterneuburg** ✉ Niedermarkt 4 ☎ 02243/32038 ⊕ www. klosterneuburg.ne. **Krems/Stein an der Donau** ✉ Undstr. 6 ☎ 02732/82676. **Melk** ✉ Babenbergerstr. 1 ☎ 02752/52307-410.

SALZBURG

Salzburg, best known as the birthplace of Wolfgang Amadeus Mozart, receives its greatest number of visitors every summer during its music festival, the world-famous Salzburger Festspiele. Dominated by a fortress on one side and the Kapuzinerberg, a small mountain, on the other, this baroque city is best explored on foot, for many of its most interesting areas are pedestrian precincts. Besides the festival, the city has innumerable other attractions. Thanks to the powerful prince-archbishops of the Habsburg era, few other places offer an equivalent abundance of baroque splendor. Many sites are identifiable from the film that made Salzburg a household name in the United States, *The Sound of Music*. No matter what season you visit, bring an umbrella: Salzburg is noted for sudden, brief downpours.

Exploring Salzburg

Numbers in the margin correspond to points of interest on the Salzburg map.

The Salzach River separates Salzburg's old and "new" towns; for the best perspective on the old, climb the Kapuzinerberg (follow pathways from Linzergasse or Steingasse). For another postcard view, look toward the fortress through the Mirabell Gardens, behind Mirabell Palace. The sweeping panorama from the fortress itself offers the reverse of both perspectives. Wander along Getreidegasse, with its quaint wrought-iron shop signs and the Mönchsberg standing sentinel at the far end. Don't neglect the warren of interconnecting side alleys: these shelter a number of fine shops and often open onto impressive inner courtyards that are guaranteed to be overflowing with flowers in summer.

⑭ Alter Markt (Old Market Square). In the heart of the Altstadt (Old City) is the Alter Markt, the old marketplace and center of secular life in past centuries. Salzburg's narrowest house is squeezed into the north side of the picturesque 17th-century square, which is filled in summer with flower stalls. Look into the former court pharmacy (Hof-Apotheke) for a touch of centuries past. ⊠ *Judeng., Getreideg., Goldg.*

❻ Carolino Augusteum Museum (Historical Museum). The city museum is devoted to art, archaeology, and fascinating musical instruments. ⊠ *Museumspl. 1* ☏ *0662/620808–200* ⊕ *www.smca.at* ☉ *Fri.–Wed. 9–5, Thurs. 9–8.*

★ **❿ Dom** (Cathedral). The cathedral is a complete aesthetic concept and one of Salzburg's most beautiful urban set pieces, whereas the sheer mass of the cathedral itself gives a suggestion of the onetime power of the prince-archbishops who ruled the region. You enter through great bronze doors. A small museum shows off centuries of church treasures. ⊠ *Dompl. 1* ☏ *0662/844189* ⊕ *www.kirchen.net* ☉ *Early May–late Oct., Mon.–Sat. 10–5, Sun. and holidays 1–6.*

★ ☾ **⓫ Festung Hohensalzburg** (Salzburg Fortress). To reach the 12th-century fortress that dominates the city, walk up the narrow Festungsgasse at the back end of Kapitalplatz. From here, you can either follow the footpath up the hill or take a five-minute ride on the funicular, or Festungsbahn. On a sunny day you can hike up Festungsgasse, turning frequently to enjoy the changing panorama of the city below. The terrace restaurant overlooks a *stunning* panorama. A main attraction is **St. George's Chapel,** built in 1501. A year later, in 1502, the chapel acquired the 200-pipe barrel organ, which is played daily in summer at 7 AM, 11 AM, and 6 PM. ⊠ *Mönchsberg 34* ☏ *0662/842430–11* ⊕ *www.salzburg-burgen. at* ☉ *Mid-Mar.–mid-June, daily 9–6; mid-June–mid-Sept., daily 8:30–8; mid-Sept.–mid-Mar., daily 9–5.*

❾ Franziskanerkloster (Franciscan Monastery). A tall, graceful spire marks this 13th-century church, whose modest Romanesque nave soars abruptly into a Gothic fan vault over the baroque altar. Check for mass—frequently one of Mozart's—on Sunday at 9 AM. ⊠ *Franziskanerg. 5* ☏ *0662/ 843629–0* ☉ *Daily 6:30 AM–7 PM.*

❷ Friedhof St. Sebastian (Cemetery of St. Sebastian). This secluded spot is the setting for the scene near the end of *The Sound of Music* when the von Trapps are nearly captured. The cemetery was commissioned in the late 16th century by Prince-Archbishop Wolf Dietrich and built in the arcaded style of an Italian *campo santo*. Wolf Dietrich's brightly tiled mausoleum is unusual for Austria. Also buried here are Mozart's widow,

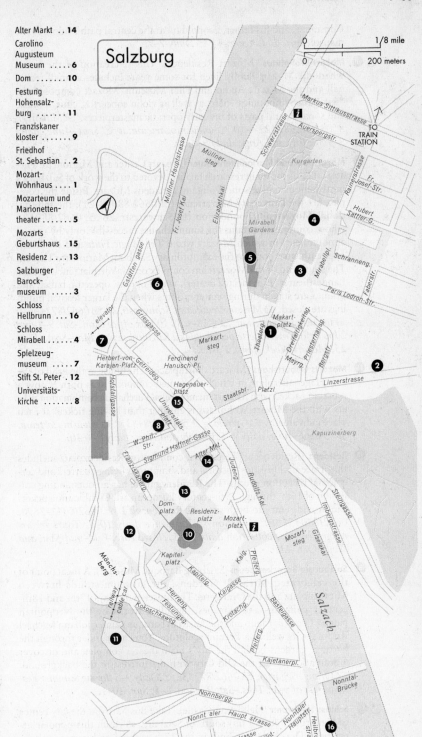

Alter Markt .. **14**

Carolino
Augusteum
Museum **6**

Dom **10**

Festung
Hohensalz-
burg **11**

Franziskaner
kloster **9**

Friedhof
St. Sebastian .. **2**

Mozart-
Wohnhaus **1**

Mozarteum und
Marionetten-
theater **5**

Mozarts
Geburtshaus . **15**

Residenz **13**

Salzburger
Barock-
museum **3**

Schloss
Hellbrunn ... **16**

Schloss
Mirabell **4**

Spielzeug-
museum **7**

Stift St. Peter . **12**

Universitäts-
kirche **8**

Salzburg

0 ___ 1/8 mile
0 ___ 200 meters

TO
TRAIN
STATION

Markus Sittikusstrasse

Auerspergstr.

Schwarzstrasse

Rainerstrasse

Fr.
Josef-Str.

Hubert
Sattler-G.

Kurgarten

Müllner-
steg

Elizabethkai

Mirabell
Gardens

Mirabellpl.

Schranneng.

Paris Lodron-Str.

Faberstr.

Fr. Josef Kai

Mülller Hauptstrasse

Gstätten gasse

elevator

Griesgasse

Markart-
steg

Makart-
platz

Theaterg.

Dreifaltigheitsg.

priesterhausg.

Mayrg.

Bergstr.

Linzerstrasse

Herbert-von-
Karajan-Platz

Ferdinand
Hanusch-Pl.

Hagenauer-
platz

Staatsbr.

Platzl

Getreideg.

Hofstallgasse

Universitäts-
platz

W. Phil.-
Str.

Sigmund Haffner-Gasse

Alter Mkt.

Judeng.

Rudolfs Kai

Kapuzinerberg

Steingasse

Franziskaberg

Dom-
platz

Residenz-
platz

Mozart-
platz

Mozart-
steg

Imbergstrasse

Giselakai

Salzach

Kapitel-
platz

Kapitelg.

Kaig.

Pfiferg.

Herreng.

Festungsg.

Kaigasse

Kokoschkaweg

Krotachg.

Basteigasse

Pfeiferg.

Kajetanerpl.

Mönchs-
berg

railway
cable car

Nonnberrg.

Nonntal-
Brücke

Nonntaler Haupt strasse

Nonntaler
Hauptstr.

Petersbrunnstrasse

Erzabt Klot-
Str.

Helbrunner
strasse

KEY

i *Tourist
Information*

Constanze, and his father, Leopold (near the central path leading to the mausoleum). ⊠ *Linzerg. 41* ⊙ *Daily 7–7.*

① Mozart-Wohnhaus (Mozart Residence). This re-creation of the house where the Mozart family lived for some years includes a small recital hall and the Mozart Audio and Film Museum. Mozart composed the "Salzburg Symphonies" here, as well as violin concertos, church music and sonatas, and parts of his early operatic masterpieces. ⊠ *Makartpl. 8* ☎ *0662/874227–40* ⊕ *www.mozarteum.at* ⊙ *Sept.–June, daily 9–5:30; July and Aug., daily 9–6:30.*

⑤ Mozarteum und Marionettentheater (Mozart Center and Marionette Theater). This is the main research facility devoted to the work of Salzburg's most famous native son, Wolfgang Amadeus Mozart. Inside the complex are the **University Mozarteum** (☎ *0662/88940–21*); the **International Mozarteum Foundation** (⊠ *Schwarzstr. 26* ☎ *0662/88940*), whose courtyard contains the summerhouse (accessible only by special appointment) in which Mozart wrote *The Magic Flute* and the **Marionettentheater,** home to the extraordinary Salzburg Marionette Theater. The south end of the Mozarteum complex on Makartplatz includes the **Landestheater** (Provincial Theater), where operas, operetta, ballet, and dramas are staged during winter months when the larger festival buildings are closed. ⊠ *Marionettentheater, Schwarzstr. 24* ☎ *0662/872406–0* ⊕ *www.marionetten.at* ✉ *€18–€35* ⊙ *Box office Mon.–Sat. 9–1 and 2 hrs before marionette performance; Salzburg season May–Sept., Dec. 25, Mozart Week (Jan.), Easter.*

⑮ Mozarts Geburtshaus (Mozart's Birthplace). The house at the head of the tiny Hagenauerplatz in which the famed composer was born is now a museum packed with Mozart memorabilia. Purchasing combination tickets with the Mozart-Wohnhaus is cheaper than buying tickets at each place individually. ⊠ *Getreideg. 9* ☎ *0662/844313* ⊕ *www.mozarteum. at* ⊙ *Sept.–June, daily 9–5:30; July and Aug., daily 9–6:30.*

⑬ Residenz (Residence). The palatial complex on Residenzplatz includes the prince-archbishops' historic and sumptuous living quarters and ceremonial reception rooms. The **Residenzgalerie** has an outstanding collection of 16th- through 19th-century European art. Combination tickets can provide entry to both sites. ⊠ *Residenzpl. 1* ☎ *0662/8042–2690; 0662/840451 art collection* ⊙ *Residence daily 10–5. Tours by arrangement. Art collection daily 10–5, closed early Feb.–mid-Mar. and Wed., Oct.–Mar.*

③ Salzburger Barockmuseum (Salzburg Baroque Museum). A focal point of the celebrated Mirabell Gardens, the museum stands between Mirabellplatz and the Orangerie. The museum displays 17th- and 18th-century paintings and sketches, including works by the Neopolitan painter Luca Giordano and the Austrian baroque painter Johann Michael Rottmayr, as well as a Bernini sculpture. You can wander through the baroque gardens behind the city's main theater complex and discover a dramatic view of the Old City with the fortress in the background. ⊠ *Orangeriegarten* ☎ *0662/877432* ⊙ *Daily 9–5 during Summer Festival; rest of year, Tues.–Sat. 9–noon, 2–5, Sun. 10–1.*

⑯ Schloss Hellbrunn (Hellbrunn Castle). Take Bus 55 from the city center to Hellbrun, 6 km (4 mi) south of Salzburg, to reach this popular attraction. The castle was built in the 17th century, and its rooms have some fine trompe-l'oeil decorations. To entertain Salzburg's great prince-archbishops, its gardens contain an ingenious system of **Wasserspiele**—hidden jets of water conceived by someone with an impish sense of humor: expect to get sprinkled by surprise. ⊠ *Fürstenweg 37, Hellweg* ☎ *0662/*

820372 ⊕ *www.hellbrunn.at* ☉ *Apr. and Oct., daily 9–4:30; May–Sept., daily 9–5:30. Evening tours in July and Aug., hourly 6–10.*

In the Hellbrunn park complex is the **Tiergarten** (zoo; ☎ 0662/820176–0 ☉ Daily 8:30–4), outstanding for the way in which the animals are housed in natural surroundings. The **Monatsschlössl**, the historic hunting lodge, houses a small folklore museum.

🐚 ❹ **Schloss Mirabell** (Mirabell Palace and Gardens). Built by Prince-Archbishop Wolf Dietrich for his mistress, the elegant complex now houses the city's registrar; many couples come here to be married. The foyer and staircase, decorated with cherubs, are splendid examples of baroque excess. The gardens are where the von Trapp children "do-re-mi-ed" in *The Sound of Music.* Outdoor concerts are held in the palace and gardens May through August, Sunday mornings at 10:30, and Wednesday evenings at 8:30. ✉ *Mirabellpl., off Makartpl.* ☎ 0662/88987–330 ☉ *Weekdays 8–6.*

🐚 ❼ **Spielzeugmuseum** (Toy Museum). Once a hospital, the Bürgerspital now houses a toy and musical instruments museum within its Renaissance arcades. There's a combined ticket with the Carolino Augusteum Museum, cathedral excavations, and the Folklore Museum at Schloss Hellbrunn. Nearby on Herbert-von-Karajan-Platz is the 15th-century royal **Pferdeschwemme** (Horse Drinking Trough). ✉ *Bürgerspitalg. 2* ☎ 0662/620808–300 ⊕ *www.smca.at* ☉ *Daily 9–5.*

🐚 ⓬ **Stift St. Peter** (St. Peter's Abbey). Late-baroque style marks this sumptuous edifice tucked beneath the mountain. Originally a Romanesque basilica, it preserves a front portal dating from 1245. Inside, the low-ceiling aisles are painted in rococo candy-box style. The cemetery lends an added air of mystery to the monks' caves cut into the cliff. The catacombs attached to the church can be visited by guided tour. ✉ *St. Peter Bezirk, just off Kapitalpl.* ☎ 0662/844578–0 ☉ *Apr.–Sept., daily 6:30 AM–7 PM; Oct.–Mar., daily 6:30–6.*

❽ **Universitätskirche** (Collegiate Church). Completed by Fischer von Erlach in 1707, this is one of the purest examples of baroque architecture in Austria. Unencumbered by rococo decorations, the modified Greek-cross plan has a majestic dignity worthy of Palladio. ✉ *Universitätspl.* ☎ 0662/841327–72 ☉ *Apr.–Oct., Mon.–Sat. 9–7, Sun. 10–7; Nov.–Mar., Mon.–Sat. 9–4, Sun. 10–4.*

Where to Eat

This is a tourist town, and popular restaurants are always crowded, so make reservations well ahead, particularly during festival times. Most restaurants are open daily during festival season.

★ **$$–$$$$** ✕ **Pfefferschiff.** The "Pepper Ship" is the top-ranked eatery in Salzburg, located just northeast of the center in the pretty rectory adjacent to a pink-and-cream chapel. Chef Klaus Fleischhaker and his wife, Petra, make sure diners feel pampered in the country-chic atmosphere, featuring polished wooden floors, antique hutches, and tables set with fine bone china. Look for scampi tempura with asparagus, lobster crepes, or olive-crusted monkfish with pesto polenta. For dessert, try the sublime rhubarb tartelette with buttermilk ice cream. A taxi is the least stressful way of getting here, but if you have your own car, drive along the north edge of the Kapuzinerberg toward Hallwang and then Söllheim. ✉ *Söllheim 3, A-5300, Hallwang* ☎ 0662/661242 ⌲ *Reservations essential* ▭ *AE.*

$$–$$$ ✕ **Stadtgasthof Blaue Gans.** In a 500-year-old building with vaulted ceilings and windows looking out onto the bustling Getreidegasse, this restaurant in the Blaue Gans hotel has been revamped to showcase an innovative style of Austrian cooking. The menu includes a basket of crispy fried chicken with greens and potato salad, herb-marinated Cornish game hen in a Riesling sauce with grilled polenta, or *Wolfsbarsch* (perch) in a cilantro-chili cream sauce, as well as traditional Austrian dishes. There are always vegetarian choices. ⊠ *Getreideg. 41–43* ☎ *0662/842491–0* ⊟ *AE, DC, MC, V* ⊗ *Closed Tues.*

$–$$$ ⨯ **St. Peter Stiftskeller.** This is one of the oldest restaurants in Europe. The courtyard, with its gray stone archways and vine-trellised walls, couldn't be more dramatic. The food, however, tends to be on the heavy side with an emphasis on pork, sauerkraut, and dumplings. Still, it's worth the experience. ⊠ *St. Peter Bezirk 4* ☎ *0662/841–2680* ⊟ *MC, V.*

$–$$ ⨯ **Krimpelstätter.** About a 15-minute walk downriver from the Altstadt, FodorsChoice this is where the locals go for traditional Salzburg cooking. The dishes ★ are served in a centuries-old building, with fetching accents provided by vaulted ceilings, leaded-glass windows, and homespun tablecloths. Start with the seasonal *Bärlauch* (wild garlic) soup, then home in on the potato goulash with chunks of country ham or the homemade pork sausage with dumplings. Augustiner beer (from the monastery next door) is fresh on tap, and there's a big shady garden for dining in summer. ⊠ *Müllner Hauptstr. 31* ☎ *0662/432274* ⊟ *No credit cards* ⊗ *Closed Sun. and Mon., Sept.–Apr.; Mon., May–Aug.*

$–$$ ⨯ **Ristorante Pizzeria al Sole.** Next to the Mönchsberg elevator, this Italian restaurant is owned by two brothers who regularly hop the border to Italy to bring back the freshest ingredients. The thin-crust pizzas are especially scrumptious, with a wide variety of toppings. Pasta dishes are numerous and delicious, such as spaghettini with tuna and black olives. Try the panna cotta with fresh strawberries for dessert. Sit upstairs in a pretty room lined with Venetian prints or in the more casual downstairs area. ⊠ *Gstätteng. 15* ☎ *0662/843284* ⊟ *AE, DC, MC, V.*

$–$$ ⨯ **Zum Fidelen Affen.** The name means "At the Merry Ape," which explains the simian motifs in this popular *Gasthaus,* dominated by a round copper-plated bar and stone pillars under a vaulted ceiling. Along with the beer on tap, the kitchen offers tasty Austrian dishes, such as Tyrolean cheese ravioli with basil and chopped, tomatoes and basil, or a big salad with strips of fried chicken in a pumpkin-seed-oil dressing. ⊠ *Priesterhausg. 8* ☎ *0662/877361* ⊟ *DC, MC, V* ⊗ *Closed Sun. No lunch.*

Where to Stay

Hotel reservations are always advisable and are imperative at festival times (both Easter and summer).

$$$$ ▥ **Goldener Hirsch.** The "Golden Stag" has the best location of all the city's luxury hotels, right down the street from Mozart's Birthplace. Big city rococo and baroque are abandoned for a delightful—and yes, gemütlich—rustic look, complete with Tyrolean woodwork, peasant-luxe furniture, and bright rag rugs. The stag motif is everywhere, even on the lamp shades, which were hand-painted by an Austrian countess. ⊠ *Getreideg. 37, A-5020* ▤ *0662/8084–0* ▤ *0662/848511–845* ⊕ *www.goldenerhirsch.com* ⇥ *69 rooms* ⌂ *2 restaurants* ⊟ *AE, DC, MC, V.*

★ **$$$$** ▥ **Sacher Salzburg.** Clientele at this beautiful hotel on the banks of the Salzach River has ranged from the Beatles and the Rolling Stones to, more recently, Hillary and Chelsea Clinton. It's owned by the Gürtler family, who also own the Hotel Sacher in Vienna. The main atrium is a symphony in marble, while the grand staircase looks like Empress Sissi could make a dazzling descent amid its ferns. Each room is different, but all are exquisite, with care and attention given to every whim or need, and the staff is warm and friendly. Room prices include a delicious buffet breakfast, complete with Sekt (Austrian sparkling wine). ⊠ *Schwarzstr. 5–7, A-5020* ☎ *0662/88977–0* 🖷 *0662/88977–14* ⊕ *www.sacher.com* ⬢ *119 rooms* ♨ *5 restaurants* ⊟ *AE, DC, MC, V.*

$$$$ 🏨 **Schloss Mönchstein.** This palatial mountain reopened in summer 2003 after being closed for renovations. Surrounded by gardens and hiking trails, the ancient, ivy-covered walls envelop luxurious rooms, some hung with tapestries and others featuring views of the woods with Salzburg in the distance. Service is pleasant and discreet. Getting in and out of town calls for a car or taxi, unless you are willing to hike into town or the nearby Mönchsberg elevator, itself an eight-minute walk away. ⊠ *Mönchsberg 26, A-5020* ☎ *0662/848555–0* 🖷 *0662/848559* ⊕ *www. monchstein.at* ⬢ *17 rooms* ♨ *Restaurant, bar* ⊟ *AE, DC, MC, V.*

Fodor'sChoice
★

★ **$$**   🏨 **Wolf-Dietrich.** Rooms in this small family-owned hotel across the river from the Altstadt are elegant, some with Laura Ashley fabrics, and have extra amenities, such as VCRs (they stock *The Sound of Music*), and attractive sitting areas. Rooms in the back look out over the looming Gaisberg and the cemetery of St. Sebastian. ⊠ *Wolf Dietrich-Str. 7, A-5020* ☎ *0662/871275* 🖷 *0662/882320* ⊕ *www.salzburg-hotel.at* ⬢ *32 rooms* ♨ *Restaurant, pool* ⊟ *AE, DC, MC, V.*

$$ 🏨 **Blaue Gans.** The "Blue Goose" has a lot of charm, and its ancient wood beams, winding corridors, and low archways add to the fun of staying here. Rooms are spacious and have contemporary furnishings, whitewashed walls with cheeky framed posters, and cheerful curtains; a few have skylights. Its location right on Getreidegasse makes this 500-year-old hotel a top choice, so reserve early. ⊠ *Getreideg. 43, A-5020* ☎ *0662/841317* 🖷 *0662/841317–9* ⊕ *www.blauegans.at* ⬢ *52 rooms* ♨ *Restaurant* ⊟ *AE, DC, MC, V.*

The Arts

Festivals

For information and tickets for the main **Salzburger Festspiele** (Salzburg Festival; ☏ Hofstallg. 1, A-5010 Salzburg 🖷 0662/8045–555 Summer Festival; 0662/8045–790 Easter Festival ⊕ www.salzburgfestival. at), held in late July and August, as well as the Easter Festival (early April) and the Pentecost Concerts (late May), write or fax ahead, as it is difficult (but not impossible) to obtain tickets for festival performances once you are in Salzburg.

Opera, Music & Art

Theater and opera are presented in the three auditoriums of the **Festspielhaus** (⊠ Hofstallg. 1 ☎ 0662/894097 ⊕ www.salzburgfestival.at). Opera, operettas, ballet, and drama are offered at the **Landestheater** (⊠ Schwarzstr. 22 ☎ 0662/871–512–21 ⊕ www.theater.co.at). Concerts are the specialty at the **Mozarteum** (⊠ Schwarzstr. 26 ☎ 0662/88940–21). Chamber music has a grand venue at the **Schloss Mirabell** (⊠ Mirabellpl., off Makartpl. ☎ 0662/88987–330). Special art exhibitions are often held in the **Rupertinum** (⊠ Wiener-Philharmoniker-G. 9 ☎ 0662/8042–2336 ⊕ www.rupertinum.at). An outstanding art venue is the **Galerie Welz** (⊠ Sigmund-Haffner-G. 16 ☎ 0662/841771–0 🖷 0662/841771–20).

Shopping

Shopping centers are on Griesgasse, Getreidegasse, and Alter Markt in the Old City and Platzl and Linzer Strasse on the other side of the river. Look for quality handicrafts at **Salzburger Heimatwerk** (⊠ Residenzpl. 9 ☎ 0662/84110–0).

Salzburg Essentials

AIRPORTS & TRANSFERS
All flights go via Salzburg Airport, 4 km (2½ mi) west of the city.
🔋 **Salzburg Airport** ☎ 0662/8580.

TRANSFERS   Bus 77 leaves for the Salzburg train station at Südtirolerplatz every 15 minutes during the day, every half hour at night until 10 PM. Transit time is about 20 minutes. At the train station, change to Bus 1 or 5 for the city center. Taxi fares from the airport to the city center run about €13–€14.

BIKE TRAVEL
Salzburg is fast developing a good network of bike paths. A detailed bicycle map from Tourist Information suggests tours that will help you get around. You can rent a bike by the day or week from Shake & Snack. Also check Veloclub Salzburger Fahrradclub. It's best to reserve in advance.
🔋 **Shake & Snack** ⊠ Kajetanerpl. 3–4 ☎ 0662/848168. **Veloclub Salzburger Fahrradclub** ⊠ Franz-Josef-Str. 23 ☎ 0662/882–7880.

BUS TRAVEL TO & FROM SALZBURG
The central bus terminal is in front of the train station, the Salzburg Hauptbahnhof. In the postal bus terminal is another bus line servicing Austrian destinations.
🔋 **StadtBus Service-Center Verkehr (main ticket office)** ⊠ Griesg. 21 ☎ 0662/4480.

BUS TRAVEL WITHIN SALZBURG
Bus and trolleybus service is frequent and reliable; route maps are available from the tourist office or your hotel. You can buy five single tickets for €1.50 each (not available in tourist offices), or a single 24-hour ticket for €5.

CAR TRAVEL
Salzburg has several Autobahn exits; study the map. Parking is available in the cavernous garages under the Mönchsberg, near the city center, and in other garages around the city; look for the large blue "P" signs.

Don't even think of traveling in Salzburg by car. The old part of the city is a pedestrian zone. Many other parts of the city have restricted parking (indicated by a blue pavement stripe), reserved either for residents with permits or for a restricted period. Get parking tickets from coin-operated dispensers on street corners; instructions are also in English.

CONSULATES
🔋 United Kingdom ⊠ Alter Markt 4 ☎ 0662/848133 🖷 0662/845563.
🔋 United States ⊠ Alter Markt 1/3 ☎ 0662/848776 🖷 0662/849777.

EMERGENCIES
🔋 Emergency Services **Ambulance** ☎ 144. **Police** ☎ 133.
🔋 Pharmacies Pharmacies (*Apotheken*) stay open nights and weekends on rotation; a sign is posted outside each pharmacy listing which are open.

ENGLISH-LANGUAGE MEDIA
BOOKS   Höllrigl sells some paperbacks in English.
🔋 **Höllrigl** ⊠ Sigmund-Haffner-G. 10 ☎ 0662/841146.

TAXIS
At festival time, taxis are too scarce to hail on the street, so order through your hotel porter or call the number below.
🔋 **Radio Cab** ☎ 0662/8111.

TOURS

BUS TOURS There are guided bus tours of the city and its environs, but buses cannot enter much of the Altstadt (Old City).

Bob's Special Tours ⊠ Rudolfskai 38 ☎ 0662/849511-0 🖷 0662/849512. **Panorama Tours** ⊠ Schranneng. 2/2 ☎ 0662/883211-0 🖷 0662/871618. **Salzburg Sightseeing Tours** ⊠ Mirabellpl. 2 ☎ 0662/881616 🖷 0662/878776.

SPECIAL-
INTEREST TOURS Many tour operators offer *Sound of Music* excursions through the city; those given by Bob's Special Tours are among the friendliest. All tour operators can organize chauffeur-driven tours for up to eight people. The tours are a good way to orient yourself. Your hotel will have details.

WALKING TOURS The folder "Salzburg—The Art of Taking It All In at a Glance" describes a one-day self-guided walking tour and is available at the Salzburg City Tourist Office.

TRAIN TRAVEL

Salzburg's main train station is at Südtirolerplatz. For train information, call the number below. For seat reservations, go to the Österreichische Bundesbahnen Zugauskunft office inside the train station.

Train Information ☎ 05/1717.

TRANSPORTATION AROUND SALZBURG

Salzburg is compact, and most distances are short. This is a city to explore on foot, but take an umbrella, as surprise showers are legendary. Consider purchasing the Salzburg Card, available at most hotels, travel agencies, and the city tourist office. *SalzburgKarten* are good for 24, 48, or 72 hours, cost €20, €28, and €34, respectively, and allow no-charge entry to most museums and sights, use of public transport, and special discount offers. Children under 15 pay half.

You can also take a *Fiaker* (horse-drawn cab); Fiakers on the Residenzplatz cost €33 (up to four people) for 20–25 minutes, €66 for 50 minutes.

TRAVEL AGENCIES

American Express ⊠ Mozartpl. 5–7 ☎ 0662/8080-0 🖷 0662/8080-9. **Columbus** ⊠ Münzg. 1 ☎ 0662/842755-0 🖷 0662/842755-5.

VISITOR INFORMATION

The Mozartplatz Information Office is open Monday–Saturday. The Central Station Information Office is open daily. The Salzburg City Tourist Office is the main tourist office. It is open weekdays 8–5 for phone calls or faxes, no walk-ins.

Information Central Station Information Office Hauptbahnhof/main train station ⊠ Platform 2A ☎ 0662/88987-330. **Mozartplatz Information Office** Stadtverkehrsbüro ⊠ Mozartpl. 5 ☎ 0662/88987-340. **Salzburg City Tourist Office** ⊠ Auerspergstr. 6 ☎ 0662/88987-0 🖷 0662/88987-435 ⊕ www.salzburginfo.at.

INNSBRUCK

Ringed by mountains and sharing the valley with the Inn River, Innsbruck is compact and very easy to explore on foot. The medieval city—it received its municipal charter in 1239—owes much of its fame and charm to its unique location. To the north, the steep, sheer sides of the Alps rise like a shimmering blue-and-white wall from the edge of the city, an awe-inspiring backdrop for the mellow green domes and red roofs of the picturesque baroque town.

Exploring Innsbruck

Numbers in the margin correspond to points of interest on the Innsbruck map.

Modern-day Innsbruck retains close associations with three historic figures: Emperor Maximilian I and Empress Maria Theresa (both responsible for much of the city's architecture), and Andreas Hofer, a Tyrolean patriot. You will find repeated references to these names as you tour the city and its historic core—the Altstadt (Old City).

8 **Annasäule** (St. Anne's Column). This memorial commemorates the withdrawal of Bavarian forces in the war of the Spanish Succession in 1703 on St. Anne's Day. From here you'll have a classic view of Innsbruck and the glorious mountains. ⊠ *Maria-Theresien-Str.*

3 **Domkirche** (Cathedral). Built in 1722 and dedicated to St. Jacob, the church has an interior with dramatic painted ceilings and a high-altar portrait of the Madonna by Lucas Cranach the Elder dating from about 1530. ⊠ *Dompl. 6* ⊙ *Sat.–Thurs. 6–noon, Fri. 2–5.*

6 **Ferdinandeum** (Tyrolean State Museum Ferdinandeum). Austria's largest collection of Gothic art is here as well as paintings from the 19th and 20th centuries. ⊠ *Museumstr. 15* ☎ *0512/59489* ⊙ *May–Sept., Sun.–Thurs. 10–5 and 7–9, Fri. and Sat. 10–5; Oct.–Apr., Tues.–Sat. 10–noon and 2–5, Sun. 10–1.*

★ **1** **Goldenes Dachl** (The Golden Roof). The ancient mansion with its goldroof (copper tiles gilded with 31 pounds of gold) balcony is the city's foremost landmark. The house was built in 1420, and the balcony, which served as a reviewing stand, was added in 1501. The building now houses a **Museum Maximilianeum** (Maximilian Museum), which focuses on the life and works of the Habsburg ruler between 1490 and 1519. The **Stadtturm**, a 15th-century city tower across the street, proffers a bird's-eye view of the old town. ⊠ *Herzog Friedrich-Str. 15* ☎ *0512/581111* ⊙ *Oct.–Apr., Tues.–Sun. 10–12:30 and 2–5; May–Sept., daily 10–6.*

9 **Helblinghaus** (Helbling House). Dating from 1560, this Gothic town house in a 1730 makeover received a facade of ornate blue-and-white rococo decoration that remains one of Innsbruck's most beautiful sights. ⊠ *Herzog Friedrich-Str.*

2 **Hofburg** (Imperial Palace). Dating from 1460, the rococo palace has an ornate reception hall, called the Hall of Giants, decorated with portraits of Maria Theresa's ancestors. ⊠ *Rennweg 1* ☎ *0512/587186* ⊙ *Daily 9–5.*

4 **Hofkirche** (Court Church). Maximilian's mausoleum is surrounded by 24 marble reliefs portraying his accomplishments, as well as 28 oversize bronze statues of his ancestors, though the emperor's body is entombed in St. George Cathedral in Weiner Neustadt. Andreas Hofer is, however, buried here. Don't miss the heavily decorated altar of the 16th-century Silberne Kapelle (Silver Chapel). ⊠ *Universitätsstr. 2* ☎ *0512/584302* ⊙ *Mon.–Sat. 9–5, July and Aug. until 5:30.*

★ **10** **Schloss Ambras** (Castle Ambras). This rambling 10th-century castle was renovated by Archduke Ferdinand II in 1556. Surrounded by acres of lush gardens and woodlands, the cheery Renaissance castle has a magnificent festival hall and an odd collection of weaponry and armaments. The castle is 3 km (2 mi) southeast of the city. To reach it without a car, take Tram 3 to Ambras, or the shuttle (€2.18 round-trip; leaves on the hour) from Maria-Theresien-Strasse 45. ⊠ *Schloss Str. 20,* ☎ *0512/348446* ⊙ *Tours Apr.–Oct., Wed.–Mon. 10–5; Dec.–Mar., 2–5* ⊙ *Closed Nov.*

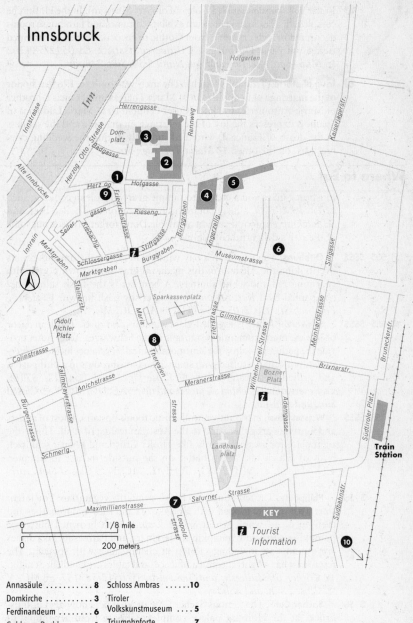

Innsbruck

⑤ Tiroler Volkskunstmuseum (Tyrolean Folk Art Museum). In the Hofkirche complex, this fascinating museum exhibits costumes and farmhouse rooms decorated in styles ranging from Gothic to rococo. There's a combined ticket with the Hofburg. ⊠ *Universitätsstr. 2* ☏ *0512/584302* ⊙ *Mon.–Sat. 9–5, July and Aug. until 5:30; Sun. 9–noon.*

⑦ Triumphpforte (Triumphal Arch). The arch was built in 1765 in honor of the marriage of Leopold (son of Maria Theresa and Francis I, brother of Marie-Antoinette, and later Kaiser Leopold II) to Maria Ludovica of Spain. It expresses the joy of the marriage on one side and the sadness at the death of Francis I, who died suddenly during the wedding celebrations, on the other. ⊠ *Maria-Theresien-Str.*

Where to Eat

Innsbruck gives you a chance to sample hearty Tyrolean cooking, such as *Tiroler G'röstl,* a tasty potato hash with onion and boiled beef, and *Schlutzkrapfen,* a local version of ravioli. Don't forget to check out some of the city's delightful coffeehouses.

$$$–$$$$ ✕ **Ottoburg.** You can sit in a bay window in one of the upstairs rooms overlooking the Altstadt in this medieval gray-stone town house with charming red-and-white shutters. A best bet is the fresh salmon accompanied by a *Kartoffelpuffer,* a big crispy hash brown. ⊠ *Herzog Friedrich-Str. 1A* ☏ *0512/584338* ⊟ *AE, DC, MC, V.*

★ $$$–$$$$ ✕ **Schwarzer Adler.** The leaded-glass windows and rustic Tyrolean decor of this intimate, romantic restaurant in the Schwarzer Adler hotel provide the perfect backdrop for a memorable meal. Specialties include *Schweinfilet* (pork fillet) stuffed with spinach and mushrooms in a puff pastry, and grilled freshwater trout. ⊠ *Kaiserjägerstr. 2* ☏ *0512/587109* ⚐ *Reservations essential* 🏠 *Jacket and tie* ⊟ *AE, DC, MC, V* ⊙ *Closed Sun. and mid-Jan.*

$$–$$$$ ✕ **Weisses Rössl.** In the authentically rustic rooms upstairs, a host of antlers and a private art gallery add to the Austrian feeling of it all. This is the right place for local standards, like Tiroler Gröstl and Wiener schnitzel, both of which taste even better on the outside terrace in summer. ⊠ *Kiebachg. 8* ☏ *0512/583057* ⊟ *AE, MC, V* ⊙ *Closed Sun., early Nov., mid-Apr.*

$–$$ ✕ **Philippine.** The tempting food here is primarily vegetarian. You might start with polenta topped with Gorgonzola and ruby-red tomatoes and then go on to whole-wheat *Schlutzkrapfen* with browned butter or pumpkin risotto with pumpkin seeds, ginger, and Parmesan. Fish dishes are a mainstay, including salmon in cream sauce with spinach. The restaurant has a light, cheerful ambience, and tables are candlelit at night. ⊠ *Corner of Müllerstr. and Tempelstr.* ☏ *0512/589157* ⊟ *MC, V* ⊙ *Closed Sun. and holidays.*

$–$$ ✕ **Sacher Café.** The famous Sacher Café of Vienna is now also in Innsbruck, at the Hofburg palace complex. Choose from a panoply of delectable pastries to go along with the excellent coffee, and sit back and enjoy the elegant red-damask surroundings. Croissant sandwiches and full meals are also offered. ⊠ *Rennweg 1* ☏ *0512/565–626* ⊟ *AE, DC, MC, V.*

$–$$ ✕ **Solo Pasta.** At this pasta boutique, the owner's Italian heritage is evident in the fresh, ample portions of authentic dishes. The lengthy wine list can be enjoyed either with a meal or in the adjoining Solo Vino bar. ⊠ *Universitätsstr. 15b* ☏ *0512/587206* ⊟ *AE, DC, MC, V.*

$ ✕ **Theresien Bräu.** This multilevel brew house in the center of town gives the appearance of the inside of a ship, and an assortment of seafaring gear is scattered throughout, such as nets, steamer trunks, and even rowboats. But the focus here is on beer, brewed right on the premises. Meals and snacks include zucchini ragout with polenta gratiné, or *Tafelspitz,* a boiled beef dish. People of all ages can be found here, but be prepared for loud music. ☒ *Maria-Theresien-Str. 51–53* ☎ *0512/587580* ▤ *AE, DC, MC, V.*

Where to Stay

$$$ 🏨 **Hilton.** This modern high-rise close to the train station offers contemporary comfort in friendly Scandinavian style. The rooms are simply furnished and efficiently modern. Try your luck in the adjacent casino. ☒ *Salurner Str. 15, A-6020* ☎ *0512/5935–0* 🖷 *0512/5935–220* ⊕ *www.hilton.com* ⇨ *172 rooms* ⚭ *2 restaurants, pool, bar* ▤ *AE, DC, MC, V.*

★ **$$–$$$** 🏨 **Goldener Adler.** Mozart, Goethe, John Glenn, and the King and Queen of Norway have all stayed here. This traditional hotel, a 600-year-old house with stone walls, winding staircases, and plentiful nooks and crannies, has mostly spacious rooms, though a few readers have complained about closetlike rooms on the upper floors. The location is ideal, in the heart of the Old City. ☒ *Herzog Friedrich-Str. 6, A-6020* ☎ *0512/586334* 🖷 *0512/584409* ⊕ *www.goldeneradler.com* ⇨ *40 rooms* ⚭ *2 restaurants* ▤ *AE, DC, MC, V.*

$$–$$$ 🏨 **The Penz.** The Penz Hotel is Innsbruck's top address. While directly within the old city, it is centuries away if measured by its ultramodern, glittering, light and glass architecture. The rooftop Sky-Bar offers food-with-a-view, with panoramic vistas of the Old City and the Alps. ☒ *Adolf-Pichler-Pl., A-6020* ☎ *0512/5657* ⊕ *www.the-penz.com* ⇨ *96 rooms* ⚭ *Restaurant, bar* ▤ *AE, DC, MC, V.*

$–$$ 🏨 **Innsbruck.** This is one of the city's newest and finest hotels. From some of the modern rooms you'll get gorgeous views of the Old City, and, from those on the river side, of the Nordkette Mountains directly behind. ☒ *Innrain 3, A-6020* ☎ *0512/59868–0* 🖷 *0512/572280* ⇨ *111 rooms* ⚭ *Restaurant, pool* ▤ *AE, DC, MC, V.*

★ **$–$$** 🏨 **Weisses Kreuz.** Occupying an honored position in the Altstadt, the White Cross is a lovely inn that dates from 1465. The rooms are simple but comfortable, with rustic furniture and lots of light wood. Mozart stayed here. ☒ *Herzog Friedrich-Str. 31, A-6020* ☎ *0512/59479* 🖷 *0512/ 59479–90* ⇨ *39 rooms, 20 with shower, 19 with bath* ⚭ *Restaurant* ▤ *AE, V.*

$ 🏨 **Tautermann.** This red-shuttered house within walking distance of the city's center is a friendly, family-run hotel with rooms in natural woods and white. Some rooms on the west side have views of the imposing Hungerburg mountain. Breakfast is included in the room rate. ☒ *Stamser Feld 5/Höttingerg, A-6020* ☎ *0512/281572* ⊕ *www.hotel-tautermann. at* ⇨ *28 rooms* ▤ *AE, DC, MC, V.*

The Arts

Most hotels have a monthly calendar of events (in English). The City Tourist Office sells tickets to most events. The leading venue for operas, musicals, and concerts is the **Tiroler Landestheater** (☒ Rennweg 2 ☎ 0512/ 52074). Other major performances are held at the **Kongresshaus** (☒ Rennweg 3 ☎ 0512/5936–0).

Shopping

The main central shopping district is concentrated around the Old City, along Maria-Theresien-Strasse, Maximilianstrasse, Anichstrasse, Burggraben, Museumstrasse, and Wilhelm-Greil-Strasse and their side streets. Here you'll discover the **Rathaus Gallery** (✉ Maria-Theresien Str. 18), an indoor mall that accommodates luxury boutiques and famous names known worldwide. The world's largest **Swarovski Crystal Gallery** (✉ Herzog-Friedrich-Str. 39) is also situated in the Old City, not far from the Rathaus Gallery. The renowned crystal manufacturer is headquartered in the nearby town of Wattens. For local handicrafts, you can try **Tiroler Heimatwerk** (✉ Meraner Str. 2–4 ☎ 0512/582320).

Innsbruck Essentials

AIRPORTS & TRANSFERS
Innsbruck Flughafen airport is 4 km (2½ mi) to the west of the city.
🛈 **Flight information** ☎ 0512/22525–304.

TRANSFERS Buses (Line F) to the city center (Maria-Theresien-Str.) run every 20 minutes and take about 20 minutes. Get your ticket from the bus driver; it costs €1.53. Taxis should take no more than 10–15 minutes into town, and the fare is between €8.72 and €10.90. Connect Transfer provides shuttle buses to and from the airport in Munich, Germany.
🛈 **Connect Transfer** ☎ 0512/343533 🖷 0512/343533-4.

BUS TRAVEL TO & FROM INNSBRUCK
The Innsbruck terminal is to the right of the main train station. Routes extend from here throughout the Tirol.
🛈 **Terminal** ✉ Südtiroler-Pl. ☎ 0512/585155.

BUS TRAVEL WITHIN INNSBRUCK
Service is frequent and efficient. Most bus and streetcar routes begin or end at Südtiroler-Platz, in front of the main train station. A bus is the most convenient way to reach the six major ski areas outside the city, and it is free when you use the special buses provided. From the Old City, the buses leave from in front of the Tiroler Landestheater, or from the corner of Innrain and Marktgraben, near the Inn River. Ask at your hotel for more information.

CAR TRAVEL
Within Innsbruck, a car is a burden except for getting out of town. Much of the downtown area is a pedestrian zone or paid-parking only; get parking vouchers at tobacco shops, coin-operated dispensers, or the City Tourist Office.

EMERGENCIES
Pharmacies (*Apotheken*) stay open nights and weekends on a rotation system. Signs outside each pharmacy, and notices in local newspapers, list which ones will be open.
🛈 **Emergency Services** **Ambulance** ☎ 144. **Police** ☎ 133.

TAXIS
Taking a taxi is not much faster than walking, particularly along the one-way streets and in the Altstadt. To order a radio cab, phone one of the numbers listed below.
🛈 **Radio Cab** ☎ 0512/1718, 0512/5311, or 0512/45500.

TOURS
BUS TOURS The Sightseer, Innsbruck's sightseeing bus, departs every half hour from the terminal on Maria Theresien Strasse opposite the Tourist Office, and visits all the city's major sights. The onboard headphones provide commentary in English and five other languages. Reservations are not required. Contact your hotel or the Tourist Office.

TRAIN TRAVEL

The city's main station is at Südtiroler-Platz, about a 10-minute walk from the Altstadt. Numbers for train information and ticket reservations are listed below.

🚆 **Ticket reservations** ☎ 0512/1700. **Train information** ☎ 0512/1717.

TRAVEL AGENCIES

🚆 **American Express** ✉ Brixnerstr. 3 ☎ 0512/582491 🖷 0512/573385. **Österreichisches Verkehrsbüro** (Austrian Travel Agency) ✉ Brixnerstr. 2 ☎ 0512/520790 🖷 0512/520-7985.

VISITOR INFORMATION

The Innsbruck Card—good for 24, 48, and 72 hours at €19, €24, and €29, respectively—gives you admission to all the museums and mountain cable cars, plus free bus and tram transportation, including the Sightseer. Österreichischer Alpenverein (Austrian Alpine Association) has information on Alpine huts and mountaineering. In the summer, they provide free guided hikes.

🚆 **Innsbruck Tourismus** City Tourist Office ✉ Burggraben 3 ☎ 0512/5356-30 🖷 0512/5356-14. **Österreichischer Alpenverein** ✉ Wilhelm-Greil-Str. 15 ☎ 0512/59547-19 🖷 0512/575528.

BALTIC STATES
ESTONIA, LATVIA, LITHUANIA

3

ESTONIA, LATVIA, AND LITHUANIA ENDURE. These tiny countries in northeastern Europe have weathered centuries of domination by Germans, Swedes, Russians, and Poles; fought countless battles to preserve at least their dignity; and won their independence twice in the 20th century. The three countries share terrain and history. Nevertheless, since breaking free of the Soviet Union in 1990 and 1991, the Baltics have been quietly reconstructing their individual national identities, societies, and economies, and each is resolute about its distinctness. While building sustainable democracies out of the rubble of post-Soviet republics, Estonia, Latvia, and Lithuania have pursued very different alliances. Estonia, with linguistic and geographic affinities to Helsinki, looks every bit as Scandinavian and Western as its neighbor across the Gulf of Finland. Latvia, with a huge Russian population, still retains some of the chaos of its former eastern nemesis but has emerged as the most cosmopolitan country of the three. Lithuania was slower in embracing the West but since 1996 has made great strides, renewing contacts and relations with Poland in an effort to hitch itself to the EU and NATO's rising star.

Although there aren't many world-famous attractions in the Baltics, the region's obscurity may actually be the best thing about it. Another plus for the English speaker is that it is becoming increasingly easy to roam the three Baltic capitals of Tallinn, Rīga (Riga), and Vilnius without encountering language barriers. The landscape itself is also free of barriers; everywhere in the Baltics you'll find unspoiled forests and beaches, as well as people whose initial aloofness toward strangers often gives way to genuine friendliness.

BALTIC STATES A TO Z

To research prices, get advice from other travelers, and book travel arrangements, visit www.fodors.com.

The following is general information on all three Baltic states; more country-specific details appear in the A to Z sections. Prices throughout the chapter are in U.S. dollars; *see* the Currency sections for press time exchange rates for the Estonian kroon, the Latvian lat, and the Lithuanian lita.

BUSINESS HOURS

Banks are open weekdays 9–4, but some open as early as 8 and close as late as 7. Most are closed on Saturday, but some stay open 9–3. Museums are generally open Wednesday–Sunday 11–5. Some stay open until

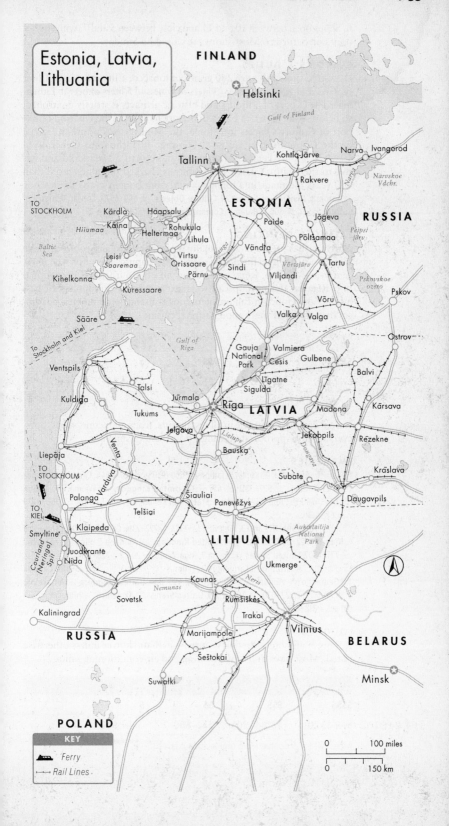

6. Shops open between 10 and 11 and close between 5 and 7, with shorter hours on Saturday. Most shops are closed on Sunday.

CUSTOMS & DUTIES

Duty-free allowances are 250 grams of tobacco, 1 liter of spirits, 1 liter of wine, and 10 liters of beer (3 liters of wine and 5 liters of beer in Lithuania). The export of antiques and historic artifacts is strictly controlled, so before you export an old item be sure to contact the Division of Export of Culture Objects in Estonia, the Ministry of Culture in Latvia, or the Committee of Cultural Heritage in Lithuania. Generally a 10%–20% duty is charged on goods more than 50 years old and native to the country; up to 100% duty is charged on goods more than 100 years old made in a foreign country but bought in the Baltics.

🚩 Estonia: **Division of Export of Culture Objects** ☎ 644-6578. Latvia: **Ministry of Culture** ☎ 7/214-100. Lithuania: **Committee of Cultural Heritage** ☎ 2/724-005.

EATING & DRINKING

Native dishes predominate: usually meat, potatoes, and root-vegetable salad. Nevertheless, the dining scene in the capitals has improved in recent years. Tallinn, Rīga, and Vilnius all offer authentic international fare. Rīga has the most upscale restaurants, whereas Vilnius has the best international food. In Tallinn international dining predominates, but diners may still find some good national cuisine.

WHAT IT COSTS In U.S. Dollars			
	$$$$	$$$	$$	$
PER PERSON	over $20	$15–$20	$8–$15	under $8

Prices are for a main course at dinner.

RESERVATIONS & DRESS Casual dress is acceptable in all restaurants. Jeans and tennis shoes, however, are not appropriate for high-priced establishments.

EMBASSIES

🚩 **Estonia Australia** ✉ Kopli 25, Tallinn ☎ 650-9308 🖷 667-8444. **Canada** ✉ Toomkooli 13, Tallinn ☎ 627-3311 🖷 627-3312. **United Kingdom** ✉ Wismari 6, Tallinn ☎ 667-4700 🖷 667-4723. **United States** ✉ Kentmanni 20, Tallinn ☎ 668-8100 🖷 668-8134.

🚩 **Latvia Australia** ✉ Raiņa 3, Rīga ☎ 722-2383 🖷 722-2314. **Canada** ✉ Doma laukums 4, Rīga ☎ 722-6315 🖷 783-0140. **United Kingdom** ✉ Alunāna 5, Rīga ☎ 777-4700 🖷 777-4707. **United States** ✉ Raiņa 7, Rīga ☎ 7036-200 🖷 728-0047.

🚩 **Lithuania Australia** ✉ Karmelitų 4/12, Vilnius ☎ 2/223-369 🖷 2/223-369. **Canada** ✉ Gedimino 64, Vilnius ☎ 2/496-853 🖷 2/496-884. **United Kingdom** ✉ Antakalnio 2, Vilnius ☎ 2/122-070 🖷 2/727-579. **United States** ✉ Akmenų 6, Vilnius ☎ 2/223-031 🖷 2/312-819.

LODGING

Rooms in all hotels listed have private bath or shower unless otherwise noted. Most have individual heating and air-conditioning units.

WHAT IT COSTS In U.S. Dollars			
	$$$$	$$$	$$	$
FOR 2 PEOPLE	over $120	$80–$120	$40–$80	under $40

Prices are for a double room and include breakfast.

PASSPORTS & VISAS

Australian, British, New Zealand, and U.S. citizens can stay in Estonia visa-free for up to 90 days. Canadian citizens need a visa to enter Estonia. Australians, Canadians, and New Zealanders need visas for Latvia; a 90-day visa can be purchased from consulates outside Latvia, and 10-day visas can be purchased for 12Ls at the Rīga Airport. Australian, British, Canadian, New Zealand, and U.S. citizens can stay in Lithuania visa-free for up to 90 days. A 10-day visa can be issued at the Vilnius Airport for 160Lt if your country of citizenship does not have a Lithuanian embassy or consulate or you are a citizen of an EU country.

VISITOR INFORMATION

🄵 **Estonia** ✉ Raekoja plats 10, Tallinn ☎ 645-7777 🖷 645-7778 ⊕ www.tourism.tallinn. ee. **Latvia** ✉ Rātslaukums 6, Rīga ☎ 702-6072 🖷 702-6068 ⊕ www.rigatourism.com. **Lithuania** ✉ Pilies 42, Vilnius ☎ 2/626470 🖷 2/620-762 ⊕ www.vilnius.lt ✉ Vilniaus 22, Vilnius ☎ 2/629-660.

WHEN TO GO

Midsummer sees an influx of tourists and an exodus by locals. For local color and temperate weather, visit in late spring or early autumn.

CLIMATE   The climate in the Baltic States is temperate but tends to be cool and damp. The rainy season is in early summer. The snowy, cold winter season lasts from November through March. Summers, though warm, are generally wet and humid. August tends to see the smallest amount of rain in all three Baltic States. The average daily temperatures for Estonia, Latvia, and Lithuania, in that order, are as follows:

Jan.	26F	−3C	May	46F	8C	Sept.	56F	13C
	28	−2		52	11		55	13
	27	−3		50	10		57	14
Feb.	24F	−4C	June	63F	17C	Oct.	45F	7C
	32	0		57	14		45	7
	24F	−4C		67F	20C		44F	6C
Mar.	32F	0C	July	65F	18C	Nov.	37F	3C
	34	1		60	16		36	2
	34	1		69	20		32	0
Apr.	43F	6C	Aug.	60F	15C	Dec.	30F	−1C
	49	9		59	15		31	−1
	48	9		62	17		30	−1

ESTONIA

The country's history is sprinkled liberally with long stretches of foreign domination, beginning in 1219 with the Danes, followed without interruption by the Germans, Swedes, and Russians. Only after World War I, with Russia in revolutionary wreckage, was Estonia able to declare its independence. Shortly before World War II, in 1940, that independence was usurped by the Soviets, who—save for a brief three-year occupation by Hitler's Nazis—proceeded to suppress all forms of national Estonian pride for the next 50 years. Estonia finally regained independence in 1991. In the early 1990s, Estonia's own Riigikogu (Parliament), not some other nation's puppet ruler, handed down from the Upper City reforms that forced Estonia to blaze its post-Soviet trail to the European Union. In 1997, the country got the nod from Brussels to join the EU in the future, an endorsement of Estonia's progress toward a sustainable market economy.

Estonia A to Z

AIR TRAVEL

There are no direct flights between Estonia and the United States. Estonian Air operates from Copenhagen, Frankfurt, Hamburg, Helsinki, Kiev, London, Moscow, Rīga, Stockholm, Vienna, Vilnius, and Warsaw. American carriers partnered with Austrian Airlines, Finnair, LOT, and SAS have good connections. Estonian Air is the national carrier. Copterline helicopters fly the 18-minute trip between Helsinki and Tallinn daily.
🛈 **Copterline helicopters** ☎ 610-1818. **Estonian Air** ☎ 631-3302.

BOAT & FERRY TRAVEL

Passenger ships—including frequent ferries and hydrofoils—connect Tallinn with Helsinki and Stockholm. Boat service to and from Tallinn is minimal and dependent on weather from October to March. Call the Tallinn Harbor for schedules; travel agencies for tickets.
🛈 **Tallinn Harbor information** ☎ 631-8550.

BUS TRAVEL

Public transportation tickets purchased from nearly any kiosk cost 10EEK. Purchased from the driver, they are 15EEK. Express tickets cost 15EEK from a kiosk or 20EEK from the driver. A single type of ticket is valid on buses, trolleys, and streetcars. A carnet of 10 tickets costs 70EEK. Upon boarding the bus, punch your ticket in the machine mounted on a pole or be fined up to 420EEK. Public transportation operates 6 AM–midnight. Intercity bus trips cost 70EEK–150EEK. For bus schedules, call the bus station.
🛈 **Bus station** ☎ 680-0900.

CAR RENTAL

Cars may be rented starting at 700EEK a day from Avis, Budget, Hertz, or National. Local agency prices start at 450EEK a day.
🛈 Major Agencies **Avis** ☎ 605-8222. **Budget** ☎ 605-8600. **Europcar** ☎ 605-8031. **Hertz** ☎ 605-8923. **National** ☎ 605-8071.
🛈 Local Agencies **Balti Autoliising** ☎ 613-1830. **Rendiauto.ee** ☎ 600-3655. **Toyota** ☎ 605-8059. **Tulika Rent** ☎ 612-0012.

CAR TRAVEL

An international or national driver's license bearing a photograph is acceptable in Estonia. Drive on the right. Most roads are not up to Western standards, but major thoroughfares tend to be in better condition than secondary roads, where potholes and unpaved ways are common. Gas costs about 10EEK per liter.

EMERGENCIES

🛈 **Police** ☎ 110. **Ambulance/Fire** ☎ 112. **Tallinn Central Hospital** ☎ 620-7015. **Doctor: Sinu Arst Family Practice** ☎ 631-5440. **Dentist: Eurodent** ☎ 611-5551. **24-Hour Pharmacy:** ✉ Tõnismägi 5 ☎ 644-2282.

HOLIDAYS

January 1; February 24 (Independence Day); Good Friday; Easter; May 1 (May Day); June 3 (Whitsuntide); June 23 (Victory Day); June 23, 24 (St. John's Day/Midsummer); August 20 (Day of Restoration and Independence); December 25, 26.

LANGUAGE

Estonian, which belongs to the Finno-Ugric family, is the official language. However, many people in cities speak English perfectly. Most Estonians will ignore attempts to communicate in Russian, though the 30% of the population that is ethnically Russian is happy to speak it.

MAIL & SHIPPING
A 20-gram letter to the United States costs 8EEK, a postcard 7.50EEK. A 20-gram letter to Europe costs 6.50EEK, a postcard 6EEK. The main post office is open weekdays 8–8, Saturday 8–6. Stamps are sold at post offices only.
🚩 **Main post office** ✉ Narva 1, Tallinn ☎ 625-7300.

MONEY MATTERS
A cup of coffee or tea costs 20EEK; a glass of beer 35EEK; a main dish at a local, medium-priced restaurant 50EEK–60EEK. Admission to museums and galleries costs 10EEK–20EEK. If you're staying in Tallinn for one to three days, the best deal is the Tallinn Card, which can be purchased at the tourist office, all points of entry, and some hotels. It allows visitors free access to public transportation, free admission to museums, a free bus and walking tour, and discounts at shops and restaurants in Tallinn.

CURRENCY The monetary unit in Estonia is the kroon, which is divided into 100 senti. There are notes of 1, 2, 5, 10, 25, 50, 100, and 500EEK and coins of 5, 10, 20, and 50 senti and 1EEK. At press time, the rate of exchange was 14.53 EEK to the U.S. dollar, 9.56EEK to the Canadian dollar, 23.93EEK to the pound sterling, 15.64EEK to the euro, 8.54 EEK to the Australian dollar, 7.91EEK to the New Zealand dollar, and 1.70EEK to the South African rand. National banks, with branches in all major and most minor cities, change cash and traveler's checks at fair commissions; most also give advances on a Visa or MasterCard. Credit cards are widely accepted in Estonia.

TAXIS
Taxis are expensive around hotels and ferry, bus, and train stations, cheaper within the city center; it's best to telephone for one. Taxi fares generally start at 6EEK or 8EEK and increase by 4EEK or 6EEK per kilometer (½ mi) in the daytime, more at night or in bad weather. Drivers are bound by law to display an operating license and a meter. In-town journeys cost up to 50EEK.
🚩 **E-takso** ☎ 605-9700. **Tulika** ☎ 612-0000.

TELEPHONES
COUNTRY & The country code for Estonia is 372. There is no city code for phone
AREA CODES numbers in Tallinn.

INTERNATIONAL 🚩 Access code **AT&T** ☎ 8–008001001.
CALLS

LOCAL CALLS Pay phones take phone cards worth 30EEK, 50EEK, or 100EEK. Buy cards at any kiosk.
🚩 **Telephone information** ☎ 626-1111.

TIPPING
At restaurants, a 10% service charge is sometimes added. An 18% VAT is also included in the price of dishes on the menu but may be listed separately on your bill. Tipping is not obligatory; for excellent service, add 10%.

TOURS
🚩 Fees & Schedules **Reisiekspert** ✉ Roosikrantsi 19 ☎ 610-8600 🖷 610-8640.

Exploring Estonia

Tallinn

Tallinn's tiny Old Town, the most impressive in the region, has romantic towers, ankle-wrenching cobblestone streets, cozy nooks, city-wall cafés, and a dozen other attractions—all within 1 square km (.4 square mi). In the 1990s, Vanalinn (the lower Old Town)—historically the domain of traders, artisans, and ordinary citizens—sprouted glitzy neon signs in otherwise charming alleys and sights. The stately, sedate Toompea (Upper Town), a hillock that was the site of the original Estonian settlement, is on the burial mound of Kalev, the epic hero of Estonia. Toompea Castle, crowning the hill, is now the seat of the country's parliament and is not open to visitors.

The 19th-century Russian Orthodox **Aleksandr Nevski Khram** (Alexander Nevsky Cathedral), with the country's largest bell, is a symbol of the centuries of Russification endured by Estonia. ⊠ *Lossi pl. 10* ☎ *644–3484* ⊙ *Daily 8–7.*

Wander through the ages in the ancient stone galleries and narrow hallways of the **Dominiiklaste Kloostri Muuseum** (Dominican Monastery Museum), founded in 1246 and now displaying 15th- and 16th-century stone carvings. At 5 PM enjoy a half-hour baroque music concert. ⊠ *Vene 16* ☎ *644–4606* ⊙ *Daily 9:30–6.*

The Lutheran **Toomkirik** (Dome Church), the oldest church in the country, was founded by the occupying Danes in the 13th century and rebuilt in 1686. ⊠ *Toom-kooli 6* ☎ *644–4140* ⊙ *Tues.–Sun. 9–5.*

The baroque **Kadriorg Palace Foreign Art Museum,** built for Catherine I by her husband Peter the Great in 1721, merits a visit not just for its impressive and thorough exhibition of 16th- to 20th-century art, but also for the palace's architectural beauty and manicured gardens. Kadriorg Palace offers a glimpse into a history from Russian imperial splendor to Soviet Socialist Realist art, with Estonian and European masterpieces along the way. ⊠ *Weizenbergi 37* ☎ *606–6400* ⊙ *Tues.–Sun. 10–7.*

★ At the southern end of the Old Town looms the magnificent, six-story tower **Kiek-in-de-Kök** (Low German for "peep in the kitchen"), so called because during the 15th century one could peer into the kitchens of lower town houses from here. The tower has a museum of contemporary art and ancient maps and weapons. ⊠ *Komandandi 2* ☎ *644–6686* ⊙ *Tues.–Fri. 10:30–6, weekends 11–4:30.*

The 15th-century **Niguliste kirik** (Church of St. Nicholas), part of the Estonian Art Museum, is famed for its fragment of a treasured frieze, Bernt Notke's (1440–1509) *Danse Macabre,* a haunting depiction of death. ⊠ *Niguliste 3* ☎ *644–9911* ⊙ *Wed.–Fri. 10–6, weekends 11:30–6.*

The stocky guardian of the northernmost point of the Old City, **Paks Margareeta** (Fat Margaret) is a 16th-century fortification named for a particularly hefty cannon it contained. Now it has a Maritime Museum and a roof with a view of Old Town. ⊠ *Pikk 70* ☎ *641–1408* ⊙ *Wed.–Sun. 10–6.*

Fodor'sChoice
★ **Raekoja Plats** (Town Hall Square) has a long history of intrigue, executions, and salt (Tallinn's main export in the Middle Ages). Take a guided tour of the only surviving original Gothic **town hall** (☎ 645–7900) in northern Europe. Old Thomas, its weather vane, has been atop the town hall since 1530. Near the center of the square, an L-shape stone marks the site of a 17th-century execution, where a priest was beheaded for

killing a waitress who had offered him a rock-hard omelet. Across the square stands the town **apothecary**, which dates from 1422. ⊠ *Raekoja plats 11* ☎ *631–4860* ⊘ *Weekdays 9–7, Sat. 9–5, Sun. 9–4.*

↺ Just a 15-minute drive from the center, the 207-acre **Rocca al Mare** (Open-air Ethnographic Museum) provides a breath of fresh air and an informative look into Estonia's past from farm architecture to World War II–era deportations. ⊠ *Vabaõhumuuseumi 12* ☎ *654–9117* ⊘ *Daily 10–6.*

$$$$ ✕ **Gloria.** The art nouveau interior compliments the French-influenced menu of high-brow European food like beef Stroganoff or tournedos Rossini. To maintain its tradition of decadence, Gloria offers a *tabacalera* (tobacco shop) complete with Cuban cigars and an extensive wine cellar. ⊠ *Müürivahe 2* ☎ *644–6950* ⌦ *Reservations essential* ⋔ *Jacket and tie* ⊟ *MC, V.*

$$–$$$ ✕ **Maiasmokk.** A top-notch restoration has revived this fine Estonian restaurant's 19th-century feel. Founded in 1864, the property has been restored to its old, refined glory, with an equally refined menu of such delicacies as lamprey, deer, wild boar, and elk, with accompaniments ranging from lingonberries to mead sauce. ⊠ *Pikk 16* ☎ *646–4070* ⌦ *Reservations essential* ⊟ *MC, V.*

$$–$$$ ✕ **Vanaema Juures.** Just as the name suggests, Grandma's Place is a cozy and homey place to sample Estonian favorites such as roast elk. Filled with antiques, sepia photographs, and the sounds of the 1920s and '30s, the restaurant gets high marks for authenticity and warmth. ⊠ *Rataskaevu 10* ☎ *626–9080* ⌦ *Reservations recommended* ⊟ *MC, V.*

$$ ✕ **Olde Hansa.** In a 15th-century building in the Old Town, this restau-
FodorśChoice rant re-creates medieval times with waiters in period costume, candlelit
★ tables, and historic Eastern European recipes for such dishes as noble-man's smoked filet mignon in mushroom sauce and wild boar with game sauce and forest berries. The honey beer is out of this world, and the old-fashioned food is always fresh and tasty. ⊠ *Vanaturg 1* ☎ *627–9020* ⊟ *MC, V.*

$ ✕ **Café Anglais.** With an excellent view of Old Town square, this second-floor café attracts a steady clientele with its nightly live jazz and refreshingly light menu of sandwiches, soups, and salads. ⊠ *Raekoja plats 14* ☎ *644–2160* ⊟ *No credit cards.*

$ ✕ **Tristan ja Isolde.** Possibly the most sedate café in Tallinn, Tristan and Isolde is inside the medieval stone walls of the Town Hall. With a dozen varieties of fresh-roasted coffee and soothing jazzy tunes on the sound system, this is a great place to relax morning, noon, or night. ⊠ *Town Hall, Raekoja Plats 1* ☎ *644–8759* ⊟ *MC, V.*

$$$$ ⊞ **Olümpia.** This high-rise has a good selection of rooms, but request one with a view of the Old Town. Amenities include a conference hall, a sauna overlooking the city, and a splendid breakfast buffet. ⊠ *Liivalaia 33, EE0001* ☎ *669–0690* ☐ *669–0691* ⊕ *www.olympia.ee* ⇥ *405 rooms* ♢ *2 restaurants, pool, 3 bars* ⊟ *AE, DC, MC, V.*

$$$$ ⊞ **Park Consul Schlössle.** In three medieval warehouses in the Old Town,
FodorśChoice Tallinn's most luxurious hotel has unparalleled service and historic
★ charm. The sauna is free for guests. ⊠ *Pühavaimu 13–15, EE10123* ☎ *699–7700* ☐ *699–7777* ⊕ *www.consul-hotels.com* ⇥ *23 rooms* ♢ *Restaurant* ⊟ *DC, MC, V.*

$$ ⊞ **Express Hotel.** Just a few minutes' walk from the center of the Old Town, the Express Hotel is extremely democratic: all rooms here are identical and cost exactly the same price. For a no-frills, good value, this is a good choice. ⊠ *Sadama 1, EE0001* ☎ *667–8700* ☐ *667–8800* ⊕ *www.olympia.ee* ⇥ *166 rooms* ♢ *Restaurant* ⊟ *AE, DC, MC, V.*

$$ ▦ **Mihkli.** The little extras like direct-dial phones, satellite TV with pay movies, and rooms for nonsmokers and allergy sufferers set apart this midrange option. Room prices in this five-story hotel on the outskirts of Old Town include breakfast and a free morning sauna. ⊠ *Endla 23, EE10122* ☎ *666–4800* 🖷 *666–4888* ⊕ *www.mihkli.ee* 🗲 *61 rooms* 🖒 *Restaurant* ▭ *AE, MC, V.*

$–$$ ▦ **Vana Tom.** This Swedish-Estonian joint venture is an excellent budget choice for its Old Town central location, spic-and-span private rooms and dormitories, and friendly service. Breakfast is included, as is a kitchen for guests. ⊠ *Väike-Karja 1, EE10140* ☎ *631–3252* 🖷 *612–0511* ⊕ *www.hostel.ee* 🗲 *9 rooms* ▭ *AE, MC, V.*

The Islands

Some 1,500 time machines float off the western coast of Estonia, embodying pre–World War II Estonia. The Soviets feared a mass exodus to the West, so these islands have largely been off-limits for the past 50 years. Only two islands, Saaremaa and Hiiumaa, are easily accessible, through port towns about 100 km (62 mi) south of Tallinn. **Kuressaare,** the capital of **Saaremaa,** is a town of only 16,000 but proudly lays claim to an almost wholly intact Gothic castle, complete with turrets and moat. Visiting the modest cliffs and beaches round out a trip to the island. **Hiiumaa,** and its center of **Kärdla,** is quieter still, with nothing more audacious than some windmills and a few birds to disturb this perfect retreat.

LATVIA

Latvia, and particularly Rīga, is fiercely distinct from the other two Baltic States. German influence was stronger here than elsewhere, because the 14th-century Knights of the Sword used this as their base. When the Soviets forcibly incorporated Latvia into the Soviet Union in 1944, the effects of Russification were more devastating. Today 45% of Latvia is Russian-speaking; in Rīga, Russians, Ukrainians, and Belorussians are the majority. This has created a palpable tension: Latvians are angered because their culture has been suppressed for 50 years, whereas Russians are frustrated with the fact that most of them have yet to be granted citizenship here.

Latvia A to Z

AIR TRAVEL

Air Baltic operates nonstop flights from Berlin, Copenhagen, Helsinki, Kiev, Moscow, Prague, Stockholm, Tallinn, Vienna, Vilnius, and Warsaw. Austrian Airlines, British Airways, Czech Airlines, Estonian Air, Finnair, Lufthansa, SAS, and LOT operate flights via Europe from the United States.

BOAT & FERRY TRAVEL

Passenger ships connect Rīga with Kiel and Lübeck (in Germany) and Stockholm.

BUS TRAVEL

Public transportation costs 20s and runs 5:30 AM–midnight. Some routes have 24-hour service. Buy tickets from the conductor on the bus. Intercity bus trips cost less than 5Ls. For bus schedules, call the toll number (20s per minute) at the bus station.
🚩 **Bus Station** ☎ 900–0009.

CAR RENTAL

Cars may be rented from 40Ls a day; lower rates are available for longer rental terms.

🖪 Major Agencies **Avis** ☎ 722-5876. **Hertz** ☎ 720-7980. **National** ☎ 720-7710.

CAR TRAVEL

An international or national driver's license bearing a photograph is acceptable in Latvia. Drive on the right. Roads are not up to Western standards. Gas costs 40s per liter.

EMERGENCIES

For medical attention in Rīga, contact the English-speaking doctors at Ars. For a 24-hour pharmacy that delivers nonprescription drugs to your door, phone Rudens aptieka.

🖪 **Police** ☎ 02. **Ambulance** ☎ 03. **Doctor: Ars** ☎ 720-1001. **Dentist: A+S Health Center** ☎ 728-9516. **Rudens aptieka** ☎ 724-4322.

HOLIDAYS

January 1; Good Friday; Easter; May 1 (Labor Day); June 23, 24 (St. John's Day/Midsummer); November 18 (Independence Day, 1918); December 24–26; December 31.

LANGUAGE

The country's official language is Latvian, which belongs to the Baltic branch of the Indo-European family of languages; the unofficial language is Russian. Most Latvians will answer you if addressed in Russian, but more and more speak perfect English.

MAIL & SHIPPING

The main post office is open weekdays 7 AM–11 PM, weekends 8 AM–10 PM.

🖪 **Main post office** ✉ Brīvības 19, Rīga ☎ 701-8738.

POSTAL RATES A 20-gram letter to the United States costs 40s, a postcard 30s. To Europe, a 20-gram letter costs 30s, a postcard 20s.

MONEY MATTERS

A cup of coffee or tea costs 40s; a glass of local beer 1Ls; a medium-priced local dish 3Ls–5Ls. Admission to museums and galleries costs around 1Ls.

CURRENCY The monetary unit in Latvia is the lat (Ls), which is divided into 100 santīmi (s). There are notes of 5, 10, 20, 50, 100, and 500 lat, coins of 1 and 2 lat and 1, 2, 5, 10, 20, and 50 santīmi. At press time, the rate of exchange was 57s to the U.S. dollar, 38s to the Canadian dollar, 95s to the pound sterling, 62s to the euro, 34s to the Australian dollar, 32s to the New Zealand dollar, and 7s to the South African rand. Banks change cash and traveler's checks at fair commissions; most also give advances on a Visa or MasterCard. Credit cards are widely accepted.

TAXIS

Taxis are expensive around Rīga's hotels and ferry, bus, and train stations, cheaper within the city center; for best results, telephone for one. The official rate is 30s per kilometer (½ mi) in the daytime and 40s at night or in bad weather. Drivers must display an operating license and a meter. Stick to the state cabs with orange and black markings. Insist that the meter be turned on; if there is no meter, choose another taxi or decide on a price beforehand. Rīga Taxi and Rīgas Taksometru Parks are by and large trustworthy taxi companies. Shared taxis accommodate up to 10 people and are cheap and comfortable. They operate on virtually every bus and trolleybus line. Fares are 20s and 30s. Passengers may embark at any regular bus stop and disembark anywhere along the route.

🚹 Rīga Taxi ☎ 800–1010. Rīgas Taksometru Parks ☎ 800–1313.

TELEPHONES

COUNTRY &
AREA CODES
The country code for Latvia is 371. Though there is no area code for numbers in Rīga, there are for other regions of the country.

INTERNATIONAL
CALLS
🚹 Access Code **AT&T** ☎ 800–2288.

LOCAL CALLS
Pay phones take phone cards worth 2, 3, or 5 Ls. Buy cards at kiosks or post offices.

🚹 Telephone information ☎ 118.

TIPPING

At restaurants, a service charge of 10% is sometimes added and an 18% V.A.T. is automatically included. Tipping is not obligatory, but for excellent service, add 10%.

TOURS

Latvia Tours offer tours of Rīga on Monday, Wednesday, and Saturday with regional tours on other days.

🚹 Fees & Schedules **Latvia Tours** ☎ 708–5057.

TRAIN TRAVEL

Electric trains are the preferable mode of transport for getting around Latvia. Tickets cost less than 5Ls. For train schedule information call Central Station.

🚹 **Central Station** ☎ 583–3095.

Exploring Latvia

Rīga

Rīga has an upscale, big-city feel unmatched in the region. The capital is almost as large as Tallinn and Vilnius combined and is the business center of the area. Original, high-quality restaurants and hotels have given Rīga something to brag about. Although Rīga's Old Town is its calling card, it is also the city of art nouveau. Long avenues of complex and sometimes whimsical Jugendstil facades hint at Rīga's grand past. Many were designed by Mikhail Eisenstein, the father of Soviet director Sergei. This style dominates the city center; you can see the finest examples at Alberta 2, 2a, 4, 6, 8, and 13; Elizabetes 10b; and Strēlnieku 4a.

The fiercely Gothic **Melngalvju Nams** (Blackheads House) was built in 1344 as a hotel for wayfaring merchants (who wore black hats). Partially destroyed during World War II and leveled by the Soviets in 1948, the extravagant, ornate building was renovated and reopened in 2000 for Rīga's 800th anniversary. The facade is a treasured example of Dutch Renaissance work. ⊠ *Strēlnieku laukums* ☎ *704–4300* 🕐 *Tues.–Sun. 10–5.*

🐾 The **Brīvdabas muzejs** (Open-air Ethnographic Museum) is well worth the 9-km (5-mi) trek from downtown. At this countryside living museum, farmsteads and villages have been crafted to look like those in 18th- and 19th-century Latvia, and costumed workers engage in traditional activities (beekeeping, smithing, and so on). ⊠ *Brīvības 440* ☎ *799–4515* 🕐 *Daily 10–5.*

★ The central **Brīvības piemineklis** (Freedom Monument), a 1935 statue whose upheld stars represent Latvia's united peoples (the Kurzeme,

Vidzeme, and Latgale), was the rallying point for many nationalist protests during the late 1980s and early 1990s. Watch the changing of the guards every hour on the hour between 9 and 6. ⊠ *Brīvības and Raiņa.*

In **Doma laukums** (Dome Square), the nerve center of the Old Town, the stately 1210 **Doma baznīca** (Dome Cathedral) dominates. Reconstructed over the years with Romanesque, Gothic, and baroque bits, this place of worship is astounding for its architecture as much as for its size. The massive 6,768-pipe organ is among the largest in Europe, and it is played nearly every evening at 7 PM. Check at the cathedral for schedules and tickets. ⊠ *Doma laukums* ☎ *721–3498* ☉ *Tues.–Fri. 1–5, Sat. 10–2.*

★ The **Okupācijas muzejs** (Latvian Occupation Museum) details the devastation of Latvia at the hands of the Nazis and Soviets during World War II as well as the Latvians' struggle for independence in September 1991. In front of the museum is a monument to the Latvian sharpshooters who protected Lenin during the 1917 revolution. ⊠ *Strēlnieku laukums 1* ☎ *721–2715* ☉ *Tues.–Sun. 11–5.*

At **Rīgas motormuzejs** (Motor Museum) the Western cars on display can impress, but the Soviet models—including Stalin's iron-plated limo and a Rolls-Royce totaled by Brezhnev himself—are the most fun. ⊠ *Eizenšteina 6* ☎ *709–7170* ☉ *Mon. 10–3, Tues.–Sun. 10–6.*

Latvia's restored 18th-century **Nacionālā Opera** (National Opera House), where Richard Wagner once conducted, is worthy of a night out. ⊠ *Box office, Aspazijas 3* ☎ *707–3777* ☉ *Daily 10–7.*

Towering **Pētera baznīca** (St. Peter's Church), originally built in 1209, had a long history of annihilation and conflagration before being destroyed most recently in 1941. Rebuilt by the Soviets, it lacks authenticity but has a good observation deck on the 200-foot spire. ⊠ *Skārņu 19* ☎ *722–9426* ☉ *Tues.–Sun. 10–7.*

The **Trīs Brāļi** (Three Brothers)—a trio of houses on Mazā Pils—show what the city looked like before the 20th century. The three oldest stone houses in the capital (No. 17 is the oldest, dating from the 15th century) span several styles, from the medieval to the baroque. The building at No. 19 is the city's **architecture museum.** ⊠ *Mazā Pils 17, 19, 21* ☎ *722–0779* ☉ *Weekdays 9–5, Sat. noon–4.*

The **Valsts mākslas muzejs** (National Art Museum) has a gorgeous interior with imposing marble staircases linking several large halls of 19th- and 20th-century Latvian paintings. ⊠ *K. Valdemāra 10a* ☎ *732–4461* ☉ *Wed.–Mon. 11–5.*

$$$ ✕ **Symposium.** One of Rīga's premier dining establishments, Symposium serves outstanding Mediterranean cuisine, with an emphasis on seafood, in a softly lit dining room. ⊠ *Dzirnavu 84/1* ☎ *724–2545* ▭ *MC, V.*

$$$ ✕ **Vincent's.** Named for van Gogh, this restaurant serves sensational international delicacies. Numbered among its clientele are Mstislav Rostropovich and José Carreras and the princes and princesses of Europe. ⊠ *Elizabetes 19* ☎ *733–2634* ▭ *MC, V.*

Fodor'sChoice ★

$$–$$$ ✕ **Charlestons.** This restaurant has achieved a level of informal class and hearty good taste from breakfast to dinner. The front café is perfect for a quiche or croissant and coffee, and the main dining room and summer terrace invite long, leisurely lunches and dinners. ⊠ *Blaumaņa 38/40* ☎ *777–0573* ▭ *MC, V.*

$ ✕ **A. Suns.** "Andalusian Dog" has long been an expat hangout in Rīga, and why not? With an art-house cinema upstairs and a breezy restaurant downstairs—with a wall of windows perfect for people-watching—the restaurant is hip and cool, with a tasty Tex-Mex menu. ⊠ *Elizabetes 83/85* ☎ *728–8418* ⊟ *MC, V.*

$ ✕ **Staburags.** In an art nouveau building in downtown Rīga, this may be the capital's best place to sample Latvian national cuisine, with such dishes as roast leg of pork, sauerkraut, all manner of potato dishes, and smoked chicken. ⊠ *Čaka 55* ☎ *729–9787* ⊟ *No credit cards.*

$$$$ 🏨 **Grand Palace Hotel.** Outstanding amenities, 19th-century furnishings, and an enviable location in the heart of Rīga make this a grand place in which to relax in luxury. ⊠ *Pils 12, LV1050* ☎ *704–4000* 🖨 *704–4001* ⊕ *www.schlossle-hotels.com* 🛏 *56 rooms* ♨ *2 restaurants* ⊟ *DC, MC, V.*

$$$ 🏨 **Konventa Sēta.** In a charming complex of buildings dating from the Middle Ages, this hotel has rooms with a clean, white Scandinavian aesthetic and medieval details. ⊠ *Kalēju 9/11, LV1050* ☎ *708–7501* 🖨 *708–7515* ⊕ *www.derome.lv* 🛏 *140 rooms* ♨ *Restaurant* ⊟ *AE, DC, MC, V.*

$$ 🏨 **Krišjānis & Ģertrūde.** Just five rooms occupy this British-style bed-and-breakfast. The friendly owners have outfitted the comfortable rooms with cable TV and coffee and tea sets. ⊠ *K. Barona 39-1, LV1011* ☎ *750–6604* 🖨 *750–6603* ⊕ *www.musbalt.com/hotel* 🛏 *5 rooms* ⊟ *MC, V.*

$$ 🏨 **Raudi un Draugi.** This small hotel affords a great location for a low price; it's efficiently run and simple. Large rooms for families are available. ⊠ *Mārstaļu 1/3, LV1050* ☎ *722–0372* 🖨 *724–2239* 🛏 *47 rooms* ⊟ *MC, V.*

Jūrmala

The Latvian name of this string of four small towns means "seaside," and for a 20-km (12-mi) stretch that is exactly what you get. Once a sought-after vacation spot for Soviet elite, this area today attracts Russian and Latvian vacationers. The beach is clean and the Soviet-era main street has been renovated. Frequent electric trains (crowded in summer) make the 40-minute trip from Rīga.

Gauja Nacionālais Parks

About one hour east of the capital, Gauja National Park is populated by friendly people and a helpful forestry staff. Latvia's deepest river valley, at 280 feet, is little more than a dip, but the gently flowing Gauja and the 13th-century ruins of **Turaidas Pils** (Turaida Castle), built by the Knights of the Sword, near Sigulda provide amusement, ancient graffiti, and a bobsled track. ⊠ *53 km (33 mi) east of Rīga; Sigulda visitor center: Pils 6* ☎ *2/971–335.*

LITHUANIA

Lithuania has historically been the invader, not the invaded. In 1386, the country formed a union with Poland, and over the following 400 years the joint kingdom stretched from the Baltic to the Black Sea. Poland took the leading role until the late 18th century, but Lithuanians still remember their time as a European superpower. Russification ensued, followed by a short period of independence (during which Kaunas was the capital, as Vilnius was occupied by Poland). Hundreds of thousands of Lithuanians were deported by the Soviets in the 1940s and 1950s, but today's population is 80% Lithuanian, with only 10% Russian-speaking. The country's Jewish population—which had thrived here since the 1400s—was decimated during World War II.

Lithuania A to Z

AIR TRAVEL
No direct flights link Lithuania and the United States. Lithuanian Airlines operates from Amsterdam, Berlin, Copenhagen, Frankfurt, Helsinki, London, Paris, Stockholm, and Warsaw. Austrian Airlines, Finnair, LOT, Lufthansa, and SAS offer good connections.

BUS TRAVEL
Public transportation costs 80c at kiosks and 75c from the driver. Buy tickets separately for buses and trolleybuses. Punch your ticket upon boarding or be fined 20Lt. Most public transportation operates 5:30 AM–midnight. Intercity bus trips cost between 8Lt and 40Lt. For bus schedules, phone Televerslas or the bus station.
▪ **Bus station** ☎ 2/162-977.

CAR RENTAL
Cars may be rented from 250Lt a day.
▪ Major Agencies **Avis** ☎ 2/306-820. **Budget** ☎ 2/230-6708. **Hertz** ☎ 2/726-940.
▪ Local Agencies **Litinterp** ☎ 2/212-3850.

CAR TRAVEL
An international or national driver's license bearing a photo is acceptable in Lithuania. Drive on the right. Main roads tend to be in good condition—better than those in Latvia or Estonia. Secondary roads, however, are commonly unpaved and have potholes. Gas costs 2.40Lt per liter.

EMERGENCIES
▪ **Police** ☎ 02. **Ambulance** ☎ 03. **Doctor: Baltic-American Clinic** ☎ 2/342-020. **Dentist: Gidenta** ☎ 2/617-143. **Pharmacy: Gedimino Vaistinė** ☎ 2/610-135.

HOLIDAYS
January 1; February 16 (Independence Day); March 11 (Restoration of Lithuania's Independence); Easter; July 6 (Day of Statehood); November 1 (All Saints' Day); December 25, 26.

LANGUAGE
Lithuanian is the official language; however, English, Russian, and, to a certain degree, Polish are spoken in Vilnius.

MAIL & SHIPPING
The main post office is open weekdays 7–7, Saturday 9–4.
▪ Post Office **Main post office** ✉ Gedimino 7 ☎ 2/616-759.

POSTAL RATES A 20-gram letter to the United States or Europe costs 1.70Lt, a postcard 1.20Lt.

MONEY MATTERS
A cup of coffee or tea costs 3Lt–5Lt; a glass of local beer 8Lt; a medium-priced dish at a local restaurant 12Lt–15Lt. Admission to museums and galleries costs about 4Lt.

CURRENCY The monetary unit in Lithuania is the lita, which is divided into 100 centas. There are notes of 1, 2, 5, 10, 20, 50, 100, and 200 litas and coins of 1, 2, and 5 litas and 1, 2, 5, 10, 20, and 50 centas. At press time, the rate of exchange was 3Lt to the U.S. dollar, 2Lt to the Canadian dollar, 5Lt to the pound sterling, 3.50Lt to the euro, 2Lt to the Australian dollar, 1.75Lt to the New Zealand dollar, and 37c to the South African rand. National banks, with branches in all major and most minor cities, change cash and traveler's checks at fair commissions; most also give advances on a Visa card. Credit cards are widely accepted.

TAXIS

Taxis in Vilnius can be expensive around hotels and the bus and train stations. It's best to telephone for one. Taxi fares generally start at 1.30Lt and increase by 65c to 1.30Lt per kilometer (½ mi) in the day-time, more at night or in bad weather. Drivers must display an operating license and a meter. In-town journeys cost up to 10Lt. Try Baltas Taxi and Vilniaus Taxi. Shared taxis accommodate up to 10 people and are cheap and comfortable. They operate on virtually every bus and trolleybus line. Fares are 1Lt to 2Lt. Passengers may embark at any regular bus stop and disembark anywhere along the route.

🚖 **Taksi Jums** ☎ 2/777-777. **Vilniaus Taxi** ☎ 2/128-888.

TELEPHONES

COUNTRY & AREA CODES
The country code for Lithuania is 370. The area code in Vilnius is 2.

INTERNATIONAL CALLS
🚖 **Access Code AT&T** ☎ 8–800/92800.

LOCAL CALLS
Pay phones accept cards worth 9Lt, 13Lt, 16Lt, and 30Lt. Buy phone cards from any post office or Lietuvos Spauda kiosk.

🚖 **Telephone information** ☎ 2/757-009.

TIPPING

At restaurants, a service charge of 7% is sometimes added. An 18% VAT is also included in the price of dishes on the menu but may be listed separately on your bill. Add 10% if you've received excellent service.

TOURS

Vilnius City Tour runs walking tours of Vilnius and minibus tours of the region.

🚖 **Fees & Schedules Vilnius City Tour** ☎ 2/615-558.

TRAIN TRAVEL

Domestic train trips cost between 8Lt and 40Lt. For schedules, call the train station. Certain trains running from Vilnius to Poland cross Belarus. Avoid these trains, as you need a Belorussian transit visa to cross a mere 48 km (30 mi) of Belarus along the way. Trains are slower and less comfortable than buses.

🚖 **Train station** ☎ 2/330-086.

Exploring Lithuania

Vilnius

What Vilnius has is *soul*. Good jazz, friendly faces, and amazingly cheap restaurants are a way of life here. The Old Town is somewhat shabby around the edges—but those deteriorating structures that have been renovated shine in baroque glory, and some that haven't been renovated house a living pulse as homes for the city's artsy squatters. Founded by Lithuanian Grand Duke Gediminas in the 14th century, Vilnius was an important center of Lithuanian, Polish, and Jewish culture until World War II. Now this former "Jerusalem of the East" is Lithuania's bustling capital—a national symbol to extradited Poles, a ghost town to the 150,000 Jews who once lived here, and home to 100,000 displaced Russians. It has museums, lush parks, a wealth of baroque churches, and myriad courtyards, many with cafés.

FodorsChoice
★
Vilnius's main cathedral, **Arkikatedra Bazilika,** has been a national symbol for centuries; inside is the dazzling 17th-century Chapel of St. Kazimieras. Originally a temple to Perkūnas, one of Lithuania's many pagan gods, the building became a church in the 13th century, when Lithua-

nia converted from paganism to Christianity; it was the last European country to do so. The cathedral was used for other purposes under Communism; the church reclaimed the cathedral in the 1980s. ⊠ *Katedros 1* 🕾 *2/611–127* ⊙ *Daily 7–7.*

★ The **Aušros Vartai** (Gates of Dawn) is the only one remaining of Vilnius's nine 16th-century gates. Beyond it to the right, a door leads to the **Chapel of Our Lady of Vilnius**, a room whose walls are covered with metal and silver hearts and that contains an icon of the Virgin Mary renowned for its healing powers. Many of the devout climb on their knees up the steps to this holy place, converted into a chapel in 1671 and remade in neoclassical style in 1829. ⊠ *Aušros Vartų* 🕾 *2/123–513.*

Visit the **Žemutinės Pilies Muziejus** (Lower Castle Museum) (🕾 2/629–988) on Cathedral Square at the foot of Castle Hill, topped by the 🕭 13th-century **Gedimino bokštas** (Gedimino Tower), once part of the city's fortifications, to see the archaeological dig of the 16th-century palace that once stood on this site. Inside the tower is the **Vilniaus Pilies Muziejus** (Vilnius Castle Museum; ⊠ Arsenalo 5 🕾 2/617–453 ⊙ Daily 11–6), which has outstanding city views.

To the east you can see the **Trijų Kryžių Kalnas** (Hill of Three Crosses), which are said to commemorate seven Franciscan monks killed on the hill by pagans; four of them were thrown into the river below (hence only three crosses).

During the early 1900s, Vilnius was Europe's major center of Yiddish education and literature. By the end of World War II, all but 600 of Vilnius's 100,000 Jews had been killed. Today the **Jewish quarter** contains almost no trace of the once-thriving culture. The single remaining **synagogue** (⊠ Pylimo 39) survived only because the Nazis used it as a medical-supply warehouse. To learn about Vilnius's Jewish heritage, visit the **Valstybinis Žydų Muziejus** (State Jewish Museum). ⊠ *Pylimo 4* 🕾 *2/ 613–003* ⊙ *Daily 2–6.*

★ In the New Town, at the **Genocido Aukų Muziejus** (KGB Museum), plaques take you through a litany of horrors in the basement of the former KGB prison. Hundreds of Lithuanians were killed here, and hundreds of thousands more were deported to Siberia by the Soviet regime during the 1940s and '50s. ⊠ *Aukų 2a* 🕾 *2/496–264* ⊙ *Tues.–Sun. 10–4.*

The amazing Gothic facade of the 16th-century **Šv Onos Bažnyčia** (St. Anne's Church) was created using 33 different types of brick. It's said that when Napoléon passed through town, he wanted to take the church back to Paris "in the palm of his hand." ⊠ *Maironio 8* 🕾 *2/611–236* ⊙ *Weekdays 6:30–8:30 PM, weekends 9–7:30.*

The baroque 17th-century **Šv Kazimiero bažnyčia** (St. Casimir's Church) is named for the city's patron saint, Prince Casimir Jagiellon. During Russia's reign a cupola replaced the familiar crown. Today the church is a popular spot for Sunday-afternoon organ recitals. ⊠ *Didžioji 34* 🕾 *2/221–715* ⊙ *Mon.–Sat. 4–6:30, Sun. 8–1:30.*

The **Šv Petro ir Povilo** (Church of Sts. Peter and Paul) has an astounding baroque interior, with nearly 2,000 ornate, white-stucco figures and an extraordinary boat-shape glass chandelier. ⊠ *Antakalnio 1* 🕾 *2/340–229* ⊙ *Mon.–Sat. 8–4:30, Sun. 10–8.*

The best collection of Lithuanian fine art is at the **Vilniaus Paveikslų Galerija** (Vilnius Picture Gallery), which displays 16th- to 19th-century paintings, as well as a number of sculptures and some early pottery and folk art. The interior of what was a palace from the 17th through the 19th centuries has been handsomely restored. ☒ *Didžioji 4* ☏ *2/124–258* ⏰ *Tues.–Sat. noon–6, Sun. noon–5.*

Vilniaus Universiteto (Vilnius University), founded by the Jesuits in 1570, is a complex of 12 courtyards. Highlights include the **observatory,** with its 18th-century zodiac engravings (note that it is not open to the public), and the Gothic **St. Johns' Church** (☏ *2/611–795*), begun in 1387. ☒ *Šv Jono 12.*

$$ ✕ **Freskos.** The dining room is furnished with antiques and props from the opera and theater. The Continental menu might offer pepper steak or grilled chicken breast salad. A salad bar, a dessert cart, and local beer are also available. ☒ *Didžioji 31* ☏ *2/618–133* ▭ *MC, V.*

$ ✕ **Prie Parlamento.** The apple crumble at this informal spot enjoys legendary status among diners; that dessert, as well as hearty English breakfasts and innovative pub grub all make for satisfying meals. Visit the cellar dance club, Ministerija, at night for drinks, pop music dancing, and a friendly crowd. ☒ *Gedimino 46* ☏ *2/496–606* ▭ *MC, V.*

$ ✕ **Ritos Sleptuvė.** Lithuanian-American Rita Dapkus, who gave up political life to cook, serves authentic Chicago-style pizza, great steaks, the best Tex-Mex in Lithuania, and Vilnius's best breakfast. ☒ *Goštauto 8* ☏ *2/626–117* ▭ *AE, MC, V.*

$ ✕ **Žaltvysklė.** Part of the Vilnius University complex of buildings, this Hungarian café has a Gothic interior. The inexpensive menu concentrates on Hungarian cuisine but also has national dishes from Lithuania and Bulgaria. ☒ *Pilies 11* ☏ *2/687–173* ▭ *MC, V.*

★ $ ✕ **Žemaičių smuklė.** The huge and delicious portions of roasted meats, fresh vegetables, and cooked potatoes, the friendly service, and the cabinlike interior and medieval summer patio make this restaurant one of the best places to sample Lithuanian cuisine. ☒ *Vokiečių 24* ☏ *2/616– 573* ▭ *MC, V.*

$$$$ ▦ **Narutis.** This Old Town hotel has spacious, well-appointed rooms. The restored building dates from the 16th century and has an unbeatable location. ☒ *Pilies 24, 2001* ☏ *2/222–894* 🖷 *2/622–882* ⤵ *30 rooms* ⌂ *2 restaurants* ▭ *AE, MC, V.*

★ $$$$ ▦ **Radisson SAS Astorija Hotel Vilnius.** Radisson-quality rooms in this late-19th-century building have a touch of the antique thrown in. As the only international chain property in town, this hotel sets the standard for service in Vilnius. ☒ *Didžioji 35/2, 2001* ☏ *2/220–110* 🖷 *2/ 221–762* ⊕ *www.radisson.com* ⤵ *120 rooms* ⌂ *Restaurant* ▭ *AE, DC, MC, V.*

$$$–$$$$ ▦ **Shakespeare Hotel.** Forgo Baltic minimalism for rich English-style comfort. Rooms here are themed around famous writers, and the design is
FodorśChoice suitably opulent. ☒ *Bernardinų 8, 2600* ☏ *2/314–521* 🖷 *2/314–522*
★ ⊕ *www.shakespeare.lt* ⤵ *31 rooms* ⌂ *Restaurant, bar* ▭ *AE, MC, V.*

$$$ ▦ **Centro Kubas.** For a taste of the Lithuanian countryside right in the middle of Old Town, Centro Kubas can't be beat. The hotel is filled with agricultural antiques and spacious rooms, and some rooms are wheelchair-accessible. ☒ *Stiklių 3, 2001* ☏ *2/660–860* 🖷 *2/660–863* ⊕ *www. centrokubas.lt* ⤵ *14 rooms* ⌂ *Restaurant* ▭ *MC, V.*

$$ ▦ **Litinterp B & B.** This bed-and-breakfast service, rental car travel agency runs a lovely guest house in the Old Town. This is a very good value for the money. ☒ *Bernardinų 7, 2600* ☏ *2/123–850* 🖷 *2/123–559* ⊕ *www.litinterp.lt* ⤵ *17 rooms* ▭ *MC, V.*

$ ▦ **JNN Hostel.** Across the river from the Old Town, this hostel has a youthful feel and impeccably clean rooms. ☒ *Ukmergės 25, 2600* ☏🖷 *2/722– 270* ⤵ *10 rooms* ⌂ *Restaurant, pool* ▭ *MC, V.*

BELGIUM
BRUSSELS, ANTWERP, GENT, BRUGGE

BELGIUM IS A CONNOISSEUR'S DELIGHT. Famous for its artistic inspiration, the land of Brueghel and Van Eyck, Rubens and Van Dyck, and Ensor and Magritte is where their best work can still be seen. Belgian culture was and remains that of a bourgeois, mercantile society. Feudal lords may have built Belgium's many castles, and the clergy its splendid churches, but merchants and craftsmen are responsible for the guild houses and sculpture-adorned town halls of Brussels, Antwerp, Gent, and Brugge.

This small country offers surprising geographic variety, from the beaches and dunes of the North Sea coast and the tree-lined canals and big sky of the "platte (flat) land" to the rolling Brueghel country around Brussels and the sheer cliffs and dense woods of the Ardennes. The state of Belgium is one of Europe's youngest, but its territory has been fought over for centuries by invaders from all sides. Julius Caesar called the Belgae the bravest of the tribes that defied the Roman legions. Since then, the land we now call Belgium has been conquered by the Franks, the dukes of Burgundy, the Spanish, the Austrians, and the French. Finally, after the defeat of Napoléon in 1815, Belgium was forcibly amalgamated with Holland into the United Kingdom of the Netherlands.

The independent state of Belgium was universally recognized in 1831 as a monarchy under its first king, Leopold I, and his heirs continue to hold the throne. The current monarch, Albert II, was crowned in 1993.

Belgium packs nearly 6 million Flemish-speaking Flemings and just over 4 million French-speaking Walloons into a country the size of Vermont or Wales. The presence of two major language communities enriches its intellectual life but also creates constant political and social tension. The creation in the mid-1990s of three largely self-governing regions—Flanders, Wallonia, and the city of Brussels, which is bilingual and multicultural—has only emphasized these divisions.

Belgium's neutrality was violated during both world wars, when much of its architectural heritage was destroyed and great suffering was inflicted by the occupying forces. This may be why Belgium, home to most of the European Union (EU) institutions, staunchly supports the EU.

BELGIUM A TO Z

To research prices, get advice from other travelers, and book travel arrangements, visit www.fodors.com.

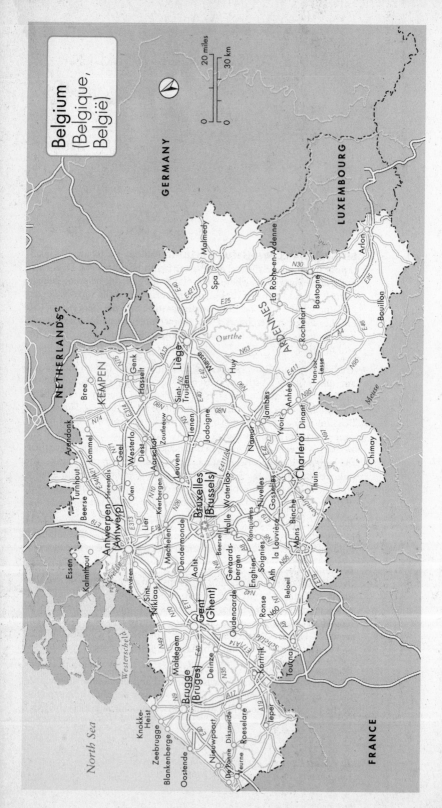

Belgium
(Belgique,
België)

North Sea
NETHERLANDS
GERMANY
LUXEMBOURG
FRANCE

20 miles
30 km

Westerschelde

Essen
Kalmthout
Knokke-Heist
Zeebrugge
Blankenberge
Oostende
De Panne
Veurne
Diksmuide
Nieuwpoort
Roeselare
Ieper
Brugge (Bruges)
Maldegem
Deinze
Gent (Ghent)
Oudenaarde
Ronse
Kortrijk
Tournai
Avondonk
Turnhout
Beerse
Herentals
KEMPEN
Bree
Geel
Olen
Lier
Westerlo
Diest
Genk
Hasselt
Aarschot
Keerbergen
Mechelen
Antwerpen (Antwerp)
Beveren
Sint-Niklaas
Dendermonde
Aalst
Leuven
Zoutleeuw
Zoutleeuw
Tienen
Jodoigne
Sint-Truiden
Liège
Huy
Spa
Malmedy
Ourthe
ARDENNES
Rochefort
Han-sur-Lesse
La Roche-en-Ardenne
Bastogne
Bouillon
Arlon
Namur
Jambes
Yvoir
Anhée
Dinant
Chimay
Thuin
Binche
Charleroi
Gosselies
La Louvière
Mons
Beloeil
Ath
Soignies
Enghien
Geraardsbergen
Ronquières
Nivelles
Halle
Waterloo
Beersel
Bruxelles (Brussels)
Lambas
Meuse
Lesse

N9
N49
A10
E40
N35
A17
A19
N8
N60
N7
N42
E429
N56
E19
N6
E42
E19
E17
E34
A21
N1
N15
N74
E314
N71
N19
N10
N26
N4
N63
N30
N25
E421
E40
E25
E411
N97
N95
E46
E25
A4
N5
E411/E44
N96
N90
08N
08N
N3
N2
A13
E313
N70

AIR TRAVEL

Belgium has no domestic air services. International flights arrive either at Brussels National Airport at Zaventem, 15 km (9 mi) northeast of Brussels, or at Brussels South Airport in Charleroi, 55 km (34 mi) south of the city.

BIKE TRAVEL

You can rent a bicycle from Belgian National Railways at 35 stations; train travelers get reduced rates. Bicycling is easy in the flat northern and coastal areas; in the hilly south and east it's more strenuous. There are bicycle lanes in many Flemish cities, where car use is being discouraged, but cycling in downtown Brussels can be downright dangerous.

BUS TRAVEL

Small towns and the outlying suburbs are served by independent transport companies De Lijn (within Flanders) and TEC (within Wallonia). Intercity bus services are rudimentary. Check at the tourist office or train station.

BUSINESS HOURS

Banks are usually open weekdays 9–4 or 4:30; some close for an hour at lunch. Currency exchange facilities (*bureaux de change* or *wisselkantoren*) are usually open evenings and weekends, but you'll get a better rate in banks. For instant cash, ATMs are nearly everywhere (but not at railway stations) and accept major credit cards. Museums are generally open 10–5 Tuesday through Sunday. Many museums will refuse to admit you after 4:15 or so. Large stores are open weekdays and Saturday from 9:30 or 10 to 6:30 or 7 and generally stay open an hour later on Friday. "Night" shops, for newspapers, tobacco, drinks, and limited grocery items, are open seven days a week from 6 PM until dawn.

CAR TRAVEL

Road signs are written in the language of the region, so you need to know that Antwerp is Antwerpen in Flemish and Anvers in French; likewise, Brugge is Bruges in French, and Brussels is Bruxelles in French and Brussel in Flemish; Gent is Gand (French). Even more confusing, Liège and Luik are the same place, as are Louvain and Leuven, and Namur and Namen. Yet more difficult is Mons (French) and Bergen (Flemish), or Tournai (French) and Doornik (Flemish). On the Brussels-Liège/Luik motorway, signs change language with alarming frequency as you crisscross the Wallonia-Flanders border. Finally, *Uitrit* is Flemish for "exit."

PARKING   On-street parking often requires you to display a ticket dispensed from not-always-obvious coin-operated machines generally in the middle of the block. Old-fashioned meters still line some streets. Many cities have "blue zones" where parking is allowed for a limited amount of time and a parking disk has to be displayed. Few parking garages stay open past 10 PM. On no account park in front of a garage or a building bearing a towing sign.

ROAD
CONDITIONS   Belgium has an excellent system of toll-free expressways. Road numbers for main roads have the prefix *N* for national roads; highways and expressways are prefixed by *A* or *E*.

RULES OF
THE ROAD   All motorists must hold a valid national or international driver's license. Drive on the right and pass on the left; passing on the right is forbidden. Seat belts are compulsory in both front and rear seats. Every car must have a triangle-shape warning sign to be used in the event of a breakdown or accident. Unless otherwise posted, traffic on the right has the right-of-way at intersections. Adhere strictly to this rule, as there are few stop or yield signs. Never, ever assume that someone with priority

will stop if you don't. Pedestrians have priority on marked crossings, and vehicles in traffic circles have priority over those entering them—even if they're coming from the right. Buses have priority over cars, and trams have absolute priority; they will ring bells or sound horns if you're obstructing them, and they will hit you if they can't stop. Maximum speed limits are 120 kph (75 mph) on highways, 90 kph (55 mph) on major roads, and 50 kph (30 mph) in cities. Lower limits are frequently imposed. The maximum permitted blood alcohol level is 0.05%, a level you can reach with two glasses of beer or one glass of wine.

CUSTOMS & DUTIES

For details on imports and duty-free limits for visitors from outside the EU, *see* Customs & Duties *in* Smart Travel Tips.

EATING & DRINKING

Most Belgians take eating seriously and are discerning about fresh produce and innovative recipes. At the top end of the scale, *menus dégustation* (tasting menus) offer a chance to sample small portions of a large selection of the chef's finest dishes. Belgian specialties include *lapin à la kriek* or *konijn met kriek* (rabbit in cherry-flavored beer), *anguilles au vert* or *paling in 't groen* (eels in a green herb sauce), *waterzooi* (a creamy fish or chicken stew), and *moules/frites* or *mossels met frieten* (fresh steamed mussels served with french fries). Other local specialties are *chicons* or *witloof* (Belgian endive); marvelous white asparagus from Mechelen, at its best in April; and *crevettes grises* or *grijze garnaaltjes* (tiny, sweet shrimp fresh from the North Sea). For lunch, cold cuts, a *croque monsieur* (grilled ham-and-cheese sandwich), and *jambon d'Ardennes* or *Ardeense ham* (smoked Ardennes ham) are popular, as is the *tartine au fromage blanc* or *boterham met platte kaas* (an open-face sandwich of dark bread with soft white cheese, served with chopped radishes and spring onions).

Fixed-price menus are widely available and often represent considerable savings. Menus and prices are posted outside most restaurants, but it's a good idea to check availability before you sit down in tourist areas. Reservations are a must in finer establishments. Few restaurants have no-smoking sections, and many welcome dogs.

Look for fixed-price menus or the daily special (*plat du jour* or *dagschotel*); if you sacrifice choice, you can eat well for less than €18 in many good restaurants.

	$$$$	**$$$**	**$$**	**$**
WHAT IT COSTS In Euros				
AT DINNER	over €30	€22–€30	€12–€22	under €12

Prices are per person for main course and include a 21% value-added tax. Belgian restaurants include a 16% service charge on all bills.

MEALTIMES Most hotels serve breakfast until 10 AM. Belgians usually eat lunch between 1 and 3 PM. The main meal of the day is dinner, eaten between 7 and 10 PM; peak dining time is now creeping closer to 9 PM.

RESERVATIONS & DRESS Jacket and tie are required only in the most exclusive establishments. Most Belgians favor casual wear; open-neck shirts, slacks, and jeans are popular with all age groups.

EMBASSIES

🏴 Australia ✉ Rue Guimard 6, 1040 Brussels ☎ 02/286-0500 ⊕ www.austemb.be.
🏴 Canada ✉ Av. de Tervueren 2, 1040 Brussels ☎ 02/741-0611 ⊕ www.ambassade-canada.be.

🏠 Ireland ✉ Ferdinand Verbiestlaan 38, 2650 Antwerp ☎ 03/289-0611.

🏠 New Zealand ✉ Sq. de Meeus 1, 7/F, 1000 Brussels ☎ 02/512-1040 🌐 www.nzembassy.com.

🏠 South Africa ✉ Rue de la Loi 26, 1000 Brussels ☎ 02/285-4400 🌐 www.ambassade.net/southafrica.

🏠 United Kingdom ✉ Rue d'Arlon 85, 1040 Brussels ☎ 02/287-6211 🌐 www.british-embassy.be.

🏠 United States ✉ Bd. du Régent 25-27, 1000 Brussels ☎ 02/508-2111 🌐 www.usembassy.be.

HOLIDAYS
January 1; Easter Monday; May 1 (Labor Day); Ascension; Pentecost or Whit Monday; July 21 (Belgian National Day); August 15 (Assumption); November 1 (All Saints' Day); November 11 (Armistice Day); December 25.

LANGUAGE
Language is a sensitive subject and exerts a strong influence on politics at the national and regional levels. There are three official languages in Belgium: French, spoken primarily in the south of the country (Wallonia); Flemish, spoken in the north (Flanders); and German, spoken in a small area near the German border. Brussels is bilingual, with both French and Flemish officially recognized, though the majority of residents are francophones. Many people speak English in Brussels and throughout Flanders; in Wallonia, English-speakers tend to be thin on the ground. Flemish and Belgian French both contain slight differences from the corresponding languages spoken in the neighboring countries to the north and south.

LODGING
As the self-proclaimed capital of Europe, Brussels attracts high-powered visitors, and many luxury hotels have been built to accommodate them. Over weekends and during July and August, business travelers are few and far between, so prices come down to €124 or less. New hotels catering to cost-conscious travelers have also been built, where doubles cost less than €76. Rates change considerably and without notice, so verify your rate when making a reservation. Hotel prices, including sales tax and service charge, are usually posted in each room.

WHAT IT COSTS In Euros			
$$$$	**$$$**	**$$**	**$**
BRUSSELS			
FOR 2 PEOPLE over €223	€161–€223	€87–€161	under €87
OTHER CITIES			
HOTELS over €186	€136–€186	€62–€136	under €62

Prices are for a standard double room, excluding a 16% service charge and a 14.9% room tax. The tax is slightly lower at suburban hotels.

B&BS   Bed-and-breakfasts are now an attractive option, thanks to self-regulation and higher standards. Contact local tourist offices.

CAMPING   Belgium is well supplied with camping and caravan (trailer) sites. For details contact the Royal Camping & Caravaning Club de Belgique. Both the Flemish and Walloon tourist offices publish guides to recommended campsites in their respective regions.

🏠 Organizations **Royal Camping & Caravaning Club de Belgique** ✉ Av. des Villas 5, Brussels ☎ 02/537-3681 🌐 www.caravanclub.nl.

HOSTELS   For information about youth hostels in Brussels and Wallonia, contact Les Auberges de la Jeunesse. For Flanders, contact Vlaamse Jeugdherbergcentrale. The youth organization Connections makes travel arrangements for young people.

🖪 Organizations **Les Auberges de la Jeunesse** ✉ Rue de la Sablonnière 28, Brussels ☎ 02/219-5676 🖷 02/219-1451 ⊕ www.laj.be. **Connections** ✉ Rue du Midi 19-21, Brussels ☎ 02/550-0100 🖷 02/512-9447 ⊕ www.connections.be. **Vlaamse Jeugdherbergcentrale** ✉ Van Stralenstraat 40, 2060 Antwerp ☎ 03/232-7218 🖷 03/231-8126 ⊕ www.vjh.be.

HOTELS   You can trust Belgian hotels, almost without exception, to be clean and of a high standard. Brugge is especially well supplied with romantic hideaways. BTR (Belgian Tourist Reservations) handles reservations free.

🖪 Organizations **BTR (Belgian Tourist Reservations)** ✉ Bd. Anspach 111, Brussels ☎ 02/513-7484 🖷 02/513-9277.

MAIL & SHIPPING

First-class (airmail) letters and postcards to the United States cost €0.84, second-class (surface) €0.57. Airmail letters and postcards to the United Kingdom cost €0.59, second-class €0.52. All international first-class mail must be marked with a blue A-PRIOR sticker (available in post offices). The central post office is open 24 hours a day, seven days a week.

🖪 Post Offices **Central post office** ✉ Av. Frosny 1, 1060 Brussels ⊕ www.post.be.

MONEY MATTERS

Costs in Brussels are roughly on a par with those in London and New York. All taxes and service charges (tips) are included in hotel and restaurant bills and taxi fares. Gasoline prices are steep, but highways are toll-free.

Cup of coffee in a café, €1.25–€1.50; glass of draft beer, €1.25–€1.75; glass of wine, about €2.97; single bus/metro/tram ride €1.24.

CURRENCY   In January 2002, Belgium, as one of the euro zone currency countries, introduced euro (€) notes and coins. Belgian francs have completely disappeared from circulation, and only the Banque Nationale will still exchange old franc notes. The euro comes in bills of 5, 10, 20, 50, 100, 200, and 500 and coins of 1, 2, 5, 10, 20, 50 cents, and 1 and 2 euros.

VALUE-ADDED   V.A.T. in Belgium is between 6% on food and clothing and 33% on luxury items. Residents outside the European Union can qualify for a V.A.T. refund but must spend €125 or more in the same shop on the same day. You must also carry the goods out of the country personally within 30 days. After you have had the invoice stamped by customs at your last port of call in the EU, you mail it back to the store of purchase, and the V.A.T. amount will be credited to your credit card or bank account.

TELEPHONES

COUNTRY &   The country code for Belgium is 32. All calls within the country must
AREA CODES   include the regional telephone code. When dialing Belgium from outside the country, drop the first zero in the regional code.

INTERNATIONAL   You can place direct calls from pay phones by using a telecard, sold at
CALLS   most tobacconists. For credit card and collect calls, dial AT&T, MCI Worldphone, or Sprint Global One. For English-language telephone assistance, dial 1405.

🖪 Access Codes **AT&T** ☎ 0800-10010. **MCI Worldphone** ☎ 0800-10012. **Sprint Global One** ☎ 0800-10014.

PUBLIC PHONES   Pay phones work mostly with telecards, available at post offices, supermarkets, neighborhood shops, railway stations, and many newsstands. Cards are sold in denominations of €5 and €10. An average local call costs €0.50. Coin-operated phones (on the platforms of metro stations) take €1 and €2 coins. All telephone numbers must be preceded by their area code prefix, regardless of the location in Belgium from where the call is made.

TIPPING
A tip (*service compris* or *service inclusief*) is always included in restaurant and hotel bills and in taxi fares. Railway porters expect €0.75 per item on weekdays and €1 per item on weekends. For bellhops and doormen, €2.50 is adequate. If no fixed price is indicated, tip washroom attendants €0.25.

TRAIN TRAVEL
Belgian Railways goes by either NMBS or SNCB, and fast and frequent trains connect all main towns and cities. Reduced tariffs are available for daily and weekend return trips, for large families, groups, senior citizens, and young people under 26. Check with the train station to see what specials are being offered. A Benelux Tourrail Pass allows unlimited travel throughout Belgium, Luxembourg, and the Netherlands for any five days over a one-month period. People under 26 can purchase a Go Pass, valid for 10 second-class, one-way trips within Belgium in a six-month period. Special weekend round-trip tickets are valid from Friday morning to Monday night: a 40% reduction is available on the first traveler's ticket and a 60% reduction on companions' tickets.

VISITOR INFORMATION
Each region has its own tourist office. The national Flemish office and the national French-speaking office are at the same address in Brussels and share a ground-floor Tourist Information Office.

Tourist Information Office ⊠ rue du Marché-aux-Herbes 63 ☎ 02/504-0390 🖷 02/504-0270 ⊕ www.tib.be.

WHEN TO GO
The tourist season runs from early May to late September and peaks in July and August, when the weather is warmest. May and September offer the advantage of generally clear skies and smaller crowds. Be prepared for rain any time of the year.

CLIMATE Temperatures range from around 65°F (18°C) in May to an average of 73°F (23°C) in July and August. In winter they drop to an average of about 43°F (6°C). Snow is unusual except in the mountains of the Ardennes, where skiing is popular. On the coast and in the Ardennes, freezing fogs can reduce visibility to 5 yards and render road surfaces glassy.

The following are the average daily maximum and minimum temperatures for Brussels.

Jan.	40F	4C	May	65F	18C	Sept.	69F	21C
	30	−1		46	8		51	11
Feb.	44F	7C	June	72F	22C	Oct.	60F	15C
	32	0		52	11		45	7
Mar.	51F	11C	July	73F	23C	Nov.	48F	9C
	36	25		4	12		38	3
Apr.	58F	14C	Aug.	72F	22C	Dec.	42F	6C
	41	5		54	12		32	0

BRUSSELS

Brussels has become synonymous with the EU, but although diplomats, politicians, lobbyists, and journalists have flocked to the city, it's far from becoming gray and faceless. Brussels's strength is its diversity. A bilingual city where French- and Dutch-speaking communities are too often divided, Brussels is home to all the cultures of Europe—east and west—as well as Americans, Canadians, Congolese, Rwandans, Vietnamese, Turks, and Moroccans. Art nouveau flourished in Brussels as nowhere else, and its spirit lives on in gloriously individualistic town houses. Away from the winding alleys of the city center, parks and squares are plentiful, and the Bois de la Cambre, at the end of avenue Louise, leads straight into a forest as large as the city itself.

Exploring Brussels

Give yourself at least two days to explore the many riches of Brussels, devoting one day to the lower town (whose cobblestones call for comfortable walking shoes) and the other to the great museums and uptown shopping streets.

Around the Grand'Place

The Grand'Place, whose gilded splendor makes it one of Europe's most impressive squares, serves as an anchor for an area where the ghosts of the past mingle with a lively contemporary scene. Narrow, cobbled streets radiate off the square, with a rich offering of cafés, restaurants, and souvenir shops.

Numbers in the margin correspond to points of interest on the Brussels map.

❾ Cathédrale des Sts-Michel-et-Gudule. The names of the archangel and an obscure 7th-century local saint have been joined for the cathedral of Brussels. Begun in 1226, it combines architectural styles from the Romanesque to full-blown Gothic. The chief treasures are the stained-glass windows inspired by the drawings of Bernard Van Orley, an early-16th-century court painter. The ornately carved pulpit (1699) depicts Adam and Eve being expelled from the Garden of Eden. ⊠ *Parvis Ste-Gudule* ☎ *02/217–8345* ☉ *Daily 7:30–6.*

★ ❿ Centre Belge de la Bande Dessinée (Belgian Comic Strip Center). This museum celebrates the comic strip, focusing on such famous Belgian graphic artists as Hergé, Tintin's creator; Morris, the progenitor of Lucky Luke; and many others. The former draper's wholesale warehouse was designed in 1903 by art nouveau pioneer Victor Horta (1861–1947). A library, a bookstore, and an airy brasserie are also here. ⊠ *Rue des Sables 20* ☎ *02/ 219–1980* ⊕ *www.brusselsbdtour.com/cbbd.htm* ☉ *Tues.–Sun. 10–6.*

❽ Galeries St-Hubert. The oldest covered shopping arcade in western Europe—and still one of its most elegant—was constructed in 1847 and is filled with shops, restaurants, and theaters. Diffused daylight penetrates the gallery from the glazed vaults, and neoclassical gods and heroes look down from their sculpted niches. The gallery is traversed by **rue des Bouchers**, which forms the main restaurant area. Caveat: the more lavish the display of food outside, the poorer the cuisine inside. ⊠ *Between rue du Marché-aux-Herbes and rue d'Arenberg.*

❻ Grand'Place. The ornate baroque guild houses here, with their burnished facades, were completed in 1695, just three years after a French bombardment destroyed everything but the Town Hall. The houses are topped by gilded statues of saints and heroes and the market square is Europe's

Fodor'sChoice
★

most sumptuous. On summer nights, music and colored light flood the entire area. Shops, restaurants, and taverns occupy most ground floors. The Maison des Brasseurs houses the **Brewery Museum** (⊠ Grand'Place 10 ☎ 02/511–4987). During Ommegang (first Tuesday and Thursday in July), a magnificent pageant reenacts Emperor Charles V's reception in the city. ⊠ *Rue au Beurre, rue du Chair et du Pain, rue des Harengs, rue de la Colline, rue de l'Étuve, rue de la Tête d'Or.*

❺ Hôtel de Ville (Town Hall). Dominating the Grand'Place, the Town Hall is around 300 years older than the guild houses that line the square. The slender central tower is topped by a statue of the archangel Michael crushing the devil under his feet. The halls are embellished with some of the finest examples of local tapestries from the 16th, 17th, and 18th centuries. ⊠ *Grand'Place* ☎ *02/279–2340* ☉ *English-speaking tours Tues. 11:30 and 3:15, Wed. 3:15, Sun. 12:15. No individual visits.*

❼ Maison du Roi (King's House). Despite the name, no king ever lived in this neo-Gothic–style palace facing the Town Hall. It contains the **Musée de la Ville de Bruxelles** (City Museum), whose collections include Gothic sculptures, porcelain, silverware, lace, and paintings such as Brueghel's *The Wedding Procession.* Don't miss the extravagant collection of some 600 costumes for the Manneken-Pis. ⊠ *Grand'Place* ☎ *02/279–4350* ☉ *Tues.–Fri. 10–5, weekends 10–1.*

❹ Manneken-Pis. The first mention of the "little man" dates from 1377, but the present version, a small bronze statue of a chubby little boy peeing, was made by Jérôme Duquesnoy in 1619. The statue is in fact a copy; the original was kidnapped by 18th-century French soldiers. ⊠ *Corner rue de l'Étuve and rue du Chêne, 3 blocks southwest of Grand'Place.*

❷ Rue Antoine Dansaert. This is the flagship street of Brussels's fashionable quarter, which extends south to the place St-Géry. Boutiques sell Belgian-designed men's and women's fashions along with other designer names. Slick restaurants, trendy bars, jazz clubs, and cozy cafés rub shoulders with avant-garde galleries and stylish furniture shops. ⊠ *Between rue Van Artevelde at Grand'Place and Porte de Flandre.*

❸ Vismet (Fish Market). The canals around which this lively quay district sprang up have been filled in, but many pricey seafood restaurants popular with residents remain. When the weather is good, tables and chairs fill the wide promenade where cargoes of fish were once unloaded. ⊠ *Quai au Bois-à-Brûler and quai aux Briques.*

Around the Place Royale

The neoclassical place Royale is home of Brussels' art museums. The rather austere Palais Royal (Royal Palace) anchors the northern end of the square.

★ ⑰ Grand Sablon. A well-to-do, sophisticated square, it's alive with cafés, restaurants, art galleries, and antiques shops, as well as an antiques market on weekends. At the upper end of the square stands the church of **Notre-Dame du Sablon,** built in flamboyant Gothic style in 1304 by the crossbowmen who used to train here. The stained-glass windows are illuminated from within at night. Downhill from the Grand Sablon stands the 12th-century church of **Notre-Dame de la Chapelle** (⊠ pl. de la Chapelle). Its Gothic exterior and surprising baroque belfry have been splendidly restored. This was the parish church of Pieter Brueghel the Elder (1520–69); he is buried here in a marble tomb.

⑮ Musée d'Art Ancien (Fine Arts Museum). The collection of old masters focuses on Flemish and Dutch paintings from the 15th to the 19th cen-

Brussels
(Bruxelles, Brussel)

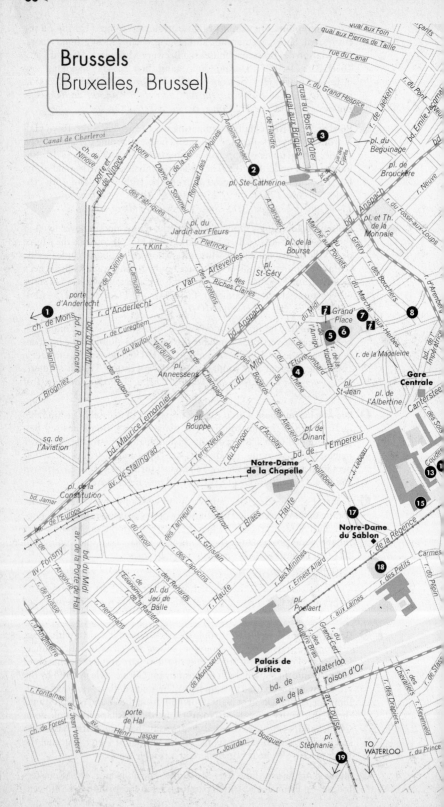

Canal de Charleroi

quai aux Foin
quai aux Pierres de Taille
rue du Canal

ch. de Ninove
porte et pl. de Ninove
r. des Fabriques

pl. du Grand Hospice
pl. du Beguinage
pl. de Brouckère

r. de Laeken
r. du Pont
r. Émile Jacqm

3

2 pl. Ste-Catherine

r. Neuve

pl. du Jardin aux Fleurs
r. Pletinckx
r. 't Kint

pl. de la Bourse
pl. St-Géry

bd. Anspach
pl. et Th. de la Monnaie
r. du Fossé-aux-Loups

porte d'Anderlecht
r. d'Anderlecht
r. de Cureghem
r. du Vautour

1 ch. de Mons
r. Plantin
r. Brogniez

8

Grand' Place **7**
5 **6**
r. de la Madeleine

Gare Centrale

4
pl. St-Jean
pl. de l'Albertine

Canterstee

pl. Rouppe
pl. de Dinant

pl. Anneessens

sq. de l'Aviation

bd. Maurice Lemonnier
av. de Stalingrad

Notre-Dame de la Chapelle

bd. de l'Empereur

pl. de la Constitution
bd. Jamar
bd. de l'Europe

r. Haute
r. Blaes

17
Notre-Dame du Sablon

r. de la Régence

Carmes

13

15

18
r. des Petits

av. Fonsny
av. de la Porte de Hal

r. des Tanneurs
r. St-Ghislain
r. des Capucins

pl. du Jeu de Balle
r. Haute

r. des Minimes
r. Ernest Allard

pl. Poelaert
r. aux Laines

Palais de Justice

ch. de Forest
porte de Hal
av. Henri Jaspar

Waterloo Toison d'Or

bd. de
av. de la

av. Louise

pl. Stéphanie

TO WATERLOO

19

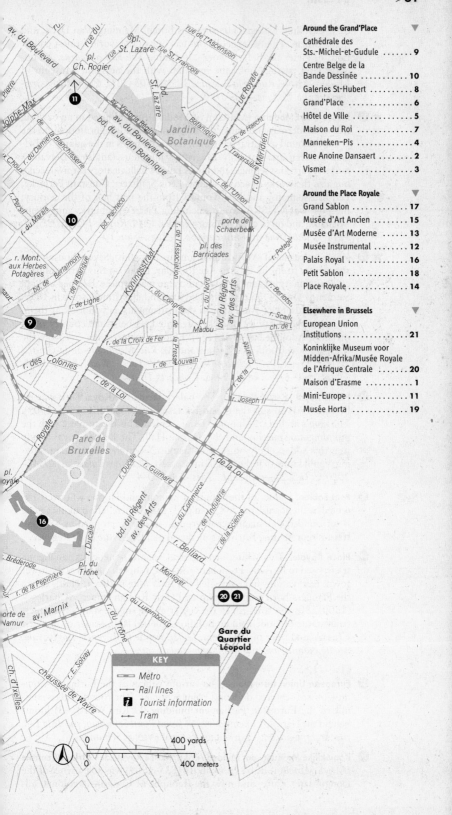

tury, including Rubens, Hieronymus Bosch, Memling, Van Dyck, and many others. The Brueghel Room has one of the world's finest collections of Pieter the Elder's works, including *The Fall of Icarus*. An underground passage links the museum with the adjacent Museum of Modern Art. ⊠ *Rue de la Régence 3* ☎ *02/508–3211* ⊕ *www.fine-arts-museum.be* ⊗ *Tues.–Sun. 10–5.*

★ ⓭ **Musée d'Art Moderne** (Museum of Modern Art). Housed in an exciting feat of modern architecture, the museum descends eight floors into the ground around a central light well. Its strength lies in the quality of Belgian modern art: not only Magritte's luminous fantasies, Delvaux's nudes in surrealist settings, and James Ensor's hallucinatory carnival scenes but also the works of artists such as Léon Spilliaert, Constant Permeke, Leo Brusselmans, and Rik Wouters from the first half of the century; the post-war COBRA group, including Pierre Alechinsky and Henri Michaux; and on to contemporary works. ⊠ *Pl. Royale 1–2* ☎ *02/508–3211* ⊕ *www.fine-arts-museum.be* ⊗ *Tues.–Sun. 10–5.*

★ ⓬ **Musée Instrumental** (Musical Instruments Museum). Seven thousand instruments, from the Bronze Age to today, make up this extraordinary collection in a glass-and-steel art nouveau masterpiece designed by Paul Saintenoy (1862–1952) for the Old England department store in 1899. Audio headsets let you listen to the instruments as you look at them. The saxophone family is well represented, as befits the country of its inventor, Adolphe Sax (1814–94). Enjoy views over the city from the sixth-floor tearoom and restaurant. ⊠ *Rue Montagne-de-la-Cour 2* ☎ *02/545–0130* ⊕ *www.mim.fgov.be* ⊗ *Tues., Wed., Fri. 9:30–5, Thurs. 9:30–8, weekends 10–5. Concerts Thurs. at 8.*

⓰ **Palais Royal** (Royal Palace). The palace facing the Royal Park was rebuilt in 1904 to suit the expansive tastes of Leopold II (1835–1909). The king's architect, Alphonse Balat, achieved his masterpiece with the monumental stairway and the Throne Hall. The Belgian royal family uses this address only on state occasions. When the Belgian flag is flying, you'll know that the king is in Brussels. ⊠ *Pl. des Palais* ☎ *02/551–2020* ⊗ *July 22–early Sept., Tues.–Sun. 10–4.*

⓲ **Petit Sablon.** Statues of the counts of Egmont and Horne, who were executed by the Spanish in 1568, hold pride of place here. The tranquil square is surrounded by a magnificent wrought-iron fence, topped by 48 small statues representing Brussels's medieval guilds. ⊠ *Rue de la Régence.*

⓮ **Place Royale.** This white, symmetrical square is neoclassical Vienna transposed to Brussels. From here you have a superb view over the lower town. Excavations have revealed the *Aula Magna* (Great Hall), where the Flanders-born king of Spain and Holy Roman emperor Charles V (1500–58) was crowned. In the center of the square stands the equestrian statue of Godefroid de Bouillon (1060–1100), leader of the First Crusade and ruler of Jerusalem. ⊠ *Jct. rue de la Régence, rue Royale, rue de Namur, and rue Montagne-de-la-Cour.*

Elsewhere in Brussels

⓴ **European Union Institutions.** The various offices of the European Commission are centered on Rond Point Schuman. The rounded glass summit of the **European Parliament building** (⊠ Rue Wiertz 43) looms behind the Gare de Luxembourg. ⊠ *Rond Point Schuman, rue de la Loi, rue Archimède, bd. Charlemagne, rue Wiertz* Ⓜ *Schuman.*

⓴ **Koninklijke Museum voor Midden Afrika/Musée Royale de l'Afrique Centrale** (Africa Museum). King Leopold II (1835–1909) was sole owner of the Congo (later Zaire, and now the Republic of Congo)—a colonial adventure that brought great wealth to the exploiters and untold misery to the exploited. He built a museum outside Brussels to house some 250,000 objects emanating from his domain. The museum has since become a leading research center for African studies. ⊠ *Leuvensesteenweg 13, Tervuren* ☎ *02/769–5211* ⊕ *www.africamuseum.be* ⊗ *Tues.–Fri. 10–5, weekends 10–6* Ⓜ *Tram 44 from place Montgomery.*

★ ❶ **Maison d'Erasme** (Erasmus House). In the middle of a nondescript neighborhood in Anderlecht, western Brussels, this remarkable redbrick 16th-century house was home to the great humanist Erasmus in 1521. Every detail is authentic, with period furniture, paintings by Holbein and Bosch, prints by Dürer, and first editions of Erasmus's works, including *In Praise of Folly.* ⊠ *Rue du Chapître 31* ☎ *02/521–1383* ⊗ *Mon., Wed., Thurs., and weekends 10–noon and 2–5* Ⓜ *St-Guidon.*

☝ ⓫ **Mini-Europe.** At the foot of the landmark **Atomium,** this popular attraction in a 5-acre park is a collection of 300 models (on a 1:25 scale) of buildings from the 15 EU countries. ⊠ *Brupark* ☎ *02/478–0550* 🎫 *€11.50* ⊗ *Oct.–Mar., daily 10–5; Apr.–June, daily 9:30–5; July and Aug., daily 9:30–8, July 17–Aug. 18 open until 11 on Fri., Sat., and Sun.; Sept., daily 9:30–5* Ⓜ *Heysel.*

★ ⓳ **Musée Horta** (Horta Museum). Victor Horta, the Belgian master of art nouveau, designed this building for himself and lived and worked here until 1919. From cellar to attic, every detail of the house displays the exuberant curves of the art nouveau style. Horta's aim was to put nature and light back into daily life, and here his floral motifs give a sense of opulence and spaciousness where in fact space is very limited. ⊠ *Rue Américaine 25* ☎ *02/543–0490* ⊗ *Tues.–Sat. 2–5:30* Ⓜ *Tram 91 or 92 from pl. Louise.*

Where to Eat

Brussels is one of the great dining cities in the world. Three thousand–odd restaurants are supplemented by a multitude of fast-food establishments and snack bars, and most cafés also offer *petite restauration* (light meals). Lip-smackingly tasty *frites* (french fries) with dollops of mayonnaise can be found at mobile friteries. Fixed-price menus, especially in top-dollar restaurants, sometimes cost only half of what you would pay dining à la carte, and the quality of your meal is likely to be just as good. There's less smoking than in the past, but no-smoking areas are rare. For price categories, *see* Eating & Drinking *in* Belgium A to Z.

$$$$
Fodor'sChoice
★ ✕ **Comme Chez Soi.** Master chef Pierre Wynants runs Brussels's most celebrated restaurant, and the array of toques and stars he has earned is well deserved. Fillet of sole with a white wine mousseline and shrimp is always on the menu, but the perfectionist owner-chef is constantly creating new masterpieces. The set menus can take a little of the sting out of the bill. The stunning art nouveau restaurant is small, so reserve well ahead; you may have to wait up to six weeks for a table. Don't be put off by the scruffy neighborhood. ⊠ *Pl. Rouppe 23* ☎ *02/512–2921* ♨ *Reservations essential* ⫟ *Jacket and tie* 🗖 *AE, DC, MC, V* ⊗ *Closed Sun. and Mon., July, and Dec. 25–Jan. 1. No lunch Sat.*

★ **$$$–$$$$** ✕ **La Truffe Noire.** Luigi Ciciriello's "Black Truffle" is a spacious eatery with cuisine that draws on classic Italian and modern French cooking. Carpaccio, prepared at the table, comes with strips of truffle and Parmesan, and main courses include pigéon de Vendé with truffles and steamed John Dory with truffles and leeks. ⊠ *Bd. de la Cambre 12* ☎ *02/640–4422* ♨ *Reservations essential* ⫟ *Jacket and tie* 🗖 *AE, DC, MC, V* ⊗ *Closed Sun., Mon. lunch, and last 3 weeks in Aug.*

★ **$$–$$$$** ✕ **Sea Grill.** Gigantic etched-glass murals convey the cool of the Arctic fjords that provide inspiration and ingredients for one of Belgium's best seafood restaurants. Chef Yves Mattagne's gift for applying meat preparations to fish is showcased in dishes like noisettes of tuna Rossini, and house classics include whole sea bass baked in salt and Brittany lobster pressed at your table. ⊠ *Radisson SAS, rue du Fossé-aux-Loups 47* ☎ *02/227–3120* 🏛 *Jacket and tie* ▭ *AE, DC, MC, V* ☉ *Closed Sun. and 4 wks in July and Aug. No lunch Sat.*

$–$$$$ ✕ **Au Vieux St-Martin.** Belgian specialties dominate the menu here, and portions are generous. The restaurant claims to have invented the now ubiquitous *filet américain* (the well-seasoned Belgian version of steak tartare). The walls are hung with bright contemporary paintings, and picture windows face the pleasant square. ⊠ *Pl. du Grand Sablon 38* ☎ *02/512–6476* ▭ *AE, MC, V.*

★ **$$$** ✕ **L'Ogenblik.** With green-shaded lamps over marble-top tables, sawdust on the floor, and ample servings, l'Ogenblik is a true bistro. The long and imaginative menu changes frequently but generally includes mille-feuille with lobster and salmon, and saddle of lamb. The kitchen stays open until midnight, making it a favorite for artists and actors. ⊠ *Galerie des Princes 1* ☎ *02/511–6151* ▭ *AE, DC, MC, V* ☉ *Closed Sun.*

$–$$$ ✕ **Aux Armes de Bruxelles.** One of the few restaurants to escape the "tourist trap" label on this hectic street, the child-friendly Aux Armes has three rooms with a lively atmosphere and cheerful service. It offers the classics of Belgian cooking—tomatoes stuffed with crevettes, waterzooi mussels steamed in white wine, and, of course, frites. ⊠ *Rue des Bouchers 13* ☎ *02/511–5550* ▭ *AE, DC, MC, V* ☉ *Closed Mon. and mid-June–mid-July.*

$–$$$ ✕ **Chez Léon.** Critics deride it as McMoules-frites, but this century-old eatery is enormously popular, with franchises across Belgium and even in Paris and Japan. The secret is heaping plates of steaming mussels, specialties such as anguilles au vert, free children's meals to those under 12, and great fries. It's loud, brightly lit, and has a charm all its own. ⊠ *Rue des Bouchers 18* ☎ *02/511–1415* ▭ *AE, DC, MC, V.*

$$ ✕ **Au Stekerlapatte.** In the shadow of the monstrous Palais de Justice, this bustling Marolles bistro is packed nightly with diners craving liberal portions of Belgian specialties. Try black pudding with caramelized apples, sauerkraut, beef fried with shallots, grilled pig's trotters, or spareribs. ⊠ *Rue des Prêtres 4* ☎ *02/512–8681* ▭ *MC, V* ☉ *Closed Sun. and Mon. July and Aug. No lunch.*

$–$$ ✕ **Chez Patrick.** This old-timer next to the Grand'Place has been dishing up good, honest Belgian food for nearly 70 years, in an unpretentious, old-fashioned setting with waitresses in black and white, and specials chalked up on the mirrors. Expect large, tasty portions of shrimp croquettes, salmon and endives cooked with beer, and chicken with *kriek* (cherry-flavored beer) and cherries. ⊠ *Rue des Chapeliers 6* ☎ *02/511–9815* ▭ *AE, DC, MC, V* ☉ *Closed Mon.*

$–$$ ✕ **Kasbah.** An Aladdin's den of stained-glass lamps and dark, sumptuous decor, this is one of the best of the capital's many North African restaurants. Steaming portions of couscous and *tajines* (Moroccan casseroles with fish or meat, usually involving fruit, vegetables, and spices) are served in this lively restaurant. ⊠ *Rue Antoine Dansaert 20* ☎ *02/502–4026* ▭ *AE, MC, V.*

★ **$–$$** ✕ **Les Salons de Wittamer.** The elegant upstairs rooms at Brussels's best-known patisserie house a stylish breakfast and lunch restaurant, where meals are topped off with a celebrated pastry or ice-cream concoction. ⊠ *Pl. du Grand Sablon 12–13* ☎ *02/512–3742* ▭ *AE, DC, MC, V* ☉ *Closed Mon.*

$–$$ ✕ **'t Kelderkerke.** This busy restaurant serves honest-to-goodness Belgian food in a 17th-century vaulted cellar on the Grand'Place. Try *stoemp et saucisses* (tasty mashed potatoes and sausages) if you aren't tempted by the excellent mussels. Open 'til 2 AM, this is a great place for a late-night feast. ⊠ *Grand'Place 15* ☎ *02/513–7344* ⌨ *Reservations not accepted* ☰ *AE, DC, MC, V.*

★ **$–$$** ✕ **Taverne Falstaff.** This huge tavern with an art nouveau interior fills up for lunch and keeps going until the wee hours. Students to pensioners consume onion soup, filet mignon, salads, and other brasserie fare. On the heated terrace, a favorite meeting point for groups, the surliness of the waiters is legendary. ⊠ *Rue Henri Maus 17–21* ☎ *02/511–8987* ☰ *AE, DC, MC, V.*

$ ✕ **Le Pain Quotidien.** These bakeries–cum–snack bars have spread like wildfire all over Brussels (and even to New York and Los Angeles) with the same formula: copious salads, hearty homemade soups, and delicious open sandwiches on farm-style bread, served at a communal table from 7:30 AM to 7 PM. ⊠ *Rue des Sablons 11* ☎ *02/513–5154* ⊠ *Rue Antoine Dansaert 16* ☎ *02/502–2361* ⌨ *Reservations not accepted* ☰ *No credit cards.*

Where to Stay

The main hotel districts are around the Grand'Place, the place de Brouck-ère, and in the avenue Louise shopping area. If you have a problem finding accommodations, go to the TIB tourist office in the Hôtel de Ville at the Grand'Place or telephone Belgian Tourist Reservations for their free service. Weekend and summer discounts, often of 50% or more, are available in almost all hotels. Most new hotels have set aside rooms or floors for nonsmokers and offer a limited number of rooms equipped for people with disabilities. For price categories, *see* Lodging *in* Belgium A to Z.

★ **$$$$** ▦ **Amigo.** Although it was built in the 1950s, this family-owned hotel off the Grand'Place has the charm of an earlier age. Each room has its own look with silk, velvet, and brocades, and most have marble bathrooms. Check for special offers when booking. Ask for a quiet room, away from the main tourist trail. ⊠ *Rue de l'Amigo 1–3, 1000* ☎ *02/ 547–4747* 🖶 *02/513–5277* ⊕ *www.hotelamigo.com* ⇱ *185 rooms, 7 suites* ⌕ *Restaurant* ☰ *AE, DC, MC, V.*

$$$$ ▦ **Brussels Hilton.** The 27-story Hilton was one of the capital's first high-rises, dating from the 1960s, and remains a distinctive landmark with great views of the inner town. Corner rooms are the most desirable; there are four floors of executive rooms and superb business facilities. The second-floor Maison du Boeuf restaurant is much appreciated by Brussels gourmets. The hotel is in the luxury avenue de la Toison d'Or and boulevard de Waterloo shopping area, overlooking the tiny Parc d'Eg-mont. ⊠ *Bd. de Waterloo 38, 1000* ☎ *02/504–1111* 🖶 *02/504–2111* ⇱ *430 rooms, 39 suites* ⌕ *2 restaurants* ☰ *AE, DC, MC, V.*

$$$$ ▦ **Conrad International.** Opened by the Hilton group in 1993, the Conrad combines the European grand hotel tradition with American tastes and amenities, and has become *the* place to stay for visiting dignitaries. Rooms are spacious, with three telephones, bathrobes, and in-room checkout. Breakfast is included. The Maison de Maître restaurant maintains the same high standard, and the large bar is pleasantly clublike. ⊠ *Av. Louise 71, 1050* ☎ *02/542–4242* 🖶 *02/542–4200* ⊕ *www.hilton.com* ⇱ *269 rooms, 20 suites* ⌕ *2 restaurants* ☰ *AE, DC, MC, V.*

$$$$ ▦ **Manos Stéphanie.** This former town house has a marble lobby, Louis XV furniture, and elegant rooms. Service is friendly, breakfast is included, and children under 12 stay free. ⊠ *Chaussée de Charleroi 28, 1060*

☎ 02/539–0250 📠 02/537–5729 ⊕ *www.manoshotel.com* ⛵ *55 rooms, 7 suites* ⚒ *Bar* ▤ *AE, DC, MC, V.*

★ $$$$ 🏨 **Le Méridien.** Conveniently located opposite the Gare Centrale, Le Méridien's marble and gilt-edged lobby recalls palatial Parisian hotels, and the restaurant sets out brightly colored Limoges china. Rooms, in dark blue or green, come with three telephones, large desks, and data ports. ✉ *Carrefour de l'Europe 3, 1000* ☎ *02/548–4211* 📠 *02/548–4080* ⊕ *www.meridien.be* ⛵ *224 rooms, 17 suites* ⚒ *Restaurant* ▤ *AE, DC, MC, V.*

$$$$ 🏨 **Le Metropole.** Built in 1895, this belle epoque masterpiece is the last trace of elegance in what was once one of Brussels's most charming squares. The lobby has a high coffered ceiling, chandeliers, and Oriental rugs, and the staircase and original elevator are as stunning as they were when Sarah Bernhardt stayed here. The theme extends to the restaurant and the café, which opens onto a heated terrace. It is planning extensive renovations in 2004. Rooms are decorated in art deco style and breakfast is included. ✉ *Pl. de Brouckère 31, 1000* ☎ *02/217–2300* 📠 *02/218–0220* ⊕ *www.metropole.be* ⛵ *400 rooms, 10 suites* ⚒ *2 restaurants* ▤ *AE, DC, MC, V.*

$$$$ 🏨 **Radisson SAS.** This excellent hotel has guest rooms decorated with great panache in four different styles: Scandinavian, Asian, Italian, and art deco. A portion of the 12th-century city wall forms part of the atrium. Children under 17 stay free. ✉ *Rue du Fossé-aux-Loups 47, 1000* ☎ *02/219–2828* 📠 *02/219–6262* ⛵ *263 rooms, 16 suites* ⚒ *2 restaurants* ▤ *AE, DC, MC, V.*

$$$ 🏨 **Le Dixseptième.** In this stylish 17th-century hotel, originally the residence of the Spanish ambassador, each room is named for a Belgian artist. Suites are up a splendid Louis XV staircase, and the standard rooms surround an interior courtyard. Whitewashed walls, bare floors, exposed beams, and colorful textiles are the style here. Some rooms have kitchenettes; suites have working fireplaces and fax machines. Breakfast is included. ✉ *Rue de la Madeleine 25, 1000, 1000* ☎ *02/517–1717* 📠 *02/502–6424* ⛵ *24 rooms, 12 suites* ▤ *AE, DC, MC, V.*

$$ 🏨 **Citadine.** This residential hotel accepts overnight guests; it's a good choice for families. The exterior is plain, but the location on the Vismet is plum. Rooms have pull-out twin beds; junior suites sleep four. All have kitchenettes. ✉ *Quai au Bois-à-Brûler 51, 1000* ☎ *02/221–1411* 📠 *02/221–1599* ⛵ *169 rooms* ▤ *AE, DC, MC, V.*

$ 🏨 **Bed & Brussels.** This upscale B&B accommodations service arranges stays with 100 host families in Brussels or surrounding areas, most of them with room to spare after children have flown the coop. Many rooms come with private bath, and breakfast with the hosts is included. ✉ *Rue Gustave Biot 2* ☎ *02/646–0737* 📠 *02/644–0114* ⊕ *www.bnb-brussels.be* ▤ *MC, V.*

$ 🏨 **Matignon.** Only the belle epoque facade of this family-run hotel opposite the Bourse was preserved when the building was converted. The lobby is tiny to make room for the bustling café-brasserie. Rooms are small but have large beds (and large TVs), and the duplex suites are good value for families. It's noisy but very central. Breakfast is included. ✉ *Rue de la Bourse 10, 1000* ☎ *02/511–0888* 📠 *02/513–6927* ⛵ *37 rooms, 9 suites* ⚒ *Restaurant* ▤ *AE, DC, MC, V.*

★ $ 🏨 **Welcome Hotel.** Owners Michel and Sophie Smeesters run this charming 15-room hotel, the smallest in Brussels. The rooms, with king- or queen-size beds, would be a credit to far more expensive establishments; it's essential to book well ahead. There's a lovely breakfast room, and Michel is also chef at the excellent seafood restaurant around the corner, La Truite d'Argent. ✉ *Rue du Peuplier 5, 1000* ☎ *02/219–*

9546 🖼 *02/217–1887* ⊕ *www.hotelwelcome.com* ⤵ *15 rooms,*
3 apartments for stays of at least one month ⌂ *Restaurant* ▤ *AE, DC,*
MC, V.

Nightlife & the Arts

The Arts

The best way to find out what's going on in Brussels—and throughout
the country—is to buy a copy of the English-language weekly the *Bulletin*. It's published every Thursday.

FILM Movies are mainly shown in their original language (indicated as v.o.,
or *version originale*). For unusual movies or screen classics, visit the **Musée
du Cinéma** (Film Museum; ⊠ rue Baron Horta 9 ☎ 02/507–8370),
where three sound films and two silents with piano accompaniment are
shown every evening. Those under 16 are not admitted.

MUSIC Free Sunday morning concerts take place at various churches, including the Cathédrale Sts-Michel-et-Gudule. Major symphony concerts
and recitals are held at the **Palais des Beaux-Arts** (⊠ rue Ravenstein 23
☎ 02/507–8200). Chamber music is best enjoyed at the intimate **Conservatoire Royal de Musique** (⊠ rue de la Régence 30 ☎ 02/511–0427).
The **Église des Minimes** (⊠ rue des Minimes 62) offers Sunday morning
concerts. **Ancienne Belgique** (⊠ bd. Anspach 110 ☎ 02/548–2424) hosts
folk, rock, pop, funk, and jazz concerts.

OPERA & DANCE The national opera company, based at the handsome **Théâtre Royal de
la Monnaie** (⊠ pl. de la Monnaie ☎ 070/233939), stages productions
of international quality. Touring dance and opera companies often perform at **Cirque Royal** (⊠ rue de l'Enseignement 81 ☎ 02/218–2015).

THEATER The **Théâtre Royal du Parc** (⊠ rue de la Loi 3 ☎ 02/505–3030) stages
productions of Molière and other French classics. Avant-garde theater
is performed at **Théâtre Varia** (⊠ rue du Sceptre 78 ☎ 02/640–8258).
Théâtre de Poche (⊠ Chemin du Gymnase 1a, in the Bois de la Cambre
☎ 02/649–1727) presents modern productions.

Nightlife

BARS There's a café on virtually every corner in Brussels, and all of them serve
beer from morning to late at night. A young crowd fills **Au Soleil** (⊠ rue
Marché au Charbon 86 ☎ 02/513–3430) in the fashionable place St-
Gery part of town. The lively **Beursschouwburg-Café** (⊠ rue Auguste Orts
22 ☎ 02/513–8290) attracts earnestly trendy young Flemish intellectuals. **Le Cirio** (⊠ rue de la Bourse 18 ☎ 02/512–1395) is a seemingly
time-warped café with 1900s-era advertisements and price lists on the
mirror-lined walls. Another 1900s-style café-bar with a lost-in-time
atmosphere is **À La Mort Subite** (⊠ rue Montagne-aux-Herbes-Potagères
7 ☎ 02/513–1318). Hang out with the cool Flemish crowd in art nouveau masterpiece **De Ultieme Hallucinatie** (⊠ rue Royale 316 ☎ 02/217–
0614). On the Grand'Place, **Le Cerf** (⊠ Grand'Place 20 ☎ 02/511–
4791) is particularly pleasant, with atmosphere and furnishings out of
the 17th century. Only a 10-minute stroll from the Grand'Place is **La Fleur
en Papier Doré** (⊠ rue des Aléxiens 53 ☎ 02/511–1659), a quaint tavern with a surrealist decor that appeals to an artsy crowd. **Rick's Café
Américain** (⊠ av. Louise 344 ☎ 02/648–1451) is a favorite with the American and British expat community. Brussels has a sizable number of "Irish"
bars, but **James Joyce** (⊠ rue Archimède 34 ☎ 02/230–9894) was the
first in Brussels and is the most genuinely Gaelic.

DANCE CLUBS Electronica fans prefer **Fuse** (⊠ rue Blaes 208 ☎ 02/511–9789), a
bunker-style techno haven with regular gay and lesbian nights. Cutting

edge **Recyclart** (✉ rue des Ursulines 25 ☎ 02/502–5734) combines art exhibitions with eclectic beats in an old railway station while trains rattle overhead. **Le Mirano Continental** (✉ Chaussée de Louvain 38 ☎ 02/227–3970) remains the glitzy hangout of choice for the self-styled beautiful people.

JAZZ Most of Brussels's dozen or so jazz haunts present live music only on certain nights; check before you go. **New York Café Jazz Club** (✉ Chaussée de Charleroi 5 ☎ 02/534–8509) is an American restaurant by day and a modern jazz hangout on Friday and Saturday evenings. **Sounds Jazz Club** (✉ rue de la Tulipe 28 ☎ 02/512–9250), a big café, emphasizes jazz-rock, blues, and other modern trends. **Travers** (✉ rue Traversière 11 ☎ 02/218–4086), a café–cum–jazz club, is a cramped but outstanding showcase for the country's leading players.

Shopping

Gift Ideas

Belgium is where the *praline*—rich chocolate filled with flavored creams, liqueur, or nuts—was invented. Try Corné Toison d'Or, Godiva, Neuhaus, or the lower-priced Leonidas, available at shops throughout the city. **Wittamer** (✉ pl. du Grand Sablon 12 ☎ 02/512–3742) is an excellent patisserie with a sideline in superb chocolates. **Pierre Marcolini** (✉ pl. du Grand Sablon 39 ☎ 02/514–1206) is the boy wonder of the chocolate world. Exclusive handmade pralines can be bought at **Mary** (✉ rue Royale 73 ☎ 02/217–4500), official purveyor of chocolates to the Belgian court.

Many stores sell crystal tableware and ornaments, including **Art & Selection** (✉ rue du Marché-aux-Herbes 83 ☎ 02/511–8448) near the Grand'Place. Only the Val-St-Lambert mark guarantees handblown, hand-carved Belgian lead crystal.

When shopping for lace, ask whether it is genuine handmade Belgian or machine-made in East Asia. **Maison F. Rubbrecht** (✉ Grand'Place 23 ☎ 02/512–0218) sells authentic Belgian lace. For a choice of old and modern lace, try **Manufacture Belge de Dentelles** (✉ Galerie de la Reine 6–8 ☎ 02/511–4477).

Markets

On Saturday (9–6) and Sunday (9–2), the upper end of the Place du Grand Sablon becomes an open-air **antiques and book market** with more than 100 stalls. The **Vieux Marché** (✉ pl. du Jeu de Balle), open daily 7–2, is a flea market worth visiting in the working-class Marolles district. To make real finds, get here early.

Shopping Districts

The shops in the **Galeries St-Hubert** sell mostly luxury goods or gift items. The **rue Neuve** and the **City 2** mall are good for less expensive boutiques and department stores. Avant-garde clothes are sold in boutiques on **rue Antoine Dansaert**, near the Bourse.

Uptown, **avenue Louise**, with the arcades Galerie Louise and Espace Louise, counts a large number of boutiques selling expensive clothes and accessories. The **boulevard de Waterloo** is home to the same fashion names as Bond Street and Rodeo Drive. The **Grand Sablon** has more charm; this is the center for antiques and art galleries.

Side Trip

Waterloo, where Napoléon was finally defeated by the British and Prussian armies on June 18, 1815, lies 19 km (12 mi) to the south of Brussels. Take the TEC bus "W" or Bus 365a from place Rouppe to the town of Waterloo. The **Waterloo Tourist Office** (⊠ Chaussée de Bruxelles 149 ☎ 02/354–9910) is in the center of town.

The **Musée Wellington** (Wellington Museum), in the former inn where General Arthur Wellesley, the first duke of Wellington, established his headquarters, displays maps and models of the battle and military memorabilia. ⊠ *Chaussée de Bruxelles 147* ☎ *02/354–7806* ⊙ *Apr.–Oct., daily 9:30–6:30; Nov.–Mar., daily 10:30–5:30.*

Just 4½ km (3 mi) south of town, and accessible by TEC Bus 365a, is the battlefield. The **Visitors' Center** has an audiovisual reconstruction, and the Panorama next door illustrates memorable phases of the battle in a huge 360-degree painting. You can hire guides to take you around the battlefield. ⊠ *Rte. du Lion 252–254, Braine–l'Alleud* ☎ *02/ 385–1912* ⊙ *Apr.–Oct., daily 9:30–6:30; Nov.–Feb., daily 10–4; Mar., daily 10:30–5* ⊠ *Guides €40 for 1 hr.*

Overlooking the battlefield is the **Butte du Lion** (The Lion Mound), a pyramid-shape mound with a 28-ton cast-iron lion. It honors the prince of Orange, leader of the Dutch-Belgian troops, who was wounded on this spot. After climbing 226 steps, you will be rewarded with a great view.

Brussels Essentials

AIRPORTS & TRANSFERS

Most international flights arrive at Brussels National Airport at Zaventem (sometimes called simply Zaventem), 15 km (9 mi) northeast of the city center. No-frills airline Ryanair runs flights to European destinations including London and Rome from Brussels South Airport in Charleroi, 55 km (34 mi) south of Brussels.

🛈 Brussels National Airport ☎ 0900–70000. Brussels South Airport ☎ 071/251211.

TRANSFERS   Shuttle trains run between Zaventem and all three main railway stations in Brussels: Midi (South), Central (Central), and Nord (North). The Airport City Express runs every 20 minutes, from about 5:30 AM to midnight. The journey takes 23 minutes. A one-way second-class ticket costs €2.10. A taxi to the city center takes about a half hour and costs about €30. The number 12 bus runs to and from the airport to the city center every 30 minutes. One-way tickets cost €3. A shuttle bus service runs between Brussels South Airport and the Gare du Midi. It leaves the station two and a half hours before each flight is due to depart. The hour-long journey costs €10 one-way.

BOAT & FERRY TRAVEL

Hoverspeed operates a Hovercraft catamaran service between Dover and Calais, carrying cars and foot passengers. Travel time is 35 minutes and there is a coach connection to Oostende. P&O North Sea Ferries operates an overnight ferry service between Hull and Zeebrugge.

🛈 Hoverspeed ☎ 44/870-5240241 in the U.K. ⊕ www.hoverspeed.co.uk. P&O North Sea Ferries ☎ 44/870-5202020 in the U.K.; 02/710-6444 in Belgium ⊕ www.ponsf.com.

BUS TRAVEL TO & FROM BRUSSELS

Eurolines operates up to three daily express services from and to Amsterdam, Berlin, Frankfurt, Paris, and London. The Eurolines Coach Station in Brussels adjoins the Gare du Nord.

🛈 Eurolines ⊠ pl. de Brouckère 50 ☎ 02/217-0025 ⊕ www.eurolines.be. Eurolines Coach Station ⊠ rue du Progrès 80 ☎ 02/203-0707.

METRO, TRAM & BUS TRAVEL WITHIN BRUSSELS

The Métro (subway), trams (streetcars), and buses (STIB/MIVB) are parts of a unified system. A single ticket, valid for one hour's travel, costs €1.40.

The best buy is a 10-trip ticket for €9.20 or a one-day card costing €3.70. Tickets are sold in metro stations and at newsstands. Single tickets can be purchased on the bus or tram.

CAR TRAVEL

If you use Le Shuttle under the English Channel or a ferry to Calais, note that the E40 (via Oostende and Brugge) connects with the French highway, cutting driving time from Calais to Brussels to less than two hours.

EMERGENCIES

Every pharmacy displays a list of pharmacies on duty outside normal hours.
🗂 Doctors & Dentists **Doctor/Pharmacy** ☎ 02/479-1818 for all-night and weekend services. **Dentist** ☎ 02/426-1026.
🗂 Emergency Services **Ambulance and Fire Brigade** ☎ 100. **Police** ☎ 101.
🗂 Hot Lines **Lost/Stolen Bank/Credit Cards** ☎ 070/344344. 24-Hour English-Speaking Info and Crisis Line ☎ 02/648-4014.
🗂 Pharmacy **Pharmacy** ☎ 0900-10500 ⊕ www.pharmacie.be.

ENGLISH-LANGUAGE MEDIA

🗂 Bookstores **The Reading Room** ⊠ av. Georges Henri 503 ☎ 02/734-7917. **Sterling Books** ⊠ rue du Fossé-aux-Loups 38 ☎ 02/223-6223. **Waterstone's** ⊠ bd. Adolphe Max 71-75 ☎ 02/219-2708.

TOURS

BUS TOURS Expertly guided half-day English-language coach tours are organized by ARAU, from March through November, including "Brussels 1900: Art Nouveau" (every Saturday) and "Brussels 1930: Art Deco" (every third Saturday). Tours (€15) begin in front of Hotel Métropole on place de Brouckère. Chatterbus tours (early June–September) include visits by minibus or on foot to the main sights. De Boeck Sightseeing Tours operates city tours with cassette commentary. It also has tours of Antwerp, the Ardennes, Brugge, Gent, Ieper, and Waterloo.
🗂 Fees & Schedules **ARAU** ⊠ bd. Adolphe Max 55 ☎ 02/219-3345 information and reservations. **Chatterbus** ⊠ rue des Thuyas 12 ☎ 02/673-1835. **De Boeck Sightseeing Tours** ⊠ rue de la Colline 8, Grand'Place ☎ 02/513-7744.

PRIVATE GUIDES Qualified guides are available for individual tours from the TIB. Three hours costs €85 for up to 20 people.
🗂 Fees & Schedules **TIB** ☎ 02/513-8940.

WALKING TOURS Chatterbus organizes visits (early June–September) on foot or by minibus to the main sights and a walking tour with a visit to a bistro. Walking tours organized by the tourist office depart from the Brussels Tourist Office (TIB) in the Town Hall, May–September, Monday–Saturday.

TAXIS

Cabs don't cruise for fares; order one from Taxis Verts or go to a cab stand. The tip is included in the fare.
🗂 Taxi Companies **Taxis Verts** ☎ 02/349-4949.

TRAIN TRAVEL

Ten Eurostar passenger trains a day link Brussels's Gare du Midi with London's Waterloo station via the Channel Tunnel in two hours, 40 minutes. A one-way trip costs €310 in business class and from €224 in economy; rail pass holders qualify for 50% discounts. Reservations are required. Check-in is 20 minutes before departure.

All rail services between Brussels and Paris are on Thalys high-speed trains (1 hr, 25 mins). A one-way trip costs €102 ("Confort 1"), €64 ("Confort 2"). Reservations are required.

Eurostar ☎ 02/528-2828 ⊕ www.eurostar.com. **Gares du Midi, Central, and Nord** Brussels ☎ 02/203-3640. **Thalys** ☎ 070/667788 information and reservations ⊕ www. thalys.com.

TRAVEL AGENCIES

Local Agent Referrals **American Express** ⊠ Houtweg 24, 1170 Brussels ☎ 02/245- 2250. **Carlson Wagonlit Travel** ⊠ bd. Clovis 53, 1040 Brussels ☎ 02/287-8811.

VISITOR INFORMATION

At Tourist Information Brussels you can buy a Tourist Passport (€7.50), a one-day public transport card that includes €50 worth of museum admissions and reductions.

Tourist Information Brussels (TIB) ⊠ Hôtel de Ville, Grand'Place ☎ 02/513-8940 🖶 02/513-8320 ⊕ www.tib.be.

ANTWERP

Antwerp's Dutch name is Antwerpen, close enough to be confused with *handwerpen*, and thereby hangs a tale. The Roman soldier Silvius Brabo is said to have cut off and flung into the water the hand of the giant who exacted a toll from boatmen on the river. *Hand* is hand, and *werpen* means "throwing." The tale explains the presence of severed hands on the city's coat of arms.

Great prosperity came to Antwerp in the 16th century, during the reign of Charles V. One hundred years later, painter Rubens and his contemporaries made the city an equally important center of the arts. Craftsmen began practicing diamond-cutting about this time, and the city is still the world leader in the diamond trade, with an annual turnover of more than $20 billion. In spite of being 88 km (55 mi) up the River Scheldt, it is Europe's second-largest port after Rotterdam. These days, the city is also known for its exceptional clothing designers; the best appear in the city's latest attraction, the Mode Museum.

Exploring Antwerp

Numbers in the margin correspond to points of interest on the Antwerp map.

The Oude Stad or Old City—a 20- to 25-minute walk or a short metro ride from Centraal Station—is the heart of Antwerp and best explored on foot. Rubens and his contemporaries seem to be everywhere, in churches, art museums, and splendid Renaissance mansions. Antwerp is also known as the City of Madonnas. You'll see a statuette of Our Lady on many a street corner.

⑫ **Centraal Station.** Leopold II (1835–1909), a monarch not given to understatement, had this station built in 1905 as a neo-baroque cathedral to the railway age, with splendid staircases and a magnificently vaulted ticket-office hall. ⊠ *Koningin Astridplein* ☎ 03/203–2040.

❷ **Grote Markt.** The heart of the Oude Stad, a three-sided square, is dominated by a huge fountain topped by a statue of Silvius Brabo, the giant-killer. The Renaissance **Stadhuis** (City Hall) flanks one side of the square, and guild houses the other two. ⊠ *Jct. Suikerrui, Oude Koornmarkt, Handschoenmarkt, Kaasrui, Hofstraat, and Nosestraat.*

❼ **Koninklijk Museum voor Schone Kunsten** (Royal Museum of Fine Arts). This huge museum south of the Oude Stad contains more than 1,500 paintings by old masters, including magnificent works by Van Eyck, Memling, Rubens, Van Dyck, Jordaens, Hals, and Brueghel. The first floor

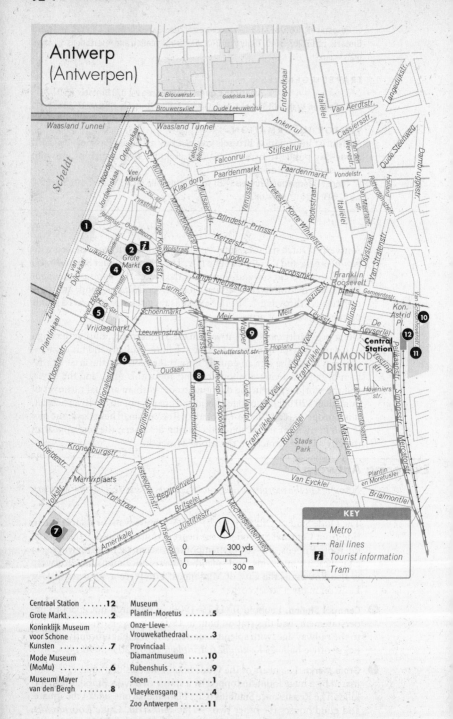

Antwerp
(Antwerpen)

has more modern paintings, including works by Magritte, Delvaux, and James Ensor. ⊠ *Leopold de Waelplaats 2* ☎ *03/238–7809* ⊕ *www. visitantwerpen.be* ⊗ *Tues.–Sun. 10–5.*

❻ Mode Museum (MoMu). Both contemporary fashion and historic clothing and textiles, including embroidery, lace, and fabric are the centerfolds of the Mode Museum, which is found in the late-19th-century Mode-Natie complex. The Flanders Fashion Institute and the reputable fashion department of the Royal Academy of Fine Arts are also here, as well as a brasserie, library, and shop. ⊠ *Nationalestraat 28* ☎ *03/470–2770* ⊕ *www.momu.be* ⊗ *Tues., Wed., and Fri.–Sun. 10–6, Thurs. 10–9.*

★ ❽ Museum Mayer Van den Bergh. A passionate 19th-century collector, Mayer Van den Bergh amassed almost 4,000 works of art, the best of which are displayed in this small museum. The masterpiece is Brueghel's great *Dulle Griet* (*Mad Meg*), an antiwar allegory. ⊠ *Lange Gasthuisstraat 19* ☎ *03/232–4237* ⊕ *www.visitantwerpen.be* 🎫 *€2.50* ⊗ *Tues.–Sun. 10–5.*

★ ❺ Museum Plantin-Moretus. This mansion was the home and printing plant of religious dissident, humanist, and printer extraordinaire Christophe Plantin (1514–89). For three centuries, beginning in 1576, the family printed innumerable Bibles, breviaries, and missals; Plantin's greatest technical achievement was the *Biblia Regia*. Two typefaces designed here, Plantin and Garamond, are still in use. Among the other treasures are portraits by Rubens as well as many first editions. Also on view are ancient presses that still work, copperplates, and old books. ⊠ *Vrijdagmarkt 22* ☎ *03/221–1450* ⊕ *www.visitantwerpen.be* ⊗ *Tues.–Sun. 10–5.*

★ ❸ Onze-Lieve-Vrouwekathedraal (Cathedral of Our Lady). You'll see the white, 404-foot spire of Antwerp's Gothic masterpiece from far away. Starting in 1352, a succession of architects worked on it for more than 200 years, but the ensemble is completely cohesive. Its paintings and statuary have repeatedly been plundered, most recently by the army of the French Revolution. The cathedral's remaining treasures include four Rubens altarpieces. His *Descent from the Cross* is flanked by panels showing Mary's visit to Elizabeth and the presentation of Jesus in the Temple; these are among the most delicate biblical scenes ever painted. ⊠ *Handschoenmarkt* ☎ *03/213–9940* ⊕ *www.dekathedraal.be* ⊗ *Weekdays 10–5, Sat. 10–3, Sun. 1–4.*

★ ❿ Provinciaal Diamantmuseum (Provincial Diamond Museum). High-tech and interactive, this diamond museum allows you to enter the fascinating world of "a girl's best friend" through an impressive image and sound display. The visit begins on the third floor, where interesting lighting, touch-screen computers, and amazing exhibits will dazzle any eye. The free audio guide explains the wonderful collections of jewelry from the 16th century through the present day. ⊠ *Koningin Astridplein 19–23,* ☎ *03/202–4890* ⊕ *www.diamantmuseum.be* ⊗ *May–Oct., daily 10–6, Nov.–Apr., daily 10–5.*

★ ❾ Rubenshuis (Rubens House). The master painter Rubens lived here from 1610 until his death in 1640. The mansion, a reconstruction based on his original designs, gives a vivid impression of the artist's life as wealthy court painter and diplomat. The mezzanine overlooks the studio where Rubens and his pupils worked. His widow promptly sold 300 paintings when he died, but a few Rubens originals do hang in the house. ⊠ *Wapper 9* ☎ *03/201–1555* ⊕ *www.visitantwerpen.be* ⊗ *Tues.–Sun. 10–5.*

❶ Steen. This 9th-century fortress is the oldest building in Antwerp. It was used as a prison for centuries, and the crucifix where condemned men said their final prayers is still in place. The Steen now houses the **Nationaal Scheepvaartmuseum** (National Maritime Museum). ⊠ *Steenplein* ☎ *03/201–9340* ⊕ *www.visitantwerpen.be* ☉ *Tues.–Sun. 10–4:45.*

❹ Vlaeykensgang. Time has stood still in this cobblestone alley in the center of town, which captures the mood and style of the 16th century. There's no better place to linger on a Monday night, when the carillon concert rings out from the cathedral.

☾ ⓫ Zoo Antwerpen. In this huge, well-designed complex, giraffes and ostriches reside in an Egyptian temple, rhinoceroses in a Moorish villa, okapis around an Indian temple. Beyond animals, attractions are a winter garden, a planetarium, an aquarium, and a good restaurant. ⊠ *Koningin Astridplein 26* ☎ *03/202–4540* ⊕ *www.zooantwerpen.be* ⊠ *€13.50* ☉ *Sept.–June, daily 10–5; July and Aug., daily 9–6:30.*

Where to Eat

Dining in Antwerp's many fine restaurants has a distinctly French flavor, making full use of the excellent ingredients from the surrounding farmland. Naturally, seafood has pride of place on the dinner tables of this port city.

★ **$$$$** ✕ **Gin Fish.** The gifted chef at this tiny restaurant in a narrow, Oude Stad street concocts such inventive dishes as grilled asparagus with fresh morels and a poached egg, and langoustines in a light curry sauce. Some say it's also the best fish restaurant in town. ⊠ *Haarstraat 9* ☎ *03/231–3207* ⚁ *Reservations essential* ⊟ *AE, DC, MC, V* ☉ *Closed Sun., Mon., and June.*

$$$$ ✕ **'t Fornuis.** In the heart of Old Antwerp, this old and cozy restaurant, decorated in traditional Flemish style, serves some of the best food in the city. The menu changes frequently, but truffled sweetbreads with wild truffle sauce is a house classic. ⊠ *Reyndersstraat 24* ☎ *03/233–6270* ⚁ *Reservations essential* ⊟ *AE, DC, MC, V* ☉ *Closed weekends and 3 wks in Aug., Dec. 25–Jan. 1.*

★ **$$–$$$$** ✕ **Sir Anthony Van Dijck.** On Antwerp's most famous alley is a classy brasserie, with an interior courtyard and tables grouped around stone pillars under high, massive beams. The menu changes monthly, but expect such items as salad *liègeoise* (with beans, boiled potatoes, and morsels of bacon), duck à l'orange, and tuna steak. There are two seatings a night. ⊠ *Vlaeykensgang, Oude Koornmarkt 16* ☎ *03/231–6170* ⚁ *Reservations essential* ⊟ *AE, DC, MC, V* ☉ *Closed Sun., Aug., Dec. 25–Jan. 1 and Easter wk.*

★ **$$–$$$** ✕ **De Kleine Zavel.** Wooden crates filled with bottles are part of the decor of this design restaurant, and may give a peek into the history of this building, which was once a hotel for shipping people. Chef Carlo Didden makes such delights as kidney of veal with mashed potatoes, spinach, and mustard sauce. ⊠ *Stoofstraat 2* ☎ *03/231–9691* ⊟ *AE, DC, MC, V* ☉ *No lunch Sat.*

$$–$$$ ✕ **Horta.** Reconstructed with the original supporting structures from the Maison du Peuple, this brasserie / restaurant includes large mustard-yellow industrial beams and windows all around. Located on the trendy Hopland street, the place has a hip air to it. The food is also a feast for the senses with delicacies such as roasted sea perch with asparagus, shiitake mushrooms, and artichokes with a warm rouille sauce. ⊠ *Hopland 2* ☎ *03/232–2815* ⊟ *AE, DC, MC, V.*

★ **$$–$$$** ✕ **Neuze Neuze.** Five tiny houses cobbled together form a handsome, split-level restaurant with whitewashed walls, dark-brown beams, and a blazing fireplace. Good choices are the grilled scallops on a bed of Belgian endive and bacon, served in a wheat-beer sauce, or the Mechelen ham finished by truffles and thin-cut vegetables. ✉ *Wijngaardstraat 19* ☎ *03/232–5783* ⊟ *AE, DC, MC, V* ۞ *Closed Sun., 1st wk in Jan., and 2 wks in July. No lunch Sat.*

$$ ✕ **Hungry Henrietta.** This stylish Antwerp institution is next to the church where Rubens is buried. You can dine in the garden when the weather's good. Fillet of salmon with endive, codfish, and loin of lamb are on the menu. ✉ *Lombardenvest 19* ☎ *03/232–2928* ⊟ *AE, DC, MC, V* ۞ *Closed Sun., Mon., and Aug.*

$$ ✕ **'t Hofke.** This restaurant is worth visiting for its location alone—it's in the Vlaeykensgang alley, where time seems to have stood still. The cozy dining room has the look and feel of a private home, and the menu includes a large selection of salads and omelets, as well as scampi in cream with cognac and calves' liver with Roquefort. ✉ *Oude Koornmarkt 16* ☎ *03/233–8606* ⊟ *AE, MC, V* ۞ *Closed Mon. and Tues.*

$–$$ ✕ **Zuiderterras.** This stark glass-and-black-metal café and restaurant was designed by avant-garde architect bOb (his spelling) Van Reeth, and resembles a docked cruise ship. While nibbling one of the inventive salads or splurging on some great waterzooi, enjoy the view of the river on one side or the cathedral and the Oude Stad on the other. ✉ *Ernest Van Dijckkaai 37* ☎ *03/234–1275* ⊟ *AE, DC, MC, V.*

Where to Stay

The Antwerp City Tourist Office keeps track of the best hotel prices and can make reservations for you up to a week in advance. Write or fax for a reservation form. It also maintains a list of some 25 recommended B&B accommodations from €30 to €50.

★ $$$$ ▥ **De Witte Lelie.** Three step-gabled 16th-century houses have been combined to make the "White Lily" Antwerp's most exclusive hotel. Personal service is the watchword in the 10-room hotel, decorated mostly in white, with colorful carpets and modern art on the walls. Sumptuous breakfasts are served on a loggia opening up on the inner courtyard. ✉ *Keizerstraat 16–18, 2000* ☎ *03/226–1966* ▤ *03/234–0019* ⊕ *www.dewittelelie.be* ↭ *4 rooms, 6 suites* ⊟ *AE, DC, MC, V.*

$$$$ ▥ **Hilton Antwerp.** Incorporating the turn-of-the-20th-century Grand Bazar building, the five stories of the Hilton are architecturally compatible with the much older buildings on Groenplaats. Rooms have three telephones, safes, and desks. Afternoon tea is served in the marble-floor lobby. The restaurant, Het Vyfde Seizoen, will satisfy gourmets. ✉ *Groenplaats, 2000* ☎ *03/204–1212* ▤ *03/204–1213* ⊕ *www.hilton.com* ↭ *193 rooms, 18 suites* ♨ *2 restaurants* ⊟ *AE, DC, MC, V.*

$$$$ ▥ **Hyllit.** The Hyllit stands on the corner of De Keyserlei, Antwerp's prestigious shopping street, with its entrance on Appelmansstraat, the gateway to the diamond district (reception on second floor). Rooms are decorated in muted colors and equipped with office-type desks. There's a rooftop buffet breakfast room and full room service. ✉ *De Keyserlei 28–30, 2018* ☎ *03/202–6800* ▤ *03/202–6890* ⊕ *www.hyllithotel.be* ↭ *71 rooms, 56 suites* ⊟ *AE, DC, MC, V.*

$$$ ▥ **Classic Hotel Villa Mozart.** This small, modern hotel in an old building in a pedestrian area could not be more central—it's next door to the cathedral. The rooms, equipped with business-class features, air-conditioning, and safes, are slightly cramped, but many overlook the cathedral. ✉ *Handschoenmarkt 3, 2000* ☎ *03/231–3031* ▤ *03/231–5685* ⊕ *www.bestwestern.be* ↭ *25 rooms* ♨ *Restaurant* ⊟ *AE, DC, MC, V.*

★ $$$ ⊞ **Firean.** An art deco gem built in 1929, Hotel Firean is family operated. There's a tiny bar–cum–breakfast room, where eggs are served in floral-print cozies. The location is not central, but a tram to Oude Stad runs outside the door. ⊠ *Karel Oomsstraat 6, 2018* ☎ *03/237–0260* ⊟ *03/238–1168* ⊕ *www.hotelfirean.com* ⇆ *9 rooms, 6 in annex next door* ⊟ *AE, DC, MC, V.*

★ $$$ ⊞ **'t Sandt.** One could never have imagined that this former soap factory would turn out to be one of Antwerp's classiest hotels. Suites and duplexes in the 19th-century neo-rococo building are lavishly appointed with a backdrop of white walls and heavy wooden beamed ceilings. Each has its own character and, accordingly, its own name, like The Cathedral Penthouse and the Waldorf Astoria Room. The garden has a view of the cathedral. ⊠ *Zand 17, B2000* ☎ *03/232–9390* ⊟ *03/232–5613* ⊕ *www.hotel-sandt.be* ⇆ *35 rooms* ⊟ *AE, DC, MC, V.*

★ $ ⊞ **Internationaal Zeemanshuis.** Originally a resting spot for seamen, the Seamen's House welcomes anyone looking for clean and affordable accommodation. Prices for single and double rooms vary depending on if you want a shower, bath, or TV and safes. The self-service restaurant appears to carry on the tradition of a friendly meeting place. ⊠ *Falconrui 221 B2000* ☎ *03/227–5433* ⊟ *03/234– 2603* ⊕ *www.zeemanshuis.be* ⇆ *114 rooms* ⌁ *Restaurant* ⊟ *AE, DC, MC, V.*

$ ⊞ **Scoutel.** This hotel, owned by the Boy Scouts and Girl Guides but open to all ages, is in a modern building five minutes' walk from Centraal Station. The double and triple rooms are simple but adequate; all have toilets and showers. Rates are lower for people under 25, and most of the guests *are* young. Breakfast and sheets are included; towels can be rented. Guests are provided with front-door keys. ⊠ *Stoomstraat 3 B2000* ☎ *03/226–4606* ⊟ *03/232–6392* ⊕ *www.vvksm.be* ⇆ *24 rooms with shower* ⊟ *V.*

Shopping

Antwerp is a fashion center second only to Milan, thanks to a group of designers who burst on the scene in the late 1980s as the Antwerp Six. Inspired by their success, other young designers have achieved prominence; check out the boutiques in the De Wilde Zee district and along Huidevetterstraat and Schuttershofstraat. Ready-to-wear by Raf Simons and Martin Margiela can be found at **Louis** (⊠ Lombardenstraat 2 ☎ 03/232–9872). **Dries Van Noten** (⊠ Kammenstraat 18 ☎ 03/470–2510) has a beautiful boutique, Modepaleis, that's not to be confused with the drab Van Noten shop opposite.

If you plan to invest in diamonds, it makes sense to do so in the world's leading diamond center. Your best bet for expert advice is **Diamondland** (⊠ Appelmansstraat 33a ☎ 03/229–2990), in whose spectacular showrooms you can see both loose and mounted diamonds.

Antwerp Essentials

AIRPORTS & TRANSFERS

Antwerp International Airport is 5½ km (3 mi) southeast of the city. There are several flights a day to and from London City Airport. Most passengers arrive via Brussels National Airport (Zaventem), which is linked with Antwerp by hourly bus service (50 minutes one-way). ⧉ **Antwerp International Airport** ☎ 03/285-6500 flight information ⊕ www.antwerpairport.be.

TRANSFERS Buses to Antwerp's Centraal Station leave every 20 minutes; travel time is about 15 minutes.

CAR TRAVEL

Expressways from Amsterdam, Eindhoven, Aachen, Liège, Brussels, and Gent converge on Antwerp's inner-city ring expressway. It's a 10-lane racetrack, so be sure you're in the correct lane well before you exit.

TOURS

BOAT TOURS Flandria operates 50-minute boat trips on the River Scheldt, departing from the Steenplein pontoon (next to the Steen) on Easter weekend and daily May through September (€7). Its boat tours of the enormous port (2½ hrs) leave from Quay 13 near Londonstraat, Easter weekend, daily May–August, and weekends in September and October (€11.50).
🚩 Fees & Schedules **Flandria** ☎ 03/231-3100 ⊕ www.flandriaboat.com.

PRIVATE GUIDES Personal guides can be engaged through the City Tourist Office, which requires a couple of days' notice. The price for two hours is €45.

TRAM TOURS Touristram operates one-hour tram tours with cassette commentary in the Oude Stad and old harbor area. Tickets (€4) are sold on the tram.
🚩 Fees & Schedules **Touristram** ✉ Groenplaats ☎ 03/480-9388 ⊕ www.touristram.be.

TRAIN TRAVEL

Frequent trains cover the distance between Antwerp (Centraal Station) and Brussels in 35 minutes.
🚩 **Centraal Station** ✉ Koningin Astridplein ☎ 03/204-2040.

TRAM TRAVEL

In the downtown area, the tram is the most convenient means of transportation. Some lines have gone underground (look for signs marked M); the most useful line runs between Centraal Station (Metro: Diamant) and the Groenplaats (for the Oude Stad). A single ride costs €1, a 10-ride ticket €7.50, and a day pass €3. For detailed transportation maps, stop at the tourist office.

VISITOR INFORMATION

🚩 **Toerisme Stad Antwerpen** (Antwerp City Tourist Office) ✉ Grote Markt 15 ☎ 03/232-0103 🖷 03/231-1937 ⊕ www.visitantwerpen.be.

GENT

Gent—also spelled Ghent and known to French-speakers as Gand—is the home of one of the world's earliest great paintings, Van Eyck's *Adoration of the Mystic Lamb*. The city center may come straight out of the Middle Ages, but this is a dynamic, modern town with a long-established rebellious streak. It was weavers from Gent, joined by others from Brugge, who took up arms to defeat the French cavalry in 1302. Charles V (1500–58) was born here, but that did not prevent an uprising against his rule (which was cruelly crushed). Centuries later, a weaver saved Gent from decline by stealing a newfangled spinning mule from England and starting Gent's industrial revolution. Later, socialists battled here for workers' rights, and Gent became the site of Belgium's first Flemish-speaking university. The militant tradition continues to this day: while the city commemorated Charles's 500th birthday in 2000, many academics and locals vehemently opposed the festivities.

Exploring Gent

The best spot to start a walk around the center is Sint-Michielsbrug (St. Michael's Bridge), with its view of Gent's three glorious medieval steeples. The closest is the severe early Gothic Sint-Niklaaskerk (St. Nicholas's Church); behind it is the Belfort (Belfry) from 1314. In the background rises the honey-colored tower of Sint-Baafskathedraal (St. Bavo's Cathedral) in Brabant Gothic. The classic walk around the Old City takes you up to the Gravensteen (Castle of the Counts) and then, on the opposite shore of the River Leie, to the Stadhuis (Town Hall) and the cathedral. Many historic buildings are lit up at night, making an evening walk a memorable experience.

The Museum voor Schone Kunsten (Fine Arts Museum) will be closed for a thorough renovation until the end of 2005. In the meantime, some parts of the collection will be shown in other museums, such as the SMAK, the Design Museum Gent, and the crypt of St. Bavo's Cathedral.

Belfort (Belfry). The power of 14th-century guilds is symbolized in this 300-foot belfry. The spire was added for the world's fair of 1913, based on the original plans. Climb the steps to the first floor and take the elevator the rest of the way to see the medieval artifacts and range of ancient bells on the second and third floors. A 52-bell carillon hangs on the top floor, but this can be visited only with a guide. ⊠ *Sint-Baafsplein* ☎ *09/269–3730* ☉ *Mid-Mar.–mid-Nov., daily 10–12:30 and 2–5:30; guided visits at 10 mins past hr, afternoons only, May–Sept.*

★ **Graslei.** This quay along the Leie River, between St. Michael's Bridge and Gras Bridge, is best seen from the Korenlei across the river. Once the center of Gent's trade, it is lined with guild houses in Romanesque, Brabant Gothic, and Renaissance style, as well as other buildings, among them the 12th-century **Koornstapelhuis** (Granary), used for 600 years.

Gravensteen. The ancient castle of the counts of Flanders hulks up like a battleship near the confluence of the Leie and Lieve Canal, the 700-year-old waterway that links the city with Brugge. First erected in 1180, the castle has been rebuilt a number of times, most recently in the 19th century. A gruesome display of torture instruments indicates how feudal power was maintained. The spinning mules that made Gent a textile center were first installed here. ⊠ *St-Veerleplein* ☎ *09/225–9306* ☉ *Daily 9–6 (Oct.–Mar. until 5).*

Museum voor Industriele Archeologie en Textiel (MIAT). The industrial archaeology and textiles museum is appropriately housed in a Lancashire-style textile mill: it houses the famous spinning mule stolen from that area of England by a Gent native, who smuggled it back to Flanders to start a rival textile industry. The cotton mill area is filled with spinning wheels and weaving machines; there are demonstrations every Tuesday and Thursday. Outside these times, just ask one of the staff for a demonstration. The museum also has a wonderful little *Cinepalace*—an old-movie theater that screens classics on the second Sunday of the month. ⊠ *Minnemeers 9, Vrijdaagmarkt* ☎ *09/269–4200* ⊕ *www.miat.gent. be* ☉ *Tues.–Sun. 10–6.*

★ **Sint-Baafskathedraal** (St. Bavo's Cathedral). In the baptistry is the stupendous 24-panel *Adoration of the Mystic Lamb,* completed in 1432 by Jan Van Eyck (1389–1441), who is said to have invented the technique of painting with oil. To the medieval viewer, the painting was a theological summation of the relationship between God and the world. The cathedral has several other treasures, notably a Rubens masterpiece, *The Conversion of St. Bavo,* in which the artist painted himself as a convert in a red cloak. ⊠ *St-Baafsplein* ☎ *09/269–2065* ⊕ *www.gent.be* ☉ *Cathedral: Apr.–Oct., daily 8:30–6, Nov.–Mar., daily 8:30–5. Chapel: Apr.–Oct., Mon.–Sat. 9:30–4:45, Sun. 1–4:30; Nov.–Mar., Mon.–Sat. 10:30–3:45, Sun. 1–3:30* ☞ *No visits to cathedral or chapel during services.*

Stedelijk Museum voor Actuele Kunst (Municipal Museum for Contemporary Art). SMAK, as it is known, has made a significant impact on Belgium's contemporary art scene since it opened in Gent's City Park back in 1999. The fascinating collection includes everything from Joseph Beuys to Francis Bacon. ⊠ *Citadelpark* ☎ *09/221–1703* 🖷 *09/221–7109* ⊕ *www. smak.be* ☾ *Tues.–Sun. 10–6* ☾ *Closed Mon.*

Stadhuis (Town Hall). The two distinct architectural styles in this 16th-century building are the result of crippling tax increases imposed by Charles V that halted construction. The older Gothic section, with its lacelike tracery, was begun early in the 16th century. The structure was finished at the end of the same century in a more sober Renaissance style. ⊠ *Botermarkt* ☎ *09/266–5222* ☾ *Guided visits only, May–Oct., Mon.–Thurs. at 3.*

Where to Eat

Gent's contribution to Belgian gastronomy is the creamy fish or chicken stew waterzooi, which most menus offer.

★ **$$$–$$$$** ✕ **Waterzooi.** This tiny restaurant stands on a square distinguished by 16th- and 17th-century buildings facing the Gravensteen. It serves such specialties as waterzooi (what else) and turbot with pepper sauce. ⊠ *Sint-Veerleplein 2* ☎ *09/225–0563* ⌂ *Reservations essential* 🏛 *Jacket and tie* ⊟ *AE, DC, MC, V* ☾ *Closed Wed., Sun., and 3 wks in July and Aug.*

$$–$$$ ✕ **Pakhuis.** This old warehouse is now an enormously popular brasserie, with marble-top tables, parquet floors, and a huge oak bar. There's an oyster bar to supplement such basic brasserie fare as knuckle of ham with mustard and steak tartare. ⊠ *Schuurkenstraat 4* ☎ *09/223–5555* ⊟ *AE, DC, MC, V* ☾ *Closed Sun.*

★ **$–$$$** ✕ **Cassis.** In a tranquil setting combining beamed ceilings, light wood, and wicker chairs, Cassis offers both traditional and modern Belgian specialties, as well as huge, inventive salads presented as artfully as a Flemish still life. ⊠ *Vrijdagmarkt 5* ☎ *09/233–8546* ⊟ *AE, MC, V* ☾ *No dinner Mon.*

$$ ✕ **'t Buikske Vol.** Trendy restaurants fill this charming residential area that historically housed textile workers, and Buikske Vol is the best among them. Well-prepared dishes include grilled turbot, fillet of beef with onion confit, and sweetbreads with rabbit. ⊠ *Kraanlei 17* ☎ *09/225–1880* ⊟ *AE, DC, MC, V* ☾ *Closed Sun., Wed., Easter wk, and 1st 2 wks of Aug. No lunch Sat.*

$–$$ ✕ **Brasserie Keizershof.** Touristy taverns are much the same all over Belgium, but this one is popular with locals, too. The daily plates are large portions of hearty Belgian food. ⊠ *Vrijdagmarkt 47* ☎ *09/223–4446* ⊟ *MC, V* ☾ *Closed Sun. and Mon.*

Where to Stay

A number of Gent hotels catering to trade-show visitors stand near the Expo Center. There are not so many in the Old City.

$$$$ 🏨 **Sofitel Gent-Belfort.** The Gent outpost of this classy and comfortable French hotel chain is a converted art nouveau building, decorated in warm brown and beige and excellently situated in the heart of the Old City. The bathrooms are palatial. ⊠ *Hoogpoort 63, 9000* ☎ *09/233–3331* 🖷 *09/233–1102* ⊕ *www.sofitel.be* ➹ *124 rooms, 3 suites* ⌂ *Restaurant* ⊟ *AE, DC, MC, V.*

$$–$$$ 🏨 **Gravensteen.** This handsome 19th-century mansion, restored to its original Second Empire style, has a superb canal-front location, a few steps from the castle of the counts. Some rooms are small but tasteful; 10 more luxurious rooms overlook the canal. ⊠ *Jan Breydelstraat 35, 9000* ☎ *09/225–1150* 🖷 *09/225–1850* ⊕ *www.gravensteen.be* 🛏 *49 rooms, 2 suites* ▭ *AE, DC, MC, V.*

$$ 🖥 **The Boatel.** Sleep aboard this friendly genuine Flemish riverboat, about a 10-minute walk from the town center. The bright, comfortable rooms are stylishly decorated, and of a good size. Breakfast is in a sunny dining area. Free parking is available on the road. ⊠ *Voorhoutkaai 44,* ☎ *09/267–1030* 🖷 *09/267–1039* ⊕ *www.theboatel.com* 🛏 *5 rooms, 2 suites* ▭ *AE, DC, MC, V.*

★ $$ 🖥 **Erasmus.** From the flagstone and wood-beam library-lounge to the stone mantels in the bedrooms, every inch of this noble 16th-century house has been scrubbed, polished, and bedecked with period ornaments. Even the tiny garden has been carefully manicured. ⊠ *Poel 25, 9000* ☎ *09/224–2195* 🖷 *09/233–4241* ⊕ *www.proximedia.com/web/hotel-erasmus.html* 🛏 *11 rooms* ▭ *AE, MC, V.*

Gent Essentials

CAR TRAVEL

Gent is just off the six-lane E40 from Brussels, which continues to Brugge and the coast. Traffic can be bumper-to-bumper on summer weekends. It is generally lighter on the E17 from Antwerp. Finding your way in and out of the city center can be extremely tricky.

TOURS

BOAT TOURS Sightseeing boats depart from landing stages at Graslei, Easter–October, and Korenlei, March–November, for 40-minute trips. Admission is €4.50 in an open boat from Graslei or Korenlei or €5 in a covered boat from Graslei.

🖪 Fees & Schedules **Sightseeing boats** ☎ 09/266–0522 Graslei ⊕ www.gent-watertoerist.be ☎ 09/223–8853; 09/229–1716 Korenlei ⊕ www.debootjesvangent.be.

WALKING TOURS A city tour departs from the tourist office in the crypt of the Belfort at 2:30 PM (weekends in April, daily May through November); it's led by Gidsenbond van Gent en Oost-Vlaanderen (GOV). For a private tour, GOV charges €50 for the first two hours, €25 per additional hour. You can make your own itinerary or choose from several themed walks. Vizit organizes entertaining walks for children and adults, full of tales of Gent's past and present. Prices range from €40 to €65.

🖪 Fees & Schedules **Gidsenbond van Gent en Oost-Vlaanderen (GOV)** ☎ 09/233–0772 🖷 09/233–0865 ⊕ www.gidsenbond-gent.be. **Vizit** ☎ 09/233–7689 🖷 09/225–2319 ⊕ www.vizit.be.

TRAIN TRAVEL

Nonstop trains depart for Gent-Sint-Pieters every half hour from Gares du Midi, Central, and Nord in Brussels. Travel time to Gent is 28 minutes.

🖪 **Station/Gare St Pieters** ⊠ Kon. Maria Hendrikaplein, Gent ☎ 09/221-4444.

TRANSPORTATION AROUND GENT

Most of the sights are within a 1-km (½-mi) radius of the Town Hall, and by far the best way to see them is on foot, as much of the city center is closed to cars. You can rent bikes at the train station or in the center. Tram numbers 1, 11, and 12 go into town—the Korenmarkt is a good place to get off. A ticket costs €1; a day pass is €5. Buy either from the ticket machine at the tram terminus next to the railway station.

VISITOR INFORMATION
The tourist office is open April–November, daily 9:30–6:30; until only
4:30 the rest of the year.
🗿 **Dienst voor Toerisme** (Tourist Office) ⊠ Belfort, Botermarkt 17A ☎ 09/266-5232
🖨 09/2256288 ⊕ www.gent.be.

BRUGGE

Brugge (or Bruges, as it is known to French- and most English-speakers) represents the flowering of commerce and culture in the Middle Ages.
The city had the good fortune to be linked with the North Sea by a navigable waterway and became a leading member of the Hanseatic League
during the 13th century. Splendid marriage feasts were celebrated here;
that of Charles the Bold, Duke of Burgundy (1433–77), to Margaret of
York in 1468 is commemorated in the annual Procession of the Holy
Blood. Disaster struck when the link with the sea silted up in the 15th
century, but this past misfortune is responsible for Brugge's present
glory: little has changed over the last 500 years in this city of interlaced
canals, making it a living museum in the best possible sense.

Exploring Brugge

*Numbers in the margin correspond to points of interest on the Brugge
(Bruges) map.*

The center of Brugge is virtually reserved for pedestrians, and its cobbled streets call for good walking shoes. Brugge draws visitors in droves,
but there's always a quiet corner away from the crowd. Try to do your
exploring in the early evening or early morning when the day-trippers
are not around and the city is at its most magical. Municipal museums
are closed on Monday but open all other days apart from Christmas
and New Year's Day. They also close early on Ascension Day, as everything comes to a standstill for the annual Procession of the Holy Blood
through the town.

★ ❿ **Begijnhof** (Beguinage). The Begijnhof has been an oasis of peace for 750
years. The first Beguines were widows of fallen crusaders. They were
not nuns but lived a devout life while serving the community. Although
the last Beguines left the enclosed area of small, whitewashed houses in
1930, a Benedictine community has replaced them, and you may join
them, discreetly, for vespers and masses in their small church. The horse
and carriage rides around the town have a 10-minute stop just outside
here—long enough for a quick look around. ⊠ *Monasterium de Wijn-
gaard, Oude Begijnhof, off Wijngaardstraat* ☎ *050/330011* ⊙ *Mar.–Nov.,
10–noon and 1:45–5; Dec.–Feb., Mon., Tues., and Fri. 10–noon, Wed.
and Thurs. 2–4.*

❶ **Belfort** (Belfry). There's a panoramic view of the town from the top of
the 285-foot-high (366 steps!) Belfort, which dominates the Markt, the
city's ancient market square. The Belfort has a carillon notable even in
Belgium, where they are a matter of civic pride. ⊠ *Markt 7* ☎ *050/448711*
⊙ *Tues.–Sun. 9:30–5.*

★ ❷ **Burg.** This magical medieval square is the focal point of ancient Brugge.
The **Stadhuis** (City Hall), a jewel of Gothic architecture in white sandstone from the 14th century, has an ornate facade adorned with statues. The Gothic Hall on the first floor is open to the public. The Stadhuis
is linked with the graceful Renaissance **Oude Griffie** (Old Recorder's
House) by a bridge arching over the narrow Blinde Ezelstraat. *Stadhuis*
⊠ *Burg 12* ☎ *050/448711* ⊙ *Tues.–Sun. 9:30–5.*

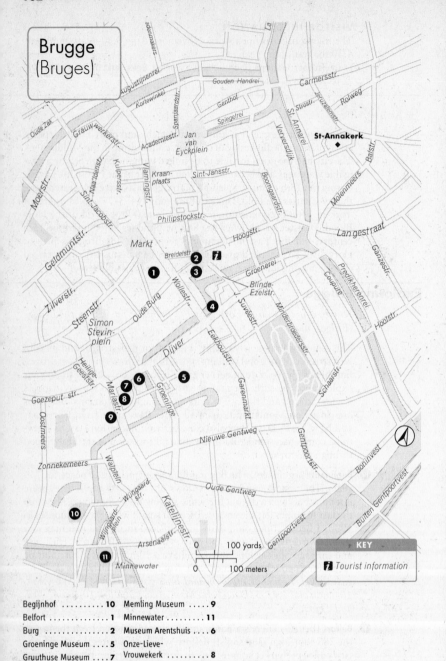

Brugge
(Bruges)

KEY

i Tourist information

★ **❺ Groeninge Museum.** This small museum enjoys a worldwide reputation for its superb collection of Flemish Primitives and includes Van Eyck's *Virgin and Canon Van der Paele,* Memling's *Moreel Triptych,* arguably his most intensely spiritual work, Hieronymus Bosch's surrealistic *Last Judgment,* and Pieter Brueghel's *Preaching of John the Baptist.* ⊠ *Dijver 12* ☎ *050/448711* ☉ *Tues.–Sun. 9:30–5.*

❼ Gruuthuse Museum. This 15th-century palace offers a glimpse into life at the powerful Burgundy court, from the kitchen downstairs to the chapel above. The gardens and canal bridge on a sunny day are beautiful. ⊠ *Dijver 17* ☎ *050/448711* ☉ *Tues.–Sun. 9:30–5.*

❸ Heilig-Bloed Basiliek (Basilica of the Holy Blood). The basilica of the Holy Blood stands on a corner of the Burg, next to the Town Hall. The lower chapel has kept its austere 12th-century Romanesque character. The upper chapel is ornate and neo-Gothic, rebuilt in the 19th century. A vial thought to contain drops of Christ's blood is displayed here every Friday. The **Heilig-Bloed Museum** (Museum of the Holy Blood) has reliquaries and paintings. The **Procession of the Holy Blood** on Ascension Day combines religious and historical pageantry in a big parade around the town. ⊠ *Burg* ☉ *Museum Apr.–Sept., daily 9:30–11:50 and 2–5:50; Oct.–Mar., daily 10–11:50 and 2–3:50* ☉ *Closed Wed. afternoon.*

★ **❾ Memling Museum.** The museum is dedicated to the work of the Brugge painter Hans Memling (c. 1430–94), among the greatest of all early Flemish painters. The six masterpieces in the museum include the altarpiece *St. John the Baptist and St. John the Evangelist* and the miniatures adorning the St. Ursula shrine. The museum is housed in the former **Sint-Janshospitaal,** where the sick were nursed for 700 years. ⊠ *Mariastraat 38* ☎ *050/448711* ☉ *Tues.–Sun. 9:30–5.*

⓫ Minnewater. This enchanting lake, created in the 13th century, was once the city harbor and more recently has been known as the Lake of Love. The 16th-century lockkeeper's house is usually surrounded by swans, one of the symbols of the city. ⊠ *Off Wijngaardplein, next to Begijnhof.*

❻ Museum Arentshuis (Brangwyn Museum). The Brugge-born English artist Frank Brangwyn (1867–1956) was one of several British Romantics who lived in the city and influenced the reconstruction of many buildings in a pseudo-Gothic style. Many of his brooding paintings of Brugge are on view here. On the ground floor is the **Kantmuseum** (Lace Museum), containing outstanding examples of a craft long and lovingly practiced in Brugge. ⊠ *Dijver 16* ☎ *050/448711* ☉ *Tues.–Sun. 9:30–5.*

❽ Onze-Lieve-Vrouwekerk (Church of Our Lady). At 381 feet, the severe spire is the tallest brick construction in the world. Inside the church, you'll find notable art—including Michelangelo's small *Madonna and Child* statue—and splendid tombs with the effigies of Duke Charles the Bold of Burgundy, who died on the battlefield in 1477, and his daughter Mary. ⊠ *Corner of Dijver and Mariastraat* ☉ *Tues.–Fri. 9:30–12:30 and 1:30–5, Sat. 9:30–12:30 and 1:30–4, Sun. 1:30–5.*

★ **❹ Reien** (Canals). The ancient canals of Brugge with their arching stone bridges can be explored both by boat and on foot along the quays. From **Steenhouwersdijk** you see the brick rear gables, which are all that remains of the old county hall. Next to the little **Huidenvettersplein,** with its 17th-century guild houses, is **Rozenhoedkaai;** from here the view of the heart of Brugge includes the pinnacles of the Town Hall, the basilica, and the belfry.

Where to Stay & Eat

Along Brugge's quiet streets you'll find some of Belgium's finest dining. The Markt, however, is ringed with unremarkable restaurants catering to the tourist trade. Many of Brugge's hotels are romantic, canal-side residences popular for second honeymoons. Prices are relatively high, but so are standards. Many hotels offer package deals.

★ **$$$$** ✕ **De Karmeliet.** Owner-chef Geert Van Hecke, one of Belgium's best chefs, works in this lovely 18th-century house. The menu from his inventive kitchen changes every two months and features such delicacies as goose liver with truffled potatoes, roast langoustines with endive in an apple-and-curry juice, and cod carpaccio with asparagus. ⊠ *Langestraat 19* ☎ *050/338259* ⚲ *Reservations essential* ⌂ *Jacket required* ▤ *AE, DC, MC, V* ⊘ *Oct.–May, no dinner Sun., closed Mon., no lunch Tues.; June–Sept., closed Sun. and Mon.*

$$-$$$$ ✕ **Breydel–De Coninc.** Famed for fresh mussels and other seafood, this simple but well-appointed restaurant stands between the Markt and the Burg. Although there are token offerings of eel and steak, the focus is on the basics—a huge crock heaped with shiny, blue-black shells. ⊠ *Breidelstraat 24* ☎ *050/339746* ▤ *MC, V.*

$-$$ ✕ **De Hobbit.** Known for its spareribs—Hobbit style (barbecued) or Thai style—this cozy restaurant is warm and inviting with flickering candles on every table and brainteaser puzzles on the place mats. You can have a second plateful of ribs for free if you're still hungry after your first; the restaurant also serves a wide variety of other food, including lamb cutlets, pasta, salads, and prawns in garlic butter. ⊠ *Kemlestraat 8 (off Steenstraat)* ☎ *050/335520* ▤ *AE, DC, MC, V.*

$ ✕ **Straffe Hendrik.** This daytime pub (it closes by 4 in winter and by 5 the rest of the year) is attached to the brewery, dating from 1546, that produces the crystal-clear beer of the same name. It also serves quite acceptable pub grub, and you can tour the facilities. The square is among Brugge's most charming. ⊠ *Walplein 26* ☎ *050/332697* ▤ *MC, V (only for amounts over €25).*

$$$-$$$$ ✕▥ **De Castillion.** This restaurant ($$$$) and hotel was the residence of 18th-century bishop Jean-Baptiste de Castillion. Fillet of venison in a Pomerol stock and turbot and scampi on a bed of tagliatelle with a curry sauce are among the offerings (reservations essential; jacket and tie required). Drinks and coffee are served in a handsome art deco salon. The guest rooms vary considerably in size, price, and style, from rustic to modern. ⊠ *Heilige Geeststraat 1* ☎ *050/343001* 🖷 *050/339475* ⊕ *www.castillion.be* ⇤ *18 rooms, 2 suites* ⚇ *Restaurant, bar* ▤ *AE, DC, MC, V* ⊘ *Restaurant closed Mon. and Tues.; no dinner Sun.*

$$-$$$$ ✕▥ **Die Swaene.** This hotel has "romantic" written all over it: canal-side location, four-poster beds, candles, and marble nymphs in every nook and cranny—in short, honeymoon heaven. The restaurant ($$$$) is a serious contender as one of the best in this gourmet city, with goose liver, sweetbreads, and grilled turbot among its treats. ⊠ *Steenhouwersdijk 1, 8000* ☎ *050/342798* 🖷 *050/336674* ⊕ *www.dieswaene-hotel.com* ⇤ *22 rooms, 2 suites* ⚇ *Restaurant, pool* ▤ *AE, DC, MC, V* ⊘ *Restaurant closed Wed., 3 wks in Jan., 3 wks in July; no lunch Thurs.*

$$ ✕▥ **'t Bourgoensche Cruyce.** In a romantic canal-side setting, this restaurant ($$$$) has salmon-and-copper decor that is reflected in the water. The cuisine is equally romantic: panfried langoustines with wild mushrooms, tournedos of salmon with bacon, turbot medallions with coriander and caramelized leeks (reservations essential). The establishment has eight cozy guest rooms furnished in traditional Flemish style; four face the canal. ✉ *Wollestraat 41* ☎ *050/337926* 🖷 *050/341968* 🛏 *8 rooms* ⚭ *Restaurant* ▤ *AE, DC, MC, V* ☉ *Restaurant closed Tues., Wed., and 1st wk in July. Hotel closed mid-Nov.–mid-Dec.*

★ **$$$$** 🏨 **De Tuilerieën.** A 15th-century mansion with Venetian glass windows has been converted into a patrician hotel and decorated with antique reproductions. Canal-side rooms have great views; courtyard rooms are quieter. ✉ *Dijver 7, 8000* ☎ *050/343691* 🖷 *050/340400* ⊕ *www. hoteltuilerieen.com* 🛏 *22 rooms, 23 suites* ⚭ *Pool* ▤ *AE, DC, MC, V.*

$$$ 🏨 **Walburg.** One of Brugge's grandest 19th-century town houses is a few blocks from the Burg. The rooms, decorated in different color schemes with period Marie Antoinette furniture and marble bathrooms, are a generous 750 square feet; the suite is twice as large. ✉ *Boomgaardstraat 13–15, 8000* ☎ *050/349414* 🖷 *050/336884* 🛏 *12 rooms, 1 suite* ⚭ *Restaurant, bar* ▤ *AE, DC, MC, V.*

★ **$$** 🏨 **Egmond.** Every room in this manorlike inn by Minnewater lake has a garden view, as well as parquet floors and the odd fireplace or dormer ceiling. The hotel near the Begijnhof is a pleasant retreat from the bustle of the center, 10 minutes away. The bathrooms are quite small. ✉ *Minnewater 15, 8000* ☎ *050/341445* 🖷 *050/342940* ⊕ *www. egmond.be* 🛏 *8 rooms* ▤ *No credit cards.*

★ **$** 🏨 **De Pauw.** At this family-run hotel, the warmly furnished rooms have names rather than numbers, and breakfast comes with six kinds of bread, cold cuts, and cheese. The two rooms that share a hall shower are a super value. ✉ *Sint-Gilliskerkhof 8, 8000* ☎ *050/337118* 🖷 *050/ 345140* ⊕ *www.hoteldepauw.be* 🛏 *8 rooms, 6 with bath* ▤ *MC, V.*

Brugge Essentials

CAR TRAVEL
Brugge is about an hour's drive from Brussels on the E40 motorway to the coast. Holiday weekend traffic is heavy. Unless you are driving to a hotel, leave your car at one of the parking lots or garages at the entrance to the Old City.

TOURS
CARRIAGE TOURS The horse-drawn carriages that congregate in the Markt are an expensive way of seeing the sights. They are available March–November, daily 10–6; a 35-minute trip will cost €27.50. The carriages take up to five people.

BOAT TOURS Boat trips along the city canals are run by several companies and depart from five separate landings. Boats ply the waters March–November, daily 10–6. They leave every 10–15 minutes, and a 30-minute trip costs €5.20.

BUS TOURS Fifty-minute minibus tours of the city center leave every hour on the hour from the Markt in front of the post office, and cost €9.50, including an audio guide in the language of your choice.

TRAIN TRAVEL
Trains run twice an hour from Brussels (Gare du Midi, Central, or Nord) to Brugge. The station is south of the canal that circles the downtown area; it is a pleasant walk from here to the Minnewater, Begijnhof, and on to the city center. Travel time from Brussels is 53 minutes. 🚩 **Brugge Train Station** ✉ Stationsplein. ☎ 050/382382.

TRANSPORTATION AROUND BRUGGE
The center of Brugge is best explored on foot, as car and bus access is severely restricted. This makes for bicycle heaven; you can either rent one at the train station (collect from the Baggage Department) or wait

until you get to the center of town. Bicycle rental information is available from the tourist office.

VISITOR INFORMATION

Contact the tourist office well in advance for tickets to the splendid Procession of the Holy Blood held on Ascension Day. It is possible to glimpse the parade going past without buying a ticket, but for a good view and a seat on one of the stands dotted around the town, you will need to book one in advance, and it's well worth it. In 2004, the procession will take place on May 20.

🚩 **Toerisme Brugge** (Brugge Tourist Office) ✉ Burg 11 ☎ 050/448686 📠 050/448600 🌐 www.brugge.be.

BULGARIA

SOFIA, THE BLACK SEA COAST, INLAND BULGARIA

WITH ITS MOUNTAINS AND SEASCAPES, modern cities, medieval villages, gorgeous countryside, thriving nightlife, eclectic and hearty cuisine, and reasonable prices, Bulgaria is a treasure waiting to be rediscovered. For adventurous souls who don't mind dealing with a few rough edges (and wrestling with Cyrillic), the country provides an extraordinary vacation destination and a chance to see history in the making.

Once among the closest allies of the former Soviet Union, Bulgaria has been struggling toward democracy and a free-market economy ever since the overthrow of its Communist regime in 1989. The struggle has paid off; continuing reforms, and the country's support of Western military operations both in the region and worldwide, led to an invitation in November 2002 to join NATO. Bulgaria has also become a serious contender for membership in the European Union.

Since 1989, Bulgarians have endured skyrocketing inflation, high unemployment, and a rapidly decreasing standard of living. In 1997, a currency board was introduced that pegged the Bulgarian lev to the deutsche mark (and, subsequently, to the euro), eliminating many uncertainties about the country's financial stability. Apart from a tangible economic improvement, Bulgaria shows an open and rather cosmopolitan image to the world. You will find Bulgarians exuberantly welcoming, especially to Western tourists.

Endowed with long Black Sea beaches, the rugged interior Balkan Range, and fertile Danube plains, Bulgaria has much to offer year-round. The Black Sea coast, the country's eastern border, is particularly alluring, with secluded coves and fishing villages built amid Byzantine and Roman ruins, and wide, shallow beaches that have been developed into resorts. The terrain of the beautiful interior is ideal for hiking and skiing. In the more remote areas hides a tranquil world of forested ridges, spectacular valleys, and small villages where donkey-drawn carts are still the primary transport.

Bulgaria was founded in AD 681 by the Bulgars, a Turkic tribe from Central Asia. Archaeological finds in Varna, on the Black Sea coast, give proof of civilization from as early as 4600 BC. Part of the Byzantine Empire from 1018 to 1185, Bulgaria was occupied by the Turks from 1396 until 1878. Today, Bulgaria has Eastern-influenced architecture, Turkish fast food, Greek ruins, Soviet monuments, and European outdoor cafés. And five hundred years of Muslim occupation and nearly half a century of Communist rule did not wipe out Christianity. The country's 120 monasteries, with their icons and numerous frescoes, chronicle the development of Bulgarian cultural and national identity.

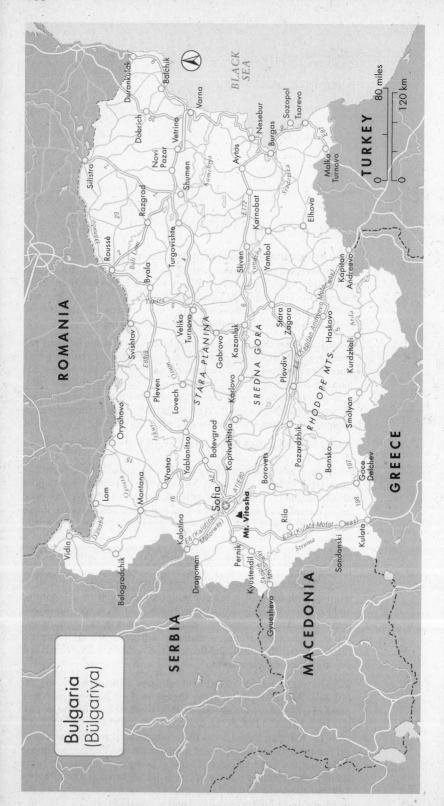

BLACK SEA

TURKEY

ROMANIA

SERBIA

MACEDONIA

GREECE

Bulgaria
(Bŭlgariya)

Durankulak
Balchik
Varna
Dobrich
Vetrino
Nesebur
Sozopol
Tsarevo
Burgas
Novi Pazar
Shumen
Aytos
Malko
Turnovo
Silistra
Razgrad
Karnobat
Roussé
Turgovishte
Sliven
Elhovo
Yambol
Byala
Kapitan
Andreevo
Svishtov
Veliko
Turnovo
Gabrovo
Kazanluk
Stara
Zagora
Pleven
Lovech
Karlovo
Plovdiv
Haskovo
Kurdzhali
Oryahovo
Botevgrad
Koprivshtitsa
Pazardzhik
Smolyan
Vratsa
Yablanitsa
Bansko
Goce
Delchev
Lom
Montana
Borovets
Sofia
Mt. Vitosha
Rila
Kulata
Kalotina
Pernik
Vidin
Dragoman
Kyustendil
Sandanski
Belogradchik
Gyuesheva

STARA PLANINA
SREDNA GORA
RHODOPE MTS.

80 miles
120 km

The capital, Sofia, sits picturesquely in a valley near Mt. Vitosha. Rich with history and culture, the city also has fine hotels and restaurants and a vibrant Mediterranean-style nightlife. Veliko Turnovo, just north of the Balkan Range in the center of the country and the capital from the 12th through 14th centuries during the Second Bulgarian Empire, still has medieval ramparts and vernacular architecture. Plovdiv, a university town southeast of Sofia, has a particularly picturesque Old Quarter as well as one of the world's best-preserved Roman amphitheaters. Varna, the site of one of Europe's first cultural settlements, is a summer beach playground and among the most important ports on the Black Sea.

BULGARIA A TO Z

To research prices, get advice from other travelers, and book travel arrangements, visit www.fodors.com.

AIR TRAVEL

Currently the only carrier within Bulgaria is Hemus Air, which has regular services to Varna, one of the major ports on the Black Sea. Flights and timetables differ depending on the season, so make sure you call to speak with an agent beforehand.

🛈 **Hemus Air** ✉ ul. Rakovski 157, Sofia ☎ 02/981-8330.

BOAT & FERRY TRAVEL

Modern luxury vessels once regularly cruised the Danube from Germany and Austria to Roussé in Bulgaria. However, the 1999 bombing of bridges over the Danube at Novi Sad, Yugoslavia, effectively blocked all river traffic. Services now run rather sporadically. Dunav Tours in Roussé handles bookings of cruises on the Danube. You can cruise between Black Sea resorts, as well as to Romania and Turkey. For information, consult the National Information and Advertising Center.

🛈 **Dunav Tours Roussé** ✉ ul. Olimpi Panov 5, Roussé ☎ 082/825-051 ⊕ www.dunavtours.bg. **National Information and Advertising Center** ✉ ul. Sveta Sofia 1, Sofia ☎ 02/987-9778 ⊕ www.bulgariatravel.org.

BUS TRAVEL

For bus trips between major Bulgarian cities you can choose among the numerous companies offering transport services. Group Travel is well established and reliable, offering service to cities all over Bulgaria. Etap Adress, with offices in more than 25 cities, owns buses in good condition, with facilities. Bus stations are generally close to the train station. Buy tickets a day or two in advance (but no more than a week). Within the cities a regular system of trams and buses operates for a single fare of 50 stotinki. In Sofia booths at bus stops sell tickets; outside the city you can pay the driver.

🛈 **Group Travel** ✉ Tsentralna Avtogara (Central Coach Station), Sofia ☎ 02/980-6336. **Etap Adress** ✉ Tsentralna Avtogara (Central Coach Station), Sofia ☎ 02/931-0494.

BUSINESS HOURS

Banks are open weekdays 9–5. Museums are usually open 9–5 but are often closed on Monday or Tuesday. Shops are open Monday–Saturday 9–7; some are open on Sunday. A few *denonoshni magazini* or *nonstops* (day-and-night minimarkets) in Sofia's city center are open 24 hours.

CAR RENTAL

Renting cars in Bulgaria is no bargain—unlike almost everything else, the cost of renting a car from a major Western firm is higher here than in other European countries. Four international car-rental firms have offices in Sofia and other major towns: Hertz, Avis, Europcar, and Budget. Their cars are generally new and in good condition but automatic transmission is almost unheard of here. Balkantourist can hire a chauffeured car for you through Budget for a fee not that much higher than the cost of a rental.

🚗 Major Agencies **Avis** ✉ Sheraton Sofia Hotel, pl. St. Nedelya 5 ☎ 02/981-1082 🌐 www. avis.bg ✉ Sofia Airport ☎ 02/945-9224. **Budget** ✉ bul. Vitosha 1 ☎ 02/987-1682 🌐 www.balkantourist.bg. **Europcar** ✉ Sofia Airport ☎ 02/981-0334. **Hertz** ✉ Sofia Airport ☎ 02/945-9217.

🚗 Local Agencies **Balkantourist** ✉ bul. Vitosha 1 ☎ 02/987-5192 🌐 www. balkantourist.bg.

CAR TRAVEL

AUTO CLUBS For motorist information contact the Bulgarian Automobile Touring Association.

🚗 In Bulgaria **Bulgarian Automobile Touring Association (SBA)** ✉ ul. Pozitano 3, Sofia ☎ 02/980-3308.

EMERGENCIES In case of breakdown call the number below. SBA trucks carry essential spares. Fiat, Ford, Volkswagen, Peugeot, and Mercedes-Benz all have car-service operations in Bulgaria. Other important numbers for drivers are the road police and ambulance.

🚗 Ambulance ☎ 150. Breakdowns ☎ 146. Road Police ☎ 165.

GASOLINE Stations are regularly spaced on main roads but may be few and far between. All are marked on Balkantourist's motoring map. A listing of 24-hour gas stations in Sofia can be found in the *Sofia City Guide* (🌐 *www.sofiacityguide.com)*, an English-language brochure for sale at news kiosks and free at major hotels.

PARKING Bulgaria's parking laws are liberal, and if there's not a place on the street, you can often park on the sidewalk. Just be sure you're not blocking a driveway or another car, and never park where there's a NO PARKING sign (a blue circle with a red line or cross through it). If you are in doubt, check with the hotel, restaurant, or sight you are visiting.

ROAD CONDITIONS Main roads are generally well maintained, although some routes are poor and narrow for the volume of traffic they have to carry. A large-scale expressway construction program has begun to link the main towns. Completed stretches run from Kalotina—on the Serbian border—to Sofia, and from Sofia to Plovdiv.

RULES OF THE ROAD Drive on the right. The speed limit is 120 kph (70 mph) on highways, 50 or 60 kph (31 or 36 mph) in built-up areas, and 80 kph (50 mph) elsewhere. You must take out collision, or Casco, insurance to drive a rented car. You are required to carry a first-aid kit, fire extinguisher, and triangle-shape breakdown sign in the vehicle. Front seat belts must be worn. The drunk-driving laws are strict—you are expected not to drive after you have had more than one drink. If you're pulled over, be prepared to pay on the spot a fine determined by the officer. When driving, *always* carry your ID card or passport, together with your driver's license (international or regular).

CUSTOMS & DUTIES

You may import duty-free into Bulgaria 250 grams of tobacco products, 1 liter of hard liquor, and 2 liters of wine. Declare items of greater value—computers, camcorders, and the like—so there will be no problems with Bulgarian customs officials on departure. Failure to declare items of value can result in a fine or even police detainment when you attempt to leave.

EATING & DRINKING

In Bulgaria you have a choice between predictable hotel dining, which often includes international fare, and more adventurous outings to restaurants or cafés, where the menu may be only in Cyrillic. The best bets are the small, folk-style restaurants called *mehanas,* which serve regional specialties, often at shared tables.

Bulgarian national dishes are closely related to their Greek and Slav counterparts: basic Balkan cooking includes lamb and potatoes, pork sausages called *kebapche,* and a popular salad called *shopska salata,* made with feta-style cheese, tomatoes, cucumbers, peppers, and onions. Bulgaria produces sumptuous fruits and vegetables. Try the rich, amber-color *bolgar* grapes and orange-red apricots. Bulgaria invented *kiselo mlyako* (yogurt), and there is excellent *tarator* (cold yogurt soup with sliced cucumber and garlic) in summer. *Banitsa* (butter, cheese, and phyllo dough pastry) is often eaten for breakfast. Syrupy baklava and chocolate or *palachinki* (nut- and honey-stuffed crepes) are favorite desserts.

Bulgarian wines are good, usually full-bodied, dry, and inexpensive. The national drink is *rakia*—either *slivova* (plum) or *grozdova* (grape) brandy—but other hard alcohol and beer are popular, too. Coffee is strong and is often drunk along with a cold beverage, such as cola, lemon drink, or mineral water.

WHAT IT COSTS In Bulgarian Leva				
	$$$$	$$$	$$	$
AT DINNER	over 18	13–18	6–12	under 6

Prices are for a main course.

RESERVATIONS & DRESS In Sofia, formal dress (jacket and tie) is customary at higher-priced restaurants. Casual dress is appropriate elsewhere.

EMBASSIES

🔒 United Kingdom ✉ ul. Moskovska 9, Sofia ☎ 02/933-9222 ⊕ www.british-embassy.bg.

🔒 United States ✉ ul. Suborna 1, Sofia ☎ 02/937-5100 ⊕ www.usembassy.bg.

HOLIDAYS

January 1; March 3 (Treaty of San Stefano Day); Orthodox Easter; May 1 (Labor Day); May 24 (Sts. Cyril and Methodius—creators of the Cyrillic alphabet—Commemoration Day); December 24–26 (Christmas); September 6 (Union Day); September 22 (Bulgarian Independence Day.)

LANGUAGE

The official language, Bulgarian, is written in Cyrillic and is close to Old Church Slavonic, the root of all Slavic languages. English, though popular with the young, is rarely understood outside major hotels and restaurants. It is essential to remember that in Bulgaria a nod of the head means "no" and a shake of the head means "yes."

LODGING

There is a wide choice of accommodations, ranging from the old, state-run hotels—most of them dating from the 1960s and '70s—to new, private hotels, apartment rentals, rooms in private homes, and campsites. Although you'll find comfortable modern chain hotels in Sofia, lodging in the countryside still tends to suffer from temperamental wiring and erratic plumbing.

At the leading hotels you can pay in either U.S. dollars or leva; the less expensive hotels accept only leva. Foreign currency can be exchanged for leva at the reception desk in most hotels.

WHAT IT COSTS In Bulgarian Leva			
	$$$$	$$$	$$	$
	SOFIA			
FOR 2 PEOPLE	over 300	150–300	80–150	under 80
	OTHER AREAS			
HOTELS	over 100	70–100	40–70	under 40

Hotel prices are for a standard double room.

APARTMENT & VILLA RENTALS   Rental accommodations are a growth industry, with planned modern complexes as well as picturesque cottages. Cooking facilities tend to be meager, though meal vouchers are often included in the deal. An English-speaking manager is generally on hand. Such accommodations usually aren't offered in Sofia but can often be found on the Black Sea coast and in Plovdiv and Veliko Turnovo.
🏠 Local Agents **Balkantour** ✉ bul. Stamboliiski 27 ☎ 02/988-5543. **Balkantourist** ✉ bul. Vitosha 1 ☎ 02/987-5192 ⊕ www.balkantourist.bg.

HOTELS   Most of the formerly government-owned or -operated hotels in Sofia, Plovdiv, and the bigger Black Sea cities have been privatized. Some state-owned hotels in smaller towns are still in the process of privatization and may be closed for renovation. Outside Sofia call ahead to hotels to get the latest information. Most hotels have restaurants and bars; the large, modern ones have swimming pools, shops, and other facilities.

PRIVATE ACCOMMODATIONS   Staying in private homes, with arrangements made by private-room agencies, is becoming a popular alternative to hotels; it not only cuts costs but also means increased contact with Bulgarians. Booking offices are in most main tourist areas. Balkantour and Balkantourist can help with Sofia lodgings. Take your own towels, soap, and other necessities.
🏠 Local Agents **Balkantour** ✉ bul. Stamboliiski 27 ☎ 02/988-5543. **Balkantourist** ✉ bul. Vitosha 1 ☎ 02/987-5192 ⊕ www.balkantourist.bg.

MAIL & SHIPPING
The postal code for Sofia is 1000. To receive mail in Bulgaria (an iffy proposition), you can have it sent to the central post office in the city where you want to pick it up, marked *poste restante* (PISMO DO POISKVANE in Bulgarian). Mail is held for one week. Do not send anything valuable in the mail and don't be surprised if your mail doesn't arrive. Pricier but more reliable is a private courier, such as DHL.
📮 Major Services **DHL Express Center** ✉ Radisson SAS Hotel, pl. Narodno Subranie 4 ☎ 02/988-2309.

POSTAL RATES   Letters up to 10 grams to North America cost 80 stotinki; to the United Kingdom, 70 stotinki. Rates change constantly with inflation, so ask for the current price at the post office.

MONEY MATTERS
The favorable exchange rate makes prices seem extremely low by international standards. The greatest expense is lodging, but it is possible to cut costs by choosing the more moderate hotels or staying in a private room in a Bulgarian house or apartment. Taxi and public transport fares, museum and theater admissions, and meal prices in most restaurants are quite low.

A trip on a tram, trolley, or bus is about 50 stotinki; a theater ticket is 3 leva–10 leva; coffee in a moderate restaurant will run about 1 lev; a bottle of wine in a moderate restaurant is 4 leva–9 leva; museum admission averages 2 leva–5 leva, guided museum tours vary between $5 and $10 (8.5 leva and 17 leva).

CREDIT CARDS   The major international credit cards are accepted in larger stores and in the most expensive hotels and restaurants, but before you place an order, check to see whether or not you can use your card. Outside Sofia, and at any small restaurant or hotel, credit cards are almost always worthless. Bring cash. If you run into a problem, Western Union has several offices in Sofia, where you can send and receive money wires.
🛈 **Western Union** ✉ ul. Rakovski 127 ☎ 02/981-7253 or 02/988-8108.

CURRENCY   The Bulgarian *lev* (BGN) is the official currency. One hundred stotinki make up 1 lev and there are bills of 1, 2, 5, 10, 20, and 50 leva (the plural) and coins of 1, 2, 5, 10, 20, and 50 stotinki. Although prices are sometimes quoted in dollars, all goods and services (except the most expensive hotels and international airline tickets) must be paid for in leva. You may import any amount of foreign currency, including traveler's checks, and exchange foreign currency at banks, hotels, airports, border posts, and the plentiful private exchange offices (which offer the best rates and take no commission). Bring new, clean U.S. bills, as counterfeiting is a common phenomenon, and torn or marked currency will be turned away. It is possible to change traveler's checks at a few select locations, such as the airport and some major hotels, but commissions are exorbitant. In small towns traveler's checks are worthless. The ATM network is well developed, with an ATM close at hand almost everywhere in the central areas of cities and larger towns. As of this writing, exchange rates were as follows: 1.70 leva to the U.S. dollar, 2.70 leva to the pound sterling, 1.94 leva to the Euro, 1.20 leva to the Canadian dollar, 1.10 leva to the Australian dollar, 1 lev to the New Zealand dollar, and 22 stotinki to the South African rand.

V.A.T.   Bulgaria has a value-added tax (V.A.T.) of 20%. You have the right to claim the V.A.T. included in the price of goods bought for personal use upon leaving the country through a local agent if each fiscal invoice for the exported goods has a V.A.T. exceeding 200 leva. V.A.T. will not be refunded for alcoholic drinks and tobacco products. Check with a customs office for details.

PASSPORTS & VISAS

All visitors need a valid passport. Americans, Canadians, and U.K. citizens do not need visas when traveling as tourists for 30 days or less. Other tourists, traveling independently, should inquire about visa requirements at a Bulgarian embassy or consulate before entering the country. Many package tours are exempt from the visa requirement.

TELEPHONES

In order to make a phone call you can choose between dialing from your room (for a surcharge) or using the *zheton-* (token-) and card-operated pay phones in the street. Zhetons can be purchased at post offices and street kiosks for 10 stotinki each and can be used for local calls only, whereas the two types of card phones, *Mobika* and *Bulfon,* can also be used for long-distance calls. Phone cards can be purchased at post offices, hotels, and numerous street kiosks. Zheton-operated phones are silver, *Mobika* phones are blue, and *Bulfon* phones are orange. Bulgarian phone numbers can be anything from three to seven digits (country, area, and cell-phone operator codes excluded).

In Sofia, direct-dial calls to the United States can be made from the international phone office (half a block west of the main post office). You can also place a call using an AT&T USA Direct international operator.

🛈 Access Codes **AT&T USA Direct** ☎ 00-800-0010.

COUNTRY & AREA CODES For international calls to Bulgaria, the country code is 359. The access code for Sofia is 2 from outside Bulgaria and 02 from within.

TIPPING

Tips are typically expected by waiters, taxi drivers, and barbers. To tip, round out the bill by 10%–15%.

TRAIN TRAVEL

In Sofia buy tickets in advance at the ticket office (in the underpass below the National Palace of Culture) to avoid long lines at the station. In other cities get your tickets at the station. It's best to take an *ekspresni* (express) or *burzi* (fast) train, as they are the fastest and most comfortable. *Putnicheski* (passengers') trains are very old and painfully slow. Trains tend to be crowded; seat reservations are obligatory on expresses. *Purva clasa* (first class) is not much more expensive than second class and is worth it. From Sofia there are several main routes: to Varna or Burgas on the Black Sea coast; to Plovdiv and beyond to the Turkish border; to Dragoman and the Serbian border; to Kulata and the Greek border; and to Roussé and the Romanian border.

TRANSPORTATION AROUND BULGARIA

Bulgaria uses the following abbreviations in addresses: *ul.* (*ulitsa*) is street; *bul.* (*bulevard*) is boulevard; *pl.* (*ploshtad*) is square. Numbers come *after* street names, unlike the order common to Western Europe and the United States. Addresses in this chapter follow the *Bulgarian* pattern.

VISITOR INFORMATION

🛈 **National Information and Advertising Center** ✉ ul. Sveta Sofia 1 ☎ 02/987-9778 🌐 www.bulgariatravel.org. **Balkantour** ✉ bul. Stamboliiski 27 ☎ 02/988-5543. **Balkantourist** ✉ bul. Vitosha 1 ☎ 02/987-5192 🌐 www.balkantourist.bg.

WHEN TO GO

The ski season lasts from mid-December through March; the Black Sea coast season runs from May through October, reaching its peak in July and August. Fruit trees blossom in April and May; in May and early June the blossoms are gathered in the Valley of Roses; in October the fall colors are at their best.

CLIMATE Summers are warm; winters are crisp and cold. The coastal areas enjoy considerable sunshine. March and April are the wettest months inland. Even when the temperature climbs, the Black Sea breezes and the cooler mountain air prevent the heat from being overwhelming.

The following are the average daily maximum and minimum temperatures for Sofia.

Jan.	35F	2C	May	69F	21C	Sept.	70F	22C
	25	−4		50	10		52	11
Feb.	39F	4C	June	76F	24C	Oct.	63F	17C
	27	−3		56	14		46	8
Mar.	50F	10C	July	81F	27C	Nov.	48F	9C
	33	1		60	16		37	3
Apr.	60F	16C	Aug.	79F	26C	Dec.	38F	4C
	42	5		59	15		28	−2

SOFIA

Bulgaria's bustling capital stands on the high Sofia Plain, ringed by mountain ranges: the Balkan Range to the north; the Lyulin Mountains to the west; part of the Sredna Gora Mountains to the southeast; and, to the southwest, Mt. Vitosha—the city's playground—which rises to more than 7,600 feet. In the 1870s Sofia was still part of the Ottoman Empire, and one mosque still remains today. Most of the city was planned after 1880, and following the destruction of World War II many of the main buildings were rebuilt in the Socialist block-housing style. The area has been inhabited for about 7,000 years, but driving in from the airport, your first impression may be of a city besieged by hasty development, dominated by an expanse of nightmarish Socialist architecture. Moving toward the center from the suburbs, however, the unpleasantness soon gives way to eclectic urban charm, spacious parks, open-air cafés, and broad streets filled with a colorful crowd.

Exploring Sofia

Numbers in the margin correspond to points of interest on the Sofia map.

There are enough intriguing museums and musical performances to merit a lengthy stay, but you can see the main city sights in two days and enjoy the serenity of Mt. Vitosha on a third day.

⑤ Banya Bashi Dzhamiya (Banya Bashi Mosque). Consisting of a large dome and a lone minaret, this distinctive building, a legacy from the centuries of Turkish rule, was built in the 16th century. Loudspeakers on the minaret call the city's Muslim minority to prayer every day. ✉ *Bul. Maria Luiza at ul. Triyaditsa.*

⑮ Borisova Gradina (Boris's Garden). Dilapidated benches, stray dogs, overflowing garbage Dumpsters, an empty lake, a dry fountain, and neglected statues of Communist leaders mar this former haven. Nevertheless, it is huge, central, and important to the city's inhabitants. The wild woods surrounding it are good for a stroll. In summer, ice-cream vendors, children in rented battery-operated minicars, an outdoor disco, and a surprisingly pristine public pool with water slides for children bring life to the park. ✉ *Bul. Bulgaria between bul. Tsar Osvoboditel and bul. Dragan Tsankov.*

⑬ Hram-pametnik Alexander Nevski (Alexander Nevski Memorial Church). The freshly gilt onion domes of this neo-Byzantine structure dominate the city. The church was built by the Bulgarian people at the beginning of the 20th century as a token of gratitude to their Russian liberators. Inside are Venetian mosaics, magnificent frescoes, and space for a congregation of 5,000. Attend a service to hear the superb choir, and, above all, don't miss the fine collection of icons in the Crypt Museum. ✉ *Pl. Alexander Nevski* ☎ *02/981–5775* ⊘ *Wed.–Mon. 10–5:30* ⊘ *Closed Tues.*

FodorsChoice
★

⑭ Narodno Subranie (National Assembly). In 1997 CNN immortalized this squat building by repeatedly broadcasting clips of Bulgarian protesters smashing the windows and attempting to drag barricaded members of the Socialist parliament onto the plaza. Topped by the Bulgarian national flag, it is adorned with an inscription reading UNITY MAKES STRENGTH, referring to the unification of the country in 1885, a few years after the Russian army and the Bulgarian people defeated the Turks. In front of the building is a monument to Russian Tsar Alexander II, known as *Tsar Osvoboditel* (The Tsar Liberator). ✉ *Bul. Tsar Osvoboditel at pl. Narodno Subranie.*

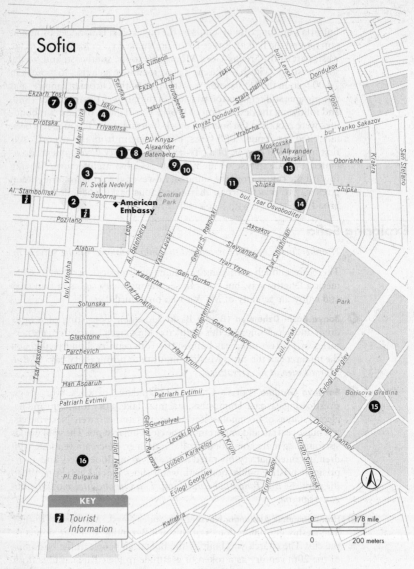

Sofia

KEY

7 Tourist
  Information

🐚 ⓲ **Natsionalen Dvorets na Kulturata** (National Palace of Culture, NDK). The large modern building has halls for conventions and cultural events, as well as the city's top-notch cinema mulitplex. Its multilevel underpass is equipped with a train-ticket office, shops, restaurants, discos, and a bowling alley. Don't miss the tallest vodka bottle in the world on the south side of the building, an entry in the *Guinness World Records* book. ✉ *Pl. Bulgaria 1.*

⓾ **Natsionalen Etnografski Muzei** (National Ethnographic Museum). The former palace of the Bulgarian tsar currently houses displays of costumes, crafts, and tools illustrating life in the country's rural areas through the 19th century. ✉ *Pl. Alexander Batenberg 1* ☎ *02/987–4191* ◷ *Weekdays 11–4.*

★ **Natsionalen Istoricheski Muzei** (National History Museum). This extraordinary museum is in a palatial mansion that was formerly the residence of deceased and controversial Communist leader Todor Zhivkov. The vast collections include priceless Thracian treasures, Roman mosaics, enameled jewelry from the First Bulgarian Kingdom (AD 600–1018), and glowing religious art that survived the centuries of Ottoman oppression. The museum is a 10-minute taxi ride from the center. City bus lines 2 and 69 pass the museum on their way out of town. ✉ *Ul. Vitoshko Lale 16* ☎ *02/955–4280* ◷ *Weekdays 9:30–6.*

❾ **Natsionalna Hudozhestvena Galeria** (National Art Gallery). In the west wing of the former tsar's palace is a collection of outstanding Bulgarian works, as well as a section devoted to foreign art. ✉ *Pl. Alexander Batenberg 1* ☎ *02/980–0093* ◷ *Tues.–Sun. 10–5:30.*

❶ **Pametnik na Sofia** (Statue of Sofia). Across the square from Partiyniyat Dom looms this imposing statue, one of the modern symbols of the city. ✉ *Pl. Alexander Batenberg.*

❽ **Partiyniyat Dom** (The Party House). The former headquarters of the Bulgarian Communist Party is prominent on a vast square. Today the parliament has its administrative offices inside the imposing Stalinist-style building; the pole on top looks bare without the gigantic red star it once supported. ✉ *Pl. Alexander Batenberg.*

❸ **Rotonda Sveti Georgi** (Rotunda of St. George). In the courtyard behind the Sheraton Hotel stands this unusual artifact, thought to be one of the oldest public buildings in Bulgaria. Built in the 4th century as a Roman temple, it has later served as both a mosque and a church. Recent restoration revealed three layers of frescoes, the earliest dating back to the 10th century. ✉ *Pl. St. Nedelya 2.*

❼ **Tsentralna Sinagoga** (Central Synagogue). This spectacular structure was erected in 1909 and has been recently refurbished. After decades of disuse it is once again open for worship, illuminated by the largest chandelier in the Balkans. ✉ *Ul. Ekzarh Yosif, behind Tsentralni Hali* ◷ *Weekdays 9–5, Sat. 9–1.*

❹ **Tsentralnata Banya** (The Central Baths). For years this former Ottoman mineral bathhouse was in ruins. Now it is being renovated to include a city museum and a hydrotherapy center. The outside of the splendid building has already been restored, displaying colorful ceramic mosaics. You can taste the hot mineral water, thought to cure respiratory diseases and ensure longevity, at the spring in the adjacent park. ✉ *Bul. Maria Luiza at ul. Triyaditsa.*

❻ **Tsentralni Hali** (Central Market Hall). The hall served as the central market during Communist times. Allowed to fall into ruin, it was closed for renovations for years. Today it is a fully functional modern indoor bazaar with cafés, restaurants, and office space that retains the bustling marketplace feel of years past. Go to the lower level to enjoy a typical Bulgarian meal amidst Roman ruins. ⊠ *Bul. Maria Luiza at ul. Ekzarh Yosif.*

② **Tsurkva Sveta Nedelya** (St. Nedelya Church). This impressive building, with its huge dome ringed by small windows, dominates the south side of St. Nedelya Square. Rebuilt after a terrorist attack in 1925, it is the latest in a series of churches that have occupied the site since the Middle Ages. ⊠ *Pl. St. Nedelya.*

⑫ **Tsurkva Sveta Sofia** (Church of St. Sofia). Dating from the 6th century, this simple brick edifice became in the mid-14th century the namesake for the city of Sofia. ⊠ *North side of pl. Alexander Nevski.*

⑪ **Tsurkva Sveti Nikolai** (Church of St. Nicholas). This ornate structure was erected between 1912 and 1914 and is commonly called The Russian Church. ⊠ *Bul. Tsar Osvoboditel at ul. Rakovski.*

Where to Eat

Sofia teems with restaurants and cafés offering high-quality but inexpensive international cuisines. If you can tolerate cigarette smoke and crowded seating, the most authentic eating experience is in a mehana, or tavern, where the music is loud and diners relax for hours over rakia and salads.

★ **$$$–$$$$** ✕ **Otvud Aleyata, Zad Shkafa** (Beyond the Alley, Behind the Cupboard). Popular with local diplomats and visiting officials, this small, upscale restaurant has innovative Bulgarian and European cuisine. There's a large selection of salads and an excellent wine list; the staff is accustomed to serving foreigners. There's a quiet patio for warm-weather dining, and in the afternoons theater performances take place upstairs in the "attic." ⊠ *Ul. Budapeshta 31* ☎ *02/983–5545 or 02/983–5581* ⌂ *Reservations essential* ▤ *DC, MC, V.*

$$–$$$$ ✕ **Restaurant Barbecue.** With a rooftop terrace for summer evenings, a cozy fireplace for winter feasts, and an indoor table-side barbecue used to grill high-quality meat and fish, this mehana is truly a fine Bulgarian restaurant. For starters, try the authentic *manastirska salata* (monastery salad), a combination of white beans, vegetables, and *pastarma* (a type of Bulgarian ham), or the mushrooms stuffed with pâté de foie gras and Roquefort. In addition to barbecued meat, fish, and chicken, they have lobster, crab, and a number of excellent veal and duck entrées. ⊠ *Ul. Tsar Ivan Assen II 38* ☎ *02/846–2802* ⌂ *Reservations essential* ▤ *No credit cards.*

$–$$$ ✕ **Flannagan's.** Though called an Irish pub, this large restaurant serves what is more traditionally considered English food. Have an English breakfast (called Irish on the menu) or a proper meal, or just go for a beer in the evening. On the ground floor of the Radisson hotel, it has a view of the whole square in front of Narodno Subranie. Half of the patrons are British or American, though journalists also frequent the place, as do Bulgarians who crave the international society and English fare. ⊠ *Radisson hotel, pl. Narodno Subranie 4* ☎ *02/933–4740* ▤ *DC, MC, V.*

$–$$ ✕ **Dani's.** Sponge-painted arty walls surround the tiny dining area of this friendly café. Don't be surprised if you find yourself sharing the large table in the middle with an ex-pat. You can choose from a list of original salad creations, pasta, or sandwiches. The soup of the day is always excellent and there is apple pie and cheesecake for dessert. In the summer you can sit on the sidewalk patio with ceramic tables in vivid colors. ⊠ *Ul. Angel Kunchev 18A* ☎ *02/987–4548* ▤ *No credit cards.*

$-$$ ✕ **Ugo.** One of a chain of pizzerias, this stylish restaurant attracts a crowd of young and trendy diners with its arty interior, round-the-clock hours, and affordable menu. Try the feta-stuffed green peppers, a typical Bulgarian invention, or choose from traditional pizzas and pasta. Inexpensive but good wine, beer, and strong liquor are also served. ⊠ *Ul. Han Krum 2* ☎ *02/989–7300* ▭ *No credit cards.*

Where to Stay

You shouldn't have trouble finding a room, even if you arrive in town without a reservation. Inexpensive lodging can be found in Sofia, though the standard Western chain hotels that cater to foreigners tend to be higher. If you are looking for budget lodging, **Balkantourist** (⊠ bul. Vitosha 1 ☎ 02/987–5192) can help you find rooms in private homes at better prices; they can also book you in a state-owned hotel.

★ $$$$ ▦ **Radisson SAS Grand Hotel.** Directly on Ploshtad Narodno Subranie and facing the Alexander Nevski Memorial Cathedral, this hotel is in the very heart of Sofia. Its proximity to the airport, the railway station, the national theater, museums, and some of the capital's best nightclubs makes it a good choice for business or leisure. The staff is fluent in English and very responsive. ⊠ *Pl. Narodno Subranie 4, 1000* ☎ *02/933–4334* ᛦ *02/933–4335* ⊕ *sas.radisson.com/sofiabg* ⫐ *136 rooms* ⌂ *2 restaurants, bar* ▭ *AE, DC, MC, V* ¡◯¡ *BP.*

$$$–$$$$ ▦ **Castle Hotel Hrankov.** At the foot of Mt. Vitosha in the suburban Dragalevtsi district, this building is a cross between a beige-and-white
FodorsChoice mountain chalet and a castle with turrets and oversize doorways. Stars
★ like Harvey Keitel, Mira Sorvino, and Jean Claude Van Damme have called it home while filming in the city. The hotel has high-quality accommodations and extensive fitness facilities; in addition, it provides shuttles to the ski slopes and helps with renting skis. ⊠ *Ul. Krusheva Gradina 53 1415* ☎ *02/932–7200* ᛦ *02/932–7327* ⊕ *www.hrankovbg.com* ⫐ *65 rooms* ⌂ *2 restaurants, 2 pools, bar* ▭ *AE, DC, MC, V* ¡◯¡ *BP.*

$$$–$$$$ ▦ **Hilton Sofia.** Right behind the National Palace of Culture (NDK), this is one of the modern architectural assets of central Sofia. Well up to Western standards of service and comfort, the hotel has all the facilities you would expect, including a multilingual staff and full business center. ⊠ *Bul. Bulgaria 1, 1421* ☎ *02/933–5000* ᛦ *02/933–5111* ⊕ *www.hilton.com* ⫐ *245 rooms* ⌂ *Restaurant, pool, bar* ▭ *AE, DC, MC, V* ¡◯¡ *BP.*

★ $$$–$$$$ ▦ **Hotel Kempinski Zografski–Sofia.** The large rooms at this luxurious highrise hotel designed in Japanese minimalist style have views of Mt. Vitosha. With audiovisual and simultaneous-translation facilities available, the hotel is a prime option for business conferences. It also has the most expensive restaurant in the entire country, Sakura, one of Bulgaria's few spots for sushi; there's also a well-regarded Italian restaurant, Parma. ⊠ *Bul. James Bourchier 100, 1407* ☎ *02/62–510* ᛦ *02/681–225* ⊕ *www.kempinski.bg* ⫐ *421 rooms* ⌂ *5 restaurants, pool, 3 bars* ▭ *AE, DC, MC, V.*

$$$–$$$$ ▦ **Sheraton Sofia Hotel Balkan.** A first-class hotel with an unbeatable central location, the Sheraton has basic (for the price) and businesslike rooms with dark-toned furnishings. Suites are done more lavishly and brightly with bigger bathtubs and views of the ploshtad Sveta Nedelya. The hotel offers free pickup from the airport upon request seven days a week. ⊠ *Pl. Sveta Nedelya 5, 1000* ☎ *02/981–6541* ᛦ *02/980–6464* ⊕ *www.starwood.com* ⫐ *188 rooms* ⌂ *3 restaurants, 3 bars* ▭ *AE, DC, MC, V* ¡◯¡ *BP.*

Nightlife & the Arts

The Arts

For a list of cultural events in Sofia, pick up a copy of *Sofia City Info Guide* from your hotel lounge or the Bulgarian *Programata,* which is distributed freely. Newsstands in Sofia carry the helpful *Sofia Echo,* an English-language newspaper that includes news and entertainment listings.

FILM Most movie theaters show recent foreign films in their original languages with Bulgarian subtitles. **The Multiplex United New Cinema** (✉ in the NDK underpass ☎ 02/951–5101) has six top-notch theaters and three cafés. You can enjoy films in 3-D in **3D Cinema Moskva** (✉ ul. Alabin 52 ☎ 02/987–3178). Smoking is allowed in **The 087-Yalta** (✉ in the underpass of the University of Sofia ☎ 02/981–6530).

GALLERIES The city has several good art galleries. The **City Art Gallery** (✉ ul. Gurko 1 ☎ 02/981–2606) has permanent exhibits of both 19th-century and modern Bulgarian paintings as well as changing exhibits showcasing contemporary artists. The **National Gallery of Foreign Art** (✉ pl. Alexander Nevski ☎ 02/980–7262) has a fine collection of Indian, African, Japanese, and Western European paintings and sculptures. The art gallery of the **Union of Bulgarian Artists** (✉ ul. Shipka 6 ☎ 02/846–7113) exhibits contemporary Bulgarian art.

MUSIC The standard of music in Bulgaria is high, whether it's performed in opera houses or symphony halls or at concerts of folk music, with its close harmonies and colorful stage displays. For ballet and opera tickets, go to the **Sofia National Opera House** (✉ ul. Vrabcha 1, at bul. Dondukov 58 ☎ 02/987–1366). Buy concert and symphony tickets at the **Zala Bulgaria** (Bulgaria Concert Hall) (✉ ul. Aksakov 1 ☎ 02/987–7656), where the Sofia Philharmonic Orchestra performs every Thursday night at 7:30.

Nightlife

BARS & NIGHTCLUBS For the latest information about the nightlife in the capital, pick up a copy of *Programata Club Guide,* a freely distributed brochure depicting the more popular bars and nightclubs, with photographs. **Backstage** (✉ bul. Vassil Levski 100 ☎ 02/846–5462) is a trendy nightclub with a spacious dance floor and quality live music. **J. J. Murphy & Co's** (✉ ul. Karnigradska 6 ☎ 02/980–2870), a genuine Irish pub, is popular with Bulgarians and the ex-pat community alike. **Mojito** (✉ ul. Ivan Vazov 12 ☎ 089–529–001), with heavy plush curtains and different music every night, is frequented by young actors who dance until dawn. **Stateside** (✉ bul. Stambolijski 34 ☎ 02/986–7983), originally owned by an American, is a low-ceiling affair with clustered tables in one chamber and live music in another, where you can enjoy an American dinner or have a drink in a prevailingly English-speaking milieu.

CASINOS Major hotels in the capital have casinos with polite English-speaking staff. Try your luck at the **International Casino Club Sheraton** (✉ pl. St. Nedelya 5, in the Sheraton hotel ☎ 02/981–5747). **Princess Casino International** (✉ Princess Hotel, bul. Maria Luiza 131 ☎ 02/931–0077) is a popular gaming spot. Gamble at **Casino** (✉ bul. James Bourchier 100, Kempinski Hotel Zografski ☎ 02/62–510).

DISCOS **Cacao** (✉ ul. Zlaten Rog 20-22) is among the trendiest dance clubs with popular European DJs behind the decks every weekend. Lively Latino music is the specialty at **Caramba** (✉ bul. Tsar Osvoboditel 4 ☎ 02/987–0778). **Chervilo** (✉ bul. Tsar Osvoboditel 9 ☎ 02/981–6633) is one of the well-established dance clubs in Sofia, drawing the capital's well-to-do twenty- and thirtysomethings. For the most adventurous, willing to taste real Bulgarian popular music, **Planeta Club** (⊠ bul. Graf Ignatiev 6 ☎ 02/987–9494) has live pop-folk performers every night.

Shopping

Department Stores

Bonjour (⊠ pl. Slaveikov 2 ⊠ ul. Alabin 93 ⊠ bul. Levski 97 ☎ no phone) stocks everything from food and wine to sporting goods, gifts, and cosmetics. The Tsentralen Universalen Magazin, better known as **TsUM** (Central Department Store ⊠ bul. Maria Luiza 2 ☎ 02/926–0600), is the closest thing to a Western-style shopping mall Bulgaria has to offer, with privately rented boutiques, cafés, and offices.

Gifts & Souvenirs

The shiny boutiques on bul. Vitosha, bul. Graf Ignatiev, and the surrounding streets are the place to go for fashion shopping. For recordings of Bulgarian music, try the underpass below the National Palace of Culture, where there are stalls selling music. Sofia has some rare antiques deals; ulitsa Rakovski is particularly full of antiques dealers.

The **Galeria Natalie** (⊠ ul. Gurko 38 ☎ 02/980–7603) carries an excellent assortment of national arts, including pottery, paintings, and a collection of handcrafted silver jewelry by Bulgarian artists. **Bulgarian Artists Magazin #10** (⊠ ul. Tsar Shishman 4 ☎ 02/980–6927) is the best of the many co-ops where Bulgarian artists display their wares; this particular shop has paintings, sculptures, hand-knitted clothes, handcrafted jewelry, and blown glass. Find arts and crafts at the shop of the **Union of Bulgarian Artists** (⊠ ul. Shipka 6). One of the most popular crafts- and souvenir-stall markets is **Nevski Pazaar,** just west of the Alexander Nevski Cathedral, with everything from antique Greek coins to original icon paintings and old Soviet whiskey flasks. For traditional Bulgarian dresses, tablecloths, and souvenirs visit the **underpass between the Presidency and the Ministerial Council.**

The Bulgarian **DIKA** (⊠ bul. Vitosha 65 ☎ 02/981–8172) has beautifully designed suits and sportswear for women. **Terranova** (⊠ bul. Vitosha at ul. Ivan Denkooglu) is great for fun, cutting-edge Italian street fashion. The four **Mason's** (⊠ ul. Solunska 34 and 39 ⊠ ul. Tsar Shishman 2 ⊠ ul. Saborna at ul. Legue, behind the Presidency) shops carry quality casual-wear collections for men, women, and children. For men's fashions, the Bulgarian **Denyl** (⊠ bul. Vitosha 43 ☎ 02/981–3998 ⊠ pl. Slaveikov 7 ☎ 02/987–3119) is a stylish alternative to pricey European designer labels.

Letostrui (⊠ ul. Rakovski 157 ☎ 02/987–3012) is a reputable (if expensive) place to start your search for antiques. For excellent regional wines and tobacco, **Bai Gencho** (⊠ bul. Yanko Sakazov 24 ⊠ ul. Rakovski 122) has one of the best selections.

Shopping Districts

Bulevard Vitosha is a lively street with many upscale shops. Moderately priced and stylish boutiques are on **ulitsa Graf Ignatiev** and **ulitsa Pirotska.** The quintessential shopping excursion is to the outdoor **Zhenski Pazaar** (⊠ ul. Stefan Stambolov, between ul. Tsar Simeon and bul. Slivnitsa), the women's market, so called for the endless stalls worked by women from neighboring villages who hawk everything from homemade brooms and lace to produce and used electronics.

Amusement Park

Sofia Land

If you are not keen on wrestling with maps and foreign traffic, **Sofia Land** (✉ bul. N. Vaptsarov) is a nice alternative to navigating the city center. In addition to a modest roller coaster, a romantic Ferris wheel, and several attractions for children, it has two restaurants, an ice-cream parlor, a bowling alley, a movie theater, and a dance club. Although far from the magnitude of American theme parks, the facilities can give you memorable, if not head-spinning, experiences.

Side Trips

Both Boyana (8 km [5 mi] southwest of Sofia) and Dragalevtsi (9 km [5½ mi] south of Sofia) are pleasant day trips to the Mt. Vitosha vicinity and can be reached by Bus 64 from Sofia.

Boyana

The little medieval **Boyana Church** is well worth a visit, as is the small, elegant restaurant of the same name, next door. The church, a historical treasure on UNESCO's World Heritage list, is closed for restoration, but a replica, complete with copies of the exquisite 13th-century frescoes, is open to visitors. ✉ *Ul. Boyansko Ezero* ⊘ *June–Aug., Thurs.–Sun. 9–1 and 2–5; Sept.–May, weekends 10–1 and 2–5.*

$–$$$ ✕ **Boyansko Hanche.** At the foot of Mt. Vitosha, this charming and authentic (but touristy) mehana has Bulgarian specialties, folk music, and dance shows with audience participation nightly at 9 PM. In the summer they have an exciting Black Sea coast fire-walking exhibition in the outdoor garden. Locals tout this mehana as the perfect spot for entertaining or holding a boisterous celebration. ✉ *Boyana district, ul. Sevastokrator Kaloyan 31* ☎ *02/856–3016* ▤ *No credit cards.*

Dragalevtsi

The **Dragalevski Manastir** (Dragalevci Monastery) stands in beech woods above the village. The complex is still used as a convent, but you can visit the 14th-century church with its outdoor frescoes. ✉ *3 km (2 mi) past Vodenicharski Mehani restaurant, Dragalevtsi.*

You can take chairlifts (beside Vodenicharski Mehani restaurant) from Dragalevtsi to the delightful resort complex of **Aleko.** In winter, it has bunny runs and sledding. In the summer, kids can run on the mountain and pick berries, hike, and look at the wildlife. From Aleko you can continue on foot for about an hour to the top of **Maluk Rezen,** the nearest peak. There are well-marked walking and ski trails.

$$–$$$ ✕ **Vodenicharski Mehani** (Miller's Tavern). Composed of three old mills linked together, this tavern, at the foot of Mt. Vitosha, serves up a folklore show and Bulgarian specialties. Try the *gyuveché* (potatoes, tomatoes, peas, and onions baked in an earthenware dish). ✉ *Dragalevtsi district (Bus 64), at southern end of town next to chairlift* ☎ *02/967–1021 or 02/967–1001* ▤ *No credit cards.*

Sofia Essentials

AIRPORTS & TRANSFERS
All international flights arrive at Sofia Airport.
🛈 **Sofia Airport** ☎ 02/937–2211; 02/937–2212 international flights; 02/937–2213 domestic flights.

TRANSFERS Bus 84 from Sofia University serves the airport. From the airport taxi stand, fares to the city center are around $24 (41 leva). If you speak some

Bulgarian and know where you're going, private taxis outside the terminal will get you there for less than half that price. Agree on the fare before starting. The Tourist Service Travel Agency operates an airport shuttle for $5 (8.5 leva) *to* the airport *from* the city center and $20 (34 leva) *from* the airport *to* the city center.

ⓘ The Tourist Service Travel Agency ⊠ ul. Rakovski 127 ☎ 02/988-8108.

BUS TRAVEL WITHIN SOFIA

Buses, trolleys, and trams run fairly often. Buy a ticket from the ticket stand near the streetcar stop and punch it into the machine on board. (Watch how other people do it.) Punch a separate ticket for larger pieces of luggage.

CAR RENTAL

You can hire a car with a driver through Balkantourist or your hotel. You can also rent a car at the airport or from one of the city's car-rental agencies.

CAR TRAVEL

From Greece, take E-79, passing through the checkpoint at Kulata; from Turkey, take E-5, passing through the checkpoint at Kapitan–Andreevo. Border crossings to Romania are at Vidin on E-79 and at Roussé on E-70.

EMERGENCIES

ⓘ Doctors & Dentists **Clinic for Foreign Citizens (St. Anna Multiprofile Medical Center)** ⊠ ul. Dimitar Mollov ☎ 02/975-9000.

ⓘ Emergency Services **Ambulance** ☎ 150. **Fire** ☎ 160. **Police** ☎ 166.

ⓘ 24-hour Pharmacies **Apteka** ⊠ pl. St. Nedelya 5 ☎ 02/950-5025.

TOURS

Guided tours of Sofia and its environs are arranged by Balkantourist or Balkantour or by major hotels. Among the possibilities are three- to four-hour tours of the principal city sights by car or minibus or a longer four- to five-hour tour that goes as far as Mt. Vitosha. As the city's sights are mostly concentrated around Ploshtad Sveta Nedelya, and are well marked, an organized tour in the center will be largely unnecessary.

TAXIS

All registered taxicabs must be yellow and should have an operating meter; rates are between 35 and 56 stotinki per 1 km (⅔ mi) and are displayed on the windows. To tip, round out the fare 5%–10%. The most reliable way to get a taxi is to order it by phone; if you hail one on the street, make sure it is a company taxi with a phone number listed on the door. Among the best established companies are Inex Taxi, Okay Supertrans, and Yes Taxi.

ⓘ **Inex Taxi** ☎ 02/91919. **Okay Supertrans** ☎ 02/973-2121. **Yes Taxi** ☎ 02/91119 or 02/91009.

TRAIN TRAVEL

ⓘ **Tsentralna Gara (Central Station)** ⊠ bul. Maria Luiza 112 ☎ 02/931-1111 or 02/932-3333. **Ticket offices** ⊠ in underpass below National Palace of Culture ☎ 02/657-185 international trains; 02/658-402 domestic trains ⊠ pl. Bulgaria 1 ☎ 02/590-136 ⊠ Rila International Travel Agency, ul. Gurko 5 ☎ 02/987-0777 or 02/987-5935.

TRANSPORTATION AROUND SOFIA

The main sights are concentrated in the center, so the best way to see the city is on foot.

TRAVEL AGENCIES

🗂 Local Agent Referrals **Carlson Wagonlit Travel** ✉ ul. Lege 10 ☎ 02/980-8126. Jamadvice **Travel & Tours** ✉ ul. Assen Zlatarov 10 ☎ 02/944-1520.

VISITOR INFORMATION

🗂 **Balkantourist** ✉ bul. Vitosha 1 ☎ 02/987-5192 ⊕ www.balkantourist.bg. **Balkantour** ✉ bul. Stamboliiski 27 ☎ 02/988-5543. *Sofia City Guide* ⊕ www. sofiacityguide.com.

THE BLACK SEA COAST

Bulgaria's most popular resort area attracts visitors from all over Europe. Its sunny, sandy beaches are backed by the easternmost slopes of the Balkan Range and, to the south, by the Strandzha Mountains. Although the tourist centers tend to be huge, state-built complexes with a somewhat lean feel, they have modern amenities. Resort complexes in the Varna region normally remain open year-round, unlike those on the southern coast, where many places shut down for the winter. In fishing villages with traditional taverns, Roman and Byzantine ruins, and peaceful swimming coves, new small, private hotels offer a welcome, affordable alternative to the resorts.

The historic port of Varna is a good center for exploration. A focal point of land and sea transportation for the region, it has museums, restaurants, and lively nightlife in summer. Albena, Zlatni Pyasutsi, and Slunchev Bryag are all modern resorts popular with Western-European and Russian tourists. Bourgas, to the south, has a rather industrial feel, but in summer numerous open-air cafés and dance clubs along the beach attract crowds of stylish and suntanned people. The fishing villages of Nesebâr and Sozopol are more attractive and tranquil. Hotels tend to be scarce in these villages, but private lodgings are easily arranged through local accommodation agencies. Besides water sports, tennis and horseback riding are available.

Varna

Bulgaria's third-largest city is easily reached by rail (about 7½ hours by express) or road from Sofia. If you plan to drive, allow time to see the **Pobiti Kamuni** (Stone Forest), a unique field of sandstone pillars just off the Sofia–Varna road between Devnya and Varna. The ancient city of Varna, named Odyssos by the Greeks, became a major Roman trading center and is now an important shipbuilding and industrial city. With its beaches and tourism, Varna has become cosmopolitan; it even holds an international film festival each August.

The **Archeologicheski Muzei** (Archaeological Museum) is one of the great—if lesser known—museums of Europe. The splendid collection includes the world's oldest gold treasures from the Varna necropolis of the 4th millennium BC, as well as Thracian, Greek, and Roman artifacts and richly painted icons. ✉ *Bul. Maria Luisa 41, in park* ☎ *052/237-057* ⊘ *Tues.–Sat. 10–5.*

The pedestrian-only **ploshtad Nezavisimost** marks the center of town. To the east, **ulitsa Knyaz Boris I** is lined with shops, cafés, and restaurants. Take a look at the lavish murals in the monumental **Tsurkva Uspenie Bogorodichno** (Cathedral of the Assumption), built between 1880 and 1886. ✉ *Pl. Mitropolit Simeon* ⊘ *Daily 7–6.*

In the extensive and luxuriant **Primorska gradina** (Seaside Park) are restaurants, an open-air theater, and the **Copernicus Astronomy Complex** (☎ 052/244–109), near the main entrance. ✉ *Southern end of bul. Primorski* ⊘ *Weekdays 8–noon and 2–5.*

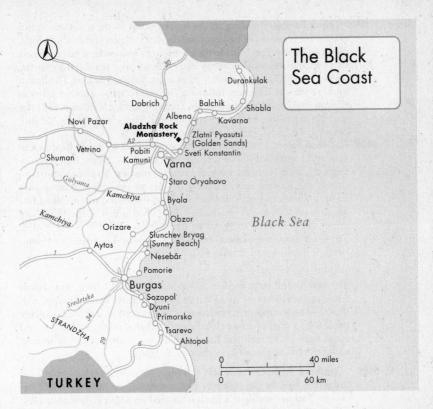

The Black Sea Coast

Durankulak
Dobrich
Balchik
6
Shabla
Albena
Kavarna
Novi Pazar
Aladzha Rock
Monastery
A2
Zlatni Pyasutsi
(Golden Sands)
Vetrino
Pobiti
Kamuni
Sveti Konstantin
Shuman
Varna
Golyama
Staro Oryahovo
Kamchiya
Byala
Kamchiya
Obzor
Black Sea
Orizare
Slunchev Bryag
(Sunny Beach)
Aytos
Nesebâr
1
Pomorie
Burgas
Sredetska
Sozopol
Dyuni
STRANDZHA
Primorsko
29
Tsarevo
6
Ahtopol

TURKEY

0 _____ 40 miles
0 _____ 60 km

Wander through the remains of the **Rimski Termi** (Roman Baths), dating from the 2nd through the 3rd centuries. Signs in English detail the various steps of the bath ritual. ⊠ *Ul. Han Krum just south of Tsurkva Sveta Bogoroditsa.*

The 1602 **Tsurkva Sveta Bogoroditsa** (Church of the Holy Virgin) is worth a look for its beautifully carved iconostasis. ⊠ *Ul. Han Krum at ul. Knyaz Alexander Batenberg.*

Running north from the cathedral is **ulitsa Vladislav Varnenchik,** with shops, movie theaters, and eateries. In the city gardens stands the **Starata Chasovnikova Kula** (Old Clock Tower; ⊠ pl. Nezavisimost), built in 1880 by the Varna Guild Association. The magnificent baroque **Dramatichen Teatur** (Drama Theater; ⊠ pl. Nezavisimost) stages local and national theater productions, as well as opera and symphonic concerts.

The restored **ulitsa Stari Druzhi** is lined with restaurants, taverns, and coffeehouses. The **Voennomorski Muzei** (Naval Museum) has displays on the early days of navigation on the Black Sea and the Danube. ⊠ *bul. Primorski 2* ☏ *052/632–018* ☉ *Tues.–Sat. 10–6.*

$$$–$$$$ ✕ **Paraklisa.** Antiquated and charming, this garden dining spot has a friendly mehana feel. The menu offers classic Bulgarian cuisine and many rakias and wines. The *pulneni chushki* (peppers stuffed with cardamom-spiced pork and rice) are especially good, though the restaurant is best known for its delicious vegetarian dishes such as *tarator* (cold garlicky yogurt and cucumber soup) and *tikvichki sus kiselo mlyako* (panfried zucchini in buttery yogurt sauce). ⊠ *Bul. Primorski 47 s/n opposite Marine Museum* ☏ *052/223–495* ▭ *No credit cards.*

$$ ✕ **Bistro Europe.** Standing on the busiest point of the main street, this restaurant is one of the best combinations of location and delicious food. You can have a seat outside under the trees and order a large portion of fresh mussels—still a rarity even here on the sea coast—that the owner himself brings every day from a small village nearby. The Italian and French specialties are following original recipes—another rarity in the country. For dessert the friendly, English-speaking waitresses will offer you an expansive list of ice creams with fruits and syrups. ⊠ *Bul. Slivnitsa 11* ☎ *052/603–950* ▤ *No credit cards.*

$$$$ ▥ **Grand Varna.** The Grand Varna is surrounded by a well-kept beach-side forest and has 24-hour room service, minibars, decent fitness equipment, and marble bathrooms. It is one of the first Black Sea resorts to deliver the Western details lacking in some of even the highest-quality Eastern European hotels. Suites have fantastic views, and it's just a few minutes on foot to the beach. ⊠ *8 km (5 mi) north of the Varna city center, dir. Sveti Konstantin (follow signs), 9006* ☎ *052/361–491* ▨ *052/ 361–920* ⊕ *www.gh-varna.com* ↴ *296 rooms, 33 suites* ♨ *3 restaurants, 3 pools, 6 bars* ▤ *AE, DC, MC, V.*

Fodor'sChoice
★

Albena

The newest and most modern Black Sea resort has a long, wide beach and clean sea. Some of its 35 hotels have extensive hydrotherapy facilities. The contemporary conveniences of this present-day tourist village come with a smaller dose of local charm, inflated prices, and menus and street signs in German and Russian. This is a resort for people seeking amenities but not necessarily the true Bulgaria.

$$–$$$$ ✕ **Hashové.** Right on the beach, this open-air restaurant has traditional Bulgarian fare. In the evenings, live entertainment includes a folk orchestra and fire-walkers; a lamb is cooked on a spit before your eyes. The bar is open all day, and the staff is attentive. ⊠ *Albena* ☎ *0579/ 629–77* ▤ *No credit cards.*

$$$$ ▥ **Dobrudzha.** Albena's most luxurious hotel is large and comfortable, with a mineral-water health spa, where you can relax in healing mud, enjoy a massage, or indulge in a curative bath. ⊠ *Bul. Bryag, off E-87, Albena exit, 9620* ☎ *0579/620–20* ▨ *0579/622–16* ⊕ *www.albena.com* ↴ *275 rooms* ♨ *2 restaurants, 3 pools, bar* ▤ *AE, DC, MC, V.*

Nesebâr

Thirty minutes by bus or car north of Bourgas is a painters' and poets' retreat. It would be hard to find a town that exudes a greater sense of age than this ancient settlement, founded by the Greeks 25 centuries ago on a rocky peninsula reached by a narrow causeway. Among its vine-covered houses are richly decorated medieval churches. Don't miss the frescoes and the dozens of small, private, cozy pubs.

$$–$$$ ✕ **Kapitanska Sreshta.** The ancient charm of this old fisherman's restaurant makes it one of the most photographed buildings in Nesebâr. Its authentic interior and top-quality seafood draw Bulgarian and foreign tourists alike, and the waiters in naval costumes provide friendly service to boisterous crowds. ⊠ *Ul. Chaika, at the pier* ☎ *0554/421–24* ▤ *No credit cards.*

Sozopol

Nestled in Byzantine ruins, the fishing port of Sozopol, with narrow, cobbled streets leading down to the harbor, was formerly known as Apollonia, the oldest of the Greek colonies in Bulgaria. It is now a popular haunt for Bulgarian and, increasingly, foreign writers and artists, who find private accommodations in the rustic Black Sea–style houses, with rough stone foundations and unpainted wood slats on the upper stories. **Lotos** (✉ ul. Moussala 7 ☎ 05514/2429) can arrange for rental of apartments and houses. Sozopol hosts the **Apollonia Arts Festival** each September, which draws musicians, playwrights, painters, dancers, and actors from all of Europe.

Black Sea Coast Essentials

TOURS

Excursions can be arranged from all resorts. There are bus excursions to Sofia from Albena and Slunchev Bryag; a one-day bus and boat trip along the Danube from neighboring resorts Zlatni Pyasutsi and Sveti Konstantin, as well as Albena; and a multiday bus tour of Bulgaria, including the Valley of Roses, departing from Zlatni Pyasutsi, Sveti Konstantin, and Albena. Contact Balkantourist for arrangements. Yacht cruises are organized by local agents.

🔳 Fees & Schedules **Balkantourist Varna** ✉ ul. Moussala 3, Varna ☎ 052/355-524.

TRANSPORTATION AROUND THE BLACK SEA COAST

Buses make frequent runs up and down the coast. Cars and bicycles can be rented. A regular boat service travels the northbound Varna–Sveti Konstantin (St. Constantine)–Zlatni Pyasutsi (Golden Sands)–Albena–Balchik route.

VISITOR INFORMATION

🔳 **Balkantourist Albena** ✉ Main Administration Bldg., Albena ☎ 0579/627–21 or 0579/621–52. **Balkantourist Burgas** ✉ Hotel Primorets, ul. Knyaz Batenberg 1, Burgas ☎ 056/843–137. **Nesebâr** ✉ Gama Tours ul. Hristo Botev 10A ☎ 0554/42–80. **Balkantourist Slunchev Bryag** ✉ Main Administration Bldg., Slunchev Bryag ☎ 0554/224–69. **Balkantourist Varna** ✉ ul. Moussala 3, Varna ☎ 052/355-524.

INLAND BULGARIA

Inland Bulgaria, despite limited hotel facilities and sometimes complicated public transportation (modern Plovdiv notwithstanding), has its own distinctive flavor. Wooded and mountainous, the interior has attractive museum villages (entire settlements are listed for preservation because of their historic cultural value) and ancient towns. The Balkan Range, or Stara Planina (old mountains), lies parallel to the lower Sredna Gora Mountains, with the verdant Rozova Dolina (Valley of Roses) between them. In the Balkan Range is the ancient capital of Veliko Turnovo; south of the Sredna Gora stretches the fertile Thracian plain, site of Bulgaria's second-largest city, Plovdiv. Between Sofia and Plovdiv lies the enchanting old town of Koprivshtitsa. Among the most popular mountain resorts are Borovets, in the Rila Mountains, and Bansko in Pirin.

Koprivshtitsa

One of Bulgaria's showpiece villages, Koprivshtitsa is set in mountain pastures and pine forests, about 3,050 feet up in the Sredna Gora range. It is 105 km (65 mi) from Sofia, reached by a minor road south from the Sofia–Kazanluk expressway. During the 19th century, Koprivshtitsa became a prosperous trading center with close ties to Istanbul. The architecture of this period, called the National Revival or Bulgarian Renaissance style, is marked by carved woodwork on broad verandas and overhanging eaves, brilliant colors, and courtyards with studded wooden gates. For centuries artists, poets, and wealthy merchants have made their homes here, and many of the historic houses are now open as museums.

$–$$ ✕📺 **Family Hotel Kalina.** Surrounded by a beautiful garden, this small hotel is in the central part of town. All rooms have balconies, private baths, telephones, and TVs. The hotel also has laundry service. For recreation, you can play table tennis or chess. ✉ *Ul. Hadzhi Nencho Palaveev 35* ☎ *07184/20–32* 🛏 *6 rooms* ⚲ *Restaurant* ▭ *No credit cards.*

$–$$ 📺 **Trayanova Kushta.** Uphill from the town square, this charming inn has rustic rooms furnished in the traditional National Revival style, with woven rugs and low beds. One room has a fireplace; all have shared baths. The intimate mehana Byaloto Konche (The White Foal) has traditional Bulgarian dishes. ✉ *Ul. Gerniloto 5, 2090* ☎ *07184/22–50* 🛏 *6 rooms with shared bath* ⚲ *Restaurant* ▭ *No credit cards.*

Troyan

Troyan is a tiny, sleepy, old place. A couple of miles from town stands the **Troyanski Manastir** (Troyan Monastery), built during the 1600s in the heart of the mountains. Its church was painstakingly remodeled during the 19th century, and its icons, wood carvings, and frescoes are classic examples of National Revival art. Here at the monastery, monks still brew the nation's most famous brand of rakia, Troyanska Slivova. ✉ *5 km (3 mi) east of Troyan* 🕐 *Daily 8–6.*

Veliko Turnovo

This town of panoramic vistas, about 200 km (124 mi) northeast of Sofia, rises up against steep mountain slopes through which the Yantra River runs its jagged course. From the 12th through 14th centuries, Veliko Turnovo was the capital of the Second Bulgarian Kingdom. Damaged by repeated Ottoman attacks, and again by an earthquake in 1913, it has been reconstructed and is now a museum city of marvelous relics. Ideally, you should begin at a vantage point above the town in order to get an overview of its design and character.

In a large, National Revival–style house, the **Muzei na Vuzrazhdaneto i Uchreditelnoto Subranie** (Museum of the National Revival and the Constitutional

Assembly) has three floors of exhibits. The first floor has a collection of medieval icons and local craftwork; the second has photos and documents detailing the national liberation movement; the third has the hall where the first Bulgarian parliament drafted the country's first constitution. ⊠ *Ul. Nicola Picolo 2* ☎ *062/29–821* ⊙ *Wed.–Sun. 9–noon and 1–6.*

Tsarevets, a hill on the east end of town, almost encircled by the Yantra River, is where the palace and patriarchate of the Second Bulgarian Kingdom stood. The area is under restoration, and steep paths and stairways allow you to view the extensive ruins of the royal palace. On summer nights a spectacular sound-and-light show brings the royal hill to life. The prominent attraction on the south side of Tsarevets is **Balduinova Kula** (Baldwin's Tower), the 13th-century prison of Baldwin of Flanders, onetime Latin emperor of Constantinople. On the west side of the hill stands the 13th-century **Tsurkva na Chetiri-desette Muchenitsi** (Church of the Forty Martyrs), with its Turnovo-school frescoes and two inscribed columns, one dating from the 9th century. On the north side of Tsarevets, the **Tsurkva na Sveti Petur i Pavel** (Church of Sts. Peter and Paul) has vigorous murals both inside and out. Across the river to the west, reached by a bridge near the Forty Martyrs, the restored **Tsurkva na Sveti Dimitur** (Church of St. Dimitrius) was built on the spot where the Second Bulgarian Kingdom was proclaimed in 1185.

Near the center of town is **ulitsa Samovodene,** lined with restored crafts workshops—a fascinating place to linger and a good place to find souvenirs, Turkish candy, or a charming café.

$–$$ ✕ **The City Pub.** If you've come to Veliko Turnovo, you can't miss this popular British pub. You can eat or drink here at any time of day and night, and it is always lively. Christmas and football championships days have witnessed dancing on tables and singing. ⊠ *Ul. Hristo Botev 15* ☎ *062/637–824* ▭ *No credit cards.*

$$$$ ▥ **Veliko Turnovo Interhotel.** In the middle of the most historic part of the town, this modern hotel has exceptional facilities. Rooms are big and airy with such amenities as TVs, phones, desks, and modern bathrooms. ⊠ *Ul. Aleksander Penchev 2, 5000* ☎ *062/621–595* 🖷 *062/639–859* 🖃 *201 rooms, 2 suites* ♨ *3 restaurants, pool, 3 bars* ▭ *AE, DC, MC, V.*

$$$–$$$$ ▥ **Hotel Millennium.** Modern and centrally situated, this hotel is a popular and less expensive alternative to the Veliko Turnovo. It has smart rooms and clean, contemporary furnishings. ⊠ *Ul. Tsanko Tserkovski 20* ☎ *062/616–01* 🖷 *062/616–01* 🖃 *16 rooms* ♨ *Restaurant, bar* ▭ *No credit cards* ⅋ *BP.*

Etur

This historic village sits on the banks of the Sivek, a small branch of the Yantra River, 9 km (6 mi) south of Gabrovo. The mill here is still powered by a stream, and local craftspeople continue to be trained in traditional skills.

Kazanluk

In this town at the eastern end of the Valley of Roses, you can trace the history of rose cultivation, Bulgaria's oldest industry. Each June the town hosts the Festival of Roses, with folk dancing, art exhibits, and rose-picking demonstrations.

Plovdiv

Bustling with college students and new businesses, Bulgaria's second-largest city, Plovdiv, is one of the oldest settlements in Europe and now a major industrial, cultural, and intellectual center. Closed to cars to preserve the original cobblestone, the breathtaking, lantern-lit **Stariat Grad** (Old Town) lies on the hillier southern side of the Maritsa River.

Below the medieval gateway of Hisar Kapiya, the **Georgiadieva Kushta** (Georgiadi House) is a grandiose example of National Revival–style architecture; it also contains a small museum dedicated to the April 1876 uprising against the Turks. ⊠ *Ul. Starinna 1* ☎ *032/623–378* ⊙ *Wed.–Sun. 9:30–12:30 and 2–5.*

The old **Kapana District** (⊠ northwest of pl. Stamboliiski) has narrow, winding streets lined with restored shops and cafés. The exquisite hilltop **Rimski amfiteatur** (Roman amphitheater), discovered and excavated in 1981, has been renovated. In summer the theater is used for dramatic and musical performances. ⊠ *Ul. Tsar Ivailo.*

The **Natsionalen Archeologicheski Muzei** (National Archaeological Museum) has a replica of the 4th-century BC Panagjuriste Gold Treasure and a wealth of ancient Thracian artifacts from Plovdiv and the surrounding region. ⊠ *Pl. Suedinenie 1* ☎ *032/624–339* ⊙ *Tues.–Sun. 9–12:30 and 2–5:30.*

The **Natsionalen Etnografski Muzei** (National Ethnographic Museum), in the former home of a Greek merchant, Arghir Kuyumdzhioglu, is an elegant example of the National Revival style, which made its first big splash in Plovdiv. The museum is filled with artifacts from that fertile period. ⊠ *Ul. Dr. Stoyan Chomakov 2* ☎ *032/624–261* ⊙ *Tues.–Sun. 9–noon and 2–5.*

The steep, narrow **ulitsa Strumna** is lined with workshops and boutiques, some reached through little courtyards. Beyond the railings and past the jewelry and leather vendors in the center of Stamboliiski Square stand the remains of the 2nd-century **Rimski stadion** (Roman stadium). ⊠ *Ul. Saborna and ul. Knyaz Alexander I.*

$$–$$$$ ✕ **Apolonia.** A spacious patio and several dining rooms in an Old Town National Revival–style house lend themselves to a leisurely meal. The food is better than average Bulgarian fare, the service is friendly, and there's an English-language menu available. There is often piano music or karaoke, as well as Internet service. Reservations are recommended. ⊠ *Ul. Vasil Kanchev 1* ☎ *032/632–699* ▤ *No credit cards.*

$$–$$$ ✕ **Alafrangite.** This charming mehana, in a restored 19th-century house with a vine-covered courtyard, is in the old part of town. One of the specialties is *kyopoolu* (vegetable puree of baked eggplant, peppers, and tomatoes). ⊠ *Ul. Kiril Nektariev 17* ☎ *032/269–595* ▤ *No credit cards.*

$–$$$ ✕ **Puldin.** On a hill in the center of old town, this folk restaurant has a romantic subterranean dining room with a waterfall and live piano music. Order the excellent *pulneni chushki* (peppers stuffed with meat, spices, and rice), served with yogurt, for a taste of Bulgarian home cooking. ⊠ *Ul. Knyaz Tseretelev 3* ☎ *032/631–720* ▤ *AE, DC, MC, V.*

$$$$ ▥ **Novotel Plovdiv.** Large, modern, and well equipped, this Novotel has all the conveniences you'd expect from a Western luxury hotel. ⊠ *Ul. Zlatyu Boyadzhiev 2, 4000* ☎ *032/652–505* 🖷 *032/551–979* ⊕ *www. plovdivhotels.com* ⤢ *315 rooms, 9 suites* ♨ *2 restaurants, pool, bar* ▤ *AE, DC, MC, V* ⏐◉⏐ *BP.*

$$$–$$$$ ▥ **Maritsa.** Centrally located, this hotel is close to the city's main attractions as well as the biggest business event in Plovdiv—the International Fair. Rooms are freshly painted, modern, and business-efficient with desks.

✉ *Bul. Tsar Boris III Obedinitel 42, 4000* ☎ *032/552–735* ⊕ *www.plovdivhotels.com* ⤴ *132 rooms, 20 suites* ♨ *Restaurant, bar* ⊟ *AE, DC, MC, V* ⊚ *BP.*

Borovets

Slightly more than 4,300 feet up the northern slopes of the Rila Mountains, this is an excellent walking center and winter-sports resort. It is well equipped with hotels, folk-style taverns, and ski schools. The winding mountain road leads back to Sofia, 70 km (43 mi) from here, past the Iskur Reservoir, the largest lake in the country.

Rila

Fodor's Choice ★ **Rilski Manastir** (Rila Monastery), founded by St. Ivan of Rila in the 10th century, lies in a steep, forested valley past the village of Rila. The monastery has suffered so frequently from fire that most of it is now a grand National Revival reconstruction, although a rugged 14th-century tower has survived. The striking mountain retreat hosts flocks of storks. Part of the complex has been turned into a museum, and some of the monks' cells are now guest rooms. You can see 14 small chapels with frescoes from the 15th and 17th centuries, a lavishly carved altarpiece in the new Church of the Assumption, the sarcophagus of St. Ivan of Rila, icons, and ancient manuscripts.

Bansko

The houses in this small, picturesque town at the foot of the Pirin Mountains may seem inaccessible with their lattice windows and heavy gates—designed to fend off Ottoman invaders—but the rooms inside these "fortresses" are delicate and beautiful, with carved ceilings and handmade rugs. Generally, these homes are not open as museums, but by planning an overnight stay, or even politely asking, you may be able to see some interiors. Tourism is booming in Bansko, with numerous plans in the works for expanding facilities. The **Tzarkvata Sveta Troitsa** (Holy Trinity Church), built in 1835, along with the tower and the town clock, is part of the architectural complex in the center of the town. ✉ *Pl. Vuzrazhdane 2.*

Privately owned bed-and-breakfasts are on almost every street, and the Vrah Vihren mountain is covered with sprawling ski resorts. The former offer small rooms and home-cooked meals, whereas the latter are usually comfortable but lack charm. Reservations are necessary at the height of ski season (March) and around December 8 (Students' Day) and New Year's.

$–$$ ✕ **Dedo Pene.** A string of cowbells clangs as you open the heavy wooden door of this traditional *krutchma* (tavern). A waitress will pour you a glass of homemade red wine before you've hung your coat on the rack. The walls are adorned with furs, stuffed bobcats, and handwoven rugs. This pagan tavern exudes authenticity (along with the aroma of uncured hides) and serves up hearty medieval meat dishes. ✉ *Southeast corner of Tsentralnia Ploshtad* ☎ *07443/50–71 or 07443/22–23* ⊟ *No credit cards.*

$$–$$$ ▥ **Pirin Hotel.** This popular hotel is large and modern, but the plain wooden furniture and wool blankets give it a state-owned feel. In the winter you can rent skis from the hotel, and you get free transport to the slopes. ✉ *Ul. Tsar Simeon 68* ☎ *07443/25–36* ⊟ *07443/42–44* ⤴ *55 rooms, 7 suites* ♨ *2 restaurants, bar* ⊟ *DC, MC, V.*

Inland Bulgaria Essentials

TOURS

Organized tours set out from Sofia, each covering different points of interest. Check with your hotel information desk or with Balkantourist or Balkantour.

TRANSPORTATION AROUND INLAND BULGARIA

Rail and bus services cover all parts of inland Bulgaria, but the best bet is to rent a car. To hire a driver, check with Balkantourist.

VISITOR INFORMATION

🛈 **Balkantourist Plovdiv** ✉ bul. Bulgaria 106 ☎ 032/632–180. **Balkantourist Veliko Turnovo** Grand Hotel Veliko Turnovo ✉ ul. Al. Penchev 2 ☎ 062/633–975. **Balkantourist Borovetz** ✉ Hotel Rila ☎ 7128/658.

CROATIA
ZAGREB, ISTRIA, DALMATIA

CROATIA'S CALM BLUE SEA, majestic mountains, and lovingly preserved historical buildings belie a checkered past. Like its Balkan neighbors, the country has a history shadowed by conflict and political strife.

The region's earliest inhabitants were the Illyrians, and two principal tribes, the Delmata and the Histri, gave their names to Dalmatia and Istria, respectively. The Greeks arrived in the 4th century BC, setting up various colonies along the coast. In the 2nd century BC, feeling threatened by the Illyrians, the Greeks called for Roman assistance, and a period of Roman expansion began.

The Romans set up military outposts and administrative centers, the most important being Pola (Pula) in Istria and Salona (Solin) in Dalmatia. In 395, Roman territory was divided into the western and eastern empires, a decisive event in Balkan history, as this same border was later to divide Catholics and Orthodox, Croats and Serbs. The 7th century saw the arrival of Slavic tribes, among them the Croats. Relations with the Latin-speaking Roman population were initially fraught, but with time the two groups assimilated.

In 910, the Croatian leader Tomislav united Dalmatia and Pannonia and with the Pope's consent took the title of king. When the Christian church split between Rome and Constantinople in 1054, Croatian royalty sided with Rome. In 1091, King Zvonimir died without heirs, and the Croatian crown was ceded to Hungary. Thus from the late 11th century to the mid-19th century, much of inland Croatia was governed by a local *ban* (viceroy), answerable to the Habsburgs.

Meanwhile the coast, Istria, and Dalmatia (excluding Dubrovnik, which remained an independent republic) came under the rule of Venice. Lying on the trade route to the Orient, port towns such as Split, Hvar, and Korčula flourished, and many of the regions' finest buildings date from this period.

By the 16th century the threat of a third Balkan presence, the Ottoman Turks, was looming on the horizon. The Venetian port towns enclosed themselves within sturdy fortifications against attack from the sea, while the Habsburgs, fearing Turkish expansion overland, created the *Vojna Krajina* (Military Frontier) and employed mercenaries to guard this buffer zone between Austria and the Turkish-occupied territory to the southeast. These recruits were predominantly Orthodox Christians fleeing the Turks in Serbia, and they enjoyed a certain autonomy until the Vojna Krajina was united with the rest of Croatia in the late 19th century. The creation of the Krajina explains the presence of the Serb communities within Croatia that became a major force during the war of the 1990s.

Venice fell in 1797, and by the 19th century all of Croatia was under Austria-Hungary. A Pan-Slavic movement was born, calling for Croats and Serbs to unite, and with the demise of the Habsburgs at the end of World War I, Croatia became part of the Kingdom of the Serbs, Croats, and Slovenes. However, Croatian nationalists soon objected to being ruled by Serbian royalty, and when the country was renamed Yugoslavia (Land of the Southern Slavs) in 1929, Ante Pavelić founded the Ustaše Croatian Liberation Movement. In 1934, Croatian and Macedonian extremists assassinated the Yugoslav king, Alexander.

After Germany declared war on Yugoslavia in 1941, Paveliča set up the Independent State of Croatia (NDH), notorious for the mass murder of Jews, Serbs, and Gypsies in the concentration camps within its borders. Out of retaliation, Josip Broz Tito founded the Partizan movement, aimed at pushing Fascist forces out of Yugoslavia. When the war ended, Tito created the Socialist Federal Republic of Yugoslavia with Croatia as one of six constituent republics. The Tito years saw a period of peace and prosperity, and during the 1960s Croatia became a popular international tourist destination.

Following Tito's death in 1980, an economic crisis set in, and relations between Croatia and the Serb-dominated Yugoslav government deteriorated. In 1989, Franjo Tudjman founded the Croatian Democratic Union (HDZ), calling for an independent Croatia, while in Serbia the nationalist leader Slobodan Milošević rose to power. The events that followed led to civil war.

In 1991, incited by Belgrade media reports that Croatia was returning to the days of the Ustaše, Croatian Serbs proclaimed the Republic of Serbian Krajina, arguing that if Croatia took autonomy from Belgrade, they would demand autonomy from Zagreb. Thanks to backing from the Serb-dominated federal Yugoslav People's Army (JNA), by the end of the year Krajina, which represented nearly one-third of Croatia, was under Serb control.

In January 1992, Croatia was recognized by the European Union, and United Nations peacekeeping troops were sent in to oversee a cease-fire. After a period of relative calm, Croat forces crossed UN lines in May 1995 and took back a Serb-held enclave in western Slavonia. Encouraged by their success, they launched the surprise *Oluja* (Operation Storm) that August, overrunning the Krajina and causing 200,000 Serbs to flee the country.

Meanwhile, there was evidence of growing corruption within the HDZ, and Croatia faced increasing international isolation for failing to respect human rights. President Tudjman's death in December 1999 saw the demise of his party. In January 2000, a new center-left alliance was voted into power, with Ivica Račan as prime minister and Stjepan Mesić as president. Mesić immediately announced that all refugees who had fled Croatia should be allowed to return to their homes, and his victory was widely welcomed in the West.

After a decade of political and economic isolation, Croatia is now back on the maps as a desirable holiday destination. Croats continue to struggle against problems of severe unemployment, low wages, and high living costs, but foreign visitors can expect more than comfortable accommodations, excellent restaurants serving fresh seasonal produce, and a stunning coastline, still as beautiful as it ever was.

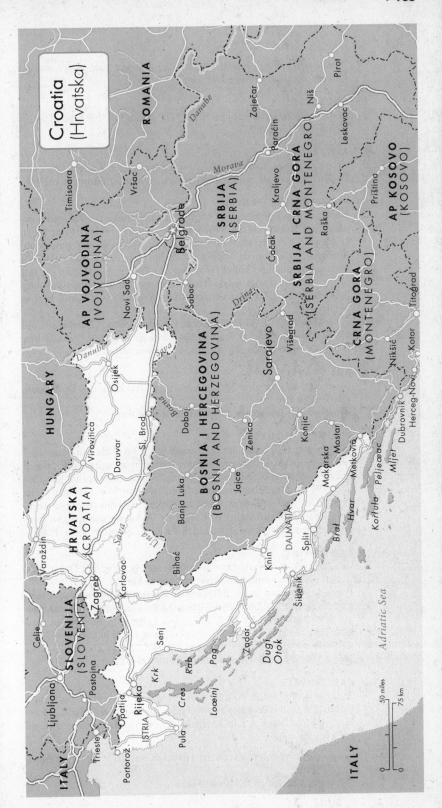

CROATIA A TO Z

To research prices, get advice from other travelers, and book travel arrangements, visit www.fodors.com.

ADDRESSES

In street addresses, the abbreviation "bb" stands for "bez broja," which means "no number."

AIR TRAVEL

Croatia Airlines operates internal services between Zagreb, Split, and Dubrovnik, as well as international services to most European capitals.

BOAT & FERRY TRAVEL

During the high season (July to August), Jadrolinija coastal ferries depart from Rijeka, in the Kvarner region, most evenings to arrive in Dubrovnik in early afternoon the following day (journey time is approximately 20 hours), stopping at Zadar, Split, Stari Grad (Island of Hvar), Korčula, and Sobra (Island of Mljet) en route. During the rest of the year the service is less frequent. Ferries are also popular routes between Italy and Croatia (particularly Ancona to Split and Bari to Dubrovnik).

⚑ **Adriatica** ☎ 39-041/781-861 in Venice, Italy ⊕ www.adriatica.it. **Jadrolinija** ☎ 051/666-111 ⊠ www.jadrolinija.hr. **Blue Line SEM Marina** ☎ 021/338-292 ⊕ www.bli-ferry.com. **SNAV** ☎ 39-081/428-5111 in Naples, Italy ⊕ www.snavali.com.

BUS TRAVEL

Buses connect Zagreb to Split, a 6-hour trip, and Zagreb to Dubrovnik, a 10½-hour trip.

⚑ **National Bus Information** ☎ 060/313-333 ⊕ www.akz.hr.

BUSINESS HOURS

In the main cities banks are open weekdays 7 AM–7 PM and Saturday 7 AM–11 AM. In smaller towns, they have shorter hours and are often closed during lunchtime. Museums vary greatly, but most are open 9 AM–2 PM and are closed on either Sunday or Monday. Many have extended hours through summer. In Zagreb, shops and department stores are open weekdays 8 AM–8 PM and Saturday 8 AM–1 PM. Along the coast, most shops are open weekdays 8 AM–1 PM and 5–8 PM, and Saturday 8 AM–1 PM.

CAR RENTAL

Avis, Budget, and Hertz have offices in Zagreb, Split, and Dubrovnik. Rental prices are similar to those in Western Europe.

⚑ **Avis** ⊠ Kršnjavoja 1, Zagreb ☎ 01/483-6006 ⊕ www.avis.hr ⊠ Hotel Marjan, obala K Branimira, Split ☎ 021/342-976 ⊠ V Nazora 9, Dubrovnik ☎ 020/422- 043. **Budget** ⊠ Praška 5, Zagreb ☎ 01/480-5687 ⊕ www.budget.hr ⊠ Hotel Marjan, obala K Branimira, Kaštela ☎ 021/345-700 ⊠ obala Stjepana Radića 20, Dubrovnik ☎ 020/418-997. **Hertz** ⊠ Mažuranićev trg 2, Zagreb ☎ 01/484-7222 ⊕ www.hertz.hr ⊠ Tomića Stine 9, Split ☎ 021/360-455 ⊠ F Supila 5 ☎ 020/425-000.

CAR TRAVEL

A car is really more trouble than it's worth in Zagreb, Split, and Dubrovnik, and is certainly not necessary for visiting the islands. However, you may want to rent a vehicle for covering the longer mainland stretches.

EMERGENCIES For motorist information contact Hrvatska Autoclub (Croatian Automobile Club).

⚑ **Hrvatska Autoclub** ☎ 987 ⊕ www.hak.hr.

GASOLINE Gas stations are open daily 7 AM–7 PM; from June to September, many stations are open until 10 PM. In the bigger cities and on main international roads some stations offer 24-hour service. All pumps sell Eurosuper 95, Super 98, Normal, and Eurodiesel.

PARKING The historic centers of walled medieval towns along the coast (Split, Hvar, Korčula, and Dubrovnik) are completely closed to traffic, putting heavy pressure on the number of parking spaces outside the fortifications.

ROAD CONDITIONS The coastal route down to Dubrovnik is scenic but tiring and can be notoriously slippery when wet. During winter, driving through the inland region of Lika, between Zagreb and Dalmatia, is occasionally made hazardous by heavy snow. It's advisable not to take a car to the islands, but if you do decide to drive, remember that the roads are narrow, twisty, and poorly maintained.

RULES OF THE ROAD Croatians drive on the right and follow rules similar to those in other European countries. Speed limits are 50 kph (30 mph) in urban areas, 80 kph (50 mph) on main roads, and 130 kph (80 mph) on motorways. Seat belts are compulsory. The permitted blood alcohol limit is 0.5%; drunk driving is punishable and can lead to severe fines.

CUSTOMS & DUTIES

Duty-free allowances for those entering the country are 200 cigarettes, 1 liter of spirits, and 2 liters of wine.

EATING & DRINKING

Formal dining takes place in a *restoran* (restaurant), whereas lighter meals accompanied by a plentiful supply of local wine are served in a more rustic *konoba* (tavern). Classic starters are *pršut* (cured ham) and *paški sir* (sheep's-milk cheese from the island of Pag), *juha* (soup), or *salata od hobotnice* (octopus salad).

In Dalmatia, the menu tends to quite basic, featuring *rižot* (risotto) followed by fresh fish prepared *na žaru* (barbecue-style) served with *blitva sa krumpirom* (Swiss chard and potatoes in olive oil and garlic). In Istria, the choice is wider and more refined: besides fish and seafood, the specialties are *tartufi* (truffles) served with either pasta (the local variation is *fuži*) or steak; the salads are exceptionally colorful, containing mixed leaves such as *rukola* (rocket) and radicchio.

Wherever you go, fish are priced by weight (Kn/kg) rather than by portion and can be divided into two categories: Class I, which encompasses quality white fish like *zubatac* (dentrix), *šampier* (John Dory), and *orada* (gilthead bream); and the cheaper Class II blue fish, including *skuše* (mackerel) and *srdele* (sardines).

Inland, meat dishes are more popular. Balkan favorites such as *janjetina* (spit-roast lamb), *kobasica* (sausage), *gulaš* (goulash), and *čevapčići* (kebobs) are widespread, and the Zagreb area is noted for *purica* (roast turkey).

Popular desserts are *palačinke* (pancakes) and baklava (just like in Greece).

WHAT IT COSTS In Croatian kuna			
$$$$	**$$$**	**$$**	**$**
AT DINNER over 80	60–80	35–60	under 35

Prices are for a main course.

EMBASSIES & CONSULATES

All the main foreign embassies are found in Zagreb; the British also have consulates in Split and Dubrovnik.

🇦🇺 **Australian Embassy** ⊠ Nova Ves 11, Zagreb ☎ 01/489–1200. **Canadian Embassy** ⊠ Prilaz Gjure Deželića 4, Zagreb ☎ 01/488–1200. **U.K. Embassy** ⊠ Vlaška 121, Zagreb ☎ 01/455–5310. **U.K. Consulate** ⊠ Bunieva Poljana 3, Dubrovnik ☎ 020/324–598 ⊠ Obala Hrvatskog Narodnog Preporoda 10, Split ☎ 021/341–464. **U.S. Embassy** ⊠ Hebrangova 2, Zagreb ☎ 01/661–2200.

LANGUAGE

The country's official language is Croatian, a Slavic language that uses the Latin alphabet. In Istria signs are posted in both Croatian and Italian, and many towns and villages have two names (one Croatian, one Italian), which can be confusing. Throughout the country, English, Italian, and German are widely spoken by people working in tourism.

LODGING

Croatia offers a wide choice of lodgings: hotels, apartments, rooms in private homes, campsites, and agritourism (working farms offering accommodation). Hotel prices tend to be on a par with those in Western Europe. You can find some excellent low-season offers, but prices skyrocket through July and August with an influx of German and Italian visitors.

Tourism started here in the late 1800s under the Habsburgs, and along the coast you'll find a number of grand hotels built for the Central European aristocracy of the time. The second stage of tourist development took place between the 1960s and 1980s in Tito's Yugoslavia. The resulting Socialist-era hotels tend to be vast, modern structures slightly lacking in soul but endowed with excellent sport and recreation facilities.

Since the opening of the Croatian property market to foreign investors, some hotels have been sold and renovated, and others are closed pending sale. In addition, a number of small, luxurious private hotels have popped up, notably in Istria.

Along the coast, tourist agencies can help you find rooms in private homes. Standards are high, and en-suite bathrooms and self-catering facilities are the norm. Host families are generally friendly and hospitable, and many visitors find a place they like, then return year after year.

WHAT IT COSTS In Croatian kuna				
	$$$$	$$$	$$	$
FOR 2 PEOPLE	over 1,200	800–1,200	550–800	under 550

Prices are for a standard double room in high season.

MAIL & SHIPPING

Airmail letters and postcards take about five days to reach other European countries and two weeks to get to Australia, Canada, and the United States. Internet cafés are popping up all over the place and can even be found in small towns on the islands. To send a postcard costs 4 Kn to Europe, 5 Kn to the United States. A letter costs 7.20 Kn to Europe, 10.20 Kn to the United States.

MONEY MATTERS

ATMS   ATMs are now found throughout the country, even on the islands.

CREDIT CARDS   Major credit cards are accepted in most shops, hotels, and restaurants.

CURRENCY
The Croatian currency is called the kuna (Kn), which is made up of 100 lipa. The kuna is not yet fully convertible, so you cannot buy the currency outside of Croatia or exchange it once outside the country.

CURRENCY EXCHANGE
You can exchange money and traveler's checks in a *banka* (bank) or *mjenjačnica* (exchange office). Rates for changing currency and traveler's checks are usually about the same.

NATIONAL HOLIDAYS
January 1 (New Year's Day), January 6 (Epiphany), Easter Sunday and Monday, May 1 (May Day), May 30 (National Day), June 22 (Anti-Fascist Day), August 5 (National Thanksgiving Day), August 15 (Assumption Day), October 8 (Independence Day), November 1 (All Saints' Day), December 25–26 (Christmas).

PASSPORTS & VISAS
Australian, Canadian, U.S., and U.K. citizens do not need visas to enter the country if they plan to stay for 90 days or less.

SAFETY
Croatia is relatively safe by Western standards, and there are no particular local scams. Violent crime is rare. Be on guard for pickpockets in crowded markets, and don't wander alone down dark streets at night.

TAXES & SERVICE CHARGES
Foreigners who spend over 500 Kn in one place can reclaim *PDV* (tax) return upon leaving the country. To do this, you need to present the receipts and the goods bought at *carina* (customs) at the airport, ferry port, or border crossing on your way out of the country.

TELEPHONES
You can make calls from the *pošta* (post office), where you enter a kiosk and pay when you have finished, or from a public telephone booth on the street, where magnetic phone cards are necessary.

COUNTRY CODE
The country code for Croatia is 385. When dialing from outside the country, drop the initial "0" from the area code.

INTERNATIONAL CALLS
To make an international call, dial "00," then the appropriate country code (Australia 61; Canada 1; U.S. 1; and U.K. 44).
International Directory Assistance ☎ 902.

LOCAL CALLS
To make a local call, dial the area code (if you are not already in that area) followed by the number you wish to reach.
Local Directory Assistance ☎ 988.

TIPPING
When eating out, if you have enjoyed your meal and are satisfied with the service, it is customary to leave a 10% tip. It is not usual to tip in cafés or bars. Maids and taxi drivers are not usually tipped. Tour guides do receive a tip, especially if they are particularly good.

TRAIN TRAVEL
Zagreb is connected to Split by rail (journey time approximately eight hours), but there is no line south of Split to Dubrovnik. International services run from Zagreb to the European cities of Ljubljana, Budapest, Belgrade, Vienna, Munich, Berlin, and Venice.
International Train Information ☎ 01/481-1892.

RAIL PASSES
The "Zone D" Interail pass is valid for Croatia, but Eurail is not.

VISITOR INFORMATION
🏛 **Croatian Tourist Board** ✉ Iblerov trg 10/4, Zagreb, 10000 ☎ 01/469-9333 ⊕ www. croatia.hr.

WHEN TO TOUR
During peak season (July and August) the coast is hot, crowded, and expensive, but it offers a good range of open-air cultural events and a vibrant nightlife to compensate. For a more peaceful holiday by the sea, try to tour in early summer (June) or late summer (September). The capital, Zagreb, remains animated the year through, with little seasonal variation in hotel prices.

ZAGREB

The capital of Croatia, Zagreb, with a population of roughly 1 million, lies between the north bank of the Sava River and the southern slopes of Mt. Medvednica. The Romans are said to have established a municipality of sorts here, but it was destroyed around AD 600, when Croatian tribes moved in.

Like so many other notable European cities, Zagreb started out as a strategic crossroads along an international river route, which was followed much later by north–south and east–west passage by road and then rail. For much of its history the city also served as a bastion on a defensive frontier, pounded for half a millennium by thundering hordes of invaders, among them Hungarians, Mongols, and Turks.

From the late Middle Ages until the 19th century, Zagreb was composed of two adjoining but separate towns situated on the high ground (Gornji Grad), one town secular, the other religious. In 1242, the secular town, named Gradec (Fortress), was burned to the ground in a wave of destruction by the Tartars, after which it locked itself up behind protective walls and towers. It is from this time that the real Zagreb (Behind the Hill) began to evolve; it was accorded the status of a free royal city in the same year by the Hungarian king Bela IV. In the 15th century, the ecclesiastical center, named Kaptol (Chapter House), also enclosed itself in defensive walls in response to the threat of a Turkish invasion.

When Zagreb became the capital of Croatia in 1557, the country's parliament began meeting alternately in Gradec and Kaptol. When Kaptol and Gradec were finally put under a single city administration in 1850, urban development accelerated. The railway reached Zagreb in 1862, linking the city to Vienna, Trieste, and the Adriatic. It was at this time that Donji Grad (Lower Town) came into being. Lying between Gornji Grad and the main train station, it was designed to accommodate new public buildings—the National Theater, the university, and various museums. Built in grandiose style and interspersed by wide tree-lined boulevards, parks, and gardens, it makes a fitting monument to the Habsburg era.

The Tito years brought a period of increasing industrialization coupled with urban expansion, as the new high-rise residential suburb of Novi Zagreb was constructed south of the Sava. In 1991, the city escaped the war of independence relatively unscathed, but for an attempted rocket attack on the Croatian Parliament building in Gradec. Zagreb did, however, suffer severe economic hardship as the country's industries collapsed, post-Communist corruption set in, and an influx of refugees—mainly Croats from Herzegovina—arrived in search of a better life.

Since 2000, public morale has picked up considerably: trendy street cafés are thriving, a number of smart new stores have opened, and the public gardens are once again carefully tended. However, underlying this apparent affluence, unemployment remains a major problem.

Exploring Zagreb

The city is clearly divided into two distinct districts: **Gornji Grad** (Upper Town) and **Donji Grad** (Lower Town). Hilltop Gornji Grad is made up of winding cobbled streets and terra-cotta rooftops sheltering the cathedral and the Croatian Parliament building, but Donji Grad is where you'll find the city's most important 19th-century cultural institutions, including the National Theater, the university, and a number of museums, all in an organized grid.

Numbers in the text correspond to numbers in the margin and on the Zagreb map.

Gornji Grad (Upper Town)

The romantic hilltop area of Gornji Grad dates from medieval times and is undoubtedly the loveliest part of Zagreb.

SIGHTS TO SEE

⑧ Crkva Svete Katerine (St. Catherine's Church). Built for the Jesuit order between 1620 and 1632, this baroque church was modeled on Giacomo da Vignola's Il Gesù in Rome. Inside, the vaults are decorated with pink and white stucco and 18th-century illusionist paintings, and the altars are the work of Francesco Robba and 17th-century Croatian artists. ⊠ *Katerinin trg* ☉ *Daily 8–8.*

⑥ Crkva Svetog Marka (St. Mark's Church). The original building was erected in the 13th century and was once the parish church of Gradec. The baroque bell tower was added in the 17th century, and the steeply pitched roof—decorated in brilliant, multicolored tiles arranged to depict the coats of arms of Zagreb on the right and the Kingdom of Croatia, Dalmatia, and Slavonia on the left—was added during reconstruction in the 19th century. ⊠ *Markov trg* ☉ *Daily 8–8.*

② Dolac (Market). Farmers from the surrounding countryside set up their stalls here daily. On the upper level, brightly colored umbrellas shade fresh fruit and vegetables on an open-air piazza, while dairy products and meats are sold in an indoor market below. ⊠ *Trg Bana Jelačića* ☉ *Weekdays 7–4, weekends 7–noon.*

⑤ Kamenita Vrata (Stone Gate). The original 13th-century city walls had four gates, of which only Kamenita Vrata remains. Deep inside the dark passageway, locals stop to pray before a small shrine adorned with flickering candles. In 1731, a devastating fire consumed all the wooden elements of the gate, except for a painting of the Virgin and Child, which was found in the ashes, remarkably undamaged. Kamenita Vrata has since become a pilgrimage site, as can be seen from the numerous stone plaques saying *hvala* (thank you). ⊠ *Kamenita.*

③ Katedrala Marijina uznesenja i Svetog Stjepana (Cathedral of the Assumption of the Blessed Virgin and St. Stephen). Built on the site of a former 12th-century cathedral destroyed by the Tartars in 1242, the present structure was constructed between the 13th and 16th centuries. The neo-Gothic facade was added by architect Herman Bolle following the earthquake of 1880, its twin steeples being the identifying feature of the city's skyline. The interior is high and bare, the main point of interest being the north wall, which bears an inscription of the 10 Commandments in 12th-century Glagolithic script. ⊠ *Kaptol 31* ☉ *Daily 8–8.*

⑨ Kula Lotršćak (Lotršćak Tower). Formerly the entrance to the fortified medieval Gradec, Kula Lotršćak now houses an art gallery. Each day

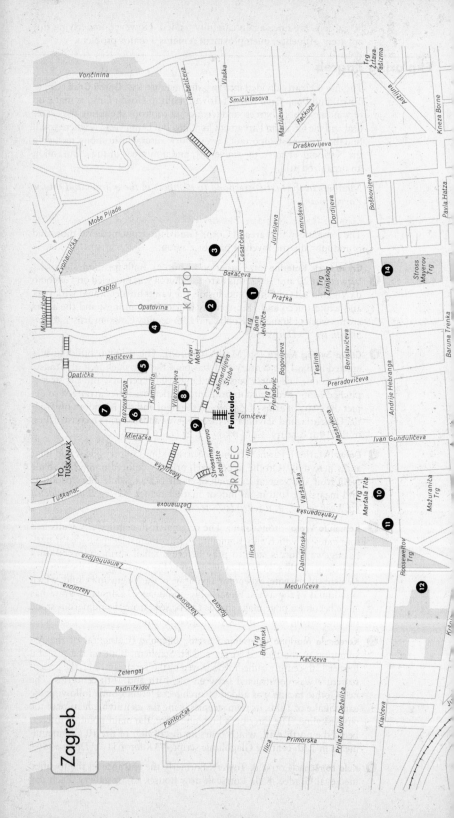

Zagreb

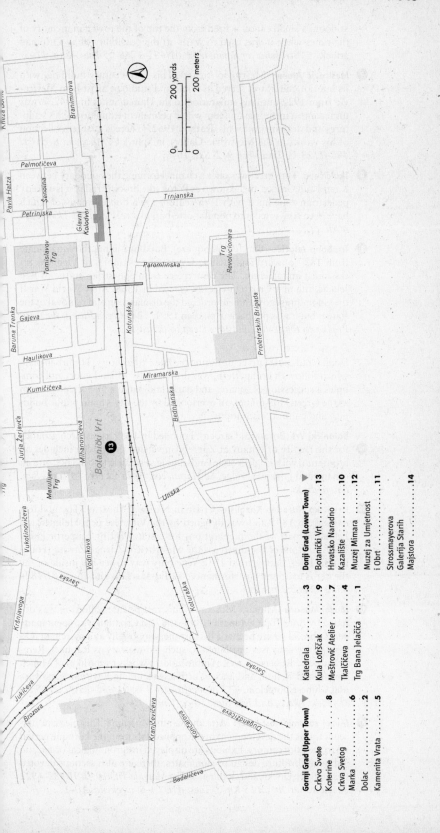

at noon, a small canon is fired from the top of the tower, in memory of the times when it was used to warn off the possibility of an Ottoman attack. ☒ *Strossmayer Šetalište* ☎ *01/485–1768* ☉ *Tues.–Sun. 11–8.*

❼ Meštrović Atelier (Meštrović Atelier). This 17th-century building, with
its interior courtyard, served as home and studio to artist Ivan Meštrović from 1922 until his emigration to the United States in 1942. It was turned into a memorial museum with a permanent exhibition of his sculptures and drawings after his death in 1962. (There is a larger collection of his works in the Meštrović Gallery in Split.) ☒ *Mletačka 8* ☎ *01/485–1123* ☉ *Tues.–Fri. 9–2, Sat. 10–6.*

❹ Tkalčićeva. This street was once a channel forming the boundary between Kaptol and Gradec, then known as Potok (the brook). Today it is a pretty pedestrian zone lined with 19th-century town houses, many of which have been converted into popular café-bars at street level. ☒ *Tkalčićeva north of Krvavi Most.*

❶ Trg Bana Jelačića (Ban Jelačić Square). Buildings lining the square date from 1827 onward and include several fine examples of Viennese Secessionist architecture. The centerpiece is an equestrian statue of Ban Jelačić, the first Croatian viceroy, erected in 1866. After World War II the Communist government ordered the dismantling and removal of the statue, but it was put back in place in 1991. ☒ *Between Ilica to the west, Praška to the south, and Jurišićeva to the east.*

Donji Grad (Lower Town)

Donji Grad came into being during the late 19th century. The urban plan, which follows a grid pattern, was drawn up by Milan Lenuci and combines a succession of squares and parks laid out in a "U" shape (known as the Green Horseshoe), all overlooked by the city's main public buildings and cultural institutions.

SIGHTS TO SEE **Botanički Vrt** (Botanical Garden). Founded in 1889 as research grounds
❸ for the faculty of botany at Zagreb University, the garden includes an arboretum with English-style landscaping, a small artificial lake, and an ornamental Japanese bridge. ☒ *Marulićeva trg 9a* ☒ *Free* ☉ *Tues.–Sun. dawn–dusk.*

❿ Hrvatsko Narodno Kazalište (Croatian National Theatre). The building dates from 1895 and was designed by the Viennese firm Hellmer and Fellner as part of the preparations for a state visit by Emperor Franz Josef. In front of the theater is the Meštrović's Zdenac Života (Fountain of Life), dating from 1912. The only way to see the inside of the theater is to attend a performance. ☒ *Trg Maršala Tita 15* ☎ *01/482–8532* ⊕ *www.hnk.hr.*

⓬ Muzej Mimara (Mimara Museum). This vast private collection was donated by Ante Topić-Mimara (1898–1987), a Croatian who spent many years abroad where he made his fortune, supposedly as a merchant. On display are canvases attributed to such old masters as Raphael, Rembrandt, and Rubens, as well as more modern works by the likes of Manet, Degas, and Renoir, and ancient artifacts including Egyptian glassware and Chinese porcelain. ☒ *Rooseveltov trg 4* ☎ *01/482–8100* ☒ *15 Kn* ☉ *Tues., Wed., and Fri.–Sun. 10–5, Thurs. 10–7.*

⓫ Muzej za Umjetnost i Obrt (Arts and Crafts Museum). This pleasant museum traces the development of the applied arts from the baroque period up to the 20th century. Exhibits are displayed in chronological order, and although furniture design predominates, there are also sections devoted to sacral art, clocks, and clothing. ☒ *Trg Maršala Tita 10* ☎ *01/482–6922* ⊕ *www.muo.hr* ☒ *15 Kn* ☉ *Tues.–Fri. 10–6, weekends 10–1.*

⑭ **Strossmayerova Galerija Starih Majstora** (Strossmayor Gallery of Old Masters). Now under the custody of the Croatian Academy of Sciences and Arts, this impressive gallery was founded in 1884. Works by Venetian Renaissance and baroque artists, such as Bellini and Carpaccio, predominate, but there are also masterpieces by Dutch painters Brueghel and Van Dyck, as well as a delightful painting of Mary Magdalene by El Greco. ⊠ *Trg Zrinjskog 11* ☎ *01/489–5111* ⊕ *www.mdc.hr* ✉ *15 Kn* ☾ *Tues. 10–1 and 5–7, Wed.–Sun. 10–1.*

Where to Eat

Traditional Zagrebian cuisine is based on roast meats with heavy side dishes such as *zagorski štrukli* (baked cheese dumplings). However, there are now a number of excellent fish restaurants in the capital, mainly owned and run by natives of Dalmatia.

$$$$ ✕ **A G Matoš Klub.** A unique first-floor view down onto the main square, coupled with a stylish modern interior and subtle lighting, makes this a memorable spot for dinner. Delectable main dishes include veal stuffed with goose liver in tarragon sauce. The entrance is difficult to find: pass through the arcade behind the Znanje bookshop, and then take the stairs next to a kiosk selling cakes and pastries. ⊠ *Gajeva 2* ☎ *01/487–2544* ⊟ *AE, DC, MC, V.*

$$$$ ✕ **Paviljon.** This chic restaurant occupies the ground floor of the charming 19th-century Art Pavilion, in front of the train station. The Italian-inspired menu includes dishes such as tagliatelli with prosciutto and asparagus as well as crispy roast duck on red cabbage with figs. The wine list is equally impressive, with a choice of Croatian, Italian, and French vintages. ⊠ *Tomislavov trg 22* ☎ *01/481–3066* ⊟ *AE, DC, MC, V* ☾ *Closed Sun.*

$$–$$$$ ✕ **Murter.** Occupying the vaulted brick cellar of a charming old building behind the cathedral, this highly regarded restaurant is renowned for Dalmatian fish dishes, but also does an excellent peppered steak. There's an open-plan kitchen, so you can watch the cooks while they work. ⊠ *Kaptol 27* ☎ *01/481–7745* ⊟ *AE, DC, MC, V* ☾ *Closed Aug. and Sun.*

$$–$$$ ✕ **Baltazar.** Behind the cathedral, Baltazar is best known for classic Balkan dishes such as *ražnjići* (mixed barbecued meats), *čevapčići* (kebobs), and *zapečeni grah* (oven-baked beans). In summer, there are tables in the vine-covered courtyard. ⊠ *Nova Ves 4* ☎ *01/466–6824* ⊟ *AE, DC, MC, V* ☾ *Closed Sun.*

$$–$$$ ✕ **Pod Gričkim Topom.** This small, informal restaurant, perched on the hillside close to the funicular station in Gornji Grad (Upper Town), affords stunning views over the city rooftops. Dalmatian cooking predominates, with dishes such as *lignje na žaru* (barbecued squid) and *crni rižot* (cuttlefish-ink risotto) that are appreciated by locals and visitors alike. ⊠ *Zakmardijeve stube 5* ☎ *01/483–3607* ⊟ *AE, DC, MC, V.*

$–$$ ✕ **Boban.** Close to Hotel Dubrovnik, Boban comprises a street-level bar and a restaurant specializing in pasta dishes in a large vaulted cellar space below. The owner, Zvonimir Boban, was captain of the Croatian national football team during the 1998 World Cup. This place is extremely popular with locals, so be prepared to line up for a table, since reservations are not accepted. ⊠ *Gajeva 9* ☎ *01/481–1549* ⊟ *AE, DC, MC, V.*

Where to Stay

Zagreb offers a good choice of large, expensive hotels geared to business travelers, but less in the way of tourist accommodations. The establishments listed here are quite central and reasonably priced.

$$$$ ⊞ **Opera Zagreb.** This colossal 17-story modern structure lies between the Mimara Museum and the Botanical Garden. Rooms are furnished with quality reproduction antiques and coordinated fabrics. There are first-rate sports and business facilities, and a hotel limousine is available for transfers to and from the airport. ⊠ *Kršnjavoga 1, 10000* ☎ *01/489–2000* 🖶 *01/489–2001* ⊕ *www.opera-zagreb.com* ⇗ *369 rooms, 36 suites* ♻ *2 restaurants, indoor pool, bar* ⊟ *AE, DC, MC, V.*

$$$ ⊞ **Hotel Dubrovnik.** Claiming the most central location in the city, just off Trg Bana Jelačića, Hotel Dubrovnik is popular with business travelers and tourists alike. The garish mirrored-glass facade conceals basic but comfortable rooms and facilities. ⊠ *Gajeva 1, 10000* ☎ *01/487–3555* 🖶 *01/481–8447* ⊕ *www.tel.hr* ⇗ *268 rooms, 8 suites* ♻ *Restaurant, bar* ⊟ *AE, DC, MC, V.*

$$$ ⊞ **Palace Hotel Zagreb.** Built in 1891 as the Schlessinger Palace and converted in 1907 to become the city's first hotel, the Palace Hotel offers romantic, old-fashioned comfort but few extras. Overlooking a green square, between the train station and the city center, it's best known by locals for the street-level Viennese-style café. ⊠ *Strossmayerov trg 10, 10000* ☎ *01/481–4611* 🖶 *01/481–1358* ⊕ *www.palace.hr* ⇗ *125 rooms, 5 suites* ♻ *Restaurant, bar* ⊟ *AE, DC, MC, V.*

$$ ⊞ **Vila Tina.** This delightful family-run hotel lies out of the center, in a peaceful side street close to Maksimir Park. Each room is individually and tastefully furnished and has extras such as fresh fruit and flowers. There's a good restaurant with a summer garden and a beautiful indoor pool. ⊠ *Bukovačka cesta 213, 10000* ☎ *01/244–5138* 🖶 *01/244–5204* ⊕ *www.vilatina.com* ⇗ *16 rooms* ♻ *Restaurant, indoor pool* ⊟ *AE, DC, MC, V.*

Nightlife & the Arts

The Zagreb entertainment scene is finally looking up. Bars, clubs, and cinemas are predominantly frequented by the city's student population, whereas the concert hall and theater remain the domain of the older generation. For information about what's on, pick up a free copy of either the monthly *Events and Performances,* published by the city tourist board, or the bimonthly English-language guide *In Your Pocket, Zagreb.*

BARS &
NIGHTCLUBS   **BP Jazz Club** (⊠ Teslina 7 ☎ 01/481–4444 ⊕ www.bpclub.hr), the capital's top venue for live jazz, is a smoky basement bar. **Bulldog** (⊠ Bogovićeva 6 ☎ 01/481–7393) is a popular split-level café-bar with a large summer terrace. **Pivnica Medvedgrad** (⊠ Savska 56 ☎ 01/617–7110) is a beer hall and microbrewery serving the best ale in town.

DISCOS   **Aquarius** (⊠ Aleja mira bb ☎ 01/364–0231 ⊕ www.aquarius.hr) is Zagreb's top club for dance, especially for disco and techno music. It overlooks Lake Jarun, 4 km (2½ mi) from the city center. **Saloon** (⊠ Tuškanac 1a ☎ 01/483–4903) is the city's most glamorous club, where you can rub shoulders with the stars and dance to commercial disco and Croatian music.

The Arts

Broadway Tkalča (⊠ Nova Ves 17 ☎ 01/486–0241) is a multiscreen cinema, in the Centar Kaptol shopping complex, behind the cathedral. Most foreign films (including those from the United States) are shown in their original language with Croatian subtitles. The **Hrvatsko Narodno Kazalište** (Croatian National Theater; ⊠ Trg Maršala Tita 15 ☎ 01/482–8532 ⊕ www.hnk.hr), a beautiful 19th-century building, hosts classical and contemporary dramas, opera, and ballet performances. **Koncertna Dvorana Vatroslav Lisinski** (Vatroslav Lisinski Concert Hall; ⊠ Stjepana Radića 4 ☎ 01/612–1166 ⊕ www.lisinski.hr), a large, modern complex with two auditoriums, is Zagreb's top venue for orchestral and classical music concerts.

Shopping

The number of Croatians who take shopping buses to Italy and Austria illustrates that this is hardly a great place for acquisitions. Clothes and household goods are still mainly imported as the country's manufacturing industries struggle to recover from the aftereffects of the war.

The capital's new shopping center, **Centar Kaptol** (⊠ Nova Ves 11), shows that things are looking up. Stores include Marks & Spencer, Kenzo, and Max & Co. The center is open Monday–Saturday 9–9, with late-night shopping until 11 on Thursday. For an authentic Croatian shopping experience, visit the **Dolac open-air market** (⊠ Trg bana Jelačića), where besides fresh fruit and vegetables there are also a number of arts-and-crafts stalls. It's open weekdays 7–4 and weekends 7–noon.

Ties may not be the most original of gifts, but few people know that the tie originated in Croatia. During the 17th century, Croatian mercenaries who fought in France sported narrow, silk neck scarfs, which soon became known to the French as *cravat* (from the Croatian *hrvat*). At **Croata** (⊠ Kaptol 13 ☎ 01/481–4600 ⊕ www.croata.hr) you can buy "original Croatian ties" in presentation boxes, accompanied by a brief history of the tie. Housed in a tastefully arranged, vaulted brick cellar, **Vinoteka Bornstein** (⊠ Kaptol 19 ☎ 01/481–2363) stocks a wide range of quality Croatian wines, olive oils, and truffle products.

Zagreb Essentials

AIR TRAVEL
There are no flights between the U.S. and Zagreb. However, the national carrier, Croatia Airlines, flies to Zagreb from Amsterdam, Brussels, Frankfurt, London, Paris, and Vienna, where connections can be made to and from U.S. flights, and major European carriers also have flights to Zagreb from their European bases. Zagreb is also a destination from most carriers in other Eastern and Central European countries.

Croatia Airlines operates at least three flights daily to Split (45 minutes) and two flights daily to Dubrovnik (50 minutes). Through summer, there is also daily service to Prague (one hour, 30 minutes) and flights several times a week to Warsaw (one hour, 40 minutes).
🛈 **Adria** ☎ 01/481-0011. **Air France** ☎ 01/456-2220. **Austrian Airways** ☎ 01/626-5900. **British Airways** ☎ 01/456-2506. **Croatia Airlines** ☎ 01/481-9633. **CŠA** ☎ 01/487-3301. **LOT** ☎ 01/483-7500. **Lufthansa** ☎ 01/456-2159. **Malev** ☎ 01/483-6935.

AIRPORTS & TRANSFERS
Zagreb Airport (ZAG) is in Pleso, 17 km (10 mi) southeast of the city.
🛈 **Zagreb Pleso Airport** ☎ 01/626-5222 general information, 01/456-2229 lost and found ⊕ www.tel.hr.

TRANSFERS A regular shuttle bus runs from the airport to the main bus station every 30 minutes from 7 AM to 8 PM and from the main bus station to the airport from 6 AM to 7:30 PM. A one-way ticket costs 25 Kn, and the trip takes 25 minutes. By taxi, expect to pay 150 Kn–200 Kn to make the same journey; the trip will take about 20 minutes.
🛈 **Airport bus** ☎ 01/615-7992.

BUS & TRAM TRAVEL WITHIN ZAGREB
An extensive network of city buses and trams runs day (4 AM–11:45 PM) and night (11:35 PM–3:45 AM). Tickets cost 6 Kn if you buy them from

a street kiosk, or 7 Kn from the driver. A full-day ticket costs 16 Kn. After you board the bus or tram, you must validate your ticket with a time stamp; tickets are good for 1½ hours. If you are caught without a valid ticket, you will be fined 150 Kn.

CAR TRAVEL

While staying in the capital you are certainly better off without a car. Split is well connected to Zagreb by train and bus, as is Dalmatia (albeit by bus only). However, a car makes your travel plans more flexible.

EMERGENCIES

🚩 Doctors & Dentists **Hitno Ponoč (Hospital)** ✉ Draškovićeva 19 ☎ 01/461–0011.
🚩 Emergency Service **Ambulance** ☎ 94. **Fire** ☎ 93. **Police** ☎ 92.
🚩 24-Hour Pharmacies **24-hour Pharmacy** ✉ Ilica 43 ☎ 01/484–8450 ✉ Ilica 301 ☎ 01/377–4423.

TAXIS

You can find taxis ranks in front of the bus and train stations, near the main square, and in front of the larger hotels. It is also possible to order a radio taxi. All drivers are bound by law to run a meter, which should start at 25 Kn and increase 7 Kn per kilometer. Each piece of luggage incurs a further 5 Kn. The night tariff operates from 10 PM to 5 AM and implies a 20% markup.
🚩 **Radio Taxi** ☎ 01/668–2505 or 01/668–2558 ⊕ www.radio-taksi-zagreb.hr.

TOURS

The Tourist Information Center is close to the train station and organizes amusing and informative guided tours of the city.
🚩 **Zagreb Tourist Information** ✉ Trg Nikole Šubića Zrinskoga 14 ☎ 01/492–1645.

TRAIN TRAVEL

The main train station lies in Donji Grad, a 10-minute walk from the center.
🚩 **Zagreb Train Station** ✉ Trg Kralja Tomislava ☎ 060/333–444 domestic train information; 01/481–1892 international train information ⊕ www.hznet.hr.

VISITOR INFORMATION

Zagreb's main tourist information center overlooks the main square.
🚩 **Zagreb Tourist Information** ✉ Trg bana Jelačića 11 ☎ 01/481–4051 ⊕ www.zagreb-touristinfo.hr.

ISTRIA

Croatia's most popular seaside resorts are found on the west coast of the Istrian peninsula, in the northwest corner of the country, south of the border with Slovenia. There's a sizable Italian minority here, and Italian influence is apparent in the architecture, the cuisine, and the local dialect.

The prettiest and best-known destinations are Rovinj and Poreč, both of which passed more than 500 years under Venetian control (1238–1797), and are today adorned with graceful campanili, loggia, and reliefs of the winged lion of St. Mark. They also offer everything you need for a restful holiday: comfortable hotels, authentic restaurants, and a wide range of sports facilities.

Rovinj

Fodor'sChoice ★ In a fantastic setting, with centuries-old red-roofed houses clustered around the hill of a former island, Rovinj is crowned by the monumental baroque Crkva Sv Eufemije (Church of St. Euphemia), which has a typical Venetian bell tower topped by a gleaming bronze figure of St. Euphemia. Far below, a wide harbor crowded with pleasure boats is rimmed with bright awnings and colorful café umbrellas. Artists, writers, musicians, and actors have long gravitated to this pretty place to carve out apartments in historic houses. Throughout the summer, the winding cobbled streets are crowded with vacationers from nearby resort developments. South of the harbor lies the beautiful landscaped park of Zlatni Rt, planted with avenues of cedars, oaks, and cypresses and offering numerous secluded coves for bathing.

Inside the 18th-century baroque **Crkva Sv Eufemije** (Church of St. Euphemia), the remains of the saint are said to lie within a 6th-century sarcophagus, which according to legend floated out to sea from Constantinople and was washed ashore in Rovinj in AD 800. ⊠ *Grisia* ⊙ *Daily 10–noon and 4–7.*

The **Akvarij** (Aquarium) displays tanks of Adriatic marine fauna and flora. It opened in 1891, making it one of the oldest institutions of its type in Europe. ⊠ *Obala G. Paliage 5* ☎ *052/804–700* ⊙ *May–Sept., daily 9–9; Oct.–Apr., by appointment only.*

Where to Stay & Eat

$$$ ✕ **Enoteca Al Gastaldo.** Walls lined with wine bottles and candlelight create a warm and intimate atmosphere in this sophisticated eatery, hidden away in the Old Town and a few blocks back from the harbor. Indulge in spaghetti with either truffles or crab, fresh fish prepared over an open fire, and a colorful rocket and radicchio salad. Round off with a glass of local *rakija.* ⊠ *Iza Kasarne 14* ☎ *052/814–109* ⊟ *AE, DC.*

$$ ✕ **Veli Jože.** This extremely popular *konoba* lies close to the seafront, at the foot of the Old Town. Specialties include *bakalar in bianco* (dried cod in white wine with onion and potatoes), *fuži* (pasta) with goulash, and roast lamb with potatoes. The house wine is excellent. ⊠ *Sv Križa 1* ☎ *052/816–337* ⊟ *AE, DC, MC, V.*

$$$$ ⌑ **Villa Angelo d'Oro.** This enchanting hotel opened in 2001 and has al-

FodorśChoice ready gained an excellent reputation. In a beautifully restored 16th-cen-

★ tury building, rooms are individually furnished with antiques and quality fabrics. Breakfast is served on a glorious garden roof terrace, and there's a high-class restaurant on the ground floor. The hotel boat and yacht are at the guests' disposal. It lies in the heart of the Old Town, one block in from the seafront. ⊠ *V Švalbe 38–42, 52210* ☎ *052/840–502* ⊟ *052/840–112* ⊕ *www.rovinj.at* ⚓ *24 rooms* ⚐ *Restaurant* ⊟ *AE, DC, MC, V.*

Poreč

A pretty, tile-roofed town on a peninsula jutting out to sea, Poreč was founded as a Roman *castrum* (fort) in the 2nd century BC. Within the historic center, the network of streets still follow the original urban layout, and Dekumanova, the Roman *decumanus* (the main traverse street), has maintained its character as the principal thoroughfare. Today it is a worn flagstone passage lined with Romanesque and Gothic mansions and patrician palaces, some of which host cafés and restaurants. Close by lies the magnificent UNESCO-listed Eufrazijeva Basilica (St. Euphrasius Basilica), Istria's prime attraction and one of the coast's major artistic showpieces. Although the town itself is small, Poreč has an ample capacity for overnight stays, thanks to the vast hotel complexes of Plava and Zelena Lagun, situated along the pine-rimmed shoreline, a short distance from the center.

★ The magnificent **Eufrazijeva Basilica** (St. Euphrasius Basilica) is among the most perfectly preserved early Christian churches in Europe. It is also one of the most important monuments of Byzantine art on the Adriatic. Built by Bishop Euphrasius in the middle of the 6th century, the basilica consists of a delightful atrium, a church decorated with stunning mosaics, an octagonal baptistery, a 16th-century bell tower, and the bishop's residence. The church interior is dominated by biblical mosaics above, behind, and around the main apse. ⊠ *Eufrazijeva* ☾ *Daily 7–7.*

Where to Stay & Eat

$$–$$$ ✕ **Peterokutna Kula.** A 15th-century pentagonal tower in the heart of the Old Town has been cleverly renovated to accommodate this sophisticated restaurant on a series of levels and terraces. House specialties include spaghetti with lobster and steak with truffles. Finish your meal with a glass of *šlivovica* (plum rakija). ⊠ *Decumanus 1* ☎ *052/451–378* ▤ *No credit cards.*

$$ ▦ **Hotel Neptun.** On the seafront promenade, where Poreč's oldest hotels are found, the Neptune was renovated in 2000 to provide smart, functional accommodations right in the center of town. ⊠ *Obala M Tita 15, 52440* ☎ *052/400–800* 🖶 *052/431–351* ⊕ *www.riviera.hr* ⇥ *145 rooms* ♨ *Restaurant* ▤ *AE, DC, MC, V.*

Istria Essentials

TOURS
Various travel agencies based in both Poreč and Rovinj offer a range of tours to the surrounding area.

TRANSPORTATION AROUND ISTRIA
Regular daily buses connect Poreč and Rovinj (journey time approximately 45 minutes).

VISITOR INFORMATION
🛈 **Poreč Tourist Information** ⊠ Zagrebačka 9, Poreč ☎ 052/451-293 ⊕ www.istria. com. **Rovinj Tourist Information** ⊠ Obala P. Budičina 12, Rovinj ☎ 052/811-566 ⊕ www.tzgrovinj.hr.

DALMATIA

Mountainous, wild, and unexploited, Dalmatia's tourist facilities may not be as sophisticated as those in Istria, but its magnificent coastal towns and rugged islands offer an unrefined Mediterranean charm all their own. The region's capital is the busy port of Split, with its historic center surrounded by the sturdy walls of an imperial Roman palace. Just a short ferry ride away lies Hvar, now the most fashionable destination on the islands, with its charming 16th-century Venetian architecture and a labyrinth of winding cobbled streets. However, for many people the highlight of the region is the majestic walled city of Dubrovnik, which was once a rich and powerful independent republic. Overlooking the sea and backed by rugged mountains, it's an unforgettable sight and probably Croatia's most photographed city. If you're traveling to Dubrovnik by coastal ferry from Split, you might choose to stop overnight in Korčula Town, on the island of Korčula, with its fine Gothic and Renaissance stone buildings bearing witness to almost 800 years of Venetian rule. If you're traveling down to Dubrovnik by road, you'll pass through a narrow coastal strip given over to Bosnia, so have your passport at hand for the border checkpoint. The stopover is inconsequential, and you are usually off after a brief passport check.

Split

Some 365 km (228 mi) south of Zagreb, Split's ancient core is so spectacular and unusual that it's more than worth the visit. The heart of the city lies within the walls of Emperor Diocletian's 3rd-century Roman palace. Diocletian, born in the nearby Roman settlement of Salona in AD 245, achieved a brilliant career as a soldier in Rome and became emperor at the age of 40. In 295, he ordered this vast palace to be built in his native Dalmatia, and when it was completed, he stepped down from the throne and retired to his beloved homeland. Upon his death, he was laid to rest in a mausoleum with the palace walls.

In 615, when Salona was sacked by barbarian tribes, those fortunate enough to escape found refuge within the stout palace walls. Thus, Diocletian's former home developed into an urban center, and by the 11th century the settlement had expanded beyond the ancient walls.

Under the rule of Venice (1420–1797), Split became one of the Adriatic's main trading ports, and the city's splendid Renaissance palaces bear witness to the affluence of those times. When the Habsburgs took control during the 19th century, an overland connection to Central Europe was established by the construction of the Split–Zagreb–Vienna railway line.

After World War II, the Tito years saw a period of rapid urban expansion: industrialization accelerated and the suburbs extended to accommodate high-rise apartment blocks. Today the historic center of Split is included on UNESCO's list of World Heritage Sites.

Dioklecijanova Palača (Diocletian's Palace). In the center of town, overlooking the seafront promenade, the palace was designed as a combination of a luxurious villa and a Roman garrison. Each of the four walls had a main gate, the largest and most important being the northern Zlatna Vrata (Golden Gate), which opened onto the road to the Roman settlement of Salona. The entrance from the western wall was the Željezna Vrata (Iron Gate), and the entrance through the east wall was the Srebrena Vrata (Silver Gate). The Mjedna Vrata (Bronze Gate) in the south wall faced directly onto the sea, and during Roman times boats would have docked here. ✉ *Obala Hrvatskog Narodnog Preporoda.*

Fodor'sChoice ★ **Galerija Meštrović** (Meßtrović Gallery). Near the Museum of Croatian Archaeological Monuments is this modern villa, which was designed by Ivan Meštrovic as his summer residence during the 1930s. Some 200 of his sculptural works in wood, marble, stone, and bronze are on display, both indoors and outside in the villa's gardens. Admission to the gallery also covers entrance to the nearby **Kaštelet** (✉ Šetalište Ivana Meštrovića 39), housing a cycle of New Testament bas-relief wood carvings that many consider Meštrović's finest work. ✉ *Šetalište Ivana Meštrovića 46* ☎ *021/358–450* ☉ *June–Oct., Tues.–Sat. 10–6, Sun. 10–3; Nov.–May, Tues.–Sat. 10–4, Sun. 10–2.*

Katedrala Sveti Dujam (Cathedral of St. Dominius). The main body of the cathedral, the chief monument on Peristil, is the 3rd-century octagonal mausoleum designed as a shrine to Emperor Diocletian. During the 7th century, refugees from Salona converted it into an early Christian church, dedicating it to Sv Duje (St. Domnius), after Bishop Domnius of Salona, one of the many Christians martyred during the late emperor's persecution campaign. If you have a head for heights, climb the elegant 200-foot Romanesque-Gothic bell tower, which was constructed in stages between the 12th and 16th centuries. ✉ *Peristil* ☉ *Daily 8–noon and 4:30–7.*

Marjan (Marjan Hill). West of the city center, a flight of steep steps lead up onto a hilly peninsula, where this much-loved park is planted with pine trees and Mediterranean shrubs. A network of paths crisscrosses the grounds, offering stunning views over the sea and islands. ✉.

Muzej Hrvatskih Arheološki Spomenika (Museum of Croatian Archaeological Monuments). A pleasant 20-minute walk along the coast, west of town, this modern building displays early Croatian religious art from the 7th through the 12th centuries. The most interesting exhibits are fine stone carvings decorated with plaitwork design, surprisingly similar to the geometric patterns typical of Celtic art. ✉ *Šetalište Ivana Meštrovića* ☎ *021/358–420* ☉ *Tues.–Sat. 9–4, Sun. 9–noon.*

Narodni Trg (People's Square). West of Peristil lies contemporary Split's main square, a pedestrianized expanse paved with gleaming white marble. Although religious activity has to this day centered on Peristil, Narodni trg became the focus of civic life during the 14th century. ✉.

Peristil (Peristyle). From Roman times up to the present day, the main public meeting place within the palace walls has been this spacious central courtyard, flanked by marble columns topped with Corinthian capitals and richly ornamented cornices linked by arches. During the Split Summer Festival, the space becomes an open-air stage hosting evening opera performances. ✉.

Zlatna Vrata (Golden Gate). Directly north of Peristil lies the most monumental of the city's four gates. Just outside the Zlatna Vrata stands Meštrović's gigantic bronze **statue of Grgur Ninski** (Bishop Gregory of Nin). During the 9th century, the bishop campaigned for the use of the Slav language in the Croatian Church, as opposed to Latin, thus infuriating Rome. Touch the big toe on his left foot for good luck. ✉ *Dioklecijanova.*

Where to Eat

As in any city of fishermen and sailors, seafood predominates here. The most popular choice is fresh fish cooked over a charcoal fire, accompanied by a bottle of Dalmatian wine.

$$–$$$$ ✕ **Konoba Varoš.** The place can seem a little dour at lunchtime but mellows when the candles are lit during the evening. The fresh fish and *pržene lignje* (fried squid) are excellent, and there's also a reasonable choice of Croatian meat dishes. The restaurant is a five-minute walk west of the center, at the foot of Marjan Hill. ✉ *Ban Mladenova 7* ☎ *021/396–138* ▭ *AE, DC, MC, V.*

$$–$$$ ✕ **Kod Jose.** This typical Dalmatian *konoba* is relaxed and romantic, with exposed stone walls and heavy wooden furniture set off by candlelight. The waiters are wonderfully discreet, and the *rižot frutta di mare* (seafood risotto) delicious. You'll find it just outside the palace walls, a five-minute walk from Zlatna Vrata (Golden Gate). ✉ *Sredmanuška 4* ☎ *021/347–397* ▭ *AE, DC, MC, V.*

$ ✕ **Pizzeria Galija.** In the city center, close to the fish market, Galija serves the best pizzas in town. The restaurant is bustling and informal, with heavy wooden tables and benches; draft beer and wine are sold by the glass. ✉ *Tončićeva 12* ☎ *021/347–932* ▭ *No credit cards.*

Where to Stay

Split still suffers from a shortage of first-class hotels, but the establishments listed here are pleasant, fairly central, and reasonably priced.

$$$ ⊞ **Hotel Park.** Now offering the best accommodation in town, Hotel Park reopened in 2001 after extensive renovation work. The building dates from 1921 and lies 10 minutes east of the city walls, overlooking Bačvice Bay. The rooms are modern and smartly furnished, and a pleasant terrace with palms offers views over the sea. ⊠ *Hatzeov Perivoj 3, 21000* ☎ *021/406–400* 🖷 *021/406–401* ⊕ *www.hotelpark-split.hr* 🛏 *54 rooms, 3 suites* ⟁ *Restaurant, bar* ▤ *AE, DC, MC, V.*

$$$ ⊞ **Hotel Split.** A 25-minute trek east of the center, Hotel Split is a white modernist building overlooking the sea. The rooms are well equipped with modern furnishings and decorated in blues and whites. There are excellent sports and business facilities. ⊠ *Put Trstenika 19, 21000* ☎ *021/303–111* 🖷 *021/303–011* ⊕ *www.hotelsplit.hr* 🛏 *135 rooms, 8 suites* ⟁ *Restaurant, pool, bar* ▤ *AE, DC, MC, V.*

$$ ⊞ **Hotel Jadran.** This small 1970s-style hotel lies close to the ACI marina and the gardens of Sveti Stipan, overlooking Zvončac Bay. A pleasant 15-minute walk along the seafront brings you to the city center. ⊠ *Sustipanjska put 23, 21000* ☎ *021/398–622* 🖷 *021/398–586* 🛏 *20 rooms* ⟁ *Pool, bar* ▤ *AE, DC, MC, V.*

Hvar

With an annual average of 2,724 hours of sunshine, Hvar bills itself as the "sunniest island in the Adriatic." It also makes visitors a sporting proposition, offering them a money-back guarantee if it snows (which has been known to happen).

FodorśChoice
★   **Hvar** is also the name of the capital, near the island's western tip. The little town rises like an amphitheater from its harbor, backed by a hilltop fortress and protected from the open sea by a scattering of small islands known as Pakleni Otoci. Through summer, the rich and famous moor their luxury yachts along the palm-lined quay. A few steps away, the magnificent main square, Trg Sveti Stjepana, the largest piazza in Dalmatia, is backed by the 16th-century Katedrala Sveti Stjepan (Cathedral of St. Stephen).

To reach Hvar Town, take an early morning Jadrolinija ferry from Split to Stari Grad (23 nautical mi) and then catch a local bus across the island, or take the afternoon catamaran service direct from Split to Hvar Town (23 nautical mi).

On the upper floor of the Arsenal is the **Kazalište** (Theater), which opened in 1612, making it the oldest institution of its kind in Croatia and one of the first in Europe. The Arsenal building, where Venetian ships en route to the Orient once docked for repairs, dates from the 13th century but was reconstructed after damage during a Turkish invasion in 1571. ⊠ *Trg Sv Stjepana* ⊙ *May–Oct., daily 9–noon and 7–9; Nov.–Apr., daily 10–noon.*

East of town, along the quay past the Arsenal, lies the **Franjevački Samostan** (Franciscan Monastery). Within its walls, a pretty 15th-century Renaissance cloister leads to the former refectory, now housing a small museum with several notable artworks. ⊠ *Obala Ivana Lučića Lavčevića bb* ☎ *no phone* ⊙ *May–Oct., daily 10–noon and 5–7.*

Where to Stay & Eat

$$–$$$$
FodorśChoice
★   ✕ **Macondo.** This superb fish restaurant lies hidden away on a narrow, cobbled street between the main square and the fortress; to find it, follow the signs from Trg Sv Stjepana. The dining room is simply furnished with wooden tables, discreet modern art, and a large open fire. The food and service are practically faultless: begin with the delicate scampi pâté, followed by a mixed seafood platter, and round off with a glass of

homemade *orahovica* (walnut rakija). ☒ *Hvar, 1 block north of Trg Sv Stjepana* ☎ *021/742–850* ⊟ *AE, DC, MC, V* ⊘ *Closed Jan.*

$$ ✕ **Bacchus.** Popular with locals, this restaurant with outdoor tables overlooking the main square stays open all year. The menu offers down-to-earth, hearty dishes such as charcoal-grilled steak and chips, with fast-moving, no-frills waiters to match. ☒ *Trg Sv Stjepana bb* ☎ *021/742–251* ⊟ *No credit cards.*

$$$ ☐ **Amfora.** A colossal white, modern structure overlooking its own bay with a pebble beach, the Amfora is backed by pine woods and lies a pleasant 10-minute walk along the coastal path from the center of town. All rooms have balconies, and there are excellent sports facilities, making this an ideal choice for families on longer stays. ☒ *Hvar, 21450* ☎ *021/741–202* 🖷 *021/741–711* ⊕ *www.suncanihvar.hr* ⇌ *373 rooms* ⌂ *Restaurant, indoor pool, bar* ⊟ *AE, DC, MC, V* ⊘ *Closed Nov.–Mar.*

$$$ ☐ **Palace.** Commanding a prime site on the edge of the main square and overlooking the harbor, the Palace remains open year-round, offering lower prices during low season. The former Venetian loggia is incorporated into the hotel and used as an elegant salon, and there's an indoor pool filled with heated seawater. ☒ *Trg Sv Stjepana, 21450* ☎ *021/741–966* 🖷 *021/742–420* ⊕ *www.suncanihvar.hr* ⇌ *76 rooms* ⌂ *Restaurant, indoor pool, bar* ⊟ *AE, DC, MC, V.*

Dubrovnik

FodorśChoice
★

Lying 216 km (135 mi) southeast of Split and commanding a splendid location overlooking the Adriatic, Dubrovnik is undoubtedly one of the world's most beautiful fortified cities. Its massive stone ramparts and splendid fortress towers curve around a tiny harbor, enclosing graduated ridges of sun-bleached orange-tile roofs, copper domes, and elegant bell towers.

Early in the 7th century AD, residents of the once Greek and later Roman Epidaurum (now the small town of Cavtat) fled the Avars and Slavs and headed north to build a new settlement on a small rocky island below the slopes of Mt. Srd. Strong walls were built to protect the city. As the town grew in importance it was called Laus and then Ragusa. This fortress city had a fleet of the fastest and most seaworthy ships of the time. On the mainland hillside opposite the island, the Slav settlement called Dubrovnik grew up along the fringe of oak forests (called *dubrava*, meaning "woodlands"). By the 12th century, the narrow channel separating the two towns was filled in, and Ragusa and Dubrovnik became one, although the city did not officially take the name Dubrovnik until 1918.

From 1358 to 1808, the city existed as a powerful independent republic, keeping its freedom by paying off would-be aggressors Venice and the Ottoman Turks. During the Middle Ages, Ragusa rivaled Venice for sea supremacy, and Ragusan caravans traded goods between Europe and the Middle East by way of Constantinople. By the 16th century, Ragusa had consulates in some 50 foreign ports along with a merchant fleet of 200 ships sailing through the Mediterranean and as far as England, the Netherlands, and eventually the New World.

The chief citizen was the Rector, elected for only a month at a time to share management of the city's business with the Grand Council and the Senate. Most of the military and naval commands were held by members of the nobility, while the increasingly prosperous middle class carried on trade.

In 1667, the city was largely destroyed by a terrible earthquake, and it was rebuilt in the baroque style. Dubrovnik lost its independence to

Napoléon in 1808, and then passed to Austria-Hungary in 1815. During the 20th century, as part of Yugoslavia, the city became a popular tourist destination. In 1979, it was listed as a UNESCO World Heritage Site. From November 1991 to May 1992, during the war of independence, the city came under heavy siege. Fortunately, the ancient fortifications stood up well to bombardments, and none of the main monuments were seriously harmed, though the terra-cotta rooftops were devastated. During the 1990s, money poured in from all over the world, and today—thanks to careful restoration work—barely any traces of war damage remain.

8 **Akvarij** (Aquarium). In front of the cathedral, a dark, narrow street leads to a cavernous space housing several small pools and 27 well-lit tanks containing a variety of fish from rays to small sharks and other underwater life such as sponges and sea urchins. Children will find the octopus, in his glass tank, either very amusing or horribly scary. ⊠ *Damjana Jude 2* ☎ *020/427–937* ⊗ *May–Sept., daily 9–8, Oct.–Apr., Mon.–Sat. 9–1.*

4 **Crkva Svetog Vlaha** (Church of St. Blaise). At the east end of Placa, this 18th-century baroque church replaced an earlier one destroyed by fire. Of particular note is the silver statue on the high altar of St. Blaise holding a model of Dubrovnik, which is paraded around town each year on February 3, the Day of St. Blaise. ⊠ *Luža* ⊗ *Daily 8–noon and 4:30–7.*

3 **Gradske Zidine** (City Walls). The highlight of any visit to Dubrovnik has to be walking a circuit of the city walls, which takes about an hour. Most of the original construction took place during the 13th century, though the walls were further reinforced with towers and bastions during the following 400 years. On average they are 80 feet high and up to 10 feet thick on the seaward side, 20 feet on the inland side. ⊠ *Placa* ⊗ *May–Sept., daily 9–6:30; Oct.–Apr., daily 9–3.*

6 **Katedrala Velika Gospa** (Cathedral of Our Lady). Close to the Bishop's Palace the cathedral was built in baroque style after the original was destroyed in the 1667 earthquake. Inside, above the main altar, is a large polyptych depicting the *Assumption of Our Lady,* attributed to Titian. The Treasury displays 138 gold and silver reliquaries, including the skull of St. Blaise in the form of a bejeweled Byzantine crown and also an arm and a leg of the saint, likewise encased in decorated golden plating. ⊠ *Bunićeva Poljana* ☎ *020/411–715* ⊗ *Daily 9–noon and 3–7.*

5 **Knežev Dvor** (Bishop's Palace). Behind the Church of St. Blaise is this exquisite bishop's palace, whose facade includes an early Renaissance arcaded loggia. The building was constructed in the 15th century but has been reconstructed several times. In the days of the Republic, the Great Council and Senate held their meetings here. Upstairs, the rector's living quarters now accommodate the **Gradski Muzej** (City Museum), containing exhibits that give a picture of life in Dubrovnik from early days until the fall of the Republic. ⊠ *Pred Dvorom 3* ☎ *020/321–422* ⊗ *Daily 9–2.*

2 **Placa.** The main thoroughfare within the Old Town walls was once the shallow sea channel separating the island of Laus from the mainland. Although the channel was filled in during the 12th century, it continued to divide the city socially for several centuries, with the nobility living in the area south of Placa and the commoners living on the hillside to the north. ⊠.

7 **Pomorski Muzej** (Maritime Museum). Directly above the aquarium, on the first floor of St. John's Fortress, this museum illustrates how rich and powerful Dubrovnik became as one of the world's most important

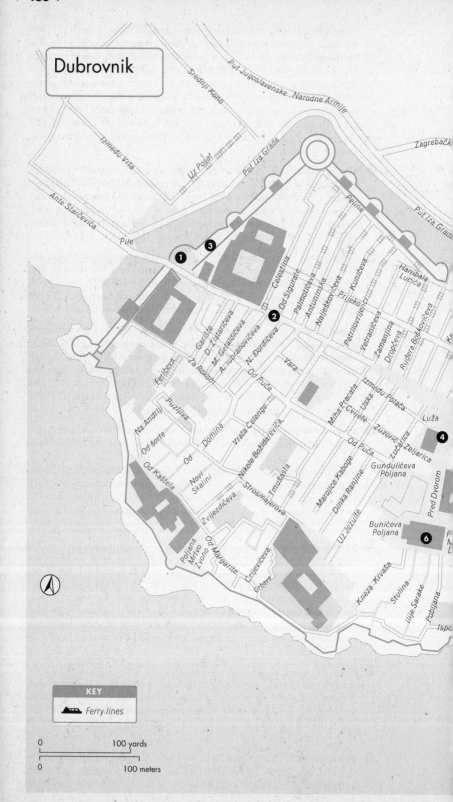

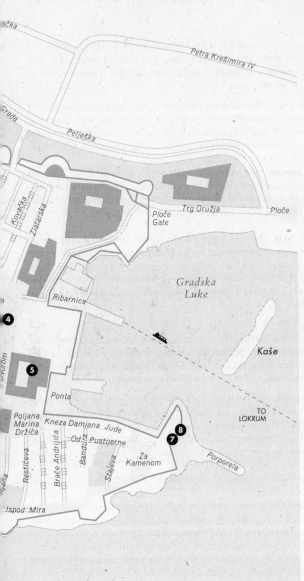

seafaring nations. On display are intricately detailed models of ships as well as engine-room equipment, sailors' uniforms, paintings, and maps. ☒ *Damjana Jude 2* ☏ *020/426–465* ☉ *Daily 9–2.*

❶ **Vrata od Pila** (Pile Gate). The main entrance to the city walls was built in 1537 and combines a Renaissance arch with a wooden drawbridge on chains. A niche above the portal contains a statue of Sveti Vlah (St. Blaise), the city's patron saint, holding a replica of Dubrovnik in his left hand. ☒ *Pile.*

Where to Eat

The narrow, cobbled street Prijeko, running parallel to Placa, is packed with mostly touristy seafood restaurants and waiters touting for customers. Less commercial and infinitely more agreeable eateries are scattered throughout the town.

$$–$$$$ ✕ **Moby Dick.** One of the many enticing restaurants that line Prijeko, Moby Dick has a sound reputation for good fresh fish and seafood. Dinner at one of the outdoor tables is a memorable event, though you may be rushed if other guests are waiting for a spot. ☒ *Prijeko 20* ☏ *020/321–170* ▤ *AE, DC, MC, V* ☉ *Closed Nov.–Mar.*

$$–$$$ ✕ **Tovjerna Sesame.** Just outside the city walls, close to Pile Gate, this romantic eatery occupies a candlelit vaulted space with bohemian decor. It's ideal for a light supper of cheese, cold meats, and colorful salad dishes with a good bottle of wine. ☒ *Dante Alighieria bb* ☏ *020/412–910* ▤ *AE, DC, MC, V.*

★ **$–$$** ✕ **Kamenica.** This informal eatery overlooks the morning market in the Old Town and remains popular for its fresh oysters and generous platters of *girice* (small fried fish) and *pržene ligne* (fried squid). It's cheap and cheerful, and if you don't like seafood, you can get a cheese omelet. ☒ *Gundulićeva Poljana 8* ☏ *No phone* ▤ *No credit cards* ☉ *No dinner Nov.–Mar.*

Where to Stay

There are no hotels within the city walls. The more exclusive places line the coastal road east of the center, offering stunning views of the Old Town and the sea, while package hotels with cheaper rooms can be found on Lapad peninsula, 3 km (2 mi) west of the center.

$$$$ ▥ **Villa Dubrovnik.** A 20-minute walk east of the center, this white modernist structure is built into the rocks, with a series of terraces and a garden coming down to a hideaway cove with a small beach. The rooms are light and airy, and there's a complimentary boat service to and from the Old Town. Airport transfer by private car is available on request. ☒ *V Bukovaca 6 20000* ☏ *020/422–933* 🖷 *020/423–465* ⊕ *www.villa-dubrovnik.hr* ⇥ *40 rooms* ⚑ *Restaurant, bar* ▤ *AE, DC, MC, V* ☉ *Closed Nov.–Mar.*

$$$$ ▥ **Villa Orsula.** Occupying a villa built in 1936, this is the most excluFodor'sChoice sive hotel in town. Beautifully furnished rooms offer magnificent views
★ over the Old Town, and a lovely terraced garden leads down to a private beach. Guests have access to recreation facilities at the much larger, neighboring Hotel Argentina, which is under the same management. ☒ *Put Frana Supila 14 20000* ☏ *020/440–555* 🖷 *020/423–465* ⊕ *www.hoteli-argentina.hr* ⇥ *12 rooms, 3 suites* ⚑ *Restaurant, pool, bar* ▤ *AE, DC, MC, V.*

$$–$$$ ▥ **Hotel Lapad.** Occupying a 19th-century building with a garden and an outdoor pool, Hotel Lapad overlooks Gruž Harbor. A boat service to nearby beaches is at guests' disposal. It stays open all year and has good discounts through low season. ✉ *Lapadska Obala 37 20000* ☎ *020/432–922* 🖷 *020/417–230* ⊕ *www.hotel-lapad.hr* 🛏 *193 rooms* ☖ *Restaurant, pool, bar* 🖃 *AE, DC, MC, V.*

Korčula

At first view, the town of Korčula seems like a much smaller version of Dubrovnik: the same high walls, the circular corner fortresses, and the church tower projecting from within an expanse of red roofs. The main difference lies in the town plan: in Korčula, narrow side streets run off the main thoroughfare at odd angles to form a herringbone pattern, preventing cold winter winds from whistling unimpeded through town. The center is small and compact and can be explored in an hour.

For eight centuries Korčula was under Venetian rule, and it shows. Inside the massive gates is a treasure trove of Gothic and Renaissance palaces and courtyards furnished with statuary, as well as a splendid 14th-century **cathedral** built from a wheat-colored stone that turns pale gold in sunlight, amber at sunset. Korčula claims to have been the birthplace of the explorer Marco Polo (1254–1324). Many historians agree that he may have been born here, since the Venetians recruited many sea captains from Dalmatia. However, **Kuća Marca Pola** (Marco Polo House), in the center of town, where he is said to have been born, was constructed hundreds of years after his death. Far more authentic is the Moreška, a colorful sword dance portraying a fictitious battle between local Christians and the Ottoman Turks for the possession of a beautiful princess: it is performed each Monday and Thursday evening from May to September just outside the city walls, next to the Land Gate. You can reach Korčula by ferry from either Dubrovnik or Split, but Dubrovnik is closer.

Where to Stay & Eat

$$–$$$
FodorsChoice
★
✕ **Adio Mare.** A long-standing favorite with locals and visitors alike, Adio Mare occupies a Gothic-Renaissance building in the Old Town near Kuća Marca Pola. There's a dining room with a high ceiling and an open-plan kitchen so you can watch the cooks while they work. The menu features down-to-earth Dalmatian meat and fish dishes. The house wine, *pošip*, is excellent. ✉ *Svetog Roka* ☎ *020/711–253* 🖃 *No credit cards* ⊘ *Closed Oct.–Apr.*

$$
🏨 **Hotel Korčula.** Built in 1871 under Austria-Hungary, the building was converted to become the island's first hotel in 1912. Exuding old-fashioned charm, it offers discreet service and a delightful seafront café terrace, ideal for watching the sunset over the water. It's the only hotel in the old town; all the others are a short distance east of the center. ✉ *Obala Dr Franje Tudmana bb, 20260* ☎🖷 *020/711–078* 🛏 *20 rooms* ☖ *Restaurant, bar* 🖃 *AE, DC, MC, V* ⦿| *BP.*

Dalmatia Essentials

AIR TRAVEL

🛪 **Croatia Airlines** ✉ Obala hrvatskog narodnog preporoda 9 Split ☎ 021/362–997 ✉ Brsalje 9, Dubrovnik ☎ 020/413–776.

AIRPORTS & TRANSFERS

In Split, you can take an airport bus into town. The airport bus goes to and picks up from Obala Lazereta, close to Split Bus Station. For your return, the airport bus leaves Split 90 minutes before each flight. A one-way ticket costs 30 Kn. Journey time is 40 minutes.

In Dubrovnik, the airport bus leaves Dubrovnik Bus Station 90 minutes before each flight. A one-way ticket costs 25 Kn. Journey time is approximately 20 minutes. It also meets all incoming flights.
🚏 **Dubrovnik Airport** ☎ 020/773-377 ⊕ www.airport-dubrovnik.hr. **Split Airport** ☎ 021/203-171 ⊕ www.split-airport.tel.hr.

TOURS
The tourist offices in Split and Dubrovnik organize informative and amusing guided tours of their respective cities.
🚏 **Dubrovnik Tourist Office** ✉ ul. Cvijete Zuzorić 1, Dubrovnik ☎ 020/426-304. **Split Tourist Information Center** ✉ Peristil bb, Split ☎ 021/342-606.

TRANSPORTATION AROUND DALMATIA
Buses make frequent runs up and down the coast, and cars are available for hire. However, the most pleasant way to travel here is by boat. During high season (July–August), Jadrolinija coastal ferries depart Split early most mornings, arriving in Dubrovnik in the mid-afternoon. From Dubrovnik, the ferries depart mid-morning to arrive in Split in the early evening (journey time approximately 8 hours in either direction). Coming and going, these ferries stop at Korčula and Stari Grad (island of Hvar). During the rest of the year, the service is less frequent. Jadrolinija runs daily local ferries from Split to Stari Grad, on the island of Hvar. The same company also runs a daily catamaran from Split direct to Hvar Town, which then continues to Vela Luka (island of Korčula).
🚏 **Jadrolinija** ✉ Dubrovnik ☎ 020/418-000 ✉ Split ☎ 021/338-333.

VISITOR INFORMATION
🚏 **Dubrovnik Tourist Office** ✉ ul. Cvijete Zuzorić 1, Dubrovnik ☎ 020/426-304. **Hvar Town Tourist Information Center** ✉ Trg Sv Stjepana 16, Hvar ☎ 021/741-059 ⊕ www.hvar.hr. **Korčula Tourist Office** ✉ Obala Dr Franje Tudjmana bb, Korčula ☎ 020/715-701. **Split Tourist Information Center** ✉ Trg Republike 2, Split ☎ 021/355-088 ⊕ www.visitsplit.com.

CYPRUS
THE REPUBLIC OF CYPRUS, NORTHERN CYPRUS

CYPRUS, ONCE A CENTER FOR THE CULT of the Greek goddess Aphrodite, is a modern island nation that retains an essentially Mediterranean character. Its 3,572 square mi (about the size of Connecticut) encompass citrus and olive groves, pine-forested mountains, and some of Europe's cleanest beaches. The easternmost island in the Mediterranean Sea, Cyprus has a 403-mi coastline and is approximately 60 mi west of Syria, 47 mi south of Turkey, and 200 mi north of Egypt. The island has a mild, typically Mediterranean climate, with an average of 340 days of sunshine a year. In winter, visitors can ski in the Troodos Mountains in morning and sunbathe on the beach in the afternoon.

Cyprus's strategic position in the eastern Mediterranean has made it subject to regular invasions by powerful empires. Greeks, Phoenicians, Assyrians, Egyptians, Persians, Romans, and Byzantines—all have either ruled or breezed through here. In 1191, Richard the Lion-Hearted, leader of the Third Crusade, took possession of Cyprus. A year later he sold Cyprus to the Knights Templar, who within a year resold it to Guy de Lusignan, the deposed King of Jerusalem. Guy's descendants ruled the island until the late 15th century, when it was annexed by the Venetians. The Turks wrested the island from Venice and ruled it from the 16th through 19th centuries. Cyprus became a British colony in 1914.

Vestiges of the diverse cultures that have ruled here dot the island, from remnants of Neolithic settlements and ancient Greek and Roman temple sites, such as the spectacular cliffside site of Kourion, to early Christian basilicas and painted Byzantine churches. Paphos has been designated a World Heritage Site by UNESCO. Kato Paphos, the lower town near the harbor, has a renowned collection of Roman mosaics. Many fortifications built by the Crusaders and the Venetians still stand throughout the island. A piece of the true cross is said to be kept in the monastery of Stavrovouni, and Paphos has the remains of a pillar to which St. Paul was allegedly tied when he was beaten for preaching Christianity.

Following independence in 1960, Cyprus became the focus of contention between Greeks and Turks—both in Greece and Turkey and in Cyprus itself. Currently some 84% of the population is Greek and 12% Turkish. Since a 1974 Turkish invasion that resulted in forced population shifts, Cyprus has been divided by a thin buffer zone—monitored by United Nations (UN) forces—between the now mainly Turkish Cypriot north and predominantly Greek Cypriot south. The zone cuts right through the capital city of Nicosia. Talks aimed at uniting the communities into one bizonal federal state have been going on for years. The north is noticeably poorer, and tourism is more developed in the south-

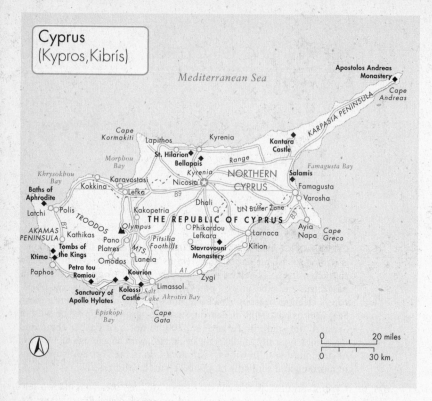

Cyprus
(Kypros, Kibrís)

Mediterranean Sea

Apostolos Andreas
Monastery

Cape
Andreas

KARPASIA PENINSULA

Cape
Kormakiti   Lapithos   Kyrenia   Kantara
                                            Castle

Morphou   Famagusta Bay
Bay   St. Hilarion
Khrysokhou   Bellapais   Range   Salamis
Bay   Karavostasi   Kyrenia   NORTHERN
Baths of   Kokkina   Nicosia   CYPRUS   Famagusta
Aphrodite   Lefka   Varosha
              B9
Latchi   Polis   Dhali   UN Buffer Zone
         TROODOS   Kakopetria   THE REPUBLIC OF CYPRUS
AKAMAS   Olympus   Phikardou   Ayia   Cape
PENINSULA Kathikas   Pano   Pitsilia   Lefkara   Larnaca   Napa   Greco
Tombs of   Platres   Foothills   Stavrovouni
Ktima   the Kings   MTS.   Monastery   Kition
         Omodos   Laneia
Paphos   Petra tou   A1
         Romiou   Kourion   Zygi
         Sanctuary of Kolossi   Limassol
         Apollo Hylates Castle Salt Akrotiri Bay
                           Lake
         Episkopi   Cape
           Bay   Gata

0   20 miles
0   30 km.

ern Republic of Cyprus. More important, entry through the Turkish-occupied north makes access to the internationally recognized Republic of Cyprus in the south impossible. Visitors to the south can visit the north for only one day, but must not have their passports stamped or they will be refused reentry.

At press time Cyprus was scheduled to join the European Union by May 2004—but without a resolution of the island's division only the Greek Cypriot south will fly the EU flag.

THE REPUBLIC OF CYPRUS

The Republic of Cyprus A to Z

To research prices, get advice from other travelers, and book travel arrangements, visit www.fodors.com.

AIR TRAVEL

There are no direct flights between Cyprus and the United States. Cyprus Airways and British Airways fly direct from London to Larnaca and Paphos. Cyprus Airways also operates from many continental and Mediterranean cities. Other carriers include KLM from Amsterdam.
🛫 British Airways ☎ 22761166. Cyprus Airways ☎ 22663054 ⊕ www.cyprusairways.com. KLM ☎ 22671616.

BOAT & FERRY TRAVEL

Passenger ships connect Cyprus (Limassol and Larnaca) with various Greek, Italian, Egyptian, and Middle Eastern ports.

BUS TRAVEL

This is the cheapest form of transportation in urban areas; the fare is 40¢. Buses operate every half hour and cover an extensive network. In Nicosia, buses run until 7:30 PM (6:30 PM October–April). In tourist areas during the summer services are extended until midnight. Intercity bus fares range between C£2 and C£3. For information on the Nicosia–Limassol–Paphos route and the Limassol–Larnaca–Ayia Napa route, call the numbers listed below.

🚌 **Nicosia–Limassol and Nicosia–Larnaka information** ☎ 22665814. **Nicosia–Paphos and Paphos–Polis information** ☎ 26936822. **Larnaka–Ayia Napa information** ☎ 23821318.

BUSINESS HOURS

BANKS & OFFICES Banks are open September–June, weekdays 8:30–12:30 and Monday afternoons 3:15–4:45; July and August, weekdays 8:15–12:30. Some have special afternoon tourist services and will cash traveler's checks weekdays 3–6 October–April, 4–7 May–August, and Saturday 8:15–12:30.

MUSEUMS & SIGHTS Museum hours vary; it pays to check ahead. Generally, museums are closed for lunch and on Sunday. Most ancient monuments are open from dawn to dusk.

SHOPS From November 1 to March 31, shops open between 8 and 9 and close as late as 7 PM Monday, Tuesday, and Thursday, 2 PM Wednesday, 8 PM Friday, and 3 PM Saturday. From April 1 to October 31, shops open between 8 and 9 and close as late as 8:30 PM Monday, Tuesday, and Thursday, 2 PM Wednesday, 9:30 PM Friday, and 5 PM Saturday. From June 15 to August 31 many shops close for the afternoon summer break daily 2–5. In tourist areas shops may stay open late and on Sunday in summer.

CAR RENTAL

Cars may be rented from C£17 per day, less off-season. Rental agencies are in all major cities as well as at the Larnaca Airport. Visitors can use a valid International Driver's License or their national driver's license, provided it is valid for the class of vehicle they rent.

CAR TRAVEL

GASOLINE Gas costs about 44¢ per liter.

ROAD CONDITIONS Main roads between large towns are good. Minor roads can be unsurfaced, narrow, and winding.

RULES OF THE ROAD Drive on the left. International traffic signs are used. The maximum speed limit is 100 kph (62 mph) on the motorways; in cities the speed limit is 50 kph (31 mph) unless otherwise posted. Use of front seat belts is compulsory. Children under the age of five are not permitted to sit in the front passenger seat.

CONSULATES, EMBASSIES & HIGH COMMISSIONS

🇨🇦 Canada **Consulate of Canada** ✉ 1 Annis Lampousas, Nicosia ☎ 22775508 🖷 22779905.

🇬🇧 United Kingdom **U.K. British High Commission** ✑ Alexandrou Palli, Box 21978, Nicosia ☎ 22861100 🖷 22861125.

🇺🇸 United States **United States Embassy** ✉ Gonia Metochiou and Ploutarchou, Egkomi, Nicosia ☎ 22776400 🖷 22780944.

CUSTOMS & DUTIES

Duty-free allowances are 250 grams of tobacco, 1 liter of spirits or 2 liters of wine, 0.6 liters of perfume, and up to C£100 in other goods (excluding jewelry). The export of antiques (items that are more than 100 years old) and historic artifacts is strictly forbidden unless a license is obtained from the Department of Antiquities in Nicosia.

🏛 **Department of Antiquities** ☎ 22865864.

EATING & DRINKING

The top hotels offer local and international food at good prices; large buffets are especially popular. Meals in local restaurants or tavernas usually start with a selection of *mezes* (appetizers), followed by kabobs, dolmas, stews, fresh fish, and various lamb dishes. Meals end with fruit or honey pastries and Greek coffee. In addition, most places serve sweet Commandaria, the world's oldest named wine. By law, all establishments must display a menu with government-approved prices, which include the 10% service charge and 5% value-added tax. Food is relatively cheap, and the quality is generally very good.

WHAT IT COSTS In Cyprus Pounds			
	$$$$	$$$	$$	$
AT DINNER	over C£12	C£7–C£12	C£5–C£7	under C£5

Prices are for a main course.

RESERVATIONS & DRESS Casual dress is acceptable in most restaurants in Cyprus, regardless of price category, although those in major hotels may require more formal clothing.

EMERGENCIES

For information in English about pharmacies that are open late and on holidays, call an area pharmacy information number, listed below by city. Medical problems can be handled in Nicosia's Nicosia General Hospital.

🚑 **Ambulance, Police, and Fire Brigade** ☎ 199 or 112. **Nicosia General Hospital** ☎ 22801400, 22801475, or 22806680. **Pharmacies open at night** ☎ 192 or automatic recording 1402 for Nicosia, 1405 for Limassol, 1404 for Larnaca, 1406 for Paphos.

HOLIDAYS

January 1; January 6 (Epiphany); February 23 (Green Monday); March 25 (Greek Independence Day); April 1 (Greek Cypriot National Day); April 11 and 12 (Greek Orthodox Easter); May 1 (Labor Day); May 31 (Pentecost Monday/Kataklysmos); August 15 (Assumption); October 1 (Cyprus Independence Day); October 28 (Greek National Day); December 24–26.

LANGUAGE

Greek is the main language, but English is widely spoken in hotels, tavernas, and other tourist haunts. Off the beaten path, creative gestures may have to do. The Republic of Cyprus government has carried out a controversial exercise to spell all place names as they are pronounced in Greek. Hence Nicosia becomes Lefkosia, Larnaca is Larnaka, Limassol is Lemesos, and Paphos is Pafos. Internationally, the original names remain, and in Cyprus both spellings are currently in use.

LODGING

All hotels listed have private bath or shower, but check when making reservations. Most have at least partial air-conditioning. In resort areas many hotel apartments have kitchens.

WHAT IT COSTS In Cyprus Pounds			
	$$$$	$$$	$$	$
FOR 2 PEOPLE	over C£80	C£60–C£80	C£40–C£60	under C£40

Prices are for a double room and include breakfast.

MAIL & SHIPPING

From September to June, main post offices are open Monday, Tuesday, Thursday, and Friday 7:30–1:30 and 3–6, Wednesday 7:30–1:30, and Saturday 8:30–10:30 AM. In July and August they are open Monday, Tuesday, Thursday, and Friday 7:30–1:30 and 4–7, Wednesday 7:30–1:30 and Saturday 8:30–10:30. Stamps are also sold at hotels, newsstands, and kiosks.

POSTAL RATES A 20-gram letter to the United States costs 41¢, a postcard 26¢. To Europe, a 20-gram letter costs 31¢, and a postcard 26¢.

MEDIA

The widely read *Cyprus Mail*, published daily, is the best source of local news in English and is available at newsstands and many hotels.

MONEY MATTERS

A cup of coffee or tea in the Republic of Cyprus costs 60¢–C£1; a glass of beer 75¢–C£1; a kabob around C£1.25–C£1.75; a bottle of local wine C£1.75–C£4.50.

CURRENCY The monetary unit in the Republic of Cyprus is the Cyprus pound (C£), which is divided into 100 cents. There are notes of C£1, C£5, C£10, and C£20 and coins of 1, 2, 5, 10, 20, and 50 Cyprus cents. The rate of exchange is approximately C£0.55 to the U.S. dollar, C£0.35 to the Canadian dollar, C£0.88 to the pound sterling, C£0.57 to the euro, C£0.31 to the Australian dollar, C£0.29 to the New Zealand dollar, and C£0.06 to the South African rand.

PASSPORTS & VISAS

No visas are necessary for holders of valid passports from the United States, Canada, the United Kingdom, or mainland European countries.

TAXIS

PRIVATE TAXIS Private taxis operate 24 hours throughout the island. They are generally very cheap within towns but far more expensive than service taxis between towns. Telephone from your hotel or hail one in the street. Urban taxis have an initial charge of C£1.25 (C£1.65 at night) and then 22¢ per kilometer (½ mi) in the daytime, 26¢ at night. Drivers are bound by law to run a meter. In-town journeys range from C£1.50 to about C£3.

SERVICE TAXIS Shared taxis accommodate four to seven passengers and are a cheap, fast, and comfortable way to travel between the main towns: Nicosia, Limassol, Larnaca, and Paphos. Tariffs are C£1.65–C£4.25. Seats must be booked by phone, and passengers may embark/disembark anywhere within the town. The taxis run every half hour (weekdays 6 AM–6 PM, until 7 PM in summer; weekends 7 AM until 5 PM). There is no service on public holidays. Various companies operate under the name "Travel & Express."

Main Number ☎ 227-77474. **Nicosia** ☎ 227-00888. **Limassol** ☎ 253-64114. **Larnaca** ☎ 246-61010. **Paphos** ☎ 269-33181.

TELEPHONES

COUNTRY & AREA CODES The country code for Cyprus is 357.

INTERNATIONAL CALLS To reach an AT&T, MCI, or Sprint long-distance operator, dial one of the access numbers listed below. Public phones may require the deposit of a coin or use of a phone card when you call these numbers.

Access Codes AT&T ☎ 080-90010. **MCI** ☎ 080-90000. **Sprint** ☎ 080-90001.

LOCAL CALLS Pay phones take 2¢, 5¢, 10¢, and 20¢ coins, but most popular these days are those taking Telecards. These have values of C£3, C£5, or C£10 and can be purchased at post offices, banks, souvenir shops, and kiosks. For telephone information, dial 192 in all towns.

TIPPING

A service charge of 10% and a 5% value-added tax (VAT) are included in all bills. If service has been especially good, add 5%.

TOURS

Licensed guides can be hired for half-day (starting at C£33) and full-day (starting at C£52) tours; a list of licensed guides is available from the Cyprus Tourism Organization. Night tours typically include dinner at a taverna, folk dancing, and bouzouki music. In seaside resorts hotels or travel agencies can arrange coastal cruises.

▸ Fees & Schedules **Cyprus Tourism Organization** ✆ Box 24942, Nicosia, 1355 ☎ 22765755 🖷 22766872.

VISITOR INFORMATION

▸ **Cyprus Tourism Organization** ✉ 13 E. 40th St., New York, 10016 ☎ 212-683-5280 ⊕ www.cyprustourism.org. **Nicosia (national office, for postal inquiries only)** ✉ Box 24535, CY 1390, ⊕ www.visitcyprus.org.cy ✉ **Nicosia** ✉ Aristokyprou 11 ☎ 22674264. **Larnaka** ✉ Plateia Vasileos Pavlou ☎ 24654322. **Larnaka International Airport** ☎ 24643576. **Limassol** ✉ Spyrou Araouzo St. ☎ 25362756. **Paphos** ✉ Gladstone St. ☎ 26932841.

WHEN TO GO

The tourist season runs throughout the year, but prices are lower November–March.

CLIMATE Spring and fall are best, usually warm enough for swimming but not uncomfortably hot. The rainy season is in January and February, and it often snows in the Troodos Mountains from January through March. July and August are always very hot and dry. The following are the average daily maximum and minimum temperatures for Nicosia.

Jan.	59F	15C	May	85F	29C	Sept.	92F	33C
	42	5		58	14		65	18
Feb.	61F	16C	June	92F	33C	Oct.	83F	28C
	42	5		65	18		58	14
Mar.	66F	19C	July	98F	37C	Nov.	72F	22C
	44	7		70	21		51	10
Apr.	75F	24C	Aug.	98F	37C	Dec.	63F	17C
	50	10		69	21		45	7

Exploring the Republic of Cyprus

Nicosia

The capital is twice divided. Its picturesque Old City is contained within 16th-century Venetian fortifications that separate it from the wide, tree-lined streets, large hotels, and high-rises of the modern section. The second division is political and more noticeable. The so-called Green Line (set up by the UN) divides the island between the Republic of Cyprus and Turkish-occupied Northern Cyprus. It is possible to arrange a day trip from the Greek to the Turkish sector through the official checkpoint in Nicosia (Ledra Palace), though it is essential to return by 5 PM. If you are late, you will not be allowed to reenter into the Republic of Cyprus. You will be forced to depart from Northern Cyprus. There are no official representatives of countries other than Turkey in the northern sector, so contact your consulate before crossing the line to confirm safety.

★ In the Greek sector **Laiki Yitonia,** at the southern edge of the Old City, is an area of winding alleys and traditional architecture that is undergoing a complete renovation. Among its important sites is the **Archbishopric,** with several museums. Tavernas, cafés, and crafts workshops line the shaded, cobbled streets. Just to the west lies Ledra Street, where modern shops alternate with yet more crafts shops. Head north to visit the tiny Greek Orthodox **Tripiotis church** (✉ Solonos 47–49), which dates from 1690 and is decorated with an ornately carved golden iconostasis and silver-covered icons.

The **Leventis Municipal Museum of Nicosia** traces the city's history from 3000 BC to the present, with exhibits on crafts and daily life. ✉ *17 Ippocratous St.* ☎ *22661475* ⊘ *Tues.–Sun. 10–4:30.*

In a wing of the archiepiscopal palace built in 1960 in neo-Byzantine style, the **Archbishop Makarios III Cultural Foundation** consists of the **Byzantine Art Museum,** with fine displays of icons spanning 1,000 years, and the **Greek War of Independence Gallery,** with maps, paintings, and mementos of 1821. ✉ *Archbishop Kyprianou Sq.* ☎ *22430008* ⊘ *Weekdays 9–4:30, Sat. 9–1.*

The **Museum of the National Struggle** has dramatic displays of the Cypriot campaigns against the British from 1955 to 1959. ✉ *Archbishop Kinyras 7* ☎ *22305878* ⊘ *Weekdays 8–2.*

★ The **Ethnographic Museum,** in the 14th-century part of the archiepiscopal palace, has demonstrations of ancient weaving techniques and displays of ceramics and olive and wine presses. ✉ *Archbishop Kyprianou Sq.* ☎ *22432578* ⊘ *Weekdays 9–5, Sun. 10–1.*

Don't miss **Ayios Ioannis** (St. John's) Cathedral, built in 1662 within the courtyard of the archiepiscopal palace. Look for the 18th-century murals illustrating important moments in Cypriot religious history and including a depiction of the tomb of St. Barnabas. ✉ *Archbishop Kyprianou Sq.* ⊘ *Weekdays 8–noon and 2–4, Sat. 8–noon.*

The **Famagusta Gate,** now a cultural center, has exhibitions, a lecture hall, and a theater. ✉ *Athina St.* ☎ *22430877* ⊘ *Weekdays 10–1 and 4–7.*

Fodor'sChoice
★ Outside the city walls stands the **Cyprus Museum.** It has archaeological displays ranging from Neolithic to Roman times. This stop is essential to an understanding of the island's ancient sites. ✉ *Museum St.* ☎ *22865888* ⊘ *Mon.–Sat. 9–5, Sun. 10–1.*

The neoclassical **Municipal Theater** (✉ Museum St. ☎ 22463028) seats 1,200 people and stages events throughout the year, including Greek-language dramas and concerts.

The lush **Municipal Gardens** (✉ opposite Cyprus Museum) are a well-maintained oasis of greenery in the city.

$$–$$$$ ✕ **Trattoria Romantica.** The fare is Italian at this distinctly friendly spot, with no shortage of advice available on any topic relating to Cyprus. There's a roaring fire in winter and service in the courtyard outside in summer. ✉ *13 Evagora Pallikaridi* ☎ *22376161* ▭ *AE, DC, MC, V* ⊘ *Closed Sun.*

$$ ✕ **Plaka Tavern.** One of the oldest eating establishments in the city, in the heart of Engomi, offers up to 30 different meze dishes, including such unusual items as snails and okra with tomatoes. ✉ *8 Stylianou Lena* ☎ *22446498* ▭ *AE, DC, MC, V.*

★ $$$$ ▤ **Cyprus Hilton.** The Hilton is among the island's best hotels, with extensive sports facilities, a skylit indoor pool, and dancing. An executive wing has business facilities. ✉ *Archbishop Makarios Ave., Box 22023,*

1516 ☎ *22377777* 🖷 *22377788* ⊕ *www.hilton.com* ⌕ *298 rooms,
17 suites* ♨ *2 restaurants, 2 pools* ▭ *AE, DC, MC, V.*

$$$$ 🏨 **Holiday Inn.** In the Old City, near commercial and historic districts,
this hotel's amenities include Japanese, international, and health-food
restaurants and a rooftop pool with a garden. ⊠ *70 Regina St., Box
21212, 1504* ☎ *22712712* 🖷 *22673337* ⊕ *www.cyprus-online.com*
⌕ *140 rooms* ♨ *4 restaurants, 2 pools* ▭ *AE, DC, MC, V.*

$$$–$$$$ 🏨 **Cleopatra Hotel.** This hostelry has a convenient location, cordial ser-
vice, and well-prepared food served poolside. ⊠ *8 Florina St., Box
21397, 1507* ☎ *22671000* 🖷 *22670618* ⊕ *www.hotelworld.com* ⌕ *89
rooms* ♨ *Restaurant, pool* ▭ *AE, DC, MC, V.*

Phikardou

In this museum village south of Nicosia, many rural houses have re-
markable woodwork; they also contain the household furnishings used
a century ago. Official tour guides are available in the village. ⊠ *Machairas
Alicosia Rd. via Klirou; 1½ km (1 mi) east of Gourri* ☎ *22634731 or
22691100 in Nicosia* ⊙ *Hrs vary.*

Ayia Napa

Much of this erstwhile fishing village, 30 km (19 mi) east of Larnaca,
has unfortunately been transformed by cheap package tourism into an
eyesore of the first magnitude. Young and frequently reckless British club-
bers, who flock here in the summer, are largely to blame. Although the
tourist authorities are hoping to change Ayia Napa's image, an over-
abundance of tacky hotels and fish-and-chip shacks—not to mention
the cavorting hordes—stand pointedly in the way. Still, the beaches are
fine, a 16th-century monastery merits a visit, and one hotel, the Nissi
Beach, is a relative haven of calm outside the town center. The Cape Greco
headland, a short drive outside Ayia Napa, is a popular spot to watch
the sunset.

$$$ 🏨 **Nissi Beach.** This modern, air-conditioned hotel is set in magnificent
gardens overlooking a sandy beach 3 km (2 mi) outside town. Some ac-
commodations are in bungalows, which do not have kitchens. Amenities include a dive shop, a health club, and more. ⊠ *Nissi Ave., Box 30010,
5340* ☎ *23721021* 🖷 *23721623* ⊕ *www.nissi-beach.com* ⌕ *270
rooms, 166 bungalows* ♨ *Restaurant, 2 pools* ▭ *AE, DC, MC, V.*

Larnaca

The seaside resort with its own airport, 51 km (32 mi) southeast of Nicosia,
has a flamboyant Whitsuntide celebration, called Cataklysmos, as well
as fine beaches, a palm-fringed seaside promenade, and a modern harbor. In the marina district, the **Larnaca Museum** displays treasures, including outstanding sculptures and Bronze Age seals. ⊠ *Kimon and Kilkis
Sts.* ☎ *24630169* ⊙ *Mon.–Wed. and Fri. 9–2:30, Thurs. 9–2:30 and
(except July and Aug.) 3–5.*

Kition, the old Larnaca of biblical times, was one of the most important
ancient city-kingdoms. Architectural remains of temples date from the
13th century BC. ⊠ *Kyman St., north of Larnaca Museum* ⊙ *Weekdays
9–2:30.*

The **Pierides Collection** is a private assemblage of more than 3,000 pieces
distinguished by its Bronze Age terra-cotta figures. ⊠ *Paul Zenon Ki-
tieos St. 4, near Lord Byron St.* ☎ *24652495* ⊙ *Mid-June–Sept.,
Mon.–Sat. 9–1 and 4–7; Oct.–mid-June, weekdays 9–1 and 3–6, Sat. 9–1.*

The **Medieval Museum** is in a 17th-century Turkish fort and has finds from
Hala Sultan Tekke and Kition. ⊠ *Within sight of marina on seafront*
⊙ *Mon.–Sat. 9–1, Sun. 11–1.*

In the town center stands one of the island's more important churches, **Ayios Lazarus** (Church of Lazarus), resplendent with icons. It has a fascinating crypt containing Lazarus's sarcophagus. ⊠ *Plateia Agiou Lazarou* ⊙ *Sept.–Mar., Mon.–Sat. 8–12:30 and 2:30–5; Apr.–Aug., Mon.–Sat. 8–12:30 and 3:30–6:30.*

★ South of Larnaca on the airport road is the 6½-square-km (2½-square-mi) **Salt Lake**. In winter it's a refuge for migrating birds. On the lake's edge a mosque stands in an oasis of palm trees guarding the **Hala Sultan Tekke**—burial place of the prophet Muhammad's aunt Umm Haram, and an important Muslim shrine. ⊠ *Salt Lake* ⊙ *Daily 9–5, summer 7:30–7:30.*

The 11th-century **Panayia Angeloktistos** church, 11 km (7 mi) south of Larnaca, has extraordinary Byzantine wall mosaics that date from the 6th and 7th centuries. ⊠ *Rte. B4, Kiti* ⊙ *Daily 8–noon, 2–4.*

On a mountain 40 km (25 mi) west of Larnaca stands the **Stavrovouni** (Mountain of the Cross) monastery. It was founded by St. Helena in AD 326; the present buildings date from the 19th century. The views from here are splendid. Ideally, you should visit the monastery in a spirit of pilgrimage rather than sightseeing, out of respect for the monks. Male visitors are allowed inside the monastery daily sunrise–sunset, except between noon and 3 (between noon and 1, Oct.–May).

$$–$$$ ✕ **Monte Carlo.** The outdoor seating at this spot along the road to the airport is on a balcony extending over the sea. Try the fish and meat mezes and casseroles. ⊠ *28 Pigiale Pasa Ave.* ☎ 24653815 ▭ *AE, DC, MC, V.*

$–$$$ ✕ **Militzis.** This restaurant is popular with locals for its homemade meze and other Cypriot specialties. ⊠ *42 Pigiale Pasa Ave.* ☎ 24655867 ▭ *AE, DC, MC, V.*

$$$$ ▦ **Golden Bay.** Comfort is paramount at this beach hotel east of the town center. All rooms have balconies and views of the sea. The extensive sports facilities make it an ideal spot. ⊠ *Larnaca-Dhekelia Rd., Box 40741, 6306* ☎ 24645444 🖷 24645451 ⊕ *www.lordos.com.cy* ⤳ *193 rooms* ♨ *2 restaurants, 2 pools* ▭ *AE, DC, MC, V.*

$$$–$$$$ ▦ **Sandy Beach Hotel.** Between Larnaca and Dhekelia, this beach hotel has a health club and tennis court. All rooms have twin beds and a partial sea view. ⊠ *Larnaca–Dekeleia Rd., 8 km (5 mi) from Larnaca, Box 40857, 6307* ☎ 24646333 🖷 24646900 ⊕ *www.sandybeachhotel. com.cy* ⤳ *205 rooms and suites* ♨ *3 restaurants, 2 pools* ▭ *AE, DC, MC, V.*

Lefkara

Some 40 km west of Larnaca, this picturesque village—one of the prettiest in Cyprus—is best known for its lace: Lefkaritika has been woven by hand here for centuries. Much of it is indeed beautiful, and most shopkeepers are willing to bargain. But considerably more evocative is the village itself, clustered on two hills and split between an upper portion, Kato Lefkara, and lower portion, Pano Lefkara. The tiny streets open up to a small plaza in front of the Church of the Holy Cross in Pano Lefkara, with a stupendous view of the surrounding sun-drenched hills.

Limassol

A major commercial port, cruise ship port of call, and wine-making center on the south coast, Limassol, 75 km (47 mi) from Nicosia, is a bustling, cosmopolitan town. Luxury hotels, apartments, and guest houses stretch along 12 km (7 mi) of seafront. The town's nightlife is among the liveliest on the island. In the center, the elegant, modern shops of Makarios

Avenue contrast with those of the old part of town, where local handicrafts prevail.

★ The 14th-century **Limassol Fort** was built on the site of a Byzantine fortification. Richard the Lion-Hearted married Berengaria of Navarre and crowned her Queen of England here in 1191. The **Cyprus Medieval Museum** in the castle displays medieval armor and relics. ⊠ *Near old port* ☎ *25330419* ⊙ *Mon.–Sat. 9–5, Sun. 10–1.*

For a glimpse of Cypriot folklore, visit the **Folk Art Museum.** The collection includes national costumes and fine examples of weaving and other crafts. ⊠ *Agiou Andreou 253* ☎ *05/362303* ⊙ *Oct.–May, Mon.–Wed. and Fri. 8:30–1:30 and 3–5:30, Thurs. 8:30–1:30; June–Sept., Mon.–Wed. and Fri. 8:30–1:30 and 4–6:30, Thurs. 8:30–1:30.*

The history of wine-making dates from at least 2000 BC in Cyprus, and many great wines (Madeira, Tokay, and others) are said to have originated from Cyprus grapes. The best-known Cypriot wine is the sweet red Commandaria, known in antiquity as "Nama." It so reminded Marc Antony of Cleopatra's kisses that he gave the whole island to his legendary lover because of it. There are dozens of other world-class wines from Cyprus. At the annual **Limassol Wine Festival** in the first half of September, local wineries offer free samples and demonstrate traditional grape-pressing methods. There are open-air music and dance performances over a period of nine days in the seaside Municipal Park. The large **KEO Winery,** just west of the town, welcomes visitors. ⊠ *Roosevelt Ave., toward the new port* ☎ *25362053* ⊙ *Tours weekdays at 10.*

A peaceful convent, **St. Nicholas of the Cats** is seemingly occupied by cats instead of nuns. According to legend, the cats are descendants of the animals St. Helena imported in the 4th century AD to whittle down the area's snake population. Their feline forebears must have done a good job, because today the dozens of cats in residence seem more inclined to laze in the sun than anything else. The little peninsula past the Akrotiri military base is still called Cape Gata (She-Cat). ⊠ *Edge of Akrotiri village.*

★ **Kolossi Castle,** a Crusader fortress of the Knights of St. John, was constructed in the 13th century and rebuilt in the 15th. ⊠ *Road to Paphos* ⊙ *June–Sept., daily 9–7:30; Oct.–May, daily 9–5.*

Fodor'sChoice The **Temple of Kourion** (Curium), west of Limassol, has Greek and Roman
★ ruins. Classical and Shakespearean plays are sometimes staged in the **amphitheater.** Next to the theater is the **Villa of Eustolios,** a summer house built by a wealthy Christian. Nearby is the partially rebuilt **Roman stadium.** The **Apollo Hylates** (Sanctuary of Apollo of the Woodlands), an impressive archaeological site, stands 3 km (2 mi) farther on. ⊠ *Main Paphos Rd.* ⊙ *June–Sept., daily 8–7:30; Oct.–May, daily 8–5.*

$$–$$$ ✕ **Porta.** A varied menu of international and Cypriot dishes, such as *foukoudha* barbecue (grilled strips of steak) and trout baked in prawn and mushroom sauce, is served in this (completely) renovated donkey stable. On many nights you'll be entertained by soft live music. ⊠ *17 Yenethliou Mitella, Old Castle* ☎ *25360339* ▭ *MC, V.*

$$–$$$ ✕ **Scottis Steak House.** Just off Makarios Avenue, the city's main thoroughfare, this restaurant serves some of the best steaks available in Cyprus. ⊠ *38 Souli St.* ☎ *25335173* ▭ *AE, DC, MC, V.*

★ $$$$ ▥ **Four Seasons Hotel.** One of the premier hotels in Cyprus, this property is not part of the international chain but offers comparable elegance. The spacious rooms have marble baths; many also have balconies with sea views. Guest services include a spa, a dive shop, a children's club, tennis and squash courts, and a gym. Furnishings lean toward the eccentric, with plenty of brightly colored carpets and fabric patterns. ⊠ *Old Limassol–Nicosia Rd., Box 57222, 3313* ☎ 25858000 🖷 25310887 ⊕ *www.fourseasons.com.cy* ⤳ *287 rooms and suites* ♨ *3 restaurants, 3 pools* 🖃 *AE, DC, MC, V.*

★ **$$$$** 🏨 **Le Meridien.** The striking lobby of this large, luxurious hotel is pink marble and glass. The amenities are first-class and include scuba diving, a kids' center, a health club, and a heated indoor pool. There's also a 3,000-square-meter indoor/outdoor thalassotherapy spa. Even if you take no spa treatments, request a room in the Royal Spa Wing—they're larger and more stylish. ⊠ *Old Limassol–Nicosia Rd., Box 56560, 3308* ☎ 25862000 🖷 25634222 ⊕ *www.lemeridien-cyprus.com* ⤳ *259 rooms, 27 suites, 43 garden villas* ♨ *3 restaurants, 2 pools* 🖃 *AE, DC, MC, V.*

$ 🏨 **Azur Beach.** This fine apartment hotel has a good sandy beach and helpful management. ⊠ *Potamios Yermasoyias, Box 51318, 3504* ☎ 25322667 🖷 25321897 ⤳ *24 1-bedroom apartments, 12 studios, 60 rooms* ♨ *2 restaurants* 🖃 *DC, MC, V.*

$ 🏨 **Continental.** A great sea view adds to the appeal of this family hotel near the Kolossi Castle. ⊠ *137 Spyros Araouzos Ave., Box 50398, 3604* ☎ 25362530 🖷 25373030 ⤳ *27 rooms* 🖃 *AE, V.*

Troodos Mountains

North of Limassol, these mountains, which rise to 6,500 feet, have shady cedar and pine forests and cool springs. Small, painted Byzantine churches in the Troodos and Pitsilia Foothills are rich examples of a rare indigenous art form. **Asinou Church,** near the village of Nikitari, and **Agios Nikolaos tis Stegis** (St. Nicholas of the Roof), south of Kakopetria, are especially noteworthy. In winter, skiers take over the mountains; **Platres,** in the foothills of Mt. Olympus, is the principal resort. At the **Kykkos** monastery, founded in 1100, the prized icon of the Virgin is reputed to have been painted by St. Luke. On the southern slopes of the Troodos is the village of Omodos, one of the prettiest in Cyprus, with whitewashed villas, narrow streets, and a broad central square. Laneia is not as beautiful but its many artisans and craftspeople make it worth a detour.

Petra tou Romiou

The legendary **birthplace of Aphrodite**—Greek goddess of love and beauty—is just off the main road between Limassol and Petra. Signs in Greek and English identify the offshore rock that is viewed from the shoreline. Park in the lot and take the passageway under the highway to the large pebble beach.

Paphos

In the west of the island and 142 km (88 mi) southwest of Nicosia, Paphos combines a seaside with stellar archaeological sites and a buzzing nightlife. Since the late 1990s it has attracted some of the most lavish resorts on the island. The modern center has a pleasant leisure harbor anchored by a medieval fortress. The surrounding area is one of the most scenic in Cyprus, especially the untrammeled Akamas Peninsula—still accessible only to off-road vehicles. In short, if you plan to spend any length of time in Cyprus, this is the place you'll want to make your base.

Fodor'sChoice Don't miss the elaborate **Roman mosaics** in the **Roman Villa of Theseus,** ★ the **House of Dionysos,** and the **House of Aion.** The impressive site is an easy walk from the harbor. ⊠ *Kato Paphos (New Paphos), near harbor* ☎ 26940217 ⊙ *June–Sept., daily 8–7:30; Oct.–May, daily 8–5.*

The **Paphos District Archaeological Museum** displays pottery, jewelry, and statuettes from Cyprus's Roman villas. ⊠ *43 Grivas Dighenis Ave., Ktima* ☎ 26940215 ⊙ *Weekdays 9–4, Sat. 9–1.*

★ There are notable 6th-century mosaics and icons in the **Byzantine Museum.** ⊠ *7 Andreas Ioannou St.* ☎ *26931393* ☉ *Weekdays 9–4, Sat. 9–1.*

The squat 16th-century **Paphos Fort** guards the entrance to the harbor; from the rooftop there's a lovely view. In early September, the fort provides the backdrop for the popular **Paphos Aphrodite Festival** (⊕ www. pafc.com.cy), a three-day festival that typically includes Italian opera.

★ ☉ *Daily 9–5, May–Oct 9–6.* The **Tombs of the Kings,** an early necropolis, date from 300 BC. The coffin niches are empty, but a powerful sense of mystery remains. ⊠ *Kato Paphos (New Paphos)* ☎ *26940295* ☉ *June–Sept., daily 8:30–7:30; Oct.–May, daily 8–5.*

The hermit and scholar Neophytos settled at what's referred to as the **Ayios Neophytos Monastery** in 1159, carving a home for himself out of the rock. Known in his time as the leading critic of Richard the Lion-Hearted and the Byzantine tax collectors, today he is best known for what became a series of grottoes hewn from the hillside rock and the evocative religious frescoes—some actually painted by Neophytos—they contain. The monastery itself, with no more than a half-dozen or so monks, is situated below the grottoes. ⊠ *Six mi north of Paphos.*

$$$ ✕ **Seven St. Georges Tavern.** This not only has the most delicious food
Fodor'sChoice in Paphos, but is also the most charming restaurant. Everyone from local
★ policemen to tourists in the know come to experience owners George and Lara's inventive Cyprus cooking, which includes a preponderance of fresh, often organic ingredients, and lots of options for vegetarians. ⊠ *Geroskipos, Paphos* ☎ *26963176* ▭ *AE, DC, MC, V* ☉ *Closed Mon.*

$–$$$ ✕ **Araouzos.** At this family-run restaurant, in the tiny village of Kathikas, about 20 mi north of Paphos, taste authentic Cyprus country cooking and experience old-fashioned hospitality. There's usually roast chicken and lots of fresh meze on the menu. Call ahead to make sure it's open on the day you plan to visit. ⊠ *In Kathikas village,* ☎ *26632076* ▭ *Cash only.*

$–$$$ ✕ **Chez Alex Fish Tavern.** The well-established tavern serves only fish (the catch of the day) and fish mezes. ⊠ *7 Constantia St., Kato Paphos* ☎ *26234767* ▭ *AE, DC, MC, V.*

$$$$ ▥ **Almyra.** Formerly the Paphos Beach Hotel, this property emerged from
Fodor'sChoice a total renovation in 2003 as a hip and family-friendly resort. There are
★ nine configurations of rooms, including several suites with private seaview terraces; all are outfitted for high-speed Internet access and some come with CD players. Furnishings throughout are decidedly contemporary, with cool fabrics and pastel colors. Among the leisure facilities are water sports, two swimming pools (one just for small children), and a spa. ⊠ *Posidonos St., Box 60136, 8125* ☎ *26933091* 🖷 *26942818* ⊕ *www.thanoshotels.com* ☞ *189 rooms and suites* ♨ *3 restaurants, 2 pools* ▭ *AE, DC, MC, V.*

$$$$ ▥ **Annabelle.** Tropical gardens, sprawling swimming pools, and com-
Fodor'sChoice fortably furnished rooms make this resort one of the area's best. Like
★ Alymra and Anassa, the property is owned by the Michaelides family, and friendly, first-rate guest services add to the appeal. ⊠ *Box 60401, 8102* ☎ *26938333* 🖷 *26945502* ⊕ *www.thanoshotels.com* ☞ *218 rooms and suites* ♨ *4 restaurants, 2 pools* ▭ *AE, DC, MC, V.*

★ $$$$ ▥ **Azia Beach Hotel.** Ninety percent of the rooms at this expansive hotel perched up on rugged cliffs have a sea view. The resort offers tennis, squash, and a health center. ⊠ *Akamas Ave., Box 62108, 8061* ☎ *26947800* 🖷 *26946883* ⊕ *www.aziahotel.com* ☞ *258 rooms* ♨ *3 restaurants, 2 pools* ▭ *AE, DC, MC, V.*

$$$$ ▥ **Coral Beach Hotel and Resort.** Just 10 minutes from the town of Paphos, this luxurious seaside hotel has Mediterranean-style rooms. Guest

facilities include a complete spa, scuba diving, and an arts and crafts workshop. ⊠ *Coral Bay, Box 62422, 8099* ☎ *26621601* 🖷 *2662930* ❧ *421 rooms* ⌂ *5 restaurants, 2 pools* ▤ *AE, DC, MC, V.*

$$$$ 🏨 **Elysium.** A Mediterranean sense of place reigns at this palatial re-
Fodor's Choice sort, which opened in 2002 near the Tombs of the Kings. Natural stone
★ and terra-cotta abound, and rooms are spacious and include studio and loft-style options. The Royal Garden villas have private pools. The spa has a colonnaded Roman-style pool and Aveda treatments. ⊠ *Queen Verenikis St., Box 60701, 8107* ☎ *26844444* 🖷 *26844333* ⊕ *www. elysium.com.cy* ❧ *250 rooms and suites* ⌂ *4 restaurants, 2 pools* ▤ *AE, DC, MC, V.*

$$$-$$$$ 🏨 **St. Georges Hotel.** This family-friendly seaside resort sits on 7 acres and has lovely landscaped gardens and views. ⊠ *Chlorakas village, Box 62372, 8063* ☎ *26951000* 🖷 *26948977* ❧ *245 rooms* ⌂ *2 restaurants, 2 pools* ▤ *AE, DC, MC, V.*

$$$ 🏨 **Amalthia Beach Hotel.** Amid banana groves, this hotel is friendly and personal. The impressive, open lobby overlooks the water, and the rooms have balconies with sea views. ⊠ *8574 Kisonerga Rd., Box 60323, 8102* ☎ *26947777* 🖷 *26945963* ⊕ *www.amalthia.com.cy* ❧ *168 rooms* ⌂ *Restaurant, 2 pools* ▤ *AE, DC, MC, V.*

$$ 🏨 **Hilltop Gardens Hotel Apartments.** All apartments have a view of the sea, just 500 yards away. Furnishings are a pleasant mixture of traditional Cypriot village style, including wooden furniture, and modern touches. ⊠ *Off Tombs of the Kings Rd., Box 60185, 8101* ☎ *26243111* 🖷 *26248229* ❧ *48 apartments* ⌂ *Pool* ▤ *AE, DC, MC, V.*

Polis

Just past the town's fishing harbor of Latchi, and 48 km (30 mi) north of Paphos, are the **Baths of Aphrodite,** a natural pool where the goddess is said to have seduced her swains. The wild, undeveloped Akamas Peninsula is perfect for a hike or jeep excursion (make inquiries for the latter in Paphos).

$$$$ 🏨 **Anassa.** *Anassa* is the Greek word for "queen," and this upscale ac-
Fodor's Choice commodation overlooks a stretch of coastline from an exclusive perch
★ filled with Greek motifs and frescoes. Suites vary in size from studios to expansive accommodations. All rooms have Mediterranean furnishings and include a private balcony or terrace. ⊠ *Polis-Baths of Aphrodite Rd., Box 66006, 8125* ☎ *26888000* 🖷 *26322900* ❧ *177 suites* ⌂ *4 restaurants, 2 pools* ▤ *AE, DC, MC, V.*

NORTHERN CYPRUS

Northern Cyprus is not a country in the strict sense of the term (see introduction to this chapter). All countries except Turkey recognize it as an illegally occupied part of the Republic of Cyprus.

Public holidays follow those in Turkey, with additional public holidays on May 1 (Labor Day), July 20 (Peace and Freedom Day), August 30 (Victory Day), October 29 (Turkish Republic Day), and November 15 ("Northern Cyprus Republic" Day). Although English is widely spoken, Turkish, not Greek, is the predominant language, and Turkish names designate the cities and towns: Nicosia is known as Lefkoşa, Kyrenia as Girne, and Famagusta as Gazimağusa. With 35,000 Turkish troops stationed in this corner of the island, visitors are advised to obey the NO PHOTOGRAPHS signs wherever they appear.

Northern Cyprus A to Z

AIR TRAVEL

Cyprus Turkish Airlines, Istanbul Airlines, and Turkish Airlines run all flights via mainland Turkey, usually with a change of plane at Istanbul. There are also nonstop flights from Adana, Ankara, Antalya, and İzmir to Ercan Airport, 24 km (15 mi) from Lefkoşa. It is not possible to enter the Republic of Cyprus from Northern Cyprus unless you are returning from a day trip from Lefkoşa.

BOAT & FERRY TRAVEL

Ferries run from Turkey: from Mersin to Gazimağusa and from Alyana, Antalya, and Tasucu to Girne.

BUS TRAVEL

Minibuses and the shared *dolmuş* (taxis) are the cheapest forms of transportation. Service is frequent on main routes. A minibus from Lefkoşa to Girne costs about $1.50 and to Gazimağusa about $1.80, with slightly lower fares if you get off before the final destination. The price of a seat in a dolmuş remains the same wherever you get off and, for the same trips, would cost approximately the same as a minibus at about $1.50 and $1.80, respectively.

BUSINESS HOURS

Shops are open in summer 8–1 and 4–7, winter 9–1 and 2–6. From May through September, most of the main tourist sites are open daily 8–7, but check before you visit.

CAR TRAVEL

See Car Travel *in* The Republic of Cyprus A to Z.

EATING & DRINKING

WHAT IT COSTS In U.S. Dollars			
$$$$	$$$	$$	$
AT DINNER over $19	$14–$19	$9–$14	under $9

Prices are for a main course.

LODGING

WHAT IT COSTS in U.S. Dollars			
$$$$	$$$	$$	$
FOR 2 PEOPLE over $150	$100–$150	$50–$100	under $50

Prices are for a double room and include breakfast.

MONEY MATTERS

Prices for food and accommodations tend to be lower than those in the Republic of Cyprus. However, with the exception of Turkish wines and spirits, most foreign drinks are slightly more expensive. A cup of coffee costs around $1, a glass of beer about $1.50. Wine is around $3 per glass. A 35-km (22-mi) taxi ride costs about $25.

CURRENCY   The monetary unit in Northern Cyprus is the Turkish lira (TL). There are bills for 100,000; 250,000, 500,000, 1,000,000, 5,000,000, and 10,000,000 TL; and coins for 10,000, 25,000, 50,000, and 100,000 TL. The Turkish lira is subject to considerable inflation, so most of the prices in this section are quoted in U.S. dollars.

VISITOR INFORMATION

🚺 **Department of Tourism Marketing** ⊠ Selçuklu Caddesi, Lefkoşa 🕾 Selçuklu Cad., Lefkoşa, KKTC, Mersin 10, Turkey ☎ 392/228-9629 🖶 392/228-9625. **Regional tourism offices** ☎ 392/366-2864 in Gazimağusa; 392/815-2145 in Girne; 392/228-9629 in Lefkoşa.

Exploring Northern Cyprus

Lefkoşa (Nicosia)

The Turkish half of the city is nominally the capital of Northern Cyprus. A walk around the Old City, within the encircling walls, is rich with glimpses from the Byzantine, Lusignan, and Venetian past. In addition to Venetian fortifications, the Old City contains the **Selimiye Mosque,** originally the 13th-century Cathedral of St. Sophia and a fine example of Gothic architecture to which a pair of minarets has been added. ⊠ *Selimiye St.* ⊙ *Oct.–Apr., weekdays 8–1 and 2–5; May–Sept., Mon. 7:30–1 and 2–6, Tues.–Fri. 7:30–2.*

Near the Girne Gate is the **Turkish Ethnographical Museum** (Mevlevi Shrine and Ethnographic Museum), the former home of the Mevlevi Dervishes, a Sufi order. The building now has a museum of Turkish history and culture. ⊠ *Girne St.* ⊙ *Oct.–Apr., weekdays 9–1 and 2–4:30; May–Sept., Mon. 7:30–1 and 2–6, Tues.–Fri. 7:30–2.*

★ $–$$ ✕ **Cyprus Kitchen.** This restaurant offers some of the finest authentic Cypriot cuisine in Northern Cyprus, with superb starters and grilled meats. The interior is crammed with mementos of village life, from a plough and loom to handicrafts. ⊠ *Atatürk Caddesi No. 39, Gönyeli* ☎ *392/ 223–1694* ▤ *MC, V* ⌂ *Reservations essential.*

Kyrenia (Girne)

Of the coastal resorts, Kyrenia (called Girne by the Turks, who have occupied the city since 1974), with its yacht-filled harbor, has always been the most appealing. There are excellent beaches to the east and west of the town. **Girne Castle,** overlooking the harbor, is Venetian. It's now the site of the **Batık Gemi Müzesi** (Shipwreck Museum), whose prize possession is the remains of a ship that sank around 300 BC. ⊙ *Daily 8–5.*

The fantastic ruins of the **St. Hilarion Kalesi** (Castle of St. Hilarion) stand on a hilltop 11 km (7 mi) southwest of Girne. It's a strenuous walk, so take a taxi (about $30 round-trip from Girne); the views are breathtaking. ⊙ *Daily 9–5.*

The romantic ruins of the former **Bella Pais Manastiri** (Abbey of Bellapais), built in the 12th century by the Lusignans, are just as impressive as those at St. Hilarion Kalesi. They lie on a mountainside 6 km (4 mi) southeast of Girne, overlooking the coastal plain. ⊙ *Daily 8:30–5.*

$ ✕ **Niazi's.** Less picturesque than the restaurants ringing the harbor, this place serves better food with excellent grilled fare, including şeftali kebab (meatballs), a Turkish Cypriot specialty, and homemade desserts. ⊠ *Kordonboyu Caddesi* ☎ *392/815–2160* ▤ *MC, V.*

$$$ 🏨 **Jasmine Court.** Next to its own beach in Girne, the luxurious hotel is a resort in its own right, with air-conditioned rooms, palm tree–shaded poolside terraces, sports facilities, a casino, and a disco. ⊠ *Temmuz Cad. 20, Girne, Mersin 10, Turkey* ☎ *392/815–1450* 🖶 *392/815–1488* ⊕ *www.lemeridien-cyprus.com* 🗗 *143 rooms* ⌂ *Restaurant, pool* ▤ *MC, V.*

$$ 🏨 **Dome Hotel.** Despite the gleaming marble of the lobby and restaurant, this doyen of Girne's hotels still has a nostalgic air of faded 1960s grandeur. Rooms on the seaside may have a slightly battered feel, but they are superbly situated, almost literally over the water. ⊠ *Kordon-*

boyu Caddesi, Girne, Mersin 10, Turkey ☎ *392/815–2453* 🖷 *392/
815–2772* ⊕ *www.domehotel.com* 🖙 *160 rooms* ⚭ *Restaurant, pool*
🖃 *MC, V.*

Famagusta (Gazimağusa)

Famagusta (Turkish: Gazimağusa), the chief port of Northern Cyprus,
has massive and well-preserved Venetian walls and the late-13th-cen-
tury Gothic Cathedral of St. Nicholas, now Lala Mustafa Pasha Mosque.
On August 1, 1571, the Venetians surrendered the town to the Turks,
ending a brutal 10-month siege and signifying the end of their rule in
Cyprus. A winged lion, symbol of the Republic of Venice, still graces
the old Sea Gate, and in a nod to Cristoforo Moro, the Venetian ad-
ministrator immortalized by Shakespeare, one of the battlements is
named Othello's Tower. The Old Town, within the walls, is the most
intriguing district to explore.

Salamis, on the seashore north of Gazimağusa, is an ancient ruined city
and perhaps the most dramatic archaeological site on the island. St. Barnabas and St. Paul arrived in Salamis and established a church near here.
Most of the ruins date from the Roman Empire, including a well-preserved theater, an amphitheater, villas, and superb mosaic floors. After
surviving earthquakes and pirate raids, the city was abandoned in the
7th century AD when the population moved to what is now Gazimağusa.
Much of the ancient city is overgrown with a tangle of bushes and dune
grass, which only serve to enhance the site's serene, poignant beauty.
⊘ *Daily 8–5.*

CZECH REPUBLIC

PRAGUE, SIDE TRIPS TO BOHEMIA & MORAVIA

FOR ALL ITS HISTORY, the Czech Republic is a very young nation. After a peaceful revolution overthrew a Communist regime that had been in power for 40 years, Czechoslovakia split in 1993 as its two constituent republics, Czech and Slovak, formed independent countries.

Formed from the ruins of the Austro-Hungarian Empire at the end of World War I, Czechoslovakia appeared to withstand the threat of divisive nationalism and brought stability to the potentially volatile region. During the difficult 1930s, the Czechoslovak republic stood as the model democracy in Central Europe. In the 1960s a courageous Slovak, Alexander Dubček, led the 1968 Prague Spring, an intense period of national renewal. Students and opponents of the Communist regime in both Prague and Bratislava toppled the ruling party in 1989.

Czechoslovakia proved to be an artificial creation that masked important and long-standing cultural differences between two outwardly similar peoples. The old Czech lands of Bohemia and Moravia, whose territory makes up most of the Czech Republic, can look to a rich cultural history that goes back a millennium, and they played pivotal roles in the great religious and social conflicts of European history. Slovakia, by contrast, languished for centuries as an agrarian outpost of the Hungarian empire. Given the state of the Slovaks' national ego, independence was probably inevitable.

Since the 1989 revolution, Prague, the Czech capital, has become one of Europe's top destinations. Forget old impressions of neglect and melancholy; Prague exudes an atmosphere of enthusiasm. Musicians and writers find new inspiration in the city that once harbored Mozart and Kafka. Spectacular Gothic, baroque, and art nouveau treasures stand in glorious counterpoint to drab remnants of socialist architecture.

Outside the capital you can discover everything from imperial spas to modern industrial cities. Don't pass up the lovely towns and castles of southern Bohemia: the Renaissance river town of Český Krumlov ranks among Central Europe's grandest sights.

CZECH REPUBLIC A TO Z

To research prices, get advice from other travelers, and book travel arrangements, visit www.fodors.com.

AIR TRAVEL

Good air service links Prague with several other towns, including Ostrava in Moravia and Bratislava and Poprad (for the High Tatras) in

Czech Republic
(Česká Republika)

Slovakia. Prices are reasonable. Make reservations at Čedok offices or directly at ČSA (Czech Airlines).

🛈 Airlines & Contacts **ČSA (Czech Airlines)** ☎ 220/104310 or 222/319995.

BUS TRAVEL

A reasonable bus network provides quicker service than trains at somewhat higher prices (low by Western standards). Buses are often full. Reserve your seat in advance, especially on long-distance routes. The Web site www.bus.cz has a searchable database to retrieve timetables for buses throughout the country (note that you should use the Czech spelling of towns, e.g., Praha instead of Prague). Most international buses arrive and depart from the main bus station, Florenc, where you'll find schedules and a few travel agencies.

BUSINESS HOURS

Banks are open weekdays 8–5. Museums are usually open Tuesday–Sunday 10–5. Shops are generally open weekdays 9–6; some close for lunch between noon and 2. Many stores, especially larger ones in the downtown area, are now open weekends.

CAR TRAVEL

EMERGENCIES Emergency road service offers help for stranded motorists.

🛈 **Emergency road service** ☎ 1230.

GASOLINE At about 100 Kč (US$3.45) a gallon, gasoline is expensive. Look for service stations along main roads on the outskirts of towns and cities.

ROAD CONDITIONS Main roads are usually good, if sometimes narrow. An expressway links Plzeň, Prague, Brno, and Bratislava. If you plan to do much exploring, pick up an *Auto Atlas,* available in bookstores and souvenir shops.

RULES OF THE ROAD Drive on the right. Speed limits are 50 kph (31 mph) in urban areas, 90 kph (55 mph) on open roads, and 130 kph (81 mph) on expressways. Seat belts are compulsory everywhere; drinking and driving is strictly prohibited. A permit sticker is required to drive on expressways and other four-lane highways. It costs 1,000 Kč per year, 200 Kč per month, or 100 Kč for 10 days. Stickers are sold at border crossings, post offices, and some service stations. The law now gives pedestrians the right of way at intersections, although most motorists ignore it.

CUSTOMS & DUTIES

You may import duty-free 200 cigarettes, 50 cigars, 1 liter of spirits, 2 liters of wine, and gifts with a total value of 1,000 Kč. Goods worth up to 3,000 Kč (approximately US$90) are not liable for duty upon arrival. Declare items of greater value (jewelry, computers, and so on) on arrival to avoid problems with customs officials on departure. You may export only antiques that are certified as not having historical value; reputable dealers will advise. Play it safe, and hang on to your receipts.

EATING & DRINKING

Dining options include restaurants; the *vinárna* (wine cellar), which covers anything from inexpensive wine bars to swank restaurants; the more down-to-earth *pivnice* or *hospody* (beer taverns); cafeterias; and coffee shops and snack bars. Be wary of food bought from street vendors, as sanitary conditions may not be ideal.

Prague ham is a favorite first course. The most typical main dish is roast pork (or duck or goose) with sauerkraut. Also try the outstanding trout, carp, and other freshwater fish. Crepes, here called *palačinky,* are ubiquitous and come with savory or sweet fillings. Dumplings in various forms, generally with a rich gravy, accompany many dishes. A typical Czech breakfast is cold cuts and spreadable cheese or jam with rolls, washed down with coffee. Privatization has brought more culinary variety, especially in Prague.

	WHAT IT COSTS In Czech Republic Koruny		
$$$$	**$$$**	**$$**	**$**
AT DINNER over 350	240–350	130–240	under 130

Prices are per person for a main course.

MEALTIMES Lunch is usually from 11:30 to 2 or 3; dinner from 6 to 9:30 or 10. At places open all day, it's easier to get a table during off-hours.

RESERVATIONS & A jacket and tie are recommended for $$$$ and $$$ restaurants. In-
DRESS formal dress is appropriate elsewhere. Make reservations at all but the humblest places during high season.

EMBASSIES
🔝 Australia **The Honorary Consulate and Trade Commission of Australia** ✉ Klimentská 10 ☎ 251-018-352.
🔝 Canada ✉ Mickiewiczova 6, Hradčany ☎ 272-101-800 ⊕ www.canada.cz.
🔝 Ireland ✉ Tržiště 13 ☎ 257/530061.
🔝 New Zealand consulate ✉ Dykova 19 ☎ 257/530061.
🔝 South Africa ✉ Ruska 65, Vršovice ☎ 267/311114.
🔝 United Kingdom ✉ Thunovská 14, Malá Strana ☎ 257/402111 ⊕ www.britain.cz.
🔝 United States ✉ Tržiště 15, Malá Strana ☎ 257/530663 ⊕ www.usis.cz.

HOLIDAYS
January 1; Easter Sunday and Monday; May 1 (Labor Day); May 8 (Liberation Day); July 5 (Sts. Cyril and Methodius); July 6 (Jan Hus); September 28 (Day of Czech Statehood); October 28 (Czechoslovak Proclamation Day); November 17 (Uprising of Students for Freedom and Democracy); December 24–26.

LANGUAGE
Czech, which belongs to the Slavic family of languages along with Russian, Polish, and Slovak, uses the Latin alphabet like English but adds special diacritical marks to make certain sounds: č is written for the "ch" sound, for instance. Unlike words in many other languages, Czech words are spelled phonetically, and the emphasis is almost always on the first syllable. You'll find a growing number of English-speakers, especially among young people and in the tourist industry. German is generally understood throughout the country.

LODGING
The Czech Republic offers everything from upscale hotels to campsites, though renovated older properties in particular have great character and style. The shortage of reasonably affordable hotel rooms is not as bad as it once was, but advance reservations are still recommended. The standards of facilities and services in the less-expensive categories hardly match those in the West, so don't be surprised by faulty plumbing or indifferent reception clerks. Unless otherwise noted, rooms include bath.

WHAT IT COSTS In Czech Republic Koruny			
$$$$	**$$$**	**$$**	**$**
PRAGUE			

FOR 2 PEOPLE	over 5,300	2,800–5,300	1,700–2,800	under 1,700
OTHER AREAS				
HOTELS	over 2,600	1,400–2,600	900–1,400	under 900

Hotel prices are for a standard double room in high season.

CAMPING Maps showing the locations of the many campgrounds around the country are available at bookstores and tourist offices. Several campgrounds in Prague operate year-round; the Prague Information Service (PIS) has a list.
📌 **Prague Information Service** ✉ Haštalská 7 ☎ 12444 ⊕ www.pis.cz.

HOSTELS IYH members can book reservations at any of more than 30 hostels across the country, including two in Prague (350 Kč and up, including breakfast), at KMC. IYH cards are also sold here (250 Kč) and at CKM Youth Travel Service.

In Prague most hostels are open to everyone and generally operate year-round. Ask at travel agencies about hostels outside Prague. Rates start at 260 Kč per person, breakfast not included, at hostels not affiliated with IYH.
📌 Organizations **CKM Youth Travel Service** ✉ Mánesova 77, Prague 1 ☎ 222/721595. **KMC** ✉ Karolíny Světlé 30, 160 00 Prague 6 ☎ 222/220081 ⊕ www.kmc.cz/English.htm.

HOTELS Bills can be paid in koruny, but most hotels accept dollars or euros, and many of the upscale ones now list rates in euros. Check to see if your hotel insists on hard currency, although this is now very rare. Some hotels refuse to accept credit cards. Breakfast is often included in the room price.

ROOMS IN PRIVATE HOMES Many travel agencies in Prague offer accommodation in private homes. Such rooms are invariably cheaper and often more comfortable than hotel rooms, though you may have to sacrifice some privacy. The largest room-finding service is probably AVE in the main and Holešovice train stations and at the airport (all branches are open daily). Insist on a room in the city center, however, or you may find yourself in a dreary, far-off suburb. Another helpful agency is City of Prague Accommodation Service. Elsewhere, look along main roads for signs that read ROOM FREE (room available) or, in German, ZIMMER FREI or PRIVATZIMMER. Offices of the travel bureau Čedok and the Prague Information Service (PIS) can also help you find private accommodations.
📌 **Ave** ☎ 224/223226 or 224/223521 ⊕ www.avetravel.cz. **Prague Information Service** ✉ Haštalská 7 ☎ 12444 ⊕ www.pis.cz.

MAIL & SHIPPING

POSTAL RATES First-class (airmail) letters to the United States and Canada cost 14 Kč for up to 20 grams; postcards cost 12 Kč. First-class (airmail) letters to the United Kingdom cost 9 Kč for up to 20 grams; postcards cost 9 Kč.

RECEIVING MAIL If you don't know where you'll be staying, American Express mail service is a great convenience, available at no charge to anyone holding an American Express credit card or carrying American Express traveler's checks. You can also have mail held *poste restante* (general delivery) at post offices in major towns, but the letters should be marked *Pošta 1*, to designate the city's main post office. The poste restante window is at the main post office in Prague. You will be asked for identification when you collect your mail.

🖪 Post Offices **American Express** ✉ Václavské náměstí 56 (Wenceslas Square). **Main Post Office** ✉ Jindřišská ul. 14, Prague.

MONEY MATTERS

Costs are highest in Prague and only slightly lower in the main Bohemian resorts and spas, though even in these places you can now find inexpensive accommodations in private homes. The least expensive area is southern Moravia. Note that many public venues in Prague and the Czech Republic continue the practice of adhering to a separate pricing system for Czechs and for foreigners. (Foreigners may be charged double or more on museum admission, for example.) This practice should end after the Czech Republic joins the European Union in 2004.

Costs: cup of coffee, 30 Kč; beer (½ liter), 19 Kč–40 Kč; Coca-Cola, 30 Kč; ham sandwich, 40 Kč; 1½-km (1-mi) taxi ride, 50 Kč–70 Kč; museum and castle admission, 20 Kč–300 Kč.

CURRENCY   The unit of currency in the Czech Republic is the crown, or koruna (plural koruny), written as Kč, and divided into 100 haléřů (hellers). There are bills of 50, 100, 200, 500, 1,000, and 5,000 koruny and coins of 50 hellers and 1, 2, 5, 10, 20, and 50 koruny. Coins of 10 and 20 hellers were phased out in 2003.

At press time, the rate of exchange was 29.50 Kč to the U.S. dollar, 19.80 Kč to the Canadian dollar, 55.19 Kč to the pound sterling, 17.85 Kč to the Australian dollar, 16.54 Kč to the New Zealand dollar, 3.62 Kč to the South African rand, and 31.80 Kč to the euro. Banks and ATMs give the best rates. Banks and private exchange outlets, which litter Prague's tourist routes, charge either a set fee or a percentage of the transaction or both. It's wise to compare. Ask exactly how much you will get back before converting your money. Signs promising no commission are often misleading. The koruna is fully convertible and can be purchased outside the country and changed into other currencies, but you should keep your receipts and convert your koruny before you leave the country just to be sure.

PASSPORTS & VISAS

ENTERING THE   CZECH REPUBLIC   United States and British citizens need only a valid passport to visit the Czech Republic as tourists. United States citizens may stay for 30 days without a visa; British citizens, six months. Canadians need a visa (C$75), which is valid for three months. Multiple entry visas cost more and are valid for six months. Australians need tourist visas to enter the Czech Republic; the visa is less expensive if obtained at a Czech embassy or consulate outside the Czech Republic; at the Czech Republic border, it costs 1,600 Kč. Even though the Czech Republic is expected to enter the European Union in 2004, passports may still be required to enter the country from other EU countries until that time.

TELEPHONES

Most people use mobile phones, so cards for working pay phones are becoming hard to find. To use a public phone, buy a phone card at a newsstand or tobacconist in the downtown area. Cards cost 175 Kč for 50 units or 320 Kč for 100 units (local calls cost one unit each). To place a call, lift the receiver, insert the card, and dial. Another option is Karta X, which comes in denominations of 300 Kč to 1,000 Kč and can be used for discount long-distance calling on any phone by entering a 14-digit number. It's available at exchange booths and newsstands.

COUNTRY &   AREA CODES   The Czech Republic's country code is 420. The country dropped regional codes and adopted a nationwide nine-digit standard in late 2002.

INTERNATIONAL CALLS
Some special international pay-phone booths in central Prague will take 5 Kč coins or accept phone cards that allow automatic dialing. You will also find coin and card booths at the main post office (Jindřišská 14, near Václavské náměstí [Wenceslas Square]); the entrance for telephone service is in this building but around the corner on Politických vězňů. The international dialing code is 00. Dial 1181 for international inquiries to the United States, Canada, or the United Kingdom. Calls can be placed using AT&T USA Direct, MCI, and Sprint international operators. International rates vary according to destination.

🏴 Access Codes **AT&T USA Direct** ☎ 0042-000101. **MCI** ☎ 0042-000112. **Sprint** ☎ 0042-087187.

TIPPING

A service charge is rarely added to restaurant bills. Give a tip for good service directly to the waiter when you pay your bill. As a rule of thumb, round up to the next multiple of 10 (i.e., if the bill comes to 83 Kč, give the waiter 90 Kč). Give 10% on big or group tabs. For taxis, consider 10% a reasonable tip. In the better hotels doormen should get 20 Kč for each bag they carry to the check-in desk; bellhops get up to 40 Kč each for taking them up to your rooms. In $$ or $ hotels plan to lug your own baggage.

TRAIN TRAVEL

The country has an extensive rail network. Fares are relatively low and trains are crowded. You have to pay a small supplement on EuroCity (EC) and InterCity (IC) trains. Most long-distance trains have dining cars; overnight trains between main centers have sleeping cars.

TRANSPORTATION AROUND THE CZECH REPUBLIC

Traveling in the Czech Republic is relatively simple once you know the basic street-sign words: *ulice* (street), abbreviated to *ul.* (note that common usage often drops ulice in a printed address), *náměstí* (square), abbreviated to *nám.*, and *třída* (avenue). In most cases blue signs on buildings mark the street address.

VISITOR INFORMATION

Many towns have an information office ("Infocentrum") or private tourist bureau, often in the main square. The ubiquitous Čedok, now a private travel agency, has offices in all larger towns.

🏴 **Čedok** main office ✉ Na Příkopě 18, 111 35 Prague 1 ☎ 224/197111.

WHEN TO GO

Organized sightseeing tours run from April or May through October (year-round in Prague). Some monuments, especially castles, either close entirely or curtail their hours in winter. Hotel rates may decrease in the off-season except during festivals. May, the month of fruit blossoms, is the time of the Prague Spring International Music Festival. Huge crowds clog Prague sites in spring, summer, and early fall.

CLIMATE
The following are the average daily maximum and minimum temperatures for Prague.

Jan.	36F	2C	May	66F	19C	Sept.	68F	20C
	25	-4		46	8		50	10
Feb.	37F	3C	June	72F	22C	Oct.	55F	13C
	27	-3		52	11		41	5
Mar.	46F	8C	July	75F	24C	Nov.	46F	8C
	32	0		55	13		36	2
Apr.	58F	14C	Aug.	73F	23C	Dec.	37F	3C
	39	4		55	13		28	-2

PRAGUE

Poets, philosophers, and residents alike have long sung the praises of Praha (Prague), also referred to as the Golden City of a Hundred Spires. Like Rome, Prague is built on seven hills, which slope gently or tilt precipitously down to the Vltava (Moldau) River. The riverside location, enhanced by a series of graceful bridges, makes a great setting for two of the city's most notable features: its extravagant, fairy-tale architecture and its memorable music. Mozart claimed that no one understood him better than the citizens of Prague, and he was only one of several great masters who lived or lingered here.

It was under Karel IV (Charles IV), in the 14th century, that Prague first became the seat of the Holy Roman Empire—virtually the capital of Western Europe—and acquired its distinctive Gothic imprint. The medieval inheritance is still here under the overlays of graceful Renaissance and exuberant baroque. Prague escaped serious wartime damage, but it didn't escape neglect. During the 1990s, however, artisans and their workers have restored dozens of the city's historic buildings with care and sensitivity.

Exploring Prague

Numbers in the margin correspond to points of interest on the Prague map.

Shades of the five medieval towns that combined to form Prague linger in the divisions of its historic districts. On the flat eastern shore of the Vltava River are three areas arranged like nesting boxes: **Josefov** (the old Jewish Quarter) within **Staré Město** (Old Town) bordered by **Nové Město** (New Town). **Malá Strana** (Lesser Quarter) and **Hradčany** (Castle District) perch along the river's hillier west bank. Spanning the Vltava is **Karlův most** (Charles Bridge), which links the Old Town to the Lesser Quarter; everything within the historic center can be reached on foot in a half hour or less from here.

Nové Město & Staré Město (New Town & Old Town)

New Town is more than 500 years old, and only new when compared with Old Town, which dates from the 12th century. Both neighborhoods have a mix of Renaissance, baroque, and modern architecture. Old Town has the slight advantage in historic sites, with its world-famous Astronomical Clock Tower and Old Town Square. New Town, with its store-packed Wenceslas Square and multiple department stores, has the lead in shopping. Almost every street in this area has a building or monument worth checking out.

⓫ Betlémská kaple (Bethlehem Chapel). The martyr and national hero Jan Hus thundered his reform teachings from the chapel pulpit during the early 15th century. The structure was rebuilt in the 1950s, but the little door through which Hus came to the pulpit is original, as are some of the inscriptions on the wall. ⊠ *Betlémské nám 5* 🎟 *30 Kč* ☉ *Apr.–Sept., daily 9–6; Oct.–Mar., daily 9–5.*

❸ Celetná ulice. Medieval kings took this street on their way to their coronation at Prague Castle. The **Royal Route** continues past the Gothic spires of the Týn Church in Old Town Square; it then crosses Charles Bridge and goes up to the castle. Along the route stands every variety of Romanesque, Gothic, Renaissance, and baroque architecture.

❿ Clam-Gallas palác (Clam-Gallas Palace). Squatting on a constricted site in the heart of the Old Town, this pompous baroque palace was designed by the great Viennese architect J. B. Fischer von Erlach. All the sculptures, including the titans that struggle to support the two doorways, are the work of one of the great Bohemian baroque artists, Matthias Braun. An exhibition hall on the first floor is open daily from 10 to 6, which is one way to peek inside the building. Another is to attend an evening concert in the large hall. ✉ *Husova 20* ⊕ *www.ahmp.cz.*

④ **Dům U černé Matky Boží** (House of the Black Madonna). This Cubist building adds a jolt to the architectural styles along Celetná ulice. In the second decade of the 20th century, several leading Czech architects boldly applied Cubism's radical reworking of visual space to structures. The Black Madonna, designed by Josef Gočár, is unflinchingly modern yet topped with an almost baroque tile roof. The building has become part of the National Gallery, with a permanent exhibit of Cubist art. ✉ *Celetná ul. (at Ovocný trh)* ⊕ *www.ngprague.cz* ۞ *Tues.–Sun. 10–6.*

⑥ **Expozice Franze Kafky** (Franz Kafka's Birthplace). A museum in the house displays photos, editions of Kafka's books, and other memorabilia from the author's life. (Kafka's grave lies in the New Jewish Cemetery at the Želivského Metro stop.) ✉ *Nám. Franze Kafky 5* ۞ *Tues.–Fri. 10–6, Sat. 10–5.*

② **Na Příkopě.** Once part of the moat surrounding the Old Town, this street is now an elegant (in places) pedestrian mall. It leads from the bottom of Wenceslas Square to the **Obecní dům** (Municipal House), Prague's most lavish art nouveau building. Tours are sometimes available; otherwise, it is difficult to see the upper floors. Evening concerts are held in the Great Hall. A bridge links it to the **Prašná brána** (Powder Tower), a 19th-century neo-Gothic restoration of the medieval original. ✉ *Nám. Republiky* ☎ *222/002101* ⊕ *www.obecnidum.cz.*

⑤ **Staroměstské náměstí** (Old Town Square). The commercial center of the
Old Town is now a remarkably harmonious hub—architecturally beautiful and relatively car-free and quiet. Looming over the center, the twin towers of **Kostel Panny Marie před Týnem** (Church of the Virgin Mary before Týn) look forbidding despite Disneyesque lighting. The large **sculptural group** in the square's center commemorates the martyr Jan Hus, whose followers completed the Týn Church during the 15th century. The white baroque **Kostel svatého Mikuláše** (Church of St. Nicholas) is tucked into the square's northwest angle. It was built by Kilian Ignatz Dientzenhofer, co-architect also of the Lesser Quarter's church of the same name. Every hour, mobs converge on the Astronomical Clock Tower of the **Staroměstská radnice** (Old Town Hall) as the clock's 15th-century mechanism activates a procession that includes the 12 Apostles. A skeleton figure of Death tolls the bell. ✉ *Pařížská, Dlouhá, Celetná, Železná, Melantrichova, and Kaprova.*

⑧ **Staronová synagóga** (Old-New Synagogue). A small congregation still attends the little Gothic Old-New Synagogue, one of Europe's oldest surviving houses of Jewish prayer. Men are required to cover their heads upon entering; skullcaps are sold for a small fee at the door. ✉ *Červená 3 at Pařížská* ☎ *222/317191* ⊕ *www.jewishmuseum.cz* ۞ *Sun.–Thurs. 9–5, Fri. 9–2.*

★ ⑨ **Starý židovský hřbitov** (Old Jewish Cemetery). The crowded cemetery is part of **Josefov**, the former Jewish Quarter, and is one of Europe's most unforgettable sights. Here, ancient tombstones lean into one another; below them, piled layer upon layer, are thousands of graves. Many gravestones—they date from the mid-14th to the late 18th centuries—are carved with symbols indicating the name, profession, and attributes of the deceased. If you visit the tomb of the 16th-century scholar Rabbi

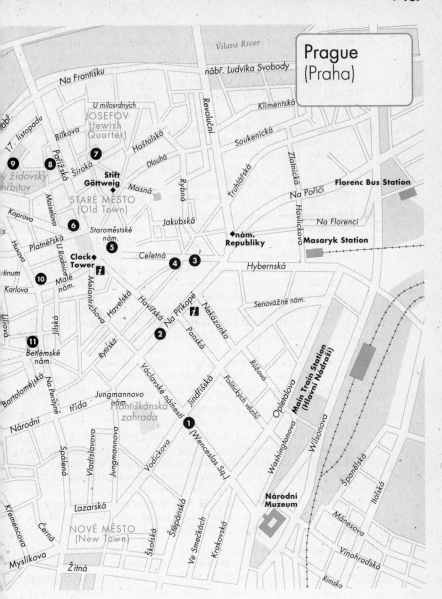

Prague (Praha)

Vltava River

nábř. Ludvíka Svobody

Na Františku

U milosrdných

Klimentská

JOSEFOV
(Jewish
Quarter)

17. listopadu

Bílkova

Pařížská

Soukenická

Haštalská

Zlatnická

Florenc Bus Station

židovský
hrbitov

Široká

Dlouhá

Truhlářská

Na Poříčí

7

9

8

Stift
Göttweig

Masná

Rybná

Havlíčkova

Na Florenci

STARÉ MĚSTO
(Old Town)

Kaprova

Maiselova

Staroměstské
nám.

Jakubská

Masaryk Station

Platnéřská

U Radnice

6

◆nám.
Republiky

Husova

tinum

Clock◆
Tower

5

Celetná

Hybernská

Karlova

Malé
nám.

10

4

3

Senovážné nám.

Melantrichova

Havelská

Havířská

Na Příkopě

Nekázanka

Jílská

11

Betlémské
nám.

Rytířská

2

Panská

Růžová

Bartolomějská

Na Perštýně

Václavské náměstí

Jindřišská

Politických vězňů

Opletalova

Main Train Station
(Hlavní Nádraží)

Wilsonova

Národní

Třída

Jungmannovo
nám.

Františkánská
zahrada

1

[Wenceslas Sq.]

Washingtonova

Spálená

Vladislavova

Jungmannova

Vodičkova

Škrétova

Španělská

Italská

Lazarská

Štěpánská

Národní
Muzeum

Manesova

Křemencova

Černá

NOVÉ MĚSTO
(New Town)

Školská

Ve Smečkách

Krakovská

Vinohradská

Myslíkova

Žitná

Rimská

Löw, you may see scraps of paper covered with prayers or requests stuffed into the cracks. In legend, the rabbi protected Prague's Jews with the help of a *golem,* or artificial man; today he still receives appeals for assistance. The same admission fee gives you access to four other sites that are all part of the Jewish Museum. ⊠ *Entrance at Pinkas Synagogue, Široká 3* ☎ *222/317191* ⊕ *www.jewishmuseum.cz* ☉ *Sun.–Thurs. 9–5, Fri. 9–2.*

❶ **Václavské náměstí** (Wenceslas Square). In the Times Square of Prague hundreds of thousands voiced their disgust for the Communist regime in November 1989 at the outset of the Velvet Revolution. The "square" is actually a broad boulevard that slopes down from the **Národní muzeum** (National Museum) and the equestrian **statue of St. Václav** (Wenceslas). ⊠ *Between Wilsonova and jct. Na příkopě and 26 Října.*

❼ **Židovské muzeum** (Jewish Museum). The rich exhibits in Josefov's Pinkas Synagogue, Maisel Synagogue, Klaus Synagogue, Ceremonial Hall, and the newly renovated Spanish Synagogue, along with the Old Jewish Cemetery, make up the museum. Jews, forced to fulfill Adolf Hitler's plan to document the lives of the people he was trying to exterminate, gathered the collections. They include ceremonial objects, textiles, and displays covering the history of Bohemia's and Moravia's Jews. The interior of the Pinkas Synagogue is especially poignant, as it is painted with the names of 77,297 Jewish Czechs killed during World War II. Pinkas Synagogue also contains a permanent exhibition of drawings by children who were interned at the Terezín (Theresienstadt) concentration camp from 1942 to 1944. *Museum ticket offices* ⊠ *U starého hřbitova 3a* ⊠ *Široká 3* ☉ *Apr.–Oct., Sun.–Fri. 9–6; Nov.–Mar., Sun.–Fri. 9–4:30; closed Sat. and Jewish holidays. Old-New Synagogue closes 2–3 hrs early on Fri.*

Karlův Most & Malá Strana (Charles Bridge & the Lesser Quarter)

Many of the houses in the charmingly quaint Lesser Quarter have large signs above the door with symbols such as animals or religious figures. These date to the time before houses were numbered, when each house was referred to by name. Aristocrats built palaces here during the 17th century to be close to Prague Castle. Many of their private gardens have evolved into pleasant public parks with strutting peacocks. Some of the former palaces have become embassies, but increased security makes it hard to have more than a quick glance at the exterior.

⓮ **Chrám svatého Mikuláše** (Church of St. Nicholas). Designed by the late-17th-century Dientzenhofer architects, father and son, this is among the most beautiful examples of the Bohemian baroque, an architectural style that flowered in Prague after the Counter-Reformation. On clear days you can enjoy great views from the tower. ⊠ *Malostranské nám.* ☉ *Sept.–May, daily 9–4; June–Aug., daily 9–6.*

⓬ **Karlův most** (Charles Bridge). As you stand on this statue-lined stone bridge, unsurpassed in grace and setting, you see views of Prague that would be familiar to its 14th-century builder Peter Parler and to the artists who started adding the 30 sculptures in the 17th century. Today, nearly all the sculptures on the bridge are skillful copies of the originals, which have been taken indoors to be protected from the polluted air. The 12th on the left (starting from the Old Town side of the bridge) depicts St. Luitgarde (Matthias Braun sculpted the original, circa 1710). In the 14th on the left, a Turk guards suffering saints. (F. M. Brokoff sculpted the original, circa 1714.) The bridge itself is a gift to Prague from the Holy Roman emperor Charles IV. ⊠ *Between Mostecká ul. on Malá Strana side and Karlova ul. on Old Town side.*

FodorśChoice ★

off the beaten path

VILLA BERTRAMKA – While in Prague, Mozart liked to stay at the secluded estate of his friends the Dušeks. The house is now a small museum packed with Mozart memorabilia. From Karmelitská ulice in Malá Strana, take Tram 12 south to the Anděl metro station; walk down Plzeňská ulice a few hundred yards, and take a left at Mozartova ulice. In the summer, there are occasional garden concerts. ✉ *Mozartova ul. 169, Smíchov* ☎ *257/318461* ⊕ *www. bertramka.cz* ⊘ *Daily 9:30–6.*

⓲ **Valdštejnská zahrada** (Wallenstein Gardens). This is one of the most elegant of the many sumptuous Lesser Quarter gardens. In the 1620s the Habsburgs' victorious commander, Czech nobleman Albrecht of Wallenstein, demolished a wide swath of existing structures to build his oversize palace with its charming walled garden. A covered outdoor stage of late-Renaissance style dominates the western end. ✉ *Entrance, Letenská 10* ⊘ *May–Sept., daily 9–7.*

Pražský Hrad & Hradčany (Prague Castle & the Castle District)

No feature dominates the city more than Prague Castle, which, because of its hilltop location, can be seen from most of the city. The neighborhood in front of the castle once housed astronomers, alchemists, counts, and clergy hoping to obtain royal favors. Some of the palaces near the castle have become museums, others are used by government ministries. A large number of churches can be found here as well. Some offer tours, others can be viewed only after early-morning religious services.

⓰ **Loreta.** This baroque church and shrine are named for the Italian town to which angels supposedly transported the Virgin Mary's house from Nazareth to save it from the infidels. The glory of its fabulous treasury is the *Sun of Prague,* a monstrance (a vessel that contains the consecrated Host and has an opening through which it can be viewed) decorated with 6,222 diamonds. Arrive on the hour to hear the 27-bell carillon. ✉ *Loretánské nám. 7* ⊘ *Tues.–Sun. 9–12:15 and 1–4:30.*

★ ⓯ **Pražský hrad** (Prague Castle). From its narrow hilltop, the monumental castle complex has witnessed the changing fortunes of the city for more than 1,000 years. The castle's physical and spiritual core, **Chrám svatého Víta** (St. Vitus Cathedral), took from 1344 to 1929 to build, so you can trace in its lines architectural styles from high Gothic to art nouveau. The eastern end, mostly the work of Peter Parler, builder of the Charles Bridge, is a triumph of Bohemian Gothic. "Good King" Wenceslas (in reality a mere prince, later canonized) has his own chapel in the south transept, dimly lit and decorated with fine medieval wall paintings. Note the fine 17th-century carved wooden panels on either side of the chancel. The left-hand panel shows a view of the castle and town in November 1620 as the defeated Czech Protestants flee into exile. The three easternmost chapels house tombs of Czech princes and kings of the 11th to the 13th centuries, although Charles IV and Rudolf II lie in the crypt, the former in a bizarre modern sarcophagus. On the southern facade of the cathedral, the 14th-century glass and quartz mosaic of the Last Judgment, long clouded over, has been restored to its original, brightly colored appearance.

Behind St. Vitus's, don't miss the miniature houses of **Zlatá ulička** (Golden Lane). Its name, and the apocryphal tale of how Holy Roman emperor Rudolf II used to lock up alchemists here until they transmuted lead into gold, may come from the gold-beaters who once lived here. Knightly tournaments often accompanied coronation ceremonies in the

Královský palác (Royal Palace), next to the cathedral, hence the broad Riders' Staircase leading up to the grandiose Vladislavský sál (Vladislav Hall), with its splendid late-Gothic vaulting and Renaissance windows. Oldest of all the castle's buildings, though much restored, is the complex of **Bazilika svatého Jiří** (St. George's Basilica and Convent). The basilica's cool Romanesque lines hide behind a glowing salmon-color baroque facade. The former convent houses a superb collection of Bohemian art from medieval religious sculptures to baroque paintings. The castle **ramparts** afford glorious vistas of Prague's fabled 100 spires rising above the rooftops. ⊠ *Approach via Nerudova, Staré zámecké schody, or Keplerova. Main castle ticket office in Second Courtyard* ☎ *224/373368* ⊕ *www.hrad.cz* ☉ *Castle: Nov.–Mar., daily 9–4; Apr.–Oct., daily 9–5. Castle gardens: Apr.–Oct., daily 9–5.*

Where to Eat

$$$$ ✕ **Peklo.** This subterranean chamber (*peklo* is the Czech word for "hell") beneath a former monastery was once a favorite drinking spot of the King Wenceslas IV. The old wine cellar has been replaced by a restaurant that offers a good selection of Czech and French wines. ⊠ *Strahovské nádvoří 1/132* ☎ *220/516652* ⊟ *AE, MC, V.*

$$$–$$$$ ✕ **Circle Line Brasserie.** Elegant yet decidedly unstuffy, this dining spot

Fodor'sChoice tucked into a restored baroque palace in Malá Strana offers delicious

★ nouvelle cuisine specialties. Appetizers and main courses may include hare terrine with sun-dried plums and apricots, roasted lamb sweetbreads with truffle sauce, and grilled veal ribs with mustard-seed sauce. A pianist plays unobtrusively each evening; and service is gracious and discreet. Smaller degustation portions of most entrees are available. ⊠ *Malostranské nám. 12* ☎ *257/530022* ⊕ *www.zatisigroup.cz* ⟡ *Reservations essential* ⊟ *AE, DC, V.*

$$$–$$$$ ✕ **Palffy palác.** The faded charm of an old-world palace makes this a lovely, romantic spot for a meal. Very good Continental cuisine is served with elegance that befits the surroundings. Try the potatoes au gratin or chicken stuffed with goat cheese. In summer, ask to dine on the terrace. Brunches here are not worth the price. ⊠ *Valdštejnská 14* ☎ *257/530522* ⊟ *MC, V.*

★ **$$$–$$$$** ✕ **U Modré Kachničky.** The exuberant, eclectic decor is as attractive as the Czech and international dishes, which include steaks, duck, and game in autumn, and Bohemian trout and carp. ⊠ *Nebovidská 6* ☎ *257/320308* ⊕ *www.umodrekachnicky.cz* ⟡ *Reservations essential* ⊟ *AE, MC, V.*

★ **$$$–$$$$** ✕ **Vinárna V Zatiší.** Continental cuisine is exquisitely prepared and presented here—fish and game specialties are outstanding, and set menus including wine are available. The wine list is extensive, with special emphasis on French vintages. Most meals are available in smaller sample portions. ⊠ *Liliová 1* ☎ *222/221155* ⟡ *Reservations essential* ⊟ *AE, MC, V.*

$$–$$$$ ✕ **U Zlaté Hrušky.** Careful restoration has returned this restaurant to its original 18th-century style. It specializes in Moravian wines, which are well matched with fillet steaks and goose liver. Dining is also available at the garden across the street in the warmer weather. ⊠ *Nový Svět 3* ☎ *220/514778* ⊕ *www.zlatahruska.cz* ⟡ *Reservations essential* ⊟ *AE, V.*

$$–$$$ ✕ **Dynamo.** With a consistent clientele of beautiful people, this little green diner is one of the trendiest spots on what is fast becoming a veritable restaurant row. Dynamo's quirky menu offers tasty variations on Continental themes, such as liver and apples on toast, and succulent eggplant filled with grilled vegetables. They also have a wide range of single malt scotches to help end the evening. ⊠ *Pštrossova 221/29* ☎ *224/932020* ⊟ *AE, MC, V.*

$$–$$$ ✕ **U Mecenáše.** This restaurant manages to be elegant despite the presence of medieval swords and battle axes. Try to get a table in the back room. The chef specializes in thick, juicy steaks served with a variety of sauces. ✉ *Malostranské nám. 10* ☎ *257/531631* ⌕ *Reservations essential* ▭ *AE, MC, V.*

$$ ✕ **Chez Marcel.** This authentic French bistro on a quiet, picturesque street offers a little taste of Paris in the center of Prague's Old Town. French owned and operated, Chez Marcel has an extensive menu suitable for lingering over a three-course meal (French cheeses, salads, pâtés, rabbit, and some of the best steaks in Prague) or just a quick espresso. ✉ *Haštalská 12* ☎ *222/315676* ▭ *No credit cards.*

$–$$$ ✕ **Novoměstský pivovar.** Always packed with out-of-towners and locals alike, this microbrewery-restaurant is a maze of rooms, some painted in mock-medieval style, others decorated with murals of Prague street scenes. Pork knee (*vepřové koleno*) is a favorite dish. The beer is the cloudy, fruity, fermented style exclusive to this venue. ✉ *Vodičkova 20* ☎ *222/232448* ⊕ *www.npivovar.cz* ▭ *AE, MC, V.*

$–$$ ✕ **Bohemia Bagel.** This casual, American-owned and child-friendly bagel shop serves a good assortment of fresh bagels with all kinds of spreads and toppings. The thick soups are among the best in Prague for the price, and the bottomless cups of coffee (from gourmet blends) are a further draw. There are now two locations. ✉ *Újezd 16* ☎ *257/310694* ⊕ *www.bohemiabagel.cz* ✉ *Masná 2* ☎ *224/812560* ▭ *No credit cards.*

$–$$ ✕ **Česká hospoda v Krakovské.** Right off Wenceslas Square, this clean pub noted for its excellent traditional fare is the place to try Bohemian duck. Pair it with cold Krušovice beer. ✉ *Krakovská 20* ☎ *222/210204* ▭ *No credit cards.*

$–$$ ✕ **Kavárna Slavia.** This legendary hangout for the best and brightest of the Czech arts world—from composer Bedřich Smetana and poet Jaroslav Seifert to then-dissident Václav Havel—offers a spectacular view both inside and out. Its art deco decor is a perfect backdrop for people-watching, and the vistas (the river and Prague Castle or the National Theater) are a compelling reason to linger over an espresso. Meals are available, but most people just come for the coffee and the view. ✉ *Smetanovo nábřeží 1012/2* ☎ *224/218493* ▭ *No credit cards.*
Fodor'sChoice ★

★ **$–$$** ✕ **Pivovarský dům.** Beer made on the premises is the main attraction here. They make not only traditional Pilsner-style but also a rotating choice of coffee, cherry, or even eucalyptus beer. The menu offers well-made traditional pub fare such as *guláš* with dumplings. Peek at the vats behind the glass to see beer fermenting. ✉ *Lipová 20* ☎ *296/216666* ▭ *No credit cards.*

$–$$ ✕ **U Sedmi Švábů.** A medieval theme accents the truly old-fashioned Bohemian fare that includes millet pudding and mead. The less adventuresome can opt for the roast meat and poultry dishes. A special knight's feast requires 24 hours' advance notice. At the bottom of the stairs you can find a dungeon. ✉ *Janský vršek 14* ☎ *257/531455* ⊕ *www.viacarolina.cz.*

$–$$ ✕ **U Zlatého Tygra.** This crowded hangout is the last of a breed of authentic Czech pivnice. The smoke and stares preclude a long stay, but it's worth a visit for such pub staples as ham and cheese plates or fried pork steak. The service is surly, but the beer is good. ✉ *Husova 17* ☎ *222/221111* ⌕ *Reservations not accepted* ▭ *No credit cards.*

$ ✕ **Country Life.** A godsend for Praguers and travelers, this health-food cafeteria offers a bounteous (and fresh) salad bar and daily rotating meat-free specials. The dining area has that rare Prague luxury for a low-end eating establishment: no blaring techno music. There's table service evenings after 6:30. It's off the courtyard connecting Melantrichova and

Michalská streets. ⊠ *Melantrichova 15* ☎ *224/213366* ▤ *No credit cards* ⊘ *Closed Sat.*

$ ✕ **U Bakaláře.** Hidden just inside a university-owned building on one of the main streets leading to Old Town Square, "at the bachelor of arts" offers some Czech standards such as meat-stuffed dumplings with sauerkraut. This is a perfect place for a quick bite while checking out the major attractions. Be aware that there is no table service. ⊠ *Celetna 13* ☎ *224/817769* ⌲ *Reservations not accepted* ▤ *No credit cards.*

Where to Stay

Many of Prague's older hotels have been renovated, and more hotels are opening in old buildings in the Old Town and Lesser Quarter, making finding a decent room much easier than it used to be. Very few hotel rooms in the more desirable districts go for less than $120 per double room in high season; most less-expensive hotels are far from the center of Prague. Private rooms and pensions remain the best budget deal.

$$$$ ▦ **Diplomat.** One of the first places to open after the Velvet Revolution, the Diplomat fuses style with Western efficiency. It's convenient to the airport: the Old Town is a 10-minute taxi or subway ride away. The hotel is modern and tasteful, with a huge, sunny lobby and comfortable rooms. ⊠ *Evropská 15, 160 00 Prague 6* ☎ *296/559111* ▤ *296/559215* ⊕ *www.diplomat-hotel.cz* ⇥ *369 rooms, 13 suites* ⌂ *2 restaurants, bar* ▤ *AE, DC, MC, V.*

$$$$ ▦ **Dům U Červeného Lva.** In Malá Strana, a five-minute walk from ★ Prague Castle's front gates, the Baroque House at the Red Lion is an intimate, immaculately kept hotel. The spare but comfortable guest rooms have parquet floors, 17th-century painted-beam ceilings, superb antiques, and all-white bathrooms with brass fixtures. The two top-floor rooms can double as a suite. There is no elevator, and stairs are steep. ⊠ *Nerudova 41, 118 00 Prague 1* ☎ *257/533832* ▤ *257/532746* ⊕ *www.hotelredlion.com* ⇥ *5 rooms, 3 suites,* ⌂ *2 restaurants* ▤ *AE, DC, MC, V.*

$$$$ ▦ **Hoffmeister.** On a picturesque (if a bit busy) corner near the Mal-
Fodor'sChoice ostranská metro station, this is one of the most stylish small hotels in
★ the city. Rooms have finely crafted wood built-ins and luxuriously appointed bathrooms. Museum-quality prints by the proprietor's father hang throughout the hotel. ⊠ *Pod Bruskou 7, 118 00 Prague 1* ☎ *251/017111* ▤ *251/017120* ⊕ *www.hoffmeister.cz* ⇥ *38 rooms* ⌂ *Restaurant, bar* ▤ *AE, DC, MC, V.*

$$$$ ▦ **Kampa.** An early baroque armory turned hotel, the Kampa is tucked away in a residential corner of the Lesser Quarter. The rooms are clean, if spare, but the bucolic setting one block from the river as well as a lovely park compensate for its relative remoteness. ⊠ *Všehrdova 16, 118 00 Prague 1* ☎ *257/320508 or 257/320404* ▤ *257/320262* ⊕ *www.bestwestern.com* ⇥ *85 rooms* ⌂ *Restaurant* ▤ *AE, DC, MC, V.*

$$$$ ▦ **Palace Praha.** The art nouveau–style palace is Prague's most elegant
Fodor'sChoice and luxurious hotel, though it now faces competition from other lux-
★ ury hotels. Rooms have high ceilings, marble baths with phones, and minibars. Its central location just off Wenceslas Square offers more convenience than local character. ⊠ *Panská 12, 110 00 Prague 1* ☎ *224/093111* ▤ *224/221240* ⊕ *www.palacehotel.cz* ⇥ *114 rooms, 10 suites* ⌂ *2 restaurants* ▤ *AE, DC, MC, V.*

$$$ ▦ **Hotel U staré paní.** The Old Lady is a delightfully cozy hotel only a five-minute walk from Old Town Square, in a renovated building on one of Prague's most atmospheric Old Town lanes. Comfortable rooms are decorated in soft tones with simple Scandinavian-style furnishings. One of Prague's best jazz clubs has concerts nightly here in the base-

ment. (Yes, it is soundproofed.) ✉ *Michalská 9, 110 00 Prague 1* ☏ *224/228090 or 224/226659* 🖷 *224/212172* 🌐 *www.ustarepani.cz* ⇨ *18 rooms* ⚭ *Restaurant* ▭ *AE, MC, V.*

$$$ 🏨 **Opera.** Once the lodging of choice for divas performing at the nearby State Theater, the Opera greatly declined under the Communists. The mid-1990s saw the grand fin-de-siècle facade rejuvenated with a perky pink-and-white paint job and the installation of bathrooms and TVs in all rooms. Comfy wing chairs add to the rooms, which are decorated in tan and white. ✉ *Těšnov 13, 110 00 Prague 1* ☏ *222/315609* 🖷 *222/311477* 🌐 *www.hotel-opera.cz* ⇨ *65 rooms, 2 suites* ⚭ *Restaurant, bar* ▭ *AE, DC, MC, V.*

$$$ 🏨 **Central.** Quite conveniently, this hotel lives up to its name, with a site near Celetná ulice and Náměstí Republiky. Rooms are sparely furnished, but all have baths. The baroque glories of the Old Town are steps away. ✉ *Rybná 8, 110 00 Prague 1* ☏ *222/321919* 🖷 *222/323100* 🌐 *www.orfea.cz* ⇨ *68 rooms* ⚭ *Restaurant, bar* ▭ *AE, MC, V.*

$$ 🏨 **Balkán.** The hotel is a spiffy yellow building on an otherwise drab street not far from the Lesser Quarter. Rooms are small, simple, and clean, with white spreads and walls, tan paneling, and lacy curtains. Request a room at the back, as the hotel is on a major street, one block from the tram stop and a large shopping and entertainment area. ✉ *Svornosti 28, 150 00 Prague 5* ☏☏ *257/327180* ⇨ *24 rooms* ⚭ *Restaurant* ▭ *AE.*

$ 🏨 **Hostel Estec.** A prefabricated, but renovated, dormitory next to the world's largest stadium and right above a large park offers fairly basic accommodation, just a 15-minute walk from Prague Castle. Bathrooms are shared; breakfast is available in a nearby restaurant for a small additional fee. ✉ *Vaníčkova 5, 160 00 Prague 6* ☏ *257/210410* ⇨ *200 rooms with shared bath* ⚭ *Bar* ▭ *AE, MC, V.*

$ 🏨 **Pension Unitas.** Operated by the Christian charity Unitas in an Old Town convent, this well-run establishment has sparely furnished rooms. Part of the facility once served as a prison, and rooms with bunk beds are available in the former cells. Reserve well in advance, even in the off-season. ✉ *Bartolomějská 9, 110 00 Prague 1* ☏ *224/221802* 🖷 *224/217555* 🌐 *www.unitas.cz* ⇨ *43 rooms with shared bath* ⚭ *Restaurant* ▭ *No credit cards.*

$ 🏨 **Penzion Sprint.** Basic, clean, no-frills rooms, most of which have their own tiny bathrooms, make the Sprint a fine budget choice. The rustic-looking pension is on a quiet residential street in the outskirts of Prague, about 20 minutes from the airport; Tram 18 rumbles directly to Old Town. ✉ *Cukrovarnická 64, 160 00 Prague 6* ☏ *233/343338* 🖷 *233/344871* 🌐 *web.telecom.cz* ⇨ *21 rooms* ⚭ *Restaurant* ▭ *AE, MC, V.*

$ 🏨 **Travellers' Hostel.** Single and double rooms are available for a reasonable price, but it costs even less to stay in the dormitory. The hostel is in the same building as a popular nightclub, Roxy, which is quite an asset if you like to stay up late. Old Town's sights are just a few feet from the door. Apartments, also a good deal, have kitchens, bathrooms, and remarkable views of the city. Breakfast and linen is included. ✉ *Dlouha 33, 110 00 Prague 1* ☏ *224/826662* 🖷 *224/826665* 🌐 *www.travellers.cz* ⇨ *5 apartments, 50 rooms with shared bath* ⚭ *Bar* ▭ *MC, V.*

Nightlife & the Arts

The Arts

Prague's cultural life is one of its top attractions—and its citizens like to dress up and participate; performances can be booked far ahead. Monthly programs of events are available at the PIS, Čedok, or hotels. The English-language newspaper *Prague Post* carries detailed entertainment listings. The main ticket agency for classical music is **Bohemia Ticket International** (⊠ Na Příkopě 16 ☎ 224/227832). **Ticketpro** (⊠ Salvátorská 10 ☎ 296/329999 ⊟ 224/814021) sells tickets for most rock and jazz events, as well as theatrical performances and some tours. Tickets for some concerts, events, and tours are available from **Ticketstream** (⊠ Koubkova 8, ☎ 224/263049). For some events, including opera, it's much cheaper to buy tickets at the box office.

CONCERTS Performances are held in many palaces and churches. Too often, programs lack originality (how many different ensembles can play the *Four Seasons* at once?), but the settings are lovely, and the acoustics can be superb. Concerts at the churches of St. Nicholas in both the Old Town Square and the Lesser Quarter are especially enjoyable. At **St. James's Church** on Malá Štupartská (Old Town) cantatas are performed amid a flourish of baroque statuary.

The excellent Czech Philharmonic plays in the intimate, lavish Dvořák Hall in the **Rudolfinum** (⊠ Nám. Jana Palacha ☎ 224/893111). The lush home of the Prague Symphony, **Smetana Hall** (⊠ Nám. Republiky 5 ☎ 222/002100), has been beautifully restored along with the rest of the Obecní dům Building, and is a suitably ornate venue for a classical concert.

OPERA & BALLET Opera is of an especially high standard in the Czech Republic. One of the main venues in the grand style of the 19th century is the beautifully restored **Národní divadlo** (National Theater; ⊠ Národní třída 2 ☎ 224/901448). The **Statni opera Praha** (State Opera of Prague; ⊠ Wilsonova 4 ☎ 224/227266), formerly the Smetana Theater, is another historic site for opera lovers. The **Stavovské divadlo** (Estates Theater; ⊠ Ovocný trh 1 ☎ 224/901448) hosts opera, ballet, and theater performances by the National Theater ensembles. Mozart conducted the premiere of *Don Giovanni* here.

PUPPET SHOWS This traditional form of Czech entertainment, generally adaptations of operas performed to recorded music, has been given new life at the **Národní divadlo marionet** (National Marionette Theater; ⊠ Žatecká 1 ☎ 224/819322).

THEATER A dozen or so professional companies play in Prague to packed houses. Nonverbal theater abounds as well, notably "black theater," a melding of live acting, mime, video, and stage trickery that, despite signs of fatigue, continues to draw crowds. The popular **Archa Theater** (⊠ Na Poříčí 26 ☎ 221/716333) offers avant-garde and experimental theater, music, and dance and hosts world-class visiting ensembles, including the Royal Shakespeare Company. The theater was very badly damaged in the floods of 2002, and the performances have been moved to other locations until repairs can be made. **Laterna Magika** (Magic Lantern; ⊠ Národní třída 4 ☎ 224/914129) is one of the more established producers of black-theater extravaganzas.

Nightlife

DISCOS & CABARET Discos catering to a young crowd blast sound onto lower Wenceslas Square. The newest dance music plays at the ever-popular **Radost FX** (⊠ Bělehradská 120, Prague 2 ☎ 224/254776).

Four clubs in one can be found at **Karlový lázně** (⊠ Novotného lávka) in a renovated spa building near the Charles Bridge. Several live acts or DJs perform nightly and a café with Internet access is open during the day.

JAZZ & ROCK CLUBS Jazz clubs are a Prague institution, although foreign customers keep them in business. Excellent Czech groups play the tiny **AghaRTA** (⊠ Krakovská

5 ☎ 222/211275 ⊕ www.arta.cz); arrive well before the 9 PM show time to get a good seat. Top jazz groups (and the odd world-music touring ensemble) play **Jazz Club U staré paní** (✉ Michalská 9 ☎ 224/228090 ⊕ www.ustarepani.cz) in Old Town. **Malostranské Beseda** (✉ Malostranské nám. 21 ☎ 257/532092 ⊕ mb.muzikus.cz) is a funky hall for rock, jazz, and folk. At **Palác Akropolis** (✉ Kubelíkova 27 ☎ 296/330913 ⊕ www.palacakropolis.cz) you can hear world music, well-known folk, rock, and jazz acts, plus DJs. **Reduta** (✉ Národní třída 20 ☎ 224/933487), the city's best-known jazz club for three decades, stars mostly local talent. Hip locals congregate at **Roxy** (✉ Dlouhá 33 ☎ 224/826296 ⊕ www.roxy.cz) for everything from punk to funk to New Age tunes.

Shopping

Many of the main shops are in and around Old Town Square and Na Příkopě, as well as along Celetná ulice and Pařížská. On the Lesser Quarter side, Nerudova has the densest concentration of shops.

Department Stores

The two adjacent modern steel-and-glass shopping complexes, **Anděl** and **Nový Smíchov** (✉ intersection of Plzeňská and Nádražní), include a Carrefour supermarket and many other stores and restaurants. **Bílá Labuť** (✉ Na Poříčí 23) is a good-value option. The biggest downtown department store is **Kotva** (✉ Nám. Republiky 8), which grows flashier and more expensive every year. The basement supermarket at **Tesco** (✉ Národní třída 26) is the best and biggest in the center of the city.

Specialty Shops

Shops specializing in Bohemian crystal, porcelain, ceramics, and antiques abound in Old Town and Malá Strana and on Golden Lane at Prague Castle. Look for the name **Dílo** (✉ Staroměstské nám. 15 ✉ U Lužického semináře 14) for glass and ceramic sculptures, prints, and paintings by local artists. **Lidová Řemesla** (✉ Jilská 22 ✉ Mostecká 17) shops stock wooden toys, elegant blue-and-white textiles, and charming Christmas ornaments made from straw or pastry. **Moser** (✉ Na Příkopě 12 ☎ 224/211293 ⊕ www.moser.cz) is the source for handmade glass.

Side Trips

The castle and spa region of Bohemia and the history-drenched villages of Moravia make excellent (and convenient) excursions from Prague. Buses or trains link the capital with every corner of the Bohemian region; transportation to towns in Moravia takes longer (three hours or more from the capital) but is also dependable.

Bohemia's Spas & Castles

The Bohemian countryside is a restful world of gentle hills and thick woods. It is especially beautiful during fall foliage season or in May, when the fruit trees that line the roads are in blossom. Two of the most famous of the Czech Republic's scores of spas lie in such settings: Karlovy Vary (Karlsbad) and Mariánské Lázně (Marienbad). During the 19th and early 20th centuries, European royalty and aristocrats came to ease their overindulged bodies (or indulge them even more) at these spas.

South Bohemia, a country of lonely castles, green hills, and quiet fishponds, is sprinkled with exquisite medieval towns, many of them undergoing much-needed rehabilitation. In such towns as Tábor, the Hussite reformist movement was born during the early 15th century, sparking a series of religious conflicts that engulfed all of Europe. Countering the Hussites from Český Krumlov was the powerful Rožmberk family, who scattered castles over the countryside and created lake-size

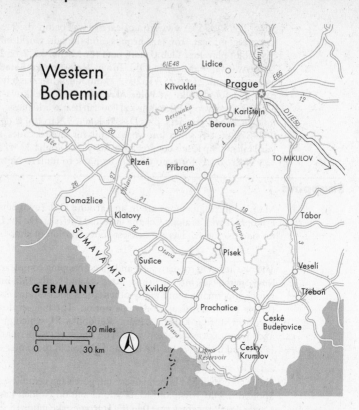

Western
Bohemia

Lidice
Prague
Křivoklát
Karlštejn
Berounka
Beroun
Mže
TO MIKULOV
Plzeň
Příbram
Domažlice
Klatovy
ŠUMAVA MTS.
Otava
Sušice
Písek
Veselí
GERMANY
Kvilda
Třeboň
Prachatice
České
Budějovice
0   20 miles
0   30 km
Český
Krumlov
Lipno
Reservoir

"ponds" in which to breed highly prized carp, still the focus of a Czech Christmas dinner.

Praguers love to spend weekends in the **Berounka Valley,** where two magnificent castles rise up over the river.

Fodor'sChoice
★
Karlštejn, less than an hour from Prague off Route E50 (direction Beroun), is an admirable restoration of the 14th-century castle built by Charles IV. It was built to protect the crown jewels of the Holy Roman Empire. Decades of renovation work on the main tower's Chapel of the Holy Rood, with its walls covered with gold leaf and semiprecious stones, have also finally been completed. There are two tours; one includes the chapel. ✉ *Karlštejn* ☎ *311/681617* ⊕ *www.hradkarlstejn.cz* ☉ *Nov.–Jan. and Mar., Tues.–Sun. 9–3; Apr. and Oct., Tues.–Sun. 9–4; May, June, and Sept., Tues.–Sun. 9–5; July and Aug., Tues.–Sun. 9–6.*

The main attractions of **Křivoklát** are its glorious woodlands, a favorite royal hunting ground in times past. The castle is about an hour from Prague. ✉ *Křivoklát* ☎ *313/558440* ☉ *Mar., Nov., and Dec., weekends 9–3; Apr. and Oct., Tues.–Sun. 9–3; May and Sept., Tues.–Sun. 9–4; June, Tues.–Sun. 9–5; July and Aug., daily 9–5.*

★ About two hours from Prague by car on Route E48, **Karlovy Vary,** or Karlsbad, was named for the Holy Roman emperor Charles IV. While he was in pursuit of a deer during a hunt, the animal supposedly led him to the main spring of Vřídlo. Over the years the spa attracted not only much of the blue blood of Europe but also leading musicians and writers. Its confident bourgeois architecture nestles in a deep, forested valley; the meandering Teplá River divides the town down the middle. The elegant, old spa part of town is lined with fanciful turn-of-the-20th-century buildings in soft colors. Four colonnades (freestanding covered pedestrian walkways)—one of wrought iron, one of carved wood, one of stone, and one of steel and glass—allow leisurely strolling and sipping of mineral waters. The waters from the spa's 12 springs are uniformly foul-tasting: sip them while nibbling rich Karlovy Vary *oplatky* (wafers), and then resort to the 13th spring, Karlovy Vary's tangy herbal liqueur known as Becherovka.

$$$$ 🏨 **Dvořák.** This Austrian-built hotel in the center of town has imaginative decor, with whimsical white furniture, pale peach walls, and lacy curtains. The view from the front rooms looks out onto the Teplá River and rose gardens in season. The staff is cheerful and utterly professional. ☒ *Nová louka 11, 360 21* ☎ *353/102111* 🖷 *353/102119* ⊕ *www.hotel-dvorak.cz* ⇨ *96 rooms, 10 suites* ⚒ *Restaurant, pool* ▭ *AE, DC, MC, V.*

$$$$ 🏨 **Grandhotel Pupp.** Founded in 1701, the Pupp still has a fine 18th-century hall, the Slavnostní sál. It's one of the oldest surviving hotels in Europe, with glittering names—past and present—in its guest register. For more elegance, request a room furnished in 19th-century period style; other rooms were redecorated in a functional way under Communism. The connecting wing, Parkhotel Pupp, offers much the same elegance at slightly lower prices. ☒ *Mírové nám. 2, 360 91* ☎ *353/109–111* 🖷 *353/224–032* ⊕ *www.pupp.cz* ⇨ *74 rooms, 28 suites, 7 apartments; additional 108 rooms and 12 apartments in the Parkhotel* ⚒ *4 restaurants, bar* ▭ *AE, DC, MC, V.*

FodorsChoice
★

$$$$ 🏨 **Thermal.** This unappealing 1970s gray high-rise is solidly anchored at one end of Karlovy Vary's colonnade. Its rooms are not special but the balconies of all front-facing rooms afford a magical view over the entire colonnade and the rolling hills of the town. The Thermal's heated outdoor pool, built into a hillside and open year-round, allows similarly gorgeous vistas. Rates are higher if spa treatments are included. ☒ *I. P. Pavlova 11, 360 00 Karlovy Vary* ☎ *359/001111* 🖷 *359/002603* ⊕ *www.thermal.cz* ⇨ *260 rooms, 13 suites* ⚒ *2 restaurants, pool* ▭ *AE, DC, MC, V.*

The sanatoriums and colonnades of **Mariánské Lázně** (Marienbad) are impressively arrayed around an oblong park. The town has one of the Czech Republic's best golf courses and hosts a PGA European Tour event. The resort is about three hours from Prague, on Route 21 off Route E50.

$$$$ 🏨 **Bohemia.** At this lemon-yellow spa resort beautiful crystal chandeliers in the main hall set the stage for a comfortable and elegant stay. The rooms are well appointed in soothing pale tones. To be really decadent, request one of the enormous suites overlooking the park. The staff can arrange spa treatments and horseback riding. ☒ *Hlavní třída 100, Mariánské Lázně, 353 01* ☎ *354/624579* 🖷 *354/610555* ⊕ *www.orea.cz* ⇨ *62 rooms, 4 suites* ⚒ *Restaurant, bar* ▭ *AE, MC, V.*

$$$$ 🏨 **Palace.** Built during the spa's heyday in 1875, this elegant five-story building is in the resort center. Turrets sprout at the top of the bright white-and-canary-yellow hotel, and the myriad balconies have swirling metal railings. Chandeliers and gold-color plating glisten in the public rooms. The comfortable guest rooms are less ostentatious, decorated in peach tones, with simple light fixtures and fluted white furniture. Complete spa services are available on-site. ☒ *Hlavní třída 67, Mariánské Lázně, 353 01* ☎ *354/658200* 🖷 *354/658151* ⊕ *www.imperial.kv.cz* ⇨ *40 rooms, 5 suites* ⚒ *Restaurant* ▭ *AE, DC, MC, V.*

★ Once the main seat of the Rožmberks, Bohemia's noblest family, **Český Krumlov** is about four hours south of Prague (on Route E55 to České Budějovice and then on Route 159). The Vltava River snakes through the town, which has steeply stacked steps on either bank linking various levels and twisting narrow lanes that converge on Náměstí Svornosti, the Old Town's main square. A number of notable Renaissance houses add an air of formality to this exquisite place. The enchanting town is home to the imposing Renaissance **Hrad** (castle), complete with romantic elevated walkways; a round, pastel-hued tower; and an 18th-century theater that still hosts performances. Tours with an English-speaking guide cost 140 Kč–180 Kč. ✉ *Latrán 1* ☎ *380/704721* ⊕ *www.ckrumlov.cz* ⊙ *Apr. and Oct., Tues.–Sun. 9–4; May–Aug., Tues.–Sun. 8–5; Sept., Tues.–Sun. 9–5.*

The **Mezinárodní kulturní centrum Egona Schieleho** (Egon Schiele Center) exhibits the work of the painter, a frequent visitor to the town, and other 20th-century artists. ✉ *Široká 70–72, Český Krumlov* ☎ *380/711224* ⊕ *www.ckrumlov.cz* ⊙ *Daily 10–6 (inquire locally about winter closures).*

$$$$ ▦ **Růže.** The stone exterior clearly shows its Renaissance monastery past, but the lobby is modern. Most of the (smallish) rooms were modernized in the '70s with violet as the color of choice; they have tiny Gothic windows. ✉ *Horní ul. 153, Český Krumlov, 381 01* ☎ *380/772100* ⊟ *380/713146* ⊕ *www.hotelruze.cz* ⇨ *71 rooms* ♨ *Restaurant, pool* ⊟ *AE, MC, V.*

★ $$ ▦ **Na louži.** Wooden shutters on the street level set the old but cared-for atmosphere of this friendly pub-restaurant and the five immaculate small rooms upstairs, which are furnished with cozy country-style beds and wardrobes. Rooms have up to four beds. ✉ *Kájovská 66, Český Krumlov, 381 01* ☎☎ *380/711280* ⊕ *www.nalouzi.cz* ⇨ *7 rooms* ♨ *Restaurant* ⊟ *No credit cards.*

After Jan Hus's death at the stake in 1415, his proto-Protestant followers established an egalitarian commune on a fortified bluff above the Lužnice River. Jan Žižka, a one-eyed general, led the zealots of **Tábor** (1½ hrs from Prague on Route E55) and shaped them into Europe's most-feared army. The town itself became a weapon of defense: its twisting streets were designed to confuse the enemy. A labyrinth of tunnels and cellars below the town served as both living quarters and link with the outer defenses. The story is told in the **Husitské muzeum** (Hussite Museum) (✉ Křivkova 31, Tábor ☎ 381/252242), which is open April–November, daily 8:30–4, and upon request December–March.

Moravian Towns

Moravia, with its peaceful villages and small towns three to four hours southeast of Prague, is the easternmost of the historic Czech Lands, sharing a lightly populated border with Bohemia.

A former center of Jewish life and learning in the Habsburg Empire, **Mikulov** (about four hours southeast of Prague on Route 620 off E55) now bears few traces of its scholarly past. Today the town is known for its wine making. During the grape harvest in October, head for the limestone hills surrounding the town—tradition dictates that a knock on the door of a private *sklípek* (wine cellar) will lead to a tasting session. The town's baroque-and-Gothic **Zámek Mikulov** (château) contains a wine-making museum where you can see a 22,000-gallon wine cask from 1643. ✉ *Zámek 5, Mikulov, 692 15* ☎ *519/510255* ⊕ *www.rmm.cz* ⊙ *Apr. and Oct., Tues.–Sun. 9–4; Mar.–Sept., Tues.–Sun. 9–5.*

$–$$ ▦ **Rohatý Krokodýl.** The classic Horned Crocodile is perfectly in keeping with the town's look in that it is a long, low white building on a street that dates from the Renaissance. Furnishings are simple, modern, and immaculate. The restaurant is outstanding. ✉ *Husova 8, Mikulov, 692 01* ☎ *519/519692* ⊟ *519/511695* ⊕ *www.rohatykrokodyl.cz* ⇨ *14 rooms* ♨ *Restaurant, bar* ⊟ *AE, MC, V.*

Amid the farmlands and industrial centers of middle Moravia, **Olomouc,** three hours from Prague on Route 462 off E50, comes as an unexpected joy. The city retains its rambling Old Town, partially circled by high brick fortifications. The Renaissance town hall and the tall, impossibly ornate Trinity Column compete for attention on **Horní náměstí,** the main square. At the eastern end of the Old Town are the neo-Gothic **Dóm svatého Václava** (Cathedral of St. Wenceslas; ⊠ Václavské nám., Olomouc), one of the glories of Moravia, and a ruined 12th-century **palace** (⊠ Dómská ul., Olomouc) with an exquisite row of Romanesque stone windows.

$$$ ⊞ **Hotel U Dómu.** This cozy, well-cared-for establishment run by the Jiříček family is steps from the cathedral. Spacious rooms (all including kitchenettes and large bathrooms) are furnished with simple, Scandinavian-style furniture, pastel carpeting, and white walls; tasteful, original watercolors decorating the rooms are by local artists. Service is friendly and obliging. ⊠ Dómská 4, Olomouc, 772 00 ☎ 585/220502 ☒ 585/ 220501 ➦ 6 rooms ⌂ Restaurant, bar ⊟ AE, MC, V.

Fodor'sChoice It is a surprise to come upon trim little **Telč,** with its neat, formal archi-
★ tecture, nestled in such bucolic countryside on Route 406 (E50 and 19). Only the Renaissance facades, each fronted by arcades and topped with rich gables, are visible, and although these are colorful, cute, and well maintained, often the buildings behind them are falling apart. The main square is a UNESCO World Heritage Site. The Renaissance theme carries over to the **Zámek Telč** (Telč Château), whose architecture and decoration form a rare pre-baroque example of stylistic unity. Two tours are offered: one that shows off the Renaissance part, another the living quarters of the last owners. ⊠ Statni Zámek Telč, Telč, 588 56 ☎ 567/ 243943 ⊕ www.zamek-telc.cz ⊙ Apr.–Oct., Tues.–Sun. 9–4.

Prague Essentials

AIRPORTS & TRANSFERS
All international flights arrive at Prague's Ruzyně Airport, about 20 km (12 mi) from downtown.
⬛ **Ruzyně Airport** ☎ 220/113314 or 221/113321 ⊕ www.csa.cz or www.prague-airport.cz.

TRANSFERS The private Cedaz minibus shuttle links the airport and Náměstí Republiky. Shuttles run every 30–60 minutes between 5:30 AM and 9 PM daily. The trip costs 90 Kč one-way and takes about 30 minutes. On regular Bus 119 the cost is 12 Kč, but you'll need to change to the metro station at the Dejvická Station to reach the center. Bus 100 also goes between the airport and the Metro Zličín stop. By taxi, expect to pay 600 Kč to the center. Only one city-authorized firm, Belinda, is permitted to have taxis waiting at the airport. (You may take any taxi *to* the airport, however, or call a taxi.)

BUS TRAVEL TO & FROM PRAGUE
The Czech bus network (ČSAD) operates from a station near Prague's main train station. Take Metro B or C to the Florenc stop.
⬛ **ČSAD** ⊠ Křižíkova 4 ☎ 222/630851 ⊕ www.jizdnirady.cz.

BUS & TRAM TRAVEL WITHIN PRAGUE
Trams are often more convenient than the metro for short hops. Most bus lines connect outlying suburbs with the nearest metro station. Trams 50–59 and buses numbered 500 and above run all night—at, however, intervals of up to an hour—after the metro stops.

CAR TRAVEL
In the center of the city, meters with green stripes let you park up to six hours; an orange stripe indicates a two-hour limit. Blue-marked

spaces are reserved for local residents. (Parking boots may be attached to offending vehicles.) There is an underground parking lot near Old Town Square.

EMERGENCIES

Be prepared to pay in cash for medical treatment, whether you are insured or not. The Lékárna U Andělais 24-hour pharmacy is near the Anděl metro station, and the Lékárna Palackého 24-hour pharmacy is located downtown.

⛨ Emergency Services **Ambulance** ☎ 155. **Police** ☎ 112.

⛨ Hospitals **American Medical Center** ✉ Janovského 48 ☎ 220/807756. **Foreigners' Department of Na Homolce Hospital** ✉ Roentgenova 2 ☎ 257/272144 or 257/272146.

⛨ 24-hour Pharmacies **Lékárna U Anděla** ✉ Štefánikova 6 ☎ 257/320918. **Lékárna Palackého** ✉ Palackého 5 ☎ 224/946982.

ENGLISH-LANGUAGE MEDIA

The Knihkupectví U černé Matky Boží is good for hiking maps and atlases; go downstairs.

⛨ Bookstores **Anagram Bookshop** ✉ Týn 4, Prague 1. **Big Ben Bookshop** ✉ Malá Štupartská 5, Prague 1. **Globe Bookstore and Coffeehouse** ✉ Pštrossova 6, Prague 1. **Knihkupectví U černé Matky Boží** ✉ Celetná ul. 34 at Ovocný trh, Prague 1. **U Knihomola** ✉ Mánesova 79, Prague 2.

SUBWAY TRAVEL

Prague's three modern metro lines are easy to use and relatively safe. They provide the simplest and fastest means of transportation, and most maps of Prague mark the routes. The metro runs from 5 AM to midnight, seven days a week.

TAXIS

Regulations have set taxi rates at 22 Kč per kilometer plus 4 Kč per minute of waiting time, with an initial fee of 30 Kč. Drivers must also display a small license, although this has not stopped fare-related problems. It is still advisable to order a taxi in advance by telephone. Try AAA for quick, reliable service. Profitaxi is also fast and efficient. Some larger hotels have their own fleets, which are a little more expensive.

Do not pick up cabs waiting at taxi stands in the tourist areas: many of these drivers have doctored their meters and have other tricks to rip you off.

⛨ Taxi Companies **AAA** ☎ 14014. **Profitaxi** ☎ 14035.

TOURS

BUS TOURS Čedok offers a daily three-hour tour of the city, starting at 10 AM from two offices. Martin-Tour offers a tour departing from Náměstí Republiky and three other Old Town points four times daily. PIS arranges guided tours at its Na Příkopě and Old Town Square locations.

Čedok's one-day tours out of Prague include excursions to the lovely medieval town of Kutná Hora, the unusual sandstone formations of the Bohemian Paradise region, famous spa towns and castles, wineries, and the Terezín Ghetto.

⛨ Fees & Schedules **Čedok** ✉ Na Příkopě 18 ☎ 224/197121 or 224/197306 ✉ Pařížská 6 ☎ 224/197618. **Martin-Tour** ☎ 224/212473. **PIS** ☎ 221/714130.

PRIVATE GUIDES Contact Čedok or PIS to arrange a personal walking tour of the city. Prices start at around 500 Kč per hour.

SPECIAL-INTEREST TOURS For cultural tours call Čedok. These include visits to the Jewish quarter, performances of folk troupes, Laterna Magika, opera, and concerts.

TRAIN TRAVEL

The main station is Hlavní Nádraží, not far from Wenceslas Square. Some international trains use Nádraží Holešovice, on the same metro line (C) as the main station.

🚉 **Domestic and international schedules** for both stations ☎ 221/111122 ⊕ www.idos. cz. **Hlavní Nádraží** ✉ Wilsonova ul. **Nádraží Holešovice** ✉ Vrbenského ul.

TRANSPORTATION AROUND PRAGUE

Public transportation is a bargain. *Jízdenky* (tickets) can be bought at hotels, newsstands, and dispensing machines in metro stations. Transport passes for unlimited use of the system for 1 day (70 Kč) up to 15 days (280 Kč) are sold at some newsstands and at the windows marked DP or JÍZDENKY in the main metro stations. Be sure to validate your pass by signing it where indicated. A basic 12 Kč ticket allows one hour's travel, with unlimited transfers (90 minutes on weekends and between 8 PM and 5 AM weekdays) on the metro, tram, and bus network within the city limits. Cheaper 8 Kč tickets are good for a tram or bus ride up to 15 minutes without transferring, or 30 minutes on the metro including transfers between lines; on the metro, though, you cannot travel more than four stops from your starting point. For the metro punch the ticket in the station before getting onto the escalators; for buses and trams punch the ticket inside the vehicle. (Enter the tram or bus through any door and stick the tickets horizontally—and gently—into the little yellow machines, which should stamp them with the date and time; it's an acquired trick of hand-eye coordination; ask for help from another passenger if your machine is not cooperating, which is often the case.) If you fail to validate your ticket, you may be fined 800 Kč by a ticket inspector, which is reduced to 400 Kč for on-the-spot payment.

Note: Prague has quite a pickpocketing racket, to which the police apparently turn a blind eye. Be very wary of raucous groups of people making a commotion as they get on and off trams and metros; generally they are working the passengers. Keep close watch on your belongings and purses on crowded streets and in crowded sites.

TRAVEL AGENCIES

🚉 Local Agent Referrals **American Express** ✉ Václavské nám. 56 ☎ 224/818205 🖨 222–211–131. **Thomas Cook** ✉ Karlova 3 ☎ 221/221055.

VISITOR INFORMATION

The English-language weekly *Prague Post* lists current events and entertainment programs.

🚉 **Čedok** main office ✉ Na Příkopě 18, near Wenceslas Sq. ☎ 224/197121 or 224/197306 ✉ Rytířská 16 ✉ Pařížská 6 ⊕ www.cedok.cz. **Prague Information Service** (PIS) ✉ Na Příkopě 20 ✉ Staroměstské nám. 22 ☎ 12444 or 221/714130.

🚉 Tourist Bureaus Outside Prague **Český Krumlov** Infocentrum ✉ Nám. Svornosti 2 ☎ 380/704622 ⊕ www.ckrumlov.cz. **Karlovy Vary** ✉ Vřídelní kolonáda ☎ 353/244097 ⊕ www.karlovyvary.cz. **Mariánské Lázně** Infocentrum ✉ Hlavní 47 ☎ 353/622474 ⊕ www.marianskelazne.cz. **Mikulov** ✉ Regional Tourist Center, Nám. 1 🖨🖨 519/510855 ⊕ www.mikulov.cz. **Olomouc** ✉ Horní nám. ☎ 585/513385 ⊕ www.olomoucko. cz. **Tábor** ✉ Žižkovo nám. 2 ☎ 381/486230 ⊕ www.tabor.cz. **Telč** ✉ Town hall, Nám. Zachariáše z Hradce 10 ☎ 567/234145 ⊕ www.telc-etc.cz.

DENMARK
COPENHAGEN, FYN & THE CENTRAL ISLANDS, JYLLAND & THE LAKES

EBULLIENCE AND A SENSE OF HUMOR have always been Danish trademarks. One might expect a country comprising more than 400 islands to develop an island mentality, but the Danes are famous for their friendliness. They even have a word—*hyggelig*—for the feeling of well-being that comes from their own brand of cozy hospitality.

The stereotype of melancholic Scandinavia simply doesn't hold here: either in the café-studded streets of the larger cities, where musicians and fruit vendors hawk their wares to passersby, or in the tiny coastal towns, where the fishing boats are as brightly painted as fire trucks. Even the country's indoor-outdoor museums, where history is brought to life in clusters of reconstructed buildings out in the open, indicate that Danes don't choose to keep experience behind glass.

This is a land of well-groomed agriculture, where every available acre is planted in orchards, forests, or crops. Nowhere are you far from water as you drive on and off the ferries and bridges linking the three regions of Jylland (Jutland), Fyn (Funen), and Sjælland (Zealand).

The surrounding sea has shaped Denmark's history. The Vikings, unparalleled seafarers, had seen much of the world by the 8th century. Today the Danes remain expert navigators, using their 7,314 km (4,544 mi) of coastline both for sport—there are regattas around Sjælland and Fyn—and for fishing and trading. Copenhagen is also proving itself as one of the most popular cruise ports in northern Europe.

Long one of the world's most liberal countries, Denmark has a highly developed social welfare system. Hefty taxes are the subject of grumbling and jokes, but Danes remain proud of their state-funded medical and educational systems.

The country that gave the world Isak Dinesen, Hans Christian Andersen, and Søren Kierkegaard has a long-standing commitment to culture and the arts. In what other nation does the royal couple translate the writings of Simone de Beauvoir, or the queen design costumes for the ballet? The Royal Danish Ballet is world renowned, and even in the provinces there are numerous theater groups and opera houses.

Perhaps Denmark's greatest charm is its manageable size, about half that of Maine or 4½ times larger than Wales (43,070 square km/16,629 square mi). The train ride from Esbjerg on the western coast of Jylland to Copenhagen on the eastern coast of Sjælland takes just over three hours, across the Storebælt Bridge. From the capital you can make comfortable, unhurried voyages by boat, car, bus, or train. Even a trip to Malmö in Sweden takes only 35 minutes by train or car since the opening of

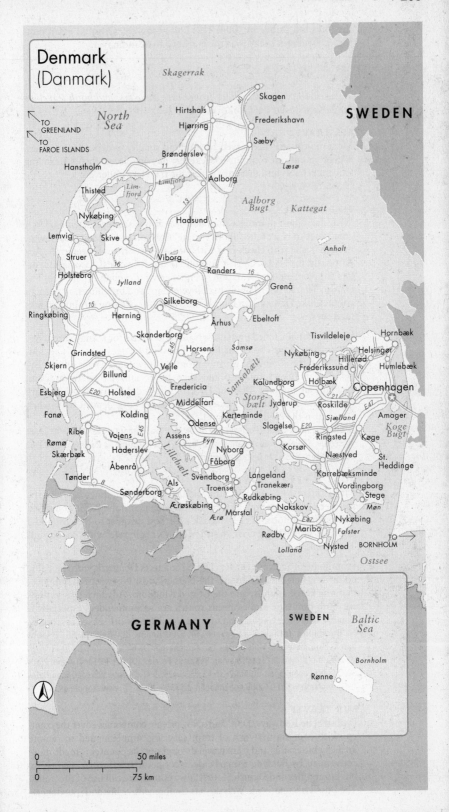

Denmark (Danmark)

Skagerrak

TO GREENLAND
TO FAROE ISLANDS

North Sea

SWEDEN

Skagen
Hirtshals
Frederikshavn
Hjørring
Sæby
Brønderslev
Hanstholm
Thisted
Limfjord
Aalborg
Læsø
Nykøbing
Hadsund
Aalborg Bugt
Kattegat
Lemvig
Skive
Struer
Viborg
Anholt
Holstebro
Jylland
Randers
Grenå
Ringkøbing
Herning
Silkeborg
Ebeltoft
Ærhus
Skanderborg
Horsens
Samsø
Grindsted
Vejle
Tisvildeleje
Hornbæk
Skjern
Billund
Fredericia
Nykøbing
Helsingør
Hillerød
Esbjerg
Holsted
Middelfart
Kalundborg
Frederikssund
Humlebæk
Fanø
Kolding
Odense
Kerteminde
Holbæk
Copenhagen
Ribe
Vojens
Assens
Fyn
Slagelse
Jyderup
Roskilde
Amager
Rømø
Haderslev
Nyborg
Sjælland
Ringsted
Køge
Koge Bugt
Skærbæk
Åbenrå
Fåborg
Korsør
Næstved
St. Heddinge
Tønder
Als
Svendborg
Langeland
Karrebæksminde
Sønderborg
Troense
Tranekær
Vordingborg
Stege
Ærøskøbing
Rudkøbing
Møn
Ærø
Marstal
Nakskov
Nykøbing
TO BORNHOLM
Rødby
Maribo
Falster
Nysted
Lolland
Ostsee

Storebælt
Samsøbælt
Lillebælt

GERMANY

SWEDEN
Baltic Sea

Bornholm
Rønne

0 — 50 miles
0 — 75 km

the Øresund Bridge in 2000. This link across the Øresund Strait reinforces Denmark's status as the entrance to Scandinavia.

DENMARK A TO Z

To research prices, get advice from other travelers, and book travel arrangements, visit www.fodors.com.

AIR TRAVEL

Most major cities are served by SAS and smaller, independent airlines. SAS offers cut-rate round-trip fares every day on selected flights, including student rebates and discount prices for travelers under 26.

SAS ☎ 70/10-20-00.

BIKE TRAVEL

With its highest point less than 600 feet above sea level, Denmark is a great place to be a cyclist. Shops renting bikes can be found in most towns, though it is wise to check first with local tourist offices for referrals. Additionally, the Dansk Cyklist Forbund (Danish Cyclists' Association) offers supplemental information to enhance your cycling experience. The Danish Tourist Board publishes bicycle maps and brochures, or you can contact Bike Denmark, a bicycle tour operator offering self-guided biking tours.

Bicycles can be carried onto most trains and ferries for a small surcharge, but cycling along the Great Belt or Øresund bridges is strictly forbidden. With the coming of warmer months, Copenhagen rolls out the Bycykler (City Bikes) and distributes them to specialized bike stands found throughout the city. Deposit DKr20 and pedal away. The bikes are often dented, but they do function. You'll get your deposit back when you return the bike to any stand.

Bike Denmark ✉ Olaf Poulsens Allé 1A, DK 3480 Fredensborg ☎ 48/48-58-00 🖶 48/48-59-00 ⊕ www.bikedenmark.com. **Dansk Cyklist Forbund** ✉ Rømersg. 7, DK 1362 Copenhagen ☎ 33/32-31-21 ⊕ www.dcf.dk.

BOAT & FERRY TRAVEL

Mols-Linien links Jylland and Sjælland, and Scandlines services the southern islands as well as Germany, Sweden, and the Baltic countries. The island of Bornholm, Denmark's farthest outpost to the east and a popular domestic tourist destination, is reachable with Bornholms Trafikken.

Scandinavian Seaways Ferries (DFDS) connects Denmark with the Baltic countries, Belgium, Germany, the Netherlands, Norway, Poland, Sweden, the Faroe Islands, and the United Kingdom. Advance reservations for both domestic and overseas routes are recommended, especially if you are traveling by car. Don't forget to ask about off-season discounts.

Bornholms Trafikken ✉ Havnen, DK 3700 Rønne ☎ 56/95-18-66 ⊕ www.bornholmstrafikken.dk. **Mols-Linien** ✉ Faergehavnen DK 8400 Ebeltoft ☎ 70/10-14-18 ⊕ www.molslinien.dk. **Scandinavian Seaways Ferries (DFDS)** ✉ Sankt Annæ Plads 30, DK 1295 Copenhagen ☎ 33/42-33-42 🖶 33/42-33-41 ⊕ www.dfds.com. **Scandlines** ✉ Dampfærgevej 10 DK 2100 Copenhagen ☎ 33/15-15-15 ⊕ www.scandlines.dk.

BUS TRAVEL

Danish State Railways (DSB) and a few private companies cover the country with a dense network of train services, supplemented in remote areas by buses. Bus and train travel throughout the country is made more convenient by Bus/Tog Samarbejde, a cooperative effort by the private bus companies and Danish State Railways to make full use of the trains. The Bus/Tog Samarbejde Web site has comprehensive bus and train timetables and route information. Bus tickets are usually sold onboard the buses immediately before departure. Ask about discounts for children, senior citizens, and groups.

Bus/Tog Samarbejde ⊕ www.rejseplan.dk. **Danish State Railways** ☎ 70/13-14-15 ⊕ www.dsb.dk.

BUSINESS HOURS

BANKS & OFFICES Banks in Copenhagen are open weekdays 9:30–4. Some branches have extended hours on Thursday until 6. Several bureaux de change, including those at Copenhagen's central station and airport, stay open until 10 PM. Outside Copenhagen, banking hours vary.

MUSEUMS & SIGHTS Museums are generally open Tuesday to Saturday from 10–3 or 11–4. Opening hours in winter are usually shorter, and some museums close entirely for the season, especially on the smaller islands. Check local papers or ask at tourist offices.

SHOPS Small shops and boutiques are open for business weekdays 10–5:30, and most stay open on Friday until 7. On Saturday, doors close at 1 or 2, though larger department stores remain open until 5. On the first Saturday of every month, most shops stay open until 4. Call ahead to verify weekend opening hours for specific stores. Grocery stores in the Nørreport neighborhood are open until 11 PM or even longer. The same goes for many kiosks in the big towns.

CAR TRAVEL

EMERGENCIES Members of organizations affiliated with Alliance International de Tourisme (AIT), including American AAA and British AA, can get technical and legal assistance from the Forenede Danske Motorejere (Danish Motoring Organization). Emergency phones can be found on all highways or you can call your car-rental company if help is needed. For immobilized motorists, Falck Redning (Falck Rescue) is available 24 hours a day to provide roadside assistance anywhere in Denmark. For emergency situations, call 112.

Falck Headquarters ⊠ Polititorvet, DK 1780 Copenhagen ☎ 70/10-20-30 emergencies; 33/15-83-20 headquarters 🖴 33/91-00-26 ⊕ www.falck.dk. **Forenede Danske Motorejere** ⊠ Firskovvej 32, DK 2800 Lyngby ☎ 70/13-30-40 🖴 45/27-09-93 ⊕ www.fdm.dk.

GASOLINE Gas costs more than DKr8 a liter (about US$5 a gallon).

PARKING In areas with signs marked PARKERING/STANDSNING FORBUDT (No Parking and No Stopping) you are allowed a three-minute grace period to load and unload. On city streets where automated parking-permit machines are used to dispense time-limited permits, be sure the ticket is clearly visible on the dashboard. When an automated permit vending machine is not available, parking disks (clock face) are used instead to indicate when the car was parked. Parking disks are available from gas stations or police stations.

ROAD CONDITIONS Roads are generally maintained in good condition and rarely suffer from traffic congestion (except around Copenhagen). Most islands are connected by toll-free bridges. The exceptions are the Storebæltsbro connecting Sjælland and Fyn, and the Øresundsbro between Copenhagen and Malmö, Sweden, which charge hefty tolls for the privilege of crossing.

RULES OF THE ROAD Anyone operating a motorized vehicle on Danish roads or highways must possess a valid driver's license. If you're using your own car, you must have a certificate of registration and national plates. A triangular hazard-warning sign is compulsory in every car and is provided with rentals. The driver and all passengers must wear seat belts whenever the vehicle is in operation, and headlights must always be on—even in the daytime. Helmets are compulsory for motorcyclists, and headlights must always be on. The prolific use of bicycles in Denmark presents a unique traffic environment. All drivers must pay special attention to cyclists who utilize the outer right lane (bicycles only!) and have the right-of-way at all intersections.

Drive on the right-hand side and give way to traffic approaching from the right. A red-and-white triangular yield sign, or a line of white triangles across the road, means you must yield to traffic on the road you are entering. Do not turn right on a red light unless there is a green arrow indicating that the turn is allowed. Speed limits are 50 kph (30 mph) in built-up areas, 100 kph (60 mph) on highways, and 80 kph (50 mph) on other roads. If you are towing a trailer, you must not exceed 70 kph (40 mph).

CUSTOMS & DUTIES
For details on imports and duty-free limits, *see* Customs & Duties *in* Smart Tavel Tips.

EATING & DRINKING
Traditional Danish food emphasizes fresh ingredients, few spices, and careful presentation. Fish and meat are both staple ingredients of the famous *smørrebrød,* which are commonly found on lunch menus throughout Denmark. Don't be fooled into thinking that this is an ordinary open-face sandwich. Nowhere else can you expect to find a slice of dark bread so dressed up with toppings and garnishes that it borders on artwork. The Danes take their smørrebrød very seriously, and they draw on generations of experience to intermingle just the right toppings to tantalize the taste buds during your midday meal. A wide selection of traditional combinations is always available, but those wishing to create their own variations should expect a raised Danish eyebrow or two for going against age-old customs. Another specialty is *wienerbrød,* a confection far superior to anything billed as Danish pastry elsewhere.

Denmark has more than 50 varieties of beer, made by a dozen or so breweries. The best-known suds are Carlsberg and Tuborg, both made by the same company. If you like harder stuff, try *snaps,* the aquavit traditionally drunk with cold food, especially herring. A note about smoking: Danes regard smoking as an inalienable right. Militant insistence that they abstain will be regarded as either hysteria or comedy. A polite tone requesting they blow their smoke away from you may prove more effective.

WHAT IT COSTS In Denmark Krone			
$$$$	**$$$**	**$$**	**$**
COPENHAGEN			
PER PERSON	over 200	150–200	100–150	under 100
OTHER AREAS			
AT DINNER	over 170	120–170	80–120	under 80

Prices are per person for a main course.

MEALTIMES The Danes start work early, which means they generally eat lunch at noon. Evening meals are also eaten early, so make sure you have dinner reservations for 9 at the latest. Bars and cafés stay open later, and most offer at least light fare.

RESERVATIONS & DRESS The Danes are fairly casual, and few restaurants require a jacket and tie. Even in the most chic establishments, the tone is elegantly casual.

EMBASSIES

All embassies are in Copenhagen.

🏴 Canada ⊠ Kristen Bernikowsg. 1, DK 1105 KBH K ☎ 33/48-32-00 ⊕ www.canada.dk.

🏴 Ireland ⊠ Østbanegade 21, DK 2100 KBH, Ø ☎ 35/42-32-33 🖷 35/43-18-58.

🏴 South Africa ⊠ Gammel Vartov Vej 8, DK 2900 Hellerup ☎ 39/18-01-55 ⊕ www. southafrica.dk.

🏴 United Kingdom ⊠ Kastelsvej 36-40, DK 2100 KBH Ø ☎ 35/44-52-00 ⊕ www. britishembassy.dk.

🏴 United States ⊠ Dag Hammarskjölds Allé 24, DK 2100 KBH Ø ☎ 35/55-31-44 ⊕ www.usembassy.dk.

HOLIDAYS

January 1; Easter (Thursday–Monday); Common Prayer (May); Ascension (40 days after Easter); June 5 (Constitution Day; shops close at noon); Whitsun/Pentecost (Sunday and Monday; 10 days after Ascension); December 24–26.

LANGUAGE

Danish is a difficult tongue for foreigners—except those from Norway and Sweden—to understand, let alone speak. Danes are good linguists, however, and almost everyone, except perhaps elderly people in rural areas, speaks English well in addition to a third language, usually French or German.

LODGING

Accommodations in Denmark range from the spare and comfortable to the resplendent. Even inexpensive hotels have invested in good materials and good, firm beds in simple designs. However, when you make reservations, pin down details so you get what you want. Many hotels are in century-old buildings; room sizes, even in top hotels, can vary enormously, and the smallest have sloping ceilings and cubbyhole-size doubles. If you have preferences, ask for them specifically and get a confirmation in writing. Many Danes prefer a shower to a bath, so if you particularly want a tub, ask for it, but be prepared to pay more. Except in the case of rentals, breakfast and taxes are usually included in prices. Check when making a reservation. Note that some hotels ask for an environmental supplement of 35 Dkr.

WHAT IT COSTS In Denmark Krone			
$$$$	**$$$**	**$$**	**$**
COPENHAGEN			
FOR 2 PEOPLE over 1,700	1,400–1,700	900–1,400	under 900
OTHER AREAS			
HOTELS over 1,400	1,200–1,400	900–1,200	under 900

Hotel prices are for a standard double room in high season.

APARTMENT & VILLA RENTALS Each year many Danes choose to rent out their summer homes, presenting an ideal opportunity for visitors who prefer to relax and take their time enjoying the peaceful countryside. Typically, a simple house accommodating four people will cost from DKr1,000 weekly up to 10 times that amount during the summer high season. Booking well in advance is advised. A number of people who regularly rent out their holiday houses have established the Association of Danish Holiday House Letters (ADHHL).

🏠 **Feriehusudlejernes Brancheforeningen (ADHHL)** ✉ Obels Have 32, DK 9000 Aalborg ☎ 96/30-22-44 🖷 96/30-22-45 ⊕ www.fbnet.dk.

B&BS Contact Dansk Bed & Breakfast to order a catalog of B&Bs for the entire country. If you want to stay in Funen and its islands, contact the Faaborg Touristbureau.

🏠 **Dansk Bed & Breakfast** ✉ Bernstorffsvej 71a, DK 2900 Hellerup ☎ 39/61-04-05 🖷 39/61-05-25 ⊕ www.bedandbreakfast.dk. **Faaborg Touristbureau** ✉ Banegaardspladsen 2A, DK 5600 Faaborg ☎ 62/61-07-07 🖷 62/61-33-37 ⊕ www.bed-breakfast-fyn.dk.

CAMPING Denmark has more than 500 approved campsites with a rating system of one, two, or three stars. You'll need either an International Camping Carnet or a Danish Camping Pass (available at any campsite and valid for one year) if you want to stay at a campsite. For more details on camping and discounts available for groups and families, contact Campingrådet.

🏠 **Campingrådet** ✉ Mosedalsvej 15, DK 2500 Valby (Copenhagen) ☎ 39/27-88-44 🖷 39/27-80-44 ⊕ www.campingraadet.dk.

FARM VACATIONS Perhaps the best way to experience how Danes live and work, farm vacations allow you to stay on a farm, sharing meals with your host family, and helping with the chores. There is a selection of packages available at varying costs, but the minimum stay is always three nights. Bed-and-breakfast is about DKr200, whereas half board, comprising an overnight with breakfast and one hot meal, costs about DKr280. The complete package or full board, including an overnight with three square meals, can also be arranged. Contact Landboferie (Holiday in the Country) for details.

🏠 **Landboferie** ✉ Ceresvej 2, 8410 Rønde ☎ 86/37-39-00 🖷 86/37-35-50 ⊕ www.bondegaardsferie.dk.

HOSTELS Youth hostels in Denmark are open to everyone regardless of age. If you have an International Youth Hostels Association card (it costs DKr160 to obtain in Denmark), the rate is roughly DKr115 for a single bed, DKr150–DKr575 for a private room accommodating up to four people. Without the card, there's a surcharge of about DKr30 per person. Prices do not include breakfast. For more information, contact Danhostel Danmarks Vandrerhjem.

🏠 **Danhostel Danmarks Vandrerhjem** ✉ Vesterbrog. 39, DK 1620 Copenhagen ☎ 33/31-36-12 🖷 33/31-36-26 ⊕ www.danhostel.dk.

HOTELS Luxury hotels, whether in the city or countryside, offer rooms of a high standard. If you choose a manor-house hotel instead, you may find yourself sleeping in a four-poster bed. Even less expensive accommodations are uniformly comfortable.

INNS For a cheaper yet still charming alternative to hotels, try one of the old *kroer* (stagecoach inns) scattered throughout Denmark. You can save money by contacting Danske Kroer & Hoteller (Danish Inns & Hotels) to invest in a book of Inn Checks, valid at any of the 83 participating inns and hotels. Each check costs about DKr675 per couple and will get you an overnight stay in a double room, including breakfast. Family checks for three (DKr775) or four (DKr875) people are also available. Order a free catalog from Danske Kroer & Hoteller, but choose carefully. The organization includes some chain hotels bereft of any inn-related charm. Some establishments will even tack on a DKr150 surcharge.

🏠 **Danske Kroer & Hoteller** ✉ Vejlevej 16, DK 8700 Horsens, Jylland ☎ 75/64-87-00 🖷 75/64-87-20 ⊕ www.krohotel.dk.

MAIL & SHIPPING

Mail can be addressed to *poste restante* and received by any post office if you don't know in advance where you'll be staying. If no post office is specified, then letters will automatically be sent to the main post office in Copenhagen.

POSTAL RATES   Surface letters, airmail letters, and postcards to non-EU countries cost DKr6.50 for 50 grams. Airmail letters and postcards within the EU cost DKr5.50. Length, width, and thickness of the package or letter affects the postage price.

🄵 Copenhagen Main Post Office ✉ Tietgensg. 37, DK 1566 Copenhagen V ☎ 80/ 20-70-30 ⊕ www.postdanmark.dk.

MONEY MATTERS

Denmark's economy is stable, and inflation remains reasonably low. The standard of living is high, but so is the cost, especially for such luxury items as alcohol and cigarettes. The steepest prices are found in Copenhagen, and the least expensive areas are Fyn and Jylland. Some sample prices: cup of coffee, DKr15–DKr25; bottle of beer, DKr20–DKr30; soda, DKr20-DKr25; ham sandwich, DKr20–DKr40; 1½-km (1-mi) taxi ride, DKr50.

CURRENCY   The monetary unit in Denmark is the krone (kr., DKr, or DKK), which is divided into 100 øre. Denmark has not adopted the euro, but the Danish krone is firmly bound to it. Exchange rates are typically about DKr7.5 to 1€. At press time (summer 2003), the krone stood at DKr8.20 to the U.S. dollar, DKr5.27 to the Canadian dollar, DKr11.71 to the pound sterling, DKr4.50 to the Australian dollar, DKr3.49 to the New Zealand dollar, and DKr1.05 to the South African rand. Most credit cards are accepted in Denmark, though it is wise to inquire about American Express and Diners Club beforehand. Traveler's checks can be cashed in banks as well as in many hotels, restaurants, and shops.

TAXES

VALUE-ADDED   Non-EU citizens can save 20% (less a handling fee) off the purchase price
TAX (V.A.T.)   if they shop in one of the hundreds of stores throughout Denmark displaying the TAX FREE SHOPPING sign. The purchased merchandise must be valued at more than DKr300. The taxes will be refunded after submitting the application with customs authorities at their final destination before leaving the EU.

TELEPHONES

COUNTRY & AREA   The country code for Denmark is 45.
CODES

DIRECTORY &   Dial 118 to speak with an operator for local assistance. Most operators
OPERATOR   are fluent in English. For an international operator, dial 113.
ASSISTANCE

INTERNATIONAL   Dial 00, then the country code, area code, and the desired number. You
CALLS   can reach AT&T, MCI, and Sprint by dialing one of the access codes.
🄵 Access Codes **AT&T** ☎ 800/10010. **MCI WorldCom** ☎ 800/10022. **Sprint** ☎ 800/ 10877.

LOCAL CALLS   Pay phones take DKr1, DKr2, DKr5, DKr10, and DKr20 coins. Area codes must be used even when calling a local number, which means dialing all eight digits for numbers anywhere within the country. Calling cards, which are sold at Danish State Railways stations, post offices, and some kiosks, are increasingly necessary as pay phones that accept coins become a thing of the past.

TIPPING

Some restaurants, usually the larger ones, will add a service charge to the price of the bill. Waiters don't expect a tip but appreciate one. A good rule of thumb is to round up the bill if the food and service merited a gratuity. Hotel porters should get around DKr5 per bag.

TRAIN TRAVEL

Hourly intercity trains connect the main towns in Jylland and Fyn to Copenhagen and Sjælland, with the most important stretches using high-speed diesel trains called IC-3s. All trains use the seven-minute tunnel crossing of the Store Bælt (Great Belt), the waterway separating Fyn and Sjælland. Seat reservations on intercity trains and IC-3s are optional, but you must have a reservation if you plan to cross the Great Belt.

Buy tickets at stations or from Arriva if you're traveling in central and northern Jutland, and the Danish State Railways (DSB) for the rest of the country.

FARES & SCHEDULES The ScanRail pass affords unlimited train travel throughout Denmark, Finland, Norway, and Sweden, as well as restricted ferry passage in and beyond Scandinavia. It is available for 5 or 10 days of travel within two months, or for 21 consecutive days. Buy the tickets in your country to save money. The passes are available in Denmark but are more expensive. Various discounts are offered to holders of the pass by hotel chains and other organizations.

🚆 **Arriva** ☎ 72/13-96-00 ⊕ www.arriva.dk. **DSB Information** ☎ 70/13-14-15 ⊕ www. dsb.dk. **ScanRail** ⊕ www.scanrail.com.

VISITOR INFORMATION

The main tourist information office is the Danish Tourist Board. Youth information is available in Copenhagen at Ungdoms Information.

🚆 **Danish Tourist Board** ✉ Danmarks Turistråd; Vesterbrogade 6D, DK 1620 Copenhagen V ☎ 33/11-14-15 🖷 33/93-14-15 ⊕ www.visitdenmark.com. **Ungdoms Information** ✉ Rådhusstr. 13, DK 1466 Copenhagen K ☎ 33/73-06-50 🖷 33/73-06-49 ⊕ www. ui.dk.

WHEN TO GO

Most travelers visit Denmark during the warmer months of July and August, but there are advantages to going in May, June, or September when sights are less crowded. Few places in Denmark are ever unpleasantly crowded, however, regardless of the season. The winter months bring short days and gloomy weather, and the Danes lose a little of their summertime extroverted mood. Many attractions close in winter.

CLIMATE The following are the average daily maximum and minimum temperatures for Copenhagen.

Jan.	36F	2C	May	61F	16C	Sept.	64F	18C
	28	-2		46	8		51	11
Feb.	36F	2C	June	67F	19C	Oct.	54F	12C
	28	-2		52	11		44	7
Mar.	41F	5C	July	71F	22C	Nov.	45F	7C
	31	-1		57	14		38	3
Apr.	51F	11C	Aug.	70F	21C	Dec.	40F	4C
	38	3		56	14		34	1

COPENHAGEN

After you arrive at Copenhagen Airport on the isle of Amager, the taxi ride into the city will not stun you with a dramatic skyline or a seething metropolis. Instead, you will be greeted by elegant spires, green copper roofs, and cobbled streets. Copenhagen is not divided like most other cities into single-purpose districts, but is instead a rich, multilayered capital where people work, play, shop, and live throughout its central core. Surrounded by water, be it sea or canal, and connected by bridges and drawbridges, it has a maritime atmosphere.

Exploring Copenhagen

Numbers in the margin correspond to points of interest on the Copenhagen map.

Copenhagen is a lively northern capital with about 1 million inhabitants. It's a city meant for walking; as you stroll through the cobbled streets and squares, you'll find that Copenhagen combines the excitement and variety of big-city life with a small-town atmosphere. If there's such a thing as a cozy metropolis, this is it.

The original city is built upon two main islands, Slotsholmen and Christianshavn, connected by drawbridges. The ancient heart of the city is intersected by two heavily peopled pedestrian streets—part of the five such streets known collectively as Strøget—and around them curls a maze of cobbled streets packed with tiny boutiques, cafés, and restaurants, all best explored on foot.

⑭ Amalienborg (Amalia's Castle). During the fall and winter, when members of the royal family return to their principal residence, the Changing of the Guard is publicly announced each day at noon with the Royal Guard and band marching through the city. Amalienborg's other big attraction is the second division of the Royal Collection (the first is at Rosenborg), housed inside the **Amalienborg Museum.** The collection includes the study of King Christian IX (1818–1906) and the drawing room of his wife, Queen Louise. **Amalienhaven** (Amalia's Gardens) includes modern sculptures and manicured flower beds. ⊠ *Amalienborg Pl., DK 1257* ☎ *33/12–08–08* ☺ *May–Oct., daily 11–4; Nov.–Apr., Tues.–Sun. 11–4.*

⑧ Børsen (Stock Exchange). This edifice is believed to be the oldest such structure still in use, though it functions only on special occasions. It was built by the 16th-century monarch King Christian IV, a scholar, warrior, and the architect of much of the city. With its steep roofs, tiny windows, and gables, the building is one of Copenhagen's treasures. ⊠ *Christiansborg Slotspl.* ☺ *Not open to public.*

㉓ Botanisk Have (Botanical Garden). Copenhagen's 25-acre botanical garden, with a spectacular Palm House containing tropical and subtropical plants, upstages the palatial gardens of **Rosenborg Slot** (Rosenborg Castle). Also on the grounds are an observatory, a geological museum, and individual houses for cacti, orchids, and carnivorous plants. ⊠ *Gothersg. 128* ☎ *35/32–22–40* ⊕ *www.botanic-garden.ku.dk* ☺ *Grounds May–Sept., daily 8:30–6; Oct.–Apr., Tues.–Sun. 8:30–4. Palm House daily 10–3. Cactus House Wed., weekends, and holidays 1–3. Orchid House Wed., weekends, and holidays 2–3. Carnivorous Plants House daily 10–3.*

㉘ Carlsberg Bryggeri (Carlsberg Brewery). Granite elephants guard the entrance to the first Carlsberg brewery, opened in 1847; inside you can visit the draft-horse stalls and **Carlsberg Visitors' Centre,** and taste the local product. ⊠ *Gl. Carlsbergvej 11* ☎ *33/27–13–14* ⊕ *www.carlsberg.dk* ☺ *Tues.–Sun. 10–4; groups book in advance* ☺ *Closed holidays and Dec. 23–31.*

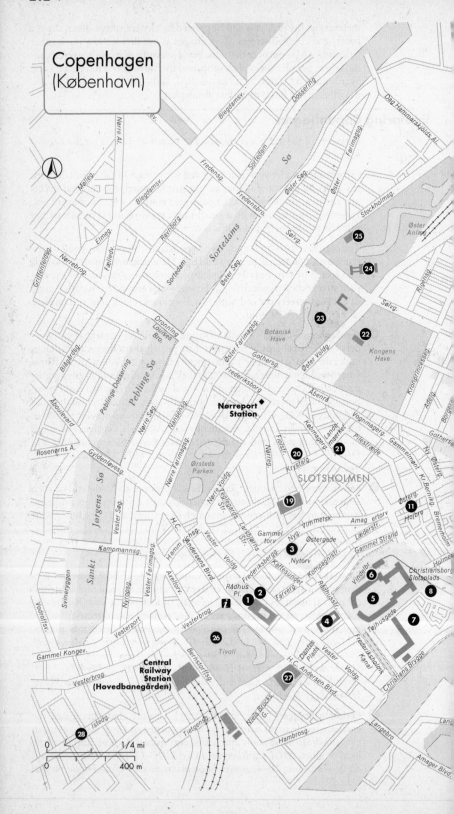

Copenhagen
(København)

①⓿ Christiania. In the 1970s, a group of locals founded Christiania as a free town, independent from Denmark. They wanted to live in a community based on peace and freedom—an idea that's been variously challenged or tolerated by the Danish authorities through the years. The colony still exists, however, and Christiania has developed into a district for cultural tourism. With guided tours, cafés, restaurants, craftsmen's workshops, and music venues, it stays lively night and day. Be aware though, that Christiania has some seedy areas, where drug dealers are known to operate. ☒ *Prinsesseg.–Bådmandsst.* ☎ *32/57–96–70 guided tours* ⊕ *www.christiania.org.*

❺ Christiansborg Slot (Christiansborg Castle). This massive gray complex, containing the Folketinget (Parliament House) and the Royal Reception Chambers, is situated on the site of the city's first fortress, which was erected in 1167 by Bishop Absalon. As a result of two disastrous fires in 1794 and 1884 that caused massive damage to the original structure, the present construction represents three architectural styles: the main building, finished in 1928, is in the new baroque style; the church shows the new classical architecture of the 19th century; and the riding ground is an example of grand 18th-century baroque. Also worth a visit are the remains of Bishop Absalon's fortress from 1167, which were excavated beneath the castle. ☒ *Christiansborg, Christiansborg Plads, DK 1218* ☎ *33/92–64–94 Christiansborg ruins; 33/37–55–00 Folketinget; 33/ 92–64–94 Royal Reception Chambers* ⊕ *www.ses.dk* ☉ *Christiansborg ruins: May–Sept., daily 9:30–3:30; Oct.–Apr., Tues., Thurs., and weekends 9:30–3:30. Folketinget: guided tours Sun. 10–4. Royal Reception Chambers: May–Sept., daily 11–3; guided tours in English.*

⑱ Den Lille Havfrue (The Little Mermaid). This statue was erected in 1913 to commemorate Hans Christian Andersen's lovelorn creation. **Langelinie,** the spit of land you follow to reach the famed nymph, is thronged with promenading Danes and tourists—many of whom are themselves more absorbing to watch than the somewhat overrated sculpture. ☒ *Langelinie promenade.*

⑯ Frihedsmuseet (Liberty Museum). Evocative displays commemorate the heroic World War II Danish resistance movement, which saved 7,000 Jews from the Nazis by hiding them and then smuggling them across to Sweden. ☒ *Churchillparken* ☎ *33/13–77–14* ⊕ *www.natmus.dk* ☉ *May–Sept. 15, Tues.–Sat. 10–4, Sun. and holidays 10–5; Sept. 16–Apr. 30, Tues.–Sat. 11–3, Sun. and holidays 11–4.*

㉕ Den Hirschsprungske Samling (Hirschsprung Collection). This cozy museum focuses on works from Denmark's golden age of painting. The mid-19th-century school of Naturalism was pioneered by C. W. Eckersberg, whose pictures contain a remarkable wealth of detail and technical skill combined with limpid, cool, luminescent color. Other prominent painters of the movement included Christian Købke and Julius Exner. The Hirschsprungske also hosts a collection of paintings by the late-19th-century artists of the Danish Skagen school. ☒ *Stockholmsg. 20* ☎ *35/ 42–03–36* ⊕ *www.hirschsprung.dk* ☉ *Thurs.–Mon. 11–4, Wed. 11–9.*

⑰ Kastellet (Citadel). Once surrounded by two rings of moats, this building was the city's main fortress during the 17th century, but, in a grim reversal during World War II, the Germans used it as one of their headquarters during their occupation of Denmark. The lovely green area around it, **Churchillparken,** cut throughout with walking paths, is a favorite among the Danes, who flock here on sunny weekends. If you have time, walk past the spired **St. Alban's,** an Anglican church at the park's entrance. ☒ *Churchillparken* ☉ *Grounds daily 6 AM–sunset.*

㉒ Københavns Synagoge (Copenhagen Synagogue). This synagogue was designed by contemporary architect Gustav Friedrich Hetsch, who borrowed from the Doric and Egyptian styles in creating the arklike structure. ✉ *Krystalg. 12* ☎ *33/12–88–86* ◷ *Daily services 4:15.*

❼ Det Kongelige Bibliotek (Royal Library). This library houses the country's largest collection of books, newspapers, and manuscripts. Look for early records of the Viking journeys to America and Greenland. A dark marble annex next door, known as the Black Diamond, houses the **National Museum of Photography.** ✉ *Søren Kierkegaards Pl. 1* ☎ *33/47–47–47* ⊕ *www.kb.dk* ◷ *Library, weekdays 10–5; Black Diamond, Mon.–Sat. 10–5.*

⑮ Kunstindustrimuseet (Museum of Decorative Art). The highlights of this museum's collection are a large assortment of European and Asian handicrafts, as well as ceramics, silver, and tapestries. The quiet library full of design tomes and magazines doubles as a primer for Danish functionalism with its Le Klint paper lamp shades and wooden desks. ✉ *Bredg. 68* ☎ *33/18–56–56* ⊕ *www.kunstindustrimuseet.dk* ◷ *Special exhibits Tues.–Fri. 10–4, weekends and holidays noon–4; permanent exhibition Tues.–Fri. 1–4, weekends and holidays noon–4.*

❷ Lurblæserne (Lur Blower Column). Topped by two Vikings blowing an ancient trumpet called a *lur,* this column was erected in 1914 and displays a good deal of artistic license: the lur dates from 1500 BC—the Bronze Age—whereas the Vikings lived a mere 1,000 years ago. The monument is a starting point for sightseeing tours of the city. ✉ *East side of Rådhus Pl.*

⑬ Marmorkirken (Marble Church). The ponderous Frederikskirke, commonly called Marmorkirken, is a baroque church that was begun in 1749 in costly Norwegian marble. It was finally completed and consecrated in 1894. Perched around the exterior are 16 statues of various religious leaders from Moses to Luther, and below them stand sculptures of outstanding Danish ministers and bishops. ✉ *Frederiksgade 4* ☎ *33/15–01–44* ⊕ *www.marmorkirken.dk* ◷ *Mon. and Tues. and Thurs. and Fri. 10–5, Wed. 10–6, weekends noon–5.*

☾ ❹ Nationalmuseet (National Museum). The extensive collections of this museum chronicle the cultural history of Denmark right up to modern times and include relics such as original Viking runic stones. Also on display are Egyptian, Greek, and Roman antiquities. The children's museum is an excellent place for kids to learn history and, although the original relics are secured behind glass, there are plenty of curiosities for kids to play with, including period clothing to dress up in and an old-world school to explore. ✉ *Ny Vesterg. 10* ☎ *33/13–44–11* ⊕ *www.natmus.dk* ◷ *Tues.–Sun. 10–5.*

⑪ Nikolaj Kirken (St. Nicholas Church). In Østergade, the easternmost of the streets that make up Strøget, you cannot miss the green spire of this building. The present structure was built in the 20th century; the previous one, dating from the 13th century, was destroyed by fire in 1728. Today the building is no longer a church but an art gallery and exhibition center. ✉ *Nikolaj Pl. 10* ☎ *33/93–16–26* ⊕ *www.nikolaj-ccac.dk* ◷ *Daily noon–5.*

★ ㉗ Ny Carlsberg Glyptotek (New Carlsberg Sculpture Museum). An elaborate neoclassical building houses one of Europe's greatest collections of Greek and Roman antiquities and sculpture. A modern wing displays an impressive pre-impressionist collection, including works from the Barbizon school; impressionist paintings, with works by Monet, Sisley, and

Pissarro; and a post-impressionist section, with 50 Gauguin paintings plus 12 of his rare sculptures. ⊠ *Dantes Pl. 7* ☎ *33/41–81–41* ⊕ *www. glyptoteket.dk* ⊙ *Tues.–Sun. 10–4.*

★ ⑫ **Nyhavn** (New Harbor). You can relax with a beer in one of the most gentrified parts of the city. Previously popular with sailors, the area's restaurants and cafés now outnumber tattoo shops. The name refers to both the street and the canal leading southeast out of Kongens Nytorv. The area still gets rowdy on long, hot summer nights, with Danes reveling against the backdrop of a fleet of old-time sailing ships and well-preserved 18th-century buildings. Hans Christian Andersen lived at numbers 18 and 20. ⊠ *East of Kongens Nytorv.*

❶ **Rådhus Pladsen** (City Hall Square). This hub of Copenhagen's commercial district is the best place to start a stroll. The Renaissance-style building dominating it is the **Rådhuset** (City Hall), completed in 1905. A statue of Copenhagen's 12th-century founder, Bishop Absalon, sits atop the main entrance. Inside, you can see the first World Clock, an astrological timepiece invented and built by Jens Olsen and set in motion in 1955. You can take a guided tour partway up the 350-foot tower for a panoramic view. ⊠ *Square in Strøget at eastern end of Vesterbrog. and western end of Frederiksbergg.* ☎ *33/66–33–66* ⊙ *Rådhus weekdays 8–5; Tower tours Oct.–May, Mon.–Sat. at noon; June–Sept., weekdays 10, noon, and 2, Sat. at noon.*

㉒ **Rosenborg Slot** (Rosenborg Castle). This Renaissance palace—built by jack-of-all-trades Christian IV—houses the Crown Jewels, as well as a collection of costumes and royal memorabilia. Don't miss Christian IV's pearl-studded saddle. ⊠ *Øster Voldg. 4A* ☎ *33/15–32–86* ⊙ *Nov.–Apr., Tues.–Sun. 11–2; May and Sept., daily 10–4; June–Aug., daily 10–5; Oct., daily 11–3.*

㉑ **Rundetårn** (Round Tower). It is said that Peter the Great of Russia drove a horse and carriage up the 600 feet of the inner staircase of this round tower, built as an observatory in 1642 by Christian IV. It's a formidable climb, but the view is worth it. At the base of the tower is the university church, Trinitas; halfway up you can take a break in the tower's art gallery. ⊠ *Købmagerg. 52A* ☎ *33/73–03–73* ⊕ *www.rundetaarn.dk* ⊙ *Tower: Sept.–May, Mon.–Sat. 10–5, Sun. noon–5; June–Aug.; Mon.–Sat. 10–8, Sun. noon–8.*

㉔ **Statens Museum for Kunst** (National Art Gallery). The original 100-year-old building and a new, modern structure house works of Danish art from the golden age (early 19th century) to the present, as well as paintings by Rubens, Dürer, the impressionists, and other European masters. The space also includes a children's museum, an amphitheater, a documentation center and study room, a bookstore, and a restaurant. ⊠ *Sølvg. 48–50* ☎ *33/74–84–94* ⊕ *www.smk.dk* ⊙ *Tues.–Sun. 10–5, Wed. 10–8.*

❸ **Strøget.** Beginning at City Hall, Frederiksberggade is the first of five pedestrian streets making up Strøget, Copenhagen's shopping district and promenade area. Stroll past the cafés and trendy boutiques to the twin squares of **Gammeltorv** and **Nytorv.** The bustling sidewalks have the festive aura of a street fair. Marking the end of Strøget is a square known as **Kongens Nytorv** (King's New Market), where you'll find **Det Kongelige Teater** (The Royal Theater).

❻ **Thorvaldsens Museum.** The 19th-century Danish sculptor Bertel Thorvaldsen, whose tomb stands in the center of the museum, was greatly influenced by the statues and reliefs of classical antiquity. In addition to his own works, the collection includes drawings and paintings by others that illustrate the influence of Italy on the artists of Denmark's golden age. ⊠ *Bertel Thorvaldsen Pl. 2* ☎ *33/32–15–32* ⊕ *www.thorvaldsensmuseum. dk* ⊙ *Tues.–Sun. 10–5.*

⓫ ㉖ **Tivoli.** Each year from May to September, about 4 million people pass
Fodor'sChoice through the gates of this unique little amusement park. More sophisti-
★ cated than a typical fun fair, Tivoli has pantomime theater on an open-air stage, elegant restaurants, and frequent classical, jazz, and rock concerts. Try to see Tivoli at least once by night when the trees, Chinese pagoda, and main fountain are brilliantly illuminated. In the month leading up to Christmas, a festive Christmas market is held at Tivoli. ⊠ *Vesterbrog. 3* ☎ *33/15–10–01* ⊕ *www.tivoli.dk* ✉ *DKr45 plus DKr10 per attraction ticket (each attraction requires from 1 to 5 tickets)* ⊙ *Mid-Apr.–mid-Sept., Sun.–Tues. 11–11, Wed. and Thurs. 11–midnight, Fri. and Sat. 11–1 AM; mid-Nov.–Dec. 23, Sun.–Wed. 11–9, Fri. and Sat. 11–10.*

❾ **Vor Frelsers Kirke** (Our Savior's Church). Legend has it that the staircase climbing up the exterior of the fantastic golden spire on this 1696 baroque structure was built spiraling in the wrong direction. The architect, upon reaching the top of his creation, realized what he had done and decided to jump to his death because of it. ⊠ *Skt. Annæg. 29* ☎ *32/57–27–98* ⊕ *www.vorfrelserskirke.dk* ⊙ *Apr.–Aug., daily 11–4:30; Sept.–Mar., daily 11–3:30* ⊙ *Tower closed Nov.–Mar., and in inclement weather.*

❿ **Vor Frue Kirke** (Church of Our Lady). This has been Copenhagen's cathedral since 1924, but the site itself has been a place of worship since the 13th century, when Bishop Absalon built a chapel here. The spare, neoclassical facade is a 19th-century innovation repairing damage suffered during Nelson's bombing of the city in 1801. If the church is open, you can see Thorvaldsen's marble sculptures of Christ and the Apostles. ⊠ *Nørregade 8* ☎ *33/37–65–40* ⊕ *www.koebenhavnsdomkirke.dk* ⊙ *Daily 8–5.*

Where to Eat

Food is one of the great pleasures in Copenhagen, and traditional Danish cuisine can span the entire spectrum of prices. You can order a light lunch of smørrebrød, snack from a store *kolde bord,* or dine on lobster, Limfjord oysters, and shrimp. You can also dig into fast food Danish-style in the form of *pølser* (hot dogs) sold from wagons on the street. Team this with pastries from one of the numerous bakeries (the shops displaying an upside-down gold pretzel), and you've got yourself a meal on the go. Many restaurants close from Christmas to the New Year.

★ **$$$$** ✕ **Kommandanten.** The 300-year-old building, once called home by the c of Copenhagen, houses Scandinavia's most celebrated restaurant. The ever varying, set-course menu follows whatever is freshest at the market, including sliced breast of guinea fowl with quail eggs or wild duck with confit. Expect adventurous French cooking of the highest caliber and impeccable service to match. If possible, book before your trip—this epicurean favorite seats only 50. ⊠ *Ny Adelgade 7* ☎ *33/12–09–90* ⊕ *www. kommandanten.dk* ⊟ *AE, DC, MC, V* ⊙ *Closed Sun. and holidays.*

$$$$ ✕ **Kong Hans Kælder.** In this hushed cloister with medieval vaulted ceil-
Fodor'sChoice ings you'll find one of the city's outstanding restaurants. The menu is
★ classic French, with a focus on the creative use of local ingredients, including mushrooms brought by bicycle from nearby forests. You haven't tasted salmon like this before, prepped for 36 hours in the restaurant's

own cold smoker. Save room for the outstanding selection of cheeses, many homemade. ✉ *Vingårdstr. 6* ☎ *33/11–68–68* ⊕ *www.konghans. dk* ⊟ *AE, DC, MC, V* ⊙ *Closed Mon. No lunch.*

$$$$ ✕ **Krogs.** Gilded mirrors, high ceilings, and 19th-century paintings make up a study in old-fashioned opulence, as does the menu here, with its grilled lobster, poached fish in Parmesan bouillon, and the locally famous bouillabaisse. Krogs' excellent reputation is reflected in its high prices. ✉ *Gammel Strand 38* ☎ *33/15–89–15* ⊕ *www.krogs.dk* ⚱ *Reservations essential* ⊟ *AE, DC, MC, V* ⊙ *Closed Sun.*

$$$ ✕ **El Mesón.** Ceiling-hung pottery, knowledgeable waiters, and a top-notch menu make this Copenhagen's best Spanish restaurant. Choose carefully for a moderately priced meal, which might include beef spiced with spearmint, lamb with honey sauce, or paella. ✉ *Hauser Pl. 12* ☎ *33/ 11–91–31* ⊟ *AE, DC, MC, V* ⊙ *Closed Sun. No lunch.*

$$$ ✕ **Els.** Said to be a favorite of the queen, Els is a piece of Danish history, largely unchanged since it first catered to the theater crowd in 1853. The flip side of the restaurant's proud past is an occasionally supercilious attitude toward foreigners, but a touch of stiffness seems in keeping with the 19th-century tiles, Renaissance-style painted muses, and the antique samovar at the bar. The fine French cooking has a focus on fish and wild game and fowl. ✉ *Store Strandstr. 3* ☎ *33/14–13–41* ⊕ *www. restaurant-els.dk* ⚱ *Reservations essential* ⊟ *AE, DC, MC, V.*

$$$ ✕ **Ida Davidsen.** Five generations old, this world-renowned lunch spot
FodorśChoice has become synonymous with smørrebrød. Choose from these creative
★ open-face sandwiches, piled high with such ingredients as pâté, bacon, and steak tartare, or even kangaroo, or try smoked duck served with a beet salad and potatoes. ✉ *St. Kongensg. 70* ☎ *33/91–36–55* ⊕ *www. idadavidsen.dk* ⚱ *Reservations essential* ⊟ *AE, DC, MC, V* ⊙ *Closed weekends and July. No dinner.*

$$$ ✕ **Le Sommelier.** Classic French country cooking is served here with a dazzling selection of wines by the glass. The steamed mussels are popular, as is homemade foie gras, and pigeon breast with mushrooms and glazed beets. Take a break from worrying about secondhand smoke and give in to the elegant surroundings. You can select from 30 brands of cigarettes to go with any of 12 varieties of coffee. ✉ *Bredg. 63–65* ☎ *33/ 11–45–15* ⊕ *www.lesommelier.dk* ⊟ *AE, DC, MC, V.*

★ **$$$** ✕ **Reinwalds.** The chairs here are exceptionally comfortable, and there's enough space between tables to afford diners some privacy. And that's just the start. The food is French, and artfully presented; the three- to five-course menu changes monthly, according to what's in season. The waiters are attentive and will help you navigate the menu. ✉ *Farveg. 15* ☎ *33/91–82–80* ⊕ *www.reinwalds.dk* ⊟ *AE, MC, DC, V* ⊙ *Closed Sun.*

$$$ ✕ **Schiøtt's.** Seasonal freshness as well as the cook's mood will each have bearing on the menu selection for this Copenhagen favorite. A cozy cellar restaurant offering superb creative fare in the Provençal style, this is an elegant experience for a very fair price. The walk along Christianshavn Canal on a warm summer night can only add pleasure to the overall experience. ✉ *Overgaden neden vandet 17* ☎ *32/54–54–08* ⊕ *www.schioetts.dk* ⊟ *AE, DC, MC, V* ⊙ *Closed Sun.*

$–$$ ✕ **Riz Raz.** An inexpensive all-you-can-eat buffet is the draw of this Middle Eastern restaurant. Health-conscious patrons fill up on lentils, bean salads, and falafel. Standouts on the menu are the grilled dishes, both meat and fish. On a corner just off Strøget, behind the church of Vor Frue Kirke, this restaurant packs in the young and old, families and singles, every night. Reservations are essential on weekends. ✉ *Kompagnistr. 20* ☎ *33/15–05–75* ✉ *Store Kannikestr. 19* ☎ *33/32–33–45* ⊕ *www.rizraz.dk* ⊟ *DC, MC, V.*

$ ✕ **Atlas Bar.** This health-food basement café serves excellent meals to a steady stream of students and hipsters. The food is mostly East Asian–influenced such as the tasty Manila Chicken. Atlas also has a large number of vegetarian dishes. ⊠ *Larsbjørnsstr. 18* ☎ *33/15–03–52* ▤ *DC, MC, V* ☉ *Closed Sun.*

$ ✕ **Molevitten.** This spacious café-restaurant-club combo serves Malaysian and other Asian-inspired dishes. A house favorite is *Laksasuppe,* a Malaysian salmon soup. Molevitten is spread over three floors and caters to brunch, lunch, and dinner crowds. After dinner on weekend evenings, the sound is turned up and it turns into a dance club. ⊠ *Nørrebrog. 13* ☎ *35/39–49–00* ⊕ *www.molevitten.com* ▤ *MC, V.*

Where to Stay

Copenhagen is well served by its hotels, which are mostly comfortable and well run. Most but not all Danish hotels include breakfast in the room rate. Summertime reservations are a good idea, but if you should arrive without one, try the hotel booking service at the Danish Tourist Board. They can also give you a "same-day, last-minute price," which is about DKr500 for a double hotel room. This service will also locate rooms in private homes, with rates starting at about DKr300 for a double. Also try the **Ungdoms Information lodging service** (⊠ Rådhusstr. 13 ☎ 33/73–06–50 ⊕ www.ui.dk) for listings of budget lodgings, or their youth information center "Use It" (⊕ www.useit.dk).

$$$$ 🏨 **Radisson SAS Scandinavia.** Strategically located on the principal route between the airport and the city center, this is one of northern Europe's largest hotels and Copenhagen's token skyscraper. A spacious lobby with cool, recessed lighting and streamlined furniture leads into the city's first and only casino. Though somewhat institutional in design, the guest rooms are large, with every modern convenience. A visit to the 25th-floor restaurant, The Dining Room (DKr200–DKr350), is a delightful experience both for its food and its view. Breakfast is not included in the rates. ⊠ *Amager Blvd. 70, DK 2300 KBH S* ☎ *33/96–50–00* 🖷 *33/96–55–00* ⊕ *www.radissonsas.com* ⤶ *542 rooms, 43 suites* ♨ *4 restaurants, indoor pool* ▤ *AE, DC, MC, V.*

★ $$$$ 🏨 **D'Angleterre.** The grande dame of Copenhagen hotels has undergone major changes but still retains its period charm. The rooms are done in pinks and blues, with overstuffed chairs and antique escritoires and armoires. Bathrooms sparkle with brass, mahogany, and marble. If you are a light sleeper, choose a back room; there is some noise from the nearby bars, and from early-morning delivery trucks. ⊠ *Kongens Nytorv 34, DK 1021 KBH K* ☎ *33/12–00–95* 🖷 *33/12–11–18* ⊕ *www.remmen.dk/hda.htm* ⤶ *118 rooms, 19 suites* ♨ *Restaurant, indoor pool* ▤ *AE, DC, MC, V.*

$$$ 🏨 **Clarion Neptun.** A central Copenhagen hotel that's been in business for nearly 150 years, the Neptun shows no signs of flagging. Rooms are decorated with blond wood. Though charming, this hotel can become very busy with tour groups. Moreover, because it's an old building, room sizes vary greatly, and so does the noise from the street. ⊠ *Skt. Annæ Pl. 18–20, DK 1250 KBH K* ☎ *33/96–20–00* 🖷 *33/96–20–66* ⤶ *133 rooms* ♨ *Restaurant, bar* ▤ *AE, DC, MC, V.*

$$$ 🏨 **71 Nyhavn.** In a 200-year-old warehouse overlooking the old ships of Nyhavn, this quiet hotel is a good choice for those seeking privacy. The maritime interiors have been preserved with their original plaster walls and exposed brick. Rooms are tiny but cozy, with warm woollen spreads, dark woods, soft leather furniture, and exposed timbers. ⊠ *Nyhavn 71, DK 1051 KBH K* ☎ *33/43–62–00* 🖷 *33/43–62–01*

⊕ *www.71nyhavnhotelcopenhagen.dk* ⇆ *150 rooms, 3 suites* ☆ *Restaurant, bar* ⊟ *AE, DC, MC, V.*

$$$ ⊡ **Phoenix Copenhagen.** This luxury hotel has crystal chandeliers and gilt touches everywhere. It's popular for business trips and with cruise passengers. Suites and executive-class rooms have Biedermeier-style furniture and 18-karat-gold-plated bathroom fixtures. Standard rooms are small, about 9 by 15 feet. If you're a light sleeper, ask for a room above the second floor to avoid street noise. ⊠ *Bredg. 37, DK 1260 KBH K* ☎ *33/95–95–00* ⊟ *33/33–98–33* ⊕ *www.phoenixcopenhagen. dk* ⇆ *206 rooms, 7 suites* ☆ *Restaurant, bar* ⊟ *AE, DC, MC, V.*

$$–$$$ ⊡ **Ascot.** A charming old building downtown, this family-owned hotel has classical columns at the entrance, and an excellent breakfast buffet. Rooms are colorful and cozy; bathrooms are on the small side. A few rooms have kitchenettes. ⊠ *Studiestr. 61, DK 1554 KBH K* ☎ *33/ 12–60–00* ⊟ *33/14–60–40* ⊕ *www.ascothotel.dk* ⇆ *161 rooms, 4 suites* ☆ *Bar* ⊟ *AE, DC, V.*

$$–$$$ ⊡ **Copenhagen Admiral.** Overlooking old Copenhagen and Amalienborg, the monolithic Admiral, with its massive stone walls and rows of tiny windows, was once a grain warehouse. It now has minimalist, airy rooms with jutting beams and modern prints. ⊠ *Toldbodg. 24–28, DK 1253 KBH K* ☎ *33/74–14–14* ⊟ *33/74–14–16* ⊕ *www.admiralhotel. dk* ⇆ *314 rooms, 52 suites* ☆ *Restaurant, bar* ⊟ *AE, DC, V.*

$–$$ ⊡ **Missionhotellet Nebo.** This budget hotel is comfortable and well maintained, with a friendly staff. The dormlike guest rooms are furnished with industrial carpeting, polished pine furniture, and soft duvet covers. Baths, showers, and toilets are clustered at the center of each hallway. There is a breakfast restaurant downstairs. ⊠ *Istedg. 6, DK 1650 KBH V* ☎ *33/21–12–17* ⊟ *33/23–47–74* ⊕ *www.nebo.dk* ⇆ *88 rooms, 40 with bath; 9 suites* ⊟ *AE, DC, MC, V.*

$ ⊡ **Cab-Inn Scandinavia.** Winter business travelers, budget-minded summer backpackers, and cost-conscious families converge on Copenhagen's answer to Japanese-style hotel minirooms. The shiplike "cabins" are brightly decorated with standard furnishings, including a small, wall-hung desk with chair. The breakfast buffet will set you back DKr50. Those wanting a little more comfort should request a Commodore Class room for an extra DKr100. ⊠ *Vodroffsvej 55, DK 1900 FR C* ☎ *35/36–11–11* ⊟ *35/36–11–14* ⊕ *www.cabinn.dk* ⇆ *201 rooms with shower* ☆ *Bar* ⊟ *AE, DC, MC, V.*

$ ⊡ **Ibis Copenhagen Triton.** Despite seedy surroundings, this streamlined hotel attracts a cosmopolitan clientele thanks to a central location in Vesterbro. The large rooms, in blond wood and warm tones, have state-of-the-art fixtures. The buffet breakfast included in the price is exceptionally generous, and the staff is friendly. There are also family rooms, each with a separate bedroom and fold-out couch. ⊠ *Helgolandsg. 7–11, DK 1653 KBH K* ☎ *33/31–32–66* ⊟ *33/31–69–70* ⊕ *www. ibishotel.dk* ⇆ *123 rooms* ☆ *Bar* ⊟ *AE, DC, MC, V.*

Nightlife & the Arts

The English-language **Copenhagen This Week** (⊕ www.ctw.dk) prints information about musical and theatrical happenings, as well as special events and exhibitions. The Web site **www.aok.dk** is a good resource for finding nightlife, bars, and cafés around Copenhagen—it also has similar information about other Danish cities. Concert and festival information is available from the **Dansk Musik Information Center** (DMIC; ⊠ Gråbrødre Torv 16 ☎ 33/11–20–66 ⊕ www.mic.dk).

Copenhagen's main theater and concert season runs from September through May, and tickets can be obtained either directly from theaters and concert halls or from ticket agencies; ask your hotel concierge for advice. **Billetnet** (☎ 70/15–65–65 ⊕ www.billetnet.dk), a box-office service available at all large post offices, has tickets for most major events. Keep in mind that same-day purchases at the box office at **Tivoli** (✉ Vesterbrogade 3 ☎ 33/15–10–12 ☺ weekdays 11–5) are half price if you pick them up after noon.

The Arts

CLASSICAL MUSIC   The **Tivoli Concert Hall** (✉ Tietensg. 20 ☎ 33/15–10–12) has more than 150 concerts each summer. There are performances by a host of Danish and foreign soloists, conductors, and orchestras.

THEATER   **Det Kongelige Teater** (The Royal Theater) (✉ Kongens Nytorv ☎ 33/69–69–33 ⊕ www.kgl-teater.dk) is the place to go for ballet or opera. If you're in search of experimental opera, then **Den Anden Opera** (✉ Kronprinsensg. 7 ☎ 33/32–38–30 ⊕ www.denandenopera.dk) is worth a visit. **London Toast Theatre** (✉ Kochsvej 18 ☎ 33/22–86–86 ⊕ www.londontoast.dk) hosts English-language theater. Modern dance is popular in Copenhagen, and **Dansescenen** (✉ Øster Fælled Torv 34 ☎ 34/35–83–00 ⊕ www.dansescenen.dk) is a good place to see it. **Kanonhallen** (✉ Øster Fælled Torv 37 ☎ 70/15–65–65 ⊕ www.kanonhallen.net) showcases up-and-coming modern dancers. **Nyt Dansk Danseteater** (✉ Guldbergsg. 29A ☎ 35/39–87–87 ⊕ www.nddt.dk) is very active in promoting Scandinavian modern dance.

Nightlife

Many of the city's restaurants, cafés, bars, and clubs stay open after midnight, some as late as 5 AM. Copenhagen is famous for jazz, but you'll find nightspots catering to musical tastes ranging from hip-hop to ballroom music. In the inner city, most discos open at 11 PM, have a cover charge (about DKr50), and charge steep prices for drinks.

JAZZ   The upscale **Copenhagen Jazz House** (✉ Niels Hemmingsensg. 10 ☎ 33/15–26–00 ⊕ www.jazzhouse.dk) draws major international names and the cream of Danish jazz. Jam sessions often take place spontaneously. It's a dimly lit, smoky place, but with ample room on two floors. **La Fontaine** (✉ Kompagnistr. 11 ☎ 33/11–60–98) is Copenhagen's quintessential jazz dive, with sagging curtains, impenetrable smoke, and crusty lounge lizards. It is a must for jazz lovers.

LIVE MUSIC   Copenhagen has a fine selection of music clubs where you can hear excellent local talent, as well as smaller or up-and-coming international acts. **Loppen** in Christiania (✉ Bådsmandsstræde 43 ☎ 32/57–84–22 ⊕ www.loppen.dk) is a medium-size concert venue where you can catch some of the bigger names in Danish music, as well as budding international artists. **Vega** (✉ Enghavevej 40 ☎ 32/25–70–11 ⊕ www.vega.dk) hosts established pop, rock, urban, and jazz artists and is a great spot for catching the next big act. It also has a dance club and bar where the action continues into the wee hours. **Rust** (✉ Guldbergsg. 8 ☎ 35/24–52–00 ⊕ www.rust.dk) and **Stengade 30** (✉ Stengade 18, [address does not match name of club] ☎ 35/36–09–38 ⊕ www.stengade30.dk) are smaller clubs, mainly featuring rock, pop, and urban acts. They double as bars that remain open through the night.

NIGHTCLUBS & DANCING   A younger crowd gets down on the floor at the fashionable **Park Café** (✉ Østerbrog. 79 ☎ 35/42–62–48 ⊕ www.parkcafe.dk). Mellower folks come for brunch when the place transforms back into a café. **Rosie McGee's** (✉ Vesterbrog. 2A ☎ 33/32–19–42 ⊕ www.rosiemcgee.dk) is a very popular Irish-style pub (but with Mexican food) that has dancing. **Sabor Latino** (✉ Vester Voldg. 85 ☎ 26/16–46–96 ⊕ www.saborlatino. dk) is a United Nations of disco, with an international crowd dancing to salsa and other Latin beats. Among the most enduring clubs is **Woodstock** (✉ Vesterg. 12 ☎ 33/11–20–71), where a mixed crowd grooves to 1960s classics.

Shopping

Strøget's pedestrian streets are synonymous with shopping.

Specialty Shops

Just off Østergade is **Pistolstræde**, a typical old courtyard filled with intriguing boutiques. Farther down the street toward the City Hall Square is a compound that includes several important stores: **Georg Jensen** (✉ Amagertorv 4 ☎ 33/11–40–80 ⊕ www.georgjensen.com), one of the world's finest silversmiths, gleams with silver patterns and jewelry. Don't miss the **Georg Jensen Museum** (✉ Amagertorv 6 ☎ 33/14–02–29), which showcases glass and silver creations ranging from tiny, twisted-glass shot glasses to an $85,000 silver fish dish. **Royal Copenhagen Porcelain** (✉ Amagertorv 6 ☎ 33/13–71–81 ⊕ www.royalcopenhagen. com) carries both old and modern china, plus porcelain patterns and figurines.

Along Strøget, at furrier **Birger Christensen** (✉ Østerg. 38 ☎ 33/11–55–55 ⊕ www.birger-christensen.com), you can peruse designer clothes and chic furs. **Illum** (✉ Østerg. 52 ☎ 33/14–40–02) is a department store that has a fine basement grocery and eating arcade. Don't confuse Illum with **Illums Bolighus** (✉ Amagertorv 10 ☎ 33/14–19–41), where designer furnishings, porcelain, quality clothing, and gifts are displayed in near-gallery surroundings. **Magasin** (✉ Kongens Nytorv 13 ☎ 33/11–44–33 ⊕ www.magasin.dk), one of the largest department stores in Scandinavia, offers all kinds of clothing and gifts, as well as an excellent grocery department.

Side Trips

Klampenborg

Just north of town, accessible by S-train or the coastal road Strandvejen, is the **Dyrehave** (Deer Park), a favorite escape for area city dwellers. What began as hunting grounds for Danish royalty is now a forest preserve of enormous beech and fir trees. Put on your walking shoes and admire the thatched cottages, the royal hunting lodge with its stone sphinxes and gods, and the roaming herds of imported deer. Tucked inside is **Bakken**, which claims to be the world's oldest amusement park. ✉ *Dyrehavevej 62, DK 2930* ☎ *39/63–73–00* ⊕ *www.bakken.dk* ☾ *Apr.–Aug.*

Helsingør

Shakespeare immortalized both the town and the castle when he chose Helsingør's **Kronborg Slot** (Kronborg Castle) as the setting for *Hamlet*. Completed in 1585, the present gabled and turreted structure is about 600 years younger than the fortress we imagine in Shakespeare's tragedy. Inside are a 200-foot-long dining hall, the luxurious chapel, and the royal chambers. The ramparts and 12-foot-thick walls are a reminder of the castle's role as a coastal bulwark—Sweden is only a couple of miles away. The castle also houses the Danish Maritime Museum, which tells the story of the Danish merchant fleet from 1400 to the present. Helsingør town—about 47 km (29 mi) north of Copenhagen—has a number of picturesque streets with 16th-century houses. From the train station there is a 20-minute walk around the harbor to the castle. ✉ *Kronborg Slot*

DK 3000 ☎ 49/21–30–78 ⊕ www.kronborg.dk ✉ DKr60 for the whole tour (Chapel, Casemates, Main Hall, and the Danish Maritime Museum) ⊙ Easter and May–Sept., daily 10:30–5; Oct. and Apr., Tues.–Sun. 11–4; Nov.–Mar., Tues.–Sun. 11–3.

Hillerød

Situated 40 km (25 mi) northwest of Copenhagen, Hillerød has Denmark's most beautiful royal residence, **Frederiksborg Slot** (Frederiksborg Castle). King Frederik II acquired this castle in 1560 and, after rebuilding it, gave his name to it. His son Christian IV demolished that structure and rebuilt it in Dutch Renaissance style. Devastated by a fire in 1859, the castle was reconstructed and now includes the **Nationalhistoriske Museum** (National History Museum). Stroll through the **Baroque Gardens**, rebuilt in 1996 in accordance with J. C. Krieger's 1725 layout, with wide waterfalls and a meticulously groomed park. ⊠ *Hillerød DK 3400 ☎ 48/26–04–39 ⊕ www.ses.dk ✉ DKr60, Baroque Gardens free ⊙ Castle Apr.–Oct., daily 10–5; Nov.–Mar., daily 10–3. Baroque Gardens May–Aug., daily 10–9; Sept. and Apr., daily 10–7; Oct. and Mar., daily 10–5; Nov.–Feb., daily 10–4.*

Humlebæk

The town, 35 km (22 mi) and a half-hour train ride from Copenhagen, is part of the "Danish Riviera" on the North Sjælland coast. Its chief ★ ☁ landmark is **Louisiana,** a world-class modern art collection set in an elegant, rambling structure with views of the sound. A combined train fare (from Copenhagen) and admission is available from DSB. A 10-minute walk from the station, the museum is also accessible by the E4 highway and the more scenic Strandvejen, or coastal road. ⊠ *Gammel Strandvej 13 ☎ 49/19–07–19 ⊕ www.louisiana.dk ✉ DKr72 ⊙ Thurs.–Tues. 10–5, Wed. 10–10.*

Roskilde

For a look into the past, head 30 km (19 mi) west of Copenhagen to the bustling market town of Roskilde. The principal city of Denmark during Viking times, it remained one of the largest towns in northern Europe through the Middle Ages. Today the legacy of its 1,000-year history lives on in its spectacular cathedral. Built on the site of one of Denmark's first churches, the **Domkirke** (cathedral) has been the burial place of Danish royalty since the 15th century. The combined effect of their tombs is striking—from the magnificent shrine of Christian IV to the simple brick chapel of Frederik IX. ⊠ *Domkirkepl. ☎ 46/ 35–16–24 ⊕ www.roskildedomkirke.dk ⊙ Oct.–Mar., Tues.–Sat. 9–9:45; Apr.–Sept., weekdays 9–4:45, Sat. 9–noon, Sun. and holidays 12:30–4:45.*

A 10-minute walk south and through the park takes you to the water FodorsChoice and the **Vikingeskibsmuseet** (Viking Ship Museum). Inside are five ★ exquisitely reconstructed Viking ships discovered at the bottom of Roskilde Fjord in 1962. ⊠ *Vindeboder 12 ☎ 46/30–02–00 ⊕ www. vikingeskibsmuseet.dk ✉ DKr60 ⊙ May–Sept., daily 9–5; Oct.–Apr., daily 10–4.*

Copenhagen Essentials

AIRPORTS & TRANSFERS

The main airport for both international and domestic flights is Kastrup International Airport, 10 km (6 mi) southeast of town.

TRANSFERS Trains from the airport's subterranean train station take 12 minutes to zip into Copenhagen's main station. Buy a ticket upstairs in the airport train station (DKr22,50); three trains an hour go into Copenhagen, and a fourth travels farther to Roskilde. Bus service to the city is frequent, but not as convenient. Bus 250S takes you to Rådhus Pladsen, the city-hall square. A taxi ride takes 15 minutes and costs about DKr170, though slightly more after 4 PM and weekends.

BIKE TRAVEL

It is estimated that more than half the 5.5 million Danish population rides bicycles regularly. Bike rental costs DKr75–DKr200 a day, though weekly rates are available, with a deposit of DKr500–DKr1,000. Contact Københavns Cykler or Østerport Cykler, both stores that belong to the Rent a Bike company.

🚲 Bike Rental **Københavns Cykler** ✉ Central Station, Reventlowsg. 11 ☎ 33/33-86-13 🌐 www.rentabike.dk. **Østerport Cykler** ✉ Oslo Plads 9 ☎ 33/33-85-13 🌐 www.rentabike.dk.

BUS & METRO TRAVEL WITHIN COPENHAGEN

Buses, suburban trains, and metro trains all operate on the same ticket system, which divides Copenhagen into three zones. Tickets are validated on both a time and a distance basis: on a basic ticket, which costs DKr15, you can travel anywhere within a single zone for an hour. You can purchase a discounted *klip kort* (clip card), equivalent to 10 basic tickets, for DKr95. Buses and suburban trains run from 5 AM (6 AM on Sunday) to 12:30 AM daily with a reduced network of buses continuing through the night. The Metro runs from 5 AM to 1 AM weekdays, and all night on weekends.

🚲 **Buses and suburban trains** ☎ 36/13-14-15 buses; 70/13-14-15 S-trains (wait for the Danish message to end and an operator will answer) 🌐 www.ht.dk; www.rejseplan.dk. **Metro** ☎ 70/15-16-15 🌐 www.m.dk.

CAR TRAVEL

Copenhagen is a city for walkers, not drivers. To maintain the charm of its pedestrian streets, the city has a complicated one-way road system and it's difficult to park. Leave your car in the garage: attractions are relatively close together, and public transportation is excellent.

EMERGENCIES

For emergency dental service you should go directly to the Tandlægevagt (Emergency Dental Clinic). It's open weekdays from 8 AM to 9:30 PM; weekends and holidays from 10 AM to noon. Expect to pay cash. Fees for the Doctor Emergency Service are also payable in cash only. The hours for this service are 4 PM to 8 AM, but house calls are made after 10 PM. You will need to make an appointment by phone. Note that nighttime visits include a DKr350 surcharge. Casualty Wards (Skadestuen) are open 24 hours.

🚑 Doctors & Dentists **Casualty Wards** ✉ Italiensvej 1, DK 2300 Amager area ☎ 32/34-35-00 ✉ Niels Andersens Vej 65, DK 2900 Hellerup ☎ 39/77-37-64 or 39/77-39-77 🌐 www.laegevagten.dk. **Doctor Emergency Service** ☎ 70/13-00-41 or 44/53-44-00. **Emergency Dental Clinic** ✉ Tandlægevagt: Oslo Plads 14, DK 2100.

🚑 Emergency Services **Auto Rescue/Falck** ☎ 70/10-20-30 🌐 www.falck.dk. **Police, fire, ambulance** ☎ 112.

🚑 24-hour Pharmacies **Steno Apotek** ✉ Vesterbrog. 6C ☎ 33/14-82-66. **Sønderbro Apotek** ✉ Amagerbrog. 158, Amager area ☎ 32/58-01-40 🌐 www.apoteket.dk.

ENGLISH-LANGUAGE MEDIA

The Copenhagen Post is a weekly newspaper covering Danish news in English. You can pick it up for DKr15 at some bookstores and information kiosks, the tourist office, and a few hotels. It has a helpful "In & Out" section with reviews and listings of entertainment events taking place in town.

🔖 Bookstores **Arnold Busck** ✉ Købmagerg. 49 ☎ 33/73-35-00 ⊕ www.arnoldbusck. dk. **Boghallen** ✉ Rådhus Pl. 37 ☎ 33/47-25-60 ⊕ www.boghallen.dk. **Copenhagen Post** ⊕ www.cphpost.dk.

TAXIS

The computer-metered Mercedeses and Volvos are not cheap. The base charge is DKr22, plus DKr10–DKr13 per kilometer (½ mi). A cab is available when it displays the green sign FRI (free); you can either hail a cab (though this can be difficult outside the center), pick one up at a taxi stand, or call the number listed below. Surcharges apply if you order a cab by night or if you are out of town.

🔖 **Taxa 4x35** ☎ 35/35-35-35 ⊕ www.35353535.dk.

TOURS

The Danish Tourist Board can recommend multilingual private guides for individual needs; travel agents have details on hiring a limousine and guide. The tourist board also has full details relating to excursions outside the city, including visits to castles (such as Hamlet's castle) and the Viking Ship Museum; they can also supply maps and brochures, and recommend walking tours.

BOAT TOURS Viewing Copenhagen from the canals is a must in the summer months. The relaxing hour-long tours give a great impression of the city; they're run by DFDS Canal Tours and depart from Nyhavn and Gammel Strand. If the weather is nice, go for a *Nettobåd* (Netto boat) tour, which departs from Holmens Church. It lasts an hour and is cheaper than Canal Tours, whose only advantage is a cover to shield against the rain (or sun). Boat tours are available April through mid-October and run every half hour from 10 to 5.

🔖 Fees & Schedules **DFDS Canal Tours** ☎ 32/64-04-31 ⊕ www.canal-tours.dk. **Nettobåd** ☎ 32/54-41-02 ⊕ www.netto-baadene.dk.

BUS TOURS Several bus tours leave from the Lur Blowers Column in Rådhus Pladsen 57, late March–September.

🔖 Fees & Schedules **Copenhagen Excursions** ☎ 32/54-06-06 ⊕ www.cex.dk. **Open Top Tours** ☎ 32/66-00-00 ⊕ www.sightseeing.dk.

TRAIN TRAVEL

Copenhagen's clean and convenient central station, Hovedbanegården, is the hub of the country's train network. Intercity express trains leave hourly, from 6 AM to 10 PM, for principal towns in Fyn and Jylland. To find out more, contact DSB.

🔖 **DSB Information** ☎ 70/13-14-15 ⊕ www.dsb.dk. **Hovedbanegården,** ✉ south of Vesterbrog ☎ 33/14-17-01 ⊕ www.hovedbanen.dk.

TRANSPORTATION AROUND COPENHAGEN

The Copenhagen Card offers unlimited travel on buses, and metro and suburban trains (S-trains) as well as admission to some 60 museums and sights throughout both metropolitan Copenhagen and Malmö, Sweden. They're valid for a limited time, though, and therefore worthwhile only if you're planning a nonstop, intense sightseeing tour. You can buy the card, which costs about DKr225 (24 hours), DKr375 (48 hours), or DKr500 (72 hours)—half price for children ages 5 to 11—at bus/train stations, tourist offices, and hotels or from travel agents.

TRAVEL AGENCIES
🎫 **Carlson Wagonlit Travel** ✉ Vester Farimagsg. 7, 2nd fl. ☎ 33/63-78-78 ⊕ www.
cwt.dk. **DSB Rejsebureau** ✉ Central Station ☎ 70/13-14-18 ⊕ www.dsb.dk. **Spies** ✉ Rådhuspl. 45-47 ☎ 70/10-42-00 ⊕ www.spies.dk.

FYN & THE CENTRAL ISLANDS

It was Hans Christian Andersen who dubbed Fyn (Funen) the Garden
of Denmark. Part orchard, part farmland, Fyn is sandwiched between
Sjælland and Jylland. With its tidy, rolling landscape, seaside towns, manor
houses, and castles, it is one of Denmark's loveliest islands. Its capital—
1,000-year-old Odense, in the north—is the birthplace of Hans Christian Andersen; his life and works are immortalized here in two museums.
Fyn is also the site of two of Denmark's best-preserved castles: 12th-
century Nyborg Slot, in the east, and 16th-century Egeskov Slot, near
Svendborg, in the south. From Svendborg it's easy to hop on a ferry and
visit some of the smaller islands, such as Tåsinge, Langeland, and Ærø,
whose main town, Ærøskøbing, seems caught in a time warp.

Many of the hotels and inns in Fyn offer off-season (October through
May) rates as well as special weekend deals. The islands also have numerous campsites and youth hostels, all clean and attractively located.
Some, like Odense's youth hostel, are set in old manor houses. Contact
local tourist offices for information.

Nyborg

This 13th-century town was Denmark's capital during the Middle Ages,
as well as an important stop on a major trading route between Sjælland
and Jylland. From 1200 to 1413, Nyborg housed the Danehof, the early
Danish parliament. Nyborg's major landmark is its 12th-century **Nyborg
Slot** (Nyborg Castle). It was here that Erik Glipping granted the first Danish constitution, the Great Charter, in 1282. ✉ *Slotsg. 34* ☎ *65/31-02-07*
⊕ *www.museer-nyborg.dk* ☉ *Mar.–May and Sept.–mid-Oct., Tues.–Sun.
10–3; June and Aug., Tues.–Sun. 10–4; July, Tues.–Sun. 10–5.*

$$$$ 🏨 **Hesselet.** This modern hotel tucked into the Fyn landscape affords
views of the Storebælt Bridge and paths down to the sea. Inside it's a
refined English-cum-Asian sanctuary with impeccable service. The guest
rooms have modern furniture, and most have splendid views. ✉ *Chris-
tianslundsvej 119, DK 5800* ☎ *65/31-30-29* 🖨 *65/31-29-58* ⊕ *www.
hesselet.dk* 🛏 *43 rooms, 3 suites* ⚃ *Restaurant, indoor pool, bar* ⊟ *AE,
DC, MC, V.*

Kerteminde

Coastal Kerteminde is Fyn's most important fishing village and a picturesque summer resort. Stroll down Langegade to see its half-timber
houses.

$$$$ ✕ **Rudolf Mathis.** You can order delectable fish and seafood specialties
and enjoy a splendid view of Kerteminde Harbor at this traditional Danish restaurant. ✉ *Dosseringen 13, 13 km (8 mi) northeast of Odense
on Rte. 165* ☎ *65/32-32-33* ⊕ *www.rudolfmathis.dk* ⊟ *AE, DC,
MC, V* ☉ *Closed Mon. and Jan. and Feb.*

Ladby

If you're a Viking enthusiast, stop in the village of Ladby to see the **Lad-
byskibet** (Ladby Ship), the 1,100-year-old underground remains of a Viking
chieftain's burial, complete with his 72-foot-long ship. The warrior was
equipped for his trip to Valhalla (the afterlife) with his weapons, four
hunting dogs, and 11 horses. ✉ *Vikingevej 123* ☎ *65/32-16-67* ⊕ *www.*

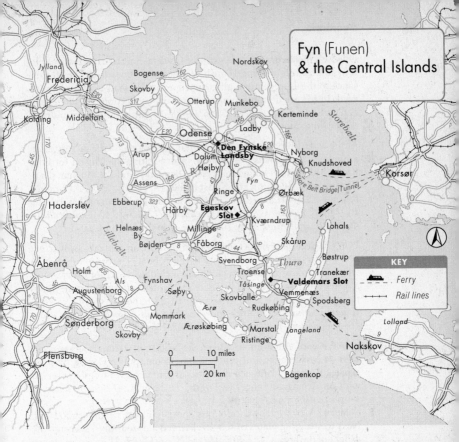

kert-mus.dk ⊗ *Mar.–May and Sept.–Oct., Tues.–Sun 10–4; June–Aug., daily 10–5; Nov.–Feb., Wed.–Sun. 11–3.*

Odense

Plan to spend at least one night in Denmark's third-largest city. In addition to its museums and pleasant pedestrian streets, Odense is a charming provincial capital. If you can't take quaintness, don't go to the **H. C. Andersens Hus** (Hans Christian Andersen House). The surrounding district has been carefully preserved, with cobbled pedestrian streets and low houses with lace curtains. Inside, exhibits use photos, diaries, drawings, and letters to convey a sense of the man and the time in which he lived. Attached to the museum is an extensive library with Andersen's works in more than 127 languages, where you can listen to fairy tales on tape. The museum includes child-friendly exhibits. ⊠ *Hans Jensenstr. 37–45* ☎ *66/14–88–14 Ext. 4611* ⊕ *www.odmus.dk* ⊗ *Mid-June–Aug., daily 9–7; Sept.–mid-June, Tues.–Sun. 10–4.*

The **Børnekulturhuset Fyrtøjet** (Children's Culture House). The Tinderbox museum includes walk-through fairy-tale exhibits as well as studios where children can draw and write their own tales and plays and then dress up and perform them. ⊠ *Hans Jensenstr. 21* ☎ *66/14–44–11* ⊕ *www.fyrtoejet.com* ⊗ *Feb.–Dec., Tues.–Sat. 10–3.*

The modern **Carl Nielsen Museet** has multimedia exhibits on Denmark's most famous composer (1865–1931) and his wife, the sculptor Anne Marie Carl-Nielsen (1863–1945). ⊠ *Claus Bergsg. 11* ☎ *66/14–88–14 Ext. 4671* ⊕ *www.odmus.dk* ⊗ *Thurs. and Fri. 4–8, Sun. and holidays noon–4.*

Odense's **Møntergården** (Museum of Cultural and Urban History) fills four houses representing Danish architectural styles from the Renaissance to the 18th century, all grouped around a shady, cobbled courtyard. Inside are dioramas, an extensive coin collection, clothing, toys, and tableaux. ✉ *Overg. 48* ☎ *66/14–88–14 Ext. 4611* ⊕ *www.odmus. dk* ⊙ *Tues.–Sun. 10–4.*

★ At the end of Brandts Passage, in what was once a textile factory, is an art gallery, the **Brandts Klædefabrik,** incorporating the **Museet for Foto Kunst** (Museum of Photographic Art), **Danmarks Grafiske Museum** (Danish Graphics Museum), and **Kunst Hallen** (Art Hall). ✉ *37–43 Brandts Passage* ☎ *Art Hall: 66/13–78–97; Museum of Photographic Art: 66/ 13–78–16; Danish Graphics Museum: 66/12–10–20* ⊕ *www.brandts. dk* ⊙ *July and Aug., daily 10–5; Sept.–June, Tues.–Sun. 10–5.*

Don't neglect **Den Fynske Landsby** (Fyn Village); an enjoyable way to get here is to travel down the Odense River by boat. The open-air museum village is made up of 20 farm buildings, including workshops, a vicarage, a water mill, and a windmill. There's a theater with summertime adaptations of Andersen's tales. ✉ *Sejerskovvej 20* ☎ *66/14–88–14 Ext. 4642* ⊕ *www.odmus.dk* ⊙ *Apr.–mid-June and mid-Aug.–Oct., Tues.–Sun. 10–5; mid-June–mid-Aug., daily 9:30–7; Nov.–Mar., Sun. 11–3.*

$$–$$$ ✕ **Le Provence.** A few minutes from the pedestrian street, this restaurant, with its cozy orange-and-yellow dining room, puts a Danish twist on Provençal cuisine, with such specialties as truffle soup or frogs' legs served with an Armagnac sauce. ✉ *Pogstr. 31* ☎ *66/12–12–96* ⊕ *www.le-provence.dk* ▭ *AE, DC, MC, V.*

$ ✕ **Målet.** A lively crowd calls this sports club its neighborhood bar. Next to steaming plates of schnitzel served a dozen ways, soccer is the delight of the house. ✉ *Jernbaneg. 17* ☎ *66/17–82–41* ⚲ *Reservations not accepted* ▭ *No credit cards.*

$$–$$$$ ▥ **First Hotel Grand.** They don't make spacious, gracious places like this anymore. Dating from 1897, the Grand offers spruced-up fin-de-siècle elegance. The green lobby is cool, with a sweeping staircase and a spectacular Pompeian-red dining room. Guest rooms are ample and comfortable. ✉ *Jernbaneg. 18, DK 5000* ☎ *66/11–71–71* ⎙ *66/14–11–71* ⊕ *www.firsthotels.com* ⇢ *138 rooms, 3 suites* ⚭ *Restaurant, bar* ▭ *AE, DC, MC, V.*

$ ▥ **Hotel Ydes.** If you're a student or are budget-conscious and tired of barracks-type accommodations, this bright, colorful hotel is a good bet. The simple, white rooms are plain but comfortable. ✉ *Hans Tausensg. 11, DK 5000* ☎ *66/12–11–31* ⎙ *66/12–14–13* ⊕ *www. ydes.dk* ⇢ *25 rooms with shower* ⚭ *Restaurant* ▭ *AE, DC, MC, V.*

Faaborg

Four times a day, the lovely little 12th-century town of Faaborg echoes with the dulcet chiming of the Klokketårnet (Bell Tower) carillon, the largest in Fyn. Dating from 1725, the **Den Gamle Gaard** (Old Merchant's House) presents the cultural history of Fyn. ✉ *Holkeg. 1* ☎ *62/ 61–33–38* ⊕ *www.fkm.nu* ⊙ *Mid-May–mid-Sept., daily 10:30–4:30, Apr.–mid-May, weekends and holidays 11–3; mid-Sept.–Oct, daily 11–3.*

The **Faaborg Museum for Fynsk Malerkunst** (Fyn Painting Museum) displays the compositions—dating mainly from 1880 to 1920—of Fyn painters. The paintings are filled with the dusky light that so often illuminates Scandinavian painting. ✉ *Grønneg. 75* ☎ *62/61–06–45* ⊕ *www.faaborgmuseum.dk* ⊙ *Apr.–Oct., daily 10–4; Nov.–Mar., Tues.–Sun. 11–3.*

$$$$ ✕▥ **Falsled Kro.** Once a smuggler's hideaway, this 500-year-old insti-
FodorśChoice tution is one of Denmark's most elegant inns. A favorite among well-
★ heeled Europeans, it has sumptuously appointed cottages with European
antiques and stone fireplaces. The restaurant combines French and Danish cuisines, employing ingredients from its own garden and markets
in faraway Lyon. ⊠ *Assensvej 513, DK 5642 Millinge, 13 km (8 mi)
northwest of Faaborg on Millinge-Assens Hwy.* ☎ *62/68–11–11*
⊕ *www.falsledkro.dk* ⮐ *19 rooms, 8 suites* ⟁ *Restaurant, bar* ▭ *AE,
DC, MC, V.*

$$–$$$$ ✕▥ **Steensgaard Herregårdspension.** A long avenue of beeches leads to
this 700-year-old moated manor house 7 km (4½ mi) northwest of
Faaborg. Rooms are elegant, with antiques, four-poster beds, and yards
of silk damask. The fine restaurant serves wild game from the manor's
own preserve. ⊠ *Steensgaard 4, DK 5642 Millinge* ☎ *62/61–94–90*
⊕ *www.herregaardspension.dk* ⮐ *18 rooms* ⟁ *Restaurant* ▭ *AE,
DC, MC, V* ☾ *Closed Jan. and Feb.*

Svendborg

The southernmost town in Fyn is the gateway to the country's south-
★ ern islands. Just north of Svendborg is **Egeskov Slot** (Egeskov Castle).
Egeskov means "oak forest," and an entire one was felled around 1540
to form the piles on which the rose-stone structure was erected. The park
contains noteworthy Renaissance, baroque, English, and peasant gar-
dens and an antique-car museum. This is still a private home, but a few
rooms, including the trophy-filled hunting room, are open to the pub-
lic. ⊠ *DK 5772, Kværndrup, 15 km/9 mi north of Svendborg* ☎ *62/
27–10–16* ⊕ *www.egeskov.com* ✉ *Castle and museum DKr130*
☾ *May–Sept., daily 10–5; July, Thurs.–Tues., 10–7, Wed. 10 AM–11 PM.*

Ærø

Take the car ferry to **Søby** at the northern tip of Ærø island, the "Jewel
of the Archipelago," where roads wend their way through fertile fields
and past thatched farmhouses. South from Søby is the charming town
of **Ærøskøbing,** on the island's north coast. Once you've spent an hour
walking through its cobbled 17th- and 18th-century streets, you'll un-
derstand its great appeal.

$$ ▥ **Ærøhus.** The half-timber building with a steep red roof looks like a
rustic cottage on the outside and a great-aunt's house on the inside. Hang-
ing pots and slanted walls highlight the public areas; pine furniture and
cheerful curtains and duvets keep the guest rooms simple and bright.
Apartments, all with kitchenettes, occupy an annex. ⊠ *Vesterg. 38, DK
5970 Ærøskøbing* ☎ *62/52–10–03* ⊕ *www.aeroehus-hotel.dk* ⮐ *67
rooms, 56 with bath; 37 apartments.* ⟁ *Restaurant* ▭ *V* ☾ *Closed Jan.*

Troense

On the island of Tåsinge, Troense is one of Denmark's best-preserved
villages. Once the home port for countless sailing ships, both Viking and,
later, commercial, the harbor today is stuffed with pleasure yachts. Dating from around 1640, **Valdemars Slot** (Valdemars Castle), now a sumptuously furnished home, is one of Denmark's oldest privately owned
castles. Upstairs rooms are appointed to the smallest detail. Downstairs
is the castle church, illuminated only by candlelight. There's a restaurant beneath the church. The sister café overlooks Lunkebugten, a bay
with one of south Fyn's best stretches of beach. ⊠ *Slotsalleen 100,
Troense* ☎ *62/22–61–06* ⊕ *www.valdemarsslot.dk* ☾ *May–Aug., daily
10–5; Sept., Tues.–Sun., 10–5; Apr. and Oct., weekends 10–5. Call to
confirm hrs.*

$$$–$$$$ ✕ **Restaurant Valdemars Slot.** Beneath the castle, this domed restaurant is all romance and prettiness, with pink carpet and candlelight. Fresh ingredients from France and Germany and game from the castle's preserve are the essentials for an ever-changing menu, which includes such specialties as venison with cream sauce and duck breast à l'orange. ⊠ *Slotsalleen 100, Troense* ☎ *62/22–59–00* ⊕ *www.valdemarsslot.dk* ▤ *AE, MC, V* ⊗ *Closed Nov.–Mar.*

Langeland

Tåsinge is connected with the island of Langeland by a causeway bridge. The largest island in the southern archipelago, Langeland is rich in relics of the past, including a castle, a thatched village, and a sculpture garden, and the beaches are worth scouting out.

Fyn & the Central Islands Essentials

TOURS

Pick up a copy of the free booklet "In the Footsteps of Hans Christian Andersen" at the Odense Tourist Board. It describes an enjoyable walking tour that you can take at your own pace. The "From Medieval Odense to the Odense of Today" tour takes place July and August, Tuesday–Thursday at 11 AM; it's also organized by the tourist board.

TRANSPORTATION AROUND FYN & THE CENTRAL ISLANDS

The best starting point is Nyborg, on Fyn's east coast, just across the Great Belt from Korsør, on Sjælland. From Nyborg, the easiest way to travel is by car, though public transportation is good. Distances on Fyn and its islands are short, but there is much to see, and you can easily spend two or three days here, circling the islands from Nyborg, or using Odense or Svendborg as a base from which to make excursions.

VISITOR INFORMATION

🚩 **Nyborg Tourist Board** ⊠ Torvet 9 ☎ 65/31–02–80 ⊕ www.nyborgturist.dk. **Odense Tourist Bureau** ⊠ Vestergade 2 ☎ 66/12–75–20 ⊕ www.visitodense.com. **South Fyn Tourist Bureau** ⊠ Centrumpl., Svendborg ☎ 62/21–09–80.

JYLLAND & THE LAKES

The peninsula of Jylland (Jutland) is the only part of Denmark that is naturally attached to the mainland of Europe; its southern boundary forms the frontier with Germany. Moors and sand dunes cover a tenth of the peninsula—the windswept landscapes of Isak Dinesen's short stories can be seen in the northwest—and the remaining land is devoted to agriculture and forestry. On the east side of the peninsula, facing Fyn, wooded fjords run inland for miles. In addition to rustic towns and flowing countryside, Jylland has numerous majestic castles, parklands, and the famed Legoland. Ribe, Denmark's oldest town, is in the south, and to the east lies Århus, Denmark's second-largest city. If you are in this region directly after touring Fyn, head northwest from Odense through Middlefart and then on to Vejle. By train, either from Odense or Copenhagen, the starting point is Kolding, to the south of Vejle.

Kolding

Don't miss the 13th-century **Koldinghus** castle, which was a royal residence during the Middle Ages. After being rebuilt in the 15th century it was destroyed by fire in the early 1800s. Modern efforts to restore Koldinghus were rewarded when it won the European Nostra Prize for restoration in 1993. Perched at the edge of the Kolding Fjord is the massive, redbrick, quadrangular fortress, centered on a courtyard. The castle floors are made of raw oak, and its walls are alternately spare and

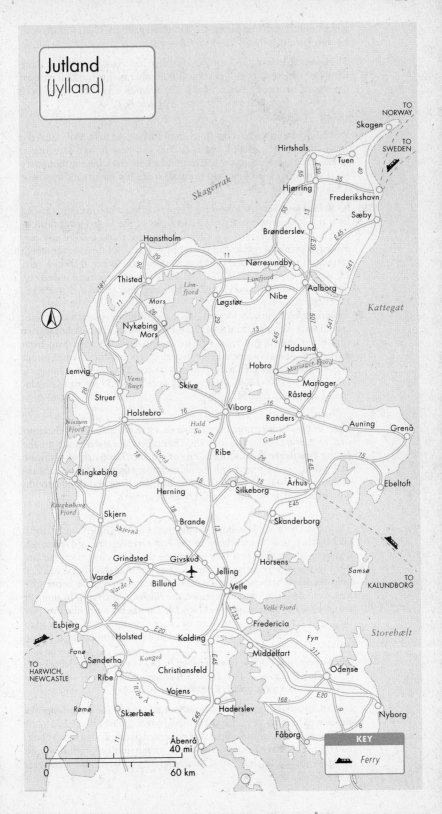

Jutland
(Jylland)

white or lined with iron plates. ⊠ *Markdanerg.* ☎ *76/33–81–00* ⊕ *www. koldinghus.dk* ◌ *Daily 10–5* ◌ *Closed Jan.*

The **Geografisk Have** (Geographical Garden) has a rose garden with more than 120 varieties, as well as some 2,000 other plants from all parts of the world, arranged geographically. ⊠ *Christian 4 Vej* ☎ *75/50–38–80* ⊕ *www.geografiskhave.dk* ◌ *May–Sept., daily 10–6.*

Vejle

Beautifully positioned on the fjord amid forest-clad hills, Vejle faces the strait that divides Jylland and Fyn. You can hear an old Dominican monastery clock chiming the hours; the clock survives, but the monastery itself was torn down long ago to make room for the town's imposing 19th-century city hall.

$$$$ 🏨 **Munkebjerg.** Seven kilometers (4½ mi) southeast of town, surrounded by a thick beech forest and majestic views of the Vejle Fjord, this elegant hotel provides privacy. Overlooking the forest, rooms are furnished in pine and soft green; the lobby is rustic. Of the two top-notch restaurants, one specializes in French cuisine, the other in Danish fare. ⊠ *Munkebjergvej 125, DK 7100* ☎ *76/42–85–00* ⊕ *www.munkebjerg. dk* ➫ *149 rooms, 2 suites* ☼ *2 restaurants, indoor pool, bar* ▭ *AE, DC, MC, V.*

$ 🏨 **Park Hotel.** Centrally located, this hotel offers very spacious rooms, considering the small stature of this establishment. The pleasant service caps off an overall enjoyable experience and ensures return visits from its patrons. Breakfast, included in the price, is bountiful. The restaurant is good though perhaps a bit thin on variety. ⊠ *Orla Lehmannsg. 5, DK 7100* ☎ *75/82–24–66* ⊕ *www.park-hotel.dk* ➫ *33 rooms* ☼ *Restaurant, bar* ▭ *AE, DC, MC, V.*

Jelling

Here are two 10th-century burial mounds, all that remains from the court of King Gorm the Old and his wife, Thyra. Between the mounds are the Jelling **Runestener** (runic stones), one of which, "Denmark's Certificate of Baptism," is decorated with the oldest known figure of Christ in Scandinavia. The stone was erected by Gorm's son, King Harald Bluetooth, who brought Christianity to the Danes in AD 960.

Silkeborg

The region between Silkeborg, on the banks of the Gudenå in Jylland's lake district, and Skanderborg to the east reveals some of Denmark's loveliest scenery. The best way to explore the area is by water; the Gudenå winds its way some 160 km (100 mi) through lakes and wooded hillsides down to the sea. You can take an excursion boat or, better still, a rare old coal-fired paddle steamer, the *Hjejlen,* which runs in summer and is based at Silkeborg. Ever since 1861 it has been paddling its way through narrow stretches of fjord where the treetops meet overhead to the foot of 438-foot Himmelbjerget at Lake Julso. You can clamber up the narrow paths through the heather and trees to the top of the hill, where there is an 80-foot tower erected in 1875 in memory of King Frederik VII. ⊠ *Havnen, DK 8600 Silkeborg* ☎ *86/82–07–66* 🖶 *86/ 82–90–10* 🎫 *Round-trip DKr90* ◌ *Mid-June–Aug.*

One of Silkeborg's chief attractions can be seen in the **Kulturhistoriske Museum** (Museum of Cultural History), which houses the 2,200-year-old Tollund Man, whose corpse was preserved naturally in a nearby bog. ⊠ *Hovedgaardsvej 7* ☎ *86/82–14–99* ⊕ *www.silkeborgmuseum.dk* ◌ *May–mid-Oct., daily 10–5; mid-Oct.–Apr., Wed. and weekends noon–4.*

Århus

Denmark's second-largest city is at its liveliest during the 10-day **Århus Festival** in late August. The event brings together everything from classical concerts to jazz and folk music, clowning, theater, exhibitions, beer tents, and sports. The town's cathedral, the 15th-century **Domkirke**, is Denmark's longest church; it contains a beautifully executed three-panel altarpiece. Whimsical sketches enliven the ceiling. ⊠ *Bispetorv* ☎ *86/12–38–45* ⊕ *www.aarhus-domkirke.dk* ⊙ *Jan.–Apr. and Oct.–Dec., Mon.–Sat. 10–3; May–Sept., Mon.–Sat. 9:30–4.*

Århus's 13th-century **Vor Frue Kirken** (Church of Our Lady), formerly attached to a Dominican abbey, has an eerie but interesting crypt church rediscovered in 1955 and dating from 1060. One of the oldest preserved stone churches in Scandinavia, the vaulted space contains a replica of an old Roman crucifix. ⊠ *Frue Kirkepl.* ☎ *86/12–12–43* ⊕ *www.aarhusvorfrue.dk* ⊙ *Sept.–Apr., weekdays 10–2, Sat. 10–noon; May–Aug., weekdays 10–4, Sat. 10–2.*

★ The town's open-air museum, the **Den Gamle By** (Old Town), is composed of 65 half-timber houses, a mill, and a millstream. The meticulously recreated period interiors range from the 15th to the early 20th century. ⊠ *Viborgvej 2* ☎ *86/12–31–88* ⊕ *www.dengamleby.dk* ⊠ *DKr75* ⊙ *Jan., daily 11–3; Feb. and Mar., daily 10–4; Apr., May, and Sept.–Oct., daily 10–5; June–Aug., daily 9–6; Nov. and Dec., daily 10–4.*

In a 250-acre forest just south of Århus, the indoor-outdoor **Moesgård Forhistorisk Museum** (Prehistoric Museum) has ethnographic and archaeological displays, including the Grauballe Man, a well-preserved, 2,000-year-old corpse. Take the Prehistoric Trail through the forest, which leads past Stone and Bronze Age displays to some reconstructed Viking-style houses. ⊠ *Moesgård Allé 20 DK 8270 Højbjerg* ☎ *89/42–45–01* ⊠ *DKr45* ⊙ *Apr.–Sept., daily 10–5; Oct.–Mar., Tues.–Sun. 10–4.*

$–$$ ✕ **Bryggeriet Sct. Clemens.** At this popular brew pub, you can sit among copper kettles and quaff the local recipe, which is unfiltered and without additives, just like in the old days. Between the spareribs and Australian steaks, you won't go hungry either. ⊠ *Kannikeg. 10–12* ☎ *86/13–80–00* ⊟ *AE, DC, MC, V.*

$$$$ ▦ **Hotel Royal.** Open since 1838, Århus's grand hotel has a stately lobby appointed with Chesterfield sofas, modern paintings, and a winding staircase. The plush guest rooms upstairs have rich drapery, furniture upholstered in velour and brocade, and marble bathrooms. ⊠ *Store Torv 4, DK 8100 Århus C* ☎ *86/12–00–11* ☐ *86/76–04–04* ⊕ *www.hotelroyal.dk* ⇥ *120 rooms, 9 suites* ⌂ *Restaurant, bar* ⊟ *AE, DC, MC, V.*

$ ▦ **Youth Hostel Pavilionen.** As in all Danish youth and family hostels, rooms here are bright and functional, and the secluded, wooded setting near the fjord is beautiful. Keep in mind that it does get noisy, with carousing business parties mixed in with budget-conscious backpackers. There's a kitchen for guests' use. The cafeteria serves breakfast only. ⊠ *Marienlundsvej 10, DK 8240 Risskov* ☎ *86/16–72–98* ☐ *86/10–55–60* ⇥ *30 rooms, 11 with shower; 4 communal showers and toilets* ⊟ *AE, MC, V* ⊙ *Closed mid-Dec.–mid-Jan.*

Aalborg

This city stands guard over the narrowest point of the Limfjord, the great waterway of northern Jylland and the gateway between north and south. Here you'll find an intriguing intermingling of ancient and modern where twisting lanes filled with medieval houses lie just adjacent to broad, modern boulevards. Jomfru Ane Gade, a tiny cobbled street in the center of Aalborg, is lined with restaurants, inns, and sidewalk cafés. The magnificent five-story **Jens Bangs Stenhus** (Jens Bang's Stone House; ⊠ Østerågade 9), dating from 1624, has a good restaurant with an excellent wine cellar. The baroque cathedral, **Budolfi Kirken** (Butolph Church; ⊠ Gammel Torv), is consecrated to English St. Butolph. The 15th-century **Helligåndskloster** (Monastery of the Holy Ghost; ⊠ C. W. Obelspl., next to Budolfi Kirken), very well preserved, is now a home for the elderly.

$$ ✕ **Spisehuset Kniv og Gaffel.** In a 400-year-old building parallel to Jomfru Ane Gade, the busy "Knife and Fork" is crammed with oak tables balancing on crazy slanting floors and lit by candles. Its year-round courtyard is a veritable greenhouse. Young waitresses negotiate the mayhem to deliver inch-thick steaks, the house specialty. ⊠ *Maren Turisg. 10* ☎ *98/16–69–72* ⊟ *DC, MC, V.*

★ $–$$ ✕ **Duus Vinkælder.** This amazing cellar is part alchemist's den, part neighborhood bar. Most people come for a drink before or after dinner, but you can also get a light bite. In summer, the menu is chiefly smørrebrød, but during the winter you can order such specialties as *pølser* (sausages), *frikadeller* (meatballs), *biksemad* (cubed potato, meat, and onion hash), and the restaurant's specialty, pâté. ⊠ *Østeråg. 9* ☎ *98/12–50–56* ⌂ *Reservations essential* ⊟ *No credit cards* ☉ *Closed Sun.*

$$$$ 🏨 **Helnan Phønix.** In a sumptuous old mansion, this hotel is popular with international and business guests. Rooms are luxuriously furnished with plump chairs and polished dark-wood furniture; in some, the original raw beams are still intact. The Brigarden restaurant serves excellent Danish cuisine. ⊠ *Vesterbro 77, DK 9000* ☎ *98/12–00–11* ⊕ *www.helnan-phonix-hotel.dk* ⟿ *210 rooms, 2 suites* ⌂ *Restaurant, bar* ⊟ *AE, DC, MC, V.*

Skagen

The picturesque streets and luminous light of the town have inspired both painters and writers. Michael and Anna Ancher, P. S. Krøyer, and other artists settled here and founded what has become known as the Skagen school of painting; you can see their work in the **Skagens Museum.** ⊠ *Brøndumsvej 4* ☎ *98/44–64–44* ⊕ *www.skagensmuseum.dk* 🎟 *DKr60* ☉ *Apr. and Oct., Tues.–Sun. 11–4; May and Sept., daily 10–5; June–Aug., daily 10–6; Nov.–Mar., Wed.–Fri. 1–4, Sat. 11–4, Sun. 11–3.*

$$ 🏨 **Brøndums Hotel.** A few minutes from the beach, this 150-year-old gabled inn is furnished with antiques and Skagen-school paintings. The 21 guest rooms in the main building, without TVs or phones, are old-fashioned, with wicker chairs, Oriental rugs, and pine and four-poster beds. The rooms in the annex are more modern. Reserve well in advance for the summer months. ⊠ *Anchersvej 3, DK 9990* ☎ *98/44–15–55* ⊕ *www.broendums-hotel.dk* ⟿ *46 rooms, 13 with bath; 3 suites* ⌂ *Restaurant, bar* ⊟ *AE, DC, MC, V.*

Viborg

Dating from the 8th century, the town started out as a trading post and a place of pagan sacrifice. Later it became a center of Christianity, with monasteries and its own bishop. The 1,000-year-old **Hærvejen,** the old military road that starts near here, was once Denmark's most important connection with the outside world. Legend has it that during the 11th century, King Canute set out from Viborg to conquer England, which he subsequently ruled from 1016 to 1035. Built in 1130, Viborg's **Domkirke** (cathedral; ⊠ Mogensg. 4 ☎ 87/25–52–50) was once the largest granite church in the world. The crypt, restored and reopened in 1876, is all that remains of the original building.

Hald Sø

There's terrific walking country beside Hald Sø (Hald Lake) and on the nearby heather-clad **Dollerup Bakker** (Dollerup Hills). At a small kiosk near the lake that sells snacks and sweets you can pick up a map.

Herning

In this old moorland town, you'll find a remarkable circular building with an exterior frieze by Carl-Henning Pedersen (b. 1913); it houses the **Carl-Henning Pedersen and Else Afelt Museum.** The museum is set within a sculpture park. ⊠ *Birk Centerpark 3* ☎ *97/22–10–79* ☉ *Nov.–Apr., Tues.–Fri. 10–5 and weekends noon–5; May and June, Sept. and Oct., Tues.–Sun. 10–5; July, daily 10–5.*

Ribe

The medieval center in Denmark's oldest town is preserved by the Danish National Trust. From May to mid-September, a night watchman walks around the town telling of its ancient history and singing traditional songs. You can see him in the main square each night at 10.

$$–$$$ ✕⬛ **Hotel Dagmar.** In the middle of Ribe's quaint center, this cozy, half-timber hotel encapsulates the charm of the 16th century, with stained-glass windows, frescoes, sloping floors, and carved chairs. The lavish rooms have antique canopy beds, fat armchairs, and chaise longues. The fine French restaurant serves such specialties as fillet of salmon in sorrel cream sauce and marinated *foie gras de canard* (duck liver). ⊠ *Torvet 1, DK 6760* ☎*75/ 42–00–33* 🖷*75/42–36–52* ⊕*www.hoteldagmar.dk* 🛏*50 rooms* ♨*Restaurant, bar* 🖃 *AE, DC, MC, V.*

Billund

★ ☮ **Legoland** is a park filled with scaled-down versions of famous things: a Statue of Liberty; a statue of Sitting Bull; a Mt. Rushmore; a safari park; even a Pirate Land—all constructed of millions of Legos. There are also exhibits of toys from pre-Lego days, including Legoland's showpiece, Titania's Palace, a sumptuous dollhouse built in 1907 by Sir Neville Wilkinson for his daughter. The park also has the double-football-field-size Castleland extravaganza, with rides and restaurants. Everything inside is made of 45 million Lego bricks, including the wizards and warlocks, dragons and knights that inhabit it. ⊠ *Normarksvej 9* ☎ *75/ 33–13–33* ⊕ *www.legoland.dk* 🎟 *DKr150* ☉ *Apr.–Oct., daily 10–8.*

Jylland & the Lakes Essentials

CAR TRAVEL

Although there is good train and bus service between all the main cities, this region is best visited by car. The delightful nearby islands are suitable only if you have ample time, as many involve an overnight stay.

TOURS

Guided tours are scarce in these parts; stop by any tourist office for maps and suggestions for walking tours. Århus also offers a Round and About the City tour, which leaves from the tourist board daily at 10 AM from mid-June to mid-August.

VISITOR INFORMATION

The Danish Tourist Board maintains a central Web site with links to all regional offices, listed below.
🏴**Nordjylland** ⊕ www.visitnord.dk. **Sydøstjylland** ⊕ www.sej.dk. **Østjylland** ⊕ www. visiteastjutland.com. **Vestjylland** ⊕ www.tgv.dk. **Aalborg** ⊠ Østeråg. 8, Aalborg ☎ 98/ 12–60–22 ⊕ www.visitaalborg.com. **Århus** ⊠ Park Allé 1, Århus ☎ 89/40–67–00 ⊕ www.visitaarhus.dk.

FINLAND

HELSINKI, THE SOUTH COAST, THE LAKELANDS, FINNISH LAPLAND

IF YOU LIKE MAJESTIC OPEN SPACES, fine architecture, and the Nordic quality of life, Finland is for you. It is a land of lakes—187,888 at the last count—and forests, whose people prize their natural surroundings while expanding the frontiers of modern design and high technology.

The music of Sibelius echoes the mood of this Nordic landscape. Both can swing from the somber nocturne of midwinter darkness to the tremolos of sunlight slanting through pine and bone-white birch, ending with the diminuendo of a sunset as it fades into the next day's dawn. Similarly, the Finnish people reflect the changing moods of their land and climate. Their affinity with nature has produced some of the world's greatest designers and architects. Many American cities have buildings designed by Alvar Aalto and the Saarinens, Eliel and his son Eero. Today Finland is also increasingly known for its high-tech achievements, especially by the mobile-phone giant Nokia.

Finnish culture has an interesting mix of rural roots and urban sophistication. Although Internet connections in Finland are more numerous per capita than almost anywhere else in the world, the country's more than 5.1 million inhabitants continue to treasure their vast silent spaces. They won't always appreciate back-slapping familiarity—least of all in the sauna, widely regarded in the land that gave the traditional bath its name as a spiritual, as well as a cleansing, experience. Nevertheless, Finns are not unlikely to strike up impromptu conversations in pubs or provide generous help for a lost tourist. Older generations are more reserved, but younger people are likely to have been abroad and almost always speak English. Although small talk does not come easily to Finns, the ice melts quickly when a visitor takes the time to express genuine interest in their country.

Until 1917 Finland (in Finnish, Suomi) was under the domination of Sweden and Russia. After more than 600 years under the Swedish crown and 100 under the tsars, the country bears marks of the two cultures, such as a small but influential Swedish-speaking minority and a smattering of onion-dome Orthodox churches. The Finns themselves, neither Scandinavian nor Slavic, are descendants of the wandering Finno-Ugric peoples, who settled on the swampy shores of the Gulf of Finland before the Christian era. Finnish is one of the Finno-Ugric languages; it is related to Estonian and, distantly, to Hungarian.

There is a tough, resilient quality to the Finns. No other people fought the Soviets to a standstill as the Finns did in the Winter War of 1939–40. They are stubborn, self-sufficient, and patriotic, yet not aggressively

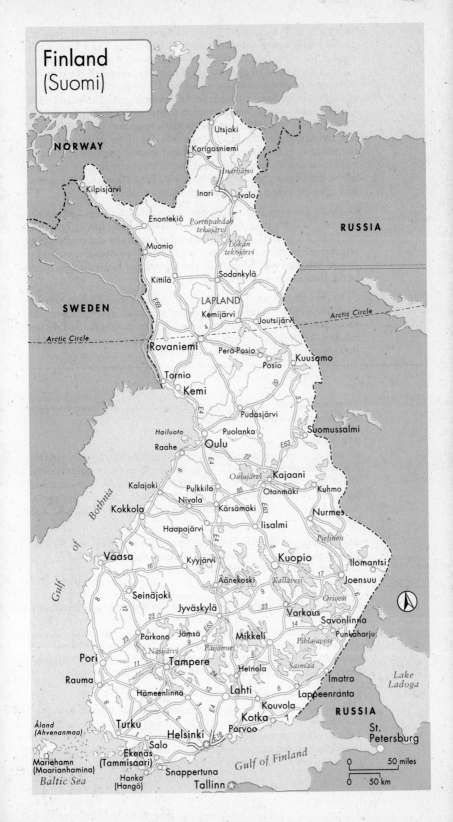

Finland
(Suomi)

NORWAY

SWEDEN

RUSSIA

Utsjoki

Karigasniemi

Inarijärvi

Kilpisjärvi

Inari

Ivalo

Enontekiö

Porttipahdan tekojärvi

Lokan tekojärvi

Muonio

Kittilä

Sodankylä

LAPLAND

Kemijärvi

Joutsijärvi

Arctic Circle

Arctic Circle

Rovaniemi

Perä-Posio

Posio

Kuusamo

Tornio

Kemi

Pudasjärvi

Suomussalmi

Hailuoto

Puolanka

Raahe

Oulu

Kalajoki

Oulujärvi

Kajaani

Kuhmo

Pulkkila

Otanmäki

Nivala

Kärsämäki

Nurmes

Kokkola

Iisalmi

Haapajärvi

Pielinen

Vaasa

Kyyjärvi

Kuopio

Ilomantsi

Äänekoski

Kallavesi

Joensuu

Seinäjoki

Orivesi

Jyväskylä

Varkaus

Savonlinna

Parkano

Jämsä

Mikkeli

Punkaharju

Pori

Näsijärvi

Päijänne

Pihlajavesi

Saimaa

Rauma

Tampere

Heinola

Imatra

Lake Ladoga

Hämeenlinna

Lahti

Lappeenranta

RUSSIA

Turku

Kouvola

Kotka

Åland
(Ahvenanmaa)

Porvoo

St. Petersburg

Helsinki

Mariehamn
(Maarianhamina)

Salo

Ekenäs
(Tammisaari)

Snappertuna

Baltic Sea

Hanko
(Hangö)

Tallinn

Gulf of Finland

Gulf of Bothnia

0   50 miles

0   50 km

nationalistic. Finland's complex relationship to the USSR once included highly beneficial trade relations, as Finland had a large ready market for its manufactured goods next door. With the fall of the USSR, Finland had to aggressively expand its exports to Western Europe and has since reached the top of lists of competitive countries, particularly in technology development. As a member of the European Union, Finland has sought to bring attention to the northern periphery of Europe and has promoted accepting its Baltic neighbors (Estonia, Latvia, and Lithuania) into the EU. Finland was one of the first countries in the world to grant women the vote, and women continue to play an important role in Finnish political life. The country has not only one of the few female presidents in the world, Tarja Halonen, but has also had a female prime minister, Anneli Jäätteenmäki.

Finland's extensive public transport system is an efficient and affordable way to cover beautiful expanses of lakeland and forest. The capital, Helsinki, with its outdoor summer bars and cafés and multilingual population, is far more cosmopolitan than it was a decade ago. An influx of Russians and Estonians is also evidence of Finland's new, more open relationship with its eastern neighbors.

"The strength of a small nation lies in its culture," noted Johan Vilhelm Snellman, Finland's leading 19th-century statesman and philosopher. As though inspired by this thought, Finns—who are among the world's top readers—continue to nurture a rich cultural climate, as is illustrated by 900 museums and a slew of summer festivals.

FINLAND A TO Z

To research prices, get advice from other travelers, and book travel arrangements, visit www.fodors.com.

AIR TRAVEL

Finnair operates an elaborate network of flights linking 24 towns in Finland. Finnair gives travelers 17–24 years old a discount on flights booked ahead, with reductions of 50%. These tickets are available at major travel agencies. One-way standby fares are also available for the same age group. Senior fares with up to 70% reductions are available to those 65 and older.

At press time several airlines such as Ryan Air, Flying Finn, and Air Finland were opening up routes within Finland and Scandinavia.
🔲 Finnair ☎ 09/818-800; 0203/140-160 in Finland.

BIKE TRAVEL

Well-marked cycle paths run into the heart of Helsinki and other towns and cities. Bikes can be rented at some youth hostels. The Finnish Youth Hostel Association offers round-trip packages from Helsinki to any of its hostel locations throughout the country, including bike rental and hostel accommodation. Packages with a regular bike: €249 (7 days) or €431 (14 days); hybrid bike: €275 (7 days) or €462 (14 days).

BOAT & FERRY TRAVEL

Helsinki and Turku have regular sea links with the Finnish Åland Islands in the Baltic Sea. Ferry and hydrofoil traffic between Helsinki and Tallinn is also convenient for one- to two-day side trips. From mid-June to mid-August you can cruise the lakes of the Finnish interior. Complete timetables are available from the Finnish Tourist Board.

BUS TRAVEL

Finland's bus system can take you virtually anywhere and has pioneered the use of "smart cards," a safe processor card that can be used to pay for bus fares all over the country on buses operated by various companies. The card can be loaded according to the number of trips or monetary value, and can be used by more than one person.

BUSINESS HOURS

BANKS & OFFICES Banks are open weekdays 9:15–4:15; at the Helsinki-Vantaa airport, daily 6:30–7:30 PM (11 PM in the transit area); exchange offices are open longer. Most ATMs are marked with an orange Otto sign and will accept major credit cards for cash withdrawals.

MUSEUMS & SIGHTS Opening hours for museums vary considerably, so check individual listings. Many museums in the countryside are open only in summer.

SHOPS Shops are generally open weekdays 9–6, Saturday 9–2. Department stores and supermarkets stay open until 8 or 9 on weekdays and 5 or 6 on Saturday. Smaller shops such as neighborhood grocery stores are often open Sunday noon–9. Shops may also open on Sunday during June, July, and August and on some other Sundays in the year—usually in December for Christmas shopping. Shops in the tunnel complex beneath Helsinki's main railway station are open daily, including holidays, until 10 PM.

CAR TRAVEL

EMERGENCIES The Automobile and Touring Club of Finland (Autoliitto) operates a 24-hour information service for club members and members of foreign auto clubs. Report accidents without delay to the insurance company listed on the rental-car documents or to the Finnish Motor Insurers' Centre (Liikennevakuutuskeskus), as well as to the police.

🛈 **The Automobile and Touring Club of Finland** ✉ Hämeentie 105 A, 00550 Helsinki ☎ 09/7258-4400, 09/7747-6400 24-hour information service 🖷 09/7258-4460 ⊕ www.autoliitto.fi. **Finnish Motor Insurers' Centre** ✉ Bulevardi 28, 00120 Helsinki ☎ 09/680-401 ⊕ www.vakes.fi/lvk.

GASOLINE Gasoline costs about €1.20 per liter.

PARKING Major cities offer multistory garages; most towns have on-street meters. In Helsinki there is no free on-street parking. In areas with no meters drivers must display a *pysäköintilippu* (parking voucher), for sale at R-kiosks and gas stations, on their dashboard.

ROAD CONDITIONS Finland has an expanding network of efficient major roads, some of which are multilane. In the north, you can expect long stretches of dirt road, which become difficult to negotiate during the spring thaw. Away from the larger towns traffic is light, but take elk and reindeer warning signs seriously.

RULES OF THE ROAD Speed limits (usually marked) are 50 kph (30 mph) in built-up areas and 80–100 kph (50–62 mph) in the country and on main roads, 120 kph (74 mph) in summer on some highways. Low-beam headlights must be used at all times outside city areas, seat belts are compulsory (for all seats), and you must carry a warning triangle in case of a breakdown.

CUSTOMS & DUTIES

For details on imports and duty-free limits, *see* Customs & Duties *in* Smart Travel Tips.

EATING & DRINKING

As in other parts of Scandinavia, the *seisovapöytä* (buffet table) is often a work of art as well as a feast. Some special Finnish dishes are *poronkäristys* (reindeer casserole); salmon, herring, and various fresh-water fish; and *lihapullat* (meatballs with a creamy sauce). In the autumn, local mushrooms such as the *suppelovahvero* (a funnel-shaped chanterelle) are a nice complement to meat and game. For a delicious dessert, try *lakka* (cloudberries), which grow above the Arctic Circle and are frequently used in sauces for ice cream. Inexpensive lunches are served in *kahvila* (coffee shops) and *baari* (usually cafés, not bars).

Prix-fixe menus, which usually include two courses and coffee, are served in many establishments and are often a good deal, particularly at lunchtime. Also, restaurants that specialize in expensive dishes such as reindeer or pheasant may have less expensive, sometimes vegetarian, options on the menu. A service charge (*palvelupalkkio*) will be included in the check. If you want to leave an additional tip—though it really isn't necessary—round the figure off to the nearest euro or two. Heavy taxation is evident in wine and hard liquor prices in restaurants. Beer is a tasty and moderately priced alternative.

WHAT IT COSTS In Euros				
	$$$$	**$$$**	**$$**	**$**
AT DINNER	over €26	€18–€26	€10–€18	under €10

Prices are per person for a main course.

MEALTIMES The Finns generally eat early at home, but restaurants run on a later schedule. Breakfast is usually from 7 to 10, lunch runs from 11 or noon to 1 or 2, and dinner from about 5 to 11 or midnight.

RESERVATIONS & Except for the most elegant establishments, where a jacket and tie are
DRESS preferred, casual attire is acceptable for restaurants in all price categories; jeans are not allowed in some more expensive dining rooms.

EMBASSIES
There are consular offices for Australia and New Zealand in Helsinki.
🔽 Canada ✉ Pohjoisesplanadi 25B, 00101 Helsinki ☎ 09/228-530.
🔽 Ireland ✉ Erottajankatu 7A, 00131 Helsinki ☎ 09/646-006.
🔽 United Kingdom ✉ Itäinen Puistotie 17, 00140 Helsinki ☎ 09/228-65100.
🔽 United States ✉ Itäinen Puistotie 14, 00140 Helsinki ☎ 09/171-931.

EMERGENCIES
🔽 **National emergency number** ☎ 112. **Police** ☎ 10022.

HOLIDAYS
January 1; January 6 (Epiphany); Good Friday, Easter, and Easter Monday; May 1 (May Day); Ascension (in May); Pentecost/Whitsunday (mid-May to early June); Midsummer (third or fourth Saturday in June); All Saints' Day (first Saturday in November); December 6 (Independence Day); December 25–26 (Christmas and Boxing Day).

LANGUAGE
The official languages of Finland are Finnish and Swedish. Only about 6% of the total population speaks Swedish, but in some areas, such as the west coast and in pockets close to Helsinki, Swedish-speakers form a local majority. English is widely spoken in Helsinki and by young Finns around the country. In Finnish Lapland the native Sámi (pronounced *Sah*-me) population speaks three different dialects of a language distantly related to Finnish. Note that the Finnish letters ä and ö and the Swedish å come at the end of the alphabet.

LODGING

Finland has accommodations of all kinds, from hotels, motels, boarding houses, B&Bs, rental chalets, and cottages, to farmhouses, youth hostels, and campsites. Standards are generally high, even in the simplest of places. Prices are for weekdays and include breakfast and service charges. Weekend and summer rates tend to be significantly lower. Most rates are listed on hotel Web sites.

WHAT IT COSTS In Euros			
$$$$	**$$$**	**$$**	**$**
HELSINKI			
FOR 2 PEOPLE over €200	€150–€200	€100–€150	under €100
OTHER AREAS			
HOTELS over €140	€115–€140	€90–€115	under €90

Hotel prices are for a standard double room in high season.

CAMPING Finland has about 350 campsites, and about 200 of them belong to the Finnish Camping Site Association network. Most sites have cabins in addition to tent and caravan/trailer pitches. An international or Scandinavian camping card is required but can be obtained at the first site for a minimal charge and is valid for one year. Finncamping checks and camping cottage checks are sold by accredited travel agents. Lists are available from the Finnish Camping Site Association.
⨍ Finnish Camping Site Association ✉ Mäntytie 7, 00270 Helsinki ☎ 09/4774-0740 🖷 09/4772-002 ⊕ www.camping.fi.

FARMHOUSE & COTTAGE RENTALS Found mainly outside Helsinki, these provide the least expensive accommodations; local tourist offices have lists of available properties. Comfortable (not luxurious) accommodations cost approximately €400–€1,000 per week for a four-person rental. A central reservations agency is Lomarengas (Finnish Country Holidays).
⨍ Lomarengas ✉ Hämeentie 105D, 00550 Helsinki ☎ 09/5766-3350 🖷 09/5766-3355 ⊕ www.lomarengas.fi.

HOSTELS Hostels range from empty schools to small manor houses. The Finnish Tourist Board and the Finnish Youth Hostel Association can provide a list of hostels. There are no age restrictions, and prices range from about €10 to €30 per bed and €10–€50 per person in single or double rooms, with a discount of €2.50 for YHA members.
⨍ Finnish Youth Hostel Association (YHA) ✉ Yrjönkatu 38B, 00100 Helsinki ☎ 09/565-7150 🖷 09/565-71510 ⊕ www.srmnet.org.

HOTELS Most hotels in Finland are modern and well equipped; a few occupy fine old manor houses. Rooms usually have a bath or shower, and virtually all hotels have saunas. Prices generally include breakfast and often a morning sauna and swim. The Finncheque voucher system offers good discounts mid-May through September. For additional information inquire at Suomen Hotellivaraukset Oy (Hotel Reservations in Finland, Ltd.).
⨍ Suomen Hotellivaraukset Oy ✉ Korkeavuorenkatu 47B, 00130 Helsinki ☎ 09/686-0330 🖷 09/686-03310.

SUMMER HOTELS Some university student housing is turned into "summer hotels" from June through August; they offer modern facilities at reasonable prices. The Finnish Youth Hostel Association publishes "Hostellit," which lists summer hotels as well as youth hostels. Free copies are available at the Finnish Tourist Board and the Finnish Youth Hostel Association.

RESERVING A
ROOM If you haven't reserved a room before arriving in Helsinki, you can make reservations through a travel agency or at the Hotel Booking Centre run by Helsinki Expert; the booking service is free by phone, fax, or e-mail; if the reservation is booked in person, the charge is €5 per room in Helsinki and the surrounding area, €7 for all other areas.
🚇 **Hotel Booking Centre** ✉ Rautatieasema (train station) central hall ☎ 09/2288-1400
🖷 09/2288-1499 ⊕ www.helsinkiexpert.fi/hotel.

MAIL & SHIPPING

If you're uncertain about where you'll be staying, have mail sent to you marked *poste restante* (general delivery) and addressed to the post office in the appropriate town or Helsinki's main post office.
🚇 **Main Post Office** ✉ Mannerheiminaukio 1A, 00100 🕭 Poste restante Helsinki 10, Elielinaukio 2F.

POSTAL RATES Airmail letters and postcards to destinations within Finland (up to 50 grams) and to all other countries (up to 20 grams) cost €0.65.

MONEY MATTERS

Prices are highest in Helsinki. The prices of many goods include an 18% sales tax; the tax on food is less.

Some sample prices include cup of coffee, €1; glass of beer, starting from €3; soft drink, €2.50; ham sandwich, €3; 2-km (1-mi) taxi ride, €6–€9 (depending on time of day).

CURRENCY The unit of currency in Finland is the euro, divided into 100 cents. There are bills of 5, 10, 20, 50, 100, and 200. Coins are 5, 10, 20, and 50 cents and 1 and 2 euros. At press time (summer 2003) the exchange rate was €0.85 to the U.S. dollar; €0.63 to the Canadian dollar; €1.42 to the pound sterling; €0.56 to the Australian dollar; €0.49 to the New Zealand dollar; and €0.11 to the South African rand. Credit cards are widely accepted, even in most taxicabs. Traveler's checks can be cashed only in banks and exchange offices.

Prepaid electronic cash cards that process even the smallest cash transactions at public pay phones, vending machines, and fast-food outlets are very popular in Finland and can be purchased at kiosks.

TAXES

Non-EU residents who purchase goods worth more than about €42 in any shop marked TAX FREE FOR TOURISTS can get a 12%–16% refund (10% on food). Show your passport and the store will give you a check for the appropriate amount, which you can cash at your final point of departure from the EU. You may be asked to show a receipt and/or the unopened item.

TELEPHONES

Telephone numbers in Finland vary in length from four to eight digits. Business phone numbers may also have special prefix codes (020 or 010), which are countrywide but are charged at only local rates.

COUNTRY &
AREA CODES The country code for Finland is 358.

INTERNATIONAL
CALLS You can dial Britain and the United States directly from anywhere in Finland. Calls to other countries can be made from telegraph offices, which are marked TELE or LENNÄTIN and are usually next to a post office. An operator will assign you a booth and collect payment at the end of the call. To dial numbers from outside Finland, omit the zero at the beginning of the city code. To make a direct international phone call from Finland, dial 999, 990, or 994, then the country code and phone

number. You can reach long-distance operators, or get help from directory assistance, by dialing one of the numbers listed below.

▮ **Access Codes AT&T** ☎ 0800–110055. **Directory assistance abroad** ☎ 020–208. **MCI** ☎ 0800–110280. **Sprint** ☎ 0800–110284.

LOCAL CALLS To avoid exorbitant hotel surcharges on calls, use public pay phones, most of which now use phone cards. For help, call local directory assistance.

▮ **Local directory assistance** ☎ 118.

PHONE CARDS Many pay phones accept only a phone card; the *Sonera Kortti, Elisa Kortti,* and other cards are available at post offices, R-kiosks, and some grocery stores. They come in increments of €6, €10, and €20. Several local phone companies also offer cards, and some pay phones accept only certain cards.

TIPPING

You can give taxi drivers small coins. Train and airport porters have a fixed charge. It's not necessary to tip hotel doormen for carrying bags to the check-in counter, but give bellhops €1–€2 for carrying bags to your room. A coat-check room fee of €1 is usually clearly posted; if not, give about €2, depending on the number in your party.

TRAIN TRAVEL

Finland's comfortable and clean rail system extends to all main centers of the country. A Finnrail Pass gives unlimited first- or second-class travel within a month for persons living permanently outside Finland. The 3-day pass costs €118 (€177 for first-class), the 5-day pass €158 (€237), and the 10-day pass €214 (€321). Children pay half fare. In Finland the Finnrail Pass is available from VR Finnish Railways.

CUTTING COSTS The ScanRail Pass allows unlimited second-class train travel throughout Denmark, Finland, Norway, and Sweden and comes in various denominations. When sold outside Scandinavia, it is valid for 5 days of travel within two months (€225), 10 days within two months (€302), or 21 days consecutively (€349). When sold in Scandinavia the periods of validity are 5 days of travel within 15 days (€225), or 21 consecutive days (€349). Discounts or free connections on certain ferries and buses are included. Certain hotel chains and organizations also offer discounts to pass holders. In the United States call Rail Europe, or DER, which also offers a 21-day pass.

▮ **DER** ☎ 800/782–2424. **Norvista** ☎ 0171/409–7334. **Rail Europe** ☎ 877/257–2887. **VR Finnish Railways** ☎ 09/3072–3706 🖷 09/3072–0111.

VISITOR INFORMATION

Many festivals are scheduled throughout the country, especially in summer. For information contact Finland Festivals.

▮ **Finnish Tourist Board Information Office** ✉ Eteläesplanadi 4, 00100 Helsinki ☎ 09/4176–9300 🖷 09/4176–9301 ⊕ www.mek.fi. **Finland Festivals** ✉ Uudenmaankatu 36D, 00120 Helsinki ☎ 09/612–6760 or 09/6126–7611 🖷 09/6126–7610 ⊕ www.festivals.fi.

WHEN TO GO

Summer is marked by long hours of sunlight and cool nights. Though many establishments close or reduce hours off-season, the advantages to off-season travel are many: fewer mosquitoes, spectacular fall foliage, and cross-country skiing.

CLIMATE You can expect warm days in Helsinki from mid-May and in Lapland from mid-June. Hot weather, with temperatures well into the 80s, is not uncommon in July and August. The midnight sun can be seen from May through July, depending on the region. Even in Helsinki, summer nights are brief and never really dark; in midwinter daylight lasts only a few hours.

The following are average daily maximum and minimum temperatures for Helsinki.

Jan.	30F	−1C	May	64F	18C	Sept.	53F	11C
	26	−3		48	9		39	4
Feb.	34F	1C	June	60F	16C	Oct.	46F	8C
	24	−4		48	9		36	2
Mar.	36F	2C	July	68F	20C	Nov.	32F	0C
	26	−3		55	13		26	−3
Apr.	46F	8C	Aug.	64F	18C	Dec.	32F	0C
	32	0		53	12		24	−4

HELSINKI

Built on the peninsulas and islands of the Baltic shoreline, Helsinki is a city of the sea. Streets curve around bays, bridges arch between islands, and ferries carry traffic to islands farther offshore. The smell of the sea hovers over the city, and there is a constant bustle in the harbors as the huge ships that ply the Baltic drop and lift anchor.

The city covers a total of 1,140 square km (433 square mi), including some 315 islands, with at least 30% of the metropolitan area reserved for parks and other open spaces. Most of Helsinki's sights, however, are crowded onto a single peninsula.

In the 16th century the Swedish king Gustav Vasa, at that time ruler of Finland as well, was determined to woo trade away from the Estonian city of Tallinn and the Hanseatic League. Helsinki was founded next to the rapids of the Vantaa River on June 12, 1550, by a group of Finns who had settled here upon the king's orders.

Over the next three centuries, Turku, on Finland's west coast, was the country's political and intellectual capital. Helsinki took center stage only when Sweden ceded Finland to Russia in 1809. Tsar Alexander I turned Finland into an autonomous grand duchy, proclaiming Helsinki its capital in 1812. Around the same time, much of Turku burned to the ground, and its university was forced to move to Helsinki. From then on Helsinki's position as Finland's first city was assured.

Just before the tsar's proclamation, a fire destroyed many of Helsinki's traditional wooden buildings, making it necessary to build a new city center. The German-born architect Carl Ludvig Engel was entrusted with the project, and thanks to him Helsinki has some of the purest neoclassical architecture in the world. Add to this foundation the stunning outlines of the Jugendstil (art nouveau) period of the early 20th century and more modern buildings designed by native Finnish architects, and you have a capital city as architecturally eye-catching as it is unlike those of the rest of Europe.

Exploring Helsinki

Numbers in the margin correspond to points of interest on the Helsinki map.

❿ **Eduskuntatalo** (Parliament House). This imposing, colonnaded, red-granite structure was built between 1927 and 1931. The legislature has one of the world's highest ratios of women to men. ⊠ *Mannerheimintie 30* ☎ *09/432–2027* ⊕ *www.eduskunta.fi.*

⑲ Finlandiatalo (Finlandia Hall). The lake Töölönlahti forms the backdrop of this important cultural venue. Architect Alvar Aalto designed this creative, marble and black-granite building to be functional: the tower and inclined roof enhance acoustics in the concert hall. ✉ *Karamzinkatu 4* ☎ *09/402–4246* ⊕ *www.finlandia.hel.fi* ☉ *Concerts usually Wed. and Thurs. night.*

Kaivopuisto (Well Park). This elegant district was favored by Russian high society during the 19th century. Now it is a residential area for diplomats and a popular strolling ground. ✉ *Close to ferry terminals, between Puistokatu and Ehrenströmintie.*

Katajanokka. Nineteenth-century brick warehouses in this district have been converted into boutiques, galleries, crafts studios, and restaurants. ✉ *East of Kanavaranta and the Orthodox cathedral.*

❸ Katumuseo/Helsingin Kaupunginmuseo (Street Museum/Helsinki City Museum). Walk down this block of Sofiankatu from the esplanade to Senate Square and step through various periods of Helsinki's history. The Helsinki City Museum, which displays art, furniture, illustrations, literature, and archives, including a model of Helsinki in the 1870s, a pharmacy, and home interiors from the 18th to the 20th centuries, is on the same street. ✉ *Sofiankatu 4* ☎ *09/169–3933* ⊕ *www.hel.fi/ kaumuseo* ☉ *Weekdays 9–5, weekends 11–5.*

❶ Kauppatori (Market Square). The colorful, bustling market beside the South Harbor attracts customers for freshly cut flowers, fruit, and vegetables, as well as handicrafts from small country villages—all sold by vendors in bright orange tents. Closer to the dock are fresh fish from the waters of the Baltic. You can't miss the curvaceous *Havis Amanda* statue watching over the busy square. ✉ *Eteläranta and Pohjoisesplanadi* ☉ *Sept.–May, weekdays 6:30–2, Sat. 6:30–3; June–Aug., weekdays 6:30–2 and 3:30–8, Sat. 6:30–3, Sun. 9–4.*

❷ Kaupungintalo (City Hall). This light-blue building on Pohjoisesplanadi (North Esplanade), the political center of Finland, is the home of city government offices. ✉ *Pohjoisesplanadi 1* ☎ *09/169–3757.*

☺ ㉔ Korkeasaari Eläintarha (Helsinki Zoo). Here snow leopards and reindeer thrive in the cold Finnish climate and children can climb on outdoor play equipment. The ferry departs from the Market Square approximately every 30 minutes from May through September. Alternatively, you can catch the bus at Erottaja or Herttoniemi (weekends), or take the metro to the Kulosaari stop, cross under the tracks, and then follow the signs 20 minutes to the zoo. ✉ *Korkeasaari Island* ☎ *09/169–5969* ⊕ *www. hel.fi/zoo* ☉ *Mar. and Apr., daily 10–6; May–Sept., daily 10–8; Oct.–Feb., daily 10–4.*

⑮ Mannerheimin patsas (statue of Marshal Mannerheim). In front of the main post office, the bronze equestrian gazes down Mannerheimintie, named in his honor. No man in Finnish history is as revered as Baron Carl Gustaf Mannerheim, the military and political leader who guided Finland through the first half of the 20th century. ✉ *Mannerheimintie.*

⑯ Nykytaiteenmuseo (Kiasma) (Museum of Contemporary Art). Praised for the boldness of its curved steel shell but condemned for its encroachment on the territory of the Mannerheim statue, this striking museum displays a wealth of Finnish and foreign art from the 1960s to the present. Look for the "butterfly" windows, and don't miss the view of Töölönlahti from the café. ✉ *Mannerheiminaukio 2* ☎ *09/1733–6501* ⊕ *www.kiasma.fi* ☉ *Tues. 9–5, Wed.–Sun. 10–8:30.*

FodorśChoice
★

10

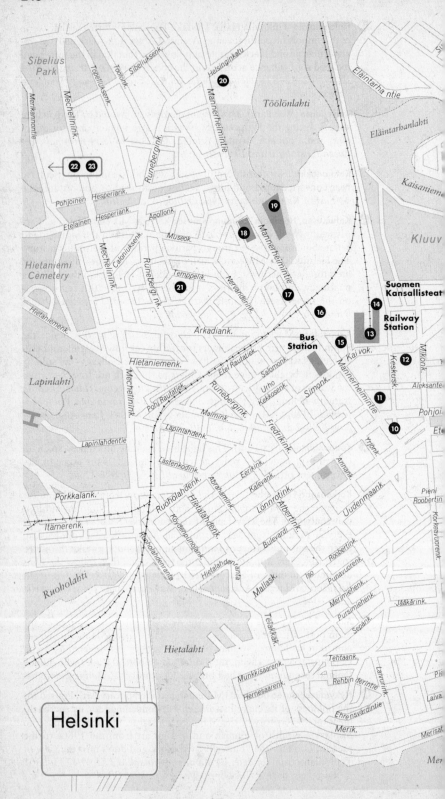

Helsinki

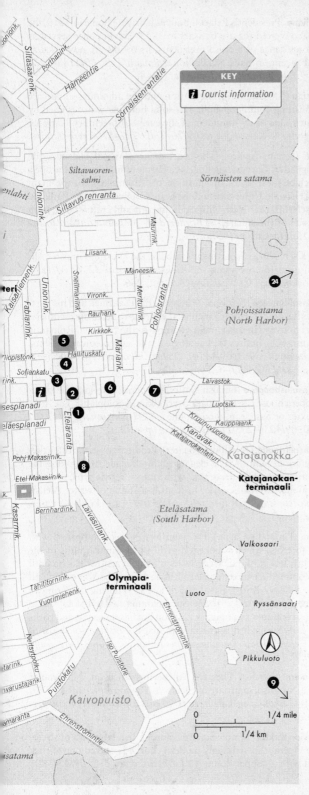

⑥ Presidentinlinna (President's Palace). Built as a private home in 1818, the palace was converted for use by tsars in 1843. Having once served as the official residence of Finnish presidents, its rooms are now used as offices and reception halls. ⊠ *Pohjoisesplanadi 1* ☎ *09/2288–1222* ⊕ *Tours by appointment, Wed. and Sat. 11–4.*

⑬ Rautatieasema (train station). The station and the adjoining square are the city's bustling commuter hub. The solid building was designed by Eliel Saarinen, one of the founders of the early-20th-century National Romantic style. ⊠ *Kaivokatu* ☎ *09/7071; 09/707–5700 reservations.*

★ ④ Senaatintori (Senate Square). The heart of neoclassical Helsinki, the square designed by Carl Ludvig Engel is a harmonious blend of Europe's ancient architectural styles. In addition to **Tuomiokirkko,** the main building of Helsinki University and the State Council Building flank the square. **Kiseleff Bazaar Hall,** with cafés and gift and crafts shops, is on the south side of the square. ⊠ *Bordered by Aleksanterinkatu to the south and Hallituskatu to the north.*

⑪ Stockmann's. This huge department store has the latest in Finnish fashion and is good for browsing. ⊠ *Aleksanterinkatu 52* ☎ *09/1211* ⊕ *www.stockmann.fi* ⊕ *Weekdays 9–9, Sat. 9–6.*

⑱ Suomen Kansallismuseo (National Museum). Eliel Saarinen and his partners blend allusions to Finnish medieval churches and castles with elements of art nouveau in this vintage example of the National Romantic style. The museum houses archaeological and ethnological exhibits. ⊠ *Mannerheimintie 34* ☎ *09/40501* ⊕ *www.nba.fi/NATMUS/Kmeng. html* ⊕ *Tues. and Wed. 11–8, Thurs.–Sun. 11–6.*

⑳ Suomen Kansallisooppera (Finnish National Opera). The splendid state-of-the-art opera house is set in a park overlooking Töölönlahti. The striking white exterior has clean, modern lines. ⊠ *Helsinginkatu 58* ☎ *09/ 4030–2210; 09/4030–2350 tours* ⊕ *www.operafin.fi.*

⑭ Suomen Kansallisteatteri (National Theater). Productions in the three theaters inside are in Finnish. The elegant granite facade overlooking the railway station square is decorated with quirky reliefs typical of the Finnish National Romantic style. In front is a statue of writer Aleksis Kivi. ⊠ *North side of Rautatientori* ☎ *09/1733–1331* ⊕ *www. nationaltheatre.fi.*

★ ⑨ Suomenlinna (Finland's Castle). Frequent ferries link Kauppatori with this island fortress, which was begun in 1748 by Finnish units of the Swedish army. Its six islands were Sweden's shield against Russia until a Swedish commander surrendered to Russia during the War of Finland (1808–19). A heavy British naval attack in 1855, during the Crimean War, damaged the fortress. Today Suomenlinna, a UNESCO World Heritage site, continues as a military garrison but has museums and parks as well. In early summer it is awash with lilacs. ⊠ *Island southeast of harbor* ☎ *09/684–1880* ⊕ *www.suomenlinna.fi* ⊕ *Tours June–Aug., daily at 10:30, 1, and 2:30.*

⑩ Svenska Teatern (Swedish Theater). All performances at this circular theater are in Swedish; many are musicals. ⊠ *Pohjoisesplanadi 2* ☎ *09/ 6162–1411* ⊕ *www.svenskateatern.fi* ⊕ *Box office daily noon–performance time.*

★ ㉑ Temppeliaukion Kirkko (Temple Square Church). In a labyrinth of streets west of the Opera, this strikingly modern church is carved out of rock and topped with a copper dome. ⊠ *Lutherininkatu 3* ☎ *09/494–698*

⊙ *Weekdays 10–8, Sat. 10–6, Sun. noon–1:45 and 3:15–5:45* ⊙ *Closed Tues. 1–2 and during weddings, concerts, and services.*

❺ **Tuomiokirkko** (Lutheran Cathedral). Completed in 1852, the domed cathedral dominates the Senaatintori and serves as a symbol of Helsinki. Organ concerts take place on Sundays at 8 PM June–August. ✉ *Yliopistonkatu 7* ☎ *09/709–2455* ⊙ *June–Aug., Mon.–Sat. 9–6, Sun. noon–4; Sept.–May, Mon.–Sat. 9–6, Sun. noon–6.*

★ ❼ **Uspenskin Katedraali** (Uspenski Cathedral). The redbrick Orthodox cathedral, completed in 1868, looms over the east side of Kauppatori. ✉ *Kanavakatu 1* ☎ *09/634–267* ⊙ *Tues.–Fri. 9:30–4, Sat. 9:30–2, Sun. noon–3.*

⓬ **Valtion Taidemuseo** (Finnish National Gallery). The best traditional Finnish art is housed in this complex, which includes the **Ateneum,** one of three museums organized under the National Gallery umbrella. The museum displays Finnish art from the 18th century to the 1960s, as well as changing shows, and has an excellent bookshop and a café. ✉ *Kaivokatu 2–4* ☎ *09/173–36401* ⊕ *www.fng.fi* ⊙ *Tues. and Fri. 9–6, Wed. and Thurs. 9–8, weekends 11–5.*

❽ **Vanha Kauppahalli** (Old Market Hall). On the western shore of the South Harbor, near the huge ferry dock for boats from Sweden, Poland, and Estonia, the brick market hall is worth a visit for its amazing spreads of meat, fish, and other delights. ✉ *Eteläranta, along the South Harbor* ⊙ *Mon.–Thurs. 8–5, Fri. 8–6, Sat. 8–3.*

Elsewhere in Helsinki

㉓ **Gallen-Kallela Museum.** Akseli Gallen-Kallela (1865–1931), one of Finland's greatest artists, lived in this studio-home, which now displays his heroic paintings and landscapes from the Golden Age of Finnish art. To get to the estate, take Tram 4 in front of the City Sokos department store on Mannerheimintie. From the Munkkiniemi stop transfer to Bus 33, or walk the 2 km (1 mi) through the woods. ✉ *Gallen-Kallelantie 27, Tarvaspää Espoo* ☎ *09/541–3388* ⊕ *www.gallen-kallela.fi* ⊙ *Mid-May–Aug., daily 10–6; Sept.–mid-May, Tues.–Sat. 10–4, Sun. 10–5.*

㉒ **Seurasaaren Ulkomuseo** (Seurasaari Open-Air Museum). Evoking the Finnish countryside within the city, this museum showcases traditional rural architecture and lifestyles on a wooded island. A highlight is the ornate **Karunan Kirkko** (Karuna Church) from 1686. Seurasaari also has a restaurant and several beaches, including a secluded clothing-optional strand. Guided tours in English are conducted at 11:30 AM and 3:30 PM. ✉ *Seurasaari, island 5 km (3 mi) west of city center; Bus 24 from Swedish Theater* ☎ *09/4050–9660 in summer; 09/4050–9574 in winter* ⊕ *www.nba.fi/museums/seuras/seurseng.htm* ⊙ *Museum June–Aug., Mon., Tues., and Thurs.–Sun. 11–5, Wed. 11–7; May 15–31 and Sept. 1–15, weekdays 9–3, weekends 11–5; Sept. 16–30, weekends 11–5.*

Where to Eat

Although Russian restaurants are among the star attractions here, do seek out Finnish specialties—pheasant, reindeer, hare, and grouse—accompanied by wild berries and exotic mushrooms. Some expensive establishments close on Sundays or weekends. For details and price-category information, *see* Eating & Drinking *in* Finland A to Z.

★ **$$$$** ✕ **Alexander Nevski.** In a city famed for fine Russian cuisine, Alexander Nevski has the best. Echoing the Russian-French style of 19th-century

St. Petersburg, the interior is dominated by palm trees and shades of green. Sample the game specialties and *blinis.* ✉ *Pohjoisesplanadi 17* ☎ *09/ 686–9560* ▭ *AE, DC, MC, V* ☾ *No lunch Sun.*

$$$$ ✕ **Savoy.** With its airy, Alvar Aalto–designed dining room overlooking the Esplanade, the Savoy is a frequent choice for business lunches. Unusual combinations include whitefish baked with liver and cabbage and baked pheasant with white turnip, apple, and truffle. ✉ *Eteläesplanadi 14* ☎ *09/684–4020* ▭ *AE, DC, MC, V* ☾ *Closed weekends.*

$$$–$$$$ ✕ **Havis Amanda.** Across the street from the *Havis Amanda* statue, this gracious restaurant, with its classic Scandinavian interior, is a seafood institution. The sophisticated menu offers local fish specialties with Continental accents. ✉ *Pohjoisesplanadi 17* ☎ *09/6869–5660* ▭ *AE, DC, MC, V* ☾ *Closed Sun. Sept.–May.*

$$$–$$$$ ✕ **Sipuli.** In a brick warehouse dating from the late 19th century, Sipuli takes its name from the golden onion-shape cupolas that adorn the Orthodox Uspenski Cathedral nearby. The food is French in style with a Finnish flair; try the fennel soup with forest mushroom ravioli. ✉ *Kanavaranta 3* ☎ *09/622–9280* ▭ *AE, DC, MC, V* ☾ *Closed weekends, except dinner for groups.*

★ $$$ ✕ **Bellevue.** Established in 1917, Bellevue is one of Helsinki's oldest Russian restaurants, in both style and cuisine. Its menu includes such classics as chicken Kiev and lamb shashlik, and innovations like stuffed pheasant in a dark vanilla sauce. ✉ *Rahapajankatu 3* ☎ *09/179–560* ▭ *AE, DC, MC, V* ☾ *No lunch weekends.*

$$–$$$ ✕ **Töölönranta.** Combining contemporary Finnish architecture and a view of Töölö Bay, the light, international cuisine here highlights wok dishes. The patio catches the evening sun. ✉ *Helsinginkatu 56* ☎ *09/ 454–2100* ▭ *AE, DC, MC, V* ☾ *Closed Sun. mid-Sept.–Apr.*

$$–$$$ ✕ **Troikka.** The Troikka takes you back to tsarist times with its plush dining room, paintings, and music. Try the *pelmeny* (small meat dumplings served with sour cream). ✉ *Caloniuksenkatu 3* ☎ *09/445–229* ▭ *AE, DC, MC, V* ☾ *Closed Sun., weekends in July.*

$$ ✕ **Kuu.** For the true character of Helsinki, try simple, friendly, and atmospheric Kuu ("Moon"), which has retained its local character since the 1960s. The menu is homey Finnish fare with monthly themes, such as elk. ✉ *Töölönkatu 27* ☎ *09/2709–0973* ▭ *AE, DC, MC, V.*

$$ ✕ **Maxill.** This café-bar hybrid is popular with the after-work crowd. The menu is light and trendy; try the salad with goat cheese croutons. ✉ *Korkeavuorenkatu 4* ☎ *09/638–873* ▭ *AE, DC, MC, V.*

★ $–$$ ✕ **Kynsilaukka /Garlic.** This cozy yet sophisticated restaurant appeals to the senses with fresh, beautifully prepared food highlighting garlic. Stellar dishes include the garlic cream soup and bouillabaisse; for dessert try the classic crepes with cloudberry sauce. A generous four-course lunch menu and the fact that it's open on holidays help make it a local favorite. ✉ *Fredrikinkatu 22* ☎ *09/651–939* ▭ *AE, DC, MC, V.*

$–$$ ✕ **Ravintola Perho.** This restaurant is associated with Helsinki's culinary school and emphasizes Finnish food; try the fish dishes and a beer from their own microbrewery. ✉ *Mechelininkatu 7* ☎ *09/5807–8600* ▭ *AE, DC, MC, V.*

$ ✕ **Zucchini.** For a vegetarian lunch or just coffee and dessert, Zucchini is a cozy hideaway with quiet music, magazines, and a few sidewalk tables. Pizzas, soups, and salads are all tasty here. ✉ *Fabianinkatu 4* ☎ *09/622–2907* ▭ *DC, MC, V* ☾ *No dinner.*

Where to Stay

Helsinki's hotels have a reputation for being extremely expensive, but this is true only of the very top stratum. Special summer and weekend offers are common. Generous breakfast buffets are nearly always included in the room price. Most hotels cater to business travelers, but standard rooms tend to be small. For details and price-category information, *see* Lodging *in* Finland A to Z.

★ **$$$$** ⊞ **Cumulus Seurahuone.** This hotel across from the train station has rooms that range from sleek and modern to formal and classic with crystal chandeliers and brass bedsteads. The winding staircase is part of its faded charm. The street-side rooms are not always quiet. ⊠ *Kaivokatu 12, 00100* ☎ *09/69141* 🖷 *09/691–4010* ⊕ *www.cumulus.fi* ⌨ *118 rooms* ♻ *Restaurant* ⊟ *AE, DC, MC, V.*

★ **$$$$** ⊞ **Hilton Helsinki Strand.** This waterfront hotel has granite and marble in the lobby and modern designer bedrooms. There is a choice of cuisines—Pamir's elegant offerings of seafood, steak, and game, or the Atrium Plaza for lighter meals. ⊠ *John Stenberginranta 4, 00530* ☎ *09/39351* 🖷 *09/393–5255* ⊕ *www.hilton.com* ⌨ *200 rooms* ♻ *2 restaurants, pool* ⊟ *AE, DC, MC, V.*

★ **$$$$** ⊞ **Hotel Kämp.** Opposite the Esplanade Park stands this splendid turn-of-the-20th-century cultural landmark. Expect the ultimate in luxury and service. ⊠ *Pohjoisesplanadi 29, 00100* ☎ *09/576–1111* 🖷 *09/576–1122* ⊕ *www.luxurycollection.com* ⌨ *179 rooms* ♻ *2 restaurants* ⊟ *AE, DC, MC, V.*

$$$$ ⊞ **Radisson SAS Hesperia Hotel Helsinki.** Built in 1972, the updated hotel remains Finnish with a modern flair. It's just a short stroll from the center of the city and has its own international nightclub. ⊠ *Mannerheimintie 50, 00260* ☎ *09/43101* 🖷 *09/431–0995* ⊕ *www.radisson.com* ⌨ *383 rooms* ♻ *Restaurant, pool* ⊟ *AE, DC, MC, V.*

$$$$ ⊞ **Rivoli Jardin.** The high-class town house is tucked into the heart of Helsinki's shopping and business center. All rooms face the courtyard, which is free of traffic noise. ⊠ *Kasarmikatu 40, 00130* ☎ *09/681–500* 🖷 *09/656–988* ⊕ *www.rivoli.fi* ⌨ *55 rooms* ⊟ *AE, DC, MC, V.*

★ **$$$$** ⊞ **Scandic Hotel Continental Helsinki.** The choice of various diplomats and dignitaries, this hotel has many in-room amenities (fax machines, printers). It's close to Finlandia Hall, the Finnish National Opera, National Museum, and the Museum of Contemporary Art; the restaurant, Olivo, serves Mediterranean dishes and has a separate wine bar. ⊠ *Mannerheimintie 46, 00260* ☎ *09/40551* 🖷 *09/4055–3255* ⊕ *www.scandic-hotels.com* ⌨ *512 rooms* ♻ *2 restaurants, pool* ⊟ *AE, DC, MC, V.*

$$$$ ⊞ **Scandic Hotel Marski.** Opposite Stockmann's department store, the Marski has suites that are the last word in modern luxury, and all rooms are soundproof, shutting out traffic noise. ⊠ *Mannerheimintie 10, 00100* ☎ *09/68061* 🖷 *09/642–377* ⊕ *www.scandic-hotels.com* ⌨ *289 rooms, 6 suites* ♻ *Restaurant* ⊟ *AE, DC, MC, V.*

$$$$ ⊞ **Sokos Hotel Torni.** Be sure to take in the striking views of Helsinki from the Atelier Bar and from the higher floors of the original part of this hotel, built in 1903. Some old-section rooms on the courtyard have high ceilings with original carved-wood details and wooden writing desks. ⊠ *Yrjönkatu 26, 00100* ☎ *09/131–131* 🖷 *09/131–1361* ⊕ *www.sokoshotels.fi* ⌨ *139 with shower, 15 with bath; 9 suites* ♻ *2 restaurants* ⊟ *AE, DC, MC, V.*

$$$ ⊞ **Cumulus Airport Hotel.** Proximity to the airport and a shuttle for the 3¼ km (2 mi) to town are the keys to this hotel. Rooms are small. ⊠ *Robert Huberintie 4, 01510 Vantaa* ☎ *09/4157–7100* 🖷 *09/4157–7101* ⊕ *www.cumulus.fi* ⌨ *260 rooms* ♻ *Restaurant, pool* ⊟ *AE, DC, MC, V.*

$$$ ⊞ **Scandic Hotel Grand Marina.** This renovated early-19th-century customs warehouse sits in the posh Katajanokka Island neighborhood. Friendly service and modern facilities have made the hotel a success.

✉ *Katajanokanlaituri 7, 00160* ☎ *09/16661* 🖷 *09/664–764* ⊕ *www.scandic-hotels.com* ⤷ *462 rooms* ♨ *2 restaurants* ▤ *AE, DC, MC, V.*

$$$ 🏨 **Scandic Hotel Kalastajatorppa Helsinki.** In the posh Munkkiniemi neighborhood by the seaside, this hotel is quiet and luxurious. The best rooms are in the seaside annex, and all are large and airy. Rooms in the main building may be equipped with bath and terrace or with showers only. ✉ *Kalastajatorpantie 1, 00330* ☎ *09/45811* 🖷 *09/45811* ⊕ *www.scandic-hotels.com* ⤷ *235 rooms, 8 suites* ♨ *2 restaurants, 2 pools* ▤ *AE, DC, MC, V.*

$$ 🏨 **Hotel Helka.** Privately owned by the Finnish YWCA, this is a pleasant, affordable alternative to the higher-price chain hotels in Helsinki. Situated in the heart of the city, the Helka is surprisingly quiet, thanks to double windows. Furnishings are in light wood and mixed pastels. The Aurinko restaurant is bright, with an open kitchen, where dishes with an international accent are prepared at reasonable prices; choose from a very good wine selection. ✉ *Pohjoinen Rautatiekatu 23A, 00100* ☎ *09/613–580* 🖷 *09/441–087* ⊕ *www.helka.fi* ⤷ *147 rooms, 3 suites* ♨ *Restaurant* ▤ *AE, DC, MC, V.*

$–$$ 🏨 **Arthur.** A property of the Helsinki YMCA, on a quiet, central street, Arthur is unpretentious and comfortable. ✉ *Vuorikatu 19, 00100* ☎ *09/173–441* 🖷 *09/626–880* ⊕ *www.hotelarthur.fi/international* ⤷ *144 rooms* ♨ *Restaurant* ▤ *AE, DC, MC, V.*

$–$$ 🏨 **Aurora.** About 2 km (1 mi) from the city center, just opposite the Linnanmäki amusement park, the hotel has reasonable prices, cozy rooms, and good facilities. ✉ *Helsinginkatu 50, 00530* ☎ *09/770–100* 🖷 *09/7701–0200* ⤷ *70 rooms* ♨ *Restaurant* ▤ *AE, DC, MC, V.*

$–$$ 🏨 **Marttahotelli.** Run by a century-old women's association, the hotel has small but pleasant rooms. It is a 10-minute walk from the railway station. ✉ *Uudenmaankatu 24, 00120* ☎ *09/618–7400* 🖷 *09/618–7401* ⊕ *www.marttahotelli.fi* ⤷ *44 rooms, 1 suite* ▤ *AE, DC, MC, V.*

$ 🏨 **Academica.** This summer hotel is a standard student dormitory during the school year. Its simple rooms and the impressive exercise facilities make this an excellent value. Rates for rooms in the new section are slightly higher. ✉ *Hietaniemenkatu 14, 00100* ☎ *09/1311–4334* 🖷 *09/441–201* ⊕ *www.hostelacademica.fi* ⤷ *215 rooms* ♨ *Pool* ▤ *AE, DC, MC, V* ⊗ *Closed Sept.–May.*

$ 🏨 **Hotelli Finn.** This small, no-frills hotel in the heart of Helsinki is an inexpensive alternative 10 minutes from the railway station. More expensive rooms have a shower; all have a toilet. Breakfast is provided for a small charge. Book well in advance. ✉ *Kalevankatu 3B, 00100* ☎ *09/684–4360* 🖷 *09/6844–3610* ⊕ *www.hotellifinn.fi* ⤷ *27 rooms* ▤ *MC, V.*

Nightlife & the Arts

The Arts

For a list of events pick up *Helsinki This Week*, available in hotels and tourist offices and on the Web at www.helsinkithisweek.net. Published every two months, *Helsinki Happens* also lists events and provides more detailed cultural background. Tickets to concerts and sports events are available from **Lippupalvelu** (☎ 0600–10800, €1 per call plus a local call charge; 3589/6138–6246 from abroad ⊕ www.lippupalvelu.fi). Call **Tiketti** (✉ Forum shopping center, Kukontori ☎ 0600/11616 €0.66, plus a local call charge ⊕ www.tiketti.fi) for tickets to music shows and other events.

CONCERTS **Finlandiatalo** (Finlandia Hall; ✉ Karamzininkatu 4 ☎ 09/402–4246) is the home of the Helsinki Philharmonic. **Savoy Theater** (✉ Kasarminkatu 46–48 ☎ 09/169–3703) presents ballet and world music. The **Sibelius Academy** (✉ Pohjois Rautatiekatu 9 ☎ 09/405–4662) hosts a program of classical music, including orchestral, choral, chamber music, and jazz, by guest artists and students. **Temppeliaukio Kirkko** (Temppeliaukion Church; ✉ Lutherinkatu 3 ☎ 09/494–698) is a favorite venue for choral and chamber music.

FESTIVALS The **Helsinki Festival** (✉ Lasipalatsi, Mannerheimintie 22–24, 00100 Helsinki ☎ 09/6126–5100 ⊟ 09/6126–5161 ⊕ www.helsinkifestival. fi), one of the largest in the Nordic region, presents music, dance, and poetry performances and art exhibits during two weeks in August and September.

THEATER Summertime productions (in Finnish or Swedish) in such bucolic settings as Suomenlinna Island, Keskuspuisto Park, Mustikkamaa Island, and the Rowing Stadium (operettas) make enjoyable entertainment. Check *Helsinki This Week* for listings. Also try the splendid **Suomen Kansallisooppera** (Finnish National Opera; ✉ Helsinginkatu 58 ☎ 09/4030–2211).

Nightlife

BARS & LOUNGES *Helsinki This Week* lists all the pubs and clubs. **Cantina West** (✉ Kasarmikatu 23 ☎ 09/622–0900) is a Tex-Mex bar and restaurant with live music Thursday–Saturday. **Kaarle XII** (✉ Kasarmikatu 40 ☎ 09/612–9990) is in one of Helsinki's striking Jugendstil buildings: the young and beautiful are drawn here for dancing on weekends. Founded in 1867, **Kappeli** (✉ Eteläesplanadi 1 ☎ 09/179–242) brews its own beer. At **Storyville** (✉ Museokatu 8 ☎ 09/408–007), jazz musicians complement New Orleans–style cuisine.

Molly Malone's (✉ Kaisaniemenkatu 1C ☎ 09/5766–7500) is a popular Irish pub. **O'Malley's** (✉ Sokos Hotel Torni, Yrjönkatu 26 ☎ 09/1311–3459) is the oldest Irish pub in Helsinki. **Angleterre** (✉ Fredrikinkatu 47 ☎ 09/647–371) is a cozy English ale house run by a cellar master and frequented by the Helsinki professional crowd. The **William K bars** (✉ Annankatu 3 ☎ 09/680–2562 ✉ Mannerheimintie 72 ☎ 09/409–484 ✉ Fredrikinkatu 65 ☎ 09/693–1427 ✉ Fleminginkatu 6 ☎ 09/821–816) around the city center have an excellent selection of European ales. **Belge Bar & Bistro** (✉ Kluuvikatu 5 ☎ 09/622–9260) serves the best of Belgian beers and light fare.

NIGHTCLUBS Helsinki's largest and most famous club is the **Hesperia Nightclub** (✉ Radisson SAS Hotel Hesperia, Mannerheimintie 50 ☎ 09/43101). **Kaivohuone** (✉ Kaivopuisto/Well Park ☎ 09/684–1530) is a summertime favorite in an attractive park.

Shopping

Department Stores

Stockmann's (✉ Aleksanterinkatu 52 ☎ 09/1211 ⊕ www.stockmann. fi) was built in 1853, and is stocked to the gills with the latest Finnish and international fashions.

Markets

In good weather you'll find a large selection of goods at the **Hietalahti Flea Market** (✉ Hietalahti at west end of Bulevardi). **Kauppatori** (✉ Market Sq.), next to the South Harbor, is an absolute must year-round.

Shopping Districts

Helsinki's prime shopping districts run along **Pohjoisesplanadi** (North Esplanade) and **Aleksanterinkatu** in the city center. Along **Pohjoisesplanadi** and **Eteläesplanadi** (bordering the gardens), you'll find Finland's design houses. Look for antiques shops in the **Kruununhaka** (behind Senate Sq.) neighborhood.

Specialty Shops

Forum (✉ Mannerheimintie 20 ☎ 09/642–210) is a modern, multistory shopping mall carrying clothing, gifts, books, and toys. The **Kiseleff Bazaar Hall** (✉ Aleksanterinkatu 22–28) has shops specializing in handicrafts, toys, knitwear, and children's items. You can shop until 10 PM in stores along the **Tunneli** (✉ underneath the train station).

Aarikka (✉ Pohjoisesplanadi 27 ☎ 09/652–277 ✉ Eteläesplanadi 8 ☎ 09/175–462) offers wooden jewelry, toys, and gifts. **Artek** (✉ Eteläesplanadi 18 ☎ 09/613–250) is known for its Alvar Aalto–designed furniture and ceramics. **Designor** (✉ Pohjoisesplanadi 25 ☎ 0204/393–501) sells household products by Arabia, Hackman, and Iittala. **Kalevala Koru** (✉ Unioninkatu 25 ☎ 09/171–520) specializes in jewelry based on ancient Finnish designs; most jewelers also sell a selection of the designs. **Union Design** (✉ Eteläranta 14, inner courtyard ☎ 09/6220–0333) is an atelier workshop of goldsmiths, silversmiths, and jewelers emphasizing limited series and unique pieces; it displays top-notch Finnish design talent. **Marimekko** (✉ Pohjoisesplanadi 31 ☎ 09/6860–2411 ✉ Pohjoisesplanadi 2 ☎ 09/622–2317 ✉ Eteläesplanadi 14 ☎ 09/170–704 ✉ Forum shopping center ☎ 09/694–1498) sells women's clothing, household items, and gifts made from its textiles. **Pentik** (✉ Mannerheimintie 5B ☎ 09/6124–0795) has tasteful pottery and household goods.

Side Trip

Hvitträsk, a dramatic and romantic log villa designed by Eliel Saarinen and his partners Herman Gesellius and Armas Lindgren, was their shared home and studio in the early 20th century and is now a museum. Art exhibitions are also held here. This forested estate 30 km (19 mi) west of Helsinki has exhibits, a restaurant, a café, a shop, and a lakeside sauna with swimming. Bus 166 will take you from Helsinki's main bus station, or take the train to Luoma and follow the signs, about 2 km (1 mi), or to Masala and take a taxi. ✉ *Luoma, Kirkkonummi* ☎ *09/4050–9630* ⊙ *June–Aug., daily 10–7; Sept., Oct., Apr., and May, daily 11–6; Nov.–Mar., Tues.–Sun. 11–5.*

Helsinki Essentials

AIRPORTS & TRANSFERS

All international flights arrive at Helsinki–Vantaa Airport.

🛈 **Helsinki-Vantaa Airport** ✉ Tuusulan Rte. ☎ 0200/14636 information ⊕ www.helsinki-vantaa.fi.

TRANSFERS   Finnair buses make the trip between Helsinki–Vantaa Airport and the city center two to three times an hour, stopping behind the Inter-Continental Helsinki and at the Finnair Terminal next to the train station. The ride takes about 35 minutes and costs €5. A local bus service (Buses 615, 617) will also take you to the train station and costs €3 for the 40-minute ride. Expect to pay between €20 and €30 for a taxi into the city center. Group taxi services such as Yellow Line take one to four people for a set fee of €18 within the Helsinki area; information is available at service desks in the arrival halls.

🛈 **Yellow Line** ☎ 0600/555-555.

BOAT & FERRY TRAVEL

Ships arriving from Rostock, Germany, and Stockholm dock at Katajanokanlaituri. Finnjet-Silja makes the trip June 3–September 11; Viking Line makes the trip year-round. Silja Line ships from Stockholm, Sweden; it arrives at Olympialaituri.

In summer regular boat service links the South Harbor Kauppatori (Market Square) with the Suomenlinna and Korkeasaari, site of Helsinki Zoo. Schedules and prices are listed on signs at the harbor.

🚢 **Finnjet-Silja** ✉ Mannerheimintie 2 ☎ 09/18–041. **Katajanokanlaituri** ✉ east side of South Harbor. **Olympialaituri** ✉ west side of South Harbor. **Silja Line** ✉ Mannerheimintie 2 ☎ 09/18–041. **Viking Line** ✉ Mannerheimintie 14 ☎ 09/12351.

BUS TRAVEL TO & FROM HELSINKI

The main long-distance bus station is Linja-autoasema (bus station). Many local buses arrive and depart from Rautatientori (Railway Station Square). For information on long-distance transport, call Matka Huolto/ Helsingin Linja-autoasema, which charges €1.15 for the call in addition to local charges.

🚌 **Matka Huolto/Helsingin Linja-autoasema** ✉ off Mannerheimintie, between Salomonkatu and Simonkatu ☎ 0200–4000 ⊕ www.matkahuolto.fi.

CONSULATES

🏛 Australia ✉ Museokatu 25B, 00100 ☎ 09/447–503.
🏛 New Zealand **Honorary Consul General of New Zealand, c/o KohdematkatKaleva** ✉ Ruoholahdenkatu 23, 00180 ☎ 020/561–5328.

EMERGENCIES

🚑 Doctors & Dentists **Dentist** ☎ 09/612–2660. **Doctor** ☎ 10023.
🚑 Emergency Services **Ambulance** ☎ 112. **Police** ☎ 112 or 10022.
🚑 24-hour Pharmacies **Yliopiston Apteekki** (University Pharmacy) ✉ Mannerheimintie 96 ☎ 0203/20200.

ENGLISH-LANGUAGE MEDIA

📚 Bookstores **Akateeminen Kirjakauppa** (Academic Bookstore) ✉ Pohjoisesplanadi 39 ☎ 09/12141. **Suomalainen Kirjakauppa** (Finnish Bookstore) ✉ Aleksanterinkatu 23 ☎ 09/651–855.

SUBWAY TRAVEL

Helsinki's subway (Metro) line runs from Ruoholahti, west of the city center, to Mellunmäki and Vuosaari, in the eastern suburbs. It operates Monday–Saturday 5:33 AM–11:23 PM, Sunday 6:38 AM–11:23 PM.

TAXIS

Taxis are all marked TAKSI. Meters start at €4, the fare rising on a per-kilometer basis and depending on the number of passengers and the time of day. A listing of all taxi companies appears in the white pages; they charge from the point of dispatch. The main phone number for taxi dispatch is listed below.

🚕 **Taxi dispatch** ☎ 0100–0700.

TOURS

BOAT TOURS J. L. Runeberg has all-day boat tours to the charming old wooden town of Porvoo, with departures at 10 AM several days a week mid-May to early September.

🚢 Fees & Schedules **J. L. Runeberg** ✉ departs from Kauppatori ☎ 019/524-3331 ⊕ www.msjlruneberg.fi.

GUIDED TOURS Guided tours are offered through Helsinki Expert. You can book one of their scheduled tours at the Helsinki City Tourist Office, or call them directly.

🚌 Fees & Schedules **Helsinki Expert** ✉ Lönnrotinkatu 7B, 00120 Helsinki ☎ 09/ 2288-1600 for scheduled city sightseeing tours; 09/2288-1222 for individualized tours; 0600-02288, €0.78 per minute plus local charge, for various tours, also outside Helsinki ⊕ www.helsinkiexpert.fi.

TRAIN TRAVEL

Helsinki's main rail gateway is the Rautatieasema (train station).

🚇 **Rautatieasema** ⊠ city center, off Kaivokatu ☎ 09/307-20902 information.

TRANSPORTATION AROUND HELSINKI

The center of Helsinki is compact and best explored on foot. If you want to use public transportation, your best buy is the Helsinki Kortti (Helsinki Card), which offers unlimited travel on city public transportation, free entry to many museums, a free sightseeing tour, and other discounts. It's available for one, two, or three days. You can buy it (for €24, €34, and €42, respectively) at some hotels and travel agencies, Stockmann's department store, the Hotel Booking Centre, some R-kiosks in the city center, and the Helsinki City Tourist Office. The Helsinki City Transport tourist ticket entitles you to unlimited travel on all buses, trams, subways, and local trains in Helsinki. It is valid for one, three, or five days and costs €4.80, €9.60, or €14.40. For timetable and ticket information for Helsinki's comprehensive and generally efficient public transport system, call the 24-hour line.

Tickets for buses, streetcars, local trains, and the subway may be purchased at subway stations, R-kiosks, and shops displaying the Helsinki city transport logo (two curving black arrows on a yellow background). Standard single tickets valid on all transport, and permitting transfers within the whole network for within an hour of the time stamped on the ticket, cost €2 and can be bought on trams and buses. Single tickets bought beforehand, at the City Transport office in the railway station tunnel or at one of the many R-kiosk shops, for example, cost €1.70. A tram-only ticket without a transfer costs €1.70, €1.20 if bought ahead of time. A 10-trip ticket sold at R-kiosks costs €15.50. Most of Helsinki's major points of interest, from Kauppatori to the Opera House, are along the 3T tram line; the Helsinki City Tourist Office distributes a free pamphlet called "Helsinki Sightseeing: 3T."

🚇 **Transportation information line** ☎ 0100-111, €0.34 plus local charge; weekdays 7-7, weekends 9-5.

TRAVEL AGENCIES

🚇 Local Agents **Finland Travel Bureau** (Suomen Matkatoimisto) ⊠ Kaivokatu 10A, PL 319, 00101 Helsinki ☎ 09/18261.

VISITOR INFORMATION

🚇 **Helsinki City Tourist Office** ⊠ Pohjoisesplanadi 19 ☎ 09/169-3757 🖷 09/169-3839 ⊕ www.hel.fi. **The Finnish Tourist Board Tourist Information Office** ⊠ Eteläesplanadi 4 ☎ 09/4176-9300 🖷 09/4176-9301 ⊕ www.mek.fi.

SOUTH COAST

A magical world of 30,000 islands stretches along Finland's coastline, forming a magnificent archipelago in the Gulf of Finland and the Baltic. On the coast, Turku, the former Finnish capital, was the main gateway through which cultural influences reached Finland over the centuries. Westward from Turku lies the rugged and fascinating Åland Islands group, an autonomous province. Many of Finland's oldest towns, chartered by Swedish kings, lie in the southwest—hence the predominance of the Swedish language here. It is a region of flat, often mist-soaked rural farmland and villages of picturesque, traditional wooden houses.

Snappertuna

Snappertuna, 70 km (43 mi) west of Helsinki, is a farming town with a proud hilltop church, a charming homestead museum, and a castle set in a small dale. The handsome, restored ruin of **Raaseporin Linna** (Raseborg Castle) is believed to date from the 12th century. In summer, concerts, dramas, and old-time market fairs are staged here. Guided tours are arranged by the local tourist office (☎ 019/278–6540). ⊠ *Keskuskatu 90* ☎ *019/234–015* ☾ *May and Aug. 16–Aug. 31, daily 10–5; June–Aug. 15, daily 10–8; Sept., weekends 10–5.*

Ekenäs (Tammisaari)

Tammisaari, more commonly known by its Swedish name, Ekenäs, has a colorful Old Quarter, 18th- and 19th-century buildings, and a lively marina. In summer the sun glints off the water and marine traffic is at its peak. The **Tammisaaren Museo** (Tammisaari Museum) is the provincial museum of western Uusimaa and provides a taste of the region's culture and history. ⊠ *Kustaa Vaasan katu 11* ☎ *019/263–3161 or 019/263–2240* ☾ *May 20–Aug. 17, daily 11–5; Sept.–May 19, Tues.–Thurs. 4–7 PM, Fri.–Sun. noon–4.*

$ ⊞ **Ekenäs Stadshotell and Restaurant.** This modern, airy hotel is set amid fine lawns and gardens right in the heart of Ekenäs. Some rooms have private balconies, and all have wide windows and comfortable modern furnishings. ⊠ *Pohjoinen Rantakatu 1, 10600 Tammisaari* ☎ *019/241–3131* 🖶 *019/246–1550* ⊕ *www.stadshotell.nu* 🛏 *16 rooms, 2 suites* ⚅ *Restaurant, pool* 🖃 *AE, DC, MC, V.*

Hanko

In the coastal town of Hanko (Hangö), you'll find long stretches of beach—about 30 km (19 mi) in total—and some of the most fanciful private homes in Finland, their porches edged with gingerbread iron- and woodwork, and whimsical towers sprouting from their roofs. Hanko is also a popular sailing center.

Fortified in the 18th century, Hanko lost its defenses to the Russians in 1854, during the Crimean War. Later Hanko became a popular spa town for Russians, then the port from which more than 300,000 Finns emigrated to North America between 1880 and 1930.

Turku

Founded at the beginning of the 13th century, Turku is the nation's oldest city and was the original capital of Finland. The city has a long history as a commercial and intellectual center; the site of the first Finnish university, it now has two major universities, the Finnish University of Turku and the Swedish-speaking Åbo Akademi. With a population of more than 170,000, Turku is the fifth-largest city in Finland; its significant commercial harbor is active year-round and is a departure point for daily ferries to Stockholm and the beautiful Åland archipelago.

Known jointly as **Aboa Vetus/Ars Nova,** the Museum of Archaeology and History and the Museum of Contemporary Art exhibit excavated medieval archaeological remains along with the modern-art collection of the former Villa von Rettig Museum. Look for Picasso's *Swordsman* as well as works by Auguste Herbin (1882–1960) and Max Ernst (1891–1976). ⊠ *Itäinen Rantakatu 4–6* ☎ *02/250–0552* ⊕ *www. aboavetusarsnova.fi* ☾ *Jan.–mid-Apr. and late Sept.–Nov., Thurs.–Sun. 11–7; Mid-Apr.–late Sept., daily 11–7; Dec., weekends 11–7* ☾ *Closed Dec. 15–Jan. 1.*

The **Luostarinmäen Käsityöläismuseo** (Luostarinmäki Handicrafts Museum) is a collection of wooden houses and buildings containing shops and workshops where traditional crafts are demonstrated and sold. ⊠ *Vartiovuorenkatu 4* ☎ *02/262–0350* ⊕ *www.turku.fi/museo* ☾ *Mid-Apr.–mid-Sept., daily 10–6; mid-Sept.–mid-Apr., Tues.–Sun. 10–3.*

Where the Aura flows into the sea stands **Turun Linna** (Turku Castle), one of the city's most important historical monuments. The oldest part of the fortress was built at the end of the 13th century, and the newer part dates from the 16th century. The vaulted chambers evoke a sense of the domestic lives of the Swedish royals. A good gift shop and a pleasant café are on the castle grounds. ⊠ *Linnankatu 80* ☎ *02/262–0300* ⊕ *www.turku.fi/museo/english/castle.htm* ۞ *Mid-Apr.–mid-Sept., daily 10–6; mid-Sept.–mid-Apr., Tues.–Sun. 10–3.*

The **Turun Taidemuseo** (Turku Art Museum) holds some of Finland's most famous paintings, including works by Akseli Gallen-Kallela, and a broad selection of turn-of-the-20th-century Finnish art and contemporary works. After extensive renovation, the museum is scheduled to return to its traditional site on the Puolalanmäki hill in time to celebrate its centenary in 2004. ⊠ *Puolalanmäki* ☎ *02/274-7570* ⊕ *www. turuntaidemuseo.fi* ۞ *June–Aug., Tues.–Thurs. 11–7, Fri.–Sun. 10–4; Sept.–May, Tues.–Thurs. 11–6, Fri.–Sun. 10–4.*

The 700-year-old **Turun Tuomiokirkko** (Turku Cathedral) remains the seat of the archbishop of Finland. Although it was partially gutted by fire in 1827, the cathedral has been completely restored. The cathedral museum includes a collection of medieval church vestments, silver chalices, and wood sculptures. ⊠ *Turun Tuomiokirkko* ☎ *02/261-7100* ⊕ *www.turunsrk.fi* ۞ *Mid-Apr.–mid-Sept., daily 9–8; mid-Sept.–mid-Apr., daily 9–7.*

$$–$$$ ✕ **Brahen Kellari.** This cellar restaurant near the main square has excellent grilled salmon and risottos, along with a diverse selection of wines. ⊠ *Puolalankatu 1* ☎ *02/232–5400* ▤ *AE, DC, MC, V.*

$$–$$$ ✕ **Suomalainen Pohja.** Next to the Turku Art Museum, this Finnish restaurant has a splendid view of an adjacent park. Seafood, poultry, and game dishes are good here; try noisettes of reindeer. ⊠ *Aurakatu 24* ☎ *02/251–2000* ▤ *AE, DC, MC, V* ۞ *Closed weekends.*

$$$–$$$$ ▣ **Park Hotel.** The castlelike Park Hotel in the heart of Turku is one of Finland's most unusual lodgings. Rooms have high ceilings and antique furniture. Visit the hotel Web site for a slide show displaying individual rooms. ⊠ *Rauhankatu 1, 20100 Turku* ☎ *02/273–2555* 🖷 *02/ 251–9696* ⊕ *www.parkhotelturku.fi* ⤶ *19 rooms* ᗡ *Restaurant* ▤ *AE, DC, MC, V.*

South Coast Essentials

AIR TRAVEL
Turku Airport is about 7 km (4½ mi) from the city center. Finnair flies to Helsinki, Mariehamn, and Stockholm.

BOAT & FERRY TRAVEL
Passenger-car ferries depart daily from Turku's harbor for Stockholm and Åland. Contact Silja Line or Viking Line for details and timetables. Their services are similar, although Viking is known for being more budget-oriented.

🗗 **Silja Line** ☎ 09/18–041 🖷 09/180–4402 ⊕ www.silja.fi. **Viking Line** ☎ 09/12351 🖷 09/647–075 ⊕ www.vikingline.fi.

BUS TRAVEL
Regular daily bus services run between Helsinki and Turku. The trip takes about 2½ hours. Turku offers a 24-hour Tourist Ticket (€4.50) for unlimited travel on local public buses; it can be purchased on board.

CAR TRAVEL

The main route between Helsinki and Turku is fast and normally traffic-free. A parallel, more picturesque route to the south takes you at a leisurely pace through the smaller towns closer to the coast.

TOURS

Turku TouRing offers area tours.

🛈 Fees & Schedules **Turku TouRing/City Tourist Information Office** ☒ Aurakatu 4, 20100 Turku ☎ 02/262-7444 🖷 02/262-7674 ⊕ www.turku.fi/turkutouring.

TRAIN TRAVEL

Turku is served by fast train services to Helsinki and Tampere several times a day. The Pendolino high-speed train also operates between Helsinki and Turku, cutting travel time to less than two hours.

VISITOR INFORMATION

🛈 **Hanko Tourist Information Office** ☐ Box 14, 5 Raatihuoneentori, 10901 Hanko ☎ 019/220-3411 🖷 019/220-3261. **Turku** Turku TouRing/City Tourist Information Office ☒ Aurakatu 4, 20100 ☎ 02/262-7444 🖷 02/233-7673.

THE LAKELANDS

In southeastern and central Finland, the light has a softness that seems to brush the forests, lakes, and islands, changing the landscape throughout the day. For centuries this beautiful region was a much-contested buffer between the warring empires of Sweden and Russia. The Finns of the Lakelands prevailed by sheer *sisu* (guts), and now their descendants thrive amid the rough beauty of the terrain.

Savonlinna

The center of Savonlinna is a series of islands linked by bridges. An open-air market flourishes alongside the main quay. Savonlinna was once the hub of the passenger fleet serving Saimaa, the largest lake system in Europe. Now cruise boats dominate lake traffic.

★ First built in 1475 to protect Finland's eastern border, the castle **Olavinlinna** rises majestically out of the lake, retaining its medieval character. It is one of Scandinavia's best-preserved historic monuments and houses two museums, one that displays items from the castle and another with icons and other Russian Orthodox items both from Finland and Russia. The **Savonlinna Opera Festival** (Opera Ticket Office ☒ Olavinkatu 27, 57130 Savonlinna ☎ 015/476-750 🖷 015/476-7540) is held in the courtyard each July. Contact the Opera Ticket Office well in advance for tickets. ☒ *10-min walk southeast from quay* ☎ *015/531-164* ⊕ *www.operafestival.fi* ☉ *June–mid-Aug., daily 10–5; mid-Aug.–May, daily 10–3.*

The **Savonlinnan maakunta museo** (Savonlinna Provincial Museum) is the home of the 19th-century steam schooners SS *Salama,* SS *Mikko,* and SS *Savonlinna.* ☒ *Riihisaari Island, near Olavinlinna* ☎ *015/571-4712* ⊕ *www.savonlinna.fi/sivistys/museo* ☉ *Mid-Aug.–June, Tues.–Sun. 11–5; July–mid-Aug., daily 11–6; boats mid-May–mid-Aug. during museum hrs.*

$$–$$$ ✕ **Majakka.** Centrally located, Majakka serves Finnish home cooking in a friendly space. Try the pepper steak in cream sauce. Reservations are essential during festival season. ☒ *Satamakatu 11* ☎ *015/531-456* 🖃 *AE, DC, MC, V.*

$$ ✕ **Paviljonki.** An affiliate of the Savonlinna restaurant school, this convenient spot just 1 km (½ mi) west of the city serves classic Finnish dishes. ☒ *Rajalahdenkatu 4* ☎ *015/574-9303* 🖃 *DC, MC, V.*

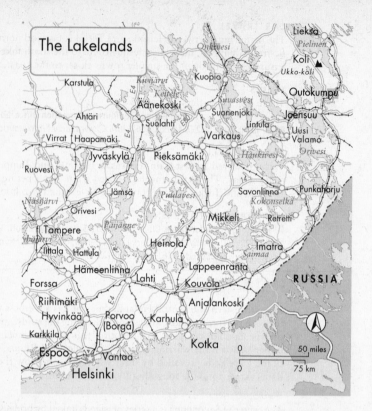

The Lakelands

$$–$$$$ ▣ **Seurahuone.** In this hotel near the market and passenger harbor, rooms are small but modern. The restaurant moves into the open air in summer. ✉ *Kauppatori 4–6, 57130* ☎ *015/5731* 🖶 *015/273–918* ⊕ *www. savonhotellit.fi* ⮐ *84 rooms* ♨ *Restaurant* ▭ *AE, DC, MC, V.*

$$$ ▣ **Spa Hotel Casino.** This hotel has a bucolic lakeside setting on an island linked by a pedestrian bridge to the center of town. Rooms are basic with brown cork floors and simple furnishings; all but one have a balcony. ✉ *Kylpylaitoksentie, Kasinosaari, 57130* ☎ *015/73950* 🖶 *015/ 272–524* ⊕ *www.lomaliitto.fi* ⮐ *80 rooms* ♨ *Restaurant, pool* ▭ *AE, DC, MC, V.*

Punkaharju

This breathtaking ridge of pine-covered rocks predates the Ice Age. Sometimes narrowing to only 25 feet, it rises out of the water to separate the lakes on either side.

Take an excursion (by boat or bus) to **Taidekeskus Retretti** (Retretti Art Center), the largest privately owned art center in Scandinavia, to see changing exhibits, multimedia programs, and children's events. ✉ *Just south of Punkaharju* ☎ *015/775–2200* 🖶 *015/644–314* ⊕ *www.retretti.fi* 🎟 *€15* ◷ *June and Aug., daily 10–5; July, daily 10–6.*

The nearby **Lusto–Suomen Metsämuseo ja Metsätietokeskus** (Lusto Finnish Forest Museum) has displays on every aspect of forestry, from the industrial to the artistic, and all sides of Finland's close relationship with its most abundant natural resource, including demonstrations and theme days. Make an appointment for a guided tour. ✉ *Lustontie 1, 58450, Punkaharju* ☎ *015/345–100* ⊕ *www.lusto.fi* ◷ *Jan.–Apr. and Oct.–Dec., Tues.–Sun. 10–5; May and Sept., daily 10–5; June–Aug., daily 10–7.*

$$–$$$ 🏨 **Punkaharju National Hotel.** Near the Retretti Art Center, this building was constructed as a gamekeeper's lodge for Tsar Nicholas I in 1845 but has since been enlarged and restored. Now it's a restful spot for a meal or an overnight visit. ⊠ *Punkaharju 2, 58450* ☎ *015/739–611* 🖶 *015/441–784* ⊕ *www.lomaliitto.fi/valtionhotelli* ⤳ *24 rooms* ♨ *Restaurant* ⊟ *AE, DC, MC, V.*

Kuopio

The 11½-hour boat trip from Savonlinna to Kuopio may be the best opportunity you'll get to appreciate the soul of the Finnish Lakelands. Meals are available on board. The boat arrives at Kuopio's passenger harbor, where you'll find a small evening market daily from 3 to 10.

★ Kuopio's tourist office is close to the **Tori** (marketplace), one of Finland's most colorful outdoor markets, which sells produce, flowers, handicrafts, and the Finnish market version of fast food: sausages and fried fish served with potatoes. Try the regional specialty, *kalakukko,* a fish and bacon pie in a rye crust. ⊠ *City center* ⊙ *May–Sept., weekdays 7–5, Sat. 7–3; Oct.–Apr., Mon.–Sat. 7–3.*

The **Ortodoksinen Kirkkomuseo** (Orthodox Church Museum) has an unusual collection of religious art from the monasteries of Karelia (the eastern province of Finland, part of which is now in Russia). ⊠ *Karjalankatu 1* ☎ *017/287–2244* ⊕ *www.ort.fi/kirkkomuseo* ⊙ *May, June, and Aug., Tues.–Sun. 10–4; July, Tues.–Sun. 11–5; Sept.–Apr., weekdays noon–3, weekends noon–5.*

Puijo Näkötorni (Puijo Tower), an observation and communications tower, is best visited at sunset, when the lakes shimmer with reflected light. It has two observation decks and a revolving restaurant on top, from which you can enjoy the views. ⊠ *3 km (2 mi) northwest of Kuopio* ☎ *017/255–5250* ⊙ *May–Aug., Mon.–Sat. 9–10, Sun. 1–8.*

Valamon Luostari (Valamo Monastery) in Heinävesi, between Varkaus and Joensuu, is a center for Orthodox religious and cultural life in Finland. Precious 18th-century icons and other sacred objects are housed in the main church and in the icon conservation center. On the grounds are a café-restaurant, hotel, and hostel accommodations. Guided tours are offered daily June through August, and at other times of year by appointment. ⊠ *Valamontie 42* ☎ *017/570–111; 017/570–1504 hotel reservations* 🖶 *017/570–1510* ⊕ *www.valamo.fi* ⊙ *Oct.–Feb., daily 8 AM–9 PM; Mar.–Sept., daily 7 AM–9 PM.*

$$–$$$ ✕ **Musta Lammas.** Finnish dishes are served in this former beer cellar. The menu is based on classic Finnish ingredients with interesting herb accents. ⊠ *Satamakatu 4* ☎ *017/581–0458* ⊟ *AE, DC, MC, V* ⊙ *Closed Sun.*

$$ ✕ **Freeport Sampo.** The specialty here is whitefish. The restaurant is down-to-earth and lively, and conveniently in the town center. ⊠ *Kauppakatu 13* ☎ *017/581–0458* ⊟ *AE, DC, MC, V.*

$$$ 🏨 **Scandic Hotel Kuopio.** The best equipped of local hotels, the Scandic has all the advantages of a lakefront location while being close to the center of town. Rooms are spacious by European standards, with parquet floors. ⊠ *Satamakatu 1, 70100* ☎ *017/195–111* 🖶 *017/195–170* ⊕ *www.scandic-hotels.com* ⤳ *134 rooms* ♨ *Pool* ⊟ *AE, DC, MC, V.*

$$ 🏨 **Hotel-Spa Rauhalahti.** Sports-oriented travelers and families flock to this high-energy hotel. Close to the lakeshore and 5 km (3 mi) from the town center, Rauhalahti offers lively activities and conveniences for all ages and interests. ⊠ *Katiskaniementie 8, 70700* ☎ *017/473–111* 🖶 *017/473–470* ⊕ *www.rauhalahti.com* ⤳ *106 rooms, 20 apartments, 26 hostel rooms* ♨ *3 restaurants* ⊟ *AE, DC, MC, V.*

Tampere

Cotton and textile manufacturers put Tampere on the map as a traditional center of industry, but the city is now known for its high-tech companies and large universities. The mobile-phone giant Nokia got its start in a small city of the same name nearby; don't be surprised to see many of the locals strolling down Tampere's compact main street, Hämeenkatu, with a *kännykä* ("little hand," or cell phone) in use. Tampere's 200,000 inhabitants also nurture an unusually sophisticated cultural environment, with the international festivals of short film (March) and theater (August) among the most popular offerings.

From about the year 1000 AD, this part of Finland was a base from which traders and hunters set out on their expeditions to the north. It was not until 1779 that a Swedish king, Gustav III, founded Tampere. A Scotsman by the name of James Finlayson came to the city in 1882 and established a factory for spinning cotton. The firm of Finlayson is still one of the country's large industrial enterprises.

An isthmus, little more than 1 km (½ mi) wide at its narrowest point, separates the lakes Näsijärvi and Pyhäjärvi, and at one spot the waters of one rush through to the other down the Tammerkoski Rapids. Their natural beauty has been preserved despite the factories on either bank, and the distinctive public buildings of the city grouped around them add to the overall effect.

The **Amurin Työläismuseokortteli** (Amuri Museum of Workers' Housing) consists of more than 30 apartments in a collection of wooden houses, plus a sauna, a bakery, a haberdashery, and more from the 1880s to the 1970s. Its café has garden seating in summer. ⊠ *Makasiininkatu 12* ☎ *03/3146–6690* ⊕ *www.tampere.fi/amuri* ☉ *Mid-May–mid-Sept., Tues.–Sun. 10–6.*

On the east side of town, the modern **Kalevan Kirkko** (Kaleva Church) is a soaring monument to light and space designed by Reima (1923–93) and Raili (b. 1926) Pietilä, the famous architect couple who also designed the Tampere city library. ⊠ *Liisanpuisto 1* ☉ *May–Aug., daily 9–6; Sept.–Apr., daily 11–3.*

The **Lenin Museo** (Lenin Museum) occupies the hall where Lenin and Stalin first met; memorabilia and temporary exhibits document the life of Lenin and the Russian Revolution. ⊠ *Hämeenpuisto 28, 3rd fl.* ☎ *03/ 276–8100* ⊕ *www.tampere.fi/culture/lenin* ☉ *Weekdays 9–6, weekends 11–4.*

The **Museokeskus Vapriikki** (Museum Centre Vapriikki) has 700,000 pieces that illustrate the city's role in Finnish history. Housed in a former factory complex that dates from the 1880s, the permanent exhibit focuses on local history, while other displays cover archaeological finds and modern art. ⊠ *Veturiaukio 4* ☎ *03/3146–6966* ⊕ *www.tampere. fi/vapriikki* ☉ *Tues., Thurs.–Sun. 10–6, Wed. 11–8.*

Among Reima Pietilä's many unusual structures in Tampere is the **Tampere pääkirjasto** (Tampere Central Library), nicknamed "metso" (wood grouse) for its unusual shape; it exhibits the Moomintroll books of Finnish author Tove Jansson. ⊠ *Pirkankatu 2* ☎ *03/314–614* ☉ *Sept.–May, weekdays 9:30–8, Sat. 9:30–3; June–Aug., weekdays 9:30–7, Sat. 9:30–3.*

The **Tuomiokirkko** (cathedral), built in 1907 in the National Romantic style, displays some of the best-known masterpieces of Finnish mural art. ⊠ *Tuomiokirkonkatu 3* ☉ *May–Aug., daily 9–6; Sept.–Apr., daily 11–3.*

The **Särkänniemi Peninsula** holds many attractions. **Särkänniemen Huvikeskus** (Särkänniemi Amusement Center) is a recreation complex made up of an amusement park, a children's zoo, a planetarium, and an aquarium with a separate "dolphinarium." Within Särkänniemi, the **Sara Hildénin Taidemuseo** (Sara Hildén Art Museum) is a striking example of Finnish architecture, displaying works by such modern artists as Chagall, Klee, Miró, and Picasso. ⊠ *Särkänniemi* 🕾 *03/248–8111; ticket sales 03/248–8212* ⊕ *www.sarkanniemi.fi* ✉ *Joint admission €27* ⊙ *Daily 11–6 (museum only; check the Web site for opening hrs of other attractions).*

Särkänniemi's 550-foot **Näsinneula Observation Tower,** the tallest in Finland, dominates the Tampere skyline. At the top are an observatory and a revolving restaurant. The contrast between the industrial maze of Tampere at your feet and the serenity of the lakes stretching out to meet the horizon is unforgettable. ⊠ *Särkänniemi* 🕾 *03/248–8111 main complex information* ⊙ *June–Aug., daily 11 AM–midnight; Sept.–Dec., Tues.–Sat. 10 AM–midnight, Sun. and Mon. 10–10; Jan.–Mar., Tues.–Sat. 10 AM–midnight, Sun. and Mon., 10–10; Apr., daily 10 AM–midnight; May 1–12, weekdays 10 AM–midnight, weekends, 11 AM–midnight; May 13–31, daily 11 AM–midnight.*

On the **"Poet's Way"** boat tour along Lake Näsijärvi, the boat passes through the agricultural parish of Ruovesi, where J. L. Runeberg, Finland's national poet, once lived. Many artists and writers spend their summers by the straits of Visuvesi. ⊠ *Finnish Silverline and "Poet's Way," Laukontori 10A3* 🕾 *03/212–4804* ✉ *Same-day round-trip fare for a boat/bus package €34, available Tues.–Sun.*

★ **$$–$$$** ✕ **Astor.** A choice of moderately priced brasserie fare and a more sophisticated menu is served in this cozy yet elegant restaurant off the main square. ⊠ *Aleksis Kivenkatu 26* 🕾 *03/260–5700* ▭ *DC, MC, V.*

$$–$$$ ✕ **Tiiliholvi.** A romantic cellar in an art nouveau building with a colorful past, Tiiliholvi offers Finnish haute cuisine and the best wine selection in town. ⊠ *Kauppakatu 10* 🕾 *03/272–0231* ▭ *AE, DC, MC, V* ⊙ *Closed Sun.*

$$ ✕ **Laterna.** In a tsarist-era hotel and once the haunt of artists and writers, Laterna serves Russian fare with a Finnish twist. Dinner is accompanied by live music in the charming main dining room and cozy side parlors. ⊠ *Puutarhakatu 11* 🕾 *03/272–0241* ▭ *AE, DC, MC, V.*

$$$$ 🏨 **Sokos Hotel Ilves.** Soaring above a restaurant and shopping island of restored warehouses near the city center, the hotel has some rooms with spectacular views of the city and Pyhäjärvi and Näsijärvi lakes. ⊠ *Hatanpään valtatie 1, 33100* 🕾 *03/262–6262* 🖷 *03/262–6264* ⊕ *www. sokoshotels.fi* ↪ *336 rooms* ♨ *3 restaurants, pool* ▭ *AE, DC, MC, V.*

$$$$ 🏨 **Sokos Hotel Tammer.** A beautiful historic hotel overlooking a park, the Hotel Tammer has a grand dining room and modern rooms. ⊠ *Satakunankatu 13, 33100* 🕾 *03/262–6265* 🖷 *03/262–6266* ⊕ *www. sokoshotels.fi* ↪ *83 rooms, 4 suites* ♨ *Restaurant* ▭ *AE, DC, V.*

$ 🏨 **Iltatähti Apartment Hotel.** In the center of town, this hotel offers pleasant and unpretentious accommodation at budget rates. ⊠ *Tuomiokirkonkatu 19, 33100* 🕾 *03/315–161* 🖷 *03/3151–6262* ⊕ *www.hoteliltatahti.fi* ↪ *40 rooms* ▭ *AE, DC, MC, V.*

Iittala

The **Iittala Lasikeskus** (Iittala Glass Center) offers museum tours for groups and has a shop. Top designers produce the magnificent glass; the seconds are bargains you won't find elsewhere. ⊠ *14500 Iittala* 🕾 *0204/ 396–230* ⊙ *Museum May–Aug., daily 10–6; Sept.–Apr., daily 10–5. Shop May–Aug., daily 9–8; Sept.–Apr., daily 10–6.*

Hämeenlinna

Hämeenlinna's secondary school has educated many famous Finns, among them composer Jean Sibelius (1865–1957). The only surviving timber house in the town center is **Sibeliuksen syntymäkoti** (Sibelius's Birth-place), a modest dwelling built in 1834. One of the rooms houses the harmonium Sibelius played as a child. ✉ *Hallituskatu 11* ☎ *03/621–2755* ⊘ *May–Aug., daily 10–4; Sept.–Apr., daily noon–4.*

Hämeen Linna (Häme Castle) is Finland's oldest castle: Swedish crusaders began building it in the 13th century. At times a granary and a prison, the lakeshore castle is now restored and open to the public for tours and exhibitions; it sits 1 km (½ mi) north of Hämeenlinna's town center. ✉ *Kustaa III:n katu 6* ☎ *03/675–6820* ⊘ *May–Aug. 14, daily 10–6; Aug. 15–Apr., daily 10–4.*

The **Hämeenlinnan Taidemuseo** (Hämeenlinna Art Museum), housed in a 19th-century granary designed by Carl Ludvig Engelas and in a sec-ond granary in the same courtyard, exhibits Finnish art from the 19th and 20th centuries and foreign art from the 17th century; works evac-uated from Vyborg in 1939 form the core of the collection. ✉ *Viipur-intie 2* ☎ *03/621–2669* ⊕ *www.hameenlinna.fi/artmuseum* ⊘ *Tues., Wed., and Fri.–Sun. noon–6, Thurs. noon–8.*

★ **$$$$** ▥ **Rantasipi Aulanko.** One of Finland's top hotels, Rantasipi Aulanko sits on the lakeshore in a beautifully landscaped park 6½ km (4 mi) from town. All rooms have wall-to-wall carpeting and overlook the golf course, the park, or the lake. ✉ *Aulanko Puisto (Aulanko Park), 13210* ☎ *03/658–801* ⊟ *03/682–1922* ⊕ *www.rantasipi.fi* ⇝ *245 rooms* ⌂ *Pool* ▤ *AE, DC, MC, V.*

Hattula

The interior of medieval **Hattulan Kirkko** (Holy Cross Church), 8 km (5 mi) north of Hämeenlinna in Hattula, has vivid frescoes of biblical scenes dating from around 1510. ✉ *Hattula* ☎ *03/672–3383 during open hrs; 03/631–1540 at other times* ⊕ *www.hattula.fi* ⊘ *May 15–Aug. 15, daily 11–5; other times by appointment.*

Riihimäki

The **Suomen Lasimuseo** (Finnish Glass Museum) in Riihimäki, 35 km (22 mi) south of Hämeenlinna, has an outstanding display on the history of glass from early Egyptian times to the present, artfully arranged in an old glass factory. ✉ *Tehtaankatu 23, Riihimäki* ☎ *019/741–7494* ⊕ *www.riihimaki.fi/lasimus* ⊘ *May–Aug., daily 10–6; Sept.–Dec. and Feb.–Apr., Tues.–Sun. 10–6* ⊘ *Closed Jan.*

$$ ✕ **Lehmushovi.** In a manor house in a park near the Glass Museum, Lehmushovi offers Finnish and international cuisine. ✉ *Lehmustie 5* ☎ *019/738–946* ⌂ *Reservations essential* ⊘ *11–6* ▤ *DC, MC, V.*

The Lakelands Essentials

AIR TRAVEL

Airports in the Lakelands are at Tampere, Mikkeli, Jyväskylä, Varkaus, Lappeenranta, Savonlinna, Kuopio, and Joensuu.

BUS TRAVEL

Buses are the best form of public transport into the region, with frequent connections to lake destinations from most major towns. The ride from Helsinki to Savonlinna takes six hours.

CAR TRAVEL

The region is vast, so the route you choose will depend on your destination. Consult Autoliitto (Automobile and Touring Club of Finland) or tourist boards for route advice.

TOURS

🖪 **Fees & Schedules Häme Tourist Service** ✉ Raatihuoneenkatu 11, 13100 Hämeenlinna ☎ 03/621-2388 🖨 03/621-2716.

TRAIN TRAVEL

Trains run from Helsinki to Lahti, Mikkeli, Imatra, Lappeenranta, Joensuu, and Jyväskylä.

TRANSPORTATION AROUND THE LAKELANDS

In Tampere you can buy a 24-hour Tourist Ticket from the city tourist office that allows unlimited travel on city transportation.

VISITOR INFORMATION

🖪 **Hämeenlinna** ✉ Raatihuoneenkatu 11, 13100 Hämeenlinna ☎ 03/621-3373. **Kuopio** ✉ Haapaniemenkatu 17, 70110 Kuopio ☎ 017/182-584. **Savonlinna** ✉ Puistokatu 1, 57100 Savonlinna ☎ 015/517-510. **Tampere** ✉ Verkatehtaankatu 2, Box 487, 33100 Tampere ☎ 03/3146-6680.

FINNISH LAPLAND

Lapland is a region of great silences, with endless forests and fells. Settlers in Finnish Lapland have walked gently and left the landscape almost unspoiled. The oldest traces of human habitation in Finland have been found in Lapland, where hoards of Danish, English, and even Arabian coins indicate active trading many centuries ago. Until the 1930s, Lapland was still largely unexploited, and any trip to the region was an expedition. Its isolation ended when the Arctic Highway was completed, connecting Rovaniemi with the Arctic Sea. Lapland covers about one-third of the total area of Finland.

Only about 4,000 native Sámi live in Lapland; the remainder of the province's population of about 200,000 is Finnish. Recent grassroots efforts to preserve Sámi language and traditions have been largely successful. Sámi craftspeople create beautiful objects and clothing out of the materials readily at hand: wood, bone, and reindeer pelts.

Although winter in Lapland brings with it the fascinating northern lights and reindeer roundups, beautiful weather often complements summer's nightless days. In early fall nature's colors (called "ruska" in Finnish) are spectacular.

Exploring Lapland

Rovaniemi

Rovaniemi is the Lapland administrative and communications hub. Nearly razed by the retreating German army in 1944, Rovaniemi is today a modern university town and business center strongly influenced by Alvar Aalto's architecture. One notable structure is the **Lappia-Talo** (Lappia House; ✉ Hallituskatu 11 ☎ 016/322-2944), an Aalto-designed concert and congress center.

★ You can get a good instant introduction to the region and its natural history at the **Arktikum** (Arctic Research Center), 1 km (½ mi) north of Lappia-Talo. It houses the Lapland Provincial Museum, with exhibits on Sámi culture. ✉ *Pohjoisranta 4* ☎ *016/317-840* ⊕ *www.arktikum.*

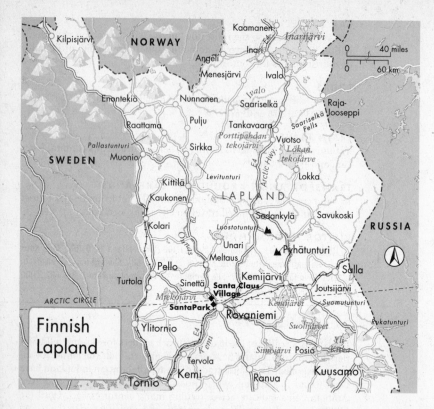

fi ✹ *June 1–15, daily 10–6; June 16–Aug. 15, daily 9–7; Aug. 16–31, daily 10–6; Sept.–Nov., Tues.–Sun. 10–6; Dec.–mid-Jan., daily 10–6; mid-Jan.–May, Tues.–Sun. 10–6.*

$$-$$$ ✕ **Fransmanni.** In the Sokos Hotel Vaakuna in downtown Rovaniemi, this restaurant specializes in international, Finnish, and Sámi dishes. ⊠ *Koskikatu 4.* ☎ *016/332–211* ▭ *AE, DC, MC, V.*

$$ ✕ **Ounasvaaran Pirtit.** This town favorite, a small restaurant decorated in traditional Lapp wooden style and focused on a welcoming open fireplace, serves traditional Finnish and Sámi fare. "Kotas," traditional Lappish huts, are available for group dining. ⊠ *Antinmukka 4* ☎ *016/369–056* ⌕ *Reservations essential* ▭ *MC, V.*

$$$ ▦ **Rantasipi Hotel Pohjanhovi.** With its pleasant location overlooking the Kemi River, this hotel is a favorite with travelers to the north. ⊠ *Pohjanpuistikko 2, 96200* ☎ *016/33711* ⎙ *016/313–997* ⊕ *www.rantasipi. fi* ⇆ *212 rooms, 4 suites* ⌂ *2 restaurants, pool* ▭ *AE, DC, MC, V.*

$$$ ▦ **Scandic Hotel Rovaniemi.** This modern hotel is in the heart of town. Some rooms have individual saunas or hot tubs. ⊠ *Koskikatu 23, 96200* ☎ *016/460–6000* ⎙ *016/460–6666* ⊕ *www.scandic-hotels.com* ⇆ *167 rooms* ⌂ *2 restaurants, bar* ▭ *AE, DC, MC, V.*

★ $$$ ▦ **Sky Hotel Rovaniemi.** The views of the town and the surrounding area are fantastic from this tranquil, full-service hotel perched on Ounasvaara Mountain, 3 km (2 mi) from town. Most rooms have saunas. ⊠ *96400* ☎ *016/335–3311* ⎙ *016/318–789* ⊕ *www.laplandhotels.com* ⇆ *47 rooms, 11 apartments* ⌂ *Restaurant* ▭ *AE, DC, MC, V.*

$$$ ▦ **Sokos Hotel Vaakuna.** The Vaakuna has small rooms in pastel shades. The club here is a center of Rovaniemi nightlife. ⊠ *Koskikatu 4, 96200* ☎ *016/332–211* ⎙ *016/332–2199* ⊕ *www.sokoshotels.fi* ⇆ *157 rooms, 2 suites* ⌂ *2 restaurants* ▭ *AE, DC, MC, V.*

$$ 🏨 **Best Western Hotel Oppipoika.** Rooms here are spacious and comfortable. The restaurant serves Lapland specialties. ✉ *Korkalonkatu 33, 96200* ☎ *016/338–8111* 🖷 *016/346–969* ⊕ *www.fintravel.com/ rovaniemi/hotel/oppipoika* 🛏 *40 rooms* 🍴 *2 restaurants, pool* 🖃 *AE, DC, MC, V.*

Arctic Circle

🏰 **SantaPark**, a Christmas theme park deep inside a rocky cavern, offers a Magic Sleigh Ride, an Elf School, and the Santa Claus Helicopter Ride, among other attractions. Take the Santa Train from the park to **Santa Claus Village**, where you can shop for gifts and have your purchases shipped with a special Santa Claus Land stamp; stop along the way at the Reindeer Park to see Santa's sleigh team. ✉ *Arctic Circle, 96930* ☎ *016/333–0000 park; 016/356–2157 village* 🖷 *016/333–0020 park; 016/356–2096 village* ⊕ *www.santapark.com* 🎫 *€20* ◷ *Park: mid-June–late Aug., daily noon–6; late Nov.–early Dec. weekdays noon–4, weekends noon–6; early Dec.–early Jan., daily noon–6; mid-Jan.–end March, Fri. and Sat. 1–5. Village: June–Aug., daily 9–7; Sept.–Nov., daily 10–5; Dec.–mid-Jan., daily 9–7; mid-Jan.–May, daily 10–5.*

Tankavaara

Tankavaara is the most accessible and best developed of several gold-panning areas in Lapland. The **Kultamuseo** (Gold Museum) tells the centuries-old story of Lapland's hardy fortune seekers. In the summer months guides will show you how to wash gold dust and tiny nuggets from the dirt of an ice-cold stream. ✉ *Arctic Hwy. 4, Kultakylä* ☎ *016/ 626–158* ⊕ *www.tankavaara.fi* ◷ *June–Aug. 15, daily 9–6; Aug. 16–Sept., daily 9–5; Oct.–May, weekdays 10–4.*

$$ ✕ **Wanha Waskoolimies.** Sámi specialties predominate at this attractive café-restaurant at the Gold Museum; try the gold prospector's reindeer steak. ✉ *Tankavaaran kultakylä* ☎ *016/626–158* 🖃 *DC, V.*

Saariselkä

From here you can set off into the true wilderness; during the snowy months, it has some of the finest cross-country and downhill skiing in Finland. More than 2,500 square km (965 square mi) of this magnificent area have been set aside as **Urho Kekkosen kansallispuisto** (Urho Kekkosen National Park; ✉ Northern Lapland Tourism, Saariseläntie 1, 99830 Saariselkä ☎ 016/668–402 🖷 016/668–403).

$$–$$$$ 🏨 **Riekonlinna.** This is the more comfortable of twin hotels on the fringes of the wilderness fells. Catering to sports enthusiasts, its facilities include a children's play room, ski maintenance, and a storage room. ✉ *99830* ☎ *016/679–4455* 🖷 *016/679–4456* ⊕ *www.riekkoparvi.fi* 🛏 *124 rooms* 🖃 *AE, DC, MC, V.*

Ivalo

Just south of here, the highway passes the **Ivalojoki** (Ivalo River). Join a canoe trip down its swift waters to Lake Inari. The modern community of Ivalo is the main center for northern Lapland.

$ 🏨 **Hotel Ivalo.** Modern and fully equipped, the Hotel Ivalo is right on the river and about 1 km (½ mi) from the village center. One of its two restaurants serves Lapland specialties. ✉ *Ivalontie 34, 99800* ☎ *016/ 688–111* 🖷 *016/661–905* ⊕ *www.hoteivalo.fi* 🛏 *94 rooms* 🍴 *2 restaurants, pool* 🖃 *AE, DC, MC, V.*

$ 🏨 **Kultahippu.** Here, next to the Ivalo River, you can patronize the "northernmost nightclub in Finland." The hotel has cozy rooms and the restaurant was given the Lappi à la Carte award. ✉ *Petsamontie 1, 99800*

☎ *016/661–825* 📠 *016/662–510* ⊕ *www.kultahippuhotel.fi* ⇝ *30 rooms* ⚭ *Restaurant* ▤ *AE, DC, MC, V.*

Inari

The huge island-studded expanses of Inarijärvi (Lake Inari), north of Ivalo, offer endless possibilities for wilderness exploration. Lakeside Inari, home of the Sámi Parliament, is a good base for summer boat excursions. Set in the oldest inhabited region of northern Lapland and named after the Lapp word for "village" or "living space," the **SIIDA Center** hosts exhibits on the Sámi people and the northern seasons. The center houses the **Saamelaismuseo** (Sámi Museum) and the **Ylä-Lapin luontokeskus** (Northern Lapland Nature Center). The Nature Center includes the **Metsähallitus** (Forest and Park Service; ☎ 0205/647–740 📠 0205/647–750), which provides camping and fishing permits and advice on exploring the wilderness. A 17-acre open-air museum is open during the summer. ⊠ *Hwy. 4 by Lake Inari* ☎ *016/665–212* 📠 *016/665–156* ⊕ *www.siida.fi* ☉ *June–Sept., daily 9–8; Oct.–May, Tues.–Sun. 10–5.*

$ 🏨 **Inarin Kultahovi.** This renovated old inn stands on the wooded bank of a swiftly flowing river. ⊠ *99870* ☎ *016/671–221* 📠 *016/671–250* ⊕ *www.saariselka.fi/kultahovi* ⇝ *29 rooms* ⚭ *Restaurant* ▤ *DC, MC, V.*

Lapland Essentials

AIR TRAVEL

Finnair domestic flights link Oulu and Rovaniemi with Ivalo, Enontekiö, Kemi, and Sodankylä. Finnair also has daily flights directly from Helsinki to Kuusamo. The SAS-owned Air Botnia also serves Lapland's airports. 🛫 **Air Botnia** ☎ 09/6151-2900.

BUS TRAVEL

Buses leave five times daily from Rovaniemi to Inari (five hours) and Ivalo (four hours). Taxi stands are at most bus stations.

CAR TRAVEL

The Arctic Highway will take you north from Rovaniemi at the Arctic Circle to Inari, just below the 69th parallel.

TOURS

For information on tours in the area, contact Lapland Travel Ltd. 🚌 **Lapland Travel Ltd.** ⊠ Koskikatu 1, Box 8156, 96101 Rovaniemi ☎ 016/332-3400 📠 016/332-3411.

VISITOR INFORMATION

🛈 **Inari and Saariselkä** Northern Lapland Tourism ⊠ Saariseläntie 1, 99830 Saariselkä ☎ 016/668-402 📠 016/668-403 ⊕ www.saariselka.fi. **Rovaniemi** ⊠ Koskikatu 1, Rovaniemi 96200 ☎ 016/346-270 📠 016/342-4650 ⊕ www.rovaniemi. fi. **Sodankylä** ⊠ Jäämerentie 3, 99600 Sodankylä ☎ 016/618-168 📠 016/613-478 ⊕ www.sodankyla.fi.

FRANCE

PARIS, THE ILE-DE-FRANCE, THE LOIRE VALLEY, NORMANDY, BURGUNDY & LYON, PROVENCE, THE CÔTE D'AZUR

11

LIKE THE HIGH-SPEED TRAINS speeding toward the Channel Tunnel, France has been on the move. This is particularly evident in Paris: in the last two decades no other European capital has seen as much building at such a pharaonic pace. I. M. Pei's glass pyramid at the Louvre and the postmodern Grande Arche de la Défense are just two examples of the architecturally dramatic monuments that have shocked purists and set the city abuzz.

But France's attachment to its heritage also persists, as major restorations of the Champs-Élysées and the Tuileries Gardens in Paris have proved. The world's most magnificent châteaux—Vaux-le-Vicomte and Fontainebleau in the Ile-de-France, Chenonceau and Chambord in the Loire Valley—have remained testaments to France's illustrious nobility and are veritable histories of France in stone. The spires of Chartres and Claude Monet's gardens in Giverny have continued to demonstrate France's glorious artistic and architectural legacy. Everywhere you go, you'll see scenery cultivated and tempered by the hand of man. The land seems to have been molded and trimmed with a strange, unerring instinct for proportion, and this celebrated Gallic measure is visible everywhere. You will be conscious of it in Notre-Dame de Paris, Versailles, the place de la Concorde, Rouen Cathedral; in hundreds of places where an unerring *sens du plastique,* or artistic sense, has managed to impart itself to stone, iron, paint, and glass in such a way that these monuments still have the power, centuries after they were created, to lift the human spirit.

If you want to experience France at its most French, first head to the storybook Loire Valley and the Ile-de-France, just to the south and north of Paris. Here, in the very heart of the country, you'll find French culture at its most elegant, pure, and refined—even the French spoken here is fabled for its beauty and diamond-cut grace. When you travel farther afield, this "Frenchness" becomes mixed in—delightfully so—with other cultural strains. If you go west to stolidly Norse Normandy, home of Camembert, calvados (apple brandy), the D-day landings, and dramatic Mont-St-Michel overlooking the English Channel (*La Manche* to the French), you'll find many remnants of the centuries-old invasions by the English and Scandinavians. If you go southeast to Burgundy, famed for its wine, you'll discover that food, art, and architecture all bear traces left by the Netherlandish courts that set up shop here during the early Renaissance era. Heading through the hills of Beaujolais, en route to Lyon, a city that competes with Paris—and Dijon—for the title of France's gastronomic capital, you'll wend your way south along the towering Rhône Valley to Provence, where the ancient Romans left an in-

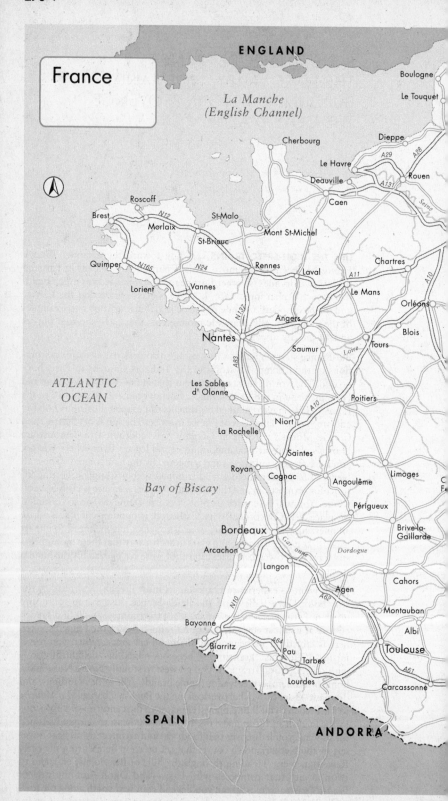

France

ENGLAND

La Manche
(English Channel)

Boulogne

Le Touquet

Dieppe

Cherbourg

Le Havre

Deauville

Rouen

A29

A28

A131

Seine

Caen

Chartres

A10

Roscoff

St-Malo

Brest

N12

Morlaix

St-Brieuc

Mont St-Michel

Rennes

Laval

A11

Quimper

N165

N24

Le Mans

Orléans

Lorient

Vannes

Angers

Blois

N137

Nantes

Saumur

Tours

Loire

A83

Les Sables
d' Olonne

Poitiers

ATLANTIC
OCEAN

A10

Niort

La Rochelle

Saintes

Royan

Cognac

Limoges

Bay of Biscay

Angoulême

C.
F.

Périgueux

Bordeaux

Brive-la-
Gaillarde

Arcachon

Garonne

Dordogne

Langon

Cahors

Agen

A62

Montauban

N10

Albi

Bayonne

Toulouse

Biarritz

A64

Pau

Tarbes

A61

Lourdes

Carcassonne

SPAIN

ANDORRA

CORSICA

Calvi
Bastia
Corte
Ajaccio
N198
Bonifacio

BELGIUM

LUXEMBOURG

GERMANY

SWITZERLAND

ITALY

Calais
Lille
Arras
Amiens
Cambrai
St. Quentin
Beauvais
Laon
Reims
Metz
Châlons-en-Champagne
Nancy
Paris
Strasbourg
Fontainebleau
Troyes
Colmar
Sens
Mulhouse
Auxerre
Belfort
Dijon
Besançon
Bourges
Nevers
Beaune
Autun
Montluçon
Mâcon
Bourg-en-Bresse
Clermont-Ferrand
Lyon
Chambéry
Aurillac
Le Puy
Grenoble
Rodez
Montélimar
Gap
Millau
Sisteron
Nîmes
Avignon
Montpellier
Aix-en-Provence
Monte Carlo
Nice
Cannes
Marseille
Narbonne
Toulon
Perpignan

A26
A16
A1
A5
A26
A4
A31
A35
A6
A36
A71
A39
A6
A72
A43
A49
A75
A57
A9
A8
A9

Rhône
Saône
Rhône

0   50 mi
0   75 km

Mediterranean Sea   *Corsica*

delible mark on the region so many centuries ago. After feasting your eyes on Provence's orange-tile roofs, the ocher earth, and bright, luminous air—so memorably captured in the paintings of Paul Cézanne—you can continue on to the Côte d'Azur, for the stars, the sun, and the beaches along the bright blue waters of the Mediterranean. In several areas here, you won't have to cross the border to feel like you're already in Italy.

The best way to get by in France is to try out a little French—a simple *"Bonjour"* (Good day) or a *"Parlez-vous anglais?"* (Do you speak English?) will go a long away. Do as the French do: you'll be surprised, for instance, at how quickly a surly waiter will melt if you fight a smirk with a smirk. Take time out from your busy sightseeing schedule to match that French passion for the daily rituals. Linger over a coffee in the afternoon or a bottle of wine at dinner and your own experience will be all the more authentic and satisfying. By the end of your stay you will probably agree with the observation that "Everyone has two countries, his or her own and France."

FRANCE A TO Z

To research prices, get advice from other travelers, and book travel arrangements, visit www.fodors.com.

AIR TRAVEL

Flying time to Paris is 7½ hours from New York, 9 hours from Chicago, and 11 hours from Los Angeles. Domestic air travel in France is less expensive than it used to be, and there are more flights all over the country; major hubs in France include Lyon, Nice, Marseille, Bordeaux, and Toulouse. A number of charter companies are cashing in on the booming inter-European travel market, offering short flights with no-frills service and exceptional fares. Within France, *easyJet* has flights from Paris to Nice and Toulouse, Aeris is a new low-cost carrier with routes from Orly Sud to Perpignan, Tarbes/Lourdes, Toulouse, and Nice, and Ryanair runs routes to Marseille and Perpignan. Train service, however, may be faster when you consider time spent getting to and from the airport.

CARRIERS Most domestic flights from Paris leave from Orly.
 ■ Contacts **Aeris** ☎ 08-20-03-77-37 ⊕ www.aeris.fr. **Air France** ☎ 800/237-2747 in the U.S., 08-20-82-08-20 in France ⊕www.airfrance.com. **EasyJet** ☎04-93-21-48-33 in France ⊕ www.easyjet.com. **Ryanair** ☎ 08-92-55-56-66 ⊕ www.ryanair.com.

AIRPORTS

The major gateways to France are the airports outside Paris: Orly and Charles de Gaulle, often referred to as Roissy.
 ■ **Charles de Gaulle/Roissy** ☎ 01-48-62-22-80 in English ⊕ www.adp.fr. **Orly** ☎ 01-49-75-15-15 ⊕ www.adp.fr.

BIKE TRAVEL

The French are great bicycling enthusiasts—witness the Tour de France—and there are many good bicycling routes in France. For about €8 a day (€12 for a 10-speed touring bike) you can rent a bike from one of 30 train stations throughout the country; you need to show your passport and leave a cash deposit of €155 or a Visa or MasterCard deposit. Tourist offices supply details on the more than 200 local shops that rent bikes, and the SNCF (⇨ Train Travel) has a brochure entitled the "Guide du Train et du Vélo," available at any train station. Bikes may be taken as accompanied luggage from any station in France; most trains in rural areas do not charge for bikes (but inquire at the SNCF ticket agencies about which ones do). Free bike space works on a first-come, first-served basis; you must take your bike to the designated compartment for loading yourself, so plan accordingly.

BOAT & FERRY TRAVEL

Canal and river vacations are popular: you can either take an organized cruise or rent a boat and plan your own leisurely route. Contact a travel agent for details or ask for a "Tourisme Fluvial" brochure in any French tourist office.

BUS TRAVEL

Because of the excellent train service, long-distance buses are rare; they're found mainly where train service is scarce. Bus tours are organized by SNCF. Long-distance routes to many European cities are covered by Eurolines.

🔖 **Eurolines** ✉ 28 av. Général-de-Gaulle, 93170 Bagnolet ☎ 08-36-69-52-52 ⊕ www. eurolines.fr Ⓜ Galliéni.

BUSINESS HOURS

BANKS & OFFICES
Banks are open weekdays 9:30–5, with variations; most close for at least an hour at lunch.

MUSEUMS & SIGHTS
The usual opening times for museums and other sights are from 9:30 to 5 or 6. Many close for lunch (noon–2). Most are closed one day a week (generally Monday or Tuesday) and on national holidays. National museums are free to the public the first Sunday of every month.

SHOPS
Shops in big towns are open from 9 or 9:30 to 7 or 8 without a lunch break; though it's still rare, an increasing number are now open on Sunday. Smaller shops often open earlier and close later but take a lengthy lunch break (12:30–3 or 4). This siesta-type schedule is more typical in the south of France. Corner grocery stores frequently stay open until around 10 PM.

CAR TRAVEL

EMERGENCIES
If your car breaks down on a highway, go to a roadside emergency telephone and call the breakdown service. If you have a breakdown anywhere else, find the nearest garage or contact the police (dial ☎ 17).

GASOLINE
Gas is expensive, especially on expressways and in rural areas. Don't let your tank get too low—you can go for many miles in the country without passing a gas station—and keep an eye on pump prices as you go. These vary enormously; from €1 to €1.20 per liter. The cheapest gas can be found at *hypermarchés* (large supermarkets).

PARKING
Parking is a nightmare in Paris and often difficult in other large towns. Meters and ticket machines (pay and display) are common: make sure you have a supply of euro coins (1 and 2 euros, plus 1, 2, 5, 10, 20, and 50 cents). Parking is free during August in certain residential areas of Paris, but be sure to check the signs. In smaller towns parking may be permitted on one side of the street only—alternating every two weeks—so pay attention to signs.

ROAD CONDITIONS
France's roads are classified into five types, numbered and prefixed *A, N, D, C,* or *V.* Roads marked *A* (Autoroutes) are expressways. There are excellent links between Paris and most French cities but poor ones between the provinces (the principal exceptions being A26 from Calais to Reims, A62 between Bordeaux and Toulouse, and A9/A8 the length of the Mediterranean coast). It's often difficult to avoid Paris when crossing France—just try to steer clear of the rush hours (7–9:30 AM and 4:30–7:30 PM). A *péage* (toll) must be paid on most expressways. The *N*

(Route Nationale) roads—which are sometimes divided highways—and *D* (Route Départementale) roads are usually wide and fast, and driving along them can be a real pleasure. Don't be daunted by the smaller *C* (Chemin Communal) and *V* (Chemin Vicinal) roads, either. The yellow regional Michelin maps—on sale throughout France—are invaluable.

RULES OF THE ROAD You may use your own driver's license in France, but you must be able to prove you have third-party insurance. Drive on the right and yield to drivers coming from the right if there is no solid white line. Seat belts are obligatory for all passengers, and children under 12 may not travel in the front seat. Speed limits are 130 kph (80 mph) on expressways, 110 kph (70 mph) on divided highways, 90 kph (55 mph) on other roads, 50 kph (30 mph) in towns. French drivers break these limits and police dish out hefty on-the-spot fines with equal abandon.

EATING & DRINKING

Eating in France is serious business, at least for two of the three meals each day. For a light meal try an informal café or brasserie (steak and french fries remains the classic) or a picnic (a baguette with ham, cheese, or pâté is a perfect combination). Reservations are advised at most restaurants, particularly in summer. French breakfasts are relatively modest—strong coffee, fruit juice if you insist, and croissants.

WHAT IT COSTS In euros			
$$$$	**$$$**	**$$**	**$**
PARIS AND THE CÔTE D'AZUR			
PER PERSON over €38	€24–€38	€14–€23	under €14
OTHER AREAS			
AT DINNER over €32	€21–€32	€12–€20	under €12

Prices are per person for a main course. Note that when prices are quoted for a restaurant that offers only prix-fixe (set-price) meals, it is given a price category that reflects this prix-fixe price, which includes tax (19.6%) and gratuity.

MEALTIMES Dinner is the main meal and usually begins at 8. Lunch begins at noon in the countryside, and 12:30 or 1 (seldom later) in towns.

RESERVATIONS & DRESS Jacket and tie are recommended for $$$$ and $$$ restaurants and at some of the more stylish $$ restaurants as well. When in doubt, it's best to dress up. Otherwise casual dress is appropriate (though be aware that casual in Paris means stylish and no shorts or sneakers).

EMBASSIES

🏛 Australia ✉ 4 rue Jean-Rey, 15ᵉ, Paris ☎ 01-40-59-33-00.
🏛 Canada ✉ 35 av. Montaigne, 8ᵉ, Paris ☎ 01-44-43-29-00.
🏛 New Zealand ✉ 7 ter rue Léonardo-da-Vinci, 16ᵉ, Paris ☎ 01-45-00-24-11.
🏛 United Kingdom **United Kingdom** ✉ 35 rue du Faubourg-St-Honoré, 8ᵉ, Paris ☎ 01-44-51-31-00.
🏛 United States **United States** ✉ 2 av. Gabriel, 8ᵉ, Paris ☎ 01-43-12-22-22; 01-43-12-23-47 in emergencies.

HEALTH

FOOD & DRINK Tap water is perfectly safe, though not always very palatable (least of all in Paris). Mineral water is a good alternative; there's a vast choice of *eaus plates* (still) and *eaux gazeuses* (fizzy).

HOLIDAYS

New Year's Day; Easter Monday; Labor Day (May 1); VE Day (May 8); Ascension (usually early May); Pentecost Monday (usually mid-

May); Bastille Day (July 14); Assumption (August 15); All Saints' Day (November 1); Armistice (November 11); Christmas.

LANGUAGE

The French study English for a minimum of four years at school and, although few are fluent, their English is probably better than the French of most Americans. English is widely understood in major tourist areas, and in most hotels there is likely to be at least one person who can converse with you. Even if your own French is rusty, try to master a few words: people will greatly appreciate your efforts.

LODGING

France's accommodations range from rambling old village inns to stylishly converted châteaux to modern hotels. Prices must, by law, be posted in the hotel room and include taxes and service. Prices are usually listed by room, not per person, and don't usually include breakfast. In smaller rural hotels, you may be expected to have your evening meal at the hotel.

The quality of accommodations, particularly in older properties, can vary greatly from room to room; if you don't like the room you're given, ask to see another. When making reservations, state your preference for *une chambre à deux lits* (twin beds) or *une chambre à grand lit* (double bed) and for *douche* (shower) or *baignoire* (bathtub)—the latter always costs more.

It's always a good idea to make hotel reservations in Paris and other major tourist destinations as far in advance as possible, especially in late spring, summer, or fall. If you arrive without a reservation, tourist offices in major train stations and most towns may be able to find a hotel for you.

WHAT IT COSTS In euros			
$$$$	**$$$**	**$$**	**$**
PARIS AND THE CÔTE D'AZUR			
FOR 2 PEOPLE	over €250	€150–€250	€100–€150	under €100
OTHER AREAS			
HOTELS	over €190	€120–€190	€60–€120	under €60

Prices are for standard double rooms in high season and include tax (19.6%) and service charges.

APARTMENT & VILLA RENTALS Renting an apartment or a *gîte* (furnished house) for a week or month can be more convenient and save you money if you're traveling with a group or family. The French Government Tourist Offices in New York and London are good sources for information about rentals. Fédération Nationale des Gîtes de France has a list of gîtes for rent: indicate the region that interests you or order the annual nationwide guide (€16).

The following agencies list houses and apartments for rent: At Home Abroad, At Home in France, Orion, Paris Appartements Services, and Ville et Village.

Rental Listings Fédération Nationale des Gîtes de France ⊠ 59 rue St-Lazare, 75009 Paris ☎ 01-49-70-75-75 📠 01-42-81-28-53 ⊕ www.gitesdefrance.fr. **Orion** ⊠ 30 pl. d'Italie, 75013 Paris ☎ 01-40-78-54-54; 800/546-4777; 212/688-9538 in the U.S. 📠 01-40-78-54-55; 212/688-9467 in the U.S. **Paris Appartements Services** ⊠ 69 rue d'Argout, 75002 ☎ 01-40-28-01-28 📠 01-40-28-92-01.

BED & BREAKFASTS   Known as *chambres d'hôte*, bed-and-breakfasts are becoming increasingly popular in rural areas and can be a great bargain. Check local tourist offices for details, or contact Fédération Nationale des Gîtes de France (⇨ Apartment & Villa Rentals), which lists B&Bs all over France.

CAMPING   A guide to France's campsites is published by the Fédération Française de Camping et de Caravaning.

🏕 **Fédération Française de Camping et de Caravaning** ✉ 78 rue de Rivoli, 75004 Paris ☎ 01-42-72-84-08 ⊕ www.campingfrance.com.

HOSTELS   Some of the hostels in France are quite nice and even have double rooms; age restrictions may apply. Contact the Fédération Unie des Auberges de Jeunesse for information.

🏠 Hostel Organizations **Fédération Unie des Auberges de Jeunesse** ✉ 27 rue Pajol, 75018 Paris ☎ 01-44-89-87-27 🖨 01-44-89-87-10 ⊕ www.fuaj.org.

HOTELS   First-time travelers to France, take note: not only are hotel rooms here small by American standards, they are also rarely as well appointed. Unless you have booked into a top-tier address, do not expect to find a spacious room with all the latest conveniences. The hotels in this chapter can be relied upon to offer clean linens, conscientious service, and considerable charm. Rest assured that the bathrooms, though sometimes small, should be clean and comfortable, but don't be surprised to find the bed a bit saggy or the carpet in the hall a little threadbare.

MAIL & SHIPPING

If you're uncertain where you'll be staying, have mail sent to American Express (if you're a card member) or Thomas Cook; mail labeled *poste restante* (general delivery) is also accepted at most French post offices.

POSTAL RATES   Letters and postcards to the United States and Canada cost €0.67 for 20 grams. Letters to the United Kingdom cost €0.46 for up to 20 grams, as do letters within France. Postcards cost €0.46 within France and to EU countries. Stamps can be bought in post offices (La Poste) and cafés sporting a red TABAC sign outside.

MONEY MATTERS

There's no way around it: France is expensive. But many travel basics—hotels, restaurants, plane, and train tickets—can be made more affordable by planning ahead, taking advantage of prix-fixe menus, and staying in smaller, family-run places. Prices are highest in Paris and on the Côte d'Azur, though even in these areas you can find reasonable accommodations and food.

Prices vary greatly depending on the region, proximity to tourist sights, and—believe it or not—whether you're sitting down (and where—inside or on the terrace) or standing up in a café. Here are a few samples: cup of coffee, €1–€3; glass of beer, €1.50–€4; soft drink, €1.50–€3; ham sandwich, €2.50–€5; 1½-km (1-mi) taxi ride, €5.

CURRENCY   France has adopted the euro (€) as its sole currency, one of the 12 European Union countries to do so. At press time (summer 2003), the exchange rate for the euro was €0.89 to the U.S. dollar, €0.64 to the Canadian dollar, €1.42 to the pound sterling, €0.58 to the Australian dollar, €0.52 to the New Zealand dollar, and €0.11 to the South African rand.

TAXES   All taxes must be included in posted prices in France. The initials TTC (*toutes taxes comprises*, which means taxes included) are sometimes included on price lists, but they are superfluous. Restaurant and hotel prices must *by law* include taxes and service charges: if they are tacked onto your bill as additional items, you should complain.

A number of shops offer VAT refunds to foreign shoppers. You are entitled to a export refund of the 19.6% tax, depending on the item purchased, but it is often applicable only if your purchases in any given store reach a minimum of €430 (for U.K. and EU residents) or €184 (for others, including U.S. and Canadian residents). In most instances, you must fill out a form at the point of purchase, which must then be tendered to a customs official at your last port of departure. Remember to ask for the refund and note that VAT refunds can't be processed after you arrive back home.

TELEPHONES

French phone numbers have 10 digits. All phone numbers have a two-digit prefix determined by zone: Paris and the Ile-de-France, 01; the northwest, 02; the northeast, 03; the southeast, 04; and the southwest, 05.

COUNTRY & AREA CODES The country code for France is 33 and for Monaco 377. To call France from the United States, dial 011 (for all international calls), then dial 33 (the country code), and the number in France, minus any initial 0. To dial France from the United Kingdom, dial 00–33, then the number in France, minus any initial 0.

INTERNATIONAL CALLS To call a foreign country from France, dial 00 and wait for the tone, then dial the country code, area code, and number. You can also contact your long-distance carrier directly and charge your call to your calling card or make a collect call.

☎ Access Codes **AT&T** ☎ 08-00-99-00-11. **MCI** ☎ 08-00-99-00-19. **Sprint** ☎ 08-00-99-00-87.

LOCAL CALLS To make calls within a region or to another region in France, simply dial the full, 10-digit number. A local call in France costs €.034 cents per minute. Cheaper rates apply between 10 PM and 8 AM and between noon Saturday and 8 AM Monday. Dial ☎ 12 for local operators.

PUBLIC PHONES The rare French person who doesn't have a mobile phone uses *télécartes* (phone cards), which you can buy just about anywhere, from post offices, tabacs, métro stations, magazine kiosks, small grocery stores, or any France Telecom office. The international rates these phone cards offer have been negotiated and are the best you will find. There are two télécartes available; *une pétite* that costs €8 for 50 units or *une grande* that costs €15 for 120 units. Scratch the card to uncover your personal PIN, dial the toll-free number and the number you wish to reach (be it local or international) and the operator will tell you the time available for your call. Note that it is virtually impossible to find a phone that will take coins.

TIPPING

The bill in a bar or restaurant includes service, but it's customary to leave some small change unless you're dissatisfied. The amount varies, from 30 cents for a beer to €1.50–€5 after a meal. Tip taxi drivers and hairdressers about 10%. Give ushers in theaters €0.50. Cloakroom attendants will expect nothing if there is a sign saying POURBOIRE INTERDIT (tipping forbidden); otherwise give them €1. Washroom attendants usually get €0.30—a sum that is often posted. Bellhops should get €1.50 per item. If you stay in a moderately priced hotel for more than two or three days, it is customary to leave something for the chambermaid—perhaps €1.50 per day. Expect to tip €1.50 for room service—but nothing is expected if breakfast is routinely served in your room. Service station attendants get nothing for giving you gas or oil, and €1–€1.50 for checking tires. Train and airport porters get a fixed sum (€1–€1.50) per bag. Museum guides should get €2–€5 after a guided tour. Tip tour guides (and bus drivers) €2 or more after an excursion.

TRAIN TRAVEL

SNCF, the French national railroad, is fast, punctual, comfortable, and comprehensive. The TGV (*Trains à Grande Vitesse*), with a top speed of 300 kph (190 mph), are the best domestic trains, heading southeast from Paris to Lyon, Marseille, the Côte d'Azur, and Switzerland; west to Nantes; southwest to Bordeaux; and north to Lille and Brussels. The TGV Méditerranée line connects Valence with Avignon, Aix, and Marseilles (with a branch line farther to Nîmes), reducing the trip from Paris to Provence from five hours to two hours and 55 minutes. TGVs require a seat reservation (easily obtained at the ticket window or from an automatic machine).

You must punch your train ticket in one of the orange machines (*composteurs*) you'll encounter alongside platforms. Slide your ticket in face-up and wait for a "clunk" sound. The ticket collectors will present you with an on-the-spot fine of €15 if your ticket hasn't been validated before boarding.

On overnight trains you choose between expensive *wagons-lits* (private sleeping cars) and *couchettes* (bunks), which sleep six to a compartment in second class and four to a compartment in first class (sheet and pillow provided) and are cheaper (€15). Ordinary compartment seats do not pull together to enable you to lie down. In summer special night trains from Paris to Spain and the Côte d'Azur are geared for a younger market, with discos and bars.

FARES & SCHEDULES As an example, the cost of a second-class ticket for the Paris–Lyon route is normally €50 but climbs to €65 during the morning and evening rush hours. Seat reservations are reassuring but seldom necessary on other French trains, except at holiday times.

CUTTING COSTS EurailPasses are valid for the entire French rail network. Various other reduced-fare passes are available from major train stations and SNCF travel agents. If France is your only destination in Europe, consider purchasing a France Rail Pass ($210–$240 per person), which allows three days of unlimited train travel in first or second class over a one-month period. Additional days may be added for extra fees in either class. Other options include the France Rail 'n Drive Pass (combining rail and rental car), France Rail 'n Fly Pass (rail travel and one air journey within France), and the France Fly, Rail 'n Drive Pass (a rail, air, and rental-car program all in one). Contact Rail Europe for more information.

When traveling together, two people (who don't have to be a couple) can get the *Prix Découverte à Deux,* which gives you a 25% discount during "périodes bleues" (blue periods; any nonholiday weekdays—calendars are available at stations). You can get a reduced rate if you are over 60. There are two options: for the *Prix Découverte Senior,* all you have to do is show a valid ID with your age and you're entitled to up to a 25% reduction in fares in first and second class. The second, the *Carte Senior* (€46) is valid for one year, and entitles you to up to a 50% discount on most trains with a minimum markdown of 25%. Young people (under 26) qualify for the *Carte 12/25* (€43), which gives 50% discounts on travel in blue periods. The *Carte Enfant +* (€55) enables children under 12—and up to four accompanying adults—to travel at 50%–75% off normal fares, depending on the travel period. The *Prix Découverte Séjour* gives a 25% discount to those traveling at least 200 km (132 mi) round-trip (during blue periods only) and staying over a Saturday night.

🚆 SNCF ✉ 88 rue St-Lazare, 75009 Paris ☎ 08-36-35-35-35 ⊕ www.sncf.com. 🚆 Rail Europe ☎ 800/942-4866 ⊕ www.raileurope.com.

VISITOR INFORMATION

France On-Call ☎ 410/286-8310, weekdays 9-7 ⊕ www.francetourism.com. **Chicago** ✉ 676 N. Michigan Ave., 60611. **London** ✉ 178 Piccadilly, W1V OAL ☎ 171/6399-3500 🖶 171/6493-6594. **Los Angeles** ✉ 9454 Wilshire Blvd., Suite 715, Beverly Hills 90212. **Montréal** ✉ 1981 av. McGill College, Suite 490, Québec H3A 2W9. **New York City** ✉ 444 Madison Ave., 16th fl., 10022.

WHEN TO GO

June and September, free of midsummer crowds, are the best months to be in France. June has the advantage of long daylight hours; slightly cheaper prices and many warm days (often lasting well into October) make September attractive. The second half of July and all of August are spoiled by inflated prices and huge crowds on the beaches, and the heat can be stifling in southern France. Paris, though pleasantly deserted, can be stuffy in August, too. Anytime between March and November offers a good chance to soak up some sun on the Côte d'Azur. The weather in Paris and the Loire is unappealing before Easter (lots of rain and chilly temperatures). If you're dreaming of Paris in the springtime, May (not April) is your best bet.

CLIMATE North of the Loire, France has a northern European climate—coldish winters, pleasant if unpredictable summers, and frequent rain. Southern France has a Mediterranean climate: mild winters; long, hot summers; and sunshine much of the year. The more Continental climate of eastern and central France is a mixture of these two extremes: winters can be very cold and summers mighty hot. France's Atlantic coast has a temperate climate even south of the Loire, with the exception of the much warmer Biarritz. The following are the average daily maximum and minimum temperatures for Paris and Marseille.

PARIS

Jan.	43F	6C	May	68F	20C	Sept.	70F	21C
	34	1		49	10		53	12
Feb.	45F	7C	June	73F	23C	Oct.	60F	16C
	34	1		55	13		46	8
Mar.	54F	12C	July	76F	25C	Nov.	50F	10C
	39	4		58	15		40	5
Apr.	60F	16C	Aug.	75F	24C	Dec.	44F	7C
	43	6		58	15		36	2

MARSEILLE

Jan.	50F	10C	May	71F	22C	Sept.	77F	25C
	35	2		52	11		58	15
Feb.	53F	12C	June	79F	26C	Oct.	68F	20C
	36	2		58	14		51	10
Mar.	59F	15C	July	84F	29C	Nov.	58F	14C
	41	5		63	17		41	5
Apr.	64F	18C	Aug.	83F	28C	Dec.	52F	11C
	46	8		63	17		37	3

PARIS

If there's a problem with a trip to Paris, it's the embarrassment of riches that faces you. No matter which Paris you choose—touristy, historic, fashion-conscious, pretentious-bourgeois, thrifty, or the legendary bohemian-arty Paris of undying attraction—one thing is certain: you will carve out your own Paris, one that is vivid, exciting, and ultimately unforgettable. Paris is a city of vast, noble perspectives and intimate, ramshackle streets, of formal *espaces vertes* (green open spaces) and quiet squares—and this combination of the pompous and the private is one of the secrets of its perennial pull.

For the first-timer, there will always be several "musts" at the top of the list, but a visit to Paris will never be quite as simple as a quick look at Notre-Dame, the Louvre, and the Eiffel Tower. Every *quartier,* or neighborhood, has its own treasures, and you should be ready to explore—a very pleasant prospect in this most elegant of cities.

Exploring Paris

Numbers in the margin correspond to points of interest on the Paris map.

As world capitals go, Paris is surprisingly compact. With the exceptions of the Bois de Boulogne and Montmartre, you can easily walk from one major sight to the next. The city is divided in two by the River Seine, with two islands (Ile de la Cité and Ile St-Louis) in the middle. The Left—or South—Bank has a more intimate, bohemian flavor than the haughtier Right Bank. The east–west axis from Châtelet to the Arc de Triomphe, via the rue de Rivoli and the Champs-Élysées, is the principal thoroughfare for sightseeing and shopping on the Right Bank.

The city is divided into 20 *arrondissements* (districts). The last one or two digits of a city zip code (e.g., 75002) will tell you the arrondissement (in this case, the 2e, or 2nd). For further help, buy the *Plan de Paris* booklet, a city map and guide with a street-name index that also shows métro stations.

The **Carté Musées et Monuments** (Museums and Monuments Pass) offers unlimited access to more than 65 museums and monuments over a one-, three-, or five-consecutive-day period; the cost, respectively, is €15, €30, and €40. Because most Paris museums cost €4–€6, you have to be a serious museum goer to make this pay off, but there is one incredible plus: you get to jump to the head of the line by displaying it.

From the Eiffel Tower to Pont de l'Alma

The Eiffel Tower lords it over this southwest area of Paris. Across the way, in the Palais de Chaillot on place du Trocadéro, are a number of museums. In this area, too, is where you get the Bateaux Mouches, the boats that ply the Seine on their tours of Paris by water.

4 **Bateaux Mouches.** These popular motorboats set off on their hour-long tours of Paris waters regularly (every half hour in summer). ⊠ *Pl. de l'Alma, 8^e* ☎ *01–40–76–99–99* ⊕ *www.bateaux-mouches.fr* Ⓜ *Alma-Marceau.*

1 **Eiffel Tower** (Tour Eiffel). What is now the worldwide symbol of Paris nearly became 7,000 tons of scrap iron when its concession expired in 1909—now much loved, it was once widely derided by Parisians as too big and too modern. Only its potential use as a radio antenna saved the day. Architect Gustave Eiffel, whose skill as an engineer earned him renown as a builder of iron bridges, created his tower for the World Exhibition of 1889. Restoration in the 1980s didn't make the elevators any faster—long lines are inevitable unless you come in the evening (when every girder is lighted in glorious detail, with a special eye-popping display that goes off on the hour)—but decent shops and two good restaurants were added. The view from 1,000 feet up will enable you to appreciate the city's layout and proportions. ⊠ *Quai Branly, 7e* ☎ *01–44–11–23–23* ⊕ *www.tour-eiffel.fr* ☉ *July and Aug., daily 9 AM–midnight; Sept.–June, daily 9 AM–11 PM* Ⓜ *Bir-Hakeim, RER: Champ-de-Mars.*

③ Musée d'Art Moderne de la Ville de Paris (City of Paris Museum of Modern Art). Both temporary exhibits and a permanent collection of top-quality 20th-century art can be found at this modern art museum. It takes over, chronologically speaking, where the Musée d'Orsay leaves off. ⊠ *11 av. du Président-Wilson, 16ᵉ* ☎ *01–53–67–40–00* ⊕ *www.paris.fr* ⊙ *Tues.–Fri. 10–5:30, weekends 10–6:45* Ⓜ *Iéna.*

② Palais de Chaillot (Chaillot Palace). This honey-color, art deco culture center facing the Seine, perched atop tumbling gardens with sculpture and fountains, was built in the 1930s. It houses three museums: the **Musée de la Marine** (Maritime Museum), with a salty collection of seafaring paraphernalia; the **Musée de l'Homme** (Museum of Mankind), with an array of prehistoric artifacts; and the **Musée des Monuments Français**, that is undergoing renovation and will re-open in 2005, when it will share space with the Institut Français d'Architecture. ⊠ *Pl. du Trocadéro, 16ᵉ* ☎ *01–44–05–72–72 Museum of Mankind; 01–53–65–69–69 Maritime Museum* ⊕ *www.mnhn.fr* ⊙ *Museum of Mankind Wed.–Mon. 9:45–5:15; Maritime Museum Wed.–Mon. 10–6* Ⓜ *Trocadéro.*

From the Louvre to the Arc de Triomphe

From the gleaming glass pyramid entrance of the Louvre, the world's greatest museum, you can see the Arc de Triomphe standing foursquare at the top of the city's most famous avenue, the Champs-Élysées. Between the Louvre and the Arc lies the city's spiritual heart—the elegant place de la Concorde.

⑤ Arc de Triomphe (Triumphal Arch). This 164-foot arch was planned by Napoléon to celebrate his military successes. Yet when Empress Marie-Louise entered Paris in 1810, it was barely off the ground. Napoléon had been dead for 15 years when the Arc de Triomphe was finished in 1836. The arch looms over place Charles-de-Gaulle, referred to by Parisians as *L'Étoile* (The Star), one of Europe's most chaotic traffic circles. Short of attempting a death-defying dash, your only way to get over to the Arc de Triomphe is to take the pedestrian underpass. France's Unknown Soldier is buried beneath the archway; the flame is rekindled every evening at 6:30. ⊠ *Pl. Charles-de-Gaulle, 8ᵉ* ☎ *01–55–37–73–77* ⊕ *www.monum.fr* ⊙ *Easter–Oct., daily 9:30 AM–11 PM; Nov.–Easter, daily 10 AM–10:30 PM* Ⓜ *Charles-de-Gaulle–Étoile.*

⑥ Champs-Élysées. The cosmopolitan pulse of Paris beats strongest along this gracefully sloping, 2-km (1-mi) avenue, originally laid out in the 1660s by André Le Nôtre as parkland sweeping away from the Tuileries. In an attempt to reestablish this thoroughfare as one of the world's most beautiful avenues, the city has planted extra trees, broadened sidewalks, refurbished art nouveau newsstands, and clamped down on garish storefronts. Ⓜ *Franklin-D.-Roosevelt, Champs-Élysées–Clemenceau.*

⑦ Grand Palais (Grand Palace). This so-called palace built for the World Exhibition of 1900 is closed for renovation until 2007, when it will re-open as a exhibition space for contemporary art. For the time being you can still visit the **Palais de la Découverte** (Palace of Discovery), with scientific and mechanical exhibits and a planetarium. ⊠ *Av. Winston-Churchill, 8ᵉ* ☎ *01–56–43–20–21* ⊙ *Palais de la Découverte Tues.–Sat. 9:30–6, Sun. 10–7* Ⓜ *Champs-Élysées–Clemenceau.*

⑧ Jardin des Tuileries (Tuileries Gardens). Immortalized in impressionist masterpieces by Monet and Pisarro, these enormous formal gardens are lined with trees, ponds, and statues. At the far end of the Tuileries, leading toward the Louvre, is the **Arc du Carrousel**, a dainty triumphal arch erected more quickly (1806–08) than its big brother at the far end of the Champs-Élysées. Ⓜ *Concorde, Tuileries.*

Paris

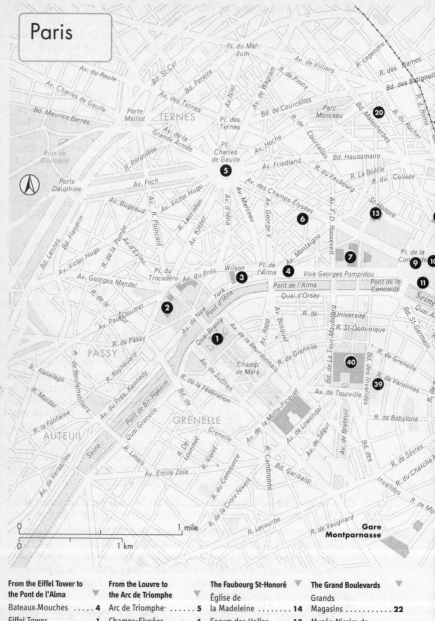

0   1 mile

0   1 km

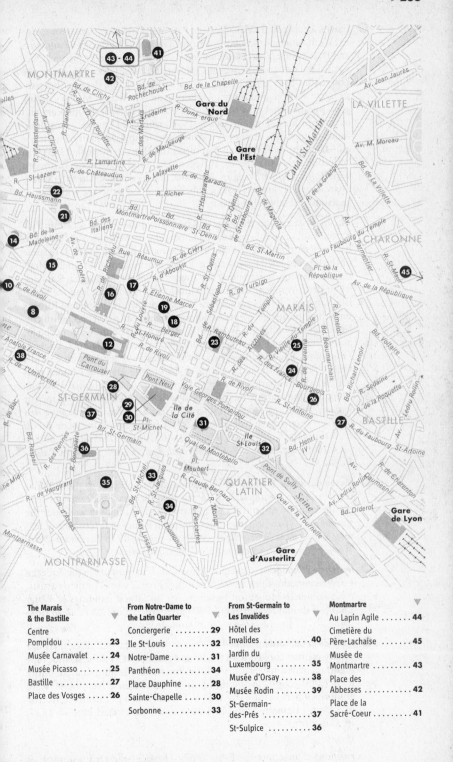

⑫ Louvre. Leonardo da Vinci's *Mona Lisa* and *Virgin and Saint Anne,* Van
Eyck's *Madonna of Chancellor Rolin,* Giorgione's *Concert Champêtre,*
and Delacroix's *Liberty Guiding the People* . . . you get the picture. Once
a royal palace, now the world's largest and most famous museum, the
Louvre has been given fresh purpose by more than a decade of expansion, renovation, and reorganization, symbolized by I. M. Pei's daring
glass pyramid that now serves as the entrance to both the museum and
an underground shopping arcade, the **Carrousel du Louvre.** Many thousands of treasures are newly cleaned and lighted, so plan on seeing it
all—from the red-brocaded Napoléon III salons to the fabled Egyptian
collection, from the 186-carat Regent Diamond to the rooms crowded
with Botticellis, Caravaggios, Poussins, and Géricaults. After all the renovations, the Louvre is now a coherent, unified structure with a more
spacious and navigable layout.

The main attraction for some is a portrait of the wife of a certain Florentine millionaire, Francesco da Gioconda, better known as Leonardo
da Vinci's *Mona Lisa* (in French, *La Joconde*), painted in 1503. In some
of the less-crowded rooms and galleries nearby Leonardo's fellow Italians are strongly represented: Fra Angelico, Giotto, Mantegna, Raphael,
Titian, and Veronese. El Greco, Murillo, and Velázquez lead the Spanish; Van Eyck, Rembrandt, Frans Hals, Brueghel, Holbein, and Rubens
underline the achievements of northern European art. The English collection is highlighted by works of Lawrence, Reynolds, Gainsborough,
and Turner. French front-runners include works by Delacroix, Poussin,
Fragonard, Chardin, Boucher, and Watteau—together with David's
Oath of the Horatii and Géricault's *Raft of the Medusa.* Famous statues include the soaring *Victory of Samothrace,* the celebrated *Venus de
Milo,* and the realistic Egyptian *Seated Scribe.* New rooms for ancient
Persian, Arab, and Greek art opened in 1997. ⊠ *Palais du Louvre (it's
faster to enter through the Carrousel du Louvre mall on rue de Rivoli
than through the pyramid),* 1ᵉʳ ☎ 01–40–20–51–51 ⊕ *www.louvre.fr*
☎ €10 ⊙ *Thurs.–Sun. 9–6, Mon. and Wed. 9* ᴀᴍ–9:45 ᴘᴍ Ⓜ *Palais-
Royal.*

⑪ Musée du Jeu de Paume. This museum, at the entrance to the Tuileries
Gardens, is an ultramodern, white-walled showcase for excellent temporary exhibits of bold contemporary art. The building was once the
spot of *jeu de paume* games (literally, palm game—a forerunner of tennis). ⊠ *1 pl. de la Concorde,* 1ᵉʳ ☎ *01–42–60–69–69* ⊙ *Tues. noon–9:30,
Wed.–Fri. noon–7, weekends 10–7* Ⓜ *Concorde.*

⑩ Musée de l'Orangerie (Orangery Museum). This museum in the Tuileries
Gardens contains fine early-20th-century French works by many artists,
most famously Monet (on view here are his largest paintings of *Water
Lilies*); it should reopen in fall 2004 after renovation. ⊠ *Pl. de la Concorde,* 1ᵉʳ ☎ *01–42–97–48–16* Ⓜ *Concorde.*

⑨ Place de la Concorde. Flanked by elegant neoclassical buildings, this huge
square is often choked with traffic and perhaps at its most scenic come
nightfall, when its beautiful florid fountains are illuminated. More
than 1,000 people, including Louis XVI and Marie-Antoinette, were
guillotined here in the early 1790s. The obelisk, a gift from the viceroy
of Egypt, originally stood at Luxor and was erected here in 1833.
Ⓜ *Concorde.*

The Faubourg St-Honoré

Fashions change, but the Faubourg St-Honoré—the area just north of
the Champs-Élysées and the Tuileries—firmly maintains its tradition
of high style. As you progress from the President's Palace, past a wealth

of art galleries and the monumental Madeleine church to the stately place Vendôme, you will see that all is luxury and refinement here. On the ritzy square, famous boutiques sit side by side with famous banks—after all, elegance and finance have never been an unusual combination. Leading names in modern fashion are found farther east on place des Victoires. Sublimely Parisian are the Palais-Royal and its elegant gardens.

⑭ Église de la Madeleine. With its rows of uncompromising columns, this church, known simply as La Madeleine, looks more like a Greek temple. Inside, the walls are richly decorated, with plenty of gold glinting through the murk. The church was designed in 1814 but not consecrated until 1842, after futile efforts to turn the site into a train station. ⊠ *Pl. de la Madeleine, 8ᵉ* ⊙ *Mon.–Sat. 7:30–7, Sun. 8–7* Ⓜ *Madeleine.*

⑱ Forum des Halles. Since the city's much-lamented central glass-and-iron market halls were torn down during the late 1960s, the area has been transformed into a trendy—albeit slightly seedy—shopping complex, the Forum des Halles. A topiary garden basks in the shadow of the nearby **Bourse du Commerce** (Commercial Exchange) and bulky church of **St-Eustache.** ⊠ *Main entrance on rue Pierre-Lescot, 1ᵉʳ* Ⓜ *Les Halles; RER: Châtelet–Les Halles.*

⑬ Palais de l'Élysée (Élysée Palace). This "palace," where the French president lives, works, and receives official visitors, was originally constructed as a private mansion in 1718 and has housed presidents only since 1873. ⊠ *55 rue du Faubourg-St-Honoré, 8ᵉ* ⊙ *Not open to the public* Ⓜ *Miromesnil.*

⑯ Palais-Royal. This erstwhile Royal Palace, built in the 1630s and now partly occupied by the Ministry of Culture, has a beautiful garden bordered by arcades and boutiques, and an adjacent courtyard with modern, candy-stripe columns by Daniel Buren. Once home to the Bourbon kings, it is now occupied by the French Ministry of Culture and private apartments, and its buildings are not open to the public. ⊠ *Pl. du Palais-Royal, 1ᵉʳ* Ⓜ *Palais-Royal.*

⑮ Place Vendôme. Mansart's rhythmically proportioned example of 17th-century urban architecture is one of the world's most opulent squares. Top jewelers compete for attention with the limousines that draw up outside the Ritz hotel. The square's central column was forged from the melted bronze of 1,200 cannons captured by Napoléon at the Battle of Austerlitz in 1805. That's Napoléon at the top, masquerading as a Roman emperor. ⊠ *Pl. Vendôme, 1ᵉʳ* Ⓜ *Tuileries.*

⑰ Place des Victoires. This circular square, now lined with many of the city's top fashion boutiques, was laid out in 1685 by Jules-Hardouin Mansart in honor of the military victories (*victoires*) of Louis XIV. The Sun King gallops along on a bronze horse in the middle. ⊠ *Pl. des Victoires, 1ᵉʳ* Ⓜ *Sentier.*

⑲ St-Eustache. This colossal church, also known as the Cathedral of Les Halles, was erected between 1532 and 1637 and testifies to the stylistic transition between Gothic and classical architecture. ⊠ *2 rue du Jour, 1ᵉʳ* Ⓜ *Les Halles; RER: Châtelet–Les Halles.*

The Grand Boulevards

Backbone of Paris's Right Bank, a wide avenue traces a continuous arc from St-Augustin, the city's grandest Second Empire church, to place de la République, whose very name symbolizes the ultimate downfall of the imperial regime. The avenue's name changes six times along the way—Parisians refer to it as the *Grands Boulevards*.

㉒ Grands Magasins (Department Stores). Paris's most venerable department stores can be found behind the Opéra: **Galeries Lafayette** has an elegant turn-of-the-20th-century glass dome, **Au Printemps** an excellent view from its rooftop cafeteria. ✉ *Bd. Haussmann, 8ᵉ* Ⓜ *Havre-Caumartin.*

★ **㉘ Musée Nissim de Camondo.** The French perfected the *art de vivre*—the art of living—in the 18th century in elegant, luxurious salons. It's all beautifully preserved and on display at this *hôtel particulier* (private mansion), magnificently furnished with beautiful furniture, *boiseries* (carved wood panels), and bibelots of the rococo and neoclassical periods. ✉ *63 rue de Monceau* ☎ *01-53-89-06-40* ⊕ *www.ucad.fr* ☼ *Wed.–Sun. 10–5* Ⓜ *Villiers.*

㉑ Opéra Garnier. Haunt of the *Phantom of the Opera*, setting for Degas's famous ballet paintings, and still the most opulent theater in the world, the original Paris opera house was the flagship building of the Second Empire (1851–70). Architect Charles Garnier fused elements of neoclassical architecture—like the bas-reliefs on the facade—in an exaggerated combination imbued with the subtlety of a Wagnerian cymbal crash. You can stroll around at leisure in the Grand Foyer, and view the super-opulent, Napoléon III–style auditorium. ✉ *Pl. de l'Opéra, 9ᵉ* ☎ *01-40-01-22-63* ⊕ *www.opera-de-paris.fr* ☼ *Daily 10–5* Ⓜ *Opéra.*

Fodor'sChoice ★

The Marais & the Bastille

The Marais is one of the city's most historic and sought-after residential districts. The gracious architecture of the 17th and early 18th centuries sets the tone. Today most of the Marais's spectacular *hôtels particuliers*—loosely translated as "mansions," the onetime residences of aristocratic families—have been restored, and many of the buildings are now museums. There are trendy boutiques and cafés among the kosher shops of the traditionally Jewish neighborhood around rue des Rosiers. On the eastern side of the neighborhood is place de la Bastille, site of the infamous prison stormed on July 14, 1789, an event that came to symbolize the beginning of the French Revolution. The surrounding Bastille quarter is filled with galleries, shops, theaters, cafés, restaurants, and bars.

㉓ Centre Pompidou. The futuristic, funnel-top Pompidou Center was built in the mid-1970s and named in honor of former French president Georges Pompidou. The center is most famous for its **Musée National d'Art Moderne** (Modern Art Museum), covering 20th-century art from Fauvism and Cubism to postwar abstraction and video constructions. Other highlights include the chic rooftop restaurant and the glass-tube elevator that snakes up the side of the building. On the sloping piazza below is the **Atelier Brancusi** (Brancusi's Studio), four reconstituted rooms crammed with works by Romanian-born sculptor Constantin Brancusi. ✉ *Pl. Georges-Pompidou, 4ᵉ* ☎ *01-44-78-12-33* ⊕ *www. centrepompidou.fr* ☼ *Wed.–Mon. 11–9* Ⓜ *Rambuteau.*

★ **㉔ Musée Carnavalet.** Two adjacent mansions in the heart of the Marais house this museum devoted to the decorative arts and the history of Paris. Along with riveting objects of the French kings, there are also magnificent 17th- and 18th-century period salons on view, including recreations of Marcel Proust's cork-lined bedroom and the late-19th-century Fouquet jewelry shop. ✉ *23 rue de Sévigné, 3ᵉ* ☎ *01-44-59-58-58* ⊕ *www. paris-france.org/musees* ☼ *Tues.–Sun. 10–5:30* Ⓜ *St-Paul.*

㉕ Musée Picasso. Housed in the scuffed yet palatial 17th-century Hôtel Salé, this museum contains the paintings, sculptures, drawings, prints, ceramics, and assorted works of art given to the government by Picasso's heirs after the painter's death in 1973 in lieu of death duties. There are works from every period of Picasso's life, as well as pieces by Cézanne, Renoir, Degas, and Matisse. ☒ *5 rue de Thorigny, 3ᵉ* ☎ *01–42–71–25–21* ⊙ *Wed.–Mon. 9:30–5:30* Ⓜ *St-Sébastien.*

㉗ Place de la Bastille. Nothing remains of the prison-fortress stormed at the outbreak of the French Revolution; the soaring **Colonne de Juillet** (July Column), topped by the figure of Liberty, commemorates Parisians killed in the long-forgotten uprising of 1830. Also on the square is the **Opéra de la Bastille,** opened in 1989 in commemoration of the Revolution's bicentennial. The **Viaduc des Arts** (Arts Viaduct), a disused railway viaduct converted into boutiques below and a planted walkway on top, leads off down avenue Daumesnil. Ⓜ *Bastille.*

★ **㉖ Place des Vosges.** The oldest monumental square in Paris—and probably still its most nobly proportioned—the place des Vosges was laid out by Henri IV at the start of the 17th century. Originally known as place Royale, it has kept its Renaissance beauty nearly intact, although its buildings have been softened by time, their pale pink brick crumbling slightly in the harsh Parisian air and the darker stone facings pitted with age. In the far corner is the **Maison de Victor Hugo** (Victor Hugo Museum), containing souvenirs of the great poet's life and many of his paintings and ink drawings. ☒ *Maison de Victor Hugo: 6 pl. des Vosges, 4ᵉ* ☎ *01–42–72–10–16* ⊕ *www.paris-france.org/musees* ⊙ *Tues.–Sun. 10–5:45* Ⓜ *St-Paul, Chemin-Vert.*

From Notre-Dame to the Latin Quarter

No matter how you first approach Paris—historically, geographically, emotionally—it is the river Seine that summons all, the Seine that harbors two islands, the Ile de la Cité and the Ile St-Louis, within the very center of Paris. Of them, it is the Ile de la Cité that forms the historic ground zero of the city. It was here that the earliest inhabitants of Paris, the Gaulish tribe of the Parisii, settled in about 250 BC. Here you'll find the great, brooding cathedral of Notre-Dame, the jewel-like Sainte-Chapelle, and the Conciergerie, last haunt of Queen Marie-Antoinette. To the east lies the smaller Ile St-Louis—one of Paris's most romantic nooks—while across the river on the Left Bank of the Seine is the bohemian Quartier Latin, with its warren of steep sloping streets, populated largely by Sorbonne students and academics.

㉙ Conciergerie. Bringing a tear to the eyes of Ancien Régime devotées, this is the famous prison in which dukes and duchesses, lords and ladies, and, most famously, Queen Marie-Antoinette were imprisoned during the French Revolution before being bundled off for their date with the guillotine. You can still see the queen's cell and chapel and the superb vaulted 14th-century **Salles des Gens d'Armes** (Hall of the Men-at-Arms). The **Tour de l'Horloge** (Clock Tower) near the entrance on quai de l'Horloge has a clock that has been ticking off time since 1370. ☒ *1 quai de l'Horloge, 1ᵉʳ* ☎ *01–53–73–78–50* ⊕ *www.monum.fr* ⊙ *Apr.–Sept., daily 9:30–6:30; Oct.–Mar., daily 10–5* Ⓜ *Cité.*

㉜ Ile St-Louis. Of the two islands in the Seine—the Ile de la Cité is to the west—it is the Ile St-Louis that best retains the loveliness of *le Paris traditionnel.* A tiny universe unto itself, shaded by trees, bordered by Seine-side quais, and overhung with ancient stone houses, the island has long been a coveted address for Parisians—Voltaire, Daumier, Cézanne, Baudelaire, Chagall, Helena Rubenstein, and the Rothschilds are just some of the lucky people who have called the St-Louis home. In summer, crowds line up for a scoop from Berthillon's ice-cream shop—savor your cone of *glace de Grande Marnier* by strolling along the isle's Seine-side streets. Ⓜ *Pont-Marie.*

★ ③ **Notre-Dame.** The cathedral of Notre-Dame remains Paris's historic and geographic heart, a place of worship for more than 2,000 years (the present building is the fourth on this site). Victor Hugo's Quasimodo sought sanctuary in its towers, kings and princes married before its great altar, and Napoléon crowned his empress here. The magnificent structure was begun in 1163, making it one of the earliest Gothic cathedrals, but wasn't finished until 1345. The interior is at its lightest and least crowded in the early morning. Window space is limited and filled with shimmering stained glass; the circular rose windows in the transept are particularly delicate. The 387-step climb up the towers is worth the effort for a perfect view of the gargoyles and Paris. ⊠ *Pl. du Parvis, 4ᵉ* ⊕ *www.monum. fr* ☉ *Cathedral daily 8–7. Towers Apr.–June, daily 9:30–7:30; July–Sept., daily 9–7:30; Oct.–Mar., daily 10–5:30* Ⓜ *Cité.*

③ **Panthéon.** This Temple to the Famous started life as a church (1758–89). Since the Revolution, the crypt has harbored the remains of such national heroes as Voltaire, Rousseau, and Zola. Its newest resident is Alexandre Dumas, whose remains were interred there in November of 2002. The austere interior is ringed with Puvis de Chavannes's late-19th-century frescoes, relating the life of Geneviève, patron saint of Paris, and contains a swinging model of the giant pendulum used here by Léon Foucault in 1851 to prove the earth's rotation. ⊠ *Pl. du Panthéon, 5ᵉ* ☎ *01–44–32–18–00* ⊕ *www.monum.fr* ☉ *Apr.–Sept., daily 9:30–6:30; Oct.–Mar., daily 10–6:15* Ⓜ *Cardinal-Lemoine; RER: Luxembourg.*

② **Place Dauphine.** At the western tail end of the Ile de la Cité, this charming plaza was built by Henri IV. The triangular place is lined with some 17th-century houses that the writer André Maurois felt represented the very quintessence of Paris and France; take a seat on the park bench and see if you agree. Ⓜ *Cité.*

③ **Sainte-Chapelle** (Holy Chapel). Not to be missed and one of the most magical sights in European medieval art, this chapel was built by Louis IX in the 1240s to house the Crown of Thorns he had bought from Emperor Baldwin. A lower chapel leads to the dazzling upper chapel, whose walls—if you can call them that—are almost completely made of stained glass. Like an enormous magic lantern, the scenes illuminate more than a thousand figures from stories of the Bible. Try to attend a candlelighted concert here. ⊠ *4 bd. du Palais, 1ᵉʳ* ☎ *01–53–73–78–52* ⊕ *www.monum.fr* ☉ *Apr.–Sept., daily 9:30–6:30; Oct.–Mar., daily 10–5* Ⓜ *Cité.*

③ **Sorbonne.** Students at Paris's ancient university—one of the oldest in Europe—used to listen to lectures in Latin, which explains why the surrounding area is known as the Latin Quarter. You can visit the main courtyard and peek into the lecture halls if they're not in use. The baroque chapel is open only during exhibitions. ⊠ *Rue de la Sorbonne, 5ᵉ* Ⓜ *Cluny–La Sorbonne.*

From St-Germain to Les Invalides

This area of the Left Bank extends from the lively St-Germain neighborhood (named for the oldest church in Paris) to the stately area around the Musée d'Orsay and Les Invalides. South of St-Germain is Montparnasse, which had its cultural heyday in the first part of the 20th century, when it was *the* place for painters and poets to live.

★ ④ **Hôtel des Invalides.** Soaring above expansive if hardly manicured lawns, Les Invalides was founded by Louis XIV in 1674 to house wounded war veterans. Les Invalides itself is an outstanding baroque ensemble, designed by Libéral Bruant. One of its two churches, the Église du Dôme, is graced by the city's most elegant dome and holds **Napoléon's Tomb,** where you can waft the fumes of hubris off the marble columns and onyx trim. The adjacent **Musée de l'Armée** has a collection of arms, armor, and uniforms, and the **Musée des Plans-Reliefs** contains a fascinating collection of old scale models of French towns. ⊠ *Pl. des Invalides, 7ᵉ* ☎ *01-44-42-37-72* ⊕ *www.invalides.org* ⊘ *Apr.–Sept., daily 10–6; Oct.–Mar., daily 10–4:30* Ⓜ *Latour–Maubourg.*

👋 ㉟ **Jardin du Luxembourg** (Luxembourg Gardens). A favorite subject for 19th-century painters, Paris's most famous Left Bank park has tennis courts, flower beds, tree-lined alleys, and a large pond (with toy boats for rent alongside). The 17th-century **Palais du Luxembourg** (Luxembourg Palace) was commissioned by Queen Maria de' Medici at the beginning of the 17th century and houses the French Senate, which is not open to the public. An adjacent wing of the palace houses the Musée de Luxembourg, open only for special exhibitions. Ⓜ *Odéon; RER: Luxembourg.*

★ ㊳ **Musée d'Orsay.** This museum, in a spectacularly converted belle epoque train station, is one of Paris's star attractions, thanks to its imaginatively housed collections of the arts (mainly French) spanning the period 1848–1914. The chief artistic attraction is its impressionist collection, which includes some of the most celebrated paintings in the world, including Manet's *Déjeuner sur l'Herbe* (*Lunch on the Grass*) and Renoir's depiction of a famous dance hall called *Le Moulin de la Galette,* to name just two among hundreds. Other highlights include art nouveau furniture and a model of the Opéra quarter beneath a glass floor. The restaurant here is set in a dazzling 19th-century foyer. ⊠ *1 rue de Bellechasse, 7ᵉ* ☎ *01-40-49-48-14* ⊕ *www.musee-orsay.fr* ⊘ *Tues., Wed., Fri., and Sat. 10–6, Thurs. 10–9:45, Sun. 9–6* Ⓜ *Solférino; RER: Musée d'Orsay.*

★ ㊴ **Musée Rodin.** The Faubourg St-Germain, studded with private mansions owned by the aristocracy and the rich, remains for the most part behind closed gates, but get a peek at this fabled neighborhood by visiting the 18th-century Hôtel Biron, onetime home of the sculptor Auguste Rodin and today a gracious stage for his work. In back is a pretty garden with Rodin works and hundreds of rosebushes. ⊠ *77 rue de Varenne, 7ᵉ* ☎ *01-44-18-61-10* ⊘ *Easter–Oct., Tues.–Sun. 9:30–5:45; Nov.–Easter, Tues.–Sun. 9:30–4:45* Ⓜ *Varenne.*

㊲ **St-Germain-des-Prés.** The oldest church in Paris was first built to shelter a relic of the true cross, brought back from Spain in AD 542. The chancel was enlarged and the church consecrated by Pope Alexander III in 1163; the church tower also dates from this period. ⊠ *Pl. St-Germain-des-Prés, 6ᵉ* ⊘ *Weekdays 8–7:30, weekends 8 AM–9 PM* Ⓜ *St-Germain-des-Prés.*

㊱ **St-Sulpice.** Dubbed the "Cathedral of the Left Bank," this enormous 17th-century church is of note for the powerful Delacroix frescoes in the first chapel on the right. The 18th-century facade was never finished, and its unequal towers add a playful touch to an otherwise sober design. ⊠ *Pl. St-Sulpice, 6ᵉ* Ⓜ *St-Sulpice.*

Montmartre

On a dramatic rise above the city is Montmartre, site of the Sacré-Coeur Basilica (try to catch a sunset or sunrise over Paris from its terrace) and a once-thriving artistic community. Visiting Montmartre means negotiating a lot of steep streets and flights of steps. Some of the avenues are now totally given over to the tourist trade, but if you wander and follow your nose, you can still find quiet corners that retain the poetry that once allured Toulouse-Lautrec and other great artists.

★ ❹❹ **Au Lapin Agile.** One of the most picturesque spots in Paris, this legendary bar-cabaret (open nights only) is a miraculous survivor from the 19th century. Founded in 1860, its adorable maison-cottage was a favorite subject of painter Maurice Utrillo, and it soon became the home-away-from-home for Braque, Modigliani, Apollinaire, Vlaminck, and most famously, Picasso. ✉ *22 rue des Saules, 18ᵉ* ☎ *01–46–06–85–87* ⊕ *www. au-lapin-agile.com* ⊙ *Tues.–Sun. 9 PM–2 AM* ▩ *€20* ⊙ *Tues.–Sat. 9 PM–2 AM* Ⓜ *Lamarck-Caulaincourt.*

❹❸ **Musée de Montmartre.** In its turn-of-the-20th-century heyday, Montmartre's historical museum quartered an illustrious group of painters, writers, and assorted cabaret artists. ✉ *12 rue Cortot, 18ᵉ* ☎ *01–46–06–61–11* ⊙ *Tues.–Sun. 11–6* Ⓜ *Lamarck-Caulaincourt.*

❹❷ **Place des Abbesses.** This triangular square is typical of the picturesque, slightly countrified style that has made Montmartre famous. The entrance to the Abbesses métro station, a curving, sensuous mass of delicate iron, is one of Guimard's two original art nouveau entrance canopies left in Paris. The innovative brick-and-concrete art nouveau church of St-Jean de Montmartre overlooks the square. Ⓜ *Abbesses.*

❹❶ **Sacré-Coeur.** Often compared to a "sculpted cloud" atop Montmartre, the Sacred Heart Basilica was erected as a sort of national guilt offering in expiation for the blood shed during the Paris Commune and Franco-Prussian War in 1870–71, and was largely financed by French Catholics fearful of an anticlerical backlash under the new republican regime. Stylistically, the somewhat bizarre Sacré-Coeur borrows elements from Romanesque and Byzantine models. The gloomy, cavernous interior is worth visiting for its golden mosaics; climb to the top of the dome for the view of Paris. ✉ *Pl. du Parvis-du-Sacré-Coeur, 18ᵉ* ⊕ *www.sacre-coeur-montmartre.com* Ⓜ *Anvers.*

❹❺ **Cimetière du Père-Lachaise** (Father Lachaise Cemetery). This cemetery forms a veritable necropolis with cobbled avenues and tombs competing in pomposity and originality. Leading incumbents include Frédéric Chopin, Marcel Proust, Jim Morrison, Edith Piaf, and Gertrude Stein. Get a map at the entrance and track them down. ✉ *Entrances on rue des Rondeaux, bd. de Ménilmontant, and rue de la Réunion; 18ᵉ* ⊙ *Apr.–Sept., daily 8–6; Oct.–Mar., daily 8–5* Ⓜ *Père-Lachaise, Gambetta, Philippe-Auguste.*

Where to Eat

Forget the Louvre, the Tour Eiffel, and the Bateaux Mouches—the real reason for a visit to Paris is to dine at its famous temples of gastronomy. Whether you get knee-deep in white truffles at Alain Ducasse or merely discover pistachioed sausage (the poor man's caviar) at a classic corner bistro, you'll discover that food here is an obsession, an art, a subject of endless debate. And if the lobster soufflé is delicious, the historic ambience is often more so. Just request Empress Josephine's table at Le Grand Véfour and find out.

Right Bank

★ $$$$ ✕ **Alain Ducasse.** You would be hard-pressed to catch the busy Alain Ducasse here these days, but it would probably be worth the wait. The rosy rococo salons have been draped with metallic organza over the chandeliers and, in a symbolic move, time stands still since all the clocks have been stopped. Overlooking the prettiest courtyard in Paris, the view is as delicious as the roast lamb garnished with "crumbs" of dried fruit or duckling roasted with fig leaves. For the price, the presentation—there are few sauce "paintings," orchid blossoms, or other visual adornments on the plate—could be enhanced. ✉ *Hotel Plaza-Athénée, 27 av. Mon-*

taigne, 8ᵉ ☎ *01–53–67–66–65* ⌖ *Reservations essential* ▭ *AE, DC, MC, V* ⊘ *Closed Sat. and Sun. No lunch Mon.–Wed.* Ⓜ *Alma-Marceau.*

★ $$$$ ✕ **Les Ambassadeurs.** Looking as if Madame de Pompadour might stroll in the door at any moment, Les Ambassadeurs offers a world of Versailles-like splendor with its marble, colored marble, even more colored marble, and gilt chandeliers. Chef Dominique Bouchet likes to mix luxe with more down-to-earth flavors: potato pancakes topped with smoked salmon, caviar-flecked scallops wrapped in bacon with tomato and basil, duck with rutabaga, turbot with cauliflower. The €62 lunch menu is well worth the splurge. ⊠ *Hôtel Crillon, 10 pl. de la Concorde, 8ᵉ* ☎ *01–44–71–16–16* ⌖ *Reservations essential* ⌂ *Jacket and tie* ▭ *AE, DC, MC, V* Ⓜ *Concorde.*

$$$$ ✕ **Le Grand Véfour.** Originally built in 1784, in the arcades of the Palais-Royal, this place is still a contender for the prize of Most Beautiful Restaurant in Paris, thanks to its 19th-century painted-glass and gilt setting. Everyone from Napoléon to Jean Cocteau has dined beneath the gilded boiseries—nearly every seat bears a plaque commemorating a famous patron. Chef Guy Martin hails from Savoie, so you'll find lake fish and mountain cheeses on the menu alongside such luxurious dishes as foie gras–stuffed raviolis. ⊠ *17 rue Beaujolais, 1ᵉʳ* ☎ *01–42–96–56–27* ⌖ *Reservations essential* ⌂ *Jacket and tie* ▭ *AE, DC, MC, V* ⊘ *Closed weekends and Aug. No dinner Fri.* Ⓜ *Palais-Royal.*

Fodor'sChoice ★

★ $$$$ ✕ **Taillevent.** Once the most traditional of all Paris luxury restaurants, this grande dame is suddenly the object of an uncharacteristic buzz, with the departure of chef Michel Del Burgo and the arrival of Alain Solivérès. Service is flawless, the 19th-century paneled salons *luxe*, the well-priced wine list probably one of the top 10 in the world—all in all, a meal here is an event. Reserve a month in advance. ⊠ *15 rue Lamennais, 8ᵉ* ☎ *01–44–95–15–01* ⌖ *Reservations essential* ⌂ *Jacket and tie* ▭ *AE, DC, MC, V* ⊘ *Closed weekends and Aug.* Ⓜ *Charles-de-Gaulle–Étoile.*

★ $$$–$$$$ ✕ **Les Élysées du Vernet.** This may be the most perfect choice for a classique blowout in Paris today, thanks to its remarkable harmonic alignment of staff, decor, and kitchen. Chef Eric Briffard triumphs with his foie gras on toast or monkfish with ginger and lime, and the dining room is graced by a magnificently beautiful *verrière* (glass ceiling) designed by Gustave Eiffel himself. This restaurant remains relatively affordable at lunch (€45 or €60 for a set menu), the wine service is outstanding, and all departing women diners are given a rose. ⊠ *Hôtel Vernet, 25 rue Vernet, 8ᵉ* ☎ *01–44–31–98–98* ⌖ *Reservations essential* ▭ *AE, DC, MC, V* ⊘ *Closed weekends, Aug., and 2 wks in Dec.* Ⓜ *George-V.*

$$$–$$$$ ✕ **Spoon, Food and Wine.** Alain Ducasse's blueprint of a bistro for the 21st century has a do-it-yourself fusion-food menu that allows you to mix and match dishes diversely American, Asian, and Italian in origin. Sign of the future? There are many salads and vegetable and grain dishes on the menu. Reservations are coveted—call a month ahead—but you can always drop in for a snack at the bar. Come late for the models and movie stars. ⊠ *14 rue de Marignan, 8ᵉ* ☎ *01–40–76–34–44* ⌖ *Reservations essential* ▭ *AE, MC, V* Ⓜ *Franklin-D.-Roosevelt.*

★ $$–$$$ ✕ **L'Astrance.** *Le Point* has called L'Astrance "a miracle," and *Le Figaro* has described it as "perfect." Much of the excitement may boil down to the fact that you get the quality of haute cuisine here without the pomposity or the crushing price tag. The food—avocado-and-crab mille-feuille, a ballotine of quail and foie gras, spiced mackerel fillet on Asian-style spinach—is fantastic. ⊠ *4 rue Beethoven, 16ᵉ* ☎ *01–40–50–84–40* ⌖ *Reservations essential* ▭ *AE, DC, MC, V* ⊘ *Closed Mon., 3 wks in Aug., and Dec. 22–Jan. 3. No lunch Tues.* Ⓜ *Passy.*

$$–$$$ ✕ **Bofinger.** Settle in to one of the tables dressed in crisp white linens, under the gorgeous art nouveau glass cupola, and enjoy fine classic

brasserie fare, such as oysters, grilled sole, or fillet of lamb. Note that the no-smoking section here is not only enforced but is also in the prettiest part of the restaurant. ⊠ *5–7 rue de la Bastille, 4ᵉ* ☏ *01-42-72-87-82* ▤ *AE, DC, MC, V* Ⓜ *Bastille.*

\$\$–\$\$\$ ✕ **La Fermette Marbeuf.** This magically beautiful belle epoque room—accidentally rediscovered during renovations in the 1970s—is a favorite haunt of French celebrities who adore the art nouveau mosaic and stained-glass mise-en-scène. The menu rolls out a solid, updated classic cuisine, such as the snails in puff pastry or the saddle of lamb with *choron* (a tomato-spiked béarnaise sauce). ⊠ *5 rue Marbeuf, 8ᵉ* ☏ *01-53-23-08-00* ▤ *AE, DC, MC, V* Ⓜ *Franklin-D.-Roosevelt.*

\$\$–\$\$\$ ✕ **Le Safran.** Passionate chef Caroll Sinclair works almost exclusively with organic produce—red mullet stuffed with cèpes mushrooms and *gigot de sept heures* (leg of lamb cooked for seven hours) are two of her signature dishes. The little room is pretty, intimate, and painted in sunny saffron. ⊠ *29 rue d'Argenteuil, 1ᵉʳ* ☏ *01-42-61-25-30* ▤ *MC, V* ☉ *Closed Sun. and 2 wks in Sept. No lunch Sat.* Ⓜ *Tuileries, Pyramides.*

★ \$\$ ✕ **L'Ardoise.** This minuscule white storefront, decorated with enlargements of old sepia postcards of Paris, is the model of contemporary bistros making waves in the city. Chef Pierre Jay's first-rate three-course menu (€30) includes a crab flan in a creamy parsley emulsion and fresh cod with grilled chorizo chips on a bed of mashed potatoes. With friendly service and a short but well-chosen wine list, L'Ardoise would be perfect if it weren't often crowded and noisy. ⊠ *28 rue du Mont Thabor, 1ᵉʳ* ☏ *01-42-96-28-18* ⌕ *Reservations essential* ▤ *MC, V* ☉ *Closed Mon., Tues., and Aug.* Ⓜ *Concorde.*

\$\$ ✕ **La Grande Armée.** The Costes brothers tapped superstar Jacques Garcia to design this brasserie near the Arc de Triomphe. Here he's unleashed an exotic Napoléon-III bordello decor—think black lacquered tables, leopard upholstery, Bordeaux velvet—for a carefully tousled clientele picking at salads, pastas, and soothing potato puree. ⊠ *3 av. de la Grande Armée, 16ᵉ* ☏ *01-45-00-24-77* ▤ *AE, DC, MC, V* Ⓜ *Charles-de-Gaulle–Étoile.*

\$–\$\$ ✕ **Café Runtz.** Next to the noted theater of Salle Favart, this friendly bistro is still gleaming from Jacques Garcia's late 1990s Weinstube makeover. Old brass gas lamps on each table and rich woodwork create a cozy, Flaubertian atmosphere. Tasty, hearty Alsatian dishes include Gruyère salad, onion tart, choucroute, and fresh fruit tarts. ⊠ *16 rue Favart, 2ᵉ* ☏ *01-42-96-69-86* ▤ *AE, MC, V* ☉ *Closed Sun. and Aug.* Ⓜ *Richelieu-Drouot.*

\$ ✕ **Chartier.** This cavernous 1896 restaurant enjoys a huge following among budget-minded students, solitary bachelors, and tourists. You may find yourself sharing a table with strangers as you study the long, old-fashioned menu of such favorites as hard-boiled eggs with mayonnaise, steak tartare, and roast chicken with fries. ⊠ *7 rue du Faubourg-Montmartre, 9ᵉ* ☏ *01-47-70-86-29* ⌕ *Reservations not accepted* ▤ *AE, DC, MC, V* Ⓜ *Montmartre.*

\$ ✕ **Le Kitch.** Fighting the good fight against ennui, this fun place is a favorite in the arty Bastille neighborhood. There's more than a touch of Pee-Wee's Playhouse here, thanks to the faux-stucco walls, plastic children's furniture, and naïf paintings of cats. The food here is mainly snacky—expect pastas and sandwiches, or a bagel with *tapenade.* ⊠ *10 rue Oberkampf, 11ᵉ* ☏ *01-40-21-94-14* ▤ *No credit cards* ☉ *No lunch weekends* Ⓜ *Oberkampf.*

\$ ✕ **Ladurée.** Pretty enough to bring a tear to Proust's eye, this ravishing *salon de thé* (tea salon) looks barely changed from 1862. You'll dote on the signature lemon-and-caramel macaroons (there are other outposts at 75 av. des Champs-Élysées and on the Left Bank at 21 rue Bonaparte). ⊠ *16 rue Royale, 8ᵉ* ☎ *01–42–60–21–79* ▭ *AE, MC, V* Ⓜ *Madeleine.*

Left Bank

$$$–$$$$ ✕ **Hélène Darroze.** Hélène Darroze has been crowned the newest female culinary star in Paris, thanks to the creative flair she has given the tried-and-true classics of southwestern French cooking, from the lands around Albi and Toulouse. You know it's not going to be *la même chanson*—the same old song—when you spot the resolutely contemporary Tse & Tse tableware and red-and-purple color scheme. The downside? Some carp that the portions are small and the service could be much better, so you might opt for the downstairs bistro, which offers the same dishes but in even smaller, tapas-style portions. ⊠ *4 rue d'Assas, 6ᵉ* ☎ *01–42–22–00–11* ▭ *AE, DC, MC, V* ☺ *Closed Sun. and Mon.* Ⓜ *Sèvres-Babylone.*

★ **$$$–$$$$** ✕ **Lapérouse.** Emile Zola, George Sand, and Victor Hugo were regulars, and the restaurant's mirrors still bear diamond scratches from the days when mistresses didn't take jewels at face value. It's hard not to fall in love with this 17th-century Seine-side town house, whose warren of intimate, boiserie-graced salons breathes history. The latest chef, Alain Hacquard, has found the right track with a daring (for Paris) spice-infused menu. ⊠ *51 quai des Grands-Augustins, 5ᵉ* ☎ *01–43–26–68–04* ⌂ *Reservations essential* ▭ *AE, DC, MC, V* ☺ *Closed Sun., 3 wks in July, and 1 wk in Aug. No lunch Sat.* Ⓜ *St-Michel.*

★ **$$$** ✕ **La Régalade.** As the leading priest who marries bistro and nouvelle cookery—who can resist his soup of lentils and puréed chestnuts poured over a mound of foie gras?—Yves Camdeborde has to satisfy the hordes who trek to the edge of town here in Montparnasse for three dinner sittings (and you still have to book at least two weeks ahead). The room, disappointingly, is no-frills. ⊠ *49 av. Jean-Moulin, 14ᵉ* ☎ *01–45–45–68–58* ⌂ *Reservations essential* ▭ *MC, V* ☺ *Closed Sun., Mon., and Aug. No lunch Sat.* Ⓜ *Alésia.*

★ **$$–$$$** ✕ **Au Bon Accueil.** To see what well-heeled Parisians eat these days, book a table here as soon as you get to town. The excellent, reasonably priced *cuisine du marché* (a daily, market-inspired menu, €25 at lunch and €29 at dinner) has made it a hit: typical of the winter fare is roast suckling pig with thyme and endives. ⊠ *14 rue de Montessuy, 7ᵉ* ☎ *01–47–05–46–11* ⌂ *Reservations essential* ▭ *MC, V* ☺ *Closed weekends and 2 wks in Aug.* Ⓜ *Pont de l'Alma.*

$$–$$$ ✕ **Brasserie de l'Ile St-Louis.** On picturesque Ile St-Louis, this outpost of Alsatian cuisine turns out *coq-au-Riesling*, omelets with Muenster cheese, and onion tarts. In warm weather, the crowds move out to the terrace overlooking the Seine and Notre-Dame. ⊠ *55 quai de Bourbon, 4ᵉ* ☎ *01–43–54–02–59* ▭ *MC, V* ☺ *Closed Wed. and Aug. No lunch Thurs.* Ⓜ *Pont Marie.*

$$–$$$ ✕ **La Coupole.** This world-renowned, cavernous spot in Montparnasse practically defines the term brasserie. It might have lost its intellectual aura since restoration (the art deco murals look better than ever), but La Coupole has been popular since the days when Jean-Paul Sartre and Simone de Beauvoir were regulars and is still great fun. Expect the usual brasserie menu—including perhaps the largest shellfish platter in Paris—choucroute, and over-the-top desserts. ⊠ *102 bd. du Montparnasse, 14ᵉ* ☎ *01–43–20–14–20* ▭ *AE, DC, MC, V* Ⓜ *Vavin.*

★ **$$** ✕ **Ze Kitchen Galerie.** If the name isn't exactly inspired, the cooking shows unbridled creativity and a sense of fun. From a deliberately deconstructed menu featuring raw fish, soups, pastas, and "à la plancha" plates, expect dishes such as a chicken wing, broccoli, and artichoke soup with lemongrass, or pork ribs with curry jus and white beans. All in all, one of the most mouth-tickling kitchens in the city. ⊠ *4 quai des Grands-Augustins, 6ᵉ* ☎ *01–44–32–00–32* ⊟ *AE, DC, MC, V* ⊘ *Closed Sun. No lunch Sat.* Ⓜ *St-Michel.*

$–$$ ✕ **Le Café des Délices.** There is a lot to like about this Montparnasse bistro, from the warm Asia-meets-Africa interior, with little pots of spices on each table, to the polished service and lip-smacking food. Drop in for the bargain €14 lunch, or indulge in à la carte dishes such as sea bream on white beans cooked with anchovy, lemon, coriander, and chili pepper. ⊠ *87 rue d'Assas, 6ᵉ* ☎ *01–43–54–70–00* ⊟ *AE, MC, V* ⊘ *Closed Aug.* Ⓜ *Vavin.*

★ **$** ✕ **Les Pipos.** The tourist-trap restaurants along romantic rue de la Montagne Ste-Genevieve are enough to make you despair—and then you stumble across this corner bistro, bursting with chatter and laughter. Slang for students of the École Polytechnique nearby, Les Pipos is everything you could ask of a Latin Quarter bistro: the space is cramped, the food substantial, and conversation flows as freely as the wine. ⊠ *2 rue de L'Ecole-Polytechnique, 5ᵉ* ☎ *01–43–54–11–40* ⊟ *No credit cards* ⊘ *Closed Sun. and 2 wks. in Aug.* Ⓜ *Maubert-Mutualité.*

Where to Stay

Right Bank

$$$$ ⊡ **Costes.** Baron de Rothschild hasn't invited you this time? No matter—just stay here at Jean-Louis and Gilbert Costes's sumptuous hotel and you won't know the difference. The darling of the fashion and media set, the place conjures up the palaces of Napoléon III, with stunning rooms swathed in rich garnet and bronze tones and luxurious fabrics. ⊠ *239 rue St-Honoré, 75001* ☎*01–42–44–50–50* ⎙*01–42–44–50–01* ⊕*www.hotelcostes.com* ⤂ *77 rooms, 5 suites* ⚬ *Restaurant, pool, bar* ⊟ *AE, DC, MC, V* Ⓜ *Tuileries.*

★ **$$$$** ⊡ **Crillon.** The Crillon began life as a regal palace designed for Louis XV in 1758 by Jacques-Ange Gabriel to preside over the north side of the fabled place de la Concorde. In 1909 it became a hostelry and since then has played host to generations of diplomats, celebrities, and refined travelers. Most rooms are lavishly decorated with rococo and Directoire antiques, crystal-and-gilt wall sconces, and gilt fittings. The sheer quantity of marble downstairs—especially in highly praised Les Ambassadeurs restaurant—is staggering. ⊠ *10 pl. de la Concorde, 75008* ☎ *01–44–71–15–00; 800/888–4747 in the U.S.* ⎙ *01–44–71–15–02* ⊕*www.crillon.com* ⤂*90 rooms, 57 suites* ⚬*2 restaurants, 2 bars* ⊟*AE, DC, MC, V* Ⓜ *Concorde.*

★ **$$$$** ⊡ **Meurice.** One of the finest hotels in the world is now even finer, thanks to the multimillion-dollar face-lift funded by the Sultan of Brunei. Few salons are as splendorous as the famous dining room here—all gilt boiseries, pink roses, and Edwardian crystal—and guest rooms, furnished with Persian carpets, marble mantelpieces, and ormolu clocks, are now more soigné than ever. ⊠ *228 rue de Rivoli, 75001* ☎ *01–44–58–10–10* ⎙*01–44–58–10–15* ⊕ *www.meuricehotel.com* ⤂ *160 rooms, 36 suites* ⚬ *2 restaurants, bar* ⊟ *AE, DC, MC, V* Ⓜ *Tuileries, Concorde.*

★ **$$$$** ⊡ **Pavillon de la Reine.** This magnificent hotel, filled with Louis XIII–style fireplaces and antiques, is in a mansion reconstructed from original 17th-century plans. Ask for a duplex with French windows overlooking the first of two flower-filled courtyards behind the historic Queen's Pavilion. ⊠ *28 pl. des Vosges, 75003* ☎ *01–40–29–19–19; 800/447–7462 in the U.S.* ⎙ *01–40–29–19–20* ⊕ *www.pavillon-de-la-reine.com* ⤂ *30 rooms, 25 suites* ⚬ *Bar* ⊟ *AE, DC, MC, V* Ⓜ *Bastille, St-Paul.*

$$$ ⊡ **Axial Beaubourg.** A solid bet in the Marais, this hotel in a 16th-century building has beamed ceilings in the lobby and in the six first-floor rooms. A top-to-bottom reworking has resulted in a sleeker, hipper interior, with higher prices to match the fancy brown fabrics and added amenities. The Centre Pompidou and the Picasso Museum are five minutes away. ⊠ *11 rue du Temple, 75004* ☎ *01–42–72–72–22* 🖷 *01–42–72–03–53* ⊕ *www.axialbeaubourg.com* 🛏 *39 rooms* ⊟ *AE, DC, MC, V* Ⓜ *Hôtel-de-Ville.*

★ $$–$$$ 🏨**Caron de Beaumarchais.** The theme of this intimate jewel is the work of Caron de Beaumarchais, who wrote *The Marriage of Figaro* in 1778. Rooms are faithfully decorated to reflect the taste of 18th-century French nobility. The second- and fifth-floor rooms with balconies are the largest; those on the sixth floor have views across Right Bank rooftops. ⊠ *12 rue Vieille-du-Temple, 75004* ☎ *01–42–72–34–12* 🖷 *01–42–72–34–63* ⊕ *www.carondebeaumarchais.com* 🛏 *19 rooms* ⊟ *AE, DC, MC, V* Ⓜ *Hôtel-de-Ville.*

$$–$$$ 🏨**Deux-Iles.** A tiny Ile St-Louis hotel, the best asset of the Deux-Iles is its lovely neighborhood setting. With red-and-gold floral fabrics and contemporary art on the walls, the rooms unsuccessfully try to mix modern and 17th-century fashions. Ask for one overlooking the little garden courtyard. In winter a roaring fire warms the basement lounge. ⊠ *59 rue St-Louis-en-l'Ile, 75004* ☎ *01–43–26–13–35* 🖷 *01–43–29–60–25* ⊕ *www. hotel-ile-saintlouis.com* 🛏 *17 rooms* ⊟ *AE, MC, V* Ⓜ *Pont-Marie.*

★ $$–$$$ 🏨**Étoile-Péreire.** Behind a quiet, leafy courtyard in the chic residential district of Parc Monceau is this unique, intimate hotel, consisting of two parts: a fin-de-siècle building on the street and a 1920s annex overlooking an interior courtyard. All of the rooms have individually decorated period or cultural themes. The copious breakfast is legendary, featuring 40 assorted jams and jellies. ⊠ *146 bd. Péreire, 75017* ☎ *01–42–67–60–00* 🖷 *01–42–67–02–90* ⊕ *www.etoileper.com* 🛏 *21 rooms, 5 suites* ♨ *Bar* ⊟ *AE, DC, MC, V* Ⓜ *Péreire.*

$$ 🏨**Bretonnerie.** This small hotel is in a 17th-century *hôtel particulier* (town house) on a tiny street in the Marais. Rooms are done in Louis XIII style, complete with upholstered walls, but vary considerably in size from spacious to cramped. ⊠ *22 rue Ste-Croix-de-la-Bretonnerie, 75004* ☎ *01–48–87–77–63* 🖷 *01–42–77–26–78* ⊕ *www.labretonnerie.com* 🛏 *22 rooms, 7 suites* ⊟ *MC, V* Ⓜ *Hôtel-de-Ville.*

$$ 🏨**Place des Vosges.** A loyal, eclectic clientele swears by this small, historic Marais hotel on a delightful street just off place des Vosges. The Louis XIII–style reception area and rooms with oak-beamed ceilings, rough-hewn stone, and a mix of rustic finds from secondhand shops evoke the old Marais. ⊠ *12 rue de Birague, 75004* ☎ *01–42–72–60–46* 🖷 *01–42–72–02–64* 🛏 *16 rooms* ⊟ *AE, DC, MC, V* Ⓜ *Bastille.*

★ $–$$ 🏨**Queen's Hôtel.** One of a handful of hotels in the tony residential district near the Bois de Boulogne, Queen's is a small, comfortable, old-fashioned hotel with a high standard of service. Each room focuses on a different 20th-century French artist. ⊠ *4 rue Bastien-Lepage, 75016* ☎ *01–42–88–89–85* 🖷 *01–40–50–67–52* ⊕ *www.queens-hotel.fr* 🛏 *21 rooms, 1 suite* ⊟ *AE, DC, MC, V* Ⓜ *Michel-Ange Auteuil.*

$ 🏨**Louvre Forum.** This friendly hotel is a find: smack in the center of town, it has clean, comfortable, well-equipped rooms at extremely reasonable prices. ⊠ *25 rue du Bouloi, 75001* ☎ *01–42–36–54–19* 🖷 *01–42–33–66–31* ⊕ *www.hotellouvreforum.com* 🛏 *27 rooms, 16 with shower* ♨ *Bar* ⊟ *AE, DC, MC, V* Ⓜ *Louvre.*

$ 🏨**Tiquetonne.** Just off marché Montorgueil and a short hoof from Les Halles, this is one of the least expensive hotels in the city center. The rooms aren't much to look at, but they're always clean. Book a room facing the quiet, pedestrian rue Tiquetonne, not the loud rue Turbigo. ⊠ *6 rue Tiquetonne, 75002* ☎ *01–42–36–94–58* 🖷 *01–42–36–02–94* 🛏 *45 rooms* ⊟ *AE, MC, V* Ⓜ *Etienne Marcel or Châtelet.*

Left Bank

$$$$ 🏨 **Pont Royal.** Once a favorite watering hole of T. S. Eliot and Gabriel Garcia Marquez, this sumptuously refurbished hotel now attracts more businessmen than writers. You can't find a more comfortable hotel, however, or a better location—a quiet street just off boulevard St-Germain. The views from the top floors are magnificent. The library-themed bar resembles a British reading room, and the Atelier Joël Robuchon restaurant is a popular luncheon spot among well-heeled locals. ⊠ *7 rue de Montalembert, 75007* ☎*01–42–84–70–00* 🖷*01–42–84–71–00* ⊕*www. hotel-pont-royal.com/hpr* 🛏*65 rooms, 10 suites* ⚐ *Restaurant, bar* ▤ *AE, DC, MC, V* Ⓜ *Rue de Bac.*

★ **$$$–$$$$** 🏨 **Hôtel d'Aubusson.** This 17th-century mansion, once setting to Paris's first literary salon, is now one of the finest *petites hôtels de luxe* in the city, with original Aubusson tapestries, Versailles-style parquet floors, and a chiseled stone fireplace. Even the small rooms are good size by Paris standards, and all are decked out in rich burgundies, greens, or blues. The 10 best rooms have canopied beds and ceiling beams. In summer, you can have your breakfast or predinner drink in the paved courtyard. ⊠ *33 rue Dauphine, 75006* ☎ *01–43–29–43–43* 🖷 *01–43–29–12–62* ⊕ *www.hoteldaubusson.com* 🛏*49 rooms* ⚐ *Bar* ▤ *AE, MC, V* Ⓜ *Odéon.*

★ **$$$–$$$$** 🏨 **Relais St-Germain.** With a gracious staff and all the countrified flowers, beams, and flea-market finds you could dream of, the Relais St-Germain oozes with traditional 17th-century flavor. The rooms, done in bright yellow-and-red printed fabrics and paints, are at least twice the size of what you find at other hotels for the same price. Breakfast is included. ⊠ *9 carrefour de l'Odéon, 75006* ☎ *01–43–29–12–05* 🖷 *01–46–33–45–30* ⊕ *www.hotel-rsg.com* 🛏 *21 rooms, 1 suite* ⚐ *Bar* ▤ *AE, DC, MC, V* Ⓜ *Odéon.*

$$$ 🏨 **Grands Hommes.** The "Great Men" this hotel has in mind are resting in peace in the Panthéon, which the Grands Hommes overlooks. The hotel's look is neo-Greek and Roman, combining plaster busts, urns, and laurel-wreath motifs with plush beige, eggplant, and burgundy fabrics. Top-floor rooms have balconies and fantastic north-facing views of the cityscape. ⊠ *17 pl. du Panthéon, 75005* ☎ *01–46–34–19–60* 🖷 *01–43–26–67–32* ⊕ *www.hoteldesgrandshommes.com* 🛏 *31 rooms* ▤ *AE, DC, MC, V* Ⓜ *RER: Luxembourg.*

$$$ 🏨 **Latour Maubourg.** In the residential heart of the 7e arrondissement, this homey and unpretentious town house accents intimacy and personalized service. Its simply furnished rooms have antique armoires, marble fireplaces, and high ceilings. ⊠ *150 rue de Grenelle, 75007* ☎*01–47–05–16–16* 🖷 *01–47–05–16–14* ⊕ *www.latour-maubourg.fr* 🛏*9 rooms, 1 suite* ▤ *MC, V* Ⓜ *La Tour–Maubourg.*

★ **$$$** 🏨 **Relais Saint-Sulpice.** A savvy clientele frequents this fashionable little hotel sandwiched between place St-Sulpice and the Luxembourg Gardens. Eclectic art objects and furnishings, some with an Asian theme, somehow pull off a unified look. The rooms, set around an ivy-clad courtyard, are understated, with simple colors and comfortable furnishings. There's a sauna downstairs, right off the breakfast salon. ⊠ *3 rue Garancière, 75006* ☎ *01–46–33–99–00* 🖷 *01–46–33–00–10* 🛏 *26 rooms* ▤ *AE, DC, MC, V* Ⓜ *St-Germain-des-Prés, St-Sulpice.*

$$ 🏨 **Bonaparte.** The congeniality of the staff only makes a stay in this intimate place more of a treat. Old-fashioned upholsteries, 19th-century furnishings, and paintings create a quaint feel in the relatively spacious rooms. And a night in the heart of St-Germain is incomparable. ⊠ *61 rue Bonaparte, 75006* ☎ *01–43–26–97–37* 🖷 *01–46–33–57–67* 🛏*29 rooms* ▤ *MC, V* Ⓜ *St-Germain-des-Prés.*

$$ 🏨 **Grandes Écoles.** Distributed among a trio of three-story buildings, the baby-blue-and-white rooms and their flowery Louis-Philippe furnishings create a grandmotherly vibe, which may not be to everyone's taste. But the verdant interior courtyard can be your second living room or a perfect breakfast spot. ✉ *75 rue du Cardinal-Lemoine, 75005* ☎ *01-43-26-79-23* 🖷 *01-43-25-28-15* ⊕ *www.hotel-grandes-ecoles. com* 🛏 *51 rooms* ▭ *MC, V* Ⓜ *Cardinal-Lemoine.*

$$ 🏨 **Hôtel du Lys.** Just climb the convoluted stairway to your room (there's no elevator) in this former 17th-century royal residence, one of the city's oldest. Well maintained by Madame Steffen, the hotel's rooms reveal unique quirks and nooks, weathered antiques and exposed beams throughout. ✉ *23 rue Serpente 75006* ☎ *01-43-26-97-57* 🖷 *01-44-07-34-90* ⊕ *www.hoteldulys.com* 🛏 *22 rooms* ▭ *MC, V* Ⓜ *St-Michel, Odéon.*

$$ 🏨 **Jardin du Luxembourg.** Blessed with a charming staff and a stylish look, this hotel is one of the most sought-after in the Latin Quarter. Rooms are a bit small (common for this neighborhood) but intelligently furnished for optimal space, and warmly decorated *à la Provençal*. Ask for one with a balcony overlooking the street. ✉ *5 impasse Royer-Collard, 75005* ☎ *01-40-46-08-88* 🖷 *01-40-46-02-28* 🛏 *27 rooms* ▭ *AE, DC, MC, V* Ⓜ *Luxembourg.*

★ **$$** 🏨 **Le Tourville.** Here is a rare find: an intimate, upscale hotel at affordable prices. Each room has crisp, virgin-white damask upholstery set against pastel or ocher walls, a smattering of antiques, original artwork, and fabulous old mirrors. ✉ *16 av. de Tourville, 75007* ☎ *01-47-05-62-62; 800/528-3549 in the U.S.* 🖷 *01-47-05-43-90* ⊕ *www.hoteltourville. com* 🛏 *27 rooms, 3 suites* 🍸 *Bar* ▭ *AE, DC, MC, V* Ⓜ *École Militaire.*

$–$$ 🏨 **Familia.** The hospitable Gaucheron family bends over backward for you. The rooms are snazzed up with murals of typical city scenes, and bathrooms have modern fixtures and tilework. Book a month ahead for one with a walk-out balcony on the second or fifth floor. ✉ *11 rue des Écoles, 75005* ☎ *01-43-54-55-27* 🖷 *01-43-29-61-77* ⊕ *www.hotel-paris-familia.com* 🛏 *30 rooms* ▭ *AE, MC, V* Ⓜ *Cardinal-Lemoine.*

$ 🏨 **Hotel du Parc Montsouris.** This modest hotel in a 1930s villa is on a quiet residential street next to the lovely Parc Montsouris on the southern edge of the city. Attractive oak pieces and high-quality French fabrics embellish the small but clean rooms. ✉ *4 rue du Parc-Montsouris, 75014* ☎ *01-45-89-09-72* 🖷 *01-45-80-92-72* ⊕ *www.hotel-parc-montsouris. com* 🛏 *28 rooms, 7 suites* ▭ *AE, MC, V* Ⓜ *Montparnasse-Bienvenue.*

Nightlife & the Arts

For detailed entertainment listings, look for the weekly magazines *Pariscope, L'Officiel des Spectacles, Zurban,* and *Figaroscope.* The **Paris Tourist Office** (☎ 08-92-68-31-12 for 24-hr English-language hot line ⊕ www.parisbienvenu.com) is a good source of information about weekly events.

Tickets can be purchased at the place of performance (beware of scalpers: counterfeit tickets have been sold); otherwise, try your hotel or a travel agency such as **Opéra Théâtre** (✉ 7 rue de Clichy, 9e ☎ 01-40-06-01-00 Ⓜ Trinité). For most concerts, tickets can be bought at the music store **FNAC** (✉ 1–5 rue Pierre-Lescot, Forum des Halles, 1er ☎ 01-49-87-50-50 Ⓜ Châtelet–Les Halles). **Virgin Megastore** (✉ 52 av. des Champs-Élysées, 8e ☎ 08-03-02-30-24 Ⓜ Franklin-D.-Roosevelt) has a particularly convenient ticket booth. Half-price tickets for same-day theater performances are available at the **Kiosques Théâtre** (✉ across from 15 pl. de la Madeleine Ⓜ Madeleine ✉ in front of the Gare Montparnasse, pl. Raoul Dautry, 14ᵉ Ⓜ Montparnasse-Bienvenüe). Both are open Tuesday–Saturday 12:30–8, Sunday 12:30–4. Expect to pay a €3 commission per ticket and to wait in line.

The Arts

CLASSICAL MUSIC & OPERA
Inexpensive organ or chamber music concerts take place in many churches throughout the city. Following are other venues for opera, orchestral concerts, and recitals. Classical- and world-music concerts are held at the **Cité de la Musique** (✉ 221 av. Jean-Jaurès, Parc de La Villette, 19ᵉ ☎ 01–44–84–44–84 Ⓜ Porte de Pantin). **Opéra de la Bastille** (✉ pl. de la Bastille, 12ᵉ ☎ 08–92–69–78–68 ⊕ www.opera-de-paris.fr Ⓜ Bastille) is the main venue for opera; however, grand opera deserves a grand house (not the modern Bastille one), so you might plan your trip around dates when the troupe presents an opera at the historic Opéra Garnier, about twice a year. The Orchestre de Paris and other leading international orchestras play regularly at the **Salle Pleyel** (✉ 252 rue du Faubourg-St-Honoré, 8ᵉ ☎ 08–25–00–02–52 Ⓜ Ternes). **Théâtre des Champs-Élysées** (✉ 15 av. Montaigne, 8ᵉ ☎ 01–49–52–50–50 Ⓜ Alma-Marceau), an art deco temple, hosts concerts and ballet.

DANCE
Opéra Garnier (✉ pl. de l'Opéra, 9ᵉ ☎ 08–92–69–78–68 ⊕ www.opera-de-paris.fr Ⓜ Opéra), the "old Opéra," now concentrates on dance. In addition to being the home of the well-reputed Paris Ballet, it also bills a number of major foreign troupes. The **Théâtre de la Ville** (✉ 2 pl. du Châtelet, 4ᵉ Ⓜ Châtelet ✉ 31 rue des Abbesses, 18ᵉ Ⓜ Abbesses ☎ 01–42–74–22–77 for both ⊕ www.chatelet-theatre.com) is the place for contemporary dance.

FILM
Paris has hundreds of cinemas. Admission is generally €7–€9, with reduced rates at some theaters on Monday. In principal tourist areas such as the Champs-Élysées and Les Halles, and on the boulevard des Italiens near the Opéra, theaters show English films marked *"version originale"* (v.o., i.e., not dubbed). Classics and independent films often play in Latin Quarter theaters. **Cinémathèque Française** (✉ 42 bd. de Bonne-Nouvelle, 10ᵉ ☎ 01–56–26–01–01 Ⓜ Bonne-Nouvelle ✉ Palais de Chaillot, 7 av. Albert-de-Mun, 16ᵉ ☎ 01–56–26–01–01 Ⓜ Trocadéro) shows classic French and international films Wednesday–Sunday.

THEATER
A number of theaters line the Grand Boulevards between Opéra and République, but there is no Paris equivalent of Broadway or the West End. Shows are mostly in French. The **Comédie Française** (✉ pl. Colette, 1ᵉʳ ☎ 01–44–58–15–15 Ⓜ Palais-Royal) performs distinguished classical drama by the likes of Racine, Molière, and Corneille. The **Théâtre de la Huchette** (✉ 23 rue de la Huchette, 5ᵉ ☎ 01–43–26–38–99 Ⓜ St-Michel) is a tiny venue where Ionesco's short plays make a deliberately ridiculous mess of the French language. The **Odéon Théâtre de l'Europe** (✉ 8 bd. Berthier, 17ᵉ ☎ 01–44–85–40–40 Ⓜ Porte de Clichy) is undergoing extensive renovations at the moment and has moved to this Clichy address until 2005.

Nightlife

BARS & CLUBS
The hottest area at the moment is around Ménilmontant and Parmentier, and the nightlife is still hopping in and around the Bastille. The Left Bank tends to be more subdued. The Champs-Élysées is making a strong comeback, though the crowd remains predominantly foreign. Gay and lesbian bars are mostly concentrated in the Marais (especially around rue Ste-Croix-de-la-Bretonnerie) and include some of the most happening addresses in the city.

If you want to dance the night away, some of the best clubs are the following: **Les Bains** (✉ 7 rue du Bourg-l'Abbé, 3ᵉ ☎ 01–48–87–01–80

Ⓜ Étienne-Marcel) opened in 1978 and back in the disco era was often featured in French *Vogue*—believe it or not, this is still a hot ticket and difficult to get past the velvet rope. **Le Nouveau Casino** (✉ 109 rue Oberkampf, 11ᵉ ☎ 01–43–57–57–40 Ⓜ St-Maur, Parmentier) will have you dancing until dawn in this electro-baroque atmosphere complete with Murano chandeliers. **Queen** (✉ 102 av. des Champs-Élysées, 8ᵉ ☎ 01–53–89–08–90 Ⓜ George-V) is one of the hottest nightspots in Paris; although it's predominantly gay, everyone else lines up to get in, too.

Paris has many bars; following is a sampling. The famous brasserie **Alcazar** (✉ 62 rue Mazarine, 6ᵉ ☎ 01–53–10–19–99 Ⓜ Odéon) comes complete with a stylish bar on the first floor, where you can sip a glass of wine under the huge glass roof. From Wednesday to Saturday a DJ spins either lounge or Latin music. Pop into the **Barrio Latino** (✉ 46–48 rue du Faubourg-St-Antoine, 12ᵉ ☎ 01–55–78–84–75 Ⓜ Bastille) for Franco-Latino opulence—red velvet couches, wide, airy atrium, warm, sexy colors—in this three-story club. **Batofar** (✉ 11 quai François-Mauriac, 11ᵉ ☎ 01–45–83–33–06 Ⓜ Quai-de-la-Gare) is an old lighthouse tug refitted to include a bar, a club, and a concert venue. **Café Charbon** (✉ 109 rue Oberkampf, 11ᵉ ☎ 01–43–57–55–13 Ⓜ St-Maur/Parmentier) is in a beautifully restored 19th-century café. **Le Fumoir** (✉ 6 rue Amiral-de-Coligny, 1ᵉʳ ☎ 01–42–92–00–24 Ⓜ Louvre) is a fashionable spot for cocktails, with comfy leather sofas and a library. **Polo Room** (✉ 3 rue Lord-Byron, 8ᵉ ☎ 01–40–74–07–78 Ⓜ George-V) is the very first martini bar in Paris; there are polo photos on the walls, regular live jazz concerts, and DJs every Friday and Saturday night. **Wax** (✉ 15 rue Daval, 11ᵉ ☎ 01–40–21–16–16 Ⓜ Bastille) is worth a visit simply for its decor—check out the orange-and-pink walls and the molded plastic banquettes by the window; DJs spin techno and house every evening.

CABARETS Paris's cabarets are household names, shunned by Parisians and beloved of foreign tourists, who flock to the shows. Prices range from €40 (simple admission plus one drink) to more than €125 (dinner plus show). **Crazy Horse** (✉ 12 av. George-V, 8ᵉ ☎ 01–47–23–32–32 Ⓜ Alma-Marceau) shows more bare skin than anyone else. **Lido** (✉ 116 bis av. des Champs-Élysées, 8ᵉ ☎ 01–40–76–56–10 Ⓜ George-V) shows are oceans of feathers and sequins. **Moulin Rouge** (✉ 82 bd. de Clichy, 18ᵉ ☎ 01–53–09–82–82 Ⓜ Blanche) has come a long way since the days of the cancan.

JAZZ CLUBS Paris is one of the great jazz cities of the world. For nightly schedules consult the magazines *Jazz Hot, Jazzman,* or *Jazz Magazine.* Nothing gets going until 10 or 11 PM, and entry prices vary widely from about €10 to €25. **New Morning** (✉ 7 rue des Petites-Écuries, 10ᵉ ☎ 01–45–23–51–41 Ⓜ Château-d'Eau) is a premier spot for serious fans of avant-garde jazz, folk, and world music. The greatest names in French and international jazz play at **Le Petit Journal** (✉ 71 bd. St-Michel, 5ᵉ ☎ 01–43–26–28–59 Ⓜ Luxembourg); it's closed Sunday.

ROCK CLUBS Lists of upcoming concerts are posted on boards in the FNAC stores. Following are the best places to catch big French and international stars: **L'Élysée Montmartre** (✉ 72 bd. Rochechouart, 18ᵉ ☎ 01–55–07–06–00 Ⓜ Anvers) is one of the prime venues for emerging French and international rock groups. **L'Olympia** (✉ 28 bd. des Capucines, 9ᵉ ☎ 01–47–42–25–49 Ⓜ Opéra) once hosted legendary concerts by Jacques Brel and Edith Piaf, but the theater has since been completely rebuilt. **Palais Omnisports de Paris-Bercy** (✉ 8 bd. de Bercy, 12ᵉ ☎ 08–25–03–00–31 Ⓜ Bercy) is the largest venue in Paris and is where top international stars perform. **Zenith** (✉ Parc de la Villette, 19ᵉ ☎ 01–42–08–60–00 Ⓜ Porte-de-Pantin) stages large rock shows.

Shopping

Boutiques

Although the born and bred French designer is a rarity these days, Paris still remains the capital of European chic. The top designer shops are found on **avenue Montaigne, rue du Faubourg-St-Honoré,** and **place des Victoires.** The area around **St-Germain-des-Prés** on the Left Bank is full of small specialty shops and boutiques, and has recently seen an influx of the elite names in haute couture. The top names in jewelry are grouped around the **place Vendôme,** and scores of trendy boutiques can be found around **Les Halles.** Between the pre-Revolution mansions and tiny kosher food stores that characterize the **Marais** are numerous gift shops and clothing stores. Search for bargains on the streets around the foot of Montmartre, or in the designer discount shops (Cacharel, Rykiel, Chevignon) along **rue d'Alésia** in Montparnasse.

Department Stores

Au Bon Marché (⊠ 24 rue de Sèvres, 7ᵉ Ⓜ Sèvres-Babylone). **Au Printemps** (⊠ 64 bd. Haussmann, 9ᵉ Ⓜ Havre-Caumartin). **Galeries Lafayette** (⊠ 40 bd. Haussmann, 9ᵉ Ⓜ Chaussée-d'Antin). **La Samaritaine** (⊠ 19 rue de la Monnaie, 1ᵉʳ Ⓜ Pont-Neuf).

Food & Flea Markets

Every *quartier* (neighborhood) has at least one open-air food market. Some of the best are on rue de Buci, rue Mouffetard, rue Montorgueil, rue Mouffetard, and rue Lepic. Sunday morning until 1 PM is usually a good time to go; they are likely to be closed Monday.

The **Marché aux Puces de St-Ouen** (Ⓜ Porte de Clignancourt), just north of Paris, is one of Europe's largest flea markets; it's open Saturday through Monday. Best bargains are to be had early in the morning. Smaller flea markets also take place at **Porte de Vanves** and **Porte de Montreuil** (weekends only).

Gifts

Old prints are sold by *bouquinistes* (secondhand booksellers) in stalls along the banks of the Seine. **Fauchon** (⊠ 30 pl. de la Madeleine, 8ᵉ Ⓜ Madeleine) is perhaps the world's most famous gourmet food shop. **Guerlain** (⊠ 47 rue Bonaparte, 6ᵉ Ⓜ Mabillon) carries legendary French perfumes. **Lavinia** (⊠ 3–5 bd. de la Madeleine, 8ᵉ ☎ 01–42–97–20–20 Ⓜ St-Augustin) has the largest selection of wine of any store in Europe— more than 6,000 wines and spirits from all over the world ranging from the simple to the sublime. **Les Salons du Palais-Royal Shiseido** (⊠ Jardins du Palais-Royal, 142 Galerie de Valois, 25 rue de Valois, 1ᵉʳ ☎ 01–49–27–09–09 Ⓜ Palais-Royal) is a magical boutique where each year Shiseido's creative genius Serge Lutens dreams up two new scents, which are then sold exclusively here. The **Musée des Arts Décoratifs** (⊠ 107 rue de Rivoli, 1ᵉʳ Ⓜ Palais-Royal) has superchic home decorations. **Sentou Galerie** (⊠ 24 rue du Pont Louis-Philippe, 4ᵉ ☎ 01–42–71–00–01 Ⓜ St-Paul) is the place to find the original gift; look for the oblong suspended crystal vases that would look great hanging above the dinner table or in front of a mirror.

Paris Essentials

AIRPORTS & TRANSFERS

International flights arrive at either Charles de Gaulle Airport (known as Roissy to the French), 24 km (15 mi) northeast of Paris, or at Orly Airport, 16 km (10 mi) south of the city. Both airports have two terminals.

TRANSFERS Both airports have train stations from which you can take the RER, the local commuter train, to Paris. The advantages of this are speed, price (€8 to Paris from Roissy, €9 from Orly via the shuttle-train Orlyval with a change to the RER at Antony), and the RER's direct link with the métro system. The disadvantage is having to lug your bags around. Taxi fares between the airports and Paris are about €25 (Orly) and €35 (Roissy), with a €1 surcharge per bag. The Paris Airports Service and PariShuttle run eight-passenger vans to any destination in Paris from Roissy (€19 for one person, €13 per person for two or more) and Orly (€17 for one, €13 per person for two or more). You need to book at least two days in advance; there are English-speaking operators.

From Roissy, Air France Buses (open to all) leave every 15 minutes from 5:40 AM to 11 PM. The fare is €10 and the trip takes from 40 minutes to 1½ hours during rush hour. You arrive at the Arc de Triomphe or Porte Maillot, on the Right Bank by the Hôtel Concorde-Lafayette. From Orly, buses operated by Air France leave every 12 minutes from 6 AM to 11 PM and arrive at the Air France terminal near Les Invalides on the Left Bank. The fare is €8, and the trip takes 30–60 minutes, depending on traffic. Alternatively, the Roissybus, operated by Paris Transport Authority (RATP), runs directly to and from rue Scribe, by the Opéra, every 15 minutes and costs €8. RATP also runs the Orlybus to and from Denfert-Rochereau and Orly every 15 minutes for €6; the trip takes around 35 minutes.

🚖 Taxis & Shuttles **Paris Airports Service** ☎ 01-55-98-10-80 🖷 01-55-98-10-89 🌐 www.parisairportservice.com. **PariShuttle** ☎ 01-43-90-91-91 🖷 01-43-90-91-10 🌐 www.parishuttle.com.

BUS TRAVEL WITHIN PARIS

Most buses run from around 6 AM to 8:30 PM; some continue until midnight. Routes are posted on the sides of buses. *Noctambus* (night buses) operate from 1 AM to 6 AM between Châtelet and nearby suburbs. They can be stopped by hailing them at any point on their route. You can use a métro ticket on the bus, or you can buy a one-ride ticket on board. You need to show weekly/monthly/special tickets to the driver; if you have individual tickets, punch one in the red and gray machines on board the bus.

CAR TRAVEL

Expressways converge on the capital from every direction: A1 from the north (225 km [140 mi] to Lille); A13 from Normandy (225 km [140 mi] to Caen); A4 from the east (500 km [310 mi] to Strasbourg); A10 from the southwest (580 km [360 mi] to Bordeaux); and A7 from the Alps and Côte d'Azur (465 km [290 mi] to Lyon). Each connects with the *périphérique*, the beltway, around Paris. Exits are named by *porte* (gateway), not numbered. The "Périphe" can be fast, but gets very busy; try to avoid it between 7:30 and 10 AM and between 4:30 and 7:30 PM. Car travel within Paris is best avoided because finding parking is difficult and there is heavy traffic for much of the day.

EMERGENCIES

Automatic phone booths can be found at various main crossroads for use in police emergencies (Police-Secours) or for medical help (Services Médicaux).

🔲 Doctors & Dentists **Dentist** ☎ 01-43-37-51-00. **Doctor** ☎ 01-43-07-77-77.
🔲 Emergency Services **Ambulance** ☎ 15 or 01-45-67-50-50. **Police** ☎ 17.
🔲 Hospitals **American Hospital** ✉ 63 bd. Victor-Hugo, Neuilly ☎ 01-46-41-25-25. **British Hospital** ✉ 3 rue Barbès, Levallois-Perret ☎ 01-47-58-13-12.

24-hour Pharmacies **Pharmacie Dérhy** ⊠ 84 av. des Champs-Élysées, 8ᵉ 01-45-62-02-41, open 24 hrs. **Pharmacie Européenne** ⊠ 6 pl. de Clichy, 9ᵉ 01-48-74-65-18 Ⓜ Place de Clichy.

ENGLISH-LANGUAGE MEDIA

Most newsstands in central Paris sell *Time, Newsweek,* and the *International Herald Tribune,* as well as the English dailies. Some English-language bookstores include the ones listed below.

Bookstores **Brentano's** ⊠ 37 av. de l'Opéra. **Galignani** ⊠ 224 rue de Rivoli. **Shakespeare & Co.** ⊠ 37 rue de la Bûcherie. **W. H. Smith** ⊠ 248 rue de Rivoli.

MÉTRO TRAVEL

Fourteen métro lines crisscross Paris and the nearby suburbs, and you are seldom more than a five-minute walk from the nearest station. It's essential to know the name of the last station on the line you take, since this name appears on all signs within the system. A connection (you can make as many as you please on one ticket) is called a *correspondance.* At junction stations illuminated orange signs bearing the names of each line terminus appear over the corridors that lead to the various correspondances.

The métro connects at several points in Paris with RER trains that race across Paris from suburb to suburb: RER trains are a sort of supersonic métro and can be great time-savers. All métro tickets and passes are valid for RER and bus travel within Paris.

Some lines and stations in the seedier parts of Paris are a bit risky at night—in particular, Line 2 (Porte-Dauphine–Nation) and the northern section of Line 13 from St-Lazare to St-Denis/Asnières. The long, bleak corridors at Jaurès and Stalingrad are a haven for pickpockets and purse snatchers. But the Paris métro is relatively safe, as long as you don't walk around with your wallet in your back pocket or travel alone (especially women) late at night.

Access to métro and RER platforms is through an automatic ticket barrier. Slide your ticket in flat and pick it up as it pops up farther along. Keep your ticket; you'll need it again to leave the RER system. Sometimes green-clad métro authorities will ask to see it when you enter or leave the station: be prepared—they aren't very friendly, and they will impose a large fine if you can't produce your ticket.

FARES & SCHEDULES The métro runs from 5:30 AM to 1:15 AM. Métro tickets cost €1.30 each, though a *carnet* (10 tickets for €9.70) is a far better value. If you're staying for a week or more, the best deal is the *coupon jaune* (weekly) or *carte orange* (monthly) ticket, sold according to zone. Zones 1 and 2 cover the entire métro network (€13 per week or €45 per month). If you plan to take a suburban train to visit monuments in the Ile-de-France, you should consider a four-zone ticket (Versailles, St-Germain-en-Laye; €22 per week) or a six-zone ticket (Rambouillet, Fontainebleau; €30 per week). For these weekly or monthly tickets, you need a pass (available from train and major métro stations), and you must provide a passport-size photograph.

Alternatively, there are one-day (*Mobilis*) and two-, three-, and five-day (*Paris Visite*) unlimited travel tickets for the métro, bus, and RER. Unlike the coupon jaune, which is good from Monday morning to Sunday evening, the latter are valid starting any day of the week and give you admission discounts to a number of museums and tourist attractions. Prices are €8.50, €14, €18.50, and €27 for Paris only; €15, €27, €38, and €46 for the suburbs, including Versailles, St-Germain-en-Laye, and Disneyland Paris.

TAXIS

Taxi rates are based on location and time. Daytime rates, A (7 AM–7 PM), within Paris are €0.55 per kilometer (½ mi), and nighttime rates, B, are around €0.90 per kilometer. Suburban zones and airports, C, are €1.10 per kilometer. There is a basic hire charge of €2 for all rides, a €0.90 supplement per piece of luggage, and a €0.75 supplement if you're picked up at an SNCF station. Waiting time is charged at €19.85 per hour. The easiest way to get a taxi is to ask your hotel or restaurant to call a taxi for you, or go to the nearest taxi stand (there's one every couple of blocks); cabs with their signs lighted can be hailed but are difficult to spot; they are not all a single, uniform color. There is an average supplement of €2.30 for a fourth passenger. It is customary to tip the driver about 10%.

TOURS

BICYCLE TOURS There are a number of companies that rent bikes for the day and organize interesting cycling tours around the city. Paris à Vélo, C'est Sympa rents bikes for €13 per day and also organizes three-hour excursions of both the heart of Paris and lesser-known sites. Mike's Bike Tours organizes guided tours of Paris daily from March to November.
 Fees & Schedules **Paris à Vélo, C'est Sympa** ⊠ 37 bd. Bourdon, 4ᵉ ☎ 01-48-87-60-01 ⊕ www.parisvelosympa.com. **Mike's Bike Tours** ⊠ 24 rue Edgar-Faure, 15ᵉ ☎ 01-56-58-10-54 ⊕ www.mikesbiketoursparis.com.

BOAT TOURS Boats depart in season every half hour from 10:30 to 5 (less frequently in winter) and cost €6–€15. Lunch or dinner tours average about €46–€90. The *Bateaux Mouches* leave from the Pont de l'Alma, at the bottom of avenue George-V. The *Bateaux Parisiens* leave from the Pont d'Iéna, by the Eiffel Tower. The *Vedettes du Pont-Neuf* set off from beneath square du Vert-Galant on the western edge of the Ile de la Cité.

BUS TOURS Bus tours of Paris provide a good introduction to the city. Tours usually start from the tour company's office and are generally given in double-decker buses with either a live guide or tape-recorded commentary. They last two to three hours and cost about €23. Tour operators also have theme tours (historic Paris, modern Paris, Paris by night) that last from 2½ hours to all day and cost up to €60, as well as excursions to Chartres, Versailles, Fontainebleau, the Loire Valley, and Mont-St-Michel (for a cost of €50–€150). Cityrama is one of the largest bus operators in Paris; it also runs minibus excursions that pick you up and drop you off at your hotel. Paris Vision is another large bus tour operator.
 Fees & Schedules **Cityrama** ⊠ 4 pl. des Pyramides, 1ᵉʳ ☎ 01-44-55-60-00. **Paris Vision** ⊠ 214 rue de Rivoli, 1ᵉʳ ☎ 08-00-03-02-14.

PRIVATE GUIDES Tours of Paris or the surrounding areas by limousine or minibus for up to seven passengers for a minimum of three hours can be organized. The cost starts at about €50 per hour. Contact Paris Major Limousines, Paris Bus, or Cityscope.
 Cityscope ⊠ 11 bis bd. Haussmann, 9ᵉ ☎ 01-53-34-11-91. **Paris Bus** ⊠ 22 rue de la Prévoyance, Vincennes ☎ 01-43-65-55-55. **Paris Major Limousines** ⊠ 14 rue Atlas, 19ᵉ ☎ 01-44-52-50-00.

WALKING TOURS Numerous special-interest tours concentrate on historical or architectural topics. Most are in French and cost between €6 and €10. Details are published in the weekly magazines *Pariscope* and *L'Officiel des Spectacles* under the heading "Conférences."

TRAIN TRAVEL

Paris has five international stations: Gare du Nord (for northern France, northern Europe, and England via Calais or the Channel Tunnel); Gare de l'Est (for Strasbourg, Luxembourg, Basel, and central Europe); Gare

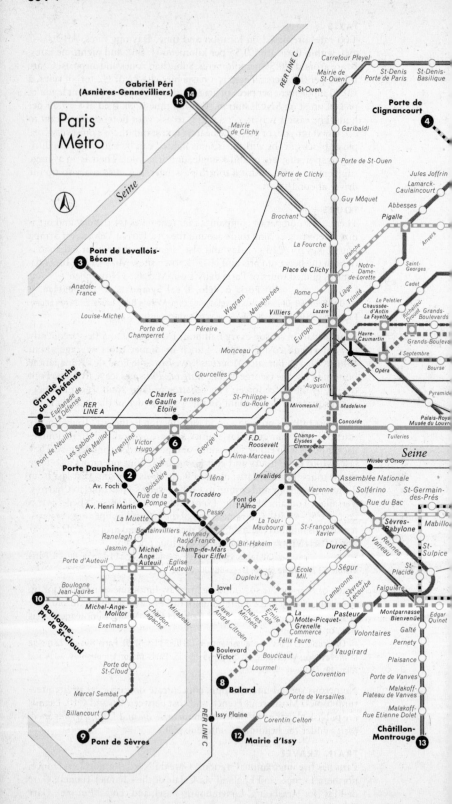

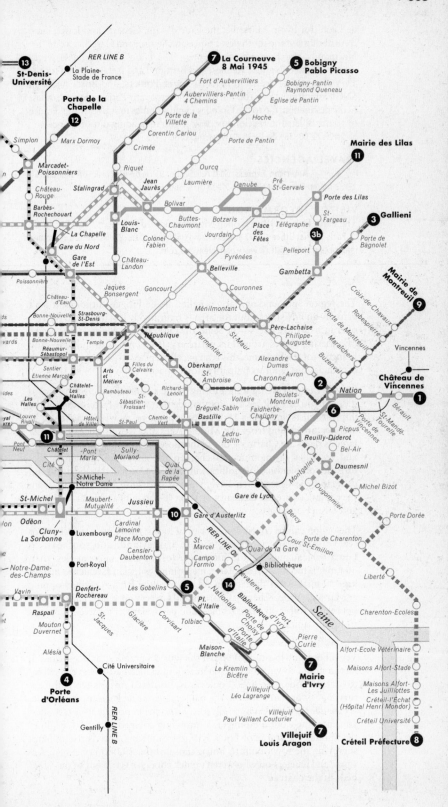

de Lyon (for Lyon, Marseille, the Côte d'Azur, Geneva, and Italy); Gare d'Austerlitz (for the southwest France and Spain); and Gare St-Lazare (for Normandy and England via Dieppe). The Gare Montparnasse serves western France (Nantes, Rennes, and Brittany) and is the terminal for the TGV Atlantic service from Paris to Tours, Poitiers, and Bordeaux. Call SNCF for information. You can reserve tickets at any Paris station regardless of the destination. Go to the Grandes Lignes counter for travel within France or to the Billets Internationaux desk if you're heading out of France.
🚉 SNCF ☎ 08-36-35-35-35 ⊕ www.sncf.com.

TRAVEL AGENCIES
🚉 Contacts **American Express** ✉ 11 rue Scribe, 9ᵉ ☎ 01-47-77-77-07. **Wagons-Lit** ✉ 32 rue du Quatre-Septembre, 2ᵉ ☎ 01-42-66-15-80.

VISITOR INFORMATION
The Paris Tourist Office is open Monday–Saturday 9–8 and Sunday 11–8.
🚉 **Paris Tourist Office** ✉ 127 av. des Champs-Élysées ☎ 08-92-68-31-12 for recorded information in English ⊕ www.parisbienvenu.com.

ILE-DE-FRANCE

The region surrounding Paris is called Ile-de-France, although it isn't actually an *île* (island). But the area is figuratively isolated from the rest of France by three rivers—the Seine, the Oise, and the Marne—that weave meandering circles around its periphery. If you are visiting Paris—and France—for the first time, this is an excellent place to get a taste of French provincial life, with its palpably slower pace.

Parts of the area are fighting a losing battle against the encroaching capital, but you can still see the countryside that was the inspiration for the impressionists and other 19th-century painters, as well as a wealth of architecture dating from the Middle Ages and Renaissance. The most famous sights are Chartres—one of the most beautiful French cathedrals—and Versailles, the monumental château of Louis XIV, the Sun King. Before the completion of Versailles, king and court resided in the delightful château of St-Germain-en-Laye, west of Paris—an easy day trip from the capital, as are the châteaux of Vaux-le-Vicomte and Fontainebleau, and Disneyland Paris.

The region can be covered in a series of loops: travel west from Paris to see Versailles and Chartres; east to Disneyland; and southeast to Fontainebleau and Vaux-le-Vicomte. Most of these sights are less than 80 km (50 mi) away from Paris, including Disneyland, which is just 32 km (20 mi) east of the city via A4 (or take the RER-A train, stopping at Marne-la-Vallée-Chessy). Chartres and Giverny are a little farther away, but they're still easily manageable—and particularly enjoyable—side trips from the capital.

Versailles

Versailles is the location of one of the world's grandest palaces—and in fact, a grand town, since the château's opulence had to have a setting to match. Wide, tree-lined boulevards, bordered by massive 18th-century mansions, fan out from the palace; avenue de Paris, in the middle, is broader than the Champs-Élysées. From the imposing place d'Armes, you enter the Cour d'Honneur, a sprawling cobbled forecourt. Right in the middle, the statue of Louis XIV, the Sun King, stands triumphant, surveying the town built to house those of the 20,000 noblemen, servants, and hangers-on who weren't quick enough to grab one of the 3,000 beds in the château.

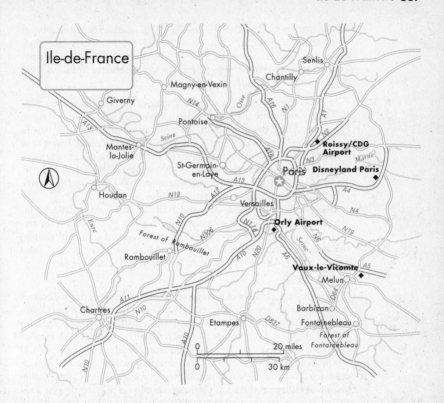

★ The **Château de Versailles** took 50 years to complete. Hills were flattened, marshes drained, forests transplanted, and water from the Seine channeled from several miles away to supply the magnificent fountains. Visit the **Grands Appartements** (State Rooms), rooms that made up the royal quarters, and the famous **Galerie des Glaces** (Hall of Mirrors), where the controversial Treaty of Versailles, asserting Germany's responsibility for World War I, was signed in 1919. Both can be visited without a guide, but you can get an audio tour in English. It was hardly surprising that Louis XIV's successors rapidly felt out of sync with the biceps-flexing baroque bombast of his great salons. Louis XV and Louis XVI preferred to cower in the **Petits Appartements** (Private Apartments), where the royal family and friends lived in relative intimacy; guided tours take you through these jewel-like rooms. Elsewhere are two showstoppers: the icily marble chapel and the magnificent opera house—one of the first oval rooms in France, built in the north wing for Louis XV in 1770.

After all this grandeur, the park outside is the ideal place to get your breath back. Although badly damaged by hurricane-force winds during a storm on Christmas 1999, the château's vast **park** remains a masterpiece of formal landscaping by Andre Le Nôtre. At one end of the Petit Canal, which crosses the Grand Canal at right angles, is the **Grand Trianon,** a scaled-down pleasure palace built in the 1680s. The **Petit Trianon,** nearby, is a sumptuously furnished 18th-century mansion that is one of the landmarks of French Neoclassicism, commissioned by Louis XV; Marie-Antoinette would flee here to avoid the stuffiness of the court. Nearby, she built the **Hameau**—a tiny village, complete with dairy and water mill, where she led a make-believe life pretending to be a shepherdess with flocks of perfumed sheep. Its fairy-tale spell is still seductive—no wonder Toni (to use the queen's nickname) didn't see the

Revolution coming. ☎ 01–30–84–76–18 ⊕ *www.chateauversailles.fr* ☉ *Château May–Sept., Tues.–Sun. 9–6; Oct.–Apr., Tues.–Sun. 9–5. Galerie des Glaces Tues.–Sun. 9:45–5. Grand Trianon and Petit Trianon Tues.–Sun. noon–5:30. Tours of Petits Appartements every 15 mins. Park daily 7* AM*–8* PM *or dusk.*

★ **$$$$** ✕ **Les Trois Marches.** If your tour of Versailles has left you feeling a little hungry and more than a little regal, promenade over to the Trianon Palace hotel and this restaurant, long recognized as one of the best in Ile-de-France. Celebrated chef Gérard Vié's take on *cuisine bourgeoise* is one of the luxest, and most delectable, around. The restaurant has a fetching and huge terrace open in pleasant weather. ✉ *1 bd. de la Reine* ☎ 01–39–50–13–21 ⌕ *Reservations essential* 🏛 *Jacket and tie* ▭ *AE, DC, MC, V* ☉ *Closed Sun., Mon., and Aug.*

$$ ✕ **Quai No. 1.** Barometers, sails, and model boats fill this small, charming seafood restaurant. In summer you can enjoy your meal on the terrace. Lobster and home-smoked salmon are specialties, and any dish on the two prix-fixe menus is a good value. ✉ *1 av. de St-Cloud* ☎ 01–39–50–42–26 ▭ *MC, V* ☉ *Closed Mon. No dinner Sun.*

Chartres

If Versailles is the climax of French secular architecture, perhaps Chartres is its religious apogee—an extraordinary fusion of Romanesque and Gothic elements brought together at a moment when the flame of medieval faith burned brightest. Long before you reach Chartres, you'll see this famous cathedral towering over the plain and wheat fields. The attractive old town, steeped in religious history and dating from before the Roman

★ conquest, is still laced with winding medieval streets. The Gothic **Cathédrale Notre-Dame** is the sixth Christian church on the site; despite a series of fires, it has remained basically the same since the 12th and 13th centuries. The **Portail Royal** (Royal Portal) on the main facade, presenting the life and triumph of the Savior, is one of the country's finest examples of Romanesque sculpture. Inside, the 12th- and 13th-century windows, many of which have been restored over the past decade, come alive even in dull weather, thanks to the deep Chartres blue of the stained glass. All the descriptive prose and poetry that have been lavished on this supreme cathedral can only begin to suggest the strange sense of the numinous that the whole ensemble imparts even to nonbelievers. The cathedral tours by local institution Malcolm Miller are legendary; you can reach him at the telephone number below. ✉ *Crypte: 16 cloître Notre-Dame* ☎ 02–37–21–56–33 ⊕ *www.ville-chartres.com* ☉ *Tours in English Mon.–Sat. noon and 2:45.*

$$$ ✕ **Vieille Maison.** In a refitted 14th-century building a stone's throw from the cathedral, the Vieille Maison serves both excellent nouvelle cuisine and traditional dishes. The menu changes regularly, but invariably includes regional specialties such as asparagus, rich duck pâté, and superb homemade foie gras. ✉ *5 rue au Lait* ☎ 02–37–34–10–67 ▭ *AE, MC, V* ☉ *Closed Mon. No dinner Sun.*

$$ ✕ **Buisson Ardent.** This attractive restaurant, in an old, oak-beamed building opposite the Vieille Maison, serves such dishes as papillotte salmon with seafood risotto and strawberry mille-feuille. ✉ *10 rue au Lait* ☎ 02–37–34–04–66 ▭ *MC, V* ☉ *Closed Wed. No dinner Sun.*

$$–$$$$ ▣ **Grand Monarque.** The most popular rooms in this 18th-century coaching inn are in a separate turn-of-the-20th-century building overlooking a garden. The hotel also has an excellent restaurant with a good choice of prix-fixe menus starting at €29. ✉ *22 pl. des Épars, 28000* ☎ 02–37–18–15–15 🖷 02–37–36–34–18 ⊕ *www.bw-grand-monarque. com* ⇲ *55 rooms* ⌕ *Restaurant, bar* ▭ *AE, DC, MC, V.*

Giverny

This small village is a place of pilgrimage for art lovers enticed by the **Maison et Jardin Claude Monet** (Monet House and Garden). The house where Monet worked and lived for more than 40 years has been faithfully restored; the kitchen with its cool blue tiles and the buttercup-yellow dining room are particularly striking. However, the real pull is the colorful garden and especially the famous lily pond with its Japanese bridge, which was one of Monet's favorite subjects. ✉ *84 rue Claude-Monet* ☎ *02–32–51–28–21* ⊕ *www.giverny.org* ⊗ *Apr.–Oct., Tues.–Sun. 10–6.*

FodorśChoice ★

After touring the painterly grounds of the Monet house, you may wish to see some real paintings at the airy **Musée Américain** (American Museum), along the same road as Monet's House. It displays works by American impressionists who were influenced by—and often studied with—Claude Monet. On-site are a restaurant and *salon de thé* (tearoom), as well as a garden "quoting" some of Monet's plant compositions. ✉ *99 rue Claude-Monet* ☎ *02–32–51–94–65* ⊕ *www.maag.org* ⊗ *Mar.–Oct., Tues.–Sun. 10–6.*

$ ✗**Jardins de Giverny.** This restaurant, with a tile-floor dining room overlooking a rose garden, is a few minutes' walk from Monet's house. Enjoy the €20 lunch menu or choose from a repertoire of inventive dishes such as foie gras spiked with calvados or scallops with wild mushrooms. ✉ *Rue du Roy* ☎ *02–32–21–60–80* ▭ *AE, MC, V* ⊗ *Closed Mon. and Dec.–Feb. No dinner Sun.–Fri.*

Fontainebleau

★

During the early 16th century the flamboyant François I transformed the medieval hunting lodge of Fontainebleau into a magnificent Renaissance palace, the **Château de Fontainebleau.** His successor, Henri II, covered the palace with his initials, woven into the *D* for his mistress, Diane de Poitiers. When he died, his queen, Catherine de' Médicis, carried out further alterations, later continued under Louis XIV. However, it was Napoléon who made a Versailles, as it were, out of Fontainebleau by spending lavishly to restore the neglected property to its former glory. Before he was exiled to Elba, he bade farewell to his Old Guard in the courtyard now known as the **Cour des Adieux** (Farewell Courtyard), with its elegant horseshoe staircase. The **Grands Appartements** (State Rooms) are the main attractions of any visit to the château; these include the **Galerie François-I** (Francis I Gallery) and a covered bridge (built 1528–30) looking out over the Cour de la Fontaine. The magnificent **Salle de Bal** (ballroom) is nearly 100 feet long, with wood paneling, 16th-century frescoes and gilding, and, reputedly, the first coffered ceiling in France, its intricate pattern echoed by the splendid 19th-century parquet floor. If you're here on a weekday, you may also be able to join a guided tour (in French) of the **Petits Appartements** (Private Apartments), used by Napoléon and Joséphine, and the **Musée Napoléon** (Napoleon Museum), which has some mementos, including the leader's imperial uniform. ✉ *Pl. du Général-de-Gaulle* ☎ *01–60–71–50–70* ⊗ *Wed.–Mon. 9:30–5.*

★ $$$$ ✗▣**Aigle-Noir.** This may be Fontainebleau's costliest hotel, but you can't go wrong if you request one of the rooms overlooking either the garden or the palace. Late-18th- or early-19th-century reproduction furniture evokes a Napoleonic mood. The restaurant, Le Beauharnais, serves subtle, imaginative cuisine; reservations are essential and jacket and tie are recommended. ✉ *27 pl. Napoléon-Bonaparte, 77300* ☎ *01–60–74–60–00* 🖨 *01–60–74–60–01* ⊕ *www.hotelaiglenoir.fr* ➥ *56 rooms* ⌂ *Restaurant, pool* ▭ *AE, DC, MC, V.*

$$–$$$ ▣**Londres.** Some balconies at this small hotel overlook the palace entrance and the Cour des Adieux; the 1830 facade is preserved by government

order. Inside, the furnishings are dominated by Louis XV accents. ✉ *1 pl. du Général-de-Gaulle, 77300* ☎*01–64–22–20–21* 🖷*01–60–72–39–16* ⊕ *www.hoteldelondres.com* 🛏 *12 rooms* ⚭ *Restaurant, bar* ▭ *AE, DC, MC, V* ⊘ *Closed 1 wk Aug., and mid-Dec.–early Jan.*

Vaux-le-Vicomte

★ The **Château de Vaux-le-Vicomte** is one of the greatest monuments of 17th-century France, dreamed up by an all-star cast of Louis Le Vau for design, André Le Nôtre in the gardens, and Charles Le Brun on all lead murals. When owner Nicolas Fouquet, the royal finance minister, threw a housewarming party in 1661, Sun King Louis XIV threw a fit of jealousy, hurled Fouquet in the slammer on trumped-up fraud charges, and promptly began building Versailles to prove just who was boss. From your point of view, though, Fouquet's *folie de grandeur* (delusions of grandeur) will probably be a treat. ☎ *01–64–14–41–90* ⊕ *www.vaux-le-vicomte.com* 🖼*€10, candlelight château visits €13* ⊘ *Mid-Mar.–Nov. 11, daily 10–6. Candlelight visits May–mid-Oct., Sat. 8 PM–midnight.*

Disneyland Paris

Get a dose of American pop culture in between visits to the Louvre and the Left Bank. Disneyland Paris is east of the capital, in Marne-la-Vallée, and easily accessible by RER from the city.

The theme park, less than 1½ km (1 mi) across, is ringed by a railroad with whistling steam engines. In the middle of the park is the soaring Sleeping Beauty Castle, surrounded by a plaza from which you can enter each of the "lands": **Frontierland, Adventureland, Fantasyland**, and **Discoveryland**. In addition, **Main Street U.S.A.** connects the castle to the entrance. Also included in the complex is **Walt Disney Studios**, an entertainment center with restaurants, shops, a post office, and a whole host of displays and demonstrations of animation, special effects, and the behind-the-scenes work at a production studio. ☎*01–60–30–60–30* ⊕*www.disneylandparis. com* 🖼 *Apr.–Oct. and Christmas period €38 (€99 for 3-day Passport); Nov.–Mar., except Christmas period, €29 (€79 for 3-day Passport); includes admission to all individual attractions within the park, but not meals* ▭ *AE, DC, MC, V* ⊘ *Mid-June–mid-Sept., daily 9 AM–10 PM; mid-Sept.–mid-June, Sun.–Fri. 10–8, Sat. 9–8; Christmas period, daily 9–8.*

$–$$$ ✕ **Disneyland Restaurants.** The park is peppered with places to eat, ranging from snack bars and fast-food joints to full-service restaurants—all with a distinguishing theme. Eateries serve nonstop as long as the park is open. ☎ *01–60–45–65–40* ▭ *AE, DC, MC, V accepted at sit-down restaurants.*

$$–$$$$ 🛏 **Disneyland Hotels.** The resort has 5,000 rooms in six hotels, all a short distance from the park, ranging from the luxurious Disneyland Hotel to the not-so-rustic Camp Davy Crockett. Free transportation to the park is available at every hotel. ⓘ *Central Reservations Office, B.P. 100, 77777 Marne-la-Vallée, cedex 4* ☎*01–60–30–60–30; 407/934–7639 in the U.S.* 🖷 *01–49–30–71–00* ⚭ *All hotels have at least 1 restaurant, pool, bar* ▭ *AE, DC, MC, V.*

Ile-de-France Essentials

The region is reached only from Paris by car and by regular RER train service. But you might find it convenient to group some sights together: Versailles and Chartres are on the Paris–Chartres train line; Fontainebleau and Vaux-le-Vicomte are within a few miles of each other.

CAR TRAVEL

The region is reached easily from Paris by car. A13 links Paris (from Porte d'Auteuil) to Versailles. You can get to Chartres on A10 from Paris (Porte d'Orléans). For Fontainebleau take A6 from Paris (Porte d'Orléans) or, for a more attractive route, take N6 from Paris (Porte de Charenton) via Melun. The 32-km (20-mi) drive along A4 from Paris to Disneyland Paris takes about 30 minutes, longer in heavy traffic. Disneyland is 4 km (2½ mi) off A4; follow the signs for the park.

TOURS

Following are two private companies that organize regular half-day and full-day tours from Paris to Chartres, Fontainebleau, and Versailles with English-speaking guides. Tours are subject to cancellation, and reservations are suggested.

Cityrama ⊠ 4 pl. des Pyramides, 1ᵉʳ, Paris ☎ 01-44-55-61-00 ⊕ www.cityrama.fr. **Paris Vision** ⊠ 214 rue de Rivoli, 1ᵉʳ, Paris ☎ 01-47-42-72-31 ⊕ www.parisvision.com.

TRAIN TRAVEL

Three lines connect Paris with Versailles; the trip takes about 30 minutes. RER-C5 to Versailles Rive Gauche station takes you closest to the château; trains from Paris (Gare Montparnasse) stop at Versailles Chantiers and continue to Chartres. Trains from Gare St-Lazare stop at La Défense en route to Versailles Rive Droite. Fontainebleau is served by 20 trains a day from Gare de Lyon; a bus leaves from the station (which is in neighboring Avon) for the château. The RER-A4 line goes to Disneyland Paris. Vaux-le-Vicomte is a 7-km (4-mi) taxi ride from the nearest station at Melun, served by regular trains from Paris and Fontainebleau. The taxi ride costs about €20.

SNCF ☎ 08-36-35-35-35 ⊕ www.sncf.com.

VISITOR INFORMATION

Espace du Tourisme d'Ile-de-France ⊠ pl. de la Pyramide-Renversée, 99 rue de Rivoli, 75001 Paris ☎ 08-03-81-80-00. **Chartres** ⊠ pl. de la Cathédrale ☎ 02-37-21-50-00 ⊕ www.ville-chartres.fr. **Disneyland Paris** ✐ B.P. 100, 77777 Marne-la-Vallée, cedex 4 ☎ 01-60-30-60-30 ⊕ www.disneylandparis.com. **Fontainebleau** ⊠ 4 rue Royale ☎ 01-60-74-99-99 ⊕ www.fontainebleau.com. **Versailles** ⊠ 2 bis av. de Paris ☎ 01-39-24-88-88 ⊕ www.versailles-tourisme.com.

THE LOIRE VALLEY

The valley watered by the broad and shallow Loire and caught in a diaphanous web of subtly shifting light is one of the most beautiful areas of France. It was here in the 15th and 16th centuries that the kings of France chose to build their fabulous châteaux *d'agrément*, or pleasure castles, which remain the chief attractions of a region rich in history. They often line the rocky banks of the Loire and its tributaries—the Rivers Cher, Indre, Vienne, and Loir (with no *e*), and in these stately houses, castles, and fairy-tale palaces, Renaissance elegance is often combined with fortresslike medieval mass. The Loire Valley was fought over by France and England during the Middle Ages until, inspired by Joan of Arc, the "Maid of Orleans" (scene of her most rousing military success), France finally managed to expel the English.

The Loire Valley's golden age came under François I, France's flamboyant contemporary of England's Henry VIII. He hired Renaissance craftsmen from Italy and hobnobbed with the aging Leonardo da Vinci, his guest at Amboise. You can see his salamander emblem in many châteaux.

Most of the sights covered here are close to the Loire River along the 170-km (105-mi) stretch between Blois and Saumur. If you're coming from Paris, Châteaudun and Vendôme make attractive stops en route to Blois. Tours, 58 km (36 mi) west of Blois, is the region's major city. Saumur, Chinon, and Amboise are the other main historic towns.

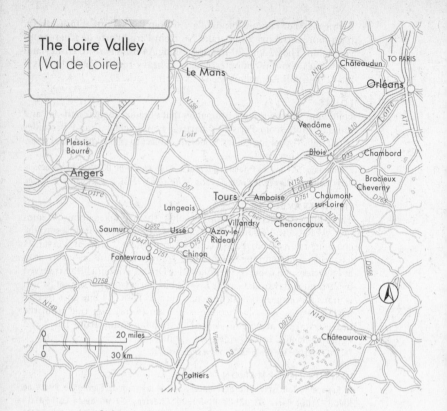

The Loire Valley
(Val de Loire)

Blois

With its forest of towers and tumbling alleyways, Blois is the most attractive of the major Loire towns. It is best known for its massive **Château de Blois,** a mixture of four different styles: Feudal (13th century), Gothic-Renaissance Transition (circa 1500), Renaissance (circa 1520), and Classical (circa 1635). ☎02–54–90–33–33 ☉ Mid-Mar.–Oct., daily 9–6; Nov.–mid-Mar., daily 9–12:30 and 2–5:30.

$$–$$$ ✕ **Au Rendez-vous des Pêcheurs.** This restaurant near the Loire, below the château, serves chef Christophe Cosme's inventive desserts and seafood specialties. ✉ 27 rue du Foix ☎ 02–54–74–67–48 ☰ AE, MC, V ☉ Closed Aug. and Sun. No lunch Mon.

$$ ✕◫ **Médicis.** Your best bet in Blois, this smart, friendly hotel 1 km (½ mi) from the château has comfortable rooms. Each is furnished differently, but all share the same joyous color scheme. Chef-owner Christian Garanger turns out innovative classic dishes—*coquilles St-Jacques* (scallops) with bitter *roquette* lettuce, for instance. ✉ 2 allée François-Ier, 41000 ☎ 02–54–43–94–04 ◱ 02–54–42–04–05 ⊕ www.le-medicis.com ⤳ 11 rooms, 1 suite ⌂ Restaurant ☰ AE, DC, MC, V ☉ Closed Jan.

Chambord

★ ℭ The largest of the Loire châteaux, the palatial **Château de Chambord** (begun in 1519) is in the heart of a vast forest. Another forest is on the roof: 365 chimneys and turrets, representing architectural self-indulgence at its least squeamish. Grandeur or a 440-room absurdity? Judge for yourself, but don't miss the superb spiral staircase—rumored to have been designed by Leonardo da Vinci—or the chance to saunter over the rooftop terrace. ☎ 02–54–50–40–28 ⊕ www.chambord.org ☉ July and Aug., daily 9–6:45; Apr.–June, Sept., and Oct., daily 9–6:15; Nov.–Mar. 9–5:15.

★ **$$** ▣ **Grand St-Michel.** Just across the lawn from the château, this place is reasonably priced and quite a delight. The grand dining room serves comfort food French style; dried flowers, mounted deer heads, and tapestries offer grace notes to its decor. Upstairs, the guest rooms are traditional, somber yet very comfortable. Unfortunately, the grand trees in front of the hotel are now so tall that only two or three rooms still offer a clear view of the château. ✉ *103 pl. St-Michel, 41250* ☎ *02–54–20–31–31* 🖷 *02–54–20–36–40* ➥ *39 rooms* ⚲ *Restaurant* ▤ *MC, V* ☯ *Closed mid-Nov.–mid-Dec.*

Amboise

This bustling town has two star attractions. The **Château d'Amboise,** dating from 1500, has splendid grounds, a rich interior, and fine views of the river from the battlements. But it wasn't always so peaceful: in 1560, more than 1,000 Protestant "conspirators" were hanged from these battlements during the Wars of Religion. ☎ *02–47–57–00–98* ⊕ *www. chateau-amboise.tm.fr* ☯ *Nov.–Mar., daily 9–noon and 2–4:45; Apr.–June, Sept. and Oct., daily 9–6; July and Aug., daily 9–7.*

☙ The **Clos-Lucé,** a 15th-century brick manor house, was the last home of Leonardo da Vinci, who was invited to stay by François I and died here in 1519. His engineering genius is illustrated by models based on his plans and sketches. ✉ *2 rue du Clos-Lucé* ☎ *02–47–57–62–88* ☯ *Sept.–June, daily 9–6; July and Aug., daily 9–7.*

$ ✕▣ **Blason.** This delightful, small hotel is two blocks behind the château. The old building has rooms of different shapes and sizes: Rooms 109 and 229 are especially nice. The pretty little restaurant has a seasonal menu that begins at €12 and might include roast lamb with garlic or medallions of pork. There's no lunch served on Wednesday or Saturday, and the restaurant is closed Tuesdays. ✉ *11 pl. Richelieu, 37400* ☎ *02–47–23–22–41* 🖷 *02–47–57–56–18* ➥ *28 rooms* ⚲ *Restaurant* ▤ *AE, DC, MC, V* ☯ *Closed mid-Jan.–mid-Feb.*

Chenonceaux

The small village of Chenonceaux, on the Cher River, is best known as the site of the "most romantic" of all the Loire châteaux. The early-16th-century **Château de Chenonceau** (without the *x*) straddles the tranquil Cher like an unfinished bridge and was the magical abode for several of France's most famous ladies, including Diane de Poitiers—who received the chateau as a gift from King Henri II, only to have to give it back to his wife, Catherine de' Medici, on his death—and Madame Dupin, the latter so beloved by the townspeople that they spared her home from destruction during the worst days of the French Revolution. Thankfully—since this is arguably the most beautiful château in France (at least from the outside), surrounded by elegant gardens and plane trees and mirrored in the river; its symmetrical style is basically Italianate in design since Catherine had Philibert de l'Orme design the signature gallery hall that spans the width of the river. Inside are fine paintings, colossal fireplaces, and richly worked ceilings, restored by the owners, the Menier family of sugar fame and fortune. A museum with wax figures depicting scenes from the château's history is in an outbuilding. Be sure to enjoy the gardens and walk along the embankment to see the Loir flowing under Chenonceau's arcades; boats are available for hire for a ride along the riverbanks. ☎ *02–47–23–90–07* ⊕ *www.chenonceau.com* ☯ *Feb.–May and Oct.–mid-Nov., daily 9–5:30; June–Sept., daily 9–7; Dec. and Jan., daily 9–4:30.*

Fodor'sChoice
★

$$ ✕▣ **Bon Laboureur.** Historic and stylish, this has been a favorite hostelry since 1882. Four generations of the Jeudi family have run this elegant inn. Rooms in the old house are comfortably traditional; those in the former stables are larger and more modern; the biggest are in the converted manor house across the street. Most are high-style, with many rooms having toile-de-jouy accents. The restaurant occupies a glowing pale-green dining room with wood beams, and offers nouvelle (and expensive) dishes that would be worthy of top Paris chefs. ⊠ *6 rue du Dr-Bretonneau, 37150* ☎ *02–47–23–90–02* 🖷 *02–47–23–82–01* ⊕ *www.amboise.com* ⇝ *24 rooms* ⚲ *Restaurant, pool, bar* ▤ *AE, DC, MC, V* ☉ *Closed Jan.–mid-Feb. and mid-Nov.–mid-Dec.*

★ **$–$$** ✕▣ **Roseraie.** What the Roseraie may lack in style, compared with its illustrious neighbor the Bon Laboureur, it makes up for with the joyful welcome of its English-speaking hosts, Laurent and Sophie Fiorito. Rooms are simple but spacious and quiet—especially those overlooking the garden—and copious meals are served in the rustic dining room. ⊠ *7 rue du Dr-Bretonneau, 37150* ☎ *02–47–23–90–09* 🖷 *02–47–23–91–59* ⊕ *www.charminghotel.com* ⇝ *17 rooms* ⚲ *Restaurant, pool, bar* ▤ *AE, DC, MC, V* ☉ *Closed mid-Nov.–Feb.*

Tours

The largest city along the Loire, with 250,000 inhabitants, Tours was extensively damaged in World War II. But the timber-frame houses in the medieval center of Tours, the attractive old quarter around place Plumereau, were tastefully restored.

The **Cathédrale St-Gatien** (1239–1484) numbers among France's most impressive churches. The influence of local Renaissance sculptors and craftsmen is evident on the facade's ornate stonework. The stained glass in the choir is particularly delicate; some of it dates from 1320. ⊠ *Rue Lavoisier* ☎ *02–47–47–05–19* ☉ *Daily 8–noon and 2–6.*

★ **$$$–$$$$** ✕▣ **Jean Bardet.** Rooms and suites at this stately Empire-style mansion, though luxurious, are on the exorbitant side. In the restaurant, Bardet, one of France's top 20 chefs, showcases produce from his rare herb and vegetable garden. Signature dishes include baby eel in red wine or oysters poached in Muscadet on a puree of watercress. Reservations are essential. The restaurant doesn't serve lunch Saturday, Monday, or Tuesday, and is closed outright on Mondays, November to March. For real style, hire Bardet's Rolls-Royce to take you on a tour of the Loire. ⊠ *Château Belmont, 57 rue Groison, 37100* ☎ *02–47–41–41–11* 🖷 *02–47–51–68–72* ⊕ *www.jeanbardet.com* ⇝ *16 rooms, 5 suites* ⚲ *Restaurant, pool* ▤ *AE, DC, MC, V* ☉ *Closed Sun. evening and Mon., Nov.–Mar.*

$$$ ▣ **Univers.** The Univers is the best hotel in central Tours. Murals in the lobby depict some of the famous people who have stayed here since it opened in 1846: Winston Churchill, Sarah Bernhardt, Maurice Chevalier, Rudyard Kipling, Ernest Hemingway, Edith Piaf, and the duke of Windsor. Rooms in this old hotel are all slightly different and all cleverly designed; wood paneling and soft colors give them warmth; most look onto the garden. ⊠ *5 bd. Heurteloup, 37000* ☎ *02–47–05–37–12* 🖷 *02–47–61–51–80* ⇝ *77 rooms, 8 suites* ⚲ *Restaurant* ▤ *AE, DC, MC, V.*

Villandry

★ The **Château de Villandry,** near the Cher River, is known for its painstakingly relaid 16th-century **gardens,** which are now the finest example of French Renaissance garden design in France. Green-thumbers flock here to gaze at the long avenues of 1,500 manicured lime trees and the gigantic terraces planted with rare species of flowers and vegetables. The château interior was restored in the mid-19th century. Note the painted and gilded ceiling from Toledo and the collection of Spanish pictures. ☎ 02–47–50–02–09 ⊕ *www.chateauvillandry.com* ☉ *Château June–Sept., daily 9–6; Oct.–mid-Nov. and mid-Feb.–May, daily 9:30–5. Gardens June–Sept., daily 9–7:30; Oct.–May, daily 9–dusk.*

Azay-le-Rideau

The fairy-tale **Château d'Azay-le-Rideau** was built in the early 16th century and was meant to evoke the distant seigneurial past, when knighthood was in flower. Its high roof and corner turrets are reflected in the Indre River, which surrounds the château like a moat. This graceful ensemble compensates for the château's spartan interior, as does the charm of the surrounding village. ☎ 02–47–45–42–04 ⊕ *www.monum.fr* ☉ *Apr.–Oct., daily 9:30–6; Nov.–Mar., daily 9:30–12:30 and 2–5:30.*

Ussé

The **Château d'Ussé**—actually in the village of Rigny-Ussé—claims to be the inspiration for the castle in Charles Perrault's fairy tale, *Sleeping Beauty.* Its bristling turrets, terraces, and forest backdrop are undeniably romantic. Be sure to visit the dainty Renaissance chapel in the park. ☎ 02–47–95–54–05 ☉ *Mid-Feb.–Mar. and Oct.–mid-Nov., daily 10–noon and 2–5:30; Apr.–May and Sept., daily 9–noon and 2–6:45; June–Aug., daily 9–6:30.*

Saumur

The prosperous town of Saumur is famous for its riding school, wines, and castle. The **Château de Saumur**—a white 14th-century castle—towers above the river. It contains two outstanding museums: the **Musée des Arts Décoratifs** (Decorative Arts Museum), featuring porcelain and enamels, and the **Musée du Cheval** (Equestrian Museum), with saddles, stirrups, skeletons, and Stubbs engravings. ⊠ *Esplanade du Château* ☎ 02–41–40–24–40 ⊕ *www.saumur-tourisme.net* ☉ *June–Sept., daily 9–6; Oct.–May, daily 9–noon and 2–5:30.*

$$–$$$ ✕▥ **Anne d'Anjou.** Close to the center of town, this hotel facing the river has a view of the château (floodlit at night) perched above. Inside the 18th-century building, the simple rooms are filled with both old furniture and contemporary decor; Room 102 has wood-panel paintings and Empire furnishings. The outstanding Les Ménestrels is one of Saumur's best restaurants. ⊠ *32 quai Mayaud, 49400* ☎ 02–41–67–30–30 🖷 02–41–67–51–00 ⊕ *www.hotel-anneanjou.com* ⇌ *45 rooms* ♨ *Restaurant* ▤ *AE, DC, MC, V.*

The Loire Valley Essentials

CAR TRAVEL

The easiest way to visit the Loire châteaux is by car; N152 hugs the riverbank and offers excellent sightseeing possibilities.

TOURS

Bus tours of the main châteaux leave daily in summer from Tours, Blois, and Saumur: Ask at the relevant tourist offices for latest times and prices. Most châteaux insist that you follow one of their tours of their interiors; try to get a booklet in English before joining the tour, as most are in French.

TRAIN TRAVEL

Trains run along the Loire Valley every two hours, supplemented by local bus services. A peaceful way to explore the region is to rent a bicycle at one of the SNCF train stations.
🚆 SNCF ☎ 08–36–35–35–35 ⊕ www.sncf.com.

VISITOR INFORMATION

🆔 Comité Régional du Tourisme Centre-Val de Loire ✉ 37 av. de Paris, 45000 Orléans. **Amboise** ✉ Quai Général-de-Gaulle ☎ 02-47-57-01-37 ⊕ www.amboise-valdeloire.com. **Blois** ✉ 3 av. du Dr-Jean-Laigret ☎ 02-54-90-41-41. **Saumur** ✉ pl. de la Bilange ☎ 02-41-40-20-60. **Tours** ✉ 78 rue Bernard-Palissy ☎ 02-47-70-37-37 ⊕ www.tourisme-touraine.com.

NORMANDY

Jutting out into the Channel, Normandy has had more connections with the English-speaking world, from the invasions of William the Conqueror to those of troops during World War II, than any other part of France. Come here not only to see historic monuments but to explore the countryside, rich with apple orchards, lush meadows, and sandy beaches.

The historic cities of Rouen and Caen, capitals of Upper and Lower Normandy respectively, are full of churches and museums. The Seine Valley is lined with abbeys and castles from all periods; along the coast are remnants of the D-Day landings. Normandy also has one of France's most enduring tourist attractions: the Mont-St-Michel, a remarkable Gothic abbey perched on a rocky mount off the Cotentin peninsula. Étretat on the Alabaster Coast and Deauville, Trouville, and Honfleur on the Côte Fleurie (Flower Coast) are among Normandy's many seaside resorts. Normandy is also recognized as one of France's finest gastronomic regions for its excellent cheeses, cider, calvados (apple brandy), and wide range of seafood dishes. The region is best visited by car, and the A13 expressway, linking Paris to Rouen and Caen, is the backbone of Normandy. At Caen it splits into the fast N13 highway, which spears on to Bayeux and up to Cherbourg; and the A84 expressway, heading southwest to Avranches near the Mont St-Michel.

Rouen

Numbers in the margin correspond to points of interest on the Rouen map.

Although blitzed during World War II, Rouen retains much medieval charm. The square where Joan of Arc was burned at the stake in 1431 has been transformed beyond recognition, but the adjacent rue du Gros-Horloge, with its giant Renaissance clock built in 1527, fires the imagination. You

❶ may be familiar with the facade of Rouen's **Cathédrale Notre-Dame** from Claude Monet's famous series of paintings. The simple Romanesque **Tour St-Romain** on the left dates from 1145 and the more intricate **Tour de Beurre** (Butter Tower) on the right was built in the 15th century in a Flamboyant Gothic style. The cast-iron steeple, the tallest in France, was added in the 19th century. The first flight of the famous **Escalier de la Librairie** (Booksellers' Stairway), attributed to Guillaume Pontifs (also responsible for most of the 15th-century work seen in the cathedral), rises from a tiny balcony just to the left of the transept. The cathedral caught fire twice during the war; Hitler ordered his troops to rescue it the first time, and the Rouennais saved it from Allied bombs the second time. ✉ *Pl. de la Cathédrale* ☎ 02–32–08–32–40 ☻ *Tues.–Sun. 8–6, Mon. 2–6.*

❷ The name of the pedestrian rue du Gros-Horloge, Rouen's most popular street, comes from the **Gros-Horloge** itself, a giant Renaissance clock; in 1527 the Rouennais had a splendid arch built especially for it. A 15th-century belfry gives you the chance to study the iron mechanism. ✉ *Rue du Gros-Horloge* ☻ *Wed.–Mon. 10–1 and 2–6.*

❸ Exactly what the shape of the modern **Église Jeanne d'Arc** (Joan of Arc Church) is supposed to represent is unclear; the flames of St. Joan's fu-

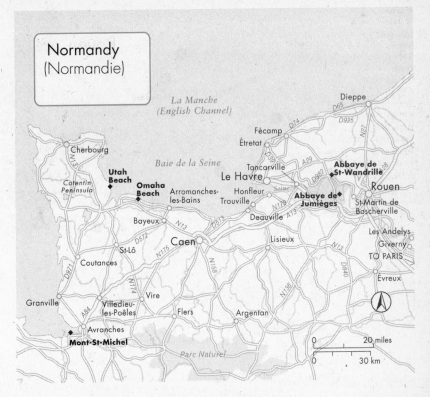

Normandy
(Normandie)

La Manche
(English Channel)

Dieppe

Fécamp
Étretat

Cherbourg

Baie de la Seine

Utah
Beach

Cotentin
Peninsula

Omaha
Beach

Arromanches-
les-Bains

Tancarville

Le Havre

Honfleur
Trouville

Deauville

Abbaye de
St-Wandrille

Rouen

Abbaye de
Jumièges

St-Martin de
Boscherville

Bayeux

Caen

Lisieux

Les Andelys
Giverny
TO PARIS

St-Lô

Coutances

Évreux

Granville

Vire

Villedieu-
les-Poêles

Flers

Argentan

Avranches
Mont-St-Michel

Parc Naturel

0   20 miles
0   30 km

neral pyre? A fish? An overturned boat? Built in 1979, in the old market square on the site of Joan of Arc's execution, this modern church showcases some pleasantly incongruous 16th-century stained glass, rescued from a church bombed in 1944. Outside, the exact spot where St. Joan was burned alive is marked by a concrete and metal cross. ⊠ *Pl. du Vieux-Marché* ☉ *Daily 10–12:15 and 2–6, except Fri. and Sun. morning.*

4 At the **Musée de la Céramique** (Ceramics Museum), you can see examples of local earthenware; Rouen used to be a renowned faience-making center, reaching its heyday in the early 18th century. ⊠ *1 rue Faucon* ☎ *02–35–07–31–74* ⊕ *www.musees-rouen.com* ☉ *Wed.–Mon. 10–1 and 2–6.*

5 The **Musée des Beaux-Arts** (Fine Arts Museum) specializes in 17th- and 19th-century French painting, with an emphasis on works by local artists and a collection of macabre paintings by Rouen-born painter Théodore Géricault. ⊠ *Square Verdrel* ☎ *02–35–52–00–62* ⊕ *www. musees-rouen.com* ☉ *Wed.–Mon. 10–6.*

6 **Abbaye St-Ouen,** an airy, beautifully proportioned 14th-century abbey-church, has splendid medieval stained glass and one of France's most sonorous 19th-century organs. ⊠ *Pl. du Général-de-Gaulle* ☎ *02–32–08–13–90* ☉ *Mid-Mar.–Oct., Wed.–Mon. 8–12:30 and 2–6; Nov.–mid-Dec. and mid-Jan.–mid-Mar., Wed. and weekends 10–12:30 and 2–6.*

7 The late-Gothic church of **St-Maclou** bears testimony to the wild excesses of Flamboyant architecture; take time to examine the central and left-hand portals of the main facade, covered with bronze lion heads and pagan engravings. Inside, note the 16th-century organ, with its Re-

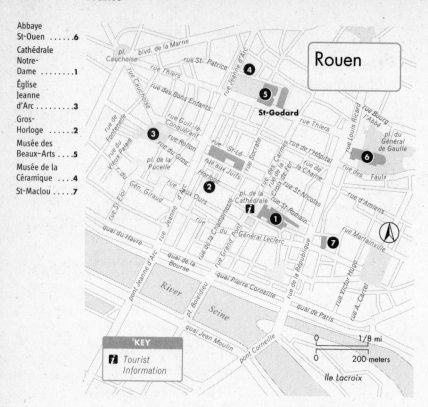

naissance wood carving, and the fine marble columns. ⊠ *Pl. St-Maclou*
☎ *02–35–71–71–72* ◷ *Mon.–Sat. 10–noon and 2–6, Sun. 3–6.*

$$$ ✕ **Couronne.** Behind a half-timber facade gushing geraniums, the "old-est inn in France," dating from 1345, is crammed with leather-uphol-stered chairs and a scattering of sculpture. The traditional Norman cuisine—lobster soufflé, sheep's feet, duck in blood sauce—makes few modern concessions. ⊠ *31 pl. du Vieux-Marché* ☎ *02–35–71–40–90*
▭ *AE, DC, MC, V.*

$–$$ ✕▦ **Vieux Carré.** This lovely little hotel with its tree-lined courtyard is in the heart of old Rouen. Rooms are small, practical, and comfortable—simply furnished with a taste for the exotic. Request one of the rooms on the third floor for a good view of the cathedral. ⊠ *34 rue Ganterie, 76000* ☎ *02–35–71–67–70* ⊟ *02–35–71–19–17* ⟿ *14 rooms* ⌂ *Restau-rant* ▭ *AE, DC, MC, V.*

$ ▦ **Cathédrale.** This appealing hotel is in a medieval building on a nar-row pedestrian street behind the cathedral (you can sleep soundly: the cathedral bells don't boom out the hour at night). Rooms are petite but neat and comfortable. ⊠ *12 rue St-Romain, 76000* ☎ *02–35–71–57–95*
⊟ *02–35–70–15–54* ⊕ *www.hotel-de-la-cathedrale.fr* ⟿ *25 rooms*
⌂ *Bar* ▭ *MC, V.*

Étretat

Claude Monet painted in Étretat as well as in Rouen and Giverny, im-mortalizing the site's rough cliff formations long before the advent of postcards. The white **Falaises d'Étretat** (Étretat Cliffs) are just as famous in France as Dover's are in England. Two immense archways—walls of stone hollowed out by the sea—lead to neighboring beaches at low tide. For a view over the bay and the **Aiguille** (Needle), which is a 300-foot spike of rock jutting out just off the coast, take the little path up the Falaise d'Aval.

$–$$ ✕ **Roches Blanches.** Just off the beach, this family-owned restaurant is a concrete, post–World War II eyesore. But the views and the superbly fresh seafood are another story. ✉ *Rue de l'Abbé-Cochet* ☎ *02–35–27–07–34* 🗖 *MC, V* ☺ *Closed Tues., Wed., and mid-Nov.–mid-Jan.*

$–$$ ✕▣ **Résidence.** This gorgeous hotel is in a 16th-century house in the heart of Étretat just 2 km (1 mi) from the sea. The cheapest rooms are just that, with both the bathroom and the shower in the hallway, although the most expensive have an in-room bathroom and a Jacuzzi. Le Salamandre, the brasserie-type restaurant on the ground floor, is rather cutting-edge for the region: all products are certified organic and farm raised. ✉ *4 bd. René-Coty, 76790* ☎ *02–35–27–02–87* 🖨 *02–35–27–17–07* ⬅ *15 rooms* ☺ *Restaurant* 🗖 *AE, MC, V.*

$$–$$$$ ▣ **Donjon.** In this charming ivy-covered château, rooms are individually furnished, spacious, and comfortable. For spectacular views of the bay, request the Oriental suite, the Horizon, or the Majorie rooms. Reliable French cuisine is served with flair in the romantic restaurant. Rooms are reserved on a half-board basis on weekends. ✉ *Chemin de St-Clair, 76790* ☎ *02–35–27–08–23* 🖨 *02–35–29–92–24* ⊕ *www.ledonjon-etretat.fr* ⬅ *21 rooms* ☺ *Restaurant, pool, bar* 🗖 *AE, DC, MC, V.*

Honfleur

Toward the end of the last century, pretty Honfleur, once an important port for maritime expeditions, became a favorite spot for vacationers and painters, including the impressionists. In summer or on weekends, be prepared for lines at restaurants and cafés. Its lively cobbled streets, harbors full of colorful yachts, and the Église Ste-Catherine—a 15th-century wooden church—make it the most attractive town on the Normandy coast.

$$–$$$ ✕ **Assiette Gourmande.** When chef Gérard Bonnefoy comes into the dining room at Honfleur's unsung top restaurant, he decides what you would enjoy after a few minutes of conversation. Maybe you'll be lucky enough to have the superb coquilles St-Jacques grilled with sautéed asparagus in a raspberry vinaigrette and orange sauce. ✉ *2 quai des Passagers* ☎ *02–31–89–24–88* 🗖 *AE, DC, MC, V* ☺ *Closed Mon. No dinner Sun. except July and Aug.*

★ $$$–$$$$ ✕▣ **Absinthe.** A 16th-century presbytery with stone walls and beamed ceilings houses a small, charming hotel. Rooms are comfortable but small, except for the attic suite, which has a private living room. The elegant reception area is adorned with an imposing stone fireplace. The restaurant is well known for its seasonal seafood dishes such as turbot grilled with leeks. ✉ *10 quai de la Quarantaine* ☎ *02–31–89–53–60* 🖨 *02–31–89–48–48* ⊕ *www.absinthe.fr* ⬅ *7 rooms* ☺ *Restaurant* 🗖 *DC, MC, V* ☺ *Closed mid-Nov.–mid-Dec.*

Trouville–Deauville

Although separated only by the little Touques River, the popular resort towns of Trouville and Deauville are vastly different in mood. Deauville is the fancier of the two, with its palaces, casino, horse racing, and film festival. Some would say all the style is artificial: the town was built from scratch in the 1860s and is invaded each weekend by wealthy Parisians (thereby earning it the title of Paris's honorary 21st arrondissement). Neighboring Trouville retains an active fishing fleet and working population and is less damaging to the wallet. Its large beach is arguably more scenic. High season is kicked off in July and culminates with the American Film Festival the first week in September. If you are planning a visit at this time, reserve in advance and request written confirmation.

$$$$ ✕⊡ **Normandy.** Well-heeled Parisians have been attracted to this imposing hotel, with its half-timber facade and underground passage to the casino, since it opened in 1912. Request a room with a sea view. Creamy sauces are much in evidence in the mouthwatering Norman dishes served in the restaurant. Ask your concierge about special guest prices at the luxurious spa. ⊠ *38 rue Jean-Mermoz, 14800 Deauville* ☎*02–31–98–66–22; 800/223–5652 for U.S. reservations* ⊟ *02–31–98–66–23* ⊕ *www. lucienbarriere.com* ⤴ *297 rooms* ⚲ *Restaurant, pool, bar* ⊟ *AE, DC, MC, V.*

$–$$ ⊡ **Carmen.** This straightforward, unpretentious little hotel is around the corner from the casino and a block from the sea. Rooms range from plain and inexpensive to comfortable and moderately priced. The owners are on hand to give advice. ⊠ *24 rue Carnot, 14360 Trouville* ☎ *02–31–88–35–43* ⊟ *02–31–88–08–03* ⤴ *18 rooms* ⚲ *Restaurant* ⊟ *AE, DC, MC, V* ☾ *Closed Jan.–mid-Feb.*

Bayeux

Bayeux, a few miles inland from the D-Day beaches, was the first French town freed by the Allies in June 1944. It's known primarily as the home

★ of the **Bayeux Tapestry,** known in French as *La Tapisserie de la Reine Mathilde* (Queen Matilda's Tapestry), which tells the epic story of William's conquest of England in 1066. You can rent headphones in English with scene-by-scene commentary. ⊠ *13 bis rue de Nesmond* ☎*02–31–51–25–50* ☾ *May–Aug., daily 9–7; Sept.–Apr., daily 9:30–12:30 and 2–6.*

Dominating the heart of Bayeux is the **Cathédrale Notre-Dame,** a harmonious mixture of Norman (Romanesque) and Gothic architecture. Note the portal on the south side of the transept, depicting the assassination of English archbishop Thomas à Becket in Canterbury Cathedral in 1170. ⊠ *Rue du Bienvenue* ☎ *02–31–92–01–85.*

The **Musée de la Bataille de Normandie** (Battle of Normandy Museum), opposite the British Military Cemetery, traces the Allied advance against the Nazis in June and July of 1944. ⊠ *Bd. du Général-Fabian-Ware* ☎ *02–31–51–46–90* ⊕ *www.mairie-bayeux.fr* ☾ *May–mid-Sept., daily 9:30–6:30; mid-Sept.–Apr., daily 10–12:30 and 2–6.*

$$–$$$ ✕ **Amaryllis.** Pascal Marie's small restaurant has three prix-fixe menus, running €11–€28. The three-course dinner may include a half-dozen oysters, fillet of sole with a cider-based sauce, and pastries or chocolate gateau for dessert. ⊠ *32 rue St-Patrice* ☎ *02–31–22–47–94* ⊟ *MC, V* ☾ *Closed Mon., Sun. evening in winter, and Jan.*

$$$$ ✕⊡ **Chenevière.** In a late-19th-century grand manor in parkland between Bayeux and the coast, this elegant hotel has rooms with modern furnishings, floor-to-ceiling windows, and flowered bedspreads. The restaurant (closed Monday and no lunch on Tuesday) serves classic Norman cuisine. ⊠ *Les Escures, 14520 Commes (9 km [5½ mi] north of Bayeux via D6)* ☎*02–31–51–25–25* ⊟*02–31–51–25–20* ⤴*21 rooms* ⚲ *Restaurant, bar* ⊟ *AE, DC, MC, V* ☾ *Closed Jan.–mid-Feb.*

$$ ⊡ **Churchill.** This friendly, family-run inn in an old town house is within walking distance of Bayeux's major attractions. Rooms vary in shape and size; furnishings are modest and functional. ⊠ *14 rue St-Jean, 14400* ☎ *02–31–21–31–80* ⊟ *02–31–21–41–66* ⤴ *32 rooms* ⊟ *AE, DC, MC, V* ☾ *Closed mid-Nov.–Feb.*

Arromanches-les-Bains

Not much remains to mark the furious fighting waged hereabouts in World War II. In the bay off Arromanches, however, some elements of the floating harbor are still visible: the best view can be had from the terraced platform on D65 above the town. A few hundred yards out to sea you can see numerous vestiges of Mulberry B, an artificial concrete harbor built for the landings. (American troops landed farther up the coast on Omaha Beach, where Mulberry A was destroyed by a storm soon after.)

The **Musée du Débarquement** (Normandy Landings Museum) on the seafront shows the D-Day landing plan and a film (in English) about the operation. ⊠ *Pl. du 6-Juin* ☎ *02-31-22-34-31* ⊙ *May–Sept., daily 9–7; Oct.–Dec. and Feb.–Apr., daily 10–12:30 and 1:30–4:30.*

$$ 🏨 **Victoria.** A well-maintained, charming stone manor, complete with chandeliered main salon, the Victoria is 2 km (1 mi) southwest of Arromanches. Request a room either on the second floor of the main house or one of the cozy, reasonably priced smaller rooms in the attic. ⊠ *Tracy-sur-Mer, 14117* ☎ *02-31-22-35-37* 🖷 *02-31-22-93-38* 🛌 *14 rooms* ▭ *MC, V* ⊙ *Closed Oct.–Mar.*

Mont-St-Michel

Fodor'sChoice
★

The fabled Mont-St-Michel, an offshore rock crowned by the spire of a medieval abbey, is perhaps the most spectacular site in France—and the most-visited outside Paris. The best views can be had on the road from Avranches, to the east. The mount's fame comes not just from its location—until a causeway was built (to be replaced in the near future by a bridge, to allow the tide to circulate), it was cut off from the mainland at high tide. Its dramatic construction dates back to the 8th century, when tons of granite were brought from the nearby Chausey Islands and hauled up the 265-foot peak. It has been a pilgrimage site ever since. The first small chapel to St. Michael, erected by the bishop of Avranches in 709, was centuries later replaced by a large church and buildings, in which for nearly 800 years Benedictine monks peacefully prayed, studied, and worked. **La Merveille** (The Wonder) is the name given to the cluster of Gothic buildings on top. What looks like a fortress is in fact a series of architectural layers that trace the evolution of French architecture from Romanesque to late Gothic. Napoléon ultimately turned it into a prison; then romantic connoisseurs had the complex restored to full medieval glory.

To view the wonders of Mont-St-Michel is not a simple matter. Entering the tiny island through a massive stone gate, you must climb its long single street, the Grand-Rue, which is at first a steep ramp and later becomes a stairway. By the time you have passed the ramparts and reached the celebrated **Escalier de Dentelle** (Lace Staircase) to the gallery of the abbey church, you have climbed no fewer than 900 steps. For most of the year Mont-St-Michel—officially a small village with a permanent population of fewer than 100—is surrounded by sandy beach. The best time to see it is during the high tides of spring and fall, when the sea comes pounding in—dangerously fast—and encircles the mount. Try to plan an overnight stay, so you can truly appreciate the peace and solitary grandeur of the mount without the daytime crowds. ☎ *02-33-89-80-00* ⊕ *www.monum.fr* ⊙ *May–Sept., daily 9:30–11:30 and 1:30–6; Oct.–Apr., Wed.–Mon. 9:30–4:30.*

★ $$–$$$ ✕🏨 **Roche Torin.** This small, ivy-clad manor house on 4 acres of parkland is a delightful alternative to the high cost of staying on Mont-St-Michel. Rooms are pleasantly old-fashioned. The restaurant (closed Tuesday, Wednesday, and Saturday lunch) serves superb seafood and chargrilled lamb. ⊠ *34 rte. de la Roche-Torin, 50220 Courtils (9 km [5½ mi] from Mont-St-Michel)* ☎ *02-33-70-96-55* 🖷 *02-33-48-35-20* 🛌 *15 rooms* ⟁ *Restaurant, bar* ▭ *AE, DC, MC, V* ⊙ *Closed Mon. and mid-Nov.–mid-Feb.*

$$ ✕⌂ **Terrasses Poulard.** This ensemble of buildings is clustered around a small garden in the middle of the mount. The rooms are some of the best—with views of the bay and rustic-style furnishings—and most spacious on the Mont, although many require you to negotiate a labyrinth of steep stairways. The restaurant's reputation derives partly from Mère Poulard's famous soufflé-like omelet and partly from its convenient location. ⊠ *Grande-Rue, 50116* ☎ *02–33–60–14–09* 🖷 *02–33–60–37–31* 🖵 *30 rooms* ⚬ *Restaurant* ▭ *AE, DC, MC, V.*

Normandy Essentials

BUS TRAVEL

For towns not covered by trains, there is a bus network; CNA covers Upper Normandy from Rouen to Le Havre; Autos-Cars Gris runs buses from Fécamp to Le Havre and Étretat; Bus Verts covers the coast from Honfleur to Caen and Bayeux and the D-Day sites.
🚍 **CNA** ☎ 02–35–52–92–92. **Autos-Cars Gris** ☎ 02–35–28–19–88. **Bus Verts** ☎ 02–31–44–77–44.

TOURS

The following companies run daily bus excursions from Paris to Mont-St-Michel for approximately €150, with a guided tour in English, meals, and admission included. This is not for the faint of heart, as buses depart Paris at 7:15 AM and return late, at 10:30 PM.
🚍 **Cityrama** ⊠ 4 pl. des Pyramides, 75001 Paris ☎ 01–44–55–61–00. **Paris Vision** ⊠ 214 rue de Rivoli, 75001 Paris ☎ 08-00-03-02-14.

TRAIN TRAVEL

Though trains leave regularly from Paris to Rouen, Caen, and Bayeux, limited connections make cross-country traveling difficult and time consuming. Visiting many of the historic monuments and towns—such as Honfleur and Mont-St-Michel, which have no train station—means using buses, which run infrequently.
🚍 **SNCF** ☎ 08-36-35-35-35 ⊕ www.sncf.com.

VISITOR INFORMATION

🚍 **Bayeux** ⊠ 3 rue St-Jean ☎ 02-31-51-28-28 ⊕ www.bayeux-tourism.com. **Deauville** ⊠ 112 rue Victor-Hugo ☎ 02-31-14-40-00. **Étretat** ⊠ pl. Maurice-Guillard ☎ 02-35-27-05-21. **Honfleur** ⊠ 9 rue de la Ville ☎ 02-31-89-23-30 ⊕ www.ville-honfleur.fr. **Mont-St-Michel** ⊠ Corps de Garde ☎ 02-33-60-14-30 ⊕ www.mont-saintmichel.com. **Rouen** ⊠ 25 pl. de la Cathédrale ☎ 02-32-08-32-40 ⊕ www.mairie-rouen.fr.

BURGUNDY & LYON

For a region whose powerful, late-medieval dukes held sway over the largest tract of Western Europe and whose current image is closely allied to its expensive wine, Burgundy is a place of surprisingly rustic, quiet charm. Its leading religious monument is the Romanesque basilica in Vézelay, once an important pilgrimage center and today a tiny village hidden in rolling hills. The heart of Burgundy is the dark, brooding Morvan Forest. Dijon, the region's only city, retains something of its medieval opulence, but its present reputation is essentially gastronomic. Top restaurants abound. The vineyards leading down toward Beaune are among the world's most distinguished and picturesque. The vines continue to flourish as you head south along the Saône Valley, through the Mâconnais and Beaujolais, toward Lyon, one of France's most appealing cities.

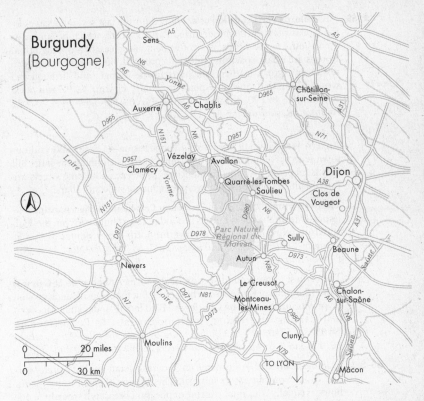

Burgundy is best visited by car. Its meandering country roads invite leisurely exploration. There are few big towns, and traveling around by train is unrewarding, especially as the infrequent cross-country trains steam along at the speed of a legendary Burgundy snail. However, the TGV (high-speed trains) zip out of Paris to Dijon (75 minutes), Mâcon (100 minutes), and Lyon (2 hours). It makes sense for Sens to be your first stop on the way down to Burgundy, as it is just 120 km (75 mi) southeast of Paris on N6—a fast, pretty road that hugs the Yonne Valley south of Fontainebleau. Take A6 if you are in a hurry. Zigzag across N6 and A6, taking the smaller roads that lead off them. A6, which turns into A7, is the highway to the Mediterranean and will take you close to Auxerre, Dijon, Beaune, Mâcon, and Lyon, then down the Rhône valley to Provence.

Sens

Sens is dominated by the 12th-century **Cathédrale St-Étienne,** which seats France's senior archbishop. This is one of the oldest cathedrals in France and has a foursquare facade topped by towers and an incongruous Renaissance campanile. The vast, harmonious interior contains outstanding stained glass of various periods. ✉ *Pl. de la République* ☎ *03–86–64–15–27.*

The roof of the 13th-century **Palais Synodal** (Synodal Palace), alongside Sens's cathedral, is notable for its red diamond-tile motif—incongruously (and misleadingly) added in the mid-19th century by medieval monument restorer Viollet-le-Duc. Annexed to the Palais Synodal is an ensemble of Renaissance buildings. Inside is a museum with archaeological finds from the Gallo-Roman period. The cathedral treasury, on the museum's second floor, is one of the richest in France. ☎ *03–86–64–46–27* ⏱ *June–Sept., daily 10–noon and 2–6; Oct.–May, Wed. and weekends 10–noon and 2–6, Mon., Thurs., and Fri. 2–6.*

★ $$ ✕▣ **Hôtel de Paris et de la Poste.** Owned for the last several decades by the Godard family, the modernized Paris & Poste, which began life as a posthouse in the 1700s, is a convenient and pleasant stopping point. Rooms are clean, spacious, and well equipped. But it is the traditional restaurant, green leather armchairs in the lounge, and little curved wooden bar that give this place its comfy charm. ⊠ *97 rue de la République, 89100* ☎ *03–86–65–17–43* 🖷 *03–86–64–48–45* 🛏 *21 rooms* ⚕ *Restaurant* ▤ *AE, DC, MC, V.*

Auxerre

Auxerre is the jewel of Burgundy's Yonne region—a beautifully laid-out town with three imposing and elegant churches climbing the large hill that is its perch over the Yonne River. Its steep, undulating streets are full of half-timber houses in every imaginable style and shape.

The town's main feature is the muscular **Cathédrale St-Étienne,** rising majestically from the squat houses around it. It was built between the 13th and 16th centuries and has a powerful north tower similar to that at Clamecy. ⊠ *Pl. St-Étienne* ☎ *03–86–52–31–68* ☉ *Easter–Nov., Mon.–Sat. 9–noon and 2–6, Sun. 2–6.*

The earliest aboveground section of the former **Abbaye de St-Germain** is the 12th-century Romanesque bell tower. But the extensive underground crypt was inaugurated by Charles the Bald in 859 and contains its original Carolingian frescoes and Ionic capitals. ⊠ *Pl. St-Germain* ☎ *03–86–51–09–74* ☉ *Guided tours of the crypt Oct.–Apr., daily at 10, 11, and 2–5; May–Sept., daily every ½ hr between 10 and 5:30.*

$$–$$$ ✕ **Jardin Gourmand.** As its name implies, this restaurant has a pretty garden where you can eat in summer. The interior of this former manor house is equally congenial. Terrine of pheasant breast is a specialty: hope that the starter of snails with barley and chanterelles is available. ⊠ *56 bd. Vauban* ☎ *03–86–51–53–52* ▤ *AE, MC, V* ☉ *Closed Mon.*

★ $ ▣ **Château de Ribourdin.** Retired farmer Claude Brodard began building his *chambres d'hôtes* (B&B) in an old stable six years ago, and the result is cozy, comfortable, and reasonably priced. Château de la Borde, named for a small manor nearby, is the smallest, sunniest, and most intimate room. ⊠ *89240 Chevannes (8 km [5 mi] southwest of Auxerre on D1)* ☎ *03–86–41–23–16* 🖷 *03–86–41–23–16* 🛏 *5 rooms* ⚕ *Pool* ▤ *No credit cards.*

Chablis

Famous for its dry white wine, Chablis makes an attractive excursion 16 km (10 mi) to the east of Auxerre, along D965. Beware of village tourist shops selling local wines at unpalatable prices. The surrounding vineyards are dramatic: their steeply banked hills stand in contrast to the region's characteristic gentle slopes.

★ $–$$ ✕▣ **Hostellerie des Clos.** The moderately priced, simple yet comfortable rooms at this inn have floral curtains and wicker tables with chairs. Most of all, come here for chef Michel Vignaud's cooking, some of the best in the region. (The restaurant is closed Wednesday.) ⊠ *18 rue Jules-Rathier, 89800* ☎ *03–86–42–10–63* 🖷 *03–86–42–17–11* 🛏 *26 rooms* ⚕ *Restaurant* ▤ *AE, MC, V* ☉ *Closed late Dec.–mid-Jan.*

Vézelay

Burgundy's leading religious monument is the Romanesque basilica in Vézelay, once an important pilgrimage center and today a somewhat isolated, scenic village set on a peak. The **Basilique Ste-Madeleine** is perched on a rocky crag, with commanding views of the surrounding countryside. It rose to fame during the 11th century as the resting place of the relics of St. Mary Magdalene and became a departure point for the great pilgrimages to Santiago de Compostela in northwest Spain. The church was rescued from decay by the 19th-century Gothic Revival architect Viollet-le-Duc and counts as one of the foremost Romanesque buildings in existence. ⊠ *Pl. de la Basilique* ☎ *03–86–33–39–50* ☸ *Daily 8–8, except during offices Mon.–Sat. 12:30–1:15 and 6–7, Sun. 11–12:15.*

$$$$ ✕🏠 **L'Espérance.** In St-Père-sous-Vézelay, a neighboring village, enjoy chef Marc Meneau's original cuisine at one of France's premier restaurants (closed Tuesday, lunch on Wednesday, and February; reservations and jacket and tie are required). A second restaurant, Le Pré des Marguerites, serves simpler, more traditional, less expensive fare. Accommodations include charming rooms overlooking the garden, full suites in a renovated mill by the trout stream, and cozy, *style-Anglaise* rooms in the annex. ⊠ *89450 St-Père-sous-Vézelay* ☎ *03–86–33–39–10* 🖷 *03–86–33–26–15* ➘ *44 rooms* ⚐ *Restaurant, pool* ▤ *AE, DC, MC, V* ☸ *Closed Feb.*

Dijon

The erstwhile wine-mustard center of the world, site of an important university, and studded with medieval art treasures, Dijon is the capital of Burgundy. Testimony to Dijon's bygone splendor is the **Palais des Ducs** (Ducal Palace), now one of France's leading art museums. The tombs of Philip the Bold and John the Fearless head a rich collection of medieval objects and Renaissance furniture. ⊠ *Cour de Bar du Palais des États* ☎ *03–80–74–52–70* ☸ *Wed.–Mon. 10–6.*

With its spindlelike towers, delicate arches gracing its facade, and 13th-century stained glass, the church of **Notre-Dame** (⊠ rue de la Préfecture) is one of the city's highlights. Among the city's oldest churches, the **Cathédrale St-Bénigne** (⊠ pl. St-Bénigne) is comparatively austere; its chief glory is the 11th-century crypt—a forest of pillars surmounted by a rotunda. The relatively new church of **St-Michel** (⊠ pl. St-Michel) is notable for its chunky Renaissance facade. Don't miss the exuberant 15th-century gateway at the **Chartreuse de Champmol** (⊠ off av. Albert 1ᵉʳ beyond the train station)—all that remains of a former charterhouse. Next to the

★ Chartreuse de Champmol is the **Puits de Moïse**, the so-called Well of Moses, with six large, realistic statues of saints that are among the most celebrated creations of the late Middle Ages. It was designed by Flemish master Claus Sluter, who also created the tombs of the dukes of Burgundy.

A leisurely trip south of Dijon in the direction of Beaune takes you through some of the world's most famous **vineyards**. Route D122 wends its way past such properties as Gevrey-Chambertin and Chambolle-Musigny, then joins N74 at Chambolle-Musigny.

$$$–$$$$ ✕ **Billoux.** Jean-Pierre Billoux's restaurant in the center of Dijon is one of the best-kept secrets of Burgundy. The house specialties are inventive, the welcome always convivial, and the wine list reads like a who's who of the region's best—but not necessarily best-known—wine makers. ⊠ *13 pl. de la Libération* ☎ *03–80–38–05–05* ⚑ *Reservations essential* ▤ *AE, DC, MC, V* ☸ *Closed Mon. No dinner Sun.*

$ ✕ **Bistrot des Halles.** Of the many restaurants in the area, this one is the best value. Well-prepared dishes range from escargots to beef bourguignon with braised endives. Dine either at the sidewalk tables or inside, where mirrors and polished wood dominate. ⊠ *8 rue Bannelier* ☎ *03–80–49–94–15* ▤ *MC, V* ☸ *No dinner Sun.*

$$–$$$ ✕🏠 **Chapeau Rouge.** A player piano in the bar and elegant staircase give this hotel a charm that the rooms, though clean and well appointed, lack. The restaurant is renowned as a haven of classic regional cuisine. ⊠ *5*

rue Michelet, 21000 ☎ *03–80–30–28–10* 🖷 *03–80–30–33–89* ⊕ *www. bestwestern.com* ⟿ *30 rooms* ♻ *Restaurant, bar* ▭ *AE, DC, MC, V.*

$$$–$$$$ 🖭 **Hôtel Sofitel Dijon–La Cloche.** The best hotel in Dijon, in use since the 19th century, La Cloche is a successful cross between luxury chain and grand hotel. Try to get a room overlooking the tranquil back garden, also the backdrop for the greenhouse restaurant La Rotonde. ⊠ *14 pl. Darcy, 21000* ☎ *03–80–30–12–32* 🖷 *03–80–30–04–15* ⊕ *www.hotel-lacloche.com* ⟿ *53 rooms, 15 suites* ♻ *2 restaurants, bar* ▭ *AE, DC, MC, V.*

Clos de Vougeot

Visit Clos de Vougeot to see its *grange viticole* (wine-making barn), surrounded by its famous vineyard. Begun by Cistercian monks during the 12th century and completed during the Renaissance, the **Château du Clos de Vougeot** is famous as the seat of Burgundy's elite company of wine lovers, the Confrérie des Chevaliers du Tastevin. They gather here in November at the start of an annual three-day festival, Les Trois Glorieuses. ☎ *03–80–62–86–09* ☉ *Apr.–Sept., daily 9–6:30; Oct.–Mar., weekdays and Sun. 9–11:30 and 2–5:30, Sat. 9–5.*

Beaune

★ Despite the hordes of tourists, Beaune remains one of the most attractive French provincial towns. The **Hospices de Beaune** (or Hôtel Dieu), founded in 1443 as a hospital, owns some of the region's finest vineyards. Its history is retraced in a museum that also has Rogier van der Weyden's Flemish masterpiece *The Last Judgment.* ⊠ *Rue de l'Hôtel-Dieu* ☎ *03–80–24–45–00* ☉ *Apr.–mid-Nov., daily 9–6:30; mid-Nov.–Mar., daily 9–11:30 and 2–5:30.*

Tapestries relating the life of the Virgin hang in Beaune's 12th-century main church, the **Collégiale Notre-Dame** (⊠ off av. de la République). In the candlelighted cellars of the **Marché aux Vins** (Wine Market) you can, for the price of admission, taste as many of the regional wines as you wish. ⊠ *Rue Nicolas Rolin* ☎ *03–80–25–08–20* ☉ *Daily 9:30–noon and 2–6.*

$$ ✕ **Écusson.** Don't be put off by its unprepossessing exterior. This is a comfortable, friendly, thick-carpeted restaurant with good-value prix-fixe menus. Showcased is chef Jean-Pierre Senelet's surefooted culinary mastery in such dishes as boar terrine with dried apricot and juniper berries. ⊠ *Pl. Malmédy* ☎ *03–80–24–03–82* ♻ *Reservations essential* ▭ *AE, DC, MC, V* ☉ *Closed Sun. No lunch Mon.*

$$ 🖭 **Hôtel de la Cloche.** In the heart of town, this welcoming hotel in a 15th-century residence has neat rooms decorated with care. The best have full baths; the smaller, delightful attic rooms have showers only. ⊠ *40–42 rue Faubourg-Madeleine, 21200* ☎ *03–80–24–66–33* 🖷 *03–80–24–04–24* ⟿ *22 rooms* ♻ *Restaurant* ▭ *AE, MC, V* ☉ *Closed late Dec.–mid-Jan.*

Cluny

Famous for its medieval abbey, which represented the finest flowering of the Romanesque style, Cluny was once the center of a vast Christian empire. Founded in the 10th century, the **Ancienne Abbaye** (Old Abbey) was the biggest church in Europe until the 16th century, when St. Peter's was built in Rome. Now in ruins, it still gives an idea of its original grandeur. The **Clocher de l'Eau-Bénite**, a majestic bell tower, crowns the only remaining part of the abbey church, the south transept. The 13th-century **farinier** (flour mill) has a fine oak and chestnut roof and a collection of Romanesque capitals from the vanished choir. The **Musée Ochier**, in the abbatial palace, contains Europe's foremost Romanesque lapidary museum. Vestiges of both the abbey and the village constructed around it are conserved here, as well as part of the monks' library. ☎ 03–85–59–12–79 ⊙ *Nov.–mid-Feb., daily 10–noon and 2–4; mid-Feb.–Mar., daily 10–noon and 2–5; Apr.–June, daily 9:30–noon and 2–6; July and Aug., daily 9–7; Sept., daily 9–6; Oct., daily 9:30–noon and 2–5.*

$$ ╳▢ **Bourgogne.** The old-fashioned hotel building, dating from 1817, stands where other parts of the abbey used to be. It has a small garden and an atmospheric restaurant serving comfort cuisine, such as *volaille de Bresse au Noilly et morilles* (Bresse chicken with vermouth and morilles [rare mushrooms]). The evening meal is mandatory in July and August, and lunch is not served on Tuesday or Wednesday. ⊠ *Pl. de l'Abbaye, 71250* ☎ *03–85–59–00–58* 🖷 *03–85–59–03–73* ⊕ *www. hotel-cluny.com* ⊅ *15 rooms* ⌂ *Restaurant, bar* ▭ *AE, DC, MC, V* ⊙ *Closed mid-Nov.–early Mar.*

Lyon

Numbers in the margin correspond to points of interest on the Lyon map.

Lyon, one of France's "second" cities, is easily accessible by car or train. Much of the city has an enchanting air of untroubled prosperity, and the dining choices are plentiful. It's easy to walk its pedestrian streets and explore its sights. If you have a few days, you can visit Vieux Lyon (Old Lyon) on the western bank of the Saône River; the old Roman district of Fourvière above it; and La Presqu'île between the Saône and the Rhône, which is the main downtown area, with shops, restaurants, bars, and theaters. For €14 you can purchase a three-day museum pass, the Clés de Lyon (keys to Lyon).

It's easy to get around the city on the subway. A single ticket costs €1.40, a 10-ticket book €9.60. A day pass for bus and métro is €4 (available from bus drivers and machines in the métro).

❶ The cliff-top silhouette of the **Basilique de Notre-Dame-de-Fourvière** is the city's most striking symbol: the 19th-century basilica is a mishmash of styles with an interior that's pure overkill. Climb the observatory heights for the view, and then go to the nearby Roman remains. ⊠ *Pl. de Fourvière* ⊙ *Basilica daily 8–noon and 2–6. Observatory Easter–Oct., daily 10–noon and 2–6; Nov.–Easter, weekends 2–6.*

❷ Two ruined, semicircular **Théâtres Romains** (Roman Theaters) are tucked into the hillside, just down from the summit of Fourvière. The **Grand Théâtre**, the oldest Roman theater in France, was built in 15 BC. The smaller **Odéon** was designed for music and poetry performances. ⊠ *Colline Fourvière* ⊙ *Daily 9 AM–dusk.*

❸ At the **Musée de la Civilisation Gallo-Romaine** (Gallo-Roman Civilization Museum), statues, mosaics, vases, coins, and tombstones from Lyon's Roman precursors are on display. ⊠ *17 rue Clébert* ☎ *04–72–38–81–90* ⊙ *Tues.–Sun. 10–5.*

❹ Housed in the city's largest ensemble of Renaissance buildings, the **Musée Historique de Lyon** (Lyon Historical Museum) has a collection of medieval sculpture, furniture, pottery, paintings, and engravings. ⊠ *1 pl. du Petit-Collège* ☎ *04–78–42–03–61* ⊙ *Wed.–Mon. 10:45–6.*

❺ The best museum in Lyon is the **Musée des Beaux-Arts** (Fine Arts Museum), with one of France's largest collections of art after that of the Louvre. It houses sculpture, classical relics, and an extensive collection of old masters and impressionists. ⊠ *20 pl. des Terreaux* ☎ *04–72–10–17–40* ⊙ *Wed.–Sun. 10:30–6.*

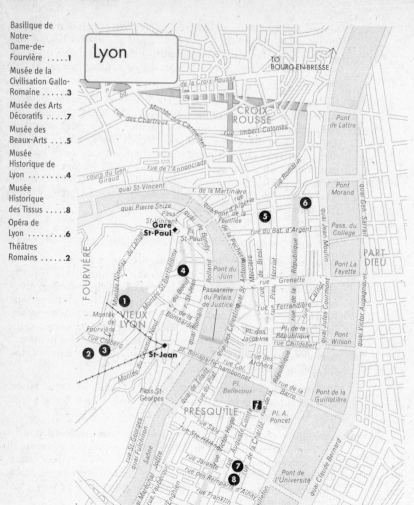

 The barrel-vaulted **Opéra de Lyon**, a reincarnation of a moribund 1831 building, was built in the early 1990s. It incorporates a columned exterior, soaring glass vaulting, neoclassical public spaces, and the latest backstage magic. ✉ *Pl. de la Comédie* ☎ *04–72–00–45–00; 04–72–00–45–45 tickets.*

★ ❼ In an 18th-century mansion, the **Musée des Arts Décoratifs** (Decorative Arts Museum) has fine collections of silverware, furniture, objets d'art, porcelain, and tapestries. ✉ *34 rue de la Charité* ☎ *04–78–38–42–00* ◷ *Tues.–Sun. 10–5:30.*

❽ On display at the **Musée Historique des Tissus** (Textile History Museum) is a fascinating exhibit of intricate carpets, tapestries, and silks—silk- and cloth-making made Lyon famous. ✉ *34 rue de la Charité* ☎ *04–78–38–42–00* ◷ *Tues.–Sun. 10–5:30.*

★ **$$$$** ✕**Les Loges.** With dazzlers like roast wild boar with rosemary raisins and poached red pears or cinnamon chicken with Swiss chard on his bill of fare, it's little wonder their creator, Nicolas Le Bec, was named Gault-Millau Chef of the Year 2002. To top it all off, mahogany chairs, modern art, and a giant medieval hearth make for a stunning setting. ⊠ *6 rue du Boeuf* ☎ *04–72–77–44–44* ⊟ *AE, DC, MC, V* ⊙ *Closed Sun., Mon., and Aug. 4–26.*

★ **$$$$** ✕**Paul Bocuse.** Whether superstar Bocuse—who kickstarted the "new" French cooking back in the 1970s—is here or not, his legendary black-truffle soup in pastry crust will be. So will the green bean–and-artichoke salad with foie gras or the Bresse chicken cooked *en vessie* (in a bladder). ⊠ *50 quai de la Plage, Collonges-au-Mont-d'Or* ☎ *04–72–42–90–90* ⚐ *Reservations essential* 🏠 *Jacket required* ⊟ *AE, DC, MC, V.*

$$–$$$ ✕**Les Muses.** High up under the glass vault of the Opéra de Lyon is this small restaurant run by Philippe Chavent. The quality of the nouvelle cuisine makes it hard to choose, but don't pass up the salmon in butter sauce with watercress mousse. ⊠ *Opéra de Lyon* ☎ *04–72–00–45–58* ⚐ *Reservations essential* ⊟ *AE, MC, V* ⊙ *Closed Sun.*

$–$$$ ✕**Brunet.** Tables are crammed together in this tiny tavern with past menus inscribed on mirrors and a few photographs. The food is good, traditional Lyonnais fare. ⊠ *23 rue Claudia* ☎ *04–78–37–44–31* ⊟ *MC, V* ⊙ *Closed Sun., Mon., and Aug.*

★ **$$$$** 🏨**Cour des Loges.** Young Lyonnais architects teamed with Italian designers to transform a former Jesuit convent of four Renaissance mansions into one of Lyon's most stylish hotels. Rooms range from fairly small to comfortably large and are either classic or contemporary in design. ⊠ *6 rue du Boeuf, 69005* ☎ *04–72–77–44–44* 🖶 *04–72–40–93–61* ⊕ *www.courdesloges.com* 🗲 *52 rooms* ♻ *Restaurant, pool, bar* ⊟ *AE, DC, MC, V.*

$$–$$$ 🏨**Grand Hôtel des Beaux-Arts.** Half of the rooms at this hotel are "inspired worlds" where an artist has developed a theme through his paintings. Some rooms are traditionally furnished. ⊠ *Rue du Président Édouard-Herriot, pl. des Jacobins, 69002* ☎ *04–78–38–09–50* 🖶 *04–78–42–19–19* ⊕ *www. accorhotels.com* 🗲 *75 rooms* ♻ *Bar* ⊟ *AE, DC, MC, V.*

★ **$–$$** 🏨**Hôtel du Théâtre.** The enthusiastic owner is sufficient enough reason to recommend this small hotel; its location and reasonable prices make it even more commendable. Rooms are simple but clean. ⊠ *10 rue de Savoie, 69002* ☎ *04–78–42–33–32* 🖶 *04–72–40–00–61* 🗲 *21 rooms* ♻ *Bar* ⊟ *AE, DC, MC, V.*

Burgundy & Lyon Essentials

AIR TRAVEL

AIRPORTS The international airport for the region is in Satolas, 26 km (16 mi) east of Lyon. Air France and other major airlines have connecting services from Paris.

🛈**Satolas** ☎ 04-72-22-72-21.

BUS TRAVEL

Local bus services are extensive; where the biggest private companies, Les Rapides de Bourgogne and TRANSCO, do not venture, the national SNCF routes (⇨ Train Travel) often do.

🛈**Les Rapides des Bourgogne** ⊠ 3 rue des Fontenottes, Auxerre ☎ 03-86-94-95-00. **TRANSCO** ⊠ rue des Perrières, Dijon ☎ 03-80-42-11-00.

CAR TRAVEL

Larger towns can be reached by train, but to see smaller towns you will want a car. A6 is the main route through the region (Lyon is 463 km [287 mi] south of Paris). N6 is a slower, prettier option.

TOURS

Write to the Comité Régional de Tourisme (Regional Committee of Tourism) for information on regional tours using Dijon as a base, including wine tastings and visits to the famous religious sites. Contact the Comité Régional du Tourisme Rhône-Alpes (Regional Committee of Tourism for Rhône-Alpes) for information on Lyon.

🛈 **Comité Régional de Tourisme** ✆ B.P. 1602, 21035 Dijon. **Comité Régional du Tourisme Rhône-Alpes** ✉ 78 rte. de Paris, 69260 Charbonnières-les-Bains ☎ 04-72-59-21-59 🖷 04-72-59-21-60 ⊕ www.rhonealpes-tourisme.com.

TRAIN TRAVEL

The TGV to Lyon leaves from Paris (Gare de Lyon) hourly and arrives in just two hours. Six TGVs also go daily between Charles de Gaulle airport and Lyon. From Lyon there is frequent train service to other points. In addition, buses leave Lyon for smaller towns in the region. Dijon has two local train routes: one linking Sens, Joigny, Montbard, Dijon, Beaune, Chalon, Tournus, and Mâcon; and the other connecting Auxerre, Avallon, Clamecy, and Nevers.

🛈 **SNCF** ☎ 08-36-35-35-35 ⊕ www.sncf.com.

VISITOR INFORMATION

🛈 **Auxerre** ✉ 1 quai de la République ☎ 03-86-52-06-19 ⊕ www.burgundy-tourism. com. **Beaune** ✉ rue de l'Hôtel-Dieu ☎ 03-80-26-21-30 ⊕ www.beaune-burgundy. com. **Cluny** ✉ 6 rue Mercière ☎ 03-85-59-05-34. **Dijon** ✉ 29 pl. Darcy ☎ 03-80-44-11-44 ⊕ www.ot-dijon.fr. **Lyon** ✉ pl. Bellecour ☎ 04-72-77-69-69 ⊕ www.lyon-france.com ✉ av. Adolphe Max near cathedral ☎ 04-72-77-69-69 ✉ Perrache train station. **Sens** ✉ pl. Jean-Jaurès ☎ 03-86-65-19-49. **Vézelay** ✉ rue St-Pierre ☎ 03-86-33-23-69.

PROVENCE

As you approach Provence there is a magical moment when the north is finally left behind: cypresses and red-tile roofs appear; you hear the jingling of cicadas and catch the scent of wild thyme and lavender—and all of this is against a backdrop of harsh, brightly lit landscapes that inspired the paintings of Paul Cézanne and Vincent van Gogh. Roman remains litter the ground in well-preserved profusion. The amphitheaters in Nîmes and Arles (both are still used for spectacles that include bullfighting), the aqueduct at Pont du Gard, and the mausoleum in St-Rémy-de-Provence are considered the best of their kind in existence.

A number of towns have grown up along the Rhône Valley owing to its historical importance as a communications artery. The biggest is bustling Marseille, but Avignon and Arles have more picturesque charm. North of Marseille lies Aix-en-Provence, with an old-time elegance that reflects its former role as regional capital. Extending the traditional boundaries of Provence westward, historic Nîmes has been included. The Côte d'Azur is also part of this region but has an identity of its own.

Avignon

A warren of medieval alleys nestling behind a protective ring of stocky towers, Avignon is where seven exiled popes camped between 1309 and 1377 after fleeing from the corruption of Rome. The dominant building within the town walls is the colossal **Palais des Papes** (Papal Palace). It's really two buildings: the severe **Palais Vieux** (Old Palace), built between 1334 and 1342 by Pope Benedict XII, a member of the Cistercian order, which frowned on frivolity; and the more decorative **Palais Nouveau** (New Palace), built in the following decade by the arty, lavish Pope Clement VI. Magnificent frescoes relieve the austere stone,

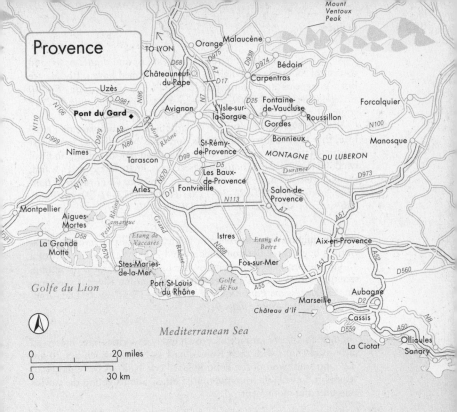

Provence

Mount Ventoux Peak

TO LYON · Orange · Malaucène · Bédoin · Carpentras · Châteauneuf-du-Pape · Uzès · Pont du Gard · Avignon · L'Isle-sur-la-Sorgue · Fontaine-de-Vaucluse · Forcalquier · Gordes · Roussillon · Bonnieux · Manosque · Nîmes · St-Rémy-de-Provence · MONTAGNE · DU LUBERON · Tarascon · Les Baux-de-Provence · Durance · Arles · Fontvieille · Salon-de-Provence · Montpellier · Aigues-Mortes · Camargue · La Grande Motte · Etang de Vaccarès · Istres · Etang de Berre · Aix-en-Provence · Stes-Maries-de-la-Mer · Fos-sur-Mer · Port St-Louis du Rhône · Golfe de Fos · Aubagne · Golfe du Lion · Marseille · Château d'If · Cassis · Mediterranean Sea · La Ciotat · Ollioules Sanary

0 — 20 miles
0 — 30 km

stripped during the Revolution. ⊠ *Pl. du Palais* ☎ *04–90–27–50–00* ⊙ *Oct.–Mar., daily 9:30–5:45; Apr.–Nov., daily 9–7; July (during theater season) 9–9.*

The 12th-century **Cathédrale Notre-Dame-des-Doms** near the Palais des Papes contains the Gothic tomb of Pope John XII. It's a marvel of stacked arches with a strong Byzantine flavor and is topped nowadays with a gargantuan Virgin Mary lantern. Beyond the cathedral is the **Rocher des Doms** (Rock of the Domes), a large park from which there are fine views of the town and the river. ⊠ *Pl. du Palais* ☎ *04–90–86–81–01* ⊙ *Mon.–Sat. 7–7, Sun. 9–7.*

The medieval **Petit Palais** (Small Palace) was once a residence for cardinals and archbishops. Nowadays it contains an outstanding collection of old masters. ⊠ *21 pl. du Palais* ☎ *04–90–86–44–58* ⊙ *Oct.–May, Wed.–Mon. 9:30–1 and 2–5:30; June–Sept., Wed.–Mon. 10–1 and 2–6.*

The 12th-century **Pont St-Bénézet** (St. Bénézet Bridge)—the "pont d'Avignon" of nursery-song fame—is an easy walk from the Petit Palais if you want a demi-inspection of the bridge (only half of it remains). ⊠ *Port du Rocher.*

$$–$$$ ✗ **La Compagnie des Comptoirs.** Glassed into the white stone of the trendy Les Cloître des Arts complex, these interiors were laid out by contemporary decorator Imaad Rahmouni. Dishes are beautifully presented and offer flavor mixtures from India, Italy, and Morocco. ⊠ *83 rue Joseph-Vernet* ☎ *04–90–85–99–04* ▤ *AE, MC, V* ⊙ *Closed Mon. Oct.–Apr.*

★ $$$$ ✗▥ **Hôtel de la Mirande.** Rich with exquisite reproduction fabrics and beeswaxed antiques, this design-mag dream of a hotel is just below the

Papal Palace. Its enclosed garden is a breakfast and dinner oasis, and its central lounge is a skylighted and jazz-warmed haven. Rooms are both gorgeous and comfortable. ☒ *Pl. de la Mirande, 84000* ☎ *04–90–85–93–93* ☒ *04–90–86–26–85* ⊕ *www.la-mirande.fr* ↩ *19 rooms, 1 suite* ♧ *Restaurant, bar* ☰ *AE, DC, MC, V.*

$–$$ ☷ **Hôtel du Blauvac.** Just off rue de la République and place de l'Horloge, this 17th-century nobleman's home has been divided into guest rooms. Many have exposed stonework, aged-oak detailing, and tall windows that look, alas, onto backstreet walls. Pretty fabrics and a warm, familial welcome more than compensate, however. ☒ *11 rue de la Bancasse, 84000* ☎ *04–90–86–34–11* ☒ *04–90–86–27–41* ⊕ *www.hotel-blauvac.com* ↩ *16 rooms* ☰ *AE, DC, MC, V.*

Pont du Gard

Twenty minutes west of Avignon looms the well-preserved Pont du Gard, a huge, three-tier aqueduct erected 2,000 years ago as part of a 48-km (30-mi) canal supplying water to Roman Nîmes. Its setting, spanning a rocky gorge 150 feet above the Gardon River, is spectacular. ☒ *Concession Pont-du-Gard* ☎ *04–66–37–50–99* ◷ *Oct.–Apr., daily 10–6; May–Sept., daily 9:30–7.*

Nîmes

Though it's a feisty rat race of a town today, few cities have preserved such visible links with their Roman past as Nîmes, which lies 20 km (12½ mi) southwest of the Pont du Gard (via N86). A three-day, €10 "passport," available from the tourist office, admits you to the town's museums and monuments.

★ In the heart of downtown Nîmes, the flawlessly preserved Roman **Arènes** (Arena) has a seating capacity of 21,000. An inflatable roof covers it in winter for concerts and exhibitions; bullfights and tennis tournaments are held in it in summer. ☒ *Bd. Victor-Hugo* ☎ *04–66–76–72–77* ◷ *May–Sept., daily 9–6:30; Oct.–Apr., daily 9–noon and 2–5.*

At the **Musée des Beaux-Arts** (Fine Arts Museum), you can admire a vast Roman mosaic and works by Poussin, Brueghel, Rubens, and Rodin. ☒ *Rue de la Cité-Foulc* ☎ *04–66–67–38–21* ◷ *Tues.–Sun. 10–6.*

The **Musée Archéologique et d'Histoire Naturelle** (Museum of Archaeology and Natural History) is rich in local finds dating from Roman antiquity. ☒ *Bd. de l'Admiral-Courbet* ☎ *04–66–76–74–80* ◷ *Tues.–Sun. 10–6.*

The **Musée du Vieux Nîmes** (Museum of Old Nîmes), in a 17th-century bishop's palace, has a vibrant display of textiles, including samples of early denim, which came from Nîmes ("de Nîmes"). The fabric was shipped to Genoa and made into pants called "de Gênes." ☒ *Pl. aux Herbes* ☎ *04–66–76–73–70* ◷ *Tues.–Sun. 10–6.*

Smack in the center of town, the **Maison Carrée** (Square House), a superb Roman temple modeled on the Temple of Apollo in Rome and dating from the 1st century AD, is now a gallery for temporary exhibitions. ☒ *Bd. Victor-Hugo* ☎ *04–66–36–26–76* ◷ *Mid-Mar.–mid-Oct., daily 9–7; mid-Oct.–mid-Mar., daily 10–5.*

★ **$$$–$$$$** ✕ **Chez Jacotte.** Duck into an Old Town back alley and into this cross-vaulted grotto that embodies Nîmes's Spanish-bohemian flair. Watch for blackboard specials such as mullet crisped in olive oil and basil or goat-cheese-and-fig gratin. ☒ *15 rue Fresque (impasse)* ☎ *04–66–21–64–59* ♧ *Reservations essential* ☰ *MC, V* ◷ *Closed Sun. and Mon. No lunch Sat.*

$$ ☷ **La Baume.** In the heart of scruffy Old Nîmes, this noble 17th-century *hôtel particulier* (mansion) has been reincarnated as a stylish hotel. The stenciled beam ceilings, cross vaults, and archways counterbalance hot ocher tones, swags of raw cotton, leather, and halogen lighting. ⊠ *21 rue Nationale, 30000* ☎ *04–66–76–28–42* 🖶 *04–66–76–28–45* ⊕ *www. new-hotel.com* 🛏 *34 rooms* ⊟ *AE, DC, MC, V.*

Arles

Charming little Arles was once considered the "Rome of the North"— thanks to the many structures built here by the ancient Romans—and it later enchanted both Gauguin and van Gogh. For €12 you can purchase a joint ticket to most of the monuments and museums.

The town's most notable sight is the 26,000-capacity **Arènes** (Arena), built in the 1st century AD for circuses and gladiator combats. ⊠ *Rond-Point des Arènes* ☎ *04–90–49–36–74* ☼ *May–Sept., daily 9–7; Oct., daily 9–noon and 2–6; Nov.–Feb., daily 10–noon and 2–5; Mar. and Apr., daily 9–noon and 2–5.*

Close by are the scanty remains of Arles's **Théâtre Antique** (Ancient Theater); the bits of marble columns scattered around the grassy enclosure hint poignantly at the theater's onetime grandeur. Today it serves as a venue for the Festival d'Arles (in July and August) and the International Photography Festival. ⊠ *Rue de la Calade* ☎ *04–90–49–36–74* ☼ *May–Sept., daily 9–7; Oct., daily 9–noon and 2–6; Nov.–Feb., daily 10–noon and 2–5; Mar. and Apr., daily 9–noon and 2–5.*

The **Museon Arlaten** (Museum of Arles), housed in a 16th-century mansion, displays costumes and headdresses, puppets, and waxworks. They were all lovingly assembled by the great turn-of-the-20th-century Provençal poet Frédéric Mistral. ⊠ *29 rue de la République* ☎ *04–90–93–58–11* ☼ *Apr.–Sept., daily 9:30–12:30 and 2–6; Oct.–Mar., Tues.–Sun. 9:30–12:30 and 2–5.*

★ Designated a world treasure by UNESCO because of its magnificent portal sculpture, the extraordinary Romanesque **Église St-Trophime** (⊠ *pl. de la République*) dates from the 11th century.

Tucked discreetly behind St-Trophime is a peaceful haven, the **Cloître St-Trophime** (St. Trophime Cloister). A Romanesque treasure worthy of the church, it is one of the loveliest cloisters in Provence. A sturdy walkway above offers good views of the town. ☎ *04–90–49–36–74* ☼ *May–Sept., daily 9–7; Oct., daily 9–6; Nov.–Feb., daily 10–5; Mar. and Apr., daily 9–6.*

The courtyard garden of the **Espace van Gogh** is impeccably restored and landscaped to match one of van Gogh's paintings. This was the hospital to which the tortured artist repaired after cutting off his earlobe, and its cloistered grounds have become something of a shrine for visitors. ⊠ *Pl. Dr-Félix-Rey.*

★ Alongside the Rhône and a little to the west of downtown is the modern **Musée de l'Arles Antique** (Museum of Ancient Arles), displaying historical artifacts excavated in the region of Arles and explicating the details of daily life in Roman times. ⊠ *Presqu'île du Cirque Romain* ☎ *04–90–18–88–88* ☼ *Mar.–Oct., daily 9–7; Nov.–Feb., daily 10–5.*

★ **$$$–$$$$** ✕ **La Chassagnette.** This fashionable dining address is sophisticated yet down-home comfortable with stone walls, burnt sienna tiles, and comfortable settees with colorful pillows. Chef Luc Rabanel serves mouthwatering open-rotisserie style prix-fixe menus that mix modern tastes with classic French-country cuisine. ⊠ *Rte. du Sambuc (13 km [8 mi] south of Arles on the D36)* ☎ *04–90–97–26–96* ⌂ *Reservations essential* ⊟ *MC, V* ☼ *Closed Tues. and Nov.–mid-Dec. No lunch Wed.*

$$ ✕ **L'Affenage.** A smorgasbord of Provençal hors d'oeuvres draws loyal locals to this former fire-horse shed. They come here for heaping plates of fried vegetables, tapenade, chickpeas in cumin, and lamb chops grilled in the great stone fireplace. ⊠ *4 rue Molière* ☎ *04–90–96–07–67* ♨ *Reservations essential* ▭ *AE, MC, V* ⊗ *Closed Sun. and 3 wks in Aug. No dinner Mon.*

$$$–$$$$ ⊡ **Nord-Pinus.** J. Peterman would feel right at home in this quintessentially Mediterranean hotel on place du Forum; Picasso certainly did. Travel relics, kilims, oil jars, wrought iron, and colorful ceramics create a richly atmospheric stage set. ⊠ *Pl. du Forum, 13200* ☎ *04–90–93–44–44* 🖷 *04–90–93–34–00* ⊕ *www.nord-pinus.com* ⇌ *25 rooms* ▭ *AE, DC, MC, V.*

$$–$$$ ⊡ **Arlatan.** Built by the counts of Arlatan, this 15th-century stone house stands on the site of a 4th-century basilica. Rows of rooms—each decorated with a chic, light hand—horseshoe around a lovely fountain courtyard. ⊠ *26 rue du Sauvage, 13200* ☎ *04–90–93–56–66* 🖷 *04–90–49–68–45* ⊕ *www.hotel-arlatan.fr* ♨ *Bar, pool* ⇌ *37 rooms, 10 suites* ▭ *AE, DC, MC, V.*

St-Rémy-de-Provence

★ Something felicitous has happened in this market town—a steady infusion of style, of art, of imagination—all brought by people with a respect for local traditions and a love of Provençal ways. Here more than anywhere you can meditate quietly on antiquity, browse through redolent markets with basket in hand, peer down the very row of plane trees you remember from a van Gogh, and also enjoy urbane galleries, cosmopolitan shops, and specialty food boutiques.

Founded in the 6th century BC, St-Rémy-de-Provence was known as Glanum to the Greeks and Romans. Its Roman **Mausolée** (Mausoleum) was erected around 20 BC, probably to the memory the emperor Caesar Augustus. The **Arc Triomphal** (Triumphal Arch) is a few decades younger but has suffered more heavily than the mausoleum. All who crossed the Alps entered Roman Glanum through this gate, decorated with reliefs of battle scenes depicting Caesar's defeat and the capture of the Gauls. Excavations of **Glanum** began in 1921, and much of the Greek and Roman towns has now been unearthed in a maze of foundations, walls, towers, and columns. The remains are less spectacular than the arch and mausoleum, but are still fascinating. ⊠ *Off D5, toward Les Baux* ☎ *04–90–92–64–04* ⊗ *Apr.–Sept., daily 9–7; Oct.–Mar., daily 9–noon and 2–5.*

You can examine many of the finds from Glanum—statues, pottery, and jewelry—at the exhibits in the **Hôtel de Sade**, a 15th- and 16th-century private manor in the center of St-Rémy. ⊠ *Rue du Parage* ☎ *04–90–92–64–04* ⊗ *Feb., Mar., and Oct., Tues.–Sun. 10–noon and 2–5; Apr.–Sept., Tues.–Sun. 10–noon and 2–6; Nov. and Dec., Wed. and weekends 10–noon and 2–5.*

★ **$–$$** ✕ **L'Assiette de Marie.** Marie Ricco is a collector, and she's turned her tiny restaurant into a bower of attic treasures. Seated at an old school desk, you choose from the day's specials, all made with Marie's Corsican-Italian touch—marinated vegetables with tapenade, a cast-iron casserole of pasta, and satiny *panetone* (flan). ⊠ *1 rue Jaume-Roux* ☎ *04–90–92–32–14* ♨ *Reservations essential* ▭ *MC, V* ⊗ *Closed Thurs. and Nov.–Mar.*

$$$–$$$$ ✕⊡ **Domaine de Valmouraine.** In this genteel inn on a broad park, overstuffed English-country decor mixes cozily with cool Provençal stone and timber. Chef Pascal Volle oversees the restaurant, which serves fresh game, seafood, local oils, and truffles. ⊠ *Petite rte. des Baux (D27)*, *13210* ☎ *04–90–92–44–62* 🖷 *04–90–92–37–32* ⊕ *www.valmouriane. com* 🖘 *14 rooms* ⚬ *Restaurant, pool* ▤ *AE, DC, MC, V.*

$$ ✕▣ **Château de Roussan.** In a majestic park, this extraordinary 18th-century château is a helter-skelter of brocantes and bric-a-brac. There are more cats and dogs than staff—but lovers of atmosphere over luxury will blossom in this three-dimensional costume-drama scene. ⊠ *Rte. de Tarascon (D99)*, *13210* ☎ *04–90–92–11–63* 🖷 *04–90–92–50–59* ⊕ *www.chateau-de-roussan.com* 🖘 *22 rooms* ⚬ *Restaurant* ▤ *AE, DC, MC, V.*

Gordes

Gordes was once an unknown, unspoiled hilltop village; it has now become a famous, unspoiled hilltop village surrounded by luxury vacation homes, modern hotels, restaurants, and B&Bs. No matter: the ancient stone village still rises above the valley in painterly hues of honey gold. The only way to see the interior of the **château** is to view its ghastly collection of photo paintings by pop artist Pol Mara, who lived in Gordes. It's worth it to see the fabulously decorated stone fireplace, created in 1541. ☎ *04–90–72–02–75* ⊘ *Wed.–Mon. 10–noon and 2–6.*

$$$ ▣ **Domaine de l'Enclos.** This cluster of stone cottages overlooking the arid hills offers privacy and autonomy as well as a warm welcome. Antique tiles and fresh faux-patinas keep it looking fashionably old. There are panoramic views and swing sets, and an aura that is surprisingly warm and familial for an inn of this sophistication. ⊠ *Rte. de Sénanque, 84220* ☎ *04–90–72–71–00* 🖷 *04–90–72–03–03* ⊕ *www. guideweb.com* 🖘 *12 rooms, 5 apartments* ⚬ *Restaurant, pool* ▤ *AE, MC, V.*

Aix-en-Provence

Few towns are as well preserved as the traditional capital of Provence: elegant Aix-en-Provence, birthplace of the impressionist Paul Cézanne and the novelist Émile Zola. The celebrated, graceful, lively avenue cours Mirabeau is the town's nerve center. It divides Old Aix in half, with narrow medieval streets to the north and 18th-century mansions to the south.

The evocative architectural mishmash that is **Cathédrale St-Sauveur** (⊠ rue Gaston-de-Saporta) houses the remarkable 15th-century *Tryptique du Buisson Ardent* (Burning Bush Triptych) by Nicolas Froment, now open to viewing only on Tuesday from 3 to 4.

The Archbishop's Palace, next to the cathedral, now contains the **Musée des Tapisseries** (Tapestry Museum). Its highlight is a magnificent series of 17 tapestries made in Beauvais that date, like the palace itself, from the 17th and 18th centuries. ⊠ *28 pl. des Martyrs de la Résistance* ☎ *04–42–23–09–91* ⊘ *Wed.–Mon. 10–5.*

The **Musée du Vieil Aix** (Museum of Old Aix), in a 17th-century mansion, displays an eclectic assortment of local treasures, from faience to *santons* (terra-cotta figurines). ⊠ *17 rue Gaston-de-Saporta* ☎ *04–42–21–43–55* ⊘ *Apr.–Oct., Tues.–Sun. 10–noon and 2:30–6; Nov.–Mar., Tues.–Sun. 10–noon and 2–5.*

At the **Atelier Cézanne** (Cézanne's Studio) no major pictures are on display, but his studio remains as he left it at the time of his death in 1906, top coat, bowler hat, ginger jar, and all. ⊠ *9 av. Paul-Cézanne* ☎ *04–42–21–06–53* ⊘ *Apr.–Sept., daily 10–noon and 2:30–6; Oct.–Mar., daily 10–noon and 2–5.*

★ **$$$$**   ✕ **Le Clos de la Violette.** Aix's best restaurant lies north of town in a residential district near the Atelier Cézanne. Chef Jean-Marc Banzo spins tradition into gold using fresh, local ingredients. ⊠ *10 av. de la Violette* ☎ *04–42–23–30–71* ⌖ *Reservations essential* 🕮 *Jacket required* ▭ *AE, MC, V* ☉ *Closed Sun. No lunch Mon. and Wed.*

$$–$$$$ ✕ **Brasserie Les Deux Garcons.** There's standard brasserie fare here—stick to the copious hot salads—but eating isn't what you come here for. It's the linen-decked sidewalk tables facing onto the cours Mirabeau, and the white-swathed waiters serving tiny espressos. There is a piano bar upstairs. ⊠ *53 cours Mirabeau* ☎ *04–42–26–00–51* ▭ *AE, MC, V.*

$$–$$$ 🛏 **Nègre-Coste.** Its prominent cours Mirabeau position and its lavish public areas make this 18th-century town house a popular hotel. Provençal decor and newly tiled bathrooms live up to the lovely ground-floor salons. Large windows open up to the cours Mirabeau, perfect for people-watching with a morning cup of coffee. ⊠ *33 cours Mirabeau, 13100* ☎ *04–42–27–74–22* 🖷 *04–42–26–80–93* ➥ *37 rooms* ▭ *AE, MC, V.*

★ **$**   🛏 **Quatre Dauphins.** In a noble hôtel particulier in the quiet Mazarin quarter, this modest but impeccable lodging has pretty, comfortable little rooms spruced up with *boutis* (Provençal quilts) and hand-painted furniture. ⊠ *55 rue Roux-Alphéran, 13100* ☎ *04–42–38–16–39* 🖷 *04–42–38–60–19* ➥ *13 rooms* ▭ *MC, V.*

Marseille

Much maligned, Marseille is often given wide berth by travelers. Their loss—the city is an eyepopper: its cubist jumbles of blinding-white stone rise up over a picture-book seaport crowned by larger-than-life neo-Byzantine churches, and the labyrinthine Old Town is painted in broad strokes of saffron and robin's-egg blue. Feisty and fond of broad gestures, Marseille is a dynamic city, as cosmopolitan now as when the Phoenicians first founded it as a trading port in 600 BC.

The picturesque Vieux Port (Old Harbor) is the heart of Marseille; avenue Canebière leads to the water's edge. A short way down the quay on the right (as you look out to sea) is the elegant 17th-century Hôtel de Ville (Town Hall). The Maison Diamantée, behind the Town Hall, is a 16th-century mansion housing the **Musée du Vieux Marseille** (Old Marseille Museum), displaying local costumes, pictures, and figurines. Unfortunately, at press time, it was closed indefinitely for renovations. ⊠ *2 rue de la Prison* ☎ *04–91–13–89–00.*

Against the backdrop of industrial docks, the various domes of Marseille's pompous, striped neo-Byzantine **Cathédrale de la Nouvelle Major** (⊠pl. de la Major) look utterly incongruous. It was built under Napoléon III—but not before he'd ordered the partial destruction of the lovely 11th-century original, once a perfect example of the Provençal Romanesque style. You can view the flashy interiors in the newer of the two churches; the medieval one is being restored.

The grid of narrow, tumbledown streets leading off rue du Panier is called simply Le Panier (The Basket). Apart from the ambience, the area is worth visiting for the elegantly restored 17th-century hospice now known as the **Centre de la Vieille Charité** (Center of the Old Charity), which houses a top-notch archaeology museum downstairs and an African and Native American art museum upstairs. ⊠ *2 rue de la Charité* ☎ *04–91–14–58–80* ☉ *May–Sept., Tues.–Sun. 11–6; Oct.–Apr., Tues.–Sun. 10–5.*

The church of **Notre-Dame-de-la-Garde,** with its great gilded statue of the Virgin, stands sentinel high over the old port below. The boggling panoply of naive ex-votos displayed inside is the main draw. ⊠ *Pl. du Colonel-Edon* ☎ *04–91–13–40–80* ⊙ *May–Sept., daily 7 AM–8 PM; Oct.–Apr., daily 7–7.*

Take time to drive the scenic 5-km (3-mi) coast road (corniche du Président-J.-F.-Kennedy) and stop at the magical **Vallon des Auffes,** a tiny castaway fishing port typical of greater Marseille. From the corniche du Président-J.-F.-Kennedy there are breathtaking views across the sea toward the rocky **Îles de Frioul,** which can be visited by ferries that leave from Vieux Port frequently throughout the day. On one, the **Chateau d'If** was the very real prison to the fictional Count of Monte Cristo.

$–$$ ✕ **Étienne.** This tiny Le Panier hole-in-the-wall has more than just a good fresh-anchovy pizza from the wood-burning oven. There is also fried squid, a slab of rare-grilled beef, and the quintessential *pieds et paquets,* Marseille's earthy classic of sheep's feet and stuffed tripe. ⊠ *43 rue de la Lorette* ☎ *No phone* ▭ *No credit cards.*

★ **$$–$$$** ▣ **Mercure Beauvau Vieux Port.** Chopin spent the night here and George Sand kept a suite in this historic hotel overlooking the Vieux Port. Real antiques, burnished wood, a touch of brass, and deep carpet underfoot give this intimate urban hotel genuine charm—and you can't beat the views from port-side balconies. At publication time, the beloved landmark is closed for renovations, but it should reopen in early 2004, and when it does, prices may well jump to the top level. ⊠ *4 rue Beauvau, 13001* ☎ *04–91–54–91–00; 800/637–2873 for U.S. reservations* 📠 *04–91–54–15–76* ⊕ *www.mercure.com* ⤳ *72 rooms* ♢ *Bar* ▭ *AE, DC, MC, V.*

Provence Essentials

BUS TRAVEL

All the major centers—Avignon, Arles, Nîmes, Aix-en-Provence—are connected by bus lines; some of these routes venture out to neighboring villages. In most cases, you can buy tickets on the bus.

CAR TRAVEL

Provence's key attractions are not far apart. Traveling by car is the most rewarding way to get around, especially if you want to go to the smaller villages and explore the landscape. Speedy highways descend from Lyon and split at Orange to go to Nîmes and Montpellier or Aix-en-Provence and Marseille en route to the Côte d'Azur.

TOURS

The tourist offices in Arles, Nîmes, Avignon, Aix-en-Provence, and Marseille all organize a full calendar of walking tours (some in summer only).

TRAIN TRAVEL

If you're limited to public transportation, Avignon makes the best base for both train and bus connections. Avignon is where the TGV from Paris and Lyon splits for either the run down to Marseille or to Montpellier. From Marseille, trains run along the coast to Nice and Monaco.
🚆 **SNCF** ☎ 08–36–35–35–35 ⊕ www.sncf.com. **TGV** ⊕ www.tgv.com.

VISITOR INFORMATION

🛈 **Aix-en-Provence** ⊠ 2 pl. du Général-de-Gaulle ☎ 04–42–16–11–61 ⊕ www. aixenprovencetourism.com. **Arles** ⊠ 35 pl. de la République ☎ 04–90–18–41–21 ⊕ www.ville-arles.com. **Avignon** ⊠ 41 cours Jean-Jaurès ☎ 04–90–82–65–11 ⊕ www. ot-avignon.fr. **Marseille** ⊠ 4 La Canebière ☎ 04–91–13–89–00 ⊕ www.marseille-tourisme.com. **Nîmes** ⊠ 6 rue Auguste ☎ 04-66-67-29-11 ⊕ www.ot-nimes.fr. **St-Rémy-de-Provence** ⊠ pl. Jean Jaurés ☎ 04-90-92-05-22 ⊕ www.saintremy-de-provence.com.

THE CÔTE D'AZUR

Few places in the world have the same pull on the imagination as France's fabled Côte d'Azur, the Mediterranean coastline stretching from St-Tropez in the west to Menton on the Italian border. Cooled by the Mediterranean in the summer and warmed by it in winter, the climate is almost always pleasant. Avoid the area in July and August, however, unless you love crowds.

The Côte d'Azur's coastal resorts may live exclusively for the tourist trade and have often been ruined by high-rises, but the hinterlands remain relatively untarnished. The little villages perched high on the hills behind medieval ramparts seem to belong to another century. One of them, St-Paul-de-Vence, is the home of the Maeght Foundation, one of the world's leading museums of modern art. Artists have played a considerable role in popular conceptions of the Côte d'Azur, and their presence is reflected in the number of art museums: the Musée Picasso in Antibes, the Musée Renoir and the Musée d'Art Moderne Méditerranée in Cagnes-sur-Mer, the Musée Jean Cocteau in Menton, and entire museums devoted to Chagall and Matisse in Nice.

Although the tiny principality of Monaco, which lies between Nice and Menton, is a sovereign state, with its own army and police force, its language, food, and way of life are French—albeit with a strong Italian accent.

The distance between St-Tropez and the border with Italy is only 120 km (75 mi), so most places are, in fact, within a day's journey. For the drama of mountains and sea, take one of the famous corniche roads, which traverse the coastline at various heights over the Mediterranean from Nice to the Italian frontier.

St-Tropez

St-Tropez was just another pretty fishing village until it was "discovered" in the 1950s by the "beautiful people," a fast set of film stars, starlets, and others who scorned bourgeois values while enjoying bourgeois bank balances. Today, its summer population swells from 6,000 to 60,000, and the top hotels and nightclubs are jammed. In winter it's hard to find a restaurant open. The best times to visit, therefore, are early summer or fall. May and June are perhaps the best months, when the town lets its hair down during two local festivals.

The **Vieux Port** (Old Harbor) is the liveliest part of town, with plenty of outdoor cafés for good people-watching. Between the old and new harbors, in a cleverly converted chapel, is the **Musée de l'Annonciade** (Annunciation Museum), a 14th-century chapel converted to an art museum that alone merits a visit to St-Tropez. Works by Signac, Matisse, Signard, and Braque, many of them painted in (and about) St-Tropez, trace the evolution of painting from impressionism to expressionism. ⊠ *Quai de l'Épi* ☎ *04-94-97-04-01* ⊙ *June–Sept., Wed.–Mon. 10–noon and 3–7; Oct.–May, Wed.–Mon. 10–noon and 2–6.*

Across place de l'Hôtel de Ville is the **Vieille Ville** (Old Town), where twisting streets, designed to break the impact of the terrible mistral (the cold, dry, northerly wind common to this region), open onto tiny squares and fountains. The long climb up to the **Citadelle** rewards you with a

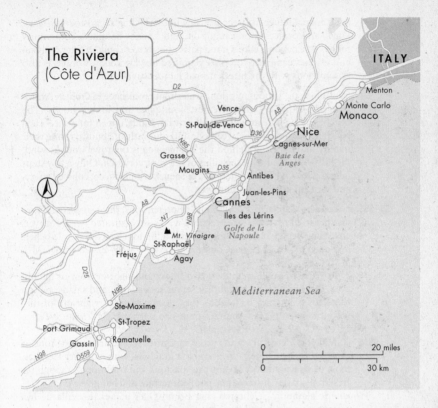

The Riviera
(Côte d'Azur)

ITALY

D2

Menton

Vence

Monte Carlo
Monaco

St-Paul-de-Vence

D36

Nice

Cagnes-sur-Mer

N85

Grasse

*Baie des
Anges*

Mougins

D35

Antibes

Juan-les-Pins

Cannes

Iles des Lérins

*Golfe de la
Napoule*

Mt. Vinaigre

St-Raphaël

Fréjus

Agay

Mediterranean Sea

Ste-Maxime

St-Tropez

Port Grimaud

Gassin

Ramatuelle

0   20 miles

0   30 km

splendid view across the gulf to Ste-Maxime, a quieter if heavily built-up and less posh family resort with a decent beach and reasonably priced hotels.

Easily visited from St-Tropez is the old Provençal town of **Ramatuelle** on a rocky spur 440 feet above the sea. Six kilometers (4 mi) north of Ramatuelle is the hilltop village of **Gassin**, a lovely place to escape the heat of the shoreline.

$$ ✕ **Le Girelier.** Like his father before him, chef Yves Rouet makes an effort to prepare Mediterranean-only fish for his buffed and bronzed clientele, who enjoy the casual sea-shanty decor and the highly visible Vieux Port terrace tables. Grilling is the order of the day; the bouillabaisse is also noteworthy. ✉ *Quai Jean-Jaurès* ☎ *04–94–97–03–87* ▭ *AE, DC, MC, V* ☼ *Closed Oct.–Mar. No lunch July and Aug.*

$$$$ ✕▣ **La Résidence de la Pinède.** This balustraded white villa and its broad annex sprawl elegantly along a private waterfront. The fair-size rooms and sunny colors add to the charms of this resort. The chef has a celebrated reputation, and you'll understand why after one taste of his truffle ravioli. ✉ *Plage de la Bouillabaisse, 83991* ☎ *04–94–55–91–00* ▤ *04–94–97–73–64* ⊕ *www.residencepinede.com* ⇝ *35 rooms, 4 suites* ♨ *Restaurant, pool, bar* ▭ *AE, DC, MC, V* ☼ *Closed mid-Oct.–mid-Apr.*

Cannes

In 1834 a chance event was to change the town of Cannes forever. Lord Brougham, Britain's lord chancellor, was en route to Nice when an outbreak of cholera forced the authorities to freeze all travel. Trapped in Cannes, he fell in love with the place and built himself a house to use as an annual refuge from the British winter. The English aristocracy, tsars, kings, and princes soon caught on, and Cannes became a community for the international elite. Grand palace hotels were built to cater to them, and Cannes came to symbolize dignified luxury. Today, Cannes is also synonymous with the International Film Festival.

Stroll along the famous mile-long waterfront promenade **La Croisette,** which strings together a series of cafés, boutiques, and luxury hotels. The beaches along here are almost all private, though open for a fee—each beach is marked with between one and four little life buoys, rating their quality and expense. Behind the promenade is the town and, beyond, the hills—studded with the villas of the very, very rich. Only a few steps inland is the Old Town, known as **Le Suquet,** with its steep, cobbled streets and its 12th-century watchtower.

$$–$$$ ✕ **Bouchon d'Objectif.** Popular and unpretentious, this tiny bistro serves inexpensive Provençal fare prepared with a sophisticated twist. An ever-changing display of photography adds a hip touch to the simple ocher-and-aqua room. ✉ *10 rue Constantine* ☎ *04–93–99–21–76* ▭ *AE, MC, V* ☉ *Closed Mon.*

$ ✕ **La Pizza.** Sprawling up over two floors and right in front of the old port, this busy Italian restaurant serves steaks, fish, and salads, but go there for what they're famous for: gloriously good right-out-of-the-woodfire-oven pizza in hungry-man-size portions. ✉ *3 quai St-Pierre* ☎ *04–93–39–22–56* ▭ *AE, MC, V.*

$$$$ ▣ **Majestic.** Classical statuary and tapestries set the aristocratic tone at this La Croisette hotel; it is grand but gracious, with a quieter feel than most of its neighbors. Rooms are spacious and traditional, though refreshingly pastel. Its romantic poolside terrace and bar give a nod to cinematic glamour. Celebrated chef Bruno Oger makes the Villa de Lys restaurant a must, and Paris brasserie Fouquet's has opened up an off-shoot here. ✉ *14 bd. de la Croisette, 06400* ☎ *04–92–98–77–00* 🖷 *04–93–38–97–90* ⊕ *www.lucienbarriere.com* ➴ *305 rooms, 23 suites* ⟑ *2 restaurants, pool, bar* ▭ *AE, DC, MC, V* ☉ *Closed mid-Nov.–Dec.*

★ $$ ▣ **Molière.** Plush, intimate, and low-key, this reasonably priced hotel has small rooms in cool shades of peach and indigo. Nearly all overlook a vast enclosed front garden. ✉ *5 rue Molière, 06400* ☎ *04–93–38–16–16* 🖷 *04–93–68–29–57* ➴ *24 rooms* ⟑ *Bar* ▭ *AE, MC, V* ☉ *Closed mid-Nov.–late Dec.*

$ ▣ **Albert Ier.** In a quiet residential area above the Forville market, this neo-deco mansion is in a tiny enclosed garden. It's a 10-minute walk downhill to La Croisette and the beach. ✉ *68 av. de Grasse, 06400* ☎ *04–93–39–24–04* 🖷 *04–93–38–83–75* ➴ *11 rooms* ▭ *MC, V.*

Antibes

On the east side of Cannes and Napoule Bay nestle Antibes and Juan-les-Pins, two villages that flow into each other with no perceptible boundary on either side of the peninsula, the Cap d'Antibes. The older Antibes dates from the 4th century BC, when it was a Greek trading port. Every morning except Monday, the market on the cours Masséna comes alive with exotic spices, hand-packed regional products, and colorful produce.

The Grimaldis, the family that rules Monaco, built the **Château Grimaldi** in the 12th century on the remains of a Roman camp. Today, the château's main attraction is the **Musée Picasso** (Picasso Museum), a bounty of the great artist's paintings, ceramics, and lithographs inspired by the sea and Greek mythology. ✉ *Pl. du Château* ☎ *04–93–90–54–20*

🕐 *June–Sept., Tues.–Sun. 10–6; Oct.–May, Tues.–Sun. 10–noon and 2–6.*

$$ ╳ **Le Brûlot.** In this busy bistro, one street back from the market, chef Christian Blancheri hoists anything from suckling pigs to apple pies in and out of his roaring wood oven. ⊠ *3 rue Frédéric-Isnard* ☎ 04–93–34–17–76 ▬ *MC, V* 🕐 *Closed Sun. No lunch Mon.–Wed.*

★ $$$$ 🏨 **Belles Rives.** Home-away-from-home for literary giant F. Scott Fitzgerald while he penned *Tender Is the Night*, the legendary Belles Rives is testament to the maxim "living well is the best revenge." Lovingly restored, this charmer proves that what's old is new again: this hotel's modern neoclassical chic draws France's stylish young set. The terrace restaurant over the water is as magical as the succulent dishes served there. ⊠ *Bd. E.-Baudoin, 06160 Juan-les-Pins* ☎ 04–93–61–02–73 🖨 *04–93–67–43–51* ⊕ *www.bellesrives.com* ↪ *45 rooms* ⌂ *2 restaurants, bar* ▬ *AE, MC, V* 🕐 *Closed late Oct.–mid-Apr.*

$$ 🏨 **Mimosa.** The fabulous setting, in a hilltop garden studded with tall palms, mimosa, and tropical greenery, makes up for the hike down to the beach. Rooms are small and modestly decorated in Victorian florals, but ask for a balcony: many look over the garden and sizable pool. ⊠ *Rue Pauline, 06160 Antibes* ☎ 04–93–61–04–16 🖨 *04–92–93–06–46* ⊕ *www.hotelmimosa.com* ↪ *34 rooms* ⌂ *Pool* ▬ *MC, V* 🕐 *Closed Oct.–Apr.*

St-Paul-de-Vence

Fodor'sChoice
★ The most popular of Provence's hilltop villages, St-Paul is nonetheless a magical place when the crowds thin. Artists—Chagall, Bonnard, and Miró—were drawn to its light, its pure air, its wraparound views, and its honey-color stone walls. Film stars loved its lazy yet genteel ways, lingering on the garden-bower terrace of the famous inn of the Colombe d'Or, and challenging the locals to a game of pétanque under the shade of the plane trees.

★ Many people come to St-Paul just to visit the **Fondation Maeght,** founded in 1964 by art dealer Aimé Maeght. It's not just a small modern art museum but an extraordinary marriage of the arc-and-plane architecture of José Sert; the looming sculptures of Miró, Moore, and Giacometti; and a humbling hilltop perch of pines, vines, and flowing planes of water. ☎ 04–93–32–81–63 ⊕ *www.fondation-maeght.com* ✉ €10 🕐 *July–Sept., daily 10–7; Oct.–June, daily 10–12:30 and 2:30–6.*

★ On the outskirts of Vence, toward St-Jeannet, the **Chapelle du Rosaire** (Chapel of the Rosary) was decorated with beguiling simplicity and clarity by Matisse between 1947 and 1951. "Despite its imperfections I think it is my masterpiece . . . the result of a lifetime devoted to the search for truth," wrote Matisse, who designed it when he was in his eighties and nearly blind. ⊠ *Av. Henri-Matisse* ☎ 04–93–58–03–26 🕐 *Tues. and Thurs. 10–11:30 and 2–5:30; Mon., Wed., and Sat. 2–5:30.*

$$$$ ╳🏨 **Colombe d'Or.** This idyllic old auberge was the heart and soul of St-Paul's artistic revival, and the cream of 20th-century France lounged together under its fig trees—Picasso and Chagall, Maeterlinck and Kipling, Marcel Pagnol and Jacques Prévert. Yves Montand and Simone Signoret met and married here, and current film stars make appearances from time to time. Rooms are smallish and a bit spartan—but where else can you enjoy your cocktail sitting under a Picasso? ⊠ *Pl. Général-de-Gaulle, 06570* ☎ 04–93–32–80–02 🖨 *04–93–32–77–78* ⊕ *www. la-colombe-dor.com* ↪ *15 rooms, 11 suites* ⌂ *Restaurant, pool, bar* ▬ *AE, DC, MC, V* 🕐 *Closed Nov.–late Dec.*

$$$$ ✕⊞ **St-Paul.** Right in the center of the labyrinth of stone alleys, with views
FodorśChoice over the ancient ramparts, this luxurious inn fills a noble 15th-century
★ house with Provençal furniture, quarried stone, and lush fabrics. The restaurant is fast acquiring a big reputation, serving sophisticated regional specialties on a candlelighted terrace with flowers spilling out from every niche. ⊠ *86 rue Grande, 06570* ☎ *04–93–32–65–25* 📠 *04–93–32–52–94* ⊕ *www.lesaintpaul.com* ☞ *15 rooms, 3 suites* ⚄ *Restaurant, bar* ⊟ *AE, DC, MC, V.*

Nice

Numbers in the margin correspond to points of interest on the Nice map.

With a population of 350,000 and its own university, Nice is the undisputed capital of the Côte d'Azur. Founded by the Greeks as Nikaia, it has lived through several civilizations and was attached to France only in 1860. It consequently has a profusion of Greek, Italian, British, and French styles and a raffish, seductive charm. It also has a labyrinthine Old Town, an opera house, museums, and flourishing markets—all strung along an open stretch of pebble beach.

❶ **Place Masséna** is a fine square built in 1815 to celebrate a local hero: one of Napoléon's most successful generals. Stroll through the Jardin
❷ Albert to get to the **Promenade des Anglais** (English Promenade), built by the English community here in 1824. Nowadays dense traffic raises the noise level, but it's a pleasant strand between town and sea with fine views of the Baie des Anges (Bay of Angels).

❸ In the **Palais Masséna** (Masséna Palace) is a museum of city history with eclectic treasures ranging from Garibaldi's death sheet to Empress Josephine's tiara. ⊠ *65 rue de France* ☎ *04–93–88–11–34* ☉ *Call for hrs; renovations pending for a 2005 reopening.*

❹ The **Musée des Beaux-Arts Jules-Chéret** (Jules Chéret Fine Arts Museum) was built in 1878 as a palatial mansion for a Russian princess. The rich collection has paintings by Sisley, Bonnard, and Vuillard; sculptures by Rodin; and ceramics by Picasso. ⊠ *33 av. des Baumettes* ☎ *04–92–15–28–28* ☉ *Tues.–Sun. 10–6.*

The cours Saleya flower market and the narrow streets in Vieux Nice (Old Nice) are the prettiest parts of town: while you're market brows-
❺ ing, stop in to see the 18th-century **Chapelle de la Miséricorde** (Chapel of the Misericord), renowned for its ornate baroque interior and sculpted decoration. At the northern end of the Old Town is the vast Italian-style
❻ **Place Garibaldi**—all yellow-ocher buildings and formal fountains. The
❼ imposing **Musée d'Art Modern** (Modern Art Museum), off place Garibaldi, has an outstanding collection of French and international abstract and figurative art from the late 1950s onward. ⊠ *Promenade des Arts* ☎ *04–93–62–61–62* ☉ *Tues.–Sun. 10–6.*

★ ❽ The **Musée du Message Biblique Marc-Chagall** (Marc Chagall Museum of Biblical Themes) has a superb, life-affirming collection of Chagall's late works, including the 17 huge canvases of *The Message of the Bible*, which took 13 years to complete. ⊠ *Av. du Dr-Ménard* ☎ *04–93–53–87–20* ☉ *Wed.–Mon. 10–6.*

★ ❾ A 17th-century Italian villa amid Roman remains contains the **Musée Matisse** (Matisse Museum), with paintings and bronzes by Henri Matisse, who lived nearly 40 years in Nice. ⊠ *164 av. des Arènes-de-Cimiez* ☎ *04–93–81–08–08* ☉ *Wed.–Mon. 10–6.*

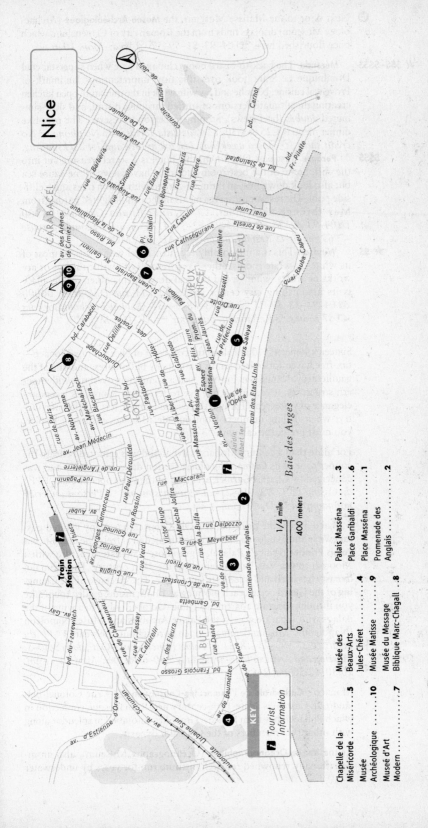

Nice

KEY

i Tourist Information

Chapelle de la Miséricorde **5**	Musée des Beaux-Arts . . . .
Musée Archéologique **10**	Musée Jules-Chéret **4**
Musée d'Art Modern **7**	Musée Matisse **9**
	Musée du Message Biblique Marc-Chagall . . **8**

Palais Masséna **3**	
Place Garibaldi **6**	
Place Masséna **1**	
Promenade des Anglais **2**	

1/4 mile

400 meters

Baie des Anges

⑩ Next door to the Matisse Museum, the **Musée Archéologique** (Archaeology Museum) displays finds from the Roman city of Cemenelum, which once flourished here. ☎ 04–93–81–59–57 ☉ Wed.–Mon. 10–6.

★ $$$–$$$$ ✕ **Mérenda.** The back-to-bistro boom climaxed here when superstar chef Dominique Le Stanc took over this tiny, unpretentious landmark of Provençal cuisine. Now he and his wife work in the miniature open kitchen creating the ultimate versions of stuffed sardines, pistou, and slow-simmered *daubes* (beef stews). Stop by in person to reserve. The prix-fixe dinner menu is €25 to €30. ⊠ *4 rue de la Terrasse* ☎ *No phone* ☐ *No credit cards* ☉ *Closed weekends, last wk in July, and 1st 2 wks in Aug.*

$$$$ ⊡ **Perouse.** Just past Old Town, this hotel is a secret treasure cut into the cliff. Some of the best rooms not only have views of the azure sea but also look down into an intimate garden with lemon trees and a cliffside pool. The restaurant serves meals in the candlelighted garden from May through September. ⊠ *11 quai Rauba-Capeau, 06300* ☎ *04–93–62–34–63* ☐ *04–93–62–59–41* ⊕ *www.hroy.com/la-perouse* ⇨ *63 rooms ⊘ Restaurant, pool* ☐ *AE, DC, MC, V.*

★ $$ ⊡ **Windsor.** This is a memorably eccentric hotel with a vision: most of its white-on-white rooms either have frescoes of mythic themes or are works of artists' whimsy. But the real draw of this otherworldly place is its astonishing city-center garden. ⊠ *11 rue Dalpozzo, 06000* ☎ *04–93–88–59–35* ☐ *04–93–88–94–57* ⊕ *www.hotelwindsor.com* ⇨ *57 rooms ⊘ Restaurant, pool, bar* ☐ *AE, DC, MC, V.*

Monaco

Sixteen kilometers (10 mi) along the coast east of Nice lies tiny Monaco—tax-free haven for retired tennis stars, lucky billionaires, and one of the gaudiest royal families in Europe. As it is completely overbuilt with modern structures, it requires a fine eye to ferret out Monaco's legendary elegance of yesteryear. Though there is no frontier, it is a different country; when dialing numbers from outside Monaco, including France, you must prefix the call with "377."

For more than a century Monaco's livelihood was centered beneath the copper roof of its **Casino.** The oldest section dates from 1878 and was conceived by Charles Garnier, architect of the Paris opera house. ⊠ *Pl. du Casino* ☎ *377/92–16–21–21* ⊕ *www.sbm.mc* ⌨ *Persons under 21 not admitted* ☉ *Daily noon–4 AM.*

Monaco Town, the principality's Old Quarter, has many vaulted passageways and exudes an almost tangible medieval feel. The magnificent **Palais Princier** (Prince's Palace), a grandiose Italianate structure with a Moorish tower, was largely rebuilt in the 19th century. The Grimaldi dynasty has lived and ruled here since 1297. The spectacle of the **Changing of the Guard** occurs each morning at 11:55; inside, guided tours take you through the state apartments (June–October only). In a wing of the palace with separate access, the **Palace Archives** and **Musée Napoléon** (Napoleonic Museum) remain open throughout the year. ⊠ *Pl. du Palais* ☎ *377/93–25–18–31* ☉ *Palais Princier June–Oct., daily 9:30–5. Museum and Archives June–Sept., daily 9:30–6:30; Oct.–May, Tues.–Sun. 10:30–12:30 and 2–5.*

Monaco's **Cathédrale de l'Immaculée-Conception** (⊠ 4 rue Colonel-Bellando-de-Castro) is a late-19th-century neo-Romanesque confection in which Philadelphia-born Princess Grace lies entombed in splendor along with other past members of the Grimaldi dynasty.

At the **Musée Océanographique** (Oceanography Museum), also an internationally renowned research institute run for years by underwater explorer Jacques Cousteau, the aquarium is the undisputed highlight. ✉ *Av. St-Martin* ☎ *377/93–15–36–00* 💶 *€11* 🕐 *July and Aug., daily 9–7:30; May, June, and Sept. daily 9–7; Oct.–Apr., daily 10–6.*

The Moneghetti area is the setting for the **Jardin Exotique** (Exotic Plants Garden), where 600 varieties of cacti and succulents cling to a vertiginous rock face overlooking the city and coast. ✉ *Bd. du Jardin Exotique* ☎ *377/93–30–33–65* 🕐 *May–Aug., daily 9–7; Sept.–Apr., daily 9–6.*

$$$$

Fodor'sChoice

★

✕ **Louis XV.** Swimming in gilt and boiseries, this sumptuous neo-baroque restaurant, in the Hôtel de Paris, stuns with royal pomp that is nonetheless upstaged by its product: the superb cuisine of Alain Ducasse and his beautifully conceived "country cooking," where ravioli with foie gras and truffles slum happily alongside salt cod and tripe. If your wallet is a fat one, this is a must. ✉ *Hôtel de Paris, pl. du Casino* ☎ *377/ 92–16–30–01* 🍴 *Reservations essential* 💳 *AE, DC, MC, V* 🕐 *Closed late Nov.–late Dec. and Tues. Sept.–mid-June. No lunch Wed. mid-June–Aug.*

$$$–$$$$

✕ **Castelroc.** With its tempting pine-shaded terrace just across from the entrance to the palace, this popular local lunch spot serves specialties of cuisine Monegasque, ranging from *anchoïade* to stockfish. ✉ *Pl. du Palais* ☎ *377/93–30–36–68* 💳 *AE, MC, V* 🕐 *Closed Sat. and Dec. and Jan.*

$$$$

🏨 **Hermitage.** A riot of frescoes and plaster flourishes embellished with gleaming brass, this landmark hotel nonetheless maintains a relatively low profile. Even if you're not staying, come to see the glass-dome art nouveau vestibule. The best rooms face the sea or angle toward the port. ✉ *Square Beaumarchais, 98005* ☎ *377/92–16–40–00* 📠 *377/ 92–16–38–52* 🌐 *www.montecarloresort.com* 🛏 *195 rooms, 32 suites* 🍴 *Restaurant, pool, bar* 💳 *AE, DC, MC, V.*

$$–$$$

🏨 **Alexandra.** The friendly proprietress, Madame Larouquie, makes you feel right at home in this central, comfortable spot. Though the color schemes clash and the bedrooms are spare, bathrooms are spacious, and insulated windows keep traffic noise out. ✉ *35 bd. Princesse-Charlotte, 98000* ☎ *377/93–50–63–13* 📠 *377/92–16–06–48* 🛏 *56 rooms* 💳 *AE, DC, MC, V.*

The Côte d'Azur Essentials

AIRPORTS
More than 30 airlines serve the International Aéroport Nice-Côte d'Azur. EasyJet and Air France flights leave for Paris several times a day.

BUS TRAVEL
Taking local buses (marked GARE ROUTIÈRE) or a guided tour is necessary to visit Grasse, Vence, and other inland areas if you're traveling by public transportation. The main routes between towns are serviced by RCA Transport (Rapides Côte D'Azur) and Phocéens Santa Azur bus companies.

🚌 **RCA Transport (Rapides Côte d'Azur)** ✉ 5 bd. Jean Jaures, Nice ☎ 04-93-85-64-44 🌐 www.rca.tm.fr. **Phocéens Santa Azur** ✉ 4 pl. Massena, Nice ☎ 04-93-13-18-20.

CAR TRAVEL
The A8 is the only way to get around the Côte d'Azur quickly (keep lots of change handy for tolls). A car is best for exploring the hill towns perched behind the Côte d'Azur.

TOURS
SNCF runs many organized tours (contact the Nice Tourist Office) to areas otherwise hard to reach. Boats operate from Nice to Marseille;

from St-Tropez to the charming Hyères Islands; and from Antibes, Cannes, and Juan-les-Pins to the Lérins Islands.

TRAIN TRAVEL

A train line follows the coast from Marseille to the Italian border, providing excellent access to the seaside resort towns.

◪ **SNCF** ☎ 08-36-35-35-35 ⊕ www.sncf.com.

VISITOR INFORMATION

◪ **Comité Régional du Tourisme Riviera Côte d'Azur** ⊠ 55 Promenade des Anglais, Nice ☎ 04-93-37-78-78 ⊕ www.crt-riviera.fr. **Antibes** ⊠ 11 pl. Général-de-Gaulle, ☎ 04-92-90-53-00. **Cannes** ⊠ Palais des Festivals, Esplanade G. Pompidou, B.P. 272 ☎ 04-93-39-24-53 ⊕ www.cannes-on-line.com. **Monaco** ⊠ 2a bd. des Moulins ☎ 377/ 92-16-61-66 ⊕ www.visitmonaco.com. **Nice** ⊠ 5 promenade des Anglais ☎ 04-92-14-48-00 ⊕ www.nicetourism.com. **St-Tropez** ⊠ quai Jean-Jaurès ☎ 04-94-97-45-21 ⊕ www.ot-saint-tropez.com.

GERMANY

MUNICH, THE BLACK FOREST, HEIDELBERG, FRANKFURT, THE RHINE, HAMBURG, BERLIN, SAXONY & THURINGIA

12

NO MATTER WHAT PART of Germany you visit, along riverbanks and within ancient towns are the thick layers of history: Roman relics keep company with medieval castles, baroque palaces with rococo chapels, and half-timbered inns with communist-era apartment blocks.

The country of oompah, cuckoo clocks, and Mercedes-Benz also gave the world Gutenberg, Luther, Bach, Beethoven, Goethe, and Marx. Germans are industrious and heavily philosophical, and they take their leisure time just as seriously. The great outdoors has always been an important escape. Crystal-clear Alpine lakes are only a short train ride from boisterous Munich. The Black Forest offers spas and hiking trails. Sprawling Berlin is filled with its own lakes and green parklands. The German trains that link these various regions are fast, clean, and punctual, and a drive on a speed limit–free autobahn will give you an idea of just how fast those BMWs and Mercedeses are built to go.

Every town and village, and many a city neighborhood, manages at least one *Fest* a year, when the beer barrels are rolled out and sausages are thrown on the grill. The seasons have their own festivities: Fasching (Carnival) heralds the end of winter; beer gardens open up with the first warm rays of sunshine; fall is celebrated with the Munich Oktoberfest; and Advent brings colorful pre-Christmas markets.

GERMANY A TO Z

To research prices, get advice from other travelers, and book travel arrangements, visit www.fodors.com.

AIR TRAVEL

Germany's national airline, Lufthansa, serves all major cities. Deutsche BA (dba), Hapag-Lloyd Express, and Germania Flug have inexpensive domestic routes.

🛫 **Deutsche BA** ☎ 01805/932-322 ⊕ www.flydba.com. **Germania Flug** ☎ 01805/107-207 ⊕ www.germania-flug.de. **Hapag-Lloyd Express** ☎ 01805/093-509 ⊕ www.hlx.com. **Lufthansa** ☎ 0180/380-3803 ⊕ www.lufthansa.com.

BIKE TRAVEL

Some of the best river bike paths are those along the Danube River, which you can meet at Regensburg or Passau, and those along the Weser River, which you can meet at Hannoversch-Münden. The *Radfährerkarten*, issued by the Bielefelder Verlaganstalt and by Haupka Verlag, are good bike travel maps available at bookstores.

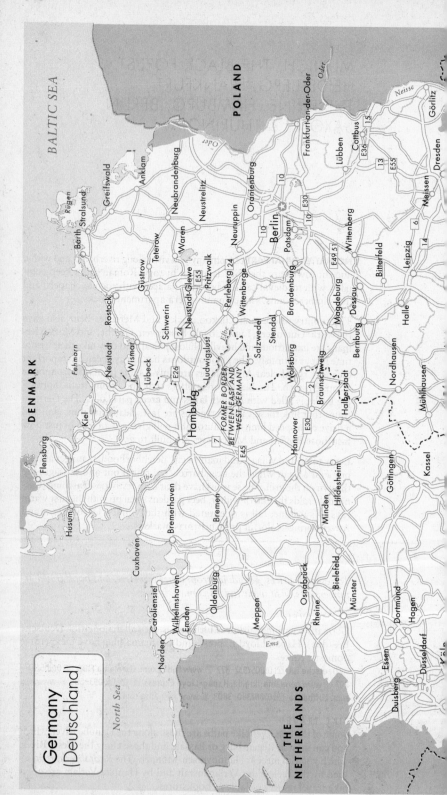

Germany
(Deutschland)

BALTIC SEA

North Sea

DENMARK

POLAND

THE
NETHERLANDS

FORMER BORDER
BETWEEN EAST AND
WEST GERMANY

Flensburg
Husum
Kiel
Neustadt
Fehmarn
Lübeck
Wismar
Schwerin
Ludwigslust
Hamburg
Neustadt-Glewe
Rostock
Güstrow
Teterow
Waren
Neubrandenburg
Anklam
Greifswald
Stralsund
Bärth
Rügen
Neustrelitz
Neuruppin
Oranienburg
Berlin
Potsdam
Frankfurt-an-der-Oder
Lübben
Cottbus
Görlitz
Dresden
Meissen
Leipzig
Bitterfeld
Wittenberg
Dessau
Halle
Bernburg
Magdeburg
Nordhausen
Mühlhausen
Halberstadt
Braunschweig
Wolfsburg
Stendal
Salzwedel
Perleberg
Pritzwalk
Wittenberge
Brandenburg
Kassel
Göttingen
Hannover
Hildesheim
Minden
Bielefeld
Osnabrück
Rheine
Münster
Dortmund
Hagen
Essen
Duisberg
Düsseldorf
Köln
Meppen
Oldenburg
Bremen
Bremerhaven
Cuxhaven
Wilhelmshaven
Emden
Norden
Carolinensiel
Neustadt

Oder
Neisse
Elbe
Ems

E26
E55
24
7
E45
E30
2
10
E49 51
E36
13
E55
6
14
24

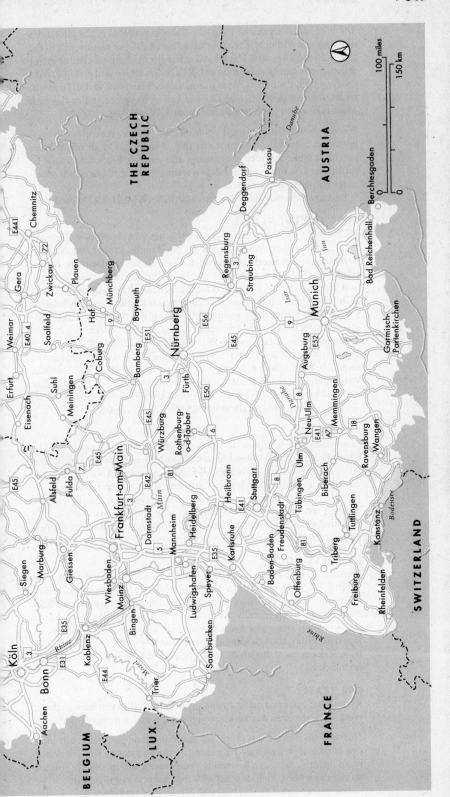

The bike-rental service of Deutsche Bahn is available in the pilot cities of Berlin and Munich. The silver bikes cost €.05 per minute, not to exceed €15 for 24 hours. The bikes are left electronically locked at major intersections and by calling in the bike's code number and giving a credit card number, the bike is yours to roll away. When you're done using it, return it to a major intersection and call in to report you're finished. Most bike shops have rentals for about €10 per day.

Bikes cannot be transported on InterCity Express trains. Bike transportation costs €3 on local trains (RB, RE, IRE). On all other trains you must make advance reservations and pay €8. Bikes can usually be transported on municipal suburban trains, trams, and buses, but sometimes you need an extra ticket. ·

🚩 **Deutsche Bahn bicycle hot line** ☎ 01805/151415; 0700/0522-5522 for rentals.

BOAT & FERRY TRAVEL

Viking River Cruises operates overnight cabin trips on rivers in Germany and Europe. The cruises, especially on the Danube, are in great demand, so **reserve several months in advance.** Köln–Düsseldorfer Deutsche Rheinschiffahrt (KD Rhine Line) offers trips of one day or less on the Rhine and Mosel. Between Easter and October there's Rhine service between Köln and Mainz, and Mosel service between Koblenz and Cochem. In summer, car ferries and passenger ships cross the Bodensee (Lake Constance), which Germany, Switzerland, and Austria border.

🚩 **KD Rhine Line** ✉ Frankenwerft 35, D-50667 Köln ☎ 0221/208-8318; 1-372/742-033 in the U.K. 🖨 0221/208-8345 ⊕ www.k-d.com ✉ in the U.S., JFO Cruise Service Corp., 2500 Westchester Ave., Purchase, NY 10577 ☎ 800/346-6525 🖨 914/696-0833. **Viking River Cruises** ✉ Hohe Strasse 68-82, D-50667 Köln ☎ 0221/258-209; 0800/258-4667 toll-free in Germany; 0207/752-0000 in the U.K. ⊕ www.vikingkd.com ✉ 21820 Burbank Blvd., Woodland Hills, CA 91367 ☎ 818/227-1234.

BUS TRAVEL

Long-distance bus services in Germany are part of the Europe-wide Europabus network. Services are neither as frequent nor as comprehensive as those on the rail system. All Europabus services have a bilingual attendant and offer small luxuries that you won't find on the more basic, though still comfortable, regular services. Travel agents and Deutsche Touring offices can provide details and take reservations.

🚩 **Deutsche Touring** (DTG) ✉ Am Römerhof 17, D-60486 Frankfurt/Main ☎ 069/790-3261 🖨 069/790-3156 ⊕ www.touring-germany.com.

BUSINESS HOURS

Banks are usually open weekdays from 8:30 or 9 to 3 or 4 (5 or 6 on Thursday). Some close from 12:30 to 1:30. Branches at airports and main train stations open as early as 6:30 AM and close as late as 10:30 PM. Museums are generally open Tuesday through Sunday 10–5. Many stay open late one night a week. Stores are allowed to be open until 8 PM on Saturday, though some shops opt to close earlier. Shops at major train stations have the latest closing hours, and are the only ones open on Sunday.

CAR TRAVEL

Know what cities and major towns are in the direction you want to drive; road signs are often marked by town names, and not route numbers.

EMERGENCIES *Notruf* signs every 2 km (1 mi) on autobahns and country roads indicate emergency telephones. By picking up the phone, you'll be connected to an operator who can determine your exact location and get you the services you need. Help is free (with the exception of materials).

🚩 **Emergency number** ☎ 01802/222-222; 222-222 from a cell phone.

GASOLINE Gas costs around €1.15 per liter—which is generally higher than in the United States.

PARKING Daytime parking in cities is very difficult, and parking restrictions are not always clearly marked. Larger parking lots have parking meters (*Parkautomaten*). After depositing enough change in a meter, you will be issued a timed ticket to display on your dashboard. In parking garages, pay immediately upon returning to retrieve your car, not when driving out. Put the ticket you received on arrival into the machine and pay the amount displayed. Retrieve the ticket and upon exiting, insert the ticket in a slot to get the barrier raised. Parking-meter spaces are free at night.

ROAD CONDITIONS The autobahn system in Germany is of the highest standard. These roads are marked either *A* (on blue signs), meaning intra-German highways, or *E* (on green signs), meaning they form part of the Europe-wide *Europastrasse* network. All autobahns are toll-free. Local roads are called *Bundesstrassen* and are marked by their number on a yellow sign.

RULES OF THE ROAD Outside of restricted zones, there's no speed limit on autobahns, although signs recommend that motorists stay below 130 kph (80 mph). Blue signs on autobahns recommend the minimum speed on that stretch. Stay in the right-hand lane on autobahns, and use the left-hand lanes only for passing. There are speed limits on other roads—100 kph (60 mph) on Bundesstrassen, 80 kph (50 mph) on country roads, between 30 kph (18 mph) and 60 kph (36 mph) in built-up urban areas. Fines for exceeding the speed limit can be heavy. Penalties for driving under the influence of alcohol are even more severe, so keep within the legal limit—.05% blood-alcohol level.

CUSTOMS & DUTIES
See Customs & Duties *in* Smart Travel Tips.

EATING & DRINKING
The range of dining experiences in Germany is vast: everything from high-priced contemporary cuisine to street-vendor *Würste* (sausages). Countrywide, seek out *Gaststätten, Gasthäuser,* or *Gasthöfe*—local inns—for traditional and regional specialties. Beer gardens in Bavaria, *Apfelwein* (alcoholic apple cider) taverns in Frankfurt, and *Kneipen* (pubs) in Berlin nearly always offer the best value and local atmosphere. Just about every town will have a *Ratskeller,* a cellar restaurant in the town hall, where exposed beams, sturdy tables, and immense portions are the rule.

Every part of the country has its local brew. Say "*Helles*" or "*Export*" if you want light beer; "*Dunkles*" if you want dark beer. *Weissbier* is a sour, refreshing beer brewed from wheat. Germany is also a major producer of wine (mostly white). All wines are graded in one of three basic categories: *Tafelwein* (table wine); *Qualitätswein* (fine wine); and *Qualitätswein mit Prädikat* (top-quality wine).

WHAT IT COSTS In Euros			
$$$$	**$$$**	**$$**	**$**
AT DINNER over €26	€20–€25	€15–€20	under €15

Prices are per person for a main course.

MEALTIMES Breakfast, served from 6:30 to 10 in hotels, often consists of cold meats, cheeses, jams, yogurt, and fruit. City cafés often serve breakfast into the afternoon. Lunch is served from around 11:30 to around 2; dinner is generally from 6 until 9:30. City and popular restaurants serve later. At lunch try the *Tageskarte,* or suggested menu, for maximum nourishment at a minimum price.

RESERVATIONS & DRESS Jacket and tie are advised for restaurants in the $$$ and $$$$ categories. In Germany, even casual attire is dressier than in the United States and Britain. Think "business casual."

EMBASSIES
Embassies are in the capital, Berlin.

🏛 Australia ✉ Wallstr. 76–79 D-10179 Berlin ☎ 030/880-0880 🖨 030/8800-88210 🌐 www.australian-embassy.de.

🏛 Canada ✉ Friedrichstr. 95, 12th floor, D-10117 Berlin ☎ 030/203-120 🖨 030/203-12121 🌐 www.canada.de.

🏛 Ireland ✉ Friedrichstr. 200, D-10117 Berlin ☎ 030/220-720 🖨 030/220-72299 🌐 www.botschaft-irland.de.

🏛 New Zealand ✉ Friedrichstr. 60, D-10117 Berlin ☎ 030/206-2110 🖨 030/206-21114 🌐 www.nzembassy.com.

🏛 South Africa ✉ Friedrichstr. 60, D-10117 Berlin ☎ 030/220-730 🖨 030/2207-3202 🌐 www.suedafrika.org.

🏛 United Kingdom ✉ Wilhelmstr. 70–71, D-10117 Berlin ☎ 030/204-570 🌐 www.britischebotschaft.de.

🏛 United States ✉ Neustädtische Kirchstr. 4–5, D-10117 Berlin ☎ 030/832-9233 🖨 030/8305-1215 🌐 www.us-botschaft.de.

HOLIDAYS
January 1; January 6 (Epiphany—Bavaria, Baden-Württemberg, and Saxony-Anhalt only); Good Friday; Easter Monday; May 1 (Worker's Day); Ascension, Pentecost Monday, in May; May 30 (Corpus Christi—south Germany only); August 15 (Assumption Day—Bavaria and Saarland only); October 3 (German Unity Day); November 1 (All Saints' Day—Baden Württemberg, Bavaria, North Rhine Westphalia, Rheinland-Pfalz, and Saarland only); December 24–26.

LANGUAGE
Among Germany's many dialects, probably the most difficult to comprehend is Bavaria's. Virtually everyone can also speak *Hochdeutsch,* the German equivalent of Oxford English. Many people under age 40 speak some English.

LODGING
The standard of German hotels, from luxury properties (of which the country has more than its fair share) to the humblest pension, is excellent. You can expect courteous service; clean and comfortable rooms; and, in rural areas especially, considerable Old German atmosphere.

The country has numerous *Gasthöfe* or *Gasthäuser* (country inns); pensions or *Fremdenheime* (guest houses); and, at the lowest end of the scale, *Zimmer,* meaning rooms, normally in private houses. Look for the sign ZIMMER FREI (rooms free) or ZU VERMIETEN (for rent). A red sign reading BESETZT means there are no vacancies.

Major hotels in cities often have lower rates on weekends or when business is quiet. If you're lucky, you can find reductions of up to 50%. Likewise, rooms reserved after 10 PM will often carry a discount. Tourist offices can provide lists of hotels offering *Pauschalangebote* (low-price inclusive weekly packages). Many winter resorts lower their rates for the periods immediately before and after the Christmas and New Year's high season.

The following chart is for hotels throughout Germany. In Berlin, Munich, and Hamburg, price categories are about €25 higher than those for other cities. Breakfast is usually, but not always, included in the room rate.

WHAT IT COSTS In Euros			
$$$$	**$$$**	**$$**	**$**
HOTELS	over €200	€150–€200	€75–€150	under €75

Hotel prices are for two people in a standard double room in high season.

APARTMENT & VILLA RENTALS Apartments and houses have reasonable rates, with reductions for longer stays. Rates for short-term stays usually include charges for gas and electricity. Local and regional tourist offices have listings for their areas.

CAMPING Some 5,500 campsites in Germany are listed, along with many other European sites, by the German Camping Club. Sites tend to be crowded in summer, so make reservations a day or two ahead. Prices at ordinary campsites range from €10 to €26 per night for two adults, a car, and a tent or trailer. Some higher-priced facilities come replete with pool, sports facilities, and entertainment programs.
🏕 **German Camping Club** (DCC) ✉ Mandlstr. 28, D-80802 Munich, ☎ 089/380–1420 🖷 089/334–737 ⊕ www.camping-club.de.

CASTLE HOTELS The prices at *Schloss*, or castle hotels, are mostly moderate; some of the simpler establishments, however, may lack some comforts, and furnishings can be basic. On the whole they're delightful, with antiques, impressive interiors, and out-of-the-way locations.
🏰 **Euro-Connection** ✉ 7500 212th St. SW, Suite 103, Edmonds, WA 98026 ☎ 800/645–3876. **Gast im Schloss Marketing** ✉ Box 1428 Niedernhausen D-65527 ☎ 06127/999–098 🖷 06127/920–822 ⊕ www.gast-im-schloss.de.

HOSTELS Germany's more than 600 *Jugendherbergen* (youth hostels) are among the most efficient and up-to-date in Europe, and many are in castles. There's an age limit of 26 in Bavaria; elsewhere, those under 20 take preference if space is limited. The DJH Service GmbH provides a complete list of German hostels. Rates at hostels average €13.30 for people under 27 and €13.30–€19 for those older (breakfast included). Accommodations can range from single-sex, dorm-style beds to rooms for couples and families. To book a hostel, you can go on DJH's Web site or call a lodging directly; it's helpful to be a member of a national hosteling association or Hostelling International (HI). Without membership, there is an extra charge, but with each overnight stay you receive a "welcome stamp." Six welcome stamps will grant you full membership in HI. Reserve well in advance for midsummer.
🏠 **Hostel Organizations DJH Service GmbH** ✉ Bismarkstr. 8 D-32754 Detmold ☎ 05231/74010 🖷 05231/740–149 ⊕ www.jugendherberge.de.

HOTELS Listings of hotels are available from DEHOGA, Germany's hotel and gastronomy federation, and from all regional and local tourist offices. Tourist offices will also make reservations for you—they usually charge a nominal fee—but may have difficulty doing so after 4 PM in peak season and on weekends. There is also an excellent, nationwide reservations service, Tourismus Service, which is open weekdays 9–6 and Saturday 9–1. In cities, trade fairs fill hotels year-round, so book well in advance.

Ringhotels are individually owned and managed, and usually fall in the medium price range. Many are in the countryside or in pretty villages. Package deals of two to three days are available. Among the most delightful places to stay and eat in Germany are the aptly named Romantik Hotels and Restaurants. All are in historic buildings and are personally run by the owners. The emphasis generally is on comfort, good food, and style.

Smaller hotels do not provide much in terms of amenities. You may even have to bring your own soap and washcloth.

🄵 **DEHOGA** ⊕ www.hotelguide.de. **Ringhotels** ✉ Belfortstr. 6–8, D-81667 Munich ☎ 089/458-7030 🖷 089/458-70331 ⊕ www.ringhotels24.de. **Romantik Hotels and Restaurants** ✉ Lyoner Stern, Hahnstr. 70, D-60528 Frankfurt/M ☎ 069/661-2340 🖷 069/6612-3456 ⊕ www.romantikhotels.com.

FARM VACATIONS Almost every regional tourist office has listings of farms, by area, offering bed-and-breakfast, apartments, or whole farmhouses to rent. The German Agricultural Association produces an annual catalog of more than 2,000 inspected and graded lodgings. It costs €9.90 and is sold in bookstores.

🄵 **German Agricultural Association (DLG)** ✉ Eschborner Landstr. 122, D-60489 Frankfurt am Main ☎ 069/247-880 🖷 069/2478-8110 ⊕ www.dlg.org.

MAIL & SHIPPING

You can arrange to have mail sent to you in care of any German post office; have the envelope marked "Postlagernd." This service is free. Alternatively, if you have an American Express card or traveler's checks, or have booked a vacation with American Express, you can have mail sent to any American Express office in Germany; there's no charge.

POSTAL RATES Airmail letters to the United States, Canada, Australia, and New Zealand cost €1.50; postcards, €1. All letters to the United Kingdom cost €0.55; postcards, €0.45.

MONEY MATTERS

The most expensive cities are Berlin, Frankfurt, Hamburg, and Munich. Costs are somewhat lower in eastern Germany, but businesses that cater specifically to visitors are increasingly charging western German rates. Some sample prices include cup of coffee €1.80; mug of beer in a beer hall, €3; soft drink, €1.80; ham sandwich, €2.80; 3-km (2-mi) taxi ride, €6.

CREDIT CARDS All major U.S. credit cards are accepted in Germany. German ATMs accept four-digit personal identification numbers.

American Express (☎ 069/97970). **Diners Club** (☎ 01805/336–696). **MasterCard** (☎ 0800/819–1040). **Visa** (☎ 0800/814–9100).

CURRENCY Germany shares a common currency, the euro (€), with 11 other countries: Austria, Belgium, Finland, France, Greece, Ireland, Italy, Luxembourg, the Netherlands, Portugal, and Spain. The euro is divided into 100 cents. There are bills of 5, 10, 20, 50, 100, and 500 euros and coins of €1 and €2, and 1, 2, 5, 10, 20, and 50 cents.

At press time (summer 2003), the exchange rate for the euro was €0.89 to the U.S. dollar, €0.62 to the Canadian dollar, €1.40 to the pound sterling, €0.56 to the Australian dollar, €0.50 to the New Zealand dollar, and €0.12 to the South African rand.

TAXES

German goods carry a 16% value-added tax (VAT). Multiply the cost of an item by .138 to determine how much of the cost is VAT. When making a purchase, ask for a Global Refund Cheque or an *Ausfuhr-Abnehmerbescheinigung* form.

TELEPHONES

COUNTRY & AREA CODES Germany's country code is 49. When calling Germany from outside the country, drop the initial 0 in the regional code. Numbers that begin 0180 cost an average of €0.12 per minute; those that begin 0190 can cost €1.85 per minute and more.

LONG DISTANCE & INTERNATIONAL CALLS

Calls can be made from just about any telephone booth, most of which are card operated. It costs only €0.13 per minute to call the United States, day or night. If you expect to do a lot of calling, international or local, purchase a telephone card. Collect calls to the United States can be made by dialing 0180/200–1033 (this is also the number to call if you have problems dialing out). For information in English dial 11837 for numbers within Germany, and 11834 for numbers elsewhere. But first look for the number in the phone book or on the Web (⊕ www.teleauskunft. de), because directory assistance costs at least €0.50, more if the call lasts more than 30 seconds.

🆔 Access Codes **AT&T** ☎ 0800-888-012. **MCI WorldCom** ☎ 0130-0012. **Sprint** ☎ 0800-888-013.

LOCAL CALLS

A local call from a telephone booth costs €.10 per minute. Drop the local area code.

TIPPING

The service charges on bills is sufficient for most tips in your hotel, though you should tip bellhops and porters; €1 per bag or service is ample. It's also customary to leave a small tip (a euro per night) for the room-cleaning staff. Whether you tip the desk clerk depends on whether he or she has given you any special service.

Service charges are included in all restaurant checks (listed as *Bedienung*), as is tax (listed as *MWST*). Nonetheless, it is customary to round small bills to the nearest euro or to leave about 10% (give it to the waiter or waitress as you pay the bill; don't leave it on the table). Table servers in bars also expect a 2%–5% tip. In taxis round up the fare about a euro as a tip.

TRAIN TRAVEL

The Deutsche Bahn is a very efficient rail service. Journeys between the centers of many cities—Munich–Frankfurt, for example—can be completed faster by rail than by plane. The Frankfurt–Hamburg InterCity Express train takes three hours, 35 minutes one-way. InterCity Night and CityNightLine trains are "rolling hotels" with dining cars and shower and lavatory in each sleeping compartment, and overnight D-class trains also have sleepers. Seat reservations (highly advisable on the high-speed InterCity, EuroCity, and InterCity Express trains) cost €2.60. City and large town stations have lockers.

CUTTING COSTS

If you plan to travel by train within a day after your flight arrives, note that Lufthansa, US Air, Delta, and Singapore Air participate in the "Rail and Fly" program with DB trains. Whatever airline you use, ask about these tickets good for rail travel.

For round-trip travel you can save 25% if you book at least three days in advance, and 40% if you book at least seven days in advance and have a Sunday in between outward and return journeys. For a one-way ticket, you can save 10% by booking at least a day in advance. There are a limited amount of seats sold at any of these discount prices, so book as early as possible. If you change your travel plans after booking, you will have to pay a fee. The surcharge for tickets bought on-board is 10% of the ticket cost, or a minimum of €5.

Children under 15 travel free when accompanied by a parent. For unrelated groups, the *Mitfahrer-Rabatt* gives up to four travelers a 50% discount when one person pays at least €15 for a second-class ticket.

The *Schönes Wochenend Ticket* (Happy Weekend Ticket) provides un-limited travel on weekends for up to five persons for as little as €3.50 per person. Groups of six or more should inquire about *Gruppen & Spar* savings.

Of all the German train classes, InterCity Express trains are the most expensive. A €3.60 surcharge (€7.20 round-trip) is added to the ticket price on all InterCity and EuroCity journeys irrespective of distance. The charge is €4.60 if paid on board the train.

A EurailPass, which you should purchase before coming to Europe, is good over the entire German rail network. There is also a German Rail Pass for travel over the entire German rail network for 4 to 10 days within a single month. A Twin Pass does the same for two people traveling to-gether and is even cheaper per person. These passes are also good for travel on tour routes, such as the ones along the Romantic Road served by Deutsche Touring and Rhine and Mosel River day cruises. These and other passes are sold by travel agents and DER Travel in the United States. 🔒 **DER Travel Services** ✉ 9501 W. Devon Ave., Rosemont, IL 60018 ☎ 800/782-2424 🖷 800/860-9944 for a brochure ⊕ www.dertravel.com. **Deutsche Bahn** (German Rail) ✉ Stephanstr. 1, D-60313 Frankfurt am Main ☎ 11861 for 24-hr hot line, roughly €0.60 per minute; 0800/150-7090 toll-free, automated service ⊕ www.bahn.de.

TRAVEL AGENTS

Deutsches Reisebüro (DER) has offices in just about every section of every German city. All offer a full range of travel services. The tours it organizes are also sold by travel agents. Euraide, in the main train sta-tion of Munich and the Zoologischer Garten station in Berlin, serves English-speaking travelers on a drop-in basis. Its Web site offers detailed advice on using train passes. 🔒 **DER Abroad** **DER Travel Services** ✉ 9501 W. Devon Ave., Rosemont, IL 60018 ☎ 800/782-2424 🖷 800/860-9944 for a brochure ⊕ www.dertravel.com. **Euraide** ⊕ www.euraide.com.

VISITOR INFORMATION

See Smart Travel Tips for the GNTB's offices outside Germany. 🔒 Tourist Information **German National Tourist Board** (GNTB) ✉ Beethovenstr. 69, D-60325 Frankfurt ☎ 069/974-640 🖷 069/751-903 ⊕ www.visits-to-germany.com. 🔒 Wine Information **Deutsches Wein Institut** ✉ Gutenbergpl. 3-5, 55116 Mainz, ☎ 06131/282-933 ⊕ www.deutschewein.de. **German Wine Information Bureau** ✉ 245 Park Ave., 39th floor, New York, NY 10167 ☎ 212/792-4134 🖷 212/792-4001 ⊕ www. germanwineusa.org.

WHEN TO GO

The main tourist season runs from May through late October, when the weather is best and hundreds of folk festivals take place. The Rhine area has wine harvest events galore in early fall; an events cal-endar from the German Wine Information Bureau can help you time your visit. Winter-sports season in the Bavarian Alps runs from Christ-mas through mid-March.

CLIMATE Germany's climate is generally temperate. Summers are usually sunny and warm, though the north half of Germany seems to have more than its share of overcast and wet days. Winters vary from mild and damp to very cold and bright. In Alpine regions spring often comes late, with snow flurries well into April. Only in southern Bavaria (Bayern) will you find strikingly variable weather, which is caused by the *Föhn*, a warm Alpine wind that brings sudden barometric changes and gives rise to clear but oppressive conditions in summer and causes snow to disappear overnight in winter.

BERLIN

Jan.	35F	2C	May	66F	19C	Sept.	68F	20C
	26	–3		47	8		50	10
Feb.	37F	3C	June	72F	22C	Oct.	56F	13C
	26	–3		53	12		42	6
Mar.	46F	8C	July	75F	24C	Nov.	45F	7C
	31	0		57	14		36	2
Apr.	56F	13C	Aug.	74F	23C	Dec.	38F	3C
	39	4		56	13		29	–1

FRANKFURT

Jan.	39F	4C	May	69F	20C	Sept.	69F	21C
	30	–1		49	9		52	11
Feb.	43F	6C	June	74F	23C	Oct.	57F	14C
	31	1		55	13		44	7
Mar.	51F	11C	July	75F	24C	Nov.	45F	7C
	37	3		58	15		37	3
Apr.	59F	15C	Aug.	76F	24C	Dec.	40F	4C
	41	5		57	14		32	0

MUNICH

Jan.	35F	1C	May	64F	18C	Sept.	67F	20C
	23	–5		45	7		48	9
Feb.	38F	3C	June	70F	21C	Oct.	56F	14C
	23	–5		51	11		40	4
Mar.	48F	9C	July	74F	23C	Nov.	44F	7C
	30	–1		55	13		33	0
Apr.	56F	14C	Aug.	73F	23C	Dec.	36F	2C
	38	3		54	12		26	–4

MUNICH

Provincial, easygoing, and wealthy, the city of beer and baroque is known for its good-natured and relaxed charm, which is known as *Gemütlichkeit*. The Bavarian city is a mix of high culture (visit its world-class opera house and art museums) and wild abandon (witness the vulgar frivolity of Oktoberfest or the very un-German high jinks of Fasching, the Bavarian version of Carnival). In the 19th century King Ludwig I of Bavaria brought much international prestige to his home city after declaring: "I want to make Munich a town that does such credit to Germany that nobody knows Germany unless he has seen Munich." He kept his promise with an architectural and artistic renaissance—before abdicating in the wake of a passionate romance with an Irish-born courtesan, Lola Montez.

Exploring Munich

Numbers in the margin correspond to points of interest on the Munich map.

Keep a map handy when walking the Old Town's jumble of pedestrian-only streets. Many shops, churches, and brew houses are packed within the triangle formed by the subway stations Odeonsplatz, Marienplatz, and Karslplatz. Once you get off at one station, you can easily walk the whole area. The major art museums are clustered just beyond the Old Town, in Maxvorstadt (use Königsplatz, Theresienstrasse, or Universität subway stations).

★ ⑯ **Alte Pinakothek** (Old Picture Gallery). This major art gallery contains celebrated old master paintings, including works by Dürer, Titian, Rem-

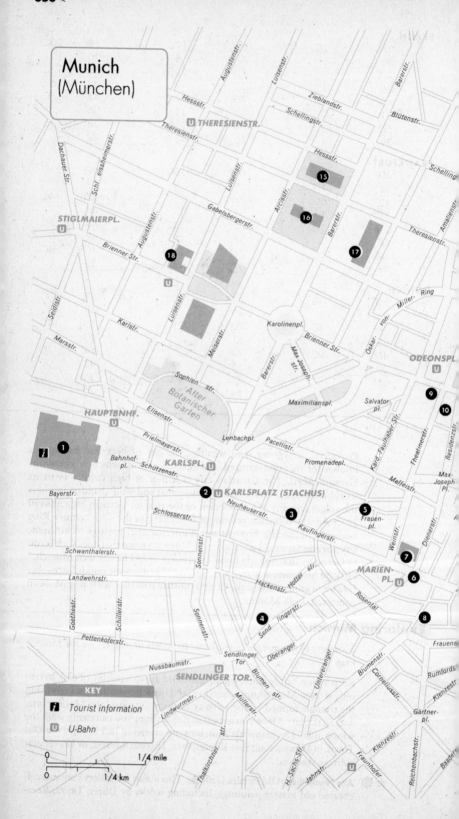

Munich (München)

THERESIENSTR.

STIGLMAIERPL.

Augustenstr.

Luisenstr.

Zieblandstr.

Schellingstr.

Blütenstr.

Barerstr.

Hessstr.

Theresienstr.

Schelling

Hessstr.

15

Arcisstr.

16

Barerstr.

17

Theresienstr.

Amalienstr.

Gabelsbergerstr.

Brienner Str.

18

Dachauer Str.

Schleissheimerstr.

Seidlstr.

Karlstr.

Luisenstr.

Meiserstr.

Karolinenpl.

Brienner Str.

Barerstr.

Max-Joseph str.

Oskar- von- Miller- Ring

ODEONSPL.

Marsstr.

Sophien str.

Alter Botanischer Garten

Maximilianspl.

Salvator-pl.

9

10

HAUPTBNHF.

Elisenstr.

Prielmayerstr.

Lenbachpl.

Pacellistr.

Promenadepl.

Theatinerstr.

Residenzstr.

Max-Joseph Pl.

i 1

Bahnhof-pl.

Schützenstr.

KARLSPL.

2

KARLSPLATZ (STACHUS)

Neuhauserstr.

3

Kaufingerstr.

Frauen-pl.

5

Kard.-Faulhaber-Str.

Maffeistr.

Dienerstr.

Bayerstr.

Schlosserstr.

Weinstr.

7

MARIEN-PL.

6

Schwanthalerstr.

Sonnenstr.

Hackenstr.

Hotter str.

Rosental

Landwehrstr.

4

Sendlingerstr.

8

Frauens

Goethestr.

Schillerstr.

Pettenkoferstr.

Sonnenstr.

Oberanger

Unteranger

Blumenstr.

Cornelius-str.

Rumfords

Klenz

Nussbaumstr.

Sendlinger Tor

SENDLINGER TOR.

Blumen str.

Gartner-pl.

KEY

i Tourist information

U U-Bahn

Lindwurmstr.

Müllerstr.

Thalkirchner str.

H.-Sachs-Str.

Jahnstr.

Fraunhofer

Klenzerstr.

Reichenbachstr.

Baader

0   1/4 mile

0   1/4 km

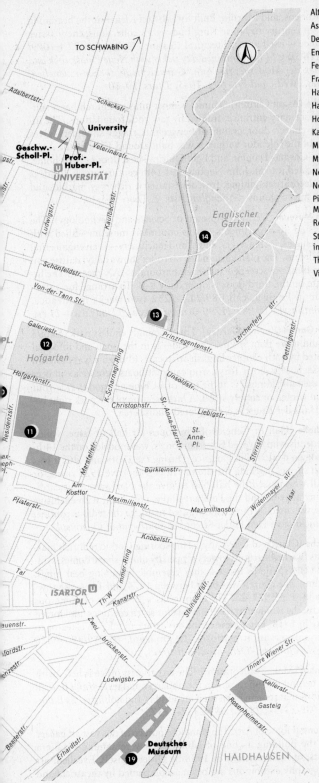

brandt, Rubens, and Murillo. Built by Leo von Klenze at the beginning of the 19th century to house King Ludwig I's collections, the massive brick edifice is itself an architectural treasure. ⊠ *Barerstr. 27* ☎ *089/ 2380–5216* ⊠ *€11 for combined day ticket with Neue Pinakothek and Pinakothek der Moderne, free Sun.* ⊕ *www.pinakotheken-muenchen. de* ⊘ *Tues., Wed., and Fri.–Sun. 10–5, Thurs. 10–10.*

★ ❹ **Asamkirche** (Asam Church). Munich's most unusual church has a suitably extraordinary entrance, framed by raw rock foundations. The insignificant church door, crammed between its craggy shoulders, gives little idea of the splendor within. It was built around 1730 by the Asam brothers—Cosmas Damian and Egid Quirin—next door to their home. They dedicated it to St. John Nepomuk, a 14th-century monk. Inside is a riot of decoration: gilding, frescoes, statuary, rich rosy marble, and billowing stucco clouds. ⊠ *Sendlingerstr.* ⊘ *Daily 9–5:30.*

★ ☺ ❶❾ **Deutsches Museum** (German Museum of Science and Technology). The six floors and 30 departments of this enormous museum—filled with aircraft, vehicles, locomotives, ships, and machinery—is an engineering student's dream. The planetarium has up to six shows daily; nature and adventure films are screened at the wraparound IMAX theater. The Internet Café on the third floor is open daily 9–3. To arrange for a two-hour tour in English, call 089/217–9252 two weeks in advance. ⊠ *Museumsinsel 1* ☎ *089/21790* ⊕ *www.fdt.de* ⊘ *Daily 9 AM–11 PM.*

☺ ❶❹ **Englischer Garten** (English Garden). This seemingly endless park (5 km/3 mi long and more than ½ km/¼ mi wide) is in the open and informal style favored by 18th-century English aristocrats (though it was designed by a Massachusetts-born Tory). You can rent boats here, relax in beer gardens (the most famous is at the foot of a Chinese pagoda), ride your bike, ski in winter, or simply stroll. A large section of the park right behind the **Haus der Kunst** is a designated nudist area.

❶⓪ **Feldherrnhalle** (Hall of Generals). This open-air hall of fame, which honors generals who have led Bavarian forces, was modeled on the 14th-century Loggia dei Lanzi in Florence. During the 1930s and '40s it was a key Nazi shrine, marking the site of Hitler's abortive 1923 rising, or *putsch*. All who passed the hall had to give the Nazi salute. Viscardigasse, a tiny alley behind the Feldherrnhalle, now lined with exclusive boutiques, was used by those who wanted to dodge the tedious routine, hence its nickname: Heil Hitler Street. ⊠ *South end of Odeonspl.*

❺ **Frauenkirche** (Church of Our Lady). This soaring Gothic redbrick masterpiece has two incongruous towers topped by onion-shape domes, symbols of the city (perhaps because they resemble brimming beer mugs, cynics claim). The church was built between 1474 and 1494; the towers were added in 1524–25. The crypt houses the tombs of numerous Wittelsbachs, the family that ruled Bavaria for seven centuries until forced to abdicate in 1918. For a view of the city, you can take an elevator to one tower's observation platform. ⊠ *Frauenpl.* ☎ *089/290–0820* ⊘ *Tower elevator Apr.–Oct., Mon.–Sat. 10–5.*

❶ **Hauptbahnhof** (Main Train Station). The city tourist office is here, with maps and helpful information. On the underground level you'll find all sorts of shops that remain open even on Sunday and holidays. ⊠ *Bahnhofpl.* ☎ *089/2333–0256 or 089/2333–0257.*

❶❸ **Haus der Kunst** (House of Art). The grandiose portico of this vast art gallery identifies the building as one of Munich's few remaining Nazi-era monuments, opened officially in 1938 by Hitler himself. Excellent art and photography exhibitions are often accompanied by theatrical and musical happenings. The oh-so-chic disco, P 1, is in the building's west wing. ☒ *Prinzregentenstr. 1* ☎ *089/211–270* ⊕ *www.hausderkunst.de* ⊙ *Daily 10–10.*

⑫ Hofgarten (Royal Garden). The formal garden was once part of the royal palace grounds. It is bordered on two sides by arcades designed in the 19th century by the royal architect Leo von Klenze. ☒ *Hofgartenstr., north of Residenz.*

❷ Karlsplatz (Charles Square). Known locally as the Stachus, this busy intersection has one of Munich's most popular fountains, a circle of water jets that cool city shoppers and office workers on hot summer days.

★ **❻ Marienplatz** (Square of Our Lady). Surrounded by shops, restaurants, and cafés, this square is named for the 1638 gilt statue of the Virgin Mary that has been watching over it for nearly four centuries. The tower of the 1474 medieval **Altes Rathaus** (Old Town Hall; ☎ 089/294–001 ⊙ Daily 10–5:30) bordering it has a little toy museum.

❸ Michaelskirche (St. Michael's Church). One of the most magnificent Renaissance churches in Germany, this spacious and handsome structure is decorated throughout in plain white stucco. It was built during the late 16th century for the Jesuits and was closely modeled on Il Gesù, the Jesuit church in Rome. More than 40 members of the Wittelsbach royal family, including King Ludwig II, are buried in the crypt. ☒ *Neuhauserstr. 6* ☎ *089/231–7060* ⊙ *Daily 8–7, except during services.*

⑮ Neue Pinakothek (New Picture Gallery). The art gallery that Ludwig I built to house his "modern" collections was destroyed during World War II and replaced by this exhibition hall in 1981. It's a superb, skylit setting for one of the finest collections of 19th-century European paintings and sculpture in the world. ☒ *Barerstr. 29* ☎ *089/2380–5195* ⊕ *www.pinakotheken-muenchen.de* ☒ *€11 for combined day ticket with Alte Pinakothek and Pinakothek der Moderne, free Sun.* ⊙ *Wed. and Fri.–Mon. 10–5, Thurs. 10–10.*

❼ Neues Rathaus (New City Hall). Munich's present city hall was built between 1867 and 1908 in the fussy, turreted, neo-Gothic style so beloved by King Ludwig II. At 11, noon, and 9 daily (also June–September at 5), the central tower's *Glockenspiel*, or chiming clock, swings into action with two tiers of dancing and jousting figures. An elevator serves an observation point near the top of one of the towers. ☒ *Marienpl.* ☎ *089/2331* ⊙ *Tower Mon.–Thurs. 9–4, Fri. 9–1.*

⑰ Pinakothek der Moderne (Modern Art Gallery). Munich's latest cultural addition is also Germany's largest museum for modern art, architecture and design. The striking glass-and-concrete complex holds four outstanding art and architectural collections, including modern art, industrial and graphic design, the Bavarian State collection of graphic art, and the Technical University's architectural museum. ☒ *Türkenstr. at Gabelsbergerstr., and Luisenstr. at Theresienstr.* ☎ *089/2380–5118* ⊕ *www.pinakothek-der-moderne.de* ☒ *€11 for combined day ticket with Neue Pinakothek and Pinakothek der Moderne, free Sun.* ⊙ *Tues., Wed., and weekends 10–5, Thurs. and Fri. 10–8.*

★ **⑪ Residenz** (Royal Palace). This mighty palace dating to the 14th century was the home of the Wittelsbach dukes for more than three centuries. Its several major attractions include the rooms of the palace itself. The **Schatzkammer** (treasury; ⊙ Apr.–Oct., Tues., Wed., Fri.–Sun. 9–6, Thurs. 9–8; Nov.–Mar., Tues.–Sun. 9–4) has as its centerpiece a small Renaissance statue of St. George, studded with 2,291 diamonds, 209 pearls, and 406 rubies. Paintings, tapestries, furniture, and porcelain are housed in the **Residenzmuseum** (☉ Apr.–Oct., Tues., Wed., Fri.–Sun. 9–6, Thurs. 9–8; Nov.–Mar., Tues.–Sun. 9–4). During the summer, chamber-music concerts take place in the inner courtyard. Also in the center of the complex is the small rococo **Altes Residenztheater/Cuvilliés Theater** (☉ Tues.–Sun. 10–4). It was built by François Cuvilliés between 1751 and 1755, and performances are still held here. The French-born Cuvilliés was a dwarf who was admitted to the Bavarian court as a decorative "bauble." Prince Max Emanuel recognized his innate artistic ability and had him trained as an architect. *Residenzmuseum* ⊠ *Max-Joseph-Pl. 3, entry through archway at Residenzstr. 1* ☎ *089/290–671* ☉ *Closed a few days in early Jan.*

★ ☺ **Schloss Nymphenburg** (Nymphenburg Palace). The summer palace of the Wittelsbachs stands magnificently in its own park in the western suburb of Nymphenburg. The oldest parts date from 1664, but the bulk of the work was undertaken during the reign of Max Emmanuel between 1680 and 1730. The interiors are exceptional, especially the **Steinerner Saal**, a rococo masterpiece in green and gold extending over two floors and richly decorated with stucco and grandiose frescoes. Summer chamber-music concerts take place here. Portraits of the many women who caught the eye of Ludwig I adorn the **Schönheits Galerie** (Gallery of Beauties). The rococo **Amalienburg** (Hunting Lodge) on the grounds was built by François Cuvilliés, architect of the theater in Munich's Residenz. The palace also contains the **Marstallmuseum** (Museum of Royal Carriages); a sleigh that belonged to Ludwig II is included among the opulently decorated vehicles. On the floor above, the **Nymphenburger Porzellan** (Nymphenburg Porcelain Gallery) exhibits porcelain produced here between 1747 and the 1920s. The **Museum Mensch und Natur** (Museum of Man and Nature) is in the north wing. Take Tram 17 or Bus 41 from the city center to the Schloss Nymphenburg stop. ⊠ *Notburgastr. at the bridge crossing the Nymphenburg Canal* ☎ *089/179–080* ☉ *Apr.–Sept., Tues.–Sun. 9–6; Oct.–Mar., Tues.–Sun. 10–4.*

⑱ **Städtische Galerie im Lenbachhaus** (Municipal Gallery). This late-19th-century Florentine-style villa is the former home and studio of the artist Franz von Lenbach (1836–1904). Inside, you'll find renowned works from the Gothic period to the present, including an exciting assemblage of art from the early-20th-century *Blaue Reiter* (Blue Rider) group: Kandinsky, Klee, Jawlensky, Macke, Marc, and Münter. The adjoining **Kunstbau** (art building), a former subway platform of the Königsplatz Station, hosts changing exhibitions of modern art. ⊠ *Luisenstr. 33,* ☎ *089/233–32000* ⊕ *www.lenbachhaus.de* ☉ *Tues.–Sun. 10–6.*

⑨ **Theatinerkirche** (Theatine Church). The church's vibrant mustard facade is eye-catching, and the chalky white, effusive stuccowork within brings a wedding cake to mind. The church, modeled after the Roman mother church, was built for the Theatine monks in the mid-17th century; its twin domes were added in the following century. ⊠ *Theatinerstr. 22* ☉ *Daily 8:45–7.*

★ **⑧** **Viktualienmarkt** (Food Market). The city's open-air market has a wide range of produce as well as benches at which to snack and quaff some beer. Whether here, or at a bakery, *do not* try to select your pickings by hand; ask for help. ⊠ *Southeast of Marienpl. via Tal or Rindermarkt* ☉ *Mon.–Sat. 7–6:30.*

Where to Eat

Munich claims some of the most noted restaurants in Germany. For local cuisine, Munich's wood-paneled, flagstone beer restaurants and halls serve food sturdy enough for the large servings of beer.

$$$$ ✕ **Am Marstall.** This restaurant has earned multiple awards for its menu, which combines the best of French and German cuisine—succulent lamb raised on salt-soaked pastures of coastal Brittany, for instance, or venison from the hunting grounds of Lower Bavaria. The prix-fixe menu runs €72–€82. ☒ *Maximilianstr. 16* ☎ *089/2916–5511* ⌂ *Reservations essential* ⛨ *Jacket and tie* ▭ *AE, MC, V* ☾ *Closed Sun. and Mon.*

$$$$ ✕ **Tantris.** Though its exalted reputation extends back to the 1970s, Tantris can thank Chef Hans Haas for maintaining its rank among the top dining establishments in Munich. He's been named the country's best chef in the past. You, too, will be impressed by the exotic nouvelle cuisine on the menu, including such specialties as shellfish and creamed potato soup, and roasted wood pigeon with scented rice. But you may wish to ignore the bare concrete surroundings and the garish orange-and-yellow decor. ☒ *Johann-Fichte-Str. 7* ☎ *089/361–9590* ⌂ *Reservations essential* ⛨ *Jacket and tie* ▭ *AE, DC, MC, V* ☾ *Closed Sun.*

FodorsChoice
★

★ **$-$$$** ✕ **Dukatz.** The high-ceilinged and light-filled *Literaturhaus* (House of Literature) hums with talk of publishing contracts and literary gossip. The excellent cuisine combines traditional German with a light Gallic touch: lamb's tripe melting in a rich champagne sauce, for instance. Some of the readable artwork is by New York artist Jennifer Holtzer, such as the statement at the bottom of your coffee cup saying, "More eroticism, gentlemen!" ☒ *Salvatorpl. 1* ☎ *089/291–9600* ▭ *No credit cards.*

★ **$-$$$** ✕ **Spatenhaus.** A view of the opera house and the royal palace complements the Bavarian mood of the wood-paneled and beamed Spatenhaus. The menu is international, with everything from artichokes to *zuppa Romana* (alcohol-soaked, fruity Italian cake-pudding). But since you're in Bavaria, try the Bavarian plate, an enormous mixture of local meats and sausages. Make reservations if you want to go after a concert or opera. ☒ *Residenzstr. 12* ☎ *089/290–7060* ▭ *AE, MC, V.*

$-$$ ✕ **Hackerhaus.** The cozy, upscale restaurant belonging to the Hacker Brewery (founded in the 15th century) has three floors of wood-paneled rooms. In summer you can order a cheese plate and beer in the cool, flower-bedecked inner courtyard; in winter, snuggle in a corner of the Ratsstube and warm up on thick homemade potato broth, followed by schnitzel and *Bratkartoffein* (panfried potatoes), or take a table in the Bürgerstube and admire the world's largest beer mug. ☒ *Sendlingerstr. 14* ☎ *089/ 260–5026* ▭ *AE, DC, MC, V.*

$-$$ ✕ **Hundskugel.** Munich's oldest tavern, dating from 1440, is also one of the city's tiniest and snuggest, so don't expect privacy. You'll share a bench-table with the regulars and dine on traditional Bavarian fare—the *Spanferkel* (roast suckling pig) is particularly good. On fine days, an equally tiny beer garden beckons. ☒ *Hotterstr. 18* ☎ *089/264–272* ▭ *No credit cards* ☾ *Closed Sun.*

$ ✕ **Andechser am Dom.** On a chilly day, heaters on the covered patio make this the liveliest restaurant surrounding the Frauenkirche. A ceiling fresco decorates the cozy inside. The place is known for its various sausages. Watch how many pretzels you gobble up from the basket the waiter brings—you'll have to confess how many you ate and pay accordingly. ☒ *Weinstr. 7A* ☎ *089/298–481* ▭ *AE, DC, MC, V.*

$ ✕ **Augustiner Keller.** This 19th-century establishment is the flagship beer restaurant of one of Munich's oldest breweries, Augustiner. The decor of the two baronial hall–like rooms emphasizes wood—from the refurbished parquet floors to the barrels from which the beer is drawn. Bavarian specialties such as *Tellerfleisch*—cold roast beef with lashings of horseradish, served on a big wooden board—fill the daily menu. ☒ *Arnulfstr. 52* ☎ *089/594–393* ▭ *AE, MC, V.*

$ ✕ **Cohen's.** You'll be well taken care of by the friendly family staff, and the homey hospitality makes this restaurant a Munich favorite. The menu includes Middle Eastern, Jewish, and German cuisine. Enjoy a standard gefilte fish doused with excellent Golan wine from Israel, or smoky baba ghanouj. The kitchen is open from 12:30 until about 10:30. Klezmer singers perform on Friday evenings. ⊠ *Theresienstr. 31 back courtyard* ☎ *089/280–9545* ⊟ *AE, MC, V.*

$ ✕ **Dürnbräu.** A fountain plays outside this picturesque old Bavarian inn. Inside, it's crowded and noisy. Expect to share a table (the 21-foot table in the middle of the place is a favorite); your fellow diners will range from businesspeople to students. The food is resolutely traditional. Try the cream of spinach soup and the boiled beef. ⊠ *Dürnbräug. 2* ☎ *089/ 222–195* ⊟ *AE, DC, MC, V.*

$ ✕ **Gasthaus Isarthor.** The communal wooden tables here host a social mix of actors, government officials, apprentice craftspeople, journalists, and retirees. Besides pork roasts, roast beef with onions, and boiled beef, the house specialty is the Augustiner beer. You can have Weisswurst and a half liter of beer for €3.40 before noon. ⊠ *Kanalstr. 2* ☎ *089/227– 753* ⊟ *MC.*

$ ✕ **Hofbräuhaus.** Crowds of singing, shouting, swaying beer drinkers fill the cavernous, smoky, stone vaults of the Hofbräuhaus. If you're not here solely to drink, try the Bavarian food in the more subdued upstairs restaurant, where the service is not so brusque. It's between Marienplatz and Maximilianstrasse. ⊠ *Platzl 9* ☎ *089/290–13610* ⌂ *Reservations not accepted* ⊟ *V.*

$ ✕ **Prinz Myshkin.** This gourmet vegetarian restaurant mixes Italian and Asian influences. You have the choice of antipasti, homemade gnocchi, tofu and stir-fried dishes, and excellent wines. If your hunger is only moderate, you can get half portions. The airy room has a majestically vaulted ceiling. ⊠ *Hackenstr. 2* ☎ *089/265–596* ⊟ *MC, V.*

Where to Stay

Munich's hotels are often full year-round. If you plan to visit during the fashion weeks in March and September or during Oktoberfest at the end of September, make reservations at least several months in advance. Munich's tourist offices will handle only written or drop-in requests for reservations assistance. Rates are often but not always lower in suburban hotels—and taking the 15-minute U-bahn or S-bahn ride into town is easy.

$$$$ ▦ **Bayerischer Hof.** Germany's most respected family-owned hotel, the Bayerischer Hof began its rich history by hosting Ludwig I's guests. Public rooms are grandly laid out with marble, antiques, and oil paintings. Laura Ashley–decorated rooms look out to the city's skyline of towers. Nightlife is built into the hotel with Trader Vic's bar, and dancing at the Night Club. ⊠ *Promenadepl. 2–6 D–80333* ☎ *089/21200* 🖷 *089/212– 0906* ⊕ *www.bayerischerhof.de* ⤴ *306 rooms, 45 suites* ♨ *3 restaurants, pool, bar* ⊟ *AE, DC, MC, V.*

★ $$$$ ▦ **Kempinski Hotel Vier Jahreszeiten.** The Four Seasons has been playing host to the world's wealthy and titled for more than a century. It has an unbeatable location on Maximilianstrasse, Munich's premier shopping street, only a few minutes' walk from the heart of the city. Elegance and luxury set the tone throughout; many rooms have handsome antique pieces. The Bistro Eck is on the main floor, and the Theater bar/restaurant is in the cellar. The afternoon tea in the poshly decorated foyer is a special treat. ⊠ *Maximilianstr. 17, D–80539* ☎ *089/21250, 516/ 794–2670 reservations in U.S.* 🖷 *089/2125–2000* ⊕ *www.kempinski-vierjahreszeiten.de* ⤴ *268 rooms, 38 suites* ♨ *2 restaurants, pool, bar* ⊟ *AE, DC, MC, V.*

$$$–$$$$ ▥ **Eden Hotel Wolff.** Chandeliers and dark-wood paneling in the public rooms underline the old-fashioned elegance of this downtown favorite (it's across from the train station and the airport bus terminal). The rooms are comfortable, and most are spacious. Dine on excellent Bavarian specialties in the intimate Zirbelstube restaurant. ⊠ *Arnulfstr. 4, D-80335* ☎ *089/551–150* ⎙ *089/5511–5555* ⊕ *www.ehw.de* ➔ *209 rooms, 7 suites* ⚇ *Restaurant* ⊟ *AE, DC, MC, V.*

$$$–$$$$ ▥ **Torbräu.** Within a handsome, century-plus-old building, this private hotel prides itself on tradition, upscale amenities, and diverse accommodations. The location is excellent, as it's midway between the Marienplatz and the Deutsches Museum (and around the corner from the Hofbräuhaus). ⊠ *Tal 41, D-80331* ☎ *089/242–340* ⎙ *089/242–34235* ⊕ *www.torbraeu.de* ➔ *89 rooms, 3 suites* ⚇ *Restaurant* ⊟ *AE, MC, V.*

$$$ ▥ **Biederstein.** The hotel is a rather uninspired block of a building, but it fits into its old Schwabing surroundings. At the rim of the Englischer Garten, the Biederstein has many advantages: peace and quiet, for one, excellent service, and comfortable, well-appointed rooms that were carefully renovated. ⊠ *Keferstr. 18, D-80335* ☎ *089/389–9970* ⎙ *089/ 389–997389* ➔ *34 rooms, 7 suites* ⚇ *Bar* ⊟ *AE, DC, MC, V.*

$$–$$$ ▥ **Advokat.** If you value the clean lines of modern taste over plush luxury, this is the hotel for you. It's within a residential neighborhood that's an easy walk from the Rathaus square and a shorter one from the subway. Between outings you can snack on the fruit plate that welcomes you upon arrival. ⊠ *Baaderstr. 1, D-80469* ☎ *089/216–310* ⎙ *089/ 216–3190* ⊕ *www.hotel-advokat.de* ➔ *50 rooms* ⊟ *AE, DC, MC, V.*

$$–$$$ ▥ **Hotel Hauser.** Close to the art museums and the Englischer Garten, this hotel is also near the shops, bars, and restaurants frequented by young Müncheners. The small, clean rooms have watercolors of the city, and amenities include a sauna and solarium. Skip the cost of breakfast and find a nearby café. ⊠ *Schellingstr. 11 80799* ☎ *089/286–6750* ⎙ *089/ 2866–7599* ⊕ *www.hotel-hauser.de* ➔ *34 rooms* ⊟ *AE, MC, V.*

$$ ▥ **Hotel Blauer Bock.** A cozy, denlike lobby and large breakfast room make this corner hostelry stand out from others in its price category. You can help yourself to drinks and pay later by an honor system. The Old Town hotel is convenient to the Viktualienmarkt, Stadtmuseum, and Marienplatz. ⊠ *Sebastianpl. 9 80331* ☎ *089/231–780* ⎙ *089/2317–8200* ➔ *75 rooms, 50 with bath* ⊟ *No credit cards.*

$ ▥ **Hotel Pension am Siegestor.** An ancient, wood-paneled elevator carries you to the fourth-floor reception area of this charming little hotel between Schwabing's main boulevard and the university quarter. Rooms on the fifth floor, tucked up under the eaves, are particularly cozy. None has a private bath, but each floor has its own bathroom. ⊠ *Akademiestr. 5, D-80799* ☎ *089/399–550 or 089/399–551* ⎙ *089/343–050* ➔ *20 rooms with shared bath* ⊟ *No credit cards.*

$ ▥ **Hotel-Pension Beck.** Rambling, friendly Beck welcomes budget-minded guests who don't mind the smoky reception area or the dog that occasionally wanders the halls. The rooms and shared bathrooms are spic-and-span. A tram line gets you to some museums and the Englischer Garten. Continental breakfast is included. ⊠ *Thierschstr. 36, D-80538* ☎ *089/220–708 or 089/221–092* ⎙ *089/220–925* ⊕ *www.bst-online. de* ➔ *44 rooms, 7 with shower* ⊟ *MC, V.*

Nightlife & the Arts

The Arts

Details of concerts and theater performances are available from the *Vorschau* or *Monatsprogramm* booklets available at most hotel reception desks. The **Gasteig Kulturzentrum** (⊠ Rosenheimerstr. 5 ☎ 089/

480–980) is the massive glass-and-brick complex on the hill above the eastern end of the Ludwigsbrücke. It's home to the Munich Philharmonic Orchestra, the main city library, and a variety of theaters, galleries, and cafés. Some hotels will make ticket reservations for you, or you can book through ticket agencies in the city center, such as **Max Hieber Konzertkasse** (✉ Liebfrauenstr. 1 ☎ 089/2900–8014). Tickets for performances at the Altes Residenztheater/Cuvilliés-Theater, Bavarian State Theater/New Residence Theater, Nationaltheater, Prinzregententheater, and Staatheater am Gartnerplatz are sold at the **central box office** (✉ Maximilianstr. 11 ☎ 089/2185–1920 ☉ Weekdays 10–6, Sat. 10–1, and one hour before curtain time).

CONCERTS & OPERA
Munich's Bavarian State Opera company is world famous, and tickets for major productions in its permanent home, the **Nationaltheater** (✉ Maximilianstr. 11 ☎ 089/2185–1920), are often difficult to come by. Try at the evening box office, which opens on the south side of the theater one hour before performances. Book far in advance through the tourist office for the annual opera festival held in July and August. Compact opera productions and plays are often performed at the **Altes Residenztheater/Cuvilliés-Theater** (✉ Max-Joseph-Pl.; entrance on Residenzstr. ☎ 089/2185–1920). **Herkulessaal in der Residenz** (✉ Hofgarten ☎ 089/2906–7263) is a leading orchestral and recital venue.

Nightlife

BARS, CABARET & NIGHTCLUBS
Alter Simpl (✉ Turkenstr. 57 ☎ 089/272–3083) turned 100 in 2002. Media types drink Guinness and Kilkenny at its square bar, and German pub food is served throughout the day and night. The **Havanna Club** (✉ Herrnstr. 3 ☎ 089/291–884) does its best to look like a run-down Cuban dive and packs in a chic clientele. **O'Reilly's Irish Cellar Pub** (✉ Maximilianstr. 29 ☎ 089/293–311) pours genuine Irish Guinness. Great Caribbean cocktails and a powerful Irish-German Black and Tan (Guinness and strong German beer) are served at the English nautical–style **Pusser's New York Bar** (✉ Falkenturmstr. 9 ☎ 089/220–500). In the Lehel district, **Scalar** (✉ Seitzstr. 12 ☎ 089/215–79–636) is designed to the last corner in modern, sleek style and draws a fairly mixed crowd of fashionable people. The bar **Schumann's** (✉ Maximilianstr. 36 ☎ 089/229–060) has a shabby New York look, but the clientele is Munich chic.

Beer Gardens

Everyone in Munich has at least one favorite beer garden, so you're in good hands if you ask someone to point you in the direction of one. Munich has very strict noise laws, so beer gardens tend to close around 11. The famous **Biergarten am Chinesischen Turm** (☎ 089/383–8730) is at the five-story Chinese Tower in the Englisher Garten. The Englisher Garten's smaller beer garden, **Hirschau** (☎ 089/369–945), has minigolf to test your skills after a few beers. It's about 10 minutes north of the Kleinhesselohersee. The **Seehaus im Englischen Garten** (☎ 089/381–6130) is on the banks of the artificial lake Kleinhesselohersee, where all of Munich converges on hot summer days (Bus Line 44, exit at Osterwaldstrasse; you can't miss it). The **Hofbräukeller** (✉ Innere Wiener Str. 19, tramway 18 to Wiener-Pl. or U-bahn 4 or 5 to Max-Weber-Pl. ☎ 089/459–9250) is a beer relative of the Hofbräuhaus. Some evenings you can move into the spacious cellar for live jazz.

DANCE CLUBS
Clubs abound in the side streets off Freilitzschstrasse, surrounding Münchener Freiheit in Schwabing. The **Skyline** (✉ Münchner-Freiheit ☎ 089/333–131) is at the top of the Hertie department store, which towers above a busy square. Bordering the Englisher Garten, **P 1** (✉ Prinzregentenstr., on west side of Haus der Kunst ☎ 089/294–252) is allegedly

the trendiest club in town; find out for yourself if you can make it past the bouncer. **Old Mrs. Henderson** (✉ Rumfordstr. 2 ☎ 089/263–469) puts on the city's best transvestite cabaret, and a mostly gay crowd packs the dance floor on weekends. The **Park-Café** (✉ Sophienstr. 7 ☎ 089/ 598–313) is one of those fashionable places where you'll have to talk yourself past the doorman to join the chic crowds inside. The **Schlachthof** (✉ Zenettistr. 8 ☎ 089/765–448) is, as the name suggests, at the slaughterhouse. The atmosphere is nevertheless very lively thanks to a mixed crowd that is not overly hip. The musical offerings are usually excellent jazz, soul, or ethnic.

Shopping

Munich has an immense central shopping area, 2 km (1 mi) of pedestrian streets stretching from the train station to Marienplatz and north to Odeonsplatz. The two main streets here are Neuhauserstrasse and Kaufingerstrasse. For upscale shopping, Maximilianstrasse, Residenzstrasse, and Theatinerstrasse are unbeatable and contain a fine array of classy and tempting stores. Schwabing, north of the university, has shops on Schellingstrasse and Hohenzollernstrasse.

Antiques

Blumenstrasse, Türkenstrasse, and Westenriederstrasse have antiques shops of every description, while those that line Prannerstrasse, behind the classy Bayerischer Hof Hotel, concentrate on treasures that usually end up in museums. The open-air Auer Dult fairs sell antiques; they're held on Mariahilfplatz at the end of April, July, and October.

Department Stores

Most of the major department stores are along Maffeistrasse, Kaufingerstrasse, and Neuhauserstrasse. **Hertie** (✉ Bahnhofpl. 7 ☎ 089/55120) is the largest and, some claim, the best department store in the city; it has a stylish delicatessen, a champagne bar, and a bistro. Upscale **Karstadt** (✉ Neuhauserstr. 18 ☎ 089/290–230) has an abundance of Bavarian arts and crafts. **Ludwig Beck** (✉ Marienpl. 11 ☎ 089/236–910) is packed from top to bottom with highly original wares—from fine feather boas to roughly finished Bavarian pottery. The collection of CDs on the upper floor is one of the finest in the city.

Gift Ideas

Dallmayr (✉ Dienerstr. 014–15 ☎ 089/21350) is an elegant gourmet food store served by efficient Munich matrons in smart blue-and-white-linen costumes. The store's famous specialty is coffee, with more than 50 varieties to blend as you wish. There's also an enormous range of breads and a temperature-controlled cigar room.

Many shops specialize in beer-related souvenirs, but **Ludwig Mory** (✉ Marienpl. 8 ☎ 089/224–542) is about the best. Munich is also the home of the famous **Porzellan Manufaktur Nymphenburg** (Nymphenburg Porcelain Factory; ✉ Odeonspl. and Briennerstr. ☎ 089/282–428 ✉ Nördliche Schlossrondell 8, in front of Schloss Nymphenburg ☎ 089/ 1791–9710).

From the end of November until December 24, Marienplatz is packed with shoppers browsing the open-air stalls of the **Christkindlmarkt** (✉ Marienpl.). Mostly Christmas ornaments are sold here (along with mulled wine). Other favorite markets for gifts are in Schwabing (Münchner-Freiheit Square) and at the Chinese Tower, in the middle of the Englischer Garten.

Side Trips

KZ–Gedenkstätte Dachau (Dachau Concentration Camp Memorial Site). Although the 1,200-year-old town of Dachau attracted hordes of painters and artists from the mid-19th century until World War I, it is now mostly known as the site of Germany's first concentration camp. Opened in 1933, the camp held more than 206,000 political dissidents, Jews, homosexuals, clergy, and other "enemies" of the Nazis; more than 32,000 prisoners died here. Photographs, contemporary documents, the few remaining cell blocks, and the grim crematorium create a somber picture of the camp. The town of Dachau is a 20-minute ride from Marienplatz on the S-2 suburban railway line. To get to the concentration camp site take Bus 724 or 726 from the train station or town center. Both stop near the entrance. If you are driving from Munich, turn right on the first country road (marked B) before entering Dachau and follow the signs. ⊠ *Alte Römerstr. 75 Dachau* ☎ *08131/669–970* ⊕ *www.kz-gedenkstaette-dachau.de* ☾ *Tues.–Sun. 9–5. Guided English tour June–Aug., Tues.–Sun. 12:30; Sept.–May, weekends 12:30.*

★ **Schloss Neuschwanstein** (Neuschwanstein Castle). The "fairy-tale" king, Ludwig II, had a deep love of theater, and his last castle soars from its mountainside like a stage creation (it was conceived by a set designer—no wonder Walt Disney used it as the model for his own Disneyland™ castle). The king spent less than six months in the country residence before his death, and the interior was never finished. Chamber concerts are held in September in the gaily decorated minstrels' hall; for details call the Verkehrsamt, Schwangau (☎ 08362/81980).

More than 1 million people pass through Neuschwanstein and Hohenschwangau, the nearby castle in which Ludwig II was born, every year. With a deposit or credit card number you can book your timed-entrance tickets in advance through **Verwaltung Hohenschwangau** (⊠ Alpseestr. 12, D-87645 Hohenschwangau ☎ 08362/930–830 🖷 0832/930–8320 ⊕ www.hohenschwangau.de). There is a €1.5 processing fee per ticket. You can cancel or change entrance times up to two hours before the confirmed entrance time. The castle lies 105 km (65 mi) southwest of Munich, and road signs to the castle read KONIGSCHLÖSSER. After parking in the village, you can take a horse-drawn carriage to the castle, or a bus to the outlook called Aussichtspunkt Jugend; from there it's only a 10-minute walk. The uphill walk from the village takes 25 minutes. ⊠*Hohenschwangau* ☾ *Guided tours Apr.–Sept., daily 8:30–5:30; Oct.–Mar., daily 10–4.*

Munich Essentials

AIRPORTS & TRANSFERS
The airport is 28 km (17 mi) northeast of the city center. 🛈 **Flughafen München** ☎ 089/97500 ⊕ www.munich-airport.de.

TRANSFERS The S-8 and S-1 suburban train lines link the airport with the main train station (Hauptbahnhof). Trains leave every 10 minutes, and the trip takes 40 minutes. Intermediate stops include the Ostbahnhof (convenient for lodgings east of the Isar River) and central Marienplatz. A one-way ticket costs €8, or €7.20 if you purchase a multiple-use "strip" ticket (you will have two strips left at the end). A family of up to five (two adults and three children under 15) can make the trip for €15 with a Tageskarte ticket (which allows travel until around 6 AM the next morning).

A taxi costs around €50. If you are driving from the airport into the city, follow the MÜNCHEN autobahn signs to A92 and A9. Once on the

A92, watch carefully for the signs to Munich; many motorists miss the sign and end up headed toward Stuttgart.

BUS TRAVEL TO & FROM MUNICH

Buses arrive and depart from an area to the west of the main train station. The actual office of the bus company, Touring GmbH, is in the northern section of the train station itself, an area referred to as the Starnberger Bahnhof.

🚌 Bus Station **Zentraler Busbahnhof** ✉ Arnulfstr. ☎ 089/545-8700.

CAR RENTAL & TRAVEL

From the north (Nürnberg, Frankfurt), leave the autobahn at the Schwabing exit and follow the STADTMITTE signs. The autobahn from Stuttgart and the west ends at Obermenzing; again, follow the STADTMITTE signs. The autobahns from Salzburg and the east, from Garmisch and the south, and from Lindau and the southwest all join up with the city beltway, the Mittlerer Ring. The city center is well posted. Once in Munich it's best to get around on foot and by public transportation.

All car rental offices in the Hauptbahnhof (train station) are in the mezzanine-level gallery above the Deutsche Bahn information and ticket center. Airport offices are in the central area, Zentralbereich.

🚗 **Avis** ✉ Airport ☎ 089/975-97600 ✉ Hauptbahnhof ☎ 089/550-2251. **Europcar** ✉ Airport ☎ 089/973-5020. **Hertz** ✉ Airport ☎ 089/978-860 ✉ Hauptbahnhof ☎ 089/550-2256. **Sixt** ✉ Airport ☎ 089/526-2525 ✉ Hauptbahnhof ☎ 089/550-2447.

CONSULATES

🏛 Canada ✉ Tal 29 ☎ 089/219-9570.
🏛 Ireland ✉ Mauerkircherstr. 1a ☎ 089/985-723.
🏛 United Kingdom ✉ Bürkleinstr. 10 ☎ 089/211-090.
🏛 United States ✉ Königinstr. 5 ☎ 089/28880.

EMERGENCIES

🏥 Dentists **Dentist** ☎ 089/723-3093.
🏥 Emergency Services **Ambulance, Fire Department, and Paramedical Aid** ☎ 112. **Police** ☎ 110.
🏥 Pharmacies **Europa-Apotheke** ✉ Schützenstr. 12, near Hauptbahnhof ☎ 089/595-423. **Internationale Ludwigs-Apotheke** ✉ Neuhauserstr. 11 ☎ 089/260-3021.

ENGLISH-LANGUAGE MEDIA

The monthly English-language magazine *Munich Found* is sold at most newspaper stands and in many hotels. It contains excellent listings, reviews restaurants and shows, and generally gives an idea of life in the city.

📚 Bookstores **Anglia English Bookshop** ✉ Schellingstr. 3 ☎ 089/283-642. **Hugendubel** ✉ Marienpl. 22, 2nd floor ☎ 089/23890 ✉ Karlspl. 3 ☎ 089/552-2530.

TAXIS

Hail taxis in the street or call for one (there's an extra charge of €1 if you call). Rates start at €2.40. Expect to pay €8–€10 for a short trip within the city. There is a €.50 charge for each piece of luggage.

🚖 ☎ 089/21610 or 089/19410.

TOURS

BIKE TOURS Cityhopper Touren offers daily escorted bike tours March–October. Bookings must be made in advance, and starting times are negotiable. Radius Touristik has bicycle tours from May through the beginning of October at 10:15 and 2; the cost, including bike rental, is €7.70. Mike's Bike Tours is run by a young American who hires German students to take visitors on a two- to three-hour spin through Munich. The tours start daily at the Old Town Hall, the Altes Rathaus, at 11:20 and 3:50. They cost €22, including bike rental. Mike also organizes walking tours for €9.

🎫 Fees & Schedules **City Hopper Touren** ☎ 089/272-1131. **Mike's Bike Tours** ☎ 089/2554-3988. **Radius Touristik** ✉ Arnulfstr. 3, opposite Platforms 30-36 in the Hauptbahnhof ☎ 089/596-113.

BUS TOURS Excursions to the Alps, to Austria, to the royal palaces and castles of Bavaria, or along the Romantic Road can be booked through DER. Panorama Tours, located next to the main train station, offers trips such as the Royal Castles Tour (Schlösserfahrt) of "Mad" King Ludwig's palaces; the cost is €41, excluding entrance fees. Bookings for both companies can also be made through all major hotels in the city. The tours depart from in front of the Hauptbahnhof outside the Hertie department store.

Panorama Tours' blue city buses operate year-round, departing from the front of the Hertie department store on Bahnhofplatz. A one-hour highlight tour leaves eight times daily. The cost is €11. A 2½-hour city tour departs daily at 10 AM and includes brief visits to the Alte Pinakothek, the Peterskirche, and Marienplatz for the glockenspiel. An afternoon tour, also 2½ hours and starting at 2:30 PM, includes a tour of Schloss Nymphenburg. The cost of each tour is €19. The München bei Nacht tour provides 4½ hours of Munich by night and includes dinner and a show at the Hofbräuhaus, a trip up the Olympic Tower to admire the lights of the city, and a final drink in a nightclub. It departs April through November, Friday and Saturday at 7:30 PM; the cost is €60.

Yellow Cab Stadtrundfahrten has a fleet of yellow double-decker buses, in which tours are offered simultaneously in eight languages. They leave hourly between 10 AM and 4 PM from the front of the Elisenhof shopping complex on Bahnhofplatz. Tours cost €9.

🎫 Fees & Schedules **DER** ✉ Hauptbahnhofpl. 2 ☎ 089/5514-0100. **Panorama Tours** ✉ Arnulfstr. 8 ☎ 089/5490-7560. **Yellow Cab Stadtrundfahrten** ✉ Sendlinger-Tor-Pl. 2 ☎ 089/303-631.

WALKING TOURS The two tourist information offices issue a free map with suggested walking tours. Two-hour tours of the old city center are given daily in summer (March–October) and on Friday and Saturday in winter (November–February). Tours organized by the visitor center start at 10:30 and 1 in the center of Marienplatz. The cost is €8. Munich Walks conducts daily tours of the old city and sites related to the Third Reich era. The cost is €10. Tours depart daily from the Hauptbahnhof, outside the EurAide office by Track 11, and also pick up latecomers outside the McDonald's at Karlsplatz.

🎫 Fees & Schedules **Munich Walks** ☎ 089/5502-9374 ⊕ www.radius-munich.com.

TRAIN TRAVEL

All long-distance services arrive at and depart from the main train station, the Hauptbahnhof. Trains to and from destinations in the Bavarian Alps usually use the adjoining Starnbergerbahnhof. For tickets and travel information, go to the station information office or try the ABR-DER travel agency.

🎫 **ABR-DER** ✉ Bahnhofpl. ☎ 089/5514-0200. **Hauptbahnhof** ✉ Bahnhofpl. ☎ 089/2333-0256; 089/2333-0257; 01805/996-633 for train schedules.

TRANSPORTATION AROUND MUNICH

Munich has an efficient and well-integrated public transportation system, consisting of the U-bahn (subway), the S-bahn (suburban railway), the Strassenbahn (streetcars), and buses. Marienplatz forms the heart of the U-bahn and S-bahn network, which operates from around 5 AM to 1 AM. An all-night tram and bus service operates on main routes within the city. For a clear explanation in English of how the system works, pick up a copy of *Rendezvous mit München,* available free of charge at all tourist offices.

As long as you are traveling in the same direction, you can transfer from one mode of transportation to another on the same ticket. You can also interrupt your journey as often as you like, and time-punched tickets are valid for up to four hours, depending on the number of zones you travel through. Fares are constantly creeping upward, but a basic *Einzelfahrkarte* (one-way ticket) costs €2 for a ride in the inner zone and €1 for a short journey of up to four stops. For two to five people on a short stay the best option is the *Partner-Tageskarte* ticket, which provides unlimited travel (maximum of two adults, plus three children under 15). It is valid weekdays from 9 AM to 6 AM the following day and at any time on weekends. The costs are €7.50 for an inner-zone ticket.

The tourist office's Welcome Card covers transport within the city boundaries and includes up to 50% reductions in admission to many museums and attractions in Munich and in Bavaria (lifts up to the Zugspitze in Garmisch-Partenkirchen, for example). The card, obtainable from visitor information offices, costs €6.50 for one day and €15.50 for three days. A three-day card for two people costs €22.50.

TRAVEL AGENCIES
Euraide serves English-speaking travelers and has an office adjacent to Track 11 in the main train station.

🚩 **American Express** ✉ Promenadenpl. 6 ☎ 089/290-900. **DER** ✉ Bahnhofpl. 2 ☎ 089/5514-0100 ✉ Münchner-Freiheit 6 ☎ 089/336-033. **Euraide** ✉ Hauptbahnhof, Room 3.

VISITOR INFORMATION
The Hauptbahnhof tourist office is open Monday–Saturday 9–8 and Sunday 10–6; the Info-Service in the Rathaus is open weekdays 10–8 and Saturday 10–4.

For information on the Bavarian mountain region south of Munich, contact the Tourismusverband München-Oberbayern.

🚩 **Hauptbahnhof** ✉ Bahnhofpl. 2 ☎ 089/2333-0123 ⊕ www.muenchen-tourist.de. **Info-Service** ✉ Marienpl. ☎ 089/2332-8242. **Tourismusverband München-Oberbayern** ✉ Bodenseestr. 113 D-81243 ☎ 089/829-2180.

THE BLACK FOREST

A little over a century ago the Black Forest (Schwarzwald) was one of the wildest stretches of countryside in Europe. But then the deep hot springs first enjoyed by the Romans were rediscovered, and small, forgotten villages became wealthy spas. The friendly and hospitable region is still extensively forested, though bouts with acid rain and a fierce windstorm in 1999 wreaked considerable havoc. The area also offers large, open valleys and stretches of verdant farmland. The Black Forest is the southernmost German wine region and the custodian of some of the country's best traditional foods. Black Forest pine cone–smoked ham and Black Forest cake—kirsch-soaked layers of chocolate cake with sour cherry and whipped cream filling—are among the most famous. The southern part of the Black Forest retains its vibrant clock-making tradition—the origin of a lucrative precision mechanics industry—and wood carving

The Black Forest (Schwarzwald)

is still a viable occupation here. Well-marked trails invite hikers in spring and fall and cross-country skiers in winter.

You can tour the region by all means of transportation, taking in parts of the Black Forest High Road, Low Road, Spa Road, Wine Road, and Clock Road. Crossing all the regions of the Black Forest, these roads start in the north in Pforzheim and go as far south as Staufen (approximately 200 km/125 mi) before descending into the Rhine Valley and returning north along the Rhine River to Baden-Baden (approximately 90 km/56 mi). The route described below begins in the northeast Black Forest and descends southward before looping back to the northwestern spa town of Baden-Baden.

Maulbronn

★ The best-preserved medieval monastery north of the Alps is **Kloster Maulbronn,** which consists of 30 buildings built between the 12th and 14th centuries. A €2.50 audio guide walks you through the church, courtyards, and the monks' and lay brothers' cloisters. An exhibition room shows the building tools and construction methods of the time. The restaurant on the grounds has been family owned since the 1600s. ✉ *Off B–35* ☎ *07043/926–610* ⊕ *www.schloesserundgarten.de* ☉ *Mar.–Oct., daily 9–5:30; Nov.–Feb., Tues.–Sun. 9:30–5.*

Pforzheim

This ancient Roman city, almost completely destroyed by World War II bombing, does not retain any old-world charm, but worth a stop is
★ the free **Schmuckmuseum** (Jewelry Museum) in the Reuchlinhaus, which has a magnificent collection of jewelry dating from 3000 BC. ✉ *Jahnstr. 42* ☎ *07231/392–126* ⊕ *www.schmuckmuseum-pforzheim.de* ☉ *Tues.–Sun. 10–5.*

Bad Liebenzell

Bathhouses were first built here in 1403, and the same hot springs still feed the modern spas. Above town, a path leads to a 13th-century tower from which a popular restaurant provides a valley view. You can take the waters at the **Paracelsusbad Lido Complex** (Paracelsus Swimming Pool Center) on the Nagold riverbank. ☒ *Off B–463* ☎ *07052/408–250* ☒ *€12.80 for 3½ hrs in sauna and baths* ☉ *Bath: Apr.–Oct., Mon.–Sat. 8 AM–9 PM, Sun. 8–8; Nov.–Mar., Mon.–Sat. 8:30 AM–9 PM, Sun. 8:30–8. Sauna: Mon.–Thurs. 1–10, Fri. 1–11, Sat. 9 AM–11 PM, Sun. 9–8, Thurs. for women only in the sauna.*

$$–$$$ ✕▨ **Kronen Hotel.** Most rooms are in a rather bland modern wing, though the Nagold River flows past it. The kitchen prides itself on its healthful cuisine with lots of fresh vegetables, herbs, and whole-grain products (one restaurant is no-smoking). A sauna and beauty spa are other amenities. ☒ *Badweg 7, D-75378* ☎ *07052/4090* ☒ *07052/409–420* ⊕ *www.kronenhotel.de* ↘ *43 rooms* ♨ *3 restaurants, pool* ▤ *AE, DC, MC, V.*

Calw

Half-timbered Calw (pronounced "calve") lies south of Bad Liebenzell. Its famous native son is Nobel Prize–winning novelist and poet Hermann Hesse (1877–1962). The **Hermann Hesse Museum** recounts the author of *Steppenwolf*'s life in photographs, manuscripts, books, and documents (English translation). ☒ *Marktpl. 30* ☎ *07051/7522* ☉ *Tues., Wed., and Fri.–Sun. 11–5, Thurs. 11–7.*

Hirsau, 3 km (2 mi) north of Calw, has the romantic ruins of a 9th-century monastery, now the setting for the Klosterspiele Hirsau (open-air theater performances) in July and August. Buy advance tickets at the **Calw tourist office** (☒ Marktbrücke 1 ☎ 07051/968–844).

★ **$$** ✕▨ **Hotel Kloster Hirsau.** This country-house hotel stands on the site of a former monastery in Hirsau, whose Gothic cloisters are still largely intact. In the restaurant, sample such regional dishes as *Fladelsuppe* (a broth soup with pancake slivers) or *Schwäbischer Rostbraten* (panfried beefsteak topped with sautéed onions). ☒ *Wildbaderstr. 2, D-75365 Calw-Hirsau* ☎ *07051/96740* ☒ *07051/967–479* ⊕ *www.hotel-kloster-hirsau.de* ↘ *40 rooms* ♨ *Restaurant, pool* ▤ *AE, MC, V.*

$$ ✕▨ **Ratsstube.** Most of the original features, including 16th-century beams and brickwork, are preserved at this historic house in Calw's center. Pastel colors brighten up the small rooms. The restaurant ($) serves such traditional German fare as *Zwiebelrostbraten* (panfried beefsteak with onions), or wild duck in orange sauce. There's a salad buffet and lunchtime specials. ☒ *Marktpl. 12, D-75365* ☎ *07051/92050* ☒ *07051/70826* ↘ *13 rooms* ♨ *Restaurant* ▤ *MC, V.*

Zavelstein

Follow signs to the tiny town of Zavelstein, 5 km (3 mi) south of Calw. It is famous for its fields of wild crocuses (*Krokuswiesen*) that bloom in March and April. A short street lined with A-frame, half-timber houses leads to the 13th-century castle, where a playground fills the moat.

Altensteig

The highway B–28 skirts beneath this ancient town, so look for the road leading up the terracelike slope. Narrow medieval streets climb to an unspoiled Old Town with half-timber houses. A 13th-century fort with a well-preserved tower houses an exceptionally nice **museum** (☎ 07453/1360 ☉ Apr.–Nov., Wed. 2–4, Sun. 2–5). It contains displays relating to life and work in the Black Forest, including the castle's own fully equipped old kitchen and wood exhibits.

Freudenstadt

This town lies at 2,415 feet, in the middle of lush farmland. Though flattened by the French two weeks before the end of World War II, it was painstakingly restored. Arcaded shops and restaurants surround the market square, the largest in Germany. The 17th-century **Protestant parish church** has an L shape and was designed with two naves but a single pulpit. The idea was that the sexes could not see each other during services. Notice the sculptures of angels along the edge of the ceiling.

$$$ ✕ **Warteck.** The lead-pane windows with stained-glass work, flowers, and beautifully upholstered banquettes create a bright setting in the two dining rooms. The modern kitchen uses only natural products and spotlights individual ingredients. A popular dish is the oxtail. In season the *Spargel* (asparagus) is dressed in an aromatic hazelnut vinaigrette. ⊠ *Stuttgarter Str. 14, D–72250* ☎ *07441/91920* ▤ *MC, V* ⊘ *Closed Tues.*

$$ ✕ **Ratskeller.** There is a modern cellar, but this restaurant with a green marble bar and pine furnishings is more a modern bistro than traditional Ratskeller. An English-language menu explains the Swabian dishes. The menu changes regularly and in season, there's venison. ⊠ *Marktpl. 8* ☎ *07441/952–805* ▤ *AE, MC, V* ⊘ *Nov.–Mar. closed Tues.*

$$ ✕▦ **Bären.** The Montigels have owned the sturdy old Gasthof Bären since 1878. Rooms are modern but contain such homey touches as farmhouse-style bedsteads and cupboards. The beamed restaurant is a favorite with locals. Its menu includes Swabian dishes (roasts in heavy sauces, fried *Maultaschen,* those giant raviolis), and lighter fare. The trout is caught locally. ⊠ *Langestr. 33, D–72250* ☎ *07441/2729* ▦ *07441/ 2887* ◁♥ *33 rooms* ◇ *Restaurant* ⊘ *Restaurant closed Fri. No lunch Mon.–Sat.* ▤ *V.*

$ ✕▦ **Hotel Adler.** Some of the very affordable rooms in this simple hotel off the main square have a balcony onto behind-the-scenes Freudenstadt. A plus is the Internet access. There are four Flammkuchen evenings a week at the restaurant. The dish is a specialty of neighboring Alsace— similar to a thin-crust pizza without tomato sauce and with toppings such as sour cream, crème fraîche, bacon, and onions. ⊠ *Forststr. 17, D–72250* ☎ *07441/91520* ▦ *07441/915–252* ⊕ *www.adler-fds.de* ◁♥ *13 rooms* ◇ *Restaurant* ▤ *MC, V.*

Baiersbronn

This mountain resort (7 km/4 mi northwest of Freudenstadt) is blessed with two of Germany's leading hotel-restaurants—both for hospitality and cuisine. Skiing, golfing, and horseback riding are among the area's activities.

★ $$$ ✕▦ **Bareiss.** This modern resort resembles a cruise ship moored on a hilltop above Baiersbronn. Inside, some guest rooms have dark-wood furniture and heavy wallpapering, whereas others have a light and airy Laura Ashley look. Its three restaurants ($$$$) range from the elegant Bareiss (where you'll find 30 brands of champagne), to the Kaminstube (which offers dining near the fireplace) to the rustic Dorfstube. The hotel itself is among the most lavish and best equipped in the Black Forest. Some suites (€382 and up in season) have their own saunas, solariums, and whirlpool baths. ⊠ *Gärtenbühlweg 14, D–07442 Mitteltal/ Baiersbronn* ☎ *07442/470* ▦ *07442/47320* ⊕ *www.bareiss.com* ◁♥ *75 rooms, 42 apartments, 10 suites* ◇ *3 restaurants, 6 pools (4 indoor), bar* ▤ *AE, DC, MC, V.*

$$ ✕▦ **Hotel Lamm.** The steep-roofed, 200-year-old building presents a clear picture of the traditional hotel within. Rooms have heavy oak fittings and some fine antiques. In winter the lounge's fireplace is a wel-

Switzerland.
get natural.

Discover Switzerland.
MySwitzerland.com

come sight when returning from the slopes (the ski lift is nearby). In its beamed restaurant ($–$$) you can order fish fresh from the hotel's trout pools. ✉ *Ellbacherstr. 4, D–72270 Mitteltal/Baiersbronn* ☏ *07442/ 4980* 🖷 *07442/49878* ⊕ *www.lamm-mitteltal.de* ⟳ *48 rooms, 6 apartments* ♿ *Restaurant, pool* ▭ *DC, MC, V.*

Wolfach

South of Freudenstadt on B–294, the cobblestone town of Wolfach has one of the only remaining glass factories in the region. The **Dorotheen-hütte** (Dorothea Blast Furnace) is one of the few places where glass is still blown using centuries-old techniques. You can watch the teams at work making vases or blowing and etching drinking glasses. The large sales room includes a Christmas display and has all kinds of excellent souvenir items. ✉ *Glashüttenweg 4* ☏ *07834/83980* 🕐 *Daily 9–4:30; shop is open until 5* 🕐 *Closed Sun. and holidays Jan.–Apr.*

Gutach

The town lies in a valley famous for its traditional costumes. If you're here on holidays (and some Sundays), you'll see the married women sporting black pom-poms on their hats to denote their matronly status (red pom-poms are for the unmarried). One of the most appealing museums ★ in the Black Forest, the **Schwarzwälder Freilichtmuseum Vogtsbauernhof** (Black Forest Open-Air Museum) has brought together farmhouses and rural buildings from all parts of the region to create a living museum of the area's architecture through the centuries. Demonstrations range from traditional dances to woodworking. ✉ *B–33* ☏ *07831/93560* ⊕ *www.vogtsbauernhof.org* 🕐 *Late Mar.–Oct., daily 9–6.*

Triberg

At the head of the Gutach Valley, the Gutach River plunges nearly 500 feet over seven huge granite steps at Triberg's **waterfall**, Germany's highest. The pleasant 45-minute walk from the center of town to the top of the spectacular falls is well signposted. You can also take a longer walk that goes by a small pilgrimage church and the old Mesnerhäschen, the sacristan's house. The ride on the **Schwarzwaldbahn** (Black Forest Railway), which passes through Triberg, is one of Germany's most scenic. It has 39 tunnels and at one point climbs 600 meters in just 11 km. It's now part of the German Railway, and you can make inquiries at any station.

The place to purchase a cuckoo clock is **Haus der 1000 Uhren** (House of 1,000 Clocks). The shop occupies two old houses right at the waterfall. A branch just off B–33 toward Offenburg in the suburb of Gremmelsbach has a huge cuckoo clock on the roof and specializes in grandfather clocks. The friendly staff is multilingual. ✉ *Hauptstr. 79-81* ☏ *07722/ 96300* 🕐 *Apr.–Oct., Mon.–Sat. 9–5, Sun. 10–4; Nov.–Mar., Mon.–Sat. 10–5, Sun. 10–4.*

★ The **Schwarzwaldmuseum** (Black Forest Museum) has exhibits related to Black Forest culture. The oldest clock on display dates from 1640; its simple wooden mechanism is said to have been carved with a bread knife. Barrel organs and fairground organs from Berlin are newcomers to the collection. ✉ *Wallfahrtstr. 4* ☏ *07722/4434* 🕐 *Apr.–Nov., daily 10–5.*

$$–$$$ ✕▥ **Romantik Parkhotel Wehrle.** The wisteria-covered facade of this large mansion dominates the town center. Rooms are individually furnished in a variety of woods with such pleasant touches as fresh flowers. The main restaurant ($$–$$$$) has international haute cuisine; the Ochsenstube ($–$$) tends toward specialties from Baden, for example, trout done a dozen different ways, all delicious. ✉ *Gartenstr. 24, D–78098 Triberg im Schwarzwald* ☏ *07722/86020* 🖷 *07722/860–290* ⊕ *www.*

parkhotel-wehrle.de ⤴ *50 rooms, 1 apartment, 1 suite* ♿ *2 restaurants, 2 pools* ☰ *AE, DC, MC, V.*

★ $ ✕▦ **Hotel-Restaurant-Pfaff.** This old post-and-beam restaurant with its blue-tile Kachelofen attracts people of all types with affordable regional specialties. Try the fresh *Forelle* (trout), either steamed or *Gasthof* (in the pan), garnished with mushrooms. The Pfaff family has owned the inn since 1882, and some rooms have balconies overlooking the famous waterfall. ⊠ *Hauptstr. 85, D–78098 Triberg* ☎ *07722/4479* 🖷 *07722/ 7897* ⊕ *www.hotel-pfaff.com* ⤴ *23 rooms* ♿ *Restaurant* ☰ *AE, D, MC, V.*

Furtwangen

The **Uhren Museum** (Clock Museum) is the largest of its kind in Germany. It charts the development of Black Forest clocks. A cabinet timepiece that weighs more than a ton makes various sounds (such as a rooster's crow in the morning) and has little mechanical figures that perform on various dates in the Christian calendar. ⊠ *Robert-Gerwig-Pl. 1* ☎ *07723/ 920–117* ⊕ *www.deutsches-uhrenmuseum.de* ⊗ *Apr.–Oct., daily 9–6; Nov.–Mar., daily 10–5.*

Titisee

The 2½-km-long (1½-mi-long) lake, set in a forest ideal for bike touring, is the star attraction of the lakeland region. It becomes invariably crowded in summer with boats and Windsurfers, and there are endless souvenir shops.

$$ ✕▦ **Romantik Hotel Adler Post.** This old, family-owned hotel is about 5 km (3 mi) east of the lake. The reception room is full of Biedermeier antiques, and the hotel's Rôtisserie zum Postillon restaurant ($–$$$) is noted for its regional cuisine. ⊠ *Hauptstr. 16, D–79822 Titisee–Neustadt* ☎ *07651/5066* 🖷 *07651/3729* ⊕ *www.adler-post-titisee.de* ⤴ *30 rooms* ♿ *2 restaurants, pool* ☰ *MC, V.*

Hinterzarten

This lovely 800-year-old town is the most popular resort for cross-country skiing and hiking in the southern Black Forest. Some buildings date from the 12th century, among them **St. Oswaldskirche** (St. Oswald's Church), built in 1146. Hinterzarten's oldest inn, **Weisses Rossle,** has operated since 1347.

★ $$$$ ✕▦ **Park Hotel Adler.** This sumptuous hotel, established in 1446, stands on 2 acres ringed by the forest. The Wirtshus restaurant ($$–$$$$) offers excellent regional fare at reasonable prices. You can also choose from a large selection of cakes. Notably, Marie Antoinette once ate here. ⊠ *Adlerpl. 3, D–79856,* ☎ *07652/1270* 🖷 *07652/127–717* ⊕ *www. parkhoteladler.de* ⤴ *46 rooms, 32 suites* ♿ *2 restaurants, pool, bar* ☰ *AE, DC, MC, V.*

$$ ▦ **Sassenhof.** Black Forest style reigns supreme here, from the wood exterior with windowboxes, to the elegant sitting areas and guest rooms with rustic, brightly painted furnishings, many of them decoratively carved. Afternoon tea, like breakfast, is included in the price. ⊠ *Adlerweg 17, D–79856* ☎ *07652/1515* 🖷 *07652/484* ⊕ *www.hotel-sassenhof.de* ⤴ *17 rooms, 6 suites* ♿ *Pool* ☰ *AE, DC, MC, V* ⊗ *Closed early June and mid-Oct.–mid-Nov.*

Schluchsee

The largest of the Black Forest lakes, mountain-enclosed Schluchsee is a diverse resort, attracting swimmers, hikers, windsurfing enthusiasts, fishers, and, in winter, skiers, skaters, and tobogganers. At 4,900 feet, the neighboring Feldberg is the region's highest mountain and offers the best downhill skiing.

$ ⊞ **Hotel Waldeck.** In summer, geraniums smother the sun-drenched balconies of the Waldeck. Walking trails begin practically at the front door, and the forest creeps up to the hotel terrace. Some rooms have traditional furnishings; others have a generic, modern look. ⊠ *Feldberg Altglashütten, D–79868* ☎ *07655/91030* 🖷 *07655/231* ⊕ *www.hotel-waldeck-feldberg. de* 🖵 *23 rooms* ⌂ *Restaurant, bar* ⊟ *DC, MC, V.*

Freiburg

Perched on the western slopes of the Black Forest, this is one of the region's largest and loveliest cities; it was founded as a free market town in the 12th century. *Bächle* (brooklets) run through many streets. The
★ city's most famous landmark is the **Münster unserer Lieben Frau** (Cathedral of Our Dear Lady), which took three centuries to build—from 1200 to 1513. Masterpieces include a 16th-century triptych by Hans Baldung Grien, and paintings by Holbein the Younger and Lucas Cranach the Elder. You can climb the tower; its spire is one of the finest in the world. ⊠ *Münsterpl.* ☎ *0761/2928–0734; 0761/388–101 tours* ⊗ *Tues.–Sat. 9:30–5, Sun. 1–5.*

A visit to the cathedral is not really complete without also exploring the **Augustinermuseum,** at the former Augustinian cloister. Original sculpture from the cathedral is on display, as well as gold and silver reliquaries. The collection of stained-glass windows is one of the most important in Germany. ⊠ *Am Augustinerpl.* ☎ *0761/201–2531* ⊗ *Tues.–Sun. 10–5.*

The Old Town is traffic-free, and every day but Sunday the square in front of the cathedral, **Münsterplatz,** teems with the town market, where you can buy everything from herbs to hot sausage. The 16th-century red Kaufhaus, with its statue-decorated facade, overlooks the square.

$$$–$$$$ ✕ **Hans Thoma Stube.** Within the luxurious Colombi Hotel, the Hans
Fodor'sChoice Thoma Stube occupies two reconstructed 18th-century farmhouse
★ rooms, lavishly furnished and decorated with Black Forest antiques. It serves local dishes such as lentil soup and venison. The cuisine in the Zirbelstube and the Falkenstube is more modern and pairs innovative sauces with traditional meat and fish dishes. ⊠ *Am Colombi Park/ Rotteckring 16, D–79098* ☎ *0761/21060* 🖎 *Reservations essential* ⊟ *AE, DC, MC, V.*

$–$$$ ✕ **Kühler Krug.** Wild game and goose liver terrine are among the specialties at this restaurant, which has even given its name to a distinctive saddle-of-venison dish. There's also an imaginative range of freshwater fish. ⊠ *Torpl. 1, Günterstal* ☎ *0761/29103* ⊟ *MC, V* ⊗ *Closed Wed.*

$ ✕ **Freiburger Salatstuben.** Vegetarian food is prepared in creative ways—try the homemade whole-wheat noodles with cauliflower in a pepper cream sauce—and served cafeteria style. Salad is priced by the gram. It gets crowded with university students at peak hours. ⊠ *Am Martinstor-Löwenstr. 1* ☎ *0761/35155* ⊟ *No credit cards* ⊗ *Closed Sun.*

$$ ✕⊞ **Oberkirchs Weinstuben.** Across from the cathedral, this wine cellar is a bastion of tradition and conviviality. Approximately 20 Baden wines are served by the glass, from white Gutedel to red Spätburgunder, many supplied from the restaurant's own vineyards. The proprietor personally bags some of the game that ends up in the kitchen ($$). Fresh trout is another specialty. Twenty-six charming guest rooms are in the Weinstuben and in a neighboring centuries-old house. ⊠ *Münsterpl. 22, D–79098* ☎ *0761/31011* 🖵 *26 rooms* ⌂ *Restaurant* ⊟ *AE, MC, V* ⊗ *Restaurant closed Sun. and late Dec.–Jan.*

$$ ✕⊞ **Rappen.** This hotel's brightly painted rooms overlook the cathedral square and marketplace with all their lively chatter. Three rooms are designated as "anti-allergy." The restaurant ($–$$) hosts market people and other locals who come in for a glass of wine in the morning (there are about 40 wines, German and French), and serves fresh vegetables, game, and fish. ✉ *Münsterpl. 13, D–79098* ☎ *0761/31353* 🖷 *0761/ 382–252* ⊕ *www.hotelrappen.de* 🛏 *24 rooms* ⚐ *Restaurant* ▭ *AE, DC, MC, V.*

$$–$$$ 🏨 **Park Hotel Post Meier.** Near the train station, the Post has been a hotel since the turn of the 20th century, with good, old-fashioned service to prove it. The art nouveau facade with stone balconies and a central copper-dome tower has earned the building protected status. A large breakfast buffet is included in the room price. ✉ *Eisenbahnstr. 35, D–79098* ☎ *0761/385–480* 🖷 *0761/31680* 🛏 *43 rooms, 2 apartments* ▭ *AE, MC, V.*

Staufen

This small town, some 20 km (12 mi) south of Freiburg, claims the inquisitive Dr. Faustus as one of its early burghers. Faustus, who reputedly made a pact with the Devil, was the subject of Goethe's 1808 drama, *Faust.* Faustus allegedly lived in Room 5 at the inn **Gasthaus zum Löwen** (✉ Hauptstr. 47) and died there of "a broken neck."

Baden-Baden

Fashionable Baden-Baden, idyllically set in a wooded valley of the northern Black Forest, sits atop the extensive hot springs that gave the city its name (*Baden* means "baths"). The Romans first exploited the springs, which were rediscovered a couple of centuries ago. By the end of the 19th century, there was scarcely a crowned head of Europe who had not dipped into the healing waters.

★ One of the grand buildings of Baden-Baden's belle epoque is the pillared 1820s **Kurhaus** (Spa), part of the complex that includes a manicured park, a theater, shops, hotels, restaurants, and Germany's oldest casino, which opened its doors in 1838. Visitors are required to sign a declaration that they enter with sufficient funds to settle subsequent debts. Passports are necessary as proof of identity and jacket and tie are required. ✉ *Kaiserallee 1* ☎ *07221/210–60* ⊙ *Sun.–Thurs. 2 PM–2 AM, Fri. and Sat. 2 PM–3 AM. Tours Apr.–Sept., daily 9:30–11:45, Oct.–Mar., daily 10–11:45 AM.*

At the famous Roman baths, the **Friedrichsbad,** you take the waters just as the Romans did—nude. The bath allows mixed nude bathing every day except on Monday and Thursday, when it is allowed only after 4 PM. The remains of the Roman baths beneath the Friedrichsbad can be visited from April through October. ✉ *Römerpl. 1* ☎ *07221/275–920* ⊙ *Mon.–Sat. 9 AM–10 PM, Sun. noon–8* ☞ *Children under 18 not admitted.*

The **Caracalla-Therme** (Caracalla Baths) are a huge, modern complex with five indoor pools, two outdoor pools, numerous whirlpools, a solarium, and a "sauna landscape"—you look out through windows at the countryside while you bake. ✉ *Römerpl. 13* ☎ *07221/275–940* ⊙ *Daily 8 AM–10 PM.*

$$–$$$$ ✗ **Le Jardin de France.** This clean, crisp little French restaurant, whose owners are Alsatian, emphasizes elegant, imaginative dining in an elegant Victorian setting. The duck might be roasted with raisins, figs, and nuts at Christmastime; the crayfish is sometimes prepared with chanterelles. ✉ *Lichtertalerstr. 13* ☎ *07221/300–7860* ▭ *AE, DC, MC, V* ⊙ *Closed Mon. No lunch Tues.*

$–$$ ✗ **Klosterschänke.** This rustic restaurant is a 10-minute drive from the center of Baden-Baden. In summer you can dine outside on a tree-covered terrace and probably will share a rough oak table with locals. The menu is surprisingly imaginative, and this is the best place for venison in season. ✉ *Landstr. 84* ☎ *07221/25854* ▭ *MC, V* ⊙ *Closed Mon. and the first 10 days in Aug. No lunch Tues.*

★ **$$$–$$$$** ✕🏨 **Hotel Der Kleine Prinz.** Delicately rendered murals depicting scenes from St. Exupéry's *The Little Prince* give a lively touch to this antiques-filled Romantik group hotel made up of two city mansions. Chef Berthold Krieger combines flair with unmistakable German thoroughness, elevating the restaurant ($$$–$$$$) to a leading position in demanding Baden-Baden. ✉ *Lichtentalerstr. 36, D–76530* ☎ 07221/3464 🖷 07221/38264 ⊕ *www.derkleineprinz.de* 🛏 *25 rooms, 15 suites* ♨ *Restaurant* ▤ AE, DC, MC, V.

★ **$$$$** 🏨 **Brenner's Park Hotel & Spa.** With some justification, this stately hotel set in a private park claims to be one of the best in the world. Behind it passes leafy Lichtentaler Allee, where Queen Victoria and Czar Alexander II, among others, strolled in their day. All the rooms and suites (the latter costing up to €680 a day) are sumptuously furnished and appointed. ✉ *Schillerstr. 6, D–76530* ☎ 07221/9000 🖷 07221/38772 ⊕ *www.brenners-park.de* 🛏 *68 rooms, 18 suites, 12 apartments* ♨ *2 restaurants, pool* ▤ AE, DC, MC.

$$ 🏨 **Merkur.** The Merkur has large and comfortable rooms. Quality is self-evident, and guests return again and again. A pretty breakfast room greets you in the morning, where a solid breakfast is provided. Ask for the special arrangements for longer stays. ✉ *Merkurstr. 8* ☎ 07221/3030 🖷 07221/303–333 ⊕ *www.hotel-merkur.com* 🛏 *44 rooms* ♨ *Restaurant* ▤ AE, D, MC, V.

$ 🏨 **Am Markt.** This 250-plus-year-old building houses a modest inn run (for more than 50 years) by the Bogner family. In the oldest part of town—a traffic-free zone—it's close to such major attractions as the Roman baths. Some rooms overlook the city. ✉ *Marktpl. 17–18, D–76530* ☎ 07221/27040 🖷 07221/270–444 🛏 *27 rooms, 12 with bath.* ▤ AE, DC, MC, V.

The Black Forest Essentials

AIR TRAVEL

The nearest airports are in Stuttgart; Strasbourg, in the neighboring French Alsace; and the Swiss border city of Basel, just 64 km (40 mi) from Freiburg.

BUS TRAVEL

The bus system works closely with the German railways to reach every corner of the Black Forest. Bus stations are usually at or near the train station. For more information on bus travel, contact the Regionalbusverkehr Südwest.

▥ Fares & Schedules **Regionalbusverkehr Südwest** Regional Bus Lines ☎ 0721/84060 in Karlsruhe.

CAR TRAVEL

The main Autobahns are the A–5 (Frankfurt–Karlsruhe–Basel), which runs through the Rhine Valley along the western length of the Black Forest; the A–81 (Stuttgart–Bodensee), in the east; and the A–8 (Karlsruhe–Stuttgart), in the north. Good two-lane highways crisscross the entire region. Taking the side roads might not save time, but they are much more interesting.

TRAIN TRAVEL

A main north–south train line follows the Rhine Valley, carrying EuroCity and InterCity trains that call at hourly intervals at Freiburg and Baden-Baden, connecting them directly with Frankfurt and many other German cities. Local lines connect most Black Forest towns, and two local east–west services, the Black Forest Railway and the Höllental Railway, are spectacular scenic runs.

VISITOR INFORMATION

For information on the northern Black Forest, contact Touristik Nördlicher Schwarzwald. For the central area, contact Schwarzwald Tourismus GmbH—Mittlerer Schwarzwald. For the southern area, contact Tourismus Südlicher Schwarzwald. The Freudenstadt tourist office can arrange hiking vacations in which your luggage is transported from hotel to hotel. **Baden-Baden** ⊠ Baden-Baden Kur-und Tourismus GmbH, Solmsstrasse 1, D-76530 ☎ 07221/275-2001 🖥 07221/275-202 ⊕ www.baden-baden.de. **Bad Liebenzell** ⊠ Kurverwaltung, Kurhausdamm 4, D-75378 ☎ 07052/4080 ⊕ www.bad-liebenzell. de. **Calw** ⊠ Stadtinformation Calw, Marktbrücke 1, D-75365 ☎ 07051/9688-10 ⊕ www. calw.de. **Freiburg** ⊠ Tourist Information, Rotteckring 14, D-79098 ☎ 0761/388-1880 ⊕ www.freiburg.de. **Freudenstadt** ⊠ Kongresse-Touristik-Kur, Marktpl. 64, D-72250 ☎ 07441/8640. **Hinterzarten** ⊠ Hinterzarten-Breitnau Tourismus GmbH, Freiburger-str. 1, D-79854 ☎ 07652/12060 ⊕ www.hinterzarten.de. **Schluchsee** ⊠ Tourist-Information, Fischbacherstr. 7, D-79859 ☎ 07656/7732 ⊕ www.schluchsee.de. **Mittlere Schwarzwald Tourismus GmbH** ⊠ Gerberstr. 8, D-77652 Offenburg ☎ 0781/923-7777 🖥 0781/923-7770 ⊕ www.schwarzwald-tourismus.com. **Titisee-Neustadt** ⊠ Tourist-Information, Strandbadstr., D-79822 ☎ 07651/98040 ⊕ www.titisee.de. **Tourismus Südlicher Schwarzwald** ⊠ Stadtstr. 2, D-79104 Freiburg ☎ 0761/218-7304 🖥 0761/218-7534 ⊕ www.schwarzwald-sued.de. **Touristik Nördlicher Schwarzwald** ⊠ Am Weisenhauspl. 26, D-75172 Pforzheim ☎ 07231/147-380 🖥 07231/147-3820 ⊕ www.noerdlicher-schwarzwald.de. **Triberg** ⊠ Tourist-Information, Luisenstr. 10, D-78098 ☎ 07722/953-230 🖥 07722/953-236 ⊕ www.triberg.de.

HEIDELBERG

Heidelberg's fame is out of all proportion to its size (population 140,000): more than 3½ million visitors crowd its narrow, twisting streets every year. Sacked twice in the late 1600s (first by Louis XIV), the old baroque town is built on the ashes of its Gothic foundations and is sandwiched between the Neckar River and hills. The entire 19th-century German Romantic movement, drawn to Heidelberg's charming Old Town, castle ruins, abandoned gardens, and university, sang its praises. Goethe and Mark Twain both fell in love here: the German writer with a beautiful young woman, the American author with the city itself. Sigmund Romberg set his operetta *The Student Prince* in the city; and it was here that Carl Maria von Weber wrote his lushly Romantic opera *Der Freischütz*.

Exploring Heidelberg

Take the Königstuhl Bergbahn (funicular) up to the famous Schloss, one of Germany's most memorable castles. (You can also hike up the winding Burgweg [castle walk] to the complex.) What's most striking about ★ the **Schloss** is its architectural variety. The oldest surviving parts date from the 15th century, though most of the castle was built in the Renaissance and baroque styles of the 16th and 17th centuries, when the castle was the seat of the Palatinate electors. There's even an English wing, built in 1612 by the elector Friedrich V for his teenage Scottish bride, Elizabeth Stuart; its plain facade and square windows are positively foreign compared to the more opulent styles of the castle. The highlight remains the Renaissance courtyard—harmonious, graceful, and ornate. The **Deutsches Apotheken–Museum** (German Apothecary Museum; ☎06221/ 25880 ⊘ daily 10–5:30), on the lower floor of the Ottheinrichsbau (Otto Heinrich Building), is filled with ancient carboys and other flagons and receptacles (each with a carefully painted enamel label), beautifully made scales, little drawers, shelves, a marvelous reconstruction of an 18th-century apothecary shop, dried beetles and toads, and a mummy with a full head of hair.

Even if you have to wait, you should make a point of seeing the **Grosses Fass** (Great Cask), the two-story-high wine barrel in the cellar, made from 130 oak trees and capable of holding 58,500 gallons. It was used to hold wines paid as taxes by winegrowers in the Palatinate. During the rule of the elector Carl Philip, the barrel was guarded by the court jester, a Tyrolean dwarf called Perkeo—when offered wine, he always answered, "*Perche no?*" ("Why not?"), hence his nickname.

In summer there are fireworks displays from the castle terrace (on the first Saturday in June and September and the second Saturday in July). In July and August the castle hosts an open-air theater festival. Performances of *The Student Prince* figure prominently. *Castle info:* ☎ *06221/ 538–431 ticket booth; 06221/53840 office ☉ Daily 8–5:30; tours in English Easter–Sept., daily at quarter past the hr 10:15–4:15; Oct.–Easter, weekdays 11:15, 12:15, 2:15, and 4:15; weekends also at 1:15 and 3:15.*

The Königstuhl funicular's next stop after the Schloss is the site of Heidelberg's other castle, **Molkenkur.** Lightning struck it in 1527, and it was never rebuilt. Today it is occupied by a restaurant with magnificent views of the Odenwald and the Rhine plain.

Heidelberg's **Marktplatz** has the 1701 Rathaus on one side, the Heiliggeistkirche on the other, and narrow side streets that should be explored. Public courts of justice were held here in the early Middle Ages, and people accused of witchcraft and heresy were burned at the stake. The baroque fountain in the middle, the Herkulesbrunnen (Hercules Fountain), is the work of 18th-century artist H. Charrasky. Until 1740 a rotating, hanging cage stood next to it. For minor crimes, people were imprisoned in it and exposed to the laughter, insults, and abuse of their fellow citizens.

The foundation stone of the **Heiliggeistkirche** (Church of the Holy Ghost) was laid in 1398, but the church was not actually finished until 1544. Unlike that of most other Gothic churches, the facade of the Heiliggeistkirche is uniform—you cannot discern the choir or naves from the outside. The gargoyles looking down on the south side (where Hauptstrasse crosses Marktplatz) are remarkable for their sheer ugliness. The church fell victim to the plundering General Tilly, leader of the Catholic League during the Thirty Years' War. Tilly loaded the church's greatest treasure—the *Bibliotheca Palatina*, at the time the largest library in Germany—onto 500 carts and trundled it off to Rome, where he presented it to the pope. At the end of the 17th century, French troops plundered the church again, destroying the family tombs of the Palatinate electors; only the 15th-century tomb of Elector Ruprecht III and his wife, Elisabeth von Hohenzollern, remains today. Just as in medieval times, there are shopping stalls between the church buttresses. ✉ *Marktpl. ☉ Apr.–Oct., Mon.–Sat. 11–5, Sun. 12:30–5; Nov.–Mar., Fri. and Sat. 11–3, Sun. 12:30–3.*

From the Old Town, walk onto the **Alte Brücke** (Old Bridge) under a portcullis spanned by two *Spitzhelm* towers (so called for their resemblance to old-time German helmets). In the west tower are three dank dungeons that once held common criminals. Between the towers are more salubrious cells that were reserved for debtors. Above the portcullis a plaque pays warm tribute to the Austrian forces who helped Heidelberg beat back a French attempt to capture the bridge in 1799. The bridge itself is the ninth to be built on this spot; ice floes and floods destroyed its predecessors. The elector Carl Theodor, who built it in 1786–88, must have been confident this one would last: he had a statue of himself erected on it, upon a plinth decorated with river gods and goddesses (symbolic of the Rhine, Danube, Neckar, and Mosel rivers). Just to be safe, he also put up a statue of a saint, St. John Nepomuk. From the center of the bridge you'll have some of the finest views of the Old Town and the castle.

For the most inspiring view of Heidelberg, find the steep, winding **Schlangenweg** (Snake Path), which begins just above the Alte Brücke. It cuts through terraced vineyards until it reaches the woods, where it crosses the **Philosophenweg** (Philosophers' Path); go right and continue through the woods to the Hölderlin Memorial, a grove traditionally frequented by poets and scholars. Try to arrive there as the sun sets and watch the red sandstone castle turn to gold.

Where to Stay & Eat

★ $-$$$ ✕ **Zur Herrenmühle.** This romantic, cozy restaurant with an idyllic court-yard began its life as a 17th-century grain mill. Fish is a specialty. Try the *Variation von Edelfischen* (medley of fine fish), served with home-made noodles. The prix-fixe menus offer good value. ✉ *Hauptstr. 239 (near Karlstor)* ☎ *06221/602–909* ▭ *AE, DC, MC, V* ☉ *Closed Sun. and Mon., and 1st half of Jan. No lunch.*

$-$$ ✕ **Zum Roten Ochsen.** Many of the rough-hewn oak tables here have ini-tials carved into them, a legacy of the thousands who have visited Hei-delberg's most famous old tavern. You can wash down simple fare, such as goulash soup and bratwurst, or heartier dishes, such as *Tellerfleisch* (boiled beef) and sauerbraten, with German wines or Heidelberg beer—evenings, to the tune of live piano music. The Red Ox has been run by the Spengel family for 164 years. ✉ *Hauptstr. 217* ☎ *06221/20977* ⚐ *Reservations essential* ▭ *No credit cards* ☉ *Closed Sun. and mid-Dec.–mid-Jan. No lunch Nov.–Mar.*

$$$-$$$$ ✕▨ **Romantik Hotel zum Ritter St. Georg.** If this is your first visit to Ger-
Fodor's Choice many, stay here. It's the only Renaissance building in Heidelberg (1592),
★ and has a top location opposite the market square in the heart of Old Town. Some rooms are more modern and spacious than others, but all are comfortable. You can enjoy German and international favorites in the restaurant Belier or in the Ritterstube ($-$$$). Both are wood pan-eled and have old-world charm. ✉ *Hauptstr. 178, D-69117* ☎ *06221/ 1350* 🖷 *06221/135–230* ⊕ *www.ritter-heidelberg.de* ◿ *39 rooms, 36 with bath, 1 suite* ⚐ *2 restaurants* ▭ *AE, DC, MC, V.*

★ $$-$$$$ ✕▨ **Hotel Die Hirschgasse.** A stunning castle view and suites decorated in Laura Ashley style mark this historical inn (1472) across the river op-posite Karlstor (15-minute walk to Old Town). Convivial Ernest Kraft and his British wife, Allison, serve upscale regional specialties and wines from the vineyard next door in the Mensurstube ($$$-$$$$), a tavern mentioned in Mark Twain's *A Tramp Abroad.* Beamed ceilings, stone walls, and deep red fabrics make for romantic dining in the elegant Le Gourmet ($$$-$$$$). ✉ *Hirschg. 3, D-69120* ☎ *06221/4540* 🖷 *06221/ 454–111* ⊕ *www.hirschgasse.de* ◿ *20 suites* ⚐ *2 restaurants* ▭ *AE, DC, MC, V* ☉ *Le Gourmet closed 2 wks in early Jan. and 2 wks in early Aug. Both restaurants closed Sun. and Mon. No lunch.*

Nightlife & the Arts

Information on all upcoming events is given in the monthly *Heidelberg aktuell,* free and available from the tourist office or on the Internet (www. heidelberg-aktuell.de). Performances are held at the castle during the an-nual **Schlossfestspiele** (☎ 06221/582–000).

On **Karlsplatz** you'll find two traditional pubs, Zum Sepp'l and Zum Roten Ochsen, where fraternity students have engaged in beer-drinking contests for the last 200-some years. The pub walls are lined with swords, trophies, faded photos, and dueling and drinking paraphernalia. Today's students hang out in the bars on **Untere Strasse**, which runs parallel to and between Hauptstrasse and the Neckar River, starting from the market square. The fanciest bars and yuppie cafés are along **Hauptstrasse.** For a terrific view, delicious drinks, and relaxing music head for the **Turm Lounge** (⊠ Alte Glockengiesserei 9 ☎ 06221/653–949), with trendy sofas and dark red walls on the seventh floor or an atmosphere shaded in deep blue on the eighth floor.

Heidelberg Essentials

AIRPORTS & TRANSFERS

From the Frankfurt airport, there's fast and easy access, by car and train, to Heidelberg. With advance reservations you can take the shuttle service TLS. The trip takes about an hour and costs €28 per person; with four people, €21.50 each. No reservations are needed for the Lufthansa Airport Bus (not restricted to Lufthansa passengers). Service is daily, on the hour, 8–1, 3–7, and 10 PM. It departs from Frankfurt airport, terminal one, Hall B, arrivals level. Exit the hall from the door closest to the *Treffpunkt* (Meeting Point) to reach the bus stop. The trip ends at the Crowne Plaza Hotel in Heidelberg and costs €19 per person.

🚹 **TLS** ☎ 06221/770–077 🖷 06221/770–070 ⊕ www.tls-heidelberg.de. **Lufthansa Airport Bus** ☎ 069/6969–4433 in Frankfurt ☎ 06221/653–256 in Heidelberg.

BUS TRAVEL TO & FROM HEIDELBERG

Europabus 189 runs the length of the Burgenstrasse daily from May through September, making stops all along the Neckar River. For information, contact Deutsche Touring (⇨ Bus Travel *in* Smart Travel Tips).

CAR TRAVEL

Heidelberg is a 15-minute drive (10 km [6 mi]) on A–656 from Mannheim, a major junction of the autobahn system. Avis, Europcar, Hertz, and Sixt all have rental offices in Heidelberg, at the Frankfurt airport and main train stations.

🚹 **Avis** ⊠ Karlsruherstr. 43, Heidelberg ☎ 06221/22215. **Europcar** ⊠ Bergheimerstr. 159, Heidelberg ☎ 06221/53990. **Hertz** ⊠ Crowne Plaza, Kurfürstenanlage 1, Heidelberg ☎ 06221/23434. **Sixt** ⊠ Eppelheimer Str. 50C, Heidelberg ☎ 06221/138–990.

TOURS

From April through October there are daily walking tours of Heidelberg in German (Thursday through Sunday in English) at 10:30 AM; tours November through March are in German only, Saturday at 10:30; the cost is €6. They depart from the Lion's Fountain on Universitätsplatz. Bilingual bus tours run April–October on Thursday and Friday at 2:30, on Saturday at 10:30 and 2:30, on Sunday at 10:30. From November through March bus tours depart Saturday at 2:30. They cost €12 and depart from Universitätsplatz. The *HeidelbergCard* costs €12 (two days) or €20 (four days) and includes free or reduced admission to most tourist attractions as well as free use of all public transportation (including the Bergbahn to the castle) and other extras, such as free guided walking tours, discounts on bus tours, and a city guidebook. It can be purchased at the tourist information office at the main train station, and at many local hotels.

TRAIN TRAVEL

Western Germany's most important rail junction is in nearby Mannheim, with hourly InterCity trains from all major German cities. Heidelberg is equally easy to get to. The super-high-speed InterCity Express service, which reaches 280 kph (174 mph), is Germany's fastest. Travel time between Heidelberg and Stuttgart is 26 minutes. Local services link many of the smaller towns.

VISITOR INFORMATION
🖼 Heidelberg Tourist Office ✉ Tourist Information am Hauptbahnhof, Willy-Brandt-Pl. 1, D-69115 ☎ 06221/19433 🖶 06221/138-8111 ⊕ www.cvb-heidelberg.de.

FRANKFURT

Originally a Roman settlement, Frankfurt later served as one of Charlemagne's two capitals (the other being Aachen). Still later, the electors of the Holy Roman Empire met here to choose and crown the emperor. In World War II Frankfurt was virtually flattened by bombs. Today it bristles with skyscrapers, visible signs of the city's role as Germany's financial capital. Five of the largest banks in Germany are headquartered here.

Exploring Frankfurt

Numbers in the margin correspond to points of interest on the Frankfurt map.

The neighborhood around the Hauptbahnhof (main train station), site of many major hotels, is mostly devoted to business, but be careful of the seedy red-light district nearby. The Old Town has some restored medieval buildings. On the south bank of the Main River, the old quarter of Sachsenhausen is full of taverns and museums. The neighborhood is the home of the famous *Apfelwein* (apple wine or cider) taverns, with long tables, backless benches, schmaltzy murals on the walls, and sing-alongs.

⑫ **Börse** (Stock Exchange). The Börse was founded by Frankfurt merchants in 1558 to establish some order in their often chaotic dealings, but the present building dates from the 1870s. ✉ *Börsenpl.* ☎ *069/21010* ⊕ *www.deutsche-boerse.com* ⊙ *Visitor's gallery: weekdays 10:30–6.*

⑬ **Fressgasse** (Pig-Out Alley). The proper name of one of the city's liveliest thoroughfares is Grosse Bockenheimer Strasse, but Frankfurters have given it this sobriquet because of the amazing choice of delicatessens, wine merchants, cafés, and restaurants. ✉ *Opernpl. to Hauptwache.*

★ ⑩ **Goethehaus und Goethemuseum.** The birthplace of Germany's most famous poet is furnished with many original pieces that belonged to his family. The adjoining museum contains manuscripts in Goethe's own hand, works of art that inspired him (he was an amateur painter), and works associated with his literary contemporaries. ✉ *Grosser Hirschgraben 23–25* ☎ *069/138–800* ⊕ *www.goethehaus-frankfurt. de* ⊙ *Apr.–Sept., weekdays 9–6, weekends 10–4; Oct.–Mar., weekdays 9–4, weekends 10–4.*

❶ **Jüdisches Museum** (Jewish Museum). In the former Rothschild Palace, this museum tells the story of Frankfurt's Jewish quarter, which prior to the Holocaust was the second-largest Jewish community in Germany. The archives include 5,000 books and a large photograph collection. ✉ *Untermainkai 14–15,* ☎ *069/212–35000* ⊕ *www. juedischesmuseum.de* ⊙ *Tues. and Thurs.–Sun. 10–5, Wed. 10–8.*

❻ **Kaiserdom** (Imperial Cathedral). Because the Holy Roman emperors were chosen and crowned here from the 16th to 18th century, the

Church of St. Bartholomew is commonly known as the Kaiserdom, even though it isn't the seat of a bishop. It was built largely between the 13th and 15th centuries, and most of its original treasures survived the bombs of World War II. The red sandstone tower (almost 300 feet high) was added between 1415 and 1514 and provides a great view of the city. Excavations in front of the main entrance revealed the remains of a Roman settlement and the foundations of a Carolingian imperial palace. ⊠ *Dompl. 1* ☎ *069/1337–6184* ⊙ *Church: Mon.–Thurs. and Sat. 9–noon and 2:30–6, Fri. and Sun. 2:30–6 (closes at 5 Oct.–Apr.). Dommuseum: Tues.–Fri. 10–5, weekends 11–5.*

❾ Karmeliterkloster (Carmelite Monastery). Secularized in 1803, the church and adjacent buildings contain the **Museum für Vor- und Frühgeschichte** (Museum of Prehistory and Early History). The **main cloister** displays the largest religious fresco north of the Alps, a 16th-century representation of Christ's birth and death. ⊠ *Karmeliterg. 1* ☎ *069/2123–5896* ⊙ *Museum and cloister: Tues. and Thurs.–Sun. 10–5, Wed. 10–8.*

❹ Leonhardskirche (St. Leonard's Church). This beautifully preserved 13th-century building with five naves has some fine old stained glass. The hanging, ornately carved piece of the ceiling vault was already a major Frankfurt tourist attraction during the 17th century. ⊠ *Am Leonhardstor and Untermainkai* ⊙ *Tues.–Sun. 10–noon and 3–6.*

★ ✋ ⓯ Naturkundemuseum Senckenberg (Natural History Museum). An important collection of fossils, animals, plants, and geological exhibits is upstaged by the famous Diplodocus dinosaur—the only complete specimen of its kind displayed in Europe. Many of the exhibits on prehistoric animals have been designed with children in mind. ⊠ *Senckenberganlage 25* ☎ *069/75420* ⊕ *www.senckenberg.uni-frankfurt.de* ⊙ *Mon., Tues., Thurs., and Fri. 9–5, Wed. 9–8, weekends 9–6.*

❺ Nikolaikirche (St. Nicholas's Church). This small red sandstone church was built in the late 13th century as the court chapel for emperors of the Holy Roman Empire. Try to time your visit to coincide with the chimes of the carillon, which rings three times a day, at 9, noon, and 5. ⊠ *South side of Römerberg* ⊙ *Oct.–Mar., daily 10–6; Apr.–Sept., daily 10–8.*

✋ ⓮ Palmengarten und Botanischer Garten (Tropical Garden and Botanical Gardens). A splendid cluster of tropical and semitropical greenhouses contains a wide variety of flora, including cacti, orchids, and palms. There is a little lake where you can rent rowboats, a play area for children, a wading pool, and a miniature railway. During most of the year there are flower shows and exhibitions; in summer, concerts are held in an outdoor music pavilion. ⊠ *Siesmayerstr. 63* ☎ *069/2123–3939* ⊙ *Feb.–Oct., daily 9–6; Nov.–Jan., daily 9–4.*

❽ Römer (City Hall). Its gabled Gothic facade with an ornate balcony is the city's official emblem. The mercantile-minded Frankfurt burghers used the complex of three patrician buildings not only for political and ceremonial purposes but also for trade fairs and other commercial ventures. Banquets to celebrate the coronations of the Holy Roman emperors were mounted starting in 1562 in the **Kaisersaal** (Imperial Hall). Impressive, full-length 19th-century portraits of the 52 emperors of the Holy Roman Empire line the walls of the banquet hall. ⊠ *West side of Römerberg* ☎ *069/2123–4814* ⊙ *Daily 10–1 and 2–5* ⊙ *Closed during official functions.*

❼ Römerberg. This restored square north of the Main River is the site of many public festivals, including the Christmas market. The fine 16th-century **Fountain of Justitia** (Justice) stands in its center. At the coro-

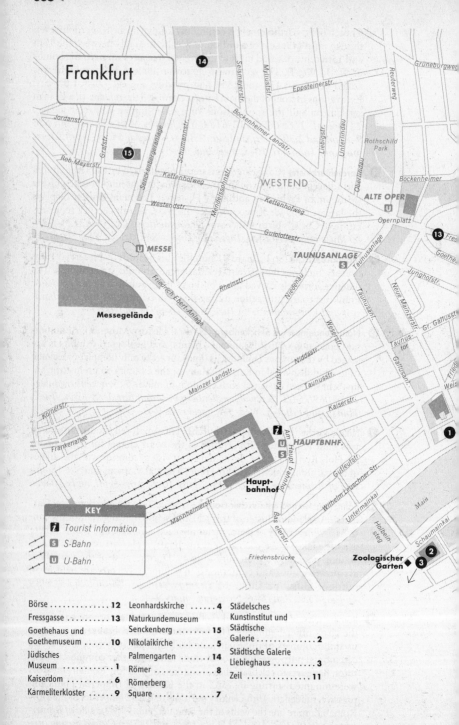

Frankfurt

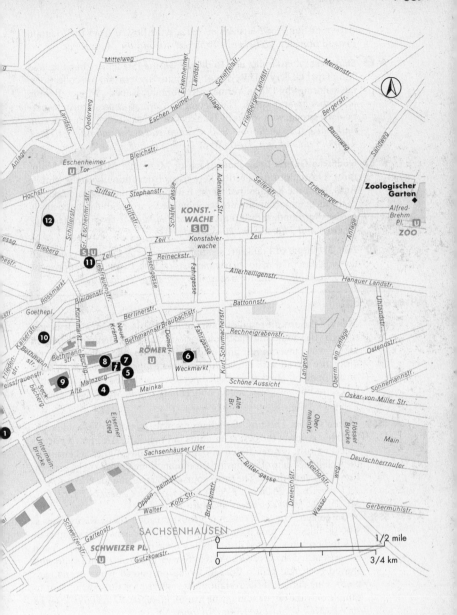

nation of Emperor Matthias in 1612, wine flowed from the fountain instead of water. ⊠ *Between Braubachstr. and the Main River.*

★ ❷ **Städelsches Kunstinstitut und Städtische Galerie** (Städel Art Institute and Municipal Gallery). This, one of Germany's important art collections, has paintings by Dürer, Vermeer, Rembrandt, Rubens, Monet, Renoir, and other great masters. The section on German expressionism is particularly strong, with works by Frankfurt artist Max Beckmann. ⊠ *Schaumainkai 63* ☎ *069/605–0980* ⊕ *www.staedelmuseum.de* ⊗ *Tues., Thurs., Fri., and Sun. 10–5, Wed. 10–8, Sat. 2–8.*

★ ❸ **Städtische Galerie Liebieghaus** (Liebieg Municipal Museum of Sculpture). The sculpture collection here spans from antiquity to the Middle Ages, from the Renaissance to the baroque era, and is considered one of the most important in Europe. Some pieces are exhibited in the lovely gardens surrounding the house. ⊠ *Schaumainkai 71* ☎ *069/2123–8617* ⊗ *Tues. and Thurs.–Sun. 10–5, Wed. 10–8.*

⓫ **Zeil.** The heart of Frankfurt's shopping district is this ritzy pedestrian thoroughfare. The major department stores lie between the Hauptwache and Konstablerwache train stations. ⊠ *East of Hauptwache.*

Where to Eat

Many of the upscale restaurants in Frankfurt serve bargain lunch menus, though you should still make reservations. At Sachsenhausen *Apfelwein* (apple-wine) taverns, just find space at one of the long tables. Foods traditionally served with apple wine include *Rippchen* (cured pork chop on a mound of sauerkraut), boiled potatoes and boiled eggs with Frankfurt's traditional green sauce, and *Handkäs mit Musik* (soft cheese, onions, vinegar, and oil on bread).

★ **$$$$** ✕ **Erno's Bistro.** This tiny, unpretentious place in a quiet Westend neighborhood is one of the best restaurants in Frankfurt. The French bistro's specialty, fish, is often flown in daily from France. When its clientele, the well-heeled elite of the business community, are unlikely to be in town, Erno's closes its doors. The three-course midday menu for €25 is a steal. ⊠ *Liebigstr. 15* ☎ *069/721–997* ⌲ *Reservations essential* ▤ *AE, DC, MC, V* ⊗ *Closed weekends and July–early Aug.*

★ **$$$–$$$$** ✕ **Gargantua.** One of Frankfurt's most creative chefs, Klaus Trebes, who doubles as a food columnist, serves new versions of German classics and French-accented dishes in this Westend dining room. His menu features such dishes as artichoke risotto with goose liver, lentil salad with stewed beef, and grilled dorado served on pureed white beans with pesto. One corner of the restaurant is reserved for those who want to sample only the outstanding wine list. ⊠ *Liebigstr. 47* ☎ *069/720–718* ▤ *AE, MC, V* ⊗ *Closed Sun. No lunch Sat.*

★ **$–$$$** ✕ **Maintower.** Atop the skyscraper that houses Hessischer Landesbank, this popular restaurant-cum-café-cum-bar captures an unbeatable view. Through 25-foot floor to ceiling windows, all of "Mainhattan" is at your feet. Prices are surprisingly reasonable, though you will have to pay €4.50 per person just to take the elevator up. The cuisine is part global, part regional. It's hard to get a table for supper, though it's less of a problem for afternoon coffee, or for spending an evening in the clouds at the bar. ⊠ *Neue Mainzer Str. 52–58* ☎ *069/3650–4770* ▤ *AE, V.*

$–$$ ✕ **Garibaldi.** The fresh pasta and friendly atmosphere are equally appealing at this Italian restaurant between the Alte Oper and Hauptwache. Selections of antipasti, seafood, pizzas, and pasta dishes are extensive, and many entrées are topped with freshly shaved truffles. Reservations

are recommended. ⊠ *Klein Hochstr. 4* ☎ *069/2199–7644* ⊟ *V*
⊘ *Closed Sun.*

$–$$ ✕ **Kangaroo's.** The main dining room of this very popular, Australia-theme restaurant is glass-roofed and lush with greenery. The decor includes highway signs warning of kangaroos ahead. The adventurous can try the Australia Platter with kangaroo, crocodile, and emu meat (but Aussies, too, eat beef, chicken, and salads). ⊠ *Rahmhofstr. 2–4* ☎ *069/282–100* ⊟ *AE, DC, MC, V.*

$ ✕ **Café Laumer.** The ambience of an old-time Viennese café, with a subdued decor and rear garden, is well preserved here. It owes its literary tradition to Theodor Adorno, a philosopher and sociologist of the Frankfurt School, who drank his daily coffee here. It's open for breakfast, lunch, and afternoon coffee and closes at 7 PM. ⊠ *Bockenheimer Landstr. 67,* ☎ *069/727–912* ⊟ *DC, MC, V* ⊘ *No dinner.*

$ ✕ **Edelweiss.** Homesick Austrians enjoy their native cuisine at this rustic restaurant with a terrace. Dishes include the genuine Wiener schnitzel, and Kaiser Franz Josef's favorite, *Tafelspitze,* made of boiled beef with a chive sauce. Then there's the roast chicken with a salad made of "earth apples" (potatoes) and the beloved *Kaiserschmarrn*: egg pancakes with raisins, apples, cinnamon, and jam. ⊠ *Schweizer Str. 96* ☎ *069/619696* ⊟ *AE, DC, MC, V* ⊘ *No lunch weekends.*

★ **$** ✕ **Wäldches.** This is Frankfurt's busiest brew pub, in a countrified location nevertheless handy to a rapid-transit station, and a favorite stop for bikers and hikers. By noon on pleasant summer Sundays, the big beer garden can be standing room only. The home-brewed light and dark beers go nicely with the German cuisine. ⊠ *Am Ginnheimer Wäldchen 8* ☎ *069/520–522* ⊟ *No credit cards* ⊘ *No lunch Oct.–Mar.*

$ ✕ **Zum Wagner.** The kitchen produces the same hearty German dishes as other apple-wine taverns, only better. Try the *Tafelspitz mit Frankfurter grüner Sosse* (stewed beef with a sauce of green herbs) or come on Friday for fresh fish. Beer and wine are served as well as cider. This Sachsenhausen classic succeeds in being touristy and traditional all at once. ⊠ *Schweizer Str. 71* ☎ *069/612–565* ⊟ *No credit cards.*

Where to Stay

Hotels in the city are expensive (many offer significant reductions on weekends) and frequently book up well in advance. The majority of the larger hotels are around the main train station, a 15- to 20-minute walk from the Old Town.

$$$$ ▨ **Hessischer Hof.** This is the choice of many businesspeople, not just because it's near the fairgrounds but for the air of class that pervades its handsome interior (the exterior is nondescript). Many of the public-room furnishings are antiques owned by the family of the princes of Hesse. Guest rooms are done in either a British or Biedermeier style. Jimmy's is one of the cult bars in town. ⊠ *Friedrich-Ebert-Anlage 40, D–60325* ☎ *069/75400* 🖷 *069/7540–2924* ⊕ *www.hessischer-hof.de* ⇗ *106 rooms, 11 suites* ⌂ *Restaurant, bar* ⊟ *AE, DC, MC, V.*

★ **$$$–$$$$** ▨ **Steigenberger Hotel Frankfurter Hof.** The Victorian Frankfurter Hof is one of the city's oldest hotels and is used to hosting heads of state. The atmosphere throughout is one of old-fashioned, formal elegance, with burnished woods, fresh flowers, and thick-carpeted hush. Although it fronts a courtyard, you must enter through a modest side entrance. ⊠ *Am Kaiserpl., D–60311* ☎ *069/21502* 🖷 *069/215–900* ⊕ *www.frankfurter-hof.steigenberger.com* ⇗ *286 rooms, 46 suites* ⌂ *3 restaurants, bar* ⊟ *AE, DC, MC, V.*

★ **$$** ▨ **Art Hotel Robert Mayer.** In a turn-of-the-20th-century villa, each room has been decorated by a different Frankfurt artist, with furniture designs by the likes of Rietveld and Frank Lloyd Wright. The room designed by Therese Traube contrasts abstract newspaper collage with a replica Louis XIV armchair. Breakfast is included in the price of the room. ☒ *Robert-Mayer-Str. 44, D–60486* ☎ *069/970–9100* 🖷 *069/ 9709–1010* ⊕ *www.art-hotel-robert-mayer.de* ➪ *11 rooms, 1 suite* 🖃 *AE, DC, MC, V.*

★ $$ 🏨 **InterCity Hotel.** If there ever was a hotel at the vortex of arrivals and departures, it's this centrally located hostelry in an elegant old-world building. It's right across the street from the main train station, and guests get a pass good for unlimited travel on local public transportation. The station's underground garage is also at your disposal. ☒ *Poststr. 8, D–60329* ☎ *069/273–910* 🖷 *069/2739–1999* ⊕ *www.intercityhotel. at* ➪ *384 rooms, 3 suites* ⚐ *Restaurant, bar* 🖃 *AE, DC, MC, V.*

★ $–$$ 🏨 **Maingau.** You'll find this pleasant hotel-restaurant in the middle of the lively Sachsenhausen quarter. Rooms are modest but spotless, comfortable, and equipped with TVs; the room rate includes a substantial breakfast buffet. Though the hotel is inexpensive, the restaurant, Maingau-Stuben, is anything but! ☒ *Schifferstr. 38–40, D–60594* ☎ *069/609– 140* 🖷 *069/620–790* ➪ *100 rooms* ⚐ *Restaurant* 🖃 *AE, MC.*

$ 🏨 **Pension Stella.** This little hostelry is in one of the most pleasant old neighborhoods in town, an area of villas between a park with a water castle and the studios of Hessischer Rundfunk. The five rooms, each with bath or shower, are comfortable and the price is right. ☒ *Frauenstein-str. 8, D–60322* ☎🖷 *069/554–026* ➪ *5 rooms* 🖃 *No credit cards.*

Nightlife & the Arts

Frankfurt was a pioneer in the German jazz scene, and also, of late, has done much for the development of techno music. In the fall the German Jazz Festival takes place in conjunction with the Music Fair. Sachsenhausen (Frankfurt's Left Bank) is a good place to start for bars, clubs, and Apfelwein taverns. The increasingly hip Nordend has an almost equal number of bars and clubs but fewer tourists.

The Arts

Tickets for most events can be purchased at the performance venue, the tourist office at Römerberg 27, or from box offices like **Frankfurt Ticket GmbH** (☒ Hauptwache Passage ☎ 069/134–0400), which handles sales for the Alte Oper, Frankfurt Opera, and the world-renowned Frankfurt Ballet (a very modern company). The most glamorous venue for classical or pop music concerts is the **Alte Oper** (Old Opera House; ☒ Opernpl. ☎ 069/134–0400). Tickets to performances can range from €10 to nearly €150.

Nightlife

Most dance and nightclubs charge entrance fees ranging from €5 to €20. Some trendy clubs, such as Living XXL and King Kamehameha, enforce dress codes banning jeans or khaki pants.

BARS & DANCE CLUBS The tiny, cozy **Balalaika** (☒ Dreikönigstr. 30 ☎ 069/612–226), in Sachsenhausen, provides intimacy and live music without charging the fancy prices you'd expect. If you're seeking something soothing, sit down at **Casablanca Bar** (☒ Parkhotel, Wiesenhüttenpl. 28 ☎ 069/26970) and listen to the tinkling of the ivories. For a strong elixir, ask the bartender to shake up a mai tai or their prizewinning Challenger. Beneath the heating pipes of a former brewery, **King Kamehameha** (☒ Hanauer Landstr. 192 ☎ 069/4800–3701) offers a quiet cocktail bar, a house band and dance floor, and a stage. The Eurotower's **Living XXL** (☒ Kaiserstr. 29 ☎ 069/242–9370) is a huge bar-restaurant. On Friday and Saturday a "subdued" disco is geared to the banking community, but the club also hosts regular gay entertainment.

JAZZ CLUBS The oldest jazz cellar in Germany, **Der Frankfurter Jazzkeller** (⊠ Kleine Bockenheimer Str. 18a ☎ 069/288–537) was founded by legendary trumpeter Carlo Bohländer. Its hot, modern jazz is often free (but the cover can also run around €20). The **Dreikönigskeller** (⊠ Färberstr. 71 ☎ 069/629–273) is patronized mostly by students, as well as a sprinkling of older hipsters, all smoking as voraciously as the musicians. **Sinkkasten** (⊠ Brönnerstr. 5–9 ☎ 069/280–385), a Frankfurt institution, is a class act for jazz, rock, pop, and African music.

Frankfurt Essentials

AIRPORTS & TRANSFERS
Frankfurt Airport, the busiest and biggest airport in mainland Europe, is 10 km (6 mi) southwest of the downtown area by the A–5 Autobahn, and has its own railway station for the high-speed InterCity (IC) and InterCity Express (ICE) trains. The airport also doubles as a shopping mall whose stores are not subject to Germany's strict closing laws.
🛈 **Flughafen Frankfurt Main** ☎ 01805/372-4636; 069/6900 from outside Germany ⊕ www.flughafen-frankfurt.de.

TRANSFERS The S–8 (S-bahn) runs from the airport to downtown, stopping at the Hauptbahnhof (main train station) and then at the central Hauptwache square. Trains run at least every 15 minutes and the ride takes about as long; the one-way fare is €3.05. A taxi from the airport into the city center normally takes around 20 minutes; allow double that during rush hours. The fare is around €15. If you're driving, take the B-43 main road, following signs for STADTMITTE (Downtown).

BUS TRAVEL TO & FROM FRANKFURT
Buses leave from the south side of the Hauptbahnhof. Tickets and information are available from Deutsche Touring.
🛈 **Deutsche Touring** ⊠ Am Römerhof 17 ☎ 069/79030.

CAR RENTAL
🛈 **Avis** ⊠ Schmidtstr. 39 ☎ 069/730-111. **Europcar** ⊠ Lyonerstr. 68 ☎ 069/6772-0291 ⊠ Frankfurt Airport Hall A, arrival level ☎ 069/697-970. **Hertz** ⊠ Hanauer Landstr. 117 ☎ 069/449-090.

CAR TRAVEL
Frankfurt is the junction of many major autobahns. The most important are the A–3, running south from Köln and then on to Würzburg, Nürnberg, and Munich; and the A–5, running south from Giessen and then on to Mannheim, Heidelberg, Karlsruhe, and the Swiss-German border at Basel. A complex series of beltways surrounds the city. If you're driving to Frankfurt on the A–5 from either north or south, exit at Nordwestkreuz and follow A–66 to the Nordend district, just north of downtown. Driving south on A–3, exit onto A–66 and follow the signs to Frankfurt-Höchst and then the Nordwestkreuz. Driving west on A–3, exit at the Offenbacher Kreuz onto A–661 and follow the signs for Frankfurt-Stadtmitte (City Center).

CONSULATES
🛈 **Australia** ⊠ Grüneburgweg 58-62 D-60322 ☎ 069/905-580.
🛈 **United Kingdom** ⊠ Bockenheimer Landstr. 42 D-60323 ☎ 069/170-0020.
🛈 **United States** ⊠ Siesmayerstr. 21 D-60323 ☎ 069/75350.

EMERGENCIES

Listings, in German, of pharmacies and doctors are available after hours through the hot line ☎ 069/011500.

🔲 Doctors & Dentists **Dental Emergencies** ☎ 069/660-7271.

🔲 Emergency Services **Fire** ☎ 112. **Medical Emergencies** ☎ 069/19292. **Police** ☎ 110.

🔲 24-hour Pharmacies ☎ 069/011500.

ENGLISH-LANGUAGE MEDIA

The American Forces Network's radio signal is full of American news, sports, and music. Its AM broadcast (primarily talk) is at 873; the FM signal (primarily music) is at 98.7.

🔲 Bookstores **British Bookshop** ✉ Börsenstr. 17 ☎ 069/280-492.

MAIL

Note that the official address for Frankfurt includes "Main" after the city name in any variety of ways—Frankfurt/Main, Frankfurt am Main, Frankfurt/M, to cite a few.

TAXIS

Cabs are not always easy to hail from the sidewalk; some stop, whereas others will pick up only from the city's numerous taxi stands or outside hotels or the train station. Fares start at €2.05 (€2.55 in the evening) and increase by a per-km (½ mi) charge of €1.48 for the first three, €1.33 thereafter. Count on paying €6.50 for a short city ride.

🔲 ☎ 069/250-001, 069/230-001, or 069/230-033.

TOURS

BOAT TOURS Day trips on the Main River and Rhine excursions run from March through October and leave from the Frankfurt Mainkai am Eiserner Steg, just south of the Römer complex.

🔲 Fees & Schedules **Frankfurter Personenschiffahrt** ✉ Mainkai 36 ☎ 069/281-884 🌐 www.aschaffenburg.personenschiffe.de.

BUS & TROLLEY TOURS Bus tours run by the tourist office and Gray Line take in all the main sights. The city transit authority runs a brightly painted old-time streetcar—the *Ebbelwoi Express* (Cider Express)—on weekend and holiday afternoons. Departures are from the Heide Strasse tram stop, near the Bornheim Mitte U-bahn station and the fare is €5. Deutsche Touring will take you outside Frankfurt to Rothenburg, Heidelberg, and the Black Forest.

🔲 Fees & Schedules **City Transit Authority** ☎ 069/2132-2425. **Deutsche Touring** ✉ Am Römerhof 17 ☎ 069/790-350. **Gray Line** ☎ 069/230-492 🌐 www.lts.de. **Main tourist office** ✉ Römerberg 27 ☎ 069/212-38708 🌐 www.tcf.frankfurt-main.de.

TRAIN TRAVEL

EuroCity and InterCity trains connect Frankfurt with all other German cities and many major European ones. The InterCity Express (ICE) line links Frankfurt with Berlin, Hamburg, Munich, and several major German cities. All long-distance trains arrive at and depart from the Hauptbahnhof.

TRANSPORTATION AROUND FRANKFURT

Frankfurt's smooth-running, well-integrated public transportation system (RMV) encompasses even regional trains. Fares for the entire system, which includes a very extensive surrounding area, are uniform, though they are based on a complex zone system. Within the time that your ticket is valid (one hour for most inner-city destinations), you can transfer from one part of the system to another.

Single, day, and group tickets are sold at vending machines at most stations and stops. A basic one-way ticket for a ride in the inner zone costs €1.90 during the peak hours of 6 AM–9 AM and 4 PM–6:30 PM weekdays. (€1.60 the rest of the time.) There is also a reduced *Kurzstrecke* ("short stretch") fare of €1.50 (€1.05 off-peak).

TRAVEL AGENCIES
🖪 **American Express International** ⊠ Theodor Heuss Allee 112 ☎ 069/97970.

VISITOR INFORMATION
The main tourist office is in the heart of the Old Town. It's open weekdays 9:30–5:30, weekends 10–4. Other information offices are in the main hall of the railroad station and at Zeil 94a. All three offices can help you find accommodations. The tourist office also sells a Frankfurt Card (€7.50 for one day, €11 for two) entitling you to unlimited travel, reduced cruise and tour fares, and half-price admission to 17 museums.
🖪 **Tourismus und Congress GmbH Frankfurt/Main** ⊠ Kaiserstr. 56 D-60329 Frankfurt am Main ☎ 069/2123-8800 ⊕ www.frankfurt.de. **Main tourist office** ⊠ Römerberg 27 ☎ 069/2123-8708.

THE RHINE

This mighty river is Germany's historic lifeline, and though it does not belong to Germany alone, the German span has the most spectacular scenery. The 190-km (120-mi) stretch between Mainz and Köln (Cologne) is known as the Middle Rhine, and the section between Bingen and Koblenz was designated a UNESCO World Heritage site in 2002. The river's banks are crowned by brooding castles and by breathtaking, vine-terraced hills that provide the livelihood for many of the villages hugging the shores. Vineyards are a legacy of the Romans, who considered the Rhine the frontier between civilization and barbaric German tribes. Rüdesheim, Bingen, Koblenz, and Köln (Cologne) remain important commercial wine centers.

The beauty, legend, and myth of the river have been a draw for centuries. The Loreley, a steep jutting slate cliff, was once believed to be the home of a beautiful and bewitching maiden who lured boatmen to a watery end in the swift currents. The Nibelungen, a Burgundian race said to have lived on its banks, serve as subjects for Wagner's epic opera cycle *Der Ring des Nibelungen* (1852–72). William Turner captured misty Rhine sunsets on canvas, and writers Goethe, Lord Byron, and Mark Twain captured the spirit of Rhine Romanticism on paper, encouraging others to follow in their footsteps.

Köln

This genial city of 1 million was first settled by the Romans in 38 BC. In the 9th century Charlemagne, the first Holy Roman Emperor, appointed Köln's first archbishop. The city's ecclesiastical heritage is one of its most striking features; it has a full dozen Romanesque churches and one of the world's largest and finest Gothic cathedrals. In the Middle Ages Köln occupied a position of greater importance in European commerce than either London or Paris.

Ninety percent of the city was destroyed in World War II, and the rush to rebuild it shows in the blocky, uninspired architecture. Whatever the city's aesthetic drawbacks, the Altstadt (Old Town), within the line of the medieval city walls, has great charm, and at night it throbs with life. Kölners put on Germany's most energetic carnival every February, an orgiastic revelry with bands, parades, and parties. Most central hotels

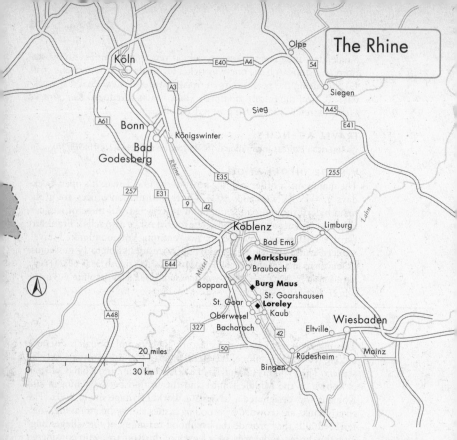

sell the KölnTourismus Card, which entitles you to a sightseeing tour, admission to all the city's museums, free city bus and tram travel, and other reductions.

★ Towering over the Old Town is the **Kölner Dom** (Cologne Cathedral), an extraordinary Gothic edifice dedicated to St. Peter and the Virgin. At 515 feet high, the two western towers of the cathedral were by far the tallest structures in the world when they were finished. The length of the building is 469 feet; the width of the nave is 148 feet; and the highest part of the interior is 139 feet. The cathedral was built to house what were believed to be the relics of the Magi, the three kings or wise men who paid homage to the infant Jesus. Today the relics are kept just behind the altar, in the same enormous gold-and-silver reliquary in which they were originally displayed. In the last chapel on the left as you face the altar is the Gero Cross, a monumental oak crucifix dating from 971 and impressive for its simple grace. More treasures can be seen in the **Domschatzkammer** (cathedral treasury; ☉ Apr.–Oct., Mon.–Sat. 9–7, Sun. 12:30–7; Nov.–Mar., Mon.–Sat. 9–4, Sun. 1–4), including the silver shrine of Archbishop Engelbert, who was stabbed to death in 1225. ✉ *Dompl.* ☎ *0221/925–84730* ⊕ *www.koelner-dom.de* ☉ *Daily 6 AM–7 PM; Dom stairwell daily 9–7; guided tours in English Mon.–Sat. 10:30 and 2:30, Sun. 2:30.*

★ The **Museum Ludwig** is dedicated to art from the beginning of the 20th century to the present day. Its pop art collection includes Andy Warhol, Jasper Johns, Robert Rauschenberg, Claes Oldenburg, and Roy Lichtenstein. The **Agfa Foto-Historama** (Agfa Photography Museum) here has one of the world's largest collections of historic photographs. ✉ *Bischofsgartenstr. 1* ☎ *0221/2212–6165* ⊕ *www.museenkoeln.de* ☉ *Tues. 10–8, Wed.–Fri. 10–6, weekends 11–6.*

★ Paintings span the years 1300 to 1900 at the **Wallraf-Richartz-Museum.** The Master of the Saint Veronica and Stefan Lochner are represented by two luminous works, *The Last Judgment* and *The Madonna in the Rose Bower.* Large canvases by Rubens, who spent his youth in Köln, hang prominently, as do outstanding works by Rembrandt, Van Dyck, Frans Hals, Tiepolo, Canaletto, and Boucher. ✉ *Martinstr. 39* ☎ *0221/ 2212-2393* ⊕ *www.museenkoeln.de* ⊙ *Tues. 10–8, Wed.–Fri. 10–6, weekends 11–6.*

★ Opposite the Dom is the **Römisch-Germanisches Museum** (Roman-German Museum), built from 1970 to 1974 around the Dionysus mosaic that was unearthed during the construction of an air-raid shelter in 1941. The huge mosaic, more than 300 feet square, once covered the dining-room floor of a wealthy Roman trader's villa. ✉ *Roncallipl. 4* ☎ *0221/ 2212-4438* ⊕ *www.museenkoeln.de* ⊙ *Tues.–Sun. 10–5.*

Though rebuilt, the **Altes Rathaus** (Old Town Hall) is the oldest town hall in Germany, dating from the 14th century. There was a seat of local government here in Roman times, and directly below the building are the remains of the Roman city governor's headquarters, the Praetorium. Standing on pedestals at one end of the town hall are figures of prophets, made in the early 15th century. Along the south wall are the *Nine Good Heroes,* carved in 1360. Charlemagne and King Arthur are among them. Beneath a small glass pyramid by the south corner of the Rathaus is the **Mikwe,** a 12th-century ritual bath from the medieval Jewish quarter. ✉ *Alter Markt* ⊙ *Mon.–Thurs. 7:30–4:45, Fri. 7:30–2.*

Köln's colorful old section near the river, the **Martinsviertel** (✉ between Lintg. and Gürzenichstr.) is an attractive combination of reconstructed, high-gabled medieval buildings; winding alleys; and tastefully designed modern apartments and business quarters. Head here at night—the place comes alive at sunset. **Gross St. Martin** (Great St. Martin) is Martinsviertel's parish church. It's the most outstanding of Köln's 12 Romanesque churches. ✉ *An Gross St. Martin 9* ☎ *0221/257–7924* ⊙ *Mon.–Sat. 10–6, Sun. 2–4.*

At the edge of Martinsviertel, within a 12th-century cathedral, the **Museum Schnütgen** is a treasure-house of medieval art from the Rhine region. Don't miss the crucifix from St. George Church or the original stained-glass windows and carved figures from the Kölner Dom. Many of the exhibits—intricately carved ivory book covers, rock-crystal reliquaries, illuminated manuscripts—require intense concentration to be appreciated. ✉ *Cäcilienstr. 29* ☎ *0221/2212–3620* ⊕ *www.museenkoeln. de* ⊙ *Tues.–Fri. 10–5 (1st Wed. of month until 8), weekends 11–5.*

The exquisite, Romanesque **St. Gereon's** church stands on the site of an old Roman burial ground, six blocks west of the train station. An enormous dome rests on walls that were once clad in gold mosaics. Roman masonry still forms part of the structure, which is believed to have been built over the grave of its namesake, the 4th-century martyr and patron saint of Köln. ✉ *Gereonsdriesch 2–4* ☎ *0221/134–922* ⊙ *Mon.–Sat. 9–12:30 and 1:30–6, Sun. 1:30–6.*

★ **$$$$** ✕ **Capricorn i Aries.** At this hip, fine-dining room, the owners personally wait on the four tables. The heavenly French cuisine with a Rhineland twist garnered them the Gault Millau Restaurant of the Year award. Just opposite, a somewhat larger brasserie serves the staples in French rural cuisine. ✉ *Alteburger Str. 34* ☎ *0221/323–182* ⌂ *Reservations essential* ▭ *AE, DC, MC, V* ⊙ *No lunch. Closed Mon., Tues.*

$$$ ✕ **Bizim.** This is one of the best Turkish restaurants in Germany. Prepare yourself for scampi with tarragon sauce, eggplant-coated lamb fillets with a garlic yogurt sauce, or quail grilled on a rosemary spit and served in its own juices. The four-course lunch menu (€28) is highly recommended. ⊠ *Weideng. 47–49* ☎ *0221/131–581* ⌖ *Reservations essential* ▤ *AE, D, MC, V* ⊙ *Closed Sun. and Mon. No lunch Sat.*

$–$$$ ✕ **Fischers Weingenuss und Tafelfreuden.** If someone were to create a shrine to wine, it would look a lot like this restaurant. Run by one of Germany's star sommeliers, the restaurant offers some 800 wines, 40 of which can be bought by the glass. The kitchen experiments with regional cuisine, with influences from France, the Mediterranean, and even Southeast Asia. The dining experience is always elegant, and an expert staff will help you pick the perfect wine for each dish. Reservations are recommended. ⊠ *Hohenstaufenring 53* ☎ *0221/310–8470* ▤ *DC, MC, V* ⊙ *Closed Sun. No lunch Sat.*

$–$$ ✕ **Paeffgen.** There is no better *Brauhaus* in Köln in which to imbibe Kölsch, the city's home brew. You won't sit long in front of an empty glass before a blue-aproned waiter sweeps by and places a full one before you. With its worn wooden decor, colorful clientele, and typical German fare (sauerbraten, *Hämmchen*, and *Reibekuchen*), Paeffgen sums up tradition—especially when compared with the trendy nightspots that surround it. ⊠ *Friesenstr. 64–66* ☎ *0221/135–461* ▤ *No credit cards.*

★ $$$–$$$$ ✕▦ **Hotel im Wasserturm.** What used to be Europe's tallest water tower is now an 11-story luxury hotel-in-the-round. The neoclassic look of the brick exterior remains and few modern architects could create a more unusual setting. The ultramodern interior was the work of the French designer Andrée Putman. The 11th-floor restaurant ($$$$) has a stunning view and offers Continental haute cuisine. ⊠ *Kayg. 2 D–50676* ☎ *0221/20080* ⎙ *0221/200–8888* ⊕ *www.hotel-im-wasserturm.de* ⤳ *48 rooms, 40 suites* ⚒ *Restaurant, bar* ▤ *AE, DC, MC, V.*

$$ ✕▦ **Chelsea.** This designer hotel has a very strong following among artists and art dealers, as well as the musicians who come to play in the nearby Stadtgarten jazz club. Breakfast is served until noon for these late-risers. The best features of the rooms are the luxuriously large bathrooms and bathtubs. The restaurant-café ($) is great for informal gatherings and for people-watching. It's 20 minutes to the city center on foot, 10 by subway or tram. ⊠ *Jülicherstr. 1 D–50674* ☎ *0221/207–150* ⎙ *0221/239–137* ⊕ *www.hotel-chelsea.de* ⤳ *36 rooms, 2 suites, 1 apartment* ⚒ *Restaurant* ▤ *AE, DC, MC, V.*

$$ ✕▦ **Hopper Hotel et cetera.** The rooms in this chicly renovated monastery are spare but not spartan, although a startlingly realistic sculpture of a bishop, sitting in the reception area, serves as a constant reminder of the building's ecclesiastic origins. The rooms are decorated with modern works by Cologne artists. The courtyard Hopper Restaurant et cetera ($–$$) serves upscale Mediterranean cuisine and has garden seating. ⊠ *Brüsselerstr. 26 D–50674* ☎ *0221/924–400* ⎙ *0221/924–406* ⊕ *www.hopper.de* ⤳ *48 rooms, 1 suite* ⚒ *Restaurant* ▤ *AE, DC, MC, V.*

★ $–$$ ▦ **Das Kleine Stapelhäuschen.** One of the few houses along the riverbank that survived World War II bombings, this is among the oldest buildings in Köln. You can't beat the location, overlooking the river and right by Gross St. Martin; yet the rooms are reasonably priced, making up in age and quaintness for what they lack in luxury. ⊠ *Fischmarkt 1–3, D–50667* ☎ *0221/257–7862* ⎙ *0221/257–4232* ⊕ *www.koeln-altstadt. de/stapelhaeuschen* ⤳ *31 rooms* ⚒ *Restaurant* ▤ *AE, MC, V.*

Bonn

The staid city of Bonn, the postwar seat of the federal government until the capital returned to Berlin in 1999, has an unhurried pace in its old markets, pedestrian malls, parks, and handsome Südstadt residential area

The town center is a car-free zone; an inner-ring road circles it with parking garages on the perimeter. A convenient parking lot is just across from the railway station and within 50 yards of the tourist office.

German history since World War II is the subject of **Haus der Geschichte** (House of History). The museum displays an overwhelming amount of original artifacts and engages various types of media. It's not all heavy either—temporary exhibits have featured political cartoonists, Miss Germany pageants, and an in-depth examination of the song "Lili Marleen," sung by troops of every nation during World War II. Historical reconstructions of typical German backyards are behind the museum. Placards are in English as well. ⊠ *Adenauerallee 250* ☎ *0228/91650* ⊕ *www.hdg.de* ☉ *Tues.–Sun. 9–7.*

The **Kunstmuseum Bonn** (Art Museum) is renowned for its contemporary art collection. The two main focuses are on Rheinish Expressionists and German art since 1945 (Beuys, Baselitz, and Kiefer, for example). Changing exhibits are generally excellent. ⊠ *Friedrich-Ebert-Allee 2* ☎ *0228/776–260* ⊕ *www.bonn.de* ☉ *Tues. and Thurs.–Sun. 10–6, Wed. until 9.*

The town of Königswinter (12 km/7 mi northeast of Bonn) has one of the most-visited castle sites on the Rhine, **Drachenfels**. Its ruins crown the highest hill in the Siebengebirge (Seven Hills), which has many hiking trails. The castle was built in the 12th century by the archbishop of Köln.

$–$$$ ✕ **Gasthaus Sutorius.** Across from the church of St. Margaretha in Königswinter, this wine tavern serves refined variations on German cuisine with a nice selection of local wines. In summer, you can eat outdoors beneath the linden trees. ⊠ *Oelinghovener Str. 7 Königswinter* ☎ *02244/912–240* ⊟ *MC* ☉ *Closed Mon. No lunch Tues.–Sat.*

$ ✕ **Em Höttche.** Travelers and Bonn residents (Beethoven was a regular) have taken sustenance at this tavern since the late 14th century, and today it offers one of the best-value lunches in town. The interior is rustic; the food stout and hearty. Reservations are recommended. ⊠ *Markt 4* ☎ *0228/690–009* ⊟ *No credit cards.*

Koblenz

This city began as a Roman camp more than 2,000 years ago and flourished thanks to its strategic location at the sharp conflux of the Rhine and Mosel rivers known as the **Deutsches Eck** (German Corner). A huge equestrian statue of Kaiser Wilhelm I, the **Kaiser-Wilhelm-Denkmal**, marks the spot. The historical sights of the **Altstadt** (Old Town) stand side by side with boutiques, pubs, and cafés near the squares Am Plan and Florinsmarkt.

Within a lovely 16th-century building near the Mosel promenade, the artworks of the **Mittelrhein Museum** span millennia. The museum sells a combo ticket with the Museum Ludwig. ⊠ *Florinsmarkt 15* ☎ *0261/129–2520* ⊕ *www.mittelrhein-museum.de* ☉ *Tues.–Sat. 10:30–5, Sun. 11–6.*

The 13th-century Deutschherrenhaus near the Rhine promenade is home to the **Museum Ludwig** and its fine collection of modern art. ⊠ *Danziger Freiheit 1* ☎ *0261/304–040* ☉ *Tues.–Sat., 10:30–5, Sun. 11–6.*

A stone's throw from the Museum Ludwig is **St. Kastor Kirche** (St. Castor's Church), stunning for its combination of Romanesque and Gothic elements. It was here that Louis the Pious negotiated plans for the Treaty of Verdun in 842. ⊠ *Kastorhof* ☉ *Daily 9–6.*

Across the river from Koblenz, on the Rhine's east bank, towers the city's most spectacular castle, **Festung Ehrenbreitstein**. The fortifications of this vast structure date from the 1100s, although the bulk of it was built during the 16th and 17th centuries. To reach the fortress take the *Sesselbahn* (cable car, €6.90 with castle visit), ferry, or Bus 9 from the train station. For the best value, purchase the combination ticket that includes the grounds, museum, and a 45-minute tour. ☎ *0261/974–2444* ☉ *Castle: Mid-Mar.–mid-Nov., daily 9:30–5. Cable car: Apr., May, and Oct., daily 10–4:50; June–Aug., daily 9–5:50; Sept., daily 10–5:50.*

$–$$ ✕ **Café Einstein.** Portraits of Einstein line the walls of this lively café-restaurant-bar just off Görresplatz. The friendly Tayhus family serves tasty fare every day, from a hearty breakfast buffet (brunch on Sunday) to late-night finger food. Fish is a specialty in summer. On the Friday and Saturday nights when there's live music, the place is packed. ☒ *Firmungstr. 30* ☎ *0261/914–4999* ▤ *DC, MC, V.*

$–$$ ▦ **Contel Hotel An Der Mosel.** The Hundertwasser-inspired, art nouveau look of this hotel is unique. Behind the colorful facade are pleasant, modern rooms (some with waterbeds). You can dine on a terrace surrounded by artificial pools and eclectic "works of art." ☒ *Pastor-Klein-Str. 19, D-56073* ☎ *0261/40650* ☒ *0261/406–5188* ⊕ *www.contel-koblenz.de* ⟳ *185 rooms, 7 apartments* ⌂ *Restaurant, bar* ▤ *AE, DC, MC, V.*

Rhine Gorge

Between Koblenz and Rüdesheim, the Rhine flows through the 65-km (40-mi) Rhine Gorge. The Rhine lives up to its legends and lore here and flows past the greatest concentration of Rhine castles, which cling to the steep, terraced slopes. The river loops at Rüdesheim and passes by the world-renowned vineyards of the Rheingau en route to Mainz.

★ **Marksburg** castle, south of Koblenz, is on the east bank of the river, 500 feet above the town of Braubach. Built in the 12th century to protect silver and lead mines in the area, it is the only land-based castle in the entire Middle Rhine Valley never to have been destroyed. Within its massive walls are a collection of weapons and manuscripts, a medieval botanical garden, and a restaurant. ☎ *02627/206* ⊕ *www.deutsche-burgen.org* ☉ *Easter–Oct., daily 10–5; Nov.–Easter, daily 11–4* ☉ *Closed last wk in Dec. Restaurant closed mid-Dec.–mid-Feb.*

The Rhine makes its largest loop just before passing the quiet old town of **Boppard,** once a bustling city of the Holy Roman Empire. Now its Roman and medieval past come to life at the site of its 4th-century fort and in a museum within the 14th-century electors' castle. Notable churches include the **Karmeliterkirche** (Carmelite Church), with two baroque altars, and the Romanesque church of **St. Severus** (1236). From Boppard there is a wonderful view across the Rhine to the ruined castles of **Liebenstein** and **Sterrenberg**. Both impressive ruins have terrace cafés.

$$–$$$ ✕▦ **Best Western Hotel Bellevue.** This turn-of-the-20th-century building along the river has an elegant white-and-yellow facade. Afternoon tea, dinner, and Sunday lunch are accompanied by piano music in the main restaurant, Le Chopin ($$$–$$$$). The restaurant Le Bristol ($–$$) offers sumptuous luncheon buffets. ☒ *Rheinallee 41–42, D-56154 Boppard* ☎ *06742/1020* ☒ *06742/102–602* ⊕ *www.bellevue.boppard.de* ⟳ *92 rooms, 1 suite* ⌂ *2 restaurants, indoor pool, bar* ▤ *AE, DC, MC, V* ☉ *Le Chopin closed Mon.; no lunch Tues.–Sat.*

$ ✕▦ **Zum weissen Schwanen.** Guests have found a warm welcome in this half-timber inn and mill just south of the Marksburg castle since 1693. Next to a 13th-century town gateway, this is a thoroughly charming place to overnight or enjoy well-prepared regional specialties ($–$$$), contemporary German cuisine, and an excellent selection of local wines. Rooms are individually decorated with period furniture ranging from Biedermeier to belle epoque. ☒ *Brunnenstr. 4, D–56338 Braubach, 12 km (7½ mi) south of Koblenz via B–42* ☎ *02627/9820* 🖶 *02627/8802* ⊕ *www.zum-weissen-schwanen.de* 🛏 *19 rooms, 1 suite* ⌕ *Restaurant, bar* 🖃 *AE, DC, MC, V* ☉ *Restaurant closed Wed. No lunch Mon.–Sat.*

St. Goar

ⓒ South of Boppard, this little town is crowded against the steep gorge cliff and shadowed by the imposing ruin of **Burg Rheinfels** (Rhine Cliff Castle), built in the mid-13th century. A battle with the French destroyed it in 1797. Inside is an exquisite model of the complete fortress. ☒ *Off Schlossberg Str.* ☎ *06741/383* ☉ *Apr.–Oct., daily 9–6; Nov.–Mar., weekends (weather permitting) 10–4.*

Just across from the town of St. Goar is **St. Goarshausen** (an hourly ferry service runs between them), which lies at the foot of two 14th-century castles whose names, **Katz** (Cat) and **Maus** (Mouse), reflect one of the many power plays on the Rhine. Katz is not open to the public, but Maus has a terrace café and falconry demonstrations. ☎ *06771/7669* ⊕ *www. burg-maus.de* ☉ *Mid-Mar.–Sept., daily at 11 and 2:30. Sun. also at 4:30.*

The **Loreley rock** is only a couple of miles from St. Goarshausen; follow the road marked with LORELEY-FELSEN signs. Here the Rhine takes a sharp turn around a rocky, shrub-covered headland. This is the narrowest and shallowest part of the Middle Rhine, full of treacherous currents. According to legend the maiden Loreley sat on the rock here, combing her golden hair and singing a song so irresistible that passing sailors forgot the navigational hazards and were swept to their deaths.

ⓒ The 10-minute film and hands-on exhibits at the **Besucherzentrum Loreley** (Visitor Center) are entertaining ways to learn about the region's flora and fauna, geology, wine, shipping, and above all, the myth of the Loreley. You can sample wines at the Vinothek, stock up on souvenirs (and euros at the ATM), and snack at the bistro before heading for the nearby vantage point at the cliff's summit. Hiking trails are signposted. ☒ *Auf der Loreley* ☎ *06771/599–093* ⊕ *www.besucherzentrum-loreley.de* ☉ *Apr.–Oct., Tues.–Sun. 10–5.*

$$$ ✕🏨 **Schloss-Hotel & Villa Rheinfels.** Directly opposite Burg Rheinfels, this hotel offers modern comfort and expansive views from the terrace of Auf Scharfeneck ($$–$$$; try to book a window alcove—Nos. 51, 52, 61, or 62). The Burgschänke in the cellar serves simpler fare. The *Wispertal Forelle* (trout from the nearby Wisper Valley) is highly recommended. ☒ *Schlossberg 47, D–56329* ☎ *06741/8020* 🖶 *06741/ 802–802* ⊕ *www.schlosshotel-rheinfels.de* 🛏 *60 rooms, 4 suites* ⌕ *2 restaurants, indoor pool, bar* 🖃 *AE, DC, MC, V.*

$–$$$ ✕🏨 **Hotel Landsknecht.** The Nickenig family makes everyone feel at home in their riverside restaurant ($–$$) and hotel north of St. Goar. In the Vinothek, you can sample the family's delicious Bopparder Hamm wines. These go well with local dishes, such as Rhine-style sauerbraten or seasonal specialties, including asparagus and game. Rooms are individually furnished and quite comfortable; some offer a Rhine view (Nos. 4, 5, and 8 are especially nice). ☒ *Rhinugerstr. (B–9), D–56329 St. Goar-Fellen* ☎ *06741/2001* 🖶 *06741/7499* ⊕ *www.hotel-landsknecht. de* 🛏 *14 rooms* ⌕ *Restaurant* 🖃 *AE, DC, MC, V* ☉ *Closed mid-Dec.–Feb.*

Shopping

The two **Montag** shops (☒ *Heerstr. 128* ☎ *06741/2488* ☒ *Schlossberg 2* ☎ *06741/93093*) sell highly esteemed "made in Germany" collectibles:

144 different beer steins; elaborate pewter drinking vessels; superb German cutlery; and a zoo of Steiff stuffed animals and teddy bears (in the Schlossberg location). Videos, CDs and cassettes highlighting the region's landscape and folk music are also for sale. They issue tax-free documents and ship worldwide.

Oberwesel

Sixteen of the original 21 towers and much of Oberwesel's town wall still stand in the shadow of Schönburg Castle. The Town of Towers is also renowned for its Riesling wines, celebrated at two lively wine festivals, the *Weinmarkt,* in early and mid-September. The **Liebfrauenkirche** (Church of our Lady), popularly known as the Red Church because of its brightly colored exterior, has a superb rood screen, masterful sculptures, tombstones and paintings, and one of Germany's oldest altars (1331).

$ ✕ **Historische Weinwirtschaft.** Tables in the flower-laden garden in front of this stone house are at a premium in the summer, yet seats in the nooks and crannies indoors are just as inviting. Ask Iris Marx, the ebullient proprietor, to translate the menu (it's in local dialect) of regional dishes. She offers country cooking at its best. The wine list features 32 wines by the glass. ⊠ *Liebfrauenstr. 17* ☎ *06744/8186* ▭ *AE, MC, V* ☉ *Closed Tues. and Jan. No lunch Mon.–Sat. May–Sept.*

$$$$ ✕▢ **Burghotel Auf Schönburg.** Part of the 12th-century Schönburg Castle complex has been lovingly restored as a romantic hotel and restaurant ($$–$$$$; closed Monday). Antique furnishings and historical rooms (library, chapel, prison tower) make for an unforgettable stay, enhanced by the extraordinarily friendly, personal service of your hosts, the Hüttls, and staff. If you have only a night or two in the area, go for this hotel's first-rate lodging, food, and wine. Luggage transfer from the parking lot below the entrance is easily arranged at the front desk. ⊠ *D–55430* ☎ *06744/93930* ▦ *06744/1613* ⊕ *www.hotel-schoenburg. com* ⤶ *20 rooms, 2 suites* ⚐ *Restaurant* ▭ *MC, V* ☉ *Hotel and restaurant closed Jan.–Mar.*

Kaub

Opposite this medieval village, south of the Lorelei on the east side of the river, is one of the most-photographed sites of the Middle Rhine region. Like a small sailing ship bristling with sharp-pointed towers, the **Pfalzgrafenstein** castle sits on a tiny island in the middle of the Rhine. Never destroyed, the Pfalz provides a good look at sparse medieval living quarters. A boat from Kaub goes to the island. ☎ *0172/262–2800* ⊕ *www.burgen-rlp.de* ☉ *Apr.–Sept., Tues.–Sun. 9–1 and 2–6; Oct.–Mar., Tues.–Sun. 9–1 and 2–5.*

$ ✕▢ **Zum Turm.** Next to a medieval *Turm* (tower) near the Rhine, this little inn offers spacious, modern guest rooms on the floors above its cozy restaurant (dinner only; closed Tuesday) and terrace. Fish, game, and produce come from either local farms or from the market halls of Paris. The daily set menus (three–six courses) are always excellent options. ⊠ *Zollstr. 50, D–56349* ☎ *06774/92200* ▦ *06774/922–011* ⊕ *www.rhein-hotel-turm.com* ⤶ *6 rooms* ⚐ *Restaurant* ▭ *DC, MC, V* ☉ *Hotel and restaurant closed 1 wk in Jan., 1 wk in Aug., and 2 wks in Nov. Restaurant closed Tues.; weekday lunch on request only Nov.–Mar.*

Bacharach

This well-preserved medieval village, complete with remains of its 14th-century walls, has been one of the Middle Rhine's most picturesque wine towns for centuries. The parish church of **St. Peter** is a good example of the transition from Romanesque to Gothic styles. From St. Peter a set of stone steps (signposted) leads to Bacharach's landmark, the sandstone ruins of the Gothic **Werner Kapelle,** highly admired for its filigree tracery. Originally a Staufen fortress (11th century), the castle lay dormant until 1925, when a youth hostel was built on the foundations. The sweeping views it affords are worth the 10-minute walk.

$–$$$ ✕ **Weinhaus Altes Haus.** Charming inside and out, this medieval half-timber house is a favorite setting for films and photos. The cheerful proprietor, Reni Weber, uses the freshest ingredients possible and buys her meat and game from local butchers and hunters. *Rieslingrahmsuppe* (Riesling cream soup), *Reibekuchen* (potato pancakes), and the hearty *Hunsrücker Tellerfleisch* (boiled beef with horseradish sauce) are favorites. She offers a good selection of wines from the family's vineyards. ⊠ *Oberstr. 61* ☏ *06743/1209* 🖃 *AE, MC, V* ⊗ *Closed Wed. and mid-Dec.–Easter.*

$ ✕ **Gutsausschank Zum Grünen Baum.** Winegrower Fritz Bastian runs this cozy tavern in a half-timber house from 1579. He is the sole owner of the vineyard Insel Heyles'en Werth, on the island opposite Bacharach. The "wine carousel" is a great way to sample a full range of flavors and styles (15 wines) under the tutelage of the congenial host. Snacks are served (from 1 PM), including homemade, air-dried *Schinken* (ham), sausages, and cheese. ⊠ *Oberstr. 63* ☏ *06743/1208* 🖃 *AE, DC, V* ⊗ *Closed Thurs. and Feb.*

Rüdesheim

Tourism and wine are the heart and soul of Rüdesheim, and best epitomized by the **Drosselgasse** (Thrush Alley). The narrow, pub-lined lane is abuzz with merrymaking from noon to well past midnight every day from Easter through October. Rüdesheim is a gateway to the Rhine Gorge region so be sure to secure lodging well in advance.

High above Rüdesheim and visible for miles stands *Germania,* a colossal female statue crowning the **Niederwald-Denkmal** (Niederwald Monument). It commemorates the rebirth of the German Empire after the Franco-Prussian War (1870–71). You can reach the monument on foot, by car (via Grabenstrasse), or by *Seilbahn* (cable car). There is also a *Sessellift* (chairlift) to and from Assmannshausen, a red wine enclave, on the west side of the hill. ⊠ *Oberstr. 37* ☏ *06722/2402* ⊕ *www.seilbahn-ruedesheim.de* ⊗ *Mid-Mar.–May and Oct., daily 9:30–4; June–Sept., daily 9:30–6:30.*

$–$$ ✕ **Rüdesheimer Schloss.** In a former tithe house built in 1729, this wine tavern specializes in Hessian cuisine and Rheingauer Riesling and Spätburgunder wines from the Breuer family's estate and other nearby wineries. The selection of older vintages is remarkable. Start with the delectable *Sauerkrautsuppe* (sauerkraut soup). Benedictine-style *Schloss Ente* (duck with dates and figs), *Ochsenbrust* (boiled breast of beef), and *Woihinkel* (chicken in Riesling sauce) are all excellent. ⊠ *Drosselg.* ☏ *06722/90500* 🖃 *AE, DC, MC, V* ⊗ *Closed Jan. and Feb., except on request.*

$$$ ✕🏨 **Hotel Krone Assmannshausen.** This elegant, antiques-filled hotel and restaurant ($$$$) in Assmannshausen offers first-class service. Classic cuisine prepared by chef Willi Mittler and wines from the family's own vineyards, as well as an overall superb collection of wines, make for very memorable meals indoors or on the terrace overlooking the Rhine. Two suites each have their own sauna. ⊠ *Rheinuferstr. 10, D–65385 Rüdesheim-Assmannshausen* ☏ *06722/4030* 🖷 *06722/3049* ⊕ *www.hotel-krone.com* ➳ *52 rooms, 13 suites* ⌂ *Restaurant* 🖃 *AE, DC, MC, V.*

★ $$ 🏨 **Breuer's Rüdesheimer Schloss.** Hosts Susanne and Heinrich Breuer have beautifully integrated modern designer decor into the historic walls of this stylish hotel. The Constantinescu Suite (No. 20) and the Rhine Suite (No. 14), with its large terrace, are especially popular; most rooms offer a vineyard view. Cellar or vineyard tours and wine tastings can be arranged. ✉ *Steing. 10, D-65385* ☎ *06722/90500* 🖷 *06722/ 47960* ⊕ *www.ruedesheimer-schloss.com* ⌖ *23 rooms, 3 suites* ⌂ *Restaurant, bar* ▤ *AE, DC, MC, V* ☾ *Closed Dec. 25–early Jan.*

Eltville

Eltville is the geographic heart of the Rheingau, 14 km (9 mi) west of Wiesbaden and 16 km (10 mi) north of Mainz. Its half-timber buildings crowd narrow streets that date from Roman times. Today the town is well known for the production of *Sekt,* sparkling German wine (champagne by any other name, though the French ensured it could not legally be called that by including a stipulation in the Treaty of Versailles in 1919). About 6 km (4 mi) from Eltville, via the village of Kiedrich, lies

★ **Kloster Eberbach** (Eberbach Abbey) in a secluded valley. The former Cistercian monastery has Romanesque and Gothic buildings that look untouched by time. Its viticultural tradition spans nearly nine centuries. You can sample wines year-round in the wine shop or restaurants on the grounds. *Stiftung Kloster Eberbach, northwest of Eltville via Kiedrich* ✉ *Postfach 1453, D–65334 Eltville* ☎ *06723/91780* ⊕ *www. klostereberbach.de* 🖭 *€3* ☾ *Easter–Oct., daily 10–6; Nov.–Easter, daily 11–4.*

The Rhine Essentials

AIRPORTS & TRANSFERS

The Rhineland is served by three international airports: Frankfurt, Düsseldorf, and Köln-Bonn. Bus and rail lines connect each airport with its respective downtown area and provide rapid access to the rest of the region.

🖪 **Flughafen Köln/Bonn (CGN)** ☎ 02203/404–00102 ⊕ www.airport-cgn.de.

BOAT & FERRY TRAVEL

Köln-Düsseldorfer Deutsche Rheinschiffahrt (KD Rhine Line) has daily cruises between Köln and Mainz from Easter through October and offers many discounts. Wednesday is family day, when children travel free with a full-fare paying adult. Those 60 and over travel for half price on Monday and Friday. On Tuesdays, two cyclists can travel for the price of one adult ticket (bike transport free). Travelers with valid rail tickets get reduced fares. Students up to 27 years old with a valid school ID get 50% off. Lastly, you can travel free on your birthday. Many smaller, family-operated boat companies offer trips as well.

From Koblenz, Personenschiffahrt Merkelbach makes round-trip castle cruises to Schloss Stolzenfels (one hour) or the Marksburg (two hours), passing by six castles en route. The Hebel-Line has Loreley Valley trips from Boppard.

🖪 **Hebel-Line** ☎ 06742/2420. **KD Rhine Line** ☎ 0221/208–8318; 800/346–6525 in the U.S. ⊕ www.k-d.com. **Personenschiffahrt Merkelbach** ☎ 0261/76810.

CAR TRAVEL

Frankfurt is 126 km (78 mi) from Koblenz, 175 km (109 mi) from Bonn, and 190 km (118 mi) from Köln (the A–3 links Frankfurt with Köln and passes near Koblenz and Bonn). The most spectacular stretch of the Rhineland is between Mainz and Koblenz, which takes in the Rhine Gorge. Highways hug the river on each bank (B–42 on the northeastern side, and B–9 on the southwestern side), and car ferries crisscross the Rhine at many points.

TRAIN TRAVEL

InterCity and EuroCity expresses connect all the cities and towns of the area. Hourly InterCity routes run between Düsseldorf, Köln, Bonn, and Mainz, with most services extending as far south as Munich and as far north as Hamburg. The Mainz–Bonn route runs beside the Rhine, providing spectacular views all the way. The city transportation networks of Bonn, Köln, and Düsseldorf are linked by the S-bahn.

VISITOR INFORMATION

The Rhineland regional tourist office, Rheinland-Pfalz-Information, provides general information on the region. The (partially) bilingual events calendar, *Veranstaltungskalender Rheinland-Pfalz Feste*, gives a comprehensive overview of wine, regional, and folk festivals, as well as cultural events. The German Wine Information Bureau has brochures on area vineyards and harvest festivals.

The Mittelrhein Burgen-Ticket, sold at 10 participating castles in the Mittelrhein area between Rüdesheim and Koblenz, offers a tremendous savings on admission fees. The cost is €14 for adults and allows free admission to the castles.

🖪**Bacharach** ✉ Tourist-Information; Oberstr. 45, D–55422 ☎ 06743/919–303 🖷 06743/ 919–304 ⊕ www.rhein-nahe-touristik.de. **Bonn** ✉ Bonn Information; Windeckstr. 2 am Münsterpl., D–53111 ☎ 0228/775–000 🖷 0228/775–077 ⊕ www.bonn.de. **Boppard** ✉ Tourist-Information; Marktpl., D–56154 ☎ 06742/3888 🖷 06742/81402 ⊕ www. boppard.de. **German Wine Information Bureau** ✉ 245 Park Ave., 39th floor, New York, NY 10167 ☎ 212/792–4134 🖷 212/792–4001 ⊕ www.germanwineusa.org. **Koblenz** ✉ Tourist-Information; Bahnhofpl. 17, D–56068 ☎ 0261/31304 🖷 0261/100–4388 ⊕ www.koblenz.de. **Köln** ✉ KölnTourismus Office; Unter Fettenhenen 19, D–50667 ☎ 0221/2213–0400 🖷 0221/2212–3311 ⊕ www.koeln.de. **Mittelrhein Burgen-Ticket** ⊕ www.burgen-am-rhein.de. **Rheinland-PfalzTourismus** ✉ Löhrstr. 103–105, D–56068 Koblenz ☎ 0261/915–200 🖷 0261/915–2040 ⊕ www.rlp-info.de. **Rüdesheim** ✉ Tourist Information; Geisenheimer Str. 22, D–65385 ☎ 06722/19433 🖷 06722/3485 ⊕ www. ruedesheim.de.

HAMBURG

Water—in the form of the Alster Lakes and the Elbe River—is Hamburg's defining feature. The city-state's official title, the Free and Hanseatic City of Hamburg, reflects its kingpin status in the medieval Hanseatic League, a union that dominated trade on the North and the Baltic seas. The city is still a major port, with 33 docks and 500 berths for oceangoing vessels. The seafaring life has created the city's most distinct attractions, including the red-light district.

Exploring Hamburg

Numbers in the margin correspond to points of interest on the Hamburg map.

Within the remaining traces of its old city walls, downtown Hamburg combines the seamiest, steamiest streets of dockland Europe with sleek avenues of shops. The city is easy to explore on foot.

⑫ Alter Botanischer Garten (Old Botanical Gardens). This green and open park in Wallringpark specializes in rare and exotic plants. Tropical and subtropical species grow under glass in hothouses, and specialty gardens—including herbal and medicinal—cluster around an old moat. ✉ *Stephanspl.* ☉ *Daily 8–6.*

★ **❼ Erotic Art Museum.** Sexually provocative art from 1520 to the present is showcased here with great taste and decorum. Photography exhibits take

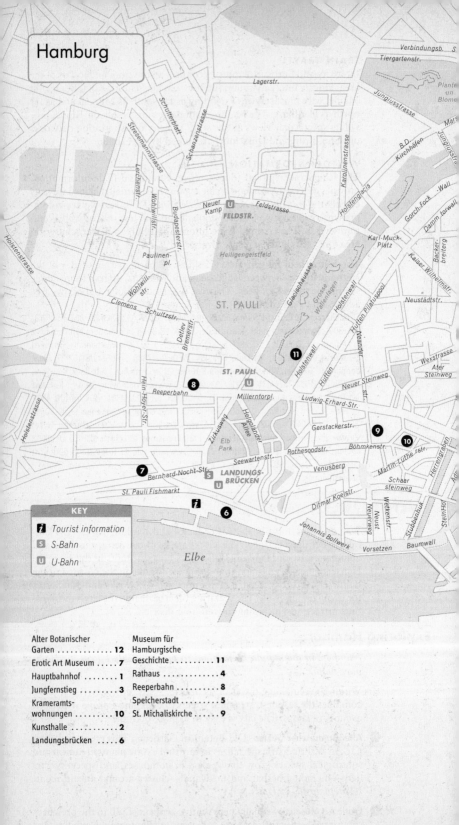

Hamburg

KEY

- **i** Tourist information
- **S** S-Bahn
- **U** U-Bahn

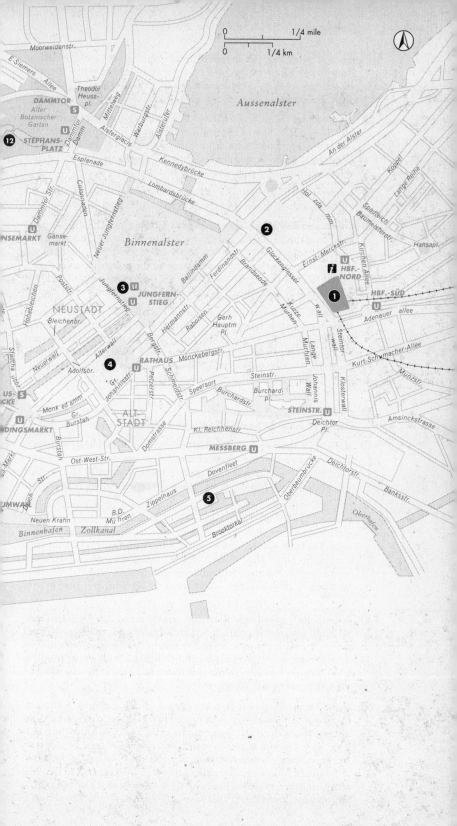

place in a building on Bernhard-Nocht-Strasse. ✉ *Nobistor 10a at Reeperbahn* ✉ *Bernhard-Nocht-Str. 69* ☎ *040/3178–4126* ⊕ *www. eroticartmuseum.de* ☞ *Minimum age 16* ☉ *Sun.–Thurs. 10 AM–midnight, Fri. and Sat. 10 AM–2 AM* Ⓜ *St. Pauli.*

❶ Hauptbahnhof (Main Train Station). The cast-iron-and-glass station is a breathtaking example of imperial German pride. It was opened in 1906 and is the largest structure of its kind in Europe. The enormous 394-foot-long structure is accentuated by a 460-foot-wide glazed roof that is supported only by pillars at each end. ✉ *Steintorpl.*

❸ Jungfernstieg. Classy jewelers and chic clothing boutiques line this wide promenade looking out over the Alster Lakes.

❿ Krameramtswohnungen (Shopkeepers' Guild Houses). The shopkeepers' guild built this tightly packed group of courtyard houses between 1620 and 1626 for members' widows. The house marked "C" is open to the public. Tour buses stop here, and some of the houses have been converted to shops. ✉ *Historic House "C," Krayenkamp 10* ☎ *040/ 3750–1988* ☉ *Tues.–Sun. 10–5.*

★ **❷ Kunsthalle** (Art Gallery). This prestigious exhibition hall's paintings include works by practically all the great northern European masters from the 14th through the 20th century. The postmodern cube-shaped building contains a modern art collection, with works by Andy Warhol, Joseph Beuys, Georg Baselitz, and David Hockney. ✉ *Glockengiesserwall* ☎ *040/4285–45765* ⊕ *www.hamburger-kunsthalle.de* ☉ *Tues., Wed., and Fri.–Sun. 10–6, Thurs. 10–9.*

❻ Landungsbrücken (Landing Bridges). Harbor cruises depart from these main terminals. ✉ *Near St. Pauli and Hafenstr.*

⓫ Museum für Hamburgische Geschichte (Museum of Hamburg History). The museum's vast collection of artifacts charts the history of Hamburg from its origins in the 9th century to the present. ✉ *Holstenwall 24* ☎ *040/4284–12380,* ⊕ *www.hamburgmuseum.de* ☉ *Tues.–Sat. 10–5, Sun. 10–6.*

★ **❹ Rathaus** (Town Hall). This pompous neo-Gothic building has 647 rooms, 6 more than Buckingham Palace. Only the state rooms are open to visitors. The large square, with its surrounding arcades, was laid out after Hamburg's Great Fire of 1842. The architects drew on St. Mark's in Venice for inspiration. ✉ *Rathausmarkt* ☎ *040/428–310* ⊕ *www. hamburg.de* ☉ *Tours Mon.–Thurs., hourly 10–3:15, Fri.–Sun., hourly 10:15–1:15.*

❽ Reeperbahn. The red-light Reeperbahn is the major thoroughfare of the St. Pauli district. It offers a broad menu of entertainment besides striptease and sex shows. Beyond this strip, St. Pauli is dominated by its riverfront, which gives it a maritime, though run-down, appeal. It is *not* advisable, however, to travel through this part of the city alone in the wee hours of the morning.

❺ Speicherstadt (Warehouse District). These harbor warehouses, with a rich overlay of gables and turrets, store and process every conceivable commodity, from coffee and spices to raw silks. You can't enter the buildings, but the nonstop activity will give you a good sense of a port at work. At **Spicy's Gewürzmuseum,** you can smell, touch and feel close to 50 spices. More than 700 objects chronicle five centuries of the once prospering spice trade in Hamburg. ✉ *Am Sandtorkai 32* ☎ *040/367–989* ⊕ *www.spicys.de* ☉ *Tues.–Sun. 10–5.*

★ ❾ **St. Michaeliskirche** (St. Michael's Church). The finest baroque church in northern Germany, St. Michael's has a distinctive 433-foot brick-and-iron tower bearing the largest tower clock in Germany, 26 feet in diameter. Just above the clock is the viewing platform, which affords a magnificent panorama. ⊠ *St. Michaeliskirche* ☏ *040/376–780* ⊕ *www. st-michaelis.de* ⊙ *Apr.–Sept., Mon.–Sat. 9–6, Sun. 12:30–6; Oct.–Mar., Mon.–Sat. 10–5, Sun. 11–5; multimedia screening Thurs. and weekends on the ½ hr, 12:30–3:30.*

Where to Eat

A flotilla of boats brings a wide variety of fish to Hamburg's harbor. One of the most celebrated of the robust local specialties is *Aalsuppe* (eel soup), a tangy concoction resembling bouillabaisse. *Räucheraal* (smoked eel) is also worth sampling. The sailors' favorite is *Labskaus,* a stew made from pickled meat, potatoes, and sometimes herring; it is usually garnished with a fried egg, sour pickles, and beets.

★ **$$$–$$$$** ✕ **Le Canard.** One of Hamburg's top restaurants, Le Canard enjoys a much-coveted location overlooking the harbor and historic vessels at Övelgönne, with enviably elegant decor and cuisine to match. Fish dishes such as panfried turbot predominate, but the roasted duck with red cabbage, traditionally served during the pre-Christmas season, is worth sampling. ⊠ *Elbchaussee 139* ☏ *040/880–5057* ⌂ *Reservations essential* ▭ *AE, DC, MC, V* ⊙ *Closed Sun.*

$$–$$$$ ✕ **Rive.** Fresh seafood, including oysters and clams, is served right at the harbor in a building representing a ship. The crowd consists mostly of media people enjoying the spectacular views. ⊠ *Van der Smissen Str. 1, Kreuzfahrt-Center* ☏ *040/3805–919* ⌂ *Reservations essential* ▭ *AE.*

$–$$$ ✕ **Fischerhaus.** Hamburg's fish market is right outside the door of this traditional old restaurant, which accounts for the variety and quality of seafood dishes on its menu. Meat eaters are also catered to, and the soups (especially fish) are legendary. It's always busy, so be sure to reserve a table and arrive on time. ⊠ *St. Pauli Fischmarkt 14* ☏ *040/314– 053* ▭ *MC, V.*

★ **$–$$$** ✕ **Weite Welt.** In an old fish smokehouse, owner Nikolaus Bornhofen's hospitality will make you feel right at home. His food, mostly fresh fish, crosses the continents (Asia and Europe). The menu is inventive and changes daily, and the theme dishes are good value. Reservations are essential on weekends. ⊠ *Grosse Freiheit 70* ☏ *040/3191–214* ▭ *No credit cards* ⊙ *No lunch.*

★ **$$** ✕ **Cox.** With its unique red leather banquettes, the reliably stylish Cox continues to attract an artsy crowd. The dishes, mostly German nouvelle cuisine, are known for the careful use of fresh produce and spices from around the globe. ⊠ *Greifswalder Str. 43* ☏ *040/249–422* ▭ *AE* ⊙ *No lunch Sun. and Mon.*

$–$$ ✕ **Eisenstein.** The daily menus or the Italian-Mediterranean dishes here are always a sure bet. The Pizza Helsinki (made with fresh tomatoes, sour cream, onions, and fresh cured salmon) is truly delicious. The crowd is upbeat and stylish, and the setting, a 19th-century industrial complex with redbrick walls, is very rustic. ⊠ *Friedensallee 9* ☏ *040/ 3904–606* ⌂ *Reservations essential* ▭ *No credit cards.*

$–$$ ✕ **Phuket.** Though it has an unimaginative name and dull facade, Phuket is by far the best Thai, or Asian for that matter, in town. The place is often jammed with Hamburgers from all districts who come to sample the hot fish dishes or the famous chicken in red wine sauce. ⊠ *Adolph-Schönfelder-Str. 33–35* ☏ *040/2982–3380* ▭ *AE, V.*

Where to Stay

Hotels are often full, and rates are high, although special weekend reductions are common.

★ **$$$** ⊡ **Side.** Premier Milanese designer Mattheo Thun was the driving force behind this architecturally sophisticated, five-star resort in the heart of the city. Whether soothed by the eggshell-white accents in your room and secluded club atmosphere in the spa, or wowed by the lobby's soaring and stark atrium or the eighth-floor lounge, you won't want to leave. ⊠ *Drehbahn 49 D–20304* ☎ *040/309–990* 🖷 *040/3099–9399* ⊕ *www.side-hamburg.de* ⤳ *158 rooms, 10 suites* ⚬ *Restaurant, bar* ▤ *AE, DC, MC, V.*

★ **$$–$$$** ⊡ **Gastwerk Hotel Hamburg.** This century-old, redbrick gas plant is the most stylish accommodation in town. Every detail has been carefully designed to please the eye. The chic furnishings mostly reflect the rooms' industrial design, but are warmed up by the use of natural materials, various woods (beech, pine), and thick carpets. The loft rooms are the best. ⊠ *Beim alten Gaswerk 3/Daimlerstr. 67 D–22761* ☎ *040/890–620* 🖷 *040/890–6220* ⊕ *www.gastwerk-hotel.de* ⤳ *122 rooms, 13 suites* ⚬ *Restaurant, bar* ▤ *AE, DC, MC, V.*

$$ ⊡ **Hotel Hafen Hamburg and Hotel Residenz Hafen Hamburg.** In a complex just across the famous St. Pauli Landungbrücken, both hotels are good value. The older Hotel Hafen Hamburg, with its smaller but nicely renovated rooms, offers a great view of the harbor, whereas the ultramodern Hotel Residenz Hafen annex has more comfort. ⊠ *Seewartenstr. 7–9 D–20459* ☎ *040/3111–3600* 🖷 *040/3111–3751* ⊕ *www.hotel-hamburg.de* ⤳ *Hotel Hafen: 230 rooms; Hotel Residenz: 125 rooms* ⚬ *Restaurant, 3 bars* ▤ *AE, DC, MC, V.*

$$ ⊡ **Hotel Village.** Red-and-black carpets and glossy wallpaper in the rooms are a nod to the hotel's past as a brothel. The service (including a 24-hour coffee bar) is extremely friendly and casual. The hotel has gained a reputation as an "in" place where celebrities can keep a low profile. ⊠ *Steindamm 4 D–20099* ☎ *040/246–137* 🖷 *040/486–4949* ⊕ *www.hotel-village.de* ⤳ *20 rooms* ▤ *AE, MC, V.*

$$ ⊡ **Kronprinz.** For its down-market location (on a busy street opposite the train station) and its moderate price, the Kronprinz is a surprisingly attractive hotel. Rooms are individually styled, modern but homey; ask for No. 45, with its mahogany and red-plush decor. ⊠ *Kirchenallee 46 D–20099* ☎ *040/243–258* 🖷 *040/280–1097* ⤳ *73 rooms* ⚬ *Restaurant* ▤ *AE, DC, MC, V.*

★ **$–$$** ⊡ **Yoho.** Centrally located between the hip Schanzenviertel and the downtown area, the new Yoho is the budget youth hostel of the 21st century. Housed in a historic, imposing villa with contemporary interior design, it offers simple yet elegant rooms with modern amenities (Internet, cable TV, phone, desk) otherwise not found in a hostel. The service is both casual and flawless, and the hotel restaurant serves a Euro-Asian breakfast. Guests under 26 receive a special rate of €57 for a single or €67 for a double room. This is the perfect place for international backpackers with an edge. ⊠ *Moorkamp 5 D–20357* ☎ *040/284–1910* 🖷 *040/2841–9141* ⊕ *www.yoho-hamburg.de* ⤳ *30 rooms* ⚬ *Restaurant* ▤ *AE, MC, V.*

★ **$** ⊡ **Hotel Terminus Garni.** This simple hotel near the central train station is popular among British and American budget travelers who appreciate its relaxed atmosphere and reliable service (the hotel is part of the Garni hotel chain). Double rooms share either a bath or shower. ⊠ *Steindamm 5 D–20999* ☎ *040/280–3144* 🖷 *040/241–518* ⊕ *www.hotel-*

terminus-hamburg.de ⤴ *20 rooms, some with shared bath, 1 apartment* ▤ *AE, DC, MC, V.*

Nightlife & the Arts

The Arts

Schmidt Theater (✉ Spielbudenpl. 24, 27–28 ☎ 040/3177–8899 or 040/3005–1400) and its sister, Schmidts Tivoli, have become Germany's most popular variety theaters. The classy repertoire of live music, vaudeville, chansons, and cabaret is hilarious and worth the cost.

The **Hamburgische Staatsoper** (✉ Grosse Theaterstr. 35 ☎ 040/356–868) is the leading northern German venue for opera and ballet. The Hamburg Ballet is directed by American John Neumeier. Both the Hamburg Philharmonic and the Hamburg Symphony Orchestra appear at the **Musikhalle** (✉ Johannes-Brahms-Pl. ☎ 040/346–920).

Nightlife

From about 10 PM on, the Reeperbahn springs to life, and *everything* is for sale. Among the Reeperbahn's even rougher side streets, the most notorious is the Grosse Freiheit, which means Great Freedom. The area is not just a red-light district, however. Side streets have a mixture of yuppie bars, restaurants, and theaters that are somewhat more refined than the seamen's bars and sex shops. Hans-Albers-Platz is a center of this revival. A real nightlife institution still going strong is the fashionable but cozy **Bar Hamburg** (✉ Rautenbergstr. 6–8 ☎ 040/2805–4880). The **Bereuther** (✉ Klosterallee 100 ☎ 040/4140–6789) is a sleek bar and club. **Docks** (✉ Spielbudenpl. 19 ☎ 040/317–8830) has a stylish bar and is Hamburg's largest venue for live music.

Hamburg Essentials

AIRPORTS & TRANSFERS

Fuhlsbüttel, Hamburg's international airport, is 11 km (7 mi) northwest of the city. The Airport-City-Bus runs nonstop to Hamburg's main train station at 30-minute intervals. Tickets are €4.60. The Airport-Express (Bus 110) runs every 10 minutes between the airport and the Ohlsdorf U- and S-bahn stations, a 15-minute ride from the main train station.
🛫 **Fuhlsbüttel** ☎ 040/50750 ⊕ www.ham.airport.de.

BUS TRAVEL TO & FROM HAMBURG

Hamburg's bus station, the Zentral-Omnibus-Bahnhof, is right behind the Hauptbahnhof (main train station).
🚌 **Zentral-Omnibus-Bahnhof (ZOB)** ✉ Adenauerallee 78 ☎ 040/247–575.

CAR TRAVEL

Hamburg is easier to handle by car than many other German cities. Incoming autobahns connect with Hamburg's three beltways, which take you smoothly to the downtown area. Follow the signs for STADTZENTRUM (downtown).
🚗 Car Rentals **Avis** ✉ Airport ☎ 040/5075–2314 ✉ Drehbahn 15–25 ☎ 040/341–651. **Hertz** ✉ Airport ☎ 040/5935–1367 ✉ Kirchenallee 34–36, opposite the Hauptbahnhof ☎ 040/280–1201. **Sixt** ✉ Airport ☎ 040/593–9480 ✉ Hauptbahnhof-Wandelhalle ☎ 040/322–419.

CONSULATES

🏛 Ireland ✉ Feldbrunnenstr. 43 ☎ 040/4418–6213.
🏛 New Zealand ✉ Domstr. 19 ☎ 040/442–5550.
🏛 United Kingdom ✉ Harvestehuder Weg 8a ☎ 040/448–0320.
🏛 United States ✉ Alsterufer 27 ☎ 040/4117–1100.

EMERGENCIES

🔂 Doctors & Dentists **Doctor** ☎ 069/19292. **Dentist** ☎ 040/11500.

🔂 Emergency Services **Ambulance and Fire Department** ☎ 112. **Medical Emergencies** ☎ 040/228-022. **Police** ☎ 110.

ENGLISH-LANGUAGE MEDIA

🔂 Bookstores **Frensche International** ✉ Spitalerstr. 26c ☎ 040/327-585.

TAXIS

Taxi meters start at €2, and the fare is €1.30–€1.50 per km or ½ mi. You can hail taxis on the street or at stands, or order one by phone.
🔂 ☎ 040/441-011, 040/686-868, or 040/666-666.

TOURS

BUS TOURS   Bus tours of the city, with a guide who rapidly describes sights in both German and English, leave from Kirchenallee (in front of the Hauptbahnhof) at regular intervals. A bus tour lasting 1½ hours sets off daily and costs €12. For €19, one of the bus tours can be combined with two one-hour boat trips on the Alster Lake and the Elbe River.
🔂 Fees & Schedules **AG Hamburg Rundfahrt** ☎ 040/641-3731.

BOAT TOURS   HADAG tours of the harbor leave every half hour in summer, less frequently during the winter, from Landungsbrücken (Piers) 1, 2, 3, and 7. The one-hour tour costs €8.50–€9. An English-language tour leaves from Pier 1 March–November, daily at noon. Warm-buffet dinner cruises (€45), including unlimited beer, depart late April to December, Saturday at 8 PM, from between Piers 6 and 9. Other watery options include renting rowboats on the Stadtpark Lake and surrounding canals. From April through October, Alster Touristik operates boat trips around the Alster Lakes and through the canals. Tours leave three times a day from the Jungfernstieg promenade in the city center. The Aussenalster 50-minute lake tour (Alster-Rundfahrt) costs €9. From May through September there's also the romantic twilight tour, called Dämmertour, every evening (September, Wednesday–Saturday at 8, €14).
🔂 Fees & Schedules **Alster Touristik** ☎ 040/357-4240. **Bordparty-Service** ✉ Landungsbrücken, Pier 9 ☎ 040/313-687. **HADAG** ☎ 040/311-7070; 040/313-130; 040/313-959; 040/3178-2231 for English-language tour.

TRAIN TRAVEL

Hamburg is a terminus for main-line service to northern Germany. All trains to German and international destinations stop at the Hauptbahnhof and regional trains also stop at Hamburg-Altona.
🔂 **Hamburg-Altona** ✉ Scheel-Plessen-Str. 17 ☎ 040/19419. **Hauptbahnhof** ✉ Steintorpl. ☎ 0180/599-6633.

TRANSPORTATION AROUND HAMBURG

The HVV, Hamburg's public transportation system, includes the U-bahn (subway), the S-bahn (suburban train), and buses. A one-way fare starts at €1.45; €2.30 covers one unlimited ride in the Hamburg city area. Tickets are available on all buses and at automated machines in all stations and at most bus stops. A *Ganztageskarte* (all-day ticket) costs €5.25. A *9 Uhr-Tageskarte* for just €4.25 is valid between 9 AM and 1 AM. If you're traveling with family or friends, a *Gruppen-* or *Familienkarte* (group or family ticket) is a good value—a group of up to five can travel for the entire day for only €7.40–€17.70 (depending on the number of fare zones the ticket covers).

Available from all Hamburg tourist offices, the Hamburg card allows free admission to state museums plus unlimited travel for 24 hours (beginning at 6 PM through 6 PM the following day) and costs €6.80 for one adult and up to three children under the age of 12. Other card combinations are available as well.

🛈 **Hamburg Passenger Transport Board (HVV)** ✉ Steinstr. 7 ☎ 040/19449 ⊕ www.hvv.de.

TRAVEL AGENCIES
🛈 **Reiseland American Express** ✉ Ballindamm 39 ☎ 040/309-080.

VISITOR INFORMATION
🛈 **Hamburg Tourist Office** ✉ Hauptbahnhof ☎ 040/3005-1200 ⊕ www.hamburg-tourism.de ✉ St. Pauli Landungsbrücken ☎ 040/3005-1200 or 040/3005-1203 ✉ Steinstr. 7 D-20015 ☎ 040/3005-1144.

BERLIN

Berlin is a city of striking modern architecture, masterworks of art and antiquity, provocative performances, raffish bars, sleek stores, canal-side cafés, and above all, history. A royal residence during the 15th century, Berlin came into its own under the rule of King Friedrich II (1712–86)—Frederick the Great—whose liberal reforms and artistic patronage led the city's development into a major cultural capital. In the 20th century Hitler and his supporters destroyed Berlin's reputation for tolerance and plunged it headlong into the war that led to its wholesale destruction, and to its eventual division by the infamous Wall in 1961. The Wall was breached in the Peaceful Revolution of 1989, and East and West are now relatively seamless. A large Turkish and European population make Berlin the most international city in Germany, and it is also the city with the most active arts and nightlife scene.

Exploring Berlin

Berlin is laid out on an epic scale but its extensive subway, bus, and streetcar (tram) services make it easy to get around. You can rely on the timetables posted at subway stations and bus and streetcar stops (the latter two marked by signs bearing the letter "H"). Board the subway in the right direction by knowing the name of the end station you're heading toward.

Western Berlin
The western districts include Charlottenburg, Tiergarten, Kreuzberg, and Schöneberg, and the entire area is best known for the constant commerce on Kurfürstendamm. The boulevard of shops, art galleries, restaurants, and bars stretches 3 km (2 mi) through the downtown.

Numbers in the margin correspond to points of interest on the Berlin map.

★ **⑭ Ägyptisches Museum** (Egyptian Museum). This small but outstanding museum is home to the portrait bust of Nefertiti known around the world. The 3,300-year-old queen is the centerpiece of a fascinating collection of Egyptian antiquities that includes some of the finest-preserved mummies outside Cairo. ✉ *Schlosstr. 70* ☎ *030/3435–7311* ⊕ *www.smpk.de* ☉ *Tues.–Sun. 10–6.*

⑰ Bildungs- und Gedenkstätte Haus der Wannsee-Konferenz (Wannsee Conference Memorial Site). On January 20, 1942, this lakeside Berlin villa hosted the conference at which Nazi leaders planned the systematic deportation and genocide of Europe's Jewish population. An exhibition documents the conference, and more extensively, the escalation of persecution against Jews, and the Holocaust itself. From the U-Bahn

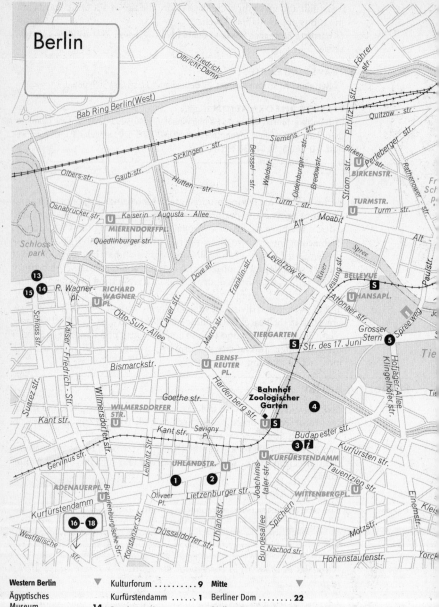

Berlin

TO SACHSENHAUSEN GEDENKSTÄTTE

FORMER LOCATION OF BERLIN WALL

FORMER LOCATION OF BERLIN WALL

FORMER LOCATION OF BERLIN WALL

KEY	
S	S-Bahn
𝑖	Tourist information
U	U-Bahn

Wannsee station take Bus 114. ✉ *Am Grossen Wannsee 56–58* ☎ *030/ 805–0010* ⊕ *www.ghwk.de* ⊙ *Mon.–Sun. 10–6.*

★ ❼ **Brandenburger Tor** (Brandenburg Gate). This is the sole remaining gate of 14 built by Carl Langhans in 1788–91, designed as a triumphal arch for King Frederick Wilhelm II. Troops paraded through the gate after successful campaigns—the last time in 1945, when victorious Red Army troops took Berlin. During Berlin's division, the gate was stranded in a no-man's-land, but it now serves as the center of festivities on Unification Day and New Year's Eve. In front of the gate is **Pariser Platz** (Paris Square), and to the south of it is Germany's national **Holocaust Mahnmal** (Holocaust Memorial). ✉ *Unter den Linden at Pariser Pl.*

⓲ **Dahlemer Museen** (Dahlem Museums). This unique complex of four museums includes the **Ethnologisches Museum** (Ethnographic Museum), famous for its artifacts from Africa, Asia, the South Seas, and the Americas. The other museums present early European cultures, ancient Indian culture, and East Asian art. ✉ *Lansstr. 8* ☎ *030/8301–438* ⊕ *www. smpk.de* ⊙ *Tues.–Fri. 10–6, weekends 11–6* Ⓜ *U-2 to Dahlem-Dorf.*

⓰ **Grunewald** (Green Forest). Together with its Wannsee lakes, this splendid forest is a popular retreat for Berliners, who come out in force, swimming, sailing their boats, tramping through the woods, and riding horseback. In winter a downhill ski run and ski jump operate on the modest slopes of Teufelsberg hill. Excursion steamers ply the Wannsee, the Havel River, and the Müggelsee. Ⓜ *S-Bahn 1 to Nikolassee or Wannsee; S-Bahn 7 to Grunewald.*

⓴⑨ **Hamburger Bahnhof, Museum für Gegenwart–Berlin** (Museum of Contemporary Art). The best place in Berlin to survey Western art after 1960 is in this light-filled remodeled 19th-century train station. You can see installations by German artists Joseph Beuys and Anselm Kiefer as well as paintings by Andy Warhol, Cy Twombly, Robert Rauschenberg, and Robert Morris. ✉ *Invalidenstr. 50–51* ☎ *030/397–83463* ⊕ *www. smpk.de* ⊙ *Tues.–Fri. 10–6, weekends 11–6.*

★ ⓫ **Haus am Checkpoint Charlie.** The seemingly homespun museum reviews events leading up to the Wall's construction and displays actual tools, equipment, records, and photographs documenting methods used by East Germans to cross over to the West. Come early to avoid the tour buses that stop here. ✉ *Friedrichstr. 43–45* ☎ *030/253–7250* ⊕ *www.mauer-museum.com* ⊙ *Daily 9 AM–10 PM.*

⓬ **Jüdisches Museum** (Jewish Museum). The history and culture of Germany's Jews from the Middle Ages through today is chronicled in this jagged building designed by architect Daniel Libeskind (who is also rebuilding the World Trade Center site in New York). Various physical "voids" represent the loss German society faces as a result of the Holocaust, and a portion of the exhibits document the Holocaust as well. You'll need at least three hours to do the museum justice. Go through the third floor quickly if you're already familiar with Jewish culture. ✉ *Lindenstr. 9–14* ☎ *030/30878–5681* ⊕ *www.jmberlin.de* ⊙ *Mon. 10–10, Tues.–Sun. 10–8.*

★ ❸ **Kaiser-Wilhelm-Gedächtniskirche** (Kaiser Wilhelm Memorial Church). Long a symbol of West Berlin, this landmark is a dramatic reminder of the futile destructiveness of war. The shell of the tower is all that remains of the 19th-century church. Adjoining it are a modern church and bell tower. ✉ *Breitscheidpl.* ☎ *030/218–5023* ⊕ *www.gedaechtniskirche. com* ⊙ *Old Tower: Mon.–Sat. 10–4, Memorial Church: daily 9–7.*

★ ❾ **Kulturforum** (Cultural Forum). With its unique ensemble of museums, galleries, and libraries, the complex is a cultural jewel. The **Gemälde-galerie** (Painting Gallery) has an extensive selection of European paintings from the 13th through 18th centuries, among them works by Rembrandt, Dürer, Cranach the Elder, and Holbein, as well as of the Italian masters—Botticelli, Titian, Giotto, Lippi, and Raphael. ✉ *Matthäikirchpl. 8* ☎ *030/2660 or 030/266–2951* ⊕ *www.smpk.de* ☉ *Tues., Wed., and Fri.–Sun. 10–6, Thurs. 10–10.*

The **Kunstgewerbemuseum** (Museum of Decorative Arts) exhibits European arts and crafts from the Middle Ages to the present. ✉ *Matthäikirchpl. 8* ☎ *030/266–2902* ⊕ *www.smpk.de* ☉ *Tues.–Fri. 10–6, weekends 11–6.*

The **Neue Nationalgalerie** (New National Gallery), designed by Mies van der Rohe, exhibits 20th-century paintings and sculpture. ✉ *Potsdamer Str. 50* ☎ *030/266–2651* ⊕ *www.smpk.de* ☉ *Tues., Wed., and Fri. 10–6, Thurs. 10–10, weekends 11–8.*

★ ❶ **Kurfürstendamm.** Ku'damm, as Berliners call the boulevard, throbs with activity day and night. The **Europa Center,** a shopping center, and Breitscheidplatz in front of it are a buzzing, central meeting point.

❽ **Potsdamer Platz.** Sony, Mercedes Benz, Asea Brown Boveri, and others maintain their company headquarters at this entirely reconstructed square, Europe's busiest plaza before World War II. The **Sony Center** is an architectural marvel designed by German-American architect Helmut Jahn. Within it, the **Filmmuseum Berlin** (✉ Potsdamer Str. 2 ☎ 030/ 300–9030 ⊕ www.filmmuseum-berlin.de ☉ Tues., Wed., and Fri.–Sun. 10–6, Thurs. 10–8) presents the history of moviemaking and memorabilia of German movie stars, including Marlene Dietrich. Also in the center is the Kaisersaal (Emperor's Hall), a café from the prewar Grand Hotel Esplanade. The **Potsdamer Platz Arkaden** houses 140 upscale shops, a musical theater, a variety stage, cafés, a movie complex, a 3D-IMAX cinema, and a casino. ✉ *Arkaden Alte Potsdamer Str. 7* ☎ *030/ 2559–2766 Arkaden* ☉ *Arkaden: weekdays 9:30–8, Sat. 9:30–4.*

★ ❻ **Reichstag** (German Parliament). The monumental building served as Germany's seat of parliament from its completion in 1894 until 1933, when it was gutted by fire under suspicious circumstances. Remodeled under the direction of British architect Sir Norman Foster, the Reichstag is once again hosting the Deutscher Bundestag, Germany's federal parliament. You can get a stunning view of Berlin from underneath the glass cupola. Lines can be long, so it's best to visit very early or very late on a weekday. ✉ *Pl. der Republik 1* ☎ *030/2273–2152* ⊕ *www. bundestag.de* ☉ *Daily 8 AM–midnight; last admission 11 PM.*

★ ⓯ **Sammlung Berggruen** (Berggruen Collection). This small museum focuses on modern art, with work from such artists as Van Gogh, Cézanne, Picasso, Giacometti, and Klee. ✉ *Schlossstr. 1* ☎ *030/3269–5815* ⊕ *www.smpk.de* ☉ *Tues.–Sun. 10–6.*

★ ⓭ **Schloss Charlottenburg.** Built at the end of the 17th century by King Frederick I for his wife, Queen Sophie Charlotte, this grand palace and its magnificent gardens were progressively enlarged for later royal residents and now include museums. The baroque apartments can be seen on tours only. ✉ *Luisenpl., U-7 subway line to Richard-Wagner-Pl. station; from station walk east along Otto-Suhr-Allee* ☎ *030/3209–1440* ⊕ *www.smpk.de* ☉ *Altes Schloss: Tues.–Fri., 9–5, weekends 10–5; New Wing: Tues.–Fri. 10–6, weekends 11–6.*

⑤ Siegessäule (Victory Column). The memorial, erected in 1873, commemorates four Prussian military campaigns. It stands at the center of the 630-acre Tiergarten (Animal Park), the former hunting grounds of the Great Elector. Climb 285 steps to see the view from its 213-foot summit. ⊠ *Am Grossen Stern* ☎ *030/391–2961* ⊘ *Nov.–Mar., daily 9:30–5; Apr.–Oct., daily 9:30–6 (last admission ½ hr before closing).*

② The Story of Berlin. Eight hundred years of the city's history, from the first settlers to the fall of the Wall, is conveyed through hands-on exhibits, film footage, and multimedia devices in this unusual venue. An eerie relic is the 1974 nuclear shelter, which you can visit by tour. Museum placards are also in English. ⊠ *Ku'damm Karree, Kurfürstendamm 207–208* ☎ *030/8872–0100* ⊕ *www.story-of-berlin.de* ⊘ *Daily 10–8 (last admission: 6).*

⑩ Topographie des Terrors (Topography of Terror). The buildings that once stood on these grounds housed the headquarters of the Gestapo, the secret security police, and other Nazi security organizations. After the war, the buildings were leveled. In 1987, the prison cellars, which are just behind a remaining stretch of the Wall, were excavated. The outdoor exhibit documents the structure of Nazi organizations, the atrocities they committed, and their victims. The free audio guide is a must. ⊠ *Niederkirchnerstr. 8* ☎ *030/2548–6703* ⊕ *www.topographie.de* ⊘ *Oct.–Apr., daily 10–5; May–Sept., daily 10–8.*

★ ④ Zoologischer Garten (Zoological Gardens). Berlin's enchanting zoo has the world's largest variety of individual types of fauna, along with a fascinating aquarium. ⊠ *Hardenbergpl. 8 and Budapester Str. 34* ☎ *030/254–010* ⊕ *www.zoo-berlin.de* ✉ *Combined ticket €13* ⊘ *Zoo: Nov.–Mar., daily 9–5; Apr.–Sept., daily 9–6:30; Oct., daily 9–6; Aquarium: daily 9–6.*

Mitte

Most of the historic architecture of the prewar capital is in the Mitte district.

Numbers in the margin correspond to points of interest on the Berlin map.

㉒ Berliner Dom (Berlin Cathedral). The impressive 19th-century cathedral with its enormous green copper dome is one of the great ecclesiastical buildings in Germany. The relatively easy climb to the dome lookout is worth it. ⊠ *Am Lustgarten* ☎ *030/2026–9136* ⊘ *Apr.–Sept., Mon.–Wed., Fri., and Sat., 9–8, Thurs. 9–10, Sun. noon–8; Oct.–Mar., Mon.–Sat. 9–7, Sun. noon–7; crypt closes 2 hrs earlier; dome open same hrs as church, weather permitting.*

㉕ Berliner Fernsehturm (Berlin TV Tower). At 1,198 feet high, eastern Berlin's TV tower is a proud 710 feet *taller* than western Berlin's. Within a disco-ball-like enclosure, the observation level affords the best view of Berlin; take a coffee break (but skip the food) in the revolving café. ⊠ *Panoramastr. 1a* ☎ *030/242–3333* ⊕ *www.berlinerfernsehturm.de* ⊘ *Nov.–Feb., daily 10 AM–midnight; Mar.–Oct., daily 9 AM–1 AM (last admission 1½ hrs before closing).*

⑳ Deutsches Historisches Museum (German Historical Museum). This magnificent baroque building, constructed in 1695–1730, was once the Prussian Zeughaus (arsenal). It now houses Germany's national history museum. The modern glass wing by I. M. Pei opened in 2003. ⊠ *Unter den Linden 2* ☎ *030/203–040* ⊕ *www.dhm.de* ⊘ *Daily 10–6.*

㉘ Gedenkstätte Berliner Mauer (Berlin Wall Memorial Site). A documentation center details the history of the Wall and the division of Germany.

You can hear radio broadcasts from both the east and west reporting the building of the Wall, as well as eyewitness accounts. Part of the memorial is the Reconciliation Church, completed in 2000 to replace the church dynamited by the Communists in 1985. The church had been walled into the "death strip" and was seen as a hindrance to patrolling it. ⊠ *Bernauer Str. 111* ☎ *030/464–1030* ⊕ *www.berliner-mauer-gedenkstaette.de* ⊗ *Wed.–Sun. 10–5.*

★ ⑲ **Gendarmenmarkt.** Anchoring this large square are the beautifully reconstructed 1818 **Schauspielhaus**, one of Berlin's main concert halls (now called the Konzerthaus), and the **Deutscher Dom and Französischer Dom** (German and French cathedrals). The **Deutscher Dom** (⊠ Gendarmenmarkt 1 ☎030/2273–0431 ⊗ Sept.–May, Tues. 10–10, Wed.–Sun. 10–6; June–Aug., Tues. 10–10, Wed.–Sun. 10–7) holds an extensive exhibition on the emergence of the parliamentary system in Germany, sponsored by the German parliament. An English audio guide covers a portion of the exhibits.

㉖ **Hackesche Höfe** (Hackesche Warehouses). Built in 1905–07, the tiled Hackesche Höfe is the finest example of art nouveau industrial architecture in Berlin. Within eight connecting courtyards are several art galleries and pricey shops. Its restaurants and theaters are a nightlife hub. ⊠ *Rosenthaler Str. 40–41* ⊕ *www.hackeschehoefe.de.*

㉑ **Museumsinsel** (Museum Island). This unique complex contains four world-class museums. The **Nationalgalerie** (National Gallery; ⊠ Bodestr.) has 19th- and 20th-century paintings and sculptures, mostly by German artists, including Caspar David Friedrich. The **Altes Museum** (Old Museum; ⊠ Am Lustgarten), a red marble, neoclassical building, was designed by Schinkel and in 1830, was the first building ever purposefully erected as a museum. It is home to artworks from ancient Greece. Etruscan art is a highlight. The **Pergamonmuseum** (Pergamon Museum; ⊠ Am Kupfergraben) takes its name from its principal exhibit, the Pergamon Altar, a monumental Greek altar dating from 180 BC. The gateways of Miletus and Ishtar are the other architectural wonders. The museums are free the first Sunday of the month. ⊠ *Museumsinsel (off Unter den Linden along the Spree Canal)* ☎ *030/209–5577 or 030/2090–5560* ⊕ *www.smpk.de* ⊗ *Pergamonmuseum: Fri.–Wed. 10–6, Thurs. 10–10; Alte Nationalgalerie and Altes Museum: Tues.–Sun. 10–6.*

㉗ **Neue Synagoge** (New Synagogue). A stunning, gilded cupola marks this landmark. The faintly Middle Eastern–looking building was completed in 1866, when its 3,200 seats made it the largest synagogue in Europe. It was destroyed on November 9, 1938 (*Kristallnacht*—Night of the Broken Glass), when Nazis vandalized, looted, and burned synagogues and Jewish shops across Germany. The exhibit on the history of the building and its congregants includes fragments of the original architecture and furnishings. ⊠ *Oranienburger Str. 28–30* ☎ *030/882–8316* ⊕ *www.cjudaicum.de* ⊗ *Oct.–Apr., Sun.–Thurs. 10–6, Fri. 10–2; May–Sept., Sun. and Tues.–Thurs. 10–6, Mon. 10–8, Fri. 10–5. Tours Wed. at 4, Sun. at 2, 4. Cupola open Apr.–late Sept.*

㉓ **Nikolaiviertel** (Nikolai Quarter). Berlin's oldest quarter is filled with shops, cafés, and restaurants. Nikolaikirchplatz has Berlin's oldest building, the **St. Nikolaikirche** (St. Nicholas's Church), dating from 1230. At Breite Strasse 35 is the **Ribbeckhaus,** the city's only surviving Renaissance structure, dating from 1624. ⊠ *Nikolaikirchpl.* ☎ *030/240–020* ⊕ *www.stadtmuseum.de* ⊗ *Tues.–Sun. 10–6.*

㉔ **St. Marienkirche** (Church of St. Mary). This medieval church, one of the finest in Berlin, is worth a visit for its late-Gothic fresco *Der Totentanz*

Fodor'sChoice
★

(*Dance of Death*). The cross on top of the church tower was an ever-lasting annoyance to Communist rulers, as its golden metal was always mirrored in the windows of the Fernsehturm TV tower, the pride of socialist construction genius. ⊠ *Karl-Liebknecht-Str. 8* ☎ *030/242–4467* ⊙ *Mon.–Thurs. 10–4, weekends noon–4; tour Mon. and Tues. at 1, Sun. at 11:45.*

Where to Eat

Typical Berliner meals include *Eisbein mit Sauerkraut* (knuckle of pork with sauerkraut), *Spanferkel* (suckling pig), Turkish *Döner kebab* (grilled lamb or chicken served with salad in a flat-bread pocket), and *Curry-wurst* (chubby and spicy frankfurters sold at wurst stands).

★ $$$$ ✗ **First Floor.** Chef Matthias Buchholz's traditional German fare has earned him high honors. The menu changes according to the season and his moods, but most of the menu items are interpretations of German dishes such as *Müritzlammrücken in Olivenkruste mit Bohnenmelange* (Müritz lamb back in olive crust, served with green beans). The four-course menu costs €66.50. ⊠ *Hotel Palace, Budapester Str. 42* ☎ *030/2502–1020* ⚘ *Reservations essential* ⊟ *AE, DC, MC, V* ⊙ *No lunch Sat.*

★ $$$$ ✗ **VAU.** The German fish and game dishes prepared by Chef Kolja Klee-berg have earned him endless praise and awards. Daring combinations include *Ente mit gezupftem Rotkohl, Quitten und Maronen* (duck with red cabbage, quinces, and sweet chestnuts) and *Steinbutt mit Kalbbries auf Rotweinschalotten* (turbot with veal sweetbread on shallots in red wine). A four-course menu runs €75; a six-course, €100. VAU's cool interior is all style and modern art. ⊠ *Jägerstr. 54/55* ☎ *030/202–9730* ⚘ *Reservations essential* ⊟ *AE, DC, MC, V* ⊙ *Closed Sun.*

★ $$$ ✗ **Borchardt.** The menu changes daily at this fashionable meeting place where columns, red plush benches, and an art nouveau mosaic create the impression of a 1920s salon. Entrées lean to French preparations. ⊠ *Französische Str. 47* ☎ *030/2038–7110* ⚘ *Reservations essential* ⊟ *AE, MC, V.*

$$–$$$ ✗ **Paris Bar.** This late-night Charlottenburg restaurant attracts a polyglot clientele of film stars, artists, and executives. The cuisine is creative but medium-quality French. ⊠ *Kantstr. 152* ☎ *030/313–8052* ⊟ *AE.*

$–$$$ ✗ **Schwarzenraben.** Berlin's successful frequent this stylish restaurant that epitomizes the rise of the New East. Though there are open spaces at the front and back, many of the tables are uncomfortably squeezed together along a long, narrow stretch. The environment is unfortunately a bit noisy. The menu, written in German and Italian, has a large selection of appetizers and presents new Italian recipes such as risotto with quail breast and leg, port wine, and goat cheese. ⊠ *Neue Schönhauser Str. 13* ☎ *030/2839–1698* ⚘ *Reservations essential* ⊟ *AE, MC, V.*

$–$$ ✗ **Hackescher Hof.** At one of the most "in" places in Mitte, the food is a mixture of German cooking and international cuisine such as Argentinian beef, grilled tuna with arugula pesto, and Wiener schnitzel. Menus are available in English and a reasonably priced breakfast is served until 1 PM during the week and 3 PM on weekends. Dinner reservations are advised. ⊠ *Rosenthaler Str. 40/41* ☎ *030/2835–293* ⊟ *AE, MC, V.*

$–$$ ✗ **Reinhard's.** Berliners of all stripes meet here in the Nikolai Quarter to enjoy the carefully prepared entrées and to sample spirits from the amply stocked bar. *Adlon* (honey-glazed breast of duck) is one of the house specialties. Reinhard's has a smaller, more elegant restaurant on the Ku'damm. ⊠ *Poststr. 28* ☎ *030/242–5295* ⊠ *Kurfürstendamm 190* ☎ *030/881–1621* ⚘ *Reservations essential* ⊟ *AE, DC, MC, V.*

$ ✗ **Café Oren.** This popular nonkosher Jewish eatery is next to the Neue Synagogue. Its vegetarian and Middle Eastern dishes round out the menu.

The restaurant buzzes with loud chatter all evening, and the atmosphere and service are friendly. The small backyard is a wonderful spot to enjoy a cool summer evening or a warm autumn afternoon. ⊠ *Oranienburger Str. 28* ☎ *030/282-8228* ▭ *AE, DC, MC, V.*

★ $ ✕ **Grossbeerenkeller.** The cellar restaurant, with its massive, dark-oak furniture and decorative antlers, is one of the most original dining spots in town. Owner and bartender Ingeborg Zinn-Baier presents such dishes as *Sülze vom Schweinekopf mit Bratkartoffeln und Remoulade* (diced pork with home fries and herb sauce). Her fried potatoes are famous. ⊠ *Grossbeerenstr. 90* ☎ *030/251-3064* ▭ *No credit cards* ☾ *Closed Sun.*

$ ✕ **Zur Letzten Instanz.** Established in 1621, Berlin's oldest restaurant combines the charming atmosphere of old-world Berlin with a limited (but tasty) choice of dishes. The emphasis here is on beer, both in the recipes and in the mug. Service can be erratic, though engagingly friendly. Chancellor Schroder treated French President Chirac to a meal here in 2003. ⊠ *Waisenstr. 14–16* ☎ *030/242-5528* ▭ *AE, DC, MC, V.*

Where to Stay

Make reservations well in advance. Prices for rooms can fluctuate wildly based on season and day of the week.

$$$$ ▦ **Kempinski Hotel Bristol Berlin.** This grand hotel in the heart of the city has the best of Berlin's shopping at its doorstep. All rooms and suites are luxuriously decorated and equipped, with marble bathrooms, cable TV, and English-style furnishings. Kids under 12 stay free if they share their parents' room. ⊠ *Kurfürstendamm 27, D-10719* ☎ *030/884-340* 🖷 *030/883-6075* ⊕ *www.kempinskiberlin.de* ⟿ *301 rooms, 52 suites* ♻ *2 restaurants, pool, bar* ▭ *AE, DC, MC, V.*

★ $$$$ ▦ **Four Seasons Hotel Berlin.** Smooth and up-to-date services, such as cell phone rentals, complement turn-of-the-20th-century luxury here. Thick carpets, heavy crystal chandeliers, and a romantic restaurant with an open fireplace make for a sophisticated and serene atmosphere. ⊠ *Charlottenstr. 49, D-10117* ☎ *030/20338* 🖷 *030/2033-6119* ⊕ *www.fourseasons.com* ⟿ *162 rooms, 42 suites* ♻ *Restaurant, bar* ▭ *AE, DC, MC, V.*

★ $$$$ ▦ **Grand Hyatt Berlin.** Europe's first Grand Hyatt is *the* address for those attending the Berlinale film festival in February. Stylish guests feel at home with a minimalist, Feng Shui–approved design that combines Japanese and Bauhaus elements. A special attraction of the first-class hotel is the top-floor spa and swimming pool, which has a great view of Berlin's skyline. ⊠ *Marlene-Dietrich-Pl. 2, D-10785* ☎ *030/2553–1234* 🖷 *030/2553–1235* ⊕ *www.berlin.grand.hyatt.com* ⟿ *325 rooms, 17 suites* ♻ *Restaurant, pool, bar* ▭ *AE, DC, MC, V.*

★ $$$$ ▦ **Hotel Adlon Berlin.** This elegant hotel next to Pariser Platz lives up to its almost mythical predecessor, the old Hotel Adlon, which, until its destruction during World War II, was considered Europe's premier resort. The city's priciest hotel has impeccable service. Guest rooms are furnished in '20s style with dark-wood trimmings and bathrooms in black marble. ⊠ *Unter den Linden 77, D-10117* ☎ *030/22610* 🖷 *030/2261–2222* ⊕ *www.hotel-adlon.de* ⟿ *255 rooms, 82 suites* ♻ *3 restaurants, pool, bar* ▭ *AE, DC, MC, V.*

$$$–$$$$ ▦ **Swissôtel Berlin.** This ultramodern hotel excels with its reputable Swiss hospitality— from accompanying guests to their floor after check-in, to equipping each room with an iron, umbrella, and Lavazza espresso machine that preheats the cups. The biggest advantage is the location at the corner of Ku'damm and Joachimsthaler Strasse. All rooms have soundproof windows, and the nightly view of the bright city lights is fantastic. ⊠ *Augsburger Str. 44 (corner of Joachimsthaler Strasse), D-10789*

Fodor's Choice
★

☎ 030/220–100 🖷 030/2201–02222 ⊕ www.swissotel.com ⟿ 316 rooms, 31 suites ⚤ Restaurant, bar ⊟ AE, DC, MC, V.

$$–$$$ ▥ **Riehmers Hofgarten.** Surrounded by the bars and restaurants of the colorful Kreuzberg district, this hotel has fast connections to the center of town. The small rooms may be too spartan for many travelers, but they are modern, quiet, and functional. The Riehmers's true appeal comes from its location in an impressive, late-19th-century apartment house. ⊠ Yorckstr. 83, D-10965 ☎ 030/7809–8800 🖷 030/7809–8808 ⊕ www. riehmers-hofgarten.de ⟿ 22 rooms ⚤ Bar ⊟ AE, MC, V.

★ **$$** ▥ **Charlottenburger Hof.** A creative flair, a convenient location across from an S-bahn station, and room computers with free Internet access make this low-key hotel a great value for no-fuss travelers. The variety of rooms can suit friends, couples, or families. Kurfürstendamm is a 10-minute walk, and the bus to and from Tegel Airport stops a block away. ⊠ Stuttgarter Pl. 14, D-10627 ☎ 030/329–070 🖷 030/323–3723 ⊕ www.charlottenburger-hof.de ⟿ 46 rooms ⚤ Restaurant ⊟ AE, MC, V.

$$ ▥ **Hotel Astoria.** You'll be well attended to in this small, privately owned and run hotel. Each room in the simple 1898 building is different, so when making a reservation, say whether you'd like a bathtub or shower. Ask about weekend specials or package deals for longer stays. The location is good for exploring the Ku'damm area, and the side street makes for a wonderful stroll. An unusual perk is free use of the Internet terminal in the lobby. ⊠ Fasanenstr. 2, D-10623 ☎ 030/312–4067 🖷 030/312–5027 ⊕ www.hotelastoria.de ⟿ 31 rooms, 1 suite ⊟ AE, DC, MC, V.

$$ ▥ **Hotel-Pension Dittberner.** The Dittberner, close to Olivaer Platz and Kurfürstendamm, is a family-run hotel in a turn-of-the-20th-century house. Some of the furniture is worn, but the warm atmosphere and the breakfast buffet more than make up for it. ⊠ Wielandstr. 26, D-10707 ☎ 030/884–6950 🖷 030/885–4046 ⟿ 21 rooms, 1 suite ⊟ No credit cards.

$–$$ ▥ **Hotel am Scheunenviertel.** This simply furnished but well-kept small hotel offers personal service and a good breakfast buffet. The biggest advantage is its location near the nightlife and cultural hot spots of the old Jewish neighborhood around the Neue Synagoge. The drawback is that it can be noisy. ⊠ Oranienburger Str. 38, D-10117 ☎ 030/282–2125 🖷 030/282–1115 ⊕ www.hotelas.com ⟿ 18 rooms with shower ⊟ AE, DC, MC, V.

$ ▥ **Mitte's Backpacker Hostel.** Accommodations are simple but creative in this orange-painted hostel, and service goes the extra mile with cheap bike rentals, free city maps, ticket services, and ride-sharing arrangements. The location is convenient for both sightseeing and nightlife, but in the evenings you can also opt to stay in for happy hour or a film. ⊠ Chauseestr. 102, D-10115 ☎ 030/2839–0965 🖷 030/2839–0935 ⊕ www.backpacker.de ⟿ 8 double rooms, 4 with bath ⚤ Bar ⊟ AE, MC, V.

Nightlife & the Arts

The Arts

The quality of opera and classical concerts in Berlin is high. If your hotel can't book a seat for you, you can go to one of several ticket agencies. **Hekticket offices** (⊠ Karl-Liebknecht-Str. 12, off Alexanderpl., ☎ 030/2431–2431 ⊠ at Zoo-Palast, Hardenbergstr. 29a ☎ 030/230–9930) offers discounted and last-minute tickets. **Showtime Konzert- und Theaterkassen** (⊠ KaDeWe, Tauentzienstr. 21 ☎ 030/217–7754 ⊠ Wertheim, Kurfürstendamm 181 ☎ 030/882–2500) has offices within the major department stores. Details about what's going on in Berlin can be found in *Berlin–Kalender,* published by Berlin's Tourism Board; the *Ex-Berliner,* a monthly English-language newspaper; and the listings magazines *tip* and *zitty,* which appear every two weeks.

CONCERTS The Berliner Philharmonisches Orchester, one of the world's best, resides at the **Philharmonie mit Kammermusiksaal** (⊠ Herbert-von-Karajan-Str. 1 ☎ 030/2548–8132 or 030/2548–8301). The **Konzerthaus Berlin** (⊠ Gendarmenmarkt ☎ 030/2030–92101 or 030/2030–92102) is a prime venue for classical music concerts.

OPERA & BALLET The **Deutsche Oper** (⊠ Bismarckstr. 34–37 ☎ 030/343–8401), by the U-bahn stop of the same name, is home to both opera and ballet. The grand **Staatsoper Unter den Linden** (⊠ Unter den Linden 7 ☎ 030/2035–4555) is Berlin's main opera house, led by Maestro Daniel Barenboim. **Komische Oper** (⊠ Behrenstr. 55–57 ☎ 030/4799–7400) presents opera and dance performances. On the day of the performance, discount tickets are sold at the box office on Unter den Linden 41.

VARIETY SHOWS The music programs in the art nouveau tent of **Bar jeder Vernuft** (⊠ Schaperstr. 24 ☎ 030/8831–582) are intimate and intellectually entertaining. The **Chamäleon Varieté** (⊠ Rosenthaler Str. 40/41 ☎ 030/2827–118) puts on hilarious shows that even non-German-speakers can appreciate. The world's largest revue is at the **Friedrichstadtpalast** (⊠ Friedrichstr. 107 ☎ 030/2326–2326), a glossy showcase famous for its female dancers. The classy **Wintergarten Varieté** (⊠ Potsdamer Str. 96 ☎ 030/2500–8888) pays romantic homage to the '20s.

Nightlife

Nightlife in Berlin is no halfhearted affair. The centers of the nocturnal scene are around Savignyplatz in Charlottenburg; the side streets of Winterfeldplatz and Nollenplatz in Schöneberg; Oranienstrasse and Wienerstrasse in Kreuzberg; Kollwitzplatz in the Prenzlauer Berg district; and Oranienburger Strasse, Rosenthaler Platz, and Hackesche Höfe in Mitte.

BARS & DANCE CLUBS A Berlin classic, **Bar am Lützowplatz** (⊠ Am Lützowpl. 7 ☎ 030/262–6807) has the longest bar counter and best-made cocktails in town. The decor and the energetic gay crowd at **Hafen** (⊠ Motzstr. 18, ☎ 030/211–4118) in Schöneberg make it ceaselessly popular and a favorite singles mixer. At 4 AM people move next door to Tom's Bar, open until 6 AM. A gay and hetero crowd mingles within the kitschy carpeted walls of rowdy **Kumpelnest 3000** (⊠ Lützowstr. 23 ☎ 030/261–6918). The historic **Leydicke** (⊠ Mansteinstr. 4 ☎ 030/216–2973) is a must for out-of-towners. The proprietors operate their own distillery and have a superb selection of sweet wines and liqueurs.

Club nights at the docked boat *Hoppetosse* (⊠ Eichenstr. 4 ☎ 030/4171–5437) most often feature reggae and Dancehall. It's a bit out of the way in Treptow, but you get a fantastic Spree Canal view from either the lower level dance floor or the top deck. The fashionable club **90 Grad** (⊠ Dennewitzstr. 37 ☎ 030/2300–5954) plays hip-hop, house, and some techno. Women go right in, but men usually have to wait outside until they get picked by the doorman. The Prenzlauer Berg beer garden **Prater** (⊠ Kastanienallee 7–9 ☎ 030/448–5688) has a year-round space to accommodate bands and crowds on its dance floors. It's near the Eberswalder U-2 subway station.

Shopping

The most popular shopping area in western Berlin is the Kurfürstendamm and its side streets, especially between Breitscheidplatz and Olivaer Platz. Large retail and department stores border Tauentzienstrasse, which starts where Ku'damm ends at Breitscheidplatz. The Mitte district's poshest wares are found along historic Friedrichstrasse, whose Friedrichstadtpassagen make up a mall-like shopping and business complex. New designer labels and trendier clothes are found in the storefronts of Mitte's Scheunenviertel, near the Hackescher Markt S-bahn station.

Antiques

Not far from Wittenbergplatz, several streets are good for antiquing, including Eisenacher Strasse, Fuggerstrasse, Keithstrasse, Kalckreuthstrasse, Motzstrasse, and Nollendorfstrasse. On weekends from 10 to 5, the lively **Berliner Trödelmarkt und Kunstmarkt** (Berlin Flea- and Art Market; ⊠ Strasse des 17. Juni) swings into action. The flea-market stands are nearer the Tiergarten S-Bahn station; the handicrafts begin past the Charlottenburg gates.

Department Stores

Galeries Lafayette (⊠ Französische Str. 23 ☎ 030/209–480), off Friedrichstrasse, carries almost exclusively French products, including designer clothes, perfume, and produce. The small but most luxurious **Department Store Quartier 206** (⊠ Friedrichstr. 71 ☎ 030/2094–6240) offers primarily French designer clothes, perfumes, and home accessories. **Galleria Kaufhof** (⊠ Alexanderpl. 9 ☎ 030/247–430) is the main department store in Mitte, on Alexanderplatz. One of Berlin's classiest department stores is the **Kaufhaus des Westens** (KaDeWe; ⊠ Tauentzienstr. 21 ☎ 030/21210); the food department occupies the whole sixth floor.

Gift & Souvenir Ideas

All the books, posters, and souvenirs focus on the city at **Berlin Story** (⊠ Unter den Linden 10 ☎ 030/2045–3842), which is open even on Sunday. Fine porcelain is sold at the **Königliche Porzellan Manufaktur** (Royal Prussian Porcelain Factory, or KPM; ⊠ KPM's store, Kurfürstendamm 27 ☎ 030/886–7210 ⊠ Unter den Linden 35 ☎ 030/206–4150 ⊠ factory salesroom, Wegelystr. 1 ☎ 030/390–090). In the homey setting of **Wohnart Berlin** (⊠ Uhlandstr. 179–180 ☎ 030/882–5252) you can imagine how the stylish European furnishings, lamps, housewares, or stationery items might suit your own pad.

Berlin Essentials

AIRPORTS & TRANSFERS

Tegel Airport is 7 km (4 mi) from downtown. Tempelhof, even closer to downtown, is used for commuter plane traffic. Schönefeld Airport is about 24 km (15 mi) from downtown; it is used primarily for charter flights to Asia and southern and eastern Europe. You can reach all three airports by calling the central service phone number.

🛈 **Central Service** ☎ 0180/500-0186 ⊕ www.berlin-airport.de.

TRANSFERS The express X9 airport bus runs at 10-minute intervals between Tegel and Bahnhof Zoologischer Garten (Zoo Station). From here you can connect to bus, train, or subway. The trip takes 25 minutes; the fare is €3.10. Alternatively, you can take Bus 128 to Kurt Schumacher Platz or Bus 109 to Jakob Kaiser Platz and change to the subway, where your bus ticket is also valid. Expect to pay about €14 for a taxi from Tegel to the western downtown area. If you rent a car at the airport, follow the signs for the Stadtautobahn into Berlin. The Halensee exit leads to Kurfürstendamm.

Tempelhof is linked directly to the city center by the U-6 subway line. From Schönefeld a shuttle bus leaves every 10–15 minutes for the nearby S-bahn station. Bus 171 also leaves every 20 minutes for the Rudow subway station. A taxi ride from the Schönefeld Airport takes about 40 minutes and will cost around €28. By car, follow the signs for Stadtzentrum Berlin.

BUS TRAVEL TO & FROM BERLIN

BerlinLinien Bus is the only intra-Germany company serving Berlin. Make reservations through ZOB-Reisebüro, or buy your ticket at their office at the central bus terminal, the Omnibusbahnhof. Only EC credit cards and cash is accepted.

🚌 **ZOB-Reisebüro** ✉ Zentrale Omnibusbahnhof, Masurenallee 4–6 at Messedamm ☎ 030/301-0380 for reservations ⊕ www.berlinlinienbus.de.

CAR RENTAL

🚗 **Avis** ✉ Tegel Airport ☎ 030/4101-3148 ✉ Tempelhof Airport ☎ 030/6951-2340 ✉ Budapester Str. 43, at Europa Center ☎ 030/230-9370. **Europcar** ✉ Tegel Airport, ☎ 030/417-8520 ✉ Kurfürstenstr. 101-104 ☎ 030/235-0640 ✉ Zentrale Omnibushahnhof, Messedamm 8 ☎ 030/306-9590. **Hertz** ✉ Tegel Airport ☎ 030/4170-4674 ✉ Budapester Str. 39 ☎ 030/261-1053. **Sixt** ✉ Tegel Airport ☎ 030/4101-2886 ✉ Nürnberger Str. 65 ☎ 030/212-9880 ✉ Kaiserdamm 40 ☎ 030/411-7087.

CAR TRAVEL

The eight roads linking the western part of Germany with Berlin have been incorporated into the countrywide autobahn network, but be prepared for traffic jams, particularly on weekends. Follow signs for BERLIN–ZENTRUM to reach downtown.

EMBASSIES

See Germany A to Z.

EMERGENCIES

Pharmacies in Berlin offer late-night service on a rotating basis. Every pharmacy displays a notice indicating the location of the nearest shop with evening hours.

🚑 Doctors & Dentists **Dentist emergency assistance** ☎ 030/8900-4333.
🚑 Emergency Services **Ambulance** ☎ 030/112. **Emergency poison assistance** ☎ 030/19240. **Pharmaceutical emergencies** ☎ 01189. **Police** ☎ 030/110.
🚑 Hospitals **Charite** ✉ Schumannstr. 20-21, Mitte ☎ 030/28020.
🚑 Hot Lines **American Hotline** ☎ 0177/814-1510 for all English-speakers. **International Emergency Hotline** ☎ 030/3100-3222 or 030/3100-3243.

ENGLISH-LANGUAGE MEDIA

The monthly *Ex-Berliner* (€2) has feature articles plus event listings.
📚 Bookstores **Dussmann Kulturkaufhaus** ✉ Friedrichstr. 90 ☎ 030/2025-2410. **Hugendubel** ✉ Tauentzienstr. 13 ☎ 030/214-060. **Marga Schoeller Bücherstube** ✉ Knesebeckstr. 33 ☎ 030/881-1112.

TAXIS

The base rate is €2.50, after which prices vary according to a complex tariff system. Figure on paying around €8 for a ride the length of the Ku'damm. If you've hailed a cab on the street and are taking a short ride of less than 2 km (1 mi), ask the driver as soon as you start off for a special fare (€3) called *Kurzstreckentarif.* You can also get cabs at taxi stands or order one by calling. U-bahn employees will call a taxi for passengers after 8 PM, and bars will often call for you late at night as well.
🚖 **Taxis** ☎ 030/210-101, 030/210-202, 030/443-322, or 030/261-026.

TOURS

BOAT TOURS Tours of downtown Berlin's Spree and Landwehr canals give you up-close and unusual views of landmarks—bring plenty of film. Tours usually depart twice a day from several bridges and piers, such as Schlossbrücke in Charlottenburg, Hansabrücke in Tiergarten, Kottbusser Brücke in Kreuzberg, Potsdamer Brücke, and Haus der Kulturen der Welt in Tiergarten. Drinks, snacks, and wursts are available during the narrated trips.

A tour of the Havel Lakes (which include Tegeler See and Wannsee) is the thing to do in summer. Trips begin at the Schlossbrücke Charlottenburg or at the Greenwich Promenade in Tegel (U-bahn station Tegel). 🛈 Fees & Schedules **Reederei Bruno Winkler** ☎030/349-9595. **Reederei Riedel** ☎030/693-4646 inner Berlin tours only. **Stern- und Kreisschiffahrt** ☎ 030/536-3600.

BUS TOURS Four companies jointly offer city tours on yellow double-decker City Circle buses, which run every 15 or 30 minutes, depending on the season. The full circuit runs two hours as does the audio guide. For €18 you can jump on and off at the 14 stops. The bus driver sells tickets. During the warmer months, the last circuit leaves at 4 PM from the corner of Rankestrasse and Kurfürrstendamm. Most companies have tours to Potsdam. Severin & Kühn also runs all-day tours to Dresden. 🛈 Fees & Schedules **Berliner Bären Stadtrundfahrten** ☎ 030/3519-5270 ⊕ www.sightseeing.de. **Berolina Berlin-Service** ☎ 030/8856-8030 ⊕ www.berolina-berlin.com. **Severin & Kühn** ☎ 030/880-4190 ⊕ www.severin-kuehn-berlin.de. **Stadtrundfahrtbüro Berlin** ☎ 030/2612-001 ⊕ www.stadtrundfahrtbuero-berlin.de.

WALKING TOURS A walking tour is one of the best ways to familiarize yourself with Berlin's history and sights, and several companies offer native English-speakers and thematic tours from which to choose. Tours usually meet at major subway stations or hostels. 🛈 Fees & Schedules **Berlin Walks** ☎ 030/301-9194 ⊕ www.berlinwalks.com. **Insider Tours** ☎ 030/692-3149 ⊕ www.insidertour.com. **Brewer's Best of Berlin** ☎ 030/9700-2906 ⊕ www.brewersberlin.com. **StattReisen** ☎ 030/455-3028 ⊕ www.stattreisen.berlin.de.

TRAIN TRAVEL

Most trains to and from Berlin pass through Bahnhof Zoo. Trains from the east usually stop first at Ostbahnhof station.

TRANSPORTATION AROUND BERLIN

The city has an excellent public transportation system: a combination of U-bahn and S-bahn lines, buses, and streetcars. For €2.20, you can buy a ticket that covers travel on the entire downtown system (fare zones A and B) for two hours. Buy a *Kurzstreckentarif* for a short trip; it allows you to ride six bus stops or three U-bahn or S-bahn stops for €1.20. The Day Card, for €5.60, is valid until 3 AM of the day of validation.

If you're caught without a validated ticket, the fine is €40. Tickets are available from vending machines at U-bahn and S-bahn stations or from bus drivers. The Berlin Tourist Office sells a Welcome Card (€19) that grants three days of free transportation and 25%–50% discounts at museums and theaters. 🛈 **Berliner Verkehrsbetriebe** (BVG; Berlin Public Transportation) ☎030/19449 ⊕www.bvg.de.

TRAVEL AGENCIES

Euroaide specifically serves English-speakers. 🛈 **Euroaide** ⊠ Hardenbergpl., inside the Zoologischer Garten train station ⊕ www.euraide.com. **Reiseland American Express Reisebüro** ⊠ Wittenbergerpl., Bayreuther Str. 37 ☎ 030/214-9830 ⊕ www.reiseland-american-express.de ⊠ Friedrichstr. 172 ☎ 030/238-4102.

VISITOR INFORMATION

The main information office of Berlin Tourismus Marketing is in the Europa Center on Breitscheidplatz; it's open 10–7 Monday–Saturday,

10–6 on Sunday. The other two branches are at the Brandenburger Tor and at the base of the Fernsehnturm (TV tower) at Alexanderplatz and are open daily 10–6. The tourist information centers have longer hours April–October. If you want materials sent to you, write to Berlin Tourismus Marketing GmbH.

The Staatliche Museen zu Berlin (state museums) sells a €6 Tageskarte and a €10 Dreitageskarte good for one- and three-day admission to all of its museums. Admission to the state museums is free on the first Sunday of the month. A free audio guide is included at all state museums. ⓘ **Berlin Tourismus Marketing GmbH** ✉ Am Karlsbad 11, D–10785 Berlin ☎ 49/700/ 8623–7546 for all calls from outside Germany; 030/250–025 for hotel, restaurant, ticket reservations; 0190/016–316 €.45 per minute, for general information 🖷 030/2500–2424 ⊕ www.berlin-tourist-information.de. **Staatliche Museen zu Berlin** ☎ 030/266–2951 operator; 030/2090–5555 recorded information ⊕ www.smpk.de.

SAXONY & THURINGIA

Saxony and Thuringia—the states' names alone conjure up images of kingdoms and forest legends, of cultural riches and booming industrial enterprises. Since German reunification, the world's admiration has returned to museum-rich Dresden (which has recovered well from the Elbe River's flooding in August 2002); the music and literary traditions of Leipzig; and Eisenach, where Martin Luther hid out in the mighty Wartburg fortress. Weimar was home to the German Enlightenment movement as well as the short-lived German democracy, the Weimar Republic.

Dresden

Saxony's capital city suffered appalling damage during World War II. It had already been long restored when the Elbe River flooded its banks in 2002, wreaking havoc on area homes and glorious rococo and baroque buildings. Thanks to dramatic rescue efforts, priceless artworks at the Zwinger and Albertinum museums were saved, and today the city is well recovered.

The magnificent **Semperoper** (Semper Opera House) was built in 1838–41 by architect Gottfried Semper. Wagner's *The Flying Dutchman* and *Tannhäuser* (conducted by the composer) and nine operas by Richard Strauss premiered here. Tickets to performances are often hard to get; try booking through your travel agent before you go or ask at your hotel. As a last resort, line up at the evening box office, the Abendkasse, left of the main entrance, about half an hour before the performance. ✉ *Theaterpl.* ☎ *0351/491–1496 tours; 0351/491–1705 tickets* ⊕ *www. semperoper.de* ☯ *Tours usually start weekdays at 1:30, 2, and 3; weekends at 10.*

★ The largely 18th-century **Zwinger** palace complex is among the greatest examples of baroque architecture in Europe. Completely enclosing a central courtyard of lawns and pools, six linked pavilions are adorned with a riot of sandstone garlands, nymphs, and other ornamentation and sculpture, created under the direction of Matthäus Daniel Pöppelmann. The complex is home to the world-renowned **Sempergalerie** (Semper Gallery), whose Gemäldegalerie Alte Meister (Gallery of Old Masters) contains works by Dürer, Holbein the Younger, Rembrandt, Vermeer, Raphael, Correggio, and Canaletto. The **Porzellansammlung** (Porcelain Collection; ☎ 0351/491–4619 ☯ Tues.–Sun. 10–6) is considered one of the best of its kind in the world. The focus, naturally, is on Dresden and Meissen china, but there are also outstanding examples of Japanese, Chinese, and Korean porcelain. ✉ *Theaterpl., follow*

Sophienstr. ☎ *0351/491–4619* ⊕ *www.skd-dresden.de* ☉ *Sempergalerie: Tues.–Sun. 10–6.*

★ Germany's greatest Protestant church, the **Frauenkirche** (Church of Our Lady), was reduced to jagged ruins after the infamous February 1945 Allied bombing raid during World War II. A painstaking reconstruction of the Frauenkirche is under way; it is hoped that it can be reconsecrated by the year 2006, the 800th anniversary of the founding of Dresden. The church has also evolved as a symbol of German–British reconciliation. Daily tours of the church's completed sections and the construction site start at entrance F of the church (northern facade). Try to avoid the always-crowded weekend tours. ⊠ *An der Frauenkirche* ☎ *0351/ 498–1131* ⊕ *www.frauenkirche-dresden.org* ☉ *Daily 10–4 (tour every hr). Call for dates and times of English-language tours.*

Dresden's leading art museum, the **Albertinum,** is housed in a massive, imperial-style building. The **Gemäldegalerie Neue Meister** (New Masters Gallery) displays outstanding 19th- and 20th-century European works. The **Grünes Gewölbe** (Green Vault; entered from Georg-Treu-Platz), named after the collection's original home in the palace of August the Strong, showcases unique objets d'art fashioned from gold, silver, ivory, amber, and other precious and semiprecious materials. Next door, the **Skulpturensammlung** (Sculpture Collection) includes ancient Egyptian and classical objects and Italian Mannerist works. ⊠ *Am Neumarkt at Brühlsche Terrasse* ☎ *0351/4914–619* ⊕ *www.skd-dresden.de* ☉ *Fri.–Wed. 10–6.*

The **Katholische Hofkirche** (Catholic Court Church) is Saxony's largest church. In the crypt are the tombs of 49 Saxon rulers and a precious vessel containing the heart of August the Strong. ⊠ *Schlosspl.* ☎ *0351/ 484–4712* ☉ *Weekdays 9–5, Sat. 10–5, Sun. noon–4:30.*

The **Sächsische Porzellanmanufaktur Dresden** (Saxonian Porcelain Company Dresden), 9 km (5½ mi) southwest of Dresden in Freital, is where Dresden's renowned porcelain is made. Exquisite examples of the porcelain are sold in all Dresden department stores, and the Freital showroom sells items as well. ⊠ *Bachstr. 16, Freital* ☎ *0351/647–1310* ⊙ *Weekdays 9–5.*

The romantic **Schloss Pillnitz** (Pillnitz Palace) was a summer retreat for King August the Strong. The palace, built in 1720–22, is surrounded by a landscaped garden and two smaller palaces, the Wasserpalais (closed Tuesday) and the Bergpalais (closed Monday). Both buildings were designed in Germany's late baroque faux–Chinese pagoda style. Today, they house the **Kunstgewerbemuseum,** which showcases not only baroque furniture and craft, but also modern design. To get here, take Tram 10 from the central train station toward Striesen, exit there and continue with Tram 12 (to Schillerplatz), change there again and take Bus 83 to Pillnitz. ⊠ *Kleinzschachwitz* ☎ *0351/261–3201* ⊕ *www. skd-dresden.de* ⊙ *May–Oct., daily 10–6.*

$–$$ ✕ **Marcolinis Vorwerk.** This old villa with a picturesque garden and art gallery is frequented by a hip crowd with a taste for fine wine. The restaurant serves Italian dishes with an original spin on meat dishes, such as veal chops served with blue cheese, or chicken baked in a honey-nut crust. In summer, terrace dining provides a spectacular view of Dresden's skyline and the Elbe River. ⊠ *Bautzner Str. 96* ☎ *0351/899–6356* ▤ *AE, DC, MC, V* ⊙ *No lunch weekdays.*

$ ✕ **Ristorante Bellotto im Italienischen Dörfchen.** This baroque structure on the Elbe was built to house Italian craftsmen working on the nearby Hofkirche. Now it's a restaurant and café, with a shady beer garden and fine river views. The Italian influence is still evident—in the decor and on the menu, where pasta dishes are heavily favored. ⊠ *Theaterpl. 3* ☎ *0351/498–160* ▤ *AE, DC, MC, V.*

★ $ ✕ **Sophienkeller.** An 18th-century beer-cellar atmosphere reigns in the basement of the Taschenberg Palace. Waitresses wear period costumes, and the furniture and porcelain are as rustic as the food is traditional, including the typically Saxon *Gesindeessen* (rye bread, panfried with mustard, slices of pork, and mushrooms, baked with cheese). The Sophienkeller is very popular with large groups; you might have to wait for a table. ⊠ *Taschenbergpalais, Taschenberg 3* ☎ *0351/497–260* ▤ *AE, DC, MC, V.*

★ $$$$ ▥ **Kempinski Hotel Taschenbergpalais Dresden.** The historic Taschenberg Palace—the work of architect Matthäus Daniel Pöppelmann—provides expensive pampering in the romantic heart of old Dresden. Rooms are as big as city apartments, and suites earn the adjective "palatial"; they are all furnished with bright elm-wood furniture and have several phone lines, as well as fax machines and data ports. ⊠ *Am Taschenberg 3, D-01067* ☎ *0351/49120* 🖷 *0351/491–2812* ⊕ *www.kempinski-dresden.de* ⇆ *188 rooms, 25 suites* ⌂ *4 restaurants, pool, bar* ▤ *AE, DC, MC, V.*

★ $$–$$$$ ▥ **artotel Dresden.** Inside the artotel are more than 600 works by Dresden-born painter and sculptor A. R. Penck, as well as designs by Italian interior architect Denis Santachiara. The hotel's heavily styled rooms and service have genuine first-class appeal at considerably lower prices. ⊠ *Ostra-Allee 33, D-01067* ☎ *0351/49220* 🖷 *0351/492–2777* ⊕ *www. artotels.de* ⇆ *155 rooms, 19 suites* ⌂ *2 restaurants, bar* ▤ *AE, DC, MC, V.*

$$ ▥ **Rothenburger Hof.** One of Dresden's smallest and oldest luxury hotels, the historic Rothenburger Hof opened in 1865 and is only a few steps away from the city's sightseeing spots. The rooms are not very large,

but they're comfortable and nicely decorated with furniture that looks antique, but, in fact, is reproduction. The breakfast buffet is rich even by German standards. ⊠ *Rothenburger Str. 15–17, D–01099* ☎ *0351/ 81260* 🖷 *0351/812–6222* ⊕ *www.dresden-hotel.de* 🛏 *26 rooms, 13 apartments* ⚏ *Bar* 🖶 *AE, MC, V.*

Leipzig

With a population of about 500,000, Leipzig is the second-largest city (after Berlin) in eastern Germany. Since the Middle Ages, it has been an important market town and a center for printing, publishing, and the fur business. Year-round trade fairs help maintain its status as a commercial hub. Yet it is music and literature that most people associate with Leipzig; Johann Sebastian Bach (1685–1750) was the organist and choir director at St. Thomas's Church, and the composer Richard Wagner was born in Leipzig in 1813. One of the greatest battles of the Napoleonic Wars, and one that led to the ultimate defeat of the French general— the Battle of the Nations—was fought here in 1813.

Leipzig's showpiece is its large **Markt** (market square). On one side of it is the Renaissance **Altes Rathaus** (Old City Hall), which houses the **Stadtgeschichtliches Museum** (City History Museum). Small streets leading off the Markt attest to Leipzig's rich trading past. Tucked in among them are glass-roofed shopping arcades. ⊠ *Markt 1* ☎ *0341/965–130* 🕙 *City Hall and museum: Tues.–Sun. 10–6.*

Mädlerpassage (Mädler Mall) is the best shopping arcade, where references to Goethe's *Faust* lurk in every marble corner. Goethe set a scene in the Auerbachs Keller restaurant here. ⊠ *Grimmaischestr.*

★ Johann Sebastian Bach worked for 27 years at **Thomaskirche** (St. Thomas's Church), composing most of his cantatas for the church's boys' choir, whose tradition continues today. ⊠ *Thomaskirchhof (just off Grimmaischestr.)* ☎ *0341/960–2855* ⊕ *www.thomaskirche.org* 🕙 *Daily 9–6. Music service Fri. 6 PM, Sat. 3 PM.*

★ **Nikolaikirche** (St. Nicholas's Church) is more impressive inside than out; it has an ornate 16th-century pulpit and an unusual diamond-pattern ceiling supported by classical pillars crowned with palm-tree-like flourishes. Demonstrations at the church in 1989 are credited with helping to bring down the Communist regime. ⊠ *Nikolaikirchhof* ☎ *0341/960–5270* ⊕ *www.nikolaikirche.de* 🕙 *Daily 10–6.*

★ The city's most outstanding museum, the **Museum der Bildenden Künste** (Museum of Fine Arts), is of international stature, especially strong in German and Dutch old masters; one of its finest collections focuses on Cranach the Elder. In the fall of 2004 it will move to its new modern construction on Katharinenstrasse. ⊠ *Grimmaischestr. 1–7* ☎ *0341/216– 990* 🕙 *Tues. and Thurs.–Sun. 10–6, Wed. 1–8.*

The **Opernhaus** (Opera House; ⊠ *Augustuspl. 12* ☎ *0345/5110–0355*) is a center of the city's music life and was the first postwar theater to be built in Communist East Germany. The **Neues Gewandhaus** (⊠ *Augustuspl. 8* ☎ *0341/127–0280*) is home to a first-class orchestra. Kurt Masur is a former director, and Herbert Blomstedt is currently at the helm.

$$$ ✕ **Kaiser Maximilian.** Leipzig's best Mediterranean restaurant serves inventive Italian and French dishes in an elegant yet modern setting, dominated by high, bare walls and black leather seats. The restaurant lies in the corner of a pleasant courtyard off Neumarkt. ⊠ *Neumarkt 9–19* ☎ *0341/998–6900* ⚐ *Reservations essential* 🖶 *AE, MC, V.*

★ $–$$ ✕ **Auerbachs Keller.** Established in 1530, this expansive cellar restaurant was already renowned before Goethe sealed its reputation in *Faust.*

Seafood, meats, gratins, and Saxon dishes get equal play. ⊠ *Mädlerpassage, Grimmaischestr. 2–4* ☎ *0341/216–100* ⚑ *Reservations essential* ⊟ *AE, DC, MC, V.*

★ **$–$$** ✕ **Barthels Hof.** The English-language menu at this restaurant in a baroque courtyard goes as far as to explain the cuisine and Leipzig's history. Waitresses wear traditional *Trachten* dresses, but the rooms look more like a modern café. The restaurant is popular with locals, especially for its breakfast. ⊠ *Hainstr. 1* ☎ *0341/141–310* ⊟ *AE, MC, V.*

$ ✕ **Paulaner Hutter Culinaria Restaurant.** Near the Markt, Munich's Paulaner brewery runs a restaurant, banquet hall, *Bierstube* (pub), and beer garden. Pizzas are served in the Bierstube and Monday's special is *Schweinshaxen mit Sauerkraut* (baked pork with sauerkraut), a mix of Bavarian and Saxon cuisine, served with a half liter of beer for €6.66. ⊠ *Klosterg. 3–5* ☎ *0341/211–3115* ⊟ *AE, DC, MC, V.*

★ **$$$$** ▣ **Hotel Fürstenhof Leipzig.** One of the country's most luxurious hotels is in the Löhr-Haus, a revered old mansion in the city center. The spacious rooms have casual cherrywood designer furniture. The incredible fitness facilities include a swimming pool, a Finnish sauna, and a Roman steam bath. ⊠ *Tröndlinring 8, D-04105* ☎ *0341/1400* 🖷 *0341/1403–700* ⊕ *www.luxurycollection.com* ⏎ *80 rooms, 12 suites* ⚑ *Restaurant, pool, bar* ⊟ *AE, DC, MC, V.*

$$ ▣ **Park Hotel-Seaside Hotel Leipzig.** A few steps from the central train station, the Park Hotel is geared primarily toward the business traveler. The modern rooms may lack some individuality and are definitely not designed for romantic weekends, but the warm service and exceptional bathrooms and swimming pool area make for a pleasant stay. The Orient Express restaurant, a reconstruction of the famous 19th-century train, is another plus. ⊠ *Richard-Wagner-Str. 7, D-04109* ☎ *0341/98520* 🖷 *0341/985–2750* ⊕ *www.seaside-hotels.de* ⏎ *281 rooms, 9 suites* ⚑ *Restaurant, pool, bar* ⊟ *AE, DC, MC, V.*

$–$$ ▣ **Ringhotel Adagio Leipzig.** Behind the facade of a 19th-century city mansion, quiet Adagio is centrally located between the Grassimuseum and the Neues Gewandhaus. All rooms are individually furnished; when making a reservation, ask for a 1920s room, which features the style of the Roaring '20s and bathtubs almost as large as a whirlpool. ⊠ *Seeburgstr. 96, D–04103* ☎ *0341/216–699* 🖷 *0341/960–3078* ⊕ *www.hotel-adagio.de* ⏎ *30 rooms, 1 suite, 1 apartment* ⊟ *AE, DC, MC, V.*

Eisenach

When you stand in Eisenach's ancient market square, it's difficult to imagine this half-timber town as an important center of the eastern German automobile industry, home of the now-shunned Wartburg. This solid, noisy staple of the East German auto trade was named after the famous castle that watches over Eisenach, atop one of the foothills of the Thuringian Forest. Today West German automaker Opel is continuing the tradition, and the GM company operates one of Europe's most modern car-assembly lines on the city's outskirts.

Fodor'sChoice ★ Begun in 1067, the mighty **Wartburg** has hosted a parade of German historical celebrities. Legend has it that this is where Walther von der Vogelweide (1170–1230), the greatest lyric poet of medieval Germany, prevailed in the celebrated *Minnesängerstreit* (minnesinger contest), which is featured in Richard Wagner's *Tannhäuser*. Within the castle's stout walls, Frederick the Wise (1486–1525) shielded Martin Luther from papal proscription from May 1521 until March 1522, even though he did not share the reformer's beliefs. Luther completed the first translation of the New Testament from Greek into German while in hiding, an act that paved the way for the Protestant Reformation. Over the centuries, souvenir hunters have scarred Luther's simple study by scratching away the plaster and much of the wood paneling.

Frederick was also a patron of the arts. Lucas Cranach the Elder's portraits of Luther and his wife are on view, as is the *Kneeling Angel,* a carving by the great 15th-century artist Tilman Riemenschneider. The 13th-century great hall is breathtaking; it's here that the minstrels sang for courtly favors. Don't leave without climbing the belvedere for a panoramic view of the Harz Mountains and the Thuringian Forest. ☎ *03691/77073* ⊕ *www.wartburg-eisenach.de* ⊘ *Nov.–Feb., daily 9–3:30; Mar.–Oct., daily 8:30–5.*

Johann Sebastian Bach was born in Eisenach in 1685. The **Bachhaus** has exhibits devoted to the entire lineage of the musical Bach family and includes a collection of historical musical instruments. ⊠ *Frauenplan 21* ☎ *03691/79340* ⊕ *www.bachhaus.de* ⊘ *Daily 10–6.*

Composer Richard Wagner gets his due at the **Reuter-Wagner-Museum,** which has the most comprehensive exhibition on Wagner's life and work outside Bayreuth. Monthly concerts take place in the old **Teezimmer** (tearoom), a hall with wonderfully restored French wallpaper. The Erard piano dating from the late 19th century is occasionally rolled out. ⊠ *Reuterweg 2* ☎ *03691/743–293* ⊘ *Tues.–Sun. 10–5.*

At Johannesplatz 9, look for what is said to be the **narrowest house** in eastern Germany, built in 1890; its width is just over 6 feet, 8 inches; its height, 24½ feet; and its depth, 34 feet.

★ **\$\$** ✕▨ **Steigenberger Hotel Thüringer Hof.** Enter the lobby of this historic 16th-century mansion, admire its huge chandelier and wooden stairways, set foot on the luxurious carpets, and you'll be instantly transported to the Middle Ages. Old sculptures and paintings accent the spacious, timeless rooms. The Galerie, serving international and local dishes with an accent on fish recipes, is one of the better restaurants in Eisenach. The rates for this quality hotel are a bargain. ⊠ *Karlspl. 11, D–99817* ☎ *03691/280* 🖷 *03691/28190* ⊕ *www.steigenberger.de* ⤢ *127 rooms, 1 suite* ♢ *Restaurant, bar* ▭ *AE, DC, MC, V.*

\$–\$\$ ✕▨ **Hotel Glockenhof.** At the base of Wartburg Castle, this former church-run hostel has blossomed into a handsome hotel, cleverly incorporating the original half-timber city mansion into a modern extension. The excellent restaurant (\$–\$\$) has been joined by a brasserie. ⊠ *Grimmelg. 4, D–99817* ☎ *03691/2340* 🖷 *03691/234–131* ⊕ *www. glockenhof.de* ⤢ *38 rooms, 2 suites* ♢ *Restaurant* ▭ *AE, MC, V.*

Saxony & Thuringia Essentials

AIR TRAVEL

It is easiest, and usually cheapest, to fly into Berlin and rent a car from there. However, Dresden Flughafen is about 10 km (6 mi) north of Dresden, and Leipzig's Flughafen Leipzig-Halle is 12 km (8 mi) northwest of the city.

🛪 **Dresden Flughafen** ☎ 0351/881-3360 ⊕ www.dresden-airport.de. **Flughafen Leipzig-Halle** ☎ 0341/224-1155 ⊕ www.leipzig-halle-airport.de.

BOAT & FERRY TRAVEL

Weisse Flotte's historic paddle-steam tours depart from and stop in Dresden, Pirna, Pillnitz, Königsstein, and Bad Schandau. Besides tours in the Dresden area, boats also go into the Czech Republic. For more information contact the Sächsische Dampfschiffahrt.

🛥 **Sächsische Dampfschiffahrt** ⊠ Hertha-Lindner-Str. 10, D-01067 Dresden ☎ 0351/ 866-090 ⊕ www.saechsische-dampfschiffahrt.de.

CAR TRAVEL

Expressways connect Berlin with Dresden (the A–13) and Leipzig (A–9). Both journeys take about two hours. The A–4 stretches east–west across the southern portion of Thuringia and Saxony.

TOURS

BUS TOURS   Contact the tourist offices in Leipzig and Dresden about the cities' English-language bus tours.

WALKING TOURS   A walking tour of Leipzig (in English) sets off from the tourist office May–September, daily 1:30; October–April, Saturday 1:30 and Sunday 10:30.

TRAIN TRAVEL

InterCity, EuroCity, and InterCity Express trains connect Dresden and Leipzig with Berlin and other major German cities, with InterRegio services completing the express network; older and slower D- and E-class trains connect smaller towns.

TRANSPORTATION AROUND SAXONY & THURINGIA

Most areas are accessible by bus, but service is infrequent and connects chiefly with rail lines. In Dresden and Leipzig public buses and streetcars are cheap and efficient.

TRAVEL AGENCY

🚩 **Reiseland American Express** ✉ Dohnaer Str. 246, D–01239 Dresden ☎ 0351/288-1109 ✉ Willy-Brandt-Pl. 5, D–04109 Leipzig ☎ 0341/961-7373 ⊕ www.americanexpress.de.

VISITOR INFORMATION

Most of the region's larger cities offer special tourist (exploring) cards such as the Dresdencard or Leipzigcard, which include discounts or special sightseeing packages for up to three days.
🚩 **Dresden** ✉ Tourist-Information, Prager Str. 10, D–01069 ☎ 0351/491-920 🖷 0351/4919-2116 ⊕ www.dresden-tourist.de. **Eisenach** ✉ Eisenach-Information, Markt 2, D–99817 ☎ 03691/79230 🖷 03691/792-320 ⊕ www.eisenach-tourist.de. **Leipzig** Leipzig Tourist Service e.V. ✉ Richard-Wagner-Str. 1, D–04109 ☎ 0341/710-4269 or 0341/710-4265 ⊕ www.leipzig.de. **Thuringia** (Thüringen State Tourism) ✉ Weimarische Str. 45, D–99099 Erfurt ☎ 0361/37420 🖷 0361/374-2299 ⊕ www.thueringen-tourismus.de.

GREAT BRITAIN

LONDON, WINDSOR TO BATH, CAMBRIDGE, YORK, THE LAKE DISTRICT, EDINBURGH

13

WHEN YOU VISIT LONDON, chances are you'll glimpse St. Paul's Cathedral riding high and white over the rooftops of the city skyline, just as it does in Canaletto's 18th-century views of the Thames. The great cathedral glows honey-gold at sunset and at night it is breathtakingly floodlighted, its details and proportions testimony to the genius of architect Christopher Wren. Then, on second glance, you'll note that St. Paul's is being nudged by modern, glittering skyscrapers, with glass-and-steel tower blocks marching two abreast the length of London Wall. The juxtaposition should give you pause: clearly, when you come to see the sights of Britain, you ought not to miss the greatest sight of all, which is the unconquered, nearly 2,000-year-long continuity of English society.

From baroque-era cathedrals to the latest postmodern structures, from prehistoric Stonehenge to Regency Bath, from one-pub Cotswold villages to London's Mod Brit restaurants, Great Britain is a spectacular tribute to the strength—and flexibility—of tradition. Here you'll find soaring medieval cathedrals; grand country mansions of the aristocracy, filled with paintings, furniture, and tapestries and set in elegantly landscaped grounds; and grim fortified castles, whose gray-stone walls held fast against all challengers. But there is more to Britain than a historical theme park aspect: many of the pleasures of exploration derive from the ever-changing variety of its countryside. A day's drive from York, for example, will take you through stretches of wild, heather-covered moorland, ablaze with color in the fall; or past the steep, sheep-dotted mountainsides of the Dales, in which isolated hamlets are scattered.

Wandering off the beaten track will allow you to discover Britain's many distinctive rural towns and villages. A medieval parish church, a high street of 18th-century buildings accented by occasional survivors from earlier centuries, and perhaps a grandiose Victorian town hall, all still in use today, convey a sense of a living past. This continuity of past into present can be generously experienced in such a celebrated place as Stratford-upon-Avon. It's even more evident in the little town of Chipping Campden, set in the rolling Cotswold Hills, or Bury St. Edmunds, in the gentle Suffolk countryside east of Cambridge. In such places the visitor's understanding is often aided by small museums devoted to local history, full of intriguing artifacts and information on trade, traditions, and social life. These towns are likely places to look for specialty goods, including knitwear, pottery, and glass, the result of increasing confidence and interest in local craftsmanship.

In contrast is the dazzling—at times hectic—pace of life in London. Today, Britain's swinging-again capital is much in the news, and the city's sizzling art, dining, style, and fashion scenes have done much to transform London's stodgy and traditional image. Thanks to such figures as artist Damien Hirst, designer-provocateur Alexander McQueen, and, of course, Tony Blair, the young(ish) prime minister, London continues to make headlines around the world. The city's turn-of-the-millennium building frenzy produced a slew of goodies, including the gigantic Tate Modern art gallery, the British Museum's sparkling glass-roofed Great Court, and many other cutting-edge museums, galleries, and bold building projects that have set the capital alight.

Finally, it is important to remember that Great Britain consists of three nations—England, Scotland, and Wales—and that 648 km (402 mi) north of London lies the capital city of Edinburgh, whose streets and monuments bear witness to the often turbulent and momentous history of the Scottish people.

GREAT BRITAIN A TO Z

To research prices, get advice from other travelers, and book travel arrangements, visit www.fodors.com.

AIR TRAVEL

Britain has an extensive network of internal air routes, run by about five different airlines. Hourly shuttle services operate every day between London and Glasgow, Edinburgh, Belfast, and Manchester. Seats are available on a no-reservations basis, and you can generally check in about an hour before flight departure time.

🛈 **British Airways** ☎ 800/247-9297 in U.S.; 0845/773-3377 in Great Britain ⊕ www.britishairways.com. **British Midland** ☎ 800/788-0555 in U.S.; 0870/607-0555 in London ⊕ www.flybmi.com. **Easyjet** ☎ 0870/600-0000 ⊕ www.easyjet.com. **Ryanair** ☎ 0871/246-0000 ⊕ www.ryanair.com. **Virgin Atlantic** ☎ 800/862-8621 in U.S.; 01293/450-150 in London ⊕ www.virgin-atlantic.com.

BIKE TRAVEL

Most towns—including London—offer bike-rental facilities. Any bike shop or tourist information center should be able to direct you to the nearest rental firm. Rental fees can be as little as £5 per day, plus a fairly large deposit, though this can often be put on your credit card. If you're planning a tour and would like information on rental shops and special holidays for cyclists, contact a VisitBritain office in the United States before you leave home. In Britain contact the Cyclists' Touring Club.

🛈 **Cyclists' Touring Club** ✉ Cotterell House, 69 Meadrow, Godalming, Surrey GU7 3HS ☎ 0870/873-0060 ⊕ www.ctc.org.uk.

BOAT & FERRY TRAVEL

Britain has more than 2,430 km (1,507 mi) of navigable inland waterways—rivers, lakes, canals, locks, and loughs—for leisure travel. Particular regions, such as the Norfolk Broads in East Anglia, the Severn Valley in the West Country, and the lochs and canals of Scotland are especially inviting. Although there are no regularly scheduled waterborne services, hundreds of yachts, canal boats, and motor cruises are available throughout the year. The Inland Waterways Association is a popular source for maps and guidebooks. British Waterways can assist with maps and information. For boat-rental operators along Britain's several

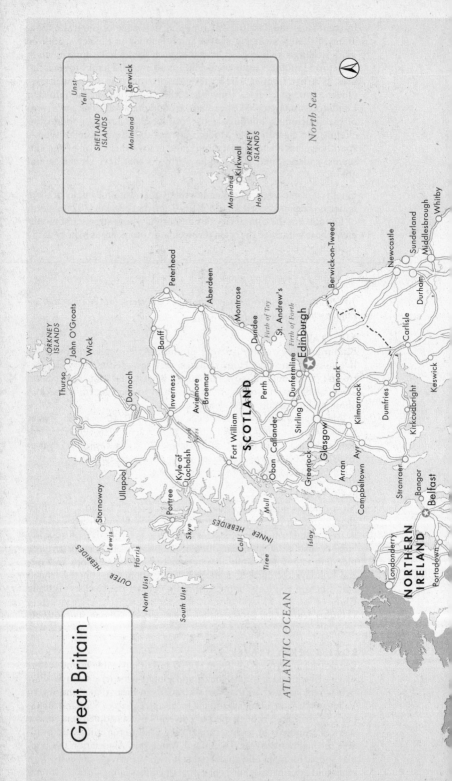

Great Britain

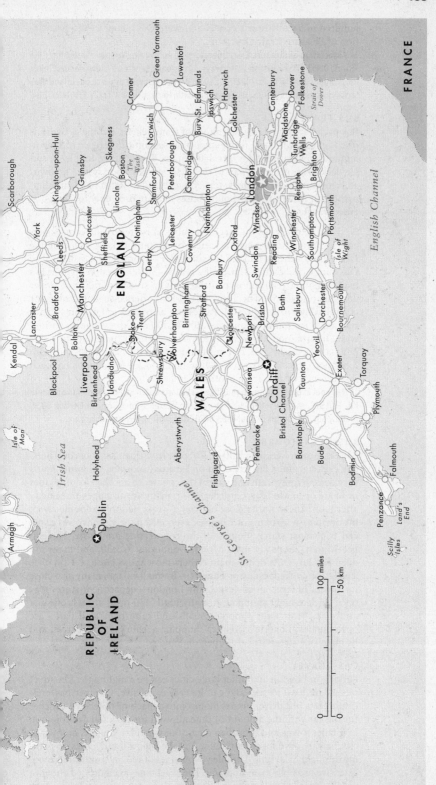

hundred miles of historic canals and waterways, contact the Association of Pleasure Craft Operators.

Association of Pleasure Craft Operators ⊠ Audley Av., Newport, Shropshire TF10 7BX ☎ 01952/813572. **British Waterways** ⊠ Customer Services, Willow Grange, Church Rd., Watford WD17 4QA ☎ 01923/201120 ⊕ www.britishwaterways.co.uk. **Inland Waterways Association** ✆ Box 114, Rickmansworth, Hertfordshire WD3 1ZY ☎ 01923/711114.

BUS TRAVEL

Bus prices are invariably half those of train tickets, and the network is just as extensive. There is one important semantic difference to keep in mind when discussing bus travel in Britain. Buses (either double- or single-decker) are generally part of the local transportation system in towns and cities and make frequent stops. Coaches, on the other hand, are comparable to American Greyhound buses and are used only for long-distance travel.

National Express has the largest number of routes of any coach operator in Britain. It also sells a variety of discount tickets, including the Discount Coachcard and the Tourist Trail Pass for overseas visitors. The Discount Coachcard (£8) provides a 20%–30% reduction on journeys made within a year and is available only to students and those under 25 years or over 50. The Tourist Trail Pass offers discounted rates for several ranges of days' travel. Passes can be bought in London's Victoria Coach Station or at any of 1,200 National Express agents nationwide. Information about all coach services, from timetables to ticket purchase by credit card, can be obtained from the National Express Information Office at Victoria Coach Station, and, for information on coach services in Scotland, from Scottish Citylink.

National Express Information Office ⊠ Victoria Coach Station, Buckingham Palace Rd., SW1 9TP ☎ 0870/580-8080 ⊕ www.nationalexpress.com. **Scottish Citylink** ⊠ St. Andrew Sq., Edinburgh, Scotland ☎ 0870/550-5050 ⊕ www.citylink.co.uk.

BUSINESS HOURS

Banks are open weekdays 9:30–4:30. Some have extended hours on Thursday evening, and a few are open on Saturday morning. Museum hours vary considerably from one part of the country to another. In large cities most are open Monday–Saturday 10–5; many are also open on Sunday afternoon. The majority close one day a week. Be sure to double-check the opening times of historic houses, especially if the visit involves a special trip; most stately houses in the countryside are closed November–March. Shops are open Monday–Saturday 9–5:30, and many are open Sunday. Outside the main centers most shops close at 1 PM once a week, often Wednesday or Thursday. In small villages many also close for lunch. In large cities—especially London—department stores stay open for late-night shopping (usually until 7:30 or 8) at least one day midweek. Most large shopping malls and suburban retail parks are open Sunday. London's premier shopping avenue, Oxford Street, and its main side streets are also open on Sunday.

CAR TRAVEL

Parking in London and other large cities can be a nightmare. On-street meters are hard to find and can be very expensive. Cheaper pay-and-display lots (the driver inserts money into a machine to receive a sticker for the car with the amount of time allowed for parking) are common in smaller towns and suburban areas. But wherever you are, in town or city, beware of yellow or red lines. A single yellow line denotes no parking during the daytime. Double yellow lines or red lines indicate a more extensive prohibition on stopping. The exact times are indicated on signs, usually attached to lampposts. Illegal parking can result in having your vehicle removed or its wheel clamped, which can lead to a great deal of inconvenience as well as a hefty fine.

In central London, where there is a good bus and underground service and taxis are plentiful, the use of a car is not recommended. A £5 "congestion charge" is now levied on all vehicles entering central London (bounded by the Inner Ring Road and visibly displayed on street signs) weekdays from 7 to 6:30, excluding bank holidays. You can pay by phone, mail, or Internet, or at retail outlets (look for signs indicating how and where you can pay). There are no tollbooths; cameras monitor the area. The penalty for not paying is stiff: £80 (£40 for prompt payment). For current information, check www.tfl.gov.uk.

EMERGENCIES The main automobile help groups are similar to the AAA in the United States. The Automobile Association runs a 24-hour breakdown service, as does the Royal Automobile Club. Most motorways have emergency phones along the route that connect the caller to the nearest police station. If you are driving extensively through Britain, membership in the AA can be useful for roadside assistance; you can also sign up through car-rental agents. If you are a member of the AAA, check your membership details, as you may be entitled to roadside assistance in Great Britain via a reciprocal agreement.

⚑ **Automobile Association** (AA) ☎ 0870/550-0600; 0990/500600 membership ⊕ www.theaa.com. **Royal Automobile Club** ☎ 0870/572-2722 ⊕ www.rac.co.uk.

GASOLINE In Britain gas (called petrol) pumps measure in liters. (There are 5 American gallons to 4 British gallons—for that amount, you will get about 20 liters.) At press time the price of gasoline was about 75p per liter for lead-free. The price generally rises in spring and autumn with government tax increases, and you'll find the cheapest prices at the supermarket pumps. Unleaded gasoline is predominant, denoted by green stickers on fuel pumps and pumplines. Premium and super premium are the two varieties, and most cars run on regular premium.

ROAD CONDITIONS Britain has superhighways (called motorways) running almost the length of the country, with links connecting them in the South, West, Midlands, and North. Motorways, given the prefix *M* on maps and road signs and shown in blue, have two or three lanes in each direction and are designed for high-speed rather than scenic travel. The other primary roads are A roads. Shown on maps as red and green lines, they connect town to town. Some bypass town centers and have fast stretches of divided (two-lane dual carriageway) highway. These are shown as thicker, black-edged lines on maps. Yellow B roads are the roads once designed for horses and carriages. Although they—and the even narrower, winding, white unclassified village roads—will allow you to see much more of the real Britain, your journey could end up taking twice the time. In remote country areas, road travel can be slow, especially in an icy winter. Good maps are available from the AA (Automobile Association) and the RAC (Royal Automobile Club); for in-depth exploring, try the Ordnance Survey 1:50,000-series maps. These show every road, track, and footpath in the country. You might also consult the useful Ordnance Survey *Motoring Atlas,* available at many bookstores.

RULES OF THE ROAD You can use either a U.S. driver's license or an International Driver's License in Britain. Drive on the left-hand side of the road and pay close attention to the varying—and abruptly changing—speed limits. Seat belts are obligatory for front-seat passengers (and backseat ones when the cars are fitted with them). In general, speed limits are 30 mph in the center of cities and built-up areas; 40 mph in suburban areas; 70 mph on motorways, divided highways, and dual carriageways; and 60 mph on all other roads. Pick up a copy of the Offical Highway Code (€1.50) at a service station, newsstand, or bookstore for all driving rules.

CUSTOMS & DUTIES

For details on imports and duty-free limits, *see* Customs & Duties *in* Smart Travel Tips.

EATING & DRINKING

British food used to be put down for its lack of imagination and its mediocrity. Today, numerous chefs have taken such giant steps that London is now one of the world's greatest cities for dining out. Across Britain, the problem may be not so much bad food as expensive food. The best of traditional British cooking, deeper into the country, uses top-quality, fresh, local ingredients: wild salmon; spring lamb; distinctive handmade cheeses; myriad, almost forgotten, fruit varieties; and countless types of seasonal vegetables. Nearly all restaurant menus include vegetarian dishes, and interesting ethnic cuisines, especially Asian, can be found on the main street of even the smaller towns and villages.

WHAT IT COSTS In pounds sterling			
$$$$	**$$$**	**$$**	**$**
AT DINNER over £22	£16–£22	£9–£15	under £9

Prices are per person for a main course.

MEALTIMES These vary somewhat, depending on the region of the country you are visiting. But in general breakfast is served between 7:30 and 9 and lunch between noon and 2 (in the North the latter meal is called dinner). Tea—a famous British tradition and often a meal in itself—is generally served between 4 and 5:30. Dinner or supper is served between 7:30 and 9:30, sometimes earlier, but rarely later outside the metropolitan areas. High tea, at about 6, replaces dinner in some areas—especially in Scotland—and in large cities, pre- and after-theater suppers are often available. Note that many upscale restaurants close for 10 days during Easter and/or Christmas and for several weeks in July, August, or September. Call ahead.

RESERVATIONS & Jacket and tie are suggested for the more formal restaurants in the top
DRESS price categories, but, in general, casual chic or informal dress is acceptable in most establishments.

EMBASSIES

🇨🇦 Canadian High Commission ✉ MacDonald House, 38 Grosvenor St., London W1X 0AB ☎ 020/7258-6600 ⊕ www.canada.org.uk. 🇺🇸 United States ✉ 24 Grosvenor Sq., London W1A 1AE ☎ 020/7499-9000 ⊕ www. usembassy.org.uk.

HOLIDAYS

Parliament isn't the only institution to decide which days are national holidays: some holidays are subject to royal proclamation. England and Wales: New Year's Day; Good Friday and Easter Monday; May Day (first Monday in May); Spring Bank Holiday (last Monday in May); August Bank Holiday (last Monday in August); Christmas Day and Boxing Day (day after Christmas).

LODGING

Accommodations in Britain range from enormous, top-quality, top-price hotels to simple, intimate farmhouses and guest houses. Note that many smaller establishments close for 10 days during Christmas and sometimes for several weeks in July or August. Call ahead.

WHAT IT COSTS In pounds sterling			
$$$$	**$$$**	**$$**	**$**
LONDON			
FOR 2 PEOPLE over £230	£160–£230	£100–£160	under £100
OTHER AREAS			
HOTELS over £150	£100–£150	£60–£100	under £60

Prices are for a double room and include all taxes.

BED & BREAKFASTS
In Britain these are small, simple establishments, not the upscale option Americans know by this name. They are inexpensive accommodations, usually in a family home. Few rooms have private bathrooms, and most bed-and-breakfasts offer no meals other than breakfast. Guest houses are a slightly larger, somewhat more luxurious, version. Both provide the visitor with an excellent glimpse of everyday British life.

CAMPING
Britain has an abundance of campsites. Some are large and well equipped; others are merely small farmers' fields, offering primitive facilities. For information contact VisitBritain in the United States or the Camping and Caravanning Club.
🚩 **Camping and Caravanning Club** ✉ Greenfields House, Westwood Way, Coventry CV4 8JH ☎ 02476/694995.

FARMHOUSES
Farmhouses rarely offer professional hotel standards, but they have a special appeal: the rustic, rural experience. Prices are generally very reasonable. A car is vital for a successful farmhouse stay. The Farm Holiday Bureau, a network of farming and country people who offer B&B accommodations, is a good source for regional tourist board–inspected and –approved properties. These properties are listed in the *Stay on a Farm* guide, produced by the bureau.
🚩 **Farm Stay UK** ✉ National Agricultural Centre, Stoneleigh Park, Kenilworth, Warwickshire CV8 2LZ ☎ 0247/669-6630 ⊕ www.farmstayuk.co.uk.

HISTORIC BUILDINGS
To spend your vacation in a Gothic temple, an old lighthouse on an isolated island, or maybe in an apartment at Hampton Court Palace, contact one of the half dozen organizations in Great Britain that have specially adapted, modernized historic buildings to rent. A leading organization that rents such buildings is the Landmark Trust; these properties do not have TVs. The National Trust, Portmeirion Cottages, and the upscale Rural Retreats also rent historic buildings.
🚩 **Landmark Trust** ✉ Shottesbrooke, Maidenhead, Berkshire SL6 3SW ☎ 01628/825925 ⊕ www.landmarktrust.co.uk. **National Trust** ⌂ Box 536, Melksham, Wiltshire SN12 8SX ☎ 01225/791199 ⊕ www.nationaltrust.org.uk. **Portmeirion Cottages** ✉ Hotel Portmeirion, Gwynedd, Wales LL48 6ET ☎ 01766/770228. **Rural Retreats** ✉ Retreat House, Station Rd., Blockley, Moreton-in-Marsh, Gloucestershire GL56 9DZ ☎ 01386/701177 ⊕ www.ruralretreats.co.uk. **Vivat Trust** ✉ 61 Pall Mall, London, SW1Y 5HZ ☎ 020/7930-8030 ⊕ www.vivat.org.uk.

HOLIDAY COTTAGES
Furnished apartments, houses, cottages, and trailers are available for weekly rental in all areas of the country. These vary from quaint, cleverly converted farmhouses to brand-new buildings set in scenic surroundings. The VisitBritain booklet "Self Catering Holiday Homes" is available from the VisitBritain office in New York. Lists of rental properties are available free of charge from local tourist information centers in Britain. Discounts of up to 50% apply during the off-season (October through March).

HOSTELS The more than 350 youth hostels throughout England, Wales, and Scotland range from very basic to very good. Many are in remote and beautiful areas; others are on the outskirts of large cities. Despite the name, there is no age restriction. The accommodations are inexpensive and generally reliable and usually include cooking facilities. For additional information, contact the YHA Headquarters.

YHA Headquarters ✉ Trevelyan House, 8 St. Stephen's Hill, St. Albans, Hertfordshire AL1 2DY ☎ 01727/855215.

HOTELS British hotels vary greatly, and there is no reliable official system of classification. Most have rooms with private bathrooms, although there are still many hotels—usually older ones—that offer some rooms with only sinks; in this case, showers and bathtubs (and toilets) are usually just down the hall. Many also have "good" and "bad" wings. Be sure to check the room before you take it. Generally, British hotel prices include breakfast, but beware: many offer only a Continental breakfast—often little more than tea and toast. A hotel that includes a traditional British breakfast in its rates is usually a good bet. Hotel prices in London can be significantly higher than in the rest of the country, and sometimes the quality does not reflect the extra cost. Tourist information centers all over the country will reserve rooms for you, usually for a small fee. Many hotels offer special weekend and off-season bargain packages.

UNIVERSITY HOUSING In larger cities and in some towns, certain universities offer their residence halls to paying vacationers. The facilities available are usually compact sleeping units, and they can be rented on a nightly basis. For information, contact the British Universities Accommodation Consortium.

British Universities Accommodation Consortium ✆ Box 1498, University Park, Nottingham NG7 2RD ☎ 01159/504571.

MAIL & SHIPPING

POSTAL RATES Airmail letters to the United States and Canada cost 45p for 10 grams; postcards, 40p; aerograms, 40p. Letters and postcards to Europe weighing up to 20 grams cost 36p. Letters within the United Kingdom: first-class, 27p; second-class and postcards, 19p.

RECEIVING MAIL If you're uncertain where you'll be staying, you can arrange to have your mail sent to American Express. The service is free to cardholders and AmEx traveler's check holders; all others pay a small fee. You can also collect letters at London's Main Post Office. Ask to have the mail addressed as the recipient's name appears on his or her passport, to *poste restante* or "to be called for" and mailed to the Main Post Office. For collection, hours are weekdays 8 AM–8 PM, Saturday 9 AM–8 PM. You'll need your passport or other official form of identification. This service can be arranged at post offices throughout Britain.

Post Offices American Express ✉ 6 Haymarket, London SW1Y 4BS. **Main Post Office** ✉ Trafalgar Square, 24–28 William IV Street, London WC2N 4DL ⊕ www.royalmail.com.

MONEY MATTERS

In general, transportation in Britain is expensive in comparison with other countries. You should take advantage of the many reductions and special fares available on trains, buses, and subways. Always ask about these when buying your ticket.

London now ranks with Tokyo as one of the world's most expensive hotel capitals. Finding budget accommodations—especially during July and August—can be difficult; you should try to book well ahead if you are visiting during these months. Dining out at top-of-the-line restaurants can be prohibitively expensive, but there are new chains of French-

Italian–style café-brasseries, along with a large number of pubs and ethnic restaurants that offer excellent food at reasonable prices.

The gulf between prices in the capital and outside is wide. Be prepared to pay a value-added tax (V.A.T.) of 17½% on almost everything you buy; in nearly all cases it is included in the advertised price.

Costs: in London, cup of coffee, £1–£2; pint of beer, £1.80–£2.20; glass of wine, £2–£4; soda, 80p–£1.50; 2-km (1-mi) taxi ride, £3; ham sandwich, £1.75–£3.50.

CURRENCY The British unit of currency is the pound sterling (£), divided into 100 pence (p). Bills are issued in denominations of £5, £10, £20, and £50. Coins are £2, £1, 50p, 20p, 10p, 5p, 2p, and 1p. Scottish banks issue Scottish currency, of which all coins and notes—with the exception of the £1 notes—are accepted in England. At press time (summer 2003) the pound stood at £0.63 to the U.S. dollar, £0.45 to the Canadian dollar, £0.41 to the Australian dollar, £0.36 to the New Zealand dollar, £0.08 to the South African rand, and £0.70 to the euro.

Traveler's checks are widely accepted in Britain, and many banks, hotels, and shops offer currency-exchange facilities. You will have to pay a £2 commission fee wherever you change them; banks offer the best rates, yet even these fees vary. If you are changing currency, you will have to pay (on top of commission) based on the amount you are changing. In London and other big cities, *bureaux de change* abound, but it definitely pays to shop around: they charge a flat fee, and it's often a great deal more than that at other establishments, such as banks. American Express foreign exchange desks do not charge a commission fee on AmEx traveler's checks. Credit cards are universally accepted, and the most commonly used are MasterCard and Visa.

VALUE-ADDED TAX (V.A.T.) Foreign visitors from outside Europe can avoid Britain's 17½% value-added tax (V.A.T.) by taking advantage of the following two methods. By the Direct Export method, the shopkeeper arranges the export of the goods and does not charge V.A.T. at the point of sale. This means that the purchases are sent on to your home separately. If you prefer to take your purchase with you, try the Retail Export scheme, run by most large stores: the special Form 407 (provided only by the retailer) is attached to your invoice. You must present the goods, form, and invoice to the customs officer at the last port of departure from the European Union. Allow plenty of time to do this at the airport, as there are often long lines. The form is then returned to the store and the refund forwarded to you, minus a small service charge. For inquiries call the local Customs and Excise office listed in the telephone directory.

TELEPHONES

COUNTRY & AREA CODES The United Kingdom's country code is 44. When dialing a number in Britain from abroad, drop the initial 0 from the local area code.

DIRECTORY & OPERATOR ASSISTANCE For information anywhere in Britain, dial ☎ 192. For the operator, dial ☎ 100. For assistance with international calls, dial ☎ 155.

INTERNATIONAL CALLS The cheapest way to make an overseas call is to dial it yourself. But be sure to have plenty of coins or phone cards close at hand. Newsdealers sell budget-rate international phone cards, such as First National and America First, which can be used from any phone by dialing an access number, then a personal identification number. After you have inserted the coins or card, dial 00 (the international code), then the country code—1 for the United States—followed by the area code and local number. You call also make calls through AT&T, MCI Worldphone, or Sprint

Global One long-distance operators. To make a collect or other operator-assisted call, dial ☎ 155.

▣ Access Codes **AT&T Direct** In the U.K., there are AT&T access numbers to dial the U.S. using three different phone types: ☎ 0500/890011 Cable & Wireless; 0800/890011 British Telecom; 0800/0130011 AT&T. **MCI Worldphone** ☎ 0800/890222. **Sprint International Access** ☎ 0800/890877.

LOCAL CALLS Public telephones are plentiful in British cities, especially London. British Telecom is gradually replacing the distinctive red phone booths with generic glass and steel cubicles, but the traditional boxes still remain in the countryside. There are three types of phones: those that accept (1) only coins, (2) only British Telecom (BT) phone cards, or (3) BT phone cards and credit cards.

The coin-operated phones are of the push-button variety; their workings vary, but there are usually instructions on each unit. Most take 10p, 20p, 50p, and £1 coins. Insert the coins *before* dialing (minimum charge is 20p). If you hear a repeated single tone after dialing, the line is busy; a continual tone means the number is unobtainable (or that you have dialed the wrong—or no—prefix). The indicator panel shows you how much money is left; add more whenever you like. If there is no answer, replace the receiver and your money will be returned.

All calls are charged according to the time of day. Standard rate is weekdays 8 AM–6 PM; cheaper rates are weekdays 6 PM–8 AM and all day on weekends. A local call before 6 PM costs 15p for three minutes; this doubles to 30p for the same from a pay phone. A daytime call to the United States will cost 24p a minute on a regular phone (weekends are cheaper), 80p on a pay phone.

AREA CODES There is one area code for London—020—followed by a prefix, either 7 (for inner London) or 8 (for outer London), before the seven-digit phone number. So, for example, for a phone call to inner London, you would dial 020/7242–4444; for outer London, 020/8242–4444. Each large city or region in Britain has its own numerical prefix, which is used only when you are dialing from outside the city. In provincial areas the dialing codes for nearby towns are often posted in the booth.

TIPPING

Some restaurants and most hotels add a service charge of 10%–15% to the bill. If this has been done, you're under no obligation to tip further. If no service charge is indicated, add 10%–15% to your total bill, unless you are unhappy with the service. Taxi drivers should also get 10%–15%, although it's not obligatory. You are not expected to tip theater or cinema ushers, elevator operators, or bartenders in pubs. Hairdressers and barbers should receive 10%–15%. If you get help from a hotel concierge, a tip of £1–£2 is appropriate.

TRAIN TRAVEL

The old single national operator British Rail (BR) has been broken up into individual private operators. Dogged by poor performance, old rolling stock, and an increase in accidents, services throughout the country are working on a major investment and overhaul program to bring the service up to safety and speed levels that used to be the bywords for excellence in previous days. For information on train travel, contact National Rail Enquiries.

The country's rail network links London with every major city in the country, and to France and Belgium via the Channel Tunnel. The most modern high-speed trains travel up to 140 mph and offer comfortable, air-conditioned cars, both first and second class, with restaurant or buffet facilities. Local train services are not as reliable, particularly around such congested city centers as London. In general, seat reservations are not necessary except during peak vacation periods and on popular medium- and long-distance routes.

FARES &
SCHEDULES
Rail fares are high when compared with those in other countries. However, the network does offer a wide, and often bewildering, range of ticket discounts. Information and tickets can be obtained from information offices in each station, Rail Travel Centres within the larger train stations, and by phone to National Rail Enquiries.

If you are planning to travel only short distances, be sure to buy inexpensive same-day round-trip tickets ("cheap day returns"). These cost only slightly more than ordinary one-way ("single"), standard-class tickets but can be used *only* after 9:30 AM and on weekends. Other special offers are regional Rover tickets, giving unlimited travel within local areas, and Saver returns, allowing greatly reduced round-trip travel during off-peak periods.

🚩 **National Rail Enquiries** ☎ 0845/748-4950 ⊕ www.nationalrail.co.uk.

VISITOR INFORMATION

🚩 **Britain Visitor Centre** ✉ 1 Regent St., Piccadilly Circus, SW1Y 4NX ☎ no phone ⊕ www.visitbritain.com.

WHEN TO GO

CLIMATE
On the whole, Britain's winters are rarely bitter, except in the north and Scotland. Wherever you are, and whatever the season, be prepared for sudden changes. Take an umbrella and raincoat wherever you go, particularly in Scotland.

The following are the average daily maximum and minimum temperatures for London.

Jan.	43F	6C	May	62F	17C	Sept.	65F	19C
	36	2		47	8		52	11
Feb.	44F	7C	June	69F	20C	Oct.	58F	14C
	36	2		53	12		46	8
Mar.	50F	10C	July	71F	22C	Nov.	50F	10C
	38	3		56	13		42	6
Apr.	56F	13C	Aug.	71F	22C	Dec.	45F	7C
	42	6		56	13		38	3

LONDON

If London, the capital of Great Britain, contained only its famous landmarks—Buckingham Palace, Big Ben, Parliament, the Tower of London—it would still rank as one of the world's great destinations. Today it occupies 600 square miles and is home to 7 million people. A city that loves to be explored, London beckons with great museums, royal pageantry, and houses that are steeped in history. Marvel at the duke of Wellington's house, track Jack the Ripper's shadow in Whitechapel, then get Beatle-ized at Abbey Road. From the East End to the West End, you'll find London is a dickens of a place.

Exploring London

Traditionally London has been divided between the City, to the east, where its banking and commercial interests lie, and Westminster, to the west, the seat of the royal court and of government. It is in these two areas that you will find most of the grand buildings that have played a central role in British history: the Tower of London and St. Paul's Cathedral, Westminster Abbey and the Houses of Parliament, Buckingham Palace, and the older royal palace of St. James's.

Those who restrict their sightseeing to the well-known tourist areas miss much of the best the city has to offer. Within a few minutes' walk of Buckingham Palace, for instance, lie St. James's and Mayfair, two neighboring quarters of elegant town houses built for the nobility during the 17th and early 18th centuries and now notable for the shopping opportunities they house. The same lesson applies to the City, where, tucked away in quiet corners, stand many of the churches Christopher Wren built to replace those destroyed during the Great Fire of 1666.

Other parts of London worth exploring include Covent Garden, a former fruit and flower market converted into a lively shopping and entertainment center where you can wander for hours enjoying the friendly bustle of the streets. Hyde Park and Kensington Gardens, by contrast, offer a great swath of green parkland across the city center, preserved by past kings and queens for their own hunting and relaxation. A walk across Hyde Park will bring you to the museum district of South Kensington, with three major national collections: the Natural History Museum, the Science Museum, and the Victoria & Albert Museum, which specializes in the fine and applied arts.

The south side of the River Thames has its treats as well. A short stroll across Waterloo Bridge brings you to the South Bank Arts Complex, which includes the Royal National Theatre, the Royal Festival Hall, the Hayward Gallery (with changing exhibitions of international art), and the National Film Theatre. Here also are the exciting reconstruction of Shakespeare's Globe theater and its sister museum, and Tate Modern in the massive former power station. The London Eye observation wheel gives the most stunning views—to the west are the Houses of Parliament and Big Ben; to the east the dome of St. Paul's looks smaller on London's changing modern architectural skyline. The Millennium Bridge leaps across the Thames like a so-called steel "blaze of light" joining Tate Modern to St. Paul's in the City. London, although not simple of layout, is a rewarding walking city, and this remains the best way to get to know its nooks and crannies. The infamous weather may not be on your side, but there's plenty of indoor entertainment to keep you amused if you forget the umbrella.

Westminster

Numbers in the margin correspond to points of interest on the London map.

Westminster is the royal backyard—the traditional center of the royal court and of government. Here, within 1 km (½ mi) or so of one another, are nearly all of London's most celebrated buildings, and there is a strong feeling of history all around you. Generations of kings and queens have lived here since the end of the 11th century—including the current monarch.

16 Banqueting House. On the right side of the grand processional avenue known as Whitehall—site of many important government offices—stands this famous monument of the English Renaissance period. Designed by Inigo Jones in 1625 for court entertainments, it is the only part of Whitehall Palace, the monarch's principal residence during the 16th and 17th centuries, that did not burn down in 1698. It has a magnificent ceiling by Rubens, and outside is an inscription that marks the window through which King Charles I stepped to his execution. ⊠ *Whitehall, SW1* ☎ *020/7930–4179* ⊕ *www.hrp.org.uk* ☉ *Mon.–Sat. 10–5*

⊘ *Closed bank holiday Mondays, Christmas week, and on short notice for banquets, so call first* Ⓤ *Charing Cross, Embankment, Westminster.*

❽ **Buckingham Palace.** Supreme among the symbols of London, indeed of Britain generally, and of the royal family, Buckingham Palace tops many must-see lists—although the building itself is no masterpiece and has housed the monarch only since Victoria moved here from Kensington Palace at her accession in 1837. Located at the end of the Mall, the palace is the London home of the queen and the administrative hub of the entire royal family. When the queen is in residence (normally on weekdays except in January, August, September, and part of June), the royal standard flies over the east front. Inside are dozens of ornate 19th-century-style state rooms used on formal occasions. The private apartments of Queen Elizabeth and Prince Philip are in the north wing. Parts of Buckingham Palace are open to the public during August and September; during the entire year, the **Queen's Gallery**, which shows treasures from the vast royal art collections. The ceremony of the **Changing of the Guard** takes place in front of the palace at 11:30 daily, April–July, and on alternate days during the rest of the year. Arrive early, as people are invariably stacked several deep along the railings, whatever the weather. ⊠ *Buckingham Palace Rd., SW1* ☎ *020/7839–1377; 020/7799–2331 24-hr information; 020/7321–2233 credit-card reservations (50p booking charge)* ⊕ *www.royal.gov.uk* ⊠ *£11.50 (prices change annually)* ⊘ *Early Aug.–early Oct. (confirm dates, which are subject to queen's mandate), daily 9:30–4:15* Ⓤ *St. James's Park, Victoria.*

⓬ **Cabinet War Rooms.** It was from this small maze of 17 bombproof underground rooms—in the back of the hulking Foreign Office—that Britain's World War II fortunes were directed. During air raids the Cabinet met here—the Cabinet Room is still arranged as if a meeting were about to convene. Among the rooms are the Prime Minister's Room, from which Winston Churchill made many of his inspiring wartime broadcasts, and the Transatlantic Telephone Room, from which he spoke directly to President Roosevelt in the White House. ⊠ *Clive Steps, King Charles St., SW1* ☎ *020/7930–6961* ⊕ *www.iwm.org.uk* ⊘ *Apr.–Sept., daily 9:30–5:15; Oct.–Mar., daily 10–5:15* Ⓤ *Westminster.*

❻ **Carlton House Terrace.** This street, a Regency-era showpiece on the Mall, was built in 1827–32 by John Nash in imposing white stucco and with massive Corinthian columns. Number 12 is home to the Institute of Contemporary Arts. ⊠ *The Mall, W1* ☎ *020/7930–3647* ⊕ *www.ica.org.uk* ⊘ *Daily noon–7:30, later for some events* Ⓤ *Charing Cross.*

⓭ **Downing Street.** Looking like an unassuming alley but barred by iron gates at both its Whitehall and Horse Guards Road approaches, this is the location of the famous **No. 10,** London's modest version of the White House, which has, at least officially, housed the prime minister since 1732. **No. 11** is traditionally the residence of the chancellor of the exchequer (secretary of the treasury), and **No. 12** is the party whips' office. Just south of Downing Street, in the middle of Whitehall, you'll see the **Cenotaph,** a stone national memorial to the dead of both world wars. At 11 AM on the Sunday closest to the 11th day of the 11th month, the queen and other dignitaries lay red poppies in tribute here. ⊠ *Whitehall, SW1* Ⓤ *Westminster.*

⓱ **Horse Guards Parade.** The former tiltyard of Whitehall Palace is the site of the annual ceremony of Trooping the Colour, when the queen takes the salute in the great military parade that marks her official birthday on the second Saturday in June (her real one is on April 21). Demand

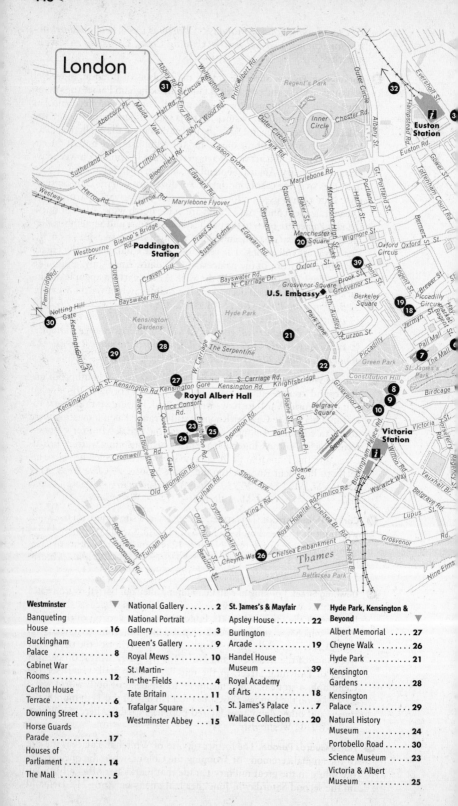

London

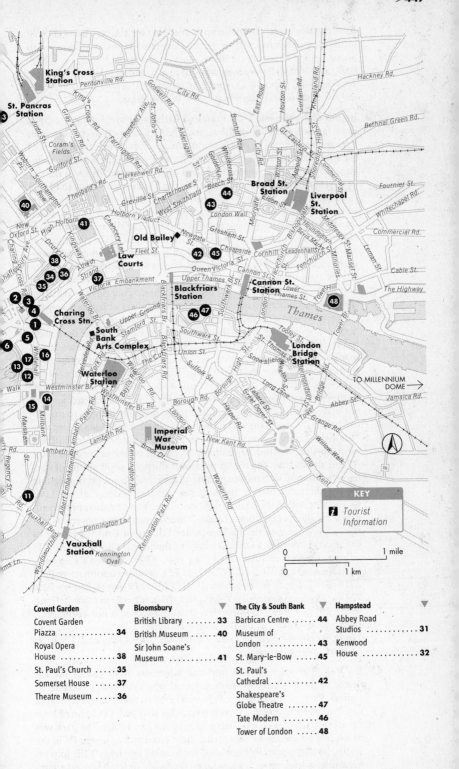

Covent Garden

Covent Garden
Piazza 34
Royal Opera
House 38
St. Paul's Church 35
Somerset House 37
Theatre Museum 36

Bloomsbury

British Library 33
British Museum 40
Sir John Soane's
Museum 41

The City & South Bank

Barbican Centre 44
Museum of
London 43
St. Mary-le-Bow 45
St. Paul's
Cathedral 42
Shakespeare's
Globe Theatre 47
Tate Modern 46
Tower of London 48

Hampstead

Abbey Road
Studios 31
Kenwood
House 32

for tickets is great, and tickets are available for the ceremony, as well as the queenless rehearsals on the preceding two Saturdays. There is also a daily guard-changing ceremony outside the guard house, on White-hall, at 11 AM (10 on Sunday)—one of London's best photo ops. ⊠ *Whitehall, opposite Downing St., SW1* ☎ *020/7414–2479 Trooping the Colour ticket information* Ⓤ *Westminster.*

⓮ **Houses of Parliament.** The Houses of Parliament are among the city's
Fodor'sChoice   most famous and photogenic sights. The Clock Tower keeps watch on
★   Parliament Square, in which stand statues of everyone from Richard the Lion-Hearted to Abraham Lincoln, and, across the way, Westmin-ster Abbey. Also known as the **Palace of Westminster,** this was the site of the monarch's main residence from the 11th century until 1512; the court then moved to the newly built Whitehall Palace. The only parts of the original building to have survived are the **Jewel Tower,** which was built in 1365 as a treasure-house for Edward III, and **Westminster Hall,** which has a fine hammer-beam roof. The rest of the structure was destroyed in a disastrous fire in 1834 and was rebuilt in the newly pop-ular mock-medieval Gothic style. Architects Sir Charles Barry and Au-gustus Pugin designed the entire place, right down to the Gothic umbrella stands. This newer part of the palace contains the debating chambers and committee rooms of the two Houses of Parliament—the Commons (whose members are elected) and the Lords (whose mem-bers are appointed or inherit their seats). There are no tours of the palace, but the public is admitted to the Public Gallery of each House; expect to wait in line for several hours (the line for the Lords is generally much shorter than that for the Commons). The most famous features of the palace are its towers. At the south end is the 336-foot **Victoria Tower.** At the other end is **St. Stephen's Tower,** or the Clock Tower, better known, but inaccurately so, as **Big Ben;** that name properly belongs to the 13-ton bell in the tower on which the hours are struck. Some say Ben was "Big Ben" Caunt, heavyweight champ; others, Sir Benjamin Hall, the far-from-slim Westminster building works commissioner of the 1850s. A light shines from the top of the tower during a night sitting of Par-liament. Be sure to have your name placed in advance on the waiting list for the twice-weekly tours of the private residence of the Lord Chancellor within the Palace of Westminster. You can also apply in ad-vance for the special "line of route" tour—open only to overseas vis-itors—by writing to the **Parliamentary Education Unit** (⊠ House of Commons Information Office, House of Commons, London SW1A 2TT) at least a month in advance of your visit. ⊠ *St. Stephen's Entrance, St. Margaret St., SW1* ☎ *020/7219–4272 Commons information; 020/ 7219–3107 Lords information; 020/7222–2219 Jewel Tower; 020/ 7219–2184 Lord Chancellor's Residence* ⊕ *www.parliament.uk* ☉ *Commons Mon.–Thurs. 2:30–10, Fri. 9:30–3 (although not every Fri.); Lords Mon.–Thurs. 2:30–10; Lord Chancellor's Residence Tues. and Thurs. 10:30–12:30* ☉ *Closed Easter wk, July–Oct., and 3 wks at Christmas* Ⓤ *Westminster.*

❺ **The Mall.** The splendid and imperial **Admiralty Arch** guards the en-trance to the Mall, the noted ceremonial way that leads alongside **St. James's Park** to Buckingham Palace. The Mall takes its name from a game called *palle maille,* a version of croquet that James I imported from France and Charles II popularized during the late 1600s. The park was developed by successive monarchs, most recently by George IV in the 1820s, having originally been used for hunting by Henry VIII. Join of-fice workers relaxing with a lunchtime sandwich, or stroll here on a sum-mer's evening when the illuminated fountains play and Westminster Abbey and the Houses of Parliament are floodlighted. Toward Buckingham

Palace, along the Mall, you'll pass the foot of the imposing **Carlton House Terrace.** ⊠ *The Mall, Cockspur St., Trafalgar Sq., SW1* Ⓤ *Charing Cross.*

★ ❷ **National Gallery.** Generally ranked right after the Louvre, the National Gallery is one of the world's greatest museums. Occupying the long neo-classical building on the north side of Trafalgar Square, it contains works by virtually every famous artist and school from the 14th through the 19th centuries. Its galleries overflow with masterpieces, including Jan van Eyck's *Arnolfini Marriage*, Leonardo da Vinci's *Burlington Virgin and Child*, Velásquez's *The Toilet of Venus* (known as "The Rokeby Venus"), and Constable's *Hay Wain*. The collection is especially strong on Flemish and Dutch masters, Rubens and Rembrandt among them, and on Italian Renaissance works. The museum's Brasserie is an excellent spot for lunch. ⊠ *Trafalgar Sq., WC2* ☎ *020/7747–2885* ⊕ *www.nationalgallery.org.uk* ⊗ *Daily 10–6, Wed. until 9 (special exhibition in Sainsbury Wing, Wed. until 10); 1-hr free guided tour of whole gallery starts at Sainsbury Wing daily at 11:30 and 2:30, and 6:30 Wed.* Ⓤ *Charing Cross, Leicester Sq.*

❸ **National Portrait Gallery.** This fascinating collection contains portraits of well-known (and not-so-well-known) Britons, including monarchs, statesmen, and writers. The gallery contains a separate research center for the study of British portraiture, a bookstore, a café, and a top-floor restaurant with viewing area across to the river. Don't miss the Victorian and early-20th-century galleries. ⊠ *2 St. Martin's Pl., at foot of Charing Cross Rd., WC2* ☎ *020/7312–2463 recorded information* ⊕ *www.npg.org.uk* ⊗ *Mon.–Wed. and weekends 10–6, Thurs. and Fri. 10–9* Ⓤ *Charing Cross, Leicester Sq.*

❾ **Queen's Gallery.** At the south side of Buckingham Palace, a splendid portico (designed by John Simpson) sets the scene for spacious galleries in classic theme. The main room, the Pennethorne Gallery, is dominated by the portrait of Charles I (Van Dyck), which almost overshadows the many works by other masters such as Holbein, Hals, Vermeer, and Rubens. Between and beneath the paintings are cabinets, vases, and silverwork. Other rooms display the finest porcelain from Delft and Sèvres. ⊠ *Buckingham Palace, Buckingham Palace Rd., SW1* ☎ *020/7321–2233* ⊕ *www.royal.gov.uk* ⊗ *Daily 10–5:30, last admission 4:30* Ⓤ *St. James's Park, Victoria.*

🖐 ❿ **Royal Mews.** Unmissable children's entertainment, this museum is the home of Her Majesty's Coronation Coach. Some of the queen's horses are stabled here, and the elaborately gilded state coaches are on view. ⊠ *Buckingham Palace Rd.* ☎ *020/7839–1377* ⊕ *www.royal.gov.uk* ⊗ *Mar.–July and Oct., daily 11–4; Aug. and Sept., daily 10–5; last admission 30 mins before closing* ⊗ *Closed royal and state occasions; call ahead* Ⓤ *St. James's Park, Victoria.*

❹ **St. Martin-in-the-Fields.** Soaring above Trafalgar Square, this landmark church may seem familiar to many Americans because James Gibbs's classical-temple-with-spire design became a pattern for churches in early Colonial America. Built in about 1730, the distinctive neoclassical church is the site for regular free lunchtime music recitals and evening concerts (tickets are available from the box office in the crypt). The crypt is a hive of activity, with a café, bookshop, plus the **London Brass-Rubbing Centre**, where you can make your own souvenir knight, lady, or monarch from replica tomb brasses for about £5. ⊠ *Trafalgar Sq., WC2* ☎ *020/ 7766–1100; 020/7839–8362 credit-card bookings for evening concerts* ⊕ *www.stmartin-in-the-fields.org* ⊗ *Church daily 8–8; crypt Mon.–Sat. 10–8, Sun. noon–6* Ⓤ *Charing Cross, Leicester Sq.*

★ ⓫ **Tate Britain.** By the river to the north of Chelsea, on traffic-laden Millbank, Tate Britain displays a vast range of modern British art. "Modern" is slightly misleading, as the gallery's collection spans from 1545 to the present, including works by Thomas Gainsborough, Sir Joshua Reynolds, and George Stubbs from the 18th century; and by John Constable, William Blake, and the Pre-Raphaelite painters from the 19th century (don't miss Millais's unforgettable *Ophelia*). Also on display is one of the highlights of the Tate's collections, the incredible Turner Bequest, consisting of the personal collection of England's greatest Romantic painter, J. M. W. Turner. The Linbury Galleries on the lower floors present changing exhibitions. Upper floors, reached by a wide, sweeping staircase, bring many works to permanent view that had previously been consigned to storage. ⊠ *Millbank, SW1* ☎ *020/7887–8000; 020/7887–8008 recorded information* ⊕ *www.tate.org.uk* ⊙ *Daily 10–5:50* Ⓤ *Pimlico.*

❶ **Trafalgar Square.** This is the center of London, as noted on a plaque on the corner of the Strand and Charing Cross Road from which distances on U.K. signposts are measured. It is the home of the **National Gallery** and of one of London's most distinctive landmarks, **Nelson's Column,** a tribute to one of England's favorite heroes, Admiral Lord Horatio Nelson, who routed the French at the Battle of Trafalgar in 1805. Constantly alive with Londoners and tourists alike, the square remains London's "living room"—great events, such as New Year's, political rallies, and sporting triumphs, always see the crowds gathering in the city's most famous square. A pedestrianization design program has joined the front of the National Gallery to the rest of the square so traffic no longer roars around the north side. Even the popular pigeons have been moved on, although some still insist on making the most of the tourists. A magic time to be here is when the lights on the gigantic Christmas tree (an annual gift from Norway in thanks for harboring its Royal Family during World War II) are illuminated. ⊠ *Trafalgar Sq., SW1* Ⓤ *Charing Cross.*

⓯ **Westminster Abbey.** It is here, in the most ancient and important of London's great churches, that Britain's monarchs are crowned. Most of the abbey dates from the 13th and 14th centuries. The main nave, which has witnessed countless splendid royal ceremonies, is packed with memories. It is also packed with crowds—so many, in fact, that there is an admission fee to the main nave (always free, of course, for participants in religious services). **Henry VII's Chapel,** an exquisite example of the heavily decorated late-Gothic style, was built in the early 1600s, and the twin towers over the west entrance are an 18th-century addition. There is much to see inside, including the tomb of the Unknown Warrior, a nameless World War I soldier buried, in memory of the war's victims, in earth brought with his corpse from France; and the famous Poets' Corner, where England's great writers—Milton, Chaucer, Shakespeare, and others—are memorialized and some are buried. Behind the high altar are the royal tombs, including those of Queen Elizabeth I and her elder sister, Mary I; her cousin, Mary, Queen of Scots; and Henry V. In the Chapel of Edward the Confessor stands the Coronation Chair.

Off the south side of the main corpus is a host of smaller abbey rooms, including the **Chapter House,** a stunning octagonal room adorned with 14th-century frescoes, where the King's Council and, after that, an early version of the Commons, met between 1257 and 1547. The **Abbey Museum** is in the undercroft and displays, among other things, a collection of macabre effigies made from the death masks and actual clothing of Charles II and Admiral Lord Nelson.

Fodor'sChoice
★

It is all too easy to forget, swamped by the crowds trying to see the abbey's sights, that this is a place of worship. Early morning is a good moment to catch something of the building's atmosphere. Better still, take time to attend a service. Photography is not permitted. ✉ *Broad Sanctuary, SW1* ☎ *020/7222–5152* ⊕ *www.westminster-abbey.org* ⊙ *Weekdays 9–4:45, Sat. 9–2:45 (last admission 1 hr before closing). Museum daily 10:30–4. Chapter House Apr.–Oct., daily 10–5:30; Nov.–Mar., daily 10–4:30* ⊙ *Abbey closed weekdays and Sun. to visitors during services* Ⓤ *Westminster.*

St. James's & Mayfair

These are two of London's most exclusive neighborhoods, where the homes are fashionable and the shopping is world class. You can start by walking west from Piccadilly Circus along Piccadilly, a busy street lined with some very English shops (including Hatchards, the booksellers; Swaine, Adeney, Brigg, the outfitters for country pursuits; and Fortnum & Mason, the department store that supplies the queen's groceries).

★ ㉒ **Apsley House (Wellington Museum).** Once known, quite simply, as No. 1, London, this was long celebrated as the best address in town. Built by Robert Adam in the 1770s, Apsley House was where the duke of Wellington lived from the 1820s until his death in 1852. It has been kept as the Iron Duke liked it, his uniforms and weapons, his porcelain and plate, and his extensive art collection displayed in opulent 19th-century rooms. Unmissable, in every sense, is the gigantic Canova statue of a nude (but fig-leafed) Napoléon Bonaparte, Wellington's archenemy. Special annual events include a commemoration of the Battle of Waterloo on and around June 18; call or check the Web site for details. ✉ *149 Piccadilly, SW1* ☎ *020/7499–5676* ⊕ *www.apsleyhouse.org.uk* ⊙ *Tues.–Sun. 11–4:30* Ⓤ *Hyde Park Corner.*

⓳ **Burlington Arcade.** This perfectly picturesque covered walkway dates from 1819. Here, shops sell cashmere sweaters, silk scarves, handmade chocolates, and leather-bound books. If not the choice shopping spot it once was, it still makes a great photo op, particularly if you can snap the uniformed beadle (he ensures that no one runs, whistles, or sings here) on duty. ✉ *Off Piccadilly, W1* Ⓤ *Piccadilly Circus.*

㊴ **Handel House Museum.** The former home of the composer, where he lived for more than 30 years until his death in 1759, celebrates his genius in its fine Georgian rooms. You can linger over original manuscripts (others are in the British Library) and gaze at portraits and art illustrating the times. Some of Handel's most famous pieces were created here, including *Messiah* and *Music for the Royal Fireworks.* ✉ *25 Brook St., W1* ☎ *020/7495–1685* ⊕ *www.handelhouse.org* ⊙ *Tues., Wed., Fri., and Sat. 10–6, Thurs. 10–8, Sun. noon–6* Ⓤ *Bond St.*

⓲ **Royal Academy of Arts.** On the north side of Piccadilly, the grand marble pile of **Burlington House** contains the offices of many learned societies and the headquarters of the Royal Academy. In addition to its permanent collection, the RA, as it is generally known, mounts a continuous program of internationally renowned loan exhibitions. Every June, the RA puts on its **Summer Exhibition,** a huge collection of sculpture and painting by Royal Academicians and a plethora of other artists working today, whose works are crammed into every nook and cranny. Craving art now? Try the shop; it's one of the best museum stores in town. ✉ *Burlington House, Piccadilly, W1* ☎ *020/7300–8000; 020/ 7300–5760 recorded information* ⊕ *www.royalacademy.org.uk* ⊙ *Sat.–Thurs. 10–6, Fri. 10–8:30* Ⓤ *Piccadilly Circus, Green Park.*

7 St. James's Palace. This historic royal palace is the current residence of the Prince of Wales. The oldest parts of the lovely brick building date from the 1530s, well before its relatively short career as the center of royal affairs—from the destruction of Whitehall Palace in 1698 until 1837, when Victoria became queen and moved the royal household down the road to Buckingham Palace. Today, the palace is closed to the public, but your viewfinder will love the picturesque exterior and regimental guard on duty. ⊠ *Friary Court, Pall Mall, SW1* Ⓤ *Green Park.*

★ **20 Wallace Collection.** A palatial town-house museum, the Wallace is important, exciting, undervisited—and free. As at the Frick Collection in New York, the setting, Hertford House itself, is part of the show—built for the duke of Manchester and now stuffed with armor, exquisite furniture, and great paintings, including Bouchers, Watteaus, Fragonard's *The Swing,* and Frans Hals's *Laughing Cavalier.* The modernized basement floor is used for educational activities, and has a Watercolour Gallery. The museum courtyard provides yet more exhibition space and an upscale restaurant. ⊠ *Hertford House, Manchester Sq., W1* ☎ *020/7935–0687* ⊕ *www.the-wallace-collection.org.uk* ☉ *Mon.–Sat. 10–5, Sun. noon–5* Ⓤ *Bond St.*

Hyde Park, Kensington & Beyond

When in need of elbow room, Londoners head for Hyde Park and Kensington Gardens. Viewed by natives as their own private backyards, they form an open swath across central London, and in and around them are some of London's most noted museums and monuments.

27 Albert Memorial. This gorgeously gilded 19th-century monument celebrates Queen Victoria's much-loved husband, Prince Albert, who died in 1861 at the age of 42. The monument, itself the epitome of high Victorian pomp and circumstance, commemorates the many socially uplifting projects of the prince, among them the Great Exhibition of 1851, whose catalog he is holding. The memorial is directly opposite the Royal Albert Hall. ⊠ *Kensington Gore* Ⓤ *Knightsbridge.*

26 Cheyne Walk. The most beautiful spot in Chelsea—one of London's most arty (and expensive) residential districts—this Thameside street is adorned with Queen Anne houses and legendary addresses. Author George Eliot died at No. 4 in 1880; Pre-Raphaelite artist Dante Gabriel Rossetti lived at No. 16. Two other resident artists were James McNeill Whistler and J. M. W. Turner. Toward the western end, outside the Church of All Saints, is a golden-face statue of the *Man for All Seasons,* Thomas More, looking beatific on a throne facing the river.

☝ 21 Hyde Park. Along with the smaller St. James's and Green parks to the east, Hyde Park started as Henry VIII's hunting grounds. Nowadays, it remains a tranquil oasis from urban London—-tranquil, that is, except for Sunday morning, when soapbox orators take over **Speakers' Corner,** near the northeast corner of the park (feel free to get up and holler if you fancy spreading your message to the masses). Not far away, along the south side of the park, is **Rotten Row,** which was Henry VIII's royal path to the hunt—*la route du roi*—hence the name. It's still used by the Household Cavalry, the queen's guard. You can see them leave on horseback, in full regalia, around 10:30 or await their exhausted return about noon. ⊠ *Bounded by the Ring, Bayswater Rd., Park La., and Knightsbridge* ☎ *020/7298–2100* ⊕ *www.royalparks.gov.uk* ☉ *Daily 5–midnight* Ⓤ *Hyde Park Corner, Lancaster Gate, Marble Arch, Knightsbridge.*

☝ 28 Kensington Gardens. More formal than neighboring Hyde Park, Kensington Gardens was first laid out as palace grounds and adjoins Kensington Palace. George Frampton's 1912 **Peter Pan,** a bronze of the boy who lived on an island in the Serpentine and never grew up, overlooks the Long Water. His creator, J. M. Barrie, lived at 100 Bayswater Road, not 500 yards from here. The **Princess Diana Memorial Playground** is designed on the theme of Barrie's Neverland. Hook's ship, crocodiles, "jungles" of foliage, and islands of sand provide a fantasy land for kids. **Round Pond** acts as a magnet for model-boat enthusiasts and duck feeders. Nearby is boating and swimming in the **Serpentine,** an S-shape lake. Refreshments can be had at the lakeside tearooms. The **Serpentine Gallery** (☎ 020/7402–6075) holds noteworthy exhibitions of modern art. ⊠ *Bounded by the Broad Walk, Bayswater Rd., the Ring, and Kensington Rd.* ⊕ *www.royalparks.gov.uk* ☉ *Daily dawn–dusk* Ⓤ *Lancaster Gate, Queensway.*

㉙ Kensington Palace. This has been a royal home since the late 17th century. From the outside it looks less like a palace than a country house, which it was until William III bought it in 1689. Queen Victoria spent a less-than-happy childhood at Kensington Palace and Princess Diana, a less-than-happy marriage. Called the "royal ghetto," the palace is home to many Windsors (they live in a distant section cordoned off from the public). Kensington Palace's state apartments have been restored to how they appeared in Princess Victoria's day. Drop in on the Orangery here for a very elegant cup of tea. ⊠ *The Broad Walk, Kensington Gardens, W8* ☎ *0870/751–5180 for advance booking and information* ⊕ *www.hrp.org.uk* 🎟 *£10.20 for tour and exhibitions* ☉ *Daily 10–5* Ⓤ *High St. Kensington.*

㉔ Natural History Museum. The outrageously ornate French Romanesque–style terra-cotta facade of this museum belies the exciting exhibits within. The Darwin Centre displays all creatures great and small in pickling jars and vats, from a tiny Seychellian frog to the giant Komodo dragon lizard. Other highlights include the myriad arthropods in the Creepy Crawlies Gallery and the Human Biology Hall's birth-simulation chamber. Helping you circumnavigate the whole are 14 daily tours from the main information desk. ⊠ *Cromwell Rd., SW7* ☎ *020/7942–5000* ⊕ *www.nhm.ac.uk* ☉ *Mon.–Sat. 10–5:50, Sun. 11–5:50* Ⓤ *South Kensington.*

㉚ Portobello Road. Northwest of Kensington Gardens is the lively **Notting Hill** district, full of stylish restaurants and cafés where some of London's trendsetters gather. The best-known attraction in this area is Portobello Road, where a lively antiques and bric-a-brac market is held each Saturday (arrive at 6 AM for the best finds); the southern end is focused on antiques, the northern end on food, flowers, and secondhand clothes. The street is also full of regular antiques shops that are open most weekdays. Ⓤ *Notting Hill Gate, Ladbroke Grove.*

㉓ Science Museum. The leading national collection of science and technology, this museum has extensive hands-on exhibits on outer space, astronomy, and hundreds of other subjects. The dramatic Wellcome Wing, a £45 million addition to the museum, is devoted to contemporary science, medicine, and technology. It also includes a 450-seat IMAX cinema. ⊠ *Exhibition Rd., SW7* ☎ *020/7942–4000* ⊕ *www.sciencemuseum.org.uk* ☉ *Daily 10–6* Ⓤ *South Kensington.*

★ ㉕ Victoria & Albert Museum. The V&A, as it is commonly known, opened during the 19th century as a museum of the decorative arts, and today it has extensive collections of costumes, paintings, jewelry, and crafts from every part of the globe. Don't miss the sculpture court, the vintage couture collections, and the great Raphael Room with its cartoons (drawings) for tapestries. The impressive British Galleries chronicle four centuries of British history, art, and design. For an overall picture, see the museum's prized treasures on a free, one-hour daily tour, at 10:30, 11:30, 1:30, and 3:30, with a 30-minute version on Wednesday evening at 7:30. The restaurant offers lunch daily, candlelighted dinners on Wednesday nights, traditional roasts on Sunday, and occasional live music. ✉ *Cromwell Rd., SW7* ☎ *020/7942–2000* ⊕ *www.vam.ac.uk* ☉ *Daily 10–5:45, Wed. and last Fri. of the month 10–10* Ⓤ *South Kensington.*

Covent Garden

The Covent Garden district—which lies just to the east of Soho—has gone from a down-at-the-heels area to one of the busiest, most raffishly enjoyable parts of the city. Continental-style open-air cafés create a very un-English atmosphere, with vintage fashion boutiques, art galleries, and street buskers attracting crowds.

㉞ Covent Garden. You could easily spend several hours exploring the block of streets north of the Strand known as Covent Garden. The heart of the area is a former wholesale fruit and vegetable market—made famous as one of Eliza Doolittle's haunts in *My Fair Lady*—established in 1656. The **Piazza**, the now-glass-covered Victorian market building, is a vibrant shopping center with numerous boutiques, crafts shops, and cafés. **The Apple Market** is a superior crafts market, and the more downscale **Jubilee Market** is south across the cobbles in Jubilee Hall. Housed in the old Flower Market at the southeast corner of the square, **London's Transport Museum** tells the story of mass transportation in the capital, with touch-screen interactive material and a Tube-driving simulator. Shops on Long Acre sell maps, art books and materials, and clothing; Neal Street establishments sell clothes, pottery, jewelry, tea, housewares, and stylish bags. ✉ *Bounded by the Strand, Charing Cross Rd., Long Acre, and Drury La., WC2* Ⓤ *Charing Cross, Covent Garden, Leicester Sq.*

㊳ Royal Opera House. This is the fabled home of the Royal Ballet and Britain's finest opera company. The glass-and-steel Floral Hall is the most wonderful feature, and visitors can wander in during the day and enjoy the piazza concourse and the Amphitheatre Bar, which gives a splendid panorama across the city, or listen to a free lunchtime chamber concert. ✉ *Bow St., WC2* ☎ *020/7240–1200 or 020/7304–4000* ⊕ *www. royaloperahouse.org* Ⓤ *Covent Garden.*

㉟ St. Paul's Church. A landmark of the Covent Garden market area, this 1633 church, designed by Inigo Jones, is known as the Actors' Church. Inside are numerous memorials to theater greats. Look for the open-air entertainers performing under the church's portico. ✉ *Bedford St., WC2* Ⓤ *Covent Garden.*

★ ㊲ Somerset House. An old royal palace once stood on the site, but the 18th-century building that finally replaced it was the work of Sir William Chambers during the reign of George III. It was built to house government offices, principally those of the Navy. Many of the gracious 18th-century chambers rooms are on view for free, including the Seamen's Waiting Hall, the Nelson Stair, and the Navy Commissioners' Barge. Lighting up the vaults is a museum of intricate works of silver, gold snuff boxes and Italian mosaics, **The Gilbert Collection** (☎ *020/7240–4080* ▦ £6, free after 4:30). **The Hermitage Rooms** (☎ *020/7845–4630* ▦ £5) also house objects with foreign origins; they are the permanent home for selected treasures from Russia's eponymous premier museum. The **Courtauld Institute of Art** (▦ £5, free Mon. 10–2 except bank holidays ☉ *Mon.–Sat. 10–6, Sun. noon–6* (last admission 5:15) occupies the northern sections of the building. Here, London's finest impressionist and postimpressionist collection spans from Bonnard to van Gogh (Manet's *Bar at the Folies-Bergère* is the star), with bonus post-Renaissance works. Arts events are held in the Italianate courtyard between the Courtauld and the rest of Somerset House. Cafés and a river terrace complete the clutch of cultural delights that visitors can reach directly by walkway from Waterloo Bridge. ⊠ *The Strand, WC2* ☎ *020/7845–4600* ⊕ *www.somerset-house.org.uk* ⊘ *Mon.–Sat. 10–6, Sun. noon–6 (last admission 5:15).*

☺ ㊱ **Theatre Museum.** A comprehensive collection of material on the history of the English theater, this museum traces the history not merely of the classic drama but also of opera, music hall, pantomime, and musical comedy. A highlight is the re-creation of a dressing room filled with memorabilia of former stars. ⊠ *Russell St., WC2* ☎ *020/7836–7891* ⊕ *www.theatremuseum.org* ⊘ *Tues.–Sun. 10–6* Ⓤ *Covent Garden.*

Bloomsbury

Bloomsbury is a semiresidential district to the north of Covent Garden that contains some spacious and elegant 17th- and 18th-century squares. It could be called the intellectual center of London, as both the British Museum and the University of London are here. The area also gave its name to the Bloomsbury Group, a clique of writers and painters who thrived here in the early 20th century.

㉝ **British Library.** Since it opened in 1759, the British Library had always been housed in the British Museum on Gordon Square—but space ran out long ago, necessitating this grand modern edifice, a few blocks north of the British Museum. The library's treasures—the Magna Carta, a Gutenberg Bible, Jane Austen's writings, Shakespeare's First Folio, and musical manuscripts by Handel and Sir Paul McCartney—are on view to the general public in the John Ritblat Gallery. ⊠ *96 Euston Rd., NW1* ☎ *020/7412–7332* ⊕ *www.bl.uk* ⊘ *Mon. and Wed.–Fri. 9:30–6, Tues. 9:30–8, Sat. 9:30–5, Sun. 11–5* Ⓤ *Euston, King's Cross.*

★ ☺ ㊵ **British Museum.** The focal point in this fabled collection of antiquities is the unmissable Great Court, where beneath a vast glass roof lies the museum's inner courtyard. The space also accommodates galleries, a computerized database for viewing the collection on screen, cafés, and shops. The museum's priceless collection of treasures includes Egyptian, Greek, and Roman antiquities; Renaissance jewelry; pottery; coins; glass; and drawings from virtually every European school since the 15th century. Some of the highlights are the **Elgin Marbles,** sculptures that formerly decorated the Parthenon in Athens; the **Rosetta Stone,** which helped archaeologists to interpret Egyptian hieroglyphs; and the JP Morgan Chase **North American Gallery,** which has one of the largest exhibitions of native culture outside the North American continent. The revered gold-and-blue Reading Room is open to the public and has banks of computers. It's best to pick one section that particularly interests you—to try to see everything would be an overwhelming and exhausting task. ⊠ *Great Russell St., WC1* ☎ *020/7636–1555* ⊕ *www.thebritishmuseum.ac.uk* ⊘ *Museum Sat.–Wed. 10–5:30, Thurs. and Fri. 10–8:30. Great Court Sun.–Wed. 9–6, Thurs.–Sat. 9–11* Ⓤ *Tottenham Court Rd., Holborn, Russell Sq.*

★ ㊶ **Sir John Soane's Museum.** On the border of London's legal district, this museum is guaranteed to induce smiles with its fairground fun-house interior, complete with concealed doors, mirrors, and split-level floors. It appears, though, that Sir John—the architect of the Bank of England who bequeathed this house to the nation—was no ordinary trickster. The space is stuffed with his diverse collection of art and artifacts, including antique busts, an ancient Egyptian sarcophagus, and early-

19th-century English paintings. ✉ *13 Lincoln's Inn Fields, WC2* ☎ *020/ 7405–2107* ⊕ *www.soane.org* ⊙ *Tues.–Sat. 10–5, also 6–9 PM 1st Tues. of every month* Ⓤ *Holborn.*

The City & South Bank

The City, the commercial center of London, was once the site of the great Roman city of Londinium. Since those days, the City has been rebuilt innumerable times, and today, ancient and modern jostle each other elbow to elbow. Several of London's most famous attractions are here, along with the adjacent area across the Thames commonly called the South Bank. Here, Shakespeare's Globe Theatre, the Tate Modern, and the British Airways London Eye—the world's largest observation wheel—draw both natives and visitors in droves.

㊹ Barbican Centre. A vast arts center, the Barbican takes its name from the watchtower that stood here during the Middle Ages. It contains a concert hall (where the London Symphony Orchestra is based), two theaters, an art gallery, a cinema, and several restaurants. The **Barbican Art Gallery** showcases modern, populist topics ranging from the Shaker movement to *Star Wars.* Also worth a look are the free displays in the Concourse Gallery. The **Barbican International Theatre Events** (BITE) calendar manages the venue's year-round dance, music, and theater performances. ☎ *020/7638–8891* ⊕ *www.barbican.org.uk* ⊙ *Barbican Centre Mon.–Sat. 9 AM–11 PM, Sun. noon–11; gallery Mon.–Sat. 10–7:30, Sun. noon–7:30* Ⓤ *Moorgate, Barbican.*

㊸ Museum of London. At **London Wall,** so called because it follows the line of the wall that surrounded the Roman settlement, the Museum of London enables you to come to grips with a great deal of the city's history. Oliver Cromwell's death mask, Queen Victoria's crinolined gowns, Selfridge's art deco elevators, and the Lord Mayor's coach are just some of the goodies here. The meticulous excavation of the Roman amphitheatre at the Guildhall is the latest and most exciting of the many archaeological finds on display. ✉ *London Wall, EC2* ☎ *020/7600–0807* ⊕ *www.museumoflondon.org.uk* ⊙ *Mon.–Sat. 10–5:50, Sun. noon–5:50* Ⓤ *Barbican.*

㊺ St. Mary-le-Bow. This landmark church has been rebuilt twice, first after the Great Fire by Christopher Wren and again after damage was sustained during World War II bombings. The peals that issue from the belfry before services are an integral part of city folklore; it is said that a Londoner must be born within the sound of Bow Bells to be a true cockney. The surrounding Cheapside district was the marketplace of medieval London (the word *ceap* is Old English for "to barter"), as the street names hereabouts indicate: Milk Street, Ironmonger Lane, and so on. ✉ *Cheapside, EC2* ☎ *020/7248–5139* ⊕ *www.stmarylebow.co.uk* ⊙ *Mon.–Thurs. 6:30–5:45, Fri. 6:30–4* Ⓤ *Mansion House.*

★ ㊷ St. Paul's Cathedral. London's symbolic heart, St. Paul's is Sir Christopher Wren's masterpiece. Its dome—the world's third largest—can be seen from many an angle in other parts of the city. The cathedral was completed in 1710 following the Great Fire. Wren was the architect who was also responsible for designing 50 parish churches in the city to replace those lost in that disaster. Fittingly, he is buried in the crypt under a simple Latin epitaph, composed by his son, which translates as: READER, IF YOU SEEK HIS MONUMENT, LOOK AROUND YOU. The remains of the duke of Wellington and Admiral Lord Nelson are also in the crypt. The cathedral has been the site of many famous state occasions, including the funeral of Winston Churchill in 1965 and the ill-fated marriage of the Prince and Princess of Wales in 1981. In the ambulatory (the area behind the high altar) is the American Chapel, a memorial to the 28,000 U.S. GIs stationed in Britain during World War II who lost their lives in active service. The greatest architectural glory of the cathedral is the dome. It consists of three distinct elements: an outer, timber-frame dome covered with lead; an interior dome built of brick and decorated with frescoes of the life of St. Paul by the 18th-century artist Sir James Thornhill; and, in between, a brick cone that supports and strengthens both. There is a good view of the church from the **Whispering Gallery**, high up in the inner dome. The gallery is so called because of its remarkable acoustics, whereby hushed words spoken on one side can be clearly heard on the other, 107 feet away. Above this gallery are two others, both external, from which there are fine views over the City and beyond. ✉ *St. Paul's Churchyard, Paternoster Sq., Ludgate Hill, EC4* ☎ *020/7236–4128* ⊕ *www.stpauls.co.uk* ⊙ *Cathedral Mon.–Sat. 8:30–4; ambulatory, crypt, and galleries Mon.–Sat. 9–5:15; shop and Crypt café also Sun. 10:30–5* Ⓤ *St. Paul's.*

★ ㊼ **Shakespeare's Globe Theatre.** This spectacular theater is a replica of Shakespeare's open-roof Globe Playhouse (built in 1599, incinerated in 1613), where most of the playwright's great plays premiered. It stands 200 yards from the original, overlooking the Thames. It was built with the use of authentic Elizabethan materials, including the first thatch roof in London since the Great Fire. Plays are presented in natural light (and sometimes rain) to 1,000 people on wooden benches in the "bays," plus 500 "groundlings," standing on a carpet of filbert shells and clinker, just as they did nearly four centuries ago. Although the main theater season runs from mid-May to mid-September, the Globe can be viewed year-round if you take the helpful tour offered by the **Shakespeare's Globe Exhibition Centre.** In addition, productions are now scheduled throughout the year in a second, indoor theater, built to a design by the 17th-century architect Inigo Jones. Call for performance schedule. ✉ *New Globe Walk, Bankside (South Bank)* ☎ *020/ 7902–1500* ⊕ *www.shakespeares-globe.org* ⊙ *Daily 10–5* Ⓤ *Black-friars, Southwark.*

㊏ ㊻ **Tate Modern.** Opposite St. Paul's Cathedral on the Thames in South Bank, this offspring of the Tate gallery resides in the 8½-acre Bankside Power Station, a dazzling, world-class venue for some of the Tate's more contemporary international treasures. Originally built in the 1930s, it was handsomely renovated to its present state by Swiss architects Herzog and de Meuron. The collection includes classic works by Matisse, Picasso, Dalí, Moore, Bacon, and Warhol, as well as creations of today's most-talked-about artists, such as Anish Kapoor's brilliant, mammoth installation/sculpture in the grand Turbine Hall. ✉ *25 Summer St., SE1* ☎ *020/7887–8000* ⊕ *www.tate.org.uk* ⊙ *Sun.–Thurs. 10–6, Fri. and Sat. 10–10* Ⓤ *Blackfriars, Southwark.*

★ ㊏ ㊽ **Tower of London.** This minicity of melodramatic towers is one of London's most famous sights and one of its most crowded, too. Come as early in the day as possible (you can buy tickets in advance at any Underground stop) and head for the Crown Jewels so you can see them before the crowds arrive. The tower served the monarchs of medieval England as both fortress and palace. Every British sovereign from William the Conqueror in the 11th century to Henry VIII in the 16th lived here, and it remains a royal palace, in name at least. The **White Tower** is the oldest and also the most conspicuous building in the entire complex. Inside, the **Royal Armouries**, England's national collection of arms and armor, occupy the ground floor. On the first floor, the **Chapel of St. John** is one of the few unaltered parts of the tower, and its simple, original architecture makes it one of the most distinctive church interiors of its time in England.

The group of buildings that make up the old **Medieval Palace** is best entered by Water Lane, beside **Traitors' Gate.** There are three towers to explore: **St. Thomas's Tower,** which contains the monarch's rooms and lobby with waterside entrance (now known as Traitors' Gate); the Wakefield Tower; and Lanthorn Tower, both of which have more royal accommodations joined by a walkway along the battlements. In the furnished rooms of the **Wakefield Tower,** costumed actors describe daily life in the Medieval Palace and its evolution over the centuries. Henry VI is alleged to have been murdered in the Wakefield Tower in 1471, during England's medieval civil war, the Wars of the Roses. Among other buildings worth seeing is the **Bloody Tower.** The little princes in the tower—the uncrowned boy-king Edward V and his brother Richard, duke of York, supposedly murdered on the orders of the duke of Gloucester, later crowned Richard III—certainly lived in the Bloody Tower and may well have died here, too. It was a rare honor to be beheaded in private inside the tower on the Scaffold Site of Tower Green; most people were executed outside, on **Tower Hill,** where the crowds could get a much better view. The church of **St. Peter ad Vincula** has the burial places of the unfortunate queens and bishops who upset the Tudor monarchy and can be seen as part of a Yeoman's Tour.

The **Crown Jewels,** a breathtaking collection of regalia, precious stones, gold, and silver, used for the coronation of the present sovereign, are housed in the **Jewel House, Waterloo Barracks.** An exhibition illustrating their history precedes the gems themselves. The Royal Scepter contains the largest cut diamond in the world. The Imperial State Crown, made for the 1838 coronation of Queen Victoria, contains some 3,000 precious stones, largely diamonds and pearls. The jewels used to be housed in the **Martin Tower** (in less secure circumstances, when daring Thomas Blood made an attempt to steal them in 1671), where an exhibit— "Crowns and Diamonds"—shows the making of the royal regalia and displays some state crowns made for earlier kings and queens. Look for the ravens near the Wakefield Tower. Their presence at the Tower is traditional, and it is said that if they leave, the Tower will fall and England will lose her greatness. ✉ *H. M. Tower of London, Tower Hill, EC3N* ☎ *0870/756–7070 recorded information and advance booking* ⊕ *www. hrp.org.uk* 🖾 *£12* ◷ *Mar.–Oct., Mon.–Sat. 9–5, Sun. 10–5; Nov.–Feb., Sun. and Mon. 10–4, Tues.–Sat. 9–4 (the Tower closes 1 hr after last admission time and all internal buildings close 30 mins after last admission)* ☞ *Yeoman Warder guides leave daily from Middle Tower, subject to weather and availability, at no charge, about every 30 mins until 3:30 in summer, 2:30 in winter* Ⓤ *Tower Hill.*

Hampstead

Hampstead is a quaint village within the city, where many famous poets and writers have lived. Today it is a fashionable residential area, with a main shopping street and some rows of elegant 18th-century houses. The heath is one of London's largest and most attractive open spaces.

③ **Abbey Road Studios.** Here, outside the legendary Abbey Road Studios (the facility is closed to the public), is the most famous zebra crossing in the world. Immortalized on the cover of the Beatles' *Abbey Road* album of 1969, this pedestrian crosswalk is a spot beloved to countless Beatlemaniacs and baby boomers, many of whom venture here to leave their signature on the white stucco fence that fronts the adjacent studio facility. Abbey Road is not in Hampstead but in adjacent St. John's Wood, an elegant residential area, a 10-minute ride on the Tube from central

London. ✉ *3 Abbey Rd., NW8* ⊕ *www.abbeyroad.co.uk* Ⓤ *St. John's Wood.*

㉜ Kenwood House. On the north side of the heath is Kenwood House, built in the 17th century and remodeled by Robert Adam at the end of the 18th century. The house contains a collection of superb paintings by Rembrandt, Turner, Reynolds, Van Dyck, and Gainsborough—and *The Guitar Player,* probably the most beautiful Vermeer in England. Unfortunately, only one grand Adam interior remains: the splendid library. The house's lovely landscaped grounds provide the setting for symphony concerts in summer. ✉ *Hampstead La., NW3* ☎ *020/8348–1286* ⊕ *www. english-heritage.org.uk* ⊗ *Easter–Aug., Sat.–Tues., and Thurs. 10–5:30, Wed. and Fri. 10:30–5:30; Dec.–Easter, Sat.–Tues., and Thurs. 10–4, Wed. and Fri. 10:30–5; Sept.–Nov., Sat.–Tues., and Thurs. 10–4, Wed. and Fri. 10:30–4* Ⓤ *Golders Green, then Bus 210.*

Greenwich

Home to a number of historical and maritime attractions, Greenwich—situated on the Thames some 8 km (5 mi) east of central London—is an ideal destination for a day out. You can get to Greenwich by Underground, by riverboat from Westminster and Tower Bridge piers, and by Thames Line's high-speed river buses.

Cutty Sark. This romantic tea clipper was built in 1869, one of many wooden tall-masted clippers to ply the seven seas trading exotic commodities in the 19th century. The *Cutty Sark,* the last to survive, was also the fastest, sailing the China–London route in 1871 in just 107 days. The photogenic vessel lies in dry dock, a museum of one kind of seafaring life—which was anything but romantic for the 28-strong crew. ✉ *King William Walk, SE10* ☎ *020/8858–3445* ⊕ *www.cuttysark. org.uk* ⊗ *Daily 10–5, last admission 4:30* Ⓤ *DLR: Cutty Sark.*

★ National Maritime Museum. This grand stone building is all glass and light within, dominated by a frigate's huge revolving propeller on show in the glassed-in courtyard. Besides containing everything to do with the sea and British sea power—from seascape paintings to scientific instruments to a collection of ships from all ages—there are the compelling stories of heroes. A gallery is devoted to Admiral Nelson, including his uniform, complete with bloodstain, worn at his death at the Battle of Trafalgar. Explorers such as Captain Cook, and Robert F. Scott of the Antarctic, are celebrated. Opportunities to grapple hands-on with maritime tasks abound, especially in the All Hands Gallery, where kids and adults alike try their skills at handling ropes and docking ferries. ✉ *Romney Rd., SE10* ☎ *020/8858–4422* ⊕ *www.nmm.ac.uk* ⊗ *Apr.–Sept. daily 10–6, Oct.–Mar. daily 10–5* Ⓤ *DLR: Greenwich.*

Old Royal Observatory. Stand astride both hemispheres in the courtyard of the Old Royal Observatory, where the prime meridian—0° longitude—is set. The observatory is at the top of the hill, behind the National Maritime Museum and Royal Naval College, in the attractive **Greenwich Park,** which was originally a royal hunting ground. Founded in 1675, the observatory has original telescopes and other astronomical instruments on display. ✉ *Greenwich Park, SE10* ☎ *020/8312–6565* ⊕ *www. rog.nmm.ac.uk* ⊗ *Oct.–Mar., daily 10–5; Apr.–Sept., daily 10–6; last admission 30 mins before closing* Ⓤ *DLR: Greenwich.*

Where to Eat

London has had a restaurant boom, or rather, a restaurant revolution. More than ever, the city loves its dining establishments—all 6,700 of them—from its "be-there" eateries to its tiny neighborhood joints, from pubs where young foodniks find their feet to swanky trendsetters where celebrity chefs launch their ego flights. After feasting on modern British cuisine, visit one (or two or three) of London's fabulous pubs for a nightcap.

Bloomsbury, Covent Garden & Soho

$$$–$$$$ ✕ **Asia de Cuba.** A trendy restaurant, in a trendy hotel, in a trendy city: Philippe Starck–designed, it's flashy and loud—check the dangly light-bulbs, Latino music, stacks of library books, portable TVs, and satin-clad pillars. The Pan-Asian fusion menu includes Thai beef salad with Asian greens and coconut and lobster with rum and red curry. It isn't cheap, but it's totally disco. ⊠ *St. Martins Lane Hotel, 45 St. Martin's La., WC2* ☎ *020/7300–5588* ▭ *AE, DC, MC, V* Ⓤ *Leicester Sq.*

★ **$$$–$$$$** ✕ **Rules.** Come, escape from the 21st century. This is probably the single most beautiful dining salon in London; oil paintings and engravings cover the lacquered yellow walls. More than 200 years old (it opened in 1798), this gorgeous institution has welcomed everyone from Dickens to the current Prince of Wales. The menu includes fine historical dishes—try the steak-and-kidney pudding for a taste of the 18th century. For a main dish, try something from the list of daily specials, which, in season, includes game from Rules' Teesdale estate. ⊠ *35 Maiden La., WC2* ☎ *020/7836–5314* ▭ *AE, DC, MC, V* Ⓤ *Covent Garden.*

★ **$$–$$$** ✕ **The Ivy.** In a wood-panel, latticed, art deco room with blinding-white tablecloths and stained glass, the theater set eat Caesar salad, kedgeree, bubble and squeak, salmon cakes, and baked Alaska. For people-watching ("Don't look now, dear, but there's Ralph Fiennes"), this is the primo spot in London. The weekend three-course lunch is a steal at £17.50. Although it's hard to get into London's favorite restaurant, try walking in off the street for a table on short notice—it's been known to work. ⊠ *1 West St., WC2* ☎ *020/7836–4751* ⌨ *Reservations essential* ▭ *AE, DC, MC, V* Ⓤ *Covent Garden.*

★ **$$** ✕ **Providores.** Kiwi Peter Gordon scores a perfect 10 with his Pacific Rim fusion food at Providores in ever-so-trendy Marylebone. Have a charming meal upstairs or go down to the relaxed ground-floor Tapa Rooms for the sweet potato and miso, the cassava fritters, and the roast *chioca* (a tuber similar to Jerusalem artichoke). ⊠ *109 Marylebone High St., W1* ☎ *020/7935–6175* ▭ *AE, MC, V* Ⓤ *Baker St.*

$–$$ ✕ **Joe Allen.** Long hours (thespians flock here after the curtains fall in Theatreland) and a welcoming interior mean New York Joe's London branch still swings after more than two decades. The fun menu helps: roasted poblano peppers and black-bean soup are typical starters; entrées include barbecued ribs and corn muffins, or monkfish with sun-dried-tomato salsa. ⊠ *13 Exeter St., WC2,* ☎ *020/7836–0651* ⌨ *Reservations essential* ▭ *AE, MC, V* Ⓤ *Covent Garden.*

★ **$** ✕ **busabe eathai.** One of Londoners' favorite cheap spots in Soho, this superior Thai canteen is fitted with rattan, benches, hardwood tables, low lights, and paper lamp shades. It's no less seductive for its communal seating. The menu includes noodles, curries, and stir-fries. Try chicken with butternut squash, cuttlefish curry, or seafood vermicelli (prawns, squid, and scallops). The mantra here is *gan gin gan yuu*, which means "as you eat, so you are." ⊠ *106–110 Wardour St., W1* ☎ *020/7255–8686* ⌨ *Reservations not accepted* ▭ *AE, MC, V* Ⓤ *Leicester Sq.*

Chelsea, Kensington & Knightsbridge

$$$$ ✕ **The Capital.** The clublike dining room has a grown-up atmosphere with formal service. Chef Eric Chavot carries out classy French cooking, and many of his dishes astonish. These include turbot with creamed baby leeks and mushroom ravioli. Desserts follow the same exciting route. Set-price menus at lunch (£26.50) make it somewhat more affordable. ⊠ *22–24 Basil St., SW3* ☎ *020/7589–5171* ⌖ *Reservations essential* ⊟ *AE, DC, MC, V* Ⓤ *Knightsbridge.*

★ $$$$ ✕ **Gordon Ramsay.** Ramsay whips up a storm with white beans, foie gras, scallops, and truffles. He's Britain's number one, and tables are booked months in advance. For £80, blow out on the seven-course option; for £65, wallow in three dinner courses; or grab lunch (£35 for three courses) for a less expensive check. ⊠ *68–69 Royal Hospital Rd., SW3* ☎ *020/7352–4441* ⌖ *Reservations essential* ⊟ *AE, DC, MC, V* ⊘ *Closed weekends* Ⓤ *Sloane Sq.*

$$$–$$$$ ✕ **Bibendum.** This converted 1911 Michelin showroom, adorned with art deco prints and brilliant stained glass, remains one of London's dining showplaces. Chef Matthew Harris cooks with Euro-Brit flair. Try deep-fried calves' brains, any of the risottos, steak *au poivre,* or milk-fed lamb with garlic and mint gravy. The £25 fixed-price lunch menu is money well spent. ⊠ *Michelin House, 81 Fulham Rd., SW3* ☎ *020/7581–5817* ⌖ *Reservations essential* ⊟ *AE, DC, MC, V* Ⓤ *South Kensington.*

$$$–$$$$ ✕ **Zafferano.** Any number of Cartier brooch–wearing Belgravians flock to Zafferano, one of London's best exponents of *cucina nuova.* The fireworks are in the kitchen, and *what* fireworks: buckwheat pasta with leek and sage, lamb cutlets with hazelnut crust and white truffle polenta. The desserts are *delizioso,* especially the poached pears and mascarpone ice cream. ⊠ *15 Lowndes St., SW1* ☎ *020/7235–5800* ⌖ *Reservations essential* ⊟ *AE, DC, MC, V* Ⓤ *Knightsbridge.*

$$–$$$$ ✕ **Zaika.** One of London's finest Indian restaurants pushes the boundaries of Indian cuisine by mixing old flavors with modern sensibilities. You can't top the *samundri Zaika* (tandoor-smoked salmon, king prawn, and swordfish), nor can you better the scallops in coconut milk, with masala mashed potato. Sign off with chocolate samosas ("chocomosas") and Indian ice cream. ⊠ *1 Kensington High St., W8* ☎ *020/7795–6533* ⌖ *Reservations essential* ⊟ *AE, MC, V* Ⓤ *High St. Kensington.*

$$–$$$ ✕ **Bluebird.** Sir Terence Conran presents a "gastrodome"—food market, fruit stand, butchers, kitchen shop, café, and restaurant. The place is blue and white, bright, and not in the least cozy, and the food can be fairly formulaic: veal kidneys and shallots, rabbit and spinach, then chocolate cake and espresso ice cream. Go for the people-watching and visual excitement; Conran's chefs tend to promise more than they deliver. ⊠ *350 King's Rd., SW3* ☎ *020/7559–1000* ⌖ *Reservations essential* ⊟ *AE, DC, MC, V* Ⓤ *Sloane Sq.*

$$–$$$ ✕ **La Poule au Pot.** One of London's most charming restaurants, La Poule au Pot is superb for proposals or romantic evenings. The "Chelsea Set"—and Americans—love this candlelighted corner of France. The country cooking is fairly good, not spectacular. The *poule au pot* (stewed chicken) and *lapin à la moutarde* (rabbit with mustard) are strong and hearty, and there are fine classics, such as beef bourguignonne and French onion soup. Service comes with bonhomie. ⊠ *231 Ebury St., SW1* ☎ *020/7730–7763* ⌖ *Reservations essential* ⊟ *AE, DC, MC, V* Ⓤ *Sloane Sq.*

$$ ✕ **The Enterprise.** Near Harrods and Brompton Cross, the Enterprise is filled with decorative types who complement the striped wallpaper, Edwardian side tables, vintage books piled up in the windows, and white linen and fresh flowers on the tables. The menu is fairly subtle—braised lamb shank with rosemary and celeriac puree—and the heartiness of the room contributes to a fun experience. ⊠ *35 Walton St., SW3* ☎ *020/7584–3148* ⊟ *AE, MC, V* Ⓤ *South Kensington.*

The City

★ **$$–$$$$** ✕ **Club Gascon.** It's hard to find a sexier scene than this in all London, with its leather-walled interior, excellent service, and courses served on slabs of rock. Club Gascon's raison d'être is foie gras, which runs through the menu from start to finish (you can even have it for dessert, with fortified wine, gingerbread, and grapes). Bliss out on roast zander or foie gras steeped in Montilla-Moriles sherry and shot through with 10-year-old Maury wine. ⊠ *57 W. Smithfield, EC1* ☎ *020/7796–0600* ⌂ *Reservations essential* ▱ *AE, MC, V* ⊙ *Closed Sun., no lunch Sat.* Ⓤ *Barbican.*

Mayfair & St. James's

$$$$ ✕ **Gordon Ramsay at Claridge's.** Sit at the chef's table, a six- to eight-
Fodor'sChoice seat booth inside the kitchen, and watch the art and intensity. Ramsay
★ is Britain's greatest chef, and Claridge's is booked six months in advance—Tony Blair came for his birthday. Try the eight-hour roast shoulder of lamb, braised halibut, or brill in red wine. Book months ahead and arrive early for dinner to have a drink at Claridge's art deco bar, the best cocktail lounge in London. They also do breakfast and bargain three-course lunches (£25). ⊠ *Claridge's Hotel, Brook St., W1* ☎ *020/ 7499–0099* ⌂ *Reservations essential* ⸙ *Jacket and tie* ▱ *AE, MC, V* Ⓤ *Bond St.*

$$–$$$$ ✕ **Locanda Locatelli.** Everything chef Giorgio Locatelli touches turns to
Fodor'sChoice gold—hence the six-week waiting list. The elegant David Collins–de-
★ signed dining room at the Churchill Inter-Continental has convex mirrors, etched glass, swivel chairs, and banquettes, and the food is accomplished. Be bold: try the ravioli osso bucco or the sweetbread with Roman *agro-dolce* (sweet and sour sauce), and choose from the all–Italian wine list. ⊠ *8 Seymour St., W1* ☎ *020/7935–9088* ⌂ *Reservations essential* ▱ *AE, MC, V* ⊙ *Closed Sun.* Ⓤ *Marble Arch.*

$$–$$$$ ✕ **Nobu.** Bulging with stars, this is a true destination restaurant. Nobuyuki Matsuhisa concocts new-style sashimi with a Peruvian touch—he sells 300 lb. of Alaskan black cod a day. Nobu is in the Metropolitan, a hip hotel, with staff, attitude, clientele, and prices to match. ⊠ *Metropolitan Hotel, 19 Old Park La., W1* ☎ *020/7447–4747* ⌂ *Reservations essential* ▱ *AE, DC, MC, V* ⊙ *No lunch weekends* Ⓤ *Hyde Park.*

★ **$$–$$$** ✕ **Le Caprice.** Secreted behind the Ritz Hotel, Le Caprice commands deep loyalty among its patrons—including Joan Collins and David Bowie—because it gets everything right: the glossy Eva Jiricna interior; the perfect service; and the menu, halfway between Euro-peasant and fashion plate. The crispy duck and watercress salad, and San Daniele ham and figs have no business being so good. ⊠ *Arlington House, Arlington St., SW1* ☎ *020/7629–2239* ⌂ *Reservations essential* ▱ *AE, DC, MC, V* Ⓤ *Green Park.*

$–$$ ✕ **Browns.** Unpretentious, crowd-pleasing, child-friendly English feeding gets done at the former establishment of the tailors Messrs. Cooling and Wells, now converted to Edwardian style by the group behind the successful Browns eateries. The classic Browns steak-and-Guinness pie is on the menu, but king prawns, lamb shanks, roasted peppers, salads, and pastas predominate. ⊠ *47 Maddox St., W1* ☎ *020/7491–4565* ▱ *AE, DC, MC, V* Ⓤ *Oxford Circus.*

Notting Hill

★ **$–$$$** ✕ **E&O.** If you like stars, you'll love E&O. Gwyneth, Madonna, and Nicole have all been drawn by its luxurious charm. The restaurant's name stands for Eastern and Oriental, and the Pan-Asian cuisine is an intelligent mix of Chinese, Japanese, Vietnamese, and Thai. Don't skip the Thai rare-beef salad with red *nam jhim* (bean sprouts) or the albacore sashimi, and remember to look up and then look away when the A-list star settles in at Table 5. ⊠ *14 Blenheim Crescent, W11* ☎ *020/7229–5454* ⌘ *Reservations essential* ☷ *AE, DC, MC, V* Ⓤ *Ladbroke Grove.*

$$ ✕ **The Cow.** Upstairs the chef whips up Anglo-French specialties for diners in this chic gastro pub, comprised of a faux-Dublin back-room bar Salmon cakes, baked brill, and cod and mash are some of the temptations offered. Notting Hillbillies love the house special: a half-dozen Irish rock oysters with a pint of Guinness. ⊠ *89 Westbourne Park Rd., W2* ☎ *020/7221–0021* ⌘ *Reservations essential* ☷ *MC, V* Ⓤ *Westbourne Park.*

South Bank

$$$–$$$$ ✕ **OXO Tower Brasserie and Restaurant.** London has a room with a view—and *such* a view. On the eighth floor of the OXO Tower near the South Bank is this elegant space serving Euro-Asian food with the latest trendy ingredients (spinach pie with quail and pumpkin salad). The ceiling slats turn from white to blue, but who notices, with the London Eye wheel and St. Paul's Cathedral across the water? The Brasserie is slightly less expensive than the restaurant; terrace tables available in summer have the best panoramas. ⊠ *Barge House St., SE1* ☎ *020/7803–3888* ☷ *AE, DC, MC, V* Ⓤ *Waterloo.*

Where to Stay

Note that although British hotels have traditionally included breakfast in their nightly tariff, many of London's most expensive establishments charge extra for breakfast.

Bayswater

$–$$ ▣ **Vancouver Studios.** This little hotel is run like an apartment building: rooms are actually studios with kitchens, and the front door has a security entry system. Each studio has daily maid service; some have working fireplaces; and there is a garden for guests to enjoy. ⊠ *30 Prince's Sq., W2 4NJ* ☎ *020/7243–1270* 🖶 *020/7221–8678* ⊕ *www.vancouverstudios.co.uk* ⇆ *45 studios* ☷ *AE, DC, MC, V* Ⓤ *Bayswater, Queensway.*

$ ▣ **Garden Court Hotel.** Built in 1870, the hotel consists of two 19th-century town houses in a quiet paved garden square. Each of the comfortable rooms has a character of its own, complete with some original Victorian fittings, and the owners are eager to please. Rooms with toilet and shower cost £30 extra, and family-size rooms are in the $$ category. ⊠ *30–31 Kensington Gardens Sq., W2 4BL* ☎ *020/7229–2553* 🖶 *020/7727–2749* ⊕ *www.gardencourthotel.co.uk* ⇆ *32 rooms, some without bath* ☷ *MC, V* Ⓤ *Bayswater, Queensway.*

Bloomsbury

$$$ ▣ **myhotel bloomsbury.** Before you arrive you'll be asked to fill out a preferences sheet so your room is just as you like it. If anything should go wrong, no need to call the front desk: just contact your personal assistant for help. Rooms are minimalist, with wooden floors and simple color schemes. Superior doubles are bigger and have separate sitting rooms. From the "jinja" spa to the library stocked with CDs, books, and free beverages, myhotel's novel approach succeeds brilliantly. ⊠ *11–13 Bayley St., Bedford Sq., WC1B 3HD* ☎ *020/7667–6000* 🖶 *020/7667–6001* ⊕ *www.myhotels.com* ⇆ *76 rooms* ⌂ *Restaurant, bar* ☷ *AE, DC, MC, V* Ⓤ *Tottenham Court Rd.*

Fodor'sChoice ★

$ ▣ **Harlingford Hotel.** The Harlingford is by far the sleekest and most contemporary of the Cartwright Gardens hotels. Bold color schemes and beautifully tiled bathrooms make this family-run hotel a bargain for contemporary style. The largest rooms sleep four and are an excellent choice for traveling families. ⊠ *61–63 Cartwright Gardens, WC1H 9EL*

☏ 020/7387–1551 🖷 020/7383–4616 ⊕ *www.harlingfordhotel.com*
⇔ *43 rooms* ⊟ *AE, DC, MC, V* Ⓤ *Russell Sq.*

Chelsea, Kensington & Holland Park

★ **$$$$** ⌹ **Blakes.** Designed by owner Anouska Hempel, each room at Blakes is a fantasy packed with precious Biedermeier, Murano glass, and modern pieces collected from all over the world. Cinematic mood lighting, with recessed halogen spots, compounds the impression that you, too, are a movie star in a big-budget biopic. The foyer sets the tone with piles of cushions, Phileas Fogg valises and trunks, black walls, rattan, and bamboo. ⊠ *33 Roland Gardens, SW7 3PF* ☏ *020/7370–6701* 🖷 *020/ 7373–0442* ⊕ *www.blakeshotels.com* ⇔ *38 rooms, 11 suites* ◊ *Restaurant, bar* ⊟ *AE, DC, MC, V* Ⓤ *South Kensington.*

★ **$$$** ⌹ **Miller's Residence.** From the moment you ring the bell and are ushered up the winding staircase flanked by antiques and curios, you know you've entered another realm where history is paramount. Run by Martin Miller of famed *Miller's Antique Price Guides,* this town house serves as his home, gallery, and B&B. Sip a complimentary evening cocktail in the long, candelighted drawing room with fireplace while mixing with other guests or the convivial staff. The rooms are named for Romantic poets. ⊠ *111A Westbourne Grove, W2 4UW* ☏ *020/ 7243–1024* 🖷 *020/7243–1064* ⊕ *www.millersuk.com* ⇔ *6 rooms, 2 suites* ⊟ *AE, DC, MC, V* Ⓤ *Notting Hill Gate.*

$$–$$$ ⌹ **Aster House.** Rooms in this delightful guest house are country casual, and the owners go out of their way to make you feel at home and answer questions. The conservatory where breakfast is served is an airy, light place, and the small garden at the back has a charming pond. Note that this is a five-story building with no elevator. ⊠ *3 Sumner Pl., SW7 3EE* ☏ *020/7581–5888* 🖷 *020/7584–4925* ⊕ *www.asterhouse.com* ⇔ *14 rooms* ⊟ *MC, V* Ⓤ *South Kensington.*

$ ⌹ **Abbey House.** This pretty, white-stucco 1860 Victorian town house is in an excellent location close to trendy Notting Hill. You can spend the cash you save by staying here in the nearby antiques shops. Rooms are spacious—with four-person rooms suitable for families—and have washbasins, but every room shares a bath with another. Note that there is no elevator. ⊠ *11 Vicarage Gate, W8 4AG* ☏ *020/7727–2594* 🖷 *020/ 7727–1873* ⊕ *www.abbeyhousekensington.com* ⇔ *16 rooms without bath* ⊟ *No credit cards* Ⓤ *High St. Kensington.*

$ ⌹ **The Vicarage.** Family-owned and set on a leafy street just off Kensington Church Street, the Vicarage occupies a large white Victorian house full of heavy and dark-stained wood furniture, patterned carpets, and brass pendant lights. All in all, it's a charmer, but it is beginning to fray around the edges. All rooms share the bathroom, but a few doubles have their own showers. ⊠ *10 Vicarage Gate, W8 4AG* ☏ *020/7229–4030* 🖷 *020/7792–5989* ⊕ *www.londonvicaragehotel.com* ⇔ *14 rooms, 8 with bath* ⊟ *No credit cards* Ⓤ *High St. Kensington.*

Knightsbridge, Belgravia & Victoria

$$$$ ⌹ **The Lanesborough.** Royally proportioned public rooms distinguish this multimillion-pound, American-run conversion of St. George's Hospital. Everything undulates with richness—moiré silks and fleurs-de-lis in the colors of precious stones, magnificent antiques and oil paintings, handwoven £250-per-square-yard carpet—as if Liberace and Laura Ashley had collaborated. To check in, sign the visitor's book, then retire to your room, where you are waited on by a personal butler. ⊠ *Hyde Park Corner, SW1X 7TA* ☏ *020/7259–5599; 800/999–1828 in U.S.* 🖷 *020/ 7259–5606; 800/937–8278 in U.S.* ⊕ *www.lanesborough.com* ⇔ *49 rooms, 46 suites* ◊ *2 restaurants, 2 bars* ⊟ *AE, DC, MC, V* Ⓤ *Hyde Park Corner.*

$$$$ ⊡ **The Rubens at the Palace.** This hotel likes to say it treats you like royalty. In fact, you're only a stone's throw from the real thing, as Buckingham Palace is just across the road. The elegant Rubens, which looks out over the Royal Mews, provides the sort of deep comfort needed to soothe away a hard day's sightseeing, with cushy armchairs crying out for you to sink into them with a cup of Earl Grey. With decent-size rooms and a location that couldn't be more central, this hotel is a favorite for many travelers. ⊠ *39 Buckingham Palace Rd., SW1W 0PS* ☎ *020/7834–6600* 🖷 *020/7233–6037* ⊕ *www.rubenshotel.com* 🛏 *160 rooms, 13 suites* ⚇ *2 restaurants, bar* ▤ *AE, DC, MC, V* Ⓤ *Victoria.*

★ **$$$–$$$$** ⊡ **The Pelham.** The Pelham looks like the country house to end all country houses. There's 18th-century pine paneling in the drawing room, flowers galore, quite a bit of glazed chintz and antique-lace bed linen, and the occasional four-poster bed and fireplace. The first-floor (American second-floor) suites are extra spacious, with high ceilings and chandeliers. ⊠ *15 Cromwell Pl., SW7 2LA* ☎ *020/7589–8288* 🖷 *020/7584–8444* ⊕ *www.firmdale.com* 🛏 *51 rooms* ⚇ *Restaurant, bar* ▤ *AE, MC, V* Ⓤ *South Kensington.*

$$$ ⊡ **Knightsbridge Hotel.** Just off glamorous Knightsbridge in quiet Beaufort Gardens, this hotel succeeds in being cheap (relatively) and chic (enormously). The balconied suites and regular rooms benefit from CD players, writing desks, and large granite and oak bathrooms. ⊠ *10 Beaufort Gardens, SW3 1PT* ☎ *020/7584–6300; 800/553–6674 in U.S.* 🖷 *020/7584–6355* ⊕ *www.knightsbridgehotel.co.uk* 🛏 *42 rooms, 2 suites* ⚇ *Bar* ▤ *AE, MC, V* Ⓤ *Knightsbridge.*

West End

$$$$ ⊡ **Brown's.** Founded in 1837 by Lord Byron's "gentleman's gentleman," James Brown, Brown's retains a cozy, oak-paneled, chintz-laden, grandfather-clock-ticking-in-the-parlor sensibility. The complex consists of 11 Georgian town houses patronized by many Anglophilic Americans—a habit established by Theodore and Franklin Delano Roosevelt. ⊠ *34 Albemarle St., W1X 4BT* ☎ *020/7493–6020* 🖷 *020/7493–9381* ⊕ *www.brownshotel.com* 🛏 *108 rooms, 10 suites* ⚇ *2 restaurants, bar* ▤ *AE, DC, MC, V* Ⓤ *Green Park.*

★ **$$$$** ⊡ **Claridge's.** Some of the world's classiest guests patronize this legendary hotel. The friendly, liveried staff is not in the least condescending, and the rooms are spacious and never less than luxurious. The grand staircase is magnificent, and the elevator contains a sofa to maximize comfort. Enjoy a cup of tea in the lounge, or retreat to the stylish bar for cocktails—or, better, to Gordon Ramsay's inimitable restaurant for dinner. ⊠ *Brook St., W1A 2JQ* ☎ *020/7629–8860; 800/637–2869 in U.S.* 🖷 *020/7499–2210* ⊕ *www.claridges.co.uk* 🛏 *203 rooms* ⚇ *Restaurant, bar* ▤ *AE, DC, MC, V* Ⓤ *Bond St.*

$$$$ ⊡ **Covent Garden Hotel.** A former 1880s hospital in the midst of artsy, boisterous Covent Garden, this hotel is the London home-away-from-home for a mélange of off-duty celebrities, actors, and style mavens. The public salons display painted silks, *style anglais* ottomans, and 19th-century Romantic oils, and are perfect places to decompress over sherry. Guest rooms are *World of Interiors* stylish, showcasing matching-but-mixed couture fabrics to stunning effect. ⊠ *10 Monmouth St., WC2H 9HB* ☎ *020/7806–1000* 🖷 *020/7806–1100* ⊕ *www.firmdale.com* 🛏 *55 rooms, 3 suites* ⚇ *Restaurant* ▤ *AE, MC, V* Ⓤ *Covent Garden.*

*Fodor's*Choice
★

★ **$$$$** ⊡ **The Savoy.** This grand hotel hosted Elizabeth Taylor's first honeymoon and poured one of Europe's first dry martinis in its American Bar, a one-time haunt of Hemingway, Fitzgerald, and Gershwin. The art deco rooms are especially fabulous, but all rooms are impeccably maintained, spacious, and elegant. A room facing the Thames costs a fortune and requires an early booking, but it's worth it. ✉ *Strand, WC2R 0EU* ☎ *020/7836–4343* 🖷 *020/7240–6040* ⊕ *www.savoy-group.com* ⇆ *263 rooms, 19 suites* ⟳ *3 restaurants, pool, 2 bars* 🖃 *AE, DC, MC, V* Ⓤ *Aldwych.*

$$$–$$$$ 🏨 **Hazlitt's.** One of the three early-18th-century houses on this site was the last home of essayist William Hazlitt (1778–1830). The hotel that now occupies the space is a disarmingly friendly place, full of personality but devoid of elevators. Robust antiques are everywhere, assorted prints crowd every wall, plants and stone sculptures occupy corners, and every room has a Victorian claw-foot bathtub. There are tiny sitting rooms, wooden staircases, and more restaurants within strolling distance than you could patronize in a year. ✉ *6 Frith St., W1V 5TZ* ☎ *020/7434–1771* 🖷 *020/7439–1524* ⊕ *www.hazlittshotel.com* ⇆ *20 rooms, 3 suites* 🖃 *AE, DC, MC, V* Ⓤ *Tottenham Court Rd.*

$$ 🏨 **Bryanston Court.** These three converted Georgian houses are decorated in a traditional English style, with fireplaces, leather armchairs, and oil portraits. The small bedrooms have pink furnishings, creaky floors, and tiny bathrooms, but they remain an excellent value for the hotel's location. Rooms at the back are quieter and face east toward the morning sun. ✉ *56–60 Great Cumberland Pl., W1H 8DD* ☎ *020/7262–3141* 🖷 *020/7262–7248* ⊕ *www.bryanstonhotel.com* ⇆ *81 rooms, 8 apartments* ⟳ *Bar* 🖃 *MC, V* Ⓤ *Marble Arch.*

$$ 🏨 **Fielding.** On a quiet pedestrian alley just steps from the Royal Opera House, this small hotel is popular with its regular, opera-loving clientele. However, there are no amenities save for the residents' bar and the coffeemakers in each room; you can get more comfort for your money elsewhere. ✉ *4 Broad Ct., at Bow St., WC2B 5QZ* ☎ *020/7836–8305* 🖷 *020/7497–0064* ⊕ *www.the-fielding-hotel.co.uk* ⇆ *24 rooms* ⟳ *Bar* 🖃 *AE, DC, MC, V* Ⓤ *Covent Garden.*

Nightlife & the Arts

The Arts

The most comprehensive list of events in the London arts scene can be found in the weekly magazine *Time Out.* The *Evening Standard* also carries listings, especially in the supplement "Hot Tickets," which comes with the Thursday edition, as do the "quality" Sunday papers and the Saturday *Independent, Guardian,* and *Times.* You can pick up the free fortnightly *London Theatre Guide* leaflet from hotels and tourist information centers.

BALLET The Royal Opera House is the traditional home of the world-famous **Royal Ballet.** As well as favorites like *The Nutcracker,* there is a spectrum of classical and innovative contemporary performances. Prices start at £3 (for ballet matinees). Bookings should be made well in advance. The **English National Ballet** (☎ 020/7632–8300) and visiting companies perform at the London Coliseum (☎ 020/7632–8300). **Sadler's Wells** (☎ 020/7863–8000) hosts regional ballet and international modern dance troupes. Prices are reasonable. A popular venue for cutting-edge modern and experimental dance is **The Place** (☎ 020/7380–1268).

CLASSICAL MUSIC Ticket prices for symphony orchestra concerts are still relatively moderate—between £5 and £35, although you can expect to pay more to hear big-name artists on tour. If you can't book in advance, arrive half an hour before the performance for a chance at returns.

The London Symphony Orchestra is in residence at the **Barbican Arts Centre** (☎ 020/7638–8891), although other top symphony and chamber orchestras also perform here. The **South Bank Centre** (☎ 020/7960–4242), which includes the **Royal Festival Hall** and the **Queen Elizabeth Hall,** is another major venue for choral, symphonic, and chamber concerts. For less expensive concert going, try the **Royal Albert Hall** (☎020/7589–8212) during the summer Promenade season (the "Proms"), when special tickets for standing room are available at the hall on the night of performance. Note, too, that the concerts are broadcast on a jumbo screen in Hyde Park, but even a seat on the grass here requires a paid ticket. The **Wigmore Hall** (☎ 020/7935–2141) is a small auditorium, ideal for recitals. Inexpensive lunchtime concerts (usually less than £5 or free) take place all over the city in smaller halls and churches, often featuring string quartets, vocalists, jazz ensembles, and gospel choirs. **St. John's, Smith Square** (☎ 020/7222–1061) offers chamber music and solo recitals. **St. Martin-in-the-Fields** (☎ 020/7839–1930) holds free lunchtime concerts.

FILM   Most big West End cinemas are in the area around Leicester Square and Piccadilly Circus. Tickets average £8. Matinees and Monday evenings are often cheaper, and some theaters offer student discounts. One of the best cinemas is the **National Film Theatre** (☎ 020/7928–3232), part of the South Bank Centre. The Regus London Film Festival is based here, and throughout the year three screens show classics, foreign-language films, documentaries, cult Hollywood features, and animation.

OPERA   The **Royal Opera House** (✉ Covent Garden ☎ 020/7304–4000) presents original-language productions in an extravagant theater. If you can't afford £100 for a ticket, consider showing up at 8 AM to purchase a same-day seat, of which a small number are offered for £30.

The **London Coliseum** (☎ 020/7632–8300) is the home of the English National Opera Company (ENO), whose productions are staged in English and are often innovative and exciting. Prices are lower than for the Royal Opera, ranging from £5 to £55. The ENO sells same-day seats for as little as £2.50.

THEATER   Most theaters have an evening performance at 7:30 or 8 Monday–Saturday, and a matinee twice a week (Wednesday or Thursday, and Saturday). Expect to pay from £10 for a seat in the upper balcony and at least £25 for a good seat in the stalls (orchestra) or dress circle (mezzanine), and more for musicals. Tickets may be booked in person at the theater box office, over the phone by credit card, or through ticket agents. **Ticketmaster** (☎ 020/7344–0055; 800/775–2525 in U.S.) sells tickets to many theaters and productions. The **SOLT** (Society of London Theatres, "TKTS") kiosk, in Leicester Square, sells half-price tickets on the day of performance for about 25 theaters; there is a £2 service charge. It's open Monday–Saturday 2–6:30, Sunday noon–3. Beware of scalpers!

London's theater life can more or less be divided into three categories: the government-subsidized national companies; the commercial, or "West End," theaters; and the fringe. The **Royal National Theatre** (NT; ☎ 020/7452–3000 box office) shares the laurels as the top national repertory troupe with the Royal Shakespeare Company. In similar fashion to the latter troupe, the NT presents plays by writers of all nationalities, ranging from the classics of Shakespeare to specially commissioned modern works. The NT is based at the South Bank Centre. The **Royal Shakespeare Company** (RSC; ☎ 020/7638–8891 box office; 01789/ 403–403 general inquiries) performs at West End venues throughout the year, and you can also see the company's productions as it tours different theaters around the country. If you're visiting London in the summer, you can book tickets at the spectacular reconstruction of **Shakespeare's Globe Theatre** (☎ 020/7401–9919 box office) on the South Bank, which offers open-air, late-afternoon performances from June through September.

The **West End theaters** stage musicals, comedies, whodunits, and revivals of lighter plays of the 19th and 20th centuries, often starring TV celebrities. Occasionally there are more serious productions, including successful performances transferred from the subsidized theaters, such as those of the RSC. The two dozen or so established **fringe theaters,** scattered around central London and the immediate outskirts, frequently present some of London's most intriguing productions, if you're prepared to overlook occasional rough staging and uncomfortable seating.

Nightlife

London's nightspots are legion; here are some of the best known. For up-to-the-minute listings, buy *Time Out* magazine.

COMEDY The best comedy in town can be found in the big, bright **Comedy Store** (✉ 1A Oxendon St., near Piccadilly Circus, SW1 ☎ 020/7344–0234).

JAZZ CLUBS **Pizza Express** (✉ 10 Dean St., W1 ☎020/7437–9595 or 020/7439–8722) is the capital's best-loved chain of pizza houses, but it is also one of London's principal jazz venues, with music every night except Mondays in the basement restaurant. Eight other branches also have live music. **Ronnie Scott's** (✉ 47 Frith St., W1 ☎ 020/7439–0747) is a legendary Soho jazz club where the food isn't great and service is slow, but where big-name international performers regularly take the stage.

NIGHTCLUBS **Café de Paris** (✉ 3–4 Coventry St., W1V 7FL ☎020/7734–7700) opened in 1914 and is one of London's most glamour-puss settings. It was once the haunt of royals and stars such as Noël Coward, Marlene Dietrich, Fred Astaire, and Frank Sinatra. **Hanover Grand** (✉ 6 Hanover Sq., W1 ☎ 020/7499–7977) is a swank and opulent big West End club that attracts TV stars and others in the entertainment business for funky U.S. garage on Friday and glam disco on Saturday. The lines outside get long, so dress up to impress the bouncers. **Ministry of Sound** (✉ 103 Gaunt St., SE1 ☎ 020/7378–6528) is more of an industry than a club, with its own record label, line of apparel, and, of course, DJs. Inside, there are chill-out rooms, dance floors, Absolut shot bars—all the club kids' favorite things. If you are one, and you have time for only one night out, make it here. **Fabric** (✉ 77A Charterhouse St., EC1 ☎ 020/7336–8898) is a sprawling subterranean club with slow, reverberating bass lines and cutting-edge music from world-class DJs. Come early on weekends to avoid a lengthy wait.

ROCK The **Forum** (✉ 9–17 Highgate Rd., Kentish Town ☎ 020/7344–0044), a little out of the way, is a premier venue for medium-to-big acts. **100 Club** (✉ 100 Oxford St., W1 ☎020/7636–0933) is a basement dive that's always been there for R&B, rock, jazz, and beer. The **Shepherds Bush Empire** (✉ Shepherds Bush Green, W12 ☎ 020/7771–2000) is a major venue for largish acts in West London. **The Borderline** (✉ Otange Yard, off Manette St., W1V ☎ 020/7734–2095) is a small but central subterranean room with fake southwestern decor that puts on Americana, blues, and indie rock.

Shopping

Shopping is one of London's great pleasures. Different areas retain their traditional specialties, and it's fun to seek out the small crafts, antiques, and gift stores, designer-clothing resale outlets, and national department-store chains.

Shopping Districts

Centering on the King's Road, **Chelsea** was once synonymous with ultrafashion; it still harbors some designer boutiques, plus antiques and home furnishings stores. A something-for-everyone neighborhood, **Covent Garden** has numerous clothing chain stores, stalls selling crafts, and shops selling gifts of every type—bikes, kites, herbs, beads, hats, you name it. **Kensington**'s main drag, Kensington High Street, is a smaller, classier version of Oxford Street, with Barkers department store, and a branch of Marks & Spencer at the eastern end. Try Kensington Church Street for expensive antiques, plus a little fashion. Venture out to the W11 and W2 neighborhoods around the Holland Park–Westbourne Grove end of **Notting Hill,** and you'll find specialty shops for clothes, accessories, and home furnishings, plus lots of fashionable bistros for sustenance. Kensington's neighbor, **Knightsbridge,** has Harrods, of course, but also Harvey Nichols, the chicest clothes shop in London, and many expensive designers' boutiques along Sloane Street, Walton Street, and Beauchamp Place. Adjacent Belgravia is also a burgeoning area for posh designer stores.

Bond Street, Old and New, is the elegant lure in **Mayfair,** with the *hautest* of haute couture and jewelry outposts, plus fine art. South Molton Street offers high-price, high-style fashion—especially at Browns—and the tailors of Savile Row are of worldwide repute. Crowded and a bit past its prime, the north end of **Oxford Street** toward Tottenham Court Rd. has tawdry discount shops sprinkled in with upmarket fashion chains. Toward Marble Arch, Selfridges, John Lewis, and Marks & Spencer are wonderful department stores. There are interesting boutiques secreted off Oxford Street, just north of the Bond Street Tube stop, in little St. Christopher's Place and Gees Court, and south of the Tube stop for chic-est South Molton Street. Check out the cobbled streets in West Soho, behind Liberty in Regent Street, for handcrafted jewelry, designer gear, and stylish cafés. Perpendicular to Oxford Street lies **Regent Street**—famous for its curving path—with the irresistible department store Liberty's, as well as Hamley's, the capital's most comprehensive toy depot. Shops around once-famous **Carnaby Street** stock designer youth paraphernalia and at least 57 varieties of T-shirts. The fabled English gentleman buys much of his gear at stores in **St. James's:** handmade hats, shirts, and shoes; silver shaving kits; and hip flasks. Here is also the world's best cheese shop, Paxton & Whitfield. Don't expect any bargains in this neighborhood.

Street Markets

Street markets are one aspect of London life not to be missed. Here are some of the more interesting markets:

Borough Market. This is a foodies' paradise with whole grain and organic products from Britain and a host of international flavors. ⊠ *Borough High St., SE1* ☉ *Fri. noon–6, Sat. 9–4* Ⓤ *London Bridge, Borough.*

Camden Lock. The volume and range of merchandise (and crowds) at this conglomeration of several markets is mind-blowing: vintage and new clothes, antiques and junk, jewelry and scarves. Hip teens use the area as a casual date spot. ⊠ *Chalk Farm Rd., NW1* ☉ *Shops Tues.–Sun. 9:30–5:30, stalls weekends 8–6* Ⓤ *Tube or Bus 24 or 29 to Camden Town.*

Camden Passage. The rows of little antiques stalls are a good hunting ground for silverware and jewelry. Stalls open Wednesday and Saturday, and there is also a books and prints market on Thursday. ⊠ *Islington, off Upper St., N1* ☉ *Wed. and Sat. 8:30–3* Ⓤ *Tube or Bus 19 or 38 to Angel.*

Covent Garden. Craft stalls, jewelry designers, clothes makers—particularly of knitwear—and other artisans congregate in the central Apple Market. The Jubilee Market, toward Southampton Street, has a worthwhile selection of vintage collectibles on Mondays. ✉ *The Piazza, WC2* ⊙ *Daily 9–5* Ⓤ *Covent Garden.*

Petticoat Lane. Look for budget-priced leather goods, gaudy knitwear, and fashions, plus cameras, videos, stereos, antiques, books, and bric-a-brac. ✉ *Middlesex St., E1* ⊙ *Sun. 9–2* Ⓤ *Liverpool St., Aldgate, Aldgate East.*

Portobello Market. Saturday is the best day for antiques, though Notting Hill is London's melting pot, becoming more vibrant throughout the week. Find fabulous small shops, trendy restaurants, and a Friday and Saturday flea market at the far end at Ladbroke Grove. ✉ *Portobello Rd., W11* ⊙ *Fri. 5 AM–3 PM, Sat. 6 AM–5 PM* Ⓤ *Tube or Bus 52 to Notting Hill Gate or Ladbroke Grove, or Bus 15 to Kensington Park Rd.*

Side Trips

Canterbury

The town of Canterbury, 56 mi (90 km) east of London, has long been a destination for day-trippers. After the 12th-century murder of Archbishop St. Thomas à Becket in the town's cathedral, thousands of Anglican pilgrims flocked here to see his shrine. Written two centuries later, Chaucer's *The Canterbury Tales* suggest the bawdier side of medieval Canterbury, which was as much a tailgate party for people on horses as it was a spiritual center. A day's journey leaves plenty of time to see the city's main sights.

★ **Canterbury Cathedral** is the focal point of the city, the nucleus of worldwide Anglicanism, and a living textbook of medieval architecture. It's also the final resting place of Thomas à Becket, who was murdered here in 1170. Although Becket's magnificent tomb was destroyed by Henry VIII in 1538, plenty of treasures remain. In **Trinity Chapel,** near the tomb's original site, you can still see a series of 13th-century stained-glass windows illustrating Becket's miracles. If time permits, also be sure to explore the **Cloisters.** Southwest of the cathedral, the immense **Christchurch Gate** was built in 1517 to celebrate the betrothal of Catherine of Aragon to Prince Arthur. When Arthur died prematurely, his younger brother, Henry VIII, took Catherine's hand. After they failed to produce a male heir, Henry divorced her, causing an irrevocable rift with the Catholic Church. ✉ *Cathedral Precincts* ☎ *01227/762862* ⊕ *www.canterbury-cathedral.org* ⊙ *Easter–Sept., Mon.–Sat. 9–6:30; Oct.–Easter, Mon.–Sat. 9–5, Sun. 12:30–2:30 and 4:30–5:30. Restricted access during services.*

The exhibits at the **Museum of Canterbury** provide an excellent overview of the city's history and architecture from Roman times to World War II. Visit early in the day to avoid the crowds. ✉ *20 Stour St.* ☎ *01227/452747* ⊕ *www.canterbury-museum.co.uk* ⊙ *June–Oct., Mon.–Sat. 10:30–5, Sun. 1:30–5; Nov.–May, Mon.–Sat. 10:30–5; last entry at 4. Closed last wk in Dec.*

Brighton

With its rich cultural mix—Regency architecture, specialty shops, sidewalk cafés, and lively arts—Brighton is an extraordinary city by the sea. For most of the 20th century the city was known for its faded glamour, but a young, bustling spirit has given a face-lift and a fresh buzz to this ever-popular resort. **Brighton Pier** follows the great tradition of amusement piers, which emerged from the county of Sussex in the 1850s. The pier is a crowded maze of arcade games, amusement-park rides, and chip shops. Built in 1866, the decaying **West Pier** (☎ *01273/321499* ⊕ *www.*

westpier.co.uk) stands just down the beach and is still for many the most recognizable landmark of the city. A renovation program has been put under pressure by storms in early 2003 that left parts of the grand old structure scattered up and down the beach. ⊠ *Waterfront along Madeira Dr.* ☎ *01273/609361* ⊕ *www.brightonpier.co.uk* ⊙ *June–Aug. daily 9 AM–2 AM; Sept.–May daily 10 AM–midnight.*

★ The most remarkable building on the Steine is the fairy-tale **Royal Pavilion.** Built by architect Henry Holland in 1787 as a simple villa, the Pavilion was transformed by John Nash between 1815 and 1823 for the Prince Regent (later George IV), who favored an exotic, eastern design with opulent Chinese interiors. Take particular note of the Music Room, styled as a Chinese-style pavilion, and the Banqueting Room, with its enormous flying-dragon "gasolier," or gaslight chandelier. The gardens, too, have been restored to Regency splendor, following John Nash's uncommonly naturalistic 1826 design. ⊠ *Old Steine* ☎ *01273/290900* ⊕ *www.royalpavilion.org.uk* ⊙ *Oct.–Mar., daily 10–5:15; Apr.–Sept., daily 9:30–5:45; last admission 45 mins before closing.*

$$ ✕ **Terre à Terre.** Exploring the outer bounds of vegetarian cuisine, Terre à Terre draws hordes of admirers to its bright, art-filled dining room. Inventive dishes like "Himmel und Erbe" (apple, potato, onion, and cheddar latkes) and an eclectic choice of salads will satisfy even the most devout carnivore. ⊠ *71 East St.* ☎ *01273/729051* ⊟ *AE, DC, MC, V* 🍴 *Reservations essential* ⊙ *No lunch Mon.*

London Essentials

AIR TRAVEL TO & FROM LONDON

International flights to London arrive at either Heathrow Airport, 24 km (15 mi) west of London, or Gatwick Airport, 43 km (27 mi) south of the capital. Most flights from the United States go to Heathrow. although Gatwick has grown from a European airport into one that serves 21 scheduled U.S. destinations. A third airport, Stansted, is to the east of the city. It handles mainly European and domestic traffic, although there is a scheduled service from New York.

TRANSFERS Airport Travel Line gives information and takes advance bookings on transfers to town and between airports, including National Express as listed below. The Heathrow Express train links the airport with Paddington Station in only 15 minutes. It costs £12, and service departs every 15 minutes from 5:02 AM to 11:47 PM. The Piccadilly Line serves Heathrow (all terminals) with a direct Underground (subway) link, and the fare is £3.70. Airbus A2 costs £8 and leaves every 30 minutes 5:30 AM–9:45 PM from Terminal 4; 5:45 AM–10:08 PM from Terminal 3, to Euston and King's Cross stations, but the trip can be lengthy, as there are around 14 other stops en route. For the same price, National Express Jetlink 777 coaches leave from the Heathrow Central Bus Station every 30 minutes from 5:40 AM to 9:35 PM and run directly to Victoria Coach Station. Cars and taxis drive into London from Heathrow, often through heavy traffic, and cost £30–£40. Add a tip of 10%–15% to the basic fare.

From Gatwick the quickest way to London is the nonstop rail Gatwick Express, costing £11 one-way and taking 30 minutes to reach Victoria Station. From 5:20 AM to 6:50 AM, trains leave every 30 minutes, then every 15 minutes until 8:50 PM, and back to every 30 minutes until the last departure at 1:35 AM. National Express Jetlink bus services from North and South terminals do not go to London, but they do stop in many other major cities, such as Bristol, Cambridge, and Oxford. From Gatwick, taxi fare is at least £50, plus tip; traffic can be very heavy.

🚌 **Airport Travel Line** ☎ 0870/574-7777. **Gatwick Express** ☎ 0845/850-1530 ⊕ www.gatwickexpress.co.uk. **Heathrow Express** ☎ 0845/600-1515 ⊕ www.heathrowexpress.co.uk. **Airbus A2** ☎ 0870/574-7777. **National Express** ☎ 0870/580-8080 ⊕ www.gobycoach.com.

BUS TRAVEL TO & FROM LONDON

The National Express coach service has routes to more than 1,200 major towns and cities in the United Kingdom. It's considerably cheaper than the train, although the trips usually take longer. Coaches depart every hour for Brighton (two hours) and Canterbury (one hour, 50 minutes).

🚌 **National Express** ✉ Victoria Coach Station, Buckingham Palace Rd., SW1 ☎ 0870/580-8080 ⊕ www.nationalexpress.com.

BUS TRAVEL WITHIN LONDON

London's bus system consists of bright red London Trasport double- and single-deckers, plus other buses of various colors from different companies. Destinations are displayed on the front and back, with the bus number on the front, back, and side. Not all buses run the full length of their route at all times. Some buses are still operated with a conductor whom you pay after finding a seat, but these days you will more often find one-person buses, in which you pay the driver upon boarding. Some buses in central London (an area bounded by Paddington, Victoria, Waterloo, and Euston Stations) now require prepurchased tickets. Machines at bus stops sell the tickets. For three-board "Bendy" buses, you must purchase tickets at the machines by the bus stops along these routes. Smoking is not allowed on any bus.

Buses stop only at clearly indicated stops. Main stops—at which buses should stop automatically—have a white sign with a red LT symbol on it. There are also request stops with red signs, a white symbol, and the word REQUEST added; at these you must hail the bus to make it stop. Although you can see much of the town from a bus, *don't* take one if you want to get anywhere in a hurry; traffic often slows travel to a crawl, and during peak times you may find yourself waiting at least 20 minutes for a bus and not being able to get on it once it arrives. If you intend to go by bus, ask at a Travel Information Centre for a free bus map.

All journeys within the central zone are 65p for short hops; for travel through any number of outer zones, add an extra 70p. A one-day pass through all zones is a good value at £2. Travelcards are good for Tube, bus, and National Rail trains in the Greater London zones. There are also a number of bus passes available for daily, weekly, and monthly use, and prices vary according to zones. A photograph is required for monthly bus passes.

🚌 **London Transport** ☎ 020/7222-1234 ⊕ www.londontransport.co.uk.

CAR TRAVEL

The best advice is to avoid driving in London because of the ancient street patterns and the chronic parking restrictions. One-way streets also add to the confusion. A £5 "congestion charge" is levied on all vehicles entering central London (bounded by the Inner Ring Road and visibly displayed on street signs) on weekdays from 7 to 6:30, excluding bank holidays. Pay in advance or on that day until 10 PM if you're entering the central zone. You can pay by phone, mail, or Internet, or at indicated retail outlets. There are no tollbooths; cameras monitor the area. For current information, check www.tfl.gov.org.uk.

EMERGENCIES

Bliss Chemist is the only pharmacy in the center of London that is open around the clock. The leading chain drugstore, Boots at Piccadilly Circus, is open until 8 PM seven days, and Boots at 151 Oxford Street is open until 8 PM on Thursday. (Note: a prescription can be filled only if issued by a British registered doctor.)

🆘 Emergency Services **Police, fire brigade, or ambulance** ☎ 999.

🆘 24-Hour Pharmacies **Bliss Chemist** ✉ 5 Marble Arch, W1, ☎ 020/7723-6116.

TAXIS

London's black taxis are famous for their comfort and for the ability of their drivers to remember the city's mazelike streets. Hotels and main tourist areas have ranks (stands) where you wait your turn to take one of the taxis that drive up. You can also hail a taxi if the flag is up or the yellow FOR HIRE sign is lighted. Fares start at £1.40 and increase by units of 20p per 281 yards or 55.5 seconds until the fare exceeds £8.60. After that, it's 20p for each 188 yards or 37 seconds. Surcharges are a tricky extra, which range from 40p for additional passengers or bulky luggage to 60p for evenings 8 PM–midnight, and until 6 AM on weekends and public holidays. At Christmas, the surcharge zooms to £2, and there's 40p extra for each additional passenger. Fares are occasionally raised from year to year. Tip taxi drivers 10%–15% of the tab.

TOURS

BOAT TOURS   In summer, narrow boats and barges cruise London's two canals, the Grand Union and Regent's Canal; most vessels operate on the latter, which runs between Little Venice in the west (the nearest Tube is Warwick Avenue on the Bakerloo Line) and Camden Lock (about 200 yards north of Camden Town Tube station). Canal Cruises offers three or four cruises daily March–October on the *Jenny Wren* and all year on the cruising restaurant *My Fair Lady*. Jason's Trip operates one-way and round-trip narrow-boat cruises on this route. Trips last 1½ hours. The London Waterbus Company operates this route year-round with a stop at London Zoo: trips run daily April–October and weekends only November–March.

All year boats cruise up and down the Thames, offering a different view of the London skyline. In summer (April–October) boats run more frequently than in winter—call to check schedules and routes. Following is a selection of the main routes. For trips downriver from Charing Cross to Greenwich Pier and historic Greenwich, call Catamaran Cruisers. Westminster Passenger Service runs from Westminster Pier and onward to Greenwich and Barrier Gardens at the Thames Barrier. Westminster Passenger Service Upriver operates through summer to Kew and Hampton Court from Westminster Pier. A Rail and River Rover ticket combines the modern wonders of Canary Wharf and Docklands development with the history of the riverside by boat. Tickets are available year-round from Westminster, Tower, and Greenwich piers, and Dockland Light Railway stations. Most launches have a public-address system and provide a running commentary on passing points of interest. Depending upon the destination, river trips may last from one to four hours.

🆘 **Canal Cruises** ☎ 020/7485-4433. **Catamaran Cruisers** ☎ 020/7987-1185 ⊕ www.catamarancruisers.co.uk. **Jason's Trip** ☎ 020/7286-3428. **London River Services** ☎ 020/7941-2400. **London Waterbus Company** ☎ 020/7482-2660. **Rail and River Rover** ☎ 020/7363-9700. **Westminster Passenger Services** ☎ 020/7930-4097 ⊕ www.wpsa.co.uk. **Westminster Passenger Service Upriver** ☎ 020/7930-2062.

BUS TOURS   There is a choice of companies, each providing daily tours, departing (8:30–9 AM) from central points, such as Haymarket (check with the individual company). You may board or alight at any of the numerous stops to view the sights, and reboard on the next bus. Tickets are bought from the driver and are good for all day, and prices vary according to the type of tour, although around £12 is the benchmark. The specialist in hop on–hop off tours is London Pride, with friendly, informative staff on easily recognizable double-decker buses. The Original London Sightseeing Tour offers frequent daily tours, departing from 8:30 AM from Baker Street (Madame Tussaud's), Marble Arch (Speakers' Corner), Piccadilly (Haymarket), or Victoria (Victoria Street) around every 12 minutes (less often out of peak summer season). The Big Bus Company runs a similar operation with Red and Blue tours. The Red Tour is a two-hour tour with 18 stops, and the Blue Tour, one hour with 13. Both start from Marble Arch, Speakers' Corner. Evan Evans offers good bus tours that also visit major sights just outside the city. Another reputable agency that operates bus tours is Frames Rickards.

🚩 **The Big Bus Company** ☎ 020/7233-9533 ⊕ www.bigbus.co.uk. **Evan Evans** ☎ 020/7950-1777 ⊕ www.evanevans.co.uk. **Frames Rickards** ☎ 020/7837-3111 ⊕ www.etmtravelgroup.com. **Original London Sightseeing Tour** ☎ 020/8877-1722. **London Pride** ☎ 020/7520-2050.

EXCURSIONS London Transport, Evan Evans, and Frames Rickards all offer day excursions (some combine bus and boat) to places of interest within easy reach of London, such as Windsor, Hampton Court, Oxford, Stratford-upon-Avon, and Bath. Prices vary and may include lunch and admission prices or admission only. Alternatively, make your own way, cheaply, to many of England's attractions on Green Line Coaches.

🚩 **Green Line Coaches** ☎ 020/8668-7261 or 0870/574-7777 ⊕ www.greenline.co.uk.

WALKING TOURS One of the best ways to get to know London is on foot, and there are many guided walking tours from which to choose. Original London Walks has theme tours devoted to the Beatles, Sherlock Holmes, Dickens, Jack the Ripper—you name it. For a more historical accent, check out the tours from Historical Walks. Peruse the leaflets in the Tourist Information Centre for special-interest tours.

🚩 **Original London Walks** ☎ 020/7624-3978 ⊕ www.walks.com. **Historical Walks** ☎ 020/8668-4019. **London Walking Forum** ⊕ www.londonwalking.com.

TRAIN TRAVEL

London is served by no fewer than 15 main-line train stations, so be certain of the station for your departure or arrival. All have Underground stops either in the train station or within a few minutes' walk from it, and most are served by several bus routes. The principal routes that connect London to other major towns and cities are on a National Rail network. Seats can be reserved in person at any Rail Travel Centre, in the station from which you depart, or by phone with a credit card.

Charing Cross Station serves southeast England, including Canterbury, Margate, Dover/Folkestone, and ferry ports. Euston/St. Pancras serves East Anglia, Essex, the Northeast, the Northwest, and North Wales, including Coventry, Stratford-upon-Avon, Birmingham, Manchester, Liverpool, Windermere, Glasgow, and Inverness, northwest Scotland. King's Cross serves the east Midlands; the Northeast, including York, Leeds, and Newcastle; and north and east Scotland, including Edinburgh and Aberdeen. Liverpool Street serves Essex and East Anglia. Paddington serves the south Midlands, west and south Wales, and the west country, including Oxford. Victoria serves southern England, including Gatwick Airport, Brighton, Dover/Folkestone and ferry ports, and the south coast. Waterloo serves the southwestern United Kingdom, including Salisbury, Portsmouth, Southampton, and Isle of Wight. Waterloo International is the terminal for the Eurostar high-speed train to Paris and Brussels.

If you're combining a trip to Great Britain with stops on the Continent, you can either drive your car onto a *Le Shuttle* train through the Channel Tunnel (35 minutes from Folkestone to Calais) or book a seat from London on the Eurostar.

FARES & SCHEDULES Generally speaking, it is less expensive to buy a return (round-trip) ticket, especially for day trips not far from London, and you should always inquire at the information office about discount fares. You can hear a recorded summary of timetable and fare information to many destinations by calling the appropriate "dial and listen" numbers listed under Rail in the telephone book. The telephone information number listed below gets you through to any of the stations.

National Rail Enquiries ☎ 0845/748-4950 ⊕ www.nationalrail.co.uk.

TRAVEL AGENCIES
American Express ✉ 30-31 Haymarket, SW1 ☎ 020/7484-9600 ✉ 89 Mount St., W1 ☎ 020/7659-0701. **Thomas Cook** ✉ 1 Woburn Pl., WC1 ☎ 020/7837-0393 ✉ 184 Kensington High St., W8, ☎ 020/7707-2300.

UNDERGROUND TRAVEL
Known as "the Tube," London's extensive Underground system is by far the most widely used form of city transportation. Trains run both below and aboveground to the suburbs, and all stations are clearly marked with the London Underground circular symbol. (A SUBWAY sign refers to an under-the-street pedestrian crossing.) Trains are all one class; smoking is *not* allowed on board or in the stations.

There are 10 basic lines—all named. The Central, District, Northern, Metropolitan, and Piccadilly lines all have branches, usually taking you to the outlying sections of the city, so be sure to note which branch is needed for your particular destination. Electronic platform signs tell you the final stop and route of the next train, and some signs indicate how many minutes you'll have to wait for the train to arrive. Begun in the Victorian era, the Underground is still being expanded and improved. The supermodern Jubilee line extension sweeps from Green Park to south of the river, with connections to Canary Wharf and the Docklands, and east to Stratford. The zippy Docklands Light Railway (DLR) runs through the Docklands to the *Cutty Sark* and maritime Greenwich.

FARES & SCHEDULES For both buses and Tube fares, London is divided into six concentric zones; the fare goes up the farther afield you travel. Ask at Underground ticket counters for the LT booklet "Fares and Tickets," which gives all details. You must buy a ticket before you travel. Many types of travel cards can be bought from Pass Agents that display the sign: tobacconists, confectioners, newsdealers, and mainline overground rail stations.

For one trip between any two stations, you can buy an ordinary single (one-way ticket) for travel anytime on the day of issue; if you're coming back on the same route the same day, then an ordinary return (round-trip ticket) costs twice the single fare. Singles vary in price from £1.60 to £3.70 for a six-zone journey. A *carnet* (£10) is a convenient book of 10 single tickets to use in Central Zone 1 only.

Travelcards allow unrestricted travel on the Tube, most buses, and national rail trains in the Greater London zones. There are different options available: an unrestricted Day Travelcard costs £5.10–£10.70; off-peak (traveling after 9:30 AM) Day Travelcards are £4.10–£5.10. Weekend Travelcards, for the two days of the weekend or on any two consecutive days during public holidays, cost £6.10–£7.60. Family Travelcards are one-day tickets for one or two adults with one to four children and cost £2.70–£3.40 per adult, including one child; each extra child must pay an additional 80p fare. Visitor Travelcards are the best bet for visitors, but they must be bought before leaving home (they're available in both the United States and Canada). They are valid for periods of three, four, or seven days ($25, $32, $49, respectively) and can be used on the Tube and virtually all buses and British Rail services in London.

From Monday through Saturday, trains begin running just after 5 AM; the last services leave central London between midnight and 12:30 AM. On Sunday, trains start two hours later and finish about an hour earlier. The frequency of trains depends on the route and the time of day, but normally you should not have to wait more than 10 minutes. A pocket map of the entire Tube network is available free from most Underground ticket counters.

🔃 **London Transport** ☎ 020/7222-1234, 24 hours ⊕ www.londontransport.co.uk or www.thetube.com. Travelers with disabilities should call for the free leaflet **"Access to the Underground"** ☎ 020/7918-3312.

VISITOR INFORMATION

Visitorcall is the London Tourist Board's 24-hour phone service. The premium-rate recorded information line has different numbers for theater, events, museums, sports, transportation around town, and so on. Call to access the list of options, or see the separate categories in the telephone directory.

🔃 **London Tourist Information Centre** ⊠ Victoria Station Forecourt. **Britain Visitor Centre** ⊠ 1 Regent St., Piccadilly Circus, SW1Y 4NX ⊙ Weekdays 9–6:30, weekends 10–4 ⊕ www.visitbritain.com. **London Tourist Board/Visitorcall** ☎ 09068/663344, calls cost 60p per minute ⊕ www.visitlondon.com.

WINDSOR TO BATH

If you follow the Thames, England's second-longest river, along its course, you embark on a journey through historic towns, verdant countryside, and some of the grandest homes ever erected. West of London, Windsor has housed the royal family since William the Conqueror. Many of England's traditions were born on or nearby the Thames: horse racing at Ascot; the Henley Royal Regatta; Oxford University; and even William Shakespeare. Blenheim Palace and Warwick Castle are emblems of grandeur in their own right, and Bath's 18th-century streets recall an age more elegant than our own. South of Stratford-upon-Avon, the Cotswolds are a verdant region of gentle hills and stone-built villages that encourage you to linger. One of Britain's grandest monuments, prehistoric Stonehenge, lies southeast of Bath.

Windsor

After seeing the castle, Windsor's main attaction, stroll around the town and enjoy the shops; antiques are sold on cobbled Church Lane and Queen Charlotte Street.

★ **Windsor Castle**, 34 km (21 mi) west of London, has housed the royal family since the 11th century. In the 14th century, Edward III revamped the old castle, building the Norman gateway, the great round tower, and new apartments. Almost every monarch since then has added new buildings or improved existing ones; over the centuries the medieval fortification has been transformed into the lavish royal palace you see today.

In the queen's state apartments, the **Grand Reception Room,** the **Green and Crimson Drawing Rooms,** and the **State and Octagonal Dining Rooms** have been restored to their former glory after the fire of 1992. The ceiling of St. George's Hall, where the queen gives state banquets, has a green

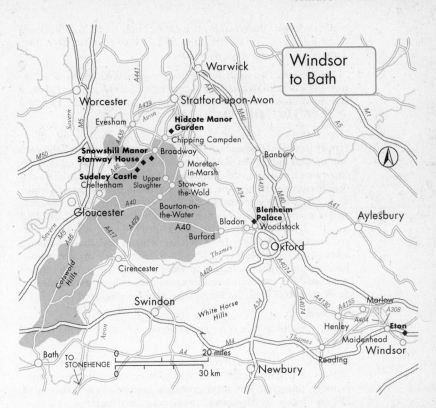

oak roof, and the largest hammer-beam roof to have been built during the 20th century looms magnificently over the 600-year-old hall. The private chapel of the royal family has also been redesigned, with a stained-glass window commemorating the fire of 1992 and the restoration work that subsequently took place. All restored rooms, except the private chapel, are open to the public. The state apartments are sometimes closed when the queen is in residence; call ahead to check.

St. George's Chapel, more than 230 feet long with two tiers of great windows and hundreds of gargoyles, buttresses, and pinnacles, is one of the noblest buildings in England. Inside, above the choir stalls, hang the banners, swords, and helmets of the Knights of the Order of the Garter, the most senior Order of Chivalry. The many monarchs buried in the chapel include Henry VIII and George VI, father of the present queen. (St. George's Chapel is closed to the public on Sunday.)

The magnificent art collection at Windsor contains paintings by such masters as Rubens, Van Dyck, and Holbein; drawings by Leonardo da Vinci; and Gobelin tapestries. There are splendid views across to Windsor Great Park, the remains of a former royal hunting forest. Make time to view **Queen Mary's Doll's House,** a charming miniature country house with every detail complete, including electricity, running water, and real books. It was designed in 1921 by architect Sir Edwin Lutyens for the present queen's grandmother. ⊠ *Windsor Castle* ☎ *020/7321–2233 for tickets; 01753/83118 for recorded information* ⊕ *www.royalresidences. com* ⊠ *£11.50* ⊙ *Mar.–Oct., daily 9:45–5:15 (last admission at 4); Nov.–Feb., daily 9:45–4:15 (last admission at 3).*

☺ An attraction to delight children (of all ages) is **Legoland,** set in woodland 3¼ km (2 mi) outside Windsor. Hands-on activities and ingenious models celebrate the versatile toy building brick. ✉ *B3202, Bracknell/ Ascot Rd.* ☎ *08705/040404* ✉ *£22.95* ⊙ *Mar.–June and Sept.–Jan., daily 10–6; July and Aug., daily 10–8.*

$ ✕ **Two Brewers.** Two small, low-ceilinged rooms make up this 17th-century pub where locals congregate (children are not welcome) over bistro-style food. Reservations are essential for the Sunday roast. ✉ *34 Park St.* ☎ *01753/855426* ✉ *AE, DC, MC, V.*

Henley

Henley has been famous since 1839 for the rowing regatta it holds each year around the first Sunday in July. The social side of the regatta is as entertaining as the races themselves; elderly oarsmen wear brightly colored blazers and boater hats, and women flaunt their smartest summer suits. The town is worth exploring for its excellent rowing museaum as well as its small but good selection of specialty shops. The Red Lion Hotel near the 200-year-old bridge has been visited by kings, dukes, and writers. The **Chantry House,** a 1420 merchant's house later converted into a school for impoverished boys, is an unspoiled example of the rare overhanging timber-frame design. **St. Mary's Church** has a 16th-century "checkerboard" tower made of alternate squares of flint and stone. ✉ *Hart St.* ☎ *01491/577062* ⊙ *Church services or by appointment.*

Oxford

Numbers in the margin correspond to points of interest on the Oxford map.

Oxford is more than a university town. It has been one of the two forerunners of English erudition since the 13th century, and the town is pristinely preserved. Tiny alleys, grimacing gargoyles, honey-color stone, and the ubiquitous "dreaming" spires make for an unforgettable experience. Oxford University comprises 40 independent colleges, and many of the magnificent chapels and dining halls are open to visitors—times and (in some cases) entry charges are displayed at the entrance lodges. Some colleges are open only in the afternoons during university semesters, when the undergraduates are in residence; college access is often restricted to the chapels, dining rooms (called halls), and libraries. All are closed during exams, usually from mid-April to late June, when the May Balls are held. The best way to gain access is to join a walking tour led by an official Blue Badge guide. These two-hour tours leave up to five times daily from the tourist office.

One of the most delightful walks through Oxford is along the **banks of the River Cherwell,** either through the University Parks area or through Magdalen College to Addison's Walk. Along the way you can watch the undergraduates idly punting a summer's afternoon away. Better still, rent one of these narrow flat-bottom boats yourself—but be warned: navigating is more difficult than it looks!

❼ Ashmolean Museum. The Ashmolean is Britain's oldest public museum, holding noted collections of Egyptian, Greek, and Roman artifacts; Michelangelo drawings; and European silverware. ✉ *Beaumont St.* ☎ *01865/278000* ⊕ *www.ashmol.ox.ac.uk* ⊙ *Tues.–Sat. 10–5, Sun. 2–5.*

❹ Balliol College. The doors between the inner and outer quadrangles of Balliol still bear the scorch marks from the flames that burned Archbishop Cranmer and Bishops Latimer and Ridley at the stake in 1555 for their Protestant beliefs. ✉ *Broad St.* ⊕ *www.balliol.ox.ac.uk* ⊙ *Daily 2–5.*

★ **❾ Bodleian Library and Radcliffe Camera.** Dating from 1602, the Bodleian is one of the oldest libraries in the world. Limited sections of the library can be visited on a **tour.** Otherwise, the general public can visit only the **Divinity School,** a superbly vaulted room with changing exhibitions of manuscripts and rare books. Part of the Bodleian is housed in the spectacular **Radcliffe Camera** and contains an unrivaled collection of manuscripts. Behind University Church, this striking English baroque structure is adorned with marble urns, massive columns, and one of the largest domes in Britain. It is not open to the public. ⊠ *Broad St.* ☎ *01865/277224 for tour information* ⊙ *Library tours Mar.–Oct., weekdays 10:30, 11:30, 2, 3, Sat. 10:30, 11:30; Nov.–Feb., weekdays 2, 3, Sat. 10:30, 11:30. Divinity School weekdays 9–4:45, Sat. 9–12:30* ☞ *Children under 14 not admitted.*

❸ **Christ Church College.** Built in 1546, Christ Church is the site of Oxford's largest quadrangle, "Tom Quad," named after the huge bell (6¼ tons) that hangs in the gate tower. Its 800-year-old chapel in one corner has been Oxford's cathedral since the time of Henry VIII. The college's medieval dining hall contains portraits of many famous alumni, including John Wesley, William Penn, and 13 of Britain's prime ministers. Lewis Carroll was a teacher of mathematics here for many years. ⊠ *St. Aldate's* ☎ *01865/286573* ⊕ *www.chch.ox.ac.uk* ⊙ *Mon.–Sat. 9:30–5:30, Sun. 2–5:30.*

Christ Church Picture Gallery. In Canterbury Quadrangle, this connoisseur's delight exhibits paintings by Tintoretto, Veronese, and Van Dyck. ⊠ *Oriel Square* ☎ *01865/276172* ⊙ *Mon.–Sat. 10:30–1 and 2–4:30, Sun. 2–4:30.*

Magdalen Bridge. At the foot of this famous Oxford landmark you can rent a punt (a shallow-bottomed boat that is poled slowly up the river) for £10 an hour. You may wish, like many an Oxford student, to spend a summer afternoon punting—while dangling your champagne bottle in the water to keep it cool. ⊠ *High St.*

★ ❶ **Magdalen College.** Founded in 1458, with an impressive main quadrangle and a supremely monastic air, Magdalen is one of the most impressive of Oxford's colleges. Scenic highlights include the Deer Park and Addison's Walk—the grounds that Cardinal Wolsey, Oscar Wilde, and Dudley Moore once called home. ⊕ *www.magd.ox.ac.uk* ⊙ *June–Sept., daily noon–6.*

❷ **New College.** Founded in 1379, the college has extensive gardens, partly enclosed by the medieval city wall, and a notorious row of gargoyles. Famous alumni include Hugh Grant and Richard Mason, who published his international best-seller, *The Drowning People,* only months after first "coming up" to Oxford. ⊠ *Holywell St.* ⊕ *www.new.ox.ac.uk* ⊙ *Easter–Sept., daily 10–5; Oct.–Easter, daily 2–4.*

❺ **Oxford Story Exhibition.** This multimedia presentation explores the university's 800-year history. ⊠ *Broad St.* ☎ *01865/728822* ⊙ *July and Aug., daily 9:30–5; Sept.–June, Mon.–Sat. 10–4:30, Sun. 11–4:30.*

❻ **Sheldonian Theatre.** Architect Christopher Wren designed this to look like a semicircular Roman amphitheater, and its front gate is topped by gigantic busts of the ancient emperors. ⊠ *Broad St.* ☎ *01865/277299* ⊙ *Mar.–mid-Nov., Mon.–Sat. 10–12:30 and 2–4:30; mid-Nov.–Feb., Mon.–Sat. 10–12:30 and 2–3:30* ⊙ *Closed 10 days at Christmas and Easter, and for student events.*

❽ **University Church.** The 14th-century tower of this central church (officially known as St. Mary the Virgin) provides a splendid panoramic view of the city's famous skyline. The Convocation House, accessible from Radcliffe Square, serves generous portions—cafeteria style—under the

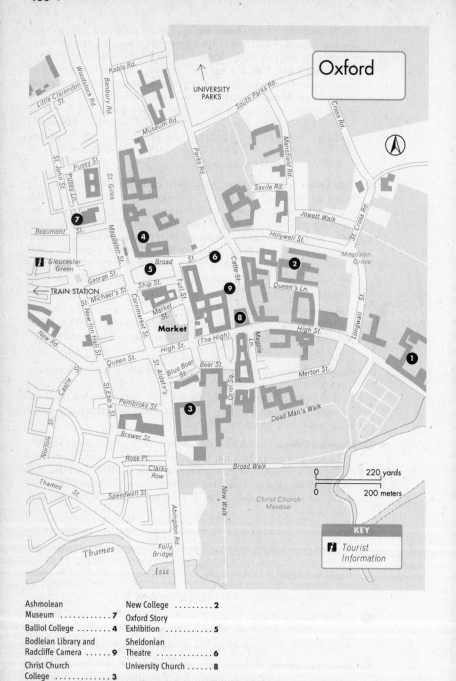

Oxford

UNIVERSITY PARKS

KEY

i *Tourist*
Information

room in which OxFam was founded. ☎ *01865/279111* ⊘ *Church and tower Sept.–June, daily 9–5 (until 4:15 in winter); July and Aug. 9–7.*

$$$–$$$$ ✕ **Gee's.** This brasserie in a conservatory, formerly a florist's shop, is just north of the town center. The menu offers French and English dishes, including a good fish selection, and the place is popular with both town and gown. ⊠ *61 Banbury Rd.* ☎ *01865/553540* ▭ *AE, MC, V.*

$ ✕ **Grand Café.** Golden-hue tiles, columns, and antique marble tables make this café both architecturally impressive and an excellent spot for a light meal or a drink. ⊠ *84 High St.* ☎ *01865/204463* ▭ *AE, MC, V.*

$$$$ ✕▣ **Le Manoir aux Quat' Saisons.** Standards run high at this 15th-cen-
Fodor'sChoice tury stone manor house, which has one of England's finest kitchens (com-
★ plete with cooking school) and luxurious rooms in styles from rococo fantasy to chic chinoiserie. Chef Raymond Blanc's epicurean touch shows at every turn. Spare yourself the trouble of deciding among the innovative French creations and treat yourself to the *menu gourmand—* eight courses for £95. ⊠ *Church Rd., Great Milton (7 mi southeast of Oxford) OX44 7PD* ☎ *01844/278881* ⎙ *01844/278847* ⊕ *www. manoir.com* ⌧ *32 rooms* ⚭ *Restaurant* ▭ *AE, DC, MC, V.*

$$$$ ✕▣ **Old Bank Hotel.** From the sleek lobby, set subtly back from High Street, to the 20th-century British paintings on display and the subdued modern furnishings in the guest rooms, the former Barclay's Bank has a cosmopolitan air. Oxford's most centrally located hotel also holds the contemporary Quod Bar and Grill. ⊠ *92–94 High St., OX1 4BN* ☎ *01865/799599* ⎙ *01865/799598* ⊕ *www.oxford-hotels-restaurants. co.uk* ⌧ *43 rooms* ⚭ *Restaurant, bar* ▭ *AE, DC, MC, V.*

★ $$$–$$$$ ▣ **Old Parsonage.** Well respected since it opened in 1660, this gabled country-house hotel is a dignified escape from the surrounding city cen-
ter. Dark-wood paneling in the lobby and tasteful chintz patterns in the rooms are far from trendy, but expeditious room service and memorable meals by an open fire keep people coming back. ⊠ *1 Banbury Rd., OX2 6NN* ☎ *01865/310210* ⎙ *01865/311262* ⊕ *www.oxford-hotels-restaurants.co.uk* ⌧ *26 rooms, 4 suites* ⚭ *Restaurant, bar* ▭ *AE, DC, MC, V.*

$$$–$$$$ ▣ **The Randolph.** Oxford's landmark hotel has undergone extensive restoration of its beautiful Victorian Gothic interior (unfortunately, this has not extended to some of the squeaky floorboards, an annoyance at night). It's across from the Ashmolean Museum. ⊠ *Beaumont St., OX1 2LN* ☎ *01865/247481* ⎙ *01865/791678* ⊕ *www.macdonald-hotels. co.uk* ⌧ *99 rooms, 10 suites* ⚭ *Restaurant, bar* ▭ *AE, DC, MC, V.*

Woodstock

★ Just outside the back gates of Blenheim Palace is the village of **Wood-stock.** Extraordinarily civilized, it is filled with beautiful shops, some el-
egant 18th-century buildings, and historic hotels, such as the **Bear** (☎ 08704/008202), the **Feathers** (☎ 01993/813158), and the **Blenheim Guest House and Tea Rooms** (☎ 01993/813814), the last set just out-
side the imperial back gates of the palace. Stay here instead of in Ox-
ford and take the 15-minute bus ride back and forth to the college town.

Since its construction in the early 18th century by architect Sir John Van-
brugh, dukes of Marlborough, Vanderbilts, and Churchills have in-
Fodor'sChoice habited **Blenheim Palace,** about 13 km (8 mi) north of Oxford on A44
★ (Woodstock Road). Upon first glace, though, the sheer English baroque grandeur—its vast pile of towers, colonnades, and porticoes—proves that it's not the most spectacular house in England just because of its his-
tory. The palace stands in 2,000 acres of beautiful gardens created by the 18th century's most gifted English landscape gardener, Capability Brown. Soldier and statesman John Churchill, first duke of Marlbor-

ough, commissioned the house on land given to him by Queen Anne as a reward for his defeat of the French at the Battle of Blenheim in 1704. The house is filled with fine paintings—don't miss the grand John Singer Sargent portrait of the ninth duke and his wife, Consuelo Vanderbilt—tapestries, and furniture. Winston Churchill, a descendant of Marlborough, was born in the palace; some of his paintings are on display, and there is an exhibition devoted to his life. A cafeteria is on the grounds, as are a famous topiary maze, a butterfly house, and other amusements. ✉ *Woodstock* ☎ *01993/811325* ⊕ *www.blenheimpalace.com* ☉ *Palace mid-Mar.–Oct., daily 10:30–4:45; grounds daily 9–4:45.*

Sir Winston Churchill (1874–1965) is buried in the nearby village of **Bladon.** His grave in the small tree-lined churchyard is all the more touching for its simplicity.

Stratford-upon-Avon

Numbers in the margin correspond to points of interest on the Stratford-upon-Avon map.

From Oxford and Blenheim, A34 runs northwest across the Cotswold Hills to Stratford-upon-Avon, the hometown of William Shakespeare. Even without its most famous son, Stratford would be worth visiting. The town's timbered buildings bear witness to its prosperity during the 16th century, when it was a thriving craft and trading center. Attractive buildings from the 18th century add to the sense of history here.

The main places of Shakespearean interest—Anne Hathaway's Cottage, Hall's Croft, Mary Arden's House, and Shakespeare's Birthplace—are run by the **Shakespeare Birthplace Trust.** They all have similar opening times, and you can get a combination ticket for them all or pay separate entry fees if you want to visit only one or two. ☎ *01789/204016* ⊕ *www.stratford-upon-avon.co.uk* ✉ *Joint ticket £13* ☉ *Shakespeare's Birthplace and Anne Hathaway's Cottage: Apr.–May, Sept., and Oct., Mon.–Sat. 9:30–5, Sun. 10–5; June–Aug., Mon.–Sat. 9–5, Sun. 9:30–5; Nov.–Mar., Mon.–Sat. 10–4, Sun. 10:30–4. Hall's Croft and Mary Arden's House: Nov.–Mar., daily 11–4; Apr.–May, Sept., and Oct., daily 11–5; June–Aug., Mon.–Sat. 9:30–5, Sun. 10–5 (last entry for all sights 30 mins before closing).*

★ ❸ **Anne Hathaway's Cottage.** Set in Shottery on the edge of the town, this is the early home of the playwright's wife. This thatched house is one of the most picturesque sights in Britain. ✉ *Cottage La., Shottery* ☎ *01789/292100.*

❺ **Guildhall Grammar School.** Along the main thoroughfare of Church Street are almshouses built by the Guild of the Holy Cross in the early 15th century. Farther along is the town school, which Shakespeare probably attended as a boy and which is still used to educate the young of Stratford. ✉ *Church St., near Chapel La.* ☎ *01789/293351* ☉ *Easter and summer school vacations, daily 10–6.*

❹ **Hall's Croft.** A fine Tudor town house, this was the home of Shakespeare's daughter Susanna and her doctor husband; it is furnished in the style of the day. The doctor's dispensary and consulting room can also be seen. ✉ *Old Town.*

❷ **Harvard House.** Next to the Garrick Inn, Harvard House is a half-timber 16th-century structure that was home to Catherine Rogers, mother of the John Harvard who founded Harvard University in 1636. Inside, the **Museum of British Pewter** displays toys, tanks, and teapots. ✉ *High St.* ☉ *May, June, and Sept.–Nov., Fri.–Sun. 11:30–4:30; July–Sept., Thurs.–Sun. 11:30–4:30.*

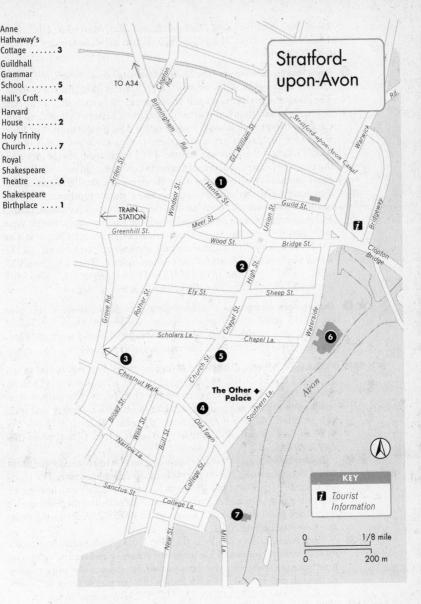

TO A34

7 **Holy Trinity Church.** Shakespeare and his wife are buried in the chancel of this sanctuary, which is down the street from Royal Shakespeare Theatre and on the bank of the Avon. ✉ *Trinity St.*

Mary Arden's House. This bucolic site in the hamlet of Wilmcote attracted attention in 2000 because the Tudor farmhouse, considered for years to have been the home of Shakespeare's mother (and so named), was discovered to have been instead the home of Adam Palmer. It was shown that Mary Arden lived in a house on Glebe Farm, which adjoins the farmhouse and is run by the Trust; this has now assumed the name Mary Arden's House. The Tudor farmhouse and farm form the **Shakespeare Countryside Museum**, with crafts exhibits, falconry demonstrations, a café, and a garden of trees mentioned in the plays. ✉ *A3400, 3 mi northwest of Stratford* ☎ *01789/204016; 01789/293455 for information on special events* ⊕ *www.shakespeare.org.uk* ⊘ *Nov.–Mar., Mon.–Sat.*

10–4, Sun. 10:30–4; Sept., Oct., Apr., and May, Mon.–Sat. 10–5, Sun. 10:30–5; June–Aug., Mon.–Sat. 9:30–5, Sun. 10–5. Last entry 30 mins before closing.

❻ Royal Shakespeare Theatre. The beloved Stratford home of the Royal Shakespeare Company (RSC) is set amid lovely gardens along the River Avon. The company performs several Shakespeare plays each season, as well as scripts by any number of other playwrights, between March and January. It is best to book well in advance for RSC productions, but a few tickets for the day of performance are always available, and it is also worth asking if there are any returns. For a fascinating insight into how the theater operates, join one of the backstage tours, led twice daily (four times on Sunday). Beside the main theater is the smaller **Swan.** Modeled on an Elizabethan theater, the Swan stages productions in the round. It also provides entry to the RSC collection of paintings, props, and memorabilia; visit it either on one of the backstage tours or on your own. Farther down Southern Lane toward Holy Trinity Church is **The Other Place,** a modern auditorium for experimental productions. ✉ *The Royal Shakespeare Theatre, Stratford-upon-Avon, Warwickshire CV37 6BB,* ☎ *01789/296655; 01789/403403 box office; 01789/403405 tours; 01789/295623 The Other Place* ∰ *www.rsc.org.uk.*

★ ❶ Shakespeare Birthplace. This holy shrine for Shakespeare lovers also contains a small museum with costumes used in the BBC's versions of the plays and an exhibition of the playwright's life and work. ✉ *Henley St.* ☎ *01789/204016* ∰ *www.shakespeare.org.uk.*

$$$$ ✕ Quarto's. Views of the River Avon and its resident swans add to the appeal of dining at this restaurant in the Royal Shakespeare Theatre. The lounge offers pretheater canapes and champagne. The menu is contemporary British so expect things like lamb with rosemary and goat cheese salad. ✉ *Royal Shakespeare Theatre, Waterside* ☎ *01789/403415* ⌂ *Reservations essential* 🗀 *AE, MC, V* ⊙ *Closed when theater is closed.*

★ $$ ✕ Lambs. Sit downstairs in the no-smoking section to appreciate the hardwood floors and oak beams of this local epicurean favorite. The modern updates of tried-and-true dishes include roast chicken with lime butter and char-grilled sausages with leek mash. The two- and three-course set menus are good deals. ✉ *12 Sheep St.* ☎ *01789/292554* ⌂ *Reservations essential* 🗀 *AE, MC, V.*

$–$$ ✕ Black Swan. Known locally as the Dirty Duck, this is one of Stratford's most celebrated pubs and has attracted actors since Garrick's days. Its little veranda overlooks the theaters and the river, and you can down an English grill specialty or a bar meal with your pint of lager. ✉ *Southern La.* ☎ *01789/297312* 🗀 *AE, MC, V* ⊙ *No dinner Sun.*

$$$–$$$$ 🛏 Shakespeare Hotel. For a touch of typical Stratford, stay at this Elizabethan town house in the heart of the town, close to the theater and to most of the attractions. The interiors have been luxuriously modernized but still retain their Elizabethan character. ✉ *Chapel St., CV37 6ER* ☎ *08704/008182* 🖷 *01789/415411* ∰ *www.heritage-hotels.com* ⇔ *74 rooms* ⌂ *Restaurant, bar* 🗀 *AE, DC, MC, V.*

$$$ 🛏 Falcon Hotel. Licensed as an alehouse since 1640, this black-and-white timber-frame hotel in the center of town retains the feeling of a friendly inn. The heavily beamed rooms in the older part are small and quaint. ✉ *Chapel St., CV37 6HA* ☎ *01789/279953* 🖷 *01789/414260* ∰ *www.regalhotels.co.uk* ⇔ *84 rooms* ⌂ *Restaurant, 2 bars* 🗀 *AE, DC, MC, V.*

$$ 🛏 Caterham House. Built in 1830, this elegantly furnished building is within an easy walk of the theater. You may spot an actor or two among the

guests. ⊠ *58 Rother St., CV37 6LT* ☎ *01789/267309* 🖷 *01789/414836*
⚲ *Bar* ⇌ *10 rooms* ▭ *MC, V.*

Warwick

Warwick, some 13 km (8 mi) north of Stratford along A46, is an unusual architectural mixture of Georgian red brick and Elizabethan half-
timbering, although some unattractive postwar developments have
★ spoiled the town center. **Warwick Castle** is one of the finest medieval structures of its kind in England, towering on a precipice above the River
Avon. Most of its features date from the 14th century. The interior contains magnificent collections of armor, paintings, and furniture, and a
waxworks display by Madame Tussaud's. Outside, peacocks strut in the
60 acres of landscaped riverside gardens. A restored Victorian boathouse
has a flora-and-fauna exhibition and a nature walk. ⊠ *Castle Hill*
☎ *01926/495421* ⊕ *www.warwick-castle.co.uk* ☉ *Apr.–Sept., daily*
10–6; Oct.–Mar., daily 10–5.

The Cotswolds

Near the spires and shires of Shakespeare Country is a region that conjures up "olde Englande" at its most blissfully rural: the Cotswolds. If
you've come in search of picture-postcard English countryside, with soft
hills and mellow stone-built villages, this is your destination. From
Stratford, take an easy detour via A3400 and B4632 into this region,
which is marked by high, bare hills patterned by patches of ancient forest and stone walls that protect the sheep that have grazed here from
the earliest times.

The gateway to the Cotswolds is **Cheltenham,** once rivaling Bath for Georgian elegance. Although much of it is marred by modern developments,
there are still some fine examples of the Regency style in its graceful secluded villas, lush gardens, and leafy crescents and squares. If you visit
this historic health resort in the spring or summer—take either M4 and
M5 north from Bath, or M5 south from Birmingham, turning east on
A40—be sure to explore elegant Lansdown Crescent, Pittville Pump
Room, Imperial Square, and Montpellier Walk. Cheltenham may look
in part like a Gilbert & Sullivan stage set, but it is also home to an **International Jazz Festival** in May and the progressive **Cheltenham Festival of Literature,** held in October.

From Cheltenham, take B4632 to reach the Cotswolds proper. Two kilo-
★ meters (1 mi) southeast of Winchcombe is **Sudeley Castle,** the home and
burial place of Catherine Parr (1512–48), Henry VIII's sixth and last
wife. Restored by the Dent-Brocklehurst family, the Tudor-age mansion
is surrounded by a spectacular rose garden, where Shakespeare performances are given in the summer. ⊠ *Winchcombe* ☎ *01242/604357*
⊕ *www.sudeleycastle.co.uk* ☉ *Castle: Apr.–late Oct., daily 11–5; gardens, grounds, plant center, and shop: early Mar.–late Oct., daily*
10:30–5:30.

★ The tiny village of Stanway is landmarked by **Stanway House,** which dates
from the Jacobean era and is familiar to many, thanks to its starring role
in many TV dramas. J. M. Barrie, author of *Peter Pan,* often rented this
house in summer, and his thatched-roof cricket pavilion adorns the
grounds. ⊠*Stanway* ☎*01386/584469* ☉*July and Aug., Tues. and Thurs.*
2–5 (other times by appt. only for groups of at least 20).

Broadway is the Cotswold town to end all Cotswold towns. William Morris first discovered this village in the late 19th century, and lovers of rural
England have journeyed here ever since to enjoy its many picturesque
houses, tea parlors, and antiques shops.

The Cotswolds in a microcosm is the idyllic town of **Chipping Campden,** announced from afar by the soaring pinnacled tower of **St. James,** one of the many wool churches built with money from wealthy wool merchants. Look for the group of almshouses built in 1624 on High Street and raised above street level and for the gabled **Market Hall,** built three years later by Sir Baptiste Hycks for the sale of local produce. The historic **Silk Mill** has been renovated for crafts shops.

★ Six kilometers (4 mi) outside Chipping Campden is **Hidcote Manor Gardens,** a 20th-century garden created around a Cotswold manor house (not open to the public). The lovely garden—which some connoisseurs consider the finest in Britain—consists of a series of open-air rooms divided by walls and hedges, each in a different style. Nearby is the fairytale hamlet of Hidcote Bartrim. ☒ *Hidcote Bartrim* ☎ *01386/438333* ⊕ *www.nationaltrust.org.uk* ☉ *Apr.–Sept., Mon.–Wed. and weekends 10:30–6:30; Oct., Mon.–Wed. and weekends 10:30–5:30; last admission 1 hr before closing.*

Stow-on-the-Wold is the highest, and largest, town in the Cotswolds. Built around a wide square, Stow's imposing golden-stone houses have been discreetly converted into a good number of quality antiques stores.

Bourton-on-the-Water is the most classic of the Cotswold "water" villages. The River Windrush runs through town, crossed by low stone bridges. Follow the stream and its ducks to the old mill, now home to
☙ the **Cotswold Motor Museum and Toy Collection,** to enjoy exhibits of more than 30 vintage cars and old advertising signage and a re-created smithy and 1940s garage. ☒ *Sherborne St.* ☎ *01451/821255* ☉ *Mid-Feb.–Oct., daily 10–6.*

$$$–$$$$ ✕🏠 **Queen's Hotel.** Overlooking Imperial Gardens from the center of Cheltenham's Promenade, this classic Regency building has welcomed visitors since 1838. Public areas and rooms are traditionally British, though there's a taste of France, too: one of the hotel's two restaurants is Le Petit Blanc, open to nonresidents and a great place to sample French provincial cooking. ☒ *The Promenade, Cheltenham GL50 1NN* ☎ *0870/4008107; 888/892–00380 toll-free in U.S.; 01242/266800 restaurant* 🖷 *01242/224145* ⊕ *www.macdonaldhotels.co.uk* ⟿ *73 rooms* ᗱ *2 restaurants* ▤ *AE, DC, MC, V.*

$–$$ ✕🏠 **Royalist Hotel.** Certified as the oldest inn in the country (AD 947), this hostelry is jammed with interesting features—witches' marks on the beams, a tunnel to the church across the road—and the owners have stylishly integrated designer bedrooms and a fine restaurant. If the set brasserie-style menu doesn't appeal, you can opt for pub grub in the adjacent Eagle and Child. ☒ *Digbeth St., Stow-on-the-Wold GL54 1BN* ☎ *01451/830670* 🖷 *01451/870048* ⊕ *www.theroyalisthotel.co.uk* ⟿ *12 rooms, 1 suite* ᗱ *2 restaurants, 2 bars* ▤ *AE, MC, V* ☉ *No dinner Sun. or Mon.*

★ **$$$$** 🏠 **Lygon Arms.** Mullioned windows, a gorgeous 17th-century stone facade, baronial fireplaces, and rooms that once sheltered Charles I and Oliver Cromwell make this one of the most luxurious hotels of the Cotswolds. On the main street of Broadway, the inn also has 3 acres of private gardens. ☒ *High St., Broadway WR12 7DU* ☎ *01386/852255, 0800/7671–7671; 800/637–2869 in U.S.* 🖷 *01386/858611* ⊕ *www.savoy-group.co.uk* ⟿ *65 rooms* ᗱ *2 restaurants, pool* ▤ *AE, DC, MC, V.*

$ 🏠 **Rooftrees.** Richly ornamented, this old Cotswold stone house has frills and flounces galore, amiable hosts, and substantial breakfasts. ☒ *Rissington Rd., Bourton-on-the-Water GL54 2DX* ☎ *01451/821943* 🖷 *01451/810614* ⟿ *3 rooms* ▤ *MC, V.*

Bath

Numbers in the margin correspond to points of interest on the Bath map.

Bath lies at the southern end of the Cotswolds (at the end of A46), some 113 km (70 mi) from Stratford. The 18th-century city, perhaps the best-preserved in Britain, is a compact place, easy to explore on foot; the museums, elegant shops, and terraces of magnificent town houses are all close to one another. Bath's golden age came about in the early 18th century when the city became England's most fashionable spa. Architect John Wood created a harmonious vision from the mellow local stone, building beautifully executed terraces and crescents throughout the city. After promenading through the town, stop at the Pump Room for either morning coffee or afternoon tea in grand surroundings.

★ **5** **Assembly Rooms.** Near the Circus, this neoclassical mansion appears frequently as a ballroom setting in Jane Austen's novels. The salons now house a **Museum of Costume** that displays dress styles from Beau Nash's day to the present. ✉ *Bennett St.* ☎ *01225/477789* ⊕ *www.museumofcostume.co.uk* ☉ *Daily 10–4:30.*

2 **Bath Abbey.** Dominating Bath's center, this 15th-century edifice of glowing stone has a splendid west front, with carved figures of angels ascending ladders on each side. There are superb fan-vaulted ceilings in the nave and a multimedia show about the abbey's history in the adjacent Heritage Vaults. ✉ *Abbey Churchyard* ☎ *01225/422462* ⊕ *www.bathabbey. org* ☉ *Abbey: Easter–Oct., Mon.–Sat. 9–6; Nov.–Easter, Mon.–Sat. 9–4:30; call for Sun. hrs. Heritage Vaults: Mon.–Sat. 10–4.*

★ **3** **Circus.** To the north of Sawclose, you can admire some of the finest Georgian architecture at Queen Square and Gay Street, but the heart of Georgian Bath is the masterful Circus, a full circle of curving, perfectly proportioned 18th-century houses. Three Georgian terraces, with a frieze running around them, surround the small garden in the center.

8 **Holburne Museum.** Housed in an elegant 18th-century building, this museum contains a superb collection of 17th- and 18th-century fine art, silverware, and decorative arts. ✉ *Great Pulteney St.* ☎ *01225/466669* ⊕ *www.bath.ac.uk/holburne* ☉ *Mid-Feb.–mid-Dec., Tues.–Sat. 10–5, Sun. 2:30–5:30.*

★ **4** **Number 1 Royal Crescent.** On Bath's most graceful crescent, this house is furnished as it might have been when Beau Nash, the master of ceremonies and arbiter of 18th-century Bath society, lived in the city. The rooms allow a delightful peek into the gracious lifestyles of the Age of Enlightenment. ☎ *01225/428126* ⊕ *www.bath-preservation-trust.org. uk* ☉ *Mid-Feb.–Oct., Tues.–Sun. 10:30–5; Nov., Tues.–Sun. 10:30–4.*

7 **Pulteney Bridge.** Florence's Ponte Vecchio inspired this 18th-century span, one of the city's most charming landmarks and the only work of Robert Adam in Bath. Little shops line the sides of the bridge. The graceful Avon flows beneath, with ornamental gardens to one side.

★ **1** **Roman Baths Museum.** The hot springs have drawn people here since prehistoric times, and the Romans built a temple in honor of their goddess Minerva and a sophisticated series of baths to make full use of the curative waters. To this day, the springs gush from the earth at a constant temperature of 115.7°F (46.5°C). Underneath the 18th-century **Pump Room,** you can see the excavated remains of almost the entire baths complex. ✉ *Abbey Churchyard* ☎ *01225/477785* ⊕ *www.romanbaths. co.uk* ☉ *Mar.–June, Sept., and Oct., daily 9–5; July and Aug., daily 9–9; Nov.–Feb., daily 9:30–4:30.*

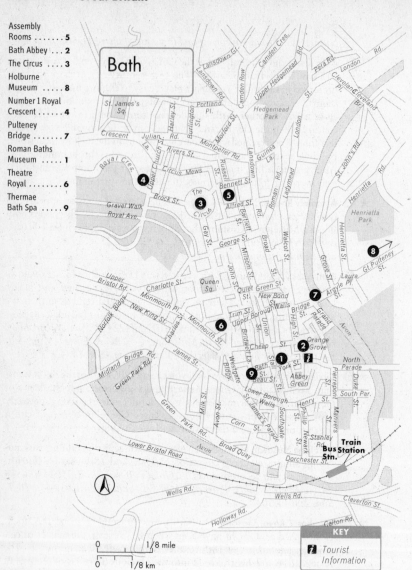

6 Theatre Royal. This theater opened in 1805 and was restored in 1982. Next door, the former home of Beau Nash—the dictator of fashion for mid-18th-century society in Bath—and his mistress, Juliana Popjoy, is now a restaurant called Popjoy's.

9 Thermae Bath Spa. This state-of-the-art complex has four luxurious floors offering all the latest spa treatments and therapies. The old Cross Bath and the Hot Bath, two 18th-century thermal baths, have been brought back into use for bathing and treatments; book in advance or call on the day. ⊠ *Hot Bath St.* ☎ *01225/477051* ⊕ *www.thermaebathspa.com* ⊙ *Daily 7 AM–10 PM.*

$$$ ✕ **Popjoy's Restaurant.** Beau Nash entertained the best of 18th-century society here, and Popjoy's retains its air of elegance. Diners can choose between dining on the ground floor or upstairs in a lovely Georgian drawing room. ☒ *Sawclose* ☎ *01225/460494* ⚖ *Reservations essential* ▤ *AE, DC, MC, V* ☯ *Closed Sun.*

$$$ ✕ **Pump Room.** In addition to the famous morning coffee, lunches, and afternoon tea served here, the restaurant is also open for evening meals (prix fixe) during the Bath Festival and in August and December. During these months, reservations are a must. There are views over the baths, and often musical accompaniment by a string trio. ☒ *Abbey Churchyard* ☎ *01225/444477* ▤ *AE, MC, V* ☯ *No dinner Sept.–Nov. or Jan.–July.*

$$–$$$ ✕ **Number 5 Bistro.** This candlelighted bistro off Pulteney Bridge has a relaxed ambience and offers tasty homemade soups or more elaborate dishes such as roast quail on wild rice and roast loin of lamb. Wednesdays are devoted to fish. ☒ *5 Argyle St.* ☎ *01225/444499* ▤ *AE, DC, MC, V* ☯ *Closed Sun. No lunch Mon.*

$$$–$$$$
Fodor'sChoice
★
✕▥ **Queensberry Hotel.** In a quiet residential street near the Circus, this intimate, elegant hotel is in three 1772 town houses built by the architect John Wood for the marquis of Queensberry. Renovations have preserved the Regency touches, and downstairs the Olive Tree restaurant serves English and Mediterranean dishes. ☒ *Russell St., BA1 2QF* ☎ *01225/447928* 🖷 *01225/446065* ⊕ *www.bathqueensberry.com* ⤳ *29 rooms* ⚘ *Restaurant* ▤ *MC, V* ☯ *Closed Dec. 24–30.*

$$–$$$ ▥ **Paradise House.** It's a steep uphill climb from the center of Bath, but you'll be rewarded by a wonderful prospect of the city from the upper stories of this Georgian guest house. There are open fires in winter and a lush, secluded garden for the spring and summer. ☒ *88 Holloway, BA2 4PX* ☎ *01225/317723* 🖷 *01225/482005* ⊕ *www.paradise-house.co.uk* ⤳ *11 rooms* ▤ *AE, DC, MC, V* ☯ *Closed last wk. in Dec.*

$ ▥ **Albany Guest House.** This homey Edwardian house, close to Victoria Park and the center of town, offers plain but comfortable rooms, of which the attic room is the largest and best. Homemade vegetarian sausages are offered at breakfast. ☒ *24 Crescent Gardens, BA1 2NB* ☎ *01225/313339* ⊕ *www.bath.org* ⤳ *4 rooms, 2 with bath* ▤ *No credit cards.*

Stonehenge

Fodor'sChoice
★
One of England's most visited and most puzzling monuments, Stonehenge is dwarfed by its lonely isolation on the wide sweep of Salisbury Plain. The great circle of stones, which lies 57 km (35 mi) southeast of Bath, is enclosed by a paved path to control the throngs of tourists, but if you visit in the early morning, when the crowds have not yet arrived, or in the evening, you can experience Stonehenge as it once was: a mystical, awe-inspiring place. Stonehenge was begun about 3000 BC, enlarged between 2100 and 1900 BC, and altered yet again by 150 BC. The original 80 bluestones (dolerite), which made up the two internal circles, were transported from the Atlantic coast of Wales. Although some of the mysteries concerning the site have been solved, the reason Stonehenge was originally built remains unknown. It is fairly certain that it was a religious site, and that worship here involved the cycles of the sun; the alignment of the stones to point to sunrise at midsummer and sunset in midwinter makes this clear. Most historians think Stonehenge may have been a kind of astronomical observatory. You can rent an audio tour, but visitors' amenities here are rather squalid; there are plans to improve them. ☒ *Junction of A303 and A344/A360, near Amesbury* ☎ *01980/624715* ⊕ *www.english-heritage.org.uk* ☯ *Mid-Mar.–May and Sept.–mid-Oct., daily 9:30–6; June–Aug., daily 9–7; mid-Oct.–mid-Mar., daily 9:30–4.*

Windsor to Bath Essentials

BUS TRAVEL

Regular long-distance services leave from Victoria Coach Station. National Express and Oxford Bus Company serve the region. The Green Line bus leaves from Eccleston Bridge, behind London's Victoria train station, *not* from the Coach Station itself. Make sure you catch the fast direct service, which takes 45 minutes and runs hourly; the local services take up to 1¼ hours.

🚌 **Green Line** ☎ 0870/608-7261 ⊕ www.greenline.co.uk. **National Express** ☎ 0870/580-8080 ⊕ www.gobycoach.com. **Oxford Bus Company** ☎ 01865/785400 ⊕ www.oxfordbus.co.uk.

CAR TRAVEL

The main highways out of London are the M4 and M40, serving Oxford, the Cotswolds, and Bath. Once you're clear of London, take to the country roads and explore tiny villages and the best of the English countryside.

TOURS

Evan Evans operates daily one-day tours to Oxford, Stratford, the Cotswolds, and Bath. Frames Rickards runs full-day sightseeing tours to Windsor, Stratford-upon-Avon, Oxford, and Bath. Golden Tours offers one-day trips to Oxford, Stratford, the Cotswolds, and Bath from London. City Sightseeing/Guide Friday has excellent open-top bus tours of Windsor, Oxford, the Cotswolds, and Shakespeare Country. Based in Oxford, Cotswold Roaming operates tours of the Cotswolds and excursions to Bath.

🚌 **City Sightseeing/Guide Friday** ☎ 01865/790522 Windsor and Oxford; 01789/294466 Stratford; 01225/444102 Bath ⊕ www.city-sightseeing.com. **Cotswold Roaming** ☎ 01865/308300 ⊕ www.oxfordcity.co.uk **Evan Evans** ☎ 020/7950-1777. **Frames Rickards** ☎ 020/7837-3111. **Golden Tours** ☎ 020/7233-7030.

TRAIN TRAVEL

Windsor is easy to reach by train from London, either from Waterloo direct to Windsor and Eton Riverside (50 minutes), or from Paddington to Windsor Central, changing at Reading (45 minutes); there are two trains per hour on each route. Regular fast trains run from Paddington to Oxford and Bath, and less frequent and slower services requiring at least one change to Stratford. An alternative route to Stratford is from London's Euston Station to Coventry, from which there are hourly bus connections on the Stratford Blue line.

🚆 **National Rail Enquiries** ☎ 0845/748-4950 ⊕ www.nationalrail.co.uk.

VISITOR INFORMATION

🚩 **Bath** ✉ Abbey Chambers, Abbey Churchyard ☎ 01225/477101 ⊕ www.visitbath.co.uk. **Cheltenham** ✉ 77 Promenade ☎ 01242/522878 ⊕ www.visitcheltenham.com. **Oxford** ✉ The Old School, Gloucester Green ☎ 01865/726871 ⊕ www.oxford.gov.uk. **Stow-on-the-Wold** ✉ Hollis House, The Square ☎ 01451/831082. **Stratford** ✉ Bridgefoot, next to Clopton Bridge ☎ 01789/293127 ⊕ www.stratford-upon-avon.co.uk. **Warwick** ✉ The Court House, Jury St. ☎ 01926/492212. **Windsor** ✉ 24 High St. ☎ 01753/743900 ⊕ www.windsor.gov.uk.

CAMBRIDGE

Cambridge, home of England's second-oldest university, is an ideal place to explore. There have been students here since the late 13th century, and virtually every generation after that has produced fine buildings, often by the most distinguished architects of its day. The result is a compact gallery of the best of English architecture. There is also good shopping in the city, and you can enjoy relaxing riverside walks. Cambridge is 87 km (54 mi) north of London, 66 km (41 mi) northwest of Colchester, and 102 km (63 mi) southwest of Norwich.

Exploring Cambridge

Numbers in the margin correspond to points of interest on the Cambridge map.

The university is in the very heart of Cambridge. It consists of a number of colleges, each of which is a separate institution with its own distinct character. Undergraduates join an individual college and are taught by professors who are known as "fellows." Each college is built around a series of courts, or quadrangles; because students and fellows live in these quadrangles, access is sometimes restricted. Visitors are not normally allowed into college buildings other than chapels, halls, and some libraries; some colleges levy an admission charge for certain buildings. Public visiting hours vary dramatically from college to college, and it's best to call ahead or to check first with the city tourist office. Some general guidelines for visiting hours, however, can be noted. Colleges close to the public during the main exam time, late May to mid-June. Termtime (when classes are in session) means October through December, January through March, and April through June, and summer term, or vacations, run from July through September. If you have time, there's no better way to absorb Cambridge's unique atmosphere than by hiring a punt at Silver Street Bridge or at Magdalene Bridge and navigating down past St. John's or upstream to Grantchester, the pretty village made famous by the poet Rupert Brooke.

⑩ **Emmanuel College.** Evident throughout much of Cambridge, the master hand of Christopher Wren designed the chapel and colonnade of Emmanuel College, founded in 1584. The college was an early center of Puritan learning; among the likenesses portrayed in stained glass in the chapel is one of John Harvard, founder of Harvard University. ⊠ *St. Andrew's St.* ☎ *01223/334200* ⊕ *www.emma.cam.ac.uk.*

★ ⑨ **Fitzwilliam Museum.** Cambridge's most renowned museum contains outstanding art collections—including paintings by Constable, Gainsborough, and the French impressionists—and antiquities, especially from ancient Egypt. ⊠ *Trumpington St.* ☎ *01223/332900* ⊕ *www.fitzmuseum. cam.ac.uk* ☉ *Tues.–Sat. 10–5, Sun. 2:15–5.*

⑤ **Kettle's Yard.** Originally a private house owned by a former curator of London's Tate Gallery, Kettle's Yard houses a fine permanent collection of 20th-century art, sculpture, furniture, and decorative arts. ⊠ *Castle St.* ☎ *01223/352124* ⊕ *www.kettlesyard.co.uk* ☉ *House: Easter–Aug., Tues.–Sun. 1:30–4:30; Sept.–Easter, Tues.–Sun. 2–4. Gallery: Tues.–Sun. 11:30–5.*

★ ❶ **King's College.** The high point of King's—and possibly of Cambridge—is its chapel, started by Henry VI in 1446 and a masterpiece of late-Gothic architecture, with a great fan-vaulted ceiling supported only by a tracery of soaring side columns. Behind the altar hangs Rubens's painting *Adoration of the Magi.* Every Christmas Eve the college choir sings the Festival of Nine Lessons and Carols, which is broadcast all over the world. The novelist E. M. Forster, author of *Howards End* and *A Passage to India,* studied at King's, as did the war poet Rupert Brooke. King's runs down to the "Backs," the tree-shaded grounds on the banks of the River Cam. ⊠ *King's Parade* ☎ *01223/331447* ⊕ *www.kings.cam.ac. uk* ☉ *Oct.–June, weekdays 9:30–3:30, Sat. 9:30–3:15, Sun. 1:15–2:15;*

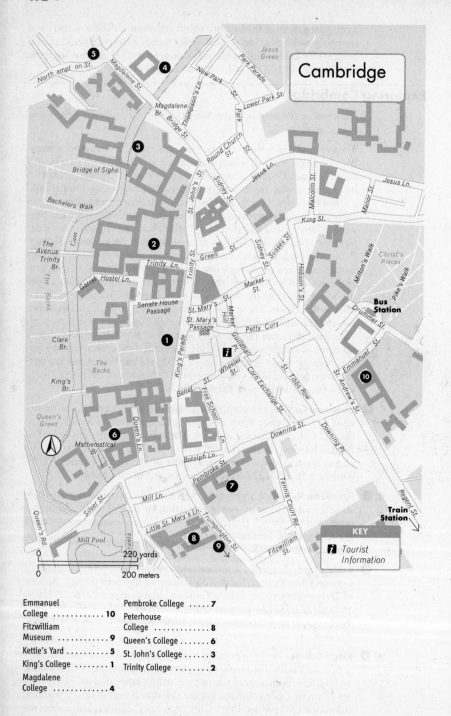

Cambridge

North ampt on St.

Magdalene St.

New Park

Park Parade

Jesus Green

Magdalene Br.

Bridge St.

Thompson's Ln.

Lower Park St.

Park St.

Round Church St.

St. John's St.

Jesus Ln.

Jesus Ln.

Malcolm St.

Manor St.

Bridge of Sighs

Bachelors Walk

Sidney St.

King St.

The Avenue Trinity Br.

The Cam

Trinity Ln.

Garret Hostel Ln.

Green St.

Sidney St.

Sussex St.

Hobson's St.

Milton's Walk

Christ's Pieces

Pike's Walk

The Backs

Senate House Passage

Market St.

Drummer St.

Bus Station

Clare Br.

St. Mary's St.

Market Hill

St. Mary's Passage

Petty Cury

King's Br.

King's Parade

i Guildhall

Wheeler St.

St. Andrew's St.

St. Emmanuel St.

The Backs

Benet St.

Free School Ln.

Corn Exchange St.

St. Tibbs Row

Queen's Green

Mathematical Br.

Queen's Ln.

Downing St.

Downing Pl.

Botolph Ln.

Pembroke St.

Tennis Court Rd.

Mill Ln.

Silver St.

Little St. Mary's Ln.

Trumpington St.

Fitzwilliam St.

Queen's Rd.

Mill Pool

220 yards

0

200 meters

Train Station

Regent St.

KEY
i Tourist Information

July–Sept., Mon.–Sat. 9:30–4:30, Sun. 1:15–2:15 and 5–5:30. Hrs vary; phone in advance.

❹ Magdalene College. Across cast-iron Magdalene (pronounced *maud*-lin) Bridge is Magdalene College, distinguished by pretty redbrick courts. It was a hostel for Benedictine monks for more than 100 years before the college was founded in 1542. The college's **Pepys Library** contains the books, diaries, and desk of the 17th-century diarist Samuel Pepys. Admission to the library is free. ⊠ *Magdalene St.* ☎ *01223/332100* ⊕ *www.magd.cam.ac.uk* ⊙ *Library: Apr.–Aug., daily 11:30–12:30 and 2:30–3:30; Oct.–mid-Mar., daily 2:30–3:30.*

❼ Pembroke College. Established in 1347, the first court of Pembroke College has some buildings dating from the 14th century. On the south side, Christopher Wren's chapel—his first major commission, completed in 1665—looks like a distinctly modern intrusion. You can walk through the college, around a delightful garden, and past the fellows' bowling green. ⊠ *Trumpington St.* ☎ *01223/338100.*

❽ Peterhouse College. Cambridge's oldest college was founded in 1281 by the bishop of Ely. Parts of the dining hall date from 1290; the late-Gothic-style chapel dates from 1632. On the river side of the buildings is a large and tranquil deer park. ⊠ *Trumpington St.* ☎ *01223/338200* ⊕ *www. pet.cam.ac.uk.*

❻ Queen's College. One of the most eye-catching colleges, Queen's is named after the respective consorts of Henry VI and Edward IV. The college's Mathematical Bridge (best seen from the Silver Street Bridge) is an arched wooden structure that was originally held together by gravity; when it was taken apart to see how Isaac Newton did it, no one could reconstruct it without using nails. The present bridge, dating from 1902, is securely bolted. ⊠ *Queen's La.* ☎ *01223/335511* ⊕ *www. quns.cam.ac.uk* ⊙ *Daily 1:45–4:30.*

❸ St. John's College. St. John's is Cambridge's second-largest college, founded in 1511 by Henry VII's mother, Lady Margaret Beaufort. The famous copy of the Bridge of Sighs in Venice is here, reaching across the Cam to the mock-Gothic New Court. ⊠ *St. John's St.* ☎ *01223/338600* ⊕ *www. joh.cam.ac.uk* ⊙ *Weekdays 10–5:30, weekends 9:30–5:30.*

❷ Trinity College. This is the largest college, with almost 700 undergraduates, established by Henry VIII in 1546. It has a handsome 17th-century great court, around which are sited the chapel, hall, gates, and a magnificent library by Christopher Wren—colonnaded and seemingly constructed as much of light as of stone. In the massive gatehouse is Great Tom, a large clock that strikes each hour and that figured in the race around the quadrangle at the heart of the movie *Chariots of Fire*. Prince Charles was an undergraduate here in the late 1960s. ⊠ *St. John's St.* ☎ *01223/338400* ⊕ *www.trin.cam.ac.uk* ⊙ *College: Mar.–Oct., daily 10–5, except exam time; Library: weekdays noon–2, Sat. in term-time 10:30–12:30; Hall and Chapel: open to visitors but hrs vary.*

★ **$$–$$$** ✕**Midsummer House.** A classy restaurant set beside the River Cam, Midsummer House is lovely in summer. Set-price menus for lunch and dinner offer a selection of robust yet sophisticated European and Mediterranean dishes. Choices might include tender lamb or the best from the fish market adorned with inventively presented vegetables. ⊠ *Midsummer Common* ☎ *01223/369299* ⚐ *Reservations essential* ▭ *AE, DC, MC, V* ⊙ *Closed Mon. No lunch Sat., no dinner Sun.*

$$ ✕**Loch Fyne Oyster Restaurant.** Part of a Scottish chain that both harvests oysters and runs seafood restaurants, this airy, casual place is across the street from the Fitzwilliam Museum and is open for breakfast, lunch, and dinner. The deservedly popular oysters and other seafood—mussels, salmon, tuna, and more—are fresh and well prepared, including the dauntingly large platters. ✉ *37 Trumpington St.* ☎ *01223/ 362433* ▭ *AE, MC, V.*

$$$ ▧ **Meadowcroft Hotel.** A pleasant 2-km (1-mi) walk from the center of Cambridge is this Victorian house where pretty rooms are filled with English antiques and print fabrics. For an extra charge, horse-drawn carriage rides tour Cambridge or nearby Grantchester. ✉ *16 Trumpington Rd., CB2 2EX* ☎ *01223/346120* 🖨 *01223/346138* ⊕ *www.meadowcrofthotel. co.uk* 🖵 *12 rooms* ⌂ *Restaurant, bar* ▭ *AE, MC, V.*

$ ▧ **Sleeperz.** This budget hostelry near the train station has small rooms with wood floors and futon beds. Most double rooms have bunk beds. These basic accommodations are recommended for those who want only a cheap, clean place to sleep. ✉ *Station Rd., CB1 2TZ,* ☎ *01223/304050* 🖨 *01223/357286* ⊕ *www.sleeperz.com* 🖵 *25 rooms* ▭ *MC, V.*

Cambridge Essentials

BUS TRAVEL TO & FROM CAMBRIDGE
There are 14 buses daily from Victoria Coach Station in London that take just under two hours.
🛈 **National Express** ☎ 0870/580–8080 ⊕ www.nationalexpress.com.

CAR TRAVEL
The main highway from London to Cambridge is the M11. The main car-rental companies have offices in Cambridge.

TOURS
BUS TOURS City Sightseeing/Guide Friday, in Cambridge, operates a city open-top bus tour every 15 minutes throughout the day (October–May, half-hourly); tickets can be bought from the driver, the office at Cambridge train station, or the Cambridge Tourist Information Center. You can join the tours at the station or at any of the specially marked bus stops throughout the city.
🛈 **City Sightseeing/Guide Friday** ☎ 01223/362444 ⊕ www.city-sightseeing.com.

WALKING TOURS The Cambridge Tourist Information Centre offers two-hour guided walking tours of the city and the colleges daily; tickets (£6.50) are available up to 24 hours in advance. Various theme tours are also offered, including combined walking-punting tours and 1½-hour evening pub tours. Booking is essential—the tours are very popular.

TRAIN TRAVEL
Half-hourly trains from London's Liverpool Street Station and King's Cross Station run to Cambridge. Because of problems with the British rail network, average journey times now vary from 1½ to 2 hours, depending on the day of week or time of day.
🛈 **National Rail Enquiries** ☎ 0845/748–4950 ⊕ www.nationalrail.co.uk.

VISITOR INFORMATION
🛈 **Cambridge Tourist Information Centre** ✉ Wheeler St., off King's Parade, CB2 3QB ☎ 01223/322640 🖨 01223/463385 ⊕ www.tourismcambridge.com.

YORK

Once England's second city in terms of population and importance, ancient York has survived the ravages of time, war, and industrialization to remain one of northern Europe's few preserved walled cities, although in terms of physical size it is considerably smaller than northern England's main cities. King George VI, father of the present queen, remarked that the history of York is the history of England. Even in a brief visit to the city, you can see evidence of life from every era since the Romans, not only in museums but also in the very streets and houses. York—41 km (25 mi) northeast of Leeds, 133 km (82 mi) south of Newcastle—is set in a fertile plain, dotted with ancient abbeys and grand aristocratic mansions, that leads westward to the hidden valleys and jagged, windswept tops of the Yorkshire Dales and northward to the brooding mass of the North York Moors.

Exploring York

Numbers in the margin correspond to points of interest on the York map.

You can get a first, memorable overview of the city by taking a stroll along the **city walls.** Originally they were earth ramparts erected by York's Viking kings to repel raiders; the present stone structure dates from the 14th century. A narrow paved walk runs along the top (originally 5 km/3 mi in circumference), passing over York's distinctive fortified gates, or "bars," and providing delightful views across rooftops and gardens.

❸ Castle Museum. A debtors' prison during the 18th century, this museum now offers a number of detailed exhibitions and re-creations, including a cobblestone Victorian street complete with crafts shops, a working water mill, and the Coppergate Helmet, a 1,200-year-old Anglo-Saxon helmet, one of only three ever found. ⊠ *Clifford St.* ☎ *01904/653611* ⊕ *www. yorkcastlemuseum.org.uk* ⊘ *Daily 9:30–5.*

❷ Jorvik. On this authentic Viking site, you can take another journey into history—whisked back in time capsules to the sights, sounds, and even the smells of a Viking street, which archaeologists have re-created in astonishing detail. ⊠ *Coppergate* ☎ *01904/653211* ⊕ *www.vikingjorvik. com* ⊘ *Apr.–Oct., daily 9–5:30; Nov.–Mar., daily 10–4:30.*

❻ Merchant Adventurers' Hall. A superb medieval building (1357–68), this hall was built and owned by one of the richest medieval guilds; it contains the largest timber-frame hall in York. ⊠ *Fossgate* ☎ *01904/ 654818* ⊕ *www.theyorkcompany.co.uk* ⊘ *Apr.–Sept., Mon.–Thurs. 9–5, Fri. and Sat. 9–3, Sun. noon–4; Oct.–Mar., Mon.–Thurs. 9–3:30, Fri. and Sat. 9–3.*

❼ National Railway Museum. Britain's national collection of locomotives forms part of this complex, the world's largest train museum. Among the exhibits are gleaming giants of the steam era, including *Mallard,* holder of the world speed record for a steam engine (126 mph). The museum lies just outside the city walls, by the train station. ⊠ *Leeman Rd.* ☎ *01904/621261* ⊕ *www.nrm.org.uk* ⊘ *Daily 10–6.*

❹ The Shambles. Within York's city walls the narrow streets still follow the complex medieval pattern. In the heart of the city is the Shambles, a particularly well-preserved example; the half-timber shops and houses have such large overhangs that you can practically reach from one second-floor window to another.

❺ Stonegate. This is a narrow pedestrian street of Tudor and 18th-century shops and courts. Along a narrow passage off Stonegate, at 52A, you will find the remains of a 12th-century Norman stone house—one of the very few surviving in England.

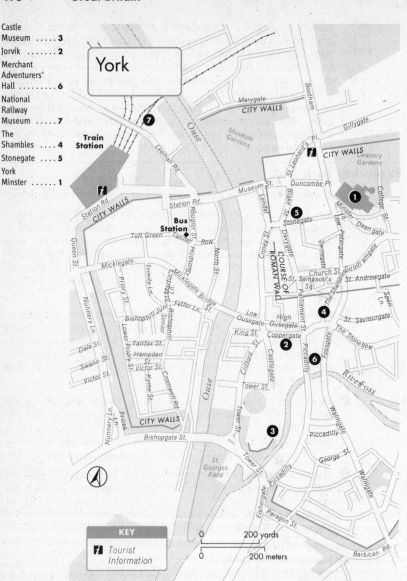

1 **York Minster.** The glory of York, this is the largest Gothic church in England and one of the finest in Europe. The 14th-century nave has soaring columns and intricate tracery, the choir screen portrays whimsical images of the kings of England, and the mighty rose window—just one of 128 stained-glass windows in the Minster—commemorates the marriage of Henry VII and Elizabeth of York. Visit the exquisite 13th-century **Chapter House** and the Roman and Saxon remains in the **Undercroft Museum and Treasury.** The 275 steps of the **Central Tower** lead to an unrivaled view of the city and the countryside beyond. The **Crypt** contains some of the cathedral's oldest and most valuable treasures, among them the Romanesque 12th-century statue of a heavy-footed Virgin Mary. ⊠ *Duncombe Pl.* ☎ *01904/557216* ⊕ *www.yorkminster.org* ☉ *Minster and Chapter House: late June–early Sept., Mon.–Sat. 7* AM*–8:30* PM*, Sun.*

noon–8:30; early Sept.–late June, Mon.–Sat. 7–6, Sun. noon–6. Under-croft, Crypt, and Central Tower: late June–early Sept., Mon.–Sat. 9:30–5:30; Sun. noon–5:30; early Sept.–late June, Mon.–Sat. 10–4:30, Sun. noon–4:30.

★ **$$** ✕ **19 Grape Lane.** The narrow, slightly cramped restaurant is housed in a typically leaning, timbered York building in the heart of town. It serves modern English food with such specials as rib-eye beef with green peppercorn sauce and wild boar sausages. The substantial puddings are always a treat. ⊠ *19 Grape La.* ☎ *01904/636366* 🖃 *MC, V* ☾ *Closed Sun. and Mon.*

★ **$** ✕ **Betty's.** At the opposite end of Stonegate from the minster, this York institution since 1912 is arranged elegantly across two large floors in a beautiful art nouveau building. Best known for its teas served with mouthwatering cakes (try the "fat rascal," a plump bun bursting with cherries and nuts), Betty's also offers light meals and exotic coffees. ⊠ *6–8 St. Helen's Sq.* ☎ *01904/659142* 🖃 *MC, V.*

$$$–$$$$ 🏠 **Dean Court.** This large Victorian house once provided accommodation for the clergy of York Minster, which looms just across the road. It now has traditionally furnished rooms with plenty of print fabrics, plump sofas, and fine views overlooking the Minster. The restaurant serves good English cuisine, including a hearty Yorkshire breakfast. ⊠ *Duncombe Pl., YO1 7EF* ☎ *01904/625082* 🖷 *01904/620305* ⊕ *www.deancourt-york.co.uk* ⇗ *40 rooms* ♿ *Restaurant* 🖃 *AE, DC, MC, V.*

$$ 🏠 **The Hazelwood.** This tall Victorian town house stands 400 yards from York Minster in a peaceful cul-de-sac, away from the noise of traffic. Rich fabrics and some handsome wood pieces adorn the rooms. The memorable breakfasts include black pudding, Danish pastries, and vegetarian sausages. ⊠ *24–25 Portland St., YO31 7EH* ☎ *01904/626548* 🖷 *01904/628032* ⊕ *www.thehazelwoodyork.com* ⇗ *14 rooms* 🖃 *MC.*

$–$$ 🏠 **Eastons.** Two Victorian houses knocked into one, Eastons retains a rich, period feel. Dark color schemes enhance the marble fireplaces, wood paneling, tiling, and antique furniture. The big sofas and affable hosts are equally welcoming. ⊠ *90 Bishopthorpe Rd., YO31 1JS* ☎ *01904/626646* 🖷 *01904/626165* ⇗ *10 rooms* 🖃 *No credit cards.*

Side Trips: Fountains Abbey & Castle Howard

★ Thirty-two kilometers (21 mi) northwest of York, along B6265, you'll find that the majestic ruins of **Fountains Abbey,** with its own high tower and soaring 13th-century arches, make a striking picture on the banks of the River Skell. Founded in 1132, the abbey still possesses many of its original buildings, and the National Trust operates informative free guided tours around them. Tours run April–October only, usually at 11, 2:30, and 3:30. The extensive ruins are set beside an 18th-century water garden and deer park, **Studley Royal,** combining lakes, ponds, and water terraces, while waterfalls splash around classical temples, statues, and a grotto. ⊠ *Off B6265* ☎ *01765/608888* ⊕ *www.fountainsabbey.org.uk* ☾ *Nov.–Jan., daily 10–4 (or dusk); Apr.–Sept., daily 10–6.*

Newby Hall—reached along pleasant country roads 5 km (3 mi) east of Fountains Abbey—has restored interiors by the 18th-century master architect Robert Adam and 25 acres of celebrated gardens. ⊠ *Skelton-on-Ure* ☎ *01423/322583* ⊕ *www.newbyhall.co.uk* ☾ *Easter–Oct., Tues.–Sun. grounds 11–5, house noon–5.*

Fodor's Choice ★ Twenty-four kilometers (15 mi) northeast of York is **Castle Howard,** one of the grandest and most opulent stately homes in Britain. Its magnificent silhouette is punctuated by stone chimneys and a graceful central dome. Many people know it best as Brideshead, the home of the Flyte family in Evelyn Waugh's tale of aristocratic woe, *Brideshead Revisited,* as much of the TV series was filmed here. The audacity and flamboyance of the great baroque house are startling, proclaiming the wealth and importance of the Howards and the utter self-assurance of its architect, Sir John Vanbrugh. Castle Howard took 60 years to build (1699–1759), and it was worth every year. A magnificent central hallway dwarfs all visitors, and there is no shortage of grandeur elsewhere: vast family portraits, delicate marble fireplaces, immense tapestries, and a great many marble busts. Outside, the stately theme continues in one of the most stunning neoclassical landscapes in England. ☒ *Coneysthorpe* ☎ *01653/648333* ⊕ *www.castlehoward.co.uk* ☒ *House and gardens £9* ☉ *House: mid-Feb.–Oct., daily 11–4; Grounds: daily 10–6:30 (or dusk).*

York Essentials

BUS TRAVEL TO & FROM YORK

National Express buses to York leave from London's Victoria Coach Station. Average travel time is 4½ hours to York.

☑ **National Express** ☎ 0870/580-8080 ⊕ www.nationalexpress.com.

CAR TRAVEL

Take the A1, the historic main route from London to the north, which branches east onto the A64 near Tadcaster for the final 19 km (12 mi) to York. Alternatively, take the M1, then the M18, and finally the A1. The drive from London takes a minimum of four hours.

TOURS

BUS TOURS City Sightseeing runs frequent city tours of York that allow you to get on and off the bus as you please (£7.50). It also conducts tours of the surrounding countryside, including Fountains Abbey and Castle Howard. Eddie Brown Tours also offers excursions to Castle Howard.

☑ **City Sightseeing** ☒ De Grey Rooms, Exhibition Sq. ☎ 01904/640896 ⊕ www.citysightseeing.co.uk. **Eddie Brown Tours** ☎ 01423/360222 ⊕ www.eddiebrowntours.com.

WALKING TOURS The York Association of Voluntary Guides arranges short walking tours around the city each morning at 10:15, with additional tours at 2:15 PM April–October, and one at 6:45 PM July–August.

☑ **York Association of Voluntary Guides** ☒ De Grey Rooms, Exhibition Sq. ☎ 01904/640780.

TRAIN TRAVEL

Great North-Eastern Railways serves York from London King's Cross. Journeys on the fastest trains take 2½ hours.

☑ **Great North-Eastern Railways** ☎ 0845/722-5225 booking line; 0845/748-4950 inquiries.

VISITOR INFORMATION

☑ ☒ De Grey Rooms, Exhibition Sq., North Yorkshire YO1 2HB ☎ 01904/621756 ☒ York Train Station ☎ 01904/621756 ⊕ www.york-tourism.co.uk.

THE LAKE DISTRICT

The poets William Wordsworth and Samuel Taylor Coleridge, and other English men and women of letters in the 19th century, found the Lake District an inspiring setting for their work, and visitors have followed ever since. Indeed, so much that is magnificent in mountain, lake, and dale is brought to bear here that entrancing vistas open out at every corner. Walking is the best way to discover the delights of this peaceful area, not the least because it has been the preferred means of travel for the district's litany of literary champions. In addition to Wordsworth and Coleridge, the list includes Thomas De Quincey, John Ruskin, Matthew Arnold, and the children's writer and artist Beatrix Potter.

The Lake District roughly 35 square mi and holding 16 major lakes and countless smaller stretches of water, lies within the county of Cumbria in the northwest of England. The major gateway from the south is Kendal; from the north, Penrith—both are on the M6 motorway. The southern lakes and valleys contain the most popular destinations, notably the largest body of water, Windermere, as well as such quintessential Lake District towns and villages as Kendal, Bowness, Ambleside, Grasmere, Elterwater, Coniston, and Hawkshead. Among the northern lakes, south of Keswick and Cockermouth, you have the best chance to get away from the crowds and soak up the Lake District experience.

Kendal

The ancient town of Kendal—113 km (70 mi) north of Manchester—was one of the most important textile centers in northern England before the Industrial Revolution. Away from the busy main road, you'll discover narrow, winding medieval streets and charming courtyards.

Take a stroll along the River Kent, where—close to the parish church—you can visit one of the region's finest art galleries at 18th-century **Abbott Hall.** Here, too, the **Museum of Lakeland Life and Industry** has interesting exhibits on blacksmithing, wheelwrighting, farming, weaving, printing, local architecture, and the curious life of Arthur Ransome (1884–1967), author of the *Swallows and Amazons* series of children's books. ⊠ *Off Highgate* ☎ *01539/722464* ⊕ *www.abbothall.org.uk* ⊙ *Apr.–Oct., daily 10:30–5; Nov.–Mar., daily 10:30–4.*

At the northern end of town, the **Kendal Museum** details splendidly the flora and fauna of the Lake District. It also contains displays on Alfred Wainwright, the region's great fell walker. His multivolume Lake District walking guides are sold in local book and gift shops. ⊠ *Station Rd.* ☎ *01539/721374* ⊕ *www.kendalmuseum.org.uk* ⊙ *Apr.–Oct., Mon.–Sat. 10:30–5; Nov.–Mar., Mon.–Sat. 10:30–4.*

$ ✕▢ **The Punch Bowl Inn.** Hidden along a country road in the hamlet of Crosthwaite, 8 km (5 mi) west of Kendal, the Punch Bowl—a coaching inn during the 17th century—delights with its inspired modern British food and comfortable rooms. Fresh fish, local lamb, warming soups, and rich desserts all hit the spot. You'll need reservations at the restaurant book a room well in advance, too. ⊠ *Crosthwaite, 5 mi west of Kendal (off A5074), LA8 8HR* ☎ *015395/68237* ▤ *015395/68875* ⯮ *3 rooms* ⟡ *Restaurant* ▭ *MC, V.*

Windermere & Bowness-on-Windermere

Fodor'sChoice Windermere, 16 km (10 mi) northwest of Kendal on the A591, makes
★ a natural touring base for the southern half of the Lake District. The town is split between the part around the station (known as Windermere) and the prettier lakeside area ½ km (¼ mi) away, called Bowness-on-Windermere. Bus 599 (every 20 minutes in summer, hourly the rest of the year), leaving from outside Windermere train station, links the two towns. The lake itself, also called Windermere, is England's largest, 18 km (11 mi) long and 2½ km (1½ mi) wide. Although Windermere's marinas and piers have some charm, you can bypass the busier stretches of shoreline by walking beyond the boathouses, which offer a fine view across the lake. A **ferry** crosses the water at this point to reach Far Sawrey

The Lake District

Beacon Pike

Blencathra

TO COCKERMOUTH

Latrigg

Castlerigg Stone Circle

Dalemain

TO PENRITH

A66

A591

A5322

A592

A591

A592

Eamont

Portinscale
Keswick

Pooley Bridge

Derwentwater

B5289

Newlands Pass

Aira Force

Buttermere Fell

Ullswater

Watendlath

Glenridding

B5289

Buttermere

Rosthwaite

Patterdale

Seathwaite

Borrowdale

Seatoller
Borrowdale
Fells

Helvellyn

Haweswater

CUMBRIA

Shap Fells

Grasmere

Langdale Fell

Scafell Pike

Grasmere

Rydal Water

Rydal Mount

Dove Cottage

A591

Elterwater

Ambleside

Lake District National Park Visitor Centre

Windermere

B5286

The Old Man of Coniston

Hawkshead

Watchgate

A591

Bowness-on-Windermere

Coniston

B5285

Windermere

Brantwood

Hill Top

Hawkshead

Kendal

Coniston Water

A5084

A593

A591

Kent

Broughton-in-Furness

Lake Side

Haverthwaite

A590

A590

A5093

Duddon Channel

A595

B5278

Hampsfield Fell

A590

Cartmel

LANCASHIRE

Cartmel Sands

B5277

A590

Morecambe Bay

A590

Barrow-in-Furness

Carnforth

A5087

M6

Morecambe

0   6 miles

0   9 km

and the road to Hawkshead; the crossing takes just a few minutes. ✆ *Ferries every 30 mins Mon.–Sat. 6:50 AM–9:50 PM, Sun. 9:10 AM–9:50 PM; winter until 8:50 PM.*

★ **$$–$$$** ✕**Porthole Eating House.** In an intimate 18th-century house in the center of Bowness, this small restaurant has a largely Italian menu with homemade pasta and excellent meat and fish dishes. In winter a large open fire adds to the ambience. ⊠ *3 Ash St., Bowness-on-Windermere* ☎ *015394/42793* ⊟ *AE, DC, MC, V* ✆ *Closed Tues. No lunch Mon., Wed., Sat.*

$$$$ ✕🔲 **Miller Howe.** This small, luxurious, white Edwardian country house
FodorsChoice is beautifully situated, with views across Windermere to the Langdale
★ Pikes. The bedrooms have exceptional individual style, and there are fresh and dried flowers everywhere. The outstanding restaurant (reservations essential; jacket and tie) is renowned for its dynamic take on British cuisine—every night is a new performance. The room rate includes breakfast and dinner. ⊠ *Rayrigg Rd., Bowness-on-Windermere LA23 1EY* ☎ *015394/42536* 🖷 *015394/45664* ⊕ *www.millerhowe.com* ⇥ *13 rooms* ⚭ *Restaurant* ⊟ *AE, DC, MC, V* ✆ *Closed Jan.*

$ 🔲 **Brendan Chase.** This well-maintained lodging is in the heart of Windermere's B&B land, not far from the train station but about 2 km (1 mi) from the lake—though some rooms have distant water views. A full breakfast (English or vegetarian) sets you up for the day. There is also a dorm room. ⊠ *1–3 College Rd., Windermere LA23 1BU* ☎ *015394/ 45638* ⇥ *8 rooms, 3 with bath* ⊟ *No credit cards.*

Brockhole

Five kilometers (3 mi) northwest of Windermere on the A591, a magnificent lakeside mansion houses the **Lake District National Park Visitor Centre,** which has fine exhibitions about the Lake District, including useful interpretative displays about the local ecology, flora, and fauna. The gardens are at their best in the spring, when fields of daffodils cover the lawns and the azaleas burst into bloom. For children there is also an adventure playground. ⊠ *Ambleside Rd.* ☎ *015394/46601* ⊕ *www.lake-district.gov.uk* ✆ *Easter–Oct., daily 10–5.*

Ambleside

The small town of Ambleside sits at the head of Lake Windermere—6½ km (4 mi) north of Brockhole, along the A591—making it a popular center for Lake District excursions. The town suffers terribly from tourist overcrowding in high season; Wednesday is particularly busy, when the local market takes place. However, it's easy enough to escape the crowds. Follow A593 west out of Ambleside and take the turning for the nearby village of **Elterwater,** a good stop for hikers. The B5343 continues west from here to **Langdale Fell,** where you can take one of several excellent walks: there are information boards at the parking places.

★ **$$–$$$** ✕ **Glass House.** This exciting conversion of an old water mill is a café by day and a thoroughly modern restaurant by night—with Mediterranean flavors, panfried fish, and char-grilled meats forming the mainstay of the menu. ⊠ *Rydal Rd.* ☎ *015394/32137* ⚭ *Reservations essential* ⊟ *MC, V* ✆ *Closed Tues. and Jan.*

$$ 🔲 **Britannia Inn.** The Britannia is a friendly inn in the heart of splendid walking country, with quaint little rooms and hearty homemade English food served in the bar. The four guest rooms across the road in the Maple Tree Corner annex are a few pounds cheaper, but you'll have to walk over to the inn for breakfast. ⊠ *Elterwater, on B5343, 6 km (4 mi) west of Ambleside, LA22 9HP* ☎ *015394/37210* 🖷 *015394/37311* ⇥ *13 rooms, 9 with shower* ⚭ *Restaurant* ⊟ *MC, V.*

$ ⌂ **3 Cambridge Villas.** Ambleside abounds with inexpensive B&Bs, but you'd be hard-pressed to find a more welcoming spot than this lofty Victorian house right in the center, with hosts who know a thing or two about local walks. ⌧ *Church St., LA22 9DL* ☎ *015394/32307* ⬓ *8 rooms, 4 with shower* ⊟ *No credit cards* ⊘ *Closed Dec. and Jan.*

Rydal Mount

If there's one poet associated with the Lake District, it is William Wordsworth, who made his home at Rydal Mount, 2 km (1 mi) northwest of Ambleside, from 1813 until his death 37 years later. Wordsworth and his family moved to these grand surroundings when he was nearing the height of his career, and his descendants still live here, surrounded by his furniture, portraits, and the 4½-acre garden laid out by the poet himself. ⌧ *Rydal* ☎ *015394/33002* ⊘ *Mar.–Oct., daily 9:30–5; Nov.–Feb., Wed.–Mon. 10–4* ⊘ *Closed 3 wks in Jan.*

Grasmere

The heart of Wordsworth country, Grasmere is one of the most typical of Lake District villages, sited on a tiny, wood-fringed lake 2 km (1 mi) north of Dove Cottage, 6½ km (4 mi) northwest of Ambleside. The town is made up of crooked lanes lined with charming slate-roof cottages. Wordsworth lived on the town's outskirts for almost 50 years—at Rydal Mount and Dove Cottage—and he, his wife, Mary, his sister, Dorothy, and his daughter Dora are buried in Grasmere churchyard.

★ **Dove Cottage** is the leading literary shrine of the Lake District. Located 2½ km (1½ mi) northwest of Rydal Mount, this was Wordsworth's home from 1799 until 1808, and the tiny house still contains many personal belongings. Your ticket includes admission to the Wordsworth Museum, which documents the contributions of Wordsworth and the Lake Poets. ⌧ *A591* ☎ *015394/35544* ⊕ *www.wordsworth.org.uk* ⊘ *Mid-Feb.–mid-Jan., daily 9:30–5.30.*

★ $$$$ ✕⌂ **White Moss House.** Wordsworth once owned this charming house, built in 1730, to overlook Rydal Water. Attention is lavished on guests, who hike to prepare for dinner in the renowned restaurant. Five courses of contemporary English cuisine always include a soup, local meat and fish, and fine British cheeses. Access to a health club is complimentary. ⌧ *A591, Rydal Water LA22 9SE* ☎ *015394/35295* ⊕ *www.whitemoss. com* ⌂ *Restaurant* ⬓ *7 rooms, 1 suite* ⊟ *MC, V.*

$ ⌂ **Banerigg House.** You don't have to spend a fortune to find appealing lakeside lodgings in Grasmere. This turn-of-the-20th-century family house, 1½ km (¾ mi) south of the village, offers well-appointed, no-smoking rooms, most with lake views. ⌧ *Lake Rd., LA22 9PW* ☎ *015394/ 35204* ⬓ *7 rooms, 5 with bath* ⊟ *No credit cards.*

Coniston

Formerly a copper-mining village, Coniston is now a small lake resort and boating center at the foot of the **Old Man of Coniston** (2,635 feet), 13 km (8 mi) south of Grasmere. Tracks lead up from the village past an old mine to the peak, which you can reach in about two hours, though many experienced hikers include the peak in an enervating seven-hour circular walk from the village.

★ Just outside Coniston is **Brantwood,** the home of Victorian artist, critic, and social reformer John Ruskin (1819–1900). Here, in the rambling white 18th-century house, you'll find a collection of Ruskin's own paintings, drawings, and books. It's an easy drive to Brantwood from Coniston, but it's much more agreeable to travel here by ferry across the lake. Services are available from the Coniston Launch (Easter–October, hourly departures; fewer sailings in winter) and the steam yacht *Gondola* (April–October, four–five trips daily), both departing from Coniston Pier. ⊠ *Brantwood* ☎ *015394/41396* ⊕ *www.brantwood. org.uk* ⊙ *Mid-Mar.–mid-Nov., daily 11–5:30; mid-Nov.–mid-Mar., Wed.–Sun. 11–4.*

Hawkshead

Just outside the attractive village of Hawkshead, **Hill Top** was the home of author and illustrator Beatrix Potter, most famous for her *Peter Rabbit* stories. Now run by the National Trust, the tiny house is a popular—and often crowded—spot; admission is strictly controlled. Avoid visiting on summer weekends and during school vacations. The house is 3 km (2 mi) south of Hawkshead on the B5285, though you can also approach via the car ferry from Bowness-on-Windermere. ⊠ *Near Sawrey, Ambleside* ☎ *015394/36269* ⊙ *Apr.–Oct., Sat.–Wed. 11–5.*

Ullswater

Hemmed in by towering hills, Ullswater, 10 km (6 mi) southwest of Penrith along A592, is the region's second-largest lake and is in a spectacular setting. Some of the finest views are from A592 as it hugs the lake's western shore, through Glenridding and Patterdale at the southern end. Here, you're at the foot of Helvellyn (3,118 feet), which lies to the west. Arduous footpaths run from the road between Glenridding and Patterdale and pass by Red Tarn, at 2,356 feet the highest Lake District tarn.

Aira Force, 8 km (5 mi) north of Patterdale, just off the A592, is a spectacular series of waterfalls pounding through a wooded ravine to feed into Ullswater. From the parking lot (parking fee charged), it's a 20-minute walk to the falls—bring sturdy shoes in wet weather. Just above Aira Force in the woods of Gowbarrow Park, William Wordsworth and his sister, Dorothy, were walking on April 15, 1802. Dorothy remarked that she had never seen "daffodils so beautiful." Wordsworth was inspired by his sister's words to write one of the best-known lyric poems in English, "I Wandered Lonely as a Cloud."

Keswick

The great Lakeland mountains of Skiddaw and Blencathra brood over the gray slate houses of Keswick (pronounced *Kezz-*ick), 22 km (14 mi) west of Ullswater, on the scenic shores of Derwentwater. Many of the best hiking routes radiate from here, so it is more of a touring base than a tourist destination. People stroll the congested, narrow streets in boots and hiking trousers, and there are plenty of mountaineering shops in addition to hotels, guest houses, pubs, and restaurants.

★ To understand why **Derwentwater** is considered one of England's finest lakes, take a short walk from the town center to the lake shore, and follow the Friar's Crag path—about 15 minutes' level walk from the center of Keswick. This pine-tree-fringed peninsula is a favorite vantage point, with its view over the lake, the surrounding ring of mountains, and many tiny wooded islands. Ahead you will see the crags that line the **Jaws of Borrowdale** and overhang a dramatic mountain ravine. Between late March and November, cruises set off every hour in each direction from a wooden dock at the lakeshore.

$$–$$$ ✕▦ **Highfield Hotel.** Overlooking the lawns of Hope Park, a few minutes' walk from lake or town, this family-run hotel harbors idiosyncratic turret rooms and a former chapel now used as a four-poster bedroom. Dinner serves Lake District delights. ⊠ *The Heads, CA12 5ER* ☎ *017687/72508* ⊕ *www.highfieldkeswick.co.uk* ⮞ *19 rooms* ♨ *Restaurant* ▭ *MC, V* ⊙ *Closed mid-Nov.–Jan.*

$–$$ ✕⊡ **Morrel's.** The relaxed kitchen in this pleasant, good-value hotel prepares innovative cuisine. Hare is served with poached pear and red currant jelly, and a trout and roast-pepper tart accompanies the roast cod. The simple but delightful bedrooms are done in cheerful prints and pastels; the top floor has great views of the fells. ✉ *34 Lake Rd., CA12 5DQ* ☎ *017687/72666* ⌂ *Restaurant* ⇝ *15 rooms* ▤ *MC, V.*

Lake District Essentials

BOAT & FERRY TRAVEL
Windermere Lake Cruises employs its handsome fleet of modern launches and vintage cruisers—the largest ships on the lake—in regular service between Ambleside, Bowness, Brockhole, and Lakeside. A Freedom of the Lake ticket (£9.50) gives unlimited travel on any of the ferries for 24 hours.

🚩 **Windermere Lake Cruises** ☎ 015395/31188 ⊕ www.windermere-lakecruises.co.uk.

BUS TRAVEL
National Express serves the region from London's Victoria Coach Station. Average travel time to Kendal is just over 7 hours; to Windermere, 7½ hours; and to Keswick, 8¼ hours.

🚩 **National Express** ☎ 0870/580-8080 ⊕ www.nationalexpress.com. **Traveline** ☎ 0870/608-2608 ⊕ www.traveline.org.uk.

CAR TRAVEL
Take M1 north from London to M6, leaving either at Exit 36, joining A590/A591 west (around the Kendal bypass to Windermere), or at Exit 40, joining A66 directly to Keswick and the northern lakes. Travel time to Kendal is about four hours, to Keswick, five or six hours. Car-rental companies are few and far between in the Lakes; rent in London or York before your trip.

Roads within the region are generally good, although many of the minor routes and mountain passes can be steep and narrow. Warning signs are normally posted if snow has made a road impassable. In July and August and during public holiday weekends, expect heavy traffic.

OUTDOORS & SPORTS
Scores of walking paths and trails originate in every hamlet, village, and town. Stores throughout the region stock equipment, books, and maps. Always check on weather conditions before setting out, as mist or rain can roll in without warning. For short, local walks, consult the tourist information centers, which can provide maps, guides, and advice. The other main source of information is the Lake District National Park Visitor Center.

TOURS
From Easter through October, the National Park Authority at Brockhole, near Windermere, arranges half-day or full-day walks that introduce you to the history and natural beauties of the Lake District. Mountain Goat Holidays provides half- and full-day minibus sightseeing tours with skilled local guides.

🚩 **Mountain Goat Holidays** ☎ 015394/45161 ⊕ www.lake-district.gov.uk. **National Park Authority** ☎ 015394/46601.

TRAIN TRAVEL
InterCity West Coast serves the region from London's Euston Station. Take an InterCity train bound for Carlisle, Edinburgh, or Glasgow, and

change at Oxenholme for the branch line service to Kendal and Windermere. Average travel time to Windermere (including the change) is 4½ hours. The Lakeside & Haverthwaite Railway Co. runs vintage steam trains in summer (and at Christmas) between Lakeside and Haverthwaite along Lake Windermere's southern tip.

National Rail Enquiries ☎ 0845/748-4950 ⊕ www.nationalrail.co.uk. **Lakeside & Haverthwaite Railway Co.** ☎ 015395/31594.

VISITOR INFORMATION

Ambleside ✉ Central Buildings, Market Cross ☎ 015394/32582. **Cumbria Tourist Board** ✉ Ashleigh, Holly Rd., Windermere, Cumbria LA23 2AQ, ☎ 015394/44444 ⊕ www.golakes.co.uk. **Grasmere** ✉ Red Bank Rd. ☎ 015394/35245. **Kendal** ✉ Town Hall, Highgate ☎ 01539/725758. **Keswick** ✉ Moot Hall, Market Sq. ☎ 017687/72645. **Windermere** ✉ The Gateway Centre, Victoria St. ☎ 015394/46499.

EDINBURGH

Scotland and England *are* different—and let no Englishman tell you otherwise. Although the two nations have been united in a single kingdom since 1603, Scotland retains its own marked political and social character, with separate legal and educational systems quite distinct from those of England and, once again, a Parliament of its own, reestablished in 1999. Charlotte Brontë once wrote, "Edinburgh is to London as poetry is to prose." One of the world's stateliest cities and proudest capitals, it is built—like Rome—on seven hills, making it the perfect backdrop for the ancient pageant of history.

Exploring Edinburgh

Numbers in the margin correspond to points of interest on the Edinburgh map.

The key to understanding Edinburgh is to make the distinction between the Old and New Towns. Until the 18th century the city was confined to the rocky crag on which its castle stands, straggling between the fortress at one end and the royal residence, the Palace of Holyroodhouse, at the other. In the 18th century, during a time of expansion known as the Scottish Enlightenment, the city fathers fostered the construction of another Edinburgh, one a little to the north. In 1767, the competition to design the New Town was won by a young and unknown architect, James Craig. His plan was for a grid of three east–west streets, balanced at each end by a grand square. The plan still survives, despite commercial pressures. Princes, George, and Queen streets are the main thoroughfares, with St. Andrew Square at one end and Charlotte Square at the other. The mostly residential New Town, with elegant squares, classical facades, wide streets, and harmonious proportions, remains largely intact and lived-in today.

Apart from the Old and New Towns in central Edinburgh, some outlying neighborhoods are also worth a visit. Leith, Edinburgh's port, throbs with chic bars and restaurants, and Duddingston has all the feel of a country village. Corstorphine is the site of Edinburgh Zoo, and in a huge stadium in Murrayfield Scotland plays its international rugby matches. Also worth a visit are Inverleith, Dean village, and Sciennes with their smart, prosperous villas.

⑫ **Arthur's Seat.** The open grounds of Holyrood Park enclose Arthur's Seat, Edinburgh's distinctive, originally volcanic 800-foot minimountain, with steep slopes and miniature crags. ✉ *Holyrood Park.*

⓱ Britannia. This excursion to a former royal yacht is an opportunity to see how the other half lives. A no-portholes-barred tour includes the queen's former sitting room as well as the engine room. ✉ *Britannia Ocean Dr., Leith., Reach Leith by walking down Leith St. and Leith Walk, from east end of Princes St. (20–30 mins); or take Lothian Bus 22* ☎ *0131/555–5566* ⊕ *www.royalyachtbrittania.co.uk* ☉ *Apr.–Sept., daily 9:30–4:30, Oct.–Mar., daily 10–3:30.*

⓰ Calton Hill. Steps and a road lead up to splendid views north across the Firth (estuary) of Forth to the Lomond Hills of Fife and south to the Pentland Hills. Among the various monuments on Calton Hill are a partial reproduction of Athens's **Parthenon,** begun in 1824 but left incomplete because the money ran out; the **Nelson Monument;** and the **Royal Observatory.** ✉ *North side of Regent Rd.* ⊕ *www.cac.org.uk.*

❾ Canongate Tolbooth. Nearly every town in Scotland once had a tollbooth; originally signifying a customhouse where tolls were gathered, the name came to mean the town hall and, later, a prison. Today, the building contains an exhibition on the history of the people of Edinburgh. Next door is the graveyard of **Canongate Kirk,** where some notable Scots, including economist Adam Smith, are buried. ✉ *Canongate* ☎ *0131/ 529–4057* ☉ *Mon.–Sat. 10–5, Sun. (during festival only) 2–5.*

★ ❶ Edinburgh Castle. The brooding symbol of Scotland's capital and the nation's martial past, the castle dominates the city center. Its attractions include the 11th-century **St. Margaret's Chapel;** the **Crown Room,** where the Regalia of Scotland are displayed; **Great Hall;** and **Queen Mary's Apartments,** where Mary, Queen of Scots, gave birth to the future King James VI of Scotland (who later became James I of England). In addition, military features include the **Scottish National War Memorial** and the **Scottish United Services Museum.** The **Castle Esplanade,** the wide parade ground at the entrance to the castle, hosts the annual Edinburgh Military Tattoo—a grand military display staged during a citywide festival every summer. ✉ *Castlehill* ☎ *0131/225–9846 for Edinburgh Castle; 0131/226–7393 for War Memorial* ⊕ *www.historic-scotland.gov. uk* ☉ *Apr.–Sept., daily 9:30–6; Oct.–Mar., daily 9:30–5.*

★ ⓮ Georgian House. Built in 1796, this house stands in Charlotte Square, the elegant urban set piece designed by Robert Adam at the west end of George Street. Graced by a palatial facade on its north side, the square is considered one of Britain's finest pieces of civic architecture. Thanks to the National Trust for Scotland, the Georgian House has been furnished in period style to show the domestic lifestyle of an affluent late-18th-century family. ✉ *7 Charlotte Sq.* ☎ *0131/225–2160* ⊕ *www. nts.org.uk* ☉ *Mar., Nov., and Dec., daily 11–3; Apr.–Oct., daily 11–5.*

❸ Gladstone's Land. This six-story property cared for by the National Trust for Scotland dates from 1620. It has an arcaded front and first-floor entrance typical of the period and is furnished in the style of a merchant's house of the time; there are magnificent painted ceilings. ✉ *477B Lawnmarket* ☎ *0131/226–5856* ⊕ *www.nts.org.uk* ☉ *Apr.–Oct., Mon.–Sat. 10–5, Sun. 2–5; last admission at 4:30.*

❺ High Kirk of St. Giles. Often called St. Giles's Cathedral, this historic structure dates from the 12th century; the impressive choir was built during the 15th century. ✉ *High St.* ☎ *0131/225–9442* ⊕ *www.stgiles.net* ☉ *May–Sept., weekdays 9–7, Sat. 9–5, Sun 1–5; Oct.–Apr., Mon.–Sat. 9–5, Sun. 1–5.*

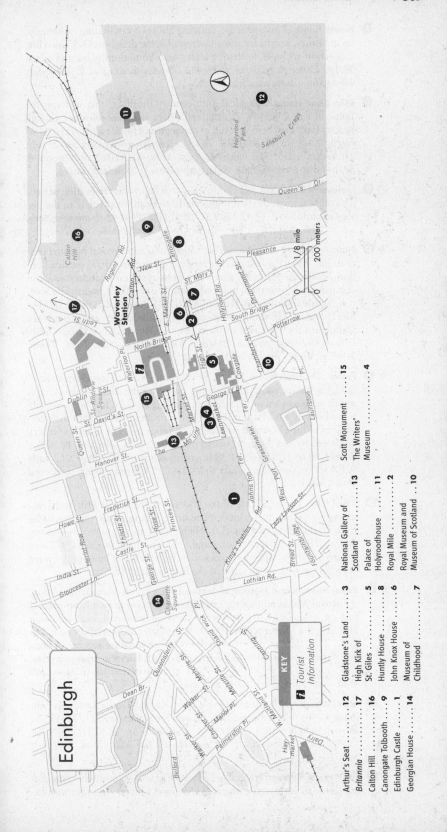

Edinburgh

KEY

i *Tourist Information*

8 **Huntly House.** This attractive building houses a fascinating museum of local history, a must for those interested in the details of Old Town life. Collection includes Scottish pottery and Edinburgh glass and silver. ⊠ *142 Canongate* ☎ *0131/529–4143* ⊕ *www.cac.org.uk* ⊗ *Mon.–Sat. 10–5, Sun. (during festival only) 2–5.*

6 **John Knox House.** A typical 16th-century dwelling, this was not the home of Knox (1514–72), Scotland's fiery religious reformer, though he may have died here. It is full of mementos of his life and career. ⊠ *45 High St.* ☎ *0131/556–2647* ⊕ *www.johnknoxhouse.org.uk* ⊗ *July, Mon.–Sat. 10–5, Sun. noon–4; Aug., Mon.–Sat. 10–7, Sun. noon–4; Sept.–June, Mon.–Sat. 10–5; last admission ½ hr before closing.*

7 **Museum of Childhood.** Even adults may well enjoy this celebration of toys. The museum was the first in the world to be devoted solely to the history of childhood. ⊠ *42 High St.* ☎ *0131/529–4142* ⊕ *www.cac.org. uk* ⊗ *Mon.–Sat. 10–5, Sun. (during festival only) 2–5.*

★ **13** **National Gallery of Scotland.** This honey-color neoclassical building contains just about the best collection of old masters in Britain outside London; Scottish painters are also well represented. It is relatively small, so you can easily tour the whole collection in a couple of hours. The **Scottish National Gallery of Modern Art** (⊠ 75 Belford Rd. ☎ 0131/556–8921) houses the national collection of 20th-century art in the Dean Gallery on the west side of town. ⊠ *The Mound* ☎ *0131/624–6200* ⊕ *www.natgalscot.ac.uk* ⊗ *Mon.–Wed. and Fri.–Sun. 10–5, Thurs. 10–7, extended hrs during the festival.*

★ **11** **Palace of Holyroodhouse.** Still the Royal Family's official residence in Scotland, the palace was built as a guest house for the Abbey of Holyrood, which was founded in 1128 by Scottish king David I. It was extensively remodeled by Charles II in 1671. The state apartments, with their collections of tapestries and paintings, can be visited. The Queen's Gallery holds exhibitions featuring works from the Royal Collection. ⊠ *Abbey Strand* ☎ *0131/556–7371* ⊕ *www.royal.gov.uk* ⊗ *Apr.–Oct., daily 9:30–5:15; Nov.–Mar., daily 9:30–3:45* ⊗ *Closed during royal and state visits.*

2 **Royal Mile.** The backbone of the Old Town, the Royal Mile starts immediately below the Castle Esplanade. It progressively changes name from Castlehill to Lawnmarket, High Street, and Canongate—leading downhill to the Palace of Holyroodhouse. The many original Old Town "closes" (narrow alleyways enclosed by high tenement buildings) reward exploration with a real sense of the former life of the city.

★ **10** **Royal Museum and Museum of Scotland.** In a lavish Victorian building, the **Royal Museum** displays extensive collections drawn from natural history, archaeology, and the scientific and industrial past. In an adjoining building, the **Museum of Scotland** concentrates on Scotland's own heritage. This state-of-the-art museum is full of intricate reconstructions and paraphernalia from the ancient Picts to the latest Scottish pop stars. ⊠ *Chambers St.* ☎ *0131/225–7534* ⊕ *www.nms.ac.uk* ⊗ *Mon. and Wed.–Sat. 10–5, Tues. 10–8, Sun. noon–5.*

15 **Scott Monument.** This unmistakable 200-foot-high Gothic spire was built in the 1840s to commemorate Scotsman Sir Walter Scott (1771–1832), the celebrated author of *Ivanhoe.* ⊠ *Princes St.* ☎ *0131/529–4068* ⊗ *Apr.–Sept., Mon.–Sat. 9–6, Sun. 10–6; Oct.–Mar., Mon.–Sat. 9–3, Sun. 10–3.*

4 **The Writers' Museum.** Housed in Lady Stair's House, a town dwelling dating from 1622, this museum evokes Scotland's literary heritage with exhibits on Sir Walter Scott, Robert Louis Stevenson, and Robert Burns. ✉ *Lady Stair's Close, Lawnmarket* ☎ *0131/529–4901* ☾ *Mon.–Sat. 10–5, Sun. (during festival only) 2–5.*

Where to Eat

Edinburgh's restaurants make the most of Scotland's excellent game, fish, shellfish, beef, and lamb.

★ **$$$–$$$$** ✕ **Martins.** Don't be put off by the forbidding facade of this fine contemporary restaurant tucked away in a little back alley between Frederick and Castle streets. All's well inside, and the food is light and delicious. Fish and game are specialties here, and the cheese board is famous. ✉ *70 Rose St., North La.* ☎ *0131/225–3106* ⌕ *Reservations essential* ▤ *AE, DC, MC, V* ☾ *Closed Sun. and Mon. No lunch Sat.*

$$$ ✕ **Oloroso.** In the heart of the New Town, this is the perfect place for a revitalizing lunch or dinner after exploring the city. Efficient service complements multicultural contemporary cooking that mixes influences from Europe and Asia. The dining room and roof terrace have stunning views across the Firth of Forth to the hills of Fife on one side, and to the castle and city rooftops on the other side. ✉ *33 Castle St.* ☎ *0131/ 226–7614* ▤ *AE, DC, MC, V.*

$$–$$$ ✕ **Howie's.** This neighborhood bistro has four branches and offers good modern Scottish fare. The steaks are tender Aberdeen beef, and the Loch Fyne herring are sweet-cured to Howie's own recipe. ✉ *29 Waterloo Pl.* ☎ *0131/556–5766* ✉ *10–14 Victoria St.* ☎ *0131/225–1721* ✉ *208 Bruntsfield Pl.* ☎ *0131/221–1777* ✉ *4–6 Glanville Pl.* ☎ *0131/313– 3334* ▤ *AE, MC, V.*

$$–$$$ ✕ **Skippers Bistro.** Once a traditional pub, this superb seafood restaurant in the port of Leith remains cozy and cluttered, with dark wood, shining brass, and lots of pictures and ephemera. Main dishes change daily but might include halibut, salmon, or monkfish in delicious sauces. Book your table ahead of time on weekends. ✉ *1A Dock Pl., Leith* ☎ *0131/554–1018* ▤ *AE, MC, V.*

$–$$ ✕ **Bann UK.** The excellent vegetarian food at this thriving restaurant off the Royal Mile is popular with young people. The light, airy dining room and wooden furniture make a pleasant setting for breakfast, tapas, sandwiches, and more substantial fare; try the enchiladas or a phyllo basket of cream cheese, herbs, and vegetables. ✉ *5 Hunter Sq.* ☎ *0131/ 226–1112* ▤ *AE, DC, MC, V.*

$–$$ ✕ **Beehive Inn.** One of the oldest pubs in the city, the Beehive snuggles in the Grassmarket, under the majestic shadow of the castle. The upstairs restaurant lies hidden in an attractive and spacious attic room, crammed with weird and wonderful junk. Open only for dinner, it features mostly steaks and fish: try the charcoal-grilled Scottish salmon. ✉ *18/20 Grassmarket* ☎ *0131/225–7171* ▤ *AE, DC, MC, V.*

Where to Stay

Many of Edinburgh's accommodations are very central, with New Town B&B establishments being especially convenient.

$$$$ ▦ **Channings.** Five Edwardian terraced houses have become an elegant boutique hotel in an upscale neighborhood minutes from Princes Street. Restrained colors, antiques, quiet rooms, and great views toward Fife (from the north-facing rooms) set the tone. The Brasserie offers excellent value, especially at lunchtime. ✉ *12–16 S. Learmonth Gardens, EH4 1EZ* ☎ *0131/332–3232* 🖷 *0131/332–9631* ⊕ *www.channings.co.uk* ▱ *46 rooms* ⏥ *2 restaurants* ▤ *AE, DC, MC, V.*

$$$$ ⌧ **The Scotsman.** When the *Scotsman* newspaper moved from these
Fodor'sChoice premises, it left behind a magnificent turn-of-the-20th-century gray
★ sandstone building with a marble staircase and ornate fireplaces and moldings. A chic and luxurious modern hotel has been created within the shell
of the old structure. Dark wood, earthy colors, and contemporary furnishings decorate the guest rooms and public spaces. ⌧ *20 N. Bridge,
EH1 1YT* ☎ *0131/556–5565* 🖷 *0131/652–3652* ⊕ *www.
thescotsmanhotel.co.uk* 🛏 *56 rooms, 12 suites* ⚐ *2 restaurants, pool,
bar* ⊟ *AE, DC, MC, V.*

$$–$$$ ⌧ **17 Abercromby Place.** A high standard is set at this Georgian terraced
B&B in the center of the New Town. There are stunning views from the
top-floor rooms. The host and the hostess both enjoy meeting guests
and are very helpful, and—unusual for this part of town—there is off-
street parking. ⌧ *17 Abercrombie Pl., EH3 6LB* ☎ *0131/557–8036*
🖷 *0131/558–3453* 🛏 *9 rooms* ⊟ *MC, V.*

★ **$$** ⌧ **Stuart House.** This classy B&B is only a 15-minute walk from the city
center in a Victorian terraced house with some fine plasterwork. The
decoration suits the structure: bold colors, floral fabrics, and generously
curtained windows combine with antique and traditional furniture to
create a sense of opulence. ⌧ *12 E. Claremont St., Canonmills, EH7
4JP* ☎ *0131/557–9030* 🖷 *0131/557–0563* ⊕ *www.stuartguesthouse.
co.uk* 🛏 *7 rooms, 2 apartments* ⊟ *AE, DC, MC, V.*

$–$$ ⌧ **The Conifers.** This trim B&B in a red-sandstone Victorian town house
north of the New Town offers simple, traditional rooms. Framed prints
of old Edinburgh scenes adorn the walls. The owner, Liz Fulton, has a
wealth of knowledge about what to see and do in Edinburgh. ⌧ *56 Pil-
rig St., EH6 5AS* ☎ *0131/554–5162* ⊕ *www.conifersguesthouse.com*
🛏 *4 rooms, 3 with bath* ⊟ *No credit cards.*

The Arts

The *List,* available from newsdealers throughout the city, as well as *What's
On* and *What's On Scotland* available from the Information Centre, carry
the most up-to-date details about cultural events. The *Scotsman,* an Edinburgh daily, also carries reviews in its arts pages on Monday and Wednesday, and daily during the festival.

EDINBURGH The **Edinburgh International Festival,** a three-week-long celebration of
FESTIVAL music, dance, and drama staged each August, draws international
artists of the highest caliber. The **Festival Fringe** (⌧ 180 High St.
☎ 0131/226–0026 🖷 0131/226–0016 ⊕ www.edfringe.com), the unruly child of the official festival, takes place about the same time and
spills out of halls and theaters all over town, offering a cornucopia of
offbeat theatrical and musical events. At the official festival you'll see
top-flight performances by established artists, whereas at a Fringe
event you might catch a new art form or a controversial new play. Advance information, programs, and ticket sales for the festival are available from the **Edinburgh International Festival Office** (⌧ Castlehill, EH1
1ND ☎ 0131/473–2020 for information; 0131/473–2000 for tickets
🖷 0131/473–2003 ⊕ www.eif.co.uk).

OTHER FESTIVALS The annual **Edinburgh Military Tattoo** (⌧ 32 Market St., EH1 1QB ☎ 0131/
225–1188 🖷 0131/225–8627 ⊕ www.edintattoo.co.uk) may not be art,
but it is certainly entertainment. This August celebration of martial
music and skills is set on the Castle Esplanade. Dress warmly for late-
evening shows. Even if it rains, the show most definitely goes on!

Edinburgh Essentials

AIR TRAVEL TO & FROM EDINBURGH

British Airways operates a shuttle service from London's Heathrow Airport to Edinburgh; reservations are not necessary. Flying time from London is one hour, 15 minutes. British Midland also flies from Heathrow. KLM UK flies from Stansted to Edinburgh. EasyJet offers bargain fares from London Luton to Edinburgh. Transatlantic flights direct to Scotland use Glasgow Airport, with regular bus and rail connections from Glasgow city center to Edinburgh. Edinburgh also has regular connections from other British airports, as well as several Continental ones.

British Airways ☎ 0845/773-3377. **British Midland** ☎ 0870/607-0500. **EasyJet** ☎ 0870/600-0000. **KLM UK** ☎ 0870/507-4074.

BUS TRAVEL TO & FROM EDINBURGH

Regular service is operated by National Express between Victoria Coach Station, London, and St. Andrew Square bus station, Edinburgh, twice a day. The journey takes approximately eight hours. National Express also connects to other British cities.

National Express ☎ 0990/808080 ⊕ www.nationalexpress.com.

BUS TRAVEL WITHIN EDINBURGH

Lothian Buses is the main provider within Edinburgh. A Day Saver Ticket (£2.20), allowing unlimited one-day travel on the city's buses, can be purchased in advance.

Lothian Buses ✉ 27 Hanover St. ☎ 0131/555-6363 ✉ Waverley Bridge ☎ 0131/555-6363 or 0131/554-4494 ⊕ www.lothianbuses.co.uk.

CAR TRAVEL

London and Edinburgh are 656 km (407 mi) apart; allow a comfortable nine hours for the drive. The principal routes to the Scottish border are the A1 (which is dual carriageway only on certain stretches), the A68, or the A7. If you want to avoid single-lane highways, you can take the eight-lane M8 (an "M" road signifies a freeway) to Glasgow and then turn south onto the M74, which becomes the M6 after it crosses the Scotland/England border. All the main car-rental agencies have offices in Edinburgh.

Driving in Edinburgh has its quirks, but competent drivers should not be intimidated. Metered parking in the center city is scarce and expensive, and the local traffic wardens are alert. Illegally parked cars are routinely towed away, and getting your car back will be expensive. After 6 PM, the parking situation improves considerably, and you may manage to find a space quite near your hotel, even downtown. If you park on a yellow line or in a resident's parking bay, be prepared to move your car by 8 AM the following morning, when the rush hour gets under way.

CONSULATES

United States ✉ 3 Regent Terr. ☎ 0131/556-8315 ⊕ www.usembassy.org.uk/scotland.

EMERGENCIES

Emergency Services Police, ambulance, fire ☎ 999.
Late-night Pharmacy Boots ✉ 48 Shandwick Pl., west end of Princes St. ☎ 0131/225-6757.

TOURS

BUS TOURS Lothian Buses runs tours in and around Edinburgh, departing from Waverley Bridge at regular intervals, from 9:30 to 5:30 daily. City Sightseeing also runs tours around Edinburgh in its open-top buses from Waverley Bridge.

🚩 **City Sightseeing** ☎ 0131/556-2244 ⊕ www.citysightseeing.com. **Lothian Buses** ✉ 27 Hanover St. ☎ 0131/555-6363 ✉ Waverley Bridge ☎ 0131/555-6363 or 0131/554-4494 ⊕ www.lothianbuses.co.uk.

TRAIN TRAVEL

Regular trains run from London's King's Cross Station to Edinburgh Waverley; the fastest journey time is just over 4½ hours.

🚩 **National Train Enquiries** ☎ 08457/484950 ⊕ www.nationalrail.co.uk.

VISITOR INFORMATION

🚩 **Edinburgh and Scotland Information Centre** ✉ 3 Princes St. ☎ 0131/473-3800 🖨 0131/473-3881 ⊕ www.edinburgh.org.

GREECE

ATHENS, THE PELOPONNESE,
MAINLAND GREECE, CORFU,
THE AEGEAN ISLANDS

14

IT MAY BE SOMEWHAT DISORIENTING for anyone conditioned by text-books, classical literature, and Keats's Grecian urn to arrive in Athens and find a modern city in full swing, with the fashionably dressed locals dodging the heavy traffic in sports cars. It takes no more than a few hours to realize that Athens is a city of dramatic juxtapositions, in which archaeological sites lie adjacent to steel-and-glass office complexes. Residents joke that you don't want to dig too deep here or you might uncover a lost ruin and find your house taken over by a museum. This dichotomy between the ancient and the new runs throughout Greece, part of the special allure of the country.

The land itself is a stunning presence, dotted with cypress groves, vineyards, and olive trees; carved into gentle bays or dramatic coves bordered with startling white sand; or articulated into hills and rugged mountain ranges that plunge into the sea. In Greece, indeed, you cannot travel far across the land without encountering the sea, or far across the sea without encountering one of its roughly 2,000 islands. Approximately equal in size to New York State, or roughly the size of England, Greece has 15,019 km (9,312 mi) of coastline, more than any other country of its size. The sea is everywhere, reaching into the shoreline like a probing hand. This natural beauty and the sharp, clear light of sun and sea, combined with plentiful archaeological treasures, make Greece one of the world's most inviting and rewarding countries to visit.

Western poetry, music, architecture, politics, medicine, law—all had their birth centuries ago in Greece. Among the mountains of mainland Greece are Mt. Olympus, whose cloud-capped peak was the fabled home of the Greek gods, and Mt. Parnassus, favorite haunt of the sun god, Apollo, and the nine Muses. Romantic and beautiful remains of the ancient past—the Acropolis and the Parthenon, the temples of Delphi, the Tombs of the Kings in Mycenae—and later Byzantine churches, Crusader castles and fortresses, and Ottoman minarets dot the country.

Of the many hundreds of islands and islets scattered across the Aegean Sea, in the east, and the Ionian Sea, in the west, fewer than 250 are still inhabited. This world of the farmer, fisherman, and seafarer has largely been replaced by the world of the tourist. More than 14 million vacationers visit Greece each year, a number more than doubling the entire native population. Once-idyllic beaches are sometimes overcrowded and noisy, and quiet fishing harbors can, in the summer, resemble flotilla-sailing centers. But traditional Greece survives: next to the new crop of pubs and bars, you'll always find an *ouzeri* (informal eateries that serve appetizers and ouzo), redolent of nostalgic charm. *Kafeneia* (Greek cof-

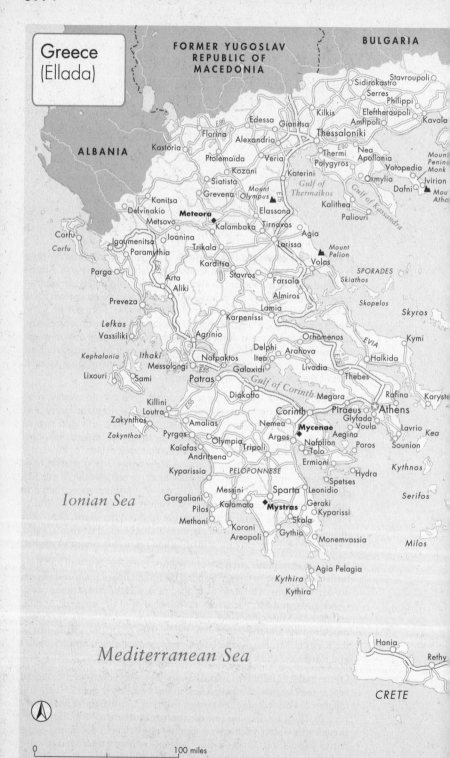

Greece
(Ellada)

FORMER YUGOSLAV
REPUBLIC OF
MACEDONIA

BULGARIA

ALBANIA

Stavroupoli
Sidirokastro
Serres
Philippi
Eleftheroupoli
Kavala
Kilkis
Amfipoli
Edessa
Gianitsa
Florina
Alexandria
Thessaloniki
Kastoria
Thermi
Nea
Apollonia
Ptolemaïda
Veria
Polygyros
Vatopedia
Mount
Penin
Monk
Kozani
Katerini
Ormylia
Dafni
Ivirion
Siatista
Mou
Athc
Grevena
Mount
Olympus
Gulf of
Thermaïkos
Gulf of Kassandra
Konitsa
Elassona
Kalithea
Paliouri
Delvinakio
Metsovo
Meteora
Kalambaka
Tirnavos
Agia
Corfu
Ioanina
Trikala
Larissa
Corfu
Igoumenitsa
Paramythia
Mount
Pelion
Parga
Karditsa
Volos
SPORADES
Stavros
Farsala
Skiathos
Arta
Aliki
Almiros
Preveza
Lamia
Skopelos
Skyros
Lefkas
Vassiliki
Karpenissi
Kephalonia
Ithaki
Agrinio
Orhamenos
EVIA
Kymi
Lixouri
Sami
Messolongi
Nafpaktos
Delphi
Arahova
Halkida
Patras
Itea
Livadia
Galaxidi
Thebes
Diakofto
Gulf of Corinth
Megara
Rafina
Killini
Corinth
Piraeus
Athens
Loutra
Nemea
Glyfada
Karyste
Zakynthos
Amalias
Mycenae
Voula
Lavrio
Pyrgos
Argos
Aegina
Poros
Kea
Zakynthos
Kaïafas
Olympia
Nafplion
Sounion
Andritsena
Tripoli
Tolo
Ermioni
Kythnos
Kyparissia
PELOPONNESE
Hydra
Spetses
Serifos
Messini
Sparta
Gargaliani
Kalamata
Mystras
Leonidio
Pilos
Geraki
Kyparissi
Methoni
Skala
Koroni
Gythio
Monemvassia
Milos
Areopoli
Agia Pelagia
Ionian Sea
Kythira
Kythira
Mediterranean Sea
Hania
Rethy
CRETE

0   100 miles
0   150 km

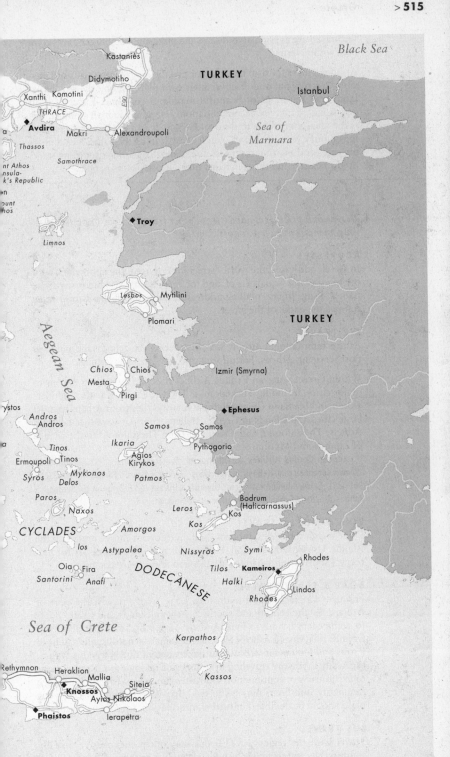

feehouses) are as popular as discos, and pizza and hamburger joints compete with tavernas.

Although mass tourism has transformed the main centers, it is still possible to strike out and discover your own place among the smaller islands and the miles of beautiful mainland coastline. Except for an occasional scarcity of accommodations, especially in high summer, this is the ideal way to see traditional Greece. If you explore this fascinating country with open eyes, you'll enjoy it in all its forms: its slumbering cafés and buzzing tavernas; its elaborate religious rituals; its stark, bright beauty; and the generosity and curiosity of its people.

GREECE A TO Z

To research prices, get advice from other travelers, and book travel arrangements, visit www.fodors.com.

ADDRESSES

In Greek addresses, the word "street" is not used; the abbreviation for the word *platia* (square) is pl, and for *agios* (saint), used in many street names, is ag. In city mailing addresses, the name of the district often follows the name of the street.

AIR TRAVEL

Athens International Airport S.A., Eleftherios Venizelos, is the main airport servicing Athens. For information *see* Athens Essentials.

CARRIERS Within Greece, Aegean Cronus Airlines flies regularly from Athens to major cities, including Thessaloniki, Rhodes, Corfu, Kavala, and Heraklion and Hania in Crete. Olympic Airways flies from Athens to most large cities and islands in Greece. Hellenic Star Airways flies between Athens, Thessaloniki, and Chios and from Thessaloniki to the islands of Limnos and Mytilini.

🛫 **Aegean Cronus Airlines** ✉ Othonos 10, Syntagma, Athens ☎ 210/998-8300 ⊕www.aegeanair.com. **Hellenic Star Airways** ✉Vouliagmenis 2, Eliniko, Athens ☎210/ 961-1881 ⊕ www.hellenicstar.com. **Olympic Airways** ✉ Filleliinon 15, Syntagma, Athens ☎ 210/966-6666 ⊕ www.olympic-airways.gr.

BIKE & MOPED TRAVEL

Dune buggies, bicycles, mopeds, and motorcycles can be rented on the islands. Use extreme caution. Helmets, technically compulsory for motorcyclists, are not usually available, and injuries are common.

BOAT & FERRY TRAVEL

Frequent car ferries and hydrofoils leave from Piraeus, the port of Athens, for the central and southern Aegean islands and Crete. Boats to such nearby islands as Evia, Andros, Mykonos, and Tinos also leave from Rafina, east of Athens. Ships to the Ionian islands usually sail from Patras and Igoumenitsa. Buy your tickets two or three days in advance, especially if you are traveling in summer or taking a car. Reserve your return journey or continuation soon after you arrive. Timetables change frequently, and boats may be delayed by weather conditions, so your plans should be flexible. For further information, *see* Athens Essentials.

BUS TRAVEL

Travel with the regional KTEL bus network is inexpensive, usually comfortable, and relatively fast. Bus timetables are available from Greek National Tourist Organization (EOT) offices. In summer and on holiday weekends, make reservations or buy tickets a few days before your planned trip. Board early, as passengers often have a loose attitude about assigned seating; if smoking bothers you, get a seat away from the driver, who is exempt from the no-smoking regulations.

🚌 KTEL ☎ 210/821-0872 ⊕ www.ktel.org.

BUSINESS HOURS

Office and shopping hours vary from season to season. Check with your hotel for up-to-the-minute information on opening and closing times.

BANKS & OFFICES Banks are open weekdays 8–2, except Friday, when they close at 1:30; they are closed weekends and public holidays. In Athens one branch of the National Bank of Greece has extended hours for foreign exchange only, Monday–Thursday 3:30–6:30, Friday 3–6:30, Saturday 9–3, Sunday 9–1. Even smaller towns have at least one bank with an ATM.

🏦 **National Bank of Greece** ⊠ Karageorgi Servias 2, Syntagma, Athens ☎ 210/334-0011.

MUSEUMS & SIGHTS Museums and archaeological sites are open 8:30–3 off-season, or winter (November–mid-April). Depending on available personnel, sites usually stay open longer mid-April–October, sometimes as late as 7 PM in July and August. Many museums are closed one day a week, usually Monday. Archaeological sites and museums are closed January 1, March 25, Good Friday morning until noon, Easter Sunday, May 1, and December 25–26; for reduced visiting hours on other holidays, check the handout from EOT.

SHOPS Shops may stay open from 9 AM to 9 PM in summer, though most stores close Monday, Wednesday, and Saturday around 3 or 4 PM. On Tuesday, Thursday, and Friday, many shops take a break and close between 3 and 5 PM. In winter (November–mid-April) hours are slightly reduced, though this changes every year. Most establishments are closed Sunday. Supermarkets are open weekdays until about 8:30 PM, with reduced hours on Saturday. In tourist areas such as Athens's Plaka, souvenir shops stay open late.

CAR TRAVEL

EMERGENCIES The Automobile and Touring Club of Greece (ELPA) assists tourists with breakdowns free of charge if they belong to the American Automobile Association or to ELPA (€115 per year, good for discounts on emergency service throughout Europe); otherwise, there is a charge. ELPA also provides tourist information to drivers.

🚗 **Automobile and Touring Club of Greece (ELPA)** ⊠ Messoghion 395, 15343 Athens ☎ 210/606-8800; 104 throughout Greece for emergency; 174 for tourist information 🖶 210/606-8981 ⊕ www.elpa.gr.

GASOLINE At press time, gas cost about €0.80–€0.90 a liter. Gas pumps and service stations are everywhere, and lead-free gas is widely available. In rural areas and on the islands many stations are closed evenings.

PARKING In Greece's half-dozen large cities, downtown street parking and lots are extremely hard to find. It's often cheaper to leave your car at the hotel and take a cab or bus. Elsewhere, parking is easy.

ROAD CONDITIONS Greece has one of the highest ratios in Europe of collisions to the number of cars on the road. The National Road can be challenging with its inadequate signposting and repair work, though rebuilding has improved it. Tolls range from €0.75 to €2.80, depending on the distance traveled. You need nerves of steel to drive in the cities, but many country roads, though narrow, are free of traffic.

RULES OF THE ROAD Non–European Union citizens must have an international driver's license. Driving is on the right, and although seat belts are compulsory, don't expect this or any other driving rule to be obeyed all the time. The speed limit is 120 kph (74 mph) on the National Road (follow the temporary speed signs where it's under repair), 90 kph (56 mph) outside built-up areas, and 50 kph (31 mph) in town.

CUSTOMS & DUTIES

For details on imports and duty-free limits, *see* Customs & Duties *in* Smart Travel Tips.

IN GREECE You may bring in only one each of such expensive portable items as camcorders and computers. You should register these with Greek customs upon arrival, to avoid any problems when taking them out of the country again. Foreign banknotes amounting to more than $2,500 must be declared for re-export, although there are no restrictions on traveler's checks; foreign visitors may export no more than €295.

EATING & DRINKING

The principal elements of Greek cuisine are fish; grilled and roasted meats, especially lamb; and fresh vegetables, such as eggplant, tomatoes, and beans, inventively combined with lots of olive oil and seasoned with lemon juice, garlic, onion, and oregano. Let your senses guide you—visit the kitchen and point to what looks appetizing; try the regional specialties and barrel wine whenever possible. Your best bet is to choose the tavernas and slightly more upscale *estiatoria* (restaurants) that are frequented by most Greeks. Both serve oven-baked dishes and stove-top stews called *magirefta,* prepared in advance and often served at room temperature. If you're in a fish taverna, ask to see the daily catch to check for freshness, choose your fish, and have it weighed before it's cooked; prices are by the kilo. Another alternative is an ouzeri or *mezedopolion,* where you order plates of appetizers, called *mezedes,* instead of an entrée. Some upscale restaurants have begun serving what could be dubbed nouvelle Mediterranean, with local ingredients unusually combined and imaginatively presented. Traditional fast food in Greece consists of the *gyro* (pronounced "*yee-*ro"), slices of grilled meat with tomato and onions in pita bread; souvlaki (shish kebab); toasted sandwiches called *tost,* which you fill from ingredients ranging from red peppers to fried bacon to smoked eggplant dip; and pastries known as *pites,* stuffed with spinach, cheese, or meat. Hamburgers and pizzas are also found everywhere.

WHAT IT COSTS In euros			
$$$$	$$$	$$	$
AT DINNER over €21	€16–€21	€10–€15	under €10

Prices are per person for a main course or, for restaurants that serve only mezedes, two mezedes.

MEALTIMES Greeks eat a light breakfast or nothing at all, but you can order breakfast in a hotel dining room until 10 (otherwise, try a café or purchase something in a bakery). Lunch in Greek restaurants is served from 12:30 until 3. Dinner begins about 9 and is served until 12:30 in Athens and until midnight outside Athens.

RESERVATIONS & In Athens, Thessaloniki, and the more touristed islands, reservations are
DRESS recommended at popular places. Throughout the Greek islands you can dress informally for dinner, even at expensive restaurants; in Athens, jackets are appropriate at the top-price restaurants. Greeks do enjoy dressing up, however, so smart casual is a good choice unless you're dining at a bar, café, or a taverna by the beach.

EMBASSIES

New Zealand maintains a consular office in Athens (⇨ Athens Essentials).

🔲 Australia ⊠ Soutsou 37 and Tsochas 24, Athens ☎ 210/645-0404 ⊕ www.ausemb.gr.

🔲 Canada ⊠ Gennadiou 4, Athens ☎ 210/727-3400 ⊕ www.dfait-maeci.gc.ca.

🔲 Ireland ⊠ Vasilissis Konstantinou 7, Athens ☎ 210/723-2771.

🔲 United Kingdom ⊠ Ploutarchou 1, Athens ☎ 210/727-2600 ⊕ www.british-embassy.gr.

🔲 United States ⊠ Vasilissis Sofias 91, Athens ☎ 210/721-2951 through 210/721-2959 ⊕ www.usembassy.gr.

HOLIDAYS

January 1; January 6 (Epiphany); Clean Monday and first day of Lent; March 25 (Independence Day); Good Friday; Greek Easter Sunday; Greek Easter Monday; May 1 (Labor Day); June 3 (Pentecost); August 15 (Assumption); October 28 (Ochi Day); December 25–26.

LANGUAGE

In Greece, the native language uses the 24-letter Greek alphabet. English is widely spoken in hotels and elsewhere, especially by young people, and even in out-of-the-way places someone is always happy to lend a helping word. In this guide names are given in the Roman alphabet according to the Greek pronunciation.

LODGING

Spartan campgrounds, family-run pensions, modern boutique hotels, and luxurious resorts complete with a pseudo-village (bakery, church, café) are some of the lodging options in Greece. If you plan to visit during Easter week (Catholic or Orthodox) or from mid-June through August, reserve well in advance. In August on the islands, even the most basic rooms are hard to find, as that's when most Greeks take their month-long vacation. Off-season, you usually can negotiate room rates.

WHAT IT COSTS In euros			
$$$$	**$$$**	**$$**	**$**
ATHENS			
FOR 2 PEOPLE over €250	€175–€250	€100–€175	under €100
OTHER AREAS			
HOTELS over €150	€100–€150	€70–€100	under €70

Prices are for a standard double room during high season, including taxes.

APARTMENT & VILLA RENTALS Most areas have pensions—usually clean and bright—and many apartments with kitchens. On islands, owners wait for tourists at the harbor, and signs in English throughout villages indicate rooms available. You can also query the tourist police or the municipal tourist information office. Accommodations are harder to find in smaller resort towns during the winter and beginning of spring. Check the rooms first, for quality and location. Also, make sure you feel comfortable with the owners if they live on the premises.

CAMPING At the numerous privately owned campgrounds, amenities range from basic to elaborate (those operated by the tourist organization are cushier than most). Contact the Greek Camping Association or the local branches of the Greek National Tourist Organization for more information.
🔲 **Greek Camping Association** ⊠ Solonos 102, 10680 Athens ☎📠 210/362-1560.

HOSTELS Hostels operate in major tourist areas but often close from season to season, so contact the Greek Youth Hostel Organization.

Greek Youth Hostel Organization ⊠ Damareos 75, 11633 Athens ☎ 210/751-9530 🖶 210/751-0616.

HOTELS

Greek hotels are classified by the government as L (for deluxe) and A (the next most luxurious category) through E (basic accommodations). Within each category quality varies greatly, but prices usually don't. Still, you may come across an A-class hotel that charges less than a B-class, depending on facilities. D- and E-class lodgings will have shared bathrooms. In this guide, hotels are classified according to price. All $$$$ and $$$ hotels are assumed to have air-conditioning, and unless indicated, all hotel rooms have private baths.

Prices quoted by hotels usually include service, local taxes, and value-added tax (V.A.T.); many include breakfast. Often you can negotiate the price, sometimes by eliminating breakfast. The official price should be posted on the back of the door or inside a closet. Booking a room through a local travel agency may reduce the price substantially. You can contact a hotel directly or write one month in advance for reservations to the Hellenic Chamber of Hotels. The chamber also has a desk inside the National Bank of Greece in Athens to help find rooms; it's open weekdays 8:30–2, Saturday 9–1. During high season, larger resort hotels may insist that you take half board (breakfast and dinner) at the hotel.

Hellenic Chamber of Hotels ⊠ Stadiou 24, 10564 Athens ☎ 210/331-0022 through 210/331-0026 🖶 210/322-5449 ⊕ http://users.otenet.gr/~grhotels ⊠ National Bank of Greece, Karageorgi Servias 2, 10564 Athens ☎ 210/323-7193.

TRADITIONAL
SETTLEMENTS

State organized, these establishments house people in buildings representative of the local architecture. Many settlements are described in a free brochure from EOT, as well as in the English-language *Traditional Inns in Greece: Alternative Forms of Tourism* (published by Vertical Advertising-Publishing), available in foreign-language bookstores in Greece.

MAIL & SHIPPING

Letters are sometimes lost in the mail; it's best to send important items registered. Most post offices are open weekdays 8–2. In Athens the main offices stay open late (weekdays 7:30 AM–8 PM, Saturday 7:30–2, Sunday 9–2). You can have your mail addressed to *poste restante* (general delivery) and sent to any post office in Greece, where you can pick it up once you show your passport. Or have it mailed to American Express offices, which you'll find in major cities and on many islands. The service is free for holders of American Express cards or traveler's checks.

American Express ⊠ Ermou 2, Athens 10563. **Athens Post Offices** ⊠ Aiolou 100, 10200 ⊠ Syntagma Square at Mitropoleos.

POSTAL RATES

Airmail letters and postcards for delivery within Europe cost €0.65 for 20 grams and €1 for 50 grams, for outside Europe €0.65 for 20 grams and €1.15 for 50 grams. All parcels must be inspected; bring them open and with wrapping materials to the nearest post office. In Athens parcels that weigh more than 2 kilograms (4½ pounds) must be brought to Mitropoleos 60 or to the Spiromiliou arcade off Voukourestiou Street.

MONEY MATTERS

On the whole, Greece offers good value compared with many other European countries. One exception is lodging in Athens, which has become very expensive because of the summer 2004 Olympics. Here are some sample prices: cup of coffee, €2.50–€3.80; bottle of beer, €2.10–€3; soft drink, €1.80; grilled cheese sandwich, €2.50; 1-km (½-mi) taxi ride, around €1.50. Admission to most museums and archaeological sites is free on Sunday from November through March.

CURRENCY The Greek monetary unit is the euro (€). Bills are in the denominations of 5, 10, 20, 50, 100, 200, and 500 euros; coins in 1, 2, 5, 10, 20, and 50 euro cents, and 1 and 2 euros. At press time, the exchange rate was about Australian $1.73, British £0.70, Canadian $1.58, New Zealand $1.95, South African R8.65 (rands), and U.S. $1.12 to the euro. Daily exchange rates are prominently displayed in banks.

SHOPPING

Prices in large stores are fixed. Bargaining may take place in small, owner-managed souvenir and handicrafts shops and in antiques shops. In flea markets bargaining is expected. You are required to have an export permit (not normally given if the piece is of any value) for antiques and Byzantine icons, but reproductions can be bought fairly cheaply, although even these require a certificate saying they are copies.

TAXES

VALUE-ADDED TAX (V.A.T.) Value-added tax, 4% for books and about 18% (13% on the Aegean Islands) for almost everything else, called FPA (pronounced fee-pee-ah) by Greeks, is included in the cost of most consumer goods and services, except groceries. If you are a citizen from a non-EU country, you may get a V.A.T. refund on products worth €118 or more (including V.A.T.) bought in Greece from licensed stores, which usually display the Tax-Free Shopping sticker. Ask the shop to complete a refund form called a Tax-Free Check, which Greek customs will stamp after viewing the item to make sure you are exporting it. Send the refund form back to the shop for repayment by check or credit card.

TELEPHONES

COUNTRY & AREA CODES The country code for Greece is 30. For Athens, or dialing within Athens, the area code is 210, and this must be added before local as well as long-distance calls. Whether you are dialing Greece from outside the country or making local or regional calls within Greece, you must dial the full 10-digit number, including the area code (which may be three, four, or five numbers).

DIRECTORY & OPERATOR ASSISTANCE For directory information, dial 131; many of the operators speak English. Many places are listed under the owner's name, not the official name, so you must know the name of the establishment's owner, even if it is a taverna or shop. For operator-assisted calls and international directory information in English, dial 161.

INTERNATIONAL CALLS Phone cards worth €3, €6, €12, or €24 can be purchased at kiosks, convenience stores, or the local OTE (Hellenic Telecommunications Organization) office, and are the easiest way to make calls from anywhere in Greece. Kiosks frequently have metered phones for long-distance calls, but their location is often on a bustling street corner. For more privacy, go to the local OTE office. There is a three-minute minimum charge for operator-assisted station-to-station and person-to-person connections. Numbers for major companies with long-distance operator assistance are listed below.
🄵 Access Codes **AT&T** ☎ 00/800-1311. **Worldphone (MCI)** ☎ 00/800-1211. **Sprint** ☎ 00/800-1411.

LOCAL CALLS Many kiosks have pay telephones for local calls only. You pay the kiosk owner €0.10 per call after you've finished, unless it was a lengthy call, in which case you pay for the number of units you racked up. It's easier to buy a phone card from an OTE office, kiosks, or convenience shops and use it at card phones. The price drops about 50% for long-distance calls daily 10 PM–8 AM; for local calls, Sundays 10 PM–8 AM.

TIPPING

By law a service charge is figured into the price of a meal, but unless the waiter was rude or inept, it is customary to leave an additional 8%–10%. During the Christmas and Greek Easter holiday periods, restaurants add an obligatory 18% holiday bonus to your bill for the waiters. Tip porters €0.60 per bag; in better hotels maids get about €1 per day. Tip the concierge €1–€3 for help received. For taxi drivers Greeks usually round off the fare to the nearest euro. Hairdressers receive 10%. In legitimate theaters tip ushers €0.50; at the cinema give €0.50 if you take a program. On cruises, cabin and dining-room stewards get about €2 per day; guides receive about the same.

TRAIN TRAVEL

The main railway line runs north from Athens, dividing into three lines at Thessaloniki. The main line continues to Skopje and Belgrade, a second line goes east to the Turkish border and Istanbul, and a third line heads northeast to Sofia, Bucharest, and Budapest. The Peloponnese in the south is served by a narrow-gauge line dividing at Corinth into the Tripoli–Kalamata section and the Patras–Kalamata section. Call the number below for general information and timetables daily 7 AM–9 PM.

FARES & SCHEDULES   🚆 **Train information** ☎ 210/529–7777 for general information; 145 for recorded departure timetable, in Greek, of trains within Greece; 147 for a Greek recording of departure times for trains to Europe.

VISITOR INFORMATION

Tourist police, at most popular tourist sites, can answer questions in English about transportation, steer you to an open pharmacy or doctor, and locate phone numbers of hotels, rooms, and restaurants. There are Greek National Tourist Organization (EOT) offices throughout the country. Often more helpful are municipal tourism offices.

WHEN TO GO

May, June, September, and October are the most temperate and least-crowded months to visit Greece. The heat can be unpleasant in late June through August, especially in Athens, although the situation is somewhat alleviated when millions leave the city in August, taking their overheated cars with them. On the islands a brisk northwesterly wind, the *meltemi*, can make life more comfortable. The winter months tend to be cold virtually everywhere but with many sunny days.

CLIMATE   The following are the average daily maximum and minimum temperatures for Athens.

Jan.	55F	13C	May	77F	25C	Sept.	84F	29C
	44	6		61	16		67	19
Feb.	57F	14C	June	86F	30C	Oct.	75F	24C
	44	6		68	20		60	16
Mar.	60F	16C	July	92F	33C	Nov.	66F	19C
	46	8		73	23		53	12
Apr.	68F	20C	Aug.	92F	33C	Dec.	58F	15C
	52	11		73	23		47	8

ATHENS

Athens is the point to which all roads lead in Greece and from which many tours take off if for no reason other than that the greatest sight of "the glory that was Greece" is here: the Parthenon and other legendary buildings of the Acropolis. But this perpetual shrine of Western civilization, set high on a rocky bluff, dominates and overlooks a 21st-century boomtown.

In 1834, when it became the capital of modern Greece, Athens had a population of fewer than 10,000. Now it houses more than a third of the entire Greek population—around 4.6 million. A modern concrete city has engulfed the old village and spreads for 388 square km (244 square mi), covering all the surrounding plain from the sea to the encircling mountains. Athens has long had problems with air pollution, traffic congestion, and inefficient bureaucracy, but preparations for the 2004 summer Olympic Games have brought sweeping changes: improved infrastructure, expanded and more environmentally friendly public transportation, and much-needed renovations to many sights and museums.

The modern city's sprawling concrete has failed to overwhelm the astonishing reminders of the legendary classical metropolis. The vibrant mix of ancient and new, and East and West, continues to make Athens one of the most exciting cities in Europe. Although Athens covers a huge area, the major landmarks of the ancient Greek, Roman, and Byzantine periods are close to the modern center. You can stroll from the Acropolis to the other sites, taking time to browse in shops and relax in cafés and tavernas along the way. The Acropolis and Filopappou, two craggy hills sitting side by side; the ancient and Roman agoras (marketplaces); and Kerameikos, the first cemetery, form the core of ancient and Roman Athens.

Exploring Athens

Numbers in the margin correspond to points of interest on the Athens map.

The central district of modern Athens is small, stretching from the Acropolis to Mt. Lycabettus, with its small white church on top. The layout is simple: three parallel streets (Stadiou, Panepistimiou, and Akademias) link two main squares (Syntagma and Omonia). Try to wander off this beaten tourist track: seeing the Athenian butchers in the central market near Monastiraki sleeping on their cold marble slabs during the heat of the afternoon siesta may give you more of a feel for the city than looking at hundreds of fallen pillars. In summer, closing times often depend on each site's available personnel, but throughout the year, arrive at least 45 minutes before the official closing time to ensure that you can buy a ticket. Flash photography is forbidden in museums.

7 **Agios Eleftherios** (St. Eleftherios). What's fascinating about the city's former cathedral is that the walls of this 12th-century Byzantine church incorporate reliefs—fanciful figures and zodiac signs—from buildings that date back to the classical period. The church is also known as Little Mitropolis and Panagia Gorgoepikoos (Virgin Who Answers Prayers Quickly), based on its 13th-century icon, said to perform miracles. ⊠ *Pl. Mitropolis* ☎ *No phone* ⊕ *www.culture.gr* ☉ *Daily 8–1; hrs depend on services.*

1 **Akropolis** (Acropolis). Even in its bleached and silent state, the Parthenon—the great temple that crowns the Acropolis, the tablelike hill that represented the "upper city" of ancient Athens—has the power to stir the heart as few other ancient relics can. Whether bathed in the sunlight of the south, or sublimely swathed in moonglow, it endures as a vital monument of ageless intellect. Well, not completely ageless. The Athenians built this complex during the 5th century BC to honor the goddess Athena, patron of the city. The first ruins you'll see are the **Propylaia,** the monumental gateway that led worshipers from the temporal world into the spiritual world of the sanctuary; now only the columns of Pentelic marble and a fragment of stone ceiling remain. Above, to the right,

Fodor'sChoice
★

Athens
(Athina)

VATHI

Tossitsa

Liossion

Aharnon

Aristoteleous

Marni

Stournara

Mager

Mezonos

Vathis
Square

Kapodistriou

Solomou

Favierou

Marni

Halkokondili

Kapodistriou

Victoros Ougo

Veranzerou

Kaningos
Square

Karaiskaki
Square

Karolou

Agiou Konstantinou

Menandrou

Sokratous

3 Septemvriou

28 Oktovriou (Patission)

Kaningos

Meg. Alexandrou

Deligiorgi

Zinonous

Omonia
Square

Panepistimiou (Venizelou)

Akademias

Kolonou

Keramikou

P. Tsaldari

Likourgou

Kotzia
Square

Stadiou

Korai

Kolokynthou

Pireos

Sokratous

Athinas

Klafthmonos
Sq.

Agisilaou

Sofokleous

Armodiou

Aristidou

Dragatsaniou

Paparigopoulou

Ch. Lada

Millerou

Eleftherias
Square
(Koumoundourou)

Epikourou

Menandrou

Aristogitonos

Evripidou

Aiolou

Miltiadou

Praxitelous

KERAMEIKOS

Psaromilingou

Dipilou

Aristofanous

Eschilou

Palados

Kolokotroni

Karageorgi
Servias

Ay. Assomaton

Sari

Leokoriou

Apostoli

Ireon
Square **6**

Miaouli

PSIRRI

Athinaidos

Perikleos

Ermou

Thissiou

5

Ermou

Monastiraki
Square

Mitropoleos

Vas. Georgio **i**

Sy

Ifestou

Adrianou

Ay. Filipou

Areos

Pandrossou

Pendeli

Mitropoleos

Nikis

Filellinon

4

Dexipou

Adrianou

7

Apollonos

Voulis

Tholos

Roman
Agora

Pelopida

Nikodimou

PLAKA

Polignotou

Panos

Kiristou

Schaliou

Adrianou

Kidathineon

Apostolos Pavlou

3

Tholou

Pritaniou

Lysiou

Tripodon

Thespidos

8

Theorias

1

ANAFIOTIKA

Vasilissis Amalias

Acropolis

2

Epimenidou

Goura

Pitakou

Vasiliss

9

10

Lysikratous

12

Vironos

Dionyssiou Areopagitou

13

Rovertou Galli

Kalisperi

11

0 220 yards

0 200 meters

stands the graceful **Naos Athenas Nikis,** or **Apterou Nikis** (Wingless Victory). The temple was mistakenly called the latter because common tradition often confused Athena with the winged goddess Nike. The elegant and architecturally complex **Erechtheion,** most sacred of the shrines of the Acropolis (later turned into a harem by the Turks), has dull, heavy copies of the caryatids (draped maidens) supporting the roof. The **Acropolis Museum** houses five of the six originals, their faces much damaged by acid rain. The sixth is in the British Museum in London.

The **Parthenonas** (Parthenon) dominates the Acropolis and indeed the Athens skyline. Designed by Ictinus, with Pheidias as master sculptor, it was completed in 438 BC and is the most architecturally sophisticated temple of that period. Even with hordes of people wandering around the ruins, it still inspires wonder. The architectural decorations were originally painted vivid red and blue, and the roof was of marble tiles. Time and neglect have given the marble pillars their golden-white shine, and the beauty of the building is all the more stark and striking. The British Museum in London houses the largest remaining part of the original 532-foot frieze (the Elgin Marbles), but Greece has long campaigned for its return. The building has 17 fluted columns along each side and eight at the ends; these were cleverly made to lean slightly inward and to bulge, counterbalancing the natural optical distortion. The Parthenon was made into a brothel by the Romans, a church by the Christians, and a mosque by the Turks. The Turks also stored gunpowder in the Propylaia. When the Propylaia was hit by a Venetian bombardment in 1687, 28 columns of the Parthenon were blown out and a fire raged for two days, leaving the temple in its present condition. Piece by piece, the entire Parthenon complex is now undergoing conservation, as part of an ambitious rescue plan launched with international support in 1983 by Greek architects; the completion date is around 2010. An elevator being added to the north side of the Acropolis for the summer 2004 Olympics should help people with mobility concerns. ⊠ *Top of Dionyssiou Areopagitou* ☎ *210/321–4172 or 210/321–0219* ⊕ *www.culture.gr* ✉ *€12 includes admission to the Theatro Dionyssou, Archaia Agora, Olimbion, Roman Agora, and Kerameikos* ☉ *Apr.–Dec., daily 8–sunset; Jan.–Mar., daily 8:30–2:30.*

❹ **Archaia Agora** (Ancient Agora). Now a sprawling confusion of stones, slabs, and foundations, this was the civic center and focal point of community life in ancient Athens, where Socrates met with his students while merchants haggled over the price of olive oil. It is dominated by the best-preserved Doric temple in Greece, the **Hephaisteion,** built during the 5th century BC. Nearby, the Stoa Attalou (Stoa of Attalos II), reconstructed in the mid-1950s by the American School of Classical Studies in Athens, houses the **Museo tis Agoras** (Museum of Agora Excavations). The museum focuses on everyday life in ancient Athens, its objects ranging from a child's terra-cotta chamber pot to the shards (*ostraka,* from which the word "ostracism" is derived) used in secret ballots to recommend the banishment of Themistocles and other powerful citizens. ⊠ *Three entrances: from Monastiraki, on Adrianou; from Thission, on Apostolos Pavlou; from the Acropolis, on descent along Ag. Apostoli* ☎ *210/321–0185* ⊕ *www.culture.gr* ☉ *Mar.–Dec., daily 8–5; Jan. and Feb., daily 8–3.*

❸ **Areios Pagos** (Areopagus). From this rocky outcrop, ancient Athens's supreme court, you can view the Propylaia, the Agora, and the modern city. Legend claims it was here that Orestes was tried for the murder of his mother, and much later St. Paul delivered his Sermon to the Unknown God. It was so moving that a senator named Dionysius converted to Christianity and became the first bishop of Athens. ⊠ *Opposite Acropolis entrance* ☉ *Daily 24 hrs.*

★ ⑲ **Benaki Museum.** Established in 1926 by an illustrious Athenian family, this museum was one of the first to place emphasis on Greece's later heritage at a time when many archaeologists were destroying Byzantine artifacts to access ancient objects. The collection (more than 20,000 items are on display in 36 rooms—and that's only a sample of the holdings) moves chronologically from the ground floor upward, from prehistory to the formation of the modern Greek state. You might see anything from a 5,000-year-old gold bowl to Lord Byron's pistols. Other parts of the collection—Islamic art, Chinese porcelain—will be displayed in branches throughout the city sometime after 2004. ⊠ *Koumbari 1, Kolonaki* ☎ *210/367–1000* ⊕ *www.benaki.gr* ☉ *Mon., Wed., Fri., and Sat. 9–5, Thurs. 9 AM–midnight, Sun. 9–3.*

⑳ **Ethniko Archaiologiko Museo** (National Archaeological Museum). The city's

FodorsChoice most important museum contains artistic highlights from every period

★ of ancient Greek civilization, from Neolithic to Roman times. Among the collection of antiquities are the sensational archaeological finds of Heinrich Schliemann in 1874 at Mycenae; 16th-century BC frescoes from the Akrotiri ruins on Santorini; and the 6½-foot-tall bronze sculpture *Poseidon,* an original work circa 470 BC that was found in the sea off Cape Artemision. The museum will close periodically through 2006 as it undergoes major expansion. ⊠ *28 Oktovriou (Patission) 44, 10-min walk north of Pl. Omonia* ☎ *210/821–7717* ⊕ *www.culture.gr* ☉ *Apr.–Oct., Mon. 12:30–7, Tues.–Fri. 8–7, weekends and holidays 8:30–3; Nov.–Mar., Mon. 11–5, Tues.–Fri. 8–5, weekends and holidays 8:30–3.*

⑯ **Goulandri Museo Kikladikis ke Ellinikis Archaias Technis** (Goulandris Mu-

FodorsChoice seum of Cycladic and Greek Ancient Art). This outstanding collection

★ spans 5,000 years and includes 350 objects from the Cycladic civilization (3000–2000 BC), with many of the marble figurines that fascinated such artists as Picasso and Modigliani. ⊠ *Neofitou Douka 4 or Irodotou 1* ☎ *210/722–8321 through 210/722–8323* ⊕ *www.cycladic.gr* ☉ *Mon. and Wed.–Sat. 10–4.*

⑨ **Irodion** (Odeon of Herod Atticus). Hauntingly beautiful, this 2nd-century AD theater was built Greek-style into the hillside but with typical Roman archways in its three-story stage building and barrel-vaulted entrances. The theater hosts Athens Festival performances from late June through September. ⊠ *Dionyssiou Areopagitou, across from Propylaia* ☎ *210/323–2771* ☉ *Open only to audiences during performances.*

★ ⑰ **Likavitos** (Mt. Lycabettus). Athens's highest hill borders Kolonaki, a residential quarter worth a visit if you enjoy window-shopping and people-watching. A steep **funicular** (⊠ Ploutarchou 1 at Aristippou ☎ 210/722–7065 ☉ Nov.–Apr., daily 9:15 AM–11:45 PM; May–Oct., daily 9:15 AM–12:45 AM; every 10 min) climbs to the summit, crowned by whitewashed Agios Giorgios chapel. The view from the top—pollution permitting—is the finest in Athens. ⊠ *Base: 15-min walk northeast of Syntagma.*

⑤ **Monastiraki.** The old Turkish bazaar area takes its name from Panayia Pantanassa Church, commonly called Monastiraki (Little Monastery). Near the church stands the Tzistarakis Mosque (1759), exemplifying the East-West paradox that characterizes Athens. The district's real draw is the Sunday flea market, centered on tiny Abyssinia Square and running along Ifestou and Kynetou streets, where Greeks bargain with wildly gesturing hands and dramatic facial expressions. Everything's for sale, from gramophone needles to old matchboxes, from nose rings to cool white linens. ⊠ *South of junction of Ermou and Athinas.*

★ ❷ **Museo Akropoleos** (Acropolis Museum). Tucked into one corner of the Acropolis, this institution displays superb sculptures, including the caryatids from the Erechtheion and a collection of colored *korai* (statues of women dedicated to Athena, patron of the ancient city). In 2004, part of the collection will move to the Neo Museo Akropoleos, at the foot of the Acropolis. The museums will operate concurrently until the new museum is completed, around 2006, when the Acropolis Museum will cose. ⊠ *Southeastern corner of Acropolis* ☏ *210/323–6665* ⊕ *www.culture.gr* ☉ *Mid-Apr.–Oct., Mon. 11–6, Tues.–Sun. 8–6; Nov.–mid-Apr., Mon. 10:30–2:30, Tues.–Sun. 8:30–3.*

⓫ **Neo Museo Akropoleos** (New Acropolis Museum). This new, state-of-the-art museum will showcase the marvelous Acropolis sculptures. It will also send a political message: Greece wants Great Britain to return the Elgin Marbles, which once stood on the Parthenon and are now in the British Museum. Britain maintains that Greece cannot adequately display the marbles; Greece says the museum answers that criticism. The museum's centerpiece will be a display of the marbles in their original order, with gaps left to indicate the sculptures still in Britain, and a glass ceiling through which you will see the temple itself. The Parthenon room is scheduled to open in summer 2004, the rest of the museum by 2006, when it will replace the older Acropolis Museum. ⊠ *Dionyssiou Areopagitou and Makriyianni* ⊕ *www.culture.gr* ☞ *Contact Acropolis Museum for updates on opening information.*

⓮ **Panathinaiko Stadio** (Panathenaic Stadium). A reconstruction of the ancient Roman stadium in Athens, this gleaming-white marble structure built for the first modern Olympic Games in 1896 seats 50,000 spectators. During the 2004 Olympics, the stadium will host archery and the marathon finish. ⊠ *Near junction Vasileos Konstantinou and Vasilissis Olgas* ☏ *No phone* ⊕ *www.culture.gr* ☉ *Weekdays 8:30–1 and 3:30–7.*

⓬ **Pili tou Adrianou** (Hadrian's Arch). Built in AD 131–32 by Emperor Hadrian to show where classical Athens ended and his new city, Hadriaopolis, began, the Roman archway with Corinthian pilasters bears an inscription on the side facing the Acropolis that reads THIS IS ATHENS, THE ANCIENT CITY OF THESEUS. The side facing the Temple of Olympian Zeus proclaims THIS IS THE CITY OF HADRIAN AND NOT OF THESEUS. ⊠ *Junction Vasilissis Amalias and Dionyssiou Areopagitou* ⊕ *www.culture.gr.*

★ ❽ **Plaka.** Stretching east from the Agora, the Plaka, almost all that's left of 19th-century Athens, is a lovely quarter of neoclassical houses, medieval churches, and many intriguing smaller sights tucked among the winding walkways. The **Museo Ellinikis Laikis Technis** (Greek Folk Art Museum; ⊠ Kidathineon 17 ☏ 210/322–9031 ☉ Tues.–Sun. 10–2) has a rich collection of embroideries, carvings, and jewelry from as long ago as 1650. The **Roman Agora** (⊠ Pelopidas and Aiolou ☏ 210/324–5220 ⊕ www.culture.gr ☉ Tues.–Sun. 8:30–3), founded by Julius Caesar and Augustus, replaced the Archaia Agora in the 1st century AD. Its highlight is the octagonal Aerides (Tower of the Winds), a 1st-century BC water clock. A visit to the delightful **Museo Ellinikon Laikon Musikon Organon** (Museum of Greek Popular Musical Instruments; ⊠ Diogenous 1–3 ☏ 210/325–0198 ☉ Tues. and Thurs.–Sun. 10–2, Wed. noon–6), around the corner from the Roman Agora, is a crash course in the development of Greek music, with three floors of instruments and headphones so you can listen to all kinds of recorded sounds, from goatskin bagpipes to the Cretan lyra (a string instrument). The **Mnimeio Lysikratous** (Monument of Lysikrates; ⊠ Herefondos and Lysikratous) is one of the few surviving tripods on which stood the award for the producer of the best play in the Dionyssia festival. Above Plaka, at the northeastern base of the Acropolis, is **Anafiotika,** the closest thing you'll find to a village in Athens. Take time to wander among its whitewashed, bougainvillea-framed houses and tiny churches.

6 **Psirri.** During the day, little in this former industrial district indicates that at night this quarter becomes a whirl of clubs and restaurants, dotted with dramatically lighted churches and lively squares. Whether you want to dance on tabletops to live Greek music, sing along with a soulful accordion player, listen to salsa in a Cuban club, or just watch the hoi polloi go by as you snack on trendy or traditional mezedes, this is the place. ✉ *Off Ermou, centered on Iroon and Ag. Anargiron Sqs.*

13 **Stiles Olymbiou Dios** (Temple of Olympian Zeus). Begun during the 6th century BC, this temple, also known as the Olymbion, was larger than all other temples in Greece when it was finally completed 700 years later. It was destroyed during the invasion of the Goths in the 4th century; only a few towering, sun-bleached columns remain. ✉ *Vasilissis Olgas 1* ☎ *210/922–6330* ⊕ *www.culture.gr* ☉ *Daily 8–5.*

18 **Syntagma** (Constitution Square). At the top of the square stands the **Vouli** (Parliament), formerly the royal palace, completed in 1838 for the new monarchy. From the Parliament you can watch the changing of the Evzone honor guard at the **Mnimeio Agnostou Stratiotou** (Tomb of the Unknown Soldier), with its text from Pericles's funeral oration and a bas-relief of a dying soldier modeled after a sculpture on the Temple of Aphaia in Aegina. The most elaborate ceremony takes place on Sunday, when the sturdy young guards don their *foustanellas* (kilts) with 400 pleats, one for each year of the Ottoman occupation. The procession usually arrives in front of Parliament at 11:15 AM. Pop into the gleaming **Stathmo Syntagma** (Syntagma metro station: at upper end of the square) to take a look at artifacts from the subway excavations and a vast cross section of earth behind glass. The cross section shows finds in chronological layers, including a skeleton in its ancient grave, traces of the 4th-century BC road to Mesogeia, and a Turkish cistern. On the southern side of Syntagma is the lush **Ethnikos Kipos** (National Garden), its dense foliage, gazebos, and trellised walkways providing a quick escape from the center's bustle. For young visitors, there are two playgrounds, a miniature zoo, duck pond, and refreshments at the stone cottage café. ✉ *Corner of Vasilissis Sofias and Vasilissis Amalias.*

10 **Theatro Dionyssou** (Theater of Dionysus). In this theater dating from about 330 BC, the ancient dramas and comedies were performed in conjunction with bacchanalian feasts. The throne in the center was reserved for the priest of Dionysus: it is adorned with regal lions' paws, and reliefs of satyrs and griffins decorate the back. ✉ *Dionyssiou Areopagitou, opposite Mitsaion* ☎ *210/322–4625* ⊕ *www.culture.gr* ☉ *Apr.–Dec., daily 8–6; Jan.–Mar., daily 8:30–2:30.*

15 **Vizantino Museo** (Byzantine Museum). This museum, part of which occupies an 1848 mansion, has a unique collection of icons, mosaics, and tapestries. Sculptural fragments provide an excellent introduction to Byzantine architecture. The museum will be closed periodically through 2006 to accommodate extensive renovations. When it finally reopens, much of the collection will be displayed for the first time, including some magnificent illuminated manuscripts. You will also be able to explore the on-site archaeological dig of Aristotle's Lyceum. ✉ *Vasilissis Sofias 22* ☎ *210/723–2178* ⊕ *www.culture.gr* ☉ *Tues.–Sun. 8:30–3.*

Where to Eat

Search for places with at least a half dozen tables occupied by Athenians—they're discerning customers.

$$$$ ✕ **Boschetto.** The restaurant near the Hilton pampers diners with its park setting, expert maître d', and creative nouvelle Italian food. The specialty here is fresh pasta, such as the shrimp cannelloni or green gnocchi with Gorgonzola sauce. Entrées may include sea bass with a potato crust or grilled wild buffalo steak with a sauce of coffee, figs, and Mavrodaphne wine. The tables tend to be close together; reserve near the window or in the courtyard during the summer. ⊠ *Alsos Evangelismos* ☎ *210/721–0893 or 210/722–7324* ♨ *Reservations essential* ⊟ *AE, V* ☉ *Closed Sun. and 2 wks in Aug. No lunch Oct.–Apr.*

$$$$ ✕ **Spondi.** The ambience here is as cool and contemporary as the cuisine. Savor the artichoke terrine with duck confit or black ravioli with honeyed leek and shrimp. Interesting entrées may include a lamb tail so tender it falls from the bone, with couscous, raisins, and cumin; and chicken with foie gras, truffles, and asparagus in porcini sauce. In good weather, you can sit in the bougainvillea-draped courtyard. ⊠ *Pirronos 5, Pangrati* ☎ *210/756–4021 or 210/752–0658* ♨ *Reservations essential* ⊟ *AE, DC, MC, V* ☉ *No lunch.*

$$$$ ✕ **Vardis.** A meal at this French restaurant is worth the trip to the northern suburb of Kifissia. The clientele may be a little sedate, but the food dazzles. The chef is committed to the classics and to quality ingredients—he brings in sweetwater crayfish from Orhomenos and tracks down rare large shrimp from Thassos island. Especially good are the caramelized lamb cutlets with morel and porcini mushrooms, and salt-crusted duck filled with foie gras and served with a sherry sauce. ⊠ *Diligianni 66, in Pentelikon Hotel, Kefalari, Kifissia* ☎ *210/623–0650 through 210/623–0656* ♨ *Reservations essential* ⊟ *AE, DC, MC, V* ☉ *Closed Sun. and Aug. No lunch.*

$$$–$$$$ ✕ **Aristera-Dexia.** Chef Chrisanthos Karalomengos' forte is fusion—artful combinations such as a tower of *haloumi* (Cypriot cheese) and feta croquettes in a melon-mirin-chili sauce, or the Greek version of sushi, raw squid on a puree of eggplant with anchovies and trout roe. The restaurant is strikingly designed, with two large partitions dividing the large room (hence the name, which means "Left-Right") and a glass runway that let you peek into the city's best wine cellar. You should take a taxi to this gritty neighborhood on the edge of the newly trendy Gazi cultural district. ⊠ *Andrónikou 3, Rouf* ☎ *210/342–2380* ♨ *Reservations essential* ⊟ *AE, MC, V* ☉ *Closed Sun. and Aug. No lunch.*

Fodor'sChoice ★

$$$–$$$$ ✕ **To Varoulko.** Chef Lefteris Lazarou is constantly trying to outdo himself, with magnificent results. You can sample such appetizers as crab salad studded with mango and grapes, with bits of leek to cut the sweetness; or fresh mullet roe laced with honey and accompanied by cinnamony cauliflower puree. This restaurant is famous for monkfish, but the many other seafood dishes include cockles steamed in Limnos sweet wine, and lobster with wild rice, celery, and champagne sauce. ⊠ *Deligeorgi 14, Piraeus* ☎ *210/411–2043 or 210/422–1283* ♨ *Reservations essential* ⊟ *AE, DC, MC, V* ☉ *Closed Sun. and Aug. No lunch.*

Fodor'sChoice ★

$$$ ✕ **Daphne's.** It may be a little ostentatious to display a laminated catalog of celebrity diners at the entrance, but Daphne's does have reason to boast. Athenians as well as luminaries from Hillary Clinton to Luciano Pavarotti have long cherished the restaurant's authentic but sophisticated take on regional Greek classics. Try the tender rabbit stewed in sweet Mavrodaphne wine, shrimp dressed in crunchy almond flakes, or pork braised with quince. In summer, diners can move from the frescoed 1830s mansion to a flower-filled courtyard. ✉ *Lysikratous 4, Plaka* ☎ *210/322–7971* ⚇ *Reservations essential* ▤ *AE, MC, V.*

$$–$$$ ✗ **Azul.** The space may be a bit cramped, but the Mediterranean food is superb. Start with salmon and trout in pastry with champagne sauce. The spaghetti *à la nona* (godmother's) with chamomile, Gorgonzola, and bacon is an unparalleled combination. Other memorable dishes are beef fillet with raisins and cedar needles, and chicken prepared with lemon leaves. In summer, Azul sets up tables outside. ✉ *Haritos 43, Kolonaki* ☎ *210/725–3817* ⚇ *Reservations essential* ▤ *AE, DC, MC, V* ⊙ *Closed last 2 wks in Aug. and Sun. Oct.–Apr. No lunch.*

$$–$$$ ✗ **Mamacas.** This was the first in a wave of "modern" tavernas now springing up all over Athens, and it helped transform the former industrial district of Gazi into one of the hippest parts of town. The cool pastel linen interior is a refreshing visual counterpart to the surrounding warehouses. Amid all this modernity, the hearty, vibrant flavors of traditional taverna food remain, although they have been tweaked with contemporary sensibility in dishes such as pork with prunes, black-eyed pea salad, and cuttlefish with spinach. ✉ *Persofonis 41, Gazi* ☎ *210/346–4984* ▤ *MC, V* ⊙ *Closed Mon.*

$$–$$$ ✗ **Tade Efi Anna.** This stylish restaurant near the end of the Ermou pedestrian zone serves regional Greek cuisine with a modern touch. The space itself is trendy, with funky lighting fixtures, loud music, and an ultracool clientele. Try the *pita Kaisarias* (the spicy, cured meat called *pastourmas* with tomato and kasseri cheese in crisp phyllo), or *melitzanes amigdalou* (sliced eggplant layered with tomatoes and cheese with a thick topping of crushed almonds). ✉ *Ermou 72, Monastiraki* ☎ *210/321–3652* ▤ *V* ⊙ *Closed Mon.*

$$ ✗ **Kollias.** Friendly owner Tassos Kollias creates his own dishes, from the humble to the aristocratic: sea urchin salad or lobster with lemon, balsamic vinegar, and a shot of honey. He's known for bringing in the best-quality catch, whether mullet from Messolonghi or oysters culled by Kalymnos sponge divers, and his prices are usually 25% lower than most fish tavernas. Call for directions—even locals get lost trying to find this obscure street in the working-class quarter of Piraeus. ✉ *Stratigou Plastira 3, near junction of Dramas and Kalokairinou, Tabouria* ☎ *210/461–9150 or 210/462–9620* ⚇ *Reservations essential* ▤ *AE, DC, MC, V* ⊙ *No lunch Mon.–Sat., no dinner Sun.*

$–$$ ✗ **Vlassis.** Relying on recipes from Thrace, Roumeli, Thessaly, and the islands, the chefs whip up Greek home cooking in generous portions. Musts are the peppery cheese dip called *tirokafteri*, pastitsio (made here with bits of lamb liver), *lahanodolmades* (cabbage leaves stuffed with minced meat), goat with oil and oregano, and octopus *stifado* (stew), tender and sweet with lots of onions. ✉ *Paster 8, Platia Mavili (near American embassy)* ☎ *210/646–3060* ⚇ *Reservations essential* ▤ *No credit cards* ⊙ *Closed Aug.–mid-Sept. No dinner Sun.*

Fodor'sChoice ★

$ ✗ **Margaro.** Near Piraeus, next to the Naval Academy, this popular, no-nonsense fish taverna serves just four items, along with excellent barrel wine: fried crayfish, fried red mullet, fried *marida* (a small white fish), and huge Greek salads. If this place is crowded, you may be asked to go into the kitchen and prepare your own salad. Tables on the terrace have a view of the port. Try to arrive between 6 and 8 PM, before Greeks eat dinner. ✉ *Hatzikyriakou 126, Piraeus* ☎ *210/451–4226* ⚇ *Reservations not accepted* ▤ *No credit cards* ⊙ *Closed 15 days at Greek Easter. No dinner Sun.*

★ **$** ✗ **O Platanos.** One of Plaka's oldest yet least touristy tavernas occupies a picturesque courtyard. The waiters are fast and the place is packed with Greeks. Don't miss the oven-baked potatoes, savory lamb fricassee, green beans in olive oil, and exceptionally cheap but delicious barrel retsina. ✉ *Diogenous 4, Plaka* ☎ *210/322–0666* ▤ *No credit cards* ⊗ *Closed Sun.*

$ ✕ **Sigalas–Bairaktaris.** Run by the same family for more than a century, this is one of the best places to eat in Monastiraki. After admiring the painted wine barrels and black-and-white stills of Greek film stars, go to the window case to view the day's magirefta—beef *kokkinisto* (stew with red sauce), spicy meat patties seasoned with clove—or sample the gyro platter. Appetizers include tiny cheese pies with sesame seeds and fried zucchini with a garlicky dip. ✉ *Pl. Monastiraki 2, Monastiraki* ☎ *210/321–3036* ▤ *AE, MC, V.*

Where to Stay

It's always advisable to reserve a room. Hotels are clustered around the center of town and along the seacoast. Modern hotels are more likely to be air-conditioned and to have double-glazed windows; the center of Athens can be so noisy that it's hard to sleep. In the year before the summer 2004 Olympics, prices have risen considerably, and they may double for the games themselves (and decline, to some degree, after the event). One benefit of the Olympics has been stylish renovations of existing hotels and the building of some new ones, including boutique hotels.

$$$$ ▦ **Andromeda Athens Hotel.** On a quiet street near the U.S. Embassy and
FodorsChoice the city's concert hall, this small luxury hotel caters to business travel-
★ ers, but all guests relish the meticulous service and sumptuous furnish-ings. During 2003, each room was renovated and refurnished according to a different theme, such as art deco, Asian, and African. All rooms have business essentials, as well as wide-screen TVs and DVD players. A new spa and fitness center are also being built. The hotel operates a property across the street with a security system and 12 stylish executive suites (one- and two-room apartments). ✉ *Timoleondos Vassou 22, Pl. Mavili, 11521* ☎ *210/641–5000* ▤ *210/646–6361* ⊕ *www.andromedaathens.gr* ⇲ *21 rooms, 8 suites, 1 penthouse* ♧ *Restaurant* ▤ *AE, DC, MC, V* ⊚ *BP.*

$$$$ ▦ **Athens Hilton.** A two-year, head-to-toe renovation completed in 2003 gave this hotel a new look that reflects the trend sweeping most of Athens's high-end properties as they prepare to face the world for the summer 2004 Olympics: all is modern, clean-lined, and uncluttered. The once-traditional lobby is a vast expanse of white marble with sleek benches. Rooms are fitted out in light wood, brushed metal, etched glass, and crisp white duvets. Facilities include an executive check-in lounge and huge conference rooms, along with a spa and the biggest pool in Athens. ✉ *Vasilissis Sofias 46, 11528* ☎ *210/728–1000, 210/728–1100 reservations* ▤ *210/333–0160* ⊕ *www.athens.hilton.com* ⇲ *498 rooms, 19 suites* ♧ *4 restaurants, pool, wading pool* ▤ *AE, DC, MC, V.*

★ $$$$ ▦ **Divani Apollon Palace.** For those who need a break from city bustle, this seaside resort is the perfect solution. Casual but sophisticated, it has excellent service and sparkling facilities. Spend an hour on the tennis court, dip into the Aegean across the street, or take the hotel shuttle to Glyfada for some serious shopping (the van continues on to downtown Athens). The airy, white-and-yellow rooms all have balconies with a sea view. Best, though, are the hotel's gleaming public spaces, the outdoor pool with hydromassage, and the Pelagos Bar with its leather sofas. ✉ *Ag. Nikolaou 10 and Iliou, Vouliagmeni, 16671* ☎ *210/891–1100* ▤ *210/ 965–8010* ⊕ *www.divaniapollon.gr* ⇲ *286 rooms, 7 suites* ♧ *2 restaurants, 2 pools (1 indoor), wading pool* ▤ *AE, DC, MC, V* ⊚ *BP.*

★ $$$$ ▦ **Grande Bretagne.** Built in 1842, the G. B. is an Athens landmark, with a guest list of more than 150 years' worth of royals, rock stars, and heads of state testifying to its colorful history. A 2003 renovation recaptured the hotel's original grandeur, restoring antiques, oil paintings, and sumptuous hand-carved details, and adding a spa, pools, and every possible modern convenience, including rooms with fax machines, photocopiers, DVD players, and Bose stereos. The only complaint is that many rooms, albeit luxuriously fitted out, are rather small. ⊠ *Vasileos Georgiou A' 1, Pl. Syntagma, 10564* ☎ *01/333–0000; 01/331–5555 through 01/331– 5559 reservations* 🖷 *01/322–8034; 01/322–2261; 01/333–0910 reservations* ⊕ *www.grandebretagne.gr* ⤳ *290 rooms, 37 suites* ⌂ *3 restaurants, 2 pools* ⊟ *AE, DC, MC, V.*

$$$$ 🖩 **Kefalari Suites.** A turn-of-the-20th-century building among the neoclassical mansions and tree-lined boulevards of the suburb of Kifissia contains imaginative theme suites with names such as Malmaison and Jaipur. The suites include kitchenettes with utensils, a modem connection, and verandas or balconies; the sundeck has a whirlpool tub. A deluxe Continental breakfast (cheese, cold cuts, cereal, yogurt, cake) is included in the room rate. ⊠ *Pentelis 1 and Kolokotroni, Kifissia, 14562* ☎ *210/623–3333* 🖷 *210/623–3330* ⊕ *www.kefalarisuites.gr* ⤳ *13 suites* ⊟ *AE, DC, MC, V* �PO *CP.*

$$$$ 🖩 **N. J. V. Athens Plaza.** The fresh, spacious rooms at this hotel right in the center of Syntagma Square are equipped with top-of-the-line amenities, including large marble bathrooms with phone extensions. Double-glazed windows and air-conditioning keep rooms peaceful and quiet. The suites on the eighth and ninth floors have breathtaking Acropolis views, and interiors decked out with designer furnishings. ⊠ *Vasileos Georgiou A' 2, Pl. Syntagma, 10564* ☎ *210/335–2400* 🖷 *210/323–5856* ⊕ *www.grecotel.gr* ⤳ *182 rooms, 15 suites* ⌂ *Restaurant* ⊟ *AE, DC, MC, V.*

$$$ 🖩 **Electra Palace.** Long the nicest hotel in Plaka, the Electra Palace has cozy rooms, a roof garden with a pool and whirlpool tub, stunning Acropolis views, and barbecues in summer; the sumptuous buffet breakfasts are among the best in the city. A head-to-toe renovation in 2003 has added an indoor pool, gym, and sauna, and rooms are being completely redecorated with new furniture. The owners are also expanding into the building next door, which they expect will add about 50 new rooms sometime in 2004. ⊠ *Nikodimou 18, Plaka, 10557* ☎ *210/337–0000* 🖷 *210/ 324–1875* ⤳ *106 rooms, 5 suites* ⌂ *Restaurant, 2 pools (1 indoor), bar* ⊟ *AE, DC, MC, V* �PO *BP.*

$$ 🖩 **Acropolis View Hotel.** Major sights are just a stone's throw away from this hotel tucked into a quiet neighborhood below the Acropolis. About half of the agreeable rooms with balconies have Parthenon views. There is a roof garden, and staff members in the homey lobby are efficient. ⊠ *Webster 10, Acropolis, 11742* ☎ *210/921–7303, 210/921–7304, or 210/921–7305* 🖷 *210/923–0705* ⊕ *www.acropolisview.gr* ⤳ *32 rooms* ⊟ *DC, MC, V* �PO *BP.*

$$ 🖩 **Art Gallery Pension.** On a side street not far from the Acropolis, this friendly, handsome house has an old-fashioned look, with family paintings on the muted white walls, comfortable beds, hardwood floors, and ceiling fans. Many rooms have balconies with views of Filopappou or the Acropolis. ⊠ *Erecthiou 5, Koukaki, 11742* ☎ *210/923–8376 or 210/ 923–1933* 🖷 *210/923–3025* ✑ *ecotec@otenet.gr* ⤳ *21 rooms, 2 suites* ⊟ *No credit cards* ☉ *Closed Nov.–Feb.*

$$ 🖩 **Athens Cypria Hotel.** A cool oasis in the city center, this hotel is a few minutes from Syntagma Square, offering a reasonably priced alternative for those who want convenience and comfort. Enter the vaguely art deco lobby from the quiet street to find simple guest rooms, done in shades of blue and furnished with basic amenities. Some of the upper floors open out onto a balcony; those on the sixth floor have Acropolis views. ⊠ *Diomias 5, Syntagma, 10557* ☎ *210/323–8034 through 210/323–8038* 🖷 *210/324–8792* 🗩 *71 rooms* ⚇ *Bar* 🖃 *AE, V* ❶❶ *BP.*

$$ 🖬 **Hotel Achilleas.** This modern, family-owned hotel just a few minutes from Syntagma has spacious, pleasant rooms with minibars, safes, and air-conditioning, unusual features in this category. Breakfast is served in an interior courtyard filled with jungly plants and marble-top blue tables. ⊠ *Lekka 21, Syntagma, 10562* ☎ *210/322–5826, 210/322–8531, or 210/323–3197* 🖷 *210/322–2412* ⊕ *www.tourhotel.gr/achilleas* 🗩 *36 rooms* 🖃 *AE, DC, MC, V* ❶❶ *CP.*

$$ 🖬 **Plaka Hotel.** Close to the ancient sights and the Monastiraki Square metro, this hotel has a roof garden overlooking the Plaka district's rooftops to the Parthenon. Double-glazed windows cut down the noise; the highest floors are the quietest. All rooms have TV and are simply furnished; those in back from the fifth floor up have the best Acropolis views. ⊠ *Kapnikareas 7 and Mitropoleos, Plaka, 10556* ☎ *210/322–2096 through 210/322–2098* 🖷 *210/322–2412* ⊕ *www.plakahotel.gr* 🗩 *67 rooms* 🖃 *AE, DC, MC, V* ❶❶ *CP.*

$–$$ 🖬 **Acropolis House.** The artists and academics who frequent this pension in a 19th-century Plaka residence appreciate its large rooms, original frescoes, and genteel owners. All rooms have private bathrooms, though about 10 have their bath immediately outside in the hallway. Rooms with air-conditioning cost extra. ⊠ *Kodrou 6–8, Plaka, 10558* ☎ *210/322–2344 or 210/322–6241* 🖷 *210/324–4143* 🗩 *20 rooms* 🖃 *V* ❶❶ *CP.*

$ 🖬 **Cecil Hotel.** A gracefully restored 1920s mansion between Monastiraki and the Central Market holds this friendly hotel with polished wood floors, spacious, high-ceilinged rooms, and cozy furnishings. All rooms have air-conditioning, and a roof garden is planned for summer 2004. ⊠ *Athinas 39, Monastiraki, 10554* ☎ *210/321–7079* 🖷 *210/321–8005* ⊕ *www.cecil-hotel.com* 🗩 *39 rooms* 🖃 *MC, V* ❶❶ *CP.*

Nightlife & the Arts

The English-language newspapers *Athens News* and *Kathemerini* (inserted in the *International Herald Tribune*) list current performances, gallery openings, and films. The magazines *Odyssey* and *Inside Out*, distributed at some hotels and available at English-language bookstores and kiosks, carry extensive information on culture and entertainment in the capital.

The Arts

The **Athens Festival** (box office ⊠ Panepistimiou 39 ☎ 210/928–2900 ⊕ www.greekfestival.gr) runs from late June through September with concerts, opera, ballet, folk dancing, and drama. Performances are in various locations, including the theater of Herod Atticus below the Acropolis and Mt. Lycabettus. Tickets range in price from €20 to €120 and are available two weeks before the performance.

Technopolis (⊠ Pireos 100, Gazi ☎ 210/346–0981), a stunningly converted foundry in a former industrial neighborhood now filled with chic galleries and restaurants, is a multipurpose arts and performance venue for everything from photography exhibits to indie music concerts.

CONCERTS Greek and international orchestras perform September through June at the **Megaron Athens Concert Hall** (⊠ Vasilissis Sofias and Kokkali ☎ 210/728–2333 through 210/728–2337 🖷 210/728–2300 ⊕ www.megaron.gr). Prices range from €18 to €90. Inexpensive and often free classical concerts are held November through May at the **Philippos Nakas Con-**

servatory (✉ Ippokratous 41 ☎ 210/363–4000 🖷 210/360–2827). Tickets cost €10 to €20.

DANCE The acclaimed **Dora Stratou Troupe** (✉ Theater, Filopappou Hill ☎ 210/324–4395 troupe's offices 🖷 210/324–6921 🌐 www.grdance.org) performs authentic Greek and Cypriot folk dances. Tickets cost €13 and are available outside the theater. Performances are from the end of May to the end of September, Tuesday–Saturday at 9:30 PM and Sunday at 8:30.

FILM Almost all Athens cinemas now show foreign films; for listings, consult the *Athens News* and the *Kathemerini* insert in the *International Herald Tribune*. Tickets run about €7 to €10. In summer, films are shown in open-air cinemas.

Nightlife

Athens has an active nightlife; most bars and clubs stay open until at least 3 AM. Drinks are rather steep (about €6–€10) but generous. Often there is a surcharge on weekends at the most popular clubs, which also have bouncers. Few clubs take credit cards for drinks. In summer most major downtown clubs move to the seaside, and some open up in new winter spaces each season. Ask your hotel for recommendations and check ahead for summer closings. For a uniquely Greek evening, visit a club featuring *rembetika* music, a type of blues, or the popular *bouzoukia* (clubs with live bouzouki music). In the larger bouzouki venues, there is usually a per-person minimum or an overpriced, second-rate prix-fixe menu; a bottle of whiskey costs about €120.

BARS & CLUBS **Bedlam** (✉ Zappio Gardens, Syntagma ☎ 210/336–9340), in lush Zappio Gardens, with tables placed among trees hung with crystals, is a glamorous escape from the city within the city. **Central** (✉ Pl. Kolonaki 14, Kolonaki ☎ 210/724–5938), open day and night, is the place to see all of Athens's beautiful people enjoying cocktails and sushi in the cool, creamy interior. **Exo** (✉ Markou Mousourou 1, Mets ☎ 210/923–5818), a downtown summer favorite, attracts a trendy, mixed-age crowd with its roof garden and spectacular Acropolis views. **Folie** (✉ Eslin 4, Ambelokipi ☎ 210/646–9852) has a congenial crowd of all ages dancing to reggae, Latin, funk, and ethnic music. **Island** (✉ Limanakia Vouliagmenis, Varkiza ☎ 210/965–3563), the summer incarnation of Central, is dreamily decked out in gauzy linens; it overlooks the Aegean. **Mommy** (✉ Delfon 4, Kolonaki ☎ 210/361–9682), a funky bar-restaurant popular with lifestyle magazine writers, has pop-art sofas, Chinese finger food, and frequent theme nights. **Plus Soda** (✉ Ermou 161, Thissio ☎ 210/345–6187), the dance temple of Athens, hires Europe's top DJs; it moves to a different spot each summer.

BOUZOUKIA **Apollon** (✉ Syngrou 259, Nea Smyrni ☎ 210/942–7580 through 210/942–7583) is one of Athens's most popular venues, showcasing singers such as dueling divas Anna Vissi and Kaiti Garbi. It's closed Monday and Tuesday. **Rex** (✉ Panepistimiou 48, Syntagma ☎ 210/381–4591) is an over-the-top laser-light show and plate-smashing extravaganza, with performances by top pop and bouzouki stars.

REMBETIKA CLUBS Rembetika, the blues sung by refugees from Asia Minor who came to Greece in the 1920s, still enthralls Greeks. At **Mnissikleous** (✉ Mnissikleous 22 and Lyceiou, Plaka ☎ 210/322–5558 or 210/322–5337), the authentic music of popular *rembetis* Bobis Goles draws audience participation. **Stoa ton Athanaton** (✉ Sofocleous 19 and Stoa Athanaton in the Central Market arcade, Omonia ☎ 210/321–4362), open day and night, is the city's premier *rembetatiko*.

House of Art (✉ Santouri 4 and Sarri, Psirri ☎ 210/321–7678) hosts small groups in a laid-back setting. **Half Note Jazz Club** (✉ Trivonianou 17, Mets ☎ 210/921–3310 or 210/923–2460) is the premier venue for international jazz and blues bands. **Parafono** (✉ Asklipiou 130, Exarchia ☎ 210/644–6512), a cozy hole-in-the-wall, has good jazz and reggae. **Rodon** (✉ Marni 24, Pl. Vathis ☎ 210/524–7427), an informal venue, showcases big names in popular music; in summer, they usually appear at the outdoor Lycabettus amphitheater. The **Rockwave Festival** (Ticket House box office ✉ Panepistimiou 42 in arcade, Syntagma ☎ 210/360–8366) takes place over three days in mid-July, usually somewhere on the Athens coast. Downtown record stores have details.

Shopping

Antiques

Pandrossou Street in Monastiraki is especially rich in shops selling small antiques and icons. Keep in mind that fakes are common and that you must have government permission to export objects from the classic, Hellenistic, Roman, or Byzantine periods. **Martinos** (✉ Pandrossou 50 ☎ 210/321–2414) attracts serious collectors looking for items such as ancient statuettes, pottery fragments, wooden dowry chests, and antique Venetian glass. **Motakis** (✉ Pl. Abyssinia 3, in basement ☎ 210/321–9005) sells antiques and other beautiful old objects. **Nasiotis** (✉ Ifestou 24, Monastiraki ☎ 210/321–2369) has interesting finds in a basement stacked with engravings, old magazines, and books, including first editions.

Flea Markets

The **Sunday-morning flea market** (✉ Pandrossou and Ifestou, Monastiraki) sells everything from secondhand guitars to Russian caviar. However little your treasured find costs, you should haggle. **Ifestou**, in Monastiraki, is the place to go weekdays for inexpensive copper wine jugs, candlesticks, and cookware.

Gift Ideas

Better tourist shops sell copies of traditional Greek jewelry; silver filigree; Skyrian pottery; onyx ashtrays and dishes; woven bags; attractive rugs, including shaggy woolen flokatis; worry beads in amber or silver; and blue-and-white amulets to ward off the *mati* (evil eye). Reasonably priced natural sponges from Kalymnos also make good gifts. **Goutis** (✉ Dimokritou 40, Kolonaki ☎ 210/361–3557) displays an eclectic assortment of costumes, embroidery, and old, handcrafted silver items. **Ilias Kokkonis** (✉ Stoa Arsakeiou 8, Omonia, enter from Panepistimiou or Stadiou ☎ 210/322–1189 or 210/322–6355) stocks any flag you've hankered after—large or small, from any country. **Mati** (✉ Voukourestiou 20, Syntagma ☎ 210/362–6238) has finely designed amulets to battle the evil eye, as well as a collection of monastery lamps and candlesticks. **Mazarakis** (✉ Voulis 31–33, Syntagma ☎ 210/323–9428) sells a large selection of flokatis and will ship.

Baba (✉ Ifestou 30, Monastiraki ☎ 210/321–9994), a hole-in-the-wall shop, sells backgammon boards and pieces in all sizes and designs. Greeks spend hours heatedly playing the game, known as *tavli*. **Loumidis** (✉ Aiolou 106, Syntagma ☎ 210/321–1540), the oldest remaining coffee roaster in Greece, is a good place to buy some freshly ground Greek coffee and the special coffeepot called *briki*.

Handicrafts

The **Kentro Ellinikis Paradosis** (Center of Hellenic Tradition; ✉ Mitropoleos 59, Monastiraki ☎ 210/321–3023) is an outlet for quality handicrafts. The **Organismos Ethnikos Pronoias** (National Welfare Organization;

⊠ Ipatias 6, and Apollonos, Plaka ☎ 210/321–8272) displays work by Greek craftspeople—stunning handwoven carpets, flat-weave kilims, hand-embroidered tablecloths, and flokatis.

At **Amorgos** (⊠ Kodrou 3, Plaka ☎ 210/324–3836) the owners make wooden furniture using motifs from regional Greek designs. They also sell needlework, handwoven fabrics, hanging ceiling lamps, shadow puppets, and other decorative accessories. The Greek cooperative **EOM-MEX** (⊠ Mitropoleos 9, Syntagma ☎ 210/323–0408) operates a showroom with folk and designer rugs made by more than 30 weavers around the country.

Jewelry

Prices for gold and silver are much lower in Greece than in many Western countries, and jewelry is of high quality. Many shops in Plaka carry original-design pieces available at a good price if you bargain hard enough. For more expensive items, the Voukourestiou pedestrian mall off Syntagma Square has a number of the city's leading jewelry shops. **Byzantino** (⊠ Adrianou 120, Plaka ☎ 210/324–6605) carries great values in gold, including pieces designed by the owners. **Fanourakis** (⊠ Patriarchou Ioakeim 23, Kolonaki ☎ 210/721–1762 ⊠ Evangelistrias 2, Mitropoleos ☎ 210/324–6642 ⊠ Panagitsas 6, Kifissia, ☎ 210/623–2334) produces some of the most original work in gold. Contemporary Athenian artists use gold like a fabric—creasing, scoring, and fluting it. The **Goulandris Cycladic Museum** (⊠ Neofitou Douka 4, Kolonaki ☎ 210/724–9706) carries modern versions of ancient jewelry designs. **LALAoUNIS** (⊠ Panepistimiou 6, Syntagma ☎ 210/361–1371) showcases pieces by Ilias Lalaounis, who takes his ideas from nature, science, and ancient Greek pieces. **Xanthopoulos** (⊠ Voukourestiou 4, Syntagma ☎ 210/322–6856) displays diamond necklaces, magnificently large gems, and the finest pearls; you can also order custom-made jewelry.

Music

Metropolis (⊠ Panepistimiou 54 ☎ 210/380–8549) is part of an excellent Greek chain; this branch sells only Greek music and stocks a wide selection.

Side Trips

Mikrolimano

The pretty, crescent-shape harbor of Mikrolimano is famous for its many seafood restaurants. Although the harbor has become increasingly touristy, its delightful atmosphere remains intact, and the harbor is crowded with elegant yachts. Terraces of lovely houses are tucked up against the hillsides. Take the metro from Monastiraki Square to the Neo Faliron station; it's only 10 minutes' walk from there.

Moni Kaisarini

★ Outside central Athens, on the slopes of Mt. Ymittos (ancient Mt. Hymettus), stands Moni Kaisariani (Kaisariani Monastery), one of the city's most evocative Byzantine remains. The well-restored 11th-century monastery, on the site of a sanctuary of Aphrodite, has some beautiful frescoes dating from the 17th century. Nearby are a basilica and a picnic site with a superb panorama of the Acropolis and Piraeus. Take a taxi or Bus 224 (in front of the Byzantine museum) to the end of the line; then walk 35 minutes along the paved road that climbs Mt. Ymittos. ⊠ Ethnikis Antistaseos ☎ 210/723–6619 ☉ Monastery Tues.–Sun. 8:30–3; grounds daily sunrise–sunset.

Athens Essentials

AIRPORTS & TRANSFERS

Athens International Airport S.A., Eleftherios Venizelos (ATH), an efficient facility opened in 2001, lies about 27 km (17 mi) southeast of Athens, in Spata, and is accessible via the city ring road, Attiki Odos.

🚩 **Eleftherios Venizelos International Airport** ✉ Spata-Elefsina Hwy., also called Attiki Othos, Spata ☎ 210/353-0000 flight information; 210/353-0445 visitor information; 210/353-0515 Lost and Found ⊕ www.aia.gr.

TRANSFERS Express buses (⇨ Bus Travel Within Athens) run between the airport and Syntagma Square, Ethnikis Aminas metro, and Piraeus. All run 24 hours and depart at 20-minute intervals. Bus E94 leaves from Ethniki Aminas metro station. Bus E95 leaves from Syntagma Square, stopping at the Hilton and the American Embassy. Bus E96 leaves from Karaiskaki Square in Piraeus, stopping at Platia Glyfada and Voula Beach. At the airport, all three buses depart from the area in front of the arrivals terminal. Tickets cost €2.90 and can be purchased from kiosks at the bus stops or on the bus. Hang on to your ticket—it acts as a travel pass and can be used on any form of public transport in Athens for 24 hours after you validate it. The trip to or from the airport takes 40 to 90 minutes, depending on traffic. All airport express buses have baggage storage areas and air-conditioning. The express buses are generally the best deal for getting into Athens. If you must take a cab, be aware that fares can top €20, especially if you have a lot of heavy baggage. An express train linking to the metro is expected to be finished by summer 2004.

BOAT & FERRY TRAVEL

Most ships serving the Greek islands dock at Piraeus (port authority), 10 km (6 mi) from the center. Boat schedules are published in *Kathemerini*, sold with the *International Herald Tribune*, and you can also call a daily Greek recording for departure times. From the main harbor you can take the nearby metro right into Omonia Square (€0.60) or Syntagma Square (change at Omonia; take the line going to Ethniki Aminas, €0.70) The trip takes 25–30 minutes. A taxi takes longer because of traffic and costs around €8. Because the driver may wait until he fills the taxi with several passengers headed in the same direction, it's faster to walk to the main street and hail a cab there. If you arrive by hydrofoil in the smaller port of Zea Marina, take Bus 905 or Trolley 20 to the Piraeus metro. At Rafina Port, which serves some of the closer Cyclades and Evia, taxis are hard to find. KTEL buses, which stop slightly uphill from port, leave every 30 minutes from about 5:30 AM until 9:30 PM and cost €1.55.

🚩 **Departure times** ☎ 143. **KTEL** ☎ 210/821-0872 ⊕ www.ktel.org. **Piraeus** ☎ 210/422-6000 through 210/422-6004. **Rafina Port** ☎ 22940/22300.

BUS TRAVEL TO & FROM ATHENS

Greek buses serving parts of northern Greece, including Thessaloniki, and the Peloponnese (Corinth, Olympia, Nafplion, Epidauros, Mycenae) arrive at Terminal A in Athens. Those traveling from Evia, most of Thrace, and central Greece, including Delphi, pull in to Terminal B; call terminals for information. From Terminal A, take Bus 051 to Omonia Square; from Terminal B, take Bus 24 downtown. To get to the stations, catch Bus 051 at Zinonos and Menandrou off Omonia Square for Terminal A and Bus 024 on Amalias Avenue in front of the National Gardens for Terminal B. International buses drop their passengers off on the street, usually in the Omonia or Syntagma Square area or at Stathmos Peloponnisos.

Most buses to the east Attica coast, including those for Sounion (€3.70 for inland route and €4.10 on coastal road) and Marathon (€2.40), leave from the KTEL terminal, which is in Platia Aigyptiou on the corner of Mavromateon and Alexandras near Pedion Areos park.

🚍 **KTEL terminal** ✉ Pl. Aigyptiou ☎ 210/821-3203 for information on bus to Sounion; 210/821-0872 for information on bus to Marathon ⊕ www.ktel.org. **Terminal A** ✉ Kifissou 100 ☎ 210/512-4910. **Terminal B** ✉ Liossion 260 ☎ 210/831-7096 Delphi; 210/831-7173 Livadia (Ossios Loukas via Distomo); 210/831-1431 Trikala (Meteora).

BUS TRAVEL WITHIN ATHENS

EOT can provide bus information, as can the Organization for Public Transportation. The office itself is open weekdays 7:30–3. The fare on buses and trolleys is €0.45–€0.75; monthly passes are sold at the beginning of each month for €17.50 (bus and trolley). Purchase tickets at curbside kiosks or from booths at terminals. Booths also provide booklets with maps of bus routes (in Greek). Validate your ticket in the orange machines when you board to avoid a €30 fine. Buses run from the center to all suburbs and nearby beaches from 5 AM until about midnight. For suburbs north of Kifissia, change at Kifissia's main square, Platia Platanou.

🚍 **Organization for Public Transportation** ✉ Metsovou 15 ☎ 185 from 7:30–3 and 7 PM–9 PM ⊕ www.oasa.gr.

CAR TRAVEL

You enter Athens by the Ethniki Odos (or National Road, as the main highways going north and south are known) and then follow signs for the center. Routes from Athens to the National Road are marked with signs in English; they usually name Lamia for the north and Corinth or Patras for the southwest.

CONSULATES

🏛 New Zealand ✉ Kifissias 268, Halandri ☎ 210/687-4700 or 210/687-4701.

EMERGENCIES

You can call an ambulance in the event of an emergency, but taxis are often faster. Most hotels will call a doctor or dentist for you; you can also contact your embassy for referrals to both. Not all hospitals are open nightly; ask your hotel to check for you, or call for a Greek listing. The *Athens News* often lists available emergency hospitals, as do most Greek newspapers. Many pharmacies in the center have someone who speaks English. For late-night pharmacies, call the information line, or check the *Athens News*. For auto accidents, call the city police.

🚑 Emergency Services **Ambulance** ☎ 166. **City Police** ☎ 100. **Coast Guard** ☎ 108. **Fire** ☎ 199. **Hospital line** ☎ 106. **Tourist police** ✉ Dimitrakopoulou 77, Koukaki ☎ 171.

💊 24-hour Pharmacies **Late-night Pharmacy Information Line** ☎ 107 information in Greek.

ENGLISH-LANGUAGE MEDIA

📚 Bookstores **Booknest** ✉ Folia tou Bibliou, Panepistimiou 25–29, Syntagma ☎ 210/322-9560. **Compendium** ✉ Nikis 28, upstairs, Syntagma ☎ 210/322-1248. **Eleftheroudakis** ✉ Nikis 4, Syntagma ☎ 210/322-9388 ✉ Panepistimiou 17 ☎ 210/331-4180. **Pantelides** ✉ Amerikis 11, Syntagma ☎ 210/362-3673.

THE OLYMPICS

The 2004 Olympics will take place in Athens from August 13 to August 29. A year before the games, the city was a gigantic construction site preparing to welcome millions of people eager to watch discus throwing in the shadow of the Parthenon or to cheer runners as they follow the original route from Marathon. Those who attend will see a city with a new airport, a new metro and tram, new highways, and many renovated hotels. By mid-2003, about 80 percent of the city's hotel rooms were already booked, and businesses from luxury hotels to souvlaki joints have indicated that they plan to raise rates—perhaps to double them or more—during the games. Visit the Athens 2004 Web site for information on every aspect of the Athens Games, and the main Olympic Web site for general information about the Olympics and links to each country's official Olympic travel agencies.

🛈 **Athens 2004** ⊕ www.athens2004.com. **Olympic Movement** ⊕ www.olympic.org.

LODGING By summer 2003, prices were skyrocketing for the decreasing number of rooms available for the Olympics. Two official Greek agencies, Alpha Filoxenia and Elliniki Filoxenia, will handle the rental of furnished homes and apartments; rates will be €30–€300 per person per day. Greek officials have also arranged for cruise ships to dock in Piraeus during the Olympics, so that people can stay in cabins. People can also stay on nearby islands such as Aegina and Hydra and take the hydrofoil to Athens. The simplest way to book accommodations—even unconventional ones—is through your country's official Olympic travel agent.

🛈 Apartment & Home Rentals **Alpha Filoxenia 2004** ✉ Panepistimiou 43, Athens ☎ 210/327-7400. **Elliniki Filoxenia** ✉ Artemidos 3, Athens ☎ 210/684-9222.

PARALYMPIC GAMES From September 17 through September 28, 2004, Athens will host the Paralympic Games, which are designed for athletes with physical disabilities. Paralympic events will take place in Olympic venues; these will be accessible for athletes and spectators with disabilities. The Athens 2004 and International Paralympic Committee Web sites have further information.

🛈 **International Paralympic Committee** ⊕ www.paralympic.org.

TICKETS The first round of Olympic ticket applications concluded in June 2003, and the balance of tickets went on sale in October 2003. Although tickets to opening and closing ceremonies and finals are expected to sell out quickly, last-minute tickets to other events will likely be available in 2004. To purchase tickets, buyers must contact their country's official Olympic ticket agencies (⇨ Travel Agencies). Other brokers may have tickets, but they will be far more expensive. During the games, any remaining tickets will be on sale in Athens. Ticket prices average around €35, though prime seats for finals and ceremonies cost between €300 and €950.

TRANSPORTATION All Olympic ticket holders are entitled to free public transportation to and from events. Shuttle buses will take you from hubs in Athens to venues outside the city. The Athens 2004 Web site will have details.

TRAVEL AGENCIES Each country has its own official Olympic travel agencies, which sell packages including tickets, accommodations, meals, transportation, and other services during and before or after the Olympics. To contact your country's official Olympic travel agencies, log on to the main Olympic Web site. From the pull-down menu, select "National Olympic Committees." Select your country and follow the links.

🛈 Official U.S. Travel Agencies **Cartan Tours** ☎ 800/360-2004 ⊕ www.cartan.com. **CoSport** ☎ 877/457-4647 ⊕ www.cosport.com.

VENUES Of the 32 Olympic venues in and around Athens, many will be temporary. The most important venue will be the Athens Olympic Sports Complex, a multi-stadium venue that will host the opening and closing ceremonies, tennis, gymnastics, swimming, diving, water polo, cycling, and the basketball finals. Architect Santiago Calatrava has designed the building and an adjoining park. After the Olympics, the complex will host cultural and sporting events. Another major venue is the enormous Hellenikon Sports Complex, on the site of the city's old airport. It will host basketball, baseball, softball, fencing, handball, hockey, and the canoe slalom. In central Athens, the Panathinaiko Stadio, which was used for the first modern Olympic Games in 1896, will be the site of archery events and the marathon finish.

🏃 Venues **Athens Olympic Sports Complex** ✉ Kifissas, next to Igiea Hospital. **Hellenikon** ✉ Poseidonos, Agios Kosmas.

SUBWAY TRAVEL

The metro system's slow, gritty Line 1, which dates from the 19th century, runs from Piraeus to the northern suburb of Kifissia, with several downtown stops. At press time, all Line 1 stations were undergoing renovations. Lines 2 and 3 opened to great fanfare in 2000. They are safe and fast but cover limited territory, mostly downtown. Extensions will be under way until 2006 and will go through all the main suburbs. By 2004, there will be stops at the major Olympic venues as well as a new airport express extension. Maps of the metro, including planned extensions, are available in stations. The fare is €0.60 if you stay only on Line 1; otherwise, it's €0.70. A daily travel pass, valid for use on all forms of public transportation, is €2.90; it's good for 24 hours after you validate it. Trains run between 5:30 AM and 11:30 PM. There is no phone number for information about the system, so check the Web site, which has updates on planned extensions.

🏃 **Metro Information** ⊕ www.ametro.gr.

TAXIS

Although you can find an empty taxi, it's often faster to call out your destination to one carrying passengers; if the taxi is going in that direction, the driver will pick you up. Most drivers speak basic English. The meter starts at €0.73, and even if you join other passengers, you must add this amount to your final charge. The minimum fare is €1.50. The basic charge is €0.23 per kilometer (½ mi); this increases to €0.44 between midnight and 5 AM or if you go outside city limits. There are surcharges for holidays (€0.50), trips to and from the airport (€1.17), and rides to, but not from, the port, train stations, and bus terminals (€0.59). There is also a €0.29 charge for each suitcase over 10 kilograms (22 pounds), but drivers expect €0.29 for each bag they place in the trunk anyway. Waiting time is €7 per hour. Make sure drivers turn on the meter and use the high tariff ("Tarifa 2") only after midnight; if you encounter trouble, threaten to go to the police. Radio taxis charge an additional €1.17 for the pickup or €2 for a later appointment. Some fairly reliable services are Ermis, Hellas, Kosmos, and Parthenon.

🏃 **Ermis** ☎ 210/411-5200. **Hellas** ☎ 210/645-7000 or 210/801-4000. **Kosmos** ☎ 1300. **Parthenon** ☎ 210/532-3300.

TOURS

BOAT TOURS   Cruises to the four most popular islands—Mykonos, Rhodes, Crete, and Santorini—usually operate from mid-March through October. Try Golden Star Cruises and Royal Olympia Cruises. Most also have downtown Athens representatives. All tour operators also offer a full-day cruise of the Saronic Gulf islands. The €75 cruise includes an on-board buffet lunch.

🏃 **Golden Star Cruises** ✉ Akti Miaouli 85, Piraeus ☎ 210/429-0650 through 210/429-0660 🖷 210/420-0660 for reservations ⊕ www.goldenstarcruises.com. **Royal Olympia Cruises** ✉ Akti Miaouli 87 ☎ 210/429-0700 for reservations 🖷 210/429-0636 for reservations ⊕ www.royalolympiacruises.com.

BUS TOURS   All travel agents (⇨ Travel Agencies) offer the same bus tours of Athens, as well as a handful of one-day excursions out of the city. The four-hour

Athens tour covers the city's major sights, including a guided tour of the Acropolis (€43). Full-day tours include excursions to Sounion (€29), Delphi and Mycenae. The Delphi and Mycenae trips cost €76 with lunch included; €66 without lunch. Evening tours of the monuments, including dinner and a floor show in Plaka, cost €47. Make reservations at your hotel or at any travel agency.

PRIVATE GUIDES All the major tourist agencies can provide English-speaking guides for personally organized tours, or call the Union of Official Guides. Hire only those licensed by EOT. A four-hour tour including the Acropolis and its museums costs about €120.

🛈 **Union of Official Guides** ✉ Apollonas 9A ☎ 210/322-9705 🖶 210/323-9200.

TRAIN TRAVEL

Athens has two railway stations, side by side, not far from Omonia Square off Deligianni Street. International trains and those coming from north of Athens use Stathmos Larissis. Trains from the Peloponnese use the ornate Stathmos Peloponnisos. Line 2 of the metro has a stop at Larissa station. As the station phones are almost always busy, it's easier to get departure times from the main information phone service and call about seat availability or buy tickets at a railway office downtown, open Monday–Saturday 8–2.

🛈 **Railway offices** ✉ Sina 6 ☎ 210/529-8910 ✉ Filellinon 17 ☎ 210/323-6747 ✉ Karolou 1 ☎ 210/529-7006 or 210/529-7007. **Stathmos Larissis** ☎ 210/529-8837. **Stathmos Peloponnisos** ☎ 210/529-8735.

TRAM TRAVEL

A tram line running from central Athens to the southern seaside suburbs was under construction at press time, with a projected completion date of summer 2004. Plans call for the tram to run between Glyfada and Fix metro stations on the outskirts of central Athens, with possible extensions to Voula and Syntagma Square. Tram tickets will be available at kiosks.

TRANSPORTATION AROUND ATHENS

Many of the sights and most of the hotels, cafés, and restaurants are within a fairly small central area. It's easy to walk everywhere, though sidewalks are often obstructed by parked cars. You can buy a monthly pass covering the metro, buses, and trolleys for €35 at the beginning of each month. Validate your ticket by stamping it in the orange machines at the entrance to the platforms, or you will be fined. Further information is at ⊕ www.oasa.gr.

TRAVEL AGENCIES

🛈 Local Agents **American Express** ✉ Ermou 2 ☎ 210/324-4975 🖶 210/322-7893. **CHAT Tours** ✉ Stadiou 4 ☎ 210/322-2886 🖶 210/323-5270. **Condor Travel** ✉ Stadiou 43 ☎ 210/321-2453 or 210/321-6986 🖶 210/321-4296. **F-Zein** ✉ Syngrou 132, 5th fl. ☎ 210/921-6285 🖶 210/922-9995. **Key Tours** ✉ Kallirois 4 ☎ 210/923-3166 🖶 210/923-2008 ⊕ www.keytours.gr. **Travel Plan** ✉ Christou Lada 9 ☎ 210/323-8801 through 210/323-8804 🖶 210/322-2152. **Trekking Hellas** ✉ Filellinon 7, 3rd floor ☎ 210/331-0323 through 210/331-0326 🖶 210/323-4548 ⊕ www.trekking.gr.

VISITOR INFORMATION

There is a visitor information office at Eleftherios Venizelos airport (⇨ Airports & Transfers).

🛈 **EOT** ✉ Tsochas 7, Ambelokipi ☎ 210/870-7000 ✉ Piraeus, EOT Building, 1st fl., Zea Marina ☎ 210/452-2591 or 210/452-2586 ⊕ www.gnto.gr.

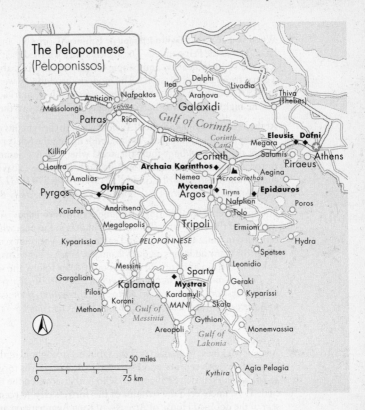

The Peloponnese (Peloponissos)

THE PELOPONNESE

Suspended from the mainland of Greece like a large leaf, the ancient land of Pelops is full of beautiful scenery—rocky coasts, sandy beaches, mountains—and fascinating ruins: temples, theaters, churches, palaces, and medieval castles. Legend and history meet as soon as you cross the isthmus of Corinth and come to Archaia Korinthos (Ancient Corinth). Mycenae, Tiryns, and Olympia are other reminders of ancient might, whereas Nafplion and Monemvassia bear the monuments of later eras. At its southern tip, the Peloponnese extends into the stark, wild lands of the Mani, and on its northwestern flank is the bustling, modern port city of Patras.

Exploring the Peloponnese

From Athens, head west across the Corinth Canal (84 km [52 mi]) to ancient Corinth. Detour off the National Road; otherwise you'll whiz over the canal and past the ancient city before you know it. Head south to Mycenae (4 km [2½ mi] off the road at Fichtion), and then turn off at Argos via Tiryns for Nafplion (63 km [39 mi] from Corinth). The ancient theater of Epidauros is another 26 km (16 mi) east. From Nafplion you can continue south through Tripoli and Sparta to Monemvassia (190 km [118 mi]), then west to Kardamyli and the Mani (60 km [37 mi]). From there the road continues north through the rugged mountains of Arcadia to ancient Olympia (190 km [117 mi]). North of Olympia (122 km [76 mi]) lies Patras, from where you can return to Athens on the National Road, an exceptionally beautiful drive along the coast. If you want to go on to Delphi, cross the gulf at Rion to Antirion en route.

Corinth

★ When you cross the **Gefira Isthmou** or Isthmos (Corinth Canal), you will have entered the Peloponnese. The ancients once winched their ships across a paved slipway nearby, and people talked for centuries about carving a canal through the limestone. The modern throughway was completed in 1893; you can watch the ships go by from a well-marked viewpoint off the highway near the narrow bridge, 197 feet above the water.

At the site of **Archaia Korinthos** (Ancient Corinth) lie remains of the Doric **Naos Apollonos** (Temple of Apollo), built during the 6th century BC and one of the few buildings that still stood when Julius Caesar decided to restore Corinth. A **museum** contains finds from the excavations. The site is 9 km (6 mi) west of Corinth. ⊠ *Off E94* ☎ *27410/31207, 27410/ 31480 (24 hrs)* ☉ *May–Oct., daily 8–7; Nov.–Apr., daily 8–6.*

Looming over ancient Corinth, the limestone **Acrocorinthos** (Acrocorinth) was one of the best naturally fortified citadels in Europe, where citizens retreated in times of invasions and earthquakes. Various excavations indicate the many additions made by Romans, Franks, Venetians, and Turks. Take a taxi from ancient Corinth (about €5) or follow the signs by car. ✥ *Take rd. outside the ticket office in Ancient Corinth, where taxis often wait for visitors, 3½ km (2 mi) up to tourist pavilion, then walk 10 mins to Acrocorinth gate* ☎ *27410/31266* ☉ *May–Oct., daily 8–7; Nov.–Apr., daily 8–5.*

Mycenae

★ Ancient Mykines (Mycenae) was the fabulous stronghold of the Achaean kings of the 13th century BC. Destroyed in 468 BC, it was forgotten until 1874, when Heinrich Schliemann, who had discovered the ruins of ancient Troy, uncovered the remains of this fortress city. Mycenae was the seat of the doomed House of Atreus—of King Agamemnon and his wife, Clytemnestra (sister of Helen of Troy), and of their ill-fated children, Orestes and Elektra. When Schliemann uncovered six shaft graves (so named because the kings were buried standing up) of the royal circle, he was certain that one was the tomb of Agamemnon. The gold masks and diadems, daggers, jewelry, and other treasures found in the graves are now in the National Archaeological Museum in Athens. The local **museum** displays other finds from the site and chronicles the excavations. Also here is the monumental **Pili ton Leonton (Lion Gate)**, dating from 1250 BC; the **castle ruins** crowning the bleak hill; and the astounding beehive tomb **Thisavros tou Atrea** (Treasury of Atreus), built into the hillside outside the massive fortification walls, all remnants of the first great civilization in continental Europe. ⊠ *Off National Rd. 7* ☎ *27510/76585, 27510/76801 through 27510/76803* ☉ *May–Oct., daily 8–7; Nov.–Apr., daily 8–5.*

Argos

One of the oldest continuously inhabited towns in Greece and prominent during the 8th century BC, Argos has a grand central square. The **archaeological museum** displays Neolithic pottery, Roman objects, and finds from the Mycenaean tombs. ⊠ *Pl. Argos at Vasilissis Olgas and Kallergi 1* ☎ *27510/68819* ☉ *Tues.–Sun. 8:30–3.*

$–$$ ✕ **I Spilia.** This countryside taverna is known for *bogana* (baby lamb slow-cooked in a sealed, wood-burning oven that gives the meat a smoky flavor). Call ahead to make sure the chef saves you some. He makes more than 30 local specialties, including wild artichoke salad, spit-roasted goat, and *tirolagana* (a fried bread made with feta and sheep's milk). ⊠ *Tripoleos 165, 3 km (2 mi) from Argos on Old Na-*

tional Rd. to Tripoli ☎ *27510/62300 or 27510/67154* ▭ *No credit cards* ⊘ *No lunch Mon.–Sat.*

Tiryns

Homer described Tirintha (Tiryns) as "the wall-girt city" for its ramparts, built of gigantic limestone blocks (the largest weighs 15 tons), which ancients thought could be handled only by giants. The remains, including the walls, date mostly from the 13th century BC, when Tiryns was one of the most important Mycenaean cities. ⊠ *On Argos–Naf-plion Rd., 4 km (2½ mi) before Nafplion* ☎ *27520/22657* ⊘ *May–Oct., daily 8–7; Nov.–Apr., daily 8:30–3.*

Nafplion

★ A favorite weekend getaway for Athenians, Nafplion is an elegant city, one of the most attractive in Greece. Brooding Venetian fortifications dominate the old part of town, which occupies a peninsula in the Gulf of Argos. Modern Greece's first king lived for a year or two within the walls of the sprawling, 18th-century hilltop fortress, **Palamidi,** when Nafplion was the capital of Greece. His courtiers had to climb almost 900 steps to reach him; you can still climb the long staircase (steps begin near the Cultural Center and the courts) or drive up the hill to the fortress. ⊠ *Above town* ☎ *27520/28036* ⊘ *May–Oct., daily 8–7; Nov.–Apr., daily 8:30–2:45; last admission 1 hr before closing time.*

Wander for at least a few hours through the narrow streets and shady squares of the **Palia Poli** (Old Town), lined with a mix of Venetian, Turkish, Frankish, and Byzantine buildings. The **Promenade,** south of the Old Town, skirts the Nafplion Peninsula and has fine sea views. The Venetian naval arsenal on the main town square houses an **archaeological museum** with Mycenaean finds, including a 7th-century BC Gorgon mask from Tiryns. ⊠ *East side of Pl. Constitution* ☎ *27520/27502* ⊘ *Tues.–Sun. 8:30–4.*

In late June, the **Festival Nafplion** stages classical music concerts in Palamidi fortress and the former Turkish mosque; for information, contact Nafplion tourist information (☎ *27520/24444*).

$$ ✕ **Savouras.** The best-known seafood taverna in town has high standards of freshness and specializes in simple but successful presentations of such specialties as mussels with cheese in tomato sauce and grilled cod, as well as more expensive choices such as red mullet and dorado. ⊠ *Bouboulinas 79* ☎ *27520/27704* ▭ *AE, MC, V.*

$ ✕ **Karamanlis.** This taverna near the courthouse is crowded at lunch with civil servants who come for its tasty magirefta. The fish soup makes a good appetizer, as do the melt-in-your-mouth *gigantes yiachni* (giant beans with fresh tomato), followed by savory *yiouvetsi* (lamb or beef baked with orzo-shape noodles). ⊠ *Bouboulinas 1* ☎ *27520/27668* ▭ *AE, MC, V.*

★ $$ ▦ **O Nausimedon.** A refurbished 19th-century residence, this lovely hotel is near the entrance of the Old Town. Most of its high-ceilinged rooms have antiques accompanied by such modern amenities as air-conditioning and TV. The quiet house sits across from the city park and has a large garden with palms. ⊠ *Sidiras Merarhias 9, 21100* ☎ *27520/ 25060* ▤ *27520/26913* ⤴ *10 rooms, 3 bungalows* ▭ *AE, V* ⦿❙ *BP.*

$–$$ ▦ **Byron.** This gracious hotel in the Old Town is in a rose-and-blue 18th-century house. Rooms include period furnishings and air-conditioning. Another building (buttercup-yellow with green shutters) has four spacious rooms, mostly decorated island-style, and also with TV and air-conditioning. You eat breakfast on a pretty terrace atop the old Turkish bath, overlooking the town and the gulf. ⊠ *Platonos 2, Platia Agios*

Spiridonos, 21100 ☎ *27520/22351* 📠 *0752/26338* ⊕*www.byronhotel. gr* ⇨ *18 rooms* ⊟ *AE, MC, V.*

Epidauros

Fodor'sChoice
★ Epidauros was the sanctuary of Asklepios, the Greek god of healing. You can visit the foundations of the temples and ancient hospital, as well as the **museum,** but the main attraction is the well-preserved 4th-century BC **open-air theater,** which seats 14,000; the acoustics are so good that you can sit in the top row and hear a whisper on stage. The **Festival of Ancient Drama** (☒ festival box office Stadiou 4, Athens ☎ 210/ 322–1459 advance tickets in Athens; 27530/22026 box office; 27530/ 22008 festival offices; 27530/41250 Micro Theatro; 210/728–2333 Megaron) in the ancient theater takes place from mid-July to mid-September; the smaller Micro Theatro (Little Theater) nearby simultaneously hosts concerts and dance performances. Tickets for the drama festival can be bought before performances or in advance from the festival box office in Athens. For the Micro Theatro, you can also contact the Megaron concert hall in Athens. ☎ *27530/22009* ⊙ *Museum: May–Oct., Tues.–Sun. 8–7, Mon. noon–7; Nov.–Apr., Tues.–Sun. 8–6, Mon. noon–6. Theater: May–Oct., daily 8–7; Nov.–Apr., daily 8–6.*

Monemvassia

Fodor'sChoice
★ The Byzantine town of Monemvassia, near the tip of a southern peninsula of the Peloponnese, clings to the side of the 1,148-foot rock that seems to blast out of the sea; in AD 375, it was separated from the mainland by an earthquake. Like Gibraltar, Monemvassia once controlled the sea lanes from western Europe to the Levant. The name *moni emvasia* (single entrance) refers to the narrow passage to this walled community. As you approach Monemvassia, the rock looks uninhabited until you suddenly see castellated walls with an opening wide enough for only one person. **Christos Elkomenos** (Christ in Chains; ☒ Pl. Tzamiou, along the main street) is said to be the largest medieval church in southern Greece. The carved peacocks are symbolic of the Byzantine era; the detached bell tower—like those of Italian cathedrals—is a sign of Venetian rebuilding in the 17th century.

The 10th-century **Agios Pavlos** (☒ across from Pl. Tzamiou), though converted into a mosque, was allowed to function as a church under the Ottoman occupation, an unusual indulgence. Up the hill from the upper town's wooden entrance gates is a rare domed octagonal church, **Agia Sofia** (☒ at top of the mountain), founded in the 13th century by Emperor Andronicus II. Follow the path to the highest point on the rock for a breathtaking view of the coast.

$–$$ ✕ **Marianthi.** You may feel as if you're dropping into someone's home at dinner here: family photos of stern ancestors hang on the walls along with local memorabilia, and someone's aunt is doing the cooking. The service is just as homey. Order the wild mountain greens, any of the fish (especially the red mullet), the addictive potato salad, and the marinated octopus sprinkled with oregano. ☒ *Old Town* ☎ *27320/61371* ⊟ *No credit cards.*

$ ▦ **Malvasia.** Three restored buildings in the Old Town make up this well-run hotel, where the rooms are tucked into nooks and crannies under
Fodor'sChoice
★ cane-and-wood or vaulted brick ceilings. Each is decorated with bright patchwork rugs, embroidered tapestries, and dark antique wood furniture. Many rooms have sea views, and some have fireplaces; all have basic cooking facilities including a refrigerator and hot plate. ☒ *Old Town, 23070* ☎ *27320/61323* 📠 *27320/61722* ⇨ *32 rooms* ♿ *Bar* ⊟ *AE, MC, V* ⑩ *CP.*

Kardamyli

Kardamyli is the gateway to the Mani, the peninsula that, on its western side, stretches from Kardamyli to Cape Tenaro, the mythical entrance to the underworld, and on its eastern side from Cape Tenaro up to Gythion. Isolated and invincible, this was the land of bandits and blood feuds. The Dorians never reached this far south, Roman occupation was perfunctory, and Christianity was not established here until the 9th century. Neither the Venetians nor the Turks could quell the constant rebellions.

The Maniotes are thought to be descended from the ancient Spartans and to have been expelled from northern Laconia by invading Slavs in the 7th century. Clans built defensive, multistory tower houses and engaged in lengthy fights over precious land in this barren landscape. Mani women were famous throughout Greece for their singing of the *moirologhi* (laments), like the ancient choruses in a Greek tragedy.

When King Otho tried to tame this incorrigible bunch in 1833, his soldiers were ambushed and held for ransom. Today, few people live in the Mani. Kardamyli has become a tourist destination for those attracted to remoteness and stark beauty, and it is an excellent base from which to explore the rest of the Mani, where you'll find beaches, hiking paths, towns of tower houses, and an overwhelming sense of emptiness.

The old section of Kardamyli is on a pine-scented hillside dotted with small clusters of **tower houses,** some of which are being restored; stone-paved paths cut through the enclave. ⊠ *Northwest of modern town.*

★ $ ✕⌂ **Lela's Taverna Pension.** Mrs. Lela is famous here for her cooking (the secret is probably in the homemade olive oil and the fresh tomatoes and herbs). On the shady, seaside terrace of this oleander-covered stone building you can savor chicken with rosemary, a light moussaka, and fish soup. Carefully chosen wines from throughout Greece are excellent accompaniments. Good-size rooms and suites above the taverna provide some of the region's nicest accommodation, with soothing sea views and furnishings that include traditional fabrics and prints of indigenous flowers. ⊠ *Seaside, above a rocky beach near old soap factory* 🕿 27210/73541 ⇌ *3 rooms, 2 suites* ♢ *Restaurant* ⊟ *No credit cards.*

Olympia

★ Just east of the modern village of Olympia, a few miles from the sea, lies **Archaia Olympia** (Ancient Olympia), where the Olympic Games were first held in 776 BC. A huge assembly hall was built here to hold the 10,000 representatives of the Arcadian League. The games continued to be celebrated every four years until AD 393, when the Roman emperor Theodosius I, a Christian, banned these "pagan rites." Women were excluded from watching the games under penalty of death; women's games were held a few weeks earlier. Archaeologists still uncover statues and votive offerings among the pine trees surrounding the **stadium,** the imposing ruins of the **Naos Dios** (Temple of Zeus), and the **Heraion** (Temple of Hera) within the sacred precinct. The **museum,** a few hundred yards north of the sanctuary, includes pedimental sculptures from the Zeus temple and the 4th-century BC head of the Hera cult statue and a well-preserved Hermes sculpted by Praxiteles, both from the Heraion. ⊠ *National Rd. 74* 🕿 *26240/22517 stadium and site; 26240/22529 museum* ⊗ *Site: May–Oct., weekdays 8–7, weekends 8:30–3; Nov.–Apr., weekdays 8–5, weekends 8:30–3. Museum: May–Oct., Mon. 12:30–7, Tues.–Fri. 8–7, weekends 8:30–3; Nov.–Apr., Mon. 10:30–5, Tues.–Fri. 8–5, weekends 8:30–3.*

A venue modeled on an ancient theater but with state-of-the-art light-ing and sound near the Olympia sanctuary hosts the summer **Festival Olympias** (☎ 26240/22250), an eclectic mix of performances. Ticket booths are located throughout the region, or call Olympia tourist in-formation.

$–$$ ✕ **O Kladeos.** Named for the river it borders, this *koutouki* (a tiny eatery) is big with locals. Sit near the fireplace in winter, in the shade of the plane tree in summer. The food is simple but classic Greek: codfish with garlic dip, fried squid, lamb in oil-oregano sauce, *saganaki* (pan-fried cheese), and charcoal-grilled dorado and shrimp. ⊠ *Ancient Olympia beside river* ☎ 26240/23322 ▤ *No credit cards* ☉ *Closed Oct.–Apr. No lunch.*

$ ✕ **Thraka.** The home-cooked food at this family-run taverna includes lahanodolmades and beef stifado made with vinegar and garlic. The two kinds of baklava are from the family's pastry shop. ⊠ *Vasiliou Bakopanou and Praxitelis Kondili* ☎ 26240/22575; 26240/22475 off-season ▤ AE, DC, MC, V ☉ Closed Nov.–Mar. (meals by special arrangement).

$$$ ▦ **Hotel Europa.** Run by the gracious Spiliopoulos family, this modern Best Western hilltop hotel overlooks the mountains of Arcadia, Alfios Valley, and the distant sea. All rooms have marble bathrooms; most face the pool, where a grill operates in summer. ⊠ *Off rd. to Ancient Olympia, at Oikismou Drouva, 27065* ☎ 26240/22650, 0624/22700, or 0624/22750 ⊟ 26240/23166 ⊕ www.bestwestern.com ⇌ 78 rooms, 2 suites ⚑ Restaurant, pool ▤ AE, DC, MC, V ⦿ BP.

$$ ▦ **Olympic Village.** Surrounded by vineyards, the hotel has simple rooms, modern baths, wooden furniture, and comfortable public spaces. The restaurant serves excellent Greek food such as *arnaki fricassee* (lamb with spinach and rice) and *giouvetsi* (beef cooked in a clay pot with vegeta-bles). ⊠ *Pyrgos–Olympia Rd. (about 300 yards from site), 27065* ☎ 26240/22211 ⊟ 26240/22812 ⇌ 60 rooms ⚑ Restaurant, pool, bar ▤ AE, MC, V ☉ Closed Nov.–Feb.

Patras

Patras, the third-largest city in Greece and its main western port, is the business hub of the Peloponnese. For the most part, Patras is a worka-day place that people rush through on their way to and from the busy port, which handles ferries to Italy and other European ports. The city's prettiest features are its arcaded streets and its squares surrounded by neoclassical buildings. The Byzantine **Kastro** (fortress), built on the site of the ancient acropolis, has a fine view along the coast. The large **Agiou Andrea** (Cathedral of St. Andrew), built in 1979 on the site of the cru-cifixion of St. Andrew, is worth exploring. The church's treasure is the saint's silver-mounted skull, returned to Patras in 1964 after 500 years in St. Peter's Cathedral, Rome. ⊠ *West side of harbor at end of Agiou Andreou* ☎ 2610/330644 ☉ Daily 7:30 AM–8 PM.

Patras stages jazz performances, chamber music concerts, and other per-formances at the **Patras International Festival** (⊠ Koryllon 2, Old Mu-nicipal Hospital, Old Town ☎ 2610/279008) in July and August.

★ **$$–$$$** ✕ **Ditis.** When the diver-owner closes up shop in summer to indulge his love of the sea, locals mourn. The humble furnishings of his fish tav-erna belie the masterful seafood dishes he prepares: delectable *kakavia* (Greek fish stew); crayfish with pepperoncini; squid that's stuffed with shrimp, cheese, peppers, and onion, then foil-wrapped and buried in the charcoal; and anchovies cooked with carrot, dill, and fennel. The fresh local fish includes sargus, pandora, swordfish, and gildhead, depend-ing on the season. ⊠ *Norman and Gambetta 44* ☎ 2610/432554 ▤ No credit cards ☉ Closed Sun. and July–Sept.

$ ✕ **Lavyrinthos (Taverna tou Antipa).** This classic taverna with wine barrels, old lamp fixtures, and a cozy loft serves such traditional Greek dishes as rabbit in lemon and pungent homemade potato salad. After your meal be sure to try a shot of *detoura,* a local liqueur similar to cognac and flavored with cinnamon and clove. ⊠ *Poukevil 44, near Pl. Vasilissis Olgas* ☏ 2610/226436 ▤ *No credit cards* ◷ *Closed Sun.*

$$$$ ▦ **Porto Rio Hotel and Casino.** Play a set of tennis or a round of beach volleyball, go for an afternoon dip, and then head for the casino at this 35-acre beachside hotel complex across from a small medieval fort at Rion, about 8 km (5 mi) east of Patras. Most rooms have outstanding views. ⊠ *Rion–Patroon National Rd., Rion 26500* ☏ 2610/992212 ⊟ *2610/992115* ⊕ *www.portorio-casino.gr* ⇨ *235 rooms, 13 suites, 48 bungalows* ᗜ *2 restaurants (1 in summer), 2 pools, bar* ▤ *AE, DC, MC, V* ⦿ *BP.*

★ $$$$ ▦ **Primarolia Art Hotel.** The furnishings at this small luxury hotel mingle disparate elements—a blue Egg chair by Arne Jacobsen, Ingo Maurer lighting, Fornasetti café tables, a Le Corbusier conference table—into a glorious visual feast that's warm, inviting, and chic. Six rooms have a sea view, and some rooms have balconies. All have showers with hydromassage, satellite TV, video telephones, and a minibar stocked with beluga caviar and oysters upon request. ⊠ *Othonos-Amalias 33, near the train station, 26223* ☏ 2610/624900 ⊟ *2610/623559* ⊕ *www. arthotel.gr* ⇨ *14 rooms* ᗜ *Restaurant, bar* ▤ *AE, DC, MC, V.*

$ ▦ **Rannia.** This hotel borders Queen Olga Square, the loveliest plaza in Patras, and is two blocks from the waterfront and within walking distance of the bus and train stations. The clean, quiet rooms all have balconies; many have air-conditioning. ⊠ *Riga Fereou 53, Pl. Vasilissis Olgas, 26500* ☏ 2610/220114 ⊞ *2610/220537* ⇨ *30 rooms* ▤ *MC, V* ⦿ *CP.*

Peloponnese Essentials

BOAT & FERRY TRAVEL

Ferries run between Athens (Piraeus) and Nafplion and Monemvassia year-round. The cities are also served by year-round hydrofoil service from Zea Marina in Athens, with a much-reduced schedule in winter, when the seas are not calm enough for the boats to operate. It's a good idea to reserve a seat in the summer.

🚩 Hydrofoils ☏ 210/418-7000. **Piraeus port authority** ☏ 210/422-6000 through 210/422-6004.

BUS TRAVEL

KTEL, the regional bus association, runs frequent service from Athens to Nafplion (where you change for Mycenae), Epidauros, Corinth, Monemvassia (with a change in Sparta), Patras, and Olympia.

🚩 KTEL ☏ 210/512-4910 or 210/512-4911 ⊕ www.ktel.org.

CAR TRAVEL

The roads are fairly good, and driving can be the most enjoyable way to see the area, once you get off the National Road.

TOURS

Available tours from Athens include one-day (€65 with lunch, €56 without lunch) or two-day (€100) trips to Mycenae, Nafplion, and Epidauros; four-day trips to those sites, as well as Olympia and Delphi (€325); and a five-day excursion to all major sites in the Peloponnese, as well as Delphi and Meteora (€425).

🚩 CHAT Tours ⊠ Xenofodos 8, Athens ☏ 210/322-2886. **Key Tours** ⊠ Kallirois 4, Athens ☏ 210/923-3166.

TRAIN TRAVEL

You can take a train from Athens to Corinth, where the route splits, heading either south to Argos and Nafplion, or west along the coast to Patras, and then south to Pyrgos and the branch line to Olympia. There is a substantial discount on round-trip tickets.

🚈 **Train information** ☎ 210/362-4402 through 210/362-4406; 210/529-7777 for general information; 145 for recorded departure timetable, in Greek, of trains within Greece.

VISITOR INFORMATION

🚈 **Nafplion** ✉ 25th Martiou across from OTE ☎ 27520/24444. **Olympia** ✉ Kondili 75 ☎ 26240/23100. **Patras** EOT ✉ Filopimenos 26 ☎ 2610/620353 ✉ Olympic Airlines, Aratou 17–19, Pl. Vasilissis Olgas ☎ 2610/222901, 2610/222902, or 2610/222903 ✉ Automobile and Touring Club of Greece, Patroon Athinon 18 ☎ 2610/425411 ☎☎ 2610/426416.

MAINLAND GREECE

The dramatic rocky heights of mainland Greece provide an appropriate setting for humanity's attempt to approach divinity. The ancient Greeks placed their gods on snowcapped Mt. Olympus and chose the precipitous slopes of Parnassus, "the navel of the universe," as the site for Delphi, their most important religious center. Many centuries later, pious Christians built a great monastery (Osios Loukas) in a remote mountain valley. Others settled on the rocky peninsula of Athos, the Holy Mountain. Later, devout men established themselves precariously on top of strange, towerlike rocks and, to be closer to God, built such monasteries as those at Meteora, which remain among the most spectacular sights in Greece.

Exploring Mainland Greece

En route to Delphi from Athens via the National Road, take the turnoff for the ancient city of Thiva (Thebes), 90 km (56 mi) northwest of Athens. After detouring to the monastery of Osios Loukas (turn off at Distomo village, 20 km [12 mi] west of Livadia), continue to Delphi. The road climbs a spur of Mt. Parnassus, past Arahova, known for its lively après-ski scene and handmade rugs of brightly colored wools; it also offers better dining and lodging options than Delphi, if you're staying in the area. From Arahova it's a short, spectacular drive through the Pleistos gorge to the ancient site (179 km [111 mi] northwest of Athens). After Delphi the road descends in sharp bends to lackluster Lamia (another 82 km [51 mi]), then heads northwest to Kalambaka and Meteora (139 km [86 mi] from Lamia).

Thiva

Thiva (Thebes), of which little remains, was the birthplace of legendary Oedipus, who unwittingly fulfilled the prophecy of the Delphic Oracle by slaying his father and marrying his mother.

Osios Loukas

★ Nestled in a serene upland valley is the monastery of Osios Loukas, a fine example of Byzantine architecture and decoration. Built during the 11th century to replace the earlier shrine of a local saint, it has some of the world's finest Byzantine mosaics. ☎ 22670/22797 ⊙ *May–mid-Sept., daily 8–2 and 4–7; mid-Sept.–Apr., daily 8–5.*

Delphi

FodorśChoice
★ At the edge of Delphi loom the Phaedriades, twin cliffs split by the Castalian spring. It was here that pilgrims to the Delphic Oracle came for purification. To the ancient Greeks Delphi was the center of the universe, because two eagles released by the gods at opposite ends of the earth

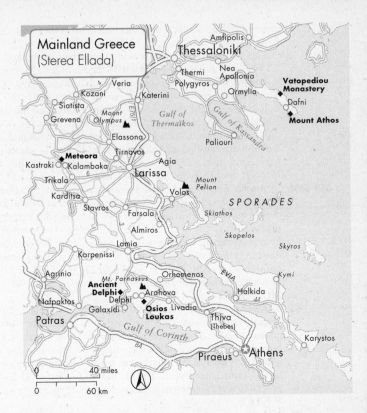

**Mainland Greece
(Sterea Ellada)**

Amfipolis
Thessaloniki
Thermi · Nea
Polygyros · Apollonia
Veria · Vatopediou
Kozani · Katerini · Ormylia · Monastery
Siatista · Dafni
Grevena · Mount · Gulf of · Mount Athos
Olympus · Thermaikos
Elassona · Paliouri
Meteora · Tirnavos
Kastraki · Kalambaka · Agia
Trikala · Larissa · Mount
Karditsa · Volos · Pelion
Stavros · SPORADES
Farsala · Skiathos
Almiros
Lamia · Skopelos
Karpenissi · Skyros
Agrinio · Mt. Parnassus · Orhomenos · Kymi
Ancient · EVIA
Delphi · Arahova · Halkida
Nafpaktos · Delphi · Livadia
Galaxidi · Osios · Thiva
Patras · Loukas · (Thebes) · Karystos
Gulf of Corinth · Piraeus · Athens

0 ___ 40 miles
0 ___ 60 km

met here. For hundreds of years the worship of Apollo and the pronouncements of the oracle made Delphi the most important religious center of ancient Greece. When ruins were first excavated in 1892, most were found to date from the 5th through the 3rd centuries BC. As you walk up the **Iera Odos** (Sacred Way) to the **Naos Apollonos** (Temple of Apollo), the **theater,** and the **stadium,** you'll see Mt. Parnassus above; silver-green olive trees below; and, in the distance, the blue Gulf of Itea. East of the main site, about 500 feet down the road, is the area with the temple of **Athena Pronaia,** from which many of the Delphi Museum's best sculptures came; the **gymnasium;** and the **Tholos,** the rotunda. If you come here in the early morning or evening, avoiding the busloads of tourists, you will feel the power and beauty of the place. ⊠ *Immediately east of Delphi modern town along road to Arahova* ☎ *22650/82312* ○ *May–Oct., weekdays 8–7, weekends 8:30–3; Nov.–Apr., daily 8:30–3.*

Don't miss the bronze charioteer (early 5th century BC) in the **Delphi Museum.** Other works of art here include a statue of Antinoüs, Emperor Hadrian's lover; fragments of a 6th-century BC silver-plated bull, the largest example of an ancient statue in precious metal; and the stone *omphalos,* representing the navel of the earth. Most of the museum, with the exception of two rooms, is closed until June 2004 for major renovations. ⊠ *Immediately east of Delphi modern town along road to Arahova* ☎ *22650/82312* ⊕ *www.culture.gr* ○ *May–Oct., weekdays 8–7, weekends 8:30–3; Nov.–Apr., daily 8:30–3.*

$–$$ ✕ **Epikouros.** In this uncluttered space with neutral color schemes, nothing detracts from the breathtaking view over the large open veranda. Even in the colder months, a clear canopy protects the seating area and allows you to take in the views year-round. Start with *horta* (freshly boiled greens drizzled with local olive oil and lemon) or the Greek salad. A must is the house specialty: wild boar stifado, a stew cooked with baby onions and tomato sauce, seasoned with bay leaves and cinnamon. ⊠ *Vasileos Pavlou and Friderikis 33* ☎ *22650/83250* ☴ *AE, MC, V.*

$ ✕ **Taverna Vakchos.** At this popular family-run taverna, owner Andreas Theorodakis keeps a watchful eye in the kitchen and on his customers. You can dine in the spacious inner dining room or on the large, flower-bedecked veranda, where you're guaranteed a stunning view. Favorite dishes include moussaka, boiled wild greens, spinach and cheese pies, and tomatoes stuffed with rice and roast chicken. In winter you can get game, such as hare, roast suckling pig, and perhaps venison. ⊠ *Apollonos 31* ☎ *22650/83186* ☴ *No credit cards.*

$$$–$$$$ ⊡ **Amalia.** Surrounded by 35 acres of gardens, this hotel built in 1965 blends seamlessly with the olive groves and pines of Delphi, and has welcomed many a famous guest over the years. Breathtaking views of Itea port and proximity to the archaeological sites add to its appeal. The public areas retain the distinctive modern style of the '60s, and guest rooms, done in earthy colors, are boxy and pleasant, with balconies and large bathrooms. ⊠ *Apollonos 1, 33054* ☎ *22650/82101* ☖ *22650/82290* ⊕ *www.amalia.gr* ⋐ *188 rooms* ♢ *Restaurant, pool, bar* ☴ *AE, DC, MC, V* ⍾ *CP.*

$$ ⊡ **Acropole.** Friendly and family-run, this hotel has a garden and a spectacular view—bare mountainside and a sea of olive groves—so that guests feel as though they're completely secluded. The rooms are freshly furnished with carved Skyrian furniture, traditional linens, and paintings of the Greek islands. Ten rooms have air-conditioning; all have satellite TV and hair dryers. ⊠ *Filellinon 13, 33054* ☎ *22650/82675* ☖ *22650/83171* ⊕ *www.delphi.com.gr* ⋐ *42 rooms* ☴ *AE, DC, MC, V* ⍾ *CP.*

$$ ⊡ **Apollo.** Owned by a husband-and-wife team, this lovely hotel has a *saloni* (living room) with a fireplace and traditional wall hangings and old prints among its carefully selected furnishings. The cheerful rooms have light-wood furniture set off by blue quilts and striped curtains, and pretty bathroom tiles. Many have wood balconies with black-iron railings. ⊠ *Vasileos Pavlou and Friderikis 59B, 33054* ☎ *22650/82580 or 22650/82244* ☖ *22650/82455* ⋐ *21 rooms* ☴ *MC, V* ⊘ *Closed weekdays Dec.–mid-Mar.* ⍾ *BP.*

★ $–$$ ⊡ **Generali Pension.** Small, well equipped, and loaded with charm, this family-run hotel is among the most delightful of its size in Greece. The individually decorated rooms have names such as Love, Company, Snow, and Helicopter. Eight have fireplaces; the larger rooms have kitchenettes, sun rooms, and two bathrooms, and can sleep up to six people. With its heated pool, wooden steam bath, and massage and aromatherapy treatments by appointment, this place is a true gem. ⊠ *Behind the local school and church of Panayia, 32004 Arahova* ☎ *22670/31529 or 22670/32287* ☖ *22670/32783* ⊘ *generalizino@yahoo.com* ⋐ *9 rooms* ♢ *Indoor pool* ☴ *No credit cards.*

Meteora

★ Kalambaka serves as the base for visits to the monasteries of Meteora, which sit atop gigantic pinnacles that tower almost 1,000 feet above the plain. Monks and supplies once reached the top on ladders or in baskets; now steps are cut into the rocks, and some monasteries can easily be reached by car. Of the original 24 monasteries, only 6 can now be visited. Appropriate dress for women requires skirts to the knee (not shorts), and men should wear long pants. The fortresslike **Varlaam monastery** (☎ *24320/22277* ⊘ May–Oct., Sat.–Thurs. 9–2 and 3:30–5; Nov.–Apr., Sat.–Wed. 10–3) is easy to reach and has beautiful Byzantine frescoes. For an idea of what living in these monasteries was like 300 years ago, climb the steep rock steps to the **Megalo Meteoron** (☎ 24320/22278 ⏱ May–Oct., Wed.–Mon. 9–1 and 3–6; Nov.–Apr., Thurs.–Mon. 9–1 and 3–5). Allow time for the trek up if it's nearing midday or evening closing time.

In Kalambaka stop at the **Koimisis tis Theotokou** (Dormition of the Virgin), built in the first half of the 12th century by Emperor Manuel Comnenus, though some historians believe it was founded during the 7th century on the site of a temple of Apollo (classical drums from columns and other fragments are incorporated into the walls). The church also has vivid 16th-century frescoes. ⊠ *North end of town; follow signs from Pl. Riga Fereou* ☎ 24320/24962 ⏱ *May–Oct., daily 7–1 and 3–7; Nov.–Apr., daily 7–10 and 3:30–6:30.*

★ $$ ╳ **Estiatorio Meteora.** A local favorite since 1925, this family restaurant on the upper square relies on the cooking of matriarch Ketty Gertzou, who prepares such dishes as *soutzoukakia* (spicy minced meat patties), lamb fricassee, stifado, *ladera* (vegetables cooked in olive oil), and chicken in wine with green peppers and garlic. ⊠ *Ekonomou 4, on Pl. Dimarchiou, Kalambaka* ☎ 24320/22316 ▭ *No credit cards* ⏱ *Closed Dec.–Mar. No dinner.*

$ ╳ **O Kipos Tou Ilia.** This simple taverna with a traditional Greek menu and a waterfall in the garden attracts everyone from visiting royalty to Olympic-medal winners. Kids get their own *paithika piata* (kids' plates). Unusual appetizers include spicy saganaki with peppers, grilled mushrooms, and fried feta. Among the main dishes are beef *stamna* (baked in a covered clay pot with herbs, potatoes, and cheese), rabbit with onions, and vegetable croquettes. ⊠ *Trikalon Rd. at the terminus of Ayia Triada, before entrance to Kalambaka* ☎ 24320/23218 ▭ V.

$ ╳ **Paradissos.** When a Greek woman cooks with *meraki* (good taste and mood), the world does indeed feel like *paradissos* (paradise). Owner Kyriakoula Fassoula serves meat dishes cooked *tis oras* (to order), such as grilled pork and lamb chops. Vegetarians can choose from eggplant *papoutsakia* (little shoes), fried zucchini with garlic sauce, and various boiled greens. ⊠ *On main rd. to Meteora across from Spania Rooms in Kastraki* ☎ 24320/22723 ▭ *No credit cards.*

★ $$$–$$$$ 🛏 **Amalia.** The area's best hotel, about 4 km (2½ mi) outside Kalambaka, is a low-lying complex with spacious, handsomely decorated public rooms with touches such as Byzantine-style frescoes, as well as a garden. The rooms are done in soothing colors and have large beds, art prints, and wooden balconies. ⊠ *15th km Trikala Kalambaka Hwy., 42200* ☎ 24320/72216; 24320/72217; 210/607–2000 *reservations* 🖶 24320/72457; 210/607–2135 *reservations* ⊕ *www.amalia.gr* ↵ *170 rooms, 2 suites* ⚖ *Restaurant, pool, bar* ▭ *AE, DC, MC, V* ⊧ *BP.*

$$ 🛏 **Hotel Antoniadis.** This reliable hotel in Kalambaka has pastel rooms with carpeting and TVs. Many rooms have a view of the Meteora monasteries. During the sweltering summers the hotel opens its rooftop pool. ⊠ *Trikalon 148, 42200* ☎ 24320/24387 or 24320/23419 🖶 24320/24319 ↵ *69 rooms* ⚖ *Restaurant, pool* ▭ V.

★ $–$$ 🛏 **Kastraki.** Step out on the balcony and bid good morning to the massive rocks that seem to loom over this great little hotel in a village on the road from Kalambaka to Meteora. All rooms have air-conditioning and a balcony and TV. The buffet breakfast (€8.50), which includes yogurt and homemade cake and fruit compotes, provides great fortification before a trek to the monastaries. ⊠ *Patriarchou Dimitriou A', 42200 Kastraki* ☎ 24320/75336 🖶 24320/75335 ↵ *28 rooms* ▭ V.

Mainland Greece Essentials

TOURS

Call travel agencies in Athens (⇨ Athens Essentials) for tours of mainland Greece, such as a two-day trip to the Meteora monasteries (€138), a three-day trip to Delphi and Meteora (€273), or a six-day excursion to northern Greece, including Delphi, Meteora, and Thessaloniki and its outlying archaeological sites (€648).

TRANSPORTATION AROUND MAINLAND GREECE

Although it's easiest to visit the region by car, there is very good train and bus service between the main towns, and between each town and Athens.

VISITOR INFORMATION

🔢 **Delphi** ✉ Vasileos Pavlou and Apollonos 11 ☎ 22650/82900 ✉ Tourist police ✉ Aggelos Sikelianou 3 ☎ 22650/82222. **Meteora** ✉ Kondili 38, Kalambaka ☎ 24320/75306 ✉ Pindou and Ioanninon, Kalambaka ☎ 24320/75100.

CORFU

Temperate, multihued Corfu—with its emerald mountains; turquoise waters lapping rocky coves; ocher and pink buildings; shimmering silver olive leaves; scarlet roses, bougainvillea, jacaranda, and lavender wisteria spread over cottages—could have inspired impressionism. The island, strategically placed in the northern Ionian Sea at the entrance to the Adriatic, opposite northwestern Greece and Albania, has a colorful history reflecting the commingling of Corinthians, Romans, Goths, Normans, Venetians, French, Russians, and British. Today, an abundance of visitors (most from England and many from Europe) enjoys, and in summer, crowds, its evocative capital city, isolated beaches, stylish restaurants, and resorts. The island combines neoclassical villas and ecosensitive resorts, horse-drawn carriages and Jaguars—simplicity and sophistication—in an alluring mix. Its desirability, however, makes it expensive. The island of Corfu is small enough to cover completely in a few days. Roads vary from gently winding to spiraling, but they're generally well marked, and all lead to Corfu town, which recalls a stage set for a Verdi opera.

Corfu Town

Fodor'sChoice
★

Along the east coast mid-island, Corfu town occupies the central prong of a three-pronged peninsula. On the southern prong is Paleopolis (Old Town) and on the northern is the Old Fortress (now the backdrop for summer sound-and-light shows), walled in the 8th century. The remains of the medieval Venetian town here are scanty. If you arrive from Igoumenitsa or Patras, on mainland Greece, your ferry will dock at the Old Port on the north side of town. The **New Fortress** (✉ on promontory northwest of the Old Fortress and medieval town) was built in 1577–78 by the Venetians and expanded by the French and the British to protect the town from a possible Turkish invasion. You can now wander through the maze of tunnels, moats, and fortifications.

The **Esplanade** (✉ between Old Fortress and Old Town), the huge, open parade ground on the land side of the canal, is central to the life of the town and is one of the most beautiful *spianadas* (esplanades) in Greece. It is bordered on the west by a street lined with seven- and eight-story Venetian and English Georgian houses, and arcades, called the **Liston** (modeled, by the French under Napoléon, on the Parisian rue de Rivoli).

Cafés spill out into the passing scene, and Corfiot celebrations, games, and trysts occur in the sun and shadows.

The oldest cultural institution in modern Greece, the **Corfu Reading Society,** contains archives (dating back several centuries) of the Ionian islands. In the early 19th century, Corfu was the literary center of Greece. One of the island's loveliest buildings, it has an exterior staircase leading up to a loggia. ☒ *Kapodistriou* ☎ *26610/39528* ☉ *Sat.–Wed. 9–1, Thurs. and Fri. 9–1 and 5–8.*

The **Garrison Church of St. George** (1830) has a fine Doric portico. In summer there's folk dancing, and in August sound-and-light shows relate the fortress's history. The views from here, east to the Albanian coast and west over the town, are splendid. ☒ *In middle of Old Fortress* ☉ *Daily 8–7.*

$$ ✕ **Aegli.** This restaurant on the Liston serves more than 100 different dishes, both local and international. The tables in front overlook the nonstop parade of people on the promenade. ☒ *Liston* ☎ *26610/31949* ▭ *AE, DC, MC, V* ☉ *Closed Dec.–Feb.*

$–$$ ✕ **Venetian Well.** On the most charming little square in the Old Town, built around a 17th-century well, this romantic restaurant seems too evocative and perfect to be true. The dining rooms in the handsome Venetian building are painted the classic Greek blue. Creative entrées might include duck with kumquats or wild boar. ☒ *Pl. Kremasti* ☎ *26610/44761* ▭ *AE, DC, MC, V.*

$ ✕ **O Yiannis.** One of the nicest restaurants in Corfu, this inexpensive place is unpretentious and full of locals. You can fill up on great barrel wine and imaginative food; try the stifado, dolmades, or *horti* (baked animal intestines). Check out the ancient photos of Corfu's old-timers. It's south of Corfu town. ☒ *Sophia Kremona and Iassonos-Sossipatrou 30, Anemomilos* ☎ *26610/31066* ⬟ *Reservations not accepted* ▭ *No credit cards.*

$$$$ ▦ **Cavalieri Hotel.** In this 17th-century, eight-story mansion, on the arcade of the Liston, get a room on the fourth or fifth floor with a number ending in 2, 3, or 4 for a breathtaking view of the Old Fortress. The building is swank yet graceful and chock-full of history. Have a drink at the usually empty but delightful English-style wood-paneled bar. Best of all is the roof garden, which offers light meals and the most remarkable view in town. ☒ *Kapodistriou 4, 49100* ☎ *26610/39041* ⎙ *26610/39336* ⊕ *www.cavalieri-hotel.com* ⬠ *50 rooms* ⬩ *Restaurant, bar* ▭ *AE, DC, MC, V.*

$$$$ ▦ **Corfu Palace.** Overlooking the bay, 100 yards from the center of town, this elegant hotel has spacious rooms decorated with white linens and Louis XIV–style furniture. Every room has a sea-view balcony and a huge marble bathroom. The hotel also has a spa and a conference center, and guests can use tennis and boating facilities nearby. ☒ *Leoforos Democratias 2, 49100* ☎ *26610/39485* ⎙ *26610/31749* ⊕ *www. corfupalace.com* ⬠ *101 rooms, 11 suites* ⬩ *2 restaurants, 2 pools (1 indoor), 2 bars* ▭ *AE, DC, MC, V.*

$$ ▦ **Hotel Bella Venezia.** This two-story Venetian building in the center of town, operated as a hotel since the 1800s, is a good value for the money. Though the hotel lacks views and a restaurant, its large lobby with a marble floor and wood-paneled ceiling, and its huge garden in which a buffet breakfast is served in season, make it quite pretty and grand. The rooms are small but tastefully furnished, and they have radios, telephones, and TVs. ☒ *Zambelli 4, 49100* ☎ *26610/20707 or 26610/44290* ⎙ *26610/20708* ✎ *belvenht@hol.gr* ⬠ *32 rooms* ▭ *AE, DC, MC, V.*

Kanoni

Outside Corfu town, at Kanoni, the site of the ancient capital, you may behold the most famous view on Corfu. A French cannon once stood in this hilly landscape, which is now built up and often noisy because of the nearby airport. From Kanoni, against the backdrop of the green slopes of Mount Ayia Deka, is the serene view of two tiny islets: One, **Moni Viahernes**, is reached by causeway. The other, **Pontikonisi** (Mouse Island), has a white convent and, beyond, tall cypresses guarding the 13th-century chapel. You can take a little launch or pedal boat to visit it—or even swim there.

Elsewhere on Corfu

In the environs outside Corfu town are two fabled palaces and gardens open to visitors: **Mon Repos**, built by Robert Adam in 1831, used by English Lord High Commissioners and birthplace of England's Prince Philip, and, in the village of Gastouri, **Achilleion**, the Greek retreat of Empress Elisabeth of Austria.

Corfu Essentials

BOAT & FERRY TRAVEL

Passenger ships stop at Corfu twice a week, April to October. Minoan Lines runs the ship service. Ferries from Igoumenitsa on the mainland leave every hour in summer and every two hours off-season, landing in Corfu town (two hours) and in Lefkimmi, at the southern tip of Corfu (45 minutes).

🚢 **Minoan Lines** ✉ Akti Poseidonos 28, Piraeus ☎ 210/419-9900 🖶 210/413-5000 ⊕ www.minoan.gr.

BUS TRAVEL

KTEL Corfu buses leave Athens three or four times a day. Bus travel on Corfu is inexpensive, and the bus network covers the island. The Spilia bus company's terminal is at the New Port. Buses also run from the San Rocco bus company's depot.

🚌 **KTEL Corfu** ☎ 26610/39985; 26610/30627; 210/512-9443 for Athens branch ⊕ www.ktel.org. **San Rocco** ✉ Pl. San Rocco, Corfu town ☎ 26610/31595. **Spilia** ✉ Avramiou, Corfu town ☎ 26610/30627.

CAR TRAVEL

By car, the best route from Athens is the National Road via Corinth to the Rion–Antirion ferry, and then to Igoumenitsa (472 km [293 mi]), where you take the ferry to Corfu. Call the Touring Club of Greece in Athens for information.

🚗 **Touring Club of Greece** ☎ 210/606-8800 ⊕ wwww.elpa.gr.

TOURS

Many agencies run half-day tours of Old Corfu town, and tour buses go daily to all the sights on the island. Tickets and information are available at travel agencies all over town.

VISITOR INFORMATION

ℹ **Greek National Tourist Organization (GNTO or EOT)** ✉ Kapodistriou 1, Corfu town ☎ 26610/37520, 26610/37638, or 26610/37639 🖶 26610/30298. **Tourist police** ✉ Kapodistriou 1 Corfu town ☎ 26610/30265.

THE AEGEAN ISLANDS

The islands of the Aegean have colorful legends of their own—the Minotaur in Crete; the lost continent of Atlantis, which some believe was Santorini; and the Colossus of Rhodes, to name a few. Mykonos,

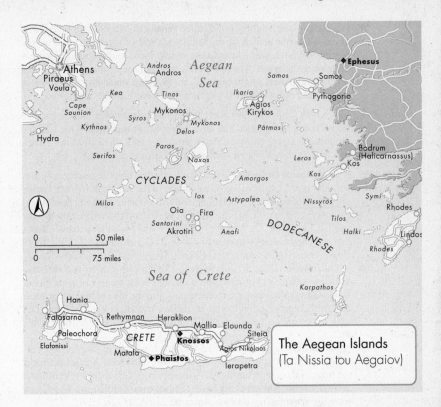

one of the islands that make up Cyclades, has windmills, dazzling white-washed buildings, hundreds of tiny red-domed churches on golden hill-sides, and small fishing harbors. Travelers to Santorini sail into a vast volcanic crater and anchor below the island's forbidding cliffs. Crete, with its jagged mountain peaks, olive orchards, and vineyards, contains the remains of the Minoan civilization. In Rhodes a bustling modern town surrounds a walled medieval city and a castle; volcanic ash has preserved a 1500 BC village in Santorini.

Mykonos

The chief village of Mykonos, also called Mykonos, is the Cyclades' best-preserved; it is a maze of narrow, flagstone streets lined with two-story whitewashed houses, many with flower-filled balconies, outdoor stair-ways, and blue or red doors and shutters. Every morning women scrub the sidewalks and streets in front of their homes, undaunted by passing donkeys. In the evening, islanders stroll down to the esplanade or wan-der the town, whose confusing layout evolved to foil pirates. During the 1960s the bohemian jet set discovered Mykonos, and many old houses are now shops, restaurants, bars, or discos; the nightlife, both gay and straight, is notorious. The rich arrive by yacht, the middle class by plane, the backpackers and Athenians by boat. It is *the* holiday desti-nation for the young, lively, and liberated.

If you stay more than a day, pay a quick visit to the **archaeological mu-seum** to get a sense of the island's history; the most significant local find is a 7th-century BC *pithos* (storage jar) showing the Greeks emerging from the Trojan Horse. ⊠ *East end of port* ☎ 22890/22325 ☉ *Tues.–Sun. 8:30–3.*

★ In a picturesque neighborhood called **Venetia** (⊠ near Mitropoeos Georgouli), or Little Venice, at the southwest end of the port, a few of the old houses have been turned into stylish bars, and wooden balconies hang over the water. From Venetia, you can see in the distance, lined up like toy soldiers on the high hill, the **Mykonos windmills**; until 40 years ago, wind power was used to grind the island's grain.

Mykoniots claim that 365 churches and chapels dot their landscape, one for each day of the year. The most beautiful, **Paraportiani** (Our Lady of the Postern Gate; ⊠ Ayion Anargyron) is really three churches imaginatively combined, like a confectioner's dream gone mad.

$$$–$$$$ ✕ **La Maison de Catherine.** One of the Cyclades' fanciest restaurants, Katerina's (as it is locally called) is surely one of the best. It showcases French dishes and also Greek specialties, and the ambience reflects this. If you are in a French mood, get the seafood soufflé; on the Greek side, try the fresh stuffed squid. The location is hidden in the Mykonos maze of streets, but everyone knows where it is. ⊠ *Agios Gerasimos* ☎ *22890/26946* ⚱ *Reservations essential* ▭ *AE, DC, MC, V* ☼ *Closed Nov.–Apr.*

Fodor'sChoice
★

$$ ✕ **Chez Maria.** Dine at this festive, 35-year-old garden restaurant—sometimes there's live music and dancing—for a sample of zesty Greek living. Octopus in wine, great cheese pies, and the fillet of beef with cheese and fresh vegetables will keep you in the mood, as will the apple tart with ice cream and walnuts. ⊠ *30 Kaloyera* ☎ *22890/27565* ▭ *AE, MC, V.*

$$ ✕ **Mamacas.** This restaurant in Mykonos town serves simple, impeccably Greek fare in a white patio under five palm trees. A good starter is the house salad, with lentils, tomatoes, beetroot, and celery; another is marinated fish. The specialty here is grilled meat of all kinds. The Greek wine list is extensive. ⊠ *Ayia Anna* ☎ *22890/26120* ▭ *AE, MC, V.*

★ **$$$$** ▥ **Cavo Tagoo.** This medley of white cubical structures perched above a small beach has been much praised for its environmentally sensitive architecture. The hotel is about 10 minutes' walk from the port; all rooms have balconies or terraces with superb sea views. Its poolside restaurant serves excellent Mediterranean cuisine. ⊠ *Road to Ayios Stefanos, 84600 Mykonos, 400 yards from town* ☎ *22890/23692* 🖷 *22890/24923* ⊕ *agn.hol.gr/hotels/cavotago* ⊠ *Athens* ☎ *210/6430233* 🖷 *2110/6445237* ↩ *68 rooms, 5 suites* ⚱ *Restaurant, saltwater pool* ▭ *AE, DC, MC, V* ☼ *Closed Nov.–mid-Apr.* ⦿ *CP.*

★ **$$$$** ▥ **Kivotos ClubHotel.** The hotel, a member of the Small Luxury Hotels of the World, has rooms that view the yachts on Ornos Bay (about 2 km [1 mi] south of Mykonos town), its own beach, fitness center, and squash court, and even a schooner you can rent for the day. Elaborate stone mosaics and much sculpture decorate the public areas, which include some pretty courtyards. The restaurant's dishes are artfully presented—the chicken stuffed with feta and tomato comes with a spoon each of fava, lentils, and *tzatziki* (yogurt-garlic dip). ⊠ *84600 Ornos Bay* ☎ *22890/24094; 210/724–6766 in Athens* 🖷 *22890/22844; 210/724–9203 in Athens* ⊕ *www.kivotosclubhotel.gr* ↩ *26 rooms, 4 suites* ⚱ *Restaurant, 2 pools* ▭ *AE, DC, MC, V* ☼ *Closed mid-Oct.–Apr.* ⦿ *BP.*

$$$$ ▥ **Ilio Maris.** The spacious lobby of this attractive hotel has painted beams, a stone floor, and whitewashed walls. But the place isn't just pretty, it's practical—you're just five minutes from Mykonos town on foot, and if you're driving you'll probably find a parking spot right out front. ⊠ *Despotiko area, 84600* ☎ *22890/23755* 🖷 *22890/24309* ⊕ *www.hotels-travel.org* ↩ *28 rooms* ⚱ *Pool* ▭ *AE, MC, V* ⦿ *BP.*

$$ ▥ **Myconian Inn.** Unpretentious and pleasant, with balconies that overlook the port, this hotel is both convenient and peaceful. Many younger people who want to be far away from the disco beat stay here. ✉ *Peta-sos, 84600 Mykonos* ☎ *22890/22663 or 22890/23420* 🖷 *22890/27269* ⊕ *www.mykonosgreece.com* ⤵ *15 rooms* 🖃 *No credit cards* ☉ *Closed Nov.–Mar.* ⵔ⃝ *BP.*

Delos

Thirty minutes by boat from Mykonos, dry little Delos was the islands' ancient religious center, sacred to Apollo and Artemis. Museum, theater, houses—the archaeological site is endlessly rich and needs exploring time. Tuesday through Sunday, **boats** (☎ 2289/22259) leave Mykonos for Delos from 8:30 to 9:30 and return from 12:30 to 1:30, depending on winds.

The **Exedra ton Leonton** (Terrace of the Lions), a weathered row of nine Naxian marble sculptures from the 7th century BC, overlooks the dried-up sacred lake; these are copies; the originals are in the on-site museum. One highlight is a group of **houses** of the Hellenistic and Roman periods, with their fine floor mosaics *in situ*.

Santorini

★ The best way to approach Santorini, or Thira, is to sail into its spectacular bay, once the vast crater of the volcano, and dock beneath its black-and-red cliffs, which rise up to 1,000 feet above the sea. Passenger ferries dock at the grungy port, Athinios, where you are met by buses, taxis, and hotel touts. The houses and churches of the main town, **Fira**, cling inside the rim in dazzling white contrast to the somber cliffs. The ride to Fira takes about a half hour, and from there you can make connections to **Oia**, or Ia, the serene town at the northern tip. Pictured on dozens of advertisements for Greece, Oia is famous for its marine sunsets. Be sure to try the local wines—a number of wineries offer tours and tastings (Antinopoulos is a good bet). The volcanic soil produces unique flavors, from light and dry to rich and aromatic.

The handsome **Museum of Prehistoric Thera** contains artifacts from Akrotiri and other excavation sites. You'll find frescoes, vases, tools, figurines—all beautifully displayed. Look for ancient Thera's symbol, the swallow. ✉ *Fira* ☎ *22860/23217* ☉ *Tues.–Sun. 8:30–3.*

The island's volcano erupted violently around 1500 BC, destroying its Minoan civilization. At **Akrotiri**, on the south end of Santorini, the remains of a Minoan city buried by volcanic ash are being excavated. The site, once a prosperous town some think is the legendary Atlantis, is remarkably well preserved. Some of its charming frescoes are in Athens, others are in the local museum. ✥ *13 km (8½ mi) south of Fira* ☎ *22860/ 81366* ☉ *Tues.–Sun. 8:30–3.*

At **Archaia Thira** (Ancient Thera), a cliff-top site on the southeast coast of the island, a town founded before the 9th century BC has a theater, agora, houses, fortifications, and temples. Though only foundations remain, it is very romantic; you can easily imagine its famed dances performed by naked youths. ✥ *South of Kamari* ☉ *Tues.–Sun. 8:30–3.*

$$$–$$$$ ✕ **1800.** Restaurants are springing up in rapidly developing Oia, but this elegant old favorite, in an atmospheric captain's mansion, remains at the very top. Veal with tomato sauce and eggplant, zucchini pie with cheese and onions—everything is good. ✉ *Main pedestrian lane, Oia* ☎ *22860/71485* 🖃 *AE, DC, MC, V* ☉ *Closed mid-Nov.–mid-Apr.*

$$–$$$ ✕ **Selene.** At this longtime favorite overlooking the bay, the creative cooking develops traditional Santorini fare into Mediterranean elegance. The fava balls with tomato caper sauce and *brodedo* (fish, squid, octopus, prawns, and other shellfish in a clay pot) are both based on local

recipes. ✉ *Fira, cliffside walkway to left of Hotel Atlantis* ☎ *22860/ 22249* ▤ *AE, MC, V* ⊘ *Closed Nov.–Mar.*

★ $$ ✕ **Camille Stefani.** One of the island's best restaurants, on the seaside walkway of the black-sand Kamari beach, below Ancient Thera, serves seafood and Greek and Continental cuisine. Begin with the lahanodolmades, a plate of fava, and moist tomato croquettes, and continue with one of the 16 versions of beef, pork, or chicken fillet. Try a glass of the mellow Santorini Lava red wine. ✉ *Beach Rd., Kamari* ☎ *22860/ 31716* ▤ *AE, DC, MC, V* ⊘ *Closed Dec.–mid-Feb.*

★ $–$$ ✕ **Nikolas.** Simple and congenial, this vintage taverna is one of the few places in town that stays open in winter. Arrive early, as the cook runs out of food around midnight. The menu on the chalkboard lists barrel wine and a delicious choice of classic Greek dishes, including stifado, stuffed cabbage rolls, and mountain greens. ✉ *Erithrou Stavrou, Fira* ☎ *2286/24550* ▤ *No credit cards.*

★ $$$$ ⌂ **Aigialos Traditional Houses.** These former cave houses have been individually redesigned with privacy, comfort, and traditional elegance in mind. Balconies overlook the bay, flowers decorate the rooms, and all the amenities are discreetly present. The restaurant is good, too. ✉ *Follow signs from Hypapantis walkway, 84700 Fira* ☎ *22860/25191 through 22860/25195* 🖷 *22860/22856* ⊕ *www.greekhotel.com* ⇌ *16 houses* ♨ *Restaurant, pool, bar* ▤ *AE, MC, V* ⊘ *Closed Nov.–mid-Apr.* ⏧| *BP.*

$$$$ ⌂ **Atlantis Villas.** If you don't mind stairs, descend to this beautiful hotel on Oia's cliffside, 600 feet above the sea, which offers separate apartments of varied configuration with splendid sunset sea views, comfort, quiet, and amenities including in-room safes. ✉ *Down from main walkway, 84702 Oia* ☎ *22860/71214* 🖷 *22860/71312* ⊕ *www.atlantisvillas. gr* ⇌ *19 houses* ♨ *Pool, bar* ▤ *AE, DC, MC, V* ⊘ *Closed mid-Oct.–mid-Apr.*

FodorsChoice ★

$$$$ ⌂ **Hotel Anteliz.** A family's cliffside house luxuriously redone with traditional white walls and dark-wood furniture, Anteliz is sparkling and isolated, but a mere 10-minute walk along the caldera from either Fira or Firostefani. You may find it hard to leave the little gated courtyard with its caldera view, or the outdoor hot tub. The spacious suites have kitchenettes and CD players. ✉ *Next to Nomikos Conference Centre, 84700 Fira* ☎ *22860/28842* 🖷 *22860/28843* ⊕ *www.anteliz.gr* ⇌ *6 suites* ♨ *Pool, bar* ▤ *MC, V.*

$$$$ ⌂ **Perivolas Traditional Houses.** Built into the cliffside at the outskirts of beautiful Oia, these authentic cave houses, some of them 200 and 300 years old, have been restored and individually decorated in Cycladic style. They overlook the sea and have kitchenettes and terraces. Check out the pool, which seems to hang over the cliff. Fashion magazines like to photograph their models here. ✉ *84702 Oia* ☎ *22860/71308* 🖷 *22860/ 71309* ⊕ *www.perivolas.gr* ⇌ *17 houses* ♨ *Pool, bar* ▤ *No credit cards* ⊘ *Closed Nov.–Mar.*

Rhodes

The large island of Rhodes, 11 km (7 mi) off the coast of Turkey, is the chief island of the Dodecanese. The northern end is one of Greece's major vacation centers. The island is large and not always beautiful, but it has fine beaches, ancient ruins, and an excellent climate. Rhodes makes a good base for visiting other islands of the Dodecanese, with their mixture of Aegean and Turkish architecture.

The town of **Rhodes** has an attractive harbor with fortifications; the gigantic, long-vanished bronze statue of the Colossus of Rhodes, incorrectly rumored to have straddled the entrance, was one of the wonders of the ancient world. The walled **Old City** is full of crooked, cobbled streets and echoes of antiquity. It's also full of the trappings of tourism, mainly evident in pubs and bars that cater to the large European market. The Old City was built by crusaders—the Knights of St. John—on the site of an ancient city. The knights ruled the island from 1309 until they were defeated by the Turks in 1522.

★ The Knights' Hospital houses the **archaeological museum,** notable for its impressive collection of ancient pottery and sculpture, including two voluptuous statues of Aphrodite. ✉ *Pl. Mouseiou (Museum Sq.)* ☎ *22410/ 27657* ⊕ *www.culture.gr* ۞ *May–Oct., Tues.–Sun. 8–6; Nov.–Apr., Tues.–Sun. 8:30–2:30.*

The medieval **Palati ton Ippoton** (Palace of the Knights), destroyed in 1856 by a gunpowder explosion, was restored by the Italians as a summer retreat for Mussolini. It is now a museum. Note its splendid Hellenistic and Roman floor mosaics. ✉ *Ippoton* ☎ *22410/23359* ⊕ *www. culture.gr* ۞ *May–Oct., Tues.–Sun. 8–7; Nov.–Apr., Tues.–Sun. 8:30–2:40.*

★ The **walls** of Rhodes's Old City are among the greatest medieval monuments in the Mediterranean. For 200 years the Knights of St. John strengthened them, making them up to 40 feet thick in places and curving the surfaces to deflect cannonballs. You can take a guided walk on about half of the 4-km (2½-mi) road along the top of the fortifications. The tour begins from the courtyard of the Palace of the Knights at the end of Ippoton street. ✉ *Old Town* ☎ *22410/23359* ۞ *Tours Tues. and Sat. at 2:45 (arrive at least 15 mins early).*

★ The enchanting village of **Lindos** ornaments the eastern coast. You can climb the winding path and steep stairs to the ruins of the ancient acropolis, **Akropoli tis Archaias Lindou.** The sight of its beautiful colonnade—part of the sanctuary to Athena Lindaia—with the sea far below is unforgettable. Look for little St. Paul's Harbor, beneath the cliffs of the acropolis; seen from above, it appears to be a lake, as rocks obscure its entrance. ✉ *Above town* ☎ *22440/31258* ۞ *May–Oct., Tues.–Sun. 8–6; Nov.–Apr., Tues.–Sun. 8:30–2:40.*

★ **$$** ✕ **Alexis.** The owners spare no effort to present the very best seafood—whether fresh lobster; mussels from nearby Simi steamed with onion, fennel, and white wine; or such specialties as sea urchin, limpets, and sea snail. ✉ *Sokratous 18, Old Town, Rhodes* ☎ *22410/29347* ⌔ *Reservations essential* ▭ *AE, MC, V* ۞ *No lunch June–Aug.*

$$ ✕ **Dinoris.** Fish of all kinds is the specialty of this longtime establishment in a cavernous hall built in 1530 as a stable for the knights. For mezedes try the variety platter of *psarokeftedakia* (fish balls made from a secret recipe), mussels, shrimp, and lobster. ✉ *Pl. Mouseiou 14A, Old Town, Rhodes* ☎ *22410/25824* ⌔ *Reservations essential* ▭ *AE, MC, V.*

★ **$$** ✕ **Palia Istoria.** Ensconced in an old house with genteel murals, this mezedopolion is a visual treat. Entrées include pork tenderloin in wine, fresh salmon in champagne sauce, and shrimp ouzo with orange juice. A taxi ride here from the center of Rhodes town costs about €4. ✉ *Mitropoleos 108, Ayios Dimitrios, Rhodes* ☎ *22410/32421* ⌔ *Reservations essential* ▭ *MC, V* ۞ *Closed mid-Dec.–mid-Jan. No lunch.*

$$ ✕ **Ta Kioupia.** Antique farm implements hang on the walls at this Rhodes landmark, and tables are elegantly set with linens, fine china, and crystal. Food arrives on large platters, and for a fixed price you select what pleases your eye: carrot bread, pine-nut salad, oven-baked meatballs with leeks, *tiropites* (four-cheese pie), and rooster kebab. ✉ *Tris, about 7 km (4½ mi) west of Rhodes town* ☎ *22410/91824* ⌔ *Reservations essential* ▭ *AE, V* ۞ *Closed Jan. No lunch.*

$ ✕ **Fotis Melathron.** Dinner is served in the courtyard of this lovely two-story stone house during summer, and in intimate dining rooms during winter. The menu changes, but you can't go wrong with the chef's suggestions, usually seafood and classics such as fried veal with sweetbreads and artichokes, and broad beans in egg and lemon sauce. ⊠ *Parodos Sokratous 41 Old Town, Rhodes* ☎ 22410/24272 ☰ *MC, V.*

★ $$$$ ⌘ **Hilton Rhodes Resort.** The buildings of this hotel zigzag down the hillside like stacked red, blue, and yellow boxes. Guest rooms, crisp and modern, have balconies, and about two-thirds have sea views. You can play tennis, jet ski and windsurf, rent a mountain bike, or just amble along in pedal boats. Linked by a pedestrian tunnel to the beach, the resort is just 4 km (2½ mi) from Rhodes town. ⬧ *Ialyssou Ave., 85100 Ixia* ☎ 22410/75000; 210/725–0920 in Athens ☒ 22410/76690; 210/725–7671 in Athens ⊕ www.rhodes.hilton.com ⇒ 402 rooms, 42 suites ♨ 3 restaurants, 3 pools ☰ AE, DC, MC, V ۞ Closed Nov.–mid-Mar.

$$$ ⌘ **Marco Polo Mansion.** Entering this converted 15th-century Ottoman mansion is like stepping into another world. The trip begins in the maze of the Old Town's colorful Turkish section, which gives a flavor of what's to come inside the hotel. Individually decorated rooms are painted in deep, warm colors; Oriental rugs adorn the pitch-pine floors; and embroidered cushions beckon from low sofas. Some of the furnishings are unusual antiques, including the large beds draped with translucent canopies. ⊠ *Aghiou Fanouriou 40–42, 85100 Rhodes* ☎ 22410/25562 ⊕ www.marcopolomansion.web.com ⇒ 3 rooms, 4 suites ♨ Bar ☰ V ⌘ CP.*

$ ⌘ **Spartalis Hotel.** A convenient refuge if you have to catch a boat from the harbor, this is in Rhodes's New Town. Many rooms in the simple but lively hotel have balconies overlooking the bay, and there is a terrace for breakfast. The rooms on the street are noisy. ⊠ *Plastira 2, 85100 Rhodes* ☎ 22410/24371 ☒ 22410/20406 ⊕ www.spartalis-hotel.com ⇒ 79 rooms ♨ Bar ☰ AE, DC, MC, V ۞ Closed Nov.–Mar.

Crete

Greece's largest island, lying in the south Aegean, was the center of Europe's earliest civilization, the Minoan, which flourished from about 2000 BC to 1200 BC. Crete was struck a mortal blow in about 1450 BC by an unknown cataclysm, perhaps political. In addition to archaeological treasures, Crete has snowcapped mountain scenery and many beach resorts, especially along the north central and northeast coasts. Western Crete, with soaring mountains, deep gorges, and rolling olive orchards, is much less visited, but is rich in Byzantine churches, Venetian monasteries, and interesting mountain villages.

The most important Minoan objects are in the **archaeological museum** in Heraklion, Crete's largest (and least attractive) city. The museum's treasures include the frescoes and ceramics from Knossos and Agia Triada depicting Minoan life, the snake goddesses, and the Phaestos disc, with Europe's first writing. ⊠ *Xanthoudidou 1, Pl. Eleftherias, Heraklion* ☎ 2810/224630 ۞ Mon. 12:30–5, Tues.–Sun. 8–5.

★ Not far from Heraklion is the partly reconstructed, sublimely evocative palace of **Knossos.** From 2000 BC to 1400 BC it was the chief site of Europe's first civilization. Note the simple throne room, with its tiny gypsum throne, pipes for running water, and splendid decorations. Its complexity and rituals probably suggested the myth of the Minotaur: the monstrous man-bull, offspring of Queen Pasiphae and a white bull, was confined by King Minos to the labyrinth. ☎ 2810/231940 ۞ May–Oct., daily 8–7; Nov.–Apr., daily 8–5.

Mallia, in addition to an extensive palace ruin, has good sandy beaches but is unattractively developed. Two other highly developed but more appealing beach resorts, Ayios Nikolaos and the nearby Elounda, lie farther east.

★ The town of **Rethymnon,** on the northwest coast, is dominated at its western end by the **Fortezza,** one of the largest and best-preserved Venetian castles in Greece. The town's old section contains carved-stone Renaissance doorways belonging to vanished mansions, fountains, wooden Turkish houses, and one of the few surviving minarets in Greece. It belongs to the **Neratzes mosque,** and you can climb its 120 steps for a panoramic view. The restored Venetian **loggia** is the clubhouse of the local nobility. The small Venetian **harbor,** with its 13th-century lighthouse, comes to life in summer, with restaurant tables cluttering the quayside.

★ **Hania,** in western Crete, is one of the most attractive towns in Greece. Work your way through the covered market, then through the maze of narrow streets to the waterfront. Walk along the inner harbor, past the Venetian arsenals and around to the old lighthouse, for a magnificent view of the town with the White Mountains looming beyond. The **archaeological museum,** in an area behind the outer harbor that is filled with Venetian and Turkish houses, contains finds from all over western Crete. Painted Minoan clay coffins and elegant Late Minoan pottery indicate the region's Bronze Age wealth. The museum building is the former Venetian church of St. Francis. ⊠ *Halidon 24* ☎ *28210/90334* ⊘ *Mon. 12:30–6, Tues.–Fri. 8–6, weekends 8:30–3.*

In summer, boat service operates along the southwest coast, stopping at **Paleochora,** the area's main resort. **Elafonissi** islet has white-sand beaches and black rocks set in a turquoise sea; to get to the island, you wade across a narrow channel. A good road on the west coast from Elafonissi north accesses beaches that are rarely crowded even in summer, including **Falasarna,** near Crete's northwest tip.

Southern Crete, separated from the north by a range of tall mountains, is relatively undiscovered, and much of the coastal plain is devoted to agriculture. **Phaistos,** an extensive Minoan palace complex, overlooks the sea and the Mesara plain from a hilltop near the market town of Mires. ⊹ *From Gortyna, cross Geropotamos River and ascend hill* ☎ *28920/42315* ⊘ *May–Sept., daily 8–7; Oct.–Apr., Mon. noon–5, Tues.–Sat. 8:30–3.*

At **Matala,** a former stopover on the hippie trail, 2nd-century AD Roman tombs are cut into the seaside cliffs. Long stretches of sandy beaches stretch on either side of Matala.

★ **$–$$** ✕ **Cavo D'Oro.** The most stylish of the handful of fish restaurants around the tiny Venetian harbor is also one of the finest restaurants in Crete. Lobster and innovative fresh fish dishes are always on the menu. The high-ceilinged, wood-paneled dining room was once a medieval storeroom, and diners also sit on the old cobbled waterfront. ⊠ *Nearchou 42–43, Rethymnon* ☎ *28310/24446* ▤ *DC, MC, V.*

$–$$ ✕ **Tamam.** An old Turkish bath has been converted to a cavernous dining room, one of the best and most atmospheric restaurants in Hania's old quarter. Specialties include peppers with grilled feta cheese and eggplant stuffed with chicken. ⊠ *Zambeliou 49, Hania* ☎ *28210/96080* ▤ *No credit cards.*

$ ✕ **Well of the Turk.** Part of the adventure is finding this restaurant on a narrow alley near the minaret in the old Arab quarter, just behind the Venetian warehouses on the harbor; you will have to ask your way, but just about everyone in the neighborhood knows this place. The food ranges from simple Greek fare—a prerequisite is the appetizer platter, a meal in itself—to some Continental dishes, such as sautéed chicken in a wine sauce. ⊠ *Kalinikou Sarpaki 1–Splantiza 3, Hania* ☎ *28210/54547* ⊟ *No credit cards.*

$$$$

Fodor'sChoice ★

🏨 **Elounda Mare.** This extraordinary Relais & Châteaux property on the Mirabello Gulf is one of the finest hotels in Greece. More than half of the rooms, all bathed in cool marble and stunningly decorated with traditional but luxurious Greek furnishings, are in villas with their own gardens and private pools. Verdant landscaping lines the shore above a sandy beach and terraced waterside lounge areas, a stone's throw from the large pool. A golf course, tennis courts, and water sports are further diversions. ⊠ *Elounda 72053* ☎ *28410/41102 or 28410/41103* 🖷 *28410/41307* ⊕ *www.elounda.com* ♬ *40 rooms, 55 bungalows* ♨ *3 restaurants, pool* ⊟ *AE, DC, MC, V* ♢ *Closed Nov.–Mar.* ⦿⦿ *BP.*

★ $$$–$$$$

🏨 **Casa Delfino.** Once part of a Venetian Renaissance palace, this tranquil hotel in the heart of Hania's Old Town still has the original stonework throughout the building and the beautiful pebble mosaic in the atrium. Cool pastel colors are used in the elegant rooms, which are set around a courtyard. Four apartments, available at a higher price, are decorated with 17th-century objects. ⊠ *Theofanous 9, Palea Poli, 73100 Hania* ☎ *28210/93098 or 28210/87400* 🖷 *28210/96500* ⊕ *www.casadelfino.com* ♬ *17 rooms, 4 suites* ⊟ *AE, DC, MC, V* ⦿⦿ *BP.*

★ $$$

🏨 **Palazzo Rimondi.** Several 15th-century houses in the heart of the old quarter make up this all-suites hotel. All of the tasteful, stylish rooms have sitting and sleeping areas and kitchenettes; many retain such architectural details as vaulted or paneled ceilings, fireplaces, and latticed Venetian windows. A courtyard with a tiny swimming pool serves as a nice retreat from the tourist clamor. ⊠ *Xanthoudidou 21, 74100 Rethymnon* ☎ *28310/51289* 🖷 *28310/51013* ✎ *rimondi@otenet.gr* ♬ *21 rooms* ♨ *Pool, bar* ⊟ *AE, DC, MC, V* ⦿⦿ *BP.*

$$$

🏨 **Villa Andromeda.** One of Hania's many charming hotels occupies a seaside, neoclassical mansion that once housed the German high command during World War II (Rommel supposedly enjoyed the plunge pool). The premises now contain large, handsomely furnished suites that surround a luxuriant garden and swimming pool or face the sea. ⊠ *150 Eleftherios Venizelos, 73100 Hania* ☎ *28210/28300 or 28210/28301* 🖷 *28210/ 28303* ✎ *vilandro@otenet.gr* ♬ *8 suites* ♨ *Pool, bar* ⊟ *DC, MC, V* ⦿⦿ *BP.*

$$

🏨 **Doma.** This converted 19th-century mansion 3 km (2 mi) from the center of Hania is as welcoming as a private home: the sitting room has a fireplace and armchairs with embroidered scarlet bolsters. The dining room, where the owner serves dinner on request, has a memorable view across the bay to the Old Town. Many rooms have air-conditioning; ask for one overlooking the garden to reduce street noise. There is an elevator. ⊠ *Eleftherios Venizelos 124, 73100 Hania* ☎ *28210/51772* 🖷 *0821/41578* ⊕ *www.hotel-doma.gr* ♬ *28 rooms* ⊟ *MC, V* ♢ *Closed Nov.–Mar.* ⦿⦿ *BP.*

Aegean Islands Essentials

AIR TRAVEL

There is frequent air service from Athens to each island, but in summer and on holidays it's vital to book well in advance. For further information, *see* Air Travel *in* Greece A to Z.

BOAT & FERRY TRAVEL

The simplest way to visit the Aegean Islands is by cruise ship. These usually stop at the four most popular islands—Mykonos, Rhodes, Crete, and Santorini. Car and passenger ferries sail to these destinations from

Piraeus. Boats for Mykonos also leave from Rafina, 32 km (20 mi) north of Athens. For ferry information, *see* Boat & Ferry Travel *in* Athens Essentials. En route from Piraeus you pass one of the great sights of Greece: the Temple of Poseidon looming on a hilltop at Cape Sounion.

TOURS

AEGEAN CRUISES From April through October many cruises go to the islands from Piraeus. Most cruise agencies also have downtown Athens representatives. For cruise information, *see* Tours *in* Athens Essentials.

VISITOR INFORMATION

🄵 **Crete** EOT ⊠ Kriari 40, Megaron Pantheon building, Hania ☎ 28210/92943 🖷 28210/92624 ⊠ Xanthoudidou 1, Heraklion ☎ 28210/228225 ⊠ Eleftherios Venizelos Paralia, Rethymnon ☎ 28310/29148 ⊠ Tourist police ⊠ Karaiskaki 60, Hania ☎ 28210/73333 ⊠ Dikaiosinis 10, Heraklion ☎ 2810/283190 ⊠ Eleftherios Venizelos Paralia, Rethymnon ☎ 28310/28156 ⊠ ELPA ⊠ G. Papandreou 46–50, Heraklion ☎ 2810/289440. **Mykonos** Hotel Reservations office ⊠ Port, next to tourist police ☎ 22890/24540 ⊠ Association of Rental Rooms and Apartments, Port, next to tourist police ☎ 22890/24860 ⊠ Tourist police ⊠ Port ☎ 22890/22482. **Rhodes** EOT ⊠ Archbishop Makarios and Papagou, Rhodes town ☎ 22410/23655 ⊠ Municipal tourism office, Platia, Rimini ☎ 22410/35945 ⊠ Tourist police, Archbishop Makarios and Papagou, entrance on Karpathou, Rhodes town ☎ 22410/27423. **Santorini tourist police** ⊠ next to KTEL bus station ☎ 22860/22649.

HUNGARY

BUDAPEST, THE DANUBE BEND, LAKE BALATON

HUNGARY SITS, proudly but precariously, at the crossroads of Central Europe, having retained its own identity despite countless invasions and foreign occupation by great powers of the East and West. Its industrious, resilient people have a history of brave but doomed uprisings: against the Turks in the 17th century, the Habsburgs in 1848, and the Soviet Union in 1956. Each upheaval has resulted in a period of readjustment, a return to politics as the art of the possible.

The 1960s and '70s saw matters improve politically and materially for most Hungarians. Communist party leader János Kádár remained relatively popular at home and abroad, allowing Hungary to improve trade and relations with the West. The bubble began to burst during the 1980s, however, when the economy stagnated and inflation escalated. The peaceful transition to democracy began when young reformers in the party shunted aside the aging Mr. Kádár in 1988 and began speaking openly about multiparty democracy, a market economy, and cutting ties with Moscow. Events quickly gathered pace, and by spring 1990, as the Iron Curtain disappeared, Hungarians went to the polls in the first free elections in 40 years. A center-right government took office, sweeping away the Communists and their renamed successor party, the Socialists, who finished fourth. Eleven years later, the nation entered the 21st century guided by an entirely new generation, the center-right FIDESZ party led by Prime Minister Viktor Orbán, only 35 years old when he was elected in 1998. Orban's FIDESZ party and its right-wing coalition were defeated in 2002, and a new and improved Hungarian Socialist Party, headed by former banker Péter Medgyessy, was elected to replace FIDESZ.

In bald mathematical terms, the total area of Hungary (Magyarország) is less than that of Pennsylvania. Two rivers cross the country: the Duna (Danube) flows from the west through Budapest on its way to the southern frontier, the smaller Tisza from the northeast across the Great Plain (Nagyalföld). Western Hungary is dominated by the largest lake in Central Europe, Lake Balaton. Although overdevelopment is advancing, the northern lakeshore is still dotted with baroque villages and old-world spas, and the surrounding hills are covered with vineyards. In eastern Hungary, the Nagyalföld is steeped in the romantic culture of the Magyars (the Hungarians' name for themselves), with its spicy food, strong wine, and proud *csikósok* (horsemen).

However, it is Budapest, a city of more than 2.5 million people, that draws travelers from all over the world. Bisected by the Danube, the city has a split personality; villas and government buildings cluster in the hills

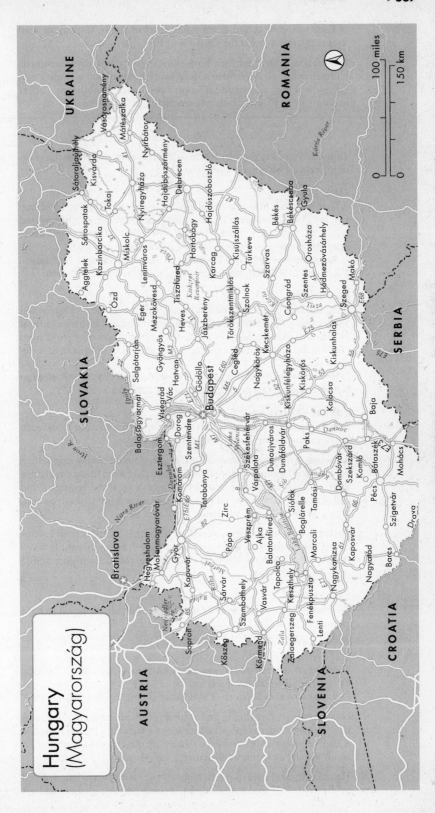

Hungary
(Magyarország)

of Buda to the west, and an imposing array of hotels, restaurants, and shopping areas crowds the flatlands of Pest.

Hungarians, known for their hospitality, enjoy talking with foreigners. Hungarians of all ages share a deep love of music, and wherever you go you will hear it, whether it's opera performed at Budapest's opera house or simply Gypsy violinists serenading you at dinner.

HUNGARY A TO Z

To research prices, get advice from other travelers, and book travel arrangements, visit www.fodors.com.

BIKE TRAVEL

A land of rolling hills and flat plains, Hungary lends itself to bicycling. For brochures and general information on bicycling conditions and suggested routes, try Tourinform or contact the Magyar Kerékpáros Túrázók Szövetsége (Bicycle Touring Association of Hungary).

🚲 **Magyar Kerékpáros Túrázók Szövetsége** ⊠ Bajcsy-Zsilinszky út 31, 2nd floor, apt. 3, Budapest ☎ 1/332-7177. **Tourinform** ⊠ Sütő u. 2, Budapest ☎ 1/438-8080.

BUS TRAVEL

Long-distance buses link Budapest with many main cities in Eastern and Western Europe. Services to the eastern part of the country leave from Népstadion Station. Services to Vienna and all points west leave from Népliget Station. Buses are inexpensive and tend to be crowded, so reserve your seat.

🚌 **Népstadion Station** ⊠ Hungária körút 46-48, Budapest ☎ 1/252-1896. **Népliget Station** ⊠ Könyves Kálmán körút 131 Budapest ☎ 1/219-8080 or 1/219-8000.

BUSINESS HOURS

BANKS & OFFICES   Banks are generally open weekdays 8–2 or 3, often with a one-hour lunch break around noon; most close at 2 on Friday.

MUSEUMS & SIGHTS   Museums are generally open 10–6 Tuesday–Sunday; many stop selling admission 30 minutes before closing. Note that some museums change their opening and closing times by an hour or so at the beginning and end of peak seasons based on visitor traffic; it's prudent to double-check hours. Many have free admission one day a week.

SHOPS   Department stores are open weekdays 10–5 or 6, Saturday until 1. Grocery stores are generally open weekdays 7–6 or 7, Saturday until 1; "non-stops" or *éjjeli-nappali* (24-hour convenience stores) are (theoretically) open 24 hours.

CAR TRAVEL

To drive in Hungary, U.S. and Canadian visitors are supposed to have an International Driver's License—although their domestic licenses are usually accepted—and U.K. visitors may use their own domestic licenses.

EMERGENCIES   The Magyar Autó Klub (Hungarian Automobile Club) runs a 24-hour Yellow Angels breakdown service.

🚗 **Magyar Autó Klub** ⊠ Francia út 38/B, Budapest ☎ 1/345-1744 or 188.

GASOLINE   Gas stations are plentiful in and around major cities, and major chains have opened modern full-service stations on highways in the provinces. A liter of *ólommentes benzin* (unleaded gasoline) costs about 235 Ft. and is usually available at all stations, as is diesel.

ROAD CONDITIONS   There are three classes of roads: highways or "motorways" (designated by the letter "M" and a single digit), secondary roads (designated by a two-digit number), and minor roads (designated by a three-digit number). Highways and secondary roads are generally well maintained. Minor roads vary; tractors and horse-drawn carts may slow you down in rural areas. Tolls on major highways help fund the upgrading of many of the country's motorways.

RULES OF THE ROAD Drive on the right. Unless otherwise noted, the speed limit in developed areas is 50 kph (30 mph), on main roads 80–100 kph (50–62 mph), and on highways 120 kph (75 mph). Speed limit signs are scarce compared with those in the United States. Seat belts are compulsory, as is the use of headlights (except in developed areas). Driving while intoxicated is prohibited—there is a zero-tolerance policy, and the penalties are severe.

CUSTOMS & DUTIES

Objects for personal use may be imported freely. If you are over 16, you may also bring in 250 cigarettes or 50 cigars or 250 grams of tobacco, plus 2 liters of wine, 1 liter of spirits, 5 liters of beer, and 0.25 liters of perfume. A customs charge is made on gifts valued in Hungary at more than 27,000 Ft.

Keep receipts of any purchases from Konsumtourist, Intertourist, or Képcsarnok Vállalat. A special permit is needed for works of art, antiques, or objects of museum value. You are entitled to a VAT refund on new goods (i.e., not works of art, antiques, or objects of museum value) valued at more than 50,000 Ft.

Hungarian Customs and Revenue Office ⊠ Hungária kürút 112–114, Budapest, ☎ 1/470–4121.

EATING & DRINKING

Although prices are steadily increasing, plenty of good, affordable restaurants offer a variety of Hungarian dishes. Meats, rich sauces, and creamy desserts predominate, but you can also find vegetarian dishes and salads, even out of season. Don't miss a chance to sample some of Hungary's excellent wines. The Villány region produces the country's tastiest reds; the best whites come from the Balaton area. Egri Bikavér, or "bull's blood," Hungary's best-known red wine, goes well with almost any meal. A regular restaurant is likely to be called either a *vendéglő* or an *étterem*. You also have the option of eating in a *büfé* (snack counter), an *eszpresszó* (café), or a *söröző* (pub). Be sure to visit a *cukrászda* (pastry shop). Keep in mind that typical Hungarian breakfasts consist of cold cuts and bread; if the start of your day requires specially prepared omelets or blueberry muffins, be sure to inquire about your hotel's breakfast offerings ahead of time.

One caveat: many restaurants have a fine-print policy of charging for each slice of bread consumed from the bread basket. General overcharging is not unheard of, either. Authorities in Budapest, however, have been cracking down on establishments reported for overcharging. Don't order from menus without prices, and don't accept dining or drinking invitations from women hired to lure people into shady situations.

Dining prices in Budapest tend to be a bit higher than elsewhere in Hungary.

WHAT IT COSTS In Hungarian Forints			
$$$$	**$$$**	**$$**	**$**
AT DINNER over 3,500	2,500–3,500	1,500–2,500	under 1,500

Prices are per person for a main course.

MEALTIMES Hungarians eat dinner early—you risk offhand service and cold food after 9 PM. Lunch, the main meal for many, is served from noon to 2. Some restaurants are introducing simple breakfast menus catering to Western travelers and expats.

RESERVATIONS & DRESS At most moderately priced and inexpensive restaurants, casual but neat dress is acceptable. Only in the most expensive Budapest establishments are a jacket and tie sometimes required.

EMBASSIES

🚩 Australia ✉ Királyhágó tér 8–9, Budapest, 1126 ☎ 1/457-9777.

🚩 Canada ✉ Budakeszi út 32, Budapest, 1121 ☎ 1/392-3360.

🚩 United Kingdom ✉ Harmincad u. 6, Budapest, 1051 ☎ 1/266-2888.

🚩 United States ✉ Szabadság tér 12, Budapest, 1054 ☎ 1/475-4400.

HOLIDAYS

January 1; March 15 (Anniversary of 1848 Revolution); Easter and Easter Monday; May 1 (Labor Day); Pentecost and Pentecost Monday; August 20 (St. Stephen's and Constitution Day); October 23 (1956 Revolution Day); November 1 (All Saints' Day); December 25, 26.

LANGUAGE

Hungarian (Magyar) tends to look and sound intimidating to English-speakers. Generally, older people speak some German, and many younger people speak at least rudimentary English, which has become the most popular language to learn. It's a safe bet that anyone in the tourist trade will speak at least one of the two languages.

LODGING

Lodging ranges from sophisticated hotels to guest houses, private rooms, and campsites.

The following price categories are for a double room with bath, including VAT but not breakfast, during the peak season; rates are markedly lower off-season and in the countryside, sometimes under 600 Ft. for two. For single rooms with bath, count on about 80% of the double-room rate. As most large hotels require payment in hard currency, rates are given in euros below.

During the peak season (June–August), full board may be compulsory at some of the Lake Balaton hotels, although this is increasingly rare. During the off-season (in Budapest, September–March; at Lake Balaton and the Danube Bend, May and September), rates can be considerably lower than those during peak season and are frequently negotiable.

WHAT IT COSTS In euros			
$$$$	**$$$**	**$$**	**$**
BUDAPEST			
FOR 2 PEOPLE over €250	€150–€250	€90–€150	under €90
LAKE BALATON AND THE DANUBE BEND			
HOTELS over €80	€50–€80	€30–€50	under €50

Hotel prices are for a standard double room in high season.

APARTMENT & VILLA RENTALS Apartments in Budapest and cottages at Lake Balaton, available for short- and long-term rental, can be the most economical lodging for families. Contact tourist offices in Hungary and abroad for rates and reservations. A Budapest apartment or a luxury cottage for two on Lake Balaton may cost anywhere from 8,000 Ft. to 18,000 Ft. a day. You can make bookings in Budapest at the Tribus Hotel Service, which is open 24 hours a day. Although some enterprising locals stand outside tourist offices and at train stations offering tourists their apartments for lower than official rates, the risk of being taken for a ride far outweighs the savings. The IBUSZ Accommodation Centre has extensive rental listings. On the Buda side, a good rental agency is Cooptourist. To-Ma Tours arranges private apartments and rooms. The apartments are remarkably spacious and resemble 1950s executive suites, without the telephone but with satellite TV and fully equipped kitchens. They're available for around $40 a night.

⚑ **Cooptourist** ✉ Bartók Béla út 4, Budapest ☎ 1/466-5349. **IBUSZ Accommodation Centre** ✉ Ferenciek tere 10, Budapest ☎ 1/485-2767 🖷 1/337-1205. **To-Ma Tours** ✉ Bartók Béla út 4, Budapest ☎ 1/353-0918 🖷 1/269-5715. **Tribus Hotel Service** ✉ Apáczai Csere János u. 1, Budapest ☎ 1/318-5776 🖷 1/317-9099 ⊕ www.tribus.hu.

GUEST HOUSES & PRIVATE LODGINGS

Also called *panziók* (pensions), small guest houses lying just outside the heart of the city or town provide simple accommodations well suited to people on a budget. These usually include a private bathroom, and many also offer breakfast. A room for two in Budapest with breakfast and private bath will cost around the equivalent of 15,000 Ft.–20,000 Ft. per night in peak season, less at other times. Arrangements can be made through local tourist offices or travel agents abroad.

In the provinces, rooms that you are offered directly are likely to be clean and in a relatively good neighborhood. Look for a placard reading either SZOBA KIADÓ or—in German—ZIMMER FREI. Rooms rent for 5,000 Ft.–8,000 Ft. a night, which usually includes the use of a bathroom but not breakfast. Reservations can also be made by any tourist office.

HOSTELS

Most hostels in Budapest are in university dorms and open only when school is not in session (typically July and August). Hostels have no age limits or membership requirements, and they offer a 10% discount to HI (Hostelling International) cardholders. Most have no curfews and offer 24-hour reception service. The Hungarian Youth Hostel Federation in Budapest publishes an informative, annual directory of hostels throughout the country and provides information. Budapest's main hostel agency, Mellow Mood Kft./Travellers' Youth Hostels, operates year-round hostels. Be sure to book in advance in summer. Hostels are uncommon outside Budapest, but some towns open their university dorms to travelers during July and August; inquire at the local tourist office.

⚑ **Hungarian Youth Hostel Federation** ✉ Almássy téri Szabadidő központ, Almássy tér 6, 4th floor, Budapest ☎ 1/352-1572. **Mellow Mood Kft./Travellers' Youth Hostels** ✉ Baross tér 15, H-1077 Budapest ☎ 1/413-2062 🖷 1/321-4851 ⊕ www.hostels.hu.

HOTELS

Don't expect a bargain on your hotel room in Budapest: high-season rates at established hotels rival those of most Western capitals. There are few expensive hotels outside Budapest, but the moderately priced hotels are generally comfortable and well run. Unless otherwise noted, breakfast is not included.

MAIL & SHIPPING

Two post offices in Budapest offer extended hours. Keleti is open daily 7 AM–9 PM. Nyugati is open Monday–Saturday 7 AM–9 PM, Sunday 8 AM–10 PM. Each is near one of Budapest's main train stations.

General delivery service is available through any post office in Budapest, including the main downtown branch; the envelope should have your name written on it, as well as "posta maradó" (poste restante) in large letters. The roman-numeral prefix listed in a Budapest street address refers to one of the city's 22 districts. Postal addresses include a zip code but not the roman numeral.

🚩 **Keleti** ✉ Baross tér 11c, Budapest ☎ 1/312–1200. **Magyar Posta 4. sz.** ✉ Városház utca 18, Budapest ☎ 1/229–3706. **Nyugati** ✉ Teréz körút 51, Budapest ☎ 1/322–1099.

POSTAL RATES

Postage for an airmail letter to the United States costs 160 Ft.; an air-mail letter to the United Kingdom and elsewhere in Western Europe costs 150 Ft. Airmail postcards to the United States cost 110 Ft. and to the United Kingdom and elsewhere in Western Europe, 100 Ft.

MONEY MATTERS

The Hungarian Forint (HUF) has held steady against most major cur-rencies in the last few years, though the weakening of the U.S. dollar has made Hungary more expensive for Americans in recent years. Nev-ertheless, even with inflation and the 25% value-added tax (VAT) in the service industry, enjoyable vacations with all the trimmings remain less expensive than in nearby Western European cities such as Vienna.

ATMS

Hundreds of ATMs have appeared throughout the capital and in other major towns. Some accept Plus network bank cards and Visa credit cards, others Cirrus and MasterCard. You can withdraw forints only (automatically converted at the bank's official exchange rate) directly from your account; most levy a 1% or $3 service charge. Many cash-exchange machines, into which you feed paper currency for forints, have also sprung up.

CURRENCY

The unit of currency is the forint (Ft.). There are bills of 200, 500, 1,000, 2,000, 5,000, 10,000, and 20,000 forints and coins of 1, 2, 5, 10, 20, 50, and 100 forints. At this writing, the exchange rate was 243 Ft. to the European euro, 226 Ft. to the U.S. dollar, 149 Ft. to the Canadian dollar, 368 Ft. to the pound sterling, and 134 Ft. to the Australian dol-lar. Always change money at a bank or an official exchange office.

TRAVELER'S CHECKS

Eurocheque holders can cash personal checks in all banks and in most hotels. Many banks now also cash American Express and Visa traveler's checks. American Express has a full-service office in Budapest, and a smaller branch on Castle Hill—in the Sissi Restaurant, closed Jan-uary–mid-March—offers only currency exchange. Hungary's first Citibank offers full services to account holders, including a 24-hour ATM.

🚩 **American Express** ✉ Deák Ferenc u. 10, Budapest ☎ 1/235–4330 travel service; 1/235–4349 cardmember services 🖷 1/267–2028 ✉ Sissi Restaurant, Dísz tér 8 ☎ 1/224–0118. **Citibank** ✉ Vörösmarty tér 4, Budapest.

PASSPORTS & VISAS

U.S., British, and Canadian citizens must carry a valid passport.

TAXES

VALUE-ADDED TAX (V.A.T.)

You are entitled to a V.A.T. (ÁFA, in Hungarian) refund on new goods (i.e., not works of art, antiques, or objects of museum value) valued at more than 50,000 Ft. (V.A.T. inclusive). Cash refunds are given only in forints. If you made your purchases by credit card, you can file for a credit to your card or to your bank account (again in forints), but this process is slow at best. If you intend to apply for the credit, make sure you get customs to stamp the original purchase invoice before you leave the country. For more information, pick up a tax refund brochure from any tourist office or hotel, or contact a tax refund agency. IBUSZ Travel Agency can assist individuals with tax refunds.

🚩 **IBUSZ Travel Agency** ✉ Ferenciak tere 10, Budapest, ☎ 1/485–2700.

TELEPHONES

COUNTRY & AREA CODES

The country code for Hungary is 36.

DIRECTORY & OPERATOR ASSISTANCE
For operator-assisted calls within Hungary, dial 191. Dial 198 for directory assistance throughout the country. Operators are unlikely to speak English. A safer bet is to consult *The Phone Book,* an English-language Yellow Pages–style telephone directory that also has cultural and tourist information; it's free in most major hotels, at many restaurants, and at English-language bookstores.

INTERNATIONAL CALLS
Direct calls to foreign countries can be made from Budapest and all major provincial towns by dialing "00" and waiting for the international dialing tone; on pay phones the initial charge is 60 Ft. Operator-assisted international calls can be made by dialing 190. To reach a long-distance operator, call AT&T, MCI, or Sprint.

🔲 **AT&T** ☎ 06-800-01111. **MCI** ☎ 06-800-01411. **Sprint** ☎ 06-800-01877.

LOCAL CALLS
The cost of a three-minute local call is 20 Ft. Pay phones use 10, 20, 50, and 100 Ft. coins. Most towns in Hungary can be dialed direct—dial 06 and wait for the buzzing tone, then dial the local number. It is unnecessary to use the city code (1) when dialing within Budapest.

Hungary's telephone system continues to be modernized, so phone numbers are subject to change—usually without forewarning and sometimes several times. A recording in Hungarian and English may provide the new number. If you're having trouble getting through, ask your concierge to check the number.

PUBLIC PHONES
Gray card-operated telephones are common in Budapest and the Balaton region. The cards—available at post offices, newsstands, and kiosks—come in units of 60 (800 Ft.) and 90 (1,800 Ft.) calls.

TIPPING

Four decades of socialism didn't alter the Hungarian habit of tipping. Hairdressers and taxi drivers expect 10%–15% tips, and porters should get a few hundred forints (the equivalent of a dollar or two). Cloakroom attendants receive 100 Ft.–200 Ft., as do gas pump attendants if they wash your windows or check your tires. Unless otherwise noted, gratuities are not automatically included in restaurant bills; when the waiter arrives with the bill, you should immediately add a 10%–15% tip to the amount and pay the waiter, as it is not customary to leave a tip on the table. If a Gypsy band plays exclusively for your table, you can leave 200 Ft. in the plate provided.

TRAIN TRAVEL

Travel by train from Budapest to other large cities or to Lake Balaton is cheap and efficient. Remember to take a *gyorsvonat* (express train) and not a *személyvonat* (local), which can be extremely slow. A *helyjegy* (seat reservation), which costs about 725 Ft., is advisable for all Inter-City trains, which provide rapid, express service among Hungary's major cities.

Only Hungarian citizens are entitled to student discounts; non-Hungarian senior citizens (men over 60, women over 55), however, are eligible for a 20% discount. For more information about rail travel, contact the MÁV Passenger Service.

🔲 Train Information **MÁV Passenger Service** ⊠ Andrássy út 35, Budapest ☎ 1/461-5500 international information; 1/461-5400 domestic information.

VISITOR INFORMATION

The main Tourinform office has a 24-hour information line; the office on Sütő is open daily from 8 to 8.

🔲 **Tourinform** ⊠ Vörösmarty tér, at Vigadó u., Budapest ☎ 1/438-8080; 06/80-660-044 24-hr automated telephone service ⊕ www.hungarytourism.hu or www.tourinform.hu ⊠ Sütő u. 2, Budapest ☎ 1/317-9800.

WHEN TO GO

Many of Hungary's major fairs and festivals take place in the spring and fall. During July and August, Budapest can be hot and the resorts at Lake Balaton crowded, so spring (May) and the end of summer (September) are the ideal times to visit.

CLIMATE The following are average daily maximum and minimum temperatures for Budapest.

Jan.	34F	1C	May	72F	22C	Sept.	73F	23C
	25	−4		52	11		54	12
Feb.	39F	4C	June	79F	26C	Oct.	61F	16C
	28	−2		59	15		45	7
Mar.	50F	10C	July	82F	28C	Nov.	46F	8C
	36	2		61	16		37	3
Apr.	63F	17C	Aug.	81F	27C	Dec.	39F	4C
	45	7		61	16		30	−1

BUDAPEST

Budapest, lying on both banks of the Danube, unites the hills of Buda and the wide boulevards of Pest. It was the site of a Roman outpost in the first century, and the modern city was not created until 1873, when the towns of Óbuda, Pest, and Buda were joined. The resulting capital is the cultural, political, intellectual, and commercial heart of the nation; for the 20% of the nation's population who live here, anywhere else is just "the country."

Much of the charm of a visit to Budapest consists of unexpected glimpses into shadowy courtyards and long vistas down sunlit cobbled streets. Although some 30,000 buildings were destroyed during World War II and in 1956, the past lingers on in the often crumbling architectural details of the antique structures that remain and in the memories and lifestyles of Budapest's citizens.

Exploring Budapest

The principal sights of the city fall roughly into three areas, each of which can be comfortably covered on foot. The Budapest hills are best explored using public transportation. Many street names have been changed since 1989 to purge all reminders of the Communist regime—you can sometimes still see the old name, negated with a victorious red *x,* next to the new. By tradition, the district number—a Roman numeral designating one of Budapest's 22 districts—precedes each address. For the sake of clarity, in this book, the word "District" precedes the number. However, if you are addressing an envelope, remember that full postal addresses do not cite this Roman numeral, as the district is indicated by the zip code. Districts V, VI, and VII are in downtown Pest; District I includes Castle Hill, the main tourist district of Buda. The maps provided by tourist offices are not very detailed, so arm yourself with one from any of the bookshops in Váci utca or from a stationery shop or newsstand.

Getting around is easier if you learn a few basic terms: *utca* (abbreviated *u.*) and *út,* which mean "street" and "road" or "avenue," respectively; *tér* or *tere* (square); and *körút* (ring road).

Várhegy

Numbers in the margin correspond to points of interest on the Budapest map.

Most of Buda's main sights are on Várhegy (Castle Hill), a long, narrow plateau laced with cobblestone streets, clustered with beautifully preserved baroque, Gothic, and Renaissance houses and crowned by the stately Royal Palace. Painstaking reconstruction work has been in progress here since the area was nearly leveled during World War II.

❺ Hadtörténeti Múzeum (Museum of Military History). The collection here includes uniforms and regalia, many belonging to the Hungarian generals who took part in the abortive uprising against Austrian rule in 1848. Other exhibits trace the military history of Hungary from the original Magyar conquest in the 9th century up to the middle of the 20th century. English-language tours can be arranged in advance. ⊠ *Tóth Árpád sétány 40* ☎ *1/356–9522* ⊕ *www.militaria.hu* ☉ *Apr.–Sept., Tues.–Sun. 10–6; Oct.–Mar., Tues.–Sun. 10–4.*

★ **❸ Halászbástya** (Fishermen's Bastion). This wondrous porch overlooking Pest and the Danube was built at the turn of the 20th century as a lookout tower to protect what was once a thriving fishing settlement. Its neo-Romanesque columns and arches frame views over the city and the river. ⊠ *East of Szentháromság tér.*

★ **❶ Királyi Palota** (Royal Palace, also known as Buda Castle). The Nazis made their final stand here and left it a blackened wasteland. Under the rubble, archaeologists discovered the medieval foundations of the palace of King Matthias Corvinus, who, in the 15th century, presided over one of the most splendid courts in Europe. The rebuilt palace is now a vast museum complex and cultural center.

The **Budapesti Történeti Múzeum** (Budapest History Museum), the southern block of the Royal Palace, displays a permanent exhibit of the city's history from Buda's liberation from the Turks in 1686 through the 1970s. The 19th- and 20th-century photos and videos of the castle, the Chain Bridge, and other Budapest monuments provide a helpful orientation to the city. Down in the cellars are the original medieval vaults of the palace, a palace chapel, and more royal relics. ⊠ *Királyi Palota (Wing E), Szt. György tér 2* ☎ *1/375–7533* ⊕ *www.btm.hu* ☉ *Mar.–mid-May and mid-Sept.–Oct., Wed.–Mon. 10–6; mid-May–mid-Sept., daily 10–6; Nov.–Feb., Wed.–Mon. 10–4.*

In the Royal Palace's northern wing, the **Ludwig Múzeum** (Ludwig Museum) houses a collection of more than 200 pieces of Hungarian and contemporary world art, including works by Picasso and Lichtenstein. ⊠ *Királyi Palota (Wing A), Dísz tér 17* ☎ *1/375–7533* ☉ *Tues.–Sun. 10–6.*

The central section of the Royal Palace houses the **Magyar Nemzeti Galéria** (Hungarian National Gallery), which exhibits a wide range of Hungarian fine art. Names to look for are Munkácsy, a 19th-century Romantic painter, and Csontváry, an early Surrealist admired by Picasso. Tours for up to five people with an English-speaking guide can be booked in advance. ⊠ *Királyi Palota (entrance in Wing C), Dísz tér 17* ☎ *1/375–7533; 1/224–3700 Ext. 423 for tours* ☉ *Mid-Mar.–Nov., Tues.–Sun. 10–6; Dec.–mid-Mar., Tues.–Sun. 10–4.*

❷ Mátyás templom (Matthias Church). This venerable church, with its distinctive roof of colored, diamond-pattern tiles and skeletal Gothic spire, dates from the 13th century. Built as a mosque by the Turks, it was destroyed and reconstructed during the 19th century, only to be bombed during World War II. Only the south porch survives from the original

FodorsChoice
★

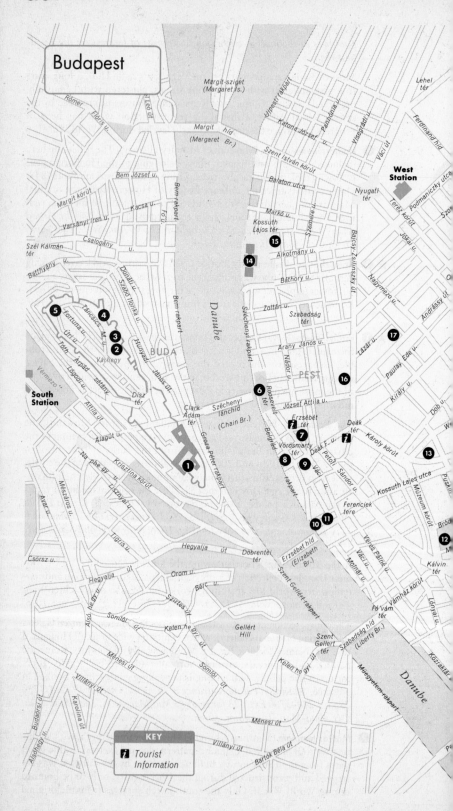

Budapest

Margit-sziget
(Margaret Is.)

Margit híd
(Margaret Br.)

West Station

Danube

BUDA

PEST

South Station

Clark Ádám tér

Széchenyi Lánchíd
(Chain Br.)

Erzsébet híd
(Elizabeth Br.)

Gellért Hill

Szabadság híd
(Liberty Br.)

Danube

KEY

Tourist Information

structure. The Habsburg emperors were crowned kings of Hungary here. High mass—in Latin—is held every Sunday at 10 AM with an orchestra and choir, and organ concerts are often held in the summer on Friday at 8 PM. Visitors are asked to remain at the back of the church during services (it's least intrusive to come after 9:30 AM weekdays and between 1 PM and 5 PM Sunday and holidays). ⊠ *Szentháromság tér 2* ☎ *1/355–5657* ☉ *Church daily 7 AM–8:30 PM. Treasury daily 9:30–5:30.*

❹ Zenetörténeti Múzeum (Museum of Music History). The handsome, 18th-century gray-stone palace that once belonged to the noble Erdődy family hosts intimate recitals of classical music and displays rare manuscripts and antique instruments. ⊠ *Táncsics Mihály u. 7* ☎ *1/214–6770* ☉ *Mid-Mar.–mid-Nov., Tues.–Fri. 10–5, weekends 10–6.*

The Heart of the City

Pest fans out from the Belváros (Inner City), which is bounded by the Kiskörút (Little Ring Road). The Nagykörút (Grand Ring Road) describes a wider semicircle from the Margaret Bridge to the Petőfi Bridge.

⓫ Belvárosi plébánia templom (Inner-City Parish Church). The oldest church in Pest dates from the 12th century. It incorporates a succession of Western architectural styles and preserves a Muslim prayer niche from the time when the Turks ruled the country. Liszt, who lived only a few yards away, often played the organ here. ⊠ *Március 15 tér 2.*

★ Korzó. This elegant promenade runs south along the Pest side of the river, providing views of Castle Hill, the Chain Bridge, and Gellért Hill on the other side of the Danube. ⊠ *from Eötvös tér to Március 15 tér.*

★ ⓱ Magyar Állami Operaház (Hungarian State Opera House). Flanked by a pair of marble sphinxes, this 19th-century neo-Renaissance treasure was the crowning achievement of architect Miklós Ybl. It has been restored to its original ornate glory—particularly inside. ⊠ *Andrássy út 22* ☎ *1/331–2550* ⊕ *www.opera.hu* ☞ *Foreign-language tours (45 mins) daily at 3 and 4; meet at the Sphinx statue in front of opera house on right-hand side.*

⓬ Magyar Nemzeti Múzeum (Hungarian National Museum). The stern, classical edifice was built between 1837 and 1847. On its steps, on March 15, 1848, Petőfi Sándor recited his revolutionary poem, "Nemzeti Dal" ("National Song"), declaring "By the God of Magyar, / Do we swear, / Do we swear, chains no longer / Will we wear." This poem, along with the "12 Points," a formal list of political demands by young Hungarians, called upon the people to rise up against the Habsburgs. Celebrations of the national holiday—long banned by the Communist regime—are now held here (and throughout the city) every year on March 15. A host of royal relics can be seen in the domed Hall of Honor. The museum's epic Hungarian history exhibition includes displays chronicling the end of Communism and the much-celebrated exodus of the Russian troops. ⊠ *Múzeum körút 14–16* ☎ *1/338–2122* ⊕ *www.hnm.hu* ☉ *Mid-Mar.–mid-Oct., Tues.–Sun. 10–6; mid-Oct.–mid-Mar., Tues.–Sun. 10–5.*

⓾ Március 15 tér (March 15 Square). This square is not particularly picturesque, but it commemorates the 1848 struggle for independence from the Habsburgs with a statue of the poet Petőfi Sándor, who died in a later uprising. On March 15, the national holiday commemorating the revolution, the square is packed with patriotic Hungarians. ⊠ *end of Apácai Csere János u. just north of Erzsébet Bridge.*

⓭ Nagy Zsinagóga (Great Synagogue). Europe's largest synagogue was built between 1844 and 1859 in a Byzantine-Moorish style. Desecrated by German and Hungarian Nazis, it underwent years of massive restorations in the post-Communist years. Liszt and Saint-Saëns are among the great musicians who once played the synagogue's grand organ. ⌧ *Dohány u. 2–8* ☏ *1/342–1335* ⊗ *Mon.–Thurs. 10–5, Fri. 10–3, Sun. 10–1.*

⑮ Néprajzi Múzeum (Museum of Ethnography). Elegant both inside and out, this museum has impressive, exhaustive exhibits—captioned in English—of folk costumes and traditions. ⌧ *Kossuth Lajos tér 12* ☏ *1/473–2400* ⊕ *www.neprajz.hu* ⊗ *Tues.–Sun. 10–6.*

Fodor'sChoice
★

⑭ Országház (Parliament). The riverfront's most striking landmark is the imposing neo-Gothic Parliament, now minus the red star on top, designed by Imre Steindl. Although it is still a workplace for the nation's legislators, the interior can be seen during regular guided tours that show off the gilded cathedral ceilings, frescoed walls, intricate glass windows, and majestic stairways (of which there are some 20 km in the building!). The highlight is the nation's Holy Crown, made for Hungary's first king, Szent István (St. Stephen), in the year 1000. The crown, Hungary's national symbol, was relocated from the National Museum and now rests on a velvet pillow flanked by two sword-wielding uniformed guards under Parliament's soaring central cupola. One-hour tours in English are held daily at 10 and 2. Purchase tickets at Gate X, to the right of the main entrance steps. You are advised to arrive at least a half hour early, and you must bring a valid passport. ⌧ *Kossuth Lajos tér* ☏ *1/441–4904 or 1/441–4415* ⊕ *www.mkogy.hu* ⊗ *Weekdays 8–6, Sat. 8–4, Sun. 8–2.*

⑥ Roosevelt tér (Roosevelt Square). On this picturesque square opening onto the Danube you'll find the 19th-century neoclassical **Magyar Tudományos Akadémia** (Hungarian Academy of Sciences) and the 1907 **Gresham Palota** (Gresham Palace), a crumbling tribute to the age of art nouveau currently undergoing massive renovations and eventually to become a Four Seasons hotel. ⌧ *at Pest end of Széchenyi lánchíd (Chain Bridge).*

★ **Széchenyi lánchíd** (Chain Bridge). The most beautiful of the Danube's eight bridges, the Széchenyi lánchíd was built twice: once in the 19th century and again after it was destroyed by the Nazis. ⌧ *Spanning the Danube between Roosevelt tér and Clark Ádám tér in District I.*

⑯ Szent István Bazilika (St. Stephen's Basilica). Massive and imposing, the 19th-century basilica is one of the landmarks of Pest. It was planned early in the 19th century as a neoclassical building, but by the time it was completed more than 50 years later, it was decidedly neo-Renaissance. The mummified right hand of St. Stephen, Hungary's first king and patron saint, is preserved in the Szent Jobb Chapel; the guard will illuminate it for you for a minimal charge. A climb up to the cupola (or a lift on the elevator) affords a sweeping city view. An ongoing, massive cleaning of the basilica's exterior, which at this writing is scheduled to be finished in 2005, has restored the marble to a sparking white. ⌧ *Szt. István tér* ☏ *1/317–2859* ⊗ *Church Mon.–Sat. 7–7, Sun 1–7. Szt. Jobb Chapel Apr.–Sept., Mon.–Sat. 9–5; Oct.–Mar., Mon.–Sat. 10–4. Cupola mid-Apr.–Oct., daily 10–5.*

Fodor'sChoice
★

⑨ Váci utca (Váci Street). Lined with expensive boutiques and dozens of souvenir shops, this pedestrian-only thoroughfare is Budapest's most upscale shopping street and one of its most kitschy tourist areas. Váci utca stretches south of Kossuth Lajos utca, making the total length extend from Vörösmarty tér to the Szabadság Bridge. ⌧ *from Vörösmarty tér to Fővám tér.*

⑧ Vigadó (Concert Hall). Designed in a striking romantic style by Frigyes Feszl and inaugurated in 1865 with Franz Liszt conducting his own *St.*

Elizabeth Oratorio, the concert hall is a curious mixture of Byzantine, Moorish, Romanesque, and Hungarian motifs, punctuated by statues of dancing figures and sturdy pillars. Brahms, Debussy, and Casals are among the musicians who have graced its stage. Mahler's Symphony No. 1 and many works by Bartók were first performed here. You can go into the lobby on your own, but the hall is open only for concerts. ⊠ *Vigadó tér 2* ☎ *1/318–9167 box office.*

⑦ Vörösmarty tér (Vörösmarty Square). In this handsome square in the heart of the Inner City, street musicians and sidewalk cafés combine to make one of the liveliest, albeit sometimes too touristy, atmospheres in Budapest. It's a great spot to sit and relax—but prepare to be approached by caricature artists and money changers. ⊠ *at northern end of Váci u.*

Hősök Tere & Városliget

Heroes' Square is the gateway to Városliget (City Park): a square km (almost ½ square mi) of recreation, entertainment, nature, and culture.

⑱ Hősök tere (Heroes' Square). Budapest's grandest boulevard, Andrássy út, ends at this sweeping piazza flanked by the Szépművészeti Múzeum and the Műcsarnok. In the center stands the 120-foot bronze **Millenniumi Emlékmű** (Millennium Monument), begun in 1896 to commemorate the 1,000th anniversary of the Magyar Conquest. Statues of Árpád and six other founders of the Magyar nation occupy the base of the monument, while Hungary's greatest rulers and princes stand between the columns on either side. ⊠ *Andrássy út at Dózsa György út.*

⑳ Műcsarnok (Palace of Exhibitions). This striking 1895 structure on Heroes' Square schedules exhibitions of contemporary Hungarian and international art and a rich series of films, plays, and concerts. ⊠ *Dózsa György út 37* ☎ *1/363–2671* ⊕ *www.mucsarnok.hu* ☾ *Tues.–Sun. 10–6.*

⑲ Szépművészeti Múzeum (Fine Arts Museum). An entire section of this Heroes' Square museum is devoted to Egyptian, Greek, and Roman artifacts, including many rare Greco-Roman ceramics. The institution's collection of Spanish paintings is among the best of its kind outside Spain. ⊠ *Dózsa György út 41* ☎ *1/363–2675* ⊕ *www2.szepmuveszeti.hu* ☾ *Tues.–Sun. 10–5:30.*

Fodor's Choice ★

★ **Városliget** (City Park). Just behind Heroes' Square, this park harbors Budapest's zoo, the state circus, an amusement park, and the outdoor swimming pool of the Széchenyi mineral baths. Inside is **Vajdahunyad Vár** (Vajdahunyad Castle), an art historian's Disneyland, created for the millennial celebration in 1896 and incorporating architectural elements typical of various periods of Hungary's history all in one complex. ⊠ *between Dózsa György út and Hungária körút, and Vágány u. and Ajtósi Dürer sor.*

Elsewhere in the City

Aquincum. The reconstructed remains of the capital of the Roman province of Pannonia, dating from the 1st century AD, lie in northern Budapest's Óbuda District. A varied selection of artifacts and mosaics has been unearthed, giving a tantalizing inkling of what life was like on the northern fringes of the Roman empire. The on-site **Aquincum Museum** displays the dig's most notable finds. ⊠ *Szentendrei út 139* ☎ *1/250–1650* ☾ *Apr. and Oct., Tues.–Sun. 10–5; May–Sept., Tues.–Sun. 10–6. Grounds open at 9.*

Jánoshegy (János Hill). A *libegő* (chairlift) will take you to the summit, the highest point in Budapest, where you can climb a lookout tower for the best view of the city. Take Bus 158 from Moszkva tér to last stop, Zugligeti út. ⊠ *Zugligeti út 97* ☎ *1/394–3764* ☾ *Mid-May–mid-Sept.,* *daily 9–6; mid-Sept.–mid-May (depending on weather), daily 9:30–4. Closed alternate Mon.*

Szobor Park (Statue Park). For a look at Budapest's too-recent Iron Curtain past, make the 30-minute drive out to this open-air exhibit cleverly nicknamed "Tons of Socialism." Forty-two Communist statues and memorials that once dominated the city have been exiled here since the political changes in 1989. You can wander among mammoth figures of Lenin and Marx while listening to songs from the Hungarian and Russian workers' movement blaring from loudspeakers. To get here by public transport, take the yellow bus (number 6) at Etele ter. ⊠ *Balatoni út, corner of Szabadkai út* ☎ *1/424–7500* ⊕ *www.szoborpark. hu* ⊗ *Daily 10–dusk.*

Where to Eat

Private restaurateurs are breathing excitement into the Budapest dining scene. You can choose from Chinese, Mexican, Italian, French, Indian, or various other cuisines—there are even vegetarian restaurants. Or you can stick to solid, traditional Hungarian fare. Be sure to check out the less expensive spots favored by locals. If you get a craving for sushi or tortellini, consult the restaurant listings in the *Budapest Sun, Where Budapest* magazine, and *Budapest in Your Pocket.*

$$$$ ✕ **Gundel.** George Lang, Hungary's best-known restaurateur, show-
Fodor'sChoice cases his country's cuisine at this turn-of-the-20th-century palazzo in
★ City Park. Dark-wood paneling, rich navy blue–and–pink fabrics, and tables set with Zsolnay porcelain make the oversized dining room plush and handsome. Violinist György Lakatos, of the Lakatos Gypsy musician dynasty, strolls from table to table playing folk music. Waiters in black tie serve traditional favorites such as tender beef tournedos topped with goose liver and forest mushroom sauce or excellent fish specialties. The most affordable choice here is one of the tasting menus, a six-course affair with complementary wines. ⊠ *Állatkerti út 2* ☎ *1/468–4040* ⚜ *Reservations essential* ⊟ *AE, DC, MC, V.*

$$–$$$$ ✕ **Kacsa.** Hungarian and international dishes with a focus on duck are done with a light touch, with quiet chamber music in the background, in this small, celebrated restaurant just a few steps from the river. Try the crisp wild duck stuffed with plums, but be wary of the pricey wine list. ⊠ *Fő u. 75* ☎ *1/201–9992* ⚜ *Reservations essential* ⊟ *AE, DC, MC, V* ⊗ *No lunch weekends.*

$$–$$$$ ✕ **Múzeum.** Named for its location just steps from the National Museum, this elegant salon with mirrors, mosaics, and swift waiters serves authentic Hungarian cuisine with a lighter touch. The salads are fresh, the Hungarian wines are excellent, and the chef dares to be creative. ⊠ *Múzeum körút 12* ☎ *1/267–0375 or 1/338–4221* ⊟ *MC, V* ⊗ *Closed Sun.*

$$–$$$$ ✕ **Tom-George.** Well situated in the heart of downtown, Tom-George is Budapest's answer to urban chic. The spacious bar blends blond wood and wicker, giving the interior a relaxed yet sophisticated feel. Minimalism at the table, though, belies exotic creativity in the kitchen, all with an Asian touch. House specialties include *nasi goreng* (Indonesian fried rice) and lamb with satay sauce. Sushi—perhaps Budapest's best—is glamorously prepared by the in-house sushi chef. ⊠ *Október 6 utca 8* ☎ *1/266-3525* ⚜ *Reservations essential* ⊟ *AE, V.*

$$–$$$ ✕ **Baraka.** The white stucco walls and airy balcony are offset by the gleam
Fodor'sChoice of varnished floorboards in this cozy and hospitable restaurant tucked
★ away on Magyar utca. The friendly husband and wife owners are never too far away, and they will tell you the source of every ingredient on the menu. The ginger-seared tuna is recommended, as is the caprese salad

with mint-basil dressing. Don't miss the unforgettable chocolate volcano for dessert. ⊠ *Magyar u. 12–14* ☎ *1/483–1355* ⌘ *Reservations essential* ▤ *AE, DC, MC, V* ⊘ *Closed Sun.*

\$\$–\$\$\$ ✕ **Kisbuda Gyöngye.** This Budapest favorite, hidden away on a small street in Óbuda, is filled with mixed antique furniture, and its walls are covered with a patchwork of antique, carved wooden cupboard doors. Try the fresh trout smothered in cream sauce with mushrooms and capers. ⊠ *Kenyeres u. 34* ☎ *1/368–6402 or 1/368–9246* ⌘ *Reservations essential* ▤ *AE, DC, MC, V* ⊘ *Closed Sun.*

★ **\$\$–\$\$\$** ✕ **Vörös és Fehér.** This smart wine bar and restaurant opened by the Budapest Wine Society is the place to enjoy Hungary's excellent vintages. Tapas-style snacks, such as smoked venison ham or marinated salmon, are perfect alongside a glass of the local favorite. The stylish wood and wrought-iron interior are all contemporary bistro, and the big glass windows facing bustling Andrássy út make you feel like you're in the center of it all. After dinner, don't miss the chance to taste some *tokaji aszú*—the celebrated Hungarian dessert wine. ⊠ *Andrássy út 41* ☎ *1/413–1545* ▤ *AE, MC, V.*

★ **\$–\$\$\$** ✕ **Náncsi Néni.** "Aunt Nancy's" out-of-the-way restaurant is irresistibly cozy. The dining room feels like a country kitchen: chains of paprikas and garlic dangle from the low wooden ceiling, and shelves along the walls are crammed with jars of home-pickled vegetables. On the Hungarian menu (which means large portions), turkey dishes are given a creative flair, such as breast fillets stuffed with apples, peaches, mushrooms, cheese, and sour cream. Special touches include an outdoor garden in summer and free champagne for all couples in love. Reservations are recommended. ⊠ *Ördögárok út 80* ☎ *1/397–2742* ▤ *MC, V.*

★ **\$–\$\$** ✕ **Café Kör.** Vaulted ceilings, low lighting, and wood floors with Oriental-style rugs render a warm and classy atmosphere. Service is excellent. The kitchen has won tremendous popularity for its lighter touch on Hungarian and Continental meat dishes and ample salads. The Kör appetizer platter, generously piled with pâtés, Brie, vegetables, goose liver, salmon, and more, is perfect for sharing. Avoid the tables by the bathroom doors and immediately at the entrance. ⊠ *Sas u. 17* ☎ *1/311–0053* ⌘ *Reservations essential* ▤ *No credit cards* ⊘ *Closed Sun.*

\$ ✕ **Tüköry Söröző.** At this traditional Hungarian spot, carnivores can sample the beefsteak tartare, topped with a raw egg; many say it's the best in town. ⊠ *Hold u. 15* ☎ *1/269–5027* ▤ *AE, MC, V* ⊘ *Closed weekends.*

Where to Stay

Some 30 million tourists come to Hungary every year, and the boom has encouraged hotel building; nearly every major Western chain has a full-service hotel here. If you arrive in Budapest without a reservation, go to the 24-hour Tribus Hotel Service or to one of the tourist offices at any of the train stations or at the airport.

\$\$\$\$ ▨ **Budapest Hilton.** Built in 1977 around a 13th-century monastery adjacent to the Matthias Church, this perfectly integrated architectural wonder overlooks the Danube from the best site on Castle Hill. Every ample room has a remarkable view. Service is of the highest caliber. ⊠ *Hess András tér 1–3, H-1014* ☎ *1/488–6600; 800/445–8667 in U.S. and Canada* ☎ *1/488–6688* ⊕ *www.danubiusgroup.com* ⤸ *295 rooms, 27 suites* △ *3 restaurants, 2 bars* ▤ *AE, DC, MC, V.*

★ **\$\$\$\$** ▨ **Hotel Inter-Continental Budapest.** This modern, riverside hotel consistently wins applause for its superior business facilities, friendly service, and gorgeous views across the Danube to Castle Hill. Sixty percent of the rooms face the river (and are slightly more expensive than those that don't). The rooms are decorated in pleasant pastels and furnished in the

Central European Biedermeier style. The bustling lobby café serves fresh pastries and sandwiches. ✉ *Apáczai Csere János u. 12–14, H-1368* ☎ *1/327–6333; 800/327–0200 in U.S.* 🖶 *1/327–6357* 🌐 *www. intercontinental.com* 🛏 *382 rooms, 16 suites* ⚭ *2 restaurants, pool, bar* 🚊 *AE, DC, MC, V.*

$$$$ 🏨 **Kempinski Hotel Corvinus Budapest.** Afternoon chamber music sets the tone at this sleek luxury hotel. Rooms are spacious, with elegant contemporary decor accented by geometric blond-and-black Swedish inlaid woods. The large, sparkling bathrooms are among the best in Budapest. ✉ *Erzsébet tér 7–8, H-1051* ☎ *1/429–3777; 800/426–3135 in U.S. and Canada* 🖶 *1/429–4777* 🌐 *www.kempinski-budapest.com* 🛏 *340 rooms, 29 suites* ⚭ *4 restaurants, pool, bar* 🚊 *AE, DC, MC, V.*

★ **$$$$** 🏨 **Le Méridien Budapest.** From Persian carpets and heavy silk draperies in the hushed lobby to polished walnut surfaces and twinkling chandeliers in the guest rooms, refined old-world elegance is everywhere. In a 1913 historic landmark building in the heart of downtown Pest, this five-star hotel is well situated for business as well as sightseeing. Breakfast and afternoon high tea are served under the lobby's soaring stained-glass cupola. ✉ *Erzsébet tér 9–10, H-1051* ☎ *1/429–5500; 800/225–5843 in U.S. and Canada* 🖶 *1/429–5555* 🌐 *www.lemeridien-hotels.com* 🛏 *192 rooms, 26 suites* ⚭ *Restaurant, pool, bar* 🚊 *AE, DC, MC, V.*

$$$ 🏨 **art'otel.** Boutique hotels may not be anything new in the West, but art'otel has the distinction of being the only one in Budapest, and it is a tribute to its class. From the multimillion-dollar art collection on the walls to the carpet and water fountains, the interior is all the work of one man, American artist Donald Sultan. Encompassing one new building and four 18th-century baroque houses on the Buda riverfront, the hotel adroitly blends old and new. Some rooms also have splendid views of Fisherman's Bastion and the Matthias Church. ✉ *Bem rakpart 16–19, H-1011* ☎ *1/487–9487* 🖶 *1/487–9488* 🛏 *156 rooms, 9 suites* ⚭ *Restaurant* 🚊 *AE, DC, MC, V.*

$$$ 🏨 **Budapest Marriott.** At this sophisticated yet friendly hotel near downtown Pest, every detail sparkles, including the marble floors and dark-wood paneling in the lobby. Stunning vistas open from every guest room, the ballroom, and even the outstanding fitness room. Most rooms have a balcony. ✉ *Apáczai Csere János u. 4, H-1052* ☎ *1/266–7000; 800/228–9290 in U.S. and Canada* 🖶 *1/266–5000* 🌐 *www.marriotthotels. com* 🛏 *351 rooms, 11 suites* ⚭ *3 restaurants* 🚊 *AE, DC, MC, V.*

$$$ 🏨 **Danubius Hotel Gellért.** Built between 1912 and 1918, Budapest's most renowned art nouveau hotel was favored by Otto von Habsburg, son of the last emperor. The Gellért is undergoing an incremental overhaul, which is refurnishing rooms in the original Jugendstil style. It's a good idea to inquire about completed rooms when you reserve. Weekend rates can be more affordable. All guests have free access to the monumental and ornate thermal baths, the most stunning in Budapest. ✉ *Gellért tér 1, H-1111* ☎ *1/385–2200* 🖶 *1/466–6631* 🌐 *www. danubiusgroup.com* 🛏 *220 rooms, 14 suites* ⚭ *2 restaurants, pool, bar* 🚊 *AE, DC, MC, V.*

FodorsChoice ★

$$$ 🏨 **Danubius Thermal Hotel Helia.** A sleek Scandinavian design and a less hectic location upriver from downtown make this spa hotel on the Danube a change of pace from its Pest peers. Rooms are reasonably spacious and furnished in the ubiquitous "Scandinavian" style popularized by IKEA. The spa facilities are the most spotlessly clean in Budapest, and an on-site medical clinic caters to English-speaking clients—including everything from electrotherapy to fitness tests. The staff is friendly and helpful, and most of the comfortable rooms have Danube views. All room rates include use of the thermal bath and free parking. ✉ *Kárpát u. 62–64, H-1133* ☎ *1/452–5800* 🖶 *1/452–5801* 🌐 *www.*

danubiusgroup.com ↘ *254 rooms, 8 suites* ⚙ *Restaurant, pool, bar* ▭ *AE, DC, MC, V.*

$$ ▢ **Carlton Budapest.** Tucked into an alley at the foot of Castle Hill, this spotless, modern hotel is a short walk via the Chain Bridge from business and shopping districts. The reception area is simply furnished in white and pale-gray contemporary shades. Rooms on the upper floors offer majestic Danube views. About half the rooms have a shower only. A buffet breakfast is included in the room price. ⊠ *Apor Péter u. 3, H-1011* ☎ *1/224–0999* 🖨 *1/224–0990* ⊕ *www.carltonhotel.hu* ↘ *95 rooms* ⚙ *Bar* ▭ *AE, DC, MC, V.*

$$ ▢ **Victoria.** The stately Parliament building is visible from every room of this intimate establishment right on the Danube. The absence of conventioneers is a plus, and the location—an easy walk from Castle Hill and downtown Pest—couldn't be better. Room rates include breakfast. ⊠ *Bem rakpart 11, H-1011* ☎ *1/457–8080* 🖨 *1/457–8088* ⊕ *www.victoria.hu* ↘ *27 rooms, 1 suite* ⚙ *Bar* ▭ *AE, DC, MC, V.*

$ ▢ **Kulturinov.** One wing of a magnificent 1902 neo-baroque castle now houses basic budget accommodations. Rooms come with two or three beds and are clean and peaceful; breakfast is included in the rates. The neighborhood—one of Budapest's most famous squares in the luxurious castle district—is magical. ⊠ *Szentháromság tér 6, H-1014* ☎ *1/355–0122* 🖨 *1/375–1886* ↘ *16 rooms* ▭ *AE, DC, MC, V.*

$ ▢ **Molnár Panzió.** Fresh air, peace, and quiet reign at this immaculate guest house high above Buda on Széchenyi Hill, 20 minutes from downtown Pest. Rooms in the octagonal main house are polyhedral, clean, and bright; most have distant views of Castle Hill and Gellért Hill, and some have balconies. Twelve rooms in a building next door are more private and have superior bathrooms. Service is friendly and professional, and the restaurant is first-rate. A Finnish sauna and garden setting add to the pension's appeal. ⊠ *Fodor u. 143, H-1124* ☎ *1/395–1873 or 1/395–1874* 🖨🖨 *1/395–1872* ⊕ *www.hotel-molnar.hu* ↘ *23 rooms* ⚙ *Restaurant* ▭ *AE, DC, MC, V.*

Fodor'sChoice
★

Nightlife & the Arts

The Arts

The English-language *Budapest Sun* has a weekly calendar of entertainment and cultural events. *Budapest in Your Pocket*, published six times a year, has a thorough list of entertainment venues. Both are available at most newsstands. Buy tickets at venue box offices, your hotel desk, many tourist offices, or ticket agencies. Arts festivals begin to fill the calendar in early spring. The season's first and biggest, the **Budapest Spring Festival** (early to mid-March), showcases Hungary's best opera, music, theater, fine arts, and dance, as well as visiting foreign artists. The weeklong **BudaFest** opera and ballet festival (mid-August) takes place at the Opera House. Information and tickets are available from ticket agencies. For music in Budapest, try the **National Philharmonic Ticket Office** (⊠ Mérleg u. 10 ☎ 1/318–0281). For various cultural events in Budapest, contact the **Vigadó Ticket Office** (⊠ Vörösmarty tér 1 ☎ 1/327–4322).

CONCERTS & MUSICALS   Several excellent orchestras, such as the Budapest Festival Orchestra, are based in Budapest. Concerts frequently include works by Hungarian composers Bartók, Kodály, and Liszt. **Liszt Ferenc Zeneakadémia** (Franz Liszt Academy of Music; ⊠ Liszt Ferenc tér 8 ☎ 1/342–0179) is Budapest's premier classical concert venue; orchestra and chamber music performances take place in its splendid main hall. Operettas and Hungarian renditions of popular Broadway musicals are staged at the **Operett Színház** (Operetta Theater; ⊠ Nagymező u. 17 ☎ 1/353–2172). Classical concerts are also held at the **Pesti Vigadó** (Pest Concert Hall;

✉ Vigadó tér 2 ☎ 1/327–4322). The **Régi Zeneakadémia** (Old Academy of Music; ✉ Vörösmarty u. 35 ☎ 1/322–9804) is a smaller venue for chamber music. The 1896 **Vígszínház** (Comedy Theater; ✉ Pannónia út 8 ☎ 1/329–2340) presents mostly musicals.

OPERA & DANCE In additional to the main venues for folk dancing, there are regular participatory folk-dance evenings—with instructions for beginners—at district cultural centers; consult the entertainment listings of *Where Budapest* and the *Budapest Sun* for schedules and locations, or check with a hotel concierge. Budapest has two opera houses, both of which stage opera and ballet. The main opera house is the gorgeous neo-Renaissance **Magyar Állami Operaház** (Hungarian State Opera House; ✉ Andrássy út 22 ☎ 1/353–0170), which is also the city's main venue for classical ballet. The rather plain **Erkel Színház** (Erkel Theater; ✉ Köztársaság tér ☎ 1/333–0540) is the State Opera's homely little theater.

From May through September, displays of Hungarian folk dancing take place at the **Folklór Centrum** (Folklore Center; ✉ Fehérvári út 47 ☎ 1/203–3868). The Hungarian State Folk Ensemble performs regularly at the **Budai Vigadó** (✉ Corvin tér 8 ☎ 1/201–3766). The young **Trafó Kortárs Művészetek Háza** (Trafo House of Contemporary Arts; ✉ Liliom u. 41 ☎ 1/456–2044) has become the hub of Budapest's modern and avant-garde dance and music productions.

Nightlife

Budapest is a lively city by night. Establishments stay open well past midnight, and Western European–style bars and British-style pubs have sprung up all over the city. For quiet conversation, hotel bars are a good choice, but beware the inflated prices. Expect to pay cash for your night on the town. The city also has its share of seedy go-go clubs and "cabarets," some of which have been shut down for scandalously excessive billing and physical intimidation and assault. Avoid places where women lingering nearby "invite" you in, and never order without first seeing the price.

BARS The most popular of Budapest's Irish pubs and a favorite expat watering hole is **Becketts** (✉ Bajcsy-Zsilinszky út 72 ☎ 1/311–1035), where Guinness flows amid polished-wood and brass decor. **Buena Vista** (✉ Liszt Ferenc tér 4–5 ☎ 1/344–6303) in the heart of the "tér"—Listz Ferenc tér—has cool jazz trios and classy bar snacks. **Café Pierrot** (✉ Fortuna u. 14 ☎ 1/375–6971) is an elegant café and piano bar on a small street on Castle Hill.

CASINOS Most casinos are open daily from 2 PM until 4 or 5 AM and offer gambling in hard currency—usually euros—only. You must be 18 to enter a casino in Hungary. The popular **Las Vegas Casino** (✉ Roosevelt tér 2 ☎ 1/317–6022) is centrally located in the Atrium Hyatt Hotel. In an 1879 building designed by the architect Miklós Ybl, who also designed the Hungarian State Opera House, the **Várkert Casino** (✉ Miklós Ybl tér 9 ☎ 1/202–4244) is the most attractive in the city.

JAZZ & DANCE CLUBS Established Hungarian headliners and young up-and-comers perform nightly at the **Jazz Garden** (✉ Veres Pálné u. 44/a ☎ 1/266–7364). Shows start at 9 PM; there is a 700-Ft. cover charge.

A welcoming, gay-friendly crowd flocks to late-night hot spot **Café Capella** (✉ Belgrád rakpart 23 ☎ 1/318–6231) for glittery drag shows (held nightly) and DJ'd club music. There's a 500-Ft. drink minimum every night, plus a cover charge (500 Ft. Wed., Thurs., and Sun., 1,000 Ft. Fri. and Sat.). **Club Seven** (✉ Akácfa 7 ☎ 1/478–9030) has more than one place to play, including an elegant cocktail bar separate from the main room, where an outgoing Hungarian crowd grooves to a mixture of live jazz, rock cover bands, and recorded dance music.

Shopping

You'll find plenty of expensive boutiques, folk art and souvenir shops, and classical record shops on or around **Váci utca**, Budapest's pedestrian-only promenade. Browsing among some of the smaller, less touristy, more typically Hungarian shops in Pest—on the **Kiskörút** (Small Ring Boulevard) and **Nagykörút** (Great Ring Boulevard)—may prove more interesting and less pricey. Artsy boutiques are springing up in the section of District V south of Ferenciek tére toward the Danube and around Kálvin tér. **Falk Miksa utca**, north of Parliament, is home to some of the city's best antiques stores. You'll also encounter Transylvanian women dressed in colorful folk costume standing on busy sidewalks selling their own handmade embroideries and ceramics at rock-bottom prices. Look for them at **Moszkva tér, Jászai Mari tér,** outside the **Kossuth tér Metro,** and around **Váci utca.**

For a Hungarian take on a most American concept, you can visit one of the many mega-malls springing up around the city. **Mammut** (⊠ Lövő-ház u. 2–6 ☎ 1/345–8020) is in central Buda, and is open on Sunday. There's also a cinema there. The **West End** (⊠ Váci út 1–3 ☎ 1/238–7777), behind Nyugati train station in downtown Pest, comes complete with a waterfall, a T.G.I. Friday's restaurant, and a multiplex cinema.

A good place for special gifts, **Holló Műhely** (⊠ Vitkovics Mihály u. 12 ☎ 1/317–8103) sells the work of László Holló, a master wood crafts-man who has resurrected traditional motifs and styles of earlier centuries. There are lovely hope chests, chairs, jewelry boxes, candlesticks, and more, all hand-carved and hand-painted with cheery folk motifs—a pre-dominance of birds and flowers in reds, blues, and greens.

Stores specializing in Hungary's excellent wines have become a trend in Budapest. Among the best of them is the store run by the **Budapest Bortársaság** (Budapest Wine Society; ⊠ Batthyány u. 59 ☎ 1/212–0262). The cellar shop, at the base of Castle Hill, always has an excellent selection of Hungary's finest wines, chosen by the wine society's discerning staff, who will happily help you with your purchases. Tastings are held Saturday afternoons from 2 to 5.

Markets

The magnificent, cavernous, three-story **Vásárcsarnok** (Central Market Hall; ⊠ Vámház körút 1–3) teems with shoppers browsing among stalls packed with salamis, red paprika chains, and other enticements. Upstairs you can buy folk embroideries and souvenirs.

A good way to find bargains (and adventure) is to make an early-morning trip out to **Ecseri Piac** (⊠ Nagykőrösi út), a vast, colorful, chaotic flea market on the outskirts of Budapest. Try to go Saturday morning, when the most vendors are out. To get there, take Bus 54 from Boráros tér. Foreigners are a favorite target for overcharging, so be tough when bargaining.

Budapest Essentials

AIR TRAVEL

The most convenient way to fly between Hungary and the United States is with Malév Hungarian Airlines' nonstop direct service between JFK International Airport in New York and Budapest's Ferihegy Airport—still the only such flight that exists. Several other airlines offer connecting service from North America, including Austrian Airlines (through Vienna), British Airways (through London), Czech Airlines (through Prague), and Lufthansa (through Frankfurt or Munich).

✈ **Austrian Airlines** ☎ 1/296-0660. **British Airways** ☎ 1/411-5555. **ČSA** (Czech Airlines) ☎ 1/318-3175. **Lufthansa** ☎ 1/429-8011. **Malév** ☎ 1/235-3535 ticketing, 1/235-3888 flight information. **Swiss** ☎ 1/328-5000.

AIRPORTS & TRANSFERS

Ferihegy Repülőtér, Hungary's only commercial airport with regularly scheduled service, is 24 km (15 mi) southeast of downtown Budapest. All non-Hungarian airlines operate from Terminal 2B; those of Malév, from Terminal 2A. (The older part of the airport, Terminal 1, no longer serves commercial flights, so the main airport is now often referred to as Ferihegy 2 and the terminals simply as A and B.)

✈ **Ferihegy Repülőtér** ☎ 1/296-9696, 1/296-8000 same-day arrival information, 1/296-7000 same-day departure information.

TRANSFERS Many hotels offer their guests car or minibus transportation to and from Ferihegy, but all of them charge for the service. You should arrange for a pickup in advance. If you're taking a taxi, allow anywhere between 25 minutes during nonpeak hours and at least an hour during rush hours (7 AM–9 AM from the airport, 4 PM–6 PM from the city).

Official airport taxis are queued at the exit and overseen by a taxi monitor; their rates are fixed according to the zone of your final destination. A taxi ride to the center of Budapest will cost around 4,500 Ft. Trips to the airport are about 3,500 Ft. from Pest, 4,000 Ft. from Buda. Avoid taxi drivers who approach you before you are out of the arrivals lounge.

Minibuses run every half hour from 5:30 AM to 9:30 PM from the Hotel Kempinski on Erzsébet tér (near the main bus station and the Deák tér metro hub) in downtown Budapest. It takes almost the same time as taxis but costs only 800 Ft.

The LRI Airport Shuttle provides convenient door-to-door service between the airport and any address in the city. To get to the airport, call to arrange a pickup; to get to the city, make arrangements at LRI's airport desk. Service to or from either terminal costs 1,800 Ft. per person; since it normally shuttles several people at once, remember to allow time for a few other pickups or drop-offs.

BIKE TRAVEL

On Margaret Island in Budapest, Bringóvár, across from the Thermal Hotel, rents four-wheeled pedaled contraptions called *Bringóhintós,* as well as traditional two-wheelers; mountain bikes cost about 850 Ft. per hour, 2,500 Ft. for 24 hours. One-speeders cost less.

🚲 **Bringóvár** ✉ Hajós Alfréd sétány 1 ☎ 1/212-0330.

BUS TRAVEL TO & FROM BUDAPEST

Most buses to Budapest from the western region of Hungary and from Vienna arrive at Népliget station. In general, buses to and from the eastern part of Hungary go from Népstadion.

🚌 **Népliget bus station** ✉ Üllői út. 131 ☎ 1/219-8080. **Népstadion bus station** ✉ Hungária Körút 46-48 ☎ 1/252-1896.

EMERGENCIES

🏥 Doctors & Dentists **R-Klinika** ☎ 1/325-9999 private English-speaking.

🏥 Emergency Services **Ambulance** ☎ 104, 1/200-0100 private English-speaking. **Police** ☎ 107.

🏥 24-hour Pharmacies **Gyógyszertár** ☎ 1/311-4439 in Pest; 1/355-4691 in Buda.

ENGLISH-LANGUAGE MEDIA

Bestsellers ⊠ Október 6 u. 11 ☎ 1/312-1295. **Central European University Academic Bookshop** ⊠ Nádor u. 9 ☎ 1/327-3096.

TAXIS

Taxis are plentiful and are a good value, but be careful to avoid the also plentiful rogue cabbies. For a hassle-free ride, avoid unmarked "freelance" taxis; stick with those affiliated with an established company. Rather than hailing a taxi in the street, your safest bet is to order one by phone; a car will arrive in about 5 to 10 minutes. The average initial charge for taxis ordered by phone is 300 Ft., to which is added about 200 Ft. per kilometer (½ mi) plus 50 Ft. per minute of waiting time. The best rates are offered by Citytaxi, where English is spoken by the dispatchers, and Főtaxi.

Citytaxi ☎ 1/211-1111. **Főtaxi** ☎ 1/222-2222.

TOURS

IBUSZ Travel and Cityrama organize a number of unusual tours, including horseback riding, bicycling, and angling, as well as visits to the National Gallery. These companies provide personal guides on request. Also check at your hotel's reception desk. Chosen Tours offers an excellent three-hour combination bus and walking tour, "Budapest Through Jewish Eyes," highlighting the sights and cultural life of the city's Jewish community.

Chosen Tours ☎ 1/355-2022). **Cityrama** ⊠ Báthori u. 22 ☎ 1/302-4382 ⊕ www.cityrama.hu. **IBUSZ Travel** ⊠ Petőfi tér 3 ☎ 1/318-5707 ⊕ www.ibusz.hu.

BOAT TOURS From April through October, boats leave from the quay at Vigadó tér on 1½-hour cruises between the railroad bridges north and south of the Árpád and Petőfi bridges, respectively. The trip, organized by MAHART Tours, runs only on weekends and holidays until late April, then once or twice a day, depending on the season; the trip costs around 1,000 Ft.

MAHART Tours ☎ 1/484-4013.

BUS TOURS Cityrama offers a three-hour city bus tour (about 6,000 Ft. per person). Year-round, IBUSZ Travel sponsors three-hour bus tours of the city that cost about 6,000 Ft; starting from Roosevelt tér (in front of the Hotel Inter-Continental), they take in parts of both Buda and Pest. Specify whether you prefer live or recorded commentary.

Cityrama ⊠ Báthori u. 22 ☎ 1/302-4382. **IBUSZ Travel** ⊠ Petőfi tér 3 ☎ 1/318-5707 ⊕ www.ibusz.hu.

SINGLE-DAY TOURS Excursions farther afield include daylong trips to the Puszta (Great Plain), the Danube Bend, the Eger wine region, and Lake Balaton. IBUSZ Travel offers trips to the Buda Hills and stays in many of Hungary's historic castles and mansions.

TRAIN TRAVEL

Call the MÁV Passenger Service for train information. Call one of the three main train stations in Budapest for information during off-hours (8 PM–6 AM): Déli, Keleti, and Nyugati. Trains for Vienna usually depart from Keleti station, those for Lake Balaton from Déli.

MÁV Passenger Service ⊠ Andrássy út 35 ☎ 1/461-5500 international, 1/461-5400 domestic **Déli** ⊠ Alkotás u. ☎ 1/375-6293. **Keleti** ⊠ Rákóczi út ☎ 1/313-6835. **Nyugati** ⊠ Nyugati tér ☎ 1/349-0115.

TRANSPORTATION AROUND BUDAPEST

The Budapest Transportation Authority (BKV) runs the public transportation system—the Metro (subway) with three lines, buses, streetcars, and trolleybuses—and it's cheap, efficient, and simple to use. Most of it closes down around 11:30 PM, but certain trams and buses run on a limited schedule all night. A *napijegy* (day ticket) costs about 925 Ft. (a *turista-jegy,* or three-day tourist ticket, costs around 1,825 Ft.) and allows unlimited travel on all services within the city limits. Metro stations or newsstands sell single-ride tickets for about 120 Ft. You can travel on all trams, buses, and on the subway with this ticket, but you can't change lines or direction.

Bus, streetcar, and trolleybus tickets must be validated onboard—watch how other passengers do it. Metro tickets are validated at station entrances. Plainclothes agents wearing red armbands spot-check frequently, often targeting tourists, and you can be fined 1,500 Ft. if you don't have a validated ticket.

TRAVEL AGENCIES

⚑ **American Express** ⊠ Déak Ferenc u. 10 ☎ 1/235-4330. **Travel One** ⊠ Nádor u. 23 ☎ 1/312-6666. **Vista Travel Center** ⊠ Andrássy út 1 ☎ 1/269-6032; 1/269-6033 air tickets; 1/328-4030 train, bus, and boat tickets and youth and student travel ⊕ www. vista.hu.

VISITOR INFORMATION

Vista Visitor Center/Café has created a uniquely welcoming environment for visitors seeking information about Budapest and Hungary. You can linger over lunch in the popular café, browse through brochures, and get information about (and make bookings for) tours, events, accommodations, and more from the young, English-speaking staff. Computer terminals are rented by the hour for Internet surfing and e-mailing; storage lockers are also available, as are international telephone stations with good rates.

The monthly *Where Budapest* magazine and the *Budapest in Your Pocket* guide are good sources. The English-language weekly *Budapest Sun* covers news, business, and culture and includes entertainment listings.

The Tourism Office of Budapest has developed the Budapest Card, which entitles holders to unlimited travel on public transportation; free admission to many museums and sights; and discounts on various purchases, entertainment events, tours, meals, and services from participating businesses. The cost is 3,950 Ft. for two days, 4,950 Ft. for three days; one card is valid for an adult plus a child under 14. Budapest Cards are sold at main metro ticket windows, tourist information offices, and hotels. IBUSZ Travel is a tour company and travel agency that organizes and runs tours all over the country but also helps book accommodations. Tourinform is the national tourism agency, which dispenses advice and information but will also help you book accommodations and transportation. You'll find Tourinform offices everywhere, not just in Budapest.

⚑ **IBUSZ Travel** ⊠ Ferenciek tere 10 ☎ 1/485-2762; 06/20-944-9091; 1/317-7767 tours and programs ⊠ Vörösmarty tér 6 ☎ 1/317-0532. **Tourinform** ⊠ Vörösmarty tér, at Vigadó u. ☎ 1/438-8080; 06/80-660-044 24-hr automated telephone service ⊠ Sütő u. 2 ☎ 1/317-9800 ⊕ www.hungarytourism.hu ⊕ www.tourinform.hu. **Tourism Office of Budapest** ⊠ Liszt Ferenc tér 11 ☎ 1/322-4098 🖶 1/342-9390 ⊠ Nyugati pályaudvar ☎ 1/302-8580 ⊠ Szentháromság tér ☎ 1/488-0453. **Tribus Hotel Service** ⊠ Apáczai Csere János u. 1 ☎ 1/318-5776 or 1/266-8042. **Vista Visitor Center/Café** ⊠ Paulay Ede u. 7 ☎ 1/267-8603.

THE DANUBE BEND

About 40 km (25 mi) north of Budapest, the Danube abandons its eastward course and turns abruptly south toward the capital, cutting through the Börzsöny and Visegrád hills. In this area, the Danube Bend, are the

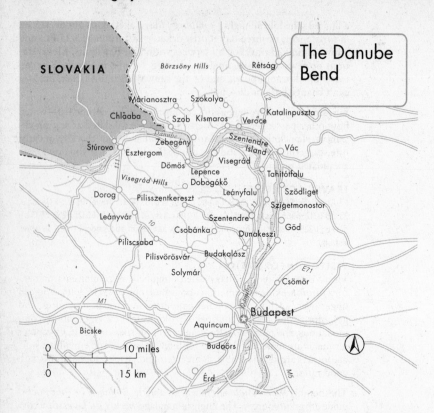

baroque town of Szentendre, the hilltop castle ruins and town of Visegrád, and the cathedral town of Esztergom.

Here, in the heartland, are traces of the country's history—the remains
of the Roman empire's frontiers, the battlefields of the Middle Ages, and
relics of the Hungarian Renaissance. Just 40 minutes or 21 km (13 mi)
north of Budapest is Szentendre, a popular day trip. To visit the entire
area, two days, with a night in Visegrád or Esztergom, is the best way
to savor its charms.

Szentendre

Fodor'sChoice
★
The lively, flourishing artists' colony of Szentendre was first settled by Serbs
and Greeks fleeing the advancing Turks in the 14th and 17th centuries.
The narrow cobbled streets are lined with cheerfully painted houses,
many now containing art galleries. Unfortunately, tacky souvenir shops
have appeared, and in summer, the streets swarm with tourists. Part of
the town's artistic reputation can be traced to the ceramic artist Margit
Kovács, whose pottery blended Hungarian folk-art traditions with motifs from modern art. The **Kovács Margit Múzeum** (Margit Kovács Museum),
in a small, 18th-century merchant's house, is devoted to her work.
⊠ *Vastag György u. 1* ☎ *26/310–244* ☉ *Mid-Mar.–Oct., daily 10–6;
Nov.–mid-Mar., Tues.–Sun. 9–5. Last tickets sold 30 mins before closing.*

The **Szabadtéri Néprajzi Múzeum** (Open-Air Ethnography Museum) re-
creates Hungarian peasant life and folk architecture of the 19th century.
Crafts demonstrations are held in summer. ⊠ *Sztaravodai út* ☎ *26/312–
304 or 26/314–456* ☉ *Apr.–Oct., Tues.–Sun. 9–5.*

$–$$ ✕ **Rab Ráby.** This popular restaurant, decorated with wood beams and
myriad eclectic antiques, is a great place for fish soup and fresh grilled

trout. Reservations are essential in summer. ✉ *Péter Pál u. 1* ☎ *26/310–819* 🍴 *AE, DC, MC, V.*

$$ 🏠 **Bükkös Panzió.** Impeccably clean, this stylishly modernized old house is on a small canal just a few minutes' walk from the town center. The narrow staircase and small rooms give it a homey feel. Rates include breakfast. ✉ *Bükkös part 16, H-2000* ☎ *26/312–021* 📠 *26/310–782* 🌐 *www.hotels.hu* ⮑ *16 rooms* ⌂ *Restaurant* 🍴 *MC, V.*

Visegrád

This hilly village presided over by a mountaintop fortress was the seat of the kings of Hungary during the 14th century. The ruins of the palace of King Matthias on the main street have been excavated and reconstructed; there are jousting tournaments on the grounds of the fortress in June and a medieval festival in July. A winding road leads up to the haunting late-medieval fortress, **Fellegvár** (Citadel), from which you have a fine view of the Danube Bend. ☎ *26/398–101* ☉ *Mid-Mar.–Oct., daily 10–5; Nov.–mid-Mar., weekends 10–3 in good weather.*

FodorsChoice
★

★ **$$$–$$$$** 🏠 **Silvanus.** Set high up on Fekete Hill, this hotel is renowned for its spectacular views and good hiking trails through the adjacent forest. The amenities include a wellness center with tepidarium (salt therapy). Rooms are bright and clean. A buffet breakfast is included in the rates. ✉ *Fekete-hegy, H-2025* ☎ *26/398–311 or 26/597–511* 📠 *26/597–516* 🌐 *www.betahotels.hu* ⮑ *94 rooms, 8 suites* ⌂ *Restaurant, indoor pool* 🍴 *AE, DC, MC, V.*

$–$$ 🏠 **Hotel Honti.** This 21-room hotel and its older, alpine-style sibling pension share the same yard in a quiet residential area, a three-minute walk from the town center. A stream running between the two houses enhances the country atmosphere. ✉ *Fő u. 66, H-2025* ☎ *26/398–120* 📠 *26/397–274* ⮑ *30 rooms, 2 suites* 🍴 *No credit cards.*

Esztergom

This primarily baroque town stands on the site of a Roman fortress. St. Stephen, the first Christian king of Hungary, was crowned here in the year 1000. The kings are long gone, but Esztergom is still the home of the archbishop of Esztergom, the cardinal primate, head of the Catholic Church in Hungary.

FodorsChoice
★

Thousands of pilgrims visit the imposing **Bazilika** (basilica), the largest in Hungary, which stands on Vár-domb (Castle Hill) overlooking the town. It was here that anti-Communist Cardinal József Mindszenty was finally reburied in 1991, ending an era of religious intolerance and persecution. The cathedral's treasury houses a valuable collection of ecclesiastical art. ✉ *Szt. István tér* ☎ *33/411–895* ☉ *Basilica Mar.–Oct., daily 7–6; Nov.–Feb., daily 7–4. Treasury Mar.–Oct., daily 9–4:30; Nov. and Dec., Tues.–Sun. 11–3:30.*

The **Keresztény Múzeum** (Museum of Christian Art) is in the Primási Palota (Primate's Palace). It is one of the finest art galleries in Hungary, with a large collection of early Hungarian and Italian paintings. The Italian collection, coupled with the early Renaissance paintings from Flanders and the Lower Rhine, provides insights into the transition of European sensibilities from medieval Gothic to the humanistic Renaissance. ✉ *Mindszenty tér 2* ☎ *33/413–880* ☉ *Mid-Mar.–mid-Oct., Tues.–Sun. 10–6; mid-Oct.–Dec., Tues.–Sun. 10–5.*

$–$$ ✕ **Primás Pince.** This restaurant's vaulted ceilings and exposed brick walls make a charming setting for refined Hungarian and Continental fare. The veal paprikas with homemade cheese curd and dill dumplings is a good, hearty bet. ✉ *Szt. István tér 4* ☎ *33/313–495* 🍴 *AE, DC, MC, V* ☉ *No dinner Jan.–Mar.*

$$ ⊞ **Ria Panzió.** In this small, friendly guest house near the cathedral, most rooms face a garden courtyard. Rates include breakfast. ⊠ *Batthyány u. 11–13, H-2500* ☎ *33/313–115* 🖷 *33/401–429* 🖘 *15 rooms* 🖃 *AE, MC, V.*

$ ⊞ **Alabárdos Panzió.** Downhill from the basilica, this cozy, remodeled house provides an excellent view of Castle Hill. Rooms (doubles and quads) are small but less cramped than at other pensions. Breakfast is included in the rates. ⊠ *Bajcsy-Zsilinszky u. 49, H-2500* 🖷🖷 *33/312–640* 🖘 *21 rooms* 🖃 *No credit cards.*

The Danube Bend Essentials

BOAT & FERRY TRAVEL
The best way to get around on the Danube is by boat or hydrofoil. The three main centers—Szentendre, Esztergom, and Visegrád—all have connections with one another and with Budapest. Contact MAHART Tours for schedules.

🖪 **MAHART Tours** ☎ 1/484–4013.

BUS TOURS
IBUSZ Travel organizes daylong bus trips from Budapest along the Danube, stopping in Esztergom, Visegrád, and Szentendre. Cityrama runs full-day bus tours to Visegrád, Esztergom, and Szentendre, returning to Budapest by boat, from May through September, Wednesday–Sunday. Both tours include lunch and admission fees.

🖪 **Cityrama** ☎ 1/302–4382. **IBUSZ Travel** ☎ 1/485–2700.

BUS TRAVEL
Regular bus service connects Szentendre, Esztergom, and Visegrád with one another and with Budapest.

TRAIN TRAVEL
Szentendre is most easily reached by HÉV commuter rail, departing from the Batthyány tér Metro in Budapest; the trip takes about 40 minutes and costs around 310 Ft.

VISITOR INFORMATION
🖪 **Grantours Esztergom** ⊠ Széchenyi tér 25, Esztergom 🖷🖷 33/413–756. **Tourinform Szentendre** ⊠ Dumsta J. u. 22, Szentendre ☎ 26/317–965.

LAKE BALATON

Lake Balaton, the largest lake in Central Europe, stretches 80 km (50 mi) across western Hungary. It is within easy reach of Budapest. Sometimes known as the nation's playground, it helps to make up for Hungary's much-lamented lack of coastline. On its hilly northern shore, ideal for growing grapes, is Balatonfüred, the country's oldest spa town.

The national park on the Tihany Peninsula is just to the south, and regular boat service links Tihany and Balatonfüred with Siófok on the southern shore. This shore is flatter and more crowded with resorts, cottages, and high-rise hotels once used as Communist trade-union retreats. The south shore's waters are shallower than those of the north: you can walk out for nearly 2 km (1 mi) before they deepen.

The region grows more crowded every year (July and August are the busiest times), but a few steps along any side road will still lead you to a serene landscape of vineyards and old stone houses. A circular tour taking in Veszprém, Balatonfüred, and Tihany could be managed in a day,

but two days, with a night in Tihany or Balatonfüred, would be more relaxed and allow for a detour to Herend and its porcelain factory.

Veszprém

★ Hilly Veszprém, though not on the lake itself, is the center of cultural life in the Balaton region. **Veszprémi Várhegy** (Castle Hill), a charming hilltop district of well-preserved buildings, is the most attractive part of town. **Hősök Kapuja** (Heroes' Gate), at the entrance to the district, houses a small exhibit on Hungary's history. Just past the gate and down a little alley to the left is the **Tűztorony** (Fire Tower); note that the lower level is medieval, whereas the upper stories are baroque. There is a good view of the town and surrounding area from the castle balcony. The tower is open May–October, daily 10–6.

Vár utca, the only street in the castle area, leads to a small square in front of the **Püspök Palota** (Bishop's Palace) and the cathedral; outdoor concerts are held here in summer. Vár utca continues past the square up to a terrace erected on the north staircase of the castle. Stand beside the modern statues of St. Stephen and his queen, Gizella, for a far-reaching view of the old quarter of town.

$–$$ ✕ **Szürkebarát Borozó.** The plain off-white walls of the Gray Monk Tavern may be less than inspiring, but the hearty Hungarian fare at this cellar restaurant in the city center more than compensates. For an unusual (but very Hungarian) appetizer, try the paprika-spiced *velős pirítós* (marrow on toast; missing from the English menu and sometimes unavailable); or for a main course, gnaw away at "Ms. Baker's Pork Hoofs." ⊠ *Szabadság tér 12* ☎ *88/327–684* ▭ *No credit cards.*

$$ ▣ **Éllő Panzió.** In this 18-room pension just southwest of the town center, you'll find ubiquitous golden lamp shades coupled with no lack of red—on the carpeting, the velvety chairs, and the curtains. Rooms in the newer annex building are more spacious than those in the chaletlike main house. Service is friendly. ⊠ *József Attila u. 25, H-8200* ☎ *88/420–097 or 88/424–118* ▤ *88/329–711* ▭ *18 rooms* ▭ *DC, MC, V.*

Herend

Herend is the home of some of Hungary's most renowned hand-painted porcelain. The **Herendi Porcelángyár** (Herend Porcelain Factory), founded in 1839, displays many rare pieces in its museum. There's an extended visitor center that includes an exhibit about the process of making porcelain, a factory shop (without any bargains, unfortunately), and a café. In the adjoining Apicus Restaurant, you can dine on priceless Herend porcelain, worth several million forints. Call ahead to confirm hours because they can vary from the official opening hours. ⊠ *Kos-*

suth Lajos u. 144 ☎ *88/261–144* ☉ *Apr.–Sept., daily 10–6; Oct.–Mar., Tues.–Sun. 10–4.*

Balatonfüred

Balatonfüred first grew famous as a spa catering to people suffering from heart disease, but thanks to its good beaches and proximity to Budapest, it's now the most popular resort on the lake. The town also lies in one of Hungary's finest wine-producing regions. In the main square, strong-smelling medicinal waters bubble up under a colonnaded pavilion. Down at the shore, the Tagore sétány (Tagore Promenade) is a wonderful place to stroll and watch the swans glide by.

★ $$–$$$$ ✕ **Baricska Csárda.** From its perch atop a hill at the southwestern end of town, this rambling, reed-thatched inn overlooks vineyards toward the river. The hearty fare includes roasted trout and *fogas* (a freshwater fish of the Balaton region) as well as desserts crammed with sweet poppy-seed filling. In summer, colorful Gypsy wedding shows are held nightly. ⊠ *Baricska dülő, off Rte. 71 (Széchenyi út) behind the Shell station* ☎ *87/343–105* ▭ *AE, V* ☉ *Closed mid-Nov.–mid-Mar.*

$–$$$ ✕ **Tölgyfa Csárda.** A prime hilltop location gives this tavern breathtaking views over the steeples and rooftops of Balatonfüred and the Tihany Peninsula. The menu and decor are the equals of a first-class Budapest restaurant, and there's live Gypsy music in the evening. ⊠ *Meleghegy Hill (at end of Csárda u.)* ☎ *87/343–036* ▭ *No credit cards* ☉ *Closed late Oct.–mid-Apr.*

$$$$ ▤ **Annabella.** The cool, spacious guest quarters in this Miami-style high-rise are especially pleasant in summer. Overlooking the Tagore Promenade and Lake Balaton, it has access to excellent water-sports facilities. All rooms have balconies; for the best vistas, request a room on a high floor with a view of the Tihany Peninsula. Room rates include breakfast. Five suites have air-conditioning. ⊠ *Deák Ferenc u. 25, H-8230* ☎ *87/342–222* ▤ *87/483–084* ⊕ *www.danubiusgroup.com* ⇘ *383 rooms, 5 suites* ⚙ *3 restaurants, 2 pools, bar* ▭ *AE, DC, MC, V* ☉ *Closed mid-Oct.–mid-Apr.*

$$ ▤ **Park.** Hidden on a side street in town but close to the lakeshore, this family-run spot is noticeably calmer than Füred's bustling main hotels. Rooms are large and bright, with high ceilings and tall windows. However, the decor is uninspired, Eastern Bloc–style, with low, narrow beds and plain upholstery. Suites have large, breezy balconies but small bathrooms. Breakfast is included in the room rates. ⊠ *Jókai u. 24, H-8230* ☎☎ *87/343–203* ⊕ *www.balaton.hu* ⇘ *38 rooms, 3 suites* ⚙ *Restaurant, bar* ▭ *No credit cards.*

Tihany

★ A short trip by boat or car takes you from Balatonfüred to the **Tihanyi fél-sziget** (Tihany Peninsula), a national park rich in rare flora and fauna. As you walk from the ferry port, follow green markers to the Oroszkút (springs) or red ones to the top of Csúcs-hegy, which has a great view of the lake.

★ The village of Tihany, with its **Bencés Apátság** (Benedictine Abbey), is on the lake's northern shore. The abbey building houses a **museum** with exhibits related to the Balaton area. Also worth a look are the pink angels painted—and seemingly floating—on the ceiling of the abbey church. Organ concerts are held weekend nights in July and the first half of August. ⊠ *Első András tér 1* ☎ *87/448–405 abbey; 87/448–650 museum* ⊕ *www.osb.hu* ☉ *May–Sept., Mon.–Sat. 9–5:30, Sun. 11–5:30; Nov.–Mar., Mon.–Sat. 10–4:30, Sun. 11–4:30; Apr. and Oct., Mon.–Sat. 10–4:30, Sun. 11–4:30.*

$–$$ ✕ **Halásztanya.** The location on a twisting, narrow street and evening Gypsy music contribute to the popularity of this restaurant, which specializes in fish. ⊠ *Visszhang u. 11* ☎ *87/448–771* ♲ *Reservations not accepted* ▤ *AE, MC, V* ⊗ *Closed Nov.–Easter.*

$–$$ ✕ **Pál Csárda.** Two thatched cottages house this simple restaurant, where cold fruit soup and fish stew are the specialties. You can eat in the garden, which is decorated with gourds and strands of peppers. ⊠ *Visszhang u. 19* ☎ *87/448–605* ♲ *Reservations not accepted* ▤ *AE, MC, V* ⊗ *Closed Oct.–Mar.*

$$$ ▦ **Kastély Hotel.** Lush landscaped gardens surround this stately neo-baroque mansion on the water's edge. Inside, it's all understated elegance; rooms have soaring ceilings and beautiful views. Next door, a newer, less attractive building houses the Kastély's sister, the Park Hotel, which has less expensive but unattractive rooms. Breakfast is included in the rates. ⊠ *Fürdő telepi út 1, H-8237* ☎ *87/448–611* ▤ *87/448–409* ⊕ *www.hotelfured.hu* ↪ *25 rooms, 1 suite* ♢ *Restaurant, bar* ▤ *AE, DC, MC, V* ⊗ *Closed mid-Oct.–mid-Apr.*

FodorsChoice
★

$$ ▦ **Kántás Pension and Restaurant.** Cozy, wood-paneled rooms are built into an attic above a popular and friendly restaurant in the heart of Tihany. Rates include breakfast. ⊠ *Csokonai út. 49, H-8237* ☎☎ *87/448–072* ↪ *6 rooms* ♢ *Restaurant* ▤ *DC, MC, V.*

Lake Balaton Essentials

CAR TRAVEL
Highway 71 runs along the northern shore; M7 covers the southern.

TOURS
IBUSZ Travel has several tours to Balaton from Budapest; inquire at the main office in Budapest. Other tours more easily organized from hotels in the Balaton area include boat trips to vineyards and folk music evenings.

🛈 **IBUSZ Travel** ☎ 1/485-2700 in Budapest ⊕ www.ibusz.hu.

TRAIN TRAVEL
Trains from Budapest serve all the resorts on the northern shore; a separate line links the resorts of the southern shore.

TRANSPORTATION AROUND LAKE BALATON
Buses connect most resorts, and regular ferries link the major ones. On summer weekends traffic can be heavy, and driving around the lake can take quite a while; because of the crowds, you should also book bus and train tickets in advance. In winter, schedules are curtailed, so check ahead.

VISITOR INFORMATION
🛈 **Balatontourist** ⊠ Tagore sétány 1, Balatonfüred ☎ 87/343-471 or 87/342-822. **Tihany Tourist** ⊠ Kossuth L. u. 11, Tihany ☎ 87/448-481. **Tourinform Tihany** Tourinform ⊠ Kossuth L. u. 20, Tihany ☎ 87/448-804. **Tourinform Veszprém** ⊠ Vár u. 4, Veszprém ☎ 88/404-548.

ICELAND
REYKJAVÍK AND THE COUNTRYSIDE

16

DON'T BE FOOLED BY ITS NAME. Iceland is anything but icy, with only 11% of the country covered by glaciers. Considering the country's high latitude, summers in Iceland are relatively warm, and the winter climate is milder than New York's. Indeed, during summer, with its lava and lushness, Iceland bears an uncanny resemblance to Hawaii, with coastal farms nestled in pastoral lowlands where livestock graze beside pristine streams.

Iceland's chilly name can be blamed on Hrafna-Flóki, a 9th-century settler who failed to store up enough fodder to see his livestock through the winter. Leaving in a huff, he passed a fjord filled with pack ice and cursed the country with a name that has stuck ever since.

The second-largest island in Europe, Iceland lies in the middle of the North Atlantic, where the warm Gulf Stream from the south meets cold currents from the north, creating a choice breeding ground for fish, which provide the nation with 70% of its export revenue. Iceland itself emerged from the bed of the Atlantic Ocean as a result of volcanic activity, which is ongoing. Every five years, on average, this fire beneath the earth breaks out in an eruption, sometimes even below glaciers. Fiery forces also heat the hot springs and geysers that bubble and spout in many parts of the country. Other geothermal water keeps public swimming pools comfortable and heats most homes and buildings, helping to keep the air smog-free.

Except for fish and agricultural products, most consumer goods are imported to Iceland, contributing to a high cost of living. Economic reforms, however, have been bringing prices down to competitive levels with those of the rest of Scandinavia, and on a par with the rest of Europe.

The first permanent settlers in Iceland came from Norway in 874, though a handful of Irish monks are thought to have arrived a century earlier. In 1262, Iceland came under foreign rule by Norway and later Denmark, and did not regain full independence until 1944. Eighty percent of the country—about the size of Ireland or the state of Virginia—is inhabited, and the population density is only three people per square km (one person per square mi). Around 60% of the country's 280,000 people live in the capital area of Reykjavík.

ICELAND A TO Z

To research prices, get advice from other travelers, and book travel arrangements, visit www.fodors.com.

AIR TRAVEL

Icelandair operates daily flights from London's Heathrow and New York's JFK airport to Keflavík Airport, 50 km (31 mi) south of Reykjavík. Domestic daily flights go to most of the larger towns. Although plane travel is expensive, special family fares, package tours, and vacation tickets are available. The airport departure fee is IKr1,250.

🔳 *Keflavik Airport* ☎ 425-0200.

BOAT & FERRY TRAVEL

The car-and-passenger ferry *Baldur,* operated by Sæferðir, links the West Fjords with the village of Stykkishólmur on the Snæfellsnes Peninsula. The ferry *Herjólfur,* operated by Samskip, travels to the Westman Islands from Þorlákshöfn on the south coast. Smyril Line calls during summer at the east coast town of Seyðisfjörður, sailing from Norway, Denmark, Scotland's Shetland Islands, and the Faroe Islands. For information, contact Smyril Line in the Faroe Islands or Norræna Terra Nova in Iceland. Information on boat trips linking several coastal spots with Ísafjörður on the West Fjords can be obtained from Vesturferðir.

🔳 *Baldur* ☎ 438-1450 at Stykkishólmur ⊕ www.saeferdir.is. *Herjólfur* ✉ Friðarhöfn, IS-900 Westman Islands ☎ 481-2800 🖶 481-2991 ⊕ www.samskip.is. **Norræna Terra Nova** (Smyril Line Ísland) ✉ Stangarhyl 3a, IS-101 Reykjavík ☎ 587-1919 🖶 587-0036. **Smyril Line** 🕾 Passenger Dept., Box 370, FO-110 Tórshavn Faroe Islands ☎ 298-345-900 🖶 298-345-950 ⊕ www.smyril-line.fo. **Vesturferðir** ☎ 456-5111 🖶 456-5185 ⊕ www.vesturferdir.is.

BUS TRAVEL

An extensive network of buses serves most parts of Iceland, though some routes operate only in summer. Many cross-country buses have bike racks. The Air Bus Rover package, available in the summer months, allows travelers to fly one-way and return by coach. The bus network is coordinated at Bifreiðastöð Íslands; its terminal is on the northern rim of Reykjavík Airport.

🔳 **Bifreiðastöð Íslands (BSÍ)** ✉ Vatnsmýrarvegur 10, Reykjavík ☎ 591-1000 🖶 591-1050 ⊕ www.BSI.is.

BUSINESS HOURS

Banks are open weekdays 9:15–4. Some branches are also open Thursday 5–6. Museums are usually open 1–4:30, but some open as early as 10 and others stay open until 7. Some may be closed Monday. Shops are open weekdays 9–6 and Saturday 10–4; shopping malls weekdays 10–7 and weekends 10–5; and grocery stores keep longer hours, including Sunday afternoon. A few supermarkets stay open daily until 11 PM.

CAR TRAVEL

An international driver's license is required. Car-rental agencies are located at most airports and in many towns, but better deals can often be had in packages from your local travel agency.

EMERGENCIES Rural service stations and garages are few and far between, but the main roads are patrolled, and fellow motorists are helpful. The general emergency number is available 24 hours throughout Iceland.

🔳 **Emergencies** ☎ 112.

GASOLINE Gasoline prices are high, IKr97–IKr106 per liter, depending on octane rating. Service stations are spaced no more than half a day's drive apart.

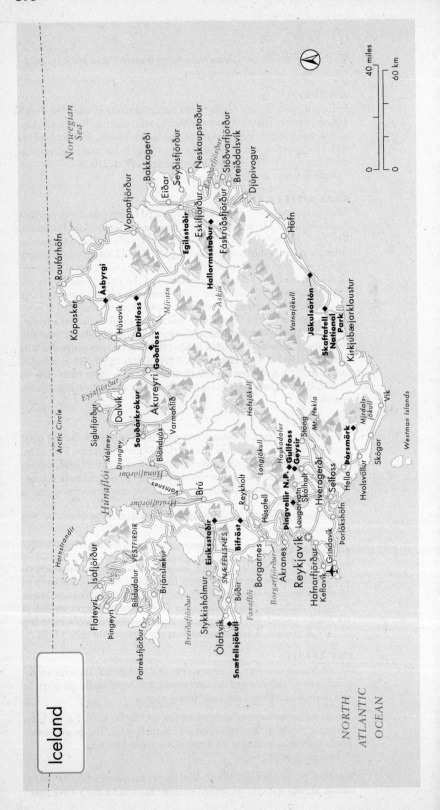

Service stations in the Reykjavík area are open Monday–Saturday 7:30 AM–7:30 PM, with some stations open as late as 11 PM; hours outside the city vary.

ROAD CONDITIONS

Most of the Ring Road, which encircles the island, is two-lane asphalt. Other roads can be bumpy, often along gravel, dirt, or lava track—but the scenery is worth it. Be alert for loose livestock. Use extra caution when approaching single-lane bridges or on blind hills (*blindhæð*). A four-wheel-drive vehicle is vital for remote roads such as those in the highlands, which may be impassable until July. If you drive over the highlands, it is best to travel in convoy, especially when crossing unbridged rivers. For information on road conditions and the availability of gasoline off the beaten track, call Vegagerð Ríkisins (Public Roads Administration).

🖅 **Vegagerð Ríkisins** ☎ 522-1000 for 24-hr road status in English ⊕ www. vegargerdin.is.

RULES OF THE ROAD

Traffic outside Reykjavík is generally light, but roads have only one lane going in each direction. Speed limits are 90 kph (55 mph) in rural areas on the Ring Road, 50 kph (30 mph) on secondary gravel roads, and 30–50 kph (20–30 mph) in urban areas. Drivers are required by law to use headlights at all times. Seat belts are required for all occupants. For more traffic rules, contact the Icelandic Traffic Council (⊕ www.umferd.is).

CUSTOMS & DUTIES

Tourists may bring in 6 liters of beer or 1 liter of wine containing up to 21% alcohol, 1 liter of liquor with up to 47% alcohol, and 200 cigarettes or 250 grams (½ lb.) of other tobacco products.

EATING & DRINKING

Restaurants are small and diverse. You can expect superb seafood, beef, and lamb, and the fresh fish is not to be missed—surely some of the best you'll ever have. In addition to a growing array of award-winning cheeses, dairy products include the unique *skýr* (pronounced "skeer"), a thick, creamy, protein-rich dairy product, which is available plain or with various fruits. Besides native cuisine, ethnic eateries range from Asian, Mexican, and Indian to French and Italian. Pizzas, hamburgers, and the tasty national version of the hot dog, with crisped onion bits, are widely available.

WHAT IT COSTS In Iceland Krónur			
$$$$	**$$$**	**$$**	**$**
AT DINNER over 3,000	2,000–3,000	1,200–2,000	under 1,200

Prices are per person for a main course.

MEALTIMES

Dinner, served between 7 and 10:30, is the main meal. A light lunch is usually served between noon and 2. Most restaurants are open from mid-morning until midnight.

RESERVATIONS & DRESS

Neat, casual dress is acceptable in all but the most expensive restaurants, where jacket and tie are recommended.

EMBASSIES

There is a Canadian consular office in Reykjavík (⇨ Reykjavík Essentials).
🖪 United Kingdom ✉ Laufásvegur 31, Reykjavík IS-101 ☎ 550-5100 ⊕ www. britishembassy.is.
🖪 United States ✉ Laufásvegur 21, Reykjavík IS-101 ☎ 562-9100 ⊕ www.usa.is.

HOLIDAYS
January 1; Maundy Thursday; Good Friday; Easter Monday; First Day of Summer (celebrated in late April—a vestige of the very optimistic Old Norse calendar); May 1 (Labor Day); Ascension (in May); Pentecost (in late May or early June); June 17 (Independence Day); Public Holiday (first Monday in August); December 24 (from noon)–26; December 31 (half-day off).

LANGUAGE
The language is Icelandic, a highly inflected North Germanic tongue that is little changed from that originally spoken by the island's Norse settlers. In fact, an official committee invents new words for modern usage to keep Icelandic pure. You'll encounter three unique letters in Icelandic: the "thorn," þ, is pronounced as a forced "th" as in "throw"; the "eth," ð, is a soft "th" as in "breath" and never starts a proper noun; the Scandinavian ligature æ is pronounced as a long "i" as in "bike." Otherwise, the "j" is pronounced as a "y." But not to worry: English proficiency is widespread, particularly among the young.

LODGING
Hotels are quiet and friendly. Reykjavík and most villages also have guest houses and private accommodations. Outside Reykjavík you'll also find some hostels and other accommodations where private baths may not be available. If you are touring Iceland on your own, get a list of hotels and guest houses in the various regions from the Tourist Information Center.

WHAT IT COSTS In Iceland Krónur			
$$$$	**$$$**	**$$**	**$**
REYKJAVÍK			
FOR 2 PEOPLE over 20,000	15,000–20,000	10,000–15,000	under 10,000
OTHER AREAS			
HOTELS over 15,000	10,000–15,000	5,000–10,000	under 5,000

Hotel prices are for a standard double room in high season.

FARM ACCOMMODATIONS Staying at farms is an excellent way to become acquainted with Iceland: some 120 participating farms are listed with Icelandic Farm Holidays. Many offer fishing, touring with a guide, and horseback riding.
🏠 **Icelandic Farm Holidays** ✉ Síðumúli 13, IS-108 Reykjavík ☎ 570-2700 🖷 570-2799 🌐 www.farmholidays.is.

HOSTELS Information on the 30 hostels around the country can be obtained from the Icelandic Youth Hostel Association.
🏠 **Icelandic Youth Hostel Association** ✉ Sundlaugavegur 34, IS-105 Reykjavík ☎ 553-8110 🖷 588-9201 🌐 www.hostel.is.

HUTS Outside Reykjavík, the Icelandic Touring Association operates a number of spartan huts for mountaineers and hikers in remote areas.
🏠 **Icelandic Touring Association** ✉ Mörkinni 6, IS-108 Reykjavík ☎ 568-2533 🖷 568-2535.

MAIL & SHIPPING
You can have your mail sent to the post office in any town or village in Iceland. In Reykjavík, have mail sent to the downtown post office.
🏠 **Downtown post office** ✉ R/O Pósthússtræti, IS-101 Reykjavík ☎ 580-1101 🕐 Weekdays 9–4:30.

POSTAL RATES Airmail letters cost IKr85 to the United States and IKr60 to Europe.

MONEY MATTERS

Like many islands, Iceland is expensive. Hotels and restaurants cost about 20% more in Reykjavík than elsewhere in the country. Interestingly, though, prestige goods, such as Armani clothes, Rolex watches, and top labels in perfumes and jewelry, are often good buys for travelers, once the value-added tax is refunded.

Some sample prices: cup of coffee or tea (with refills) or soft drink, IKr150; bottle of beer, IKr300; sandwich or snack, IKr350; 3-km (2-mi) taxi ride, IKr750.

CURRENCY The Icelandic monetary unit is the króna (plural krónur), which is abbreviated kr locally and IKr or ISK internationally. Coins are the IKr1, 5, 10, 50, and 100. Krónur bills come in denominations of 500, 1,000, 2,000, and 5,000. At press time, the rate of exchange was IKr78 to the U.S. dollar, IKr52 to the Canadian dollar, IKr123 to the pound sterling, IKr84 to the euro, IKr47 to the Australian dollar, IKr44 to the New Zealand dollar, and IKr10 to the South African rand.

CURRENCY
EXCHANGE Most major foreign currency is easily exchanged for krónur at Icelandic banks, but Icelandic money is virtually unavailable abroad. Almost all businesses accept major credit cards, even for small amounts. Currency exchange is also provided by the Change Group, open June–August, daily 8:30–6, and September–May, weekdays 9–5, Saturday 10–2. In the summer, the Change Group's office at the airport is open 24 hours every day. The Change Group is also the agent for Western Union in Iceland.
🏢 **Change Group** ✉ Bankastræti 2, Reykjavík ☎ 552-3735.

TAXES

VALUE-ADDED
TAX (V.A.T.) A 24.5% *virðisaukaskattur* (value-added tax, or V.A.T.), abbreviated VSK, applies to most goods and services. It's usually included in the price tag, tacitly making up 19.68% of the total; if not, that fact must be stated. Foreign visitors can claim a partial refund on the V.A.T., or 15% of the purchase price, provided they bought at least IKr4,000 worth of goods at one time. Souvenir stores issue "tax-free checks" that simplify collecting the V.A.T. rebates as you depart Iceland, at the international airport terminal or ferry building. To qualify, keep your purchases (except woolens) in tax-free packages, and show them to customs officers along with a passport and the tax-free check.
🏢 **Iceland Refund** ✉ Bæjarhraun 8, IS-220 Hafnarfjörður ☎ 564-6400 🖷 564-3600
🌐 www.icelandrefund.com.

TELEPHONES

Iceland's phone system is entirely digital and is part of the Nordic Mobile Telephone (NMT) system and the GSM global cellular phone network. Coverage for phones with NMT or GSM capability includes all but the remotest areas of Iceland. Iceland has one of the highest percentages of cellular phones per capita in the world, with 248,000 cellphone subscriptions for a population of 280,000. When calling Icelandic numbers whose prefix is 800, the charge is the same, regardless of where you're calling from within the country. A novel result of Iceland's small size and patronymic system (last names are derived from the first name of the father) is that the country's phone books are organized by first names rather than last.

COUNTRY &
AREA CODES The country code for Iceland is 354. All the country's local numbers are seven digits, with the first three giving a rough idea of location in lieu of area codes. Except for the country's 800 numbers, distance determines the cost of the call. Non-800 numbers starting with 8 often indicate cellular phones.

INTERNATIONAL CALLS For assistance with overseas calls dial 1811; for direct international calls dial 00. You can reach AT&T World Traveler, MCI World Phone, and Sprint International FONCARD by dialing their access codes. 🚹 Access Codes **AT&T World Traveler** ☎ 00800-22255288. **MCI World Phone** ☎ 800-9002. **Sprint International FONCARD** ☎ 800-9003.

LOCAL CALLS Pay phones usually take IKr10, IKr50, and IKr100 coins and are found in hotels, some shops, and post offices; outdoor telephone booths are scarce. Phone cards in the value of IKr500, IKr1,000, and IKr2,000 are sold at post offices, hotels, and some stores. For information and operator assistance with local calls dial 118; for collect calls 1811.

TIPPING

Tipping is not customary in Iceland.

VISITOR INFORMATION

🚹 **Icelandic Tourist Board** ✉ Gimli, Lækjargata 3, IS-101 Reykjavík ☎ 535-5500 🖷535-5501 🌐www.icetourist.is. **City of Reykjavík Tourist Information Center** ✉Bankastræti 2, IS-101 Reykjavík ☎ 562-3045 🖷 562-3057 🌐 www.tourist.reykjavik.is.

WHEN TO GO

Although it is a great year-round destination, Iceland is easiest to visit from May to mid-November. From June through July, the sun barely sets, and it never gets dark. In December the sun shines for only three hours a day, but on clear, cold nights anytime from September through March you may see the northern lights dancing among the stars.

CLIMATE Weather in Iceland is unpredictable: in June, July, and August, sunny days alternate with spells of rain showers and chilling winds, or even snow in the highlands. Winter temperatures fluctuate wildly around freezing, often getting as high as 50°F (10°C) or as low as −14°F (−10°C). In general, the climate in the north is stable and continental, in the south fickle and maritime.

Below are average daily maximum and minimum temperatures for Reykjavík.

Jan.	35F	2C	May	50F	10C	Sept.	52F	11C
	28	−2		39	4		43	6
Feb.	37F	3C	June	54F	12C	Oct.	45F	7C
	28	−2		34	7		38	3
Mar.	39F	4C	July	57F	14C	Nov.	39F	4C
	30	−1		48	9		32	0
Apr.	43F	6C	Aug.	56F	14C	Dec.	36F	2C
	33	1		47	8		29	−2

REYKJAVÍK

Reykjavík has a small, generally safe city center, clean air, and plenty of open spaces. The name means "Smokey Bay" and was coined when surprised Vikings saw steam rising from geothermal springs in the area. Today most of the buildings in this, the world's northernmost capital, are heated geothermally and the tap water is natural hot water, recognizable by its sulphurous odor. For a city of 112,000, Reykjavík offers an astonishingly wide range of artistic events—the main cultural season is winter, but plenty goes on in summer as well. In June of even-numbered years, Reykjavík hosts a two-week arts festival with a strong international flavor. Most nightlife is in or near the city center; it's liveliest on weekends. If weather is good, this can make for a carnival-like atmosphere, with hundreds or even thousands spilling into Lækjartorg Square when pubs begin closing in the wee hours.

Exploring Reykjavík

Numbers in the margin correspond to points of interest on the Reykjavík map.

Old Midtown, the capital's original core, is the city's highlight, with classic buildings, a park, museums, shops, galleries, and a plethora of cafés. Between World War II and the mid-1960s, a middle belt of residential neighborhoods, such as Vesturbær, was established. Extending from the once separate community of Seltjarnarnes, well west of Old Midtown, to the salmon-populated Elliðaá River in the east, these areas have small, inviting parks. Besides lovely flower beds and large trees (by Icelandic standards), homes present the Icelandic flair for wildly colored rooftops. Since the late 1960s, suburbs such as the sprawling Breiðholt have sprung up outside town. These austere areas offer few attractions, other than showing how a lot of the modern population lives. Old Midtown can be browsed on foot; elsewhere, the city's bus system is an efficient, inexpensive option.

A practical option for visitors is purchase of a Reykjavík Tourist Card at the Tourist Information Center. The card permits unlimited bus use and admission to any of the capital area's seven pools, the Reykjavík Zoo, and eight of the city's museums—you can buy it for one (IKr1,000), two (IKr1,500), or three days (IKr2,000).

⑱ Árbæjarsafn (Open-Air Folk Museum). This authentic "village" of relocated 18th- and 19th-century houses, 20 minutes southeast of downtown, is well worth the trip. ✉ *Kistuhylur 4, Árbær* Ⓜ *Bus 4, 10, or 110 from Hlemmur bus station* ☎ *577–1111* ✆ *IKr500* ⊙ *June–Aug., Tues.–Fri. 10–5, weekends 10–6.*

⑭ Arnarhóll. A statue of the Viking **Ingólfur Arnarson,** whose family first settled Iceland in 874, dominates this hill, which overlooks the bay. To the north is the ultramodern, glossy-black **Seðlabanki** (Central Bank). Behind Ingólfur is the copper-green **High Courts** building nestled beside the **National Theater** and old **Library,** dating from the early 20th century. ✉ *Arnarhóll.*

⑰ Ásmundarsafn (Ásmundur Sveinsson Sculpture Museum). Some originals by this sculptor (1896–1982), depicting ordinary working people, myths, and folktale episodes, are exhibited in the museum's gallery and studio as well as in the surrounding garden and chosen spots in Reykjavík. ✉ *Sigtún, 5-min ride from Hlemmur Station on Bus 5* ☎ *553–2155* ✆ *IKr500 (admission ticket valid for entry to Reykjavík Art Museum's two other sites—Hafnarhús and Kjarvalsstaðir—on the same day)* ⊙ *June–Sept., daily 10–4; Oct.–May, daily 1–4.*

★ ② Austurvöllur (East Field). This green square in Old Midtown is truly the heart of Reykjavík. The 19th-century **Alþingishús** (Parliament House), one of the oldest stone buildings in Iceland, faces the square and houses meetings of the world's oldest operating parliament, which dates from 930. A statue of Jón Sigurðsson (1811–79), the nationalist who led Iceland toward independence, stands in the square's center. ✉ *Bounded by Kirkjustræti and Pósthússtræti.*

❽ Bernhöftstorfa. Picturesque, two-story, mid-19th-century wooden houses typify this small hill, which rises from Lækjargata, the main street linking the peaceful park by Tjörnin Lake with the busy city center. One

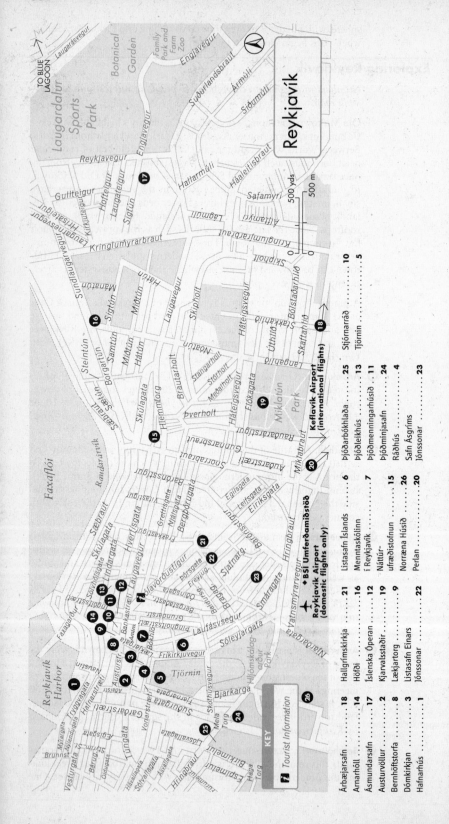

corner of the lake is fed by warm water that does not freeze, creating a destination for birds year-round. ⊠ *Just east of Lækjargata and just south of Bankastræti.*

❸ Dómkirkjan (Lutheran Cathedral). This 18th-century stone church, with a treasured baptismal font carved by sculptor Bertel Thorvaldsen (1768/70–1844), stands by Kirkjustræti, or Church Street. ⊠ *Lækjargata 14, Austurvöllur* ☎ *520–9700* ☉ *Weekdays 10–5* ☉ *Closed during services.*

★ **❶ Hafnarhús** (Harbor House, Reykjavík Art Museum). A former warehouse in the port of Reykjavík, Hafnarhús now serves as the main building of the city's art museum. The six exhibition halls over two floors exhibit works by Icelandic and international artists, as well as the hundreds of works that make up the museum's Erró Collection, by expatriate Icelandic pop artist Erró. ⊠ *Tryggvagata 17* ☎ *511–5155* ☒ *Kr500 (admission ticket valid for entry to Reykjavík Art Museum's two other sites—Ásmundarsafn and Kjarvalsstaðir—on the same day)* ☉ *Daily 10–5.*

㉑ Hallgrímskirkja (Hallgrímur's Church). Forty years in the making, this church was finally completed in the 1980s. Its 210-foot gray concrete tower, visible from almost anywhere in the city, is open to the public, allowing a panoramic view of the city and its expansive suburbs. ⊠ *Top of Skólavörðustígur* ☎ *551–0745* ☒ *Admission to the tower IKr300* ☉ *May–Sept., daily 9–6; Oct.–Apr., daily 9–5.*

⑯ Höfði. Mikhail Gorbachev and Ronald Reagan met here for the Reykjavík Summit of 1986. Rumored to be haunted, the house now serves as a venue for city functions. It is decorated with some of the city's art and opens to the public in summer, on the first Sunday of each month. ⊠ *Near junction of Borgartún and Nóatún.*

⑫ Íslenska Óperan (Icelandic Opera). Reminiscent of old-fashioned movie houses, this building was, in fact, Iceland's first cinema. The resident company performs here in winter. ⊠ *Ingólfsstræti* ☎ *511–6400.*

⑲ Kjarvalsstaðir (Reykjavík Art Museum). This municipal art museum, named for Jóhannes Kjarval (1885–1972), the nation's best-known painter, displays the artist's lava landscapes and images of mystical beings. It also shows works by contemporary Icelandic artists and great masters, as well as visiting exhibits. ⊠ *Flókagata, Miklatún Park* ☎ *552–6131* ☒ *Kr500 (admission ticket valid for entry to Reykjavík Art Museum's two other sites—Ásmundarsafn and Hafnarhús—on the same day)* ☉ *Daily 10–5.*

❾ Lækjartorg (Brook Square). A focal point of Old Midtown, this square opens onto **Austurstræti**, a semipedestrian shopping street. ⊠ *Junction of Bankastræti and Lækjargata.*

㉒ Listasafn Einars Jónssonar (National Gallery of Einar Jónsson). Cubic and fortresslike, this building was once the home and studio of Iceland's leading early-20th-century sculptor (1874–1954). His monumental works explore mystical subjects. The sculpture garden (entrance from Freyjugata) is always open. ⊠ *Njarðargata* ☎ *551–3797* ⊕ *www.skulptur.is* ☒ *IKr400; sculpture garden free* ☉ *June–mid-Sept., Tues.–Sun. 2–5; mid-Sept.–Nov. and Feb.–May, weekends 2–5.*

❻ Listasafn Íslands (National Gallery). A collection of Icelandic art fills the stately white building overlooking Tjörnin Lake. ⊠ *Fríkirkjuvegur 7* ☎ *515–9600* ⊕ *www.listasafn.is* ☒ *IKr400* ☉ *Tues.–Sun. 11–5.*

❼ Menntaskólinn í Reykjavík (Reykjavík Grammar School). Many graduates from the country's oldest educational institution, established in 1846, have gone on to dominate political and social life in Iceland. ⊠ *Corner of Amtmannsstígur and Lækjargata.*

⓯ Náttúrufræðistofnun (Museum of Natural History). One of the last great auks is on display here, along with other exhibits that focus on Icelandic natural history. ⊠ *Hlemmur 5 (entry from Hverfisgata)* ☎ *590–0500* ⊕ *www.ni.is* ⊠ *IKr300* ⊙ *May–Aug., Tues., Thurs., and weekends 1–5; Sept.–Apr., Tues., Thurs., and weekends 1:30–4.*

㉖ Norræna Húsið (Nordic House). Designed by Finnish architect Alvar Aalto, this blue-and-white cultural center hosts exhibitions, lectures, and concerts; it has a library and a coffee shop. ⊠ *Sæmundargata* ☎ *551–7030* ⊕ *www.nordice.is* ⊠ *IKr300; vestibule exhibitions free* ⊙ *Exhibitions daily 2–7, coffee shop daily 9–5.*

⓴ Perlan (The Pearl). The gleaming glass dome perches like a space station on a hill atop six huge hot-water tanks that provide hot water for much of the capital area. Paths in the wooded slopes and the warm effluent water at the shoreline draw many locals for sport and relaxation. Two man-made geysers—one inside, erupting frequently, and Strókur on the south slope, spouting without pumps on the same pressure and release system as in natural geysers—complement the site. Also inside you'll find a balcony with splendid views, a coffee shop, an ice-cream bar, and a fine restaurant. ⊠ *Öskjuhlíð Hill* ☎ *562–0200* ⊙ *Daily 10 AM–11 PM.*

㉕ Þjóðarbókhlaða (National and University Library). Clad in red aluminum, this park-side edifice is hard to miss. It houses a substantial collection of books and manuscripts. ⊠ *Arngrímsgata 3 (corner of Birkimelur and Hringbraut)* ☎ *563–5600* ⊕ *www.bok.hi.is* ⊙ *Weekdays 9–7, Sat. 10–5.*

⓭ Þjóðleikhús (National Theater). The interior of this structure reflects the basalt lava columns that are typical in Icelandic geology. It is a venue for the biennial Reykjavík Arts Festival and, from fall to spring, diverse cultural events and drama. ⊠ *Hverfisgata 19* ☎ *585–1200 or 551–1200.*

⓫ Þjóðmenningarhúsið (National Culture House). Crests on the facade of this impressive classic building, once the National Library, name prominent Icelandic literary figures. Lavishly restored, it now houses diverse changing cultural exhibits. ⊠ *Hverfisgata 15* ☎ *545–1400* 🖷 *545–1420* ⊕ *www.thjodmenning.is* ⊠ *IKr300* ⊙ *Daily 11–5.*

㉔ Þjóðminjasafn (National Museum). On display are Viking artifacts, national costumes, weavings, carvings, and silver. ⊠ *Suðurgata 141* ☎ *530–2200* ⊕ *www.natmus.is* ⊙ *Mid-May–mid-Sept., Tues.–Sun. 11–5; mid-Sept.–mid-May, Tues., Thurs., and weekends noon–5.*

❹ Ráðhús (Reykjavík City Hall). Inside are a tourist information desk, a large-scale relief map of Iceland, and a coffee shop. Modern architecture and nature meet here—not only with Tjörnin Lake to the south, but with water seeping over moss on the building's north wall. ⊠ *Vonarstræti and Tjarnargata* ☎ *563–2000 main switchboard; 563–2005 tourist information* ⊙ *Mid-May–mid-Sept., weekdays 8:20–4:30, weekends noon–6; mid-Sept.–mid-May, weekdays 8:20–4:30, Sat. noon–6; coffee shop, weekdays 10:30–6, weekends noon–6.*

㉓ Safn Ásgríms Jónssonar (Ásgrímur Jónsson Collection). Works by this well-regarded post-impressionist painter (1876–1958) are displayed in his house, left otherwise untouched since his death. ⊠ *Bergstaðastræti 74* ☎ *515–9600* ⊠ *Free* ⊙ *By appointment.*

❿ Stjórnarráð (Government House). Once a jail, this white, 18th-century building now houses the offices of Iceland's prime minister. ⊠ *Lækjartorg, on seaward side of Bankastræti.*

★ **Bláa Lónið** (The Blue Lagoon). A dip in the Blue Lagoon, a natural hot spring close to the Keflavik airport, is one of the highlights of a visit to Iceland. The spring keeps a temperature of around 40°C (104°F) year-round, and is warmer as you get closer to the source. Once your body gets over the shock of the dramatic change in temperature you can enjoy the benefits of the waters. Made up of two-thirds salt water and one-third freshwater, the lagoon is high in silica and algae, substances known for their natural healing powers. There are various spa services available, and you can get Blue Lagoon skin care products in the gift shop. Þingvallaleið has scheduled coach services between the Main Bus Station in Reykjavík (BSÍ) and the Blue Lagoon for IKr850, one way. The bus leaves at 10, 1:30, 3:15, 5:15, and 6. ⊠ *Grindavík* ☎ *420–8800* ⊕*www.bluelagoon.is* ⊠*IKr980* ☉ *Mid-May–Aug., daily 9–9; Sept.–mid-May, daily 10–7:30.*

★ ❺ **Tjörnin.** This natural, shallow lake is a haven for a variety of birds, from majestic swans to elegant Arctic terns. In colder winters, skaters venture out onto it. At the south end of the lake, **Hljómskálagarður Park** is a fine spot to relax. ⊠ *Bounded by Tjarnargata/Bjarkargata on west and Fríkirkjuvegur/Sóleyjargata on east.*

Where to Eat

Most Reykjavík restaurants offer excellent seafood and lamb dishes. Winter menus often include game, such as goose, ptarmigan, or reindeer. Lavish winter holiday buffets offer innumerable varieties of seafood, meats, and desserts. Evening reservations are necessary on weekends in the better restaurants. Some offer discounts at lunch, or daily specials or tourist menus that may beat some entrée prices. For details and price-category definitions, *see* Eating & Drinking *in* Iceland A to Z.

$$$$ ✕ **Gallery at Hótel Holt.** The walls of this distinguished hotel dining room are covered with Icelandic art from the owner's private collection. You can indulge in such mouthwatering seafood as gravlax and grilled halibut, and there's a fabulous wine list to match. ⊠ *Hótel Holt, Bergstaðastræti 37* ☎ *552–5700* ▤ *AE, DC, MC, V.*

★ **$$$$** ✕ **Perlan.** In this rather formal revolving restaurant under "The Pearl" dome, you may pay a bit more for the food—including Icelandic fish and lamb dishes—but the splendid view, especially at sunset, justifies the expense. ⊠ *Öskjuhlíð* ☎ *562–0200* ▤ *AE, DC, MC, V* ☉ *No lunch.*

$$$–$$$$ ✕ **Siggi Hall á Óðinsvéum.** Iceland's own celebrity chef, Siggi Hall, reigns at this intimate hotel restaurant creating delicious and innovative offerings of fish, lamb, and, in season, game. ⊠ *Óðinstorg* ☎ *511–6677* ⊕*www. siggihall.is* ▤ *AE, DC, MC, V* ᴥ *Reservations essential.*

$$$ ✕ **Við Tjörnina.** Imaginatively prepared seafood is the draw here, including marinated cod cheeks and, in season, *tindabikkja* (starry ray). The restaurant is on the second floor of a typical early-20th-century house clad in corrugated iron. Lunch specials are enticing and good value. ⊠ *Templarasund 3* ☎ *551–8666* ᴥ *561–8666* ⊕ *www.islandia. is/~vidtjornina* ▤ *MC, V.*

$$ ✕ **Potturinn og pannan.** This cozy restaurant on the edge of the downtown area has a varied menu of seafood, lamb, beef, pork, and chicken, as well as an ever-popular salad bar. ⊠ *Brautarholt 22* ☎ *551–1690* ▤ *DC, MC, V.*

$$ ✕ **Þrír Frakkar hjá Úlfari.** Housed in an unassuming building in an older part of town, this restaurant serves traditional Icelandic food. The emphasis is on seafood; try the novelty whale-meat sushi. The bright annex overlooks a tiny, tree-filled park. ⊠ *Baldursgata 14* ☎ *552–3939* ⊕ *www.3frakkar.com* ▤ *DC, MC, V.*

$ ✕ **Solon Islandus.** Once a paint shop, this building is now home to a thriving café with menu items showing influence from Mexico to Japan. On Thursdays, live jazz upstairs adds even more flavor. ⊠ *Bankastræti 7a* 🕾 *562–3232* 🖃 *MC, V.*

Where to Stay

Hotels run the gamut from elegant to simple, classic to modern. For details and price-category definitions, *see* Lodging *in* Iceland A to Z.

★ $$$$ 🏨 **Hótel Holt.** In a quiet, residential neighborhood, the Holt has superb service, and its Gallery restaurant is exquisite. Rooms are on the small side but, like the aptly named restaurant, are decorated with works by leading Icelandic artists from the largest privately owned art collection in Iceland. ⊠ *Bergstaðastræti 37, IS-101* 🕾 *552–5700* 🖷 *562–3025* ⊕ *www. holt.is* 🛏 *42 rooms, 12 suites* ♨ *Restaurant* 🖃 *AE, DC, MC, V.*

$$$$ 🏨 **Radisson SAS Saga Hótel.** All rooms above the fourth floor have spectacular views. Hillary Clinton and her entourage stayed here during an official visit, occupying nearly 200 rooms. The hotel has a full range of services, and there are museums, shops, and restaurants nearby. ⊠ *Hagatorg, IS-107* 🕾 *525–9900* 🖷 *525–9909* 🛏 *211 rooms, 9 suites* ♨ *2 restaurants* 🖃 *AE, DC, MC, V.*

$$$–$$$$ 🏨 **Hótel Borg.** Elegant art deco rooms retain their original style but are equipped with CD players and coffeemakers. The upper floors expansion has individually styled rooms, including a luxurious tower suite. ⊠ *Pósthússtræti 11, IS-101* 🕾 *551–1440* 🖷 *551–1420* ⊕ *www. hotelborg.is* 🛏 *51 rooms, 5 suites* ♨ *Restaurant* 🖃 *AE, DC, MC, V.*

$$–$$$ 🏨 **Hotel Nordica, Icelandair Hotel.** With its in-house fitness club and spa, this hotel pampers its guests with spa therapies and personal trainers. Rooms in the boxy layer-cake building with blue panels and glass are appealingly decorated in neutral colors; those facing north have a view of Mount Esja. ⊠ *Suðurlandsbraut 2, IS-108* 🕾 *505–0950* 🖷 *505–0955* ⊕ *www.icehotel.is* 🛏 *284 rooms, 12 suites* ♨ *Restaurant* 🖃 *AE, DC, MC, V.*

$$ 🏨 **FossHótel Lind.** Though indulging in few frills, the Lind has comfortable rooms. It's near the Hlemmur bus station and a 15-minute walk from downtown. ⊠ *Rauðarárstígur 18, IS-105* 🕾 *562–3350* 🖷 *562–3351* ⊕ *www.fosshotel.is* 🛏 *56 rooms* ♨ *Restaurant* 🖃 *DC, MC, V.*

$$ 🏨 **Hotel Leifur Eiríksson.** Across from Reykjavík's biggest church, this hotel is convenient to countless boutiques, galleries, and city attractions. ⊠ *Skólavörðustígur 45, IS-101* 🕾 *562–0800* 🖷 *562–0804* ⊕ *www. hotelleifur.is* 🛏 *47 rooms* ♨ *Bar* 🖃 *MC, V.*

$$ 🏨 **Hótel Reykjavík.** This hotel's unimposing facade incorporates a vertical wedge of windows to channel light inward; rooms have smart, Nordic-style furnishings. A hidden wing has now added more than two dozen rooms to this conveniently located hotel. ⊠ *Rauðarárstígur 37, IS-105* 🕾 *562–6250* 🖷 *562–6350* ⊕ *www.hotelreykjavik.is* 🛏 *79 rooms, 6 suites* ♨ *2 restaurants* 🖃 *DC, MC, V.*

$–$$ 🏨 **Tower Guesthouse.** Stylishly decorated apartment units are convenient to the shopping street Laugavegur, but quietly tucked a block away. Have breakfast or unwind on the balconies, one of which has a Jacuzzi open to all guests. ⊠ *Grettisgata 6, IS-101* 🕾 *896–6694* 🖷 *552–5581* ⊕ *www.towerguesthouse.homestead.com* 🛏 *3 apartments* ♨ *Kitchens* 🖃 *MC, V.*

$ 🏨 **Hotel Garður.** A student dormitory convenient to the National Museum and downtown, it is open as a hotel only from June through August. The rooms are basic but modern. Book through City Hotel. ⊠ *Hringbraut, IS-107* 🕾 *511–1155 City Hotel* 🖷 *552–9040 City*

Hotel ⊕ *www.icelandichotels.is* ↩ *44 rooms with shared bath* ☰ *AE, DC, MC, V.*

Nightlife & the Arts

BARS
Despite its size, Reykjavík has a very large and active bar scene. Bar of the moment is **Kaffibarinn** (⊠ Bergstadastræti 1 ☎ 551–1588), partly owned by Damon Albarn from the Brit pop group Blur. The line to get in usually reaches around the block, and the names on the VIP list alone can fill up the place. Lots of candles give the bar a cozy feel, and the music ranges from Latin to hip-hop, house, and funk. The trendy **Rex Bar** (⊠ Austurstræti 9 ☎ 551–9111) was designed by Sir Terence Conran. A well-dressed crowd hangs out in the minimalist ground floor bar and the "Mafia Room" downstairs. **Astro Bar** (⊠ Austurstræti 22 ☎ 552–9222), like the Rex Bar, is another British-design addition to the Reykjavík bar scene; it's a popular haunt of local and visiting celebrities, and the dance floor gets very crowded. The **Kaffibrennslan** (⊠ Pósthússtræti 9 ☎ 561–3600) is a laid-back bar with café-style tables and a large selection of beers.

CLASSICAL MUSIC
& OPERA
The Icelandic Symphony Orchestra, **Sinfóníuhljómsveit Íslands** (⊠ Hagatorg ☎ 545–2500 ⊕ www.sinfonia.is), has a very ambitious program with about 60 concerts each season. Icelandic Opera, **Íslenska Óperan** (⊠ Ingólfsstræti ☎ 511–6400 ⊕ www.opera.is), puts on series of evening opera performances, but also has a popular afternoon concert series.

FILM
All foreign language films in Iceland are subtitled in Icelandic. Movies and show times are listed on the cinema's own Web sites. **Saga-Bíó** (⊠ Álfabakki 8 ☎ 587–8900) and **Kringlubíó** (⊠ Kringlan Shopping Center ☎ 588–0800) are both owned by Samfilm (⊕ www.samfilm.is). **Háskólabíó** (⊠ Hagatorg ☎ 530–1919 ⊕ www.kvikmyndir.is) and **Laugarásbíó** (⊠ Kleppsvegur ☎ 553–2075 ⊕ www.laugarasbio.is) show a good selection of new movies.

Shopping

The main shopping street starts at Lækjartorg, heads east up the hill as Bankastræti, and continues on to become Laugavegur where the street Skólavörðustígur angles down from the facade of Hallgrímskirkja. Skólavörðustígur has been reborn as a center for distinctive custom jewelry, Icelandic-designed fashions, arts, crafts, and leatherwork.

At the **Handknitting Association of Iceland** (⊠ Skólavörðustígur 19 ☎ 552–1890) you can buy high-quality hand knits through a cooperative. The **Kringlan Mall** (⊠ junction of Miklabraut and Kringlumýrarbraut) offers indoor shelter for shopping when the cold winds blow outside. **Rammagerðin** (⊠ Hafnarstræti 19 ☎ 551–1122) stocks a wide range of Icelandic clothes and souvenirs. For other bargains, try the weekend flea market, **Kolaportið** (⊠ Harborside in the Customs House on Geirsgata), between 11 and 5.

Reykjavík Essentials

AIRPORTS & TRANSFERS
Flights from the United States and Europe arrive at Keflavík Airport, 50 km (31 mi) south of Reykjavík. Reykjavík Airport is the central hub of domestic air travel in Iceland.
🛈 **Keflavík Airport** ☎ 425-0600. **Reykjavík Airport** ☎ 569-4100.

TRANSFERS
FlyBus (by the company Kynnisferðir) automatically connects with all flights to and from Keflavík. The trip into town takes 45 minutes and

costs IKr1,000. The terminus is at Hótel Loftleiðir, with requested stops at most major hotels. Call the day before to request a pickup at your hotel, 2½ hours before scheduled flight departure. A taxi ride from Keflavík Airport to downtown Reykjavík costs around IKr8,600.

FlyBus ☎ 562-1011.

BUS TRAVEL TO & FROM REYKJAVÍK

Central Reykjavík is served by two bus stations: Lækjartorg and Hlemmur. These punctuate the popular shopping street, Laugavegur, near its west end and midpoint.

BUS TRAVEL WITHIN REYKJAVÍK

Buses run from 7 AM to around midnight, some slightly later on weekends. The flat fare for Reykjavík and suburbs is IKr220 for adults. Exact change may be required. Strips of tickets are available from bus drivers and at stations. If you need to change buses, ask for a *skiptimiði* (free transfer ticket, pronounced *skiff*-ti-mi-thi).

CONSULATES

Canada ✉ Suðurlandsbraut 10, IS-101 ☎ 568-0820.

EMERGENCIES

Many pharmacies are open at night and on weekends. Lyf & heilsa apotek has two relatively convenient locations, listed below. The Háaleitisbraut branch is open until midnight. Further information can be obtained by calling the medical information line.

Doctors & Dentists Dentist ☎ 575-0505 for recorded information in Icelandic. **Doctor** ☎ 1770, weekdays 5 PM–8 AM and weekends 24 hours.

Emergency Services Police, ambulance, fire ☎ 112.

Late-night Pharmacies Lyf & heilsa apotek ✉ Austerver, Háaleitisbraut 68 ☎ 581-2101 ✉ Domus Medica, Egilsgötu 3 ☎ 563-1000. **Pharmacy information** ☎ 581-2101 until midnight; after midnight call 1770.

ENGLISH-LANGUAGE MEDIA

Bookstores Bókabúð Steinars ✉ Bergstaðastræti 7 ☎ 551-2030. **Eymundsson-Penninn** ✉ Austurstræti 18 ☎ 511-1130. **Mál og menning** ✉ Suðurlandsbraut 12 ☎ 522-2000.

TAXIS

Rates start at about IKr400; few in-town taxi rides exceed IKr900.

BSR ☎ 561-0000 or 561-1720. **Hreyfill** ☎ 588-5522. **Borgarbíll** ☎ 552-2440.

TOURS

SINGLE- & MULTIPLE-DAY TOURS

Most longer tours operate between June and September and cost from IKr25,000 to IKr150,000 per person, including accommodations and three meals a day. On some tours you'll stay in hotels, on others in tents. Such tours typically last from 3 to 19 days. One-day tours from Reykjavík include above all the classic circle to Gullfoss Waterfall, the hotspring area at Geysir, and the founding site of Parliament at Þingvellir and costs around IKr6,100. A sightseeing tour around Reykjavík costs around IKr2,400. Tours can be booked through bus companies, airlines, and travel agencies. For information on reliable tour operators, contact the Icelandic Tourist Board.

TRAVEL AGENCIES

Guðmundur Jónasson Travel ✉ Borgartún 34, IS-105 ☎ 511-1515 🖷 511-1511 ⊕ www.gjtravel.is. **Iceland Excursions Allrahanda** ✉ Funahöfdi 17, IS-110 ☎ 540-1313 🖷 540-1310 ⊕ www.icelandexcursions.is. **Reykjavík Excursions–Kynnisferðir** ✉ Vesturvör 6, IS-200 Kópavogur ☎ 580-5400 🖷 564-4776 ⊕ www.re.is.

THE COUNTRY

Incredible natural contrasts appear throughout Iceland's beautiful countryside. Magnificent, diverse fjords impart a scenic wrinkle to all coasts except the south, which is marked by spacious plains, foothills, and bizarre black sands crowned by pristine white glaciers. The interior highlands, a challenge to reach, are raw wonderlands of panorama and solitude. You are never far from cool waterfalls, steamy hot springs, or snow-capped summits.

The amount of countryside you can cover depends on time. And there's plenty of that during the summer midnight sun. Trips from Reykjavík can easily be expanded to several rewarding days in the neighboring southern or western regions. To circle the country via the Ring Road (Road 1), allow at least a week, so you have time to explore spectacular attractions along the way. There can be up to 170 km (105 mi) between towns and gas stations.

The South

You reach the rich piedmont and coastal farmlands of the south by descending the plateau east of Reykjavík along the Ring Road. Look offshore toward the southeast on your way down, and you may see Vestmannaeyjar (the Westman Islands) in the distance. Once down, you'll quickly come upon the village of Hveragerði, noted for greenhouses and health retreats. Larger Selfoss is 15 minutes away and straddles the Ölfusá River. Much farther east you reach tiny Skógar, and you'll have lots of time to practice pronouncing it before you reach Kirkjubæjarklaustur (hint: *keer*-kyew-*bye*-yar-kler-ster). Next you'll reach the stunning **Skaftafell National Park.** But should you see a 50-year-old yellow jeep en route, show some tolerance, since the driver is nearing 90 (that's years, not mph) and is one of two bachelor brothers whose huge farmstead is at the awesome bluffs of Lómagnúpur. The region is anchored at Höfn (harbor) í Hornafjörður. This whole area, laced by major glacial rivers and some of the country's best-known waterfalls, like majestic Gullfoss, Europe's largest waterfall, which plunges 105 feet into a deep canyon, and pure-white Skógafoss, is charged with geothermal springs, such as Geysir, namesake for spouting springs the world over. The original Geysir is a little tired these days, but nearby Strokkur spouts its stuff more regularly.

Crowning the countryside are noteworthy peaks. Mt. Hekla, once said to be where lost souls were banished, is alive and well, and the volcanic network under Europe's largest glacier, Vatnajökull, is also active. Resulting meltwater from an eruption pushed forward huge boulders and expanded the vast black sands of Skeiðarársandur, which cover a sizable part of the central south coast. Skiers, snowmobilers, and ice climbers find thrills at Vatnajökull, the world's largest temperate glacier. Don't miss the unique geology, flora, and fauna of Skaftafell National Park, with Hvannadalshnjúkur, Iceland's highest peak, just beyond its borders.

Hveragerði

Hveragerði, about 40 km (25 mi) east of Reykjavík, has hot springs and fruit and vegetable greenhouses. An unabashed tourist stop is the greenhouse **Eden,** where homegrown bananas have astonished visitors for years.

\$\$\$–\$\$\$\$ 🏨 **Hótel Örk.** Few hotels match the extras here, which include tennis courts, a pool, golf, and a sauna. Meals in the ground-floor restaurant are reasonable. Staff can book "spa cure" retreat packages at the nearby health clinic. ✉ *Breiðamörk 1, IS-810* ☎ *483–4700* 🖨 *483–4775* 🌐 *www.keyhotel.is* 🛏 *85 rooms* ⚑ *Restaurant, pool* ☰ *MC, V.*

$ ⊡ **Ból Youth Hostel & Ljósbrá Guesthouse.** Rooms in the hostel have up to five beds and share kitchen facilities. The guest house has five doubles with bath. Staff are a trove of information. ⊠ *Hveramörk 14, IS-810* ☎ *483–4198 hostel; 483–4588 guest house* ⊟ *483–4088* ⊕ *www. hotelljosbra.is* ⤶ *Youth hostel 12 rooms, 32 beds; guest house 5 rooms with bath, 3 with shared bath* ⊟ *MC, V.*

Selfoss

Selfoss, on the turbulent Ölfusá River, is the south's largest community. With many diverse services, it is home to the nation's largest dairy plant.

$$$ ⊡ **Hótel Selfoss.** On the glacial riverbanks, this hotel is a perfect base for visits to inland sites or the coast. The restaurant is the town's best eatery. ⊠ *Eyravegur 2, IS-800* ☎ *482–2500* ⊟ *482–2524* ⊕ *www. icehotel.is* ⤶ *100 rooms* ⚮ *Restaurant* ⊟ *MC, V.*

Skógar

Skógar, 120 km (75 mi) east of Selfoss, is near one of the country's most picturesque waterfalls, **Skógafoss.** What you see from the bottom is the final drop in a series of cascades and rapids that reward the hiker. The town also boasts one of the country's best rural museums, **Byggðarsafniði Skógar** (⊠ just east of Hótel Edda Skógar), whose curator is a walking encyclopedia and has been commended for his efforts with the Falcon Medal of Honor, the nation's highest distinction.

$$$ ⊡ **Hótel Edda Skógar.** Close to the Skógafoss waterfall, and near a dramatic glacial backdrop, this airy summer hotel has views of the sea and lush green slopes. ⊠ *Skógar, IS-861* ☎ *487–8870; 505–0910 off-season* ⊟ *487–8871* ⤶ *34 rooms* ⚮ *Restaurant, pool* ⊟ *MC, V* ☉ *Closed Sept.–mid-June.*

Kirkjubæjarklaustur

Aptly named Kirkjubæjarklaustur (or "church farm cloister") was the site of a medieval convent. When the volcano Laki erupted in 1783, producing the greatest amount of lava from a single eruption in recorded history, its deposits reshaped the landscape. A tiny chapel commemorates the pastor whose prayers are said to have stopped the lava before it reached these habitations. Two lovely nearby waterfalls and a first-rate August chamber-music festival are among local attractions. At the foot of Systrafoss waterfalls, beneath the town bluffs, visit **Kirkjubæjarstofa** (Kirkjubæjar Center; ⊠ Klausturvegur 2, IS-880 ☎ 487–4645) for exhibits on regional nature and culture.

$$$ ⊡ **Hotel Kirkjubæjarklaustur, Icelandair Hotel.** This excellent facility is open year-round. For liquid and solid refreshment, head to the bar and restaurant in the spacious newer building. ⊠ *Klausturvegur 6, IS-880* ☎ *487–4900* ⊟ *487–4614* ⊕ *www.icehotel.is* ⤶ *57 rooms* ⚮ *Restaurant, pool* ⊟ *MC, V.*

Skaftafell National Park

Near the foot of Skaftafellsjökull Glacier, you can hike from lowland sands into lush foothills, and on to hidden glacial canyons and stunning mountaintops. If you're lucky, you will glimpse Iceland's highest summit, Hvannadalshnjúkur Peak, rising 6,950 feet just outside the park borders.

★ About 32 km (20 mi) east of the park is the adventure world of **Jökul-sárlón,** where you can tour the glacial lagoon's eerie ice floes by boat.

$$–$$$ ⊡ **Hótel Skaftafell.** Near Skaftafell National Park, this hotel has an unmatched setting. Rooms come in three varieties: contemporary with private bath, spartan without bath, and, last, without bed linens for which you provide a sleeping bag. The latter two share bathrooms, but kitchen facilities are a plus. ✉ *Freysnes, Öræfi, IS-785* ☎ *478–1945* 🖶 *478–1846* ⊕ *www.hotelskaftafell.is* 📞 *42 rooms* ☆ *Restaurant* 🖃 *AE, MC, V.*

$ 🏕 **Skaftafell National Park Campground and Service Center.** This spacious campground has excellent facilities. It's open year-round for camping, although the facilities are available only from May to September. ✉ *Skaftafell National Park, 2 km (1.2 mi) off Ring Rd.* 1 ☎ *478–1627* 🖃 *MC, V.*

Höfn

Höfn, the major port community of the southeast, offers fine views of Europe's largest glacier, **Vatnajökull**, equal in size to all the glaciers on the European mainland and 3,000 feet deep at its thickest point, and the adjacent mountains.

$–$$$ ✕ **Kaffi Hornið.** Despite its name, which means Coffee Corner, this is more than just a coffee spot. Buffets, a salad bar, and piping-hot soups make this log-cabin eatery popular with locals and travelers alike. ✉ *Hafnarbraut 42* ☎ *478–2600* 🖃 *MC, V.*

$$$$ 🏨 **Hótel Höfn.** With splendid views of both mountains and sea, this hotel also has impeccable rooms. There's an emphasis on dining, whether in the upper-level restaurant, where sumptuous buffets and reindeer steak may be found, or in the ground-level bistro, where you can have lobster 101 ways (almost). ✉ *Vikurbraut 24, IS-780* ☎ *478–1240* 🖶 *478–1996* ⊕ *www.hotelhofn.is* 📞 *36, 32 with bath* ☆ *2 restaurants* 🖃 *MC, V.*

$$$–$$$$ 🏨 **FossHótel Vatnajökull.** This hotel with spectacular views of the glacier has a nationwide reputation for quality accommodations and excellent cooking. ✉ *Lindarbakki, Hornafjörður, IS-781* ☎ *478–2555* 🖶 *562–4001* ⊕ *www.fosshotel.is* 📞 *26 rooms* ☆ *Restaurant* 🖃 *MC, V* ⊙ *May 15–Sept. 25.*

Westman Islands

This cluster of islets off Iceland's south coast again became the focus of world attention when Keiko, the Orca whale that starred in the movie *Free Willy*, was brought to **Heimaey**, the largest of the Westman Islands. In a roomy sea pen he has thrived from the day he arrived. Reluctant to take advantage of the attempts to set him free, Keiko kept returning to his sea pen every time his caretakers released him, but has been spending longer and longer periods of time out at sea, sometimes up to 40 days at a time before returning to the pen. If all goes according to plan, Keiko may become a roving ambassador for Heimaey.

Heimaey has one of Iceland's best natural-history museums, the **Fiska-og náttúrugripasafn** (Fish and Nature Research Center); its reliable work was pivotal in returning Keiko to the Icelandic waters from which he was taken in the 1970s. ✉ *Heiðarvegur 12* ☎ *481–1997* 💳 *IKr 300* ⊙ *May–Aug., daily 11–5; Sept.–Apr., weekends 3–5.*

On the first weekend of August, thronging islanders celebrate the 1874 grant of Icelandic sovereignty with a three-day **festival** on Heimaey. The population and hundreds of visiting revelers move into a tent city in **Herjólfsdalur** (Herjólfur's Valley), a 10-minute stroll west of town, for a raucous extended weekend of bonfires, fireworks, dance, and song.

The nearby **Surtsey**, which erupted onto the scene as a new island in 1963, is preserved for ecological research and is closed to the public.

The East

Bustling fishing towns and villages dot Iceland's east coast. As names such as Stöðvarfjörður, Fáskrúðsfjörður, and Reyðarfjörður testify, each village has its own fjord. Farming thrives in the valleys, which enjoy almost Continental summers.

Djúpivogur

Some of the oldest buildings in Djúpivogur, a trading post since the 1500s, date from the Danish monopoly that ended in 1855. One, **Langa-Búð** (✉ Second house inland from the pier ☎ 478–8220), besides being a local museum and coffee shop, pays tribute to the late master wood-carver and sculptor Ríkarður Jónsson, whose ornate rococo mirror frame, done to complete his apprenticeship, would fit handsomely in any Tuscan palace. Nearby, pyramidal Mt. Búlandstindur, legendary as a force of mystical power, rises to 6,130 feet.

$$ ▨ **Hótel Framtíð.** A large dining room, where fish is the forte, and an annex, all in square-hewn Finnish timber, give this friendly harborside hotel a country look. ✉ *Vogaland 4, IS-765* ☎ *478–8887* ᕻ *478–8187* ⊕ *www.simnet.is/framtid* ⇗ *18 rooms* ⌂ *Restaurant* ▤ *AE, MC, V.*

$ ▨ **Berunes Youth Hostel.** This hostel offers lodging for 34 people in two-, three-, and four-person rooms. There are two separate cottages for five and seven people. Reserve in advance fall–spring. Note that you have to pay a supplement for bed linen, breakfast, and a private room. ✉ *Beruneshreppur, IS-765* ☎☎ *478–8988* ⊕ *www.simnet.is/berunes* ⇗ *34 beds* ▤ *MC, V.*

Breiðdalsvík

Commerce in this tiny village of a few hundred souls dates from 1883. The hamlet offers stores, a hotel, and boats.

$$ ▨ **Hótel Bláfell.** The hotel has a cozy, rustic interior and a homey restaurant with wonderful food. ✉ *Sólvellir 14, IS-760* ☎ *475–6770* ᕻ *475–6668* ⊕ *www.centrum.is/~blafell* ⇗ *24 rooms, 17 with bath* ⌂ *Restaurant* ▤ *MC, V.*

Seyðisfjörður

Although it's hard to believe now, the quaint village of Seyðisfjörður was one of Iceland's major trading ports in the 1800s, when tall sailing ships plied the crowded fjord. Beautiful wooden houses and buildings in Norwegian style attest to its affluent past. Nowadays in summer, the ferry *Norröna* cruises regularly into harbor from Europe. Summer Wednesday-evening concerts and exhibitions abound; for information contact the tourist office.

$$ ▨ **Hótel Seyðisfjörður.** In a classic Norse-style wooden house, this hotel overlooking the dramatic fjord puts out a varied buffet on summer Wednesdays, accompanied by live music. Rooms are tidy and cozy but not lavish. ✉ *Austurvegur 3, IS-710* ☎ *472–1460* ᕻ *472–1570* ⇗ *9 rooms* ⌂ *Restaurant* ▤ *MC, V.*

Egilsstaðir

Egilsstaðir, commercial hub of the eastern sector, has an airport equipped for international flights. The town straddles the Ring Road and lies on the eastern shore of Lake Lögurinn, reputed home of a wormlike serpent that guards a treasure chest. Named **Lagarfljótsormurinn**, like the monster, a pleasure ship now plies the glacially murky waters, scanning for supernatural spouts of steam. ✉ *Main River Bridge* ☎ *471–2900* ᕻ *471–2901* ⊕ *www.ormur.is.*

The nation's largest forest, **Hallormsstaðarskógur**, is 25 km (15 mi) south of Egilsstaðir. Native birch and planted aspen, larch, and spruce have grown tall here. The woods are ideal for walkers and horseback riders. Cross the valley bridge from the forest to visit **Skriðuklaustur** (☎ 471–2990), an unusual stone-covered mansion built by the writer

Gunnar Gunnarsson, and donated by him to the state for an agricultural research station and visiting artist's residence.

\$\$-\$\$\$\$ 🏨 **Hótel Hérað, Icelandair Hotel.** With views of the nearby meadows and glacial lake, this modern hotel is convenient to Egilsstaðir's shops and the town pool. ✉ *Miðvangur 5–7, IS-700* ☎ *471–1500* 🖷 *471–1501* 🌐 *www.icehotel.is* 🛏 *36 rooms* ⚥ *Restaurant, bar* ▭ *MC, V.*

\$\$ 🏨 **Fosshotel Valaskjálf.** In the heart of Egilsstaðir, Fosshotel Valaskjálf is a good base for exploring the Eastern fjords and Iceland's largest forest. The staff will help organize such activities as river rafting, horseback riding, and jeep safaris. ✉ *Skaógarlönd 3, IS-700* ☎ *471–1000* 🖷 *562–4001* 🛏 *22 rooms, 17 with bath* ⚥ *Restaurant, bar* ▭ *MC, V.*

The North

The north coast is deeply gouged by fjords, from Vopnafjörður in the east to Hrútafjörður (Rams' Fjord) in the west. In fact, Eyjafjörður, the country's longest, dips far inward to Akureyri, the "Capital of the North." In the region's midsection, large, well-established farms, some dating from Viking times, have thrived in fertile valleys, whose rivers attract salmon fishers.

Húsavík

★ Húsavík is a charming port with a uniquely painted timber church. Handy to nearby winter sports, it is also a base for summer hiking. Whale watchers have had amazing success (99%) on tours aboard restored oak boats. The **Hvalamiðstöð á Húsavík** (Húsavík Whale Center) has exhibits on Iceland's history as a whaling nation and on the biology of these behemoths. ✉ *Gamli Baukur* ☎ *464–2520* 🌐 *www.nordursigling.is* 🎟 *IKr 400* ⊙ *May and Sept., daily 10–5; June–Aug. daily 9–9.*

★ The true jewel of this area is **Mývatn,** a lake surrounded by fascinating "false" and eruptive craters, as well as varied, abundant bird life. More duck species nest here than at any other lake on earth, and the harlequin duck and Barrow's goldeneye exist nowhere else in Europe. Bring head nets if you visit in summer, because the lake is rightly named for midges.

In the region around Mývatn, shrub lands, lava barrens, and black sands are traversed by rivers with impressive waterfalls. It was to this area NASA's Apollo 11 crew came in the late 1960s to train, before setting off for the moon. At **Goðafoss** (Waterfall of the Gods), the leader of the pagan Norse faith at Parliament in the year 1000 tossed his religious icons into the waterfall to signal his acceptance of Christianity. Thundering **Dettifoss** on Jökulsá (Glacier River), southeast of Húsavík via the Tjörnes Peninsula, is Europe's most powerful waterfall, and its lengthy canyon is a national park. Also protected is the nearby hollow of **Ásbyrgi,** which, according to legend, is a giant hoofprint left by Sleipnir, the eight-legged horse of the ancient Norse god Óðinn.

\$\$\$ 🏨 **Hótel Gígur.** You can enjoy the delightful dining area at this hotel, with stunning views of the lake and landscape. ✉ *Skútustaðir, IS-660* ☎ *464–4455* 🖷 *462–4279* 🌐 *www.keahotel.is* 🛏 *37 rooms* ⚥ *Restaurant* ▭ *DC, MC, V* ⊙ *Closed Sept.–mid-May.*

\$\$\$ 🏨 **Hótel Húsavík.** Two eateries and plenty of help in booking area day tours make this hotel, within walking distance of the harbor, an attractive option. ✉ *Ketilsbraut 22, IS-640* ☎ *464–1220* 🖷 *464–2161* 🌐 *www.fosshotel.is* 🛏 *44 rooms* ⚥ *Bar* ▭ *AE, D, MC, V.*

\$\$\$ 🏨 **Hótel Reynihlíð.** This well-situated, comfortable hotel provides an information service and restaurant for hungry travelers. The on-site eatery, Gamli Bærinn, is a friendly café by day, congenial pub by night. ✉ *Mý-*

vatn, IS-660 Reykjahlíð ☎ *464–4170* 🖶 *464–4371* ⊕ *www.reynihlid. is* 🖂 *41 rooms* ⚲ *Restaurant* ▭ *AE, DC, MC, V.*

$$ 🏨 **Hótel Reykjahlíð.** This peaceful hotel is on the shore of Lake Mývatn, and bird-watchers can spot many of the lake's species right from their windows. Rooms have baths and all essentials, but nature supplies the luxury here. 🖂 *Mývatn, IS-660 Reykjahlíð* ☎ *464–4142* 🖶 *464–4336* ⊕ *www.reykjahlid.is* 🖂 *9 rooms* ⚲ *Restaurant* ▭ *MC, V.*

Akureyri

Akureyri's natural surroundings are unrivaled. Several 18th- and 19th-century wooden houses give the city a sense of history, as well as architectural variety. Lystigarðurinn (Arctic Botanic Gardens) has more than 400 species of flora native to Iceland and neighboring Greenland. 🖂 *Eyrarlandsholt* ⊙ *June–Sept., Fri. 8 AM–10 PM, weekends 9 AM–10 PM.*

With the northernmost 18-hole golf course in the world, Akureyri hosts the **Arctic Open Golf Tournament** during the unending days of midsummer. For details, contact local tourist information.

$$$$ 🏨 **Hótel KEA.** Centrally located at the end of a pedestrian shopping lane, this first-class hotel has an excellent ground-level restaurant, Rósagarðurinn, serving haute cuisine. Room furnishings are elegant mahogany. 🖂 *Hafnarstræti 87–89, IS-602* ☎ *460–2000* 🖶 *460–2060* ⊕ *www.hotelkea.is* 🖂 *73 rooms* ⚲ *Restaurant* ▭ *AE, DC, MC, V.*

$$$ 🏨 **Hótel Edda.** This summer hotel in a school dormitory is known for quality service and good meals. 🖂 *Eyrarlandsvegur, IS-600* ☎ *461–1434* 🖶 *461–1423* ⊕ *www.hoteledda.is* 🖂 *79 rooms, 14 with bath* ⚲ *Restaurant* ▭ *MC, V.*

$$$ 🏨 **Lykilhótel Norðurland.** Rooms here are pleasantly decorated with Danish furnishings. The sitting room has an impressive view. 🖂 *Geislagata 7, IS-600* ☎ *462–2600* 🖶 *462–7962* ⊕ *www.keyhotel.is* 🖂 *34 rooms* ⚲ *Restaurant* ▭ *MC, V.*

$ 🏨 **Hostelling in Akureyri.** Accommodations run from bunks for those with sleeping bags, to separate, completely equipped cottages that sleep six comfortably. Kitchen facilities are available. 🖂 *Stórholt 1, IS-600* ☎ *462–3657 or 894–4299* 🖶 *461–2549* ⊕ *www.hostel.is* 🖂 *20 rooms without bath* ⊙ *Closed Dec. 16–Jan. 9* ▭ *MC, V.*

Sauðárkrókur

In summer, boat trips from the coastal town of Sauðárkrókur to Drangey and Málmey islands offer striking views of the fjord and bird cliffs.

$$$ 🏨 **Fosshótel Áning.** Views from the tidy, austere rooms of this summer hotel are of either the nearby mountains or the fjord. Hiking, golfing, horseback riding, boat touring, and river rafting can be arranged from here. 🖂 *Sæmundarhlíð, IS-550* ☎ *453–6717* 🖶 *562–4001* ⊕ *www. fosshotel.is* 🖂 *71 rooms* ⚲ *Restaurant* ▭ *MC, V.*

The West

At Iceland's dragon head—the rugged fjords at Europe's western tip—seabirds vastly outnumber people. Due south is the long arm of Snæfellsnes Peninsula, with the awe-inspiring Snæfellsjökull volcano. South of that peninsula lies Borgarfjörður, where wide farmlands steeped in the history of the Viking sagas still fire the imagination of visitors.

Ísafjörður

The uncrowned capital of the West Fjords and one of the most important fishing towns in Iceland hosts a renowned Easter week ski meet. With its quaint buildings and lively cultural activities, the town is a convenient jumping-off point for tours to Hornstrandir, the splendidly peaceful, desolate coast north of the 66th parallel that is inhabited by millions of seabirds.

$$$ ⬚ **Hótel Ísafjörður.** A stone's throw from the sea, this hotel is great for families. The modern structure is decorated in Scandinavian style, and the restaurant offers haute cuisine, with delicious emphasis on fresh seafood. ⊠ *Silfurtorg 2, IS-400* ☎ *456–4111* 🖷 *456–4767* ⊕ *www. hotelisafjordur.is* ⚓ *32 rooms* ⚭ *Restaurant* ⊟ *AE, DC, MC, V.*

Stykkishólmur

Stykkishólmur is an active small port community, with a beautifully sheltered harbor. Classic timber houses, many lovingly restored, and some dating from as early as 1828, reveal its distinguished past, when many of the now-abandoned islets of Breiðafjörður were settled.

$$ ✕ **Narfeyrarstofa.** This charming, tiny eatery in an old timber building serves homemade quiches, coffee, light entrées, and desserts daily until midnight in summer. In winter it's purely a coffee and dessert spot, but impromptu live music can spring up almost anytime. ⊠ *Aðalgata 3* ☎ *438–1119* ⊟ *MC, V.*

$$$ ⬚ **Hótel Stykkishólmur.** The town's largest hotel has views of the harbor and neighboring mountains. The restaurant features lamb, seafood, and, in season, puffin and other seabirds. ⊠ *Borgarbraut 6, IS-340* ☎ *430–2100* 🖷 *430–2101* ⚓ *33 rooms* ⚭ *Restaurant* ⊟ *MC, V.*

Snæfellsjökull

Literally the high point on Snæfellsnes Peninsula is Snæfellsjökull, the entrance in Jules Verne's novel *Journey to the Center of the Earth.* This stupendous, glacier-covered, conical summit, according to local legend, possesses supernatural energies and is home to hidden folk.

Ólafsvík

Commerce has been carried on in this village, under the north shoulder of Snæfellsjökull, since 1687. From here you can hike to the top of the glacier or arrange snowmobile tours.

$$$ ⬚ **Hótel Ólafsvík.** This family-style harborside hotel has a charming restaurant that serves fresh local fare such as trout and halibut. ⊠ *Ólafsbraut 20, IS-355* ☎ *436–1650* 🖷 *436–1651* ⚓ *29 rooms, 18 with bath* ⚭ *Restaurant* ⊟ *AE, MC, V.*

The Countryside Essentials

TOURS

Aptly named Iceland Adventure can arrange a wide variety of exciting tours, be it glacier jeep safaris, skiing, snowmobiling, or river rafting. 🔲 **Iceland Adventure** ☎ 591-1026 🖷 591-1050 ⊕ www.adventure.is.

TOURS IN THE SOUTH Boat tours can be arranged on arrival at the Jökulsárlón glacial lagoon between May and September. Jórvík Aviation offers spectacular sightseeing flights around and to Skaftafell National Park or can be chartered to anywhere in the country. Öræfaferðir, a father-son outfit, puts together tours ranging from ice climbing to hiking Iceland's highest mountain, to seal- and bird-watching. Toppferðir has four-wheel-drive glacier tours leaving from Hotel Vatnajökull.
🔲 **Jökulsárlón** ☎ 478-2122. **Jórvík Aviation** ⊠ Reykjavík Airport ☎ 533-1500 🖷 533-1509 ⊕ www.jorvik.is. **Öræfaferðir** ⊠ Hofsnes, IS-785 Öræfi ☎ 854-0894 ⊕ www.hofsnes.com. **Toppferðir** ⊠ Lindarbakki, Höfn in Hornafjörður ☎ 4487-5530.

TOURS IN THE NORTH In Húsavík, Norðursigling–North Sailing offers whale-watching aboard classic oak ships.
🔲 **Norðursigling–North Sailing** ⚓ Gamli Baukur, IS-640 Húsavík ☎ 464-2350.

Sæferðir runs boat tours. Snowmobile trips to the top of Snæfellsjökull are arranged for groups at Snjófell. West Tours runs adventure trips to isolated parts of the West Fjords.

▪ **Sæferðir** ✉ Smiðjustígur 3, Stykkishólmur ☎ 438-1450. **Snjófell** ✉ Arnarstapi ☎ 435-6783 ⊕ www.snjofell.is. **West Tours** ☎ Aðalstræti, Ísafirði ☎ 456-5111.

VISITOR INFORMATION

▪ **Akureyri** ✉ Hafnarstræti 82 ☎ 462-7733. **Egilsstaðir** ✉ Kaupvangur 10 ☎ 471-2320 ⊕ www.east.is. **Höfn** ✉ Hafnarbraut 52 ☎ 478-1500. **Húsavík** ✉ Húsavíkurstofa Garðarsbraut 5 ☎ 464-3800. **Ísafjörður** ✉ Aðalstræti 7 ☎ 456-5121. **Kirkjubæjarklaustur** ✉ Klausturvegur 10 ☎ 487-4620. **Mývatn** ✉ Verslunin STRAX ☎ 464-4390. **Ólafsvík** ✉ Pakkhúsið ☎ 436-1543. **Selfoss** ✉ Þingvellir National Park ☎ 482-2660. **Seyðisfjörður** ✉ Austurvegur 42 ☎ 472-1551 ⊕ www.sfk.is.

IRELAND

DUBLIN, DUBLIN TO CORK, CORK TO GALWAY, GALWAY TO DONEGAL, NORTHERN IRELAND

17

FOR A SMALL ISLAND COUNTRY isolated on the westernmost extreme of the continent, Ireland has nevertheless managed to strut its way around the European stage. Economically it has outperformed the major European powers over the past decade; politically its influence is minimal and yet everyone knows of the Irish, and they all cast a slightly envious eye at this mysterious island of romance.

The booming economy has heralded a level of prosperity and development never before enjoyed, particularly in the capital city of Dublin. One-third of the country's very young population lives in the city, which is as much a college town as a center of government. Galleries, art-house cinemas, elegant shops, coffeehouses, and restaurants are springing up on almost every street. Along with an influx of immigrants from all corners of the globe, these factors are transforming the provincial capital that once suffocated Joyce into a city almost as cosmopolitan as the Paris to which he fled.

The pace of life outside Dublin is more relaxed. Indeed, the farther you travel from the metropolis, the more you'll be inclined to linger. Apart from such sporting attractions as championship golf, horse racing, angling, and the native games of hurling and Gaelic football, the thing to do in Ireland is to stop, take a deep breath of some of the best air in the Western world, and look around.

The lakes of Killarney—a chain of azure lakes surrounded by wild, boulder-strewn mountains—are justifiably among the country's most famous attractions. The Ring of Kerry is a gift from the gods to touring motorists, an out-and-back daylong adventure through lush green mountain and valley, and on down to the sea. By contrast, the lunar landscape of County Clare's eerie limestone desert, the Burren, must be explored on foot if you're to enjoy its rare alpine and Mediterranean flowers. Likewise, if you want to stand on the summit of the Cliffs of Moher to watch the Atlantic breakers bite into the ancient rocks 710 feet below, you'll have to get out of your car—even in the rain, and it often rains in Clare. If you love history, there are plenty of delightful castles and great stately houses peppering the banks of the old River Shannon, the spine of the nation. Throughout the country, prehistoric and early Christian ruins and remains hint at the awesome age of civilization on this ancient island. Alternatively, you could just visit a bookstore and pick up anything by the great writers of Ireland; let James Joyce, William Butler Yeats, John Millington Synge, or Seamus Heaney be your travel guide as you seek out the places made famous in their works.

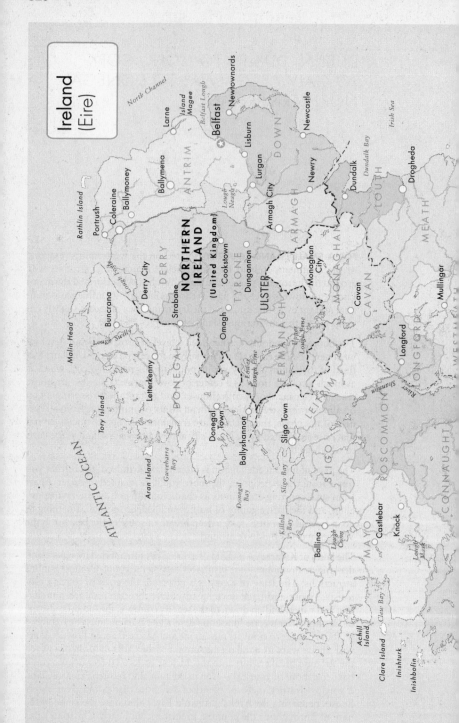

Ireland
(Eire)

North Channel

Island
Magee

Belfast Lough

Irish Sea

Rathlin Island

Larne

Newtownards

Portrush
Ballymoney
Ballymena

Belfast

Newcastle

ANTRIM

Coleraine

Lisburn

DOWN

Dundalk Bay

Lough
Neagh

Lurgan

Drogheda

Malin Head

Derry City

NORTHERN
IRELAND
(United Kingdom)

Cookstown

Armagh City

Newry

Dundalk

LOUTH

MEATH

Buncrana

DERRY

Strabane

TYRONE

Dungannon

ARMAGH

MONAGHAN

Lough Foyle

Lough Swilly

Letterkenny

Omagh

ULSTER

Monaghan
City

Cavan

Mullingar

Tory Island

DONEGAL

Upper
Lough Erne

CAVAN

LONGFORD

WESTMEATH

Gweebarra
Bay

Aran Island

Donegal
Town

Ballyshannon

Lower
Lough Erne

FERMANAGH

Longford

Donegal
Bay

Sligo Town

LEITRIM

River Shannon

ROSCOMMON

Sligo Bay

SLIGO

CONNAUGHT

Killala
Bay

Ballina

Castlebar

Knock

MAYO

Lough
Conn

Lough
Mask

Achill
Island

Clew Bay

Clare Island

Inishturk

Inishbofin

ATLANTIC OCEAN

IRELAND A TO Z

To research prices, get advice from other travelers, and book travel arrangements, visit www.fodors.com.

ADDRESSES

We've tried to provide full addresses for hotels, restaurants, and sights, though many of Ireland's villages and towns are so tiny they barely have street names, much less house numbers. If in doubt, ask for directions.

AIR TRAVEL

Distances are not great in Ireland, so airplanes play only a small role in internal travel. There are daily flights from Dublin to Derry, Shannon, Cork, Waterford, Kerry, Knock, and Galway; all flights take about 30 minutes. There is frequent service to the Aran Islands, off Galway Bay, from Connemara Airport in Galway; the flight takes about six minutes.

BIKE TRAVEL

Biking can be a great way to get around Ireland. For information about renting bikes, contact Bord Fáilte. Rates average €12.70 per day or €63.50 per week. You must pay a €63.50 deposit. Be sure to make reservations, especially in July and August. If you rent a bike in the Republic, you may *not* take it into Northern Ireland; nor may you take a bike rented in Northern Ireland into the Republic.

BOAT & FERRY TRAVEL

Exploring Ireland's lakes, rivers, and canals is a delightful, offbeat way to get to know the country. Motor cruisers can be chartered on the Shannon, the longest river in Ireland. Bord Fáilte has details of the wide choice of trips and operators available. For drifting through the historic Midlands on the Grand Canal and River Barrow, contact Celtic Canal Cruisers.

🖪 **Celtic Canal Cruisers** ⊠ 24th Lock, Tullamore, Co. Offaly ☎ 0506/21861 ⊕ www.celticcanalcruisers.com.

BUS TRAVEL

Bus Éireann (Irish Bus) runs bus service in the Republic. The 15-day Rambler ticket gives unlimited travel by bus in the Republic and is an excellent value at €145. It can be purchased from any city bus terminal and is valid for travel on any 15 days in a 30-day period. The provincial bus system operated by Bus Éireann is widespread—more so than the train system—although service can be infrequent in remote areas. In Northern Ireland, all buses are operated by the state-owned Ulsterbus.

🖪 **Bus Éireann** ☎ 01/836-6111. **Ulsterbus** ☎ 028/9033-3000.

BUSINESS HOURS

Banks are open weekdays 10–4 and until 5 on Thursday. In small towns they may close for lunch from 12:30 to 1:30. Museums are usually closed on Mondays but open Tuesday–Saturday 10–5, and Sunday 2–5. Shops are open Monday–Saturday 9–5:30, closing earlier on Tuesday, Wednesday, or Saturday, depending on the locality. Most shops, however, remain open until 9 PM on Thursday.

CAR TRAVEL

PARKING Parking in towns (especially Dublin) can be difficult. Signs with the letter P indicate parking lots, but if there's a stroke through the P, keep away or you'll collect a stiff fine, normally around €19.05. After 6 PM, restrictions are lifted.

ROAD
CONDITIONS

Ireland is one country in which a car is more or less essential to really get around. Despite improvements in public transportation, both the train and bus networks are limited, and many of the most intriguing regions are accessible only by car. Distances in Ireland seem short, but roads are narrow and often twisting and hilly, and side attractions are numerous, so you should aim for a daily mileage of no more than 240 km (149 mi). You'll find that driving past an ever-changing and often dramatic series of unspoiled landscapes is very much part of the fun. Outside the cities, the traffic is normally light, though you can easily find yourself crawling down country lanes behind an ancient tractor or a flock of sheep.

All principal roads are designated by the letter N, meaning National Primary Road. Thus, the main highway north from Dublin is N1, the main highway northwest is N2, and so on. Divided highways, or motorways—designated by blue signs and the letter M—take the place of some N roads. They are the fastest way to get from one point to another, but use caution, as they can end as abruptly as they begin. Road signs are usually in both Irish and English; in isolated parts of the northwest and Connemara, most are in Irish only, so make sure you have a good road map. A sensible rule to follow at unmarked intersections is to keep going straight if there's no sign directing you to do otherwise. Distances on the green signposts are in kilometers; white signposts give distances in miles.

RULES OF
THE ROAD

Driving is on the left. There is a general speed limit of 96 kph (60 mph) on most roads; in towns, the limit is 48 kph (30 mph). In some areas, the limit is 64 kph (40 mph); this is always clearly posted. At traffic circles (roundabouts), which are the main form of interchange, traffic from the right takes priority. Seat belts must be worn by the driver and front-seat passengers. Children under 12 must ride in the back. The drunk-driving laws are strict, limiting the driver to less than one pint of beer.

CUSTOMS & DUTIES

For details on imports and duty-free limits, *see* Customs & Duties *in* Smart Travel Tips.

EATING & DRINKING

Ireland is in the throes of a food revolution. Many of today's Irish chefs are young and have traveled widely and absorbed the best influences of Europe, North America, and the Pacific Rim. The result is a pan-European cuisine that has moved beyond the age-old roast-beef-and-Yorkshire-pudding habit of the old Anglo-Irish country houses. In its place an innovative, indigenous style is emerging, marrying simple treatments of traditional courses—nettle soup, oysters, wild salmon—with more exotic dishes featuring unusual combinations of the best local, often organic, ingredients.

Despite the introduction of café society and sushi bars, there are many examples of traditional cooking, particularly in pubs serving lunches of Irish stew, boiled bacon and cabbage, or steamed mussels. Pubs are one of the pillars of Irish society, worth visiting as much for conversation and music as for a good drink. Ireland is the home of Guinness, a pitch-black, malted stout—one of the great beers of the world.

Hotel dining rooms vary in quality, but the best country-house hotels offer some of the finest dining in Europe.

Prices are per person for a dinner main course. Sales tax is included in the price. Many places add a 10%–15% service charge—if not, a 10% tip is fine. For the Northern Ireland dining price chart, *see* Northern Ireland Essentials.

WHAT IT COSTS In Euros			
$$$$	$$$	$$	$
AT DINNER	over €26	€18–€26	€12–€18	under €12

Prices are per person for a main course.

MEALTIMES　Always check breakfast times in advance. It's usually 7 to 10, but some hotels serve from 7 to 11. Most offer a full Irish breakfast, with cereal followed by bacon, eggs, sausage, and, sometimes, black-and-white pudding. Lunch, from noon to 2 (or even 3), is a leisurely affair. Some hotels serve afternoon tea and scones. Most people go out for dinner after 8; if you want to eat earlier, watch for early-bird menus, typically served from 6:30 to 7:30.

RESERVATIONS &　People dress up for dinner at the top restaurants, but a jacket is ordi-
DRESS　narily sufficient. Ties are rarely essential. Nice casual wear is usually acceptable at all other places.

EMBASSIES
For information on consulates in Northern Ireland, *see* Northern Ireland Essentials.
🚩 Australia ✉ Fitzwilton House, Fitzwilton Terr., Dublin 2 ☎ 01/676-1517.
🚩 Canada ✉ 65 St. Stephen's Green, Dublin 2 ☎ 01/478-1988.
🚩 South Africa ✉ Alexandra House, 2nd fl., Earlsfort Terrace, Dublin 2 ☎ 01/661-5553.
🚩 United Kingdom ✉ 31 Merrion Rd., Dublin 2 ☎ 01/205-3700.
🚩 United States ✉ 42 Elgin Rd., Ballsbridge, Dublin 4 ☎ 01/668-8777.

HOLIDAYS
January 1; March 17 (St. Patrick's Day); April 9 (Good Friday); April 12 (Easter Monday); May 5 (May Day); June 2 and August 2 (summer bank holidays); October 25 (October Holiday); and December 25–26 (Christmas and St. Stephen's Day). In Northern Ireland, May 31 (spring bank holiday), July 12 (Battle of the Boyne), and August 30 (summer bank holiday) are holidays. June 7, August 2, and October 25 are not holidays in Northern Ireland.

LANGUAGE
Officially, Irish (Gaelic) is the first language of the Republic, but the everyday language of the vast majority of Irish people is English. The Gaeltacht (pronounced "*gale*-tocked")—areas in which Irish *is* the everyday language of most people—constitutes only 6% of the land, and all its inhabitants are, in any case, bilingual. Except for isolated parts of the northwest and Connemara, where many signs are not translated, most signs in the country are written in English, with an Irish translation. There is one important exception to this rule, with which you should familiarize yourself: FIR (pronounced "fear") and MNÁ (pronounced "muh-*naw*") translate, respectively, into "men" and "women."

LODGING
Accommodations in Ireland range from deluxe castles and stately homes to thatched cottages and farmhouses to humble bed-and-breakfasts. Standards everywhere are high, and they—along with prices—continue to rise. The days of considering Ireland your basic bargain destination are long gone. Pressure on hotel space reaches a peak between June and September, but it's a good idea to make reservations in advance at any time of the year, particularly at the more expensive spots. Accommodations are more economical in winter, although some—particularly in the west and the northwest—are closed from October through March.

Prices are for two people in a double room, based on high-season (June–mid-September) rates, including value-added tax (V.A.T.) and service charges. For the Northern Ireland lodging price chart, *see* Northern Ireland Essentials.

WHAT IT COSTS In euros			
$$$$	**$$$**	**$$**	**$**
HOTELS	over €200	€150–€200	€100–€150	under €100

Prices are for two people in a standard double room in high season.

BED & BREAKFASTS Bed-and-breakfast means just that. The bed can vary from a four-poster in the wing of a castle to a feather bed in a whitewashed farmhouse or the spare bedroom of a modern home. Rates are generally around €32 per person, though these can vary significantly. Although many larger B&Bs have rooms with bath or shower, in some you'll have to use the bathroom in the hall.

CAMPING Ireland has many beautifully sited campgrounds and trailer parks, but be prepared for wet weather. All are listed in *Caravan and Camping in Ireland,* available from Bord Fáilte.

GUEST HOUSES Some smaller hotels are graded as guest houses. To qualify, they must have at least five bedrooms, but in major cities they often have many more. A few may have restaurants; those that do not will often provide evening meals by arrangement. Otherwise these rooms can be as comfortable as those of a regular hotel, and in major cities they offer very good value for the money, compared with the $ hotels.

HOTELS In general, hotels charge per person. In most cases (but not all, especially in more expensive places), the price includes a full breakfast. Value-added tax (V.A.T.) is included, but some hotels—again, usually the more expensive ones—add a 10%–15% service charge. This should be mentioned in their price list. If it's not, a tip of between 10% and 15% is customary—if you think the service is worth it. In $$ and $ hotels, be sure to specify whether you want a private bath or shower; the latter is cheaper. Off-season (October–May) prices are reduced by as much as 25%.

RESERVING A ROOM Rooms can be reserved directly from the United States and elsewhere; ask your travel agent for details. Local tourist board offices can also make reservations, as can Bord Fáilte's (the Irish Tourist Board, pronounced "Board *Fall*-cha") Central Credit Card Reservations Service. Bord Fáilte has an official grading system and publishes a detailed price list of all approved accommodations, including hotels, guest houses, farmhouses, B&Bs, and hostels. No hotel may exceed this price without special authorization from Bord Fáilte; prices must also be displayed in every room. Don't hesitate to complain either to the manager or to Bord Fáilte, or both, if prices exceed this maximum.

🔧 Toll-Free Numbers **Bord Fáilte Central Credit Card Reservations Service** ✉ Suffolk St., Dublin 2 ☎ 1800/668-668 in Ireland; 800/398-4376 in U.S. 🖷 01/605-7787.

MAIL & SHIPPING
🔧 **General Post Office** ✉ O'Connell St., Dublin 1 ☎ 01/705-7000.

POSTAL RATES Airmail rates to the United States and Canada are €0.60 for letters and postcards. Letters and postcards to Britain and continental Europe cost €0.40. Rates in Northern Ireland are 43p for letters and postcards to the United States and Canada. To the United Kingdom and the Irish Republic, rates are 26p for first-class letters and 20p for second class.

MONEY MATTERS

Dublin is expensive—an unfortunate state of affairs that manifests itself most obviously in hotel rates and restaurant menus. You can generally keep costs lower if you visit Ireland on a package tour. Alternatively, consider staying in a guest house or a B&B; they provide an economical and atmospheric option. The rest of the country—with the exception of the better-known hotels and restaurants—is less expensive than Dublin. That the Irish themselves complain bitterly about the high cost of living is partly attributable to the rate of value-added tax (V.A.T.)—a stinging 21% on "luxury" goods and 13½% on hotel accommodations. A double room in a moderately priced Dublin hotel will cost about €114, with breakfast; the current rate for a country B&B is around €32 per person. Modest, small-town hotels generally charge around €50 per person.

Sample prices include cup of coffee, €1; pint of beer, €3; Coca-Cola, €1.20; a sandwich, €2.30; 2-km (1-mi) taxi ride, €5.10. Prices are about 10% higher in Dublin.

CURRENCY The Irish Republic is a member of the European Monetary Union (EMU) and the euro is legal tender. Euro notes come in denominations of €500, €200, €100, €50, €20, €10, and €5. The euro is divided into 100 cents and coins are available as €2 and €1, and 50, 20, 10, 5, 2, and 1 cent. Northern Ireland uses British currency; euros are not accepted. Although the euro is the only legal tender in the Republic, U.S. dollars and British currency are often accepted in large hotels and shops licensed as "bureaux de change." Banks give the best rate of exchange. There is likely to be some variance in the rates of exchange between Ireland and the United Kingdom (which includes Northern Ireland). Change U.K. pounds at a bank when you get to Ireland (note that pound coins are not accepted). The rate of exchange at press time was €0.94 to the U.S. dollar, €0.61 to the Canadian dollar, €1.51 to the pound sterling, €0.55 to the Australian dollar, €0.52 to the New Zealand dollar, and €0.11 to the South African rand.

TAXES

VALUE-ADDED TAX (V.A.T.) Visitors from outside Europe can take advantage of the "cash-back" system on value-added tax (V.A.T.) in two ways. The first is by having your invoice receipt stamped by customs on departure and mailing it back to the store for V.A.T. refund. You must, however, verify at the time of purchase that the store operates by this system. The second and more popular option is to use one of the private cash-back companies, which charge a commission.

TELEPHONES

COUNTRY & AREA CODES The country code for the Republic of Ireland is 353; for Northern Ireland it's 44.

INTERNATIONAL CALLS In the Republic and Northern Ireland, calls to the United States and Canada can be made by dialing 001 followed by the area code. For calls to the United Kingdom, dial 0044 followed by the number, dropping the beginning zero. For long-distance operators, call one of the service providers below.

🖪 Access Codes **AT&T** ☎ 800/550-000. **MCI** ☎ 800/551-001. **Sprint** ☎ 800/552-001.

LOCAL CALLS Pay phones can be found in all post offices and most hotels and bars, as well as in street booths. Local calls cost €0.25 for three minutes, calls within Ireland cost about €1 for three minutes, and calls to Britain cost about €2.50 for three minutes. Telephone cards are available at post offices and most newsdealers. Prices range from €2.55 for 10 units to

€10.15 for 50 units. Card-operated booths are as common as coin-operated booths. Rates go down by about a third after 6 PM and all day Saturday and Sunday. Northern Ireland is part of the United Kingdom telephone system; a local call costs 10p.

TIPPING

Some hotels and restaurants will add a service charge of about 12% to your bill, so tipping isn't necessary unless you've received particularly good service. But if there is no service charge, you might want to add a minimum of about 10% to the total. You don't tip in pubs, but if there is waiter service in a bar or hotel lounge, leave about €0.60. Tip taxi drivers about 10% of the fare if the taxi has been using its meter. For longer journeys, where the fare is agreed upon in advance, a tip will not be expected unless some kind of commentary (solicited or not) has been provided. In luxury hotels, porters and bellhops will expect €1.30; elsewhere, €0.65 is adequate. Hairdressers normally expect a tip of about €1.30.

TRAIN TRAVEL

The Irish Republic's train services are generally reliable, reasonably priced, and comfortable, though trains in Ireland travel more slowly than in other places in Europe. Iarnód Éireann (Irish Rail) and Bus Éireann are independent components of the state-owned public transportation company Coras Iompair Éireann (CIE). All the principal towns are easily reached from Dublin, though services between provincial cities are roundabout. To reach Cork City from Wexford, for example, you have to go via Limerick Junction. It is often quicker, though perhaps less comfortable, to take a bus. Most mainline trains have one standard class. Round-trip tickets are usually cheapest.

CUTTING COSTS Eurailpasses are not valid in Northern Ireland. The Irish Explorer Rail & Bus Pass, for use on Ireland's railroads, bus system, or both, covers all the state-run and federal railways and bus lines throughout the Republic of Ireland. It does not apply to the North or to transportation within the cities. The Emerald Isle Card offers unlimited bus and train travel anywhere in Ireland and Northern Ireland, valid within cities as well. In Northern Ireland, Rail Runabout tickets entitle you to seven days' unlimited travel on scheduled rail services April–October. Even if you have a rail pass, be sure to book seats ahead of time.
🚆 **Iarnód Éireann** ☎ 01/836-6222 ⊕ www.irishrail.ie. **Translink** ☎ 028/9089-9411 ⊕ www.translink.co.uk.

VISITOR INFORMATION

For information on travel in the Irish Republic, contact the headquarters of the Irish Tourist Board.
🚆 **Irish Tourist Board (Bord Fáilte)** ✉ Baggot St. Bridge, Dublin 2 ☎ 1850/230-330
🖨 01/602-4100 ⊕ www.ireland.travel.ie.

WHEN TO GO

June to mid-September is Ireland's high season, but the country's attractions are not as dependent on the weather as those in most other northern European countries, and the scenery is just as attractive in the off-peak times of fall and spring.

CLIMATE In all seasons you can expect rain, although the sun is often out moments after a squall passes. Winters are mild though wet; summers can be warm and sunny, but there's always the risk of a sudden shower. No one ever went to Ireland for a suntan. The following are the average daily maximum and minimum temperatures for Dublin.

Jan.	46F	8C	May	60F	15C	Sept.	63F	17C
	34	1		43	6		48	9
Feb.	47F	8C	June	65F	18C	Oct.	57F	14C
	35	2		48	9		43	6
Mar.	51F	11C	July	67F	19C	Nov.	51F	11C
	37	3		52	11		39	4
Apr.	55F	13C	Aug.	67F	19C	Dec.	47F	8C
	39	4		51	11		37	3

DUBLIN

Europe's most intimate capital has changed forever—the soul of the Republic of Ireland has experienced the nation's most dramatic period of transformation since the Georgian era. For the last decade, Dublin has ridden the back of its "Celtic Tiger" economy, and massive construction cranes hover over both shiny new hotels and old Georgian houses. Irish culture became hot: patriot Michael Collins became a Hollywood box-office star, Frank McCourt's *Angela's Ashes* conquered best-seller lists in the United States and was made into a movie, and *Riverdance* became a worldwide old-Irish mass jig. Because of these and other attractions, travelers are coming to Dublin in ever-greater numbers, so don't be surprised if you stop to consult your map in Temple Bar—the city's most happening neighborhood—and are swept away by the ceaseless flow of bustling crowds. Dublin has become a colossally entertaining, engaging city—all the more astonishing considering its gentle size. The quiet pubs and little empty backstreets might be harder to find now that Dublin has been "discovered," but a bit of effort and research can still unearth the old "Dear Dirty Dumpling," a city that Joyce was so fond of.

Exploring Dublin

Numbers in the margin correspond to points of interest on the Dublin map.

Originally a Viking settlement, Dublin sits on the banks of the River Liffey, which divides the city north and south. The liveliest round-the-clock spots, including Temple Bar and Grafton Street, are on the south side, although several construction projects on the north side have helped to reinvigorate these areas. The majority of the city's most notable buildings date from the 18th century—the Georgian era—and, although many of its finer Georgian buildings disappeared in the redevelopment of the '70s, enough remain to recall the elegant Dublin of centuries past. Dublin is small as capital cities go, with a compact downtown area, and the best way to soak in the full flavor of the city is on foot. Literary Dublin can still be recaptured by following the footsteps of Leopold Bloom's progress, as described in James Joyce's *Ulysses*. Trinity College, alma mater of Oliver Goldsmith, Jonathan Swift, and Samuel Beckett, among others, is a green, Georgian oasis, alive with students.

South of the Liffey

South of the Liffey are graceful squares and fashionable terraces from Dublin's elegant heyday, and, interspersed with some of the city's leading sights, this area is perfect for an introductory city tour. You might begin at O'Connell Bridge—as Dublin has no central focal point, most natives regard it as the city's Piccadilly Circus or Times Square—then head south down Westmoreland Street to Parliament House. Continue on to Trinity College—the Book of Kells, Ireland's greatest artistic treasure, is on view here—then eastward to Merrion Square and the National Gallery; south to St. Stephen's Green and Fitzwilliam Square; west to Dublin's two beautiful cathedrals, Christ Church and St. Patrick's; and end with dinner in a Temple Bar restaurant overlooking the Liffey.

❷ Bank of Ireland. With a grand facade of marble columns, the Bank of Ireland is one of Dublin's most striking buildings. Across the street from the front entrance to Trinity College, the Georgian structure was once the home of the Irish Parliament. Built in 1729, it was bought by the Bank of Ireland in 1803. Hurricane-shape rosettes adorn the coffered ceiling in the pastel-hued, colonnaded, clerestoried main banking hall, once the Court of Requests, where citizens' petitions were heard. Just down the hall is the original House of Lords, with tapestries, an oak-paneled nave, and a 1,233-piece Waterford glass chandelier; ask a guard to show you in. Visitors are welcome during normal banking hours; a brief guided tour is given every Tuesday at 10:30, 11:30, and 1:45. ⊠ *2 College Green* ☎ *01/677–6801* ۞ *Mon.–Wed. and Fri. 10–4, Thurs. 10–5; Arts Center Tues.–Fri. 10–4, Sat. 2–5, Sun. 10–1.*

⑰ Christ Church Cathedral. You'd never know from the outside that the first Christianized Danish king built a wooden church at this site in 1038; thanks to the extensive 19th-century renovation of its stonework and trim, the cathedral looks more Victorian than Anglo-Norman. Stone construction was begun in 1172 by Strongbow, a Norman baron and conqueror of Dublin for the English crown. The vast, sturdy **crypt,** with its 12th- and 13th-century vaults, is Dublin's oldest surviving structure and the building's most notable feature. At 6 PM on Wednesday and Thursday you can enjoy a choral evensong. ⊠ *Christ Church Pl. and Winetavern St.* ☎ *01/677–8099* ۞ *Weekdays 9:45–5, weekends 10–5.*

⑯ City Hall. Facing the Liffey from the top of Parliament Street, this grand Georgian municipal building (1769–79), once the Royal Exchange, was designed by Thomas Cooley. It has a central rotunda encircled by 12 columns, a fine mosaic floor, and 12 frescoes depicting Dublin legends and ancient Irish historical scenes. The building now holds an exhibition tracing the evolution of Ireland's 1,000-year-old capital. ⊠ *Dame St.* ☎ *01/672–2204* ⊕ *www.dublincorp.ie* ۞ *Mon.–Sat. 10–5:15, Sun. 2–5.*

⑮ Dublin Castle. The film *Michael Collins* captures this structure's near-indomitable status in the city. Just off Dame Street behind City Hall, the grounds of the castle encompass a number of buildings, including the **Record Tower,** a remnant of the original 13th-century Norman castle that was the seat of English power in Ireland for almost 7½ centuries, as well as various 18th- and 19th-century additions. The lavishly furnished **state apartments** are now used to entertain visiting heads of state. Guided tours run every half hour, but the rooms are closed when in official use, so call first. The **Castle Vaults** now hold an elegant little patisserie and bistro. The castle is also the home of the **Chester Beatty Library.** Among the library's exhibits are clay tablets from Babylon dating from 2700 BC, Japanese color wood-block prints, Chinese jade books, and Turkish and Persian paintings. ⊠ *Castle St.* ☎ *01/677–7129* ⊕ *www.dublincastle.ie* ۞ *Weekdays 10–5, weekends 2–5.*

❹ Dublin Civic Museum. Built in 1765–71 as an assembly house for the Society of Artists, the museum displays drawings, models, maps of Dublin, and other civic memorabilia. ⊠ *58 S. William St.* ☎ *01/679–4260* ۞ *Tues.–Sat. 10–6, Sun. 11–2.*

★ ❸ Grafton Street. Open only to pedestrians, brick-lined Grafton Street is one of Dublin's vital spines: it's the most direct route between the front door of Trinity College and Stephen's Green; the city's premier shopping street, off which radiate smaller streets housing stylish shops and pubs; and home to many of the city's street musicians and flower sell-

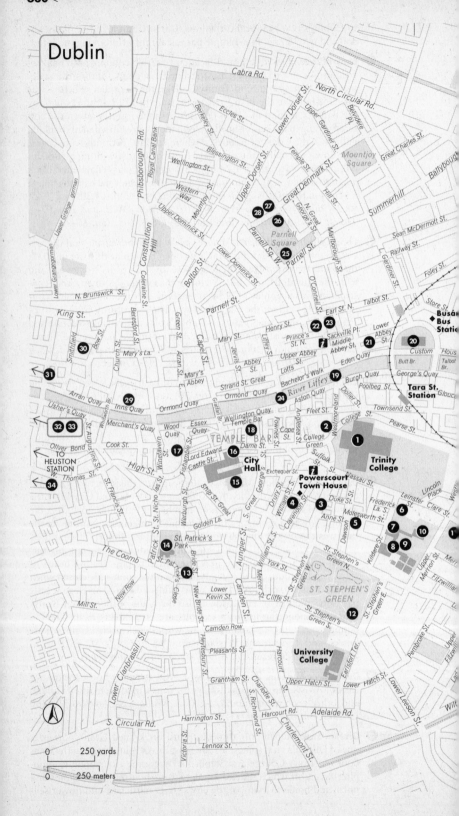

Dublin

ers. Browse through the Irish and international designer clothing and housewares at **Brown Thomas,** Ireland's most elegant department store. The **Powerscourt Town House** is a shopping arcade installed in the covered courtyard of one of Dublin's most famous Georgian mansions.

6 Heraldic Museum. If you're a Fitzgibbon from Limerick, a Cullen from Waterford, or a McSweeney from Cork, chances are your family designed, begged, borrowed, or stole a coat of arms somewhere along the way. The Heraldic Museum has hundreds of family crests, flags, coins, stamps, and silver, all highlighting the uses and development of heraldry in Ireland. ⊠ *2 Kildare St.* ☎ *01/661–4877* ⊘ *Mon.–Wed. 10–8:30, Thurs. and Fri. 10–4:30, Sat. 10–12:30; guided tours by appointment.*

9 Leinster House. When it was built in 1745 it was the largest private residence in Dublin. Today it is the seat of Dáil Éireann (pronounced "Dawl Erin"), the Irish House of Parliament. The building has two facades: the one facing Merrion Square is designed in the style of a country house; the other, on Kildare Street, is in the style of a town house. ⊠ *Kildare St.* ☎ *01/618–3000* ⊕ *www.irlgov.ie* ⊘ *Tours Mon. and Fri. by appointment (when Parliament is not in session).*

13 Marsh's Library. A short walk west from Stephen's Green and accessed through a tiny but charming cottage garden lies a gem of old Dublin: the city's—and Ireland's—first public library, opened in 1701 to "All Graduates and Gentlemen." Its interior has been left practically unchanged since it was built—it still contains "cages" into which scholars who wanted to peruse rare books were locked. ⊠ *St. Patrick's Close* ☎ *01/454–3511* ⊕ *www.kst.dit.ie* ⊘ *Mon. and Wed.–Fri. 10–12:45 and 2–5, Sat. 10:30–12:45.*

★ **11 Merrion Square.** Created between 1762 and 1764, this tranquil Georgian square is lined on three sides by some of Dublin's best-preserved Georgian town houses. Even when the flower gardens are not in bloom, the vibrant green grounds, dotted with sculpture and threaded with meandering paths, are worth a walk. **No. 1,** at the northwest corner, was the home of Sir William and Speranza Wilde, Oscar's parents. ⊠ *East end of Nassau St.* ⊘ *Daily sunrise–sunset.*

★ **10 National Gallery of Ireland.** On the west side of Merrion Square, this 1854 building contains the country's finest collection of old masters—treasures include Vermeer's *Woman Writing a Letter* (twice stolen from Sir Alfred Beit and now safe at last), Gainsborough's *Cottage Girl,* and Caravaggio's *The Arrest of Christ.* The gallery's restaurant is one of the city's best spots for an inexpensive, top-rate lunch. The new Millennium Wing, a standout of postmodern architecture in Dublin, also houses part of the permanent collection, and stages major international traveling shows. Free guided tours are available on Saturday at 3 PM and on Sunday at 2:15, 3, and 4. ⊠ *Merrion Sq. W* ☎ *01/661–5133.* ⊕ *www.nationalgallery.ie* ⊘ *Mon.–Wed., Fri., and Sat. 10–5:30, Thurs. 10–8:30, Sun. 2–5.*

7 National Library. The collections here include first editions of every major Irish writer. Temporary exhibits are held in the entrance hall, off the colonnaded rotunda. The main reading room, opened in 1890, has a dramatic dome ceiling. The library also offers a free genealogical consultancy service that advises you on how to trace your Irish ancestors. ⊠ *Kildare St.* ☎ *01/661–8811* ⊕ *www.nli.ie* ⊘ *Mon.–Wed. 10–9, Thurs. and Fri. 10–5, Sat. 10–1.*

8 National Museum. On the other side of Leinster House from the National Library, the museum is most famous for its spectacular collection of Irish artifacts from 7000 BC to the present, including the Tara Brooch, the

Ardagh Chalice, the Cross of Cong, and a fabled hoard of Celtic gold jewelry. Upstairs, Viking Age Ireland is a permanent exhibit on the Norsemen, featuring a full-size Viking skeleton, swords, leather works recovered in Dublin and surrounding areas, and a replica of a small Viking boat. ⊠ *Kildare St.* ☎ *01/660–1117* ⊕ *www.museum.ie* ⊙ *Tues.–Sat. 10–5, Sun. 2–5.*

⑲ O'Connell Bridge. Strange but true: the main bridge spanning the Liffey is wider than it is long. The north side of the bridge is dominated by an elaborate memorial to Daniel O'Connell, "The Liberator," erected as a tribute to the great 19th-century orator's achievement in securing Catholic Emancipation in 1829. Today **O'Connell Street,** one of the widest in Europe, is less a street to loiter in than to pass through on your way to elsewhere. **Henry Street,** to the left just beyond the General Post Office, is, like a downscale Grafton Street, a busy pedestrian thoroughfare where you'll find throngs of Dubliners out doing their shopping. A few steps down Henry Street off to the right is the colorful **Moore Street Market,** where street vendors recall their most famous ancestor, Molly Malone, by singing their wares—mainly flowers and fruit—in the traditional Dublin style.

⑤ Royal Irish Academy. The country's leading learned society houses important manuscripts in its 18th-century library. Just below the academy is the **Mansion House,** the official residence of the Lord Mayor of Dublin. Its Round Room, the site of the first assembly of Dáil Éireann in January 1919, is now used mainly for exhibitions. ⊠ *19 Dawson St.* ☎ *01/676–2570* ⊕ *www.ria.ie* ⊙ *Weekdays 9:30–5.*

⑭ St. Patrick's Cathedral. Legend has it that St. Patrick baptized many converts at a well on the site of the cathedral in the 5th century. The building dates from 1190 and is mainly early English Gothic in style. At 305 feet, it is the longest church in the country. In the 17th century Oliver Cromwell, dour ruler of England and no friend of the Irish, had his troops stable their horses in the cathedral. It wasn't until the 19th century that restoration work to repair the damage was begun. St. Patrick's is the national cathedral of the Anglican Church in Ireland and has had many illustrious deans. The most famous was Jonathan Swift, author of *Gulliver's Travels,* who held office from 1713 to 1745. Swift's tomb is in the south aisle. Memorials to many other celebrated figures from Ireland's past line the walls. "Living Stones" is the cathedral's permanent exhibition celebrating St. Patrick's place in the life of the city. Matins (9:45 AM) and evensong (5:35 PM) are still sung on most days, a real treat for the music lover. ⊠ *Patrick St.* ☎ *01/453–9472* ⊕ *www. stpatrickscathedral.ie* ⊙ *May and Sept.–Oct., weekdays 9–6, Sat. 9–5, Sun. 10–11 and 12:30–3; June–Aug., weekdays 9–6, Sat. 9–4, Sun. 9:30–3 and 4:15–5:15; Nov.–Apr., weekdays 9–6, Sat. 9–4, Sun. 10–11 and 12:45–3.*

⑫ St. Stephen's Green. Dubliners call it simply Stephen's Green; green it is—strikingly so, year-round (you can even spot a palm tree or two). Among the park's many statues are a memorial to Yeats and another to Joyce by Henry Moore. The north side is dominated by the magnificent **Shelbourne Méridien Hotel.** A drink in one of its two bars, or afternoon tea in the elegant Lord Mayor's Room is the most financially painless way to soak in the old-fashioned luxury.

★ ⑱ Temple Bar. Dublin's hippest neighborhood—bordered by Dame Street to the south, the Liffey to the north, Fishamble Street to the west, and Westmoreland Street to the east—is the city's version of the Latin Quarter, the playing ground of "young Dublin." Representative of the improved fortunes of the area, with its narrow, winding pedestrian-only cobblestone streets, is the **Clarence** (⊠ 6–8 Wellington Quay ☎ 01/670–9000), a favorite old Dublin hotel now owned by Bono and the Edge of U2. The area is chock-full of small hip stores, art galleries, and inexpensive restaurants and pubs. The **Irish Film Centre** (⊠ 6 Eustace St. ☎ 01/679–5744) is emblematic of the area's vibrant mix of high and alternative culture.

❶ Trinity College. Ireland's oldest and most famous college is the heart of college-town Dublin. Trinity College, Dublin (officially titled Dublin University but familiarly known as Trinity), was founded by Elizabeth I in 1592 and offered a free education to Catholics—providing they accepted the Protestant faith. As a legacy of this condition, until 1966 Catholics who wished to study at Trinity had to obtain a dispensation from their bishop or face excommunication. Today more than 70% of Trinity's students are Catholics, an indication of how far away those days seem now.

Fodor'sChoice ★

The pedimented, neoclassical Georgian facade, built between 1755 and 1759, consists of a magnificent portico with Corinthian columns. The design is repeated on the interior, so the view from outside the gates and from the quadrangle inside is the same. On the quad's lawn are statues of two of the university's illustrious alumni—statesman Edmund Burke and poet Oliver Goldsmith. Other famous students include the philosopher George Berkeley (who gave his name to the northern California city), Jonathan Swift, Thomas Moore, Oscar Wilde, John Millington Synge, Bram Stoker, Edward Carson, and Samuel Beckett. The 18th-century building on the left, just inside the entrance, is the **chapel.** There's an identical building opposite, the **Examination Hall.** The oldest buildings are the library in the far right-hand corner, completed in 1712, and a 1690 row of redbrick buildings known as the **Rubrics,** which contain student apartments.

Ireland's largest collection of books and manuscripts is housed in **Trinity College Library,** entered through the library shop. Its principal treasure is the Book of Kells, generally considered the most striking manuscript ever produced in the Anglo-Saxon world. Only a few pages from the 682-page, 9th-century gospel are displayed at a time, but an informative exhibit has reproductions of many of them. At peak hours you may have to wait in line to enter the library; it's less busy early in the day. Don't miss the grand and glorious Long Room, an impressive 213 feet long and 42 feet wide, which houses 200,000 volumes in its 21 alcoves. ☎ 01/677–2941 ⊕ www.bookofkells.ie ☉ Mon.–Sat. 9:30–4:45, Sun. noon–4:30.

In the Thomas Davis Theatre in the Arts Building, **"Dublin Experience"** is an audiovisual presentation devoted to the history of the city over the last 1,000 years. ☎ 01/677–2941 ☉ Late May–Oct., daily 10–5; shows every hr on the hr.

North of the Liffey

The Northside city center is a mix of densely thronged shopping streets and slightly run-down sections of once-genteel homes, which are now being bought up and renovated. There are some classic sights in the area, including gorgeous Georgian monuments—the Custom House, the General Post Office, Parnell Square, and Dublin City Gallery The Hugh Lane—and two landmarks of literary Dublin, the Dublin Writers Museum and the James Joyce Cultural Center, hub of Bloomsday celebrations. A good way to begin is by heading up O'Connell Street to Parnell Square and the heart of James Joyce Country.

㉑ Abbey Theatre. Ireland's national theater was founded by W. B. Yeats and Lady Gregory in 1904. Works by Yeats, Synge, O'Casey, Kavanagh, and Friel have premiered here. The original building was destroyed in a fire in 1951; the present, rather austere theater was built in 1966. It has some noteworthy portraits and mementos in the foyer. Seats are usually available for about €15; all tickets are €10 for Monday performances. ⊠ *Lower Abbey St.* ☎ *01/878–7222* ⊕ *www.abbeytheatre.ie.*

⑳ Custom House. Extending 375 feet on the north side of the Liffey, this is the city's most spectacular Georgian building (1781–91), the work of James Gandon, an English architect. The central portico is linked by arcades to the pavilions at each end. A statue of Commerce tops the graceful copper dome; additional allegorical statues adorn the main facade. Republicans set the building on fire in 1921, but it was completely restored; it now houses government offices and a visitor center tracing the building's history and significance, and the life of Gandon. ⊠ *Custom House Quay* ☎ *01/876–7660* ☾ *Mid-Mar.–Oct., weekdays 10–12:30, weekends 2–5; Nov–mid-March., Wed.–Fri. 10–12:30, Sun. 2–5.*

★ ㉘ Dublin City Gallery The Hugh Lane. The imposing Palladian facade of this town house, once the home of the Earl of Charlemont, dominates the north side of Parnell Square. Sir Hugh Lane, a nephew of Lady Gregory (Yeats's patron), collected impressionist paintings and 19th-century Irish and Anglo-Irish works. Among them are canvases by Jack Yeats (W. B.'s brother) and Paul Henry. The late Francis Bacon's partner donated the entire contents of the artist's studio to the Hugh Lane Gallery, where it has been reconstructed. ⊠ *Parnell Sq.* ☎ *01/874–1903* ⊕ *www. hughlane.ie* ☾ *Tues.–Thurs. 9:30–6, Fri. and Sat. 9:30–5, Sun. 11–5.*

★ ㉗ Dublin Writers Museum. Two restored 18th-century town houses on the north side of Parnell Square, an area rich in literary associations, lodge one of Dublin's finest cultural sights. Rare manuscripts, diaries, posters, letters, limited and first editions, photographs, and other mementos commemorate the lives and works of the nation's greatest writers, including Joyce, Shaw, Wilde, Yeats, and Beckett. The bookshop and café make this an ideal place to spend a rainy afternoon. ⊠ *18–19 Parnell Sq. N* ☎ *01/872–2077* ⊕ *www.visitdublin.com* ☾ *June–Aug., Mon.–Sat. 10–6, Sun. 11–5; Sept.–May, Mon.–Sat. 10–5, Sun. 11–5.*

㉒ General Post Office. The GPO (1818), still a working post office, is one of the great civic buildings of Dublin's Georgian era, but its fame derives from the role it played during the Easter Rising. Here, on Easter Monday, 1916, the Republican forces stormed the building and issued the Proclamation of the Irish Republic. After a week of shelling, the GPO lay in ruins; 13 rebels were ultimately executed. Most of the original building was destroyed; only the facade—you can still see the scars of bullets on its pillars—remained. ⊠ *O'Connell St.* ☎ *01/872–8888* ⊕ *www.anpost.ie* ☾ *Mon.–Sat. 8–8, Sun. 10:30–6:30.*

㉔ Ha'penny Bridge. This heavily trafficked footbridge crosses the Liffey at a prime spot: Temple Bar is on the south side, and the bridge provides the fastest route to the thriving Mary and Henry Street shopping areas to the north. Until early in this century, a half-penny toll was charged to cross it. Yeats was one among many Dubliners who found this too high a price to pay—more a matter of principle than of finance—and so made the detour via O'Connell Bridge.

㉖ Parnell Square. This is the Northside's most notable Georgian square and one of Dublin's oldest. Some of the brick-face town houses have larger windows than others—some fashionable hostesses liked passersby to be able to peer into the first-floor reception rooms and admire the distinguished guests.

㉕ Rotunda Hospital. Founded in 1745 as the first maternity hospital in Ireland or Britain, the Rotunda is now most worth a visit for its **chapel,** with elaborate plasterwork, appropriately honoring motherhood. The **Gate Theatre,** housed in an extension, attracts large crowds with its fine repertoire of classic Irish and European drama. ⊠ *Parnell St.* ☎ *01/873–0700.*

★ ㉓ The Spire. Also known as the Monument of Light, The Spire was originally planned as part of the city's millennium celebrations. Ian Ritchie's spectacular 395-foot-high monument was finally erected at the beginning of 2003. Though christened "The Stiletto in the Ghetto" by some local wags, most agree the needlelike sculpture is the most exciting thing to happen to Dublin's skyline this century. The stainless steel structure is seven times taller than the nearby GPO. ⊠ *O'Connell St.*

Dublin West

If you're not an enthusiastic walker, hop a bus or find a cab to take you to these sights in westernmost Dublin.

㉙ Four Courts. Today the seat of the High Court of Justice of Ireland, the Four Courts are James Gandon's second Dublin masterpiece, built between 1786 and 1802. The courts were destroyed during the Troubles of the 1920s and restored by 1932. Its distinctive copper-covered dome atop a colonnaded rotunda makes this one of Dublin's most recognizable buildings. You are allowed to listen in on court proceedings, which can often be interesting, educational, even scandalous. ⊠ *Inns Quay* ☎ *01/872–5555* ⊕ *www.courts.ie* ⊗ *Daily 10:30–1 and 2:15–4.*

★ ㉞ Guinness Brewery and Storehouse. Founded by Arthur Guinness in 1759, Ireland's all-dominating brewery is on a 60-acre spread west of Christ Church Cathedral. It is the most popular tourist destination in town. The brewery itself is closed to the public, but the Storehouse is a spectacular tourist attraction with a high-tech exhibition about the brewing process of the "dark stuff." In a cast-iron and brick warehouse, it covers six floors built around a huge central glass atrium. But without doubt the star attraction is the top-floor **Gravity Bar,** with its 360°, floor-to-ceiling glass walls and a stunning view over the city. The funky new Guinness Shop on the ground floor is full of lifestyle merchandise. ⊠ *St. James's Gate* ☎ *01/408–4800* ⊕ *www.guinness.com* ✉ €*13.50* ⊗ *Apr.–Sept., Mon.–Sat. 9:30–7, Sun. 11–5; Oct.–Mar., daily 9:30–5.*

㉝ Kilmainham Gaol. This grim, forbidding structure was where leaders of the 1916 Easter Rising, including Pádrig Pearse and James Connolly, were held before being executed. A guided tour and a 30-minute audiovisual presentation relate a graphic account of Ireland's political history over the past 200 years from a Nationalist viewpoint. ⊠ *Inchicore Rd.* ☎ *01/453–5984* ⊕ *www.heritageireland.ie* ⊗ *Apr.–Sept., daily 9:30–5; Oct.–Mar., Mon.–Sat. 9:30–4, Sun. 10–5.*

㉚ Old Jameson Distillery. The birthplace of one of Ireland's best whiskeys has been fully restored and offers a fascinating insight into the making of *uisce batha,* or "holy water." There is a 40-minute guided tour of the old distillery, a 20-minute audiovisual tour, and a complimentary tasting. ⊠ *Bow St.* ☎ *01/807–2355* ⊕ *www.irish-whiskey-trail.com* ⊗ *Daily 9–6, tours every ½ hr.*

★ ㉛ Phoenix Park. Europe's largest public park encompasses 1,752 acres of verdant lawns, woods, lakes, playing fields, a zoo, a flower garden, and two residences—those of the president of Ireland and the ambassador for the United States. A 210-foot-tall obelisk, built in 1817, commemorates the Duke of Wellington's defeat of Napoléon. It is a runner's paradise, but Sunday is the best time to visit, when all kinds of games are likely to be in progress.

★ ㉜ **Royal Hospital Kilmainham.** A short ride by taxi or bus from the city center, this structure is regarded as the most important 17th-century building in Ireland. Completed in 1684 as a hospice for soldiers, it survived into the 1920s as a hospital. The ceiling of the Baroque chapel is extraordinary. It now houses the **Irish Museum of Modern Art,** which displays works by such non-Irish greats as Picasso and Miró but concentrates on the work of Irish artists. ⊠ *Kilmainham La.* ☎ *01/612–9900* ⊕ *www. modernart.ie* ☉ *Tues.–Sat. 10–5:30, Sun. noon–5:30; Royal Hospital tours every ½ hr; museum tours Wed. and Fri. at 2:30, Sat. at 11:30.*

Where to Eat

Beyond the restaurants recommended here, the area between Grafton Street and South Great George's Street has many to offer, as does Temple Bar, just across Dame Street. It's also worth checking out suburban villages like Ranelagh, Blackrock, and Sandycove for good local restaurants.

$$$$ ✕ **The Commons Restaurant.** This restaurant is in a large, elegant room with French windows in the basement of Newman House, where James Joyce was a student in the original premises of University College Dublin. The seasonal menu encompasses a light treatment of classic themes. ⊠ *85–86 St. Stephen's Green* ☎ *01/478–0530* ▤ *AE, DC, MC, V* ☉ *Closed weekends.*

$$$$ ✕ **Patrick Guilbaud.** Everything is French here, including the eponymous Fodor'sChoice owner, his chef, and the maître d'. Guillaume Le Brun's cooking is a flu-
★ ent expression of modern French cuisine—not particularly flamboyant, but coolly professional. ⊠ *Merrion Hotel, 21 Upper Merrion St.* ☎ *01/ 676–4192* ▤ *AE, DC, MC, V* ☉ *Closed Sun. and Mon.*

★ $$$$ ✕ **Thornton's.** If you are passionate about food, this place is mandatory— owner Kevin Thornton has forged a reputation as one of the very best chefs in Ireland. The dining room is simply decorated—there's little to distract you from the exquisite food. ⊠ *Fitzwilliam Hotel, St. Stephen's Green,* ☎ *01/454–9067* ⌂ *Reservations essential* ▤ *AE, DC, MC, V* ☉ *Closed Sun. and Mon.*

$$$–$$$$ ✕ **Chapter One.** In the vaulted, stone-walled basement of the Dublin Writers Museum, this is one of the most notable restaurants in Northside Dublin. Typical dishes include roast venison with mustard and herb lentils and roast beetroot. ⊠ *18–19 Parnell Sq.* ☎ *01/873–2266* ▤ *AE, DC, MC, V* ☉ *Closed Sun. and Mon. No lunch Sat.*

$$–$$$$ ✕ **Brownes Brasserie.** Huge mirrors reflect the light from crystal chandeliers onto jewel-colored walls and upholstery. The food is rich and heartwarming, with classics such as Irish smoked salmon and confit of duck with lentils. ⊠ *22 St. Stephen's Green* ☎ *01/638–3939* ▤ *AE, DC, MC, V* ☉ *No lunch Sat.*

$$–$$$ ✕ **Bruno's.** At this French–Mediterranean bistro on one of the busiest corners in Temple Bar, enjoy simple but stylish dishes: starters include feuilleté of crab meat and saffron sauce, and main dishes include roast scallops with Jerusalem artichoke purée and warm smoked bacon. ⊠ *30 Essex St. E* ☎ *01/670–6767* ▤ *AE, DC, MC, V* ☉ *Closed Sun.*

$$–$$$ ✕ **Caviston's.** The Cavistons have been dispensing recipes for years from their fish counter and delicatessen in Sandycove, just south of the ferry port of Dun Laoghaire, 30 minutes by taxi or DART train south of Dublin. The fish restaurant next door is a lively and intimate spot for lunch, but you should book in advance. ⊠ *59 Glasthule Rd., Dun Laoghaire*

☎ 01/280–9120 ▤ MC, V ⊘ Closed Sun., Mon., and late Dec.–early Jan. No dinner.

$$–$$$ ✕ **Eden.** This popular brasserie-style restaurant overlooking one of Temple Bar's main squares turns out good contemporary cuisine, such as vegetarian buckwheat pancake filled with garlic, spinach, and cheddar, and duck leg confit with lentils. Try to go when there are open-air movies in the square. ✉ Meeting House Sq. ☎ 01/670–5372 ⚭ Reservations essential ▤ AE, MC, V.

★ **$$–$$$** ✕ **La Stampa.** One of the most dramatic dining rooms in Dublin, La Stampa has huge gilt mirrors and elaborate candelabra that are gloriously over the top. The menu changes frequently to reflect an eclectic, international style. For a main course you may get rack of organic lamb with braised beans, tomatoes, and rosemary jus, or roast scallops with artichoke mash and a tomato vinaigrette. ✉ 35 Dawson St. ☎ 01/677–8611 ▤ AE, DC, MC, V ⊘ No lunch.

$$–$$$ ✕ **The Lord Edward.** Creaking floorboards and an old fireplace give the impression of being in someone's drawing room at this restaurant, one of the oldest in the city. Start with classic fish dishes such as prawn cocktail or smoked salmon, followed by fresh and simply cooked Dover sole, salmon, or lobster. ✉ 23 Christ Church Pl. ☎ 01/454–2420 ▤ AE, DC, MC, V ⊘ No lunch Sat. Closed Sun.

$ ✕ **Milano.** In a well-designed dining room with lots of brio, choose from a tempting array of inventive, thin-crust pizzas. ✉ 38 Dawson St. ☎ 01/670–7744 ✉ 19 Essex St. E ☎ 01/670–3384 ✉ 38–39 Lower Ormond Quay ☎ 01/872–0003 ✉ IFSC, Clarion Quay ☎ 01/611–9012 ▤ AE, DC, MC, V.

Pub Food

Most pubs serve food at lunchtime, some throughout the day. Food ranges from hearty soups and stews to chicken curries, smoked salmon salads, and sandwiches. Expect to pay €5.10–€7.60 for a main course. Larger pubs tend to take credit cards.

✕ **Davy Byrne's.** James Joyce immortalized Davy Byrne's in Ulysses. Nowadays it's more akin to a cocktail bar than a Dublin pub, but it's good for fresh and smoked salmon, salads, fresh oysters, and a hot daily special. ✉ 21 Duke St. ☎ 01/671–1298.

✕ **Old Stand.** Conveniently close to Grafton Street, the Old Stand serves grilled food, including steaks. ✉ 37 Exchequer St. ☎ 01/677–7220.

✕ **Porterhouse.** Ireland's first brew pub has an open kitchen and a dazzling selections of beers—from pale ales to dark stouts. ✉ 16–18 Parliament St. ☎ 01/679–8847.

✕ **Stag's Head.** The Stag's Head is a favorite of Trinity students and businesspeople, who come for one of the best pub lunches in the city. ✉ 1 Dame Ct. ☎ 01/679–3701.

✕ **Zanzibar.** This is a spectacular and cavernous bar that looks as though it might be more at home in downtown Marakesh. While away an afternoon on one of its wicker chairs. ✉ 34–35 Lower Ormond Quay ☎ 01/878–7212.

Cafés

Though Dublin has nowhere near as many cafés as pubs, it's easier than ever to find a good cup of coffee at most hours of the day or night.

✕ **Bewley's Coffee House.** The granddaddy of the capital's cafés, Bewley's has been supplying Dubliners with coffee and buns for more than a century. ✉ 78 Grafton St. ✉ 12 Westmoreland St. ☎ 01/677–6761 for both.

✕ **Kaffe Moka.** One of Dublin's hottest haunts for the caffeine-addicted, this spot has three hyperstylish floors and a central location in the heart of the city center. ✉ *39 S. William St.* ☎ *01/679–8475.*

✕ **Thomas Read's.** By day it's a café, by night a pub. Its large windows overlooking a busy corner in Temple Bar make it a great spot for people-watching. ✉ *1 Parliament St.* ☎ *01/671–7283.*

Where to Stay

On the lodging front Dublin is in the midst of a major hotel boom. For value, stay in a guest house or a B&B; both tend to be in suburban areas—generally a 10-minute bus ride from the center of the city. **Bord Fáilte** can usually help find you a place to stay if you don't have reservations.

$$$$ ⊞ **Conrad Dublin International.** A subsidiary of Hilton Hotels, the Conrad is aimed at the international business executive. The seven-story redbrick and smoked-glass building is just off Stephen's Green. The spacious rooms are done in light brown and pastel greens. Alfie Byrne's, the main bar, attempts to re-create a traditional Irish pub. ✉ *Earlsfort Terr., Dublin 2* ☎ *01/676–5555* 🖷 *01/676–5424* ⊕ *www.conrad-international. ie* ⇥ *182 rooms, 9 suites* ♢ *2 restaurants, bar* ▤ *AE, DC, MC, V.*

$$$$ ⊞ **Hibernian.** An early-20th-century Edwardian nurses' home was converted into this hotel, retaining the distinctive red-and-amber brick facade. Every room is a different shape, though all are done in light pastels with deep-pile carpets. Public rooms are slightly small but are attractive in cheerful chintz and stripes. ✉ *Eastmoreland Pl., off Upper Baggot St., Dublin 4* ☎ *01/668–7666* 🖷 *01/660–2655* ⊕ *hibernianhotel. com* ⇥ *40 rooms* ♢ *Restaurant, bar* ▤ *AE, DC, MC, V.*

$$$$ ⊞ **Jurys and the Towers.** These adjacent seven-story hotels, a short cab ride from the center of town, are popular with businesspeople and vacationers. Both have more atmosphere than most comparable modern hotels, though the Towers has an edge over Jurys, which is older, larger, and less expensive. ✉ *Pemroke Rd., Ballsbridge, Dublin 4* ☎ *01/660–5000* 🖷 *01/ 660–5540* ⊕ *www.jurys.com* ⇥ *Jurys: 300 rooms, 3 suites. The Towers: 100 rooms, 5 suites* ♢ *3 restaurants, pool* ▤ *AE, DC, MC, V.*

$$$$ ⊞ **Merrion.** Four exactingly restored Georgian town houses make up part
FodorsChoice of this luxurious hotel. The stately rooms have been richly appointed
★ in classic Georgian style down to the last detail. Leading Dublin restaurateur Patrick Guilbaud's eponymous restaurant is here. ✉ *21 Upper Merrion St., Dublin 2* ☎ *01/603–0600* 🖷 *01/603–0700* ⊕ *www. merrionhotel.com* ⇥ *127 rooms, 18 suites* ♢ *2 restaurants, 2 bars* ▤ *AE, DC, MC, V.*

★ $$$$ ⊞ **Shelbourne Méridien Hotel.** Old-fashioned luxury prevails at this magnificent showplace, which has presided over Stephen's Green since 1824. Each room has its own fine, carefully selected furnishings. Those in front overlook the green; rooms in the back are quieter. The restaurant, 27 The Green, is one of the most elegant rooms in Dublin; Lord Mayor's Room, off the lobby, serves a lovely afternoon tea. ✉ *27 Stephen's Green, Dublin 2* ☎ *01/663–4500; 800/543–4300 in U.S.* 🖷 *01/661–6006* ⊕ *www.shelbourne.ie* ⇥ *181 rooms with bath, 9 suites* ♢ *2 restaurants, pool, 2 bars* ▤ *AE, DC, MC, V.*

$$$$ ⊞ **Westbury.** This comfortable, modern hotel has a spacious main lobby furnished with antiques and large sofas, where you can have afternoon tea. Rooms are rather utilitarian; the suites, which combine European decor with Japanese prints and screens, are more inviting. The flowery Russell Room serves formal lunches and dinners. ✉ *Grafton St., Dublin 2* ☎ *01/679–1122* 🖷 *01/679–7078* ⊕ *www.jurysdoyle.com* ⇥ *203 rooms, 8 suites* ♢ *2 restaurants, bar* ▤ *AE, DC, MC, V.*

$$$–$$$$ ⌂ **Chief O'Neill's.** This modern hotel—named after a 19th-century Cork-man who became chief of police in Chicago—has a huge lobby-bar area looking out onto a cobbled courtyard. Smallish, high-tech rooms all have chrome fixtures and minimalist furnishings. Top-floor suites have delightful rooftop gardens with views of the city on both sides of the Liffey. ⊠ *Smithfield Village, Dublin 7* ☎ *01/817–3838* 🖷 *01/817–3839* ⊕ *www.chiefoneills.com* ⇗ *70 rooms, 3 suites* ⌂ *Restaurant, bar* ⊟ *AE, DC, MC, V.*

★ **$$$–$$$$** ⌂ **Number 31.** Two strikingly renovated Georgian mews are connected via a small garden to the grand town house they once served; together they form a marvelous guest house a short walk from Stephen's Green. Owners Deirdre and Noel Comer offer gracious hospitality and made-to-order breakfasts. ⊠ *31 Leeson Close, Dublin 2* ☎ *01/676–5011* 🖷 *01/676–2929* ⊕ *www.number31.ie* ⇗ *18 rooms* ⊟ *AE, MC, V.*

★ **$$–$$$** ⌂ **Ariel Guest House.** Dublin's leading guest house is in a tree-lined suburb, a 10-minute walk from Stephen's Green, and close to a DART stop. Rooms in the main house are lovingly filled with antiques; those at the back of the house are more spartan; all are immaculate. Owner Michael O'Brien is a helpful and gracious host. ⊠ *52 Lansdowne Rd., Dublin 4* ☎ *01/668–5512* 🖷 *01/668–5845* ⊕ *www.ariel-house.com* ⇗ *40 rooms* ⌂ *Wine bar* ⊟ *MC, V.*

$$–$$$ ⌂ **Mount Herbert Hotel.** Close to the luxury hotels in the tree-lined inner suburb of Ballsbridge, a 10-minute DART ride from Dublin's center, the Loughran family's sprawling accommodation is popular with budget-minded visitors. Rooms are small, but have all the necessary amenities. There's no bar on the premises, but there are plenty to choose from nearby. ⊠ *7 Herbert Rd., Ballsbridge, Dublin 4* ☎ *01/668–4321* 🖷 *01/660–7077* ⊕ *www.mountherberthotel.ie* ⇗ *200 rooms* ⌂ *Restaurant* ⊟ *AE, DC, MC, V.*

$$–$$$ ⌂ **Paramount.** This medium-size hotel at the heart of Temple Bar has kept its classy Victorian facade. The bedrooms are all dark woods and subtle colors, very 1930s. If you're fond of a tipple try the hotel's art deco Turks Head Bar and Chop House. ⊠ *Parliament St. and Essex Gate, Dublin 2* ☎ *01/417–9900* 🖷 *01/417–9904* ⊕ *www.paramounthotel. ie* ⇗ *70 rooms* ⌂ *Restaurant, bar* ⊟ *AE, DC, MC, V.*

$$ ⌂ **Central Hotel.** Established in 1887, this grand, old-style redbrick hotel is in the heart of the city. Rooms are small but have high ceilings and tasteful furnishings. The Library Bar on the second floor is one of the best spots in the city for a quiet pint. ⊠ *1–5 Exchequer St., Dublin 2* ☎ *01/679–7302* 🖷 *01/679–7303* ⊕ *www.centralhotel.ie* ⇗ *67 rooms, 3 suites* ⌂ *Restaurant, 2 bars* ⊟ *AE, DC, MC, V.*

$ ⌂ **Avalon House.** Many young, independent travelers rate this cleverly restored, Victorian redbrick building the most appealing of Dublin's hostels. A five-minute walk from Grafton Street and 5–10 minutes from some of the city's best music venues, it has a mix of dormitories, rooms without bath, and rooms with bath. The Avalon Café serves food until 10 PM, but is open as a common room after hours. ⊠ *55 Aungier St., Dublin 2* ☎ *01/475–0001* 🖷 *01/475–0303* ⊕ *www.avalon-house.ie* ⇗ *312 beds* ⌂ *Restaurant, bar* ⊟ *AE, MC, V.*

$ ⌂ **Jurys Christchurch Inn.** Expect few frills at this functional budget hotel (part of an otherwise upscale hotel chain), where there's a fixed room rate for up to three adults or two adults and two children. The biggest plus: the pleasant location, facing Christ Church Cathedral and within walking distance of most city-center attractions. Rooms are in pastel colors. The bar serves a pub lunch, and the restaurant, breakfast and dinner. ⊠ *Christchurch Pl., Dublin 8* ☎ *01/454–0000* 🖷 *01/454–0012* ⊕ *www. jurys.com* ⇗ *182 rooms* ⌂ *Restaurant, bar* ⊟ *AE, DC, MC, V.*

Nightlife & the Arts

The weekly magazines *In Dublin* and the *Big Issue* (at newsstands) contain comprehensive details of upcoming events, including ticket availability. *The Event Guide* also lists events and is free at many pubs and cafés. In peak season, consult the free Bord Fáilte leaflet "Events of the Week."

Cabarets

The following all have cabaret shows, with dancing, music, and traditional Irish song; they are open only in peak season (roughly May–October; call to confirm): **Abbey Tavern** (✉ Howth, Co. Dublin ☎ 01/839–0307). **Burlington Hotel** (✉ Upper Leeson St. ☎ 01/660–5222). **Clontarf Castle** (✉ Castle Ave., Clontarf ☎ 01/833–2321). **Jurys Hotel** (✉ Pembroke Rd., Ballsbridge ☎ 01/660–5000).

Classical Music

The **National Concert Hall** (✉ Earlsfort Terr. ☎ 01/475–1666), just off Stephen's Green, is the place to hear the National Symphony Orchestra of Ireland and is Dublin's main theater for classical music of all kinds. **St. Stephen's Church** (✉ Merrion Sq. ☎ 01/288–0663) has a regular program of choral and orchestral events.

Nightclubs

The **POD** (✉ Harcourt St. ☎ 01/478–0166) is the city's hippest spot for twentysomethings. **Rí Ra** (✉ Dame Court ☎ 01/677–4835) means "uproar" in Irish, and on most nights the place does go a little wild; it's one of the best spots for no-frills, fun dancing in Dublin. **Sugar Club** (✉ Lower Lesson St. ☎ 01/678–7188) is a refreshing mix of cocktail bar, nightclub, and performance venue. The place is know for its smooth Latin sounds and plush surroundings.

Pubs

Check advertisements in evening papers for folk, ballad, Irish traditional, or jazz music performances. The pubs listed below generally have some form of musical entertainment. The **Brazen Head** (✉ 20 Lower Bridge St. ☎ 01/677–9549)—Dublin's oldest pub, dating from 1688—has music every night. **Chief O'Neill's** (✉ Smithfield Village ☎ 01/817–3838) has an open, airy bar-café. The **Cobblestone** (✉ N. King St. ☎ 01/872–1799) is a glorious house of ale in the best Dublin tradition. **Doheny & Nesbitt's** (✉ 5 Lower Baggot St. ☎ 01/676–2945) is frequented by local businesspeople, politicians, and legal eagles. In the **Horseshoe Bar** (✉ Shelbourne Méridien Hotel, St. Stephen's Green ☎ 01/676–6471) you can eavesdrop on Dublin's social elite. **Kehoe's** (✉ 9 S. Anne St. ☎ 01/677–8312) is popular with students, artists, and writers. Locals and tourists bask in the theatrical atmosphere of **Neary's** (✉ 1 Chatham St. ☎ 01/676–2807). **O'Donoghue's** (✉ 15 Merrion Row ☎ 01/661–4303) has some form of musical entertainment on most nights. The **Palace Bar** (✉ 21 Fleet St. ☎ 01/677–9290) is a journalists' haunt.

Theaters

Ireland has a rich theatrical tradition. The **Abbey Theatre** (✉ Marlborough St. ☎ 01/878–7222) is the home of Ireland's national theater company, its name forever associated with J. M. Synge, W. B. Yeats, and Sean O'Casey. The **Peacock Theatre** is the Abbey's more experimental small stage. The **Gaiety Theatre** (✉ S. King St. ☎ 01/677–1717) shows musical comedy, opera, drama, and revues. The **Gate Theatre** (✉ Cavendish Row, Parnell Sq. ☎ 01/874–4045) is an intimate spot for modern drama and plays by Irish writers. The **Olympia Theatre** (✉ Dame St. ☎ 01/677–7744) has comedy, vaudeville, and ballet performances. The **Project Arts Centre** (✉ 39 E. Essex St. ☎ 01/679–6622) is an established fringe theater.

Shopping

The rest of the country is well supplied with crafts shops, but Dublin is the place to seek out more specialized items—antiques, haute couture, designer ceramics, books and prints, silverware and jewelry, and designer hand-knit items.

Shopping Centers & Department Stores

The shops north of the river—many of them chain stores and lackluster department stores—tend to be less expensive and less design-conscious. The one exception is the **Jervis Shopping Center** (⌧ Jervis St. at Mary St. ☎ 01/878–1323), a major shopping center with chain stores as well as smaller boutiques. **Arnotts** (⌧ Henry St. ☎ 01/805–0400) is Dublin's largest department store and carries a good range of cut crystal. **Brown Thomas** (⌧ Grafton St. ☎ 01/605–6666) is Dublin's most elegant department store. **St. Stephen's Green Center** (⌧ St. Stephen's Green ☎ 01/478–0888) contains 70 stores in a vast Moorish-style glass-roof building.

Shopping Districts

Grafton Street is the most sophisticated shopping area in Dublin's city center. **Francis Street** and **Dawson Street** are the places to browse for antiques. **Nassau Street** and **Dawson Street** are for books; the smaller side streets are good for jewelry, art galleries, and old prints. The pedestrianized **Temple Bar** area, with its young, offbeat crowd, has a number of small art galleries, specialty shops (music and books), and inexpensive, trendy clothing shops. The area is further enlivened by buskers (street musicians) and street artists.

Bookstores

Fred Hanna's (⌧ 29 Nassau St. ☎ 01/677–1255) sells old and new books, with a good choice of books on travel and Ireland. **Hodges Figgis** (⌧ 56–58 Dawson St. ☎ 01/677–4754) is Dublin's leading independent, with a café on the first floor. **Hughes & Hughes** (⌧ St. Stephen's Green Centre ☎ 01/478–3060) has strong travel and Irish-interest sections. There is also a store at Dublin Airport. **Waterstone's** (⌧ 7 Dawson St. ☎ 01/679–1415) is the Dublin branch of the renowned British chain.

Gift Items

Blarney Woollen Mills (⌧ Nassau St. ☎ 01/671–0068) has a good selection of tweed, linen, and woolen sweaters. **Dublin Woolen Mills** (⌧ Metal Bridge Corner, 41 Lower Ormond Quay ☎ 01/677–5014), at Ha'penny Bridge, sells hand-knit and other woolen sweaters at competitive prices. **Kevin & Howlin** (⌧ Nassau St. ☎ 01/677–0257) carries tweeds for men. **Kilkenny Shop** (⌧ Nassau St. ☎ 01/677–7066) is good for contemporary Irish-made ceramics, pottery, and silver jewelry. **McDowell** (⌧ 3 Upper O'Connell St. ☎ 01/874–4961), in business for more than 100 years, is a popular jewelry shop. **Tierneys** (⌧ St. Stephen's Green Centre ☎ 01/478–2873) carries a good selection of crystal, china, claddagh rings, pendants, and brooches.

Outdoor Markets

Bric-a-brac is sold at the **Liberty Market** on the north end of Meath Street, open on Friday and Saturday 10–6, Sunday noon–5:30. **Moore Street** (⌧ Henry St.), a large mall behind the Ilac Center, is open from Monday to Saturday 9–6; stalls lining both sides of the street sell fruits and vegetables. The indoor **Mother Redcap's Market**, opposite Christ Church, is open Friday, Saturday, and Sunday 10–5; come here for antiques and other finds.

Side Trips

The **Hill of Tara**, 33 km (21 mi) northwest of Dublin, was the religious and cultural capital of Ireland in ancient times. Its importance waned with the arrival of Christianity in the 5th century, and today its crest is, appropriately enough, crowned with a statue of the man who brought Christianity to Ireland—St. Patrick.

It was in the 8th-century abbey in **Kells**, 64 km (40 mi) north of Dublin, that the Book of Kells was completed; a facsimile can be seen in **St. Columba's Church**. Among the remains of the abbey are a well-preserved round tower and a rare example of a stone-roof church dating from the 9th century.

Dublin Essentials

AIRPORTS & TRANSFERS

All flights arrive at Dublin Airport, 10 km (6 mi) north of town.
🅵 ☎ 01/814-1111.

TRANSFERS Express buses leave every 20 minutes from outside the Arrivals door for the central bus station in downtown Dublin. The ride takes about 30 minutes, depending on the traffic, and the fare is €5. If you have time, take a regular bus for €1.30. A taxi ride into town will cost from €17 to €19, depending on the location of your hotel; be sure to ask in advance if the cab has no meter.

BOAT & FERRY TRAVEL

Irish Ferries has a regular car and passenger service directly into Dublin port from Holyhead in Wales. Stena Sealink docks in Dublin port (3½-hour service to Holyhead) and in Dun Laoghaire (High Speed Service, known as HSS, which takes 99 minutes). Prices and departure times vary according to season, so call to confirm. In summer, reservations are strongly recommended. Dozens of taxis wait to take you into town from both ports, or you can take DART or a bus to the city center.
🅵 **Irish Ferries** ⊠ Merrion Row ☎ 01/661-0511. **Stena Sealink** ⊠ Ferryport, Dun Laoghaire ☎ 01/204-7777.

BUS TRAVEL TO & FROM DUBLIN

The central bus station is Busaras; some bus lines also terminate near O'Connell Bridge. Bus Éireann provides express and provincial service.
🅵 **Busaras** ⊠ Store St. near the Custom House. **Bus Éireann** ☎ 01/836-6111.

BUS TRAVEL WITHIN DUBLIN

Dublin Bus provides city service, including transport to and from the airport. Most city buses originate in or pass through the area of O'Connell Street and O'Connell Bridge. If the destination board indicates AN LÁR, that means that the bus is going to the city center. Timetables (€3.20) are available from Dublin Bus; the minimum fare is €0.70.
🅵 **Dublin Bus** ⊠ 59 Upper O'Connell St. ☎ 01/873-4222.

CAR TRAVEL

The main access route from the north is N1; from the west, N4; from the south and southwest, N7; from the east coast, N11. All routes have clearly marked signs indicating the center of the city: AN LÁR. The M50 motorway encircles the city from Dublin Airport in the north to Tallaght in the south.

The number of cars in Ireland has grown exponentially in the last few years, and nowhere has their impact been felt more than in Dublin, where the city's complicated one-way streets are often congested. Avoid driving a car in the city except to get into and out of it, and be sure to ask your hotel or guest house for clear directions when you leave.

EMERGENCIES

🎦 Doctors & Dentists **Dentist: Dublin Dental Hospital** ☎ 01/662-0766. **Doctor: Eastern Help Board** ☎ 01/679-0700.

🎦 Emergency Services **Ambulance** ☎ 999. **Police** ☎ 999.

🎦 Pharmacies **Hamilton Long** ☎ 01/874-8456.

TAXIS

Official licensed taxis, metered and designated by roof signs, do not cruise; they can be found beside the central bus station, at train stations, at O'-Connell Bridge, Stephen's Green, College Green, and near major hotels. The initial charge is €2.30, with an additional charge of about €2 per 2 km (1 mi) thereafter (make sure the meter is on). Hackney cabs, which also operate in the city, have neither roof signs nor meters and will sometimes respond to hotels' requests for a cab. Negotiate the fare before your journey begins.

TOURS

BUS TOURS Bus Éireann runs day trips to all the major sights around the capital. Gray Line Tours organizes bus tours of Dublin and its major sights; they also have daylong tours into the surrounding countryside and longer tours elsewhere (the price for excursion tours includes accommodations, breakfast, and admission). Dublin Bus runs a continuous guided open-top bus tour (€12) that allows you to hop on and off the bus as often as you wish and visit some 15 sights along its route.

🎦 **Bus Éireann** ☎ 01/836-6111. **Dublin Bus** ☎ 01/873-0000. **Gray Line Tours** ☎ 01/670-8822.

SPECIAL INTEREST TOURS Elegant Ireland arranges tours for groups interested in architecture and the fine arts; these include visits with the owners of some of Ireland's stately homes and castles.

🎦 **Elegant Ireland** ☎ 01/475-1665.

WALKING TOURS The tourist office has leaflets giving information on a selection of walking tours, including "Literary Dublin," "Georgian Dublin," and "Pub Tours." Bord Fáilte has a "Tourist Trail" walk, which takes in the main sites of central Dublin and can be completed in about three hours, and a "Rock 'n Stroll" tour, which covers the city's major pop and rock music sites.

TRAIN TRAVEL

Irish Rail provides train service throughout the country. Dublin has three main stations. Connolly Station is the departure point for Belfast, the east coast, and the west. Heuston Station is the departure point for the south and southwest. Pearse Station is for Bray and connections via Dun Laoghaire to the Liverpool-Holyhead ferries.

An electric train commuter service, DART, serves the suburbs out to Howth, on the north side of the city, and to Bray, County Wicklow, on the south side. Fares are about the same as for buses. Street-direction signs to DART stations read STAISIUN/STATION.

🎦 **Connolly Station** ⊠ At Amiens St. **Heuston Station** ⊠ At Kingsbridge. **Irish Rail** ⊠ 35 Lower Abbey St. ☎ 01/836-6222 information. **Pearse Station** ⊠ On Westland Row.

TRAVEL AGENCIES

🎦 **American Express** ⊠ 116 Grafton St. ☎ 01/677-2874. **Thomas Cook** ⊠ 118 Grafton St. ☎ 01/677-1721.

VISITOR INFORMATION

In addition to the visitor information offices in the entrance hall of the headquarters of Bord Fáilte, Dublin Tourism has visitor information at the airport (Arrivals level), open daily 8 AM–10 PM; and at the Ferryport, Dun Laoghaire, open daily 10 AM–9 PM.

DUBLIN TO CORK

One good way to see the country is to drive southwest from Dublin to Cork, the Republic's second-largest city. On the way, you'll see the lush green fields of Ireland's famous stud farms and imposing Cashel, where Ireland built its reputation as the "Land of Saints and Scholars" while most of Europe was slipping into the Dark Ages.

Naas

The road to Naas (pronounced "*nace*") passes through the area known as the Pale—that part of Ireland in which English law was formally acknowledged up to Elizabethan times. The aesthetically mundane seat of County Kildare and a thriving market town in the heartland of Irish Thoroughbred country, Naas is full of pubs filled with jockeys discussing the merits of their stables. Naas has its own small racecourse, but **Punchestown Racecourse** (⊠ 3 km [2 mi] from Naas) has a wonderful setting amid rolling plains and is famous for its steeplechases.

The Curragh

The Curragh, 8 km (5 mi) southwest of Naas, just beyond the end of the bypass M7 and bisected by the main N7 road, is the biggest area of common land in Ireland, containing about 31 square km (12 square mi) and devoted mainly to grazing. It's also Ireland's major racing center, and home of the **Curragh Racecourse** (☏ 045/441205), where the Irish Derby and other international horse races are run. In addition, the Irish army trains here, at the **Curragh Main Barracks.**

Kildare Town

The thriving economy of Kildare, 5 km (3 mi) from the Curragh on M7, is based on horse breeding. The town is also where St. Brigid founded a religious settlement in the 5th century; **St. Brigid's Cathedral** (⊠ off Market Sq.) is a restoration of a 13th-century building.

If you're a longtime horse aficionado, or are just curious, the **National Stud Farm,** a main center of Ireland's racing industry, is well worth a visit. Also on the grounds, the **National Stud Horse Museum** recounts the history of the horse in Ireland. ⊠ *South of Kildare Town about 2½ km (1½ mi), clearly signposted to left of market square* ☏ *045/521617* ⊕ *www.irish-national-stud.ie* ⊙ *Mid-Feb.–mid-Nov., daily 9:30–6.*

★ The elegant **Japanese Gardens,** adjacent to the National Stud Farm, were laid out between 1906 and 1910 and are considered among the finest in Europe. ⊠ *South of Kildare Town about 2½ km (1½ mi), clearly signposted to left of market square* ☏ *045/521617* ⊕ *www.irish-national-stud.ie* ⊙ *Mid-Feb.–mid-Nov., daily 9:30–6.*

Cashel

Cashel is a market town on the busy Cork–Dublin road, which, in spite of the incessant heavy traffic running through it, retains some interesting Victorian shopfronts on its Main Street. The town has a lengthy history as a center of royal and religious power.

★ The awe-inspiring, oft-mist-shrouded **Rock of Cashel** is one of Ireland's most-visited sites. The rock itself, which is a short walk from the north of the town, rises as a giant, circular mound 200 feet above the surrounding plain; it is crowned by a tall cluster of gray monastic remains. The kings

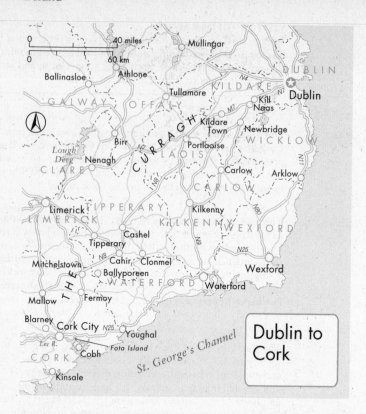

Dublin to
Cork

of Munster held it as their seat for about seven centuries, and it was here that St. Patrick reputedly plucked a shamrock from the ground, using it as a symbol to explain the mystery of the Trinity, giving Ireland, in the process, its universally recognized symbol. ☎ 062/61437 ⊕ *www. heritageireland.ie* ☉ *Mid-Mar.–mid-June, daily 9:30–5:30; mid-June–mid-Sept., daily 9–7:30; mid-Sept.–mid-Mar., daily 9:30–4:30.*

$$$ ✕ **Chez Hans.** Enjoy fresh local produce cooked with a French accent in this converted chapel at the foot of the famous rock. ⊠ *Rockside* ☎ 062/61177 ☲ *MC, V* ☉ *Closed Sun., Mon., and first 3 wks in Jan. No lunch.*

★ **$$$–$$$$** ✕▨ **Cashel Palace.** This magnificently restored 18th-century bishop's palace in the center of town has great views of the Rock of Cashel from its back rooms. Inexpensive light meals are served all day in its bistro-style cellar restaurant. ⊠ *Main St., Co. Tipperary* ☎ 062/62707 ☱ *062/ 61521* ⊕ *www.cashel-palace.ie* ⇆ *23 rooms* ♨ *2 restaurants, bar* ☲ *AE, DC, MC, V.*

Cahir

Cahir (pronounced "care") is a popular stopping place to break the Dublin–Cork journey. **Cahir Castle,** the town's main attraction, is a massive limestone structure dating from 1164 and built on rock in the middle of the river. There are guided tours and an audiovisual display in the lodge. ☎ 052/41011 ⊕ *www.heritageireland.ie* ☉ *Mid-Mar.–mid-June and mid-Sept.–mid-Oct., daily 10–5:30; mid-June–mid-Sept., daily 9–7:30; mid-Oct.–mid-Mar., daily 9:30–4:30.*

$ ▨ **Kilcoran Lodge Hotel.** This handsome, sprawling, former 19th-century hunting lodge sits amid beautiful countryside 6 km (4 mi) outside Cahir on the main Cork–Dublin (N8) road. Rooms facing the front have the best views of the beautiful, heather-covered slopes; all have Victorian-style furnishings and comfortable beds. ⊠ *Cahir, Co. Tipperary* ☎ *052/41288* 🖷 *052/41994* ⊕ *www.tipp.ie* ⤳ *23 rooms* ⚏ *Restaurant, indoor pool, bar* ⊟ *AE, DC, MC, V.*

Cork City

The road enters Cork City along the banks of the River Lee. In the center of Cork, the Lee divides in two, giving the city a profusion of picturesque quays and bridges. The name Cork derives from the Irish *corcaigh* (pronounced "corky"), meaning a marshy place. The city received its first charter in 1185 and grew rapidly during the 17th and 18th centuries with the expansion of its butter trade. It is the major metropolis of the south, and with a population of about 175,000, the second-largest city in Ireland.

The main business and shopping center of Cork lies on the island created by the two diverging channels of the Lee, and most places of interest are within walking distance of the center. **Patrick Street** is the focal point; here you'll find the city's major department stores, **Roches** and **Brown Thomas.** If you look up above the plate-glass shop facades, you'll see examples of the bowfront Georgian windows that are emblematic of old Cork.

The famous bell tower of **St. Anne's Church**, the 120-foot **Shandon Steeple,** is on a hill across the river to the north of Cork's main shopping area. Shaped like a pepper pot, it houses the bells immortalized in the song "The Bells of Shandon." You can climb the tower and ring the bells over Cork. ⊠ *Church St.* ◷ *May–Oct., Mon.–Sat. 9:30–5; Nov.–Apr., Mon.–Sat. 10–3:30.*

The liveliest place in town to shop is the pedestrian-only **Paul Street** area, parallel to the northwest side of Patrick Street. Housed in the 1724 building that was once the city's Custom House, the **Crawford Municipal Art Gallery** at the top of Paul Street has an excellent collection of 18th- and 19th-century views of Cork and adventurous exhibits by modern artists. ⊠ *Emmet Pl.* ☎ *021/427–3377* ⊕ *www.synergy.ie/crawford* ◷ *Weekdays 9–5, Sat. 9–1.*

\$\$\$–\$\$\$\$ ✕ **The Ivory Tower.** Seamus O'Connell, the young chef-owner of this restaurant off Patrick Street, concocts such adventurous dishes as blackened shark with banana ketchup, or wild duck with vanilla, sherry, and jalapeños. The bare boards and stick-back chairs are offset by original works of art. ⊠ *35 Princes St.* ☎ *021/427–4665* ⊟ *AE, MC, V* ◷ *Closed Sun. and Mon.*

★ **\$–\$\$** ✕ **Isaac's.** In an old warehouse, this popular spot has modern art on the walls and Mediterranean-influenced food. Excellent local produce is used in such starters as warm potato salad with smoked bacon and black pudding. ⊠ *48 MacCurtain St.* ☎ *021/450–3805* ⊟ *MC, V.*

\$\$\$ ✕🏠 **Jurys.** Beside the River Lee, a five-minute walk from the city center, this modern, two-story structure of smoked glass and steel is a popular local meeting place. The Glandore Restaurant serves an à la carte menu with the emphasis on fresh local produce. Rooms are spacious, with the best ones overlooking the internal patio garden and pool. ⊠ *Western Rd., Co. Cork* ☎ *021/427–6622* 🖷 *021/427–4477* ⊕ *www.jurysdoyle.com* ⤳ *188 rooms* ⚏ *2 restaurants, indoor pool* ⊟ *AE, DC, MC, V.*

★ **\$\$\$\$** 🏠 **Hayfield Manor.** This fine luxury hotel is built to resemble a classic Georgian country house. It's beside the university campus, five minutes' drive from the city center. ⊠ *Perrott Ave., off College Rd., Co. Cork*

☎ 021/431–5600 🖨 021/431–6839 ⊕ www.hayfieldmanor.ie ⇴ 53 rooms ⚬ Restaurant, indoor pool, bar ⊟ AE, DC, MC, V.

$$ 🖳 **Hotel Isaac's.** This stylish city-center hotel has bright and cheerful rooms, with polished wood floors and rustic pine furniture. ⊠ 48 MacCurtain St., Co. Cork ☎ 021/450–0011 🖨 021/450–6355 ⊕ www.isaacs.ie ⇴ 36 rooms with bath ⚬ Restaurant ⊟ AE, MC, V.

Cobh & Fota Island

If you're from the United States and have Irish roots, chances are your ancestors were among the thousands who sailed from the port of Cork. Cobh (pronounced "cove"), as it is known nowadays, is an attractive, hilly town, dominated by its 19th-century cathedral. From Cork, follow the signposts for Waterford on N25 along the northern bank of the River Lee. Alternatively, a suburban rail service leaves from Cork's **Kent Station** (☎ 021/450–6766 schedule) with stops in Cobh and Fota Island.

★ In the old Cobh railway station, the **Queenstown Story** re-creates the experience of the emigrants who left the town between 1750 and the mid-20th century. It also tells the stories of the great transatlantic liners, including the *Titanic,* whose last port of call was Cobh, and the *Lusitania,* which was sunk by a German submarine off this coast on May 7, 1915. ☎ 021/481–3591 ⊕ www.cobhheritage.com ⊘ Feb.–Nov., daily 10–6.

Fota House, an 18th-century hunting lodge in the classical Regency style, is the centerpiece of a large estate on Fota Island. The house is surrounded by a magnificent arboretum (☎ 021/481–5543 ⊕ www.fotahouse.com ⊘ House Mon.–Sat. 10–6, Sun. 11–6). Also on the estate is the 238-square-km (70-acre) **Fota Wildlife Park,** an important breeding center for cheetahs and wallabies. ☎ 021/481–2678 ⊕ www.fotawildlife.ie ⊘ Mid-Mar.–Sept., daily 10–6.

★ **$$$$** ✕🖳 **Ballymaloe House.** One of Ireland's best-known and most-admired country houses, Ballymaloe is the home of the Allen family, who will welcome you with gracious aplomb. Each guest room is an elegant variation on country-house style. Myrtle, the doyenne of Irish cooking, presides over the outstanding dining room. ⊠ 29 km (18 mi) east of Cobh, Shanagarry, Midleton ☎ 021/465–2531 🖨 021/465–2021 ⊕ www.ballymaloe.ie ⇴ 32 rooms ⚬ Restaurant, pool ⊟ AE, DC, MC, V.

Blarney

Just north of Blarney is **Blarney Castle**—or what remains of it: the ruined central keep is all that's left of this mid-15th-century stronghold. The walls of the castle contain the famed **Blarney Stone,** in a wall below the castle's battlements; kissing the stone, it is said, endows you with the fabled "gift of gab." To kiss the stone, you must lie down on the battlements and lean your head way back. Nobody knows how the tradition originated, but Elizabeth I is credited with giving the word "blarney" to the language when, commenting on the unfulfilled promises of Cormac MacCarthy, Lord Blarney of the time, she remarked, "This is all Blarney; what he says he never means." ☎ 021/438–5252 ⊕ www.blarneycastle.ie ⊘ Mon.–Sat. 9 AM–sundown, Sun. 9–5:30.

Dublin to Cork Essentials

AIRPORTS

Cork Airport, 5 km (3 mi) south of Cork City on the Kinsale road, is used primarily for flights to and from the United Kingdom. Regular 30-minute internal flights are scheduled between Shannon and Dublin, Shannon and Cork, and Cork and Dublin.

🛈 **Cork Airport** ☎ 021/431-3131.

BIKE TRAVEL
🚲 Bike Rentals **Rothar Cycle Tours** ✉ 2 Bandon Rd., Cork City ☎ 021/431-3133.

BUS TRAVEL
Bus Éireann operates Expressway services from Dublin to Cork City.
🚌 **Bus Éireann** ☎ 01/836-6111 Dublin; 061/313333 Limerick; 021/450-8188 Cork; 066/23566 Tralee. **Cork City Main Bus Terminal** ✉ Parnell Pl. ☎ 021/450-8188.

CAR TRAVEL
From Dublin, pick up N8 in Portlaoise for Cork City (257 km [160 mi]); the journey time is about 3½ hours. A car is the ideal way to explore this area. Roads are generally narrow, two-lane motorways. All the main car-rental firms have desks at Cork Airport. Be sure to get a map of Cork City's complicated one-way street system.

TOURS
Arrangements Unlimited can arrange special-interest tours of the region for small or large groups. Bus Éireann operates a number of city tours and regional excursions from Parnell Place in Cork City.
🚌 **Arrangements Unlimited** ✉ 1 Woolhara Park, Douglas, Cork City, Co. Cork ☎ 021/429-3873 🖨 021/429-2488 ⊕ www.arrangements.ie. **Bus Éireann** ☎ 021/450-6066 ⊕ www.buseireann.ie.

TRAIN TRAVEL
The terminal in Cork City is Kent Station. There is direct service from Dublin and Tralee, and a suburban line to Cobh.
🚆 **Kent Station** ☎ 021/450-6766 information.

VISITOR INFORMATION
🚌 **Cahir** ✉ Castle St., Co. Tipperary ☎ 052/41453; open April–September. **Cashel** ✉ Town Hall, Co. Tipperary ☎ 062/61333 🖨 062/61789; open April–September. **Cork City** ✉ Grand Parade, Cork City ☎ 021/425-5100 ⊕ www.corkkerry.ie; open year-round.

CORK TO GALWAY

The trip from Cork north to Galway is about 300 km (186 mi) and includes stops in Killarney and Limerick. The Shannon region around Limerick is littered with castles, both ruined and restored. Along the way, the Cork–Killarney road passes through the west Cork Gaeltacht—a predominantly Irish-speaking region—and begins its climb into the Derrynasaggart Mountains.

Killarney & Environs

Killarney itself is an undistinguished market town, well developed to handle the crowds that gather here in peak season. They come to drink in the famous scenery, located out of town toward the lakes that lie in a valley running south between the mountains. Much of Killarney's lake district is within **Killarney National Park**. At the heart of the park is the 10,000-acre **Muckross Estate**, which is open daily, daylight hours. Cars are not allowed in the estate, so if you don't want to walk, rent a bicycle in town or take a trip in a jaunting car—a small two-wheel horse-drawn cart whose operators can be found at the gates to the estate and in Killarney. At the center of the estate is **Muckross House**, a 19th-century manor that contains the Kerry Country Life Experience. On the adjoining grounds is an old-world farm. ☎ 064/31440 ⊕ *www.muckross-house.ie* ⊗ *Sept.–June, daily 9–5:30; July and Aug., daily 9–7* ⊗ *Closed 1 wk at Christmas.*

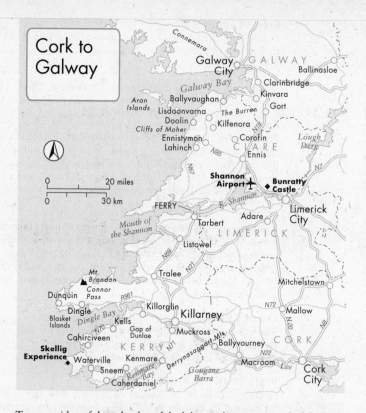

Cork to
Galway

To get an idea of the splendor of the lakes and streams—and of the massive glacial sandstone and limestone rocks and lush vegetation that characterize the Killarney district—take a daylong tour of the **Gap of Dunloe**, as well as **the Upper Lake, Long Range, Middle and Lower lakes, and Ross Castle.** The central section, the Gap of Dunloe, is not suitable for cars, but horses and jaunting cars are available at **Kate Kearney's Cottage** (☎ 064/44146), which marks the entrance to the gap.

$$–$$$ ✕ **Dingles.** The warm welcome supplied by Gerry Cunningham at his rustic restaurant in Killarney's center will make you feel like a local. His wife, Marie, creates such tasty dishes as baked crab and prawn au gratin or roast rack of Kerry lamb. ⊠ *40 New St.* ☎ *064/31079* ▭ *AE, DC, MC, V* ☺ *Closed Nov.–Mar. No lunch.*

$$–$$$ ✕ **Gaby's Seafood.** Tile floors, pine booths, and red gingham tablecloths are the hallmarks of this cheerful, informal Killarney restaurant. Fresh seafood simply prepared is the specialty. ⊠ *17 High St.* ☎ *064/32519* ▭ *AE, DC, MC, V* ☺ *No lunch. Closed Sun.*

★ $$$$ ✕▦ **Aghadoe Heights.** Its location on a bluff translates into unforgettable lake views—especially from the aerie of the famous hotel restaurant, Frederick's. The luxurious interior is a pleasant combination of the antique and the modern. ⊠ *Aghadoe Heights, 4 km (2½ mi) outside Killarney on the Tralee side, signposted off the N22, Co. Kerry* ☎ *064/31766* 🖷 *064/31345* 🌐 *www.aghadoeheights.com* 🛏 *72 rooms, 3 suites* ♨ *Restaurant, bar* ▭ *AE, DC, MC, V.*

$$ ▦ **Arbutus.** A good budget hotel in the town center, Arbutus has been in the same family since it was built more than 60 years ago. Ask for a room in the newer, second-story section. Its quiet bar draws a local crowd. ⊠ *College St., Killarney, Co. Kerry* ☎ *064/31037* 🌐 *www.arbutuskillarney.com* 🖷 *064/34033* 🛏 *36 rooms* ♨ *Restaurant, bar* ▭ *AE, DC, MC, V.*

Ring of Kerry

Running along the perimeter of the Iveragh Peninsula, the dramatic Ring of Kerry is probably the single most popular tourist route in Ireland. Stunning mountain and coastal views are around almost every turn. The only drawback: on a sunny day, it seems like half the tourists in Ireland are here. It's a daylong drive (176 km [109 mi] round-trip) from Killarney; leave by N71 (the Kenmare road).

Kenmare

Kenmare is a small, mainly 19th-century market town at the head of Kenmare Bay. Across the water, as you drive out along the Iveragh Peninsula, are views of the gray-blue mountain ranges of the Beara Peninsula.

$$$$
Fodor'sChoice
★
⊠✗ **Park Hotel.** Spacious rooms with late-Victorian antiques and Italian marble–tile bathrooms distinguish this fine country-house hotel. Local ingredients and seafood star on the restaurant's sophisticated Irish-Continental menu (a jacket and tie are required). ⊠ *Kenmare, Co. Kerry* ☎ *064/41200* 🖷 *064/41402* ⊕ *www.parkenmare.com* 🛏 *50 rooms* ☼ *Restaurant, bar* ☰ *AE, DC, MC, V* ☼ *Closed Jan.–mid-Apr.*

Sneem

Sneem, on the estuary of the River Ardsheelaun, is one of the prettiest villages in Ireland. Look for "the pyramids" (as they are known locally), 12-foot-tall, traditional stone structures that look old but were completed in 1990 by Kerry-born artist James Scanlon.

Caherdaniel

The **Derrynane House** was once the home of the 19th-century politician and patriot Daniel O'Connell, "The Liberator." The south and east wings of the house are open to visitors and still contain much of the original furniture and other items associated with him. ☎ *066/947–5113* ⊕ *www. heritageireland.ie* ☼ *Jan.–Mar., Nov., and Dec., weekends 1–5; Apr. and Oct., Tues.–Sun. 1–5; May–Sept., Mon.–Sat. 9–6, Sun. 11–7.*

Dingle Area

If time and weather are on your side, turn off the main Killorglin–Tralee road and make a tour of the **Dingle Peninsula**—one of the wildest and least-spoiled regions of Ireland. Take in **Connor Pass, Mount Brandon, Gallarus Oratory,** and stop in **Dunquin** to hear some of Ireland's best traditional musicians.

Dingle Town itself is a handy touring base with crafts shops, seafood restaurants, and pubs; still, its main streets—the Mall, Main and Strand streets, and the Wood—can be covered in less than an hour. For an adventure off the beaten path, take a boat ride to the **Blasket Islands** and spend a few blissful hours wandering along the cliffs.

★ **$$$–$$$$**
✗ **Beginish.** The food at this outstanding Dingle Town restaurant imaginatively interprets French nouvelle cuisine; specialties include local lobster and honey-glazed duck breast with apple and Calvados sauce. ⊠ *Green St.* ☎ *066/915–1588* ☰ *AE, DC, MC, V* ☼ *Closed Mon. and mid-Dec.–mid-Feb. No lunch.*

$$$$
⊠✗ **Dingle Skellig.** This hotel-restaurant, a five-minute walk from the town center, is a showcase of Irish craft, art, and design. More than half the spacious rooms have sea views (ask for these when reserving). The Coastguard Restaurant is the town's only water's-edge eatery; seafood is the specialty. ⊠ *Dingle Town, Co. Kerry* ☎ *066/915–0200* 🖷 *066/ 915–1501* ⊕ *www.dingleskellig.com* 🛏 *116 rooms* ☼ *Restaurant, indoor pool* ☰ *AE, DC, MC, V* ☼ *Closed last wk in Dec. and Jan.*

$–$$
⊠ **Greenmount House.** This impeccably kept, modern B&B a short walk from the town center is renowned for its imaginative breakfasts. ⊠ *Gor-*

tanora, Dingle Town, Co. Kerry ☎ *066/915–1414* 🖷 *066/915–1974*
⊕ *www.greenmounthouse.com* ⏤⤴ *9 rooms* ▤ *MC, V.*

Tralee

County Kerry's capital and its largest town, Tralee has neither ruins nor
quaint architecture, yet it makes a go at attracting visitors. Tralee has
long been associated with its annual festival, during which, every September, a young woman of Irish descent is chosen to be the "Rose of
Tralee." The **Kerry County Museum**, Tralee's major cultural attraction,
traces the history of Kerry's people from 5000 BC to the present. ✉ *Ashe
Memorial Hall, Denny St.* ☎ *066/712–7777* ⊕ *www.kcmuseum.com*
⊙ *Sept.–July, Mon.–Sat. 10–6; Aug., Mon.–Sat. 10–8.*

Adare

Adare is one of Ireland's most picture-perfect towns. A bit of England
in the Old Sod, it has storybook thatch-roof cottages and Tudor-style
churches. Visit the **Adare Heritage Centre** for a look back at the town's
picturesque history. A seasonal tourist office is open here May through
October. ✉ *Main St.* ☎ *061/396666* ⊙ *May–Sept., daily 9–6; Oct.–Apr.,
daily 10–5.*

★ **$$$–$$$$** ▣ **Dunraven Arms.** Although Adare Manor, a Tudor-Gothic castle just
across the road, is swankier, you get a warmer welcome at this old coach-
ing inn. It's a handy first stop when arriving at Shannon Airport, about
40 km (25 mi) northwest. Guest rooms, decorated with antiques, are
comfortable. ✉ *Adare, Co. Limerick* ☎ *061/396633* 🖷 *061/396541*
⊕ *www.dunravenhotel.com* ⏤⤴ *76 rooms* ♨ *Restaurant, indoor pool,
bar* ▤ *AE, DC, MC, V.*

Limerick City

Limerick is an industrial port and the third-largest city in the Republic
(population 75,000). The area around the cathedral and the castle is the
old part of the city, dominated by mid-18th-century buildings with fine
Georgian proportions. Economic investment is helping to spiff up its
former image as an unattractive city marked by high unemployment and
a high crime rate. Frank McCourt's 1996 memoir *Angela's Ashes*—set
in Limerick, where McCourt grew up desperately poor—has also helped
to pique interest in the city.

★ **Bunratty Castle** is one of three castles in the area that has nightly me-
dieval banquets. The castle, once the stronghold of the princes of
Thomond, is the most complete and—despite its Ye Olde World ban-
quets—authentic medieval castle in Ireland, restored in such a way as
to give an idea of life during the 15th and 16th centuries. The **Folk Park**
on its grounds has farm buildings and crafts shops typical of the 19th
century. ✉ *18 km (10 mi) west of Limerick City on N18* ☎ *061/361511*
⊕ *www.shannonheritage.com* ⊙ *Daily 9:30–dusk (last entry 1 hr be-
fore closing).*

In the Old Customs House on the banks of the Shannon in the city cen-
ter, the **Hunt Museum** has the finest collection of Celtic and medieval trea-
sures outside the National Museum in Dublin. ✉ *Rutland St.* ☎ *061/
312833* ⊕ *www.ul.ie/~hunt* ⊙ *May–Sept., Mon.–Sat. 10–5, Sun. 2–5;
Oct.–Apr., Tues.–Sat. 10–5, Sun. 2–5.*

Built by the Normans in the early 1200s, **King John's Castle** still bears
traces on its north side of the 1691 bombardment. Climb the drum tow-
ers for a good view of the town and the Shannon. Inside, exhibitions il-
lustrate the history of Limerick. ✉ *Castle St.* ☎ *061/411201* ⊕ *www.
shannonheritage.com* ⊙ *Apr.–Sept., daily 9:30–5; Oct.–Mar., week-
ends 9:30–5.*

★ **$$$$** 🏨 **Castletroy Park.** High standards of comfort are the rule at this well-designed modern hotel on the outskirts of town. ✉ *Dublin Rd., Co. Limerick* 🕾 *061/335566* 🖷 *061/331117* 🌐 *www.castletroy-park.ie* ⟿ *107 rooms* 🍴 *2 restaurants, indoor pool* ☱ *AE, DC, MC, V.*

$$ 🏨 **Greenhills.** This suburban, modern low rise is convenient for Shannon Airport and also makes a good touring base. The friendly owner-manager welcomes families. ✉ *Ennis Rd., Co. Limerick* 🕾 *061/453033* 🖷 *061/453307* 🌐 *www.greenhillsgroup.com* ⟿ *55 rooms* 🍴 *Restaurant, indoor pool* ☱ *AE, DC, MC, V.*

Ennis

Ennis, 37 km (23 mi) northwest of Limerick, and the principal town of County Clare, is a pleasant if unremarkable market town that's often bustling. It has always fostered traditional music, especially fiddle playing, and step dancing; at the end of May, it's the gathering place for the **Fleadh Nua** (pronounced "fla-nooa"), a festival of Irish music.

$$$ ✕🏨 **Lynch West County.** This lively modern hostelry is a popular stopping point on the Limerick–Galway road and is a five-minute walk from Ennis's historic town center. It caters to both vacationers and business travelers. Boru's Porterhouse serves traditional Irish fare, including local steak and seafood. ✉ *Clare Rd., Ennis, Co. Clare* 🕾 *065/682–8421* 🖷 *065/682–8801* 🌐 *www.lynchotels.com* ⟿ *152 rooms* 🍴 *2 restaurants, 3 indoor pools* ☱ *AE, DC, MC, V.*

Corofin

If you're searching for your Irish roots, Corofin's **Clare Heritage Center** has a genealogical service and information about doing research yourself. It also has displays on the history of the West of Ireland in the 19th century. 🕾 *065/683–7955* ⏱ *Apr.–Oct., daily 10–6; Nov.–Mar. (genealogy service only), weekdays 9–5; museum by appointment.*

Lisdoonvarna

Lisdoonvarna is a small spa town with several sulfurous and iron-bearing springs. Its buildings reflect a mishmash of mock-architectural styles, which, depending on your taste, is either lovably kitschy or unappealingly tacky. The town has developed something of a reputation over the years as a matchmaking center, with bachelor farmers and single women converging here each year in late September for a Bachelors' Festival.

$$–$$$ ✕🏨 **Sheedy's Restaurant and Country Inn.** Originally a 17th-century farmhouse, this small, friendly, family-run hotel is only a short walk from both the town center and spa wells. Rooms are spotlessly clean and well cared for. Creative French-Irish cuisine is served at the moderately priced restaurant, and there is an informal Seafood Bar beside the lobby. ✉ *Co. Clare* 🕾 *065/707–4026* 🖷 *065/707–4555* 🌐 *www.sheedyscountryhouse. com* ⟿ *11 rooms* 🍴 *Restaurant, bar* ☱ *AE, DC, MC, V* ⏱ *Closed Oct.–Mar.*

$$ ✕🏨 **Ballinalacken Castle.** It's not a castle but a converted Victorian shooting lodge on 100 acres of wildflower meadows, commanding a breathtaking view of the Atlantic. Rooms are modest but full of character. Local seafood, lamb, and beef are prepared by a stylish and imaginative chef. ✉ *Co. Clare* 🕾 *065/707–4025* 🖷 *065/707–4025* 🌐 *www. ballinalackencastle.com* ⟿ *12 rooms* 🍴 *Restaurant* ☱ *AE, DC, MC, V* ⏱ *Closed early Oct.–Easter.*

The Burren

In the northwest corner of County Clare, the Burren (from the Irish word for "stony rock") is a strange, rocky limestone district—and a superb nature reserve, with a profusion of wildflowers that are at their best in late May. Huge colonies of birds—puffins, kittiwakes, shags, guillemots,

and razorbills—nest along its coast. The **Burren Center** explains the extraordinary geology and wildlife of the area in a simple audiovisual display. ☒ *Kilfenora* ☎ *065/708–8030* ⊕ *www.theburrencentre.ie*
⊘ *Mid-Mar.–May, Sept., and Oct., daily 9:30–5; June–Aug., daily 10–6.*

The Cliffs of Moher

One of Ireland's most breathtaking natural sites, the majestic Cliffs of
Moher rise out of the sea in a wall that stretches over an 8-km (5-mi)
swath and as high as 710 feet. **O'Brien's Tower** is a defiant, broody sentinel built at their highest point. The **visitor center,** at the base of the
cliffs, beside the parking lot, has a tearoom and is a good refuge from
passing rain squalls. It's open daily 9:30–5:30. On a clear day the Aran
Islands are visible from the cliffs, and in summer there are regular day
trips to them from **Doolin,** a tiny village that claims three of the best
pubs in Ireland for traditional music.

Ballyvaughan

A pretty waterside village with views of Galway Bay and the Aran Islands, Ballyvaughan makes a good base for exploring the Burren. At
nearby **Aillwee Cave,** you can take a guided tour into the underworld of
the Burren, where 3,415 feet of cave, formed millions of years ago, can
be explored. ☎065/707–7036 ⊕*www.aillweecave.ie* ⊘ *Early Mar.–June*
and Sept.–early Nov., daily 10–6 (last tour at 5:30); July and Aug., daily
10–7 (last tour at 6:30).

$$ ☷ **Hyland's Burren Hotel.** Travelers have been looked after for 250 years
at this comfortable, family-run coaching inn. The cheerful, unpreten-
tious restaurant specializes in local seafood and lamb. ☒*Co. Clare* ☎*065/*
707–7037 ☎ *065/707–7131* ⊕ *www.hylandsburren.com* ⇖ *31 rooms*
♿ *Restaurant* ▤ *AE, MC, V.*

Kinvara

The picture-perfect village of Kinvara is worth a visit, thanks to its gor-
geous bay-side locale, great walking and sea angling, and numerous pubs.
The town is best known for its early August sailing event, **Cruinniú na**
mBád (Festival of the Gathering of the Boats). On a rock north of Kin-
vara Bay, the 16th-century **Dunguaire Castle** stands commanding the ap-
proaches from Galway Bay. ☒ *Co. Galway* ☎ *091/637108* ⊕ *www.*
shannonheritage.com ⊘ *May–Sept., daily 9:30–5; banquets at 5:30*
and 8:30.

Clarinbridge

Clarinbridge hosts Galway's annual **Oyster Festival,** which is held in
September and features the superlative products of the village's oyster
beds.

$$ ✕ **Moran's Oyster Cottage.** This waterside traditional thatched cottage
is one of Ireland's simplest yet most famous seafood eateries. The spe-
cialty here is oysters, but crab, prawns, mussels, and smoked salmon
are also served. ☒ *The Weir, Kilcolgan* ☎ *091/796113* ▤ *AE, MC, V.*

Cork to Galway Essentials

AIRPORTS

The most convenient international airport is Shannon, 25 km (16 mi)
east of Ennis. Galway Airport, at Carnmore, near Galway City, is used
mainly for internal flights.

🛈 **Galway Airport** ☎ 091/752874. **Shannon Airport** ☎ 061/471444.

BUS TRAVEL

Bus Éireann operates Expressway services from Dublin to Limerick City and Tralee and from Dublin, Cork City, and Limerick City to Ennis and Galway City. Information is also available at local tourist offices.
🚌 **Bus Éireann** ☎ 01/836-6111, 061/313-333, 021/450-8188, or 066/712-3566.

CAR RENTAL

To rent a car at Shannon Airport call Avis or Budget; both agencies have offices in Killarney as well.
🚌 **Avis** ✉ Killarney ☎ 064/36655 ✉ Shannon Airport ☎ 061/471094. **Budget** ✉ Killarney ☎ 064/34341 ✉ Shannon Airport ☎ 061/471361.

CAR TRAVEL

Though it's possible to explore the region by local and intercity bus services, you will need plenty of time; a car makes getting around much easier.

TOURS

Bus Éireann organizes day tours by bus from the Killarney and Tralee train stations; check with the tourist office or rail station for details. Destination Killarney arranges tours of Killarney and the Gap of Dunloe. Shannon Castle Tours has "Irish Nights" in Bunratty Folk Park or takes you to a medieval banquet at Bunratty Castle.
🚌 **Destination Killarney** ☎ 064/32638. **Shannon Castle Tours** ☎ 061/360788.

TRAIN TRAVEL

Trains run from Cork to Tralee, via Killarney, and from Cork to Limerick City. Trains for Galway City leave from Dublin's Heuston Station.

VISITOR INFORMATION

All visitor information offices are open weekdays 9–6 and Saturday 9–1.
🚌 **Ennis** ✉ Arthur's Row, Town Centre, Co. Clare ☎ 065/682-8366. **Killarney** ✉ Aras Fáilte, Beech Rd. ☎ 064/31633 📠 064/34506 🌐 www.corkkerry.ie. **Limerick City** ✉ Arthur's Quay ☎ 061/317522 📠 061/317939 🌐 www.shannon-dev.ie/tourism. **Shannon Airport** ☎ 061/471664. **Tralee** ✉ Ashe Memorial Hall ☎ 066/7121288.

GALWAY TO DONEGAL

The trip from Galway to Donegal takes you through the rugged landscape of Connemara to the fabled Yeats country in the northwest and then skirts the borders of Northern Ireland. Although it passes through some of the wildest, loneliest, and most dramatic parts of Ireland, it takes in Galway City, which today has become a hip mini-Dublin.

Galway City

As almost any Galwegian will tell you, theirs is the fastest-growing city in all of Ireland. Nonetheless, its heart is a warren of compact streets. The city's medieval heritage is everywhere apparent, particularly in and around its main pedestrian-oriented street—the name of which changes from Williamsgate to William to Shop to High to Quay. For many Irish people, Galway is a favorite weekend getaway—it's in a beautiful spot, on the north shore of Galway Bay, where the River Corrib flows from Lough Corrib out into the sea. It's also a university town: University College Galway (or UCG as it's locally known) is a center for Gaelic culture. The town, too, has long attracted writers, artists, and musicians, who keep the traditional music pubs lively year-round—the de facto centers of culture.

On the west bank of the Corrib estuary, just outside of the town walls, is **Claddagh,** said to be the oldest fishing village in Ireland. **Salthill Prom-**

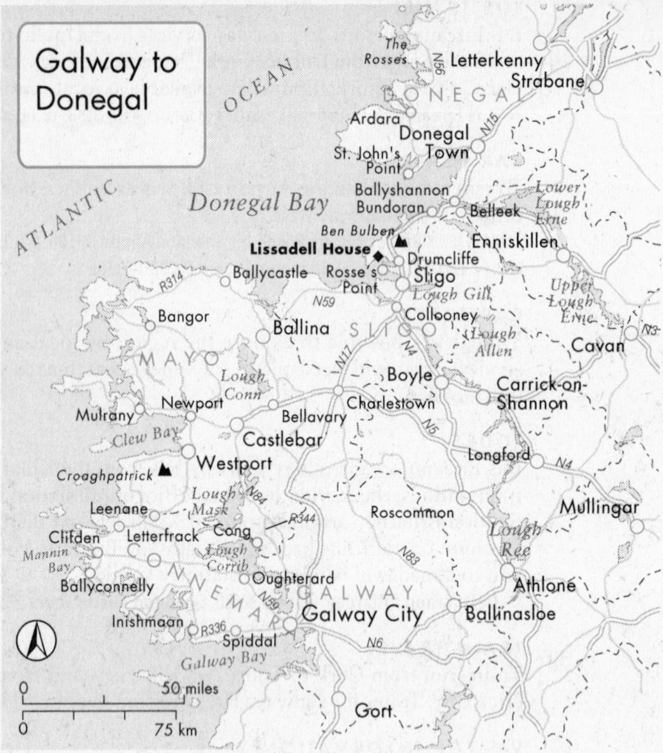

enade is the place "to sit and watch the moon rise over Claddagh, and see the sun go down on Galway Bay"—in the words of the city's most famous song.

$$–$$$$ ✕ **Malt House.** This cheerful pub-restaurant tucked away in an alley off High Street in the center of Old Galway has long been popular for good food—steaks, rack of lamb, prawns panfried in garlic butter—served in pleasantly informal surroundings. ✉ *Olde Malte Mall, High St.* ☎ *091/567866* ▭ *AE, DC, MC, V* ⏲ *Closed Sun.*

$$$ ✕ **Kirwan's Lane Creative Cuisine.** This restaurant serves a bistro-style menu in striking minimalist surroundings. Rack of lamb comes with sweet-potato mash, and fresh local cod fillet is accompanied by spring onion risotto. ✉ *Kirwan's La.* ☎ *091/568266* ▭ *AE, MC, V.*

$–$$$ ✕ **McDonagh's Seafood Bar.** An old Galway institution in the heart of the pedestrianized town center, this is part fish-and-chips bar, part serious seafood restaurant; try the famous Galway oysters here. ✉ *22 Quay St.* ☎ *091/565001* ▭ *AE, DC, MC, V* ⏲ *No dinner Sun.*

$$$$ 🏨 **Ardilaun House.** This lovely 19th-century house is in a quiet, tree-lined suburb, midway between the city center and the Salthill promenade. For views of the bay, book an even-numbered room on the top floor; other rooms, which are just as pleasant, overlook the flower garden. ✉ *Taylor's Hill, Co. Galway* ☎ *091/521433* 📠 *091/521546* 🌐 *www.ardilaunhousehotel.ie* ⇆ *81 rooms, 7 suites* 🛎 *Restaurant, indoor pool, 2 bars* ▭ *AE, DC, MC, V.*

$$$–$$$$ 🏨 **Galway Great Southern.** Expect to rub elbows with many native Irish visiting Galway at this grand, old-fashioned hotel presiding over Eyre Square. Rooms have high ceilings and Georgian-style furniture. A pianist often graces the spacious lobby, which, like the two bars, is a popular gathering spot. ✉ *Eyre Sq., Co. Galway* ☎ *091/564041* 📠 *091/*

566704 ⊕ *www.gshotels.com* ⇋ *99 rooms* ⌂ *Restaurant, indoor pool, 2 bars* ▤ *AE, DC, MC, V.*

$$$ ⊡ **Jurys Galway Inn.** At the foot of Galway's busy main Quay Street, this modern, four-story hotel offers good-quality budget accommodations. Each room is big enough for three adults or two adults and two children. ⊠ *Quay St., Co. Galway* ☎ *091/566444* 🖷 *091/568415* ⊕ *www.jurysdoyle.com* ⇋ *128 rooms* ⌂ *Restaurant, bar* ▤ *AE, DC, MC, V.*

The Aran Islands

Jutting from a belligerent ocean, the Aran Islands—Inishmore, Inishmaan, and Inisheer—are remote western outposts of the ancient province of Connaught. The islands have been populated for thousands of years, and the Irish-speaking inhabitants have adhered to the traditions of their ancestors. The best time to visit the islands is May and early June, when the unusual, Burren-like flora is at its best and before the bulk of tourists arrive.

★ **Rossaveal,** a port on the coast road beyond Spiddal, is the handiest port for a trip to the Aran Islands, 48 km (30 mi) off the coast. **Inis Meáin (Inishmaan),** the middle island, is the most unspoiled of the three; it's here that the traditional Aran lifestyle is most evident. Boats depart for Inishmaan from Rossaveal and less frequently from Galway. You can also fly daily from the **Connemara Airport** (☎ 091/593–034 ⊕ www.aran-islands.com).

Connemara

Bordered by the long expanse of Lough Corrib on the east and the deeply indented, jagged coast of the Atlantic on the west, rugged, desolate western County Galway is known as Connemara. It's an area of spectacular, almost myth-making geography—of glacial lakes; gorgeous, silent mountains; lonely roads; and hushed, uninhabited boglands. In the midst of this wilderness, you'll find few people. In the off-season, especially, you're far more likely to come across sheep than another car.

Two main routes—one inland, the other coastal—lead through Connemara. To take the inland route, leave Galway City on the well-signposted outer-ring road and follow signs for N59—Moycullen, Oughterard, and Clifden. If you choose to go the coastal route, you'll travel due west from Galway City to Rossaveal on R336 through Salthill, Barna, and Spiddal.

Clifden

The principal town of Connemara, Clifden has an almost alpine setting, nestling on the edge of the Atlantic with a spectacular mountain backdrop. A good selection of small restaurants, lively bars with music most nights in the summer, some very pleasant accommodations, and excellent walks make the town a popular base, especially in July and August. A short (2-km [1-mi]) walk along the beach road through the grounds of the ruined **Clifden Castle** is the best way to explore the seashore.

Kylemore Abbey, about 15 minutes from Clifden on N59, is one of the most photographed castles in all of Ireland. The vast Gothic Revival, turreted, gray-stone castle was built as a private home between 1861 and 1868. Today it's the home of Benedictine nuns. Three reception rooms and the main hall are open to the public, as are a crafts center and simple cafeteria. ⊠ *Kylemore* ☎ *095/41146* ⊕ *www.kylemoreabbey.com* ⊙ *Crafts shop mid-Mar.–Nov., daily 10–6; cafeteria Easter–Nov., daily 9:30–6; grounds Easter–Nov., daily 9 AM–dusk; exhibition and gardens Easter–Nov., daily 9–5:30.*

$$$ ✕⊡ **Erriseask House.** This rambling, modern house, on the rocky shore of Mannin Bay, is a stylish, comfortable accommodation. Owner-chef Stefan Matz has won many awards for his fine cooking; freshly turf-smoked fillet of beef is a house specialty. ⊠ *Ballyconneely, Co. Galway* ☎ *095/23553* 🖷 *095/23639* ⊕ *www.erriseask.connemara-ireland.com* ⇨ *8 rooms, 5 suites* ♢ *Restaurant* ⊟ *MC, V* ☯ *Closed Jan.–mid-Feb.*

Letterfrack

The 5,000-acre **Connemara National Park** lies just southeast of the village of Letterfrack (14 km [9 mi] north of Clifden on N59). The park's **visitor center** covers the area's history and ecology. You can also get details on the many excellent walks and beaches in the area. ☎ *095/ 41054* ⊕ *www.heritageireland.ie* ☯ *Park daily. Visitor center Apr., May, and Sept.–mid-Oct., daily 10–5:30; June, daily 10–6:30; July and Aug., daily 9:30–6:30.*

★ $$$$ ✕⊡ **Renvyle House.** The extraordinary setting—a lake at the front door and the Atlantic Ocean at the back—distinguishes this country house. The elegant rooms all have breathtaking views. The cheerful, softly lighted restaurant's table d'hôte menu emphasizes fresh local fish and lamb. ⊠ *Renvyle, Co. Galway* ☎ *095/43511* 🖷 *095/43515* ⊕ *www.renvyle. com* ⇨ *65 rooms* ♢ *Restaurant, pool* ⊟ *AE, DC, MC, V* ☯ *Closed Jan.–mid-Feb.*

Westport

Westport is a quiet, mainly 18th-century town overlooking Clew Bay—a wide expanse of water studded with nearly 400 islands. The distinctive silhouette of **Croagh Patrick,** a 2,540-foot mountain, dominates the town. Today some 25,000 pilgrims climb it on the last Sunday in July in honor of St. Patrick, who is believed to have spent 40 days fasting on its summit in AD 441. Whether he did or not, the climb is an exhilarating experience and can be completed in about three hours; it should be attempted only in good weather, however.

$$$ ✕ **Quay Cottage.** On the harbor front, a short distance from the town center, this tiny cottage decorated with a nautical theme is both an informal wine bar and a seafood restaurant. ⊠ *The Harbour* ☎ *098/26412* ⊟ *AE, MC, V* ☯ *Closed Jan. No lunch.*

$$$ ⊡ **Delphi Lodge.** In the heart of spectacular mountains-and-lakes scenery, this sporting lodge is heavily stocked with fishing paraphernalia. The owner, Peter Mantle, is a valuable storehouse of information and stories. ⊠ *6 km (4 mi) off N59, northwest of Leenane, Co. Mayo* ☎ *095/ 42211* 🖷 *095/42296* ⊕ *www.delphilodge.ie* ⇨ *12 rooms* ♢ *Restaurant, bar* ⊟ *MC, V* ☯ *Closed mid-Dec.–mid-Jan.*

$$$ ⊡ **Olde Railway Hotel.** This Victorian hotel on the town center's tree-lined mall offers both character and comfort. ⊠ *The Mall, Co. Mayo* ☎ *098/25166* 🖷 *098/25090* ⊕ *www.anu.ie/railwayhotel* ⇨ *15 rooms* ♢ *Restaurant* ⊟ *AE, DC, MC, V.*

Sligo Area

County Sligo is noted for its seaside resorts, the famous golf course at Rosses Point (just outside Sligo Town), and its links with Ireland's most famous 20th-century poet, W. B. Yeats. **Sligo Town** is the best place to begin a tour of Yeats Country. In the throes of an economic boom, Sligo retains all the charm of smaller, sleepier villages, yet by day it's as lively and crowded as Galway City. The **Model and Niland Centre** houses collections of works by the poet's brother, Jack B. Yeats, and a fine collection of early-20th-century Irish art, as well as memorabilia of Yeats the poet. The latter's grave is in Drumcliff, beneath the slopes of Ben

Bulben, just north of town. ⊠ *The Mall* ☎ *071/41405* ⊘ *Daily 10–5 and during performances.*

★ From Sligo Town, you can take a boat or drive up to **Lough Gill** and see the **Lake Isle of Innisfree** and other places immortalized in Yeats's poetry. Fourteen kilometers (9 mi) northwest of Sligo Town is **Lissadell House**, a substantial mansion dating from 1830 that appears prominently in Yeats's writings. It was the home of Constance Gore-Booth, later Countess Markeviecz, who took part in the 1916 uprising. ☎ *071/63150* ⊕ *www.ireland-northwest.travel.ie* ⊘ *June–mid-Sept., Mon.–Sat. 10:30–12:30 and 2–4:30.*

$$$ ✕ **Bistro Bianconi.** The decor is all white, with blond wood and white-tile floors. The food is a colorful array of pizzas, baked in the wood-burning oven with toppings both traditional and innovative. ⊠ *44 O'Connell St., Sligo Town* ☎ *071/41744* ⊟ *AE, MC, V* ⊘ *Closed Sun.*

$$$–$$$$ ✕⊡ **Markree Castle.** This 17th-century, family-owned hotel in a castle is on a pastoral, 1,000-acre estate. Public rooms share a comfortable informality; guest rooms are idiosyncratic. The kitchen offers up an excellent table d'hôte menu, and on Sunday a traditional lunch attracts a sizable, family-oriented crowd. ⊠ *Off N4, south of Sligo Town, Collooney, Co. Sligo* ☎ *071/67800* 🖶 *071/67840* ⊕ *www.markreecastle. ie* 🛏 *30 rooms* ⚲ *Restaurant* ⊟ *AE, DC, MC, V.*

Donegal Town

Donegal is the gateway to the magnificent Northwest, with its rugged coastline and dramatic highlands. The town is centered on the triangular Diamond, where three roads converge (N56 to the west, and N15 to the south and the northeast) and the mouth of the River Eske pours gently into Donegal Bay. Near the north corner of the Diamond is **Donegal Castle,** built by clan leader Hugh O'Donnell in the 1470s. Ruins of the **Franciscan abbey,** founded in 1474 by Hugh O'Donnell, are a five-minute walk south of town at a spectacular site perched above the Eske.

$ ✕ **Blueberry Tea Room.** This pleasant restaurant and café is just across the street from Donegal Castle. ⊠ *Castle St.* ☎ *073/972–2933* ⊟ *V* ⊘ *Closed Sun. mid-Sept.–May.*

$$$$ ✕⊡ **St. Ernan's House.** On its own wooded tidal island in Donegal Bay,
FodorsChoice five minutes south of town, St. Ernan's is one of the most spectacularly
★ situated country houses in all of Ireland. Guest rooms are simple but elegant, with antiques and views of the bay. Dinner in the intimate dining room is prepared in Irish country-house style. ⊠ *St. Ernan's Island, Co. Donegal* ☎ *073/972–1065* 🖶 *073/972–2098* ⊕ *www.sainternans. com* 🛏 *10 rooms* ⚲ *Dining room* ⊟ *MC, V* ⊘ *Closed Nov.–Easter.*

$$ ✕⊡ **Castle Murray House Hotel.** The original house has been extended and modernized to take full advantage of the exceptional panoramic views of the bay and distant mountains. The restaurant serves superb French cuisine. ⊠ *21 km (13 mi) west of Donegal Town, St. John's Point, Dunkineely, Co. Donegal* ☎ *073/37022* 🖶 *073/37330* 🛏 *10 rooms* ⚲ *Restaurant* ⊟ *MC, V* ⊘ *Closed mid-Jan.–mid-Feb., Mon. and Tues. Oct.–mid-Jan. and mid-Feb.–Easter.*

Galway to Donegal Essentials

BIKE TRAVEL

Bikes can be rented from Celtic Cycles, Gary's Cycles, or John Mannion.
🚴 Bike Rentals **Celtic Cycles** ⊠ Victoria Pl., Galway City ☎ 091/566–606. **Gary's Cycles** ⊠ Quay St., Sligo ☎ 071/45418. **John Mannion** ⊠ Railway View, Clifden ☎ 095/21160.

BUS TRAVEL

Bus Éireann travels all over the region. McGeehan Coaches services County Donegal locally.

🚩 **Bus Éireann** ☎ 01/836-6111. **McGeehan Coaches** ☎ 075/46150.

CAR RENTAL

🚩 **Avis** ☎ 091/568886. **Budget** ☎ 091/564570 or 091/566376. **Murray's** ☎ 091/562222.

TAXIS

Taxis do not operate on meters; agree on the fare beforehand.

TOURS

CIE Tours International operates day tours of Connemara out of Galway City and bus tours into the Donegal highlands from Sligo train station; details are available from local tourist offices. Bus Éireann and Gray Line organize tours of the Boyne Valley and County Meath out of Dublin.

🚩 **Gray Line** ☎ 01/661-9666.

TRAIN TRAVEL

Trains to Galway, Westport, and Sligo operate from Dublin's Heuston or Connolly (Sligo) station. There is no train service north of Sligo.

VISITOR INFORMATION

All tourism offices are open weekdays 9–6 and Saturday 9–1.

🚩 **Galway City** ✉ Off Eyre Sq. ☎ 091/537700 ⊕ www.irelandwest.ie. **Sligo Town** ✉ Temple St. ☎ 071/61201 ⊕ www.ireland-northwest.travel.ie. **Westport** ✉ James St. ☎ 098/25711.

NORTHERN IRELAND

Northern Ireland, a province ruled by the United Kingdom, has some of the most unspoiled scenery you could hope to find—the granite Mountains of Mourne; the Giant's Causeway, made of extraordinary volcanic rock; more than 320 km (200 mi) of coastline with long, unspoiled beaches and hidden coves; and rivers and island-strewn lakes that provide fabled fishing grounds, among them the largest freshwater lake in Europe, Lough Neagh. Northern Ireland also holds a great legacy in its celebrated descendants. Nearly one in six of the more than 4½ million Irish who made the fateful journey across the Atlantic to seek their fortune in the New World was from Ulster, and of this group (and from their family stock) more than a few left their mark in the United States: Davy Crockett, President Andrew Jackson, President Woodrow Wilson, General Stonewall Jackson, financier Thomas Mellon, merchant Paul Getty, writers Edgar Allan Poe and Mark Twain, and astronaut Neil Armstrong.

Belfast is the capital of Northern Ireland. A great Victorian success story, the city was once an industrial boomtown whose prosperity was built on trade—especially linen and shipbuilding (this is where the *Titanic* was built). You'll find some of the warmest, wryest people in all of Ireland here, a fair amount of construction, and, most of all, a palpable will to move beyond the infamous Troubles that plagued the city, and all of Northern Ireland, for almost three decades. With an ongoing, albeit uncertain, peace agreement in Northern Ireland since 1997, Nationalists and Unionists have been working together for the betterment of the province.

Belfast is fairly compact; its center is made up of roughly three contiguous areas that are easy to navigate on foot, though from the south end to the north it's about an hour's leisurely walk. At Belfast's southern end, the **Queen's University area** is easily the most appealing part of the city. This is where you'll find the university, the Botanic Gardens, fine 19th-century buildings, and many good pubs, restaurants, and B&Bs. Between University Street and Shaftesbury Square is the **Golden Mile,** with hotels, major civic and office buildings, and some restaurants, cafés, and stores. City Hall marks the northern boundary of the Golden Mile and the southern end of the (theoretically) pedestrian-only **Central District,** which extends from Donegall Square north almost to St. Anne's Cathedral; this is the old heart of Belfast and has the highest concentration of retail outlets that Belfast has to offer. Behind St. Anne's is the **Cathedral Quarter,** a maze of cobbled streets that the city plans to transform over the next few years.

$$$ ✕ **Deane's.** Celebrated Chef Michael Deane serves up delicious contemporary cuisine at his two-story restaurant—a brasserie downstairs and formal restaurant upstairs—in the center of Belfast. Deane's tastes are eclectic and Thai influences (he worked in Bangkok) particularly shine. Squab is a Deane specialty, and the ravioli of lobster is a standout. ✉ *34–40 Howard St.* ☎ *028/9033–1134 restaurant; 028/9056–0000 brasserie* ▤ *AE, MC, V* ☺ *Restaurant closed Sun.–Tues. Brasserie closed Sun.*
FodorsChoice ★

★ **$$–$$$** ✕ **Aldens.** East Belfast was a gastronomic wilderness until this modernist restaurant opened with chef Cath Gradwell at the helm, producing an opulent menu at some of the most reasonable prices in town. The set dinner menus from Monday to Thursday are £15.95 for three courses. The mood is relaxed, the staff friendly, and the wine list one of the best around. Try the roast Dublin Bay prawns to start, and grilled quails with wild cranberry compote and baked polenta for a main course. Reservations are recommended. ✉ *229 Upper Newtownards Rd., Belfast* ☎ *028/9065–0079* ▤ *AE, DC, MC, V* ☺ *No lunch weekends. No dinner Sun.*

$$–$$$ ✕ **Cayenne.** Celebrity TV chefs Paul and Jeanne Rankin run this Golden Mile spot. Cayenne serves up fusion cuisine with an Asian twist; main dishes range from coconut-crusted cod, to duck with wild rice pancakes, and Donegal wild salmon with hazelnut beurre blanc. Open until 11:15 PM on Friday and Saturday, this is an excellent choice for a late meal after taking in an opera or concert. ✉ *Shaftesbury Sq. at end of Great Victoria St.* ☎ *028/9033–1532* ▤ *AE, DC, MC, V* ☺ *No lunch Sat.*

$$$$ ▥ **The McCausland Hotel.** Clean, simple lines and an aura of sumptuous minimalism are the hallmarks of this pair of 1867 grain warehouses, which have been turned into a luxury hotel. Each comfortable, contemporary guest room is well equipped with VCR and CD player. ✉ *34–38 Victoria St., Belfast, Co. Antrim BT1 3GH* ☎ *028/9022–0200* 🖷 *028/9022–0220* ⊕ *www.slh.com* ⇄ *60 rooms* ⚏ *2 restaurants, bar* ▤ *AE, DC, MC, V.*

$$ ▥ **Ash-Rowan Guest House.** This outstanding B&B in a spacious Victorian home has guest rooms decorated in tasteful, individual styles; each has a private bath and TV. It was the marital home of Thomas Andrews, the designer of the ill-fated *Titanic.* ✉ *12 Windsor Ave., BT9 6EE* ☎ *028/9066–1758* 🖷 *028/9066–3227* ⇄ *5 rooms with bath* ⚏ *Restaurant, bar* ▤ *MC, V* ☺ *Closed Christmas wk.*
FodorsChoice ★

$$ ▥ **Madison's.** A few minutes' walk from the university, this hotel is done in a modish Barcelona-inspired take on art nouveau. Rooms, in cool yellows and rich blues, are sparely furnished but comfortable. ✉ *59 Botanic Ave., BT7 1JL* ☎ *028/9050–9800* 🖷 *028/9050–9808* ⊕ *www. madisonshotel.com* ⇄ *35 rooms with bath* ⚏ *Restaurant, bar* ▤ *AE, MC, V.*

Northern Ireland Essentials

AIRPORTS
Belfast International Airport at Aldergove is the North's principal air arrival point, 30½ km (19 mi) from Belfast. Belfast City Airport is the second airport, 6½ km (4 mi) from the city; it receives flights only from the United Kingdom.

🛪 **Belfast City Airport** ☎ 028/9093-9093 ⊕ www.belfastcityairport.com. **Belfast International Airport at Aldergove** ☎ 028/9448-4848 ⊕ www.bial.co.uk.

BUS TRAVEL
Ulsterbus runs a direct service between Dublin and Belfast. Questions regarding Ulsterbus, or any other bus service in Northern Ireland, can be dealt with by the central call center of Translink. The Republic's Bus Éireann also runs direct services between Dublin and Belfast.

🚌 **Bus Éireann** ☎ 01/836-6111 in Dublin ⊕ www.buseireann.ie. **Translink** ☎ 028/9066-6630 ⊕ www.translink.co.uk.

CAR RENTALS
All the major car-rental agencies have branches at Belfast International Airport; some also have branches at Belfast City Airport. If you're planning to take a rental car across the border into the Republic, inform the company and check its insurance procedures.

CAR TRAVEL
Many roads from the Republic into Northern Ireland were once closed for security reasons, but all are now open, leaving you with a score of legitimate crossing points to choose from. Army checkpoints at all approved frontier posts are rare, and few customs formalities are observed. The fast N1/A1 road connects Belfast to Dublin (160 km [100 mi]) with an average driving time of just over two hours.

CONSULATES
🏴 Canada ✉ 35 The Hill, Groomsport BT19 6JS ☎ 028/9127-2060.
🏴 New Zealand ✉ New Balance House, 118A Lisburn Rd., Glenavy Co. Antrim BT29 4NY ☎ 028/9264-8098.
🏴 United States ✉ Queen's House, 14 Queen St., Belfast BT1 6EQ ☎ 028/9032-8239.

EATING & DRINKING
Prices are per person for a dinner main course. Sales tax is included in the price. Many places add a 10%–15% service charge—if not, a 10% tip is fine.

WHAT IT COSTS In U.K. pounds			
$$$$	**$$$**	**$$**	**$**
AT DINNER over £18	£12–£18	£7–£12	under £7

Prices are per person for a main course.

EMERGENCIES
🚑 **Ambulance, police, fire, and coast guard** ☎ 999 toll-free in all of Northern Ireland. **Belfast's main police station** ✉ 6-10 N. Queen St. ☎ 028/9065-0222.

LODGING
Prices are for two people in a double room, based on high season (June–mid-September) rates, including value-added tax (V.A.T.) and service charges.

WHAT IT COSTS In U.K. pounds			
$$$$	**$$$**	**$$**	**$**
HOTELS	over £120	£90–£120	£60–£90	under £60

Hotel prices are for two people in a standard double room in high season.

TOURS

Citybus runs three Belfast city tours. Ulsterbus operates half-day or full-day trips (June–September) from Belfast to surrounding areas. Historical Pub Tours of Belfast offers walking tours of the city's pubs on Tuesday at 7 PM and Saturday at 4 PM.

🖪 Fees & Schedules **Citybus** ☎ 028/9066-6630 ⊕ www.translink.co.uk. **Historical Pub Tours of Belfast** ☎ 028/9268-3665. **Ulsterbus** ☎ 028/9033-7004 ⊕ www.translink.co.uk.

TRAIN TRAVEL

The Dublin–Belfast Express train, run jointly by Northern Ireland Railways and Iarnród Éireann (Irish Rail), travels between the two cities in about two hours. Eight trains (check timetables, as some trains are much slower) run daily in both directions (three on Sunday) between Dublin and Belfast's misnamed Central Station. A free shuttle bus service from Belfast Central Station will drop you off at City Hall or Ulsterbus's city-center Europa Buscentre. You can change trains at Central Station for the city-center Great Victoria Street Station, which is adjacent both to the Europa Buscentre and the Europa Hotel.

🖪 **Central Station** ✉ E. Bridge St. ☎ 028/9089-9411. **Europa Buscentre** ☎ 028/9066-6630. **Great Victoria Street Station** ✉ Great Victoria St. ☎ 028/9066-6630. **Iarnród Éireann** ☎ 027/9066-6630. **Northern Ireland Railways** ☎ 028/9089-9411.

VISITOR INFORMATION

Northern Ireland Tourist Board Information Centre can provide contact information for local branches throughout Northern Ireland.

🖪 **Northern Ireland Tourist Board Information Centre** ✉ 35 Donegall Pl., BT1 5AU ☎ 028/9023-1221 or 028/9024-6609 📠 028/9031-2424 ⊕ www.discovernorthernireland.com.

ITALY

ROME, FLORENCE, TUSCANY, MILAN, VENICE, CAMPANIA

WHERE ELSE IN EUROPE can you find the blend of great art, delicious food and wine, and human warmth and welcome that awaits you in Italy? This Mediterranean country has made a profound contribution to Western civilization, producing some of the world's greatest thinkers, writers, politicians, saints, and artists. Impressive traces of their lives and works can still be seen in Italy's great buildings and enchanting countryside.

The whole of Italy is one vast attraction, but the triangle of its most-visited cities—Rome (Roma), Florence (Firenze), and Venice (Venezia)—represents the great variety found here. In Rome, especially, you can feel the uninterrupted flow of the ages, from the classical era of the ancient Romans to the bustle and throb of contemporary life being lived in centuries-old settings. Florence is the jewel of the Italian Renaissance, which is evident in the formal grandeur of its palaces and piazzas and the sumptuous villas in the surrounding countryside. Venice, by contrast, seems suspended in time, the same today as it was when it held sway over the eastern Mediterranean. Each of these cities reveals a different aspect of the Italian character: the baroque exuberance of Rome, Florence's Renaissance harmony, and the dreamy sensuality of Venice.

Trying to soak up Italy's rich artistic heritage poses a challenge. The country's many museums and churches draw hordes of visitors, all wanting to see the same thing at the same time. From May through September, the Sistine Chapel, Michelangelo's *David*, Piazza San Marco, and other key sights are more often than not swamped by tourists. Try to see the highlights at off-peak times. If they are open during lunch, this is often a good time. Seeing some attractions—such as the gleaming facades of Rome's glorious baroque churches and fountains—does not require waiting in long lines.

Making the most of your time in Italy doesn't mean rushing through it. To gain a rich appreciation for the country, don't try to see everything at once. Practice the Italian-perfected *il dolce far niente*—the sweet art of idleness. Skip a museum to sit at a table in a pretty café and enjoy the sunshine and a cappuccino. Art—and life—is to be enjoyed, and the Italians can show you how.

ITALY A TO Z

To research prices, get advice from other travelers, and book travel arrangements, visit www.fodors.com.

AIR TRAVEL

Alitalia and some privately owned companies, such as Meridiana and Air One, in addition to other European airlines, provide service throughout Italy. Most of them offer several types of discount fares; inquire at travel agencies or at Alitalia agencies in major cities.

BOAT & FERRY TRAVEL

Ferries connect the mainland with all the major islands. Car ferries operate to Sicily, Sardinia, Elba, Ponza, Capri (though taking a car here is not advised), and Ischia, among other islands. Lake ferries connect the towns on the shores of the Italian lakes: Como, Maggiore, Garda, and Iseo.

BUS TRAVEL

Regional bus companies provide service throughout Italy. Route information and timetables are usually available either at tourist information offices and travel agencies, or at bus company ticket offices. One of the interregional companies providing long-distance service is SITA.
📶 SITA ☎ 800/373760 toll-free.

BUSINESS HOURS

Banks are open weekdays 8:30–1:30 and 2:45–3:45. Churches are usually open from early morning to noon or 12:30, when they close for about two hours or more, opening again in the afternoon until about 7 PM. National museums (*musei statali*) are usually open from about 9 AM until about 8 PM and are often closed on Monday. Private museums often have different hours, which may vary according to season. Most major archaeological sites are open every day from early morning to dusk, except some holidays. At all museums and sites, ticket offices close an hour or so before official closing time. Always check with the local tourist office for current hours and holiday closings. Shops are open, with individual variations, from 9 to 1 and from 3:30 or 4 to 7:30 or 8, although in most tourist areas, many stay open through lunchtime. They are open Monday–Saturday but close for a half day during the week; for example, in Rome most shops are closed on Monday morning, although food shops close on Thursday afternoon in fall–spring. Most shops, including food shops, close Saturday afternoon in July and August. Some tourist-oriented shops and department stores in downtown Rome, Florence, and Venice are open all day, every day.

CAR TRAVEL

The extensive autostrada network (toll superhighways) connecting all major towns is complemented by equally well maintained but toll-free *superstrade* (express highways), *strade statali* (main roads), and *strade provinciali* (secondary roads). The Autostrada del Sole (A1) crosses the country from north to south, connecting Milan to Naples. From Salerno, the A3 brings you farther south to Reggio Calabria. The A4 from west to east connects Turin to Trieste.

All highways are clearly signposted and numbered. The ticket issued on entering an autostrada must be returned on leaving, along with the toll. On some shorter autostrade, mainly connections, the toll is payable on

666 <

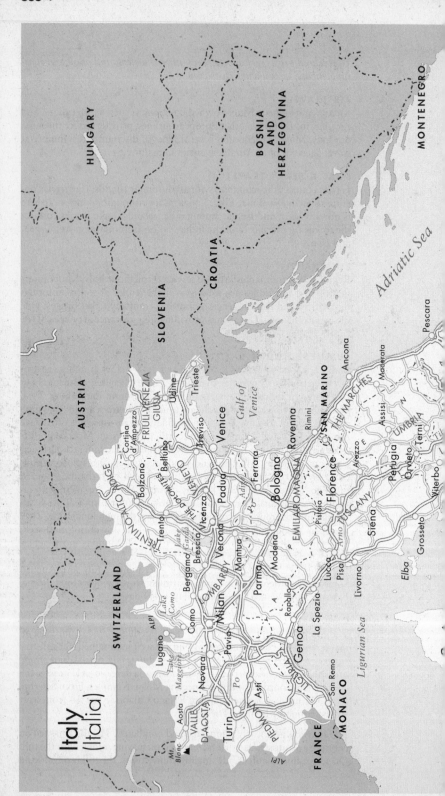

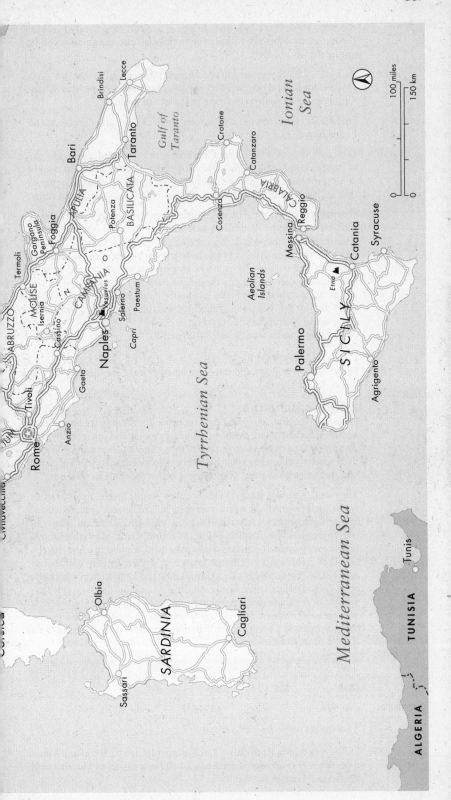

entering. Have small bills and change or a credit card handy for tolls. If paying by credit card, simply slip in the card and the amount will be automatically charged.

Parking is greatly restricted in the center of most cities. Parking in a Zona Disco is for limited periods. City garages cost up to €25 per day. Check with your hotel to determine the best place to park.

EMERGENCIES Dial 803/116 for towing and repairs. Dial 113 for an ambulance and highway police.

GASOLINE Gas costs about €1.05 per liter. Except on the autostrade, most gas stations are closed Sunday; they also close from 12:30 PM to 3:30 PM and at 7 PM for the night. Many stations have automatic self-service pumps that accept bills of 5, 10, 20, and 50 euros; most also take credit cards.

RULES OF THE ROAD Driving is on the right. The speed limit on an autostrada is 130 kph (81 mph). It is 110 kph (70 mph) on state and provincial roads, unless otherwise marked. Other regulations are largely as in the United States except that the police have the power to levy severe on-the-spot fines. Italians drive fast and impatiently; don't be surprised when, on a winding two-lane highway, drivers zip into the ongoing-traffic lane to pass you if you are going too slowly. Call the Automobil Club Italiano (ACI, daily 8 AM–8 PM) for information in English about rules of the road, road conditions, car insurance, and travel tips.

🛈 **Automobil Club Italiano** ☎ 06/49982389 or 1518.

CUSTOMS & DUTIES

For details on imports and duty-free limits in Italy, *see* Customs & Duties *in* Smart Travel Tips.

EATING & DRINKING

Generally speaking, a *ristorante* pays more attention to its appearance and service than does a *trattoria,* which is simpler and often family run. An *osteria* used to be a simple tavern, though now the term may be used to designate a chic and expensive eatery. A *tavola calda* offers hot dishes and snacks, with seating. A *rosticceria* offers the same to take out.

The menu is always posted in the window or just inside the door of an eating establishment. Note whether there are charges for *coperto* (cover) and *servizio* (service), which will increase your check amount. The coperto charge has been abolished in many eating places. Many restaurants offer a *menù turistico,* usually a complete meal, limited to a few entrées, at a reasonable price (including taxes and service, usually with beverages extra). Tap water is safe in large cities and almost everywhere else unless noted *non potabile.* Bottled mineral water is available everywhere, *gassata* or *frizzante* (with bubbles) or *non gassata* (without bubbles). If you prefer tap water, ask for *acqua semplice.* Note that many restaurants close from Christmas through the first week in January and for a good part of August.

WHAT IT COSTS In euros			
	$$$$	**$$$**	**$$**	**$**
AT DINNER	over €22	€17–€22	€12–€17	under €12

Prices are per person for a main course.

MEALTIMES Lunch is served in Rome from 1 to 3, dinner from 8 to 10:30 and sometimes later. Service begins and ends a half hour earlier in Florence and Venice and later in the south.

RESERVATIONS &
DRESS
Except for restaurants in the $$$$ and occasionally in the $$$ categories, where jacket and tie are advisable, neat, casual attire is acceptable.

HOLIDAYS

January 1; January 6 (Epiphany); Easter Sunday and Monday; April 25 (Liberation Day); May 1 (May Day); August 15 (Assumption, known as Ferragosto); November 1 (All Saints' Day); December 8 (Immaculate Conception); December 25–26.

The feast days of patron saints are observed locally. Many businesses and shops may be closed in Florence, Genoa, and Turin on June 24 (St. John the Baptist); in Rome on June 29 (Sts. Peter and Paul); in Palermo on July 15 (Santa Rosalia); in Naples on September 19 (San Gennaro); in Bologna on October 4 (San Petronio); in Trieste on November 3 (San Giusto); and in Milan on December 7 (St. Ambrose). Venice's feast of St. Mark is April 25, the same as Liberation Day, and the city also celebrates November 21 (Madonna della Salute).

LANGUAGE

Italy is accustomed to English-speaking tourists, and in major cities you will find that many people speak at least a little English. In smaller hotels and restaurants and on public transportation, knowing a few phrases of Italian comes in handy.

LODGING

Italy, especially Rome, Florence, and Venice, offers a good choice of accommodations, though rooms tend to be small. Room rates are on a par with those of most European capitals, although porters, room service, and in-house laundering are disappearing in all but the most elegant hotels. Taxes and service are included in the room rate. Although breakfast is usually quoted in the room rate, it's actually an extra charge that you can decline. Make your preference clear when booking or checking in. Air-conditioning also may be an extra charge. Specify if you care about having either a bathtub or shower, as not all rooms have both. In $$ and $ places, showers may be the drain-in-the-floor type guaranteed to flood the bathroom. In older hotels room quality may be uneven; if you don't like the room you're given, ask for another. This applies to noise, too; some front rooms are bigger and have views but get street noise. Train stations in major cities have hotel-reservation service booths.

WHAT IT COSTS In euros			
$$$$	**$$$**	**$$**	**$**
ROME, FLORENCE, VENICE, MILAN			
FOR 2 PEOPLE over €300	€225–€300	€150–€225	under €150
OTHER AREAS			
HOTELS over €210	€160–€210	€110–€160	under €110

Hotel prices are for two people in a standard double room in high season.

RENTALS &
AGRITOURISM
Short or long rental stays in town apartments or in rural villas or farms are a good option for families traveling with children and others who value independence and want a taste of living Italian-style. Agritourism, or the practice of staying on a working farm, usually for a week or more, is growing in popularity in rural areas throughout Italy, especially in Tuscany and Umbria. Agritourism accommodations range in style from rustic simplicity to country chic, and prices vary accordingly. Contact local APT tourist offices or visit the multilingual Web site, www.agriturist.it.

You can also buy *Agriturism,* available in major bookstores; it's in Italian but has pictures and international symbols describing facilities.

CAMPING Italy has a wide selection of campgrounds, and the Italians themselves have taken to camping, which means that beach or mountain sites will be crammed in July and August. A *carnet* (permit) is required in most campgrounds; get one from your local association before leaving home. You can buy a campsite directory such as the detailed multilingual guide published by the Touring Club Italiano or the more evocative *Guida ai Campeggi in Italia* (published by Demetra in Italian only but with international symbols), with color pictures of the most popular resorts. Alternatively, you can obtain *Campeggiare in Italia,* the free directory of campsites published by the Federazione Italiana dei Campeggiatori by mail from the organization.

 Federazione Italiana del Campeggio ⊠ Via Vitt. Emanuele 11 50041 Calenzano, Florence ☎ 055/882391 �🖷 055/8825918 ⊕ www.federcampeggio.it.

HOTELS Italian hotels are classified by regional tourist boards from five-star (deluxe) to one-star (modest hotels and small inns). The established price of the room appears on a rate card on the back of the door of your room or inside the closet door, though you may be able to get a lower rate by asking. Any variations above the posted rate should be cause for complaint and should be reported to the manager and the police. Standards in one-star hotels are very uneven. At best, rooms are usually spotlessly clean but basic, with showers and toilets down the hall.

Low-season rates do not officially apply in Rome, Florence, and Milan, but you can usually bargain for discounted rates in Rome and Milan in summer and during weekends (when business travelers are few) and in Florence in winter. Ask for *"la tariffa scontata."* You can save on hotel accommodations in Venice and in such resorts as Sorrento and Capri during their low seasons—the winter (with the exception of Christmas holidays and Carnevale in Venice), early spring, and late-autumn months.

MAIL & SHIPPING

The Italian mail system is notoriously erratic and can be excruciatingly slow. Allow up to 15 days for mail to and from the United States and Canada and about a week to and from the United Kingdom and within Italy. Posta Prioritaria (stationery and small packages up to 2 kilograms) and the more expensive Postacelere (up to 20 kilograms) are special-delivery services from the post office that guarantee delivery within 24 hours in Italy and three to five days abroad.

Correspondence can be addressed to you in care of the Italian post office. Letters should be addressed to your name, "c/o Ufficio Postale Centrale," followed by "Fermo Posta" on the next line, and the name of the city (preceded by its postal code) on the next. You can collect it at the central post office by showing your passport or photo-bearing ID and paying a small fee. American Express also has a general-delivery service. There's no charge for cardholders, holders of American Express Traveler's checks, or anyone who booked a vacation with American Express.

POSTAL RATES Airmail letters and postcards (lightweight stationery) to the United States and Canada cost €.52 for the first 20 grams; for heavier stationery you should go to the post office. Always stick the blue airmail tag on your mail, or write "Airmail" in big, clear characters to the side of the address. Postcards and letters (for the first 20 grams) to any EU country, including Italy, cost €.41.

Posta Prioritaria (stationery and small packages up to 2 kilograms) and the more expensive Postacelere (up to 20 kilograms) are special delivery services from the post office that guarantee delivery within 24 hours in Italy and three to five days abroad. Lightweight stationery sent as Posta Prioritaria to the United States and Canada costs €.77 (for the first 20 grams, double that for parcels up to 100 grams); to the United Kingdom, Italy, and all other EU countries it costs €.62. As regular stamps are not valid for this service, make sure you buy the special golden Posta Prioritaria stamps. Postacelere rates to the United States and Canada are between €23.76 (€15.49 to the United Kingdom and Europe) for parcels up to 500 grams (a little over a pound) and €184.90 (€76.44 to the United Kingdom and Europe) for packages weighing 20 kilos.

You can buy stamps at tobacconists and post offices.

🚩 **Informazioni Poste Italiane** ☎ 160, €.31 for information in Italian about rates and local post offices' opening hours; 800/160000 toll-free for information about Postacelere ⊕ www.poste.it.

MONEY MATTERS

Venice, Milan, Florence, and Rome are the more expensive Italian cities to visit. Taxes are usually included in hotel bills; there is a 20% tax on car rentals, usually included in the rates. A cup of espresso enjoyed while standing at a bar costs from €.60 to €.80, the same cup served at a table, triple that. At a bar, beer costs about €3.70, a soft drink €1.40–€2. A *tramezzino* (small sandwich) costs about €2, a more substantial one about €3. You will pay about €10 for a short taxi ride. Admission to a major museum is about €8.

CREDIT CARDS Credit cards are generally accepted in shops and hotels but may not always be welcome in restaurants. When you wish to leave a tip beyond the 15% service charge that is usually included with your bill, leave it in cash rather than adding it to the credit card slip.

CURRENCY The euro is the main unit of currency in Italy, as well as in 11 other European countries. Under the euro system, there are eight coins: 1, 2, 5, 10, 20, and 50 *centesimi* (cents), at 100 centesimi to the euro, and 1 and 2 euros. There are seven notes: 5, 10, 20, 50, 100, 200, and 500 euros. At press time, the exchange rate was about 0.94 euros to the U.S. dollar; 0.61 euros to the Canadian dollar; 1.52 euros to the pound sterling; 0.55 euros to the Australian dollar; 0.51 euros to the New Zealand dollar; and 0.10 euros to the South African rand.

SALES TAX Foreign tourists who have spent more than €155 (before tax) in one store can obtain a refund of Italy's value-added tax (IVA). At the time of purchase, with passport or ID in hand, ask the store for an invoice describing the article or articles and the total euro amount. If your destination when you leave Italy is a non-EU country, you must have the invoice stamped at customs upon departure from Italy; if your destination is another EU country, you must obtain the customs stamp upon departure from that country. Once back home—and within 90 days of the date of purchase—you must send the stamped invoice back to the store, which should forward the IVA rebate directly to you. If the store participates in the Europe Tax-Free Shopping System (those that do display a sign to the effect), things are simpler. To calculate the price without IVA, you don't subtract 20% from the price on the label, which already includes IVA. Instead, you need to subtract roughly 16.5%. Transaction fees, which go to the companies providing the tax-free service, are 3%–4%, so in this case you should expect to get only about 13% of the purchase price back.

TELEPHONES

The country code for Italy is 39. Do not drop the 0 in the regional code when calling Italy.

To place an international call, insert a phone card, dial 00, then the country code, area code, and phone number. To reach an operator for collect calls, dial 170 and 172/3535 if you're having difficulty with an international call. The cheaper and easier option, however, is to use your AT&T, MCI, or Sprint calling card. You can also purchase a phone card at a tobacconist. The best card for calling North America or Europe is the Europa card, which gives you a local number to dial and a PIN. The card is sold in units of three hours (with the €5 card) or six hours (with the €10 card).

🛈 Access Codes **AT&T Direct** ☎ 800/172-444. **MCI WorldPhone** ☎ 800/172-401 or 800/172-404. **Sprint International Access** ☎ 800/172-405.

Prepaid *carte telefoniche* (calling cards) are prevalent throughout Italy. You can buy the card (values vary) at post offices, tobacconists, most news stalls, and bars. Tear off the corner of the card and insert it in the telephone's slot. When you dial, the card's value appears in the window. After you hang up, the card is returned so you can use it until its value runs out.

SAFETY

Always be on guard against pickpockets and purse snatchers in the main tourist cities, particularly in crowded buses and trains in Rome, Milan, and Naples, and on board the vaporetti in Venice; in Naples, it's advisable to carry your bags on the side facing away from the street, as purse snatchers here more often than not ride scooters. Especially in Rome and Florence, watch out for bands of Gypsy children, expert at lifting wallets. Keep the children at a distance, and don't be shy about shouting at them to stay away. Small cities and towns are usually safe.

TIPPING

Tipping practices vary depending on where you are. Italians tip smaller amounts in small cities and towns, often not at all in cafés and taxis north of Rome. The following guidelines apply in major cities.

In restaurants a 15% service charge is usually added to the total; it's customary to give the waiter an additional 5%–10%, depending on the service and on the quality of the meal. Charges for service are included in all hotel bills, but smaller tips to staff members are appreciated. In general, in a $$ hotel, chambermaids should be given about €.75 per day, or about €4.50–€5 a week; bellhops should get €1. Tip at least €1 for room service and valet service. Tip breakfast waiters €.25 per day per table (at end of stay). These amounts should be increased by 40% in $$$ hotels, doubled in $$$$ hotels. Give the concierge about 15% of the bill for services. Tip doormen about €.50 for calling a cab.

Taxi drivers are happy with 5%–10%, although Italians rarely tip them. Porters at railroad stations and airports charge a fixed rate per suitcase; tip an additional €.50 per person, more if the porter is very helpful. Tip service-station attendants €1 if they are especially helpful. Tip guides about €1.50 per person for a half-day tour, more if they are very good.

TRAIN TRAVEL

The fastest trains on the Trenitalia, the Italian State Railways, are the Eurostar trains, operating on several main lines, including Rome–Milan via Florence and Bologna. Supplement is included in the fare; seat reservations are mandatory at all times. Ask for seats located away from the smoking car, as the poorly designed partitions are not smoke-proof. To avoid having to squeeze through narrow aisles, board only at your car (look for the number on the reservation ticket). Car numbers are displayed on their exterior. Next-fastest trains are the Intercity (IC) trains, for which you pay a supplement and for which seat reservations may be required and are always advisable. *Diretto* and *Interregionale* trains usually make more stops and are a little slower. *Regionale* and *Locale* trains are the slowest; many serve commuters. For train information, call Trenitalia or visit the Web site.

You can buy tickets and make seat reservations at travel agencies up to two months in advance, thereby avoiding lines at station ticket windows or automated ticket vendors. All tickets must be date-stamped in the small yellow or red machines near the tracks before you board. Once stamped, tickets are valid for six hours on distances of less than 200 km (124 mi) or for 24 hours on distances of 200 km or more. If you wish to stop along the way and your final destination is more than 200 km away, you can stamp the ticket a second time before it expires to extend its validity to a maximum of 48 hours from the time it was first stamped. You can get on and off at will for the duration of the ticket's validity. If you don't stamp your ticket in the machine, you must actively seek out a conductor to validate the ticket on the train for an extra fee. If you merely wait in your seat for him to collect your ticket, unless the train is overcrowded, you risk a heavier fine. You will pay a hefty surcharge if you purchase your ticket on board the train. Tickets for destinations within a 200-km (124-mi) range can be purchased at any *tabacchi* (tobacconist) inside the station. There is a refreshment service on most long-distance trains. Trains are very crowded at holiday times; always reserve. Traveling by night is inexpensive, but never leave your belongings unattended and make sure the door of your compartment is locked.

🚈 Trenitalia ☎ 166/105050 🌐 www.trenitalia.it.

VISITOR INFORMATION
Information is available at regional and local agencies, either the Azienda di Promozione Turistica (APT) or the Ente Provinciale per il Turismo (EPT), as well as municipal tourist offices and others known as Informazione e Accoglienza Turistica (IAT) or Pro Loco in small towns.

WHEN TO GO
The best months for sightseeing are April–June, September, and October, which are usually pleasant and not too hot.

CLIMATE In general the northern half of the peninsula and the entire Adriatic Coast, with the exception of Apulia, are rainier than the rest of Italy. In Venice, fog and high tides are likely to be part of the landscape between November and February. The hottest months are July and August, when brief afternoon thunderstorms are common in inland areas. Winters are relatively mild in most places on the tourist circuit, but there are always some rainy spells. The following are average daily maximum and minimum temperatures for Rome and Milan.

ROME

Jan.	52F	11C	May	74F	23C	Sept.	79F	26C
	40	5		56	13		62	17
Feb.	55F	13C	June	82F	28C	Oct.	71F	22C
	42	6		63	17		55	13
Mar.	59F	15C	July	87F	30C	Nov.	61F	16C
	45	7		67	20		49	9
Apr.	66F	19C	Aug.	86F	30C	Dec.	55F	13C
	50	10		67	20		44	6

MILAN

	°F	°C		°F	°C		°F	°C
Jan.	40F	5C	May	74F	23C	Sept.	75F	24C
	32	0		57	14		61	16
Feb.	46F	8C	June	80F	27C	Oct.	63F	17C
	35	2		63	17		52	11
Mar.	56F	13C	July	84F	29C	Nov.	51F	10C
	43	6		67	20		43	6
Apr.	65F	18C	Aug.	82F	28C	Dec.	43F	6C
	49	9		66	16		35	2

ROME

For 2,500 years, emperors, popes, and the citizens of the ages have left their mark on Rome, and the result is like nothing so much as a hustling, bustling open-air museum. Most of the city's major sights are in the *centro storico* (historic center), which lies between the long, straight Via del Corso and the Tevere (Tiber River), and the adjacent area of *Roma antica* (ancient Rome), site of the Foro Romano (Roman Forum) and Colosseo (Colosseum). The best way to discover the city is to wander, taking time to notice the layers of history that make Rome unique. On your way between monuments and museums note the changing architectural landscape: the soft curves of medieval Rome, which covered the horn of land that pushes the Tiber toward the Vatican and extended across the river into Trastevere, and the formal elegance of Renaissance Rome, which was erected upon medieval foundations and extended as far as the Vatican, with showcase villas created in what were then the outskirts of the city.

Exploring Rome

Numbers in the margin correspond to points of interest on the Rome map.

The layout of the centro storico is irregular, but several landmarks serve as orientation points to identify the areas that most visitors come to see: the Colosseo, Pantheon, Piazza Navona, St. Peter's Basilica, the Spanish Steps, and the Baths of Caracalla. You'll need a good map to find your way around; newsstands offer a wide choice. Much of your sightseeing in the historic center can, and should, be done on foot, since most automobile traffic is barred during the day. To move between the center and sites that are farther afield, take taxis, buses, or the metro. If you are in Rome during a hot spell, do as the Romans do: start out early in the morning, have a light lunch and a long siesta during the hottest hours, then resume sightseeing in the late afternoon and end your evening with a leisurely meal outdoors, refreshed by cold Frascati wine and the *ponentino,* the cool evening breeze.

Ancient Rome

The geographic center of the city is at Piazza Venezia, site of the late-19th-century monument to the first king of a united Italy, Vittorio Emanuele II. The most evocative ruins of the ancient city extend from the Campidoglio across the Foro Romano to the Colosseo and the Terme di Caracalla and include the Palatino and Circo Massimo. This is one of the world's most striking and significant concentrations of historic remains; stand at the back of the Campidoglio overlooking the Roman Forum and take in 2,500 years of history at a glance.

8 **Arco di Costantino** (Arch of Constantine). The best preserved of Rome's triumphal arches, this 4th-century monument commemorates Constantine's victory over Maxentius at the Milvian Bridge. Just before this battle in AD 312, Constantine had a vision of a cross in the heavens and heard the words: "In this sign thou shalt conquer." The victory led not only to the construction of this majestic marble arch but also to a turning point in the history of Christianity: soon afterward a grateful—and converted—Constantine decreed that it was a lawful religion and should be tolerated throughout the empire. His newfound faith didn't seem to cure his imperial sticky fingers, however; the arch's decorations were pilfered from monuments to earlier emperors. ⊠ *Piazza del Colosseo.*

❷ Campidoglio (Capitoline Hill). The majestic ramp and beautifully proportioned piazza are the handiwork of Michelangelo (1475–1564), who also designed the facades of the three palaces that face this square on Capitoline Hill. Palazzo Senatorio, at the center, is still the ceremonial seat of Rome's City Hall; it was built over the Tabularium, where ancient Rome's state archives were kept. The statue at the center of the square is a copy of an ancient Roman bronze of Marcus Aurelius (AD 120–180). The Capitoline Museums, the two palaces flanking the Senatorio, house the original. ⊠ *Piazza del Campidoglio.*

★ ❻ Colosseo (Colosseum). Massive and majestic, this ruin is ancient Rome's hallmark monument, inaugurated in AD 80 with a program of games and shows that lasted 100 days. Before the imperial box, gladiators would salute the emperor and cry, *"Ave, imperator, morituri te salutant"* ("Hail, emperor, men soon to die salute thee"); it is said that when one day they heard the emperor Claudius respond, "Or maybe not," they became so offended that they called a strike. The Colosseum could hold more than 50,000 spectators; it was faced with marble, decorated with stuccos, and had an ingenious system of awnings to provide shade. It was built in just eight years. The Colosseum takes its name from a colossal, 118-foot statue of Nero that once stood nearby. ⊠ *Piazza del Colosseo,* ☎ 06/39967700 ⊕ *www.archeorm.arti.beniculturali.it* ⊗ *Tues.–Sun. 9–4:30.*

❼ Domus Aurea. Nero's "Golden House" is a sprawling example of the excesses of Imperial Rome. After fire destroyed much of the city in AD 64, Nero took advantage of the resultant open space to construct a palace so large that contemporary accounts complained his house was bigger than the rest of the city. One wing of the building was given over to public functions, and the other served as the emperor's private residence. More than 150 rooms have been excavated (although only a few are open to the public), revealing a subterranean trove of ancient Roman architecture and some well-preserved Roman paintings decorating the walls. ⊠ *Via della Domus Aurea,* ☎ *06/39967700 reservations* ⊕ *www.archeorm.arti.beniculturali.it* ⊗ *Wed.–Mon. 9–7:45.*

❺ Foro Romano (Roman Forum). Rome's foundations as a world capital and crossroads of culture are to be found here—literally. Excavations have shown that this site was in use as a burial ground as far back as the 10th century BC, hundreds of years before Rome's legendary founding by Romulus. But the Forum gained importance (and the name in use today) during Roman and Imperial times, when this marshy hollow was the political, commercial, and social center of Rome, and by extension, of the ancient world. The majestic ruins of temples and palaces visible today are fragments of the massive complex of markets, civic buildings, and houses of worship that dominated the city in its heyday. Wander down the **Via Sacra**, which runs the length of the Roman Forum, and take in the timeless view; then climb the **Colle Palatino** (Palatine Hill), where the emperors had their palaces and where 16th-century cardinals strolled in elaborate Renaissance gardens. From the *belvedere* (overlook) you have a good view of the **Circo Massimo** (Circus Maximus).

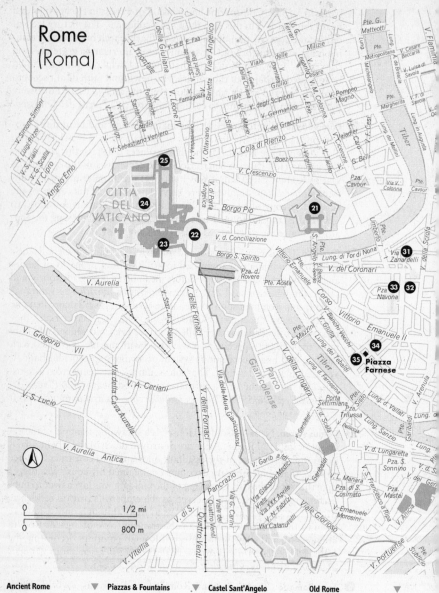

Rome
(Roma)

CITTÀ DEL VATICANO

V. Aurelia

V. Gregorio VII

Parco Gianicolense

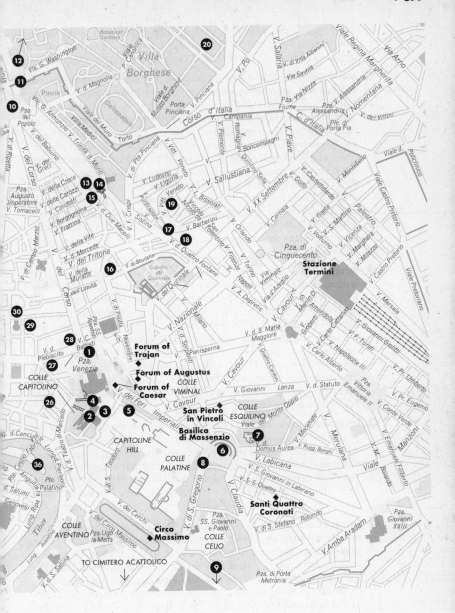

Audio guides are available at the bookshop–ticket office at the Via dei Fori Imperiali entrance. ⊠ *Entrances at Via dei Fori Imperiali and Piazza del Colosseo,* ☎ *06/39967700* ⊕ *www.pierreci.it* ⊙ *Daily 9–4:30.*

❸ **Musei Capitolini** (Capitoline Museums). The **Museo Capitolino** and **Palazzo dei Conservatori,** the palaces flanking Palazzo Senatorio on the Campidoglio, form a single museum holding some fine classical sculptures, including the gilded bronze equestrian statue of Marcus Aurelius that once stood on the pedestal in the piazza, as well as the *Dying Gaul,* the *Capitoline Venus,* and a series of portrait busts of ancient philosophers and emperors. In the courtyard of Palazzo dei Conservatori on the right of the piazza are mammoth fragments of a colossal statue of the emperor Constantine (circa 280–336). Inside are splendidly frescoed salons still used for municipal ceremonies, as well as sculptures and paintings. Don't miss the superb baroque painting collection in the Pinacoteca, which holds masterpieces by Caravaggio and Rubens, among other stars. ⊠ *Piazza del Campidoglio,* ☎ *06/39967800* ⊕ *www.pierreci.it* ⊙ *Tues.–Sun. 9–8.*

Fodor'sChoice
★

❶ **Piazza Venezia.** Considered the geographical heart of the city, the square is dominated by the **Monumento a Vittorio Emanuele II,** or Altare della Patria (Victor Emmanuel Monument, or Altar of the Nation), the enormous marble monument (1911) honoring the first king of unified Italy, Vittorio Emanuele II (1820–78). Climb to the top of the "Vittoriano" for a stunning panorama over Rome. The piazza takes its name from the smaller but more historically important Palazzo Venezia, once Mussolini's headquarters. His most famous speeches were delivered from its balcony to the roaring crowds below. ⊠ *Square at intersection of Via del Corso, Via del Plebiscito, and Via del Fori Imperiali,* ⊙ *Tues.–Sun. 10:30–1 hr before sunset.*

❹ **Santa Maria d'Aracoeli.** The 13th-century church on the Campidoglio can be reached by a long flight of steep stairs or, more easily, by way of the stairs on the far side of the Museo Capitolino. Stop in to see the medieval pavement, the Renaissance gilded ceiling that commemorates the victory of Lepanto, and the Pinturicchio (1454–1513) frescoes. ⊠ *Piazza Aracoeli,* ☎ *06/6798155* ⊙ *Oct.–May, daily 7–noon and 4–6; June–Sept., daily 7–noon and 4–6:30.*

❾ **Terme di Caracalla** (Baths of Caracalla). The scale of the towering ruins of ancient Rome's most beautiful and luxurious public baths hint at their past splendor. Inaugurated by Caracalla in AD 217, the baths were used until the 6th century. An ancient version of a swank athletic club, the baths were open to all, though men and women used them separately; citizens could bathe, socialize, and exercise in huge pools and richly decorated halls and libraries. ⊠ *Via delle Terme di Caracalla 52* ☎ *06/ 39967700* ⊕ *www.pierreci.it* ⊙ *Mon. 9–2, Tues.–Sun. 9–4.*

Piazzas & Fountains

The lush park of Villa Borghese is dotted with pines and fountains and faux neoclassical-style ruins. It is a happy conjunction of the pleasure gardens and palaces of Renaissance prelates on the site of ancient Roman villas. It also holds the world-class museums of the Galleria Borghese and Villa Giulia. The Pincio, the ancient Pincian Hill, is a belvedere over the city and a vantage point over elegant pedestrian Piazza del Popolo, below. Via del Corso, with its many midrange shops, runs straight to Piazza di Venezia and is intersected with upscale shopping streets, including Via Condotti, which lead to the bustle of the Piazza di Spagna. The scene at the nearby Fontana di Trevi is equally crowded, forcing the wishful to toss their coins into the fountain from center field.

★ **⑯ Fontana di Trevi** (Trevi Fountain). A spectacular fantasy of mythical sea creatures and cascades of splashing water, this fountain is one of Rome's baroque greats. The fountain as you see it was completed in the mid-1700s, but there had been a drinking fountain on the site for centuries. Pope Urban VIII (1568–1644) almost sparked a revolt when he slapped a tax on wine to cover the expenses of having the fountain repaired. Legend has it that a coin tossed into the fountain ensures a return trip to Rome. ⊠ *Piazza di Trevi.*

★ **⑳ Galleria Borghese.** At the southeast corner of Villa Borghese, a park studded with pines and classical statuary, is this gallery created by Cardinal Scipione Borghese in the early 17th century as a showcase for his fabulous collection of ancient sculpture and baroque painting. Highlights of the collection are the seductive reclining statue of Pauline Borghese by Canova (1757–1822) and some extraordinary works by Bernini (1598–1680), including the virtuoso *Apollo and Daphne.* The painting collection is no less impressive, with works by Caravaggio (1573–1610), Raphael (1483–1520), and Titian (circa 1488–1576), but the palace's restored magnificence is such that it would be a must-see even if it were empty. ⊠ *Piazza Scipione Borghese 5, off Via Pinciana* ☎ *06/8548577 information; 06/328102 reservations* ⊕ *www.galleriaborghese.it information or www.beniculturali.it ticketing* ⊘ *Tues.–Sun. 9–7; reservations required, entrance every 2 hrs.*

⑮ Keats–Shelley Memorial House. To the right of the Spanish Steps is the house where Keats (1795–1821) died; the building is now a museum dedicated to English Romanticism and Keats and Shelley memorabilia. It also houses a library of works by Romantic authors. ⊠ *Piazza di Spagna 26, next to the Spanish Steps* ☎ *06/6784235* ⊕ *www.keats-shelley-house.org* ⊘ *Weekdays 9–1 and 3–6, Sat. 11–2 and 3–6.*

⑫ Museo Etrusco di Villa Giulia (Etruscan Museum of Villa Giulia). Pope Julius III (1487–1555) built this gracious Renaissance villa as a summer retreat. It's been turned into a fine museum dedicated to the Etruscans, central Italy's pre-Roman inhabitants. The collection, a well-explained cross section of Etruscan statuary and sculpture, provides an introduction to this complex and ancient culture that is an interesting counterpoint to the city's usual emphasis on Imperial and Papal Rome. ⊠ *Piazzale di Villa Giulia 9* ☎ *06/32810* ⊕ *www.beniculturali.it* ⊘ *Tues.–Sun. 8:30–7:30.*

⑱ Palazzo Barberini (Barberini Palace). Rome's most splendid 17th-century palace houses the **Galleria Nazionale di Arte Antica.** Its gems include Raphael's *La Fornarina* and many other fine paintings, some lavishly frescoed ceilings, and a suite of rooms decorated in 1782 on the occasion of the marriage of a Barberini heiress. ⊠ *Via Barberini 18* ☎ *06/32810* ⊕ *www.galleriaborghese.it* ⊘ *Tues.–Sun. 9–7.*

⑰ Piazza Barberini. This busy crossroads is marked by two Bernini fountains: the saucy **Fontana del Tritone** (Triton Fountain) in the middle of the square and the **Fontana delle Api** (Fountain of the Bees) at the corner of Via Veneto. Decorated with the heraldic Barberini bees, the shell-shape fountain bears an inscription that was immediately seen as an unlucky omen by the superstitious Romans: it proclaimed that the fountain had been erected in the 22nd year of the reign of Pope Urban VIII, who commissioned it, whereas in fact the 21st anniversary of his election was still some weeks away. The incorrect numeral was hurriedly erased, but to no avail: Urban died eight days before the beginning of his 22nd year as pontiff. ⊠ *Square at intersection of Via del Tritone, Via Vittorio Veneto, and Via Barberini.*

⑩ **Piazza del Popolo.** Designed by neoclassical architect Giuseppe Valadier in the early 1800s, this circular square is one of the largest and airiest in Rome. It's a pleasant spot for an afternoon stroll. The 3,000-year-old obelisk in the middle of the square, brought to Rome from Egypt by the emperor Augustus, once stood in the Circus Maximus. ⊠ *Southern end of Via Flaminia and northern end of Via del Corso.*

⑬ **Piazza di Spagna.** The square is the heart of Rome's chic shopping district and a popular rendezvous spot, especially for the young people who throng the **Spanish Steps** on evenings and weekend afternoons. In the center of the elongated square, at the foot of the Spanish Steps, is the **Fontana della Barcaccia** (Old Boat Fountain) by Pietro Bernini (Gian Lorenzo's father). ⊠ *Southern end of Via del Babuino and northern end of Via Due Macelli.*

⑲ **Santa Maria della Concezione.** In the crypt under the main Capuchin church, skeletons and scattered bones of some 4,000 Capuchin monks are arranged in odd decorative designs, intended as a macabre reminder of the impermanence of earthly life. ⊠ *Via Veneto 27* ☎ *06/4871185* ☼ *Fri.–Wed. 9–noon and 3–6.*

⑪ **Santa Maria del Popolo.** This medieval church rebuilt by Gian Lorenzo Bernini in baroque style is rich in art; the pièces de résistance are two stunning Caravaggios in the chapel to the left of the main altar. ⊠ *Piazza del Popolo,* ☎ *06/3610836* ☼ *Mon.–Sat. 7–7, Sun. 8–2 and 4:30–7:30.*

★ ⑭ **Scalinata di Trinitá dei Monti** (Spanish Steps). The 200-year-old stairway got its nickname from the nearby Spanish Embassy to the Holy See (the Vatican), though it was built with French funds in 1723 as the approach to the French church of **Trinità dei Monti** at the top of the steps. Rome's classic picture-postcard view is even more lovely when the steps are banked with blooming azaleas, from mid-April to mid-May. ⊠ *Piazza di Spagna and Piazza Trinità dei Monti.*

Castel Sant'Angelo & the Vatican

Given that the Vatican has many of Rome's (and the world's) greatest art treasures, as well as being the spiritual home of a billion Catholics, this area of the city is full of tourists and pilgrims almost year-round. Between the Vatican and the once-moated bulk of Castel Sant'Angelo, the pope's covered passageway flanks an enclave of workers and craftspeople, the old Borgo neighborhood, whose workaday charm is beginning to succumb to gentrification.

㉑ **Castel Sant'Angelo** (Sant'Angelo Castle). Transformed into a formidable fortress, this castle was originally built as the tomb of Emperor Hadrian (AD 76–138) in the 2nd century AD. In its early days it looked much like the Augusteo (Tomb of Augustus), which still stands in more or less its original form across the river. Hadrian's Tomb was incorporated into the city's walls and served as a military stronghold during the barbarian invasions. According to legend it got its present name in the 6th century, when Pope Gregory the Great, passing by in a religious procession, saw an angel with a sword appear above the ramparts to signal the end of the plague that was raging. Enlarged and fortified, the castle became a refuge for the popes, who fled to it along the Passetto, an arcaded passageway that links it with the Vatican.

Inside the castle are ancient corridors, medieval cells, and Renaissance salons, a museum of antique weapons, courtyards piled with stone cannonballs, and terraces with great views of the city. The highest terrace of all, under the bronze statue of the legendary angel, is the one from which Puccini's heroine Tosca threw herself to her death. **Ponte Sant'Angelo,** the ancient bridge spanning the Tiber in front of the castle, is decorated with lovely baroque angels designed by Bernini. ⌧ *Lungotevere Castello 50* ☎ *06/39967700* ⊕ *www.pierreci.it* ⊘ *Tues.–Sun. 9–8.*

24 **Giardini Vaticani** (Vatican Gardens). The attractively landscaped gardens can be seen in a two-hour tour that shows you a few historical monuments, fountains, and the lovely 16th-century house of Pius IV (1499–1565), designed by Pirro Ligorio (1500–83), as well as the Vatican's mosaic school. Vistas from within the gardens give you a different perspective on the basilica itself. Reserve two or three days in advance. ⌧ *Centro Servizi, south side of Piazza San Pietro* ☎ *06/ 69884466* 🖷 *06/69885100* ⊕ *www.vatican.va* 🖅 *€9 for the Gardens tour; €19 for Gardens and Sistine Chapel* ⊘ *Mon.–Sat.*

25 **Musei Vaticani** (Vatican Museums). One of the world's greatest collections of Western art, the holdings of the Vatican Museum are an embarrassment of riches that include Ancient Egyptian sarcophagi, Greek and Roman statuary, paintings by Giotto, Leonardo, and Raphael, and Michelangelo's magnificent frescoes in the Sistine Chapel. The nearly 8 km (5 mi) of displays are said to represent only a small part of the Vatican's holdings. The museums are almost unavoidably overwhelming and include the famed **Cappella Sistina** (Sistine Chapel). In 1508 Pope Julius II (1443–1513) commissioned Michelangelo to paint the more than 10,000 square feet of the chapel's ceiling. For four years Michelangelo dedicated himself to painting in the fresco technique, over wet plaster, and the result is one of the Renaissance's masterworks. Cleaning has removed centuries of soot and revealed the original and surprisingly brilliant colors of the ceiling and the *Last Judgment.* The chapel is almost always unpleasantly crowded—try to avoid the tour groups by going early or late. A pair of binoculars and an illustrated or audio guide will contribute greatly to understanding and appreciating the work.

A complete list of the great works on display would go on for pages; don't-miss highlights, however, certainly include the Egyptian collection, the Roman mosaics and wall paintings, and the great classical- and Hellenistic-style statuary in the Belvedere Courtyard, including the *Laocoön,* the *Belvedere Torso* (which inspired Michelangelo), and the *Apollo Belvedere.* The **Stanze di Raffaello** (Raphael Rooms) are decorated with masterful frescoes, and there are more of Raphael's works in the **Pinacoteca** (Picture Gallery). Bored children may perk up in the whimsical **Sala degli Animali,** a seemingly forgotten room full of animal statuary. ⌧ *Viale Vaticano* ☎ *06/69884947* ⊕ *www.vatican.va* ⊘ *Easter week and mid-Mar.–Oct., weekdays 8:45–4:45 (no admission after 3:45), Sat. and last Sun. of month 8:45–1:45 (no admission after 12:30); Nov.–mid-Mar. (except Easter week), Mon.–Sat. and last Sun. of month 8:45–1:45 (no admission after 12:30). Note: Ushers at the entrance of St. Peter's Basilica and the Vatican Museums will not allow entry to persons with inappropriate clothing (no bare knees, shoulders, or low-cut shirts).*

22 **Piazza San Pietro** (St. Peter's Square). Gian Lorenzo Bernini designed this vast, circular piazza in the 17th century with an eye to the dramatic contrast between the dark, narrow medieval streets of the area and the wide open space of the piazza, presided over by the magnificence of St. Peter's Basilica. Unfortunately for art history, Mussolini had his own ideas about dramatic effect, which led him to raze much of the medieval neighborhood around the square to create Via della Conciliazione, the broad avenue that leads to the square today. Other aspects of Bernini's vision of architectural harmony remain, however: look for the stone disks in the

Fodor'sChoice ★

pavement halfway between the fountains and the obelisk. From these points the colonnades seem to be formed of a single row of columns all the way around. The square was designed to accommodate crowds, and it has held up to 400,000 people at one time. At noon on Sunday when he is in Rome, the pope appears at his third-floor study window in the **Palazzo Vaticano,** to the right of the basilica, to bless the crowd in the square, and in warm months he blesses visitors from a podium on the basilica steps on Wednesday mornings. ⊠ *End of Via Conciliazione.*

Since the Lateran Treaty of 1929, Vatican City has been an independent and sovereign state, which covers about 108 acres and is surrounded by thick, high walls. Its gates are watched over by the Swiss Guards, who still wear the colorful dress uniforms based on a Michelangelo design. Sovereign of this little state is the pope of the Roman Catholic Church. For many visitors a **papal audience** is the highlight of a trip to Rome. Mass audiences take place on Wednesday morning in the square or in a modern audience hall (capacity 7,000) off the left-hand colonnade. Tickets are necessary. For audience tickets write or fax well in advance indicating the date you prefer, language you speak, and hotel in which you will stay. Or, apply for tickets in person on the Monday or Tuesday before the Wednesday audience. ⊠ *Tickets: Prefettura della Casa Pontificia, 00120 Vatican City* ☎ *06/69883273* 🖷 *06/69885863* ⊙ *Mon.–Sat. 9–1.*

★ ㉓ **St. Peter's Basilica** (Basilica di San Pietro). In its staggering grandeur and magnificence, St. Peter's Basilica is best appreciated as the lustrous background for ecclesiastical ceremonies thronged with the faithful. The original basilica was built in the early 4th century AD by the emperor Constantine, above an earlier shrine that supposedly marked the burial place of St. Peter. After more than 1,000 years, the decrepit old basilica had to be torn down. The task of building a new, much larger one took almost 200 years and employed the genius of many of the Renaissance's greatest architects, including Alberti (1404–72), Bramante (1444–1514), Raphael, Peruzzi (1481–1536), Antonio Sangallo the Younger (1483–1546), and Michelangelo, who died before the dome he had planned could be completed. The structure was finally finished in 1626.

The most famous work of art inside is Michelangelo's *Pietà* (1498), in the first chapel on the right as you enter the basilica. Michelangelo carved four statues of the Pietà, or Mary cradling her dead son; this one is the earliest and best known, two others are in Florence, and the fourth, the *Rondanini Pietà,* is in Milan. At the end of the central aisle is the bronze statue of St. Peter, its foot worn by centuries of reverent kisses. The bronze throne above the altar in the apse was created by Bernini to contain a simple wood-and-ivory chair believed to have once belonged to St. Peter. Bernini's baldachin over the papal altar was made with bronze stripped from the dome of the Pantheon at the order of Pope Urban VIII, one of the powerful Roman Barberini family. His practice of plundering ancient monuments for material with which to carry out his grandiose decorating schemes inspired the famous quip "*Quod non fecerunt barbari, fecerunt Barberini*" ("What the barbarians didn't do, the Barberinis did").

As you stroll up and down the aisles and transepts, notice the fine mosaic copies of famous paintings above the altars, the monumental tombs and statues, and the fine stuccowork. Stop at the **Museo Storico** (Historical Museum), which contains some priceless liturgical objects. ⊙ *Apr.–Sept., daily 9–6; Oct.–Mar., daily 9–5.*

The entrance to **Le Sacre Grotte Vaticane** (Tombs of the Popes) is in one of the huge piers under the dome, next to the central altar. It's best to leave this visit for last, as the crypt's only exit takes you outside the church. It occupies the area of the original basilica, over the necropolis (left beyond Arco delle Campane entrance to Vatican), the ancient burial ground where evidence of what may be St. Peter's burial place has been found. ☉ *Apr.–Sept., daily 7–6; Oct.–Mar., daily 7–5.*

To see the **roof and dome** of the basilica, take the elevator or climb the stairs in the courtyard near the exit from the Vatican Grottoes. From the roof you can climb a short interior staircase to the base of the dome for an overhead view of the basilica's interior. Then, and only if you are in good shape, you should attempt the very long, strenuous, and claustrophobic climb up the narrow stairs to the balcony of the lantern atop the dome, where you can look down on the Giardini Vaticani (Vatican Gardens) and out across all of Rome. ✉ *Entrance in courtyard to the left as you leave the basilica* ☉ *Daily 8–5. Closed during ceremonies in the piazza.*

Free 60-minute tours of St. Peter's Basilica are offered in English daily (Monday–Saturday usually starting about 10 AM and 3 PM, Sunday at 2:30 PM) by volunteer guides. They start at the information desk under the basilica portico. At the Ufficio Scavi you can book special tours of the necropolis. Note that entry to St. Peter's, the Musei Vaticani, and the Gardens is barred to those wearing shorts, miniskirts, sleeveless T-shirts, and otherwise revealing clothing. Women can cover bare shoulders and upper arms with scarves; men should wear full-length pants or jeans. ✉ *Piazza San Pietro* ☎ *06/69884466; 06/69885318 necropolis* ⊕ *www. vatican.va* ☉ *Apr.–Sept., daily 7–7; Oct.–Mar., daily 7–6. Closed during ceremonies in the piazza. Apply for a special tour a few days in advance to Ufficio Scavi, or try in morning for the same day. Office: Mon.–Sat. 9–5.*

Old Rome

The land between the Corso and the Tiber bend is packed with churches, patrician palaces, baroque piazzas, and picturesque courtyards, with Piazza Navona as a magnificent central point. In between are narrow streets and intriguing little shops, interspersed with eating places and cafés that are a focus of Rome's easygoing, itinerant nightlife.

㉞ **Campo de' Fiori** (Field of Flowers). This wide square is the site of Rome's best-loved morning market, a crowded and colorful circus of fruits, flowers, and fish, raucously peddled daily 9–2. If you'd rather watch than participate in the genial chaos, sit at one of the casual cafés that line the square. The hooded bronze figure brooding over the piazza is philosopher Giordano Bruno (1548–1600), who was burned at the stake for heresy here in 1600. ✉ *Piazza Campo dei Fiori.*

㉗ **Chiesa del Gesù.** This huge 16th-century church is a paragon of the baroque style and the tangible symbol of the power of the Jesuits, who were a major force in the Counter-Reformation in Europe. Its interior gleams with gold and precious marbles, and it has a fantastically painted ceiling that flows down over the pillars, merging with painted stucco figures to complete the three-dimensional illusion. ✉ *Piazza del Gesù* ☎ *06/697001* ☉ *Daily 7–noon and 4–7.*

㉖ **Fontana delle Tartarughe** (Turtle Fountain). The winsome turtles that are this 16th-century fountain's hallmark are thought to have been added around 1658 by Bernini as a low-budget way to bring the Renaissance fountain into the baroque. Visit it on a stroll through Rome's former Jewish Ghetto, an atmospheric old neighborhood with medieval inscriptions and friezes on the buildings on Via Portico d'Ottavia, and the remains of the Teatro di Marcello (Theater of Marcello), a theater built by Julius Caesar to hold 20,000 spectators. ✉ *Piazza Mattei.*

28 Galleria Doria Pamphili. You can visit this formidable palazzo, still the residence of a princely family, to view the gallery housing the family's art collection, which includes works by Velázquez and Bernini. ✉ *Piazza del Collegio Romano 2* ☎ *06/6797323* ⊕ *www.doriapamphilj.it* ⊙ *Fri.–Wed. 10–5.*

36 Isola Tiberina. Built in 62 BC, Rome's oldest bridge, the **Ponte Fabricio,** links the Ghetto neighborhood on the Tiber's left bank to this little island, with a hospital and the church of San Bartolomeo. The island has been dedicated to healing ever since a temple to Aesculapius was erected here in 291 BC. **Ponte Cestio** links the island with the Trastevere neighborhood on the right bank.

> **off the beaten path**
>
> **OSTIA ANTICA** (Ancient Ostia) – The well-preserved Roman port city of Ostia Antica, near the sea, is now a vast archaeological park just outside Rome, a lovely day trip into the ancient past. Wander through ancient markets and ruined houses, or bring a picnic and enjoy the sea breeze. There's regular train service from the Ostiense Station (Piramide Metro B stop). ✉ *Via dei Romagnoli, Ostia Antica, not far from Fiumicino Airport* ☎ *06/56358099* ⊕ *www.itnw.roma.it* ⊙ *Tues.–Sun. 8:30–5.*

31 Palazzo Altemps. A 15th-century patrician dwelling, the palace is a showcase for the sculpture collection of the **Museo Nazionale Romano** (National Museum of Rome). Informative labels in English make it easy to appreciate such famous sculptures as the intricate carved reliefs on the *Ludovisi Sarcophagus* and the *Galata,* representing the heroic death of a barbarian warrior. ✉ *Piazza Sant'Apollinare 46* ☎ *06/39967700* ⊕ *www.archeorm.arti.beniculturali.it* ⊙ *Tues.–Sun. 9–7:45.*

35 Palazzo Farnese. Now the French Embassy, one of the most beautiful of Rome's many Renaissance palaces dominates Piazza Farnese, where Egyptian marble basins from the Terme di Caracalla have been transformed into fountains. Note the unique brickwork patterns on the palace's facade. ✉ *Piazza Farnese.*

★ **30 Pantheon.** Lauded for millennia for its architectural harmony, the Pantheon is no less impressive in the 21st century. Built in 27 BC by Augustus's general Agrippa and totally rebuilt by Hadrian in the 2nd century AD, this unique temple (consecrated as a church in the Middle Ages) is a mustsee. Notice the equal proportions of the height of the dome and the circular interior—unlike most angular buildings, the Pantheon is designed after a globe. The oculus, or opening in the ceiling, is meant to symbolize the all-seeing eye of heaven; in practice, it illuminates the building and lightens the heavy stone ceiling. In earlier times the dome was covered in bronze, which was later pilfered to construct the baldachin over the altar in St. Peter's. ✉ *Piazza della Rotonda* ☎ *06/68300230* ⊙ *Mon.–Sat. 8:30–7:30, Sun. 9–6, holidays 9–1.*

★ **33 Piazza Navona.** This elongated 17th-century piazza traces the oval form of the underlying Circus of Diocletian. At the center, Bernini's lively **Fontana dei Quattro Fiumi** (Four Rivers Fountain) is a showpiece. The four statues represent rivers in the four corners of the world: the Nile, with its face covered in allusion to its then-unknown source; the Ganges; the Danube; and the Rio de la Plata, with its hand raised. You may hear the legend that this was Bernini's mischievous dig at Borromini's design of the façade of the church of **Sant'Agnese in Agone,** from which the statue seems to be shrinking in horror. In point of fact, the fountain was created in 1651; work on the church's façade began a year or two later. ⊠ *North of Corso Vittorio Emanuele and west of Corso Rinascimento.*

㉜ San Luigi dei Francesi. The clergy of San Luigi considered Caravaggio's roistering and unruly lifestyle scandalous enough, but his realistic treatment of sacred subjects—seen in three paintings here—was just too much for them. They rejected his first version of the altarpiece and weren't particularly happy with the other two works either. Thanks to the intercession of Caravaggio's patron, an influential cardinal, they were persuaded to keep them—a lucky thing, since they are now recognized to be among the artist's finest paintings. Have some coins handy for the light machine. ⊠ *Piazza San Luigi dei Francesi* ☎ *06/688271* ☉ *Fri.–Wed. 8:30–12:30 and 3:30–5, Thurs. 8:30–12:30.*

㉙ Santa Maria sopra Minerva. Rome's only major Gothic church takes its name from the temple of Minerva over which it was built. Inside are some beautiful frescoes by Filippino Lippi (circa 1457–1504); outside in the square is a charming elephant by Bernini carrying an obelisk on its back. ⊠ *Piazza della Minerva* ☎ *06/6793926* ☉ *Daily 7:30–7.*

Where to Eat

Rome has no shortage of restaurants, and what the city lacks in variety of fare is made up for by overall quality. Don't make the mistake of assuming that expensive restaurants serve better or more authentic food; in Rome, you may pay top dollar for nothing more than a flourish of linen and silver. Some of Rome's prime restaurants are worth the expense, but you'll often do better at a more unassuming trattoria or osteria. Romans eat out a lot, and there's Italian fast food that caters to workers on lunch breaks. These places serve anything from a fruit salad and fresh spinach to lasagna and deep-fried cod fillets. Unfortunately, non-Italian cuisines haven't really caught on in Rome, although there are a few excellent Eritrean and Ethiopian places near Termini and some less appealing Chinese restaurants throughout the center. That old Roman standby, the paper-thin, crispy wood-oven pizza, is a low-budget favorite among locals and travelers alike, as is its to-go cousin, the heartier *pizza al taglio.* During August and over Christmas many restaurants close for vacation.

★ **$$$$** ✕ **La Pergola.** High atop Monte Mario, the Cavalieri Hilton's rooftop restaurant has a commanding view of the city below. Trompe-l'oeil ceilings and handsome wood paneling combine with low lighting to create a feeling of intimacy. Celebrated wunder-chef Heinz Beck brings Rome its finest example of Mediterranean *alta cucina* (haute cuisine); dishes are balanced and light, and presentation is striking. For a window table, reserve a month in advance; otherwise, two weeks. ⊠ *Cavalieri Hilton, Via Cadlolo 101* ☎ *06/3509221* ⌂ *Reservations essential* 🏛 *Jacket and tie* ⊟ *AE, DC, MC, V* ☉ *Closed Sun. and Mon. and 2 wks in Dec. No lunch.*

$$$–$$$$ ✕ **Papà Baccus.** Italo Cipriani, owner of Rome's best Tuscan restaurant, takes his meat as seriously as any Tuscan, using real Chianina beef for the house special, *bistecca alla fiorentina* (grilled, thick bone-in steak). If you're avoiding beef, you can sample such dishes as Tuscan bean soup and the sweet and delicate prosciutto from Pratomagno. The welcome here is warm, the service excellent, and the interior elegant. ⊠ *Via Toscana 36* ☎ *06/42742808* ⊟ *AE, DC, MC, V* ⌂ *Reservations essential.*

$$$–$$$$ ✕ **Il Simposio di Costantini.** At the classiest wine bar in town—done out in wrought-iron vines, wood paneling, and velvet—choose from about 30 wines in *degustazione* (available by the glass) or order a bottle from a list of more than 1,000 Italian and foreign labels sold in the shop next door. Food is appropriately fancy: marinated and smoked fish, designer salads, fine cured meats, terrines and pâtés, and stellar cheeses. ⊠ *Piazza Cavour 16* ☎ *06/3211502* ▤ *AE, DC, MC, V* ⊘ *Closed Sun. and last 2 wks of Aug. No lunch Sat.*

★ **$$–$$$** ✕ **Antico Arco.** Antico Arco has won the hearts of foodies from Rome and beyond. The menu changes with the season, but you may find such delights as *flan di taleggio con salsa di funghi* (taleggio flan with mushrooms), or a *carré d'agnello* (rack of lamb) with foie gras sauce and pears in port wine. Don't miss dessert, especially the chocolate soufflé with melted chocolate center. ⊠ *Piazzale Aurelio 7* ☎ *06/5815274* ⚐ *Reservations essential* ▤ *AE, DC, MC, V* ⊘ *No lunch. Closed Sun. and 2 wks in Aug.*

$$–$$$ ✕ **Checchino dal 1887.** Carved out of a hillside made of potsherds from Roman times, Checchino serves the most traditional Roman cuisine—carefully prepared and served without fanfare—in a clean and sober environment. You can try the different meats that make up the soul of Roman cooking, including *trippa* (tripe) and *coratella* (sweetbreads). There's also plenty to choose from for those uninterested in innards. ⊠ *Via di Monte Testaccio 30* ☎ *06/5746318* ▤ *AE, DC, MC, V* ⊘ *Closed Mon., Aug., and during Christmas. No dinner Sun.*

★ **$$–$$$** ✕ **Sangallo.** Small and intimate, this is an old-fashioned restaurant where the owner buys the fish himself and where dinner is meant to last all night. The traditional menu leans heavily toward the gourmet, with dishes like oysters tartare, snapper with foie gras, Texas steaks, and a fixed-price menu based on truffles. There are few tables in the tiny dining room, so make sure to book ahead. ⊠ *Vicolo della Vaccarella 11/A* ☎ *06/6865549* ▤ *AE, DC, MC, V* ⊘ *Closed Sun., 1 wk in Jan., and 2 wks in Aug. No lunch Mon.*

$–$$$ ✕ **Myosotis.** Myosotis does things the old-fashioned way: with hand-rolled pastas, fresh-baked bread, and olive oil brought direct from the owner's farm in Umbria. The vast menu is a selection of updated takes on classic ingredients, as in the *vellutata di ceci e funghi porcini* (chickpea and porcini mushrooms soup), or a time-honored *spigola* (sea bass) filleted and served *in crosta di patate* (in a potato crust). ⊠ *Via della Vaccarella 3/5* ☎ *06/6865554* ▤ *AE, DC, MC, V* ⊘ *Closed Sun., no lunch Mon.*

$$ ✕ **Dal Bolognese.** This classic restaurant is a trendy choice for a leisurely lunch between sightseeing and shopping. Contemporary paintings decorate the dining room, but the real attraction is the lovely piazza—prime people-watching real estate. As the name of the restaurant promises, the cooking here adheres to the hearty tradition of Bologna, with delicious homemade *tortellini in brodo* (tortellini in broth), fresh pastas in creamy sauces, and *bollito misto* (steaming trays of boiled meats). ⊠ *Piazza del Popolo 1* ☎ *06/3611426* ▤ *AE, D, MC, V* ⊘ *Closed 3 wks in Aug. No lunch Mon. or Tues.*

$–$$ ✕ **Dal Toscano.** The hallmarks of this great family-run Tuscan trattoria near the Vatican are friendly and speedy service, an open wood-fired grill, and such classic dishes as *ribollita* (a dense bread and vegetable soup) and the prized bistecca alla fiorentina. Wash it all down with a strong Chianti. All desserts are homemade and delicious. ⊠ *Via Germanico 58* ☎ *06/39725717* ▤ *DC, MC, V* ⊘ *Closed Mon., Aug., and 2 wks in Dec.*

$ ✕ **Alfredo e Ada.** There's no place like home, and you'll feel like you're back there from the moment you squeeze into a table at this hole in the wall just across the river from Castel Sant'Angelo. There's no menu, just plate after plate of whatever Ada thinks you should try, from hearty, classic pastas to *involtini di vitello* (savory veal rolls with tomato) and homemade sausage. Sit back and enjoy—it's all good. ☒ *Via dei Banchi Nuovi 14* ☎ *06/6878842* ▤ *No credit cards* ☉ *Closed weekends.*

$ ✗ **Arancia Blu.** Owner and chef Fabio Passan has a mission: to prove that "vegetarian cuisine" isn't an oxymoron. Start with a leek-and-almond quiche or lemon-ricotta ravioli with squash and sage, and move on to *polpettine vegetali* (meatless meatballs) with a tomato–coriander seed sauce. Gourmet palates will be tickled by the selections of coffee and olive oil, and by the chocolate tasting—14 varieties in all. Vegan and wheat-free dishes are available on request. ☒ *Via dei Latini 65* ☎ *06/ 4454105* ▤ *No credit cards* ☉ *No lunch.*

$ ✗ **Perilli.** A bastion of authentic Roman cooking and trattoria charm since 1911 (the interior has changed very little), this is the place to go to try rigatoni *con pajata* (with veal intestines)—if you're into that sort of thing. Otherwise the carbonara and *all'amatriciana* (spicy tomato sauce with pancetta) are classics. The house wine is a golden nectar from the Castelli Romani. ☒ *Via Marmorata 39* ☎ *06/5742415* ▤ *AE, DC, MC, V* ☉ *Closed Wed.*

Where to Stay

Hotels listed are within walking distance of at least some sights and handy to public transportation. Those in the $$ and $ categories do not have restaurants but serve Continental breakfast. Rooms facing the street may get traffic noise throughout the night, and few hotels in the lower price categories have double-glazed windows. Ask for a quiet room—or bring earplugs. Always make reservations, even if only a few days in advance. Always inquire about discounts. Should you find yourself in Rome without a hotel booking, contact **HR** (☒ Termini Station; Aeroporto Fiumicino ☎ 06/6991000), a reservation service. **EPT** (☒ Via Parigi 5 ☎ 06/48899253 ☐ 06/4819316 ☒ Near Piazza della Repubblica ☒ Aeroporto Fiumicino ☎ 06/65956074 ☒ Stazione Termini ☎ 06/ 4871270), the local tourist office, may be able to help with hotel reservations.

★ $$$$ ⊞ **Eden.** The historic Eden, a haunt of Hemingway, Ingrid Bergman, and Fellini, merits superlatives for dashing elegance and stunning vistas of Rome from the rooftop restaurant and bar (also from some of the most expensive rooms). Precious but discreet antique furnishings, fine linen sheets, and marble baths whisper understated opulence. ☒ *Via Ludovisi 49, 00187* ☎ *06/478121* ☐ *06/4821584* ⊕ *www.hotel-eden.it* ⇗ *112 rooms, 14 suites* ♢ *Restaurant, bar* ▤ *AE, DC, MC, V* ⵙ *EP.*

$$$–$$$$ ⊞ **Scalinata di Spagna.** An old-fashioned pensione loved by generations of romantics, this tiny hotel is booked solid for months ahead. Its location at the top of the Spanish Steps, inconspicuous little entrance, quaint hodgepodge of old furniture, and view from the terrace where you breakfast make it seem like your own special, exclusive inn. ☒ *Piazza Trinità dei Monti 17 00187* ☎ *06/6793006* ☐ *06/69940598* ⊕ *www. hotelscalinata.com* ⇗ *16 rooms* ▤ *AE, D, MC, V.*

★ $$$ ⊞ **Farnese.** An early-20th-century mansion, the Farnese is in a quiet but central residential district. Art deco–style furniture is mixed with enchanting fresco decorations amid its compact rooms, plenty of lounge space, and a roof garden. ☒ *Via Alessandro Farnese 30 00192* ☎ *06/ 3212553* ☐ *06/3215129* ⇗ *23 rooms* ♢ *Bar* ▤ *AE, DC, MC, V* ⵙ *EP.*

★ $$–$$$ ⊞ **Britannia.** A quiet locale off Via Nazionale is only one of the attractions of this small, special hotel, where you will be coddled with luxurious touches such as English-language dailies and local weather reports delivered to your room each morning. The well-furnished rooms (two with a rooftop terrace), frescoed halls, and lounge (where a rich breakfast buffet is served) attest to the fact that the management really cares about superior service and value. ☒ *Via Napoli 64, 00184* ☎ *06/4883153* 🖨 *06/4882343* ⊕ *www.hotelbritannia.it* 🛏 *32 rooms, 1 suite* ♨ *Bar* ☱ *AE, DC, MC, V.*

$$–$$$ 🖭 **Residenza Paolo VI.** Located inside the Vatican walls, the Paolo VI (pronounced Paolo Sesto, Italian for Pope Paul VI) is a convenient base for seeing St. Peter's and the Vatican sights. Rooms in this former monastery have plain furniture and marble floors, but their simplicity is balanced out by the wonderful roof terrace with a view of the basilica. Breakfast is an American-style buffet. ☒ *Via Paolo VI 29, 00193* ☎ *06/68134108* 🖨 *06/6867428* ⊕ *www.residenzapaolovi.com* 🛏 *29* ♨ *Bar* ☱ *AE, D, MC, V.*

$$ 🖭 **Amalia.** Handy to St. Peter's, the Vatican, and the Cola di Rienzo shopping district, this small hotel is owned and operated by the Consoli family—Amalia and her brothers. On several floors of a 19th-century building, it has large rooms with functional furnishings, TVs, minibars, pictures of angels on the walls, and gleaming marble bathrooms (hair dryers included). The Ottaviano stop of Metro A is a block away. ☒ *Via Germanico 66 00192* ☎ *06/39723356* 🖨 *06/39723365* ⊕ *www. hotelamalia.com* 🛏 *30 rooms, 25 with bath or shower* ☱ *AE, MC, V.*

$$ 🖭 **La Residenza.** A converted town house near Via Veneto, this hotel offers good value and first-class comfort at reasonable rates. Public areas are spacious, and guest rooms are comfortable and have large closets and TVs. The hotel's clientele is mainly from the United States. Rates include a generous buffet breakfast. ☒ *Via Emilia 22 00187* ☎ *06/4880789* 🖨 *06/485721* ⊕ *www.thegiannettihotelsgroup.com* 🛏 *28 rooms* ♨ *Bar* ☱ *AE, MC, V.*

$$ 🖭 **Romae.** Near Termini Station, this midsize hotel has clean, spacious rooms with light-wood furniture and small but bright bathrooms. The congenial, helpful management offers special winter rates and welcomes families. Low rates that include breakfast and free Internet access make this a good deal. ☒ *Via Palestro 49, 00185* ☎ *06/4463554* 🖨 *06/4463914* ⊕ *www.hotelromae.com* 🛏 *32 rooms* ☱ *AE, MC, V.*

★ $ 🖭 **Margutta.** This small hotel near the Spanish Steps and Piazza del Popolo has an unassuming lobby but bright, attractive bedrooms with wrought-iron bedsteads and modern baths. ☒ *Via Laurina 34 00187* ☎ *06/3223674* 🖨 *06/3200395* 🛏 *24 rooms* ☱ *AE, DC, MC, V.*

$ 🖭 **Panda.** This is one of the best deals in the neighborhood—particularly remarkable given that the neighborhood is Via della Croce, one of the chic shopping streets around the Spanish Steps. Guest rooms are outfitted in terra-cotta and wrought iron; they're smallish, but quiet, thanks to double-glazed windows. Pay even less by sharing a bath, and in low season, you may have it to yourself. ☒ *Via della Croce 35, 00187Piazza di Spagna* ☎ *06/6780179* 🖨 *69942151* 🛏 *20 rooms, 14 with bath* ☱ *MC, V.*

Nightlife & the Arts

You will find information on scheduled events and shows at the main APT office and other tourist booths. The monthly booklet *Un Ospite a Roma,* free from concierges at some hotels, is another source of information, as is *Wanted in Rome,* published every other Wednesday and available at newsstands. There are listings in English in the back of the weekly *roma c'è* booklet, with handy price and opening hours information for each listing; it is published on Wednesdays and sold at newsstands. If you want to go to the opera, the ballet, or a concert, it's best to ask your concierge to get tickets for you. You can buy some online or at box offices a few days before performances.

The Arts

CONCERTS The main year-round classical concert series in Rome is organized by the **Accademia di Santa Cecilia** (✉ Via della Conciliazione 4 ☎ 06/68801044 ⊕ www.santacecilia.it) near the Vatican. With the 2002 opening of the **Auditorium-Parco della Musica** (✉ Via de Coubertin 15 ☎ 06/80693444; 06/68801044 for information and tickets ⊕ www.musicaperroma.it), Rome has three concert halls, with state-of-the-art acoustics, that host the symphonic music season of the Accademia di Santa Cecila and other important classical, jazz, rock, and pop concerts.

FILM There is one entirely original-language movie theater in Rome, the **Pasquino** (✉ Piazza Sant'Egidio 10, near Piazza Santa Maria in Trastevere ☎ 06/5815208). Otherwise both the **Metropolitan** (✉ Via del Corso 7, off Piazza del Popolo ☎ 06/32600500) and the **Warner Village Moderno** (✉ Piazza della Repubblica 45-46 near the station, ☎ 06/47779202) have one screen dedicated to English-language films from September to June. Programs are listed in Rome's daily newspapers and *roma c'è.* Several other movie theaters now show at least one film in English from time to time; look for *versione originale* (original version) in the listings.

OPERA The opera season runs from November or December through May, and performances are staged in the **Teatro dell'Opera** (✉ Piazza Beniamino Gigli 8, ☎ 06/481601; 06/48160255 for tickets). From May through August performances are held in various outdoor venues, such as the Stadio Olimpico. Smaller opera companies put up their own low-budget, high-quality productions in various venues. Look for posters advertising performances.

Nightlife

Rome's "in" nightspots change frequently, and many fade into oblivion after a brief moment of glory. The best places to find an up-to-date list are the weekly entertainment guide "Trovaroma," published each Thursday in the Italian daily *La Repubblica,* and *roma c'è,* the weekly guide sold at newsstands.

BARS Chic wine bars are drawing more and more trendy Romans all the time. Try the area between the Tiber and Campo de' Fiori or the area west of Piazza Navona for a bit of bar-hopping. One of the grandest places for a drink in well-dressed company is **Le Grand Bar** (✉ Via Vittorio Emanuele Orlando 3 ☎ 06/47091) in the St. Regis Grand Hotel. **Jazz Café** (✉ Via Zanardelli 12 ☎ 06/68210119), near Piazza Navona, is an upscale watering hole with good live music downstairs. A classic choice for a cocktail or evening drink is **Bar della Pace** (✉ Via della Pace 5 ☎ 06/6861216) in the ultra-happening area of town west of Piazza Navona. In summer the atmospheric leafy piazza is excellent for both stargazing and people-watching. **Trinity College** (✉ Via del Collegio Romano 6, near Piazza Venezia ☎ 06/6786472) has two floors of Irish pub trappings, with happy chatter and background music until 3 AM.

DISCOS & NIGHTCLUBS A good area for nightclubs is Testaccio (across the river from Trastevere) and its winding Via di Monte Testaccio, which is literally lined with discos and live music clubs that cater to all tastes. **Suite** (✉ Via degli Orti di Trastevere 1 ☎ 06/5861888) is a hip nightclub in Trastevere with a sleek, futuristic interior. You might spot an American celeb at **Gilda** (✉ Via Mario de' Fiori 97 ☎ 06/6784838), with a disco, piano bar, and live music. It's closed Monday and jackets are required. Just as exclusive is **Bella Blu** (✉ Via Luciani 21 ☎ 06/3230490), a club in Parioli that caters to Rome's elite.

MUSIC CLUBS   For the latest jazz, independent, and ethnic sounds try the **La Palma Club** (✉ Via Giuseppe Mirri 35, ☎ 06/43599029), which, despite its off-the-beaten-track location in the Tiburtino district, has become synonymous with quality and an uncanny ability to woo the best names on the international music scene. Live performances of jazz, soul, and funk by leading musicians draw celebrities to **Alexanderplatz** (✉ Via Ostia 9, in the Vatican area ☎ 06/39742171). The music starts about 10 PM, and you can have supper while you wait.

Shopping

Via Condotti, directly across from the Spanish Steps, and the streets running parallel to Via Condotti, as well as its cross streets, form the most elegant and expensive shopping area for clothes and accessories in Rome—head here first for top Italian and European designer shops. Lower-price fashions are on display at shops on **Via Frattina** and **Via del Corso**. Romans in the know do much of their shopping along **Via Cola di Rienzo** and **Via Nazionale**. For prints, browse among the stalls at **Piazza Fontanella Borghese** or stop in at the shops in the Pantheon area. For minor antiques, **Via dei Coronari** and other streets around Piazza Navona and Campo de' Fiori are good. High-end antiques dealers are situated in **Via del Babuino** and its environs. The open-air markets in **Campo de' Fiori** and in other neighborhoods throughout the city provide an eyeful of typically Roman color. For local artisans making and selling their wares, try the area northwest of Campo de' Fiori and the winding medieval streets of **Trastevere**.

Rome Essentials

AIRPORTS & TRANSFERS

Rome's principal airport is Aeroporto Leonardo da Vinci, usually known as Fiumicino. The smaller Ciampino, on the edge of Rome, is used as an alternative by international and domestic lines, especially for charter flights.

🛫 **Aeroporto Leonardo da Vinci** ✉ 29 km/18 mi southeast of Rome at Fiumicino ☎ 06/65951 ⊕ www.adr.it. **Ciampino** ☎ 06/794941 flight information ⊕ www.adr.it.

TRANSFERS   Two trains link downtown Rome with Fiumicino: inquire at the airport (EPT tourist information counter in the International Arrivals hall or train information counter near the tracks) to determine which takes you closest to your destination in Rome. The 30-minute nonstop Airport–Termini express goes directly to Track 22 at Termini Station, Rome's main train station, well served by taxis and hub of metro and bus lines. Departures from the airport begin at 8 AM and run hourly, with the final departure at 8 PM. Trains from Termini Station to the airport run every half hour, from 6:37 AM until 11:37 PM. Tickets cost €8.80. The other airport train, FM1, leaves from the same tracks and runs from the airport to Rome and beyond, serving commuters as well as air travelers. The main stops in Rome are at Trastevere (35 minutes), Ostiense (40 minutes), and Tiburtina (50 minutes); at each you can find taxis and bus and/or metro connections to other parts of Rome. The FM1 trains run from Fiumicino between 6:28 AM and 1:28 AM, with departures every 20 minutes, a little less frequently in off-hours; the schedule is similar going to the airport. Tickets cost €2.27. For either train, buy your ticket at a vending machine or at ticket counters at the airport and at some stations (Termini Track 22, Trastevere, Tiburtina). At the airport, stamp the ticket at the gate. Remember when using the train at other stations to stamp your ticket in the little yellow or red machine near the track before you board. During the night, take COTRAL buses from the airport to Tiburtina Station in Rome (45 minutes); they depart from in front of the International Arrivals hall at 1:15, 2:15, 3:30, and 5 AM. Buses leave Tiburtina Station for the airport at 12:30, 1:15, 2:30, 3:45, and 5 AM. Tickets either way cost €3.60.

A taxi to or from Fiumicino costs about €50, including extra charges for baggage and off-hours. At a booth inside the terminal you can hire a four- or five-passenger car with driver for a little more. If you decide to take a taxi, use only the yellow or the newer white cabs, in line at the official stand outside the terminal; make sure the meter is running. Gypsy cab drivers solicit your business as you come out of customs; they're not reliable, and their rates are usually much higher. Ciampino is connected with the Anagnina Station of the Metro A by bus (runs every half hour). A taxi between Ciampino and downtown Rome costs about €30.

BIKE & MOPED TRAVEL

Pedaling through Villa Borghese, along the Tiber, out on the Via Appia Antica, and through the city center when traffic is light is a pleasant way to see the sights, but remember: Rome is hilly. Rental concessions are at the Piazza di Spagna and Piazza del Popolo metro stops, and at Piazza San Silvestro and Largo Argentina. You will also find rentals at Viale della Pineta and Viale del Bambino on the Pincio, inside Villa Borghese. Collalti, just off Campo de' Fiori, leases and repairs bikes. St. Peter's Motor Rent carries bikes and mopeds. You can also rent a moped or scooter and mandatory helmet at Scoot-a-Long.

🚲 Bike & Moped Rentals **Colatti** ✉ Via del Pellegrino 82 ☎ 06/68801084. **Scoot-a-Long** ✉ Via Cavour 302 ☎ 06/6780206. **St. Peter Moto** ✉ Via di Porta Castello 43 ☎ 06/6875714 or 06/4885485 ✉ Via Fosse di Castello 7 ☎ 06/6874909.

BUS & TRAM TRAVEL WITHIN ROME

Orange ATAC city buses (and a few streetcar lines) run from 5:30 AM to midnight, with night buses (indicated N) on some lines. Bus lines 116, 117, and 119, with compact electric vehicles, make a circuit of limited but scenic routes in downtown Rome. They can save you from a lot of walking, and you can get on and off as you please.

🚌 **ATAC urban buses** ☎ 800/431784.

CAR TRAVEL

If you come by car, put it in a parking space (and note that parking in central Rome is generally either metered or prohibited) or a garage, and use public transportation. If you must park in a metered (blue-outlined) space, buy credits at the blue machines near parking areas, scratch off the time you've paid for, and display them on your dashboard. If you plan to drive into or out of the city, take time to study your route, especially on the GRA (Grande Raccordo Anulare, a beltway that encircles Rome and funnels traffic into the city, not always successfully). The main access routes to Rome from the north are the A1 autostrada from Florence and Milan, and the Aurelia highway (SS 1) from Genoa. The principal route to or from points south, such as Naples, is the A2 autostrada.

EMBASSIES

🏛 Canada ✉ Via G. B. de Rossi 27, Rome ☎ 06/445981.
🏛 United Kingdom ✉ Via XX (pronounced "Venti") Settembre 80a ☎ 06/4825441.
🏛 United States ✉ Via Veneto 121 ☎ 06/46741.

EMERGENCIES

Pharmacies are open 8:30–1 and 4–8. Some stay open all night, and all open Sunday on a rotation system; a listing of the neighborhood pharmacies open all night is posted at each pharmacy. The number below gives an automated list of three open pharmacies closest to the telephone from which you call. When calling for ambulance service, say *Pronto Soccorso* ("emergency room") and be prepared to give your address.

Emergencies Ambulance ☎ 118. **General Emergencies** ☎ 113. **Police** ☎ 112.

Hospitals Rome American Hospital ✉ Via Emilio Longoni 69, Tor Sapienza ☎ 06/22551 ⊕ www.rah.it. **Salvator Mundi Hospital** ✉ Viale delle Mura Gianicolensi 66, Monte Verdi Vecchio ☎ 06/588961 ⊕ www.smih.pcn.net.

24-hour Pharmacies Farmacia della Stazione ✉ Piazza Cinquecento 51 ☎ 06/4880019. **Internazionale** ✉ Piazza Barberini 49 ☎ 06/4825456.

ENGLISH-LANGUAGE MEDIA

Bookstores Anglo-American Bookstore ✉ Via della Vite 102 ☎ 06/6795222 ⊕ www.aab.it. **Corner Bookstore** ✉ Via del Moro 45, Trastevere ☎ 06/5836942. **Economy Book and Video Center** ✉ Via Torino 136 ☎ 06/4746877 ⊕ www.booksitaly. com. **Feltrinelli International** ✉ Via Emanuele Orlando 78/81 ☎ 06/4870171. **Open Door Bookshop** secondhand books ✉ Via Lungaretta 23 ☎ 06/5896478.

METRO TRAVEL

The metro (subway) is a fast and easy way to get around, but it does-n't serve many of the areas you'll probably want to visit, particularly Old Rome. It opens at 5:30 AM, and the last train leaves each terminal at 11:30 PM. Metro A runs from the eastern part of the city to Termini Station and past Piazza di Spagna and Piazzale Flaminio to Ottaviano-S. Pietro, near St. Peter's and the Vatican museums. Metro B serves Termini, the Colosseum, and Tiburtina Station (where the FM1 Fiumicino Airport train stops).

TAXIS

Taxis wait at stands and, for a small extra charge, can also be called by telephone. They're very difficult to hail, but you can try to flag down taxis whose roof lights are illuminated. The meter starts at €2.33 during the day, €4.91 after 10 PM, and €3.36 on Sundays and holidays. There's a supplement of €1.04 for each piece of baggage. Note that these charges do not appear on the meter. If you take a taxi at night and/or on a Sunday, or if you have baggage or have had the cab called by phone, the fare will legitimately be more than the figure shown on the meter.

☎ 06/3570, 06/5551, 06/4994, or 06/6645.

TOURS

Most operators offer half-day excursions to Tivoli to see the Villa d'Este's fountains and gardens; Appian Line and CIT run half-day tours to Tivoli that also include Hadrian's Villa and its impressive ancient ruins. Operators also offer all-day excursions to Assisi, to Pompeii and/or Capri, and to Florence. For do-it-yourself excursions to Ostia Antica and other destinations, pick up information at the APT information offices. American Express, Appian Line, ATAC, and CIT all offer orientation tours of Rome.

American Express ☎ 06/67641. **Appian Line** ☎ 06/487861. **Carrani** ☎ 06/4880510. **CIT** ☎ 06/4620311.

WALKING TOURS Enjoy Rome offers walking and bicycling tours in English, including a nighttime tour of Old Rome. All About Rome, Scala Reale, Through Eternity, and Walks of Rome all offer a range of English-language tours.

All About Rome ☎ 06/7100823. **Enjoy Rome** ☎ 06/4451843. **Scala Reale** ☎ 06/4745673 or 800/732-2863 Ext. 4052 ⊕ www.scalareale.org. **Through Eternity** ☎ 06/7009336 ⊕ www.througheternity.com. **Walks of Rome** ☎ 06/484853.

TRAIN TRAVEL

Termini Station is Rome's main train terminal, although the Tiburtina, Ostiense, and Trastevere stations serve some long-distance trains, many commuter trains, and the FM1 line to Fiumicino Airport. For train information call the toll-free number below, or try the English-speaking personnel at the information office in Termini, or at any travel agency. Tickets and seats can be reserved and purchased at travel agencies bearing the FS (Ferrovie dello Stato) emblem. Tickets are sold up to two months in advance. Short-distance tickets are also sold at tobacconists and ticket machines in the stations.

🚆 **Trenitalia** ☎ 166/105050 ⊕ www.trenitalia.it.

TRANSPORTATION AROUND ROME

Rome's transportation system includes buses and trams (ATAC), metro and suburban trains and buses (COTRAL), and some other suburban trains (Trenitalia) run by the state railways. A ticket valid for 75 minutes on any combination of buses and trams and one admission to the metro costs €.75 (time-stamp your ticket when boarding the first vehicle; you're supposed to stamp it again if you board another vehicle just before the ticket runs out, but few do). Tickets are sold at tobacconists, newsstands, some coffee bars, automated ticket machines in metro stations, some bus stops, and at ATAC and COTRAL ticket booths. A BIG tourist ticket, valid for one day on all public transport, costs €3.10. A weekly ticket (Settimanale, also known as CIS) costs €12.40 and can be purchased only at ATAC and metro booths.

TRAVEL AGENCIES

🚩 **American Express** ✉ Piazza di Spagna 38 ☎ 06/67641. **CIT** ✉ Piazza della Repubblica 64 ☎ 06/4620311 ⊕ www.citonline.it. **CTS** ✉ Via Genova 16 ☎ 06/4620431 ⊕ www.cts.it for youth and budget travel and discount fares.

VISITOR INFORMATION

🚩**APT** Rome Provincial Tourist Agency, main office ✉ Via Parigi 5, 00185 ☎ 06/36004399 ✉ Termini Station ☎ 06/47301 ✉ Leonardo da Vinci (Fiumicino) Airport ☎ 06/ 65951. **City tourist information booths** ✉ Largo Goldoni, corner of Via Condotti ✉ Via del Corso in the Spanish Steps area ✉ Via dei Fori Imperiali, opposite the entrance to the Roman Forum ✉ Via Nazionale, at Palazzo delle Esposizioni ✉ Piazza Cinque Lune, off the north end of Piazza Navona; Piazza Sonnino, in Trastevere ⊕ www. romaturismo.it.

FLORENCE

The birthplace of the Renaissance and one of Europe's preeminent treasures, Florence draws visitors from all over the world. Lining the narrow streets of the historic center are 15th-century palazzi whose plain and sober facades often give way to delightful courtyards. The classical dignity of the High Renaissance and the exuberant invention of the baroque are mostly absent in Florentine buildings; here, the typical exterior gives nothing away of the treasures contained within.

Exploring Florence

Numbers in the margin correspond to points of interest on the Florence map.

Founded by Julius Caesar, according to legend, Florence was built in the familiar grid pattern common to all Roman colonies. Except for the major monuments, which are appropriately imposing, the buildings are low and unpretentious and the streets are narrow. At times Florence can be a nightmare of mass tourism. Plan, if you can, to visit the city in late fall, early spring, or even in winter to avoid the crowds.

Piazza del Duomo & Piazza della Signoria

The area between Piazza del Duomo and Piazza della Signoria constitutes the core of the centro storico. Piazza del Duomo has been the center of Florence's religious life for centuries; work began on the Duomo
in 1296, and the structure that sprang from the site is testament to religious fervor and a wealthy populace. Via Calzaiuoli links this piazza
to Piazza della Signoria, the center of Florentine government since the
end of the 13th century. The piazza is lined with Renaissance sculpture
(some originals, some copies). The Galleria degli Uffizi, next to Palazzo
Vecchio, houses one of the most important collections of Renaissance
paintings in the world.

★ ❸ **Battistero** (Baptistery). In front of the Duomo is the octagonal baptistery, one of the city's oldest (modern excavations suggest its foundations
date from the 4th to 5th and the 8th to 9th centuries) and most beloved
buildings. The interior dome mosaics are famous but cannot outshine
the building's renowned gilded bronze east doors (facing the Duomo),
the work of Lorenzo Ghiberti (1378–1455). The ones you see at the Baptistery, however, are copies; the originals are preserved in the Museo dell-
l'Opera del Duomo. ⊠ *Piazza del Duomo* ☎ *055/2302885* ⊕ *www.
operaduomo.firenze.it* ⊗ *Mon.–Sat. noon–7, Sun. 8:30–2.*

❷ **Campanile** (Bell tower). This early-14th-century bell tower, designed by
Giotto (circa 1267–1337), is richly decorated with colored marble and
sculpture reproductions; the originals are in the Museo dell'Opera del
Duomo. The 414-step climb to the top is less strenuous than that to the
cupola on the Duomo. ⊠ *Piazza del Duomo* ☎ *055/2302885* ⊕ *www.
operaduomo.firenze.it* ⊗ *Daily 8:30–7:30.*

★ ❶ **Duomo.** The Cattedrale di Santa Maria del Fiore is dominated by a
cupola representing a landmark in the history of architecture. Work began
on the cathedral in 1296 under the supervision of master sculptor and
architect Arnolfo di Cambio, and its construction took 140 years to complete. Gothic architecture predominates; the facade was added in the 1870s
but is based on Tuscan Gothic models. Inside, the church is cool and
austere, a fine example of the architecture of the period. Take a good
look at the frescoes of equestrian figures on the left wall of the nave:
the one on the right is by Paolo Uccello (1397–1475), the one on the
left by Andrea del Castagno (circa 1419–57). The dome frescoes by Vasari
take second place to the dome itself, Brunelleschi's (1377–1446) greatest architectural and technical achievement. The dome was also the inspiration for the one Michelangelo designed for St. Peter's in Rome and
even for the dome of the Capitol in Washington. You can visit early medieval and ancient Roman remains of previous constructions excavated
under the cathedral. And you can climb to the top of the dome, 463 exhausting steps up between the two layers of the double dome for a fine
view. ⊠ *Piazza del Duomo* ☎ *055/2302885* ⊕ *www.operaduomo.
firenze.it* ⊗ *Crypt: weekdays 10–5:40, Sat. 8:30–5:40, first Sat. of the
month 8:30–4. Cupola: weekdays 8:30–7, Sat. 8:30–5:40, first Sat. of
the month 8:30–4. Duomo: weekdays 10–5, Sat., 10–4:45, Sun. 3:30–4:45,
first Sat. of the month 10–3:30.*

❾ **Galleria degli Uffizi** (Uffizi Gallery). The Uffizi was built to house the administrative offices of the Medici, onetime rulers of the city. Later their
fabulous art collection was arranged in a gallery on the top floor, which
was opened to the public in the 17th century—making this the world's
first modern public gallery. It comprises Italy's most important collection of paintings, with the emphasis on Italian art from the 13th to 16th
centuries. Make sure you see the *Ognissanti Madonna* by Giotto (circa
1267–1337), and look for Botticelli's (1445–1510) *Birth of Venus* and

Fodor'sChoice
★

Primavera in Rooms X–XIV, Michelangelo's *Holy Family* in Room XXV, and works by Raphael next door in Room XXVI. In addition to its art treasures, the gallery offers a magnificent close-up view of the Palazzo Vecchio tower from the coffee bar. Avoid long lines at the ticket booths by purchasing tickets in advance from Consorzio ITA. ☒ *Piazzale degli Uffizi 6* ☏ *055/23885* ☒ *Advance tickets, Consorzio ITA, Piazza Pitti 1, 50121* ☏ *055/294883* ⊕ *www.uffizi.firenze.it* ☒ *€8.50, (€1.55 reservation fee)* ☉ *Tues.–Sun. 8:15–6:50.*

❽ Mercato Nuovo (New Market). This open-air loggia was completed in 1551. Beyond the slew of souvenir stands, its main attraction is a copy of Pietro Tacca's bronze *Porcellino* (though it means *Little Pig,* it's actually a wild boar) on the south side, dating from around 1612 and copied from an earlier Roman work now in the Uffizi. The *Porcellino* is Florence's equivalent of the Trevi Fountain: put a coin in his mouth, and if it lands properly, it means that one day you'll return to Florence. ☒ *Via Por San Maria at Via Porta Rossa* ☉ *Market: Mon. 1–7, Tues.–Sat. 8–7.*

★ ❹ Museo dell'Opera del Duomo (Cathedral Museum). The museum contains some superb sculptures by Donatello (circa 1386–1466) and Luca della Robbia (1400–82)—especially their *cantorie,* or singers' galleries—and an unfinished *Pietà* by Michelangelo that was intended for his own tomb. ☒ *Piazza del Duomo 9* ☏ *055/2302885* ⊕ *www.operaduomo.firenze. it* ☉ *Mon.–Sat. 9:30–7:30, Sun. 9–1:40.*

❿ Museo di Storia della Scienza (Museum of the History of Science). You don't have to know a lot about science to appreciate the antique scientific instruments presented here in informative, eye-catching exhibits. From astrolabes and armillary spheres to some of Galileo's own instruments, the collection is one of Florence's lesser-known treasures. ☒ *Piazza dei Giudici 1* ☏ *055/265311* ⊕ *www.imss.fi.it* ☉ *Oct.–May, Mon. and Wed.–Sat. 9:30–5, Tues. 9:30–1, 2nd Sun. of month 10–1; June–Sept., Mon. and Wed.–Fri. 9:30–5, Tues. and Sat. 9:30–1.*

❺ Orsanmichele (Garden of St. Michael). For centuries this was an odd combination of first-floor church and second-floor granary. Today it serves as a museum, and the statues in the niches on the exterior (many of which are now copies) constitute an anthology of the work of eminent Renaissance sculptors, including Donatello, Ghiberti, and Verrocchio (1435–88). The tabernacle inside is an extraordinary piece by Andrea Orcagna (1320–68). Many of the original statues can be seen in the Museo di Orsanmichele contained within. At press time the museum was closed for restoration; check with the Tourist Information office for details. ☒ *Via dei Calzaiuoli; museum entrance at via Arte della Lana* ☏ *055/284944* ☉ *Weekends 9–1 and 4–6; guided tours weekdays at 9, 10, and 11* ☉ *Closed 1st and last Mon. of month.*

❼ Palazzo Vecchio (Old Palace). Also called Palazzo della Signoria, this massive, fortresslike city hall was begun in 1299 and was taken over, along with the rest of Florence, by the Medici. Inside, the impressive, frescoed salons and the *studiolo* (little study) of Francesco I are the main attractions. ☒ *Piazza della Signoria* ☏ *055/2768465* ☉ *Mon.–Wed., Fri., and Sat. 9–7, Thurs. and Sun. 9–2.*

❻ Piazza della Signoria. This is the heart of Florence and the city's largest square. In the pavement in the center of the square a plaque marks the spot where Savonarola, the reformist Dominican friar who urged Florentines to burn their pictures, books, musical instruments, and other worldly objects, was hanged and then burned at the stake as a heretic in 1498. The square, the Fontana di Nettuno (Neptune Fountain) by Ammanati (1511–92), and the surrounding cafés are popular gathering

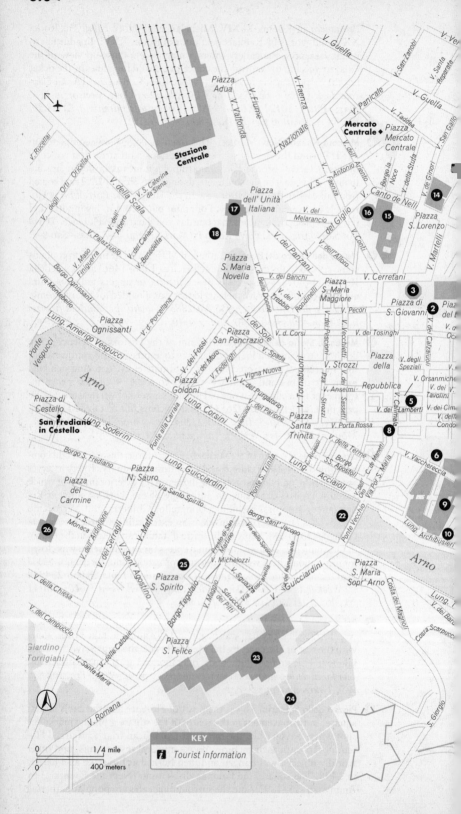

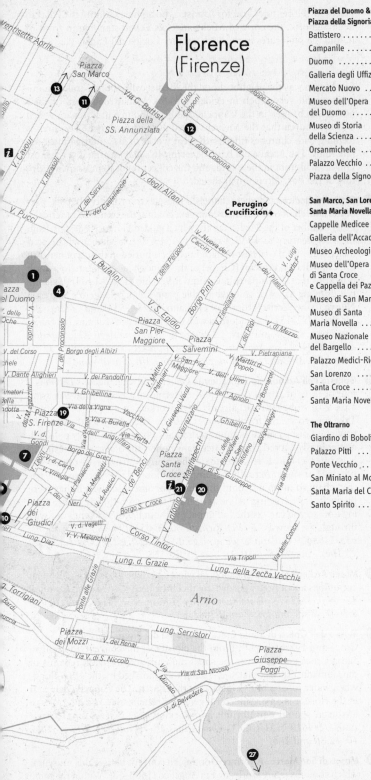

Florence (Firenze)

places for Florentines and for tourists who come to admire the Palazzo della Signoria, the copy of Michelangelo's *David* standing in front of it, and the sculptures in the 14th-century Loggia dei Lanzi.

San Marco, San Lorenzo, Santa Maria Novella, Santa Croce

San Marco was the neighborhood the Medici called home, and their imprint is still very much in evidence today. Visual reminders of their power can be seen in the Cappelle Medicee and in San Lorenzo, which was the church that the Medici viewed as their very own. This area is teeming with churches filled with great works of art, and two must-see museums. The Accademia has Michelangelo's *David*, arguably the most famous sculpture in the world, and the collection of Renaissance sculpture at the Bargello is unparalleled.

★ ⓰ **Cappelle Medicee** (Medici Chapels). These extraordinary chapels, part of the church of San Lorenzo complex, contain the tombs of practically every member of the Medici family, which guided Florence's destiny from the 15th century to 1737. Cosimo I (1519–74), a Medici whose acumen made him the richest man in Europe, is buried in the crypt beneath the **Cappella dei Principi** (Chapel of the Princes), and Donatello's tomb is next to that of his patron, Cosimo il Vecchio (1389–1464). Upstairs is a dazzling array of colored marble panels. Michelangelo's **Sagrestia Nuova** (New Sacristy) tombs of Giuliano (1478–1534) and Lorenzo de' Medici (1492–1519) are adorned with the justly famed sculptures of *Dawn* and *Dusk, Night* and *Day.* ⊠ *Piazza di Madonna degli Aldobrandini* ☎ *055/294883 reservations* ⊕ *www.sanlorenzo.com* ☉ *Daily 8:15–5; closed 1st, 3rd, and 5th Mon. and 2nd and 4th Sun. of month.*

★ ⓫ **Galleria dell'Accademia** (Accademia Gallery). Michelangelo's *David* is a tour de force of artistic conception and technical ability, for he was using a piece of stone that had already been worked on by a lesser sculptor. Take time to see the forceful *Slaves,* also by Michelangelo; their rough-hewn, unfinished surfaces contrast dramatically with the highly polished, meticulously carved *David.* Michelangelo left the *Slaves* "unfinished," it is often claimed, to accentuate the figures' struggle to escape the bondage of stone. Actually, he simply abandoned them because his patron changed his mind about the tomb monument for which they were planned. Try to be first in line at opening time or go shortly before closing time so you can get the full impact without having to fight your way through the crowds. ⊠ *Via Ricasoli 60* ☎ *055/294 883 reservations; 055/2388609 Galleria* ⊕ *www.mega.it* ✉ *€8.50, €1.55 reservation fee* ☉ *Tues.–Sun. 8:15–6:50.*

⓬ **Museo Archeologico** (Archaeological Museum). Fine Etruscan and Roman antiquities and a pretty garden are the draw here. ⊠ *Via della Colonna 38* ☎ *055/23575* ⊕ *www.mega.it* ☉ *Mon. 2–7, Tues. and Thurs. 8:30–7, Wed. and Fri.–Sun. 8:30–2.*

⓴① **Museo dell'Opera di Santa Croce e Cappella dei Pazzi** (Museum of Santa Croce and Pazzi Chapel). From the cloister of the convent adjacent to Santa Croce you can visit the small museum and see what remains of the Cimbaue crucifix that was irreparably damaged by the 1966 flood, when water rose to 16 feet in parts of the church. The **Cappella dei Pazzi** in the cloister is an architectural gem by Brunelleschi. The interior is a lesson in spatial equilibrium and harmony. ⊠ *Piazza Santa Croce* ☎ *055/244619* ☉ *Mar.–Oct., Thurs.–Tues. 10–7; Nov.–Feb., Thurs.–Tues. 10–12:30 and 3–6.*

⓭ **Museo di San Marco.** A former Dominican convent houses this museum, which contains many works by Fra Angelico (1400–55). Within the same walls where the unfortunate Savonarola, the reformist friar, later contemplated the sins of the Florentines, Fra Angelico went humbly about his work, decorating many of the otherwise austere cells and corridors with brilliantly colored frescoes on religious subjects. Look for his masterpiece, the *Annunciation.* Together with many of his paintings arranged on the ground floor, just off the little cloister, they form a fascinating collection. ☒ *Piazza San Marco 1* ☎ *055/2388608* ☉ *Weekdays 8:15–1:50, Sat. 8:15–6:50, Sun. 8:15–7* ☉ *Closed 2nd and 4th Mon. of month, and 1st, 3rd, and 5th Sun. of month.*

⑱ Museo di Santa Maria Novella. Adjacent to the church, this museum is worth a visit for its serenity and the faded Paolo Uccello frescoes from Genesis, as well as the **Cappellone degli Spagnoli** (Spanish Chapel), with frescoes by Andrea di Buonaiuto. The museum is closed for restoration and due to reopen in September 2003; contact the Tourist Information office for details. ☒ *Piazza Santa Maria Novella 19* ☎ *055/282187.*

★ ⑲ Museo Nazionale del Bargello. This grim, fortresslike palace served in medieval times as the residence of Florence's chief magistrate and later as a prison. It is now filled with Italian Renaissance sculpture, including masterpieces by Donatello, Verrocchio, Michelangelo, and other major sculptors. The Bargello also has an eclectic collection of antique arms and ceramics. ☒ *Via del Proconsolo 4* ☎ *055/2388606* ⊕ *www.arca. ne* ☉ *Daily 8:15–1:50* ☉ *Closed 2nd and 4th Mon. of month and 1st, 3rd, and 5th Sun. of month.*

⑭ Palazzo Medici-Riccardi. Few tourists know about Benozzo Gozzoli's (1420–97) glorious frescoes in the tiny second-floor chapel of this palace, built in 1444 by Michelozzo for Cosimo de' Medici (Il Vecchio, 1389–1464). Glimmering with gold, they represent the journey of the Magi as a spectacular cavalcade with cameo portraits of various Medici and the artist himself. ☒ *Via Cavour 1* ☎ *055/2760340* ☉ *Thurs.–Tues. 9–7.*

⑮ San Lorenzo. The facade of this church was never finished, but the Brunelleschi interior is elegantly austere. Stand in the middle of the nave at the entrance, on the line that stretches to the high altar, and you'll see what Brunelleschi achieved with the grid of inlaid marble in the pavement. Every architectural element in the church is placed to create a dramatic effect of single-point perspective. The **Sagrestia Vecchia** (Old Sacristy), decorated with stuccoes by Donatello, is attributed to Brunelleschi. ☒ *Piazza San Lorenzo* ☎ *055/290184* ☉ *Church: Mon.–Sat. 7–noon and 3:30–5:30, Sun. 3:30–5. Old Sacristy: Mon.–Sat. 8–noon and 3:30–5:30, Sun. 3:30–5:30. Closed Dec. and Jan.*

★ ⑳ Santa Croce. The mighty church of Santa Croce was begun in 1294 and has become a pantheon for Florentine greats; monumental tombs of Michelangelo, Galileo (1564–1642), Machiavelli (1469–1527), and other Renaissance luminaries line the walls. Inside are two chapels frescoed by Giotto and another painted by Taddeo Gaddi (1300–66), as well as an *Annunciation* and crucifix by Donatello. But it is the scale of this grandiose church that proclaims the power and ambition of medieval Florence. ☒ *Piazza Santa Croce 16* ☎ *055/244619* ☉ *Mar.–Oct., Mon.–Sat. 9:30–5:30, Sun. 3–5:30; Nov.–Feb., Mon.–Sat. 9:30–noon and 3–5:30, Sun. 3–5:30.*

⑰ Santa Maria Novella. A Tuscan interpretation of the Gothic style, this handsome church should be seen from the opposite end of Piazza Santa Maria Novella for the best view of its facade. Inside are some famous frescoes, especially Masaccio's (1401–28) *Trinity,* a Giotto crucifix in the sacristy, and Ghirlandaio's frescoes in the **Capella Maggiore** (Main

Chapel). ✉ *Piazza Santa Maria Novella* ☏ *055/210113* ✆ *Mon.–Thurs. and Sat. 9:30–5, Fri. and Sun. 1–5.*

The Oltrarno

The Oltrarno, which means "beyond the Arno," is on the south side of the Arno. It's a neighborhood filled with artisans' workshops, and in that respect, it has changed little since the Renaissance. The gargantuan Palazzo Pitti stands as a sweeping reminder of the power of the Medici family, and there are some lovely Renaissance churches, terrific restaurants, and first-rate shoe stores—all reason enough to cross over and explore.

㉔ **Giardino di Boboli** (Boboli Gardens). The main entrance to this park on a landscaped hillside is in the right wing of Palazzo Pitti. Laid out in 1549, the gardens were for Cosimo I's wife, Eleanora da Toledo, who made the palazzo her home. They were further developed by later Medici dukes. ✉ *Enter through Palazzo Pitti* ☏ *055/294883* ✆ *Apr.–Oct., daily 8:15–5:30; Nov.–Mar., daily 8:15–4:30* ✆ *Closed 1st and last Mon. of each month.*

Fodor's Choice
★

㉓ **Palazzo Pitti.** This enormous palace is a 16th-century extravaganza the Medici acquired from the Pitti family after the latter had gone deeply into debt to build the central portion. The Medici enlarged the building, extending its facade along the immense piazza. Solid and severe, it looks like a Roman aqueduct turned into a palace. The palace houses several museums: the **Museo degli Argenti** (Silver Museum) displays the fabulous Medici collection of objects in silver and gold; another has the collections of the **Galleria d'Arte Moderna** (Gallery of Modern Art). The most famous museum, though, is the **Galleria Palatina** (Palatine Gallery), with an extraordinary collection of paintings, many hung frame-to-frame in a clear case of artistic overkill. Some are high up in dark corners, so try to go on a bright day. ✉ *Piazza Pitti* ☏ *055/294883* ⊕ *www. thais.it* ✆ *Museo degli Argenti: Mon.–Sun. 8:15–1:50; closed 2nd and 4th Sun. and 1st, 3rd, and 5th Mon. of month. Galleria Palatina: Nov.–Mar., Tues.–Sat. 8:15–6:50, Sun. 8:15–6:50; Apr.–Oct., Tues.–Sat. 8:15–10, Sun. 8:15–7.*

★ **㉒** **Ponte Vecchio** (Old Bridge). Florence's oldest bridge appears to be just another street lined with goldsmiths' shops until you get to the middle and catch a glimpse of the Arno below. Spared during World War II by the retreating Germans (who blew up every other bridge in the city), it also survived the 1966 flood. It leads into the **Oltrarno**, where fascinating artisans' workshops preserve the feel of old, working-class Florence. ✉ *East of Ponte Santa Trinita and west of Ponte alle Grazie.*

㉗ **San Miniato al Monte.** One of Florence's oldest churches, this charming green-and-white marble Romanesque edifice is full of artistic riches, among them the gorgeous Renaissance chapel where a Portuguese cardinal was laid to rest in 1459 under a ceiling by Luca della Robbia. ✉ *Viale Galileo Galilei, or take stairs from Piazzale Michelangelo* ☏ *055/ 2342731* ✆ *Daily 8–6:30.*

㉖ **Santa Maria del Carmine.** The church is of little architectural interest but of immense significance in the history of Renaissance art. It contains the celebrated frescoes painted by Masaccio, Masolino, and Filippino Lippi in the **Cappella Brancacci.** The chapel was a classroom for such artistic giants as Botticelli, Leonardo da Vinci (1452–1519), Michelangelo, and Raphael, since they all came to study Masaccio's realistic use of light and perspective and his creation of space and depth. ✉ *Piazza del Carmine* ☏ *055/2382195* ✆ *Mon. and Wed.–Sat. 10–5, Sun. 1–5.*

㉕ Santo Spirito. Its plain, unfinished facade is less than impressive, but this church is important because it is one of Brunelleschi's finest architectural creations. It contains some superb paintings, including a *Madonna* by Filippino Lippi. Santo Spirito is the hub of a colorful, trendy neighborhood of artisans and intellectuals. An outdoor market enlivens the square every morning and some Sunday afternoons, pigeons, pet owners, and pensioners take over. ⊠ *Piazza Santo Spirito* ☎ *055/210030* ☺ *Church: Thurs.–Tues. 8:30–noon and 4–6, Wed. 8:30–noon and 4–7; museum: Tues.–Sun. 10–2.*

Where to Eat

Mealtimes in Florence are from 1 to 2:30 and 8 to 9 or later. Reservations are always advisable; to find a table at inexpensive places, get there early.

★ $$$$ ✕ **Cibrèo.** The food at this classic Florentine trattoria is fantastic, from the first bite of seamless, creamy *crostini di fegatini* (savory Tuscan chicken liver spread on grilled bread) to the last bite of one of the melt-in-your-mouth-good desserts. If you thought you'd never try tripe, let alone like it, this is the place to lay any doubts to rest: the cold tripe salad with parsley and garlic is an epiphany. ⊠ *Via Andrea del Verrocchio 8/r* ☎ *055/2341100* ⌲ *Reservations essential* ⊟ *AE, DC, MC, V* ☺ *Closed Sun. and Mon., July 25–Sept. 5, and Dec. 31–Jan. 7.*

$$$$ ✕ **Enoteca Pinchiorri.** A sumptuous Renaissance palace with high, frescoed ceilings and bouquets in silver vases is the setting for this restaurant, one of the most expensive in Italy. Some consider it one of the best, and others consider it an expensive, non-Italian rip-off: prices are high and portions are small. Fish, game, and meat dishes are always on the menu, along with pastas such as the *ignudi*—ricotta and cheese dumplings with a lobster fricassee. ⊠ *Via Ghibellina 87* ☎ *055/242777* ⌲ *Reservations essential* ⊟ *AE, MC, V* ☺ *Closed Sun. and Aug. No lunch Mon.*

★ $$$$ ✕ **Taverna del Bronzino.** Would you like to have a sophisticated meal in a 16th-century Renaissance artist's studio? This restaurant, the former studio of Santi di Tito, a student of Bronzino's, has a simple formality, with white tablecloths and place settings. The classic Tuscan food, however, is superb, and the presentation is often dramatic. A wine list of solid, affordable choices rounds out the menu. The service is outstanding. Reservations are advised, especially for eating at the wine cellar's only table. ⊠ *Via delle Ruote 25/r* ☎ *055/495220* ⊟ *AE, DC, MC, V* ☺ *Closed Sun. and Aug.*

★ $$-$$$ ✕ **Beccofino.** Forget the fact that the noise levels in this place often reach the pitch of the Tower of Babel. Concentrate, instead, on the food, which might be the most creative in town. The interior has a pale-wood serpentine bar separating the ochre-walled wine bar from the green-walled restaurant. Chef Francesco Berardinelli has paid some dues in the United States, and it shows in his food, which is inventive although the results taste wholly and wonderfully Italian. The wine bar offers a shorter and less expensive menu; in the summer, you can enjoy this food on an outdoor terrace facing the Arno. ⊠ *Piazza degli Scarlatti 1/r (Lungarno Guicciardini)* ☎ *055/290076* ⌲ *Reservations essential* ⊟ *MC, V* ☺ *Closed Mon. Nov.–Mar.*

★ $$-$$$ ✕ **La Giostra.** La Giostra, which means "carousel" in Italian, is owned and run by Prince Dimitri Kunz d'Asburgo Lorena. It feels like a club, with white walls and tablecloths and dim lighting accented with a few tiny blue lights twinkling on the ceiling. Try the unusually good pastas, maybe the *carbonara di tartufo*, decadently rich spaghetti with eggs and white truffles. Leave room for dessert: this might be the only show in town with a sublime tiramisu and a wonderfully gooey Sacher torte. ⊠ *Borgo Pinti 12/r* ☎ *055/241341* ▱ *AE, DC, MC, V.*

★ **$$–$$$** ✕ **Le Fonticine.** The area around the train station is not noted for its fine dining options, and this place provides a welcome oasis. It combines the best of two Italian cuisines: owner Silvano Bruci is from Tuscany and his wife, Gianna, is from Emilia-Romagna. Start with the mixed-vegetable antipasto plate and then move on to any of their house-made pastas. The feathery light tortelloni *nostro modo* are stuffed with fresh ricotta and served with a tomato and cream sauce, and should not be missed. The interior of the restaurant, filled with the Brucis' painting collection, provides a cheery space for this soul-satisfying food. ⊠ *Via Nazionale 79/r,* ☎ *055/282106* ▱ *AE, DC, MC, V* ☉ *Closed Sun. and Mon., Dec. and Aug.*

$–$$$ ✕ **Finisterrae.** Four large, dramatically lit rooms, with colorful walls dotted with maps detailing various Mediterranean towns, lend an aura of romance to this spot. There may not be a prettier restaurant in town. The eminently affordable menu offers a little bit from Lebanon, Spain, France, Morocco and, yes, Italy. The Spanish options are particularly fine, especially the *filetto al cabrales* (beef with Spanish blue cheese and port). The seductive bar, with its expert barmen, is dimly lit with low-slung seats; they'll even provide tobacco if you want to light up one of the hookahs. ⊠ *via de' Pepi 3/5r* ☎ *055/2638675* ▱ *MC, V* ☉ *Closed Mon. and Nov.–Mar.*

★ **$–$$** ✕ **Osteria de'Benci.** Just a few minutes from Santa Croce, this charming osteria serves some of the most eclectic food in Florence. Try the spaghetti *dell'ubriacone* (literally "drunken spaghetti," cooked in red wine). The grilled meats are justifiably famous, such as the *carbonata,* a succulent piece of grilled beef served rare. When it's warm, you can dine outside with a view of the 13th-century tower belonging to the prestigious Alberti family. The English-speaking staff shouldn't scare you off: Florentines *do* eat here. ⊠ *Via de'Benci 11-13/r* ☎ *055/2344923* ▱ *AE, DC, MC, V* ☉ *Closed Sun.*

$ ✕ **La Casalinga.** "Casalinga" means "housewife," and this place has all the charm of a 1950s kitchen with Tuscan comfort food to match. Tables are set close together and the place is usually jammed, and with good reason. The menu is long, portions are plentiful, and service is prompt and friendly. If you eat ribollita anywhere in Florence, eat it here—it couldn't be more authentic. ⊠ *Via Michelozzi 9/r* ☎ *055/218624* ▱ *AE, DC, MC, V* ☉ *Closed Sun., 1 wk at Christmas, 3 wks in Aug. No lunch in July.*

Where to Stay

Hotel rooms are at a premium in Florence for most of the year. Reserve well in advance. If you arrive without a reservation, the **Consorzio ITA office** (⊠ Stazione Centrale di Santa Maria Novella) in the train station, open 8:20 AM–9 PM, can help you, but there may be a long line (take a number and wait). Now that much traffic is banned in the centro storico, many central hotel rooms are quieter. Local traffic and motorcycles can still be bothersome, however, so check the decibel level before you settle in. From November through March, ask for special low winter rates.

★ **$$$$** ▥ **Brunelleschi.** Architects united a Byzantine tower, a medieval church, and a later building in a stunning structure in the very heart of the centro storico to make this unique hotel. Medieval stone walls and brick arches contrast pleasantly with the plush, contemporary furniture. The comfortable, soundproof rooms are done in coordinated patterns and soft colors. ⊠ *Piazza Sant'Elisabetta 3/r (off Via dei Calzaiuoli), 50122* ☎ *055/27370* ▤ *055/219653* ⊕ *www.hotelbrunelleschi.it* ⇆ *96 rooms, 7 junior suites* ⌂ *Restaurant, bar* ▱ *AE, DC, MC, V.*

★ **$$$$**   🏠 **Excelsior.** Florentine hotels do not get much more exquisite or expensive than this. Rooms are decorated in Empire style but still feel up-to-date. High ceilings, dramatic views of the Arno, patterned rugs, and tasteful prints lend the rooms a sense of extravagant well-being. Public rooms have stained glass and acres of Oriental carpets strewn over marble floors. The opulence of 19th-century Florentine antiques is set off by charming old prints of the city and long mirrors. ✉ *Piazza Ognissanti 3, 50123* ☎ *055/264201* 🖷 *055/210278* ⊕ *www.westin.com* ↩ *155 rooms, 16 suites* ♿ *Restaurant, bar* 🚭 *AE, DC, MC, V.*

$$$$ 🏠 **Grand.** This Florentine classic provides all the luxuries. Rooms are furnished in either Renaissance or Empire style; the former have deep, richly hued damask brocades and canopied beds, the latter a lovely profusion of crisp prints and patterned fabric offsetting white walls. The overall effect is sumptuous, as is the view of either the Arno or a small courtyard lined with potted orange trees. Avoid the piano bar, which is high-priced karaoke. ✉ *Piazza Ognissanti 1, 50123* ☎ *055/288781* 🖷 *055/217400* ⊕ *www.grandhotelflorence.com* ↩ *107 rooms* ♿ *Restaurant, bar* 🚭 *AE, DC, MC, V.*

$$$$ 🏠 **Hotel Savoy.** From the outside, it looks very much like the turn-of-the-19th-century building that it is. But step inside this hotel in the heart of the centro storico and sleek minimalism prevails. Sitting rooms have a funky edge with cream-colored walls dotted with contemporary prints and photographs. Many rooms, decorated in muted colors, with clean lines and soaring ceilings, overlook Piazza Repubblica and have views of the Duomo's cupola. ✉ *Piazza della Repubblica 7, 50123* ☎ *055/27351* 🖷 *055/2735888* ⊕ *www.roccofortehotels.com* ↩ *98 rooms, 9 suites* ♿ *Restaurant, bar* 🚭 *AE, DC, MC, V.*

$$$$ 🏠 **Lungarno.** Rooms and suites in this hotel across the Arno from the Palazzo Vecchio and the Duomo have private terraces jutting out over the river. The chic interior approximates a breezily elegant home, with lots of crisp white fabrics trimmed in blue. Four suites in a 13th-century tower preserve exposed stone walls and old archways. More than 100 paintings and drawings—from Picassos to Cocteaus—hang in hallways and bedrooms. ✉ *Borgo San Jacopo 14, 50125* ☎ *055/27261* 🖷 *055/268437* ⊕ *www.lungarnohotels.com* ↩ *60 rooms, 13 suites* ♿ *Restaurant, bar* 🚭 *AE, DC, MC, V.*

★ **$$$–$$$$**   🏠 **Monna Lisa.** Housed in a 15th-century palazzo, parts of which date from the 13th century, this hotel retains some of its original coffered wood ceilings, as well as its original marble staircase. The rooms are on the small side, but they are tastefully decorated. The public rooms are decorated in a 19th-century style. ✉ *Borgo Pinti 27, 50121* ☎ *055/2479751* 🖷 *055/2479755* ⊕ *www.monnalisa.it* ↩ *45 rooms* ♿ *Bar* 🚭 *AE, DC, MC, V.*

★ **$$$**   🏠 **Hermitage.** This place is centrally located and, given the price, a great bargain. All rooms are hung with lively wallpaper; some have views of the Palazzo Vecchio and others of the Arno. The rooftop terrace, where you can breakfast or enjoy a cocktail, is decked with flowers. The lobby feels like a friendly living room, with warm yellow walls. ✉ *Vicolo Marzio 1 (Piazza del Pesce, Ponte Vecchio), 50122* ☎ *055/287216* 🖷 *055/212208* ⊕ *www.hermitagehotel.com* ↩ *27 rooms, 1 suite* 🚭 *MC, V.*

★ **$$–$$$**   🏠 **Beacci Tornabuoni.** Florentine pensioni do not come any more classic than this. In a 14th-century palazzo, it has old-fashioned style and just enough modern comfort to keep you happy. The sitting room has a large fireplace, the terrace has a tremendous view of some major Florentine monuments, and the wallpapered rooms are inviting. On Monday, Wednesday, and Friday nights from May to October, the dining room opens, serving Tuscan specialties. ✉ *Via Tornabuoni 3 50123* ☎ *055/*

212645 🖨 055/283594 ⊕ *www.bthotel.it* ⇌ *28 rooms* ♿ *Restaurant, bar,* ☰ *AE, DC, MC, V.*

$$ 🏨 **Loggiato dei Serviti.** Occupying a 16th-century former monastery, this attractively spare Renaissance building was originally a refuge for traveling priests. Vaulted ceilings, tasteful furnishings (some antique), canopied beds, and rich fabrics give you the feel of Old Florence while you enjoy modern creature comforts. ✉ *Piazza Santissima Annunziata 3, 50122* ☎ *055/289592* 🖨 *055/289595* ⊕ *www.loggiatodeiserviti.it* ⇌ *29 rooms* ☰ *AE, DC, MC, V.*

★ **$$** 🏨 **Morandi alla Crocetta.** This charming and distinguished residence near Piazza Santissima Annunziata was once a monastery, and access is up a flight of stairs. It is furnished in the classic style of a Florentine home, and guests are made to feel like friends of the family. Small and exceptional, it is also a good value and must be booked well in advance. ✉ *Via Laura 50, 50121* ☎ *055/2344747* 🖨 *055/2480954* ⊕ *www.hotelmorandi.it* ⇌ *10 rooms* ☰ *AE, DC, MC, V.*

$$ 🏨 **Nuova Italia.** Near the main train station and within walking distance of the sights, this homey hotel in a dignified palazzo is run by a genial English-speaking family. Rooms are simply furnished, and the triple-glazed windows ensure restful nights. ✉ *Via Faenza 26, 50123* ☎ *055/268430* 🖨 *055/210941* ⇌ *20 rooms* ☰ *AE, MC, V.*

$$ 🏨 **Porta Faenza.** A hospitable Italian-Canadian couple owns and manages this conveniently positioned hotel near the station. Spacious rooms in Florentine style and sparkling bathrooms that, though compact, have such amenities as hair dryers make this a good value. The staff is helpful and attentive to your needs. ✉ *Via Faenza 77, 50123* ☎ *055/284119* 🖨 *055/210101* ⊕ *www.hotelportafaenza.it* ⇌ *25 rooms* ☰ *AE, DC, MC, V.*

$$ 🏨 **Villa Azalee.** A five-minute walk from the train station and a short distance from the Fortezza da Basso (site of the Pitti fashion shows), this 19th-century villa deftly recalls its previous incarnation as a private residence. Some rooms have private terraces, many have views of the hotel's flower-filled garden. ✉ *Viale Fratelli Rosselli 44, 50123* ☎ *055/214242* 🖨 *055/268264* ⊕ *www.villaazalee.it* ⇌ *25 rooms* ☰ *AE, DC, MC, V.*

★ **$–$$** 🏨 **Bellettini.** This small, central hotel occupies two floors of an old but well-kept building near San Lorenzo, in an area with many inexpensive restaurants. Rooms are large, with traditional Venetian or Tuscan furnishings, and bathrooms are modern. The management is friendly and helpful. ✉ *Via dei Conti 7, 50123* ☎ *055/213561* 🖨 *055/283551* ⊕ *www.firenze.net* ⇌ *27 rooms, 4 without bath* ☰ *AE, DC, MC, V.*

$ 🏨 **Albergo Losanna.** Most major sights are within walking distance of this tiny pensione just within the viale. Despite its dated feel, the property is impeccably kept. Guest rooms have high ceilings: try to get one facing away from the street—you won't have a view but you will get a quiet night's sleep. ✉ *Via V. Alfieri 9, 50121* ☎🖨 *055/245840* ⇌ *8 rooms, 3 with bath* ☰ *MC, V.*

$ 🏨 **Alessandra.** The location, a block from the Ponte Vecchio, and ample rooms make this a good choice for basic accommodations at reasonable rates. The English-speaking staff makes sure guests are happy. ✉ *Borgo Santi Apostoli 17, 50123* ☎ *055/283438* 🖨 *055/210619* ⊕ *www.hotelalessandra.com* ⇌ *26 rooms, 18 with bath, 1 suite, 1 apartment* ☰ *AE, MC, V* ⊗ *Closed Dec. 10–26.*

Nightlife & the Arts

The Arts

FILM You can find movie listings in *La Nazione*, the daily Florence newspaper. On Monday and Tuesday, first-run English-language films are shown at the **Odeon** (✉ Piazza Strozzi).

MUSIC Most major musical events are staged at the **Teatro Comunale** (✉ Corso Italia 12 ☎ 055/211158). The box office (closed Sunday and Monday) is open from 9 to 1 and a half hour before performances. It's best to order your tickets by mail, however, as they're difficult to come by at the last minute. Amici della Musica (Friends of Music) puts on a series of concerts at the **Teatro della Pergola** (✉ Box office: Via della Pergola 10a/r ☎ 055/2479651 ⊕ www.pergolafirenze.it). For information on concerts contact the **Amici della Musica** (✉ Via Alamanni 39 ☎ 055/210804) directly.

Nightlife

BARS **Negroni** (✉ Via dei Renai 17/r ☎ 055/243647) is exactly where you want to be at cocktail hour if you're young, or simply young at heart. **Rex** (✉ Via Fiesolana 23–25/r, Santa Croce ☎ 055/2480331) is trendy, with an artsy crowd.

NIGHTCLUBS **Central Park** (✉ Via del Fosso Macinante 2 ☎ 055/353505) is a great spot if you want to put on your dancing shoes. **Maracaná** (✉ Via Faenza 4 ☎ 055/210298) is a restaurant and pizzeria serving Brazilian specialties; at 11 PM, it transforms itself into a cabaret floor show and then into a disco until 4 AM. Remember to book a table if you want to eat. Young, up-to-the-minute Florentines drink and dance 'til the wee hours at **Maramao** (✉ Via dei Macci 79/r ☎ 055/244341), which opens at 11 PM and doesn't really get going until much before 2. Those craving a night out with less raucous live music might check out **Jazz Club** (✉ Via Nuova de' Caccini 3, corner of Borgo Pinti ☎ 055/2479700). It's situated, appropriately enough, in a smoky basement. **Yab** (✉ Via Sassetti 5/r ☎ 055/215160) is one of the largest clubs, with a young clientele. Popular especially on Tuesday and Thursday nights, it packs in locals and foreigners.

Shopping

Markets

Don't miss the indoor, two-story **Mercato Centrale** (✉ Piazza del Mercato Centrale), near San Lorenzo, open in the morning Monday–Saturday. The **Mercato di San Lorenzo** (✉ Piazza San Lorenzo and Via dell'Ariento) is a fine place to browse for buys in leather goods and souvenirs; it's open March–December, daily 8–7; January–February, Tuesday–Saturday 8–7, June–September, Sunday 8–7.

Shopping Districts

Via Tornabuoni is the high-end shopping street. **Via della Vigna Nuova** is just as fashionable. Goldsmiths and jewelry shops can be found on and around the **Ponte Vecchio** and in the **Santa Croce** area, where there is also a high concentration of leather shops and inconspicuous shops selling gold and silver jewelry at prices much lower than those of the elegant jewelers near Ponte Vecchio. The convent of **Santa Croce** (✉ Via San Giuseppe 5/r ✉ Piazza Santa Croce 16) houses a leather-working school and showroom. Antiques dealers can be found in and around the center but are concentrated on **Via Maggio** in the Oltrarno area. **Borgo Ognissanti** has shops selling period decorative objects.

Florence Essentials

ADDRESSES

It is easy to find your way around in Florence: major sights can be explored on foot, as they are packed into a relatively small area. Wear comfortable shoes. The system of street addresses is unusual, with commercial addresses (those with an *r* in them, meaning *rosso*, or red) and residential addresses numbered separately (32/r might be next to or a block away from plain 32).

AIRPORTS & TRANSFERS

The airport that handles most arrivals is Aeroporto Galileo Galilei, more commonly known as Aeroporto Pisa-Galilei. Some domestic and European flights use Florence's Aeroporto Vespucci.

🛪 **Aeroporto Galileo Galilei** ✉ Pisa 🕾 050/500707 ⊕ www.pisa-airport.com. **Aeroporto Vespucci** ✉ Peretola 🕾 055/373498 ⊕ www.safnet.it.

TRANSFERS Pisa-Galilei Airport has a direct train service to the Stazione Centrale di Santa Maria Novella. There are hourly departures throughout the day, and the trip takes about 60 minutes. When departing, you can buy train tickets for the airport and check in for all flights leaving from Aeroporto Pisa-Galilei at the Florence Air Terminal at Track 5 of Santa Maria Novella. Aeroporto Vespucci is connected to downtown Florence by SITA bus.

BIKE & MOPED TRAVEL

🛪 Bike & Moped Rentals **Alinari** ✉ Via Guelfa 85/r 🕾 055/280500.

BUS TRAVEL TO & FROM FLORENCE

For excursions outside Florence, to Siena, for instance, you take SITA near the Stazione Centrale di Santa Maria Novella. The CAP bus terminal is also near the train station.

🛪 **Lazzi Eurolines** ✉ Via Mercadante 2, 🕾 055/363041 ⊕ www.lazzi.it. **SITA** bus terminal ✉ Via Santa Caterina da Siena 17 🕾 055/214721 ⊕ www.sita-on-line.it.

BUS TRAVEL WITHIN FLORENCE

Bus maps and timetables are available for a small fee at the Azienda Trasporti Autolinee Fiorentine city bus information booths. The same maps may be free at visitor information offices. ATAF city buses run from about 5:15 AM to 1 AM. Buy tickets before you board the bus; they are sold at many tobacco shops and newsstands. The cost is €1 for a ticket good for one hour, and €3.90 for four one-hour tickets, called a *multiplo*. A 24-hour tourist ticket (*turistico*) costs €4.

🛪 **Azienda Trasporti Autolinee Fiorentine** (ATAF) ✉ near Stazione Centrale di Santa Maria Novella ✉ Piazza del Duomo 57/r 🕾 800/019794 toll-free.

CAR TRAVEL

The north–south access route to Florence is the Autostrada del Sole (A1) from Milan or Rome. The Florence–Mare autostrada (A11) links Florence with the Tyrrhenian coast, Pisa, and the A12 coastal autostrada. Parking in Florence is severely restricted.

CONSULATES

🛪 United Kingdom ✉ Lungarno Corsini 2 🕾 055/284133.
🛪 United States ✉ Lungarno Vespucci 38 🕾 055/2398276.

EMERGENCIES

Pharmacies are open Sunday and holidays by rotation. Signs posted outside pharmacies list those open all night and on weekends. The pharmacy at Santa Maria Novella train station is always open.

🛪 Doctors & Dentists **Tourist Medical Service** ✉ Via Lorenzo il Magnifico 59 🕾 055/475411.
🛪 Emergency Services **Ambulance** 🕾 118. **Police** 🕾 113.

ENGLISH-LANGUAGE MEDIA

🛪 Bookstores **BM Bookshop** ✉ Borgo Ognissanti 4/r 🕾 055/294575. **Paperback Exchange** ✉ Via Fiesolana 31/r 🕾 055/2478154. **Edison** ✉ Piazza della Repubblica 27/r 🕾 055/213110.

TAXIS

Taxis wait at stands throughout the centro storico; you can also telephone them. Hailing taxis from the street is not done in Florence. Use only authorized cabs, which are white with a yellow stripe or rectangle on the door. The meter starts at €2.30, with extra charges for nights, holidays, or radio dispatch.

🚖 ☎ 055/4798 or 055/4390.

TOURS

BUS TOURS A bus consortium (through hotels and travel agents) offers tours in air-conditioned buses covering the important sights in Florence with a trip to Fiesole. The cost is about €25 for a three-hour tour, including entrance fees, and bookings can be made through travel agents.

Operators offer a half-day excursion to Pisa, usually in the afternoon, costing about €25, and a full-day excursion to Siena and San Gimignano, costing about €35. Pick up a timetable at ATAF information offices near the train station or at SITA. Also inquire at the APT tourist office.

TRAIN TRAVEL

The main station is Stazione Centrale di Santa Maria Novella. Florence is on the main north–south route between Rome, Bologna, Milan, and Venice. High-speed Eurostar trains reach Rome in less than two hours and Milan in less than three.

🚉 **Stazione Centrale di Santa Maria Novella** ☎ 8488/88088 toll-free.

TRAVEL AGENCIES

🚉 **American Express** ⊠ Via Dante Alighieri 22/r ☎ 055/50981. **CIT Italia** ⊠ Piazza Stazione 51/r ☎ 055/284145. **Micos Travel Box** ⊠ Via dell'Oriuolo 50–52/r ☎ 055/2340228.

VISITOR INFORMATION

🚉 **Azienda Promozione Turistica (APT)** ⊠ Via Cavour 1/r, 50100 ☎ 055/290832.

TUSCANY

Tuscany is a blend of rugged hills, fertile valleys, and long stretches of sandy beaches that curve along the west coast of central Italy and fringe the pine-forested coastal plain of the Maremma. The gentle, cypress-studded green hills may seem familiar: Leonardo da Vinci and Raphael often painted them in the backgrounds of their masterpieces. Cities and towns here were the cradle of the Renaissance, which during the 15th century flourished most notably in nearby Florence. Come to Tuscany to enjoy its graceful, good living, and, above all, its unparalleled artistic treasures, many still in their original tiny old churches and patrician palaces.

Lucca

Any tour of Tuscany should include Lucca, with its handful of marvelously elaborate Romanesque churches and late-19th-century and early-20th-century Liberty facades along the Fillungo, its main shopping thoroughfare. Cars are not allowed in the historic center, making the city a pleasure to explore. For that very reason it's an excellent alternative to, or side trip from, Pisa, just 22 km (14 mi) away. First enjoy the views of Lucca and countryside from the parklike 16th-century ramparts. Then visit the churches that look suspiciously like oversized marble wedding cakes. Fanciful colonnettes decorate the facade of the 11th-century **Duomo**; inside is the 15th-century tomb of Ilaria del Carretto by Jacopo della Quercia (1374–1438). ⊠ *Piazza San Martino* ☎ *0583/490530* ⊙ *Duomo: weekdays 7–5:30, Sat. 9:30–6:45, Sun. 11:30–11:50 and 1–5:30. Tomb: Nov.–Mar., weekdays 9:30–4:45, Sat. 9:30–6:45, Sun.*

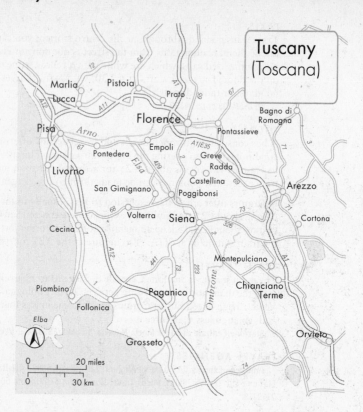

Tuscany
(Toscana)

Marlia · Pistoia · Prato · Bagno di Romagna
Lucca · Florence · Pontassieve
Pisa · Arno · Empoli · Greve · Radda
Pontedera · Livorno · Castellina · Poggibonsi · Arezzo
San Gimignano · Volterra · Siena · Cortona
Cecina · Montepulciano
Piombino · Paganico · Chianciano Terme
Follonica · Orvieto
Elba · Grosseto

0   20 miles
0   30 km

11:30–11:50 and 1–4:45; Apr.–Oct., weekdays 9:30–5:45, Sat. 9–6:45, Sun. 9–10, 11:30–noon, and 1–5:45.

Piazza del Anfiteatro Romano preserves the oval form of the Roman amphitheater over which it was built; there is a bustling outdoor market here on weekdays. The church of **San Frediano** is graced with an austere facade ornamented by 13th-century mosaic decoration. Inside, check out the exquisite reliefs by Jacopo della Quercia in the last chapel on the left and the bizarre mummy of St. Zita, patron saint of domestic servants. ⊠ *Piazza San Frediano* ⏱ *Mon.–Sat. 8:30–noon and 3–5, Sun. 10:30–5.*

One of the most fanciful facades in central Italy can be seen on the front of the church of **San Michele in Foro,** adorned with a marriage of arches and columns crowned by a statue of St. Michael. The church is an exceptional example of the Pisan Romanesque style and the decorative flair peculiar to Lucca. ⊠ *Piazza San Michele* ⏱ *Daily 7:40–noon and 3–6.*

The **Villa Reale** (Royal Villa), at Marlia, 8 km (5 mi) west of Lucca, was once the home of Napoléon's sister and has been restored by the Counts Pecci-Blunt. It is celebrated for its spectacular gardens, originally laid out in the 16th century and redone in the middle of the 17th century. Gardening buffs adore the legendary **Teatro di Verdura,** a theater carved out of hedges and topiaries; a music festival is usually held here during July and August. ⊠ *Via Villa Reale, Marlia* ☎ *0583/30108* ⊕ *www.comunedicapannori.it* ⏱ *Mar.–Nov., tours at 10, 11, noon, 3, 4, 5, and 6; Dec.–Feb., open by appointment only.*

★ **$$** ✕ **bucadisantantonio.** It's been around since 1782, and you can understand why. The staying power of the place is the result of its superlative Tuscan food, brought to the table by staff that doesn't miss a beat. The white-walled interior, hung with copper pots and brass musical instruments, is classy and comfortable. The menu ranges from the simple but blissful *tortelli lucchesi al sugo* (meat-stuffed pasta with a tomato and meat sauce) to such daring dishes as roast *capretto* (kid) with herbs. ✉ *Via della Cervia 3* ☎ *0583/55881* 🖃 *AE, DC, MC, V* ☺ *Closed Mon., 2 wks in Jan., and 2 wks in July. No dinner Sun.*

$ ✕ **Osteria del Neni.** Tucked into a side street just a block away from San Michele, this cozy, delightful little place serves tasty treats. The walls are a warm orange, and the dining room is dotted with wooden tables. All the pasta is made in-house, and if you're lucky enough to find *ravioli, spinaci e anatra in salsa di noci* (ravioli stuffed with duck and spinach in a creamy but light walnut sauce), by all means order it. The menu changes regularly; in the summer, the splendid food can be enjoyed alfresco. ✉ *Via Pescheria 3* ☎ *0583/492 681* ✍ *Reservations essential* 🖃 *MC, V* ☺ *Closed Sun. and Jan.*

★ $$$$ ✕🏨 **Locanda l'Elisa.** Surrounded by rosemary, lavender, and azaleas, this hotel preserves the intimacy of a well-furnished home: it's decorated in Empire style with 19th-century furniture, prints, and fabrics. The attached restaurant serves Luccan specialties and elevates them to new heights. ✉ *Via Nuova per Pisa 1951, 55050* ☎ *0583/379737* 🖴 *0583/ 379019* ⊕ *www.lunet.it* 🛏 *3 rooms, 8 suites* ⚲ *Restaurant, pool* 🖃 *AE, DC, MC, V* ☺ *Closed Jan. 7–Feb. 7.*

★ $$$ 🏨 **Palazzo Alexander.** This small, elegant boutique hotel, tucked into a quiet side street, is a stone's throw from San Michele in Foro. The building, dating from the 12th century, has a level of luxury that would have been familiar to the Lucchesi nobility: timbered ceilings, warm yellow walls, and brocaded chairs adorn the public rooms, and the motif is carried into the guest rooms, all of which have high ceilings and that same glorious damask. ✉ *Via S. Giustina 48, 55100* ☎ *0583/583571* 🖴 *0583/583610* ⊕ *www.palazzo-alexander.com* 🛏 *9 rooms, 3 suites, 1 apartment* ⚲ *Bar* 🖃 *AE, DC, MC, V.*

Pisa

If you cut through the kitschy atmosphere around the Leaning Tower, Pisa has much to offer. Its cathedral-baptistery-tower complex in Piazza dei Miracoli is among the most dramatic in Italy, and Piazza dei Cavalieri is a superb example of a Renaissance piazza. Pisa's treasures are more subtle than Florence's, to which it is inevitably compared. Pisa usually emerges the loser, and it shouldn't. Though it sustained heavy damage during World War II, many of its beautiful Romanesque structures are still preserved.

The **Battistero** (Baptistery) in front of the cathedral is known for its graceful form and for the pulpit carved by Giovanni Pisano's father, Nicola (1220–78). The Baptistery was begun in 1153 but not completed until around 1400. Ask one of the ticket takers if he'll sing for you inside the Baptistery; the acoustics are remarkable. A €3 gratuity is appropriate. ✉ *Piazza dei Miracoli* ⊕ *www.duomo.pisa.it* ☺ *June 22–Sept. 21, daily 8–7:40; Sept. 22–Dec. 21 and Mar. 22–June 21, daily 9–5:40; Dec. 22–Mar. 21, daily 9–4:40.*

The **Camposanto** (Cemetery) is said to be filled with earth brought back from the Holy Land by Crusaders. Important frescoes, notably the *Drunkenness of Noah* by Renaissance artist Benozzo Gozzoli and a 14th-century *Triumph of Death*, are within. ✉ *Piazza dei Miracoli* ⊕ *www. duomo.pisa.it* ☺ *June 22–Sept. 21, daily 8–7:40; Sept. 22–Dec. 21 and Mar. 22–June 21, daily 9–5:40; Dec. 22–Mar. 21, daily 9–4:40.*

★ Pisa's **Duomo** is elegantly simple, its facade decorated with geometric and animal shapes. The cavernous interior is supported by 68 columns, and the pulpit is a prime example of Giovanni Pisano's work and one of the major monuments of the Italian Gothic style. The lamp suspended across from the pulpit is known as Galileo's Lamp; it's said to have inspired his theories on pendular motion. ⊠ *Piazza del Duomo* ⊕ *www. duomo.pisa.it* ⊘ *June 22–Sept. 21, Mon.–Sat. 10–7:40, Sun. 1–7:40; Mar. 22–June 21 and Sept. 22–Dec. 21, Mon.–Sat. 10–7:40, Sun. 1–7:40; Dec. 22–Mar. 21, Mon.–Sat. 10–12:45, Sun. 3–4:45.*

⓫ **Leaning Tower.** The Leaning Tower (Torre Pendente) provided the final grace note for the complex comprising the Duomo, Baptistery, and the Camposanto. Construction started in 1174, and the lopsided settling was evident by the time work began on the third story. After years of being closed, it is once again open to the public for climbing. Legend holds that Galileo conducted an experiment on the nature of gravity by dropping metal balls from the top of the 187-foot-high tower; historians say this legend has no basis in fact (which is not quite to say that it is false). ⊠ *Campo dei Miracoli* ☎ *050/560547* ⊕ *http://torre.duomo.pisa.it* ✉ *€15, reservations 050/835013 or www.duomo.pisa.it (€17 online)* ⊘ *Nov.–Mar., daily 9–5:50; Apr.–Oct., daily 8–8.*

★ **$$** ✕ **La Mescita.** This cheerful trattoria has high, vaulted brick ceilings and stencilled walls lined with colorful contemporary prints. What better place for the tasty and inventive food on offer: the *tagliolini con ragù bianco di anatra* (house-made thin noodles with minced duck in a delicate white wine sauce) is extraordinary. ⊠ *Via Cavalca 2* ☎ *050/544294* ▱ *AE, DC, MC, V* ⊘ *Closed last 3 wks in Aug., 3 wks in Jan., and Mon. No lunch weekdays.*

$–$$ ✕ **Osteria dei Cavalieri.** This charming osteria, a few steps from Piazza dei Cavalieri, is reason enough to come to Pisa. On offer are exquisitely grilled fish dishes, vegetarian dishes, and *tagliata*, thin slivers of rare beef. Finish your meal with a lemon sorbet bathed in Prosecco, and walk away feeling that you've eaten like a king at plebeian prices. ⊠ *Via San Frediano 16* ☎ *055/580858* ▱ *AE, DC, MC, V* ⊘ *Closed Sun. and July 25–Aug. 25. No lunch Sat.*

Chianti

Directly south of Florence is the Chianti district, one of Italy's most famous wine-producing areas; its hill towns, olive groves, and vineyards are quintessential Tuscany. Many British and northern Europeans have relocated here, drawn by the unhurried life, balmy climate, and charming villages; there are so many Britons, in fact, that the area has been nicknamed Chiantishire. Still, it remains strongly Tuscan in character, and you'll be drawn to the views framing vine-quilted hills and elegantly elongated cypress trees.

The sinuous SS222, known as the Strada Chiantigiana, runs from Florence through the heart of Chianti. Its most scenic section connects Strada in Chianti, 16 km (10 mi) south of Florence, and Greve in Chianti, 11 km (7 mi) farther south.

If there is a capital of Chianti, it is **Greve,** a friendly market town with no shortage of cafés, enoteche (wine bars), and crafts shops lining its main piazza. The sloping, asymmetrical Piazza Matteotti is attractively arcaded and has a statue of Giovanni da Verrazano (circa 1480–1528), the explorer who discovered New York harbor, in the center.

With its magnificent views, **Panzano** is one of the prettiest stops in Chianti. The town centerpiece is the church of Santa Maria Assunta, where you can see an *Annunciation* attributed to Michele di Ridolfo del Ghirlandaio (1503–77).

Radda in Chianti sits on a hill separating Val di Pesa from Val d'Arbia. It's one of many tiny Chianti villages that invite you to stroll through its steep streets and follow the signs that point you toward the *camminamento*, a covered medieval passageway circling part of the city inside the walls. In Piazza Ferrucci, you'll find the Palazzo del Podestà, or Palazzo Comunale, the city hall that has served the people of Radda for more than four centuries. It has 51 coats of arms embedded in its facade.

$$ ✕ **Oltre il Giardino.** An ancient stone house has been converted into a tasteful dining area with a large terrace and spectacular views of the valley. Try to book a table in time to watch the sunset. The menu captures a little more fantasy than typical Tuscan cuisine. Try the *tagliatelle all'anatra* (a flat noodle tossed with a savory duck sauce) or the *peposo* (a beef stew laced with black pepper). On weekends, reservations are a must. ⊠ *Piazza G. Bucciarelli 42, Panzano* ☎ *055/852828* ▤ *DC, MC, V* ☺ *Closed Mon. and Nov.*

$ ✕ **Osteria Le Panzanelle.** Nada Michelassi and Silvia Bonechi combined their accumulated wisdom in the hotel and restaurant worlds to create this hospitable place a few minutes outside Radda. Its small but carefully crafted menu has typical tastes of Tuscany, such as the exquisite *trippa alla fiorentina* (tripe in a tomato sauce). Then there are unexpected treats like *crostone con salsiccia fresca* (toasted bread with fresh sausage). The restaurant consists of two small, simple rooms and some outdoor tables. The wine list is particularly strong on local vintages—in this case, Chianti Classico and Super Tuscans. ⊠ *Località Lucarellia 29, Radda in Chianti* ☎ *0577/733 511* ▤ *MC, V* ☺ *Closed Mon.*

$$$–$$$$ ✕▦ **Relais Fattoria Vignale.** On the outside, it's an unadorned manor house with an annex across the street. Inside, it's refined country-house comfortable, with terra-cotta floors, sitting rooms, and nice stone- and woodwork. White rooms with exposed brick and wood beams contain simple wooden bed frames and furniture, charming rugs and prints, and modern white-tile bathrooms. The grounds, lined with vineyards and olive trees, are equally inviting, with lawns, terraces, and a pool. The sophisticated Ristorante Vignale ($$$) serves excellent wines and Tuscan specialties; the in-house enoteca ($$$), simpler Tuscan fare. ⊠ *Via Pianigiani 9, 53017 Radda in Chianti* ☎ *0577/738300 hotel; 0577/738094 restaurant; 0577/738701 enoteca* ▤ *0577/738592* ⊕ *www.vignale.it* ↝ *35 rooms, 5 suites* ♨ *2 restaurants, pool, bar* ▤ *AE, DC, MC, V* ☺ *Closed 3 wks. in Jan., restaurant closed Thurs., enoteca closed Wed.*

$$–$$$$ ▦ **Villa Vignamaggio.** This historic estate has guest rooms and apartments in a villa, as well as two small houses and a cottage on the grounds. The villa, surrounded by manicured classical Italian gardens, dates from the 14th century but was restored in the 16th. It's reputedly the birthplace of Mona Lisa, the woman later made famous by Leonardo da Vinci. The place also does tastings of its very fine wine; inquire at reception to organize a tasting. ⊠ *Via Petriolo 5, 50022 Greve in Chianti* ☎ *055/854661* ▤ *055/8544468* ⊕ *www.vignamaggio.com* ↝ *2 rooms, 15 apartments, 1 cottage, 2 houses* ▤ *DC, MC, V* ☺ *Closed Dec. 23–Jan. 6.*

$ ▦ **Castello Vicchiomaggio.** Formerly a fortified castle, this building, now a prestigious wine estate with a tasting facility, dates from 956 and was rebuilt during the Renaissance. Throughout the nine apartments and two farmhouses is wonderful heavy wooden furniture, in keeping with the estate's history. The restaurant serves homemade pastas and specialties such as *stracotto*, beef cooked in the farm's own prizewinning Chianti Classico. ⊠ *Via Vicchiomaggio 4, 50022 Greve in Chianti* ☎ *055/*

854079 🗎 *055/853911* ⊕ *www.vicchiomaggio.it* ⇗ *8 apartments, 2 farmhouses* ⌂ *Restaurant, pool* ▤ *MC, V.*

Siena

One of Italy's best-preserved medieval towns, Siena is rich in both works of art and expensive antiques shops. Built on three hills, it is not an easy town to explore, for everything you'll want to see is either up or down a steep hill or stairway and many hotels are outside the old walls. But it is worth every ounce of effort. Siena was a center of learning and art during the Middle Ages, and many of the public buildings and churches are worth visiting. You can buy a combined ticket for admission to the Biblioteca Piccolomini, Museo dell'Opera del Duomo, and the Battistero.

One of the finest Gothic cathedrals in Italy, Siena's **Duomo** is unique in displaying a mixture of religious and civic ornamentation on both its interior and exterior. The lovely inlaid marble floors and Nicola Pisano's (circa 1220–1284) pulpit, carved between 1266 and 1268, are highlights. The animated frescoes of scenes from the life of Pope Pius II in the **Biblioteca Piccolomini** (Piccolomini Library) were painted by Pinturicchio. ✉ *Piazza del Duomo* ☎ *0577/283048* ⊕ *www.operaduomo.it* ⊙ *Duomo: Nov.–mid-Mar., Mon.–Sat. 7:30–5, Sun. 2–5; mid-Mar.–Oct., Mon.–Sat. 7:30–7:30, Sun. 2–7:30. Biblioteca Piccolomini: Nov.–mid-Mar., Mon.–Sat. 10–1 and 2–5, Sun. 2–5; mid-Mar.–Oct., Mon.–Sat. 9–7:30, Sun. 2–7:30.*

The **Museo dell'Opera Metropolitana** (Cathedral Museum) contains some fine works of art, notably a celebrated *Maestà* by Duccio di Buoninsegna. ✉ *Piazza del Duomo* ☎ *0577/283048* ⊕ *www.operaduomo. it* ⊙ *Nov.–mid-Mar., daily 9–1:30; mid-Mar.–Sept., daily 9–7:30; Oct., daily 9–6.*

★ The 13th-century **Palazzo Pubblico** (City Hall) dominates Piazza del Campo and houses the **Museo Civico** (Civic Museum), where there are noteworthy frescoes. ✉ *Piazza del Campo* ☎ *0577/292226* ⊕ *www. comune.siena.it* ⊙ *Nov.–Mar. 15, daily 10–5:30; Feb. 16–Mar. 15, daily 10–6:30, Mar.–Oct., daily 10–7.*

★ Fan-shape, sloping **Piazza del Campo** is Siena's main center of activity, with 11 streets leading into it. Farsighted planning has preserved it as a medieval showpiece. This is the venue for the famous **Palio**, a breakneck, 90-second horse race that takes place twice each year, on July 2 and August 16. The **Torre del Mangia** (Bell Tower) of the Palazzo Pubblico offers a wonderful view (you'll have to climb 503 steps to reach it, however). ✉ *Piazza del Campo* ⊙ *Daily 10–1 hr before sunset.*

$$$$ ✕ **Antica Trattoria Botteganova.** Just outside the city walls, north toward Chianti, the Botteganova is arguably the best restaurant in Siena. The interior, with high vaulting, is relaxed yet classy, and the service is first-rate. Clean flavors, balanced combinations, and inviting presentations are the trademarks here. The menu changes every two months to reflect the season's bounty; three different tasting menus are also available. ✉ *Strada per Montevarchi, SS408, 2 km (1 mi) north of Siena* ☎ *0577/ 284230* ▤ *AE, DC, MC, V* ⊙ *Closed Mon.*

★ **$–$$** ✕ **Enoteca I Terzi.** Owner Michele Incarnato happily calls his place "anarchic" because it offers a little bit of everything—leisurely or quick business lunches for the locals, lavish dinners, and significant snacks in between. On the ground floor of a 12th-century tower, it is much more than a wine bar, although it is hard to beat for a good glass of wine from a lengthy and carefully chosen list. The pasta specials change daily; you'll be blessed if *pici all'anatra e funghi* (thick spaghetti with a duck and mushroom sauce) is on the menu. ⊠ *Via dei Termini 7* ☎ *0577/44329* 🖃 *AE, DC, MC, V* ⊗ *Closed Sun.*

★ **$$$$** 🏨 **Certosa di Maggiano.** A 14th-century Carthusian monastery less than 2 km (1 mi) southeast of Siena has been converted into a luxury oasis furnished in impeccable style. The bedrooms have every comfort. In warm weather breakfast is served on the patio. Half board is required during high season, which increases the cost of the stay. ⊠ *Via Certosa 82, 53100* ☎ *0577/288180* 🖷 *0577/288189* ⊕ *www.certosadimaggiano.it* ◁ *6 rooms, 11 suites* ♣ *Restaurant, pool* 🖃 *AE, MC, V.*

$$$$ 🏨 **Park.** Just outside the walls of the old city, this is a handsome and sprawling 15th-century villa on its own well-equipped grounds, with a 9-hole golf course. The furnishings in the public areas strike an elegant balance between antique charm and patrician comfort. Guest rooms have bold, dark fabrics and modern appointments. ⊠ *Via Marciano 18, 53100* ☎ *0577/44803* 🖷 *0577/49020* ⊕ *www.parkhotelsiena.it* ◁ *64 rooms, 1 suite* ♣ *Restaurant, pool, bar* 🖃 *AE, DC, MC, V.*

★ **$$$** 🏨 **Palazzo Ravizza.** There might not be a more romantic and pretty place in the center of Siena than this quietly charming pensione just outside Porta San Marco and a short 10-minute walk to the Duomo. Rooms have high ceilings, antique furniture, big windows, and bathrooms decorated with hand-painted tiles. The restaurant offers up tasty Tuscan classics, which can be eaten outdoors when it's warm. ⊠ *Pian dei Mantellini, 34, 53100* ☎ *0577/280462* 🖷 *0577/221597* ⊕ *www.palazzoravizza.it* ◁ *40 rooms, 4 suites* ♣ *Restaurant* 🖃 *AE, DC, MC, V.*

$ 🏨 **Antica Torre.** A cordial young couple runs this hotel in a restored centuries-old tower that is a 10-minute walk from Piazza del Campo. Rooms are smallish and are furnished sparingly but tastefully. Beam ceilings throughout and original brick vaults here and there are reminders of the tower's venerable history. ⊠ *Via Fieravecchia 7, 53100* ☎☎ *0577/222255* ◁ *8 rooms* 🖃 *AE, DC, MC, V.*

San Gimignano

San Gimignano of the Beautiful Towers—to use its original name—is perhaps the most delightful of the Tuscan medieval hill towns, 31 km (20 mi) northwest of Siena. There were once more than 70 tall towers here, symbols of power for the wealthy families of the Middle Ages. Fifteen still stand, giving the town its unique skyline. The main street leads directly from the city gates to Piazza della Cisterna, with a quaint wellhead, and Piazza del Duomo.

The walls of the **Collegiata** (church), and those in the **Cappella di Santa Fina** (Chapel of St. Fina), are decorated with radiant frescoes by Domenico Ghirlandaio. The frescoes in the Collegiata itself include Bartolo di Fredi's cycle of scenes from the Old Testament on the left nave wall, which date from 1367. Taddeo di Bartolo's otherworldly *Last Judgment,* on the arch just inside the facade, depicts distorted and suffering nudes—avant-garde stuff for the 1390s. ⊠ *Piazza del Duomo* ☎ *0577/ 940316* ⊗ *Mar.–Oct., weekdays 9:30–7:30, Sat. 9:30–5, Sun. 1–5; Nov.–Jan. 20, Mon.–Sat. 9:30–5, Sun. 1–5* ⊗ *Closed Jan. 21–Feb. 28.*

$$–$$$ ✕ **Bel Soggiorno.** Bel Soggiorno is attached to a small hotel. It has fine views, refectory tables set with linen and candles, and leather-covered chairs. The menu, which changes frequently, has such treats as *sorpresa in crosta* (spicy rabbit stew in a bread crust). ⊠ *Via San Giovanni 91* ☎ *0577/ 940375* 🖃 *AE, DC, MC, V* ⊗ *Closed Wed. and Jan. 6–Feb. 28.*

$ ✕ **Enoteca Gustavo.** The ebullient Maristella Becucci reigns supreme in this tiny little wine bar (three small tables in the back, two in the bar, two bar stools) serving divine, and ample, crostini. The *crostino con carciofini e pecorino* (toasted bread with artichokes topped with semi-aged pecorino) packs a punch. So too does the selection of wines by the glass: the changing list has about 16 reds and wines, mostly local, all good. The cheese plate is a bit more expensive than the other offerings, but it's worth it. ⊠ *Via San Matteo 29* ☎ *0577/940057* ⌕ *Reservations not accepted.* ☰ *MC, V* ⊘ *Closed Tues.*

$$ 🏨 **Pescille.** This rambling stone farmhouse, about 3 km (2 mi) outside San Gimignano, with a good view of the town, has been restored as a hotel and furnished in attractive, chic rustic style. ⊠ *Località Pescille, 53037* ☎ *0577/940186* 🖷 *0577/940186* 🛏 *38 rooms, 12 suites* ⌕ *Pool, bar* ☰ *AE, DC, MC, V* ⊘ *Closed Nov.–Mar.*

Arezzo

To appreciate Arezzo you have to delve into the town's centro storico, ignoring the industrialized suburbs. The city is one of Italy's three major gold jewelry production centers. In the old, upper town are medieval and Renaissance buildings and a piazza that is a compendium of several eras. Tuscan art treasures abound in Arezzo, including frescoes by Piero della Francesca (1420–92), stained glass, and ancient Etruscan pottery. The poet Petrarch (1304–74), the artist Vasari (1511–74), and the satirical author Pietro Aretino (1492–1556) were born and raised in Arezzo's centro storico.

The fine Gothic **Duomo** is decorated with richly colored 16th-century stained-glass windows and a fresco of a somber Magdalene by Piero della Francesca. ⊠ *Piazza del Duomo* ☎ *0575/23991* ⊘ *Daily 7–12:30 and 3–6:30.*

Piazza Grande is an attractive, sloping square where an extensive open-air fair of antiques and old bric-a-brac is held the first weekend of every month. The shops around the piazza also specialize in antiques, with prices lower than those you will encounter in Florence. The colonnaded apse and bell tower of the Romanesque church of **Santa Maria della Pieve** grace one end of this pleasant piazza. ⊠ *Corso Italia* ☎ *0575/377678* ⊘ *Daily 8–12:30 and 3–6:30.*

★ In the church of **San Francesco** are famous frescoes by Piero della Francesca, depicting *The Legend of the True Cross* on three walls of the choir. They were painted between 1452 and 1466 and are a stunning display of his skill and genius. Admission is limited to 25 people at a time, and reservations are required. ⊠ *Via Cavour* ☎ *0575/ 900404* ⊕ *www.pierodellafrancesca.it* ⊘ *Nov.–Mar., weekdays, 9–5:30, Sat. 9–5, Sun. 1–5; Apr.–Oct., weekdays 9–6:30, Sat. 9–5:30, Sun. 1–5:30.*

$ ✕ **La Torre di Gnicche.** If you're looking for a small, intimate place with Italian home cooking, grab a light lunch or dinner here. This one-room eatery, seating about 30, is part of a Renaissance palazzo. The short menu includes assorted crostini, sensational *delicatezze sott'olio* (vegetables in oil), cheese plates, and an earthy *polpettone* (meat loaf). The formidable and eminently affordable wine list makes eating ribollita a heightened experience. ⊠ *Piaggia San Martino 8* ☎ *0575/352 035* ☰ *MC, V* ⊘ *Closed Wed.*

$$ 🏨 **Calcione Country and Castle.** The elegant Marchesa Olivella Lotter-inghi della Stufa has turned her 600-year-old family homestead into a

Fodor'sChoice

★ top-notch agriturismo. Think sophisticated rustic; many of the apartments have open fireplaces, the houses have a private pool (the rest share the estate pool), and there are private lakes for fishing and windsurfing. Calcione is convenient to Arezzo, Siena, San Gimignano, and the delights of Umbria. During high season, from June to September, a one-week stay is mandatory. ⊠ *Lucignano, 52046* ☎ *0575/837100* 🖷 *0575/*

837153 ⊕ *www.calcione.com* ✒ *2 houses, 1 cottage, 6 apartments* ♨ *3 pools* ▭ *No credit cards* ⊘ *Nov.–Mar.*

Cortona

Cortona, about 30 km (19 mi) south of Arezzo, has a peculiarly Tuscan brand of charm. This well-preserved, unspoiled medieval hill town is known for its excellent small museum and a number of fine antiques shops, as well as for its colony of foreign residents. The approach to Cortona from the east passes the Renaissance church of **Santa Maria del Calcinaio**. The heart of Cortona is formed by **Piazza della Repubblica** and the adjacent **Piazza Signorelli**.

The **Museo Diocesano** (Diocesan Museum) houses an impressive number of large and splendid paintings by native son Luca Signorelli (circa 1450–1523), as well as a beautiful *Annunciation* by Fra Angelico. ✉ *Piazza del Duomo 1* ☎ *0575/62830* ⊘ *Nov.–Mar., Tues.–Sun. 10–1 and 3–5; Apr.–Sept., Tues.–Sun. 9:30–1 and 3:30–7.*

$–$$ ✕ **Osteria del Teatro.** Just up the street from Teatro Signorelli, this small osteria is lined with photographs from theatrical productions spanning several decades. The food is deliciously simple—try the *filetto in crema di tartufo* (beef in a creamy tartufo sauce). ✉ *Via Maffei 5* ☎ *0575/ 630556* ▭ *AE, DC, MC, V* ⊘ *Closed Wed. and 2 wks in Nov.*

$$$$ ✕▥ **Il Falconiere.** Run by the husband-wife team of Riccardo and Silvia Baracchi, this heavenly hotel, just minutes outside Cortona, consists of rooms in an 18th-century villa and suites in the *chiesetta* (little church) once belonging to an obscure 19th-century Italian poet and hunter. If you desire a little bit more privacy, you can stay at Le Vigne del Falco at the opposite end of the property, where most of the rooms are suites with their own entrances, and all of them have a grand view of the plain below. The restaurant's inventive menu is complemented by the wine list, the product of Silvia's extensive sommelier training. ✉ *Località San Martino 370, 52044* ☎ *0575/612679* 🖨 *0575/612927* ⊕ *www. ilfalconiere.com* ✒ *13 rooms, 6 suites* ♨ *Restaurant, 2 pools, bar* ▭ *AE, DC, MC, V.*

FodorsChoice ★

Tuscany Essentials

BUS TRAVEL

Buses are a good alternative to driving; the region is crisscrossed by bus lines, which in some cases offer more frequent local service than trains, especially from Florence to Prato, a half-hour trip, and from Florence to Siena, which can take from 1¼ (by express bus) to 2 hours.

CAR TRAVEL

The best way to see the region is by car, taking detours to hill towns and abbeys. Roads throughout Tuscany are in good condition, though often narrow. The A1 autostrada links Florence with Arezzo and Chiusi (where you turn off for Montepulciano). A toll-free superstrada links Florence with Siena. For Chianti wine country scenery, take the SS222 south of Florence through the undulating hills between Strada in Chianti and Greve in Chianti.

TOURS

American Express operates one-day excursions to Siena and San Gimignano out of Florence. CIT Italia operates regional tours, too. ▣ **American Express** ✉ Via Dante Alighieri 22/r ☎ 055/50981. **CIT Italia** ✉ Piazza Stazione 51/r ☎ 055/284145.

TRAIN TRAVEL

The main train network connects Florence with Arezzo and Prato. Another main line runs to Pisa, and a secondary line goes from Prato to the coast via Lucca. Trains also connect Siena with Pisa, a two-hour ride. ⓕ ☎ 8488/888088 toll-free.

VISITOR INFORMATION

ⓕ **Arezzo** ✉ Piazza della Repubblica 22 ☎ 0575/377678 ⊕ www.apt.arezzo.it. **Cortona** ✉ Via Nazionale 42 ☎ 0575/630352 ⊕ www.cortonaweb.it. **Lucca** ✉ Piazza Santa Maria 125 ☎ 0583/99931 ⊕ www.lucca.tourist.it. **Pisa** ✉ Via Cammeo 2 ☎ 050/560464 ⊕ www.pisa.turismo.toscana.it. **Pistoia** ✉ Palazzo dei Vescovi ☎ 0573/21622 ⊕ www.comune.pistoia.it. **Prato** ✉ Piazza delle Carceri 15 ☎ 0574/24112 ⊕ www.prato.turismo.toscana.it. **San Gimignano** ✉ Piazza del Duomo ☎ 0577/940008 ⊕ www.sangimignano.com.

MILAN

Milan, capital of all that is new in Italy, has a history spanning at least 2,500 years. Its fortunes, both as a great commercial trading center and as the object of regular conquest and occupation, are readily explained by its strategic position at the center of the Lombard Plain.

Exploring Milan

Numbers in the margin correspond to points of interest on the Milan map.

Virtually every invader in European history—Gaul, Roman, Goth, Longobard, and Frank—as well as a long series of rulers from France, Spain, and Austria, has taken a turn at ruling Milan. So if you are wondering why so little seems to have survived from antiquity, the answer is simple—war. Thanks to the Visconti and Sforza families, however, there are still great Gothic and Renaissance treasures to be seen, including the spectacular Duomo and Leonardo da Vinci's unforgettable *Last Supper*. And thanks to Milan's new dynasties—Armani, Prada, Versace—the city now dazzles as the design and fashion center of the world. Just a few steps from the impossibly chic shops of the *quadrilatero d'oro*, the golden quadrangle of style, stands La Scala, Europe's most important opera house.

❼ **Basilica di Sant'Ambrogio** (Basilica of St. Ambrose). Noted for its medieval architecture, the church was consecrated by St. Ambrose in AD 387 and is the model for all Lombard Romanesque churches. Ancient pieces inside include a remarkable 9th-century altar in precious metals and enamels and some 5th-century mosaics. ✉ *Piazza Sant'Ambrogio* ☎ *02/86450895* ☉ *Mon.–Sat. 7–noon and 2:30–7, Sun. 7–1 and 3–8.*

❺ **Castello Sforzesco.** Surrounded by a moat, this building is a somewhat sinister 19th-century reconstruction of the imposing 15th-century fortress built by the Sforzas, who succeeded the Viscontis as lords of Milan. It now houses collections of sculptures, antiques, and ceramics, including Michelangelo's *Rondanini Pietà*, his last work, left unfinished at his death. ✉ *Piazza Castello* ☎ *02/86461404* ☉ *Tues.–Sun., 9–5:30.*

★ ❶ **Duomo.** The massive Duomo, a mountain of marble fretted with statues, spires, and flying buttresses, sits—in all its Gothic drama—in the heart of Milan. The **Madonnina**, a gleaming gilt statue on the highest spire, is a city landmark. Take the elevator or walk up 158 steps to the roof for a view of the Lombard Plain and the Alps beyond. Dating from the 4th century, the **Baptistery** ruin is beneath the piazza; enter through the Duomo. ✉ *Piazza del Duomo* ☎ *02/86463456* ☉ *Mid-Feb.–mid-Nov., daily 9–5:45; mid-Nov.–mid-Feb., daily 9–4:15.*

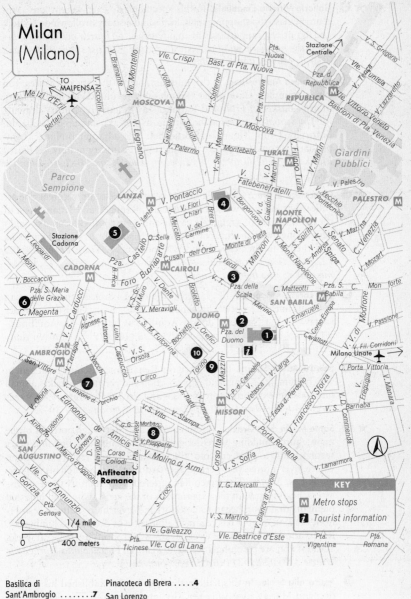

**Milan
(Milano)**

KEY

M Metro stops

i Tourist information

★ ❷ **Galleria Vittorio Emanuele.** In this spectacularly extravagant late-19th-century, glass-top shopping mall, locals and visitors stroll, window-shop, and sip pricey cappuccinos at trendy cafés. ⊠ *Piazza del Duomo, beyond the northern tip of cathedral's facade* ⊙ *Most shops 9:30–1 and 3:30–7, others later or all day.*

❿ **Pinacoteca Ambrosiana.** In this museum, one of the city's treasures, you can contemplate Caravaggio's simple—yet revolutionary in the history of art—*Basket of Fruit* and Raphael's awesome preparatory drawing for *The School of Athens* in the Vatican, as well as paintings by Leonardo, Botticelli, Luini, Titian, and Brueghel. The adjacent Biblioteca Ambrosiana is considered to be the oldest public library in Italy. ⊠ *Piazza Pio XI 2* ☏ *02/806921* ⊙ *Museum: Tues.–Sun. 10–5:30. Library: Mon.–Sat. 9:30–5.*

★ ❹ **Pinacoteca di Brera** (Brera Painting Gallery). One of Italy's great fine art collections includes works by Mantegna, Raphael, and Titian. Most of the paintings are of a religious nature and were confiscated and brought here during the 19th century when many religious orders were suppressed and their churches closed under Napoleon. ⊠ *Via Brera 28* ☏ *02/722631* ⊕ *www.brera.beniculturali.it* ⊙ *Tues.–Sun. 8:30–7:15, last admission 45 min before closing.*

❽ **San Lorenzo Maggiore** (St. Lorenzo the Elder). Sixteen ancient Roman columns line the front of this sanctuary; 4th-century Christian mosaics survive in the **Cappella di San Aquilino** (Chapel of St. Aquilinus). ⊠ *Corso di Porta Ticinese 39* ☏ *02/89404129* ⊙ *Church: daily 7:30–12:30 and 2–6:45. Mosaics: daily 9:30–12:30 and 2–6:30.*

❾ **San Satiro** (St. Satyr). This church is a Renaissance architectural gem in which Bramante's command of proportion and perspective makes a small interior seem extraordinarily spacious and airy. ⊠ *Via Torino 9* ⊙ *Weekdays 7:30–11:30 and 3:30–6:30, weekends 9–noon and 3:30–7.*

★ ❻ **Santa Maria delle Grazie** (Madonna of Grace). Although portions of the main church building were designed by Bramante, the building plays second fiddle to the **Cenacolo Vinciano**, the former rectory next door, where, over a three-year period, Leonardo da Vinci painted his megafamous *Last Supper.* The fresco has suffered more than its share of disasters, beginning with the experiments of the artist, who used untested pigments that soon began to deteriorate. Nevertheless, after a restoration, the *Last Supper* has regained a measure of clarity and luminosity. Reservations can be made weekdays 9–6 and Saturday 9–2; call weeks ahead if you are planning a weekend visit. ⊠ *Piazza Santa Maria delle Grazie 2* ☏ *02/89421146* ⊙ *Tues.–Sun. 8–7.*

❸ **Teatro alla Scala.** In this hallowed space, Verdi established his reputation and Maria Callas sang her way into opera lore. The opera house was closed in 2002 for renovations, with a reopening planned for December 7, 2004. In the meantime, performances are held at the Teatro Arcimboldi on the outskirts of Milan, and the **Museo Teatrale** (Theatrical Museum) is temporarily housed in Palazzo Busca, directly across from the *Last Supper.* ⊠ *Theater: Piazza della Scala* ☏ *02/8053418* ⊙ *Theater closed for renovations.* ⊠ *Museum: Corso Magenta 71* ☏ *02/4691249* ⊙ *Daily 9–6.*

Where to Eat

The lakes north of Milan contain Italy's freshest waters, and the plains to the south claim the country's best pastureland. You can be sure that city restaurants—among the most elegant, most creative in Europe—

make good use of this superior selection of fish and meats, pairing the cuisine with the crisp wines of the region.

$$$$ ✕ **Don Carlos.** This restaurant near La Scala is nothing like its indecisive operatic namesake: flavors are bold, and the presentation is precise and full of flair. Walls are hung with sketches of the theater, and the aria recordings are every bit as well chosen as the wine list. ✉ *In the Grand Hotel et de Milan, Via Manzoni 29* ☎ *02/723141* ✎ *Reservations essential* ▱ *AE, DC, MC, V* ☙ *Closed Mon., Aug., Dec. 15–Jan. 7. No lunch.*

$$$$ ✕ **Savini.** Savini is a Milanese institution, with red carpets and cut-glass chandeliers characteristic of its late-19th-century roots. Stick with the standards: the Milanese specialty *risotto al salto* (cooked as a pancake, grilled in the pan) is excellent here, as are the *cotoletta di vitello* (breaded veal cutlet) and osso buco. ✉ *Galleria Vittorio Emanuele* ☎ *02/72003433* ✎ *Reservations essential* ▱ *AE, DC, MC, V* ☙ *Closed Sun. and 3 wks mid-Aug.*

★ **$$$** ✕ **Boeucc.** Milan's oldest restaurant, opened in 1696, is in a square not far from La Scala. The opulent interior has come a long way from its basement origins (*boeucc,* pronounced "birch," is old Milanese for *buco,* or hole). You'll savor such dishes as penne *al branzino e zucchini* (with sea bass and zucchini) and *gelato di castagne con zabaglione caldo* (chestnut ice cream with hot zabaglione). ✉ *Piazza Belgioioso 2* ☎ *02/76020224* ✎ *Reservations essential* ▱ *AE* ☙ *Closed Sat., Aug., and Dec. 24–Jan. 2. No lunch Sun.*

$$$ ✕ **Joia.** At this haute-cuisine restaurant near Piazza della Repubblica, delicious vegetarian dishes are artistically prepared by chef Pietro Leemann. The menu is ever-changing, using fresh, seasonal produce; a favorite item is ravioli with basil, potatoes, pine nuts, and crisp green beans. A fish menu is also available. ✉ *Via Panfilo Castaldi 18* ☎ *02/29522124* ▱ *AE, DC, MC, V* ☙ *Closed weekends, Aug., and Dec. 24–Jan. 8.*

$$ ✕ **Antica Trattoria della Pesa.** Fin-de-siècle furnishings, dark-wood paneling, and old-fashioned lamps still look much as they must have when this eatery opened 100 years ago. It's authentic Old Milan, and the menu is right in line, offering risotto, minestrone, and osso buco. ✉ *Viale Pasubio 10* ☎ *02/6555741* ▱ *AE, DC, MC, V* ☙ *Closed Sun., Aug., and Dec. 24–Jan. 6.*

$$ ✕ **Trattoria Milanese.** Between the Duomo and the Basilica of Sant'Ambrogio, this small, popular trattoria has been run by the same family in the same location since 1933. It's invariably crowded, especially at dinner, when the regulars love to linger. Food is classic regional in approach, and the risotto is reliable. ✉ *Via Santa Marta 11* ☎ *02/86451991* ▱ *AE, DC, MC, V* ☙ *Closed Tues., Aug., and Dec. 24–Jan. 6.*

★ **$** ✕ **Da Abele.** The superb risotto dishes at this neighborhood trattoria change with the season, and there may be just two or three on the menu at any one time—order them all. It's a relaxed place with informal service, and the prices make it well worthwhile. Located outside the touristed center of town, this trattoria is convenient by subway. ✉ *Via Temperanza 5* ☎ *02/2613855* ▱ *AE, DC, MC, V* ☙ *Closed Mon., Aug., and Dec.15–Jan. 7. No lunch.*

$ ✕ **La Bruschetta.** The wood oven of this tiny, bustling Duomo-area pizzeria is in full view of its contented patrons. Along with first-class pizza, specialties from Tuscany and other parts of Italy are available: try the spaghetti *alle cozze e vongole* (with mussels and clams) or the grilled and skewered meats. ✉ *Piazza Beccaria 12* ☎ *02/8692494* ▱ *AE, MC, V* ☙ *Closed Mon., 3 wks in Aug., and late Dec.–early Jan.*

Where to Stay

Rome may be Italy's administrative and political capital, but Milan is its bustling business heart. As such, hotels are plentiful, with excellent standards and efficient service. Stay as close to the city center as possible, and book well in advance.

$$$$ 🏨 **Four Seasons.** The elegant restoration of a 15th-century monastery in the middle of Milan's most exclusive shopping district has produced a gem—for which you'll pay dearly. The hotel blends European sophistication with American comfort. Individually furnished rooms have opulent marble bathrooms; most rooms face a quiet courtyard. ✉ *Via Gesù 8, 20121* ☎ *02/77088* 🖷 *02/77085000* ⊕ *www.fourseasons.com* ✍ *93 rooms, 25 suites* ⚒ *2 restaurants, bar* ☴ *AE, DC, MC, V.*

★ $$$$ 🏨 **Grand Hotel Duomo.** Just 20 yards from the cathedral, this hotel's first-through third-floor rooms all overlook the church's Gothic gargoyles and pinnacles. The rooms are spacious and furnished in a snappy, contemporary style. ✉ *Via San Raffaele 1, 20121* ☎ *02/8833* 🖷 *02/86462027* ⊕ *www.grandhotelduomo.com* ✍ *162 rooms* ⚒ *3 restaurants, bar* ☴ *AE, DC, MC, V.*

★ $$$$ 🏨 **Westin Palace.** The Palace is Milan's premier hotel for business, offering unequaled comfort and connectivity (high-speed Internet access is available in every room). Don't be fooled by the functional 1950s-era exterior: guest rooms are elegantly outfitted with antiques, and bathrooms are lined with handsome marble. ✉ *Piazza della Repubblica 20, 20124* ☎ *02/63361* 🖷 *02/654485* ⊕ *www.westin.com* ✍ *244 rooms* ⚒ *2 restaurants, bar* ☴ *AE, DC, MC, V.*

$$$ 🏨 **Hotel Spadari Al Duomo.** This intimate boutique hotel near the Duomo and the Pinacoteca Ambroseum museum has its own private art collection. Junior suites on the 7th floor have views of the cathedral. ✉ *Via Spadari 11, 20123* ☎ *02/72002371* 🖷 *02/861184* ⊕ *www.spadarihotel.com* ✍ *40 rooms, 3 suites* ⚒ *Bar* ☴ *AE, DC, MC, V.*

$$ 🏨 **Antica Locanda Leonardo.** Convenient to the *Last Supper,* and close to the city center, this small hotel looks out onto a peaceful inner courtyard. The friendly staff is happy to provide information about getting tickets to the opera, soccer games, and other Milan events. ✉ *Corso Magenta 78, 20123* ☎ *02/463317* 🖷 *02/48019012* ⊕ *www.leoloc.com* ✍ *20 rooms* ⚒ *Bar* ☴ *AE, DC, MC, V* ☉ *Dec. 27–Jan. 5 and 3 wks in Aug.*

$$ 🏨 **Ariston.** This hotel near the Duomo was built according to bio-architectural principles, with nontoxic building materials used wherever possible. The attitude is warm and informal. The buffet breakfast includes organic foods, free Internet access is available in the lobby, and bicycles are available in summer. ✉ *Largo Carrobbio 2, 20123* ☎ *02/72000556* 🖷 *02/72000914* ⊕ *www.brerahotels.com* ✍ *46 rooms* ⚒ *Bar* ☴ *AE, DC, MC, V* ☉ *Closed Aug.*

$$ 🏨 **Canada.** This friendly, small hotel is close to Piazza Duomo on the edge of a district full of shops and restaurants. It offers modern comforts at a reasonable price. ✉ *Via Santa Sofia 16, 20121* ☎ *02/58304844* 🖷 *02/58300282* ⊕ *www.canadahotel.it* ✍ *35 rooms* ⚒ *Bar* ☴ *AE, DC, MC, V.*

★ $$ 🏨 **London.** The London's polite, efficient staff hosts its many English-speaking patrons in well-appointed, comfortable rooms. It has convenient access to Milan's main sights. ✉ *Via Rovello 3, 20121* ☎ *02/72020166* 🖷 *02/8057037* ⊕ *www.hotellondonmilano.com* ✍ *29 rooms* ⚒ *Bar* ☴ *MC, V* ☉ *Closed Aug. and Christmas wk.*

$ 🏨 **San Francisco.** In a residential area between the central station and the university, this medium-size hotel is handy to metro stations on two lines (Loreto or Piola stop). The management is friendly, the rooms are bright and clean, and there's a charming garden. ⊠ *Viale Lombardia 55, 20131* ☎ *02/2361009* 🖷 *02/26680377* ⊕ *www.hotel-sanfrancisco. it* ⤻ *31 rooms* ▭ *AE, DC, MC, V.*

Nightlife & the Arts

The Arts

The Teatro alla Scala is closed for restorations, but opera buffs can still see the company perform at **Teatro degli Arcimboldi** (⊠ Viale dell' Inovazione and Via Piero Calidrola) in the Bicocca neighborhood. The opera schedule—which runs between December 7 (St. Ambrose Day) and May—is interspersed with ballets and concerts. You can get information about performances and purchase tickets at the La Scala Web site (⊕ www.teatroallascala.org) or by using the automated phone reservation system (☎ 02/860775). For further information, consult the listings in the monthly *Milano Mese,* free at APT (tourist board) offices.

Nightlife

Head off to the Navigli or Brera district to have a drink or take advantage of one of the many happy hours that run from around 6:30 to 9:30. **El Brellin** (⊠ Vicolo Lavandai, at Alzaia Naviglio Grande ☎ 02/58101351) is one of many bars in the Navigli district; it's closed Sunday evening but offers one of Milan's increasingly popular brunches on Sunday afternoon. **La Banque** (⊠ Via Bassano Porrone 6 ☎ 02/86996565), near Piazza La Scala, is an exclusive and expensive bar, disco, and restaurant popular for anything from an aperitivo to a night out on the town. **Le Scimmie** (⊠ Via Ascanio Sforza 49 ☎ 02/89402874) delivers cool jazz in a laid-back space. **Magazzini Generali** (⊠ Via Pietrasanta 14 ☎ 02/55211313), in an old warehouse, is a fun, futuristic place to dance and to hear concerts. It's closed on Sunday. For a quieter evening, the cinema **Mexico** (⊠ Via Savona, 57 ☎ 02/48951802), although a bit out of the way, frequently shows films in English. **Nordest Caffe** (⊠ Via P. Borsieri 35 ☎ 02/69001910) is an elegant bar with jazz concerts Wednesday and Thursday nights and classical music on Friday. It's closed on Saturday. Check out **Orient Express** (⊠ Via Fiori Chiari 8 ☎ 02/8056227) in the Brera quarter for a bite to eat and live music.

Shopping

Milan is one of the world's capitals of fashion—designer shops (with designer price tags) line nearly every street in the city center. The most exclusive labels can be found in the *quadrilatero d'oro* (golden quadrangle) defined by **Via Monte Napoleone, Via Manzoni, Via della Spiga,** and **Via Sant'Andrea.** If you are more interested in bargain shopping than window-shopping, head for **Corso Buenos Aires,** near the central train station.

Milan Essentials

AIR TRAVEL TO & FROM MILAN

As Lombardy's capital and the most important financial and commercial center in northern Italy, Milan is well connected with Rome and Florence by fast and frequent rail and air service. Flights in and out of Milan during winter months are often prone to delay because of heavy fog.

AIRPORTS & TRANSFERS

Aeroporto Malpensa (MXP), well outside the city, services all intercontinental flights, as well as many European and domestic flights.

Aeroporto Milano Linate (LIN), closer to downtown, handles the remainder of European and domestic traffic.

⚡ Aeroporto Malpensa ✉ 50 km (30 mi) northwest of Milan ☎ 02/74852200 ⊕ www.sea-aeroportimilano.it. **Aeroporto Milano Linate** ✉ 10 km (7 mi) east of Milan ☎ 02/74852200.

TRANSFERS The *Malpensa Express* train connects Malpensa Airport with the Cadorna train station near downtown Milan. The 40-minute train ride costs €9 (€12 round-trip), leaving Cadorna every half hour (5:50 AM–8:20 PM) and leaving Malpensa every half hour (6:45 AM–9:45 PM). Buses run on the same route outside of these hours. In addition, buses connect both airports with *Stazione Centrale,* Milan's central train station. The fare from Malpensa is €5; from Linate it's €4. A taxi to the center of Milan costs about €70 from Malpensa or €20 from Linate. Shuttle buses (€8) run every 90 minutes between the two airports.

⚡ *Malpensa Express* ☎ 02/27763. **Malpensa Shuttle Buses** ☎ 02/58583158.

CAR TRAVEL

Several major autostrada routes cross at Milan, all connected by the circular *tangenziale* that surrounds the city. The A4 runs west to Turin and east to Venice; A1 leads south to Bologna, Florence, and Rome; A7 angles southwest down to Genoa. Parking is difficult in Milan's center—park on the outskirts and use public transportation.

CONSULATES

⚡ Canada ✉ Via Vittor Pisani 19 ☎ 02/67581.
⚡ United Kingdom ✉ Via San Paolo 7 ☎ 02/723001.
⚡ United States ✉ Via Principe Amedeo 2 ☎ 02/290351.

EMERGENCIES

⚡ Doctors & Dentists Hospital and Doctor ☎ 113.
⚡ Emergency Services Ambulance ☎ 118. **Carabinieri (Military Police)** ☎ 112. **Police** ☎ 113.

SUBWAY TRAVEL

Milan's subway network, the Metropolitana, is modern, fast, and easy to use. Trains runs every five minutes from 6 AM to midnight; signs marked MM indicate stations. Tickets are sold at newsstands, tobacconists, and machines at larger stops (some of which require exact change). The fare is €1 for travel within the center of Milan; passes for 24 hours of unlimited travel are available at the Duomo Station for €3. Buses follow the subway routes aboveground for about an hour after the subway closes.

⚡ Azienda Trasporti Milanesi (ATM) information office ✉ Mezzanine of the Duomo Station ☎ 800/016857 ⊕ www.atm-mi.it.

TAXIS

Taxicabs wait at stands or can be called in advance; they are difficult (but not impossible) to flag down off the street.

⚡ Radiotaxi ☎ 02/5353 or 02/8585.

TOURS

Three-hour morning sightseeing tours depart Tuesday–Sunday from Piazzetta Reale, next to the Duomo, at 9:30; they cost about €35 and are run by Autostradale Viaggi. Tickets can be purchased from the APT offices or aboard the bus. In addition, APT offices offer three-hour walking tours of the city, held Monday mornings at 10. Guided tours to city museums (many of which do not have their own guides) and other Milan and nearby artistic and architectural attractions are also organized by the APT.

TRAIN TRAVEL

The main train station is Milano Centrale. Several smaller stations handle commuter trains. Rapid Intercity trains connect Rome and Milan daily, stopping in Florence and/or Bologna; a nonstop Intercity leaves Rome or Milan morning and evening, and the trip takes about four hours. Information on train hours can be found on the FS–Trenitalia Web site.

Milano Centrale ✉ Piazzale Duca d'Aosta, about 3 km (2 mi) northwest of the Duomo ☎ 848/888088. **Trenitalia** ☎ 848/888088 ⊕ www.trenitalia.com.

TRAVEL AGENCIES

American Express Travel Agency ✉ Via Brera 3 ☎ 02/72003693. **Compagnia Italiana Turismo (CIT)** ✉ Galleria Vittorio Emanuele ☎ 02/863701.

VISITOR INFORMATION

APT Offices ✉ Via Marconi 1 (Piazza Duomo) ☎ 02/72524300 ✉ Stazione Centrale ☎ 02/72524370 ⊕ www.milanoinfotourist.it.

VENICE

It was called La Serenissima Repubblica, the majestic city that for centuries was the unrivaled mistress of trade between Europe and the Far East, and the staunch bulwark of Christendom against the tides of Turkish expansion. Venice is a labyrinth of narrow streets and waterways, and though many of its magnificent palazzi could use a face-lift, shabby here is magically transformed into beauty and charm. Romance is everywhere is Venice, especially at night when starlight dances on the water and streetlights all but revive those gargoyles glaring down from centuries-old facades. Venice's glory days as a wealthy city-state may be only a a memory, but art and fantasy live on, and with a courtesan's guile, they'll seduce your eye and your very soul.

Exploring Venice

Numbers in the margin correspond to points of interest on the Venice map.

To enjoy the city you will have to come to terms with the crowds of day-trippers, who take over the center around San Marco from May through September and during Carnevale. Venice is cooler and more welcoming in early spring and late fall. Romantics like the winter, when streets are often deserted and a haunting melancholy descends with the sea mist on *campi* (squares) and canals. Piazza San Marco is the pulse of Venice, but after elbowing the crowd to visit the Basilica di San Marco and the Doge's Palace, strike out on your own—let your feet and your eyes pick a direction. You won't be disappointed.

Piazza San Marco & the San Polo Neighborhood

Piazza San Marco put Venice on the world voyagers' grand tour circuit centuries before mass tourism crammed the square with more than 100,000 people in a single day (during Carnevale). San Marco is a great place to begin exploring monuments and streets packed with boutiques and expensive shops, but whatever you do, don't stop here; the less crowded, more affordable San Polo district, with its lively backstreets, can be even more fun to explore on foot.

★ ❸ **Basilica di San Marco** (St. Mark's Basilica). When the Doge's agents returned from Egypt in the 9th century with the stolen corpse of St. Mark the Evangelist, a church was built. That building burned to the ground, but the relics of the city's patron saint survived. Today they rest in an 11th-century structure, a blend of Byzantine, Gothic, and Renaissance

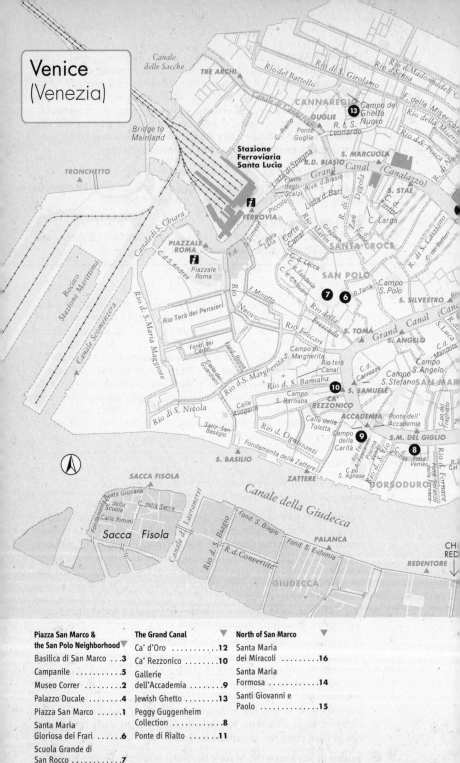

Venice (Venezia)

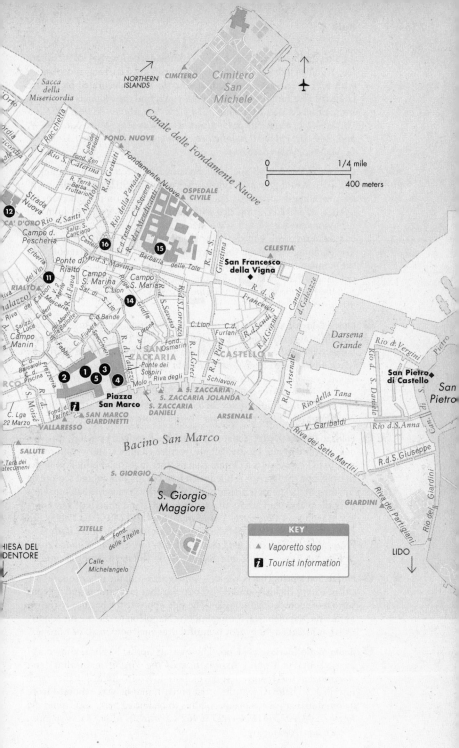

NORTHERN ISLANDS

CIMITERO

Cimitero San Michele

Sacca della Misericordia

Orto

cordia

cordia

Canale delle Fondamente Nuove

0   1/4 mile
0   400 meters

C. d. Racchetta

FOND. NUOVE

Ci Copoladi Gesuiti

Rio S. Caterina

Fond. Zen

R. Terra Barba Fruttarioli

Fondamente Nuove

R.d.Gesuiti

Rio della Panada

OSPEDALE CIVILE

Strada Nuova

12 CA' D'ORO

Campo d. Pescheria

Saliz. S. Canciano

C. Castelli

Rio d. Santi

Apostoli

C.d. Squero

C.d. Testa

Erberia

C. d. Vin

16

C.d. Fava

C.d.lela Mendicanti

15

Barbaria delle Tole

CELESTIA

Ginstina

R. d. S.

San Francesco della Vigna

11 RIALTO

Rio d.S. Marina

Campo S. Marina

Sal. di S. Lio

Campo S. Maria

S. Severo

C.d. Fava

R. d. S. Francesco

R. d. S.

Canale d. Galeazze

Darsena Grande

Rio d. Vergini

San Pietro di Castello

San Pietro

Ponte di Rialto

Palazzo

Riva del Carbon

C.d. Mercerie

C.d. Bande

Garba

S. Lorenzo

C. Lion

C.d. Furlani

R.d.Scudi

R.d.Gorna

Rio della Tana

S. Daniele

V. Garibaldi

Rio d.S. Anna

Catt.

Pietro

Salizz. S. Luca

C. dell' Oro

C.d. Fiubera

Specchieri

C.d. Bande

R.d. Valaresso

Fond. Osmarin

R.d.Greci

Schiavoni

R.d. Arsenale

Riva dei Sette Martiri

R. d. S. Giuseppe

2

1

3

SAN ZACCARIA

Ponte dei Sospiri

S. ZACCARIA

ARSENALE

GIARDINI

Campo Manin

Frezzeria

5

4

Molo

Riva degli

S. ZACCARIA JOLANDA

S. ZACCARIA DANIELI

i

Piazza San Marco

SAN MARCO GIARDINETTI

C. Lga 22 Marzo

VALLARESSO

Bacino San Marco

Riva dei Partigiani

Rio dei Giardini

LIDO

SALUTE

Tera dei Catecumeni

S. GIORGIO

S. Giorgio Maggiore

GIARDINI

ZITELLE

Fond. delle Zitelle

CHIESA DEL REDENTORE

Calle Michelangelo

KEY

▲ Vaporetto stop

i Tourist information

architectural elements, beneath a ceiling adorned with 43,055 square feet of golden mosaics. Don't miss the **Pala d'Oro,** a dazzling gilded screen with 1,927 precious gems. Riding atop the richly decorated facade are copies of four famous bronze horses; you'll find the originals up a steep staircase in **Museo Marciano.** ⊠ *Piazza San Marco* ☎ *041/5225205* ☉ *May–Oct., Mon.–Sat. 9:45–5, Sun. 2–5; Nov.–Apr., Mon.–Sat. 9:45–4, Sun. 2–4; last entry 30 min before closing; tours June–Aug., Mon.–Sat* Ⓥ *Vallaresso/San Zaccaria.*

★ ☾ ❺ **Campanile.** Venice's original brick bell tower (325 feet tall, plus the angel) had been standing nearly 1,000 years when in 1902, practically without warning, it collapsed. The new tower, rebuilt on the old plan, reopened in 1912. During the 15th century, clerics guilty of immoral behavior were suspended in wooden cages from the tower, some forced to subsist on bread and water for as long as a year, others left to starve. The stunning view from the tower includes the Lido, the lagoon, and the mainland as far as the Alps, but, strangely enough, none of the myriad canals that snake through the city. ⊠ *Piazza San Marco* ☎ *041/ 5224064* ☉ *June–Sept., daily 9–sunset or 9 PM; Oct.–May, 9–4; last entry 30 min before closing.*

❷ **Museo Correr.** Exhibits in this museum of Venetian art and history range from the absurdly high-soled shoes worn by 16th-century Venetian ladies (who walked with the aid of a servant) to Jacopo de' Barbari's (circa 1440–1515) huge *Grande Pianta Prospettica*, detailing in carved wood every inch of 16th-century Venice. Through Correr, you can access the **Museo Archeologico** and the **Biblioteca Marciana.** ⊠ *Piazza San Marco, Ala Napoleonica* ☎ *041/5225625* ☉ *Apr.–Oct., daily 9–7; Nov.–Mar., 9–5; last tickets sold 1½ hrs before closing.*

★ ❹ **Palazzo Ducale** (Doge's Palace). During the Republic's heyday, this was combination White House, Senate, torture chamber, and prison rolled into one. The facade is a Gothic-Renaissance fantasia of pink-and-white marble, and the interior is filled with frescoes, paintings, and sculptings by some of the greatest artists of the times. Don't miss the balcony view over the piazza and across the water to the island church of San Giorgio Maggiore. ⊠ *Piazzetta San Marco* ☎ *041/5224951* ▱ *Piazza San Marco museums: €9.50. Musei Civici: €15.50* ☉ *Apr.–Oct., daily 9–7; Nov.–Mar., 9–5; last tickets sold 1½ hrs before closing. Guided tours in English: Tues.–Thurs. and Sat. 11:30* Ⓥ *Vallaresso/San Zaccaria.*

★ ☾ ❶ **Piazza San Marco.** This is Venice's only *piazza*—all the other squares are called *campi* (fields)—and it's so popular that pedestrians and pigeons seem to be competing for space. The side opposite the basilica is known as the **Ala Napoleonica,** a wing built by Napoléon to enclose the square, or what he called "the most beautiful drawing room in all of Europe."

❻ **Santa Maria Gloriosa dei Frari.** The soaring Gothic basilica, known as I Frari, contains Titian's *Assumption of the Virgin* (main altar) and *Madonna di Ca' Pesaro* (left nave), both loved from the day they were unveiled. So beloved was the artist himself, that he was exhumed from a communal grave for plague victims to be buried here. ⊠ *Campo dei Frari* ☎ *041/2728618; 041/2750462 Chorus.* ☉ *Mon.–Sat. 9–6, Sun. 1–6* Ⓥ *San Tomà.*

❼ **Scuola Grande di San Rocco.** Venice's *scuole* (plural) weren't schools, but benevolent fraternities that helped society's neediest. Following in San Rocco's footsteps, this wealthy group helped the sick. Tintoretto painted more than 60 canvases for the scuola during the 1500s, among which the *Crucifixion* in the Albergo (off the great hall) is said to be his masterpiece. ⊠ *Campo San Rocco, San Polo 3052,* ☎ *041/5234864* ☉ *Nov.*

3–Mar. 27, daily 10–4; Mar. 28–Nov. 2, 9–5:30; last entrance ½ hr before closing V *San Tomà.*

The Grand Canal

The canal may be called Canalazzo by Venetians, but to the rest of the world, it's the Grand Canal. Here 200 opulent and fantastic palazzi, born of a culture obsessed with opulence and fantasy, appear by day in all their architectural splendor. By night, they appear like a voyeur's dream come true. Take a 45-minute ride aboard vaporetto Line 1 from the train station to San Marco (4 km or 2½ mi) and do try to grab one of the seats in the prow, from which you'll have an unobstructed view.

★ **12 Ca' d'Oro.** This lovely Venetian Gothic palace got its name from the pure gold that once embellished its facade. Today it houses the **Galleria Franchetti,** a fine collection of tapestries, sculptures, and paintings. ⊠ *Calle Ca' d'Oro, Cannaregio 3933,* ☎ *041/5222349* ◷ *Mon. 8:15–2, Tues.–Sun. 8:15–7:15; last entry 30 min before closing* V *Ca' d'Oro.*

★ **10 Ca' Rezzonico.** Designed by Baldassare Longhena in the 17th century, this mansion was completed nearly 100 years later and became the last home of English poet Robert Browning (1812–89). The **Museo del Settecento Veneziano** (Museum of Venice in the 1700s) feels like you've dropped into an old Venetian palazzo, with period furniture, tapestries, and gilded salons. Recent donations added nearly 300 paintings, most from Venetian schools of artists. There's also a restored apothecary, complete with powders and potions. ⊠ *Fondamenta Rezzonico, Dorsoduro 3136* ☎ *041/2410100.* ◷ *Apr.–Oct., Wed.–Mon. 10–6; Nov.–Mar., Wed.–Mon. 10–5; last entry 1 hr before closing* V *Ca' Rezzonico.*

★ **9 Gallerie dell'Accademia.** (Accademia Gallery). Trace the development of Venetian painting and the changes in the city itself as you explore the world's most extensive collection of Venetian art. From Byzantine roots, explore the art of Venice through the centuries. On view are paintings by Jacopo Bellini, father of Venetian Renaissance (1400–1471), his son Giovanni (1430–1516); Giorgione's *Tempest*; Titian's *Presentation of the Virgin,* and several works by Tintoretto (1518–94). Don't miss *Feast in the House of Levi* that got Veronese branded (1528–88) a heretic. ⊠ *Campo della Carità* ☎ *041/5222247; 041/5200345 reservations* ⊕ *www.gallerieaccademia.org* ◷ *Mon. 8:15–2, Tues.–Sun. 8:15–7:15* V *Accademia.*

13 Jewish Ghetto. The quiet island neighborhood gave the world the word "ghetto" and still houses Jewish institutions. It also has Europe's highest density of ancient synagogues, each one a unique cross-cultural creation. At the **Museo Ebraico,** you'll discover the history of Jewish culture within the Republic. ⊠ *Campo del Ghetto Nuovo, Cannaregio 2902/B,* ☎ *041/715359* ⊕ *www.museoebraico.it* ◷ *Oct.–May, Sun.–Fri. 10–5:45; June–Sept., Sun.–Fri. 10–6:45. Last hourly tour at 5:30 in summer (at 4:30 in winter) on Fri. at sunset* V *San Marcuola or Guglie.*

8 Peggy Guggenheim Collection. Peggy Guggenheim was one of the 20th century's greatest art collectors. At Palazzo Venier, her former Grand Canal home, you'll see works by Picasso, Kandinsky, Magritte, Motherwell, Pollock, and Ernst (at one time her husband). ⊠ *Calle San Cristoforo, Dorsoduro 701* ☎ *041/2405411* ⊕ *www.guggenheim-venice.it* ◷ *Nov.–Mar., Wed.–Mon. 10–6; Apr.–Oct., Wed.–Fri., Sun., and Mon. 10–6, Sat. 10–10* V *Accademia.*

★ **11 Ponte di Rialto** (Rialto Bridge). The late-16th-century competition to design a stone bridge across the Grand Canal (replacing earlier wooden versions) attracted the best architects of the period, including Michelangelo, Palladio, and Sansovino, but the job went to the appropriately named Antonio da Ponte. His pragmatic design included 90 feet of shop space and was high enough for galleys to pass beneath; it also kept decoration and cost to a minimum at a time when the Republic's coffers were suffering from wars with the Turks and loss of its Eastern trading monopoly. The bridge offers one of the city's most famous views: the Grand Canal alive with gondola and motorboat traffic. Don't miss the Rialto's fruit and vegetable market and its *pescheria,* where fish have been bartered for 1,000 years. Ⓥ *Rialto/San Silvestro.*

North of San Marco

Put away your map and let yourself get lost in the picturesque neighborhoods north of San Marco. Here, where low-key shops, bakeries, and tiny watering holes haven't yet been replaced by tourist stops, wooden boats still line jade-green canals and residents of less palatial homes still hang their laundry to dry in the breeze.

⑯ **Santa Maria dei Miracoli.** Tiny, yet perfectly proportioned, this Renaissance jewelbox is sheathed in marble outside and decorated inside with exquisite marble reliefs. Architect and illusionist Pietro Lombardo varied color on the exterior to create the effect of greater distance, and used extra pilasters so the building's canal side looks longer than it is. ⊠ *Campo Santa Maria Nova* ☎ *041/2750462 Chorus* ☉ *Mon.–Sat. 10–5, Sun. 1–5* Ⓥ *Rialto.*

⑭ **Santa Maria Formosa.** Mauro Coducci built this 15th-century marble church atop 11th-century foundations. Visit Bartolomeo Vivarini's *Our Lady of Mercy* and Jacopo Palma il Vecchio's *Santa Barbara,* then enjoy the cafés and produce market in the bustling square. ⊠ *Campo Santa Maria Formosa* ☎ *041/5234645* ☉ *Mon.–Sat. 10–5, Sun. 1–5* Ⓥ *Rialto.*

⑮ **Santi Giovanni e Paolo.** While Franciscan friars were laboring away on their church in San Polo, the Dominicans were similarly busy in Castello. *San Zanipolo,* as Venetians call it, contains a wealth of artwork and the tombs of 25 doges. In the campo rides **Bartolomeo Colleoni** (1400–75), Venice's most famous mercenary, immortalized on horseback. ⊠ *Campo dei Santi Giovanni e Paolo* ☎ *041/5235913* ☉ *Mon.–Sat. 7:30–12:30 and 3:30–6, Sun. 3–6* Ⓥ *Fondamente Nuove /Rialto.*

Venetian Lagoon

The perfect vacation from your Venetian vacation is an escape to the lagoon islands. Let a vaporetto whisk you away from busy streets and into the world of Murano's glassworks, Burano's wonderland houses painted a riot of colors, and Torcello, dreamily romantic and lushly green.

Burano. Centuries ago, lace-making rescued the economy of this former fishing village. At the **Museo del Merletto** (Museum of Lace), you can watch women carrying on the lace-making tradition. They sometimes have pieces for sale, but don't expect bargains—handmade Burano lace costs $1,000 to $2,000 for a 10-inch doily. ⊠ *Piazza Galuppi 187* ☎ *041/730034* ☉ *Apr.–Oct., Wed.–Mon. 10–5; Nov.–Mar., Wed.–Mon. 10–4.*

★ ☾ **Murano.** During the 13th century, the Republic, concerned about fires, moved its **glassworks** to Murano. Factories that you can visit line the **Fondamenta dei Vetrai,** the canalside walkway leading from the Colonna vaporetto landing. The glass collection at **Museo Vetrario** ranges from priceless antiques to equally expensive modern pieces. ⊠ *Fondamenta Giustinian 8* ☎ *041/739586* ☉ *Apr.–Oct., Thurs.–Tues. 10–5; Nov.–Mar., Thurs.–Tues. 10–4.*

Basilica dei Santi Maria e Donato has an elaborate mosaic floor that dates from 1140 and a wooden ship's keel roof. ⊠ *Fondamenta Giustinian,* ☎ *041/739056* ⊗ *Daily 8–noon and 4–7.*

Torcello. This is where some of the first Venetians landed in their flight from the barbarians, 1,500 years ago. During the 16th century the island had 10 churches and 20,000 inhabitants; today you'll be lucky to see one of the island's 16 residents. The 11th-century **Santa Maria Assunta** testifies to Torcello's former wealth. The Byzantine mosaic *Last Judgment* shows sinners writhing, and the Madonna looks down from her field of gold. Do climb the **Campanile** for an incomparable view of the lagoon wetlands. ☎ *041/730119* ⊗ *Apr.–Oct., daily 10:30–6; Nov.–Mar., 10–5.*

Where to Eat

Venetians love seafood, and it figures prominently on most restaurant menus, sometimes to the exclusion of meat dishes. Fish is generally expensive, and you should remember when ordering that the price given on menus for fish as a main course is often per 100 grams, not the total cost of what you are served, which could be two or three times that amount. *Sarde in saor* (fried sardines marinated with onions, vinegar, pine nuts, and raisins) is a tasty traditional dish that can cost as little as a pizza. City specialties also include *pasta e fagioli* (pasta and bean soup), risotto, and the delicious *fegato alla veneziana* (calves' liver with onions) served with grilled polenta.

$$$$ ✕ **Osteria Da Fiore.** Long a favorite with Venetians, Da Fiore has been discovered by tourists, so reservations are imperative. It's known for its excellent seafood, which might include such specialties as *pasticcio di pesce* (fish pie) and *seppioline* (little cuttlefish). Not easy to find, it's just off Campo San Polo. ⊠ *Calle dello Scaleter, 2202/A San Polo* ☎ *041/721308* ⚐ *Reservations essential* ▭ *AE, DC, MC, V* ⊗ *Closed Sun. and Mon., Aug. 10–early Sept., and Dec. 25–Jan. 15.*

$$$–$$$$ ✕ **Da Arturo.** This tiny eatery on the Calle degli Assassini has the distinction in Venice of *not* serving seafood. On offer are tasty, tender, meat courses in generous portions, such as the subtly pungent *braciola alla veneziana* (pork chop schnitzel with vinegar), and an authentic creamy homemade tiramisu to finish. Vegetarian Venetians and visitors make their way here as well, as the antipasti and *primi* offerings are more than hospitable. ⊠ *Calle degli Assassini, 3656 San Marco* ☎ *041/5286974* ⚐ *Reservations essential* ▭ *No credit cards* ⊗ *Closed Sun., 10 days after Carnevale, and 4 wks in Aug.*

★ **$$$–$$$$** ✕ **Alle Testiere.** A strong local following can make it tough to get one of the five tables at this tiny trattoria near Campo Santa Maria Formosa. Chef Bruno Gavagnin's dishes stand out for lightness and balance: try the *gnocchetti con moscardini* (little gnocchi with tender baby octopus), the linguine with *coda di rospo* (monkfish), or the carpaccio special of the day. The well-assembled wine list is particularly strong on local whites. ⊠ *Calle del Mondo Novo, 5801 Castello* ☎ *041/5227220* ⚐ *Reservations essential* ▭ *MC, V* ⊗ *Closed Sun. and Mon.*

$$–$$$$ ✕ **Fiaschetteria Toscana.** Contrary to what the name suggests, there's nothing Tuscan about this restaurant's menu. It was formerly a storehouse for Tuscan wine and oil, and it's worth a trip for its cheerful and courteous service, fine *cucina* (cooking), and noteworthy cellar. Gastronomic highlights include a light *tagliolini neri al ragù di astice* (thin spaghetti served with squid ink and mixed with a delicate lobster sauce), and *zabaione* (zabaglione). ⊠ *Campo San Giovanni Crisostomo, 5719*

Cannaregio ☎ 041/5285281 ⊟ AE, DC, MC, V ⊘ Closed Tues. and 4 wks in July and Aug. No lunch Mon.

★ $$ ✕ **L'Incontro.** A faithful clientele, attracted by flavorful Sardinian food, flocks to this place. Starters include Sardinian sausages, but you might sample the delicious traditional primi like *culingiones* (large ravioli filled with pecorino, saffron, and orange peel). Don't miss the herb-crusted meat dishes such as *coniglio al mirto* (rabbit baked on a bed of myrtle sprigs) and the *costine d'agnello con rosmarino e mentuccia* (baby lamb's ribs with rosemary and wild mint). ⊠ *Rio Terrà Canal, 3062/ A Dorsoduro* ☎ 041/5222404 ⊟ AE, DC, MC, V ⊘ Closed Mon., Jan., and 2 wks in Aug. No lunch Tues.

★ $–$$ ✕ **Vini da Gigio.** A quaint, friendly, family-run trattoria on the quay side of a canal just off the Strada Nuova, da Gigio is very popular with Venetians and other visiting Italians, who appreciate the affable service; the well-prepared homemade pasta, fish, and meat dishes; the imaginative and varied cellar; and the high-quality draft wine. It's good for a simple lunch at tables in the barroom. ⊠ *Fondamenta de la Chiesa, 3628/ A Cannaregio* ☎ 041/5285140 ⊟ AE, DC, MC, V ⊘ Closed Mon., 3 wks in Jan. and Feb., 1 wk in June, and 3 wks in Aug. and Sept.

$ ✕ **Alla Madonna.** At times it seems there are more foreigners eating here than locals, but this osteria is hard to beat for quality and price. In short, it's a rare Venetian bargain. The *granseola* (spider crab) is a real winner; make sure to ask for some extra virgin olive oil. And try to save room for the tiramisu. ⊠ *Calle della Madonna, 594 San Polo* ☎ 041/ 5223824 ⊟ AE, MC, V ⊘ Closed Wed. and Aug.

★ $ ✕ **Bancogiro.** Here's a place to consider if you're tired of typical Venetian food. Yes, fish is on the menu—the *mousse di gamberoni con salsa di avocado* (shrimp mousse with an avocado sauce) provides a tasty diversion. But you can also sample offbeat offerings such as the Sicilian-style *sarde incinte* (stuffed, or "pregnant," sardines). Set in the heart of the Rialto market in a 15th-century loggia, the restaurant's tables are upstairs in a carefully restored no-smoking room with a partial view of the Grand Canal. ⊠ *Campo San Giacometto 122 (under the porch), Santa Croce* ☎ 041/5232061 ⊟ No credit cards ⊘ Closed Mon. No dinner Sun.

Where to Stay

Space in the time-worn but renovated palaces-cum-hotels is at a premium in this city, and even in the best hotel, rooms can be small and offer little natural light. Preservation restrictions on buildings often preclude the installation of such things as elevators and air-conditioning. On the other hand, Venice's luxury hotels can offer rooms of fabulous opulence and elegance, and even in the more modest hotels you can find comfortable rooms of great charm and character, sometimes with stunning views. Venice attracts visitors year-round, although the winter months, with the exception of Carnevale time, are generally much quieter, and most hotels offer lower rates during this period. It is always worth booking in advance, but if you haven't, AVA (Venetian Hoteliers Association) booths will help you find a room after your arrival in the city.

$$$$ ▦ **Danieli.** Parts of this rather large hotel are built around a 15th-century palazzo bathed in sumptuous Venetian colors. The downside is that the Danieli also has several modern annexes that some find bland and impersonal, and the lower-price rooms can be exceedingly drab. Still, celebrities and English-speaking patrons crowd its sumptuous four-story-high lobby, chic salons, and dining terrace with a fantastic view of St. Mark's Basin. ⊠ *Riva degli Schiavoni, 4196 Castello, 30122*

☎ *041/5226480* 🖷 *041/5200208* ⊕ *www.luxurycollection.com* ⌁ *221 rooms, 12 suites* ⚒ *Restaurant, bar* ▤ *AE, DC, MC, V.*

$$$$ ⌂ **Gritti Palace.** This haven of pampering luxury is like an aristocratic private home, with fresh flowers, fine antiques, lavish appointments, and attentive service. The dining terrace overlooking the Grand Canal is best in the evening when boat traffic dies down. ⊠ *Campo Santa Maria del Giglio, 2467 San Marco, 30124* ☎ *041/794611* 🖷 *041/5200942* ⊕ *www.luxurycollection.com* ⌁ *87 rooms, 6 suites* ⚒ *Restaurant, bar* ▤ *AE, DC, MC, V.*

$$$$ ⌂ **Hotel Londra Palace.** The hotel's 100 windows overlook the lagoon and the island of San Giorgio, which imparts a hearty dash of sunlight to many of its finely decorated rooms. The view must have been pleasing to Tchaikovsky, who wrote his 4th Symphony here in 1877. Neoclassical-style public rooms, with splashes of blue and green glass suggesting the sea, play nicely off guest rooms, with their fine fabric, damask drapes, Biedermeier furniture, and Venetian glass. ⊠ *Riva degli Schiavoni, 4171 Castello, 30122* ☎ *041/5200533* 🖷 *041/5225032* ⊕ *www.hotelondra.it* ⌁ *36 rooms, 17 suites* ⚒ *Restaurant, bar* ▤ *AE, DC, MC, V.*

★ **$$$$** ⌂ **il Palazzo at the Bauer.** A $38 million restoration has turned il Palazzo into the ultimate word in luxury. Bevilacqua and Rubelli fabrics cover the walls, and no two rooms are decorated the same. Il Palazzo is separate from the Bauer Hotel, but both have rooms with high ceilings, Murano glass, marbled bathrooms, and damask drapes. The outdoor hot tub on the 7th floor offers wonderful views of La Serenissima. ⊠ *Campo San Moisè, 1459 San Marco, 30124* ☎ *041/5207022* 🖷 *041/5207557* ⊕ *www.bauervenezia.it* ⌁ *35 rooms, 40 suites* ⚒ *Restaurant, bar* ▤ *AE, DC, MC, V.*

★ **$$$$** ⌂ **Metropole.** Guests can step from their water taxi or gondola into the lobby of this small, well-run hotel, rich in precious antiques and just five minutes from Piazza San Marco. Many rooms have a view of the lagoon and others overlook the garden at the back. ⊠ *Riva degli Schiavoni, 4149 Castello, 30122* ☎ *041/5205044* 🖷 *041/5223679* ⊕ *www. hotelmetropole.com* ⌁ *43 rooms, 26 suites* ⚒ *Restaurant, bar* ▤ *AE, DC, MC, V.*

$$$ ⌂ **American.** At first sight, it's hard to pick out this quiet, family-run hotel from the houses along the fondamenta: there are no lights, flags, or big signs on the hotel's yellow stucco facade. Rooms vary in size and shape, but sage green and delicate pink fabrics and lacquered Venetian-style furniture are found throughout. ⊠ *San Vio, 628 Dorsoduro, 30123* ☎ *041/5204733* 🖷 *041/5204048* ⊕ *www.hotelamerican.com* ⌁ *28 rooms, 2 suite* ▤ *AE, DC, MC, V.*

$$$ ⌂ **Hotel Pausania.** From the moment you ascend the grand staircase rising above the fountain of this 14th-century palazzo, you sense the combination of good taste and modern comforts that characterize this hotel. Light-shaded rooms are spacious, with comfortable furniture and carpets with rugs thrown over them. Some rooms face the small canal (which can become a bit noisy early in the morning) in front of the hotel, and others look out over the large garden courtyard. ⊠ *Fondamenta Gherardini, 2824 Dorsoduro, 30123* ☎ *041/5222083* 🖷 *041/5222989* ⊕ *www.hotelpausania.it* ⌁ *26 rooms* ⚒ *Bar* ▤ *AE, MC, V.*

$$ ⌂ **Hotel Antico Doge.** If you're looking for a small, intimate hotel in a quiet, central location, look no further. This delightful palazzo once belonged to Doge Marino Falier; since then, it's been modernized with lovely results: some rooms have canopy beds or baldacchini; all have fabric walls and hardwood floors. On a small canal, only minutes away from San Marco and the Rialto Bridge, this is an oasis of tranquillity. An ample buffet breakfast is served in a room with a frescoed ceiling and Murano chandelier. ⊠ *Campo SS. Apostoli, Cannaregio 5643, 30131* ☎ *041/ 241 1570* 🖷 *041/244 3660* ⊕ *www.anticodoge.com* 🛏 *13 rooms, 2 suites* ♿ *Bar* ☰ *AE, DC, MC, V.*

$$ 🏨 **Paganelli.** The lagoon views here so impressed Henry James that he described the Paganelli in the preface to his *Portrait of a Lady*. This enchanting small hotel on the waterfront near Piazza San Marco is tastefully decorated in the Venetian style. The quieter annex in Campo San Zaccaria is a former convent, and some rooms preserve the original coffered ceilings. ⊠ *Riva degli Schiavoni, 4687 Castello, 30122* ☎ *041/ 5224324* 🖷 *041/5239267* ♿ *Bar* ☰ *AE, MC, V.*

$$ 🏨 **Wildner.** Right between the superdeluxe Danieli and Londra Palace hotels, this pleasant, unpretentious, family-run pensione enjoys the same views. The rooms are spread over four floors (no elevator), half with a view of San Giorgio and half looking out onto the quiet Campo San Zaccaria. The no-nonsense interior has parquet floors, solid, dark furniture, and brown leather headboards. White curtains and creamy bedspreads enhance the Wildner's simplicity. ⊠ *Riva degli Schiavoni, 4161 Castello, 30122* ☎ *041/5227463* 🖷 *041/2414640* ⊕ *www. veneziahotels.com* 🛏 *16 rooms* ☰ *AE, DC, MC, V.*

$–$$ 🏨 **Agli Alboretti.** The Alboretti is one of the many hotels clustered at the foot of the Ponte dell'Accademia. Its unpretentious, rather small rooms are blessed with plenty of light. Some steep climbing might be part of your stay, as there are four floors and no elevator. In warm weather, breakfast is served in an inner courtyard under a rose bower; a small terrace with potted plants is open during the warmer months. ⊠ *Rio Terrà Foscarini, 884 Dorsoduro, 30123* ☎ *041/5230058* 🖷 *041/5210158* ⊕ *www. aglialboretti.com* 🛏 *20 rooms* ♿ *Restaurant, bar* ☰ *AE, DC, MC, V.*

$–$$ 🏨 **La Calcina.** The Calcina sits in an enviable position along the sunny
FodorśChoice   Zattere, with views across the wide Giudecca Canal. A stone staircase
★   (no elevator) leads to the rooms upstairs, with shiny wooden floors, original art deco furniture and lamps, and firm beds. Some rooms suffer from a lack of storage space, and anyone staying in a single room should note that a few of the rooms have a shared bath. ⊠ *Zattere 780 Dorsoduro, 30123* ☎ *041/5206466* 🖷 *041/5227045* ⊕ *www.lacalcina.com* 🛏 *29 rooms, 26 with bath; 5 suites* ♿ *Restaurant* ☰ *AE, DC, MC, V.*

★ $ 🏨 **Dalla Mora.** On a quiet lane beyond the main flow of traffic, this hotel occupies two simple, well-maintained houses, both with a view. The tiny, cheerful entrance hall leads upstairs to a terrace lined with potted geraniums—a perfect place to catch the breeze on summer evenings. Rooms are spacious, with basic wooden furniture and tile floors. The annex across the street has rooms without private bathrooms and others with only showers and sinks. The excellent price and good views make this an especially attractive place to stay if you're on a budget. ⊠ *Off Salizzada San Pantalon, 42 Santa Croce, 30135* ☎ *041/710703* 🖷 *041/723006* 🛏 *14 rooms, 6 with bath* ☰ *MC, V.*

Nightlife & the Arts

To find out what's going on, pick up a *Guest in Venice* booklet, free at hotels, or *Venezia News,* which is sold at newsstands. Both have information in English (and Italian) concerning concerts, opera, ballet, theater, exhibitions, movies, sports, and clubs. They also print schedules for the busiest vaporetto and bus lines, and the main trains and flights from Venice.

The Arts

Venice is a stop for major traveling exhibits, from ancient Mayan to contemporary art. In odd-numbered years, from mid-June to early

November, the **Biennale dell'Arte** attracts several hundred contemporary artists from around the world. Biennale also holds the Venice International Film Festival each August as well as numerous music and dance events throughout the year. ✉ *Ca' Giustinian* ☎ *041/5218711* 🖷 *041/5227539* ⊕ *www.labiennale.org.*

CONCERTS Biennale Musica spotlights contemporary music, and clubs around town occasionally have jazz and Italian pop, but the vast majority of music played in Venice is classical, with Vivaldi (Venice's star composer) usually featured. You'll find posters and costumed youth pitching concerts, but especially worth seeking out are **L'Offerta Musicale** (☎ 041/5241143 call for information) and **Gruppo Accademia di San Rocco,** which performs at **Scuola di San Rocco** (☎ 041/5234864 or 041/962999). Travel agency **Kele e Teo** (✉ Ponte dei Bareteri, between San Marco and Rialto ☎ 041/5208722) handles tickets for a number of orchestras. A great source of information is **Vivaldi** (✉ Fontego dei Tedeschi 5537, opposite Rialto Post Office ☎🖷 041/5221343), which sells CDs by local groups and often has tickets available.

OPERA **Teatro La Fenice,** one of Italy's oldest opera houses, has witnessed memorable premieres, including Verdi's 1853 first-night flop of *La Traviata.* It has also endured its share of disasters, like the fire of January 1996, which badly damaged it. Until La Fenice rises again, as its name (*The Phoenix*) promises, opera, symphony, and ballet events alternate between the **Teatro Malibran** (✉ Campo San Giovanni Crisostomo) and the tent-like **Palafenice** (✉ Tronchetto parking area). Visit (⊕ www.teatrolafenice. it) for a calender of performances or to buy tickets for either venue. Tickets are available at the theater one hour before show time. Information and tickets are also available through **Vela** (✉ Piazzale Roma or Calle dei Fuseri ☎ 899/909090).

Nightlife

Hybrid **Caffè Blue** (✉ San Pantalon ☎ 041/710227) reserves one bar for whiskey drinkers and also serves afternoon tea from a samovar. It's open noon 'til 2 AM and has live music on Friday. Lido's summery **Discoteca Acropolis** (✉ Lungomare 22 ☎ 041/5260466) beach disco has a terrace bar and occasional live music. Near Accademia Gallery, **Piccolo Mondo** (✉ Dorsoduro 1056/A ☎ 041/5200371) has a tiny dance floor open until 4 AM. **Martini Scala Club** (✉ Campo San Fantin ☎ 041/5224121), attached to the elegant restaurant of the same name, serves full meals until 2 AM and has live music until 3:30 AM.

Shopping

At **Gilberto Penzo** (✉ Calle Seconda dei Saoneri, 2681 San Polo ☎ 041/719372 ⊕ www.veniceboats.com) you'll find small-scale models of gondolas and their graceful oarlocks known as *forcole.* **Norelene** (✉ Calle della Chiesa, 727 Dorsoduro, near the Peggy Guggenheim Collection ☎ 041/5237605) has hand-painted fabrics that make wonderful wall hangings or elegant jackets and chic scarves. In San Marco, **Venetia Studium** (✉ Calle Larga XXII Marzo ☎ 041/5229281 ⊕ www.venetiastudium.com) is famous for Fortuny-inspired lamps and elegant scarves.

Glass

There's a lot of cheap, low-quality Venetian glass for sale around town; if you want something better, try **l'Isola** (✉ Campo San Moisè, 1468 San Marco ☎ 041/5231973), where Carlo Moretti's contemporary designs are on display. **Domus** (✉ Fondamenta dei Vetrai, Murano ☎ 041/739215), on Murano, has a good selection of glass objects.

Shopping Districts

Le Mercerie, the **Frezzeria**, and **Calle dei Fabbri** are some of Venice's busiest shopping streets and lead off of Piazza San Marco.

Venice Essentials

AIRPORTS & TRANSFERS

Aeroporto Marco Polo ✉ 10 km (6 mi) north of Venice on the mainland ☎ 041/2609260 flight information.

TRANSFERS
The cheapest, most direct airport transfer to historic Venice is Alilaguna. The company's free airport shuttle bus takes you to the dock, where for €10 per person, including bags, you board one of the boats that leave hourly (until midnight). The trip to Piazza San Marco takes an hour, and you will stop at the Lido on the way. Blue ATVO buses run nonstop to Piazzale Roma in 25 minutes and cost €2.70. Yellow ACTV local buses (Line 5) cost €.77, but you must buy tickets before boarding, and large bags can be awkward during rush hour. From Piazzale Roma you can catch a vaporetto to your hotel. Private water taxis, called *motoscafi*, should carry four persons and four bags to a single stop for €78, but agree on the price before boarding. Land taxis cost about €30.
Alilaguna ☎ 041/5235775. **Radio Taxi** ☎ 041/936222 **Motoscafo** ☎ 041/5415084 airport transfers.

BOAT & FERRY TRAVEL

BY GONDOLA
If you can't leave Venice without a gondola ride, take it in the evening, when traffic has died down and palace windows are illuminated. Let the gondolier know that you want to see the *rii*, or smaller canals, as well as the Grand Canal. The fixed minimum is €62 for 50 minutes with a nighttime supplement of €15.50, but agree on prices before getting into the boat.

BY TRAGHETTO
Few tourists know about the two-man gondola ferries that cross the Grand Canal at various fixed points. At €.40, they're the cheapest and shortest gondola ride in Venice, but they can save a lot of walking. Look for TRAGHETTO signs and hand your fare to the gondolier when you board.

BY VAPORETTO
ACTV water buses serve several routes daily and after 11 PM provide limited night service. Some cover the Grand Canal, and others circle the city or connect Venice with lagoon islands. One ride costs €3.10, but tourist tickets are a better deal: buy a 24-hour ticket for €9.30, three days for €18.08, and seven days for €30.99. Remember to validate your ticket in the yellow box before boarding, and if you board without a ticket, buy one immediately. Line information is posted at landings, and complete timetables are sold at ticket booths for €.50. Landings are marked with name and line number, but check before boarding, particularly with lines 1 and 82, to make sure the boat is going in your direction.

Line 1, the Grand Canal local, calls at every stop between Piazzale Roma and San Marco (about 45 minutes), then continues to the Lido. Lines 41 (counterclockwise) and 42 (clockwise) circle the island and connect San Zaccaria with Murano. Lines 51 and 52 are express boats between the train station and the Lido. In one direction, Line 82 is the Grand Canal express; in the other direction, it stops at Tronchetto parking, Zattere, and Giudecca before arriving at San Zaccaria. Line N runs from midnight to 6 AM, stopping at the Lido, Vallaresso, Accademia, Rialto, the train station, Piazzale Roma, Giudecca, and San Zaccaria, then making the return trip in reverse order.

BY WATER TAXI Motoscafi, or water taxis aren't cheap; you'll spend about €48 for a short trip in town, €60 to the Lido, and €75 per hour for an island visit. Luggage handling, waiting time, early or late hours, and even ordering a taxi from your hotel can add expense so always agree on price first.

ACTV ☎ 041/5287886 ⊕ www.actv.it. **Motoscafo** ☎ 041/5224281 or 041/5222303. **Vela Information and Tickets** ☎ 041/2714747 or 899/909090 €.40/min ⊕ www.velaspa.com.

CAR TRAVEL

PARKING If you bring a car to Venice, you will have to pay for a garage or parking space. Ignore anyone trying to flag you down with offers of parking and hotels. Drive directly to one of the parking garages.

Parking at Autorimessa Comunale costs €18.59 for 24 hours. The private Garage San Marco costs €19 for up to 12 hours, and €26 for 12–24 hours. To reach Tronchetto parking (€18 for 1–24 hours), watch for signs as you cross the bridge from the mainland; you'll have to turn right before you get to Piazzale Roma. Many hotels have discounts with garages; get a voucher when you check in and present it when you pay the garage. Line 82 connects Tronchetto with Piazzale Roma and Piazza San Marco, but if there's thick fog or extreme tides, a bus will take you to Piazzale Roma. Garage San Marco and Autorimessa Comunale accept reservations.

Autorimessa Comunale ⊠ Piazzale Roma, end of S11 road, ☎ 041/2727301, ⊕ www.asmvenezia.it. **Garage San Marco** ⊠ Piazzale Roma 467/F, turn right into bus park, ☎ 041/5232213 ⊕ www.garagesanmarco.it. **Tronchetto** ☎ 041/5207555.

CONSULATES

United Kingdom ⊠ Campo della Carità, near Gallerie dell'Accademia ☎ 041/5227207.

EMERGENCIES

The U.K. Consulate or your hotel can recommend doctors and dentists. Venice's pharmacies are open 9–12:30 and 3:30–7:30, and they take turns staying open lunches, nights, weekends, and holidays.

Emergency Services Ambulance ☎ 118. **Carabinieri** ☎ 112. **General emergencies** ☎ 113.

TOURS

BOAT TOURS Boat tours to Murano, Burano, and Torcello islands leave various docks around San Marco daily. These 3- to 3½-hour trips cost €15–€17 and can be annoying, often pressuring you to buy at showroom prices even higher than normal. From April to October trips depart at 9:30 and 2:30, and from November to March they leave at 2.

More than a dozen major travel agents have grouped together to form the Consorzio San Marco, which provides frequent, quality tours of the city. Serenaded gondola trips, with or without dinner (€68/31), can be purchased at any of their offices or at American Express. Tours leave at 7:30 PM and 8:30 PM May–September; at 7:30 PM in April and October; and at 3:30 PM November–March.

American Express ⊠ Salizada San Moisè, San Marco 1471 ☎ 041/5200844 🖷 041/5229937. **Consorzio San Marco** ☎ 041/2406712.

WALKING TOURS The Consorzio San Marco offers a two-hour walking tour of the San Marco area (€24), which ends with a glassblowing demonstration (no Sunday tour in winter). From April to October, there's also an afternoon walking tour that ends with a gondola ride (€29). Venicescapes, an Italo-American cultural association, focuses itineraries on history and culture as well as tourist sights. Venice à la Carte customizes tours specifically to clients' needs. Both cater only to small groups (two to eight people), and reservations are recommended during busy seasons.

🔲 **Albatravel** ✉ Calle dei Fabbri, San Marco 4538 ☎ 041/5210123 🖨 041/5200781. **Consorzio San Marco** ☎ 041/2406712. **Venice à la Carte** ☎ 349/1447818 🖨 240/208-7273 in U.S. 🌐 www.tourvenice.org. **Venicescapes** 🖨🖨 041/5206361 🌐 www.venicescapes.org.

TOURS OF THE
SURROUNDING
REGION American Express and other agencies offer excursions in the Veneto region. Tuesday, Thursday, and Saturday from March to October you can take a boat trip to Padua along the Brenta River, stopping at three Palladian villas and returning to Venice by bus for €62 per person (€86 with lunch). Wednesday's Palladio Tour by eight-person minibus includes villas and Vicenza (€108 per person).

The Hills of the Veneto minibus tour visits Marostica, Bassano del Grappa, and Asolo, with a vineyard stop along Strada del Prosecco for wine tasting (Tuesday, Thursday, and weekends; €104 per person; lunch €13). Monday and Friday you can cool off with the scenic Dolomite Mountains Tour. You'll see Titian's birthplace—Pieve di Cadore—and Cortina d'Ampezzo (€113 includes a packed lunch). Reservations for all tours are suggested during high season.

🔲 **American Express** ✉ Salizada San Moisè, San Marco 1471, ☎ 041/5200844 🖨 041/5229937.

PRIVATE GUIDES Pick up a list of more than 100 licensed guides from the tourist information office or the guides' association. Two-hour tours with an English-speaking guide for up to 30 people start at €113. Agree on a total price before you begin, as there are some hidden extras. Guides are of variable quality.

🔲 **Guides' Association** ✉ San Marco 750, near San Zulian ☎ 041/5209038 🖨 041/5210762.

TRAIN TRAVEL

Venice has rail connections with every major city in Italy and Europe. Some continental trains do not enter historic Venice but stop at the mainland Mestre Station. All trains traveling to and from Venice Santa Lucia stop at Mestre, so it's not difficult to hop on the next passing train, but if you upgrade from regional train to Intercity or Eurostar, don't forget to buy a *supplemento* or you can be fined. You'll also be fined if you forget to purchase and validate train tickets in the yellow machines found on or near platforms. Venice Station is well equipped with tourist information, a baggage depot, and free hotel booking. Just outside, nearly every vaporetto line has a landing to take you to your hotel's neighborhood. Be prepared with advance directions from the hotel and a good map.

🔲 **APT** ☎ 041/5298727. **Trenitalia** ☎ 892021 local call in Italy 🌐 www.trenitalia.it.

TRANSPORTATION AROUND VENICE

Venice has more than 100 islands, in excess of 400 bridges, and few straight lines. The city's house-numbering seems nonsensical, and the *sestieri* (six districts) of San Marco, Cannaregio, Castello, Dorsoduro, Santa Croce, and San Polo all copy each other's street names. Traveling by vaporetto can be bewildering, and often you're forced to walk, whether you want to or not. Yellow signs, posted on many corners, point toward major landmarks—San Marco, Rialto, Accademia—but you won't find them deep in residential neighborhoods. Three ways to enjoy yourself more are to wear comfortable shoes, buy a good map at a newsstand, and accept the fact that you will get lost.

TRAVEL AGENCIES

Gran Canal ⊠ Ponte del Ovo, San Marco 4759 near Rialto Bridge ☎ 041/2712111 🖷 041/5223380. **Kele e Teo** ⊠ Ponte dei Bareteri, San Marco 4930 between San Marco and Rialto ☎ 041/5208722 🖷 041/5208913 also handles train tickets.

VISITOR INFORMATION

The train station branch of the Venice Tourist Office is open daily 8–6:30; other branches generally open at 9:30. Vela's Hello Venezia Center is open 8 AM–8 PM.

Venice Tourist Offices ⊕ www.turismovenezia.it ⊠ Train Station ☎ 041/5298727 ⊠ Procuratie Nuove San Marco 71/F, near Museo Correr ☎ 041/5298740 ⊠ Venice Pavilion, near Giardini Reali ☎ 041/5225150 ⊠ Garage Comunale ☎ 041/2411499 ⊠ Summer only: S. Maria Elisabetta 6/A ☎ 041/5265721. **Vela** ☎ 041/2714747 or 899/909090 €.40/min.

Associazione Veneziana Albergatori, an association of hotel keepers, operates a booking service by phone, fax, and at booths around Venice. There's a kiosk inside Santa Lucia train station (open 8 AM–9 PM), one at Marco Polo Airport (open 8 AM–10 PM), and one kiosk in each of the two Piazzale Roma parking garages (open 9 AM–10 PM). This service is free, but you'll pay a deposit (€11–€47 per person; V and MC accepted), which will be deducted from your hotel bill. Another service, **Venezia Sì,** makes free reservations by phone Monday–Saturday 9–7.

Reserving a Room AVA Booths ⊠ Piazzale Roma ☎ 041/5231397 and 041/5228640 ⊠ Train station ☎ 041/715288 and 041/715016 ⊠ Marco Polo Airport ☎ 041/5415133. **Venezia Sì** ☎ 800/843006 in Italy (toll-free, Mon.–Sat. 9 AM–7 PM); 0039/0415222264 from abroad 🖷 0039/0415221242.

CAMPANIA

Campania, the region composed of Naples, the Amalfi coast, and the surrounding sun-drenched area, is where most people's preconceived ideas of Italy become a reality. You'll find beaches, good food that relies heavily on tomatoes and mozzarella, acres of classical ruins, and gorgeous scenery. The exuberance of the locals doesn't leave much room for efficient organization, however, and you may have to revise your concept of time; here minutes dilate into hours at the drop of a hat.

Once a city that rivaled Paris as a brilliant and refined cultural capital, Napoli (Naples) today is afflicted by acute urban decay and chronic delinquency. You need patience, stamina, and a degree of caution to visit Naples on your own, but it's worth it for those who have a sense of adventure and the capacity to discern the enormous riches the city has accumulated in its 2,000-year history.

If you want the fun without the hassle, skip Naples and head for Sorrento, Capri, and the Amalfi coast, legendary haunts of the sirens who tried to lure Odysseus off course. Sorrento is touristy but has some fine old hotels and beautiful views; it's a good base for a leisurely excursion to Pompeii. Capri is a pint-size paradise, though sometimes too crowded for comfort, and the Amalfi coast offers enchanting towns and spectacular scenery.

Naples

Founded by the Greeks, Naples became a playground of the Romans and was ruled thereafter by a succession of foreign dynasties, all of which left traces of their cultures in the city and its environs. The most splendid of these rulers were the Bourbons, who were responsible for much of what you will want to see in Naples. Among the greatest relics of Bourbon powers in Naples is the 17th-century **Palazzo Reale** (Royal Palace),

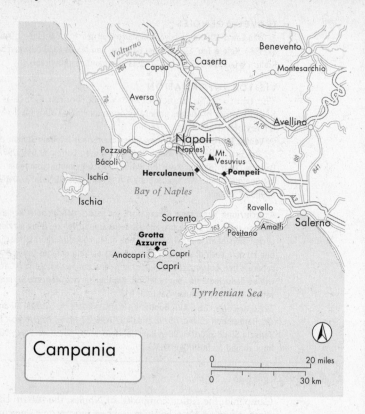

Campania

| 0 | 20 miles |
| 0 | 30 km |

still furnished in the lavish baroque style that suited them so well. ⊠ *Piazza del Plebiscito* ☎ 081/7944021 ⊙ *Thurs.–Tues. 9–8.*

On the heights of the Vomero Hill, the bastions of **Castel Sant'Elmo** occupy an evocative position with distant views over Naples and its bay. You can reach it by the **Montesanto funicular,** near Piazza Dante. ⊠ *Largo San Martino* ⊙ *Tues.–Sun. 9–7.*

Also known as the Maschio Angioino, the massive stone **Castel Nuovo** (New Castle) was built by the city's Aragon rulers in the 13th century; inside, the city's **Museo Civico** (Civic Museum) comprises mainly local artwork from the 15th to the 19th centuries, and there are also regular exhibitions. ⊠ *Castel Nuovo, Piazza Municipio* ☎ 081/7952003 ⊙ *Castle: Mon.–Sat. 9–7. Courtyard only: Sun. 9–1.*

The **Certosa di San Martino,** a Carthusian monastery restored in the 17th century, contains an eclectic collection of Neapolitan landscape paintings, royal carriages, and *presepi* (Christmas crèches). Check out the view from the terraced gardens at the back of the monastery. The museum lies on the Vomero Hill, near the Castel Sant'Elmo. ⊠ *Museo Nazionale di San Martino* ☎ 081/5781769 ⊙ *Tues.–Fri. 8:30–7:30, weekends 9–7:30.*

★ The **Museo Archeologico Nazionale** (National Archaeological Museum) is in the throes of a long-awaited renovation program, but is still open to the public. It holds one of the world's great collections of antiquities. Greek and Roman sculptures, vividly colored mosaics, countless objects from Pompeii and Herculaneum, and an equestrian statue of the Roman emperor Nerva are all worth seeing. ⊠ *Piazza Museo* ☎ *081/ 440166* ☉ *Wed.–Mon. 9–7.*

★ The **Museo di Capodimonte** is housed in an 18th-century palace built by Bourbon king Charles III and surrounded by a vast park that affords sweeping views of the bay. The picture gallery is devoted to work from the 13th to 18th centuries, including many familiar works by Dutch and Spanish masters, as well as by the great Italians. Other rooms contain an extensive collection of porcelain and majolica from the various royal residences, some produced in the Bourbons' own factory right here on the grounds. ⊠ *Parco di Capodimonte* ☎ *081/7499111* ☉ *Tues.–Sun. 8:30–7:30.*

Santa Chiara was built during the early 1300s in Provençal Gothic style. A favorite Neapolitan song celebrates the quiet beauty of its cloister, decorated in delicate floral tiles. ⊠ *Piazza Gesù Nuovo* ☎ *081/5526209* ☉ *Apr.–Sept., daily 8:30–noon and 4–7; Oct.–Mar., daily 8:30–noon and 4–6.*

Via Toledo, also known as Via Roma, is flanked by 17th-century *palazzi* and is great for strolling, shopping, and people-watching. The church **Gesù Nuovo,** with oddly faceted stone facade and elaborate baroque interior, is off Via Toledo. ⊠ *Piazza Gesù Nuovo* ☎ *081/5518613* ☉ *Mon.–Sat. 6:30–12:45 and 4:15–7:30, Sun. 6:30–1:30.*

$$$ ╳ **La Sacrestia.** This lovely restaurant above Mergellina has a fine view from the delightful summer terrace. Traditional Neapolitan specialties of the day might be baked or steamed sea bass and linguine *in salsa di scorfano* (with scorpion-fish sauce). ⊠ *Via Orazio 116* ☎ *081/7611051* ▭ *AE, DC, MC, V* ☉ *Closed Sun. in July and Aug. and 2 wks in mid-Aug. No lunch Mon., no dinner Sun.*

$$–$$$ ╳ **La Stanza del Gusto.** The name means "The Room of Taste," and this restaurant lives up to the billing. A minute's walk from some of the city's busiest streets, it feels removed from the hectic world outside. This is the place to try both imaginative Mediterranean cuisine and the great Neapolitan stalwarts. ⊠ *Vicoletto Sant'Arpino 21* ☎ *081/401578* ▭ *DC, MC, V* ⌂ *Reservations essential* ☉ *Closed Sun., Mon., and Aug. Lunch by appointment only.*

$$ ╳ **Ciro a Santa Brigida.** Tables at this no-frills restaurant are arranged on two levels. This is the place to try traditional Neapolitan *sartù di riso* (a rich rice dish with meat and peas) and *melanzane alla parmigiana* or *polpette alla Ciro* (meatballs). There's pizza, too. ⊠ *Via Santa Brigida 71, off Via Toledo* ☎ *081/5524072* ▭ *AE, DC, MC, V* ☉ *Closed Sun. and 2 wks in Aug.*

$$$$ ▦ **Excelsior.** On the shore drive, the Excelsior has splendid views of the bay from its front rooms. Spacious bedrooms are furnished in informal floral prints or more formal Empire style; all have a comfortable, traditional air. The salons are formal, with chandeliers and wall paintings, and the Terrazza restaurant enjoys stupendous views. ⊠ *Via Partenope 48, 80121* ☎ *081/7640111* 🖷 *081/7649743* ⊕ *www.prestigehotels.it* ⇌ *136 rooms* ⌂ *Restaurant* ▭ *AE, DC, MC, V.*

$$ ⊡ **Chiaja.** A two-minute walk away from Piazza Plebiscito and the Royal Palace, the Chiaja occupies a spruce 18th-century *palazzo*, part of which includes a historic brothel. Although there's no sea view, the location is central and rooms are charming and reasonably priced. ⊠ *Via Chiaja 216, 80121* ☎ *081/415555* 🖷 *081/422344* ⊕ *www.hotelchiaia.it* ⤳ *27 rooms* ▤ *AE, DC, MC, V.*

$$ ⊡ **Rex.** On the first two floors of an art nouveau building, the hotel, in a fairly quiet spot near the Santa Lucia waterfront, reveals a haphazard collection of 1950s modern, fake period pieces, and some folk art. ⊠ *Via Palepoli 12, 80132* ☎ *081/7649389* 🖷 *081/7649227* ⊕ *www.hotel-rex.it* ⤳ *34 rooms* ▤ *AE, DC, MC, V.*

Herculaneum

★ Hercules is reputed to have founded Herculaneum (Ercolano), just 10 km (6 mi) southeast of Naples. The elite Roman resort was devastated by the same volcanic eruption that buried Pompeii in AD 79. Excavations have revealed that many died on the shore while attempting to escape. A short time after the eruption, a slow-moving mud slide embalmed the entire town by covering it with a 36-foot-deep blanket of volcanic ash and ooze. Though devastating for Herculaneum's residents, it preserved the site in pristine condition for nearly two millennia. ⊠ *Corso Ercolano* ☎ *081/8575347* ⊕ *www.pompeiisites.org* ☉ *Apr.–Oct., daily 8:30–7:30 (ticket office closes at 6); Nov.–Mar., daily 8:30–5 (ticket office closes at 3:30).*

Pompeii

★ An estimated 2,000 of Pompeii's residents perished on that fateful August day in AD 79. The ancient city of Pompeii was much larger than Herculaneum, and excavations have progressed to a much greater extent, though the remains are not as well preserved because of some 18th-century scavenging for museum-quality artwork, most of which is displayed in Museo Archeologico Nazionale in Naples. This prosperous Roman city had an extensive forum, lavish baths and temples, and patrician villas richly decorated with frescoes. It's worth hiring an audio guide to the site (ID card required) to gain an understanding of the ruins and their importance. Be sure to see the **Villa dei Misteri** (Villa of the Mysteries), with 1,900-year-old frescoes that retain rich detail and color depth. ⊠ *Pompeii Scavi* ☎ *081/8575347* ⊕ *www.pompeiisites.org* ☉ *Apr.–Oct., daily 8:30–7:30 (ticket office closes at 6); Nov.–Mar., daily 8:30–5 (ticket office closes at 3:30).*

Sorrento

In the not-too-distant past, small Sorrento was a genteel resort for the fashionable elite. Now the town, 28 km (17 mi) southwest of Pompeii, has spread out along the crest of its fabled cliffs. The once-secret haunts of the few tourists who came for the magnificent coastline have been long discovered, and they are now ravaged by package tours. But nothing can dim the delights of the marvelous climate and view of the Bay of Naples. For the best views go to the **Villa Comunale**, near the old church of San Francesco (in itself worth a visit), planted with flowering vines. **Museo Correale**, in an attractive 18th-century villa, retains a collection of decorative arts and paintings of the Neapolitan school. ⊠ *Via Correale* ☎ *081/8781846* ☉ *Wed.–Mon. 9–2.*

$$$–$$$$ ✕ **Antica Trattoria.** Garden dining at this homey, hospitable spot is a joy in summer. Classic *pennette al profumo di bosco* (minipenne with a creamy mushroom and ham sauce), fish, and *gamberetti freschi all'Antica Trattoria* (shrimp in a tomato sauce) are among the house specialties. ⊠ *Via Giuliani 33* ☎ *081/8071082* ▤ *AE, DC, MC, V* ☉ *Closed Mon. and 4 wks in Jan. and Feb.*

$–$$ ✕ **Parrucchiano.** One of the town's oldest and best restaurants, Parruc-chiano has greenhouse-type dining rooms dripping with vines and dot-ted with plants. For antipasti, try the *panzerotti* (pastry crust filled with mozzarella and tomato) and, for a main course, the *scaloppe alla sor-rentina* (cutlets with mozzarella and tomato). ⊠ *Corso Italia 71* ☏ *081/ 8781321* ⊟ *MC, V* ☉ *Closed Wed. Nov.–Mar.*

$ ✕ **Trattoria da Emilia.** You can sit outside here, right on the Marina Grande, and watch the life of the port go by. This simple, rustic restau-rant with wooden tables has been run by Donna Emilia and her offspring since 1947 and provides typical Sorrento home cooking and a relaxed atmosphere. Fried seafood is the specialty. ⊠ *Via Marina Grande 62* ☏ *081/8072720* ⊟ *No credit cards* ☉ *Closed Tues. Oct.–Mar. No dinner.*

$$$$ ▦ **Bellevue Syrene.** This exclusive hotel is set in a cliff-top garden close to the center of Sorrento. It retains its solid, old-fashioned comforts and sumptuous charm, with Victorian nooks and alcoves, antique paintings, and exuberant frescoes. ⊠ *Piazza della Vittoria 5, 80067* ☏ *081/ 8781024* ⊟ *081/8783963* ⊕ *www.bellevuesyrene.it* ⥿ *76 rooms* ⌂ *Restaurant* ⊟ *AE, DC, MC, V.*

$$$$ ▦ **Excelsior Vittoria.** In the heart of Sorrento, this hotel right on the cliff has art nouveau furnishings, some of which are grand, although faded. Tenor Enrico Caruso's bedroom is preserved as a relic; guest bedrooms are spacious and elegant in a late-19th-century style. ⊠ *Piazza Tasso 34, 80067* ☏ *081/8071044* ⊟ *081/8771206* ⊕ *www.exvitt.it* ⥿ *109 rooms* ⌂ *Restaurant, pool* ⊟ *AE, DC, MC, V.*

$$ ▦ **Settimo Cielo.** This is an excellent choice if you want to stay on the seafront without breaking your budget. The beach is steps away. Rooms are simple, modern, and all sea-facing. ⊠ *Via Capo 27, 80060* ☏ *081/ 8781012* ⊟ *081/8073290* ⊕ *www.hotelsettimocielo.com* ⥿ *20 rooms* ⌂ *Restaurant, pool* ⊟ *AE, DC, MC, V* ☉ *Closed Nov.–mid-Mar.*

$ ▦ **Mignon Meublé.** A good find for this price category and central lo-cation, this friendly hotel is simple but stylish. Rooms are spacious and homey, and breakfast is brought to you. It's a popular place, so book well in advance. ⊠ *Via Sersale 9, 80067* ☏ *081/8073824* ⊟ *081/ 5329001* ⥿ *23 rooms* ⊟ *AE, DC, MC, V.*

Capri

No matter how many day-trippers crowd onto the island, no matter how touristy certain sections have become, Capri remains one of Italy's loveliest places. Incoming visitors disembark at Marina Grande, from where you can take some time out for an excursion to the **Grotta Az-zurra** (Blue Grotto). Be warned that this is one of the country's all-time great rip-offs: motorboat, rowboat, and grotto admissions are charged separately, and if there's a line of boats waiting, you'll have little time to enjoy the grotto's marvelous colors. At Marina Grande you can also take a boat excursion around the island. A funicular railway or bus ser-vice takes you up to the deliberately commercial and self-consciously picturesque **Capri Town**, where you can stroll through the Piazzetta, a choice place from which to watch the action and window-shop in ex-pensive boutiques. The **Giardini di Augusto** (Gardens of Augustus; ⊠ Via Matteotti) has gorgeous views. To get away from the crowds, hike to

★ **Villa Jovis,** one of the many villas that Roman emperor Tiberius built on the island. The walk takes about 45 minutes, with pretty views all the way and a final spectacular vista of the entire Bay of Naples and part of the Gulf of Salerno. ⊠ *Villa Jovis, Via Tiberio* ☏ *081/8370381* ☉ *Daily 9–1 hr before sunset.*

You can take the bus or a jaunty open taxi to Anacapri and look for the little church of **San Michele,** where a magnificent, hand-painted majolica tile floor shows you an 18th-century vision of the Garden of Eden. ⊠ *Piazza Nicola* ⊙ *Easter–Oct., daily 9–7; Nov.–Easter, daily 9:30–5.*

Villa San Michele is the charming former home of Swedish scientist-author Axel Munthe. ⊠ *Via Axel Munthe* ☎ *081/837401* ⊕ *www. sanmichele.org* ⊙ *May–Sept., daily 9–6; Nov.–Feb., daily 10:30–3:30; Mar., daily 9:30–4:30; Apr. and Oct., daily 9:30–5.*

★ **$$$–$$$$** ✕ **La Capannina.** One of Capri's finest restaurants, La Capannina is only a few steps from the busy social hub of the Piazzetta. It has a discreet covered veranda—open in summer—for dining by candlelight; most of the regulars avoid the stuffy indoor rooms. The specialties are homemade ravioli and *linguine con lo scorfano* (flat spaghetti with scorpion fish). Look for the authentic Capri wine with the house label. ⊠ *Via Botteghe 12 bis and 14* ☎ *081/8370732* ⊟ *AE, DC, MC, V* ⊙ *Closed mid-Nov.–mid-Mar. (except a week at New Year), and Wed. in Mar. and Oct.–mid-Nov.*

$$ ✕ **Al Grottino.** This small, family-run restaurant, with a handy location near the Piazzetta, displays autographed photographs of celebrity customers. House specialties are gnocchi with tomato sauce and mozzarella and *linguine ai gamberetti* (linguine with shrimp sauce). ⊠ *Via Longano 27* ☎ *081/8370584* ⊟ *AE, MC, V* ⊙ *Closed Tues. and Nov. 3–Mar. 20.*

★ **$$** ✕ **Da Tonino.** It is well worth making the short detour off the beaten track to the Arco Naturale to be pampered by its creative chef Tonino. The emphasis here is on land-based dishes; try the *terrina di coniglio* (rabbit terrine) or ask for the pigeon dish with pesto, rosemary, and pine nuts, accompanied by wine from a well-stocked cellar. ⊠ *Via Dentecala 34, Capri Town* ☎ *081/8376718* ⊟ *AE, DC, MC, V* ⊙ *Closed Jan. 10–Mar. 15.*

★ **$$$$** ✕☐ **Villa Brunella.** The restaurant of this family-run hotel is on the lane leading to Punta Tragara and the Faraglioni. From that level you descend to the rooms and the pool on lower levels. Furnishings are tastefully casual and comfortable, the views serendipitous. ⊠ *Via Tragara 24, 87003* ☎ *081/8370122* ⊠ *081/8370430* ⊕ *www.villabrunella.it* ☜ *20 rooms* △ *Restaurant, pool* ⊟ *AE, DC, MC, V* ⊙ *Closed Nov.–Mar.*

$$$$ ☐ **Quisisana.** This is one of Italy's poshest hotels, and it is right in the center of the town of Capri. The rooms are spacious, and many have arcaded balconies with views of the sea; the interior is traditional or contemporary, with some antiques. From the small terrace at the entrance you can watch all Capri go by, but the enclosed garden and pool in the back are perfect for getting away from it all. The bar and restaurant are casual but very elegant. ⊠ *Via Camerelle 2, 80073* ☎ *081/8370788* ⊠ *081/8376080* ⊕ *www.quisi.com* ☜ *149 rooms* △ *Restaurant, bar* ⊟ *AE, DC, MC, V* ⊙ *Closed Nov.–mid-Mar.*

$$–$$$ ☐ **Villa Sarah.** Just a 10-minute walk from the Piazzetta, the Sarah is a whitewashed Mediterranean villa with a garden and bright, simply furnished rooms. ⊠ *Via Tiberio 3/A, 87003* ☎ *081/8377817* ⊠ *081/ 8377215* ⊕ *www.villasarah.it* ☜ *20 rooms* △ *Bar* ⊟ *AE, DC, MC, V* ⊙ *Closed Nov.–Mar.*

Positano

★ Positano's jumble of pastel houses topped by whitewashed cupolas clings to the mountainside above the sea. The town—the prettiest along this stretch of coast—attracts a sophisticated group of visitors and summer residents who find that its relaxed and friendly feel more than compensates for the sheer effort of moving about this exhaustingly vertical town, most of whose streets are stairways. A former fishing village, the town has opted for the more regular and lucrative rewards of tourism and fashion. Practically every other shop is a boutique displaying locally made casual wear. The beach is the town's focal point, with a little promenade and a multitude of café-restaurants.

$$–$$$ ✕ **Donna Rosa.** This minimalist little hideaway in one-street Montepertuso, the hamlet high over Positano, is original. Everybody gets into the act: Mamma does the creative cooking, to order; Pappa "makes noise"; and the daughters rule out front—Rosa is the namesake donna. Homemade pasta is the house specialty, along with the delectable desserts, which may include walnut or strawberry mousse and *crostata all'arancio* (orange tart). Reservations are essential at dinner. ⊠ *Via Montepertuso* ☎ *089/811806* ⊟ *AE, DC, MC, V* ☉ *Closed Mon.*

$$$$ ⊞ **Le Sirenuse.** The most fashionable hotel in Positano, in an 18th-century villa, has been in the same family for eight generations. The hotel is set into the hillside overlooking Positano's harbor. Most of the bedrooms face the sea. Because of the hotel's location, the dining room is like a long, closed-in terrace overlooking the village of Positano. The cuisine ranges from acceptable to excellent. ⊠ *Via Cristoforo Colombo 30, 84017* ☎*089/875066* 🖷*081/811798* ⊕*www.sirenuse.it* ⟿*60 rooms* ♧ *Restaurant* ⊟ *AE, DC, MC, V.*

$$$$ ⊞ **San Pietro.** Perched on the side of a cliff, this opulent hotel is eclectic and airy, with unusual antiques and, everywhere, hanging bougainvillea. The guest rooms are tastefully appointed, but the stupendous window views steal the show. The light, open dining room is verdant with plants. An elevator takes guests to the hotel's small beach area. ⊠ *Via Laurito 2, 84017* ☎ *089/875455* 🖷 *089/811449* ⊕ *www.ilsanpietro. it* ⟿ *60 rooms* ♧ *Restaurant* ⊟ *AE, DC, MC, V* ☉ *Closed Nov.–Mar.*

$$$$ ⊞ **Palazzo Murat.** The location is perfect, in the heart of town, near the beachside promenade and set within a walled garden. The old wing is a historic palazzo, with tall windows and wrought-iron balconies; the newer wing is a whitewashed Mediterranean building with arches and terraces. You can relax in antiques-strewn lounges or on the charming vine-draped patio. ⊠ *Via dei Mulini 23, 84017* ☎ *089/875177* 🖷 *089/ 811419* ⊕ *www.palazzomurat.it* ⟿ *31 rooms* ♧ *Restaurant* ⊟ *AE, DC, MC, V* ☉ *Closed Jan.–mid-Mar.*

$$ ⊞ **La Fenice.** This tiny and unpretentious hotel beckons with bougainvillea-laden vistas, castaway cottages, and a turquoise pool, all perched over a private beach. Guest rooms—accented with coved ceilings, whitewashed walls, and native folk art—are simple havens of tranquillity (book the best, those closest to the sea, only if you can handle *very* steep walkways). Situated on the peaceful outskirts of town, this is, happily, open year-round. ⊠ *Via G. Marconi 4, 84017* ☎ *089/875513* 🖷 *089/811309* ⟿ *15 rooms* ♧ *Pool* ⊟ *No credit cards.*

Amalfi

The coastal drive down to the resort town of Amalfi provides some of Italy's most dramatic and beautiful scenery. Amalfi itself is a charming maze of covered alleys and narrow byways straggling up the steep mountainside. The piazza just below the cathedral forms the town's heart—a colorful assortment of pottery stalls, cafés, and postcard shops grouped around a venerable old fountain. The exterior of the **cathedral** is its most impressive feature. The **cloisters**, with whitewashed arches and palms, are worth a glance, and the small **museum** in the adjoining basilica could inspire you to climb up all those stairs. ☎ *089/871059* ☉ *Duomo, cloister, and museum: Mar.–June and Oct., daily 9–7; July–Sept., daily 9–9; Nov.–Feb., daily 10–12:30 and 2:30–5:30.*

$$$–$$$$ ✕ **La Caravella.** Tucked away under some arches lining the coast road, the Caravella has a pleasant interior decorated with paintings of old Amalfi. It's small and intimate, and proprietor Franco describes the cuisine as *sfiziosa* (taste tempting). Specialties include *linguine alla colatura di alici* (linguine with anchovies), which is based on a medieval recipe, and *calamari ripieni* (stuffed squid). ✉ *Via M. Camera 12* ☎ *089/871029* ▭ *AE, MC, V* ⊘ *Closed Tues. and Nov.*

★ $$$$ ⌂ **Santa Caterina.** A large mansion perched above terraced and flowering hillsides on the coast road just outside Amalfi proper, the Santa Caterina is one of the best hotels on the entire coast. The rooms are tastefully decorated, and most have small terraces or balconies with great views. There are lounges and terraces for relaxing, and an elevator whisks guests down to the seaside saltwater pool, bar, and swimming area. Amid lemon and orange groves are two romantic villa annexes. ✉ *Strada Amalfitana 9, 84011* ☎*089/871012* ⎙*089/871351* ⊕*www.hotelsantacaterina.it* ⇌*66 rooms* ⚭ *Restaurant, pool* ▭ *AE, DC, MC, V.*

Ravello

★ Ravello is on a high mountain bluff overlooking the sea 8 km (5 mi) north of Amalfi. The road up to it is a series of switchbacks, and the village itself clings precariously on the mountain spur. The village flourished during the 13th century and then fell into a tranquillity that has remained unchanged for the past six centuries. The town center is Piazza del Duomo, with its **cathedral,** founded in 1087. Note the fine bronze 12th-century doors and, inside, two pulpits richly decorated with mosaics: one depicts the story of Jonah and the whale; the other, more splendid mosaic is carved with fantastic beasts and rests on a pride of lions. Composer Richard Wagner once stayed in Ravello, and today there is a Wagner festival every summer on the garden terrace of the 11th-century **Villa Rufolo.** There is a Moorish cloister with interlacing pointed arches, beautiful gardens, an 11th-century tower, and a belvedere with a fine view of the coast. ✉ *Piazza Vescovado* ☎ *089/857657* ⊘ *Daily 9–sunset.*

At the entrance to the **Villa Cimbrone** complex is a small cloister that looks medieval but was actually built in 1917, with two bas-reliefs: one representing nine Norman warriors, the other illustrating the seven deadly sins. The long avenue leads through peaceful gardens scattered with grottoes, small temples, and statues to a belvedere and terrace where, on a clear day, the view stretches out over the Mediterranean Sea. ✉ *Via Santa Chiara 26* ☎ *089/857459* ⊘ *Daily 9–sunset.*

$$$$ ⌂ **Hotel Palumbo.** Occupying a 12th-century patrician palace outfitted with antiques and modern comforts, this elegant hotel has the feel of a lovely private home. It has beautiful garden terraces, breathtaking views, and a sumptuous upstairs dining room. In summer, you can descend to a villa at sea level and be pampered in the hotel's coastal retreat. Note that half board is compulsory except in winter, when the restaurant is closed. ✉ *Via San Giovanni del Toro 16, 84010* ☎ *089/857244* ⎙*089/858133* ⊕ *www.hotel-palumbo.it* ⇌ *20 rooms* ⚭ *Restaurant* ▭ *AE, DC, MC, V.*

Campania Essentials

AIR TRAVEL

There are several daily flights between Rome and Aeroporto Capodichino, 8 km (5 mi) north of downtown Naples. From May through September there's direct helicopter service between Capodichino and Capri or Ischia.

🛈 **Aeroporto Capodichino** ☎ 081/7896259. **Cab Air** ☎ 081/5844355 or 081/2587110.

18

BOAT & FERRY TRAVEL

Most boats and hydrofoils for the islands and the Sorrento Peninsula leave from the Molo Beverello Pier, near Naples's Piazza Municipio; there's also a hydrofoil station at Mergellina Pier. Passenger and car ferry service is frequent. Note that you cannot take cars onto Capri.

🚢 Hydrofoils **Alilauro** ☎ 081/5522838. **Caremar** ☎ 081/5513882. **Navigazione Libera del Golfo (NLG)** ☎ 081/5527209. **SNAV** ☎ 081/7612348.

🚢 Passenger & Car Ferries **Caremar** ☎ 081/5513882. **Navigazione Libera del Golfo (NLG)** ☎ 081/5527209.

BUS TRAVEL

🚌 **SITA** ☎ 081/5522176 ⊕ www.sita-on-line.it.

CAR TRAVEL

The Naples–Pompeii–Salerno toll road has exits at Herculaneum and Pompeii and connects with the tortuous coastal road to Sorrento and the Amalfi coast at the Castellammare exit. Parking within Naples is not recommended: window smashing and robbery are not uncommon.

TOURS

One-, two-, or three-day guided tours of the area depart from Rome. From Naples you can choose from half-day and all-day tours on the mainland and to the islands.

🚍 **American Express** ✉ Rome ☎ 06/67641. **Appian Line** ✉ Rome ☎ 06/487861. **Carrani** ✉ Rome ☎ 06/4880510 or 06/4742501. **Milleviaggi** ✉ Riviera di Chiaia 252, Naples ☎ 081/7642064. **Tourcar** ✉ Piazza Matteotti 1, Naples ☎ 081/5520429 ⊕ www.tourcar.it.

TRAIN TRAVEL

Many trains run between Rome and Naples from the Stazione Centrale every day; Intercity trains make the journey in less than two hours. There are several stations in Naples, and a network of suburban trains connects the city with diverse points of interest in Campania, most usefully the Circumvesuviana line, which runs to Herculaneum (Ercolano), Pompeii, and Sorrento. Naples has two *Metropolitane* (subways); the state-of-the-art Linea 2 links the Archaeological Museum and Piazza Dante area with the Vomero suburb, and the older, less regular Linea 1 crosses the city from east to west. The fare is €.77.

🚆 **Circumvesuviana line** ☎ 081/7722444 ⊕ www.vesuviana.it. **Stazione Centrale** ✉ Piazza Garibaldi, Naples ☎ 848/888088 ⊕ www.fs-on-line.it.

VISITOR INFORMATION

🛈 **Capri** ✉ Marina Grande pier ☎ 081/8370634 ✉ Piazza Umberto I, Capri Town ☎ 081/8370686 ⊕ www.capritourism.com. **Naples** EPT ✉ Piazza dei Martiri 58 ☎ 081/4107211 ⊕ www.ept.napoli.it ✉ Stazione Centrale ☎ 081/268779 ✉ Stazione Mergellina ☎ 081/7612102 ✉ Aeroporto Capodichino ☎ 081/7805761 ✉ Azienda Autonoma di Soggiorno, Cura e Turismo, AASCT ✉ Via San Carlo 9 ☎ 081/402394 ✉ Piazza del Gesù ☎ 081/5523328. **Sorrento** ✉ Via De Maio 35 ☎ 081/8074033 ⊕ www.sorrentotourism.com.

LUXEMBOURG

WHEN YOU TRY TO LOCATE LUXEMBOURG ON A MAP, look for "Lux," at the heart of Western Europe. Even abbreviated, the name runs over—west into Belgium, east into Germany, south into France—as the country's influence has done for centuries. The Grand Duchy of Luxembourg is a Rhode Island–size land that contains variety and contrasts out of all proportion to its size.

Luxembourg has a wild and beautiful highland country studded with castles rich in history. It has legendary vineyards producing great wines and a lovely farmland called Le Bon Pays. And, of course, it has its capital Luxembourg City—or *Luxembourg Ville* to the locals—with an ancient fortress towering above the south-central plain. Seen through early morning mists, Luxembourg City revives the magic of Camelot. Yet it is actually the nerve center of a 1,000-year-old seat of government and a bustling and important element of the European Union (EU).

One of the smallest countries in the United Nations, Luxembourg comprises only 2,586 square km (998 square mi). It is dwarfed by its neighbors, and from its history of invasion, occupation, and siege, you might think the land was veined with gold. Starting in AD 963, when Charlemagne's descendant Sigefroid started to build his castle atop the promontory of the Bock, the duchy encased itself in layer upon layer of fortifications until by the mid-19th century its very impregnability was considered a threat. The Castle of Luxembourg was ultimately dismantled in the name of peace, and the country's neutrality was "guaranteed" by the 1867 Treaty of London. But the Grand Duchy was to be invaded twice again, in 1914 and 1940. After World War II, Luxembourg joined its neighbors in establishing NATO and the European Economic Community, and set down banking laws that attracted financial institutions from all over the world, enough to rival Switzerland. The wooded Plateau Kirchberg in Luxembourg City was razed in the mid-1960s to make way for the seat of several EEC institutions, including the Court of Justice and the European Investment Bank. These days, the city is heavily populated by EU *fonctionnaires*. The entire country now flaunts new wealth, new political muscle, and the highest per capita income in Europe.

There is an old saying that describes the life of the Luxembourgers (or Luxembourgeois, if you prefer the more elegant French appellation): "One Luxembourger, a rose garden; two Luxembourgers, a kaffeeklatsch; three Luxembourgers, a band." This is a country of parades and processions, good cheer, and a hearty appetite for beer and Moselle wine. In its traditions, values, and politics, Luxembourg remains more conservative than its neighbors. This may occasionally seem stifling to the

Luxembourg

BELGIUM

GERMANY

Wemperhaardt
Heinerscheid
Wincrange
Clervaux
Wiltz
Wilwerwiltz
Vianden
Esch-sur-Sûre
Bourscheid
Diekirch
Bigonville
Ettelbruck
Beaufort
Echternach
Martelange
Romach
Berg
Larochette
PETITE
SUISSE
LUXEM-
BOURGEOISE
Rosport
Useldange
Mullerthal
Mompach
Redange
Mersch
Wasserbillig
Septfontaines
Junglinster
Koerich
Grevenmacher
Steinfort
Sandweiler
Wormedange
Luxembourg
Hamm
Ehnen
Pétange
Kleinmacher
Remich
Differdange
Bech
Esch
Mondorf
Schengen
Rumelange
Dudelange
FRANCE

KEY
Rail lines

younger generation of Luxembourgeois, but to the majority of their elders these attitudes express the age-old national motto, *Mir wëlle bleiwe wat mir sin.* ("We want to remain what we are.")

LUXEMBOURG A TO Z

To research prices, get advice from other travelers, and book travel arrangements, visit www.fodors.com.

BUSINESS HOURS

BANKS & OFFICES Banks are generally open weekdays 8:30–7, though some close for lunch (noon–2). In Luxembourg City, the exchange desk at the railway station is open daily 9–9. There is also a currency exchange booth at the airport that is open daily.

MUSEUMS & SIGHTS Most museums are closed Monday, and in the countryside some also close for lunch (noon–2).

SHOPS Shops and department stores are generally open Monday 2–6 and Tuesday–Saturday 9–6. Some close for lunch (noon–2). A few small family businesses are open Sunday 8–noon. Large supermarkets are generally open weekdays until 8.

CUSTOMS & DUTIES

For information on customs regulations, *see* Customs & Duties *in* Smart Travel Tips.

EATING & DRINKING

Restaurants in Luxembourg combine Gallic quality with Teutonic quantity. The best deals are at lunch, when you can find a plat du jour or *menu* (two or three courses included in the price) at bargain rates. Pizzerias, found everywhere, offer an inexpensive alternative. Service (10%) and sales tax (3%) are included in quoted prices.

WHAT IT COSTS In euros			
$$$$	$$$	$$	$
AT DINNER over €32	€25–€32	€17–€25	under €17

Prices are per person for a main course.

MEALTIMES Most hotels serve breakfast until 10. Luxembourgers shut down their computers at noon to rush home for a two-hour lunch. Dinner is generally eaten between 7 and 10.

RESERVATIONS & DRESS Stylish, casual dress is expected in most restaurants; when in doubt, err on the side of formality. In expensive French restaurants, jacket and tie is a given.

EMBASSIES
🏳 Ireland ✉ 28 Rte. D' Arlon ☎ 4506101.
🏳 United Kingdom ✉ Bd. F. D. Roosevelt 14 ☎ 229864.
🏳 United States ✉ Bd. Emmanuel Servais 22 ☎ 460123.

HOLIDAYS
January 1; Carnival (mid-February to early March); Easter Monday; May 1 (May Day); Ascension (mid- to late May); Pentecost Monday; June 23 (National Day); August 15 (Assumption); November 1 (All Saints' Day); December 25–26. When a holiday falls on a Sunday, the following Monday is automatically a national holiday.

LANGUAGE
Native Luxembourgers speak three languages fluently: Luxembourgian (a Germanic language salted with French), German, and French. Many also speak English.

LODGING
Price categories are for a double room. Service (10%) and sales tax (3%) are included in posted rates. Check for special rates when making reservations.

WHAT IT COSTS In euros			
$$$$	$$$	$$	$
HOTELS over €223	€149–€223	€74–€149	under €74

Prices are for a standard double room.

CAMPING The Grand Duchy is probably the best-organized country in Europe when it comes to camping. It offers some 120 sites, all with full amenities. Listings are published annually by the National Tourist Office.

HOSTELS Inexpensive youth hostels are plentiful; many are housed in historic buildings and there is no age limit for guests. For information, contact Centrale des Auberges Luxembourgeoises.
🏳 **Centrale des Auberges Luxembourgeoises** ✉ 24/26, place del la Gare, L-1616 Luxembourg Ville ☎ 26293500 ⊕ www.youthhostels.lu.

HOTELS Most hotels in Luxembourg City are relatively modern and range from the international style to smaller, family-run establishments. Many hotels offer reduced rates on weekends.

MAIL & SHIPPING

Mail can be sent in care of BBL Travel American Express. This service is free for holders of American Express credit cards or traveler's checks.
⚑ BBL Travel American Express ✉ 3 rue Jean Piret, L-2350 Luxembourg Ville.

POSTAL RATES Airmail postcards and letters to North America weighing less than 20 grams cost €0.62. Letters and postcards to the United Kingdom cost €0.45.

MONEY MATTERS

Luxembourg has a high standard and cost of living. Prices in the countryside are slightly lower than in Luxembourg City. Sample prices include cup of coffee, €1.35–€2; glass of beer, €1.35–€1.75; movie admission, €6.20–€7.45; 5-km (3-mi) taxi ride, €20.

CURRENCY Luxembourg's unit of currency is the euro (€). Currency is issued in bills of 500, 200, 100, 50, 20, 10, and 5 euros, coins of 2 and 1 euros, and coins of 50, 20, 10, 5, 2, and 1 cents.

At press time (spring 2003), the exchange rate was €1.09 to the U.S. dollar, €0.63 to the Canadian dollar, €1.44 to the pound sterling, €0.56 to the Australian dollar, €0.51 to the New Zealand dollar, and €0.12 to the South African rand.

TAXES

VALUE-ADDED TAX (V.A.T.) Purchases of goods for export may qualify—after a certain amount—for a value-added tax (called TVA, or *taxe sur la valeur ajoutée*) refund of 15%. Check with the retailer.

TELEPHONES

To place operator-assisted calls, dial 0010.

COUNTRY & AREA CODES The country code for Luxembourg is 352. Note that there are no area codes.

INTERNATIONAL CALLS To reach an AT&T, MCI, or Sprint long-distance operator, dial one of the access codes below.
⚑ Access Codes AT&T ☎ 0800-20111. **MCI** ☎ 0800-0112. **Sprint** ☎ 0800-20115.

LOCAL CALLS You can find public phones on the street and in city post offices. A local call costs a minimum of €0.20 from a public phone. Post offices sell phone cards, called Telekaarten, in denominations from €10 to €50, which can be used in nearly all the country's phone booths. Many public phone booths no longer accept coins.

TIPPING

In hotels and restaurants, taxes and service charges are included in the bill. If you wish to tip further, round off the total to the nearest €1 or add about €5 per €100. Bellhops and doormen appreciate a tip of €1 to €2. Porters at the railway station charge €1.50 per bag, to a maximum of €4. Taxi drivers expect a tip; add about 15% to the amount on the meter.

VISITOR INFORMATION

⚑ Office National du Tourisme (National Tourist Office) ✉ Main branch, Gare Centrale ☎ 481199 ✉ Head office, B.P. 1001, L-1010 Luxembourg Ville ☎ 428282-10 📠 428282-38 ⊕ www.ont.lu ✉ Airport branch ☎ 4282-8221.

WHEN TO GO

The main tourist season in Luxembourg is from early May through October, with spring and fall the most rewarding seasons to travel.

CLIMATE In general, temperatures in Luxembourg are moderate. Be sure to pack rain gear. In the hilly north there is frequently snow in winter. The following are the average daily maximum and minimum temperatures for Luxembourg.

Jan.	37F	3C	May	65F	18C	Sept.	66F	19C
	29	−1		46	8		50	10
Feb.	40F	4C	June	70F	21C	Oct.	56F	13C
	31	−1		52	11		43	6
Mar.	49F	10C	July	73F	23C	Nov.	44F	7C
	35	1		55	13		37	3
Apr.	57F	14C	Aug.	71F	22C	Dec.	39F	4C
	40	4		54	12		32	0

LUXEMBOURG CITY

As you arrive in the capital of Luxembourg from the airport and cross the vast span of the Grande Duchesse Charlotte Bridge, you are greeted by an awe-inspiring panorama of medieval stonework fortifications fronted by massive gates. Then, after a left turn into avenue de la Porte Neuve and a right onto boulevard Royal, you're back in the 21st century of BMW and Mercedes cars and glass-and-concrete office buildings. A block away, in the Old City, the sedate pace of a provincial picture-book town delightfully returns. Across the Alzette River on the Plateau Kirchberg is a huge campus of European Union institutions, as well as several banks, the sports and cultural center, the 10-screen Utopolis cinema complex, and the city's major shopping center, Auchan.

Exploring Luxembourg City

Numbers in the margin correspond to points of interest on the Luxembourg City map.

The military fortifications and the Old Town, with its cobbled streets and inviting public squares, make for terrific exploring. In 1994 UNESCO declared these areas part of the world's cultural heritage.

★ ⑭ **Bock.** This stony promontory is Luxembourg's raison d'être. Jutting dramatically above the valley, the Bock once supported the castle built by the first duke of Luxembourg in AD 963. Taking in vertiginous views of the valley, you'll see the **Plateau du Rham** across the way, on the right and, before it, the massive towers of Duke Wenceslas's fortifications, which were built in 1390. The blocklike *casernes* (barracks) were added during the 17th century by the French. From the Bock you can gain access to 18th-century military tunnels. At the entrance, the **Crypte Archéologique du Bock** (Archaeological Crypt) offers a brief audiovisual history of Luxembourg from the 10th to 15th centuries. ⊠ *Montée de Clausen* ☎ 226753 ⊗ *Mar.–Oct., daily 10–5.*

❽ **Boulevard Royal.** Luxembourg's mini–Wall Street, once the site of the fortress's main moat, curves around the west and north sides of the Old Town. It is lined with as many of the duchy's 220 financial institutions as could be crowded into five blocks.

❺ **Casemates de la Pétrusse** (Pétrusse Casemates). During the many phases of the fortress-city's construction, the rock itself was hollowed out to form a honeycomb of underground passages. Those facing the Pétrusse Valley date from the 17th-century Spanish occupation. ⊠ *Pl. de la Constitution* ☎ 461046 ⊗ *Easter and Whitsun weekends and July–Sept., daily 11–4.*

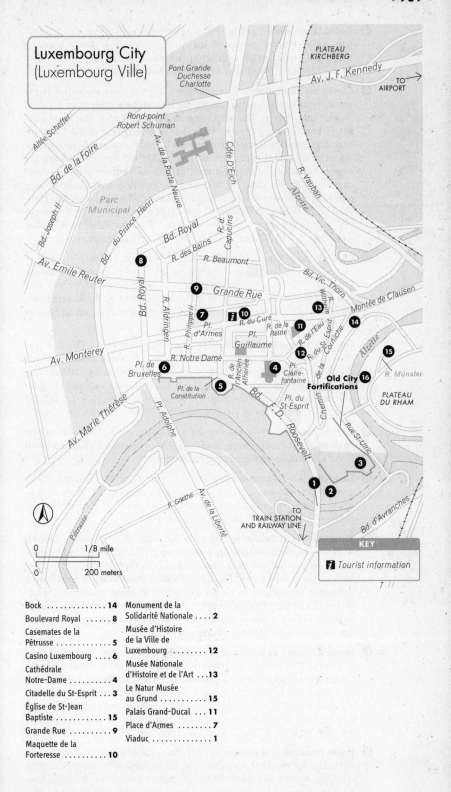

Luxembourg City
(Luxembourg Ville)

PLATEAU KIRCHBERG

Av. J. F. Kennedy

TO AIRPORT

Pont Grande Duchesse Charlotte

Rond-point Robert Schuman

Allée Scheffer

Bd. de la Foire

Av. de la Porte Neuve

Côte D'Eich

R. Vauban

Alzette

Parc Municipal

Bd. Joseph II

Bd. du Prince Henri

Bd. Royal

R. d. Capucins

Av. Emile Reuter

R. des Bains

R. Beaumont

Bd. Vic. Thorn

Montée de Clausen

8

9 Grande Rue

R. Aldringen

R. Philippe II

7 Pl. d'Armes

i

10 R. du Curé

R. Wiltheim

13

14

Av. Monterey

R. Notre Dame

Pl. Guillaume

R. de la Reine

11

R. de l'Eau

R. du St-Esprit

Corniche

15

R. Münster

Pl. de Bruxelles

6

R. de l'Ancien Athénée

4 Cathédrale

Pl. Claire-fontaine

12

Chemin de la

16 Old City Fortifications

Av. Marie Thérèse

Pl. de la Constitution

5

Bd. F. D. Roosevelt

Pl. du St-Esprit

Rue St-Ulric

PLATEAU DU RHAM

Pl. de la Constitution

R. Goethe

Av. de la Liberté

Pétrusse

3

1

2

TO TRAIN STATION AND RAILWAY LINE

Bd. d'Avranches

0 — 1/8 mile
0 — 200 meters

6 **Casino Luxembourg.** Far from being a gaming establishment, this gracious hall, where Franz Liszt played his last public concert, is now a gallery where contemporary art exhibitions are mounted. ⊠ *Rue Notre-Dame 41* ☎ *225045* ◷ *Wed. and Fri.–Mon. 11–6, Thurs. 11–8.*

4 **Cathédrale Notre-Dame.** Luxembourg's 17th-century cathedral is the scene of national pilgrimage during the two weeks beginning on the third Sunday after Easter. The pilgrimage honors the Virgin Mary and celebrates her for saving the city from the bubonic plague in the 14th century. The cathedral has an extravagantly carved portal and a fine baroque organ gallery, both the work of Daniel Müller. In the crypt are the tombs of members of the present ruling Nassau-Weilburg dynasty as well as that of John the Blind (1296–1346), the gallant count of Luxembourg and king of Bohemia who fell at the Battle of Crécy during the Hundred Years' War. ⊠ *Rue Notre-Dame (crypt entrance bd. F. D. Roosevelt)* ◷ *Crypt Easter–Oct., weekdays 10–5, Sat. 8–6, Sun. 10–6; Nov.–Easter, weekdays 10–11:30 and 2–5, Sat. 8–11:30 and 2–5, Sun. 10–5.*

3 **Citadelle du St-Esprit** (Citadel of the Holy Spirit). This 17th-century citadel was built during a French occupation by Maréchal Vauban (1633–1707), Louis XIV's chief military engineer. From the "prow," take in a panoramic view of the three spires of the cathedral, the Alzette River, and the white tower of the European Parliament secretariat. ⊠ *Plateau du St-Esprit.*

15 **Église de St-Jean Baptiste** (Church of St. John the Baptist). This baroque church on the shore of the Alzette River was formerly part of a Benedictine abbey. Among its treasures are a cycle of the stations of the cross made of Limoges enamel and a Black Madonna once thought to provide protection against the plague. The riverside passageway outside the church has a wonderful view of the cliffs. ⊠ *Rue Münster.*

9 **Grande Rue.** The city's main upscale shopping street runs west to east from boulevard Royal to rue du Fossé. The pedestrian mall is lined with luxury boutiques and tempting patisseries.

10 **Maquette de la Forteresse** (Scale Model of the Fortress). This model is a copy of one (now in Paris) made of the fortress-city for Napoléon in 1804, when the fortified complex was in its glory. ⊠ *Rathskeller, rue du Curé* ☎ *222809* ◷ *May–Sept., daily 10–5.*

2 **Monument de la Solidarité Nationale** (Monument to National Unity). This moving memorial honors Luxembourg's World War II casualties— young men who had been conscripted into the German army after Hitler annexed the Grand Duchy—as well as those killed or imprisoned following the general strike protesting the German occupation. Luxembourg was the only country during the war to resist in this way. Within the stark walls is a small, stained-glass chapel housing a symbolic tombstone. ⊠ *Kanounenhiwel, Plateau du St-Esprit.*

★ **12** **Musée d'Histoire de la Ville de Luxembourg** (Luxembourg City Historical Museum). This interactive museum, a marriage of ancient buildings and contemporary technology, explores the city's history over 1,000 years. You'll descend in time and space in a panoramic elevator the size of an exhibition hall. You'll also receive an electronic card to use the many touch-sensitive screens in your language of choice. ⊠ *Rue du St-Esprit 14* ☎ *47963061* ◷ *Tues., Wed., and Fri.–Sun. 10–6, Thurs. 10–8.*

13 **Musée Nationale d'Histoire et de l'Art** (National Museum of History and Fodor'sChoice ★ Art). Also known as the *Staatsmusée*, the impressively monolithic main wing incorporates elements of the previous 18th-century building into its elegant mix of glass and steel. The collection focuses on the prehistoric eras, Gallo-Roman history, and the Middle Ages; it also holds a small sample of painting and sculpture from the 15th through the 21st century. The highlight is a huge Roman mosaic unearthed in nearby Vichten. ⊠ *Marché aux Poissons* ☎ *4793301* ⊕ *www.mnha.lu* ⊗ *Tues.–Sun. 10–5, two Thurs. per month 10–8.*

★ ⑯ **Le Natur Musée au Grund** (Museum of Natural History). This building, dating from 1308, was once a women's prison and now houses collections and displays that explain the environment, past and present. The museum stands on the bank of the Alzette River in the heart of the **Grund** neighborhood; to get here in comfort, take the elevator from the Plateau du St-Esprit. ⊠ *Rue Münster 25* ☎ *462233–1 information* ⊕ *www.mnhn. lu* ⊗ *Mid-Sept.–mid-May, Tues.–Fri. 2–6, Sat. 10–6; mid-May–mid-Sept., Tues.–Sun. 10–6.*

⑪ **Palais Grand-Ducal** (Palace of the Grand Dukes). Parts of the city residence of the grand ducal family date from the 16th century, notably the section that once served as the town hall. A distinct Spanish-Moorish influence is obvious in the elaborate facade. Tickets for guided tours (often sold out) are available only at the City Tourist Office. ⊠ *Rue du Marché-aux-Herbes* ⊗ *Guided tours only; mid-June–mid-Aug., in English, weekdays 1–4, Sat. 10.*

⑦ **Place d'Armes.** Lined with symmetrical plane trees and strung with colored lights, this is the city's liveliest and most welcoming square. A bandstand (concerts are often held here on summer evenings), sidewalk cafés, fast-food joints, and a twice-monthly flea market constantly lure natives and tourists alike. From its southeast corner, a short passage leads to the more dignified **Place Guillaume,** with the Hôtel de Ville (Town Hall); there's a farmers' market Wednesday and Saturday mornings. Next, as you continue southeast, comes the elegant, sloping **Place Clairefontaine,** adorned with a graceful statue of the much-loved Grande Duchesse Charlotte, who ruled from 1919 to 1964.

① **Viaduc.** The 19th-century bridge is also known as the *Passerelle* (footbridge), although it carries vehicular traffic from the railway station. A good starting point for exploring Luxembourg City, it spans the valley of the Pétrusse (now more a brook than a river), which has become a beautiful park. ⊠ *From av. de la Gare to Plateau du St-Esprit.*

Where to Eat

Leading chefs are taking traditional Luxembourg specialties—*jambon d'Ardennes* (raw-smoked ham served cold with pickled onions), *treipen* (blood pudding), and *écrevisses* (crayfish)—and giving them all a newer-than-now nouvelle spin. In the process, Luxembourg City is becoming a true capital *gastronomique.* Note that many upscale places offer a reasonably priced menu at lunch.

$$$$
Fodor'sChoice
★
✕ **Clairefontaine.** The tastefully discreet luxury of this restaurant on the city's most attractive square draws government ministers, visiting dignitaries, and well-heeled gourmands. Chef-owner Tony Tintinger's inspirations include foie gras specialties and innovative dishes such as wild turbot poached in smoked milk with truffles and eggs. ⊠ *Pl. de Clairefontaine 9* ☎ *462211* ⚑ *Reservations essential* ⚏ *Jacket and tie* ▭ *AE, DC, MC, V* ⊗ *Closed 2 wks in Aug., first wk in Nov., and Sun. No lunch Sat.*

★ **$$$$**
✕ **Jan Schneidewind.** The chef-owner of this tiny bistro serves excellent stuffed North Sea crab, bouillabaisse, and other seafood specialties. In August, this is virtually the only top-rank restaurant in town that stays

open. ✉ *Rue du Curé 20* ☎ *222618* ▭ *AE, DC, MC; V* ⊙ *Closed Mon. and 2 wks in Sept. No lunch weekends.*

★ **$$$** ✕**Le Bouquet Garni.** A short walk from the Palais Grand-Ducal, this charming French restaurant in a wonderfully restored 18th-century building is one of the city's best dining experiences. Chefs Lysiane and Thierry Duhr serve original dishes such as pigeon breast in caramelized *soja* sauce. ✉ *Rue de l'Eau 32* ☎ *262006* ▭ *AE, DC, MC, V* ⊙ *Closed Dec. 24–Jan. 4. Closed Sun. No lunch Sat.*

$$$ ✕**La Lorraine.** Outstanding seafood is the specialty of this restaurant strategically situated on the Place d'Armes. A retail shop around the corner carries many of the same fresh ingredients used by the chef, as well as some preserved specialties of the house. Roasted lobster or chicken in a salt and herb crust are good bets. ✉ *Pl. d'Armes 7* ☎ *471436* ▭ *AE, DC, MC, V* ⊙ *Closed Sun. and Aug.*

$$ ✕**Chiggeri.** In the heart of the Old Town, Chiggeri offers both bistro and fine dining and is famous for its ever-changing wine list that features more than 2,200 different wines. ✉ *Rue du Nord 15* ☎ *229936* ▭ *AE, DC, MC, V.*

★ **$$** ✕**Ristorante Roma.** Luxembourg's first Italian restaurant, the Roma has been serving classic Italian food in an unpretentious, inviting atmosphere since the 1950s. Local favorites include the paper-thin carpaccio and fresh pasta. ✉ *Rue Louvigny 5* ☎ *223692* ▭ *AE, MC, V* ⊙ *Closed Mon. No dinner Sun.*

$–$$ ✕**Mousel's Cantine.** Right next to the great Mousel brewery, this comfortable café serves heaping platters of local specialties—braised and grilled ham, sausage, broad beans, and fried potatoes—accompanied by crockery steins of creamy *Gezwickelte Béier* (unfiltered beer). ✉ *Montée de Clausen 46* ☎ *470198* ▭ *MC, V* ⊙ *Closed Sun. and 3 wks in Aug.*

★ **$** ✕**Ems.** Everybody in town vies for one of the vinyl booths in this unpretentious establishment. Its vast portions of mussels in a rich wine-and-garlic broth are best accompanied by french fries and a bottle of sharp, cold, and inexpensive Auxerrois or Rivaner. Ems is open until 1 AM. Reservations are essential on weekends. ✉ *Pl. de la Gare 30* ☎ *487799* ▭ *AE, DC, MC, V* ⊙ *No lunch Sat.*

$ ✕**Oberweis.** Luxembourg's most famous patisserie also serves light lunches. You select your meal at the counter (quiche lorraine, spinach pie, and the like), and it is served at your table. ✉ *Grande Rue 19–20* ☎ *470703* ⊕ *www.oberweis.lu* ▭ *AE, DC, MC, V* ⊙ *Closed Sun.*

Where to Stay

Hotels in the city center are more convenient to exploring than those clustered around the train station. There are also large, modern hotels near the airport and on the Plateau Kirchberg.

$$$$ ▦ **Cravat.** This charming Luxembourg relic straddles the valley and the Old Town in the best location in the city. Corridors have a dated air, but guest rooms are fresh and welcoming in a variety of tastefully retro styles. The art deco coffee shop has been updated but still draws hat-wearing ladies to tea. You can dine in the brasserie La Taverne, or have cocktails in the bar Le Trianon. The restaurant Le Normandy offers upscale French cuisine. ✉ *Bd. F. D. Roosevelt 29, L-2450* ☎ *221975* ⊟ *226711* ⊕ *www.hotelcravat.lu* ⤳ *60 rooms* ♨ *2 restaurants, bar* ▭ *AE, DC, MC, V.*

$$$$ ▦ **Le Royal.** For luxury, Le Royal is the hands-down best choice. Rooms
FodorśChoice vary in style from airy spaces in shades of white to warm burgundy-and-
★ green decor. Each floor has a genteel lobby; there's also a health club, an exotic winter garden, and a posh restaurant. The hotel's at the edge of the Old Town, within steps of parks and shopping. ✉ *Bd. Royal 12,*

L-2449 ☎ 2416161 🖶 225948 ⊕ *www.hotelroyal.lu* 📞 *190 rooms, 20 suites ⚲ 2 restaurants, indoor pool* 🖃 *AE, DC, MC, V.*

$$$ 🏨 **Parc Belair.** This privately owned, family-run hotel a few blocks from the city center stands on the edge of the Parc de Merl. The warm beige rooms have parquet floors and birchwood furniture; those on the park are the quietest. A substantial buffet breakfast is included. The restaurant serves dinner only. ✉ *Av. du X Septembre 109, L-2551* ☎ *4423231* 🖶 *444484* ⊕ *www.hpb.lu* 📞 *52 rooms, 19 suites ⚲ Restaurant* 🖃 *AE, DC, MC, V.*

★ $$ 🏨 **La Cascade.** A turn-of-the-20th-century villa is now a hotel of considerable charm, with fresh, comfortable rooms in flowery pastels. There's a good French restaurant and a lovely terrace overlooking the Alzette River. A bus stops outside to take you to the city center, just over 2 km (1 mi) away. ✉ *Rue de Pulvermuhl 2, L-2356* ☎ *428736* 🖶 *424788* 📞 *9 rooms ⚲ Restaurant* 🖃 *AE, DC, MC, V.*

$$ 🏨 **Ibis.** The hotel is across the street from the airport, with direct access to the motorway. You can walk from the airport or call the hotel to send its free shuttle. Not strong on personality—rooms contain the standard Ibis modular suite that verges on plastic—it does provide honest value for the money. Family rooms sleeping up to four are available. The forest begins just behind the hotel. ✉ *Rte. de Trèves, L-2632 Findel* ☎ *438801* 🖶 *438802* ⊕ *www.ibis.com* 📞 *120 rooms ⚲ Restaurant* 🖃 *AE, DC, MC, V.*

$$ 🏨 **Italia.** This is a find: a former private apartment house converted into hotel rooms, some with stucco detailing and vintage cabinetry. Rooms are solid and freshly furnished, all with beige tile bathrooms. The restaurant of the same name downstairs is one of the city's better Italian eateries. ✉ *Rue d'Anvers 15–17, L-1130* ☎ *4866261* 🖶 *480807* 📞 *20 rooms ⚲ Restaurant* 🖃 *AE, DC, MC, V.*

$$ 🏨 **Sieweburen.** At the northwestern end of the city is this attractively rustic hotel, opened in 1991. There's a playground in front and woods border the property in the back. The brasserie-style tavern, older than the rest of the hotel, is hugely popular, especially when its terrace is open. ✉ *Rue des Septfontaines 36, L-2534* ☎ *442356* 🖶 *442353* 📞 *14 rooms ⚲ Restaurant* 🖃 *MC, V* ⊗ *Closed 3 wks late Dec.–early Jan.*

$ 🏨 **Carlton.** In this vast 1918 hotel near the train station you'll find roomy, quiet quarters. The beveled glass and the oak parquet and terrazzo floors are original—but so are the toilets, all down the hall. Each room has antique beds, floral-print comforters, and a sink; wooden floors, despite creaks, are spotless. ✉ *Rue de Strasbourg 9, L-2561* ☎ *299660* 🖶 *299664* 📞 *50 rooms without bath, 8 with shower* 🖃 *No credit cards.*

Shopping

Luxembourg City's principal shopping areas comprise the **Grande Rue** and its side streets, the **Gare** (train station) area, and the **Auchan** shopping center on Plateau Kirchberg. Jewelry and designer fashions are particularly well represented. Luxembourg chocolates, called *knippercher,* are popular purchases at the best pastry shops. Luxembourg's most famous product is porcelain from **Villeroy & Boch** (✉ Rue du Fossé 2 ☎ 463343 ✉ Factory outlet, Rue Rollingergrund 330 ☎ 46821359). Feast your eyes on their tableware, crystal, and cutlery at the glitzy main store; then buy—at a 20% discount—at the excellent second-quality factory outlet to the northwest of the city center.

Side Trips

The northern highlands that compose the celebrated Ardennes plateau were the hunting ground of emperors and dukes and have been fought over from time immemorial to World War II. Castles punctuate its hills and dominate the valleys; rocky rivers and streams pour off its slopes. In contrast, the Petite Suisse, to the northeast of the capital, is a more gentle retreat. It's a hilly area of leafy woods, rushing brooks, and old farms, ideal for rustic picnicking and great hiking. An easy hour's drive from Luxembourg City will take you to any of the towns except Clervaux, which is a bit farther.

Echternach

Echternach's cobbled market square is a mix of Gothic arcades and medieval town houses. The River Sûre here forms the border with Germany, and large numbers of tourists cross over on weekends. Some 15,000 pilgrims participate every year in a dancing procession on the Tuesday after Pentecost, ending at the **Basilique St-Willibrord** (⊠ Porte St-Willibrord), whose crypt, open daily 9:30–6:30, contains the tomb of the great English missionary St. Willibrord (658–739).

Painstakingly detailed reproductions of the illuminated manuscripts of the Echternach School are displayed in the **Musée de l'Abbaye** (Abbey Museum). ⊠ *Parvis de la Basilique 11* ☎ *727472* ☉ *Palm Sun.–June, Sept., and Oct., daily 10–noon and 2–6; July and Aug., daily 10–6.*

Diekirch

In the Ardennes, Diekirch has a lovely little Romanesque church, **Église St-Laurent** (St. Lawrence's Church), with Merovingian tombs, and (south of town) the **Devil's Altar**, a Celtic dolmen. The **Musée National d'Histoire Militaire** (National Military History Museum) mainly commemorates the Battle of the Bulge, the last German counteroffensive, which began just before Christmas 1944. ⊠ *Bamertal 10* ☎ *808908* ☉ *Apr.–Oct., daily 10–6; Nov.–Mar., daily 2–6.*

Vianden

★ The medieval **Château de Vianden** is the most romantic sight in the Grand Duchy. Rearing up on a hill above the tiny village, and replete with conical spires and massive bulwarks, it vividly recalls Luxembourg's feudal past. ⊠ *Grande Rue* ☎ *8341081* ⊕ *www.castle-vianden.lu* ☉ *Apr.–Sept., daily 10–6; Mar. and Oct., daily 10–5; Nov.–Feb., daily 10–4.*

Clervaux

Surrounded by deep-cleft hills, the town is noted for the 12th-century **Château de Clervaux,** which has become the permanent home for Luxembourg-born Edward Steichen's "Family of Man." This photo essay on the human condition was put together in 1955 by Steichen from more than 2 million photographs by professionals and amateurs. It was first shown in a phenomenally successful exhibition at the Museum of Modern Art in New York; it then toured the world for eight years and was finally donated to the Grand Duchy in 1964. ⊠ *Grande Rue* ☎ *929657* ☉ *Mar.–June and Sept.–Dec., Tues.–Sun. 10–6, July and Aug., daily 10–6.*

Bourscheid

★ The romantic ruins of the **Château de Bourscheid** loom 500 feet above the River Sûre, commanding three valleys. Restorations have made the ruin's rambling towers and walls more accessible. ⊠ *Bourscheid Moulin-Plage* ☎ *990570* ☉ *Apr., daily 11–5; May, June, and Sept., daily 10–6; July and Aug., daily 10–7; Oct., daily 11–4; Nov.–Mar., weekends and holidays 11–4.*

Moselle

On the eastern border with Germany, this wide river turns into Luxembourg's seaside during the summer, with promenading and jet-skiing. The banks of the river are covered with vineyards where the

Luxembourg Moselle wine and sparkling wine (*crement*) are produced. Famous for sparkling wines, the **Bernard Massard** cellars are open for tours and tastings. ⊠ *8 rue Pont, Grevenmacher* ☎ *750545228* ⊙ *Apr.–Oct., daily 9:30–6, Nov.–Mar., reservations only.*

The valley can be best appreciated from aboard the **MS *Princess Marie-Astrid,*** which cruises along the Moselle. ⊠ *Rte. du Vin 10, Grevenmacher* ☎ *758275.*

Luxembourg City Essentials

AIRPORTS & TRANSFERS

All international flights arrive at Luxembourg's Findel Airport, 6 km (4 mi) northeast of the city.
🚹 **Findel Airport** ☎ 47/982315.

TRANSFERS Bus 9 links the airport, the city center, and the main bus depot, next to the train station. Tickets cost €4.60. A taxi costs €18–€20.

BIKE TRAVEL

Bicycling is an excellent way to see the city and outlying areas. Bikes can be rented in Luxembourg City at Vélo en Ville from March through October.
🚹 **Bike Rentals** **Vélo en Ville** ⊠ Bisserwee 8 ☎ 222753.

BUS TRAVEL WITHIN LUXEMBOURG CITY

Luxembourg City has highly efficient bus service. Information can be found at Aldringen Center, an underground station off boulevard Royal. A 10-ride book of tickets costs €9.20.

CAR TRAVEL

PARKING On-street parking in Luxembourg City is difficult. If you're in Luxembourg for a day, use one of the underground parking lots or park at the Parking Glacis next to the Municipal Theater, five minutes' walk from the city center. If you arrive from the west, use the free Parking Stade (opposite the Stadium) on Route d'Arlon and take the shuttle bus (€4.60) to town. If you arrive from France, look for the park-and-ride facility Sud (south); from Germany, look for Kirchberg-FIL.

EMERGENCIES

Pharmacies in Luxembourg stay open nights on a rotation system; see signs listing late-night facilities outside each pharmacy.
🚹 **Ambulance, Dentist, Doctor** ☎ 112. **Police** ☎ 113.

ENGLISH-LANGUAGE MEDIA

For books and magazines in English, try English Shop. The English-language paper *Luxembourg News*, published on Thursday, is available from newsdealers in the city.
🚹 **Bookstores** **English Shop** ⊠ 16, rue Victor Hugo ☎ 224925.

TAXIS

Taxi stands are near the Gare Centrale and the main post office; it is almost impossible to hail one in the street.
🚹 **Taxi dispatch** ☎ 480058 or 482233.

TOURS

BUS TOURS Sales-Lentz runs 2¼-hour city bus tours, mid-March–mid-November, from the war memorial on place de la Constitution and from the bus station. A 4¾-hour tour to Château de Vianden takes place on weekends May–September.
🚹 **Sales-Lentz** ☎ 232211.

TRAIN TOURS Pétrusse Express guided minitrain tours of the Old Town and the Pétrusse Valley run from the place de la Constitution mid-March–October.
🚃 **Pétrusse Express** ☎ 461617.

WALKING TOURS A guided walking tour called "City Promenade," given on Monday, Wednesday, and weekends at 2 from November to Easter, and daily from Good Friday to October at 3, leaves from Place d'Armes. The "Wenzel Walk," a guided tour offered Easter–October daily at 3, covers 1,000 years of history in 100 minutes. The walk starts at the Bock promontory and leads over medieval bridges and past ancient ruins. You can also rent audio headsets for an individual recorded tour throughout the year.
🚃 **Luxembourg City Tourist Office** ☎ 222809.

TRAIN TRAVEL

Luxembourg is served by frequent direct trains from Paris (four hours) and Brussels (three hours). From Amsterdam (six hours), the journey is via Brussels. There are connections from most German cities via Koblenz. Outside Luxembourg City, three major train routes extend to the north, south, and east. All services are from the Gare Centrale.
🚃 **Gare Centrale** ✉ Pl. de la Gare ☎ 4990–4990.

TRAVEL AGENCIES

🚃 **BBL Travel American Express** ✉ 3 rue Jean Piret ☎ 4924041. **Carlson/Wagonlit** ✉ Grande Rue 105 ☎ 460315. **Connections** ✉ Grande Rue 70 ☎ 229933, including youth travel.

VISITOR INFORMATION

The Luxembourg Card provides admission to 40 major attractions in the capital and countryside and use of public transport throughout the Grand Duchy from mid-April to October 31. It costs €9 for one day, €16 for two days, and €22 for three days; family cards are twice the price. Cards can be bought in hotels and tourist offices.
🚃 **Luxembourg City Tourist Office** ✉ Pl. d'Armes ☎ 222809. **Beaufort** ✉ Rue de l'Église 9 ☎ 836081. **Bourscheid** ✉ Château ☎ 990564. **Clervaux** ✉ Château ☎ 920072. **Diekirch** ✉ Esplanade 1 ☎ 803023. **Echternach** ✉ Porte St-Willibrord, Basilique ☎ 720230. **Vianden** ✉ rue du Vieux Marché 1A ☎ 834257.

THE NETHERLANDS
AMSTERDAM; HISTORIC HOLLAND; THE HAGUE, DELFT & ROTTERDAM

THE BUCOLIC IMAGES of windmills and wooden shoes that brought tourism here in the decades after World War II have little to do with the Netherlands today. Sure, tulips grow in abundance in the bulb district of Noord- and Zuid-Holland provinces, but today's Netherlands is no backwater operation: this tiny nation has an economic strength and cultural wealth that far surpass its size and population.

Sophisticated, modern Netherlands has more art treasures per square mile than just about any other country on Earth, as well as a large number of ingenious, energetic citizens with a remarkable commitment to quality, style, and innovation. The 33,393 square km (16,033 square mi) of the Netherlands are just about half the area of the state of Maine or half the area of Scotland, and its population of nearly 16 million is slightly smaller than that of the state of Texas or twice the population of London. With a history of successful seafaring merchants, the country is still one of the world's most important distribution and transport hubs, and its banks have invested this wealth around the world. The country encourages internal accomplishments as well, particularly of a cultural nature. In the country, within a 120-km (75-mi) radius, are 10 major art museums and several smaller ones that together contain the world's richest and most comprehensive collection of Western art masterpieces from the 15th to 20th centuries. In the same small area are a half-dozen performance halls offering music, dance, and internationally known performing arts festivals.

The marriage of economic power and cultural wealth is nothing new to the Dutch; during the 17th century, for example, money raised through their colonial outposts overseas was used to buy or commission portraits and paintings by young artists such as Rembrandt, Hals, Vermeer, and Van Ruysdael. But it was not only the arts that were encouraged: the Netherlands was home to the philosophers Descartes, Spinoza, and Comenius; the jurist Grotius; the naturalist Van Leeuwenhoek, inventor of the microscope; and others like them who flourished in the country's enlightened tolerance. The Netherlands continues to subsidize its thinkers, artists, and performers, supporting an educational system in which creativity in every field is respected and nourished.

The Netherlands is the delta of Europe, located where the great Rhine and Maas rivers and their tributaries empty into the North Sea. Near the coast, it is a land of flat fields and interconnecting canals; in the center it is surprisingly wooded; and in the far south are rolling hills. About half of the Netherlands is below sea level.

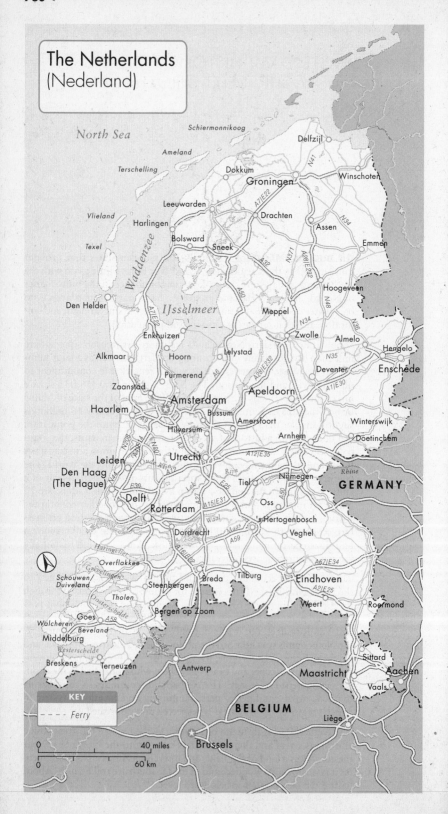

The Netherlands
(Nederland)

North Sea

Schiermonnikoog

Delfzijl

Ameland

Dokkum

Groningen

Winschoten

Terschelling

Leeuwarden

N41

A7|E22

Drachten

Assen

N34

Vlieland

Harlingen

Bolsward

Emmen

Texel

Sneek

A28|E232

A32

Hoogeveen

Den Helder

IJsselmeer

Meppel

N371

N48

Zwolle

N34

Almelo

Enkhuizen

N36

Hengelo

Alkmaar

Hoorn

Lelystad

N35

Deventer

Enschede

Purmerend

A6

A28|E232

A1|E30

Zaanstad

Apeldoorn

Haarlem

Amsterdam

Bussum

Winterswijk

Hilversum

Amersfoort

Arnhem

Doetinchem

Leiden

Utrecht

A12|E35

Rhine

GERMANY

Den Haag
(The Hague)

Tiel

Nijmegen

Delft

A15|E31

Oss

Rotterdam

Waal

's-Hertogenbosch

Dordrecht

A59

Veghel

Overflakkee

A67|E34

Breda

Tilburg

Eindhoven

Steenbergen

A2|E25

Roermond

Goes

Bergen op Zoom

Weert

Middelburg

Sittard

Aachen

Breskens

Terneuzen

Antwerp

Maastricht

Vaals

BELGIUM

Liège

0 _____ 40 miles

0 _____ 60 km

Brussels

Amsterdam is the focal point of the country's culture, as well as of a 60-km (37½-mi) circle of cities, known as the Randstad (agglomeration of cities), that includes the Hague (the Dutch seat of government and the world center of international justice), Rotterdam (the industrial center of the Netherlands and the world's largest port), and the historic cites of Haarlem, Leiden, Delft, and Utrecht.

The northern and eastern provinces are rural and quiet; the southern provinces that hug the Belgian border are lightly industrialized and sophisticated. The great rivers that cut through the heart of the country provide both geographical and sociological borders. The area "above the great rivers," as the Dutch phrase it, is peopled by tough-minded and practical Calvinists; to the south are more ebullient Catholics. A tradition of tolerance pervades this densely populated land; aware that they cannot survive alone, the Dutch are bound by common traits of ingenuity, personal honesty, and a bold sense of humor.

THE NETHERLANDS A TO Z

To research prices, get advice from other travelers, and book travel arrangements, visit www.fodors.com.

AIR TRAVEL

KLM Royal Dutch Airlines, under the banner of CityHopper, operates several domestic services connecting Amsterdam to Maastricht, Eindhoven, and Rotterdam. In this small country, however, you'd probably travel just as fast by car or train.

🛈 KLM/CityHopper ☎ 020/474-7747 ⊕ www.klm.nl.

BIKE TRAVEL

The Netherlands is a cyclist-friendly country with specially designated cycle paths, signs, and picnic areas. Bikes can be rented at train stations in most cities and towns, and Dutch trains are cycle-friendly, too, with entryways designed to accommodate bicycles. You will need an extra ticket for the bike, however. There are some restrictions on carrying bicycles on trains, so check first. Advice on rentals and routes is available from offices of the Netherlands Board of Tourism in North America or in the Netherlands, or from local tourist offices.

BUS TRAVEL

The Netherlands has an excellent bus network between and within towns. Bus excursions can be booked on the spot and at local tourist offices. In major cities, the best buy is a *strippenkaart* ticket (€6.20), which can be used for all bus, tram, and metro services. Each card has 15 strips, which are canceled either by the driver as you enter the bus or by the stamping machine at each door of the tram. More than one person can travel on a strippenkaart. You can buy it at train stations, post offices, some tourist offices, many newsstands, and in Amsterdam at the public transport (GVB) ticket office in the plaza in front of the central railway station. A *dagkaart,* a travel-anywhere ticket (€5.50, one day; €8.80, two days; €11.30, three days), covers all urban bus and streetcar routes. The Amsterdam Transport Pass gives you unlimited use of all forms of public transport, including the canal bus, for a day (€19). National public transport information is available from the number listed below, at a cost of €0.50 per minute.

🛈 National public transport information ☎ 0900/9292.

BUSINESS HOURS

BANKS & OFFICES Banks are open weekdays 9–4. Some banks are closed Monday mornings. GWK Border Exchange Offices at major railway stations are generally open Monday–Saturday 8–8, Sunday 10–4. GWK offices at border checkpoints are generally open 8–8 and at Schiphol Airport 7 AM–10 PM.

MUSEUMS & SIGHTS Museums in Amsterdam are open daily. Elsewhere they close on Monday, but there are exceptions, so check with local tourist offices. In rural areas, some museums close or operate shorter hours in winter. Usual hours are 10–5.

SHOPS Shops are open weekdays and Saturday 8:30 or 9 to 5:30 or 6, but outside the cities some close for lunch; many shops don't open until 1 PM on Monday. In major cities there is usually late-night shopping until 9 PM on Thursday or Friday. Sunday opening, from noon to 5, varies from city to city.

CAR TRAVEL

EMERGENCIES Experienced, uniformed mechanics of the *Wegenwacht* patrol the highways in yellow cars 24 hours a day. Operated by the Royal Dutch Touring Club (ANWB), the patrol's members will help if you have car trouble. On major roads, ANWB also maintains phone boxes from which you can call for assistance. Otherwise call the number listed below. To use these services, you may be asked to take temporary membership in ANWB.

🚗 **ANWB** ☎ 0800/0888.

GASOLINE Gas (*benzine* in Dutch) is unleaded and costs around €1.30 per liter for regular, €1.20 for super, and €0.85 for diesel.

PARKING Parking in the larger towns is difficult and expensive, with illegally parked cars quickly towed away or subject to a wheel clamp. Fines for recovery or release from a clamp can top €136. Consider parking on the outskirts and using the efficient public transportation. Watch for blue P&R (Park and Ride) signs on ring roads and approach roads to major towns.

ROAD CONDITIONS The Netherlands has one of the best road systems in Europe. Multilane expressways (toll-free) link major cities, but the smaller roads and country lanes provide more picturesque routes. In towns, many streets are narrow, and you'll have to contend with complex one-way systems and cycle lanes. Be particularly vigilant for cyclists; they're ubiquitous, and they assume you'll give them the right of way. Information about weather and road conditions—in Dutch—can be obtained by calling the number below (€0.35 per minute).

🚗 **Weather and road condition information** ☎ 0900/9622.

RULES OF THE ROAD In the Netherlands your own state or national driver's license is acceptable. Driving is on the right. The speed limit on expressways is 100 kph (62 mph) or 120 kph (75 mph); outside built-up areas it is 80 kph (50 mph); on city streets and in residential areas it is 50 kph (30 mph) or less, according to the signs. Note that slow traffic from the right has the right-of-way in urban areas and local roads. On traffic circles, drivers in the circle have the right-of-way. Front-seat passengers are required to wear a seat belt, and all other passengers are required to use available seat belts.

CUSTOMS & DUTIES

For details on imports and duty-free limits, *see* Customs & Duties *in* Smart Travel Tips.

EATING & DRINKING

The Dutch enjoy a wide variety of cuisines, from traditional Dutch to Indonesian—the influence of the former Dutch colony. Breakfast includes several varieties of bread, butter, jam, ham, cheese, chocolate, boiled eggs, juice, and steaming coffee or tea. Lunch tends to be a *broodje* (sandwich) from the great selection of delicatessens. Dutch specialties for meals later in the day include *erwtensoep* (rich, thick pea soup with pieces of tangy sausage or pigs' knuckles) and *stamppot* (mashed potatoes and greens with *worst* [sausage]); both are usually served only in winter. *Haring* (herring) is particularly popular, especially the "new herring" caught between May and September and served raw, with a garnish of onions and pickles. At Indonesian restaurants, the chief item is *rijsttafel* (rice table), a meal made up of rice and 20 or more small meat, seafood, or vegetable dishes, many of which are hot and spicy. Eating places range from snack bars, fast-food outlets, and modest local cafés to haute cuisine restaurants of international repute. Of special note are the *bruin cafés* (brown cafés), characterful, traditional pubs that normally serve snack-type meals. They are so named because of the rich wooden furnishings and—some say—the centuries-old pipe-tobacco stains on the ceilings. The indigenous Dutch liquor is potent and warming *jenever* (gin), both "old" (matured) and "young."

WHAT IT COSTS In euros			
$$$$	**$$$**	**$$**	**$**
AMSTERDAM, ROTTERDAM, AND THE HAGUE			
PER PERSON over €36	€25–€36	€14–€24	under €14
OTHER AREAS			
AT DINNER over €30	€23–€30	€12–€22	under €12

Prices are per person for a main course.

MEALTIMES   Lunchtime is between 12:30 and 1. The Dutch eat dinner around 6 or 7, especially in the country and smaller cities, so many restaurants accept final orders at 9 PM and close about 10. In larger cities dining hours vary, and some restaurants stay open until midnight.

RESERVATIONS &   Jacket and tie are advised for restaurants in the $$$$ and $$$ categories.
DRESS   The tolerant Dutch accept casual outfits in most eateries.

EMBASSIES
All embassies are in the Hague.
- Australia ⊠ Carnegielaan 4 ☎ 070/310-8200.
- Canada ⊠ Sophialaan 7 ☎ 070/311-1600.
- Ireland ⊠ Dr. Kuyperstraat 9 ☎ 070/363-0993.
- New Zealand ⊠ Carnegielaan 10 ☎ 070/346-9324.
- South Africa ⊠ Wassenaarseweg 40 ☎ 070/392-4501.
- United Kingdom ⊠ Lange Voorhout 10 ☎ 070/427-0427.
- United States ⊠ Lange Voorhout 102 ☎ 070/310-9209.

HOLIDAYS
New Year's Day; Easter; Queen's Day (April 30); Ascension (mid-May); Pentecost/Whitsunday and Whitmonday (late May); Christmas; and Boxing Day (day after Christmas).

LANGUAGE
Dutch is a difficult language for foreigners, but the Dutch are fine linguists, so almost everyone speaks at least some English, especially in larger cities and tourist centers.

LODGING

The Netherlands has accommodations covering the full spectrum from the luxurious, Dutch-owned international Golden Tulip hotel chain to traditional, small-town hotels and family-run guest houses. For adventurous travelers, the provinces abound with modest hostels, campgrounds, and rural bungalows. Accommodations are tight from Easter to summer, especially in Amsterdam, so early booking is advised.

WHAT IT COSTS In euros				
	$$$$	**$$$**	**$$**	**$**
AMSTERDAM, ROTTERDAM, AND THE HAGUE				
FOR 2 PEOPLE	over €350	€180–€350	€105–€180	under €105
OTHER AREAS				
HOTELS	over €200	€165–€200	€90–€165	under €90

Prices are for two people sharing a double room in high season.

BED & BREAKFASTS VVV provides lists of bed-and-breakfasts and "pension" accommodations, which can be much cheaper than hotel accommodations and introduce you to Dutch domestic life in the flesh. Bed & Breakfast Holland also provides B&B addresses in cities and rural areas around the country.
🚩 **Bed & Breakfast Holland** ⊠ Theophile de Bockstraat 3, 1058 TV, Amsterdam ☎ 020/615-7527 🖷 020/669-1573. **VVV** ☎ 0900/400-4040.

HOTELS Dutch hotels are generally clean, if not spotless, no matter how modest their facilities, and service is courteous and efficient. There are many moderate and inexpensive hotels, most of which are relatively small. In the provinces, the range of accommodations is more limited, but there are friendly, inexpensive family-run hotels that are usually centrally located. Some have good—if modest—dining facilities. Hotels generally quote room prices for double occupancy, and rates often include breakfast, service charges, and value-added tax (V.A.T.). The prime tourist season in the Netherlands runs from April through October and peaks during school vacation periods (Easter, July, and August), when hotels may impose a 20% surcharge.

To book hotels in advance, you can use the free Netherlands Reservation Center. For a small fee, tourist offices can usually make reservations at short notice. Bookings must be made in person, however.
🚩 **Netherlands Reservation Center** ☎ 0299/689144 ⊕ www.hotelres.nl.

MAIL & SHIPPING

If you're uncertain where you'll be staying, have mail sent to "poste restante, Hoofd Postkantoor" in major cities along your route (making sure that your name and initials are clear and correctly spelled), or to American Express offices, where a small fee is charged on collection to non–American Express customers.

POSTAL RATES Airmail letters to the United States cost €0.75 for the first 20 grams; postcards cost €0.54; an aerogram (called *priority blad*) costs €0.50. Airmail letters to the United Kingdom cost €0.59 for the first 20 grams; postcards cost €0.54; an aerogram costs €0.50.

MONEY MATTERS

The Netherlands is prosperous, with a high standard of living, so overall costs are similar to those in other northern European countries. Prices for hotels and services in major cities are 10%–20% higher than those in rural areas. Amsterdam and the Hague are the most expensive.

Hotel and restaurant service charges and the 6% value-added tax (V. A.T.) are usually included in the prices quoted. Some sample prices include half bottle of wine, €11; glass of beer, €1.50; cup of coffee, €2; ham and cheese sandwich, €2.25; 2-km (1-mi) taxi ride, €6.50.

CURRENCY The Netherlands is one of 12 nations that have adopted the euro, the European Union currency, written as euro or simply €.

At press time (summer 2003), the exchange rate for the euro was €0.89 to the U.S. dollar, €0.64 to the Canadian dollar, €1.40 to the pound sterling, €0.56 to the Australian dollar, €0.50 to the New Zealand dollar, and €0.12 to the South African rand.

VALUE-ADDED TAX (V.A.T.) Stores carrying the TAX FREE SHOPPING sign guarantee that you can get a V.A.T. (value-added tax, called BTW in Holland) refund by means of a Global Refund check, which you request from the salesperson. Stores without this sign may be willing to privately arrange to help you receive the refund, but this is an unwieldy procedure and not likely to happen. Purchases of goods in one store on one day amounting to €136 or more qualify for a V.A.T. refund of 19%, less a service charge. After the refund check has been validated by customs at the airport, you can submit it when you leave the Netherlands or exit the European Union, or by mail, and the refund will be credited to your credit card within five weeks. This arrangement is valid only if you export the goods within three months after date of purchase.

TELEPHONES

COUNTRY & AREA CODES The country code for the Netherlands is 31. When dialing a number in the Netherlands from outside the country, drop the initial 0 from the local area code.

INTERNATIONAL CALLS Direct-dial international calls can be made from any phone booth. To reach an AT&T, MCI (called WorldPhone in the Netherlands), or Sprint operator, dial one of the access codes below.
🔢 Access Codes **AT&T** ☎ 0800/022-9111. **MCI** ☎ 0800/022-9122. **Sprint** ☎ 0800/022-9119.

LOCAL CALLS All towns and cities have area codes that are used only when you are calling from outside the area. All public phone booths require phone cards, which may be purchased from post offices, railway stations, and newsdealers in €5 and €10 amounts. Most operators speak English. Dial 0900–8418 for international assistance (€1.15 per minute).

TIPPING

Hotels and restaurants almost always include 10%–15% service and 6% V.A.T. in their charges. Give a doorman €1.50 for calling a cab. Bellhops in first-class hotels should be tipped €1 for each bag they carry. Hat-check attendants expect at least €0.50, and washroom attendants get €0.25. Taxis in almost every town have a tip included in the meter charge, but round the fare to the next euro nevertheless.

TRAIN TRAVEL

Fast, frequent, and comfortable Nederlandse Spoorwegen trains operate throughout the country. All trains have first- and second-class cars, and many intercity trains have buffet or dining-car services. Sometimes one train contains two separate sections that divide during the trip, so be sure you are in the correct car for your destination.

National public transportation information and route advice for door-to-door travel is available from the number below, at a cost of €0.50 per minute. A booklet, *Holland by Train,* is available at train stations.

CUTTING COSTS To get the best value out of rail travel, purchase a pass. The Benelux Tourrail can be bought abroad, but the other passes are available only in the Netherlands. Popular options are a Weekendretour (weekend round-trip valid from Friday evening to Monday morning), Dagkaart (one-day, travel-anywhere train ticket), or an OV-Dagkaart (one-day, travel-anywhere ticket for the train, bus, tram, and metro). The Railrunner ticket allows children to travel under adult supervision for just €1. From July through August, you can purchase a Zomertoer (summer tour) ticket for three days' travel within a 10-day period. You need your passport when you purchase these tickets. Ask about these fares at railway information bureaus or local tourist offices.

🚹 **National public transport information** ☎ 0900/9292. **Nederlandse Spoorwegen** ✉ Antwoordnummer 4470 3500 VE Utrecht ⊕ www.ns.nl.

VISITOR INFORMATION

The VVV (acronym for the Vereniging voor Vreemdelingenverkeer, or national tourist offices) has branches in smaller towns; the information line below costs €0.55 per minute.

The *Museumjaarkaart,* which can be purchased from most museums and all VVV tourist offices, provides a year's free or discounted admission to almost 450 museums throughout the country. It costs €35, €15 if you're under 25. A photo and passport are required for purchase. Nearly all museums participate.

🚹 **Netherlands Board of Tourism** ✍ Box 458, 2260 MG Leidschendam, Holland ☎ 070/370-5705 🖷 070/320-1654 ⊕ www.holland.com. **VVV** ☎ 0900/400-4040.

WHEN TO GO

Dutch bulb fields bloom from late March to the end of May. June is the ideal time to catch the warm weather and miss the crowds, but every region of the Netherlands has its season. Delft is luminous after a winter storm, and fall in the Utrecht countryside can be as dramatic as it is in New England.

CLIMATE Summers are generally warm, but beware of sudden showers and blustery coastal winds. Winters are chilly and wet but are not without clear days. If the canals freeze over, they immediately fill with keen skaters, the learners pushing along chairs. After a cloudburst, notice the watery quality of light that inspired Vermeer and other great Dutch painters. The following are the average daily maximum and minimum temperatures for Amsterdam.

Jan.	40F	4C	May	61F	16C	Sept.	65F	18C
	34	1		50	10		56	13
Feb.	41F	5C	June	65F	18C	Oct.	56F	13C
	34	1		56	13		49	9
Mar.	47F	8C	July	70F	21C	Nov.	47F	8C
	38	3		59	15		41	5
Apr.	52F	11C	Aug.	68F	20C	Dec.	41F	5C
	43	6		59	15		36	2

AMSTERDAM

Amsterdam has as many facets as a 40-carat diamond polished by one of the city's gem cutters: a font for artistic geniuses such as Rembrandt and van Gogh; a cornucopia bursting with parrot tulips; and a social scene that takes in cozy bars, brown cafés, and outdoor markets. While impressive gabled houses bear witness to the golden age of the 17th century, their upside-down reflections in the city's canal waters below symbolize the contradictions within broader Dutch society. With a mere 730,000 friendly souls and with almost everything a scant 10-minute bike ride away, Amsterdam is actually more of a village—albeit a largish global one—that packs the cultural wallop of a megalopolis.

Exploring Amsterdam

The old heart of the city consists of canals, with narrow streets radiating out like the spokes of a wheel. The hub of this wheel and the most convenient point to begin sightseeing is Centraal Station (Central Station). Across the street, in the same building as the Old Dutch Coffee House, is a tourist information office. The Rokin, once an open canal, is the main route from Central Station via the Dam to the Muntplein. Amsterdam's key points of interest can be covered within two or three days, including visits to one or two of the important museums and galleries. Small and densely packed, the city center is divided into districts that are easily covered on foot.

Around the Dam

The Dam (Dam Square) is the official center of town. It traces its roots to the 12th century, when wanderers from central Europe floated their canoes down the Amstel River and stopped to build a dam. Soon this muddy mound became the focal point of the small city of Amstelledamme and the location of the local weigh house. From these inauspicious beginnings, by the 17th century Amsterdam had developed into one of the richest and most powerful cities in the world.

Numbers in the margin correspond to points of interest on the Amsterdam map.

⑭ **Anne Frankhuis** (Anne Frank House). Immortalized by the poignant diary kept by the young Jewish girl from 1942 to 1944, when she and her family hid here from the German occupying forces, this canal-side house also has an educational exhibition and documents about the Holocaust and civil liberty. Consider visiting during summer evenings to avoid the crowds. ⊠ *Prinsengracht 267* ☎ *020/556–7100* ⊕ *www. annefrank.nl* ☉ *Apr. and June–Aug., daily 9–9; May, daily 9–7; Sept.–Mar., daily 9–7* ☉ *Closed Yom Kippur.*

FodorsChoice ★

⑩ **Beurs van Berlage** (Berlage's Stock Exchange). This impressive building, completed in 1903, was designed by Hendrik Petrus Berlage, whose aesthetic principles were to guide modernism. The sculpture and rich decoration of the plain brick interior are among modernism's embryonic masterpieces. It now houses two concert halls, a large exhibition space, and its own museum, which offers the chance to climb the 138-foot-high tower for its superb views. ⊠ *Damrak 277* ☎ *020/530–4141* ⊕ *www.beursvanberlage.nl* ☉ *Museum Tues.–Sun. 11–5.*

① **Centraal Station** (Central Station). The flamboyant redbrick and stone portal was designed by P. J. H. Cuijpers and built in 1884–89. Cuijpers's other significant contribution to Amsterdam's architectural heritage is the Rijksmuseum. ⊠ *Stationsplein.*

⑪ **Dam** (Dam Square). This is the broadest square in the old section of the town. Fishermen used to come here to sell their catch. Today it is a busy crossroads, circled with shops and bisected by traffic; it is also a popular spot for outdoor performers. At one side of the square stands a simple monument to Dutch victims of World War II. Eleven urns contain soil from the 11 provinces of the Netherlands, and a 12th contains soil from the former Dutch East Indies, now Indonesia. ⊠ *Junction of Rokin, Damrak, Moses en Aaronstraat, and Paleisstraat.*

Amsterdam

❻ De Waag (The Weigh House). Dating from 1488, when it was built as a city gate, this turreted, redbrick monument dominates the Nieuwmarkt (New Market) in the oldest part of Amsterdam. It became a weigh house and was once the headquarters for ancient professional guilds. The magnificently restored **Theatrum Anatomicum,** up the winding stairs, was added in 1691 and set the scene for Rembrandt's painting the *Anatomy Lesson of Dr. Tulp.* The upper floors are now home to the media lab of the Society for Old and New Media, which hosts occasional conferences and exhibitions. Downstairs is a grand café and restaurant. ✉ *Nieuwmarkt 4* ☎ *020/557-9898* ⊕ *www.waag.org.*

⓭ Het Koninklijk Paleis te Amsterdam (Royal Palace in Amsterdam). The vast, well-proportioned classical structure dominating the Dam was completed in 1655. It is built on 13,659 pilings sunk into the marshy soil. The great pediment sculptures are an allegorical representation of Amsterdam surrounded by Neptune and mythological sea creatures. Filled with opulent 18th- and early 19th-century furnishings, it is the official royal residence but is used only on high state occasions. ✉ *Dam* ☎ *020/624-8698* ⊕ *www.koninklijkhuis.nl* ☉ *July and Aug., daily 12:30–5; May, June, Sept., and Oct., irregular Tues.–Thurs. 1–4. Call for detailed annual schedule. Closed for state events.*

❾ Museum Amstelkring. The facade carries the inscription *"Ons Lieve Heer Op Solder"* ("Our Lord in the Attic"). In 1578 Amsterdam embraced Protestantism and outlawed the church of Rome. The municipal authorities were so tolerant that secret Catholic chapels were allowed to exist; at one time there were 62 in Amsterdam alone. One such chapel was established in these three buildings—one canal-side house with two adjoining houses in the alley—built around 1661. Services were held in the attics regularly until 1888, the year the St. Nicolaaskerk was consecrated for Catholic worship. Of interest are the baroque altar with its revolving tabernacle, the swinging pulpit that can be stowed out of sight, and the upstairs gallery with its displays of religious artifacts. The authentic 17th-century merchant's living quarters are extremely rare. ✉ *Oudezijds Voorburgwal 40* ☎ *020/624-6604* ⊕ *www.museumamstelkring.nl* ☉ *Mon.–Sat. 10–5, Sun. and holidays 1–5.*

☝ ❺ Nederlands Scheepvaartmuseum (Netherlands Maritime Museum). This former naval warehouse maintains a collection of restored vessels and a replica of a three-masted trading ship from 1749. The museum explains the history of Dutch shipping, from dugout canoes right through to modern container ships, with maps, paintings, and models. ✉ *Kattenburgerplein 1* ☎ *020/523-2222* ⊕ *www.scheepvaartmuseum.nl* ☉ *Mid-June–mid-Sept., daily 10–5; mid-Sept.–mid-June* ☉ *Closed Mon.*

☝ ❸ NEMO Science & Technology Center. Renzo Piano, architect of the Centre Pompidou in Paris, designed this interactive museum. Hands-on exhibits cover topics from elementary physics to the latest technological gadgets. The rooftop terrace offers a panoramic view across the city. ✉ *Oosterdok 2* ☎ *0900/919–1100, €0.35 per min* ⊕ *www.e-nemo.nl* ☉ *Tues.–Sun. 10–5.*

⓬ Nieuwe Kerk (New Church). This huge Gothic structure was gradually expanded until 1540, when it reached its present size. Gutted by fire in 1645, it was reconstructed in an imposing Renaissance style, as interpreted by strict Calvinists. The superb oak pulpit, the 14th-century nave, the stained-glass windows, and the great organ are all noteworthy. As befits the Netherlands' national church, it is the site of all coronations and the 2001 royal wedding between Prince Willem Alexander and Princess Maxima. In democratic Dutch spirit, the church is also used as a meeting place, has a lively café, and hosts temporary exhibitions and concerts. ☒ *Dam* ☎ *020/638–6909* ⊕ *www.nieuwekerk.nl* ☉ *Mon.–Wed. and Fri.–Sun. 10–6; Thurs. 10–10.*

❽ Oude Kerk (Old Church). The city's oldest house of worship dates from the early 14th century, but it was badly damaged by iconoclasts after the Reformation. The church still retains its original bell tower and a few remarkable stained-glass windows. Rembrandt's wife, Saskia, is buried here. ☒ *Oudekerksplein 23* ☎ *020/625–8284* ⊕ *www.oudekerk.nl* ☉ *Mon.–Sat. 11–5, Sun. 1–5.*

❼ Rosse Buurt (Red-Light District). This area is defined by two of the city's oldest canals. In the windows at canal level, women in sheer lingerie slouch, stare, or do their nails. The area can be shocking, but is generally safe, although midnight walks down dark side streets are not advised. If you do explore the area, watch for purse snatchers and pickpockets. ☒ *Bordered by Oudezijds Voorburgwal and Oudezijds Achterburgwal.*

❹ Scheepvaarthuis (Shipping Offices). Designed by J. M. der Mey and the Van Gendt brothers in the early 1910s, this office building is the earliest example of the Amsterdam School's unique building style. The fantastical facade is richly decorated in brick and stone, with lead and zinc roofing pouring from on high. ☒ *Prins Hendrikkade 108–119.*

❷ Schreierstoren. This lookout tower was erected on the harbor in 1486 as the endpoint of the city wall. The term *schreiren* suggests the Dutch word for "wailing," and hence the folklore arose that this Weeping Tower was where women came to cry when their sailor husbands left for sea. The word *schreier* actually comes from the Old Dutch word for "sharp corner"—the building's rounded harbor face forms a sharp corner with its straight street face. A tablet marks the point from which Henrik (aka Henry) Hudson set sail on the *Half Moon* on April 4, 1609, on a voyage that eventually took him to what is now New York and the river that bears his name. ☒ *Prins Hendrikkade 94–95.*

⑮ Westerkerk (West Church). The church's 279-foot tower is the city's highest; it also has an outstanding carillon. Rembrandt and his son Titus are buried in the church, which was completed as early as 1631. In summer you can climb to the top of the tower for a fine view over the city. ☒ *Prinsengracht 281 (corner of Westermarkt)* ☎ *020/624–7766* ☉ *Church: Apr.–Sept., weekdays 11–3; July and Aug., weekdays 11–3, Sat. 11–3. Tower: June–Sept., daily 10–5. Closed during private services.*

South of the Dam

From the south of Dam Square to Museumplein lies the artistic heart of Amsterdam, with its wealth of museums and fine architecture. The Golden Bend, the grandest stretch of canal in town, has some of the finest mansions built by Amsterdam's prosperous merchants.

⑯ Amsterdam Historisch Museum (Amsterdam Historical Museum). The museum traces the city's history from its origins as a fishing village, through the 17th-century golden age of material and artistic wealth, to the decline of the trading empire during the 18th century. In the courtyard off Kalverstraat, a striking Renaissance gate guards a series of tranquil inner courtyards. In medieval times, this area was an island devoted to piety. Today the bordering canals are filled in. ☒ *Kalverstraat 92* ☎ *020/523–1822* ⊕ *www.ahm.nl* ☉ *Weekdays 10–5, weekends 11–5.*

★ **⑰ Begijnhof** (Beguine Court). This enclosed square of almshouses, founded in 1346, is a surprising oasis of peace just a stone's throw from the city's hectic center. The Beguines were women who led a form of convent life, often taking the vow of chastity. The last Beguine died in 1974, and her house, No. 26, has been preserved as she left it. Dating from the 15th century, No. 34 is the oldest house and the only one to retain its wooden Gothic facade. A small passageway and courtyard link the Begijnhof to the Amsterdam Historisch Museum. The small **Engelse Kerk** (English Church) across from here at No. 48 dates from 1400. This church was given to Amsterdam's English and Scottish Presbyterians early in the 17th century. On the church wall and in the chancel are tributes to the Pilgrim Fathers, who sailed from Delftshaven (in Rotterdam) to the New World in 1620. Opposite the church is another of the city's secret Catholic chapels, whose exterior looks as though it were two adjoining houses, built in 1671. At press time, the future of public access to the Begijnhof was unclear; please contact VVV Amsterdam for updated information. ✉ *Enter at Begijnhof 29* ☎ *020/623–3565* ⊕ *www. begijnhofamsterdam.nl* ۞ *Daily 9–11AM; contact VVV Amsterdam for access information.*

㉑ **Bloemenmarkt** (Flower Market). Here floating stalls carry a bright array of freshly cut flowers and foliage, as well as an enviable variety of bulbs and plants. ✉ *Along Singel Canal, from Muntplein to Koningsplein* ۞ *Mon.–Sat. (occasionally Sun.) 8:30–6.*

★ ⑲ **Gouden Bocht** (Golden Bend). The Herengracht (Gentlemen's Canal) is the city's most prestigious canal. The stretch of the canal from Leidsestraat to Vijzelstraat is named for the sumptuous patrician houses that line it. Seventeenth-century merchants moved here from the Amstel River to escape the by-products of their wealth: noisy warehouses, unpleasant brewery smells, and the risk of fire in the sugar refineries. The houses display the full range of Amsterdam architectural detailing, from gables in a variety of shapes to elaborate Louis XIV–style cornices and frescoed ceilings. They are best seen from the east side of the canal. ✉ *Herengracht, Leidsestraat to Vijzelstraat.*

⑳ **Munttoren** (Mint Tower). Built in 1620 at this busy crossroads, the graceful tower that was later added to this former royal mint has a clock and bells that still seem to mirror the golden age. There are frequent carillon recitals. ✉ *Muntplein.*

㉒ **Museum Willet-Holthuysen.** Built in 1690, the elegant residence was bequeathed to the city of Amsterdam on condition that it be retained as a museum. It provides a peek into the lives of the city's well-heeled merchants. ✉ *Herengracht 605* ☎ *020/523–1822* ⊕ *www.willetholthuysen. nl* ۞ *Weekdays 10–5, weekends 11–5.*

⑱ **Spui** (Sluice). In the heart of the university area, the lively square was a center for revolutionary student rallies in 1968. Now you'll find bookstores and bars, including cozy brown cafés. ✉ *Junction of Nieuwezijds Voorburgwal, Spuistraat, and Singel Canal.*

Jewish Amsterdam

The original settlers in the Jodenbuurt (old Jewish Amsterdam) were wealthy Sephardic Jews from Spain and Portugal, later followed by poorer Ashkenazic refugees from Germany and Poland. At the beginning of the 20th century this was a thriving community of Jewish diamond polishers, dyers, and merchants.

㉓ **Jodenbreestraat.** During World War II this street marked the southwestern border of the *Joodse wijk* (Jewish neighborhood), then a Nazi-controlled ghetto surrounded by barbed wire. The character of the area was largely destroyed by construction of both the Metro and the Muziektheater/Stadhuis complex. However, you can still find a flavor of times past by wandering around the quaint and peaceful canals and streets. ✉ *Jodenbreestraat, between the Rechtboomssloot and the Oude Schans.*

②⑦ Joods Historisch Museum (Jewish Historical Museum). This complex of four synagogues, the oldest dating from 1671, opened in 1987 as a unique museum. The succession of synagogues was gradually constructed to accommodate Amsterdam's growing community of Jews, many of whom had fled from oppression and prejudice elsewhere. Before the war, there were about 120,000 Jews here, but only 20,000 of them survived the Nazis and the war. Founded by American and Dutch Jews, the museum displays religious treasures in a clear cultural and historical context. Because the synagogues lost most of their treasures in the war, their architecture and history are more compelling than the exhibits. ✉ *Nieuwe Amstelstraat 1* ☎ *020/626–9945* ⊕ *www.jhm.nl* ☉ *Daily 11–5* ☉ *Closed Yom Kippur.*

②⑤ Muiderstraat. This pedestrian area east of Waterlooplein retains much of the neighborhood's historic charm. Notice the gateways decorated with pelicans, symbolizing great love; according to legend, the pelican will feed her starving young with her own blood. ✉ *Muiderstraat/Waterlooplein.*

★ **②④ Museum het Rembrandthuis** (Rembrandt's House). From 1639 to 1658, Rembrandt lived at Jodenbreestraat 4. For more than 20 years he used the ground floor as living quarters; the sunny upper floor was his studio. The museum has a superb collection of his etchings as well as work by his contemporaries. The modern wing next door houses a multimedia auditorium, two exhibition spaces, and a shop. ✉ *Jodenbreestraat 4–6* ☎ *020/520–0400* ⊕ *www.rembrandthuis.nl* ☉ *Mon.–Sat. 10–5, Sun. 1–5.*

②⑧ Muziektheater/Stadhuis (Music Theater/Town Hall complex). Amsterdammers come to the Town Hall section of the building by day to obtain driver's licenses, pick up welfare payments, and get married. They return by night to the rounded, marble-clad facade overlooking the Amstel River to see opera and ballet performed by the Netherlands' national companies. You can wander into the Town Hall for a look at some interesting sculptures and other displays. A guided tour of the Muziektheater takes you around the dressing rooms, dance studios, backstage, and even to the wig department. ✉ *Amstel 3/Waterlooplein 22* ☎ *020/551–8117; 020/551–8103 tour information* ⊕ *www.muziektheater.nl* ☉ *Guided tours Sat. at 3.*

★ **②⑥ Portugese Israelitische Synagoge** (Portuguese Israelite Synagogue). As one of Amsterdam's five neighboring synagogues, this was part of the largest Jewish religious complex in Europe. The beautiful, austere interior of the 17th-century building is still intact, even if the building itself is marooned on a traffic island. ✉ *Mr. Visserplein 3* ☎ *020/624–5351* ⊕ *www.esnoga.com* ☉ *Apr.–Oct., Sun.–Fri. 10–4; Nov.–Mar., Sun.–Thurs. 10–4, Fri. 10–3* ☉ *Closed Jewish holidays.*

The Museum Quarter

Amsterdam's wealth of art—from Golden Age painters, through van Gogh, up to the present day—is concentrated on the area around the grassy Museumplein, which also serves as the transition point between the central canal area and the modern residential sections of the city. The nearby Leidseplein is dotted with cafés and discos and attracts young visitors to the city.

③② Concertgebouw (Concert Hall). The sounds of the country's foremost orchestra resonate in this imposing, classical building. The smaller of the two auditoriums is used for chamber music and solo recitals. The main hall hosts world-class concerts. ✉ *Concertgebouwplein 2–6* ☎ *020/671–8345* ⊕ *www.concertgebouw.nl.*

㉞ Leidseplein. This square is the pulsing heart of the city's nightlife. In summer you can enjoy the entertainment of street performers on the many café terraces. ✉ *Junction of Leidsestraat, Marnixstraat, and Weteringschans.*

㉙ Rijksmuseum (State Museum). This, the most important Dutch museum, was founded in 1808, but the current, rather lavish building dates from 1885 and was designed by the architect of Central Station, P. J. H. Cuijpers. The museum's fame rests on its unrivaled collection of Dutch 16th- and 17th-century masters. Rembrandt's masterpiece, the *Night Watch*, concealed during World War II in a cave in Maastricht, was misnamed because of its dull layers of varnish; in reality it depicts the Civil Guard in daylight. Also worth searching out are Frans Hals's family portraits, Jan Steen's drunken scenes, Van Ruysdael's romantic but menacing landscapes, and Vermeer's glimpses of everyday life bathed in his limpid light. A complete renovation and restructuring of the Rijksmuseum will close much of it until 2008. However, the museum's most famous works will still be on view in the Philips Wing. ✉ *Stadhouderskade 42* ☎ *020/674–7047* ⊕ *www.rijksmuseum.nl* ☉ *Daily 10–5; only the Philips Wing open during renovations.*

Fodor's Choice ★

㉛ Stedelijk Museum (Museum of Modern Art). Renovations are planned for 2004 and beyond, which will likely close the museum. When it is open, the Stedelijk has a stimulating collection of modern art and ever-changing displays of the works of contemporary artists, including Cézanne, Chagall, Kandinsky, and Mondrian. ✉ *Paulus Potterstraat 13* ☎ *020/573–2911* ⊕ *www.stedelijk.nl* ☉ *Closed for renovations until further notice.*

★ **㉚ Van Gogh Museum.** This museum contains the world's largest collection of the artist's works—200 paintings and nearly 500 drawings—as well as works by some 50 of his contemporaries. The main building was designed by Gerrit Rietvelt and completed in 1972. A wing, designed by Japanese architect Kisho Kurokawa, was added later to exhibit van Gogh's prints and accommodate temporary exhibitions, which focus on art from the late 19th and early 20th centuries. ✉ *Paulus Potterstraat 7* ☎ *020/570–5252* ⊕ *www.vangoghmuseum.nl* ☉ *Daily 10–6.*

㉝ Vondelpark. Amsterdam's central park is an elongated rectangle of paths, lakes, and pleasant, shady greenery. A monument honors the 17th-century epic poet Joost van den Vondel, after whom the park is named. There are special children's areas with paddling pools and sandboxes. From June through August, the park hosts free outdoor concerts and plays Wednesday–Sunday. ✉ *Stadhouderskade* ⊕ *www.openluchttheater.nl.*

The Jordaan

㉟ Jordaan. In this old part of Amsterdam the canals and side streets are named for trees, flowers, and plants. When it was the French quarter of the city, the area was known as *le jardin* (the garden), a name that over the years has become Jordaan. The best time to explore the district is in the evening or on a Sunday morning. The Jordaan has attracted many artists and is something of a bohemian quarter, where run-down buildings are being converted into restaurants, antiques shops, boutiques, and galleries. ✉ *Bordered by Prinsengracht, Lijnbaansgracht, Brouwersgracht, and Elandsgracht.*

Where to Eat

Health-conscious Amsterdammers prefer set menus and early dinners. For traditionalists the NEDERLANDS DIS soup tureen sign is a promise of regional recipes and seasonal ingredients. For a superbly luxurious culinary experience try the restaurant at Blake's Hotel, which is one of the city's best.

$$$–$$$$ ✕ **Dynasty.** Surrounded by luxurious Oriental furniture and murals, you can savor dishes from Thailand, Malaysia, and China. Main-course delicacies include mixed seafood in banana leaves and succulent duck and lobster on a bed of watercress. In one of the city's most active nightlife areas, it can get very busy, but service is always impeccable. ⊠ *Reguliersdwarsstraat 30* ☎ *020/626–8400* ☰ *AE, DC, MC, V* ☾ *Closed Tues. No lunch.*

★ $$$–$$$$ ✕ **Excelsior.** The restaurant at the Hôtel de l'Europe offers a varied menu of French cuisine based on local ingredients. There are no fewer than 15 splendid set menus. Service is discreet and impeccable, and the view over the Amstel River, to the Muntplein on one side and the Muziektheater on the other, is the best in Amsterdam. ⊠ *Hôtel de l'Europe, Nieuwe Doelenstraat 2–8* ☎ *020/531–1705* ⌕ *Reservations essential* ⌂ *Jacket required* ☰ *AE, DC, MC, V* ☾ *No lunch weekends.*

★ $$$–$$$$ ✕ **La Rive.** The light French cuisine, with an awe-inspiring "truffle menu" of dishes prepared with exotic (and expensive) ingredients, can be tailored to meet your every whim. Epicureans should inquire about the "chef's table": with a group of six you can sit at a table alongside the open kitchen and watch chefs prepare and describe each of your courses. At this world-class restaurant, you can also enjoy the city's most elegant view of the river Amstel. ⊠ *Amstel Inter-Continental Hotel, Professor Tulpplein 1* ☎ *020/622–6060* ⌂ *Jacket and tie* ☰ *AE, DC, MC, V.*

$$$–$$$$ ✕ **Oesterbar.** The "Oyster Bar" specializes in seafood—grilled, baked, or fried. The upstairs dining room is more formal than the downstairs bistro, but prices don't vary. The sole is prepared in four different ways, or you can try local specialties such as halibut and eel; oysters are a stimulating, if pricey, appetizer. ⊠ *Leidseplein 10* ☎ *020/623–2988* ☰ *AE, DC, MC, V.*

★ $$$ ✕ **De Silveren Spiegel.** In an alarmingly crooked 17th-century house, you can have an outstanding meal while you enjoy the personal attention of the owner at one of just a small cluster of tables. Local ingredients such as Texel lamb and wild rabbit are cooked with subtlety and flair. ⊠ *Kattengat 4–6* ☎ *020/624–6589* ☰ *AE, MC, V* ☾ *Closed Sun.*

$$–$$$ ✕ **Blauw aan de Wal.** At the end of a cul-de-sac, the hidden courtyard and flowering garden forms an oasis of peace in the busy red-light district. The French/Italian courses and legendary warm chocolate tart make this an "in" spot with foodies. The ground floor is a completely no-smoking area—a rarity in Amsterdam. ⊠ *O.Z. Achterburgwal 99* ☎ *020/330–2257* ⌕ *Reservations essential* ☰ *AE, MC, V* ☾ *Closed Sun.*

$$–$$$ ✕ **D' Theeboom.** Just behind the Dam, the ground floor of this historic canal-side warehouse has been converted into a stylish, formal restaurant. The seasonal menu might include a delicious parcel of vegetables flavored with a selection of mushrooms, followed by carefully prepared red mullet with a saffron sauce. ⊠ *Singel 210* ☎ *020/623–8420* ☰ *AE, DC, MC, V* ☾ *No lunch.*

★ $$–$$$ ✕ **Long Pura.** Lonny Gerungan's family have been cooks on Bali for generations—even preparing banquets for visiting Dutch royals. His plush restaurant in Amsterdam, draped in silky fabrics, serves the finest authentic Indonesian cuisine. Even the simplest rijsttafel is a feast of more than 15 delicately spiced dishes. ⊠ *Rozengracht 46–48* ☎ *020/623–8950* ☺ *Reservations essential* ▭ *AE, DC, MC, V.*

$$–$$$ ✕ **Segugio.** Finely prepared meals served in this stylish and spacious interior include unusual risottos, white truffles, seafood, and game. The restaurant's name means "research," and the staff pride themselves on seeking out hard-to-find regional Italian ingredients. ⊠ *Utrechtsestraat 96* ☎ *020/330–1503* ▭ *AE, MC, V* ☺ *Closed Sun.*

$$ ✕ **In de Waag.** The lofty, beamed interior below the Theatrum Anatomicum has been converted into a grand café and restaurant. The reading table harbors computer terminals for Internet enthusiasts. Dinnertime brings a seasonal selection of hearty cuisine to be savored by candlelight. ⊠ *Nieuwmarkt 4* ☎ *020/422–7772* ▭ *AE, DC, MC, V.*

★ **$$** ✕ **L'Indochine.** This is one of the city's first ventures into Vietnamese cuisine, and the chef's skillful preparation of the freshest ingredients, some specially imported, has been an immediate success. Sample the healthful, mint-flavored spring rolls or the meatier seared prawn and beef skewers to start, followed by lightly fried fish with vegetables in a subtly spiced sauce. ⊠ *Beulingstraat 9* ☎ *020/627–5755* ☺ *Reservations essential* ▭ *AE, DC, MC, V* ☺ *Closed Mon. No lunch.*

★ **$$** ✕ **Pier 10.** This former shipping office is on a pier behind Centraal Station. The candlelighted interior and unusual view—be certain to book a table in the "glass room" overlooking the river—makes this a popular spot for romantic dining. The food is international, with a French influence. Dinner splits into two distinct shifts, so lingering is not an option. ⊠ *De Ruyterkade, pier 10* ☎ *020/624–8276* ☺ *Reservations essential* ▭ *AE, DC, MC, V.*

$$ ✕ **Puyck.** Owner/chef Jacob Preyde's new restaurant is a sensation on Fodor'sChoice the Amsterdam scene. His French-Asian-Caribbean fusion dishes are prepared with exotic herbs and spices. Even top wines are affordable, due to a fixed cork charge. Attractive paintings, oak flooring, and an open kitchen enhance the experience. ⊠ *Ceintuurbaan 147* ☎ *020/676–7677* ▭ *MC, V* ☺ *Closed Sun. and Mon. No lunch.*

$–$$ ✕ **De Knijp.** Dutch food and French bistro fare are served here in a traditional Dutch environment. The mezzanine level is especially cozy. Alongside tamer dishes, there are seasonal specialties including wild boar, ham with red cabbage, and fillet of hare. After-midnight dinner draws concert goers and performers from the neighboring Concertgebouw. ⊠ *Van Baerlestraat 134* ☎ *020/671–4248* ☺ *Reservations not accepted* ▭ *AE, DC, MC, V.*

$–$$ ✕ **Rose's Cantina.** Rose's fills a sad Tex-Mex void in the Amsterdam dining market, but connoisseurs should prepare themselves to deem the food merely "sufficient." In addition to heaps of food, this place has buckets of lethal margaritas and a noise level that careens up the decibel scale. ⊠ *Reguliersdwarsstraat 38* ☎ *020/625–9797* ☺ *Reservations essential on weekends* ▭ *AE, DC, MC, V.*

$–$$ ✕ **Walem.** At this popular, all-day grand café, elegant breakfast and brunch options are served on chic *ciabatta* (a crispy, white Italian bread). At dinnertime the chefs prepare up-to-the-minute fusion cooking with a French influence—and affix a higher price tag. ⊠ *Keizersgracht 449* ☎ *020/625–3544* ▭ *AE, MC, V.*

$ ✕ **Het Gasthuys.** In this bustling restaurant you'll be served handsome portions of traditional Dutch home cooking—choice cuts of meat with excellent fries and piles of mixed salad. Sit at the bar or take a table high up in the rafters at the back. In summer the enchanting terrace on the canal side opens. ⊠ *Grimburgwal 7* ☎ *020/624–8230* ▭ *No credit cards.*

$ ✕ **Song Kwae.** The traditional offerings in Amsterdam's Chinatown, based around the Nieuwmarkt and Zeedijk, have now been complemented by a surge of Thai restaurants, and this buzzing joint offers speedy service and quality food for a budget price. Alongside the traditional red and green Thai curries and the stir-fry options, there are specialties such as green papaya salad with crab. ⊠ *Kloveniersburgwal 14* ☎ *020/624–2568* ☰ *AE, DC, MC, V.*

Where to Stay

$$$$ ⊞ **Amstel Inter-Continental.** Amsterdam's grande dame first opened in 1867.
Fodor'sChoice   The spacious rooms have Oriental rugs, brocade upholstery, Delft lamps,
★   and a color scheme inspired by the warm, earthy tones of Makkum pottery. The Amstel is frequented by many of the nation's top businesspeople and sometimes hosts members of the royal family. ⊠ *Professor Tulpplein 1, 1018 GX* ☎ *020/622–6060* 🖷 *020/622–5808* ⊕ *www.intercontinental.com* ⇋ *55 rooms, 24 suites* ⚇ *Restaurant, pool* ☰ *AE, DC, MC, V.*

$$$$ ⊞ **Blake's.** British designer Anouska Hempel's luxury hotel continues to be an "in" spot. The beautifully appointed interior has an Oriental influence, and the entire hotel and courtyard offer serenity in a bustling city. The restaurant is one of Amsterdam's best, with a Thai/French fusion kitchen. ⊠ *Keijzersgracht 384, 1016 GB* ☎ *020/530–2010* 🖷 *020/530–2030* ⊕ *www.slh.com* ⇋ *22 rooms, 19 suites* ⚇ *Restaurant* ☰ *AE, DC, MC, V.*

★ **$$$$**   ⊞ **Grand Amsterdam.** Parts of this elegant building, which used to serve as Amsterdam's city hall, date from the 16th century, but most of it belongs to the early 20th, when the country's best artists and architects were commissioned to create a building the city could be proud of. Features include a mural by Karel Appel, Jugendstil stained-glass windows, Gobelin tapestries, and palatially luxurious reception areas and rooms. The kitchen of the brasserie-style restaurant, Café Roux, is supervised by the incomparable Albert Roux. ⊠ *Oudezijds Voorburgwal 197, 1012 EX* ☎ *020/555–3111* 🖷 *020/555–3222* ⊕ *www.thegrand.nl* ⇋ *160 rooms, 6 suites, 16 apartments* ⚇ *Restaurant, pool* ☰ *AE, DC, MC, V.*

★ **$$$$**   ⊞ **Hôtel de l'Europe.** Behind the stately facade of this late-19th-century building is a full complement of modern facilities, as befits a hotel often ranked among the world's best. Large, bright rooms overlooking the Amstel are done in pastel colors; others have warm, rich colors and antiques. In addition to its world-renowned Excelsior restaurant, the hotel houses a sophisticated fitness center. ⊠ *Nieuwe Doelenstraat 2–8, 1012 CP* ☎ *020/531–1777* 🖷 *020/531–1778* ⊕ *www.leurope.nl* ⇋ *80 rooms, 20 suites* ⚇ *2 restaurants, pool* ☰ *AE, DC, MC, V.*

★ **$$$$**   ⊞ **Pulitzer.** The Pulitzer is one of Europe's most ambitious hotel restorations, using the structures of a block of 25 17th- and 18th-century merchants' houses. The refined interior is marked by a modern art gallery and lovingly restored brickwork and oak beams. No two of the split-level rooms are alike, and many have antique furnishings to match period architectural features. ⊠ *Prinsengracht 315–331, 1016 GZ* ☎ *020/523–5235* 🖷 *020/627–6753* ⊕ *www.luxurycollection.com* ⇋ *224 rooms, 6 suites* ⚇ *Restaurant* ☰ *AE, DC, MC, V.*

$$–$$$$ ⊞ **NH Grand Hotel Krasnapolsky.** This fine hotel is enhanced by the Winter Garden restaurant, which dates from 1818. The large-scale expansion into neighboring buildings has provided space for extensive conference and business facilities and an amazing selection of additional restaurants. The cosmopolitan atmosphere carries through all the well-equipped rooms, with styles ranging from Victorian to art deco. ⊠ *Dam 9, 1012 JS* ☎ *020/554–9111* 🖷 *020/622–8607* ⊕ *www.krasnapolsky.nl* ⇋ *431 rooms, 7 suites, 36 apartments* ⚇ *7 restaurants* ☰ *AE, DC, MC, V.*

$$$ ⊞ **Ambassade.** With its beautiful canal-side location, its Louis XV–style decoration, and its Oriental rugs, the Ambassade seems more like a stately home than a hotel. Breakfast is served in an elegant room overlooking the canal. For other meals, the neighborhood has a good choice of restaurants. ⊠ *Herengracht 341, 1016 AZ* ☎ *020/555-0222* 🖷 *020/ 555-0277* ⊕ *www.ambassade-hotel.nl* 🛏 *51 rooms, 7 suites, 1 apartment* 🖃 *AE, DC, MC, V.*

$$–$$$ ⊞ **Canal House Hotel.** The Irish owners of this canal-side hotel have opted for antiques rather than TVs as furnishings, producing a real sense of stepping back in time. Spacious rooms overlook the canal or the atmospheric garden. A hearty Dutch breakfast served in the breakfast room is included in the price. Children under age 12 are not permitted. ⊠ *Keizersgracht 148, 1015 CX* ☎ *020/622-5182* 🖷 *020/624-1317* ⊕ *www.canalhouse.nl* 🛏 *26 rooms* 🖃 *AE, DC, MC, V.*

$$–$$$ ⊞ **Seven Bridges Hotel.** Named for the view from its front steps, this small canal-house hotel has rooms decorated with individual flair. Oriental rugs warm wooden floors, and there are comfy antique armchairs and marble washstands. The Rembrandtsplein is nearby. For a stunning view, request a canal-side room, but make sure to reserve weeks in advance. One of the pleasures here is breakfast in bed. ⊠ *Reguliersgracht 31, 1017 LK* ☎ *020/623-1329* 🛏 *8 rooms* 🖃 *AE, DC, MC, V.*

★ $$ ⊞ **Agora.** The cheerful bustle of the nearby Singel flower market carries over to this small hotel in an 18th-century house. Rooms are light and spacious, and some are decorated with vintage furniture; the best overlook the canal and the university. The Agora has a considerate staff, and the neighborhood is relaxed. Book well in advance. ⊠ *Singel 462, 1017 AW* ☎ *020/627-2200* 🖷 *020/627-2202* ⊕ *www.hotelagora. nl* 🛏 *15 rooms, 13 with bath or shower* 🖃 *AE, DC, MC, V.*

$$ ⊞ **Hotel de Filosoof.** On a quiet street near Vondelpark, the hotel attracts artists, thinkers, and people looking for something a little unusual. Each room is decorated in a different philosophical or cultural motif— such as an Aristotle room and a Goethe room adorned with texts from *Faust.* A large Dutch breakfast is included in the price. ⊠ *Anna van den Vondelstraat 6, 1054 GZ* ☎ *020/683-3013* 🖷 *020/685-3750* ⊕ *www. hotelfilosoof.nl* 🛏 *38 rooms* 🖃 *AE, MC, V.*

$$ ⊞ **Hotel Washington.** On a peaceful street, the hotel is just a few blocks from the Museum District and the Concertgebouw. Many of the world's top musicians find it the ideal place to reside when performing in Amsterdam. Period furniture and attentive service lend this small establishment a homey feel. All except the cheaper upper-floor rooms have bath or shower and toilet. ⊠ *Frans van Mierisstraat 10, 1071 RS* ☎ *020/679- 6754* 🖷 *020/673-4435* 🛏 *21 rooms, 19 with bath or shower* 🖃 *AE, DC, MC, V.*

$ ⊞ **Amstel Botel.** The floating hotel moored near Central Station is an appropriate place to stay in watery Amsterdam. The rooms are small and basic, but the large windows offer fine views across the water to the city. Make sure you don't get a room on the land side of the vessel, or you'll end up staring at a postal sorting office. ⊠ *Oosterdokskade 2–4, 1011 AE* ☎ *020/626-4247* 🖷 *020/639-1952* ⊕ *www.amstelbotel.com* 🛏 *175 rooms* 🖃 *AE, DC, MC, V.*

$ ⊞ **Hotel Acro.** This friendly tourist hotel is on a quiet street within easy walking distance to the main museums and the Vondelpark. The light blue rooms are clean and pleasant. ⊠ *Jan Luykenstraat 44, 1071 CR* ☎ *020/662-5538* 🖷 *020/675-0811* ⊕ *www.acro-hotel.nl* 🛏 *65 rooms* 🖃 *AE, DC, MC, V.*

Nightlife & the Arts

The Arts

The arts flourish in cosmopolitan Amsterdam. The best source of information about performances is the monthly English-language *Day by Day in Amsterdam*, published by the VVV tourist office, where you can also secure tickets for the more popular events. *De Uitkrant* is available in Dutch and covers practically every event. You can also find the latest information and make personal or phone bookings for a small charge at the **Amsterdam Uitburo** (⊠ Stadsschouwburg, Leidseplein 26 ☎ 0900/ 0191, €0.40 per min ⊕ www.uitlijn.nl ☉ Daily 9–9).

FILM The greatest concentration of movie theaters is around Leidseplein and near Muntplein. Most foreign films are subtitled rather than dubbed. Conveniently located close to Leidseplein, **City 1–7** (⊠ Kleine Gartmanplantsoen 13–25 ☎ 0900/1458, €0.35 per min for recorded info) has seven screens. **Pathe de Munt** (⊠ Vijselstraat 15 ☎ 0900/1458, €0.35 per min for recorded info) is the largest multiplex cinema in Amsterdam, with 13 screens.

MUSIC The **Concertgebouw** (⊠ Concertgebouwplein 2–6 ☎ 020/671–8345) is the home of one of Europe's finest orchestras. A smaller hall in the same building hosts chamber music, recitals, and even jam sessions. Ticket prices for international orchestras are high, but most concerts are good value, and Wednesday lunchtime concerts at 12:30 are free. The **Muziekgebouw** (⊠ Piet Heinkade 1 ☎ 020/668–1805 ⊕ www.muziekgebouw.nl) is opening to the public in mid-2004. The huge structure is intended to serve as a venue for all types of music; it also contains a documentation center, rehearsal spaces, and rooms for classes and workshops. A spectacular glass facade overlooks IJ river.

OPERA & BALLET The Dutch national ballet and opera companies perform in the **Muziektheater** (⊠ Waterlooplein 22 ☎ 020/625–5455 ⊕ www.hetmuziektheater. nl). Guest companies from other countries perform here during the Holland Festival in June. The country's smaller regional dance and opera companies usually include performances at the **Stadsschouwburg** (City Municipal Theater; ⊠ Leidseplein 26 ☎ 020/624–2311 ⊕ www. stadsschouwburgamsterdam.nl) in their schedules.

THEATER **Boom Chicago** (⊠ Leidseplein Theater, Leidseplein 12 ☎ 020/423–0101 ⊕ www.boomchicago.nl) offers improvised comedy with a local touch. For experimental theater, contemporary dance, and colorful cabaret in Dutch, catch the shows at **Felix Meritis** (⊠ Keizersgracht 324 ☎ 020/ 623–1311 ⊕ www.felix.meritis.nl).

Nightlife

Amsterdam has a wide variety of dance clubs, bars, and exotic shows. The more respectable—and expensive—after-dark activities are in and around Leidseplein and Rembrandtsplein; fleshier productions are on Oudezijds Achterburgwal and Thorbeckeplein. Most bars are open Sunday to Thursday to 1 AM and later on weekends; clubs stay open until 4 AM or later and at least 5 AM on weekends. On weeknights very few clubs charge admission, though the livelier ones sometimes ask for a "club membership" fee of €15 or more. Watch out around the red-light district, where street touts will offer tempting specials for louche clubs with floor shows—the experience may turn out to cost more than you bargained for.

CAFÉS & BARS Amsterdam, and particularly the Jordaan, is renowned for its brown cafés. There are also grand cafés, with spacious interiors, snappy table service, and well-stocked reading tables. Two other variants of Amsterdam's buzzing bar scene are the *proeflokalen* (tasting houses) and *brouwerijen* (breweries). The Dutch have a relaxed tolerance of soft drugs like marijuana and hashish, which can be encountered in "coffee shops" with the green leaves of the marijuana plant showing in the window.

Among more fashionable cafés is **Café Nielsen** (✉ Berenstraat 19 ☎ 020/330–6006), serving delicious, healthful lunches. Everything here is fresh and organic, with plenty of vegetarian and vegan dishes. The beamed interior of **De Admiraal Proeflokaal en Bar Spijshuis** (✉ Herengracht 319 ☎ 020/625–4334) is an intimate setting in which to enjoy the Jenevers and unique liqueurs. **De Gijs** (✉ Lindegracht 249 ☎ 020/638–0740) is an atmospheric brown café. **De Jaren** (✉ Nieuwe Doelenstraat 20 ☎ 020/625–5771), a spacious grand café with a canal-side terrace, attracts young businesspeople, arts and media workers, and other trendy types. At the **Rooie Nelis** (✉ Laurierstraat 101 ☎ 020/624–4167), you can spend a rainy afternoon chatting with friendly strangers over homemade meatballs and a beer or apple tart and coffee. **Tweede Kamer** (✉ Heisteeg 6, just off the Spui ☎ 020/422–2236), named after the Dutch parliament's lower house, offers chess and backgammon in a convivial, civilized atmosphere permeated with the smoke of hemp.

CASINO   **Holland Casino** (✉ Max Euweplein 62 ☎ 020/521–1111), just off Leidseplein, has blackjack, roulette, and slot machines in elegant, canalside surrounds. You'll need your passport to get in, and although you don't have to wear a tie, sneakers will not get you past the door; the minimum age is 18.

DANCE CLUBS   Dance clubs tend to fill up after midnight. The cavernous **Escape** (✉ Rembrandtsplein 11–15 ☎ 020/622–1111) has taken on a much hipper mantle. The **iT** (✉ Amstelstraat 24 ☎ 020/489–7285) has gay nights on Saturday; it's primarily straight on Friday—but could never be accused of being straitlaced. **Seymour Likely Lounge** (✉ Nieuwezijds Voorburgwal 161 ☎ 020/420–5663) has a lively, trendy crowd hopping to the latest music.

GAY & LESBIAN NIGHTLIFE   Amsterdam has a vibrant gay and lesbian community. **Spijker** (✉ Kerkstraat 4 ☎ 020/620–5919) is a popular late-night bar with a sociable pool table and pinball machine. **Café Rouge** (✉ Amstel 60 ☎ 020/420–9881) has traditional Dutch oompapa music and frivolity. The **Amstel Taverne** (✉ Amstel 54 ☎ 020/623–4254) is the oldest existing gay bar in Amsterdam and is an early-evening venue. The trendy set prevails at bars along the Reguliersdwarsstraat. A mixed blend of nationalities and ages meets early in the evening at **April** (✉ Reguliersdwarsstraat 37 ☎ 020/625–9572). The **You II** (✉ Amstel 178 ☎ 020/421–0900) is an all-women disco open Thursday to Sunday. The lesbian community meets at the **Saarein II** (✉ Elandsstraat 119 ☎ 020/623–4901), a traditional bar in the Jordaan.

The **Gay & Lesbian Switchboard** (☎ 020/623–6565) has friendly operators who provide up-to-the-minute information on events in the city, as well as general advice for gay or lesbian visitors. The **COC** (✉ Rozenstraat 14 ☎ 020/626–3087), the Dutch lesbian and gay organization, operates a coffee shop and hosts a popular Saturday night women-only disco.

JAZZ CLUBS   The **Bimhuis** (✉ Oude Schans 73–77 ☎ 020/623–3373) offers the best jazz and improvised music in town. The adjoining BIM café has a magical view across the Oude Schans canal.

ROCK CLUBS   **Melkweg** (✉ Lijnbaansgracht 234 ☎ 020/531–8181) is a major rock and pop venue with a large auditorium; it also has a gallery, theater, cinema, and café. The **Paradiso** (✉ Weteringschans 6–8 ☎ 020/626–4521 ⊕ www.

paradiso.nl), converted from a church, is a vibrant venue for rock, New Age, and even contemporary classical music.

Shopping

Department Stores

De Bijenkorf (⊠ Dam 1), the city's number one department store, is excellent for contemporary fashions and furnishings. **Maison Bonneterie** (⊠ Rokin 140) is gracious, genteel, and understated. The well-stocked departments of **Vroom & Dreesmann** (⊠ Kalverstraat 203) carry all manner of goods.

Gift Ideas

DIAMONDS Since the 17th century, "Amsterdam cut" has been synonymous with perfection in the quality of diamonds. At the diamond-cutting houses, the craftsmen explain how a diamond's value depends on the four c's—carat, cut, clarity, and color—before encouraging you to buy. There is a cluster of diamond houses on the Rokin. **Amsterdam Diamond Centre** (⊠ Rokin 1–5 ☎ 020/624–5787) is the largest institution on the Rokin and offers free tours. You can take a free guided factory tour at **Gassan Diamonds** (⊠ Nieuwe Uilenburgerstraat 173–175 ☎ 020/622–5333).

PORCELAIN The Dutch have been producing Delft, Makkum, and other fine porcelain for centuries. **Hogendoorn & Kaufman** (⊠ Rokin 124 ☎ 020/638–2736) sells pieces ranging from affordable, hand-painted, modern tiles to expensive Delft blue-and-white pitchers, as well as quality crystal.

Markets

The **Bloemenmarkt** (flower market) on the Singel canal near the Muntplein is world-famous for its bulbs, many certificated for export, and cut flowers. Amsterdam's lively **Waterlooplein flea market,** open Monday–Saturday 9–5, next to the Muziektheater, is the ideal spot to rummage for secondhand clothes, inexpensive antiques, and other curiosities. In summer, you'll find etchings, drawings, and watercolors at the Sunday **art markets** on Thorbeckeplein and the Spui. There are as many English-language books as Dutch ones for browsing at the **book market** on the Spui, every Friday 10–6. A small but choice **stamp market,** open Wednesday and Saturday 1–4, is held on the Nieuwezijds Voorburgwal. **Kunst & Antiekmarkt De Looier** (De Looier Art & Antiques Market; ⊠ Elandsgracht 109 ☎ 020/624–9038 ⊕ www.looier.nl) is a bustling, warrenlike indoor market, with myriad stalls selling everything from expensive antiques and art to kitschy bric-a-brac; it's open Saturday to Thursday 11–5.

Shopping Districts

Leidsestraat, Kalverstraat, Utrechtsestraat, and Nieuwendijk, Amsterdam's chief shopping districts, have largely been turned into **pedestrian-only areas,** but watch out for trams and bikes nevertheless. The imposing **Kalvertoren shopping mall** (⊠ Kalverstraat near Munt) has a rooftop restaurant with magnificent views of the city. **Magna Plaza shopping center** (⊠ Nieuwezijds Voorburgwal 182), built inside the glorious turn-of-the-last-century post office behind the Royal Palace at the Dam, is *the* place for A-to-Z shopping in the huge variety of stores. The **Spiegelkwartier** (⊠ Nieuwe Spiegelstraat and Spiegelgracht), just a stone's throw from the Rijksmuseum, is Amsterdam's antiques center, with galleries for wealthy collectors as well as old curiosity shops. **P. C. Hooftstraat,** and also Van Baerlestraat and Beethovenstraat, are the homes of haute couture and other fine goods. **Rokin** is hectic with traffic and houses a cluster of boutiques and renowned antiques shops selling 18th- and 19th-century furniture, antique jewelry, art deco lamps, and statuettes.

The **Jordaan** to the west of the main ring of old canals, and the quaint streets crisscrossing these canals, is filled with trendy small boutiques and unusual crafts shops. The tax-free shopping center at **Schiphol Airport** is often lauded as the world's best.

Side Trips

Zaanse Schans
Set 24 km (10 mi) north of Amsterdam and near the town of Zaandam, this small village contains working windmills and restored wooden houses dating from the 17th and 18th centuries. Clog makers, cheese makers, bakers, and other craftsmen are at work, providing a fascinating look at life as it was lived in "olde Hollande." ☎ *075/6168218* ⊕ *www.zaanseschans.nl* ⊙ *Apr.–Oct., daily 8:30–6, Oct.–Apr., daily 8:30–5.*

Zuiderzee Museum
Fifty kilometers (30 mi) northeast of Amsterdam, the historic town of Enkhuizen has been transformed into a famous indoor and open-air museum that gives a dazzling glimpse into the folkloric past of an old Zuiderzee town. Among the many restored 19th-century houses, craftsmen ply their trade and children can don traditional costumes and play old Dutch games. The NS train service offers a delightful day trip to Zuiderzee using an old-fashioned steam locomotive and boat which travel past the picturesque towns of Medemblik and Hoorn. ☎ *0228/351111* ⊕ *www.zuiderzeemuseum.nl* ⊙ *Indoor museum, daily 10–5; outdoor museum, Apr.–Oct., daily 10–5.*

Amsterdam Essentials

AIRPORTS & TRANSFERS
Most international flights arrive at Amsterdam's Schiphol Airport. Immigration and customs formalities on arrival are relaxed, with no forms to be completed.

TRANSFERS   The best link is the direct rail line to the central train station, where you can get a taxi or tram to your hotel. The train runs every 10 to 15 minutes throughout the day and takes about a half hour. Make sure you buy a ticket before boarding, or ruthless conductors will impose a fine. Second-class single fare is €3.10. Taxis from the airport to central hotels cost about €35.

BIKE TRAVEL
Rental bikes are widely available for around €6.50 per day with a €50 deposit and proof of identity. Several rental companies are close to the central train station; ask at tourist offices for details. Lock your bike to something immovable whenever you park it. Also, check with the rental company to see what your liability is under their insurance terms. MacBike has various rental points around the center.
🚲 MacBike ⊠ Mr. Visserplein 2 ☎ 020/620-0985 ⊠ Marnixstraat 220 ☎ 020/626-6964 ⊠ Stationsplein 12 ☎ 020/624-8391.

BOAT & FERRY TRAVEL
A day pass for the Canalbus costs €15 and provides unlimited travel on the canals with stops at major points of interest between the central train station to the Rijksmuseum. The Museum Boat (€13.25) stops near major museums. Water taxis are more expensive than land taxis: standard-size water taxis—for up to eight people—cost €75 for a half hour, and €60 per half hour thereafter. They offer different types of catering

services and are a popular way to enjoy the city or celebrate special occasions.

🚌 **Canalbus** ✉ Nieuwe Weteringschans 24 ☎ 020/623-9886. **Museum Boat** ✉ Prinshendrikkade 26 ☎ 020/530-1090. **Water taxis** ☎ 020/535-6363 ⊕ www.water-taxi.nl.

CAR TRAVEL

The city's concentric ring of canals, one-way systems, hordes of cyclists, and lack of parking facilities make driving here unappealing. It's best to put your car in one of the parking lots on the edge of the old center and abandon it for the rest of your stay.

CONSULATES

🏛 United Kingdom ✉ Koningslaan 44 ☎ 020/676-4343.
🏛 United States ✉ Museumplein 19 ☎ 020/575-5309.

EMERGENCIES

The Central Medical Service supplies names and opening hours of pharmacists and dentists, as well as doctors, outside normal surgery hours.
🏛 Doctors & Dentists **Central Medical Service** ☎ 020/592-3434.
🏛 Emergency Services **Ambulance, Fire, Police, and Rescue** ☎ 112.

ENGLISH-LANGUAGE MEDIA

🏛 Bookstores **American Book Center** ✉ Kalverstraat 185 ☎ 020/625-5537. **Athenaeum Boekhandel** ✉ Spui 14 ☎ 020/622-6248. **English Bookshop** ✉ Lauriergracht 71 ☎ 020/626-4230. **Waterstone's** ✉ Kalverstraat 152 ☎ 020/638-3821.

TAXIS

Taxis are expensive: a 5-km (3-mi) ride costs around €12. Taxis are not usually hailed on the street but are picked up at stands near stations and other key points, where you will see a yellow column. You can order a taxi by dialing Taxi Centrale. Always check that the meter is set to "tariff 1" for daytime fares; "tariff 2" is for evening.
🏛 **Taxi Centrale** ☎ 020/677-7777.

TOURS

BICYCLE TOURS From April through October, guided bike tours are an excellent way to discover Amsterdam. There are also supervised tours to the idyllic countryside and quaint villages just north of the city. The three-hour city tour costs €17, and the six-hour countryside tour costs €22.50, arranged by Yellow Bike Guided Tours.
🏛 **Yellow Bike Guided Tours** ✉ Nieuwezijds Kolk 29 ☎ 020/620-6940 ⊕ www.yellowbike.nl.

BOAT TOURS The most enjoyable way to get to know Amsterdam is on a boat trip along the canals. Departures are frequent from points opposite Central Station, along the Damrak, and along the Rokin and Stadhouderskade (near the Rijksmuseum). For a tour lasting about an hour, the cost is around €8.50, but the student guides expect a small tip for their multilingual commentary. A candlelight dinner cruise costs upward of €24. Trips can be booked through the tourist office.

The Museum Boat combines a scenic view of the city with seven stops near 20 museums. Tickets, good for the day and including discounted entry to museums, are €13.25. At Canal-Bike, a pedal boat for four costs €28 per hour.
🏛 **Canal-Bike** ✉ corner of Leidsestraat and Keizersgracht ✉ Leidsekade ✉ Stadhouderskade opposite Rijksmuseum ✉ Prinsengracht opposite Westerkerk ☎ 020/623-9886 ⊕ www.canal.nl. **Museum Boat** ✉ Prinshendrikkade 26 ☎ 020/530-1090.

BUS TOURS Guided bus tours provide an excellent introduction to Amsterdam. Bus-and-boat tours with Canalbus include the inevitable trip to a diamond factory. Costing €30, a comprehensive, 2½-hour tour can be booked through Key Tours.

🎫 **Key Tours** ✉ Dam 19 ☎ 020/623-5051. **Canalbus** ✉ Weteringschans 24 ☎ 020/623-9886 ⊕ www.canal.nl.

WALKING TOURS Amsterdam is a compact city of narrow streets and canals, ideal for exploring on foot. The tourist office issues seven excellent guides in English that detail self-guided walking tours around the center.

TRAIN TRAVEL
The city has excellent rail connections with the rest of Europe. Central Station is in the center of town.

🎫 **Central Station** ✉ Stationsplein ☎ 0900/9296 international service information, €0.35 per min and sometimes a long wait.

TRANSPORTATION AROUND AMSTERDAM
A zonal fare system is used for the public transportation system, which includes metro, tram, and bus. Tickets (starting at €1.60) are available from automated dispensers on the metro or from the drivers on trams and buses; or buy a money-saving strippenkaart. Even simpler is the dagkaart, which covers all city routes for €5.50. These discount tickets can be obtained from the main GVB ticket office (open weekdays 7 AM–9 PM and weekends 8 AM–9 PM), in front of Central Station, and from many newsstands, along with route maps of the public transportation system.

TRAVEL AGENCIES
🎫 **American Express** ✉ Damrak 66 ☎ 020/504-8787. **Holland International** ✉ Damrak 90 ☎ 020/555-0808. **Key Tours** ✉ Dam 19 ☎ 020/623-5051.

VISITOR INFORMATION
VVV Amsterdam Tourist Office has offices at Schiphol Airport, at Stationsplein 10, in front of Central Station in the Old Dutch Coffee House, as well as one in the station itself. The information number, listed below, costs €0.55 per minute, and the electronic queue has a long wait.

🎫 **VVV Amsterdam Tourist Office** ✉ Schiphol Airport ✉ Stationsplein 10, in front of Central Station in the Old Dutch Coffee House ✉ Spoor 2 (Platform 2) inside the station ☎ 0900/400-4040 ⊕ www.amsterdamtourist.nl.

HISTORIC HOLLAND

Between the historic towns, you'll see some of the Netherlands' windmill-dotted landscape and pass through centers of tulip growing and cheese production. Apeldoorn is 90 km (56 mi) east of Amsterdam along Highway A1, where Hoge Veluwe National Park and the palace of Het Loo are day trips in themselves. Amersfoort is an optional stop on the way. Arnhem, 15 km (9 mi) south of Apeldoorn on the A90, has a child-friendly open-air museum and is the location of one of the most famous battles of World War II. The historically important centers of Utrecht, Gouda, and Leiden form an arc from the Groene Hart (Green Heart) of Holland toward the coast. Utrecht is 40 km (25 mi) southeast of Amsterdam on the A2. West of Utrecht, 36 km (22 mi) along the A12, you'll come to Gouda. The ancient city of Leiden is north on N11. The bulb fields of Lisse are halfway between Haarlem and Leiden, taking the N208 or the H206 coastal route. Haarlem, with its major museums, is 20 km (12 mi) directly west of Amsterdam on the A5.

Amersfoort
Although Amersfoort, east of Amsterdam on the way to Apeldoorn, is now a major industrial town, it has managed to retain much of its me-

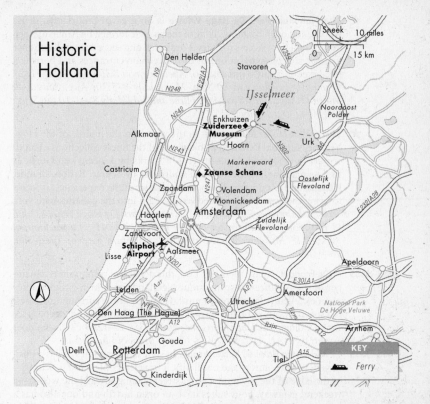

dieval character and charm. It was the birthplace of painter Piet Mondrian. A double ring of canals surrounds the town's old center. **Hovik** canal was once the harbor and loading quay. The **Koppelport** (✉ Kleine Spui), an imposing water gate across the Eem, dates from 1400. Turreted **Kamperbinnenpoort** (✉ Langstraat) is a land gate from the 15th century. The graceful 335-foot-high **Onze Lieve Vrouwetoren** (Tower of Our Lady; ✉ Breestraat), on a Gothic church, has musical chimes that ring every Friday between 10 and 11 AM.

Museum Flehite, with its unusual medieval collections, gives insight into the history of the town. In the associated **St. Pieters-en-Bloklands Gasthuis,** a hospice founded in 1390, are a chapel and a medieval room. ✉ *Westsingel 50* ☎ *033/461–9987* ⊕ *www.museumflehite.nl* ۩ *Tues.–Fri. 11–5, weekends 1–5.*

The **Culinair Museum Marienhof** (Culinary Museum), a convent during the 15th century, traces the history of eating and drinking from prehistoric times, to the Roman period, through to the present day, sometimes accompanied by tasty demonstrations. ✉ *Kleine Haag 2* ☎ *033/463–1025* ۩ *Daily by appointment only.*

Apeldoorn

★ The main attraction at Apeldoorn is the **Paleis Het Loo.** Built during the late 17th century for William III, this former royal palace was the summer residence for the House of Orange from 1684 to 1972. It has been beautifully restored to illustrate the domestic surroundings enjoyed by the monarchs for more than three centuries. Royal memorabilia, silver, and ceramics are displayed, and there is a collection of old royal cars and carriages in the stables. ✉ *Koninklijkpark 1* ☎ *055/577–2448* ⊕ *www.paleishetloo.nl* ۩ *Tues.–Sun. 10–5.*

★ The **Nationale Park De Hoge Veluwe** is an area of moorlands, dense woods, and open meadows lying in the triangle formed by Arnhem, Apeldoorn, and Ede. Access for cars is restricted and there is a small entrance fee, but you can park at one of the three main entrances and borrow a free bike. ✛ *5 km (3 mi) south of Apeldoorn on N304* ☎ *0318/591627* ⊕ *www.hogeveluwe.nl* ⊗ *Nov.–Mar., daily 9–5:30; Apr., daily 8–8; May and Aug., daily 8 AM–9 PM; June and July, daily 8 AM–10 PM; Sept., daily 9–8; Oct., daily 9–7.*

★ The **Kröller-Müller Museum** lies in the woods in the middle of the Hoge Veluwe National Park and displays one of the finest collections of modern art in the world. It possesses 278 works by Vincent van Gogh, as well as paintings, drawings, and sculptures by Seurat, Redon, Braque, Picasso, and Mondrian. The building is part of the experience; it seems to bring the museum's wooded setting right into the galleries with you. ⊠ *Houtkampweg 6, Otterlo, in Nationale Park De Hoge Veluwe, 5 km (3 mi) from Apeldoorn on N304* ☎ *0318/591241* ⊕ *www.kmm.nl* ⊡ *€10* ⊗ *Museum: Tues.–Sun. 10–5, sculpture garden: Tues.–Sun. 10–4:30.*

$$$–$$$$ ✕ **De Echoput.** Near Paleis Het Loo, this delightful restaurant is a member of the Alliance Gastronomique Néerlandaise, which is a guarantee of an excellent, classic French meal. Game from the surrounding forest is a specialty. An attractive terrace overlooks fountains and greenery for summer dining. ⊠ *Amersfoortseweg 86* ☎ *055/519–1248* ⊛ *Reservations essential* ▭ *AE, DC, MC, V* ⊗ *Closed Mon. No lunch Sat.*

$$$–$$$$ ▦ **Bilderberg Hotel de Keizerskroon.** In style and amenities this is a business hotel; in comfort and cordiality, a traveler's hotel; and in setting—at the edge of the town on a quiet street leading toward the woods—a weekend getaway. Four suites have an open hearth and one also has a hot tub. ⊠ *Koningstraat 7, 7315 HR, Apeldoorn* ☎ *055/521–7744* ▦ *055/521–4737* ⊕ *www.keizerskroon.nl* ⇆ *89 rooms, 5 suites* ⌕ *Restaurant, pool* ▭ *AE, DC, MC, V.*

Arnhem

☣ If you have children in tow, consider a visit to the **Nederlands Openluchtmuseum** (Open-Air Museum) in Arnhem. In a 44-acre park, the curators have brought together more than 80 original buildings and furnishings from all over the Netherlands to establish a comprehensive display of Dutch rural architectural styles and to depict traditional ways of living since 1650. There are farmhouses and barns, workshops, and windmills—even a *HollandRama* mobile time-capsule tour. An indoor exhibition space and panoramic theater accommodates visitors when the weather is inclement. ⊠ *Schelmseweg 89* ☎ *026/357–6111* ⊕ *www. openluchtmuseum.nl* ⊡ *€11.20* ⊗ *Apr.–Oct., daily 10–5.*

FodorsChoice ★ (margin)

Utrecht

The city of Utrecht was formerly the academic and religious center of the Netherlands. The gabled houses of Nieuwegracht, the canals with their sluice gates, the 13th-century wharves and storage cellars of Oudegracht, and an abundance of Gothic churches are just some of the city's key attractions. Utrecht hosts a number of internationally respected festivals, especially the annual Holland Festival of Early Music in the last week of August. If you arrive by rail, you pass through the enormous and ugly Vredenburg shopping center on the way to the beautiful, tree-lined Old Town.

The main cathedral square is a good point for orientation. The **Domkerk** is a late-Gothic cathedral with a series of fine stained-glass windows. Across the way, the **Domtoren** (Cathedral Tower; ⊗ Apr.–Oct., weekdays 10–5, weekends noon–5; Nov.–Mar., weekends noon–5) was connected to the cathedral until a freak tornado destroyed part of the nave in 1674. The bell tower is the country's tallest, and its 465 steep steps lead to a magnificent view. A guide is essential in the tower's labyrinth of steps and passageways. ⊠ *Domplein* ☎ *030/231–0403* ⊙ *Tours on the hr: May–Sept., weekdays 10–5, Sat. 10–3:30, Sun. 2–4; Oct.–Apr., weekdays 11–4, Sat. 11–3:30, Sun. 2–4.*

★ � The **Rijksmuseum van Speelklok tot Pierement** (National Museum of Mechanical Musical Instruments) is devoted to music machines—from music boxes to street organs and even musical chairs. During the tour, music students play some of the instruments. ⊠ *Buurkerkhof 10* ☎ *030/231–2789* ⊕ *www.museumspeelklok.nl* ⊙ *Tues.–Sat. 10–5, Sun. noon–5.*

The **Museum Catharijneconvent** (Catherine's Convent Museum) contains the country's largest display of medieval art in addition to its collection of holy relics and vestments. ⊠ *Lange Nieuwstraat 38* ☎ *030/231–7296* ⊕ *www.catharijneconvent.nl* ⊙ *Tues.–Fri. 10–5, weekends 11–5.*

The **Centraal Museum** houses a rich collection of contemporary art, especially applied arts, and exhibits about the city. There is a Viking ship (discovered in 1930), a 17th-century dollhouse with period furniture, porcelain, and miniature old master paintings. Several pieces by architect and designer Gerrit Rietveld are displayed in the museum. ⊠ *Nicolaaskerkhof 10* ☎ *030/236–2362* ⊕ *www.centraalmuseum.nl* ⊙ *Tues.–Sun. 11–5.*

An important part of the Centraal Museum's collection is the **Rietveld-Schröderhuis** (Rietveld-Schröder House), a 15-minute walk away in Utrecht's eastern suburbs. In 1924, architect Gerrit Rietveld, working with Truus Schröeder, designed what is considered to be the architectural pinnacle of de Stijl ("the" Style). The use of primary colors (red, yellow, blue) and black and white, as well as the definition of interior space, remains unique and innovative today. ⊠ *Prins Hendriklaan 50a* ☎ *030/236–2310* ⊙ *Wed.–Sat. 11–5.*

$$–$$$ ✕**Polman's Huis.** A comfortable, classic café welcomes you to this restaurant; beyond, the spacious dining room has an incredibly high, cherub-decked ceiling. Attentive service accompanies well-prepared international cuisine, influenced by Mediterranean palates. ⊠ *Keistraat 2* ☎ *030/231–3368* ⊟ *MC, V.*

$–$$ ✕**De Soepterrine.** This snug restaurant offers 10 varieties of steaming homemade soups, including Dutch specialties such as thick erwtensoep. Each bowl comes with crusty bread and herb butter. Quiches and generous salads fill up extra corners. ⊠ *Zakkendragerssteeg 40* ☎ *030/231–7005* ⚌ *Reservations not accepted* ⊟ *AE, DC, MC, V.*

$$–$$$ ▦**Malie Hotel.** The Malie is a 15-minute walk from the old center, in two 19th-century row houses on a quiet, leafy street. Rooms are vividly decorated and furnished in the classical style. The breakfast room overlooks a garden and terrace. ⊠ *Maliestraat 2, 3581 SL* ☎ *030/231–6424* 🖷 *030/234–0661* ⊕ *www.maliehotel.nl* ⟿ *45 rooms* ☖ *Bar* ⊟ *AE, DC, MC, V.*

Gouda

Just a short walk from the railway station, the **Stadhuis** (City Hall) stands in fairy-tale Gothic majesty in the middle of the market square. The facade dates from 1450. Quirky mechanical figures in a mechanical clock to the right of the main entrance stir into action every hour, depicting Floris V granting Gouda its city rights in 1272. A special event held on the second Tuesday in December each year is **Kaarsjesavond** (Candle

Night), when the city is illuminated by thousands of candles, an important local product, and enlivened with culinary and musical festivities.

Gouda is perhaps most famous for its cheeses, and brightly colored farm wagons arrive loaded with them for the morning **Kaasmarkt** (Cheese Market; ☉ June–Aug., Thurs. 10–12:30). In the baroque **Waag** (Weigh House) to the side of the marketplace, the **Kaasexposeum** (Cheese Exhibition) explains the history of cheese and dairy products. ⊠ *Markt 35–36* ☎ *0182/529996* ☉ *Apr.–Oct., Mon.–Sat. 10–5, Sun. noon–5.*

Sint Janskerk (Church of St. John) has the longest nave in the country, primarily built during the 16th century. There are 64 glorious stained-glass windows depicting biblical and historical scenes, which you can examine through a telescope. The oldest windows date from 1555 and survived the bombardments of World War II in bombproof bunkers. The modern window memorializing the Holocaust is extremely moving. ⊠ *Achter de Kerk 16* ☎ *0182/512684* ⊕ *www.st-janskerkgouda.nl* ☉ *Mar.–Oct., Mon.–Sat. 9–5; Nov.–Feb., Mon.–Sat. 10–4.*

The **Stedelijk Museum Het Catharina Gasthuis** (Catharina Hospice Municipal Museum) is a former poorhouse and hospital. Housed in a complex of historic buildings, exhibits include period furniture, galleries of paintings and prints, a former chapel with religious art, and a medieval torture chamber. ⊠ *Oosthaven 10/Achter de Kerk 14* ☎ *0182/588440* ☉ *Mon.–Sat. 10–5, Sun. noon–5.*

Leiden

Leiden is renowned for its spirit of religious and intellectual tolerance and for its university and royal connections. The university was founded by William the Silent as a reward to Leiden for its victory over the Spanish in the 1573–74 siege. During the war the dikes were opened and the countryside flooded so the rescuing navy could sail right up to the city walls. The unusual **De Burcht** (The Keep; ⊠ Burgsteeg 14), a man-made mound that formed part of the city's early fortifications, affords a spectacular view of the city.

The Pilgrims stayed in Leiden before they set out for Delftshaven on the first stage of their arduous voyage to the New World. Leiden is becoming known as Pilgrim City because of its wealth of historically interesting material relating to the Pilgrims. A good starting point for a tour is the **Pilgrim Archives**, housed in the exhibition space of the Stadsarchief (City Record Office). Knowledgeable personnel are on hand to help with research. There is a multimedia presentation in addition to original documents and a model of the *Mayflower.* ⊠ *Vliet 41–43* ☎ *071/516–5355* ⊕ *www.pilgrimarchives.nl* ☉ *Tues.–Sat. noon–4.*

The **Leiden American Pilgrim Museum** displays a historic furniture collection in a 16th-century house, along with copies of documents relating to the Pilgrims. The American curator offers guided tours of the city's Pilgrim sights. ⊠ *Beschuitsteeg 9* ☎ *071/512–2413* ☉ *Wed.–Sat. 1–5.*

★ Founded in 1590, the **Hortus Botanicus** (Botanical Garden) is among the oldest in the world. The highlights are ancient trees, a faithful reconstruction of a 16th-century garden, an herb garden, a Japanese garden, and an orangery. ⊠ *Rapenburg 73* ☎ *071/527–7249* ⊕ *www. hortusleiden.nl* ☉ *Mar.–Oct., daily 10–6; Nov.–Feb., Sun.–Fri. 10–4.*

☋ **Naturalis** (National Museum of Natural History) displays superb collections of minerals, fossils, insects, and stuffed birds and animals. The collections have been growing since Leiden University scientists started the museum in 1820, and now you will have the natural wonders of the world explained with the help of the latest technology. ⊠ *Darwinweg*

☎ *071/568–7600* ⊕ *www.naturalis.nl* ⊙ *Tues.–Sun. 10–6; during school holidays, daily 10–6.*

Stedelijk Museum De Lakenhal (Cloth Hall Municipal Museum), a textile and antiques museum and art gallery, occupies a classical building constructed in 1639 for cloth merchants. Pride of place in the collection goes to the Dutch 16th- and 17th-century paintings, with works by Steen, Dou, Rembrandt, and, above all, Lucas van Leyden's *Last Judgment* (1526)—the first great Renaissance painting executed in what is now the Netherlands. Other rooms are devoted to furniture and to the history of Leiden's medieval guilds. Exhibitions of modern art are a regular feature. ⊠ *Oude Singel 28–32* ☎ *071/516–5360* ⊕ *www.lakenhal. nl* ⊙ *Tues.–Fri. 10–5, weekends and holidays noon–5.*

☾ **Molenmuseum de Valk** (Windmill Museum of the Falcon) is housed in a windmill built in 1743, which was worked by 10 generations of millers until 1964. The seven floors contain the original machinery, an old forge, and living quarters. ⊠ *2E Binnenvestgracht 1* ☎ *071/516–5353* ⊕ *home. wanadoo.nl/molenmuseum* ⊙ *Tues.–Sat. 10–5, Sun. 1–5.*

St. Pieterskerk (St. Peter's Church) is associated closely with the Pilgrims, who worshiped here, and with their spiritual leader, John Robinson, who is buried here. ⊠ *Pieterskerkhof 1A* ☎ *071/512–4319* ⊕ *www. pieterskerk.com* ⊙ *Daily 1:30–4, except when the church is used for private services.*

A narrow street by the **Jan Pesijnhofje Almshouse** (⊠ Kloksteeg 21), dating from 1683, leads to the tree-lined **Rapenburg** canal, crossed by triple-arch bridges and bordered by stately 18th-century houses.

The **Rijksmuseum van Oudheden** (National Museum of Antiquities) is the country's leading archaeological museum. Some of the exhibits to look out for among the 6,000 objects on display are the collection of 13 ancient Egyptian human mummies, monumental Roman portraits, and a complete set of 4th-century Greek armor. ⊠ *Rapenburg 28* ☎ *071/516– 3163* ⊕ *www.rmo.nl* ⊙ *Tues.–Fri. 10–5, weekends and holidays noon–5.*

$–$$ ✕ **Annie's Verjaardag.** A vaulted cellar full of students and a canal-side terrace make Annie's attractive in all weather. The selection of salads and baguettes is usually accompanied by a daily special, such as mussels or jugged hare. ⊠ *Hoogstraat 1a* ☎ *071/512–5737* ⌓ *Reservations not accepted* ▭ *MC, V.*

$–$$ ✕ **Stadscafé Restaurant van der Werff.** From the art nouveau interior you can see the De Valk windmill framed across the water. The restaurant serves café fare throughout the day, and on Sunday afternoons the place swings to live jazz. In the evening there is an appetizing and adventurous dinner menu based on French cuisine. ⊠ *Steenstraat 2* ☎ *071/ 513–0335* ▭ *AE, DC, MC, V.*

$–$$ ▥ **Hotel De Doelen.** The spartan decor of this small hotel is in keeping with its origins as a 17th-century patrician's house, but the rooms are comfortable and modern. ⊠ *Rapenburg 2, 2311 EV* ☎ *071/512–0527* ▥ *071/512–8453* ⊕ *www.dedoelen.com* ⤶ *16 rooms* ▭ *AE, DC, MC, V.*

$–$$ ▥ **Nieuw Minerva.** This family-run hotel is a conversion of six 16th-century buildings. The original part is decorated in Old Dutch style. The newer part is better equipped but has slightly less character. Many rooms overlook a quiet tributary of the Rhine. The restaurant serves an excellent three-course tourist menu with vegetarian, meat, and fish selections. ⊠ *Boommarkt 23, 2311 EA* ☎ *071/512–6358* ▥ *071/514– 2674* ⊕ *www.nieuwminerva.nl* ⤶ *38 rooms, 1 suite* ⌂ *Restaurant* ▭ *AE, DC, MC, V.*

Lisse

Keukenhof, a 70-acre park and greenhouse complex, is planted each year to create a special exhibition of springtime flowering bulbs in 79 acres of landscaped gardens situated between Amsterdam, Leiden, and Haarlem. The world's largest flower show draws huge crowds to its woodland walks, greenhouse pavilions, and regimental lines of tulips, hyacinths, and daffodils. The Zomerhof (Summer Garden) displays summer bulbs and tuberous plants such as lilies, anemones, begonias, and canna, as well as perennials. ⊠ *Lisse, N208* ☎ *0252/465555* ⊕ *www.keukenhof. nl* ☜ *€11.50* ⊘ *Late Mar.–late May, daily 8–7:30; early Aug.–mid-Sept., daily 9–6.*

Aalsmeer

Flowers are big business to the Dutch, and the Netherlands has the world's largest complex of flower auction houses. The biggest of these facilities—it also is the largest in the world—is the **Bloemenveiling** (Flower Auction) in Aalsmeer, close to Schiphol International Airport and Amsterdam. In a building the size of 145 soccer fields, five auction rooms function simultaneously. Get here early; it's all over by 10 AM. ⊠ *Legmeerdijk 313* ☎ *0297/392185* ⊕ *www.aalsmeer.com* ⊘ *Weekdays 7:30–11 AM.*

Haarlem

With buildings notable for their secret inner courtyards and pointed gables, Haarlem resembles a 17th-century canvas by Frans Hals, the city's greatest painter. The area around the **Grote Markt** (Market Square) provides an architectural stroll through the 17th and 18th centuries.

The **Vleeshal** (Meat Market), near the Stadhuis (City Hall), dates from the early 1600s and has an especially fine gabled front. It now serves as an additional exhibition space for the Frans Hals Museum. ⊠ *Grote Markt 16* ⊘ *Tues.–Sat. 11–5, Sun. and holidays noon–5.*

The **Grote Kerk** (Great Church) is also known as St. Bavo, to whom it is dedicated. Rebuilt between 1400 and 1550 after sustaining severe fire damage in 1328, it houses one of the world's finest organs, which has 5,000 pipes and was played by both Mozart and Handel. An annual organ festival is held here in July. ⊠ *Grote Markt* ☎ *023/533–0877* ⊘ *Apr.–Aug., Mon.–Sat. 10–4; Sept.–Mar., Mon.–Sat. 10–3:30.*

★ The **Teylers Museum** claims to be the oldest museum in the country. It was founded by a wealthy merchant in 1778 as a museum of science and the arts and has old showcases filled with mineral specimens as well as an intriguing collection of historic scientific instruments. It also has a fine collection of the Hague school of painting as well as drawings and sketches by Michelangelo, Raphael, and other non-Dutch masters. As the canvases in this building are shown in natural light, try to visit on a sunny day. ⊠ *Spaarne 16* ☎ *023/531–9010* ⊕ *www.teylersmuseum. nl* ⊘ *Tues.–Sat. 10–5, Sun. and holidays noon–5.*

★ The **Frans Hals Museum,** in what was a 17th-century hospice, contains a marvelous collection of works by Hals. His paintings of the guilds of Haarlem are particularly noteworthy. The museum also has works of the artist's 17th-century contemporaries and an extensive contemporary collection. ⊠ *Groot Heiligland 62* ☎ *023/511–5775* ⊕ *www. franshalsmuseum.nl* ⊘ *Tues.–Sat. 11–5, Sun. and holidays noon–5.*

$–$$ ✕ **Café Restaurant Brinkman.** This elegant, classic grand café overlooks the magnificent Grote Kerk. You can while away the afternoon over a single coffee or choose from a wide menu of casseroles and grills with salad. ⊠ *Grote Markt 9–13* ☎ *023/532-3111* ▭ *AE, DC, MC, V.*

$$$–$$$$ ⊡ **Golden Tulip Lion d'Or.** Just five minutes from the old city center and conveniently near the railway station, this comfortable but unprepossessing hotel offers spacious guest rooms and meeting rooms. ⊠ *Kruisweg 34–36, 2011 LC* ☎*023/532–1750* 📠*023/532–9543* ⊕*www.goldentulip. nl* ⮔ *34 rooms, 4 suites* △ *Restaurant* ▤ *AE, DC, MC, V.*

Historic Holland Essentials

CAR TRAVEL

The most convenient way to explore the countryside is by rented car from Amsterdam. All the towns listed above can also be reached by bus or train. Check with the tourist office in Amsterdam for help in planning your trip, or inquire at Central Station.

TOURS

The towns of Historic Holland are covered, in various combinations, by organized bus tours out of Amsterdam. Brochures for tour operators are available from the VVV Amsterdam Tourist Offices. The VVV office in Utrecht organizes several excursions, including a boat trip along the canals and a sightseeing flight over the city. There are also day trips to country estates, castles, and gardens.

VISITOR INFORMATION

In towns such as Apeldoorn and Gouda, which have few good hotels, B&B accommodations can be booked through the VVV. Calls to the 0900 numbers below cost €0.45–€0.50 per minute.

🛈 **Amersfoort** VVV ⊠ Stationsplein 9–11 ☎ 0900/112–2364. **Apeldoorn** VVV ⊠ Stationstraat 72 ☎ 0900/168–1636. **Arnhem** VVV ⊠ Stationsplein 45 ☎ 0900/202–4075. **Gouda** VVV ⊠ Markt 27 ☎ 0900/468–3288. **Haarlem** VVV ⊠ Stationsplein 1 ☎ 0900/616–1600. **Leiden** VVV ⊠ Stationsweg 2d ☎ 0900/222–2333. **Lisse** VVV ⊠ Grachtweg 53 ☎ 0252/414262. **Utrecht** VVV ⊠ Vredenburg 90 ☎ 0900/414–1414.

THE HAGUE, DELFT & ROTTERDAM

The royal, diplomatic, and governmental seat of Den Haag, or 's-Gravenhage (the Hague), is the Netherlands' most dignified and spacious city. Its close neighbor is the leading North Sea beach resort of Scheveningen. Also nearby are Delft, a historic city with many canals and ancient buildings, and the energetic and thoroughly modern international port city of Rotterdam.

These cities are all linked by excellent train service. The Hague and Delft, only 14 km (9 mi) from each other, are both about 60 km (37 mi) southwest of Amsterdam and can be reached within an hour by fast, frequent trains. Rotterdam is a quarter of an hour farther.

By road the Hague is 50 km (31 mi) southwest of Amsterdam using the A4, then the A44. Delft is 60 km (37 mi) southwest of Amsterdam on the A4, then the A13, via the Hague. The A13 is also the trunk road to Rotterdam, 13 km (8 mi) farther south. Rotterdam is just 73 km (45 mi) south of Amsterdam.

The Hague

During the 17th century, when Dutch maritime power was at its zenith, the Hague was known as "the Whispering Gallery of Europe" because it was thought to be the secret manipulator of European politics. The Hague remains a powerful world diplomatic and juridical capital, as well as the seat of government for the Netherlands.

★ The gracious **Binnenhof** (Inner Court) complex is the site where William II built a castle when he adopted the Hague, then surrounded by for-

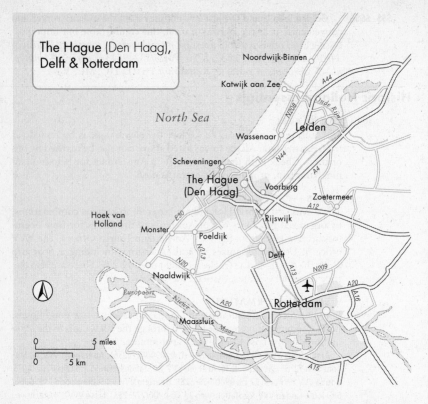

The Hague (Den Haag), Delft & Rotterdam

North Sea

Noordwijk-Binnen
Katwijk aan Zee
Wassenaar
Leiden
Scheveningen
The Hague (Den Haag)
Voorburg
Zoetermeer
Hoek van Holland
Monster
Poeldijk
Rijswijk
Delft
Naaldwijk
Europoort
Rotterdam
Maassluis

0   5 miles
0   5 km

est, as the base for his hunting activities in 1250. It is now surrounded by early classical buildings that serve as offices for politicians working in the neighboring Parliament buildings. At the center is the imposing late-13th-century **Ridderzaal** (Knights' Hall). Inside are vast beams spanning a width of 59 feet, flags, and stained-glass windows. The city's heart is the **Hofvijver** (Court Pond), which was originally a protective moat and is now a reflecting pond filled with water lilies. Tours of the government buildings are conducted in English by **Stichting Bezoekerscentrum Binnenhof** (Binnenhof Visitors Center), just to the right of the Ridderzaal. ⊠ *Binnenhof 8a* ☎ *070/364–6144 tour reservations* ☉ *Mon.–Sat. 10–3:45; tours by appointment only.*

★ The **Mauritshuis** (Maurits' House), a small, perfectly proportioned neoclassical palace on the far side of the Binnenhof, dates from 1644. This former royal residence is one of the finest small art museums in the world. It contains a feast of art from the 17th century, including six works by Rembrandt van Rijn. Of these the most powerful is the *Anatomy Lesson*, a theatrical work depicting a dissection of the lower arm. Also here are the celebrated *Girl with a Pearl Earring* and the glistening *View of Delft* by Jan Vermeer, the painter famous for his brilliant ability to capture the fall of light. ⊠ *Korte Vijverberg 8* ☎ *070/302–3456* ⊕ *www.mauritshuis.nl* ☉ *Tues.–Sat. 10–5, Sun. 11–5.*

Lange Voorhout is a large L-shape boulevard close to the Mauritshuis and Parliament buildings. During the 19th century, horse-drawn trams clattered along its cobbles and deposited dignitaries outside the various palaces, which are now primarily inhabited by embassies. The **Hoge Raad** (Supreme Court; ⊠ Lange Voorhout 34) once belonged to William I, the first king of the Netherlands. With its redbrick stepped gable, the

Rode Kruis (Dutch Red Cross) headquarters, in a former servants' house at No. 6, seems out of place on this stately avenue.

Escher in Het Paleis (Escher in the Palace), a former royal residence, is now a museum dedicated to the work of world-famous Dutch graphic artist M. C. Escher. ⊠ *Lange Voorhout 74* ☎ *070/362–4061* ⊕ *www. escherinhetpaleis.nl* ⊗ *Tues.–Sun. 11–5.*

The **Kloosterkerk** (Cloister Church), built in 1400, is the Hague's oldest church. In spring the adjoining square is covered with yellow and purple crocuses; on Thursday in summer it is the setting for a colorful antiques market. ⊠ *Lange Voorhout 4, corner of Parkstraat.*

Panorama Mesdag is a 400-foot painting-in-the-round that shows the nearby seaside town of Scheveningen as it looked in 1880. Hendrik Mesdag, a marine painter, used the muted colors of the Hague school in his calming seascape, as well as special perspective techniques. ⊠ *Zeestraat 65* ☎ *070/364–4544* ⊕ *www.mesdag.nl* ⊗ *Mon.–Sat. 10–5, Sun. noon–5.*

Museum Mesdag, the painter's former home, contains works by H. W. Mesdag and members of the Hague school interspersed with those of Corot, Courbet, and Rousseau. These delicate landscapes represent one of the finest collections of Barbizon School painting outside France. ⊠ *Laan van Meerdervoort 7f* ☎ *070/362–1434* ⊕ *www.museummesdag. nl* ⊗ *Tues.–Sun. noon–5.*

The **Vredespaleis** (Peace Palace) is a monument to world peace through negotiation. Following the first peace conference at the Hague in 1899, the Scottish-American millionaire Andrew Carnegie donated $1.5 million for the construction of a building to house an international court. The interior and furniture display an eclectic mix of works donated by participating nations from around the world. The **International Court of Justice,** which rules on disputes between countries, has its headquarters here. ⊠ *Carnegieplein 2* ☎ *070/302–2323* ⊕ *www.icj-cij.org* ⊗ *Tours May–Oct., weekdays 10, 11, 2, 3; Nov.–Apr., weekdays 11, 2, 3; reservations required.*

★ The **Gemeentemuseum Den Haag** (Hague Municipal Museum) houses the world's largest collection of work by painter Piet Mondrian, including his last, unfinished work, *Broadway Boogie Woogie,* acquired in 1998 for $20 million. The exhibition traces Mondrian's stylistic development from figurative painting to refined, minimalist abstraction. The Hague School of painters is also amply represented, as well as the CoBrA artist Karel Appel. In addition to magnificent Arts and Crafts collections, there are two vast collections of musical instruments. H. P. Berlage's 1935 yellow-brick building itself is a fascinating example of the International Style. ⊠ *Stadhouderslaan 41* ☎ *070/338–1111* ⊕ *www. gemeentemuseum.nl* ⊗ *Tues.–Sun. 11–5.*

ⓒ **Madurodam,** between the Hague and Scheveningen, is a miniature Netherlands where the country's important buildings are duplicated at a scale
Fodor'sChoice
★ of 1:25. No detail has been forgotten, from the lighthouse and 4½-km (3-mi) train track to the hand-carved furniture in the gabled houses. ⊠ *George Maduroplein 1* ☎ *070/416–2400* ⊕ *www.madurodam.nl* 🎫 *€11* ⊗ *Sept.–mid-Mar., daily 9–6; mid-Mar.–June, daily 9–8; July and Aug., daily 9 AM–10 PM.*

$$–$$$ ✕ **Sequenza.** Good food in an intimate, relaxed setting is what draws customers here. The menu consists of Spanish and French dishes, which vary daily depending on seasonal favorites like fresh fish and game. ⊠ *Spui*

224 ☎ 070/345–2853 ◬ *Reservations essential* ▤ *AE, DC, MC, V* ◷ *Closed Sun. and Mon. No lunch.*

★ **$–$$$** ✕ **Bistro-mer.** A notch above most other seafood restaurants in the Hague, Bistro-mer has a menu that ranges from the North Sea to the Mediterranean. Start with a selection of the three types of oysters on the half shell. Portions are generous, and the food is cooked to perfection. There's a wood-paneled dining room for snug winter meals and an attractive glassed-in terrace for the summer. ⊠ *Javastraat 9* ☎ *070/ 360–7389* ▤ *AE, DC, MC, V* ◷ *Closed Mon. No lunch weekends.*

$–$$$ ✕ **Oni.** This is one of the country's best Japanese restaurants. In ultra-modern, minimalist surroundings, all attention is focused on the cuisine. The attentive staff serves a royal selection of bento boxes, vegetarian dishes, and seafood with unique sauces. ⊠ *Prinsestraat 35* ☎ *070/ 364–5240* ▤ *AE, MC, V* ◷ *Closed Mon. No lunch.*

$$ ✕ **Le Haricot Vert.** What was built in 1638 as a staff house for the nearby palace is today an intimate, candlelighted restaurant in the city center. Succulent meats swimming in sauce appear on large plates with a colorful tangle of vegetables. Leave room for one of the sinfully laden dessert platters. ⊠ *Molenstraat 9a–11* ☎ *070/365–2278* ▤ *AE, DC, MC, V* ◷ *No lunch Sun.–Wed.*

$$$–$$$$ ⬚ **Hotel Des Indes.** At the end of one of the Hague's most prestigious squares, this hotel offers supreme grace and gentility. The once-private mansion was built for grand balls and entertainments; the rooms are arranged around the glamorous, marble-pillared foyer. For more than 100 years it has hosted ambassadors and kings, dancers and spies. Rooms are spacious and classically styled; one suite offers a spectacular view across the city toward the coast. The historic restaurant, frequented by diplomats, serves French-style haute cuisine. ⊠ *Lange Voorhout 54–56, 2514 EG* ☎ *070/361–2345* ▤ *070/361–2350* ⊕ *www. desindes.com* ⥽ *70 rooms, 6 suites* ◬ *Restaurant* ▤ *AE, DC, MC, V.*

$$–$$$ ⬚ **Golden Tulip Hotel Corona.** Overlooking a charming square in the center of the city, this hotel has rooms decorated in a restful scheme of white, cream, and dove gray. Mouthwatering dishes from its excellent Restaurant Marc Smeets include lamb with forest mushrooms and wild duck with sage and thyme. The lunch menu includes sandwiches and light meals. ⊠ *Buitenhof 39–42, 2513 AH* ☎ *070/363–7930* ▤ *070/ 361–5785* ⊕ *www.corona.nl* ⥽ *32 rooms, 4 suites* ◬ *Restaurant, bar* ▤ *AE, DC, MC, V.*

$–$$ ⬚ **Hotel Sebel.** This hotel is in a largely residential district between the city center and the Peace Palace. The rooms are invitingly spacious and light and have marble bathrooms. ⊠ *Zoutmanstraat 40, 2518 GR* ☎ *070/345–9200* ▤ *070/345–5855* ⊕ *www.hotelsebel.nl* ⥽ *27 rooms* ▤ *AE, DC, MC, V.*

Scheveningen

Scheveningen is adjacent to the Hague on the North Sea coast, with the **Scheveningse Bosjes** (Scheveningen Woods) separating it from the capital. A fishing village since the 14th century, Scheveningen became a popular beach resort in the 19th century. The beach itself, protected from tidal erosion by stone jetties, slopes gently into the sea in front of a high promenade that protects the boulevard and everything behind it from winter storms. During the summer, cafés and restaurants line the sandy beach, but you can escape to quieter environs by walking north of the pier along miles of untouched beach.

The **Pier,** completed in 1962, stretches 1,220 feet into the sea. The four circular buildings at its end contain a sun terrace and restaurant, an observation tower, an amusement center with a children's play area, and an underwater panorama. ⊠ *Northern end of Strandweg.*

☺ **Sea Life Scheveningen** on the beachfront is an ingeniously designed aquarium complex with a transparent underwater tunnel. You walk through it as if you were on the sea floor, with sharks and conga eels swimming inches above your head. Rays, octopuses, and other marine animals can be viewed in 40 aquariums. ⊠ *Strandweg 13* ☎ *070/354–2100* ⊕ *www. sealife.nl* ☾ *Sept.–June, daily 10–6; July and Aug., daily 10–8.*

$$$$ ⊞ **Steigenberger Kurhaus Hotel.** At the turn of the last century this imposing hotel stood alone at the center of the beach as a fashionable resort. The ballroom is still the hotel's focal point, with an extravagantly decorated ceiling, under which you can enjoy a superb lunch. Rooms have tasteful, modern furnishings. The Vitalizee spa, alongside the hotel's panoramic sea-view terrace, has a suite of saunas and steam rooms, as well as massage, restorative therapies, and beauty treatments. The spa is open to guests and nonguests alike. ⊠ *Gevers Deynootplein 30, 2586 CK* ☎ *070/416–2636; 070/416–6500 spa* 🖷 *070/416–2646* ⊕ *www.kurhaus.nl* 🛏 *245 rooms, 10 suites* ☾ *2 restaurants* ▤ *AE, DC, MC, V.*

Delft

Probably no town in the Netherlands is more intimate, more attractive, or more traditional than this minimetropolis, whose famous blue-and-white earthenware is popular throughout the world. Compact and easy to explore despite its web of canals, Delft is best discovered on foot—although canal-boat excursions are available April through October and horse-drawn trams leave from the marketplace. Every canal and street is lined with attractive Gothic and Renaissance houses.

In the marketplace, the only lively spot in this tranquil town, stands the **Nieuwe Kerk** (New Church), built in the 14th century with tall Gothic spire and a 48-bell carillon. The crypt has been the final resting place for all members of the Dutch royal family since the mid-16th century. ⊠ *Markt* ☎ *015/212–3025* ☾ *Tower: Mar.–Oct., Mon.–Sat. 9–6; Nov.–Feb., Mon.–Sat. 11–4.*

The **Stedelijk Museum Het Prinsenhof** (Prinsenhof Municipal Museum) was formerly the Convent of St. Agatha, founded in 1400; William of Orange was murdered here in 1584. The chapel dates from 1471; its interior is remarkable for the wooden statues under the vaulting ribs. Today the Prinsenhof's collection includes 16th- and 17th-century paintings by Delft masters, local silverware, and Delft ceramics. The **Museum Nusantara,** part of the same complex, has a collection of objects from the former Dutch colonies in Indonesia. ⊠ *St. Agathaplein 1* ☎ *015/260–2358* ⊕ *www.gemeentemusea-delft.nl* ☾ *Tues.–Sat. 10–5, Sun. 1–5.*

The **Oude Kerk** (Old Church), a vast Gothic monument from the 13th century, overlooks the Oude Delft canal, the city's oldest waterway. The beautiful tower, surmounted by a brick spire, lists somewhat alarmingly. ⊠ *Heilige Geestkerkhof* ☎ *015/212–3015* ☾ *Apr.–Nov., Mon.–Sat. 9–6.*

The timbered rooms of the **Lambert van Meerten Museum** have been filled with an extensive collection of old Dutch and foreign tiles and Delft pottery since the museum was founded in the home of this successful 19th-century industrialist in 1908. ⊠ *Oude Delft 199* ☎ *015/260–2358* ☾ *Tues.–Sat. 10–5, Sun. 1–5.*

When decorated porcelain brought to the Netherlands from China on East India Company ships during the 17th century became so popular that Dutch potters felt their livelihood threatened, they set about creating pottery to rival the Chinese product. This resulted in Delftware.

Only two manufacturers still make hand-painted Delftware, and at both workshops tours allow you to see the craftspeople at work. **Koninklijke Porceleyne Fles** (✉ Rotterdamsweg 196 ☎ 015/256–9204 ⊕ www. royaldelft.com) first opened in 1653 and has plenty of blue-and-white porcelain ware out to tempt all shoppers. **De Delftse Pauw** (✉ Delftweg 133 ☎ 015/212–4920) admits visitors for free and puts on a painting demonstration.

$$–$$$$ ✕ **L'Orage.** This canal-side restaurant serves delicious fish steeped in tantalizing sauces. The work of chef-owner Jannie Munk is influenced by French cuisine, but she bases many of her dishes on recipes from her native Denmark. Main courses might include grilled red bass served on a bed of risotto and sun-dried tomatoes. ✉ *Oude Delft 111B* ☎ *015/ 212–3629* ⚲ *Reservations essential.* ▭ *AE, DC, MC, V* ☉ *Closed Mon. No lunch.*

$$ ✕ **Spijshuis De Dis.** Seafood is a house specialty at this favorite neighborhood spot, where a friendly staff serves typically Dutch cuisine. The mussels with garlic sauce are delicious, and you can try such delicacies as roast quail. Lunch is served only to groups of 20 or more. ✉ *Beestenmarkt 36* ☎ *015/213–1782* ⚲ *Reservations essential for lunch* ▭ *AE, MC, V* ☉ *Closed Wed.*

$$ ▦ **Hotel De Ark.** This bright, airy hotel in the center of old Delft comprises four 17th-century canal houses joined so nearly every room has a view of either the canal or the garden in back. Rooms are clean and modern. ✉ *Koornmarkt 59–65, 2611 EC* ☎ *015/215–7999* 🖷 *015/ 214–4997* ⊕ *www.deark.nl* ➳ *28 rooms, 9 apartments* ▭ *AE, DC, MC, V.*

★ $$ ▦ **Hotel de Plataan.** Converted from a rather grand old post office building, the hotel was decorated by a local artist in 1950s-style cream and Bordeaux red. Studio rooms have a kitchen nook. The classic Grand Café Quercus serves drinks and snacks. ✉ *Doelenplein 10, 2611 BP* ☎ *015/ 212–6046* 🖷 *015/215–7327* ⊕ *www.hoteldeplataan.nl* ➳ *21 rooms, 3 suites* ▭ *AE, DC, MC, V.*

$$ ▦ **Hotel Leeuwenbrug.** On one of the prettiest canals in Delft, this traditional Dutch family-style hotel is in a former patrician mansion and an annex. The mansion is simpler, with smaller rooms; the annex is more contemporary and businesslike. You can breakfast overlooking the canal; rooms on the top floor of the annex overlook the city. ✉ *Koornmarkt 16, 2611 EE* ☎ *015/214–7741* 🖷 *015/215–9759* ⊕ *www. leeuwenbrug.nl* ➳ *36 rooms* ▭ *AE, MC, V.*

Rotterdam

Rotterdam is one of the few thoroughly modern cities in the Netherlands and the site of the world's largest and busiest port. Art lovers know the city for its extensive and outstanding collection of art; philosophers recall it as the city of Erasmus. Representative of the city's adventuresome modern architecture is the **Erasmusbrug** (Erasmus Bridge), an extraordinary, single-span pylon bridge over the Maas River, nicknamed "the Swan." This forms the main link with the **Kop van Zuid,** Rotterdam's phenomenal redevelopment project in former docklands on the south bank.

In the city center a most intriguing "forest" of cube-shape apartments balances on concrete stilts, all conceived in the mind of architect Piet Bloom. Collectively, the complex is known the Blaakse Bos (Blaakse Forest). One of these precarious-looking houses, the **Kijk-Kubus** (Show Cube), just east of the center, is open to the public. ✉ *Overblaak 70* ☎ *010/414–2285* ⊕ *www.kubuswoning.nl* ☉ *Daily 11–5.*

The biggest surprise in Rotterdam is the remarkable 48-km-long (30-mi-long) **Europoort** (Europort; ⊠ Willemsplein), which handles more than 300 million tons of cargo every year and more ships than any other port in the world. It is the delta for three of Europe's most important rivers: the Rhine, the Waal, and the Maas. You can get to the piers by tram or metro (blue line to Leuvehaven). A 1¼-hour harbor tour illuminates Rotterdam's vital role in world trade.

You can also survey the harbor from the vantage point of the **Euromast** observation tower. Get there via the RET metro red line to Dijkszicht. ⊠ *Parkhaven 20* ☎ *010/436–4811* ⊕ *www.euromast.nl* ✆ *Oct.–Mar., daily 10–5; Apr.–Sept., daily 10–7; July and Aug., Tues.–Sat. 10 AM–10:30 PM.*

The **Maritiem Museum Rotterdam** (Rotterdam Maritime Museum) is a sea lover's delight, appropriately perched at the head of Leuvehaven harbor. The hodgepodge of cranes, barges, steamships, and old shipbuilding machinery nearby looks like a maritime junkyard and is still a work in progress. Moored in the inner harbor adjacent to the museum is the historic 19th-century Royal Dutch Navy warship *De Buffel*. Within the museum are exhibits devoted to the history and activity of the great port outside. ⊠ *Leuvehaven 1* ☎ *010/413–2680* ⊕ *www.maritiemmuseum. nl* ✆ *Sept.–June, Tues.–Sat. 10–5, Sun. 11–5; July and Aug., Mon.–Sat. 10–5, Sun. 11–5.*

The **Museumpark,** an easy stroll along the canal from Eendrachtsplein metro station, is a welcome contrast to the industrial might of the Europoort and the Netherlands' maritime history. Three of Rotterdam's art institutions are sited around these landscaped gardens. The **Boijmans Van Beuningen Museum** has a section that includes the work of Brueghel, Bosch, and Rembrandt, as well as a renowned print gallery with works by artists such as Dürer and Cézanne. Dalí and Magritte mix with the impressionists in the Modern Arts collection. ⊠ *Museumpark 18–20* ☎ *010/ 441–9400* ⊕ *boijmans.kennisnet.nl* ✆ *Tues.–Sat. 10–5, Sun. 11–5.*

The **Nederlands Architectuurinstituut** (Netherlands Institute of Architecture), designed by Jo Coenen, hosts innovative exhibitions and lectures in the fields of architecture, urban and rural planning, and interior design from the 1800s to the present. ⊠ *Museumpark 25* ☎ *010/440– 1200* ⊕ *www.nai.nl* ✆ *Tues.–Sat. 10–5, Sun. 11–5.*

The **Kunsthal** (Art Hall) in Museumpark mounts all manner of major temporary exhibitions—from prehistoric bones, to private collections of Dutch impressionist works, to avant-garde rows of compact cars. ⊠ *Westzeedijk 341* ☎ *010/440–0300* ⊕ *www.kunsthal.nl* ✆ *Tues.–Sat. 10–5, Sun. 11–5.*

Delfshaven—spelled Delftshaven when the Pilgrims set sail from here— is the last remaining nook of old Rotterdam. Rows of gabled buildings and a windmill line the waterfront. Today Delfshaven is strewn with trendy galleries, cafés, and restaurants. ⊠ *From Delfshaven metro station, double back along Schiedamseweg, then turn right down Aelbrechtskolk, Voorhaven.*

Set near the southeast edge of Rotterdam, **Kinderdijk** is home to one of Holland's most beloved photo-ops. Here, the tiny village of Alblasserdam sports 19 windmills, the largest number found in any place in the world. The mills date from 1740 and are in full sail operation on the Dutch National Windmill Day (second Saturday in May) and on Saturday afternoons from 2 PM to 5 PM in July and August (the interior of one mill is open 9:30 AM to 5:30 PM daily from April through September). A short boat trip that passes all the windmills is available May to September and the mills are romantically floodlit during the evenings of the first week of September. Buses run to Kinderdijk from Rotterdam's suburban Lombardijen station. ☎ *078/6917405* ⊕ *www. kinderdijk.nl.*

$$$–$$$$ ✕**Parkheuvel.** This restaurant, run by chef-owner Cees Helder, is said to be popular among the harbor barons, who can oversee their dockside territory from the bay windows of the tastefully modern, semicircular building. Luxuries such as truffle are added to the freshest ingredients, with the day's menu dictated by the availability of the best produce at that morning's markets. ⊠ *Heuvellaan 21* ☎ *010/436– 0530* 🍴 *Jacket required* ⊟ *AE, DC, MC, V* ⊘ *Closed Sun. No lunch Sat.*

$$–$$$ ✕**Loos.** This stylish café is in one of the city's few remaining old neighborhoods. The fare is adventurous French-influenced Dutch, with such dishes as braised calf's tail with truffle sauces or sea bass stir-fried with vegetables. ⊠ *Westplein 1* ☎ *010/411–7723* ⊟ *AE, MC, V* ⊘ *No lunch weekends.*

$$–$$$ ✕**Parkzicht.** Beside a lake in the city's Maas Park, this airy 19th-century building has the sunniest terrace in town. Take time for a lazy lunch or high tea in the casual brasserie, join the trendy for a cocktail at the marble bar, or revel in a full dinner from the cosmopolitan menu in the upstairs restaurant. Influences run from Sumatra to Norway. ⊠ *Kievitslaan 25* ☎ *010/436–8888* ⊟ *AE, DC, MC, V* ⊘ *Closed Sun. No lunch Sat.*

$$$ 🏨**Hotel Inntel Rotterdam.** Right on the riverside, with a view of the landmark Erasmus Bridge, this location is ideal to get a feel for this world port. Le Papillon has great views of the harbor and serves traditional French cuisine. ⊠ *Leuvehaven 80, 3011 EA* ☎ *010/413–4139* 🖷 *010/ 413–3222* ⊕ *www.hotelinntel.com* ⤱ *149 rooms* ♨ *Restaurant, pool* ⊟ *AE, DC, MC, V.*

$$$ 🏨**NH Atlanta Rotterdam.** Close to the river and at the heart of the shopping district, this hotel is a surprisingly beautiful art deco building in the midst of postwar architecture. The Sakura serves Japanese fare, whereas more traditional meals are available in the brasserie. ⊠ *Coolsingel/Aert van Nesstraat 4, 3012 CA* ☎ *010/206–7800* 🖷 *010/413–5320* ⊕ *www.nh-hotels.com* ⤱ *215 rooms* ♨ *2 restaurants* ⊟ *AE, DC, MC, V.*

$$–$$$ 🏨**Bilderberg Parkhotel.** Within walking distance of all Rotterdam's neighborhoods, this hotel was built as a town house in the late 19th-century, though it now incorporates a colossal steel-faced tower. The Restaurant 70 serves a fusion of new style, global, and traditional cuisines in the classical surroundings of the old wing of the hotel. ⊠ *Westersingel 70, 3015 LB* ☎ *010/436–3611* 🖷 *010/436–4212* ⊕ *www. parkhotelrotterdam.nl* ⤱*187 rooms, 2 suites* ♨ *Restaurant* ⊟ *AE, DC, MC, V.*

$–$$$ 🏨**Hotel New York.** The towers of the Hotel New York have been a feature of Rotterdam's skyline for almost a century. In the days of transatlantic liners, the building was the head office of the Holland-America Line. Some rooms retain the original walnut paneling and restored art nouveau carpets, whereas others are modern in design. Downstairs, the huge café-restaurant serves everything from English afternoon tea to myriad varieties of oysters. ⊠ *Koninginnenhoofd 1, 3072 AD* ☎ *010/ 439–0500* 🖷 *010/484–2701* ⊕ *www.hotelnewyork.nl* ⤱ *72 rooms* ♨ *Restaurant* ⊟ *AE, DC, MC, V.*

$ 🏨**Grand Hotel Central.** For the traveler on a budget, this basic hotel is a reasonable bet and ideally located for access to the city's shops, restaurants, and museums. Rooms in this late-19th-century building are spacious and airy with simple modern furniture. Breakfast is served in the large dining room. ⊠ *Kruiskade 12, 3012 EH* ☎ *010/414–0744* 🖷 *010/ 412–5325* ⌁ *64 rooms* ☰ *AE, DC, MC, V.*

The Hague, Delft & Rotterdam Essentials

EMERGENCIES

The Doctors Telephone supplies names and opening hours of pharmacists and dentists, as well as doctors, outside normal surgery hours. 🛈 **Ambulance, Fire, Police, and Rescue** ☎ 112. **Doctors Telephone** ☎ 070/346-9669 in the Hague, 9 PM-7 AM; 010/4201100 in Rotterdam.

TOURS

BOAT TOURS   In Scheveningen there are fishing-boat tours around the Dutch coast; Sportsviscentrum Trip offers circle tours and seasonal fishing expeditions. In Delft, the tourist office organizes boat tours along the unspoiled canal system. Spido Rondvaarten, the main boat company, lets you cruise the port of Rotterdam on a basic tour of 1¼ hours (year-round). You can also choose one that lasts as long as 7½ hours (midsummer only). The pier can be reached by taking the RET metro blue line toward Spijkenisse to the Leuvehaven station and walking to the end of the boulevard.
🛈 **Spido Rondvaarten** ⊠ Willemsplein ☎ 010/413-5400 ⊕ www.spido.nl. **Sportsvis-centrum Trip** ⊠ Dr. Lelykade 3 ☎ 070/354-1122.

BUS TOURS   Sightseeing tours of the Hague can be arranged by or through the main VVV tourist office next to the train station. The three-hour Royal Tour by bus, which departs from this office at 1 PM Thursday–Saturday from April to September, takes passengers past Queen Beatrix's residences and stops at the Ridderzaal (Knight's Hall) and Panorama Mesdag.

WALKING TOURS   Scheveningen is for walkers. The Scheveningen VVV office has information about coastal strolls. Delft is best seen on foot.

TRANSPORTATION AROUND THE HAGUE, DELFT & ROTTERDAM

The Hague and Delft are compact enough to be explored on foot. Scheveningen is reached from the Hague's center by bus or tram; public transportation is more convenient than driving because of severe parking problems at the resort. The RET metro is an easy-to-use option for getting around Rotterdam; the two main branches (north–south and east–west) cross in the heart of the business district.

VISITOR INFORMATION

Calls to VVV 0900 numbers cost €0.35–€0.45 per minute.
🛈 **The Hague** VVV ⊠ Babylon Center, Koningin Julianaplein 30, next to Den Haag CS train station ☎ 0900/340-3505. **Rotterdam** VVV ⊠ Coolsingel 67 ☎ 0900/403-4065. **Scheveningen** VVV ⊠ Gevers Deynootweg 1134 ☎ 0900/340-3505.

NORWAY

ON NORWAY'S DRAMATIC WEST COAST, deep fjords knife into steep mountain ranges. Inland, cross-country ski trails follow frozen streams, and downhill trails slice through forests that are carpeted with wildflowers and berries in summer. In older villages, wooden houses spill down toward docks where Viking ships were once moored. Small fishing boats, pleasure craft, and large industrial oil tankers dot the maritime horizon.

Inhabited since 1700 BC, Norway is today a peaceful nation, but from the 8th to the 10th century AD the Vikings marauded as far afield as Seville and the Isle of Man and engaged in vicious infighting at home. This fierce spirit remained alive, despite Norway's subsequent centuries of subjugation by the Danes and Swedes. Independence came early in the 20th century but was tested during World War II, when the Germans occupied the country. Norwegian Resistance fighters rose to the challenge, eventually sabotaging Nazi efforts to develop atomic weapons.

The foundations for modern Norwegian culture were laid in the 19th century, during the period of union with Sweden, which lasted until 1905. Oslo blossomed at this time, and Norway produced its three greatest men of arts and letters: composer Edvard Grieg (1843–1907), playwright Henrik Ibsen (1828–1906), and painter Edvard Munch (1863–1944). Other notable Norwegians of this period were the polar explorers Roald Amundsen and Fridtjof Nansen.

The fjords, however, are Norway's true claim to fame. They were formed during an ice age a million years ago, when the ice cap created enormous pressure by burrowing deep into existing mountain-bound riverbeds. There was less pressure along the coast, so the entrances to most fjords are shallow, about 500 feet, whereas inland depths reach as much as 4,000 feet. Although Norway's entire coastline is notched with fjords, the most breathtaking sights are on the west coast between Stavanger and Trondheim, and the northern Helgeland coastline to the Lofoten Islands. From the sheltered villages deep in fjord country to the wildest windswept plateaus in Finnmark, Norway's natural beauty captivates both visitors and residents, transforming many into serious outdoor enthusiasts.

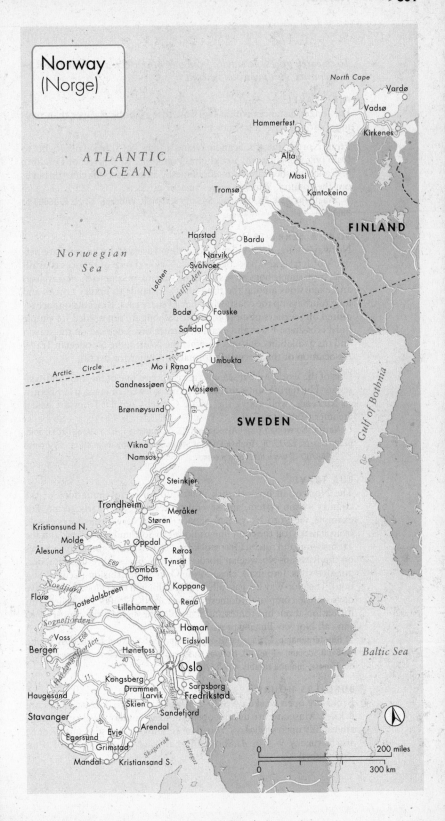

Norway
(Norge)

ATLANTIC OCEAN

North Cape

Vardø

Vadsø

Hammerfest

Kirkenes

Alta

Masi

Tromsø

Kantokeino

FINLAND

Norwegian Sea

Harstad

Bardu

Narvik

Svolvær

Lofoten

Vestfjorden

Bodø

Fauske

Saltdal

Arctic Circle

Mo i Rana

Umbukta

Sandnessjøen

Mosjøen

Brønnøysund

E6

SWEDEN

Gulf of Bothnia

Vikna

Namsos

Steinkjer

Trondheim

Meråker

Støren

Kristiansund N.

Molde

Ålesund

70

Oppdal

Røros

Tynset

E69

Dombås

Otta

Koppang

Nordfjord

Florø

Jostedalsbreen

Lillehammer

Rena

Sognefjorden

E68

Voss

Lake Mjøsa

Hamar

Eidsvoll

Bergen

Hønefoss

Hardangerfjorden

40

Oslo

11

Kongsberg

Drammen

Larvik

Sarpsborg

Fredrikstad

Haugesund

Skien

Stavanger

Sandefjord

Evje

Arendal

Egersund

Grimstad

Mandal

Kristiansand S.

Skagerrak

Kattegat

Baltic Sea

0		200 miles
0		300 km

NORWAY A TO Z

To research prices, get advice from other travelers, and book travel arrangements, visit www.fodors.com.

AIR TRAVEL

For longer distances within Norway, flying can be cheaper than renting a car or taking a train or bus.

CARRIERS From North America, Scandinavian Airlines (SAS) has daily flights to Oslo (via Copenhagen, Stockholm, Frankfurt, Reykjavík, or London). SAS and Braathens are the major domestic airlines, serving cities throughout the country. Widerøe serves smaller airports.
🇳 **Braathens ASA** 🕾 81520000. **SAS** 🕾 81520400. **Widerøe** ✉ 🕾 67116000 or 81001200.

BOAT & FERRY TRAVEL

Norway's long, fjord-indented coastline is served by an intricate network of ferries and passenger ships. A wide choice of services is available, from simple hops across fjords (saving many kilometers of traveling) and excursions among the thousands of islands to luxury cruises and long journeys up the coast. Most ferries carry cars. Reservations are required on journeys of more than one day but are not needed for simple fjord crossings. Fares and exact departure times depend on the season and the availability of ships. Contact the *Nortra,* the Norwegian Travel Association or the Norway Information Center for details.

One of the world's great sea voyages is aboard one of the mail-and-passenger Hurtigruta ships that run up the Norwegian coast from Bergen to Kirkenes, well above the Arctic Circle. Contact Tromsø Coastal Steamer Company.
🇳 **Nortra** (Norwegian Travel Association) ✉ Drammensvn. 40, Postboks 2893, Solli, 0230 Oslo 🕾 22925200. **Tromsø Coastal Steamer Company** main office, ✉ Tromsø 🕾 77648200 ⊕ www.hurtigruten.com.

BUS TRAVEL

The Norwegian bus network makes up for some limitations of the country's train system, and several routes are particularly scenic. For example, the Nord-Norge Buss Service (North Norway Bus Service) goes from Fauske (on the train line to Bodø) to Sortland; from Sortland the Tromsø–innland rutebil (Tromsø–inland coach) goes right up to Kirkenes on the Russian–Norwegian border. In Oslo, buses leave from Bussterminalen (Bus Terminal), close to the Oslo Sentralstasjon (Central Station). The Nor-Way BusPass allows you unlimited travel for 21 successive days on the company's domestic lines for NKr 2,300. For general information about bus routes and schedules throughout the country, you can call Norway Bussekspress.
🇳 **Bussterminalen** ✉ Galleriet Oslo, Schweigaardsgt. 10. **Nord-Norge Buss Service** ✉ 8400 Sortland 🕾 76111111. **Norway Bussekspress** 🕾 81544444 ⊕ www.nor-way. no. **Tromsø-innland rutebil** 🕾 77852100.

BUSINESS HOURS

Banks are open weekdays 8:30–3:30; from June to August, hours are 8:15–3. Museums are usually open Tuesday–Sunday 10–3 or 4. Shops are usually open weekdays from 9 or 10 until 6 (Thursday until 7 or 8) and Saturday 9–3 or 4. Shopping malls are often open until 8 on weeknights.

CAR TRAVEL

EMERGENCIES   Norges Automobil Forbund (NAF), the Norwegian Automobile Association, patrols main roads and has emergency telephones on mountain roads. For NAF 24-hour service, dial the number listed below.

🚗 **Norges Automobil Forbund** ✉ Storgt. 2, 0155 Oslo ☎ 81000505 or 22341400 🌐 www.naf.no.

PARKING   Street parking in cities and towns is clearly marked. There are also municipal parking lots. You cannot park on main roads or on bends. Check the leaflet "Parking in Oslo," available free from the tourist office, at toll stations, and at the City Hall; or ask at your hotel.

RENTALS   Car rentals are available throughout the country. International companies like Avis and Hertz operate in the major cities.

🚗 **Avis Bilutleie** ✉ Oslo Lufthavn ☎ 64810660 ✉ Oslo Sentrum ☎ 23239200. **Hertz Bilutleie** ✉ Oslo Lufthavn ☎ 64810550 ✉ Oslo Sentrum ☎ 22210000.

ROAD CONDITIONS   Away from the major routes, especially in the mountains and fjords, roads can be narrow and winding, so don't expect to average more than 50–70 kph (30–40 mph), especially in fjord country. Even the best roads suffer from frost, and mountain passes may be closed in winter. Snow tires (preferably studded) are advised in winter in most areas.

RULES OF THE ROAD   Driving is on the right. The speed limit is 90 kph (55 mph) on highways, 80 kph (50 mph) on main roads, 50 kph (30 mph) in towns, and 30–40 kph (18–25 mph) in residential areas. The use of headlights at all times is mandatory. For assistance contact Norges Automobil Forbund. Remember to yield to the vehicle approaching from the right. Passing areas on narrow roads are marked with a white M (for *møteplass*) on a blue background.

CUSTOMS & DUTIES

Residents of non-European countries who are over 18 may import duty-free into Norway 400 cigarettes or 500 grams of other tobacco products. Residents of European countries who are over 18 may import 200 cigarettes or 250 grams of other tobacco goods. Anyone can bring in souvenirs, gifts, perfume, and eau de cologne to a value of NKr 5,000 after being out of the country for more than 24 hours. Within 24 hours, you may bring in goods duty-free valued up to NKr 2,000. Anyone over 20 may bring in 1 liter of liquor, 1 liter of wine, and 2 liters of beer or 2 liters of wine and 2 liters of beer. Travelers who are at least 18 years old may bring in 2 liters of wine and 2 liters of beer.

EATING & DRINKING

The Norwegian diet emphasizes protein and carbohydrates. Breakfast is usually a large buffet of smoked fish, cheeses, sausage, cold meats, and whole-grain breads accompanied by tea, coffee, or milk. Lunch is simple, usually *smørbrød* (open-face sandwiches). Restaurant and hotel dinners are usually three-course meals, often starting with soup and ending with fresh fruit and berries. Meals are generally expensive, so take hotel breakfast when it's offered. Spirits are not served on Sunday, although beer and wine are available in most establishments. Alcohol is very expensive and, except in restaurants, is sold only during strictly regulated hours at state-owned *vinmonopol* stores. Note that laws relating to drinking and driving are very strict.

WHAT IT COSTS In Norwegian Kroner			
$$$$	**$$$**	**$$**	**$**
AT DINNER	over 250	150–250	100–150	under 100

Prices are per person for a main course.

MEALTIMES — Lunch is from noon to 3 at restaurants featuring a *koldtbord*—a Scandinavian buffet, primarily for special occasions and visitors, but locals generally eat lunch anywhere between 11:30 and 1. Dinner has traditionally been early, but in hotels and major restaurants it is now more often from 6 to 11.

RESERVATIONS & DRESS — Unless otherwise indicated, jacket and tie or high-fashion casual wear is recommended for restaurants in the $$$$ and $$$ price categories; during the summer, neat casual dress is acceptable in most places.

EMBASSIES
Australia, Ireland, New Zealand, and South Africa have consular offices in Oslo (⇨ Oslo Essentials).
Canada ⊠ Wergelandsvn. 7, 0244 Oslo ☏ 22995300.
United Kingdom ⊠ Thos. Heftyesgt. 8, 0244 Oslo ☏ 23132700.
United States ⊠ Drammensvn. 18, 0244 Oslo ☏ 22448550.

HOLIDAYS
January 1; Palm Sunday; Good Friday; Easter Sunday and Monday; May 1 (Labor Day); May 17 (Constitution Day); Ascension (mid-May to early June); Pentecost Sunday and Monday (late May to early June); December 25–26. Many restaurants and hotels close during the Easter holidays and Christmas holidays, between Christmas and New Year's.

LANGUAGE
There are two official forms of the Norwegian language, *bokmål* and *nynorsk,* along with many dialects. As is typical of Scandinavian languages, Norwegian's additional vowels—æ, ø, and å—come at the end of the alphabet in the phone book.

English is the main foreign language taught in schools, and movies, music, and TV reinforce its popularity. It is widely spoken by people in larger cities and most commercial establishments.

LODGING
Prices quoted in this chapter are summer/weekend rates and include breakfast, service, and taxes. Overnight rates during the week can be NKr 200–NKr 300 higher.

WHAT IT COSTS In Norwegian Kroner			
$$$$	**$$$**	**$$**	**$**
MAJOR CITIES			
FOR 2 PEOPLE	over 1,500	1,200–1,500	800–1,200	under 800
OTHER AREAS			
HOTELS	over 1,000	850–1,000	650–850	under 650

Prices are for two people in a standard double room in high season.

CABIN & HOME RENTALS — Norwegians escape to *hytter* (mountain cabins) whenever they have the chance. Stay in one for a week or two and you'll see why—magnificent scenery, pure air, edible wild berries, and a chance to hike, fish, or cross-country ski. For information on renting cabins, farms, or private homes, write to Den Norske Hytteformidling A. S. An increasingly popular alternative is to rent a *rorbu* (fisherman's cabin) in the northerly Lofoten Islands. Contact Destination Lofoten.

🔹 **Den Norske Hytteformidling A.S.** 🗗 Box 309, Sentrum, 0103 Oslo ☎ 22356270 🌐 www.hytte.com. **Destination Lofoten** 🗗 Box 210, 8301 Svolvær ☎ 76069800 🌐 www.lofoten.info.

CAMPING   There are more than 1,000 registered campsites in the country, many in spectacular surroundings. Prices vary according to the facilities provided: a family with a car and tent can expect to pay about NKr 80–NKr 150 per night. Some campsites have log cabins available from between NKr 20 and NKr 600 per night. *Camping Norway* is available from tourist offices and the Norges Automobil Forbund.

🔹 **Norges Automobil Forbund (NAF)** ✉ Storgt. 2, 0105 Oslo ☎ 22341400 🌐 www.naf.no.

HOSTELS   Norway has about 100 hostels; some are schools or farms in winter.

🔹 **Norske Vandrerhjem (NoVa)** ✉ Dronningensgt. 26, 0154 Oslo ☎ 23139300 🌐 www.vandrerhjem.no.

HOTELS   Accommodations in Norway are usually well kept, and smaller establishments are often family-run. Service is attentive and considerate, right down to blackout curtains to block out the midnight sun. The Fjord Pass, which costs about NKr 100, is valid for two adults and children under 15, for discounts at 200 hotels, inns, cottages, and apartments. Hotels in larger towns have special summer rates from late June to early August, and some chains have their own discount offers—see Norway's annual accommodation guide at tourist offices. Discounts in smaller hotels are offered to guests staying several days; meals are then included in the rate.

🔹 **Fjord Pass** 🗗 Fjord Tours, Bergen ☎ 55557660 🌐 www.fjordpass.no.

MAIL & SHIPPING

Opening times for post offices vary throughout the country, but in general they are weekdays 9–5 and Saturday 10–2. Post offices cash traveler's checks, exchange foreign currency, and provide postal services. All mailing addresses in Norway include a four-digit zip code. The Oslo Hoved Post Kontor (Oslo Main Post Office) is open weekdays 8–7, Saturday 10–3.

🔹 **Oslo Hoved Post Kontor** ✉ Dronningensgt. 15 ☎ 23147820.

POSTAL RATES   Letters and postcards to the United States cost NKr 10 for the first 20 grams. The rate within Europe varies between NKr 5 and NKr 8 for the first 20 grams.

MONEY MATTERS

Norway has a high standard—and cost—of living, but there are ways to save money by taking advantage of special offers for accommodations and travel during the tourist season and on weekends.

Some sample prices include cup of coffee, NKr 25; ½ liter of beer, NKr 35–NKr 55; soft drink, NKr 20–NKr 35; ham sandwich, NKr 30–NKr 50.

CURRENCY   The unit of currency in Norway is the krone, written as NOK (bank designation), NKr, or kr. The krone is divided into 100 øre. Bills of NKr 50, 100, 200, 500, and 1,000 are in general use. Coins are in denominations of 50 øre and 1, 5, 10, and 20 kroner. Credit cards are accepted in most hotels, stores, restaurants, and many gas stations and garages, but generally not in smaller shops and inns in rural areas.

SHOPPING

Prices of handmade articles are government controlled, and selection is widest in Oslo, so that's the best place to do your shopping. Pewter, silver, glass, sheepskin, leather, painted-wood decorations, kitchenware, knitwear, and wall hangings all make special souvenirs.

TAXES

TAX-FREE Residents of countries outside of Norway, Sweden, Finland, or Denmark, intending to take their purchases out of the country, will get the Norwegian Value-Added Tax (MOMS) refunded when leaving the country. You must clearly mention this in the shop when the purchase is being made so your Global Refund Cheque (export document) is properly filled in. For more information, contact Global Refund Norge.

🖪 **Global Refund Norge AS** ☎ 67156010.

TELEPHONES

COUNTRY & AREA CODES The international country code for Norway is 47.

DIRECTORY & OPERATOR ASSISTANCE For local information, dial 1880. For international information, dial 1881.

INTERNATIONAL CALLS Cheap rates for international calls apply only after 10 PM. International calls can be made from any pay phone. For calls to North America, dial 00–1, then the area code and number. When dialing the United Kingdom, omit the initial zero of the area code. To reach an AT&T or MCI WorldCom operator, dial one of the access codes below.

🖪 Access Codes **AT&T** ☎ 80019011. **MCI WorldCom** ☎ 80019912.

LOCAL CALLS Domestic rates are reduced 5 PM–8 AM weekdays and all day on weekends. Area codes are not used in Norway. The cost of calls within the country varies according to distance: in Oslo, the cost goes up according to the amount of time used after the three-minute flat fee. The Oslo phone book has dialing information in English.

PUBLIC PHONES Avoid using room phones in hotels. In public booths you can find card phones or coin phones. Be sure to read the instructions; some phones require the coins to be deposited before dialing, some after. You can buy telephone cards at Narvesen kiosks or at the post office. The minimum deposit is NKr 5, depending on the phone.

TIPPING

A 10%–12% service charge is added to most bills at hotels and restaurants. If you have had exceptional service, give an additional 5%–10% tip. Round off a taxi fare to the next higher unit, or a little more if the driver has been particularly helpful with luggage. If the porter helps with your luggage, give NKr 15–NKr 20. Tip with kroner only.

TRAIN TRAVEL

Trains are punctual and comfortable, and most routes are scenic. Lines fan out from Oslo and leave the coastline (except in the south) to buses and ferries. Reservations are required on all *ekspresstog* (express trains) and night trains. The Oslo–Bergen route is especially beautiful, and the Oslo–Trondheim–Bodø route takes you within the Arctic Circle. Do not miss the side trips from Myrdal to Flåm from the Oslo–Bergen line and Dombås to Åndalsnes from the Oslo–Trondheim line. NSB trains leave Oslo from Oslo Central Station.

FARES & SCHEDULES Two types of ScanRail passes, good in Norway, Sweden, Denmark, and Finland, are available, offering unlimited travel on a given number of travel days within a specified period (on 5 days out of 15 or 21 consecutive days). These are available in Norway through NSB, the Nor-wegian State Railways. A Norway Rail Pass, also available from NSB, offers a choice of one or two weeks unlimited rail travel or three travel days within a month within Norway. Reduced fares during off-peak times ("green" routes) are also available if booked in advance.

🚉 **NSB (Norwegian State Railways)** ✉ Oslo ☎ 81500888 ⊕ www.nsb.no. **Oslo Central Station** ✉ Jernbanetorget, beginning of Karl Johans Gt.

VISITOR INFORMATION

🚉 **Nortra (Norwegian Travel Association)** ✉ Drammensvn. 40, Postboks 2893, Solli, 0230 Oslo ☎ 22925200. **Tourist Information** ✉ Fridtjof Nansens Plass 5, 0160 Oslo ☎ 23117880 ⊕ www.visitoslo.com ✉ Oslo Central Station, Jernbanetorget 2. **Trafikanten** ✉ Oslo Central Station, east of Strandgt. ☎ 177 for Oslo public transportation, 81500176 ⊕ www.trafikanten.no.

WHEN TO GO

Norway is an important winter sports destination. January, February, and early March are good skiing months. Avoid late April, when sleet, rain, and repeated thaws may ruin the good skiing snow and leave roads—and spirits—in bad shape. The country virtually closes down for the five-day Easter holiday, when Norwegians make their annual migration to the mountains. In May the days are long and sunny, cultural life is going strong, and *Syttende mai* (Constitution Day, May 17), with all its festivities, is worth a trip in itself. Norwegians tend to take their vacations in July and the first part of August. Summers are generally mild. With the midnight sun, even in the "southern" city of Oslo, night seems more like twilight around midnight, and dawn comes by 2 AM. The weather can be fickle, and rain gear and sturdy waterproof shoes are recommended even in summer.

OSLO

Oslo is the capital of Norway with approximately 515,000 inhabitants, just over 10% of Norway's entire population. As far north as Helsinki, St. Petersburg, and Anchorage, Oslo is Scandinavia's sunniest capital. Founded in 1000 AD, Oslo survived the Black Death of 1328, losing 50% of its residents, only to burn to the ground in the great fire of 1624.

The city was rebuilt and renamed Christiania by King Christian IV of Denmark and Norway. After Norway's union with Sweden was dissolved in 1905 and the country gained its independence, the original Viking name Oslo was reinstated by an act of Parliament in 1925. Compared with worldly Scandinavian capitals Stockholm and Copenhagen, Oslo was once considered very provincial. Since the late 1990s, though, Oslo has been emerging as a world-class city, adopting café culture, international restaurants, shops, music, films, and festivals galore. Oslo is known the world over for the Nobel Peace Prize, awarded every December 10, and for the Holmenkollen Ski Festival.

Exploring Oslo

Numbers in the margin correspond to points of interest on the Oslo map.

The downtown area is compact, but the city limits include forests, fjords, and mountains, giving Oslo a pristine airiness that complements its urban dignity.

In fact, within its 454-square-km (175-square-mi) area are 242 square km (93 square mi) of forest, 8 square km (3 square mi) of parkland and recreational areas, and some 40 island and 343 inland lakes. Ex-

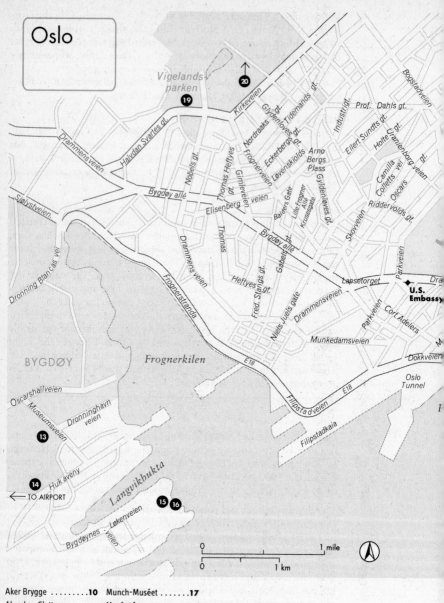

Oslo

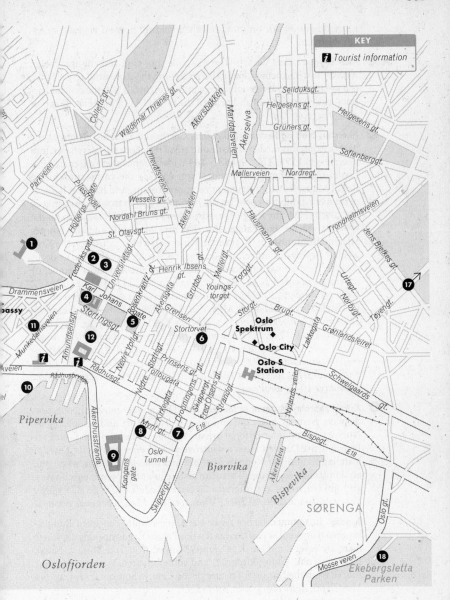

plore downtown or on foot, and then venture beyond via bus, street-car, or train.

★ ⑩ **Aker Brygge** (Aker Wharf). The quayside shopping and cultural center, with a theater, cinemas, and galleries among the stores and restaurants, is a great place to linger late into summer nights. It's in the central harbor—the heart of Oslo and head of the fjord. ⊠ *Off Dokkvn.* ⊕ *www. akerbrygge.no.*

⑨ **Akershus Slott og Festning** (Akershus Castle and Fortress). Right at the harborfront, this medieval castle and royal residence was developed into a fortress in 1592. Then in 1637–1648, it was rebuilt into a Renaissance castle. On summer guided tours, you can see the castle church, the Royal Mausoleum, government reception rooms, and banquet halls. A permanent exhibition profiles the history of the fortress. A changing of the guard (HM The King's Guards) takes place at 1:30 PM. Also on the grounds are the **Forsvarsmuséet** (Defense Museum) and the **Norges Hjemmefrontmuseum** (Resistance Museum), which focuses on the Norwegian Resistance movement during the World War II German occupation. The Nazis set up headquarters on this site and had a number of patriots executed here. ⊠ *Festningspl.* ☎ *22412521; 23093582 Forsvarsmuséet; 23093138 Hjemmefrontmuseum* ⊕ *www.nhm.mil.no* ☉ *Castle May 2–mid-Sept., Mon.–Sat. 10–4, Sun. 12:30–4. Fortress June 16–Aug. 17, weekdays 9–5, weekends 11–5; rest of year, weekdays 9–4, weekends 11–4. Forsvarsmuséet June–Sept., weekdays 10–6, weekends 11–4; Oct.–May, weekdays 10–3, weekends 11–4. Norges Hjemmefrontmuseum mid-Apr.–mid-June, Mon.–Sat. 10–4, Sun. 11–4; mid-June–Sept., weekdays 10–5, Sat. 10–4, Sun. 11–4; Oct.–mid-Apr., weekdays 10–3, weekends 11–4.*

⑦ **Astrup Fearnley Museum of Modern Art.** This private museum collection displays postwar and contemporary works of art and sculptures by Norwegian and international artists. Among its best-known pieces are British artist Damien Hirst's controversial *Mother and Child Divided* installation and Jeff Koons's *Michael Jackson and Bubbles* white and gold porcelain sculpture. There are also regular temporary exhibitions, and guided tours are offered. ⊠ *Grev Wedels Pl. 9* ☎ *22936060* ⊕ *www.af-moma.no* ☉ *Tues., Wed., and Fri. 11–5, weekends noon–5.*

Bygdøy. In summer, ferries make the seven-minute run from Rådhus-bryggen (City Hall Wharf) across the fjord to the Bygdøy peninsula, where there are several museums (⇨ *Fram-Muséet, Kon-Tiki* Muséet, Norsk Folkemuseum, Vikingskiphuset) and some beaches. You can also take Bus 30 from the National Theater or the Central Station. ☉ *Ferries run May–Sept., daily every ½ hr 8:15–5:45.*

★ ❶ **Det Kongelige Slottet** (The Royal Palace). Right at the end of Karl Johans Gate, the vanilla-and-cream–colored neoclassical palace is a symbol of Oslo. Completed between 1824 and 1848, it is understated and unpretentious. The surrounding park is open to the public. During the summer, the palace is open only for special guided tours. The changing of the guard takes place daily at 1:30. ⊠ *Drammensvn. 1* ☉ *Late June–mid-Aug., daily; guided English tours at 2 and 2:20 PM.*

⑱ **Ekebergsletta Parken.** The oldest traces of human habitation in Oslo are the 5,000-year-old stone carvings across the road from this park; they are marked by a sign reading FORTIDSMINNE (ancient monument). ⊠ *Karlsborgvn.; take Trikk (Tram) 18 or 19 east from National Theater or Oslo Central Station to Sjømannsskolen stop.*

⑯ Fram-Muséet (*Fram* Museum). Housed in a triangular building, the entire famed Arctic exploration ship *Fram,* built in 1892, is exhibited with its original interior and inventory. The ship was used on expeditions by Fridtjof Nansen (1893–96), Otto Sverdrup (1898–1902), and Roald Amundsen (1910–12). ⊠ *Bygdøynes* ☏ 23282950 ⊕ *www.fram. museum.no* ⊗ *Mar.–Apr., daily 11–3:45; May, Sept., and Oct., daily 10–4:45; June–Aug., daily 9–6:45; Nov.–Feb., weekdays 11–2:45, weekends 11–3:45.*

② Historisk Museum (Historical Museum). In addition to displays of daily life and art from the Viking period, the museum has an ethnographic section with a collection related to the great polar explorer Roald Amundsen, the first man to reach the South Pole. ⊠ *Frederiksgt. 2* ☏ 22859912 ⊕ *www.uk.uio.no* ⊗ *Mid-May–mid-Sept., Tues.–Sun. 10–4; mid-Sept.–mid-May, Tues.–Sun. 11–4.*

Karl Johans Gate (Karl Johan's Street). Oslo's main street runs right through the center of town, from the Oslo Central Station uphill to the Royal Palace. Half its length is closed to automobiles, but it still bustles with many of the city's shops and outdoor cafés.

Ibsen-museet (The Ibsen Museum). Famed Norwegian dramatist Henrik Ibsen, known for *A Doll's House* and *Peer Gynt* among many other classic plays, spent his final years here in the apartment on the second floor, until his death in 1906. Huge, intense portraits of Ibsen and his archrival, August Strindberg, face each other in the study. On his desk still sits his "devil's orchestra," a playful collection of frog- and troll-like figurines that inspired him. In spring and autumn, there are special evening lectures and performances. ⊠ *Arbiensgt. 1* ☏ 22552009 ⊕ *www.ibsen.org* ⊗ *Tues.–Sun. only guided tours, at noon, 1, and 2.*

★ ⑮ Kon-Tiki Museum (*Kon-Tiki* Museum). This museum is dedicated to late adventurer Thor Heyerdahl's many expeditions. His famous *Kon-Tiki* raft, in which he crossed the Pacific in 1947, and his papyrus boat *RA II* from 1970 are on view, as well as the *Tigris,* built in 1978, which he sailed from Iraq to Pakistan, and then to Africa. ⊠ *Bygdøynesvn. 36* ☏ 22036540 ⊕ *www.kon-tiki.no* ⊗ *Tues., Wed., and Fri. 11–3, Thurs. 11–7, weekends noon–4.*

Kunstindustrimuseet (Museum of Applied Art). Rich Baldishol tapestries from 1100, Norwegian dragon-style furniture, and royal Norwegian apparel (including wedding dresses) make this museum a real treat. It focuses on Norwegian and international applied art, fashion, and design from the 7th century to the present. There are also impressive collections of silver, glass, and porcelain. ⊠ *St. Olavs Gt. 1* ☏ 22036540 ⊕ *www.kunstindustrimuseet.no* ⊗ *Tues., Wed., and Fri. 11–3, Thurs. 11–7, weekends noon–4.*

⑯ Munch-Muséet (Munch Museum). In 1940, four years before his death, Edvard Munch bequeathed a vast collection of his works of art to the city; the museum opened in 1963, the centennial of his birth. Although only a fraction of its 22,000 items—books, paintings, drawings, prints, sculptures, and letters—are on display, you can still get a sense of the tortured expressionism that was to have such an effect on European painting. ⊠ *Tøyengt. 53* ☏ 23241400 ⊕ *www.munch.museum.no* ⊗ *June–mid-Sept., daily 10–6; mid-Sept.–May, Tues.–Fri. and Sat. 10–4, Sun. 11–5* Ⓜ *Bus 29 from Rådhuset or T-bane from Nationaltheatret to Tøyen in northeast Oslo.*

Fodor'sChoice ★

⑧ Muséet for Samtidskunst (Museum of Contemporary Art). Housed in the Norwegian art nouveau former Bank of Norway building, the museum displays Norwegian and international contemporary art. There are also a library, a cafeteria, and a bookstore. ✉ *Bankpl. 4* ☏ *22862210* ⊕ *www.museet.no* ◷ *Tues., Wed., and Fri. 10–5, Thurs. 10–8, Sat. 11–4, Sun. 11–5. Guided tours weekends at noon.*

❸ Nasjonalgalleriet (The National Gallery). Norway's largest public gallery houses a selection of Norwegian and international art, up to 1945. The major works of the National Romantic period or "golden period" of Norwegian painting are emphasized here. The collection includes Edvard Munch's iconic painting, *The Scream.* ✉ *Universitetsgt. 13* ☏ *22200404* ⊕ *www.nasjonalgalleriet.no* ◷ *Mon., Wed., and Fri., 10–6, Thurs. 10–8, weekends 10–4.*

❹ Nationaltheatret (National Theater). Statues of Bjørnstjerne Bjørnson, the nationalist poet who wrote Norway's anthem, and Henrik Ibsen, who wrote the plays *Peer Gynt, A Doll's House,* and *Hedda Gabler,* watch over Nationaltheatret. Ibsen worried that his works, packed with allegory, myth, and sociological and emotional angst, might not have appeal outside Norway. As it happened, they changed the face of modern theater around the world. ✉ *Stortingsgt. 15* ☏ *22412710* ⊕ *www. nationaltheatret.no.*

★ ☺ ⓭ Norsk Folkemuseum (Norwegian Folk Museum). Take the ferry from Rådhusbryggen (City Hall Wharf) and walk up a well-marked road to see sod-roofed farmhouses that have been collected from all over the country and reassembled here. A whole section of 19th-century Oslo was also moved here, as was a 12th-century wooden stave church. ✉ *Museumsvn. 10* ☏ *22123700* ⊕ *www.norskefolke.museum.no* ◷ *Mid-Sept.–mid-Dec., weekdays 11–3, weekends 11–4; mid-May–mid-Sept., daily 10–6.*

Norsk Sjøfartsmuseum (Norwegian Maritime Museum). The story of coastal Norway, its culture and traditions, is explored at this museum. Exhibits have a maritime theme, from fishing boats and paintings of fishermen braving rough seas, to intricate ship models. Take time to experience the coast and sea in Ivo Caprino's breathtaking, supervideograph, panoramic movie *The Ocean: A Way of Life.* ✉ *Bygdøynesveien 37* ☏ *24114150* ⊕ *www.norsk-sjofartsmuseum.no* ◷ *Oct.–mid-May, Fri.–Wed. 10:30–4, Thurs. 10:30–6; mid-May–Sept., daily 10–6.*

Oslo Bymuseum (Oslo City Museum). Oslo has changed and evolved greatly over its 1,000-year history. In Frogner Manor House, the two-floor meandering exhibition covers Oslo's prominence in 1050, the Black Death that came in 1349, the great fire of 1624 and subsequent rebuilding, and the urban development of the 20th century. Guided tours, a multimedia show, and city walks are available. ✉ *Frognerveien 67* ☏ *23284170* ⊕ *www.oslobymuseum.no* ◷ *Jan.–June, Tues.–Fri, 10–4, weekends 11–4; July–Sept., Tues.–Fri. 10–6, weekends 11–5; Oct.–Dec., Tues.–Sun. 10–4.*

❻ Oslo Domkirke (Oslo Cathedral). Consecrated in 1697 and subsequently much renovated, this rather austere cathedral is modest compared with those of other European capitals. The interior, however, is rich with treasures such as the baroque carved-wood altarpiece and pulpit. The ceiling frescoes by Hugo Lous Mohr were done after WWII. ✉ *Stortorvet 1* ☏ *23314600* ◷ *Daily noon–6.*

★ ⓬ Rådhuset (City Hall). Designed by architects Arnstein Arneberg and Magnus Poulsson, the impressive redbrick City Hall opened officially on May 15, 1950. The courtyard friezes portraying scenes from Norwegian folklore literally pale in comparison with the marble-floored inside halls, where murals and frescoes bursting with color depict daily life, historical events, and Resistance activities in Norway. The elegant main hall has been the venue for the Nobel Peace Prize ceremony since 1991. ⊠ *Rådhuspl.* ☎ *23461600* ⊘ *May–Sept., daily 9–5, Oct.–Apr., daily 9–4. Guided tours weekdays at 10, noon, and 2 (daily during June and July).*

⓫ **Stenersenmuséet** (The Stenersen Museum). The museum has a collection of Norwegian art from 1850 to 1970, with works by Amaldus Neilsen, Ludvig O. Ravensberg, and Rolf E. Stenersen. In addition, there are special exhibitions, generally in photography and Nordic modern art. ⊠ *Munkedamsv. 15* ☎ *23493600* ⊕ *www.stenersen.museum.no* ⊘ *Tues. and Thurs. 11–7; Wed., Fri., and weekends, 11–5.*

❺ **Stortinget** (Parliament). Built in 1866 by Swedish architect Emil Langelot, this bow-front, yellow-brick building is open to visitors by request when Parliament is not in session. A guide will take you around the frescoed interior and into the debating chamber. ⊠ *Karl Johans Gt. 22* ☎ *22313050* ⊘ *Guided tours July and Aug.; public gallery, weekdays when Parliament is in session.*

⓳ **Vigelandsparken** and **Vigelandsmusset** (Vigeland's Park, also known as Frogner Park and Vigelands Museum). Called Frogner Park by locals, Vigelandsparken is Oslo's most-visited attraction. It has 212 bronze, granite, and wrought-iron sculptures by Gustav Vigeland (1869–1943). Two works in particular continue to spark metaphysical ruminations: *Wheel of Life,* a circle in stone depicting the stages of human life, and *The Monolith,* nearly 50 feet high and covered with more than 100 linked human forms. The nearby Vigeland Museum, open-air restaurants, tennis courts, and swimming pools provide additional diversions. ⊠ *Vigelandsparken, Kirkevn. and Middelthunsgt.* ☎ *22542530* Ⓜ *Trikk 12 or 15 or T-bane train 1, 2, 3, 4, or 5 to Majorstuen.*

★ ⓮ **Vikingskiphuset** (Viking Ship Museum). Three remarkably intact 9th-century ships last used by Vikings on the shores of the Oslofjord as royal burial chambers are the treasures of this cathedral-like museum. Also on display are riches that accompanied the royal bodies on their last voyage. The ornate craftsmanship evident in the ships and jewelry dispels any notion that the Vikings were skilled only in looting and pillaging. ⊠ *Huk Av. 35* ☎ *22135280* ⊕ *www.uio.no/vikingskiphuset* ⊘ *May–Oct., daily 9–6; Oct.–May, daily 11–4.*

Elsewhere in Oslo

⓴ **Holmenkollbakken Skimuseum and Jump Tower.** Distinctive in the city's skyline, Oslo's Holmenkollen ski jump holds a special place in the hearts of Norwegians. The 1892 ski jump was rebuilt for the 1952 Winter Olympics and is still a popular site for international competitions like the Holmenkollen Ski Festival in March. The Holmenkollen National Ski Arena is open year-round. The ski museum, carved into rock at its base, traces the history of the sport back 4,000 years. You can take a trip up to the observation tower. The scenic half-hour subway ride from downtown Oslo to the ski jump sweeps up behind the city. ⊠ *Kongevn. 5* ☎ *22923200* ⊕ *www.skiforeningen.no* ⊘ *Jan.–Apr. and Oct.–Dec., daily 10–4; May and Sept., daily 10–5; June–Aug., daily 9–8* Ⓜ *Frognerseter/Holmenkollen T-bane train from Nationaltheatret, to Holmenkollen; walk uphill to the jump.*

Where to Eat

The Oslo restaurant scene is vibrant. The city's chefs have embraced international trends but at the same time take pride in traditional Norwegian cuisine. Traditional or contemporary, international or gourmet, food in Oslo is often based on produce from the country's waters and farmland. Menus change daily, weekly, or seasonally in many Oslo restaurants.

For details and price-category information, *see* Eating & Drinking *in* Norway A to Z.

★ $$$$ ✕ **Bagatelle.** Chef and owner Eyvind Hellstrøm has established an international reputation for his modern Norwegian French-inspired cuisine. The who's who of Norwegian society dine at his restaurant, where the three-, five-, and seven-course menus change daily. The elegant interior is formal, and complemented by the impeccable service. ✉ *Bygdøy allé 3* ☎ *22446397* ☰ *AE, DC, MC, V* ☺ *Closed Sun., and mid-July–mid-Aug. No lunch.*

★ $$$$ ✕ **Oro.** A Mediterranean restaurant, this is where chef Terje Ness practices her culinary artistry. Gourmet diners book months in advance for the Taste of Oro, a 7- or 12-course dinner. Dishes include grilled scallops with eggplant and orange, turbot with lentils and capers, and for dessert Chocolate Oro, chocolate mousse with passion fruit topped with gold leaf. Next door is **Plata,** a chocolate-brown-colored Spanish tapas bar. There's also a delicatessen selling top-quality products. ✉ *Tordenskjolds Gt. 6* ☎ *23010240* ☝ *Reservations essential* ☰ *AE, DC, MC, V* ☺ *Closed Sun. No lunch Sat.*

★ $$$–$$$$ ✕ **Lofoten Fiskerestaurant.** Named for the Lofoten Islands off Norway's northwest coast, this is one of Oslo's best fish restaurants. It has views of the harbor, and a minimalist interior. From January through March, try the cod served with its own liver and roe; from April through September, the shellfish; and from October through December, the lutefisk. ✉ *Stranden 75, Aker Brygge* ☎ *22830808* ☰ *AE, DC, MC, V.*

$$–$$$ ✕ **Bistro Brocade.** Walk into this new bistro in Oslo's hip Grünerløkka neighborhood, and the mood is unmistakably French. Edith Piaf's singing and French accordion music drift by. Glossy, dark wood glistens on wall paneling and tabletops. Antique brass Lyon lamps cast soft, romantic light. The menu is classic French with a few nods to Norway. ✉ *Thorvald Meyers Gt. 40* ☎ *22654752* ☰ *AE, DC, MC, V.*

$$–$$$ ✕ **A Touch of France.** Two blocks behind the Parliament, this inviting wine bistro is straight out of Paris. The waiters' long, white aprons; the art nouveau decor; old French posters; and closely packed tables all add to the illusion. The tempting menu includes a steaming hot bouillabaisse. ✉ *Øvre Slottsgt. 16* ☎ *23100165* ☰ *AE, DC, MC, V.*

$–$$$ ✕ **Sushi & Wok.** Sushi bars have established themselves in Oslo, and this one at the city's harborfront is one of the finest. Among the recommended dishes are nigiri-sushi and makimono. Sushi Happy Hour, between 4 and 7 every evening, has three specially priced meals. ✉ *Bryggetorget, 7 Aker Brygge* ☎ *22836351* ☰ *DC, MC, V.*

$–$$ ✕ **Brasserie 45.** Overlooking the fountain on Karl Johans Gate, this candlelighted brasserie has a Scandinavian feel to match its cuisine. Fish dishes such as grilled salmon and catfish are its signatures. ✉ *Karl Johans Gt. 45 (upstairs)* ☎ *22413400* ☰ *AE, DC, MC, V.*

★ $–$$ ✕ **Dinner.** The bland name belies the fact that this is one of the best places in Oslo for Chinese food, as well as dishes that combine Norwegian and Cantonese styles. The three-course Peking duck is a specialty. Try the platter of seafood in chili-pepper sauce. ✉ *Stortingsgt. 22* ☎ *23100466* ☰ *AE, DC, MC, V* ☺ *No lunch.*

$ ✕ **Kaffistova.** Norwegian homemade cooking is served cafeteria style at this downtown restaurant. Everyday specials in generous portions include soup and a selection of entrées, including a vegetarian dish. ✉ *Rosenkrantz Gt. 8* ☎ *22429974* ☰ *AE, DC, MC, V.*

Where to Stay

Lodging in the capital is expensive. Prices for downtown accommodations are high, even for bed-and-breakfasts, although just about all hotels have weekend, holiday, and summer rates (25%–50% reductions). Taxes and service charges are included, unless otherwise noted. Breakfast is usually included also, but be sure to ask before booking your room. If you arrive and need a hotel the same day, ask about last-minute prices, which are generally discounted. The helpful accommodations bureau of the **Touristinformation** (⇨ Visitor Information *in* Oslo Essentials) in the Oslo Central Station can help you find a room; apply in person and pay a fee of NKr 20. For details and price-category information, *see* Lodging *in* Norway A to Z.

★ $$$–$$$$ **Radisson SAS Plaza Hotel.** Striking on the Oslo skyline, this is Northern Europe's largest hotel. It has a reputation for excellent service, and there's easy access to buses, trains, and airport transportation. Reserve a room on the top floor for magnificent, bird's-eye views of the city. ✉ *Sonja Henies pl. 3, 0134* ☎ *22058000* 🖷 *22058010* ⊕ *www.radissonsas.com* ✏ *673 rooms, 20 suites* ⚑ *2 restaurants, indoor pool, bar* ⊟ *AE, DC, MC, V.*

★ $$$–$$$$ **Rica Hotel Bygdøy Allé.** Although in a big city, this hotel is intimate and personal. One of its main attractions is its location in the Frogner neighborhood, within walking distance of Vigelandsparken and close to the National Gallery, the Royal Palace, Aker Brygge, exclusive shops, and cafés. Guest rooms are individually decorated. ✉ *Bygdøy Allé 53, 0265* ☎ *23085800* 🖷 *23085808* ⊕ *www.rica.no* ✏ *57 rooms* ⚑ *Restaurant, bar* ⊟ *AE, DC, MC, V.*

★ $$–$$$$ **Clarion Royal Christiania Hotel.** What was once bare-bones housing for 1952 Olympians is now a luxury hotel. Although the original plain exterior has been retained, inside many rooms were renovated in 2001 using feng shui principles. The new rooms have white walls that contrast with the mahogany furniture. ✉ *Biskop Gunnerus Gt. 3, 0106* ☎ *23108000* 🖷 *23108080* ⊕ *www.royalchristiania.no* ✏ *505 rooms, 91 suites* ⚑ *Restaurant, indoor pool, bar* ⊟ *AE, DC, MC, V.*

$$–$$$$ **Frogner House.** In the heart of Oslo's West End, this charming, small hotel is popular among business travelers. The five-story redbrick and stone building went up in 1890 as an apartment house and now sits inconspicuously amid rows of other turn-of-the-20th-century town houses. It has a reputation for its quiet rooms, which even have TVs with Internet and e-mail access. ✉ *Skovvn. 8, 0257* ☎ *22560056* 🖷 *22560500* ⊕ *www.frogner-house.com* ✏ *60 rooms, 8 suites* ⊟ *AE, DC, MC, V.*

$$–$$$ **Gabelshus.** With only a discreet sign above the door, this ivy-covered brick house in a posh residential area is one of Oslo's most personal hotels. The lounges are filled with antiques, some in the National Romantic style, but the rooms are plain. ✉ *Gabelsgt. 16, 0272* ☎ *22552260* 🖷 *23276560* ⊕ *www.gabelshus.no* ✏ *43 rooms* ⊟ *AE, DC, MC, V.*

$$ **First Hotel Millennium.** This boutique hotel has its own comfortable, downtown chic. All the simple dark blue, green, and yellow decorated rooms have bathtubs. Several rooms are geared toward women and come with a bathrobe, skin products, and women's magazines. The main-floor lounge has games, a music room, Internet access, and a library. The restaurant-bar, Primo, serves an impressive, international menu including quail and swordfish. ✉ *Tollbugt. 25, 0157* ☎ *21022800* 🖷 *21022830* ⊕ *www.firsthotels.com* ✏ *112 rooms with bath, 10 suites* ⚑ *Restaurant, bar* ⊟ *AE, DC, MC, V.*

★ $$ **Rainbow Cecil.** A short walk from Parliament, this modern hotel is a less expensive, centrally located option. Although the rooms are basic, they are perfectly suited to the active, on-the-go traveler. The second floor opens onto a plant-filled atrium, the hotel's "activity center." In the morning it's a breakfast room, but in the afternoon it becomes a lounge, serving coffee, juice, and fresh fruit, with newspapers available in many languages. ⊠ *Stortingsgt. 8, 0130* ☏ *23314800* 🖷 *23314850* ⊕ *www.rainbow-hotels.no* ⤵ *112 rooms, 2 suites* 🖃 *AE, DC, MC, V.*

$-$$ 🖾 **Cochs pensjonat.** A stone's throw from the Royal Palace, this no-frills guest house offers reasonably priced lodging in comfy, but rather spartan rooms. All rooms have TVs, but no phone. Most of the 88 rooms have en suite bathrooms; some have kitchenettes. No meals are served. ⊠ *Parkvn. 25, 0350* ☏ *23332400* 🖷 *23332410* ⊕ *www.virtualoslo.com/cochs_pensjonat* ⤵ *88 rooms* 🖃 *MC, V.*

$-$$ 🖾 **Teaterbåten Innvik.** A B&B on a boat docked at Oslo's Bjørvika provides alternative, spartan accommodations for budget travelers. Nordic Black Theater owns and operates the boat, and aspiring actors often work on board. In summer there are sail-in movies, an outdoor café, and live music. ⊠ *Bjørvika, Oslo, 0166* ☏ *24103000* ⊕ *www.msinnvik.no* ⚖ *Restaurant* 🖃 *AE, DC, MC, V.*

$ 🖾 **Haraldsheim.** Named for King Harald, Oslo's hilltop hostel is Europe's largest. Opened in 1954, it has maintained an old-fashioned, typical Scandinavian style. Most of the large rooms have their own toilet and shower, and have four beds. Bring your own sheets or rent them here. A supermarket is close by and local transit is easily accessible. ⊠ *Haraldsheimvn. 4, 0409* ☏ *22222965* 🖷 *22221025* ⤵ *71 rooms, 40 with bath* 🖃 *MC, V.*

Nightlife & the Arts

The Arts

Considering the city's small population, Oslo has a surprisingly rich arts scene. Check the English-language monthly *What's On in Oslo,* available at the Touristinformation (⇨ Visitor Information *in* Oslo Essentials).

FILM All films are screened in the original language with Norwegian subtitles. Oslo has one of Europe's best cinema collections, with 30 screens. Call ☏ 82030000 for schedules for most of the city's theaters. For alternative and classic films, try **Cinemateket** (⊠ Dronningensgt. 16 ☏ 22474505), the city's only independent cinema.

MUSIC **Oslo Konserthus** (Oslo Concert Hall) (⊠ Munkedamsvn. 14 ☏ 23113100 ⊕ www.oslokonserthus.no) is the home of the Oslo Philharmonic. A smaller hall in the same building has folk dancing, held Monday and Thursday at 9 PM in July and August. At **Den Norske Opera** (The Norwegian Opera House; ⊠ Storgt. 23 ☏ 23315000), performances usually start at 7:30; it's closed in July and August. **Herr Nilsen** (⊠ C. J. Hambros pl. 5 ☏ 22335405) is an atmospheric bar with some of the best jazz acts in Norway. **Oslo Spektrum** (⊠ Sonja Henies pl. 2 ☏ 22052900) is a large indoor show and concert venue. **Rockefeller/John Dee** (⊠ Torggt. 16 ☏ 22203232) has concerts featuring well-known pop and rock acts.

THEATER Winter is *the* cultural season, when the **Nationaltheatret** (National Theater; ⇨ Exploring Oslo) presents modern plays (all in Norwegian), classics, and a good sampling of Ibsen. The modern theater complex **Det Norske Teatret** (The Norwegian Theater; ⊠ Kristian IV's Gt. 8 ☏ 22424344) has musicals and plays (all in Norwegian).

Nightlife

NIGHTCLUBS, **Barock-Restauranthuset** (⊠ Universitetsgt. 26 ☏ 22424420), complete
BARS & PUBS with elegant chandeliers and blaring techno-pop, is where Oslo's young

and beautiful people choose to dance. Media people and students hang out at **Galleriet** (✉ Kristian IV's Gt. 12 ☎ 22422936), a three-story disco with live music sessions on the third floor. **Karl Johans Gate** is a lively neighborhood into the wee hours, with a good selection of music cafés and clubs, as well as more conventional nightspots. Dress codes apply at **Lipp** (✉ Olav V's Gt. 2 ☎ 22824060), a popular upscale predinner-drinks bar (for people over 24); Lipp's restaurant serves international cuisine. **Smuget** (✉ Rosenkrantz Gt. 22 ☎ 22425262) is a combination discotheque and bar with live rock and blues bands most nights of the week.

Shopping

Many of the larger stores are in the pedestrian-only areas between Stortinget and the cathedral. Regular opening hours for shops are 10 until 5 or 6 on weekdays, 7 or 8 on Thursday, and 2 or 3 on Saturday. Check out the many shops and department stores on **Majorstuen** and **Bogstadveien–Hegdehaugsveien;** Majorstuen starts at the T-bane station of the same name and Bogstadveien runs down to Parkveien and the castle. **Aker Brygge,** on the waterfront, used to house Oslo's shipyards; it's now a self-contained complex of theaters, cinemas, entertainment, 35 restaurants, clubs, and bars, as well as 60 shops, food stores, cafés, and galleries. **Stortorvet** has several department stores, a flower market, and small lanes full of shops and boutiques. **Karl Johans Gate** has been the city's main street for more than 100 years. Beginning at Oslo Central Station and running to the Royal Palace, it has a vast selection of Norwegian and international shops. Near Nationaltheatret station, **Vikaterassen** has 60 shops, 18 restaurant-cafés, two nightclubs, Cinema Vika Kino, the Stenersen Museum, Oslo Konserthus, and lots of parking. **Grünerløkka,** often referred as Oslo's Greenwich Village, is considered very hip and has interesting restaurants, shops, galleries, and cafés.

Department Stores & Malls

Byporten (✉ Jernbanetorget 6 ☎ 23362160), open weekdays 10–9 and Saturday 10–6, is a modern complex with a number of eateries and 75 shops, including a well-stocked delicatessen and upscale housewares stores. **Glasmagasinet** (✉ Stortorvet 9 ☎ 22908900), open weekdays 10–7 and Saturday 10–6, has a large assortment of wares in 50 different stores, including souvenirs, glassware, and silver and pewter jewelry. Oslo's largest shopping mall, **Oslo City** (✉ opposite Central Station ☎ 22938050), open weekdays 9–9 and Saturday 9–7, has more than 100 stores and businesses, including a bank, a travel agency, and a grocery store on the lower level. **Paléet** (✉ Karl Johans Gt. 37–43 ☎ 22417086), open weekdays 10–8 and Saturday 10–5, is an elegant indoor shopping center with 45 shops and 12 restaurants. **Steen & Strøm** (✉ Kongensgt. 23 ☎ 22100250), open weekdays 10–7 and Saturday 10–6, is an exclusive department store with six floors and 58 different shops plus a cafeteria.

Side Trips

Høvikodden

By the Oslo Fjord, 15 minutes from the city center, **Henie-Onstad Kunstsenter** (Henie-Onstad Museum of Modern Art) has Norway's largest collection of international modern art. It was a gift from the late Norwegian skater Sonja Henie and her husband, shipowner Niels Onstad. The impressive permanent collection of works include Munch, Picasso, Bonnard, and Matisse. Guided tours are available. Added attractions are a library, sculpture park, museum shop, and Kafe Bølgen & Moi. ✉ *About 12 km (7 mi) southwest of Oslo on E18* ☎ 67804880 ⊕ *www. henieonstad.no* ⊙ *Tues.–Thurs. 10–9, Fri.–Mon. 11–6.*

Vinterbro

🎡 **Tusenfryd** is Norway's largest amusement park, with more than 50 attractions, including carousels, a roller coaster, games, an outdoor stage, shops, and restaurants. Don't miss **Vikingelandet** (Viking Land), which re-creates life during the time of the Vikings, with trading centers, boat-building, a blacksmith, jewelry making, and farm animals. One of the "Vikings" will also help you try your talent as an archer, or you can join "Leif Eriksson" on an expedition in the depths of a mountain cave. ⊠ *1433 Vinterbro, about 20 km (12 mi) southeast of Oslo on E18* ☎*64976497* ⊙ *Tusenfryd May–early June and mid-Aug.–mid-Sept., weekends 10:30–7; early June–mid-Aug., daily 10:30–7. Vikingelandet 2 wks in mid-June, weekdays 10:30–3, weekends 1–7; last wk in June–mid-Aug., daily 1–7.*

Lillehammer

At the top of the long finger of Lake Mjøsa, Lillehammer is reached by train from the Central Station in about two hours. A paddle steamer, D/S *Skibladner*, travels the length of the lake (six hours each way) in summer, making several stops. At the site of the 1994 Winter Olympics, Lillehammer's Olympic bobsled track, **Hunderfossen** (⊠ about 5 km [3 mi] north of town), is open for runs; you can book at the **Lillehammer Tourist Office** (⊠ Lilletorget ☎ 61259299 or 81548170). Lillehammer 🎡 is also home of **Maihaugen,** one of the largest open-air museums in northern Europe. More than 100 old buildings have been relocated here, along with workshop interiors, antique tools, and the like. ⊠ *Maihaugvn. 1* ☎ *61288900* ⊕ *www.maihaugen.museum.no* ⊙ *Mid-May–May 31 and mid-Aug.–Sept., daily 10–5; June–mid-Aug., daily 9–6.*

Oslo Essentials

AIRPORTS & TRANSFERS
Gardermoen Airport, 37 km (23 mi) north of Oslo, is Oslo's main airport.
🛈 **Gardermoen Airport** ☎ 81550250 flight information ⊕ www.osl.no.

TRANSFERS Taxis between downtown and Gardermoen cost between NKr 700 and NKr 800. Flybussen (airport bus) takes about 40 minutes from Galleri Oslo shopping center, stopping at Jernbanetorget (Oslo Central Station); the fare is NKr 55. The high-speed Airport Express Train carries passengers from Central Station to Gardermoen in 20 minutes; a one-way fare is NKr 120.
🛈 **Flybussen** ☎ 82054301.

CONSULATES
🛈 Australia ⊠ Jernbanetorget 2, 0106 Oslo ☎ 22479170.
🛈 Ireland ⊠ Haakon VII's Gt. 1, 5 etg., 0283 Oslo ☎ 22017200.
🛈 New Zealand ⊠ Billingstadsletta 19 B, 1396 Billingstad ☎ 66775330.
🛈 South Africa ⊠ Drammensvn. 88C, 0271 Oslo ☎ 22273220.

EMERGENCIES
🛈 Doctors & Dentists **Dentist** ☎ 22673000.
🛈 Emergency Services **Ambulance and Medical Assistance** ☎ 113. **Fire, Accidents, and Serious Pollution** ☎ 110. **Police-Immediate Assistance** ☎ 112.
🛈 Hospitals **Oslo Kommunale Legevakt** (Municipal Medical Emergency Service) ☎ 22118080.
🛈 24-hour Pharmacies **Jernbanetorgets Apotek** ☎ 22412482.

ENGLISH-LANGUAGE MEDIA

Bookstores **ARK Qvist** ✉ Drammensvn. 16 ☎ 22542600. **Nomaden** ✉ Uranienborgvn 4 ☎ 22562530. **Norli** ✉ Universitetgt. 24 ☎ 22004300. **Tanum** ✉ Karl Johans Gt. 37–41 ☎ 22411100.

TAXIS

Taxis can be hailed on the street when the roof light is on, found at taxi stands, or ordered by phone, though during peak hours you may have to wait. Do not accept rides in unlicensed taxis.

OsloTaxi ☎ Sentralen 02323.

TOURS

CITY TOURS Båtservice Sightseeing has a bus tour, five cruises, and one combination tour. HMK Sightseeing offers several bus tours in and around Oslo. Starting at noon and continuing at 45-minute intervals until 10 PM, the Oslo Train, which looks like a chain of dune buggies, leaves Aker Brygge for a 30-minute ride around the town center. Ask at the Norway Information Centre (⇨ Visitor Information).

Båtservice Sightseeing ✉ Rådhusbryggen 3 ☎ 23356890 ⊕ www.boatsightseeing. com. **HMK Sightseeing** ✉ Hegdehaugsvn. 4 ☎ 23157300 ⊕ www.hmk.no.

PRIVATE GUIDES The Touristinformation can provide an authorized city guide for your own private tour. OsloTaxi also gives private tours. Or Guideservice A/S is another option.

Guideserve A/S ✉ Akershusstranda 35 ☎ 22427020 ⊕ www.guideservice.no.

SPECIAL- INTEREST TOURS The Touristinformation arranges four- to eight-hour motor safaris through the forests surrounding Oslo. Sightseeing by helicopter with Pegasus helicopter is an unforgettable way to see the Norwegian capital.

Pegasus helicopter ✉ Gardermoen Vest, 2061 Gardermoen ☎ 64819200 ⊕ www. pegasus-as.no.

TRAIN TRAVEL

Trains on international or domestic long-distance and express routes arrive at Oslo's Central Station. Suburban trains depart from the Central Station, Stortinget, and Nationaltheatret stations.

Central Station ✉ East of Strandgt.

TRANSPORTATION AROUND OSLO

If you're using public transportation only occasionally, you can get tickets (NKr 20) at bus and subway (T-bane) stops. The Dags Kort (Day Card) and the 7-Dagers Kort (seven-day card) are valid for unlimited travel on all public transport, including the summer ferries to Bygdøy, Hovedøya, Langøya, and Gressholmen. The Flexikort gives you eight rides on the subway, bus, or *trikk* (the name given to Oslo's extensive tram network), including transfers. The tickets vary in price and can be purchased from attendants, machines, or Trafikanten. For information on public transportation, call Trafikanten.

Trafikanten ✉ Jernbanetorvet 1, by Oslo Central Station ☎ 81500176.

TRAVEL AGENCIES

Local Agents **Bennett** ✉ Linstowsgt. 6 ☎ 22597800. **Berg-Hansen Reisebyrå** ✉ Kongensgt. 6 ☎ 81550290. **Winge** American Express ✉ Karl Johans Gt. 33–35 ☎ 22004500.

VISITOR INFORMATION

The Oslo Pass—valid for one, two, or three days—entitles you to free admission to museums, sights, and swimming pools; public transit within Zone 4 (not valid on night bus/tram); free parking in municipal parking lots; and discounts for various tours, shops, and services. You can purchase the card at Oslo's tourist information offices and hotels. A one-day card costs NKr 190; two-day, NKr 280; three-day, NKr 370. These prices cover a family of two adults and two children.

🎏 **Nortra** (Norwegian Travel Association) ✉ Drammensvn. 40, Postboks 2893, Sentrum, 0230 Oslo ☎22925200. **Oslo Promotion–Oslo Visitors and Convention Bureau** ✉Tourist Information by City Hall or Oslo Central Station ☎ 23117880 ⊕ www.visitoslo.com.

THE NORTH SEA ROAD

Route E18 parallels the coast of Sørlandet, or Southern Norway, south of Oslo toward the sun-kissed summer capital Kristiansand. Beyond the city, the coast curves west and north to Stavanger. After Flekkefjord, follow the coast road (Route 44) past the fishing port of Egersund to Ogna, and then on to Stavanger. Sørlandet's whaling business has given way to canneries, lumber, paper production, and petrochemicals. Yet the beauty of this 608-km (380-mi) route remains, and you'll find seaside towns, rocky headlands, and stretches of forest. Travel between towns takes less than an hour in most cases. South of Stavanger is flat and stony Jæren, the largest expanse of level terrain in this mountainous country. The mild climate and the absence of good harbors caused the people here to turn to agriculture, and the miles of stone walls are a testament to their labor. It is also possible to reach Stavanger on an inland route through Telemark.

Drammen

Drammen lies on the bank of the wide Drammen River, 45 km (28 mi) long and popular for its salmon and trout fishing. The river was the city's main street during the centuries when the production of wood products (paper and cellulose) was the chief industry in Drammen. From May 10 through August you can join a five-hour guided tour aboard the 114-year-old sailing ship **Christiane** (☎ 95887560 tours), which sails south from Drammen to the attractive little village of Holmsbu. Holmsbu has a restaurant overlooking the small harbor and a number of attractive arts-and-crafts shops.

The center of Drammen has a great variety of shops and restaurants. **Bragernes Torg** is home to a sizable farmers' market. This large square is lined by several buildings dating from just after 1866, when a huge fire devastated the entire district. **Drammens Teatret,** also built after the great fire, has an impressive collection of ceiling paintings and crystal chandeliers. Designed by Emil Langlet, it was completed in 1870 and is a working theater and conference venue.

$$ ✕ **Spiraltoppen Café.** You'll find excellent views and food here atop Bragernes Hill. ✉ *Bragernesåsen* ☎ *32263761* ⌂ *Reservations not accepted* ⊟ *AE, DC, MC, V.*

$$ 🏨 **Rica Park Hotel.** This comfortable hotel has a central location close to the station. ✉ *Gamle Kirkepl. 3, 3019* ☎ *32263600* 🖷 *32263777* ⊕ *www.rica.no* 🛏 *96 rooms, 2 suites* ⌂ *2 restaurants* ⊟ *AE, DC, MC, V.*

Åsgårdstrand

Edvard Munch spent seven summers in **Munchs lille hus** (Munch's Little House), his summer house and studio. Now a museum, it was here that he painted *Girls on the Bridge* and earned a reputation as a ladies' man. ✉*Munchsgt.* ☎*33082131* ⊙ *May and Sept., weekends 11–7; June–Aug., Tues.–Sun. 11–7.*

Tønsberg

Tønsberg was founded in AD 871; it is the site of the Oseberg Viking ship, discovered in 1903. Shipping, commerce, and culture prospered

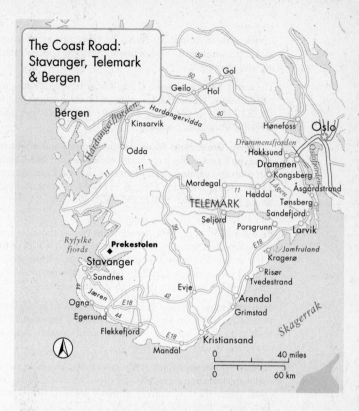

The Coast Road: Stavanger, Telemark & Bergen

in Tønsberg from the Viking Age until the rise of Oslo as Norway's capital during the 14th century. During the 1700s, Tønsberg had a resurgence as a thriving whaling port. Today, on steep **Slottsfjellet** (Castle Hill; ⊠ Next to Tønsberg train station), the ruins of **Tønsberghus**, an extensive fortress and abbey, evoke the Middle Ages, when Tønsberg was the administrative center for the Norwegian kings. A model of Tønsberghus stands in the lookout tower. The tower also affords a panoramic view of Oslo fjord and the surrounding mountains.

Sandefjord

Attractive Sandefjord is a port that served as the base for the Norwegian whaling fleet until after World War II, when large-scale competition from the Soviet Union and Japan made the operation uneconomical. The port remains a busy depot for timber shipping.

★ $$–$$$$ ✕ **Ludl's Gourmet Odd Ivar Solvold.** Norwegian celebrity chef Solvold has taken over chef Ludl's duties preparing fish specialties in one of the best restaurants outside Oslo. Solvold is a former three-time national culinary champion and it shows. He is famous for his seafood, so try his grilled crayfish, turbot, catfish, scallops, and mussels. ⊠ *Rådhusgt. 7* ☎ *33462741* ☐ *AE, DC, MC, V* ⊘ *Closed Sun.*

★ $$$ 🏨 **Rica Park Hotel.** The imposing Rica Park, one of the best hotels in Norway, overlooks Sandefjord's harbor. The rooms are large and comfortable, and the service is flawless. ⊠ *Strandpromenaden 9, 3200* ☎ *33447400* 🖷 *33447500* 🌐 *www.rica.no* ➪ *179 rooms* ⌂ *Restaurant* ☐ *AE, DC, MC, V.*

Larvik

Larvik is the terminus for ferries to Frederikshavn, Denmark. It once looked to whaling for its livelihood but now concentrates on lumbering and ferrying.

The **Larvik Sjøfarts Museum** (Larvik Maritime Museum), in the former customhouse, chronicles Larvik's seafaring history. ⊠ *Kirkestredet 5* 🕾 *33130404* ☉ *Mid-May–June and mid-Aug.–Sept., Sun. noon–5; July–mid-Aug., daily noon–5.*

$$ 🏨 **Quality Grand Hotel Farris.** Spotless rooms and attentive service are what you'll find at this large hotel overlooking the fjord. Sample the local fish soup and smoked meat platters in the hotel's restaurant. ⊠ *Storgt. 38–40, 3256* 🕾 *33187800* 🖷 *33187045* ⊕ *www.choice.no* 🛏 *88 rooms* ☖ *Restaurant* ☰ *AE, DC, MC, V.*

Arendal

Between 1850 and 1886, Arendal was one of the most important seafaring towns in Scandinavia. You can still discern a bit of that era in the tidy cottages and grandiose captains' houses within shouting distance of the docks. Explore Arendal's **Tyholmen Quarter,** the oldest part of the town, for a glimpse into this 19th-century world.

Arendals Rådhus (Arendal's City Hall) was created by the Danish architect Peder Krog Bonsach Jessen and constructed between 1812 and 1815. Built as a private home for one of Arendal's wealthy shipowners, it was converted to City Hall in 1844.

$$ ✕ **Madam Reiersen.** Good, traditional rustic fare is served at this informal waterfront restaurant. Reservations are essential on summer weekends, when there is a great atmosphere and live music. ⊠ *Nedre Tyholmsvn. 3* 🕾 *37021900* ☰ *AE, DC, MC, V.*

$$$$ 🏨 **Clarion Tyholmen Hotel.** This hotel is in the heart of the Old Town, which is filled with brightly painted houses. The views of the fjord are splendid. ⊠ *Teaterpl. 2, 4801* 🕾 *37026800* 🖷 *37026801* ⊕ *www. choice.no* 🛏 *60 rooms* ☖ *2 restaurants* ☰ *AE, DC, MC, V.*

Kristiansand

The largest town in Sørlandet, Kristiansand has important air, sea, road, and rail links. It was laid out in the 17th century in a grid pattern, with the imposing **Christiansholm Festning** (fort) guarding the eastern harbor approach.

☾ The open-air **Vest-Agder Fylkesmuseum** (County Museum) has 30 old buildings and farms rebuilt in the local style of the 18th and 19th centuries. ⊠ *Kongsgård, Rte. E18, east of Kristiansand* 🕾 *38090228* ⊕ *www. museumsnett.no/vafymuseum* ☉ *June–late Aug., Mon.–Sat. 10–6, Sun. noon–6; late Aug.–May, Sun. noon–5.*

The **Kristiansand Kanonmuseum** (Cannon Museum) shows the cannon that the occupying Germans rigged up during World War II. There are also bunkers with related military artifacts on display. ⊠ *South of town, off E39* 🕾 *38085090* ☉ *May–mid-June, Sept., and Oct., Thurs.–Sun. 11–6; mid-June–Aug., daily 11–6.*

☾ **Kristiansand Dyreparken** (Kristiansand Zoo) has five separate parks, including a water park (bring bathing suits and towels); a forested park; an entertainment park; a theme park; and a zoo, which contains an enclosure for Scandinavian animals such as wolves and moose, and a large breeding ground for Bactrian camels. The theme park, **Kardemomme By** (Cardamom Town), is named for a book by Norwegian illustrator and writer Thorbjørn Egner. A new attraction, My Africa, allows you to move along a bridge observing native savanna animals such as giraffe and zebras. The park is 11 km (6 mi) east of town. ⊠ *4609 Kardemomme By* ☎ *38049725* ⊕ *www.dyreparken.no* ⊠ *NKr 200* ⊙ *Mid-May–Sept., weekdays 10–7; Oct.–mid-May, daily 10–3:30.*

$$-$$$ ✕ **Sjøhuset.** This restaurant began life as a salt warehouse in 1892. The white-trimmed red building has since developed a well-earned reputation for its seafood. Take a summer seat on the patio and dine on fresh lobster. ⊠ *Østre Strandgt. 12a* ☎ *38026260* ⚓ *Reservations not accepted* ⊟ *AE, DC, MC, V.*

$$$-$$$$ ⬚ **Rica Dyreparken Hotel.** Built like Noah's Ark, this family-friendly hotel is designed to delight children of all ages. The animals in the neighboring park have inspired the interior design with tiger-stripe chairs, paw prints, and rooms named after them. Children have cozy bunk beds, their own playroom, and a cinema on board the ark. ⊠ *Dyreparken Kristiansand, 4609* ☎ *38146400* 🖷 *38146401* ⊕ *www. rica.no* ⟿ *160 rooms* ⚙ *Restaurant, bar* ⊟ *AE, DC, MC, V.*

Mandal

Norway's southernmost town is famous for its beach, salmon, and 18th- and 19th-century houses. Seafood lovers flock here for the shellfish festival held on the second weekend in August.

Flekkefjord

The road climbs and weaves its way through steep, wooded hills before descending to the fishing port of Flekkefjord, with its charming **Hollenderbyen,** or Dutch Quarter.

Ogna

Ogna is known for the stretch of unspoiled sandy beach that has inspired so many Norwegian artists, among them Kitty Kjelland.

Stavanger

Stavanger has always prospered from the riches of the sea. During the 19th century, it was the sardine capital of the world. A resident is a called a Siddis, from S(tavanger) plus *iddis,* which means "sardine label," the city's symbol. Since the discovery of oil in the North Sea in the 1960s, Stavanger has been at the center of the oil boom. Today, the cosmopolitan city is Norway's fourth largest, with a vibrant cultural life. Roam its cobblestone streets or harborfront and you're likely to spot many cozy cafés and fine restaurants, as well as lively clubs and pubs.

Stavanger's Anglo-Norman **Domkirke** (cathedral), next to the central market, was established in 1125 by the English bishop of Winchester. Norway and England had strong trading and ecclesiastical links throughout the Middle Ages. ⊠ *City center, next to pond, Breiavatnet.*

Ledaal is a fine patrician mansion where the royal family resides when visiting Stavanger. ⊠ *Eiganesvn. 45* ☎ *51520618* ⊕ *www.stavanger. museum.no* ⊙ *Mid-June–mid-Aug., daily 11–4; mid-Aug.–mid-June, Sun. 11–4.*

Resembling a shiny, offshore oil platform, the **Norsk Oljemuseum** explains how oil forms, its exploration, production, uses, and impact on Norway's economy and environment. Interactive multimedia exhibits accompany original artifacts, models, and films. The museum café serves delicious light meals. ⊠ *Kjeringholmen, Stavanger Havn* ☎ *51939300* ⊕ *www.norskoljemuseu.no* ⊙ *June–Sept. daily 10–7; Oct.–May, Mon.–Sat. 10–4, Sun. 10–4.*

Breidablikk manor house, designed by the architect Henrik Nissen, was built by a Norwegian shipping magnate in 1882. An outstanding example of Norwegian "Swiss-style" chalet architecture, the property has been perfectly preserved inside and out. The rich interiors, complete with antiques, give an idea of how a well-to-do family would have lived in the late 19th century. ⊠ *Eiganesvn. 40A* ☏ *51526035* ⊕ *www.stavanger. museum.no* ⊙ *Mid-June–mid-Aug., daily 11–4; mid-Aug.–mid-June, Sun. 11–4.*

The **Norsk Hermetikkmuseum** (Norwegian Canning Museum) in the heart of Old Stavanger is a reconstructed sardine factory that was in use between 1890 and 1920. ⊠ *Øvre Strandgt. 88A* ☏ *5184270089* ⊕ *www. stavanger.museum.no* ⊙ *Mid-June–mid-Aug., daily 11–4; early June and late Aug., Mon.–Thurs. 11–3, Sun. 11–4; Sept.–May, Sun. 11–4 or by appointment.*

The **Ryfylke fjords** north and east of Stavanger form the southern end of the fjord country. The city is a good base for exploring this region, with the "white fleet" of low-slung sea buses making daily excursions into even the most distant fjords of Ryfylke. Great for a heart-stopping view is **Prekestolen** (Pulpit Rock), a huge cube of rock with a vertical drop of 2,000 feet. You can join a tour to get here or you can do it on your own from mid-June to late August by taking the ferry from Fiskepiren across Hildefjorden to Tau, riding a bus to the Pulpit Rock Lodge, and walking 1½ to 2 hours to the rock.

$$–$$$$ ✕ **Craigs Kjøkken & Bar.** The Oklahoman proprietor Craig Whitson is known locally for his eccentric personality and panache. His wine and culinary expertise is apparent in his collection of more than 600 bottles of wine and his seasonal, eclectic menu, ranging from Mediterranean to Asian. ⊠ *Breitorget* ☏ *51939590* ⊕ *www.craigs.no* ⊟ *AE, DC, MC, V.*

$$–$$$$ ✕ **Straen Fiskerestaurant og Akevitt bar.** Facing Vågen quay, this fish restaurant is cozy, with white tablecloths and walls strewn with memorabilia. The most popular dishes are salmon soup, cream of shellfish soup, grilled monkfish, and lutefisk. Try the three-course meal of the day for the best value. Choose from the 30 aquavits to accompany your food. ⊠ *Nedre Strandgt. 15* ☏ *51843700* ⊕ *www.herlige-stavanger.com* ⊟ *AE, DC, MC, V.*

$–$$$ ✕ **N.B. Sørensens Dampskibsexpedition.** This historic wharf house was once the waiting room for steamships crossing the Atlantic to North America. Emigrants' tickets, weathered wood, nautical ropes, old photographs, and gaslights make you feel as though you're about to make the voyage yourself. Today it's a popular waterfront restaurant and bar known for its Norwegian and international menu. ⊠ *Skagen 26* ☏ *51843820* ⊕ *www.herlige-stavanger.com* ⊟ *AE, DC, MC, V.*

$$–$$$$ ▦ **Skagen Brygge Hotell.** A Stavanger symbol, this classic hotel's white wooden wharf houses are common on city postcards and photographs. Deep blue–accented, wood-beamed rooms have charming irregular shapes. Ask for a room facing the harbor and watch the world dock outside your window. ⊠ *Skagenkaien 30, 4004* ☏ *51850000* ⊟ *51850001* ⊕ *www.skagenbrygghotell.no* ⊰ *110 rooms, 2 suites* ⊟ *AE, DC, MC, V.*

The North Sea Road Essentials

BUS TRAVEL

Local buses cover the entire route, but they take much longer than the train. For details on fares and schedules, check with the tourist offices listed below or the Norway Information Centre in Oslo (⇨ Visitor Information *in* Oslo Essentials).

CAR TRAVEL

Driving gives you the chance to stop at coastal villages that are either not served by trains or have only sporadic service. The route is simple: E18 as far as Flekkefjord, then Route 44 to Stavanger.

TOURS

Several special summer guided tours operate in and around Stavanger, Lysefjorden, and Preikestølen. Fjordhopping allows hopping on and off tourist ferries and express boats in Lysefjorden for two days for 200 NKr. **Rødne Clipper Fjord Sightseeing** ⊠ Skagenkaien 18 ☎ 51895202 ⊕ www.rodne. no. **Fjordhopping** ⊕ www.fjordhopping.com. **FjordTours Panorama** ⊠ Brønngt. 95 ☎ 51537340 ⊕ www.fjordpanorama.no.

TRAIN TRAVEL

The Sørland line leaves from Oslo Central Station and goes all the way to Stavanger via Kristiansand. It has five departures daily to Kristiansand; three continue to Stavanger. The Oslo–Drammen stretch is an engineering feat that includes Norway's longest tunnel, an 11-km (7-mi) bore through sheer rock.

VISITOR INFORMATION

Arendal ⊠ Friholmsgt. 1 ☎ 37005544. **Drammen** ⊠ Rådhuset ☎ 32806210. **Destinasjon-Sørlandet Kristiansand** ⊠ Vestre Strandgt. 32 ☎ 38121314 ⊕ www.sorlandet. com. **Larvik** ⊠ Storgt. 48 ☎ 33139100. **Mandal** ⊠ Bryggetgt. ☎ 38278300. **Stavanger** ⊠ Rosenkildetorget 1 ☎ 51859200 ⊕ www.visitStavanger.com. **Tønsberg** ⊠ Nedre Langgt. 36B ☎ 33310220.

THROUGH TELEMARK TO BERGEN

Bergen is Norway's second-largest city. To get here from Oslo, drive west through Telemark, a region marked by steep valleys, pine forests, lakes, and fast-flowing rivers full of trout. Morgedal, the cradle of skiing, is here. At the Haukeligrend crossroads, Route 11 really begins to climb, and you'll see why the Norwegians are so proud of keeping this route open all year. Hardangervidda, a wild mountain area and national park, was the stronghold of Norway's Resistance fighters during World War II. Farther west is the beautiful Hardangerfjord. Few places on earth match western Norway—the fabled land of the fjords—for spectacular scenic beauty.

Fjord transportation is good, as crossing fjords is a necessary as well as scenic way to travel in Norway. Hardangerfjorden, Sognefjord, and Nordfjord are three of the deepest and most popular.

One way to enjoy Telemark is to take a boat trip on the **Telemark Canal,** a heritage watercourse that cuts 105 km (65 mi) through the county from the coast to the foothills of the Hardanger highlands. The canal has 18 lock systems and is lined with pathways for cyclists. The lakes and views toward the mountains are breathtaking. Contact **Telemark Reiser** (⌂ Box 3133, Handelstorget, 3707 Skien ☎ 35900030 ☎ 35900021) for more information.

Kongsberg

Kongsberg, founded in 1624 next to the fast-flowing Lågen River as a silver-mining town, is one of the gateways to Telemark. Forests give way to rocky peaks and desolate spaces farther into the plateau. Although there is no more mining, the old mines at Saggrenda are open for guided tours; contact the tourist office (⇨ Visitor Information *in* Through Telemark to Bergen Essentials). In the town center is an 18th-century rococo church, which reflects the town's former source of wealth: silver.

The **Norsk Bergverksmuseum** (Norwegian Mining Museum) includes the Sølvverkets Samlinger (Silver Mines Collection), the **Kongsberg Skimuseum** (Ski Museum), and **Den Kongelige Mynts Museum** (Royal Mint Museum). ⊠ *Hyttegt. 3* ☎ *32723200* ⊕ *www.bvm.museum.no* ⊙ *Mid-May–June, daily 10–4; July–mid-Aug., daily 10–5; mid-Aug.–Sept., daily noon–4; Oct.–mid-May, Sun. noon–4. Otherwise by appointment.*

Heddal

★ Heddal is the first stop in Telemark. Here you'll find the **Heddal Stavkirke** (Heddal Church), Norway's largest stave church, built in 1147. Stave churches are built with wooden planks staked vertically into the ground or base and usually have some carved ornamentation on the doors and around the aisle. These churches date from the medieval period and are found almost exclusively in southern Norway. ☎ *35020400* ⊕ *www. kirker.net/heddal* ⊙ *Mid-May–mid-June and mid-Aug.–mid-Sept., daily 10–5; mid-June–mid-Aug., daily 9–7.*

Seljord

The attractive village of Seljord, on a lake of the same name, has ornamented wooden houses and a medieval church. The countryside by the lake is richer than that on the Telemark plateau; meadows and pastureland run down to the lakefront. Before you descend toward Seljord, you'll see the Lifjell area's highest peak, **Røydalsnuten** (4,235 feet), on the left.

Kinsarvik

The attractive village of Kinsarvik is on the Sørfjord. For the best view of the junction of the Sørfjord and the mighty Hardangerfjord, take the ferry to Utne. On the dramatic 30-minute ferry crossing, you will come to understand why this area was such a rich source of inspiration for Romantic composer Edvard Grieg.

★ $$$$ ▥ **Utne Hotel.** The white frame house dates from 1722, making this hotel one of the oldest in Norway. The wood-paneled, hand-painted dining room is decorated with copper pans, old china, and paintings. ⊠ *5797 Utne* ☎ *53666983* 🖷 *53666950* ⛂ *22 rooms with bath or shower* ⚭ *Restaurant* ⊟ *AE, DC, MC, V.*

$$$ ▥ **Best Western Kinsarvik Fjord Hotel.** This handsome family-run hotel near the busy ferry port offers good views of Hardangerfjord and the glacier. The rooms are bright and spacious. ⊠ *5780 Kinsarvik* ☎ *53663100* 🖷 *53667433* ⊕ *www.nettvik.no/handelskleiva/bestwestern* ⛂ *70 rooms* ⚭ *Restaurant* ⊟ *AE, DC, MC, V.*

Bergen

Norway's second-largest city, Bergen, the city of seven mountains, has earned many titles: *Trebyen* (Wooden City) for her many wooden houses; *Regnbyen* (Rainy City) for the 200 days of rain every year; and *Fjordbyen* (Fjord City) for being the capital of the fjords. Olav Kyrre, King of Norway, founded the city in 1070, and it was the capital in the 13th century. Bergen's harbor made it an important commercial and military center, and it served as a vital link in the Hanseatic League (a chain of European and Baltic cities with shared trading agreements) in the Middle Ages. Today its economic life is centered around the North Sea oil industry and its proud natives continue to think of Oslo as a dour provincial town.

Much of medieval Bergen has survived. Seven surrounding mountains set off the weathered wooden houses, cobbled streets, and Hanseatic-era warehouses of **Bryggen** (the harbor area).

The best way to get a feel for Bergen's medieval trading heyday is to visit the **Hanseatisk Museum.** One of the oldest and best-preserved of

Bergen's wooden buildings, it is furnished in 16th-century style. ⊠ *Finnegårdsgt. 1* ☎ *55314189* ⊕ *www.hanseatisk.museum.no* ☾ *June–Aug., daily 9–5; Oct.–Apr., Tues.–Sat. 11–2, Sun. noon–5; May and Sept. daily 11–2.*

☾ The **Bergen Aquarium** overlooks the approach to the port of Bergen. Seals and penguins cavort in large pools, and the aquarium has one of Europe's most impressive collections of fish and marine invertebrates. There is also a spectacular video-in-the-round film on Norway's coastal flora and fauna. ⊠ *Nordnesbakken 4* ☎ *55557171* ⊕ *www.akvariet. com* ☾ *May–Oct., daily 9–8; feedings times noon, 3, 6; Nov.–Apr., daily 10–6; feeding times noon and 3.*

From behind Bryggen you can walk through the meandering back streets to the popular **Fløybanen** (Fløyen Funicular), which climbs a steep 1,070 feet to the top of Fløyen, one of the seven mountains guarding the city. ⊠ *Øvregt.* ☾ *May–Sept., weekdays every ½ hr 7:30 AM–11 PM, Sat. 8 AM–midnight, Sun. 9 AM–midnight.*

★ **Damsgaard Manor** is in the suburb of Laksevaag, 10 minutes by bus outside Bergen. Once the most splendid in the area, the house has been restored with gardens replanted as they might have been 200 years ago. ☎ *55325108* 🖶 *55940870* ☾ *Late May–Aug., Tues.–Sun. 10–5; Sept.–late May, tours by appointment. Guided tours available.*

★ $$$–$$$$ ✕ **Fiskekrogen.** Right at the fish market, the Fish Hook is the quintessential fish restaurant. A charming blue-and-white interior and open kitchen give a rustic look. Stick to seafood dishes such as the grilled monkfish in a goat cheese sauce, or the mixture of catfish, salmon, shellfish, and mussels with vegetables. ⊠ *Target 2* ☎ *55559655* ⌁ *Reservations essential* ⊟ *AE, DC, MC, V.*

$$–$$$ ✕ **Mago Restaurant & Café.** The name is Italian for "magician," and this is a magical health-kick of a restaurant. British chef Simon Warhurst creates sumptuous yet healthful dishes based on ecologically balanced ingredients. Try the Pretzel Logic (free-range chicken breast stuffed with avocado and Parma ham, oven roasted with sweet mango and chili sauce). ⊠ *Neumanns Gate 5* ☎ *55962980* ⊟ *AE, DC, MC, V.*

$$$$ ▥ **Radisson SAS Royal Hotel.** Right on Bryggen, this hotel was opened in 1982 where old warehouses once stood. Dark wood and light gold walls decorate the small but comfortable rooms. The Café Royal restaurant serves meals and light snacks. ⊠ *Bryggen, 5003* ☎ *55543000* 🖶 *55324808* ⊕ *www.radisson.no* ⇗ *273 rooms* ♨ *3 restaurants, indoor pool* ⊟ *AE, DC, MC, V.*

★ $$–$$$$ ▥ **Clarion Hotel Admiral.** Called "the hotel with the sea on three sides," Clarion Hotel Admiral is situated harborside with views of the Fish Market and Mt. Floien. Rooms have an art nouveau style. ⊠ *C. Sundsgt. 9–13, 5004 Bergen* ☎ *55236400* 🖶 *55236464* ⊕ *www.admiral.no* ⇗ *210 rooms* ♨ *Restaurant, bar* ⊟ *AE, DC, MC, V.*

Hardangerfjord

Hardanger fjord, known as the Garden of Fjord Norway, is a name Norwegians identify with blossoms and fruit. The mild climate and clear, light summer nights are ideal for berries and fruit like apples and cherries. Famed Norwegian composer Edvard Grieg got inspiration for some of his finest masterpieces here. Springtime is the most stunning season here, with fruit trees abloom against the backdrop of blue fjord, snow-topped mountains, and foaming waterfalls. Beginning early May, the cherry and plum flowers can be seen and later in the month, pink apple blossoms. Then cherries come in July and early August followed by plums, pears, and apples from mid-August to late October. Farmers sell fresh fruit at farm shops or fruit storehouses, and many open their farms for sightseeing and refreshments.

Through Telemark to Bergen Essentials

AIR TRAVEL
Flesland Airport is 20 km (12 mi) south of Bergen.

BUS TRAVEL
Buses in the region rarely run more than twice a day; schedules are available at tourist offices or Nor-Way Bussekspress. All buses serving the Bergen region depart from Bergen's central bus station.
🚍 **Central bus station** ✉ Strømgaten 8 ☎ 177. **Nor-Way Bussekspress** ✉ Bussterminalen, Galleri Oslo ☎ 23002400; 81544444 within Norway.

CAR TRAVEL
E18 stretches from Oslo to Drammen and Route 11 from Drammen to Haukeli. From Haukeli to Kinsarvik you take Route 13. After the ferry crossing, Kinsarvik–Utne–Kvandal, follow Route 7 to Bergen.

TOURS
Bergen is the gateway to the fjords, and excursions cover most towns in the western part of the region as well as the fjords farther north. Contact the tourist information offices (⇨ Visitor Information) for details of these constantly changing tours.

TRAIN TRAVEL
For Bergen, the Bergensbanen has five departures daily, plus an additional one on Sunday, in both directions on the Oslo–Bergen route. The only train service in the southern part of Telemark is the Oslo–Stavanger line (via Kristiansand).

VISITOR INFORMATION
🚍 **Bergen** ✉ Vaagsallmeningen 1 ☎ 55552000 ⊕ www.visitBergen.com. **Kinsarvik** ✉ Public Library bldg. ☎ 53663112; open mid-June–mid-August. **Kongsberg** ✉ Storgt. 35 ☎ 32735000.

ABOVE BERGEN: THE FAR NORTH

The fjords continue northward from Bergen all the way to Kirkenes, on Norway's border with the Republic of Russia. In the north you can hike, climb, fish, bird-watch (seabirds), see Samiland—the land of the Sami ("Lapps")—and experience the unending days of the midnight sun in June and July. The Lofoten Islands present the grand face of the Lofoten Wall—a rocky massif surrounded by the sea and broken into six pieces. Svolvær, the most populated island, has a thriving summer artists' colony. It's also known for Lofotfisket, a winter cod-fishing event. Cheaper accommodations are the rule in the north, whether you stay in hotels, cabins, campsites, guest houses, or *rorbuer*—fishermen's huts next to the sea with modern facilities.

Sognefjorden
Stunning Sognefjorden, Europe's longest fjord, stretches 200 km (124 mi) deep into the country and meets **Jotunheimen National Park**, Norway's highest and wildest mountains, and **Jostedalsbreen National Park**, the largest European glacier at 500 square km (193 square mi). In the summer, mountain-sport enthusiasts flock here to climb, hike, and glacier walk. The Glacier Center, **Breheimsenteret** (☎ 57683250 ⊕ www.jostedal.com), is the Jostedalsbreen National Park's visitor center, with fascinating exhibitions on glaciers.

Norsk Bremuseum (Norwegian Glacier Museum) is one of Norway's most innovative museums, in gorgeous Fjærland. You can study glaciers up close and conduct your own experiments with 1,000-year-old glacial ice. Take time to watch Ivo Caprino's panorama film of Jostedal Glacier. ☒ *6848 Fjærland* ☎ *57693288* ⊕ *www.bre.museum.net.*

$–$$$$ ⊡ **Turtagrø Hotel.** Turtagrø is called the cradle of mountain sports in Norway. Shaped like a mountain, the hotel has lots of white and heavy oak furniture. Rooms have very comfortable beds and black-and-white photographs depicting mountain sports. Sign up for glacier walking, mountain tracking, or a climbing trip. ☒ *6877 Fortun* ☎ *57680800* ☒ *57680801* ⊕ *www.turtagro.no* ↙ *74 rooms* ♺ *Restaurant, bar* ▭ *AE, DC, MC, V.*

Ålesund

★ Ålesund's pride is its unique, internationally recognized collection of art nouveau buildings constructed between 1904 and 1907 after the Great Fire. Romantic and colorful, these buildings line the narrow streets of the old town. Also attractive is **Brosundet** (the old harbor). This area on the west coast of Norway was one of the first places exposed after the Ice Age. Excavations in the Skjonghelleren cave on the nearby island of Valderøy have given evidence of Stone Age settlements that lived off plentiful fishing. Even today, much of the town's income derives from the fishing industry. *Klipfisk* (split, dried cod), which is exported worldwide, is the main ingredient for *bacalao,* a popular local dish whose name derives from the Portuguese for salted cod, and whose preparation was learned from Portuguese fishermen.

Atlantic Sea Park, 3 km (2 mi) west of Ålesund, is northern Europe's largest aquarium specializing in coastal and fjord fish. ☎ *70107060* ⊕ *www. atlanterhavsparken.no* ⊙ *Mid-June–mid-Aug., weekdays and Sun. 10–7, Sat. 10–5; mid-Aug.–mid-June, Mon.–Sat. 11–4, Sun. noon–5.*

$$ ✕ **Fjellstua.** This mountaintop restaurant has tremendous views over the surrounding peaks, islands, and fjords. The main dining room serves the widest variety of dishes and homemade desserts. ☒ *Fjellstua* ☎ *70126582* ▭ *AE, DC, MC, V* ⊙ *Closed mid-Dec.–early Feb.*

$$$ ⊡ **Quality Scandinavie Hotel.** The building dates from 1905. The rooms are decorated in blue, peach, and green, with reproduction Biedermeier furniture. ☒ *Løvenvoldgt. 8, 6002* ☎ *70123131* ☒ *70132370* ⊕ *www. choice.no* ↙ *65 rooms* ♺ *2 restaurants* ▭ *AE, DC, MC, V.*

Trondheim

Trondheim sits at the southern end of Norway's widest fjord, Trondheimsfjord. This water-bound city, the third largest in the country, is a major high-tech center for research and education. Historically, it is where all the country's kings have been crowned or blessed, and the crown jewels are on view. It has a historic fish market worth seeing, as well as Scandinavia's two largest wooden buildings. One is a student dormitory and the other is the rococo **Stiftsgården**, built between 1774 and 1778, which today is the official royal residence in Trondheim. This late-baroque building gives an insight into 18th-century Trondheim.

Construction of Scandinavia's largest medieval building, **Nidaros Domkirke** (Nidaros Cathedral), first started in 1070, but it suffered numerous fires and was not completed until 1969. The cathedral has been attracting pilgrims since the 11th century, following the miraculous preservation of the body of King Olaf Haraldsson, who died in 1030. He was worshipped as a saint soon after his death, and he is the patron saint of Norway. The national crown jewels are exhibited here. ☒ *Kongsgårdsgt. 2* ☎ *73538480* ⊕ *www.nidarosdomen.no* ⊙ *Late June–late Aug., week-*

days 9–6, Sat. 9–2, Sun. 1–4; late Aug.–mid-Sept. and May–late June, weekdays 9–3, Sat. 9–2, Sun. 1–4; mid-Sept.–Apr., weekdays noon–2:30, Sat. 11:30–2, Sun. 1–3.

★ **NTNU Vitenskapsmuseet** (The NTNU Science Museum) is Norway's oldest institution of science. Exhibitions focus on natural history, flora and fauna, minerals and rocks, as well as church history, southern Sami culture, and archaeology. ⊠ *Erling Skakkes Gt. 47* ☎ *73592145* ⊕ *www. ntnu.no/vmuseet* ⊙ *Late Apr.–mid-Sept. weekdays 9–4, weekends 11–4; mid-Sept.–late Apr., Tues.–Fri. 9–2, weekends noon–4.*

At Ringve Gård, one of the traditional country estates, **Ringve Museum** is Norway's national museum of music and musical instruments, with collections from around the world. ⊠ *Lade Allé* ☎ *73922411* ⊕ *www. ringve.com* ⊙ *Mid-Dec.–mid-May, Sun. 11–4; Mid-May–June 21, daily 11–3; June 22–Aug. 10, daily 11–5; Aug. 11–mid-Sept., daily 11–3; mid-Sept.–mid-Dec., Sun. 11–4.*

★ **$$–$$$** ✕ **Bryggen.** An elegant country-style refurbished warehouse, Bryggen is one of the city's standouts. The international menu uses seasonal Norwegian ingredients such as fish and reindeer. The wine list is extensive, with many French and Italian choices. ⊠ *Øvre Bakklandet 66* ☎ *73874242* ⊟ *AE, DC, MC, V.*

$$$–$$$$ 🏨 **Radisson SAS Royal Garden Hotel.** Right on the river, this glass house hotel has superb service and a lush interior with an atrium full of marble and colorful plants. The rooms have blue and red tones. ⊠ *Kjøpmannsgt. 73* ☎ *73803000* 🖨 *73803050* ⊕ *www.radissonsas.com* 🛏 *298 rooms, 9 suites* ⌂ *Restaurant, indoor pool* ⊟ *AE, DC, MC, V.*

Bodø

The last stop on the European rail system, Bodø is the first major town above the Arctic Circle and, with its 42,000 inhabitants, the second-largest city in northern Norway. Bodø's modern airport has frequent flights daily serving most of the country. *Hurtigruten* (the Coastal Express ship) calls here and a ferry will take you from Bodø straight to the Lofoten Islands. For boat excursions to coastal bird colonies on **Værøya**, Bodø is also the best base. The city was bombed by the Germans in 1940, but postwar reconstruction gave rise to the bustling modern city center, replete with lively shopping streets, a marina, and good restaurants and accommodations. A war memorial stands outside the stunning, contemporary **Bodø Domkirke** (Bodø Cathedral), its spire separated from the main building; inside are rich modern tapestries.

A giant propeller marks **Norsk Luftfartssenter** (Norwegian Aviation Museum). In the high-ceilinged rotunda exhibition hall, you'll first learn about man's primeval dream of flight. Go up into the control tower to see the wild northern Norway landscape. Take a turn at the flight simulator and feel the real-life rush of flight. ⊠ *Olav V's Gt.* ☎ *75507850 or 75507851* ⊕ *www.aviation-museum.com* ⊙ *Mid-June–mid-Aug., weekdays and Sun. 10–7, Sat. 10–5; mid-Aug.–mid-June, weekdays 10–4, weekends 11–5.*

Saltstraumen, the world's strongest tidal current, has inspired tales of ships' being sucked down in its maelstrom (whirlpool). It is one of nature's wonders as well as a paradise for anglers. Saithe is the local specialty, and the biggest ever caught with a rod was caught here. The Experience Center has a café and shop. ⊠ *33 km (20 mi) south of Bodø* ☎ *75560655* ⊙ *June–Aug. 24, daily 11–6.*

Kjærringøy Gamle Handelssted (Old Kjærringøy Trading Post) is 40 km (25 mi) north of Bodø. It has one of Norway's most important collections of buildings preserved from the 19th century, capturing part of the history of north Norwegian coastal life and culture. (☎ 75511257 ⏱ Late May–late Aug., daily 11–5).

$$$–$$$$ ▨ **Landego Fyr.** This red-and-white-striped, cast-iron lighthouse, built in 1901, has stunning views. A thrilling 30-minute boat ride across Landegode Fjord gets you here; the staff greets you as you arrive and makes you feel right at home. Stay in one of the simple, sky blue rooms in the old house, where the lighthouse keeper, his family, and staff lived. Landego is open to individual guests in July and August; the rest of the year is primarily booked by groups. ⊠ *Eggsløysa Island* ☎ *75584644 or 75519100* ⊕ *www.skagen-hotel.no* ⇆ *14 rooms* ♨ *Restaurant* ▤ *AE, DC, MC, V.*

$$$–$$$$ ▨ **Skagen Hotel.** Every room here varies in personality, from bold and artsy to understated and elegant. The service is superb and the mood intimate and warm. Every afternoon, the English-style library has complimentary waffles and coffee. The hotel has a special wireless Internet service (Wi-Fi) *kveldsmat* supper. ⊠ *Nyholmsgata 11* ☎ *75519100* 🖷 *75519101* ⊕ *www.skagen-hotel.no* ⇆ *70 rooms, 2 suites* ♨ *Restaurant* ▤ *AE, DC, MC, V.*

Lofoten Islands

★ The Lofoten Islands archipelago is a 190-km (118-mi) chain of mountaintops rising from the bottom of the sea north of Bodø. In recent years, tourism has exploded on Lofoten, including fishing competitions, midnight sun golf, mountain climbing, bird-watching, and sea kayaking. Most often the accommodations are varying standards of rorbuer in fishing villages and fjords. Between January and March, thousands of fishermen from all over the country head for Lofoten to the annual Lofoten Fishery, the world's largest annual cod-fishing event. **Svolvær,** the main town and administrative center for the villages on Lofoten Islands, is connected with the other islands by express boat and ferry, and by coastal steamer and air to Bodø. It has a thriving summer art colony.

🖰 **Lofotr** (Viking Museum of Borg; ⊠ 8360 Bøstad ☎ 76084900 ⊕ www. lofotr.no), 67 km (42 mi) south of Svolvær on Route E10, has a reconstruction of a Viking chieftain's homestead. The year AD 900 is re-created inside, with a flickering fireplace and oil lamps. You may also bump into the chieftain himself; he tells many stories of raids and expeditions. The midnight sun is visible in Lofoten from May 27 to July 17. The best places to view it are Unstad and Eggum on **Vestvågøy** and Gimsøy and Laukvik on **Vågan.** It is also worth taking a fishing boat trip to see the impressive **Refsvikhula Cave.**

Narvik

Narvik is a rebuilt city, an ice-free seaport, and a major iron ore shipping center. An excellent railway connects it to the mines across the Swedish border. **Krigsminnemuséet** (War Memorial Museum) has gripping displays on wartime intrigue and suffering. ⊠ *Kongensgt. near the main sq.* ☎ *76944426* ⏱ *Mar.–mid-June and mid-Aug.–Sept., daily 11–3; mid-June–mid-Aug., Mon.–Sat. 10–10, Sun. 10–4; tours arranged by appointment Oct.–Feb.*

The Nordland Red Cross War Memorial Museum. In April–May 1940, the Battle of Narvik and the fight for the iron ore ended with the city being razed and five years of German occupation. The museum recounts the war through exhibitions of photographs and military equipment. ⊠ *Kongensgt. near the main sq.* ☎ *76944426* ⏱ *Mar.–May and Sept., daily 10–4; June–Aug., daily 10–10.*

$$ ⊞ **Inter Nor Grand Royal Hotel.** An eager-to-please staff serves you at this handsome hotel near the train station. There are many possibilities for skiing and fishing nearby, as well as whale safaris. ⊠ *Kongensgt. 64, 8500* ☎ *76941500* ☏ *76977007* ☞ *107 rooms* ♨ *2 restaurants* ⊟ *AE, DC, MC, V.*

Tromsø

Farther north on the mainland is Tromsø, self-dubbed "the Paris of the North" for its nightlife inspired by the midnight sun. Looming over the remote Arctic university town are 6,100-foot peaks with permanent snow-caps. Tromsø trails off into the islands: half the 50,000 inhabitants of the town live offshore. Every January, the Northern Lights Festival, **Nordlysfestivalen** (☎ 77689070 ⊕ www.nordlysfestivalen.no), celebrates one of the city's natural attractions. Be sure to see the spectacular **Ishavskatedral** (Arctic Cathedral), with its eastern wall made entirely of stained glass. Coated in aluminum, the **Tromsø bridge** has triangular peaks that make a bizarre mirror for the midnight sun.

Part of Tromsø University, **Tromsø Museum** concentrates on science, the Sami, and northern church art. ⊠ *Lars Thøringsvei 10, Folkeparken (take Bus 28)* ☎ *77645000* ⊙ *June–Aug., daily 9–8; Sept.–May, Mon., Tues., Thurs., and Fri. 8:30–3:30, Wed. and Sat. noon–3, Sun. 11–4.*

$$–$$$$ ⊞ **Rica Ishavshotel.** Shaped like a ship, Tromsø's snazziest hotel is right at the harbor and stretches over the sound toward Ishavskatedralen. Nautical-style wood furnishings evoke the life of the sea. Guests represent a mix of business executives, tourists, and scientists on conference. Inquire about special summer and weekend prices. ⊠ *Sjøgt. 7, 9001* ☎ *77600000* ☏ *77685474* ⊕ *www.rica.no* ☞ *195 rooms* ♨ *3 restaurants* ⊟ *AE, DC, MC, V.*

Hammerfest

With 10,000 inhabitants, Hammerfest is the world's northernmost town. Founded in 1789, it is an elegant, festive-looking port. In the late 19th century fire consumed it, and years later, defeated German troops destroyed the town as they retreated. Modern Hammerfest is the natural starting point for exploring Finnmark.

Discover **Sami culture** and try traditional Sami food on a trip to a *mikkelgammen* (Sami turf hut) just outside town through Hammerfest Turist AS (☎ 78412185). The city is also home to the **Isbjørn Klubben** (Royal and Ancient Polar Bear Society), which has taxidermic displays of polar bears and other Arctic animals. ⊠ *Town Hall ground floor* ☎ *78413100* ⊕ *www.hammerfest-turist.no/polarbear* ⊙ *June–Aug., weekdays 7–7; Sept.–May, daily 11:30–1:30.*

Far North Essentials

AIR TRAVEL
Flesland Airport is 20 km (12 mi) south of Bergen.

BOAT & FERRY TRAVEL
One of the best ways to travel in northern Norway is aboard a *Hurtigruta* (contact Tromsø Coastal Steamer Company for information), which starts out in Bergen and turns around 2,000 nautical km (1,250 nautical mi) farther north at Kirkenes. Many steamers run this route, so you can stay in port for any length of time and pick up the next one coming through. Major tourist offices have schedules, and reservations are essential as far as a year in advance (⇨ Visitor Information).
₤ Tromsø Coastal Steamer Company ☎ 77648200.

TOURS

Bergen is the gateway to the fjords, and excursions cover most towns in the western part of the region as well as the fjords farther north. Contact the tourist information offices (⇨ Visitor Information) for details.

TRAIN TRAVEL

A major train route runs from Oslo to Trondheim, then to Bodø. From Bodø tours go to the Lofoten Islands by ferry. To reach the Nordkapp (North Cape), the northernmost mainland point in Europe, you must continue your trip by bus from Fauske. With a ScanRail pass you get a 50% discount on buses. From Narvik a train to Sweden departs twice a day. In summer a day trip through wild and beautiful scenery takes you to the Swedish border. Schedule and fare information is available from the tourist office at Narvik (⇨ Visitor Information).

VISITOR INFORMATION

🄵 Ålesund ✉ Rådhuset ☎ 70125804. **Bodø** ✉ Sjøgt. 21 ☎ 75548000. **Fjord Norway** ☎ 55550730 ⊕ www.fjordnorway.no. **Hammerfest** ✉ 9600 ☎ 78412185. **Harstad** ✉ Torvet 8 ☎ 77063235. **Lofoten Islands** ✉ 8300 Svolvær ☎ 76073000. **Narvik** ✉ Kongensgt. 66 ☎ 76946033. **Sognefjorden** ✉ Sogndal ☎ 57673083 ⊕ www. sognefjorden.no. **Tromsø** ✉ Storgt. 61 ☎ 77610000. **Trondheim** ✉ Munkegt. 19 ☎ 73929394.

POLAND

WARSAW, KRAKÓW & ENVIRONS, GDAŃSK & THE NORTH

POLES ARE FOND OF QUOTING, with a wry grimace, the old Chinese curse, "May you live in interesting times." The times were certainly interesting in the 1990s. Poland, the home of the Solidarity political-labor-social movement that sent shock waves through the Soviet Bloc in 1980, was the first Eastern European state to shake off Communist rule. But as the grimace implies, being on the firing line of history—something that the Poles are well used to—can be uncomfortable. Poles in the new millennium are looking forward to membership in the European Union (EU) to gain the stability that eluded their nation in the 20th century.

You will be constantly reminded in Poland that the return to free-market capitalism after more than 45 years of state socialism is an experiment on an unprecedented scale that has brought hardships for millions but also benefits for a growing percentage of the population. Poland's 39 million inhabitants are still suspended between the Old World and the New, and the images can be contradictory and confusing. Bright, new, privately owned shops with smiling assistants often carry on business in shabby buildings that have not been renovated for decades. Billboards advertise goods that many Poles cannot afford. However, sweeping reform programs in the fields of education, health care, and social security are under way.

The official trappings of the Communist state were quickly dismantled after the Solidarity victory in the 1989 elections. But Communism never sat easily with the Poles. It represented yet another stage in their age-old struggle to retain their identity in the face of pressure from large and powerful neighbors to the west and east. Since its foundation as a unified state on the great north European plain in the 10th century, Poland has stood at the heart of Europe, precisely at the halfway point on a line drawn from the Atlantic coast of Spain to the Ural Mountains. This has never been an enviable position. During the Middle Ages Poland fought against a strong German military advance. In the golden age of Polish history during the 16th and 17th centuries—of which you will be reminded by splendid Renaissance buildings in many parts of the country—Poland pushed eastward against her Slavic neighbors, taking Kiev and dreaming of a kingdom that stretched from the Baltic to the Black Sea. By the end of the 18th century Poland's territories were divided among the Austrian, Prussian, and Russian empires. In the 20th century Poland fell victim to peculiarly vicious forms of dictatorship—from both the right and the left: the brutal Nazi occupation and imposition of Soviet rule.

Poland
(Polska)

0   100 miles

0   150 km

Whereas Poland's ancient cities—Kraków, Warsaw, Gdańsk—tell much of the tale of European history and culture, its countryside offers unrivaled opportunities to escape from the present. The Soviet-imposed government dropped attempts to collectivize agriculture in the 1950s and left the Polish farmer to tend his small, uneconomical plot, leaving rural Poland in something of a time warp. Cornflowers still bloom, storks perch atop untidy nests by cottage chimneys, and you may still come across horsepower in the four-legged variety. Although the Poles have a certain wary reserve, they will win you over with their strong individualism—expressed through their well-developed sense of humor and their capacity for conviviality.

It's likely to take several generations before the physical and psychological traces of 45 years of Soviet rule fade, and at least 15 years until Poland "catches up" with the poorest EU member in terms of standard of living. Nevertheless, Poland became a NATO member in 1997 and is one of 10 Central European countries fast-tracked for European Union membership, slated to join in May 2004.

POLAND A TO Z

To research prices, get advice from other travelers, and book travel arrangements, visit www.fodors.com.

AIR TRAVEL

LOT, Poland's national airline, operates daily flights linking eight main cities: Warsaw, Kraków, Gdańsk, Wrocław, Szczecin, Poznań, Katowice, and Rzeszów. Fares begin at about $80 round-trip from Warsaw. Tickets and information are available from LOT or any travel agent. Be sure to book well in advance, especially for the summer season.

🛫 **LOT Polish Airlines** ☎ 0801/300-952; 800/223-0593 in U.S. ⊕ www.lot.com.

BUS TRAVEL

PKS is the national bus company. Polski Express is privately owned and much nicer. Both offer long-distance service to most cities. Express buses, on which you can reserve seats, are often faster than trains. For really out-of-the-way destinations, the bus is often the only means of transportation. Bus stations are usually near railway stations. Tickets and information are best obtained from any travel agency, hotel, or the bus station itself.

🚌 **PKS** ☎ 022/823-63-94 ⊕ www.pks.pl. **Polski Express** ☎ 022/620-03-30 ⊕ www. pex.civ.com.pl.

BUSINESS HOURS

Banks are open weekdays 8 or 9 until 3 or 6. Museum hours vary greatly but are generally Tuesday–Sunday 10–5. Food shops are open weekdays 7–7, Saturday 7–1 or 2; many are now open on Sunday, and there are a few all-night stores in most central shopping districts. Other stores are open weekdays 11–7 or 10–6 and Saturday 9–1 or 2.

CAR TRAVEL

EMERGENCIES Poland's Motoring Association (PZMot) offers breakdown, repair, and towing services to members of various international insurance organizations; check with Orbis before you leave home. Carry a spare-parts kit.

🚗 **Emergency road help** ☎ 981. **PZMot** ☎ 022/629-83-36; 9637 countrywide for emergency roadside assistance ⊕ www.pzm.pl. **Orbis** ✉ Ul. Marszałkowska 142 ☎ 022/ 827-80-31.

GASOLINE The price of gas is about zł 3.70 for a liter of high-octane fuel. Filling stations are located every 30 km (19 mi) or so and are usually open 6 AM–10 PM. More and more bright, clean, full-service 24-hour stations are opening each year, and they're often accompanied by fast-food restaurants or grocery stores.

ROAD CONDITIONS Despite the extensive road network, steadily increasing traffic and the lack of divided highways make driving in Poland inconvenient if not dangerous. Minor roads tend to be narrow and encumbered with horse-drawn carts, bicycles, and pedestrians. If you're in a hurry, stick to roads marked E (express roads that in theory lead to a Polish border) or A (domestic express roads). New international highways are under construction.

RULES OF THE ROAD Driving is on the right. The speed limit is 110 kph (68 mph) on highways, 60 kph (37 mph) on roads in built-up areas, and 50 kph (30 mph) in the metropolitan Warsaw area. A built-up area is marked by a white rectangular sign with the name of the town on it. It is illegal to use cellular phones while driving.

CUSTOMS & DUTIES
Persons over 18 may bring in, duty-free, personal belongings, including musical instruments, one computer, one radio, one camera with 24 rolls of film, up to 250 cigarettes, 50 cigars, 1 liter of spirits, and 2 liters of wine. Additional goods with a collective value of $75 may be brought into the country. The foreign currency limit is $5,200, and you must declare on arrival any foreign currency you are carrying.

🛈 **Customs information** ☎ 022/650-28-73 Warsaw.

EATING & DRINKING
Polish food and drink are basically Slavic with Baltic overtones. The emphasis is on soups and meat (especially pork), as well as freshwater fish. Cream is a staple, and pastries are rich and often delectable. The most popular soup is *barszcz* (known to many Americans as borscht), a clear beet soup often served with such Polish favorites as sausage, cabbage, potatoes, sour cream, and coarse rye bread. Other typical dishes are pierogi, which may be stuffed with savory or sweet fillings; *gołąbki* (cabbage leaves stuffed with minced meat); *bigos* (sauerkraut with meat and mushrooms); and *flaki* (a tripe soup). Polish beer is excellent; vodka is a specialty and is often downed before, during, and after meals.

Zajazdy (roadside inns) and *bar mleczny* (milk bars), which are often less expensive than regular restaurants, serve more traditional food. As elsewhere in Central Europe, cafés are a way of life in Poland and often serve delicious homemade pastries and ice cream.

WHAT IT COSTS In złotys			
$$$$	**$$$**	**$$**	**$**
WARSAW/KRAKÓW			
PER PERSON over zł 50	zł 36–zł 50	zł 15–zł 35	under zł 15
OTHER AREAS			
AT DINNER over zł 35	zł 21–zł 35	zł 10–zł 20	under zł 10

Prices are per person for a main course.

MEALTIMES Poles eat their main meal around 2 PM, with a light supper about 8. Restaurants—especially in major cities—open around noon for lunch and serve dinner between 7 and 10. Although many restaurants in the provinces close around 10, more cosmopolitan establishments stay open until 11 or later. Most hotel restaurants serve the evening meal until 10:30.

RESERVATIONS & DRESS In Warsaw and Kraków jacket and tie are customary at $$$ and $$$$ restaurants. Casual dress is appropriate elsewhere.

EMBASSIES
All embassies are in Warsaw.

🛈 Australia ✉ Ul. Nowogrodzka 11 ☎ 022/521-34-34 ⊕ www.australia.pl.
🛈 Canada ✉ Al. Jerozolimskie 123 ☎ 022/584-31-00 ⊕ www.canada.pl.
🛈 United Kingdom ✉ Al. Róż 1 ☎ 022/628-10-01 ⊕ www.britishembassy.pl.
🛈 United States ✉ Al. Ujazdowskie 29-31 ☎ 022/628-30-41 ⊕ www.usinfo.pl.

HEALTH
Tap water in major cities is unsafe to drink, so ask for bottled mineral water. Beware of meat dishes served in cheap snack bars.

HOLIDAYS

New Year's Day; Easter Monday; Labor Day (May 1); Constitution Day (May 3); Corpus Christi (early to mid-June); Assumption (August 15); All Saints' Day (November 1); Independence Day (November 11; rebirth of the Polish state in 1918); Christmas; and Boxing Day (day after Christmas).

LANGUAGE

Polish is a Slavic language that uses the Roman alphabet but has several additional characters and diacritical marks. Because it has a high incidence of consonant clusters, most English speakers find it a difficult language to decipher, much less pronounce. Many older Poles speak German; the younger generation usually knows some English. In larger cities English is increasingly common, especially in hotels, but you may have difficulty in the countryside.

LODGING

Lodging options are getting better and better, although travelers seeking elegant accommodations have fewer options to choose from than in more popular cities in Central Europe like Prague. The following prices are in U.S. dollars; many hotels in Poland quote prices in American dollars or euros.

WHAT IT COSTS In U.S. dollars			
$$$$	**$$$**	**$$**	**$**
HOTELS over $200	$100–$200	$50–$100	under $50

Prices are for two people in a double room with a bath or shower, including breakfast.

APARTMENT & VILLA RENTALS
Rooms can be arranged in advance or on your own through a travel agent, or on the spot at the local tourist information office. Villas, lodges, rooms, or houses are available. Daily rates vary from about $8 for a room to more than $150 for a villa.

HOTELS
The government rates hotel accommodations from one to five stars. Orbis hotels, owned by the state tourist office and currently undergoing privatization, have almost all been accorded three or four stars and guarantee a reasonable standard of cleanliness and service (although they tend to lack character). Most of them range in price from $$ to $$$$; the chain includes a number of foreign-built luxury hotels. Orbis hotels face competition from a growing number of privately owned lodgings, often part of international chains and mostly in the top price range. Discounts on various ranges of hotels and castles throughout the country are offered at www.hotelspoland.com.

Municipal hotels and Dom Turysty hotels are run by local authorities or the Polish Tourist Association. They are often rather old and can have limited bath and shower facilities. Standards are improving as many undergo renovations; prices are in the $$ category.

ROADSIDE INNS
Many roadside inns are quite attractive, offering inexpensive food and guest rooms at moderate rates.

MAIL & SHIPPING

POSTAL RATES
Airmail letters abroad cost about zł 2.50 (depending on weight); postcards, zł 2.20. Most post offices are open weekdays 8–8. At least one post office is open 24 hours in every major city. In Warsaw the 24-hour post office is at ulica Świętokrzyska 31.

MONEY MATTERS

The Polish złoty is fairly strong and stable, with an annual inflation rate of about 2%. Prices are highest in the big cities, especially Warsaw. Although you can still get good value for your money in Poland, prices are likely to increase with the country's pending accession to the EU.

Sample prices include a cup of coffee, zł 3–zł 10; a bottle of beer, zł 4–zł 10; a soft drink, zł 2–zł 5; a ham sandwich, zł 4–zł 6; a 2-km (1-mi) taxi ride, zł 4–zł 6.

CREDIT CARDS Major credit cards are accepted in all major hotels, in the better restaurants and nightclubs, and for other tourist services. In small cafés and shops, especially in the provinces, credit cards are not accepted.

CURRENCY The monetary unit in Poland is the złoty (zł), which is divided into 100 groszy (gr). There are notes of 10, 20, 50, 100, and 200 złotys, and coins in values of 1, 2, and 5 złotys and 1, 2, 5, 10, 20, and 50 groszys. The złoty is exchangeable at a free-market rate in banks and at *kantory* (private exchange bureaus), which sometimes offer slightly better rates than banks do and are usually open until 8 PM. There are also cash machines (*bankomat*) throughout the country that accept most major credit cards as long as you have a personal identification number (PIN).

At press time (spring 2003), the exchange rate for the złoty was zł 4.44 to the euro, zł 3.85 to the U.S. dollar, zł 2.84 to the Canadian dollar, zł 6.43 to the pound sterling, zł 2.56 to the Australian dollar, zł 2.26 to the New Zealand dollar, and zł 0.50 to the South African rand.

VALUE-ADDED TAX (V.A.T.) A 22% value-added tax (V.A.T.) is applied to most goods and services, but a refund is available for visitors. You should retain your receipts, accompanied by V.A.T. refund forms from the shop where you bought the goods. You must spend zł 200 in a given shop on a given day to be eligible for the refund. Present the receipts and forms to the refund service at any border or the Warsaw or Kraków airport when leaving the country in order to receive V.A.T. reimbursement.

PASSPORTS & VISAS

Citizens of the United States and the United Kingdom do not need visas for entry to Poland; Canadian citizens and citizens of other countries must apply to the Polish Consulate General in any country. (Canadians must pay the equivalent of C$89–C$207 for single- and multiple-entry visas.) Visitors who are required to have visas must complete one application form and provide two photographs; allow one to two weeks for processing. Visas for Canadians are issued for 180 days but can be extended in Poland through the local province police headquarters.

TELEPHONES

COUNTRY & AREA CODES The international country code for Poland is 48. When dialing a number in Poland from outside the country, drop the initial 0 from the local area code. Calls from one Polish city to another require that an additional prefix be dialed before the area code (you can choose between 1033, 1044, or 1055, corresponding to different phone companies); however, this does not apply when using public phones or making international calls.

DIRECTORY & OPERATOR ASSISTANCE For local directory information, dial ☎ 913; for Poland-wide directory information and dialing codes, dial ☎ 912; for international information and codes, dial ☎ 908.

INTERNATIONAL CALLS Post offices and first-class hotels have booths at which you can use your calling card or pay after completing your call. If you need to place a call on a calling card, various international operators can be reached from Poland.

☎ Access Codes **AT&T USA Direct** ☎ 0800/111-1111. **MCI** ☎ 0800/111-2122. **Sprint Global One** ☎ 0800/111-3115.

LOCAL & LONG-DISTANCE CALLS Most public phones in Poland now take phone cards, and not coins. Older, blue phones take magnetic cards. Newer, silver phones are gradually replacing the old ones and operate on electronic chip cards. Either can be used for both local and long-distance calls. The cards, which cost zł 11.30, zł 20.40, or zł 37.20, depending on how much time you are purchasing, are sold at kiosks, post offices, and hotels. When making a long-distance call, dial 0, wait for the dial tone, and then dial the rest of the number.

TIPPING

It is customary to round up on bills, for a total of not more than about 10% for waiters. For taxi drivers, round upward to the nearest złoty or two. Hotel porters, concierges, and doormen get about zł 5. Tour guides should get at least zł 10.

TRAIN TRAVEL

Poland's PKP railway network is extensive and relatively inexpensive. Most trains have first- and second-class accommodations. The fastest trains are Intercity and express trains, which require reservations. Orbis and other travel agents furnish information, reservations, and tickets. If you're traveling on overnight trains, reserve a berth in a first- or second-class car. Some long-distance trains carry buffet cars.

Polish trains run at three speeds—*ekspresowy* (express), *pośpieszny* (fast), and *osobowy* (slow)—and fares vary accordingly.

VISITOR INFORMATION

There is no national tourist office in Poland. State-run tourist offices are listed in individual cities' Essentials sections.

WHEN TO GO

The main tourist season runs from May through September. The best times for sightseeing are late spring and early fall. Major cultural events usually take place in the cities during the fall.

CLIMATE The early spring is often wet and windy. Below are the average daily maximum and minimum temperatures for Warsaw.

Jan.	32F	0C	May	67F	20C	Sept.	66F	19C
	22	–6		48	9		49	10
Feb.	32F	0C	June	73F	23C	Oct.	55F	13C
	21	–6		54	12		41	5
Mar.	42F	6C	July	75F	24C	Nov.	42F	6C
	28	–2		58	16		33	1
Apr.	53F	12C	Aug.	73F	23C	Dec.	35F	2C
	37	3		56	14		28	–3

WARSAW

Over the centuries, Warsaw has repeatedly had to rebuild and reinvent itself. Nearly annihilated in World War II, the city rose like a phoenix from the ashes during the 1950s and 1960s. Soviet austerity demanded that much of the reconstituted city be erected in postwar "functional" styles, but proud architects managed to raise and re-create the Old Town with brick-by-brick precision. Stalin added a dollop of Socialist

Realism to the skyline, directing construction of the period's pièce de résistance and the city's enduring landmark, the Palace of Culture and Science. Somewhat drab and decaying for decades, Warsaw is finally experiencing another rebirth, this one bringing a receptiveness to experimentation in its cultural pursuits as well as a face-lift of its facades.

Exploring Warsaw

Numbers in the margin correspond to points of interest on the Warsaw map.

The sights of Warsaw are all relatively close to one another, making most attractions accessible on foot. A walking tour of the old historic district takes about two hours. A walk along the former Royal Route—the Trakt Królewski—which stretches south from Castle Square down Krakowskie Przedmieście, through Nowy Świat, and on along Aleje Ujazdowskie, considered by many locals to be Warsaw's finest street, is also worthwhile. Lined with magnificent buildings and embassies, it has something of a French flavor. The Muranów district is the site of Jewish Warsaw.

Stare Miasto (Old Town) & Nowe Miasto (New Town)

Both Old and New Town lay in rubble after the war; Varsovians painstakingly rebuilt these districts, reconstructing them after consulting old prints and paintings. The remarkable result is an area whose picturesque tenement houses are painted in warm pastel colors. If you did not know their tragic history, you would think these buildings dated back hundreds of years.

❸ **Archikatedralna Bazylika świętego Jana** (Cathedral of St. John). Dating from the 14th century, this is the oldest church in Warsaw. Several Polish kings were crowned here. ⊠ *Ul. Świętojańska 8.*

❼ **Barbakan** (Barbican). This pinnacled redbrick gate is a fine example of a 16th-century defensive fortification. From here you can see the partially restored wall that was built to enclose the Old Town. ⊠ *Ul. Freta.*

❿ **Kościół Najświętszej Marii Panny** (St. Mary's Church). The oldest church in the New Town, St. Mary's was built as a parish church for the district by the princes of Mazovia in the early 15th century. It has been destroyed and rebuilt many times throughout its history. ⊠ *Przyrynek 2.*

❻ **Muzeum Historyczne Warszawy** (Historical Museum of Warsaw). Four Renaissance mansions on the north side of Old Town Square house this excellent museum. The 20-minute movie *Warsaw Remembers* describes the history of Warsaw using mostly old footage. It is shown in English every day at noon. ⊠ *Rynek Starego Miasta 28* ☎ *022/635–16–25* ⊕ *um.warszawa.pl/muzeum_historyczne* ☉ *Tues. and Thurs. 11–5:30, Wed. and Fri. 11–3:30, weekends 10:30–4.*

❺ **Muzeum Literatury Adama Mickiewicza** (Adam Mickiewicz Museum of Literature). This museum, dedicated to Poland's greatest Romantic poet, who lived from 1798 to 1855, has manuscripts, mementos, and portraits of many Polish writers. ⊠ *Rynek Starego Miasta 20* ☎ *022/831–40–61* ☉ *Mon., Tues., and Fri. 10–3, Wed., Thurs., and Sat. 11–6, Sun. 11–5.*

❽ **Muzeum Marii Skłodowskiej-Curie** (Marie Curie Museum). This house was the birthplace of the great physicist and chemist who won two Nobel Prizes (1903 and 1911) and discovered the elements radium and polonium (named after Poland). ⊠ *Ul. Freta 16* ☎ *022/831–80–92* ☉ *Tues.–Sat. 10–4, Sun. 10–2.*

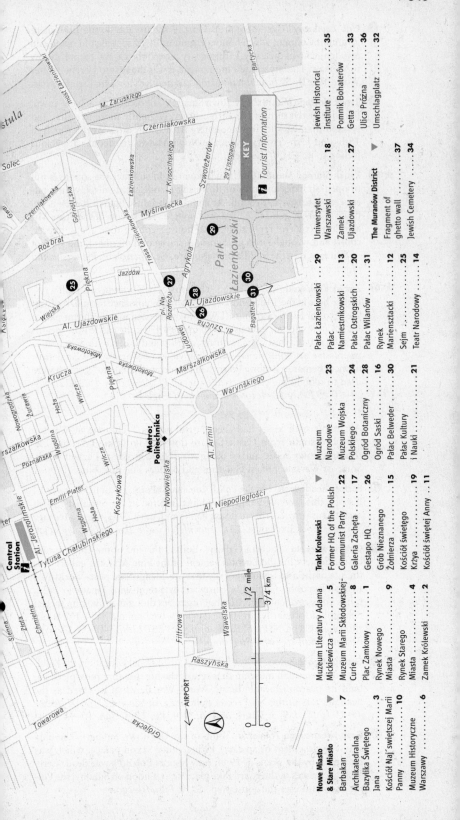

❶ Plac Zamkowy (Castle Square). On the square stands the prominent **Zygmunt Column,** which honors Zygmunt III Wasa, king of Poland and Sweden, who in the early 17th century moved the capital from Kraków to Warsaw. The city's oldest monument, it was the first to be rebuilt after World War II. ✉ *Junction ul. Miodowa and Krakowskie Przedmieście.*

❾ Rynek Nowego Miasta (New Town Square). The center of the New Town, founded at the turn of the 15th century, is slightly more irregular and relaxed than its Old Town counterpart. Rebuilt after World War II in 18th- and 19th-century styles, the **Nowe Miasto** district has a spacious feeling to it. ✉ *Off ul. Freta.*

★ **❹ Rynek Starego Miasta** (Old Town Square). In summer the square is full of open-air cafés and tubs of flowering plants; artists display their talents for tourists year-round. At night the brightly lighted Rynek is the place to go for good food and atmosphere. The streets of the **Stare Miasto** have colorful replica-medieval houses, cobblestone alleys, uneven roofs, and wrought-iron grillwork. A statue of a mermaid, the symbol of Warsaw, is in the middle of the square. ✉ *Junction ul. Piekarska and ul. Świętojańska.*

★ **❷ Zamek Królewski** (Royal Castle). The princes of Mazovia first built a residence here in the 14th century; its present Renaissance form dates from the reign of King Zygmunt III Waza, who needed a magnificent palace for his new capital. Reconstructed in the 1970s, the castle now gleams as it did in its earliest years, with gilt, marble, and wall paintings; it houses impressive art collections—including views of Warsaw by Canaletto's nephew Bernardo Bellotto (known in Poland as "Canaletto"), which were used to rebuild the city after the war. ✉ *Pl. Zamkowy 4* ☎ *022/657–21–70* ⏱ *Daily 10–4; tours available in English.*

Trakt Królewski (The Royal Route)

All towns with kings had their "royal routes." The one in Warsaw stretched south from Castle Square down Krakowskie Przedmieście, through Nowy Świat, and on along Aleje Ujazdowskie to Łazienki Park. Some of Warsaw's finest churches and palaces line this route.

㉒ Former headquarters of the Polish Communist Party. In an ironic twist of history, this large, solid, gray building, erected in the Socialist-Realist architectural style, came to house banks and, until 2001, the pre-teenage Warsaw Stock Exchange. ✉ *Corner al. Jerozolimskie and Nowy Świat.*

⑰ Galeria Zachęta (Zachęta Gallery). Built at the end of the 19th century by the Society for the Encouragement of the Fine Arts, the gallery was the site of the assassination of the first president of the post–World War I Polish Republic, Gabriel Narutowicz, by a right-wing fanatic in 1922. It has no permanent collection but organizes thought-provoking special exhibitions (primarily modern art) in lofty, well-lighted halls. The bookshop is excellent. ✉ *Pl. Małachowskiego 3* ☎ *022/827–58–54* ⊕ *www. zacheta.art.pl* ⏱ *Tues.–Sun. noon–8.*

㉖ Gestapo Headquarters. Now the Ministry of National Education, the building houses a small museum that recalls the horrors that took place behind its peaceful facade during World War II, when it served as the headquarters of the Nazi secret police. ✉ *Al. Szucha 25* ☎ *022/629–49–19* ⏱ *Wed. 9–5, Thurs. and Sat. 9–4, Fri. 10–5, Sun. 10–4.*

⑮ Grób Nieznanego Żołnierza (Tomb of the Unknown Soldier). The only surviving fragment of an early 18th-century Saxon palace, which was blown up by the Nazis in 1944, now honors Poland's war dead. Ceremonial changes of the guard take place here at noon on Sunday; the Polish army still uses the goose step. ✉ *Pl. Piłsudskiego.*

⑲ Kościoł świętego Krzyża (Holy Cross Church). The heart of the great Polish composer Frédéric Chopin is immured in a pillar inside this baroque church. Opposite the church is a statue of the astronomer Nicolaus Copernicus, another famous Pole. ⊠ *Krakowskie Przedmieście 3.*

⑪ Kościół świętej Anny (St. Anne's Church). Originally constructed in 1454, this church was rebuilt in high-baroque style in the 17th century. A plaque on the wall outside marks the spot where Pope John Paul II celebrated mass in 1980, during his first visit to Poland after his election to the papacy. ⊠ *Krakowskie Przedmieście 68.*

★ **㉓ Muzeum Narodowe** (National Museum of Warsaw). The spacious, skylighted museum has an impressive collection of 19th-century Polish and European paintings, Gothic icons, and works from antiquity. ⊠ *Al. Jerozolimskie 3* ☎ *022/621–10–31* ⊕ *www.mnw.art.pl* ☉ *Tues., Wed., and Fri. 10–4, Thurs. noon–5, weekends 10–4.*

㉔ Muzeum Wojska Polskiego (Polish Army Museum). With exhibits of weaponry, armor, and uniforms tracing Polish military history across the past 10 centuries, it captures the romance of the subject. If the museum is closed, stroll past the gates to see the military helicopters, airplanes, and tanks parked outside. ⊠ *Al. Jerozolimskie 3* ☎ *022/629–52–71* ☉ *May–Sept., Wed.–Sun. 11–5; Oct.–Apr., Wed.–Sun. 11–4.*

㉘ Ogród Botaniczny (Botanical Gardens). These beautiful plantings belonging to Warsaw University were laid out in 1818. Note the neoclassical **observatory**. ⊠ *Al. Ujazdowskie 4* ☎ *022/628–75–14* ☉ *Daily dawn–dusk.*

⑯ Ogród Saski (Saxon Gardens). French and Saxon landscape gardeners designed the palace park; the gardens contain 18th-century sculptures, a man-made pond, and a sundial. ⊠ *Corner ul. Marszałkowska and ul. Królewska.*

㉚ Pałac Belweder (Belvedere Palace). This 18th-century former residence and office of the president was vacated in 1994 by former president Lech Wałesa, who declared Pałac Namiestnikowski the official presidential residence after the fall of Communism. It is currently closed to the public. ⊠ *Ul. Belwederska 2.*

㉑ Pałac Kultury i Nauki (Palace of Culture and Science). With ironic humor, locals tell you that the best vantage point from which to admire their city is from the 30th-floor viewing platform on the 42-story Palace of Culture and Science. Why? Because it is the only point from which you can't see the Palace of Culture and Science. This wedding-cake-style skyscraper was a personal gift from Stalin. It is Warsaw's best example of early 1950s "Socialist Gothic" architecture. ⊠ *Pl. Defilad 1* ☎ *022/620–02–11* ☉ *Daily 9–6.*

★ **㉙ Pałac Łazienkowski** (Łazienki Palace). Set inside the wonderfully landscaped French-style **Park Łazienkowski,** the palace, a gem of the Polish neoclassical style, was the private residence of Stanisław August Poniatowski (1732–98), the last king of Poland. It overlooks a lake stocked with huge carp. At the impressionistic Chopin monument nearby, open-air concerts take place on summer Sunday. ⊠ *Ul. Agrykola 1* ☎ *022/621–62–41* ☉ *Tues.–Sun. 10–3:15.*

⑬ Pałac Namiestnikowski (Namiestnikowski Palace). Built during the 17th century by the Radziwiłł family (into which Jacqueline Kennedy's sister, Lee, later married), this palace at one time functioned as the administrative office of the czarist occupiers. In 1955 the Warsaw Pact was signed here, and now the palace serves as the official residence of

Poland's president. In the forecourt is an equestrian statue of Prince Józef Poniatowski, a nephew of the last king of Poland, and one of Napóleon's marshals. The building is closed to the public and heavily guarded. ✉ *Krakowskie Przedmieście 46–48.*

⑳ Pałac Ostrogskich (Ostrogski Palace). Headquarters of the Chopin Society, the 17th-century mansion towers impressively above the street. The best approach is along the steps from ulica Tamka. In the 19th century the Warsaw Conservatory was housed here (Paderewski was one of its students); now used for Chopin concerts, it has a small museum with mementos of the composer. ✉ *Ul. Okólnik 1* ☎ *022/827–54–71* ⊙ *Mon.–Wed., Fri., and Sat. 10–2, Thurs. noon–6.*

★ ㉛ Pałac Wilanów (Wilanow Palace). Built by King Jan Sobieski, who in 1683 stopped the Ottoman advance on Europe at the Battle of Vienna, the palace later passed into the hands of Stanisław Kostka Potocki. Potocki amassed a major art collection, laid out the palace gardens, and opened Poland's first public museum here in 1805. The palace still contains much of the original furniture; there's also a striking display of 16th- to 18th-century Polish portraits on the first floor. Outside, to the left of the main entrance, is a romantic park with pagodas, summerhouses, and bridges overlooking a lake. There's also a **gallery** of contemporary Polish art on the grounds, and the stables to the right of the entrance house a **poster museum.** ✉ *Ul. Wiertnicza 1, 10 km (6 mi) south of town center* ☎ *022/ 842–81–01* ⊕ *www.wilanow-palac.art.pl* ⊙ *Palace Tues.–Sun. 9:30–2:30, Sun. until 6 PM mid-June–mid-Sept.; park daily 9–dusk.*

⑫ Rynek Mariensztacki (Mariensztat Square). At the bottom and to the left of a steeply sloping, cobbled street lies a quiet, leafy 18th-century square that is worth a detour. ✉ *Ul. Bednarska.*

㉕ Sejm. The Polish Houses of Parliament, with their round, white debating chamber, were built in the 1920s, after the rebirth of an independent Polish state. The building is not open to the public. ✉ *Ul. Wiejska 4–6.*

⑭ Teatr Narodowy (Opera House and National Theater). This columned theater, built in the 1820s and reconstructed after World War II, has a grand dome that is adorned inside with abstract constellation art. The **Museum Teatralne** (Museum of Theatre; ☎ 022/826–52–13), on the first floor, is open Friday through Wednesday 10–2. ✉ *Pl. Teatralny* ☎ *022/ 629–02–08.*

⑱ Warsaw University. Established in 1816, the university has been a center for independent political thinking; most student protests have started here. Near the university, in the small garden opposite ulica Bednarska, stands a monument to the great Polish poet Adam Mickiewicz. It was here that Warsaw University students gathered in March 1968, after a performance of Mickiewicz's until-then banned play, *Forefathers' Eve,* and set in motion the events that led to the toppling of Poland's long-time Communist leader Władysław Gomułka. ✉ *Krakowskie Przedmieście 26–28* ☎ *022/620–03–81* ⊕ *www.uw.edu.pl.*

㉗ Zamek Ujazdowski (Ujazdów Castle). Reconstructed in the 1980s, this is now home of the **Center for Contemporary Art,** which hosts a variety of exhibitions by Polish, European, and North American artists. The terrace in back overlooks formal gardens laid out down to the Vistula. ✉ *Al. Ujazdowskie 6* ☎ *022/628–12–71* ⊕ *csw.art.pl* ⊙ *Tues.–Thurs. and weekends 11–5, Fri. 11–9.*

The Muranów District

The Muranów district is the historic heart of the prewar Warsaw Jewish district and ghetto under the Nazi regime. In April 1943 the Jewish resistance began the Warsaw Ghetto uprising, which was suppressed by the Nazis with unbelievable ferocity; the Muranów district was flattened. Today there are mostly just bleak gray apartment blocks here.

㊲ Fragment of ghetto wall. In the courtyard of this building, through the archway on the right, stands a 10-foot-tall fragment of the ghetto wall that existed for one year from November 1940. ✉ *Ul. Sienna 55.*

㉞ Jewish Cemetery. This active cemetery is an island of continuity amid destruction. It survived the war and, although badly neglected during the postwar period, is gradually being restored. Fine 19th-century headstones testify to the Jewish community's important role in Polish history and culture. ✉ *Ul. Okopowa 49–51.*

㉟ Jewish Historical Institute. Some 3 million Polish Jews were put to death by the Nazis during World War II, ending the enormous Jewish contribution to Polish culture, tradition, and achievement. The institute houses a genealogy project that acts as a clearinghouse of information on archival sources and on the history of towns and villages in which Polish Jews lived. The institute also contains a **museum** with displays of photographs and artifacts recalling a lost world. The nearby Sony building stands on the site of Warsaw's largest synagogue, which was blown up by the Nazis in May 1943 as a finale to the liquidation of the Jewish ghetto. ✉ *Ul. Tłomackie 3* ☏ *022/827–92–21* ⊕ *www.jewishinstitute. org.pl* ☉ *Tues.–Fri. 10–6.*

㉝ Pomnik Bohaterów Getta (Monument to the Heroes of the Warsaw Ghetto). The simple monument to the heroes of the Warsaw Ghetto uprising is a slab of dark granite with a bronze bas-relief. A monument— inscribed in Hebrew and Polish—also marks the site of the house at ulica Miła 18 in which the command bunker of the uprising was concealed. ✉ *Ul. Zamenhofa, between ul. Anielewicza and ul. Lewartowskiego.*

㊱ Ulica Próżna. This is the only thoroughfare in Jewish Warsaw where tenement buildings have been preserved on both sides of the street. The Lauder Foundation plans to restore the street to its original state. No. 9 belonged to Zelman Nożyk, founder of the ghetto synagogue.

㉜ Umschlagplatz. From this rail terminus, hundreds of thousands of the ghetto's inhabitants were shipped in cattle cars to the extermination camp of Treblinka, about 100 km (60 mi) northeast of Warsaw. The school building to the right of the square was used to detain those who had to wait overnight for transport, and the beginning of the rail tracks survives on the right. At the entrance to the square is a memorial gateway, erected in 1988 to commemorate the 45th anniversary of the uprising. The first names of deportees are inscribed on the walls. ✉ *Ul. Stawki and ul. Dzika.*

Where to Eat

Interesting and ethnically diverse restaurants have sprung up over the city in the past few years, yet some of the most atmospheric dining rooms are still to be found on and around the Rynek Starego Miasta. For the higher-price dining spots, it is essential to make reservations, which can be done by telephone (or by your hotel receptionist if you don't speak Polish).

★ **$$$$** ✕ **Belvedere.** You could not find a more romantic setting for lunch or dinner than this elegant restaurant in the New Orangery at Łazienki Park. The traditional Polish menu offers dishes prepared with a variety of fresh mushrooms and a delicious roast boar. ✉ *Łazienki Park, ul. Agrykola 1, enter from ul. Parkowa* ☏ *022/841–48–06* ⚑ *Reservations essential* ▭ *AE, DC, MC, V.*

★ $$$–$$$$ ✕ **Dom Restauracyjny Gessler.** Three restaurants make up this establishment; the brick cellar, bathed in candlelight, serves traditional Polish recipes while music students often entertain. The ground floor houses a café and the first floor specializes in European cuisine. ⊠ *Rynek Starego Miasta 19–21* ☎ *022/831–44–27* ⌂ *Reservations essential* ⊟ *AE, DC, MC, V.*

$$$–$$$$ ✕ **Fukier.** This long-established wine bar (with a 15th-century wine cellar) has become a fascinating network of elaborately decorated dining rooms, specializing in Polish cuisine with a European twist. Follow the steak, served on a grill, with one of the rich cream gâteaux. ⊠ *Rynek Starego Miasta 27* ☎ *022/831–10–13* ⊟ *AE, DC, MC, V.*

$$–$$$$ ✕ **Café Ejlat.** A Warsaw institution owned by the Polish-Israeli Friendship Society has a menu rich in traditional Jewish dishes (including a halvah dessert) and contemporary Polish cuisine. ⊠ *Al. Ujazdowskie 47* ☎ *022/628–54–72* ⌂ *Reservations essential* ⊟ *AE, DC, MC, V.*

$$–$$$$ ✕ **Qchnia Artystyczna.** The vegetarian dishes on the menu are creative and filling at this artsy eatery at the back of the Ujazdowski Castle. Unfortunately, the service is terrible. Sample the *naleśniki* (crepes stuffed with sweet cheese or fruit). In summer, outdoor tables overlook the park. ⊠ *Zamek Ujazdowski, Al. Ujazdowskie 6* ☎ *022/625–76–27* ⊟ *AE, DC, MC, V.*

★ $$–$$$$ ✕ **Restauracja Polska.** This restaurant is the place to be seen in Warsaw these days and, decorated with antique furnishings and bouquets of flowers, it is also a treat for the senses. The specialty here is nouvelle Polish cuisine, and the service is excellent. You can't go wrong with any of the dishes, but try the royal carp with sour cream sauce, an update of the country's classic Christmas dish. ⊠ *Nowy Świat 21* ☎ *022/826–38–77* ⊟ *AE, DC, MC, V.*

$$–$$$ ✕ **Czytelnik.** Intellectuals and politicians from the Parliament next door hang out at this cafeteria-style restaurant-café with homemade, upscale milk-bar cuisine: classic Polish soups, such as tomato and mushroom, and cutlets of various meats, from veal to pork to chicken. ⊠ *Ul. Wiejska 12a* ☎ *022/628–14–41* ⊟ *No credit cards* ◷ *No dinner.*

$$–$$$ ✕ **Studio Buffo.** Just steps from the Sheraton, this fashionable restaurant offers patio dining in summer. The constantly changing menu is mainly a twist on classic Polish dishes. ⊠ *Ul. Marii Konopnickiej 6* ☎ *022/626–89–07* ⊟ *AE, DC, MC, V.*

Where to Stay

Orbis hotels are reliable, offering standardized, functional rooms. Most show signs of wear, but bathrooms are usually up to Western European standards. Some hotels have lower prices during the winter months. Private accommodations are cheap and hospitable. Information and reservations are available through the Center for Tourist Information. **Bureau of Private Accommodations** (⊠ Ul. Krucza 17 ☎ 022/628–75–40) arranges for rooms in private homes.

$$$$ 🏨 **Le Royal Méridien Bristol.** This is Warsaw's most exclusive and luxurious hotel, where heads of state and celebrities stay when visiting the
Fodor'sChoice city. It was built in 1901 and once partially owned by Ignacy Paderewski, the pianist who was Poland's prime minister in 1919–20. The decidedly Polish Sunday brunch includes a caviar bar. ⊠ *Krakowskie Przedmieście 42–44, 00–325* ☎ *022/625–25–25* 🖷 *022/625–25–77* ⊕ *www.bristol.polhotels.com* ⇌ *163 rooms, 43 suites* ⌂ *2 restaurants, pool, bar* ⊟ *AE, DC, MC, V.*

$$$$ 🏨 **Marriott.** This Marriott's 40 stories (20 make up the hotel; the rest are office and retail shopping space) make it one of the tallest buildings

in Warsaw. Its Italian restaurant, Parmizzano's, is among the best of its kind in the city. Café Vienna, on the mezzanine level, is a popular meeting place. ⊠ *Al. Jerozolimskie 65–79, 00–697* ☎ *022/630–63–06* 🖷 *022/830–03–11* ⊕ *www.marriotthotels.com* ➘ *487 rooms, 34 suites* ♨ *3 restaurants, pool, 3 bars* 🖃 *AE, DC, MC, V.*

★ **$$$$** 🖾 **Sheraton.** Halfway down the Royal Route from the Old Town, this hotel stands near the Parliament and Embassy Row. Some of the tastefully decorated and generously sized rooms overlook a beautiful square. The well-trained staff makes this hotel the friendliest in Warsaw. ⊠ *Ul. Prusa 2, 00–493* ☎ *022/657–61–00* 🖷 *022/657–62–00* ⊕ *www.sheraton. pl* ➘ *331 rooms, 21 suites* ♨ *3 restaurants* 🖃 *AE, DC, MC, V.*

$$$–$$$$ 🖾 **Holiday Inn.** Opposite Warsaw's Central Station, this friendly hotel avoids some of the standard chain-hotel impersonality. A tree-filled, steel-and-glass conservatory fronts the building up to the third floor. ⊠ *Ul. Złota 48, 00–120* ☎ *022/697–39–99* 🖷 *022/697–38–99* ⊕ *www. sixcontinenthotels.com* ➘ *365 rooms* ♨ *3 restaurants, 2 bars* 🖃 *AE, DC, MC, V.*

$$$ 🖾 **Hotel Europejski.** This late-19th-century hotel has views overlooking the Royal Route. Rooms are spacious, and the location is so good that you may not mind the slightly shabby furnishings. ⊠ *Krakowskie Przedmieście 13, 00–065* ☎ *022/826–50–51* 🖷 *022/826–11–11* ⊕ *www. orbis.pl* ➘ *224 rooms, 13 suites* ♨ *Restaurant* 🖃 *AE, DC, MC, V.*

$$ 🖾 **Dom Chłopa.** This renovated 1950s hotel has bright, pine-furnished rooms with gleaming bathrooms. It is a five-minute walk from the primary shopping streets and the National Philharmonic. If you don't mind the noisy clientele of the nightclub on the ground floor, it's a good value. ⊠ *Pl. Powstańców Warszawy 2, 00–030* ☎ *022/625–15–45* 🖷 *022/625–21–40* ➘ *282 rooms* ♨ *Restaurant, bar* 🖃 *AE, DC, MC, V.*

$$ 🖾 **MDM.** The rooms are slightly dreary, with brown bedspreads, but the place is clean and the bathrooms are up to Western standards. For a downtown hotel, you can't beat the price. The central location can be noisy, so request a room on one of the higher floors. ⊠ *Pl. Konstytucji 1, 00–647* ☎ *022/621–62–11* 🖷 *022/621–41–73* ⊕ *www.mdm.hotel.pl* ➘ *105 rooms, 5 suites* ♨ *2 restaurants* 🖃 *AE, DC, MC, V.*

Nightlife & the Arts

The Arts

The monthly *Warsaw Insider* (⊕ www.warsawinsider.com), available at most major hotels, is the best English-language source. If you read Polish, *Gazeta Wyborcza* and the monthly *IKS* (*Informator Kulturalny Stolicy*) or *City Magazine* have extensive listings. Tickets can be ordered at your hotel, at the theater, or through the ticket office of **ZASP** (⊠ Al. Jerozolimskie 25 ☎ 022/621–93–83).

CONCERTS The **National Philharmonic** (⊠ Ul. Sienkiewicza 10 ☎ 022/826–72–81) is Poland's best concert hall. The **Royal Castle** (⊠ Pl. Zamkowy 4 ☎ 022/657–21–70) has regular concerts in its stunning Great Assembly Hall. In summer free Chopin concerts are held at the Chopin monument in **Łazienki Park** on Sunday.

OPERA **Teatr Wielki** (⊠ Pl. Teatralny 1 ☎ 022/826–32–88) hosts the Grand Theater of Opera and Ballet. Its stage is one of Europe's largest. The beautiful, intimate **Opera Kameralna** (Warsaw Opera House; ⊠ Al. Solidarności 76b ☎ 022/625–7510) theater is not to be missed.

THEATERS There are still 17 major theaters in Warsaw, despite large cuts in state funding, attesting to Poles' love of this art form. The **Globe Theatre Group** (☎ 022/620–44–29) has a varied contemporary English-language repertory. **Teatr Narodowy** (✉ pl. Teatralny 1 ☎ 022/826–32–88) is the oldest in Poland; it opened in 1765. **Żydowski Theater** (✉ Pl. Grzybowski 12/16 ☎ 022/620–70–25), Warsaw's Jewish Theater, stages performances in Yiddish.

Nightlife

BARS **Harenda** (✉ Krakowskie Przedmieście 4/6, enter from ul. Obożna ☎ 022/ 826–29–00), with an outdoor terrace in summer, is open until 3 AM; jazz is played almost every night in the cellar bar. **Soma** (✉ Ul. Foksal 19 ☎ 022/828–21–33) is a bright, spacious bar-restaurant with comfy couches reminiscent of trendy spots found in London or New York. The Irish-owned **Morgan's** (✉ Ul. Okólnik 1 ☎ 022/826–81–38), below the Pałac Ostrogskich, stays open until the wee hours.

CAFÉS Warsaw's *kawiarnia* (cafés), which move outdoors in summer, are busy meeting places, serving coffee and pastries in Central European, Viennese style. **Café Blikle** (✉ Nowy Świat 35 ☎ 022/826–66–19) is a traditional, fashionable hangout on Warsaw's main shopping street; try the *pączki* (Polish doughnuts). **Cafe Brama** (✉ ul. Marszałkowska 8 ☎ 022/ 629–65–36) serves great food and coffee; the café's ban on cell phones fosters a quiet, conversation-friendly atmosphere. **E. Wedel** (✉ Ul. Szpitalna 8 ☎ No phone), a venerable Warsaw institution, is best known for its thick, incredibly rich hot chocolate. The large glass facade of the **Modulor Café** (✉ Pl. Trzech Krzyży 8 ☎ 022/627–26–04) makes this the place to see and be seen. It serves good coffees and salads. The tiny, fourtable café **Pożegnanie z Afryką** ("Out of Africa"; ✉ Ul. Freta 4/6 ☎ no phone) has aromatic coffees from all over the world but a limited selection of pastries. If you're craving a Starbucks-style experience, then **TriBeCa Coffee** (✉ Ul. Bracka 22 ☎ no phone) is your place.

DANCE CLUBS The cavernous **Ground Zero** (✉ Ul. Wspólna 62 ☎ 022/625–43–80), a former bomb shelter, is a large, crowded bilevel disco. **Labirynt** (✉ Ul. Smolna 12 ☎ 022/826–22–20) plays mainstream pop and dance for an upscale crowd and has a two-lane bowling alley. The elegant **Piekarnia** (✉ Ul. Młocińa 11 ☎ 022/636–49–79) is where local and international DJs come to play.

JAZZ CLUBS Hotel Bristol's plush **Column Bar** (✉ Krakowskie Przedmieście 42/44 ☎ 022/625–25–25) has live jazz on Friday nights. The cozy **Kawiarnia Literacka** (✉ Krakowskie Przedmieście 87/89 ☎ 022/826–5784) has classic jazz on Sunday evenings.

Shopping

Nowy Świat, Krakowskie Przedmieście, and ulica Chmielna are lined with boutiques selling good-quality leather goods, silver and amber jewelry, clothing, and trinkets. For the best selection of Polish wood carvings, including animals and nativity scenes, go to **Arex** (✉ Ul. Chopina 5B ☎ 022/629–66–24). Try the **Cepelia stores** (✉ Pl. Konstytucji 5 ☎ 022/621–26–18 ✉ Rynek Starego Miasta 10 ☎ 022/831–18–05) for handicrafts such as glass, enamelware, amber, and handwoven wool rugs. **Desa** (✉ Ul. Marszałkowska 34 ☎ 022/621–66–15 ✉ Nowy Świat 51 ☎ 022/827–47–60) specializes in antiques, but note that objects from before 1945 cannot be legally exported. **Galeria Plakatu** (✉ Rynek Starego Miasta 23 ☎ 022/831–93–06) has an excellent selection of Polish posters, many of which celebrate National Theater performances.

Warsaw Essentials

AIRPORTS & TRANSFERS

International flights arrive at Warsaw's Okęcie Airport just southwest of the city. Terminal 1 serves international flights; Terminal 2, next door, serves domestic flights.

🛈 **Okęcie Airport** ☎ 022/650-42-20 or 0800/244-855 ⊕ www.porty-lotnicze.com.pl.

TRANSFERS The AIRPORT–CITY bus (zł 5.60–zł 10) leaves every 20 minutes from Platform 4 outside Terminal 1 and passes many downtown hotels on its route. The trip takes about 25 minutes. Bus 175 (zł 2.40) departs every 15 minutes and also runs past almost all major downtown hotels.

Avoid at all costs taxi drivers who approach you inside and those parked outside the arrivals hall. Your best bet is to go upstairs to the departure drop-off and hail a taxi (if the driver cannot take you, ask him to call one) or call for a radio taxi (fare about zł 25). Some of the hotels will also pick you up (fare about zł 35).

🛈 **Radio taxi** ☎ 022/919.

BUS TRAVEL TO & FROM WARSAW

Dworzec PKS Zachodni is Warsaw's main bus terminal and serves most long-distance routes.

🛈 **Dworzec PKS Zachodni** ⊠ Al. Jerozolimskie 144 ☎ 022/823-63-94.

BUS, TRAM & SUBWAY TRAVEL WITHIN WARSAW

Though often crowded, trams and buses are the cheapest way of getting around. A ticket, valid for a daytime ride, costs zł 2.40. Night buses run between 11:15 PM and 4:45 AM and require three tickets. Tickets may be bought in advance from Ruch newsstands or from bus drivers. You must validate the ticket in a machine on the tram or bus when you get on; watch how others do it. Beware of professional pickpockets.

Warsaw's only subway line runs from the southern suburbs to the city center (Kabaty to Ratusz, at Plac Bankowy). It is clean and fast and costs the same as the tram and bus. Tickets are electronically canceled once you enter the turnstiles. Trains run from 5 AM to 11:30 PM, every five minutes during rush hours and every 15 minutes during off-peak hours.

CAR TRAVEL

A car is more a nuisance than a convenience in the city, due to scarce parking and frequent traffic snarls. Seven main access routes lead to the center of Warsaw. Highways E30 and E77 are the main arteries from the west. Street parking costs zł 1.40 per hour.

CONSULATES

🛈 **United Kingdom** ⊠ Ul. Emilii Plater 28 ☎ 022/625-30-99.

EMERGENCIES

Call the number listed below for an ambulance and doctor, or call your embassy or the American Medical Center. Pharmacies in Warsaw stay open late on a rotational system. Signs listing the nearest open facility are posted outside every pharmacy. There is also a 24-hour pharmacy upstairs in the Central Train Station.

🛈 **Emergency Services Ambulance and Doctor** ☎ 999. **American Medical Center (AMC)** ⊠ Ul. Wilcza 23, Suite 29 ☎ 0602/243-024, 24-hr service. **Police** ☎ 997.
🛈 **24-hour Pharmacies** ⊠ Central Train Station, Al. Jerozolimskie 54 ☎ 022/825-69-84.

ENGLISH-LANGUAGE BOOKSTORES

🛈 **Bookland** ⊠ Al. Jerozolimskie 61 ☎ 022/625-41-46. **Empik** ⊠ Nowy Świat 15-17 ☎ 022/625-67-94 ⊠ Ul. Marszałkowska 116-122 ☎ 022/627-43-65.

TAXIS

Taxis are still relatively cheap—about zł 3.60 for the first kilometer (½ mi) and zł 1.60 for each additional kilometer—and are readily available at taxi stands. Beware of any that just have a TAXI sign on the top of the car with no company name—they do not have meters and may rip you off. Most major hotels have their own monogrammed fleets, but expect to pay more than you would for the efficient radio taxi service, which is also considerably cheaper than taxis at stands.
▪ **Radio taxi** ☎ 022/919.

TOURS

Bus tours of the city depart in the morning and afternoon from major hotels. Mazurkas Travel offers an excellent selection of tours around the city. Orbis also has half-day excursions into the surrounding countryside. Our Roots conducts four-hour tours of Jewish Warsaw.

Horse-drawn carriages can be rented at a negotiated price at the Old Town Market Square or Castle Square. Prices vary, but the average rate is zł 60 for a ride around the entire Old Town area.
▪ **Mazurkas Travel** ⊠ Ul. Długa 8/14 ☎ 022/635-66-33. **Orbis** ⊠ Ul. Marszałkowska 142 ☎ 022/827-80-31. **Our Roots** ⊠ Ul. Twarda 6 ☎ 022/620-05-56.

TRAIN TRAVEL

Trains to and from Western Europe and domestic lines arrive at Warszawa Centralna in the center of town. For tickets contact a travel agent or your hotel, or go to the train station.
▪ **Dworzec Centralny** (Central Station) ⊠ Al. Jerozolimskie 54 ☎ 022/620-03-61 domestic train information; 022/620-45-12 international train information.

TRAVEL AGENCIES

▪ **American Express** ⊠ Ul. Sienna 39 ☎ 022/581-51-00 ⊠ Marriott Hotel, Al. Jerozolimskie 65/79 ☎ 022/630-69-52 ☎ 022/625-40-30 for lost or stolen cards, 6 AM–2 AM. **Carlson/Wagonlit Travel** ⊠ Nowy Świat 64 ☎ 022/826-04-31. **Orbis Travel Office** ⊠ Ul. Marszałkowska 142 ☎ 022/827-80-31. **Our Roots–Jewish Information and Tourist Bureau** ⊠ Ul. Twarda 6 ☎ 022/620-05-56.

VISITOR INFORMATION

▪ **Center for Tourist Information** ⊠ Pl. Zamkowy 1 ☎ 022/635-18-81. **Warsaw Tourist Information Office** ⊠ Dom Chłopa, Pl. Powstańców Warszawy 2 ☎ 022/625-15-45.

KRAKÓW

Kraków, the ancient capital of Poland (before gracefully relinquishing the honor to Warsaw in 1609) and seat of one of the oldest universities in Europe, miraculously escaped devastation during World War II. Preserved like an insect in amber, Kraków's Old Town with its fine ramparts, towers, facades, and churches, illustrating seven centuries of Polish architecture, has earned a listing by UNESCO as one of the 12 great historic cities of the world. Refreshingly provincial, with a decidedly bohemian attitude, Kraków does not rush into the 21st century, but lives at its own leisurely pace.

The city's location—about 270 km (167 mi) south of Warsaw—makes it a good base for hiking and skiing trips in the mountains of southern Poland. Within exploring range from Kraków are the Polish shrine to the Virgin Mary at Częstochowa, and a grim reminder of man's capacity for inhumanity at Auschwitz (Oświęcim).

Exploring Kraków

Numbers in the margin correspond to points of interest on the Kraków map.

In Kraków, all roads lead to Rynek Główny, with all major sights within walking distance. Each of the three basic districts for touring—the Old Town, the Jewish quarter, and the Wawel—can be seen in a half day or so, but more time can easily be spent.

❶ Barbakan (The Barbican). This imposing, round, redbrick 15th-century fortress was part of the old city defense system. It stands in Planty Park, which, circling the Old Town, replaces the old walls, which were torn down in the mid-19th century. ⊠ *Ul. Basztowa.*

❷ Brama Floriańska (St. Florian's Gate). The surviving fragment of the city wall opposite the Barbakan, where students and amateur artists like to hang their paintings for sale in the summer, contains the Renaissance-period Municipal Arsenal, now one of Kraków's exhibition spaces. ⊠ *Ul. Pijarska.*

★ ❾ Collegium Maius. The pride of the oldest building of the world-renowned **Jagiellonian University**, founded in 1364, is the Italian-style arcaded courtyard. A **museum** (☎ 012/422–05–49 ⊙ Mon.–Thurs. 11–3, Sat. 11–1:30) contains the so-called Jagiellonian globe, the first on which the American continents were shown, as well as astronomy instruments from the time of Copernicus, Kraków's most famous graduate. ⊠ *Ul. Jagiellońska 15* ⊙ *Courtyard Mon.–Sat. 8–6.*

★ ❺ Kościół Mariacki (Church of Our Lady). Every hour, four short bugle calls drift down from the spire of this church. The notes are a centuries-old tradition that honors a trumpeter whose throat was pierced by an enemy arrow as he was warning his fellow citizens of an impending Tartar attack. Inside the church is a 15th-century wooden altarpiece—the world's largest and arguably one of the most magnificent—carved by Veit Stoss. The saints' faces are reputedly those of local burghers. ⊠ *Rynek Główny* ⊙ *Altar Mon.–Sat. 11:30–6, Sun. 2–6.*

⓫ Kościół na Skałce (Church on the Rock). Standing on the Vistula embankment south of Wawel Hill, this church is the center of the cult of St. Stanisław, an 11th-century bishop and martyr. From the 19th century on, it became the last resting place for well-known Polish writers and artists. ⊠ *Between ul. Skałeczna and ul. Paulińska on the Vistula.*

★ ❸ Muzeum Czartoryskich (Czartoryski Museum). This branch of the National Museum, partially housed in the **Municipal Arsenal**, has one of the best art collections in Poland. Among its treasures is Leonardo da Vinci's *Lady with an Ermine.* ⊠ *Ul. Św. Jana 19* ☎ 012/422–55–66 ⊙ *Tues. and Thurs. 9–3:30, Wed. 11–6, Sat. 10–3:30.*

❼ Muzeum Narodowe (National Museum). The highlights of this museum are Polish art nouveau and 20th-century paintings, as well as historic arms and uniforms. ⊠ *Al. 3 Maja 1* ☎ 012/634–33–77 ⊙ *Tues. and Thurs.–Sun. 10–3:30, Wed. 10–6.*

⓬ Ratusz (City Hall of Kazimierz). The 15th-century building presides over the Kazimierz district of Kraków, which was once a town in its own right, chartered in 1335 and named for its founder, Kazimierz the Great. Today the former seat of government houses **Muzeum Etnograficzne** (Ethnographic Museum), which displays a well-mounted collection of regional folk art. ⊠ *Pl. Wolnica* ☎ 012/430–55–63 ⊙ *Mon. 10–6, Wed.–Fri. 10–3, weekends 10–2.*

Kraków

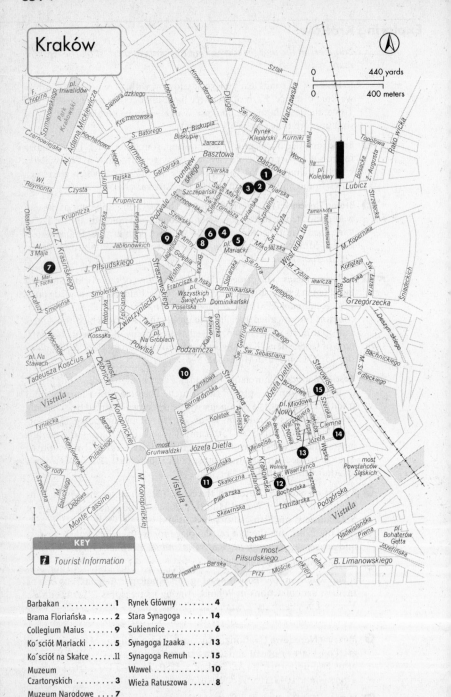

0 — 440 yards
0 — 400 meters

KEY

🛈 Tourist Information

4 **Rynek Główny** (Main Market Square). Europe's largest medieval mar-
Fodor'sChoice   ketplace is on a par in size and grandeur with St. Mark's Square in Venice.
★   Although there are a few flower sellers who remain as reminders of the
square's once-bustling commercial activity, the Rynek mainly serves as
a large outdoor patio for the cafés that line its perimeter. ⊠ *Center of
Old Town at ul. Floriańska and ul. Św. Anny.*

14 **Stara Synagoga** (Old Synagogue). This synagogue was built in the 15th
century and reconstructed in Renaissance style following a fire in 1557.
Here, in 1794, Tadeusz Kościuszko successfully appealed to the Jewish
community to join in the national insurrection. The synagogue now houses
the **Museum of the History and Culture of Kraków Jews.** ⊠ *Ul. Szeroka 24* ☎ *012/422–09–62* ☽ *Wed., Thurs., and weekends 9–3, Fri.
11–6* ☽ *Closed 1st weekend of month.*

6 **Sukiennice** (Cloth Hall). In the center of the main square stands a covered market hall built in the 14th century but remodeled during the Renaissance. The ground floor is still in business, selling trinkets and
folk-art souvenirs. On the second floor, in a branch of the **National Museum** (☎ 012/422–11–66), there's a collection of 19th-century Polish
paintings. ⊠ *Rynek Główny* ☽ *Tues. and Thurs. 11–6, Wed. 9–3:30,
weekends 10–3:30.*

13 **Synagoga Izaaka.** This Renaissance synagogue has Roman columns separating the women's gallery from the main room. Two documentaries,
The Jewish District of Kraków (1936) and *Removal to the Kraków Ghetto*
(1941), are continuously shown at the site. ⊠ *Ul. Kupa 18* ☎ *012/602–
300–277* ☽ *Sun.–Fri. 9–7, except Jewish holidays.*

15 **Synagoga Remuh.** This tiny 16th-century synagogue is still used for worship. The cemetery, used by the Jewish community from 1533 to 1799,
is the only well-preserved Renaissance Jewish burial ground in Europe.
The so-called new cemetery, established in 1800, is on ulica Miodowa
and contains many old headstones. ⊠ *Ul. Szeroka 40* ☽ *Sun.–Fri. 9–4,
except Jewish holidays.*

10 **Wawel.** This impressive castle complex of Gothic and Renaissance build-
Fodor'sChoice   ings stands on fortifications that date from the 8th century. Inside the
★   castle is a **museum** with an exotic collection of Asian tents captured from
the Turks at the Battle of Vienna in 1683, as well as rare 16th-century
Flemish tapestries. **Katedra Wawelska** (Wawel Cathedral) is where, until
the 18th century, Polish kings were crowned and buried. Until 1978 the
cathedral was the principal church of Archbishop Karol Wojtyła, later
Pope John Paul II. ⊠ *Ul. Grodzka* ☎ *012/422–51–55* ⊕ *www.cyf-kr.
edu.pl/wawel* ☽ *Tues.–Sat. 9:30–3, Sun. 10–3.*

8 **Wieża Ratuszowa** (Town Hall Tower). Across from the Cloth Hall this
is all that remains of the 16th-century town hall. A climb up the winding staircase give you a good view of the town square from the two observation levels. ⊠ *Rynek Główny.*

Where to Eat

$$$–$$$$ ✕ **Copernicus.** This top-class restaurant in a hotel by the same name in
one of Kraków's loveliest corners, at the foot of Wawel Hill, will de-
light you with its elegant and imaginative menu, cosmopolitan yet with
traditional Polish accents. Although expensive, it is worth every złoty.
⊠ *Ul. Kanonicza 16* ☎ *012/421–10–44* ♵ *Reservations essential*
⊟ *AE, DC, MC, V.*

$$$–$$$$ ✕ **Pod Róża.** Built in the converted courtyard of a tenement house,
Fodor'sChoice Under the Rose is airy, spacious, and elegant, all under a glass roof. A
★ seasonally changing, contemporary menu is matched by impeccable
service; there is nightly live piano music. The chefs make their own pas-
tas, ice cream, and bread. Adjoining is a sister restaurant, Amarone, with
slightly cheaper Italian cuisine. ⊠ *Ul. Floriańska 14* ☎ *012/424–33–81*
⌁ *Reservations essential* ▭ *AE, DC, MC, V.*

$$–$$$$ ✕ **Chłopskie Jadło.** This is the place for authentic Polish cuisine. The interior is a maze of rooms, each decked out like a Polish farmhouse with
benches and chunky wooden picnic tables. The soups are outstanding;
try the *żurek* (sour cream soup). ⊠ *Św. Agnieszki 1* ☎ *012/421–85–20*
⌁ *Reservations essential* ▭ *AE, DC, MC, V.*

★ **$$–$$$$** ✕ **Pod Aniołami.** In summer the restaurant is in a courtyard; in win-
ter it moves into a cozy cellar, which is purported to have once been
an alchemist's lab. The country-style kitchen turns out homemade bread
and hearty entrées. The chef will roast an entire pig for a group.
⊠ *Ul. Grodzka 35* ☎ *012/421–39–99* ⌁ *Reservations essential* ▭ *No
credit cards.*

★ **$–$$$** ✕ **Cherubino.** The menu here is a combination of Polish and Tuscan cui-
sine. The decor is cozy and imaginative: you can choose to dine under
a winged boat or in one of four beautifully restored 19th-century carriages. ⊠ *Św. Tomasza 15* ☎ *012/429–40–07* ▭ *AE, DC, MC, V.*

$$ ✕ **Jama Michalikowa.** Kraków's most famous café is well worth a visit
for its historical and aesthetic quality, if not for the service. ⊠ *Ul. Flo-
riańska 45* ☎ *012/422–15–61* ▭ *No credit cards.*

$$ ✕ **Loch Camelot.** This little café, a favorite of Cracovians and visitors alike,
is decorated with folk and naive art, and filled to the brim most of the
time. If you can get a table and a waiter's attention, there's hardly a better place to get a glass of wine and soak up the lively atmosphere. It's
also open in the morning for coffee. ⊠ *Św. Tomasza 17* ☎ *022/421–
01–23* ▭ *No credit cards.*

Where to Stay

In spite of the new hotels that appear every year, the unceasing popularity of Kraków as a tourist destination makes it essential to book well
in advance, especially during the summer. Rooms facing the street in the
Old Town may be noisy at night.

$$$$ ▣ **Grand.** An air of Regency elegance predominates at this late-19th-
century hotel in the Old Town, although some art nouveau stained-glass
windows have been preserved on the first floor. Rooms have reproduction period furniture, and the banquet room has its own miniature hall
of mirrors. ⊠ *Ul. Sławkowska 5–7, 31–016* ☎ *012/421–72–55* 🖶 *012/
421–83–60* ⊕ *www.grand.pl* 🛏 *56 rooms* ⌂ *Restaurant, bar* ▭ *AE,
DC, MC, V.*

★ **$$$–$$$$** ▣ **Amadeus Hotel.** A stone's throw from the Rynek, this small hotel is
among Kraków's newest. In style and ambience, it claims inspiration
from Wolfgang Amadeus Mozart. ⊠ *Ul. Mikołajska 20, 30–027* ☎ *012/
429–60–70* 🖶 *012/429–60–62* ⊕ *www.hotel-amadeus.pl* 🛏 *22 rooms*
⌂ *Restaurant* ▭ *AE, DC, MC, V.*

$$$–$$$$ ▣ **Holiday Inn.** The four-star Holiday Inn Kraków resides in a refurbished
and extended block of historic tenement houses. The hotel is next to
the main post office, just outside the Planty ring, within walking dis-
tance of the Market Square. ⊠ *Ul. Wielopole 4, 31–072* ☎ *012/619–
00–00* 🖶 *012/619–00–05* ⊕ *www.krakow.globalhotels.pl* 🛏 *164 rooms*
⌂ *Restaurant* ▭ *AE, DC, MC, V.*

$$$–$$$$ 🏨 **Hotel Copernicus.** A tastefully adapted medieval tenement house, this
FodorsChoice hotel is in the oldest and, arguably, the most charming street in Kraków.
★ Traces of history remain in Renaissance portals, wall paintings, and floor
mosaics, although all rooms are happily modern: air-conditioned and
equipped with minibars, TVs, and whirlpool baths. ⊠ *Ul. Kanonicza
16, 31–002* ☎ *012/424–34–00* 🖶 *012/424–34–05* ⊕ *www.hotel.com.
pl* ↩ *37 rooms* ⚄ *Restaurant, pool* ☰ *AE, DC, MC, V.*

$$$ 🏨 **Francuski.** This small, turn-of-the-20th-century hotel stands on a
quiet street just inside the Old Town's ramparts. The atmosphere is in-
timate and the service friendly. The sweeping spiral staircase leads to
rooms that are small but elegant. The restaurant is tranquil and plush.
⊠ *Ul. Pijarska 13, 31–015* ☎ *012/422–51–22* 🖶 *012/422–52–70*
⊕ *www.orbis.pl* ↩ *42 rooms* ⚄ *Restaurant, bar* ☰ *AE, DC, MC, V.*

$$$ 🏨 **Pod Różą.** The management is still proud that both Chopin and Czar
Alexander I slept here. More recently, it has welcomed presidents and
royals. Housed in a 14th-century building, the hotel offers spacious, high-
ceilinged rooms on the fashionable shopping street Floriańska. ⊠ *Ul.
Floriańska 14, 31–021* ☎ *012/424–33–00* 🖶 *012/424–33–51* ⊕ *www.
hotel.com.pl* ↩ *54 rooms* ⚄ *2 restaurants* ☰ *AE, DC, MC, V.*

$$ 🏨 **Pollera.** This 150-year-old hotel is a bit on the shabby side but is a
good value because of its location and original art nouveau decor. ⊠ *Ul.
Szpitalna 30, 31–024* ☎ *012/422–10–44* 🖶 *012/422–13–89* ↩ *42
rooms* ⚄ *Restaurant* ☰ *AE, DC, MC, V.*

Side Trips

Oświęcim (Auschwitz)

Sixty kilometers (38 mi) west of Kraków is Oświęcim, better known by
its German name, Auschwitz. Here 4 million victims, mostly Jews, were
executed by the Nazis in the Auschwitz and Birkenau concentration camps.
Auschwitz is now a museum, with restored crematoria and barracks housing dramatic displays of Nazi atrocities. The buildings at **Birkenau,** a
15-minute walk away, have been left just as they were found in 1945
by the Soviet Army. Oświęcim itself is an industrial town with good connections from Kraków; buses and trains leave Kraków periodically, and
signs in town direct visitors to the former camp. ⊠ *Ul. Więźniów
Oświęcimia 20* ☎ *033/843–21–33* ⊕ *www.auschwitz-muzeum.oswiecim.
pl* ⊗ *Daily 8–dusk.*

Wieliczka

About 12 km (7½ mi) southeast of Kraków, this is the oldest salt mine
in Europe, in operation since the 13th century. The mine is on the UN-
ESCO World Cultural Heritage list and is famous for its miles of salty
corridors and chambers, including the magnificent underground chapel
hewn from crystal rock, the **Chapel of the Blessed Kinga,** named after a
beatified 14th-century Polish queen. ⊠ *Ul. Daniłowicza 10* ☎ *012/278–
73–34* ⊕ *www.kopalnia-wieliczka.pl* ⊗ *Apr.–Oct., daily 7:30–7:30;
Nov.–Mar., daily 8–4.*

Częstochowa

Nearly 120 km (74 mi) from Kraków and reachable by regular trains
and buses, Częstochowa is the home of the holiest shrine in a country
that is some 95% Catholic. Inside the 14th-century **Pauline Monastery**
on Jasna Góra (Hill of Light) is the *Black Madonna of Częstochowa,* a
painting of the Madonna and child attributed by legend to St. Luke. Here
an invading Swedish army met heroic resistance from the Poles in 1655.
⊠ *Al. Najświętszej Marii Panny 1.*

Kraków Essentials

AIR TRAVEL

Kraków can be reached by plane with direct flights from many major European cities and most Polish cities.

🛈 **Pope John Paul II Kraków-Balice Airport** ☎ 012/411-67-00 ⊕ www.lotnisko-balice.pl.

BUS TRAVEL

Express bus service runs regularly between Kraków and most Polish cities. All buses arrive at the main PKS station, just across from the train station on plac Kolejowy.

🛈 **Kraków Main PKS Station** ✉ Ul. Worcella ☎ 012/9316.

CAR TRAVEL

By car Kraków can be reached on major highways—E7 direct from Warsaw and E40 from Częstochowa, and a car is invaluable when making any side trips from the city. Much of Kraków's Old Town is closed to automobile traffic.

CONSULATE

🛈 United States ✉ Ul. Stolarska 9 ☎ 012/429-66-55 🖶 012/421-82-92.

TOURS

Bus or walking tours of Kraków and its environs are provided by Orbis and other travel agencies. Jardan Tours specializes in "Schindler's List" tours. Horse-drawn carriages can be rented at the main market square for a negotiated price.

🛈 **Jardan Tours** ✉ Ul. Szeroka 2 ☎ 012/421-71-66. **Orbis** ✉ Rynek Główny 41 ☎ 012/422-40-35 ✉ Al. Marszałka F. Focha 1 ☎ 012/421-98-80.

TRAIN TRAVEL

Trains link Kraków with most major destinations in Poland; the station, Kraków Główny, is in the city center near the Old Town.

🛈 **Kraków Główny** ✉ Pl. Dworkowy 1 ☎ 012/9436.

VISITOR INFORMATION

🛈 **Częstochowa** Częstochowa Informacja Turystyczna ✉ Al. Najświętszej Marii Panny 64 ☎ 034/324-13-60. **Kraków** ✉ Jewish Cultural Center, ul. Rabina Mieselsa 17 ☎ 012/423-55-95 ✉ Cultural Information Center, ul. Św. Jana 2 ☎ 012/421-77-87 ⊕ www.karnet.krakow2000.pl ✉ Tourist Information Office, Rynek Główny, Sukiennice 1/3 ☎ 012/422-60-91 ✉ Tourist Information Point, ul. Szpitalna 25 ☎ 012/432-01-10.

GDAŃSK & THE NORTH

In contrast to Kraków and the south, Poland north of Warsaw is a land of castles, dense forests and lakes, fishing villages, and beaches. If you don't have a car, consider going straight to Gdańsk and making excursions from there.

Exploring Gdańsk & the North

By car from Warsaw, follow routes E77 and E62 through Płock. Continue through Włocławek to Toruń, where you can stay overnight. The route leading north from Toruń to Gdańsk passes through some of the oldest towns in Poland. Along the way are many medieval castles, manor houses, and churches that testify to the wealth and strategic importance of the area. Two short detours are a must: one is to Kwidzyn, to see the original 14th-century castle and cathedral complex. The other is to Malbork, a medieval castle.

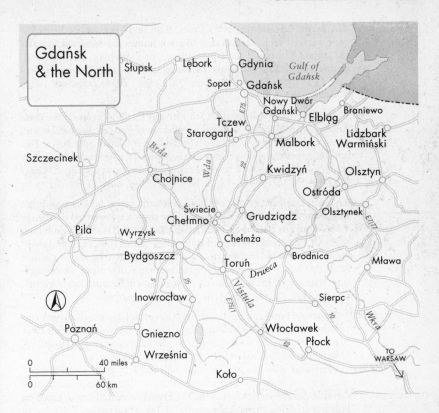

For a different route back to Warsaw, follow highway E77 southeast along the edge of Poland's scenic lake district. The area is rich in natural and historic attractions. A side trip 42 km (26 mi) east of Ostróda takes you to the medieval town of Olsztyn.

Gdańsk

Gdańsk, once the Free City of Danzig, contains one of Poland's beautifully restored Old Towns, displaying a rich heritage of Gothic, Renaissance, and Mannerist architecture. In 1997 Gdańsk celebrated its 1,000th anniversary. This is where the first shots of World War II were fired and where the first free trade union in the Soviet bloc, Solidarity, was born after strikes in August 1980. The city's Old Town has a wonderful collection of historic town houses and narrow streets. The splendid shopping strand, ulica Długa, and Długi Targ (Long Market) are great starting points for walks into other districts. The evocative Pomnik Solidarności (Solidarity Monument)—erected in honor of workers killed by the regime during strikes in 1970—stands outside the former Lenin shipyards. The nearby town of Sopot is Poland's most charming prewar seaside resort.

★ The largest brick church in the world and the largest church in Poland, the **Kościół Najświętszej Marii Panny** (St. Mary's Church) can hold 25,000 people. The 14th-century structure underwent major restoration after World War II, and 15 of its 22 altars have been relocated to museums in Gdańsk and Warsaw. The highlight of a visit is climbing the hundreds of steps up the church tower, where the view is sensational. The church also contains a 500-year-old, 25-foot-high astronomical clock that has been restored to working order after years of neglect. ⊠ *Podkramarska 5.* ⊙ *Daily 9–5.*

The **Żuraw Gdański** (Harbor Crane), built in 1444, was medieval Europe's largest and oldest crane. Today it houses the **Muzeum Morskie** (Maritime Museum), with a collection of models of the ships constructed in the Gdańsk Shipyards since 1945. ⊠ *Ul. Ołowianka 9–13* ☎ *058/301–86–11* ☉ *Oct.–June, Tues.–Sun. 10–4; July–Sept., daily 10–4.*

★ Built over a period from the 15th through the 17th century, the **Dwór Artusa** (Artus Mansion) displays a collection of Renaissance furnishings, paintings, holy figures, and the world's largest Renaissance stove. This and the other stately mansions on the Długi Targ are reminders of the traders and aristocrats who once resided in this posh district. ⊠ *Długi Targ 43* ☎ *058/346–33–58* ☉ *Tues.–Sat. 10–4, Sun. 11–4.*

The city's northern district of Oliwa is worth visiting for its magnificent
★ **Katedra w Oliwie** (Oliwa Cathedral). The church was erected during the 13th century as part of a Cistercian monastery; it has since been rebuilt many times in a hodgepodge of styles from Gothic to Renaissance to rococo. The cathedral houses one of the most impressive organs you're ever likely to hear or see, incorporating more than 6,000 pipes. Demonstrations of the organ are given hourly on weekdays in summer, less frequently on weekends and the rest of the year. ⊠ *Ul. Cystersów 10.*

★ $$$$ ✕ **Tawerna.** For traditional Polish and Germanic dishes such as pork cutlets and seafood, try this well-established restaurant overlooking the river. It's touristy, but the food is delicious. ⊠ *Ul. Powroźnicza 19–20, off Długi Targ* ☎ *058/301–41–14* ▭ *AE, DC, MC, V.*

$$$$ ✕ **Villa Hestia.** Built in 1894, the Sopot villa that houses this elegant restaurant is an architectural and artistic treasure. The atmosphere is comfortable and the service is superb. The French-accented menu, based on Polish specialties, changes seasonally. ⊠ *Ul. Władysława IV 3/5, Sopot* ☎ *058/551–21–00* ▭ *AE, DC, MC, V.*

$$$–$$$$ ✕ **Euro.** Paisley prints and dark wood give this restaurant a tasteful look, matched by its classic menu. The pork chop stuffed with plums is a regional dish. ⊠ *Ul. Długa 79/80* ☎ *058/305–23–83* ▭ *AE, DC, MC, V.*

$$$ ✕ **Retman.** This restaurant, with ornate furniture and stained-glass windows, takes you back to the 18th century. The food includes Old Gdańsk–style cuisine and specialty fish dishes. ⊠ *Ul. Stągiewna 1* ☎ *058/301–92–48* ▭ *AE, DC, MC, V.*

$$$ ▥ **Hanza.** This luxury hotel overlooks the picturesque harbor in Gdańsk. Warm colors and recessed lighting soften the ultramodern interiors. The increasingly popular restaurant specializes in Continental cuisine. ⊠ *Ul. Tokarska 6, 80–888* ☎ *058/305–34–27* ⎙ *058/305–33–86* ⊕ *www.hanza-hotel.com.pl* ⤲ *60 rooms* ⏅ *Restaurant, bar* ▭ *AE, DC, MC, V.*

$$$ ▥ **Mercure Hewelius.** This 18-story hotel is within walking distance of the Old Town and is also close to the train and bus stations. The spacious, blandly furnished rooms have most modern conveniences. ⊠ *Ul. Heweliusza 22, 80–861* ☎ *058/321–00–00* ⎙ *058/301–19–22* ⊕ *www.orbis.pl* ⤲ *281 rooms* ⏅ *Restaurant* ▭ *AE, DC, MC, V.*

★ $$–$$$ ▥ **Grand.** With its magnificent location on the Bay of Gdańsk in the charming German-era seaside resort of Sopot, this prewar hotel is well worth the short commute. The rooms could have been restored more authentically, but the view from the restaurant is great. ⊠ *Ul. Powstańców Warszawy 12/14, 81–718 Sopot* ☎ *058/551–00–41* ⎙ *058/551–61–24* ⊕ *www.orbis.pl* ⤲ *112 rooms* ⏅ *Restaurant* ▭ *AE, DC, MC, V.*

$$–$$$ ▥ **Novotel Marina.** This modern high-rise hotel is a short taxi ride from the center of Sopot. The hotel is on the beach, and upper floors have ocean views. ⊠ *Ul. Jelitkowska 20, 80–342* ☎ *058/558–91–00* ⎙ *058/*

553–04–60 ⊕ *www.orbis.pl* ↪ *176 rooms* ♨ *Restaurant, pool* ▭ *AE, DC, MC, V.*

Olsztyn

Olsztyn, which was badly damaged during World War II, is more of a jumping-off point for the Mazurian Lakes region than a place of interest in its own right. The **Rynek** (marketplace) in the Old Town is worth a short stroll.

The town's 14th-century **castle** contains a museum dedicated to local culture and **Copernicus's quarters** on the first floor, where he lived for three years. ✉ *Ul. Zamkowa 1* ☎ *089/527–95–96* ☉ *Castle Tues.–Sun. 9–3, museum Tues.–Sun. 10–4.*

$$ ▥ **Orbis Novotel.** This typical Polish hotel from the 1970s is the most comfortable lodging in the area, set in beautiful surroundings on the shores of Lake Ukiel. Water sports and horseback-riding facilities are nearby. ✉ *Ul. Sielska 4A, 10–802* ☎ *089/522–05–00* 🖷 *089/527–54–03* ⊕ *www.orbis.pl* ↪ *97 rooms* ♨ *Restaurant* ▭ *AE, DC, MC, V.*

Malbork

★ This huge, redbrick, turreted castle was one of the most powerful strongholds in medieval Europe. From 1308 to 1457 it was the residence of the Grand Masters of the Teutonic Order. The Teutonic Knights were a thorn in Poland's side until their defeat at the Battle of Grunwald in 1410. A museum inside Malbork Castle displays beautiful examples of amber—including lumps as large as melons and pieces containing perfect specimens of prehistoric insects. ✉ *Rte. 50, 58 km (36 mi) southeast of Gdańsk* ☎ *055/272–33–64* ⊕ *www.malbork.pl* ☉ *Oct.–Apr., Tues.–Sun. 9–3; May–Sept., Tues.–Sun. 9–7.*

Toruń

Toruń, birthplace of Nicolaus Copernicus, is a medieval city that grew wealthy because of its location on the north–south trading route along the Vistula. Toruń's **Old Town,** placed on the UNESCO World Cultural Heritage List, is a blend of Gothic buildings—churches, the town hall, and burghers' residences—and Renaissance and baroque patrician houses. The town hall tower, built in 1274, is the oldest in Poland.

★ Toruń's most famous native son is celebrated at the **Muzeum Mikołaja Kopernika** (Nicolaus Copernicus Museum), which occupies the house where Copernicus was born (in 1473) and lived until he was 17 years old. The rooms have been restored with period furnishings, some of which belonged to the Copernicus family. ✉ *Ul. Kopernika 15/17* ☎ *056/622–67–48* ☉ *Tues.–Sun. 10–4.*

$–$$ ✗ **Zajazd Staropolski.** Excellent meat dishes and soups are served in a restored 17th-century interior. The restaurant, which is part of a small hotel, is only one block from Toruń's Old Town Square. ✉ *Ul. Żeglarska 10/14* ☎ *056/622–60–60* ▭ *AE, DC, MC, V.*

$$ ▥ **Helios.** This friendly, medium-size Orbis hotel in the city center is within convenient walking distance of the Old Town. Request a room with a renovated bathroom—it's worth the higher rate. ✉ *Ul. Kraszewskiego 3, 87–100* ☎ *056/619–65–50* 🖷 *056/655–54–29* ⊕ *www.orbis.pl* ↪ *108 rooms* ♨ *Restaurant, pool* ▭ *AE, DC, MC, V.*

$$ ▥ **Kosmos.** A functional 1960s hotel, Kosmos is near the Vistula River, in the city center. ✉ *Ul. Popiełuszki 2, 87–100* ☎ *056/622–89–00* 🖷 *056/622–13–41* ⊕ *www.orbis.pl* ↪ *58 rooms* ♨ *Restaurant, pool* ▭ *AE, DC, MC, V.*

Gdańsk & the North Essentials

GETTING AROUND

Gdańsk is a major transportation hub, with an international airport just outside town (and good bus connections to downtown) and major road and rail connections with the rest of the country.

TOURS

Orbis and other travel agencies arrange group and individual package tours of Toruń, Gdańsk, Poznań, and the surrounding areas.

VISITOR INFORMATION

🛈 **Gdańsk** ✉ Ul. Długa 45 ☎ 058/301-93-27. **Olsztyn** ✉ Orbis, ul. Dąbrowszczaków 1 ☎ 089/527-46-74. **Płock** ✉ Ul. Tumska 4 ☎ 024/262-94-97. **Toruń** ✉ Rynek Staromiejski 1 ☎ 056/622-37-46 ✉ Orbis, ul. Mostowa 7 ☎ 056/655-48-63.

PORTUGAL
LISBON, THE ESTORIL COAST, SINTRA, QUELUZ & THE ALGARVE

CLINGING TO THE WESTERN CUSP of the continent, Portugal is one of Europe's great surprises. It is a land of fine food and wine, spectacularly sited castles, medieval hilltop villages, and excellent beaches.

The landscape unfolds in astonishing variety from a mountainous, green interior to a sweeping coastline—Celtic, Roman, and Islamic influences are evident in the land, its people, and their tongue. Given Portugal's long Atlantic coastline, it isn't surprising that most of its tumultuous history has revolved around the sea. From the charting of the Azores archipelago in 1427 to their arrival in Japan in 1540, Portuguese explorers unlocked the major sea routes to southern Africa, India, eastern Asia, and the Americas. The great era of exploration, known as the *descobrimentos,* reached its height during the 15th century under the influence of Prince Henry the Navigator. But the glories of the Portuguese empire were relatively short-lived, and the next several centuries saw dynastic instability, extravagant spending by feckless monarchs, natural disasters, and foreign invasion. Order was finally imposed in the 20th century by the drastic solution of a right-wing dictatorship. The regime lasted more than 40 years, until a bloodless coup established democracy in 1974 and the process of modernization began.

Today Portugal is a stable country, its people keen to share in the prosperity offered by developments within the European Union (EU). Political confidence couldn't have been maintained without improvements in the economy, and there have been great strides forward since 1974—the highway system, in particular, has been completely overhauled as EU money has been used to modernize the country's infrastructure.

Lisbon, Portugal's centuries-old capital, is an engaging mixture of modernity and mellow age, where graceful old buildings hold their own with modern high-rises. The city's coastal and wooded environs give it an added dimension. Following its 1994 stint as the European City of Culture, Lisbon moved firmly into the international limelight by hosting Expo '98, the last great World Exposition of the 20th century. A startling regeneration program has improved the city center, its transportation, and public buildings. At the former Expo site—reclaimed shore northeast of the city's center—now the Parque das Nações (Park of the Nations), are riverside restaurants, exhibitions, concerts, a cable-car ride, and the stupendous Lisbon Oceanarium, the Expo's centerpiece.

The sun-swept beaches of the Algarve in the country's south are some of Europe's most popular vacation areas. Off the beaten track, you can catch glimpses of a traditional life and culture, shaped by memories of empire and tempered by the experience of revolution.

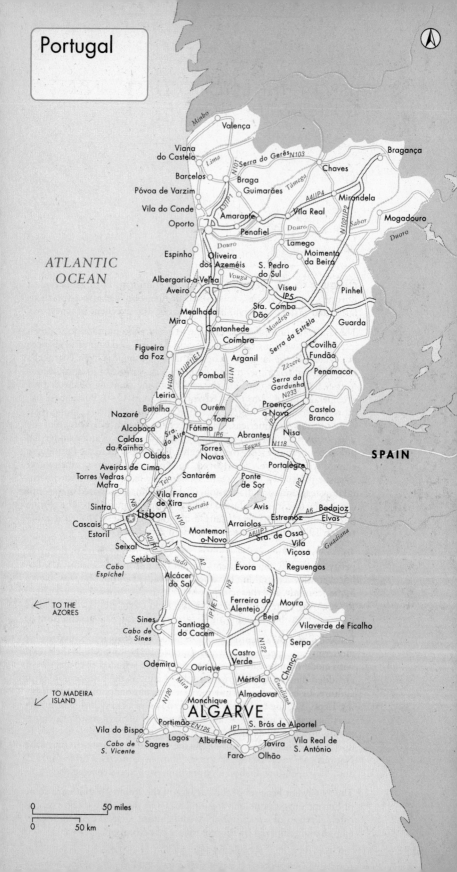

PORTUGAL A TO Z

To research prices, get advice from other travelers, and book travel arrangements, visit www.fodors.com.

AIR TRAVEL

CARRIERS Domestic air travel options are limited and expensive, given the distances involved. You're better off renting a car or taking the train or bus, unless time is an issue. TAP Air Portugal and PGA (Portugália Airlines) fly between Lisbon, Oporto, and Faro; SATA Air Açores flies between Lisbon and the Azores; and Aerocondor and Omni have some intercity flights.

 Aerocondor ☎ 21/445-76-00 in Portugal ⊕ www.aerocondor.com. **OMNI** ☎ 21/445-86-00 in Portugal ⊕ www.omni.pt. **PGA** ☎ 21/842-55-59 in Portugal ⊕ www.pga.pt. **SATA Air Açores** ☎ 296/20-97-57 in Portugal ⊕ www.virtualazores.com/sata. **TAP Air Portugal** ☎ 800/221-7370 in U.S.; 0845/601-0932 in U.K.; 21/841-50-00 in Portugal ⊕ www.tap-airportugal.pt.

BUS TRAVEL

Bus service within Portugal is fairly comprehensive, and in some places, such as the Algarve, buses are the main form of public transportation. Some luxury coaches even have TVs and food service—a comfortable way to travel. Two of the largest bus companies are Rede Expressos and Eva Transportes.

Lisbon's main bus terminals are at the Oriente train station and the Arco do Cego. Note that bus travel can be slow; it can also be difficult to arrange on your own. For schedules within Portugal it's best to inquire at tourist information offices, since routes and companies change frequently, and bus company personnel rarely speak English. Most travel agents can sell you a bus ticket in advance; it's always wise to reserve a ticket at least a day ahead, particularly in summer for destinations in the Algarve.

 Bus Companies **Eva Transportes** ⊕ www.eva-bus.com. **Rede Expressos** ⊕ www.rede-expressos.pt.

 Bus Terminals **Arco do Cego** ✉ Av. Duque de Ávila, 12. **Oriente** ✉ Parque das Nações.

BUSINESS HOURS

Many businesses, particularly those outside of urban areas, close between 1 and 3 and then open again until 6 or 7. Shopping malls in Lisbon and other cities remain open until 10 PM or midnight and are often open on Sunday.

Government offices are typically open weekdays 9–noon and 2–5, and banks are open weekdays 8:30–3. Most gas stations on main highways are open 24 hours. In more rural areas, stations will be open 7 AM to 10 PM. Museums and palaces generally open at 10, close for lunch from 12:30 to 2, and then reopen until 5; a few, however, remain open at midday. Many are closed on Monday, though some close on Tuesday or Wednesday. Pharmacies are usually open weekdays 9–1 and 3–7 and Saturday 9–1. When they're closed, pharmacies display a card on their doors indicating where to find a nearby pharmacy that's open all night or on Sunday.

CAR TRAVEL

EMERGENCY All large garages in and around towns have breakdown services, and
SERVICES you'll see orange emergency (SOS) phones along turnpikes and highways. The national automobile organization, Automóvel Clube de Por-

tugal, provides reciprocal membership with AAA and other European automobile associations.

🅵 **Automóvel Clube de Portugal** ☎ 21/942-91-03 for breakdowns south of Pombal; 22/834-00-01 for breakdowns north of Pombal ⊕ www.acp.pt.

GASOLINE Gas stations are plentiful. Prices are controlled by the government and are the same everywhere. At press time (summer 2003) gasoline cost €1.01 a liter (approximately ¼ gallon) for 98 octane, €0.96 for 95 octane *sem chumbo* (unleaded), and €0.70 for diesel. Credit cards are frequently accepted at gas stations.

PARKING Parking lots and underground garages abound in major cities, but those in Lisbon and Oporto are pricey. It's often difficult to find a parking space near city-center hotels, though increasing numbers of parking meters are improving the situation.

ROAD Major EU-funded work has been done on Portugal's highway system; CONDITIONS commercially operated *autoestradas* (toll roads with four or more lanes identified with an "A" and a number) link the principal cities, including Oporto, with Lisbon and Faro, circumventing congested urban centers. Many main national highways (labeled with "N" and a number) have been upgraded to toll-free, two-lane roads identified with "IP" (Itinerário Principal) and a number. Highways of mainly regional importance have been upgraded to IC (Itinerário Complementar). Roads labeled with "E" and a number are routes that connect with the Spanish network. Because road construction is still under way, you may find that one road has several designations—A, N, IP, E, etc.—on maps and signs.

Heading out of Lisbon, there's good, fast access to Setúbal and to Évora and other Alentejo towns, although rush-hour traffic on the Ponte 25 de Abril (25th of April Bridge) across the Rio Tejo (Tagus River) can be frustrating. An alternative is taking the 17-km-long (11-mi-long) Ponte Vasco da Gama (Europe's second-longest water crossing after the Chunnel) across the Tejo estuary to Montijo; you can then link up with southbound and eastbound roads. Signposting on these fast roads isn't always adequate, so keep your eyes peeled for exits and turnoffs.

Tolls seem steep in Portugal, but time saved by traveling the autoestradas usually makes them worthwhile. Minor roads are often poor and winding with unpredictable surfaces. The local driving may be faster and less forgiving than you're used to, and other visitors in rental cars on unfamiliar roads can cause problems: drive carefully.

RULES OF Driving is on the right. At the junction of two roads of equal size, traf-
THE ROAD fic coming from the right has priority. Vehicles already in a traffic circle have priority over those entering it from any point. The use of seat belts is obligatory. Horns shouldn't be used in built-up areas, and you should always carry a reflective red warning triangle for use in a breakdown, your driver's license, and proof of car insurance. The speed limit on turnpikes is 120 kph (74 mph); on other roads it's 90 kph (56 mph), and in built-up areas, 50 kph–60 kph (30 mph–36 mph).

Billboards warning you not to drink and drive dot the countryside. Penalties for driving under the influence of alcohol are severe, so keep within the legal limit—.05% blood-alcohol level. Portuguese drivers are notoriously rash, and the country has one of the highest traffic fatality rates in Europe—drive carefully.

CUSTOMS & DUTIES

For details on imports and duty-free limits, *see* Customs & Duties *in* Smart Travel Tips.

🖪 **Direção Geral das Alfândegas e dos Impostos Especiais sobre o Consumo** ⊠ Rua da Alfândega, 5, 1149-006 Lisbon ☎ Blue Line: 21/881-38-18 ⊕ www.dgaiec.min-financas.pt.

EATING & DRINKING

Although Portugal's plush, luxury restaurants can be good, they seldom measure up to their counterparts in other European countries. The best food tends to be found in the moderately priced and less expensive spots. Lower priced *tascas* (taverns, or bistros) and small, sometimes family-run restaurants are where discerning Lisboners go for a good meal. *Cervejarias* (pub-restaurants) and *marisqueiras* specialize in seafood. The food is usually good in these places, but however proletarian the trappings, seafood is always pricey. Shellfish (*mariscos*) is expensive and is often sold by weight in restaurants. This means that if you indulge in lobster, crab, prawns, and the like without watching the scales in an otherwise modestly priced eatery, you can end up paying more than you would for a non-*marisco* meal in a $$$$ place.

Restaurants featuring charcoal-grilled meats and fish, called *churasqueiras,* are popular (and often economical) options, and the Brazilian *rodízio*-type restaurant, where you are regaled with an endless offering of spit-roasted meats, is entrenched in Lisbon, Oporto, and the Algarve. Restaurant prices fall appreciably when you leave the Lisbon, Oporto, and Algarve areas, and portion sizes increase the farther north you go.

While you ponder the menu, you may be served an impressive array of appetizers. If you eat any of these, you'll probably be charged a small fee called a *couberto* or *couvert.* If you don't want these appetizers, you're perfectly within your rights to send them back. As in many European countries, Portuguese restaurants serve an *ementa* (or *prato*) *do dia,* or set menu. This can be a real bargain—usually 80% of the cost of three courses ordered separately.

WHAT IT COSTS In euros			
	$$$$	**$$$**	**$$**	**$**
AT DINNER	over €21	€14–€21	€7–€14	under €7

Prices are per person for a main course.

MEALTIMES Breakfast is the lightest meal—most hotels serve it until 10. Lunch, the main meal of the day, is served between noon and 2:30, although office workers in cities often grab a quick sandwich in a bar instead of stopping for a big meal. At about 5 there's a break for coffee or tea and a pastry; dinner is eaten around 8. Unless otherwise noted, the restaurants listed in this guide are open daily for lunch and dinner.

PAYING A surprising number of restaurants in Portugal still don't accept credit cards. Always check first, or you may end the evening washing dishes.

RESERVATIONS & DRESS Neatness suffices for all but the most formal occasions; jacket and tie are advised for city restaurants in the $$$$ category; otherwise, casual dress is fine.

SPECIALTIES Portugal has a rich, varied gastronomy. The Portuguese introduced coriander, pepper, ginger, curry, saffron, and paprika to Europe as a result of their explorations and establishment of trade routes. They brought back tea from the Orient—it was the 11th-century Portuguese princess Catherine of Bragança, wife of England's King Charles II, who popularized the aromatic beverage in England—coffee and peanuts from Africa, and pineapples, tomatoes, and potatoes from the New World.

The country's many rivers and its proximity to the sea mean that there's an abundance of seafood dishes: be sure to try the *caldeirada* (seafood stew) and fresh *sardinhas assadas* (grilled sardines). *Lulas recheadas,* squid stuffed with sausage and rice, is a unique combination of texture and flavor. Chicken and pork are good everywhere, and the mention of golden and crunchy *leitão da bairrada* (roast suckling pig) in the north is enough to give anyone an appetite. Sautéed or grilled *bife á português* (steak), often cooked in a port-wine sauce, is served throughout the country. *Bacalhau* (codfish) can be served 365 different ways (or so legend has it). Soups of all kinds are popular, and most restaurants serve *caldo verde,* a filling blend of shredded cabbage, potatoes, and slices of *chouriço* (smoked pork sausage). The famous pork-and-clam dish called *porco á Alentejana* is made with diced marinated pork and clams and served with potatoes or rice. Desserts tend to be sweet and egg-based; *pudim flan,* a caramel custard, is practically a national passion.

WINE, BEER & SPIRITS   The Portuguese climate and soil, combined with literally thousands of years of experience (it is believed that wine history in the Iberian Peninsula dates back to the year 2000 BC), make Portuguese wines some of the finest in the world. There are 47 wine regions throughout the country. Among the most popular are Bairrada from the Coimbra/Aveiro region, Ribatejo and Liziria from the Ribatejo region, and the reds from the Dão region. In the Minho area, in the northwest, the light, sparkling *vinho verde* (green wine, named not for its color but for the fact that it's drunk early and doesn't improve with age) is also popular, especially on hot days. For the most part you can find a large variety of Portuguese wines (from different regions) wherever you go in the country. Prices in restaurants can vary quite a lot, but there is always the *vinho da casa* (house wine), which is perfectly drinkable in most restaurants.

The leading brands of Portuguese beer—including Super Bock, Crystal, Sagres, and Imperial—are available on tap and in bottles or cans. They're made with fewer chemicals than the average American beers, and are on the strong side with a good, clean flavor. Local brandy—namely Macieira and Constantino—is cheap, as is domestic gin, although it's marginally weaker than its international counterparts.

As long as you're 16 (the legal drinking age) or older, you can buy alcohol at shops, supermarkets, bars, and restaurants.

Spirit Divino ⊕ www.spiritdivino.com. **Instituto do Vinho do Porto** ⊕ www.ivp. pt. **Real Companhia Velha** ⊕ www.realcompanhiavelha.pt. **Comissão de Viticultura da Região dos Vinhos Verdes** ⊕ www.vinhoverde.pt.

Embassies

Australia ✉ Av. da Liberdade, 200, 2nd fl., 1250-147 Lisbon ☎ 21/310-15-00 🖷 21/310-15-55 ⊕ http://www.portugal.embassy.gov.au/.

Canada ✉ Av. da Liberdade, 198-200, 1269-121 Lisbon ☎ 21/316-46-00 🖷 21/316-46-92.

United Kingdom ✉ Rua de São Bernardo, 33, 1249-082 Lisbon ☎ 21/392-40-00 🖷 21/392-41-85 ⊕ www.uk-embassy.pt/framset.shtml.

United States ✉ Av. das Forças Armadas, 1600-081 Lisbon ☎ 21/727-33-00 or 21/770-22-22 🖷 21/727-91-09 ⊕ www.american-embassy.pt.

HOLIDAYS

New Year's Day (January 1); Mardi Gras (also known as Carnaval; the day before Ash Wednesday); Good Friday; Easter Sunday; Liberty Day (April 25); Portuguese Labor Day (May 1); Corpus Christi (Corpo de Deus) (May 30); Camões Day (June 10); Assumption Day (August 15); Proclamation of Portuguese Republic (October 5); All Saints' Day (November

1); Restoration of Portuguese Independence (December 1); Feast of Immaculate Conception (December 8); Christmas Day (December 25).

If a national holiday falls on a Tuesday or Thursday, many businesses also close on the Monday or Friday in between, for a long weekend called a *ponte* (bridge). There are also local holidays when entire towns, cities, and regions grind to a standstill. Check the nearest tourist office for dates.

LANGUAGE

Portuguese is spoken by 200 million people around the world. It can be difficult to pronounce and understand. If, however, you have a fair knowledge of a Latin language, you may be able to read a little Portuguese. Any attempt you make to speak Portuguese will be well received. In large cities and major resorts many people speak English and, occasionally, Spanish or French.

LODGING

Portugal has some of the lowest room rates in Europe. Nonhotel options include small family-owned *pensões* (pensions), *estalagens* (country inns), rooms in country manor houses, villas, holiday apartments, and luxury *pousadas* (tourist hotels) in historic buildings. Rates depend on location and time of year. In the Algarve in winter, particularly January through March, room prices drop by as much as 40%. Book ahead in summer and at Easter and Christmas.

Tourist offices can help with reservations and provide free lists of the local hostelries. If you arrive at a resort in summer without a reservation, you may be offered an inexpensive *quarto* (room) near a rail or bus station; always see the room before agreeing to take it.

WHAT IT COSTS In euros				
	$$$$	$$$	$$	$
HOTELS	over €275	€175–€275	€75–€175	under €75

Prices are for two people in a standard double room in high season.

COUNTRY HOUSES Throughout the country, though particularly in the north, many rural and manor houses have been remodeled to receive small numbers of guests (from 1 to 10 rooms) in a venture called *Turismo no Espaço Rural* (TER). These guest houses are in bucolic settings, near parks or monuments or in historic *aldeias* (villages). Breakfast is always included in the price. You can request more information at regional tourism bureaus, or contact the Central Nacional de Turismo no Espaço Rural (National Center for Rural Tourism), which serves as a clearinghouse for information from several organizations involved in this endeavor.

🖪 **Central Nacional de Turismo no Espaço Rural** ✉ Praça da República, 4990 Ponte de Lima ☏ 258/74-16-72, 258/74-28-27, or 258/74-28-29 ⊕ www.center.pt. **TURIHAB** ⊕ www.turihab.pt.

HOTELS Portugal has many excellent and reasonably priced hotels, though good properties can be hard to come by in remote inland areas. The government officially grades accommodations with one to five stars or with a category rating. Ratings, which are assigned based on the level of comfort and the number of facilities offered, can be misleading, as quality is difficult to grade. In general, though, the system works.

Most hotel rooms have such basic amenities as a private bathroom and a telephone; those with two or more stars may also have air-conditioning, cable or satellite TV, a minibar, and room service. (Note that all hotels listed in this guide have private bath unless otherwise indicated.)

Contact the Portuguese National Tourist Office for a countrywide lodging directory.

High season means not only the summer months, but also the Christmas and New Year's holiday period on Madeira, Easter week throughout the country, and anytime a town is holding a festival. In the off-season (generally November through March), many hotels reduce their rates by as much as 30%–40%.

🏷 **Mais Turismo** ⊕ www.hotelguide.pt. **Portuguese National Tourist Office** ✉ 590 5th Ave., New York, NY 10036 ☎ 212/354-4403 or 212/354-4404 ⊕ www.portugalinsite.pt.

POUSADAS The term "pousada" is derived from the Portuguese verb *pousar* (to rest). Portugal has a network of more than 40 of these state-run hotels, which are in restored castles, palaces, monasteries, convents, and other charming buildings. Each pousada is in a particularly scenic and tranquil part of the country and is tastefully furnished with regional crafts, antiques, and artwork. All have restaurants that serve local specialties; you can stop for a meal or a drink without spending the night. Rates are reasonable, considering that most pousadas are four- or five-star hotels and a stay in one can be the highlight of a visit. They're extremely popular with foreigners and Portuguese alike, and some have 10 or fewer rooms; make reservations well in advance, especially for stays in summer. Also check for seasonal and senior-citizen discounts, which can be as high as 40%.

🏷 **Pousadas de Portugal** ✉ Av. Santa Joana Princesa, 10, 1749-090 Lisbon ☎ 21/844-20-01 🖶 21/844-20-85 ⊕ www.pousadas.pt.

SPAS Portugal has a profusion of *termas* (thermal springs), whose waters reputedly can cure anything that ails you. In the smaller spas, hotels are rather simple; in the more famous ones, they're first-class. Most are open from May through October.

🏷 **Associação das Termas de Portugal** ✉ Av. Miguel Bombarda 110, 2 Dt., 1050-167 Lisbon ☎ 21/794-05-74 🖶🖶 Linha Termas: 21/797-13-38 🖶 21/793-82-33 ⊕ www.termasdeportugal.pt.

MAIL & SHIPPING

You can expect a letter to take 7–10 days to reach the United States, Australia, or New Zealand and 4–5 days to the United Kingdom or elsewhere in the European Union. All post is sent airmail unless otherwise specified.

The Portuguese postal service—the CTT—has a Web site with some limited information in English.

You can have mail sent care of American Express; call for lists of offices in Portugal. Elsewhere in the country, post offices in major towns have "held mail" services (you simply have letters sent to you labeled *poste restante* at a particular post office address).

🏷 **American Express** ☎ 800/543-4080 ⊕ www.americanexpress.pt. **CTT** ⊕ www.ctt.pt.

MONEY MATTERS

Lisbon isn't as expensive as most other international capitals, but it's not the extraordinary bargain it used to be. The coastal resort areas from Cascais and Estoril down to the Algarve can be expensive, though there are lower-price hotels and restaurants catering mainly to the package-tour trade. If you head off the beaten track you'll find substantially cheaper food and lodging.

Transportation is still cheap in Portugal when compared with the rest of Europe. Gas prices are controlled by the government, and train and bus travel are inexpensive. Highway tolls are steep but may be worth the cost if you want to bypass the small towns and villages. Flights within the country are costly.

Here are some sample prices. Coffee in a bar: €0.50 (standing), €0.70 (seated). Draft beer in a bar: €0.50 (standing), €0.65 (seated). Bottle of beer: €0.70. Port: €1.50–€10, depending on brand and vintage. Table wine: €5.50 (bottle), €3 (half bottle), €0.60 (small glass). Coca-Cola: €1. Ham-and-cheese sandwich: €1.50. One-kilometer (½ mi) taxi ride: €2.50. Local bus ride: €1. Subway ride: €0.60. Ferry ride in Lisbon: €1.65–€1.80, one-way, depending on destination. Opera or theater seat: €10–€60, depending on show and location. Nightclub cover charge: €10–€25. Fado performance: €15 for just a show or €25–€40 for dinner and a show. Movie ticket: €3.25–€4.75 (the lowest price indicated can be paid on Mondays at most cinemas). Foreign newspaper: €1.50–€2.50.

CURRENCY Portugal is one of the European Union countries, which use a single currency—the euro (€). Coins are issued in denominations of 1, 2, 5, 10, 20, and 50 euro cents. Notes are issued in denominations of €5, 10, 20, 50, 100, 200, and 500.

SHOPPING
Bargaining is not the practice in city stores or shops, though it is sometimes possible in flea markets and antiques shops. The Centro de Turismo Artesanato ships goods abroad. By air to the United States, parcels take about three weeks; by sea, two months.

🄵 **Centro de Turismo e Artesanato** ✉ Rua Castilho, 61 B, 1250-068 Lisbon ☎ 21/386-08-79 ⊕ www.mateus-shop.com.

TAXES
SALES TAX Value-added tax (IVA, pronounced *ee-vah*, in Portuguese) is 12% for hotels. By law prices must be posted at the reception desk and should indicate whether tax is included. Restaurants are also required to charge 12% IVA. Menus generally state at the bottom whether tax is included (*IVA incluido*) or not (*mais 12% IVA*). When in doubt about whether tax is included in a price, ask: *Está incluido o IVA?*

A number of Portuguese stores, particularly large ones and those in resorts, offer a refund of the 19% IVA on single items worth more than €80. Be sure to ask for your tax-free check; you show your passport, fill out a form, and the store mails you the refund at home.

TELEPHONES
All phone numbers have nine digits, the first two being the area code in or around Lisbon and Oporto, the first three anywhere else in the country. All fixed-phone area codes begin with 2; mobile numbers, which also have nine digits, begin with 9. The country code for Portugal is 351.

DIRECTORY & OPERATOR ASSISTANCE For general information, dial 118 (operators often speak English). The international information and assistance numbers are 171 for operator-assisted calls, 172 for collect calls, and 177 for information (the operators speak English).

INTERNATIONAL CALLS Calling abroad is expensive from hotels, which often add a considerable surcharge. The best way to make an international call is to go to the local telephone office and have someone place it for you. Every town has such an establishment, and big cities have several. When the call is connected, you'll be directed to a quiet cubicle and charged according to the meter. If the price is €10 or more, you can pay with Visa or MasterCard. Lisbon's main phone office is in the Praça dos Restauradores, right off the Rossio.

To make an international call yourself, dial 00 followed directly by the country code (1 for the United States and Canada, 44 for the United Kingdom, 61 for Australia, and 64 for New Zealand) and the area code and number. The Portuguese telephone directory contains a list of all of the principal world country codes and the codes for principal cities.

🖪 Access Codes **AT&T Direct** ☎ 800/80-01-28 in Portugal; 800/222-03-00 for other areas. **MCI WorldPhone** ☎ 800/80-01-23 in Portugal; 800/444-41-41 for other areas. **Sprint International Access** ☎ 800/80-01-87 in Portugal; 800/877-46-46 for other areas.

LONG-DISTANCE CALLS
To make calls to other areas within Portugal, precede the provincial code with 0 (most phone booths have a chart inside listing the various province codes). The 0 is unnecessary when dialing from outside Portugal.

PUBLIC PHONES
You can ask to use the phone in cafés or bars, where they're often metered. The waiter or bartender will charge you after you've finished, though expect to pay a higher rate than the one you would pay in a public phone booth.

The easiest way to call from a public booth is to use a *Telecom Card PT* (calling card), which you can buy at post offices, newspaper shops, and tobacconists for either €3, €6, or €10. The phones that accept them have digital readouts, so you can see your time ticking away. Instructions in several languages, including English, are posted in the booths. With coin-operated phones you insert coins and wait for a dial tone. The minimum cost for a local call is €0.20; it's €0.50 to call another area, for which you must dial the area code. Some public booths are payable with credit cards (Visa and MasterCard). You can also find booths that enable you not just to phone, but also to access the Internet and send e-mail. Fifteen minutes of Internet navigation costs €0.63. You can find these booths at the Lisbon airport, Amoreiras shopping centre, and *Forum Telecom, Picóas.*

🖪 **Portugal Telecom** ⊕ www.telecom.pt/uk.

TIPPING
Service is included in café, restaurant, and hotel bills, but waiters and other service people are poorly paid, and you can be sure your contribution will be appreciated. If, however, you received bad service, never feel obligated (or intimidated) to leave a tip. An acceptable tip is 10%–15% of the total bill, and if you have a sandwich or *petiscos* (appetizers) at a bar, leave less, just enough to round out the bill to the nearest €0.50. Cocktail waiters get €0.30–€0.50 a drink, depending on the bar.

Taxi drivers get about 10% of the meter; more for long rides or extra help with luggage (note that there's also an official surcharge for airport runs and baggage). Hotel porters should receive €1 a bag; a doorman who calls you a taxi, €0.50. Tip €1 for room service and €1–€2 per night for maid service. Tip a concierge for any additional help he or she gives you.

Tip tour guides €2–€5, depending on how knowledgeable they are and on the length of the tour. Ushers in theaters or bullfights get €0.50; barbers and hairdressers (for a wash and a set) at least €1. Washroom attendants are tipped €0.50.

TRAIN TRAVEL
Portugal's train network covers most of the country, though it's thin in the Alentejo region. The cities of Lisbon, Coimbra, Aveiro, and Oporto are linked by the fast, extremely comfortable Alfa Pendular (tilt train) services. Most other major towns and cities are connected by InterCidades trains, which are reliable, though slower and less luxurious than

the Alfa Pendular trains. The regional services that connect smaller towns and villages tend to be infrequent and slow, with stops at every station along the line.

The standards of comfort vary from Alfa Pendular train luxury—with air-conditioning, food service, and airline-type seats—to the often spartan conditions on regional lines. All InterCidades trains have bar and restaurant facilities, but the food is famously unappealing. A first-class ticket will cost you 40% more than a second-class one and will buy you extra leg and elbow room but not a great deal more on the Alfa Pendular and InterCidades trains. The extra cost is definitely worth it on most regional services, however. Smoking is restricted to special carriages on all trains in Portugal. A 10% discount is given when buying a two-way ticket. Children and people over 65 years old are given a discount of 50%.

RESERVATIONS Advance booking isn't required on Portuguese trains but is definitely recommended in the case of popular services like the Alfa Pendular trains. Reservations are also advisable for other trains if you want to avoid long lines in front of the ticket window on the day the train leaves. You can avoid a trip out to the station to make the reservation by booking through a travel agent, or by purchasing through a cashpoint or ATM. Tickets can be bought 30 days in advance at any CP (Portuguese train company) counter or travel agency, or 21 days in advance at any cashpoint.

SCHEDULES If you speak Portuguese, you can call the general information number of the Caminhos de Ferro Portugueses (CP) for schedule and other information. Otherwise check the Web site, or head to a train station information desk for a printed timetable.

🚊 CP ☎ 21/888-40-25; Call Center: 808/20-82-08, 7 AM-11 PM ⊕ www.cp.pt.

VISITOR INFORMATION
🚊 **Green Line** ☎ 800/29-62-96 tourist help line within Portugal.

WHEN TO GO
Peak season begins in spring and lasts through the autumn. In midsummer it's never unbearably hot (except in parts of the Algarve and on the mainland plains); along the coast, cool breezes often spring up in the evening. In the Algarve, springtime begins in February with a marvelous range of wildflowers. Late September and early October herald Indian summer, which ensures warm sunshine through November. Hotel prices are greatly reduced between November and February, except in Lisbon, where business visitors keep rates uniformly high throughout the year. Winter is mild and frequently rainy.

CLIMATE 🚊 The following are average daily maximum and minimum temperatures for Lisbon.

LISBON

Jan.	57F	14C	May	71F	21C	Sept.	79F	26C
	46	8		55	13		62	17
Feb.	59F	15C	June	77F	25C	Oct.	72F	22C
	47	8		60	15		58	14
Mar.	63F	17C	July	81F	27C	Nov.	63F	17C
	50	10		63	17		52	11
Apr.	67F	20C	Aug.	82F	28C	Dec.	58F	15C
	53	12		63	17		47	9

LISBON

Spread out over a string of hills on the north bank of the Tagus River estuary, Portugal's capital presents unending treats for the eye. Its wide boulevards are bordered by black-and-white mosaic sidewalks made of small cobblestones called *calçada*. Modern, pastel-color apartment blocks vie for attention with some of Europe's finest art nouveau structures. Tiled facades glint in the sun. Winding, hilly streets provide scores of vantage points with spectacular views of the river and the city.

With a population of around a million, Lisbon is a small capital by European standards. Its center stretches north from the spacious Praça do Comércio, one of the largest riverside squares in Europe, to the Rossio, a smaller square lined with shops and sidewalk cafés. This district, known as the Baixa (Lower Town), is one of the earliest examples of town planning on a large scale. The grid of parallel streets between the two squares was built after an earthquake and tidal wave destroyed much of the city in 1755. The Alfama, the old Moorish quarter that survived the earthquake, lies just east of the Baixa, and the Bairro Alto—an 18th-century quarter of restaurants, bars, and clubs—just to the west; Belém, a historic riverside district with restaurants, museums, palaces, and famed tourist sights like the Mosteiro dos Jerónimos, lies another 5 km (3 mi) to the west. Northeast of the center, the riverside Parque das Nações has the Lisbon Oceanarium—Europe's largest aquarium.

Exploring Lisbon

Numbers in the margin correspond to points of interest on the Lisbon map.

Lisbon is not easy to explore on foot. The steep inclines of many streets present a tough challenge to the casual visitor, and places that appear to be close to one another on a map are sometimes on different levels. But the effort is worthwhile—judicious use of trams, the funicular railway, and the majestic city-center *elevador* (vertical lift) makes tours enjoyable even on the hottest summer day.

Castelo de São Jorge & the Alfama

The Moors, who imposed their rule on most of the southern Iberian Peninsula during the 8th century, left a subtle but enduring mark on Lisbon. Their most visible traces are in the medina-like pattern of narrow streets found in the Alfama, the quarter of narrow alleys that clusters around St. George's Castle and occupies the approximate site of the old Moorish settlement. Though the area is relatively compact, it is notoriously easy to get lost among the jumble of little streets and whitewashed houses with flower-laden balconies and red tile roofs. Its down-to-earth charm is most apparent in June, during the festivals of the Santos Populares (Popular Saints), when the entire quarter turns out to eat, drink, and be merry. The best way to tour the area is to take a taxi, Tram 12 and 28, or Bus 37 up to the castle and then walk down.

❶ Castelo de São Jorge (St. George's Castle). Only vestiges remain of the ancient Roman, Visigothic, and Moorish origins of Lisbon's oldest monument, destroyed and rebuilt time and again over the centuries. Nevertheless, this is Lisbon's birthplace and it is a pleasant spot from which to survey the city. Inside the main gate are well-tended grounds and terraces with panoramic city views. There's also a 25-minute multimedia show, *Olisipónia* (€1.50), about the history of Lisbon. ⊠ *Entrances at Rua do Chão da Feira, Largo Rodrigo de Freitas, Rua de Santa Cruz, Rua das Cozinhas, and Largo do Menino de Deus* ☎ *21/887–72–44*

FodorsChoice ★

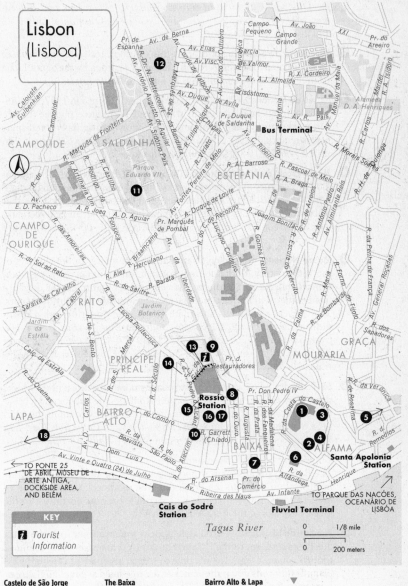

Lisbon (Lisboa)

KEY

ⓘ Tourist Information

for Olisipónia ⊕ *www.atl-turismolisboa.pt* ⊙ *Gardens and Belvederes: Mar.–Oct., daily 9–9; Nov.–Feb., daily 9–6; Olisipónia: daily 10–1 and 2–5:30, last admissions 12:30 and 5.*

❷ **Miradouro de Santa Luzia.** Stop at this overlook for sweeping views of the Alfama and the Tagus River. The terrace garden by the Santa Luzia Church catches the sun all day. ⊠ *Largo de Santa Luzia.*

❸ **Museu da Marioneta** (Puppet Museum). When it opened in 1987, this museum sparked new interest in traditional Portuguese puppet theater. The workmanship that went into the creation of the puppets on display here is remarkable. ⊠ *Convento das Bernardas, Rua da Esperança, 146* ☎ *21/394–28–10* ⊙ *Tues.–Sun. 10–1 and 2–6.*

❹ **Museu-Escola de Artes Decorativas** (Museum of Decorative Arts). In a splendid 17th-century mansion with period furnishings, this museum has temporary exhibits of art and furniture. It also conducts workshops that teach traditional handicrafts—bookbinding, carving, and cabinetmaking. ⊠ *Largo das Portas do Sol, 2* ☎ *21/881–46–00* ⊕ *www.fress.pt* ⊙ *Tues.–Sun. 10–5.*

❺ **Museu Nacional do Azulejo** (National Tile Museum). In the cloisters of the 16th-century Madre de Deus convent, this museum has a highly esteemed collection of 15th- to 21st-century tiles that traces the development of the art in Portugal from its introduction into Iberia by the Moors. The convent church has an ornate 18th-century interior with a splendid rococo altarpiece. ⊠ *Rua da Madre de Deus, 4 (Bus 104 or 105 from Santa Apolónia station)* ☎ *21/814–77–47* ⊕ *www.mnazulejo-ipmuseus.pt* ⊙ *Tues. 2–6, Wed.–Sun. 10–6* ⊙ *Closed Mon.* ✉ *Free entrance on Sun. and holidays until 2 PM.*

★ ❻ **Sé** (Cathedral). Founded in 1150 to commemorate the defeat of the Moors three years earlier, the Sé has an austere Romanesque interior and a beautiful 13th-century cloister. The treasure-filled sacristy contains the relics of St. Vincent. ⊠ *Largo da Sé* ☎ *21/886–67–52* ⊙ *Cathedral: Tues.–Sat. 9–7, Sun. and Mon. 9–5. Cloister and sacristy: daily 10–1 and 2–6.*

The Baixa & the Modern City

The Baixa, Lisbon's main shopping and banking district, opens on its northwestern end into the Praça dos Restauradores, the beginning of modern Lisbon, with Avenida da Liberdade running northwest to the green expanses of the Parque Eduardo VII.

❾ **Avenida da Liberdade.** A stroll along the city's main avenue from the Praça dos Restauradores to the Parque Eduardo VII takes about 30 minutes, though you may want to take time to stop at an open-air café in the esplanade that runs down the center of the tree-lined avenue. ⊠ *Between Praça dos Restauradores and Parque Eduardo VII.*

❼ **Baixa** (Lower Town). The Baixa once housed trades and crafts now reflected in the street names: Rua dos Sapateiros (Cobblers' Street), Rua da Prata (Silversmiths' Street), and Rua do Ouro (Goldsmiths' Street). Scattered throughout are shoe shops, glittering jewelry stores, and a host of cafés and delicatessens that sell wines, cheeses, and pastries. ⊠ *Between the river and Rossio.*

❿ **Chiado.** This chic district is home to some of the city's most fashionable shops. Rua Garrett, the Chiado's principal street, is lined with old department stores and a series of comfortable, turn-of-the-20th-century, wood-paneled coffee shops. Chiado's most famous café is the **Brasileira** (⊠ Rua Garrett, 120 ☎ 21/346–95–41), which has a life-size statue of one of Portugal's great poets, Fernando Pessoa, seated at one of the side-walk tables. ⊠ *Western side of Baixa.*

★ ⑫ **Museu Calouste Gulbenkian.** One of Europe's finest collections of art and artifacts, collected by Armenian oil magnate Calouste Gulbenkian (1869–1955), is housed at this museum. The collection includes masterpieces by Rubens, Rembrandt, Gainsborough, and Rodin; Persian carpets; Chinese porcelain; ancient Egyptian art; Greek and Roman coins; and a room of Lalique jewelry. Two performance halls host concerts and ballet productions. ⊠ *Av. de Berna, 45-A* ☎ *21/782–30–00* ⊕ *www.museu.gulbenkian.pt* ☉ *Tues.–Sun. 10–6* Ⓜ *Metro: São Sebastião or Praça de Espanha.*

⑪ **Parque Eduardo VII** (Edward VII Park). The city's main park was named in honor of King Edward VII of England, who visited Lisbon in 1903. Rare flowers, trees, and shrubs thrive in the greenhouses. ☎ *21/388–22–78 for information on greenhouses* ☉ *Park: daily dawn–dusk. Greenhouses: Apr.–Sept., daily 9–5:30; Oct.–Mar., daily 9–4:30* Ⓜ *Metro: Parque or Marquês de Pombal.*

⑧ **Rossio.** Lisbon's main square since the Middle Ages is officially known as Praça Dom Pedro IV (whom the central statue commemorates), but is almost always referred to as *Rossio,* which loosely translates to "Common Square." Renowned sidewalk cafés line the east and west sides of the square. ⊠ *Praça Dom Pedro IV.*

Bairro Alto & Lapa

Lisbon's Bairro Alto (Upper Town) is largely made up of 18th- and 19th-century buildings crowding narrow streets that house an exciting mixture of restaurants, theaters, nightclubs, fado houses, bars, and antiques shops. You can access the district by funicular railway and by street elevator.

⑯ **Convento do Carmo.** (Carmelite Convent). The sacristy and nave of this church, the only sections to survive the 1755 earthquake, house the quirky **Museu Arqueológico do Carmo** (Archaeological Museum), filled with everything from Roman coins to medieval sarcophagi. ⊠ *Largo do Carmo* ☎ *21/347–86–29* ☉ *May–Sept., daily 10–6; Oct.–Apr., daily 10–5* ☉ *Closed Mon.* Ⓜ *Metro: Baixa-Chiado.*

⑬ **Elevador da Glória.** One of the finest approaches to the Bairro Alto is via the funicular railway, which dates to 1885, in the northwest corner of Praça dos Restauradores. The ascent takes about two minutes; you are let out at the São Pedro de Alcântara Miradouro, facing the castle and the Alfama. ⊠ *Calçada da Glória* ☎ *21/363–20–44* ☉ *Daily 7 AM–12:55 AM.*

⑰ **Elevador de Santa Justa.** The elevator—enclosed in a Gothic-style tower created by Raul Mésnier de Ponsard, a Portuguese protégé of Gustave Eiffel—connects the Bairro Alto with Rua da Santa Justa in the Baixa. ⊠ *Rua Aurea and Rua de Santa Justa* ☎ *21/361–30–54* ☉ *Mon.–Sat. 7 AM–11 PM, Sun. and holidays 9 AM–11 PM.*

⑮ **Igreja de São Roque.** The plain exterior of the Church of St. Roque (16th century) belies its rich interior. Its flamboyant 18th-century **Capela de São João Baptista** (Chapel of St. John the Baptist) is adorned with rare stones and mosaics that resemble oil paintings. The **Museu de Arte Sacra** (Museum of Sacred Art) displays 16th- to 18th-century paintings. ⊠ *Largo Trindade Coelho* ☎ *21/323–53–83 for church; 21/323–53–82 for museum* ☉ *Church daily 8:30–5, museum daily 10–5* Ⓜ *Metro: Baixa-Chiado.*

⑭ Instituto do Vinho do Porto (Port Wine Institute). Inside the cozy, club-like lounge you can sample the different types and vintages of Portugal's most famous beverage from the institute's formidably stocked cellars. ⊠ *Solar do Vinho do Porto, Rua de São Pedro de Alcântara, 45* ☎ *21/347–57–07 or 21/347–57–08* ⊕ *www.ivp.pt* ⊙ *Mon.–Sat. 11 AM–midnight* ⊙ *Closed Sun.* Ⓜ *Metro: Restauradores (then take Elevador de Glória).*

⑱ Museu Nacional de Arte Antiga (National Museum of Art). A beautiful collection of Portuguese art, mainly 12th–19th century, is exhibited at this museum in the Lapa district, midway between the Baixa and Belém. Much of the collection was collected from convents in 1834 after a new law forced many of them to close. Highlights are the St. Vincent Altarpiece (1467–70) by Nuno Gonçalves, Dürer's *St. Jerome*, and the Japanese lacquered *namban* screens depicting the arrival of the Portuguese in Japan in the 16th century. ⊠ *Rua das Janelas Verdes* ☎ *21/391–28–00* ⊕ *21/397–37–03* ⊙ *Tues. 2–6, Wed.–Sun. 10–6* ⊙ *Closed Mon.*

Belém
Numbers in the margin correspond to points of interest on the Belém map.

For the best examples of the uniquely Portuguese, late-Gothic architecture known as Manueline, head for Belém (the Portuguese word for Bethlehem), on the riverside at the southwestern edge of Lisbon. If you're traveling in a group of three or four, taxis are the cheapest way to get here; otherwise take the train from Cais do Sodré to Belém station or Tram 15 from the Praça do Comércio for a more colorful, though bumpier, journey.

⑲ Mosteiro dos Jerónimos. This monastery was conceived by King Manuel I at the end of the 15th century. Construction began in 1501, and took almost a century to complete. It is now considered a shining example of the Manueline style, and was named a UNESCO World Cultural Heritage Site in 1984. ⊠ *Praça do Império* ☎ *21/362–00–34* ⊕ *www.mosteirojeronimos.pt* ⊙ *May–Sept., Tues.–Sun. 10–6:30; Oct.–Apr., Tues.–Sun. 10–5* ⊙ *Closed Mon.*

Fodor'sChoice
★

⑳ Museu de Marinha (Maritime Museum). Portugal's long seafaring tradition is reflected in this huge collection of exhibits ranging from early maps, model ships, and navigational instruments to fishing boats and royal barges. ⊠ *Praça do Império* ☎ *21/362–00–19* ⊙ *June–Sept., Tues.–Sun. 10–6; Oct.–May, Tues.–Sun. 10–5* ⊙ *Closed Mon.*

㉓ Museu Nacional dos Coches (National Coach Museum). One of the largest collections of coaches in the world is on display at this former riding school. The most elaborate exhibits are three golden baroque coaches made in Rome for King John V in 1716. ⊠ *Praça Afonso de Albuquerque* ☎ *21/361–08–50* ⊕ *Adults €3; free Sun. and holidays until 2 PM* ⊙ *Tues.–Sun. 10–6* ⊙ *Closed Mon.*

㉑ Padrão dos Descobrimentos. (Monument to the Discoveries). This landmark was erected in 1960 by architect Cotinelli Telmo and sculptor Leopoldo de Almeida to commemorate the 500th anniversary of D. Henrique's death, and as a modern tribute to the seafaring explorers. A tall, white, angular slab at the water's edge, it overlooks what was the departure point for many a voyage. Take the elevator to the top for river views. ⊠ *Av. de Brasília* ☎ *21/303–19–50* ⊙ *Tues.–Sun. 9–5.*

㉔ Palácio Nacional da Ajuda. Once a royal residence, the Ajuda Palace now contains a collection of 15th- and 20th-century paintings, furniture, and tapestries. Guided tours are available on request. ⊠ *Largo da Ajuda* ☎ *21/*

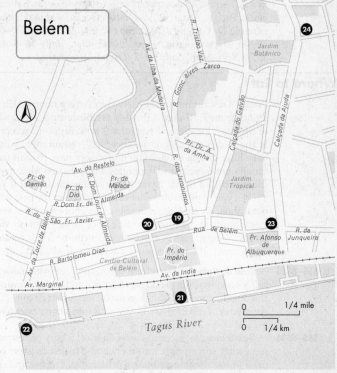

363–70–95 ⊕ *www.cidadevirtual.pt/palacio-ajuda* ⊗ *Thurs.–Tues. 10–4:30.*

★ ㉒ **Torre de Belém.** With ornate balconies and domed turrets, the Belém Tower is one of the finest Manueline structures in the country—and a masterpiece of early-16th-century military architecture. Built on a basalt outcrop more than 200 meters (656 feet) out in the water, the tower originally guarded the river approach to Lisbon. Land-reclamation works carried out over the centuries have brought the riverbank up to its doorstep. ⊠ *Av. de Brasília* ☎ *21/362–00–34* ⊕ *www. mosteirojeronimos.pt* ⊗ *Oct.–Apr., Tues.–Sun. 10–5; May–Sept., Tues.–Sun. 10–6:30.*

Parque das Nações

To prepare for the World Exposition in 1998, Lisbon's officials wisely kept in mind not only the immediate needs of the event, but also the future needs of the city. The result is Parque das Nações, a revitalized district on the banks of the Rio Tejo, 5 km (3 mi) northeast of Lisbon's center. Today it has apartment buildings, office complexes, hotels, restaurants, bars, and stores surrounded by landscaped parkland. It's also home to a marina; the Pavilhão Atlântico, a venue for major cultural and sporting events; the Bowling Internacional de Lisboa (BIL), Portugal's largest bowling alley; and the Feira Internacional Lisboa (FIL) convention center. The area is easy to reach: take the subway to Oriente; or if you're driving, take the 16-km (9-mi) Ponte Vasco da Gama (Vasco da Gama Bridge), which spans the Tagus.

Oceanário de Lisboa (Lisbon Oceanarium). This glass-and-stone structure, rising from the river and reached by footbridge, is the largest aquarium in Europe, with 25,000 fish, seabirds, and mammals. It is the first aquarium to incorporate selected world ocean habitats (North Atlantic, Pacific, Antarctic, and Indian Ocean) within one complex. ⊠ *Esplanada D. Carlos I (Doca dos Olivais)* ☎ *21/891–70–02 or 21/891–70–06* ⊕ *www.oceanario.pt* ⊘ *Apr.–Oct., daily 10–8 (last admission at 7); Nov.–Mar., daily 10–7 (last admission at 6).*

Where to Eat

Lisbon's restaurants usually serve lunch from noon or 12:30 until 3 and dinner from 7:30 until 11; many establishments are closed on Sunday or Monday. Inexpensive restaurants typically don't accept reservations. In the traditional *cervejarias* (beer hall–restaurants), which frequently have huge dining rooms, you'll probably have to wait for a table, but usually not more than 10 minutes. In the Bairro Alto, many of the reasonably priced *tascas* (taverns) are on the small side: if you can't grab a table, you're probably better off moving on to the next place. Throughout Lisbon, dinner attire is usually casual, but exceptions are noted below. Restaurants in the low to middle price range often provide an *ementa turistica* (tourist menu), especially at lunchtime. These meals vary in quality but generally include three courses, a drink, and coffee.

$$$–$$$$ ✕ **Casa da Comida.** The refined decor, complete with indoor garden, perfectly complements the polished service and quality cuisine at this longstanding feature on Lisbon's gourmet restaurant circuit. ⊠ *Travessa das Amoreiras, 1* ☎ *21/388–53–76* ⌂ *Reservations essential* ▭ *AE, DC, MC, V.*

$$$–$$$$ ✕ **Gambrinus.** An inconspicuous door off a busy pedestrian street leads somewhat surprisingly into the wood-paneled comfort of one of Portugal's most notable traditional restaurants. The fish and shellfish dishes are highly favored, and the select wine list focuses on long-established Portuguese labels. ⊠ *Rua Portas de S. Antão, 23–25* ☎ *21/342–14–66* ▭ *AE, DC, MC, V.*

$$$–$$$$ ✕ **Tagide.** Restrained elegance, impeccable service, and top-level traditional Portuguese cuisine are the keynotes here. Try to secure a window table with a view over the Baixa quarter and the river. ⊠ *Largo Academia das Belas Artes, 18–20, at bottom of Rua Ivens* ☎ *21/342–07–20* ⌂ *Reservations essential* ▭ *AE, DC, MC, V* ⊘ *Closed Sun. No lunch Sat.*

★ $$$–$$$$ ✕ **Tavares.** Lisbon's oldest and most aristocratic restaurant was founded in 1784. Today it pleases customers with superb, French-inspired fare and an excellent wine list. The sole cooked in champagne sauce is a classic, and there are game birds available in season, served roasted in a rich wine sauce. Portuguese tastes can be assuaged by the bacalhau or the *sopa Alentejana* (Alentejo-style soup that's a concoction of garlic, bread, and egg). ⊠ *Rua Misericórdia, 35–37* ☎ *21/347–09–06 or 21/342–11–12* ⌂ *Reservations essential* ⌗ *Jacket and tie* ▭ *AE, DC, V* ⊘ *Closed Sat. No lunch Sun.*

$$–$$$$ ✕ **Bica do Sapato.** Installed like many of its new-wave brethren in a converted dockside warehouse, this airy restaurant, a favorite with TV stars and other trendy celebrities, serves food that is perfectly in sync with its contemporary lines: light and imaginative variations on traditional basics. ⊠ *Av. Infante Dom Henrique, Armazém B, Cais da Pedra (just in front of Sta. Apolónia Train Station)* ☎ *21/881–03–20* ▭ *AE, DC, MC, V* ⊘ *No dinner Sun. and Mon.*

★ $$–$$$$ ✕ **Pap' Açorda.** Art and media types scramble for the closely packed tables in this former bakery at the heart of the Bairro Alto. Portuguese classics are skillfully and imaginatively adapted to modern tastes. The *açorda*, a bread-based seafood dish, is legendary among Bairro Alto gourmets. ⊠ *Rua da Atalaia, 57* ☎ *21/346–48–11* ⌂ *Reservations essential* ⊟ *AE, DC, MC, V.*

$$$
Fodor'sChoice
★

✕ **Bota Alta.** Lines form outside the door by 8 PM at this small tavern, one of the Bairro Alto's oldest and most popular restaurants. The menu focuses on traditional Portuguese dishes, among them a famed *Amei-joas à Bulhão Pato* (clams steamed in a garlic and coriander sauce), *Bacalhau Real* (fried codfish and onions in port wine and brandy), and *Carne de Porco à Alentejana* (pork sautéed with clams in white wine with garlic), which is one of the best in Lisbon. ⊠ *Travessa da Queimada, 35–37* ☎ *21/342–79–59* ⊟ *AE, DC, MC, V* ☉ *Closed Sun. No lunch Sat.*

$$–$$$
Fodor'sChoice
★

✕ **A Travessa.** In an old monastery (17th–18th century) hidden away in the Madragoa quarter, this inviting bistro is on every Lisbon gourmet's phone list. Fresh fish dishes are popular and, as one of the owners is Belgian, Saturday nights are dedicated to mussels. Reservations are recommended. ⊠ *Travessa do Convento das Bernardas, 12* ☎ *21/394–08–00* ⊟ *AE, MC, V* ☉ *Closed Sun. No lunch Sat.*

$$–$$$
Fodor'sChoice
★

✕ **Sua Excêlencia.** At this cozy, family-run restaurant, you won't find any menus. Instead, the English-speaking owner will describe what is available from a short but tempting list of imaginatively prepared dishes, many based on traditional Portuguese regional recipes. ⊠ *Rua do Conde, 34* ☎ *21/390–36–14* ⊞ *21/396–7585* ⊟ *MC, V* ☉ *Closed Wed. and Sept. No lunch weekends.*

$$

✕ **As Barrigas.** The house specialty is a rich *arroz de polvo* (rice with octopus). Also on the menu are a number of fresh fish dishes, steak, and other Bairro Alto tavern standards. And the name? It means "the stomachs," owing to the large portions. ⊠ *Travessa da Queimada, 31* ☎ *21/347–12–20* ⊟ *V.*

$$

✕ **Comida de Santo.** Lively Brazilian music and genuine Brazilian food served in a dining room decorated with tropical motifs ensure a steady repeat clientele. You have to ring the bell for entrance. ⊠ *Calçada Engenheiro Miguel Pais, 39* ☎ *21/396–33–39* ⌂ *Reservations essential* ⊟ *AE, DC, MC, V.*

$$

✕ **Sinal Vermelho.** At this update of a traditional *adega* (tavern), the split-level dining room is tiled, and the food is thoroughly Portuguese, but the prints on the wall are modern, the clientele firmly professional, and the wine list extensive. Consider starting with a plate of clams drenched in oil and garlic and follow it with a fresh seafood dish; the meat dishes are less inspiring, although if you feel daring, you might try the tripe or the kidneys. ⊠ *Rua das Gáveas, 89* ☎ *21/346–12–52* ⌂ *Reservations essential* ⊟ *AE, MC, V* ☉ *Closed Sun. No lunch Sat.*

$–$$

✕ **Cervejaria Trindade.** The Trindade is a classic 19th-century cervejaria, with colorful tiles, vaulted ceilings, and frenetic service. You can pop in for a beer and a snack or eat a full meal. Hearty dishes such as *açorda* and steaks form the mainstay; if you opt for the grilled seafood, the tab will jump dramatically. The terrace is an enjoyable spot for dining in summer. ⊠ *Rua Nova da Trindade, 20 C* ☎ *21/342–35–06* ⊟ *AE, DC, MC, V.*

$–$$

✕ **1° de Maio.** Based on recipes from Portugal's rural heartland, the dishes at this former tavern in Bairro Alto are the work of Sr. and Sra. Santos, a husband and wife team of culinary genius. The wine list puts fancier restaurants to shame, and Sr. Santos is on hand with expert guidance. ⊠ *Rua da Atalaia, 8* ☎ *21/342–68–40* ⊟ *AE, MC, V* ☉ *Closed Sun. No dinner Sat.*

Where to Stay

★ **$$$$**

▨ **Four Seasons Hotel The Ritz Lisbon.** One of the finest hotels in Europe, the Ritz, in the heart of the city, is renowned for excellent service. The large, handsomely decorated guest rooms have terraces, and the public rooms are ornate, with tapestries, antique reproductions, and fine paintings. The hotel also provides a spa with an 18-meter swimming pool as well as four treatment rooms. ⊠ *Rua Rodrigo da Fonseca, 88, 1099-039* ☎ *21/381–14–42* 📠 *21/383–16–88* ⊕ *www.fourseasons.com/lisbon* 🛏 *264 rooms, 20 suites* ⌂ *Restaurant, bar* ⊟ *AE, DC, MC, V* |O| *EP* Ⓜ *Metro: Marquês de Pombal.*

$$$$ 🛌 **Lapa Palace.** Built in 1870 as the private residence of the Count of
Fodor'sChoice Valença, the Lapa Palace is in a unique old Lisbon quarter, amidst em-
★ bassies and regal homes. The luxurious guest rooms, suites, and public rooms run the gamut from neoclassical opulence to English country-house charm. ⊠ *Rua Pau de Bandeira, 4, 1249-021* ☎ *21/394–94–94* 📠 *21/395–06–65* ⊕ *www.lapa-palace.com* 🛏 *91 rooms, 18 suites* ⌂ *3 restaurants, 2 pools (1 indoor), bar* ⊟ *AE, DC, MC, V* |O| *BP.*

★ **$$$–$$$$** 🛌 **Tivoli Lisboa.** Facing Lisbon's main avenue, this comfortable, well-run establishment has a large public area furnished with inviting armchairs and sofas. The guest rooms are all pleasant, but those in the rear are quieter. ⊠ *Av. da Liberdade, 185, 1269-050* ☎ *21/319–89–00* 📠 *21/319–89–50* ⊕ *www.tivolihotels.com* 🛏 *299 rooms, 30 suites* ⌂ *Restaurant, pool, 2 bars* ⊟ *AE, DC, MC, V* |O| *BP* Ⓜ *Metro: Avenida.*

★ **$$$** 🛌 **Hotel Lisboa Plaza.** The staff at this family-owned hotel behind Avenida da Liberdade is friendly and helpful. The rooms are comfortable and pleasant and the bathrooms well stocked. Although it's not included in the room rate, the buffet breakfast is excellent. ⊠ *Travessa do Salitre, 7, 1269-066* ☎ *21/321–82–18* 📠 *21/347–16–30* ⊕ *www.heritage.pt* 🛏 *94 rooms, 12 suites* ⌂ *Restaurant, bar* ⊟ *AE, DC, MC, V* |O| *EP* Ⓜ *Metro: Avenida.*

★ **$$–$$$** 🛌 **As Janelas Verdes.** This late-18th-century mansion has marvelously restored, individually furnished rooms. You can eat breakfast in an ivy-covered patio garden. Reservations are vital at this hotel; it's as popular as it is small. ⊠ *Rua das Janelas Verdes, 47, 1200-670* ☎ *21/396–81–43* 📠 *21/396–81–44* ⊕ *www.heritage.pt* 🛏 *17 rooms* ⌂ *Bar* ⊟ *AE, DC, MC, V* |O| *EP* Ⓜ *Metro: Cais do Sodré.*

$$–$$$ 🛌 **Hotel Britania.** Dating from the 1940s and designed by a famous Portuguese modernist architect, Cassiano Branco, the Hotel Britania is decked out in genuine period surroundings. It is on a quiet street, off the Avenida da Liberdade, and has the feeling of an exclusive club. ⊠ *Rua Rodrigues Sampaio, 17, 1150-278* ☎ *21/315–50–16* 📠 *21/315–50–21* ⊕ *www.heritage.pt* 🛏 *30 rooms* ⌂ *Bar* ⊟ *AE, DC, MC, V* |O| *BP* Ⓜ *Metro: Avenida.*

★ **$$–$$$** 🛌 **Pensão Residencial York House.** This atmospheric residential pension, built as a convent in the 17th century, is in a shady garden at the top of a long flight of steps. It has a good restaurant, and full or half board is available. Book well in advance: the place is small and has a loyal following. ⊠ *Rua das Janelas Verdes, 32, 1200-691* ☎ *21/396–24–35* 📠 *21/397–27–93* ⊕ *www.yorkhouselisboa.com* 🛏 *34 rooms* ⌂ *Restaurant, bar* ⊟ *AE, DC, MC, V* |O| *BP.*

$$ 🛌 **Albergaria Senhora do Monte.** The terraces of the four junior suites have some of the loveliest views in town. Other rooms in this small, unpretentious hotel are less exalted, and cheaper; the top-floor restaurant has a wide picture window. ⊠ *Calçada do Monte, 39, 1170-250* ☎ *21/886–60–02* 📠 *21/887–77–83* ⊕ *www.maisturismo.pt.sramonte* 🛏 *24 rooms, 4 suites* ⌂ *Bar* ⊟ *AE, DC, MC, V* |O| *BP.*

$$ 🛌 **Aparthotel VIP Eden.** This nine-floor *apart'hotel*, in one of Lisbon's main downtown squares, offers fully furnished and equipped apartments for one to four people. The rooms are bright and modern, and the building itself is a 1930s architectural landmark. ⊠ *Praça dos Restauradores, 24, 1250-187* ☎ *21/321–66–00* 📠 *21/321–66–66* ⊕ *www.*

viphotels.com ⇱ *75 studios, 59 1-bedroom apartments* ⛄ *Pool, bar* ⊟ *AE, MC, V* ⭕ *EP* Ⓜ *Metro: Restauradores.*

$$ ⊞ **Casa de São Mamede.** One of the first private houses to be built in Lisbon after the 18th-century earthquake, São Mamede has been handsomely restored and transformed into a relaxed guest house. You're just a 10-minute walk from the Bairro Alto or a long, steep hike from the metro. ⊠ *Rua da Escola Politécnica, 159, 1250-100* ☎ *21/396–31–66* 🖷 *21/395–18–96* ⇱ *28 rooms* ⊟ *No credit cards* ⭕ *CP* Ⓜ *Metro: Avenida.*

$$ ⊞ **Flamingo.** A good-value choice near the top of the Avenida da Liberdade, this hotel has simply furnished, slightly old-fashioned rooms; those in the front are noisy. ⊠ *Rua Castilho, 41, 1250-068* ☎ *21/384–12–00* 🖷 *21/384–12–08* ⊕ *www.bestwestern.com* ⇱ *39 rooms* ⛄ *Restaurant, bar* ⊟ *AE, DC, MC, V* ⭕ *BP* Ⓜ *Metro: Marquês de Pombal.*

$ ⊞ **Albergaria Residencial Insulana.** One of a series of long-standing, modest hotels in Baixa's shopping area, near St. George's Castle, the Insulana has the edge over most and generally has space even when others are full—possibly because it's a little hidden away, up two flights of stairs through a clothes shop. Rooms are dark and dated, but clean; ask for a room at the rear to minimize disturbance from street noise. ⊠ *Rua da Assunção, 52, 1100-044* ☎ *21/342–31–31* 🖷 *21/342–89–24* ⊕ *www.insulana.cjb.net* ⇱ *32 rooms* ⛄ *Bar* ⊟ *AE, DC, MC, V* ⭕ *CP* Ⓜ *Metro: Baixa-Chiado.*

$ ⊞ **Ibis Lisboa Saldanha.** Frills are not on the menu in this practical modern hotel, but in terms of comfort, service, and location, the value could hardly be better. The rooms are small, but adequately equipped. The buffet breakfast is extra. ⊠ *Av. Casal Ribeiro, 23, 1000-090* ☎ *21/319–16–90* 🖷 *21/319–16–99* ⊕ *www.ibishotel.com* ⇱ *116 rooms* ⛄ *Restaurant* ⊟ *AE, DC, MC, V.*

Nightlife & the Arts

Lisbon has a thriving arts-and-nightlife scene. There are listings of concerts, plays, and films in the monthly *Agenda Cultural* and the quarterly *Unforgettable Lisboa* booklets, both available from the tourist office. Also, the Friday editions of both the *Diário de Notícias* and *O Independente* newspapers have separate magazines with entertainment listings. Although written in Portuguese, listings are fairly easy to decipher.

Free recitals take place regularly at the Igreja do Carmo and Igreja de São Roque in the Bairro Alto, and at the Sé. All films shown in Lisbon appear in their original language accompanied by Portuguese subtitles, and you can usually find the latest Hollywood releases playing around town. There are dozens of movie houses throughout the city, including a couple on Avenida da Liberdade. Some theaters are in preserved art deco buildings and are attractions in their own right.

The Arts

The **Teatro Nacional de São Carlos** (⊠ Rua Serpa Pinto, 9 ☎ 21/325–30–45 or 21/325–30–46 ⊕ www.saocarlos.pt) hosts an opera season October through May.

The prime mover behind Lisbon's artistic and cultural scenes is the **Fundação Calouste Gulbenkian** (⊠ Av. de Berna, 45A ☎ 21/782–37–00 ⊕ www.gulbenkian.pt), which not only presents exhibitions and concerts in its buildings but also sponsors events throughout the city. The **Centro Cultural de Belém** (⊠ Praça do Império ☎ 21/361–24–00 ⊕ www.ccb.pt) puts on a full range of reasonably priced concerts and exhibitions, featuring national and international artists and musicians. Plays are performed in Portuguese at the **Teatro Nacional de Dona Maria II** (⊠ Praça Dom Pedro IV ☎ 21/712–03–00 ⊕ www.teatro-dmaria.pt),

Lisbon's principal theater. Performances are given August through June, and there are occasional foreign-language productions, too.

A modern cinema complex in the **Amoreiras** (✉ Av. Eng. Duarte Pacheco ☎ 21/381–02–40) shopping complex has 10 screens. There are multi-screen movie theaters at **Colombo** (✉ Av. Lusíada ☎ 21/711–36–00) and **Centro Comercial Vasco da Gama** (✉ Av. D. João II ☎ 21/892–22–80) malls. Portugal's national film theater, the **Cinemateca Portuguesa** (✉ Rua Barata Salgueiro, 39 ☎ 21/352–31–80 ⊕ www.cinemateca.pt), has screenings Monday through Saturday at 6:30 and 9:30. This is the place to catch contemporary Portuguese films and art-house reruns.

Nightlife

Lisbon bars and discos open late (10 PM). On weekends the mobs are shoulder to shoulder in the street, as each passing hour heralds a move to the next trendy spot. Many places are dark and silent on Sunday; Monday, Tuesday, and (sometimes) Wednesday are also popular nights to close. For a less boisterous evening out, visit a café-bar or an *adega típica* (traditional wine cellar) that has fado shows. Still other venues host a variety of live events, from rock 'n' roll to African music.

DANCE CLUBS & BARS   The **Pavilhão Chinês** (✉ Rua Dom Pedro V, 89 ☎ 21/342–47–29) bar is a good jumping-off place for an excursion into the Bairro Alto neighborhood. Not far from the Pavilhão Chinês, **Trumps** (✉ Rua Imprensa Nacional, 104B ☎ 21/397–10–59 ⊕ www.trumps.pt) is the city's biggest gay disco.

Bar Salsa Latina (✉ Cais de Alcântara ☎ 21/395–05–50) is the place to go for the Latin American beat. Dancing, some nights to live music, begins at around 10:30. **Kapital** (✉ Av. 24 de Julho, 68 ☎ 21/395–59–63) is typical of the high-fashion, high-price venues down on the avenida; its terrace is its nicest feature. It's rumored that John Malkovich is one of the owners of the hot club **Lux** (✉ Av. Infante D. Henrique, near Sta. Apolónia ☎ 21/882–08–90 ⊕ www.luxfragil.com), which is in a remodeled riverside warehouse.

MUSIC CLUBS   Fado is a haunting music rooted in African slave songs. During colonial times it was exported to Portugal; later, Lisbon's Alfama was recognized as the birthplace of the style, and today most performances occur in the Bairro Alto. In the *adegas típicas,* food and wine are served, and fado plays late into the night: the singing starts at 10 or 11, and the adegas often stay open until 3 AM. It's becoming increasingly difficult to find an authentic adega; ask around for a recommendation. Note that some establishments charge (according to the night and who is playing) a minimum food and drink consumption charge, usually around €10–€15.

One of the oldest fado clubs, **Adega do Machado** (✉ Rua do Norte, 91 ☎ 21/322–46–40), is busy every night but Monday, when it's closed. For fado at budget prices, consider a meal in the **Adega do Ribatejo** (✉ Rua Diário de Notícias, 23 ☎ 21/346–83–43), a popular local haunt, where there's live entertainment nightly. **Parreirinha d'Alfama** (✉ Beco do Espírito Santo, 1 ☎ 21/886–82–09) is a little club owned by Fado legend Argentina Santos. She doesn't sing very often herself these days but the club hires many other highly rated singers.

Shopping

Districts

The **Chiado** quarter is one of Lisbon's best shopping districts, with some of the city's oldest and most prestigious shops and an upscale shopping center with a large FNAC bookstore. The **Baixa,** from Restauradores Square down to the River Tagus, is a popular shopping area. Designer boutiques and trees line the **Avenida da Liberdade,** north of the Baixa. On Avenida Engenheiro Duarte Pacheco, west of Parque Eduardo VII, the blue-and-pink towers of the **Amoreiras Shopping Center** dominate the Lisbon skyline. **Colombo,** in the suburb of Benfica and reached directly by metro (Col. Militar–Luz), is the largest shopping mall on the Iberian Peninsula. The big **Vasco da Gama** mall in Parque das Nações is airy and attractive.

Flea Markets

The best-known flea market is the **Feira da Ladra** (✉ Campo de Santa Clara), or "Thieves' Market," held Tuesday and Saturday from 9 AM to 6 PM from October to March, and until 8 PM from April through September.

Every Sunday the **Feira de Domingo** (Sunday Market) is held in the Parque das Nações, near the waterfront on Rua da Pimenta. Though easy to spot, it is not always in the same place on the street. Call the Parque das Nações information office for the exact location (☎ 21/891–9333).

Specialty Stores

HANDICRAFTS For embroidered goods and baskets from the Azores, stop by **Casa Regional da Ilha Verde** (✉ Rua Paiva de Andrade, 4 ☎ 21/342–59–74). **Casa Ribeiro da Silva** (✉ Travessa Fiéis de Deus, 69) is the place for handcrafted pottery. The **Fábrica Sant'Ana** (✉ Rua do Alecrim, 95 ☎ 21/342–25–37), founded in the 1700s, sells wonderful hand-painted ceramics and tiles based on antique patterns; the pieces sold here may be the finest in the city. Portugal's most famous porcelain producer, **Vista Alegre** (✉ Largo do Chiado, 20–23 ☎ 21/346–14–01 ⊕ www.va.empresas.com), established its factory in 1824. A visit to the flagship store is a must. **Viúva Lamego** (✉ Largo do Intendente, 25 ☎ 21/885–24–08 ✉ Calçada do Sacramento, 29 ☎ 21/346–96–92) sells the largest selection of tiles and pottery in Lisbon—and at competitive prices.

JEWELRY & ANTIQUES For antique silver and jewelry visit **António da Silva** (✉ Praça Luís de Camões, 40 ☎ 21/342–27–28). **Ourivesaria Sarmento** (✉ Rua Aurea, 251 ☎ 21/342–67–74), one of the city's oldest goldsmiths, produces characteristic Portuguese gold- and silver-filigree work.

LEATHER GOODS You'll find fine leather handbags and luggage at **Casa da Sibéria** (✉ Rua Augusta, 254 ☎ 21/342–56–79). Visit **Luvaria Ulisses** (✉ Rua do Carmo, 87 ☎ 21/342–02–95) for leather gloves.

Lisbon Essentials

AIRPORTS & TRANSFERS

International and domestic flights land at Lisbon's small, modern Aeroporto de Lisboa, also known as Aeroporto de Portela, 7 km (5 mi) north of the city. There's a tourist office here as well as a currency exchange bureau.

🛈 **Aeroporto de Portela** ☎ 21/841-35-00 or 21/841-37-00 🖶 21/841-36-75.

AIRPORT TRANSFERS There are no trains or subways between the airport and the city, but getting downtown by bus or taxi is simple and inexpensive. A special bus, Aerobus 91, runs every 20 minutes, 7 AM–9 PM, from outside the airport into the city center. Tickets, which you buy from the driver, cost €2.29 or €5.49 and allow one or three days of travel, respectively, on all Lisbon's buses and trams; TAP passengers can claim a free ride by showing their boarding pass. Taxis in Lisbon are relatively cheap, and the airport is so close to the city center, that many visitors make a bee-line straight for a cab (lines form at the terminal). To avoid any hassle over fares you can buy a prepaid voucher (which includes gratuity and luggage charges) from the tourist office booth in the arrivals hall.

BUS TRAVEL TO & FROM LISBON

Lisbon has two main bus terminals: Arco do Cego and Estação Oriente. The major national and international companies operate out of these two stations. Neither has a central information number; you have to call the individual bus companies. Rede Expressos is one of the companies at Arco do Cego. Renex operates out of Estação Oriente.

Rede Express ☎ 21/358-14-60 ⊕ www.rede-expressos.pt. **Renex** ☎ 21/894-02-85 and 21/894-08-88.

BUS TRAVEL WITHIN LISBON

City buses are operated by the public transportation company Carris and run 6:30 AM to midnight. Each stop is posted with full details of routes. For a spectacular journey across the Ponte 25 de Abril over the Rio Tejo take a bus from Praça de Espanha to Costa da Caparica or Setúbal. You can buy tickets for buses, elevadors, and funiculars at Carris kiosks in the Praça de Figueira, at the foot of the Elevador de Santa Justa, in the Santa Apolónia and Cais do Sodré railway stations, and elsewhere around town. When boarding, simply insert your ticket in the ticket-punch machine behind the driver and wait for the pinging noise. You can pay with cash once on board (have small change on hand if possible), but it's twice the price.

Carris ☎ 21/361-30-54 ⊕ www.carris.pt.

CAR RENTAL

Avis ✉ Av. Praia da Vitória, 12 C ☎ 21/351-45-60; 21/843-55-50 airport branch; 0800/20-10-02 ⊕ www.avis.com.pt. **Budget** ✉ Rua Castilho ☎ 21/386-05-16; 21/849-55-23; 21/847-88-03 airport branch ☎ 21/383-09-78 ⊕ www.budgetportugal.com. **Europcar** ✉ Av. António Augusto de Aguiar, 24 C/D ☎ 21/353-51-15; 21/840-11-63 airport; 21/886-15-73 Santa Apolónia station; 21/894-60-71 Gare do Oriente ⊕ www.europcar.pt. **Hertz** ✉ Rua do Castilho, 72 ☎ 21/381-24-30; 21/849-27-22 airport branch; 800/22-12-31.

CAR TRAVEL

Avoid driving around Lisbon yourself. Most central streets are choked with traffic during the day and parking spaces are always hotly contested; taxi drivers are skilled at navigating the one-way street system.

EMERGENCIES

Hours of operation and listings of pharmacies that stay open late are posted on most pharmacy doors. Local newspapers also carry a current list of pharmacies that have extended hours. In town, useful pharmacy addresses include those of Farmácia Azevedo Filhos, Farmácia Barral, and Farmácia Durão.

Emergency Services Red Cross Ambulances ☎ 21/942-11-11. **Fire** ☎ 21/342-22-22. **General emergencies** ☎ 112. **Police** ☎ 21/346-61-41. **Tourism Police** ✉ Rua Capelo, 13, near Teatro de São Carlos ☎ 21/346-61-41.

Hospitals British Hospital ✉ Rua Saraiva de Carvalho, 49 ☎ 21/394-31-00. **Clínica Médica International de Lisboa** ✉ Rua António Augusto de Aguiar, 40, R/C-E ☎ 21/315-16-68 ⊕ www.cmil.pt. **Hospital Santa Maria** ✉ Av. Prof. Egas Moniz ☎ 21/780-50-00 ⊕ www.hsm.pt. **Hospital de São Francisco Xavier** ✉ Est. Forte A. Duque ☎ 21/300-03-00 ⊕ www.hsfxavier.min-saude.pt. **Hospital São José** ✉ Rua José A. Serrano ☎ 21/884-10-00.

METRO TRAVEL

The metro operates 6:30 AM to 1 AM. Individual tickets cost €0.55; a 10-ticket strip, a *caderneta*, costs €4.50. There's also a one-day (€1.40) or seven-day (€4.80) Pase Metropolitano (Metro Pass) for use just on the metro system. Insert your ticket in the ticket-punch machine at the barrier.

🚇 **Metro Lisboa–Public Relations** ☎ 21/350-01-15, 21/350-01-16, or 21/350-01-17 🌐 www.metrolisboa.pt.

TAXIS
Lisbon taxis are cream-color. When the TAXI sign on the roof is lighted, the taxi is for hire. When only a green light is showing, the taxi is in use. Many city squares have taxi stands, or you can flag one down (on streets where stopping is allowed).

The meter starts at €1.80 during the day and €2.15 at night. The price per kilometer during the day on weekdays is €0.33; it rises to €0.39 evenings and weekends. Supplementary charges are added for luggage and if you phone for a cab (€0.75). The meter generally isn't used for journeys outside Lisbon, so you'll have to agree on a fare. Also available is the Taxi Voucher, a service at the Lisbon airport. This service is available to passengers arriving at Lisbon who wish to travel by taxi. The price of this voucher depends on the distance or length of time of the trip, as well as on the type of service required: normal or personalized (driver who speaks foreign languages and is trained as a tourist guide). On sale at ASKME-Tourist Offices (☎ 21/844-6473).

TOURS
BUS TOURS   Many companies organize half-day bus tours of Lisbon and its environs and full-day trips to more distant places of interest. Reservations can be made through any travel agency or hotel; some tours will pick you up at your door. A half-day tour of Lisbon will cost about €28. A full-day trip north to Obidos and Fátima will run about €75 and a full day east on the "Roman Route" to Évora about €70 (including lunch).

🚌 **Cityrama** ✉ Av. Praia da Vitória, 12 B ☎ 21/319-10-90 🌐 www.cityrama.pt. **Gray Line Tours** ✉ Av. Praia da Vitória, 12 B ☎ 21/319-10-90 🌐 www.grayline.com. **Top Atlântico** ✉ Av. Duque de Loulé, 108 ☎ 21/310-88-00; Call Centre 808/21-02-10 🌐 www.topatlantico.com.

PRIVATE GUIDES   For personal guides, contact Lisbon's main tourist office or the Syndicate of Guide Interpreters. It can provide an English-speaking guide for half-day (around €55) or full-day (around €95) tours; the price remains the same for up to 20 people. Office hours are weekdays 9–1 and 2–5:30.

🚶 **Sindicato Nacional das Actividades Turísticas, Tradutoras e Intérpretes** (Syndicate of Guide Interpreters) ✉ Rua do Telhal, 4 1150-346 ☎ 21/346-71-70 🖷 21/342-32-98.

TRAIN TRAVEL
International trains from Paris and Madrid arrive at the spectacular Estação Oriente, which has bus, subway, and taxi connections to all parts of the city. They continue on to the older terminal, just east of the city center. To get from Santa Apolonia to the central Praça dos Restauradores by public transport, take Bus 9, 39, 46, or 90.

🚆 **Estação Barreiro** ☎ 21/206-46-36. **Estação Lisboa Oriente** ☎ 21/892-03-16. **Estação Rossio** ☎ 21/346-50-22; toll-free 800/20-09-04. **Estação Santa Apolónia** ☎ 21/881-62-42.

TRAVEL AGENCIES
You can save yourself a lot of time by buying train or bus tickets from travel agencies, which often employ English-speaking staffers. Major agencies include Abreu, American Express/Topatlântico, and Marcus & Harting.

📋 **Abreu** ✉ Av. da Liberdade, 160 ☎ 21/323-02-00 🖶 21/323-02-09. **Topatlântico** ✉ c/o Topatlântico, Av. Duque de Loulé, 108 ☎ 21/310-88-00; Call Center 808/21-02-10. **Marcus & Harting** ✉ Praça D. Pedro IV, 45-50 ☎ 21/346-92-71 🖶 21/347-02-74.

VISITOR INFORMATION

The Lisbon branch of Portugal's tourist office—Investimentos, Comércio e Turismo de Portugal (ICEP)—is open daily 9–8. It's in the Palácio Foz, at the Baixa end of Avenida da Liberdade. There's also a branch at the airport that's open daily 6 AM to midnight. A much more rewarding place to get information is the Lisboa Welcome Centre, though you may have to wait patiently in a long line. The good news is that the information desk, which is open daily 9–8, is in a small complex with a café, a restaurant, a gallery, and a few shops. For general inquiries, you can try the Linha Verde Turista toll-free number.

For information on all the facilities and events at the Parque das Nações, stop at the information desk on Alameda dos Oceanos, in front of the Vasco da Gama center. The desk is open daily 9:30–8.

📋 **ICEP** ✉ Palácio Foz, Praça dos Restauradores ☎ 21/346-63-07; 21/849-43-23 to airport branch. **Lisboa Welcome Centre** ✉ Rua do Arsenal, 15 ☎ 21/031-27-00 🌐 www.atl-turismolisboa.pt. **Linha Verde Turista** ☎ 800/29-62-96. **Parque das Nações Information** ☎ 21/891-93-33 🌐 www.parquedasnacoes.pt.

THE ESTORIL COAST, SINTRA & QUELUZ

Extending 32 km (20 mi) west of Lisbon is a river and seaboard stretch of coastline known as the Costa do Estoril—the Estoril Coast, whose string of beaches has long served as a summer playground for Lisboners and tourists. The food here is some of the region's best, and sporting possibilities abound: golf courses, horseback riding, fishing, tennis, swimming, mountain climbing, hang gliding, and 4×4 excursions. Beaches vary in quality and cleanliness, though more and more display the blue flag of the Council of Europe, which sets high standards for unpolluted water and sand. The waters off Cascais and Estoril are calm. To the north, around Guincho's rocky promontory and along the Praia de Maçãs coast, the Atlantic is often windswept and rough—good for surfing and windsurfing.

To the north of Cascais and Estoril lie the mountains of Sintra and to the northeast, the historic 18th-century Queluz Palace. Set back from the modern coastal developments, the villas and luxury *quintas* (country properties) of the wealthy still populate the Sintra hills and secluded parts of Estoril and Cascais.

Estoril

Despite latter-day development, the more secluded parts of Estoril, 26 km (16 mi) west of Lisbon, are still filled with grand homes and gardens. Many of the mansions date from the 19th century, when the town was a favorite escape for the European aristocracy. Estoril's blue-blooded air has dissolved somewhat, but it's still a cosmopolitan place of considerable charm. The best and longest local beach is in adjoining Monte Estoril.

The biggest casino in Europe, **Estoril Casino**, with gaming rooms, restaurants, floor shows, and bars, is not just the hub of Estoril's nightlife; it also houses one of Portugal's major art galleries and hosts cultural events ranging from craft shows to the ballet. Admission to the casino complex and the 1,300 slot machines is free, but the traditional gaming rooms are made up of two distinct areas, one of which is open to

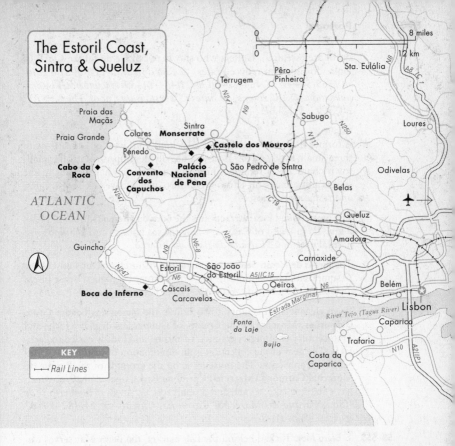

The Estoril Coast, Sintra & Queluz

ATLANTIC OCEAN

KEY

--- Rail Lines

the general public and the other a reserved VIP room. Reservations are essential for the restaurant and floor show. For €20 you can see the show and have one drink on the house; €52 buys you entrance to the show and dinner. ⊠ *Praça José Teodoro dos Santos* ☎ *21/466–77–00* ⊕ *www. casino-estoril.pt* ⊘ *Daily 3* PM*–3* AM; *floor show nightly at 11* ▭ *AE, DC, MC, V.*

$$$–$$$$ ✕ **Restaurant Cimas.** You're in for a good meal at this restaurant, which has been in business for more than 50 years. Surroundings are baronial, with plenty of burnished wood, heavy drapes, and oak beams. The menu is an international hybrid: choose from game in season, fresh fish, chicken curry, even Indonesian *saté* (skewered, charcoal-broiled meats served with a peanut sauce). ⊠ *Av. Sabóia, 9, Monte Estoril* ☎ *21/468–04–13* ⊕ *www.cimas.pt* ▭ *AE, DC, MC, V* ⊘ *Closed Sun.*

$$–$$$$ ✕ **A Choupana.** Just outside town toward Lisbon, this restaurant overlooks the beach, putting its picture windows to good use with views of Cascais Bay. You can sample high-quality fresh seafood and other local dishes such as the cataplana of chicken and clams. ⊠ *Estrada Marginal, São João de Estoril* ☎ *21/468–30–99* ▭ *AE, DC, MC, V.*

$$–$$$ ✕ **Restaurante Costa do Estoril.** One of the best deals in the area, this restaurant specializes in charcoal-grilled fish and has a terrace for warm-weather dining. ⊠ *Av. Amaral, 2765 Estoril* ☎ *21/468–18–17* 🖷 *21/487–15–90* ▭ *AE, MC, V* ⊘ *Closed Mon.*

★ **$$** ✕🏨 **Hotel Palácio.** Exiled European courts waited out World War II in this luxurious 1930s hotel. Several of the well-appointed, Regency-style guest rooms have balconies, and public areas are adorned with monumental columns and chandeliers: A comfortable bar has views over the outdoor pool to the town's central park. There's no more-elegant spot in town to dine than the Four Seasons Grill ($$$; reservations and a smart outfit are essential). Golfers who stay here can tee up on the Clube de Golfe do Estoril at reduced rates. ⊠ *Rua do Parque, Parque do Estoril 2769-504* ☎ *21/464–80–00* 🖷 *21/464–81–59* ⊕ *www.hotel-estoril-palacio.pt* ⇗ *132 rooms, 30 suites* ♨ *2 restaurants, pool, 3 bars* ⊟ *AE, DC, MC, V* ⭗⊙ *BP.*

Cascais

★ A former fishing village, Cascais (3¼ km [2 mi] west of Estoril)—with three small, sandy bays—is now a heavily developed resort. Its small-town character is retained, however, around the harbor and in the streets and squares off Largo 5 Outubro, which have lace shops, cafés, and restaurants galore.

The most-visited local attraction is the **Boca do Inferno** (Mouth of Hell), 2 km (1¼ mi) west of Cascais, where the sea pounds into an impressive natural grotto. ⊠ *Estrada da Boca do Inferno.*

The **Igreja de Nossa Senhora da Assunção** (Church of Our Lady of the Assumption) has paintings by the 17th-century Portuguese artist Josefa de Óbidos. ⊠ *Largo da Assunção* ☎ *No phone* ⊙ *Daily 9–1 and 5–8.*

In an elegant 19th-century town house, the **Museu dos Condes Castro Guimarães** (Museum of the Counts of Guimarães) displays 18th- and 19th-century paintings, ceramics, furniture, and locally excavated artifacts. The gem of the collection is an illumination of Lisbon in a 16th-century manuscript. The museum is on the grounds of the **Parque do Marechal Carmona** (Marechal Carmona Park), open daily 9–6, which has a shallow lake, a café, and a small zoo. ⊠ *Av. Rei Humberto II de Itália, Parque do Marechal Carmona, Cascais* ☎ *21/482–54–07* ⊙ *Tues.–Sun. 10–5.*

$$–$$$ ✕ **Beira Mar.** Tucked behind the fish market, the Beira Mar serves traditional Portuguese seafood dishes. Watch the scales when choosing shellfish—it's often sold by weight and can be pricey. The atmosphere is comfortable and unpretentious. ⊠ *Rua das Flores, 6* ☎ *21/483–01–52* ⊟ *AE, DC, MC, V* ⊙ *Closed Tues.*

★ **$$$–$$$$** ✕🖬 **Hotel Albatroz.** The most luxurious of Cascais's hotels, this charming old house sits atop a rocky outcrop that was converted from an aristocrat's summer residence. The restaurant ($$–$$$$; reservations and dressy-casual attire are essential) offers superior sea views and specializes in fish dishes, like grilled sole or baked cod stuffed with ham. ⊠ *Rua Frederico Arouca, 100, 2750-353* ☎ *21/484–73–80* 🖷 *21/484–48–27* ⊕ *www.albatrozhotels.com* ⇗ *37 rooms, 3 suites* ♨ *Restaurant, saltwater pool, bar* ⊟ *AE, DC, MC, V* ⭗⊙ *EP.*

$$$–$$$$ 🖬 **Farol Design Hotel.** This remodeled 19th-century mansion lies so close to the marina you can practically touch the sea. Rooms were individually designed by some of the most distinguished Portuguese fashion designers and stylists. ⊠ *Av. Rei Humberto II de Itália, 7 2750* ☎ *21/483–01–73* 🖷 *21/483–64–61* ✉ *faroldh@mail.telepac.pt* ⇗ *30 rooms, 3 suites* ♨ *Restaurant, saltwater pool, bar* ⊟ *AE, DC, MC, V.*

$$–$$$ 🖬 **Baía.** In the center of town, this hotel looks directly out onto the old harbor and the little crescent of sand known as the fishermen's beach. The rooms are small, but well equipped and attractive, and some have balconies with views over the harbor. ⊠ *Av. dos Combatentes da Grande Guerra, 2754-509* ☎ *21/483–10–33* 🖷 *21/483–1095* ⊕ *www.hotelbaia. com* ⇗ *113 rooms* ♨ *Restaurant, pool, bar* ⊟ *AE, DC, MC, V.*

Guincho

A superb wide beach overlooked by several seafood restaurants rests at Guincho, 11 km (7 mi) northwest of Cascais. Waves from the Atlantic pound onto the sand here even on the calmest of days, providing perfect conditions for windsurfing. But beware: the undertow at Guincho beach is notoriously dangerous, and even strong swimmers should take heed.

$$–$$$$ ✕▥ **Fortaleza do Guincho.** Along one of the most beautiful stretches of Portugal's Atlantic coast sits this exquisite hotel, a former fort. The rooms are small but luxurious, and decorated in a mixture of period styles; the views they afford of the rocky shoreline are spectacular. The spacious and elegant restaurant ($$$$) is the hub of the establishment. The cooking is nouveau-ish French, coordinated by Strasbourg chef and restaurateur Antoine Westermann. ⊠ *Estrada do Guincho, 2750-642* ☎ *21/487–04–91* 🖷 *21/487–04–31* ⊕ *www.guinchotel.pt* ⤴ *29 rooms* ⚒ *Restaurant* ▤ *AE, DC, MC, V.*

$–$$ ✕▥ **Estalagem do Forte Muchaxo.** This inn is nestled in the rocks over Guincho beach. Although most of the rooms have ocean views, those at the back overlook the nearby hills; the beach itself is just steps away. Much of the building is rustic, with stone floors, wood paneling, and maritime bric-a-brac. In the well-known restaurant ($$–$$$), fish specialties such as *caldeirada* (fish stew) are the order of the day. Meals are a little overpriced, and service isn't always top-notch, but what you're ultimately paying for is the unrivaled view through picture windows. ⊠ *Praia do Guincho, 2750-642* ☎ *21/487–02–21* 🖷 *21/487–04–44* ⤴ *60 rooms* ⚒ *Restaurant, saltwater pool, bar* ▤ *AE, DC, MC, V* ◯▮ *BP, MAP, FAP.*

Sintra

★ One of Portugal's oldest towns, Sintra—30 km (19 mi) northwest of Lisbon, and 13 km (8 mi) north of Estoril—was the summer residence of early Portuguese kings and aristocrats. By the 18th and 19th centuries its charms became widely known, as English travelers, poets, and writers—including an enthusiastic Lord Byron—were drawn by the region's beauty. On the second or fourth Sunday of the month, the Feira de São Pedro, known as the Sintra Fair by local English-speakers, takes place in the nearby village of São Pedro de Sintra, 2 km (1¼ mi) to the southeast.

The 8th-century **Castelo dos Mouros** (Moorish Castle) defied invaders until it was conquered by D. Afonso Henriques, Portugal's first king, in 1147. Follow the steep, partially cobbled road up to the ruins or rent a horse-drawn carriage in Sintra. From the castle's serrated walls, you can see why its Moorish architects chose the site: the views falling away on all sides are breathtaking. ⊠ *Estrada da Pena* ☎ *21/923–73–00* ⊕ *www.parquesdesintra.pt* ◯ *Daily: May–mid-June 9–7; mid-June–mid-Sept., 9–8; mid-Sept.–Oct., 9–7; Nov.–Apr., 9:30–6. Last admission 1 hr before closing.*

★ At the center of the Old Town stands the 14th-century **Palácio Nacional de Sintra** (Sintra Palace). This twin-chimney building, a combination of Moorish and Gothic architectural styles, was once the summer residence of the House of Avis, Portugal's royal family. Today it's a museum exhibiting fine examples of Moorish-Arabic *azulejos* (tiles). ⊠ *Praça da República* ☎ *21/910–68–40* ◯ *Thurs.–Tues. 10–5:30 (last admission at 5).*

Fodor'sChoice
★ The **Palácio Nacional de Pena** (Pena Palace), an extravaganza built by the king consort Ferdinand of Saxe-Coburg in 1840, is a cauldron of clashing styles, from Arabian to Manueline, and was home to the last kings of Portugal. The surrounding park is filled with trees and flowers brought from every corner of the Portuguese empire by Dom Fernando, consort to Dona Maria II, in the 1840s. It's a long but pleasant climb from Sintra to the palace—about 4 km (2½ mi). There's hourly bus service from

the Sintra train station and town center. ⊠ *Estrada da Pena* ☎ *21/910–53–40* ⊙ *Mid-Sept.–mid-June, Tues.–Sun. 10–5:30, last admission 4:45; mid-June–mid-Sept., Tues.–Sun. 10–7, last admission 6:15.*

Museu de Arte Moderna (Sintra Museum of Modern Art). The Berardo collection of modern European and American art, one of the finest private assemblages of modern painting and sculpture in Europe, is displayed here. ⊠ *Av. Heliodoro Salgado* ☎ *21/924–81–70 or 21/924–81–76* ⊕ *www.malhatlantica.pt* ⊠ *Adults €3, Wed. free* ⊙ *Tues.–Sun. 10–6.*

Palácio Quinta da Regaleira. Masonic symbolism and the mystical ideas of the Knights Templar are represented at this romantic palace built by a Portuguese lawyer who made his fortune in Brazil at the turn of the 20th century. Its turrets, gargoyles, and mysterious Well of Initiation would surely have delighted Charles Addams. ⊠ *Quinta da Regaleira, 2710-567 Sintra* ☎ *21/910–66–50* ⊠ *Adults €5, guided visits range from €10 to €20* ⊙ *June–Sept. tours daily 10–5, every 30 mins; tours less frequently Oct.–May.*

$$–$$$$ ✕ **Tacho Real.** Sintra locals come to this restaurant, at the top of a steep flight of steps, for a celebratory night out. They can count on confident, traditional dishes cooked with panache. Lamb, *leitão* (suckling pig), steaks, and game in season are all on the menu. ⊠ *Rua do Ferraria, 4* ☎ *21/923–52–77* ⊟ *AE, MC, V* ⊙ *Closed Wed.*

$–$$ ✕ **Alcobaça.** The friendly owner bustles around to make sure guests are well served in this simple restaurant on a town-center side street. Try the excellent grilled chicken, *arroz de marisco,* or tasty fresh clams *bulhão pato* (in garlic sauce). ⊠ *Rua das Padarias, 7–11* ☎ *21/923–16–51* ⊟ *MC, V.*

$$$ ✕⌂ **Hotel Palácio de Seteais.** Formerly a palatial residence, this luxuri-
FodorśChoice ous hotel 1 km (½ mi) from Sintra was built by the Dutch consul in Por-
★ tugal in the 18th century. Its stately rooms are decorated with delicate wall and ceiling frescoes. The restaurant ($$–$$$; reservations essential; dressy attire requested) serves set, four-course, Continental meals. ⊠ *Rua Barbosa do Bocage, 8, 2710-517* ☎ *21/923–32–00* ⊞ *21/923–42–77* ⊕ *www.tivolihotels.com* ⟿ *30 rooms, 1 suite* ⟐ *Restaurant, pool, bar* ⊟ *AE, DC, MC, V* ⟐⊙ *BP.*

$$$ ✕⌂ **Lawrence's Hotel.** When this 18th-century inn reopened as a luxury hotel late in the 20th century, the U.S. secretary of state and the Netherlands' Queen Beatrix were among the first guests. The intimate rooms are bathed in light from French windows, and deluxe touches such as heated towel racks and crested linens abound. At Lawrence's Restaurant ($$$–$$$$; reservations recommended) specialties might include fish soup *en croûte* with coriander, roast duck, and a dessert flambéed at your table. ⊠ *Rua Consigliéri Pedroso, 38–40, 2710-550* ☎ *21/910–55–00* ⊞ *21/910–55–05* ⊕ *www.portugalvirtual.pt* ⟿ *11 rooms, 5 suites* ⟐ *Restaurant, bar* ⊟ *AE, DC, MC, V* ⟐⊙ *BP.*

$$$ ⌂ **Tivoli Sintra.** From its perch in the center of Sintra, the Tivoli has views over the nearby valleys. The smart rooms provide space and comfort in equal measure. ⊠ *Praça da República, 2710-616* ☎ *21/923–72–00* ⊞ *21/923–72–45* ⊕ *www.tivolihotels.com* ⟿ *77 rooms* ⟐ *Restaurant, bar* ⊟ *AE, DC, MC, V* ⟐⊙ *BP.*

★ **$$** ⌂ **Quinta das Sequóias.** Located down a side road, this lovely manor house is a good touring base. After a day of sightseeing you can unwind in the gardens, which include a Jacuzzi, and a terrace. (Note that there's a two-night minimum stay in peak season, and that dinner must be ordered in advance. Reservations are essential.) ⊠ *2 km (1 mi) from Sintra, past the Palácio de Seteais (Box 4), 2710-801* ☎ *21/924–38–21 or 21/923–*

03–42 ☐ *21/910–60–65* ⊕ *www.quintadassequoias.com* ↘ *6 rooms* ♨ *Pool, bar* ⊟ *AE, DC, MC, V* ⨯⨪ *BP.*

Queluz

The town of Queluz, 15 km (9 mi) east of Sintra and the same distance northwest of Lisbon, is accessible by train directly from Lisbon or by way of the IC19/N249 road, which runs between Lisbon and Sintra.

★ Once you turn off the main road, it's hard to miss the magnificent **Palácio Nacional de Queluz** (Queluz Palace). Inspired in part by Versailles, the salmon-pink rococo palace begun by Dom Pedro III in 1747 was completed 40 years later. The landscaping and waterways are the work of the French designer Jean-Baptiste Robillon. The palace is now used for formal banquets and music festivals and houses visiting heads of state. A display of the elegant formal horsemanship known as haute ècole dressage, an art for which Portuguese riders are famed, is held in the gardens every Wednesday. ⊠ *Largo do Palacio Nacional* ☎ *21/434–38–60* ⊠ *Adults €3* ☉ *Wed.–Mon. 10–5, last admission 4:30.*

$$ ✕⊞ **Pousada de Dona Maria I.** Marble hallways lined with prints of Old
Fodor'sChoice   Portugal give way to high-ceilinged rooms with 18th-century reproduction
★   furniture in these former servants' quarters beneath the clock tower opposite the Queluz Palace. Across the street, in an 18th-century palace kitchen, is the Cozinha Velha restaurant ($$–$$$$; reservations essential), where the Portuguese specialties on the ever-changing menu are occasionally tempered by a French touch. ⊠ *Rte. IC19, 2745-191* ☎ *21/435–61–58* ☐ *21/435–61–89* ⊕ *www.pousadas.pt* ↘ *24 rooms, 2 suites* ♨ *Restaurant, bar* ⊟ *AE, DC, MC, V* ⨯⨪ *BP.*

The Estoril Coast, Sintra & Queluz Essentials

BUS TRAVEL TO & FROM THE ESTORIL COAST, SINTRA & QUELUZ

The best way to reach Cascais, Estoril, and Sintra is by train from Lisbon, but there are some useful bus connections between towns. The bus terminal outside the train station at Cascais has summer service to Guincho (15-minute trip) and Sintra (40 minutes). From the bus terminal outside the Sintra train station, there's year-round service to Cascais and Estoril (1 hour), and to the Moorish Castle and Pena Palace.
🚍 **Cacilhas bus terminal** ⊠ Largo Alfredo Diniz ☎ No phone. **Cascais bus terminal** ☎ 21/483–63–57. **Palmela bus station** ⊠ Largo do Chafariz D. Maria I ☎ 21/235–00–78. **Sesimbra bus station** ⊠ Av. da Liberdade ☎ 21/223–30–71. **Setúbal bus station** ⊠ Av. 5 de Outubro, 44 ☎ 265/52–50–51.

CAR TRAVEL

Fast highways connect Lisbon with Estoril (A5/IC15) and Setúbal (A2/IP1), and the quality of other roads in the region is generally good. Take care on hilly and coastal roads, though, and if possible, avoid driving out of Lisbon at the start of a weekend or public holiday or back in at the end. Both Rio Tejo bridges—especially the Ponte 25 de Abril but also the dramatic Ponte Vasco da Gama—can be very slow. Parking can be problematic, too, especially in the summer along the Estoril Coast. When you do park, *never* leave anything visible in the car, and it's wise to clear out the trunk as well.

TOURS

ORIENTATION   Most travel agents and large hotels in Lisbon or its environs can reserve
TOURS   a place on a guided tour for you. Cityrama has half-day trips to Queluz, Sintra, and Estoril and a tour of the area's royal palaces (each €65–€70); nine-hour tours of Mafra, Sintra, and Cascais (€70–€75 including

lunch); and even an evening visit to Estoril's famous casino (€82.30 including dinner). Gray Line Tours has half-day trips into the Arrábida Mountain range and to local crafts centers for around €50.

For guided tours of the Sintra area, ask at the tourist information center, which has current schedules and can sell tickets. Half-day tours typically encompass visits to all the principal sights and a wine tasting in Colares.

🖪 **Cityrama/Gray Line Tours** ⊠ Av. Praia da Vitória, 12-B, 1049-054 Lisbon ☎ 21/319-10-90; 21/319-10-91; 21/319-10-92; Tours Info 21/386-43-22 🖶 21/356-06-68 ⊕ www.cityrama.pt.

TRAIN TRAVEL

Electric commuter trains travel the entire Estoril Coast, with departures every 15 to 30 minutes from the waterfront Cais do Sodré station in Lisbon, west of the Praça do Comércio. The scenic trip to Estoril takes about 30 minutes, and four more stops along the seashore bring you to Cascais, at the end of the line. A one-way ticket to either costs €1.20; service operates daily 5:30 AM–2:30 AM. Trains from Lisbon's Rossio station, between Praça dos Restauradores and the Rossio, run every 15 minutes to Queluz (a 20-minute trip) and on to Sintra (40 minutes total). The service operates 6 AM–2:40 AM, and one-way tickets cost €1 to Queluz-Massamá, €1.20 to Sintra.

🖪 **Fertagus** ☎ 21/294-97-00. **Rail information line** ☎ 21/888-40-25 ⊕ www.cp.pt.

VISITOR INFORMATION

🖪 **Câmara Municipal de Cascais** ⊠ Rua Visconde da Luz, 14 ☎ 21/486-82-04. **Junta de Turismo da Costa do Estoril** ⊠ Arcadas do Parque, 2769-503 Estoril ☎ 21/466-38-13 or 21/468-70-44 🖶 21/467-22-80 ⊕ www.costa-do-estoril.pt. **Câmara Municipal de Sintra** ⊠ Praça da República, 23, 2710-611 Sintra ☎ 21/923-11-57 or 21/923-38-12 ⊠ Sintra train station, Av. Miguel Bombarda, 2710-590 Sintra ☎ 21/924-16-23.

THE ALGARVE

The Algarve, Portugal's southernmost region, encompasses 240 km (150 mi) of sun-drenched coastline. Vacationers head here for clean, sandy beaches, top-quality sports facilities, fine hotels, championship golf courses, Mediterranean-type weather, and colorful local markets and cafés. Heavily developed since the 1960s, apartment complexes, hotels, and restaurants crowd every bay and cliff top in certain areas. Still, some fishing villages and secluded beaches remain untouched. The drive to Albufeira from Lisbon takes about three hours; allow another hour to reach either Faro or Lagos. (Regional authorities have been working to improve directional signs along roads, but signposting remains inadequate.)

Monte Gordo

Pine woods and orchards break up the flat landscape around Monte Gordo, a town near the Spanish border 4 km (2½ mi) west of Vila Real de Santo António. Brightly colored houses dot the streets, which are laid out in an 18th-century grid pattern similar to that of the Baixa district in Lisbon. There's a long stretch of beach here, but beaches to the west, such as Praia Verde and Manta Rota, are equally attractive. You should have little trouble finding a spot on the sand, perhaps for a lunch of grilled sardines at one of the numerous beach-side bistros.

$–$$ ✕ **Mota.** The Mota is a lively, unpretentious seafood restaurant with a covered terrace right on the ocean. ⊠ *Praia de Monte Gordo* ☎ *281/ 51–23–40* ▤ *No credit cards.*

$$ ▣ **Alcazar.** Unusual architecture and interior design mark this engaging hotel. The sinuous arches and low molded ceilings suggest the in-

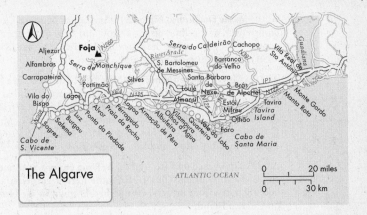

side of a cave or an Arab tent. ⊠ *Rua de Ceuta, 9, 8900-435* ☎ *281/51–01–40* 🖷 *281/51–01–49* ➥ *119 rooms* ♨ *Restaurant, 2 pools, bar* 🖃 *AE, DC, MC, V* ⓧ⊙ *BP, MAP.*

Tavira

A tuna fishing port at the mouth of the River Gilão, 20 km (12 mi) west of Monte Gordo, Tavira has cobbled streets, a seven-arch Roman bridge, old Moorish defense walls crowning the central hill, and several artistic and historical churches. Of particular interest is Santa Maria do Castelo (St. Mary of the Castle), where the sons of King João I were knighted in the early 15th century for their part in taking the North African city of Ceuta from the Moors. Ferries (€0.80–€0.90 round-trip) to sand beaches on nearby Ilha de Tavira (Tavira Island) are available from the jetty at Quatro Águas (2 km [1 mi] east of town center). Boats leave every 10 minutes or so July through August, and less frequently in other months, depending on demand. Another ferry runs from June 1 until September 15 near the fishing port of Tavira to the same sand beaches on nearby Ilha de Tavira. The boats leave every 30 minutes (€1 round-trip).

Olhão

Founded in the 18th century, this fishing port 22 km (14 mi) west of Tavira is notable for North African–style cube-shaped whitewashed buildings and for some of the best food markets in the Algarve (near the harbor). Ferries to the islands of Armona and Culatra, both of which have excellent beaches, are available from the jetty east of the town gardens. Schedules are available at the tourist office.

Faro

Founded by the Moors, Faro—provincial capital of the Algarve—was taken by Afonso III in 1249, ending the Arab domination of Portugal. Nine kilometers (6 mi) west of Olhão, it's a fairly modern city, full of restaurants with international cuisines.

★ The best of the sights in Faro is surely the **Capela dos Ossos** (Chapel of the Bones) in the **Igreja do Carmo** (Carmelite Church), decorated with more than 1,000 skulls and bones of parishioners and monks. ⊠ *Largo do Carmo* ☎ *No phone* ⊙ *Weekdays 10–1 and 3–5, Sat. 10–1.*

★ In the older district, called the **Cidade Velha,** you can see remnants of medieval walls and gates. One of the gates, the **Arco da Vila,** with a white marble statue of St. Thomas Aquinas at the top, leads to the restored Gothic **Sé** (Cathedral), surrounded by orange trees in the grand Largo da Sé (Cathedral Square). The cathedral is open Monday through Saturday 10–5 or 6, and Sunday 8–1 for services.

At the **Museu Etnográfico Regional** (Ethnological Museum), lace making, embroidery, and fishing displays show just how much the Algarve has changed over the years. ⊠ *Praça da Liberdade, 2* ☎ *289/82–76–10* ⊙ *Weekdays 9–12:30 and 2–5:30.*

The Old Town's **Museu Municipal** (Municipal Museum), in a former convent, has a section devoted to the Roman remains found at the nearby archaeological site of Milreu. ⊠ *Largo D. Afonso III, 14* ☎ *289/89–74–00* ⊠ *Museum €1, Old Town guided tour €1, Museum plus Old Town Tour €1.50* ⊙ *June–Sept., Mon. and Sat. 2:30–6, Tues.–Fri. 10–6; Oct.–May, Mon. and Sat. 2–5:30, Tues.–Fri. 9:30–5:30.*

A large sand beach on Faro Island, the **Praia de Faro,** is connected to the city of Faro by bridge (Bus 16 from the harbor gardens). Or you can take the ferry from the jetty below the old town to the beach at Farol on Culatra Island.

$$–$$$$ ✕ **Camané.** Carlos Manuel Martins and his wife, Graça, have made this Faro restaurant facing the lagoon (ria de Faro) a seafood mecca. Algarve desserts, like the *tarte de amêndoa* (almond tart), an open pastry with a rich almond-and-egg filling, are especially good. Reservations are recommended for dinner. ⊠ *Praia de Faro, Av. Nascente* ☎ *289/81–75–39* ⊟ *AE, DC, MC, V* ⊙ *Closed Mon.*

$–$$ ✕ **Taska.** Mere mention of this small, cozy, family-run restaurant makes mouths water; the wide selection of seafood and market-fresh produce draws diners from far beyond the boundaries of Faro. ⊠ *Rua do Alportel, 38* ☎ *289/82–47–39* ⊟ *No credit cards* ⊙ *Closed Sun.*

★ $$–$$$ 🏨 **Hotel Apartamento La Reserve.** High-class apartments and duplexes with verandas and sea views are available at this intimate luxury hotel in the hills of Santa Barbara. Just 10 km (6 mi) inland from Faro, the property's facilities include a tennis court and a surrounding 6-acre park. The restaurant serves elegant Continental cuisine with a French accent. ⊠ *Santa Bárbara de Nexe, Sítio da Igreja, 8000-712 Faro* ☎ *289/99–94–94* 🖶 *289/99–94–02* 🛏 *12 studios, 8 duplexes* ⌂ *Restaurant, pool* ⊟ *AE, DC, MC, V.*

$$ 🏨 **Hotel Eva.** This modern, well-appointed hotel overlooking the yacht basin has rooms with spacious balconies that face the sea. There's a shuttle to the beach. ⊠ *Av. da República, 1, 8000-078* ☎ *289/80–33–54* 🖶 *289/80–23–04* ⊕ *www.tdhotels.pt* 🛏 *135 rooms, 13 suites* ⌂ *Restaurant, pool, bar* ⊟ *AE, DC, MC, V* ¶⊙ *BP, MAP, FAP.*

Estói

The charming village of Estói, 9 km (5½ mi) north of Faro, on a signposted branch road off the N2, is the setting for the 18th-century **Palácio do Visconde de Estói** (Palace of the Counts of Estói). The palace is closed to the public, but you can tour its gardens. ⊠ *Rua da Barroca* ☎ *28/999–72–82* ⊙ *Tues.–Sat. 9–12:30 and 2–5:30.*

Extensive Roman ruins at **Milreu** include a temple and mosaic fragments adorning some 3rd-century baths. ⊠ *Estrada Nacional 2, Nó do Infante* ☎ *289/99–74–87* ⊙ *May–Sept., Tues.–Sun. 9:30–12:30 and 2–6; Oct.–Apr., Tues.–Sun. 9:30–12:30 and 2–5.*

Loulé

Once a Moorish stronghold, the market town of Loulé, in the hills 17 km (10 mi) northwest of Faro, along the N125–4, is now best known for its crafts and the decorative white chimneys of its houses. You can usually see coppersmiths and leather workers toiling in their workshops along the narrow streets.

You can visit the partially restored ruins of the medieval Saracen **Castelo de Loulé,** which houses the town's archaeological and historical museum, the Museu Arqueológical de Loulé. ⊠ *Rua D. Paio Peres Correia, 17* ☎ *289/40–06–42* ⊘ *Weekdays 9–5:30, weekends 10–2.*

The restored 13th-century **Igreja Matriz** (Parish Church) has handsome tiles, wood carvings, and an unusual wrought-iron pulpit. ⊠ *Largo Pr. C. da Silva* 🕾 *No phone* ⊘ *Mon.–Sat. 9–noon and 2–5:30.*

Almancil

This small town, 10 km (6 mi) northwest of Faro, is rather nondescript but is worth a visit for its baroque church and for the two major resorts in the area: the Vale de Lobo resort sits in exclusive isolation on a beach about 2 km (1 mi) southwest of Almancil. The grand Quinta do Lago resort, famed for its golf, tennis, horseback riding, and water-sports facilities, is southeast of Almancil.

One of the best reasons to visit Almancil is the 18th-century baroque **Igreja de São Lourenço** (Church of Saint Lawrence)—filled with blue-and-white tile panels and intricate gilt work. The cottages beside it have been transformed into a lovely art gallery. ⊠ *N125, 3 km (2 mi) east of Almancil proper* ☎ *28/939–54–75* ⊘ *Chapel Mon. 2–6, Tues.–Sat. 10–1.*

$$–$$$$ ✕ **Gigi.** You have to walk 400 meters (¼ mi) across a wooden footbridge that begins near the Hotel Quinta do Lago entrance (at the end of Rua André Jordão) to reach this famed beachside restaurant, but seafood lovers from around the world make the effort. Preparation is simple but masterly. Accompanying salads are skillfully constructed to harmonize with the food, and so is the wine list. ⊠ *Praia da Quinta do Lago* ☎ *96/ 404–50–78* ♨ *Reservations essential* 🖃 *AE, DC, MC, V* ⊘ *Closed Oct.–Feb.*

★ $$$$ ✕🖾 **Le Meridien Dona Filipa & San Lorenzo Golf Course.** On extensive, beautifully landscaped grounds near the beach, this lavish hotel has first-rate service, tennis courts, and discounts for nearby golf courses. Dining choices ($$$–$$$$) include the Dom Duarte restaurant, which has a Portuguese menu; the Primavera, which serves Italian cuisine; and the Grill, which offers local and international fare. ⊠ *Vale do Lobo* ⌖ *8135–901* ☎ *289/35–72–00* 🖶 *289/35–72–01* ⊕ *www.lemeridien.com* ❧ *147 rooms* ♧ *2 restaurants, pool, 2 bars* 🖃 *AE, DC, MC, V* ⊗ *BP.*

$$$$ 🖾 **Hotel Quinta do Lago.** Green hills, pine woods, and golf courses surround this secluded and luxurious hotel on the rim of the Ria Formosa Natural Park, the wetland nature reserve that extends along the coast almost to the Spanish border. Most rooms have balconies with views over the Ria Formosa lagoon and the Atlantic Ocean. Superb Venetian dishes are served in the elegant Ca d'Oro restaurant ($$$–$$$$); the equally classy Brisa do Mar ($$$–$$$$) focuses on more local culinary matters. ⊠ *Quinta do Lago, 8135–024* ☎ *289/35–03–50* 🖶 *289/ 39–63–93* ⊕ *www.quintadolagohotel.com* ❧ *132 rooms, 9 suites* ♧ *2 restaurants, 2 pools (1 indoor), 3 bars* 🖃 *AE, DC, MC, V* ⊗ *BP, MAP.*

Vilamoura

A highly developed resort 10 km (6 mi) west of Almancil, Vilamoura is replete with luxury hotels, a casino, a large yacht marina, several golf courses, a major tennis center, and one of Europe's largest shooting centers. The beach is splendid, and there's more sand 4 km (2½ mi) to the east at the neighboring market town of Quarteira, a quiet fishing village turned bustling high-rise resort.

$$$–$$$$ ✕🖾 **Tivoli Marinotel.** The luxurious Marinotel overlooks Vilamoura's marina. Its rooms are well equipped, its facilities are wide ranging, and activities available at the marina include sailboat and motorboat excursions,

deep-sea fishing trips, and scuba diving. Many people think this hotel has the best places to eat ($$$–$$$$) in town: the Grill Sirius, overlooking the boats, specializes in fish and has live music; the Aries restaurant faces the hotel gardens and serves top-quality international dishes. ⊠ *Vilamoura Marina, 8126-901* ☎ *289/30–33–03* 🖷 *289/30–33–45* ⊕ *www.tivolihotels.com* 🛏 *393 rooms* ♨ *2 restaurants, 2 pools (1 indoor), 2 bars* ⊟ *AE, DC, MC, V* ⊠ *BP, MAP, FAP.*

$$$ 🏨 **Hotel Dom Pedro Golf.** Part of a highly successful vacation complex, the Dom Pedro is close to the casino, not far from a splendid beach, and five minutes from the marina. Rooms are attractively furnished, and there's a garden in which to relax. The hotel also has a comprehensive range of facilities. ⊠ *Rua Atlântico, 8125-478* ☎ *289/30–07–00* 🖷 *289/30–07–01* ⊕ *www.dompedro.com* 🛏 *261 rooms* ♨ *Restaurant, 2 pools, bar* ⊟ *AE, DC, MC, V* ⊠ *BP, MAP, FAP.*

Albufeira

Like many Algarve towns, Albufeira, 10 km (6¼ mi) west of Vilamoura, was a sleepy fishing village that mushroomed into a large and popular resort. But with its steep, narrow streets and hundreds of whitewashed houses clutching the slopes, Albufeira retains a distinctly Moorish flavor. The town has a lively fish market (open daily), caves and grottoes along its coast, and an active nightlife.

$$$–$$$$ ✕ **A Ruina.** A rustic restaurant on the beach, built on several levels, this is the place for good views and charcoal-grilled seafood. ⊠ *Cais Herculano, Praia dos Pescadores* ☎ *289/51–20–94* ⊟ *AE, MC, DC, V.*

$$–$$$ ✕ **La Cigale.** Nine kilometers (5½ mi) east of Albufeira proper, overlooking its own little beach, this restaurant—one of the best—offers both French and Portuguese cuisines. ⊠ *Praia de Olhas d'Agua* ☎ *289/50–16–37* ⊟ *DC, MC, V* ☺ *Closed Dec.–Feb.*

$$ ✕ **Cabaz da Praia.** From its cliff-side terrace, this long-established restaurant has a spectacular view of the main beach. There's fine French-Portuguese cooking here—fish soup, imaginative fish plates, and chicken with seafood. ⊠ *Praça Miguel Bombarda 7* ☎ *289/51–21–37* ⊟ *AE, MC, V* ☺ *Closed Thurs. No lunch Sat.*

★ **$$$–$$$$** 🏨 **Sheraton Algarve Hotel.** On a spectacular cliff-top site by the sea 8 km (5 mi) east of town, this hotel blends Moorish courtyards, fountains, and terraces, with fine Portuguese tiles and furnishings. The hotel has a sauna, a 9-hole golf course, tennis courts, and access by an exterior elevator to the beach. A buffet breakfast is included. ⊠ *Praia da Falésia, Box 644, 8200-909* ☎ *289/50–01–00* 🖷 *289/50–19–50* ⊕ *www.pinecliffs.com* 🛏 *215 rooms* ♨ *2 restaurants, 3 pools (1 indoor), 3 bars* ⊟ *AE, DC, MC, V* ⊠ *BP, MAP, FAP.*

$$ 🏨 **Hotel Vila Galé Cerro Alagoa.** Guest rooms here are smartly decorated and have private balconies, some with sea views. It's about a ½-km (¼-mi) walk to downtown Albufeira, or you can take the courtesy bus, which also stops at local beaches. ⊠ *Rua do Município, 26, 8200-916* ☎ *289/58–31–00* 🖷 *289/58–31–99* ⊕ *www.vilagale.pt* 🛏 *310 rooms* ♨ *Restaurant, 2 pools* ⊟ *AE, DC, MC, V.*

Armação de Pêra

The straggling resort of Armação de Pêra, 14 km (9 mi) west of Albufeira, has one of the longest beaches in the Algarve, a wide, sandy strand with a pretty promenade. Local boats take sightseers on cruises to the caves and grottoes along the shore.

$–$$ ✕ **The Beach Bar.** A famed lunchtime venue, this beach spot doesn't do dinners, but serves its lunch menu until 9 PM. Fish is the specialty, and it has the best paella for miles around. ⊠ *Praia Grande* ☎ *28/231–69–66* ⊟ *No credit cards.*

$$$$ ⊞ **Vila Vita Parc.** The pampering begins as soon as you pass through the wrought-iron gates. Fireplaces, dark woods, and the aura of an exclusive oasis fill this superb cliff-top resort. There is golf and tennis, and landscaped gardens wind down to two sequestered beaches. ⊠ *Armação de Pêra, Porches, 8400-450* ☎ *282/31–02–00* 🖷 *282/31–53–33* ⊕ *www.vilavitaparc.com* ⤴ *91 rooms, 74 suites* ♨ *6 restaurants, 3 pools (1 indoor), 8 bars* ▭ *AE, DC, MC, V* ⑩ *BP, MAP, FAP.*

$$–$$$ ⊞ **Hotel Garbe.** The bar, lounge, and restaurant all have terraces that provide views of the sea at this low-rise, gleaming white hotel. Rooms are modern and smartly furnished. Steps lead from the hotel down to the beach. ⊠ *Apartado 1, 8365-909* ☎ *282/32–02–60* 🖷 *282/31–50–87* ⊕ *www.hotelgarbe.com* ⤴ *152 rooms* ♨ *2 restaurants, pool, 2 bars* ▭ *AE, MC, V* ⑩ *BP, MAP, FAP.*

Portimão

Portimão, 15 km (9 mi) west of Armação de Pêra, is the most important fishing port in the Algarve; it's cheerful and busy, with shops and open-air cafés. Even before the Romans arrived, there was a settlement here at the mouth of the River Arade. At restaurants along the quay you can sample the local specialty: charcoal-grilled sardines with chewy fresh bread and red wine.

$$ ✕ **A Lanterna.** On the main road just over the bridge from Portimão, this well-run restaurant serves exceptional fish soup and smoked swordfish, both genuine Algarvian treats. Other seafood specialties are worthy, too. ⊠ *Parchal* ☎ *282/41–44–29* ▭ *MC, V* ☯ *Closed Sun.*

★ $$ ✕⊞ **Le Meridien Penina Golf and Resort.** On 360 manicured, secluded acres off the main road between Portimão and Lagos, this golf hotel with attentive service has an impressive range of activities, a health club, an elegant interior, and a number of rooms with balconies and views of the Serra de Monchique. The beautifully landscaped golf courses were designed by Henry Cotton; greens fees are waived for hotel guests. There's a choice of five restaurants ($$$–$$$$), including the Grill Room, which serves excellent Portuguese dishes, and the Sagres Restaurant, with lively theme evenings. ⊠ *Box 146, Penina, 8501-952* ☎ *282/42–02–00* 🖷 *282/42–03–00* ⊕ *www.lemeridien.com* ⤴ *196 rooms* ♨ *5 restaurants, pool, 2 bars* ▭ *AE, DC, MC, V* ⑩ *BP, MAP, FAP.*

Praia da Rocha

Now dominated by high-rise apartments and hotels, this was the first spot in the Algarve (3 km [2 mi] south of Portimão) to be developed as a resort. On its sheltered beach of fine sand, excellent for swimming and sunbathing, is a wall of huge, colored rocks worn into odd shapes by sea and wind.

$–$$$ ✕ **Safari.** This lively cliff-top restaurant has a distinctly African flavor. Seafood and Angolan dishes are the best choices: try the chicken curry or one of the charcoal grills. Enjoy your meal on the terrace. ⊠ *Rua António Feu, 8500-805 Portimão* ☎ *282/42–35–40* ▭ *AE, DC, MC, V.*

$$$ ⊞ **Hotel Algarve-Casino.** A modern hotel, the Algarve-Casino has sizable rooms and an attentive staff. Leisure facilities, including windsurfing, deep-sea fishing, tennis, and golf, are within easy reach and there's access to the beach below the hotel's cliff-side perch. The casino has international shows and gaming rooms. ⊠ *Av. Tomás Cabreira, 8500-802* ☎ *282/40–20–00* 🖷 *282/40–20–99* ⊕ *www.solverde.pt* ⤴ *209 rooms* ♨ *3 restaurants, 2 pools* ▭ *AE, DC, MC, V* ⑩ *BP, MAP.*

★ $$ ⊞ **Bela Vista.** Traditional tiles and stained-glass panels infuse this small beachfront hotel with charm. You can relax on the terrace overlooking the beach, and enjoy live music performances in summer. ⊠ *Av. Tomás*

Cabreira, 8500-802 ☎ *282/45–04–80* 🖨 *282/41–53–69* ⊕ *www. hotelbelavista.net* 🛏 *14 rooms, 2 suites* 🛎 *Bar* 🖃 *AE, DC, MC, V* ⃝❘ *BP.*

Silves

Once the Moorish capital of the Algarve, Silves, 18 km (11 mi) northeast of Portimão, along the N124-1, ceased to be important after it was almost completely destroyed by the 1755 earthquake. The 12th-century
★ sandstone **fortaleza** (fortress), with its impressive parapets, was restored in 1835 and still dominates the area from its rocky heights above the town. ☎ *282/44–56–24* ⊙ *June–Sept., daily 9–8 (last admission 7:30); Oct.–May, daily 9–6 (last admission 5:30).*

The 14th- to 15th-century **Antiga Sé Catedral de Silves** (Silves Old Cathedral) was built just after the Portuguese Christian army conquered Silves in the 13th century. ⊠ *Rua da Sé* ☎ *No phone* ⊙ *Mon.–Sat. 9–6:30, Sun. 8:30–1.*

The **Museu Municipal de Arqueologia** (Archaeological Museum) is divided into four periods: Prehistoric, Roman, Islamic, and Portuguese. It displays one of the most notable and recent archaeological discoveries—a 12th-century well-cistern. ⊠ *Rua das Portas de Loulé* ☎ *282/44–48–32* ⊙ *Mon.–Sat. 9–6.*

Lagos

Lagos, the western terminus of the coastal railway that runs from Vila Real de Santo António, is a bustling holiday resort of pedestrian streets lined with shops, restaurants, and bars. It's still an important fishing port, though it's the nearby cove beaches that attract the crowds. The prettiest, the Praia de Dona Ana, is a 3-km (2-mi) walk from town. Lagos has a venerable history (Henry the Navigator maintained a base here), most evident in its imposing **city walls**, which still survive, and its 17th-century harbor-side **Forte Ponta da Bandeira.** ⊠ *Av. dos Descobrimentos* ☎ *282/76–14–10* ⊙ *Tues.–Sun. 9:30–12:30 and 2–5.*

The 18th-century baroque **Igreja de Santo António** (Church of St. Anthony) is renowned for its exuberant carved and gilt wood decoration. The **Museu Regional** (Regional Museum) at the church displays mosaics and archaeological and ethnographical items. ⊠ *Entrance via Museu Regional on Rua General Alberto Silveira* ☎ *282/76–23–01* ⊙ *Tues.–Sun. 9:30–12:30 and 2–5.*

\$\$–\$\$\$ ✕ **No Patio.** As its name implies (*no patio* means "on the patio"), this restaurant has a lovely outdoor patio. Run by a Danish couple, Bjarne and Gitte, the restaurant serves international dishes with a Scandinavian flair. Tenderloin of pork with a sherry-mushroom sauce is a house specialty. ⊠ *Rua Lançarote de Freitas, 46* ☎ *282/76–37–77* 🖃 *AE, MC, DC, V* ⊙ *Closed Sun. and Mon.*

\$–\$\$ ✕ **Dom Sebastião.** Charcoal-grilled fish and shellfish are the star attractions at this cheerful restaurant. The long wine list has been carefully selected to complement the fare. ⊠ *Rua 25 de Abril, 20* ☎ *282/76–27–95* ⊕ *www.marinario.com* 🖃 *AE, DC, MC, V.*

★ **\$\$** 🏨 **Hotel Tivoli de Lagos.** In the very heart of the ancient and picturesque resort town, the Tivoli de Lagos was planned with all the character and charm of a small village set in its own gardens. The rooms, suites, restaurants, bars, the various and spacious living rooms, arcades, patios and swimming pools all flow into each other, creating a unique welcoming atmosphere. ⊠ *Rua António Crisógono Santos, 8600-678* ☎ *282/79–00–79* 🖨 *282/79–03–45* ⊕ *www.tivolihotels.com* 🛏 *324 rooms* 🛎 *4 restaurants, 3 pools, 3 bars* 🖃 *AE, DC, MC, V.*

Sagres

Historians now agree that Prince Henry the Navigator's legendary school of navigation at Sagres is just that: mostly legend. But the 15th-century visionary who opened the era of Portuguese discoveries did have a base in nearby Lagos, and it is not difficult to imagine him standing here, on the windy headland, contemplating uncharted seas. Sagres is 30 km (19 mi) west of Lagos; take the N268 south from the N125 at Vila do Bispo.

★ A small road leads across a promontory above the sea through the tunnel-like entrance to the **Fortaleza de Sagres** (Sagres Fortress). The ruins of this 15th- to 16th-century fort about 1 km (¾ mi) from the village have been transformed into a modern structure that houses an exhibition center and a cafeteria. Nevertheless, the Sagres site retains a particular magic. A cobblestone wind compass, 43 meters (141 feet) in diameter, is still visible on the flat ground beside the fortress. Archaeologists and historians quibble about its date, but some think the compass was used as a navigational tool by Prince Henry. The crashing of waves and howl of the wind create an apt background for thoughts about Portugal's nautical history. You can also explore the restored 16th-century chapel of Nossa Senhora da Graça or watch fishermen cast their long lines from the surrounding cliffs. ☎ *282/62–01–40* ☒ *€3* ☉ *May–Sept., daily 10–8:30; Oct.–Apr., daily 10–6:30.*

$$ ✕⊡ **Pousada do Infante.** Views of the sea and craggy rock cliffs are spectacular at this sprawling pousada. Moderate-size rooms are well appointed and have small balconies. The service and the Portuguese food in the well-respected restaurant ($$–$$$$) are accomplished; expect seafood specials such as fried squid or clams with pork, and, for dessert, almond cake. ☒ *On headland between fishing harbor and Praia da Mareta, 8650-385* ☎ *282/62–02–40* ☐ *282/62–42–25* ⊕ *www.pousadas.pt* ⇲ *39 rooms* ⚙ *Restaurant, bar* ☰ *AE, DC, MC, V* ⏐◯⏐ *BP.*

Fodor'sChoice
★

Cabo de São Vicente

Fodor'sChoice
★
Sometimes called *o fim do mundo* (the end of the world), Cabo de São Vicente (Cape St. Vincent), 6 km (4 mi) west of Sagres, is the southwesternmost point in Europe and offers sweeping views. The lighthouse, open to the public, is said to have the strongest reflectors in Europe, casting a beam some 96 km (60 mi) out to sea.

Algarve Essentials

AIR TRAVEL TO & FROM THE ALGARVE
TAP Air Portugal has regular daily service from Lisbon and Oporto. Flying time from Lisbon to Faro is 45 minutes; from Oporto, 90 minutes.
🔌 **TAP Air Portugal** ☎ 289/81-85-38.

BUS TRAVEL TO & FROM THE ALGARVE
Daily bus and rail service connects Lisbon with the major towns in the Algarve; trips take four to six hours.

CAR TRAVEL
The main east–west highway in the Algarve is the two-lane N125, extending from Vila Real de Santo António, on the Spanish border, to Sagres. It doesn't run right along the coast, but has turnoffs to beachside destinations. A four-lane motorway, the IP1/E1, several miles inland, runs parallel to the coast from the suspension bridge at the Spanish border west to Albufeira, where it joins the main road to Lisbon.

TOURS

Organized guided bus tours of some of the more noteworthy villages and towns depart from Faro, Vilamoura, Albufeira, Portimão, and Lagos.

VISITOR INFORMATION

Albufeira ✉ Rua 5 de Outubro ☎ 289/58-52-79. **Armação de Pêra** ☎ 282/31-21-45. **Faro** ✉ Airport ☎ 289/81-85-82 ✉ Rua da Misericórdia, 8-12 ☎ 289/80-36-04. **Lagos** ✉ Sitio de São João ☎ 282/76-30-31. **Loulé** ✉ Edifício do Castelo ☎ 289/46-39-00. **Monte Gordo** ✉ Av. Marginal ☎ 281/54-44-95. **Olhão** ✉ Largo Sebastião Martins Mestre, 6A ☎ 289/71-39-36. **Portimão** ✉ Av. Zeca Afonso ☎ 282/53-18-00. **Praia da Rocha** ✉ Av. Tomás Cabreira ☎ 282/41-91-32. **Silves** ✉ Rua 25 de Abril ☎ 282/44-22-55. **Tavira** ✉ Rua da Galeria, 9 ☎ 281/32-25-11.

ROMANIA

BUCHAREST, THE BLACK SEA COAST & DANUBE DELTA, TRANSYLVANIA

CONSIDERED ONE OF THE MOST BEAUTIFUL countries in Eastern Europe, Romania has villages where traditional customs still reign and cities, such as Sibiu, Sighişoara, and Braşov, with intact medieval sections. More than 2,000 monasteries, including the famed Painted Monasteries of Bucovina, await visitors, as do Transylvania's Saxon-influenced fortified churches. Palaces and castles range from 14th- and 15th-century fortresses straight out of Gothic novels to fairy tale–like Peleş, built in the 19th century. Hardly a town or city lacks an ethnographic museum showcasing regional costumes, carpets, ceramics, embroidery, and festival masks. Ecotourists should head for the Danube Delta, Europe's largest wetlands reserve and habitat of 300 bird species. The fir-covered Carpathians are the backdrop for glorious mountain drives, hiking trails, and skiing, and to the east the Black Sea attracts hearty beachgoers. Bucharest's 19th-century mansions, museums, and wide boulevards retain the French cultural influence for which the city has long been known. If you are on a Dracula quest, you can trace the path of the fictious count and his real-life inspiration, Prince Vlad Ţepeş.

Romania borders Ukraine, Moldova, Bulgaria, Serbia, Hungary, and the Black Sea, and includes the provinces of Wallachia, Moldavia, and Transylvania. People here trace their heritage to the Dacians, a Thracian tribe, and conquering Roman legions. The language, in fact, is Latin-based, and the country is often tagged the "Latin Island of Eastern Europe." Other influences have shaped Romania, as well, and struggles against foreign invaders were many and furious. During the medieval period, Saxons settled in Transylvania and built powerful market towns, including Braşov and Sibiu. Bucharest has long enjoyed a strong French cultural influence, which you will note in many of its buildings, parks, and avenues. Some of the most renowned monasteries were erected by 15th- and 16th-century princes in gratitude for victories against the Ottoman Turks. For centuries, until 1918, the Austro-Hungarian empire dominated Transylvania; this date marks the unification of the three provinces at the end of World War I. Today, Hungarian Romanians account for about 8% of the country's population.

Between 1866 and 1947, Romania was ruled by kings. In 1945, the Communists achieved control of the government and stayed in power until the 1989 revolution, which overthrew dictator Nicolae Ceauşescu. Romania established a multiparty system with an elected president, a two-chamber parliament, and a constitution guaranteeing individual rights. The country has embraced capitalism, as evidenced by an ever-expanding network of shops, restaurants, hotels, bed-and-breakfast es-

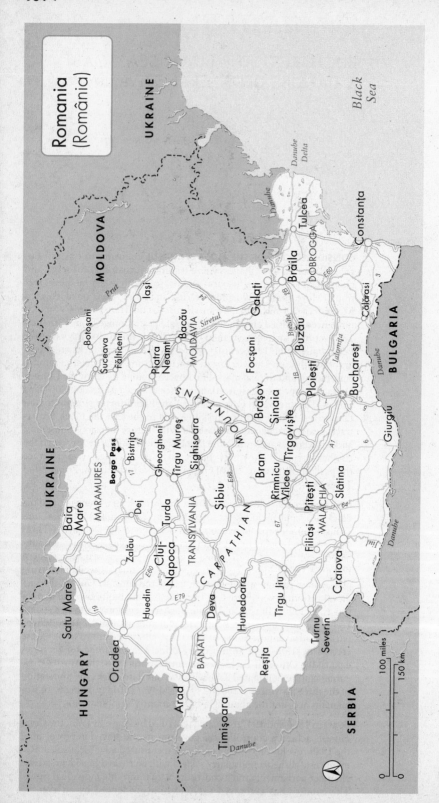

Romania
(România)

UKRAINE

Black
Sea

MOLDOVA

Danube Delta

Danube

Tulcea

Brăila

Galați

DOBROGGA

Constanța

E60

Călărasi

BULGARIA

Botoșani

Suceava
Fălticeni

Iași

Prut

Bacău

Siretul

MOLDAVIA

Focșani

Buzău

Bârlad

Ploiești

Bucharest

Ialomița

Danube

Piatra
Neamț

MOUNTAINS

Brașov
Sinaia

Târgoviște

A1

Giurgiu

Bistrița

Borgo Pass

Gheorgheni

Târgu Mureș

Sighișoara

Bran

Rîmnicu
Vîlcea

Pitești

Slătina

WALACHIA

E68

E60

17

16

MARAMUREȘ

Baia
Mare

Dej

Turda

Cluj-
Napoca

TRANSYLVANIA

Sibiu

67

Filiași

64

Craiova

Dir

Danube

Zalău

Huedin

E60

E79

Deva

Hunedoara

CARPATHIAN

Târgu Jiu

Turnu
Severin

Satu Mare

UKRAINE

HUNGARY

Oradea

Arad

BANAT

Deva

Reșița

Timișoara

Danube

SERBIA

100 miles

150 km

tablishments, travel agencies, and clubs. Major industries include chemicals, metal processing, textiles, lumber and furniture production, and agriculture.

Political and economic reforms have not been unqualified successes, and as in many changing economies, some people have been left behind. You may encounter beggars in some cities. Your charitable impulses are best directed toward the elderly, whose pensions have not kept up with inflation; do not display money or valuables around younger, more assertive beggars. Violent crime against tourists is virtually unknown, though you should be alert for pickpockets and scams. Hospitality enjoys a long tradition here, and most visitors return home rather overwhelmed by the friendliness of the average Romanian. In small towns and villages, it is not unusual to be invited into homes for strong coffee, cake, and *țuica,* a wicked plum brandy. Even in bustling cities, most people will pause to help with directions and information. Food, entry fees, hotels outside the capital, souvenirs, and transportation remain quite reasonable by Western standards. The exceptions are car rentals, gas, and upscale lodgings in Bucharest, which are on a par with pricey European and American cities.

ROMANIA A TO Z

To research prices, get advice from other travelers, and book travel arrangements, visit www.fodors.com.

AIR TRAVEL

Tarom, the Romanian national carrier, operates flights from Bucharest's Otopeni Airport to many Romanian cities. You can call to reserve a flight or make reservations at travel agencies. Angel Airlines serves several major domestic destinations from Bucharest's Baneasa Airport.

🛈 **Angel Airlines** ✉ Str. C. Bălcescu 18 Bucharest ☎ 021/231-5945 ⊕ angelairlines. ro. **Tarom** ✉ Splaiul Independenței 17 Bucharest ☎ 021/337-0220; central reservations 9361 in Bucharest; 021/337-2037 outside Bucharest ⊕ www.tarom.ro.

BOAT & FERRY TRAVEL

Many U.S. and European tour operators offer multicountry Danube River cruises, which call at Romanian ports. Passenger service operates from Galați and Tulcea to some points in the Danube Delta.

BUS TRAVEL

An upgraded fleet has made intercity bus travel more comfortable, but obstacles remain, especially for foreigners. Pickup points, rather than stations, are the norm, and schedules are not readily available. Trains are a better choice.

BUSINESS HOURS

Banks are open weekdays 9–noon only, but major cities have ATMs. Exchange office hours vary, but most are open weekdays 9–5 and Saturday 9–1; some are open until 7 on Saturday and a few are open on Sunday until 1. Most museums are open Tuesday–Sunday 10–5. Shops generally are open weekdays 9–6 and Saturday 9–2.

CAR TRAVEL

Foreign visitors staying more than 30 days need an International Driver's Permit. Otherwise, your regular license will suffice.

GASOLINE There is no lack of gas stations, including those offering 24-hour service, along major roads and in towns. Many have convenience stores attached and some have two-star motels adjacent. Most stations sell regular (90-octane), premium (98-octane), *motorina* (diesel), and *fară plumb* (unleaded). Gas averages $2.20 per gallon.

A network of main roads covers the country, though the majority allow for only a single lane in each direction. Potholes are common, and some side roads are not paved. Progress may be impeded by slow-moving trucks and horse-drawn wagons. At night, the situation becomes doubly hazardous due to poorly lighted or unlighted roads and vehicles.

Drive on the right and observe the speed limits: 30 kph (19 mph) in built-up areas, 50 kph (30 mph) within city limits, 80 kph (50 mph) on main roads, and 100 kph (60 mph) on multilane highways. Road signs are the same as in Western Europe. Driving after drinking any amount of alcohol is prohibited, and seat belts are obligatory in the front seat of vehicles. Spot checks are frequent, but police are generally courteous to foreigners. At unmarked intersections, traffic coming from the right has priority. When asking directions, refer to major towns ahead, rather than the road's official number.

CUSTOMS & DUTIES

Foreigners' bags seldom are inspected. By law, you may bring in 200 cigarettes, 2 liters of liquor, and 4 liters of wine or beer. You may import duty-free gifts up to a value of $1,200. An antique taken out of Romania must have a receipt and a document, available from the store, stating that the item is not part of the national patrimony. Keep exchange receipts if you want to change money back into your own currency.

EATING & DRINKING

International and ethnic restaurants abound in major cities, but expect less variety elsewhere. Menus tend to be meat-oriented, emphasizing pork, though other choices are available. Typically, you order each food item individually. Traditional Romanian dishes include *mămăligă* (polenta), *sarmale* (cabbage rolls filled with meat and rice), *ciorbă* (a slightly sour soup stock), *mititei* (spicy sausages), and *clătite* (pancakes filled with cheese, jam, or chocolate). The familiar alcoholic and nonalcoholic drinks are available, as is bottled water. Romanian wines can be very good.

Due to inflation, prices fluctuate. Therefore, prices are given in the more constant U.S. dollar. Your bill will be in lei.

WHAT IT COSTS In U.S. dollars			
$$$$	**$$$**	**$$**	**$**
AT DINNER over $15	$8–$15	$4–$8	under $4

Prices are per person for a main course.

Most restaurants open before noon and serve until 11 PM or later. Eateries in small towns close earlier.

Jacket and tie are advised for upscale restaurants and business lunches and dinners; otherwise, casual dress is appropriate. Though seldom required, dinner reservations are wise at better restaurants.

EMBASSIES & CONSULATES

🏛 Australian Consulate ⊠ B-dul. Unirii 74 Bucharest ☎ 021/320-9826 🖨 021/320-9823.

🏛 Canada ⊠ Str. N. Iorga 36, Bucharest ☎ 021/307-5000 🖨 021/307-5014.

🏛 United Kingdom ⊠ Str. J. Michelet 24, Bucharest ☎ 021/201-7200 🖨 021/201-7317.

🏛 United States ⊠ Str. Tudor Arghezi 7–9, Bucharest ☎ 021/210-4042 🖨 021/211-3360.

HOLIDAYS

January 1–2; Orthodox Easter Sunday and Monday (moveable holiday in March, April, or May); May 1 (Labor Day); December 1 (National Day); December 25–26.

LANGUAGE

If you speak a Romance language, Romanian is likely to sound pleasantly familiar. Both French and English are widely spoken.

LODGING

Accommodations include everything from chain hotels to small, attractive inns (in prime tourist areas, such as Transylvania and Bucovina) to bed-and-breakfasts to monasteries. Facilities at individual monasteries range from basic rooms to attractive units constructed especially for tourists. It's wise to book such stays through a Romanian travel agency, as English may not be spoken at the monastery. For all properties, rates are quoted for double rooms, and breakfast, often a buffet, is almost always included in the price. Although Bucharest hotel prices are comparable to Western Europe, you'll find that rates outside the capital are reasonable. Unless you're in a major city, credit cards or traveler's checks are seldom accepted, so make sure you have enough cash.

WHAT IT COSTS In U.S. dollars				
	$$$$	**$$$**	**$$**	**$**
	BUCHAREST			
FOR 2 PEOPLE	over $200	$150–$200	$80–$150	under $80
OTHER AREAS	over $95	$70–$95	$35–$70	under $35

Prices are for two people in a standard double room in peak season, including breakfast.

HOTELS — Most international chains are present in Bucharest, and the number of properties in the under-$100 category has increased. Continental Hotels, a Romanian chain with more than 10 properties around the country, provides reliable accommodations at reasonable prices. Away from tourist and business centers, most hotels date to the Communist era, so expect clean rooms with private baths, but not much character. The usual ranking system of one to five stars is in place and room rates are posted. Hotels are licensed, assigned stars, and periodically inspected by the Ministry of Tourism through its department of licensing and compliance. At four- and five-star properties, you can expect such amenities as multiple restaurants and, most likely, a pool and fitness center. Lower-end hotels usually have a breakfast room, but not a restaurant, and some staff may not speak English.

PRIVATE ACCOMMODATIONS — The bed-and-breakfast concept has taken off. Look for *camere libere* (rooms available) signs. Homes displaying the green ANTREC logo have been approved by this organization and provide a comfortable room, shared bath, and two meals for $12 to $25 per person. Hosts may not speak English.

ANTREC (National Association of Rural, Ecological and Cultural Tourism) ✉ Str. Maica Alexandra 7 Bucharest ☎🖷 021/223-7024 ⊕ www.antrec.ro.

MAIL & SHIPPING

Postal codes exist but mail may be delivered without. A better and more reliable option, however, is to have mail sent to your hotel.

POSTAL RATES — A letter to North America costs 80¢, a postcard 73¢. Within Europe, the postcard rate is 42¢, the letter rate 45¢. Stamps may be purchased at post offices, from your hotel concierge, and at some newsstands. Mailboxes are red metal with *Poşta Romană* in yellow.

MONEY MATTERS

Because of inflation, prices in lei change often; therefore, prices throughout this chapter are given in the more stable U.S. dollar equivalents. The cost of luxury hotels, upscale restaurants, and gasoline can equal prices in Western Europe; rental cars are higher. A meal in a nice restaurant typically runs no more than $5 per person, and a bottle of Romanian wine averages $3 in a restaurant and $1.50 in a store. A bottle of Romanian beer is about 45¢, and a 2-liter bottle of mineral water costs 55¢. Museum entries range from 30¢ to $1.85, and concert tickets run 65¢–$4.95. A gallon of gasoline averages $2.20.

CREDIT CARDS & TRAVELER'S CHECKS Credit cards are accepted in most hotels, better restaurants, and some shops in cities accustomed to tourists and business travelers. Do not count on using credit cards elsewhere. Traveler's checks can be cashed only at banks, major hotels in large cities, and selected exchange bureaus. Banks charge a commission. The American Express representative in Bucharest is Marshal Turism. This firm can issue checks and replace lost ones, but will not cash checks.

🖪 **Marshal Turism** ⊠ B-dul. Magheru 43 Bucharest ☎ 021/223-1204.

CURRENCY The unit of currency is the *leu* (plural *lei*), which is circulated in denominations of 2,000-, 10,000-, 50,000-, 100,000-, and 500,000-lei notes, and 500-, 1,000-, and 5,000-lei coins. At press time (summer 2003), the official exchange rate was about 34,000 lei to the U.S. dollar, 23,000 lei to the Canadian dollar, 53,000 lei to the pound sterling, and 36,000 lei to the euro.

The many exchange bureaus (*casa de schimb valutar*) offer the best rates. Most do not charge commission. Rates are posted outside; make sure you're reading *cumpărare* (buying) rates. Never change money on the street; it's illegal, plus you're likely to be cheated. Retain exchange receipts if you want to convert lei back into your own currency upon departure. Payment for all goods and services should be made in lei, but some establishments accept major foreign currencies. In cities, tipping in dollars or euros is not a problem.

VALUE-ADDED TAX (V.A.T.) Romania has a 19% sales tax. To obtain a refund, keep your original receipts and ask each store for a stamped V.A.T. refund form. Refund offices are located at all border crossing points, including Otopeni International Airport. Customs officers may ask to see the items for which the refund is claimed.

PASSPORTS & VISAS

Citizens of the United States, Canada, and Great Britain need only a valid passport to enter Romania for up to 90 days. Citizens of Australia and New Zealand must obtain visas, but no photos or applications are required. The cost is equivalent to $25 plus a $6 consular tax. Those on organized tours pay only $1 with proof of prior payment for services.

SHOPPING

In Romania, you can easily go on a shopping spree and still not spend a lot of money. Each region has its own patterns and colors in handwoven carpets and embroidered items, including blouses, tablecloths, scarfs, and bedspreads. Other handmade items include masks, icons painted on glass or wood, ceramics, and painted or beaded eggs. The quality of workmanship is high. Monastery and museum shops and Artizanat stores are good places for such purchases. Crystal and glassware are also good buys.

TELEPHONES

COUNTRY & AREA CODES
The country code for Romania is 40. When dialing Romania from outside the country, drop the initial 0 from regional codes.

INTERNATIONAL CALLS
Direct-dial international calls can be made from most hotels, phone companies, and orange public phones found throughout the country. A phone card is necessary for public phones. To place long-distance calls out of Romania, dial 00, then the country code, and the number. To access AT&T, MCI, or Sprint, dial the numbers below.

🎦 Access Codes **AT&T** ☎ 021/800-4288. **MCI** ☎ 021/800-1800. **Sprint** ☎ 021/800-0877. **International information** ☎ 971.

LOCAL CALLS
To make a long-distance call within Romania, dial 02, the regional area code, and the number. Orange public phones require a phone card (*cartela telefonică*), which can be purchased at post offices, telephone companies, and many stationery stores. Phone cards come in values of 50,000, 100,000, and 200,000 lei.

The area code for Bucharest is 21. Dial 931 for directory assistance. For assistance in a region other than the one from which you are calling, dial 02 + the area code + 931. Not all operators speak English; your hotel can help.

TIPPING

Tipping has become the norm in cities and tourist areas. Tip 5%–10% of restaurant bills and in bars if you're occupying a table. Rounding up the taxi fare is adequate.

TOURS

Guided tours of specific regions or around the country are offered by local travel agencies (*agenția de turism*). If you have a particular interest (churches and monasteries, Dracula, ecotourism, Jewish heritage, health spas, vineyards, skiing, medieval sites, traditional villages, handicrafts), agencies can create individual itineraries.

TRAIN TRAVEL

The extensive network of trains run by Romanian Railways (CFR) covers the country, making this the best choice for public transportation. In Bucharest, most trains operate in and out of Gara de Nord. Trains are categorized as *Inter-City* (newest and fastest), *rapid, accelerat,* and *persoane*; the latter are slow, making many stops. Fares are inexpensive, so opting for first class is wise. Compartments are clean and reasonably comfortable, but toilets are abominable. A *vagon de dormit* (sleeper) or cheaper *cușeta,* with bunk beds, are available on longer journeys. International trains connect Bucharest to such points as Budapest, Istanbul, Prague, Sofia, and Vienna. Tickets are sold at stations one hour before departure. It's best to reserve a seat in advance; this must be done at a train agency (advance booking office).

Current timetables (*mersul trenurilor*) are clearly posted in stations and train agencies. Some helpful vocabulary: *plecare or pl.* (departure time), *sosire or sos* (arrival time), *de la* (from or starting point), *până* (to or last stop), and *linia* (track). If you book a reserved seat, you'll receive more than one small cardboard ticket (*bilet*); the second will indicate the train number (*nr. trenului)*), carriage or car (*vagon*), and seat number (*loc.*).

🎦 **Agenția de Voiaj CFR** (advance booking office) ⊠ Str. Domnița Anastasia 10-14 Bucharest ☎ 021/313-2643 ⊕ www.cfr.ro. **Gara de Nord** ⊠ B-dul. Gării de Nord Bucharest ☎ 021/223-0880.

VISITOR INFORMATION

🛈 **Romania Tourist Information Office** ✉ Str. Apolodor 17, 5th floor, Bucharest ☎ 021/410-1262 ⊕ www.romaniatourism.com. The Romanian National Tourist Office in your home country is an excellent source of information, maps, and brochures. In Romania, consult local travel agencies for hotel, restaurant, and excursion suggestions.

WHEN TO GO

Romania is at its best during the spring and fall. Many Black Sea hotels are open only June through September. Carpathian Mountain spots, such as Poiana Braşov and Sinaia, offer skiing in winter and hiking and other outdoor activities in summer. Folkloric festivals take place throughout the year, especially in summer and between Christmas and New Year's.

CLIMATE The Romanian climate is temperate and generally free of extremes, but snow as late as April is not unknown, and the lowlands can be very hot in midsummer. The following are the average daily maximum and minimum temperatures for Bucharest.

Jan.	34F	1C	May	74F	23C	Sept.	78F	25C
	19	–7		51	10		52	11
Feb.	38F	4C	June	81F	27C	Oct.	65F	18C
	23	–5		57	14		43	6
Mar.	50F	10C	July	86F	30C	Nov.	49F	10C
	30	–1		60	16		35	2
Apr.	64F	18C	Aug.	85F	30C	Dec.	39F	4C
	41	5		59	15		26	–3

BUCHAREST

According to legend, a shepherd named Bjucur settled on the site where Romania's capital now stands. The name Bucureşti was bequeathed by Vlad Ţepeş, the 15th-century prince who was the model for Bram Stoker's fictional *Dracula*. Two centuries later, in 1659, this citadel on the Dâmboviţa River became the capital of the province of Wallachia and, later—when the three provinces united into one country in 1918—the national capital. Bucharest gradually developed into a center of trade and gracious living, with ornate and varied architecture; landscaped parks; busy, winding streets; and wide boulevards. Before World War II, the city was known as the "Paris of the East," and although the comparison is less apt today, traces of its past glory remain.

During the Communist era (1945–89), dictator Nicolae Ceauşescu determined to remake Bucharest after his own vision, concentrating all government buildings and apartments for officials in one area. This led to the forced displacement of thousands of people and the demolition of many early houses, churches, synagogues, and other structures. Piaţa Unirii (Unirii Plaza) was the hub of his enormously expensive and impractical goal. With the exception of the mammoth Palace of Parliament, the buildings erected during this period are of no touristic interest. However, Bucharest still has numerous examples of fine 19th- and early-20th-century architecture, two particularly lovely parks (Cişmigiu and Herăstrău), and many sites of historic and cultural interest.

Exploring Bucharest

After admiring the fine structures around Piaţa Revoluţiei, including Creţulescu Church, the Romanian Athenaeum, the National Library, and the former royal palace (now the National Art Museum), stroll north along Calea Victoriei with its many old mansions. Soon you'll come to

Şoseaua Kiseleff and the marvelous Museum of the Romanian Peasant. Continue along, and visit the vast Museum Village in Herăstrău Park.

Knowing basic street sign words can help you find your way around. Strada, usually abbreviated as Str., means "street." Bulevard and "bule-vardul," abbreviated as B-dul, translate into boulevard. Calea means "way," and piaţa is a plaza or square.

A second sightseeing route leads west from Piaţa Universităţii along B-dul. Republicii past the University of Bucharest's 19th-century build-ings. Turn south on Calea Victoriei to visit the National History Museum and to explore the Lipscani area, the oldest part of the city. Be sure to stop at the Curtea Veche and Stavropoleos churches. A museum devoted to the history of Romania's Jewish community is not far from Lipscani. A long walk west or short metro ride brings you to the huge Palace of Parliament and Cotroceni Palace. The Eroilor metro stop on Line M1 places you midway between the two attractions.

Numbers in the margin correspond to points of interest on the Bucharest map.

⑰ Arcul de Triumf (Arch of Triumph). Commemorating the 1877 War for Independence and those who died in World War I, this monument re-sembles its Parisian namesake. ⊠ *Head of Şos. Kiseleff.*

★ **⑬ Ateneul Român** (Romanian Athenaeum). This 19th-century concert hall, home to the George Enescu Philharmonic Orchestra, has a baroque dome and classical columns. Attend a concert to view the splendid interior, as the building is often locked at other times. ⊠ *Str. Franklin 1* ☎ *021/ 315–6875.*

⑪ Biserica Creţulescu (Creţulescu Church). Dating from the early 17th cen-tury, this redbrick church next to the former palace has lovely, albeit faded interior frescoes and an ornate iconostasis (screen separating the altar from the nave). ⊠ *Piaţa Revoluţiei* ☉ *Daily 6 AM–7 PM.*

❺ Biserica Curtea Veche (Old Court Church). The oldest church in Bucharest is ocher in color with crosshatched onion domes. This important cen-ter of worship was founded in the 16th century beside the Princely Court, also known as the Curtea Veche, or the Old Court. ⊠ *Str. Selari* ☉ *Daily 6 AM–7 PM.*

❽ Biserica Stavropoleos (Stavropoleos Church). This small, exquisite church combines late-Renaissance and Byzantine styles with elements of Ro-manian folk art. Inside are superb wood and stone carvings and a gold-leaf iconostasis covered with religious art. ⊠ *Str. Stavropoleos* ☉ *Daily 6 AM–7 PM.*

Fodor'sChoice ★

❻ Curtea Veche (Old Court). Dracula fans can check out the ruins of the palace built by Vlad Ţepeş, the 15th-century prince on whom the fic-tional count was based. There's a small museum. ⊠ *Str. Franceză 27– 31* ☎ *021/314–0375* ☉ *Mon.–Sat. 9–3.*

❹ Hanul lui Manuc (Manuc's Inn). Built in 1808 for traveling merchants, this inn still functions as a hotel. Although the rooms are less than ap-pealing, the timbered architecture with a covered walkway is interest-ing, and the courtyard is a pleasant spot for a drink. ⊠ *Str. Franceză 62–64* ☎ *021/313–1415.*

❾ Lipscani. A maze of narrow, dirty streets, Lipscani is the center of Old Bucharest. The charming **Hanul cu Tei**, a rectangular courtyard between Strada Lipscani and Strada Blănari, houses dozens of art and antiques shops.

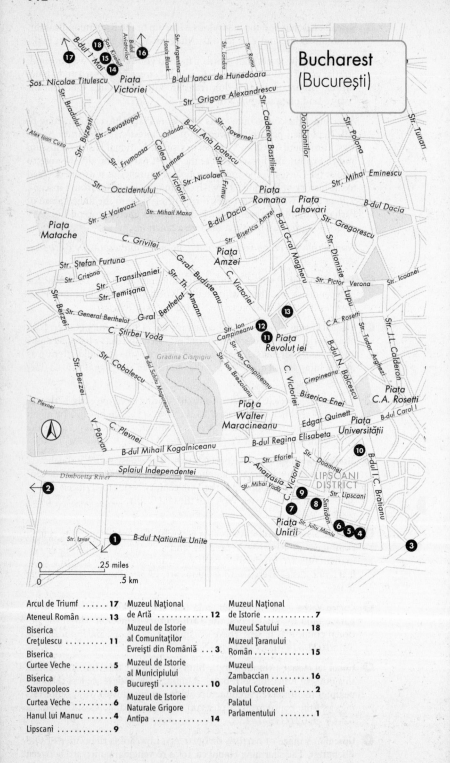

Bucharest
(Bucureşti)

③ Muzeul de Istorie al Comunitaților Evreiești din România (Museum of the History of the Jewish Community in Romania). Housed in a 1850s synagogue, this museum traces the history of Romania's Jewish population, using portraits, printed matter, and other memorabilia. ⊠ *Str. Mămulari 3* ☎ *021/311–0870* ⊘ *Mon., Wed., and Sun. 9–1, Thurs. 9–noon and 3–6.*

⑩ Muzeul de Istorie al Municipiului București (Bucharest History Museum). The artifacts and art on display in this neo-Gothic mansion, the former Șuțu Palace, capture the rich history of Romania's capital from ancient times to World War I. ⊠ *B-dul. Brătianu 2* ☎ *021/315–6858* ⊘ *Wed.–Sun. 9–5.*

⑭ Muzeul de Istorie Naturală Grigore Antipa (Natural History Museum). Natural wildlife exhibits from Romania and other realms are on display in realistic settings. ⊠ *Șos. Kiseleff 1* ☎ *021/312–8826* ⊘ *Tues.–Sun. 10–5.*

⑫ Muzeul Național de Artă (National Art Museum). Sculptures by Brancuși and paintings from the Brueghel school are among the works of Romanian and other European masters displayed in 15 rooms of the former royal palace. Five branch museums are nearby. ⊠ *Calea Victoriei 49–53* ☎ *021/313–3030* ⊕ *art.museum.ro* ⊘ *Wed.–Sun. 10–6.*

⑦ Muzeul Național de Istorie (National History Museum). This vast, somewhat dreary museum contains an enormous collection that spans the time from the Neolithic period to the 1920s. The Treasury has a stunning trove of gold objects—royal crowns, weapons, plates, and jewelry—dating from Roman days to the present. ⊠ *Calea Victoriei 12* ☎ *021/315–8207* ⊕ *www.mnir.ro* ⊘ *Wed.–Sun. 10–5.*

⟳ ⑱ Muzeul Satului (Village Museum). This open-air museum in Herăstrău
Fodor'sChoice Park introduces the varied architectural styles of Romania's traditional
★ houses, workshops, and churches. The structures, some complete with regional furnishings, have been assembled here from around the country. ⊠ *Șos. Kiseleff 28–30* ☎ *021/222–9110* ⊘ *Nov.–Mar., daily 9–5; Apr.–Oct., daily 9–8.*

⑮ Muzeul Țăranului Român (Museum of the Romanian Peasant). Some
Fodor'sChoice 90,000 traditional costumes, icons, carpets, and other artifacts from rural
★ life are vividly displayed, along with interiors from two 19th-century wooden churches. A shop sells fine handicrafts. ⊠ *Șos. Kiseleff 3* ☎ *021/212–9663* ⊘ *Tues.–Sun. 10–6.*

⑯ Muzeul Zambaccian (Zambaccian Museum). This unassuming, though lovely, Romanian home contains an impressive collection of art: works by Romanian artists hang alongside paintings by Cézanne, Matisse, Pissarro, and Renoir—all gathered by Armenian-Romanian businessman K. H. Zambaccian. ⊠ *Str. Muzeul Zambaccian 21* ☎ *021/230–1920* ⊘ *Apr.–Oct., Wed.–Sun. 11–7; Nov.–Mar., Wed.–Sun. 10–6.*

★ ② Palatul Cotroceni (Cotroceni Palace). Situated near the Botanical Gardens, this grand building was once the royal residence. Lavish furnishings, art, and personal effects offer a glimpse into the lives of Romania's former kings and queens. Guides are required (no additional charge) for the one-hour tour. It's wise to call for reservations. ⊠ *B-dul. Geniului 1* ☎ *021/221–1200* ⊕ *www.ici.ro* ⊘ *Tues.–Sun. 9:30–4:30.*

★ ① Palatul Parlamentului (Palace of Parliament). This mammoth structure, the second largest building in the world after the Pentagon, was the vision of former dictator Ceaușescu. Today, it houses the country's Parliament. From the 24-karat gold on the ceilings to a huge handwoven carpet, every detail is Romanian. Reservations are required for the 45-minute tour of the ground-floor rooms. ⊠ *Calea 13 Septembrie* ☎ *021/311–3611* ⊘ *Daily 10–4.*

Where to Eat

Bucharest's restaurant boom has given rise to a host of attractive establishments offering tasty food. In addition to restaurants, you'll find no shortage of food kiosks, cafés, grills, and fast-food chains. No-smoking sections are virtually nonexistent.

$$$–$$$$ ✕ **Casa Caragiale.** Named for 19th-century playwright Ion Luca Caragiale, this restaurant presents French taste treats. Vocalists and a keyboardist entertain. ⊠ *Str. Ion Luca Caragiale 21–23* ☎ *021/211–1518* ▭ *MC, V.*

$$$–$$$$ ✕ **Casa Doina.** Two dining salons serve Continental dishes in this 19th-century villa, while a traditional *cramă* (wine cellar) offers more casual fare. A Gypsy band plays evenings. ⊠ *Şos. Kiseleff 4* ☎ *021/222–6717* ▭ *AE, DC, MC, V.*

$$$–$$$$ ✕ **Casa Vernescu.** Dine in a magnificent 19th-century mansion surrounded by gilded moldings, frescoes, and marble columns. The French dishes are superbly prepared and presented. ⊠ *Calea Victoriei 133* ☎ *021/231–0220* ▭ *AE, DC, MC, V.*
FodorśChoice ★

$$–$$$ ✕ **Aquarium.** The interior of this Italian restaurant is light and airy, and the menu presents tempting pasta, fish, and meat dishes. The food quality is high. ⊠ *Str. Alecu Russo 4* ☎ *021/211–2820* ▭ *AE, MC, V.*

★ **$$–$$$** ✕ **Silviu's.** Enjoy carefully prepared Italian specialties in a setting filled with art and antiques. Silviu's offers two dining salons, private rooms, and an outdoor pavilion. ⊠ *Str. Louis Pasteur 44* ☎ *021/410–9184* ▭ *MC, V.*

$–$$ ✕ **Bistro Atheneu.** This Parisian-style bistro has a varied menu with dishes ranging from traditional Romanian favorites to tasty Greek salads. A musical duo plays evenings. ⊠ *Str. Episcopiei 3* ☎ *021/313–4900* ▭ *No credit cards.*

$–$$ ✕ **Burebista.** Handicrafts cover the walls and woolly sheepskins the chairs, and the menu is as Romanian as the furnishings. Servers wear traditional garb, and musicians play folk tunes each evening. ⊠ *Calea Moşilor 195* ☎ *021/201–9704* ▭ *MC, V.*

$–$$ ✕ **Club Contele Dracula.** At this unique theme restaurant, every item, from service plates to the three dining salons, relates to the fictional Dracula or to 15th-century prince Vlad Ţepeş. You'll find tasty Transylvanian and wild game dishes on the menu. Some evenings, the count rises from his cellar coffin to mingle with guests. ⊠ *Splaiul Independenţei 8A* ☎ *021/312–1353* ▭ *AE, MC, V.*
FodorśChoice ★

Where to Stay

New hotels are opening at a brisk pace in Bucharest, and older properties have undergone renovation. In all hotel categories, you can expect that reception and at least some restaurant staff speak English.

$$$$ ⊡ **Athenée Palace Hilton.** Guest rooms at this historic hotel are bright and attractive; the staff is young and enthusiastic. ⊠ *Str. Episcopiei 1–3* ☎ *021/303–3777* ⊟ *021/315–2121* ⊕ *www.hilton.com* ⇝ *257 rooms, 15 suites* ⌂ *3 restaurants, 2 bars* ▭ *AE, DC, MC, V.*
FodorśChoice ★

★ **$$$$** ⊡ **Inter-Continental.** Right in the heart of the business district, this hotel remains Bucharest's tallest building. Furnishings are elegant, and service is punctual and correct. ⊠ *B-dul. Nicolae Bălcescu 4* ☎ *021/310–2029* ⊟ *021/312–0486* ⊕ *www.interconti.com* ⇝ *404 rooms, 19 suites* ⌂ *3 restaurants, pool, bar* ▭ *AE, DC, MC, V.*

$$$ 🖥 **București.** Well-located for both business and sightseeing, this property offers spacious guest rooms and a restaurant notable both for food and service. ✉ *Calea Victoriei 63–81* ☎ *021/312–7070* 🖷 *021/312– 0927* ⊕ *www.hbu.ro* ➹ *415 rooms, 31 suites* ⛬ *2 restaurants, pool* 🖃 *AE, MC, V.*

★ **$$–$$$**   🖥 **Helveția.** Fine furnishings and art characterize this white marble property near Herăstrău Park. ✉ *Piața Charles de Gaulle 13* ☎ *021/ 223–0566* 🖷 *021/223–0567* ⊕ *helvetia.netvision.net.il* ➹ *24 rooms, 6 suites* ⛬ *Restaurant, bar* 🖃 *AE, DC, MC, V.*

$$ 🖥 **Flanders.** In a quiet neighborhood close to the city center you'll find this attractive small hotel with Scandinavian-style furniture. Rates drop on weekends. ✉ *Str. Ștefan Mihăileanu 20* ☎ *021/327–6572* 🖷 *021/ 327–6573* ➹ *7 rooms, 1 suite* ⛬ *Restaurant, bar* 🖃 *AE, DC, MC, V.*

$ 🖥 **Batiștei.** Though on the small side, guest rooms have balconies and other amenities. The hotel has no elevator. It is, however, centrally located. ✉ *Str. Emanuel Bacaloglu 2* ☎ *021/314–9022* 🖷 *021/314–0887* ➹ *29 rooms, 2 suites* ⛬ *Restaurant* 🖃 *AE, DC, MC, V.*

Nightlife & the Arts

The Arts

Ateneul Român (✉ Str. Franklin 1 ☎ 021/315–6875) is Bucharest's concert hall, where the George Enescu Philharmonic Orchestra performs regularly. At the **Teatrul Național,** the National Theater (✉ Piața Universității ☎ 021/314–1717), you can see performances by the Ion Dacian Operetta. The **Opera Română** (✉ B-dul. M. Kogălniceanu 70–72 ☎ 021/313–1857) stages operas and ballet. **Sala Radio** (✉ Str. Berthelot 60–64 ☎ 021/314–6800) hosts classical concerts by local and visiting musicians.

Nightlife

Bucharest has no lack of clubs and bars, including less reputable ones, so choose your nightspot carefully. Even in the best places, do not expect a smoke-free environment. Foreign films are shown in their original language with Romanian subtitles. **Green Hours** (✉ Calea Victoriei 120 ☎ 021/211–9592) has live jazz and the occasional classical guitar. The interior of **Once Upon a Time** (✉ Str. Gheorghe Manu 334 ☎ 0722/ 654–191) replicates a 1930s town, incongrously paired with loud techno music. Expect a crowd if you take to the small, but popular dance floor at **Planters** (✉ Str. Mendeleev 10 ☎ 021/659–7606). **Tunnel Club** (✉ Str. Academiei 19–21 ☎ 021/312–6971) has catacomb-like rooms and good dance music. Enjoy a drink plus pop and dance tunes at **Yellow Bar** (✉ Str. Edgar Quinet 10 ☎ 021/310–1351).

Casinos proliferate in Bucharest. At **Casino Palace** (✉ Calea Victoriei 133 ☎ 021/231–0220 ⊕ www.casinopalace.ro) you can enjoy all the usual games of chance amid opulent surroundings. Photo identification is required for entry. The elegant Casa Vernescu restaurant is in the same building.

The Bucharest Mall's 10-screen **Hollywood Multiplex** (✉ Calea Vitan 55–59 ☎ 021/327–7030) has the best sound and picture quality, and the most comfortable seats.

Shopping

For traditional handicrafts, look for Artizanat stores. Romania is known for its handmade carpets; most are woven in monasteries or in private homes, and each region claims distinctive designs and colors. For handicrafts, visit the shop connected to **Muzeul Țăranului Român,** the Museum of the Romanian Peasant (⊠ Şos. Kiseleff 3 ☎ 021/212–9663 ☉ Tues.–Sun. 10–6). **Muzeul Satului,** the Village Museum (⊠ Şos. Kiseleff 28–30 ☎ 021/222–9110 ☉ Nov.–Mar., daily 9–5; Apr.–Oct., daily 9–8), an open-air museum, sells handicrafts. **Romartizana** (⊠ Calea Victoriei 16–20 ☎ 021/314–0770) sells traditional handmade carpets. Crystal and porcelain can be great values in Romania. **Sticerom** (⊠ Str. Selari 9–11 ☎ 021/315–7504) carries a good selection. You can watch glassblowers ply their trade in the shop's courtyard weekdays 9:30–5:30 and Saturday 9:30–2. The many galleries and shops surrounding the courtyard at **Hanul cu Tei** (⊠ off Str. Lipscani) sell art and antiques.

The four-story **Bucharest Mall** (⊠ Calea Vitan 55–59) houses some 70 stores, 20 restaurants, a supermarket, and a 10-screen cinema. The **World Trade Center** (⊠ B-dul. Expoziţiei 2) has some nice small stores in a galleria attached to the Sofitel Hotel. The department store–like **Unirea Shopping Center** (⊠ Piaţa Unirii 1) can supply all your basic needs from groceries to CDs to furniture. The outdoor market at **Piaţa Amzei,** just east of Calea Victoriei, bustles with animated locals bargaining for fresh produce, cheese, and flowers.

Bucharest Essentials

AIR TRAVEL TO & FROM BUCHAREST
Most international flights to Romania land at Bucharest's Otopeni Airport, 16 km (9 mi) north of the city.

AIRPORTS & TRANSFERS
TRANSFERS   Bus 783 runs between the airport and Piaţa Unirii every 15 minutes between 5:30 AM and 11 PM, stopping at main squares along the way. Buses are crowded and attract pickpockets. Taxi drivers at the airport seek business aggressively, and bargaining is essential. Major hotels will arrange a car and driver on request.
🛈 **Otopeni Airport** ☎ 021/204-1000.

BUS, TRAM & TROLLEY BUS TRAVEL WITHIN BUCHAREST
Surface transit is extensive, but vehicles tend to be crowded and can be difficult to cope with if you don't speak Romanian. Route maps are not readily available. A one-way ticket (*una călătorie*) costs 15¢ and is purchased at kiosks near bus stops; validate the ticket on board. There are also *abonamente* (day and week passes). Maxi taxis (minibuses that stop on request) and express buses (which require a special magnetic card) operate, but they, too, pose difficulties for foreigners. Surface transport operates between 5:15 AM and 11:30 PM.

CAR TRAVEL
Four main routes lead in and out of the city: E70 west to the Hungarian border, E60 north via Braşov, E70/E85 south to Bulgaria, and E85/60 east to Constanţa and the coast. Streets in Bucharest have few signs and many are one-way. City driving is not for the fainthearted.

EMERGENCIES
Each sector of Bucharest has one or more 24-hour pharmacies; inquire at your hotel.
🛈 **Emergency Services Police** ☎ 955. **Ambulance** ☎ 961. **Fire** ☎ 981.

SUBWAY TRAVEL
Bucharest's metro (*metrou*) is fast, efficient, and easy to use. Purchase a two-ride (37¢), day (45¢), 10-trip ($1.25), or monthly ($3.85) card in any station. Route maps are found in city maps and in *Bucharest: What, Where, When,* distributed free in most hotels. Route maps also are posted on plat-

forms and in cars. Stations are marked with a blue and white sign showing a large M. Trains operate between 5 AM and 11:30 PM.

TAXIS

Although posted rates are quite reasonable (16¢ initial charge, plus 16¢ per km), many drivers inflate prices or have rigged meters. Ask your hotel or restaurant for the approximate fare, then negotiate a fixed price before entering the taxi, or call one of the reputable companies, such as Alfa, Cristaxi, Meridian, and Titan.

🛈 **Alfa** ☎ 9481. **Cristaxi** ☎ 9421. **Meridian** ☎ 9444. **Titan** ☎ 9661.

TOURS

City tours take in most of the sites described in ⇨ **Exploring Bucharest.** Visits to outlying palaces and to Snagov Monastery, reputed burial place of Vlad Ţepeş, also are offered. Contact local travel agencies for itineraries and prices.

TRAIN TRAVEL

Most international and domestic trains operate from Gara de Nord. For advance bookings and information, go to Agenţia de Voiaj CFR.

🛈 **Gara de Nord** ⊠ B-dul. Gării de Nord ☎ 021/223-0880. **Agenţia de Voiaj CFR** ⊠ Str. Domniţa Anastasia 10-14 ☎ 021/313-2643.

TRAVEL AGENCIES

In recent years, agencies have proliferated, especially in Bucharest. Some have limited expertise, so it's important to choose carefully. The following are well-established firms with English-speaking staff accustomed to working with foreigners. They offer a variety of tours in Bucharest and around the country.

🛈 **Accent Travel & Events** ⊠ Str. Episcopiei 5, Suite 2 ☎ 021/314-1980 📠 021/314-1981 ⊕ www.accenttravel.ro. **Atlantic Tour** ⊠ Calea Victoriei 202 ☎ 021/312-7757 📠 021/312-6860 ⊕ www.atlantic.ro. **Romantic Travel** ⊠ Str. Prof. Dr. Mihail Georgescu 24 ☎ 021/326-3036 📠 021/326-3037 ⊕ www.romantic.ro.

TRANSPORTATION AROUND BUCHAREST

Bucharest is a sizable city, but its historic section and most sights can be explored on foot. (You might opt for the metro or a taxi, however, to reach Palatul Cotroceni or Muzeul Satului.) The streets are generally safe at night, but do watch out for potholes and vehicles without headlights.

VISITOR INFORMATION

The English-language publications *Bucharest: What, Where, When* and *Bucharest in Your Pocket* provide a wealth of information about sights, restaurants, and entertainment. The former is available free in most hotels, and the latter is sold in bookstores for $2.45. Also consult travel agencies, hotels, and the Romanian National Tourist Office in your home country.

THE BLACK SEA COAST & DANUBE DELTA

The southeastern Dobrogea region, only 45 minutes by plane from Bucharest (210 km by road), has been important throughout Romania's long history. Within a clearly defined area are the historic port of Constanţa; Romania's Black Sea coast; the Murfatlar vineyards (one of the most prestigious of Romania's many wine-growing regions and producers); Roman, Greek, and earlier ruins; and the Danube Delta, Europe's largest wetlands reserve.

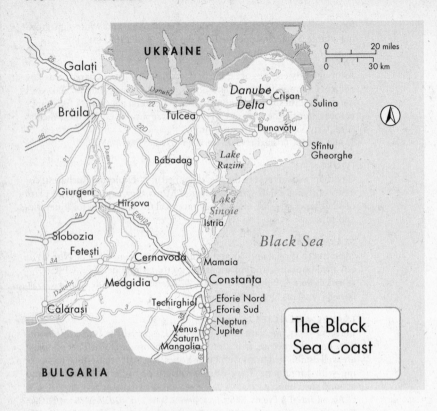

The Black Sea Coast

Black Sea Coast

A string of seaside hotels extends north and south of Constanța. New properties, plus the refurbishment of older ones, have raised standards overall. Health spas, primarily for the treatment of medical ills (balneology), are attached to many hotels. Beaches are sandy but are generally crowded. Most properties close from October through May. Romania's Black Sea primarily attracts European groups looking for relatively inexpensive sun and sea vacations, but after a hectic sightseeing schedule, you might enjoy a few days' relaxation here. Constanța and the surrounding area offer Roman artifacts and worthwhile museums.

\$\$\$\$ ☒ **Iaki.** Owned by the soccer star Hagi, this year-round beachside property includes a fitness center and health spa that offers Ana Aslan anti-aging treatments. Rates drop mid-September–May. ⊠ *Mamaia 8741* ☎ *0241/831–025* 🖷 *0241/831–169* ⊕ *www.iaki.ro* ⇆ *28 rooms, 32 suites* ⟁ *2 restaurants, 3 bars, 2 pools* ⊟ *AE, DC, MC, V.*

\$\$\$\$ ☒ **President.** This year-round hotel, right on the beach, incorporates archaeological remains into its public areas. Balconies in the guest rooms overlook the sea. Rates drop October–May. ⊠ *Str. Teilor 6 Mangalia* ☎ *0241/755–695* 🖷 *0241/755–861* ⊕ *www.hpresident.com* ⇆ *64 rooms, 1 suite* ⟁ *2 restaurants, bar* ⊟ *AE, MC, V.*

\$\$\$–\$\$\$\$ ☒ **Best Western Savoy.** Open year-round, this property is on the beach. Guest rooms are spacious and have balconies and sea views. Nautical sports are available, as is a fitness center. An orchestra entertains in the evenings at the terrace restaurant. ⊠ *Mamaia 8741* ☎ *0241/831–426* 🖷 *0241/831–266* ⊕ *www.savoyhotel.ro* ⇆ *115 rooms, 16 suites* ⟁ *2 restaurants, pool, 2 bars* ⊟ *AE, DC, MC, V.*

\$\$–\$\$\$ ☒ **Dorna.** This hotel near the beach has cozy rooms with balconies; it's under the same ownership as the Guci in Constanța. ⊠ *Mamaia 8741*

🏨 *0241/831–639* ⊕ *www.blackseahotels.ro* ⇌ *146 rooms, 3 suites* ♨ *Restaurant, pool, 2 bars* ▭ *AE, MC, V* ☉ *June–Sept. 15.*

Constanţa

Known as Tomis in antiquity, legend has it that Constanţa was founded by survivors of a battle with the Argonauts. The Roman poet Ovid was exiled here in AD 8; his statue stands in a main square. Much of ancient Tomis remains unexcavated. If you're curious about Romanian wine, consider driving 20 or 30 minutes from here to the Murfatlar vineyards—considered one of the best producers in the country.

Famous for its large mosaic floor, **Edificiul Roman cu Mozaic** (Roman Mosaic Building) is a Roman complex of warehouses and shops from the 4th century (⊠ Piaţa Ovidiu 1 ☎ 0241/618–763 ☉ June–Aug., daily 8–7; Sept.–May, Tues.–Sun. 9–5). The **Parcul Arheologic** (Archaeology Park; ⊠ B-dul. Republicii) contains artifacts from the 3rd and 4th centuries, including the remains of Roman baths. **Muzeul Naţional de Istorie şi Arheologie** (National History and Archaeological Museum) displays artifacts from Greek, Roman, and Daco-Roman civilizations. (⊠ Piaţa Ovidiu 12 ☎ 0241/618–763 ☉ June–Aug., daily 9–8; Sept.–May, Tues.–Sun. 9–5). Culture buffs shouldn't miss **Muzeul Artă Populară** (Ethnographic Museum) with its display of regional handicrafts and costumes (⊠ B-dul. Tomis 32 ☎ 0241/6 16–133 ☉ June–Aug., daily 9–7:30; Sept.–May, daily 9–5).

$$ ✗ **Cazino.** Dine by the seaside at this ornately decorated, turn-of-the-20th-century former casino. Seafood dishes are the house specialty. ⊠ *B-dul. Elisabeta 2* ☎ *0241/617–416* ▭ *No credit cards.*

★ **$$$–$$$$** 🏨 **Capri.** Light, airy, and filled with plants, this centrally located hotel has a Mediterranean air and friendly service. ⊠ *Str. Mircea cel Batrân 109* ☎ *0241/553–090* 🏨 *0241/550–993* ⇌ *16 rooms, 8 suites* ♨ *Restaurant, pool, bar* ▭ *AE, DC, MC, V.*

★ **$$–$$$** 🏨 **Guci.** Guest rooms at this centrally located property are attractive and welcoming. The restaurant serves Mexican and international food. ⊠ *Str. Răscoalei 23* ☎ *0241/695–500* 🏨 *0241/638–426* ⊕ *www.blackseahotels. ro* ⇌ *10 rooms, 10 suites* ♨ *Restaurant, bar* ▭ *AE, MC, V.*

Tulcea

Tulcea is the main town of the Danube Delta and the gateway to the region. Built on seven hills and influenced by Turkish architectural styles, it is home to some modest Roman remains, a 19th-century mosque, and several museums.

Muzeul Deltei Dunării (Danube Delta Museum) provides a good introduction to the flora, fauna, and way of life of the communities in the region. ⊠ *Str. Progresului 14* ☎ *0240/515–866* ☉ *June–Aug., daily 8–8; Sept.–May, daily 10–6.*

$$ 🏨 **Delta.** On the bank of the Danube, this hotel, the best in town, is popular with tour groups. Guest rooms have balconies. ⊠ *Str. Isaacei 2* ☎ *0240/514–720* 🏨 *0240/516–260* ⇌ *114 rooms, 3 suites* ♨ *Restaurant, bar* ▭ *MC, V.*

The Danube Delta

The **Delta Dunării** (Danube Delta), Europe's largest wetlands reserve, covers approximately 5,000 square km (2,000 square mi) of eastern Romania. As the Danube approaches the end of its 2,860-km (1,773-mi) journey to the Black Sea, it divides into three branches. The northernmost branch forms the border with Ukraine, the middle arm leads to the busy port of Sulina, and the southernmost arm meanders toward the little port of Sfântu Gheorghe. From these channels, countless canals widen into tree-fringed lakes, pools filled with water lilies, and reeded islands.

A UNESCO World Heritage Site, the delta shelters some 300 bird species, including Europe's largest pelican colonies and numerous varieties of migratory birds, some from as far away as China and India. May and September are ideal bird-watching months. The region is also home to 160 species of fish, 800 plant families, and fishing villages where the Lipoveni, who immigrated centuries ago from Russia, live in traditional reed cottages.

From Tulcea, you can travel by boat to villages such as Crişan, Uzlina, Sulina, and Sfântu Gheorghe, all deep in the delta. From these points, you can explore small waterways either with local fisherfolk or in boats arranged by your lodging. Facilities are limited to small hotels and pensions that often do not respond to individual inquiries, so it's best to book through a travel agency in Constanţa or Bucharest. Tour operators also run day trips from Constanţa to Tulcea, including a boat excursion. Fishing programs can be arranged.

Black Sea Coast & Danube Delta Essentials

TOURS

Travel agencies organize day and multi-day excursions from Black Sea hotels and Constanţa. Programs typically include the following attractions: the Danube Delta; the Murfatlar vineyards, situated west of Constanţa and widely regarded as one of Romania's most prestigious wine producers; the Grecian ruins of Istria, the coastal region's major Greek settlement until the 7th century AD and where today, the remains of temples to various deities still stand; and the 1st century AD triumphal marble monument of an armored warrior, erected in 109 AD at Adamclisi, southwest of Constanţa, to memorialize Emperor Traian's defeat of the Dacians.

TRANSPORTATION AROUND THE BLACK SEA COAST & DANUBE DELTA

Constanţa is reached easily by car, train, or plane from Bucharest. By car, follow Route E60; the trip takes about three hours. In summer, 10 trains per day make the three-hour trip, three per day in other seasons. Tarom, the national airline, offers daily service in summer and several flights per week the rest of the year; the flight takes 45 minutes. For regional sightseeing, hire a car or taxi or join an organized tour.

TRAVEL AGENCIES

Constanţa travel agencies can help with hotels, transportation, and regional or more extensive sightseeing. **Danubius** ✉ B-dul. Ferdinand 36 ☎ 0241/615-686 🖷 0241/618-010 ⊕ www.danubius.ro. **Latina** ✉ B-dul. Ferdinand 70 ☎ 0241/639-713 🖷 0241/693-107. **Mamaia Tours** ✉ Str. Ştefan cel Mare 55 ☎☎ 0241/612-511.

VISITOR INFORMATION

The English-language publication *Constanţa: What, Where, When* is available free at most hotels. **Info Litoral** (Tourist Information Center) ✉ Str. Traian 36, Bl. 1, C1, Apt. 31, Constanţa ☎ 0241/555-000 🖷 0241/555-111 ⊕ www.infolitoral.ro.

TRANSYLVANIA

Transylvania, Romania's western province, contains some of Europe's most beautiful and unspoiled villages and rural landscapes. Cities such as Sibiu, Braşov, and Sighişoara have intact medieval sections. The forested Carpathian Mountains, which separate Transylvania from Wallachia and Moldavia, shielded the province from invasion during the Middle Ages. Germans and Hungarians settled here during this period and built castles and fortified churches. Although many ethnic Germans emigrated in the 1980s, Transylvania is still home to the majority of Hungarian Romanians. In some areas, such as the city of Miercurea Ciuc, signs are in both Romanian and Hungarian. Much of Romania's Gypsy, or Roma, population also lives in Transylvania. In the 10th and 11th centuries, Gypsies left their home in northern India and eventually arrived in Europe. Today, this ethnic group is found in most European countries.

It's easy to base yourself in a major center, such as Braşov or Sibiu, and explore the countryside on day trips. On the other hand, if you have a car or enough time to take public buses, you can immerse yourself in village life by overnighting in private homes.

Sinaia

Prior to World War II and the abdication of Romania's royal family, Sinaia was a summer retreat for the aristocracy. Less than a two-hour drive from Bucharest, the town is now a popular getaway for city dwellers. On the mountainside remain many grand summer homes, mostly late-19th and early-20th-century buildings, as well as the **Mănăstirea Sinaia** (Sinaia Monastery), dating from 1695. ⊙ *7 AM–7 PM.*

FodorśChoice ★ Just up the hill from the monastery is **Castelul Peleş** (Peleş Palace), a 19th-century Bavarian-style palace that served as the summer residence of Romania's first Hohenzollern king, Carol I. The 106 rooms are ornately decorated. You must join a tour, available in English, to view the interior. Photography is not permitted. ⊠ *Str. Peleşului 2* ☎ *0244/312–184* ⊙ *Wed.–Sun. 9–5.*

You'll find **Pelişor** (Little Peleş), the summer home of King Ferdinand, Carol's heir, just above Peleş Palace. Tours in English are available. ⊠ *Str. Peleşului* ☎ *0244/312–184* ⊙ *Wed. and Fri.–Sun. 9:30–4, Thurs. noon–4.*

The **teleferic,** or cable car, takes you up the mountain for panoramic views of the Carpathians and the town. Return by cable car or hike down. ⊠ *Behind Hotel Montana* ⊙ *Daily 8–4.*

★ **$$$** ▦ **Holiday Inn Resort Sinaia.** Guest rooms surround an atrium and have balconies. In addition to an on-site spa, which has health and beauty treatments, you can expect glorious mountain views from the restaurant. ⊠ *Str. Toporaşilor 1A* ☎ *0244/310–440* 🖷 *0244/310–551* 🛏 *128 rooms, 10 suites* ⌂ *Restaurant, pool, bar* ▭ *AE, MC, V.*

$–$$ ▦ **Economat.** Built in the same Bavarian style as nearby Peleş Palace, this simple, comfortable hotel is surrounded by mountains. The restaurant serves Romanian specialties. ⊠ *Str. Peleşului 2* ☎ *0244/314–151* 🖷 *0244/311–150* 🛏 *26 rooms, 8 suites* ⌂ *Restaurant, bar* ▭ *MC, V.*

Bran

A gloomy, well-preserved medieval fortress, **Castelul Bran** (Castle Bran) is hyped as Dracula's castle. In reality, the castle of Vlad Ţepeş lies in mountaintop ruins in the Argeş Valley. Still, Bran is well worth a visit. Tours in English are available. ⊠ *Str. Traian Moşoiu 495–498 Bran* ☎ *0268/238–333* ⊙ *Tues.–Sun. 8–4:30.*

Braşov & Poiana Braşov

To enjoy Braşov, stroll through **Piaţa Sfatului,** the bustling cobblestone square at the heart of the old Saxon city, formerly an important medieval trade center. **Muzeul de Istorie Braşov,** or Braşov History Museum (⊠ Piaţa Sfatului ⊙ Tues.–Sun. 10–6), dates from 1420 and was once the town hall. Just off Piaţa Sfatului, the Gothic **Biserica Neagră** (Black Church) acquired its name after a fire in 1689 left the walls darkened. It houses 119 Turkish carpets, gifts from long-ago merchants, and a 4,000-pipe organ. At the opposite end of the square from the church, **Strada Republicii** is a shop-filled pedestrian street.

For a fine view of Braşov, ride the **Telecabina Tâmpa** (✉ Aleea T. Brădiceanu ☉ Tues.–Sun. 9:30–5), a cable car that runs to the top of Mount Tâmpa. Just below the entrance to the cable car, the remains of the old city wall include **Bastionul Ţesătorilor** (Weaver's Bastion), now a museum. In a strategic position overlooking the city, the **Cetate,** or Citadel (✉ Dealul Cetăţii), was part of Braşov's medieval fortifications.

If time allows, visit the fortified **Saxon churches** in Hărman, 12 km (7.2 mi) northeast of Braşov, and Prejmer, 3 km (1.8 mi) farther east. Both are UNESCO World Cultural Heritage sites. If you don't have a car, you can make arrangements with a travel agency in Braşov or hire a taxi for the trip.

A 15-minute drive or bus ride from the city leads to **Poiana Braşov,** a mountaintop ski and summer resort with several excellent restaurants and hotels. Poiana Braşov has some of Romania's best skiing and hiking trails.

$–$$ ✕ **Coliba Haiducilor** (Outlaws' Hut). The walls of this restaurant—one
FodorsChoice of Romania's most famous eateries—are covered with dried peppers,
★ corncobs, and animal pelts. The dishes are traditional, as are the waiters' outfits and the tunes you'll hear the musicians play. ✉ *Poiana Braşov* ☎ *0268/262–137* ⚅ *Reservations essential* ☐ *No credit cards.*

★ **$–$$** ✕ **Şura Dacilor** (Dacians' Shed). Built to resemble a traditional Romanian hunting lodge, this restaurant serves game, special cheeses, and freshly baked bread. ✉ *Poiana Braşov* ☎ *0268/262–327* ☐ *No credit cards.*

$$$$ ▥ **Miruna.** Flowers and artwork enhance this cheery property. Most guest rooms have balconies, and several have skylights. Rates are lower April–December. ✉ *Poiana Braşov* ☎ *0268/262–120* 🖷 *0268/262–035* ⊕ *www.hotelmiruna.ro* 🛏 *3 rooms, 11 suites, 2 villas* ⚅ *Restaurant, bar* ☐ *AE, MC, V.*

$$$$ ▥ **Tirol.** A Romanian-Swiss joint venture, this Tyrolean-style hotel has
FodorsChoice a cozy lobby, a superb restaurant, and attractive guest rooms, most with
★ balconies. It's under the same ownership as Bucharest's Helvetia Hotel. ✉ *Poiana Braşov* ☎ *0268/262–453* 🖷 *0268/262–439* 🛏 *54 rooms, 4 suites* ⚅ *Restaurant, bar* ☐ *MC, V.*

$$–$$$ ▥ **Alpin.** Expect marvelous views from most guest rooms at this alpine-style hotel, which is within walking distance of ski lifts and the bus stop for Braşov. The hotel is popular with families. ✉ *Poiana Braşov* ☎ *0268/262–343* 🖷🖷 *0268/262–435* 🛏 *125 rooms, 4 suites* ⚅ *Restaurant, pool, bar* ☐ *MC, V.*

Sighişoara

FodorsChoice Sighişoara's stone towers and spires can be seen from a great distance.
★ Each July, a Medieval Festival, with people in period costume, re-creates Sighişoara's past. Contact the Romanian National Tourist Office in your home country for exact dates.

Above the modern town is an exceptionally well-preserved medieval **citadel,** which you enter through an arched entryway at the base of the 14th-century clock tower. Wooden figures symbolizing the days of the week, peace, justice, and even an executioner move in and out of the clock on the hour. Within the clock tower, the **Muzeul de Istorie,** or History Museum, (✉ Piaţa Muzeului 1 ☉ Mon.–Sat. 9–5:30, Sun. 9–3:30) includes a torture chamber and medieval arms. From the gallery at the top, you can view the historic district's terra-cotta roofs and the citadel's eight additional remaining towers.

From the citadel, follow the narrow, cobbled streets lined with faded pink, green, and ocher houses until you come to **Pasajul Scărilor** (Students' Passage), a 175-step covered staircase. The 17th-century passageway leads to **Biserica din Deal** (Church on the Hill), a 14th-century Gothic church that is heavily buttressed and has interior frescoes. Behind the Biserica din Deal, the **Cimitirul German,** or German Cemetery (⊠ Str. Școlii.), stretches across the hillside to the ancient wall of the citadel, bearing testament to the town's Saxon settlers.

$–$$ ✕ **Restaurantul Vlad Dracul.** The presumed birthplace of Vlad Țepeș is a popular spot for a break or a meal of traditional Romanian food. ⊠ *Piața Muzeului 6* ☎ *0265/771–596* ▭ *No credit cards.*

Sibiu

Founded in the 12th century, Sibiu was a major Saxon center. The Old Town's architecture recalls the days when rich and powerful guilds dominated trade. Sections of the medieval wall still guard the historic area, where narrow streets are lined with steep-roofed 17th-century buildings with "eyebrow" windows (gable overhangs) before opening onto vast, church-dominated squares.

The old part of the town centers on **Piața Mare** (Great Square), with its painted 17th-century houses. The **Biserica Romano Catolică** (Roman Catholic Church), a high-baroque structure, stands right in the Great Square. The **Muzeul Brukenthal,** or Brukenthal Museum (☎ 0269/211–699 ☉ Tues.–Sun. 9–5 ⊕ www.brukenthal.verena.ro), on the Great Square, has an impressive collection of silver, paintings, and religious art.

Behind Piața Mare are two other important squares. In the northwest corner of **Piața Mica** (Small Square), you'll find a fine wrought-iron bridge nicknamed *Podul Minciunilor* (Liars' Bridge). Tell a lie while standing on it, and the bridge will collapse, or so the tale goes. In Piața Huet, another square, the tile-covered spires of **Biserica Evanghelică** (Evangelical Church) sparkle in the sun.

A short drive brings you to **Muzeul Civilzației Populare Tradiționale Astra** (Traditional Folk Civilization Museum), a 200-acre outdoor exhibit of original rural structures. (⊠ Calea Rășinari ☎ 0269/218–195 ☉ May–Aug., Tues.–Sun. 10-6; Sept.–Apr., Tues.–Sun. 9–5.) In the nearby village of **Sibiel, Muzeul de Icoane pe Sticlă** (Icons on Glass Museum) houses some 700 icons. ⊠ *Str. Bisericii 326* ☎ *0269/552–536* ☉ *Daily 8–8.* Returning to Sibiu, turn off at the village of **Cristian** to see its 14th-century fortified church.

★ $ ✕ **Crama Sibiul Vechi** (Old Sibiu Wine Cellar). Waiters in traditional garb serve Romanian specialties while singers render old tunes. Embroidered scarves and ceramic plates cover the brick walls. ⊠ *Str. Papiu Ilarian 3* ☎ *0269/431–971* ▭ *No credit cards.*

$$ ▦ **Continental.** Only a 10-minute walk form the historic section, this property, part of Romania's largest chain, is right on the main road into town. Rooms are comfortable, and the staff is helpful. ⊠ *Calea Dumbrăvii 2–4* ☎ *0269/218–100* ☏ *0269/210–125* ⊕ *www.continentalhotels.ro* ⤳ *169 rooms, 13 suites* ⚭ *Restaurant, bar* ▭ *AE, DC, MC, V.*

★ $$ ▦ **Împăratul Romanilor** (Roman Emperor). Just a block from Piața Mare, this 16th-century structure has been an inn since 1772. The elegant lobby and guest rooms are furnished with antique reproductions, and the restaurant has a retractable glass ceiling. ⊠ *Str. Nicolae Bălcescu 4*

FodorsChoice
★

FodorsChoice
★ $

☎ *0269/216–500* 🖨 *0269/213–278* 🛏 *64 rooms, 32 suites* ⚱ *Restaurant, bar* 🖃 *MC, V.*

Transylvania Essentials

CAR TRAVEL

From Bucharest, Route E60 runs north through Sinaia to Braşov and Sighişoara. Take Route 14 southwest from Sighişoara or E68 west from Braşov to reach Sibiu.

TOURS

Many American and European tour operators run tours of Transylvania, as do travel agencies in Bucharest. Some tours have a *Dracula* focus, and they visit sites relevant to the fictional count and the 15th-century prince, Vlad Ţepeş. It's best to contact a reputable travel agency in Bucharest for itineraries and fees.

TRAIN TRAVEL

Train service between Bucharest and major Transylvanian cities is frequent: close to 20 trains a day to Braşov (2½ hours) and around 10 to Sibiu (5 hours) and Sighişoara (4 hours). Approximately 10 trains per day travel between Braşov and Sibiu (2 hours), even more between Braşov and Sighişoara (1½ hours). All trip times mentioned are for *InterCity* and *rapid* trains. Braşov-bound trains stop at Sinaia.

VISITOR INFORMATION

The English-language publications *Brasov: What, Where, When* and *Transylvania in Your Pocket* have hotel, restaurant and sightseeing information. The former is available free at most hotels, and the latter may be purchased at bookstores and kiosks for $1.10.

🚩 **Tourist Information Office** ✉ Str. Nicolae Bălcescu 7, Piaţa Mare, Sibiu ☎ 0269/211–110 ⊕ www.primsb.ro.

SLOVAKIA
BRATISLAVA, THE HIGH TATRAS & EASTERN SLOVAKIA

SLOVAKIA IS STEEPED IN A FOLK TRADITION that originated in the agrarian countryside—pottery, music, wood carving, embroidery—and is still largely untouched by westernization. Seven decades of common statehood with the Czechs ended in 1992 and was just a part of the history of the people living from east of the Tatra Mountains to the Danube River.

Slovaks speak a language closely related to Czech and Polish. United with fellow Slavs briefly during the 9th century as part of the Great Moravian Empire, the area was conquered a century later by the Magyars and remained under Hungarian rule until 1918. During this time, Rusyns from the east populated the foothills of the Carpathian Mountains (the majority of which are now in the Ukraine). After the Tatar invasions of the 13th century, many Saxons were invited to resettle the land and develop the economy. During the 15th and 16th centuries, Romanian shepherds migrated from Walachia into Slovakia. The merging of these varied groups with earlier Slav inhabitants enriched the native folk culture.

Bratislava was once a city filled with picturesque streets and Gothic churches. Some old buildings were destroyed to make way for Communist "progress," but the Old Town center retains much of its charm. Plaster ornamentation on the remaining buildings has been repaired and many sport a new coat of pastel paint. In the pedestrian zone near the Danube, whimsical bronze statues seem to walk arm and arm down the street or pop out of an imaginary manhole.

The peaks of the High Tatra Mountains are an international draw for hikers and skiers. The smallest alpine range in the world, the rugged mountains rise magnificently from the foothills of northern Slovakia. The area's subtler attractions, including the exquisite medieval towns of the Spiš region below the Tatras and the beautiful 18th-century wood churches farther east, are definitely worth the trip.

SLOVAKIA A TO Z

To research prices, get advice from other travelers, and book travel arrangements, visit www.fodors.com.

ADDRESSES
The most common words on street signs are *ulica* (street, abbreviated *ul.*) and *námestie* (square, abbreviated *nám.*).

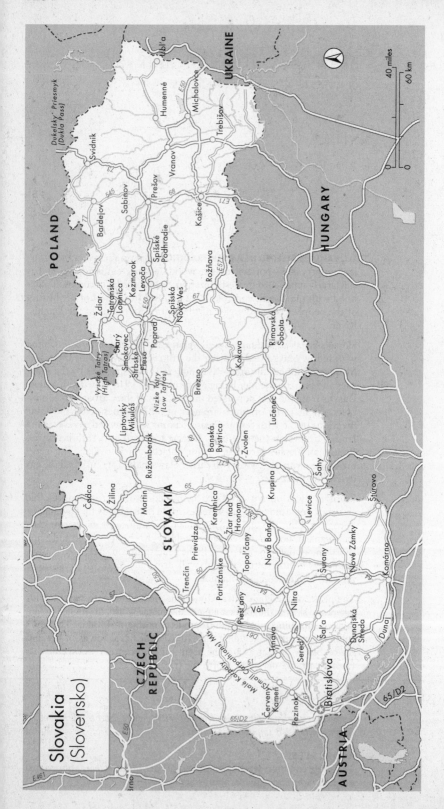

Slovakia
(Slovensko)

POLAND

UKRAINE

HUNGARY

AUSTRIA

CZECH REPUBLIC

SLOVAKIA

Dukelský Priesmyk
(Dukla Pass)

Ubl'a

Humenné

Michalovce

Trebišov

Svidník

Vranov

Prešov

Sabinov

Bardejov

Košice

Spišské
Podhradie

Rožňava

Levoča

Kežmarok

Tatranská
Lomnica

Ždiar

Spišská
Nová Ves

E571

Rimavská
Sobota

Poprad

Starý
Smokovec

Štrbské
Pleso

Vysoké Tatry
(High Tatras)

Nízke Tatry
(Low Tatras)

Brezno

Kokava

Liptovský
Mikuláš

Ružomberok

Banská
Bystrica

Zvolen

Lučenec

Šahy

Žilina

Čadca

Martin

Kremnica

Žiar nad
Hronom

Krupina

Levice

Štúrovo

Prievidza

Topol'čany

Nová Baňa

Trenčín

Partizánske

Piešt'any

Nitra

Šurany

Nové Zámky

Komárno

Váh

Malé Karpaty
(Little Carpathians)

Tmava

Sered

Šal'a

Dunajská
Streda

Dunaj

Červený
Kameň

Pezinok

Bratislava

65/D2

E461

AIR TRAVEL

A few airlines fly into Bratislava; most fly into nearby Vienna, Austria. Sky Europe has daily flights between Bratislava and Košice.

BUS TRAVEL

Bus and tram service in Bratislava is very cheap and reasonably frequent; you can use it to reach any of the places in the tours below. The bus network in the rest of Slovakia is dense, but service to the smaller towns can be infrequent.

BUSINESS HOURS

Banks are open weekdays 8–4. Museums are usually open Tuesday–Sunday 10–5. Shops are generally open weekdays 9–6 and stay open slightly later on Thursday; a few close between noon and 2. Many are also open Saturday 9–noon (department stores 9–4) and, in big cities, on Sunday.

CAR RENTAL

Though not cheap, a rented car is the most convenient way to explore Slovakia beyond Bratislava. Rates run from 1,200 Sk to 3,000 Sk per day. Hertz and Avis have counters at the airport. The locally owned Advantage Car Rental will pick you up at the airport or your hotel.

🚗 **Advantage Car Rental** ✉ Box 151, Bratislava, 85299 ☎ 02/6241-0510 or 02/6383-5831 🌐 www.autopozicovna.sk. **Avis** ✉ Letisko M.R. Štefánika, Bratislava ☎ 02/5341-6111 🌐 www.avis.sk. **Hertz** ✉ Letisko M.R. Štefánika, Bratislava ☎ 02/4364-0562 or 02/4363-6662 🌐 www.hertz.sk.

CAR TRAVEL

EMERGENCIES If your car breaks down and you need help, call the 24-hour repair service, Autoklub Slovakia Assistance. If you have an accident, call the police.

🚗 **Ambulance** ☎ 155. **Autoklub Slovakia Assistance** ☎ 124. **Police** ☎ 158.

GASOLINE Gasoline is expensive. Finding a station in Bratislava can be challenging; filling up on the freeway as you approach the city is easier. Lead-free gasoline is known as *natural*.

ROAD CONDITIONS Decent highways link Bratislava with Prague and Budapest. From Bratislava to Poprad, about half the journey is over multilane highway, and construction continues to complete the link. As you travel east in Slovakia, roads get narrower but are generally good. Although you might find yourself behind a horse cart on a mountain road in the Tatras, a car is still the best way to get around.

RULES OF THE ROAD Drive on the right. Speed limits are 60 kph (37 mph) in built-up areas, 90 kph (55 mph) on open roads, 110 kph (68 mph) on expressways, and 130 kph (80 mph) on four-lane highways. Seat belts are compulsory; drinking and driving is strictly prohibited.

CUSTOMS & DUTIES

U.S. or European Union citizens over 18 years old can bring in 250 cigarettes (or their equivalent in tobacco), 2 liters of wine, 1 liter of spirits, and ½ liter of perfume.

There is no limit on the amount of goods purchased for noncommercial use, but to be on the safe side, keep all receipts. You can officially export antiques (items more than 50 years old) only with the written approval of the Ministry of Culture as authenticated by the Slovak National Museum.

🚗 **Ministry of Culture** ✉ Nám. SNP 33 ☎ 02/5939-1411 🌐 www.mksr.sk.

EATING & DRINKING

In Slovakia you can choose between restaurants, *vináreň* (wine bars that serve meals), taverns, cafeterias, and a growing number of coffee shops and snack bars.

Slovakia's food is a combination of its neighbors' cuisines. The long-shared history with Hungary and Austria gives traditional Slovak cuisine a bit more flair than that of the Czech Republic, though it is just as meat-heavy. Hungarian paprika–laced stews with sour cream sauces are served (if you're lucky) with *halušky* (small dumplings). *Bryndzové halušky*, the country's unofficial national dish, is a tasty and filling mix of these dumplings (similar to Italian gnocchi or German spaetzle) covered in soft cheese made from sheep's milk and a little bacon. Pork, veal, and turkey cutlets can all be had fried Viennese schnitzel–style. Vegetarians don't have many options, though marinated vegetable salads are normally available. For dessert, be sure to try *palacinky*, delicious crepes stuffed with fruit and cream, jam, or chocolate.

Prices are reasonable by American standards, even in the more expensive restaurants.

WHAT IT COSTS In Slovak koruny			
$$$$	**$$$**	**$$**	**$**
AT DINNER over 400	250–400	150–250	under 150

Prices are per person for a main course.

MEALTIMES   Lunch is usually from 11:30 to 2 or 3, dinner from 6 to 9:30 or 10. Some places are open all day, and in Bratislava it may be easier to find a table at trendier establishments during off-hours.

RESERVATIONS & DRESS   A jacket is suggested for higher-price restaurants. Otherwise, casual dress is acceptable.

EMBASSIES

🏛 Canada ✉ Mostova 2 ☎ 02/5920-4031 🖨 02/5443-4227 🌐 www.canada.cz.
🏛 United Kingdom ✉ Panská 16 ☎ 02/5998-2000 🖨 02/5998-2237 🌐 www.britemb.sk.
🏛 United States ✉ Hviezdoslavovo nám. 4 ☎ 02/5443-0861 🖨 02/5441-8861 🌐 www.usis.sk.

HOLIDAYS

January 1 (day of founding of the Slovak Republic); January 6 (12th Night); Good Friday and Easter Monday; May 1 (Labor Day); May 8 (Liberation of the Republic); July 5 (Sts. Cyril and Methodius); August 29 (anniversary of the Slovak National Uprising); September 1 (Constitution Day); September 15 (Our Lady of Sorrows); November 1 (All Saints' Day); December 24–26.

LANGUAGE

Slovak, a western Slavic tongue related to both Czech and Polish, is the official language of Slovakia. English is increasingly popular.

LODGING

A multimillion-dollar refurbishment of a huge old luxury hotel on a main square in Bratislava has set the pace for the capital's hotel prices. Room rates are high, as in Western Europe, but amenities aren't universally on par. Hotels in the Tatras are not much less expensive, but rates drop dramatically in eastern Slovakia, where it's possible to find accommodation in buildings that date from as far back as the 16th century (the decor is usually strangely modern). Inexpensive private rooms and apartments are available through travel agencies across the country. Room shortages in the mountains are common from January to February and July to August, so make reservations well in advance.

Prices are for peak season double rooms, sometimes including breakfast.

WHAT IT COSTS In Slovak koruny			
$$$$	$$$	$$	$
HOTELS over 6,000	3,500–6,000	1,500–3,500	under 1,500

Prices are per person for a standard double room in high season.

HOTELS Satur, the national tourist agency, officially grades hotels from one to four stars, but their standards are not as exacting as a Michelin rating. Pensions are small inns that mostly include breakfast in their prices.

ROOMS IN PRIVATE HOMES Travel agencies can help you find a private room in a house in Bratislava and other cities. Standards vary widely, and you may have to sacrifice some privacy (shared entrances, phone lines, and bathrooms, for example). You can also find rooms by looking for signs in windows, especially in the Tatras, that read ROOM FREE or ZIMMER FREI, in German.

MAIL & SHIPPING

POSTAL RATES First-class (airmail) letters and postcards (up to 20 grams) cost 21 Sk to send to the United States and Canada, and 16 Sk to send to the United Kingdom.

RECEIVING MAIL Mail can be marked *poste restante* and sent to the main post office in Bratislava.
🏛 **Main Post Office** ✉ Hlavná pošta, Nám. SNP 35 ☎ 02/5939-3111.

MONEY MATTERS

Costs are highest in Bratislava and only slightly lower in the High Tatra resorts and main spas. The least expensive areas are central and eastern Slovakia.

Cup of coffee, 15 Sk; beer (½ liter), 20 Sk–40 Sk; glass of wine, 20 Sk–40 Sk; pastry, 30 Sk; 2-km (1-mi) taxi ride, 150 Sk. Admission to museums and castles ranges from 20 Sk to 100 Sk.

CURRENCY The unit of currency in Slovakia is the crown, or koruna, written as Sk, and divided into 100 halierov. There are bills of 20, 50, 100, 200, 500, 1,000, and 5,000 Sk, and coins of 10, 20, and 50 halierov and 1, 2, 5, and 10 Sk.

At press time (summer 2003), the rate of exchange was 38 Sk to the U.S. dollar, 26 Sk to the Canadian dollar, 60 Sk to the pound sterling, 41 Sk to the euro, 23 Sk to the Australian dollar, 21 Sk to the New Zealand dollar, and 5 Sk to the South African rand.

PASSPORTS & VISAS

ENTERING SLOVAKIA Entry without a visa is permitted for citizens of the United States (up to 30 days), United Kingdom (six months), and Canada (90 days). Citizens of Australia and New Zealand need a visa for any visits.

TELEPHONES

COUNTRY & AREA CODES The country code for Slovakia is 421. When dialing a number from outside the country, drop the initial zero from the city code. When dialing a number from within the same city, drop the city code.

INTERNATIONAL CALLS You can dial many countries, including North America and the United Kingdom, from public pay phones. You can also call from Telefón/Telegraf, a public communications office with phone booths inside and out. It's open weekdays 7 AM–9 PM, weekends 8 AM–8 PM. International calls can also be placed through AT&T, Sprint, and MCI.

☎ Access Codes **AT&T** ☎ 0800/000101. **MCI** ☎ 0800/000112. **Sprint** ☎ 042/187187. **Telefón/Telegraf** ✉ Kolárska 12, Bratislava ☎ 0149 international inquiries.

LOCAL CALLS Pay phone calls cost 4 Sk. Some machines take coins, but many accept only phone cards. You can buy one at most newsstands or at any post office. For information, call ☎ 120 or 121.

TIPPING

Although many Slovaks still tip in restaurants by rounding up the bill to the nearest multiple of 10, higher tipping is beginning to catch on. For good service, 10% is considered an appropriate gratuity on very large tabs. Tip porters and room service 20 Sk. In taxis round up the bill to the nearest multiple of 10. Give tour guides and helpful concierges between 20 Sk and 30 Sk for services rendered.

TRAIN TRAVEL

Frequent train service is available to the largest cities, including Bratislava, Poprad, Prešov, and Košice, with connections to smaller towns. Make sure to take the express trains marked "R" or the fast Intercity trains (IC) if you don't want to stop in every village. Reliable, if slow, electric rail service connects Poprad with the resorts of the High Tatras.

VISITOR INFORMATION

Satur is the official national tourist agency for Slovakia. Most cities also have a tourist information center that can help reserve hotels and private rooms as well as offer city tours.

☎ **Satur** ✉ Jesenského 5, Bratislava ☎ 02/5441-0133 or 02/5441-0129 🖷 02/5441-0138 🌐 www.satur.sk ✉ Miletičova 1 ☎ 02/5542-2828 or 02/5542-2664.

WHEN TO GO

Organized sightseeing tours generally run from April or May through October. In winter, some attractions, especially castles, either close entirely or have shorter hours. Hotel rates drop during the off-season except during festivals. In winter (December–February), skiers from all over Eastern Europe crowd the slopes and resorts of the High Tatra Mountains. Visit the mountains in late spring (May or June) or fall (October–November) and you will have the hotels and restaurants pretty much to yourself.

CLIMATE The following are the average daily maximum and minimum temperatures for Bratislava.

Jan.	36F	2C	May	70F	21C	Sept.	72F	22C
	27	–3		52	11		54	12
Feb.	39F	4C	June	75F	24C	Oct.	59F	15C
	28	–2		57	14		45	7
Mar.	48F	9C	July	79F	26C	Nov.	46F	8C
	34	1		61	16		37	3
Apr.	61F	16C	Aug.	79F	26C	Dec.	39F	4C
	43	6		61	16		32	0

BRATISLAVA

The Starý mesto (Old Town) in Bratislava is quaint and compact. Many building facades have been restored with a fresh coat of pastel-color paint and a bright café or shop in the streetside storefront. Across the Danube and in the newer parts of town is the unfortunate Communist legacy—seas of gray, concrete-block apartment buildings and faded supermodern structures like the Nový most (New Bridge), which resembles a UFO on stilts. The hillsides surrounding the town are dotted with homes and gardens, and with parks and forests for stolling.

Exploring Bratislava

Numbers in the margin correspond to points of interest on the Bratislava map.

Head toward the Danube River to discover the Gothic and Renaissance architectural treasures of the Old Town. It's mainly a pedestrian-only zone. Walking between the major sites will take a few hours tops.

⑩ Dóm svätého Martina (St. Martin's Cathedral). Construction of this massive Gothic church, with its 280-foot gold-trimmed steeple, began in the 14th century. Between the 16th and 19th centuries, 17 Hungarian monarchs were crowned here. ⊠ *Rudnayovo nám.* ☎ *02/5443–1359* ⊘ *Weekdays 10–11:30 and 2–6, Sat. 10–noon, Sun. 2–4:30.*

❼ Hlavné námestie (Main Square). This enchanting square in the Old Town is lined with old houses and palaces that represent architectural styles, from Gothic (No. 2), through baroque (No. 4) and rococo (No. 7), to a wonderfully decorative example of art nouveau (No. 10). Booths in the center sell local handicrafts. ⊠ *Bordered by Radničná ul. and Rybárska brána.*

❾ Hrad (Castle). Bratislava's castle has been continually rebuilt since its original foundations were laid in the 9th century. Hungarian kings expanded the castle into a royal residence, and the Habsburgs turned it into a successful defense against the Turks. Its current design dates from the 17th century, although the existing castle was completely rebuilt after a fire in 1811. Inside, the **Slovenské národné múzeum** (Slovak National Museum) displays crafts, furniture and clocks, and silver. ⊠ *Zámocká ul.* ☎ *02/5934–1626* ⊘ *Castle and museum: Tues.–Sun. 9–5.*

❷ Hurbanovo námestie (Hurban Square). Between a café and a shoe store hides an entrance to the Old Town. A small bridge decorated with statues of St. John Nepomuk and St. Michael crosses over the old moat into the intricate barbican and through Michalská brána (Michael's Gate). ⊠ *Junction of Obchodná, Suché mýto, Michalská, and Námestie SNP.*

❹ Jezuitský kostol (Jesuit Church). Wild with baroque detailing on the inside, this church was built by Protestants who, in 1636, received an imperial concession for a place of worship on the condition that it have no tower. ⊠ *Kostolna 1* ☎ *no phone.*

❽ Kostol Klarisiek (Church and Monastery of the Poor Clares). This 14th-century early-Gothic church exterior is small but still imposing because of its richly decorated spire. A mendicant order, the Poor Clares were forbidden from building a steeple atop the church, so they sidestepped the rules and built one against a side wall in the 15th century. The church is now a concert hall. ⊠ *Farská ul.* ☎ *No phone.*

❸ Michalská brána (Michael's Gate). Topped with a copper onion dome and a statue of St. Michael, this 500-year-old gate is the only remainder of Bratislava's three original city entrances. The tower affords a good view over the Old Town, and inside is a display of ancient weapons and town fortifications. ⊠ *Michalská 24* ☎ *02/5443–3044* ⊘ *Wed.–Mon. 10–4:30.*

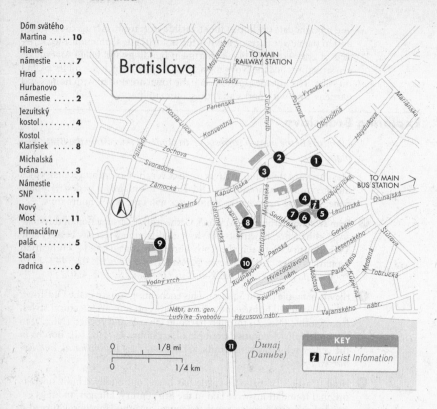

● **Námestie SNP** (SNP Square). A monument here commemorates the Slovenské Národné Povstanie (SNP, Slovak National Uprising). The anti-Nazi Resistance movement involved partisan fighting in Slovakia's mountainous areas during the final years of World War II. On December 31, 1992, this square was the center of the celebration when at midnight Slovakia became an independent nation. ⊠ *Bordered by Obchodná ul. and Poštová ul.*

🤚 ⑪ **Nový Most** (New Bridge). This futuristic bridge with slanting supports has a disc-shape restaurant and observation platform aloft. (Many Slovaks think it resembles a spaceship.) Opened in 1972, the bridge was formerly known as Most SNP. ⊠ *Between Staromestská ul. and Panónska cesta* ☾ *Daily 8 AM–10 PM.*

❺ **Primaciálny palác** (Primates' Palace). The elegance of the palace's pale pink, classical facade dominates the square. Following Napoléon's victory at the Battle of Austerlitz, Napoléon and Habsburg emperor Francis I signed the Peace of Bratislava of 1805 in the dazzling Hall of Mirrors. ⊠ *Primaciálne nám. 1* ☎ *02/5443–5151 or 02/5935–6166* ☾ *Tues.–Sun. 10–5.*

❻ **Stará radnica** (Old Town Hall). A colorful jumble of Gothic and Renaissance arcades, archways, and audience halls developed gradually over the 13th and 14th centuries from a number of burghers' houses. Walk through the vaulted passageway with early Gothic ribbing into a cheerful Renaissance courtyard. Toward the back is the entrance to the **Mestské Múzeum** (City Museum), which documents Bratislava's storied past. ⊠ *Primaciálne nám.* ☎ *02/5443–5800* ☾ *Tues.–Sun. 10–5.*

Where to Eat

Hotel restaurants in the capital city are undoubtedly the fanciest, and most expensive, though not always the best (the Carlton Hotel being a notable exception). Trendy bar-restaurants and ethnic cuisine alternatives have begun to appear around the Old Town, but there are still many boring pork-and-potatoes places to weed through.

$$$-$$$$ ✕ **Koliba Expo.** If you're not going on to the Tatras, be sure to take the 10-minute taxi ride up Kamzik hill to experience a traditional mountain *koliba* (open grill) restaurant. Chicken is roasted for close to an hour over a fire pit in the dining room, and other grilled dishes include pork kabobs and flank steak. Hunting trophies hang below the steep roofline, which is slanted to keep snow off. Slovak folk music fills the air nightly. ⊠ *Kamzikov vrch* ☎ *02/5477–1781* ▭ *MC, V.*

$$-$$$ ✕ **Hradná Vináreň.** Dine on the summer terrace (May to August) to enjoy the excellent view of the Old Town. When the weather turns colder, head indoors to the room with soaring Gothic arches and chandeliers. Sip one of the large selection of Slovak and Hungarian wines while you peruse an occasionally inventive menu. Would you like to try ostrich in a cream sauce? If not, you can always choose the hearty Slovak pasta standby: halušky with bacon and soft Lipatur cheese. ⊠ *Mudroňova 1* ☎ *02/ 5934–1563* ▭ *AE, DC, MC, V.*

$$-$$$ ✕ **Leberfinger.** Rumor has it that Napoléon once stopped at this roadside tavern. The 50-item menu is traditionally Slovak: try the *kapustné strapačky* (sauerkraut and pasta flakes topped with tangy sheep's cheese). There are also some vegetarian options, such as the oddly named *hájnikov tanier* (gamekeeper's plate), a potato pancake filled with vegetables, mushrooms, and cheese. The place is kid-friendly, with a play corner inside and seesaws outside. It's across the Danube from the Old Town, on the riverbank adjacent to a major city park. ⊠ *Viedenská cesta 257* ☎ *02/6231–7590* ▭ *DC, MC, V.*

★ $$-$$$ ✕ **Traja Musketieri.** A Middle Ages–theme cellar restaurant and bar, Three Musketeers overflows with diplomats, expats, and trendy locals served by waiters costumed as barmaids and stable boys. The menu is more contemporary: salmon in a caviar sauce, venison medallions in a wine reduction, pasta Alfredo with spinach noodles and garlic. Top it all off with a decent house red. ⊠ *Sládkocicova 7* ☎ *02/5413–1026* ▭ *AE, DC, V.*

$-$$$ ✕ **Café Meyer.** Sample the Austrian influence on Pressburg (as Bratislava was known in German) at a rebuilt café on the sight of an original. Cases filled with a great variety of delicious fruit- and cream-filled confections are a reminder of former owner Julius Meyer, a candy supplier to the Austrian emperor's court in the late 1800s. Want more than a sweet snack? Try a dinner of Wiener schnitzel or a hot strudel filled with vegetables, cabbage, spinach, or meat. In nice weather you can sit outside under umbrellas on the pedestrian square. ⊠ *Hlavné nám. 4* ☎ *02/5441–1741* ▭ *MC, V.*

★ $$ ✕ **Modrá Hviezda.** Candlelight flickers on the barrel-vaulted ceilings of this intimate, family-owned wine cellar in the side of the castle hill. *Mamičkina špecialita* (Mama's specialty) is a favorite: the beef medallions topped with a sour cream sauce and lingonberries go well with the *krokety* (potato croquettes). ⊠ *Beblavého 14* ☎ *02/5443–2747* ▭ *No credit cards* ☼ *Closed Sun.*

Where to Stay

Hotels in the Old Town tend to be expensive, though only one or two have high enough levels of luxury to warrant the prices. If you have a car, a pension or hotel outside the center is worth considering. To beat the costs, you can arrange to rent a room in a private house through a travel agency like Satur or the Bratislava Information Service. Be sure to ask for a place near the city center or on a hillside and avoid the fringe areas, which are filled mostly with ugly apartment block housing.

$$$$ 🏨 **Danube.** The design of this French-run hotel on the banks of the Danube echoes the river's flowing shape and blue accents. Pastels decorate the modern rooms and the gleaming public areas. Business facilities here are everything you would expect from a large international chain. ✉ *Rybné nám. 1, 81102* ☎ *02/5934–0000* 🖷 *02/5441–4311* ⊕ *www.hoteldanube. com* 🖙 *264 rooms, 16 suites* ♻ *2 restaurants, pool, bar* ⊟ *AE, DC, MC, V.*

$$$$ 🏨 **Radisson SAS Carlton Hotel.** Everything about the place screams lux-
Fodor'sChoice ury, from the gilt mirrors and mahogany-panel walls in the Library Bar
★ to the perfectly seared three-peppercorn fillet in the restaurant, Brasserie at the Opera. Traditional rooms have a Louis XIV style, with antique reproductions, plush carpeting, and muted tones; business rooms are boldly modern with primary colors and black accents on sculptural furniture. This refurbished grand dame sits opposite the Opera House in the Old Town. ✉ *Hviezdoslavovo nám. 3, 81102* ☎ *02/5939–0000* 🖷 *02/ 5939–0010* ⊕ *www.radissonsas.com* 🖙 *163 rooms, 5 suites* ♻ *Restaurant, bar* ⊟ *AE, DC, MC, V.*

$$$ 🏨 **Hotel Pension No. 16.** Looking for character and hominess? Try this sprawling bed-and-breakfast in a quiet residential neighborhood a short drive from the castle. Rooms are individually decorated with honey-color wood floors and ceiling panels. The apartments, which have kitchenettes, are a good deal. ✉ *Partizánska 16A 81103* ☎ *02/5441–1672* 🖷 *02/5441–1298* ⊕ *www.internet.sk* 🖙 *11 rooms, 5 apartments* ⊟ *AE, MC, V* ⦿ *BP.*

$$$ 🏨 **Perugia.** Bratislava's only boutique hotel is a pink plaster jewel in the Old Town pedestrian zone (taxis can get you here, and it's best not to have a car). The clean, pastel rooms open onto an interior courtyard with a large skylight. ✉ *Zelená 5 81101* ☎ *02/5443–0719* 🖷 *02/ 5443–1821* ⊕ *www.perugia.sk* 🖙 *13 rooms, 1 suite* ♻ *Restaurant* ⊟ *AE, DC, MC, V* ⦿ *BP.*

$$ 🏨 **Hotel West.** Relax in a forest setting atop a hill with great views and recreation like walking in the woods and horseback riding. Though only a short drive to the city, it remains above all the hubbub. The furniture is plain, mostly Scandinavian modern. The property has been adopted by the Best Western chain. ✉ *Kamzik Les, 83329* ☎ *02/5478–8693* 🖷 *02/ 5477–7781* ⊕ *www.hotel-west.sk* 🖙 *40 rooms, 9 suites* ♻ *Restaurant, pool, bar* ⊟ *AE, V.*

★ $ 🏨 **Grémium.** This tiny pension with very basic rooms is above an Old Town art gallery. The friendly staff serves a terminally hip, arty clientele. All rooms have showers, not tubs. ✉ *Gorkého ul. 11, 81103* ☎ *02/5413–1026* 🖷 *02/5443–0653* 🖙 *5 rooms, 1 suite* ♻ *Restaurant* ⊟ *AE, MC, V* ⦿ *CP.*

Nightlife & the Arts

For listings of weekly music, club nights, and theater, look in Bratislava's English-language newspaper, the *Slovak Spectator* (www.slovakspectator. sk), or check out the monthly list in *Kam v Bratislave*. Both are available at newsstands, hotels, and tourist offices.

The Arts

The **Slovenská filharmónia** (Slovak Philharmonic Orchestra; ✉ Medená 3 ☎ 02/5443–3351 or 02/5443–3352 ⊕ www.filharm.sk) stages excellent concerts at the rococo Reduta Theater. **Slovenské národné divadlo** (Slovak National Theater; ✉ Hviezdoslavovo nám. 1 ☎ 02/5443–3890 or

02/5443–3771 ⊕ www.snd.sk) presents high-quality opera, operettas, and ballet performances at bargain prices compared with Western Europe.

Nightlife

Bratislava's club scene is lacking, but there are numerous pubs and cafés in the Old Town where you can stop and quaff a pint. In October, the city hosts an extensive annual jazz festival at performance venues citywide. Good Guinness beer is served at the Irish pub **Dubliner** (⊠ Sedlárska ul. 6 ☎ 02/5441–0706). The tiny **Jazz Cafe** (⊠ Ventúrska 5 ☎ 02/5443–4661) is one of the few year-round jazz clubs in Bratislava. Listen to live Slovak folk music and learn traditional dances on scheduled nights at **V-Club** (⊠ Nám. SNP 12 ☎ 02/5296–6936). Or just drop in for a drink and pop music other evenings.

Shopping

Folk-art and souvenir shops line Obchodná ulica (Shopping Street) as well as Hlavné Námestie.

"Unusual" and "fun" are words often used to describe the designer jewelry and clothing, ceramic pieces, and other works of art at the trendy **Dielo** (⊠ Nám. SNP 12 ☎ 02/5296–8648 ⊠ Obchodná 27 ☎ 02/5443–4568 ⊠ Obchodná 33 ☎ 02/5293–2433). **Folk, Folk** (⊠ Rybárska Brána 2 ☎ 02/5443–4874) deals in Slovak folk art, including crystal, pottery, handwoven tablecloths, wooden articles, and dolls in folk costumes. **ÚLǓV** (⊠ Nám. SNP 12 ☎ 02/5292–3802) has hand-painted table pottery and vases, wooden figures, and folk costumes.

Bratislava Essentials

AIR TRAVEL

Few carriers fly into Bratislava. The Czech national airline, ČSA, flies from Prague to Bratislava and Košice. Sky Europe flies to Bratislava from Milan, Munich, Berlin, and Zurich. Slovak Airlines flies from Bratislava to Moscow. Vienna, Austria, is only an hour away and serves most international destinations.

Sky Europe connects Bratislava and Košice.

⌚ Carriers **ČSA** ⊠ Šturova 13 ☎ 02/5296–1042 ⊕ www.czech-airlines.com. **Sky Europe** ⊠ Ivanská cesta 26 ☎ 02/4850–1111 ⊕ www.skyeurope.com. **Slovak Airlines** ⊠ Trnavská cesta 56 ☎ 02/4445–0096 ⊕ www.slovakairlines.sk.

AIRPORTS & TRANSFERS

Although few airlines provide direct service to Bratislava's M.R. Štefánika Airport, Vienna's Schwechat Airport is only about 60 km (37 mi) to the west and is served by most international carriers.

⌚ **Letisko M.R. Štefánika** ⊠ Ivanská cesta ☎ 02/4857–3353. **Flughafen Wien Schwechat** ⊠ 1300 Wien Flughafen, Vienna, Austria ☎ 431/70070 ⊕ english.viennaairport.com.

TRANSFERS   A taxi ride from the Bratislava airport to the town center should cost no more than 200 Sk. Eight buses a day make the bus connection between Vienna's airport and Bratislava's main bus station for about €10. A Slovak cab ride to Vienna's airport could cost as little as 2,000 Sk.

⌚ **Airport bus connection** ☎ 02/5557–1312 ⊕ english.viennaairport.com.

BOAT TRAVEL

Hydrofoils travel the Danube between Vienna and Bratislava (1 hr, 40 min, €21) and Budapest and Bratislava (4 hr, €68) from May to September. Boats depart from the eastern bank of the Danube near Mostová and Va-

janského nábrežie. Purchase tickets at the dock at least one hour prior to departure for the 9:30 AM trip to Budapest or the 5:30 PM trip to Vienna.
🚩 Slovenská plavba a pristavý ✉ Fajnorovo nábr. 2 ☎ 02/5293-3518 or 02/5293-2226.

BUS TRAVEL

Three buses a day make the five-hour journey from Prague to Bratislava. From Vienna, there are eight buses a day departing Autobusbahnhof Wien Mitte; the trip takes an hour or so, depending on the lines at the border. The main *Autobusová Stanica* (Bus Station) in Bratislava is outside the city center; take Trolley 207 or 208 to Mierové námestie or 202 to the Tesco department store.
🚩 Autobusová Stanica ✉ Mylinské nivy 31 ☎ 0984/222222 or 0984/333333 ⊕ www. busy.sk.

BUS TRAVEL WITHIN BRATISLAVA

Bus, trolleybus, and tram service in Bratislava is cheap, fairly frequent, and convenient for getting to the main sights. Buy your ticket ahead of time at a newsstand or an automated ticket dispenser and validate it when you get on board. A 30-minute ride with transfers is 14 Sk, a 24-hour ticket is 75 Sk, and a 48-hour ticket is 140 Sk.

CAR TRAVEL

Good highways link Prague and Bratislava via Brno (D1 and D2); the 315-km (195-mi) journey takes about 3½ hours. The 60-km (37-mi) trip from Vienna (A4 and then Route 8) takes 1–1½ hours.

Bratislava's Old Town is compact and sights can be reached on foot, so a car is not necessary. Driving can be difficult in town because of congestion and because parking spaces are at a premium. Watch out for no-parking zones or your car may be booted and you will have to pay a hefty fine to have the device removed.

EMERGENCIES

🚩 Emergency Services **Ambulance** ☎ 155. **Police** ☎ 158.
🚩 Hospital **Fakultna nemonica L. Derera** ✉ Limbova 3 ☎ 02/5954-1111 or 02/5941-4111.
🚩 24-hour Pharmacy **Pharmacia** ✉ Palackého 10 ☎ 02/5441-9665.

ENGLISH-LANGUAGE MEDIA

🚩 Bookstores **Eurobooks** ✉ Jesenského 5-9 ☎ 02/5441-7959.

TOURS

The best tours of Bratislava are given by Bratislavská informačná služba (Bratislava Information Service, BIS). They have scheduled English-language tours May to September, and they can arrange an individual guide for a reasonable price. Both BIS and Satur offer one-day tours of castles and the Small Carpathian Mountains close to Bratislava.

TRAIN TRAVEL

Bratislava's main train station is Hlavná stanica. Reasonably efficient train service connects Prague and Bratislava (5–6 hours). There are several trains a day to and from Vienna (just over 1 hour) and Budapest (3 hours), and one train from Krakow to Bratislava (5½ hours). Take the Intercity trains (IC) because they make fewer stops and better time. To travel the 2 km (1 mi) to the Old Town, take Tram 1 to Poštová ulica or take a taxi.
🚩 Hlavná Stanica ✉ Predstaničné nám. ☎ 02/5058-7565 ⊕ www.zsr.sk.

VISITOR INFORMATION

The downtown BIS can help you find a private room or a hotel, as can the smaller office at the train station. The country's national travel agency, Satur, books private accommodations as well as air, rail, and bus tickets.

📘 **BIS** ✉ Klobučnícka 2 ☎ 02/5443-3715 or 02/5443-4059 ✉ Hlavná stanica, Predstaničné nám. ☎ 02/5249-5906. **Satur** ✉ Jesenského 5 ☎ 02/5441-0133 or 02/5441-0129.

THE HIGH TATRAS & EASTERN SLOVAKIA

A visit to the Vysoké Tatry (High Tatras) alone would make a trip to Slovakia worthwhile. Although the range is relatively compact (just 32 km [20 mi] from end to end), its peaks seem a bit wilder and more starkly beautiful than those of the Alps. The highest is Gerlachovský štít, at 8,710 feet; some 20 others exceed 8,000 feet. The area has an extensive system of hiking trails so you can explore that beauty.

To the southeast of the High Tatras lies Slovakia's Spiš region, which seldom appears on tourist itineraries. Isolation has its advantages, however. Baroque and Renaissance facades in painted stone and local wood dominate well-preserved old town squares like those in Levoča.

Farther to the east in the foothills of the Carpathian Mountains, the influences of Byzantium are strongly felt. Drive through the villages near the Polish and Ukrainian borders to see the legacy of 17th- and 18thcentury Greek Catholic (Uniate) and Orthodox wooden churches with onion domes. The splendid walled town of Bardejov makes the best center from which to explore. In contrast to these more romantic images, Nazi and Soviet tanks, trenches, and planes are kept in the area as a reminder of the fighting that took place in 1944 at the Dukelský Priesmyk (Dukla Pass).

Levoča

Fodor'sChoice
★ One of the most famous medieval Spiš towns is Levoča, which is still partially surrounded by walled fortifications. Striking Gothic-on-Renaissance buildings populate the main square, Námestie Majstra Pavla.

Kostol svätého Jakuba (St. Jacob's Church) on the main square has an astounding concentration of Gothic religious art, including work by Spiš artist Pavol of Levoča. His carved-wood high altar is said to be the world's largest and incorporates a magnificent limestone relief of the Last Supper. ✉ *Nám. Majstra Pavla 3* ☎ *053/451-2347* ⊙ *June–Aug., daily 9–5:30; Sept.–May, Tues.–Sun. 8:30–4.*

Check out the great views from one of the largest castles in Europe, **Spišský hrad** (Spiš Castle), just 16 km (10 mi) east from Levoča along Route 18. The sprawling fortifications first built in the 1200s are mostly in ruins, but in the section that has been preserved, a museum houses a collection of torture devices. ✉ *Rte. 18, on hill above town of Spišské Podhradie* ☎ *053/451-2786* ⊙ *June–Aug., daily 9–6; May, Sept., and Oct., Tues.–Sun. 9–6; Nov.–Apr., Tues.–Sun. 9–3.*

Where to Stay

$$ 🏨 **Hotel Satel.** This beautiful 18th-century mansion is flanked by other old buildings on the town square. An interior courtyard retains its original character and has an ornate fountain. The contemporary room decor can be a bit gaudy—particularly the peach lacquer headboards. ✉ *Nám. Majstra Pavla 55, 05401* ☎ *053/451-2943* 🖨 *053/451-4486* ⊕ *www.satel-slovakia.sk* 🛏 *21 rooms, 2 suites* ⟨ *Restaurant, bar* ⊟ *AE, DC, MC, V.*

The High Tatras & Eastern Slovakia

★ **$–$$** 🏨 **Arkada Hotel.** An interesting history and reasonable prices make this hotel a standout. In the 17th century, this 13th-century building became the first printing shop in the Austro-Hungarian Empire. The large, bright rooms—some with arched ceilings—are done mostly in contemporary neutrals. ✉ *Nám. majstra Pavla 26, 05401* ☎ *053/451–2255* 🛏 *23 rooms, 3 apartments* ♨ *Restaurant, bar* 🖃 *AE, MC, V* 🍴 *BP.*

Smokovec

Smokovec is really three resorts in one: Starý (Old), Nový (New), and Horný (Upper), all a stone's throw from one another. Starý Smokovec is an excellent place to start exploring the hiking trails in the Tatras. Some of the more traveled paths lead to waterfalls, a turn-of-the-20th-century chalet, and alpine lakes. Walk up to Hrebienok and you can take a funicular back to town. The multipurpose **Tatrasport** (✉ Starý Smokovec ☎ 052/442–5241 🌐 www.tatry.net/tatrasport), opposite the bus station, provides numerous services, including ski lessons, ski rental, sleigh rides, mountain guides, horseback riding, river rafting, spa services, babysitting, and a restaurant.

Where to Stay & Eat

$$–$$$ ✗ **Restaurant Koliba.** This restaurant's koliba turns out excellent beef, venison steak with cranberry sauce and red wine, and *kapustová polievka* (sauerkraut soup with mushrooms and sausage). A local cimbalom (a dulcimerlike folk instrument) band plays here nightly. ✉ *Starý Smokovec, downhill from train station* ☎ *052/442–2204* 🖃 *No credit cards* ⊘ *Closed Sun.*

★ **$$–$$$** 🏨 **Grand Hotel.** The golden Tudor-style facade of the town's oldest hotel has an air of faded fin-de-siècle elegance. Large guest rooms have high ceilings; ask for one with a balcony. You can fill up on the buffet breakfast before heading out to hike or rent skis here. ⊠ *Starý Smokovec, 06201* ☎ *052/442–2154* 🖷 *052/442–2157* ⮑ *79 rooms, 52 with bath; 5 suites* ♿ *Restaurant, pool, bar* 🖃 *AE, DC, MC, V* ⭐ *BP.*

Tatranská Lomnica

On the eastern end of the electric rail line, Tatranská Lomnica has a near-perfect combination of peace and convenience. Moreover, the cable car behind the Grandhotel Praha brings some of the best walks in the Tatras to within 10 minutes or so of your hotel door.

The **Magistrale** trail (24 km [15 mi]) begins behind the Grandhotel Praha. Take the small cable car to Skalnaté Pleso, from which the trail skirts the peaks along the tree line with spectacular views, which you can reach with relatively little exertion. Consider making a reservation at Skalnaté Pleso for the large cable car that takes you up to **Lomnický štít** (8,635 feet), the second-highest peak in the range. You're permitted to linger on the limited walkways near the observatory at the top for only 30 minutes, after which you take the cable car back down. Tickets sell out quickly each morning, and your hotel staff can help you book.

Where to Stay & Eat

★ **$$–$$$$** ✕ **Zbojnícka Koliba.** Gypsy music plays in the dark log tavern with rustic decor that specializes in *kurča* (chicken) cooked on a spit. To take the edge off your hunger while you wait, order the *bryndza* (a spreadable cheese made from sheep's milk), served with onions and pieces of bacon to spread on bread. The *varené vino* (hot spiced wine) tastes especially good on a cold day. ⊠ *Below Grandhotel Praha* ☎ *052/446–7630* 🖃 *No credit cards* ⊙ *No lunch.*

★ **$$–$$$** 🏨 **Grandhotel Praha.** The multiturreted, turn-of-the-20th-century, cream-color building has red roof tiles and intricate ironwork balconies painted a burnt orange. Built in 1905, the hotel is one of the wonders of the Tatras. Public rooms retain an old-world elegance but renovated guest rooms in blond wood and teal seem incongruous. ⊠ *Tatranská Lomnica, 05960* ☎ *052/446–7941* 🖷 *052/446–7891* ⊕ *www.tatry.sk/grandpraha.html* ⮑ *83 rooms, 7 suites* ♿ *Restaurant, bar* 🖃 *AE, DC, MC, V.*

Bardejov

Bardejov is a great surprise, tucked away in this remote corner of Slovakia yet possessing one of the nation's most enchanting town squares. Indeed, Bardejov owes its splendors to its location, astride the ancient trade routes to Poland and Russia. On the south side of the square is the **Šarišské múzeum** (Icon Museum), filled with icons from the 16th to 19th century and multipanel alter screens from the region's Orthodox and Greek Catholic churches. ⊠ *Radničné nám. 13* ☎ *054/474–6038* ⊙ *Tues.–Sun. 8–noon and 12:30–4.*

Don't miss the *skansen* (open-air village museum) 4 km (2½ mi) north in Bardejovské Kupele. Nineteenth- and early-20th-century wooden buildings have been relocated to the **Múzeum ludovej architektúry** (Museum of Vernacular Architecture), including a small wooden church from Zboj. Inside the houses, storage barns, and craft shops are the furnishings and tools of village life. Park in the town lot and follow signs up the hill to the museum. ⊠ *Bardejovské Kupelé* ☎ *054/472–2072* ⊙ *Daily 8:30–noon and 12:30–5.*

Old **Wooden Churches** in the area are still in use in their original village settings. Look for the onion domes as you drive or pick up the booklet *Wooden Churches Near Bardejov* at hotels and bookstores. ✛ *Off Rte. 545 and Rte. 77.*

Where to Stay & Eat

★ $$ ✕🏠 **Hotel Bellevue.** On a hill above the center, this hotel affords splendid views. Elegant, contemporary cherrywood furnishings are upholstered in botanical prints with deep greens and earth tones. Heat radiates from below the ceramic-tile floors. Locals often clog up the bar, and the adjoining restaurant menu uses an impressive number of vegetables—uncommon in this area—in dishes such as turkey breast stuffed with asparagus. ⊠ *Off Rte. 525, Mihalov, 08501* ☎ *054/472–6099* 🖨 *054/ 472–8404* ⊕ *www.bellevuebardejov.sk* 🛏 *25 rooms, 3 apartments* ⟁ *Restaurant, pool, bar* ⊟ *MC, V* ⊙⟋ *BP.*

The High Tatras & Eastern Slovakia Essentials

ADDRESSES

Many towns in this region have no formal street names; instead, they have signs pointing to hotels, restaurants, and museums.

AIR TRAVEL

Sky Europe flies from Košice to Bratislava and to Prague. ČSA also connects Košice with Prague.

🛉 Carriers **ČSA** ⊠ Juzna 2, Košice ☎ 55/678–2490 ⊕ www.czech-airlines.com. **Sky Europe** ⊠ Košice-Barca Letisko, Košice ☎ 02/4850–4850 central reservations ⊕ www. skyeurope.com.

CAR RENTAL

A rental car can run about 2,500 Sk per day, but it provides the best way to see the region. Hertz and Avis have offices at Košice's airport.

🛉 Agencies **Avis** ⊠ Letisko Košice-Barca, Košice ☎ 055/643-3099. **Hertz** ⊠ Letisko Košice-Barca, Košice ☎ 055/789-6041.

CAR TRAVEL

Driving is the quickest and most convenient way to see eastern Slovakia—sometimes it's the only way to reach small villages. Route 537 is the main road between Poprad and the High Tatras resort towns. Route 68 connects Košice with Bardejov. You can take the same route to Highway E50 and east to Levoča.

TOURS

Satur's seven-day Grand Tour of Slovakia, which leaves from Bratislava every other Saturday from June through September, stops in the High Tatras and a few other towns in eastern Slovakia. The Satur office in Starý Smokovec is also helpful in arranging tours of the Tatras and the surrounding area.

🛉 **Satur** ⊠ Miletičova 1, Bratislava ☎ 02/5542-2828 ⊠ Starý Smokovec ☎ 052/ 442-2710.

TRAIN & BUS TRAVEL

Trains and buses run frequently from Bratislava to Poprad on weekdays and less often on weekends. The electric trains that travel between Poprad and the resort towns in the High Tatras leave from the upper platforms of Poprad's main train station, Železničná stanica Poprad-Tatry.

🛉 **Železničná stanica Poprad-Tatry** ⊠ Wolkerova 496 ☎ 052/7166-8484 ⊕ www.zsr.sk.

VISITOR INFORMATION

🛉 **Bardejov Spirit** ⊠ Radničné nám. 21 ☎ 054/472-6273 ⊕ www.bardejov.sk. **Slovakoturist** ⊠ Horný Smokovec ☎ 052/442-2031. **Tourist Information Center** ⊠ Nám. majstra Pavla 58, Levoča ☎ 053/451-3763 ⊕ www.levoca.sk ⊠ Tatranská Lomnica ☎ 052/ 446-7951.

SLOVENIA

SURGING PEAKS, MYSTERIOUS CAVES, the majestic Old Town of Ljubljana, and a coast dotted with well-preserved Venetian cities of old are the attractions of Slovenia. The combination of Alpine, plain, and coastal geography allows both morning skiing high in the Julian Alps and views of sunset on the Adriatic on the same day. Slovenes' love of their natural surroundings is reflected in the motto they use for their country (fully half of which is covered by forests): "A Green Piece of Europe."

Slovenia's northern border is lined with the jagged peaks of the Karavanke Mountains. The Julian Alps, capped by majestic Mt. Triglav (Three Heads), which rises to 9,393 feet, dominate the northwest. Eastward, the mountains gradually descend to the great Hungarian plain. Lovely lakes nestle in thickly wooded mountain valleys, and vineyards cover low-lying hills farther east.

Slovenia has from earliest times been a frontier region. The Romans came from the coast and marched north; Germanic tribes propelled themselves south. Later Slovenia became a province of Charlemagne's empire; next it served as the Habsburg Empire's bulwark against the Turks. The years during World War II, when Slovenia was annexed by Hitler and Mussolini, were filled with both heroic and unspeakable acts. After World War II, as part of Yugoslavia, Slovenia was at the vanguard of the movement toward democracy and self-determination following Tito's death.

The 2 million Slovenes held a national referendum on December 23, 1990, voting for sovereignty and independence from Yugoslavia, and proclaimed their independence on June 25, 1991. Slovenia gained recognition from other nations and soon set about becoming an active member of the family of European states; in 2004 it is scheduled to become a member of the European Union. Following 500 years as part of the Austro-Hungarian Empire, Slovenes have perfectly combined Austrian efficiency and organization with a genuine and captivating Slavic friendliness. Slovenia's small size (about half the area of Switzerland) can be an advantage: from the centrally located capital, Ljubljana, everything in the country is no more than a three-hour drive away.

SLOVENIA A TO Z

To research prices, get advice from other travelers, and book travel arrangements, visit www.fodors.com.

AIR TRAVEL
There are no direct flights between Slovenia and the United States. Adria Airways, the Slovene national airline, offers regular flights to most

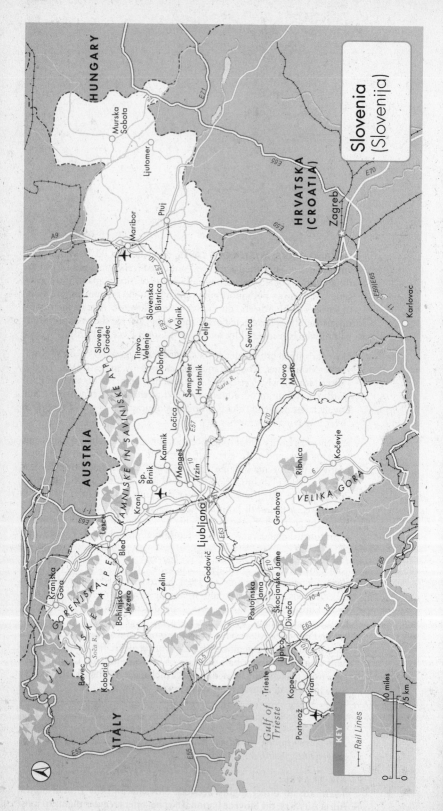

Slovenia
(Slovenija)

HUNGARY

Murska
Sobota

Ljutomer

Ptuj

Maribor

HRVATSKA
(CROATIA)

Zagreb

Karlovac

A9

E57

Slovenska
Bistrica

Sloveni
Gradec

Titovo
Velenje

Vojnik

Celje

Sevnica

Dobrna

Šempeter

Hrastnik

Novo
Mesto

Sava R.

AUSTRIA

Ločica

E57

Kamnik

Mengeš

Trzin

Grahova

Ribnica

Kočevje

VELIKA GORA

Sp.
Brnik

Kranj

Lesce

Bled

Ljubljana

E63

Godovič

Želin

Kranjska
Gora

Bohinjsko
Jezero

Soča R.

Postojnska
Jama

Škocjanske Jame

Divača

E70

E63

Bovec

Kobarid

Lipica

Trieste

Kopar

Piran

Portorož

Gulf of
Trieste

ITALY

E55

GORENJSKE ALPE

JULIJSKE ALPE

KAMNIŠKE IN SAVINJSKE ALPE

E55

KEY

Rail Lines

0   10 miles

0   5 km

major European cities. Austrian Airlines has daily flights from Vienna.

🛫 **Adria Airways** ✉ Gosposvetska 6, 1000 Ljubljana ☎ 01/431-1855 🌐 www.adria.si.

BOAT & FERRY TRAVEL

From early March to late October the *Prince of Venice* hydrofoil makes regularly scheduled trips between Venice and Portorož.

From mid-July to mid-September, the Italian firm Adriatica runs a round-trip service from Trieste, calling at Piran and stopping at several towns on the Croatian Adriatic coast.

🛫 **Adriatica** Maona ✉ Cankarievo nab. 7, 6330 Piran ☎ 05/673-1290. *Prince of Venice* Kompas Turizem ✉ Obala 41, 6320 Portorož ☎ 05/617-8000.

BUS TRAVEL

Intercity bus service is regular, cheap, and efficient, reaching even the most outlying mountain villages. For information contact the Ljubljana bus station.

🛫 **Ljubljana bus station** ✉ Trg OF 5 ☎ 01/090-4230.

BUSINESS HOURS

Most banks are open weekdays 9–noon and 2–4:30, Saturday 9–11. You can also change money at exchange desks in hotels, gas stations, tourist agencies, supermarkets, and small exchange offices. The main museums are open Tuesday–Sunday 10–6. Larger shops are open Monday–Saturday 10–6, whereas smaller ones may open only 10–2. Most are closed Sunday.

CAR TRAVEL

An international driver's license is required in Slovenia. Rental for a mid-size car costs about €100 for 24 hours, with unlimited mileage.

GASOLINE   Gasoline costs SIT185 per liter and is readily available.

ROAD CONDITIONS   Main roads between large towns are comparable to those in Western Europe. Highways charge a toll depending on route and distance traveled. A tunnel speeds traffic through the Karavanke Alps between Slovenia and Austria. From Vienna the passage is by way of Maribor to Ljubljana, with a highway from Graz to Celje. Slovenia's roads also connect with Italy's autostrada highway system.

RULES OF THE ROAD   Slovenes drive on the right. Speed limits are 60 kph (37 mph) in urban areas and 120 kph (74 mph) on motorways. Local drivers are courteous by European standards.

CUSTOMS & DUTIES

Duty-free allowances are 1 carton of cigarettes, 1 liter of spirits, 2 liters of wine. The export of historical artifacts is strictly forbidden.

EATING & DRINKING

When you look at a menu remember two key words: "regional" and "seasonal." This is the best way to eat in Slovenia. There are no pretensions at the table, and full respect is paid to traditional peasant dishes. To really get down to basics, eat in a country *gostilna* (inn). Typical dishes are *krvavice* (black pudding) served with *žganci* (polenta) or sausages served with sauerkraut. Fresh Adriatic calamari is widely available on Slovenian menus. Another favorite is *bograč*, a peppery stew similar to Hungarian goulash, made from either horse meat or beef. Coffee shops serve the delicious calorie-laden *prekmurska gibanica*, a layered cake combining curd cheese, walnuts, and poppy seeds. Another national favorite is *potica*, a rolled cake filled with either walnuts, chocolate, poppy seeds, or raisins. Slovenes enjoy drinking and produce some excellent wines, notably the red *Teran* and the white *Laški Rizling*.

WHAT IT COSTS In Slovenian tolars			
$$$$	$$$	$$	$
AT DINNER over 3,000	2,000–3,000	1,000–2,000	under 1,000

Prices are per person for a main course.

RESERVATIONS & DRESS Casual dress is acceptable in many restaurants in Slovenia, but Slovenes do tend to dress more formally when going out for the evening.

EMBASSIES
Australia maintains a consulate in Ljubljana.

🏠 Canada ✉ Miklošičeva 19 ☎ 01/430-3570 🖨 01/430-3575.
🏠 United Kingdom ✉ Trg Republike 3/IV ☎ 01/200-3910 🖨 01/425-0174.
🏠 United States ✉ Prešernova 31 ☎ 01/200-5500 🖨 01/200-5555.

HOLIDAYS
January 1–2; February 8 (Prešeren Day, Slovene cultural day); Easter; April 27 (National Resistance Day); May 1–2 (Labor Day); June 25 (Slovenia National Day); August 15 (Assumption); October 31 (Reformation Day); November 1 (All Saints' Day); December 25; December 26 (Independence Day).

LANGUAGE
Slovene is the chief language. In the eastern part of the country signs are posted in Slovene and Hungarian; on the Adriatic coast both Slovene and Italian are officially used. English, German, and Italian are spoken in many places.

LODGING
Don't expect Slovenia to be a cheap option: prices are comparable to those in Western Europe. During the high season (June–September), many hotels, particularly on the coast, are fully booked.

WHAT IT COSTS In euros			
$$$$	$$$	$$	$
HOTELS over €200	€150–€200	€80–€150	under €80

Prices are for two people in a standard double room in high season.

APARTMENT & VILLA RENTALS This can be the cheapest option, especially for stays of a week or more. Prices vary depending on region and season. Contact local tourist information centers for details.

HOSTELS During the summer break, university dorms in Ljubljana and Maribor are open to visitors. There are also a number of youth hostels, generally in country areas, that cater to hikers. For further information, contact the Slovenian Tourist Board.

HOTELS Many hotels are clean, smartly furnished, and well run. Establishments built under socialism are equipped with extras such as saunas and sports facilities but tend to be gargantuan structures lacking in soul. Hotels dating from the turn of the 20th century are more romantic. Most establishments add a 30% surcharge for stays of fewer than three days.

TOURIST FARMS Staying on a working farm offers the chance to experience rural life firsthand. "Agritourism" is growing in popularity, especially in Triglav Na-

tional Park. This is an ideal solution for families with children. Contact the Association of Tourist Farms of Slovenia.
🖪 **Association of Tourist Farms of Slovenia** ✉ Trnoveljska 1, 3000 Celje 🖨🖨 03/491-6480.

MAIL & SHIPPING
Post offices are open weekdays 8–6, Saturday 8–noon. Stamps are also sold at hotels, newsstands, and kiosks.

POSTAL RATES Airmail postage to the United States is SIT190 for a letter, SIT150 for a postcard. Airmail postage in Europe is SIT130 for a letter, SIT120 for a postcard.

MONEY MATTERS
Costs in general are comparable to those in Western Europe. Notable exceptions are public transportation, alcohol, and cigarettes, all of which are cheaper here. Typical prices are as follows: cup of coffee, SIT250; glass of beer, SIT400; slice of cake, SIT500; bottle of house wine, SIT2,000; sandwich, SIT500; admission to museums, SIT500–SIT1,000.

CURRENCY The monetary unit in Slovenia is the Slovenian tolar (SIT). One Slovenian tolar is divided into 100 stotin. There are notes of SIT10, SIT20, SIT50, SIT100, SIT200, SIT500, SIT1,000, SIT5,000, and SIT10,000, and coins of 1, 2, and 5 Slovenian tolar and 50 stotin.

Exchange rates at press time (summer 2003) were SIT213 to the U.S. dollar, SIT143 to the Canadian dollar, SIT334 to the British pound sterling, SIT228 to the European euro.

PASSPORTS & VISAS
No visas are necessary for holders of valid passports from the United States, Canada, the United Kingdom, mainland European countries, Australia, New Zealand, or the Republic of Ireland. South African nationals, however, must have a three-month tourist visa.

TELEPHONES
COUNTRY CODE The country code for Slovenia is 386.

INTERNATIONAL CALLS To make international calls, dial 00 and then the appropriate country code. International calls can be made from local pay phones or at the post office. To call collect, dial 901. For international directory inquiries, dial 989.

LOCAL CALLS Pay phones take telephone cards, available at post offices and kiosks. Lower rates apply from 10 PM to 7 AM and all day Sunday. For local directory inquiries dial 988.

TIPPING
Tax is already included in listed prices. Tips are not included in bills, so a 10% tip is customary; if service is especially good, tip 15%.

TRAIN TRAVEL
The internal rail network is limited, but trains are cheap and efficient. Daily trains link Slovenia with Austria, Italy, Hungary, and Croatia. Many are overnight trains with sleeping compartments. For information contact the Ljubljana Train Station.
🖪 **Ljubljana Train Station** ✉ Trg OF 6 🖨 01/291-3332.

TRANSPORTATION AROUND SLOVENIA
In Slovenian the words for street (*ulica*) and drive (*cesta*) are abbreviated *ul.* and *c. Nabrežje* (abbreviated *nab.*) means "embankment." The word for square is *trg*.

VISITOR INFORMATION

Each region has its own tourist information center (TIC).

Slovenian Tourist Board ⊠ Dunajska 156, 1000 Ljubljana ☎ 01/589-1840 🖶 01/589-1841 ⊕ www.slovenia-tourism.si.

WHEN TO GO

The tourist season runs throughout the year, though prices tend to be lower from November through March. Late spring and fall are best—usually warm enough for swimming, but not uncomfortably hot.

CLIMATE   Weather in Slovenia can vary greatly, depending upon what part of the country you are in. Temperatures are colder and there is more precipitation in the Alpine regions, although the summers on the coast can be quite hot. Ljubljana and the Pannonian plain have less extreme variations in weather. The following are the average daily maximum and minimum temperatures for Ljubljana.

Jan.	36F	2C	May	67F	19C	Sept.	69F	20C
	23	−5		45	7		49	9
Feb.	40F	4C	June	73F	22C	Oct.	58F	14C
	25	−3		52	11		41	5
Mar.	50F	10C	July	77F	25C	Nov.	44F	6C
	31	0		55	12		31	0
Apr.	57F	13C	Aug.	77F	25C	Dec.	37F	2C
	37	2		55	12		26	−3

LJUBLJANA

The capital of the republic of Slovenia is on occasion referred to as "Ljubljana the beloved," a play on words: *Ljubljena* means "beloved"; change one letter, and you have the name Ljubljana.

In 34 BC, the Romans founded Emona on this site. Traces of the Roman occupation have been preserved in sections of walls and a complex of foundations complete with mosaics. Slovenes settled here in the 7th century. Later, under the German name Laibach, this became the capital of the Duchy of Carniola, which in 1335 passed into the hands of the House of Habsburg. From then until the end of World War I Ljubljana remained part of the Habsburg Empire. In 1849 the railway linking Vienna and Trieste reached Ljubljana, establishing it as a major center of commerce, industry, and culture.

Influences from the past are apparent in the Ljubljana of today, although you will have to pass through concentric circles like the growth rings of a tree in order to reach the romantic heart of the original Old Town. Vast industrial complexes and high-rise apartments form the outermost ring. "Downtown," composed mainly of modern office buildings, is also spread out.

To reach the old, romantic Ljubljana, follow one of the city's main commercial streets, Miklošičeva Cesta, south from the railway station, eventually passing a series of palatial three- and four-story structures in florid art nouveau style (Jugendstil), topped by cupolas, spires, and ornate statuary, with facades adorned with extravagant arches, balustrades, and curlicue details. Miklošičeva reaches the River Ljubljanica at Prešernov trg, the square named for Slovenia's greatest poet, France Prešeren (1800–49), whose bronze statue stands here. This expansive, traffic-free square, the banks of the river, and old Ljubljana are the places where this lively city is at its most animated. The narrow cobblestone passageways through the medieval quarter and its 19th-century adjuncts evoke a calmer, quieter time. Here students pedal bicycles to and from classes. Along Mestni and Stari trgs green hills rise straight up behind the curve of steeply pitched tile roofs.

Exploring Ljubljana

Numbers in the margin correspond to points of interest on the Ljubljana map.

⓭ Cankarjevo Nabrežje. Numerous cafés line this pretty riverside walkway. When the weather is good, tables are placed outside overlooking the water. ⊠ *Between Tromostovje and Čevljarski Most.*

❶ Centromerkur. This magnificent Vienna Secessionist–style building, dating from 1903, is the oldest department store in town. The entrance, off Prešernov trg, has a flaring iron butterfly-wing portal and is topped by a statue of Mercury. Inside, extraordinarily graceful curved wrought-iron stairways lead to upper floors. ⊠ *Trubarjeva 1* ☎ *01/426–3170.*

⓮ Čevljarski Most (Shoemaker's Bridge). Linking the old and new sides of town, this romantic pedestrian bridge was built in 1931 to plans by the architect Jože Plečnik (1872–1957). The name is derived from an older wooden structure that once stood here and was lined with cobblers' huts. ⊠ *Pod Tranco.*

❷ Franciskanska Cerkev (Franciscan Church). This massive, pink, high baroque church was built between 1646 and 1660. The main altar, by Francesco Robba (1698–1757), dates from 1736. The three sets of stairs in front are a popular meeting place for students. ⊠ *Prešernov trg 4* ☾ *Daily 8–6.*

⓬ Gornji trg. This cobbled street, with some of the capital's finest restaurants, rises up above the Old Town and leads to the wooded parkland surrounding the castle. ⊠ *End of Stari trg leading up toward the castle.*

❼ Grad (Castle). Ljubljana's castle sits up on a hill and affords magnificent views over the river and the Old Town's terra-cotta rooftops, spires, and green cupolas. On a clear day the distant Julian Alps are a dramatic backdrop. The castle walls date from the early 16th century, but the tower was added in the mid-19th century. The surrounding park was landscaped by Plečnik in the 1930s. The ramparts shelter a café and summer terrace. ⊠ *Uphill from Vodnikov trg via Studentovska Ul.* ☎ *01/432–7216* ☾ *Apr.–Oct., daily 9 AM–11 PM; Nov.–Mar., daily 10–7.*

⓯ Križanke Poletno Gledališče (Monastery of the Holy Cross Summer Theater). The annual International Summer Festival and the Jazz Festival are both held in this unusual open-air theater. Set in the courtyard of an 18th-century monastery, the space was adapted to plans drawn up by the architect Jože Plečnik and completed in 1976 after his death. There is seating for 1,400 and a movable roof in case it rains. ⊠ *Trg Francoske Revolucije.*

❾ Magistrat (Town Hall). Guarded by an austere facade, this building hides delightful secrets within. The walls of the internal courtyard are animated with murals depicting historic battles for the city, and a statue of Hercules keeps company with a fountain bearing a Narcissus figure. ⊠ *Mestni trg 1.*

❿ Mestni trg (Town Square). This cobbled, traffic-free square extends into the oldest part of the city. Colorful baroque town houses, now divided

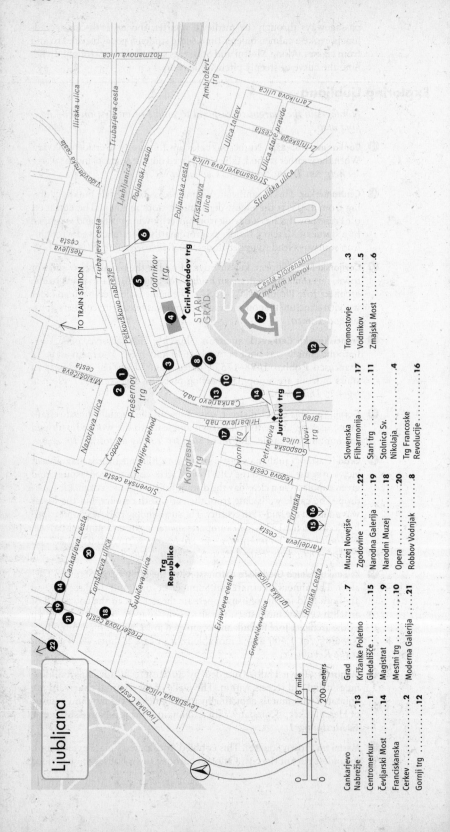

Ljubljana

into functional apartments, present marvelously ornate facades; carved oak doors with great brass handles are framed within columns, and upper-floor levels are decorated with balustrades, statuary, and intricate iron-work. Narrow passageways connect with inner courtyards in one direction and run to the riverfront in the other. Street-level floors contain boutiques, antiques shops, and art galleries. ⊠ *Junction of Ciril-Metodov trg, Stritarjeva ul., and Stari trg.*

㉑ **Moderna Galerija** (Modern Gallery). The strikingly modern one-story structure contains paintings, sculpture, and prints by Slovenian 20th-century artists. In odd-numbered years it also hosts the International Biennial of Graphics, an exhibit of artwork by leading artists from as far afield as the United States, South America, and Japan. ⊠ *Cankarjeva 15* ☎ *01/251–4106* ⊙ *Tues.–Sat. 10–6, Sun. 10–1.*

㉒ **Muzej Novejše Zgodovine** (Museum of Modern History). The permanent exhibition on Slovenes in the 20th century takes you from the days of Austria-Hungary to World War II, through the victory of the Partisan liberation movement and the ensuing Tito period, and up to the present day. Relics and memorabilia are combined with a dramatic sound and video presentation. You'll find the museum in a pink-and-white baroque villa in Tivoli Park. ⊠ *Celovška 23* ☎ *01/300–9610* ⊙ *Tues.–Sun. 10–6.*

⑲ **Narodna Galerija** (National Gallery). The imposing turn-of-the-20th-century building has a survey of Slovene art from the 13th through the early 20th century. ⊠ *Prešernova 24* ☎ *01/426–3109* ⊙ *Tues.–Sun. 10–6.*

⑱ **Narodni Muzej** (National Museum). A 5th-century BC bronze urn known as the Vace Situle is the centerpiece here. Discovered in Vace, Slovenia, it is a striking example of Illyrian workmanship. ⊠ *Prešernova 20* ☎ *01/241–4400* ⊙ *Tues., Wed., and Fri.–Sun. 10–6, Thurs. 10–8.*

⑳ **Opera.** This neo-Renaissance palace with an ornate facade topped by an allegorical sculpture group was erected in 1892. The Opera, site of the Slovene National Opera and Ballet Theater, was originally built for the Theater of the County of Carniola during the time when, as part of the Austro-Hungarian Empire under the Habsburgs, Ljubljana was the county's administrative center. ⊠ *Župančičeva 1* ☎ *01/425–4840* ⊙ *Weekdays 11–1 and 1 hr before performances.*

⑧ **Robbov Vodnjak** (Robba's Fountain). When the Slovenian baroque sculptor Francesco Robba saw Bernini's *Fountain of the Four Rivers* on Piazza Navona during a visit to Rome, he was inspired to create this allegorical representation of the three main Kranjska rivers—the Sava, the Krka, and the Ljubljanica—that flow through Slovenia. ⊠ *Mestni trg.*

⑰ **Slovenska Filharmonija** (Slovenian Philharmonic Hall). The hall was built in 1891 for one of the oldest music societies in the world, established in 1701. Associates of the orchestra have included Haydn, Brahms, Beethoven, Mahler, and Paganini. ⊠ *Kongresni trg 10* ☎ *01/241–0800.*

⑪ **Stari trg** (Old Square). More a narrow street than a square, Stari trg is lined with cafés and small restaurants; in good weather tables are set out on the cobblestones. ⊠ *Between Mestni trg and Gornji trg.*

④ **Stolnica Sv. Nikolaja** (Cathedral of St. Nicholas). This proud baroque cathedral overshadows the daily market on Vodnikov trg. Building took place between 1701 and 1708, and in 1836 the cupola was erected. In 1996, in honor of the pope's visit, new bronze doors were added: the main door tells the story of Christianity in Slovenia, and the side door portrays the history of the Ljubljana Diocese. ⊠ *Dolničarjeva 1* ⊙ *Daily 7–noon and 3–7.*

16 **Trg Francoske Revolucije** (French Revolution Square). When Napoléon took Slovenia he made Ljubljana the capital of his "Illyrian Provinces." This square is dominated by Plečnik's **Ilirski Steber** (Illyrian Column), erected in 1929 to commemorate that time. ⊠ *Junction of Rimska c. and Vegova c.*

3 **Tromostovje** (Triple Bridge). This monumental structure spans the River Ljubljanica from Prešernov trg to the Old Town, taking the fortress on 1,233-foot-high Grajski Hrib (Castle Hill) as its backdrop. The three bridges started as a single span, but in 1931 the two graceful outer arched bridges, designed by Plečnik, were added. ⊠ *Prešernov trg at north end; Stritarjeva ul. at Cankarjevo nab. at south end.*

5 **Vodnikov trg** (Vodnik Square). The big and bustling flower, fruit, and vegetable market is held here Monday through Saturday from 7 to 6. An elegant riverside colonnade designed by Plečnik runs the length of the market, and a bronze statue of the Slovene poet Valentin Vodnik, after whom the square is named, overlooks the scene. ⊠ *Resljeva c. and Poljanska c.*

6 **Zmajski Most** (Dragon's Bridge). Four fire-breathing winged dragons crown the corners of this spectacular concrete-and-iron structure. ⊠ *Resljeva c.*

Where to Eat

You can eat exceptionally well in Ljubljana, but it won't be cheap. At some of the better restaurants the menu may verge on nouvelle cuisine, with seasonal dishes that make the best of local fish, game, and produce. Slovenian interest in foreign cuisines is growing; good Mexican, Spanish, Moroccan, and Greek restaurants are new fixtures in the city. For a lunchtime snack visit the Vodnikov market. Choose from tasty fried squid and whitebait in the riverside arcade by the fish section or freshly baked pies and cakes at the bakeries on the square.

$$$–$$$$ ✕ **AS.** This refined restaurant is tucked away in a courtyard near FodorsChoice Prešernov trg. AS is the place to try innovative fish dishes (priced by the ★ dekagram) and pasta specialties, all complemented by a first-rate wine list. The surroundings are old-fashioned, but the dishes are creative and modern. If you're reluctant to leave, move on to the after-hours bar in the basement. ⊠ *Knafljev prehod* ☎ *01/425–8822* ✍ *Reservations essential* ⊟ *AE, DC, MC, V.*

★ **$$$–$$$$** ✕ **Pri sv. Florijanu.** On Gornji trg, on the way to the castle, this popular restaurant serves up a new generation of Slovenian cuisine with a French touch. In every season the chef seems to have the right touch with Slovenia's bounty; porcini mushroom risotto and pumpkin ravioli in the fall, asparagus soup and *motovílec* (lamb's lettuce) salad in the spring. The service is both inviting and discreet. ⊠ *Gornji trg 20* ☎ *01/251–2214* ⊟ *AE, DC, MC, V.*

$$$ ✕ **Špajza.** A few doors away from Pri sv. Florijanu, you'll find a restaurant with a series of romantic candlelighted rooms and bohemian furnishings. The menu has local specialties like *Kraši pršut* (Karst air-dried ham) and scampi tails, as well as an inspired selection of salads. The tiramisu is exceptional. ⊠ *Gornji trg 28* ☎ *01/425–3094* ⊟ *AE, MC, V* ☉ *Closed Sun.*

$$ ✕ **Jo Peña's Cantina y Bar.** Slovenians interpret Mexican cuisine with enthusiasm in this lively and popular downtown restaurant. Bright colors, cold beer, and a friendly staff evoke memories of your best Mexican vacation. Chimichangas and tortillas don't disappoint, and guacamole—

freshly prepared table-side—is a visual treat. ✉ *Cankarjeva 6* ☎ *01/421–5800* ▭ *AE, MC, V* ⊙ *Mon.–Thurs. 10 AM–midnight, Fri. and Sat. 10–1 AM, Sun. noon–10.*

$$ ✕ **Pivnica Kratchowill.** First and foremost a microbrewery, Kratchowill also has good food. The interior is modern, but the menu is classic: beer sausage and sauerkraut, game dishes, tasty pastas, and a salad bar. The beer is brewed according to old Czech recipes. It's near the train and bus stations. ✉ *Kolodvorska 14* ☎ *01/433–3114* ▭ *AE, DC, MC, V.*

$$ ✕ **Zlata Ribica.** An ideal stop after a visit to the Sunday flea market, this popular bar and bistro is frequented by boisterous stallholders and antiques buffs. The fare includes black pudding, squid, and mushroom omelets. In the spring, tables outside are packed with locals eating fried calamari and drinking white wine spritzers. ✉ *Cankarjevo nab. 5* ☎ *01/252–1367* ▭ *AE, DC, MC, V* ⊙ *No dinner weekends.*

Where to Stay

The hotels listed here are clustered conveniently around Miklošičeva cesta, the main axis running from the train station down to the Triple Bridge. Ljubljana is expensive, but standards are high. In summer you can opt for private accommodation or university dorms for better deals; ask at the **TIC kiosk** (☎ 01/433–9475) in the train station.

$$$ **Hotel Lev.** The Hotel Lev is five minutes from the city center, though soundproof windows keep traffic from spoiling the comfort. Rooms are done in soothing pastel tones and many have stunning views of Tivoli Park and the Julian Alps outside of Ljubljana. Parking is free, and you'll have easy access to all major highways. The sushi restaurant is popular with locals. ✉ *Vošnjakova 1, 1000* ☎ *01/433–2155* 🖷 *01/434–3350* 🌐 *www.hotel-lev.si* *170 rooms* *Restaurant* ▭ *AE, DC, MC, V.*

$$–$$$ Fodor's Choice ★ **Grand Hotel Union.** The pricier Executive section of this bustling hotel complex in central Ljubljana is in a magnificent Secessionist-style building; the interior and furnishings remain typically turn-of-the-20th-century Vienna. The Comfort section is in an attached modern building overlooking a pleasant courtyard with a fountain. All hotel facilities are shared and have been modernized with great care. ✉ *Miklošičeva 1–3, 1000* ☎ *01/308–1270* 🖷 *01/308–1015* 🌐 *www.gh-union.si* *297 rooms, 12 suites* *2 restaurants, pool* ▭ *AE, DC, MC, V.*

$$ **Pension Mrak.** This friendly pension offers good value with simple but comfortable rooms and a decent restaurant. It is on a quiet side street, close to the Križanke Summer Theater. ✉ *Rimska 4, 1000* ☎ *01/421–9600* 🖷 *01/421–9655* 🌐 *www.daj-dam.si* *30 rooms* *Restaurant* ▭ *AE, DC, MC, V.*

$–$$ **Hotel Turist.** Although the rooms are basic, this hotel has the only budget-priced accommodations within the city center; it's also close to the bus and train stations. In summer breakfast is served in the terrace restaurant. ✉ *Dalmatinova 15, 1000* ☎ *01/432–9130* 🖷 *01/234–9140* 🌐 *www.hotelturist.si* *119 rooms* *2 restaurants* ▭ *AE, DC, MC, V.*

Nightlife & the Arts

The Arts

Ljubljana's **International Summer Festival,** running through July and August, is held in Plečnik's open-air Križanke theater. Musical, theatrical, and dance performances attract acclaimed artists from all over the world. ✉ *Trg Francoske Revolucije 1–2* ☎ *01/241–6000.*

The **Jazz Festival** runs through June. *Box Office,* ✉ *Cankarjev Dom, Prešernova 10* ☎ *01/241–7100.*

Nightlife

Slovenes old and young alike enjoy music and a few drinks, especially at tables down by the river in nice weather. The bars and clubs listed here are all within walking distance of the center. Long-standing **Jazz Club Gajo** (⊠ Beethovnova 8 ☎ 01/425–3206) is an intimate place to hear top international jazz talent. **K4** (⊠ Kersnikova 4 ☎ 01/431–7010), a student-run nightclub attached to the university, is something of an institution, attracting a young and alternative crowd.

Club-cum-restaurant **Bachus Center** (⊠ Kongresni trg 3 ☎ 01/241–8244) is filled with zebra print bar stools and serves the trendiest cocktails. With a large terrace and glamorous clientele, **Cafe Maček** (⊠ Krojaška 5 ☎ 01/425–3791) is *the* place to be seen down by the river. Hip newcomer **Cafe Galerija** (⊠ Mestni trg 5 ☎ 01/241–1770) serves stylish cocktails by candlelight in a North Africa–inspired hideout.

Shopping

The Sunday-morning flea market is held on Cankarjevo nabrežje, near the Triple Bridge.

Ljubljana Essentials

AIR TRAVEL TO & FROM LJUBLJANA

Ljubljana's airport is at Brnik, 22 km (14 mi) north of the city. A shuttle bus runs between the airport and Ljubljana and other nearby destinations.

🛈 **Brnik Airport** ☎ 04/206-1981.

BUS TRAVEL WITHIN LJUBLJANA

Tokens are sold at kiosks and post offices. As you board the bus, drop your token into the box by the driver. The cost is a little higher if you pay in change. During the day, buses operate every half hour and cover an extensive network; at night they are less frequent.

CONSULATES

🛈 **Australia** ⊠ Trg Republike 3/XII ☎ 01/425-4252 🖷 01/426-4721.

EMERGENCIES

🛈 **Ambulance and Fire Emergencies** ☎ 112. **Emergency Road Assistance** ☎ 987. **Lekarna Miklošič Pharmacy** ⊠ Miklošičeva 24, Ljubljana ☎ 01/231-4558. **Ljubljana Emergency Medical Services** ☎ 01/232-3060. **Police Emergencies** ☎ 113.

ENGLISH-LANGUAGE MEDIA

MK Knjigarna Konzorcij has a good selection of English books and magazines on the upper floor.

🛈 **Bookstores MK Knjigarna Konzorcij** ⊠ Slovenska 29 ☎ 01/425-0196.

TAXIS

Private taxis operate 24 hours a day. Telephone from your hotel or hail one in the street. Drivers are bound by law to display and run a meter.

🛈 **Private taxis** ☎ 01/9700 through 01/9709.

TOURS

Informative and amusing sightseeing walks, organized by Ljubljana Promotion Center (⊕ www.ljubljana-tourism.si), depart from the Magistrat (Town Hall) June, Mon.–Thurs. 5 PM, Fri.–Sun. 11 AM and 5 PM; July and Aug., daily 11 AM and 5 PM; Sept., Mon.–Thurs. 5 PM, weekends 11 AM and 5 PM; October–May, weekends at 11 AM.

🛈 **Fees & Schedules Magistrat** (Town Hall) ⊠ Mestni trg 1.

TRAIN TRAVEL

The train station, close to the city center, has a tourist office to help travelers find accommodations in hotels, pensions, and apartments.

🚉 **Train station** ✉ Trg OF 6 ☎ 01/291-3332.

VISITOR INFORMATION

🚉 **Turistično Informacijski Center** (Tourist Information Center (TIC)) ✉ Stritarjeva ☎ 01/306-1215 🌐 www.ljubljana-tourism.si.

TRIGLAV NATIONAL PARK & THE SOČA VALLEY

Northwest of Ljubljana lies a region of mountain and lakeside resorts complete with thermal springs, ski trails, and historic religious shrines. The Julian Alps, lying at the junction of the borders of Italy, Austria, and Slovenia, are contained within Triglav National Park. Lake Bohinj and the small waterside settlement of Ribčev Laz are also within the national park, though Lake Bled and the town of Bled lie just outside the park's boundary. The Alpine village of Kranjska Gora is situated on the rim of the park. The Soča River begins within the park, then flows southwest to form the beautiful Soča Valley. The river passes through Kobarid and snakes south before crossing over into Italy (where it's known as the Isonzo). The region has unspoiled countryside and magnificent mountain walks, many on well-marked trails. Local tourist information centers can supply maps and further details.

Bled

Bled, 50 km (31 mi) northwest of Ljubljana, is among the most magnificently situated mountain resorts in Europe. The healing powers of its thermal springs were known during the 17th century; in the early 19th century the aristocracy arrived to bask in Bled's tranquil Alpine surroundings. Many hotels and recreational outlets operate here, and facilities for rowing, hiking, swimming, boating, biking, tennis, and horseback riding are available. In winter there's skiing and ice-skating at the nearby high-altitude resort of Zatrnik.

Blejsko Jezero (Lake Bled), surrounded by forests, is nestled within a circle of mountains, with a castle on one side and a promenade beneath stately chestnut trees on the other. Horse-drawn carriages clip-clop along the promenade while swans glide on the water. On a minuscule island in the lake the lovely **Cerkov Svetega Martina** (St. Martin's Pilgrimage Church) rises from within a circle of red roofs and trees. Graceful, old-fashioned canopied wooden boats called *pletna*, propelled by oarsmen standing aft, carry passengers to the island.

☙ The stately 16th-century **Grad** (Castle) perches above the lake at the summit of a steep cliff, against the backdrop of the Julian Alps and Mt. Triglav. You can climb up to the castle for fine views of the lake, the resort, and the surrounding countryside. Inside is an exhibit tracing the development of the castle through the centuries, with archaeological finds and period furniture. ☎ 04/574-1230 ☉ *Mar.–Oct., daily 8–7; Nov.–Feb., daily 9–4.*

☙ The **Vintgar Gorge** was cut between precipitous cliffs by the clear river Radovna, which flows over numerous waterfalls and through pools and rapids. A signed path up the gorge leads over bridges and along wooden walkways and galleries. ✉ *5 km (3 mi) northeast of Bled on road to Pokljuka/Zg. Gorje.*

★ **$$$** ✕ **Gostilna Lectar.** This warm, country-inn restaurant serves an impressive selection of traditional dishes. For a cross section of the local cuisine, try the pumpkin soup, the Peasant's Plate (buckwheat dumplings, mixed smoked meats, potatoes, and fresh steamed vegetables), and the apple strudel. The restaurant is 9 km (5½ mi) south of Bled on the E61. ⊠ *Linhartov trg 2 Radovljica* ☎ *04/531–5642* ⊟ *AE, DC, MC, V.*

$$ ✕ **Gostilna pri Planincu.** This friendly joint is busy year-round. Locals meet here to enjoy morning coffee or a bargain set-menu lunch, or just to drink the cheapest beer in town. While rowdy farmers occupy the front bar, lovers share a candlelighted supper in the dining room. Portions are "for people who work all day": roast chicken and chips, steak and mushrooms, black pudding and turnips. Walnut *štrukle* (dumplings) are served with cream. ⊠ *Grajska 8* ☎ *04/574–1613* ⊟ *AE, DC, MC, V.*

★ **$$$** ▦ **Grand Hotel Toplice.** This old-fashioned, ivy-covered resort hotel has been favored by British travelers since the 1920s. Directly on the lake, the main building has balconies and big windows from which you can take in dramatic views of the castle and the Julian Alps. The rooms, the lounges, and the bar are all furnished with antiques and heirloom rugs. ⊠ *C. Svobode 20, 4260* ☎ *04/579–1000* ▤ *04/574–1841* ⊕ *www.hotel-toplice.com* ⇆ *206 rooms* ⚬ *3 restaurants, bar* ⊟ *AE, DC, MC, V* ⫽◯⫽ *BP.*

$$$ ▦ **Vila Bled.** Late Yugoslav president Tito was the gracious host to numerous 20th-century statesmen at this former royal residence, amid 15 acres of gardens overlooking the lake. It was converted into a luxurious small-scale hotel in 1984 and became part of the Relais & Chateaux association in 1987. Among the elegant touches are hand-embroidered linen sheets, art deco furnishings, antique rugs, and Asian vases. ⊠ *C. Svobode 26, 4260* ☎ *04/579–1500* ▤ *04/574–1320* ⊕ *www.vila-bled.com* ⇆ *10 rooms, 20 suites* ⚬ *Restaurant, bar* ⊟ *AE, DC, MC, V* ⫽◯⫽ *BP.*

$ ▦ **Bledec Youth Hostel.** Just 5 minutes from the lake and 10 minutes from the castle, Bledec is one of the cleanest and most comfortable youth hostels in Europe. Rooms have mostly three or four beds; there are no private double rooms. ⊠ *Grajska 17, 4260* ☎ *04/574–5250* ▤ *04/574–5251* ⊕ *www.mlino.si* ⇆ *13 rooms (all with shared baths)* ⚬ *Restaurant, bar* ⊟ *MC* ⊙ *Closed Nov.* ⫽◯⫽ *BP.*

Bohinjsko Jezero

A 26-km (16-mi) drive west from Bled will take you to Bohinjsko Jezero (Lake Bohinj) in Triglavski Narodni Park (Triglav National Park). In a valley surrounded by the steep walls of the Julian Alps, at an altitude of 1,715 feet, this deep-blue, 4½-km-long (3-mi-long) lake is even more dramatically situated than Bled and not nearly as developed.

At the lakeside, the small, exquisite 15th-century Gothic church of **Sveti Janez** (St. John), with a fine bell tower, contains a number of notable 15th- and 16th-century frescoes. ⊙ *Daily 9–noon and 4–7.*

At the west end of the lake a cable car leads up **Mt. Vogel** to a height of 5,035 feet. Here you have spectacular views of the Julian Alps massif and the Bohinj Valley and lake. From the cable-car base the road continues 5 km (3 mi) beyond the lake to the point where the waters of the Savica make a tremendous leap over a 195-foot waterfall.

$ ▦ **Hotel Bellevue.** As the name suggests, the Bellevue affords wonderful views of the lake, so request a room that allows you to see it. Agatha Christie fell in love with this old-fashioned hotel and stayed one month here while working on *Murder on the Orient Express.* ⊠ *Ribčev Laz*

65, 4265 Bohinj ☎ *04/572–3331* 🖷 *04/572–3684* 📞 *76 rooms* ♨ *2 restaurants, bar* ⊟ *AE, DC, MC, V* ⏚⧫ *BP.*

Kranjska Gora

Kranjska Gora, 39 km (24 mi) northwest of Bled, is one of the largest winter tourist centers in Slovenia, overseen by some of the country's highest peaks. In summer the resort caters mainly to hiking and mountaineering enthusiasts.

From Kranjska Gora head south over the **Vršič Pass**, 5,252 feet above sea level. You'll then descend into the beautiful Soča Valley, winding through the foothills to the west of Triglav Peak and occasionally plunging through tunnels.

Kobarid

Along the magnificent turquoise-color Soča River, running parallel to the Italian border, is the pretty market town of Kobarid, 41 km (25 mi) from Kranjska Gora.

In the center of town the **Kobariški muzej** (Kobarid Museum) gives a 20-minute presentation of the tragic fighting that took place here during World War I, as recorded in Hemingway's *A Farewell to Arms.* ⊠ *Gregorčičeva 10* ☎ *05/389–0000* ⊗ *Daily 9–7.*

$$ ✕🏨 **Hotel Hvala.** Delightful and family-run, this welcoming hotel is

FodorśChoice known locally for its restaurant, Restauracija Topli Val, which serves

★ local trout and freshwater crayfish, as well as mushrooms and truffles in season. Italians drive over the border just to eat here. ⊠ *Trg Svobode 1, 5222* ☎ *05/389–9300* 🖷 *05/388–5322* ⊕ *www.topli-val-sp.si* 📞 *28 rooms, 4 suites* ♨ *Restaurant* ⊟ *AE, DC, MC, V* ⏚⧫ *BP.*

Triglav National Park & the Soča Valley Essentials

BIKE TRAVEL

You can rent mountain bikes at Bohinjsko Jezero through Alpinum.
🏷 Bike Rentals **Alpinum** ⊠ Ribčev Laz 50 ☎ 04/572-3446 ⊕ www.alpinum.net.

BUS TRAVEL

Hourly buses link Ljubljana to Bled, Bohinjsko Jezero, and Kranjska Gora. There are several buses daily from Ljubljana to Kobarid.

CAR TRAVEL

From Ljubljana a toll road (E63) runs 42 km (26 mi) northwest past Kranj; from there road E651 leads to the resorts of Bled and Kranjska Gora.

TOURS

Alpinum organizes guided mountain-hiking and climbing tours in Triglav National Park, as well as rafting and kayaking trips down the Soča River. Slovenijaturist arranges a trip on a steam locomotive, following the Bohinj line, which runs through the Soča Valley, operating every Thursday mid-June to mid-September.
🏷 **Alpinum** ☎ 04/572-3446. **Slovenijaturist** ☎ 01/234-4829.

VISITOR INFORMATION

🏷 **Bled** ⊠ C. Svobode 15, 4260 Bled ☎ 04/574-1122 ⊕ www.bled.si. **Bohinjsko Jezero** ⊠ Ribčev Laz 48, 4265 Bohinjsko Jezero ☎ 04/574-6010 ⊕ www.bohinj.si. **Kobarid** ⊠ Trg Svobode 2, 5222 Kobarid ☎ 05/389-9200. **Kranjska Gora** ⊠ Tičarjeva 2, 4280 Kranjska Gora ☎ 04/588-1768 ⊕ www.kranjska-gora.si.

ADRIATIC COAST
& KARST HINTERLAND

Adriatic Coast

Backed by hills planted with olive groves and vineyards, this tiny strip of coast, only 42 km (26 mi) long, is dominated by the towns of Koper, Piran, and Portorož. Following centuries under the Republic of Venice, the region remains culturally and spiritually connected to Italy. The best Venetian architecture of the area can still be seen in the delightful medieval town of Piran. Portorož is a more commercial resort, and Koper is Slovenia's largest port.

Piran

The jewel of the Slovenian coast, the medieval walled Venetian town of Piran stands compact on a small peninsula, capped by a neo-Gothic lighthouse and presided over by a hilltop Romanesque cathedral. Narrow, winding, cobbled streets lead to the main square, Trg Tartini, which in turn opens out onto a charming harbor.

★ $-$$ 🏨 **Hotel Tartini.** The old facade hides a modern interior with a spacious central atrium. Most rooms have terraces with views of surrounding red-tile roofs or the harbor. The location, overlooking the piazza Trg Tartini, is out of this world. ✉ *Trg Tartini 15, 6330* ☎ *05/671–1666* 📠 *05/671–1665* 📑 *43 rooms, 2 suites* 🍴 *Restaurant* ☰ *AE, DC, MC, V.*

Portorož

Known for its thermal spas, Portorož has a pleasant Mediterranean climate. Its location on a south-facing slope keeps the city warm and blocks cold northern air even in winter. In summer vacationers fill the town in pursuit of the pleasures of the sea and the healing spas.

★ $$-$$$ ✕ **Ribič.** Two kilometers (1 mi) down the coast from Portorož at Seča, Ribič may just be the best fish restaurant in the area. Specialties include baked sea bass with porcini mushrooms, and risotto Alpe Adria, which combines wild mushrooms from the Alps and fresh scampi from the Adriatic. In summer you can eat in the garden. ✉ *Seča* ☎ *05/677–0790* ☰ *AE, DC, MC, V* ☺ *Closed Tues.*

$$ 🏨 **Hotel Palace.** At this modern hotel resort complex the elegant thermal spa center offers massages and medical treatments. Rooms are comfortable, the service professional. ✉ *Obala 45, 6320* ☎ *05/696–1025* 📠 *05/696–9003* 📑 *150 rooms* 🍴 *Restaurant, 2 pools (1 indoor)* ☰ *AE, DC, MC, V.*

Karst Hinterland

The name of this limestone plateau between Ljubljana and the coast is the source of the word "karst," which describes a geological phenomenon whose typical features include sinkholes, underground caves, and streams.

Postojnska Jama

Postojnska Jama (Postojna Cave) is one of the largest networks of caves in the world, with 23 km (14 mi) of underground passageways. A miniature train takes you through the first 7 km (4½ mi) to reveal a succession of well-lighted rock formations. This strange underground world is home of the snakelike "human fish," on view in an aquarium in the Great Hall. Eyeless and colorless because of countless millennia of life in total darkness, these amphibians can live for up to 60 years. Temperatures average 8°C (46°F) year-round, so in summer have a jacket handy or rent a woolen cloak at the entrance. Tours leave every half hour in summer, hourly the rest of the year. ✉ *Jamska c. 30, Postojna* ☎ *05/ 700–0100* ⊘ *May–Sept., daily 9–6; Apr. and Oct., daily 10–4; Nov.–Mar., weekdays 10–2, weekends 10–4* 🎫 *SIT2,600.*

Škocjanske Jame

The Škocjanske Jame (Škocjan Caves) at Matavun, near Divača, is on UNESCO's list of World Natural and Cultural Heritage sites. These caves require walking, but the beauty of the caverns makes the effort worthwhile. Here, the Reka River thunders along an underground channel, amid a wondrous world of stalactites and stalagmites. One-hour tours leave hourly. ✉ *Matavun 12, 6215 Divača* ☎ *05/763–2840* ⊘ *June–Sept., daily 10, 11:30, 1–5 (tours leave hourly); Apr., May, Oct., tours daily at 10, 1, and 3:30; Nov.–Mar., tours weekdays at 10, weekends at 10 and 3.*

Lipica

The **Kobilarna Lipica** (Lipica Stud Farm) in Sežana is the birthplace of the Lipizzaner white horses. Founded in 1580 by the Austrian archduke Karl II, the farm still supplies Lipizzaners to the Spanish Riding School in Vienna. Lipica has developed into a modern sports complex, with two hotels, an indoor riding arena, a swimming pool, and a golf course. The stables are open to the public, and riding classes are available. ✉ *Lipica 5, 6210 Sežana* ☎ *05/739–1580* ⊕ *www.lipica.org* ⊘ *Stables, July and Aug., daily 9–6; Apr.–June, Sept., and Oct., daily 10–5; Nov.–Mar., daily 11–3. Dressage performances June–Oct., Tues., Fri., and Sun. at 3.*

Adriatic Coast & Karst Hinterland Essentials

BOAT & FERRY TRAVEL
See Boat & Ferry Travel *in* Slovenia A to Z.

BUS TRAVEL
Buses connect the region to Ljubljana and to Trieste in Italy. For information contact Lucija Bus Station, which serves Portorož and the coast.
🚌 **Lucija Bus Station** ☎ 05/677-0468.

CAR TRAVEL
A drive of 52 km (32 mi) west from Ljubljana on the toll road (marked A-10) will bring you to the Karst region; 125 km (78 mi) southwest of Ljubljana (via the A-10) lies the Adriatic Coast.

TRAIN TRAVEL
All trains from Ljubljana to Venice pass through the Karst region, stopping at Postojna, Divača, and Sežana. A train from Ljubljana to Koper serves the coast.

VISITOR INFORMATION
Along the coast, private lodgings provide a cheap alternative to hotels. Owners usually live on the ground floor and let rooms or apartments upstairs. Contact local tourist information centers for details.
🚌 **Lipica** ✉ Lipica 5 ☎ 05/739-1580. **Piran** ✉ Trg Tartini 2 ☎ 05/673-0220. **Portorož** ✉ Obala 16 ☎ 05/674-0231. **Postojna** ✉ Jamska c. 30 ☎ 05/720-1061.

MARIBOR & PTUJ

During the 1st century AD, Poetovio, now known as Ptuj, was the largest Roman settlement in the region. Much later, in the 13th century, Maribor was founded. Originally given the German name Marchburg, the city took its Slavic name in 1836. For centuries the two towns competed for economic and cultural prominence, with Maribor finally gaining the lead in 1846, when a new railway line connected the city to Vienna and Trieste.

Maribor

More geared toward business travelers than tourists, Maribor is Slovenia's second-largest city. However, the Old Town has retained a core of ornate 18th- and 19th-century town houses, typical of imperial Austria, and is worth a visit. The heart of the Old Town is **Rotovški trg,** with the **Kužno Znamenje** (Plague Memorial) at its center and overlooked by the proud 16th-century Renaissance **Rotovž** (Town Hall).

From Rotovški trg, a number of traffic-free streets lead down to a riverside promenade, known as **Lent.** It is lined with bars, terrace cafés, restaurants, and boutiques.

A little way upstream from the riverside promenade, an old vine, **Stara Trta,** carefully trained along the facade of a former inn, is believed to date back to the 16th century and thus to be the oldest continuously producing vine in Europe. ⊠ *Vojasniska 8.*

Inside the **Vodni Stolp** (Water Tower), a former defense tower, is the **Vinoteka Slovenskih Vin** (Slovenian Wine Shop). Here you can sample from and purchase more than 500 different Slovenian vintages. ⊠ *Usnjarska 10* ☎ *02/251–7743.*

The **Grad** (castle) has Renaissance and baroque elements grafted onto its original Gothic core, built in 1478. Within the castle is the **Pokrajinski Muzej** (Regional Museum), with regional costumes and uniforms, Roman relics, an art gallery, and a collection of arms and armor. The main salon, where Franz Liszt (1811–86) gave recitals, is decorated with frescoes and ceiling paintings. ⊠ *Grajska ul. 2* ☎ *02/228–3551* ☉ *Mid-Apr.–Nov., Tues.–Sat. 9–5, Sun. 10–2.*

$$$ ✕ **Toti Rotovž.** Close to the Town Hall and Plague Memorial, this building has been restored to reveal vaulted brick ceilings and terra-cotta floors. The ground-level restaurant serves typical Slovenian dishes, and the *klet* (wine cellar) in the basement cooks up barbecued steaks. ⊠ *Glavni trg 14* ☎ *02/228–7650* 🖃 *AE, DC, MC, V.*

$ 🏨 **Hotel Orel.** The four-story prewar building on the main square has a pleasant restaurant at street level. The rooms are acceptable, and the service is friendly. ⊠ *Grajski trg 3a, 2000* ☎ *02/251–6700* 🖷 *02/251–8497* 🛏 *146 rooms, 7 suites* ⚭ *Restaurant* 🖃 *AE, DC, MC, V.*

Ptuj

Ptuj, built beside the Drava River and crowned by a hilltop castle, hits the national news each year in February with its extraordinary carnival celebration, known as Kurentovanje. South of Ptuj lie the hills of Haloze, famous for quality white wines.

Ptujski Grad (Ptuj Castle) stands at the top of a steep hill in the center of town. Planned around a baroque courtyard, the castle has a museum with musical instruments, an armory, 15th-century paintings, and period furniture. ⊠ *Grajska Raven* ☎ *02/771–3081* ☉ *Mid-Apr.–mid-Oct., daily 9–6; mid-Oct.–mid Apr., daily 9–4.*

★ **Vinska Klet** (Ptuj Wine Cellars) offers a tasting session with five different wines, bread, and cheese, plus a bottle to take home. Tour the underground cellars and enjoy a sound and video presentation that takes you through the seasons of wine making at the vineyards. The wines stocked here come predominantly from the Haloze Hills. ⊠ *Trstenjakova 6* ☎ *02/787–9810* ☉ *Daily 8–6; tasting sessions Fri.–Sun. 11 AM (daily for groups, but call first).*

Maribor & Ptuj Essentials

AIR TRAVEL
🛪 **Maribor Airport** ☎ 02/629-1790.

CAR TRAVEL
To reach Maribor from Ljubljana take the E57; to reach Ptuj turn off at Slovenska Bistrica.

TRAIN TRAVEL
Regular service links Ljubljana and Maribor; several international trains continue to Graz and Vienna. Change at Pragersko for Ptuj. For information contact Maribor Train Station.
🚆 **Maribor Train Station** ☎ 02/292-2100.

VISITOR INFORMATION
In summer, Maribor university dorms are open to visitors, offering a cheap alternative to hotels. Ask at the tourist information center for details.
🛈 **Maribor** ✉ Partizanska 47 ☎ 02/234-6611 ⊕ www.maribor.si. **Ptuj** ✉ Slovenski trg 14 ☎ 02/771-5691 ⊕ www.ptuj.si.

SPAIN

MADRID, CASTILE, BARCELONA, ANDALUSIA, COSTA DEL SOL & GIBRALTAR

MUCH MORE THAN flamenco, bullfights, and white hillside villages, modern Spain has everything from cutting-edge art museums to quaint fishing ports, green highland valleys, soaring cathedrals, medieval towns, designer cuisine, spirited nightlife, and an immense treasury of painting and sculpture.

As most Hispanists are quick to point out, Spain is really several countries in one, each with its own proud culture and character, its own distinctive cuisine, even its own language. Andalusia, in the south, comes closest to postcard images of Spain: rolling hills dotted with whitewashed villages and olive trees. Andalusia's capital, Seville, is known for flamenco music and dance; for beautiful women dressed in ruffled polka-dot dresses at its April Fair; and for the solemn processions of penitents during Semana Santa (Holy Week). The region is also marked by its Moorish heritage, and remnants of its Islamic past abound, from the red-and-white-striped arches of Córdoba's mosque to Spain's most visited monument, Granada's Alhambra Palace. Andalusia is known for tapas; provincial specialties include mounds of fried fish and shellfish called *frituras,* olives, cured ham, and the sherries of Jerez. On the Andalusian coast, the famed Costa del Sol, you can join the jet set at Marbella.

Spain's vast center is still shaped by its role as a battlefield for centuries of contests between Moorish and Christian armies. Turreted castles overlook the bleak plains of Castile–La Mancha, the land of Don Quixote, and Castile–León, once known as Old Castile. And in Castile you'll discover Toledo, where Jews, Moors, and Christians lived and worked together before the Christian Reconquest that concluded in the late 15th century. Castile is studded with medieval jewels, including Segovia, the university city of Salamanca, and the fortress town of Ávila. The people of central Spain are simple, warm, and hearty—not unlike their cuisine (think roast lamb or suckling pig accompanied by powerful red wines from the Valdepeñas or Ribera del Duero regions).

At the hub of it all is Madrid, one of the liveliest capitals in Europe. Madrid is the seat of the Spanish government, a center for the national media, and the home of dozens of embassies, but its sophistication is largely a veneer. Scratch the surface, and beyond Madrid's designer boutiques and chic restaurants you'll find a simple Castilian town. Life here is lived in cafés and rustic taverns; all it takes to become a local is to duck inside.

Madrid is also a magnet for art lovers, with three world-class museums—the Prado, the Reina Sofía, and the Thyssen-Bornemisza—all along a

1-km (½-mi) stretch of leafy promenade. The city's restaurants serve fine cuisine from all of Spain's regions but are probably best known for their seafood, which arrives daily from the coasts and has earned landlocked Madrid an affectionate reputation as Spain's first port.

Catalonia—with a population of 6 million Catalan speakers—is Spain's richest and most industrial region. Its capital, Barcelona, rivals Madrid for power and is generally regarded as the winner in culture and style. Barcelona's tree-lined streets, art nouveau architecture, and renovated waterfront still gleam from the scouring they received for the 1992 Summer Olympics—an event that not only focused the world's attention on this Mediterranean port but also provided the city with new museums, sports facilities, and restaurants. The spirit of modernist architect Antoni Gaudí lives on both in his Sagrada Família church, which is still unfinished, and in the Catalan passion for radical, playful design. Barcelona's 2004 Forum de les Cultures has sparked a new round of construction and renovation in the ultramodern Diagonal Mar District.

Since joining the European Union (EU) in 1986, Spain has become one of the most technologically up-to-date countries in Europe. The most obvious improvement for travelers is the nationwide network of superhighways and the high-speed AVE train linking Seville and Córdoba to Madrid. The Madrid–Barcelona AVE line is scheduled to be completed in late 2004. Happily, Spain's uniqueness has not been tossed aside. Real siestas are on the wane these days, but shops still close at midday, and three-hour lunches are commonplace. Young adults still live with their parents until marriage. Bullfights continue despite protests from animal-rights activists. And flamenco is making a strong comeback.

Most exciting for anyone vacationing in Spain is the nationwide insistence on enjoying life. Whether that means strolling in the park with the family on a Sunday afternoon, lingering over a weekday lunch, or socializing with friends until dawn, a zest for living life to its fullest is Spain's greatest contribution to Europe.

SPAIN A TO Z

To research prices, get advice from other travelers, and book travel arrangements, visit www.fodors.com.

ADDRESSES
In addresses, the word *Calle* (street) is abbreviated C. Addresses with the abbreviation s/n mean *sin numero,* or "without number."

AIR TRAVEL
Domestic airfares are high by U.S. standards, although deregulation is pushing prices lower. A frequent shuttle service connects Madrid and Barcelona.

CARRIERS Iberia and its subsidiary Aviaco operate a wide network of domestic flights, linking Spain's major cities and the Balearic Islands. Iberia has its own offices in most major Spanish cities and acts as agent for Aviaco. You can also book flights at most travel agencies. Air Europa offers slightly cheaper service on domestic flights. Spanair is another Spanish domestic airline offering good regional rates. For information on other airlines' flights to and within Spain, call the airline itself, or call the Madrid airport and ask for the airline.

🛪 **Air Europa** ☎ 902/401501 ⊕ www.air-europa.com. **Iberia** ✉ Velázquez 130, Madrid ☎ 902/400500 ⊕ www.iberia.com. **Madrid-Barajas Airport** ☎ 91/305-8343 through 91/305-8346. **Spanair** ☎ 902/131415 ⊕ www.spanair.com.

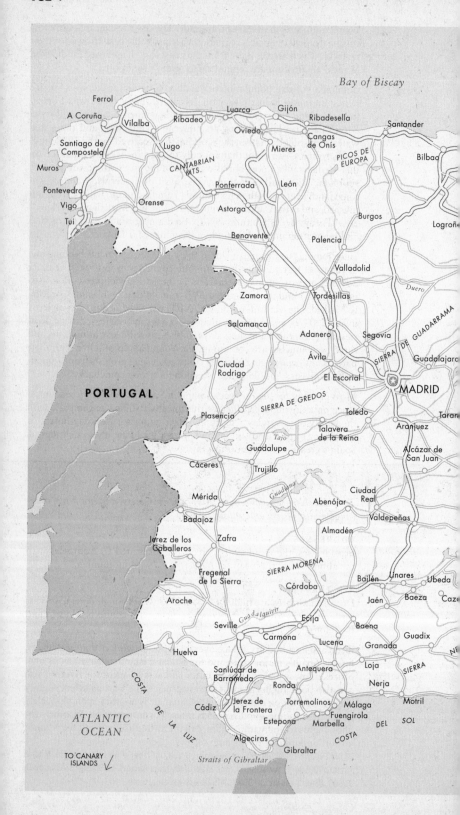

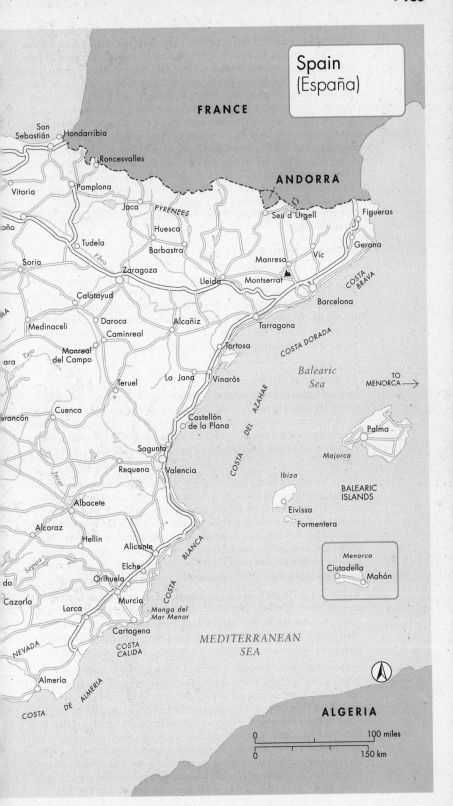

Spain (España)

FRANCE

ANDORRA

San Sebastián
Hondarribia
Roncesvalles
Vitoria
Pamplona
Jaca
PYRENEES
ño
Tudela
Huesca
Barbastro
Soria
Zaragoza
Lleida
Seu d'Urgell
Figueras
Manresa
Vic
Gerona
Montserrat
COSTA BRAVA
Calotayud
Daroca
Caminreal
Alcañiz
Barcelona
Medinaceli
Tarragona
Monreal del Campo
Tortosa
COSTA DORADA
ara
Tajo
Teruel
La Jana
Vinaròs
Balearic Sea
TO MENORCA →
rancón
Cuenca
Castellón de la Plana
COSTA DEL AZAHAR
Palma
Sagunto
Majorca
Requena
Valencia
Ibiza
BALEARIC ISLANDS
Albacete
Eivissa
Formentera
Alcaraz
Hellín
Alicante
COSTA BLANCA
Menorca
Ciutadella
Mahón
da
Elche
Orihuela
Cazorla
Murcia
Manga del Mar Menor
MEDITERRANEAN SEA
Lorca
Cartagena
COSTA CALIDA
NEVADA
Almería
ALGERIA
COSTA
DE ALMERIA

Ebro

Júcar

Segura

0   100 miles
0   150 km

BUS TRAVEL

Spain has an excellent bus network. There is no national or nationwide bus company, but Enatcar is a consortium of individual, regional bus companies that together cover most of the country. There are also numerous local companies. Buses tend to be more frequent than trains, are sometimes cheaper, and often allow you to see more of the countryside. Some of those on major routes are now quite luxurious; but although they designate no-smoking seats, it's hard to cordon smoke in a bus, so you may be in for a smokier ride than you're used to. On major routes and at holiday times, buy your ticket a day or two in advance. Some cities have central bus stations, but in many of these, including Madrid and Barcelona, buses leave from various boarding points; always check with the local tourist office. Unlike train stations, bus stations usually have facilities for luggage storage.

🚍 **Enatcar main office** ✉ Estación Sur de Autobuses, Calle Méndez Álvaro, Madrid ☎ 91/754-9950.

BUSINESS HOURS

Banks are open Monday–Saturday 8:30 or 9 until 2 from October through June; in summer they are closed on Saturday. Hours for museums and churches vary; most are open in the morning, but most museums close one day a week, often Monday. Stores are open weekdays from 9 or 10 until 1:30 or 2, then in the afternoon from around 5 to 8. Larger department stores and supermarkets do not close at midday. In some cities, especially in summer, stores close on Saturday afternoon.

CAR TRAVEL

GASOLINE All rental cars use unleaded gas (*sin plomo*). Gas costs about €1 per liter for super (98 octane) and €.90 per liter for regular (95 octane). Many stations are self-service, though prices are the same as those at full-service stations, and there's no need to tip for a simple fill-up. You simply unhook the nozzle, pump the gas, and then pay. At night, however, you must pay before you fill up. All gas stations accept credit cards.

PARKING Check locally for parking restrictions. A yellow line along the curb indicates a no-parking zone. Blue markings in the street indicate a metered parking area. Look for the nearest meter, insert coins to cover the time you plan to park, and place the receipt in a visible spot inside the windshield. Beware of parking in no-parking zones or in areas where parking is allowed for residents only; cars are towed promptly. Thefts are common, so it's safer to leave your car in one of the many staffed parking lots; charges are reasonable.

ROAD CONDITIONS Roads marked *A* are four-lane highways, which can be either toll roads (*autopista*) or freeways (*autovía*). N stands for national or main roads and C for country roads. Spain's huge road-improvement scheme has been largely completed, but many N roads are still single-lane, and the going can be slow. Tolls vary but are high.

RULES OF THE ROAD Spaniards drive on the right. The use of horns and high-beam headlights is forbidden in cities. Front seat belts are compulsory; children under age 10 may not ride in front seats. At traffic circles, cars already in the circle have right of way. Motorists entering freeways should not expect other vehicles to merge left or give way; a full stop is often required before entering traffic. Your home driver's license is essential and must be carried with you at all times, along with your insurance card and vehicle registration. If you are bringing your own car into Spain, you will also need an International Driver's License and a proof-of-insurance Green Card. Speed limits are 120 kph (74 mph) on autopistas, 100 kph (62 mph) on N roads, 90 kph (56 mph) on C roads, and 60 kph (37 mph) in cities unless otherwise signposted.

CUSTOMS & DUTIES

For details on imports and duty-free limits, *see* Customs & Duties *in* Smart Travel Tips.

EATING & DRINKING

Spain offers a choice of restaurants, tapas bars, and cafés. Restaurants are strictly for lunch and dinner; they do not serve breakfast. Tapas bars are ideal for a glass of wine or beer accompanied by appetizers. Cafés, called *cafeterías*, are basically coffee shops that serve snacks, light meals, tapas, and pastries along with coffee, tea, and alcoholic drinks. They also serve breakfast.

Spanish restaurants are officially classified from five forks down to one fork, with most places earning two or three forks. Prices are for one dinner entrée. Sales tax (IVA) is usually included in the menu price; check the menu for *IVA incluído* or *IVA no incluído*. When it's not included, an additional 7% will be added to your bill. Most restaurants have a prix-fixe menu called a *menú del día*, generally available only at lunch. *Menús* are usually the cheapest way to eat; à la carte dining is more expensive. Service charges are generally included in your bill, though leaving 5%–10% extra is customary.

WHAT IT COSTS In Euros			
$$$$	**$$$**	**$$**	**$**
MAJOR CITIES*			
AT DINNER over €25	€18–€25	€12–€18	under €12
OTHER AREAS			
AT DINNER over €20	€15–€20	€10–€15	under €10

Prices are per person for a main course. *Major cities are Barcelona and Madrid. Other areas includes the colony of Gibraltar.

MEALTIMES   Mealtimes in Spain are much later than in any other European country. Lunch begins between 1:30 and 2 in the afternoon. Dinner is usually available from 8:30 on, but it's more often taken at 9:30 or 10, especially in larger cities and resorts. Lunch is the main meal. Tapas bars are busiest between noon and 2 and from 8 PM on. Cafés are usually open from around 8 AM to midnight.

RESERVATIONS &   In $$$$ restaurants, jacket and tie are not uncommon but are by no means
DRESS   the norm. Generally, casual, though stylish, dress is fine.

EMBASSIES

The following countries also maintain consular offices in Barcelona.

🇦🇺 Australia ⊠ Plaza del Descubridor Diego de Ordás 3, Madrid ☎ 91/441-9300.
🇨🇦 Canada ⊠ Núñez de Balboa 35, Madrid ☎ 91/431-4300.
🇳🇿 New Zealand ⊠ Plaza de La Lealtad 2, Madrid ☎ 91/523-0226.
🇬🇧 United Kingdom ⊠ Fernando el Santo 16, Madrid ☎ 91/700-8200.
🇺🇸 United States ⊠ Serrano 75, Madrid ☎ 91/577-4000.

HEALTH

FOOD & DRINK   Tap water is safe to drink in all but the remotest villages. In Madrid tap water is excellent; in Barcelona it's safe and getting tastier. However, most Spaniards drink bottled mineral water; ask for either *agua sin gas* (without bubbles) or *agua con gas* (with bubbles). A good paella should be served only at lunchtime and should be prepared to order (usually 30 minutes); beware of paella dinners (tourist traps), the frozen offerings of *paelladors,* any restaurant with a pictorial menu out front, or prices that look too good to be true.

HOLIDAYS

New Year's; Epiphany (January 6); Good Friday; Easter; May Day (May 1); St. James's Day (July 25); Assumption (August 15); National Day (October 12); All Saints' Day (November 1); Constitution (December 6); Immaculate Conception (December 8); Christmas. Local holidays vary from one Autonomous Community, or province, to another.

LANGUAGE

Spanish (called Castellano, or Castilian) is spoken and understood throughout Spain. However, the Basques speak Euskera; in Catalonia, you'll hear Catalan; and in Galicia, Gallego. If you don't speak Spanish, you should have little trouble finding people who speak English in major cities and coastal resorts, but you won't necessarily be able to count on the bus driver or the passerby on the street. Fortunately, Spanish is fairly easy to pick up, and your efforts to speak the local tongue will be graciously received.

LODGING

Spain has lots of different accommodations, including luxury palaces, medieval monasteries, converted 19th-century houses, modern hotels, coastal high-rises, and inexpensive hostels in family homes. Rates are generally quoted per room, not per person. Single occupancy of a double room costs 80% of the usual price. Breakfast is rarely included in the quoted room rate. The quality of rooms, particularly in older properties, can be uneven; always ask to see your room *before* you sign the acceptance slip. If you want a private bathroom in a less expensive hotel, state your preference for shower or bathtub; the latter usually costs more, though many hotels have both. All hotels and hostels are listed with their rates in the annual *Guía de Hoteles,* available from bookstores and kiosks or for perusal in local tourist offices.

WHAT IT COSTS In Euros			
$$$$	$$$	$$	$
MAJOR CITIES*			
HOTELS over € 225	€150–€ 225	€80–€150	under €80
OTHER AREAS			
FOR 2 PEOPLE over €180	€100–€180	€60–€100	under €60

Prices are for two people in a standard double room in high season, excluding tax and breakfast. *Major cities are Barcelona and Madrid. Other areas includes the colony of Gibraltar.

APARTMENT &   Villas are plentiful all along the Mediterranean coast. A few agencies
VILLA RENTALS   rent cottages in Cantabria and Asturias, on the north coast; check with the Tourist Office of Spain.

HOSTELS   *Hostales* are rated from three stars to one star; these are not the youth hostels associated with the word in most countries but are usually family homes converted to provide accommodations in one part of the building. A three-star hostel is usually comparable to a two-star hotel; two- and one-star hostels offer basic accommodations.

HOTELS Hotels are officially classified from five stars (the highest) to one star. Although quality is a factor, the ratings mainly indicate the number of facilities in each hotel. A hotel with an *R* on its blue plaque is classified as a *residencia* and may offer breakfast and cafeteria facilities. The main hotel chains are Barceló, Husa, Iberotel, Meliá Sol, NH, Tryp, and the state-run *paradores* (paradors). Holiday Inn, InterContinental, and Forte also own some of the best hotels in Madrid, Barcelona, and Seville; these, as well as the paradors, and the Estancias de España, a group of lodgings in historic buildings, usually have the most character. The others mostly provide clean, comfortable accommodations in the two- to four-star range.

At many hotels, rates can vary dramatically according to the time of year. The hotel year is divided into *temporada alta, media,* and *baja* (high, mid-, and low season, respectively); high season usually covers summer, Easter, and Christmas plus the major fiestas. The value-added tax, called IVA, is rarely included in the quoted room rates, so expect an additional 7% to be added to your bill. Service charges are not included.

PARADORS Spain has about 85 state-owned and -run paradors (upmarket hotels), many of which are in magnificent medieval castles or convents. Most are relatively luxurious but moderately priced. All have restaurants that specialize in regional delicacies, and you can stop in for a meal or a drink without spending the night. Breakfast, however, is an expensive buffet, and you'll do better to go down the street for a cup of coffee and a roll. Paradors are often booked far in advance. For more information or to make reservations, contact the central reservations office, Paradores, which also has extensive information on—and can reserve—other fine lodgings.

🚹 **Paradores** ✉ Requena 3, Madrid 28013 ☎ 91/516-6666 🖷 91/516-6657 ⊕ www.parador.es.

MAIL & SHIPPING

Mail can be sent to American Express offices around Spain, as well as to Spanish post offices, addressed to *lista de correos* (poste restante) in a town you'll be visiting. The address should include the name of the province in parentheses—e.g., Marbella (Málaga). You'll need to show your passport to claim your mail. American Express charges $2 per letter for noncardholders.

POSTAL RATES To the United States, airmail letters up to 20 grams and postcards each cost €.80. To the United Kingdom and other European countries (both EU and non-EU), letters up to 20 grams and postcards each cost €.54. Within Spain, letters and postcards each cost €.28. Mailboxes are yellow with red stripes; use the slot marked EXTRANJERO for mail going abroad. Buy your *sellos* (stamps) at a *correos* (post office) or in an *estanco* (tobacco shop).

MONEY MATTERS

The cost of living in Spain is on a par with that of most other European nations. However, currency fluctuations have increased the buying power of those visiting from North America and the United Kingdom. A cup of coffee costs between €.75 and €1; a glass of wine in a bar, €.60–€1; a sandwich, €2–€3; a local bus or subway ride, €.75–€1.20; a 2-km (1-mi) taxi ride, about €3.

CREDIT CARDS Most hotels, restaurants, and stores accept credit cards. Visa is the most widely accepted card, followed by MasterCard (also called EuroCard in Spain).

CURRENCY The euro is Spain's standard currency, and banks and ATMs dispense all money in euros. Euro notes come in denominations of 5, 10, 20, 50, 100, 200, and 500; coins are worth 1 cent of a euro, 2 cents, 5 cents, 10 cents, 20 cents, 50 cents, 1 euro, and 2 euros. At press time (summer 2003), the exchange rate was €.86 to the U.S. dollar, €.63 to the Canadian dollar, €1.40 to the pound sterling, €.56 to the Australian dollar, €.50 to the New Zealand dollar.

You may take any amount of foreign currency in bills or traveler's checks into Spain, as well as any amount of euros. When leaving Spain you may take out only €3,000 or the equivalent in foreign currency, unless you can prove you declared the excess at customs on entering the country.

CURRENCY The word to look for is CAMBIO (exchange). Most Spanish banks take
EXCHANGE a 1½% commission, though some less scrupulous places charge more. Hotels offer rates lower than banks, but they rarely charge a commission, so you may well break even. Restaurants and stores generally do not accept payment in dollars or traveler's checks. If you have a credit card with a personal identification number, you'll have no trouble drawing cash from automated teller machines.

TAXES

VALUE-ADDED Value-added tax, called IVA, is levied on most goods and services. It's
TAX (V.A.T.) 7% at hotels and restaurants and 16% on goods and car rentals.

A number of shops, particularly large stores and boutiques in holiday resorts, participate in Global Refund (formerly Europe Tax-Free Shopping), a V.A.T. refund service that makes getting your money back relatively hassle-free. On purchases of more than €90, you're entitled to a refund of the 16% tax (there is no refund for the 7% tax). Ask for the Global Refund form (called a Shopping Cheque) in participating stores. You show your passport and fill out the form; the vendor then mails you the refund, or you present your original receipt to the V.A.T. office at the airport when you leave Spain. (In both Madrid and Barcelona, the office is near the duty-free shops. Save time for this process, as lines can be long.) Customs signs the original and either refunds your money on the spot in cash, or sends it to their central office to process a credit-card refund. Credit-card refunds take a few weeks.

TELEPHONES
The country code for Spain is 34.

DIRECTORY & For the operator and directory information for any part of Spain, dial
OPERATOR 1–1818. The international information and assistance operator is at
ASSISTANCE 1–18–25 (some operators speak English). If you're in Madrid, dial 1008 to make collect calls to countries in Europe; 1005 for the rest of the world.

INTERNATIONAL You can call abroad from any pay phone marked TELÉFONO INTERNA-
CALLS CIONAL. Some are coin-operated, but it is best to purchase a *tarjeta telefónica* (telephone card), available at most newsdealers and many shops. A few public phones also accept credit cards. Dial 00, then dial 1 for the United States, 0101 for Canada, or 44 for the United Kingdom, followed by the area code and number. For lengthy calls, go to the *telefónica,* a phone office found in all sizable towns: here an operator assigns you a private booth and collects payment at the end of the call. This is the cheapest and by far the easiest way to call overseas, and you can charge calls costing more than €3 to Visa or MasterCard. Private long-distance companies, such as AT&T, MCI, and Sprint, have special access numbers.

🖪 Access Codes **AT&T** ☎ 900/990011. **MCI** ☎ 900/990014. **Sprint** ☎ 900/990013.

LOCAL CALLS Note that to call anywhere within Spain—even locally—you need to dial the area code first. All provincial codes begin with a 9.

PUBLIC PHONES Most pay phones have a digital readout, so you can see your money ticking away. You need at least €.20 for a local call, €.50 to call another province, and at least €.60 if you are calling a Spanish cell phone. Some pay phones take only phone cards, which can be purchased at any tobacco shop in various denominations.

TIPPING

Spanish waiters, porters, and taxi drivers appreciate being tipped, but they don't expect American rates. By law, restaurants and hotels are not allowed to add a service charge to your bill, but, confusingly, your bills for both will probably say *servicios e impuestos incluídos* (service and tax included). In restaurants, ignore this unhelpful snippet and leave 10% if you've had a full meal. In humbler eateries, bars, and cafés, leave 5%–10% or round the bill up to the nearest €1. Tip taxi drivers 10%. Train and airport porters usually operate on a posted, fixed rate per bag, around €1. Hotel porters get €.50 for carrying bags, and waiters get the same for room service. If you stay in a hotel more than two nights, it's customary to tip the maid €1.

TRAIN TRAVEL

The Spanish railroad system—usually known by its initials, RENFE—operates several different types of trains: Talgo (ultramodern), electric unit expresses (ELT), diesel rail cars (TER), and ordinary *expresos* and *rápidos*. A few lines, such as the narrow-gauge FEVE routes along the north coast and the Costa Blanca, do not belong to the RENFE network and do not accept international rail passes. The high-speed AVE connects Madrid with Cordoba and Sevilla in less than three hours. By late 2004 Barcelona and Madrid will be connected in just over three hours by AVE.

CUTTING COSTS The RENFE Tourist Card, on sale to anyone who lives outside Spain, buys you unlimited distance over 3, 5, or 10 days' travel. Contact the Tourist Office of Spain for a list of agencies or call RENFE.

FARES & SCHEDULES Fares are determined by the kind of train as well as the distance traveled. Of the long-distance trains, Talgos are by far the quickest, most comfortable, and most expensive of the lot; *expresos* and *rápidos* are the slowest and cheapest. The high-speed Alto *Velocidad Español* (AVE) runs between Madrid and Seville in just 2½ hours, with a stop in Córdoba; fares vary, but the AVE can cost almost as much as flying.

🚆 **RENFE** ☎ 34/902/240202 from outside Spain; 902/240202 from Spain.

VISITOR INFORMATION

Before you go, consult the Tourist Office of Spain in your home country or on the World Wide Web. The site ⊕ www.okspain.org provides a basic introduction; the Spain-based ⊕ www.tourspain.es is more sophisticated. Both are run by Turespaña, the head tourist office in Spain. For general information on travel within Spain, call Turespaña's information line.

🚩 **Turespaña** ☎ 901/300600.

🚩 Offices **Chicago** ⊠ Water Tower Pl., 845 N. Michigan Ave., Suite 915-East, Chicago, IL 60611 ☎ 312/642-1992. **Los Angeles** ⊠ 8383 Wilshire Blvd., Suite 960, Beverly Hills, CA 90211 ☎ 213/658-7188. **Miami** ⊠1221 Brickell Ave., Suite 1850, Miami, FL 33131 ☎ 305/358-1992. **New York** ⊠ 666 5th Ave., 35th floor, New York, NY 10103 ☎ 212/265-8822. **Canada** ⊠ 2 Bloor St. W, Suite 3402, Toronto, Ontario M4W 3E2 ☎ 416/961-3131. **United Kingdom** ⊠ 22-23 Manchester Sq., London W1M 5AP, U.K. ☎ 0207/486-8077.

WHEN TO GO

The tourist season runs from Easter to mid-October. Seasonal events can clog parts of the country, and major fiestas, such as Pamplona's San-fermines (July 6–15), cause prices to soar. Semana Santa (Holy Week) takes place anywhere from late March to mid-April; this is the time to catch some of Spain's most spectacular fiestas.

CLIMATE   The best months for sightseeing are May, June, September, and early Oc-tober, when the weather is usually pleasant and sunny without being unbearably hot. In July and August, avoid Madrid and the inland cities of Andalusia, where the heat can be stifling and many places close down at 1 PM. Air-conditioning is not widely used. The one exception to Spain's high summer temperatures is the north coast, where the cli-mate is similar to that of northern Europe. The following are average daily maximum and minimum temperatures for Madrid.

Jan.	47F	9C	May	70F	21C	Sept.	77F	25C
	35	2		50	10		57	14
Feb.	52F	11C	June	80F	27C	Oct.	65F	18C
	36	2		58	15		49	10
Mar.	59F	15C	July	87F	31C	Nov.	55F	13C
	41	5		63	17		42	5
Apr.	65F	18C	Aug.	85F	30C	Dec.	48F	9C
	45	7		63	17		36	2

MADRID

Dead center in the heart of Spain at 2,120 feet above sea level, Madrid is the highest capital in Europe and one of the continent's most excit-ing cities. Madrid's famous museum mile has more masterpieces per foot than anywhere else in the world. Home of Spain's royal court for the last 500 years, the city's regal palaces and gardens conceal a villagelike medieval Madrid with narrow lanes and red-tiled roofs. This is all in contrast to the rowdy Madrid one finds after midnight, when the ac-tion really begins; Madrileños are vigorous, joyful people, famous for their defiance of the need for sleep.

Exploring Madrid

Numbers in the margin correspond to points of interest on the Madrid map.

You can see important parts of the city in one day if you stop only to visit the Prado and Royal Palace. Two days should give you time for browsing. You can begin in the Plaza Atocha (Glorieta del Emperador Carlos V), at the bottom of the Paseo del Prado.

★ ❶   **Centro de Arte Reina Sofía** (Queen Sofía Arts Center). Spain's Queen Sofía opened this center in 1986, and it quickly became one of Europe's most dynamic venues—a Spanish rival to Paris's Pompidou Center. A con-verted hospital, the center houses painting and sculpture, including works by Joan Miró and Salvador Dalí as well as Picasso's *Guernica,* the painting depicting the horrific April 1937 carpet bombing of the Basque country's traditional capital by Nazi warplanes aiding Franco in the Span-ish Civil War. ⊠ *Main entrance, C. de Santa Isabel 52* ☎ *91/467–5062* ⊙ *Mon. and Wed.–Sat. 10–9, Sun. 10–2:30.*

❿   **Convento de las Descalzas Reales** (Convent of the Royal Barefoot Nuns). This convent, founded by Juana de Austria, daughter of Charles V, is still in use. Over the centuries, the nuns—daughters of royalty and no-bility—have endowed it with an enormous wealth of jewels, religious ornaments, superb Flemish tapestries, and the works of such master painters as Titian and Rubens. A bit off the main track, it's one of Madrid's better-kept secrets. Your ticket includes admission to the nearby, but less interesting, **Convento de la Encarnación.** ⊠ *Plaza de las Descalzas 3* ☎ *91/454–8809 information* ⊗ *Tues.–Thurs. and Sat. 10:30–12:45 and 4–5:45, Fri. 10:30–12:45, Sun. 11–1:45.*

⑦ Fuente de la Cibeles (Fountain of Cybele). Cybele, the Greek goddess of fertility and unofficial emblem of Madrid, languidly rides her lion-drawn chariot here, watched over by the mighty Palacio de Comuni-caciónes, a splendidly pompous, cathedral-like post office. Fans of the home football team, Real Madrid, used to celebrate major victories by splashing in the fountain, but police now blockade it during big games. The fountain stands in the center of **Plaza de la Cibeles,** one of Madrid's great landmarks. ⊠ *C. de Alcalá.*

Las Ventas. Formally known as the Plaza de Toros Monumental, this is Madrid's bullring. You can buy tickets here before the fight or, for a 20% surcharge, at the agencies that line Calle Victoria, off Carrera de San Jerónimo near Puerta del Sol. During the bullfighting season corridas are held on Sunday and sometimes also on Thursday; starting times vary between 5 PM and 7 PM. The height of the taurine calendar comes with the San Isidro Festival in May, with five weeks of daily bullfights. ⊠ *Alcalá 237* ☎ *91/356–2200* ⊗ *Mar.–Oct.* Ⓜ *Ventas.*

★ ② Museo del Prado (Prado Museum). On the old cobblestone section of the Paseo del Prado you'll find Madrid's number one cultural site and one of the world's most important art museums. Plan to spend at least a day here; it takes at least two days to view the museum's treasures properly. Brace yourself for crowds. The greatest treasures—the Velázquez, Murillo, Zur-barán, El Greco, and Goya galleries—are all on the upper floor. Two of the best works are Velázquez's *La Rendición de Breda* and his most famous work, *Las Meninas,* awarded a room of its own. The Goya galleries contain the artist's none-too-flattering royal portraits, his exquisitely beautiful *Marquesa de Santa Cruz,* and his famous *La Maja Desnuda* and *La Maja Vestida,* for which the 13th duchess of Alba was said to have posed. Goya's most moving works, the *Second of May* and the *Fusillade of Moncloa,* or *Third of May,* vividly depict the sufferings of Madrid patriots at the hands of Napoléon's invading troops in 1808. Before you leave, feast your eyes on Hieronymus Bosch's flights of fancy, *Garden of Earthly Delights,* and the triptych the *Hay Wagon,* both on the ground floor. The museum is adding a new wing, designed by Rafael Moneo, much of which will be occupied by long-forgotten masterpieces by Zurbarán and Pereda. ⊠ *Paseo del Prado s/n* ☎ *91/330–2800* ⊗ *Tues.–Sun. 9–7.*

④ Museo Thyssen-Bornemisza. This museum, in the elegant Villahermosa Palace, has plenty of airy spaces and natural light. The ambitious collection—800 paintings—traces the history of Western art through examples from each important movement, beginning with 13th-century Italy. Among the museum's gems are the *Portrait of Henry VIII,* by Hans Holbein. Two halls are devoted to the impressionists and postimpressionists, with works by Pissarro, Renoir, Monet, Degas, van Gogh, and Cézanne. The more recent paintings include some terror-filled examples of German expressionism, but these are complemented by some soothing Georgia O'Keeffes and Andrew Wyeths. ⊠ *Paseo del Prado 8* ☎ *91/ 369–0151* ⊗ *Tues.–Sun. 10–7.*

★ ⑬ Palacio Real (Royal Palace). This magnificent granite-and-limestone pile was begun by Philip V, the first Bourbon king of Spain, who was always homesick for his beloved Versailles and did his best to re-create its op-

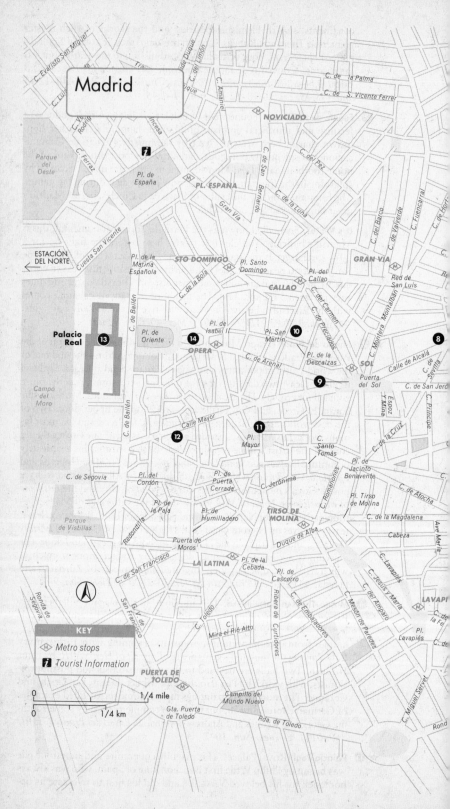

Madrid

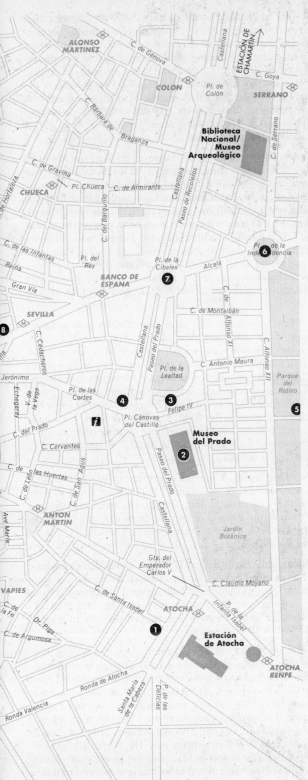

ulence and splendor. Judging by the palace's 2,800 rooms, with their lavish rococo decorations, precious carpets, porcelain, timepieces, mirrors, and chandeliers, his efforts were successful. From 1764, when Charles III first moved in, until the coming of the Second Republic and the abdication of Alfonso XIII in 1931, the Royal Palace proved a very stylish abode for Spanish monarchs; today, King Juan Carlos, who lives in the far less ostentatious Zarzuela Palace outside Madrid, uses it only for official state functions. ⊠ *Bailén s/n* ☎ *91/454–8800* ⊙ *Apr.–Sept., Mon.–Sat. 9–6, Sun. 9–3; Oct.–Mar., Mon.–Sat. 9:30–5, Sun. 9:30–2* ⊙ *Closed during official receptions.*

★ ♥ ❺ **Parque del Retiro** (Retiro Park). Once a royal retreat, Retiro is Madrid's prettiest park. Visit the beautiful rose garden, **La Rosaleda;** enjoy street musicians and magicians; row a boat around El Estanque; and wander past the park's many statues and fountains. Look particularly at the monumental **statue of Alfonso XII,** one of Spain's least notable kings (though you wouldn't think so from the statue's size), or wonder at the **Monument to the Fallen Angel**—Madrid claims the dubious honor of being the only capital to have a statue dedicated to the Devil. The **Palacio de Velázquez** and the beautiful, glass-and-steel **Palacio de Cristal,** built as a tropical plant house during the 19th century, now host occasional art exhibits. ⊠ *Between C. Alfonso XII and Avda. de Menéndez Pelayo below C. de Alcalá.*

⓬ **Plaza de la Villa** (City Square). This plaza's notable cluster of buildings includes some of the oldest houses in Madrid. The **Casa de la Villa,** Madrid's city hall, was built in 1644 and has also served as the city prison and the mayor's home. Its sumptuous salons are occasionally open to the public; ask about guided tours, which are sometimes given in English. An archway joins the Casa de la Villa to the **Casa Cisneros,** a palace built in 1537 for the nephew of Cardinal Cisneros, primate of Spain and infamous inquisitor general. Across the square is the **Torre de Lujanes,** one of the oldest buildings in Madrid; it once imprisoned Francis I of France, archenemy of the emperor Charles V. ⊠ *C. Mayor between C. Santiago and C. San Nicolás.*

★ ⓫ **Plaza Mayor** (Main Square). Without a doubt the capital's architectural showpiece, the Plaza Mayor was built in 1617–19 for Philip III—the figure astride the horse in the middle. The plaza has witnessed the canonization of saints, the burning of heretics, fireworks, and bullfights, and it is still one of Madrid's great gathering places. ⊠ *South of C. Mayor, west of Cava San Miguel.*

❻ **Puerta de Alcalá** (Alcalá Gate). Built in 1779 for Charles III, the grandiose gateway dominates the Plaza de la Independencia. A customs post once stood beside the gate, as did the old bullring until it was moved to its present site, Las Ventas, in the 1920s. At the beginning of the 20th century, the Puerta de Alcalá more or less marked the eastern edge of Madrid. ⊠ *Plaza de la Independencia.*

❾ **Puerta del Sol** (Gate of the Sun). The old gate disappeared long ago, but you're still at the very heart of Madrid here, and indeed at the very heart of Spain: kilometer distances for the whole nation are measured from the zero marker, a brass plaque on the south sidewalk. The square was expertly revamped in 1986 and now accommodates a copy of **La Mariblanca** (a statue that adorned a fountain here 250 years ago), a statue of Carlos III on horseback, and, at the bottom of Calle Carmen, the much-loved statue of the **bear and strawberry tree.** The Puerta del Sol is inextricably linked with the history of Madrid and of Spain; a half century ago, a generation of literati gathered in Sol's long-gone cafés to thrash out the burning issues of the day. Nearly 200 years ago, the square witnessed the patriots' uprising immortalized by Goya in his painting *The Second of May.* ⊠ *Meeting of C. Mayor and C. Alcalá.*

8 **Real Academia de Bellas Artes de San Fernando** (St. Fernando Royal Academy of Fine Arts). Often overlooked in favor of the Prado, the Reina Sofia, and the Thyssen, this surprisingly comprehensive collection covers the masters (Murillo, Zurbarán, Ribera, El Greco, Velázquez, and Goya) and also houses some 19th- and 20th-century work (Zuloaga, Sorolla). ⊠ *Alcalá 13* ☎ *91/522–0046* ⊙ *Tues.–Fri. 9:30–7, Sat.–Mon. 9:30–2.*

3 **Ritz.** Alfonso II built Madrid's grande dame in 1910, when he realized that his capital had no hotels elegant enough to accommodate his wedding guests. The garden is a wonderfully aristocratic—if wildly overpriced—place to lunch in summer. ⊠ *Plaza de Lealtad 5.*

14 **Teatro Real** (Royal Theater). This neoclassical theater was built in 1850 and has long been a cultural center. Replete with golden balconies, plush seats, and state-of-the-art stage equipment for operas and ballets, the theater is a modern showpiece with its vintage appeal intact. ⊠ *Plaza de Isabel II* ☎ *91/516–0600.*

Where to Eat

For details and price-category definitions, *see* Eating & Drinking *in* Spain A to Z. Note that some restaurants close for Holy Week.

★ **$$$$** ✕ **La Broche.** Sergi Arola, who trained with celebrity chef Ferran Adriá, has added his own twists and innovations to those of the Catalan master and vaulted directly to the top of Madrid's dining charts. The minimalist dining room clears the decks for maximum taste bud protagonism—a lucky thing, as you'll want to concentrate on the hot-cold counterpoints of your codfish soup with bacon ice cream or the marinated sardine with herring roe. ⊠ *Miguel Angel 29* ☎ *91/399–3437* ⚌ *Reservations essential* ⊟ *AE, DC, MC, V* ⊙ *Closed weekends, Easter week, and Aug.*

$$$$ ✕ **Lhardy.** This place looks pretty much the same as it must have on day one (September 16, 1839) with its dark-wood paneling, brass chandeliers, and red-velvet chairs. Most diners come for the traditional *cocido a la madrileña* (garbanzo-bean stew) and *callos a la madrileña* (tripe in spicy sauce). The dining rooms are upstairs; the ground-floor entry doubles as a delicatessen and stand-up coffee bar that fills up on chilly winter mornings with shivering souls sipping steaming-hot *caldo* (chicken broth) from silver urns. ⊠ *Carrera de San Jerónimo 8* ☎ *91/521–3385* ⊟ *AE, DC, MC, V* ⊙ *No dinner Sun.*

$$$$ ✕ **Zalacaín.** A deep-apricot color scheme, set off by dark wood and gleaming silver, makes this restaurant look like an exclusive villa. Zalacaín introduced nouvelle Basque cuisine to Spain in the 1970s and has since become a Madrid classic. Splurge on such dishes as prawn salad in avocado vinaigrette, scallops and leeks in Albariño wine, and roast pheasant with truffles. ⊠ *Álvarez de Baena 4* ☎ *91/561–4840* ⚌ *Reservations essential* ⏢ *Jackets required* ⊟ *AE, DC, V* ⊙ *Closed Sun., Easter wk, and Aug. No lunch Sat.*

$$$–$$$$ ✕ **La Trainera.** This place is all about fresh seafood. With a nautical style and a maze of little dining rooms, this informal restaurant has reigned as the queen of Madrid's fish houses for decades. Shellfish are served by weight, and although Spaniards often share several plates of delicacies as their entire meal, the grilled hake, sole, or turbot makes an unbeatable second course. ⊠ *Lagasca 60* ☎ *91/576–8035* ⊟ *AE, MC, V* ⊙ *Closed Sun. and Aug.*

$$$–$$$$ ✕ **Pedro Larumbe.** This excellent restaurant is atop the ABC shopping center. It has a lovely summer roof terrace, which is glassed in for the winter, and an Andalusian patio. Owner-chef Pedro Larumbe is famous for the presentation of his modern dishes, such as lobster salad. ✉ *Serrano 61/Castellana 34* ☎ *91/575–1112* ⊟ *AE, DC, MC, V* ⊙ *Closed Sun. and 15 days in Aug. No lunch Sat.*

$$$–$$$$ ✕ **Viridiana.** This black-and-white place has the relaxed pace of a mellow bistro. Iconoclast chef Abraham García creates a new menu every two weeks, dreaming up such varied fare as red onions stuffed with *morcilla* (black pudding), soft flour tortillas wrapped around marinated fresh tuna, and filet mignon in white-truffle sauce. ✉ *Juan de Mena 14* ☎ *91/523–4478* ⚘ *Reservations essential* ⊟ *AE, DC, MC, V* ⊙ *Closed Sun. and Aug.*

$$–$$$ ✕ **Asador Fronton 1.** Long established in Tirso de Molina and now with two branches in northern Madrid, this popular Basque restaurant serves some of the most outstanding meat and fish in the city. The huge chunks of delicious steak, seared on a charcoal grill and then lightly sprinkled with sea salt, are for two or more. Order lettuce hearts or a vegetable to accompany. ✉ *Tirso de Molina 7 (rear, upstairs)* ☎ *91/369–1617* ⚘ *Reservations essential* ⊟ *AE, DC, MC, V* ⊙ *Closed Sun.*

★ **$$–$$$** ✕ **Botín.** Just below Plaza Mayor, this is Madrid's oldest (1725) and most famous restaurant. The food is traditionally Castilian, as are the wood-fire ovens used for cooking. *Cochinillo asado* (roast suckling pig) and *cordero asado* (roast lamb) are the specialties. The restaurant, a Hemingway favorite featured in the final scene of *The Sun Also Rises*, is somewhat touristy, but it's still fun. ✉ *Cuchilleros 17* ☎ *91/366–4217* ⚘ *Reservations essential* ⊟ *AE, DC, MC, V.*

★ **$$–$$$** ✕ **El Cenador del Prado.** The innovative menu has French and Asian touches, as well as exotic Spanish dishes that rarely appear in restaurants. The house specialty is *patatas a la importancia* (sliced potatoes fried in a sauce of garlic, parsley, and clams); other possibilities are shellfish consommé with ginger ravioli, veal and eggplant in béchamel, and venison with prunes. ✉ *C. del Prado 4* ☎ *91/429–1561* ⊟ *AE, DC, MC, V* ⊙ *Closed Sun. and Aug. 1–15. No lunch Sat.*

★ **$$–$$$** ✕ **La Gamella.** Some of the American-born former chef Dick Stephens's dishes—Caesar salad, hamburger, steak tartare—are still on the reasonably priced menu at this perennially popular dinner spot. The new selections are a fusion of Asian, Mediterranean, and American dishes. ✉ *Alfonso XII 4* ☎ *91/532–4509* ⊟ *AE, DC, MC, V* ⊙ *Closed Sun. and last 2 wks in Aug. No lunch Sat.*

$–$$ ✕ **La Cava Real.** Wine connoisseurs love the intimacy of this small, elegant restaurant and bar—Madrid's first true wine bar when it opened in 1983. There are a staggering 350 wines from which to choose, including 50 by the glass. The charming, experienced maître d', Chema Gómez, can help you select. Chef Javier Collar designs good-value set menus around wines. ✉ *Espronceda 34* ☎ *91/442–5432* ⚘ *Reservations essential* ⊟ *AE, DC, MC, V* ⊙ *Closed Sun. and Aug.*

$–$$ ✕ **La Trucha.** This Andalusian deep-fry specialist is one of the happiest places in Madrid. The house specialty, the *trucha a la truchana* (crisped trout stuffed with ample garlic and diced jabugo ham) is a work of art. *Chopitos* (baby squid), *pollo al ajillo* (chunks of chicken in crisped garlic), and *espárragos trigueros* (wild asparagus) are among the star entrées. The Nuñez de Arce branch is usually less crowded. ✉ *Manuel Fernandez y Gonzalez 3* ☎ *91/429-3778* ✉ *Nuñez de Arce 6* ☎ *91/532–0890* ⊟ *AE, MC, V* ⊙ *Nuñez de Arce branch closed Sun., Mon., and Aug.*

★ **$** ✕ **Casa Mingo.** This Asturian cider tavern is built into a stone wall beneath the Norte train station. The nearby Ermita de San Antonio de la Florida with its famous Goya frescoes and Casa Mingo are a classic

Madrid combination. Succulent roast chicken, sausages, and salad are the only offerings, along with *sidra* (hard cider). The long plank tables are shared with other diners, and in summer, tables are set out on the sidewalk. ⊠ *Paseo de la Florida 2* ☎ *91/547–7918* ⟁ *Reservations not accepted* ⊟ *No credit cards.*

$ ✕ **Nabucco.** With pastel-washed walls and subtle lighting from gigantic, wrought-iron candelabras, this pizzeria and trattoria is a trendy but elegant haven in gritty Chueca. The spinach, ricotta, and walnut ravioli is heavenly, and this may be the only Italian restaurant in Madrid where you can order barbecued-chicken pizza. ⊠ *Hortaleza 108* ☎ *91/ 310–0611* ⊟ *AE, MC, V.*

Where to Stay

For details and price-category definitions, *see* Lodging *in* Spain A to Z.

★ $$$$ ▦ **AC Santo Mauro.** Once the Canadian embassy, this turn-of-the-20th-century neoclassical mansion is now an intimate luxury hotel. The architecture is accented by contemporary furniture (such as suede armchairs). The best rooms are in the main building; the others are in a new annex and are split-level, with stereos and VCRs. Request a room with a terrace overlooking the gardens. ⊠ *Zurbano 36, 28010* ☎ *91/319–6900* 🖷 *91/308–5477* ⊕ *www.ac-hoteles.com* ⟿ *50 rooms, 4 suites* ⟁ *Restaurant, pool, bar* ⊟ *AE, DC, MC, V.*

$$$$ ▦ **Ritz.** Alfonso XIII, about to marry Queen Victoria's granddaughter, encouraged the construction of this hotel, the most exclusive in Spain, for his royal guests. Opened in 1910 by the king himself, the Ritz is a monument to the belle epoque, its salons furnished with rare antiques, hand-embroidered linens, and handwoven carpets. Most rooms have views of the Prado. The restaurant, Goya, is famous. ⊠ *Plaza Lealtad 5, 28014* ☎ *91/701–6767* 🖷 *91/701–6776* ⊕ *www.ritz.es* ⟿ *167 rooms* ⟁ *Restaurant, bar* ⊟ *AE, DC, MC, V.*

$$$$ ▦ **Villa Magna.** The concrete facade here gives way to an interior furnished with 18th-century antiques. Prices are robust, but it's hard to find flourishes such as a champagne bar and—in the largest suite in Madrid— a white baby-grand piano. All rooms have large desks, and all bathrooms have fresh flowers. One restaurant, Le Divellec, has walnut paneling and the feel of an English library, and you can dine on its garden terrace in season. The other restaurant, the Tsé-Yang, is Madrid's most exclusive for Chinese food. ⊠ *Paseo de la Castellana 22, 28046* ☎ *91/431–2286* 🖷 *91/575–3158* ⊕ *www.madrid.hyatt.com* ⟿ *164 rooms, 18 suites* ⟁ *2 restaurants, 2 bars* ⊟ *AE, DC, MC, V.*

$$$$ ▦ **Villa Real.** For a medium-size hotel that combines elegance, modern amenities, friendly service, *and* a great location, look no further: the Villa Real faces Spain's parliament and is convenient to almost everything. The simulated 19th-century facade gives way to an intimate lobby with modern furnishings. Many rooms are split-level, with a small sitting area. Some suites have whirlpool baths. ⊠ *Plaza de las Cortes 10, 28014* ☎ *91/ 420–3767* 🖷 *91/420–2547* ⊕ *www.derbyhotels.es* ⟿ *94 rooms, 20 suites* ⟁ *Restaurant, bar* ⊟ *AE, DC, MC, V.*

★ $$$$ ▦ **Westin Palace.** Built in 1912, Madrid's most famous grand hotel is a belle epoque creation of Alfonso XIII. The guest rooms meet today's highest standards; banquet halls and lobbies have been beautified; and the facade has been finely restored. The Palace is more charming and stylish than ever—and although the glass dome over the lounge remains exquisitely original, the windows in the guest rooms are now double-glazed. ⊠ *Plaza de las Cortes 7, 28014* ☎ *91/360–8000* 🖷 *91/360–8100* ⊕ *www.palacemadrid.com* ⟿ *465 rooms, 45 suites* ⟁ *2 restaurants, bar* ⊟ *AE, DC, MC, V.*

$$$ ⌨ **Reina Victoria.** Madrid's longtime favorite among bullfighters, this gleaming white Victorian building across the square from the Teatro Español has been transformed over the last decade into an upscale and modern establishment. The pervasive taurine theme is most concentrated in the bar. The best rooms are on the top floors, providing the most insulation from noise and great views over the rooftops and the theater. ⌧ *Plaza Santa Ana 14, 28012* ☎ *91/531–4500* 🖷 *91/522–0307* ⮐ *195 rooms* ⌂ *Bar* ▤ *AE, DC, MC, V.*

$$ ⌨ **Carlos V.** If you like to be right in the center of things, hang your hat at this classic hotel on a pedestrian street: it's just a few steps away from the Puerta del Sol, Plaza Mayor, and Descalzas Reales convent. A suit of armor guards the tiny lobby, and crystal chandeliers add elegance to the second-floor lounge. All rooms are bright and carpeted, and the doubles with large terraces are a bargain. ⌧ *Maestro Victoria 5, 28013* ☎ *91/531–4100* 🖷 *91/531–3761* ⊕ *www.carlosv.com* ⮐ *67 rooms* ▤ *AE, DC, MC, V.*

$$ ⌨ **El Prado.** Wedged in among the classic buildings of Old Madrid, this slim hotel is within stumbling distance of Madrid's best bars and nightclubs. Rooms are soundproof, with double-pane glass, and are surprisingly spacious. Appointments include pastel floral prints and gleaming marble baths. ⌧ *Prado 11, 28014* ☎ *91/369–0234* 🖷 *91/429–2829* ⊕ *www.hotelgreenprado.com* ⮐ *47 rooms* ▤ *AE, DC, MC, V.*

$$ ⌨ **Inglés.** This hotel was once a favorite with writers and artists, including Virginia Woolf. Though dreary, the rooms are comfortable enough, and the location is key: a short walk from the Puerta del Sol in one direction, the Prado in the other. Inexpensive restaurants and distinctive bars are close at hand. ⌧ *Echegaray 8, 28014* ☎ *91/429–6551* 🖷 *91/420–2423* ⮐ *58 rooms* ⌂ *Bar* ▤ *AE, DC, MC, V.*

$$ ⌨ **Liabeny.** A large, paneled lobby leads to bars, a restaurant, and a café in this 1960s hotel, centrally located near an airy plaza (and several department stores) between Gran Vía and Puerta del Sol. The large, comfortable rooms have floral fabrics and big windows; interior and top-floor rooms are the quietest. ⌧ *Salud 3, 28013* ☎ *91/531–9000* 🖷 *91/532–5306* ⊕ *www.liabeny.es* ⮐ *222 rooms* ⌂ *Restaurant, 2 bars* ▤ *AE, DC, MC, V.*

$$ ⌨ **Mora.** You'll find this cheery hotel, with a sparkling, faux-marble lobby and bright, carpeted hallways, across the Paseo del Prado from the Botanical Garden. Rooms are simple but large and comfortable. Those on the street have great views of the garden and Prado through soundproof, double-pane windows. For breakfast and lunch, the attached café is excellent, affordable, and popular with locals. ⌧ *Paseo del Prado 32, 28014* ☎ *91/420–1569* 🖷 *91/420–0564* ⮐ *62 rooms* ▤ *AE, DC, MC, V.*

Nightlife & the Arts

The Arts

Details of all cultural events are listed in the daily newspaper *El País* and in the weekly *Guía del Ocio.* Two English-language publications, the *Broadsheet* and *In Spain,* are available free in Irish pubs and other expat hangouts and detail mainly expat activities.

CONCERTS & OPERA　Madrid's main concert hall is the **Auditorio Nacional de Madrid** (⌧ Príncipe de Vergara 146 ☎ 91/337–0100). Beneath the Plaza de Colón, the underground **Centro Cultural de la Villa** (⌧ Plaza de Colón s/n ☎ 91/480–0300 information; 902/10–1212 tickets) hosts all kinds of performances, from gospel, spiritual, and blues festivals to Celtic dance. For opera, catch a performance at the legendary **Teatro Real** (⌧ Plaza de Isabel II ☎ 91/516–0660), whose splendid facade dominates the Plaza de Oriente.

FILM Foreign films are mostly dubbed into Spanish, but movies in English are listed in *El País* or *Guía del Ocio* under "VO" (*versión original*). A dozen or so theaters now show films in English. **Alphaville** (✉ Martín de los Héros 14, off Plaza España ☎ 91/559–3836) shows films in English. **Renoir Plaza de España** (✉ Martín de los Héros 12, off Plaza España ☎ 91/559–5760) is an old favorite, and shows films in VO. The **Filmoteca Cine Doré** (✉ Santa Isabel 3 ☎ 91/369–1125) is a city-run institution showing different classic English-language films every day. Your best bet for first-run films in the original language is the **Multicines Ideal** (✉ Doctor Cortezo 6 ☎ 91/369–2518).

THEATER Most theaters have two curtain times, at 7 PM and 10:30 PM, and close on Monday. Tickets are inexpensive and often easy to come by on the night of the performance. The **Centro Cultural de la Villa** (☎ 91/575–6080), beneath the Plaza Colón, stages theater and musical events. In summer, check listings for open-air events in Retiro Park. The **Círculo de Bellas Artes** (✉ Marqués de Casa Riera 2, off Alcalá 42 ☎ 91/360–5400) houses a leading theater. **Sala Triángulo** (✉ Zurita 20 ☎ 91/530–6891) is one of the many fringe theaters in Lavapiés and is definitely worth a detour if you understand Spanish. *Zarzuela,* a combination of light opera and dance that's ideal for non–Spanish-speakers, is performed at the **Teatro Nacional Lírico de la Zarzuela** (✉ Jovellanos 4 ☎ 91/524–5400) October to July. The **Teatro Español** (✉ Príncipe 25 on Plaza Santa Ana ☎ 91/429–6297) stages Spanish classics. The **Teatro María Guerrero** (✉ Tamayo y Baus 4 ☎ 91/319–4769), the home of the Centro Dramático Nacional, stages plays from García Lorca to Els Joglars.

Nightlife

BARS & CAFÉS The most traditional and colorful taverns are on Cuchilleros and Cava San Miguel, just west of Plaza Mayor, where you'll find **mesónes** with such names as Tortilla, Champiñón, and Boqueron. These are the places to start your evening out in Madrid; many serve tapas and *raciónes* and close around midnight, when crowds move on to bars and nightclubs. Wander the narrow streets between Puerta del Sol and Plaza Santa Ana in Old Madrid—most are packed with traditional tapas bars. Once lined with turn-of-the-20th-century bars playing guitar or chamber music, Calle Huertas now has more nightclubs than any other street in Madrid. Just off Alonso Martínez, Plaza Santa Bárbara is packed with fashionable bars and beer halls. Stroll along Santa Teresa, Orellana, Campoamor, or Fernando VI and take your pick. Madrid has no lack of old-fashioned cafés, with dark-wood counters, brass pumps, and marble-top tables.

The **Cervecería Alemana** (✉ Plaza Santa Ana 6 ☎ 91/429–7033) is a beer hall founded more than 100 years ago by Germans and patronized, inevitably, by Ernest Hemingway. **El Abuelo** (✉ Victoria 6 ☎ 91/532–1219), or Grandpa, serves only two tapas but does them better than anyone else: grilled shrimp and shrimp sautéed in garlic. For a more tranquil place try the lovely, old tiled bar **Viva Madrid** (✉ Fernández y González 7 ☎ 91/429–3640) early in the evening.

Casa Alberto (✉ C. Huertas 18 ☎ 91/429–9356), a quiet restaurant-tavern with brick walls, has a good selection of draft beers, and tapas. **La Fídula** (✉ C. Huertas 57 ☎ 91/429–2947) often has live classical music. For zest, try the disco **La Fontanería** (✉ Huertas 38 ☎ 91/369–4904), where the action lasts until 4 AM.

The **Cervecería Santa Bárbara** (☎ 91/319–0449), in the plaza itself, is one of the most colorful, a popular beer hall with different tapas. **Café Comercial** (✉ Glorieta de Bilbao 7 ☎ 91/521–5655) is a classic. **Café Gijón** (✉ Paseo de Recoletos 21 ☎ 91/521–5425) is a former literary hangout that offers a cheery set lunch; it's now one of many cafés with summer terraces that dot the Castellana and Paseo de Recoletos. **El Espejo** (✉ Paseo de Recoletos 31 ☎ 91/308–2347) has art nouveau furnishings and an outdoor terrace in summer.

DISCOS & NIGHTCLUBS

Nightlife—or *la marcha,* as the Spanish fondly call it—reaches legendary heights in Spain's capital. Smart, trendy dance clubs filled with well-heeled Madrileños are everywhere. For adventure, try the scruffy bar district in Malasaña, around the Plaza Dos de Mayo, where smoky hangouts line Calle San Vicente Ferrer. The often seedy haunts of Chueca, a popular gay area, can be exciting (watch your purse), but classy cafés and trendy live music venues occasionally break up the alleys of tattoo parlors, boutiques, techno discos, and after-hours clubs.

Amadis (✉ Covarrubias 42, under Luchana Cinema ☎ 91/446–0036) has concerts, dancing, and telephones on every table, encouraging people to call each other with invitations to dance. You must be over 25 to enter. Salsa is a fixture in Madrid; check out the most spectacular moves at **Azúcar** (✉ Paseo Reina Cristina 7 ☎ 91/501–6107). **Ave Nox** (✉ Lagasca 31 ☎ 91/576–9715) is a torrid music bar–disco in a converted chapel, complete with vaulted ceiling, choir loft, and all. **Changó** (✉ Covarrubias 42 ☎ 91/446–0036), named for the Cuban Santería Zeus, is a mega-disco with savage go-go-dancers. **El Clandestino** (✉ Barquillo 34 ☎ 91/521–5563) is a low-key bar-café with impromptu jam sessions. Madrid's hippest club for wild, all-night dancing to an international music mix is **El Sol** (✉ C. Jardines 3 ☎ 91/532–6490). **Fortuny** (✉ Fortuny 34 ☎ 91/319–0588) attracts a celebrity crowd, especially in summer, when the lush outdoor patio is open. The door is ultraselective. **Joy Eslava** (✉ Arenal 11 ☎ 91/366–3733), a downtown disco in a converted theater, is an old standby. Stop into the baroque **Palacio de Gaviria** (✉ Arenal 9 ☎ 91/526–6069), a restored 19th-century palace with a maze of rooms that have been turned into a disco, mainly for foreigners. **Pachá** (✉ Barceló 11 ☎ 91/447–0128), one of Spain's infamous chain discos, is always energetic. **Torero** (✉ Cruz 26 ☎ 91/523–1129) is for the beautiful people—a bouncer allows only those judged *gente guapa* (beautiful people) to enter.

FLAMENCO

Madrid has lots of flamenco shows, some good, but many aimed at the tourist trade. Dinner tends to be mediocre and overpriced, though it ensures the best seats; otherwise, opt for the show and a *consumición* (drink) only, usually starting around 11 PM and costing €20–€25.

Arco de Cuchilleros (✉ Cuchilleros 7 ☎ 91/364–0263) is one of the better and cheaper venues in the city to view flamenco. **Café de Chinitas** (✉ Torija 7 ☎ 91/559–5135) is expensive, but offers the best flamenco dancing in Madrid. **Casa Patas** (✉ Cañizares 10 ☎ 91/369–0496) is a major showplace; it offers good, if somewhat touristy, flamenco and tapas, all at reasonable prices. **Corral de la Morería** (✉ Morería 17 ☎ 91/365–8446) invites well-known flamenco stars to perform with the resident group. One of Madrid's prime flamenco showcases—and less commercial than the traditional and better known *tablaos*—**Las Carboneras** (✉ Plaza del Conde de Miranda 1 ☎ 91/542–8677) presents young artists on their way up as well as more established stars on tour. Shows are staged nightly from 10:30 PM to 2 AM.

JAZZ CLUBS

Seasonal citywide festivals present excellent artists; check the local press for listings and venues. The city's best-known jazz venue is **Café Central** (✉ Plaza de Angel 10 ☎ 91/369–4143). **Café del Foro** (✉ San Andrés 38 ☎ 91/445–3752) is a friendly club with live music nightly. **Clamores** (✉ Albuquerque 14 ☎ 91/445–7938) is known for its great champagne list. **Populart** (✉ Huertas 22 ☎ 91/429–8407) has blues, Brazilian music, and salsa.

Shopping

The main shopping area in central Madrid surrounds the pedestrian streets Preciados and Montera, off the Gran Vía between Puerta del Sol and Plaza Callao. The Salamanca district, just off the Plaza de Colón, bordered roughly by Serrano, Goya, and Conde de Peñalver, is more elegant and expensive; just west of Salamanca, the shops on and around Calle Argensola, just south of Calle Génova, are on their way upscale. Calle Mayor and the streets to the east of Plaza Mayor are lined with fascinating old-fashioned stores straight out of the 19th century.

Antiques

The main areas for antiques are the Plaza de las Cortes, Calle Prado, the Carrera San Jerónimo, and the Rastro flea market, along the Ribera de Curtidores and the courtyards just off it.

Fashion

Calle Serrano has the widest selection of smart boutiques and designer fashions—think Prada, Armani, and DKNY, as well as renowned Spanish designers, such as Josep Font-Luz Diaz. Upscale shopping centers have exclusive shops stocked with unusual clothes and gifts.

Adolfo Dóminguez (✉ Serrano 96 ☎ 91/576–7053 ✉ C. Ortega y Gasset 4 ☎ 91/576–0084), one of Spain's top designers, has several boutiques in Madrid. **Jesús del Pozo** (✉ Almirante 9 ☎ 91/531–3646) is one of Spain's premier young fashion designers, a scion of Spanish style for both men and women. **Loewe** (✉ Serrano 26 and 34 ☎ 91/577–6056 ✉ Gran Vía 8 ☎ 91/532–7024) is Spain's most prestigious leather store. **Sybilla** (✉ Jorge Juan 12 ☎ 91/578–1322) is the studio of Spain's best-known woman designer, who designs fluid dresses and hand-knit sweaters in natural colors and fabrics.

Los Jardines de Serrano (✉ C. Goya and Claudio Coello) has smart boutiques. For street-chic fashion closer to medieval Madrid, check out the **Madrid Fusion Centro de Moda** (✉ Plaza Tirso de Molina 15 ☎ 91/369–0018), where up-and-coming Spanish labels like Instinto, Kika, and Extart fill five floors with faux furs, funky jewelry, and the city's most eccentric selection of shoes. **Zara** (✉ ABC, Serrano 61 ☎ 91/575–6334 ✉ Gran Vía 34 ☎ 91/521–1283 ✉ Princesa 63 ☎ 91/543–2415) is for men, women, and children with trendy taste and slim pocketbooks.

Department Stores

Centro Comercial ABC (✉ Paseo de la Castellana 34) is a four-story mall with a large café. **El Corte Inglés** (✉ Preciados 3 ☎ 91/531–9619 ✉ Goya 76 and 87 ☎ 91/432–9300 ✉ Princesa 56 ☎ 91/454–6000 ✉ Serrano 47 ☎ 91/432–5490 ✉ Raimundo Fernández Villaverde 79 ☎ 91/418–8800 ✉ La Vaguada Mall ☎ 91/387–4000) is Spain's largest chain department store, with everything from auto parts to groceries to fashions. The British chain **Marks & Spencer** (✉ Serrano 52 ☎ 91/520–0000 ✉ La Vaguarda Mall ☎ 91/378–2234) is best known for its woolens and underwear, but most shoppers head straight for the food shop in the basement. **FNAC** (✉ Preciados 28 ☎ 91/595–6100) is filled with books, music, and magazines from all over the world.

Food & Flea Markets

El Rastro, Madrid's most famous flea market, operates on Sunday from 9 to 2 around the Plaza de Cascorro and the Ribera de Curtidores. A **stamp and coin market** is held on Sunday morning in the Plaza Mayor.

Mornings, take a look at the colorful food stalls inside the 19th-century glass-and-steel **San Miguel** market, also near the Plaza Mayor. There's a **secondhand-book market** most days on the Cuesta Claudio Moyano, near Atocha Station.

Gift Ideas

Madrid is famous for handmade leather boots, guitars, fans, and capes. **Seseña** (⊠ Calle de la Cruz 23 ☎ 91/531–6840) has outfitted international celebrities in wool and velvet capes since the turn of the 20th century. **Tenorio** (⊠ Plaza de la Provincia 6 ☎ No phone) is where you'll find one dedicated shoemaker who makes country boots (similar to cowboy boots) to order. The hitch is he needs five to six months to complete a pair. The boots start at €1,200.

Casa de Diego (⊠ Puerta del Sol 12 ☎ 91/522–6643), established in 1853, has fans, umbrellas, and classic Spanish walking sticks with ornamented silver handles. The British royal family buys autograph fans here—white kid-skin fans for signing on special occasions. **José Ramirez** (⊠ C. La Paz 8 ☎ 91/531–4229) has provided Spain and the rest of the world with guitars since 1882, and his store includes a museum of antique instruments. Carefully selected handicrafts from all over Spain—ceramics, furniture, glassware, rugs, embroidery, and more—are sold at **Artespaña** (⊠ Hermosilla 14 ☎ 91/435–0221). **Casa Julia** (⊠ Almirante 1 ☎ 91/522–0270) is an artistic showcase, with two floors of tasteful antiques, paintings by up-and-coming artists, and furniture in experimental designs.

Madrid Essentials

AIRPORTS & TRANSFERS

Barajas Airport, 16 km (10 mi) northeast of town just off the NII Barcelona Highway, receives international and domestic flights. Info-Iberia, at the airport, dispenses information on arrivals and departures. 🛂 **Barajas Airport** ☎ 91/305-8343 or 91/393-6000. **Info-Iberia** ☎ 91/329-5767.

TRANSFERS The fastest and most convenient way to get to and from the Madrid airport is the Line 8 metro running every few minutes daily from 6:30 AM to 1 AM between Barajas and Nuevos Ministerios. This run costs €1.10 and takes 12 minutes.

For a mere €3, there's a convenient bus to the central Plaza Colón, where you can catch a taxi to your hotel. Buses leave every 15 minutes between 4:45 AM and 2 AM (slightly less often very early or late in the day). Watch your belongings, as the underground Plaza Colón bus station is a favorite haunt of purse snatchers and con artists.

The metro is a bargain at €1.10 per ticket (or €5.20 for a 10-trip ticket that can also be used on city buses), but you have to change trains twice to get downtown, and the trip takes 45 minutes.

The most expensive route into town (and depending on traffic, not necessarily the fastest) is by taxi (about €20 plus tip in traffic). Pay the metered amount plus the €2 surcharge and €1 for each suitcase. By car take the NII (which becomes Avenida de América) into town, head straight into Calle María de Molina, then turn left on either Calle Serrano or the Castellana.

BUS TRAVEL TO & FROM MADRID

Madrid has no central bus station. Check with the tourist office for departure points for your destination. The Estación del Sur serves Toledo, La Mancha, Alicante, and Andalusia. Auto-Rés serves Extremadura,

Cuenca, Salamanca, Valladolid, Valencia, and Zamora; Auto-Rés has a central ticket and information office, just off Gran Vía, near the Hotel Arosa. The Basque country and most of north-central Spain are served by Continental Auto. For Ávila, Segovia, and La Granja, use Empresa La Sepulvedana. Empresa Herranz serves El Escorial and the Valley of the Fallen. La Veloz serves Chinchón.

🚍 **Auto-Rés** ✉ Plaza Conde de Casal 6 ☎ 91/551-7200 Ⓜ Conde de Casal ✉ Central ticket office, Salud 19 ☎ 91/551-7200. **Continental Auto** ✉ Alenza 20 ☎ 91/530-4800 Ⓜ Ríos Rosas. **Empresa Herranz** ✉ 3 Moncloa Bus Terminal ☎ 91/890-4100 Ⓜ Moncloa. **Empresa La Sepulvedana** ✉ Paseo de la Florida 11 ☎ 91/530-4800 Ⓜ Norte. **Estación del Sur** ✉ Méndez Álvaro s/n ☎ 91/468-4200 Ⓜ Palos de la Frontera. **La Veloz** ✉ Avda. Mediterraneo 49 ☎ 91/409-7602 Ⓜ Conde de Casal.

BUS TRAVEL WITHIN MADRID

Red city buses run from about 6 AM until midnight, and cost €1.10 per ride. After midnight, buses called *buyos* (night owls) run out to the suburbs from Plaza de Cibeles for the same price. Signs at every stop list all other stops by street name, but they're hard to comprehend if you don't know the city well. Pick up a free route map from EMT kiosks on the Plaza de Cibeles or the Puerta del Sol, where you can also buy a 10-ride ticket called a Metrobus (€5.20) that's equally valid for the metro. Drivers will generally make change for anything up to a €20 note. If you've bought a 10-ride ticket, step just behind the driver and insert it in the ticket-punching machine until the mechanism rings. If you speak Spanish, call for information (☎ 91/406–8810).

CAR TRAVEL

The main roads are as follows: north–south, the Paseo de la Castellana and Paseo del Prado; east–west, Calle de Alcalá, Gran Vía, and Calle de la Princesa. The M30 circles Madrid, and the M40 is an outer ring road about 12 km (7 mi) farther out. For Burgos and France, drive north up the Castellana and follow the signs for the NI. For Barcelona and Barajas Airport, head up the Castellana to Plaza Dr. Marañón, then right onto María de Molina and the NII; for Andalusia and Toledo, head south down Paseo del Prado, and then follow the signs to the NIV and N401, respectively. For Segovia, Ávila, and El Escorial, head west along Princesa to Avenida Puerta de Hierro and onto the NVI–La Coruña.

EMERGENCIES

The general emergency number in all EU nations (akin to 911 in the United States) is 112. A list of pharmacies open 24 hours (*farmacias de guardia*) is published daily in *El País*. The Madrid Police has a special phone service in several languages for tourists. Your complaint will be sent to the nearest police station where the crime took place, and you will have two days to drop by the station and sign the report.

🚨 Emergency Services **Ambulance** ☎ 91/522-2222. **Red Cross Ambulance** ☎ 092 **Police** ☎ 091 emergencies. **Police line for tourists** ☎ 902/102112.

🏥 Hospitals **Hospital 12 de Octubre** ✉ Carretera de Andalucía, Km 5.4 ☎ 91/390-8000. **Hospital Ramon y Cajal** ✉ Carretera de Colmenar, Km 9 ☎ 91/336-8000. **La Paz Ciudad Sanitaria** ✉ Paseo de la Castellana 261 ☎ 91/358-2600.

ENGLISH-LANGUAGE MEDIA

The International Bookshop carries secondhand books only.

📚 Bookstores **Booksellers** ✉ José Abascal 48 ☎ 91/442-8104. **Casa del Libro** ✉ Gran Vía 29 ☎ 91/521-4898. **International Bookshop** ✉ Campomanes 13 ☎ 91/541-7291.

METRO TRAVEL

The metro offers the simplest and quickest means of transport and operates from 6 AM to 1:30 AM. Metro maps are available from ticket offices, hotels, and tourist offices. The flat fare is €1.10 a ride; a 10-ride ticket costs €5.20 and is also valid for buses. Carry some change for the ticket machines, especially after 10 PM; the machines make change and allow you to skip long ticket lines.

SIGHTSEEING TOURS

Julià Tours, Pullmantur, and Trapsatur all run the same city orientation tours, conducted in Spanish and English. Reserve directly with their offices, through any travel agent, or through your hotel. Departure points are the addresses listed below, though you can often arrange to be picked up at your hotel. The Madrid Visión bus makes a one-hour tour of the city with recorded commentary in English. No reservation is necessary; catch the bus in front of the Prado every 1½ hours beginning at 10 AM daily (9:30 in summer). There are no buses on Sunday afternoon. A day pass, which allows you to get on and off at various attractions, is €13.

Julià Tours, Pullmantur, and Trapsatur also run full- or half-day trips to El Escorial, Ávila, Segovia, Toledo, and Aranjuez, and in summer to Cuenca and Salamanca. Summer weekends, the popular *Tren de la Fresa* (Strawberry Train) takes passengers from the old Delicias Station to Aranjuez (known for its production of strawberries and asparagus) on a 19th-century train. Tickets can be obtained from RENFE offices, travel agents, and the Delicias Station (Paseo de las Delicias 61). Other one- or two-day excursions by train are available on summer weekends. Contact RENFE for details.

Julià Tours ⊠ Gran Vía 68 ☎ 91/559-9605. **Madrid Visión** ☎ 91/779-1888). **Pullmantur** ⊠ Plaza de Oriente 8 ☎ 91/541-1807. **RENFE** ⊠ Alcalá 44 ☎ 902/240202 ⊕ www.renfe.es/ingles. **Trapsatur** ⊠ San Bernardo 23 ☎ 91/542-6666.

WALKING TOURS The Municipal Tourist Office leads English-language tours of Madrid's Old Quarter every Saturday morning at 10. The *ayuntamiento* (city hall) has a popular selection of Spanish bus and walking tours under the name Descubre Madrid. Walking tours depart most mornings and visit many hidden corners as well as major sights; options include Madrid's Railroads, Medicine in Madrid, Goya's Madrid, and Commerce and Finance in Madrid. Schedules are listed in the "Descubre Madrid" leaflet available from the municipal tourist office. Tickets can be purchased at the Patronato de Turismo. If you want a personal tour with a local guide, contact the Asociación Profesional de Informadores.

Asociación Profesional de Informadores ⊠ Ferraz 82 ☎ 91/542-1214 or 91/541-1221. **Municipal Tourist Office** ⊠ Plaza Mayor 3. **Patronato de Turismo** ⊠ C. Mayor 69 ☎ 91/588-2900.

TAXIS

Taxis are one of Madrid's few truly good deals. They work under three different tariff schemes. Tariff 1 is valid in the city center from 6 AM to 10 PM; meters start at €1.45 and add €.67 per kilometer (½ mi). Supplemental charges include €4 to or from the airport, and €2 from bus and train stations. Tariff 2 is from 10 PM to 6 AM in the city center (and from 6 AM to 10 PM in the suburbs) and the meter runs faster and charges more per kilometer. Tariff 3 runs at night beyond the city limits. All tariffs are listed on the taxi window.

Taxi stands are numerous, and taxis are easily hailed in the street—except when it rains, at which point they're exceedingly hard to come by. Available cabs display a LIBRE sign during the day, a green light at night. No tip is expected, but if you're inspired to give one, €.5 is about right for shorter rides; you may want to go as high as 10% for a trip to the airport. You can call a cab through Tele-Taxi, Radioteléfono Taxi, or Radio Taxi Gremial.

🚩 **Radio Taxi Gremial** ☎ 91/447-5180. **Radioteléfono Taxi** ☎ 91/547-8200. **Tele-Taxi** ☎ 91/371-2131.

TRAIN TRAVEL

Madrid has three railroad stations: Chamartín, Atocha, and Norte, the last primarily for commuter trains. Chamartín, in the northern suburbs beyond the Plaza de Castilla, is the main station, with trains to Portugal, France, and the north (including Barcelona, Ávila, Salamanca, Santiago, and La Coruña, San Sebastián, Burgos, León, and Oviedo). Most trains to Valencia, Alicante, and Andalusia leave from Chamartín but stop at the Atocha Station as well. Atocha sends trains to Segovia, Toledo, Extremadura, Lisbon, El Escorial, and southern and eastern cities such as Seville, Granada, Málaga, Córdoba, Valencia, and Castellón. A convenient metro stop (Atocha RENFE) connects the Atocha rail station to the city subway system. The Atocha Station, a spectacular, late-19th-century greenhouse, is Madrid's terminal for high-speed AVE service to Córdoba and Seville and service to Zaragosa and Lleida.

For all train information call or visit the RENFE offices, open weekdays 9:30–8. Ask for an English operator. You can also charge tickets to your credit card and even have them delivered to your hotel. There's another RENFE office in the international arrivals hall at Barajas Airport, or you can purchase tickets at any of the three main stations or from travel agents displaying the blue and yellow RENFE sign.

🚩 **Atocha** ✉ Glorieta del Emperador Carlos V, southern end of Paseo del Prado ☎ 91/328-9020. **Chamartín** ✉ Avda. Pío XII ☎ 91/315-9976. **RENFE** ✉ Alcalá 44 ☎ 902/240202 ⊕ www.renfe.es/ingles.

TRANSPORTATION AROUND MADRID

Madrid is a fairly compact city, and most of the main sights can be visited on foot. If you're staying in one of the modern hotels in northern Madrid, however, off the Castellana, you may need to use the bus or subway.

TRAVEL AGENCIES

🚩 **American Express** ✉ Plaza de las Cortes 2 ☎ 91/743-7740. **Carlson Wagons-Lits/Viajes Ecuador** ✉ Paseo de la Castellana 96 ☎ 91/563-1202 ⊕ www.viajesecuador.net. **Carlson Wagons-Lits** ✉ Condesa de Venadito 1 ☎ 91/724-9900. **Pullmantur** ✉ Plaza de Oriente 8 ☎ 91/541-1807.

VISITOR INFORMATION

Madrid Provincial Tourist Office is the best place for comprehensive information. The municipal tourist office is centrally located, but hordes of tourists tend to deplete its stock of brochures. Other tourist offices are at the International Arrivals Hall in Barajas Airport and at Chamartín train station.

🚩 **Madrid Provincial Tourist Office** ✉ Duque de Medinaceli 2 ☎ 91/429-4951. **Municipal Tourist Offices** ✉ Plaza Mayor 3 ☎ 91/588-1636 ✉ International Arrivals Hall, Barajas Airport ☎ 91/305-8656 ✉ Chamartín train station ☎ 91/315-9976 ⊕ www.munimadrid.es.

CASTILE

The beauty and romantic histories of the towns around Madrid rank them among Spain's greatest sights. Historic Toledo, Spain's former capital; the great palace-monastery of El Escorial; Segovia's Roman aqueduct and fairy-tale Alcázar; the imposing medieval walls of Ávila; and

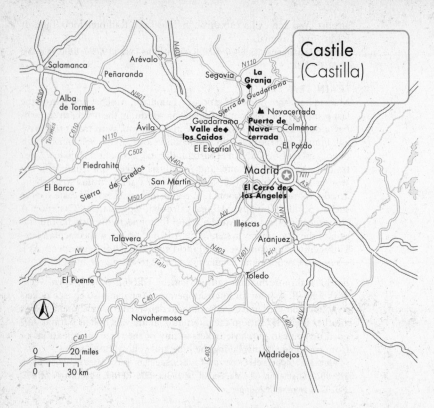

the magnificent Plaza Mayor of the old university town of Salamanca all lie within an hour or two of the capital.

All these towns, with the possible exception of Salamanca, are easy day trips from Madrid. But if you've had your fill of Spain's booming capital, you'll find it far more rewarding to leave Madrid altogether and tour from one town to another, spending a night or two in classically Spanish Castile (Castilla). After the day-trippers have gone home, you can enjoy the real charm of these provincial communities and wander at leisure through their medieval streets.

Toledo

If you're driving, head south from Madrid on the N401. About 20 minutes from the capital, look left for a prominent rounded hill topped by a statue of Christ. This is **El Cerro de los Ángeles** (Hill of the Angels), the geographical center of the Iberian Peninsula. After 90 minutes of drab, industrial scenery, the unforgettable silhouette of Toledo suddenly rises before you, with the imposing bulk of the Alcázar and the slender spire of its cathedral dominating the skyline. This former capital, where Moors, Jews, and Christians once lived in harmony, is now a living national monument, holding all the elements of Spanish civilization in hand-carved, sun-mellowed stone. For a stunning view of Toledo as El Greco knew it, begin with a panoramic drive around the Carretera de Circunvalación, crossing over the Alcántara bridge and returning by way of the bridge of San Martín. As you gaze at the city rising like an island in its own bend of the Tagus, you may notice how little its skyline has changed in the four centuries since El Greco painted *Storm over Toledo.*

Toledo is a small city steeped in history and full of magnificent buildings. It was the capital of Spain under both Moors and Christians until Philip II moved the capital to Madrid in 1561. Begin your visit with a drink in one of the many terrace cafés on the central **Plaza Zocódover**; study a map and try to get your bearings, for a veritable labyrinth confronts you as you try to find your way to Toledo's great treasures. While here, search the square's pastry shops for Toledo's typical *mazapanes* (marzipan candies).

Toledo's 13th-century **cathedral** is one of the greatest in Spain, and the seat of the Cardinal Primate. Somber but elaborate, it blazes with jeweled chalices, gorgeous ecclesiastical vestments, historic tapestries, some 750 stained-glass windows, and paintings by Tintoretto, Titian, Murillo, El Greco, Velázquez, and Goya. The cathedral has two surprises: a **Mozarabic chapel**, where mass is still celebrated on Sunday according to an ancient Mozarabic rite from the days of the Visigoths (AD 419–711); and its unique **Transparente**, an ornate baroque roof that gives a theatrical glimpse of heaven as the sunlight pours down through a hole to a mass of figures and clouds. ⊠ *Arco de Palacio 2* ☎ *925/222241* ۞ *Mon.–Sat. 10:30–6:30, Sun. 3–6.*

The tiny chapel of **Santo Tomé**, which houses El Greco's (1541–1614) masterpiece the *Burial of the Count of Orgaz*, captures some of the incredible spirit of the Greek painter who adopted Spain, and Toledo in particular, as his home. Do you recognize the sixth man from the left in the painting's earthly contingent? Or the young boy in the left-hand corner? The first is El Greco himself, the second his son Jorge Manuel—embroidered on the boy's handkerchief you'll see *1578*, the year of his birth. ⊠ *Pl. del Conde 4* ☎ *925/256098* ⊕ *www.santotome.org* ۞ *Mar.–mid-Oct., daily 10–6:45; mid-Oct.–Feb., daily 10–5:45.*

The **Casa de El Greco** (El Greco's House) has copies of the artist's works. The museum next door contains some originals, including a panorama of Toledo with the Hospital of Tavera in the foreground. The house itself, however, is closed indefinitely for restoration. ⊠ *Samuel Levi s/n* ☎ *925/224046.*

The splendid **Sinagoga del Tránsito** (Tránsito Synagogue) was commissioned in 1366 by Samuel Levi, chancellor to Peter the Cruel. The synagogue bears Christian and Moorish as well as Jewish influences in its architecture and decoration; notice the Stars of David interspersed with the arms of Castile and León. The small **Museo Sefardí** (Sephardic Museum) chronicles Toledo's former Jewish community. ⊠ *Samuel Levi s/ n* ☎ *925/223665* ۞ *Tues.–Sat. 10–2 and 4–6, Sun. 10–2.*

Santa María la Blanca (St. Mary the White) was originally a synagogue, founded in 1203. It was consecrated as a church in the early 15th century when it was stormed by a Christian mob led by St. Vincent Ferrer. Except for the 16th-century altarpiece, however, the architecture is neither Jewish nor Christian, but Moorish: the interior has five naves, horseshoe arches, and capitals decorated with texts from the Koran. ⊠ *Reyes Católicos 4* ☎ *925/227257* ۞ *Daily 10–1:45 and 3:30–6 ('til 7 July and Aug.).*

San Juan de los Reyes, a convent church in western Toledo, was erected by Ferdinand and Isabella to commemorate their victory at the Battle of Toro in 1476, and was intended to be their burial place. The building is largely the work of architect Juan Guas, who considered it his masterpiece and asked to be buried here himself. In true plateresque fashion, the white interior is covered with inscriptions and heraldic motifs.

✉ *Reyes Católicos 17* ☎ *925/223802* ☉ *Apr.–Oct., daily 10–7; Nov.–Mar., daily 10–6.*

In a beautiful Renaissance hospital with a stunning classical-plateresque facade, the **Museo de la Santa Cruz**, unlike Toledo's other sights, is open all day (limited hours Monday) without a break. The light and elegant interior has changed little since the 16th century, the main difference being that works of art have replaced the hospital beds; among the displays is El Greco's *Assumption* of 1613, the artist's last known work. A small **Museo de Arqueología** (Museum of Archaeology) is in and around the hospital's delightful cloister, off which is a beautifully decorated staircase by Alonso de Covarrubias. ✉ *Cervantes 3* ☎ *925/221036* ☉ *Mon.–Sat. 10–6:30, Sun. 10–2.*

Outside the walls beyond the imposing Puerta Nueva de Bisagra, Toledo's main northern gate, built in 1550 by Spanish architect Alonso de Covarrubias (1488–1570), is the **Hospital de Tavera.** Begun by Bustamente in 1541 and finished by the Vergara brothers and Covarrubias, this unfinished and slightly dilapidated complex is full of character. The evocatively ramshackle **Museo de Duque de Lema** occupies its southern wing. The museum's miscellaneous collection includes a painting by the 17th-century artist José Ribera, and the monumental chapel holds El Greco's final painting, the *Baptism of Christ* and the carved marble tomb of Cardinal Tavera, the last work of Alonso de Berruguete. For some bizarre acoustical effects, don't miss the crypt downstairs. ✉ *Cardenal Tavera 2* ☎ *925/220451* ☉ *Daily 10–1:30 and 3:30–6.*

$$–$$$ ✕ **Asador Adolfo.** Steps from the cathedral but discreetly hidden away, this restaurant has an old, intimate interior whose wood-beam ceiling was painted in the 14th century. The emphasis is on fresh produce and traditional Toledan food. The *tempura de flor de calabacín* (zucchini-blossom tempura in saffron sauce) is a tasty starter; a flavorful entrée is the *solomillo de cerdo* (pork loin with wild mushrooms and black truffles). ✉ *Granada 6* ☎ *925/227321* ⌂ *Reservations essential* ▭ *AE, DC, MC, V* ☉ *Closed Mon. No dinner Sun.*

$$–$$$ ✕ **Cason de los López de Toledo.** A vaulted foyer leads to an enclosed patio with marble statues, twittering caged birds, a fountain, and abstract religious paintings. The market-based menu has the finest Castilian and Continental cuisine. Starters such as garlic-ravioli soup are followed by hearty second courses, including braised rabbit with sesame sauce and mashed potatoes. ✉ *Sillería 3* ☎ *925/254774* ▭ *AE, DC, MC, V.*

$$–$$$ ✕ **Venta de Aires.** This century-old inn on the edge of town, not far from the Tajo River, is where Toledanos go to eat partridge. Steaks and lamb are also expertly prepared. ✉ *Circo Romano 35* ☎ *925/220545* ▭ *AE, DC, MC, V.*

$$ ✕ **La Abadía.** Perfect for a light lunch, a sandwich, or a round of tapas, this stylish bar-restaurant has vaulted stone ceilings and a huge, old wooden door. The dining room downstairs specializes in shish kebabs, grilled meats, and salads. ✉ *Plaza San Nicolás, Núnez de Arce 3* ☎ *925/251140* ▭ *MC, V.*

★ **$$** ✕🛏 **Hostal del Cardenal.** Built in the 18th century as a summer palace for Cardinal Lorenzana, this quiet and beautiful hotel has rooms with antique furniture. Some rooms overlook the hotel's wooded garden, which lies at the foot of the town's walls. The restaurant has a long-standing reputation; dishes are mainly local, and in season you'll find delicious asparagus and strawberries from Aranjuez. ✉ *Paseo Recaredo 24, 45004* ☎ *925/224900* 🖷 *925/222991* ⊕ *www.hostaldelcardenal.com* ⇖ *27 rooms* ⌂ *Restaurant* ▭ *AE, DC, MC, V.*

$$$ ▦ **Parador de Toledo.** This modern building on Toledo's outskirts has an unbeatable panorama of the town. The architecture and furnishings nod to the traditional Toledan style, emphasizing brick and wood. ⊠ *Cerro del Emperador s/n, 45001* ☎ *925/221850* 🖷 *925/225166* ⊕ *www.parador.es* ↩ *76 rooms* ♨ *Restaurant, pool, bar* ⊟ *AE, DC, MC, V.*

$$$ ▦ **Hotel Pintor El Greco.** Next door to the painter's house-museum, this friendly hotel occupies what was once a 17th-century bakery. The modern interior is warm and clean, with tawny colors and antique touches, like exposed-brick vaulting. ⊠ *Alamillos del Transito 13, 45002* ☎ *925/285191* 🖷 *925/215819* ⊕ *www.hotelpintorelgreco.com* ↩ *33 rooms* ⊟ *AE, DC, MC, V.*

El Escorial

In the foothills of the Guadarrama Mountains, 50 km (31 mi) northwest of Madrid and 120 km (74 mi) from Toledo, stands the Monastery of San Lorenzo del Escorial, the burial place of Spanish kings and queens. Built by the religious fanatic Philip II as a memorial to his father, Charles V, El Escorial is a vast, rectangular structure, conceived and executed with a monotonous magnificence worthy of the Spanish royal necropolis. It was designed by Juan de Herrera, Spain's greatest Renaissance architect. The **Pantéon Real** (Royal Pantheon) contains the tombs of all the monarchs since Carlos I save three. Only those queens who bore sons who were later crowned lie in the same crypt; the others, along with royal sons and daughters who never ruled, lie in the nearby **Panteón de los Infantes** (Princes' Pantheon). The monastery's other highlights are Philip II's magnificent **library,** with 40,000 rare volumes and 2,700 illuminated manuscripts (including the diary of St. Teresa), and the **royal apartments.** Compare the spartan private apartment of Philip II, including the simple bedroom in which he died in 1598, with the beautiful carpets, porcelain, and tapestries with which his less austere successors embellished the rest of his somber commission. ⊠ *Junction of Rtes. C600 and M505, northwest of Madrid* ☎ *91/890–5905* ⊕ *www.patrimonionacional.es* ☉ *Oct.–Mar., Tues.–Sun. 10–6; Apr.–Sept., Tues.–Sun. 10–7; last entry 1 hr before closing.*

★ $$$–$$$$ ✕ **Charolés.** The meat dishes at this elegant restaurant are famous throughout the region; try the *charolés a la pimienta* (peppered steak). Fresh fish is brought in daily from Spain's north coast. In summer you can dine on a terrace above the street. ⊠ *Floridablanca 24* ☎ *91/890–5975* ♨ *Reservations essential* ⊟ *AE, DC, MC, V.*

$$$ ✕ **Parrilla Príncipe.** The scents of roast kid, lamb, chicken, and pork sausage draw crowds with big appetites to this specialist in succulent barbecue. Airier and more modern that most local taverns, the restaurant also has vegetarian paella and pasta on its menu. ⊠ *Floridablanca 6* ☎ *91/890–1611* ⊟ *AE, DC, MC, V* ☉ *Closed Tues.*

$$ ✕ **Mesón de la Cueva.** Founded in 1768, this atmospheric mesón has several small, rustic dining rooms. ⊠ *San Antón 4* ☎ *91/890–1516* ⊟ *MC, V* ☉ *Closed Mon.*

$$$ ▦ **Victoria Palace.** The rooms at the back of this grand old hotel near the monastery have balconies and a splendid view toward Madrid. There's also a garden. ⊠ *Juan de Toledo 4, 28200* ☎ *91/896–9890* 🖷 *91/896–9896* ↩ *87 rooms* ♨ *Pool* ⊟ *AE, DC, MC, V.*

$$ ▦ **Miranda Suizo.** With its dark-wood fittings, marble café tables, and main-street location, this charming hotel is straight out of the 19th century. The guest rooms are comfortable, and the Taberna del Alabardero restaurant is a cozy place to dine. ⊠ *Floridablanca 18, 28200* ☎ *91/890–4711* 🖷 *91/890–4358* ↩ *52 rooms* ♨ *Restaurant* ⊟ *AE, DC, MC, V.*

Segovia

★ The golden-stone market town of Segovia has outstanding medieval and Roman monuments, embroideries, and textiles, and excellent food.

The majestic **Roman aqueduct,** its huge granite blocks held together without mortar, greets you at the entrance to Segovia. At its foot is a small bronze statue of Romulus and the wolf, presented by Rome in 1974 to commemorate the 2,000-year history of Spain's greatest surviving Roman monument.

The **Ronda de Santa Lucía** leads to the most romantic view of the Alcázar, perched high on its rock like the prow of a mighty ship. Return via the Carretera de los Hoyos for yet another magical view, this time of the venerable cathedral rising from the ramparts.

Calle Real, the main shopping street, passes the Romanesque church of **San Martín,** with a porticoed outer gallery.

Plaza Mayor, with colorful ceramics shops (good bargains) and pleasant cafés, is set against a backdrop of ancient arcaded houses and one of the loveliest Gothic cathedrals in Spain.

Segovia's **cathedral** was the last Gothic cathedral to be built in Spain (the first was in nearby Ávila). Begun in 1525 by order of Charles V, it has a golden and harmonious interior, illuminated by 16th-century Flemish windows. Its museum, off the cloister, has the first book printed in Spain (1472) and a 17th-century ceiling paneled in white and gold, a splendid example of Mudéjar *artesonado* work. ⊠ *Marqués del Arco 1, Plaza Mayor* ☏ *921/462205* ☽ *June–Sept., daily 10–7; Oct.–May, daily 10–6* ☽ *Closed Wed. afternoon.*

The turreted **Alcázar** is largely a fanciful re-creation from the 1880s; the original 13th-century castle was destroyed by fire in 1862. However, the view from its ramparts—and, even better, from its tower if you can manage the 156 steps—is breathtaking. The Alcázar served as a major residence of the Catholic Monarchs; here Isabella met Ferdinand, and from here she set out to the Plaza Mayor to be crowned queen of Castile. The interior successfully illustrates the dawn of Spain's golden age. ⊠ *Pl. de la Reina Victoria Eugenia* ☏ *921/460759* ⊕ *www. alcazardesegovia.com* ☽ *May–Sept., daily 10–7; Oct.–Apr., Mon.–Thurs. 10–6, Fri.–Sun. 10–7.*

$$–$$$ ✕ **Casa Duque.** At the end of Segovia's main shopping street, this restaurant has several floors of beautifully decorated traditional dining rooms. There's a local vibe, and the food is pure Castilian—roasts are the house specialty. ⊠ *Cervantes 12* ☏ *921/462487* ♨ *Reservations essential* ▤ *AE, DC, MC, V.*

$$–$$$ ✕ **La Oficina.** Traditional Castilian dishes are served here in two delightful dining rooms that date from 1893. ⊠ *Cronista Lecea 10* ☏ *921/460286* ▤ *AE, DC, MC, V.*

★ **$$–$$$** ✕ **Mesón de Cándido.** Tucked cozily under the aqueduct, Segovia's most prestigious restaurant benefits from the ban on traffic by the monument. The dining rooms are full of medieval objects and Castilian memorabilia. Specialties are *cochinillo asado* (roast suckling pig) and cordero asado, both succulent. Terrace dining is available in summer. ⊠ *Plaza Azoguejo 5* ☏ *921/425911* ♨ *Reservations essential* ▤ *AE, DC, MC, V.*

★ **$$–$$$** ✕ **Mesón de José María.** With a lively bar, this mesón is hospitable, and its passionately dedicated owner is devoted to maintaining traditional Castilian specialties while concocting innovations of his own. The menu changes by the season. The large, old-style, brightly lighted dining room is often packed, and the waiters are uncommonly friendly. Although it's a bit touristy, it's equally popular with locals. ⊠ *Cronista Lecea 11* ☎ 921/466017 ⊟ *AE, DC, MC, V.*

★ **$$$** ✕🖼 **Parador Nacional de Segovia.** To the north of town, this modern parador offers comfortable, spacious rooms and both indoor and outdoor pools. The views of the city are magnificent, especially at sunset. The rooms are light, with generous amounts of glass. The restaurant serves excellent Castilian food. ⊠ *Carretera de Valladolid s/n (off the N601 toward Valladolid), 40003* ☎ 921/443737 🖷 921/437362 ⊕ *www. parador.es* 🛏 *113 rooms* ♿ *Restaurant, 2 pools (1 indoor)* ⊟ *AE, DC, MC, V.*

$$ 🖼 **Infanta Isabel.** Right on a corner of the Plaza Mayor, this small, central hotel has a Victorian sensibility and great views of the cathedral. Guest rooms are light, with painted white furnishings. ⊠ *Isabel la Católica, 40001* ☎ 921/461300 🖷 921/462217 ⊕ *www.hotelinfantaisabel.com* 🛏 *37 rooms* ♿ *Restaurant* ⊟ *AE, DC, MC, V.*

$-$$ 🖼 **Las Sirenas.** A few steps from the Plaza Mayor, this elegant hotel is in one of Segovia's best locations. The furnishings are slightly faded, but old-fashioned charm and splendid views of the church of Millín make it a hard-to-beat value. ⊠ *Juan Bravo 30, 40001* ☎ 921/462663 🖷 921/462657 🛏 *39 rooms* ⊟ *AE, DC, MC, V.*

Ávila

At nearly 4,100 feet above sea level, Ávila is the highest provincial capital in Spain. Alfonso VI and his son-in-law, Count Raimundo de Borgoña, rebuilt the town and walls in 1090, bringing it permanently under Christian control. It is these walls, the best-preserved military installations of their kind in Spain, that give Ávila its special medieval quality. Thick and solid, with 88 towers tufted with untidy storks' nests, they stretch for 2½ km (1½ mi) around the entire city and make an ideal focus for the start of your visit. For a superb overall view, drive out to the **Cuatro Postes** (Four Posts), ¾ km (½ mi) out on the road to Salamanca. Ávila's other claim to fame is St. Teresa the Mystic, who lived much of her life here in the 16th century.

The **Basílica de San Vicente,** just outside the walls, is one of Ávila's finest Romanesque churches, erected on the spot where St. Vincent and his sisters Sabina and Cristeta were martyred in AD 306. Here, too, St. Teresa is said to have experienced the vision that told her to reform the Carmelite order. ⊠ *Plaza de San Vicente* ☎ 920/255230 ☉ *Daily 10–1:30 and 4–6:30.*

Ávila's oldest and most rewarding ecclesiastical monuments predate St. Teresa. The impregnable hulk of the **cathedral** resembles a fortress as much as a house of God. Though of Romanesque origin—the Romanesque sections are recognizable by their red-and-white stonework—it is usually cited as Spain's first Gothic cathedral. Inside is the ornate alabaster tomb of Cardinal Alonso de Madrigal, a 15th-century bishop whose swarthy complexion earned him the nickname of El Tostado (the toasted one). ⊠ *Pl. de la Catedral s/n* ☎ 920/211641 ☉ *June–Aug., weekdays 10–7, Sat. 10–6:30, Sun. noon–6; Sept.–May, weekdays 10–5, Sat. 10–6, Sun. noon–5.*

The **Convento de Santa Teresa** stands on the site of the saint's birthplace, with an ornate baroque chapel and a museum with some of Teresa's relics: her rosary, books, walking stick, sandal sole, and preserved ring finger. ⊠ *Pl. de la Santa s/n* ☎ 920/211030 ☉ *Daily 10–1:30 and 3:30–5:30* ☉ *Closed Mon. Oct.–Easter.*

The **Monasterio de Santo Tomás** was built between 1482 and 1493 by Ferdinand and Isabella, who used it as a summer palace. It houses the tomb of their only son, Prince Juan, who died at the age of 19 while a student at Salamanca, and the tomb of the notorious Inquisitor General Tomás de Torquemada. ⊠ *Pl. de Granada 1* ☎ *920/220400* ⊙ *Cloister; daily 10–1 and 4–8, museum: Tues.–Sun. 11–1 and 4–6.*

You can relax in the pleasant **Plaza de Santa Teresa,** with outdoor cafés and a statue of the saint erected for Pope John Paul's visit in 1982.

★ **$$–$$$** ✕ **El Molino de la Losa.** Nearly straddling the serene Adaja River, with one of the best views of the town walls, this restaurant occupies a 15th-century mill, the working mechanism of which has been well preserved and provides much distraction for those seated in the animated bar. Lamb is roasted in a medieval wood oven, and trout comes from the river; try the beans from nearby El Barco (*judías de El Barco*). The garden has a small playground for children. ⊠ *Bajada de la Losa 12* ☎ *920/211101 or 920/211102* ▤ *AE, MC, V* ⊙ *Closed Mon.*

$–$$ ✕ **Mesón del Rastro.** In a wing of the medieval Palacio Abrantes, this restaurant has an attractive Castilian interior with exposed stone walls and beams, low lighting, and dark-wood furniture. Try the lamb and El Barco beans; also worthwhile is the *caldereta de cabrito* (goat stew). The place suffers somewhat from its popularity with tour buses, and service is sometimes slow and impersonal. ⊠ *Pl. Rastro 1* ☎ *920/211218* ▤ *AE, DC, MC, V.*

★ **$$$** ▦ **Palacio de los Velada.** A beautifully restored 16th-century palace houses Ávila's top hotel, right in the heart of the city, beside the cathedral. You can relax between sightseeing excursions in the lovely palace courtyard. The attractive rooms are modern and comfortable, and have all the amenities. ⊠ *Plaza de la Catedral 10, 05001* ☎ *920/255100* ▤ *920/254900* ⊕ *www.veladahoteles.com* ↘ *145 rooms* ⌂ *Restaurant, bar* ▤ *AE, DC, MC, V.*

$$–$$$ ▦ **Parador de Ávila.** This is a restored 18th-century building attached to the town walls, with a leafy garden that leads to the ramparts. The interior is unusually warm, in tawny tones, and public rooms are convivial. Guest rooms have terra-cotta tile floors and leather chairs; bathrooms are spacious, gleamingly modern, and fashionably designed. ⊠ *Marqués Canales de Chozas 2, 05001* ☎ *920/211340* ▤ *920/226166* ⊕ *www.parador.es* ↘ *61 rooms* ⌂ *Restaurant, bar* ▤ *AE, DC, MC, V.*

$$ ▦ **Hospedería La Sinagoga.** This small, new hotel—in what was once a medieval synagogue—is a gem. The original columns in the entry, the stairway that once led to the Jewish baths, and the stone and exposed brick walls of certain rooms are all that remain of the original structure in this sleek combination of modern and medieval. ⊠ *Reyes Catolicos 22, 05001* ☎ *920/352321* ▤ *920/353474* ⊕ *www.lasinagoga.com* ↘ *22 rooms* ▤ *AE, DC, MC, V.*

Salamanca

★ Salamanca is an ancient and gorgeous city, and even your first glimpse of it is bound to be unforgettable. In the foreground as you approach is the sturdy 15-arch Roman bridge, and above this—dominating the view—soar the city's old houses and the golden walls, turrets, and domes of its plateresque cathedrals. The word *plateresque* comes from *plata* (silver), implying that the stone is chiseled and engraved as intricately as that delicate metal. Today, as centuries ago, the University of Salamanca is the dominant influence here, creating an intellectual vibe and a stimulating arts scene.

The west facade of the Dominican **Convento de San Esteban** (Monastery of St. Stephen) is superbly plateresque. ⊠ *Pl. Concilio de Trento* ☎ *923/215000* ⊗ *Daily 9–1 and 4–8 (4–6 in winter).*

Salamanca has two distinct, adjoining **cathedrals,** the **Catedral Vieja** (Old Cathedral) and the grandly carved **Catedral Nueva** (New Cathedral). Inside the sturdy Romanesque walls of the Old Cathedral is a stunning altarpiece with 53 painted panels. Within the splendid **cloister** are a worthy collection of religious art and the **Capilla de Santa Bárbara** (Chapel of St. Barbara, or Degree Chapel), where anxious students sought help the night before their final exams. ⊠ *Plá y Deniel s/n* ☎ *923/217476* ⊗ *New Cathedral: Mon.–Sat. 9–6, Sun. 9:30–2; Old Cathedral: Mon.–Sat. 10–5:30, Sun. 10–2.*

Founded by Alfonso IX in 1218, Salamanca's **Universidad** (University) is to Spain what Oxford is to England. On the famous facade of the **Escuelas Mayores** (Medieval University), a profusion of plateresque carving surrounds the medallions of Ferdinand and Isabella. See if you can find the famous frog and skull, said to bring good luck to students taking exams. Inside, the **Sala de Fray Luis de León** (Friar Luis's Lecture Room) has been untouched since the days of that great scholar, and the prestigious **library** holds some 50,000 parchment and leather-bound volumes. ⊠ *Patio de Las Escuelas* ☎ *923/294550 Ext. 1150* ⊗ *Weekdays 9:30–1:30 and 4–7:30, Sat. 9:30–1:30 and 4–7, Sun. 10–1:30.*

The elegant, 18th-century **Plaza Mayor** is Salamanca's crowning glory. Built by Alberto and Nicolás Churriguera, it is widely thought the most beautiful Plaza Mayor in Spain. Here you can browse in stores offering typical *charro* jewelry (silver and black flower beads), head down the adjoining streets in search of colorful tapas bars, or just relax and watch the world go by at an outdoor café.

$$$$ ✕ **Chez Victor.** If you're tired of Castilian cuisine, try this chic place, where chef-owner Victoriano Salvador adapts French food to Spanish tastes. Sample the *carrillada de buey braseada con jengibre* (cheek of beef braised in ginger) and outstanding desserts, especially the raspberry-walnut *tarta de chocolate* (chocolate pie) with fresh whipped cream. ⊠ *Espoz y Mina 26* ☎ *923/213123* ⊟ *AE, DC, MC, V* ⊗ *Closed Mon. No dinner Sun. Closed Aug.*

★ **$$–$$$** ✕ **Chapeau.** This chic spot offers both meat and fish carefully roasted in its wood-fire ovens. Try the *pimientos rellenos* (stuffed peppers) and, for dessert, the orange mousse. ⊠ *Gran Vía 20* ☎ *923/211–726* ⊟ *AE, DC, MC, V* ⊗ *Closed Sun. and Aug.*

$–$$ ✕ **Río de la Plata.** This tiny, long-standing basement restaurant just off Calle de San Pablo retains a warm, old-fashioned character; it has a fireplace and is frequented by locals. The food, good-quality fish and meat, is simple but carefully prepared. ⊠ *Plaza del Peso 1* ☎ *923/219005* ⊟ *AE, DC, MC, V* ⊗ *Closed Mon. and July.*

$$$ 🏨 **Gran Hotel.** The grande dame of Salamanca's hotels offers stylishly baroque lounges and refurbished, yet old-fashioned, oversize rooms, just steps from the Plaza Mayor. ⊠ *Poeta Iglesias 5, 37001* ☎ *923/213500* 🖷 *923/213500* ⊕ *www.helcom.es* ⇆ *136 rooms* ⌂ *Restaurant, bar* ⊟ *AE, DC, MC, V.*

$$$ 🏨 **NH Palacio de Castellanos.** Housed in an immaculately restored 15th-century palace, this hotel has an exquisite interior patio and an equally beautiful restaurant. ⊠ *San Pablo 58, 37008* ☎ *923/261818* 🖷 *923/261819* ⊕ *www.nh-hoteles.com* ⇆ *62 rooms* ⌂ *Restaurant* ⊟ *AE, DC, MC, V.*

$–$$ 🏨 **Hostal Plaza Mayor.** Steps from the Plaza Mayor, this agreeable hostelry has small but modern rooms. The potential drawback is noise on Friday and Saturday nights, when student *tunas* (strolling musicians) sing guitar ballads at nearby cafés until the wee hours. Reserve in advance. ✉ *Plaza del Corrillo 20, 37008* ☎ *923/262020* 🖷 *923/217548* 🛏 *19 rooms* ♿ *Restaurant* 🖃 *MC, V.*

Castile Essentials

BUS TRAVEL

All towns are linked by buses; local tourist offices can advise on schedules. Each town has a central bus station.

🚌 **Ávila** ✉ Avda. de Madrid ☎ 920/220154. **Salamanca** ✉ Filiberto Villalobos 71 ☎ 923/236717. **Segovia** ✉ Paseo Ezequiel González ☎ 921/427707. **Toledo** ✉ Ronda de Castilla la Mancha, off the road from Madrid ☎ 925/215850.

CAR TRAVEL

The N403 from Toledo to Ávila passes through spectacular scenery in the Sierra de Gredos, as does the C505 from Ávila to El Escorial. From El Escorial to Segovia, both the Puerto de León and Puerto de Navacerrada mountain passes offer magnificent views. The N501 from Ávila to Salamanca takes you across the tawny plain of Castile.

TRAIN TRAVEL

Trains to Toledo leave from Madrid's Atocha Station; to Salamanca from Chamartín Station; and to Ávila, Segovia, and El Escorial from both stations, although sometimes more frequently from Chamartín. For schedules and reservations call RENFE. Within the region, there's a direct train line from El Escorial to Ávila and Salamanca; otherwise, train connections are poor, and you'll do better by bus.

🚆 **RENFE** ☎ 902/2400202 ⊕ www.renfe.es.

VISITOR INFORMATION

🚌 **Ávila** ✉ Plaza de la Catedral 4 ☎ 920/211387. **El Escorial** ✉ Floridablanca 10 ☎ 91/890-1554. **Salamanca** ✉ Casa de las Conchas, Rúa Mayor s/n ☎ 923/268571 ✉ Information booth, Plaza Mayor. **Segovia** ✉ Plaza Mayor 10 ☎ 921/460334 ✉ Plaza del Azoguejo 1 ☎ 921/462-906. **Toledo** ✉ Puerta de Bisagra ☎ 925/220843.

BARCELONA

As the capital of Catalunya (Catalonia), 2,000-year-old Barcelona commanded a vast Mediterranean empire when Madrid was still a dusty Moorish outpost on the Spanish steppe. Relegated to second-city status only after Madrid was chosen as site of the royal court in 1561, Barcelona more than rivals Madrid for architecture, culture, commerce, and nightlife. Industrious, creative, and playful in even parts, the citizens of this thriving metropolis are proud to have and use their own language: street names, museum exhibits, newspapers, radio programs, and movies are all in Catalan. An important milestone here was the city's long-awaited opportunity to host the Olympic Games in summer 1992, an event of singular importance in Barcelona's modernization. Ring roads, highways, a renovated port and beaches, and the creation of an entire neighborhood in what used to be the run-down industrial district of Poble Nou were among Barcelona's main 1992 achievements. Preparations for the 2004 Forum de les Cultures have gone even further in creating an entire new city, Diagonal Mar, on the city's eastern Mediterranean waterfront. The Gothic Quarter's narrow alleys, the elegance and distinction of the moderniste (a Spanish and mainly Catalan version of art nouveau) Eixample, and the many fruits of Gaudí's whimsical imagination make Barcelona's two millenniums of art and architecture a world center for design.

Exploring Barcelona

Numbers in the margin correspond to points of interest on the Barcelona map.

It should take you two full days of sightseeing to complete the following tour. The first part covers the Gothic Quarter, the Picasso Museum, and Las Ramblas. The second part takes you to Passeig de Gràcia and the church of the Sagrada Família; and the third, to Montjuïc.

The Barri Gòtic (Gothic Quarter) & Las Ramblas

★ ❶ **Catedral de la Seu** (Cathedral). Citizens of Barcelona gather on Sunday morning to dance the *sardana*, a symbol of Catalan identity, on Plaça de la Seu, in front of the cathedral. The elaboraté Gothic structure was built between 1298 and 1450, though the spire and Gothic facade were not added until 1892. Inside, highlights are the beautifully carved **choir stalls**; Santa Eulàlia's tomb in the crypt; the battle-scarred crucifix from Don Juan's galley in the naval battle of Lepanto, in the **Capella de Lepanto** (Lepanto Chapel); and the cloisters. ⊠ *Plaça de la Seu* ☎ *93/315–2213* ⊙ *Daily 7:45–1:30 and 4–7:45.*

⓬ **Gran Teatre del Liceu.** Barcelona's famous opera house was gutted by fire in 1994 but, phoenixlike, reopened five years later, a modern replica of its original self. Built between 1845 and 1847, the Liceu was famed as one of the world's most beautiful opera houses, with ornamental gilt and plush red-velvet fittings. Anna Pavlova danced here in 1930, and Maria Callas sang here in 1959. The restored building has recovered much of its original charm with a state-of-the-art technical infrastructure as well. The downstairs Espai Liceu provides the city with daily cultural and commercial interaction with its opera house: a cafeteria; a shop specializing in opera-related gifts, books, and recordings; a circular concert hall that can accommodate 50; and a *Mediateca* (music library) with recordings and films of past opera productions. ⊠ *La Rambla 51–59* ☎ *93/485–9900* ⊕ *www.liceubarcelona.com* ⊙ *Daily at 10 AM.*

❾ **Monument a Colom** (Columbus Monument). You can ride an elevator to the top for a commanding view of the city and port. Columbus faces out to sea, pointing, ironically, east toward Naples. Nearby you can board the cable car to cross the harbor to Barceloneta or catch it in the other direction up Montjuïc. ⊠ *Portal de la Pau s/n* ☎ *93/302–5224* ⊙ *Weekdays 10–1:30 and 3–6:30, weekends 10–6:30.*

⓯ **Museu d'Art Contemporani de Barcelona** (MACBA; Barcelona Museum of Contemporary Art). Designed by American Richard Meier, the contemporary-art museum is an important addition to Barcelona's treasury of art and architecture. In the once rough-and-tumble Raval district, it and the neighboring **Centre de Cultura Contemporànea** (CCCB; Center for Contemporary Culture) have reclaimed important buildings and spaces as part of the city's renewal of its historic quarters and traditional neighborhoods. ⊠ *Plaça dels Àngels* ☎ *93/412–0810* ⊙ *Weekdays 11–7, Sat. 10–8, Sun. 10–3.*

❷ **Museu Frederic Marès.** Here you can browse for hours among the miscellany assembled by sculptor-collector Frederic Marès, including everything from polychrome wood crucifixes to hat pins, pipes, and walking sticks. ⊠ *Plaça Sant Iu 5* ☎ *93/310–5800* ⊙ *Tues.–Wed. and Fri.–Sat. 10–7, Thurs. 10–5, Sun. 10–3.*

❿ **Museu Marítim** (Maritime Museum). Housed in the 13th-century Drassanes Reiales (Royal Shipyards), this museum is packed with ships, figureheads, and nautical paraphernalia. You can pore over early navigation

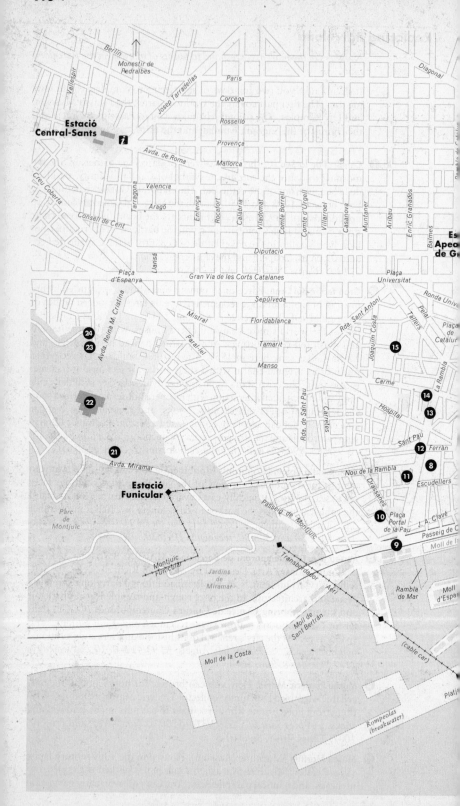

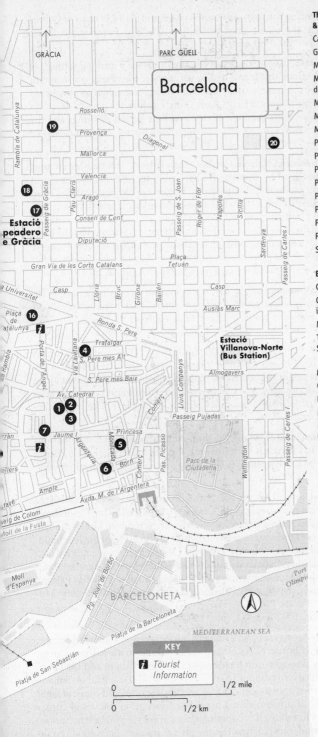

charts, including a map by Amerigo Vespucci and the 1439 chart of Gabriel de Valseca, the oldest chart in Europe. ✉ *Plaça Portal de la Pau 1* ☎ *93/342–9920* ⊙ *Daily 10–7.*

★ ⑤ **Museu Picasso.** Two 15th-century palaces provide a striking setting for these collections of Picasso's early art, donated by Picasso's secretary and then by the artist himself. The works range from childhood sketches to exhibition posters done in Paris shortly before the artist's death. In rare abundance are the Rose Period and Blue Period paintings and the variations on Velázquez's *Las Meninas.* ✉ *Carrer Montcada 15–19* ☎ *93/319–6310* ⊙ *Tues.–Sat. 10–8, Sun. 10–3.*

★ ④ **Palau de la Música Catalana** (Catalan Music Palace). This flamboyant tour de force designed by Domènech i Muntaner in 1908 is the flagship of Barcelona's moderniste architecture. Wagnerian cavalry explodes from the right side of the stage while flowery maidens languish on the left; an inverted stained-glass cupola overhead seems to offer the manna of music straight from heaven, and even the stage is dominated by the busts of muselike art nouveau instrumentalists. *Box office* ✉ *Sant Francesc de Paula 2 (off Via Laietana, around a corner from the hall itself)* ☎ *93/ 295–7200* ⊙ *English-language tours daily at 10:30, 2, and 3.*

⑭ **Palau de la Virreina.** Built by a onetime Spanish viceroy to Peru in 1778, this building is now a major exhibition center. Check to see what's showing while you're in town. ✉ *Rambla de les Flors 99* ☎ *93/301–7775* ⊙ *Mon. 4:30–9, Tues.–Sat. 10–2 and 4:30–9, Sun. 10–2.*

★ ⑪ **Palau Güell.** Gaudí built this mansion between 1886 and 1890 for his patron, Count Eusebi de Güell. Gaudí's artful creation of light in the dark Raval neighborhood is one of the highlights in this key visit along the Ruta Modernista. The playful rooftop will remind you of the later Gaudí of Parc Güell. ✉ *Nou de la Rambla 3–5* ☎ *93/317–3974* ⊙ *Weekdays 10–2 and 4–7:30.*

⑯ **Plaça de Catalunya.** This intersection, interesting mainly for its various sculptures and statues, is the transport hub of the modern city. Café Zurich, at the top of Las Ramblas, is Barcelona's most popular meeting point. ✉ *Top of Las Ramblas.*

③ **Plaça del Rei.** Several historic buildings surround what is widely considered the most beautiful square in the Gothic Quarter. Following Columbus's first voyage to America, the Catholic Monarchs received him in the **Saló de Tinell**, a magnificent banquet hall built in 1362. Other ancient buildings around the square are the **Palau del Lloctinent** (Lieutenant's Palace); the 14th-century **Capella de Santa Àata** (Chapel of St. Agatha), built right into the Roman city wall; and the **Palau Padellàs** (Padellàs Palace), which houses the **Museu d'Història de la Ciutat** (City History Museum). ✉ *Palau Padellàs, Carrer del Veguer 2* ☎ *93/315–1111* ⊙ *Tues.–Sat. 10–2 and 4–8, Sun. 10–2.*

⑧ **Plaça Reial.** An elegant and symmetrical 19th-century arcaded square, Plaça Reial is bordered by elegant ocher facades with balconies overlooking the wrought-iron Fountain of the Three Graces and the lampposts designed by Gaudí in 1879. The place is most colorful on Sunday morning, when crowds gather to sell and trade stamps and coins; at night it's a center of downtown nightlife. **Bar Glaciar**, on the uphill corner toward Las Ramblas, is a booming beer station for young internationals. The **Taxidermist**, across the way, is the square's only good restaurant, and **Tarantos** and **Jamboree** are top venues for jazz, flamenco, and rock. ✉ *C. Colom, off Las Ramblas.*

7 **Plaça Sant Jaume.** This impressive square in the heart of the Gothic Quarter, originally the Roman Forum 2000 years ago, was built in the 1840s, but the two imposing buildings facing each other across it are much older. The 15th-century **ajuntament** (city hall) has an impressive black-and-gold mural (1928) by Josep María Sert (who also painted the murals in New York's Waldorf-Astoria) and the famous **Saló de Cent,** the first European parliament, from which the Council of One Hundred ruled the city from 1372 to 1714. To visit the interior, check with the protocol office. The **Palau de la Generalitat,** seat of the Autonomous Catalonian Government, is a 15th-century palace open to the public on special days or by arrangement. ✉ *Junction of C. de Ferràn and C. Jaume I.*

13 **Rambla St. Josep.** This stretch of the Rambla is one of the most fascinating. The colorful paving stones on the Plaça de la Boquería were designed by Joan Miró. Glance up at the swirling moderniste dragon on the **Casa Bruno Quadras** and the art nouveau street lamps; then take a look inside the **Boquería market** and the **Antiga Casa Figueras,** a vintage art nouveau pastry shop on the corner of Petxina, with a splendid mosaic facade. ✉ *Between Plaça de la Boquería and Rambla de les Flors.*

★ **6** **Santa Maria del Mar** (St. Mary of the Sea). Simply the best example of Mediterranean Gothic architecture, this church is widely considered Barcelona's loveliest. It was built between 1329 and 1383 in fulfillment of a vow made a century earlier by James I to build a church for the Virgin of the Sailors. The structure's simple beauty is enhanced by a colorful rose window and slender soaring columns. ✉ *Plaça Santa Maria* ⊙ *Weekdays 9–1:30 and 4:30–8.*

Eixample

Above the Plaça de Catalunya you enter modern (post-1860) Barcelona and an elegant area known as the Eixample (literally, "widening"), built in the late 19th century as part of the city's expansion scheme. Much of the building here was done at the height of the moderniste movement, a Spanish and mainly Catalan version of art nouveau, whose leading exponents were the architects Lluís Domènech i Montaner, Josep Puig i Cadafalch, and Antoni Gaudí. The main thoroughfares are the Rambla de Catalunya and the Passeig de Gràcia, both lined with some of the city's most elegant shops and cafés. Moderniste houses are among Barcelona's drawing cards.

★ **19** **Casa Milà.** This Gaudí house is known as **La Pedrera** (stone quarry). Its remarkable curving stone facade, with ornamental balconies, ripples its way around the corner of the block. In the attic of La Pedrera is the superb **Espai Gaudí,** Barcelona's only museum dedicated exclusively to the architect's work. ✉ *Passeig de Gràcia 92* ☎ *93/484–5995* ⊙ *Casa Milà: daily 10–8; guided tours weekdays at 6 PM, weekends at 11 AM; Espai Gaudí and rooftop: July–Sept., also open 9 PM–midnight with bar and live music.*

18 **Casa Montaner i Simó–Fundació Tàpies.** This former publishing house exhibits the work of preeminent contemporary Catalan painter Antoni Tàpies, as well as temporary exhibits. On top of the building is a tangle of metal entitled *Núvol i Cadira* (*Cloud and Chair*). ✉ *Carrer d'Aragó 255* ☎ *93/487–0315* ⊙ *Tues.–Sun. 10–8.*

17 **Mançana de la Discòrdia** (Block of Discord). The name is a pun on the Spanish word *manzana,* which means both "block" and "apple." The houses here are quite fantastic: the floral **Casa Lleó Morera** (No. 35) is by Domènech i Montaner, the pseudo-Flemish **Casa Amatller** (No. 41) is by Puig i Cadafalch, and No. 43 is Gaudí's **Casa Batlló.** ✉ *Passeig de Gràcia, between Consell de Cent and Aragó.*

★ ➋ **Temple Expiatori de la Sagrada Família** (Expiatory Church of the Holy Family). Barcelona's most eccentric landmark was designed by Gaudí, though only one tower was standing upon his death in 1926. Gaudí's intent was to evangelize with stone, to create an entire history of Christianity on the building's facade. The angular figures on the southwestern Passion Facade by sculptor Joseph Maria Subirach are a stark contrast to Gaudí's Nativity Facade on the opposite lateral facade. Don't miss the museum, with Gaudí's scale models, or the elevator to the top of one of the towers for a magnificent view of the city. Gaudí is buried in the crypt. ⊠ *Plaça de la Sagrada Familia* ☎ *93/207–3031* ☉ *Nov.–Mar. and Sept.–Oct., daily 9–6; Apr.–Aug., daily 9–8.*

Montjuïc

The hill of Montjuïc is thought to have been named for the Jewish cemetery once located here. Montjuïc has a fortress, delightful gardens, a model Spanish village, an illuminated fountain, the Mies van der Rohe Pavilion, Caixaforum, and a cluster of museums. The 1992 Olympics were held in the Olympic stadium here.

➋ **Caixaforum** (Casaramona). Built as a factory in 1911 by architect Josep Puig i Cadafalch, this redbrick art nouveau fortress was opened in early 2002 as a center for art exhibits, concerts, lectures, and other cultural events. The restoration is a paradigmatic example of the fusion of modern design and traditional architecture. ⊠ *Av. Marquès de Comillas 6–8* ☎ *93/476–8600* ☉ *Tues.–Sun. 10–8.*

★ ➋ **Fundació Miró** (Miró Foundation). A gift from the artist Joan Miró to his native city, this is one of Barcelona's most exciting galleries, with much of its exhibition space devoted to Miró's droll, colorful works. ⊠ *Avda. Miramar 71* ☎ *93/329–1908* ☉ *Tues.–Wed., Fri., and Sat. 10–7, Thurs. 10–9:30, Sun. 10–2:30.*

➋ **Mies van der Rohe Pavilion.** The reconstructed Mies van der Rohe Pavilion—the German contribution to the 1929 Universal Exhibition, reassembled between 1983 and 1986—is a stunning "less is more" study in interlocking planes of white marble, green onyx, and glass: Barcelona's aesthetic antonym for the moderniste Palau de la Música. ⊠ *Av. Marquès de Comillas s/n* ☎ *93/423–4016* ☉ *Daily 10–8.*

★ ➋ **Museu Nacional d'Art de Catalunya** (National Museum of Catalan Art). In the **Palau Nacional** atop a long flight of steps up from the Plaça Espanya, this collection of Romanesque and Gothic art treasures, medieval frescoes, and altarpieces—most from small churches and chapels in the Pyrenees—is simply staggering. The museum's last renovation was directed by architect Gae Aulenti, who also remodeled the Musée d'Orsay, in Paris. ⊠ *Mirador del Palau 6* ☎ *93/423–7199* ☉ *Tues., Wed., Fri., and Sat. 10–7, Thurs. 10–9, Sun. 10–2:30.*

Elsewhere in Barcelona

Barceloneta. Take a stroll around what was once the fishermen's quarter, built in 1755. Hike out to the end of the *rompeolas* (breakwater), extending 4 km (2½ mi) southeast into the Mediterranean, for a panoramic view of the city and a few breaths of fresh air. The modernized port has one of Europe's best aquariums; the Maremagnum shopping center; an IMAX wide-format cinema; the World Trade Center business development; and numerous bars and restaurants. The 1992 Olympic Village, now a hot tapas and nightlife spot, is up the beach to the north and is easily identifiable by the enormous, gold, Frank Gehry–designed fish sculpture next to the Hotel Arts. ⊠ *East of Estació de França and Ciutadella Park.*

Gràcia. This small, once-independent village within the city is a warren of narrow streets whose names change at every corner. Tiny shops sell everything from old-fashioned tin lanterns to feather dusters. Gaudí's first house, at Carrer de les Carolines 24–26; Plaça Rius i Taulet, with its clock tower; and the Llibertat and Revolució markets are key sights. ⊠ *Around C. Gran de Gràcia above Diagonal.*

Monestir de Pedralbes. This is one of Barcelona's best visits, a onetime Clarist convent with a triple-tier cloister and now home of the Thyssen-Bornemisza collection of early paintings. ⊠ *Baixada Monestir 9* ☎ *93/ 203–9282* ⊙ *Tues.–Sun. 10–2.*

★ **Parc Güell.** This park in the upper part of town above Gràcia is Gaudí's magical attempt at creating a garden city. ⊠ *C. D'Olot s/n* ⊙ *May–Aug., daily 10–9; Sept.–Apr., daily 10–7.*

Port Vell. The Old Port now includes an extension of the Rambla, the **Rambla de Mar,** which crosses the inner harbor from just below the Columbus Monument. This boardwalk connects the Rambla with the **Moll d'Espanya,** which in turn comprises a shopping mall, restaurants, an aquarium, a cinema, and two yacht clubs. A walk around Port Vell leads past the marina to Passeig Joan de Borbó, both lined with restaurants and their outdoor tables. From here you can go south out to sea along the *rompeolas,* a 3-km (2-mi) excursion, or north (left) down the San Sebastián beach to the Passeig Marítim, which leads to the **Port Olímpic.** The **Golondrinas** boats tour the harbor and up the coast past the Olympic Port.

Sarrià. Originally an outlying hamlet overlooking the city, Sarrià retains a distinctive village charm. ⊠ *North of the western end of the Diagonal (best reached by the Sarrià train from Plaça Catalunya to the Reina Elisenda stop).*

Where to Eat

For details and price-category definitions, *see* Eating & Drinking *in* Spain A to Z.

★ **$$$$** ✕ **Can Gaig.** This exquisite Barcelona favorite is famous for superb design *and* cuisine. Market-fresh ingredients and experimental cooking are based on ancient recipes from Catalan home cooking, and the menu balances seafood and upland specialties, game, and domestic raw materials. Try the *perdiz asada con jamón ibérico* (roast partridge with Iberian ham). ⊠ *Passeig de Maragall 402* ☎ *93/429–1017* 🖷 *93/429–7002* 🍴 *Reservations essential* ⊟ *AE, DC, MC, V* ⊙ *Closed Mon., Holy Week, and Aug.*

★ **$$$$** ✕ **Comerç 24.** Artist, aesthete, and chef Carles Abellan playfully reinterprets traditional Catalan favorites at this minimalist treasure. Try the *arròs a banda* (paella without the morsels), *tortilla de patatas* (potato omelet), and, for dessert, a postmodern version of the traditional afterschool snack of chocolate, olive oil, salt, and bread. The menu is far out, but always hits the mark. ⊠ *Carrer Comerç 24* ☎ *93/319–2102* 🍴 *Reservations essential* ⊟ *AE, DC, MC, V* ⊙ *Closed Sun.*

$$$$ ✕ **Jean Luc Figueras.** Every restaurant Figueras has touched has shot straight to the top. This one, installed in an elegant Gràcia town house that was once couturier Cristóbal Balenciaga's studio, may be the best of all. The taster's menu is an extra $20 or so, but it's the best choice. ⊠ *C. Santa Teresa 10* ☎ *93/415–2877* 🍴 *Reservations essential* ⊟ *AE, DC, MC, V* ⊙ *Closed Sun. No lunch Sat.*

★ **$$$$** ✕ **Tram-Tram.** At the end of the old tram line above the village of Sarrià, Isidre Soler and his stunning wife, Reyes, have put together one of

Barcelona's finest culinary offerings. Try the taster's menu and you might score cod medallions or venison filet mignons. Reservations are a good idea, but Reyes can almost always invent a table. ⊠ *Major de Sarrià 121* ☏ *93/204–8518* ▭ *AE, DC, MC, V* ⊘ *Closed Sun. and late Dec.–early Jan. No lunch Sat.*

★ $$$–$$$$ ✕ **Botafumeiro.** Barcelona's most exciting Galician spot is open continuously from 1 PM to 1 AM and always filled with ecstatic people in mid-feeding frenzy. The main attraction is the *mariscos Botafumeiro,* a succession of myriad plates of shellfish. Try the half rations at the bar, such as *pulpo a feira* (squid on potato) or *jamón bellota de Guijuelo* (acorn-fed ham from a town near Salamanca). ⊠ *Gran de Gràcia 81* ☏ *93/218–4230* ▭ *AE, DC, MC, V.*

★ $$$–$$$$ ✕ **Can Majó.** On the beach in Barceloneta is one of Barcelona's premier seafood restaurants. House specialties include *caldero de bogavante* (a cross between paella and lobster bouillabaisse) and *suquet* (fish stewed in its own juices), but whatever you choose will be excellent. In summer, the terrace overlooking the Mediterranean is the closest you can come to beachside dining. ⊠ *Almirall Aixada 23* ☏ *93/221–5455* ▭ *AE, DC, MC, V* ⊘ *Closed Sun. and Mon.*

$$$–$$$$ ✕ **Casa Calvet.** This art nouveau space in Antoni Gaudí's 1898–1900 Casa Calvet is Barcelona's only opportunity to break bread in one of the great modernist's creations. The dining room is a graceful and spectacular design display, and the cuisine is light and Mediterranean with more contemporary than traditional fare. ⊠ *Casp 48* ☏ *93/412–4012* ▭ *AE, DC, MC, V* ⊘ *Closed Sun. and Aug. 15–31.*

$$$–$$$$ ✕ **El Racó de Can Freixa.** This is one of Barcelona's hottest restaurants, with young chef Ramón Freixa taking the work of his father, José María, in new directions. The cuisine is innovative and yet traditionally Catalan; try one of the game specialties in season. One specialty is *peus de porc en escabetx de guatlle* (pig's feet with quail in a garlic-and-parsley gratin). ⊠ *Sant Elíes 22* ☏ *93/209–7559* ⌔ *Reservations essential* ▭ *AE, DC, MC, V.*

$$$–$$$$ ✕ **El Tragaluz.** *Tragaluz* means skylight—literally, "light-swallower"—an excellent choice if you're on a design high. The sliding roof opens to the stars, and the furnishings by Javier Mariscal (creator of 1992 Olympic mascot Cobi) reflect Barcelona's passion for playful design. The Mediterranean cuisine is light and innovative. ⊠ *Passatge de la Concepció 5* ☏ *93/487–0196* ▭ *AE, DC, MC, V* ⊘ *Closed Jan. 5. No lunch Mon.*

$–$$ ✕ **Agut.** Simple, hearty Catalan fare awaits you in this unpretentious restaurant in the lower reaches of the Gothic Quarter. Founded in 1924, this place continues to be popular. There's plenty of wine to go with the traditional home cooking. ⊠ *Gignàs 16* ☏ *93/315–1709* ▭ *AE, MC, V* ⊘ *Closed Mon. and July. No dinner Sun.*

$–$$ ✕ **El Convent.** Behind the Boqueria market, this traditional restaurant offers good value. Catalan home cooking, such as *faves a la catalana* (broad beans stewed with sausage), comes straight from the Boqueria. The intimate balconies and dining rooms have marble-top tables for 2 or 20. ⊠ *Jerusalem 3* ☏ *93/317–1052* ▭ *AE, DC, MC, V.*

Where to Stay

Hotels around Las Ramblas and in the Gothic Quarter have generous helpings of old-fashioned charm but are weaker on creature comforts; those in the Eixample are mostly '50s or '60s buildings, often more recently renovated; and the newest hotels are out along the Diagonal or beyond, with the exception of the Hotel Arts, in the Olympic Port. The Airport and Sants Station have hotel-reservation desks. For details and price-category definitions, *see* Lodging *in* Spain A to Z.

$$$$
Fodor'sChoice
★
Claris. Widely considered Barcelona's best hotel, this wonderful place is a fascinating mélange of design and tradition. The rooms come in 60 different modern layouts, some with restored 18th-century English furniture and some with contemporary furnishings from Barcelona's endlessly playful legion of lamp and chair designers. Lavishly endowed with wood and marble, the hotel also has a Japanese water garden and a rooftop pool. The restaurant East 47 is stellar. ⊠ *Carrer Pau Claris 150, 08009* ☎ *93/487–6262* 🖷 *93/215–7970* ⊕ *www.derbyhotels.es* ⤴ *80 rooms, 40 suites* ♨ *2 restaurants, pool, bar* ☰ *AE, DC, MC, V.*

$$$$
Fodor'sChoice
★
Condes de Barcelona. Reserve well in advance—this is one of Barcelona's most popular hotels. The pentagonal lobby has a marble floor and the original columns and courtyard from the 1891 building. The newest rooms have hot tubs and terraces overlooking interior gardens. An affiliated fitness club nearby has golf, squash, and swimming. The restaurant, Thalassa, is excellent. ⊠ *Passeig de Gràcia 75, 08008* ☎ *93/467–4780* 🖷 *93/467–4785* ⊕ *www.condesdebarcelona.com* ⤴ *183 rooms* ♨ *Restaurant, pool, bar* ☰ *AE, DC, MC, V.*

$$$$
Hotel Arts. This luxurious Ritz-Carlton monolith overlooks Barcelona from the Olympic Port, providing views of the Mediterranean, the city, and the mountains behind. A short taxi ride from the center of the city, the hotel is virtually a world of its own, with three restaurants (one specializing in California cuisine), an outdoor pool, and the beach. ⊠ *C. de la Marina 19–21, 08005* ☎ *93/221–1000* 🖷 *93/221–1070* ⊕ *www. harts.es* ⤴ *397 rooms, 59 suites, 27 apartments* ♨ *3 restaurants, pool, bar* ☰ *AE, DC, MC, V.*

$$$$
Fodor'sChoice
★
Majestic. On Barcelona's most stylish boulevard, surrounded by fashion emporiums, you'll find this near-perfect place to stay. The building is part Eixample town house and part modern extension, but each room is stylishly decorated. The superb restaurant, Drolma, is a destination in itself. ⊠ *Passeig de Gràcia 70, 08008* ☎ *93/488–1717* 🖷 *93/488–1880* ⊕ *www.hotelmajestic.es* ⤴ *273 rooms, 30 suites* ♨ *2 restaurants, pool, bar* ☰ *AE, DC, MC, V.*

$$$$
Princesa Sofía. This modern high-rise has everything from shops to the 19th-floor Top City, with breathtaking views. The rooms, decorated in soft colors, are ultracomfortable. ⊠ *Plaça Pius XII 4, at Av. Diogonal, 08028* ☎ *93/508–1000* 🖷 *93/508–1001* ⊕ *www.interconti.com* ⤴ *475 rooms, 25 suites* ♨ *3 restaurants, 2 pools (1 indoor), bar* ☰ *AE, DC, MC, V.*

★ **$$$$**
Rey Juan Carlos I–Conrad International. Towering over the western end of Barcelona's Avinguda Diagonal, this luxury hotel is also an exciting commercial complex where you can even buy or rent a fur or limousine. The lush garden, which includes a pond with swans, has an Olympic-size swimming pool, and the green expanses of Barcelona's finest in-town country club, El Polo, are beyond. ⊠ *Av. Diagonal 661–671, 08028* ☎ *93/364–4040* 🖷 *93/364–4232* ⊕ *www.hrjuancarlos.com* ⤴ *375 rooms, 37 suites* ♨ *2 restaurants (3 in summer), pool, 2 bars* ☰ *AE, DC, MC, V.*

★ **$$$$**
Ritz. Founded in 1919 by Caesar Ritz, this grande dame of Barcelona hotels has been restored to the splendor of its earlier years. The imperial lobby is at once loose and elegant; guest rooms contain Regency furniture, and some have Roman baths and mosaics. Service is generally excellent. ⊠ *Gran Via 668, 08010* ☎ *93/318–5200* 🖷 *93/318–0148* ⊕ *www.ritzbcn.com* ⤴ *122 rooms* ♨ *Restaurant, bar* ☰ *AE, DC, MC, V.*

$$$–$$$$
Fodor'sChoice
★
Colón. Charming and intimate, this Barcelona standby across from the cathedral overlooks weekend sardana dancing, Thursday antiques markets, and, of course, the floodlighted cathedral by night. Rooms are comfortable and tasteful. Rooms with views of the cathedral are better

and more expensive. Considering its combination of comfort, style, and location it may be the best place to stay in Barcelona. ⊠ *Av. Catedral 7 08002* ☎ *93/301–1404* 🖷 *93/317–2915* ⊕ *www.hotelcolon.es* 🛏 *147 rooms* ⚬ *Restaurant, bar* ⊟ *AE, DC, MC, V.*

$$ 🏨 **Gran Vía.** This 19th-century town house is a moderniste enclave, with an original chapel, hall-of-mirrors breakfast room, ornate moderniste staircase, and belle epoque phone booths. Guest rooms have plain alcoved walls, bottle-green carpets, and Regency-style furniture; those overlooking Gran Via itself have better views but are quite noisy. ⊠ *Gran Via 642, 08007* ☎ *93/318–1900* 🖷 *93/318–9997* ⊕ *www.nnhotels.es* 🛏 *53 rooms* ⊟ *AE, DC, MC, V.*

$$ 🏨 **San Agustí.** Just off the Rambla in the leafy square of the same name, this place has long been popular with musicians performing at the Liceu opera house. Rooms are small but pleasantly modern, with plenty of fresh wood and clean lines. There is a cafeteria here. ⊠ *Pl. de San Agustín 3, 08001* ☎ *93/318–1658* 🖷 *93/317–2928* ⊕ *www.hotelsa.com* 🛏 *77 rooms* ⚬ *Bar* ⊟ *AE, DC, MC, V.*

$–$$ 🏨 **Continental.** This modest hotel stands at the top of the Rambla, below Plaça de Catalunya. Space is tight, but rooms manage to accommodate large, firm beds. It's high enough over the Rambla to escape street noise, so ask for a room overlooking Barcelona's most emblematic street. This is a good place to read *Homage to Catalonia*, as George Orwell stayed here with his wife in 1937. ⊠ *Rambla 138, 08002* ☎ *93/301–2570* 🖷 *93/302–7360* ⊕ *www.hotelcontinental.com* 🛏 *35 rooms* ⊟ *AE, DC, MC, V.*

$ 🏨 **Jardí.** Perched over the traffic-free and charming Plaça del Pi and Plaça
FodorśChoice ⭐ Sant Josep Oriol, this chic budget hotel has rooms with views of the Gothic church of Santa Maria del Pi. All rooms have pine furniture and small bathrooms. With five floors and an elevator, this is not the Ritz, and it can be noisy in summer, but it's still a great value. ⊠ *Pl. Sant Josep Oriol 1, 08002* ☎ *93/301–5900* 🖷 *93/342–5733* ⊕ *www.hoteljardi.com* 🛏 *40 rooms* ⊟ *AE, DC, MC, V.*

Nightlife & the Arts

The Arts

To find out what's on, look in the daily papers or the weekly *Guía del Ocio. Actes a la Ciutat* is a weekly list of cultural events published by City Hall and available from its information office on Plaça Sant Jaume, or at the Palau de la Virreina. *El País* lists all events of interest on its *agenda* page.

CONCERTS   Musical events are held in some of Barcelona's finest early architecture, such as the medieval shipyards, **Drassanes,** the church of **Santa Maria del Mar,** or the **Monestir de Pedralbes.** The **Auditori de Barcelona** (⊠ Carrer Lepant 150, near Plaça de les Glòries ☎ 93/247–9300) has a full program of classical music, with occasional jazz and pop thrown in. The **Liceu** (⊠ La Rambla 51–59 ☎ 93/485–9913), Barcelona's opera house, is alive and thriving. The art nouveau **Palau de la Música** is not to be missed for the music and the venue itself. Sunday-morning concerts (11 AM) are a local tradition (⊠ Sant Francesc de Paula 2 ☎ 93/295–7200).

DANCE   **El Mercat de les Flors** (⊠ Lleida 59 ☎ 93/426–1875), not far from Plaça d'Espanya, always has a rich program of modern dance and theater. **L'Espai de Dansa i Mùsica de la Generalitat de Catalunya** (⊠ Travessera de Gràcia 63 ☎ 93/414–3133), usually listed simply as L'Espai (The Space), is Barcelona's prime venue for ballet and contemporary dance. **Teatre Tivoli** (⊠ Casp 8 ☎ 93/412–2063), just above Plaça de Catalunya, hosts major ballet and flamenco troupes.

FILM Many if not most Barcelona theaters show foreign movies in their original languages—indicated by "VO" (*versión original*). The Olympic Port's 15-screen **Icaria Yelmo** (✉ Salvador Espriu 61 ☎ 93/221–7585) shows everything in VO. **Renoir Les Corts** (✉ Eugeni d'Ors 12), near the Corte Inglés Diagonal, has four VO theaters. The Gràcia neighborhood's **Verdi** (✉ Verdi 32 ☎ 93/237–0516) is a standard VO cinema favorite. **Verdi Park** (✉ Torrijos 49 ☎ 93/238–7990) in the Gràcia neighborhood is a popular spot.

THEATER Most plays are in Catalan, but top Spanish productions also open in Barcelona. **El Mercat de les Flors** holds theater and dance performances. The **Teatre Lliure** (✉ Montseny 47, Gràcia ☎ 93/218–9251) has top theater, dance, and musical events. The **Teatre Nacional de Catalunya** (✉ Plaça de les Arts 1 ☎ 93/900–121133) covers everything from Shakespeare to ballet to avant-garde theater. **Teatre Poliorama** (✉ Rambla Estudios 115 ☎ 93/317–7599), on the upper Rambla, holds excellent theater performances. **Teatre Romea** (✉ Hospital 51 ☎ 93/317–7189) is a traditional haven for dramatic events. **Teatre Tívoli** (✉ Casp 10 ☎ 93/412–2063) stages flamenco, ballet, and plays.

Nightlife

BARS *Xampanyerías,* or champagne bars serving sparkling Catalan *cava*, are a Barcelona specialty. **El Xampanyet** (✉ Montcada 22 ☎ 93/319–7003), near the Picasso Museum, serves cava, cider, and tapas. **La Cava del Palau** (✉ Verdaguer i Callis 10 ☎ 93/310–0938), near the Palau de la Música, has a wide selection of cavas, wines, and cocktails.

You'll find the **Passeig del Born**, near the Picasso Museum, is lined with cocktail bars. **Dry Martini** (✉ Aribau 162 ☎ 93/217–5072) has more than 80 different gins. **El Copetín** (✉ Passeig del Born 19 ☎ 93/317–7585) looks exciting and has good cocktails. **Miramelindo** (✉ Passeig del Born 15 ☎ 93/319–5376) offers a large selection of cocktails, and often has live jazz. Stylish **El Paraigua** (✉ Plaça Sant Miquel, behind City Hall ☎ 93/217–3028) serves cocktails, along with classical music.

Ambitiously named **La Vinya del Senyor** (Lord's Vineyard; ✉ Pl. de Santa Maria 5 ☎ 93/310–3379), across from Santa Maria del Mar, has a new wine list every fortnight. **Cal Pep** (✉ 8 Plaça de les Olles ☎ 93/319–6183), near Santa Maria del Mar, is a popular spot, with the best and freshest selection of tapas. **Sagardi** (✉ Argenteria 62 ☎ 93/319–9993), near Santa Maria del Mar, is one of many, uniformly good, Basque taverns. **El Irati** (✉ Cardenal Casañas 17 ☎ 93/302–3084), just off Plaça del Pi, is a good, if usually overcrowded, Basque bar. **Ciudad Condal** (✉ Rambla de Catalunya 24 ☎ 93/412–9414), at the intersection of Gran Via and Rambla Catalunya, has lots of appetizing morsels. **Cata 1.81** (✉ Valencia 181 ☎ 93/322–6818) is a wine taster's delight—with designer cuisine to match. **La Santa Maria** (✉ Comerç 17 ☎ 93/315–4536) serves postmodern morsels at bar and table.

CABARET **Barcelona City Hall** (✉ Rambla de Catalunya 2–4, access through New Canadian Store ☎ 93/317–2177) presents sophisticated cabaret in a beautiful music hall.

CAFÉS The **Café de l'Opera** (✉ Rambla 74 ☎ 93/317–7585), across from the Liceu opera house, is a perennial hangout, open daily until 2 AM. **Café Zurich** (✉ Plaça de Catalunya 1 ☎ 93/302–4140), at the head of Las Ramblas, is Barcelona's number one rendezvous spot. **Carrer Petritxol** (from Portaferrissa to Plaça del Pi) is famous for its *chocolaterías* (serving hot chocolate, tea, coffee, and pastries) and tearooms. Picasso hung out at **Els Quatre Gats** (✉ Montsió 3 ☎ 93/302–4140), which is a great place to people-watch.

A line forms at **Bikini** (✉ Deu i Mata 105, at Entença ☎ 93/322–0005) on festive Saturday nights. **Costa Breve** (✉ Aribau 230 ☎ 93/414–2778) welcomes all ages, even those over 35. **Danzatoria** (✉ Avda. Tibidabo 61 ☎ 93/211–6261), a fusion of Salsitas and Partycular, is a "multi-space" with five venues. At **Luz de Gas** (✉ Muntaner 246 ☎ 93/209–7711), live guitar and soul shows are followed by dance music and wild abandon. **Oliver y Hardy** (✉ Diagonal 593, next to Barcelona Hilton ☎ 93/419–3181) is popular with over-35s. **Otto Zutz** (✉ Lincoln 15, below Via Augusta ☎ 93/238–0722) is a top spot. **Sala Razzmatazz** (✉ Almogavers 122 ☎ 93/320–8200) offers Friday and Saturday disco madness 'til dawn. Weeknight concerts include international stars such as Ani diFranco and Enya. **Torres de Avila** (✉ Marquès de Comillas 25 ☎ 93/424–9309), in Pueblo Espanyol, is wild and woolly until daylight on weekends. **Up and Down** (✉ Numancia 179 ☎ 93/280–2922), pronounced "pendow," is a lively classic for elegant carousers.

El Patio Andaluz (✉ Aribau 242 ☎ 93/209–3378) is a solid option but rather expensive. **Los Tarantos** (✉ Plaça Reial 17 ☎ 93/318–3067) is the most happening flamenco spot. **El Tablao del Carmen** (✉ Arcs 9, Poble Espanyol ☎ 93/325–6895) hosts touring troupes up on Montjüic.

La Cova del Drac (✉ Vallmajor 33 ☎ 93/200–7032) is Barcelona's most traditional jazz venue. The Gothic Quarter's **Harlem Jazz Club** (✉ Comtessa Sobradiel 8 ☎ 93/310–0755) is small but sizzling. **Jamboree** (✉ Plaça Reial 17 ☎ 93/301–7564), downstairs from Los Tarantos, has regular jazz performances featuring top musicians from New York and all over the world.

Shopping

Elegant shopping districts are the Passeig de Gràcia, Rambla de Catalunya, and the Diagonal. For more affordable, old-fashioned, and typically Spanish-style shops, explore the area between the Rambla and Via Laietana, especially around Carrer de Ferràn. The area around Plaça del Pi from Boquería to Portaferrisa and Canuda is well stocked with youthful fashion stores and imaginative gift shops.

El Triangle mall in Plaça de Catalunya includes FNAC, Habitat, and the Sephora perfume emporium. **Les Glories** (✉ Avda. Diagonal 208, Plaça de les Glories ☎ 93/486–0639) is near the *encants*, Barcelona's flea market. **L'Illa** (✉ Diagonal 545, between Numancia and Entenza ☎ 93/444–0000) has everything from FNAC to Decathlon to Marks & Spencer. **Maremagnum** (✉ Moll d'Espanya s/n, Port Vell ☎ 93/225–8100) is well stocked with shops. **Carrer Tuset**, north of Diagonal between Aribau and Balmes, has many small boutiques.

Antiques

Carrer de la Palla and Banys Nous, in the Gothic Quarter, are lined with antiques shops. An **antiques market** is held every Thursday in front of the cathedral. The **Centre d'Antiquaris** (✉ Passeig de Gràcia 57 ☎ 93/215–4499) has some 75 antiques stores. **Gothsland** (✉ Consell de Cent 331 ☎ 93/488–1922) specializes in moderniste designs.

Boutiques

Fashionable boutiques line Passeig de Gràcia and Rambla de Catalunya. Others are on Gran Via between Balmes and Pau Claris, and on the Diagonal between Ganduxer and Passeig de Gràcia. **Adolfo Domínguez** (✉ Passeig de Gràcia 89, Valencia 245 ☎ 93/487–3687) is one of Spain's most popular clothing designers. **Joaquín Berao** (✉ Rosselló 277 ☎ 93/218–6187) is a top jewelry designer. **La Manual Alpargartera**

(✉ Avinyó 7), just off Carrer Ferran, is a lovely shop specializing in hand-made rope-soled sandals and espadrilles.

Loewe (✉ Passeig de Gràcia 35, Diagonal 570 ☎ 93/216–0400) is Spain's top leather store. Lovers of fine stationery will linger in the Gothic Quarter's **Papirum** (✉ Baixada de la Llibreteria 2), a tiny, medieval-tone shop with exquisite hand-printed papers, marbleized blank books, and writing implements. **Zapata** (✉ Buenos Aires 64, at Diagonal ☎ 93/430–4785) is a major jewelry dealer.

Department Stores

With four locations in Barcelona alone, **El Corte Inglés** (✉ Plaça de Catalunya 14 ☎ 93/302–1212 ✉ Porta de l'Angel 19–21 ☎ 93/306–3800 ✉ Avda. Francesc Macià 58 ☎ 93/419–2020 ✉ Diagonal 617, near María Cristina metro stop ☎ 93/419–2828) is Spain's great consumer emporium. Both Plaça de Catalunya's Mançana de Oro (aka El Triangle) and L'Illa have FNAC stores.

Food & Flea Markets

The **Boqueria Market** (✉ Las Ramblas between Carme and Hospital) is an exuberant cornucopia, a colorful display of both food and humanity; it's open every day except Sunday. **Els Encants** (✉ End of Dos de Maig, on the Plaça Glòries Catalanes), Barcelona's wild-and-woolly flea market, is held every Monday, Wednesday, Friday, and Saturday 8–7. **Sant Antoni Market** (✉ End of Ronda Sant Antoni) is an old-fashioned food and clothes market, best on Sunday when there's a **secondhand-book market** with old postcards, press cuttings, lithographs, and prints. There's a **stamp and coin market** (✉ Plaça Reial) on Sunday morning. An **artists' market** (✉ Placeta del Pi, off Las Ramblas and Boquería) sets up on Saturday morning.

Gifts

A number of stores and boutiques specialize in design items (jewelry, furnishings, knickknacks). **Xavier Roca i Coll** (✉ Sant Pere mes Baix 24, off Via Laietana ☎ 93/215–1052) specializes in silver models of Barcelona's buildings. **Art Escudellers** (✉ C. Escudellers 5, Barri Gòtic) has ceramics from all over Spain, with more than 140 different artisans represented and maps showing where the work is from. Don't miss the art gallery and wine, cheese, and ham tasting bar downstairs.

Bd (Barcelona Design; ✉ Mallorca 291293 ☎ 93/458–6909) sells reproduction furniture from many designers. **Dos i Una** (✉ Rosselló 275 ☎ 93/217–7032) is a good source for clever gifts. **Vinçon** (✉ Passeig de Gràcia 96 ☎ 93/215–6050) has a huge selection of stylish housewares.

Barcelona Essentials

AIRPORTS & TRANSFERS

All international and domestic flights arrive at El Prat de Llobregat airport, 14 km (8½ mi) south of Barcelona just off the main highway to Castelldefels and Sitges. For information on arrival and departure times, call the airport or Info-Iberia.

🛈 **El Prat de Llobregat** ☎ 93/478-5000 or 93/478-5032. **Info-Iberia** ☎ 93/412-5667.

TRANSFERS The airport-to-city train leaves every 30 minutes between 6:30 AM and 11 PM, costs €2.50, and reaches the Barcelona Central (Sants) Station in 15 minutes and Plaça de Catalunya, in the heart of the old city (at the head of Las Ramblas), in 20–25 minutes. From there a short taxi ride of €3–€6 will take you to most of central Barcelona's hotels. The Aerobus service connects the airport with Plaça de Catalunya every 15 minutes between 6:25 AM and 11 PM; the fare of €3 can be paid with all international credit cards. A taxi from the airport to your hotel, including airport and luggage surcharges, will cost about €20.

BOAT & FERRY TRAVEL

Golondrinas (harbor boats) make short trips from the Portal de la Pau, near the Columbus Monument. The fare is €4.50 for a 30-minute trip. Departures are Holy Week–September, daily 11–7; October–Holy Week, weekends and holidays only 11–5. It's closed December 16–January 2. A one-way ticket lets you off at the end of the breakwater for a 4-km (2½-mi) stroll, surrounded by the Mediterranean, back into Barceloneta.
🚢 Golondrinas ☎ 93/442-3106.

BUS TRAVEL TO & FROM BARCELONA

Barcelona's main bus station is Estació del Nord, east of the Arc de Triomf. The Estació Autobuses de Sants also dispatches long-distance buses—Julià runs buses to Zaragoza and Montserrat, and Alsina Graëlls runs to Lérida and Andorra. Buses also depart from the depots of Barcelona's various private bus companies. Rather than pound the pavement (or the telephone, usually futile because of overloaded lines) trying to sort out Barcelona's complex and confusing bus system, go through a travel agent, who can quickly book you the best bus passage to your destination.
🚌 Alsina Graëlls ⊠ Ronda Universitat 4 ☎ 93/265-6866. **Estació Autobuses de Sants** ⊠ C. Viriato, next to Sants Central train terminal ☎ 93/490-0202. **Estació del Norte** ⊠ End of Avda. Vilanova ☎ 93/893-5312. **Julià** ⊠ Ronda Universitat 5 ☎ 93/317-6454.

BUS TRAVEL WITHIN BARCELONA

City buses run from about 5:30 or 6 AM to 10:30 PM, though some stop earlier. There are also night buses to certain destinations. The flat fare is €1. Route plans are displayed at bus stops. For multiple journeys you can purchase a *tarjeta multiviatge,* good for 10 rides, at the transport kiosk on Plaça de Catalunya (€6).

CONSULATES

🏛 Australia ⊠ Gran Vía Carles III 98 ☎ 93/330-9496.
🏛 Canada ⊠ Elisenda de Pinós ☎ 93/204-2700.
🏛 New Zealand ⊠ Travessera de Gràcia 64 ☎ 93/209-0399.
🏛 United Kingdom ⊠ Diagonal 477 ☎ 93/419-9044.
🏛 United States ⊠ Passeig Reina Elisenda 23 ☎ 93/280-2227.

EMERGENCIES

The general emergency number in all EU nations (akin to 911 in the United States) is 112.
🏥 Doctors & Dentists **Medical emergencies** ☎ 061.
🏥 Emergency Services **Police** ☎ 091 National Police; 092 Municipal Police. **Tourist Attention** ⊠ La Rambla 43 ☎ 93/317-7016 24-hr assistance for crime victims.
🏥 24-hour Pharmacies **Pharmacies** ☎ 010.

ENGLISH-LANGUAGE MEDIA

BOOKS BCN Books is one of Barcelona's top spots for books in English. Come In is another good option for English books. El Corte Inglés sells English guidebooks and novels, but the selection is limited. For variety, try English Bookshop. The bookstore at the Palau de la Virreina has good books on art, design, and Barcelona.
🏛 Bookstores **BCN Books** ⊠ Aragó 277 ☎ 93/487-3123. **Come In** ⊠ Provença 203 ☎ 93/253-1204. **English Bookshop** ⊠ Entençan 63 ☎ 93/425-4466.

SUBWAY TRAVEL

The metro is the fastest and easiest way to get around. You can pay a flat fare of €1 or buy a tarjeta multiviatge, good for 10 rides (€6). Maps of the system are available at main metro stations and branches of the Caixa savings bank.

TAXIS

Taxis are black and yellow. When available for hire, they show a LIBRE sign in the daytime and a green light at night. The meter starts at €3 (which lasts for six minutes), and there are supplements for luggage, night travel, Sunday and holidays, and rides from a station or to the airport. There are cab stands all over town, and you can also hail cabs on the street. To call a cab, try one of the numbers listed below, 24 hours a day.

24-hr Service ☎ 93/387-1000, 93/490-2222, or 93/357-7755.

TOURS

BUS TOURS City sightseeing tours are run by Julià Tours. Pullmantur also has city sightseeing. Tours leave from the terminals listed below, though you may be able to arrange a pickup at your hotel. Both agencies offer the same tours at the same prices. A morning sightseeing tour visits the Gothic Quarter and Montjuïc; an afternoon tour concentrates on Gaudí and the Picasso Museum. You can visit Barcelona's Olympic sites from May through October.

Fees & Schedules Julià Tours ⊠ Ronda Universitat 5 ☎ 93/317-6454. **Pullmantur** ⊠ Gran Viá de les Corts Catalanes 635 ☎ 93/318-5195.

SINGLE-DAY Trips out of town are run by Julià Tours and Pullmantur. The principal
TOURS attractions are a half-day tour to Montserrat to visit the monastery and shrine of the famous Black Virgin; a full-day trip to the Costa Brava resorts, including a boat cruise to the Medes Isles; and, from June through September, a full-day trip to Andorra for tax-free shopping. If you are not an EU citizen, bring your passport with you.

WALKING TOURS La Ruta del Modernisme (the Modernism Route), created by Barcelona's *ajuntament* (city hall), connects four key art nouveau sites: the Palau de la Música, the Fundació Tàpies, the Museu d'Art Modern (in Ciutadella), and the Museo de Zoologia (in Doménech i Muntaner's Castell dels Tres Dragons en la Ciutadella). Guided tours, some in English, are given at the Palau de la Música. Buy your tickets at Casa Amatller, open Monday through Saturday 10–7, Sunday 10–2. The price, €3, gets you 50% discounts at all nine locations.

The bookstore in the Palau de la Virreina rents cassettes whose walking tours follow footprints painted on sidewalks—different colors for different tours—through Barcelona's most interesting areas. The do-it-yourself method is to pick up the guides produced by the tourist office, *Discovering Romanesque Art* and *Discovering Modernist Art,* which have art itineraries for all of Catalonia. El Consorci Turisme de Barcelona (Barcelona Tourism Cortium) leads walking tours of the Gothic Quarter in English at 10 AM on Saturday. The tour costs €6 and includes a visit to the Town Hall.

Fees & Schedules Casa Amatller ⊠ Passeig de Gràcia 41 ☎ 93/488-0139. **El Consorci Turisme de Barcelona** ⊠ Plaça de Catalunya 17, lower level ☎ 906/301282. **Palau de la Virreina** ⊠ La Rambla 99.

TRAIN TRAVEL

The Sants Central Station at Plaça Països Catalans is Barcelona's main train station, serving international and national destinations as well as suburban areas. The old and elegant Estació de França (Avda. Marquès de l'Argentera) now serves only certain points in Spain. Inquire at the tourist office to get current travel information and to find out which station you need. Many trains also stop at the Passeig de Gràcia underground station (at C. Aragó), which is closer to the Plaça de Catalunya

and Rambla area than Sants. Tickets and information are available here, but luggage carts are not. You can also get information on fares and schedules from RENFE with their 24-hour hot line.
🚇 RENFE ☎ 902/240202.

TRAMS & CABLE CARS

The Montjuïc Funicular is a cog railroad that runs from the junction of Avenida Parallel and Nou de la Rambla to the Miramar Amusement Park on Montjuïc; it's open 10:45 AM–8 PM, except in summer (late June to mid-September), when it runs 11 AM–10 PM. A *teleferico* (cable car) runs from the amusement park up to Montjuïc Castle October–June 21, weekends 11–2:45 and 4–7:30; June 22–September, daily 11:30–9.

The Transbordador Aeri Harbor Cable Car runs from Miramar on Montjuïc to the Torre de Jaume I across the harbor on Barcelona *moll* (quay), and on to the Torre de Sant Sebastià at the end of Passeig Joan de Borbó in Barceloneta. You can board at either stage. Hours are October–June, weekdays noon–5:45, and weekends noon–6:15; and July–September, daily 11–8. A round-trip ticket costs €9 (one-way €7.50).

To reach Tibidabo summit, take either Bus 58 or the Ferrocarrils de la Generalitat train from Plaça de Catalunya to Avenida Tibidabo, then the *tramvía blau* (blue tram) to Peu del Funicular, and the *Tibidabo Funicular* from there to the Tibidabo Fairground. The funicular runs every half hour from 7:15 AM to 9:45 PM.
🚇 El Consorci Turisme de Barcelona ✉ Plaça de Catalunya 17, lower level ☎ 906/301282.

TRANSPORTATION AROUND BARCELONA

Modern Barcelona, the Eixample—above the Plaça de Catalunya—is built on a grid system; the Gothic Quarter, from the Plaça de Catalunya to the port, is a warren of narrow streets. Almost all sightseeing can be done on foot, but you may need to use taxis, the metro, or buses to link certain areas, depending on how much time you have. The **Bus Turistic** offers 27 stops at major tourist sights for €15. The two circuits (red for upper Barcelona, blue for the lower city) coincide (for transfers from one line to the other) at Plaça Catalunya, Avinguda Diagonal, and Passeig de Gràcia. The bus originates in Plaça Catalunya and runs from 9 AM to 8 PM.

Turisme de Barcelona sells the very worthwhile Barcelona Card, which costs €17 for 24 hours, €20 for 48 hours, €23 for 72 hours, and €27 for five days. Travelers get unlimited travel on all public transport as well as discounts at 27 museums, 10 restaurants, 14 leisure spots, 20 stores, and various other services including walking tours, the airport shuttle, the bus to Tibidabo, and the Tombbus between Barcelona's key shopping areas.
🚇 Turisme de Barcelona ☎ 93/368-9732 ⊕ www.barcelonaturisme.com.

TRAVEL AGENCIES

🚇 Local Agents **American Express** ✉ Roselló 257, corner of Passeig de Gràcia ☎ 93/217-0070. **Bestours** ✉ Diputació 241 ☎ 93/487-8580. **Viajes Iberia** ✉ Rambla 130 ☎ 93/317-9320. **Wagons-Lits Cook** ✉ Passeig de Gràcia 8 ☎ 93/317-5500.

VISITOR INFORMATION

El Prat Airport and Centre d'Informació Turística have general information on Catalonia and Spain. The other offices listed below focus mostly on Barcelona. You can also get general information on the city by dialing 010.
🚇 **Ajuntament** ✉ Pl. Sant Jaume 1, Barri Gòtic. **Centre d'Informació Turistic de Barcelona** ✉ Plaça de Catalunya 17, lower level ☎ 906/301282 🖷 93/304-3155. **Estació**

de Sants ⊠ Pl. Països Catalans s/n, Eixample ☎ 93/491-4431. **Centre d'Informació Turística** ⊠ Palau Robert, Passeig de Gràcia 107, at Diagonal ☎ 93/238-4000. **El Prat Airport** ☎ 93/478-4704. **Palau de Congressos** during special events and conferences ⊠ Avda. María Cristina ☎ 93/423-3101 Ext. 8356. **Palau de la Virreina** ⊠ Rambla de les Flors 99 ☎ 93/301-7775.

ANDALUSIA

Stretching from the dark mountains of the Sierra Morena in the north, west to the plains of the Guadalquivir valley, and south to the mighty, snowcapped Sierra Nevada, Andalusia (Andalucía) rings with echoes of the Moors. Creating a kingdom they called Al-Andalus, these North African Muslims ruled southern Spain for almost 800 years, from their conquest of Gibraltar in 711 to their expulsion from Granada in 1492. To this day the cities and landscapes of Andalusia are rich in their legacy: Córdoba's breathtaking mosque, Granada's magical Alhambra Palace, and Seville's landmark Giralda tower were the inspired creations of Moorish architects and craftsmen working for Al-Andalus's Arab emirs. Outside the cities, brilliant white villages—with narrow streets, heavily grilled windows, and whitewashed facades, all clustered around cool private patios—and the wailing songs of flamenco, vaguely reminiscent of the muezzin's call to prayer, all stem from centuries of Moorish occupation.

The downside to a visit here, especially to Seville, is that petty crime is not uncommon, and thieves often prey on tourists. Purse-snatching and thefts from cars, even when drivers are in them, are depressingly familiar. *Always* keep your car doors *and* trunk locked. *Never* leave valuables in your car. Leave your passport, traveler's checks, and credit cards in your hotel's safe, *never* in your room. Don't carry expensive cameras or wear jewelry. Take only the minimum amount of cash with you.

Seville

Numbers in the margin correspond to points of interest on the Seville map.

Lying on the banks of the Guadalquivir River, 538 km (334 mi) southwest of Madrid, Seville (Sevilla)—Spain's fourth-largest city and the capital of Andalusia—is one of the most alluring cities in Europe. Famous in the arts as the home of the sensuous Carmen and the amorous Don Juan—and celebrated in real life for its spectacular Semana Santa (Holy Week) processions and April Fair—Seville is the urban embodiment of Moorish Andalusia.

★ ❷ **Alcázar.** The high, fortified walls of this Moorish palace belie the exquisite delicacy of its interior. It was built by Pedro the Cruel—so known because he murdered his stepmother and four of his half brothers—who lived here with his mistress, María de Padilla, from 1350 to 1369. Don't mistake this for a genuine Moorish palace, as it was built more than 100 years after the reconquest of Seville; rather, its style is Mudéjar—built by Moorish craftsmen working under orders of a Christian king. Pedro's Mudéjar palace centers on the beautiful **Patio de las Doncellas** (Court of the Damsels), whose name pays tribute to the annual gift of 100 virgins to the Moorish sultans whose palace once stood here. Resplendent with lacelike stucco and gleaming *azulejo* (tile) decorations, the patio is immediately reminiscent of Granada's Alhambra and is in fact the work of Granada artisans. Opening off this patio are the **Salón de Embajadores,** where Charles V married Isabel of Portugal, and the apartments of María de Padilla.

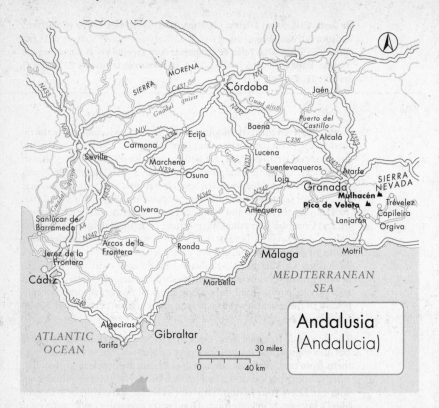

Occupying the upper floors of the Alcázar are the **Estancias Reales** (Royal Chambers), which are the apartments still used by Spain's king Juan Carlos I and his family when they visit Seville. For an additional admission price, you can take the guided tour of the dining room and other protocol rooms and the king's office. Tours, in the morning only, are every half hour in summer and every hour in winter. Next door to Pedro's palace, the Renaissance **Palacio de Carlos V** has a collection of Flemish tapestries.

The fragrant **Alcázar Gardens** are planted with jasmine and myrtle; there's also an orange tree said to have been planted by Pedro the Cruel, and a lily pond well stocked with fat, contented goldfish. The end of your visit brings you to the **Patio de las Banderas** for an unrivaled view of the Giralda. ⊠ *Pl. del Triunfo* ☎ *95/450–2324* ⊕ *www.patronato-alcazarsevilla.es* ⊙ *Apr.–Sept., Tues.–Sat. 9:30–8, Sun. 9:30–6; Oct.–Mar., Tues.–Sat. 9:30–6, Sun. 9:30–2:30.*

★ ❸ **Barrio de Santa Cruz.** With its twisting alleyways, cobbled squares, and whitewashed houses, this intriguing neighborhood is the perfect spot for an operetta. Once the home of Seville's Jewish population, it was much favored by 17th-century nobles and today includes some of the most expensive properties in Seville. Romantic images of Spain come to life here: every house gleams white or deep ocher, wrought-iron grilles adorn the windows, and balconies and patios are bedecked with flowers. Ancient bars nestle side by side with antiques shops. Don't miss the bar **Casa Román,** in Plaza de los Venerables, its ceilings hung thick with some of the best hams in Seville; or the **Hostería del Laurel,** next door, where in summer you can dine in one of the loveliest squares in the city. Souvenir shops and excellent ceramics shops surround the **Plaza Doña**

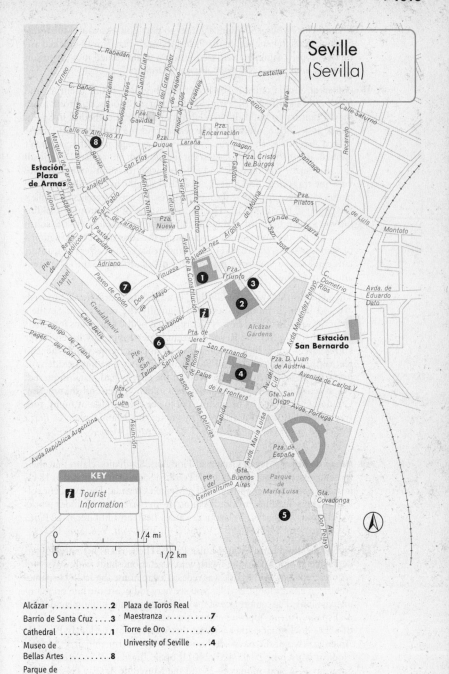

Seville
(Sevilla)

Elvira, where young Sevillanos gather to play guitars around the fountain and azulejo benches. In the **Plaza Alianza,** with its well-stocked antiques shops, a simple crucifix hangs on a wall, framed in a profusion of bougainvillea. ✉ *North of Alcázar Gardens.*

★ ❶ **Cathedral.** Seville's massive cathedral was begun in 1402, a century and a half after Ferdinand III seized Seville from the Moors, and took more than a century to build. It's the largest and highest cathedral in Spain, the largest Gothic building in the world, and the world's third-largest church after St. Peter's in Rome and St. Paul's in London. As if that weren't enough, it has the world's largest carved wooden altarpiece. Despite all this, the inside can be dark and gloomy, with too many overly ornate baroque trappings. Seek out the beautiful Virgins by Murillo and Zurbarán. In a silver urn before the high altar rest the precious relics of Seville's reconquerer, Ferdinand III. The mortal vestiges of Christopher Columbus are said to be enshrined in the flamboyant mausoleum in the south aisle. Borne aloft by statues representing the four medieval kingdoms of Spain, perhaps the voyager has found peace at last, after the transatlantic quarrels that carried his body from Valladolid to Santo Domingo and from Havana to Seville.

The cathedral's tower, the **Giralda,** is a splendid example of Moorish art and is the symbol of Seville. Originally the minaret of Seville's great mosque, the Giralda was incorporated by the Christians into their new cathedral after the Reconquest and later topped by a bell tower and weather vane. In place of steps, 35 sloping ramps climb the 230 feet to the viewing platform; St. Ferdinand is said to have ridden his horse to the top to admire the view of the city he had just conquered. Seven centuries later, your view of the Golden Tower and shimmering Guadalquivir is just as beautiful. Try to see the Giralda at night, too, when floodlights cast a different magic on this Islamic gem. ✉ *Plaza Virgen de los Reyes* ☎ *95/4214971* ⊙ *Cathedral: Mon.–Sat. 11–5, Sun. 2–6, and for mass.*

❽ **Museo de Bellas Artes** (Museum of Fine Art). Sevillanos claim that their museum is second only to Madrid's Prado in Spanish art. Opened in 1841, it occupies the former convent of La Merced Calzada. The excellent collection, presented in chronological order on two floors, includes works by Murillo, Zurbarán, Velázquez, Valdés Leal, and El Greco. ✉ *Plaza del Museo* ☎ *95/422–0790* ⊙ *Tues. 3–8, Wed.–Sat. 9–8, Sun. 9–3.*

❺ **Parque de María Luisa** (María Luisa Park). The gardens here are a wonderful blend of formal design with wild vegetation, shady walkways, and sequestered nooks. The park was redesigned to house the 1929 Hispanic-American exhibition; the villas you see here today are the fair's remaining pavilions. The centerpiece of the exhibition was the monumental **Plaza de España.** At the opposite end of the park you can feed the hundreds of white doves that gather around the fountains of the lovely **Plaza de América.** Two of the pavilions house the **Museo Arqueológico** (Archaeological Museum; ☎ 95/423–2401), open Tuesday 3–8, Wednesday–Saturday 9–8, and Sunday 9–2; and the **Museo de Artes y Costumbres Populares** (Museum of Folklore; ☎ 95/423–2576), open Wednesday–Saturday 9–8, Sunday 9–2. ✉ *Park entrance, Glorieta San Diego.*

❼ **Plaza de Toros Real Maestranza** (Maestranza Bullring). Sevillanos have spent many a thrilling Sunday afternoon in this bullring, built between 1760 and 1763. Corridas (bullfights) are held from Easter through October; the best are during the April Fair. Buy tickets in advance at the ring or from the kiosks on Calle Sierpes (these charge a commission). You can visit the ring and the small **museum** year-round. ✉ *Paseo de*

Colón 12 ☎ *95/422–4577* ⊙ *Daily 9:30–2 and 3–7 (mornings only on bullfight days).*

❻ **Torre de Oro** (Tower of Gold). Built by the Moors in 1220, this 12-sided structure is visible from both sides of the river. During the day you can enjoy a nice view from the tower, which also houses a small naval museum. ⊠ *Paseo de Colón, between C. Santander and C. Almirante Lobo* ☎ *95/422–2419* ⊙ *Tues.–Fri. 10–2, weekends 11–2.*

❹ **University of Seville.** Between the Alcázar gardens and the Parque María Luisa stands what used to be the Real Fábrica de Tabacos (Royal Tobacco Factory). Built between 1750 and 1766, the factory employed some 3,000 *cigarreras* (female cigar makers) less than a century later, including, of course, the heroine of Bizet's opera *Carmen*, who rolled her cigars on her thigh. The enormous building has been the Seville university's home since the 1950s. ⊠ *C. San Fernando* ☎ *95/455–1000* ⊙ *Weekdays 9–8:30.*

Seville's regular flamenco clubs cater largely to tourists and cost around €25 per person, but their shows are colorful and serve as a good introduction for the uninitiated. You'll find **El Arenal** (⊠ Rodo 7 ☎ 95/421–6492) in the back of the picturesque Mesón Dos de Mayo. Catch flamenco and other regional dances nightly at **El Patio Sevillano** (⊠ Paseo de Colón 11 ☎ 95/421–4120), which mainly serves tour groups. **Los Gallos** (⊠ Plaza Santa Cruz 11 ☎ 95/421–6981), an intimate club in the heart of the Barrio Santa Cruz, offers fairly pure flamenco.

★ **$$$$** ✗ **Egaña-Oriza.** This is one of Seville's most fashionable and acclaimed restaurants. The menu, which changes with the seasons, might include *lomos de lubina con salsa de erizos de mar* (sea bass with sea-urchin sauce) or *solomillo con foie natural y salsa de ciruelas* (fillet steak with foie gras and plum sauce). ⊠ *San Fernando 41* ☎ *95/422–7211* ▭ *AE, DC, MC, V* ⊙ *Closed Sun. and Aug. No lunch Sat.*

★ **$$$** ✗ **La Albahaca.** In an attractive old house in the heart of the Barrio Santa Cruz, this place has plenty of style and original, imaginative cuisine. The menu changes seasonally, but there will always be some variation on *lubina al horno* (baked sea bass) and the restaurant's star dish, *foie de oca salteado* (lightly sautéed goose liver perfumed with honey vinegar). ⊠ *Plaza Santa Cruz 12* ☎ *95/422–0714* ▭ *AE, DC, MC, V* ⊙ *Closed Sun.*

★ **$$$** ✗ **Poncio.** Named for the seaman who first sighted the New World, this happy place combines Andalusian tradition with a French flair. Chef Willy Moya trained in Paris and blends local and cosmopolitan cuisine flawlessly. Try the *salmorejo encapotado* (roughly chopped gazpacho topped with diced egg and chunks of acorn-fed ham), or the *besugo con gambitas* (sea bream with shrimp). ⊠ *C. Victoria 8* ☎ *954/340010* ▭ *AE, DC, MC, V.*

$$$ ✗ **Taberna del Alabardero.** Installed in a 19th-century mansion near the Plaza Nueva, this restaurant is also a hotel with seven guest rooms. Preceded by a courtyard and a bar, the dining area is decorated in Sevillian tiles. Modern dishes include *bacalao fritado con manitas guisadas con Pedro Ximénez* (fried cod with pig's trotters stewed in Pedro Ximénez wine) or *ensalada de espárragos verdes naturales con bogavante* (fresh green asparagus with lobster). ⊠ *Zaragoza 20* ☎ *954/560637* ▭ *AE, DC, MC, V* ⊙ *Closed Aug.*

★ **$$–$$$** ✗ **Mesón Don Raimundo.** In an old convent close to the cathedral, this restaurant has a decidedly Sevillian style. The bar is the perfect place to sample some splendid tapas, and the restaurant, when not catering to tour groups, is one of Seville's most delightful. ⊠ *Argote de Molina 26* ☎ *95/422–3355* ▭ *AE, DC, MC, V.*

$$ ✕ **El Bacalao.** This popular fish restaurant, opposite the church of Santa Catalina, occupies an Andalusian house decorated with ceramic tiles. As the name suggests, the house specialty is bacalao. They once claimed to prepare it 101 different ways, but have since lost count. Try it *con arroz* (with rice) or *al pil-pil* (fried in oil with garlic). ✉ *Plaza Ponce de León 15* ☎ *95/421–6670* ▭ *AE, DC, MC, V* ☉ *Closed Mon., late July, and early Aug.*

★ $$ ✕ **Enrique Becerra.** Excellent tapas await at this cozy restaurant in a white-washed house with wrought-iron window grilles. Locals meet at the lively, crowded bar, decorated with ceramic tiles. The menu focuses on traditional, home-cooked Andalusian dishes, such as *pez espada al amontillado* (swordfish cooked in dark sherry) and *rape al azafrán* (monkfish in saffron sauce). ✉ *Gamazo 2* ☎ *95/421–3049* ▭ *AE, DC, MC, V* ☉ *Closed Sun.*

$–$$ ✕ **El Corral del Agua.** You'll find this place in a restored 18th-century house on one of the prettiest streets in the Barrio Santa Cruz. The restaurant is centered around a delightful patio decorated with a profusion of potted plants and a central fountain. The menu specializes in Andalusian food prepared with modern flair. ✉ *Callejón del Agua 6* ☎ *95/422–4841 or 95/422–0714* ▭ *AE, DC, MC, V* ☉ *Closed Sun. Closed Jan. and Feb.*

$ ✕ **San Marco.** In an old neoclassical house in the shopping district, this Italian restaurant has a leafy patio, and a menu that combines Italian, French, and Andalusian cuisine. The restaurant now has four satellites, but this one, the original, is the most charming. ✉ *Cuna 6* ☎ *95/421–2440* ✍ *Reservations essential* ▭ *AE, DC, MC, V.*

★ $$$$ ▥ **Alfonso XIII.** Inaugurated by King Alfonso XIII on April 28, 1929, this grand hotel is a splendid, historical Mudéjar Revival palace, built around a huge central patio surrounded by ornate brick arches. The public rooms have marble floors, wood-panel ceilings, heavy Moorish lamps, stained glass, and ceramic tiles in the typical Sevillian colors. ✉ *San Fernando 2, 41004* ☎ *95/491–7000* 🖷 *95/491–7099* ⊕ *www.westin.com* ➴ *127 rooms, 19 suites* ⌖ *2 restaurants, pool, bar* ▭ *AE, DC, MC, V.*

$$$$ ▥ **Meliá Colón.** Built for the 1929 Exhibition, the grand old Colón has a white-marble staircase that leads up to the central lobby—which has a magnificent stained-glass dome and crystal candelabra. The old-fashioned rooms are elegantly furnished with silk drapes and bedspreads and wood fittings. ✉ *Canalejas 1, 41001* ☎ *954/505599* 🖷 *954/220938* ⊕ *www.solmelia.com* ➴ *204 rooms, 14 suites* ⌖ *Restaurant, bar* ▭ *AE, DC, MC, V.*

★ $$$–$$$$ ▥ **Los Seises.** The combination of modern and Renaissance architecture in this hotel—in a section of Seville's 16th-century Palacio Episcopal (Bishop's Palace)—is striking. A pit in the center of the basement restaurant reveals the building's foundations and some archaeological finds, including a Roman mosaic. The rooftop pool and summer restaurant are in full view of the Giralda. ✉ *Segovia 6, 41004* ☎ *95/422–9495* 🖷 *95/422–4334* ⊕ *www.hotellosseises.com* ➴ *40 rooms, 2 suites* ⌖ *Restaurant, pool* ▭ *AE, DC, MC, V.*

$$$ ▥ **Bécquer.** Right near the main shopping district, this hotel has marble floors, dark wood, and leather furniture in its public areas, which include a small sitting room dedicated to the poet Gustavo Adolfo Bécquer. The guest rooms have floral prints, matching woven bedspreads, and carved-wood headboards. There's also a cafeteria. ✉ *Reyes Católicos 4, 41001* ☎ *954/228900* 🖷 *954/214400* ⊕ *www.hotelbecquer.com* ➴ *137 rooms, 2 suites* ⌖ *Bar* ▭ *AE, DC, MC, V.*

$$$ ▥ **Doña María.** This is one of Seville's most charmingly old-fashioned hotels, and it's not far from the cathedral. Some rooms are small and plain; others are tastefully furnished with antiques. Room 310 has a four-

poster double bed, and 305 has two single four-posters; both have spacious bathrooms. There's also a rooftop pool with a good view of the Giralda, just a stone's throw away. ✉ *Don Remondo 19, 41004* ☎ *954/224990* ☎ *954/219546* ⊕ *www.hdmaria.com* ⌁ *67 rooms* ☆ *Pool* ⊟ *AE, DC, MC, V.*

$$$ ⊞ **Inglaterra.** Next door to the British consulate, this is a historic British outpost in Spain. The rooms are traditional, understated, and relaxing. Those on the fifth floor have large balconies. The on-site Trinity Irish Pub lends a literary twist to this family-run enterprise. The second-floor dining room overlooks orange trees and the busy Plaza Nueva, as does La Galería, which serves some of Seville's finest Andalusian and Mediterranean cuisine. ✉ *Pl. Nueva, 41001* ☎ *954/224970* ☎ *954/561336* ⊕ *www.hotelinglaterra.es* ⌁ *109 rooms* ☆ *Restaurant, bar* ⊟ *AE, DC, MC, V.*

$$$ ⊞ **Las Casas de la Judería.** This labyrinthine hotel occupies three of the barrio's old palaces, each arranged around inner courtyards. Ocher predominates in the palatial common areas; the spacious guest rooms are dressed in tasteful pastels and decorated with prints of Seville. The hotel is tucked into a passageway off the Plaza Santa María. ✉ *Callejón de Dos Hermanas 7 41004* ☎ *954/415150* ☎ *954/422170* ⌁ *103 rooms, 3 suites* ☆ *Restaurant* ⊟ *AE, DC, MC, V.*

★ **$$** ⊞ **Hotel Amadeus.** With pianos in the soundproof rooms and a music room off the central patio and lobby, this acoustical oasis is ideal for touring professional musicians and music fans in general. The breakfast terrace on the roof terrace overlooks the Judería and the Giralda. The 18th-century palace has been charmingly restored and equipped with modern amenities. ✉ *Calle Farnesio 6, 41004* ☎ *95/450–1443* ☎ *95/450–0019* ⊕ *www.hotelamadeussevilla.com* ⌁ *14 rooms* ⊟ *AE, DC, MC, V.*

$$ ⊞ **Simón.** In a rambling turn-of-the-19th-century town house, this hotel is a good choice for inexpensive, basic accommodation near the cathedral. The spacious, fern-filled, azulejo-tiled patio makes a fine initial impression; the elegant marble stairway and high-ceilinged and pillared dining room are cool and stately spaces. The rooms are less grand, but the mansion's traditional style permeates the house. ✉ *García de Vinuesa 19, 41001* ☎ *95/422–6660* ☎ *95/456–2241* ⊕ *www.hotelsimonsevilla. com* ⌁ *29 rooms* ⊟ *AE, DC, MC, V.*

Carmona

Thirty kilometers (19 mi) east of Seville, the NIV brings you to Carmona. This unspoiled Andalusian town of Roman and Moorish origin has a wealth of Mudéjar and Renaissance churches and streets filled with whitewashed houses. At the entrance to the town stands the church of **San Pedro**, begun in 1466, whose extraordinary interior is an unbroken mass of sculptures and gilded surfaces and whose tower, erected in 1704, is an unabashed imitation of Seville's Giralda. Opposite this is the **Alcázar de Abajo** (Lower Fortress), a Moorish fortification built on Roman foundations. In the tower beside the gate is the tourist office. Carmona's most affecting monument is its splendid **Roman necropolis**, where in huge underground chambers some 900 family tombs, dating between the 2nd and 4th centuries AD, were chiseled out of the rock. ✉ *C. Enmedio* ☎ *95/414–0811* ⊙ *Mid-June–mid-Sept., Tues.–Sat. 9–2, Sun. 10–2; mid-Sept.–mid-June, Tues.–Fri. 9–5, weekends 10–2.*

$$$$ ⊞ **Casa de Carmona.** One of the most original hotels in Spain is in a 16th-century palace, elegantly decorated with fine art, rich fabrics, and antiques. The small pool is in a cool Moorish-style patio. Note, however, that staff can be indifferent and maintenance uneven. ✉ *Pl. de Lasso 1*

41410 ☎ 95/419–1000 🖷 95/419–0189 ⊕ *www.casadecarmona.com*
🖙 *31 rooms, 1 suite* ♧ *Restaurant, pool, bar* ☰ *AE, DC, MC, V.*

$$–$$$ ✕🖽 **Alcázar de la Reina.** Stylish and contemporary, this hotel has public areas that incorporate three bright and airy courtyards, with marble floors and pastel walls. Guest rooms are spacious and comfortable. The elegant Ferrara serves tasty Spanish dishes. ⊠ *Pl. de Lasso 2, 41410* ☎*95/419–6200* 🖷 *95/414–0113* ⊕ *www.alcazar-reina.es* 🖙 *66 rooms, 2 suites* ♧ *Restaurant, pool, bar* ☰ *AE, DC, MC, V.*

★ **$$$** 🖽 **Parador Alcázar del Rey Don Pedro.** The beauty of this modern parador is its splendid, peaceful location, in the ruins of the old Moorish Alcázar on top of the hill above Carmona. The views across the vast fertile plain below are magnificent. ⊠ *Alcázar, 41410* ☎ *95/414–1010* 🖷 *95/414–1712* 🖙 *63 rooms* ♧ *Restaurant, pool* ☰ *AE, DC, MC, V.*

Jerez de la Frontera

One hundred kilometers (60 mi) south of Seville, Jerez is world headquarters for sherry. The word *sherry,* first heard in Great Britain in 1608, is in fact an English corruption of this town's old Moorish name, Xeres; today, names such as González Byass and Domecq are just as inextricably linked with Jerez. The town's wine-making tradition dates from Roman times and continued under the Moors despite the Koran's condemnation of alcohol.

At any given time more than half a million barrels of sherry are maturing in Jerez's vast, aboveground wine cellars. Most *bodegas* (wineries) welcome visitors, but it's wise to phone ahead for an appointment.

Domecq (☎ 956/151000) is Jerez's oldest bodega (1730) and makes sherry as well as the world's best-selling brandy, Fundador. You can tour the prestigious **González Byass** (☎ 956/357000), home of Tío Pepe. **John Harvey** (☎ 956/346004) makes the best-selling Harvey's Bristol Cream, a sweet sherry. **Sandeman** (☎ 956/301100) is a winery famous for its man-in-a-cape logo and Royal Corregidor sherry, their masterpiece.

The **Real Escuela Andaluza del Arte Ecuestre** (Royal Andalusian School of Equestrian Art) stands on the grounds of the Recreo de las Cadenas, a splendid 19th-century palace. Every Thursday (Tuesday and Thursday in summer) the Cartujana horses—a cross between the native Andalusian workhorse and the Arabian—and skilled riders in 18th-century riding costume demonstrate intricate dressage techniques and jumping in the spectacular show. Reservations are essential for the shows. On weekdays you can visit the stables and tack room, watch the horses being schooled, and witness rehearsals. ⊠ *Avda. Duque de Abrantes* ☎ *956/319635* ⊙ *Shows Nov.–Feb., Thurs. at noon; Mar.–Oct., Tues. and Thurs. at noon.*

★ **$$** ✕ **La Mesa Redonda.** Owner José Antonio Valdespino spent years researching the classic recipes once served in aristocratic Jerez homes, and now his son, José, presents them in this small, friendly restaurant off Avenida Alcalde Alvaro Domecq. The eight tables are surrounded by shelves lined with cookbooks. Ask the chef's mother, Margarita—who has an encyclopedic knowledge of Spanish wines—what to eat. ⊠ *Manuel de la Quintana 3* ☎ *956/340069* ☰ *AE, DC, MC, V* ⊙ *Closed Sun. and mid-July–mid-Aug.*

$–$$ ✕ **Gaitán.** Within walking distance of the riding school, this restaurant has white walls and brick arches decorated with colorful ceramic plates and photos of famous guests. It's crowded with businesspeople at lunchtime. The menu is Andalusian, with a few Basque dishes thrown in. *Setas* (wild mushrooms) make a delicious starter in season; follow them with cordero asado in a sauce of honey and Jerez brandy. ⊠ *Gaitán 3* ☎ *956/345859* ⊟ *AE, DC, MC, V* ⊘ *No dinner Sun.*

★ **$$$** ⊞ **Royal Sherry Park.** Set back from the road in an unusually large, tree-filled garden, this modern hotel is designed around several patios filled with exotic foliage. The sunny hallways are hung with contemporary paintings. Rooms are bright and airy, and most have balconies overlooking the garden. ⊠ *Avda. Alvaro Domecq 11 Bis, 11405* ☎ *956/317614* 🖷 *956/311300* ⊕ *www.sherryparkhotel.com* ⇥ *173 rooms* ♧ *Restaurant, 2 pools (1 indoor)* ⊟ *AE, DC, MC, V.*

$–$$ ⊞ **Ávila.** This friendly hostel on a side street off Calle Arcos offers affordable central lodgings. The rooms have basic furnishings and tile floors; beds are European twin-size. A TV lounge and a small bar and breakfast room adjoin the lobby. ⊠ *Ávila 3, 11401* ☎ *956/334808* 🖷 *956/336807* ⇥ *32 rooms* ♧ *Bar* ⊟ *AE, DC, MC, V.*

Córdoba

Numbers in the margin correspond to points of interest on the Córdoba map.

One of Spain's oldest cities, Córdoba is the greatest urban embodiment of Andalusia's Moorish heritage. Moorish emirs and caliphs held court here from the 8th to the 11th century. The city became one of the Western world's greatest centers of art, culture, and learning, and an oasis of tolerance and cooperation where Moors, Christians, and Jews lived together in peace.

❺ **Alcázar de los Reyes Cristianos** (Fortress of the Christian Monarchs). Built by Alfonso XI in 1328, the Alcázar is a Mudéjar-style palace with splendid gardens. (The original Moorish Alcázar stood beside the Mezquita, on the site of the present Bishop's Palace.) This is where, in the 15th century, the Catholic Monarchs held court and launched their conquest of Granada. Boabdil was imprisoned here for a time in 1483, and for nearly 300 years the Alcázar served as a base for the Inquisition. ⊠ *Plaza Campo Santo de los Mártires* ☎ *957/421015* ⊘ *Apr.–Sept., Tues.–Sat. 10–2 and 6–8, Sun. 9:30–3; Oct.–Mar., Tues.–Sat. 10–2 and 4:30–6:30, Sun. 9:30–2:30.*

❷ **Judería.** The medieval Jewish quarter is packed with houses, museums, and monuments that tell the story of Córdoba's rich past. The municipal tourist office is on the **Plaza Judá Leví.** From here, wander along Calle Albucasis and Calle Tomás Conde to the Plaza Maimónides, where you'll find the **Bullfighting Museum.** Head up Calle Judíos, where you will pass the statue of the great Jewish philosopher **Maimónides;** farther up is the **Zoco,** a former Arab souk that has pleasant shops and stalls, and a bar that opens in summer. Finally, you reach the **Synagogue.** ⊠ *Around C. Judíos.*

★ ❶ **Mezquita** (Mosque). Founded by Abd ar-Rahman I (756–788), Córdoba's justly famous mosque was completed by Al Mansur (976–1002) around 987. Inside you'll face a forest of gleaming pillars of precious marble, jasper, and onyx, rising to the red-and-white horseshoe arches characteristic of Moorish architecture. Not even the Christian cathedral that Charles V built in its midst—and later regretted—can detract from the extraordinary art of the Moorish craftsmen. The mosque once housed the original copy of the Koran and a bone from the arm of the prophet Mohammad, relics that drew thousands of pilgrims before St. Ferdinand reconquered Córdoba for the Christians in 1236. The building opens onto the **Patio de los Naranjos** (Orange Tree Courtyard) and the bell tower, which was the mosque's minaret. Near the mosque, the

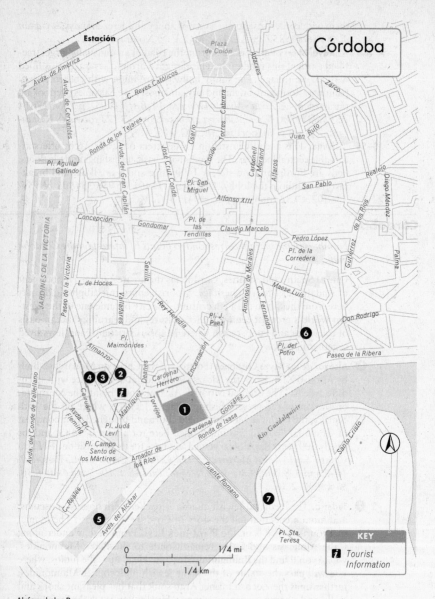

Estación

Plaza de Colón

Córdoba

Avda. de América

Avda. de Cervantes

C. Reyes Católicos

Ronda de los Tejares

Avda. del Gran Capitán

José Cruz Conde

Osario

Conde · Torres · Cabrera

Cardenal y Morand

Alfaros

Juan Rufo

Zarco.

Realejo

Diego Méndez

Pl. Aguilar Galindo

JARDINES DE LA VICTORIA

Concepción

Gondomar

Pl. San Miguel

Alfonso XIII

Claudio Marcelo

San Pablo

Pedro López

Gutiérrez de los Ríos

Palma

Pl. de las Tendillas

Pl. de la Corredera

Paseo de la Victoria

L. de Hoces

Sevilla

Rey Heredia

Valladares

Ambrosio de Morales

C.S. Fernando

Maese Luis

Don Rodrigo

Pl. J. Páez

Pl. Maimónides

Almanzor

Encarnación

6

Pl. del Potro

Paseo de la Ribera

Cerrajón

Avda. Dr. Fleming

Deanes

Cardenal Herrero

4 **3** **2**

i

Manríquez

Torrijos

1

Cardenal González

Ronda de Isasa

Río Guadalquivir

Santo Cristo

Pl. Judá Leví

Pl. Campo Santo de los Mártires

Amador de los Ríos

Avda. del Conde de Vallellano

C. Reales

Avda. del Alcázar

Puente Romano

5

7

Pl. Sta. Teresa

0 ———— 1/4 mi

0 ———— 1/4 km

streets of Torrijos, Cardenal Herrero, and Deanes are lined with shops specializing in local handicrafts, especially the filigree silver and embossed leather for which Córdoba is known. ☒ *Torrijos and Cardinal Herrero* ☎ *957/470512* ☉ *Mon.–Sat. 10–7 (5 in winter), Sun. for morning mass and 3:30–7 (5 in winter).*

❻ Museo de Bellas Artes. Córdoba's Museum of Fine Arts belongs to a former Hospital de la Caridad (Charity Hospice) founded by Ferdinand and Isabella, who twice received Columbus here. The collection includes paintings by Murillo, Valdés Leal, Zurbarán, Goya, and Sorolla. Across the courtyard from the entrance is a museum devoted to the early-20th-century Córdoba artist and folk hero **Julio Romero de Torres** (free Fri.; closed at lunchtime), who specialized in nude portraits of demure Andalusian temptresses. ☒ *Off Pl. del Potro* ☎ *957/473345* ☉ *Tues. 3–8, Wed.–Sat. 9–8, Sun. 9–3.*

❸ Museo Taurino (Museum of Bullfighting). Two delightful old mansions house this well-presented collection of memorabilia, paintings, and posters by early-20th-century Córdoban artists. Some rooms are dedicated to great Córdoban *toreros*—one holds the hide of the bull that killed the legendary Manolete in 1947. ☒ *Plaza Maimónides* ☎ *957/ 201056* ☉ *Tues.–Sat. 10–2 and 4:30–6:30 (6–8 in July and Aug.), Sun. 9:30–2:30.*

❹ Synagogue. Córdoba's was the only synagogue in Andalusia to survive the expulsion of the Jews in 1492. One of only three remaining ancient synagogues in Spain—the other two are in Toledo—it has Hebrew and Mudéjar stucco tracery and a women's gallery. ☒ *C. Judíos* ☎ *957/ 202928* ☉ *Tues.–Sat. 10–2 and 3:30–5:30, Sun. 10–1:30.*

❼ Torre de la Calahorra. The tower on the far side of the Puente Romano (Roman Bridge) was built in 1369 to guard the entrance to Córdoba. It now houses the **Museo Vivo de Al-Andalus** (Museum of Al-Andalus), with films and audiovisual guides (in English) on Córdoba's history and its greatest Christian, Muslim, and Jewish thinkers. Climb the narrow staircase to the top of the tower for the view of the Roman bridge and city on the other side of the Guadalquivir. ☒ *Avda. de la Confederación* ☎ *957/293929* ☉ *May–Sept., daily 10–2 and 4:30–8:30; Oct.–Apr., daily 10–6. Last tour 1 hr before closing.*

$$$–$$$$
Fodor'sChoice
★
✕ **El Caballo Rojo.** Royalty and society folk frequent this place in the Judería, one of the most famous traditional restaurants in Andalusia. The interior resembles a leafy Andalusian patio, and the elegant dining room is furnished with stained glass, dark wood, and gleaming marble. The restaurant serves traditional specialties, such as *rabo de toro* (oxtail stew), and dishes inspired by Córdoba's Moorish and Jewish heritage. ☒ *Cardenal Herrero 28* ☎ *957/478001* ⊕ *www.elcaballorojo.com* ⊟ *AE, DC, MC, V.*

$$$ ✕ **La Almudaina.** This attractive restaurant is in a 15th-century house and former school that overlooks the Alcázar at the entrance to the Judería. It has an Andalusian patio; the interior and the cooking are both typical of Córdoba. ☒ *Campo Santo de los Mártires 1* ☎ *957/474342* ⊟ *AE, DC, MC, V* ☉ *Closed Sun. June 15–Aug. No dinner Sun.*

★ **$$–$$$** ✕ **Bodegas Campos.** A block east of the Plaza del Potro, this former wine cellar is now a warren of barrel-heavy dining rooms and leafy courtyards. Regional dishes include *ensalada de bacalao y naranja* (salad of salt cod and orange with olive oil) and *solomillo al oloroso con foie y setas* (sirloin with foie and mushrooms in sherry). ☒ *Los Lineros 32* ☎ *957/497643* ⊟ *AE, MC, V* ☉ *No dinner Sun.*

★ $$–$$$ ✕ **El Churrasco.** In the heart of the Judería, this atmospheric restaurant has a patio and a colorful tapas bar. The steak is the best in town, and the grilled fish is fresh. Specialties are *churrasco* (a pork dish in pepper sauce) and an excellent *salmorejo*. In a separate house, two doors down the street, is the restaurant's formidable wine cellar, which is also a small museum. Ask your waiter to take you there. ⊠ *Romero 16* ☎ *957/290819* ⊕ *www.elchurrasco.com* ⊟ *AE, DC, MC, V* ⊘ *Closed Aug.*

$$–$$$ ✕ **Taberna Casa Pepe de la Judería.** This three-floor labyrinth of elegant rooms and leafy patios is just around the corner from the mosque, toward the Judería. In summer (May–October) the rooftop opens for barbecues, and there is live Spanish guitar music. In winter the tables on the patio are individually heated with charcoal braziers. ⊠ *Romero 1, off Deanes* ☎ *957/200744* ⊕ *www.casapepedelajuderia.com* ⊟ *AE, DC, MC, V.*

$$$ ⌂ **Conquistador.** This contemporary hotel on the east side of the mosque is built in Andalusian Moorish style, with a charming patio and ceramic details. Rooms at the front have small balconies overlooking the mosque, which is floodlighted at night. ⊠ *Magistral González Francés 15, 14003* ☎ *957/481102* ⊟ *957/474677* ⊕ *www.hotel-conquistador.com* ⌲ *99 rooms, 3 suites* ⊟ *AE, DC, MC, V.*

★ $$$ ⌂ **NH Amistad Córdoba.** This stylish hotel is built around two former 18th-century mansions that overlook the Plaza de Maimónides. (You can also enter through the old Moorish walls on Calle Cairuan.) It has a Mudéjar courtyard, carved-wood ceilings, and a plush lounge area. The rooms are large and comfortable. The newer wing has a more modern look, with Norwegian wood. ⊠ *Plaza de Maimónides 3, 14004* ☎ *957/420335* ⊟ *957/420365* ⊕ *www.nh-hoteles.com* ⌲ *84 rooms* ⌂ *Restaurant* ⊟ *AE, DC, MC, V.*

$–$$ ⌂ **Mezquita.** Ideally located next to the mosque, this hotel occupies a restored 16th-century home. The public areas are dappled with bronze sculptures on Andalusian themes that reflect the owner's penchant for collecting antiques. The best rooms face the interior patio. There's a dining room here; the only real drawback overall is the lack of parking. ⊠ *Plaza Santa Catalina 1, 41003* ☎ *957/475585* ⊟ *957/476219* ✉ *hotelmezquita@wanadoo.es* ⌲ *21 rooms* ⊟ *AE, DC, MC, V.*

Granada

Numbers in the margin correspond to points of interest on the Granada map.

The graceful city of Granada, 166 km (103 mi) southeast of Córdoba, rises onto three hills dwarfed by the mighty snowcapped peaks of the Sierra Nevada, on which lie the highest roads in Europe. Atop one of these hills, the pink-gold Alhambra Palace, at once terribly imposing yet infinitely delicate, gazes out across the rooftops and gypsy caves of the Sacromonte to the fertile plain, rich in orchards, tobacco fields, and poplar groves. Granada was the Moors' last stronghold; the city fell to the Catholic Monarchs in January 1492.

❹ **Albaicín.** Narrow streets wind up steep slopes in the old Moorish quarter, a fascinating mixture of dilapidated white houses and beautiful *cármenes* (a local term for flower-covered villas). Make your way up to the plaza in front of **San Nicolás** church for an unforgettable view of the Alhambra—particularly at night, when the palace is floodlighted.

★ ❺ **Alhambra.** On a hill overlooking Granada is the grandest and most stunning Moorish monument in Andalusia. Entrance to the interior palace of the Alhambra is restricted to 350 people every half hour, so it's wise to reserve them up to a year in advance through any branch of the **Banco Bilbao Vizcaya** (BBV; ⊠ Plaza Isabel Católica 1 ☎ 913/

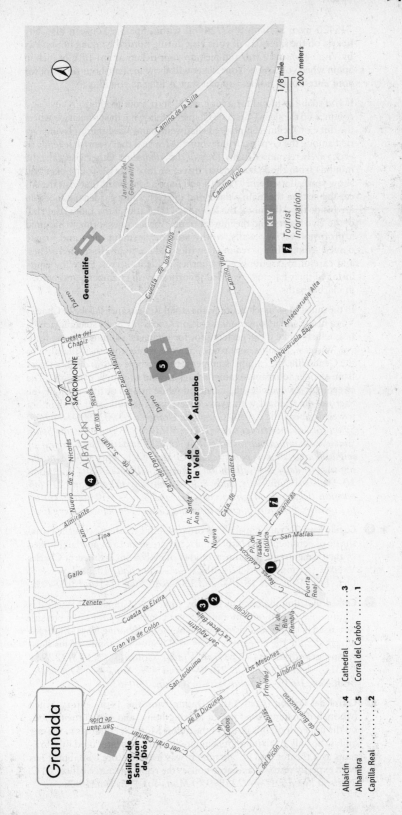

Granada

Basílica de
San Juan
de Diós

Generalife

Jardines del
Generalife

Camino de la Silla

Camino Viejo

KEY
ℹ Tourist
Information

Cuesta del
Chapiz

TO
SACROMONTE

ALBAICÍN

Cuesta de los Chinos

Paseo Padre Manjón

Antequeruela Alta

Antequeruela Baja

Camino Viejo

5

Alcazaba

Torre de
la Vela

Carr. del Darro

Pl. Santa
Ana

Cta. de Gomérez

C. de S. Nicolás

C. do S. Juan de los Reyes

Cam. Nuevo de S. Nicolás

Almirante

Tina

Gallo

Zenete

Cuesta de Elvira

Gran Vía de Colón

San Agustín

La Cárcel Baja

3
2

Pl.
Nueva

Reyes Católicos

Pl. de
Isabel la
Católica

1

C. Pavaneras

C. San Matías

Oficios

Puerta
Real

Pl. de
Bib-
Rambla

Los Mesones

Alhóndiga

San Jerónimo

Pl.
Trinidad

C. de Beatasuesso

C. de la Duquesa

Pl.
Lobos

Tablas

C. del Gran Capitán

C. del Picón

San Juan de Diós

1/8 mile
200 meters

Albaicín . . . . **4**   Cathedral **3**
Alhambra . . . . **5**   Corral del Carbón **1**
Capilla Real **2**

745420 from abroad; 902/224460 within Spain). You can also buy tickets on the same day of your visit during normal banking hours. Pay by Visa or MasterCard, and pick up your tickets at any BBV branch in Spain when you arrive. Your ticket will show the half-hour time slot for your entry; once inside, you can stay as long as you like.

If you're in the mood for a long walk, start from the Plaza Nueva and continue up the steep Cuesta de Gomérez, following the promenade where the duke of Wellington planted shady elms and Washington Irving tarried among the Gypsies, from whom he learned the Moorish legends so evocatively recounted in his *Tales of the Alhambra*. Otherwise, take the minibus from the Plaza Nueva, drive, or take a taxi. Your ticket will show your allotted entry time (if you have a long wait, first visit the **Alcazaba** next to the main palace, and the Generalife gardens). Once you are inside the Alhambra, the legends of the Patio of the Lions, the Hall of the Two Sisters, and the murder of the Abencerrajes spring to life amid a profusion of lacy walls, frothy stucco, gleaming tiles, and ornate domed ceilings. In this realm of myrtles and fountains, festooned arches, and careful inscriptions, every corner holds its secret. Here the emirs installed their harems, awarded favorites lavish chambers, and bathed in marble baths.

In the midst of so much delicacy, the stolid Renaissance **Palace of Charles V** is a heavy and incongruous intrusion saved only by its splendid acoustics, which make it the perfect spot for Granada's summer music festival. Wisteria, jasmine, and roses line your route from the Alhambra to the **Generalife,** the caliphs' summer retreat, where crystal drops shower from slender fountains against a background of stately cypresses. The sweeping view includes the clustered white houses of the Albaicín; the Sacromonte, riddled with gypsy caves; and the bulk of the Alhambra towering above the city. ⊠ *Cuesta de Gomérez* ☎ *902/224460 within Spain for advance ticket sales (BBV); 91/3465936 from outside Spain* ⊕ *www.alhambra-patronato.es (booking information and prices) or www.alhambratickets.com (tickets)* ☉ *Mar.–Oct., daily 8:30–2 (morning ticket); daily 2–8 (afternoon ticket); floodlighted visits Tues.–Sat. 10–11:30 PM. Nov.–Feb., daily 8:30–2 (morning ticket); daily 2–6 (afternoon ticket); floodlighted visits Fri. and Sat. 8–9:30 PM. Ticket office opens ½ hr before opening time and closes ½ hr before closing time.*

★ ❷ **Capilla Real** (Royal Chapel). This ornate Gothic masterpiece is the burial shrine of Ferdinand and Isabella, placed here since 1521 and later joined by their daughter Juana la Loca, mother of Holy Roman Emperor Charles V. ⊠ *C. Oficios* ☎ *958/229239* ☉ *Mar.–Sept., daily 10:30–1 and 4–7; Oct.–Feb., Mon.–Sat. 10:30–1 and 3:30–6:30, Sun. 11–1 and 3:30–6:30.*

❸ **Cathedral.** Commissioned in 1521 by Charles V, Granada's cathedral is a grandiose and gloomy monument, not completed until 1714 but still surpassed in beauty and historic value by the neighboring Royal Chapel—which, despite the emperor's plans, still houses the tombs of his illustrious grandparents. ⊠ *Gran Vía de Colón 5* ☎ *958/222959* ☉ *Mar.–Sept., Mon.–Sat. 10:30–1 and 4–7, Sun. 4–7; Oct.–Feb., Mon.–Sat. 10:30–1:30 and 3:30–6:30, Sun. 3:30–6.*

❶ **Corral del Carbón** (Coal Yard). Dating from the 14th century, when Moorish merchants used it as a lodging house and stored their goods on the upper floor, this is one of the oldest Moorish buildings in the city and is the only Arab inn of its kind in Spain. It was later used by Christians as a theater, and at one time it was used to store coal, but it has been expertly restored and now houses the regional tourist office. ⊠ *C. Mariana Pineda* ☎ *958/225990* ☉ *Mon.–Sat. 9–8, Sun. 10–2.*

The province of Granada was the home of the poet Federico García Lorca. García Lorca was born on June 5, 1898, in the village of **Fuentevaqueros**, 10 km (6 mi) west of Granada. Lorca's childhood home is now a **museum** (✉ Poeta García Lorca 4 ☎ 958/516453). On the outskirts of Granada is the Lorca family's summer residence, **Huerta de San Vicente** (✉ Parque Federico García Lorca ☎ 958/258466), now also a museum and a cultural center with exhibits on Lorca and his time. Nine kilometers (5½ mi) northeast of Granada is **Viznar**, where the poet was executed at the outbreak of the Spanish Civil War in 1936. He is probably buried here, in a common grave; a memorial park commemorates him.

There are several "impromptu" flamenco shows in the caves of the Sacromonte, but these can be little more than tourist traps. Go only if you're accompanied by a Spanish friend who knows his or her way around or with a tour organized by a local agency. **Jardines Neptuno** (✉ C. Arabial ☎ 958/522533) is a colorful flamenco club catering mainly to tourists. **Reina Mora** (✉ Mirador de San Cristóbal ☎ 958/401265), though somewhat smaller than Jardines Neptuno, offers regular flamenco shows known as tablaos.

$$$ ✕ **Cármen de San Miguel.** Hidden down a lane, in a villa on the Mauror hill above the Realejo, this restaurant has a spacious dining room and Andalusian-style terrace that would merit a visit just for the view over the city. The food—a mixture of Andalusian traditional and creative cuisine by chef David Reyes—also merits the highest marks. Try the *pichón asado con anís estellado y puré de castãnas* (roast squab with aniseed and chestnut sauce). ✉ *Paseo de Torres Bermejas 3* ☎ *958/226723* ▭ *AE, MC, V* ✆ *Closed Sun.*

$$–$$$ ✕ **El Huerto de Juan Ranas.** Gastronomically a cut above most Albaicín terrace restaurants, this intimate spot has only two or three difficult-to-secure outside tables. Views of the Alhambra from inside are excellent, though temperatures can soar in summer. The cuisine is Moorish and Spanish, ranging from *pastilla* (sweet and salty meat in puff pastry) to *croquetas de perdiz y jamón ibérico* (partridge and ham croquettes). Reservations are essential between Easter and October. ✉ *Atarazana Vieja 6-8* ☎ *958/286925* ▭ *AE, MC, V* ✆ *Closed Mon.*

$–$$ ✕ **Mirador de Morayma.** It's difficult to find this spot on the northeastern end of the Albaicín, and it might appear closed (ring the doorbell), but your efforts will be splendidly rewarded. This is Granada's most classic cármen. Terrace views of the Alhambra are magical. The food is mediocre, but the value, considering the location, is excellent. ✉ *Pianista García Carrillo 2* ☎ *958/228290* ▭ *958/228125* ✍ *Reservations essential* ▭ *AE, DC, MC, V* ✆ *Closed Sun.*

$$$–$$$$ 🏨 **Parador de Granada.** This is Spain's most expensive and popular
Fodor'sChoice   parador, and it's right on the Alhambra precincts. The building is soul-
★   stirring and gorgeous: a former Franciscan monastery built by the Catholic Monarchs after they captured Granada. If possible, go for a room in the old section where there are beautiful antiques, woven curtains, and bedspreads. The rooms in the newer wing are simpler, although still very charming. Reserve four to six months in advance. ✉ *, 18009* ☎ *958/221440* ▭ *958/222264* ⊕ *www.parador.es* ✒ *36 rooms, 2 suites* ⚘ *Restaurant, bar* ▭ *AE, DC, MC, V.*

★ $$$ 🏨 **Alhambra Palace.** This flamboyant, ocher-red, Moorish-style palace was built around 1910 and sits halfway up the hill to the Alhambra. Furnishings include rich carpets, tapestries, and Moorish tiles. The best rooms overlook the town. ✉ *Peña Partida 2, 18009* ☎ *958/221468* ▭ *958/226404* ⊕ *www.h-alhambrapalace.es* ✒ *122 rooms, 13 suites* ⚘ *Restaurant* ▭ *AE, DC, MC, V.*

$$$ ☒ **Casa Morisca.** Once a 15th-century Morisco building, this house was transformed into a hotel by its architect owner, who was given the 2001 National Restoration Award for this project. It has three floors and a central courtyard with a small pond and well. All rooms have Andalusian- and Moroccan-wood furniture and some have views of the Alhambra. ☒ *Cuesta de la Victoria 9, 18010* ☎ *958/215796* 🖶 *958/215* ⊕ *www.casamorisca.com* 🛏 *9 rooms, 2 suites* ☰ *AE, DC, MC, V.*

$$–$$$ ☒ **América.** This simple but charming hotel occupies a magnificent spot within the Alhambra precincts. You can linger over breakfast on a delightful patio. It's popular, so reserve months in advance. ☒ *Real de la Alhambra 53, 18009* ☎ *958/227471* 🖶 *958/227470* 🛏 *14 rooms, 1 suite* ⚬ *Restaurant* ☰ *MC, V* ⊙ *Closed Nov.–Feb.*

$$–$$$ ☒ **Palacio de Santa Inés.** This small hotel is in the heart of the Albaicín, on the two upper floors of a converted 16th-century palace. Each room is uniquely decorated with tasteful antiques and low-key modern art, and some rooms have views of the Alhambra. ☒ *Cuesta de Santa Inés 9, 18010* ☎ *958/222362* 🖶 *958/222465* 🛏 *9 rooms, 2 suites* ☰ *AE, DC, MC, V.*

$$–$$$ ☒ **Reina Cristina.** This hotel is in an old house near the lively Plaza de la Trinidad. A marble stairway leads to the rooms, which are simply but cheerfully furnished with red curtains and red-and-white-checkered bedspreads. ☒ *Tablas 4, 18002* ☎ *958/253211* 🖶 *958/255728* ⊕ *www.hotelreinacristina.com* 🛏 *43 rooms* ⚬ *Restaurant* ☰ *AE, DC, MC, V.*

Andalusia Essentials

BUS TRAVEL

Most bus service from Madrid to Andalusia operates out of the Estación del Sur.

Seville has two bus stations. Estación del Prado de San Sebastián has services to Córdoba, Granada, and eastern Andalusia. Estación Plaza de Armas, closer to downtown, has links to western Andalusia and Madrid. In Granada, the main bus station is on Carretera de Jaén. Córdoba's bus station is next to the AVE high-speed train station.

🚌 **Córdoba bus station** ☒ Glorieta de las Tres Culturas ☎ 957/404040. **Estación del Prado de San Sebastián** ☒ C. Manuel Vázquez Sagastizábal s/n ☎ 95/441-7111. **Estación Plaza de Armas** ☒ Cristo de la Expiración, by Cachorro Bridge ☎ 95/490-8040. **Granada main bus station** ☎ 958/185010.

CAR TRAVEL

By car, follow the NIV, which takes you through the scorched orange plains of La Mancha to Córdoba, then along the Guadalquivir River to Seville. The N323 road, which splits from the NIV at Bailén, takes you past lovely olive groves and rolling hills to Granada. Four-lane highways make traveling between the main cities in Andalusia much safer and quicker than relying on secondary roads, and as a result, the scenic routes are less congested. Driving is the best way to enjoy the scenery, although parking is a problem in cities and towns of any size. In cities, seek hotels with parking facilities or use underground parking lots.

TOURS

Guided tours of Seville, Córdoba, and Granada are run by Pullmantur, which has offices in major Spanish cities. Trapsatur has organized tours to southern Spanish destinations, departing from Madrid. In Seville, you may find group excursions to the sherry bodegas and equestrian museum in Jerez.

🚌 **Pullmantur** ☎ 91/541-1807. **Trapsatur** ☎ 91/542-6666.

TRAIN TRAVEL

Seville, Córdoba, and Granada all lie on direct train routes from Madrid. Service is frequent from both Chamartín and Atocha stations in Madrid and includes overnight trains (to Seville and Granada), slower day trains, and express Talgos. In addition, the high-speed AVE train connects Seville, Córdoba, and Atocha Station on entirely new track; it's more expensive than any other train, but it's a pleasant whiz of a ride and cuts the interprovince travel time down to 2½ hours.

Seville and Córdoba are linked by direct train service. Buses are a better choice between either town and Granada, as trains are relatively slow and infrequent and often involve a time-consuming change. Seville's main train station is Santa Justa. Granada's train station is at the end of Avenida Andaluces. Córdoba's train station is on the Glorieta de las Tres Culturas. For general information, call RENFE.

Córdoba train station ☎ 957/400202. **Granada train station** ☎ 958/271272. **RENFE** ☎ 902/240202. **Santa Justa** ✉ Avda. Kansas City ☎ 95/454-0202.

VISITOR INFORMATION

Córdoba ✉ Plaza de Judá Leví ☎ 957/200522. **Granada** ✉ Plaza Mariana Pineda 10 ☎ 958/223528 ✉ Corral del Carbón, C. Mariana Pineda ☎ 958/225990. **Jerez** ✉ Larga 35 ☎ 956/331150. **Seville** ✉ Avda. Constitución 21 ☎ 95/422-1404 ✉ Costurero de la Reina, Paseo de las Delícias 9 ☎ 95/423-4465.

COSTA DEL SOL & GIBRALTAR

The Costa del Sol's impoverished fishing villages of the 1950s are now retirement colonies and package-tour havens for northern Europeans and Americans. Fear not; behind the concrete monsters are old cottages, villas, and gardens resplendent with jasmine and bougainvillea. The sun still sets over miles of beaches, and the lights of small fishing craft still twinkle in the distance. The primary diversion here is indolence—swimming and sunning—but when you need something to do, you can head inland to historic Ronda and the white villages of Andalusia or take a day trip to Gibraltar.

Nerja

Nerja is a small but expanding resort town that so far has escaped the worst excesses of development. Its growth has been largely confined to village-style complexes outside town, such as El Capistrano. There's pleasant bathing here, though the sand is gray and gritty. The **Balcón de Europa** is a fantastic lookout, high above the sea. The **Cuevas de Nerja** (a series of stalactite caves) lie off the road to Almuñecar and Almería; a kind of vast underground cathedral, they contain the world's largest known stalactite (203 feet long). ☎ 95/252-9520 ☉ Daily 10–2 and 4–6:30 (4–8 in July and Aug.).

$$ ✕ Casa Luque. One of Nerja's most authentic Spanish restaurants, this place is in an old Andalusian house behind the Balcón de Europa church. The menu has dishes from northern Spain, often of Basque or Navarrese origin, with an emphasis on meat and game; good fresh fish is also on offer. Ask to sit on the patio during the summer. ✉ Pl. Cavana 2 ☎ 952/521004 ═ AE, DC, MC, V ☉ Closed Wed.

$$-$$$ ✕▣ Parador de Nerja. On a cliff's edge is this modern parador, with rooms that have balconies overlooking a garden and the sea. Rooms in the newer, single-story wing open onto their own patios; some have whirlpool baths. An elevator descends to the rocky beach. The restaurant is known for its fish; offerings might include *pez espada a la naranja* (swordfish in orange sauce) or giant *langostino* (shrimp). ✉ Almuñecar 8, 29780

Costa del Sol

☎ 95/252–0050 🖨 95/252–1997 ⊕ *www.parador.es* ⇆ *73 rooms* ♨ *Restaurant, pool* ⊟ *AE, DC, MC, V.*

$$ 🏨 **Paraiso del Mar.** An erstwhile private villa was expanded to accommodate this 12-room hotel perched on the edge of a cliff overlooking the sea east of the Balcón de Europa. Inside it's bright and cheerful. Some rooms have terraces, four have hot tubs, and most have sea views; prices vary accordingly. ⊠ *Prolongación del Carabeo 22, 29780* ☎ *95/ 252–1621* 🖨 *95/252–2309* ⇆ *9 rooms, 3 suites* ♨ *Pool* ⊟ *AE, DC, MC, V* ⊘ *Closed mid-Nov.–mid-Dec.*

Málaga

Málaga (544 km/337 mi south of Madrid) is a busy port city with ancient streets and lovely villas surrounded by exotic foliage. The central Plaza de la Marina, overlooking the port, is a pleasant place for a drink. The main shops are along the Calle Marqués de Larios.

Málaga's **cathedral,** built between 1528 and 1782 on the site of the former mosque, is unfinished, its construction funds having mysteriously dried up. (One story has it that the money was donated instead to the American Revolution.) Because it's missing one of its twin towers, the cathedral is known as *La Manquita* (the one-armed lady). The lovely, enclosed choir, which somehow survived the burnings of the civil war, is the work of the great 17th-century artist Pedro de Mena. The adjoining **museum** has art and religious artifacts. ⊠ *C. de Molina Larios* ☎ *95/ 221–5917* ⊘ *Mon.–Sat. 10–6:45.*

The **Alcazaba** (fortress) was begun in the 8th century, when Málaga was the most important port in the Moorish kingdom. The inner palace dates from the 11th century, when the Moorish emirs camped out here for a time after the breakup of the caliphate in Córdoba. ☒ *Entrance on Alcazabilla* ☉ *Oct.–Mar., Wed.–Mon. 8:30–7; Apr.–Sept., Wed.–Mon. 9:30–8.*

It takes some energy to climb from the Alcazaba to the summit of **Gibralfaro.** (You can also drive, by way of Calle Victoria, or take the parador minibus that leaves roughly every 1½ hours from near the cathedral on Molina Lario.) Gibralfaro's fortifications were built for Yusuf I in the 14th century—the Moors called it Jebelfaro, which means "rock of the lighthouse," after the beacon that stood here to guide ships into the harbor and warn of invasions by pirates. The beacon is gone, but the parador makes a delightful place for a drink or a meal and has some stunning views. ☉ *Daily 9–6.*

$$$–$$$$ ✗ **Café de Paris.** The owner of this stylish restaurant in the Paseo Marítimo area is one of Spain's most awarded chefs. Specialties may include *rodaballo* (turbot) or *lubina* (sea bass) or, in meats, *solomillo de buey* (beef fillet). ☒ *C. Vélez Málaga 8* ☎ *95/222–5043* ⌨ *Reservations essential* ▤ *AE, DC, MC, V* ☉ *Closed Mon. No dinner Sun.*

$$–$$$ ✗ **Antonio Martín.** This local institution founded in 1886 is right on the beach, one block east of the lighthouse, with a large terrace (glassed in during winter) overlooking the sea. Variations on local dishes mark the culinary theme, with specialties including *zarzuela de pescado y mariscos de la Bahía* (seafood stew) and *solomillo de cerdo estilo Montes de Málaga* (pork fillet Málaga style). ☒ *Plaza la Malagueta* ☎ *95/222–7382* ▤ *AE, D, MC, V.*

$$–$$$ ✗ **El Chinitas.** Decorated with tiles, this place sits at one end of Pasaje Chinitas, Málaga's most *típico* street. The tapas bar is popular, especially for its cured ham. Try the *sopa viña AB,* a fish soup flavored with sherry and thickened with mayonnaise, and consider *solomillo al vino de Málaga,* fillet steak in Málaga wine sauce. ☒ *Moreno Monroy 4* ☎ *95/221–0972* ▤ *AE, DC, MC, V.*

$–$$ ✗ **La Cancela.** In an alley off Calle Granada, at the top of Molina Larios, this pretty bistro serves standard Spanish food, such as *riñones al jerez* (kidneys sautéed with sherry) and *cerdo al vino de Málaga* (pork with Málaga wine sauce). The two dining rooms are crowded with birdcages, potted plants, and plastic flowers. In summer, tables appear on the sidewalk for outdoor lunches. ☒ *Denís Belgrano 5* ☎ *95/222–3125* ▤ *AE, DC, MC, V* ☉ *Closed Wed. No dinner Mon.*

$$$ ✗▦ **Parador de Málaga–Gibralfaro.** Surrounded by pine trees on top of Gibralfaro, 3 km (2 mi) above the city, this cozy, gray-stone parador has spectacular views of Málaga and the bay. Rooms are attractive—with blue curtains and bedspreads, and woven rugs on bare tile floors—and are considered the best in Málaga. Reserve well in advance. The restaurant serves regional and international food. ☒ *Monte de Gibralfaro, 29016* ☎ *95/222–1902* 🖷 *95/222–1904* ⊕ *www.parador.es* ⤶ *38 rooms* ⌖ *Restaurant, pool, bar* ▤ *AE, DC, MC, V.*

$$$ ▦ **Larios.** This stylish hotel is in an elegant, restored building on the central Plaza de la Constitución. Rooms have light wood, cream-color fabrics, and black-and-white photographs. ☒ *Marqués de Larios 2, 29005* ☎ *95/222–2200* 🖷 *95/222–2407* ⊕ *www.hotel-larios.com* ⤶ *34 rooms, 6 suites* ⌖ *Restaurant* ▤ *AE, DC, MC, V.*

$$ ▦ **Don Curro.** Just around the corner from the cathedral, this family classic is going through continual renovations, but an old-fashioned air permeates the wood-paneled common rooms, the fireplace lounge, and the somewhat stodgy wood-floor guest rooms. The best rooms are in the new wing, at the back of the building. ☒ *Sancha de Lara 7, 29015* ☎ *95/ 222–7200* 🖷 *95/221–5946* ⊕ *www.hoteldoncurro.com* ⤶ *112 rooms, 6 suites* ⌖ *Restaurant* ▤ *AE, DC, MC, V.*

$$ ⊞ **Venecia.** This four-story hotel has a central location on the Alameda Principal, next to the Plaza de la Marina. The rooms are simply furnished but spacious. ⊠ *Alameda Principal 9, 29001* ☎ *95/221–3636* 📠 *95/ 221–3637* 🛏 *40 rooms* ⊟ *AE, DC, MC, V.*

Torremolinos & Benalmádena

As you approach Torremolinos through an ocean of concrete blocks, it's hard to grasp that it was once an inconsequential fishing village. Now it's a grossly overdeveloped resort. The town center is full of overpriced bars and restaurants. Far more attractive is the district of **La Carihuela,** farther west, below the Avenida Carlota Alexandra—here you'll find some old fishermen's cottages, excellent seafood restaurants, and a traffic-free esplanade for an enjoyable stroll on a summer evening. La Carihuela merges with the coastal resort of Benalmádena-Costa, which has a lively yacht harbor and marina; at the western end of the resort is the Casino Torrequebrada, and inland is the surprisingly unspoiled village of Benalmádena itself.

$$–$$$ ✗ **Casa Guaquin.** Widely known as the best seafood restaurant in the popular Carihuela district of Torremolinos, this place on a seaside patio serves changing daily catches and stalwarts, such as *coquinas al ajillo* (wedge-shell clams in garlic sauce). ⊠ *Paseo Marítimo 63* ☎ *95/238–4530* ⊟ *AE, MC, V* 🕙 *Closed Mon. and mid-Dec.–mid-Jan.*

$$–$$$ ✗ **Juan.** If you want a great place to dine in summer—on a sunny outdoor patio facing the sea—this place is ideal. Specialties include the great Costa del Sol standbys: *sopa de mariscos* (shellfish soup), *dorada al horno* (oven-roasted giltheads), and *fritura malagueña* (Málaga's fried fish). ⊠ *Paseo Marítimo 28, La Carihuela* ☎ *95/238–5656* ⊟ *AE, DC, MC, V.*

$$ ✗ **Mar de Alborán.** This top-class restaurant is right next to the Benalmádena yacht harbor. The cheerful dining room is further illuminated by picture windows. Fish dishes, such as the Basque-inspired *lomo de merluza con kokotxas y almejas* (hake with cheek morsels and clams), are an imaginative switch from standard Costa fare. Meat and fowl are also also well represented. ⊠ *Avda. de Alay 5* ☎ *95/244–6427* ⊟ *AE, MC, V* 🕙 *Closed Mon. No dinner Sun.*

$$ ✗ **Ventorillo de la Perra.** This old inn (built in 1785) is 3 km (2 mi) from the center of Torremolinos, on the road inland to Arroyo de la Miel. A cozy, rustic vibe prevails in both the dining room and the bar. The menu mixes Malagueño specialties and general Spanish fare with international favorites. ⊠ *Avda. Constitución, Arroyo de la Miel* ☎ *95/244–1966* ⊟ *AE, DC, MC, V* 🕙 *Closed Mon.*

$$$ ⊞ **Tropicana.** On the beach at the far end of the Carihuela is this comfortable, relaxing resort hotel. The tropical theme is carried throughout, from the leafy gardens and kidney-shape pool to the rooms, which have ceiling fans and marble floors. ⊠ *Trópico 6, 29620* ☎ *95/238–6600* 📠 *95/238–0568* 🛏 *84 rooms* ⟨ *Pool* ⊟ *AE, DC, MC, V.*

$ ⊞ **Miami.** In an old Andalusian villa in a shady garden west of the Carihuela, this place is an oasis in the desert of concrete. ⊠ *Aladino 14, 29620* ☎📠 *95/238–5255* 🛏 *26 rooms* ⟨ *Pool* ⊟ *No credit cards.*

Fuengirola & Mijas

Head west from Torremolinos for the similar but more staid resort of Fuengirola, a retirement haven for Britons and Americans. A short drive from Fuengirola up into the mountains takes you to the picturesque and ★ oft-photographed village of **Mijas.** Though the vast and touristy main square may seem like an extension of the Costa's tawdry bazaar, Mijas does have hillside streets of whitewashed houses whose authentic village tone survived the tourist boom of the '60s largely unscathed. You can visit the bullring, the nearby church, and the chapel of Mijas's patroness, and the Virgen de la Peña (to the side of the main square).

$$$–$$$$ ✕ **Mirlo Blanco.** Here, in a large Andalusian town house overlooking the square, you can sample Basque dishes, such as *txangurro* (crab) and *merluza a la vasca* (hake with asparagus, eggs, and clam sauce). Inside it's pleasantly busy; in warm weather, you can dine on the terrace overlooking the square in Mijas. ⊠ *Plaza Constitución 13* ☎ 95/248–5700 ▭ *AE, DC, MC, V* ⊗ *Closed Jan.*

$$ ✕ **Portofino.** This lively restaurant, one of Fuengirola's best, is camouflaged among the brash souvenir shops and fast-food joints on the seafront promenade, just east of the port. The menu is international. ⊠ *Paseo Marítimo Rey de España 29* ☎ 95/247–0643 ▭ *AE, DC, MC, V* ⊗ *Closed Mon. No lunch July–mid-Sept.*

★ $$$$ ▥ **Byblos Andaluz.** You won't miss any comforts in this luxury spa hotel, amid a huge garden of palms, cypresses, and fountains. The restaurant, Le Nailhac, is known for its French cuisine. ⊠ *Mijas-Golf, Fuengirola 29640* ☎ 95/247–3050 ◱ 95/247–6783 ⊕ *www.byblos-andaluz.com* ⤳ *108 rooms, 36 suites* ◬ *2 restaurants, 2 pools* ▭ *AE, DC, MC, V.*

$$$ ▥ **Mijas.** This beautifully situated hotel at the entrance to Mijas has views of the hillsides stretching down to Fuengirola and the Mediterranean. ⊠ *Urb. Tamisa, 29650* ☎ 95/248–5800 ◱ 95/248–5825 ⊕ *www.hotasa.es* ⤳ *197 rooms, 4 suites* ◬ *Restaurant, 2 pools* ▭ *AE, DC, MC, V.*

Marbella & Estepona

Marbella is the most fashionable resort area on the Costa del Sol. It smacks a bit of the Florida land boom, and the town's otherwise charming ancient Moorish quarter is crowded with upscale boutiques and T-shirt-and-fudge shops; but when people speak of Marbella, they refer both to the town and the resorts. These stretch some 8 km (5 mi) east of town, between the highway and the beach, and west to San Pedro de Alcántara and Estepona. If you're vacationing in southern Spain, this is the place to stay.

Marbella's Golden Mile (which is, in fact, 5 km/3 mi), with its mosque, Arab banks, and residence of Saudi Arabia's King Fahd, illustrates the ever-growing influence of wealthy Arabs in this playground of the rich. In the plush marina, **Puerto Banús**, flashy yachts, fashionable people, and expensive restaurants form a glittering parade that outshines even St. Tropez.

Estepona is set back from the main highway and lacks the hideous high-rises of Torremolinos and Fuengirola. It's not hard to see the original outlines of this old fishing village. Wander the streets of the Moorish village, around the central food market and the church of **San Francisco**, and you'll find a pleasant contrast to the excesses up the coast.

$$$$ ✕ **La Meridiana.** This is a favorite with the local jet set. It's famous for its original Bauhaus architecture and the superb quality and freshness of the ingredients the chef uses. ⊠ *Camino de la Cruz* ☎ 95/277–6190 ◬ *Reservations essential* ▭ *AE, DC, MC, V* ⊗ *Closed Jan. No lunch.*

$$$–$$$$ ✕ **El Portalón.** This attractive restaurant combines hearty Castilian roasts and innovative *cocina de mercado*, based on whatever ingredients are freshest at the market. ⊠ *Carretera de Cádiz, Km 178* ☎ 95/282–7880 ▭ *AE, DC, MC, V.*

$$$-$$$$ ✕ **Santiago.** This busy place on the seafront promenade is known as the best fish restaurant in Marbella. Try the *ensalada de langosta* (lobster salad), followed by *besugo al horno* (baked red bream). ⊠ *Paseo Marítimo 5* ☎ *95/277–0078* ▭ *AE, DC, MC, V* ⊘ *Closed Nov.*

$$$$ ▦ **Kempinski.** On the beach just east of Estepona, this luxurious, ocher resort hotel looks like a combination of the Moroccan casbah and the hanging gardens of Babylon, surrounded by tropical gardens. Rooms are spacious and luxurious, with balconies overlooking the sea. ⊠ *Playa del Padrón, Carretera N340, Km 159, 29680* ☎ *95/280–9500* 🖷 *95/ 280–9550* ⊕ *www.kempinski-spain.com* 🖘 *131 rooms, 17 suites* ♨ *Restaurant, pool* ▭ *AE, DC, MC, V.*

$$$$ ▦ **Las Dunas.** This spectacular hotel rises like a multicolor apparition next to the beach midway between Estepona and Marbella. The place is palatial, and the large guest rooms are bright and airy, with large easy chairs, hemp carpets, and light-green furniture. ⊠ *La Boladilla Baja, Carretera de Cádiz, Km 163, 29689* ☎ *95/279–4345* 🖷 *95/279–4825* ⊕ *www.las-dunas.com* 🖘 *34 rooms, 39 suites, 33 apartments* ♨ *2 restaurants, pool* ▭ *AE, DC, MC, V.*

★ $$$$ ▦ **Le Méridien Los Monteros.** This deluxe hotel offers top-notch facilities, including an 18-hole golf course, tennis, horseback riding, and dining in the famous El Corzo Grill. ⊠ *Urb. Los Monteros, Carretera N340, Km 187, 29600* ☎ *95/277–1700* 🖷 *95/282–5846* ⊕ *www.monteros.com* 🖘 *159 rooms, 10 suites* ♨ *3 restaurants, 3 pools* ▭ *AE, DC, MC, V.*

★ $$$$ ▦ **Marbella Club.** The grande dame of Marbella attracts an older clientele. The bungalow-style rooms run from small to spacious, and the furnishings vary considerably, from regional to modern, so specify the type you prefer. The grounds are exquisite. ⊠ *Carretera de Cádiz, Km 178, 29600* ☎ *95/282–2211* 🖷 *95/282–9884* ⊕ *www.marbellaclub.com* 🖘 *90 rooms, 36 suites, 10 bungalows* ♨ *Restaurant, 2 pools* ▭ *AE, DC, MC, V.*

★ $$$$ ▦ **Puente Romano.** A spectacular, modern hotel and apartment complex of low, white stucco buildings 3¼ km (2 mi) west of Marbella (on the road to Puerto Banús), this "village" has a Roman bridge on its beautiful grounds, as well as a tennis club, squash courts, and a nightclub. ⊠ *Carretera de Cádiz, Km 177, 29600* ☎ *95/282–0900* 🖷 *95/277–5766* ⊕ *www.puenteromano.com* 🖘 *175 rooms, 99 suites* ♨ *3 restaurants, 2 pools* ▭ *AE, DC, V.*

$$$-$$$$ ▦ **El Fuerte.** The best of the few hotels in the center of Marbella, this one has comfortable rooms with sea views. The 1950s-style building sits in a large garden with an outdoor pool. ⊠ *Avda. El Fuerte s/n, 29600* ☎ *95/286–1500* 🖷 *95/282–4411* ⊕ *www.hotel-elfuerte.es* 🖘 *261 rooms, 2 suites* ♨ *Restaurant, pool* ▭ *AE, DC, MC, V.*

Ronda

You arrive in Ronda (61 km/38 mi northwest of Marbella) via a spectacular mountain road from San Pedro de Alcántara, between Marbella and Estepona. Ronda is one of the oldest towns in Spain and the last stronghold of the storied Andalusian bandits. The town's most dramatic feature is its ravine, known as **El Tajo,** which is 915 feet across and divides the old Moorish town from the "new town" of El Mercadillo. Spanning the gorge is the amazing **Puente Nuevo,** built between 1755 and 1793, whose parapet provides dizzying views of the River Guadalevin, far below. Ronda's breathtaking location and ancient houses are its chief attractions. Stroll the old streets of **La Ciudad;** drop in at the historic **Reina Victoria** hotel, built by the English from Gibraltar as a fashionable resting place on their Algeciras–Bobadilla railroad line. Visit the **bullring,** one of the oldest and most beautiful in Spain; Ronda's most famous native son, Pedro Romero (1754–1839), father of modern bullfighting, is said to have killed 5,600 bulls here during his 30-year career. The **museum** (☎ 95/287–4132) inside has posters dating from the very first fights held in this ring in May 1785. The ring is privately owned now, but three or four fights are still held in the summer; tickets are exceedingly difficult to come by. It's open daily 10–6 and 10–8 in July and August. Above all, don't miss the cliff-top walk and the gardens of the **Alameda del Tajo** (Tajo Park), where you can enjoy one of the most dramatic views in all of Andalusia.

★ **$$$–$$$$** ✕ **Tragabuches.** This restaurant around the corner from Ronda's Parador and the tourist office has an interesting style, which, like the food, combines traditional and modern ingredients. Try the *menú de degustación,* a taster's menu of five courses plus two desserts. ⊠ *José Aparicio 1* ☎ *95/ 219–0291* ▭ *AE, DC, MC, V* ☉ *Closed Mon. No dinner Sun.*

$–$$ ✕ **Pedro Romero.** Named after the father of modern bullfighting, this restaurant opposite the bullring is packed with colorful taurine objects. Bulls peer down at you as you tuck into the *sopa del mesón* (house soup), *rabo de toro* (oxtail), or *perdiz estofada con salsa de vino blanco y hierbas* (partridge stewed in white wine and herb sauce). ⊠ *Virgen de la Paz 18* ☎ *95/287–1110* ▭ *AE, DC, MC, V.*

$$$ ✕🏨 **Parador de Ronda.** The exterior of this parador is the old town hall, perched at the very edge of the Tajo gorge, but only the shell of the building remains—inside, the design is daringly modern. The spacious rooms have enormous bathrooms. The famous restaurant serves a gazpacho based on green peppers, a regional specialty; for dessert, try the chef's own *helado de aceite de oliva* (olive oil ice cream). ⊠ *Pl. de España, 29400* ☎ *952/877500* 🖷 *952/878188* ⊕ *www.parador.es* ⟿ *70 rooms, 8 suites* ⌂ *Restaurant, pool* ▭ *AE, DC, MC, V.*

$$–$$$ 🏨 **Reina Victoria.** Built in 1906 by the Gibraltar British as a weekend stop on the rail line between Algeciras and Bobadilla, this classic Spanish hotel rose to fame in 1912, when the ailing German poet Rainer Maria Rilke came here to convalesce. Rilke's room has been preserved as a museum. The views from the cliff-top gardens, hanging over a 500-foot-deep gorge, are particularly dramatic. ⊠ *Av. Doctor Fleming 25, 29400* ☎ *952/871240* 🖷 *952/871075* ⊕ *www.ronda.ne* ⟿ *89 rooms* ⌂ *Restaurant, pool* ▭ *AE, DC, MC, V.*

Casares

Nineteen kilometers (11¾ mi) northwest of Estepona, the mountain village of Casares lies high in the Sierra Bermeja. Streets lined with ancient white houses perch on the slopes beneath a ruined Moorish castle. Stop for a breather, admire the view of the Mediterranean, and check out the village's thriving ceramics industry.

$–$$ 🏨 **Casares.** This place has rustic rooms in a typical mountain village and splendid views over the valley. The restaurant (closed Thursday) serves typical upland Andalusian food. ⊠ *Copera 52, 29690* ☎ *95/289–5211* 🖷 *95/289–4227* ⟿ *17 rooms* ⌂ *Restaurant* ▭ *AE, DC, MC, V.*

Gibraltar

Numbers in the margin correspond to points of interest on the Gibraltar map.

Gibraltar is the only colony in Europe. It was captured by the British in 1704, and Spain has been claiming it back ever since. To enter Gibraltar, simply walk or drive across the border at **La Línea** and show your passport. There may be border delays for cars, and traffic in Gibraltar is congested, so unless you have a good reason for driving it is best to leave your car in a guarded parking lot in La Línea, walk across the border, and take a taxi or bus from there. Once you reach Gibraltar the official language is English, and the currency is the British pound, although the euro is also widely accepted.

The Rock of Gibraltar acquired its name in AD 711, when it was captured by the Moorish chieftain Tarik at the beginning of the Arab invasion of Spain. It became known as Jebel Tariq (Rock of Tariq), later corrupted to Gibraltar. After successive periods of Moorish and Spanish domination, Gibraltar was captured by an Anglo-Dutch fleet in 1704 and ceded to the British by the Treaty of Utrecht in 1713. This tiny British colony, whose impressive silhouette dominates the strait between Spain and Morocco, is a rock just 5⅕ km (3⅗ mi) long, ¾ km (½ mi) wide, and 1,394 feet high.

7 **Apes' Den,** near the Wall of Charles V, can be reached by car or cable car. The famous Barbary apes are a breed of cinnamon-color, tail-less monkeys, natives of the Atlas Mountains in Morocco. Legend holds that as long as the apes remain, the British will continue to hold the Rock. Winston Churchill himself ordered the maintenance of the ape colony when its numbers began to dwindle during World War II.

14 **Catalan Bay.** If you turn left (east) at Devil's Tower Road just after you enter Gibraltar, you'll reach a small fishing village founded by Genoese settlers during the 18th century and now one of the Rock's most picturesque resorts.

11 **Gibraltar Museum.** Exhibits recall the history of the Rock throughout the ages. ⊠ *Bomb House La.* ☎ *9567/74289* ⊕ *www.gibraltar.gi* ⊗ *Weekdays 10–6, Sat. 10–2.*

13 **Great Siege Tunnel.** These huge galleries at the northern end of the Rock were carved out during the Great Siege of 1779–83, when the French and Spanish attacked. In 1878 the governor, Lord Napier of Magdala, entertained ex-president Ulysses S. Grant here at a banquet in St. George's Hall. From here the Holyland Tunnel leads out to the east side of the Rock, above Catalan Bay.

4 **Jews' Gate.** Drive down Engineer Road for an unbeatable lookout point over the docks and Bay of Gibraltar to Algeciras. Here you can access the **Upper Nature Preserve,** which includes St. Michael's Cave, the Apes' Den, the Great Siege Tunnel, and the Moorish Castle. The preserve is open daily 9:30–sunset.

10 **Koehler Gun.** Standing in Casemates Square, this is an impressive example of the type of gun developed during the Great Siege. ⊠ *Northern end of Main St.*

6 **Ladbroke International Casino.** Perched above the Alameda Gardens, the casino is open for gaming daily until 4 AM. Dress is "smart casual," and children under age 18 are not permitted. ⊠ *Europa Rd.* ☎ *9567/76666.*

12 **Moorish Castle.** This refuge was built by chieftain Tarik's successors in the 11th century. The **Tower of Homage,** the only bit remaining, was rebuilt by the Moors in 1333. Admiral Rooke hoisted the British flag from its top when he captured the Rock in 1704, and it has flown here ever since. ⊠ *Willis Rd.*

8 **Nefusot Yehudada Synagogue.** The synagogue is worth a look for its inspired design. ⊠ *Line Wall Rd.*

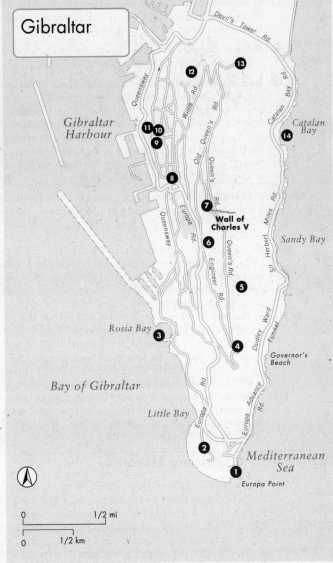

Gibraltar

*Gibraltar
Harbour*

*Catalan
Bay*

**Wall of
Charles V**

Sandy Bay

Rosia Bay

*Governor's
Beach*

Bay of Gibraltar

Little Bay

*Mediterranean
Sea*

Europa Point

0   1/2 mi

0   1/2 km

① **Punta Grande de Europa** (Europa Point). Stop here at the Rock's southernmost tip to admire the view across the strait to the coast of Morocco,
22½ km (14 mi) away. You are standing on what in ancient times was
called one of the two Pillars of Hercules. (The second pillar was just across
the water, in Morocco—a mountain between the cities of Ceuta and Tangier.) Plaques explain the history of the gun installations here.

③ **Rosia Bay.** This is where Admiral Nelson's flagship, HMS *Victory*, was
towed after the Battle of Trafalgar, in 1805. Aboard were the battle's
casualties, now buried in **Trafalgar Cemetery** (⊠ southern edge of town),
and the body of Nelson himself, preserved in a barrel of rum. Nelson
was taken to London for burial in St. Paul's Cathedral. ✣ *From Europa Flats, follow Europa Rd. back along the Rock's western slopes.*

⑤ St. Michael's Cave. A series of underground chambers adorned with sta-
lactites and stalagmites, the cave is a wonderful place to see concerts,
ballet, and drama. ✉ *Off Queen's Rd.*

② Shrine of Our Lady of Europe. The shrine has been venerated by sailors
since 1462. ✉ *West of Europa Point.*

⑨ Town of Gibraltar. Britain's dignified Regency architecture blends with
the shutters, balconies, and patios of southern Spain in this colorful, congested confluence. The tourist office is on Cathedral Square. Apart
from the shops, restaurants, and pubs that beckon on busy Main Street,
you'll want to see the **Governor's Residence,** with the ceremonial Changing of the Guard and Ceremony of the Keys. The changing of the guard
takes place daily, every 80 minutes between 9 AM and 5 PM, and the ceremony of the keys is held twice annually.

$$–$$$ ✕ **La Bayuca.** One of the Rock's best-established restaurants, this place
is renowned for its onion soup and Mediterranean dishes. ✉ *21 Turn-
bull's La.* ☎ *9567/75119* 🖃 *AE, DC, MC, V* ⊘ *Closed Tues. No lunch
weekends.*

$$$$ 🏨 **The Eliott.** The Rock's most modern hotel is right in the center of the
town. The rooms are functional and comfortable. The higher the room,
the better the view over the Bay of Gibraltar. ✉ *2 Governor's Parade*
☎ *9567/70500* 🖷 *9567/70243* ⊕ *www.gibraltar.gi* ↩ *107 rooms, 7
suites* ↻ *2 restaurants, pool, 2 bars* 🖃 *AE, DC, MC, V.*

★ $$$ 🏨 **The Rock.** Overlooking the town and harbor, this refurbished hotel
is spiffy enough to qualify as an international hotel while preserving some-
thing of its colonial English background. Pink, peach, and a beach
theme predominate in the rooms and restaurant, which have ceiling fans.
✉ *3 Europa Rd.* ☎ *9567/73000* 🖷 *9567/73513* ⊕ *www.blandgroup.
gi* ↩ *112 rooms, 8 suites* ↻ *Restaurant, pool, bar* 🖃 *AE, DC, MC, V.*

$$$ 🏨 **Bristol.** This colonial-style hotel is in the heart of town, just off Gibral-
tar's main street. Rooms are large and comfortable, and the tropical gar-
den is a haven if you're craving some isolation. ✉ *10 Cathedral Sq.* ☎ *9567/
76800* 🖷 *9567/77613* ↩ *60 rooms* ↻ *Pool* 🖃 *AE, DC, MC, V.*

Costa del Sol & Gibraltar Essentials

AIR TRAVEL
Daily flights on Iberia and Aviaco connect Málaga with Madrid and
Barcelona. Air Europa and Spanair also schedule wallet-friendly flights.
Iberia, British Airways, and numerous charter airlines offer frequent ser-
vice from London; most other major European cities also have direct
air links. You'll have to connect in Madrid if you're flying from the United
States. Flights leave London for Gibraltar daily; as yet there are no flights
from Spanish airports.

AIRPORTS & TRANSFERS
Málaga Airport is 12 km (7 mi) west of the city.
🛈 **Málaga Airport** ☎ 95/204-8804.

TRANSFERS   City buses run from the Málaga Airport to the city every 30 minutes,
6:30 AM–midnight, and cost €1. Portillo bus company has frequent service from the airport to Torremolinos. A suburban train serving Málaga,
Torremolinos, and Fuengirola also stops at the airport every half hour,
though the station is a long walk from the terminal.
🛈 **Portillo** ☎ 95/236-0191.

BUS TRAVEL
Buses are the best means of transportation along the Costa del Sol (as
well as from Seville or Granada). Málaga's long-distance station is on

the Paseo de los Tilos; nearby, on Muelle de Heredía, a smaller station serves suburban destinations. The main bus company serving the Costa del Sol is Portillo. Alsina-Gräells goes to Granada, Córdoba, Seville, and Nerja.

Alsina-Gräells ☎ 95/231-8295 at the station. **Málaga main bus station** ☎ 95/235-0061. **Portillo** ☎ 95/236-0191.

TOURS

There are plenty of bus tours from Spanish cities. Pullmantur and many smaller agencies run daily tours to Gibraltar (except Sunday) from most Costa del Sol resorts. Portillo runs an inexpensive daily tour to Gibraltar from the Torremolinos bus station, and you can always take the regular Portillo bus to La Línea and walk across the border.

Numerous companies, including Pullmantur, lead one- and two-day excursions from all Costa del Sol resorts to such places as Seville, Granada, Córdoba, Ronda, Gibraltar, and Tangier. Your hotel desk or any travel agent can arrange a reservation.

TRAIN TRAVEL

From Madrid, Málaga is served by half a dozen rapid trains daily. The train station in Málaga is a 15-minute walk from the city center, across the river. Call RENFE for general information.

Málaga train station ✉ Explanada de la Estación ☎ 95/236-0202. **RENFE** ☎ 902/240202.

VISITOR INFORMATION

The most helpful tourist offices (by far) are in Málaga and Marbella. The Málaga office covers the entire province.

Estepona ✉ Paseo Marítimo Pedro Manrique ☎ 95/280-0913. **Fuengirola** ✉ Avda. Jesús Santos Rein 6 ☎ 95/246-7457. **Gibraltar** ✉ Cathedral Sq. ☎ 9567/74950. **Málaga** ✉ Pasaje de Chinitas 4 ☎ 95/221-3445 ✉ Avda. Cervantes 1, Paseo del Parque ☎ 95/260-4410. **Marbella** ✉ Glorieta de la Fontanilla ☎ 95/282-2818. **Nerja** ✉ Puerta del Mar 2 ☎ 95/252-1531. **Ronda** ✉ Plaza de España 1 ☎ 95/287-1272. **Torremolinos** ✉ Ayuntamiento, Plaza Blas Infante ☎ 95/237-9511.

SWEDEN

STOCKHOLM, UPPSALA & THE FOLKLORE DISTRICT, THE WEST COAST & THE GLASS COUNTRY

28

THE NATURAL BEAUTY OF SWEDEN, with its glaciated mountains, vast forest tracts, thousands of lakes and rivers, and unspoiled archipelagoes, stands in stark contrast to the cosmopolitan lifestyle of Swedish towns and cities.

Sweden is Europe's fourth-largest country, encompassing an area of 449,964 square km (173,731 square mi). Watch its geography change dramatically as you travel from the barren Arctic north to the fertile plains of the south, a distance measuring nearly 1,600 km (1,000 mi). Despite its large size, Sweden has a population of only 8.9 million. The railway line that runs 2,128 km (1,322 mi) from Trelleborg, in the far south, to Riksgränsen, in the north, is the world's longest stretch of continuously electrified track. Traveling it takes more than 35 hours.

Sweden is a land of contrasts. It has short, warm summers and long, dark, cold winters. Ancient Viking rune stones and 19th-century landmarks coexist with modern skyscrapers. Socialism exists side by side with royalism. Shop windows, full of the latest in consumer goods, attract shoppers who are as at home in the city as they are in the countryside. Swedes seem to like this diversity, big-city living contrasting with the silence of the countryside. Sweden is also a clean country; it is possible to fish for salmon and trout right in the center of Stockholm, just a stone's throw away from the Royal Palace. In downtown Malmö, startlingly large hares hop around in the parks.

Once the dominant power of the Nordic region, Sweden has always been politically independent. During the cold war, it was largely successful in retaining its position as a neutral trading partner of both superpowers. The economic recession of the late 1980s forced Sweden to rethink its comprehensive welfare system, and changes were made down to its very foundations. When the country developed one of Europe's largest budget deficits, the fragile conservative coalition that had defeated the long-incumbent Social Democrats in 1991 attempted further cutbacks. The Social Democrats' power was restored in 1994, but cutbacks have continued at an ever-increasing pace. Sweden joined the European Union (EU) in January 1995, following a closely won referendum, but it did not adopt the euro as its national currency. Although the domestic benefits of membership have been slow in showing themselves, Sweden has quickly become an influential member of this often divided organization.

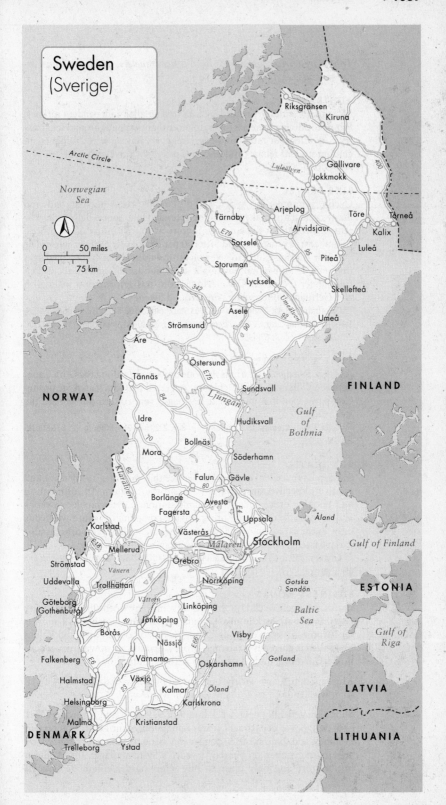

SWEDEN A TO Z

To research prices, get advice from other travelers, and book travel arrangements, visit www.fodors.com.

AIR TRAVEL

Most major cities are served by SAS and smaller, independent airlines. From Stockholm, there are flights to more than 30 points around the country. SAS offers cut-rate round-trip fares every day on selected flights, including student rebates and discount prices for travelers under 26.

🛪 **SAS** ☎ 0770/727727.

BIKE TRAVEL

Cycling is popular in Sweden, and the country's uncongested roads and many cycle paths make it ideal for extended bike tours. Bicycles can be rented throughout the country; inquire at tourist information offices. Rental costs average around SKr 100 per day or SKr 500 per week. The Swedish Touring Club can give you information about cycling packages that include bike rental, overnight accommodation, and meals. Cykelfrämjandet (National Cycle Association) has information in English and German about cycling trips around Sweden.

🚲 **Cykelfrämjandet** ✉ Tulegatan 43, 113 53 Stockholm ☎ 08/54591030 🖨 08/54591039. **Swedish Touring Club** ✉ Amiralitetsbachan 1, Box 25, 101 20 Stockholm ☎ 08/4632200 or 020/292929 🖨 08/6781958.

BOAT & FERRY TRAVEL

A classic Swedish boat trip is the four-day journey along the Göta Canal between Göteborg and Stockholm, operated by Göta Canal Steamship Company. Children must be at least eight years old to ride aboard the steamship.

🚢 **Göta Canal Steamship Company** ✒ Box 272, 401 24 Göteborg ☎ 031/806315 🖨 031/158311.

BUS TRAVEL

Sweden has excellent express bus service that provides inexpensive and relatively speedy transportation around the country. An information and booking office is at Stockholm's station, Cityterminalen. Swebus and Wasatrafik run daily; other private companies operate weekends only. In the far north, postal buses delivering mail to remote areas also carry passengers, providing an offbeat, inexpensive journey.

🚌 **Cityterminalen** ✉ Klarabergsviadukten 72 ☎ 0200/218218 wait on the line for English service.

BUSINESS HOURS

BANKS & OFFICES Banks are open weekdays 9:30 to 3; some stay open until 5 in larger cities. Banks at Stockholm's Arlanda Airport and Göteborg's Landvetter Airport are open every day, with extended hours. Forex and Valuta Specialisten currency-exchange offices operate in downtown Stockholm, Göteborg, and Malmö, also with extended hours.

MUSEUMS & Museum hours vary widely, but most are open weekdays 10 to 4 or 10 SIGHTS to 5, weekends 11 to 4; many close on Monday.

SHOPS Shops are generally open weekdays 9 or 9:30 to 6 and Saturday 9 to 1 or 9 to 4. Some department stores remain open until 8 or 9 on certain evenings, and some are also open Sunday noon to 4 in major cities. Many supermarkets open on Sunday. Sweden's Systembolaget, the state-run liquor store and only place to buy wine, hard alcohol, or class III (medium-strength) beer, is open weekdays 10 to 6 and Saturday 10 to 2. Expect a long line on Friday evenings.

CAR TRAVEL

EMERGENCIES The Larmtjänst organization, run by a confederation of Swedish insurance companies, provides 24-hour breakdown service.

🖪 **Larmtjänst** ☎ 08/7837000 Stockholm headquarters.

GASOLINE Sweden has some of the highest gasoline prices in Europe, SKr 9–SKr 10 per liter. Gas stations are self-service: pumps marked SEDEL are automated and accept SKr 20 and SKr 100 bills; pumps marked KONTO are also automated and accept credit cards; gas purchased at pumps marked KASSA is paid for at the cash desk.

PARKING Park on the right-hand side of the road if you want to park overnight. Be sure not to do so the night the street is being cleaned; circular signs with a red border indicate when this occurs. Timed ticket machines and, sometimes, meters operate in larger towns, usually between 8 AM and 6 PM. The fee varies from about SKr 5 to SKr 40 per hour; parking is free on weekends. Parking garages in urban areas are mostly automated, often with machines that accept credit cards; LEDIGT on a garage sign means space is available. On the street, a circular sign with a red border and a red diagonal on a blue background means parking is prohibited; a yellow rectangle with a red border means restricted parking. Beware: fines for parking violations are very high in Sweden. City "Trafikkarta" maps, available at many gas stations, include English explanations of parking signs and systems.

ROAD CONDITIONS Sweden has an excellent network of more than 80,000 km (50,000 mi) of highways. The fastest routes are those with numbers prefixed with an *E* (for "European"). All main and secondary roads are well surfaced, but some minor roads, particularly in the north, are gravel.

RULES OF THE ROAD Drive on the right. No matter where you sit in a car, you must wear a seat belt. You must also have at least low-beam headlights on at all times (in a Swedish car these will always come on automatically when you start the motor). Signs indicate five basic speed limits, ranging from 30 kph (19 mph) near school or playground areas to 110 kph (68 mph) on long stretches of *E* roads.

CUSTOMS & DUTIES

For details on imports and duty-free limits, *see* Customs & Duties *in* Smart Travel Tips.

EATING & DRINKING

Traditional Swedish restaurants are giving way to myriad international culinary influences. Fast-food outlets abound, but you will find places to suit even the most fickle palates and every budget, from top-class establishments to less expensive places for lunch or a snack.

Restaurants all over the country specialize in *husmanskost* (home cooking), based on traditional Swedish recipes. Sweden is world famous for its *smörgåsbord,* a word now internationally used as a synonym for diversity. This tempting buffet of hot and cold dishes has an emphasis on seafood, especially herring. You can usually find an authentic smörgåsbord, and eat as much as you wish, for SKr 200–SKr 300. Hotels sometimes serve a smörgåsbord-style breakfast, often included in the room price.

Service charges and *moms* (value-added tax) are included in the check, but it is common to tip 5%–10%.

WHAT IT COSTS In Swedish Kronor			
$$$$	**$$$**	**$$**	**$**
AT DINNER	over 350	250–350	120–250	under 120

Prices are per person for a main course.

MEALTIMES   Swedes eat early. Lunch is served from 11 AM, and outside the main cities restaurants often close at 9 PM or don't even open for dinner.

RESERVATIONS &
DRESS   Except in the most formal restaurants, where a jacket and a tie are preferable, casual—or casual chic—attire is perfectly acceptable.

EMBASSIES
🇫 Australia ✉ Sergelstorg 12, Stockholm ☎ 08/6132900.
🇫 Canada ✉ Tegelbacken 4, Stockholm ☎ 08/4533000.
🇫 Ireland ✉ Östermalmsg. 97, Stockholm ☎ 08/6618005.
🇫 United Kingdom ✉ Skarpög. 6–8, Stockholm ☎ 08/6713000.
🇫 United States ✉ Strandv. 101, Stockholm ☎ 08/7835300.

HOLIDAYS
January 1; January 6 (Epiphany); Good Friday; Easter Monday; May 1 (Labor Day); Ascension (in May); June 21 (Midsummer Evening); June 22 (Midsummer Day); All Saints' Day (first Saturday in November); December 24–26.

LANGUAGE
Swedish is closely related to Danish and Norwegian. After "z," the Swedish alphabet has three extra letters, "å," "ä," and "ö." Note that the letter *w* is pronounced like a *v* and both letters are listed under *v* in telephone directories and other alphabetical listings. Most Swedes speak English.

LODGING
Sweden offers a variety of accommodations from simple bed-and-breakfasts, campsites, and hostels to hotels of the highest international standard. Major hotels in larger cities cater mainly to business clientele and can be expensive; weekend rates are more reasonable. Prices are usually on a per-room basis and include all taxes, service charges, and breakfast. Apart from the more modest inns and the cheapest budget establishments, private baths and showers are standard. Whatever their size, Swedish hotels provide scrupulously clean accommodation and courteous service. Sweden virtually shuts down during the entire month of July, so make your hotel reservations in advance, especially if you're staying outside the city areas during July and early August.

WHAT IT COSTS In Swedish Kronor			
$$$$	**$$$**	**$$**	**$**
HOTELS	over 2,700	1,800–2,700	1,000–1,800	under 1,000

Prices are for two people in a standard double room in high season.

CAMPING   Camping is popular in Sweden. About 750 officially approved sites dot the country, most next to the sea or a lake and offering such activities as windsurfing, horseback riding, and tennis. They are generally open June to September, although some stay open year-round. A free, abbreviated list of sites is published in English by the Sveriges Campingvårdernas Riksförbund (Swedish Campsite Owners' Association).
🇫 **Sveriges Campingvårdernas Riksförbund** 🖉 Box 255, 451 17 Uddevalla ☎ 0522/642440 🖨 0522/642430.

CHALET RENTALS Accommodations can often be arranged on the spot at tourist offices for 250 chalet villages, all with high standards. Scandinavian Seaways in Göteborg arranges package deals that combine a ferry trip from Britain across the North Sea and a stay in a chalet village.

🏠 **Scandinavian Seaways** ☎ 031/650600.

HOTELS You can contact major hotel groups through their central reservations services: Best Western hotels can be found throughout the country. Radisson SAS has high-quality hotels, often in city centers. Scandic is one of Sweden's largest hotel chains. Sweden Hotels has about 100 independently owned hotels and its own classification scheme—A, B, or C—based on facilities.

You'll find comprehensive information about hotel facilities and prices in the official annual guide *Hotels in Sweden*, published by and available free from the Swedish Travel and Tourism Council. Countryside Hotels, 40 select resort hotels, may be restored manor houses or centuries-old inns. Hotellcentralen is an independent agency that makes advance telephone reservations for hotels in Stockholm.

🏠 **Best Western** ☎ 08/56629370 or 020/792752. **Countryside Hotels** ⌂ Box 69, 830 13 Åre ☎ 0647/50680 🖷 0647/51920. **Hotellcentralen** ✉ Central Station, 111 20 ☎ 08/7892456 🖷 08/7918666. **Radisson SAS** ☎ 020/797592. **Scandic** ☎ 08/51751700. **Sweden Hotels** ☎ 08/7017900.

MAIL & SHIPPING

If you're uncertain where you will be staying, have your mail addressed to *poste restante* and sent to S-101 10 Stockholm. Collection is at Post Office Stockholm 1. American Express offers a poste-restante service free to cardholders and for a small fee to others.

🏠 **Post Office Stockholm 1** ✉ Drottningg. 53 ☎ 08/7814682.

POSTAL RATES Airmail letters and postcards to the United States, Canada, and Europe weighing less than 20 grams cost SKr 10.

MONEY MATTERS

Sweden is looked upon as an expensive country, although prices are generally in line with the European average. Restaurant prices can be high, but bargains exist: in cities look for the lunch *dagens rätt* (dish of the day) for about SKr 60–SKr 70. Also, check for a recommended two- or three-course menu. Hotels are at their priciest fall through spring; many have special low summer and weekend winter rates. Heavy taxes and excise duties make liquor prices among the highest in Europe.

Some sample prices: cup of coffee, SKr 15–SKr 25; beer, SKr 39–SKr 60 soda, SKr 20–SKr 30; ham sandwich, SKr 25–SKr 50; 2-km (1-mi) taxi ride, SKr 60–SKr 80 (depending on the taxi company, day, and time).

CURRENCY The unit of currency in Sweden is the krona (plural kronor), which is divided into 100 öre and is written as SKr, SEK, or kr. Coins come in values of 50 öre and 1, 5, or 10 kronor; bills come in denominations of 20, 100, 500, and 1,000 kronor. Traveler's checks and foreign currency can be exchanged at banks all over Sweden and at post offices displaying the NB EXCHANGE sign. At press time (summer 2003), the exchange rate was SKr 8.01 to the U.S. dollar, SKr 5.65 to the Canadian dollar, SKr 13.41 to the pound sterling, SKr 9.10 to the euro, SKr 5.08 to the Australian dollar, SKr 4.75 to the New Zealand dollar, and SKr 1.05 to the South African rand.

SHOPPING

Swedish goods are internationally renowned for their style and quality, especially clothing, furniture, and interior design items, such as plastic kitchen tools, glassware, stainless steel, pottery, and ceramics. Textiles are also of exceptional quality. You will find a wide selection of top-quality goods, including Swedish-designed clothing, at such major stores as NK, PUB, and Åhléns City in Stockholm. Other clothing stores nationwide are H&M, jc, Vero Moda, and MQ.

For glassware at bargain prices, head for the Glass Country. The major glassworks have large factory outlets where you can pick up seconds at prices well below normal retail. For textiles, the best centers are Borås and Ullered, not far from Göteborg. In rural areas, head to the local Hemslöjd crafts centers for high-quality clothing, woodwork, and needlework.

TAXES

VALUE-ADDED TAX (V.A.T.)
Many Swedish shops participate in the tax-free shopping program, enabling visitors to claim a refund of most of the *moms* (value-added tax) paid, a rate of about 25%. Participating shops display a distinctive black, blue, and yellow sticker in the window. (Some stores offer the service only on purchases amounting to more than SKr 200.) The cashier will wrap and seal your purchase and give you a Tax-Free Shopping Check equivalent to the tax paid minus a handling charge. This check can be cashed when you leave Sweden and show your unopened packages, either at the airport or aboard ferries. If you're packing your purchases in a suitcase, you can show them at the Tax-Free Counter at Arlanda Airport's check-in lobby and get your refund before you check your luggage. You need your passport when making your purchase and claiming your refund.

TELEPHONES

COUNTRY & AREA CODES
The country code for Sweden is 46. When dialing Sweden from outside the country, drop the first zero in the regional telephone code.

DIRECTORY & OPERATOR ASSISTANCE
For international calls, the operator assistance number is ☎ 0018; directory assistance, which costs SKr 16 per minute, is ☎ 118119. Within Sweden, dial ☎ 90200 for operator assistance and ☎ 118118 for directory assistance (this service costs SKr 11 per minute).

INTERNATIONAL CALLS
These can be made from any pay phone. For calls to the United States and Canada, dial 00, then 1 (the country code), then wait for a second dial tone before dialing the area code and number. When dialing the United Kingdom, omit the initial zero on area codes. You can make international calls from Telebutik offices. AT&T, MCI, and Sprint all offer long-distance service from Sweden.
🔊 Access Codes **AT&T** ☎ 020/795611. **MCI** ☎ 020/795922. **Sprint** ☎ 020/799011.

LOCAL CALLS
Telephone numbers beginning with 020 are toll-free within Sweden. Telephone numbers beginning with 0771 are charged at local rate.

PUBLIC PHONES
Sweden has plenty of pay phones; to use them you'll need SKr 1, SKr 5, or SKr 10 coins, as a local call costs SKr 2. You can also purchase a *telefonkort* (telephone card) from a Telebutik, hospital, or *Pressbyrån* store for SKr 35, SKr 60, or SKr 100. The card can provide a savings if you make numerous domestic calls and is indispensable when you're faced with one of the many public phones that accept only cards.

TIPPING

Tipping in Sweden has become more common. At hotels it is customary to tip the porter about SKr 5 per item. For taxi rides, SKr 5–SKr 10 is usual. When dining out, you are often made to check your coat, regardless of whether you wish to do so; the tip (or cost) for this is usually SKr 10.

TRAIN TRAVEL

Frequent trains link Stockholm with Göteborg and Malmö. First- and second-class cars are available on all main routes, and sleeping cars are available in both classes on overnight trains. Most long-distance trains have a buffet car and a playground car for kids. Seat reservations are advisable, and on some trains—indicated with *R, IN,* or *IC* on the timetable—mandatory. Reservations can be made right up to departure. *Couchette* reservations on the regular train cost SKr 95 and beds from SKr 180. The Swedish rail network also operates high-speed X2000 trains from Stockholm to Göteborg, Falun, Malmö, Jönköping, and Sundsvall, and from Göteborg to Malmö.

CUTTING COSTS   There is a 50% discount on *röda platser* ("red," or off-peak, seats) booked at least seven days in advance. ScanRail passes allow unlimited train travel throughout Sweden, as well as to Denmark, Finland, and Norway. Limited ferry passage in and beyond Scandinavia is also included. The pass is available for 21 days, or 5 days of travel within 15 days.
Reservations ☎ 0771/757575.

TRANSPORTATION AROUND SWEDEN

The basic street-sign terms you'll come across are *gatan* (street, abbreviated to *g.*), *vägen* (road, abbreviated to *v.*), and *gränd* (lane, shortened to *gr.*).

VISITOR INFORMATION

Swedish Travel and Tourism Council ✉ Kungsg. 36, Box 3030, 103 61 Stockholm ☎ 08/7255500 🖷 08/7255531 🌐 www.visit-sweden.com.

WHEN TO GO

The tourist season runs from mid-May through mid-September; many attractions, however, close in late August, when the schools reopen at the end of the Swedish vacation season. July is the Swedish vacation month, and some local restaurants and privately run shops close for the duration. The weather can be glorious in the spring and fall, when fewer visitors are around.

CLIMATE   Sweden has typically unpredictable northern European summer weather, but as a general rule it is likely to be warm but not hot from May until September. In Stockholm, the weeks just before and after midsummer have almost 24-hour light, and in the far north, above the Arctic Circle, the sun doesn't set between the end of May and the middle of July.

The following are the average daily maximum and minimum temperatures for Stockholm.

Jan.	30F	−1C	May	58F	14C	Sept.	60F	15C
	23	−5		43	6		49	9
Feb.	30F	−1C	June	67F	19C	Oct.	49F	9C
	22	−5		51	11		41	5
Mar.	37F	3C	July	71F	22C	Nov.	40F	5C
	26	−4		57	14		34	1
Apr.	47F	8C	Aug.	68F	20C	Dec.	35F	3C
	34	1		55	13		28	−2

STOCKHOLM

Stockholm stands on 14 islands surrounded by water so clean that you can fish and swim in the heart of the city. This cultivated, civilized city has many parks, squares, and wide streets, providing welcome calm in what has become a bustling metropolis. Modern glass-and-steel buildings abound in the city center, but you are seldom more than a five-minute walk from twisting, medieval streets and water views.

The first written mention of Stockholm dates from 1252, when a powerful regent named Birger Jarl built a fortified castle here. The strategic position, where the fresh waters of Lake Mälaren meet the brackish Baltic Sea, prompted King Gustav Vasa to take over the city in 1523, and King Gustavus Adolphus to make it the heart of an empire a century later.

During the Thirty Years' War (1618–48), Sweden became an important Baltic trading state, and the city gained a reputation as a commercial center. By the beginning of the 18th century, however, Swedish influence had begun to wane, and Stockholm's development slowed. It did not pick up again until the Industrial Revolution, when the hub of the city moved north from the Gamla Stan (Old Town) area.

Exploring Stockholm

Numbers in the margin correspond to points of interest on the Stockholm map.

Stockholm's main attractions are concentrated in a relatively small area, and the city itself can be explored in just a few days. If you have only limited time in Stockholm, give priority to a tour of Stockholm's Gamla Stan (Old Town), a labyrinth of narrow medieval streets, alleyways, and quiet squares on the island just south of the city center. Be sure to visit the large island of Djurgården. Although it's only a short walk from the city center, the most pleasant way to approach it is by ferry from Skeppsbron, in Gamla Stan.

13 **Gröna Lund Tivoli.** Stockholm's only amusement park is an annual favorite, drawing huge crowds every year. Traditional attractions and sideshows rub shoulders with 21st-century, pulse-racing rides, guaranteed to leave your knuckles white. ⊠ *Djurgårdsv.* ☎ *08/58750100* ⊕ *www.tivoli.se* ☉ *May–Sept., daily. Hrs vary; call ahead.*

9 **Historiska Museet** (Historical Museum). The museum houses some remarkable gold and silver treasures dating from the Swedish Viking era. ⊠ *Narvav. 13–17* ☎ *08/51955600* ⊕ *www.historiska.se* ☉ *Tues.–Sun. 11–5.*

10 **Junibacken.** This fairy-tale house lets you travel in small carriages through Fodor'sChoice the world of children's book writer Astrid Lindgren, creator of the irrepressible character Pippi Longstocking. ⊠ *Galärvarsv.* ☎ *08/58723000* ⊕ *www.junibacken.se* ☉ *June–Aug., daily 9–6; Sept.–May, Wed.–Sun. 10–5.*

3 **Kungliga Slottet** (Royal Palace). Visit at noon and watch the time-honored yet now purely ceremonial changing of the smartly dressed guards. Fodor'sChoice You can wander at will into the palace courtyard and the building itself. The **Livrustkammaren** (Royal Armory) has an outstanding collection of weaponry and royal regalia. The **Skattkammaren** (Treasury) houses the Swedish crown jewels, including the regalia used for the coronation of King Erik XIV in 1561. You can also visit the **Representationsvåningen** (State Apartments), where the king swears in each successive government. ⊠ *Gamla Stan* ☎ *08/4026130* ⊕ *www.royalcourt. se* ☉ *Sept.–May 14, daily 10–4; May 15–Aug., Tues.–Sun. noon–3* ☞ *Prices and hrs subject to change; call ahead.*

6 **Kungsträdgården** (King's Garden). Originally built as a royal kitchen garden, Kungsträdgården was turned into a public park in 1562. In summer you can watch people playing open-air chess with giant chess pieces.

In winter the park has a skating rink. ⊠ *Between Hamng. and the Royal Opera in the city center.*

8 **Moderna Museet** (Museum of Modern Art). Housed in an ultramodern building designed by Rafael Moneo, the museum displays works by Picasso, Kandinsky, Dalí, Brancuşi, and other international artists. You can also view paintings and sculptures created by prominent Swedish artists. ⊠ *Skeppsholmen* ☏ *08/51955200* ⊕ *www.modernamuseet.se* ⊗ *Tues.–Thurs. 11–10, Fri.–Sun. 11–6.*

7 **National Museum.** The works of important old masters, including Rembrandt, Goya, Degas, and those of many Swedish artists line the walls here. There is a wide selection of prints and drawings, as well as a permanent design exhibition. ⊠ *Södra Blasieholmshamnen* ☏ *08/51954300* ⊕ *www.nationalmuseum.se* ⊗ *Jan.–Aug., Tues. 11–8 and Wed.–Sun. 11–5; Sept.–Dec., Wed. and Fri.–Sun. 11–5, Thurs. 11–8.*

☾ 11 **Nordiska Museet** (Nordic Museum). The museum shows how Swedes have lived during the past 500 years. On permanent display are peasant costumes, folk art, and items from the Sami (Lapp) culture. On the ground floor, there's a delightful "village life" play area. ⊠ *Djurgårdsv. 6–16* ☏ *08/5195600* ⊕ *www.nordm.se* ⊗ *Tues. and Thurs. 10–8, Wed. and Fri.–Sun. 10–5.*

2 **Riddarholms Kyrkan** (Riddarholm Church). A legion of Swedish kings is buried in this magnificent sanctuary, a Grey Friars monastery dating from 1270. ⊠ *Riddarholmen, Gamla Stan* ☏ *08/4026130* ⊗ *May–Aug., daily 10–4; Sept., weekends noon–3.*

★ ☾ 14 **Skansen.** More than 150 reconstructed traditional buildings from all over Sweden, handicraft displays, and demonstrations form this large, open-air folk museum. There is a zoo, with native Scandinavian lynx, wolves, bears, and elk, as well as an aquarium and an old-style *tivoli* (amusement park). Snack kiosks and a pleasant restaurant make it easy to spend a whole day. ⊠ *Djurgårdsslätten 49–51* ☏ *08/4428000* ⊕ *www.skansen.se* ⊗ *Oct.–Apr., daily 10–4; May, daily 10–8; June–Aug., daily 10–10; Sept., daily 10–5* ☞ *Prices and hrs subject to change; call ahead.*

1 **Stadshuset** (City Hall). Architect Ragnar Östberg's ornate 1923 facade is a Stockholm landmark. Lavish mosaics adorn the walls of the **Gyllene Salen** (Golden Hall), and the **Prinsens Galleri** (Prince's Gallery) holds a collection of large murals by Prince Eugen (1865–1947), brother of King Gustav V. Take the elevator halfway up, and then climb the rest of the way to the top of the 348-foot tower for a magnificent view of the city. ⊠ *Hantverkarg. 1* ☏ *08/50829058* ⊗ *Guided tours only. Tours in English, June–Aug., daily 10, 11, noon, and 2; Sept., daily 10, noon, and 2; Oct.–May, daily 10 and noon.*

FodorsChoice ★

4 **Storkyrkan** (Cathedral). In this 15th-century Gothic cathedral is the *Parhelion,* a painting of Stockholm dating from 1520, the oldest in existence. ⊠ *Trångsund 1* ☏ *08/7233016* ⊗ *Sept.–Apr., daily 9–4; May–Aug., daily 9–6.*

5 **Stortorget.** In 1520 Danish king Christian II ordered a massacre in this square. The event triggered a revolt and the founding of the sovereign state of Sweden. ⊠ *Just southwest of Kungliga Slottet.*

12 **Vasamuseet** (Vasa Museum). The 17th-century warship *Vasa* sank ignominiously in Stockholm Harbor on its maiden voyage in 1628 because it was not carrying sufficient ballast. Forgotten for centuries, the largely intact vessel was recovered from the sea in 1961 and now stands sentinel over the harbor in this striking museum; film presentations and ex-

FodorsChoice ★

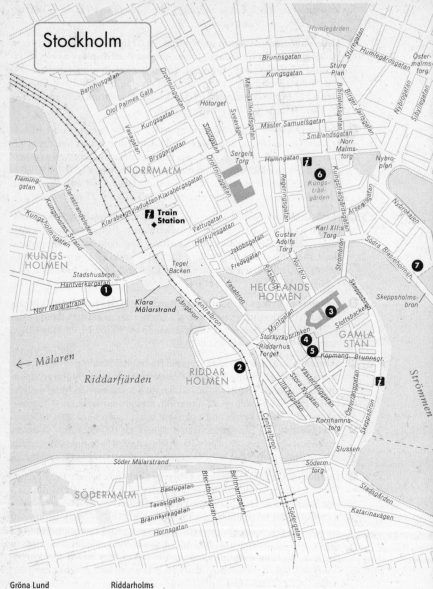

Stockholm

NORRMALM

Humlegården

Brunnsgatan

Kungsgatan

Sture
Plan

Österns-
malms-
torg

Humlegårdsgatan

Barnhusgatan

Olof Palmes Gata

Hötorget

Sveavägen

Malmskillnadsgatan

Master Samuelsgatan

Smålandsgatan

Droffninggatan

Kungsgatan

Storgatan

Norr
Malms-
torg

Nybro-
plan

Vasagatan

Bryggargatan

Sergels
Torg

Hamngatan

Regeringsgatan

f

6
Kungs-
trädgården

Fleming-
gatan

Klarabergsviadukten Klarabergsgatan

Droffninggatan

Vattugatan

Karl XII:s
Torg

Kungsholms Strand

Klarastrandsleden

f **Train
Station**

Herkulesgatan

Jakobsgatan

Gustav
Adolfs
Torg

Fredsgatan

Vasabron

Strömbron

Södra Blasieholmsh.

Nybrokajen

7

Kungsholmsgatan

KUNGS-
HOLMEN

Tegel
Backen

HELGEANDS
HOLMEN

Skeppsbron

Skeppsholms-
bron

Stadshusbron

Hantverkargatan

1

Klara
Mälarstrand

Gångbron

Centralbron

Myntgatan

Storkyrkobrinken

3

Slottsbacken

GAMLA
STAN

Norr Mälarstrand

Riddarhus
Torget

4
5

Köpmang. Brunnsgr.

f

← Mälaren

RIDDAR
HOLMEN

2

Västerlånggatan

Stora Nygatan

Lilla Nygatan

Österlånggatan

Skeppsbron

Strömmen

Riddarfjärden

Kornhamns-
torg

Slussen

Centralbron

Söder Mälarstrand

Söderm.
torg

Stadsgården

SÖDERMALM

Bastugatan

Blecktornsgränd

Bellmansgatan

Tavastgatan

Brännkyrkagatan

Hornsgatan

Katarinavägen

Södergatan

hibits are also on-site. ✉ *Galärvarvet* ☎ *08/51954800* ⊕ *www. vasamuseet.se* ☉ *Thurs.–Tues. 10–5, Wed. 10–8. English tours available year-round, throughout the day.*

🔟 **Waldemarsudde.** Once the summer residence of Prince Eugen, this museum has a significant collection of Nordic paintings dating from 1880 to 1940, as well as the prince's own works. ✉ *Prins Eugensv. 6* ☎ *08/ 54583700* ⊕ *www.waldemarsudde.com* ☉ *May–Aug., Tues., Wed., and Fri.–Sun. 11–5, Thurs. 11–8; Sept.–Apr., Tues., Wed., and Fri. 11–4, Thurs. 11–8, weekends 11–5.*

Elsewhere in Stockholm

Bergianska Botaniska Trädgården (Bergianska Botanical Garden). North of the city center, this garden and greenhouse has plants from all over the world. The **Victoria House** has the world's largest display of water lilies. ✉ *Frescati* ☎ *08/162853* ⊕ *www.bergianksa.se* ☉ *Greenhouse: daily 11–5. Herbal Garden: May–Sept., daily 8–5; Oct.–Apr., weekends 11–4. Victoria House: May–Sept., daily 11–5. Park: daily.*

🔟 **Kaknästornet** (Kaknäs TV Tower). Just shy of 511 feet, the tower on Gärdet is the tallest structure in Scandinavia. From its top you have a magnificent view of the city and the surrounding archipelago. Facilities include a cafeteria, restaurant, and gift shop. ✉ *Mörkakroken off Djurgårdsbrunsv, Bus 69 from Sergels Torg* ☎ *08/7892435* ☉ *June–Aug., daily 9 AM–10 PM; Sept.–May, daily 10–9.*

Where to Eat

Stockholm has one of the highest densities of restaurants per capita in Europe. If you're looking for value dining, make lunch your big meal.

$$$$ ✕ **Edsbacka Krog.** Fifteen kilometers (10 mi) north of Stockholm, in a storybook inn that dates from the 1600s, this restaurant is one of the country's finest. Expect Swedish cuisine taken to new heights here. Service is impeccable, and the chef is known to send out small complimentary dishes during a meal. ✉ *Sollentunav. 220* ☎ *08/963300* ⚋ *Reservations essential* ▭ *AE, DC, MC, V* ☉ *Closed Sun. No lunch Mon. and Sat.*

$$$–$$$$ ✕ **Den Gyldene Freden.** This restaurant dates from 1722 and was once a favorite haunt of Stockholm's artists and composers. Every Thursday the Swedish Academy, the group of writers, artists, and scholars that chooses the Nobel Prize winners each year, meets for dinner on the second floor. The food is a combination of French and Swedish, with delicious results. ✉ *Österlångg. 51* ☎ *08/249760* ▭ *AE, DC, MC, V* ☉ *Closed Sun. and July. No lunch weekdays.*

$$$–$$$$ ✕ **Wedholms Fisk.** You can get only fresh fish and shellfish at this austerely traditional, high-ceilinged restaurant near Berzelli Park, across from the Royal Dramatic Theater. The tartare of salmon and the grilled sole are noteworthy, and portions are generous. The Scandinavian artwork on display is part of the owner's personal collection. ✉ *Nybrokajen 17* ☎ *08/6117874* ▭ *AE, DC, MC, V* ☉ *Closed Sun. and July.*

$$–$$$$ ✕ **Operakällaren.** One of Stockholm's best-known traditional restaurants is found in the elegant Opera House. With both Scandinavian and Continental cuisine on its menu, it is famed for its smörgåsbord, available from June 1, with seasonal variations, through Christmas. In summer you can dine on the veranda. ✉ *Operahuset, Jakobs Torg 2* ☎ *08/ 6765800* ▭ *AE, DC, MC, V* ☉ *Main dining room closed July.*

★ $$$ ✕ **Bon Lloc.** With a crew of internationally renowned chefs, an elegant and spacious dining area, and a creative Mediterranean-influenced menu, this restaurant has established itself as one of the hottest in town.

The extensive wine list offers an excellent selection of European wines. ⊠ *Regeringsg. 111* ☎ *08/6606060* ♣ *Reservations essential* ▤ *AE, DC, MC, V* ☺ *Closed Sun.*

★ **$$$** ✕ **Fredsgatan 12.** Young chef Melker Andersson works his magic at this stylish restaurant, creating dishes with Swedish, East Asian, and European overtones that defy convention and positively demand enjoyment. The earth-tone dining room is the perfect arena in which Andersson and his team serve what is arguably some of the best food in the capital. ⊠ *Fredsgatan 12* ☎ *08/248052* ♣ *Reservations essential* ▤ *AE, DC, MC, V* ☺ *Closed Sun.*

$$$ ✕ **Gondolen.** Suspended under the gangway of the Katarina elevator at Slussen square, this contemporary restaurant has a magnificent view over the harbor, Mälaren, and the Baltic. The cuisine is international with prix-fixe menus available. ⊠ *Stadsgården 6* ☎ *08/6417090* ▤ *AE, DC, MC, V* ☺ *Closed Sun.*

$$$ ✕ **Stallmästaregården.** This historic inn with an attractive courtyard
Fodor'sChoice and garden sits in Haga Park, just north of Norrtull, about 15 minutes'
★ drive from the city center. In summer fine French and Swedish cuisine is served in the tented courtyard overlooking the beautiful Brunnsviken lake. ⊠ *Norrtull near Haga* Ⓜ *Bus 52 to Stallmästaregården* ☎ *08/ 6101300* ▤ *AE, DC, MC, V* ☺ *Closed Sun.*

$$–$$$ ✕ **Sturehof.** Opened before the turn of the 20th century, Sturehof is one of Sweden's oldest fish restaurants. A pub was added in the 1990s, but the nautical theme of the main restaurant has been carefully preserved. ⊠ *Stureplan 2* ☎ *08/4405730* ▤ *AE, DC, MC, V.*

$–$$ ✕ **Il Conte.** This warm, Italian restaurant close to Strandvägen, Stockholm's most elegant avenue, has delicious Italian food and wine, served by an attentive staff. The restaurant is tastefully decorated. ⊠ *Grevg. 9* ☎ *08/6612628* ♣ *Reservations essential* ▤ *AE, DC, MC, V* ☺ *Call for closing dates.*

$–$$ ✕ **Koh Phangan.** Creative food is served until midnight at this lively Thai restaurant, where you'll be seated in individual "huts," each with a special name and style. Sign up for a table on the chalkboard next to the bar when you arrive. Although you can expect a wait on weekends, it's well worth a visit for the food and the imaginative interior. ⊠ *Skånag. 57* ☎ *08/6425040* 🖷 *08/6426568* ▤ *AE, DC, MC, V.*

$ ✕ **Örtagården.** One floor up from Östermalms Saluhall market is this attractive vegetarian restaurant in an early-20th-century building. An all-you-can-eat buffet of soups, salads, hot dishes, and homemade bread is served, accompanied by a bottomless cup of coffee to wash it all down. ⊠ *Nybrog. 31* ☎ *08/6621728* ▤ *AE, MC, V.*

Where to Stay

Stockholm has plenty of hotels in higher price brackets, but summer rates—some as much as 50% off—can make even very expensive hotels affordable. The major chains also have bargain plans on weekends throughout the year and weekdays in summer.

More than 50 hotels offer the "Stockholm Package," providing one night's lodging for between SKr 398 and SKr 890 per person, including breakfast and a Stockholmskortet, which grants unlimited transportation on city subway, bus, and rail services, and free admission to several museums and sightseeing trips. The package is available June through mid-August, at Christmas and Easter, and Friday through Monday year-round; get details from Hotellcentralen and American Express travel agency. If you arrive in Stockholm without a hotel reservation, Hotellcentralen can arrange accommodation for you.

$$$$ **Berns Hotell.** This cozy yet ultramodern hotel occupies a grand mid-
19th-century building. Rooms are chintz-free and have cherrywood
furniture. The restaurant and bar, which are joint ventures with well-
known British restaurateur Terence Conran, serve creative Swedish cuisine in dramatic spaces that contrast modern Swedish furniture design
with the hotel's original opulent interior. ⊠ *Näckströmsg. 8, 111 47*
☎ *08/56632000* 🖷 *08/56632201* ⊕ *www.berns.se* ⤶ *65 rooms*
⌂ *Restaurant* ⊟ *AE, DC, MC, V.*

Fodor's Choice
★

$$$$ **Grand.** Each year the Grand accommodates Nobel Prize winners. The
waterfront hotel dates from 1874 and stands opposite the Royal Palace
in the center of town, a testament to a period of gilt trim, stuccowork,
and ornate furnishings. Request a room with a view of the water. The
two excellent restaurants—French and Swedish—have harbor views, and
the bar serves light snacks. ⊠ *Blasieholmshamnen 8, 103 27* ☎ *08/
6793500* 🖷 *08/6118686* ⊕ *www.grandhotel.se* ⤶ *307 rooms, 20
suites* ⌂ *2 restaurants* ⊟ *AE, DC, MC, V.*

$$$–$$$$ **Hotel Birger Jarl.** Just outside the city center, this contemporary hotel
has colorful rooms created by some of Sweden's top designers. The beds
have duvets and down pillows. Special business rooms with ISDN con-
nections and lots of outlets are designed for the convenience of the work-
ing traveler. ⊠ *Tuleg. 8, 104 32* ☎ *08/6741800* 🖷 *08/6737366* ⊕ *www.
birgerjarl.se* ⤶ *225 rooms* ⊟ *AE, DC, MC, V.*

$$$–$$$$ **Nordic Hotel.** This is actually two hotels—Nordic Light and Nordic
Sea—in one, on opposite sides of the street. Nordic Light focuses on sim-
plicity. Rooms are a mix of dark wood, gray flannel, and black-and-white
tile. Nordic Sea uses lighter wood and has a Mediterranean theme, with
lots of blue fabric and mosaic tiles. The lobby has Stockholm's only "ice
bar," where you can sip vodka from ice glasses, standing at ice tables
in temperatures of -5 degrees Celsius. ⊠ *Vasaplan, 101 37* ☎ *08/
50563000* 🖷 *08/50563060* ⊕ *www.nordichotels.se* ⤶ *542 rooms* ⌂ *2
bars* ⊟ *AE, DC, MC, V.*

$$$–$$$$ **Radisson SAS Strand.** The stylish rooms signify the grace of this 1912
hotel. No two rooms are alike, but all have antiques, colorful furnish-
ings, and lots of natural light. The restaurant serves Italian food and a
superb wine list. ⊠ *Nybrokajen 9, 103 27* ☎ *08/50664000* 🖷 *08/
50664001* ⊕ *www.radissonsas.com* ⤶ *148 rooms* ⌂ *Restaurant* ⊟ *AE,
DC, MC, V.*

$$$–$$$$ **Scandic Hotel Sergel Plaza.** In Stockholm's financial district, Sergel Plaza
has comfortable rooms, a piano bar just behind the bright, spacious lobby,
an executive floor, a casino, and a body care center. The restaurant serves
international haute cuisine. ⊠ *Brunkebergstorg 9, 103 27* ☎ *08/
51726300* 🖷 *08/5172631* ⊕ *www.scandic-hotels.com* ⤶ *405 rooms,
11 suites* ⌂ *Restaurant, bar* ⊟ *AE, DC, MC, V.*

$$$ **Amaranten.** Not far from the central train station, Amaranten is a large,
modern hotel. Rooms with air-conditioning and soundproofing are
available at a higher rate. ⊠ *Kungsholmsg. 31, 104 20* ☎ *08/6925200*
🖷 *08/6526248* ⊕ *www.firsthotels.com* ⤶ *410 rooms* ⌂ *Restaurant,
pool* ⊟ *AE, DC, MC, V.*

$$$ **Continental.** In the city center across from the train station, the Con-
tinental is considered one of the best hotels in town for the business trav-
eler, with its conference rooms and business center, and is especially popular
with Americans. ⊠ *Klara Vattugr. 4, 101 22* ☎ *08/51734200* 🖷 *08/
51734211* ⊕ *www.scandic-hotels.com* ⤶ *268 rooms* ⌂ *Restaurant*
⊟ *AE, DC, MC, V.*

★ $$$ **Diplomat.** This elegant hotel, in an early-20th-century town house near
the city center, has magnificent views of central Stockholm. Rooms
overlooking the water have no bathroom doors, allowing you to soak
in the tub while taking in the view. Be sure to check out the cocktail bar

on the second floor, a piece of Stockholm social history. ✉ *Strandv. 7C, 104 40* ☎ *08/4596800* 🖷 *08/4596820* ⊕ *www.diplomathotel.com* ⇦ *133 rooms* ☖ *Restaurant* 🖃 *AE, DC, MC, V.*

$$$ 🏨 **Lydmar Hotel.** This modern, design-conscious hotel is popular with the cool set. Rooms are stark and come with DVD and CD players and wide-screen TVs. The lobby lounge is alive nearly every night with the latest DJs and live musicians. ✉ *Stureg. 10, 114 36* ☎ *08/56611300* 🖷 *08/56611301* ⊕ *www.lydmar.se* ⇦ *56 rooms, 5 junior suites* 🖃 *AE, DC, MC, V.*

$$$ 🏨 **Stockholm Plaza Hotel.** On one of Stockholm's foremost streets for shopping and entertainment, this turn-of-the-20th-century building has an old-style elegance. Rooms are spacious and decorated in warm colors. ✉ *Birger Jarlsg. 29, 103 95* ☎ *08/56622000* 🖷 *08/56622020* ⊕ *www.elite.se* ⇦ *151 rooms* ☖ *Restaurant, bar* 🖃 *AE, DC, MC, V.*

$$–$$$ 🏨 **Gamla Stan.** This quiet and welcoming hotel in a former 17th-century residence gives you the feeling of being someone's houseguest. Each room is decorated in a different style. ✉ *Lilla Nyg. 25, 111 28* ☎ *08/7237250* 🖷 *08/7237259* ⊕ *www.rica.cityhotels.se* ⇦ *51 rooms* 🖃 *AE, DC, MC, V.*

$$ 🏨 **August Strindberg.** A narrow, frescoed corridor leads from the street to the flagstone courtyard, into which the hotel's restaurant expands in summer. Parquet flooring and high ceilings distinguish the rooms, which are otherwise plainly furnished. Kitchenettes are available; some rooms can be combined into family apartments. The four floors have no elevator. ✉ *Tegnérg. 38, 113 59* ☎ *08/325006* 🖷 *08/209085* ⇦ *19 rooms* ☖ *Restaurant* 🖃 *AE, DC, MC, V.*

$$ 🏨 **Örnsköld.** Just behind the Royal Dramatic Theater in the heart of the city, this gem has the feel of an old private club, with a brass-and-leather lobby and Victorian-style furniture in the moderately spacious, high-ceilinged rooms. Rooms over the courtyard are quieter, but those facing the street are sunnier. ✉ *Nybrog. 6, 114 34* ☎ *08/6670285* 🖷 *08/6676991* ⇦ *30 rooms* 🖃 *AE, MC, V.*

Fodor'sChoice
★

$$ 🏨 **Reisen.** A 17th-century building on the waterfront, Reisen has been a hotel since 1819. It has a fine restaurant, a grill, tea and coffee service in the library, and a piano bar. The swimming pool was installed beneath surviving medieval arches in the structure's foundations. ✉ *Skeppsbron 12–14, 111 30* ☎ *08/223260* 🖷 *08/201559* ⇦ *114 rooms* ☖ *3 restaurants, pool* 🖃 *AE, DC, MC, V.*

$–$$ 🏨 **Långholmen.** This former prison (built in 1724) was converted into a combined hotel and hostel in 1989. The island on which it sits has popular beaches and a prison museum. ✉ *Långholmen, Box 9116, 102 72* ☎ *08/6680500* 🖷 *08/7208575* ⊕ *www.langholmen.se* ⇦ *101 rooms* ☖ *3 restaurants* 🖃 *AE, DC, MC, V.*

$ 🏨 *Gustav af Klint.* A hotel ship moored at Stadsgården quay, near Slussen subway station, the *Gustav af Klint* is divided into a hotel and a hostel. The rooms are small but clean, with bunk-style beds in both the hotel and hostel rooms; the shared bathrooms are easily accessible. You can dine on the deck in summer. ✉ *Stadsgårdskajen 153, 116 45* ☎ *08/6404077* 🖷 *08/6406416* ⇦ *8 hotel cabins, 120 hostel beds* ☖ *Restaurant* 🖃 *AE, MC, V.*

Nightlife & the Arts

The Arts

Stockholm's theater and concert season runs from September through May, so you won't find many big-name artists in summer. For a list of events, pick up the free magazine *What's On*, available throughout the city and from hotels and tourist information offices. For tickets to theaters and shows, try **Biljettdirekt** at Sweden House or any post office.

CONCERTS The city's main concert hall is **Konserthuset** (✉ Hötorget 8 ☎ 08/102110), home of the Stockholm Philharmonic Orchestra. Look in the local press for events at **Berwaldhallen** (✉ Strandv. 69 ☎ 08/7841800), a concert hall downtown. In summer many city parks have free concerts; listings appear in the "Events" section of *What's On* or in local newspapers.

FILM English and American films predominate, screened with the original soundtrack and Swedish subtitles. Programs are listed in the local evening newspapers, although movie titles are usually given in Swedish. **Filmstaden Sergel** (✉ Hötorget ☎ 08/56260000) has 18 cinemas under one roof. There are also a number of theaters on Kungsgatan. Most cinemas take reservations over the phone, and the latest releases may well be sold out. The city's annual **Stockholms Filmfestival** is held in early November, screening films from all over the world.

OPERA **Operan** (Royal Opera House; ✉ Jakobs Torg 2 ☎ 08/248240) lies just across the water from the Royal Palace and puts on world-class performances. The season runs from mid-August to early June. The exquisite **Drottningholms Slottsteater** (Drottningholm Court Theater; ✉ Drottningholm ☎ 08/6608225) presents opera, ballet, and orchestral music from May to early September; the original 18th-century stage machinery is still used in these productions. Drottningholm, the royal residence, is reached by subway and bus or by special theater-bus (which leaves from the Grand Hotel or opposite the Central Train Station). Boat tours run here in summer.

THEATER Stockholm has some 20 theaters. **Kungliga Dramatiska Teatern** (Royal Dramatic Theater; ✉ Nybroplan ☎ 08/6670680), better known as the Dramaten, with great gilded statues at Nybroplan, stages international productions in Swedish. **Vasa Teatern** (✉ Vasag. 19–21 ☎ 08/102363 last-minute bookings) produces whimsical Swedish comedies. Musicals are presented regularly at several city theaters. Productions by the **English Theatre Company** are occasionally staged at various venues in Stockholm; check the local press for details.

Nightlife

BARS & The Red Room, on the second floor of the renovated restaurant-bar **Berns'**
NIGHTCLUBS **Salonger** (✉ Berzelli Park 9 ☎ 08/56632000), is where playwright August Strindberg once held court. **Café Opera** (✉ Operahuset, Gustav Adolfs Torg ☎ 08/6765807) is a favorite meeting place of the suit-and-tie set; at the waterfront end of Kungsträgården, it has the longest bar in town, plus dining, roulette, and dancing after midnight. **Mosebacke Etablissement** (✉ Mosebacke Torg 3 ☎ 08/6419020) is a combined indoor theater and outdoor café with a spectacular view of the city. Royalty and other dignitaries mingle at **Riche** (✉ Birger Jarlsg. 4 ☎ 08/54503560); the grand bar's pedigree stretches back to 1893. **O Bar** (✉ Stureplan 2 ☎ 08/4405730), inside Restaurant Sturehof, is great for live soul and hip-hop music. **Sture Compagniet** (✉ Stureg. 4 ☎ 08/6117800) is good for drinking and dancing. **Olssons Skor** (✉ Odeng. 41 ☎ No phone) is a former shoe shop, now a dark, hip bar mixing the best cocktails in town.

Pubs abound in Stockholm. Watch for happy hour, when drinks are cheap. Irish beer enthusiasts rally at **Dubliner** (✉ Smålandsg. 8 ☎ 08/6797707). **Bishops Arms** (✉ Bellmansg. 12 ☎ 08/55692118) is an English-style pub with a huge collection of whiskey and ale. The **Tudor Arms** (✉ Grevg. 31 ☎ 08/6602712) is just as popular as when it opened in the '70s.

CABARET Stockholm's biggest nightclub, **Börsen** (⊠ Jakobsg. 6 ☎ 08/7878500), has high-quality Swedish and international cabaret. **Wallmans Salonger** (⊠ Teaterg. 3 ☎ 08/6116622) provides an unforgettable cabaret experience; reservations are essential.

DANCING **Bäckahästen** (⊠ Kungsg. 56 ☎ 08/4115180) is lively on weekends, catering to a slightly older crowd. **Karlson & Co** (⊠ Kungsg. 56 ☎ 08/54512140) is a pub, restaurant, and nightclub for the middle-age set. **Residence** (⊠ Birger Jarlsg. 29 ☎ 08/201411) pulls in all ages with music from the '70s and '80s.

JAZZ CLUBS **Fasching** (⊠ Kungsg. 63 ☎ 08/53482960) is Stockholm's most popular jazz club, offering both jazz and soul. **Nalens** (⊠ Stora Nyg. 5 ☎ 08/4533434) is a mellow jazz and dance club with events four or five nights a week. Tickets for concerts are available through **BiljettDirekt** (☎ 077/1707070); most shows cost SKr 150–SKr 200 or less.

Shopping

Department Stores

NK (⊠ Hamng. 18–20 ☎ 08/7628000) is a high-class galleria. **PUB** (⊠ Hötorget ☎ 08/4021611) has 42 boutiques. **Åhléns City** (⊠ Klarabergsg. 50 ☎ 08/6766000) is a traditional department store with lots of Swedish and international name brands.

Food & Flea Markets

For a high-class Swedish food market with such specialties as marinated salmon and reindeer, try **Östermalms Saluhall** (⊠ at Östermalmstorg). Another good bet is **Hötorgshallen** (⊠ at Hötorget), which is filled with butcher shops, coffee and tea shops, and fresh fish markets. It's located under Filmstaden Sergel.

Glassware

Duka (⊠ Sveav. 24/26 ☎ 08/104530) specializes in crystal as well as porcelain. **Gustavsbergs Fabriksbod** (⊠ Odelbergs Väg 13, Gustavsberg ☎ 08/57035655), just outside the city, is a factory shop of quality. For the best buys try **Nordiska Kristall** (⊠ Kungsg. 9 ☎ 08/104372).

Handicrafts

For unique Swedish stationery and office supplies in fun colors and styles go to **Ordning & Reda** (⊠ Hamng. 18–20 ☎ 08/7628462) in NK department store. Kitchen supplies and interior design items by some of Sweden's best designers are available at **Designtorget** (⊠ Kulturuset Sergelstorg 3 ☎ 08/50831520). A good center for all kinds of Swedish wood and metal handicrafts is **Svensk Hemslöjd** (⊠ Sveav. 44 ☎ 08/232115). **Vista** (⊠ Kungsg. 55 ☎ 08/214726) has Swedish folk costumes and handicrafts from different parts of Sweden. For elegant home furnishings and timeless fabrics, try **Svenskt Tenn** (⊠ Strandv. 5A ☎ 08/6701600), best known for its selection of designer Josef Franck's furniture and fabrics.

Shopping Districts

Shop 'til you drop means hitting the stores along **Hamngatan** and **Biblioteksgatan** with a vengeance. The **Gamla Stan** area is best for antiques shops, bookshops, and art galleries. **Sturegallerian** (⊠ Stureg.) is an elegant covered shopping gallery on the site of the former public baths at Stureplan.

Side Trips

Skärgården

★ You could sail forever among the 24,000 islands of Stockholm's Skärgården (archipelago). If you don't have a boat, purchase the *Båtluffarkortet* (Inter-Skerries Card, SKr 385), which gives you 16 days' unlimited travel on Waxholmsbolaget (Waxholm Steamship Company) boats. Get the card at the Excursion Shop at the Stockholm Tourist Centre or at the Waxholm Steamship Company terminal.

Fjäderholmarna

The group of four islands known as Fjäderholmarna (the Feather Islets) lies only 20 minutes by boat from the city center. They were formerly a restricted military zone but are now a haven of restaurants, cafés, a museum depicting life in the archipelago, an aquarium with many species of Baltic marine life, handicraft studios, shops, and a pirate-ship playground. Boats leave for the islands from Slussen, Strömkajen, and Nybroplan (April 29–September 17). For boat information and time schedules contact the **Strömma Kanalbolaget** (Strömma Canal Company). Tourism information is available from the **Fjäderholmarna Information Service** (☎ 08/7180100).

Mariefred

★ In Mariefred, on the southern side of Lake Mälaren, about 64 km (40 mi) from Stockholm, **Gripsholm Slott** (Gripsholm Castle), with its drawbridge and four massive round towers, is one of Sweden's most romantic castles. King Gustav Vasa built the present structure in 1577. It now houses the state portrait collection. ☎ *0159/10194* ⊕ *www.royalcourt.se* ⊗ *May–Aug., daily 10–4; Sept., Tues.–Sun. 10–4; Oct.–Apr., weekends noon–3.*

An unforgettable boat journey on the restored vintage steamer *Mariefred*, the last coal-fired ship on Lake Mälaren, is the best way to get to Gripsholm, but you can also take the train. ✉ *Boat departs quay next to City Hall* ☎ *08/6698850* 🕮 *SKr 170 round-trip* ⊗ *Mid-May–late Aug., Tues.–Sun. 10 AM (returns 4:30).*

Skokloster

Built by the Swedish field marshal Carl Gustav Wrangel, **Skokloster** (Skokloster Castle) contains many of his trophies from the Thirty Years' War. The palace, about 70 km (44 mi) from Stockholm in Skokloster, also displays one of the largest private collections of arms in the world, as well as some magnificent Gobelin tapestries. Next door to the palace is a **motor museum** housing Sweden's largest collection of vintage cars and motorcycles. ☎ *018/386077* ⊗ *May–Aug., daily 11–4; Apr., Sept., and Oct., weekdays 1–2, weekends noon–3.*

Skokloster is easily reached by boat. The route follows the narrow inlets of Lake Mälaren along the "Royal Waterway." It stops at **Sigtuna**, Sweden's oldest town. You can get off the boat here to look around, taking in the medieval ruins and an 18th-century town hall. For boat information, contact the **Strömma Kanalbolaget.** ✉ *Boats depart from Stadshusbron (City Hall Bridge)* ☎ *08/58714000* 🕮 *SKr 200 round-trip* ⊗ *Early June–mid-Aug., Tues.–Thurs. and weekends.*

Stockholm Essentials

AIRPORTS & TRANSFERS

International flights arrive at Arlanda Airport. For information on arrival and departure times, call the individual airlines.

🏢 Arlanda Airport ✉ 40 km/25 mi north of city ☎ 08/7976000 ⊕ www.arlanda.com.

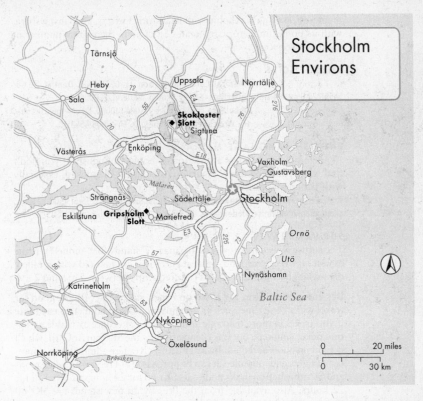

Stockholm Environs

TRANSFERS The airport is linked to Stockholm by a major highway as well as a high-speed train that costs SKr 125 one-way and takes 20 minutes. Families can get a group rate for SKr 240. Trains leave every 15 minutes 6 AM–7 PM and then twice an hour 7–11 PM. Buses, called Flygbusarna, depart for Cityterminalen from the international and domestic terminals every 10–15 minutes between 6:30 AM and 11 PM. The ride costs SKr 80 per person and takes about 40 minutes. A bus-taxi package is available from the bus driver at prices ranging from SKr 150 per person to SKr 220; additional passengers in a group pay only the bus portion of the fare. Ask the bus driver for details. A taxi directly from the airport will cost around SKr 350–SKr 430 (before you get into the taxi, ask the driver if he offers a fixed-price airport-to-city rate). Look for Taxi Stockholm, Taxi 020, and Taxi Kurir cabs, and ask the cab line attendant for help since illegal taxis abound.

BOAT & FERRY TRAVEL

🚢 **Strömma Kanalbolaget** (Strömma Canal Company) ✉ Boats depart from Stadshusbron (City Hall Bridge) ☎ 08/58714000 🌐 www.strommakanalbolaget.com. **Waxholmsbolaget** (Waxholm Steamship Company) ✉ Terminal, Strömkajen, in front of Grand Hotel ☎ 08/6795830 🌐 www.waxholmbolaget.se.

BUS TRAVEL TO & FROM STOCKHOLM

All major bus lines arrive at the Cityterminalen, next to the train station. Bus tickets are also sold at the railroad reservations office.

BUS TRAVEL WITHIN STOCKHOLM

The Stockholm Transit Authority, known as the SL, operates both the bus and subway systems. Tickets for the two networks are interchangeable. The comprehensive bus network serves out-of-town points of interest, such as Waxholm, with its historic fortress, and Gustavsberg, with its porcelain factory. In greater Stockholm there are a number of night-bus services.

EMERGENCIES

Doctors & Dentists **Medical Care Information** ☎ 08/320100. **Dentist** ☎ 08/54551220 8 AM–9 PM. **Private clinic** ✉ City Akuten ☎ 08/4122960.

Emergency Services **Ambulance** ☎ 112. **Police** ☎ 08/4010000, 112 emergencies only.

24-hour Pharmacies **C. W. Scheele** ✉ Klarbergsg. 64 ☎ 08/4548130.

ENGLISH-LANGUAGE MEDIA

BOOKS Akademibokhandeln has a selection of books in English. If you don't find what you need there, Hedengrens is also well stocked, especially with fiction and poetry.

Bookstores **Akademibokhandeln** ✉ Mäster Samuelsg. 32 ☎ 08/6136100 ⊕ www.akademibokhandeln.se. **Hedengrens** ✉ Sturepl. 4/Sturegalerian ☎ 08/6115132.

SUBWAY TRAVEL

The subway system, known as T-banan (*T* stands for "tunnel"), is the easiest way to get around. Station entrances are marked with a blue T on a white background. Trains run frequently between 5 AM and 2 AM.

Bus and subway fares are based on zones, starting at SKr 20, good for travel within one zone, such as downtown, for one hour. You pay more if you travel in more than one zone. Single tickets are available at station ticket counters, but it is cheaper to buy the SL Tourist Card, which is valid on buses and the subway and also gives free admission to a number of sights and museums. It can be purchased at Pressbyrån newsstands and SL information desks and costs SKr 80 for 24 hours or SKr 150 for 72 hours. Also available from the Pressbyrån newsstands are SKr 60 coupons, good for at least 10 bus or subway rides in the central zone. The Stockholmskortet (Stockholm Card) also grants unlimited transportation on city subway, bus, and rail services, plus free admission to more museums than the SL Tourist Card, and several sightseeing trips.

TAXIS

Typically, a trip of 10 km (6 mi) will cost about SKr 120 between 9 AM and 4 PM on weekdays, SKr 130 on weekday nights, and SKr 150 on weekends. It can be difficult to hail a taxi on the street, so call ahead if possible. Taxi Stockholm is one of the city's biggest taxi companies. Taxikurir also serves the greater Stockholm area, as does Taxi 020.

Taxi 020 ☎ 020/939393. **Taxikurir** ☎ 08/300000. **Taxi Stockholm** ☎ 08/150000.

TOURS

BOAT TOURS Take a boat trip through the archipelago with the Strömma Kanalbolaget (Strömma Canal Company) or the Waxholmsbolaget (Waxholm Steamship Company). Trips range from one to three hours each way. One-day excursions include Waxholm, Utö, Sandhamn, and Möja. Conventional sightseeing tours include a one-hour city tour run by Strömma Kanalbolaget and leaving from the Nybroplan quay every hour on the half hour between 10:30 and 5:30 in summer. Don't miss the boat trip to the 17th-century palace of Drottningholm. Trips depart every hour on the hour from 10 to 4 and at 6 PM during the summer from City Hall Bridge (Stadshusbron). Other trips go from Stadshusbron to the ancient towns of Sigtuna and Vaxholm. By changing boats you can continue to Uppsala to catch the train back to Stockholm. Information is available from the boat companies or the Stockholm Tourist Centre at Sweden House.

Strömma Kanalbolaget ✉ Boats depart from Stadshusbron [City Hall Bridge] ☎ 08/58714000 ⊕ www.strommakanalbolaget.com. **Waxholmsbolaget** ✉ Terminal, Strömkajen, in front of Grand Hotel ☎ 08/6795830 ⊕ www.waxholmbolaget.se.

ORIENTATION TOURS
More than 35 different tours—on foot or by boat, bus, or a combination of these—are available throughout the summer. Some take only 30 minutes, others an entire day. A 90-minute coach tour, costing SKr 130, runs daily. Tickets are available from the Excursion Shop at Stockholm Tourist Centre.

PRIVATE GUIDES
Guide Centralen at the Stockholm Information Service offers individual guides and group bookings.

🏠 **Guide Centralen** ✉ Sweden House, Hamng. 27, Box 7542, 103 93 ☎ 08/7892496.

SPECIAL-INTEREST TOURS
Special-interest tours in the Stockholm area include spending a weekend at a cabin in the archipelago, renting a small fishing or sailing boat, visiting the Gustavsberg porcelain factory, and more. Call the Stockholm Tourist Centre at Sweden House for details.

TRAIN TRAVEL

Both long-distance and commuter trains arrive at Stockholm Central Station on Vasagatan, a main boulevard in the heart of the city. For information and ticket reservations 6 AM–11 PM, call the train information number below. There is a ticket and information office at the station where you can make reservations. Automated ticket-vending machines are also available.

Commuter trains run by the Stockholm Transit Authority (SL) travel from Stockholm Central Station to a number of nearby locales, including Nynäshamn, a departure point for ferries to the island of Gotland. Trains also run from the Slussen station to the fashionable seaside resort of Saltsjöbaden.

🏠 **Stockholm Central Station** ✉ Vasag. ☎ 0771/757575 ⊕ www.sj.se.

TRANSPORTATION AROUND STOCKHOLM

Maps and timetables for all city transportation are available from the Stockholm Transit Authority (SL) information desks.

Stockholmskortet (Stockholm Card) grants unlimited transportation on city subway, bus, and rail services, and free admission to 70 museums and several sightseeing trips. The card costs SKr 220 for 24 hours, SKr 380 for two days, and SKr 540 for three days. It is available at the tourist information centers at Sweden House, Kaknästornet (TV Tower), and at Hotellcentralen at the central train station.

🏠 **Stockholm Transit Authority** ✉ Sergels Torg; Stockholm Central Station; Slussen in Gamla Stan ☎ 08/6001000 information ⊕ www.sl.se.

TRAVEL AGENCY

🏠 **American Express** ✉ St. Eriksg. 117 ☎ 08/4295600 🖶 08/4294343.

VISITOR INFORMATION

🏠 **Stockholm Tourist Centre/Excursion Shop** ✉ Sweden House, Kungsträdgården, Hamng. 27 ☎ 08/7892490. **Stockholm Information Service** ✉ Sweden House, Box 7542, 103 93 ☎ 08/7892400 ⊕ www.stockholmtown.com. City Hall summer only ✉ Hantverkarg. 1 ☎ 08/50829000. **Kaknästornet** ✉ TV Tower, Ladugårdsgärdet ☎ 08/7892435. **Fjäderholmarna** ☎ 08/7180100.

UPPSALA & THE FOLKLORE DISTRICT

The Folklore District is essentially the provinces of Dalarna and Värmland. With its rural landscape, it is the best place to discover some of the country's most ancient traditions. Dalarna, which has its own special style of handicrafts, can be reached via the ancient city of Uppsala. Return to Stockholm through the Bergslagen region, the heart of the centuries-old Swedish iron industry.

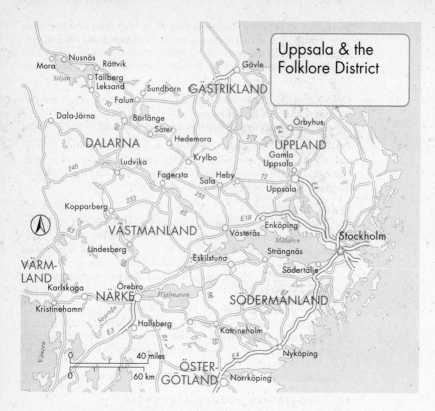

Uppsala & the
Folklore District

Nusnäs
Mora   Rättvik   Gävle
Siljan   Tällberg
Leksand   Sundborn   GÄSTRIKLAND
Falun
Dala-Järna   Borlänge   Örbyhus
Säter
DALARNA   Hedemora   UPPLAND
Krylbo   Gamla
Ludvika   Uppsala
Fagersta   Heby
Sala   Uppsala
Kopparberg
VÄSTMANLAND   Enköping
Lindesberg   Västerås   Stockholm
Mälaren
VÄRM-   Eskilstuna   Strängnäs
LAND   Karlskoga   Örebro   Södertälje
NÄRKE   Hjälmaren   SÖDERMANLAND
Kristinehamn
Hallsberg   Katrineholm
0   40 miles
0   60 km   ÖSTER-   Nyköping
GÖTLAND   Norrköping

Uppsala

Fodor's Choice   Uppsala is well worth exploring. **Gamla Uppsala** (Old Uppsala) is dom-
★   inated by three huge burial mounds dating from the 5th century. The
first Swedish kings, Aun, Egil, and Adils, are all buried here. The church
next to the burial mounds was the seat of Sweden's first archbishop and
was built on the site of a former pagan temple. **Historiskt Center** (Historical Center; ☎ 018/239300 ☉ May–Sept., daily 10–5; Oct.–Apr.,
Tues.–Sun. 10–5), a museum next to the church, displays archaeological finds from the burial mounds and attempts to separate fact from myth
of the local history. At the adjacent Odinsborg restaurant you can sample local mead brewed from a 14th-century recipe.

The impressive **Domkyrka** (cathedral), with its twin towers dominating
the skyline, has been the seat of the archbishop of the Swedish church
for 700 years. Its present appearance owes much to major restoration
work completed during the late 19th century. At the **Cathedral Museum**
in the north tower, you can see one of Europe's finest collections of ecclesiastical textiles. ⊠ Domkyrkoplan ☎ 018/187201 ☉ Cathedral:
daily 8–6. Museum: May–Aug., Mon.–Sat. 10–5, Sun. 12:30–5; Sept.–Apr.,
Tues.–Sat. 11–3, Sun. 12:30–3.

Strategically positioned atop a hill, the august **Uppsala Slott** (Uppsala Castle) was built in the 1540s by King Gustav Vasa. Having broken his ties
with the Vatican, the king was eager to show who was actually running
the country; he even arranged to have the cannons aimed at the archbishop's palace. ⊠ Borggården ☎ 018/7272482 ☉ Mid-Apr.–mid-
June, daily 11–3; mid-June–mid-Aug., daily 10–5.

One of the most famous people to emerge from Uppsala was Carl von
Linné, known as Linnaeus. A professor of botany during the 1740s, he

developed the system of plant and animal classification still used today. Visit the **gardens** he designed, as well as his former residence, Linné Trädgården (Linné Gardens), now a museum. ⊠ *Svartbäcksg. 27* ☎ *018/ 109490 garden; 018/136540 museum* ⊙ *Garden: May–Aug., daily 9–9; Sept., daily 9–7. Museum: June–Aug., Tues.–Sun. noon–4; May and Sept., weekends noon–4.*

$$–$$$ ✕ **Hambergs Fisk.** As the name suggests, this modern, airy restaurant specializes in fish. After you have sampled the wonderful menu, you can head to the in-house deli and buy fresh fish and other fine foods. ⊠ *Fyris Torg 8* ☎ *018/710050* ▤ *AE, DC, MC, V.*

$$ ⊞ **Grand Hotel Hörnan.** Opened in 1906, the Grand Hotel Hörnan is in the city center near the train station. It has views of the castle and the cathedral. ⊠ *Bangårdsg. 1, 753 20* ☎ *018/139380* ⎙ *018/120311* ⊕ *www.eklundshof.se* ↩ *37 rooms* ▤ *AE, DC, MC, V* ⊙ *Closed July.*

$–$$ ⊞ **First Hotel Linné.** The stark white, simple interior of this stone hotel belies its warmth and comfort. The lush gardens are a joy in the summer, the roaring fire one in the winter. Rooms are furnished with plain wood furniture and light fabrics. Uppsala's only wine bar can be found on the ground floor, with more than 200 wines by the glass from which to choose. ⊠ *Skolg. 45, 750 02* ☎ *018/102000* ⎙ *018/137597* ⊕ *www. firsthotels.com* ↩ *116 rooms* ▤ *AE, DC, MC, V.*

Säter

Säter, one of the best-preserved wooden villages in Sweden, sits northwest of Uppsala on the way to Dalarna in farming country.

Falun

Falun is the center of Sweden's copper mining history, once the key to the country's great wealth. Here you can visit the **Falu Koppargruva** (Great Pit), a hole created in 1687 when an abandoned copper mine collapsed. There are working mines in the area and guided tours (requiring good shoes) into some of the old shafts. ⊠ *Ask at tourist board on Stora Torget (main square) for directions* ☎ *023/711475* ⊙ *May–Aug., daily 10–4:30; Sept.–mid-Nov. and Mar.–Apr., weekends 12:30–4:30.*

The **Stora Kopparberg Museum** tells the story of the local mining industry. ☎ *023/15825 or 023/711475* ⊙ *May–Aug., daily 10–4:30; Sept.–Apr., daily 12:30–4:30.*

$$ ⊞ **Hotel Winn.** In the town center, this cozy hotel built in traditional Dalarna style is filled with antiques. ⊠ *Bergskolegr. 7, 791 26* ☎ *023/ 63600* ⎙ *023/22524* ⊕ *www.swedenhotels.se* ↩ *88 rooms* ⚑ *Restaurant* ▤ *AE, DC, MC, V.*

$ ⊞ **Hotel Falun.** This is a basic hotel—built in the 1950s in the center of town—that's comfortable and bright, with lots of light wood furnishings. ⊠ *Centrumhuset, Trotzg. 16, 791 71* ☎ *023/29180* ⎙ *023/13006* ⊕ *www. hotelfalun.nu* ↩ *27 rooms, 15 with shower* ▤ *AE, DC, MC, V.*

Sundborn

Just outside Falun, at Sundborn, is the former home of Swedish artist Carl Larsson, **Carl Larsson Gården.** You can see a selection of the artist's paintings, which owe much to local folk-art traditions. The house has a beautiful setting, on a lakeside. Larsson's great-grandchildren still use it on occasion. ⊠ *Carl Larssonsv. 12* ☎ *023/60053 summer; 023/60069 winter* ⊕ *www.clg.se* ⊙ *Tours May–Sept., daily 10–5, every 10 min.*

FodorsChoice ★

Tällberg

The tiny village of Tällberg on the shores of Lake Siljan, with its flower-strewn meadows and old wooden houses, is for many the center of the Dalarna region.

$$ 🏨 **Åkerblads.** Near the shores of Lake Siljan, the hotel offers a genuine
Fodor's Choice   experience of rural Sweden. In a typical Dalarna farmstead, parts of which
★   date from the 16th century, it is run by the 19th generation of the
Åkerblad family and has been a hotel since 1910. The restaurant serves
superb dishes made from local fish and game. ⊠ *Sjögatu, 793 70*
☎ *0247/50800* 🖷 *0247/50652* ⊕ *www.akerblads-tallberg.se* 🛏 *58
rooms with bath, 6 rooms with shared bath* ⚴ *Restaurant* ⊟ *AE, DC,
MC, V.*

Mora

Mora was the home of the artist Anders Zorn (1860–1920), famous for
his distinctive and tasteful paintings of robust, naked women in rural
surroundings. His house and **Zorn Museet** (Zorn Museum), exhibiting
his paintings, are open to the public. ⊠ *Vasag. 36* ☎ *0250/16560*
⊕ *www.zorn.se* ⊙ *House: guided tours only; call for information and
times. Museum: mid-May–mid-Sept., Mon.–Sat. 9–5, Sun. 11–5; mid-
Sept.–mid-May, Mon.–Sat. noon–5, Sun. 1–5.*

$$ 🏨 **Siljan.** Named for the nearby lake, Siljan is a small but up-to-date
hotel. Many rooms have a lake view. ⊠ *Morag. 6, 792 01* ☎ *0250/13000*
🖷 *0250/13098* ⊕ *www.swedenhotels.se* 🛏 *42 rooms, 40 with shower*
⚴ *Restaurant* ⊟ *AE, DC, MC, V.*

Rättvik

At midsummer in Rättvik, hundreds of people wearing traditional costumes arrive in longboats to attend midsummer church services—a
time-honored tradition. Twelve-man longboat races are held in summer.
The *Gustav Vasa* vintage steamboat has trips with nightly dancing and
prawn dinners.

Nusnäs

Nusnäs is the home of the brightly colored Dalarna handmade wooden
horses, known as *Dalahästar.* Red or blue and painted with traditional
floral patterns, the only real Dala horses are made here. Fashion affects
even this tradition, though, and unpainted or single-color horses are becoming increasingly popular. One of the biggest workshops is **Nils Ols-
son** (⊠ Edåkersv. 17 ☎ 0250/37200).

Ludvika

This town is an important center of the old Bergslagen mining region,
which stretches from the forests of Värmland in the west to the coastal
gorges in the east. Ludvika has a notable open-air mining museum, the
Gammelgården. ⊠ *Nilsnilsg. 7* ☎ *0240/10019* ⊙ *June–Sept. 3, daily 11–6.*

Music and poetry festivals are held in memory of local poet Dan Andersson in nearby towns. Visit the **Dan Andersson Museum** to learn more
about his work. You can also follow signposts to his former home, **Lu-
osastugan** (Luosa Cottage; ☎ 0240/86050), open mid-May to August,
daily 11–5. ⊠ *Engelbrektsg. 8* ☎ *0240/10016* ⊙ *May–Aug., Tues.–Sat.
10–5; Sept.–Apr., Tues.–Sat. 10–2.*

$–$$ 🏨 **Grand.** This modern-style hotel has a central location. ⊠ *Eriksg. 6,
771 31* ☎ *0240/18220* 🖷 *0240/611018* ⊕ *www.grand-elektra.se* 🛏 *102
rooms* ⚴ *Restaurant* ⊟ *AE, DC, MC, V.*

$ 🏨 **Rex.** Built in 1960, the Rex is a basic modern hotel near the city cen-
ter. ⊠ *Engelbrektsg. 9, 771 30* ☎ *0240/13690* 🛏 *28 rooms, 15 with
shower* ⊟ *AE, DC, MC, V* ⊙ *Closed 1 wk in July.*

Örebro

Örebro nestles on the western edge of Lake Hjälmaren. It received its
charter in the 13th century, becoming an important trading center for
the farmers and miners of the Bergslagen region. Rising from a small

island in the Svartån (Black River), right in the center of town, is the imposing **Örebro Slott** (Örebro Castle), parts of which date from the 13th century. The castle is now the residence of the regional governor and has an excellent restaurant, Slottskrogen. ⊠ *Kanslig.* ⊕ *www.orebro. se* ⊙ *Call Örebro Tourist Information for opening hrs.*

$$ ✕ **Drängen.** Decorated in the style of an old Swedish farmhouse, this eccentric restaurant serves a fine mix of international and traditional cuisine. ⊠ *Oskarstorget 1* ☎ *019/323296* ⊟ *AE, DC, MC, V.*

$–$$ 🏨 **Elite Stora Hotellet.** Across the street from the castle on the Svartån, this hotel is one of the oldest in Sweden, dating from 1858. All rooms are individually furnished. It has a cozy cellar restaurant, the Slottskällaren, and an English pub, the Bishop's Arms. ⊠ *Drottningg. 1, 701 45* ☎ *019/156900* 🖷 *019/156950* ⊷ *103 rooms* ⟁ *Restaurant, bar* ⊟ *AE, DC, MC, V.*

Uppsala & the Folklore District Essentials

BUS TRAVEL

For information about bus travel, call Dalatrafik, the region's traffic information center.
🚌 **Dalatrafik** ☎ 020/232425 ⊕ www.dalatrafik.se.

CAR TRAVEL

A car will give you the flexibility to explore some attractions not so easily accessible by public transportation. The drive to Uppsala from Stockholm, via the E4, is about 71 km (44 mi).

TOURS

Uppsala is compact enough to explore on foot, and guided sightseeing tours are available; call the Guide Service at the Uppsala Tourist Information office. For guided tours of the district, contact the Falun tourist office, which has both package tours and personalized services.
🚶 **Guide Service** ☎ 018/7274800.

TRAIN TRAVEL

The train from Stockholm to Uppsala takes only 50 minutes, and service is fairly frequent.

VISITOR INFORMATION

🏢 **Falun** ⊠ Stora Torget ☎ 023/83050 ⊕ www.falun.se. **Ludvika** ⊠ Fredsg. 10 ☎ 0240/86050 ⊕ www.ludvika.se. **Mora** ⊠ Ångbåtskajen ☎ 0250/592020 ⊕ www. mora.se. **Örebro** ⊠ Slottet ☎ 019/212121 ⊕ www.orebro.se. **Rättvik** ⊠ Torget ☎ 0248/ 797210 ⊕ www.rattvik.se. **Uppsala** ⊠ Fyris Torg 8 ☎ 018/7274800 ⊕ www.uppsala. se.

THE WEST COAST & THE GLASS COUNTRY

Göteborg (Gothenburg) is an important Swedish port on the North Sea. North and south of the city lie scenic stretches of the country's western coast, where you'll find the history-rich town of Helsingborg and the booming city of Malmö. Inland are the lakes and forests of the Glass Country, and beyond stands the medieval fortress town of Kalmar, on the east coast.

Göteborg

Sweden's second-largest city is an eclectic mix of industrial waterfront, elegant modern city, with broad avenues and green parks, and restored working-class quarter, now bohemian shopping area; all within short walking distance. The city was laid out during the 17th century by Dutch architects, who gave it its extensive network of straight streets divided by canals. Only one major canal survives; you can explore it by sightseeing boat. Gothenburgians fondly refer to these short and squat (so they can pass under the city's 20 low bridges) boats as *paddan* (toads).

Fodor's Choice You can embark for the one-hour boat tour at the **Paddan terminal.**
★ ✉ *Kungsportsplatsen* ☉ *Departures late Apr.–late June and mid-Aug.–early Sept., daily 10–5; late June–mid-Aug., daily 10–9; early Sept.–Oct. 1, daily noon–3* ☉ *Closed Oct.–late Apr.* Running through the heart of Göteborg is **Kungsportsavenyn**, commonly called Avenyn (the Avenue). This broad, tree-lined boulevard is lined with many boutiques and eateries. Avenyn ends at **Götaplatsen**, which has a **grand theater**, a **concert hall**, an **art museum**, and a **library** that has a wide selection of English-language newspapers.

⊙ Just a stone's throw away from Götaplatsen is the **Liseberg amusement park**, the largest of its kind in the Nordic region. Liseberg is an excellent place to take kids, and its downtown location makes it convenient for a quick visit. ✉ *Öregrytev. 5* ☎ *031/400100* ⊕ *www.liseberg.se* ☉ *Late Apr., weekends 11–8; May and June, Mon.–Thurs. 3–11, Fri. and Sat. 11–11, Sun. 11–8; July–mid-Aug., Sun.–Thurs. 11–11, Fri. and Sat. 11–midnight; mid-Aug.–Sept., Fri. 5–11, Sat. 11–11, Sun. 11–8.*

Trädgårdsföreningen (Garden Association) maintains an attractive park with a magnificent Palm House, built in 1878, and a Butterfly House containing 40 different species. ✉ *Just off Kungsportsavenyn* ☎ *031/ 7411111 Butterfly House* ☉ *Park: daily 9 AM–sundown. Palm House: daily 10–4. Butterfly House: Oct.–Mar., Tues.–Sun. 10–3; Apr., Tues.–Sun. 10–4; May and Sept., daily 10–4; June–Aug., daily 10–5.*

For shopping, try **Nordstan** (✉ entrances on Köpmansg., Nils Ericsonsg., Kanaltorgsg., and Östra Hamng.), a covered complex of shops near the train station.

$$–$$$ ✕ **Fond.** The bright, spacious interior and the simple wooden tables give
Fodor's Choice this restaurant the feel of an informal brasserie-style restaurant. It's all
★ the more surprising then when you discover that Steffan Karlsson and his team of young chefs produces some of the best food in town. Dishes like deep-fried crayfish with black pepper carrots and orange cream or lobster, scallop, and eel with sauerkraut and parsnip broth are highlights. The wine list and the excellent restaurant staff complete the experience. ✉ *Götaplatsen* ☎ *031/812580* ⌨ *Reservations essential* ⊟ *AE, DC, MC, V.*

$–$$ ✕ **Noon.** Combining Swedish and Asian styles in both its menu and its interior design, Noon has excellent seafood and noodle dishes, served in a sleek, modern space. ✉ *Viktoriag. 2* ☎ *031/138800* ⊟ *AE, DC, MC, V* ☉ *No lunch weekends; no lunch weekdays Sept.–May.*

$$$ ▦ **Elite Plaza.** One of the smartest hotels in the city, the Plaza is an ar-
Fodor's Choice chitectural treasure from 1889, complete with original stucco ceilings
★ and English mosaic floors, and given a sympathetic restoration in 2000. Modern art adorns the walls and all rooms come with state-of-the-art facilities. Avoid rooms on the fifth floor, as these are in a modern extension, which lacks the charm of the original building. ✉ *Västra Hamng. 3, 404 22* ☎ *031/7204000* ⊟ *031/7204010* ⊕ *www.elite.se* ⇆ *144 rooms* ⌂ *Restaurant, bar* ⊟ *AE, DC, MC, V.*

★ **$–$$** ▦ **Eggers.** Dating from 1859, this Best Western has more character than other hotels in the city. Most rooms are furnished with antiques. ✉ *Drottningtorget, 401 25* ☎ *031/806070* ⊟ *031/154243* ⊕ *www. hoteleggers.se* ⇆ *67 rooms* ⌂ *Restaurant* ⊟ *AE, DC, MC, V.*

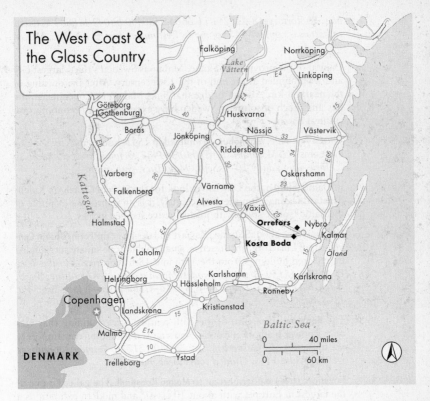

**The West Coast &
the Glass Country**

$–$$ **Liseberg Heden.** Not far from the Liseberg amusement park, this is a modern family hotel. ⊠ *Sten Stureg., 411 38* ☎ *031/7506900* 🖷 *031/7506930* 🗗 *159 rooms* ⚒ *Restaurant* ⊟ *AE, DC, MC, V.*

Helsingborg

Helsingborg, with its twin town, Helsingør (Elsinore in Shakespeare's *Hamlet*), across the Öresund, is a small town with a rich history dating to the 10th century. Today it comprises a busy industrial waterfront, charming pedestrian streets, and large parks.

All that remains of Helsingborg's castle is **Kärnan** (The Keep). It stands in a park and offers fine views over the Öresund from the top. ⊠ *Slottshagen* ☎ *042/105991* ⊙ *June–Aug., daily 10–7; Apr., May, and Sept., daily 9–4; Oct.–Mar., Tues.–Sun. 10–3.*

★   **Sofiero Slott** (Sofiero Castle), built in 1864 in the Dutch Renaissance style, is a haven for more than 300 kinds of rhododendron, a large English garden, and art exhibitions. A café (open April through September) and a fine restaurant (open March through December) are on the grounds. ⊠ *Sofierov. (on the road to Laröd)* ☎ *042/137400 or 042/140440* ⊕ *www.helsingborg.se* ⊙ *Apr.–Sept., daily 10–6; guided tours only. Park open year-round.*

$$–$$$ ✕ **Gastro.** A long leather banquette divides this stylish, dark wood and **Fodor'sChoice** blue-painted modern dining room into two halves; one a bar area, the ★   other with more formal seating. The kitchen produces international fare with Swedish influences. Fish and seafood are the stars. ⊠ *Södra Storgatan 11–13* ☎ *042/243470* ⊟ *AE, DC, MC, V* ⊙ *Closed Sun.*

★ $–$$ **Grand Hotel.** One of Sweden's oldest hotels, this hotel maintains its long-standing reputation for excellence. Antiques and fresh flowers fill the hotel, which is convenient to the railway station and ferry terminals. ⊠ *Stortorget 8–12, 251 11* ☎ *042/380400* 🖷 *042/118833* ⊕ *www. radissonsas.com* 🛏 *117 rooms* ♨ *Restaurant, bar* ⊟ *AE, DC, MC, V.*

Malmö

Capital of the province of Skåne, Malmö is Sweden's third-largest city and was founded at the end of the 13th century. After the opening of the nearly 8-km (5½-mi) bridge that links Malmö to Copenhagen, the city and much of southern Sweden have experienced an economic and cultural boom.

The city's castle, **Malmöhus,** completed in 1542, houses the city's major museums. ⊠ *Malmöhusv.* ☎ *040/344437* ⊕ *www.museer.malmo.se* ☉ *June–Aug., daily 10–4; Sept.–May, Tues.–Sun. noon–4.*

In Gamla Staden, the Old Town, look for the **St. Petri Church** on Kalendegatan. Dating from the 14th century, it is an impressive example of the Baltic Gothic style, with its distinctive stepped gables.

Fodor'sChoice
★

You can learn about Scandinavian art and design at the **Form/Design Centre** just off Lilla Torg, an attractive, small cobblestone square surrounded by restored buildings from the 17th and 18th centuries. ⊠ *Lilla Torg* ☎ *040/6645150* ⊕ *www.formdesigncenter.com* ☉ *Aug.–June, Tues., Wed., and Fri. 11–5, Thurs. 11–6, Sat. 10–4, Sun. noon–4; July, Tues.–Fri. 11–5, Sat. 10–4.*

★

The **Rooseum,** in a turn-of-the-20th-century brick building that was once a power plant, is one of Sweden's most outstanding contemporary art museums. ⊠ *Gasverksg. 22* ☎ *040/121716* ⊕ *www.rooseum.se* ☉ *Tues.–Sun. 11–5. Guided tours weekends at 2.*

Fodor'sChoice
★

For more (free) modern art go to **Malmö Konsthall.** The gallery is one of the largest in Europe, with about 10 classic and modern exhibitions a year. Other activities at the gallery include theater performances, film presentations, and poetry readings. The café and bookstore are excellent. ⊠ *St. Johannesg. 7* ☎ *040/341286* ⊕ *www.konsthallen.com* ☉ *Thurs.–Tues. 11–5, Wed. 11–10.*

Rådhuset (Town Hall), dating from 1546, dominates Stortorget, a huge, cobbled market square in Gamla Staden.

$–$$$
Fodor'sChoice
★

✕ **1r.o.k.** The name is an abbreviation for "one room and a kitchen," but this is in fact two restaurants: an informal, lively brasserie and a more serious dining room. Both serve superb, innovative food based on local specialties such as seafood and goose. ⊠ *St. Pauli Kyrkogata 11* ☎ *040/302024* ⊟ *AE, DC, MC, V* ☉ *Closed Sun.*

$$$

🏨 **Radisson SAS Hotel.** Only a five-minute walk from the train station, this modern luxury hotel has rooms decorated in several styles: Scandinavian, Asian, and Italian. The restaurant serves Scandinavian and Continental cuisine, and there's a cafeteria for quick meals. ⊠ *Österg. 10, 211 25* ☎ *040/6984000* 🖷 *040/6984001* ⊕ *www.radissonsas.com* 🛏 *221 rooms* ♨ *Restaurant, bar* ⊟ *AE, DC, MC, V.*

Jönköping

Jönköping is an attractive town on the southern shore of Lake Vättern. It is distinguished not only by its age—it celebrated the 700th anniversary of its founding in 1984—but also as the birthplace of the match-manufacturing industry, established here in the 19th century. **Tändsticksmuseet** (Match Museum), built on the site of the first factory, has exhibits on the development and manufacture of matches. ⊠ *Tändsticksgr. 7* ☎ *036/105543* ☉ *June–Aug., weekdays 10–5, weekends 10–3; Sept.–May, Tues.–Thurs. noon–4, weekends 11–3.*

★ **$-$$** ✕ **Mäster Gudmunds Källare.** This particularly inviting restaurant is nestled beneath the vaults of a 16th-century-style cellar and is only two minutes from the train station. The cuisine is typically Swedish. ⊠ *Kapellg. 2* ☏ *036/100640* ⊟ *AE, DC, MC, V.*

$-$$ ⊞ **John Bauer Hotel.** This modern hotel, named for a local artist famous for his fairy-tale depictions of trolls and mystical landscapes, lies close to the center of town and overlooks Munksjön Lake. ⊠ *Södra Strandg. 15, 550 02* ☏ *036/349000* 🖷 *036/349050* ⊕ *www.johnbauer.se* ⇄ *100 rooms* ♨ *Restaurant* ⊟ *AE, DC, MC, V.*

Växjö

The hub of Sweden's Glass Country is Växjö, the main town in Kronoberg County. Some 10,000 Americans visit Växjö each year, drawn here by a desire to see where their ancestors emigrated from in the 19th century. The **Utvandrareshus** (Emigrants' House; ⊠ Vilhelm Mosbergsg. 4 ☏ 0470/20120), in the town center, tells the story of the immigration period, when close to a million Swedes—a fourth of the entire population—set sail for the promised land across the sea. People of Swedish descent can trace their ancestry in a research center.

Swedish glass manufacture dates from the middle of the 16th century, when Venetian glassblowers were first invited to the Swedish court. The dense forests between Växjö and Kalmar were seen as an unlimited supply of wood for firing furnaces, and by the 18th century glassmaking had become a major industry in Sweden. All the major Swedish glass companies still operate in this area, and their plants are open to the public. The factory shops sometimes give huge discounts. Be sure to visit Fodor'sChoice **Orrefors** (⊠ Follow signposts ☏ 0481/34195 ⊕ www.orrefors.se) for ★ quality Swedish crystal. **Kosta Boda** (⊠ Follow signposts ☏ 0478/34500 tours ⊕ www.kostaboda.se) has been producing fine glassware for more than 200 years.

$$ ⊞ **Elite Statshotel.** This conveniently located traditional hotel is now part of the Swedish Elite group. The building dates from 1853; the rooms themselves are modern but classic. The hotel has a cozy Irish pub and two restaurants. ⊠ *Kungsg. 6, 352 33* ☏ *0470/13400* 🖷 *0470/44837* ⊕ *www.elite.se* ⇄ *124 rooms* ♨ *2 restaurants* ⊟ *AE, DC, MC, V.*

$ ⊞ **Esplanad.** This small family hotel in the center of town offers basic amenities. ⊠ *Norra Esplanaden 21A, 352 31* ☏ *0470/22580* 🖷 *0470/ 26226* ⇄ *27 rooms* ⊟ *MC, V.*

Kalmar

Fodor'sChoice In this bustling coastal town the imposing 12th-century **Kalmar Slott** ★ (Kalmar Castle) stands as a reminder of the time when Kalmar was the "lock and key" of Sweden. Situated on the eastern coast, it was often attacked by Baltic raiders. Most of the present-day castle dates from the days of King Gustav Vasa, who rebuilt the fortress in the 16th century. ⊠ *Slottsv.* ☏ *0480/451490* ⊕ *www.kalmarslott.kalmar.se* ☉ *Apr., May, and Sept., daily 10–4; June and Aug., daily 10–5; July, daily 10–6; Oct.–Mar., daily 11–3:30.*

$-$$ ⊞ **Scandic Stadshotellet.** In the center of town, this large hotel is decorated in a traditional English style. Rooms are smart and spacious. The main building dates from 1907. ⊠ *Stortorget 14, 392 32* ☏ *0480/ 496900* 🖷 *0480/496910* ⊕ *www.scandic-hotels.com* ⇄ *139 rooms* ♨ *Restaurant* ⊟ *AE, DC, MC, V.*

$-$$ ⊞ **Slottshotellet.** Occupying a gracious old house on a quiet street, this hotel faces a waterfront park and is a few minutes' walk from both the train station and Kalmar Castle. Inside, the facilities are modern, but the furnishings are traditional. Restaurant service is offered on the terrace in summer. ✉ *Slottsv. 7, 392 33* ☎ *0480/88260* 🖷 *0480/88266* ⊕ *www.romantikhotels.com* ⤴ *36 rooms* ♨ *Restaurant* 🖃 *AE, DC, MC, V.*

The West Coast & the Glass Country Essentials

AIR TRAVEL

SAS operates hourly flights to Göteborg from Stockholm's Arlanda Airport between 7 AM and 10 PM on weekdays, less frequently on weekends. The flight takes 55 minutes.

CAR TRAVEL

Göteborg is 478 km (297 mi) west of Stockholm along the E20. Malmö is 620 km (386 mi) from Stockholm. Take the E4 to Helsingborg, then the E6/E20 to Malmö and Lund. If you're approaching from Copenhagen, take the Öresund Bridge.

TOURS

Summer sightseeing tours around Göteborg usually begin at the city tourist office on Kungsportsplatsen 2 (reserve tickets at the office in advance). Tour boats run frequently in summer; a central reservations service will book you with either Paddans Sightseeing or Börjessons Sightseeing. Helsingborg and Malmö also offer summer sightseeing tours, arranged through the local tourist information.

🖪 **Central reservations service** ☎ 031/609660.

TRAIN TRAVEL

Regular trains departs from Stockholm's Central Station for Göteborg, Helsingborg, and Malmö. High-speed X2000 trains travel between Stockholm and Göteborg and Stockholm and Malmö. A train service also runs from Copenhagen to Malmö over the Öresund Bridge. Trains depart every 20 minutes.

TRANSPORTATION AROUND THE WEST COAST & THE GLASS COUNTRY

In Göteborg, the best and cheapest way to get around is with the Göteborg Card. It provides free travel on all public transportation, free parking, and free admission to the Liseberg amusement park and all city museums. The card costs SKr 175 for 24 hours.

VISITOR INFORMATION

🖪 **Göteborg** ✉ Kungsportsplatsen 2 ☎ 031/612500 ⊕ www.goteborg.com. **Helsingborg** ✉ Stortorget Södra Storg. 1 ☎ 042/104350 ⊕ www.visit.helsingborg.se. **Jönköping** ✉ Juneporten ☎ 036/105050 ⊕ www.jonkoping.se. **Kalmar** ✉ Larmg. 6 ☎ 0480/15350 ⊕ www.kalmar.se. **Malmö** ✉ Central Station ☎ 040/341200 ⊕ www.malmo.se. **Växjö** ✉ Kungsg. 11 ☎ 0470/41410 ⊕ www.turism.vaxjo.se.

SWITZERLAND

ZÜRICH, GENEVA, LUZERN, LUGANO, BERN, ZERMATT

THE PARADOX OF SWITZERLAND is its penchant for both high-tech efficiency and rustic flavor. Not far from the hum of commerce in the streets of Zürich you can listen to the tinkle of cowbells on the slopes of the Klewenalp. While fur-wrapped and bejeweled socialites shop in Geneva, the women of Appenzell, across the country, stand beside their husbands on the Landsgemeinde-Platz, raising their hands to vote in local elections—a right they won only in 1991. Alcohol here is measured with scientific precision into glasses marked for 1 or 2 deciliters (⅓ or ⅔ ounces), and the local wines come in graduated carafes reminiscent of laboratory beakers.

Switzerland combines most of the attractions of its larger European neighbors—Alpine grandeur, urban sophistication, ancient villages, exhilarating ski slopes, and all-around artistic excellence. It's the heartland of the Reformation, the homeland of William Tell; its cities are full of historic landmarks, its countryside strewn with castles. The varied cuisine reflects French, Italian, and German influences. All these assets have made Switzerland a major tourist destination, and the Swiss are delighted to pave the way.

SWITZERLAND A TO Z

To research prices, get advice from other travelers, and book travel arrangements, visit www.fodors.com.

AIR TRAVEL

CARRIERS Swiss International Airlines (SIA or Swiss) connects airports in Zürich, Basel, and Geneva, servicing local airports and various Continental cities as well, including Rome, Barcelona, Berlin, Amsterdam, and London. The airline's in-house tour operator, Swisspack, arranges flexible packages for the independent traveler who flies at least one way between North America and Europe on Swiss. "Fly-Rail Baggage" allows SIA passengers departing Switzerland to check their bags at any of 120 rail or postal bus stations throughout the country; luggage is automatically transferred to the airplane. At many Swiss railway stations, passengers may complete all check-in procedures for SIA flights, including picking up their boarding pass and checking their bags.

🛫 **Swiss** ☎ 800/221-4750 in U.S.; 0845/6010956 in U.K. **Swisspack** ✉ 106 Calvert St., Harrison, NY 10528 ☎ 800/688-7947.

BIKE TRAVEL

Bikes can be rented at some 200 train stations and returned to most stations. (If you return a bike to a station other than the one from which

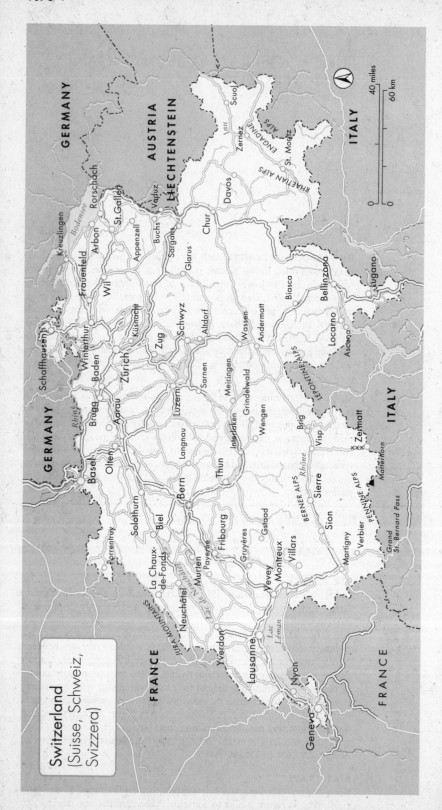

Switzerland
(Suisse, Schweiz, Svizzera)

you rented it, there's a service charge of 6 SF per bike if you've notified the station where you've rented in advance and double that if you have not.) Rates for standard or mountain bikes are 30 SF per day, and 210 SF per week. Individuals must make a reservation by 6 PM the day before they plan to use the bike, groups a week in advance.

BOAT & FERRY TRAVEL

Drifting across a Swiss lake and stopping off here and there at picturesque villages makes for a relaxing day trip, especially on one of the elegant old paddle steamers. Trips are scheduled on most of the lakes year-round. Unlimited travel is free to holders of the Swiss Pass. For those not traveling by train, there is also a Swiss Boat Pass (35 SF), which allows half-fare travel on all lake steamers for the entire calendar year. If you don't hold one of the passes, a day pass for all lines costs 66 SF for first class and 44 SF for second class. For the many short-hop trips also available, prices vary accordingly.

🏠 **Schifffahrtsgesellschaft des Vierwaldstettersees** ✉ Werftstr. 5, Box 4265, CH-6002 Luzern ☎ 041/3676767 🖷 0413676868 ⊕ www.lakelucerne.ch.

BUS TRAVEL

Switzerland's famous yellow postal buses (called *postauto* or *postcar*) link main cities with villages. Both postal and city buses follow posted schedules to the minute. Routes and timetables can be found in train timetable books, available in post offices. The Swiss Pass allows you unlimited travel on postal buses, which venture well beyond the rail routes.

BUSINESS HOURS

Banks are open weekdays 8:30–4:30 or 5 but are often closed at lunch. Many museums close on Monday—check locally. Shops are generally open 8–noon and 1:30–6:30, though some are open weekday evenings until 8. Some close Monday morning and at 4 or 5 on Saturday. In cities, many large stores do not close for lunch. All shops are closed on Sundays except those in resort areas during high season and in the Geneva and Zürich airports and train stations.

CAR TRAVEL

EMERGENCIES   Assistance is available by telephone: dial 140 and ask for *Strassenhilfe/Secours routier.*

GASOLINE   *Sans plomb* or *bleifrei* (lead-free) gasoline costs 1.29 SF per liter; super costs 1.31 SF per liter.

PARKING   Areas are clearly marked and parking times are signposted. Blue and red zones, which require a *disque* to be displayed in the windshield, are slowly being replaced by metered white zones. Some machines in these zones simply accept coins and dispense tickets. At others, you'll need to punch in your parking space number, then add coins. The parking ticket may or may not have to be placed in your car window; this information is noted on the machine or ticket. The disques (provided in rental cars or available from banks, tourist offices, or police stations) must be placed clearly in the front window. Make sure that the arrow on the disque is indicating the proper arrival time; the arrow will also indicate the corresponding departure time so you will know how long you may use the space. Parking in public lots normally costs about 2 SF per hour.

ROAD CONDITIONS   Conditions are usually excellent due to well-surfaced roads. Note that roads—especially in the mountains—wind about considerably. Don't plan to achieve high average speeds. When estimating likely travel times, look carefully at the map: there may be only 32 km (20 mi) between one point and another, but there could also be a mountain pass along the way. Switzerland has a well-developed highway network, though some notable gaps still exist in the south along an east–west line, roughly between Lugano and Sion. Under some mountain passes, there are tunnels through which cars are transported by train while passengers remain inside—an experience not unlike riding through the world's longest car wash. A combination of steep or winding routes and hazardous weather conditions may close some roads during the winter. Dial 163 for bulletins and advance information on road conditions.

RULES OF THE ROAD
The Swiss drive on the right. Priority is given to the driver on the right except in roundabouts. In built-up areas, the speed limit is 50 kph (30 mph), and on main highways, it's 120 kph (75 mph). On other roads outside built-up areas, the limit is 80 kph (50 mph). Pass on the left only. Fines for speeding are exorbitant and foreigners are required to pay on the spot—in cash. Children under seven are not permitted to sit in the front seat. The use of seat belts in both the front and rear seats is mandatory. Driving with parking lights is prohibited, and the use of headlights is mandatory during heavy rain and in road tunnels. To use the main highways, you must display a sticker, or *vignette,* which you can buy for 40 SF from Switzerland Tourism before you leave home, at the border stations when you enter the country, or at post offices and most gas stations. Cars rented in Switzerland already have these stickers. Traffic going up a mountain has priority, except when postal buses are coming down (signs showing a yellow post horn against a blue background indicate that postal buses have right-of-way). During the winter, snow chains are advisable—sometimes mandatory. They can be rented in all areas, and snow-chain service stations have signs reading SERVICE DE CHAÎNES À NEIGE or SCHNEEKETTENDIENST.

CUSTOMS & DUTIES

For details on imports and duty-free limits, *see* Customs & Duties *in* Smart Travel Tips.

EATING & DRINKING

Switzerland produces great cheeses—Gruyère, Emmentaler, Appenzeller, and Vacherin—that form the basis of many dishes. Raclette is cheese melted over a fire and served with potatoes and pickles. Fondue is either a bubbling pot of melted cheeses flavored with garlic and kirsch, into which you dip chunks of bread or boiled potatoes, or a pot of boiling broth (*chinois*) or oil (*bourgignon*) into which you dip various meats. *Rösti* is grated potato sautéed until golden brown. Other Swiss specialties are *geschnetzeltes Kalbfleisch* (veal bits in cream sauce with mushrooms), Italian-style polenta in the Ticino, and fine game in autumn. A wide variety of Swiss sausages or air-dried beef with *pommes frites* (french fries) and salad makes for filling, inexpensive meals, and in every region the breads are varied and superb. Fresh or smoked fish from the many lakes is always a treat.

Dining options range from luxury establishments to modest cafés and *Stübli* (tavern-cafés) specializing in local cuisine. In resorts especially, most restaurants are associated with hotels, and the half-pension plan includes a hot meal in the room rate. Watch for *Tagesteller* or *plats du jour* (prix-fixe lunch platters or menus), enabling you to a taste of the best restaurants without paying high à la carte rates.

WHAT IT COSTS in Swiss francs			
$$$$	**$$$**	**$$**	**$**
ZÜRICH/GENEVA/RESORT AREAS			
PER PERSON over 50	30–50	20–30	under 20
OTHER AREAS			
AT DINNER over 40	30–40	20–30	under 20

Prices are per person for a main course at dinner.

MEALTIMES At home, the main Swiss meal of the day is lunch, followed by a light snack in the evening. Restaurants are open at midday and at night; often limited menus are offered all day. Dinner is served around 6 or 7 PM in the Germanic regions, a bit later in the French- and Italian-speaking areas.

RESERVATIONS & Jacket and tie are suggested for restaurants in the $$$$ and $$$ cate-
DRESS gories (except in more relaxed ski resorts); casual dress is acceptable elsewhere.

EMBASSIES
For the New Zealand consulate, *see* Geneva Essentials.
🏳 Australia ✉ Chemin des Fins 2, Geneva ☎ 022/7999100.
🏳 Canada ✉ Kirchenfeldstr. 88, Bern ☎ 031/3573200.
🏳 Ireland ✉ Kirchenfeldstr. 68, Bern ☎ 031/3521442.
🏳 South Africa ✉ Alpenstr. 29, Bern ☎ 031/3501313.
🏳 United Kingdom ✉ Thunstr. 50, Bern ☎ 031/3597700.
🏳 United States ✉ Jubiläumsstr. 93, Bern ☎ 031/3577011.

HOLIDAYS
New Year's (January 1–2); Good Friday; Easter Sunday and Monday; Ascension; Whitsunday, Pentecost; National Day (August 1); Christmas (December 25–26). Note that May 1 (Labor Day) is celebrated in most cantons, but not all.

LANGUAGE
French is spoken in the southwest, around Lake Geneva (Lac Léman), and in the cantons of Fribourg, Neuchâtel, Jura, Vaud, and the western portion of Valais; Italian is spoken in the Ticino; and German is spoken everywhere else—in more than 70% of the country, in fact. (Keep in mind that the Swiss versions of these languages can sound very different from those spoken in France, Italy, and Germany.) The Romance language called Romansh has regained a firm foothold throughout the Upper and Lower Engadine regions of the canton Graubünden, where it expresses itself in five different dialects. English is spoken widely. Many signs are in English as well as in the regional language, and all hotels, restaurants, tourist offices, train stations, banks, and shops have at least a few English-speaking employees.

LODGING
Hotels and inns here are famous for cleanliness and efficiency, and the notoriously high prices do mirror the quality you'll receive in return. Pick up the "Schweizer Hotelführer" ("Swiss Hotel Guide") from Switzerland Tourism for 15 SF. The guide lists all members of the Swiss Hotel Association (SHA).

Some hotels may still practice the old tradition of separate beds or, at best, a double with separate bedding. For a standard double bed, request a "French bed" or a *lit matrimonial*. Service charges and taxes are included in the price quoted. Continental breakfast is usually included.

In resorts especially, half pension (choice of a noon or evening meal) is often encouraged and included in the room price. If you choose to eat à la carte or elsewhere, the management, if notified in advance, will usually reduce your price.

WHAT IT COSTS In Swiss francs			
$$$$	$$$	$$	$
ZÜRICH/GENEVA/RESORT AREAS			
HOTELS over 350	250–350	150–250	under 150
OTHER AREAS			
FOR 2 PEOPLE over 300	200–300	120–200	under 120

Prices are for two people in a double room with bath or shower, including taxes, service charges, and Continental breakfast.

HOTELS The Swiss Hotel Association grades from one to five stars. Always confirm the price before you register, and check the posted price in your room. Often, rates will be quoted on a per-person basis; single rooms are about two-thirds the price of doubles, but this can vary considerably. Romantik Hotels and Restaurants and Relais & Châteaux have premises in either historic houses or houses with some special character. First-class Relais du Silence hotels are usually isolated in a peaceful setting. The E&G (*einfach und gemütlich,* or "Simple and Cozy") Swiss Budget Hotels are dependable small hotels, boardinghouses, and mountain lodges.

🔳 **Swiss Budget Hotels** ☎ 0848/805508 ⊕ www.rooms.ch. **Relais & Châteaux** ☎ 800/735-2478 in U.S.; 00800/20000002 in Switzerland ⊕ www.relaischateaux. com. **Romantik Hotels and Restaurants** ☎ 049/0696612340 main office in Germany ⊕ www.romantikhotels.com.

MAIL & SHIPPING

You can have your mail, marked *poste restante* or *postlagernd,* sent to any post office in Switzerland. The sender's name and address must be on the back, and you'll need identification to collect it.

POSTAL RATES Mail rates are divided into first-class "A" (air mail) and second-class "B" (surface). Letters and postcards to the United States up to 20 grams cost 1.80 SF first-class, 1.40 SF second-class; to the United Kingdom, 1.30 SF first-class, 1.20 SF second-class.

MONEY MATTERS

You'll pay more for luxury here than in almost any other European country, and Switzerland's exorbitant cost of living makes travel noticeably expensive. You'll find plenty of reasonably priced digs and eats, however, if you look for them.

Zürich and Geneva are Switzerland's priciest cities, followed by Basel, Bern, and Lugano. Price tags at resorts—especially the better-known Alpine ski centers—rival those in the cities. Off the beaten track and in the northeast, prices drop considerably.

Some sample prices include cup of coffee, 3 SF; bottle of beer, 3.50 SF; soft drink, 3.50 SF; sausage and Rösti, 16 SF; 2-km (1-mi) taxi ride, 12 SF (more in Geneva, Lugano, Zürich).

CREDIT CARDS Most major credit cards are generally, though not universally, accepted at hotels, restaurants, and shops. Traveler's checks are almost never accepted outside banks and railroad station change counters.

CURRENCY The unit of currency is the Swiss franc (SF), divided into 100 centimes (in Suisse Romande) or rappen (in German Switzerland). There are coins of 5, 10, 20, and 50 rappen/centimes and of 1, 2, and 5 francs. Bills come in denominations of 10, 20, 50, 100, 200, and 1,000 francs. Many stores in the major cities accept payment in euros; change is given in Swiss francs. At press time (sumer 2003) the Swiss franc stood at 1.38 SF to the U.S. dollar, 0.93 SF to the Canadian dollar, 1.48 SF to the euro, 0.83 SF to the Australian dollar, 0.75 SF to the New Zealand dollar, and.017 SF to the South African rand.

TAXES

A 7.6% value-added tax (V.A.T.) is included in the price of all goods. Nonresidents spending at least 400 SF (including V.A.T.) at one time at a particular store may get a V.A.T. refund. To obtain a refund, pay by credit card; at the time of purchase, the store clerk should fill out and give you a red form and keep a record of your credit card number. When leaving Switzerland, you must hand deliver the red form to a customs officer—at the customs office at the airport or, if leaving by car or train, at the border. Customs will process the form and return it to the store, which will refund the tax by crediting your card.

TELEPHONES

COUNTRY & The country code for Switzerland is 41, for Liechtenstein 423. When
AREA CODES dialing Switzerland from outside the country, drop the initial zero from the area code.

INTERNATIONAL To dial international numbers directly from Switzerland, dial 00 before
CALLS the country's code. If a number cannot be reached directly, dial 1141 for a connection. Dial 1159 for international numbers and information. International access codes will put you directly in touch with an operator who will place your call. Calls to the United States and Canada cost 0.12 SF per minute; calls to the United Kingdom, Australia, and New Zealand cost 0.25 SF per minute. International telephone rates are lower on weekends.
🔖 Access Codes **AT&T** ☎ 0800/890011. **MCI WorldCom** ☎ 0800/890222. **Sprint** ☎ 0800/899777.

PUBLIC PHONES Since the cell phone boom, the number of public phone booths in Switzerland has been drastically reduced, but they can still be found at train stations, town centers, and in shopping districts. Calls from booths are far cheaper than those made from hotels. A phone card, available in 5 SF, 10 SF, and 20 SF units at the post office, kiosk, or train station, allows you to call from any public phone. Note that very few public phones accept coins.

TIPPING

Although restaurants include service charges of 15% along with the taxes in bills, a small tip is still expected: a bit of change for a light meal, 1 to 2 SF for a modest meal, 5 to 10 SF for a first-class meal, and at least 10 SF at an exclusive gastronomic mecca. When possible, tip in cash. Elsewhere, give bathroom attendants 1 SF and hotel maids 2 SF. Theater and opera-house ushers get 2 SF. Hotel porters and doormen should get about 2 SF per bag in an upscale hotel, 1 SF elsewhere. Airport porters receive 5 SF per bag.

TRAIN TRAVEL

Swiss trains are swift (except through the mountains), immaculate, and punctual. Don't linger between connections: Swiss Federal Railways (CFF/SBB) runs a tight ship. A useful booklet, "Swiss Travel System," available from Switzerland Tourism, describes passes, itineraries, and discounts available to rail travelers. Apply for tickets through your travel agent or Rail Europe.

Inter-City or Express trains are the fastest, stopping only at principal towns. A *Regionalzug/Train Régional* is a local train, often affording the most spectacular views. Seat reservations are useful during rush hours and high season, especially on international trains and in second class. Travelers holding tickets or passes on Swiss Federal Railways can forward their luggage to their final destination.

The Holiday Pass gives unlimited free regional travel for three or seven consecutive days on many rail routes and local bus routes and a 30% to 50% discount on PTT buses and other lines. Available at the tourist office or train station, they cost 46 SF for three days, 66 SF for seven days.

The Swiss Card, which can be purchased in the United States through Rail Europe, is valid for 30 days and grants full round-trip travel from your arrival point to any destination in the country, plus a half-price reduction on any further excursions during your stay (170 SF second-class, 242 SF first-class). For more information, get the free "Swiss Travel System" or "Discover Switzerland" brochure from Switzerland Tourism. You can also get information from Swiss Federal Railways line.

CUTTING COSTS | The Swiss Pass is the best value, offering unlimited travel on Swiss Federal Railways, postal buses, boats, and the local bus and tram services of 36 cities. It also gives reductions on many privately owned railways, cable cars, and funiculars. Available from Switzerland Tourism and from travel agents outside Switzerland, the card is valid for 4 days, 15 days, or one month. There is also a three-day Flexi Pass, which offers the same unlimited travel options as a regular Swiss Pass for any three days within a month. A 15% discount is offered for the Swiss Pass and the Flexi Pass for two or more people. The STS Family Card is issued free of charge, upon request; it allows children up to age 16 to travel free with a parent. In some popular tourist areas Regional Holiday Season Tickets are available, providing discounts on fares. Prices vary widely, depending upon the region and period of validity.

FARES & SCHEDULES | If you plan to use the trains extensively, get a comprehensive timetable (*Offizieles Kursbuch* or *Horaire*), which costs 16 SF, or a portable, pocket version called the *Reka* for 14 SF. Both are available from either Rail Europe or Swiss Federal Railways.
Rail Europe ✉ 226–230 Westchester Ave., White Plains, NY 10604 ☎ 800/438-7245. **Swiss Federal Railways** ☎ 0900/300300, 1.19 SF/min ⊕ www.sbb.ch.

VISITOR INFORMATION
Switzerland Tourism ✉ Tödistr. 7, Postfach, CH-8027 Zürich ☎ 01/2881111 🖷 01/2881205 ⊕ www.myswitzerland.com. **Switzerland Tourism London** ✉ 10 Wardour St., W1D 6QF London ☎ 00800/10020030 🖷 00800/10020031. **Switzerland Tourism New York** ✉ 608 Fifth Ave., New York, NY 10020 ☎ 877/794-8037 🖷 212/262-6116.

WHEN TO GO
Winter sports begin around Christmas and usually last until mid-April, depending on snow conditions. The countryside is a delight in spring, when wildflowers are in bloom, and foliage colors (and clear skies) in fall rival those in New England. In the Ticino, or the Italian-speaking region, and around Lake Geneva (Lac Léman), summer often lingers with warm weather in September and October.

CLIMATE | Summer is generally warm and sunny, though the higher you go, the cooler it gets. Winter is cold everywhere: in low-lying areas it is frequently damp and foggy or overcast and rainy, while in the Alps above 1,000–1,200 meters (3,600–4,200 feet) days are either brilliantly clear and cold, or snowy.

In summer and winter, some areas of Switzerland are subject to an Alpine wind that blows from the south and is known as the *Föhn*. It brings clear warm weather. The wind that blows from the north is called the *Bise* and can create very cool summer days; in winter, it chills to the bone. The only exception to these more general weather patterns is the Ticino; protected by the Alps, it has a positively Mediterranean climate—even in winter.

The following are the average daily maximum and minimum temperatures for Zürich.

Jan.	36F	2C	May	67F	19C	Sept.	69F	20C
	26	–3		47	8		51	11
Feb.	41F	5C	June	73F	23C	Oct.	57F	14C
	28	–2		53	12		43	6
Mar.	51F	11C	July	76F	25C	Nov.	45F	7C
	34	1		56	14		35	2
Apr.	59F	15C	Aug.	75F	24C	Dec.	37F	3C
	40	–4		56	14		29	–2

ZÜRICH

Stroll around on a fine spring day and you'll ask yourself if this city, with its glistening lake, swans on the river, sidewalk cafés, and hushed old squares of medieval guild houses, can really be one of the great business centers of the world. There's not a gnome—a mocking nickname for a Swiss banker—in sight. For all its economic importance, this is a place where people enjoy life.

Zürich started in 15 BC as a Roman customs post on the Lindenhof overlooking the Limmat River, but its growth really began around the 10th century AD. It became a free imperial city in 1336, a center of the Reformation in 1519, and gradually assumed commercial importance during the 1800s. Today the Zürich stock exchange is the fourth largest in the world, and the city's extraordinary museums and galleries and luxurious shops along the Bahnhofstrasse, Zürich's 5th Avenue, attest to its position as Switzerland's cultural—if not political—capital.

Exploring Zürich

Numbers in the margin correspond to points of interest on the Zürich map.

Although Zürich is Switzerland's largest city, it has a population of only 360,000 and is small enough to be explored on foot. The Limmat River, crisscrossed with lovely low bridges, bisects the city. On the left bank are the Altstadt (Old Town), the polished section of the old medieval center; the Hauptbahnhof, the main train station; and the Bahnhofplatz, a major urban crossroads and the beginning of the world-famous luxury shopping street, Bahnhofstrasse. The right bank, divided into the Oberdorf (Upper Village), toward Bellevueplatz, and the Niederdorf (Lower Village), around the Central, is young and lively and buzzes on weekends. The latest addition to the city's profile is Zürich West, an industrial neighborhood that's quickly being reinvented. Amid the cluster of cranes, former factories are being turned into spaces for restaurants, bars, art galleries, and dance clubs. Construction and restoration will most likely be ongoing well into 2006.

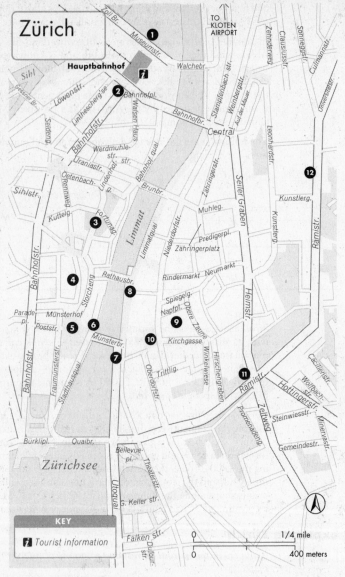

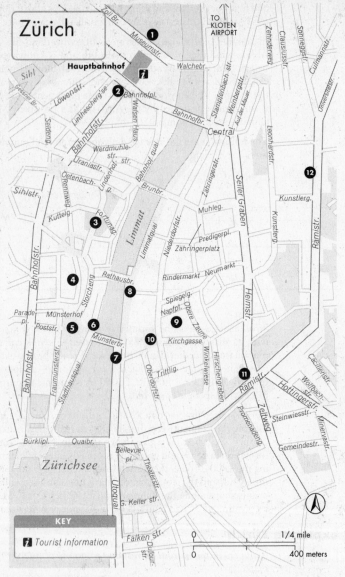 **Altstadt.** Zürich's medieval core is a maze of well-preserved streets and buildings easily explored on foot in a few hours. The area stretches from Bahnhofplatz to Bürkliplatz on the left bank. On the right bank of the city's historic center is a livelier section known as the **Niederdorf,** which reaches from Central to Bellevueplatz.

 Bahnhofstrasse. Zürich's principal boulevard offers concentrated luxury shopping, while much shifting and hoarding of the world's wealth takes place discreetly behind the upstairs windows of the banking institutions. ⊠ *Runs north–south, west of Limmat.*

★ **Fraumünster.** Of the church spires that are Zürich's signature, the Fraumünster's is the most delicate, a graceful sweep to a narrow spire. The Romanesque, or pre-Gothic, choir has stained-glass windows by

Chagall. ✉ *Stadthausquai* 🕐 *May–Sept., Mon.–Sat. 9–6; Mar.–Apr. and Oct., Mon.–Sat. 10–5; Nov.–Feb., Mon.–Sat. 10–4.*

⑫ Graphische Sammlung (Graphic Collection). This impressive collection of the Federal Institute of Technology displays portions of its vast holdings of woodcuts, etchings, and engravings by European masters such as Dürer, Rembrandt, Goya, and Picasso. ✉ *Rämistr. 101* 📞 *01/6324046* 🕐 *Mon.–Tues. and Thurs.–Fri. 10–5, Wed. 10–7.*

★ **⑩ Grossmünster** (Great Church). In the 3rd century AD, St. Felix and his sister Regula were martyred nearby by the Romans. Legend maintains that having been beheaded, they then walked up the hill carrying their heads and collapsed on the spot where the Grossmünster now stands. On the south tower of this 11th-century structure you can see a statue of Charlemagne (768–814), who is said to have founded the church when his horse stumbled on the same site. In the 16th century, the Zürich reformer Huldrych Zwingli preached sermons here that were so threatening in their promise of fire and brimstone that Martin Luther himself was frightened. ✉ *Zwinglipl.* 📞 *01/2513860* 🕐 *Mid-Mar.–Oct., daily 9–6; Nov.–mid-Mar., daily 10–5.*

★ **⑪ Kunsthaus.** With a varied, high-quality permanent collection of paintings—medieval, Dutch and Italian baroque, and impressionist—the Kunsthaus is Zürich's best art museum. There's a rich collection of works by Swiss artists, though some could be an acquired taste. Besides those of Ferdinand Hodler (1853–1918), there are darkly ethereal paintings by Johann Heinrich Füssli and a terrifying *Walpurgisnacht* by Albert Welti. Other European artists, including Picasso, Klee, Degas, Matisse, Kandinsky, Chagall, and Munch, are satisfyingly represented. ✉ *Heimpl. 1* 📞 *01/2538484* 🌐 *www.kunsthaus.ch* 🕐 *Tues.–Thurs. 10–9, Fri.–Sun. 10–5.*

③ Lindenhof. A Roman customhouse and fortress and a Carolingian palace once stood on the site of this quiet square overlooking both sides of the river. A fountain commemorates the day in 1292 when Zürich's women saved the city from the Habsburgs. As the story goes, the town was on the brink of defeat when its women donned armor and marched to the Lindenhof. On seeing them, the enemy thought they were faced with another army and promptly beat a strategic retreat. ✉ *Bordered by Fortunag. to west and intersected by Lindenhofstr.*

⑧ Rathaus (Town Hall). Zürich's 17th-century town hall is strikingly baroque, with its interior as well preserved as its facade. There's a richly decorated stucco ceiling in the Banquet Hall and a fine ceramic stove in the government council room. ✉ *Limmatquai 55* 🕐 *Tues., Thurs., and Fri. 10–11:30 AM.*

④ St. Peters Kirche (St. Peter's Church). Zürich's oldest parish church, dating from the early 13th century, has the largest clock face in Europe. ✉ *St. Peterhofstatt* 🕐 *Weekdays 8–6, Sat. 8–4.*

★ **① Schweizerisches Landesmuseum** (Swiss National Museum). In a gargantuan neo-Gothic building, this museum possesses an enormous collection of objects dating from the Stone Age to modern times, including costumes, furniture, early watches, and a great deal of military history, including thousands of toy soldiers reenacting battles. ✉ *Museumstr. 2* 📞 *01/2186511* 🌐 *www.musee-suisse.ch* 🕐 *Tues.–Sun. 10:30–5.*

⑦ Wasserkirche (Water Church). This is one of Switzerland's most delicate late-Gothic structures; its stained glass is by Augusto Giacometti. ✉ *Limmatquai 31* 🕐 *Tues. and Wed. 2–5.*

6 **Zunfthaus zur Meisen.** Erected for the city's wine merchants during the 18th century, this baroque guildhall today houses the Landesmuseum's exquisite ceramics collection. ✉ *Münsterhof 20* ☎ *01/2212807* ⊕ *www.musee-suisse.ch* ⊙ *Tues.–Sun. 10:30–5.*

Where to Eat

Since the mid-1990s, new restaurants, both Swiss and international, have been sprouting up all over town. The newcomers tend to favor lighter cuisine and bright rooms, frequently open to the street. Prices are often steep; for savings, watch for posted Tagesteller lunches.

$$$$ ✕ **Petermann's Kunststuben.** This is one of Switzerland's culinary desti-
FodorśChoice nations, and although it's south of the city center—in Küssnacht on the
★ lake's eastern shore—it's more than worth the 8-km (5-mi) pilgrimage. The ever-evolving menu may include lobster with artichoke and almond oil or Tuscan dove with pine nuts and herbs. Come here for serious, world-class food—and prices to match. ✉ *Seestr. 160, Küssnacht* ☎ *01/9100715* ⌀ *Reservations essential* ▭ *AE, DC, MC, V* ⊙ *Closed Sun. and Mon., 2 wks in Feb., and 3 wks in late summer.*

★ **$$$–$$$$** ✕ **Kronenhalle.** From Stravinsky, Brecht, and Joyce to Nureyev, Deneuve, and Saint-Laurent, this beloved landmark has always drawn a stellar crowd for its genial, formal but relaxed atmosphere; hearty cooking; and astonishing collection of 20th-century art. Try the roast chicken with garlic and rosemary, or lobster thermidore with *Spätzli* (tiny dumplings). Have a cocktail in the adjoining bar: anyone who's anyone in Zürich drinks here. ✉ *Rämistr. 4* ☎ *01/2516669* ⌀ *Reservations essential* ▭ *AE, DC, MC, V.*

$$$–$$$$ ✕ **Veltliner Keller.** Though its rich, carved-wood decor borrows from Graubündner Alpine culture, this ancient dining spot is no tourist-trap transplant: the house, built in 1325, has functioned as a restaurant since 1551. There is a definite emphasis on the heavy and the meaty, but the kitchen is flexible and reasonably deft with more modern favorites as well: sole in creamed pepper sauce, osso buco with saffron rice, and dessert mousses. ✉ *Schlüsselg. 8* ☎ *01/2254040* ▭ *AE, DC, MC, V* ⊙ *Closed weekends.*

$$–$$$ ✕ **La Salle.** This is a favorite of theatergoers heading for the Schiffbauhalle Theater, as it conveniently shares the same building. The glass, steel and concrete interior mixes well with the brick elements left from the original building. Elegantly dressed patrons enjoy delicate dishes such as breaded lamb fillet or sole in coconut-vanilla sauce, beneath an enormous Murano glass chandelier. A smaller version of the menu is available at the bar. ✉ *Schiffbaustr. 4* ☎ *01/2587071* ▭ *AE, DC, MC, V.*

★ **$$–$$$** ✕ **Oepfelchammer.** This was once the haunt of Zürich's beloved writer Gottfried Keller, and it still draws unpretentious literati. The bar is dark and riddled with graffiti, with sagging timbers and slanting floors; the welcoming little dining rooms have carved oak paneling, coffered ceilings, and damask linens. The traditional meats—calves' liver, veal, tripe in white wine sauce—come in generous portions; salads are fresh and seasonal. It's always packed and service can be slow. ✉ *Rindermarkt 12* ☎ *01/2512336* ▭ *MC, V* ⊙ *Closed Sun. and Mon.*

★ **$$–$$$** ✕ **Zunfthaus zur Zimmerleuten/Küferstube.** While the pricier Zunfthaus upstairs is often overwhelmed with conference crowds, at basement level a cozy, candlelighted haven dubbed "Coopers' Pub" serves meals in a dark-beamed, Old Zürich setting. Standard dishes have enough novelty to stand apart: strawberry risotto with asparagus, roasted duck breast in mango sauce, and homemade cinnamon ice cream with wine-poached pears. ✉ *Limmatquai 40* ☎ *01/2505363* ▭ *AE, DC, MC, V.*

$–$$ ✕ **Adler's Swiss Chuchi.** Right on the Niederdorf's busy main square, Hirschenplatz, this squeaky-clean, Swiss-kitsch restaurant has an airy, modern decor, with carved fir, Alpine-rustic chairs. The fondue stands out among the good home-cooked national specialties. Excellent lunch menus are rock-bottom cheap and served double-quick. ✉ *Roseng. 10* ☎ *01/2669666* ▭ *AE, DC, MC, V.*

★ **$–$$** ✕ **Bierhalle Kropf.** Under the mounted boar's head and restored century-old murals, businesspeople, workers, and shoppers share crowded tables to feast on generous portions of traditional Alamannic cuisine, in which no part of an animal is ever wasted. Whether pig's knuckles or ribs, liver dumplings or one of the huge selection of sausages—add potatoes on the side and wash it down with a foamy local lager. ✉ *In Gassen 16* ☎ *01/2211805* ▭ *AE, DC, MC, V* ☉ *Closed Sun.*

$–$$ ✕ **Reithalle.** In a downtown theater complex behind the Bahnhofstrasse, this old military horse barn is now a noisy and popular restaurant, with candles perched on the mangers and beams and heat ducts exposed. Young locals share long tables arranged mess-hall style to sample French and Italian specialties, many vegetarian, and an excellent, international blackboard list of wines. ✉ *Gessnerallee 8* ☎ *01/2120766* ▭ *AE, MC, V.*

★ **$–$$** ✕ **Zeughauskeller.** Built as an arsenal in 1487, this enormous stone-and-beam hall offers truly affordable *Zurigschnätzlets* (sliced veal in mushroom sauce) and a variety of beers and wines amid comfortable, friendly chaos. The waitstaff is harried and brisk, especially at lunchtime, when the crowd is thick with locals—don't worry, just roll up your sleeves and dig in. ✉ *Bahnhofstr. 28, at Paradepl.* ☎ *01/2112690* ▭ *AE, DC, MC, V.*

$ ✕ **Les Halles.** This old warehouse space in Zürich West is enhanced with an eclectic mix of antiques and '50s collectibles. The fare is health conscious, made from organic ingredients sold in the attached health food store; try the couscous with vegetables or the chicken with peppers, tomatoes, and eggplant. ✉ *Pfingstweidstr. 6* ☎ *01/2731125* ▭ *AE, DC, MC, V.*

Where to Stay

Zürich has an enormous range of hotels, from chic and prestigious to modest. Deluxe hotels—the five-star landmarks—average between 500 SF and 800 SF per night for a double, and you'll be lucky to get a shower and toilet in your room for less than 160 SF. The Dolder Grand, one of the country's landmark hotels, will be closed for a major renovation beginning in summer 2004; for updates see their Web site, www.doldergrand.ch.

★ **$$$$** ▥ **Baur au Lac.** This is the highbrow patrician of Swiss hotels, with luxurious but low-key facilities—like the Rolls-Royce limousine service. Its broad back is turned to the commercial center, whereas its front rooms overlook the lake, canal, and manicured lawns of the hotel's private park. The decor is posh, discreet, and firmly fixed in the Age of Reason. ✉ *Talstr. 1, CH-8022* ☎ *01/2205020* 🖶 *01/2205044* ⊕ *www.bauraulac. ch* ⇌ *108 rooms, 17 suites* ⌕ *2 restaurants, bar* ▭ *AE, DC, MC, V.*

★ **$$$$** ▥ **Florhof.** In a quiet residential area by the Kunstmuseum, this is an anti-urban hotel—a gentle antidote to the bustle of downtown commerce. This Romantik property pampers guests with its polished wood, bluewillow fabrics, and wisteria-sheltered garden. ✉ *Florhofsg. 4, CH-8001* ☎ *01/2614470* 🖶 *01/2614611* ⊕ *www.florhof.ch* ⇌ *33 rooms, 2 suites* ⌕ *Restaurant* ▭ *AE, DC, MC, V.*

$$$$ ▥ **Splügenschloss.** Befitting its age (built in 1897 in the art nouveau style), this Relais & Châteaux property maintains its ornate, antiques-filled decor. One room is completely paneled in Alpine-style pine; others are decorated in fussy florals. Its location (a 10-minute walk from Paradeplatz) may be a little out of the way for sightseeing, but those who appreciate atmosphere will find it worth the effort. ⊠ *Splügenstr. 2, CH-8002* ☎ *01/ 2899999* 🖷 *01/2899998* ⊕ *www.splugenschloss.ch* ➯ *50 rooms, 2 suites* ⚴ *Restaurant, bar* ☰ *AE, DC, MC, V.*

$$$$
Fodor'sChoice
★

🖾 **Widder.** One of the city's most captivating hotels, the Widder revels in the present while preserving the past. Ten adjacent medieval houses were gutted and combined to create it. Behind every door is a fascinating mix of old and new—a guest room could pair restored 17th-century frescoes with a leather bedspread and private fax. ⊠ *Rennweg. 7, CH-8001* ☎ *01/2242526* 🖷 *01/2242424* ⊕ *www.widderhotel.ch* ➯ *42 rooms, 7 suites* ⚴ *2 restaurants, bar* ☰ *AE, DC, MC, V.*

★ **$$$$**
🖾 **Zum Storchen.** In a stunning central location, tucked between Fraumünster and St. Peters Kirche, this 600-year-old structure has become an impeccable modern hotel. It has warmly appointed rooms, some with French windows opening over the Limmat, and a lovely restaurant with riverfront terrace seating. ⊠ *Weinpl. 2, CH-8001* ☎ *01/2272727* 🖷 *01/ 2272700* ⊕ *www.storchen.ch* ➯ *73 rooms* ⚴ *Restaurant, bar* ☰ *AE, DC, MC, V.*

$$$–$$$$
🖾 **Haus zum Kindli.** This charming little bijou hotel could pass for a model Laura Ashley home, with every cushion and bibelot as artfully styled as a magazine ad. The result is welcoming, intimate, and a sight less contrived than most cookie-cutter hotels. At the Opus restaurant downstairs, guests get 10% off menu prices, though you may have to vie with locals for a table. ⊠ *Pfalzg. 1, CH-8001* ☎ *01/2115917* 🖷 *01/2116528* ➯ *21 rooms* ⚴ *Restaurant* ☰ *AE, DC, MC, V.*

$$–$$$
🖾 **Rössli.** This ultrasmall but friendly hotel is in the heart of Oberdorf. The chic white-on-white decor mixes stone and wood textures with bold textiles and mosaic bathrooms. Extras include safes and bathrobes—unusual in this price range. Some singles are tiny, but all have double beds. The top-floor suite has its own roof terrace. ⊠ *Rösslig. 7, CH-8001* ☎ *01/2567050* 🖷 *01/2567051* ⊕ *www.hotelroessli.ch* ➯ *16 rooms, 1 suite* ⚴ *Bar* ☰ *AE, DC, MC, V.*

$–$$
🖾 **Leoneck.** From the cowhide-covered front desk to the edelweiss-print curtains, this budget hotel wallows in its Swiss roots but balances this with no-nonsense conveniences: tile baths (with cow-print shower curtains) and built-in pine furniture. It's one stop from the Central tram stop, two from the Hauptbahnhof. ⊠ *Leonhardst. 1, CH-8001* ☎ *01/ 2542222* 🖷 *01/2542200* ⊕ *www.leoneck.ch* ➯ *65 rooms* ⚴ *Restaurant* ☰ *AE, DC, MC, V.*

$
🖾 **Limmathof.** This spare but welcoming city hotel inhabits a handsome historic shell and is ideally placed on the Limmatquai, minutes from the Hauptbahnhof. Rooms have tile bathrooms and plump down quilts. There's an old-fashioned *Weinstube* (wine bar), as well as a vegetarian restaurant that doubles as the breakfast room. ⊠ *Limmatquai 142, CH-8023* ☎ *01/2676040* 🖷 *01/2620217* ➯ *62 rooms* ⚴ *Restaurant* ☰ *AE, DC, MC, V.*

Nightlife & the Arts

Zürich's nightlife scene is largely centered in the Niederdorf area on the right bank of the Limmat. The small city supports a top-ranked orchestra, an opera company, and a theater. For information on goings-on, check *Zürich News*, published weekly in English and German. Also check "Züri-tipp," a German-language supplement to the Friday edition of the daily newspaper *Tages Anzeiger*. Tickets to opera, concert, and theater events can also be bought from the tourist office. **Ticketcorner** (☎ 0848/800800) allows you to purchase advance tickets by phone for almost any event.

Musik Hug (✉ Limmatquai 28–30 ☎ 01/2694100) can make reservations for selected events. **Jecklin** (✉ Rämistr. 30 ☎ 01/2537676) sells tickets for all major concert events, plus its own productions, which showcase small classical concerts and independent artists.

The Arts

During July or August, the **Theaterspektakel** takes place, with circus tents housing avant-garde theater and experimental performances on the lawns by the lake at Mythenquai. The Zürich Tonhalle Orchestra, named for its concert hall **Tonhalle** (✉ Claridenstr. 7 ☎ 01/2063434), was inaugurated by Brahms in 1895 and enjoys international acclaim. Tickets sell out quickly, so book directly through the Tonhalle. The music event of the year is the **Züricher Festspiele,** hosted by the Tonhalle. From late June to mid-July, orchestras and soloists from all over the world perform and plays and exhibitions are staged. Book well ahead. Details are available from the Tonhalle ticket office or on-line (⊕ www.zuercher-festspiele.ch).

Nightlife

BARS & LOUNGES   Not just for intellectuals, **I.Q.** (✉ Hardstr. 316 ☎ 01/4407440) has a good selection of whiskies. The **Jules Verne Panorama Bar** (✉ Uraniastr. 9 ☎ 01/2111155) shakes up cocktails with a wraparound downtown view. The narrow bar at the **Kronenhalle** (✉ Rämistr. 4 ☎ 01/2511597) draws mobs of well-heeled locals and internationals. Serving a young, arty set until 4 AM, **Odéon** (✉ Am Bellevue ☎ 01/2511650) is a cultural and historic landmark (Mata Hari danced here and James Joyce scrounged drinks).

DANCING   The medieval-theme **Adagio** (✉ Gotthardstr. 5 ☎ 01/2063666) offers classic rock, jazz, and tango to well-dressed thirtysomethings. **Kaufleuten** (✉ Pelikanstr. 18 ☎ 01/2253333) is a landmark dance club that draws a well-dressed, upwardly mobile crowd. **Mascotte** (✉ Theaterstr. 10 ☎ 01/2524481) draws all ages on weeknights, and a young crowd on weekends, for funk and soul.

JAZZ CLUBS   **Moods** (✉ Schiffbaustr. 6 ☎ 01/2768000) hosts international and local acts in the hip new Zürich West district. The **Widder Bar** (✉ Widderg. 6 ☎ 01/2242411), in the Hotel Widder, attracts local celebrities with its 800-count "library of spirits" and international jazz groups.

Shopping

One of the broadest assortments of watches in all price ranges is available at **Bucherer** (✉ Bahnhofstr. 50 ☎ 01/2112635). **Heimatwerk** (✉ Rudolf-Brun Brücke, Rennweg 14 and Bahnhofstr. 2 ☎ 01/2178317) specializes in Swiss handicrafts, all of excellent quality. **Jelmoli** (✉ Seideng. 1 ☎ 01/2204411), Switzerland's largest department store, carries a wide range of tasteful Swiss goods. You can snag some of last season's fashions at deep discounts at **Check Out** (✉ Tödistr. 44 ☎ 01/2027226), which jumbles chichi brands on thrift shop–style racks. If you have a

★   sweet tooth, stock up on truffles at **Sprüngli** (✉ Paradepl. ☎ 01/2244711). The renowned chocolatier **Teuscher** (✉ Storcheng. 9 ☎ 01/2115153) concocts a killer champagne truffle. For the latest couture, go to one of a dozen **Trois Pommes** (✉ Weggengasse 1 ☎ 01/2124710) boutiques featuring top-name designers such as Versace and Armani.

Side Trip from Zürich: Liechtenstein

For an international day trip out of Zürich, dip a toe into tiny Liechtenstein: there isn't room for much more. Just 80 km (50 mi) southeast on the Austrian border, this miniature principality covers a scant 158 square km (61 square mi). An independent nation since 1719, Liechtenstein has a customs union with Switzerland, which means they share trains, currency, and diplomats—but not stamps, which is why collectors prize the local releases. It's easiest to get there by car, since Swiss trains pass through without stopping. If you're using a train pass, ride to Sargans or Buchs. From there, local postal buses deliver mail and passengers across the border to Liechtenstein's capital, Vaduz.

Exploring Liechtenstein

Green and mountainous, with vineyards climbing its slopes, greater Liechtenstein is best seen by car; however, the postal buses are prompt and their routes are extensive.

VADUZ In fairy-tale Vaduz, Prince Johannes Adam Pius still lives in the castle, a massive 16th-century fortress perched high on the cliff above the city. Only honored guests of the prince tour the interior, but its exterior and the views from the grounds are worth the climb. In the modern town center, head for the tourist information office to have your passport stamped with the Liechtenstein crown.

The black polished-concrete block that houses the **Kunstmuseum Liechtenstein** (Liechtenstein Museum of Art) contains paintings, sculpture, and installations, charting the course of modern art from the Barbizon school of 1830 to more recent artists such as Joseph Beuys. It also showcases various segments of Prince Johannes Adam Pius's vast collection, mostly 14th- to 19th-century paintings with a focus on the Flemish school: Rembrandt, Reubens, Van Dyck. ⊠ *Städtle 32* ☎ *2350300* ⊕ *www.kunstmuseum.li* ⊘ *Tues., Wed., and Fri.–Sun. 10–5, Thurs. 10–8.*

The **Briefmarkenmuseum** (Stamp Museum) attracts philatelists from all over the world to see the 300 frames of beautifully designed and relatively rare stamps. ⊠ *Städtle 37* ☎ *2366105* ⊘ *Apr.–Oct., daily 10–noon and 1:30–5:30; Nov.–Mar., daily 10–noon and 1:30–5.*

BEYOND VADUZ In **Schaan**, just north of Vaduz, visit the Roman excavations and the parish church built on the foundations of a Roman fort. For spectacular views of the Rhine Valley, drive southeast of the capital to the chalets of picturesque **Triesenberg**. **Malbun** is a sun-drenched ski bowl with comfortable slopes and a low-key ambience.

Where to Stay & Eat

★ **$–$$** ✕ **Wirthschaft zum Löwen.** It may be tiny, but Liechtenstein has a cuisine of its own, and this is the place to try it. In a farmhouse on the Austrian border, the friendly Biedermann family serves pungent *Sauerkäse* (sour cheese) and *Käseknöpfli* (cheese dumplings), plus lovely meats and the local crusty, chewy bread. ⊠ *Schellenberg* ☎ *3731162* ▤ *No credit cards.*

★ **$$–$$$** ✕▦ **Real.** Surrounded by slick modern decor, you'll find rich, old-style Austrian-French cuisine in all its buttery glory. It's prepared by Martin Real, son of the unpretentious former chef Felix Real—who, in his retirement, presides over the 20,000-bottle wine cellar. The menu offers game, seafood, soufflés, and an extraordinary wine list. Downstairs is a more casual Stübli for those who don't feel like getting dressed up. Upstairs is a baker's dozen of small, airy rooms. ⊠ *Städtle 21, Vaduz FL-9490* ☎ *2322222* ▤ *2320891* ⊕ *www.hotel-real.li* ⟿ *11 rooms, 2 suites* ⟁ *Restaurant* ▤ *AE, DC, MC, V.*

$$$$ ▦ **Park-Hotel Sonnenhof.** A garden oasis commanding a superb view of the valley and mountains beyond, this hillside retreat in a residential district offers discreet luxury minutes from downtown Vaduz. Some rooms open directly onto the lawns; others have balconies. The excellent restaurant serves light French cuisine. ⊠ *Mareestr. 29, Vaduz FL-9490*

Fodor'sChoice
★

☎ *2321192* 🖨 *2320053* ⊕ *www.relaischateaux.ch/sonnenhof* ⇆ *17 rooms, 12 suites* ⚬ *Restaurant, pool* ▤ *AE, DC, MC, V.*

$$ 🍽 **Engel.** On the main tourist street, its café bulging with bus-tour crowds, this simple hotel manages to maintain a local, comfortable ambience. ⊠ *Städtle 13, Vaduz FL-9490* ☎ *2361717* 🖨 *2331159* ⇆ *20 rooms* ⚬ *2 restaurants* ▤ *AE, DC, MC, V.*

Liechtenstein Essentials

TELEPHONES
Liechtenstein now has its own country code, 423; from Switzerland call 00423 plus the local number.

VISITOR INFORMATION
🛈 **Liechtenstein Tourist office** ⊠ Städtle 37, Box 139, FL-9490 ☎ 2396300 ⊕ www.liechenstein.li.

Zürich Essentials

AIRPORTS & TRANSFERS
Unique Zürich Airport (ZRH), 11 km (7 mi) north of Zürich is Switzerland's most important airport. Several airlines fly directly to Zürich from major cities in the United States, Canada, and the United Kingdom.
🛈 **Unique Zürich Airport** ☎ 0900/300313.

TRANSFERS You can take a Swiss Federal Railways feeder train directly from the airport to Zürich's Hauptbanhof (main train station). Tickets cost 5.40 SF one way, and trains run every 10–15 minutes, arriving in 10 minutes. The Airport Shuttle costs about 22 SF per person for a one-way tirp and runs roughly every half hour to a series of downtown hotels.
🛈 **Airport Shuttle** ☎ 01/3001410.

BUS TRAVEL TO & FROM ZÜRICH
All bus services to Zürich will drop you at the Hauptbahnhof (main train station), which is between Museumstrasse and Bahnhofplatz.

BUS TRAVEL WITHIN ZÜRICH
ZVV (Zürich Public Transport) buses and trams run daily from 5:30 AM to midnight. On Friday and Saturday nights buses run every two hours until morning to major towns within the Canton of Zürich. Before you board, you must buy your ticket from one of the vending machines found at every stop. An all-day pass is a good buy at 7.20 SF. Free route plans are available from ZVV offices and larger kiosks. The tourist office sells the ZürichCARD, which allows unlimited travel for 24 hours (15 SF) or 72 hours (30 SF), including free admission to 43 museums and discounts at restaurants and nightclubs.

CAR TRAVEL
Highways link Zürich to France, Germany, and Italy. The quickest approach is from Germany; the A5 autobahn reaches from Germany to Basel, and the A2 expressway leads from Basel to Zürich. The A3 expressway feeds into the city from the southeast.

CONSULATES
🛈 **United Kingdom** ⊠ Minervastr. 117, Zürich ☎ 01/3836560.

EMERGENCIES
🛈 **Doctors & Dentists** Doctor/Dentist Referral ☎ 144.
🛈 **Emergency Services** Ambulance ☎ 144. Police ☎ 117.
🛈 **24-hour Pharmacies** Bellevue ⊠ Theaterstr. 14 ☎ 01/2525600.

ENGLISH-LANGUAGE MEDIA
🔳 Bookstores The **Bookshop** ✉ Bahnhofstr. 70 ☎ 01/2110444. **Payot** ✉ Bahnhofstr. 9 ☎ 01/2115452.

TAXIS
Taxis are very expensive, with an 8 SF minimum.

TOURS
BUS TOURS The daily "Trolley Zürich" tour (32 SF) gives a good general tour of the city in two hours. "Zürich's Surroundings" covers more ground and includes an aerial cableway trip to Felsenegg; it takes three hours and costs 45 SF for adults. The daily "Cityrama" tour hits the main sights, then visits Rapperswil, a nearby lakeside town; it costs 45 SF. All tours start from the Hauptbahnhof. Contact the tourist office for reservations. This tourist office service also offers day trips by coach to Luzern; up the Rigi, Titlis, or Pilatus mountains; and the Jungfrau.

WALKING TOURS Two-hour walking tours (20 SF) organized by the tourist office start at the train station. Times for groups with English-language commentary vary, so call ahead.

TRAIN TRAVEL
Zürich is the northern crossroads of Switzerland, with swift and punctual trains arriving from Basel, Geneva, Bern, and Lugano. All routes lead to the Hauptbahnhof (main train station).
🔳 **Hauptbahnhof** ✉ Between Museumstr. and Bahnhofpl. ☎ 0900/300300.

TRAVEL AGENCIES
🔳 **Imholz Reisen** ✉ Central 2 ☎ 01/2675050. **Kuoni Travel** ✉ Bahnhofpl. 7 ☎ 01/2243333.

VISITOR INFORMATION
🔳 **Zürich Tourist Information** ✉ Hauptbahnhof ☎ 01/2154000 🌐 www.zuerich.com. **Hotel reservations** ☎ 01/2154040 🔳 01/2154044.

GENEVA

Geneva shares most of its borders, as well as its language, with France. It also commands postcard-perfect views of the French Alps from its position at the southwestern tip of Lac Léman (Lake Geneva). The combination of Swiss efficiency and French savoir faire gives the city a chic polish; the infusion of international blood from the United Nations adds a cosmopolitan heterogeneity rarely seen in a population of only 180,000.

Geneva was known for enlightened tolerance long before the International Red Cross was founded here (1864) or the League of Nations moved in (1919). The city gave refuge to religious reformers Calvin and Knox and sheltered the writers Voltaire, Hugo, Balzac, and Stendhal. Rousseau was born here; Byron, Shelley, Wagner, and Liszt all fled to Geneva from scandal at home.

The city's history as a crossroads stretches back further still. Geneva controlled the only bridge over the Rhône north of Lyon when Julius Caesar breezed through in 58 BC; the early Burgundians and bishop-princes who succeeded the Romans were careful to maintain this control. Calvin's rejection of Catholicism in the 16th century transformed Geneva into a stronghold of Protestant reform. The fiercely independent city-state fell to the French in 1798, then made overtures to Bern as Napoléon's star waned. Geneva joined the Swiss Confederation as a canton in 1814.

Exploring Geneva

Numbers in the margin correspond to points of interest on the Geneva map.

Lac Léman bisects Geneva's *centre ville* with graceful precision, then tapers off into the River Rhône. The historic Rive Gauche (Left Bank, on the south shore) mixes museums, shopping streets, and cobbled Old Town alleyways. The International Area, the train station, and sumptuous waterfront hotels dominate the Rive Droite (Right Bank, on the north shore). Most of the main neighborhoods are easily toured on foot. The International Area, on the northern edge of the city, is a short bus or cab ride from downtown.

⑫ **Auditoire de Calvin** (Protestant Lecture Hall). The Scots reformer John Knox preached here from 1556 to 1559 and Jean Calvin taught missionaries his doctrines of puritanical reform in this sober Gothic chapel. English, Dutch, and Italian services are held every Sunday at 11. ⊠ *1 pl. de la Taconnerie* ☎ *022/9097000* ☉ *Variable.*

★ ⑩ **Cathédrale Saint-Pierre** (St. Peter's Cathedral). Construction began in 1160 and lasted 150 years, by which time this towering Romanesque cathedral had acquired Gothic accents. Its huge neoclassical facade was added in 1750. The nave's austerity reflects its 1536 conversion from a Catholic cathedral to a Protestant church; Calvin's followers removed statuary and frescoes like those now restored to the Chapel of the Maccabees. The bird's-eye view from the north tower is worth the climb. ⊠ *Cour Saint-Pierre* ☎ *022/3117575* ☉ *June–Sept., daily 9:30–5:30; Oct.–May, Mon.–Sat. 10–noon and 2–5, Sun. noon–5:30.*

⑭ **Collections Baur.** Alfred Baur's trove of lovingly preserved Chinese and Japanese ceramics spans more than 10 centuries. Jades from China, lacquerware and sword-fittings from Japan, stoneware tea services, and age-old smoking paraphernalia round out the largest collection of Asian art in Switzerland. ⊠ *8 rue Munier-Romilly* ☎ *022/7043282* ⊕ *www.collections-baur.ch* ☉ *Tues.–Sun. 2–6.*

⑦ **Hôtel de Ville** (City Hall). The cantonal government now inhabits this elegant, vaulted compound, Geneva's political seat since 1455. Sixteen countries signed the first Geneva Convention in the ground-floor **Alabama Hall** on August 22, 1864, and the League of Nations convened its first assembly here in 1920. The tourist office includes the complex on its weekday morning walking tours of the Old Town. ⊠ *2 rue de l'Hôtel-de-Ville* ☎ *022/9097000.*

⑧ **Maison Tavel** (Tavel House). Geneva's oldest house traces the development of life in the city from the 14th to the 19th century. Several rooms have period furnishings; others display artifacts ranging from medieval graffiti to a gigantic model of Geneva's pre-1850 defense walls. Don't miss the little room full of photographs. ⊠ *6 rue du Puits-St-Pierre* ☎ *022/4183700* ⊕ *mah.ville-ge.ch* ☉ *Tues.–Sun. 10–5.*

★ ⑤ **Monument de la Réformation** (Wall of the Reformers). Conceived on a grand scale and erected between 1909 and 1917, this phalanx of enormous granite statues pays homage to the 16th-century religious movement spearheaded by Guillaume Farel, Jean Calvin, Théodore de Bèze, and John Knox. It's flanked by memorials to Protestant kingpins Ulrich Zwingli and Martin Luther. ⊠ *Parc des Bastions.*

⑬ **Musée d'Art et d'Histoire** (Museum of Art and History). Switzerland's largest collection of Egyptian art, 17th-century weapons, and an impressive array of Alpine landscape paintings crown this museum's extensive archaeo-

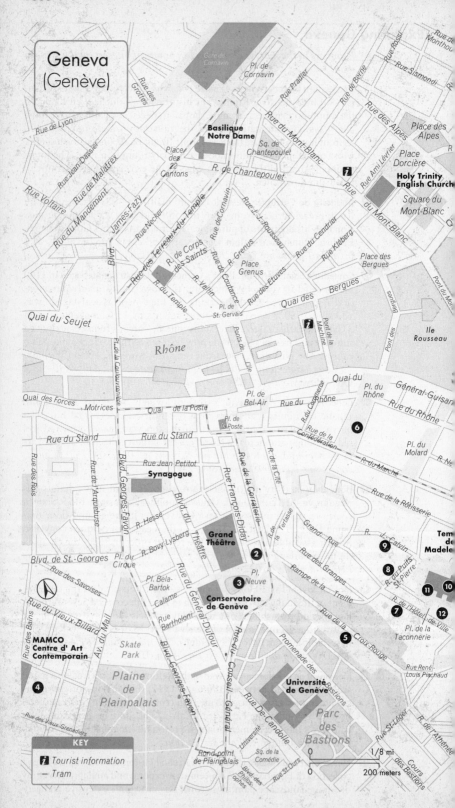

Geneva
(Genève)

Rue des Grottes

Rue de Lyon

Gare de
Cornavin

Pl. de
Cornavin

Rue Pradier

Rue de Berne

Rue des Alpes

Rue Rossi

Rue de Monthou

Rue Sismondi

R

**Basilique
Notre Dame**

Rue du Mont-Blanc

Place des
Alpes

Place
Dorcière

R

Rue Jean-Dassier

Rue de Malatrex

Place
des
22
Cantons

Sq. de
Chantepoulet

R. de Chantepoulet

Rue Ami-Lévrier

**Holy Trinity
English Church**

Rue Voltaire

Rue du Mandement

James-Fazy

Rue Necker

Rue J.-J.-Rousseau

Rue de Cornavin

Rue du Cendrier

Rue Kléberg

Rue du Mont-Blanc

Square du
Mont-Blanc

Rue des Terreaux-du-Temple

R. de Corps
des Saints

R. Grenus

Place
Grenus

Place des
Bergues

Blvd.

R. du Temple

R. Vallin

Rue de Coutance

Rue des Etuves

Pont du Mont

Pl. de
St. Gervais

Quai des   Bergues

Pont des

Ile
Rousseau

Quai du Seujet

Rhône

Ponts de l'Ile

Pont de la
Machine

Pont des

Quai des Forces

Motrices

Quai   de la Poste

Pl. de
Bel-Air

Rue du   Rhône

Quai du
Rhône

Pl. du
Rhône

Général-Guisan

Rue du Rhône

Pl. de la Couronne

Pl. de
la Poste

R. du Commerce

Rue de la
Confédération

6

Pl. du
Molard

R. Ne

Rue du Stand

Rue des Rois

Rue de l'Arquebuse

Blvd. Georges-Favon

Rue Jean-Petitot

Synagogue

R. Hesse

Blvd. du Théâtre

Rue François-Diday

Rue de la Corraterie

R. de la Cité

R. du Marché

Rue de la Rôtisserie

Rue du Stand

R. Bovy-Lysberg

**Grand
Théâtre**

R. de la Terrasse

Grand-Rue

R. J.-Calvin

Tem
de
Madele

Blvd. de St.-Georges

Pl. du
Cirque

Pl. Béla-
Bartók

Calame

Rue du Général-Dufour

2

Pl.
Neuve

3

**Conservatoire
de Genève**

Rue des Granges

Rampe de la

Treille

R. du Puits-
St-Pierre

R. de l'Hôtel-de-Ville

9

8

11

10

7

12

Rue des Bains

Rue des Savoises

Rue du Vieux-Billard

Av. du Mall

Rue
Bartholoni

Skate
Park

Rue de la   Croix-Rouge

Pl. de la
Taconnerie

5

**MAMCO
Centre d' Art
Contemporain**

4

*Plaine
de
Plainpalais*

Blvd. Georges-Favon

Rue Du-Conseil-Général

Promenade des Bastions

**Université
de Genève**

Rue René-
Louis Piachaud

Rue St-Léger

R. de l'Athénée

Rue des Vieux-Grenadiers

Université

Rond-point
de Plainpalais

Sq. de la
Comédie

Rue des
aignes

Rue St-Ours

Rue De-Candolle

*Parc
des
Bastions*

Cours des Bastions

0   1/8 mi

0   200 meters

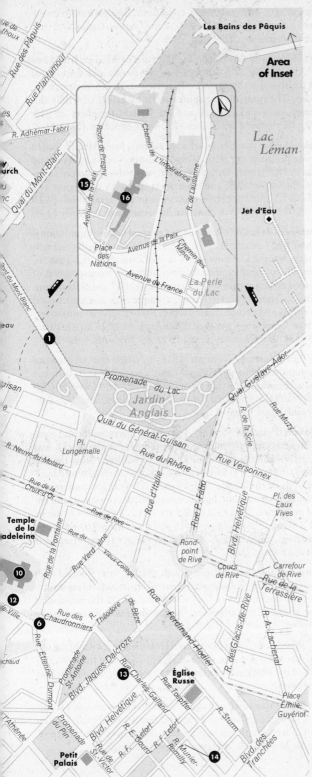

logical, applied arts, and beaux arts collections. The enormous building that houses them dates from 1910. ✉ *2 rue Charles-Galland* ☎ *022/ 4182600* ⊕ *mah.ville-ge.ch* ⊙ *Tues.–Sun. 10–5.*

❹ Musée d'Art Moderne et Contemporain (Museum of Modern and Contemporary Art; MAMCO). Concrete factory floors and fluorescent lighting set the tone for this gritty collection of stark, mind-stretching, post-1965 art. The museum juxtaposes work by artists of wildly different cultures and politics. ✉ *10 rue des Vieux-Grenadiers* ☎ *022/ 3206122* ⊕ *www.mamco.ch.* ⊙ *Tues.–Fri. noon–6, Sat. and Sun. 11–6.*

★ **❾ Musée Barbier-Mueller** (Barbier-Mueller Museum). Josef Mueller began to acquire fine primitive art from Africa, Oceania, Southeast Asia, and the Americas in 1907; today his family's vast, inspired collection of sculpture, masks, shields, textiles, and ornaments spans six continents and seven millennia. A small selection is on view at any given time. ✉ *10 rue Calvin* ☎ *022/3120270* ⊕ *www.barbier-mueller.ch* ⊙ *Daily 11–5.*

★ ☾ **❶❺ Musée International de la Croix-Rouge et du Croissant Rouge** (International Red Cross and Red Crescent Museum). State-of-the-art media technology illuminates human kindness in the face of disaster in this custom-built bunker. The sometimes grim displays include a reconstruction of a 9- by 6½-foot concrete prison cell that once held 17 political prisoners. The Mur du Temps (Wall of Time), a simple time line punctuated by armed conflicts and natural disasters, puts the overall story into sobering perspective. Commentary is available in English. ✉ *17 av. de la Paix* ☎ *022/7489525* ⊕ *www.micr.org* ✉ *10 SF* ⊙ *Wed.–Mon. 10–5.*

❷ Musée Rath (Rath Museum). Dating to 1826, the oldest fine-art museum in Switzerland hosts up to three major exhibitions each year. Its focus ranges from archaeology to contemporary art. ✉ *1 pl. Neuve* ☎ *022/ 4183340* ⊕ *mah.ville-ge.ch* ✉ *Up to 10 SF* ⊙ *Tues. and Fri.–Sun. 10–5, Wed. and Thurs. noon–9.*

❶❻ Palais des Nations (Palace of Nations). The core of this monumental compound, the largest center for multilateral diplomacy in the world, was built in the early 1930s to house the League of Nations. Now the European headquarters of the United Nations, it hosts scores of world leaders and hundreds of thousands of delegates each year for conferences on human rights, disarmament, humanitarian aid, development, and environmental protection. ✉ *14 av. de la Paix* ☎ *022/9074896* ⊕ *www. unog.ch* ✉ *8.50 SF* ⊙ *Apr.–June, Sept., and Oct., daily 10–noon and 2–4; July and Aug., daily 10–5; Nov.–Mar., weekdays 10–noon and 2–4* ⊙ *Closed last 2 wks of Dec.*

★ **❻ Place du Bourg-de-Four.** Once a Roman cattle market, later flooded with Protestant refugees, this quintessential Genevois crossroads mixes scruffy bohemia, genteel tradition, and slick gentrification. ✉ *Intersection of rue Verdaine, rue des Chaudronniers, rue Étienne-Dumont, and rue de l'Hôtel-de-Ville.*

❸ Place Neuve. Aristocratic town houses overlook the Musée Rath, the operatic Grand Théâtre, the Conservatoire de Musique, and the wrought-iron entrance to the Parc des Bastions. ✉ *Intersection of bd. du Théâtre, rue de la Corraterie, rue de la Croix-Rouge, and rue Bartholoni.*

❶ Pont du Mont-Blanc (Mont-Blanc Bridge). Mont Blanc hovers like a sugar-dusted meringue in the distance and the **Jet d'Eau**, Europe's tallest fountain, gushes 475 feet into the air in plain view of this major traffic artery. ✉ *Joins rue du Mont-Blanc and quai Général-Guisan.*

★ ☾ ⑪ **Site Archéologique** (Archaeological Site). Archaeologists found multiple layers of history underneath the Cathédrale Saint-Pierre in 1976; ongoing excavations have so far yielded remnants of two 4th-century Christian sanctuaries, mosaic floors, and an 11th-century crypt. ⊠ *Cour St-Pierre* ☎ *022/3117575* ☉ *June–Sept., Tues.–Fri. 11–5, weekends 11–5:30; Oct.–May, Tues.–Fri. 2–5, weekends 1:30–5:30.*

Where to Eat

Geneva's local cuisine is earthy and rich; look for *cardon* (cardoon, an artichokelike vegetable) baked with cream and Gruyère, lake fish such as *omble* (char) and *perche* (perch), *longeole* (unsmoked pork sausage with cabbage and fennel), *fricassée de porc* (pork simmered in wine), and *la chasse* (wild game). Menus vary with the seasons and many restaurants close on weekends.

$$$$ ✕ **Domaine de Châteauvieux.** Philippe Chevrier's kitchen, at the heart of FodorśChoice Geneva's wine country, has a glowing (and growing) reputation for its ★ simple, elegant, unpretentious quality. Seasonal dishes highlight asparagus in spring, seafood in summer, game come October, and truffles in winter; the cellar houses top local vintages. Ancient beams, antique wine presses, and a summer terrace overlooking the vineyards complete the country setting; a warm welcome is assured. ⊠ *Peney-Dessus, Satigny* ☎ *022/7531511* ⚄ *Reservations essential* ▭ *AE, DC, MC, V* ☉ *Closed Sun. and Mon.*

$$$$ ✕ **Le Lion d'Or.** Cologny is Geneva's Beverly Hills with a view, and this culinary landmark takes full advantage of its real estate; picture windows and the summer terrace overlook the city at sunset. Cardons served au gratin with truffles and roasted sea bass are perennial favorites. The dessert cart favors luscious cream and chocolate confections. ⊠ *5 pl. Pierre-Gautier, Cologny* ☎ *022/7364432* ▭ *AE, DC, MC, V* ☉ *Closed weekends.*

★ $$$ ✕ **Bistrot du Boeuf Rouge.** The menu at this brisk bistro offers rich, unadulterated Lyonnaise cuisine. The tender filet mignon barely requires a knife; the andouillettes, *boudin noir* (blood sausage) with apples, and citrus mousse are all superlative. Each dish is presented on a decorated silver tray. ⊠ *17 rue Alfred-Vincent* ☎ *022/7327537* ▭ *AE, DC, MC, V* ☉ *Closed weekends.*

★ $$$ ✕ **La Favola.** Run by a Ticinese chef from Locarno, this quirky little restaurant may be the most picturesque in town. The tiny dining room, at the top of a vertiginous spiral staircase, strikes a delicate balance between rustic and fussy. The food mixes country simple and city chic: homemade pastas melt on the tongue, the carpaccio is paper thin, and the tiramisu is divine. ⊠ *15 rue Calvin* ☎ *022/3117437* ▭ *No credit cards* ☉ *Closed Sun. and June–Sept. No lunch Sat. Oct.–May.*

★ $$$ ✕ **Le Vallon.** A rosy facade and hanging grapevines set the scene at this century-old village restaurant. Everything on the elegant seasonal menu is made in-house, warm melted chocolate with gingerbread crowns the dessert selection, and the summer terrace, out back, wraps diners in a virtual tunnel of bucolic foliage. ⊠ *182 rte. de Florissant, Conches* ☎ *022/3471104* ▭ *AE, DC, MC, V* ☉ *Closed weekends.*

$$–$$$ ✕ **Chez Léo.** Daniel Carugati's tiny, smoky, sunny corner bistro serves a variety of homemade ravioli and tortellini and a noteworthy *tarte au citron* (lemon tart). Intense, trendy locals descend on the old-fashioned bentwood-and-posters setting for lunch, then linger over coffee. ⊠ *9 rond-point de Rive* ☎ *022/3115307* ▭ *MC, V* ☉ *Closed Sun. No dinner Sat.*

$$–$$$ ✕ **Le Lyrique.** Portraits of Beethoven, Verdi, Strauss, and Liszt watch from under wedding-cake ceilings as pretheater diners choose homemade pasta with scampi, summer gazpacho, or a nuanced steak tartare. The

croissants served from 7 AM are buttery and rich; the Place Neuve setting and the dessert cart make for a terrific afternoon tea. ⊠ *12 bd. du Théâtre* ☎ *022/3280095* ⊟ *AE, DC, MC, V* ⊙ *Closed weekends.*

$$–$$$ ✕ **L'Opéra Bouffe.** The mood is casual-chic and friendly, with wine racks stretched floor to ceiling, classical music in the background, and opera posters on the walls. The Syrian chef rolls out subtle updates of traditional bistro fare. ⊠ *5 av. de Frontenex* ☎ *022/7366300* ⊟ *AE, DC, MC, V* ⊙ *Closed Sun. and Mon. No lunch Sat.*

$$ ✕ **L'Echalotte.** Artists and journalists jostle for space on the polished wood banquettes, and the seasonal menu spans from vegetarian options to the namesake *onglet a l'echalotte* (steak in shallot butter). Service is jovial and prompt. ⊠ *17 rue des Rois* ☎ *022/3205999* ⊟ *MC, V* ⊙ *Closed weekends.*

Where to Stay

Hotel prices in Geneva are similar to those in most European capitals, but many establishments offer weekend deals and group rates. The city is a popular convention center, so be sure to book well in advance; large events can suddenly fill entire hotels.

$$$$ ▦ **Des Bergues.** Creamy fabrics, graceful statues, and unpretentious, friendly service give the oldest of Geneva's grand hotels an inner glow. The sumptuous marble bathrooms and Louis-Philippe elegance mesh seamlessly with such modern conveniences as private fax machines and modem connections. ⊠ *33 quai des Bergues, CH-1201* ☎ *022/9087000* 🖨 *022/9087090* ⊕ *www.hoteldesbergues.com* ↴ *107 rooms, 15 suites* ♨ *2 restaurants, bar* ⊟ *AE, DC, MC, V.*

Fodor'sChoice ★

$$$$ ▦ **President Wilson.** Huge, fragrant flower arrangements punctuate the public areas of this expansive hotel; 17th-century tapestries, colorful paintings, and Greco-Roman stonework complement green marble and sleek wood throughout. Many of the stylish, modern rooms have sweeping views of the lake, Cologny, or the French Alps. ⊠ *47 quai Wilson, CH-1211* ☎ *022/9066666* 🖨 *022/9066667* ⊕ *www.hotelpwilson.com* ↴ *207 rooms, 23 suites* ♨ *2 restaurants, pool, bar* ⊟ *AE, DC, MC, V.*

$$$–$$$$ ▦ **Ambassador.** Don't let the airport-lounge lobby fool you—each room in this central Right Bank hotel is fresh, colorful, and full of natural light. Many of the huge doubles would be called suites elsewhere, and bathrooms gleam with white tile. The seventh floor offers early morning sun and Old Town views. ⊠ *21 quai des Bergues, CH-1211* ☎ *022/9080530* 🖨 *022/7389080* ⊕ *www.hotel-ambassador.ch* ↴ *86 rooms* ♨ *Restaurant* ⊟ *AE, DC, MC, V.*

★ $$$ ▦ **Cornavin.** The comic book character Tintin made this hotel famous with *L'Affaire Tournesol* (*The Sunflower Affair*). It's now modernized with a spectacular glassed-in breakfast hall, sleek cherrywood furniture, frosted-glass bathroom walls, and panoramic top-floor views. ⊠ *Gare de Cornavin, CH-1201* ☎ *022/7161212* 🖨 *022/7161200* ⊕ *www.fassbind-hotels.ch* ↴ *162 rooms, 4 suites* ⊟ *AE, DC, MC, V.*

$$–$$$ ▦ **Le Montbrillant.** Front rooms in this family-run hotel behind the train station have a terrific view of the TGV train arriving from Paris; double-glazed windows keep it quiet. Nineteenth-century beams and stone walls accent rose fabrics and blue-gray trim throughout. ⊠ *2 rue de Montbrillant, CH-1201* ☎ *022/7337784* 🖨 *022/7332511* ⊕ *www.montbrillant.ch* ↴ *58 rooms, 24 studios* ♨ *2 restaurants, bar* ⊟ *AE, DC, MC, V.*

$$ ▦ **Suisse.** Colorful trompe l'oeil scenes decorate the elevator doors, and a model tall ship or clipper guards the landing on each floor of this stylish, if rough-edged, corner hotel facing the train station. The lobby is sponge-painted in peach; ask for a room facing rue du Mont-Blanc if you prefer silence to sun. ☒ *10 pl. de Cornavin, CH-1201* ☎ *022/7326630* 🖷 *022/7326239* ⊕ *www.hotel-suisse.ch* ⇥ *57 rooms* ⊟ *AE, DC, MC, V.*

$-$$ 🏠 **Bel'Espérance.** The Salvation Army owns this former *foyer pour* **Fodor'sChoice** *dames* (ladies' boardinghouse) tucked away near place du Bourg-de-Four. ★ Its spectacular terrace, bright yellow-and-blue rooms, and graceful Louis Philippe–style breakfast salon put it on a par with much pricier hotels. Monthly rates, no-smoking rooms, self-service laundry facilities, and communal kitchen space are available—alcohol is not. ☒ *1 rue de la Vallée, CH-1204* ☎ *022/8183737* 🖷 *022/8183773* ⊕ *www.hotel-bel-esperance.ch* ⇥ *38 rooms, 2 studios* ⊟ *AE, DC, MC, V.*

$ 🏠 **St-Gervais.** Red tartan carpeting and fresh, creamy linen warm the garretlike rooms in this old Right Bank inn. The tiny, wood-paneled café on the ground floor doubles as a breakfast room. Most major bus lines stop just around the corner. ☒ *20 rue des Corps-Saints, CH-1201* ☎ *022/7324572* ⇥ *21 rooms, 1 with bath, 1 with shower* ⊟ *AE, DC, MC, V.*

Nightlife & the Arts

Widely available is the tourist office's free *Genève Agenda*, which lists concerts, performances, museums, restaurants, and clubs each week in French and English. The French and English monthly *Genève Le Guide* (⊕ www.le-guide.ch) profiles current film, theater, music, dance, and museum events and provides a map. Tourist information booths and some hotels offer free copies.

The Arts

The **Grand Théâtre** (☒ pl. Neuve ☎ 022/4183130 ⊕ www.geneveopera.ch) stages full-scale operas, ballets, and recitals from September through June. **Victoria Hall** (☒ 14 rue du Général-Dufour ☎ 022/4183500 ⊕ www.ville-ge.ch) is home to L'Orchestre de la Suisse Romande (☎ 022/8070017 ⊕ www.osr.ch), which punctuates its performances of 20th-century classical music with older crowd-pleasers; its season runs from September to June.

Nightlife

The **Griffin's Club** (☒ 36 bd. Helvétique ☎ 022/7351218) has a dress code and celebrity regulars. **L'Interdit** (☒ 18 quai du Seujet ☎ 022/7389091) alternates high-voltage techno with flamboyant disco classics. **La Clémence** (☒ 20 pl. du Bourg-de-Four ☎ 022/3122498) fills its tiny bar space with university students and overflows into the street. Rarefied opulence and long drinks lure the jet set to **Le Baroque** (☒ 12 pl. de la Fusterie ☎ 022/3110515). Luxury hotels such as the **President Wilson** (☒ 47 quai Wilson ☎ 022/9066666) provide piano bars with quiet settings and pricey cocktails. The **Spring Bros. Pub** (☒ 23 Grand-Rue ☎ 022/3124008) serves Guinness and Strongbow on tap.

Geneva Essentials

AIR TRAVEL TO & FROM GENEVA

SIA operates direct service from New York City, frequent shuttle flights to its hub in Zürich, and regular connections to Basel, Lugano, and most major European cities. Continental also flies direct from New York (Newark). British Airways and EasyJet fly direct from London.

AIRPORTS & TRANSFERS

Geneva's airport, Cointrin (GVA), lies 5 km (3 mi) northwest of the city center.

🛈 **Cointrin** ☎ 022/7177111 ⊕ www.gva.ch.

Cointrin has a direct rail link with the Gare Cornavin, Geneva's main train station. Trains run about every 15 minutes from 5:30 AM to midnight. The trip takes six minutes; the fare is 5.20 SF. Regular city bus service between the airport departure level and downtown takes about 20 minutes and costs 2.20 SF. Taxis are plentiful but expensive; you'll pay at least 40 SF to reach the city center, plus 1.50 SF per bag.

🚆 **Gare Cornavin** ☎ 0900/300300. **Taxi-Phone** ☎ 022/3314133.

BUS TRAVEL TO & FROM GENEVA

Long-distance bus lines use the Gare Routière de Genève (bus station).

🚌 **Gare Routière de Genève** ✉ pl. Dorcière ☎ 022/7320230 ⊕ www.coach-station. com.

BUS TRAVEL WITHIN GENEVA

Buses and trams operate every few minutes on all city routes. Buy a ticket from the vending machine at the stop before you board (instructions are in English). The 2.20 SF fare will let you transfer between buses, trams, and the Mouettes Genevoises harbor ferries for one hour. A *carte journalière*, available for 6 SF from the vending machines and the Transports Publics Genevois booths at the train station and cours de Rive, buys all-day unlimited city-center travel. Travel with a Swiss Pass is free.

🚌 **Transports Publics Genevois** ☎ 022/3083434 ⊕ www.tpg.ch.

CAR TRAVEL

Geneva's long border with France makes for easy access from the south; Chamonix, Annecy, Lyon, and Grenoble are all one to two hours away on the French A40 (l'Autoroute Blanche). The Swiss A1 expressway is Geneva's northern link to Lausanne and the rest of Switzerland.

CONSULATES

🏛 Australia ✉ 2 chemin des Fins ☎ 022/7999100.
🏛 Canada ✉ 5 av. de l'Ariana ☎ 022/9199200.
🏛 New Zealand ✉ 2 chemin des Fins ☎ 022/9290350.
🏛 United Kingdom ✉ 37–39 rue de Vermont ☎ 022/9182400.
🏛 United States ✉ Consular Agent, 7 rue Versonnex ☎ 022/8405161 or 022/8405160.

EMERGENCIES

🚑 Doctors & Dentists **Médecins Urgence** ☎ 022/3222020.
🚑 Emergency Services **Ambulance** ☎ 144. **Fire** ☎ 118. **Police** ☎ 117.
🚑 Hospitals **Hôpital Cantonal** ✉ 24 rue Micheli-du-Crest ☎ 022/3723311 ⊕ www. hcuge.ch.
🚑 24-hour Pharmacies **Pharmacies** *de garde* ☎ 111.

TAXIS

Taxis are clean and the drivers are polite, but expect a 6.30 SF minimum charge plus 2.70 SF per kilometer (½ mi) traveled. In the evening and on Sunday, the rate climbs to 3.30 SF per kilometer.

🚕 **Taxi-Phone** ☎ 022/3314133.

TOURS

BOAT TOURS Belle epoque steamships owned by the Compagnie Générale de Navigation ply the lake all year. Swissboat operates guided lake cruises daily from April to October. Les Mouettes Genevoises conduct warm-weather tours of the Rhône and lower lake.

🚢 **Compagnie Générale de Navigation** ☎ 0848/811848 ⊕ www.cgn.ch. **Les Mouettes Genevoises** ☎ 022/7322944 ⊕ www.mouettesgenevoises.ch. **Swissboat** ☎ 022/7324747 ⊕ www.swissboat.com.

BUS-AND-MINITRAIN TOURS
Two-hour bus-and-minitrain tours of Geneva, operated by Key Tours, leave from the place Dorcière bus station daily at 2 PM year-round as well as at 10 AM May–October and 3:15 PM July and August. You may opt to catch the minitrain (independent of the bus tour) at place Neuve for a trip around the Old Town, on the quai du Mont-Blanc for a tour of the Right Bank parks, or in the Jardin Anglais for a ride along the Left Bank quais.

🖪 **Key Tours** ☎ 022/7314140 ⊕ www.keytours.ch.

WALKING TOURS
The tourist office organizes a two-hour walk through the Old Town every Saturday at 10 AM as well as Monday to Friday at 10 AM between June 15 and October 1. A shorter walk takes place year-round at 6:30 PM on Tuesdays and Thursdays. Private tours are available upon request from the Service des Guides at the tourist information booth on rue du Mont-Blanc, as are English-language audio tours of the Old Town. Rental of the map, cassette, and player costs 10 SF plus a 50 SF deposit.

🖪 **Service des Guides** ☎ 022/9097030.

TRAIN TRAVEL

Direct express trains from most Swiss cities arrive at the Gare Cornavin every hour. The French TGV provides a fast link to Paris; the Cisalpino connects Geneva with Milan and Venice.

🖪 **Gare Cornavin** ✉ pl. de Cornavin ☎ 0900/300300 ⊕ www.cff.ch.

VISITOR INFORMATION

🖪 **Genève Tourisme** ✉ 18 rue du Mont-Blanc ☎ 022/9097000 ⊕ www.geneve-tourisme.ch ✉ Cointrin arrivals terminal ☎ 022/7178083 ✉ Pont de la Machine ☎ 022/3119827. **Information by mail** ✉ Case Postale 1602, CH-1211, Genève ☎ 022/9097000 🖷 022/9097011.

LUZERN

As you cruise down the leisurely sprawl of the Vierwaldstättersee (Lake Luzern), mist rising off the gray waves, mountains—great loaflike masses of forest and stone—looming above the clouds, it's easy to understand how Wagner could have composed his *Siegfried Idyll* while in his lake-side mansion. This is inspiring terrain, romantic and evocative. When the waters roil up you can hear the whistling chromatics and cymbal clashes of Gioacchino Rossini's thunderstorm from his 1829 opera, *Guillaume Tell*. It was on this lake, after all, that William Tell—the beloved, if legendary, Swiss national hero—supposedly leaped from the tyrant Gessler's boat to freedom. And it was in a meadow nearby that three furtive rebels and their cohorts swore an oath by firelight and planted the seed of the Swiss Confederation.

Exploring Luzern

Numbers in the margin correspond to points of interest on the Luzern map.

Luzern's Old Town straddles the waters of the River Reuss where it flows out of the Vierwaldstättersee, its more concentrated section occupying the river's right bank. There are a couple of passes available for discounts for museums and sights in the city. One is a museum pass that costs 29 SF and grants free entry to all museums for one month. If you are staying in a hotel, you may also want to pick up a special visitor's card; once stamped by the hotel, it entitles you to discounts at most museums and other tourist-oriented businesses as well. You can get both passes at the tourist office.

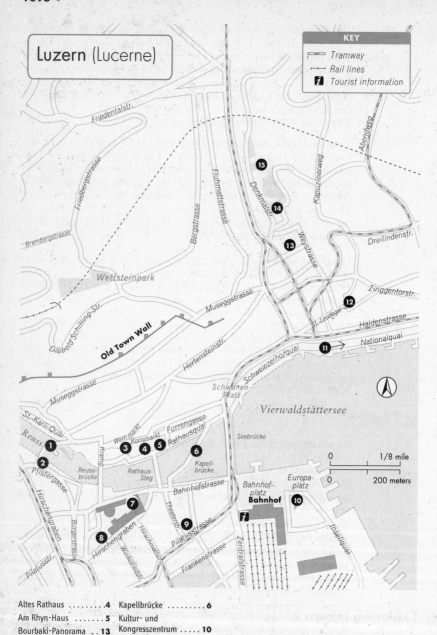

Luzern (Lucerne)

KEY
- Tramway
- Rail lines
- *i* Tourist information

Friedentalstr.

Friedbergstrasse

Bergstrasse

Brambergstrasse

Fluhmattstrasse

Denkmalstr.

Weystrasse

Dreilindenstr.

Abendweg

Kapuzinerweg

15

14

13

12

Zinggentorstr.

Wettsteinpark

Museggstrasse

Diebold-Schilling-Str.

Old Town Wall

St. Leodegar-Str.

Haldenstrasse

Hertensteinstr.

Schweizerhofquai

Nationalquai

11

Museggstrasse

Schwanen-Platz

Vierwaldstättersee

St.-Karli-Quai

Reuss

Weinmarkt

Furrengasse

Kornmarkt

Rathausquai

Seebrücke

1

2

Pfistergasse

Kramg.

Reuss-brücke

Rathaus-Steg

3 4 5

6

Kapell-brücke

Bahnhofstrasse

Bahnhof-platz

Europa-platz

0   1/8 mile

0   200 meters

Hirschengraben

Burgerstrasse

7

Theaterstr.

Sammlung

9

Pilatusstrasse

Bahnhof

i

10

Inseliquai

Pilatusstr.

8

Hirschengraben

Hirschmattstr.

Winkelriedstr.

Frankenstrasse

Zentralstrasse

④ Altes Rathaus (Old Town Hall). This relic overlooking the River Reuss was built between 1602 and 1606 in the late-Renaissance style. ✉ *Rathausquai, facing north end of bridge, Rathaus-Steg.*

⑤ Am Rhyn-Haus (Am Rhyn House). Also known as the Picasso Museum, the compact Renaissance-style building has an impressive collection of late paintings by Picasso. ✉ *Furreng. 21* ☎ *041/4101773* ⊕ *www. kulturluzern.ch/picasso-museum* ⊘ *Apr.–Oct., daily 10–6; Nov.–Mar., daily 11–5.*

⑬ Bourbaki-Panorama. Surrounded by a modern glass cube, this enormous conical wooden structure was created in 1876–78 as a genuine tourist attraction. Its roof covers a sweeping, wraparound epic painting of the French Army of the East retreating into Switzerland at Verrières—a famous episode in the Franco-Prussian War. ✉ *Löwenpl.* ☎ *041/4123030* ⊕ *www.bourbaki.ch* 📷 *7 SF* ⊘ *Daily 9–6.*

⑧ Franziskanerkirche (Franciscan Church). More than 700 years old, this church retains its 17th-century choir stalls and carved wooden pulpit despite persistent modernization. ✉ *Franziskanerpl., just off Münzg.*

⑮ Gletschergarten (Glacier Garden). The bedrock of this 19th-century tourist attraction, dramatically pocked and polished by Ice Age glaciers, was excavated between 1872 and 1875. A private museum on the site has impressive relief maps of Switzerland. ✉ *Denkmalstr. 4* ☎ *041/ 4104340* ⊕ *www.gletschergarten.ch* 📷 *9 SF* ⊘ *Mar., daily 10–5; Apr.–Oct., daily 9–6; Nov.–Feb., Tues.–Sun. 10–5.*

② Historisches Museum (Historical Museum). Dating from 1567, this building was an armory and today exhibits city sculptures, Swiss arms, and flags; reconstructed rooms depict rural and urban life. ✉ *Pfisterg. 24* ☎ *041/2285424* ⊕ *www.hmluzern.ch* ⊘ *Tues.–Fri. 10–noon and 2–5, weekends 10–5.*

⑫ Hofkirche (Collegiate Church). Founded in 750 as a monastery, this Gothic structure was destroyed by fire in 1633 and rebuilt in late-Renaissance style. The 80-rank organ (1650) is one of Switzerland's finest. ✉ *St. Leodegarstr. 13.*

⑦ Jesuitenkirche (Jesuit Church). Constructed in 1666–77, this baroque edifice reveals a symmetrical entrance flanked by two onion-dome towers, added in 1893. The vast interior is a rococo explosion of gilt, marble, and epic frescoes. ✉ *Bahnhofstr., west of Rathaus-Steg.*

FodorśChoice ★

★ **⑥ Kapellbrücke** (Chapel Bridge). This 14th-century bridge snaking diagonally across the water first served as a rampart in case of attacks from the lake. Its shingled roof and grand stone water tower (now housing a souvenir stand) are to Luzern what the Matterhorn is to Zermatt—but considerably more vulnerable, as was proved by a fire in 1993. Almost 80% of this fragile monument was destroyed, including many of the 17th-century paintings inside; the original 110 gable panels painted by Heinrich Wägmann in the 17th century have been replaced with polychrome copies. The paintings depict historic scenes, legendary exploits of the city's patron saints—St. Leodegar and St. Mauritius—and coats of arms of local patrician families. ✉ *Between Seebrücke and Rathaus-Steg bridges, connecting Rathausquai and Bahnhofstr.*

★ **⑩ Kultur- und Kongresszentrum** (Culture and Convention Center). Architect Jean Nouvel's masterful design fits this glass-and-steel building smoothly into its ancient milieu; immense sheets of glass mirror the picture-postcard surroundings. Its concert hall has perfect acoustics. ✉ *Europapl.* ☎ *041/2267070* ⊕ *www.kkl-luzern.ch.*

★ ⓮ **Löwendenkmal** (Lion Monument). The evocative monument commemorates the 760 Swiss guards and their officers who died defending Louis XVI of France at the Tuileries in Paris in 1792. Carved out of a sheer sandstone face by Lucas Ahorn of Konstanz, this 19th-century wonder is a simple image of a dying lion, his chin sagging on his shield, a broken stump of spear in his side. The Latin inscription translates: "To the bravery and fidelity of the Swiss." ⊠ *Denkmalstr.*

➒ **Sammlung Rosengart** (Rosengart Collection). The entire Rosengart collection of painting spanning the French movements of the late 19th to 20th centuries is always on display here, heavy on Picasso, Klee, and the impressionists. ⊠ *Pilatustr. 10* ☎ *041/2201660* ⊕ *www.rosengart. ch* ☉ *Apr.–Oct., daily 10–6; Nov.–Mar., daily 11–5.*

➊ **Spreuerbrücke.** This narrow, all-wood covered bridge dates from 1408. In its center is a lovely 16th-century chapel looking back on the Old Town. Its interior gables hold a series of eerie, well-preserved paintings by Kaspar Meglinger of the *Dance of Death*; they date from the 17th century, though their style and inspiration—tracing to the plague that devastated Luzern and all of Europe during the 14th century—are medieval. ⊠ *Connecting Zeughaus Reuss-Steg and Mühlenpl.*

★ ⓫ **Verkehrshaus.** Easily reached by steamer, car, or Bus 8 or 6, the Swiss Transport Museum is almost a world's fair in itself, with a complex of buildings and exhibitions, including dioramas, live demonstrations, an IMAX theater, and a "Swissorama" (360° screen) film about Switzerland. Every mode of transit is discussed, from stagecoaches and bicycles to jumbo jets and space capsules. ⊠ *Lidostr. 5* ☎ *041/3757575* ⊕ *www.verkehrshaus.org* 🎫 *21 SF* ☉ *Apr.–Nov. 1, daily 9–6; Nov. 2–Mar., daily 10–5.*

➌ **Weinmarkt** (Wine Market). Surrounded by buildings frescoed in 16th-century style, the loveliest of Luzern's squares drew visitors from across Europe from the 15th to the 17th century to witness its passion plays. Its Gothic central fountain depicts St. Mauritius, patron saint of warriors. ⊠ *Sq. just west of Kornmarkt, north of Metzgerrainle.*

Where to Stay & Eat

Rooted in the German region of Switzerland and surrounded by farmland, Luzern's native cuisine is best described as down-home and hearty. The city takes pride in its *Kügelipaschtetli,* puff pastry nests filled with tiny veal meatballs, mushrooms, cream sauce, occasionally raisins, and bits of chicken, pork, or sweetbreads. Lake fish such as *Egli* (perch), *Hecht* (pike), *Forelle* (trout), and *Felchen* (whitefish) are often sautéed and sauced with tomatoes, mushrooms, and capers.

Unlike most other Swiss cities, Luzern has its high and low seasons, and lodgings drop prices considerably in winter.

★ $$$–$$$$ ✕ **Galliker.** Step past the ancient facade into an all-wood room roaring with local action. Brisk, motherly waitresses serve fresh *Kutteln* (tripe) in rich white wine sauce with cumin seeds; real *Kalbskopf* (chopped fresh veal head) served with heaps of green onions and warm vinaigrette; and the famous simmered-beef pot-au-feu. ⊠ *Schützenstr. 1* ☎ *041/2401002* ▤ *AE, DC, MC, V* ☉ *Closed Sun., Mon., and mid-July–mid-Aug.*

★ $$$–$$$$ ✕ **Rotes Gatter.** This chic restaurant in the Des Balances hotel has a combination as desirable as it is rare: soigné decor, shimmering river views, and a sophisticated menu with fish dishes such as trout with peppers and leeks, or the house specialty, meat and fish fondue. There's a more casual, less-expensive bistro area as well. ⊠ *Weinmarkt* ☎ *041/4182828* 🖃 *AE, DC, MC, V.*

$$–$$$ ✕ **Pfistern.** One of the architectural focal points of the Old Town waterfront, this floridly decorated former guildhall offers a good selection of moderately priced meals in addition to higher-priced standards. Lake fish and *Pastetli* (meat pies made with puff pastry) are good local options. ⊠ *Kornmarkt 4* ☎ *041/4103650* 🖃 *AE, DC, MC, V.*

$$–$$$ ✕ **Rebstock/Hofstube.** Across from the Hofkirche, this kitchen offers modern, international fare, including rabbit and ostrich. The lively bentwood brasserie hums with locals lunching by the bar, while the more formal, old-style restaurant glows with wood whitewash under a low-beam herringbone-pattern ceiling. ⊠ *St. Leodegarpl. 3* ☎ *041/4103581* 🖃 *AE, DC, MC, V.*

$$$$ ✕🏨 **Palace Hotel.** This waterfront hotel drinks in the broadest possible lake views. Built in 1906, it has been brilliantly refurbished so that its classical look has a touch of postmodernism. Rooms are large enough for a game of badminton, and picture windows afford sweeping views of Lake Luzern and Mt. Pilatus. The hotel's elegance infuses its excellent restaurant, Jasper, as well. ⊠ *Haldenstr. 10, CH-6002* ☎ *041/ 4161616* 🖷 *041/4161000* ⊕ *www.palace-luzern.com* ➯ *178 rooms, 45 suites* ♢ *Restaurant, bar* 🖃 *AE, DC, MC, V.*

$$$$ 🏨 **Château Gütsch.** Any antiquity in this "castle" (built as a hotel in 1888) is strictly contrived, but honeymooners, groups, and determined romantics in search of a storybook Europe enjoy the Disneyland-like experience. The turrets and towers are worthy of mad Ludwig of Bavaria; a hodge-podge of relics lines the cellars, crypts, and corridors; and beyond the magnificent hilltop site is a private forest. ⊠ *Kanonenstr., CH-6002* ☎ *041/2494100* 🖷 *041/2494191* ⊕ *www.chateau-guetsch.ch* ➯ *28 rooms, 3 suites* ♢ *2 restaurants, pool* 🖃 *AE, DC, MC, V.*

★ **$$$$** 🏨 **Des Balances.** This 19th-century riverfront property gleams with style. State-of-the-art tile baths, up-to-date pastel decor, and one of the best sites in Luzern (in the heart of the Old Town) make this the slickest in its price class. The restaurant, Rotes Gatter, is so good, you may want to eat every meal in the hotel. ⊠ *Weinmarkt, CH-6000* ☎ *041/ 4182828* 🖷 *041/4182838* ⊕ *www.balances.ch* ➯ *50 rooms, 7 suites* ♢ *Restaurant* 🖃 *AE, DC, MC, V.*

$$$$ 🏨 **The Hotel.** Ultrahip elements mark this Jean Nouvel design, including metal block cupboards, puffy chairs and a movie still on the ceiling of each room. An Asian/French fusion restaurant serves the city as well as hotel guests. ⊠ *Sempacherstr. 14, CH-6002* ☎ *041/2268686* 🖷 *041/ 2268690* ⊕ *www.the-hotel.ch* ➯ *10 rooms, 15 suites* ♢ *Restaurant, bar* 🖃 *AE, DC, MC, V.*

FodorsChoice ★

★ **$$$$** 🏨 **Wilden Mann.** The city's best-known hotel offers its guests a gracious and authentic experience of Old Luzern, with stone, beams, brass, and burnished wood everywhere. Standard rooms have a prim 19th-century look. The hotel's reputation is matched by its restaurants. ⊠ *Bahnhofstr. 30, CH-6003* ☎ *041/2101666* 🖷 *041/2101629* ⊕ *www.wilden-mann. ch* ➯ *42 rooms, 8 suites* ♢ *2 restaurants* 🖃 *AE, DC, MC, V.*

$$$ 🏨 **Krone.** Spotless and modern, this hotel softens its edges with pastel linens and walls; along the interior walls you may find a stone prayer shrine retained from the original structure. The rooms facing the Weinmarkt have high ceilings and tall windows. Rooms to the back are less bright but a little larger. The restaurant has a no-alcohol policy. ⊠ *Weinmarkt 12, CH-6004* ☎ *041/4194400* 🖷 *041/4194490* ⊕ *www.krone-luzern.ch/index_e.html* ➯ *25 rooms* ♢ *Restaurant* 🖃 *AE, DC, MC, V.*

$$ 🏨 **Schlüssel.** This spare, no-nonsense little lodging on the Franziskanerplatz attracts young bargain hunters. It's a pleasant combination of tidy, modern touches (quarry tile, white paint) and antiquity: you can have dinner in a low, cross-vaulted "crypt" and admire the fine old lobby beams. ☒ *Franziskanerpl. 12, CH-6003* ☎ *041/2101061* 🖷 *041/ 2101021* 📞 *10 rooms* ⌂ *Restaurant* ☱ *AE, DC, MC, V.*

★ **\$\$** 🏨 **Tourist.** Anything but a backpackers' flophouse, this cheery dormlike spot has a terrific setting around the corner from the Old Town. The coed four-bed, shared-bath dorms (sex-segregated in high season) draw sociable travelers with their rock-bottom prices; there are also seven private-bath doubles. ☒ *St. Karli Quai 12, CH-6003* ☎ *041/4102474* 🖷 *041/4108414* ⊕ *www.touristhotel.ch* 📞 *35 dormitory rooms, 7 doubles with bath* ☱ *AE, DC, MC, V.*

Nightlife & the Arts

For information on performances, consult the German-English *Luzern City Guide,* published seasonally and available at the tourist office.

The Arts

The **Luzerner Symphonieorchester** (LSO) offers a season of concerts from October through June in the **Kultur- und Kongresszentrum. Lucerne Festival** (☒ Hirschmanttstr. 13, CH-6002 Luzern ☎ 041/2264400) events throughout the year take place at the Kultur- und Kongresszentrum.

Nightlife

BARS & LOUNGES The beautiful **Meridiani** (☒ Klosterstr. 12 ☎ 041/2404344) pours everything from coffee to cognac. The **Opus** (☒ Bahnhofstr. 16 ☎ 041/ 2264141) specializes in fine wines by the glass. The **Palace Hotel** (☒ Haldenstr. 10 ☎ 041/4161616) has two American-style bars.

CASINO The most sophisticated nightlife in Luzern is found in the **Casino** (☒ Haldenstr. 6 ☎ 041/4185656), a turn-of-the-20th-century building on the northern shore by the grand hotels. You can visit the Gambling Room, dance in the **Vegas** club, or have a Swiss meal in **Le Chalet** while watching a folklore performance.

FOLKLORE **Nightboat** (☒ Landungsbrücke 6 ☎ 041/3194978) sails nightly May through September at 8:45 PM, with drinks, meals, and a folklore show. The **Stadtkeller** (☒ Sternenpl. 3 ☎ 041/4104733) transports you to the Valais Alps for cheese, yodeling, and dirndled dancers.

Shopping

Luzern no longer produces embroidery or lace, but you can find Swiss crafts of the highest quality, and watches in all price categories. **Bucherer** (☒ Schwanenpl. 5 ☎ 041/3697700) represents Piaget and Rolex. **Gübelin** (☒ Schweizerhofquai 1 ☎ 041/4105142) is the exclusive source for Audemars Piguet, Patek Philippe, and its own house brand. **Ordning & Reda** (☒ Hertensteinstr. 3 ☎ 041/4109506) is a Swedish stationer whose store is filled with brightly colored, handmade, recycled paper products. At **Sturzenegger** (☒ Schwanenpl. 7 ☎ 041/4101958), you'll find St.-Gallen–made linens and embroidered niceties.

Luzern Essentials

AIRPORTS & TRANSFERS

The nearest international airport is Unique Zürich Airport, 54 km (33 mi) northeast of Luzern. SIA flies in most often from the United States and the United Kingdom. Easy rail connections, departing hourly, whisk you on to Luzern within 50 minutes.

🛈 **Unique Zürich Airport** ☎ 0900/571060.

BOAT & FERRY TRAVEL

Some of Luzern's most impressive landscapes can be seen from the deck of one of the cruise ships that ply the Vierwaldstättersee. Boats operate on a standardized, mass-transit-style schedule, crisscrossing the lake and stopping at scenic resorts and historic sites. The Swiss Pass entitles you to free rides; the Swiss Boat Pass gives you a discount.

Schiffahrtsgesellschaft des Vierwaldstättersees ☎ 041/3676767.

BUS TRAVEL WITHIN LUZERN

The city bus system offers easy access to sights throughout the urban area. If you're staying in a Luzern hotel, you will be eligible for a special Guest-Ticket, offering unlimited rides for three days for a minimal fee of 12 SF.

CAR TRAVEL

It's easy to reach Luzern from Zürich by road, approaching from the national expressway A3 south, connecting to the A4 via the secondary E41, in the direction of Zug, and continuing on A4 to the city (roads are well marked). Approaching from the southern St. Gotthard Pass route, or after cutting through the Furka Pass by rail ferry, you'll descend below Andermatt to Altdorf, where a view-stifling tunnel sweeps you through to the shores of the lake and on to the city. Arriving from Basel in the northwest, it's a clean sweep on the A2 into Luzern. In case of emergencies or auto breakdowns, contact the Tourist Club of Switzerland or the Swiss Automobile Club.

Swiss Automobile Club ☎ 041/4203333. Tourist Club of Switzerland ☎ 140.

EMERGENCIES

Doctors & Dentists **Medical, dental, and pharmacy referral** ☎ 111.
Emergency Services **Police** ☎ 117.

TAXIS

Given the small scale of the Old Town and the narrowness of most of its streets, taxis can prove a pricey encumbrance.

TOURS

WALKING TOURS The tourist office guides a two-hour walk with English commentary.

TRAIN TRAVEL

Luzern functions as a rail crossroads, with express trains connecting every half hour from Zürich and hourly from Geneva, the latter with a change at Bern or Olten. For rail information, call the Swiss Federal Railways.

Swiss Federal Railways ☎ 0900/300300 ⊕ www.sbb.ch.

TRANSPORTATION AROUND LUZERN

Luzern's modest scale allows you to explore most of the city easily on foot, but you will want to resort to mass transit to visit such noncentral attractions as the Verkehrshaus (Swiss Transport Museum).

VISITOR INFORMATION

Luzern Tourist Information ⊠ Zentralstr. 5, in the Hauptbahnhof ☎ 041/2271717.
Central Switzerland Tourism Association (Verkehrsverband Zentralschweiz) ⊠ Alpenstr. 1, Luzern ☎ 041/4184080 ⊕ www.centralswitzerland.ch.

LUGANO

Because of the beautiful, sparkling bay of the Lago di Lugano and dark, conical mountains rising up on either side, Lugano is often referred to as "the Rio of the Old World." The largest city in the Ticino—Switzerland's Italian-speaking region—Lugano has not escaped some of the overdevelopment inevitable in a successful resort town. There's bumper-to-bumper traffic, much of it manic Italian–style; and concrete high-rise hotels crowd the waterfront, with balconies skewed to a view no matter what the aesthetic cost.

Even so, the view from the waterfront is unforgettable, the boulevards are fashionable, and the Old Quarter is still reminiscent of sleepy old towns in Italy. And the sacred *passeggiata*—the early evening stroll to see and be seen—asserts the city's true personality as a graceful, sophisticated old-world resort—not Swiss, not Italian . . . just Lugano.

Exploring Lugano

Numbers in the margin correspond to points of interest on the Lugano map.

8 Castagnola Parks. The **Parco degli Ulivi** (Olive Park) spreads over the lower slopes of Monte Brè and offers a romantic landscape of silvery olive trees mixed with cypress, laurel, and wild rosemary; you enter it from the Gandria footpath (Sentiero di Gandria). **Parco San Michele** (St. Michael Park), also on Monte Brè, has a public chapel and a broad terrace that overlooks the city, the lake, and, beyond, the Alps. From Cassarate, walk up the steps by the lower terminus of the Monte Brè funicular.

3 Cattedrale di San Lorenzo (St. Lawrence Cathedral). The graceful Renaissance facade faces a lovely view and inside are noteworthy frescoes. ⊠ *Via Cattedrale.*

★ **2 Chiesa di Santa Maria degli Angioli** (Church of St. Mary of the Angels). Dating from 1455, this church has frescoes of the Passion and Crucifixion by Bernardino Luini (1475–1532). ⊠ *Piazza Luini.*

1 Giardino Belvedere (Belvedere Gardens). Mixed in with palms, camellias, oleanders, and magnolias are 12 modern sculptures. At the west end there's public bathing on the Riva Caccia. ⊠ *Quai Riva Antonio Caccia* ☉ *Daily.*

10 Lido. Along the lake, the municipal stretch of sandy beach includes several swimming pools (heated in spring and autumn) and a restaurant. ⊠ *Entrance on right off Viale Castagnola* ☎ *091/9714041* ☉ *May and Sept., daily 9:30–7; June–Aug., daily 9–7:30.*

5 Museo Cantonale d'Arte (Cantonal Art Museum). A group of three palaces dating from the 15th to the 19th century was adapted for this museum. Its exhibits span paintings, sculpture, and photography, including some important avant-garde works. The permanent collection holds works by Klee, Turner, Degas, Renoir, and Hodler as well as contemporary Ticinese artists. Descriptive material is available in English. ⊠ *Via Canova 10,* ☎ *091/9104780* ⊕ *www.museo-cantonale-arte.ch* ☉ *Tues. 2–5, Wed.–Sun. 10–5.*

7 Museo Cantonale di Storia Naturale (Cantonal Museum of Natural History). This museum in the Parco Civico has exhibits on the region's fossils, plants, and mushrooms. ⊠ *Viale Cattaneo 4 (on the grounds of the Parco Civico)* ☎ *091/9115380* ☉ *Tues.–Sat. 9–noon and 2–5.*

6 Parco Civico (Town Park). With its cacti, exotic shrubs, and more than 1,000 varieties of roses, this first-rate park also holds fountains, statues, an aviary, a tiny "deer zoo," and a fine view of the bay from its peninsula. Music and events take place here during fair-weather months. **Villa Ciani** has paintings and sculptures from Tintoretto to Giacometti. ⊠ *Area south of Viale Carlo Cattaneo, east of Piazza Castello.*

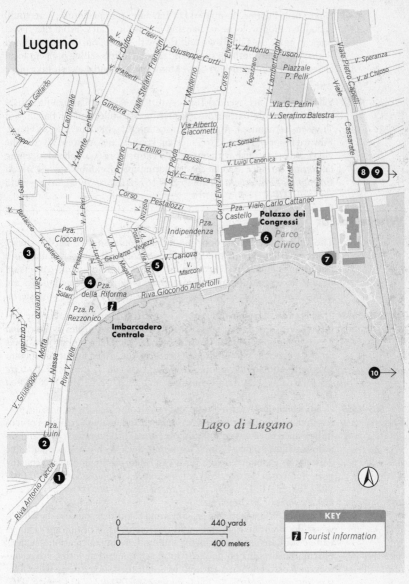

Lugano

Lago di Lugano

KEY

🛈 *Tourist information*

0 —————— 440 yards
0 —————— 400 meters

★ ❹ **Piazza della Riforma.** Stronghold of Lugano's Italian culture, here you'll encounter modish locals socializing in outdoor cafés. From the piazza one can enter the **Old Town** and follow the steep, narrow streets lined with chic Italian clothing shops and small markets selling pungent local cheeses and porcini mushrooms. Many festivals and concerts take place here. ⊠ *Town center.*

★ ❾ **Villa Favorita.** This splendid 16th-century mansion in Castagnola houses a portion of the extraordinary private art collection of Baron von Thyssen-Bornemisza. Among the artists represented are Lucian Freud, Edward Hopper, Franz Marc, Jackson Pollock, and Andrew Wyeth. The villa gardens are lush with native and exotic flora. Call ahead; opening hours and entrance fees can change during special exhibitions. ⊠ *Strada Castagnola, Via Rivera 14* ☎ *091/9716152* ⊠ *10 SF* ☉ *Easter–Oct., Fri.–Sun. 10–5.*

Where to Eat

The Ticinese were once poor mountain people, so their cuisine shares the earthy delights of the Piemontese: polenta, gnocchi, game, and mushrooms. But as in all prosperous resorts, the mink-and-Vuarnets set draws the best in upscale international cooking. Prix-fixe lunches are almost always cheaper, so dine as the Luganese do—before your siesta.

★ **$$$–$$$$** ✕ **Al Portone.** Silver and lace dress up the stucco and stone, but the ambience here is strictly easygoing. Chef Roberto Galizzi creates *nuova cucina* (nouvelle cuisine, Italian-style) with ambition and flair, putting local spins on classics such as fillet of bison with artichokes, grilled turbot with potato spaghetti, and squid ravioli. ⊠ *Viale Cassarate 3, Lugano-Cassarate* ☎ *091/9235511* ⚲ *Reservations essential* ⊟ *AE, DC, MC, V* ☉ *Closed Sun. and Mon.*

$$$–$$$$
FodorśChoice
★
✕ **Santabbondio.** Ancient stone and terra-cotta blend with pristine pastels in this upgraded grotto, where superb and imaginative new Franco-Italian dishes are served in intimate, formal little dining rooms and on a flower-filled terrace. Watch for honey duck with black pepper, olive gnocchi, or eggplant ravioli. It's a cab ride from town, toward the airport, but worth the trip. ⊠ *Via Fomelino 10, Lugano-Sorengo* ☎ *091/ 9932388* ⊟ *AE, DC, MC, V* ☉ *Closed Sun., Mon., 1st wk in Jan., and last wk in Feb. No lunch Sat.*

$$$ ✕ **Orologio.** White fabric covers tables and chairs that stand on dark hardwood floors in this very open and minimalist-style restaurant. The attentive staff are quick at bringing out modern Italian creations, such as porcini mushrooms on butter lettuce, salmon ravioli with fresh tomatoes, and osso buco in a garlic crust—but they soon disappear and let you linger over coffee. ⊠ *Via Nizzola 2,* ☎ *091/9232338* ⊟ *AE, DC, MC, V* ☉ *Closed Sun.*

★ **$$–$$$** ✕ **Locanda del Boschetto.** The grill is the first thing you see in this no-nonsense restaurant specializing in simple but sensational seafood *alla griglia* (grilled). Crisp linens contrast with rustic wood touches, and the low-key service is helpful and down-to-earth. ⊠ *Via al Boschetto 8* ☎*091/ 9942493* ⊟ *AE, DC, MC, V* ☉ *Closed Mon. and first 2 wks of Nov.*

$–$$ ✕ **Grotto Figini.** This restaurant is in a short stretch of woods on a hill in Gentilino, above Lugano-Paradiso. Locals gather here for a *boccalino* (ceramic vessel) of good merlot and a satisfying, rib-sticking meal of polenta and grilled meats. ⊠ *Via ai Grotti* ☎ *091/9946497* ⊟ *V* ☉ *Closed Mon. and mid-Dec.–Feb.*

★ **$–$$** ✕ **La Tinera.** This tiny tavern crowds loyal locals, tourists, and families onto wooden benches for authentic regional specialties, hearty meats, and pastas. It's tucked down an alley off Via Pessina in the Old Town.

Wine is served in traditional ceramic bowls. ⊠ *Via dei Gorini 2* ☎ *091/ 9235219* ⊟ *AE, DC, MC, V* ☉ *Closed Sun. and Aug.*

Where to Stay

There are few inexpensive hotels in downtown Lugano, but a brief drive into the countryside increases your options. Since this is a summer resort, many hotels close for the winter, so call ahead.

★ **$$$$** 🏨 **Ticino.** This 500-year-old palazzo, protected as a historical monument, is in the heart of the Old Town, just steps away from the funicular to the railway station. Shuttered windows look out from every room onto a glassed-in garden and courtyard, and vaulted halls are lined with art and antiques. There is a two-night minimum stay. ⊠ *Piazza Cioccaro 1, CH-6901* ☎ *091/9227772* 🖷 *091/9236278* ⊕ *www.romantikhotels. com/lugano* ⟿ *18 rooms, 2 suites* ♨ *Restaurant* ⊟ *AE, DC, MC, V* ☉ *Closed Jan.*

$$$$ 🏨 **Villa Principe Leopoldo/Hotel Montalbano.** A Relais & Châteaux prop-
Fodor'sChoice erty, this garden mansion sits on the Collina d'Oro (Golden Hill), of-
★ fering guests magnificent lake, garden, or pool views. There are scads of facilities, including a fitness room, sauna, and tennis. ⊠ *Via Montalbano 5, CH-6900* ☎ *091/9858855* 🖷 *091/9858825* ⊕ *www.leopoldo. ch* ⟿ *70 rooms, 4 suites* ♨ *3 restaurants, pool* ⊟ *AE, DC, MC, V.*

$$$–$$$$ 🏨 **Du Lac.** This discreet, simple hotel gives you true lakefront luxury for your money—all rooms face the lake. The hotel has a private swimming area on the lake, plus a number of such pampering facilities as a sauna and massage. ⊠ *Riva Paradiso 3, CH-6902 Lugano-Paradiso* ☎ *091/ 9864747* 🖷 *091/9864748* ⊕ *www.dulac.ch* ⟿ *52 rooms, 1 suite* ♨ *Restaurant, pool* ⊟ *AE, DC, MC, V* ☉ *Closed Jan.–mid-Mar.*

$$–$$$ 🏨 **International au Lac.** This big, friendly hotel classic is half a block from the lake, with many lake-view rooms. It's next to Santa Maria degli Angioli, on the edge of the Old Town. ⊠ *Via Nassa 68, CH-6901* ☎ *091/ 9227541* 🖷 *091/9227544* ⊕ *www.hotel-international.ch* ⟿ *80 rooms* ♨ *Restaurant, pool* ⊟ *AE, DC, MC, V* ☉ *Closed Nov.–Easter.*

★ **$$** 🏨 **Park-Hotel Nizza.** This former villa affords panoramic views from its perch on the lower slopes of San Salvatore; it's an uphill hike from town. The mostly small rooms are decorated in styles ranging from repro-antique to modern; there is no extra charge for lake views. A cozy bar overlooks the lake, and the restaurant serves vegetables from its own garden and even wine from its own vineyards—alfresco, when weather permits. There are some no-smoking rooms, and one of the restaurants is no-smoking as well. A shuttle provides service to the nearby town Paradiso and the Old Town. ⊠ *Via Guidino 14, CH-6902* ☎ *091/9941771* 🖷 *091/9941773* ⊕ *www.villanizza.com* ⟿ *29 rooms* ♨ *2 restaurants, pool, bar* ⊟ *AE, MC, V* ☉ *Closed mid-Dec.–mid-Mar.*

$$ 🏨 **Zurigo.** Handy to parks and shopping, this hotel has bright and modern rooms with white tile bathrooms. There's a nice garden in front, too. ⊠ *Corso Pestalozzi 13, CH-6900* ☎ *091/9234343* 🖷 *091/9239268* ⊕ *www.hotelzurigo.ch* ⟿ *40 rooms* ⊟ *AE, DC, MC, V* ☉ *Closed Dec. and Jan.*

$–$$ 🏨 **San Carlo.** The San Carlo offers one of the better deals in this high-priced town: it's small, clean, and quiet. The location is great, too—right on the main pedestrian shopping street, a block from the waterfront, and just 150 yards from the funicular that takes you to the railway station. ⊠ *Via Nassa 28, CH-6901* ☎ *091/9227107* 🖷 *091/9228022* ⟿ *22 rooms* ⊟ *AE, DC, MC, V.*

$ 🏨 **Dischma.** The welcoming owners of this hotel make it a bargain worth seeking out. The rooms are clean and bright, with flowers on the balconies; public rooms are a riot of colors, souvenirs, and knickknacks.

The restaurant is no-smoking (rare in these parts). ✉ *Vicolo Geretta 6, CH-6902 Lugano-Paradiso* ☎ *091/9942131* 🖷 *091/9941503* ⊕ *www. hotel-dischma.ch* ⇆ *35 rooms* 🍴 *Restaurant* ▭ *AE, MC, V* ⊗ *Closed Dec.–Feb.*

Lugano Essentials

AIRPORTS & TRANSFERS

SIA offers short domestic flights to Aeroporto Lugano-Agno (LUG) from Zürich, Geneva, Basel, and Bern, as well as from Paris, Nice, Rome, Florence, and Venice. The nearest intercontinental airport is Malpensa, about 50 km (31 mi) northwest of Milan, Italy.

🚹 Aeroporto Lugano-Agno Airport ☎ 091/6101111. Malpensa ☎ 02/74852200.

TRANSFERS | The aptly named Shuttle Bus offers service (20 SF) between the airport and central Lugano, 7 km (4 mi) away. A taxi ride costs about 30 SF to the center.

🚹 Shuttle Bus ☎ 079/2214243.

BOAT & FERRY TRAVEL

Cruise-boats make excursions around the bay to the romantic fishing village of Gandria and to the Villa Favorita. You may use these like public transit, following a schedule and paying according to distance, or look into special tickets: seven consecutive days' unlimited travel costs 62 SF, three days' travel within a week costs 51 SF (with half price for the other four days), and an all-day pass costs 34 SF.

🚹 Società Navigazione Lago di Lugano ☎ 091/9715223 ⊕ www.lakelugano.ch.

BUS TRAVEL WITHIN LUGANO

Well-integrated services run regularly on all local routes. Buy your ticket from the machine at the stop before you board.

CAR TRAVEL

There are fast, direct highways from both Milan and Zürich. If you are planning to drive from Geneva, dial 163 for weather and road conditions beforehand. Once you're there, Lugano's maze of winding, often one-way streets makes public transportation or taxis preferable.

EMERGENCIES

🚹 Dentists **Dental clinic** ☎ 091/9350180.
🚹 Emergency Services **Ambulance** ☎ 144. **Police** ☎ 117.
🚹 Hospitals **Civic Hospital** ☎ 091/8116111.

TAXIS

Though less expensive than in Zürich or Geneva, taxis are still not cheap, with a 10 SF minimum.

🚹 ☎ 091/9712121 or 091/9931616.

TOURS

The tourist office has information about hiking tours into the mountains surrounding Lugano; it provides a wonderful packet of topographical maps and itineraries. There are bus trips to Locarno, Ascona, Lake Como, Lake Maggiore, Milan, Venice, St. Moritz, Florence, the Alpine passes, and the Italian market in Como.

TRAIN TRAVEL

There's a train from Zürich every hour; the trip takes about three hours. If you're coming from Geneva, you can catch the Milan express at various times, changing at Domodossola and Bellinzona. During the day, there's a train every hour from Milan's Stazione Centrale; the trip takes about 1½ hours. Always keep passports handy and confirm times with the Swiss Federal Railways.

🏢 Swiss Federal Railways ☎ 0900/300300 ⊕ www.cff.ch.

VISITOR INFORMATION

🏢 Lugano Tourism ⊠ Palazzo Civico, Riva Albertolli, CH-6901 ☎ 091/9133232 🖷 091/9227653 ⊕ www.lugano-tourism.ch.

BERN

No cosmopolitan nonsense here: the mascot is a common bear, the annual fair celebrates the humble onion, and the president is likely to take the tram to work. Walking down medieval streets past squares teeming with farmers' markets, you might forget the city of Bern is the federal capital—indeed, the geographic and political hub—of a sophisticated nation.

Bern earned its pivotal position with a combination of muscle and influence dating from the 12th century, when the Holy Roman emperor Berchtold V established a fortress on this gooseneck in the River Aare. By the 15th century the Bernese had overcome the Burgundians to expand their territories west to Geneva. Napoléon suppressed them briefly—from 1798 until his defeat in 1815—but by 1848 Bern was back in charge as the capital of the Swiss Confederation.

Today it's not the massive Bundeshaus (Houses of Parliament) that the city is known for, however, but rather its perfectly preserved arcades and fountains—all remnants of its heyday as a medieval power. They're the reason UNESCO granted Bern World Cultural Heritage status.

Exploring Bern

Numbers in the margin correspond to points of interest on the Bern map.

Bern's easily walkable streets run in long parallels east to the Old Town. The original city was founded in a bend of the river and grew westward; those stages of growth are marked by three "towers"—the Zeitglockenturm, the Käfigturm, and the Christoffelturm. The city is crisscrossed by *Lauben* (arcades) that shelter stores of every kind and quality. On Tuesday and Saturday mornings merchant stalls of produce, flowers, cheese, meat, and household items pack the plazas and walkways.

Hundreds of steps below the hyperactive City Center and along the river front lies the Matte, a bohemian district of compact town houses and converted warehouses known for its own distinctive dialect. To get to the cluster of museums in Kirchenfeld, on the opposite side of the river, you can walk across the Kirchenfeldbrücke or hop on a tram.

★ ❾ **Bärengraben** (Bear Pits). According to legend, Berchtold V named Bern after the first animal he killed while hunting. It was a bear; in those days the woods were full of them. Live mascots have been on display in the city since the late 1400s. ⊠ *East end of Nydeggbrücke* ☉ *June–Sept. daily 8–5:30; Oct.–May daily 9–4.*

★ ⓭ **Bernisches Historisches Museum** (Historical Museum). This castlelike Victorian building houses 15th-century Flemish tapestries and Bernese sculptures as well as 15th- and 16th-century stained-glass windows. Don't miss the novel three-way portrait of Calvin, Zwingli, and Luther. ⊠ *Helvetiapl. 5* ☎ *031/3507711* ☉ *Tues. and Thurs.–Sun. 10–5, Wed. 10–8.*

❸ **Bundeshaus** (Parliament House). This hulking, domed building is the beating heart of the Swiss Confederation and meeting place of the National Council and Council of States. Free tours include entry to the parlia-

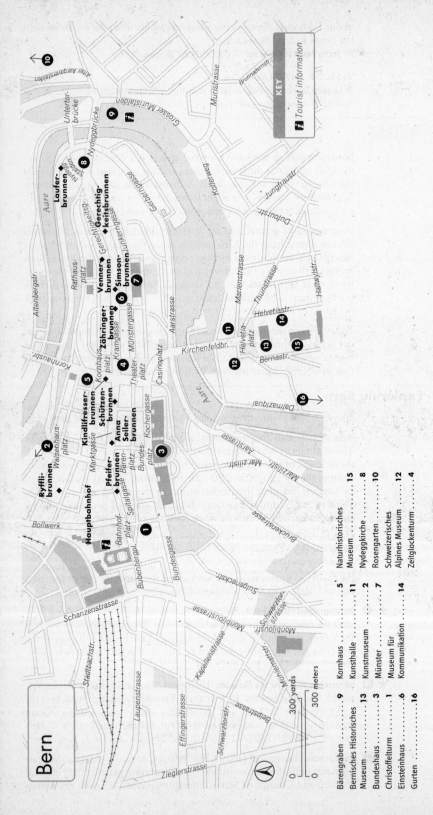

Bern

KEY

i Tourist information

mentary chambers when the council is not in session. Otherwise you can observe proceedings from the public gallery. ⊠ *Bundespl.* ☎ *031/ 3228522* ☉ *Tours weekdays at 9, 10, 11, 2, 3, and 4; passport or ID required for entry.*

❶ Christoffelturm (Christoffel Tower). Remains of the city's 14th-century third gate were uncovered in the train station during construction of a pedestrian passageway. ⊠ *Christoffelunterführung, southernmost entrance to Bahnhofpl.*

❻ Einsteinhaus (Einstein's House). For a bit of intellectual history, you can visit the apartment and workplace of Albert Einstein. It was during his stay here, from 1903 to 1905, that the 26-year-old published his *Special Theory of Relativity.* ⊠ *Kramg. 49,* ☎ *031/3120091* ☉ *Tues.–Fri. 10–5, Sat. 10–4* ☉ *Closed Dec. and Jan.*

★ ☺ ⓰ Gurten. Reach this park with a panoramic view by taking the three-minute trip on the bright red funicular or climbing a steep pathway through woods and pastures. A diagram on the east side points out more than 200 peaks on snowcapped mountains. Reward any climb with a meal at one of the restaurants. ⊠ *Wabern, tram stop Gurtenbahn* ☎ *031/ 9703333* ⊕ *www.gurtenpark.ch* ☉ *Funicular: Mon.–Sat. 7:10 AM–11:40 PM, Sun. 7:40 AM–10:10 PM.*

❺ Kornhaus (Granary). At various times a granary, a post office, and a beer hall, this cellar with a magnificent vaulted ceiling now houses a popular restaurant, Kornhauskeller. ⊠ *Kornhauspl. 18* ☎ *031/3129110* ☉ *Tues.–Fri. 10–7, weekends 10–5.*

⓫ Kunsthalle (Art Gallery). This groundbreaking contemporary art venue displays the works of living artists, usually before you've heard of them. Built in 1918 in heroic classical style to boost local artists—Kirchner, Klee, Hodler—it grew to attract the young Kandinsky, Miró, Cy Twombly—and a parade of newcomers of strong potential. ⊠ *Helvetiapl. 1* ☎ *031/3510031* ⊕ *www.kunsthallebern.ch* ☉ *Tues. 10–7, Wed.–Sun. 10–5.*

★ ❷ Kunstmuseum (Art Museum). Established for the promotion of Swiss artists, this landmark art museum houses an exceptional group of works by Ferdinand Hodler, including some enormous allegories. There is also an impressive collection of old masters and impressionists and a constant turnover of temporary exhibitions. Fans of Paul Klee have hit the jackpot: the world's largest collection of his work, with more than 2,000 pieces. Renzo Piano's center dedicated to Klee's work opens in 2005 outside the city center in Schöngrün. ⊠ *Hodlerstr. 8–12* ☎ *031/3280944* ⊕ *www.kunstmuseumbern.ch* ☉ *Tues. 10–9, Wed.–Sun. 10–5.*

★ ❼ Münster (Cathedral). Begun in 1421, Bern's famous cathedral was planned on lines so spacious that half the population could worship in it at one time; its construction went on for centuries. It has an outstanding painted portal (1490) depicting the Last Judgment, and stunning stained-glass windows, both originals and period reproductions. The steeple, added in 1893, is the tallest in Switzerland. Climb to the top of the tight spiral staircase for a panoramic view. ⊠ *Münsterpl. 1* ☎ *031/3120462* ☉ *Easter–Oct., Tues.–Sat. 10–5, Sun. 11:30–5; Nov.–Easter, Tues.–Fri. 10–noon and 2–4, Sat. 10–noon and 2–5, Sun. 11:30–2.*

⓮ Museum für Kommunikation (Museum of Communication). This museum dedicated to communication—from signaling by bonfire through the transmission of complex digital information—features interactive exhibits, artifacts related to the history of the post and telecommunications, and the world's largest public display of stamps. ✉ *Helvetiastr. 16* ☎ *031/3575555* ⊕ *www.mfk.ch* ⊙ *Tues.–Sun. 10–5.*

★ ⑮ **Naturhistorisches Museum** (Museum of Natural History). This slick and spacious natural history museum, considered one of Europe's finest, features enormous wildlife dioramas, exhibits on master builders, and a splendid collection of Alpine minerals. ✉ *Bernastr. 15* ☎ *031/3507111* ⊙ *Mon. 2–5, Tues., Thurs., and Fri. 9–5, Wed. 9–6, weekends 10–5.*

⑧ **Nydeggkirche** (Nydegg Church). Built between 1341 and 1571 on the foundations of Berchtold V's ruined fortress, this ancient church marks the founding place of Bern. ✉ *Nydegg.* ⊙ *Mon.–Sat. 10–noon and 2–5:30, Sun. 10–noon.*

⑩ **Rosengarten** (Rose Garden). This splendidly maintained garden features a riot of color from April to October, with 27 types of rhododendrons, 200 roses, and 200 irises. There's also a panoramic view of the bridges, roofs, and major buildings of downtown Bern. ✉ *Alter Aargauerstalden/Laubeggstr.* ⊙ *Daily sunrise–sunset.*

⑫ **Schweizerisches Alpines Museum** (Swiss Alpine Museum). This museum of the Alps, known for its topographical maps and reliefs, also covers the histories of mountain climbing and life in the mountains. There are fine old photos and a magnificent Hodler mural of the tragic conquest of the Matterhorn. ✉ *Helvetiapl. 4* ☎ *031/3510434* ⊕ *www. alpinesmuseum.ch* ⊙ *Mon. 2–5, Tues.–Sun. 10–5.*

★ ④ **Zeitglockenturm** (Clock Tower). This mighty landmark, Bern's oldest building, was built as a city gate in 1191 but was transformed by the addition of an astronomical clock on its east side in 1530. At five minutes before the hour, every hour, a delightful group of mechanical figures parades out of the clock. ✉ *Kramg. between Theaterpl. and Kornhauspl.* ⊙ *Tours May–Oct. at 4:30.*

Where to Eat

Although Bern teeters between two cultures politically, Teutonic conquers Gallic when it comes to cuisine. Dining here is usually a down-to-earth affair, with Italian home cooking a popular alternative to meat and potatoes. Specialties include the famous *Bernerplatte* (sauerkraut with boiled beef, pork, sausages, ham, and tongue), normally served in heaping portions, and the Berner version of *Ratsherrtopf* traditionally enjoyed by the town councillors: veal shank cooked in white wine, butter, and sage.

$$$$ ✕ **Bellevue-Grill.** When Parliament is in session, this haute-cuisine landmark turns into a political clubhouse. The menu leans to luxury; unusual dishes might include beef fillet with truffle pasta or roast breast of duck with a hint of coffee in the sauce. In summer, seating moves to the upper-level terrace overlooking the Aare. ✉ *Kocherg. 3–5* ☎ *031/ 3204545* ⌂ *Reservations essential* ▭ *AE, DC, MC, V.*

★ $$$$ ✕ **Schultheissenstube.** The intimate, rustic dining room of the Schweizerhof hotel may look less like a gastronomic haven than a country pub, but this is formal dining at its best. The cooking is sophisticated, international, and imaginative, such as sautéed wild turbot with two sauces—apple fennel and braised chicory—or roasted reindeer with cumin cabbage. Men are required to wear a jacket. ✉ *Schweizerhof hotel, Bahnhofpl. 11* ☎ *031/3268080* ⌂ *Reservations essential* ▭ *AE, DC, MC, V* ⊙ *Closed Sun., July, and Aug.*

★ $$$–$$$$ ✕ **Kornhauskeller.** Entering the Kornhauskeller is like entering a cathedral, except that the spectacular vaulted ceilings and frescoes are all underground. Now a restaurant serving classic Mediterranean cuisine, this historic building is worth a stop if only for a glass of wine. ⊠ *Kornhauspl. 18* ☏ *031/3277272* ▭ *AE, DC, MC, V.*

★ **$$$-$$$$** ✕ **Zimmermania.** This deceptively simple bistro in an Old Town side street has been in business for more than 150 years and is a local favorite for French bourgeois cooking. Try duck breast with rose hip and cassis sauce or *Kalbsleberli* (calves' liver) and Rösti. A European-only wine list focuses on France with vintages in all price ranges. ⊠ *Brunng. 19* ☏ *031/3111542* ▭ *AE, MC, V* ☾ *Closed Sun. and Mon.*

$$-$$$ ✕ **Harmonie.** Cheese specialties: fondue, *käseschnitte* (open-face, melted cheese sandwich), and *chäshörnli* (macaroni and cheese) are legendary at this well-trodden address. Regional recipes of pork, veal, and tripe accompanied by Spätzli are equally notable. A small outdoor patio catches a slice of sun and is great for viewing pedestrian activity. ⊠ *Hotelg. 3* ☏ *031/3112780* ▭ *AE, MC, V.*

★ **$$-$$$** ✕ **Lorenzini.** Politicos, bankers, and urbanites hold standing reservations at this sleek second-floor restaurant known for its pastas and risottos. Osso buco and scallopini are constant requests. The café-bar downstairs draws a young and chic crowd for *prosecco, panini,* and espresso. ⊠ *Theaterpl. 5/Hotelg. 8* ☏ *031/3117850* ▭ *AE, DC, MC, V* ☾ *Closed Sun.*

$-$$$ ✕ **Markthalle.** Within this multilevel marketplace across from the train station is a variety of cuisines—pasta, tapas, curry dishes, seafood, and wok specialties. It's not a true food court, but a collection of individual restaurants, with anything from starched linen to stand-up counters, intermingled with shops and flower stalls. Mille Sens, the anchor eatery, has a Vinotek, where you can sample and select a wine to go with your Mediterranean meal. ⊠ *Bubenbergpl. 9* ☏ *031/3292929* ▭ *AE, DC, MC, V* ☾ *Closed Sun.*

$-$$ ✕ **Menuetto.** A sophisticated and imaginative cooking team of naturalists prepares traditional dishes like Cordon Bleu and Stroganoff with tofu and zesty sauces. The vegetarian menu mixes rich soups and garden salads with ethnic foods and pasta. Homemade fruit ice creams and organic wines complement the meals. A no-smoking section with skylights and greenery adds to the fresh atmosphere. ⊠ *Münsterg. 47/Herreng. 22* ☏ *031/3111448* ▭ *AE, DC, MC, V* ☾ *Closed Sun. and holidays.*

Where to Stay

There's no shortage of hotels in all price ranges in Bern, except when Parliament is in session (March, June, September, and December). Those not in the Old Town or city center are a pleasant walk or a short tram or bus ride away.

$$$$ ▣ **Hotel Bellevue Palace.** Similar in proportion and stateliness to nearby FodorsChoice government buildings, the grand hotel (owned by the Confederation) is ★ the hub of Swiss politics, diplomatic entertaining, and social celebration. Old-world moldings, hand-cast plaster, marble, and stained glass hide an infrastructure of state-of-the-art technology that keeps these elegant spaces humming. Guest rooms mix contemporary and antiquity: minimalist Oriental bed coverings, flat-screen wall-mounted TVs, and authentic period furniture. Oversize baths of stone, tile, and glass retain privacy behind original detail crafted doors. Rooms above the Aare get views of the Bernese Alps. ⊠ *Kocherg. 3–5, CH-3001* ☏ *031/3204545* ⎙ *031/3114743* ⊕ *www.bellevue-palace.ch* ⮑ *100 rooms, 30 suites* ⎯ *Restaurant, bar* ▭ *AE, DC, MC, V.*

★ **$$$$** ▣ **Schweizerhof.** Intimate and sophisticated, this landmark is steeped in tradition. City movers and shakers circulate through the lobby on their way to the bustling Arcady bar and the popular restaurants. Rich greens and blues with accents of gold and yellow dominate the spacious rooms;

original pieces of art and Edwardian furnishings add an individual touch. Soundproof windows block out noise from the train station and tram circle outside the entrance. ✉ *Bahnhofpl. 11, CH-3001* ☎ *031/ 3268080* 🖷 *031/3268090* ⊕ *www.schweizerhof-bern.ch* ⤸*72 rooms, 12 suites* ⚲ *2 restaurants, bar* ⊟ *AE, DC, MC, V.*

$$$ 🏨 **Allegro.** This cutting-edge hotel caters to guests who prefer everything modern and accessible, including direct connection to the Kursaal, the city's grand casino and conference center. "Comfort" rooms have streamlined modular furniture, Internet TV, contemporary art, plus baths trimmed in marble. "Panorama" rooms are outfitted similarly with vistas toward the mountains. The Penthouse floor, requiring elevator key access, has a spacious lounge area and balconies with the best views in town. ✉ *Kornhausstr. 3, CH-3000* ☎ *031/3395500* 🖷 *031/3395510* ⊕ *www.allegro-hotel.ch* ⤸ *167 rooms, 4 suites* ⚲ *4 restaurants, 2 bars* ⊟ *AE, DC, MC, V.*

$$$ 🏨 **Bären/Bristol.** In the hub of shopping, banking, and government, these Best Western properties connected on one level are dependable business-class hotels with fresh, modern rooms decorated in blues and yellows. The hotels share amenities, including a computer room. Locals drop in for their morning espresso and after-work glass of wine sipped beneath humorous bear paintings. ✉ *Bären: Schauplatzg. 4, CH-3011* ☎ *031/3113367; 800/780–7234 in U.S.* 🖷 *031/3116983* ⤸ *57 rooms* ⊕ *www.baerenbern.ch* ✉ *Bristol: Schauplatzg. 10, CH-3011* ☎ *031/ 3110101; 800/780–7234 in U.S.* 🖷 *031/3119479* ⊕ *www.bristolbern. ch* ⤸ *92 rooms* ⊟ *AE, DC, MC, V.*

★ **$$$** 🏨 **Belle Epoque.** This novel hotel is more suggestive of fin-de-siècle Paris than Germanic Bern. The arcaded row house is filled with art nouveau antiques. Light fixtures by Daum and Gallé and an evocative tile mural in the restaurant are eye-catching. Guest rooms have a historic look with up-to-date features including ultramodern baths and Internet access. ✉ *Gerechtigkeitsg. 18, CH-3011* ☎ *031/3114336* 🖷 *031/3113936* ⊕*www.belle-epoque.ch* ⤸*15 rooms, 2 suites* ⚲*2 restaurants, bar* ⊟*AE, DC, MC, V.*

★ **$$** 🏨 **Zum Goldenen Adler.** From the outside, this 1764 building looks like a patrician town house, but its interior is modern and modest, with severe Formica furniture. The ambience is comfortable and familial nonetheless; it's been in the same family for 100 years. ✉ *Gerechtigkeitsg. 7, CH-3011* ☎ *031/3111725* 🖷 *031/3113761* ⤸ *16 rooms* ⚲ *Restaurant, bar* ⊟ *AE, DC, MC, V.*

$ 🏨 **Goldener Schlüssel.** This little hotel is midway between the Rathaus and the Zytglogge in the heart of Old Town. The good, inexpensive restaurant serves specialties like bratwurst with Rösti and *Suure Mocke,* a marinated roast beef served with mashed potatoes. ✉*Rathausg. 72, CH-3011* ☎ *031/3110216* 🖷 *031/3115688* ⊕ *www.goldener-schluessel.ch* ⤸ *29 rooms, 21 with bath* ⚲ *Restaurant* ⊟ *AE, MC, V.*

$ 🏨 **Marthahaus.** This cheery pension stands at the end of a quiet cul-de-sac in a residential neighborhood, equidistant from the train station and the heart of Old Town. The comfortable rooms are bright and sunny. A computer with Internet access is available for use by guests. From the train station, take Bus 20 across the Lorraine bridge to the first stop, Gewerbeschule. ✉ *Wyttenbachstr. 22a, CH-3013* ☎ *031/3324135* 🖷 *031/3333386* ⤸ *38 rooms, 6 with bath* ⊟ *MC, V.*

Nightlife & the Arts

The monthly *what's: on* lists special events, concerts, entertainment, museum exhibits, and a variety of telephone numbers. Portions of the text are in English. The booklet is free from Bern Tourismus and hotels.

Be forewarned: dance clubs often also have a separate "cabaret," but don't expect Liza Minnelli; it's normally a strip joint.

The Arts

The **Bern Symphony Orchestra** (☎ 031/3114242 tickets) is the city's most notable musical institution. Concerts are held at the Casino or the Münster. A five-day **International Jazz Festival** (✉ Bärenpl. 8 ☎ 031/3362539) takes place in early May, with tickets available through TicketCorner (☎ 031/3362539), at the train station, or TicketLine (☎ 084/8800800).

Bern's resident opera company and ballet perform at the **Stadttheater** (✉ Kornhauspl. 20 ☎ 031/3295151); tickets are sold next door (Kornhauspl. 18) weekdays 10–6:30, Saturday 10–4, Sunday 10–12:30.

Nightlife

BARS & LOUNGES Contemporary spaces like **Andriano's** (✉ Theaterpl. 2 ☎ 031/3188831) abound, doubling as gathering places for a coffee during the day and drinks until late at night. For history, head for **Klötzlikeller** (✉ Gerechtigkeitsg. 62), said to be the oldest wine bar in Bern. Plush leather seating keeps a chic crowd lingering over cocktails at **Le Nouveau du Théâtre** (✉ Hotelg. 10 ☎ 031/3185067).

DANCING **Guayas** (✉ Parkterrasse 16 ☎ 031/3187075) plays a variety of music from hip-hop to Latin and hosts after-hours parties that go until dawn. One of the biggest and hottest spots in town is **Toni's the Club** (✉ Aarbergerg. 35 ☎ 031/3115011), with two bars and two dance floors.

Bern Essentials

AIRPORTS & TRANSFERS

Bern's small airport (BRN), 9 km (5½ mi) south of the city in Belp, has flights to and from most European capitals. A convenient shuttle bus running between the airport and the train station costs 14 SF, a taxi about 35 SF.

🚩 **Bern-Belp Airport** ☎ 031/9602111.

BUS TRAVEL WITHIN BERN

The bus and tram service in Bern is excellent; fares range from 1.50 SF to 2.40 SF. Buy individual tickets from the dispenser at the tram or bus stop. Visitor cards for unlimited rides are available for 7 SF a day at the tourist office in the Hauptbahnhof or at the public-transportation ticket office on Bankgässchen (from the train station follow signs for Bus 13). A Swiss Pass allows you to travel free.

CAR TRAVEL

Bern is connected conveniently by expressway to Basel and Zürich via A1, to the Berner Oberland via A6, and to Lac Léman and thus Lausanne, Geneva, and the Valais via A12. The city's many pedestrian zones make parking in city garages a necessity. Electronic signs on incoming thoroughfares give up-to-the minute counts on space availability.

EMERGENCIES

🚩 Doctors & Dentists **Emergency medical, dental, and pharmacy referrals** ☎ 0900/576747.

🚩 Emergency Services **Ambulance** ☎ 144. **Police** ☎ 117.

TAXIS

Taxis are expensive; it costs around 18 SF just to travel from the train station to the end of Old Town.

TOURS

A two-hour multilingual bus tour covering Bern's principal sights is offered by the tourist office for 25 SF.

From June to September a multilingual 1½-hour tour of the Old Town is offered daily at 11 AM and costs 14 SF. Contact the tourist office. A brochure describing all 13 historic fountains is a good self-guided option.

TRAIN TRAVEL

Bern is a major link between Geneva, Zürich, and Basel, and Intercity trains, which make the fewest stops, leave almost every hour from the Hauptbahnhof. Bern is the only European capital to have three high-speed trains: the ICE from Berlin takes 9 hours; the TGV from Paris takes 4½ hours; and the Pendolino from Milan takes 3–4 hours.

🚇 **Hauptbahnhof** ☎ 0900/300300 costs 1.19 SF per min.

VISITOR INFORMATION

The Bern Tourismus location at the Bear Pits offers a multimedia history of Bern.

🚇 **Bern Tourismus** ✉ Hauptbahnhof, Bahnhofpl. ☎ 031/3281212 🌐 www.bernetourism.ch.

ZERMATT

The ultimate Swiss-Alpine experience is bundled in one tidily wrapped package in Zermatt (5,300 feet): spectacular mountains, a roaring stream, a state-of-the-art transport network, and a broad range of high-quality accommodations—some of them rich in rusticity—plus 230 km (143 mi) of downhill runs and 7 km (4 mi) of cross-country trails. But its greatest claim to fame remains the Matterhorn (14,690 feet), which attracts swarms of package-tour sightseers pushing shoulder to shoulder to get yet another shot of this genuine wonder of the Western world. Excursions to the Klein Matterhorn and Gornergrat are particularly spectacular.

Exploring Zermatt

Zermatt lies in a hollow of meadows and trees ringed by mountains—among them the broad **Monte Rosa** (14,940 feet), with its tallest peak, the **Dufourspitze** (at 15,200 feet, the highest point in Switzerland), of which visitors hear relatively little, so all-consuming is the cult of the **Matterhorn**. Walking down the main street, Bahnhofstrasse, you'll be deluged by Matterhorn images: on postcards, on beer steins, on candy wrappers. Yet the Matterhorn deserves idolatry: though it has become an almost self-parodying icon, like the Eiffel Tower or the Statue of Liberty, this distinctive, snaggletoothed pyramid thrusting upward in solitary splendor is even more impressive than the photographs suggest.

Despite its celebrity mountain, Zermatt remains a resort with its feet on the ground. It is as protective of its regional quirks as it is of its wildlife and its tumbledown *mazots* (grain-storage sheds raised on stone bases to keep the mice away), which hunker between the glass-and-concrete chalets like old tenements trapped between skyscrapers. Car-free streets twist past weathered wood walls and flower boxes until they break into open country that inevitably slopes uphill.

The cog railway between Visp and Zermatt began disgorging summer tourists in 1891, but it was not until 1927 that it also plowed through in wintertime. What had drawn the first tourists and made Zermatt a household word was Edward Whymper's spectacular—and catastrophic—

conquest of the Matterhorn in 1865. Whymper and his band of six managed to reach the summit, but then tragedy struck. On the treacherous descent, four of the men lost their footing and snapped their safety rope, pulling one another 4,000 feet to their death. One of the bodies was never recovered, but the others remain in the grim little cemetery behind the church in the village center.

It's quite simple to gain the broader perspective of high altitudes without risking life or limb: the train trip up the **Gornergrat** (10,269 feet) on the **Gornergratbahn,** does double duty as ski transport and sightseeing excursion. Completed in 1898 and the highest exposed rail system in Europe, it connects out of the main Zermatt station and climbs slowly up the valley to the **Riffelberg,** which at 8,471 feet offers wide-open views of the Matterhorn. From **Rotenboden,** at 9,248 feet, a short downhill walk leads to the **Riffelsee,** with its pristine reflections of the famous peak. At the end of the 9-km (5½-mi) line, passengers pour onto the observation terraces of the Gornergrat to take in majestic views of Gorner glacier, the Matterhorn, Monte Rosa, and scores of other peaks. Bring warm clothes and sturdy shoes. ⌧ *63 SF round-trip; 38 SF one-way up and ski or hike down* ⊙ *Departures every 24 mins 7* AM–6 PM.

Skiing

Zermatt's skiable terrain lives up to its reputation: the 70 lift installations are capable of moving well over 50,000 skiers per hour to reach approximately 250 km (156 mi) of marked pistes—if you count those of Cervinia in Italy. This royal plateau has several less-than-perfect features, however, not least of which is the separation of the skiable territory into three sectors. **Sunegga-Blauherd-Rothorn** culminates at an elevation of 10,170 feet. **Gornergrat-Stockhorn** (11,155 feet) is the second. The third is the region dominated by the **Klein Matterhorn**; to go from this sector to the others you must return to the bottom of the valley and lose considerable time crossing town to reach the lifts to the other elevations. The solution is to ski for a whole day in the same area, especially during high season (mid-December to the end of February, or even until Easter if the snow cover is good). A one-day lift ticket costs 64 SF; a six-day pass costs 318 SF. A hands-free "Smart Card" makes payment and lift access a breeze. A **ski school** (Skischulbüro; ☎ 027/9662466) runs during the high season.

Where to Stay & Eat

Perched at the German end of the equally French canton of Valais, Zermatt offers a variety of French and German cooking, from veal and Rösti to raclette and fondue. Specialties often feature pungent mountain cheese: Käseschnitte, for instance, are substantial little casseroles of bread, cheese, and often ham, baked until the whey saturates the crusty bread and the cheese browns to gold. Air-dried beef is another Valais treat; it's served in thin, translucent slices, with gherkins and crisp pickled onions.

At high season—Christmas and New Year's, Carnaval to Easter, and late summer—Zermatt's high hotel prices rival those of Zürich and Geneva. But most hotels include half pension in their price, serving breakfast and your choice of a noon or evening meal. Hotels that call themselves "garni" do not have a full kitchen and serve only breakfast and sometimes light snacks. In Zermatt street addresses are rarely used; family and chalet names take precedence. Find your way to hotels using signposts that mark the destination that could be on a main street, side alley, or path.

$$–$$$ ✕ **Grill-Room Stockhorn.** The tantalizing aromas of pungent cheese and roasting meat on the open grill should sharpen your hunger the moment you step inside this low-slung restaurant decked out with mountain memorabilia. This is a great place to fortify yourself with regional dishes; the service and the clientele are equally lively. ☎ 027/9671747 ▤ AE, MC, V ☾ Closed mid-May–mid-June and Oct.

$$–$$$
FodorsChoice
★ ✕ **Zum See.** In a hamlet (little more than a cluster of mazots) of the same name, this restaurant turns out inventive meals that merit acclaim. Although it's in the middle of nowhere (walk or ski down from lift station Furi), it overflows until late afternoon with skiers and hikers sunning on the terrace or packed into the 400-year-old log house. Hosts Max and Greti Mennig masterfully prepare regional specialties such as venison salad with wild mushrooms and herbed goat cheese ravioli. Don't expect to arrive unannounced and get a table; cell phone–toting regulars call in their reservation. ✉ Zum See ☎ 027/9672045 ▤ MC, V ☾ Closed Apr.–June and Oct.–mid-Dec.

★ $–$$ ✕ **Findlerhof.** This mountain restaurant in tiny Findeln is perched high between the Sunnegga and Blauherd ski areas. The Matterhorn views from the wraparound dining porch are astonishing, the food surprisingly fresh and creative. Franz and Heidi Schwery tend their own Alpine garden to provide lettuces for their salads and berries for vinaigrettes and fruit tarts. The *Matterkuchen*, a bacon and leek quiche, will fortify you for the 30- to 40-minute walk to the village. ✉ Findeln ☎ 027/9672588 ▤ MC ☾ Closed May–mid-June and mid-Oct.–Nov.

$ ✕ **Whymperstube.** This little restaurant is in the Hotel Monte Rosa. Here, plates of melted raclette and bubbling pots of fondue are delivered to tightly packed tables by an agile waitstaff. Imagine the climber's stories that must have echoed within these walls. ✉ Bahnhofstr. ☎ 027/9672296 ▤ AE, DC, MC, V.

★ $$$$ ✕▣ **Monte Rosa.** This was the first inn in Zermatt and the home base of Edward Whymper when he conquered the Matterhorn in 1865. Behind its graceful shuttered facade you will find an ideal balance between history and modern convenience in the burnished pine, beveled glass, flagstone floors, and restored Victorian dining hall. Dinner is a five-course candlelight affair that could have been styled for a Merchant-Ivory film. The bar is an après-ski must. Guests have access to the sports facilities at Mont Cervin, and all Seiler restaurants on the members' "Dine-Around" plan. ✉ CH-3920 ☎ 027/9663333 ▤ 027/9671160 ☞ 44 rooms, 5 suites ♨ Restaurant, bar ▤ AE, DC, MC, V.

$$$–$$$$ ✕▣ **Grand Hotel Schöegg.** Above the valley floor, accessible through a tunnel and private elevator, the Relais & Châteaux affiliate owns some of the village's premier views. The interiors are richly decorated with patina woods rubbed to a sheen and ornately painted ceilings; sumptuous fabrics and touches of wrought iron add to the elegance. The Gourmetstübli is one of the haute dining addresses in town serving au courant dishes like rabbit ravioli with fig beurre blanc or lobster cooked in soy butter accompanied by bok choy and a mix of Chinese noodles. ✉ CH-3920 ☎ 027/9663434 ▤ 027/9663435 ⊕ www.schonegg.ch ☞ 37 rooms, 2 suites ♨ 2 restaurants, 2 bars ▤ AE, DC, MC, V ☾ Closed late Apr.–late May and Oct.–Nov.

★ $$$–$$$$ ✕▣ **Julen.** This hotel has shunned the usual regional kitsch in favor of a century-old spruce-wood decor coupled with primary-color carpets and silk curtains. A three-floor sports center includes an elaborate Roman bath room. Besides a restaurant serving international cuisine, there's a welcoming Stübli with unusual dishes prepared with lamb from local family-owned flocks. ✉ CH-3920 ☎ 027/9667600 ▤ 027/9667676 ☞ 27 rooms, 5 suites ♨ 2 restaurants, pool, bar ▤ AE, DC, MC, V.

★ $$$$ ☒ **Mont Cervin Hotel and Residences.** One of the flagships of the Seiler dynasty, this is a sleek, luxurious, and urbane mountain hotel. Built in 1852, it's unusually low slung for a grand hotel, with dark beams and classic decor. Rooms are impeccably decorated in primary colors that mix stripes and plaids; many have views of the Matterhorn. Luxurious apartments across the street are accessible through a handy tunnel. ☒ *CH-3920* ☎ *027/9668888* 🖷 *027/9672878* 🛏 *100 rooms, 15 suites, 24 apartments* ☄ *2 restaurants, pool, bar* ▤ *AE, DC, MC, V* ☯ *Closed May–mid-June and mid-Oct.–Nov.*

$$$–$$$$ ☒ **Apartmenthotel Zurbriggen.** Sleeping under the roof of Olympic medalist Pirmin Zurbriggen's six-unit apartment house may not make you a better skier, but the view will elicit dreams of starting gates and downhill races. Flexible configurations can sleep a couple or expand to include a pack of friends. Near the cable car to Klein Matterhorn, this ultramodern glass structure with clean interiors of larch and chrome has all the amenities of a boutique hotel. Fully stocked kitchenettes and wellness facilities add to your comfort. ☒ *CH-3920* ☎ *027/9663838* 🖷 *027/ 9663839* ⊕ *www.zurbriggen.ch* 🛏 *6 apartments* ☄ *Pool* ▤ *AE, DC, MC, V.*

$$ ☒ **Mischabel.** One of the least, if not *the* least, expensive hotels in this pricey resort town, the Mischabel provides comfort, atmosphere, and a central location few places can match at twice the price: southern balconies frame a perfect Matterhorn view—the higher the floor, the better. Creaky, homey, and covered with *Arvenholz* (Alpen pine) aged to the color of toffee, its rooms have sinks only and share the linoleum-lined showers on every floor. A generous daily menu, for guests only, caters to families and young skiers on the cheap. ☒ *CH-3920* ☎ *027/ 9671131* 🖷 *027/9676507* 🛏 *28 rooms* ☄ *Restaurant* ▤ *MC, V.*

$$ ☒ **Romantica.** Among the scores of anonymously modern hotels cloned all over the Zermatt plain, this modest structure has an exceptional location directly above the town center. Its tidy, bright gardens and flower boxes, its game trophies, and its old-style granite stove give it personality, and the plain rooms benefit from big windows and balconies. You can also stay in one of the two, 200-year-old, tiny (but charming) *Walliserstadel* huts in the hotel's garden. Views take in the mountains, though not the Matterhorn, over a graceful clutter of stone roofs. ☒ *CH-3920* ☎ *027/9662650* 🖷 *027/9662655* 🛏 *13 rooms* ☄ *Bar* ▤ *AE, DC, MC, V.*

Nightlife

If you can find a space, squeeze into **Elsie's Place** (☎ 027/9672431), a rustic hut across from the church, for an aged scotch or double martini. Snacks and light meals replace dinner. **GramPi's Bar** (☎ 027/ 9677788), in an area locals call the Bermuda Triangle because of the concentration of nightspots, is a lively, young people's bar with dancing downstairs. For a double dose of folklore song and dance, an evening at the **Schweizer Stübli** (☎ 017/9676767), in the Hotel Schewizerhof, is full of rowdy sing-alongs and accordion music. **T-Bar** (☎ 027/9674000), below the Pollux hotel, plays more varied music than the generic disco of most ski resort nightspots.

Zermatt Essentials

AIR TRAVEL
The airports of Zürich and Geneva are roughly equidistant from the nearby town of Brig, which is well connected by train, but by approaching from Geneva you can avoid crossing mountain passes.

CAR TRAVEL

Zermatt is a car-free resort isolated at the end of the Mattertal, a rugged valley at the eastern end of the Alpine canton of Valais. A good mountain highway cuts south through the Mattertal valley from Visp, the crossroads of the main Valais east–west routes. You can drive up the valley as far as Täsch, but there you must abandon your car in a parking lot and catch the train for the cogwheel climb into Zermatt.

EMERGENCIES

🔁 Emergency Services **Ambulance** ☎ 144. **Police** ☎ 117.

TRAIN TRAVEL

The Brig-Visp-Zermatt Railway, a private narrow-gauge system, runs from Brig to Visp, connecting on to Zermatt. All major rail routes connect through Brig, whether you approach from Geneva or Lausanne in the west, from the Lötschberg line that tunnels through from Kandersteg and the Bernese Oberland, or from the connecting Simplon Pass from Italy. The SBB provides information on all train service.

TRANSPORTATION AROUND ZERMATT

Electric taxi shuttles and horse-drawn carriages operated by hotels are the only means of transportation, but the village is relatively small and easily covered on foot. A sophisticated network of cable cars, lifts, cog railways, and even an underground metro carries you above the village center into the wilderness for hiking and skiing.

VISITOR INFORMATION

🔁 **Verkehrsbüro Zermatt** ✉ Bahnhofpl., CH-3920 ☎ 027/9678100 🌐 www.zermatt.ch.

TURKEY

ISTANBUL, THE AEGEAN COAST, THE MEDITERRANEAN COAST, CENTRAL ANATOLIA & CAPPADOCIA

30

TURKEY IS ONE PLACE to which the phrase "East meets West" really applies. It's especially true in Turkey's largest city, Istanbul, that the continents of Europe and Asia come together, separated only by the Bosporus, which flows 29 km (18 mi) from the Black Sea to the Sea of Marmara. On the vibrant streets of this city of 12 million people, miniskirts and trendy boots mingle with head scarves and prayer beads.

Although 97% of Turkey's landmass is in Asia, Turkey began facing west politically in 1923, when Mustapha Kemal, better known as Atatürk, founded the modern republic. He transformed the remnants of the shattered Ottoman Empire into a secular state with a Western outlook. So thorough was this changeover—culturally, politically, and economically—that in 1987, 49 years after Atatürk's death, Turkey applied to the European Union (EU) for full membership and in December 1999 was finally listed as an official candidate. However, its prospects look dim until Turkey's government implements reforms toward greater democratization as requested by the EU. Full membership is also likely to depend on the resolution of a number of long-standing problems, including 15 years of rampant inflation, social polarization over the role of Islam in public life, and the recognition of minority rights.

For 16 centuries Istanbul, originally known as Byzantium, played a major part in world politics: first as the capital of the Eastern Roman Empire, when it was known as Constantinople, then as capital of the Ottoman Empire, the most powerful Islamic empire in the world, when it was renamed Istanbul. Atatürk moved the capital to Ankara at the inception of the Turkish Republic.

The legacies of the Greeks, Romans, Ottomans, and numerous other civilizations have made the country a vast outdoor museum. The most spectacular of the reconstructed classical sites are along the western Aegean coast and the southwest Mediterranean coast, which are lined with magnificent sandy beaches and sleepy little fishing villages, as well as busy resorts with sophisticated facilities for travelers.

If you have an extra five to seven days, an excursion inland to central Anatolia and the eroded lunar valleys of the Cappadocia area will give you a glimpse at some of the enormous diversity of the landscapes and people of Turkey.

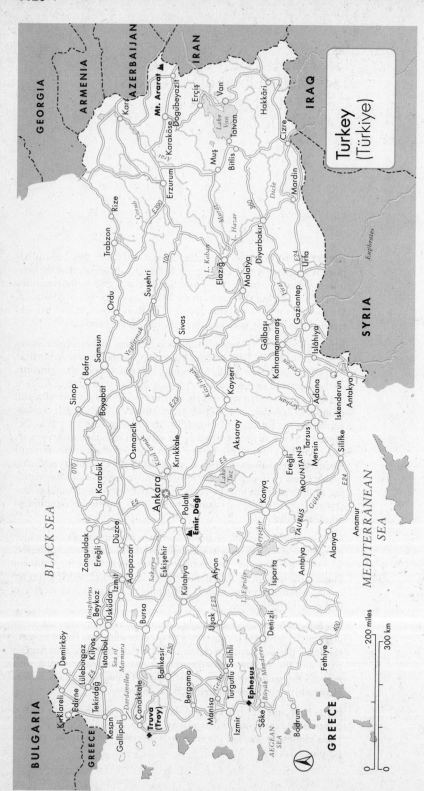

TURKEY A TO Z

To research prices, get advice from other travelers, and book travel arrangements, visit www.fodors.com.

AIR TRAVEL

CARRIERS   Turkish Airlines operates an extensive domestic network. There are at least 14 flights daily on weekdays between Istanbul and Ankara, as well as less-frequent flights to other major cities. In summer additional flights between the cities and coastal resorts are added.

🛪 **Turkish Airlines (THY)** ⊠ Taksim Sq., Istanbul ☎ 212/444-0849; 212/663-6363 reservations.

CHECK IN &   Try to arrive at the airport at least 45 minutes before your flight, be-
BOARDING   cause security checks, which are rigidly enforced, can be time-consuming. Checked luggage is placed on trolleys on the tarmac and must be identified by boarding passengers before it is put on the plane. Unidentified luggage is left behind and checked for bombs or firearms.

BOAT & FERRY TRAVEL

A car ferry and cruise service is operated out of Istanbul by Turkish Maritime Lines. Cruises are in great demand, so make your reservations well in advance through the main office in Istanbul. The Black Sea Ferry sails from May through September from Istanbul to Samsun and Trabzon and back, from Karaköy Dock in Istanbul. One-way fares to Trabzon are about $30 for a reclining seat, $60–$90 for cabins, and $90 for cars. The Istanbul-to-İzmir car ferry departs once a week. The price of a one-way ticket with meals included varies between $60 and $85, plus $60 for a car.

🛥 **Turkish Maritime Lines** ⊠ Rıhtım Cad. 1, Karaköy ☎ 212/249-9222 or 212/249-9222.

BUS TRAVEL

Buses, which are run by private companies, are much faster than trains and provide excellent, inexpensive service. Buses are available, almost around the clock, between all cities and towns. They are fairly comfortable and many are air-conditioned. Companies have their own fixed fares for different routes. Istanbul to Ankara, for instance, varies from $15 to $20, and Istanbul to İzmir varies from $20 to $25. *Şişe suyu* (bottled water) is included in the fare. You can purchase tickets at stands in a town's *otogar* (central bus terminal) or at branch offices in city centers. All seats are reserved. There are small variations in fares among the different companies, but it is usually worth paying the 3%–5% extra for companies such as Varan, Ulusoy, and Kamil Koç, which offer no-smoking seating. Many buses between major cities are double-deckers and all of those operated by the larger companies have toilets. For very short trips or getting around within a city, use minibuses or a *dolmuş* (shared taxi). Both are inexpensive and comfortable.

BUSINESS HOURS

BANKS & OFFICES   Banks are generally open weekdays 8:30 or 9–12:30 and 1:30–5, although increasingly banks are remaining open at lunchtime. Foreign exchange bureaus normally remain open from 9:30 or 10 AM to 6 PM.

MUSEUMS &   Museums are generally open Tuesday–Sunday 9:30–4:30. Palaces are
SIGHTS   open Friday–Wednesday 9:30–4:30. Mosques are usually open to the public, except during *namaz* (prayer hours), which are observed five times a day. These times are based on the position of the sun, so they vary throughout the seasons between the following hours: sunrise (5–7), lunchtime (noon–1), afternoon (3–4), sunset (5–7), bedtime (9–10). Prayers last 30–40 minutes.

SHOPS Most shops are open Monday–Saturday 9:30–7. There are some exceptions in the major shopping areas in large cities and resort areas, where shops stay open until 9 PM. Most are closed Sunday, although small grocery stores and a few other stores in the main shopping areas remain open seven days a week.

CAR TRAVEL

EMERGENCIES If your car breaks down, Turkish mechanics in the villages will usually manage to get you going again, at least until you reach a city for full repairs. In the cities, entire streets are given over to car-repair shops. Prices are not high, but it's good to give a small tip to the person who does the repair work. If you're not in the shop during the repairs, take all car documents with you. The Touring and Automobile Club gives information about driving in Turkey and has a repair service.

🚗 **Touring and Automobile Club (TTÖK)** ☎ 212/282-8140.

GASOLINE Throughout the country Shell, Total, Elf, and British Petroleum, as well as two Turkish oil companies, have gas stations that are open 24 hours on the main highways. Others are open from 6 AM to 10 PM.

ROAD CONDITIONS Turkey has 37,500 km (25,000 mi) of well-maintained, paved highways, but signposts are few, lighting is scarce, and city traffic is chaotic. City streets and highways are jammed with vehicles operated by high-speed drivers who constantly blast their horns. In Istanbul avoid the many small one-way streets; you never know when someone is going to barrel down one of them in the wrong direction. Better yet, use public transportation or take taxis. Parking is a big problem in the cities and larger towns.

RULES OF THE ROAD The best way to see Turkey is by car, but be warned that it has one of the highest accident rates in Europe. In general, Turkish driving conforms to Mediterranean customs, with driving on the right and passing on the left. But watch out for drivers passing on a curve or on the top of a hill. Other hazards are carts and motorcycles weaving in and out of traffic. Archaeological and historical sites are indicated by yellow signposts. Seat belts are required in the front seats.

CUSTOMS & DUTIES

Turkish customs officials rarely look through tourists' luggage on arrival. You are allowed to bring in 400 cigarettes, 50 cigars, 200 grams of tobacco, 1.5 kilograms of instant coffee, 500 grams of tea, and 2.5 liters of alcohol. An additional 600 cigarettes, 100 cigars, or 500 grams of tobacco may be imported if purchased at the Turkish duty-free shops on arrival. Register all valuable personal items in your passport on entry. Goods at duty-free shops in airports are usually less expensive here than in duty-free shops in other European airports or in-flight offerings. Turkey is extremely tough on anyone attempting to export antiques without authorization or on anyone caught with illegal drugs, regardless of the amount.

EATING & DRINKING

The Turkish people are justly proud of their cuisine. In addition to the blends of spices used, the food is also extremely healthful—full of fresh vegetables, yogurt, legumes, and grains, not to mention fresh seafood, roast lamb, and kebabs made of lamb, beef, or chicken. Because Turkey is predominantly Muslim, pork is not readily available. But there's plenty of alcohol, including local beer and wine, which are excellent and inexpensive. Particularly good wines are Villa Doluca and Kavaklidere, available in *beyaz* (white) and *kırmızı* (red). The most popular beers are Efes Pilsen and Troy. Miller, Carlsberg, and Becks are also now brewed locally under license, and are widely available. In major cities and large hotels it's usually possible to find imported beers from Europe and the United States. The national alcoholic drink, *rakı*, is made from grapes and aniseed. Turks mix it with water or ice and sip it throughout their meal or serve it as an aperitif.

Many hotel restaurants have English-language menus and usually serve a bland version of Continental cuisine. Foreign fast-food chains are also becoming increasingly widespread. Far more adventurous and tasty are meals in *restorans* and *lokantas* (Turkish restaurants). Most lokantas do not have menus because they serve only what's fresh and in season, which varies daily. At lokantas you simply sit back and let the waiter bring food to your table, beginning with a tray of *mezes* (appetizers). You point to the dishes that look inviting and take as many as you want. Then you select your main course from fresh meat or fish—displayed in glass-covered refrigerated units—which is then cooked to order, or from a steam table laden with casseroles and stews. For lighter meals there are *kebabcıs*, tiny restaurants specializing in kebabs served with salad and yogurt, and *pidecis*, selling *pides*, a pizzalike snack of flat bread topped with butter, cheese, egg, or ground lamb and baked in a wood-burning oven.

Prices are for a main course at dinner. For meals including mezes the overall cost of the meal per person will be approximately twice the price of the main course.

WHAT IT COSTS In U.S. dollars			
$$$$	**$$$**	**$$**	**$**
MAJOR CITIES*			
AT DINNER	over $20	$12–$20	$6–$12	under $6
OTHER AREAS			
AT DINNER	over $17	$10–$17	$5–$10	under $5

Prices are per person for a main course. *Major cities include Istanbul.

MEALTIMES Lunch is generally served from noon to 3 and dinner from 7 to 10. In cities you can find restaurants or cafés open almost any time of day or night, but in villages, finding a restaurant open at odd hours can be a problem. In more conservative areas restaurants often close during daylight hours in the Islamic holy month of Ramadan (in autumn), when most Muslims fast.

RESERVATIONS & DRESS If you're going to a fancy restaurant, jacket and tie are appropriate. Informal dress is acceptable at restaurants in all other price categories.

EMBASSIES
Consular offices are in Istanbul. *See* Istanbul Essentials for additional information.

HEALTH
Although tap water is heavily chlorinated, it's often not safe to drink—and even when it is, it's often unpalatable. Play it safe and drink *maden suyu* (bottled mineral water) or regular *şişe suyu* (bottled water).

HOLIDAYS
New Year's; Kurban Bayramı, an important sacrificial feast celebrating Abraham's willingness to sacrifice his son to God (January 31–February 4); National Sovereignty and Children's Day (April 23); National

Youth and Sports Day (May 19); Victory Day (August 30); Republic Day (October 29); Şeker Bayramı, "Sugar Feast," a three-day celebration marking the end of Ramadan (November 13–16).

The Islamic religious holidays of Şeker Bayramı and Kurban Bayramı follow the lunar calendar and move forward by approximately 10 days each year. The dates given above are for 2004. Many shops and most companies close at midday on the day before the official beginning of Şeker Bayramı and Kurban Bayramı.

LANGUAGE

Atatürk launched language reforms that replaced Arabic script with the Latin-based alphabet. English and German are widely spoken in cities and resorts. In villages and remote areas you'll have a hard time finding anyone who speaks anything but Turkish. Try learning a few basic Turkish words; your efforts will be appreciated. Living Language, a division of Random House, Inc., sells a 60-minute program called *In-Flight Turkish* to get you started.

LODGING

Accommodations range from international luxury chains in Istanbul, Ankara, and İzmir to comfortable, family-run *pansiyons* (guest houses). Plan ahead for the peak summer season, when resort hotels are often booked solid by tour companies. Turkey does not have central hotel reservations offices.

Hotels are officially classified in Turkey as HL (luxury), H1 to H5 (first- to fifth-class); motels, M1 to M2 (first- to second-class); and P, pansiyons. The classification is misleading because the lack of a restaurant or a lounge automatically relegates the establishment to the bottom of the ratings. A lower-grade hotel may actually be far more charming and comfortable than one with a higher rating. There are also many local establishments that are licensed but not included in the official ratings list. You can obtain their names from local tourist offices.

Rates vary from $10 to more than $200 a night for a double room. In less expensive hotels the plumbing and furnishings will probably leave much to be desired. You can find very acceptable, clean double rooms with bath for between $30 and $70, with breakfast included. Room rates are displayed in the reception area. It is accepted practice in Turkey to ask to see the room in advance.

Prices are for two people in a double room, including breakfast, 17% value-added-tax (V.A.T.), and a 10%–15% service charge.

WHAT IT COSTS In U.S. dollars			
$$$$	**$$$**	**$$**	**$**
MAJOR CITIES*			
FOR 2 PEOPLE over $200	$100–$200	$60–$100	under $60
OTHER AREAS			
FOR 2 PEOPLE over $150	$100–$150	$50–$100	under $50

Hotel prices are for two people in a standard double room in high season, excluding tax and breakfast. *Major cities include Istanbul.

MAIL & SHIPPING

Post offices are painted bright yellow and have PTT (Post, Telegraph, and Telephone or PTT) signs on the front. The major ones are open Monday–Saturday 8 AM–9 PM, Sunday 9–7. Smaller branches are usually open Monday–Friday 8–4:30.

If you're uncertain where you'll be staying, have mail addressed to *poste restante* and sent to Merkez Postanesi (central post office) in the town of your choice.

MONEY MATTERS

Turkey is among the least expensive of the Mediterranean countries. Prices in this chapter are quoted in U.S. dollars, which indicate the real cost to you more accurately than do the constantly increasing lira prices. (Exchange rates often move by 30%–40% or more per year.)

Coffee can range from about 50¢ to $2.50 a cup, depending on whether it's the less expensive Turkish coffee or American-style coffee and whether it's served in a luxury hotel or a café; tea, 20¢–$2 a glass; local beer, $1–$5; soft drink, $1–$4; lamb shish kebab, $2–$7; taxi, approximately $1.30 for 2 km (1 mi). Taxi prices are 50% higher between midnight and 6 AM.

CURRENCY The monetary unit is the Turkish lira (TL), which comes in bank notes of 250,000, 500,000, 1,000,000, 5,000,000, 10,000,000, and 20,000,000. Coins come in denominations of 25,000, 50,000, 100,000, and 250,000. The high rate of inflation means that Turkish lira depreciates by 30%–40% a year against major currencies. At press time (March 2003), the exchange rate was 1,707,017 TL to the U.S. dollar, 1,162,449 TL to the Canadian dollar, 2,667,338 TL to the pound sterling, 1,831,971 TL to the euro, 1,018,243 TL to the Australian dollar, 955,366 TL to the New Zealand dollar, and 217,420 TL to the South African rand. Major credit cards and traveler's checks are widely accepted in hotels, shops, and expensive restaurants in cities and resorts but rarely in villages and small shops and restaurants.

There are no problems changing money back from Turkish lira to other currencies. But because the value of Turkish currency can sometimes fall significantly over a very short period, it is advisable to change enough money for only a few days at a time.

Foreign exchange bureaus are now widespread in Turkey's major cities and resorts (they usually have a sign saying DÖVIZ, Turkish for "Foreign Exchange"). Exchange rates are usually displayed just inside the door. Rates may vary slightly between exchange bureaus but are always better than bank rates and considerably more attractive than rates offered in hotels.

PASSPORTS & VISAS

U.S. citizens not arriving on a cruise line need visas. These are most easily obtained at the port of entry—just be sure to have cash (U.S. $20). Canadian tourists do not need visas. Visas are required if you're from the United Kingdom—obtain them at the port of entry for £10 or from any Turkish consulate (the rate will be somewhat higher).

SHOPPING

The best part of shopping in Turkey is visiting the *bedestans* (bazaars), brimming with copper and brass wares, hand-painted ceramics, alabaster and onyx goods, fabrics, richly colored carpets, and relics and icons trickling in from the former Soviet Union. The key word for shopping in the bazaars is "bargain." You must be willing to bargain, and bargain hard. It's great fun once you get the hang of it. As a rule of thumb offer 50% less after you're given the initial price and be prepared to go up by about 25%–30% of the first asking price. It is often advisable to get up to leave, as the best price is invariably the one called after you as you disappear around the corner. You can always think about it for two minutes and, if you are happy about it, return and accept. It's both bad manners and bad business to underbid grossly or to start bargaining if you're not serious about buying. Outside the bazaars prices are usually fixed, although in resort areas some shopkeepers may be willing to bargain if you ask for a "better price." Part of the fun of roaming through the bazaars is having a free glass of çay (tea), which vendors will offer you whether you're a serious shopper or just browsing. Beware of antiques: chances are you will end up with an expensive fake, but even if you do find the genuine article, it's illegal to export antiques of any type. If you decide to buy something that looks antique, ask for documentation from the seller that the item is not an antique.

TAXES

Value-added tax (V.A.T.) is nearly always included in the price. You can claim back the V.A.T. if you buy articles from authorized shops. The net total value of articles subject to V.A.T. on your invoice must be more than a specified amount, depending on the nature of the goods, and these articles must be exported within three months of purchase. The invoice must be stamped by customs. Otherwise, mail the stamped invoice back to the dealer within one month of departure and the dealer should send back a check.

TELEPHONES

All telephone numbers in Turkey have seven local digits plus three-digit city codes. Intercity calls are preceded by 0. The code for the European side of Istanbul is 212; be sure to dial the country code first if you are calling from outside Turkey; otherwise you may reach New York City! To call Asian Istanbul, dial 216.

Turkey's three main GSM mobile telephone service providers have reciprocal agreements with most of their European counterparts, enabling subscribers to use the Turkish GSM network during their stay in the country. But most subscribers to U.S. and Canadian cellular telephone service providers are currently unable to connect to the Turkish network.

COUNTRY & AREA CODES
The country code for Turkey is 90. When dialing a number in Turkey from outside the country, drop the initial 0 from the local area code.

INTERNATIONAL CALLS
For all international calls dial 00, then dial the country code, area or city code, and the number. You can use the higher-price cards for this, or reach an international operator by dialing ☎ 132. To reach a long-distance operator call AT&T, MCI, or Sprint.
🔲 Access Codes **AT&T** ☎ 00800-12277. **MCI** ☎ 00800-11177. **Sprint** ☎ 00800-14477.

LOCAL CALLS
Pay phones are blue, push-button models. Most now take phone cards, or occasionally credit cards. However, particularly away from large cities, you can still find the old-type phones which take jetons (tokens). Multilingual directions are posted in many phone booths.

Telephone cards are available at post offices in small denominations. They can also often be purchased for just a little more from street booths. Tokens are available for local and long-distance calls. If you need operator assistance for long-distance calls within Turkey, dial ☎ 131. For intercity calls, dial 0, then dial the city code and the number.

Telephone numbers in European and Asian Istanbul have different codes: the code for European Istanbul (for numbers beginning with 2, 3, 5, 6, or 8) is 0/212; for Asian Istanbul (for numbers that start with 3 or 4), dial 0/216.

TIPPING

Except at the cheapest restaurants, a 10%–15% charge is added to the bill. As the money does not necessarily find its way to the waiter, leave an additional 10% on the table or hand it to the waiter. In top restaurants waiters expect tips of between 10% and 15%. Hotel porters expect between $1 and $4 and the chambermaid about $2. Taxi drivers don't expect tips, although they are becoming accustomed to foreigners' giving them something. Round off the fare to the nearest 500,000 TL. At Turkish baths the staff that attends you expects to share a tip of 30%–35% of the bill. Don't worry about missing them—they'll be lined up expectantly on your departure.

TRAIN TRAVEL

Although there are trains labeled EXPRESS, the term is usually a misnomer. These trains have several long-distance routes, but they tend to be slow. The best daily trains between Istanbul and Ankara are the *Başkent Expres* and the *Fatih Expres*. The overnight *Yataklı Ankara Expres* has luxurious sleeper cars; the *Anadolu Expres* has cheaper, less comfortable berths. There are overnight trains to Pamukkale as well as daily trains to Edirne from Sirkeci station in Istanbul. Dining cars on some trains have waiter service and serve surprisingly good and inexpensive food.

FARES & SCHEDULES Train fares tend to be lower than bus fares. Seats on the best trains, as well as those with sleeping berths, should be reserved in advance. In railroad stations, buy tickets at windows marked ANAHAT GISELERI. Travel agencies carrying the TCDD (State Railways) sign and some post offices sell train tickets, too.

WHEN TO GO

The tourist season runs from April through October. July and August are the busiest and warmest months. April–June and September–October are the best months to visit archaeological sites or Istanbul and the Marmara area because the days are cooler and the crowds are smaller.

CLIMATE The Mediterranean and Aegean coasts have mild winters and hot summers. You can swim in the sea from late April through October. The Black Sea coast is mild and damp, with a rainfall of 90 inches a year.

The following are the average daily maximum and minimum temperatures for Istanbul.

Jan.	46F	8C	May	69F	21C	Sept.	76F	24C
	37	3		53	12		61	16
Feb.	47F	9C	June	77F	25C	Oct.	68F	20C
	36	2		60	16		55	13
Mar.	51F	11C	July	82F	28C	Nov.	59F	15C
	38	3		65	18		48	9
Apr.	60F	16C	Aug.	82F	28C	Dec.	51F	11C
	45	7		66	19		41	5

ISTANBUL

Istanbul is noisy, chaotic, and exciting. Spires and domes of mosques and medieval palaces dominate the skyline. At dawn, when the muezzin's call to prayer rebounds from ancient minarets, many people are heading home from the nightclubs and bars, whereas others are kneeling on their prayer rugs, facing Mecca.

Day and night, Istanbul has a schizophrenic air. Women in jeans, business suits, or elegant designer outfits pass women wearing the long skirts and head coverings that villagers have worn for generations. Donkey-drawn carts vie with old Chevrolets and Pontiacs or shiny Mercedes and BMWs for dominance of the loud, narrow streets. The world's most fascinating Asian bazaar competes with Western boutiques for your time and attention.

Exploring Istanbul

Istanbul's Asian side is filled with Western-style sprawling suburbs, while its European side contains Old Istanbul—a wonderland of mosques, opulent palaces, and crowded bazaars. The Golden Horn, an inlet 6½ km (4 mi) long, flows off the Bosporus on the European side, separating Old Istanbul from New Town. The center of New Town is Beyoğlu, a district filled with a combination of modern and turn-of-the-20th-century hotels, banks, and shops grouped around Taksim Square. There are three bridges spanning the Golden Horn: the Atatürk, the Galata, and the Haliç.

The historic Galata Bridge (the original structure has been replaced by a modern drawbridge) is a central landmark and a good place to get your bearings. From here, you can see the city's layout and its seven hills. The bridge will also give you a taste of Istanbul's frenetic street life. It's filled with peddlers selling everything from pistachio nuts and spices to curly-toed slippers fancy enough for a sultan; fishermen grill their catch on coal braziers and sell them to passersby. None of this sits well with motorists, who blast their horns constantly, usually to no avail. If you want to orient yourself in a quieter way, take a boat trip from the docks on the Eminönü side of the Galata Bridge up the Bosporus.

Old Istanbul (Sultanahmet)
Numbers in the margin correspond to points of interest on the Istanbul map.

The triangular peninsula of Old Istanbul contains most of the oldest sites in Istanbul. Its boundaries of water on two sides and the ancient walls on the other are identical to those of the ancient city first laid out by the Emperor Constantine nearly 1,700 years ago. Although a couple of broad modern highways now cut a swathe through its tumble of stone and concrete buildings, most of Old Istanbul's narrow streets twist and turn over the city's seven hills as they have done for centuries.

★ ❷ **Arkeoloji Müzesi** (Archaeological Museum). This museum houses a fine collection of Greek and Roman antiquities, including finds from Ephesus and Troy. Admission to the Archaeological Museum is also good for entrance to the **Eski Şark Eserleri Müzesi** (Museum of the Ancient Orient), with Sumerian, Babylonian, and Hittite treasures; and the **Çinili Köşkü** (Tiled Pavilion), which houses ceramics from the early Seljuk and Osmanli empires. ⊠ *Gülhane Park* ☎ *212/520–7740* ☉ *Tues.–Sun. 9:30–5.*

❸ **Aya Sofya** (Hagia Sophia, Church of the Divine Wisdom). One of the world's greatest examples of Byzantine architecture, it was built in AD 532 under the supervision of Emperor Justinian. The third church on the site, it took 10,000 men five years to complete it. The first was built in 360; both it and its successor were destroyed by fire. The dome of the current church was the world's largest until the dome at St. Peter's Basilica was built in Rome 1,000 years later. Aya Sofya was the cathedral of Constantinople for nearly 1,000 years, surviving earthquakes and looting crusaders until 1453, when it was converted into a mosque by Mehmet the Conqueror. Minarets were added by succeeding sultans. Aya Sofya originally had many mosaics depicting Christian scenes, which were plastered over by Süleyman I, who felt they were inappropriate for a

Fodor'sChoice
★

mosque. In 1935 Atatürk converted Aya Sofya into a museum. Shortly after that American archaeologists discovered the mosaics, which were restored and are now on display. According to legend, the Sacred Column in the north aisle "weeps water" that can work miracles. It's so popular that over the centuries believers have worn a hole through the marble and brass column. ⊠ *Aya Sofya Meyd.* ☎ *212/522–1750* ☾ *Tues.–Sun. 9–4.*

⑤ Hippodrome. Once a Byzantine stadium with 100,000 seats, this was the focal point for city life, including chariot races, circuses, and public executions. Disputes between rival groups of supporters of chariot teams often degenerated into violence. In AD 531, 30,000 people died in the Hippodrome in what came to be known as the Nike riots. The original shape of the Hippodrome is still clearly visible. The monuments that can be seen today—the **Dikilitaş** (Egyptian Obelisk), the **Örme Sütun** (Column of Constantinos), and the **Yılanlı Sütun** (Serpentine Column) taken from the Temple of Apollo at Delphi in Greece—formed part of the central barrier around which the chariots raced. ⊠ *Sultanahmet Meyd.*

⑨ İstanbul Üniversitesi (Istanbul University). The main campus of one of Istanbul's leading universities is worth visiting for its magnificent Ottoman gateway and quiet walkways. ⊠ *Fuat Paşa Cad., Beyazit* ☾ *Daily dawn–dusk.*

★ **⑧ Kapalı Çarşısı** (Grand Bazaar, also known as the Covered Bazaar). This maze of 65 winding, covered streets hides 4,000 shops, tiny cafés, and restaurants, and is believed to be the largest number under one roof anywhere in the world. Built by Mehmet the Conqueror in the 1450s, it was ravaged by two modern-day fires, one in 1954 that nearly destroyed it and a smaller one in 1974. In both cases the bazaar was quickly rebuilt. It's filled with thousands of curios, including carpets, fabrics, clothing, brass ware, furniture, icons, and gold jewelry. ⊠ *Yeniçeriler Cad. and Fuatpaşa Cad.* ☾ *Apr.–Oct., Mon.–Sat. 8:30–7; Nov.–Mar., Mon.–Sat. 8:30–6:30.*

★ **⑪ Mısır Çarşısı** (Egyptian Bazaar). Built during the 17th century to provide rental income for the upkeep of the Yeni Mosque, the Egyptian Bazaar was once a vast pharmacy, filled with bags overflowing with herbs and spices for folk remedies. Today, you're more likely to see bags full of fruit, nuts, royal jelly from the beehives of the Aegean coast, and white sacks spilling over with culinary spices. Some shopkeepers will offer you tastes of energizing pastes, such as *macun,* as well as dried fruits or other Turkish delights. Nearby are colorful fruit and fish markets. ⊠ *Sabunchanı Sok., Eminönü* ☾ *Mon.–Sat. 8–7.*

★ **⑩ Süleymaniye Cami** (Mosque of Süleyman). Sinan, the 16th-century architectural genius who masterminded more than 350 buildings and monuments under the direction of Süleyman the Magnificent, designed this mosque. It is his grandest and most famous monument. The mosque serves as the burial site of both Sinan and his patron, Süleyman. ⊠ *Süleymaniye Cad., near Istanbul University's north gate* ☾ *Daily except during prayer hrs.*

④ Sultan Ahmet Cami (Blue Mosque). With its shimmering blue tiles, 260 stained-glass windows, and six minarets, Sultan Ahmet is as grand and beautiful a monument to Islam as Aya Sofya was to Christianity. Mehmet Ağa, also known as Sedefkar (Worker of Mother of Pearl), built the mosque during the reign of Sultan Ahmet I in eight years, beginning in 1609, nearly 1,100 years after the completion of Aya Sofya. His goal was to surpass Justinian's masterpiece, and some believe he succeeded. Press through the throngs and enter the mosque at the side entrance that

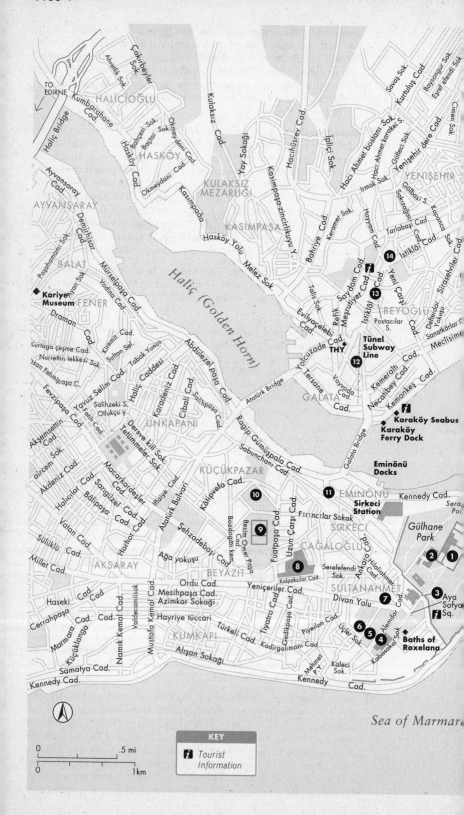

Sea of Marmara

KEY

i Tourist
Information

0   .5 mi

0   1km

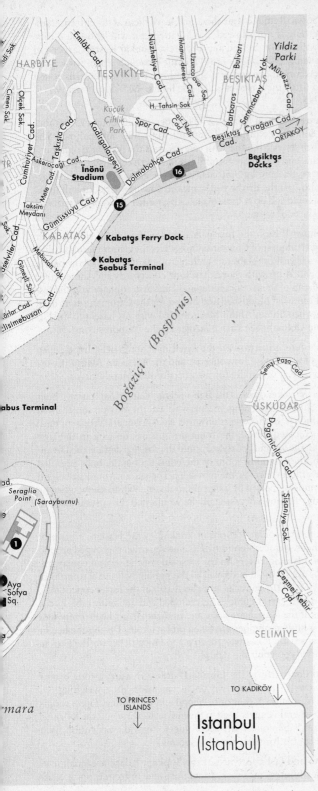

faces Aya Sofya. Remove your shoes and leave them at the entrance. Immodest clothing is not allowed, but an attendant will lend you a robe if he feels you are not dressed appropriately. **Hünkar Kasrı** (Carpet and Kilim Museum; ☎ 212/518–1330) is in the mosque's stone-vaulted cellars and upstairs at the end of a stone ramp, where the sultans rested before and after their prayers; call for hours. ✉ *Sultanahmet Meyd.* ⏱ *Daily 9–5.*

★ ❶ **Topkapı Saray** (Topkapı Palace). The number one attraction in Istanbul stands on Seraglio Point in Old Istanbul, known as Sultanahmet. The palace, which dates from the 15th century, was the residence of a number of sultans and their harems until the mid-19th century. To avoid the crowds try to get here by 9:30 AM, when the gates open. If you're arriving by taxi, tell the driver you want the Topkapı Saray in Sultanahmet, or you could end up at the remains of the former Topkapı bus terminal on the outskirts of town.

Sultan Mehmet II built the first palace during the 1450s, shortly after the Ottoman conquest of Constantinople. Over the centuries, sultan after sultan added ever more elaborate architectural fantasies, until the palace eventually ended up with more than four courtyards and some 5,000 residents, many of them concubines and eunuchs. Topkapı was the residence and center of bloodshed and drama for the Ottoman rulers until the 1850s, when Sultan Abdül Mecit moved with his harem to the European-style Dolmabahçe Palace farther up the Bosporus coast.

In Topkapı's outer courtyard are the **Aya İrini** (Church of St. Irene), open only during festival days for concerts, and the **Merasim Avlusu** (Court of the Janissaries), originally for members of the sultan's guard.

Adjacent to the ticket office is the **Bab-i-Selam** (Gate of Salutation), built in 1524 by Süleyman the Magnificent, who was the only person allowed to pass through it. In the towers on either side, prisoners were kept until they were executed beside the fountain outside the gate in the first courtyard. In the second courtyard, amid the rose gardens, is the **Divan-i-Humayun,** the assembly room of the council of state, once presided over by the grand vizier (prime minister). The sultan would sit behind a latticed window, hidden by a curtain so no one would know when he was listening, although occasionally he would pull the curtain aside to comment.

One of the most popular sections of Topkapı is the **Harem,** a maze of nearly 400 halls, terraces, rooms, wings, and apartments grouped around the sultan's private quarters on the west side of the second courtyard. Forty rooms are restored and open to the public. Next to the entrance are the quarters of the eunuchs and about 200 of the lesser concubines, who were lodged in tiny cubicles, as cramped and uncomfortable as the main rooms of the Harem are large and opulent. Tours begin every half hour. Only a limited number are taken on each tour. During the height of the tourist season it is advisable to try to buy a ticket for the Harem tour soon after you enter the palace.

In the third courtyard is the **Hazine Dairesi** (Treasury), four rooms filled with jewels, including two uncut emeralds, each weighing 3½ kilograms (7.7 pounds), that once hung from the ceiling. Here, too, is the dazzling emerald dagger used in the movie *Topkapı* and the 84-carat "Spoonmaker" diamond that, according to legend, was found by a pauper and traded for three wooden spoons.

In the fourth and last courtyard of the Topkapı Palace are small, elegant summer houses, mosques, fountains, and reflecting pools scattered amid the gardens on different levels. Here you will find the **Rivan Köşk**, built by Murat IV in 1636 to commemorate the successful Rivan campaign. In another kiosk in the gardens, called the **İftariye** (Golden Cage), the closest relatives of the reigning sultan lived in strict confinement under what amounted to house arrest. Such confinement began in the 1800s after the old custom of murdering all possible rivals to the throne had been abandoned. The confinement of the heirs apparently helped keep the peace, but it deprived them of any chance to prepare themselves for the formidable task of ruling a great empire. ✉ *Topkapı Palace* ☎ *212/512–0480* ☉ *Wed.–Mon. 9–5.*

⑥ Türk Ve İslâm Eserleri Müzesi (Museum of Turkish and Islamic Arts). The museum is housed in Ibrahim Paşa Palace, once the grandiose residence of the son-in-law and grand vizier of Süleyman the Magnificent, Ibrahim Paşa, who was executed when he became too powerful for Süleyman's liking. The collection gives a superb insight into the lifestyles of Turks of every level of society, from the 8th century to the present. ✉ *Atmeydanı 46, Sultanahmet* ☎ *212/518–1805 or 212/518–1806* ☉ *Tues.–Sun. 9–4:30.*

★ **⑦ Yerebatan Sarnıcı** (Sunken Cistern, also known as the Basilica Cistern). This underground cistern was probably first excavated by Emperor Constantine in the 4th century and then enlarged by Emperor Justinian in the 6th century. It has 336 marble columns rising 26 feet to support Byzantine arches and domes. The cistern was always kept full as a precaution against long sieges. Its echoing vastness and the reflections of the columns in the dark water give it a haunting, cathedral-like beauty, and it is a welcome relief from the heat and noise aboveground. ✉ *Yerebatan Cad.* ☎ *212/522–1259 or 212/522–1570* ☉ *Daily 9–5:30.*

New Town

New Town is the area on the northern shore of the Golden Horn, the waterway that cuts through Istanbul on the European side of the Bosporus. The architecture reflects the city's steady expansion north over the last century. Most of the buildings in Beyoğlu, the neighborhood closest to the Golden Horn, date from the late 19th and early 20th century. The faded grandeur of their ornate stone facades recalls a time when Istanbul was one of the most cosmopolitan cities in the world and more than half of its population was non-Turkish. The majority of the buildings to the north in Taksim and Nişantaşı are made from concrete and date from the 1970s and 1980s, while farther north are the modern skyscrapers of glass and steel housing the city's current business district.

⑭ Çiçek Pasajı (Flower Arcade). Here is a lively blend of restaurants, bars, and street musicians. ✉ *Çiçek Pasajı, off İstiklâl Cad., Galatasaray.*

★ **⑮ Dolmabahçe Cami** (Dolmabahçe Mosque). Founded by Valide Sultan Bezmialem, mother of Abdül Mecit I, it was completed in 1853; the 88-foot-tall clock tower was built a year later. ✉ *Dolmabahçe Cad.* ☉ *Daily except during prayer hrs.*

⑯ Dolmabahçe Sarayi (Dolmabahçe Palace). Built in 1853, this was, until the declaration of the modern republic in 1923, the residence of the last sultans of the Ottoman Empire. It was also the residence of Atatürk, who died here in 1938. The palace, floodlit at night, is an extraordinary mixture of Hindu, Turkish, and European styles of architecture and interior design. Queen Victoria's contribution to the lavishness was a chandelier weighing 4½ tons. Tours of the palace take about 80 minutes. ✉ *Dolmabahçe Cad.* ☎ *212/258–5544* ☉ *Apr.–Oct., Tues., Wed., and Fri.–Sun. 9–4; Nov.–Mar., Tues., Wed., and Fri.–Sun. 9–3.*

⑫ **Galata Kulesi** (Galata Tower). It was built by the Genoese in 1349 as part of the fortifications for their quarter of the Byzantine city. In this century it served as a fire lookout until 1960. Today it houses a restaurant and nightclub and a viewing tower from which you can see out across the Golden Horn to Old Istanbul and beyond to the Sea of Marmara. ⊠ *Büyük Hendek Cad., Galata* ☏ *212/293–8180* ⊗ *Daily 9–8.*

⑬ **İstiklâl Caddesi.** Formerly known as La Grande Rue de Pera, İstiklâl Caddesi was the most fashionable street in the city during the 19th and early 20th centuries. Pedestrianized and lined with shops, restaurants, banks, and cafés in turn-of-the-20th-century buildings, the street teems with every human element in Turkey's cultural melting pot, dodging the restored 19th-century tram that runs from Tünel to Taksim Square. In the side streets are Greek and Armenian churches, bars, cafés, and other establishments. ⊠ *İstiklâl Cad., Beyoğlu.*

Where to Eat

Most major hotels have dining rooms serving bland international cuisine. It's far more rewarding to eat in Turkish restaurants.

$$$ ✕ **Tuğra.** This spacious and luxurious restaurant in the historic Çırağan Palace serves the most delectable of long-savored Ottoman recipes, including slices of tender beef cooked in paper, air-dried beef cooked in vine leaves, and quince tart in cinnamon syrup. The Bosporus view is framed by the palace's marble columns; the high ceilings support dazzling glass chandeliers. ⊠ *Çırağan Cad. 84, Beşiktaş* ☏ *212/258-3377* ⌂ *Reservations essential* ⌐ *Jacket required* ⊟ *AE, DC, MC, V* ⊗ *Closed Mon. No lunch.*

$$-$$$ ✕ **Le Select.** In an elegant villa in the upmarket Levent neighborhood, this restaurant lives up to its name by offering a sumptuous selection of Turkish, French, and Russian cuisines. House specialties include marinated salmon, sea bass with thyme, and steak in wine sauce. ⊠ *Manolya Sokak 21, Levent* ☏ *212/268-2120* ⌂ *Reservations essential* ⊟ *AE, DC, MC, V.*

$$ ✕ **Divan.** Enjoy Turkish and international haute cuisine, elegant surroundings, and excellent service at this restaurant in the Divan hotel. Specialties include *islim kebap* (lamb covered with eggplant and served with Turkish rice). ⊠ *Cumhuriyet Cad. 2, Elmadağ* ☏ *212/231-4100 or 212/231-4070* ⊟ *AE, DC, MC, V* ⊗ *Closed Sun.*

$$ ✕ **Dört Mevsim.** The "Four Seasons," which occupies a large Victorian building, is noted for its blend of Turkish and French cuisine and for the friendliness and cheerful service of its owners, Gay and Musa, an Anglo-Turkish couple that opened it in 1965. You'll find them in the kitchen overseeing such delights as shrimp in cognac sauce and baked marinated lamb. ⊠ *İstiklâl Cad. 509, Beyoğlu* ☏ *212/293-3941* ⊟ *AE, DC, MC, V.*

$$ ✕ **Hamdi.** Spread over three floors, this place specializes in spicy meat dishes from southeastern Turkey, including eggplant, plum, and pistachio kebabs. In summer dine on its rooftop terrace with superb views across the Golden Horn toward the Galata Tower. Ask for a table at the front. ⊠ *Kalcın Sokak 17, Tahmis Caddesi, Eminönü* ☏ *212/512-5424 or 212/526-1242* ⌂ *Reservations essential* ⊟ *AE, MC, V.*

★ **$$** ✕ **İmroz.** Tucked away in a side street behind similar restaurants behind the Balık Pazarı (Fish Market) in Beyoğlu is one of the last Greek tavernas in Istanbul. On the menu you'll find high-quality fish and meat dishes. Wooden tables and faded photographs contribute to the cozy, relaxed mood. In summer you can dine at tables set out on the street. ⊠ *Nevizade Sokak 24, Beyoğlu* ☏ *212/249-9073* ⊟ *No credit cards.*

$$ ✕ **Körfez.** The specialty here is seafood, with such dishes as bass baked in salt. The garden setting on the waterfront is very romantic, and the restaurant has a boat that ferries you across the Bosporus from Rumeli Hisarı. ⊠ *Körfez Cad. 78, Kanlıca* ☎ *216/413–4314* ⊛ *Reservations essential* ⊟ *AE, DC, MC, V* ☉ *No lunch Mon.*

$$ ✕ **Rejans.** Founded by two Russians and a Crimean fleeing the Bolshevik Revolution, and now run by their widows, this place has excellent Russian food and lemon vodka, as well as Turkish dishes. The interior has remained basically unchanged since the 1930s. During World War II, when Turkey remained neutral, diplomats and spies from the Allies and Axis powers used to dine here, glowering at each other from different tables. ⊠ *Emir Nevrut Sok. 17, İstiklâl Cad., Beyoğlu* ☎ *212/ 244–1610 or 212/243–3882* ⊛ *Reservations essential* ⊟ *AE, MC, V* ☉ *Closed Sun.*

$$ ✕ **Yakup 2.** This smoky hole-in-the-wall is a favorite with Istanbul's bohemian community of artists and musicians. Its mezes, from Albanianstyle fried liver to stuffed peppers, *börek* and octopus salad, are so appetizing that you may find you have no room for a main course. ⊠ *Asmalımescit Sokak 35, Tünel* ☎ *212/249–2925* ⊟ *AE, MC, V.*

$–$$ ✕ **Beyti.** This classy, sprawling eatery is famous for inventing the *beyti kebabı* (spicy, skewered meatballs wrapped in pita), but also serves other tasty meat dishes and salads. Over the last 55 years it has grown from a couple of chairs and a table to a dozen ornately decorated rooms and an airy terrace; the photographs of previous diners that line the entrance are like a who's who list of the last half century. ⊠ *Orman Caddesi 8, Florya* ☎ *212/663–2992* ⊟ *MC, V* ☉ *Closed Mon.*

$–$$ ✕ **Develi Restaurant.** Dishes from southeast Anatolia, which are traditionally more spicy than those from the west of the country, are the specialty here, at one of the oldest and best kebab restaurants in Istanbul (established in 1912). Also expect great views across the Marmara. Try the *patlıcan kebap* (kebab with eggplants) or the *fıstıklı kebap* (kebab with pistachios). ⊠ *Balıkpazarı, Gümüşyüzük Sok. 7, Samatya* ☎ *212/ 529–0833* ⊟ *AE, MC, V.*

$–$$ ✕ **Hacı Salih.** This charming, tiny, family-run lunch place has only 10 FodorśChoice tables, so you may have to line up and wait—but it's worth it. Traditional Turkish food is the rule, with special emphasis on vegetable and lamb dishes, which change daily. Alcohol is not served. ⊠ *Anadolu Pasajı 201, off İstiklâl Cad., Beyoğlu* ☎ *212/243–4528* ⊟ *AE, MC, V* ☉ *Closed Sun. No dinner.*

★ **$–$$** ✕ **Hacıbaba.** This large, cheerful-looking place has a summer terrace overlooking an old Greek church. Fish, meat, and plenty of vegetable dishes are on display for your selection. Before you choose your main course, you'll be offered a tray of mezes that can be a meal in themselves. ⊠ *İstiklâl Cad. 49, Taksim* ☎ *212/244–1886 or 212/245–4377* ⊟ *AE, MC, V.*

Where to Stay

The top hotels are mainly around Taksim Square in New Town. Hotels generally include the 15% V.A.T. and a service charge of 10%–15% in the rate. In Old Istanbul, the Aksaray, Laleli, Sultanahmet, and Beyazit areas have many conveniently located, inexpensive small hotels and family-run pansiyons.

$$$$ ▦ **Çirağan Palace.** The 19th-century Ottoman palace is the city's most FodorśChoice luxurious hotel. The location is exceptional—it's right on the Bosporus, and the pool is on the water's edge. Most rooms are in the new wing (ask for one here), though there are 12 suites in the palace. ⊠ *Çirağan Cad. 84, Beşiktaş, 80700* ☎ *212/258-3377* 🖷 *212/259-6686* ⊕ *www.*

ciraganpalace.com ⌨ *315 rooms, 31 suites* ♨ *6 restaurants, pool* ☰ *AE, DC, MC, V.*

$$$$ ⊡ **Divan Hotel.** Quiet, but close enough to Taksim Square, this renovated old hotel has some rooms with terraces overlooking the Bosporus. All are clean and functionally furnished and a favorite with business travelers. The restaurant is renowned for impeccably prepared Turkish and international dishes. ✉ *Cumhuriyet Cad. 2, Elmadağ, 80200* ☎ *212/ 231–4100* 🖷 *212/248–8527* ⊕ *www.divanoteli.com.tr* ⌨ *154 rooms, 13 suites* ♨ *3 restaurants* ☰ *AE, DC, MC, V.*

$$$$ ⊡ **Istanbul Hilton.** One of the best hotels in the chain, it offers a combination of comfort and local color, with reception and public areas decorated with Turkish rugs and large brass urns. Ask for a room overlooking the Bosporus. ✉ *Cumhuriyet Cad., Harbiye, 80200* ☎ *212/315–6000* 🖷 *212/241–4165* ⊕ *www.hilton.com* ⌨ *498, 7 suites* ♨ *3 restaurants, 2 pools* ☰ *AE, DC, MC, V.*

★ **$$$$** ⊡ **Pera Palas.** A grand hotel with a genuinely Turkish feel, the Pera Palas was built in 1892 to accommodate guests arriving on the *Orient Express.* Everyone who was anyone stayed here, from Mata Hari to Agatha Christie to visiting heads of state. Although it has been modernized for comfort, the hotel has retained its original Victorian elegance. Many old features, such as a magnificent antique elevator, are still in working order. ✉ *Meşrutiyet Cad. 98, Tepebaşı, 80050* ☎ *212/251–4560* 🖷 *212/ 251–4089* ⊕ *www.perapalas.com* ⌨ *145 rooms* ♨ *Restaurant* ☰ *AE, DC, MC, V.*

$$$$ ⊡ **Richmond.** A turn-of-the-20th-century building on İstiklâl Caddesi was renovated to create this comfortable hotel. Downstairs is the Lebon patisserie, a remake of the 19th-century pastry shop that once operated here and an excellent place to watch the world pass by. ✉ *İstiklâl Cad. 445, Tepebaşı, 80070* ☎ *212/252–5460* 🖷 *212/252–9707* ⌨ *104 rooms, 2 suites* ♨ *2 restaurants* ☰ *AE, V.*

★ **$$$$** ⊡ **Swissôtel.** Near the city center in a hilltop wood, this hotel has superb views across the Bosporus and beyond to the Sea of Marmara. It also has lavish amenities, including excellent sports facilities and French, Turkish, Japanese, Chinese, and Swiss cuisines at its many restaurants. ✉ *Bayıldım Cad. 2, Maçka, 80680* ☎ *212/326–1100* 🖷 *212/316– 1122* ⊕ *www.swissotel.com* ⌨ *585 rooms* ♨ *6 restaurants, 2 pools* ☰ *AE, DC, MC, V.*

$$$ ⊡ **Ayasofya Pansiyons.** These guest houses are part of an Automobile Club project to restore a little street of historic wooden houses along the outer wall of Topkapı Palace. One of the houses has been converted into a library and the rest into pansiyons, furnished in late Ottoman style. In summer, tea and refreshments are served in the gardens. ✉ *Soğukçeşme Sok., Sultanahmet, 34400* ☎ *212/513–3660* 🖷 *212/513–3669* ⌨ *63 rooms, 6 suites* ♨ *2 restaurants* ☰ *AE, MC, V.*

$$$ ⊡ **Hyatt Regency.** This massive but tasteful pink building, reminiscent of Ottoman splendor, houses an upscale hotel. Many rooms have views of the Bosporus. The furnishings are a combination of earth tones in many textures. At the restaurants you'll get Asian, Turkish, and Italian food. ✉ *Taşkışla Cad., Taksim, 80090* ☎ *212/225–7000* 🖷 *212/368– 1000* ⊕ *www.istanbul.hyatt.com* ⌨ *360 rooms, 28 suites* ♨ *3 restaurants, pool* ☰ *AE, DC, MC, V.*

★ **$$$** ⊡ **Yeşil Ev.** Practically next door to the Blue Mosque, the restored 19th-century "Green House" is decorated in old-fashioned Ottoman style with lace curtains and latticed shutters. Its high-walled garden restaurant is a peaceful oasis in the midst of frenetic Istanbul. ✉ *Kabasakal Cad. 5, Sultanahmet, 34400* ☎ *212/517–6786* 🖷 *212/517–6780* ⌨ *19 rooms with shower* ♨ *Restaurant* ☰ *AE, MC, V.*

$$ ⊞ **Büyük Londra.** This six-story, mid-19th-century hotel has aged grace-fully. The rooms are small and comfortably worn, the furnishings heavy and traditional. The dark woods and velvet drapes used in the high-ceilinged lobby and dining room evoke an Ottoman Victorian era. ⊠ *Meşrutiyet Cad. 117, Tepebaşı, 80050* ☎ *212/293–1619 or 212/245–0670* 🖨 *212/245–0671* 🔁 *48 rooms, 8 suites* ⚑ *Restaurant* ▭ *AE, MC, V.*

$$ ⊞ **Hotel Empress Zoe.** Named for an empress who ruled Byzantium dur-ing the 11th century, this unusual property is decorated with murals and paintings in that era's style. Rooms, of varying configurations, are brightened with colorful embroidered textiles. The American owner, Ann Nevans, can help you with your itinerary. ⊠ *Akbıyık Cad., Adliye Sok. 10, Sultanahmet, 34400* ☎ *212/518–2504 or 212/518–4363* 🖨 *212/518–5699* ⊕ *www.emzoe.com* 🔁 *19 rooms, 3 suites* ▭ *MC, V.*

FodorsChoice
★

$–$$ ⊞ **Berk Guest House.** Cheerful Güngör and Nevim Evrensel run this clean, comfortable pansiyon in a converted private home. There is a small lounge inside and a terrace offers beautiful views across the Sea of Mar-mara. Two of the rooms also have balconies overlooking a garden; all rooms have showers. ⊠ *Kutlugün Sok. 27, Sultanahmet, 34400* ☎ *212/516–9671* 🖨 *212/517–7715* ⊕ *www.berkguesthouse.com* 🔁 *9 rooms* ▭ *No credit cards.*

$ ⊞ **Hotel Barin.** Modern, clean, and comfortable, this place makes up in convenience, functionality, and friendliness what it lacks in character. The hotel caters to business travelers as well as tourists. ⊠ *Fevziye Cad. 7, Şehzadebaşı, 34470* ☎ *212/513–9100 or 212/513–1333* 🖨 *212/526–4440* ⊕ *www.barinhotel.com* 🔁 *65 rooms, 3 suites* ⚑ *Restaurant* ▭ *AE, MC, V.*

Nightlife & the Arts

The Arts

For tickets to the **Istanbul International Festival**—held late June through mid-July and attracting internationally renowned artists and perform-ers—contact the **Istanbul Foundation for Culture and Arts** (⊠ Kültür ve Sanat Vakfı, İstiklâl Cad., Luvr Apt. 146, Beyoğlu, 80070 ☎ 212/293–3133). Tickets can also be purchased at ticket booths outside some of the venues. Performances, which include modern and classical music, ballet, opera, and theater, are given throughout the city in historic build-ings. The season at the city of Istanbul's **Cemal Reşit Rey Concert Hall** (☎ 212/231–5498) runs from September through May and includes clas-sical, jazz, and rock music, as well as ballet performed by visiting and local groups.

CONCERTS From October through May, the Istanbul State Symphony gives per-formances at the main concert hall, **Atatürk Kültür Merkezi** (⊠ Box of-fice, Taksim Sq. ☎ 212/251–5600); tickets are also available here for concerts at Cemal Reşit Rey Concert Hall. Ballet and dance companies perform at this hall, too.

Nightlife

BARS **Bebek Bar** (⊠ Bebek Ambassadeurs Hotel, Cevdet Paşa Cad. 113, Bebek ☎ 212/263–3000) has views over the Bosporus and draws locals from the neighborhood and nearby Bosporus University. Sophisticated **Beyo-ğlu Pub** (⊠ İstiklâl Cad. 140/7, Beyoğlu ☎ 212/252–3842), behind an arcade off İstiklâl Caddesi, has a pleasant garden and a discreet indoor bar. **Hayal Kahvesi** (⊠ Büyük Parmakkapı Sok. 19, Beyoğlu ☎ 212/244–2558) is a bohemian side-street bar with wooden furniture, lace curtains, and live music. The fin-de-siècle style of the **Orient Express Bar** (⊠ Pera Palas Hotel, Meşrutiyet Cad. 98, Tepebaşı ☎ 212/251–4560) distills the style and sensibility of Old Istanbul with the lingering presence of the rich, powerful, and famous who once played here. With its British pub character and imported beers and malt whiskies, the **Sherlock Holmes** (✉ Çalıkuşu Sokak 5 ☎ 212/281–6372) has become a popular haunt for local yuppies and expatriates alike. **Kehri Bar** (✉ Divan Hotel, Cumhuriyet Caddesi 2, Taksim ☎ 212/231–4100) resonates with the latest in Turkish music, including live pop and jazz bands.

DANCE CLUBS   **Çubuklu 29** (✉ Paşabahçe Yolu, Çubuklu ☎ 216/322–2829), by the Bosporus on the Asian side, is open mid-June–September. **Jukebox** (✉ Nizamiye Caddesi 14, Talimhane ☎ 212/292–3656) has the best local and visiting foreign DJs. Even with its spacious dance floor, the club is usually packed on weekends. **Hayal Kahvesi** (✉ Burunbahçe, Çubuklu ☎ 216/413–6880), a huge, restaurant-bar-disco complex on the Asian shore of the Bosporus, has dancing to live jazz or rock on Friday or Saturday (summer only). The loud and lively three-story **Kemancı Rock-Bar** (✉ Taksim Sitesi, Sıraselviler 69, Taksim ☎ 212/245–3048 or 212/251–3015) is a favorite with students, who dance to live rock and blues bands. **Les Ambassadeurs** (✉ Bayıldım Caddesi 2, Maçka ☎ 212/326–1100) under the Swissôtel plays rock and jazz and usually has live music on weekends.

JAZZ CLUBS   **Q Jazz Bar** (✉ Çırağan Cad. 84, Beşiktaş ☎ 212/236–2489 or 212/236–2121), the Çırağan Hotel's luxurious jazz bar, has some of the classiest music in town—at equally classy prices. **Gossip** (✉ Hyatt Regency Hotel, Takışla, Taksim ☎ 212/225–7000) is open every night except Monday and often features live jazz by American and European artists.

NIGHTCLUBS   **Galata Tower** (✉ Kuledibi ☎ 212/245–1160) serves dinner followed by a Turkish show and dancing. **Kervansaray** (✉ Cumhuriyet Cad. 30, Elmadağ ☎ 212/247–1630) has dining, dancing, and belly-dancing shows. The revue at **Orient House** (✉ Tiyatro Cad. 27, Beyazıt ☎ 212/517–3488) is the spot for some of Istanbul's best-known belly dancers and folk dances from around Turkey.

Shopping

Districts & Malls

In New Town, stores and boutiques line İstiklâl Caddesi, which runs off Taksim Square, and Rumeli, Halaskargazi, and Valikonağı Caddeleri, north of the Istanbul Hilton. Two streets in the Kadıköy area with good shops are Bağdat and Bahariye Caddeleri. **Akmerkez**, the newest of the malls in Etiler, has luxury and designer wear. **Ataköy Shopping and Tourism Center** is a large mall near the airport. In Altunizade on the Asian side, the slick **Capitol** mall has movies and entertainment, too.

Markets

The **Grand Bazaar** has all things Turkish—carpets, brass, copper, jewelry, textiles, and leather goods. **Tünel Square,** a quick Metro ride up from Karaköy, is a quaint group of stores with old prints, books, and artifacts. **Çukurcuma,** in the back streets of Beyoğlu, contains several shops specializing in maps and odds and ends from the late 19th and early 20th centuries. **Balıkpazarı** (fish market) is in Beyoğlu Caddesi, off İstiklâl Caddesi. A bustling clutter of narrow covered streets, Balıkpazarı contains stalls and tiny stores, selling everything from spices, vegetables, and fruit to fish, cooked meats, and even pork. Turkish traders are joined by new arrivals from eastern Europe and the former Soviet Union at a flea market held in **Beyazıt Square,** near the Grand Bazaar, every Sunday starting at about 10 AM; here you can find everything from cheap electronic goods to Russian boots and hats. A crafts market, with street entertainment, is open on Sunday along the Bosporus at **Ortaköy.** A weekend crafts market takes place on **Bekar Sokak,** off İstiklâl Caddesi.

Istanbul Essentials

AIRPORTS & TRANSFERS
All international and domestic flights arrive at Istanbul's Atatürk Airport. For arrival and departure information call the individual airline or the airport's information desk listed below.

🛈 **Atatürk Airport** ☎ 212/252-1106.

TRANSFERS Shuttle buses run every 30 minutes from the airport's international and domestic terminals to the Turkish Airlines (THY) terminal in downtown Istanbul, at Cumhuriyet Caddesi, near the THY Taksim office. Buses depart for the airport from the same address. Allow at least 45 minutes for the bus ride. Plan to be at the airport two hours before your international flight because of the lengthy security and check-in procedures. The ride from the airport into town takes from 30 to 40 minutes, depending on traffic. Taxis charge about $15 to Taksim Square and $10 to Sultanahmet.

🛈 **THY Taksim office** ☎ 212/245-2454.

BOAT & FERRY TRAVEL
Many ferries run between the Asian and European continents. Deniz otobüsü (sea buses) run between the continents and, in summer, to destinations such as the Princes' Islands; they are fast and efficient. For an inexpensive ride take the boat in the direction of Anadolu Kavağı, along the Bosporus to its mouth at the Black Sea. The boat leaves year-round from Dock No. 5 at the Eminönü Docks, next to the Galata Bridge on the Old Istanbul side, at 10:35 AM and 1:35 PM, with two extra trips on weekdays and four extra trips on Sunday, April through September. The fare is $6 (round-trip). The trip takes 1¾ hours one-way. You can disembark at any of the stops and return by land if you wish. Regular ferries depart from Kabataş Dock, near Dolmabahçe Palace on the European side, to Üsküdar on the Asian side; and also from Eminönü Docks 1 and 2, near Sirkeci Station.

🛈 **Deniz otobüsü** ☎ 216/362-0444. **Karaköy port** ☎ 212/244-4233.

BUS TRAVEL TO & FROM ISTANBUL
Buses arrive in Istanbul at Esenler terminal, northwest of the city center. From the terminal, the major bus companies offer free minibus service to centers such as Sultanahmet, Taksim, and Aksaray. The Hızlı Tren (rapid train) also connects the terminal to Aksaray, though it is often very crowded and can be extremely hot in summer. A few buses from Anatolia arrive at Harem terminal, on the eastern shore of the Bosporus. If you arrive with baggage, it is much easier to take a taxi, which will cost about $10 to Taksim from the Esenler terminal and about $6 to Old Istanbul.

BUS TRAVEL WITHIN ISTANBUL
You need to buy a ticket before boarding a bus. Individual tickets or books of 10 can be purchased at ticket stands around the city. Shoeshine boys or men on the street will also sell them to you for a few cents more. Fares are about 40¢ per ride. On the city's orange privatized buses (Halk Otobüsü), you pay for tickets on the bus. The London-style red double-deckers operate along a scenic route between Sultanahmet and Emigran on the Bosporus and between Europe and Asia and cost about $1 one-way.

CAR TRAVEL

If you drive in from the west, take the busy E5 highway, also called Londra Asfaltı, which leads from Edirne to Atatürk Airport and on through the city walls at Cannon Gate (Topkapı). E5 heading out of Istanbul leads into central Anatolia and on to Syria. You can also take one of the numerous car ferries that ply the Sea of Marmara and the Dardanelles from Kabataş Dock, or try the overnight ferry to İzmir, which leaves from Sarayburnu.

CONSULATES

🏛 Australia ✉ Tepecik Yokuşu 58, Etiler, 80630 ☎ 212/257-7050.
🏛 Canada ✉ Büyükdere Cad. 107/3, Bengün Han, 80300, Gayrettepe ☎ 212/272-5174.
🏛 Ireland ✉ Honorary, Cumhuriyet Cad. 26, Harbiye, 80200 ☎ 212/246-6025.
🏛 United Kingdom ✉ Meşrutiyet Cad. 34, Tepebaşı, 80050, Beyoğlu ☎ 212/334-6400.
🏛 United States ✉ Meşrutiyet Cad. 104-108, Tepebaşı, 80050, Beyoğlu ☎ 212/251-3602.

EMERGENCIES

Dial ☎ 118 for information on 24-hour pharmacies in each neighborhood; a notice in the window of every pharmacy lists the name and address of the nearest all-night shop. For a doctor, call one of the hospitals below.

🏛 Emergency Services **Ambulance** ☎ 112. **Tourism Police** ☎ 212/527-4503.
🏛 Hospitals **American Hospital** ✉ Güzelbahçe Sok. 20, Nişantaşı, 80200 ☎ 212/231-4050 through 212/231-4069. **International Hospital** ✉ Yesilyurt ☎ 212/663-3000.

ENGLISH-LANGUAGE MEDIA

🏛 Bookstores **D & R** ✉ Nispetiye Cad., Etiler ☎ 212/263-2914. **Homer** ✉ Yeni Çarşı Cad. 28A, Galatasaray ☎ 212/249-5902. **Pandora** ✉ Büyükparmakkapı Sok. 3 ☎ 212/243-3503 or 212/243-3504. **Robinson Crusoe** ✉ İstiklâl Cad. 389, Tünel ☎ 212/293-6968 or 212/293-6977.

TAXIS

Taxis are inexpensive and metered. As most drivers do not speak English and may not know the street names, write down the street you want, the nearby main streets, and the name of the area. Although tipping is not expected, you should round off the fare to the nearest 500,000 TL.

DOLMUŞ These are shared taxis operating between set destinations throughout the city. Dolmuş stops are indicated by a blue-and-white sign with a large D. The destination is shown on either a roof sign or a card in the front window. Until the mid-1990s all the dolmuş were classic American cars from the 1950s, but they have now been nearly all replaced by modern yellow minibuses.

TRAIN TRAVEL

Trains from the west arrive at Sirkeci Station in Old Istanbul. Eastbound trains to Anatolia depart from Haydarpaşa Station on the Asian side.
🏛 **Haydarpaşa Station** ☎ 216/336-0475. **Sirkeci Station** ☎ 212/527-0050 or 212/527-0051.

TRANSPORTATION AROUND ISTANBUL

The best way to get to the various magnificent monuments in Sultanahmet in Old Istanbul is to walk; they're all within easy distance of one another. A tram system runs from Topkapı, via Sultanahmet, to Sirkeci. The Tünel, a tiny underground train, is handy for getting up the steep hill from Karaköy to the bottom of İstiklâl Caddesi. It runs every 10 minutes and costs about 40¢. Trams run the length of İstiklâl Caddesi from Taksim to Tünel and cost about 40¢.

TRAVEL AGENCIES

Tours can be arranged through travel agencies. Most companies have a half- or full-day Classical Tour. The half-day tour includes Aya Sofya, the Museum of Turkish and Islamic Arts, the Hippodrome, Yerebatan Saray, and the Blue Mosque; the full-day tour, in addition to the above sights, includes Topkapı Palace, the Süleymaniye Mosque, the Covered or Egyptian Bazaar, and lunch.

Local Agents Fest ✉ Barbaros Apt. Barbaros Bulvarı 44, Balmumcu ☎ 212/234-1200. **Intra** ✉ Halaskargazi Cad. 111/2, Harbiye ☎ 212/247-8174 or 212/240-3891. **Plan Tours** ✉ Cumhuriyet Cad. 131/1, Elmadağ ☎ 212/230-2272 or 212/230-8118. **Setur** ✉ Cumhuriyet Cad. 107, Harbiye ☎ 212/230-0336. **Türk Express** American Express Travel Service representative ✉ Istanbul Hilton, Cumhuriyet Cad., Harbiye ☎ 212/241-0248 or 212/241-0249. **Vip Tourism** ✉ Cumhuriyet Cad. 269/2, Harbiye ☎ 212/241-6514.

VISITOR INFORMATION

Opening hours for tourist offices tend to vary according to the season, and usually change every year. Most are generally open from 9 to 6.

Atatürk Airport ☎ 212/663-0793. **Istanbul Hilton** ☎ 212/233-0592. **Karaköy Yolcu Salonu** International Maritime Passenger Terminal ☎ 212/249-5776. **Pavilion** ✉ Divan Yolu Cad. 3, Sultanahmet ☎ 212/518-1802 or 212/518-8754.

THE AEGEAN COAST

Some of the finest ancient Greek and Roman cities, including the fabled Pergamum, Ephesus, Aphrodisias, and Troy, are found in this region of Turkey. Watch for the ubiquitous bright-yellow road signs pointing to historic sites or to those currently undergoing excavation. There are so many Greek and Roman ruins, in fact, that some haven't yet been excavated and others are going to seed. Grand or small, all the sites are best visited early in the morning or late in the afternoon, when crowds are smaller. Escape the heat of the day on one of the sandy beaches along the coast.

It makes sense to begin your exploration of the Aegean Coast in the north at inland Bursa, moving west to Gallipoli and Çanakkale at the Dardanelles. Farther south, past Troy, is the city of İzmir. Follow the southern coast down to Bodrum, with a detour inland to the ruins at Aphrodisias and the natural hot springs of Pamukkale. You'll need 8–10 days to cover the region thoroughly.

Bursa

The first capital of the Ottoman Empire, Bursa used to be known as Yeşil (Green) Bursa. Thanks to rapid growth, hastily built concrete apartment blocks now surround the city. The city center, however, has retained the many trees and parks and **Yeşil Cami** (Green Mosque) and **Yeşil Türbe** (Green Mausoleum) that gave it its nickname. Both mosque and mausoleum derive their names from the green tiles that line their interiors. ✉ Yeşil Cad. (Green Ave.) ☾ Daily except during prayer hrs.

The town square, called Heykel, which means "statue," is named for its statue of Atatürk. Off Heykel is the **Ulu Cami** (Great Mosque) with its distinctive silhouette of 20 domes. ✉ Atatürk Cad. ☾ Daily except during prayer hrs.

Bursa is the site of **Uludağ** (Great Mountain), Turkey's most popular ski resort. To fully appreciate why the town is called Green Bursa, take a ride on the teleferik (cable car; Namazgah Cad.) up the mountain for a panoramic view.

$$ ✕ **Cumurcul.** This restaurant in a converted old house is a local favorite. Grilled meats and fish are attentively prepared, and there are plenty of

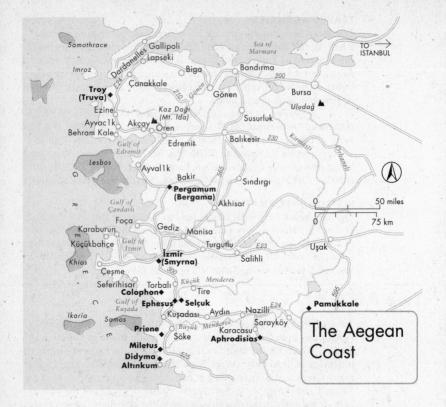

The Aegean Coast

cold and hot mezes, including *avcı böreği* (hunter's pie), a deep-fried or oven-baked pastry filled with meat or cheese, to choose from. ⊠ *Çekirge Cad.* ☎ *224/235–3707 or 224/235–3373* ▤ *AE, MC, V.*

$ ✕ **Kebabcı İskender.** Bursa is famous for the namesake dish served in this 140-year-old restaurant. The *İskender kebab* (Alexander's kebab) includes slivers of skewer-grilled meat and pita bread immersed in a rich tomato sauce and topped with hot butter and yogurt. ⊠ *Ünlü Cad. 7, Heykel* ☎ *224/221–4615* ▤ *AE, MC, V.*

★ $$$$ ▦ **Çelik Palace.** After you've indulged at this posh hotel's restaurant, casino, and clubs, enjoy a dip in the domed, Roman-style thermal pool fed by local hot springs. The place has a lively 1930s design scheme, and some rooms have balconies. ⊠ *Çekirge Meyd. 79, 16000* ☎ *224/233–3800* 🖶 *224/236–1910* ⊕ *hotels.wec-net.com.tr/emek* ⤵ *161 rooms, 6 suites* ♨ *Restaurant* ▤ *AE, DC, MC, V.*

$ ▦ **Ada Palas.** Thermal baths are on every floor of this Çekirge hotel, and the price is lower than that at the nearby Çelik. Rooms are unexceptional and don't have air-conditioning, but are in good shape. ⊠ *Murat Cad. 21, Çekirge, 16000* ☎ *224/233–3990* 🖶 *224/236–4656* ⤵ *39 rooms* ♨ *Restaurant* ▤ *AE, MC, V.*

Çanakkale & Gallipoli

Çanakkale is the guardian of the Dardanelles, the narrow straits that separate Europe from Asia and connect the Aegean Sea with the Sea of Marmara. This strategic point has been fought over since the days of the Trojan War. During World War I Britain and France tried to breach Çanakkale's defenses in the unsuccessful Gallipoli campaign. They were defeated by the strategy of Mustafa Kemal—the man who would later be called Atatürk. Thirty-one beautifully tended **military cemeteries** of the Allied dead from World War I dot the battlefields.

Nowadays Çanakkale is a drab agricultural center and garrison town, but it serves as the gateway to historic Gallipoli, on the north side of the Dardanelles. At Cape Helles there is a massive, four-pillared memorial to Turkey's war dead. Half-day excursions to Gallipoli are organized by **Troy-Anzac Tours** (✉ İskele Meyd., south side near clock tower, Çanakkale ☎ 286/217–5849).

$$ 🏨 **Akol.** This modern hotel is perched on the waterfront in Çanakkale. The lobby is bright and full of cool white marble and brass fixtures. The rooms are fitted with green carpeting and furnished with wooden tables, chairs, and dressers. Ask for a room with a terrace overlooking the Dardanelles. ✉ *Kordonboyu, Çanakkale, 17100* ☎ *286/217–9456* 🖨 *286/217–2897* ⊕ *www.hotelakol.com* 🛏 *135 rooms, 2 suites* ⌂ *Restaurant, pool* ▤ *MC, V.*

$$ 🏨 **Büyük Truva.** Near the center of Çanakkale, the Truva is an excellent base for sightseeing. Rooms are clean and functional and have large windows. The older section at the front of the hotel has views across the Dardanelles. ✉ *Cevatpaşa Mah. Mehmet Akif Ersoy Cad. 2 Kordonboyu, Çanakkale, 17100* ☎ *286/217–1024* 🖨 *286/217–0903* 🛏 *66 rooms, 3 suites* ⌂ *Restaurant* ▤ *AE, MC, V.*

Troy

Long thought to be simply an imaginary city from Homer's *Iliad*, **Troy** (Truva in Turkish, Ilion in Greek) was excavated in the 1870s by Heinrich Schliemann, a German amateur archaeologist. He also found the remains of nine successive civilizations, one on top of the other, dating back 5,000 years. Considering Troy's fame, the site is surprisingly small. It's best to take a guided tour to appreciate fully the significance of this discovery and the unwavering passion of the man who proved that Troy was not just another ancient myth. ✉ *Follow signs from Rte. E87, 32 km (20 mi) south of Çanakkale* ☉ *Daily 8–7.*

$$ 🏨 **Tusan.** Along the beachfront north of Troy at Güzelyalı, and framed by a pine forest, this is one of the most attractive hotels in the area. The two-story stucco-and-brick structure has nondescript rooms, but the location is superb. Reserve well in advance. ✉ *Güzelyalı, 17001* ☎ *286/232–8746* 🖨 *286/232–8226* ⊕ *www.tusanhotel.com* 🛏 *64 rooms* ⌂ *Restaurant* ▤ *AE, MC, V* ☉ *Closed Nov.–Mar.*

Ayvalık

The charming, sleepy coastal resort just south of the Gulf of Edremit has some of the best examples of 19th-century Greek domestic architecture found anywhere in the Aegean. From Ayvalık you can take boats to **Ali Bey Adası**, a tiny island with pleasant waterfront restaurants, and to the Greek island of Lesbos.

$–$$ 🏨 **Örtünç.** This complex of 22 bungalows in an orchard on Ali Bey Adası also has its own beach. The rooms are functional, with sparse furnishings, but the hotel is in a wonderfully tranquil spot, which makes up for it. ✉ *Ali Bey Adası, 10400* ☎ *266/327–1120* 🖨 *266/327–2082* 🛏 *22 rooms* ⌂ *Restaurant* ▤ *MC, V* ☉ *Closed Oct.–Mar.*

$ 🏨 **Yalı Pansiyon.** This pension in a restored 19th-century house has its own beach and shaded waterfront garden. The rooms are basic but clean. Book ahead to make sure of getting one with bathroom en suite. ✉ *PTT Arkası 25, 10400* ☎ *266/312–2423 or 266/312–3819* 🛏 *8 rooms* ▤ *No credit cards* ☉ *Closed Nov.–Mar.*

Pergamum

The windswept ruins of Pergamum (Bergama in Turkish) are among the most spectacular in Turkey. Pergamum's glory peaked during the Greek Attalid dynasty (241 BC–133 BC), when it was one of the world's most magnificent architectural and artistic centers—especially under the rule of Eumenes II, who lavished his great wealth on the city. When the mad Attalus III died, he bequeathed the entire kingdom to Rome.

Because the attractions are spread out over several miles, it's best to take a taxi from one site to the next. The most noteworthy places are the Asklepieion, the Ethnological Museum, the Red Hall, and the Acropolis. The most famous building at the Acropolis is the library, which once contained a collection of 200,000 books, all on papyrus. The library's collection was second only to the one in Alexandria, Egypt. ⊗ *Apr.–Oct., daily 8:30–6:30; Nov.–Mar., daily 8:30–5:30.*

$ ✕ **Pergamon Restaurant.** This inexpensive eatery on the main street serves an excellent selection of kebabs and starters, including local specialties—such as tasty spicy meatballs *Bergama köftesi*—at tables set amid potted plants around a small indoor pond filled with plump goldfish. ✉ *Bankalar Caddesi 5* ☎ *232/633–4343* ⊟ *No credit cards.*

$ ▦ **Asude Hotel.** Some of the rooms at the front of this clean, no-frills hotel on the outskirts of town have distant views of the ancient ruins of Pergamum. The restaurant serves a passable selection of grilled meats. ✉ *İzmir Asfaltı No. 93, Fatih Mah., Bergama, 35700* ☎ *232/633–3179* 🖶 *232/632–0512* ⤢ *52 rooms* ⚲ *Restaurant, bar* ⊟ *MC, V.*

$ ▦ **Hotel İskender.** Although it's plain and modern, this place is in the center of town and has air-conditioning. The outdoor restaurant serves tasty fresh mezes and grilled foods. ✉ *İzmir Cad. Ilica Önü Mev., Bergama, 35700* ☎ *232/633–2123 or 232/632–9710* 🖶 *232/632–9711* ⤢ *60 rooms, 4 suites* ⚲ *2 restaurants* ⊟ *AE, MC, V.*

İzmir

Turkey's third-largest city is also its most Mediterranean. Called Smyrna by the Greeks, it was a vital trading port that was often ravaged by wars and earthquakes. The city was almost completely destroyed by a fire in 1922 during the final stages of Turkey's War of Independence against Greece. It was quickly rebuilt and became known by its Turkish name, İzmir. Today it's a lively, modern city filled with wide boulevards, apartment houses, and office buildings. At the center of the city is **Kültürpark**, a large green park that is the site of İzmir's industrial fair from late August to late September (a time when most hotels are full).

Atop İzmir's highest hill is the **Kadifekale** (Velvet Fortress), built in the 3rd century BC by Lysimachos. It is easily reached by dolmuş and is one of the few ancient ruins that was not destroyed in the fire. At the foot of İzmir's highest hill is the restored **Agora**, the market of ancient Smyrna. A modern-day marketplace is in **Konak Square**, a maze of tiny streets filled with shops and covered stalls. ⊗ *Mon.–Sat. 8–8.*

$$$$ ▦ **İzmir Hilton.** At 34 stories, this is one of the tallest buildings on the Aegean coast. Striking and modern, the structure looms over the city center. From the 10-story atrium to the rooftop restaurant, the public spaces are suitably grand. Guest rooms are plush. ✉ *Gazi Osman Paşa Bul. 7, 35210* ☎ *232/497–6060* 🖶 *232/449–6000* ⊕ *www.hilton.com* ⤢ *381 rooms* ⚲ *4 restaurants, pool* ⊟ *AE, DC, MC, V.*

$$$–$$$$ ▦ **Best Western Hotel Konak.** This hotel right on the water has lots of cool marble and greenery. Guest rooms have big windows with views. The city's museums are within easy walking distance. ✉ *Mithatpasa Cad. 128, 35210* ☎ *232/489–1500 or 232/489–1125* 🖶 *232/489–1709* ⊕ *www. bestwestern.com* ⤢ *82 rooms, 4 suites* ⚲ *Restaurant* ⊟ *AE, MC, V.*

Kuşadası

One of the most popular tourist resorts in the Mediterranean, Kuşadası has grown in 30 years from a fishing village into a sprawling town. Although geared to serving thousands of tourists who visit the nearby ruins and beaches, the busy town maintains an easy pace.

\$\$ ✕ **Alize.** A five-minute walk from the waterfront, this excellent bistro more than makes up for its lack of sea view with superb meat, fish, and pasta dishes and live acoustic music in the evenings. It's a favorite hangout for locals, particularly the young trendy set. ⊠ *Karagöz Sok. 67, Sağlık Cad.* ☎ *256/612–0769* ▭ *MC, V.*

\$–\$\$ ✕ **Ali Baba Restaurant.** The focus is on fish at this simply styled (starched white tablecloths, wooden chairs) waterfront spot with a peaceful view of the bay. Try the marinated octopus salad or the fried calamari, followed by a grilled version of whatever has just been caught. ⊠ *Belediye Turistik Çarşısı 5* ☎ *256/614–1551* ⚐ *Reservations essential* ▭ *AE, MC, V.*

★ **\$\$\$** ⌂ **Kismet.** Run on a grand scale, this hotel is surrounded by beautifully maintained gardens and sits on a promontory overlooking the marina on one side and the Aegean on the other. Ask for rooms in the garden annex. Reservations are a must. ⊠ *Akyar Mev., Türkmen Mahallesi, 09400* ☎ *256/613–1203* ⊟ *256/612–7244* ⊕ *www.kismet.com.tr* ⛳ *101 rooms, 3 suites* ⚐ *2 restaurants* ▭ *MC, V.*

\$\$ ⌂ **Club Kervansaray.** In a refurbished 300-year-old caravansary, this hotel in the center of town is Ottoman in style and loaded with charm. Its restaurant has a floor show and there's dancing after dinner in the palm-fringed courtyard, where the camels were once kept. ⊠ *Atatürk Bul. 2, 09400* ☎ *256/614–4115* ⊟ *256/614–2423* ⊕ *www.kusadasihotels.com/caravanserail* ⛳ *26 rooms, 1 suite* ⚐ *Restaurant* ▭ *AE, DC, MC, V.*

\$ ⌂ **Efe Otel.** On the waterfront just beyond the path to Pigeon Island you'll find this small, clean, and comfortable hotel. The rooms are nondescript, with bare walls and low beds with wooden frames, but you can compensate by asking for one with a balcony and a view over Pigeon Island. ⊠ *Guvercin Ada Cad. 37, 09400* ☎ *256/614–3661 or 256/614–3662* ⊟ *256/614–3662* ⛳ *44 rooms, 1 suite* ⚐ *Restaurant* ▭ *AE, MC, V.*

Ephesus & Selçuk

Ephesus is the showpiece of Aegean archaeology and one of the grandest reconstructed ancient sites in the world. Created by the Ionians in the 11th century BC, Ephesus became a powerful trading port and the sacred center for the cult of Artemis, Greek goddess of chastity, the moon, and hunting. The Ionians built a temple in her honor, one of the Seven Wonders of the Ancient World. Later the city received a visit from St. Paul, who spent two years preaching here and established one of the first Christian communities on the Aegean coast. Over the centuries, heavy silting of the old port finally led to the city's abandonment; the ancient site now lies 3 km (2 mi) inland. Allow yourself one full day for Ephesus. The city is especially appealing out of season, when it can seem like a ghost town with its shimmering, long, white marble road grooved by chariot wheels. Some of the splendors here include the two-story Library of Celsus; houses of nobles, with their terraces and courtyards; a 25,000-seat amphitheater, still used today during the Selçuk Ephesus Festival of Culture and Art; remains of the municipal baths; and a brothel. ⊠ *4 km (2½ mi) west of Selçuk on Selçuk–Ephesus Rd.* ☎ *232/892–6402* ☉ *Apr.–Sept., daily 8:30–6; Oct.–Mar., daily 8:30–5.*

In Selçuk, east of Ephesus, on Ayasoluk Hill, stands the restored **Basilica of St. John** (St. Jean Anıtı), containing the tomb of the apostle. Near the entrance to the basilica is the **Ephesus Museum**, with two statues of Artemis and marvelous frescoes and mosaics. ☉ *Basilica and museum Tues.–Sun. 8:30–6.*

St. Paul and St. John preached in both Ephesus and Selçuk and changed the cult of Artemis into the cult of the Virgin Mary. **Meryemana,** 5 km (3 mi) from Ephesus, has the **House of Mary,** thought by some to have been the place where St. John took the mother of Jesus after the crucifixion and from which some believe she ascended to heaven. ☉ *Daily 7:30–sunset.*

$$ 🏨 **Kale Han.** In two refurbished stone buildings is one of the nicest hotels in town, run by a very welcoming family. Rooms are simple, with bare, whitewashed walls and dark timber beams. Ask for one facing the castle behind the hotel. The restaurant is open around the clock. ⊠ *Atatürk Cad. 49, Selçuk, 35920* ☎ *232/892–6154* 🖷 *232/892–2169* ⊕ *www. kalehan.com* 🔊 *40 rooms, 4 suites* 🍴 *Restaurant, pool* ▤ *MC, V.*

$ 🏨 **Victoria Hotel.** Rooms in this tidy, cheerful hostelry in the center of town have whitewashed walls and honey-color wooden trim. In summer most have delightful views of storks nesting on a nearby aqueduct. The restaurant is a good bet for traditional Turkish fare. ⊠ *Cengiz Topel Cad. 4, Selçuk, 35920* ☎ *232/892–3203* 🖷 *232/892–3204* 🔊 *24 rooms* 🍴 *Restaurant* ▤ *No credit cards.*

Priene

Priene, which sits atop a steep hill, was an artistic and cultural center during the Hellenistic period. Its main attraction is the **Temple of Athena,** with five fluted columns and a backdrop of mountains and the fertile plains of the Meander River. The city also has a small amphitheater, gymnasium, council chambers, marketplace, and stadium. ☉ *Daily 8:30–6.*

Miletus

A thriving port made Miletus one of the greatest commercial centers of the ancient Greek world. It was the first Greek city to use coins for money. It also became an Ionian intellectual center and the home of such philosophers as Thales, Anaximander, and Anaximenes, all of whom made contributions to mathematics and the natural sciences. The city's most magnificent building is the **Great Theater,** a remarkably intact amphitheater built by the Ionians and enlarged by the Romans to seat 25,000. Climb to the highest seats in the amphitheater for a view across the city to the bay. ☉ *Tues.–Sun. 8:30–6.*

Didyma

Once home to one of the most famous oracles in the ancient world, Didyma was a sanctuary dedicated to Apollo. It's possible to follow the 32-km (20-mi) path of what was known as the Sacred Way, leading from the coast at Miletus to the site of the oracle at Didyma's **Temple of Apollo.** Under the temple courtyard is a network of corridors whose walls would throw the oracle's voice into deep and ghostly echoes. The messages would then be interpreted by the priests. Fragments of bas-relief include a gigantic head of Medusa and a small statue of Poseidon and his wife, Amphitrite. ☉ *Daily 8:30–6.*

Pamukkale

The place first appears as an enormous chalky-white cliff rising some 330 feet from the plains. Mineral-rich volcanic spring water cascades over basins and natural terraces, crystallizing into white stalactites—curtains of solidified water seemingly suspended in air. The hot springs in the area were popular with the ancient Romans, who believed them to have curative powers. People still believe that the waters cure various ailments, including rheumatism. Accommodations are in the nearby village of Karahayıt, 3 km (2 mi) from the springs, where several hotels have their own thermal pools. You can see the remains of Roman baths among the ruins of nearby **Hierapolis.**

★ It's best to stay in Karahayıt overnight before heading on to the ruins of **Aphrodisias,** a city of 60,000 dedicated to Aphrodite, the Greek goddess of love and fertility. It thrived from 100 BC to AD 500. Aphrodisias is reached via Karacasu, a good place to stop for lunch; fresh trout is the local specialty. Aphrodisias is filled with marble baths, temples, and theaters, all overrun with wild blackberries and pomegranates. Across a field sprinkled with poppies and sunflowers is a well-preserved **stadium,** which was built for 30,000 spectators.

$$$ 🏨 **Polat Thermal Hotel.** Clean, spacious, and comfortable, with numerous facilities, this place is almost a thermal resort in itself. It includes a scattering of one- and two-story buildings around a large outdoor pool. ⊠ *Karahay, Denizli, 20227* ☎ *258/271–4111* 📠 *258/271–4092* ⇥ *288 rooms, 7 suites* ⚖ *2 restaurants, 3 pools (2 indoor)* ⊟ *MC.*

Aegean Coast Essentials

BUS TRAVEL

Bus is the best way to get around—most people in Turkey do not own cars, and buses are the primary mode of transportation. All the towns are served by direct bus routes, and there are connecting services to the ancient sites.

CAR TRAVEL

The main intercity roads are fine, but minor roads are more rustic, and present a little more of a challenge to your car. The E24 from Çanakkale follows the coast until it turns inland at Kuşadası to meet the Mediterranean again at Antalya.

TOURS

Travel agencies in all the major towns organize tours of the historic sites. Travel agencies along Teyyare Caddesi in Kuşadası arrange escorted tours to Ephesus; Priene, Miletus, and Didyma; and Aphrodisias and Pamukkale.

VISITOR INFORMATION

🏢 **Ayvalık** ⊠ Yat Limanı Karşısı, 10400 ☎ 266/312–2122. **Bergama** ⊠ Hükümet Binası, Zemin Kat, B Blok, 35700 ☎ 232/633–1862. **Bursa** ⊠ Ulu Cami Parkı, Orhangazi Alt Geçidi No 1, 16020 ☎ 224/220–1848. **Çanakkale** ⊠ İskele Meyd. 67, 17000 ☎ 286/217–1187. **Çeşme** ⊠ İskele Meyd. 8, 35948 ☎ 232/712–6653. **İzmir** ⊠ Gaziosmanpaşa Bul. 1/C, 35340 ☎ 232/489–9278. **Kuşadası** ⊠ İskele Meyd., 09400 ☎ 256/614–1103.

THE MEDITERRANEAN COAST

Until the mid-1970s, Turkey's southwest coast was inaccessible to all but the most determined travelers in four-wheel-drive vehicles or on the backs of donkeys. Today, well-maintained highways wind through the area, and jets full of tourists arrive at the Dalaman Airport.

Thanks to strict developmental control, the area has maintained its Turkish flavor, with low, whitewashed buildings and tile roofs. The beaches are clean, and you can swim and snorkel in turquoise waters so clear that it is possible to see fish 20 feet below. There are excellent outdoor cafés and seafood restaurants, and no shortage of nightlife. But the region isn't just about untainted beaches and charming fishing villages. It also contains ancient cities of Greek, Roman, Arab, Seljuk, Armenian, crusader, and Byzantine vintage.

Seven full days should give you enough time to travel the 560-km (347-mi) route from Bursa to Antalya, stopping at the highlights in between.

The Mediterranean Coast

TO ANKARA
Afyon

Izmir
Turgutlu Salihli
TO ISTANBUL
Uşak

Küçük Menderes
E23

♦ Ephesus
E24

Büyük Menderes
Denizli Burdur

♦ Miletus
Milás Isparta
Milás
400 Yeşilova

♦ Halikarnas Mugla
Bodrum
Termessos,
Perge, Aspendos

Kos Datça Marmaris Lake Köyceğiz Kaunus Tefenni
Cnidos Bozburun Dalyan Dalaman

G R E E C E Fethiye Antalya
Kemer
♦ Pinara
Letoön ♦ Kinik **Phaselis**
♦ Xanthos
Aegean Rhodos **Patara ♦** Kalkan Finike
Sea Kaş Kale Demre
Uçağız

Mediterranean Sea

0   50 miles
0   75 km

Bodrum

Sitting between two crescent-shape bays, Bodrum, known as Halicarnassos in antiquity, was one of the first Greek colonies in Asia, founded around 1000 BC. In modern times it has long been the favorite haunt of the Turkish upper classes. Today the elite are joined by thousands of foreigners, and the area is rapidly filling with hotels and guest houses, cafés, restaurants, and discos. Many compare it to St. Tropez on the French Riviera. Fortunately, it is still beautiful and unspoiled, with gleaming, whitewashed buildings covered with bougainvillea and magnificent unobstructed vistas of the bays. People flock to Bodrum not for its beach, which is a disappointment, but for its fine dining and nightlife. Beautiful **beaches** can be found in the outlying villages on the peninsula—Torba, Türkbükü, Yalıkavak, Turgutreis, Akyarlar, Ortakent, Bitez, and Gümbet. Easy to reach by minibus or dolmuş, these villages are about an hour's drive away and have clean hotels and plenty of outdoor restaurants.

One of the outstanding sights in Bodrum is **Bodrum Kalesi** (Bodrum Castle), known as the Castle of St. Peter. Standing between the two bays, the castle was built by crusaders during the 15th century. It has beautiful gardens and a **Sualtı Arkeoloji Müzesi** (Museum of Underwater Archaeology). ⊠ *Kale Cad.* ☎ *252/316–2516* ⊗ *Winter 8–5; summer 8–7.*

$$ ✕ **Amphora.** In a gorgeous location—an old stone building decorated with kilims and fishing gear, opposite the marina at the edge of town—this eatery offers dazzling options of 20 or so mezes (including eggplant pureed, sautéed with garlic, or in tomato sauce) and two dozen kinds of kebabs. ⊠ *Neyzen Tevfik Cad. 172* ☎ *252/316–2368* ⌂ *Reservations essential* ▭ *MC, V.*

$$ ✕ **Kortan.** This seaside fish restaurant with white tablecloths and candles has outdoor seating with views of Bodrum's castle and the Greek island of Kos off the coast. The better dishes include fish kebabs, calamari, octopus salad, and whatever the catch of the day happens to be, usually grilled. ⊠ *Cumhuriyet Cad. 32* ☎ *252/316–1241* ♧ *Reservations essential* 🖃 *AE, MC, V.*

$$ 🏨 **Ayaz Hotel.** Less than a five-minute drive east of Bodrum harbor, this hotel on a small bay has its own gardens and a beach with a bar where you can listen to the waves. The guest rooms are done in contemporary style and have balconies and sea views. ⊠ *On Gümbet Bay, 48400* ☎*252/316–1174 or 252/316–2956* 🖷 *252/316–4751* ⏎ *96 rooms* ♧ *Restaurant, pool, bar* 🖃 *MC, V.*

$$ 🏨 **Hotel Anka.** This hilltop hotel, just 2 km (1 mi) from the city center, has commanding views of the Bodrum bay. Rooms, which are in whitewashed bungalows, are simple and clean, and have balconies. ⊠*Eskiçeşme Mah. Asarlık Mev., Gümbet, 48400* ☎ *252/317–2171* 🖷 *252/317–2161* ⏎ *83 rooms, 2 suites* ♧ *Restaurant, pool* 🖃 *AE, MC, V.*

$$ 🏨 **Manastır Hotel Bodrum.** The bar in this comfortable whitewashed-stucco Mediterranean-style hotel was once the site of a monastery. Front rooms have balconies and overlook the Petronion; all are cool and spacious, with whitewashed walls and tasteful, modern furnishings. ⊠ *Barış Sitesi Mev., Kumbahçe, 48400* ☎ *252/316–2854* 🖷 *252/316–2772* ⏎ *59 rooms, 14 suites* ♧ *2 restaurants, pool* 🖃 *AE, DC, MC, V.*

Marmaris

Built on the site of the ancient Greek city of Phryscus, Marmaris has developed into a sophisticated resort with boutiques, elegant restaurants, plenty of nightlife, and some of the best sailing in the Mediterranean. Nearby are quiet villages that are easy to reach by boat or taxi. The remains of Phryscus can be seen on **Asar Tepe,** a hill 1½ km (1 mi) north of the modern town.

★ At **Knidos,** on the end of the peninsula, you can see the ruins of Aphrodite's circular temple and an ancient theater. By road Knidos is a very rough 108 km (67 mi) from Marmaris; it's easier and quicker to take a boat. **Turunç,** 16 km (10 mi) from Marmaris, is also worth a day trip, especially for its beaches.

Dalyan

Tombs from the Carian civilization of the first millennium BC are carved into the cliff that rises behind the Dalyan River in the fishing town of Dalyan, 20 minutes' drive from the airport in Dalaman. The town is a good base for exploring the 4th-century BC city of **Kaunos,** 10 km (6 mi) to the west. It costs about $20 to rent a boat with a boatman to sail from Dalyan to the ruins and unspoiled İstuzu beach. You can also reach freshwater **Lake Köyceğiz** by boat through the reed beds of the Dalyan delta. This entire area is a wildlife preserve, filled with such birds as kingfishers, kestrels, egrets, and cranes.

$$ 🏨 **Dalyan Hotel.** Comfortable and clean, with views across Lake Köyceğiz to the tombs, this place is surrounded by trees on the shore of the lake. It has an excellent restaurant and a friendly, attentive staff that organizes hiking, bicycling, and motorcycling trips on nearby mountain paths. ⊠ *Yalı Sok., Maras Mahalli, Dalyan, 48840* ☎ *252/284–2239 or 252/284–3344* 🖷 *252/284–2240* ⏎ *20 rooms with shower* ♧ *2 restaurants, pool* 🖃 *AE, MC, V.*

$$ 🏨 **Osmanlı Hanı.** Beautifully ensconced among trees and lawns around the pool is this collection of whitewashed, two-story units built in the form of old Ottoman houses. The hotel is just 100 yards from the estuary, and there's a courtesy boat to the nearby beach. ⊠ *Sokak 55,*

Gulpınar Mahallesi, Dalyan, 48840 ☎ *252/284–4498 or 252/284–
4750* 🖨 *252/284–4751* 🛏 *14 suites* ♨ *Restaurant, pool* ☰ *MC, V*
⊘ *Closed Nov.–Apr.*

$ 🏨 **Hotel Özay.** Lush greenery and palm trees surround this quiet, mod-
ern, efficiently run lakeside hotel. Its indoor café is in a garden draped
with vines, bougainvillea, and jasmine, and the restaurant is better than
average. Daily boat tours of the lake are available, and Turkish belly-
dancing shows take place at night. ⊠ *Kordon Boyu 11, Köyceğiz,
48800* ☎ *252/262–4300* 🖨 *252/262–2000* 🛏 *32 rooms, 2 suites*
♨ *Restaurant, pool* ☰ *MC, V.*

Ölü Deniz

One of Turkey's greatest natural wonders is Ölü Deniz, an azure lagoon
flanked by long, white beaches. There are a few wooden chalets in
campgrounds and one beachfront hotel. Opposite the beach are small
restaurants with rooftop bars, many with live music all night long.

★ $$–$$$ ✕ **Ölü Deniz.** The name of this domed restaurant with wicker chairs and
wooden floors means "white dolphin." One of the most picturesque
restaurants in the area, it's right on a promontory overlooking the sea.
Continental and Turkish cuisines are imaginatively prepared and presented. ⊠ *On bay of Belcekiz, near Padirali* ☎ *252/617–0068* ☰ *No
credit cards* ⊘ *Closed Nov.–Mar.*

$–$$ ✕ **Asmali Restaurant.** In addition to homemade dishes that vary daily,
this family-run restaurant serves cold mezes, grilled meats, and fish. It
has a beautiful garden terrace with overhanging vines. ⊠ *On road to
Meri Oteli* ☎ *No phone* ☰ *No credit cards.*

$$ 🏨 **Meri Oteli.** On a steep incline above the lagoon, this hotel is made up
of a series of bungalows with rooms that are a bit down-at-the-heel though
clean. But it's the only place to stay at the lagoon. Look for signs for
Meri. ⊠ *Fethiye, 48300* ☎ *252/617–0001* 🖨 *252/617–0010* ⊕ *www.
hotelmeri.com* 🛏 *94 rooms, 1 suite* ♨ *2 restaurants, pool* ☰ *MC, V.*

Pinara

In ancient times Pinara was one of the most important cities of the for-
mer Roman province of Lycia. Near the ruins of the ancient city, up a
steep and strenuous dirt road, are nearly 200 Roman tombs cut hon-
eycomb-fashion into the face of the cliffs. ⊠ *Southeast of Fethiye, near
Rte. 400* ⊘ *Daily 8:30 AM–sunset.*

Xanthos

Xanthos was one of the leading cities of the Roman province of Lycia.
Its inhabitants developed a fearsome reputation for bravery, twice burn-
ing down their own city rather than surrender. The ruins of the city lie
down a rough road, but it's still well worth the bumpy ride to see the
acropolis, the Tomb of Harpies, some plaster-cast reliefs, and ruins of
some Byzantine buildings. ⊠ *Off Rte. 400 from Kinik* ⊘ *Daily 8:30
AM–sunset.*

Patara

Two thousand years ago, Patara, port city of Xanthos, was among the
busiest ports in the region. Hannibal and St. Paul both visited, and St.
Nicholas, the future Santa Claus, was born here. Today you will find
ruins scattered around the marshes and sand dunes. The area's long, wide
beaches remain unspoiled despite the fact that they attract hundreds of
Turkish families and tourists.

Kalkan

With its red-tile roofs and waterfront restaurants, Kalkan is a perfect
Mediterranean fishing village. Nearby beaches have made it a popular
base for exploring the region.

$–$$ ⊞ **Kalkan Han.** This rambling, clean-lined, restored Ottoman cara-vansary in the back part of the village has a roof terrace with sweeping views of the bay. It's a splendid place to enjoy breakfast, and is perfect after dark when it becomes the Star Bar. ⊠ *Köyiçi Mev., 07960* ☎ *242/ 844–3151* 🖷 *242/844–2059* 🛏 *6 rooms, 4 suites* ⧄ *Restaurant* ⊟ *No credit cards* ⊘ *Closed Nov.–Apr.*

$ ⊞ **Hotel Pirat.** This large, modern hotel, a cluster of three-story build-ings, occupies a beautiful spot right on the harbor. It's just a short walk from the swimming platform. Each room has its own private terrace; ask for one overlooking the water. ⊠ *Kalkan Marina, 07960* ☎ *242/ 844–3178* 🖷 *242/844–3183* 🛏 *136 rooms, 25 suites* ⧄ *2 restaurants, 3 pools* ⊟ *AE, MC, V.*

Kaş

Kaş is rapidly developing from a sleepy resort into a major yachting cen-ter. There are still plenty of old-fashioned, budget-price pansiyons, but luxury hotels have replaced many of the tiny houses on the hills. One of the attractions here is a day trip by boat to the underwater city of **Kekova,** where you can look overboard and see ancient Roman and Greek columns that were once part of a thriving city before the area was flooded. Kekova is especially popular with scuba divers and snorkelers; to scuba dive or fish in this area, you must get a permit from the direc-torate of the harbor and from the directorate of the ministry of tourism. Boats leave daily at 9:30 and cost about $15.

$$ ✕ **Mercan.** Good, basic Turkish food in an open-air setting is what you should expect at this place on the eastern side of the harbor. The menu includes whole lamb on a spit, fish, and lobster, and vegetarian choices. The water is so close you can hear fish jumping as you watch the ex-cursion boats head out to sea. ⊠ *Hükümet Cad., Cumhuriyet Meyd.* ☎ *242/836–1209* ⊟ *MC, V.*

$$–$$$ ⊞ **Hadrian Hotel.** Magnificent sea views characterize this hotel built in the traditional Kaş style on the rocky southern tip of the Çukurbağ penin-sula. In summer the hotel's whitewashed walls are covered in purple bougainvillea. There is a swimming platform so you can dive straight into the sea. ⊠ *Çukurbağ Yarımadası 45, Kaş, 07580* ☎ *242/836– 2856* 🖷 *242/836–1387* 🛏 *10 rooms, 4 suites* ⧄ *Pool* ⊟ *AE, MC, V.*

Phaselis

Phaselis is the site of some of the most romantic ruins in Turkey, with jumbles of stones dating from the 7th century BC through the Roman period. Overgrown streets descend to the sparkling waters of the Mediter-ranean, which are ideal for swimming.

Kemer

This town is a center of intensive tourist development, with hotels and restaurants, a well-equipped marina, and club-style holiday villages that may make you forget you're in Turkey.

Antalya

The resort of Antalya is a good base for several worthwhile excursions to major **archaeological sites** at Perge, Aspendos, Side, and Termessos. The city, built around a restored harbor, is filled with narrow streets lined with small houses, restaurants, and pansiyons. On the hilltop are tea gardens where you can enjoy tea made in an old-fashioned samovar and look across the bay to the Taurus Mountains. To the right of the port is the 13th-century **Yivli Minare** (Fluted Minaret).

The first-rate **Antalya Müzesi** (Antalya Museum) displays Turkish crafts, costumes, and artifacts of the classical Greek and Roman eras. ⊠ *Konyaaltı Cad., west of town* ☎ *242/241–4528* ⊘ *Tues.–Sun. 9–6.*

$$ ✕ **Kırk Merdiven Restaurant.** You can reach this restaurant—once the barn of an Ottoman house—from the marina by climbing the 40 stairs from which it takes its name. Choose from the high-quality meats, fish, and large selection of mezes and salads, and eat either inside or in the garden. The restaurant is in the Kaleiççi neighborhood in the Selçuk Mahallesi district. ⊠ *Musalla Sok: 2, Kaleiçi, Selçuk Mah.* ☎ *242/242–9686* ▤ *MC, V.*

★ **$$$$** ▦ **Talya.** At this luxurious resort you reach the private beach by taking an elevator down the side of the cliff. Every angle gives a view of the sea. Rooms are spacious, with big beds and terraces. The hotel is usually full in high season, so plan ahead. ⊠ *Fevzi Çakmak Cad. 30, 07100* ☎ *242/248–6800* 🖷 *242/241–5400* ⊕ *www.talya.com.tr* ☙ *204 rooms* ♨ *3 restaurants, pool* ▤ *AE, DC, MC, V.*

$$ ▦ **Tütav Türk Evleri.** Part of the old Kaleiçi district, this hotel consists of a row of restored 19th-century Turkish houses joined together. Well-tended gardens surround the inn; its popular restaurant serves French-inspired cuisine and is known for its delectable fish stew. ⊠ *Mermerli Sok. 2, 07100* ☎ *242/248–6478 or 242/248–6591* 🖷 *242/241–9419* ☙ *19 rooms, 1 suite* ♨ *Restaurant, pool* ▤ *AE, MC, V.*

Termessos

Writers in antiquity referred to Termessos as the "Eagle's Nest." It's not hard to see why. The only access is a stiff but rewarding climb up a steep, rocky path. But from the ruins, right on top of the mountain, you can expect views that are among the most dramatic in Turkey. Much of the site is romantically but inconveniently overgrown, and large areas, including virtually the entire Roman city, have never been excavated. You can see an amphitheater built on the mountainside. Organized tours to Termessos leave from Antalya. ⊠ *Korkuteli, Rte. 350 off Rte. E87, northwest of Antalya* ☉ *Daily 9–5:30.*

Perge

The ruins of the ancient city of Perge, northeast of Antalya, include a superb amphitheater, well-preserved thermal baths, a restored colonnaded street, and a Roman basilica where St. Paul gave his first sermon, in AD 45. ⊠ *North off Rte. 400 at Aksu turnoff* ☉ *Daily 9–5:30.*

Aspendos

★ This site contains Turkey's best-preserved Roman amphitheater. The acoustics are so fine that modern-day performers don't need microphones or amplifiers. ⊠ *North off Rte. 400 at turnoff past Belkis* ☉ *Daily 9–5:30.*

Mediterranean Coast Essentials

BOAT & FERRY TRAVEL

There are many coves and picnic areas along the coast, accessible only by boat. For a small fee local fishermen will take you to and from the coves; you can also take one of the many water taxis. Or charter a small yacht, with or without skipper, at the marinas in Bodrum and Marmaris. One of the most enjoyable ways to see the coast is to take a one- or two-week cruise on a *gulet,* a wooden craft with a full crew.

CAR TRAVEL

Although the highways between towns are well maintained, the smaller roads are usually unpaved and very rough.

VISITOR INFORMATION

🗗 **Antalya** ⊠ Cumhuriyet Cad., Özel İdare Altı 2, 07040 ☎ 242/241-1747. **Bodrum** ⊠ Barış Meyd. 12, 48400 ☎ 252/316-1091. **Dalaman** ⊠ Dalaman Airport, 48770 ☎ 252/792-5291. **Datça** ⊠ İskele Mah. Hükümet Binası, 48900 ☎ 252/712-3163 or 252/712-3546.

Kaş ⊠ Cumhuriyet Meyd. 5, 07580 ☎ 242/836-1238. **Marmaris** ⊠ İskele Meyd. 2, 48700 ☎ 252/412-1035.

CENTRAL ANATOLIA & CAPPADOCIA

The archaeological sites of Central Anatolia abound with well-preserved Roman architecture. Cappadocia, an area in the eastern part of Anatolia filled with ruins of ancient civilizations, has changed little over the centuries. People still travel between their farms and villages in horse-drawn carts, women drape their houses with strings of apricots and peppers for drying in the sun, and nomads pitch their black tents beside sunflower fields and cook on tiny fires that send smoke billowing through the tops of the tents.

Ankara

From the time it was founded in about 1200 BC through its gradual decline under the Ottomans, Ankara, now Turkey's capital, had an illustrious yet strife-filled existence. By the early 20th century it was little more than a dusty provincial town, the perfect site for Atatürk to build his new capital and establish the new Turkish Republic. Today it is a bureaucrats' city, with functional, uninspired architecture and straight, broad roads. Although it is less frenetic than Istanbul, it is not as orderly as it was a decade ago, and traffic and overcrowding are becoming serious problems.

It was at the **Cumhuriyet Müzesi** (Republic Museum,; ⊠ Cumhuriyet Bul. off Ulus Meyd. ☎ 312/310–5361) in 1920 that Atatürk was elected chairman of the Grand National Assembly, which would organize the new nation. Housed in a restored 15th-century *bedestan* (covered bazaar and Fodor'sChoice inn) is the superb **Ankara Anadolu Medeniyetleri Müzesi** (Museum of ★ Anatolian Civilizations). The museum is small but packed with masterpieces from the Neolithic and Bronze ages and through the Assyrian, Phrygian, Urartu, Hellenistic, and Roman eras. The heart of the museum is its comprehensive collection of Hatti and Hittite artifacts, dating from the dawn of the second millennium BC. There are also small statues, jewels worked in gold and iron, combs and needles, as well as wonderful bas-relief carvings in stone. The addition in 1998 of several frescoes from the site of Çatal Höyük (first occupied in the 7th millennium BC) offers an opportunity to view art that adorned the walls of homes in the oldest settled community in the world. ⊠ *Gözcü Sok.* ☎ *312/ 324–3160* ☉ *Daily 9–4:30.*

★ $$$$ ▦ **Ankara HiltonSA.** This luxurious 16-story hotel in a quiet, hilly neighborhood on Embassy Row provides many amenities and a view to boot. Expect the standards of comfort and style that you've come to expect from Hiltons the world over, but without many distinguishing characteristics to show that you're in Turkey. ⊠ *Tahran Cad. 12, Kavaklıdere, 06700* ☎ *312/468–2888* ☏ *312/468–0909* ⊕ *www.hilton.com* ⤳ *324 rooms* ◊ *2 restaurants* ⊟ *AE, DC, MC, V.*

$$ ▦ **Kent Hotel.** A cheerful, helpful staff distinguishes this hotel in the heart of the city, near the main shopping and business areas. Rooms are pleasant and comfortable, if nondescript. ⊠ *Mithatpaşa Cad. 4, Sıhhiye, 06540* ☎ *312/435–5050* ☏ *312/434–4657* ⤳ *120 rooms* ◊ *Restaurant, bar* ⊟ *AE, DC, MC, V.*

★ $$ ▦ **King Hotel.** On a quiet street near the Turkish Grand National Assembly, this place is a favorite both with returning businessmen and with tourists or Turks visiting Ankara. The central location, helpful staff, above-average restaurant, and clean rooms with standard furnishings all make this hotel a great deal. ⊠ *Güvenlik Cad. 13, Aşağıayrancı, 06540*

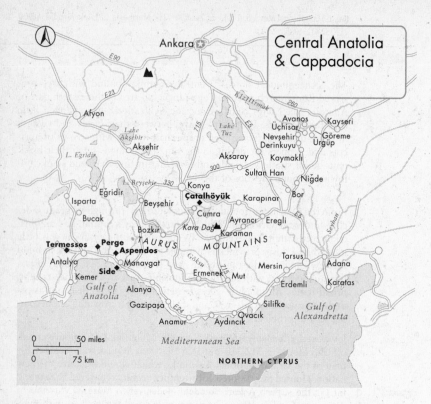

Central Anatolia & Cappadocia

☎ *312/418–9099* 🖶 *312/417–0382* 🛏 *36 rooms* ♨ *Restaurant* 🖃 *AE, DC, MC, V.*

Konya

Konya has always been the religious capital of Turkey. During the Ottoman Empire it was the center of the Islamic mystical order known to the West as the whirling dervishes. The order was founded in the 13th century by Celaleddin Rumi, or Mevlâna, a Muslim mystic, who said, "There are many ways of knowing God. I choose the dance and music." The **Mevlâna Müzesi** (Mevlâna Museum; ✉ Mevlâna Meyd. ☎ 332/331–1215) contains the **Mevlâna Türbesi** (Tomb of Mevlâna Celaleddin) as well as displays that illustrate the dervishes' way of life. You can still see the dervishes whirl to the sounds of a flute at the annual commemorative rites held in Konya in early December. Tickets are available from travel agencies or from the Konya tourist information office.

$ ✕ **Hanedan.** Kebabs are the order of the day at Hanedan. Highly recommended are the *tandır* (baked lamb) and the *inegöl köfte* (grilled meatballs). ✉ *Mevlâna Cad. No. 2* ☎ *332/351–4546* 🖃 *No credit cards.*

Cappadocia

Over the centuries the softness of the volcanic rock in the Cappadocia region has been ideal for hollowing out cave dwellings and forming defenses against invading armies. They were begun as early as the 5th century BC. From the 7th through the 10th centuries AD, inhabitants of the Christian kingdom of Cappadocia took refuge from Arab raiders in about 40 underground cities, with some structures as deep as 20 stories underground. The largest of these cities housed 20,000 people. Each had dormitories, dining halls, sewage disposal systems, ventilation chimneys, a cemetery, and a prison. Large millstones sealed off the entrances from enemies.

The magical landscape of Cappadocia consists roughly of the triangular area between Kayseri in the east, Nevşehir in the center, and Niğde in the south. Within that triangle Ürgüp is the center from which to explore the villages on your own or to arrange tours; it is the best place to shop. Because the Cappadocia area is so vast, you'll need at least two days to see the main sights.

In the ruins of the underground city of **Derinkuyu** (✉ Rte. 765, 30 km [19 mi] south of Nevşehir ☎ 384/381–3194) is an unusual Greek church carved out of rock. Equipped with a flashlight, explore the stairways and ★ corridors of the underground city of **Kaymaklı** (✉ Rte. 765, 21 km [13 mi] south of Nevşehir ☎ 384/218–2500). Both cities are open daily 8–5.

Some of the earliest relics of Christianity can be found in the **Göreme Valley,** a couple of miles east of Nevşehir. There are dozens of old churches and monasteries covered with frescoes honeycombed through ★ the soft rock. For a history of the area, visit the **Göreme Açık Hava Müzesi** (Göreme Open-Air Museum). Signs provide information about the site, but bring a flashlight—most churches are illuminated only by the natural light that seeps in. The oldest rock church dates from the 4th century, although frescoes first appeared in the 8th century. ✉ *1 km (½ mi) outside Göreme village on Ürgüp road.* ⊙ *Daily 8:30–5:30.*

$$$$ 🏨 **Ataman.** Run by a tourist guide and his wife, this hotel is built into the face of a rock. Rooms are connected by mazelike corridors and are individually decorated with kilims and handicrafts. Rates include breakfast and dinner. ✉ *Göreme, 50180* ☎ *384/271–2310* 🖷 *384/271–2313* 🌐 *www.atamanhotel.com* 🍴 *38 rooms* ♨ *Restaurant* 🖃 *MC, V.*

$$–$$$ 🏨 **Yunak Evleri.** For the ultimate Cappadocia experience try this hotel, which has been formed by joining together six ancient cave houses, some of which date back 1,500 years. The houses combine modern comforts with traditional kilims and elegant wooden furniture. ✉ *Yunak Mahallesi, Ürgüp, 50400* ☎ *384/341–6920* 🖷 *384/341–6924* 🌐 *www.yunak.com* 🍴 *27 rooms* ♨ *Restaurant* 🖃 *MC, V.*

Central Anatolia & Cappadocia Essentials

BUS TRAVEL

A good bus network links most towns and cities, and fares are reasonable, so take the bus if possible. If you want to visit the region's main sights, buses and minibuses are definitely your best (and least expensive) bets. However, if you want to explore the landscape—and there are many interesting rock formations outside the main sites—then you should hire a car.

CAR TRAVEL

There are good roads between Istanbul and the main cities of Anatolia—Ankara, Konya, and Kayseri. The highways are generally well maintained and lead to all the major sites. Minor roads are full of potholes and are very rough. On narrow winding roads, look out for oncoming trucks.

TOURS

If you are driving, consider hiring a guide for about $15 to $30 a day. Local tourist offices and hotels can recommend guides and excursions. Taxi drivers are usually willing to take you to historical sites out of town for reasonable fares.

TRAIN TRAVEL

Although there is frequent train service between the big cities (Istanbul and Ankara), it's almost nonexistent between small towns. Trains take longer than buses, even from the big cities, and are less comfortable.

VISITOR INFORMATION

🏛 **Aksaray** ✉ Ankara Cad. Dinçer Apt. 2/2, 68000 ☎ 382/212-5651. **Ankara** ✉ Gazi Mustafa Kemal Bul. 121, Tandoğan, 06050 ☎ 312/229-2631. **Kayseri** ✉ Kağnı Pazari 61, 38000 ☎ 352/222-3903. **Konya** ✉ Mevlâna Cad. 65, Karatay, 42030 ☎ 332/351-1074. **Nevşehir** ✉ Atatürk Bul., 50130 ☎ 384/213-3659. **Ürgüp** ✉ Kayseri Cad. 37, 50200 ☎ 384/341-4059.

VOCABULARY

DUTCH

English	Dutch	Pronunciation

Basics

English	Dutch	Pronunciation
Yes/no	Ja, nee	yah, nay
Please	Alstublieft	**ahls**-too-bleeft
Thank you	Dank u	**dahnk** oo
Excuse me, sorry	Pardon	pahr-**don**
Good morning	Goede morgen	**hoh**-deh **mor**-ghen
Goodbye	Dag	dah

Numbers

1	Een	ehn
2	Twee	tveh
3	Drie	dree
4	Vier	veer
5	Vijf	vehf
6	Zes	zehss
7	Zeven	**zeh**-vehn
8	Acht	ahkht
9	Negen	**neh**-ghen
10	Tien	teen

Days of the Week

Sunday	zondag	**zohn**-dagh
Monday	maandag	**mahn**-dagh
Tuesday	dinsdag	**dinns**-dagh
Wednesday	woensdag	**voons**-dagh
Thursday	donderdag	**don**-der-dagh
Friday	vrijdag	**vreh**-dagh
Saturday	zaterdag	**zah**-ter-dagh

Useful Phrases

Do you speak English?	Spreekt U Engels?	sprehkt oo **ehn**-gls
I don't understand.	Ik begrijp het niet.	ihk be-**ghrehp** het neet
I don't know.	Ik weet niet.	ihk **veht** ut neet
I'm American/ English.	Ik ben Amerikaans/ Engels.	ihk ben am-er-ee-**kahns**/**ehn**-gls
Where is . . .	Waar is . . .	vahr iss

the train station?	het station?	heht stah-**syohn**
the post office?	het postkantoor?	het **pohst**-kahn-tohr
the hospital?	het ziekenhuis?	het **zeek**-uhn-haus
Where are the restrooms?	Waar is de WC?	**vahr** iss de **veh**-seh
Left/right	Links/rechts	leenks/rehts
How much is this?	Hoeveel kost dit?	hoo-**vehl** kohst deet
It's expensive/ cheap	Het is te duur/ goedkoop	het ees teh **dour**/ **hood**-kohp
I am ill/sick.	Ik ben ziek.	ihk behn zeek
Help!	Help!	help
Stop!	Stoppen!	**stop**-pen

Dining Out

Bill/check	De rekening	de **rehk**-en-eeng
Bread	Brood	brohd
I'd like to order	Ik wil graag bestellen	ihk veel khrah behs-**tell**-en
Menu	Menu/kaart	men-**oo**/kahrt
Napkin	En servet	ehn ser-**veht**
Please give me . . .	Mag ik [een] . . .	mahkh ihk [ehn]

FRENCH

English	French	Pronunciation

Basics

Yes/no	Oui/non	wee/nohn
Please	S'il vous plaît	seel voo **play**
Thank you	Merci	mair-**see**
Excuse me, sorry	Pardon	pahr-**dohn**
Good morning/ afternoon	Bonjour	bohn-**zhoor**
Goodbye	Au revoir	o ruh-**vwahr**
Mr. (Sir)	Monsieur	muh-**syuh**
Mrs. (Ma'am)	Madame	ma-**dam**
Miss	Mademoiselle	mad-mwa-**zel**

Numbers

1	Un	uhn
2	Deux	deuh
3	Trois	twah
4	Quatre	**kaht**-ruh
5	Cinq	sank
6	Six	seess
7	Sept	set
8	Huit	wheat
9	Neuf	nuf
10	Dix	deess

20	Vingt	vehn
21	Vingt-et-un	vehnt-ay-**uhn**
50	Cinquante	sang-**kahnt**
100	Cent	sahn
1,000	Mille	meel

Days of the Week

Sunday	dimanche	dee-**mahnsh**
Monday	lundi	luhn-**dee**
Tuesday	mardi	mahr-**dee**
Wednesday	mercredi	mair-kruh-**dee**
Thursday	jeudi	zhuh-**dee**
Friday	vendredi	vawn-druh-**dee**
Saturday	samedi	sahm-**dee**

Useful Phrases

Do you speak English?	Parlez-vous anglais?	par-lay **voo** ahn-**glay**
I don't understand.	Je ne comprends pas.	zhuh nuh kohm-**prahn** pah
I don't know.	Je ne sais pas.	zhuh nuh say **pah**
I'm American/ British.	Je suis américain/ anglais.	zhuh sweez a-may-ree-**kehn**/ahn-**glay**
Yesterday	Hier	yair
Today	Aujourd'hui	o-zhoor-**dwee**
Tomorrow	Demain	duh-**mehn**
What is it?	Qu'est-ce que c'est?	kess-kuh-**say**
Where is . . .	Où est . . .	oo ay
the train station?	la gare?	la gar
the subway station?	la station de métro?	la sta-**syon** duh may-**tro**
the post office?	la poste?	la post
the bank?	la banque?	la bahnk
the hospital?	l'hôpital?	lo-pee-**tahl**
Where are the rest rooms?	Où sont les toilettes?	oo sohn lay twah-**let**
Left/right	A gauche/à droite	a goash/a drwaht
I'd like . . .	Je voudrais . . .	zhuh voo-**dray**
a room	une chambre	ewn **shahm**-bruh
I'd like to buy . . .	Je voudrais acheter . . .	zhuh voo-**dray** ahsh-**tay**
How much is it?	C'est combien?	say comb-bee-**ehn**
A little/a lot	Un peu/beaucoup	uhn peuh/bo-**koo**
More/less	Plus/moins	plu/mwehn
I am ill/sick.	Je suis malade.	zhuh swee ma-**lahd**
Help!	Au secours!	o suh-**koor**
Stop!	Arrêtez!	a-reh-**tay**

Dining Out

A bottle of . . .	Une bouteille de . . .	ewn boo-**tay** duh
Bill/check	L'addition	la-dee-see-**ohn**
Bread	Du pain	dew pan
Dish of the day	Le plat du jour	luh plah dew **zhoor**
Fixed-price menu	Le menu	luh muh-**new**
I'd like to order.	Je voudrais commander.	zhuh voo-**dray** ko-mahn-**day**
Is service/the tip included?	Est-ce que le service est compris?	ess kuh luh sair-**veess** eh comb-**pree**
Menu	La carte	la cart
Napkin	Une serviette	ewn sair-vee-**et**
Please give me . . .	Donnez-moi . . .	doe-nay-**mwah**
Waiter!/Waitress!	Monsieur!/ Mademoiselle!	muh-**syuh**/ mad-mwa-**zel**
Wine list	La carte des vins	la cart day **van**

GERMAN

English	German	Pronunciation

Basics

Yes/no	Ja/nein	yah/nine
Please	Bitte	**bit**-uh
Thank you (very much)	Danke (vielen Dank)	**dahn**-kuh (**fee**-lun dahnk)
Excuse me	Entschuldigen Sie	ent-**shool**-de-gen zee
Good day	Guten Tag	**goo**-ten tahk
Good bye	Auf Wiedersehen	auf **vee**-der-zane
Mr./Mrs.	Herr/Frau	hair/frau
Miss	Fräulein	**froy**-line

Numbers

1	Ein(s)	eint(s)
2	Zwei	tsvai
3	Drei	dry
4	Vier	fear
5	Fünf	fumph
6	Sechs	zex
7	Sieben	**zee**-ben
8	Acht	ahkt
9	Neun	noyn
10	Zehn	tsane

Days of the Week

Sunday	Sonntag	**zone**-tahk
Monday	Montag	**moan**-tahk
Tuesday	Dienstag	**deens**-tahk

Wednesday	Mittwoch	**mit**-vokh
Thursday	Donnerstag	**doe**-ners-tahk
Friday	Freitag	**fry**-tahk
Saturday	Samstag/ Sonnabend	**zahm**-stakh/ **zonn**-a-bent

Useful Phrases

Do you speak English?	Sprechen Sie Englisch?	**shprek**-un zee **eng**-glish?
I am American/ British.	Ich bin Amerikaner(in)/ Engländer(in).	ich bin a-mer-i-**kahn**-er(in)/**eng**-glan-der(in)
Where are the rest rooms?	Wo ist die Toilette?	vo ist dee twah-**let**-uh
Left/right	links/rechts	links/rechts
Where is . . .	Wo ist . . .	**vo** ist
the train station?	der Bahnhof?	dare **bahn**-hof
the subway station?	die U-Bahn-Station?	dee oo-bahn-**staht**-sion
the post office?	die Post?	dee **post**
the bank?	die Bank?	dee **banhk**
the hospital?	das Krankenhaus?	dahs **krahnk**-en-house
I'd like to have . . .	Ich hätte gerne . . .	ich **het**-uh **gairn**-uh . . .
a room	ein Zimmer	ine **tsim**-er
a ticket	eine Karte	I-nuh **cart**-uh
How much is it?	Wieviel kostet das?	**vee**-feel **cost**-et dahs?
I am ill/sick.	Ich bin krank.	ich bin krahnk
Help!	Hilfe!	**hilf**-uh
Stop!	Halt!	hahlt

Dining Out

A bottle of . . .	Eine Flasche . . .	I-nuh **flash**-uh
Bill/check	Die Rechnung	dee **rekh**-nung
Do you have . . . ?	Haben Sie . . . ?	**hah**-ben zee
I'd like to order . . .	Ich möchte bestellen . . .	ich **mush**-tuh buh-shtel-en . . .
Menu	Die Speisekarte	dee **shpei**-zeh-car-tuh
Napkin	Die Serviette	dee zair-vee-**eh**-tuh

ITALIAN

English	Italian	Pronunciation

Basics

Yes/no	Sí/No	see/no
Please	Per favore	pear fa-**vo**-ray
Thank you	Grazie	**grah**-tsee-ay
You're welcome	Prego	**pray**-go

Excuse me, sorry	Scusi	**skoo**-zee
Good morning/afternoon	Buon giorno	bwohn **jor**-no
Good evening	Buona sera	**bwoh**-na **say**-ra
Good bye	Arrivederci	a-ree-vah-**dare**-chee
Mr. (Sir)	Signore	see-**nyo**-ray
Mrs. (Ma'am)	Signora	see-**nyo**-ra
Miss	Signorina	see-nyo-**ree**-na
Hello (over the phone)?	Pronto?	**proan**-to

Numbers

1	Uno	**oo**-no
2	Due	**doo**-ay
3	Tre	tray
4	Quattro	**kwah**-tro
5	Cinque	**cheen**-kway
6	Sei	say
7	Sette	**set**-ay
8	Otto	**oh**-to
9	Nove	**no**-vay
10	Dieci	dee-**eh**-chee
20	Venti	**vain**-tee
50	Cinquanta	cheen-**kwahn**-ta
100	Cento	**chen**-to
10,000	Diecimila	dee-eh-chee-**mee**-la
100,000	Centomila	chen-to-**mee**-la

Days of the Week

Sunday	domenica	doe-**men**-ee-ca
Monday	lunedì	loo-neh-**dee**
Tuesday	martedì	mahr-teh-**dee**
Wednesday	mercoledì	mare-co-leh-**dee**
Thursday	giovedì	jo-veh-**dee**
Friday	venerdì	ven-air-**dee**
Saturday	sabato	**sah**-ba-toe

Useful Phrases

Do you speak English?	Parla inglese?	**par**-la een-**glay**-zay
I don't understand.	Non capisco.	non ka-**peess**-ko
I don't know.	Non lo so.	noan lo **so**
I'm American/British.	Sono americano/a Sono inglese.	**so**-no a-may-ree-**kah**-no/a **so**-no een-**glay**-zay
What is it?	Che cos'è?	kay ko-**zay**
Where is . . .	Dov'è . . .	doe-**veh**
the train station?	la stazione?	la sta-tsee-**oh**-nay

the subway station?	la metropolitana?	la may-tro-po-lee-**tah**-na
the post office?	l'ufficio postale?	loo-**fee**-cho po-**stah**-lay
the bank?	la banca?	la **bahn**-ka
the hospital?	l'ospedale?	lo-spay-**dah**-lay
Where are the rest rooms?	Dov'è il bagno?	doe-**vay** eel **bahn**-yo
Left/right	A sinistra/a destra	a see-**neess**-tra/ a **des**-tra
I'd like . . .	Vorrei . . .	vo-**ray**
a room	una camera	**oo**-na **kah**-may-ra
How much is it?	Quanto costa?	**kwahn**-toe **coast**-a
A little/a lot	Poco/tanto	**po**-ko/**tahn**-to
More/less	Più/meno	pee-**oo**/**may**-no
I am sick.	Sto male.	sto **mah**-lay
Help!	Aiuto!	a-**yoo**-toe
Stop!	Alt!	ahlt

Dining Out

A bottle of . . .	Una bottiglia di . . .	**oo**-na bo-**tee**-lee-ah dee
Bill/check	Il conto	eel **cone**-toe
Fixed-price menu	Menù a prezzo fisso	may-**noo** a **pret**-so **fee**-so
I'd like . . .	Vorrei . . .	vo-**ray**
Is service included?	Il servizio è incluso?	eel ser-**vee**-tzee-o ay een-**kloo**-zo
Menu	Il menù	eel may-**noo**
Napkin	Il tovagliolo	eel toe-va-lee-**oh**-lo
Waiter/Waitress	Cameriere/ cameriera	ka-mare-**yer**-av/ ka-mare-**yer**-a
Wine list	La lista dei vini	la **lee**-sta **day**-ee **vee**-nee

SPANISH

English	Spanish	Pronunciation

Basics

Yes/no	Sí/no	see/no
Please	Por favor	pohr fah-**vohr**
Thank you (very much)	(Muchas) gracias	(**moo**-chas) **grah**-see-as
You're welcome	De nada	deh **nah**-dah
Excuse me	Con permiso	con pehr-**mee**-so
Good morning!	¡Buenos días!	**bway**-nohs **dee**-ahs
Goodbye!	¡Adiós!/ ¡Hasta luego!	ah-dee-**ohss**/ ah-stah-**lwe**-go
Mr./Mrs.	Señor/Señora	sen-**yor**/sen-**yohr**-ah

Miss	Señorita	sen-yo-**ree**-tah
Hello (on the telephone)	Diga	**dee**-gah

Numbers

1	Un, uno	oon, **oo**-no
2	Dos	dohs
3	Tres	tress
4	Cuatro	**kwah**-tro
5	Cinco	**sink**-oh
6	Seis	saice
7	Siete	see-**et**-eh
8	Ocho	**o**-cho
9	Nueve	new-**eh**-veh
10	Diez	dee-**es**
20	Veinte	**vain**-teh
50	Cincuenta	seen-**kwen**-tah
100	Cien	see-**en**
500	Quinientos	keen-**yen**-tohss
1,000	Mil	meel

Days of the Week

Sunday	Domingo	doh-**meen**-goh
Monday	Lunes	**loo**-ness
Tuesday	Martes	**mahr**-tess
Wednesday	Miércoles	me-**air**-koh-less
Thursday	Jueves	hoo-**ev**-ess
Friday	Viernes	vee-**air**-ness
Saturday	Sábado	**sah**-bah-doh

Useful Phrases

Do you speak English?	¿Habla usted inglés?	**ah**-blah oos-**ted** in-**glehs**
I don't understand (you).	No entiendo.	no en-tee-**en**-doh
I don't know.	No sé.	no seh
I am American/British.	Soy americano (americana)/inglés(a).	soy ah-meh-ree-**kah**-no (ah-meh-ree-**kah**-nah)/in-**glehs** (ah)
Yes, please/No, thank you	Sí, por favor/No, gracias	**see** pohr fah-**vor**/no **grah**-see-ahs
Yesterday/today/tomorrow	Ayer/hoy/mañana	ah-**yehr**/oy/mahn-**yah**-nah
What is it?	¿Qué es esto?	keh es **es**-toh
Where is . . .	¿Dónde está . . .	**dohn**-deh es-**tah**
the train station?	la estación del tren?	la es-tah-see-**on** del **train**
the subway station?	la estación del metro?	la es-ta-see-**on** del **meh**-tro

the post office?	la oficina de correos?	la oh-fee-**see**-nah deh-koh-**reh**-os
the bank?	el banco?	el **bahn**-koh
the hospital?	el hospital?	el ohss-pee-**tal**
the bathroom?	el baño?	el **bahn**-yoh
Left/right	Izquierda/derecha	iss-key-**er**-dah/ dare-**eh**-chah
I'd like . . .	Quisiera . . .	kee-see-**ehr**-ah
a room.	un cuarto/una habitación.	oon **kwahr**-toh/ **oo**-nah ah-bee-tah-see-**on**
I'd like to buy . . .	Quisiera comprar . . .	kee-see-**ehr**-ah kohm-**prahr**
How much is it?	¿Cuánto cuesta?	**kwahn**-toh **kwes**-tah
A little/a lot	Un poquito/ mucho	oon poh-**kee**-toh/ **moo**-choh
More/less	Más/menos	mahss/**men**-ohss
Please call a doctor.	Por favor llame un medico.	pohr fah-**vor** ya-meh oon **med**-ee-koh
Help!	¡Ayuda!	ah-**yoo**-dah

Dining Out

A bottle of . . .	Una bottella de . . .	**oo**-nah bo-**teh**-yah deh
A glass of . . .	Un vaso de . . .	oon **vah**-so deh
Bill/check	La cuenta	lah **kwen**-tah
Bread	El pan	el pahn
Menu of the day	Menú del día	meh-**noo** del **dee**-ah
Fixed-price menu	Menú fijo o turistico	meh-**noo fee**-hoh oh too-**ree**-stee-coh
Is the tip included?	¿Está incluida la propina?	es-**tah** in-cloo-ee-dah lah pro-**pee**-nah
Menu	La carta, el menú	lah **cart**-ah, el meh-**noo**
Napkin	La servilleta	lah sehr-vee-**yet**-ah
Please give me	Por favor déme	pohr fah-**vor deh**-meh
Waiter!/Waitress!	¡Por favor Señor/Señorita!	pohr fah-**vor** sen-**yor**/ sen-yor-**ee**-tah

INDEX